THE HARPERCOLLINS ENCYCLOPEDIA OF CATHOLICISM

THE
HARPERCOLLINS
ENCYCLOPEDIA OF
CATHOLICISM

GENERAL EDITOR
Richard P. McBrien

ASSOCIATE EDITORS

HAROLD W. ATTRIDGE   JOHN R. DONAHUE   JOHN F. LAHEY

MICHAEL J. BUCKLEY   REGIS A. DUFFY   RICHARD A. McCORMICK

JOHN C. CAVADINI   KEITH J. EGAN   THOMAS F. O'MEARA

REGINA A. COLL   MICHAEL J. HIMES   ROBERT F. TAFT

LAWRENCE S. CUNNINGHAM   ROBERT A. KRIEG   JOSEPH P. WAWRYKOW

JAY P. DOLAN   CATHERINE MOWRY LaCUGNA

HarperSanFrancisco
A Division of HarperCollins*Publishers*

PUBLICATION STAFF

SENIOR EDITOR John B. Shopp

ASSISTANT EDITOR Steven Anderson

PRODUCTION EDITOR Mimi Kusch

COPYEDITORS Ann Moru, Pam Suwinsky, Nancy Haught

PRODUCTION COORDINATORS Virginia Rich, Jennifer Boynton, Lisa Zuniga

PROOFREADERS Annelise Zamula, Steven Anderson, Beverly M. Brazauskas

EDITORIAL ASSISTANT Judith Kleppe

PHOTO RESEARCHERS Photosearch, Inc.

DESIGN Design Office, Bruce Kortebein, Peter Martin, Mary Faria, Marilyn Perry

DESIGN MANAGER Martha Blegen

TYPESETTER Auto-Graphics, Inc.

TEXT PRINTER AND BINDER R. R. Donnelley & Co.

Scripture quotations are from the New Revised Standard Version of the Bible, copyright © 1989 by the Division of Christian Education of the National Council of the Churches of Christ in the USA. Used by permission. All rights reserved; quotations from the documents of Vatican II are reprinted with permission of America Press, Inc., 106 West 56th Street, New York, NY 10019. Copyright © 1966. All rights reserved; the text of the Outline from the English translation of *Rite of Christian Initiation of Adults*, copyright © 1985, is reprinted with permission of the International Committee on English in the Liturgy, Inc. All rights reserved.

Photograph and illustration credits begin on page 1347.

FIRST EDITION

Library of Congress Cataloging-in-Publication Data
The HarperCollins encyclopedia of Catholicism / general editor,
Richard P. McBrien ; associate editors, Harold W. Attridge ...
[et al.]. — 1st ed.
p.   cm.
ISBN 0–06–065338–8 (cloth: alk. paper)
1. Catholic Church—Encyclopedias. I. McBrien, Richard P.
II. Attridge, Harold W.
BX841.H37 1995
282'.03—dc20   94–39972
                                     CIP

00 01 02 03 04   RRD(C)   14 13 12 11 10 9 8

This edition is printed on acid-free paper that meets the American National Standards Institute Z39.48 Standard.

CONTENTS

CONTRIBUTORS

STEPHEN A. ALLEN, M.M.S.,
PH.D. CAND.
  Medieval Institute
  University of Notre Dame
  Notre Dame, Indiana

CHARLOTTE A. AMES, M.A.,
M.L.S.
  Catholic Americana Librarian
  University of Notre Dame
  Notre Dame, Indiana

MICHAEL F. ANDREWS, S.J.,
PH.L.
  Instructor in Philosophy
  Fairfield University
  Fairfield, Connecticut

BENEDICT M. ASHLEY, O.P.,
PH.D.
  Professor Emeritus of Moral
    Theology
  Aquinas Institute of Theology
  St. Louis, Missouri

HAROLD W. ATTRIDGE, PH.D.
  Professor of New Testament and
  Dean, College of Arts and
    Letters
  University of Notre Dame
  Notre Dame, Indiana

STEVEN M. AVELLA, PH.D.
  Associate Professor of History
  Marquette University
  Milwaukee, Wisconsin

JOHN F. BALDOVIN, S.J., PH.D.
  Associate Professor of Historical
    and Liturgical Theology
  Jesuit School of Theology at
    Berkeley/Graduate
    Theological Union
  Berkeley, California

KATHARINE S. BARRETT,
M.DIV.
  Director of Religious Education,
    Campus Ministry
  University of Notre Dame
  Notre Dame, Indiana

GREGORY BAUM, D.TH.
  Professor of Religious Studies
  McGill University
  Montreal, Quebec, Canada

MICHAEL R. BEGGS, M.A.,
PH.D. CAND.
  Department of Theology
  University of Notre Dame
  Notre Dame, Indiana

THOMAS E. BLANTZ, C.S.C.,
PH.D.
  Professor of History
  University of Notre Dame
  Notre Dame, Indiana

JOSEPH BLENKINSOPP, D.PHIL.
  John A. O'Brien Professor of
    Biblical Studies
  University of Notre Dame
  Notre Dame, Indiana

CHRISTOPHER O. BLUM, M.A.,
PH.D. CAND.
  Graduate Program in History
    and Philosophy of Science
  University of Notre Dame
  Notre Dame, Indiana

THÉRÈSE MARIE BONIN, PH.D.
  Assistant Professor of
    Philosophy
  Duquesne University
  Pittsburgh, Pennsylvania

JOSEPH A. BRACKEN, S.J.,
PH.D.
  Professor of Theology
  Xavier University
  Cincinnati, Ohio

PAUL F. BRADSHAW, D.D.
  Professor of Liturgy
  University of Notre Dame
  Notre Dame, Indiana

BEVERLY M. BRAZAUSKAS,
M.ED., M.A.
  Religious Education Consultant
  Silver Burdett Ginn
  South Bend, Indiana

PAMELA BRIGHT, PH.D.
  Associate Professor of Historical
    Theology
  Concordia University
  Montreal, Quebec, Canada

MICHAEL J. BUCKLEY, S.J.,
PH.D.
  Professor of Systematic
    Theology
  Director, Jesuit Institute
  Boston College
  Chestnut Hill, Massachusetts

JEFFREY M. BURNS, PH.D.
  Archivist, Archdiocese of San
    Francisco
  Menlo Park, California

DAVID B. BURRELL, C.S.C.,
PH.D.
  Hesburgh Professor of
    Philosophy and Theology
  University of Notre Dame
  Notre Dame, Indiana

SUSAN M. CALEF, M.A., PH.D.
CAND.
  Department of Theology
  University of Notre Dame
  Notre Dame, Indiana

EDMUND CAMPION, M.A.
(CANTAB.)
  Associate Professor of History
  Catholic Institute of Sydney
  Sydney, New South Wales,
    Australia

KATHLEEN CANNON, O.P.,
D.MIN.
  Concurrent Associate Professor
    of Theology and Associate
    Provost
  University of Notre Dame
  Notre Dame, Indiana

GEORGE L. CAREY, PH.D.
  Archbishop of Canterbury
  Primate of All England and
    Metropolitan
  Lambeth Palace
  London, England

MARIA LUIZA CARRANO, M.A.
Assistant Professional Specialist
University of Notre Dame
Notre Dame, Indiana

JOHN C. CAVADINI, PH.D.
Associate Professor of Theology
University of Notre Dame
Notre Dame, Indiana

SARA C. CHARLES, M.D.
Professor of Clinical Psychiatry
University of Illinois School of
Medicine at Chicago
Chicago, Illinois

KEVIN J. CHRISTIANO, PH.D.
Associate Professor of Sociology
University of Notre Dame
Notre Dame, Indiana

ANDREW D. CIFERNI,
O.PRAEM., PH.D.
Associate Professor of Liturgy
Washington Theological Union
Silver Spring, Maryland

FRANCIS X. CLOONEY, S.J.,
PH.D.
Associate Professor of Theology
Boston College
Chestnut Hill, Massachusetts

AELRED CODY, O.S.B., S.T.D.,
S.S.D.
Editor, *Catholic Biblical
Quarterly*
St. Meinrad Archabbey
St. Meinrad, Indiana

REGINA A. COLL, C.S.J., ED.D.
Director, Field Education
Department of Theology
University of Notre Dame
Notre Dame, Indiana

ADELA YARBRO COLLINS,
PH.D.
Professor of New Testament
University of Chicago
Chicago, Illinois

JOHN J. COLLINS, PH.D.
Professor of Hebrew Bible
University of Chicago
Chicago, Illinois

RAYMOND F. COLLINS, S.T.D.
Dean, School of Religious
Studies
The Catholic University of
America
Washington, D.C.

MARIE A. CONN, PH.D.
Assistant Professor of Religious
Studies
Chestnut Hill College
Philadelphia, Pennsylvania

MARTIN F. CONNELL, M.A.,
PH.D. CAND.
Department of Theology
University of Notre Dame
Notre Dame, Indiana

JAMES T. CONNELLY, C.S.C.,
PH.D.
Associate Professor of History
University of Portland
Portland, Oregon

MICHAEL L. COOK., S.J. TH.D.
Professor of Religious Studies
Gonzaga University
Spokane, Washington

M. SHAWN COPELAND, PH.D.
Associate Professor of Theology
Marquette University
Milwaukee, Wisconsin

JAMES A. CORIDEN, J.C.D., J.D.
Professor of Canon Law
Washington Theological Union
Silver Spring, Maryland

ANN HIRSCHMAN
COTTINGHAM, M.A.R., PH.D.
CAND.
Department of Theology
University of Notre Dame
Notre Dame, Indiana

STEVEN D. CRAIN, PH.D.
Adjunct Assistant Professor of
Theology
University of Notre Dame
Notre Dame, Indiana

PAUL G. CROWLEY, S.J., PH.D.
Assistant Professor of Religious
Studies
Santa Clara University
Santa Clara, California

LAWRENCE S. CUNNINGHAM,
PH.D.
Professor and Chair of Theology
University of Notre Dame
Notre Dame, Indiana

CHARLES E. CURRAN, S.T.D.
Elizabeth Scurlock Professor of
Human Values
Southern Methodist University
Dallas, Texas

ROBERT EMMETT CURRAN,
S.J., PH.D.
Associate Professor of History
Georgetown University
Washington, D.C.

FREDERICK J. CWIEKOWSKI,
S.S., S.T.D.
Professor of Systematic
Theology
St. Patrick's Seminary
Menlo Park, California

BRIAN E. DALEY, S.J., D.PHIL.
Associate Professor of Historical
Theology
Weston Jesuit School of
Theology
Cambridge, Massachusetts

NANCY A. DALLAVALLE, PH.D.
Assistant Professor of Religious
Studies
Fairfield University
Fairfield, Connecticut

CORNELIUS F. DELANEY, PH.D.
Professor of Philosophy
University of Notre Dame
Notre Dame, Indiana

ANGEL DELGADO-GOMEZ,
PH.D.
Associate Professor of Spanish
University of Notre Dame
Notre Dame, Indiana

TERRENCE E. DEMPSEY, S.J.,
PH.D.
Assistant Professor of Artistry
and Director, Museum of
Contemporary Religious Art
St. Louis University
St. Louis, Missouri

DANIEL DiDOMIZIO, S.T.D.
Professor of Religious Studies
Cardinal Stritch College
Milwaukee, Wisconsin

JOSEPH A. DI NOIA, O.P., PH.D.
Professor of Theology
Dominican House of Studies
Washington, D.C.

WILLIAM J. DOHAR, C.S.C.,
PH.D.
Associate Professor of History
University of Notre Dame
Notre Dame, Indiana

JAY P. DOLAN, PH.D.
Professor of History
University of Notre Dame
Notre Dame, Indiana

JOHN R. DONAHUE, S.J., PH.D.
Professor of New Testament
Jesuit School of Theology at
Berkeley/Graduate
Theological Union
Berkeley, California

MARY ANN DONOVAN, S.C.,
PH.D.
Professor of Historical Theology
Jesuit School of Theology at
Berkeley/Graduate
Theological Union
Berkeley, California

LEONARD DOOHAN, S.T.D.
Professor of Religious Studies
and Dean, Graduate School
Gonzaga University
Spokane, Washington

MARGARET DORGAN, D.C.M.,
A.B.
John of the Cross Monastery
Hermitage
Orland, Maine

ELIZABETH A. DREYER, PH.D.
Associate Professor of
Ecclesiastical History
Washington Theological Union
Silver Spring, Maryland

REGIS A. DUFFY, O.F.M., S.T.D.
Associate Professor of Theology
University of Notre Dame
Notre Dame, Indiana

CHRISTIAN Y. DUPONT, M.A.,
PH.D. CAND.
Department of Theology
University of Notre Dame
Notre Dame, Indiana

KEITH J. EGAN, PH.D.
Professor and Chair of Religious
Studies
Saint Mary's College
Notre Dame, Indiana

E. ROZANNE ELDER, PH.D.
Director, Institute of Cistercian
Studies
Western Michigan University
Kalamazoo, Michigan

VIRGILIO ELIZONDO, S.T.D.
Professor of Pastoral Theology
Mexican American Cultural
Center
San Antonio, Texas

MICHAEL E. ENGH, S.J., PH.D.
Associate Professor of History
Loyola Marymount University
Los Angeles, California

MARY EWENS, O.P., PH.D.
Executive Director, Conrad N.
Hilton Fund for Sisters
Los Angeles, California

MICHAEL B. FABRY, M.A., PH.D.
CAND.
Systematic and Philosophical
Theology
Graduate Theological Union
Berkeley, California

MICHAEL A. FAHEY, S.J.,
DR.THEOL.
Dean, Faculty of Theology
University of St. Michael's
College
Toronto, Ontario, Canada

JAMES W. FELT, S.J., PH.D.
Jesuit Community Professor of
Philosophy
Santa Clara University
Santa Clara, California

BARBARA A. FINAN, PH.D.
Associate Professor of Theology
Ohio Dominican College
Columbus, Ohio

MITCH FINLEY, M.A.
Author and Speaker
Spokane, Washington

EUGENE J. FISHER, PH.D.
Associate Director, Secretariat
for Ecumenical and
Interreligious Affairs
National Conference of Catholic
Bishops
Washington, D.C.

JOSEPH A. FITZMYER, S.J.,
PH.D.
Professor Emeritus of Biblical
Studies
The Catholic University of
America
Washington, D.C.

DARLENE K. FLAMING, M.DIV.,
PH.D. CAND.
Department of Theology
University of Notre Dame
Notre Dame, Indiana

PETER W. FLINT, PH.D.
Professor of Biblical Studies
Southwestern College
Phoenix, Arizona

GERALD P. FOGARTY, S.J.,
PH.D.
Professor of Religious Studies
and History
University of Virginia
Charlottesville, Virginia

J. MASSYNGBAERDE FORD, PH.D.
Professor of New Testament
University of Notre Dame
Notre Dame, Indiana

JOHN T. FORD, C.S.C., S.T.D.
Professor of Theology and
Associate Dean, School of
Religious Studies
The Catholic University of
America
Washington, D.C.

MARK R. FRANCIS, C.S.V.,
S.L.D.
Assistant Professor of Liturgy
Catholic Theological Union
Chicago, Illinois

RICHARD R. GAILLARDETZ,
PH.D.
Assistant Professor of
Systematic Theology
University of St. Thomas School
of Theology
Houston, Texas

CLARENCE GALLAGHER, S.J.,
J.C.D.
Professor of Oriental Canon Law
Pontifical Oriental Institute
Rome, Italy

MICHAEL O. GARVEY, B.A.
Assistant Director, Public
Relations and Information
University of Notre Dame
Notre Dame, Indiana

THOMAS W. GEDEON, S.J., B.A.
Executive Director, Retreats
International
Notre Dame, Indiana

PHILIP GLEASON, PH.D.
Professor of History
University of Notre Dame
Notre Dame, Indiana

GEORGE E. GRIENER, S.J., TH.D.
Assistant Professor of
Systematic Theology
Jesuit School of Theology at
Berkeley
Berkeley, California

COLLEEN M. GRIFFITH, TH.D.
Lecturer in Pastoral Theology
Boston College
Chestnut Hill, Massachusetts

DANIEL P. GRIGASSY, O.F.M., PH.D.
Assistant Professor of Word and
Worship
Washington Theological Union
Silver Spring, Maryland

THOMAS H. GROOME, ED.D.
Professor of Theology and
Religious Education
Institute of Religious Education
and Pastoral Ministry
Boston College
Chestnut Hill, Massachusetts

RICHARD M. GULA, S.S., PH.D.
Professor of Moral Theology
St. Patrick's Seminary
Menlo Park, California

ROGER HAIGHT, S.J., PH.D.
Professor of Systematic and
Historical Theology
Weston Jesuit School of
Theology
Cambridge, Massachusetts

RONALD P. HAMEL, PH.D.
Senior Associate
The Park Ridge Center
Chicago, Illinois

MICHAEL S. HAMILTON, M.A.
Coordinator, Pew Scholars
Program
University of Notre Dame
Notre Dame, Indiana

G. SIMON HARAK, S.J., PH.D.
Associate Professor of
Theological Ethics
Fairfield University
Fairfield, Connecticut

ROBERT F. HARVANEK, S.J., PH.D.
Professor Emeritus of
Philosophy
Loyola University of Chicago
Chicago, Illinois

ADRIAN HASTINGS, D.D.
Emeritus Professor of Theology
University of Leeds
Leeds, England

JOHN F. HAUGHT, PH.D.
Professor of Theology
Georgetown University
Washington, D.C.

JOHN C. HAWLEY, PH.D.
Associate Professor of English
Santa Clara University
Santa Clara, California

PETER HEBBLETHWAITE, M.A. (D. 1994)
Vatican Affairs Writer
National Catholic Reporter
Oxford, England

J. BRYAN HEHIR, TH.D.
Professor of the Practice in
Religion and Society
Harvard Divinity School
Cambridge, Massachusetts

JAMES HENNESEY, S.J., PH.D.
Rector, Jesuit Community
St. Peter's College
Jersey City, New Jersey

MARY CATHERINE HILKERT, O.P., PH.D.
Associate Professor of
Systematic Theology
Aquinas Institute of Theology
St. Louis, Missouri

KENNETH R. HIMES, O.F.M., PH.D.
Associate Professor of Moral
Theology
Washington Theological Union
Silver Spring, Maryland

MICHAEL J. HIMES, PH.D.
Associate Professor of Theology
Boston College
Chestnut Hill, Massachusetts

BRADFORD E. HINZE, PH.D.
Associate Professor of Theology
Marquette University
Milwaukee, Wisconsin

MARK D. HOLTZ, M.M.S., PH.D. CAND.
Medieval Institute
University of Notre Dame
Notre Dame, Indiana

FRANCIS J. HOUDEK, S.J., PH.D.
Assistant Professor of Historical
and Systematic Theology
Jesuit School of Theology at
Berkeley
Berkeley, California

JOHN W. HOUGHTON, PH.D.
Instructor of English
Mary Institute and St. Louis
Country Day School
St. Louis, Missouri

JOHN M. HUELS, O.S.M., J.C.D.
Associate Professor of Canon
Law
Catholic Theological Union
Chicago, Illinois

GERARD JACOBITZ, M.A., PH.D. CAND.
Department of Theology
University of Notre Dame
Notre Dame, Indiana

JOSEPH JENSEN, O.S.B., S.T.D.
Associate Professor, School of
Religious Studies and
Executive Secretary, Catholic
Biblical Association
The Catholic University of
America
Washington, D.C.

ELIZABETH A. JOHNSON, C.S.J., PH.D.
Professor of Systematic
Theology
Fordham University
Bronx, New York

KATHRYN L. JOHNSON, M.PHIL.
Assistant Professor of Historical
Theology
Louisville Presbyterian
Theological Seminary
Louisville, Kentucky

PHYLLIS H. KAMINSKI, PH.D.
Assistant Professor of Religious
Studies
Saint Mary's College
Notre Dame, Indiana

CHRISTOPHER J. KAUFFMAN, PH.D.
Catholic Daughters of the
Americas Professor of Church
History
The Catholic University of
America
Washington, D.C.

EILEEN F. KEARNEY, PH.D.
Associate Professor of the
History of Theology
Saint Xavier College
Chicago, Illinois

ANTHONY W. KEATY, M.A.,
PH.D. CAND.
Department of Theology
University of Notre Dame
Notre Dame, Indiana

THOMAS G. KELLIHER, JR.,
M.A., PH.D. CAND.
Department of History
University of Notre Dame
Notre Dame, Indiana

DAVID F. KELLY, PH.D.
Professor of Theology and
Health Care Ethics
Duquesne University
Pittsburgh, Pennsylvania

EUGENE C. KENNEDY, PH.D.
Professor of Psychology
Loyola University of Chicago
Chicago, Illinois

ROBERT P. KENNEDY, M.A.,
PH.D. CAND.
Department of Theology
University of Notre Dame
Notre Dame, Indiana

ROBERT T. KENNEDY, J.U.D.
Associate Professor of Canon
Law
The Catholic University of
America
Washington, D.C.

ROBERT A. KRIEG, C.S.C., PH.D.
Associate Professor of Theology
University of Notre Dame
Notre Dame, Indiana

DANIEL KROGER, O.F.M., PH.D.
Professor of Christian Ethics
Our Lady of Angels Seminary
Quezon City, Philippines

JOHN S. KSELMAN, S.S., PH.D.
Associate Professor of Old
Testament
Weston Jesuit School of
Theology
Cambridge, Massachusetts

HANS KÜNG, DR.THEOL.
Professor of Ecumenical
Theology and Director,
Ecumenical Institute
for Ecumenical Research
University of Tübingen
Tübingen, Germany

CATHERINE MOWRY LaCUGNA,
PH.D.
Professor of Theology
University of Notre Dame
Notre Dame, Indiana

ALICE L. LAFFEY, S.S.D.
Associate Professor of Old
Testament
College of the Holy Cross
Worcester, Massachusetts

JOHN F. LAHEY, C.S.C., J.C.D.
Assistant Professional Specialist
Department of Theology
University of Notre Dame
Notre Dame, Indiana

MATTHEW L. LAMB,
DR.THEOL.
Professor of Theology
Boston College
Chestnut Hill, Massachusetts

DERMOT A. LANE, S.T.D.
Lecturer in Confessional
Theology
Irish School of Ecumenics
Dublin, Ireland

JOHN P. LANGAN, S.J., PH.D.
Rose Kennedy Professor of
Christian Ethics
Kennedy Institute of Ethics
Georgetown University
Washington, D.C.

MICHAEL G. LAWLER, PH.D.
Professor of Theology
Creighton University
Omaha, Nebraska

DONAL P. LEADER, C.F.C.,
PH.D.
Academic Director, Marino
Institute of Education
Dublin, Ireland

JAMES LE GRYS, PH.D.
Managing Editor, The Thomist
Washington, D.C.

BLAKE LEYERLE, PH.D.
Assistant Professor of Early
Christian History
University of Notre Dame
Notre Dame, Indiana

ALISON LIDSTAD, M.A.
South Bend, Indiana

GERARD H. LUTTENBERGER,
C.M., S.T.D.
Professor of Systematic
Theology
Seminary of the Immaculate
Conception
Huntington, New York

GARY MACY, PH.D.
Professor of Religious Studies
University of San Diego
San Diego, California

EDWARD J. MALATESTA, S.J.,
S.S.D.
Director, Ricci Institute
University of San Francisco
San Francisco, California

ELENA MALITS, C.S.C., PH.D.
Professor of Religious Studies
Saint Mary's College
Notre Dame, Indiana

MARTIN E. MARTY, PH.D.
Professor of Religious History
The Divinity School, University
of Chicago
Chicago, Illinois

MARCHITA B. MAUCK, PH.D.
Professor of Art History
Louisiana State University
Baton Rouge, Louisiana

RICHARD P. McBRIEN, S.T.D.
Crowley-O'Brien-Walter
Professor of Theology
University of Notre Dame
Notre Dame, Indiana

RICHARD A. McCORMICK, S.J.,
S.T.D.
John A. O'Brien Professor of
Christian Ethics
University of Notre Dame
Notre Dame, Indiana

ELIZABETH McDONOUGH, O.P.,
J.C.D.
Canonical Consultant
Archdiocese of Washington
Washington, D.C.

ANNE C. McGUIRE, M.A., PH.D.
CAND.
Department of Theology
University of Notre Dame
Notre Dame, Indiana

MARY J. McKAY, C.S.J., PH.D.
Assistant Professor of Religious
Studies
Mount St. Mary's College
Los Angeles, California

ELIZABETH McKEOWN, PH.D.
Associate Professor of Theology
Georgetown University
Washington, D.C.

GERALD McKEVITT, S.J., PH.D.
Professor of History
Santa Clara University
Santa Clara, California

R. EMMET McLAUGHLIN, PH.D.
Associate Professor of Religious
Studies
Villanova University
Villanova, Pennsylvania

PATRICIA McNEAL, PH.D.
Director of Women's Studies
Indiana University at South
Bend
South Bend, Indiana

MARY JO MEADOW, S.F.C.C.,
PH.D.
Professor of Psychology and
Director of Religious Studies
Mankato State University
Mankato, Minnesota

JOHN ALLYN MELLOH, S.M.,
PH.D.
Director, John S. Marten
Program in Homiletics and
Liturgics
University of Notre Dame
Notre Dame, Indiana

MARK MILLER, C.SS.R, PH.D.
Director
Redemptorist Bioethic
Consultancy for Western
Canada
Edmonton, Alberta, Canada

VINCENT J. MILLER, M.A.,
PH.D. CAND.
Department of Theology
University of Notre Dame
Notre Dame, Indiana

GEORGE MINAMIKI, S.J., PH.D.
Associate Professor Emeritus of
Classical/Oriental Language
and Literature
University of Notre Dame
Notre Dame, Indiana

WILSON D. MISCAMBLE, C.S.C.,
PH.D.
Associate Professor and Chair of
History
University of Notre Dame
Notre Dame, Indiana

NATHAN D. MITCHELL
Associate Director of Research,
Center for Pastoral Liturgy
University of Notre Dame
Notre Dame, Indiana

SANDRA YOCUM MIZE, PH.D.
Assistant Professor of Religious
Studies
University of Dayton
Dayton, Ohio

DOMINIC V. MONTI, O.F.M.,
PH.D.
Associate Professor of
Ecclesiastical History
Washington Theological Union
Silver Spring, Maryland

CATHERINE M. MURPHY, M.A.,
PH.D. CAND.
Department of Theology
University of Notre Dame
Notre Dame, Indiana

JEROME MURPHY-O'CONNOR,
O.P., TH.D.
Professor of New Testament
École Biblique et Archéologique
Française
Jerusalem, Israel

SUSAN E. MYERS, M.A., PH.D.
CAND.
Department of Theology
University of Notre Dame
Notre Dame, Indiana

W. DAVID MYERS, PH.D.
Assistant Professor of History
Fordham University
Bronx, New York

JOHN J. NAVONE, S.J., TH.D.
Professor of Biblical Theology
Gregorian University
Rome, Italy

PAUL R. NELSON, PH.D.
Director for Worship
Evangelical Lutheran Church in
America
Chicago, Illinois

JEROME H. NEYREY, S.J., PH.D.
Professor of New Testament
University of Notre Dame
Notre Dame, Indiana

JON NILSON, PH.D.
Associate Professor of Theology
Loyola University of Chicago
Chicago, Illinois

LAWRENCE M. NJOROGE, PH.D.
Chair, Department of Education
Catholic University of Eastern
Africa
Karen, Nairobi, Kenya

DAVID J. O'BRIEN, PH.D.
Professor of History
College of the Holy Cross
Worcester, Massachusetts

STEPHEN J. OCHS, PH.D.
Chair, History Department
Georgetown Preparatory School
North Bethesda, Maryland

GERALD G. O'COLLINS, S.J.,
PH.D.
Professor of Fundamental
Theology
Gregorian University
Rome, Italy

KEVIN G. O'CONNELL, S.J.,
PH.D.
Provincial Offices
New England Province of the
Society of Jesus
Boston, Massachusetts

MARVIN R. O'CONNELL, PH.D.
Professor of History
University of Notre Dame
Notre Dame, Indiana

DAVID K. O'CONNOR, PH.D.
Associate Professor of
Philosophy
University of Notre Dame
Notre Dame, Indiana

MICHAEL E. O'KEEFFE, PH.D.
Assistant Professor of Religious
Studies
Mercyhurst College
Erie, Pennsylvania

JOHN W. O'MALLEY, S.J., PH.D.
Professor of Church History
Weston Jesuit School of
Theology
Cambridge, Massachusetts

THOMAS F. O'MEARA, O.P.,
PH.D.
William K. Warren Professor of
Theology
University of Notre Dame
Notre Dame, Indiana

MARY AQUIN O'NEILL, R.S.M.,
PH.D.
Director, Mount St. Agnes
Theological Center for
Women
Baltimore, Maryland

LADISLAS ORSY, S.J., D.C.L.
Professor Emeritus of Canon
Law
The Catholic University of
America
Washington, D.C.

KENAN B. OSBORNE, O.F.M.,
DR.THEOL.
Professor of Systematic
Theology
Franciscan School of Theology/
Graduate Theological Union
Berkeley, California

CAROLYN OSIEK, R.S.C.J., TH.D.
Professor of New Testament
Catholic Theological Union
Chicago, Illinois

JAMES M. O'TOOLE, PH.D.
Associate Professor of History
University of Massachusetts–
Boston
Boston, Massachusetts

RONALD A. PACHENCE, PH.D.
Professor of Religious Studies
University of San Diego
San Diego, California

KIM PAFFENROTH, M.T.S.,
PH.D. CAND.
Department of Theology
University of Notre Dame
Notre Dame, Indiana

ROBERT S. PELTON, C.S.C.,
S.T.D.
Faculty Fellow
Helen Kellog Institute for
International Studies
University of Notre Dame
Notre Dame, Indiana

PHEME PERKINS, PH.D.
Professor of Theology
Boston College
Chestnut Hill, Massachusetts

MICHAEL PHAYER, PH.D.
Professor of History
Marquette University
Milwaukee, Wisconsin

MARY ALICE PIIL, C.S.J., PH.D.
Professor of Liturgy
Seminary of the Immaculate
Conception
Huntington, New York

MICHAEL D. PLACE, S.T.D.
Research Theologian to the
Curia
Archdiocese of Chicago
Chicago, Illinois

FRANCES FORDE PLUDE, PH.D.
Associate Professor of
Communications
Notre Dame College of Ohio
South Euclid, Ohio

ERIC PLUMER, M.A. (OXFORD)
Teaching Fellow
University of Notre Dame
Notre Dame, Indiana

JANICE M. POORMAN, M.A.
Assistant Dean, Graduate School
University of Notre Dame
Notre Dame, Indiana

MARK L. POORMAN, C.S.C.,
PH.D.
Assistant Professor of Theology
University of Notre Dame
Notre Dame, Indiana

STEPHEN J. POPE, PH.D.
Associate Professor of Theology
Boston College
Chestnut Hill, Massachusetts

JEAN PORTER, PH.D.
Associate Professor of Christian
Ethics/Moral Theology
University of Notre Dame
Notre Dame, Indiana

HERMANN J. POTTMEYER,
DR.THEOL., LIC.PHIL.
Professor of Fundamental
Theology
Ruhr-Universität
Bochum, Germany

THOMAS J. POUNDSTONE,
M.A., PH.D. CAND.
Department of Theology
University of Notre Dame
Notre Dame, Indiana

F. CLARK POWER, ED.D.
Associate Professor, Program of
Liberal Studies
University of Notre Dame
Notre Dame, Indiana

WALTER H. PRINCIPE, C.S.B.,
M.S.D.
Professor Emeritus of Theology
Pontifical Institute of Mediaeval
Studies
University of Toronto
Toronto, Ontario, Canada

LOUISE PROCHASKA, S.N.D.,
PH.D.
Assistant Professor of Theology
Notre Dame College of Ohio
South Euclid, Ohio

JAMES H. PROVOST, J.C.D.
Professor of Canon Law
The Catholic University of
America
Washington, D.C.

JOHN F. QUINN, PH.D.
Assistant Professor of History
Salve Regina University
Newport, Rhode Island

MARGARET M. QUINN, C.S.J.,
PH.D.
Archivist, Congregation of
Sisters of St. Joseph
Brentwood, New York

KATHLEEN L. RILEY, PH.D.
Adjunct Assistant Professor of
History
Canisius College
Buffalo, New York

RONALD G. ROBERSON, C.S.P.,
S.E.O.D.
Formation Team
St. Paul's College
Washington, D.C.

JOHN R. SACHS, S.J.,
DR.THEOL.
Associate Professor of Theology
Weston Jesuit School of
Theology
Cambridge, Massachusetts

ANTHONY J. SALDARINI, PH.D.
Professor of New Testament and
Judaism
Boston College
Chestnut Hill, Massachusetts

T. HOWLAND SANKS, S.J.,
PH.D.
Professor of Theology
Jesuit School of Theology at
Berkeley
Berkeley, California

EDWARD B. SCHARFENBERGER,
J.C.L.
Judicial Vicar
Diocese of Brooklyn
Brooklyn, New York

DAVID L. SCHINDLER, PH.D.
Gagnon Professor of
Fundamental Theology
John Paul II Institute for Studies
on Marriage and Family
Washington, D.C.

GERALD W. SCHLABACH,
M.A.T.S., PH.D. CAND.
Department of Theology
University of Notre Dame
Notre Dame, Indiana

SANDRA M. SCHNEIDERS,
I.H.M., S.T.D.
Professor of New Testament
Studies and Christian
Spirituality
Jesuit School of Theology at
Berkeley/Graduate
Theological Union
Berkeley, California

ROBERT SCHREITER, C.PP.S.,
DR.THEOL.
Professor of Doctrinal Theology
Catholic Theological Union
Chicago, Illinois

BONAVENTURE SCULLY, C.F.X.,
M.S.
Adjunct Instructor, Freshman
Writing Program
University of Notre Dame
Notre Dame, Indiana

MARK SEARLE, DR.THEOL.
(D. 1992)
Associate Professor of Liturgical
Studies
University of Notre Dame
Notre Dame, Indiana

SOPHIA SENYK, O.S.B.M.,
S.E.O.D.
Professor of Church History
Pontifical Oriental Institute
Rome, Italy

ROBERT W. SHAFFERN, PH.D.
Visiting Assistant Professor of
History
University of Notre Dame
Notre Dame, Indiana

PHILIP F. SHELDRAKE, M.TH.
Lecturer in Church History
Cambridge Theological
Federation
Cambridge, England

ANTHONY F. SHERMAN
Adjunct Professor of Liturgy
Seminary of the Immaculate
Conception
Huntington, New York

MICHAEL A. SIGNER, PH.D.
Abrams Professor of Jewish
Thought and Culture
University of Notre Dame
Notre Dame, Indiana

CONSTANTINE SIMON, S.J.,
S.E.O.D.
Professor of Church History
Pontifical Oriental Institute
Rome, Italy

KEVIN J. SMANT, PH.D.
Adjunct Associate Professor of
History
Indiana University at South
Bend
South Bend, Indiana

JOANMARIE SMITH, C.S.J.,
PH.D.
Professor of Pastoral Theology
Methodist Theological School in
Ohio
Delaware, Ohio

RALPH F. SMITH, PH.D.
(D. 1994)
Associate Professor of Liturgics
Wartburg Theological Seminary
Dubuque, Iowa

THOMAS A. SMITH, PH.D.
Associate Professor of Historical
Theology
Loyola University
New Orleans, Louisiana

MARINA B. SMYTH, PH.D.
Librarian, Medieval Institute
University of Notre Dame
Notre Dame, Indiana

GRAYDON F. SNYDER, TH.D.
Professor of New Testament
Chicago Theological Seminary
Chicago, Illinois

THOMAS W. SPALDING, C.F.X.,
PH.D.
Professor of History
Spalding University
Louisville, Kentucky

J. MICHAEL STEBBINS, PH.D.
Senior Fellow
Woodstock Theological Center
Georgetown University
Washington, D.C.

GREGORY E. STERLING, PH.D.
Assistant Professor of New
Testament and Christian
Origins
University of Notre Dame
Notre Dame, Indiana

WILLIAM R. STOEGER, S.J.,
PH.D.
Staff Astrophysicist
Vatican Observatory Research
Group
Steward Observatory
University of Arizona
Tucson, Arizona

THOMAS F. STRANSKY, C.S.P.
Rector, Ecumenical Institute for
Theological Studies (Tantur)
Jerusalem, Israel

JOHN J. STRYNKOWSKI, S.T.D.
Professor of Systematic
Theology
Seminary of the Immaculate
Conception
Huntington, New York

SUSAN M. ST. VILLE, M.A.,
PH.D. CAND.
Assistant Professor of Religion
St. Lawrence University
Canton, New York

FRANCIS A. SULLIVAN, S.J.,
S.T.D.
Professor Emeritus of Theology
Gregorian University
Rome, Italy
and Adjunct Professor of
Ecclesiology
Boston College
Chestnut Hill, Massachusetts

ANNE MARIE SWEET, O.S.B.,
PH.D.
Mount St. Scholastica Convent
Atchison, Kansas

JAMES H. SWETNAM, S.J.,
D.PHIL.
Professor of New Testament
Greek
Pontifical Biblical Institute
Rome, Italy

ROBERT F. TAFT, S.J., S.E.O.D.
Professor of Oriental Liturgy
Pontifical Oriental Institute
Rome, Italy

CAROL A. TAUER, PH.D.
Professor of Philosophy
College of St. Catherine
St. Paul, Minnesota

GEORGE H. TAVARD, A.A.,
S.T.D.
Distinguished Professor of
Theology
Marquette University
Milwaukee, Wisconsin

JEAN M. ROGER TILLARD, O.P.,
TH.D.
Professor of Dogmatic Theology
Dominican Faculty of Theology
Ottawa, Ontario, Canada

MARY KATHERINE TILLMAN,
PH.D.
Associate Professor, Program of
Liberal Studies
University of Notre Dame
Notre Dame, Indiana

THOMAS H. TOBIN, S.J., PH.D.
Associate Professor of Theology
Loyola University of Chicago
Chicago, Illinois

KERN R. TREMBATH, PH.D.
Assistant Chairman,
Department of Theology
University of Notre Dame
Notre Dame, Indiana

ROBERT F. TRISCO, S.T.D.,
HIST.ECCL.D.
Professor of Church History and
American History
The Catholic University of
America
Washington, D.C.

EUGENE ULRICH, PH.D.
Professor of Hebrew Scriptures
University of Notre Dame
Notre Dame, Indiana

JAMES C. VANDERKAM, PH.D.
Professor of Hebrew Scriptures
University of Notre Dame
Notre Dame, Indiana

JEFFREY T. VANDERWILT, M.A.,
PH.D. CAND.
Department of Theology
University of Notre Dame
Notre Dame, Indiana

JACINTA VAN WINKEL, M.A.
Associate Professor of Theology
Carlow College
Pittsburgh, Pennsylvania

JAIME R. VIDAL, PH.D.
Associate Professor of Hispanic
Ministry
Pontifical College Josephinum
Columbus, Ohio

PATRICIA MARY VINJE, O.C.V.,
PH.D.
Milwaukee, Wisconsin

BENEDICT VIVIANO, O.P.,
PH.D.
Professor of New Testament
École Biblique et Archéologique
Française
Jerusalem, Israel

JAMES K. VOISS, S.J., S.T.L.,
PH.D. CAND.
Department of Theology
University of Notre Dame
Notre Dame, Indiana

ANNE M. VOLK., M.DIV.
Assistant, Sex Offense Services
South Bend, Indiana

CHRYSOGONUS WADDEL,
O.C.S.O., S.TH.L.
Professor of Liturgy, Monastic
History, and Medieval
Spirituality
Our Lady of Gethsemani Abbey
Trappist, Kentucky

MICHAEL WALDSTEIN, PH.D.,
TH.D.
Assistant Professor of New
Testament
Program of Liberal Studies
University of Notre Dame
Notre Dame, Indiana

LINDA WALL, M.DIV.
Pastoral Minister
Christ Church Newman Center
St. Cloud State University
St. Cloud, Minnesota

JAMES J. WALTER, PH.D.
Professor of Christian Ethics
Loyola University of Chicago
Chicago, Illinois

JOSEPH P. WAWRYKOW, PH.D.
Associate Professor of History of
Christianity
University of Notre Dame
Notre Dame, Indiana

JOHN F. WELCH, O.CARM.,
PH.D.
Professor of Spirituality
Washington Theological Union
Silver Spring, Maryland

JOHN P. WELLE, PH.D.
Associate Professor of Italian
University of Notre Dame
Notre Dame, Indiana

JANET M. WELSH, O.P., M.A.,
PH.D. CAND.
Department of History
University of Notre Dame
Notre Dame, Indiana

JAMES F. WHITE, PH.D.
Professor of Liturgical Studies
University of Notre Dame
Notre Dame, Indiana

JOSEPH M. WHITE
Research Associate
POLIS Research Center
Indiana University–Purdue
University
Indianapolis, Indiana

TODD DAVID WHITMORE,
PH.D.
Assistant Professor of Social
Ethics
University of Notre Dame
Notre Dame, Indiana

CORINNE WINTER, M.A., PH.D.
CAND.
Assistant Professor of Theology
St. Ambrose University
Davenport, Iowa

JAMES A. WISEMAN, O.S.B.,
S.T.D.
Associate Professor of Theology
The Catholic University of
America
Washington, D.C.

PAUL J. WOJDA, PH.D.
Assistant Professor of Theology
University of St. Thomas
St. Paul, Minnesota

SUSAN K. WOOD, S.C.L., PH.D.
Associate Professor of Theology
Saint John's University
Collegeville, Minnesota

MICHAEL S. WOODWARD,
PH.D.
Professor of History
University of Northern Colorado
Greeley, Colorado

LAWRENCE G. WRENN, J.C.D.
  Judicial Vicar
  Court of Appeals, Province of
    Hartford
  Hartford, Connecticut

JOHN H. WRIGHT, S.J., S.T.D.
  Professor Emeritus of
    Systematic Theology
  Jesuit School of Theology at
    Berkeley
  Berkeley, California

JOHN H. YODER, DR.THEOL.
  Professor of Theology
  University of Notre Dame
  Notre Dame, Indiana

KATHERINE TEPAS YOHE,
PH.D.
  Assistant Professor of Theology
  LaSalle University
  Philadelphia, Pennsylvania

RANDALL C. ZACHMAN, PH.D.
  Assistant Professor of
    Reformation Studies
  University of Notre Dame
  Notre Dame, Indiana

FOREWORD

The Catholic Church and the religious tradition it embodies have been twenty centuries in the making. Today we stand on the threshold not only of a new century but of a new millennium. It is particularly fitting, therefore, that this extraordinary compendium of Catholic belief and practice should be published at this time.

The *HarperCollins Encyclopedia of Catholicism* will afford the many thousands who consult it a splendid opportunity to grasp the full sweep of Catholic life and history: its doctrines and theologies, its religious orders and spiritualities, its liturgies and devotions, its sacraments and creeds, its councils and synods, its literature and art, its music and sculpture, its sacred objects and sacred texts, its rules and regulations, its heresies and schisms, its saints and sinners, its good popes and bad.

One is struck by the enormous sweep of the encyclopedia's content. There are feature articles on major doctrinal and moral issues such as the papacy and grace, abortion and social justice. There are entries on celebrated and obscure saints alike: Augustine of Hippo and Thomas Aquinas, as well as Abbo of Fleury and John Leonardi; Catherine of Siena and Teresa of Ávila, as well as Anastasia and Maria Mazzarello. There seems to be an endless stream of short articles on items many of us older Catholics, with deep roots in the pre–Vatican II period, will have long forgotten about: custody of the eyes, the maniple, interdict, *Liber Usualis,* and spiritual bouquet, to name only a few. This is a veritable treasury of facts and information. The most assiduous student of Catholicism, inside and outside the Church, will be hard-pressed to name a relevant topic, large or small, that hasn't been included in this book.

I am impressed, however, not only by the encyclopedia's comprehensiveness, but also by its clarity and balance. Definitions are to the point. Descriptions are always pertinent and informative. Explanations are presented objectively, without the intrusion of the author's own opinions or preferences. While the encyclopedia is not slavishly literal when it comes to the Church's official teachings, it takes care to present those teachings in their fullness and, where relevant, to summarize the theological discussions that have so often swirled around those teachings. Although the many hundreds of articles are written by people who are experts in their fields, the presentations are accessible to the average reader, which is most of us. No one, not even a scholar who has been a lifelong Catholic, knows everything there is to know about Catholicism. We all have something to learn or to discover anew. This volume, then, is for everyone, and the editors and the publishers have done well remembering that vast audience for whom it has been written.

Although an encyclopedia of Catholicism, the book is ecumenical in the range of topics it treats, the manner in which its addresses them, and the authors it has selected to write them. I am especially impressed that two of my good friends in the ecumenical world have contributed major articles: George L. Carey, the Archbishop of Canterbury, has written a particularly illuminating piece on Anglicanism, and Martin E. Marty, of the University of Chicago, has produced a wonderfully instructive and fair-minded entry on Protestantism. But other Anglicans and Protestants have also contributed to the book, and so has Rabbi Michael Signer, the Abrams Professor of Jewish Thought and Culture at the University of Notre Dame.

Which raises one final point. I am particularly proud of the fact that so much of the creative thought and scholarly energy that went into this remarkable volume have their source right here at Notre Dame. The general editor, Father Richard McBrien, and the great majority of the associate editors are members of the Notre Dame faculty. Even the few associate editors who are not currently on the Notre Dame faculty once were. Many of the contributors of individual articles are also associated with Notre Dame in one way or another. It is fitting, in my judgment, that the University of Notre Dame should have played so prominent a role in the production of this encyclopedia. Few institutions around the world are so closely identified with Catholicism, and few institutions have so great a responsibility to accurately reflect and effectively communicate the riches of that tradition to a broader public. This book does that very well indeed.

I would be remiss if I did not conclude, on behalf of all who will profit spiritually and intellectually from this encyclopedia, with a word of sincere thanks to the General Editor, Father Richard McBrien. Without his inspiration, his planning, and his long days and nights of writing, rewriting, and editing over a span of years, this wonderful gift to all of us would never have seen the light of day. Scholarship is a lonely task, but good scholarship in a work of high quality and great need is a gift beyond all calculation. But then, as John Henry Cardinal Newman said, "Calculation never made a hero." Richard McBrien, in producing this unique encyclopedia, is indeed a rare hero.

THEODORE M. HESBURGH, C.S.C.
President Emeritus
University of Notre Dame

INTRODUCTION

T he purpose of this encyclopedia is to provide a convenient and reliable source of information regarding every aspect of Catholicism, past and present, in clear, accessible prose for the widest possible audience. That purpose may seem, at first glance, too ambitious, but readers will find in this volume some 4,200 carefully edited, alphabetically arranged entries of varying lengths, totaling more than 800,000 words, written by 280 experts covering a vast range of topics in Catholic theology, doctrine, biblical scholarship, history, culture, ministries, governing structures, worship, sacramental life, spirituality, art, architecture, literature, and canon law. Some individual entries are illustrated and the volume itself is enhanced by color and black-and-white photographs, maps, tables, charts, and drawings. The encyclopedia is intended for nonspecialists, including scholars in one field who are nonspecialists in others: teachers and students at all levels, clergy, religious, lay ministers, seminarians, journalists, those in such professions as law and medicine, as well as the general public, Catholic and non-Catholic alike.

In preparing such a resource, we have tried as far as possible to avoid technical language. Where we could not do so, we have taken care to define terms and to explain references with which general readers might not be familiar. When foreign words are used, the language is identified and translated, and, where appropriate, a pronunciation is provided.

We have also tried to make each entry self-sufficient. Throughout the volume we have employed the principle of "one-stop shopping." Readers are usually not required to consult four or five other entries just to understand all the key terms and references in the entry initially consulted. The purpose of the many cross-references, therefore, is only to assist readers who want to have a fuller description and explanation of related topics.

SCOPE

The encyclopedia focuses on a subject that is at once particular and universal. It is particular in that Catholicism refers to a specific religious tradition, a specific religious community, and a specific way of life. But Catholicism is also universal, as the literal meaning of the word suggests. It is in principle open to all reality: to every truth, every value, every culture, every human experience.

Insofar as Catholicism is a particular tradition, community, and way of life, the encyclopedia defines and describes topics that are associated with Catholicism exclusively or at least primarily. Thus, there are entries on religious orders such as the Jesuits, Benedictines, Franciscans, Dominicans, and Carmelites; on popes such as Damasus I, Leo the Great, Gregory VII, Pius XII, John XXIII, and John Paul II; on theological and doctrinal topics such as apostolic succession, papal primacy, infallibility, the seven sacraments, the Immaculate Conception; on saints such as Francis of Assisi, Catherine of Siena, Thomas Aquinas, Elizabeth Ann Bayley Seton, Ignatius of Loyola, and Thérèse of Lisieux; on literature such as *Introduction to the Devout Life, Imitation of Christ, Ascent of Mount Carmel, Rule of St. Benedict,* and *Spiritual Exercises;* on devotions such as the Rosary, Stations of the Cross, Benediction, and holy hour; on ecumenical councils such as Nicaea, Trent, Vatican I, and Vatican II; on organizations such as Christian Family Movement, Catholic Theological Society of America, Opus Dei, and the National Conference of Catholic Bishops; on structures such as the College of Cardinals, the Roman Curia, and the World Synod of Bishops; on institutions such as the University of Notre Dame, Georgetown University, St. Patrick's Cathedral, and the Abbey of Our Lady of Gethsemani; on Marian topics such as the virgin birth, Mediatrix, apparitions, the Assumption, and Mariology; and on Eastern Catholicism's rites, churches, liturgies, canon law, and people.

But insofar as Catholicism is a catholic reality—both universal and inclusive—it is open to, and draws from, the spiritual riches of Orthodox, Anglican, Protestant, Oriental, Jewish, Muslim, Buddhist, and other religious traditions. Accordingly, the encyclopedia has entries on Martin Luther, John Calvin, Ulrich Zwingli, Menno Simons, Sergius of Radonezh, Photius, Thomas Cranmer, Moses Maimonides, the Koran, and the ecumenical movement. There are separate entries, for example, on Protestantism, written by Martin E. Marty, and on Anglicanism, written by the Archbishop of Canterbury, George L. Carey. There are entries as well on art, science, music, and literature: on Michelangelo, Raphael, Dante Alighieri, Leonardo da Vinci, Wolfgang Amadeus Mozart, Czeslaw Milosz, Flannery O'Connor, Evelyn Waugh, and Graham Greene. And there are entries on Catholicism throughout the world: in particular countries, in particular regions, and on particular continents—all with appropriate statistical information.

RANGE OF THE ARTICLES

Readers will find entries that discuss major topics in greater depth, that provide accurate and useful biographical information on a wide assortment of persons, living and dead, and that offer precise information regarding the myriad of details that constitute the nature and function of Catholicism. Thus, in the "A's" alone there are lengthier entries on abortion, Catholicism in Africa, Americanism, Anointing of the Sick, Apostles' Creed, Assumption of the Blessed Virgin Mary, Catholicism in Australia, and authority. There are biographical entries on Peter Abelard,

Lord John Acton, Karl Adam, St. Agatha, St. Agnes, St. Margaret Mary Alacoque, St. Albertus Magnus, Pope Alexander VI, St. Aloysius Gonzaga, St. Alphonsus Liguori, St. Ambrose of Milan, St. Angela Merici, St. Athanasius, and St. Augustine of Hippo. And there are more pointed identifications and explanations of such items as abbey nullius, abstinence, acolyte, *ad limina* visit, affective prayer, *akolouthia*, altar society, ambo, amice, anaphora, anathema, angel, annulment, apostasy, apostolic delegate, archimandrite, asperges, and auxiliary bishop. But these are only samples. There are nearly 350 separate entries under "A" alone.

The diversity and variable lengths of the many entries suggest that the volume, although self-described as an encyclopedia, combines the advantages of both an encyclopedia and a dictionary.

FORMAT: ENTRIES, ILLUSTRATIONS, AND TABLES

Each entry has the same basic structure. The entry title is followed by a fragment of a sentence that defines the topic or that indicates what is most important or most central to it. When the entry is biographical, the person's years of birth and death are given first. In a few instances where experts differ, we have allowed inconsistencies to stand, as a reminder that our knowledge of the ancient and medieval world remains imperfect. If the person is a saint, the feast day is given at the end of the entry. When there is need for assistance with pronunciation, the name or item is also spelled phonetically. If it involves a foreign word or words, the etymology is given: the language is identified and the word or words are translated. Just as the encyclopedia employs a "one-stop shopping" approach in each entry, so it presumes nothing in the case of language and terms employed. Cross-references are provided at the end of most entries, and subheads within the entry and brief bibliographies at the end are provided for longer entries. In summary, the encyclopedia always tries to put readers first. Everything is designed to make this resource as easy as possible to use and to understand and as attractive as possible to the eye.

For that reason, the volume is also amply illustrated. There are color and black-and-white photographs and drawings of major monuments, persons, events, and objects. Since Jesus Christ is at the heart and center of the Catholic and Christian faith, he is the one most fully featured in the color photographs. And since his mother, the Blessed Virgin Mary, is also so important a part of Catholic faith, devotion, art, statuary, and music, she, too, is featured in classic and contemporary forms alongside the other great saints of the Catholic tradition.

In addition, there is a time line to assist readers in placing persons and events in the wider context of Church and secular history. Tables accompany various entries to provide both supplementary information and convenient reference points. Thus, the entry on angels has a table listing and describing the nine different categories of celestial beings. The entry on ecumenical council lists all twenty-one councils and provides thumbnail sketches of their proceedings. The very brief entry on pope is followed by an extensive and detailed table that does more than simply list, telephone-directory style, all two hundred and sixty-two popes with the years in which they occupied the Chair of Peter. The list of popes is one of the many unique features of this encyclopedia. The name of each pope is accompanied by a brief sketch of the most important accomplishments of his pontificate or some other form of identification to distinguish him from the many others who have filled the same office. Where there are apparent discrepancies in the numbering of various popes (for example, should it be Pope Felix II or Pope Felix III?), the discrepancies are explained. There is also a list of antipopes under the antipope entry. There is a list of the social encyclicals of the popes under the entry "encyclicals, social"; a complete listing of the Church's liturgical calendar for Sundays and feasts alike under the entry "liturgical calendar"; a listing of patron saints and saints associated with special needs under the entry "saints, patron"; and a detailed, annotated listing of every congregation, tribunal, office, and department of the Roman Curia under the entry of the same name. Entries on hymns, prayers, and creeds are often accompanied by the full or partial text of each.

STYLE

Gender-inclusive language has been employed throughout. We believe that its appropriateness no longer requires explanation or defense. Readers will notice that sometimes the adjective "Roman" modifies the noun "Catholic," and many other times it does not. This is because not all Catholics are Roman Catholic. There are millions of Catholics in various Eastern-rite traditions who are also in communion with the Bishop of Rome and are an integral part of that particular communion of churches known as the Catholic Church. When the reference is limited to Catholics of the Roman or Latin rite, it will read "Roman Catholic." When the reference is to the whole Catholic communion of churches or to the worldwide Catholic community, it will read simply "Catholic." And all this is said without prejudice to the desire of many Orthodox, Oriental, Anglican, and Protestant Christians to embrace the name "Catholic" for themselves as well. "Catholic" is by its very nature an inclusive, not exclusive, term. Although the references in this encyclopedia have the Catholic Church, that is, the communion of churches in union with the Bishop of Rome, in mind, we explicitly embrace those other Christians who wish to be included as well, particularly because so much of the material in this volume is historically antecedent to the East-West Schism with roots in the mutual excommunications of 1054 and to the Reformation within the Western Church in the sixteenth century.

The designations B.C. (before Christ) and A.D. (*anno Domino*, Lat., "in the year of the Lord") are used in this encyclopedia rather than B.C.E. (before the common era) and C.E. (of the common era) because B.C. and A.D. are still the most widely recognized way of identifying historical dates. We do not thereby depreciate the arguments of those who employ the newer designations on the ground that they display greater sensitivity to the ecumenical and interfaith character of the religious and secular communities today.

Finally, the New Revised Standard Version (NRSV) of the Bible is employed, in almost every instance, throughout the encyclopedia, not only for consistency's sake but also because of the NRSV's standing in both the scholarly and ecclesiastical communities. This newest of translations has been approved for liturgical use in the United States, Canada, and other English-speaking countries.

EDITORS AND CONTRIBUTORS

The 280 contributors and 17 associate editors of this volume represent a wide range of specializations, interests, and experiences on the academic, professional, and pastoral spectra and also a wide range of religious affiliations on the ecumenical and interfaith spectra. Our contributors are Roman Catholic, Eastern-rite Catholic, Anglican, Protestant, and Jewish. Their entries have been submitted from countries all around the globe: Kenya, Italy, France, Germany, England, Ireland, Australia, Canada, Israel, the Philippines, as well as the United States.

The contributors and editors were chosen not only because of their own scholarly and pastoral expertise but also because of their ability to translate their scholarship into accessible language and concepts for the sake of nonspecialist readers. Many of them have already established themselves as scholars of national and international stature, having published numerous books and articles over the years. Others are younger scholars and professionals, some in their early years of teaching and research; others are still at the stage of doctoral studies; and others are in various nonacademic positions, pastoral and professional alike. The contributors also span the attitudinal spectrum. Ideology does not inform the individual entries. Each contributor was specifically charged with the task of being informative, clear, and objective. Personal views and opinions were to be excluded; editorializing was to have no place in the entries; and scholarly debates were to be avoided. Official and theologically mainstream positions were to be preferred. As far as possible, that mandate has been honored by the contributors, the editors, and the publisher alike. This encyclopedia, therefore, has no point of view other than its central, underlying conviction that the multifaceted reality of Catholicism deserves to be examined and explained accurately, fairly, and comprehensively. We believe the encyclopedia has succeeded in that regard.

THE NOTRE DAME CONNECTION

Although this encyclopedia is not the production of the University of Notre Dame, even casual readers will not fail to notice a very strong connection between the volume, its editors, and its contributors, and the university itself. The general editor and thirteen of the associate editors are currently affiliated with Notre Dame. Indeed, twelve of the thirteen are members of the university's department of theology, one the current chair and another the former chair. Of the four other associate editors, three were members of the Notre Dame faculty at the time the encyclopedia was conceived, planned, and launched, and the fourth continues to serve on a regular basis as a visiting faculty member. Given the status of the University of Notre Dame as perhaps the best-known Catholic university in the world and given our own proud identification with it, we believe that the Notre Dame connection enhances the credibility of this volume as a compendium of information regarding the Catholic Church, past and present. On the other hand, we wish to make it clear that the University of Notre Dame has provided no official sponsorship to this project beyond the fact that so many of its editors and contributors are members of the Notre Dame faculty and staff. We are honored, of course, by the contributions of so many Catholic scholars and experts from other Catholic colleges, universities, and seminaries, as well as by the contributions of non-Catholics, Christian and non-Christian alike.

ACKNOWLEDGMENTS

There remains only the traditionally agreeable task of expressing appreciation to those who, beyond the contributors and editors, have made this encyclopedia possible. Without the inspiration, support, and editorial guidance of those at HarperCollins in San Francisco, there would be no *HarperCollins Encyclopedia of Catholicism*. We are indebted to many, to be sure, but if any are to be singled out, then surely that list must include John Shopp, our senior editor, who assumed the major editorial and supervisory responsibility on behalf of the publisher, and Steven Anderson, assistant editor, who managed the long and laborious copy-editing process from beginning to end. I should also like to pay a special word of tribute to Janice Johnson, a former executive editor at Harper-Collins, who, along with John Shopp, first proposed this project to its eventual general editor in the fall of 1989. On the Notre Dame side of the operation, two names stand out beyond those of the editors themselves. The general editor's secretary, Donna Shearer, managed the project from the outset through correspondence, telephone calls, filing, and various forms of record-keeping—all integrated in a highly sophisticated computerized system, which she alone came to understand and master. Her contribution was at once invaluable and irreplaceable. And the President Emeritus of the University of Notre Dame, Theodore M. Hesburgh, C.S.C., contributed the Foreword. It was through his inspiration and leadership that Notre Dame became the kind of university it is today, and it is his own personal embodiment of the ideals of Catholicism that has set a high standard for all others, inside and outside that community.

We trust that the final product more than amply justifies all the labor and energy that went into this volume since its original conception over five years ago.

RICHARD P. McBRIEN
General Editor

ABBREVIATIONS

OT	Old Testament	Arab.	Arabic
NT	New Testament	Aram.	Aramaic
NRSV	New Revised Standard Version	Arm.	Armenian
RSV	Revised Standard Version	Fr.	French
KJV	King James Version	Ger.	German
NIV	New International Version	Gk.	Greek
St.	Saint	Heb.	Hebrew
Bl.	Blessed	It.	Italian
ch(s).	chapter(s)	Lat.	Latin
v(v).	verse(s)	Old Eng.	Old English
n(n).	note(s), number(s)	Old Fr.	Old French
can(s).	canon(s)	Pol.	Polish
D	Denzinger, *Enchiridion Symbolorum*	Port.	Portuguese
DS	Denzinger-Schoenmetzer, *Enchiridion Symbolorum*	Russ.	Russian
ca.	circa	Sp.	Spanish
		Slav.	Slavic
		Syr.	Syriac

The following abbreviations are used for the books of the Bible:

OLD TESTAMENT

Gen	Genesis	Sir	Sirach (Ecclesiasticus)
Exod	Exodus	Isa, Dt-Isa, Tr-Isa	Isaiah, Deutero-Isaiah, Trito-Isaiah
Lev	Leviticus	Jer	Jeremiah
Num	Numbers	Lam	Lamentations
Deut	Deuteronomy	Bar	Baruch
Josh	Joshua	Let Jer	Letter of Jeremiah
Judg	Judges	Ezek	Ezekiel
Ruth	Ruth	Dan	Daniel
1-2 Sam	1-2 Samuel	Pr Azar	Prayer of Azariah
1-2 Kgs	1-2 Kings	Sus	Susanna
1-2 Chr	1-2 Chronicles	Bel	Bel and the Dragon
Ezra	Ezra	Hos	Hosea
Neh	Nehemiah	Joel	Joel
Tob	Tobit	Amos	Amos
Jdt	Judith	Obad	Obadiah
Esth, Add Esth	Esther, Additions to Esther	Jonah	Jonah
1-2 Macc	1-2 Maccabees	Mic	Micah
Job	Job	Nah	Nahum
Ps(s)	Psalm(s)	Hab	Habakkuk
Prov	Proverbs	Zeph	Zephaniah
Eccl	Ecclesiastes	Hag	Haggai
Song	Song of Solomon	Zech, Dt-Zech	Zechariah, Deutero-Zechariah
Wis	Wisdom of Solomon	Mal	Malachi

NEW TESTAMENT

Matt	Matthew	1-2 Thess	1-2 Thessalonians
Mark	Mark	1-2 Tim	1-2 Timothy
Luke	Luke	Titus	Titus
John	John	Phlm	Philemon
Acts	Acts of the Apostles	Heb	Hebrews
Rom	Romans	Jas	James
1-2 Cor	1-2 Corinthians	1-2 Pet	1-2 Peter
Gal	Galatians	1-2-3 John	1-2-3 John
Eph	Ephesians	Jude	Jude
Phil	Philippians	Rev	Revelation (Apocalypse)
Col	Colossians		

PRONUNCIATION KEY

SYMBOL	SOUND	SYMBOL	SOUND
a	cat	ng	sing
ah	father	o	hot
ahr	lard	oh	go
air	care	oi	boy
aw	jaw	oo	foot
ay	pay	*oo*	boot
b	bug	oor	poor
ch	chew	or	for
d	do	ou	how
e, eh	pet	p	pat
ee	seem	r	run
f	fun	s	so
g	good	sh	sure
h	hot	t	toe
hw	whether	th	thin
i	it	*th*	then
i̱	sky	ts	tsetse
ihr	ear	tw	twin
j	joke	uh	ago
k	king	uhr	her
kh	ch as in German *Buch*	v	vow
ks	vex	w	weather
kw	quill	y	young
l	love	z	zone
m	mat	zh	vision
n	not		

TIME LINE

Catholic and Secular Persons, Events, and Developments

TIME LINE *Catholic and Secular Persons, Events, and Developments*

CATHOLICISM

1–100		100
Death and Resurrection of Jesus Christ (ca. 33)	Pope Clement I (ca. 91–ca. 101)	Irenaeus (ca. 130–ca. 200)
	Primacy of Rome recognized (end of century)	Pope Victor I (189–98)
Paul's three missionary journeys (ca. 46–ca. 58)		*Didache* (uncertain date)
"Council" of Jerusalem (ca. 49)		Gnosticism (into 3d century), Adoptionism, Docetism (into 3d century), Montanism
Local persecutions of Christians: emperors Nero (ca. 64), Domitian (ca. 81–ca. 96), Trajan (ca. 98–117)		Development of synods (local and provincial)
Peter and Paul martyred in Rome (ca. 64)		
Destruction of the Temple (70)		
The Four Gospels (ca. 70–end of century)		

WORLD HISTORY

1–100	100
Roman emperors: Tiberius (14–37), Caligula (37–41), Claudius (41–54), Nero (54–68), Domitian (ca. 81–ca. 96)	Roman emperors: Trajan (ca. 98–117), Antoninus Pius (138–61), Marcus Aurelius (161–80), Septimus Severus (193–211)

Origen (ca. 185–ca. 254)

Decian (249–51) and Valerian (257–58) persecutions

Anthony of Egypt (ca. 251–356): beginnings of eremetical life

Pope Stephen I (254–57)

Cyprian of Carthage (d. ca. 258)

Period of toleration under Roman emperors (258–ca. 300)

Manichaeism (into 4th century)

Pachomius (ca. 290–ca. 347): beginnings of cenobitic life/monasticism

Athanasius (ca. 296–373)

Diocletian persecution (303–13)

Edict of Constantine (313)

Arianism

Council of Nicaea I (325)

St. Peter's Basilica constructed (ca. 330)

Ambrose (ca. 339–97): conversion of Augustine (387)

Cappadocians: Gregory of Nazianzus (329–90), Basil (ca. 330–79), Gregory of Nyssa (ca. 330–ca. 395)

Jerome (ca. 342–420): the Vulgate

Pope Damasus I (366–84)

Apollinarianism

Council of Constantinople I (381): Nicene-Constantinopolitan Creed

Donatism

Roman emperors: Decius (249–51), Gallus (251–53), Valerian (253–60), Gallienus (260–68), Diocletian (284–305)

Partition of Roman Empire into West and East (285)

Constantine the Great (306–37): sole emperor

Seat of Roman Empire moved to Constantinople (331)

Empire splits again into West and East (340)

Barbarian migrations begin (ca. 375–ca. 568)

Theodosius the Great (392–95): last ruler of united empire

CATHOLICISM

400   **500**

Pelagianism

Augustine of Hippo (354–430)

Patrick (ca. 390–ca. 461): mission to Ireland (ca. 431)

Pope Innocent I (401–17)

Augustine's *City of God* (412)

Nestorianism

Council of Ephesus (431)

Pope Leo the Great (440–61)

Monophysitism

Council of Chalcedon (451)

Acacian Schism (482–519)

Pope Gelasius I (492–96)

Benedict of Nursia (ca. 480–ca. 547)

Monte Cassino founded (ca. 525)

Church of Santa (Hagia) Sophia, Constantinople, consecrated (538)

Council of Constantinople II (553)

Isidore of Seville (ca. 560–636)

Pope Gregory the Great (590–604)

Augustine of Canterbury (d. ca. 605): mission to Britain (596)

WORLD HISTORY

400   **500**

Barbarian migrations continue

Visigoths invade Italy (401)

Alaric captures and sacks Rome (410)

Vandals sack Rome (455)

End of Western Roman emperors (476)

Theodoric founds Ostrogoth kingdom of Italy (493)

Clovis, king of the Franks, converts to Christianity (496)

Justinian the Great (527–65)

Rome and Naples annexed to Byzantium (553)

Lombards drive Byzantines from northern Italy (565)

CATHOLICISM

900   **1000**

Monastery of Cluny founded (909)

Hungary is Christianized (ca. 942)

Monastery on Mount Athos founded (962)

Poland is Christianized (966)

Pope Benedict VII (974–83)

Prince Vladimir of Kiev introduces Christianity into Russia (ca. 988)

First formal canonization (993)

Peter Damian (1007–72)

Camaldolese founded (ca. 1012)

Anselm of Canterbury (1033–1109)

Pope Leo IX (1049–54)

Monasticism established in Russia (ca. 1051)

East-West Schism (1054)

Pope Nicholas II (1058–61)

Pope Gregory VII (1073–85)

Dictatus Papae (1075)

Carthusians founded (1084)

First Crusade (1096–1099)

Cistercians founded (1098)

WORLD HISTORY

900   **1000**

Arabs expelled from central Italy (916)

Otto I crowned Holy Roman emperor by Pope John XII (962)

Otto II crowned Holy Roman emperor by Pope John XIII (967)

Otto III crowned Holy Roman emperor by Pope Gregory V (996)

Muslims sack the Church of the Holy Sepulchre in Jerusalem (1009)

Battle of Hastings (1066)

Henry IV excommunicated by Pope Gregory VII (1076)

Henry IV is absolved by the pope at Canossa (1077)

Henry IV again deposed and excommunicated (1080)

Henry IV storms Rome, imprisons the pope (1084)

Crusaders capture Jerusalem (1099)

Bernard of Clairvaux
(1090–1153)

Peter Abelard (1079–1142)

Thomas Becket (ca. 1118–70)

Premonstratensians
(Norbertines) founded (1120)

Lateran Council I (1123)

Pope Innocent II (1130–43)

Lateran Council II (1139)

Decree of Gratian (ca. 1140)

Second Crusade (1146–48)

Carmelite order founded (ca.
1154)

Pope Alexander III (1159–81)

Lateran Council III (1179)

Notre Dame Cathedral, Paris,
consecrated (1182)

Third Crusade (1189–92)

Scholasticism (12th and 13th
centuries)

Albigensianism (late 12th century until end of 14th century)

Dominic de Guzman
(1170–1221)

Francis of Assisi (1181/2–1226)

Alexander of Hales (ca.
1186–1245)

Pope Innocent III (1198–1216)

Albertus Magnus (ca.
1200–1280)

Fourth–Seventh Crusades
(1202–54)

Franciscan order founded (1209)

Dominican order founded (1215)

Lateran Council IV (1215)

Bonaventure (ca. 1217–74)

Henry V crowned Holy Roman
emperor by Pope Paschal II
(1111)

Lothar III crowned Holy Roman
emperor by Pope Innocent II
(1133)

Frederick Barbarossa crowned
Holy Roman emperor by Pope
Hadrian IV (1155)

Thomas Becket murdered in
Canterbury Cathedral (1170)

Crusaders capture
Constantinople, establish Latin
empire (1204)

Pope Innocent III places England
under interdict (1208)

England and Ireland become
papal fiefs (1213)

Magna Carta (1215)

Marco Polo to China (1271–95)

Crusades formally end (1291)

CATHOLICISM

1200	1300	1400
(continued)	Pope Celestine V (1294)	Joan of Arc (1412–31)
Thomas Aquinas (ca. 1225–74)	Pope Boniface VIII (1294–1303)	Council of Constance (1414–18)
Pope Gregory IX (1227–41)	Growth of mysticism	Pope Martin V (1417–31)
Papal Inquisition established (1233)	*Unam Sanctam* (1302)	Council of Basel-Ferrara-Florence-Rome (1431–45)
Council of Lyons I (1245)	Avignon papacy (1309–77)	Pope Pius II (1458–64)
Augustinian Hermits founded (1256)	Council of Vienne (1311–12)	Erasmus (ca. 1469–1536)
Chartres Cathedral consecrated (1260)	Pope Benedict XII (1334–42)	Spanish Inquisition established (1479)
Meister Eckhart (ca. 1260–1327)	Catherine of Siena (1347–80)	Pope Alexander VI (1492–1503)
Duns Scotus (ca. 1265–1308)	Great Western Schism (1378–1417)	
Dante Alighieri (1265–1321)		
Council of Lyons II (1274)		

WORLD HISTORY

1300	1400
Hundred Years War begins (1337)	Henry V defeats the French at Agincourt (1415)
Black Death in Europe (1347–49)	Louvain University founded (1425)
Byzantines lose last possession in Asia Minor to Turks (1390)	Constantine XI Palaeologus, last Byzantine emperor (1448–53)
	Fall of Constantinople to the Turks (1453)
	End of Hundred Years War (1453)
	Gutenberg Bible (1456)
	Lorenzo de' Medici rules Florence (1469–92)
	Moorish kingdom ends in Spain (1492)

1500

Thomas More (1478–1535)

Ignatius of Loyola (1491–1556)

Pope Julius II (1503–13)

Francis Xavier (1506–52): missions to India (1542–45, 1548–49) and Japan (1549)

Lateran Council V (1512–17)

Pope Leo X (1513–21)

Teresa of Ávila (1515–82)

Reformation begins (1517)

Peter Canisius (1521–97)

Pope Hadrian VI (1522–23)

English Reformation begins (1534)

Society of Jesus (Jesuits) founded (1534)

Pope Paul III (1534–49)

John of the Cross (1542–91)

Robert Bellarmine (1542–1621)

Council of Trent (1545–63)

Jesuit mission to Japan (1548)

Francisco de Suárez (1548–1617)

Index of Forbidden Books established (1557)

Pope Pius V (1566–72)

Francis de Sales (1567–1622)

Jesuit mission in China (1582)

1500

Christopher Columbus discovers America (1492)

Pope Alexander VI divides New World between Spain and Portugal (1493)

Explorers: Vasco da Gama (1469–1524), Ferdinand Magellan, (1480–1521), Francis Drake (1540–96)

Michelangelo (1475–1564)

Copernican theory (1512)

Sack of Rome by imperial troops; Pope Clement VII imprisoned (1527)

Thomas More executed (1535)

Mary succeeds Edward VI (1553)

Elizabeth I succeeds Mary (1558)

Roman catacombs discovered (1578)

Gregorian calendar adopted (1582)

Defeat of the Spanish Armada (1588)

CATHOLICISM

1500   **1600**

(continued)

Pope Sixtus V (1585–90)   Vincent de Paul (ca. 1580–1660)   Pope Innocent XI (1676–89)

Vatican Library opens (1588)   Bernini (1598–1680)   Gallicanism (1682–1789)

Union of Brest (1596)   Baroque Catholicism
                                 (ca. 1600–ca. 1750)

                                 John Eudes (1601–80)

                                 Jean Jacques Olier (1608–57)

                                 Blaise Pascal (1623–62)

                                 St. Peter's Basilica, Rome, conse-
                                 crated (1626)

                                 Jacques Bossuet (1627–1704)

                                 Jansenism (ca. 1640–ca. 1800)

                                 Chinese rites controversy (1645)

                                 Trappist order founded (1664)

WORLD HISTORY

1600

Jesuit missionary Matteo Ricci
admitted to Peking (1601)

Queen Elizabeth I dies (1603)

First African slaves brought to
North America (1619)

Peter Minuit buys island of
Manhattan for $24 (1626)

Galileo imprisoned (1633)

Harvard College founded (1636)

Isaac Newton (1642–1727)

Peace of Westphalia (1648)

1700 | **1800**

Baroque Catholicism continues (1700–ca. 1750)

Pope Clement XI (1700–21)

Pope Benedict XIV (1740–58)

Jesuits suppressed (1773)

John Carroll, first bishop consecrated in U.S. (1790)

Catholic Romanticism

Johann Adam Möhler (1796–1838)

Pope Pius VII (1800–23)

John Henry Newman (1801–90)

Catholic Emancipation Act, England (1829)

University of Notre Dame founded (1842)

Pope Pius IX (1846–78)

Dogma of the Immaculate Conception (1854)

Syllabus of Errors (1864)

Vatican Council I (1869–70)

Loss of the Papal States (1870)

Pope Leo XIII (1878–1903)

Vatican archives opened to scholars (1881)

Rerum Novarum (1891)

Condemnation of Americanism (1899)

Missionary renewal

1700 | **1800**

Boston Tea Party (1773)

Declaration of Independence (1776)

U.S. Constitution (1788)

George Washington, first U.S. president (1789–97)

French Revolution (1789)

Rosetta Stone found in Egypt (1799)

Thomas Jefferson, U.S. president (1801–1809)

Louisiana Purchase (1803)

Napoleon crowned king of Italy (1805), annexes Papal States (1809), is defeated at Waterloo (1815)

Charles Darwin (1809–82)

Karl Marx (1818–83)

Communist Manifesto (1848)

Italy proclaimed a kingdom (1861)

American Civil War (1861–65)

U.S. Emancipation Proclamation (1863)

Dominion of Canada established (1867)

Kulturkampf in Prussia (1871)

CATHOLICISM

1900

Modernism

Dorothy Day (1897–1980)

Pope Pius X (1903–14)

Karl Rahner (1904–84)

Oath against Modernism (1907)

Pope Benedict XV (1914–22)

Thomas Merton (1915–68)

Code of Canon Law (1917)

Oscar Arnulfo Romero (1917–80)

Pope Pius XI (1922–39)

Lateran Treaty (1929)

Pope Pius XII (1939–58)

Dogma of the Assumption (1950)

Pope John XXIII (1958–63)

Vatican Council II (1962–65)

Pope Paul VI (1963–78)

Humanae Vitae (1968)

Pope John Paul I (1978)

Pope John Paul II (1978–)

Revised Code of Canon Law (1983)

Catechism of the Catholic Church (1992)

WORLD HISTORY

1900

Sigmund Freud (1856–1939)

Commonwealth of Australia established (1901)

New Zealand attains Dominion status (1907)

First World War (1914–18)

Russian Revolution (1917)

Irish Free State established (1922)

Franklin D. Roosevelt elected U.S. president (1932)

Adolf Hitler, German chancellor (1933)

Spanish Civil War (1936–39)

Second World War (1939–45)

United Nations charter (1945)

Cold War (1945–89)

Republic of Ireland established (1949)

John F. Kennedy assassinated (1963)

Vietnam War (1965–73)

Communism collapses (1989)

Aaron, high priest and ancestor of all legitimate priests according to Israelite tradition. He was the elder brother of Moses (Exod 6:20; 7:7). Aaron assisted Moses in his mission to Pharaoh, the Exodus from Egypt, and during the wandering in the wilderness. That not all the references to Aaron are favorable (e.g., his role in the golden calf incident, Exod 32–34) reflects the struggles within priestly families resulting in the eventual ascendancy of the Aaronite branch. In Heb 5:1–10 Aaron is the type, or foreshadowing, of Jesus as high priest of the new dispensation. *See also* priesthood.

Benedictine abbey in Ettal, Bavaria, Germany.

Abba (ah'buh; Aram., "father"), title used to address God, often used in a familiar sense, as in "my father." Such intimate language for addressing God characterized the prayers of Jesus and his followers. The Aramaic term is explicitly attributed to Jesus in the account of his prayer at Gethsemane in Mark 14:36. It may underlie Jesus' address to God now preserved in Greek, e.g., in the Lord's Prayer in Matt 6:9 and Luke 11:2 or the prayer of John 17:1. The Aramaic word was certainly used in the prayers of early Christians, to which Paul refers in Rom 8:15 and Gal 4:6.

abbé (Fr., "father"), abbot or superior of a monastery of men. In the sixth century, the term was applied in France to every person who wore the dress of a secular ecclesiastic. During the following centuries, the use of *abbé* was further extended to clerics engaged as professors or tutors, even if they were not ordained. *See also* monastery.

abbess, superior of a group of twelve or more nuns. A term originally used only for Benedictines, it is the feminine form of "abbot" and is an elected office. During the feudal period, abbesses exercised temporal, spiritual, and quasiepiscopal power. They were usually of noble rank and sat in parliaments and councils, recognizing no authority under the pope. At times they governed double monasteries of both monks and nuns. *See also* abbey; abbot; double monasteries; nun.

abbey, autonomous monastery of at least twelve religious, governed by an abbot or abbess. Benedict of Nursia founded the first abbey at Monte Cassino near Rome in the sixth century. By 1415, there were over fifteen thousand abbeys following his rule. Abbeys were usually established on arable land because they were intended to be self-sufficient centers of prayer, productivity, and communal harmony.

Abbeys were also centers of culture, learning, and social progress. Monks established schools, copied and illuminated manuscripts, improved farming methods, and organized early cooperative farming. They developed the first hospitals in the West because of their care of the sick on pilgrimage. *See also* monastery.

abbey nullius, an abbey that has territory exempt from the jurisdiction of the local bishop; it is the equivalent of a diocese. The abbot fulfills the responsibilities of the bishop within the territory. Since 1976 there were to be no new such abbeys established; "territorial" abbeys, a similar entity, are allowed in the 1983 code of canon law. *See also* abbey; abbot nullius; diocese.

Abbo of Fleury, St., ca. 945–1004, abbot of Fleury (Saint-Benoît-sur-Loire), writer, canonist, and monastic reformer. Having entered Fleury as a child, Abbo studied in Paris, Reims, and Orléans, taught in England at Ramsey, and helped Oswald, archbishop of York, to introduce into England the reforms of the monastery of Cluny. After returning to France in 988, he was elected abbot of Fleury. As abbot, he served as a mediator between the king and the pope, also promoting monastic independence from secular and episcopal control. His writings cover a number of subjects, including the relationship of papal and royal power, the history of the popes, lives of the Desert Fathers, logic, grammar, and *computus* (calendrical science). He was killed in a revolt in 1004 while implementing reforms at the abbey of La Réole. Feast day: November 13. *See also* Fleury.

abbot (Aram., *abba*, "father"), the leader of a male

monastic community. The abbot is considered a supreme moderator of his religious institute in canon law. He is given a special blessing at his installation. *See also* monastery; monasticism.

abbot nullius, the leader of an abbey nullius (a territory not under the jurisdiction of the local bishop). The abbot nullius is not only, as an abbot, the ordinary (local authority) of the religious for whom he is responsible, but he is also the ordinary for laypersons living within his jurisdiction. *See also* abbey nullius.

abbot primate, the leader of the Benedictine order. The position is one that carries with it more moral authority than of power of governance because each Benedictine monastery is virtually independent of the other monasteries and, on most matters, immediately subject to the Holy See. *See also* Benedictine order.

abbuna (ah-boon'ah; Arab., "our father"), common Arabic title for a priest, adopted also in Ethiopia (*abun*) for metropolitans and eminent ecclesiastics.

abdication, an earlier term for the renunciation of ecclesiastical office, used when the prevailing model of office was monarchical. The current term is "resignation," and its use in canon law indicates movement away from such a model. *See also* resignation.

abduction, impediment of, the canonical prohibition of the retention of a woman against her will for the purpose of eliciting matrimonial consent. Canon law (can. 1089) establishes this action as invalidating a marriage because the consent of the woman is not freely given. The use of the term "rape" for the impediment of abduction is now outdated. *See also* marriage law.

Abelard, Peter, 1079–1142, French theologian and logician. Born at Le Pallet outside of Nantes in Brittany, Abelard initially intended to pursue a career as a teacher of logic. He studied with the foremost dialecticians of his day: first with the nominalist Roscelin of Compiègne at Loches and later with the Neoplatonist philosopher William of Champeaux in Paris. Abelard's insightful critique of William's philosophical realism brought him fame and students. He taught logic at Melun, Corbeil, Paris, and Mont-Sainte-Geneviève. While teaching, he began publishing commentaries on Aristotle's logical writings.

Abelard's significance as a teacher and twelfth-century intellectual extends beyond his influence on the development of logical theory. His interest in applying methods of dialectical inquiry to Christian doctrine, especially the Trinity, marked a turning point in his life. In ca. 1112 he studied with Anselm of Laon, the most celebrated theologian of the early twelfth century. Dissatisfied with Anselm's methods, Abelard returned to Paris determined to bring systematic and critical inquiry to influence biblical exegesis and the development of doctrine. Henceforth, Abelard was dedicated to teaching both theology and logic.

Another event significantly affected Abelard's life and thought. While teaching at Notre Dame in Paris, Abelard met Heloise, the niece of Fulbert, canon of the cathedral of Notre Dame. He became her tutor, friend, and lover. Héloïse bore a son, Astralabe, and although she and Peter married, Fulbert ordered that Abelard be castrated. In 1118, both Héloïse and Abelard entered cloistered religious life. Abelard's narrative, *The Story of My Misfortunes,* records their tragic story. For over eight hundred years, this text has provided generations with a powerful and enduring paradigm of star-crossed lovers.

While in residence at the Royal Abbey of St.-Denis (1118–22), Abelard designed the ways in which scientific methods of inquiry and textual analysis could be applied to sacred literature. He composed *Sic et Non,* a text that, in its prologue, explicitly sets forth guidelines and principles for interpreting difficult or contradictory teachings. He also wrote his first theological treatise on the Trinity, the *Theologia Summi Boni (A Theology of the Highest Good).* Though the work was condemned at the Council of Soissons (1121), Abelard revised it during the next twenty years, republishing it first as the *Theologia Christiana (Christian Theology),* and finally as the *Theologia Scholarium (Theology of the Scholars).*

Despite numerous setbacks, the last decade or so of Abelard's life was especially creative, including a brief period as abbot of St. Guildas, an unruly community near Vannes in Brittany. During the 1130s he wrote prolifically and founded an order of nuns at the Paraclete, the land and oratory along the banks of the Ardusson near Quincy in Troyes. Abelard composed numerous works for them: a treatise on the origin of nuns (Letter 7), a rule of life (Letter 8), a collection of sermons, and one of hymns. He taught them how to read Scripture, urged them to study its languages (Letter 9), resolved a series of questions concerning problematic biblical passages (*Problemata Heloissae*), and brought his own skill to bear upon the difficult Hexaemeron, the Genesis account of the creation of the universe in six days. At about the same time, Abelard composed a brilliant, literal commentary on Paul's Letter to the Romans, wrote an ethical treatise known as the *Scito Teipsum (Know Thyself)*, and wrote a *Dialogue of a Philosopher with a Jew and with a Christian*.

Abelard's insistence upon the primacy of dialectic for theological reflection continued to threaten others, and in 1140 his teaching was again the subject of conciliar condemnation, at Sens. Abelard intended to appeal his case to the pope but ill health forced him to abandon the journey to Rome. Befriended by Peter the Venerable, he retired first to Cluny and then to a smaller priory at St. Marcel-sur-Saone, where he died. *See also* Héloïse; Paraclete, the; Scholasticism; Trinity, doctrine of the. *EILEEN KEARNEY*

abjuration, the formal denial of beliefs contrary to the official teaching of the Catholic Church previously held by non-Catholic Christians before they are received into the Catholic Church. Mandated by the 1917 code of canon law, it is no longer required.

ablution, a ritual of purification or cleansing. Ritual cleansings with water or blood are viewed in many religious traditions as means of purifying persons or objects. In the Roman tradition, the baptismal bath and the *Asperges* rite of sprinkling holy water on the congregation at the beginning of Mass were associated with a cleansing from sin. Ablutions were also found at the Offertory and Post-Communion in the Mass.

The term "ablution" is no longer used in reformed rites. However, ritual gestures of washing are found at both the Preparation of Gifts and Post-Communion in the Order of Mass. *See also* asperges; holy water.

abomination of desolation, or "desolating sacrilege," the desecration of the Jerusalem Temple by pagan ruler Antiochus IV Epiphanes in 167 B.C. (Dan 9:27; 11:31; 12:11; 1 Macc 1:54). In Mark 13:14 and Matt 24:15 Jesus utters the phrase, most likely as a prophecy after the fact (Lat., *vaticinium ex eventu*), in reference either to the attempt of the Roman emperor Caligula to erect his statue in the Temple (A.D. 40) or to the destruction of the Temple by the Roman general Titus in A.D. 70.

abortion, termination of pregnancy at a gestational age or by a method that ordinarily precludes survival of the embryo or fetus.

Historical Background: Catholic Church teaching on abortion has its roots in two disparate sources: the Hebrew tradition and Jewish law as expressed in the Torah, the first five books of the Bible, and classical Greek philosophy, particularly the metaphysics and anthropology of Aristotle.

The Hebrew tradition places heavy weight on one verse of the Torah, Exod 21:22, that is the only Scriptural text explicitly dealing with abortion in Jewish law. (In the text the Hebrew word is *yasa*, "to go out," and it is consistently translated as "miscarriage," not "abortion.") This text prescribes the penalty to be imposed if, as a result of a fight, a pregnant woman is injured and suffers a miscarriage. The assailant must pay damages (i.e., "fined what the woman's husband demands") for causing the death of the fetus. This penalty is differentiated from the penalty for causing the death of the woman herself, which is a capital crime requiring "life for life" (21:23).

Hebrew scholars have consistently interpreted this text to mean that the fetus is not a full human being as the mother is. Jewish teaching requires a high degree of respect for the potential life of the fetus, but does not regard it as fully human until birth.

The Septuagint (Greek) translation of Exodus (third century B.C.) presents a different version of the situation described in Exod 21:22. The text distinguishes between a formed and an unformed fetus. If the assailant causes the death of an unformed fetus, he must pay a fine. But if the fetus has already taken bodily form, then he is guilty of a capital crime.

The Septuagint translators may have been influenced by Greek philosophy, particularly that of Aristotle. According to Aristotle's philosophy of natural beings, hylomorphism, the soul is the life principle that animates the body. A soul can animate only the sort of body that is appropriate to that soul. Thus a plant is animated by a vegetative soul, an animal by a sensitive soul, and a human body by a rational human soul. In applying this theory to human fetal development, Aristotle concluded that a human fetus could acquire a human soul (that is, be a true human being) only when it had developed human bodily form. Referring to evidence from observation of aborted fetuses, Aristotle set this time at forty days after conception for a male and ninety for a female.

The Jewish tradition of respect for prenatal human life, and the Aristotelian theory of delayed animation of the human fetus, formed the backdrop for Christian views on abortion. However, even in the earliest years of the Christian tradition, abortion at any gestational age was regarded as a grave sin. Documents of the first and early second centuries, for example, the *Didache* and the *Letter of Barnabas,* categorically prohibited abortion. Athenagoras (second century) stated that those who use abortifacients are as guilty before God as those who commit homicide. Early Christian writers made their points strongly to distinguish Christian morality from that of the dominant Roman culture.

By the third and fourth centuries, however, there was speculation and debate among Christian scholars as to the time at which the fetus achieves human status. Latin Church Fathers Jerome (d. 420) and Augustine (d. 430) both taught that abortion is not homicide until the "scattered elements" are formed into a body. Basil (d. 379), a Greek Church Father, criticized the "fine distinction" between formed and unformed fetuses as malicious, and described all who procure abortion as murderers. The weight given to the Septuagint translation of Exodus, and the assessment of Aristotle's theory of delayed animation, influenced the course of such debates up to the nineteenth century.

The Significance of Ensoulment: In the early Christian centuries, several theories of the origin of the human soul were propounded. Among these was creationism, which held that each human soul was created out of nothing by God and infused into the developing human embryo at an appropriate time.

By the twelfth century, the creationist view had gained the ascendancy. When Gratian codified canon law (ca. 1140), he explicitly adopted creationism and also stated that the soul is not infused until the fetus is formed. From that time until 1869, Catholic canon law distinguished between the unensouled and ensouled fetus in assessing the gravity of abortion. The penalty for procuring the abortion of an ensouled fetus was excommunication. Up until 1869 no canonical penalty was imposed for abortion of an unensouled fetus, though early abortion was still considered to be a serious sin, just as contraception was.

Aristotle's hylomorphic theory was explicitly in-

corporated into the theological writings of Thomas Aquinas (d. 1274). In his monumental *Summa Theologiae,* Aquinas reiterated Aristotle's description of successive souls, first vegetative, then sensitive, then rational, which informed the developing embryo and fetus. The theology and philosophy of Thomas Aquinas have been given official sanction by the Catholic Church, including papal approbation. However, on the matter of the succession of souls animating the human fetus, Catholic authorities today regard Aquinas's views as erroneous.

Catholic teaching continues to maintain the doctrine of the special creation of the human soul by God. In its authoritative teaching, it leans to the view that the soul is infused into the zygote at the time of conception. Removal of the canonical distinction between unensouled and ensouled fetuses in 1869 was related to the clarification at that time of the biological process of fertilization. The new knowledge seemed to give support to acceptance of immediate ensoulment at fertilization.

In its *Declaration on Abortion* (1974), the Sacred Congregation for the Doctrine of the Faith asserts that the fertilized egg "would never be made human if it were not human already." However, the congregation also notes the continuing debate on the time of ensoulment, and, in a footnote, recognizes that Catholic authors are still in disagreement on this point.

The Catholic Church does not have an authoritative position on the time of ensoulment that must be held by all Catholics. Rather, while allowing and even encouraging debate on this metaphysical point, the Church asserts a moral position it regards as unquestionable: even though we are not certain when the soul is infused, hence when a human being truly exists, it is gravely sinful even to risk committing murder. Hence it is seriously wrong to terminate the life of a human zygote, blastocyst, embryo, or fetus.

Conflicts with the Mother's Welfare: While the early Christian tradition made some distinction between the formed and the unformed fetus, abortion was sinful in either case. The first deviation from this view, given a situation of danger to the mother, was enunciated in the early fourteenth century. The Dominican theologian John of Naples argued that it would be permissible to abort an unformed or unanimated fetus to save the life of the mother. Since the unanimated fetus was not yet a human being, it was acceptable to sacrifice it in order to save a fully human life. The noted Jesuit theologian Thomas

Sanchez (d. 1610) discussed the matter in detail, supporting John of Naples's position with two main arguments: Since the same procedure kills the fetus and saves the mother, it is permissible if the intended effect is to save the mother. Furthermore, in this situation the fetus can be considered an aggressor against the life of the mother, and thus self-defense justifies taking its life.

Therapeutic abortion to save the life of the mother was not officially condemned by the Catholic Church until the latter half of the nineteenth century. In response to several specific questions directed to it, the Holy Office condemned craniotomy of the fetus to save the mother's life, and later condemned any direct attack on the life of the fetus.

These condemnations have been reiterated by popes in the twentieth century. Pope Pius XI in his encyclical on marriage (*Casti Connubi*, 1930) stated that no reason can excuse the direct killing of the innocent, and that self-defense could not be invoked since the fetus was not an unjust aggressor. After Vatican Council II (1962–65) described abortion as an "unspeakable crime," Pope Paul VI (in the encyclical that sustained the Church's prohibition of artificial contraception) asserted that "directly willed and procured abortion, even if for therapeutic reasons, [is] to be absolutely excluded as licit" (*Humanae Vitae*, 1968).

Two apparent exceptions to this absolute prohibition have been approved. These exceptions have been allowed on grounds that the abortion in question is not a direct attack on the fetus, but an indirect and unintended effect of a legitimate medical procedure. Thus the conditions of the double effect principle are satisfied, and the procedure is morally permissible.

The two exceptions are these: If a pregnant woman suffers from uterine cancer, the diseased uterus may be removed even though the surgery places the fetus into an environment where it cannot survive. The death of the fetus is an indirect and unintended effect of surgery to remove a diseased organ, the uterus. In the second case, ectopic pregnancy, surgery prior to viability of the fetus was condemned by the Holy Office in 1902. Later, however, the Jesuit theologian T. L. Bouscaren wrote convincingly (in 1933) that the tube or organ in which the fetus was lodged could be considered pathological. Thus its removal, even with the fetus inside, could be defended on the same basis as the removal of a cancerous uterus. The Church has adopted Bouscaren's position, but in its official documents it has never approved removal of the fetus from within the tube because that would be viewed as a direct abortion.

Alternate Approaches to Conflict Situations: Within mainstream contemporary Catholic theology, several alternate approaches to conflict situations have been proposed. One group of theologians suggests that the approved exceptions to the prohibition of abortion simply express the basic Christian conviction that abortion is wrong except when it is necessary to save a life. Holding to the essence of this conviction is more important than invoking the distinction between direct and indirect intentions. This position has been enunciated publicly even by members of the Catholic hierarchy, including the Belgian bishops in 1973. The statement of Bishop Josef Stimpfle of Augsburg is typical: "He who performs an abortion, except to save the life of the mother, sins gravely."

A second alternate approach retains the principle of double effect but applies it differently. For example, the American moral philosopher German Grisez argues that in case of threat to the mother's life, it is not the death of the fetus but its removal from her body that saves her. One can remove the fetus without intending its death, and hence, according to this interpretation, abortion to save the mother's life is justifiable.

A third approach to conflict situations suggests that we use the same criteria regarding abortion dilemmas that we use in other situations where the Catholic Church justifies the deliberate taking of human life. One comparison involves the concept of aggressor. In dealing with an adult aggressor, one may defend oneself even though the aggressor is not responsible or blameworthy, say if the aggressor were mentally ill or severely retarded. One does not have to submit to an aggressor merely because he or she is incapable of bearing responsibility for his or her actions. Hence, one should not have to submit to the presence of a fetal aggressor who is physically causing one grave harm.

More complex comparisons involve the reasoning used by the Church to justify going to war and killing members of the enemy forces. While a country must have serious reasons for entering into combat, these reasons may include defense of territory or property, defense of basic human rights, and defense of national self-determination. Surrender to the enemy may avert loss of life, but a nation is not morally required to give up all interests other than life itself. Analogously, it could be argued that the pregnant woman's interest in physical or mental health, not simply in life itself, could justify causing the death of a human who is a serious threat to her well-being.

Alternate Views of the Status of the Fetus: Just as Catholic theologians, both historical and contemporary, suggest alternate approaches to conflict situations, so they also present a range of views regarding the ontological status of the embryo and fetus. As noted earlier, speculation as to the time at which the prenatal human becomes a full human being (i.e., is ensouled) extends back at least to Jerome and Augustine.

In contemporary Catholic theology, the predominant view is that ensoulment takes place at conception. This view supports the authoritative moral teaching that human life may not be destroyed at any time after fertilization. Biological information on the reproductive process indicates that the union of egg and sperm marks the beginning of a new human life, genetically distinct from either of its parents, and genetically unique (apart from twinning). The fact that this life has an internal principle that guides its self-development indicates that its soul (life principle) must be present from the beginning. Proponents of this view argue that the human embryo would not have the potential to develop through higher stages to rationality if it did not already possess a rational soul to direct this development.

A growing number of Catholic theologians, however, maintain that it is unlikely that a full human being is present before approximately fourteen days' gestational age. They recognize that biology provides a complex body of data, not easily interpretable in metaphysical terms, and that a careful look at these data supports delayed rather than immediate ensoulment. The biological facts cited are: (1) Up until about fourteen days, twinning of the embryo is possible, and at least through the morola stage, several embryos may aggregate ("recombine") to form one embryo. Thus we do not have an individuated human organism at this stage. An entity open to twinning and recombination cannot have a human soul because souls neither split, fuse, nor expire. (2) Before the process of differentiation begins, the entity has a cellular form of life, where each cell has equal potential to develop into any tissue or organ of the fetus, or more likely, not to become part of the fetus at all. Only through differentiation does the cellular mass come to exhibit the characteristics of a unified human organism. (3) Between fertilization and the completion of implantation, a large

proportion of embryos, generally estimated at over fifty percent, are discarded naturally. Jesuit theologian Karl Rahner (d. 1984) asks whether it is reasonable to maintain that over half of all human beings live and die without anyone's knowing of their existence.

The view that ensoulment occurs only after fourteen days' gestation is expanded by other authors, who argue for later ensoulment on the basis of arguments like these: The hylomorphic theory of Aristotle and Thomas Aquinas, approved by the Church, holds that the soul is the life-principle of a body suited to it. A rational or human soul can be infused only into a body that has reached an appropriate level of development. The characteristic of rationality requires some sort of brain structure, since reason operates through the organ of the brain in humans. Authors making this argument differ as to what level of brain structure would be required for the soul to be present.

Such metaphysical opinions do not contradict authoritative Catholic teaching, as noted in the Vatican *Declaration on Abortion*. It is, however, contrary to Catholic moral teaching to destroy the embryo at any time after fertilization, because one then assumes the risk of killing a possible human being.

Catholic Teaching and Abortion Legislation: Catholic teaching regarding the morality of abortion is clear, but what is demanded of Catholics in the political arena is not so clear. Catholic doctrine does not require Catholics to insist that all their moral values be incorporated into the secular law. Particularly in a pluralist country like the United States, there are Catholic moral teachings—regarding divorce and birth control, for example—that Catholics do not attempt to impose by law.

The Catholic hierarchy has treated abortion differently on grounds that it is the taking of a human life, and that because of the heinousness of killing, it cannot be permitted in a society ruled by law. In a small number of cases, local bishops have tried to enforce this position by declaring that Catholic public figures who defend or support a public policy of choice on abortion may not receive Holy Communion or speak at official Catholic functions.

Catholic bishops as well as theologians disagree as to the appropriateness of such sanctions. Most bishops rely on persuasion and exhortation, regarding them as more effective than penalties imposed on specific individuals.

Within a pluralist society, an individual may utilize political strategies that do not fully express that individual's conscientious moral beliefs, since political deliberation must incorporate questions such as these: What is the best public policy that can be achieved in the current actual situation? Is it better to accept a compromise (prohibition of some abortions, regulation to discourage abortion, energetic efforts to make abortion unnecessary) rather than to insist on an absolute position that cannot prevail? Would an absolute legal prohibition of abortion be unenforceable, hence be like Prohibition, which failed as a move to outlaw alcoholic beverages because it did not represent a consensus? Does an unenforceable law bring about more harm than good, for example, the breakdown of respect for law in general?

The moral teaching of the Catholic Church on abortion is clear. The most effective political role for the Catholic hierarchy, for Catholic public figures, and for Catholics in general, however, is neither clear nor clearly prescribed by Catholic doctrine. *See also* civil law and morality; medical ethics; reproductive technologies; sexual morality.

Bibliography

Connery, John, S.J. *Abortion: The Development of the Roman Catholic Perspective.* Chicago: Loyola University Press, 1977.

Coughlan, Michael J. *The Vatican, the Law and the Human Embryo.* Iowa City: University of Iowa Press, 1990.

Grisez, Germain G. *Abortion: The Myths, the Realities, and the Arguments.* New York: Corpus Books, 1970.

Jung, Patricia Beattie, and Thomas A. Shannon. *Abortion & Catholicism: The American Debate.* New York: Crossroad, 1988.

Noonan, John T., ed. *The Morality of Abortion: Legal and Historical Perspectives.* Cambridge, MA: Harvard University Press, 1970.

CAROL A. TAUER

Abraham (Heb., "father of a multitude"), Hebrew patriarch. The traditions about Abram, later Abraham, are contained in Gen 11:26–25:11, beginning with the call to leave his Mesopotamian homeland and go to another country and ending with his death at the age of one hundred and seventy-five. The principal theme is the promise of land and descendants, a theme repeated many times in the course of the ancestral histories. The first is deferred, since Abraham secures only a burial site in Canaan (Gen 23), and the second is assured after Abraham demonstrates heroic faith in his willingness to sacrifice his son Isaac (Gen 22, the *akedah,* or binding of Isaac). These promises are secured by covenant (Gen 15; 17) but their fulfillment lies in the future. Early Christians also looked to Abraham as their father (e.g., Rom 11:1) and as a heroic model of faith (Gal 3:6–9; Rom 4: Heb 11:8–12). *See also* patriarch [biblical].

abrogation, the complete revocation of an ecclesiastical law. This can be done expressly by the competent lawgiver (the pope, the local bishop, or other religious authority), by a new law that is entirely contradictory to the standing law, or by new laws that so completely reorganize the subject matter of the law as to make the two incompatible (cf. can. 20).

absence, leave of. *See* leave of absence [from religious life].

absenteeism, also known as nonresidency, the absence of a cleric from his post, a matter of grave concern to ecclesiastical reformers. From the twelfth to the eighteenth centuries, 10 to 25 percent of all Catholic clergy were absent from their parishes, either illegally or by dispensation, in order to further their education, to hold other employment, or because they held a number of noncompatible benefices (pluralism).

absolutes, moral, ways of being and acting that will always, everywhere, and for everyone be morally obligatory.

Moral absolutes have been questioned from several fronts. Situation ethics has questioned whether it is possible to have any universal norms since each person, action, and situation is unique and discontinuous. In Catholicism, the use of transcendental Thomism has brought a respect for the historicity of human nature and the processive character of knowing.

Official Catholic teachings witness to moral absolutes, and the consensus of moral theologians confirms that witness. Yet the type of norm that can be so regarded is controversial. Catholic moral theology distinguishes two broad types of moral norms, formal and material. The absoluteness of only the latter is questioned.

Formal norms express values that are constitutive of what it means to be human and so are universal among humankind. They are very general and do not have specific content, e.g., "do good and avoid evil," "be just," "be loving," and "do not be selfish."

Another type of formal norm uses synthetic terms (compact value terms) that cover the objective morality of the act by specifying the action and also including the relevant circumstantial factors. Examples are "do not murder," "do not commit adultery," "do not lie," and "do not steal." These norms forbid illicit killing, illicit sex, telling an illicit untruth, or taking what one has no right to. The issue with these terms is how intention and circumstances are to be related so that one can tell which acts of killing count as murder, which appropriations are theft, etc.

Material norms, by contrast, describe actions apart from circumstances: "do not use artificial contraception," "do not masturbate," "do not abort a fetus." Whether this type of norm can be absolute is a point of controversy. Some moralists argue that since material norms do not include circumstantial factors, they point only to actions that generally ought to be avoided as harmful for human nature, but not absolutely so. What is at stake is not the general obligation to avoid these acts, but the nature of the circumstantial factors in the less than ideal situations that count for a justifiable exception to the norm. Official Catholic teaching, however, has specified certain acts as intrinsically evil in themselves and so always immoral independently of circumstances.

Some other material norms, while not absolute in theory, do highlight values that will generally take precedence and, for all practical purposes, ought to be preferred, e.g., "noncombatants are to be immune from attack in war" and "render help to one in extreme distress." These are "virtually exceptionless" material norms because they leave us with no practical options. They protect values that nearly always take precedence even if this precedence cannot be demonstrated absolutely.

So affirming that some norms are absolute does not mean that all are. The critical issues underlying the formulation of a universal, absolute norm are an understanding of human nature and how well we know objective morality in order to express universally what nature demands. *See also* moral theology.

RICHARD A. MCCORMICK

absolution, the formula used by a priest in the sacramental ritual of Reconciliation. A spoken formula began to appear in the ninth century; until then a laying on of hands by a bishop or priest with no spoken words was the customary sign of reconciliation with God and with the Church. In Western churches the acceptable spoken form of priestly absolution became indicative: i.e., I absolve you; in Eastern churches the acceptable form became subjunctive: i.e., May God forgive you. Both forms, each in its respective rite, are valid. In the Middle Ages, when a spoken form of absolution began to form an integral part of the sacrament, theologians debated whether a priest "declared" sins forgiven, or "caused" such forgiveness. This debate was mirrored in discussions by medieval canon lawyers, many of whom viewed priestly absolution as a judicial act. The Council of Trent (1545–63) taught that priestly absolution was not merely an announcement of the gospel, but an effective part of God's own forgiving grace. In the post–Vatican II renewed ritual, the absolution prayer clearly states this interaction of priestly words and God's grace. The absolution prayer first recalls God's creative work, the salvific work of Jesus, and the effective presence of the Holy Spirit in the Church. Only on the basis of God's saving history does the priest then conclude: I absolve you from your sins. In this prayer both the priest and the penitent participate in the grace of God's saving history. *See also* confession, auricular; general absolution; Reconciliation.

abstinence, generically speaking, the act of voluntary forbearance. The term can apply to everything from not partaking of alcoholic beverages to restraint in sexual matters as a private act of penance for a certain period of time.

Most commonly in Catholicism the term applies to practice of not eating flesh meats for determined periods. In some religious communities this is done on a regular basis (e.g., certain monastic communities always abstain from meat; others only on certain days of the week). For centuries the Catholic laity abstained from meat products each Friday, but that rule was mitigated in 1966. Catholics now abstain from meat on Ash Wednesday, Fridays during Lent, and on Good Friday.

Orthodox Christians observe a much more rigorous Lenten abstinence that extends beyond meat to dairy products and the use, for example, of certain condiments such as oil on food. *See also* fasting; penance.

Acacianism, fifth-century split between Rome and Constantinople over a theological document that seemed, to Rome, to make too many concessions to Monophysitism, which held that in Christ there was only one divine nature; also called the Acacian Schism. In A.D. 482, Acacius, patriarch of Constantinople (472–89), tried to resolve the Monophysite controversy by writing, with Peter Mongus, the *Henoticon,* the Decree of Union, which attempts to state the Church's teaching about Jesus Christ by appealing to the first three ecumenical councils but omitting the Council of Chalcedon. While condemning Nestorius and Eutyches, the *Henoticon* does not mention the two natures of Christ. It was subsequently promulgated for Egypt by Emperor Zeno (474–91), but it was unacceptable both to Pope Felix III and also to the Monophysite Egyptians. The schism began in 484 when the pope excommunicated Acacius for acknowledging Peter Mongus as the patriarch of Alexandria. Despite the efforts of Acacius's successors to become reconciled with Rome, the schism continued until 519 when it was resolved by Emperor Justin I (518–27). *See also* Monophysitism.

academic freedom, the protection given to teaching and research in higher education. General agreement exists that higher education needs an atmosphere of freedom in which to accomplish its purpose, but different understandings of academic freedom exist throughout the world and within North America.

General Understandings: Despite these different understandings, higher education within the United States agrees on an operative approach to academic freedom as found in the 1940 Statement of Principles on Academic Freedom and Tenure issued by the Association of American Colleges and the American Association of University Professors (AAUP). Well over one hundred professional academic societies have subscribed to this statement and American colleges and universities accept its principles and incorporate them into their governing documents.

The 1940 statement bases academic freedom on the common good of society, which depends upon the free search for truth and its expression. Academic freedom covers the full area of a professor's work—teaching, research and publication, and extramural utterances. Correlative duties are mentioned in each area. Tenure, which is conferred after a probationary period of no more than seven years in the institution, serves as the primary functional safeguard of academic freedom, but academics in their probationary period enjoy the same academic freedom as tenured faculty members. A tenured professor can be terminated only for "adequate cause" (incompetence, moral turpitude, *bona fide* financial exigency) in accord with elaborate due-process procedures calling for a faculty committee of peers to judge the case in the first instance, with the final decision made by the governing body on the basis of the record. The 1940 statement recognizes that "limitations of academic freedom because of religious or other aims of the institution should be clearly stated in writing at the time of appointment."

Subsequent AAUP interpretive comments point out that most church-related institutions no longer need or desire any limitations and the organization itself does not now endorse such departures.

The historical context of interference in the hiring and firing of faculty by interests outside the university such as churches, state legislators, or monetary benefactors of the institution shaped the theory and practice of academic freedom as developed by the academy in the United States. This approach to academic freedom is pragmatic, procedural, and partial. The 1940 statement presents no in-depth theoretical discussion of academic freedom, lays heavy emphasis on the procedures and processes to be employed, and covers only the threat to academic freedom coming from people outside the academy. However, the framers of this statement deserve great credit because American higher education has universally approved and accepted what they proposed.

The acceptance of full academic freedom for Catholic institutions of higher learning means that Church authorities cannot directly interfere in the hiring, promoting, tenuring, or dismissing of faculty members. Today the primary tension exists in the area of theology, in which scholars might criticize some aspect of hierarchical teachings. Hierarchical teaching authorities of the Church can declare the positions of a certain professor to be heretical or not in accord with Catholic teaching, but Church authorities cannot directly intervene in the academy.

Just as academic freedom in general finds its justification in the common good of society, so academic freedom for Catholic higher education finds its justification in the common good of the Church. Academic freedom, despite the mistakes that Catholic scholars can and will make, best serves the good of the Catholic Church wherever it is engaged in higher education.

Two different positions, both within the pale of the AAUP approach to academic freedom, exist with regard to the understanding of the competency because of which a Catholic theologian can be dismissed. Catholic theology constitutes a legitimate academic or university discipline with a distinctive methodology, including due respect for hierarchical teaching. A scholar who does not employ the proper method can be judged to be incompetent. Others acknowledge nothing distinctive about the competency of the Catholic theologian as such.

Historical Development: Before 1965 Catholic higher education in the United States did not want academic freedom for itself and strongly opposed academic freedom existing in other American institutions of higher learning. What explains the Catholic opposition to academic freedom in its own colleges and universities and even in secular and other private institutions?

From a theological perspective, Catholics believed they had the truth and the God-given hierarchical teaching authority to proclaim that truth. From a philosophical perspective, Catholic Scholasticism maintained that the human mind can know the truth in general and even the existence of God. A classicism that saw truth as eternal, immutable, and unchangeable supported these theological and philosophical positions. From an educational perspective, Catholic colleges understood themselves as part of the pastoral ministry of the Church, trying to increase the knowledge of faith and ensure the eternal salvation of the students. From a cultural perspective, Catholics tended toward a ghetto mentality and disapproved of the secularism and liberalistic individualism present in American society and illustrated by academic freedom.

By the end of the 1960s and the early 1970s the mainstream of Catholic higher education had fully accepted and incorporated the understanding and practice of academic freedom for itself. The transformation was dramatic, quick, and total. In the summer of 1967 twenty-six leaders of Catholic higher education, meeting as a local region of the International Federation of Catholic Universities under the presidency of Theodore M. Hesburgh of Notre Dame, issued the Land O' Lakes Statement. The opening paragraph clearly makes the point: "To perform its teaching and research functions effectively the Catholic university must have a true autonomy and academic freedom in the face of authority of whatever kind, lay or clerical, external to the academic community itself." Many reasons helped to explain the sudden and massive change with regard to academic freedom. The Second Vatican Council (1962–65) brought about significant changes within Catholicism, especially the recognition of historical consciousness as affecting theology and the understanding of faith so that theology, like the Church itself, is constantly in need of a self-critical attitude. The council passed a historical document accepting religious freedom for the first time (Declaration on Religious Freedom); emphasized the legitimate autonomy and independence of earthly affairs, institutions, and sciences; stressed the need for dialogue with all other people; and even spoke about a lawful freedom of inquiry, thought, and expression (Pastoral Constitution on the Church in the Modern World, n. 62). Significant changes had also been occurring in Catholic higher education, which from the 1950s onward was becoming more self-critical, more professional, more conscious of its role as a college or university, and more connected with public and other private institutions of higher learning. In the post–World War II period Catholics entered fully into the mainstream of American life and culture and were more accepting of American institutions and practices (without, however, losing their critical awareness). Financial considerations also played a role, for Catholic higher education could not prosper without some government aid. Although government aid to Catholic grammar schools and high schools was ruled to be unconstitutional, the U.S. Supreme Court in the *Tilton* case in 1971 accepted the constitutionality of government aid for the particular Catholic colleges in question for a number of reasons, including the fact that they do not proselytize and that they accept the principles of academic freedom.

The Current Situation: Since the 1970s the mainstream of Catholic higher education has continued to support the principles and practice of academic freedom, although a very few smaller schools have not accepted full academic freedom. Many theoreticians have supported the general position of Catholic higher education, but a few theologians, philosophers, and educators have strongly disputed the compatibility of academic freedom with Catholic higher education.

The leadership of Catholic higher education has made strenuous and heretofore successful efforts to acquire and sustain the support of the U.S. Catholic bishops for their position. In the contemporary conservative Church climate, with different attempts to control theologians, some bishops have endorsed the need to limit academic freedom. Since 1967 the Vatican has been skeptical about academic freedom and has never firmly approved it, but Church authorities have not interfered with the practice of academic freedom in Catholic higher education in the United States. In 1990 the Vatican finally issued a long-awaited apostolic constitution for Catholic higher education, *Ex Corde Ecclesiae*. The presidents of Catholic colleges and universities have generally welcomed the document, which, by allowing adaptations to local conditions, customs, and civil law, provides a basis for Catholic institutions to continue as they are. Other commentators point out some problems. The document theoretically limits academic freedom by truth and the common good, sees local bishops not as external to the college or university but as participants in the institution, and includes canonical provisions for those who teach theology in Catholic higher education. The National Conference of Catholic Bishops was given the task of devising norms applicable to Catholic institutions of higher learning in the United States. Meanwhile, Catholic higher education strongly endorses and supports academic freedom, but the future could bring some problems. *See also* Catholic colleges and universities—statistics; Catholicism and education.

Bibliography

American Association of University Professors (AAUP). *Policy Documents and Reports.* 1990 ed. Washington: American Association of University Professors, 1990.

Annarelli, James John. *Academic Freedom and Catholic Higher Education.* New York: Greenwood, 1987.

Curran, Charles E. *Catholic Higher Education, Theology, and Academic Freedom.* Notre Dame, IN: University of Notre Dame Press, 1990.

Worgul, George S., Jr., ed. *Issues in Academic Freedom.* Pittsburgh: Duquesne University Press, 1992.   CHARLES E. CURRAN

a cappella (ah kah-pel'lah; It., "in chapel [style]"), music sung without instrumental accompaniment; the traditional manner in which plain chant is sung in the liturgy. *See also* chant, plain.

Acarie, Bl. Barbe, 1566–1618, French mystic. After thirty years of a happy marriage and six children, she entered the Discalced Carmelites as a lay sister and was given the name Mary of the Incarnation. Madame Acarie was a cousin of Cardinal Pierre de Bérulle, and she received spiritual direction from Francis de Sales. More than anyone she was responsible for the introduction into France of the Discalced Carmelite nuns; for this she has been known as the "mother and foundress of Carmel in France." Acarie's three daughters became Carmelite nuns. She was beatified in 1791. *See also* Carmelite order.

accident, a term used by Scholastic theologians and philosophers (in the eleventh to fourteenth centuries) to refer to the outward appearance of created reality, in contrast to "substance" or essence that gives being to everything that exists. According to these medievals, who were influenced by Aristotle, the way things appear to our senses of sight, touch, taste, smell, and hearing constitute their accidents.

The most important accidents are quantity and quality (absolute accidents) and action, affection, and position in space and time (relative accidents). This medieval philosophical division of human reality into accidents and substance helped Thomas Aquinas develop his understanding of Christ's presence in the Eucharist through transubstantiation: the essence or substance of the bread and wine is transformed by the words of consecration at Mass into the essence or substance of the body and blood of Christ, while the accidents, or appearance of bread and wine, remain. *See also* substance; transubstantiation.

acclamation, a brief phrase or sentence sung or recited by the congregation during a liturgical assembly. The two most important acclamations are the Gospel acclamation, which is comprised of sung Alleluias followed by a verse, often from Scripture, and the Memorial acclamation, an acclamation sung during the Eucharistic Prayer. Acclamations range from one word, "Amen," or "Alleluia," to single-sentence expressions of praise, "Thanks be to God," or "Praise to you, Lord Jesus Christ." Acclamations are not hymns like the Gloria in Excelsis. They are not litanies like the Agnus Dei, responses, or prayers. Instead, they function as a form of praise directly addressed to God or to Christ by the congregation.

accommodation of Scripture. *See* Scripture, accommodation of.

acculturation, a term from cultural anthropology that is now used in connection with forms of the liturgy. It is one of two possible ways that worship may be adapted. A first way, accommodation, refers to making adjustments in the liturgy without necessarily referring to the culture of a people. Acculturation is a preliminary process in which worship is adapted to a particular culture in an external or a partial way while respecting the unique character of the Roman liturgy. Acculturation may deal with either the stylistic characteristics or with the theological emphasis of the Roman liturgy. Thus, the intellectual and sober expressions of a Roman eucharistic prayer might be changed to a more affective way of addressing God. The theological meaning of the priesthood might be represented by names for leadership in a local culture. After an initial mistrust of anything pagan, the Church began to use certain elements from pagan culture and religion (e.g., showing reverence by kissing an object or the Christian transformation of a pagan feast). Missionary efforts were sometimes accompanied by attempts at acculturation of worship. Matteo Ricci (d. 1610), for example, received permission in the seventeenth century from Rome to adapt Christian worship to the Chinese language and dress. Vatican II (1962–65) once again encouraged use of the particular genius and talents of various cultures (Constitution on the Sacred Liturgy, n. 37). The council gave broad guidelines for such adaptation: anything that is not intrinsically bound to error or superstition and that is in accord with the authentic spirit of the liturgy may be used. *See also* inculturation.

Achilleus, St. (akh-il-lay'uhs), martyr. Nothing certain is known of this martyr whose tomb was in the Roman catacombs of Domitilla. Feast day (with St. Nereus): May 12.

acolyte (Gk., *akolouthein,* "to follow"), a minister at the altar who assists the bishop, priest, or deacon. The acolyte's role consists of lighting and carrying candles in the procession and in ministering wine and water at Mass. The acolyte may serve as extraordinary minister of Holy Communion. In the early Church (third and fourth centuries), acolytes also assisted the celebrant in breaking the bread for distribution to the faithful and in carrying Communion to the sick. Canonically, the office of acolyte was termed a minor order until 1972 when Pope Paul VI, in a papal decree known as a *motu proprio,* reclassified it as a ministry. *See also* minor orders; server, altar.

acquired right, a vested right, obtained through a completed legal transaction, actually exercised by either a physical or a juridical person (legal entity) in canon law. The canonical tradition affords a measure of protection for acquired rights when new laws are established (e.g., can. 4). *See also* rights and obligations in canon law.

Acta Apostolicae Sedis (ahk'tah ah-poh-stoh' lee-chay say'dihs; Lat., "Acts of the Apostolic See"), also known by its abbreviation A.A.S., the official journal of the Holy See, containing the laws, pronouncements, and addresses of the pope and the principal documents issued by the various dicasteries, or departments, of the Vatican. In accord with the September 29, 1908, constitution of Pope Pius X, *Promulgandi,* the A.A.S. has been published regu-

larly since January 1909 as the official publication of the Holy See. It replaced the *Acta Sanctae Sedis,* which, though similar in content to the A.A.S., lacked its official character.

Universal Church laws are promulgated in the A.A.S.; they ordinarily take effect three months after the date of publication, unless another date is specified or it is evident from the nature of the matter that the law should take effect immediately. Most of the contents of the A.A.S. are not legal in nature and do not require promulgation. *See also* Holy See.

Acta Sanctae Sedis (ahk'tah sahnk'tay say'dihs; Lat., "Acts of the Holy See"), also known by its abbreviation A.S.S., a monthly journal published in Rome from 1865 through 1908. Like the *Acta Apostolicae Sedis,* it contained the legislative and administrative acts published by the Holy See, but it lacked the latter journal's official character until Pope Pius X made it "authentic and official" in 1904. The original title of the A.S.S. was *Acta ex iis decerpta, quae apud S. Sedem geruntur in compendium opportune redacta et illustrata* (Lat., "a compendium of documents produced by the Holy See and appropriately edited and explained"). This title was later abbreviated to *Acta Sanctae Sedis. See also* Holy See.

Action Française, French political movement begun in the late nineteenth century. Characterized as intensely nationalistic, it emphasized Catholicism as an important component of French culture, even though the most important spokesman for the movement, Charles Maurras (d. 1951), was not a believer. Condemned by Pope Pius XI in 1926, Action Française still had many sympathizers among the French. Its ideas were especially prominent among the leaders of the puppet government of Vichy after the fall of France at the beginning of the Second World War. The movement's chauvinism and anti-Semitism attracted a certain kind of Catholic mind in France that could accept neither the French Revolution nor the rising power of the Left. *See also* France, Catholicism in.

Acton, Lord John, 1834–1902, English historian. A student of Ignaz von Döllinger at Munich and a member of Parliament for Carlow (1859–65), he collaborated with John Henry Newman in editing *The Rambler,* a liberal Catholic publication which Acton closed after the "Syllabus of Errors" in 1864. An outspoken critic of Roman curial power, the centralization of authority in the papacy, and the

Vatican's preoccupation with the preservation of the Papal States, he strongly opposed Vatican I's declaration of papal infallibility as a threat to individual consciences. His reports from Vatican Council I were published by Döllinger as *Letters from Rome on the Council by Quirinus.* Acton's lay status preserved him from canonical reprisals after the council. From 1896 to 1901, he was the first Regius Professor of Modern History at Cambridge, where he coordinated the writing of *The Cambridge Modern History.* *See also* Vatican Council I.

acts, human, those actions of human beings over which they have dominion, that is, ones they do deliberately. These are actions that are freely chosen and for which the person is responsible. "Human acts" are often distinguished from the "acts of a human," which are not free but are done by humans. The analysis of human acts reveals an extraordinary complexity which, however, should not detract from the essential unity of a person acting. Many aspects of a particular human act may be distinguished: perception of, desire for, deliberation about an end; consent to, decision about, and choice of an end; and implementation of the choice. Each of these distinguishable aspects, and others, may be more or less present in a single human act. Furthermore, in describing a human act three difficulties should be kept in mind. First, providing an exact description of an act as human is not always easy, and this has important implications for morality. For example, although the term "murder" always designates an evil, one may be excused for killing another human during war. Second, the intentional purpose behind an action is essential to its full description. "Eating" can be a mindless activity in front of a television, or part of a family celebration. Third, a "single" human act like eating or murder can also be analyzed into any number of human acts; the lifting of a fork or the pulling of a trigger is a human act, but it is also a part of a larger act.

actual grace. *See* grace, actual.

actual sin, a deliberate choice of a morally wrong action, as distinct from a sinful habit (vice) and from original sin. Actual sin is a freely chosen activity of the whole personality against the will of God, as manifested in Christian revelation and in the goodness and order of creation. True actual sin, which is serious and not venial in nature, involves, negatively, a refusal to do the good and, positively,

the deliberate choice of a moral direction away from God's plan. Knowledge, emotions, and circumstances condition the freedom necessary for actual sin. Unlike Protestantism's emphasis upon an essentially sinful human condition, Catholicism focuses upon the moral specificity of individual human acts and upon the psychological and social context and impact of those acts. *See also* mortal sin; sin; venial sin.

A.D. (Lat., *anno Domini,* "in the year of the Lord"), the current designation for the Christian era, based on the calculation of the date of the birth of Jesus by the sixth-century Russian monk Dionysius Exiguus. It is now known that this calculation was off by several years, since Jesus was born before the death of Herod the Great in 4 B.C. In deference to those of other faiths, many now prefer B.C.E. and C.E. *See also* C.E.

Adalbert of Magdeburg, St., d. 981, missionary and first archbishop of Magdeburg. Sent by Otto the Great to evangelize the Russians under the Christian Princess Olga, he was forced to flee when her pagan son Svyatoslav took the throne. As archbishop of Magdeburg, he was given jurisdiction over the Slavs. Feast day: June 20.

Adalhard, St., also known as Adelard, 753–827, monk, cousin of the emperor Charlemagne, patron saint of gardeners. Born in France, he had a reputation for concern for the poor and the sick and for love of learning and teaching. Feast day: January 2.

Adam (Heb., *'adam,* "[hu]man"), the first man. According to Gen 2–5 Adam was created first from the clay of the earth (he is said to have lived for 930 years); from his rib the first woman was later made, also in the image of God. After his wife, Eve, succumbed to temptation, Adam joined her in disobeying the command not to eat of the forbidden fruit and was cursed to work the ground. Adam is mentioned infrequently in the Bible after Gen 5, but Sir 49:16 places him above every creature. In the NT (Rom 5:12–21; 1 Cor 15:21–22) Paul presents a contrast between Adam and Christ: everyone dies as a result of Adam's sin, but in Christ all will be made alive. *See also* Adam and Eve; Eve; original justice; original sin.

Adam, Karl, 1876–1966, German Catholic theologian. Ordained a priest for the diocese of Regensburg in 1900, he received his doctorate in theology from the University of Munich in 1904 and subsequently published books and articles in patristics, especially on the theology of Augustine of Hippo. After teaching at the University of Munich and the University of Strasbourg, he joined the faculty of the University of Tübingen (1919–48) and immediately found himself at home within the Catholic Tübingen school. Adam's writings helped to prepare the way for the Second Vatican Council (1962–65). *The Spirit of Catholicism* (1924) presents the Church as a community, specifically, in terms of the Pauline metaphor of the body of Christ. *Christ Our Brother* (1926), *The Son of God* (1933), and *The Christ of Faith* (1954) emphasize the humanity of Jesus Christ. *One and Holy* (1948) develops an ecumenical theology. Adam's writings were read by Catholics around the world, influencing such people as Dorothy Day, Walter Kasper, Flannery O'Connor, Pope Paul VI, Karl Rahner, and Edward Schillebeeckx.

Adam and Eve, the first human creatures. The story of Adam and Eve, their creation, sin, and demise is recounted in Genesis 2–3. God formed Adam from the clay of the earth and brought him to life by breathing into his nostrils. The name *'ādām,* derived from the Hebrew word *'adāmāh* (earth), is

Adam and Eve covering their nakedness in shame, a consequence of their sin of disobedience in the garden of Eden; detail from the sarcophagus of a fourth-century Roman prefect, located in the Vatican.

the generic word for human being and came to be used as a proper name. Eve, Adam's wife, was formed from his rib when no other creature proved to be a suitable companion. Because she was to be the "mother of all the living," her name, *hawwah,* is derived from the Hebrew word for life, *hayyim* (Gen 3:20).

After their creation, God placed Adam and Eve in the Garden of Eden, instructing them to care for it and forbidding them to eat of the tree in the middle of the garden. At the persuasion of the serpent, Eve ate of the tree. She gave some of its fruit to her husband, who also ate of it. As a result of their sin of disobedience, Adam and Eve were expelled from the garden and subjected to various afflictions.

Numerous motifs found in other ancient Near Eastern literature are evident in this biblical story that explains not only the origins of humanity, but also marriage, suffering and death, and the afflictions of labor. In Pauline theology, the sin of Adam is seen as the origin of all human sin, an interpretation that gave rise to the subsequent development of the doctrine of original sin (Rom 5:12). *See also* original sin.　　　　　　　　　　ANNE M. SWEET

Adamnan of Iona, St., or Adomán of Iona (Gaelic), ca. 625–704, ninth abbot of Iona. According to Bede, when Adamnan visited Northumbria in the late 680s he became convinced of the superiority of the nineteen-year cycle for calculating the date of Easter; though his own monastery retained the eighty-four-year cycle, his Easter reform was successful among Irish churches that were not dependent on Iona. Adamnan wrote a *Life of Columba* (the founder of Iona) and a treatise on the Holy Land, *De Locis Sanctis.* The Synod of Birr (697) promulgated *Cáin Adomnáin,* Adomnán's Law, for the protection of clerics, women, and children against acts of violence. Feast day: September 23. *See also* Iona.

Adam of Marsh, d. 1259, English theologian. A student of Robert Grosseteste, in 1247 he became the first Franciscan master at Oxford. Firmly committed to Franciscan piety, in 1241 he urged Pope Gregory IX not to mitigate the Rule of St. Francis. Known for his erudition and reputation, he served the English king Henry III, the popes, and the English episcopate as adviser. His best-known writings are 247 edited letters, which offer considerable insight into the thirteenth-century English church. *See also* England, Catholicism in; Franciscan spirituality.

Adam of St. Victor, ca. 1110–ca. 1180, liturgical poet. Born in Brittany or Britain and educated at Paris, where he entered the abbey of St. Victor (ca. 1130), he is noted for his composition of liturgical poems known as Sequences, which precede the Alleluia. These poems follow a typological pattern that unites figures within the Hebrew Scriptures with Christian figures, including Mary. He was dependent in his theology on that of Hugh of St. Victor, who held that the visible both reveals and conceals the invisible. *See also* typology; Victorines.

Adela, St., d. ca. 734, abbess. She became a nun after the death of her husband and founded a Benedictine monastery near Trier, where she was its first abbess. She is not venerated liturgically. Feast day: December 24.

Adelaide, St., d. ca. 999, widow of Roman emperor Otto the Great. She helped lead the Roman Empire through three generations, restored monasteries, and worked for the conversion of Slavs. Feast day: December 16.

Ad Gentes Divinitus (ahd jen'tez di-vin'ee-toos). *See* Decree on the Church's Missionary Activity.

adiaphora (ahd-ee-ahf'uh-ruh; Gk., "things indifferent"), a term for things neither commanded nor forbidden by God. Drawing upon Paul's Letters (e.g., Rom 14:17; 1 Cor 6:12; 8:8; Gal 5:6; Col 2:20), Protestant Reformers used the term to describe nonessential points that they were willing to concede to the Catholics in the interest of peace and union. In the Augsburg Interim Philipp Melanchthon and others accepted the Latin liturgy, Confirmation, the Feast of Corpus Christi, Extreme Unction, fasting, and the jurisdiction of bishops. These concessions led to the adiaphoristic controversies that split the Lutheran church in the second half of the sixteenth century. *See also* Reformation, the.

Adjutor, St., d. 1131, patron saint of yachtsmen. As a Crusader, he was captured by the Muslims but escaped. He became a monk and lived the life of a recluse. Feast day: April 30.

ad limina apostolorum (ahd li'mee-nah ahpaws-toh-law'room). *See ad limina* visit.

ad limina visit (Lat., *ad,* "to"; *limina,* "threshold"), the visit each diocesan bishop is regularly required to make to Rome, where he meets personally with the pope and with various officials of the Roman Curia, the Church's central administration. It originated in pilgrimages made by bishops of the Roman province to the threshold of the tombs of the two great apostles, Peter and Paul, for their veneration. Currently it is a canonical obligation for every bishop who presides over a particular diocese and is to be fulfilled personally by the bishop or, if impeded, by his coadjutor bishop, an auxiliary bishop, or a designated priest of his diocese (Code of Canon Law, can. 400). The visit is considered as strengthening the bond of hierarchical communion and as witnessing to the catholicity of the Church and the unity of the episcopal college, while providing an opportunity for bishops to discuss personally with the pope any particular matters of concern in their own dioceses (*Pastor Bonus,* 1988, n. 10.28–32; appendix i.) Six months prior to his *ad limina* visit, the diocesan bishop submits to the Holy See a report on the state of the diocese in accord with the 1988 Directory for the "Ad Limina Visit," issued by the Congregation for Bishops. *See also Pastor Bonus.*

Adonai (ah'dohn-i; Heb., "Lord"; the plural majestic form used here is translated "My great Lord"), name for God. The culture of the ancient Near East attached particular importance to personal names because they gave access to, and perhaps control over, another. To lose one's name was to lose one's life. Out of profound reverence to God, the name YHWH (pronounced "Yahweh"), which occurs in the Hebrew text of the OT, was never said. In the postexilic period *Adonai* was gradually substituted for the name Yahweh. In the texts of the Hebrew Bible, the vowel signs proper to Adonai were attached to the consonants YHWH. *See also* Yahweh.

adoption, a metaphor used to describe the relationship between God and God's chosen people, particularly in Paul's Letters. In Rom 9:4 Paul remarks that Israel enjoyed "adoption," perhaps alluding to passages in which Israel is called the son of Yahweh (e.g., Exod 4:22; Deut 14:1; Isa 43:6; Jer 31:9; Hos 11:1). According to Paul, Christ came so that gentile Christians might also receive the status of God's adopted children (Gal 4:5), evident when they call on God as Father (Gal 4:6). Adoption is received in its fullest sense when redemption is complete (Rom 8:23). Adopted status is intimately connected with the gift of God's spirit (Rom 8:15), a gift for which some have been chosen and foreordained (Eph 1:5).

adoption, impediment of, in canon law invalidating obstacle to a marriage in which an adopted person wishes to marry an adopted parent, grandparent, or sibling (can. 1094). *See also* marriage law.

Adoptionism, eighth-century doctrine first condemned by Pope Adrian in 794 because of its proclamation of a dual sonship of Christ, one natural, the other adopted. Though its origins go back to the writings of Paul of Samosata, Adoptionism was first officially taught by Elipandus, archbishop of Toledo, Spain (ca. 785), who declared that as the eternally begotten Logos, Christ is the natural Son of God, but that as human and Son of Mary, Christ is merely the adopted Son of God. After much controversy, Charlemagne assembled a council at Frankfurt (794), which summarized the error of Adoptionism as ascribing sonship to a nature instead of to a person and thereby undermining orthodox teaching about the substantial reality of Jesus Christ as truly God and truly human. Even after its initial condemnation by Adrian, Adoptionism made several reappearances and was condemned again by councils at Friuli, Italy (796), Rome (799), and Aix-la-Chapelle (800). Then during both the twelfth and fourteenth centuries, new forms of Adoptionism emerged and were condemned. Pope Alexander III (d. 1181) rejected the Adoptionist formulations of Abelard, Folmar of Trier, and Gilbert of Porrée, who had concluded that Jesus Christ in his human nature was only the adopted Son of God. Finally, two centuries later, even the declaration that Jesus Christ is simultaneously the natural and adopted Son of God was condemned, for espousing any form of Adoptionism would have been implying that the one person of Jesus Christ is in his humanity not truly one with the Father. *See also* Christology; Incarnation, the; Jesus Christ. JANICE POORMAN

adoration, one of the highest attitudes of prayer. It is a religious act performed by the whole person, body, mind, and soul, wherein God alone is praised as the supreme source and object of all that exists. Before Vatican II (1962–1965) adoration pertained principally to eucharistic devotion. It was the gazing in reverence upon the exposed or elevated eucharistic bread or wine. Adoration was a component of every Eucharist when the consecrated bread and cup were elevated during the Eucharistic Prayer and be-

fore Communion. By extension, adoration was and remains a central part of Forty Hours devotions, Benediction of the Blessed Sacrament, and Holy Hours. Some communities of vowed religious practice a "Perpetual Adoration."

During the late Middle Ages, the theology of eucharistic adoration became quite influential. Religious piety centered on the practices of "ocular communion," receiving Christ through the eyes, if not upon the tongue. The adoration of Christ in his manifestation in the eucharistic elements has been ecumenically troublesome. The sixteenth-century Reformers objected that the Eucharist was instituted by Christ for eating and not for worshiping, that Christ was in heaven and not upon the altar. The Catholic Church teaches that every Eucharist is ordered toward the worship of God and the communion of the faithful, and ultimately, toward salvation in God. Eucharistic adoration can be viewed as a prolongation of the time of Christ's most intimate presence to the Church. However, adoration of the Real Presence must always be secondary to its reception as spiritual nourishment. *See also* Benediction; Blessed Sacrament; Eucharist; *latria*.

JEFFREY T. VANDERWILT

Adoro te devote (ah-doh'roh tay day-voh'teh; Lat., "I devotedly adore you"), Latin hymn attributed to Thomas Aquinas (1225–74). Legend suggests that Thomas wrote this hymn, one of five in honor of the Eucharist, for the Feast of Corpus Christi, established by Pope Urban IV in 1264. English texts of this hymn and its traditional tune may be found in most Catholic hymnals (see also *Catholic Source Book,* Dubuque: Brown-ROA, 1990, p. 329).

Adrian I. *See* Hadrian I.

Adrian VI. *See* Hadrian VI.

Adrian of Canterbury, St., d. ca. 710, African who as abbot of Nerida, near Naples, accompanied St. Theodore to England when he had been appointed archbishop of Canterbury. As abbot of Sts. Peter and Paul (later St. Augustine's) in Canterbury for thirty-nine years, he advanced the monastery as a center of learning. Feast day: January 9.

Advent (Lat., *adventus,* "coming"), the four-week season beginning with First Evening Prayer of the Sunday that falls on or closest to November 30 and ending with First Evening Prayer of Christmas. This season of joyful expectation has a twofold character: it prepares for the commemoration of the Incarnation celebrated during the Christmas season, and it looks forward to Christ's Second Coming at the end of time.

The remote origins of Advent are Spanish and Gallican. The Council of Saragossa (380) reminded the laity of the obligation for daily church attendance from December 17 through January 6. Hilary of Poitiers (d. ca. 367) attests to a Gallican three-week period of preparation for Epiphany. In fifth-century Gaul a three-day-a-week fast began on or near St. Martin's Day (November 11) and extended to Christmas. These pieces of evidence, however, are insufficient to establish the earlier theory that Advent began as a catechumenal period prior to Epiphany baptisms. By 384 in Spanish jurisdictions baptisms took place on Epiphany, but also on Christmas. More probably the pre-festival preparation counterpoised the pagan Saturnalia festivals, a holiday leisure season that church leaders feared could be misused.

The Gallican fasts may have derived from Celtic monastic practices; a synod at Tours (567) prescribed fasts for monks and a council at Macon in 581 ordered an Advent fast for the laity. Gallican Advent, lasting from four to six weeks, took on a penitential character similar to early medieval Lent.

In fourth-century Rome there is a pre-Christmas fast (though not necessarily related to the feast) and Ember days, quarterly fasts. The real architect of Roman Advent practice was Gregory the Great (d. 604), who fixed the season at four weeks (though the Gelasian Sacramentary provides for six Sundays), composed seasonal prayers and antiphons, and arranged the Mass and Office lectionary. Ember day texts and the later-added (seventh-century) "O Antiphons" exemplify joyful preparation for the Nativity.

The Roman liturgy exported to Gaul in the ninth century was enriched there by eschatological themes and also by penitential elements. The fusion of Gallican and Roman Advents returned to Rome by the twelfth century, providing the basis for today's Advent.

General Norms for the Liturgical Year and Calendar preserve the two-fold focus of Advent: the first two Sundays highlight Christ's Second Coming; the last two, incarnational themes, with the fourth Sunday adverting to Mary. *See also* Christmas; liturgical year.

JOHN A. MELLOH

advocate, approved expert at canon law appointed by a party or sometimes by judicial mandate to safeguard the rights of a party in a canonical process. Advocates, unlike a proxy, offer professional counsel, make arguments, and may be several. The qualifications are majority age, good reputation, canonical expertise, mandate, and approval by the diocesan bishop, who may allow non-Catholics to serve.

Advocatus Diaboli (ahd-voh-kah'too*s* dee-ah' boh-lee). *See* promoter of justice.

Aegidius Romanus (ay-jee'dee-*oo*s roh-mah' noos). *See* Giles of Rome.

Aelfric, also called "the Grammarian," ca. 950–1020, abbot of Eynsham. Active in the tenth-century English Benedictine reform, Aelfric was educated at Winchester, served as master of the monastic school at Cerne Abbas, and became abbot of Eynsham in 1005.

A distinctive prose stylist, Aelfric wrote several collections of homilies and composed pastoral letters for his contemporary bishops. His *Colloquy*, a beginner's school text in Latin, gives us many glimpses of everyday life in his time.

During the English Reformation, Aelfric's homilies were used to attack the doctrines of transubstantiation and the Immaculate Conception: this application ignores the historical context of his ideas. *See also* Benedictine order.

Aelred of Rievaulx, St., ca. 1110–67, abbot of the Cistercian monastery of Rievaulx, England (1147–67). Born at Hexham, Aelred spent several years with the Scottish court before joining the Cistercians in 1134. He is best known for *The Mirror of Charity*, a defense of the Cistercian life requested by Bernard of Clairvaux, and *On Spiritual Friendship*, patterned after Cicero's dialogue on friendship. Spiritual friendships are described as inspired by God and a means to holiness. Aelred's meditations on the life of Christ are forerunners of the method of imagining oneself in Christ's presence found in Ignatius of Loyola's *Spiritual Exercises*. Feast day: March 3.

Aeterni Patris (ay-tair'nee pah'trees; Lat., "Of the eternal Father"), encyclical of Leo XIII, August 4, 1879, calling for the revival of Thomism as the philosophy best able to provide the principles capable of organizing theology into a coherent and unified body of knowledge. Leo required that Thomistic philosophy be taught in seminaries as the foundation for theological studies and that academies for scholarly research in Thomism be established. The encyclical interpreted Thomism through nineteenth-century neo-Thomist lenses; it deprecated post-Cartesian philosophy and modern science as tainted with skepticism and so incapable of attaining truth or entering into a fruitful relationship with theology. *See also* Aquinas, St. Thomas; Thomism.

affective prayer, prayer that engages the emotions or feelings in a positive, loving way; prayer of the heart. There has been a recovery of interest recently in the affective dimension of prayer in Catholic spirituality. Often in the past, the role of feeling in prayer was misunderstood, neglected, and, in some instances, feared. Feelings were thought to be dangerous, requiring strict forms of control through fasting and self-denial. Recent developments in psychology emphasize the wholeness and integrity of the human person, paving the way for a similar understanding of prayer and the spiritual life. Affections are no longer ignored but nurtured and allowed to work in harmony with other aspects of the human person.

Most of the mystics experienced God in profoundly affective ways. Leading names in the tradition include Augustine, Anselm, Bernard of Clairvaux, Francis of Assisi, Hadewijch of Antwerp, Bonaventure, Teresa of Ávila, and John of the Cross. In the fourth century, Augustine knew how important it was to be moved deeply by the love of God, and in his *Confessions* he consciously seeks to move his readers to that end.

In the Bible, the Psalms and the Canticle of Canticles are examples of affective prayer. Powerful feelings of love and affection are experienced as in intimate friendship and marital love. The Christian becomes the lover of Christ who seeks God's presence and who is on fire with the desire to do God's will and unconsolable when God seems withdrawn. The soul feels dissolved in God's love and ardently desires that others experience God in a similar way.

In affective prayer, one is touched, moved, affected by divine and human love. Examples of such feelings include compassion for the suffering of Jesus and for others, awe at the beauty of creation, praise, thanksgiving, joy, resolve to live a good life. One might meditate on a text or image and pause when one's heart stirs with feeling and reaches out in love

to God. One can experience such feelings, allow them to deepen and to motivate virtuous action on behalf of the world. *See also* prayer.

ELIZABETH DREYER

affectivity, that aspect of experience that refers to feeling and emotion. Affectivity varies from warm feelings to passion toward an object of desire to revulsion from an object of aversion. Feelings can be fleeting, or can be developed and deepened over a lifetime, or can reflect the basic orientation of one's life. Examples of affectivity that express liking are love, joy, and awe. Aversion produces feelings such as sorrow, fear, anger, and jealousy. Affective interior dispositions are often accompanied by physiological changes such as tears, increased body temperature, rapid heartbeat, or muscle tension. Feelings also provide energy for action. One's affective dispositions provide momentum and zest for life. Affectivity and cognition are inextricably linked and ideally work in harmony and mutual correction. Cognition is associated with reason, knowledge, clarity; affectivity with the will, value, mystery. A common symbol of affectivity is the heart and a frequent name for the Christian God is Love.

affinity. *See* consanguinity.

affirmative judgment, in canon law judicial pronouncement favoring the rights asserted or declaration sought in the complaint of the petitioner. Only with moral certitude derived from the acts and the proofs may judges render an affirmative decision.

affusion, a method of baptizing a person by pouring water over his or her head. With the passing of time, affusion replaced immersion as the accepted mode of initiation. In the Rite of Christian Initiation of Adults (RCIA) and in Baptism for Children, affusion is the alternate form of Baptism; both rituals mention immersion first. In some modern fonts, adult candidates stand in a pool of water, partially immersed and water is poured over their heads. *See also* Baptism.

Africa, Catholicism in. The twentieth century has witnessed the rapid growth of African Catholicism, especially in the sub-Saharan region. To appreciate this increase, it is helpful to view it against overall population increase, total Christian expansion, and the spread of Islam.

Statistics: In 1900 Africa had an estimated population of 108 million. This grew to over 460 million by 1980. Projections in the *World Christian Encyclopedia* (1982) indicate that by the year 2000, the continent will be the home of over 800 million, nearly 10 percent of humanity.

In 1900 about 10 million Africans (11 percent) were Christian. This figure rose to approximately 203 million or 44 percent in 1980. It is estimated that in 2000, Africa will have a little over 393 million Christians, representing over 48 percent of the continent's population.

There were about 35 million African Muslims (32 percent) in 1900. The number grew to 190 million or 41 percent in 1980. Indications are that as the twentieth century closes, Islam will have 339 million followers, constituting about 42 percent of the continental population.

Africa had only 2 million Catholics in 1900, less than 2 percent of the total. The figure rose to 77 million or 17 percent in 1980. Projections suggest that in 2000, Africa will be the home of 152 million Catholics, or 18 percent. By the year 2000, therefore, Catholicism will have grown from less than 2 to nearly 20 percent, the biggest gain by any single denomination on the continent.

History: The history of Catholicism in Africa may be considered in three main periods. The first saw a vibrant Church in Roman North Africa from the second to the seventh centuries. Little is known of its origins. During the great persecution by the emperor Diocletian (d. 305) beginning in 303, the Church historian Eusebius (d. 340) relates that he witnessed Christians being martyred in the hundreds around Alexandria. This Catholicism produced Clement (d. 215), leader of the school of Christian instruction in Alexandria. Beside providing martyrs and scholars, this Catholicism also con-

Pope John Paul II blesses Catholics during a 1993 visit to Uganda, where there are over 8 million Catholics comprising about 40 percent of the total population.

tributed to the development of the monastic movement.

North African Catholicism was steeped in several theological controversies. Some of its members insisted that those who had given up the faith, especially in times of persecution, needed a second baptism before readmission. Proponents of this view, called Donatists, were vigorously opposed by Augustine of Hippo (d. 430). This Catholicism also contended with the Monophysites, who held that Jesus' human nature was totally absorbed by the divine Person. The monks who had sought solitude in the Egyptian desert were particularly emphatic about Christ's divinity. The Monophysites in North Africa held to their view, even after the Council of Chalcedon (451) taught that Jesus Christ was truly God and truly a human being, whose two natures were united in one divine person.

In the fifth century Roman rule was crumbling in its African frontiers. Hordes of Vandals from Europe arrived in 429 to misrule the territory for over a century. When the Arabs came in the seventh century, bringing with them newly founded Islam, African Catholicism was already in decline. It was soon displaced by the faith of the new rulers.

A second period of Catholicism began in the fifteenth century when Portuguese explorers and traders, accompanied by missionaries, sailed down the West African coast searching for a sea route to India. Along with their desire for wealth and adventure, the Portuguese were also looking for the legendary Prester John, priest and king of Ethiopia in deepest Africa, a reputed sworn enemy of both Islam and "paganism."

The Portuguese crown, at whose behest these mariners sailed, was itself obeying papal orders. In his bull *Romanus Pontifex* of January 8, 1455, Pope Nicholas V (1447–55) gave all Africa forever to the Portuguese king Alfonso V (1432–81) and his successors "out of [the] plenitude of the Apostolic power." This document gave the monarch permission to enslave all Saracens and "pagans." For the next two centuries, this policy determined Portuguese missionary activity in Africa.

Portuguese caravels sailed the West African coast, with Diego Cão as captain, and reached the Kongo River in 1483. But Cão found neither Christians nor Muslims to be fought. Instead, the captain met Nzinga Nkuwu, king of the Kongo, a polygamist who was willing to work with the strange men from the sea. Shortly, Cão arranged for the Portuguese crown to send builders to enlarge the king's palace.

Nkuwu, having been instructed by the Franciscans, embraced the faith and was baptized in 1491. A subsequent quarrel between Nkuwu and the missionaries saw the latter depart temporarily.

By now the slave trade was fast becoming a menace. Nkuwu's African successor, who took a Portuguese name, Alfonso I (ruled 1506–43), was willing but unable to curb it. His attempts to forge direct diplomatic relations with the papacy failed.

Sailing along the East African coast, Portuguese mariners and missionaries encountered Islam. For two centuries both cross and crescent were locked in battle for the political, commercial, and religious control of the eastern shores.

Aided by the crown, the Portuguese Augustinians built several places of worship along the eastern coast, chief among them a monastery in Mombasa. Since the missionaries found the coast already Islamized, they made few converts. There was little effort to win followers beyond the coastal strip. Hence the friars ended up ministering to Portuguese sailors and their mixed-race offspring.

In 1593 the Portuguese built Fort Jesus in Mombasa, their headquarters. African and Arab resentment against Portuguese rule resulted in an uprising in 1631 led by Dom Jerónimo Chingulia, a former Catholic. Upon reverting to Islam as Yusuf bin al-Hasan, he massacred all but five Portuguese in Mombasa. Over 250 Christians were killed. In 1636 the Augustinian order requested that the Vatican take the first steps to declare the slain Christians martyrs and saints, but the process was soon stopped.

After the Mombasa massacre the Portuguese regained control. But in 1696 Saif bin Sultan of Oman, a staunch Muslim, personally sailed down to Mombasa with three thousand men and attacked Fort Jesus, which fell in December 1698. The Portuguese were finally dislodged from East Africa north of Mozambique, and with them Catholicism.

Between 1500 and 1700 Catholicism failed on both coasts of Africa mainly because it came under the wing of an imperial power that was resented by the people it sought to rule. Moreover, far from lifting a finger against the slave trade, many missionaries compromised the gospel by becoming slaveholders. Also, on the east coast, Islam provided too formidable a challenge and eventually carried the day.

The third and most recent period of Catholicism in Africa began around the 1850s and continues to the present. The middle of the nineteenth century witnessed one of the greatest Catholic missionary awakenings of all time. Many new congregations and missionary associations were started with the aim of evangelizing Africa.

Such was the case of the White Fathers founded by Bishop (later Cardinal) Charles Lavigerie (1825–92), who was appointed bishop of Algiers in 1867. A man of great energy, Lavigerie had a missionary plan of converting Africa, both Muslim and "pagan" alike, from north to south. To facilitate Catholicism's southward expansion, he founded the *Pères Blancs* (White Fathers) in 1868, today known as the Society of Missionaries of Africa.

Lavigerie, the builder, constructed monumental stone structures such as Notre Dame d'Afrique in Algiers, the Basilica of St. Louis at Carthage, and the Cathedral of St. Vincent de Paul in Tunis. These churches were used by expatriate Catholics during the colonial period until national independence came in the 1950s. Today they are government museums. While Lavigerie's efforts seem to have borne no lasting fruit in North Africa, the labors of his missionaries south of the Sahara are much in evidence in the countless small Christian communities that were founded.

Another group founded to evangelize Africa was the Congregation of the Holy Ghost Fathers, which was reorganized in 1839 by Francis Libermann (1802–52), a French Jew who had converted to Catholicism. Members of his congregation have ministered in West and East Africa since the nineteenth century. One of them, Bishop Joseph Shanahan of southern Nigeria, built the largest private school system in Africa at the turn of the century.

A feature common to missionary groups that have made a major impact in Africa is the contribution of women religious to the proclamation and witness of the gospel. Soon after founding the White Fathers, Lavigerie established the White Sisters, also known as the Missionary Sisters of Our Lady of Africa, with the cooperation of Mother Marie Salome in 1869. And when the Holy Ghost missionaries began their work in East Africa in 1863, they invited the Daughters of Mary from France, and later the Precious Blood Sisters from Germany and the Institute of the Blessed Virgin Mary, commonly called the Loreto Sisters, from Ireland to work alongside them. Archbishop (later Cardinal) Herbert Vaughan (1832–1903) of Westminster founded the Mill Hill Missionaries in 1866 and shortly afterward established the Franciscan Missionary Sisters of St. Joseph. And after Daniel Comboni (1831–81), a diocesan priest, founded the Verona Fathers in 1867, he started the Missionary Sisters of Verona in 1872 for the same African mission field. Canon Joseph Allamano (1851–1926) followed a similar pattern. Having founded the Institute of the Consolata Fathers in 1902, he set up the Consolata Sisters in 1910.

Challenges: African Catholicism faces major challenges. The rate of conversions far outstrips that of ordinations. The result is that many communities cannot celebrate the Sunday Eucharist, often having to wait weeks or even months before a priest can visit. Meanwhile, a catechist leads them in a celebration of the Liturgy of the Word. African Catholicism currently depends on the catechist, but unfortunately not on the Eucharist.

Given this pastoral challenge, African Catholicism has rediscovered small Christian communities comparable to the base ecclesial communities of Latin America. During their plenary meeting in Nairobi in 1976, the bishops of central and eastern Africa (AMECEA) gave pastoral priority to the support of small Christian communities. Characterized by the gift of sharing (koinonia), these churches are reminiscent of the communities Paul mentions in his Letters, e.g., 1 Corinthians and Ephesians.

Another challenge is inculturation. In many respects African Catholicism today resembles that of its founders, especially in art, architecture, liturgy, and theology. The dominance of the European spirit in African Catholicism may have prompted Pope Paul VI to challenge the African Church to cultivate a soul of its own. Speaking to African bishops at Kampala, Uganda, in 1969 the pope said: "You may, and you must have an African Christianity."

Breakaway churches are a major feature of Protestant Christianity in Africa. According to the *World Christian Encyclopedia,* there were about six thousand independent churches on the continent in the mid-1960s. Remarkably, this phenomenon has hardly affected African Catholicism, a fact acknowledged by Catholic and non-Catholic writers alike. But if African Catholicism has not lost many followers through church breakaways, it has begun to experience considerable desertions to new Christian fundamentalist groups that have been sweeping much of sub-Saharan Africa in the last three decades of the twentieth century.

A further challenge is the place of women in Church and society, a concern expressed by several bishops at a synod of the African Church held in Rome in 1994. If women have lower status than men in many parts of the world, this is eminently true in Africa. To its credit, missionary Catholicism has done much to uplift the African woman, especially through modern education and medicine. Perhaps no one single factor has influenced the improvement of the indigenous woman's lot more than the contribution of women religious from Europe and North America. The African Church faces the task of continuing to address this problem.

In the final decade of the twentieth century, leaders of African Catholicism have spoken up increasingly for social justice. This is a welcome development in a continent where the disparity between rich and poor, and between the powerful and the powerless has been so great. *See also* Africa, Church in Roman; Donatism; Holy Ghost Fathers; Islam; Portugal, Catholicism in; White Fathers.

Bibliography

Barrett, David B. *World Christian Encyclopedia.* Nairobi: Oxford University Press, 1982.

Boulaga, Eboussi F. *Christianity Without Fetishes: An African Critique and Recapture of Christianity.* New York: Orbis Books, 1984.

Donders, Joseph G. *Non-Bourgeois Theology: An African Experience of Jesus.* New York: Orbis Books, 1985.

Hastings, Adrian. *African Catholicism: Essays in Discovery.* London: SCM Press, 1989.

Nyamiti, Charles. *Christ as Our Ancestor.* Harare: Mambo, 1986.

LAWRENCE NJOROGE

Africa, the Church in Roman, the Church in the Roman province of Africa, a province established in the first century by Augustus on the ruins of the old Punic colony. Christianity flourished in Roman Africa in hundreds of communities in what are today the Islamic nations of Tunisia, Algeria, and Morocco. In general, its ecclesiastical divisions followed those of the imperial divisions under Diocletian and stretched from the Gulf of Tunis in the east to the Atlantic in the west: Tripolitana, Byzacena, Africa Proconsularis, Numidia, and Mauretania. The archaeological evidence of these Christian communities is found in an abundance of mosaics, in the extensive catacombs of Hadrumetum (Sousse), and in the ruins of vast basilican complexes near the Mediterranean coast, through the mountains of the interior, to the borders of the Sahara. Just as impressive is the literary legacy of this lively and factious church, reflected in the writings of its bishops, Cyprian of Carthage, Augustine of Hippo, and a host of others, as well as in a confident and articulate laity: martyrs like Perpetua in the second century, and theologians like Tyconius in the fourth century. These Christian communities shared in the urban sophistication, as well as in the rich agricultural development, of the region. They were part of a cosmopolitan mix of native Berber, surviving Punic elements, and Greek culture, together with the strong Latin component contributed by the pervasive presence of the imperial administration and the descendants of the Roman veterans who had settled as colonists after the reestablishment of the region by Augustus.

The Conflict with Donatism: While scholars debate the provenance of African Christianity, the earliest written evidence is the *Acts of the Scillitan Martyrs* (180). It is significant that this document already marks a tension with imperial authorities that was to characterize the whole course of African Christianity. The *Passion of Perpetua and Felicitas* (203) and the writings of Tertullian witness to the persecutions in the early years of the third century. The writings of Cyprian referring to the severe persecutions of the African church under the Roman emperors Decius (249–251) and Valerian (257–258), together with numerous other martyr acts, make one of the richest collections of the genre in the early Church. The documents collected by Optatus of Milevis in the fourth century evidence the disruption of church life and the deep divisions in the community occasioned by the persecution of Diocletian (302–304). Even after the Edict of Toleration by Constantine (313), the African church experienced internal dissension related to imperial measures. Constantine summoned the Council of Arles (314) to hear the case between Catholics and Donatists, and instructed governors to preside at provincial hearings in Africa. The Emperor Constans sent the legates Paul and Macarius to enforce church unity (348), but their harsh measures deepened the schism. The emperor Julian allowed the return of Parmenian, the exiled Donatist bishop of Carthage (362–392). Parmenian's intellectual and administrative gifts galvanized the Donatist communities so that at Augustine's return to Africa in 388, large sections of African Christianity were dominated by Donatism. Powerful Donatist bishops like Optatus of Thamugadi in Numidia sided with the rebels in an uprising against the imperial authorities (395–398). This action set in motion a series of confrontations between Catholics and Donatists, in which Augustine played a leading part and which culminated in the Council of Carthage (411), resulting in an imperial proscription against the Donatists. The final act of imperial politics that impinged upon church life in Africa was the attack on the Arian Vandals (534) by Justinian's general, Belisarius, who restored the Catholic ascendency. The next two centuries saw an impressive building program overseen by the Byzantine authorities. Christianity in Roman Africa crumbled under the onslaught of the Arab invasions at the end of the seventh century, although there is isolated evidence of continuing church life for the next five hundred years.

The Ecclesiology of the Roman African Church: In spite of its demise, the Church of Roman Africa left an indelible impression on Latin Christianity. The basic contribution lies in the area of ecclesiology. The attention of African theologians was focused upon the significance of Baptism for the unity, the holiness, the catholicity and the apostolicity of the Church. The many African treatises on Baptism from Cyprian, struggling with the problem of the readmission to the Church of those who had lapsed in the persecutions, to Augustine, arguing against the Donatists, reflect the struggles of the community to express their understanding of a Church made holy by the one Spirit in Baptism and yet a community that was a locus of forgiveness and reconciliation. The lively and often disputatious correspondence between the sees of Carthage and Rome helped to clarify the relationship between local churches and Rome. This is evident not only in the mid-third-century disputes between Cyprian of Carthage and Pope Stephen I, but more importantly in the ruling of the Council of Carthage (419) on the question of appeals from a local church to the Ro-

Roman Africa encompassed in part the territory now occupied by the Islamic countries of Tunisia, Algeria, and Morocco. Among the places of major importance were Hippo, where Augustine (d. 430) served as bishop, and Carthage, where the most famous bishop was Cyprian (d.258). Carthage was the site of several councils, including one in 411 that condemned Donatism—a schismatic movement that plagued the Church of Roman Africa—and another in 419 that contested the jurisdictional claims of Rome over Africa. Imperial and papal influence ended with the Arab invasions in the late seventh century.

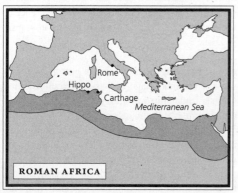

ROMAN AFRICA

man see. The ruling of the African council was incorporated into later collections of canon law. African translations of the Septuagint (the Greek version of the Hebrew Bible) and of the books of the NT, together called the Vetus Latina (the Old Latin version of the Bible), were being read in the churches in the second century. Augustine refers to the resistance of his congregation to the introduction of Jerome's Vulgate. The methods of scriptural interpretation in Africa had reached high levels of articulation, as in the *Book of Rules* of Tyconius, even before Augustine wrote what was to become a classic study of scriptural interpretation, *On Christian Doctrine*. Finally, it was in the African church that the Latin language became an expressive vehicle for Christianity, both at the technical theological level as early as Tertullian, and at the popular level in the sermons of Augustine. *See also* Africa, Catholicism in; Augustine of Hippo, St.; Cyprian of Carthage, St.; Donatism; *lapsi;* persecutions; Septuagint.

Bibliography

Brown, Peter. *Augustine of Hippo: A Biography.* Berkeley, CA: University of California Press, 1967.

———. *Religion and Society in the Age of St. Augustine.* New York: Harper & Row, 1972.

Frend, W. H. C. *The Donatist Church.* Oxford: Clarendon Press, 1952.

Hinchliff, Peter B. *Cyprian of Carthage and the Unity of the Christian Church.* London: Geoffrey Chapman, 1974.   PAMELA BRIGHT

African-American Catholics. *See* black Catholics.

agape (ah-gah'pay; Gk., "love"), word meaning "love," used in the NT. Appearing in the synoptic Gospels in Matt 24:12 and Luke 11:42, it is related to the verb "to love" used in the "great commandment" to love God and neighbor (Mark 12:28; Matt 22:39–40) and in Jesus' injunction to love even one's enemies (Matt 5:43). Early Christian authors regularly designate agape as the hallmark of Christian life. For Paul agape is the saving will that God has shown humankind (Rom 5:5, 8; 9:13, 25) through Christ and the Spirit. It is also what human beings owe to God and to one another (Rom 13:10; Gal 5:13). Paul links it with faith and hope but deems it greater than either (1 Cor 13:13). For John, agape defines the new commandment of Jesus (John 13:35). It binds Jesus and the believer (John 15:9–10), and is epitomized in the act of self-giving for one's friends (John 15:13). It in fact defines God (1 John 4:8) and that which unites the believer to God (1 John 4:16).

Agape came to be used for a special meal, a "love feast" in which both divine and human love were manifested in sharing and fellowship. Originally there seems to have been no distinction between community meals and the Eucharist (1 Cor 11:17–34). The two are distinguished by the early second century (Jude 12; Ignatius, *Smyrn.* 8.2). By the end of the century community meals are widely practiced (Tertullian *Apology* 39; Clement of Alexandria *Paedagogue* 2.1; Hippolytus *Apostolic Tradition* 26.1.2). The practice of the agape meal was eventually excluded from churches. *See also* Eucharist.

HAROLD W. ATTRIDGE

Agapitus, St., d. 536, pope from May 535 to April 536. He traveled to Constantinople and successfully deposed the Monophysite patriarch Anthimus, replacing him with Mennas, but he was unsuccessful in dissuading Justinian from invading Italy. Agapitus established his house library as a center for learning. Feast day: September 20 (Western); April 17 (Eastern).

Agatha, St., virgin martyr. Executed in the Decian persecution (A.D. 251) in Sicily, she is widely venerated there. She is patron saint of both Palermo and Catania. Feast day: February 5.

Agatho, St., ca. 577–681, pope from 678 to 681. The Council of Constantinople III (680–81) incorporated two of his letters in its decrees. These letters affirm, against Monothelitism, two wills in Christ and contain statements relevant to the doctrine of papal infallibility. Agatho does not include the *Filioque* (Lat., "and the Son") in his citation of the creed. Feast day: January 10 (Western); February 20 (Eastern). *See also* Monothelitism.

age, impediment of, in canon law invalidating obstacle to marriage; a man may not marry before age sixteen, a woman before age fourteen. Although marriage at such early ages is not common in many societies today, these limits are set with reference to the usual age of puberty (can. 1094). *See also* marriage law.

age of reason, the time when a person begins to show a minimal stage of personal responsibility. Church leadership has never indicated a specific age; commonly, Catholics consider age 6–8 as the age of reason. Until the year 1000, First Communion in the West was given to newly baptized infants; today Confirmation and first Eucharist are often given prior to first Confession with the revised Rite of Christian Initiation of Children. Currently, more attention is given by Church leadership to the relationship of various developmental stages of an individual's spiritual growth.

aggiornamento (ah-jawhr-nah-men'toh; It., "bringing up to date"), a term that has become synonymous with the Church renewal initiated by Pope John XXIII and the Second Vatican Council (1962–65). *Aggiornamento* called for a new openness on the part of the Church toward the world, and toward other Christian churches and non-Christian religions, using "the medicine of mercy" rather than condemnation as the means of promoting the Church's teachings and wisdom. *Aggiornamento* also called for the internal reform and renewal of the Church, especially in its liturgical life. At the final session of the council, Pope Paul VI offered a new definition: "From now on *aggiornamento* will signify for us a widely undertaken quest for a deeper understanding of the spirit of the council and the faithful application of the norms it has happily and prayerfully provided." *See also* Vatican Council II.

Agnes, St., virgin martyr. Nothing is known beyond her third-century death. A century later the daughter of Constantine erected a basilica over her tomb in Rome. Feast day: January 21.

Agnes of Assisi, St., 1197–1253, abbess. Sister of Clare of Assisi, she entered religious life under the inspiration of Francis of Assisi. Feast day: November 16. *See also* Francis of Assisi, St.,

agnosticism, the position that confines knowledge to sense experience or the empirically verifiable. Consequently, agnostics, in rejecting positive knowledge of anything beyond sense experience, reject the possibility of supernatural knowledge, especially any knowledge of the existence of God.

While the philosophical underpinnings for agnosticism were in place with the rejection of the speculative by Immanuel Kant (1724–1804), the term itself, coined by T.H. Huxley in 1869, refers to the rejection of metaphysics as "Gnosticism." The nineteenth-century debate focused on the fundamental limitations of human knowing and thus ruled out either positive or negative statements on the existence of God. Consequently, agnosticism is not the same as atheism but is rather a form of scepticism, specifically, a scepticism that rejects metaphysics.

Agnosticism can also appear in company with religious belief as the view that since God is unknown or unknowable, religious faith cannot and should not attempt to engage in apologetics. For the "religious agnostic" of the nineteenth century, the profession of agnosticism was meant to highlight that the "leap of faith" (belief in this unknowable God) is not a rational move, but a position borne of faith alone or moral necessity (the latter being Kant's resolution).

Vatican I (1869–70) reaffirmed the Catholic tradition that God's existence is knowable by natural reason alone (see Wis 13; Rom 1:20). This is not the same as affirming the knowability of God's essence (what God is), which abides as incomprehensible mystery. Rather, the Catholic objection to agnosticism is a theologically grounded refusal to privatize the objective claim of faith upon humanity. *See also* atheism; faith and reason; God. NANCY DALLAVALLE

Agnus Dei (ahn'yoos day'ee; Lat., "Lamb of God"). 1 Latin title for the litany sung by the congregation at Mass during the final preparations for Holy Communion. Introduced into the Roman rite during the seventh century, the Lamb of God litany accompanies the final preparations of the eucharistic foods. Ordinarily sung three times, the text, "Lamb of God, who takes away the sins of the world, have mercy on us" is concluded the third time with, "grant us peace." 2 Agnus Dei also refers to small pieces of wax cut from the paschal candle, stamped with the image of a lamb, blessed by the pope, and distributed to various individuals during the first year of the pontificate and every seven years thereafter. *See also* Lamb of God.

Agobard, St., 769–840, archbishop of Lyons. Born in Spain, Agobard moved to Lyons by 792, and became its forty-seventh bishop in 816. Agobard supported a rebellion by the sons of Emperor Louis the Pious and was compelled to take refuge in Italy with one of them, Lothair I, from 835 to 837. Among his works are treatises against the Adoptionist Felix of Urgel and on *The Insolence of the Jews*. Feast day: June 6. *See also* Adoptionism; Felix of Urgel.

agrapha (ah'grah-fah; Gk., "unwritten things"), sayings attributed to Jesus but not recorded in the NT. Many were transmitted orally and then preserved in the works of patristic authors such as Justin Martyr and Clement of Alexandria and in apocryphal Gospels such as the *Gospel of Thomas*.

Agrypnia (ah-grip-nee'ah). *See* All-Night Vigil.

Aidan of Iona, St., d. 651, monk and bishop of Lindisfarne. Sent from Iona at the request of King Oswald of Northumbria, he was consecrated a bishop in 635, taking Lindisfarne as his see. Since he did not know the English language, the king (who had been recalled from exile among the Irish) translated as Aidan preached. Aidan was a holy man who succeeded in spreading Christianity and monasticism throughout the region, as Bede willingly acknowledged despite his distaste for the Irishman's mistaken views on the dating of Easter. Feast day: August 31. *See also* Lindisfarne.

AIDS (Acquired Immune Deficiency Syndrome), a fatal disease resulting from HIV (human immunodeficiency virus) infection. It represents the most serious health disaster in the United States since the influenza epidemic of 1918 and is now worldwide in scope. HIV is spread by sexual contact, parenteral exposure (needle sharing, blood transfusions), and perinatal exposure (transplacental and/or intrapartum transmission).

Pope John Paul II in an address to the Catholic Health Association (Phoenix, September 14, 1987) referred to the "moral obligation and social responsibility to help those who suffer" from AIDS by showing the "compassion of Christ and his Church." The problem of prevention and containment has centered on the means to be used. While stressing the desirability of abstinence as the only medically reliable and morally acceptable means, some Catholics believe that prophylactics are acceptable when all other preventive means will foreseeably fail. The U.S. Catholic bishops, however, have generally opposed this course.

aisle (īl), the areas within a church building on either side of the nave (the main part of the church where the laity sit) between the exterior walls and the columns; also the walkways, defined by pews, extending from the doors to the sanctuary. Some authorities claim the second usage is incorrect, saying that the term "center aisle" is contradictory.

Akathistos (ah-kah'-this-tohs; Gk., "not seated"), ancient Byzantine poem in honor of Mary, comprising twelve poetic refrains (*kontakion*) each followed by its strophe (*ikos*), chanted standing (whence the name) during Matins of the fifth Saturday of Lent or on other occasions as a devotional office. It was composed to commemorate the miraculous liberation of Constantinople from the invasions of the Persians and Avars in 626.

akolouthia (ah-koh-*loo*-thee'uh; Gk., "order," "rite"), Byzantine-rite term for a particular rite or office (the *akolouthia* of Baptism), for the proper variable parts of the offices of a day or feast (the *akolouthia* of Christmas), or for the common of a category of saint (the *akolouthia* of a martyr).

Alacoque, St. Margaret Mary, 1647–90, French mystic, chief founder of devotion to the Sacred Heart. Born a peasant in Burgundy, she entered the Visitation convent at Paray-le-Monial in 1671. She had difficulty adapting to the pace of life in the convent and its active prayer style, and provoked the jealousy of some of the sisters. On December 27, 1673, Margaret Mary began to experience a series of revelations in which Jesus told her about his loving heart. She informed her spiritual adviser that the Lord was asking her to promulgate devotion to the heart of Jesus in reparation for humanity's indifference to God. She also claimed that Jesus told her the approval of her superiors was necessary for all her undertakings so that Satan would not mislead her, because he had no power over those who act out of obedience. She encouraged the reception of the Eucharist on the First Friday of each month in reparation for sins and a prayer vigil every Thursday night in honor of Jesus' agony in Gethsemane. She also asked the Church to observe the feast of the Sacred Heart on the Friday after the Octave of Corpus Christi. Her religious community was initially suspicious of her requests but her confessor, Claude la Colombière, sought ecclesiastical approval for them. Colombière's memoirs disclosed the revelatory origin of Margaret Mary's devotion to the Sacred Heart. She was canonized in 1920. Feast day: October 16. *See also* First Fridays; Sacred Heart, devotion to the.

Alan of Lille, ca. 1120–1202/3, Cistercian lay brother, theologian, poet, preacher, and canonist. After preaching against heresy in southern France, he lived his final days as a Cistercian lay brother. He was a prolific and original writer highly influenced by the Platonic thought of the time. His works are varied and include allegorical poems, handbooks on sermons and preaching, a dictionary of biblical language, and a work refuting not only Christian heresies, but Judaism and Islam as well.

Alaric, ca. 370–410, Visigothic conqueror of Rome. A former ally, Alaric began to attack the empire in the East ca. 395; unable to take Constantinople, he moved on to Illyria, where he was made imperial *magister militum* (virtually a military governor) by 401 and received a huge bribe around 407. Satisfied by neither title nor gold, he besieged Rome in 408 and 409. Negotiations for further bribes collapsed in 410, and Alaric sacked the city in August. *See also* Visigoths.

alb (Lat., *albus,* "white"), a long white linen tunic worn by priests, deacons, and other ministers for liturgical functions. The alb, which may be fastened at the waist by a cincture, is fashioned after the Greco-Roman *tunica talaris,* an everyday garment that reached to the ankles. The custom of wearing albs for liturgy was established by the sixth century. *See also* vestments.

Alba Iulia (yoo lee-ah). *See* Pseudo-Synod of Alba Iulia.

Alban, St., ca. third century, protomartyr of Roman Britain. A pagan soldier at Verulamium (modern St. Alban's), he sheltered a Christian priest during a persecution and was so moved by the Christian message that he was baptized and, posing as the priest, martyred. Feast day: June 20.

Albanian Byzantine Catholics, Albanian Orthodox or their descendants who became Catholic but retained their Byzantine heritage. The first such community was a small mission along the coast of Epirus, which existed from 1628 until 1765. A second group was established ca. 1900 by a former Albanian Orthodox priest, George Germanos. By 1912 his community numbered about 120 and was centered in the village of Elbasan. In 1938 monks from the Italo-Albanian monastery at Grottaferrata came to assist the community, which by 1945 had about 400 members. The group vanished after 1967 when Albania was declared an atheist state, and there is no indication that it has been reestablished after the fall of Communism.

Alberic of Molesmes, St., d. 1109, a hermit who in 1098, along with Stephen Harding (d. 1134) and Robert of Molesmes (d. 1111), founded a new monastery at Cîteaux, the motherhouse of the Cistercians. Feast day: January 26. *See also* Cîteaux.

Albert the Great. *See* Albertus Magnus, St.

Albertus Magnus, St. (Lat., "Albert the Great"), ca. 1200–80, German Dominican bishop, philosopher, theologian, Doctor of the Church, and patron saint of natural scientists.

Life: Albert the Great probably received training in the liberal arts at Padua, where he would have seen newly translated works of Aristotle. Upon entering the Dominican order, probably in his thirties, he studied theology and then lectured in German Dominican priories. In the early 1240s, he went to the University of Paris for further study; there he found more newly available Peripatetic texts (derived from the school of Aristotle), whose contents he absorbed with astonishing rapidity. He was a master of theology at Paris from 1245 until 1248, when he was asked to establish the Dominicans' international house of studies at Cologne. In addition to his speculative genius, Albert possessed diplomatic and administrative skills, so that his teaching and writing were frequently interrupted by practical demands. Besides often being called upon to settle conflicts or give counsel, he was provincial of the German Dominicans from 1254 to 1257, and bishop of Regensburg from 1260 to 1262 (a position he

Alb

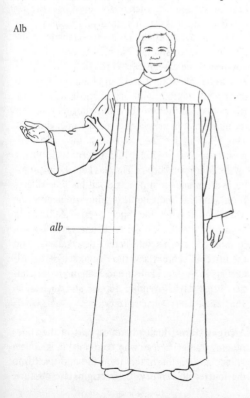

alb

Albertus Magnus, teacher of fellow Dominican Thomas Aquinas; fifteenth-century painting by Fra Angelico, Museum of St. Mark, Florence.

accepted only at the pope's command, resigning as soon as possible). Once rid of the bishopric, he seems to have resumed writing and teaching in various German Dominican houses until shortly before his death, when his memory failed. His unusual scientific interests guaranteed that legends of black magic would grow up around him and that occult books would be ascribed to him. Consequently, his beatification was delayed until 1622, and his canonization until 1931.

Thought: Asked by fellow Dominicans for help understanding Aristotelian physics, Albert undertook to make that and all of Aristotelian learning intelligible to those whose academic language was Latin. Over the course of some twenty years (ca. 1250–70), he paraphrased the known works of Aristotle, together with some spurious works. But he did not simply repeat Aristotle. Rather, he presented the best of the living Peripatetic school, adding whole books when Peripatetics had contributed to sciences about which Aristotle had not written and correcting Aristotle in light of later Peripatetics and of his own occasional experiments and abundant observations (because Dominicans were not allowed horses, Albert had time to examine animals, plants, stones, and the like as he crossed Europe on foot). Furthermore, when faced with philosophical arguments opposed to faith, he respected the autonomy of secular sciences and addressed the arguments philosophically, showing how they were inconclusive or faulty on philosophical grounds, whereas sound philosophy never contradicts revelation.

Thus, while a number of his contemporaries toyed with heresy or issued blanket condemnations of the new learning, Albert showed concretely how room could be made for Aristotle within the Church's intellectual tradition.

However comprehensive Albert's explanation of Aristotelian learning, he insisted that it could not represent the whole of philosophy, since complete philosophers must know Plato too. Indeed, most Peripatetics Albert read were somewhat Platonic, with the result that his Aristotelian encyclopedia exhibits Neoplatonic traits. So, too, do his numerous theological works, where Augustine and Pseudo-Dionysius lend their authority to this tendency.

Albert complained that his fellow religious were uninterested in learning about things they thought irrelevant to salvation; he himself cultivated all branches of philosophy, because he found vestiges of the creator in all creatures. He also held that training in these secular sciences was invaluable for theologians. Therefore, in 1259, while heading a commission on study in the Dominican order, he saw to it that Dominican students would be taught philosophy. This was unheard of, since both canon law and the Dominican constitutions made it quite hard for religious to pursue secular studies; still, he himself, though a master of theology, had already dared lecture on Aristotle's ethics and zoology.

Legacy: While Albert has been overshadowed by his most famous student, Thomas Aquinas, this was not always the case: Albert is the only philosopher ever to be called "the Great," and he was called that during his lifetime, contrary to medieval custom. His respect for the autonomy of philosophy and his recognition of the services it could render theology were taken up by Thomas, who studied under Albert from 1246 to 1252, while Albert was lecturing on the Dionysian corpus; Thomas kept a copy of Albert's Dionysian commentaries all his life. Albert's Dionysian and Neoplatonic leanings influenced the Rhineland mystics too; such people as Heinrich Suso, Johannes Tauler, Meister Eckhart, and Jan van Ruysbroeck are his intellectual descendants. And the fifteenth century saw the rise of self-styled Albertists in German, Polish, and Bohemian universities. Feast day: November 15. *See also* Aquinas, St. Thomas; Aristotle; Dominican order.   *THÉRÈSE BONIN*

Albigensians, dualist heretics, part of the wide-ranging Cathari heresy, who flourished in southern France and northern Italy from the mid-twelfth to the fourteenth century. Their origins are obscure:

they may have been influenced by the Bogomils of Bulgaria, who in turn were dependent upon earlier Manichees, or they may have been an independent dualist movement. Their dualism is both cosmological and anthropological. A good God, who created the angels and human souls, and an evil God, Satan, who created the physical world, battle for control of the cosmos. Human salvation is a process of becoming aligned with the good God by liberating the soul from the contamination of the flesh. As a result, they championed an austere asceticism, rejecting all sexual activity and the eating of meat, eggs, and milk and practicing rigorous fasts, sometimes unto death. Their religious beliefs were seen as a challenge to both the secular and the ecclesiastical orders. They refused to bear arms or swear oaths and rejected both the Catholic hierarchy and its sacraments.

They developed their own ecclesiastical organization, dividing their territory into dioceses paralleling the Catholic and distinguishing in their own ranks between the Pure, or Perfect, and their less advanced followers. Only Perfect souls could hope to transcend the cycle of death and reincarnation. Those whom the Perfect deemed fit to achieve their more lofty status were initiated through a rite of laying on of hands, called *consolamentum* (Lat.). As itinerant preachers, the Albigensians won many adherents among the poor, who were impressed by their sharp renunciation of the world and their condemnation of the wealthy and powerful.

The Catholic Church took a number of measures to regain Albigensian territory. The Cistercian and then Dominican preaching campaign of the late twelfth and early thirteenth centuries proved ineffective, giving way to the Albigensian Crusade and Inquisition, which eventually overcame the Albigensian threat. *See also* Cathari; Crusades; dualism; Inquisition; Manichaeism.   MICHAEL WOODWARD

alcoholism, an addiction with genetic, biological, and social dimensions, progressive through varying degrees of dependency. Characteristics include a preoccupation with alcohol, drinking more than intended and over a longer period, giving up important activities to drink, and drinking even though it causes problems. Disposing factors include personal susceptibility (physical/genetic and/or psychological), environmental stress (economic, relational), and the availability of alcohol. The alcoholic becomes increasingly controlling and inflexible, while the habit is enabled by a system of denial and role-playing maintained by family and friends. Alcohol becomes the system's central organizing principle. Dependency is progressively destructive and often fatal.

Researchers reflect that modern culture does not provide a sense of place in the cosmos or a sense of self-assurance. Drugs or alcohol promise to alleviate or numb the corresponding deep feelings of anxiety.

As seen in Augustine's *Confessions,* no amount of will power, promises, or resolutions can liberate one from such addictive patterns. Thus, successful programs such as Alcoholics Anonymous (AA), founded by Bill W[ilson], have counseled a Twelve-Step program that centers around surrender of the will to a Higher Power and active participation in recovery communities. Some have suggested parallels between such communities and the base communities of Latin America, though the emphases of the base communities on Scripture and structural analysis are absent.

The late Father Ed Dowling told his friend Bill W. of similarities between AA's Twelve Steps and Ignatius of Loyola's "Rules for the Discernment of Spirits." The life of Matt Talbot is often invoked among recovering Catholic alcoholics. *See also* base communities; discernment of spirits; Talbot, Matt. SIMON HARAK

Alcuin (al'kwin), ca. 730–804, deacon, abbot of Tours, and teacher. Born in Anglo-Saxon Northumbria and educated in the cathedral school at York, Alcuin became its master in 778. Moving to Aachen at Charlemagne's request in 782 to be master of the palace school, he was made abbot of Tours in 796.

An active educator, Alcuin prepared *On Grammar, On Rhetoric and the Virtues, On Dialectic,* and *On Orthography,* textbooks melding the best classical and patristic materials. He served the king as a general adviser, drafting royal letters and taking a leading role in the literary circle in which Charlemagne was known as "David," the royal poet, and Alcuin himself as "Flaccus," after the Roman poet Q. Horatius Flaccus (Horace). Alcuin's poem on the church of York survives, along with a number of other verses and an extensive correspondence.

Alcuin also pursued more narrowly theological interests, including regularization of the biblical text and preparation of biblical commentaries. He was once credited with most of the liturgical reforms of Charlemagne's reign, but this position is not now generally accepted. He played a prominent role in the Adoptionist and iconoclastic controversies, setting out the Carolingian party line at the

Council of Frankfurt (794) and writing tracts against the Spanish heresy of Adoptionism (that Christ is only the adopted son of God). *See also* Adoptionism; iconoclasm.

Alexander II [Anselm of Lucca, not to be confused with his nephew, St. Anselm of Lucca, d. 1088], d. 1073, pope from 1061 to 1073. A member of the reforming party of Hildebrand (later Pope Gregory VII) and elected with his support, Alexander renewed and enforced decrees regarding simony and clerical celibacy and forbade lay investiture, pressing forward his agenda with legates sent out widely over Europe. Emperor Henry IV did not confirm Alexander's election but from late 1061 supported the antipope Honorius II (d. 1072). Alexander approved the conquest of England by William I (1066) and encouraged latinization of Greek sees in Italy and the reconquest of Muslim dominions; but he intervened on behalf of the Jews in France and Spain, insisting that they not be mistreated, explicitly invoking the precedent of Pope Gregory the Great (d. 604). *See also* celibacy, clerical; investiture controversy; Jews, Catholicism and; latinization; simony.

Alexander III [Orlando Bandinelli], ca. 1105–81, scholar, diplomat, and canon lawyer, and pope from 1159 to 1181. Before his election, he taught at the University of Bologna and wrote a famous commentary on the *Decretum* of Gratian as well as a scholastic treatise, the *Sententiae Rolandi Bonoienses Magistri,* one of the principal witnesses to the theological school of Abelard (d. 1142). Under Pope Hadrian IV (d. 1159) he served as chancellor (1153) and on numerous occasions as his legate. Although elected by a majority, from 1160 Emperor Frederick Barbarossa supported a succession of three antipopes (Victor IV, Paschal III, and Callistus III), remaining in schism until 1177. From 1162 to 1165 Alexander lived in France, and from 1167 (when Frederick occupied Rome) to 1177, in Benevento. For Alexander's support of the Lombard communes against Frederick, the new city Alessandria was named after him. He is also remembered for having imposed penance (1172) on Henry II for the murder of Thomas Becket. In 1179 he presided over the Third Lateran Council. *See also Decretum Gratianum;* Lateran councils.

Alexander V [Peter of Candia], ca. 1339–1410, antipope from 1409 to 1410. Born in Crete, he joined the Franciscans and became Master of Theology at the University of Paris (1381). Later, he was named archbishop of Milan (1402) and cardinal and papal legate of Lombardy (1403). Originally obedient to Rome during the Great Schism, Peter opposed Gregory XII's refusal to convene a reform council and helped assemble the Council of Pisa (1409), for which he gave the keynote address. In 1409 the twenty-two cardinals at the council attempted to resolve the schism by deposing the two rival claimants and electing Peter as pope (June 26, 1409). As Alexander V, he sought to weaken his two rivals and end the schism by shrewd distribution of benefits. To strengthen papal authority, Alexander dissolved the council after promising to work for reform. He died ten months later without achieving either unity or reform.

The validity of Alexander's election has not been recognized by the Catholic Church because the Council of Pisa was not convened by a pope. *See also* Great Schism; Pisa, Council of.

Alexander VI [Rodrigo Borgia], 1431–1503, pope from 1492 to 1503. Born in Valencia, Spain, he was one of the Renaissance popes notorious for lavishness and personal immorality. Despite a private life that produced four children, including Lucrezia Borgia and Macchiavelli's idol Cesare Borgia, Rodrigo was elected pope, reportedly through bribery. He was notable for aggrandizing his family's power through Cesare's military skill and Lucrezia's marriages. As pope he was first allied with Isabella and Ferdinand of Spain and the kingdom of Naples. After Charles VIII of France invaded Italy (1494), Alexander's policies and troops helped drive them out (1495). After 1497 he drew closer to French king Louis XII. With Louis's help, Alexander and Cesare successfully unified the four Papal States under Cesare's control. Alexander's death ended Cesare's rule.

Alexander's open immorality and lavish patronage of the Roman Renaissance sparked a struggle with the Florentine reformer Savonarola, ending in Savonarola's excommunication and execution by fire. Despite his lax morals and unabashed exploitation of the papacy to the advantage of the Borgia family, Alexander VI cannot be completely condemned. He was a generous patron of Renaissance art and architecture, commissioning Michelangelo's *Pietà,* the restoration of Castel Sant'Angelo, and the refurbishing of the papal apartments. Finally, he promoted the evangelization of the New World and his papal line of demarcation (1493) helped ensure

Pope Alexander VI, the most notorious of the "bad popes"; fifteenth-century mural in the Borgia apartment, Vatican.

peace between Castile and Portugal in their new colonies in Asia and America. *See also* Renaissance.

Alexander VII [Fabio Chigi], 1599–1667, pope from 1655 to 1667. Born in Siena, Fabio was a brilliant student, receiving a doctorate in theology in 1626 and embarking on a diplomatic career in the papal service. Upon becoming bishop of Nardo, he was also ordained a priest. Pope Urban VIII named him papal nuncio to Cologne, and he represented the papacy at the negotiations of the Peace of Westphalia ending the Thirty Years' War (1618–48). Pope Innocent X named him secretary of state in 1651 and made him a cardinal in 1652. In 1655 he succeeded Innocent as Alexander VII. As pope, he patronized scholarship and the arts, commissioning the Bernini Colonnade at St. Peter's, but his papacy was marred by conflict with Louis XIV of France, who seized Avignon and forced Alexander into the Peace of Pisa in 1664. The most significant events of Alexander's reign concerned the Jansenists. As secretary of state he had encouraged Innocent X to condemn the five propositions of Jansenism as found in Cornelius Jansen's *Augustinus*. These propositions held that human beings cannot fulfill God's commandments without a special grace, and that the operation of grace is irresistible. The brilliant Jansenist Antoine Arnauld, while agreeing that the propositions were heretical, convinced Innocent that they were not actually found in that book. As pope,

Alexander went ahead and condemned the *Augustinus* in 1665. *See also* Jansenism.

Alexander of Alexandria, St., d. 328, bishop of Alexandria from 312 to 328. After some toleration, he led a local synod (319) to depose Arius, one of his presbyters (priests), for denying the true divinity of Christ. At the Council of Nicaea (325), Alexander, with his deacon Athanasius, decisively opposed the teachings of Arius. Feast day: February 26 (Western); May 29 (Greek); April 22 (Coptic). *See also* Arianism; Arius; Nicaea, First Council of.

Alexander of Hales, ca. 1185–1245, English Franciscan theologian, known as the "Irrefutable Doctor." Born in England, he was a regent master of theology at the University of Paris beginning in 1220. His entrance into the Franciscan order in 1236 brought the Franciscans his chair in theology. His vast literary production, much indebted to the writings of Augustine, includes numerous disputed questions and a lengthy *Gloss* on the *Sentences* of Peter Lombard. The large *Summa Theologica* ascribed to him is in fact a collaborative work prepared by disciples familiar with his thought. Alexander exerted tremendous influence on Franciscan scholastic theology until the time of Duns Scotus (d. 1308). Perhaps his most significant contribution came in his championing of the *Sentences* as a favored scholastic teaching text; he is also responsible for the division of the Lombard's chapters into "distinctions." *See also* Scholasticism.

Alexander of Jerusalem, St., d. ca. 251, bishop and confessor. Together with Theoctistus, bishop of Caesarea, Alexander invited Origen, still a layman, to preach, later (ca. 230) ordaining him priest. A confessor under the persecution of Septimus Severus, Alexander died in prison during the persecution of Decius, the Roman Emperor (249–51). Feast day: March 18 (Western); December 12 (Eastern). *See also* Origen.

Alexandria, metropolis founded ca. 332 by Alexander the Great at the mouth of the Nile, the most illustrious center of Greek culture in the Roman Empire, and third of the five ancient patriarchal sees (after Rome and Constantinople). Traditionally founded by St. Mark, the see of Alexandria gained prominence through its famous catechetical school (headed by such teachers as Origen and Didymus the Blind), and its succession of powerful bishops, from Dionysius, Peter, and Athanasius to Theophilus and Cyril. The Council of Nicaea (325) ranked the see of Alexandria as second only to Rome, although the Council of Constantinople (381) ranked it third after Constantinople. The see of Alexandria had direct jurisdiction over all of Egypt, Libya, and the Pentapolis, while the Ethiopian church, from its rise in the mid-fourth century, was also dependent on the patriarch of Alexandria.

Alexandrian influence was dominant at the Councils of Nicaea, Constantinople, and Ephesus (431). But when the Council of Chalcedon (451) deposed Cyril's Monophysite successor Dioscorus (444–51, d. 454), the great majority of Alexandrian and indeed Egyptian Christians refused to accept the council and retained their Monophysite sympathies. By 565, the end of the reign of the emperor Justinian, the Coptic church had developed a hierarchy independent of Constantinople or Rome, and it continues, as the Coptic Orthodox church, to represent the great majority of Egyptian Christians to this day. There are three other patriarchal sees of Alexandria: the Coptic Catholic (uniat), the Eastern (Greek) Orthodox, and the Melchite (Melkite) Catholic church. *See also* Alexandria, school of; Antioch, school of; Athanasius, St.; Chalcedon, Council of; Coptic Catholic Church; Cyril of Alexandria, St.; Egypt; Monophysitism. *DARLENE K. FLAMING*

Alexandria, school of, both a theological tradition and the catechetical school (Gk., *didaskaleion*) with which it was associated. The earliest known Christian teachers in Alexandria were the Gnostics Basilides and Valentinus, who taught in the first part of the second century, but when more orthodox teachers appeared somewhat later—first the shadowy Pantaenus and then Clement of Alexandria (ca. 150–215)—they retained the typical Alexandrian predilection toward speculation, philosophical discourse, and allegorical exegesis. Clement defended the goodness of creation against the Gnostics, teaching that philosophy had prepared the Greeks for Christ as Mosaic law had prepared the Jews. A fragment from the historian Philip of Side (d. after 439) lists Clement, after Athenagoras and Pantaenus, as a teacher in the catechetical school at Alexandria, but it is unclear whether these early figures taught privately or in a school sponsored by the Church.

Clearly, however, Origen, the next teacher on Philip's list, was assigned by the bishop Demetrius to direct a catechetical school. Origen divided the school into two levels, reserving the higher for himself and giving the elementary level to Heraclas, a Christian philosopher who was his student. At odds with Demetrius, Origen left Alexandria permanently ca. 231. Heraclas, who concurred in Demetrius's condemnation and succeeded him as bishop, was appointed in Origen's place, but the school retained Origen's stamp for the rest of its existence. Although generally renouncing some of Origen's more adventuresome speculations (e.g., the preexistence of souls), it retained his emphasis on allegorical exegesis and on the divinity of Christ. The school and the episcopate remained closely linked, four of its directors (Heraclas, Dionysius, Achillas, and Peter) becoming bishops, but with the death of Didymus the Blind (398), who had been appointed director by Athanasius, the school began to fade from view, perhaps a victim of the anti-Origenism of Theophilus (bishop from 385 to his death in 412).

Nevertheless, the distinctive Alexandrian "Word/flesh" (*Logos/sarx*) Christology, evolved from the time of Athanasius but with roots as early as Clement, survived and developed into the fifth century and later. The most extreme version of this Christology was the heretical doctrine of Apollinarius of Laodicea (d. 392) who taught that the Word simply replaced the human soul in Christ, so that the Christ was without qualification "one nature," that of the Word "incarnate" ("in flesh"). In the fifth century, in the person of Cyril of Alexandria (d. 444), a modified form of this Christology came into conflict with the "two nature," "Word/man" (*Logos/anthropos*) scheme of the school of Antioch. Cyril succeeded in having Nestorius, patriarch of Constantinople, condemned at the Council of Ephesus (431). Cyril was himself able to compromise with John of Antioch (433), and the spirit of this compromise was upheld in the formula subsequently promulgated by the Council of Chalcedon (451), but a great majority of the Egyptian church rejected Chalcedon and drifted into schism, reaffirming its traditional Christology under the form of Monophysitism. *See also* Antioch, school of; Apollinarius of Laodicea; Athanasius, St.; Chalcedon, Council of; Christology; Clement of Alexandria; Cyril of Alexandria, St.; Logos; Monophysitism; Origen. *JOHN C. CAVADINI*

Alexandrian rite, common if inaccurate name for the liturgical tradition of Egypt, especially the Orthodox Greek rite of the patriarchal see of Alexandria. In the fourth and fifth centuries the pure monastic offices of the desert tradition of Lower Egypt had a seminal influence on the formation of monastic common prayer in the East and the West. After the Council of Chalcedon in 451, the Alexandrian rite continued in use among the Greek-speaking Orthodox of Egypt, while related liturgical uses celebrated in Coptic by the Coptic-speaking monks and populace who rejected Chalcedon developed into the Coptic rite. The Alexandria Greek rite fell into disuse when the Orthodox patriarchate of Alexandria abandoned it in favor of the Byzantine rite around the twelfth century. *See also* Eastern rites; rite.

Alfred the Great, 849–899, king of Wessex (England). Youngest son of King Aethelwulf, Alfred succeeded his brother Aethelred (871) in the midst of the Danish invasions. Though heavily outnumbered, Alfred eventually forced the Danish king Guthrum to agree to a peace and be baptized (879).

Concerned about ignorance among the clergy and religious, Alfred translated into the vernacular the *Pastoral Care* of Gregory the Great, Augustine's *Soliloquies,* Boethius's *Consolation of Philosophy,* and the first fifty psalms. He also sponsored translations of Orosius's *History Against the Pagans* and Bede's *Ecclesiastical History.* A biography by his friend Asser, bishop of St. Asaph's, survives.

Alfrink, Bernard Jan, 1900–87, former cardinal-archbishop of Utrecht and primate of The Netherlands. Ordained in 1924, he was professor of Sacred Scripture at major seminaries (Utrecht, 1933–45; University of Nijmegen, 1945–51) until he was ordained bishop in 1951. He served as archbishop of Utrecht from 1955 to 1976. Created cardinal in 1960, he was a leading progressive at the Second Vatican Council.

alienation of property, the canonical term for the transfer of ownership of Church property by sale, gift, or exchange, of temporal goods, tangible or intangible. Canon law requires approval by various levels of authority, e.g., the diocesan bishop or the Holy See, depending upon the value of the property to be alienated (can. 1291). Without the requisite approvals, the attempted alienation is canonically null and void, often giving rise to Church-state conflicts when the canonically invalid transaction is civilly valid. In addition to the sanction of invalidity, canon law provides that those who attempt to alienate Church property without the requisite approvals are subject to canonical penalties (can. 1296). The same approvals are required for the canonical valid-

ity of transactions other than alienation that entail risk of serious harm to the economic condition of the ecclesiastical entity (e.g., parish, diocese, school), also known as a juridical person, such as mortgaging property, making unsecured loans, or accepting gifts with burdensome conditions attached. *See also* juridical person.

aliturgical days, days of fasting and penance, like Good Friday in the Roman rite, when the Eucharist may not be celebrated. The prohibition goes back at least to the Council of Laodicea in Asia Minor (ca. 360–90), which forbade Mass during Lent except on Saturdays and Sundays. This prohibition has remained in force for all of Lent in most Eastern rites, where the Eucharist is considered festive and incompatible with days of penance. The Byzantine rite has a Presanctified Liturgy or Communion service celebrated on Wednesdays and Fridays of Lent. Most other Eastern rites once had such a service for use at least in monasteries but later abandoned it. Some Byzantine Catholic churches have also abandoned their heritage in favor of Latin usage in this regard. *See also* fast days; penance.

Allatius, Leo (al-lay'shee-uhs), 1586–1669, Greek Catholic humanist and alumnus of the Greek College in Rome. An outstanding Byzantinist, he held various Vatican posts and was first Custodian of the Vatican Library, for which he collected numerous Greek and Syriac manuscripts. He published numerous, still valuable works in Latin and Italian on the Byzantine church, its liturgy, and church buildings and left innumerable unpublished writings preserved in the Vatican Library.

allegory (Gk., *allos,* "other"; *agoreuō,* "speak aloud"), an extended metaphor in which objects, persons, and actions in a narrative serve as symbols for meanings outside the narrative itself. Though the term is not used in the Septuagint, nor does the Hebrew Bible have an exact correspondence, certain texts are generally called allegories, e.g., the allegories of the trees (Judg 9:7–15) and of the vineyard (Isa 5:1–6). In Gal 4:24, Sarah and Hagar refer allegorically to the earthly and heavenly Jerusalem, and the images of Jesus in the Gospel of John (vine, branches, good shepherd) are allegorical. In subsequent interpretation the allegorical sense refers to the deeper symbolic meaning behind the literal meaning of a text (e.g., the Good Samaritan is Jesus coming to the aid of wounded humanity). Allegory develops into a literary genre where a complete theological worldview unfolds in narratives such as Dante's *The Divine Comedy* or Bunyan's *Pilgrim's Progress.*

alleluia (ah'le-loo'yah; Heb., "Praise God"), expression of praise occurring in the Psalms, in the "heavenly liturgy" of Rev 19:2–6, and sung during Christian worship. Alleluias are sung at Mass before the Gospel (as the Gospel acclamation), and in the antiphons (verses sung before and after psalms and as a refrain between psalm verses) and Psalms of the Liturgy of the Hours. Alleluia is not sung during Lent. *See also* psalmody; Psalms, the.

All-Night Vigil (Gk., *agrypnia;* Slav., *vsenoshchnoe bdenie*), Byzantine-rite monastic vigil, of Palestinian origin, comprising Vespers and *orthros* (Matins, Lauds), along with the entire Psalter and all nine canticles of the canon of *orthros.* It is celebrated in monasteries Saturday nights and the vigils of certain feasts and, in abbreviated form, also in Russian parishes.

allocution, papal, an address or talk given by the pope to a department of the Roman Curia or to some other group of persons. Ordinarily a papal allocution does not contain material of legislative import but merely expresses the pope's thoughts or opinions on any particular topic.

All Saints, Feast of, feast celebrated in the West on November 1. Originally the word "saint" was synonymous with "martyr," i.e., someone who witnesses faith in Christ even to death. After a martyr's death, local Christians endeavored to bury the body in a tomb that would be accessible to the faithful. On the anniversary of the martyr's death, Christians would gather to pray and celebrate the Eucharist "in memory of those athletes who have gone before, and to train and make ready those who are to come hereafter" (*Mart. Pol.,* second century). Eventually, the memorial celebration of martyrs occurred in local churches that did not have tombs. By the fifth century, there was already a feast of "all saints" in the East, on the Friday of Easter week. By the eighth century, the church of "St. Mary to the Martyrs" in Rome seems to have celebrated a similar feast. In the ninth century, Pope Gregory IV changed the date of the feast to November 1. From the beginning, those who had endured torture for the faith but had not died ("confessors") were treated with great respect. Eventually Christians who led heroic gospel-inspired lives were often acclaimed after their death as a saint by a local church. The theology and the celebration of the feast emphasize the bond between those Christians already with God and those still on earth. The feast points to our ultimate goal—to be with God. *See also* saints; saints, devotion to.

All Souls, Feast of, feast celebrated on November 2 since the eleventh century for deceased Christians that they "may rest in peace." At an early date, Christians had the custom of remembering their dead. Third-century Christian writers like Tertullian spoke of an intermediate place of rest where the faithful waited until the final judgment. In the same century there seems to have been some idea of deceased Christians who need purification before seeing God. From the eleventh to the thirteenth centuries, the feast spread throughout Europe until it was finally adopted in Rome. The feast involves several beliefs: that some Christians while dying in peace with Christ might still need some purification, that the prayers and good deeds of the living help those who have died, and that there is an intermediate place between heaven and hell. The Eastern Church has usually insisted upon the need for growth in seeing God as characteristic of this intermediate state while the Roman Catholic Church tended to emphasize the penal character of this state. The liturgy itself is the best guide to the meaning of this feast. The liturgical readings point to Christ as the hope of the living and the dead. The liturgical prayers see new life in Christ as God's promise that enables the Christian to face death with faith and hope. Ultimately the feast complements that of All Saints in proclaiming that all those who love God, whether living or dead, are united in a living communion with Christ and one another. *See also* communion of saints; eternal life.

almsgiving (Gk., *eleemosyne,* "pity"), a freewill gift for those in need. The giving of alms is linked to the love or charity commanded by Jesus (Luke 18:22) and to the example of the disciples in the early Church (Acts 9:36; 24:17). Paul encouraged the cheerful giving of alms in his exhortation to the Corinthians on behalf of a collection he was taking up for impoverished members of the Church (1 Cor 9). In the first three centuries, alms were brought to the Eucharist for later distribution by the deacons. By the fourth century, bishops frequently collected offerings and established charitable endowments used for building hospitals and establishing other institutions to help the poor, orphans, widows, the imprisoned, and the sick. Almsgiving is considered a corporal work of mercy by the Church and a penitential act that is especially appropriate during the Lenten season. Like prayer and fasting, almsgiving encourages believers to direct their attention to God, to recall their dependence on God's gifts, and to share in Jesus' ministry of feeding the hungry (Mark 6:34–44; 8:1–10) and healing the sick (Matt 14:34–36). Through the giving of alms, Catholics believe that they are participating in Christ's work to establish God's kingdom of justice and peace. Vatican II (1962–65) reaffirmed the Church's constant tradition of almsgiving in its call for economic solidarity among all peoples of the world (Pastoral Constitution on the Church in the Modern World, nn. 83–90). *See also* mercy, corporal works of.

Aloysius Gonzaga, St., 1568–91, patron saint of youth. Heir to an Italian principality, Aloysius was prepared by his father for a military career. In 1581 he joined the court of Philip II of Spain, where he decided to enter the Society of Jesus, a decision his father opposed until 1585, when Aloysius renounced his inheritance to undertake the novitiate in Rome. He studied philosophy at the Roman College and took his final vows in 1587. He then studied theology, but, while nursing the sick during the plague in Rome in 1591, he contracted the disease and died after a three-month struggle. His spirituality was marked by a strong devotion to the Eucharist, interior prayer, and charitable service to others. Aloysius was canonized in 1726 and declared patron saint of youth in 1926 as a model of purity especially for young men who enter holy orders. Feast day: June 21.

Alphege of Canterbury, St., 954–1012, Benedictine monk, abbot near Bath, bishop of Winchester (984), and archbishop of Canterbury (1006). He was captured and killed by the Danes. Feast day: April 19. *See also* Canterbury.

Alphonsus Liguori, St. (lee-goohr'ee), 1696–1787, founder of the Congregation of the Most Holy Redeemer (Redemptorists) in 1732 and cofounder of the Redemptoristines, a contemplative order, in 1750. He was canonized in 1839 and is the patron saint of moral theologians.

Born of an aristocratic family in Naples, Alphon-

Alphonsus Liguori, outstanding eighteenth-century theologian whose influence on Catholic moral theology continues to this day.

sus began a career as a gifted lawyer. A crisis from a fixed court case turned him away from worldly "justice" to the Lord's service as a priest. After working among the poorest and most abandoned in Naples, Alphonsus discovered that the peasants of the countryside were even more bereft of spiritual care. Breaking from his close family ties, he founded the Redemptorists in the town of Scala to instruct the country poor in their faith, especially through the preaching of parish missions. Alphonsus expended incalculable energy preaching God's love for all, holding to the teaching that God willed the salvation of everyone and gave grace accordingly. He used his considerable musical and artistic talents to encourage a strong devotional life. He would not allow his preachers to use the flowery preaching style customary at the time, but demanded a simplicity and zeal that could move both the hearts and convince the minds of ordinary people. Although he tried to avoid episcopal office, he was made bishop of Saint Agatha of the Goths, a country diocese northeast of Naples, in 1762 by Pope Clement XIII. There Alphonsus concentrated upon educating his people, reforming his seminary, and developing a strong devotional life among clergy and laity. His care for the poor was never greater than during the winter famine of 1763, when he literally emptied the bishop's residence to feed whoever came. In his diocese alone was there no starvation.

Alphonsus, who vowed never to waste a moment's time, was one of the great Catholic authors of the eighteenth century. He wrote over a hundred works: devotional literature, instructions for priests and religious, responses against enemies of the Church, and his *Theologia Moralis.* The latter work Alphonsus revised and reprinted nine times during his life. Despite his own personal struggles with scruples, Alphonsus fought a strenuous battle against the rigorist forces of Jansenism, which portrayed God as stern, demanding, and condemnatory. Jansenists made the moral law a harsh, overbearing master and, in horror at human sinfulness, decried frequent reception of the sacraments as unworthy. In contrast, Alphonsus developed his moral theology out of the best tradition of the Church but also with his compassionate experience of common people. In challenging the Jansenist rigorism, or probabiliorism, which effectively demanded a following of the law in virtually all doubtful situations, he also avoided the opposite extreme of permissiveness or laxism. Alphonsus eventually called his position "equiprobabilism," mostly to avoid accusations of a probablism that allowed the following of a moral opinion for which a sound, even if less probable, argument could be constructed. Alphonsus's balanced moral reasoning provided the basis for one prominent stream of Catholic moral theology for the next two hundred years. In 1871 he was declared a Doctor of the Church, a sign of highest praise for his faith-filled contribution to the moral instruction of the faithful. *See also* equiprobabilism.

MARK MILLER

altar (awl'tuhr), the central table in a church building, the locus of the sacramental presence of Christ.

The Bible: In the OT, the altar is presented as a small mound of stones upon which the flesh of sacrificed animals could be roasted (see Gen 8:20). In Exod 20:24, the commandment to offer sacrifices to God upon an altar is given at the same time the Ten Commandments are delivered. Before the Israelites entered the promised land, they were ordered to tear down the altars of the Canaanites, to destroy their cult (Exod 34:13).

The English word "altar" translates two Greek terms, *bômos,* the altar of non-Christian cults, and *thusiasterion,* the altar of God. The distinction originated in the Septuagint where the *bômos* of idols is

A simply adorned, freestanding altar, during Mass in a church in Puerto Rico.

contrasted to *thusiasterion* of Israel's God. God commanded that the altars of the cults of false gods be destroyed (Amos 7:9). Again, in Judg 6:25, Gideon is told to destroy his father's altar to Baal and to erect "an altar to the Lord ... in proper order."

The altars of false gods are ordered to be struck down, as in Judg 6:25. The altar is a place for God's people to gather, as in Joel 2:17. Ps 26:6 makes the altar the location of God's forgiveness and mercy. In 1 Kgs 13:2, it is the place where God's word is preached, even when that word is a prophecy against Temple authorities.

In the NT, the attitude of Jesus to the Temple cult is unclear. According to the Gospels he never repudiated the ritual worship of his Jewish contemporaries. During the "cleansing of the Temple" (see Matt 21:12–17; Mark 11:15–19; Luke 19:45–48; John 2:14–17) Jesus affirmed the Temple as a "house of prayer," even as he condemned the unjust business practices of the Temple merchants.

Much Christian typology of the altar derives from the book of Revelation. The altar of the heavenly liturgy symbolizes the place of the sacrifice of the Lamb. When the angel offers incense upon the altar, the prayers of God's people are said to ascend (Rev 8: 3). The altar is the place where the sacrifices of the martyrs are conjoined to the sacrifice of Christ: "I saw under the altar the souls of those that who had been slaughtered for the word of God" (Rev 6:9).

Church History: In the first two centuries of the early Church, Christians gathered in "house churches" or Christian "synagogues." Archaeological evidence indicates that the altar was less a cultic "high place" (Lat., *ara*) than it was a simple, wooden *mensa* (Lat., "table"). In the house church of Dura-

Europos, an ancient city in the Syrian desert, the altar was situated upon a platform a single step above the rest of the assembly hall. Most likely it was made of wood and it served, as all altars, the functional purpose of providing a place upon which to set the gifts of bread and wine.

From the early third century, Christians erected altars over the burial places of martyrs. On these altars, they celebrated the *refrigeria* (Lat.), or funeral feasts. The custom led not only to the practice of sealing relics within or beneath altars, but also to the erection of whole churches over the tombs of martyrs. St. Peter's Basilica in Rome is the most famous example.

During the Reformation, the cultic significance of the altar was challenged. Some reformers encouraged the destruction of stone altars, replacing them with wooden "communion tables." Because an altar was understood to be a place of sacrifice, and because the theology of sacrifice in the Eucharist was unacceptable to the sixteenth-century reformers, the idea of stone altars in their churches was abhorrent to them. Catholic response to the Protestant antisacrificial polemic may be seen in the baroque elaboration of altar and reredos behind the altar, triumphantly exemplified in the altars of artists such as Giovanni Bernini (d. 1680).

Altars built in twentieth-century churches are far less grandiose. *Environment and Art in Catholic Worship* (EACW) states, "The altar, the holy table, should be the most noble, the most beautifully designed and constructed table the community can provide" (n. 71). "The holy table . . . should not be elongated, but square or slightly rectangular, an attractive, impressive, dignified, noble table, constructed with solid and beautiful materials, in pure and simple proportions" (n. 72). Nothing extrinsic to the celebration is to be placed upon the altar—no flowers, candles, crosses, decorations, papers, or cruets. It is to be freestanding, centrally located, and within the visible and audible range of every member of the worshipping community.

The altars in Catholic churches are consecrated in a solemn ceremony conducted by a bishop. They generally contain a small depository of the relics of a saint. They are anointed by the consecrating bishop with chrism, the perfumed oil ordinarily used for Confirmation. Five crosses are traced with chrism upon the table, one in each of the four corners and in the center.

Altars are accorded the honors due a symbol of Christ's presence. At the beginning of Mass, the altar is greeted with a kiss. It may be honored with incense at several times during the Mass. The ordinary reverence for the altar, when the sacrament is not present upon it, is a deep bow. *See also* Eucharist; priesthood; sacrifice.   *JEFFREY T. VANDERWILT*

altar bread, the bread used at the altar for the celebration of the Eucharist. It must be unleavened, made of wheat flour and water, with no additives. It must also have the appearance of real food and be large enough to be broken and distributed to at least some of the communicants present at the Mass. For validity, the bread must be made substantially of wheat flour without notable additives such as honey, eggs, or milk, which would alter its character as bread. In many churches, especially with large congregations, a small flat wafer, called a "host," is the common form of altar bread. In the Eastern churches leavened bread is used. *See also* host.

altar cloth, a piece of linen that covers an altar completely. The use of altar cloths in Christian liturgy dates to the fourth century. By the eighth century, as many as four cloths were used to protect the altar in case of spillage. The cloth on top came to be known as the corporal, since it held the Body (*Corpus*) of Christ. In the beginning the altar was simply the wooden table used for the eucharistic meal. Not until the fourth century was it constructed of stone and rendered immovable. In some instances it was free-standing in the middle of the sanctuary, but when the altar was situated against the wall, the cloth that had originally covered the whole altar became the antependium or frontal, since only the altar front could then be covered. After Vatican II (1962–65), when altars again became free-standing, altar cloths returned to their original function of covering the whole table. *See also* altar.

altar society, a parish group of women who helped care and provide for the altar and the sanctuary area around it. In some parishes the group was also called the "rosary and altar society," or the "tabernacle society." The group assumed responsibility for preparing the sanctuary for Mass and special services. Each society usually elected its own leaders, with one of the parish's priests serving as chaplain.

The altar society decorated and cared for objects and articles used for Mass. Some of their tasks included: dusting and cleaning the area around the altar; polishing the candlesticks; cleaning the linen used for the altar; caring for the priest's vestments; buying flowers; and arranging decorations. The society sometimes organized a festival and other social events to help raise money for the church. Since the Second Vatican Council other parish associations, worship committees, and sacristans have replaced altar societies in most parishes. *See also* altar; sanctuary.

altar stone. 1 The fixed, immovable table of the altar, which is made of one piece of solid stone. 2 The movable altar, which is a solid slab of stone about eight by ten inches long, inserted into the altar table. The altar stone, in both instances, contains the relics of saints, a custom dating to the early Church when the liturgy was celebrated on the tombs of the martyrs. For a time after Vatican II (1962–65), the use of the altar stone was considered optional, but the revised Code of Canon Law indicates that this custom must be revered (can. 1237.2). *See also* altar.

altar wine, the wine used at the altar for the celebration of the Eucharist. It must be made from the fruit of the vine, namely, from grapes. It is not permitted to use wine not made from grapes, wine that has become so sour that it has become vinegar, or wine that is diluted with 50 percent or more of water. According to Church law, the use of such wines would render the sacrament invalid, i.e., the wine could not be changed into the Blood of Christ.

A small amount of water is mixed with the wine by the deacon or priest at Mass. Originally this was done to dilute the wine, but Christian tradition assigned it various symbolic meanings; among them are the union of Christ with his people, and the union of the divine and the human in Christ.

Alumbrados (ah-luhm-brah'dohs), Spanish term from the Latin *Illuminati* for a group of individuals in sixteenth-century Spain claiming direct divine illumination and valuing inward prayer alone. Thinking the sacraments, the saints, and perhaps even Christ superfluous, some experienced mystical trances after which they claimed complete freedom from sin; this was sometimes interpreted as a license for immoral behavior. Followers of Erasmus and even Ignatius of Loyola were arrested by the Inquisition as suspected Alumbrados.

Amalarius of Metz, ca. 775–ca. 850, archbishop and liturgist. Having studied in one of Alcuin's schools (at Aachen or at Tours), Amalarius was

archbishop of Trier and then ambassador to Constantinople (813–14). In 835, Louis the Pious appointed him to administer the archdiocese of Lyons in place of the exiled Bishop Agobard. In 838, the Synod of Quiercy, led by the deacon Florus of Lyons and urged on by letters from Agobard, condemned Amalarius's liturgical innovations as well as his claim that the Canon of the Mass includes two sacrifices in sequence, one for the dead and one for all sinners. After the Council of Aachen in 817, Amalarius apparently helped compile collections of rules for canons (diocesan priests attached to a cathedral church) and nuns. His great work is the *Liber Officialis* (first edition ca. 823), which helped to popularize the allegorical interpretation of Christian worship by granting each detail of vesture and action a mystical significance. *See also* liturgy, theology of.

Amand, St., ca. 584–ca. 679, monk, missionary, known as "the Apostle of Belgium." Born in France, he became a monk in 604, lived as a hermit, and was consecrated a missionary bishop (with no diocese) in 629. He founded numerous monasteries in Belgium and spent his last years as an abbot. Feast day: February 6.

ambo (Gk., *ambon,* "pulpit"), Byzantine-rite term for the pulpit and, after the pulpit fell into disuse, for the semicircle on the sanctuary platform jutting out into the nave before the central doors of the iconostasis (altar screen), where the litanies and Gospel are proclaimed. The ambo was originally a huge pulpit in the center of the nave; it and the bema (sanctuary) were the two focal points of the liturgy, and processions back and forth between the two were a standard part of the ritual. The eucharistic liturgy opened and closed at the ambo; litanies, diptychs, and the Scriptures were proclaimed there; and special rites such as imperial coronation, the exaltation of the cross, and the promulgation of councils and their anathemas took place there. Preaching, however, was usually done from the throne in the apse. *See also* lectern; pulpit.

Ambrose of Milan, St., ca. 339–97, bishop of Milan and Doctor of the Church. Elected bishop when Milan was the seat of the Roman government and he was a still-unbaptized rising government official, Ambrose dedicated himself to scriptural study, theological advocacy, pastoral guidance, and diplomacy, all of which formed his legacy.

Ambrose devoted to his ministry resources from

an aristocratic background. Classically educated at a time when knowledge of Greek was declining in the Western Church, he channeled much Eastern Christian theology and especially exegesis into the Latin tradition. His allegorical readings of Scripture, the OT in particular, combined with his rhetorical skill made him a compelling preacher in his time. In his *Confessions,* Augustine writes that Ambrose's sermons contributed to his decision to be baptized. Ambrose's ethical teaching, notably *On the Duties of the Clergy,* both continued classical themes and supported the growing ascetical movement, while his contributions to Latin hymnody were substantial in themselves.

In relations with Roman civil authority Ambrose was unyielding. In 386 he physically occupied the Milan basilica to protest and effectively end its government-countenanced use in Arian worship. His opposition helped uphold the exclusion of the pagan Altar of Victory from its traditional place of honor in the Roman senate. In two encounters with Theodosius, Ambrose enforced his position that the emperor was not "above" the Church but "within" it and thus subject to its discipline. As bishop, he deterred the emperor from rebuilding a synagogue destroyed by a Christian mob and subjected him to penance for punishing an unrelated riot with a massacre. Ambrose's authority made his legacy powerful in medieval relations between Church and state. Feast day: December 7.   KATHRYN L. JOHNSON

Ambrosiana, a famous library in Milan founded in 1609 by Cardinal Federico Borromeo, cousin of Charles Borromeo. Named after Ambrose, patron saint of Milan, the Ambrosiana contains over ten thousand manuscripts from the fourth to the sixteenth century, written in Latin, Greek, Arabic, and Hebrew as well as in European vernacular languages. Microfilms of its holdings are now housed at the University of Notre Dame.

Ambrosian chant. *See* chant, Ambrosian.

Ambrosian rite, the liturgical forms associated with the Italian city of Milan. The rite is attributed to Milan's patron bishop, Ambrose (ca. 340–97), but it predates him in development and origin. The Ambrosian rite is similar in most respects to its "sister," the Roman rite. Three significant variations are noted. Baptism is performed by immersion and has included a rite of footwashing. The litany, or Prayer of the Faithful, is chanted by the deacon. The proces-

sion of the gifts, the Offertory, precedes the creed and does not follow it as in the Roman rite. The Ambrosian rite has been reformed in recent decades according to the mandate of Vatican II (1962–65).

Ambrosiaster, anonymous fourth-century scriptural commentator. Erasmus (d. 1536) coined the name "Ambrosiaster" when he argued that a commentary on the Letters of St. Paul long attributed to Ambrose must be by another author. A collection of questions on the OT and the NT ascribed to Augustine is also Ambrosiaster's. *See also* Scripture, interpretation of.

ambry. *See* aumbry.

ambulatory (Lat., *ambulare,* "to walk"), covered walkway around the periphery of the apse of a church. The ambulatory permitted access to chapels radiating out from the walkway for Mass or to visit reliquaries housed in the chapel. The twelfth-century ambulatory of St.-Denis (Paris) marks the beginning of the Gothic style of architecture.

amen (ah'men or ay'men; Heb., "firm," "established with certainty"), word said as the formal conclusion to liturgical prayer. Uttering the word constitutes the acceptance of a claim. In the NT, "amen" is frequently attributed to Jesus and is translated, "truly" or "verily," as in the idiom, "Truly, truly, I say to you. . . ." According to Justin Martyr (d. ca. 165), "amen" concludes the prayers of Christians, preeminently the Eucharistic Prayer. Justin gave the word its popular meaning, "so be it" (Gk., *genoito*). Amen is the chief means by which members of the congregation join themselves to the prayer and praise of the Church.

America, a weekly journal published by the Jesuits of the United States and Canada. Founded in 1909 by the Jesuits of the United States, this periodical reviews literature, education, science, the arts, secular news, and ecclesiastical developments. The journal has been jointly published with the Jesuits of Canada since 1957.

American Board of Catholic Missions, fundraising organization for the support of the missions. Founded in 1919 and reorganized in 1924, the board, under the supervision of the hierarchy, raises and administers funds for American missions. The board now uses 40 percent of the money collected each year on Mission Sunday for mission work with underprivileged groups; the remainder is allocated for general missionary purposes. *See also* missions.

American Catholic Historical Association, society to promote the study of Catholic history. Founded in Cleveland, Ohio, in 1919 by Peter Guilday, professor of Church history at The Catholic University of America, with the collaboration of the rector, Bishop Thomas J. Shahan, the association promotes historical scholarship of the Catholic Church. Affiliated with the American Historical Association, it publishes the *Catholic Historical Review,* originally established by Guilday in 1915. From an original membership of Catholics who were historians, it now includes all those whose interest is Catholic history; two non-Catholics, including one woman, have served as presidents. In 1992, its membership exceeded one thousand.

American Catholic spirituality. *See* spirituality, American Catholic.

Americanism, an ill-defined movement, associated with efforts to adapt Catholicism to American culture, condemned by *Testem Benevolentiae* in 1899.

Background: In the 1890s, a series of issues divided the American Catholic Church. First, under the leadership of Archbishop John Ireland of St. Paul, Cardinal James Gibbons of Baltimore, Bishop John J. Keane, first rector of The Catholic University of America, and Monsignor Denis J. O'Connell, rector of the American College in Rome, a group of American prelates sought to accommodate Catholicism to American culture and to Americanize immigrant Catholics. In 1890, Ireland praised the state's right to educate and, in 1891, arranged to lease his parochial schools to the public school board. He also supported the prohibition of the use of German as the language of instruction in German-American parochial schools. German-American Catholics and Archbishop Michael A. Corrigan of New York represented Ireland's plan as surrendering to the state the Church's right to educate. In addition, James Gibbons defended the Knights of Labor, an early labor union, and Ireland was later instrumental in having Edward McGlynn, a priest of New York excommunicated for disobedience and social activism, reconciled to the Church through Archbishop Francesco Satolli. To win Vatican approval of his program, however, Ireland had

to agree to accept Satolli as the first permanent apostolic delegate to the American hierarchy in 1893.

A second factor was the support the Americanizing party gave to the separation of Church and state. When Gibbons, as a newly created cardinal, took possession of his titular parish in Rome in 1887, he had praised the American system, which not only guaranteed the Church its freedom, but also provided an opportunity to cooperate with Protestant denominations. In 1893, he, Ireland, and Keane all participated in the World's Parliament of Religions, an early ecumenical meeting in Chicago. Their opponents and the Vatican thought that such gatherings implied religious indifference. Moreover, Pope Leo XIII issued his apostolic letter *Longingua Oceani,* rejecting the American separation of Church and state as an ideal for other nations. The pope then demanded the resignations of O'Connell from the American College in 1895 and of Keane from The Catholic University of America in 1896.

European Controversy over Americanism: The tension in the United States crossed the Atlantic through the controversy over the thought of Isaac Hecker, founder of the Paulists. Untrained in Thomistic theology, then prevalent in the Church, Hecker frequently used nontechnical language in his writings, especially when speaking of the indwelling of the Holy Spirit. His biography by Walter Elliott, C.S.P., caused little comment in the United States when it was published in 1891. But when it was translated into French in 1897, with an introduction by Félix Klein of the Institut Catholique of Paris, Hecker became the model for the priest of the future, more at home in the marketplace than in the cloister, optimistic that Americans would be converted if only Catholic teaching were presented in a positive light emphasizing "active" over "passive" virtues and even praising "natural" virtues.

The controversy now formally became known as Americanism. Ireland's speeches in favor of the separation of Church and state and of republican government had already been translated in France, where Catholics were then trying, unsuccessfully, to carry out the papal call to rally to the Third Republic. In Italy, translations of his speeches were accommodated to a constitutional monarchy by omitting his references to republican government. The U.S. separation of Church and state, moreover, was transformed into the basis for ending the Roman Question, the dispute between the Holy See and the Italian government over the territorial claims of the Holy See following the loss of the Papal States.

As Europeans debated over Hecker and Americanism, O'Connell delivered a speech at the Fourth International Catholic Scientific Congress at Fribourg, Switzerland, in August 1897. In his "New Idea in the Life of Father Hecker," he distinguished between "political" and "ecclesiastical" Americanism. The first, he argued, flowed from "the order of ideas" in the Declaration of Independence, culminating in the words: "all men are created equal and are endowed by their Creator with certain unalienable rights." He noted that this idea was derived from British and American common law, which acknowledged the rights of subjects even prior to the forming of a government. To this he contrasted Roman public law, which envisioned subjects as recipients of rights from the state. Common law, he argued, so closely approximated the dignity conferred on the Christian in Baptism that the Church could well adopt it as its own.

O'Connell's treatment of "ecclesiastical Americanism" touched on the more delicate topic of relations between Church and state. Although American Catholics had consistently supported the American separation of Church and state, in 1864 Pius IX's "Syllabus of Errors" condemned the proposition that the Church should be separated from the state and the state from the Church. At that time, Bishop Félix Dupanloup of Orléans, France, popularized the distinction that what the pope was condemning was an absolute, a "thesis," to which there could be no exception, but the pope was not making the contrary, the union of Church and state, the Catholic thesis. Rather, the thesis was the harmony that should exist between Church and state and the "hypothesis" was the application of that harmony in the real order. Archbishop Martin J. Spalding of Baltimore used this distinction in a pastoral letter widely distributed in the United States and among Roman officials. Gibbons reflected this distinction in his 1887 address. By 1897, however, a different theological interpretation was dominant. The condemned thesis remained the same as it did for Dupanloup, but now the Catholic thesis became the union of Church and state. The "hypothesis" was whatever could be tolerated while working toward the full implementation of the thesis.

For O'Connell, ecclesiastical Americanism resulted from Hecker's recognition that the First Amendment prevented any church from being established and recognized the Church's freedom. But his interpretation of the "thesis" led him into controversy. While accepting the thesis "of the legal union of Church and state," he declared that in practice it had diminished the Church's freedom. Inconsistently, he then argued that the American hypothesis worked as well for the Church as any other system.

O'Connell's address became a principal interpretation of authentic Americanism, but it joined Ireland's speeches and the biography of Hecker as the targets of increasing attacks. In the spring of 1898, Father Charles Maignen wrote a series of articles in *La Vérité* challenging the orthodoxy of the Americanists. He claimed that Ireland would soon be deposed and Gibbons given a coadjutor. Keane, he said, had been forced to resign from The Catholic University for heresy, and O'Connell denied the teaching of the Syllabus. As European Catholics debated Americanism, moreover, the United States declared war on Spain. The shift from a war of ideas to a shooting war shaped the final stages of the reaction against Americanism.

Vatican Investigation and *Testem Benevolentiae*: Maignen published his articles as a book entitled *Le Père Hecker: c'est-il un saint?* After Cardinal François-Marie Richard of Paris, under the influence of the Sulpicians, denied the book an *imprimatur* (Lat., "it may be printed"), official ecclesiastical approval for the publication of a book, Maignen obtained one from Father Alberto Lepidi, the Master of the Sacred Palace, who thus appeared to lend the aura of papal approval to Maignen's attacks. Gibbons, Ireland, and Keane wrote protests to Rome, while O'Connell fought the battle personally. On several occasions, he met Lepidi and explained in writing what he meant by Americanism but then found these personal letters published by Maignen in *La Vérité*.

During the summer of 1898, the Vatican examined several different questions. Leo XIII appointed commissions to investigate Americanism, the orthodoxy of Marie-Joseph Lagrange, and his *Révue biblique,* and the theories of evolution of Father John Zahm, of the University of Notre Dame. Each of these questions challenged traditional Catholic interpretations of doctrine and were seen by some European observers as closely interrelated. On January 22, 1899, Leo issued his apostolic letter *Testem Benevolentiae.* He stated that the controversy arose over the translation of the life of Hecker into a "foreign language," but he addressed the letter to Gibbons in Baltimore. Making no mention of Church-state relations, he condemned those who denigrated religious vows or "watered down" doctrine to gain converts. He challenged Hecker's use of the term "active" and "passive" virtues on the grounds that Thomas Aquinas made all virtues active. He commended Hecker's emphasis on the indwelling of the Holy Spirit and quoted the declaration of the Second Council of Orange (529) that the Spirit's illumination was essential for one to consent to the saving gospel. If the pope implied that he thought the Americanists might be semi-Pelagians condemned at Orange, he removed all doubt when he challenged those who praised "natural virtues," which implied that "nature ... with grace added to it, [was] weaker than when left to its own strength."

The papal letter was a caricature of American thought. In France, Klein termed Americanism a "phantom heresy." The U.S. reaction followed the earlier divisions in the hierarchy. Gibbons, Ireland, and their supporters denied that heresy ever existed. Those archbishops who had been neutral simply acknowledged receiving the letter. But archbishops Frederick Katzer of Milwaukee and Corrigan of New York thanked the pope for thwarting the heresy by exercising his infallible magisterium. In Italy, the bishops of the provinces of Turin and Vercelli, where support was strong for the monarchy, likewise thanked the pope for his "infallible" pronouncement (it was not, in fact, infallible according to the criteria set down by Vatican Council I in 1870).

In the United States, the condemnation of Americanism had two major effects. First, American Catholic support of the First Amendment fell under suspicion until the Second Vatican Council (1962–65). Second, American Catholic intellectual life, only in its infancy, was stifled for more than a generation, especially when Modernism, which bore some similarities, was condemned by Pope Pius X in 1907. *See also* Church and state; Gibbons, James; Hecker, Isaac Thomas; Ireland, John; Keane, John Joseph; Knights of Labor; O'Connell, Denis Joseph; Spalding, Martin John; *Testem Benevolentiae;* United States of America, Catholicism in the.

Bibliography

Fogarty, Gerald P. *The Vatican and the American Hierarchy from 1870 to 1965.* Collegeville, MN: Liturgical Press/Michael Glazier, 1985.
McAvoy, Thomas T. *Great Crisis in American Catholic History, 1895–1900.* Chicago: Henry Regnery, 1957. GERALD P. FOGARTY

amice (a'miss; Lat., *amictus,* "cloak"), a rectangular piece of linen worn by a priest or deacon around the neck and shoulders to protect the outer liturgical vestments from soil. During the Middle Ages, the amice, which was worn over the alb or linen tunic, partially covered the head until the stole and

Amice

chasuble (outer vestment) were in place. The use of the amice is only optional when the alb completely covers the minister's street clothing. *See also* vestments.

ampulla (ahm'poo-lah, Lat., "vase"), small jar for liquids. Used in the ancient Church to carry oil from lamps that burned near the tombs of martyrs. Today the term applies to the container of oil used for liturgical and sacramental anointings, e.g., at Baptism and Confirmation. *See also* chrism; oil; oil of catechumens; oil of the sick.

Anabaptism (Gk., "rebaptism"), a name referring to the conviction that those Christians who were baptized as infants need to be baptized again as adults, since it is only as adults that they can make a true commitment to Jesus Christ. This belief in adult Baptism gained its strongest expressions in the Radical Reformation of the sixteenth century, under the leadership of such figures as Conrad Grebel (1498–1526), Menno Simons (1496–1561), Thomas Munzer (1490–1525), Caspar Schwenckfeld (1489–1561) and Michael Servetus (1511–53). Their respective groups agreed on the following: the baptism of adults as a repentance of sin and a confession of faith in Christ; a necessary joining of faith and good works for salvation; the strict adherence to the specific teachings of the NT as theological and ethical rules for living (e.g., "turn the other cheek"); a refusal of military service owing to the rejection of territorial Christianity and allegiance to a state or government; a refusal to own private property and to charge interest on loans.

Anabaptism flourishes in the 1990s among the Mennonites, the Amish, the Hutterites, the Quakers, and some Baptist denominations. Because of its stress on adult confession of faith, Anabaptism has had a strong influence on shaping the notion that the Church is a voluntary association of deeply committed Christians. *See also* Baptism; Reformation, the; sectarianism.

Anacletus, St., also known as Cletus, d. ca. 91, traditionally regarded as the third Bishop of Rome, from ca. 79 to 91. He is credited with dividing Rome into twenty-five parishes. Feast day (until 1969): April 26.

analogy, a comparison in the form "A is to B as C is to D," e.g., "God is to the world as the artist is to her work."

All theological language is analogous since we can compare God only to the created things we know; we cannot speak of God except in human terms. The Fourth Lateran Council (1215) declared that "No similarity can be found so great but that the dissimilarity is even greater" (DS 806). Thus every similarity between God and creatures (God is wise; humans are wise) is understood to include a greater dissimilarity (God's wisdom is unlike human wisdom in that it infinitely surpasses it). Thomas Aquinas (d. 1274) is particularly well known for developing the role of analogy in theological discourse. *See also* language, religious.

anamnesis (ah-nam'nee-sis; Gk., "memorial"), liturgical term applied in the Latin rite to the prayer following the consecration of the Eucharist. At one time this prayer in the Latin rite was referred to as the *post pridie* (Lat., "after the day before") or the *post secreta* (Lat., "after the secret") prayer. The *anamnesis,* in which the Church recalls Jesus' death, Resurrection, and Ascension, is a memorial of the whole Paschal Mystery, that redemptive act of Christ which is at the heart of every eucharistic liturgy. The function of the *anamnesis* is twofold: it recalls something which was done in the past, while at the same time it renders that memorialized action present in the eucharistic celebration. In the Jewish tradition, remembering is always linked with some kind of action. *Anamnesis* has this sense: it is not only remembering something past, but representing that past action before God so that it becomes present. Thus, the *anamnesis* serves to bring out a basic aspect of the liturgy: through the Eucharist, the worshiping community both recalls Christ's death and Resurrection and makes Christ's sacrifice sacramentally present on earth. *See also* Eucharistic Prayer.

Ananias, St. (an-uh-ni'uhs), a member of the earliest Christian community at Damascus. According to Acts 9:10–18 and 22:12, Ananias, prompted by a divine message, visited Paul after his blinding vision on the Damascus road, restored Paul's sight, and baptized him. Feast day: January 25.

anaphora (a-nah'for-uh; Gk., "offering"), the Canon of the Mass or the Eucharistic Prayer, a term more commonly used in reference to Eastern rites. The *anaphora* is the principal prayer of the eucharistic liturgy; it extends from the opening dialogue between priest and people to the final doxology and amen. In the *anaphora,* the Church recalls the whole saving act of Christ by recalling the Last Supper and Christ's sacrificial death; it calls down the Holy Spirit; and it consecrates the bread and wine as the body and blood of Christ. The Church does all this in a spirit of praise and thanksgiving to God. In the West, the revised Roman Missal of Pope Paul VI uses the term *prex eucharistica* (Lat.), eucharistic prayer; the *anaphora* in Eastern liturgies is sometimes used more broadly to include additional elements before or after the Eucharistic Prayer. *See also* eucharistic prayer.

Anastasia, St., ca. 304, martyr commemorated in the Eucharistic Prayer of the Mass. In the late fifth century her relics were transferred to, and venerated in, Constantinople's church of the Anastasis (Gk., "resurrection"), and for many centuries thereafter the pope celebrated Mass in her Roman church each Christmas (her feast day until 1969). Feast day (in the East): December 22.

Anastasius I, St., d. 401, pope from 399 to 401 and friend of Paulinus of Nola and Jerome. Anastasius pronounced against Origen's teaching in three letters, although the precise value of the condemnation, which seems based on relatively slight acquaintance with Origen's writings, is uncertain. He also wrote against Donatism, which insisted on the rebaptism of those who left the Church and later returned, to the Council of Carthage (401). Feast day: April 27. *See also* Donatism; Origen.

Anastasius Bibliothecarius (bib-lee-oh-teh-kahr'ee-uhs), also called Anastasius the Librarian, ca. 815–79, official in the Roman church. Created cardinal ca. 847, Anastasius had been deposed by 854. Briefly antipope during 855, he later became an abbot and papal librarian. He opposed Photius of Constantinople and assisted Western delegates at the Eighth Ecumenical Council, Constantinople IV (869–70). Noted for his knowledge of Greek, he translated the *Acts* of this, as well as of the Seventh Ecumenical Council, into Latin. *See also* Constantinople, councils of.

Anastasius of Hungary, St., d. ca. 1040, Bohemian who became the first abbot of St. Martin's in Pannonhalma, Hungary, and later under King Stephen of Hungary the first archbishop of Hungary. Feast day: November 12 (or August 14). *See also* Hungary, Catholicism in.

anathema (Gk. "accursed," "separated from the fold"), a formula for excommunication. It carries a much stronger connotation than exclusion from eucharistic communion, extending to exclusion from the ecclesial community itself. "Anathema" as used in conciliar canons means that a teaching is condemned as heretical and that its contradictory is defined as revealed truth.

Etymologically, the term originally meant "votive offering," but came to refer to a cursed offering to the anger of God rather than a holy offering to the divinity. The term occurs in the OT with its original positive meaning in Judith 16:19. In Deut 7:26 the term means "set apart for destruction." The Israelites themselves are declared anathema ("devoted to destruction") when they fall into idolatry in Deut 13:17.

Anathema occurs six times in the NT: in Luke 21:5 it carries the original sense of offering in the Temple; in 1 Cor 12:3; 16:22; Gal 1:8–9, and Rom 9:3 it refers to a curse; Acts 23:14 refers to a solemn oath sworn under pain of anathema.

The formula as it appears in Gal 1:8–9 is used by church councils beginning in the fourth century. In this context the word occurs for the first time in the canons of the Council of Elvira (ca. 300), although it is not certain whether it carried the meaning of separation from the ecclesial community. Up until the sixth century, the term referred to a solemn excommunication. In the following centuries metropolitan bishops used it against obstinate sinners and hardened criminals. When minor excommunication was

An anchor-cross with fish, an early symbol for Christ; stone carving in the Roman catacomb of St. Priscilla.

suppressed in 1869, the word "anathema" became equivalent to excommunication.

According to the 1917 Code of Canon Law anathema refers to solemn excommunication by which a person is excluded from the community of the faithful, especially if it is assessed with the formulas and the ceremonies contained in the Roman Pontifical (can. 2257). Excommunication, the most severe of penalties, does not affect membership in the Church through the theological virtues and sanctifying grace. Moreover, membership in the Church that results from the indelible character of Baptism is not superseded by the penalty of excommunication. It does cut a person off from external union with the Church, from the external use of sacred things, and also from participation in the spiritual benefits obtained from divine worship. The reference to anathema does not occur in the 1983 Code of Canon Law. *See also* excommunication.   SUSAN K. WOOD

anchor-cross, Christian symbol. Frequently found inscribed in marble in catacomb art, the anchor was a symbol of hope (see Heb 6:19–20) in early Christian iconography. Some anchors have shanks that look like crosses; this may have been another meaning attached to the anchor. *See also* cross.

anchorite, anchoress, a person dedicated to a life of strict solitude and penance. Because they are not allowed to leave their dwellings, anchorites often have their cells attached to the church sanctuary so they may receive the Eucharist through a window; their meals are passed through a different window. In addition to a life of prescribed prayer and fasting, these solitaries study, write books, sew clothing for the poor, and offer spiritual advice to visitors through a veiled window. Prophetic witness and compassion characterize this canonical form of consecrated life. *See also* monasticism.

Ancyra (ahn-si̧'ruh), Ankara, city in present-day Turkey. Ancyra was the site of two fourth-century church councils. In 314 a council of bishops met there to discuss the problems of reconciling Christians who had lapsed from their faith during persecution. In 358 a council of anti-Nicene semi-Arians met to condemn extreme Arian views as well as the definitions of the ecumenical Council of Nicaea (325). *See also* Arianism; Nicaea, First Council of; semi-Arianism.

André Bessette, Bl., 1845–1937, Canadian Holy Cross laybrother noted for his devotion to St. Joseph. He inspired the building of the Oratory of St. Joseph on Mount Royal in Montreal. Feast day: January 6.

Andrew, St., one of Jesus' first disciples, whose Greek name means "manly." He and his brother, Simon Peter, came from Bethsaida, on the northeast shore of the Sea of Galilee (John 1:44), but they lived at nearby Capernaum (Mark 1:29), where they worked as fishermen (Mark 1:16). As a disciple of John the Baptist, Andrew learned of Jesus, to whom he brought Peter (John 1:40). Andrew is prominent in all lists of the twelve apostles (Matt 10:2; Mark 3:18; Luke 6:14; Acts 1:13).

Andrew appears in several episodes of the NT. Before the feeding miracle, he notes the boy with the loaves and fish (John 6:8). With Philip, the only other apostle with a Greek name, he brings to Jesus the request of the Greeks who seek him (John 12:22). With Peter, James, and John, he asks Jesus about Jerusalem's fate (Mark 13:3).

Second-century apocryphal acts tell of missionary adventures. The *Acts of Andrew and Matthias* recounts Andrew's rescue of Matthias from cannibals. The *Acts of Andrew,* surviving in a Latin translation by Gregory of Tours (538–94) and in Greek fragments, reports miracles performed in Greece and Asia Minor. The account of Andrew's crucifixion at Patras, Greece, on an X-shaped cross also circulated independently.

Later legend reports that Regulus translated Andrew's bones to St. Andrews, Scotland. Andrew's head, brought to Rome from Amalfi by Crusaders in 1461, was returned to Constantinople by Pope Paul VI.

Andrew is the patron saint of fishermen, Scotland, Greece, and Russia. Feast day: November 30. *See also* apostle; Twelve, the.   HAROLD W. ATTRIDGE

Andrew Dung-Lac, St., priest and martyr, one of many Vietnamese martyrs killed between 1820 and 1862. Feast day (with others): November 24.

Andrew Kim Taegon, St., the first native Korean priest. The son of Christian converts, he was martyred in 1846 and canonized by Pope John Paul II in 1984. Feast day: September 20. *See also* Korea, Catholicism in.

Andrew of Crete, St., ca. 660–740, archbishop of Crete. Born in Damascus, then a monk at Jerusalem, he represented Theodore, patriarch of Constantinople, at the Council of Constantinople III (680–81), although he had at first been a Monothelite, believing that there was only one divine will in Christ. One of the greatest orators of the Byzantine church, Andrew delivered elegant homilies on such subjects as the birth and dormition of Mary, the lives of saints and martyrs, and the Gospels. He is especially remembered as a poet; his "Grand Canon" is a penitential work of 250 stanzas. Feast day: July 4 (East). *See also* Monothelitism.

Andrew of St. Victor, d. 1176, exegete who wrote commentaries on most books of the Hebrew Scriptures. Probably born in England, he went to Paris, where he entered the abbey of St. Victor, later serving as abbot at Wigmore on the Welsh border. He was influenced by Hugh of St. Victor's emphasis on the importance of the literal sense of Scripture as the foundation for understanding the spiritual and moral senses. Like his teacher Hugh, Andrew consulted contemporary Jews, recording their interpretations. Richard of St. Victor wrote *De Emmanuele* condemning Andrew's acceptance of Jewish teachings about Isa 7:14. *See also* Scripture, senses of; Victorines.

Andronicus, St., d. fifth century, patron saint of silversmiths. A silversmith by trade, he and his wife Athanasia entered the monastic life in Egypt after the death of their children, his wife assuming the identity of a man. After living separately for twelve years, they went on pilgrimage together to Jerusalem and upon their return joined a monastery near Alexandria. Andronicus, however, had not recognized his companion as his wife. Upon her death in the monastery a note she left behind revealed to him her true identity. Andronicus died a week later and the two were buried together. Feast day: October 9.

angel (Heb., *mal'āk*, Gk., *angelos,* "messenger"), a spiritual supernatural being who acts as a messenger of God. Contrary to artistic convention depicting them as winged, angels are represented in the Bible in the guise of human beings. They are sent to announce the birth of a child and its future destiny (Gen 16:11; 18:9–15; Judg 13:3–5; Luke 1:11–20; 2:8–14); they intercede before God and intervene in human affairs sometimes to protect (Gen 22:11; 48:16; Exod 14:19; Ps 91:11), sometimes to execute judgment (2 Sam 24:16; 2 Kgs 19:35; Ezek 9:1–2). This view of angels and their functions probably goes back to the common ancient Near Eastern representation of the heavenly court with the high god surrounded by ministers who discharge these and other functions; compare the prophet Micaiah's vision of the heavenly court in session (1 Kgs 22:19–23) and Isaiah's vision of the enthroned God of Israel surrounded by the seraphim (Isa 6:1–13). Angels are therefore also known as "sons of God," i.e., divine beings (Gen 6:1–4; Job 38:7), and "holy ones." In some instances, e.g., the angel who guides Israel through the wilderness (Exod 23:20–23; 33:2), the

Conventional depiction of an angel complete with wings and trumpet; in the church of San Angelo in Formis, Capua, Italy.

distinction between the divine agent and God himself is somewhat blurred.

In the postbiblical period, especially in apocalyptic writings, we find a great increase in the number and activity of angelic beings. At this stage there is a tendency to identify them by name and arrange them in hierarchical order, and a distinction is made between good and evil angels. This is not so apparent in the biblical period when Satan or the adversary is mentioned only in three postexilic texts (Job 1–2; Zech 3:1–2; 1 Chr 21:1). The evil spirits most frequently encountered in postbiblical texts, including the Dead Sea Scrolls, are Belial (Beliar) and Asmodeus, and their numbers coalesce into a mighty army that will be engaged in the final struggle with the forces of good, e.g., in the Qumran War Scroll (1QM 15:1–16:1). Scholars have rightly suspected the influence of foreign ideas, especially from ancient Persia, in these developments.

The NT offers no new perspective on this belief in angelic beings, both good and evil. Jesus speaks often of angels (e.g., Luke 12:8–9), and the angel Gabriel announces the births of the Baptist (Luke 1:11–20) and of Jesus (1:26–38). An angel assists Jesus in his agony in Gethsemane (Luke 22:43), and another angel removes the stone from the tomb of Jesus (Matt 28:2–3). An angel announces the message of the Resurrection to the women who come to the tomb (Matt 28:1–7). Angels are part of the heavenly court at the Last Judgment (Matt 13:39–41; 25:31–46). All of this corresponds to popular Jewish belief at that time, the only dissenters being the Sadducees, who denied the existence of angels.

In later Christian thought speculation on angels was influenced as much by philosophical speculation as by reflection on the biblical materials. Christian theologians writing under the influence of Platonic philosophy tended to view angels as entities intermediate in their degree of perfection between God and the visible, material reality. Speculations along these lines gave rise to theories of the hierarchy of the angels, as, for example, in the writings of Pseudo-Dionysius. In later medieval thought, particularly in the thought of Aquinas, speculation on the nature of angels provided an occasion for much fruitful reflection on the nature of thought and action and the relation of mental states to embodiment in time. The famous quibble over the number of angels that can dance on the head of a pin was intended as a logical exercise and not as a serious problem. *See also* archangel; guardian angel.

JOSEPH BLENKINSOPP

THE CELESTIAL HIERARCHY

The order of the celestial hierarchy is given in slightly different forms in various early Christian sources, including Ambrose, Jerome, Pope Gregory the Great, Isidore of Seville, and John of Damascus. However, it was Denys (also know as Dionysius) the Areopagite (d. ca. 500) who was given what is closest to a definitive list in his *Celestial Hierarchy,* where the nine choirs of celestial beings are ranked in three hierarchies, each containing three choirs. In the Middle Ages Denys's speculative doctrine was developed by the Scholastics and found its way into the works of Peter Lombard, Albertus Magnus, Bonaventure, Duns Scotus, and Thomas Aquinas.

I. 1. Seraphim	According to Isa 6:2–7, each in this highest category has six wings: "with two they covered their faces, and with two they covered their feet, and with two they flew." As the seraphs surround the throne of the Lord, they call to one another: "Holy, holy, holy is the Lord of hosts; the whole earth is full of his glory," lines that are incorporated into the liturgy at the beginning of the Eucharistic Prayer.	
2. Cherubim	According to Gen 3:24 and Ezek 28:14, the cherubim function as attendants of God, guarding, for example, the garden of Eden after Adam and Eve had been expelled from it. Representations of two of them in gold were placed in Solomon's Temple at Jerusalem, facing one another at either end of the mercy seat, the cover of the ark of the covenant (Exod 25:18–22).	
3. Thrones	They are mentioned in Col 1:16 as part of God's creation in Christ. According to Jewish legend there are seventy such beings. Some are numbered among the fallen angels. The dominant characteristic of those in heaven is steadfastness. It is through the thrones, Denys the Areopagite says, that God brings his justice to bear upon us.	
II. 4. Dominations	Also known as dominions (Col 1:16), according to Denys the Areopagite they regulate angels' duties and through them the majesty of God is manifested. Their emblems of authority are scepters and orbs.	
5. Virtues	According to Hebrew lore, their principal duty is to work miracles on earth. The two angels ("two men in white robes") standing by the apostles at the moment of Jesus' ascension into heaven are traditionally regarded as virtues (Acts 1:10).	
6. Powers	Mentioned in Col 1:16, according to Denys the Areopagite they thwart the efforts of demons to overthrow the world. For Pope Gregory the Great, they preside over the demons. In Eph 6:12, however, they are regarded as evil and under the control of the devil: "the cosmic powers of this present darkness." They are also listed among those who cannot "separate us from the love of God in Christ Jesus our Lord" (Rom 8:38–39).	
III. 7. Principalities	Their principal function, according to tradition, is the protection of religion. According to Denys the Areopagite, they watch over the leaders of the people and inspire them to make right decisions. They are also linked with the powers to include evil as well as good spirits (Eph 6:12; 2:2). The word "principalities" (Gk., *archai*) is rendered as "rulers" in English.	
8. Archangels	The "chief angels" (Gk.) are, according to Denys the Areopagite, the messengers who bear divine decrees. The word occurs twice in the NT: in Jude 9, where Michael is referred to as the archangel who "contended with the devil," and in 1 Thess 4:16, where there is a reference to "the archangel's call" that will come on the day the Lord returns from heaven. In Christian tradition Gabriel and Raphael are also considered archangels. Gabriel assists Daniel in the understanding of his visions (Dan 8:15; 9:21) and announces the conception of Jesus in Mary's womb (Luke 1:11; 1:26). Raphael is one of the seven archangels (called "angels" in the text) who stands in the presence of God (Tob 12:12, 15). *1 Enoch* names the seven as Uriel, Raguel, Michael, Seraqael, Gabriel, Haniel, and Raphael.	
9. Angels	Although referred to frequently in the Bible, very few are actually named, Satan being one. Angels perform many different functions. In addition to those mentioned above for archangels, angels as divine agents execute judgment, lead, protect and heal, and intercede with God on behalf of humans. Guardian angels do not constitute a separate choir.	

Angela Merici, St. (may-ree'chee), 1474–1540, founder of the Ursulines. Born in the Republic of Venice, she received a vision in 1506 to found a society of virgins in Brescia. She moved to that city in 1516 and by 1531 had begun to gather young women. In 1535 she formed twenty-five followers into the Company of St. Angela, the first order for the teaching of young girls. No formal vows were taken, but their rule prescribed virginity, poverty, and obedience. Each member remained with her family evangelizing her relatives, acquaintances, and neighbors. St. Angela was canonized in 1807. Feast day: January 27. *See also* Ursulines.

Angela of Foligno, Bl., ca. 1248–1309, Italian mystic and Franciscan tertiary. Around the age of forty, Angela formed the desire to abandon the worldly life, eventually living as a Franciscan tertiary after the death of her husband and children. Her many visions, recorded by the Franciscan brother Arnold in her *Book of Visions and Instructions,* include a twenty-step plan of penitence and meditations on the Lord's Prayer, the Eucharist, the Crucified Christ, and the mystical life, the culmination of which is mystical marriage with God. She was beatified in the seventeenth century. Feast day: February 28.

Angelica, Mother, b. 1923, American religious broadcaster and founder of EWTN (Eternal Word Television Network). She is a member of the Franciscan Nuns of the Most Blessed Sacrament and a former member of the Order of St. Francis and of the Discalced Carmelites of Perpetual Adoration. The EWTN studio is on the grounds of Our Lady of the Angels Monastery, which Mother Angelica had established in 1962 in Irondale, Alabama. EWTN's first program was presented on August 15, 1981.

Angelic Doctor, colloquial designation of the Scholastic theologian Thomas Aquinas (d. 1274), who wrote so well and abundantly about the angels and who seemed to approximate their intelligence. *See also* Aquinas, St. Thomas.

Angelico, Bl. Fra [Fra Giovanni da Fiesole], ca. 1400–55, Florentine painter of the early Renaissance. Nicknamed "Angelico" (the angelic painter), also known as "Il Beato" (It., "Blessed"), he was a Dominican whose paintings of the Virgin were influenced by the theological doctrine of the "garden of the soul" of his prior at San Marco, Antoninus of

Florence. Fra Angelico's importance lies in his unparalleled use of color to create a naturalism of pictorial space and atmospheric effects. His notable works include the *Annunciation* (ca. 1434, Cortona, Italy), *Descent from the Cross* (ca. 1434, San Marco, Florence), and the frescoes in the monastic cells at San Marco in Florence (1438–45).

Angélique, Mère (mair ahn-jay-leek'). *See* Arnauld, Jacqueline Marie Angélique.

Angelus, a devotion that honors the Incarnation three times a day at the tolling of church or chapel bells. The name derives from the Latin phrase *Angelus Domini* ("Angel of the Lord"), which introduces the prayer: "The angel of the Lord declared to Mary, and she conceived of the Holy Spirit." This versicle and response is followed by the Hail Mary, then two more versicles and responses: "Behold the handmaid of the Lord, be it done unto me according to your word." "The Word was made flesh, and dwelt among us." Each of these biblical texts is also followed by a Hail Mary. The devotion is completed by a prayer addressed to God that recalls the "Incarnation, made known by the message of an angel. . . ." During Eastertide, the Angelus is replaced by a similar devotion, the Regina Coeli ("Queen of Heaven").

The origin of this prayer is obscure. Historians seem to agree, however, that the custom began with the practice of the evening tolling of the bell for Compline in monasteries or the tolling of the bell for curfew. The practice may go back as far as the tenth century in England. By the thirteenth century, people were being exhorted to follow the Franciscan custom of reciting three Hail Marys at the ringing of the evening bell. Indulgences were attached to the practice in the fourteenth century. The devotion was finalized as we know it today during the sixteenth century. *See also* Incarnation, the; Marian devotions.

anger. *See* capital sins.

Anglicanism, a term that pertains to the Anglican Communion. The communion was described by the Lambeth Conference of 1930 as "a fellowship within the One, Holy, Catholic and Apostolic Church of those duly constituted dioceses, provinces or regional Churches in communion with the See of Canterbury." The archbishop of Canterbury is regarded as "*primus inter pares*" (Lat. "first among equals") of the Anglican archbishops (primates).

Anglicans comprise between seventy to eighty

million members worldwide. As the name suggests, Anglicanism originated in England. Christianity was probably brought to England by soldiers or traders. England's first martyr was Alban (d. ca. 203), a Roman officer who refused to renounce Christ. Early in the sixth century, Celtic missionaries evangelized from the north. Notable among them was St. Columba, who settled on the island of Iona. He died in 597. Exactly eight days later, St. Augustine and a small party of Benedictine monks, sent by Pope Gregory the Great, landed on the Kent coast. After an abortive start, Augustine established his mission with a monastic community at Canterbury.

At the Synod of Whitby (663) the two forms of Christianity, Celtic and Roman, settled their differences, resulting in the unity of the Church under the authority of the pope. Catholic Christianity was further consolidated through the organizing ability of Theodore, appointed archbishop in 669, at the age of 66. He divided England into dioceses and created the parish system, thus providing for sacramental and spiritual nourishment for all people.

In the sixteenth century the Church in England separated from Rome, partly for theological reasons and partly for political ones. The theology of Martin Luther and other Reformers influenced English theologians in Cambridge and Oxford. The issues they debated included: (1) authority—how is it defined and how do papal and biblical authority relate? (2) justification—is faith or works the ground of salvation; are the sacraments the means to, or the results of, salvation? (3) priesthood—what is the relationship between the offering of the Eucharistic sacrifice, the finished work of Christ and the priesthood of the ordained ministry?

Henry VIII's political defiance of the pope and separation from him led to the suppression of Roman Catholicism in Britain. Under Henry and the following sovereigns, deep hostility led to persecution for both Catholics and Protestants. Queen Elizabeth gave protection to a "reformed" Church of England under the temporal authority of the sovereign and with the archbishop of Canterbury its spiritual head. For three hundred years Roman Catholicism was driven underground but it never died out.

England exploited its position as a seafaring nation and settled in many different parts of the world—the West Indies, Americas, Canada, India, and the Far East. Anglican missionaries were among the first to emigrate to minister to the English communities and to win others for Christ.

Bishops were appointed and men ordained to build up the Church. By the middle of the nineteenth century, it was evident that there was a need for the many autonomous dioceses to consult with each other. In 1867 the archbishop of Canterbury called a conference at his London home in Lambeth. The Lambeth Conference gathers all bishops together every ten years for fellowship, prayer, and theological discussion. Seventy bishops met at Lambeth Palace in 1867. The 1988 conference called together more than five hundred bishops, who met at the University of Kent and Canterbury Cathedral. Today the Anglican Communion has become worldwide in character. English is no longer the universal language of the communion—Spanish, French, Arabic, and many other languages are spoken in Anglican congregations around the world.

Doctrine: Anglicanism maintains that its doctrine is both catholic and reformed. It is catholic because it holds firmly to Christian fundamentals expressed in the Nicene-Constantinople Creed and in the early Church Fathers and because it retains many of the traditions associated with the Catholic Church. Its liturgy and Ordinal (ordination ritual) testify to this inheritance. Anglicanism is reformed because it affirms the primacy of Scripture in determining doctrine, repudiates the jurisdiction of the pope over the Church of England, and places salvation by faith through grace at the center of its thinking.

In 1888 the third Lambeth Conference set out the Anglican understanding of what is essential to the life and unity of the Church in the so-called Lambeth Quadrilateral. It embraced: (i) the Holy Scriptures as the record of God's revelation; (ii) the Nicene and Apostles' creeds as the rules of faith; (iii) the divinely instituted sacraments of Baptism and the Lord's Supper; (iv) the historic episcopate locally adopted.

The claim to be both reformed and catholic is upheld by a belief that the Church must be as comprehensive as possible. Visitors to different Anglican churches are often struck by the great variations between traditions. Evangelical Anglicans, generally "low church," emphasize preaching. The middle of the way, or broad church, is noted for its affirmation of the mind. The Anglo-Catholic wing, deeply influenced by Cardinal John Henry Newman (d. 1890) and the Oxford movement, is strikingly similar to Roman Catholicism.

Unity: In spite of events that forced Anglicans and Roman Catholics apart, relations today are strong and cordial. At the Second Vatican Council (1962–65), the Catholic Church recognized the closeness of Anglicanism to its own life. Among the separated churches that guard, in part, the Catholic tradition and structures, the Anglican Communion "occupies a special place" (Decree on Ecumenism, n. 13). Dialogues began with the meeting in Rome between Pope Paul VI and Archbishop Michael Ramsey in 1966. The establishment of the Anglican/ Roman Catholic International Commission (ARCIC) resulted in statements of agreement on the Eucharist (1971), the ministry (1973), and authority (1976 and 1981). These statements were published in the *Final Report of ARCIC,* which has been submitted to both churches for response. The Anglican Communion, at the 1988 Lambeth Conference, declared that the statements on the Eucharist and ministry and ordination were "consonant in substance with the faith of Anglicans" and recognized the convergence in understanding on authority. In 1991, the Catholic Church also found much it could agree with but wanted certain points relating to both Eucharistic doctrine and the ministry of the priesthood clarified. A Second Commission (ARCIC II) has made significant progress on shared understanding of justification by faith through grace and on the communion of the Church. The commission is looking now at questions of ethics.

While the dialogue continues to deepen understanding between communions, the Catholic Church acknowledges the "obstacle" to growth in communion occasioned by the Anglican ordination of women to the priesthood and episcopate. The Church of England approved the ordination of women in 1992.

In addition to its dialogue with the Roman Catholic Church, the Anglican Communion is committed to "all round" and "all level" ecumenism. Bilateral international conversations are taking place between Anglicans and Orthodox churches, Lutherans, Methodists, and Old Catholics. Anglicans also play a significant role within the World Council of Churches. In every region of the world, Anglicans seek to develop relationships with other Christians and to live in closer communion on the basis of agreement in faith. *See also* England, Catholicism in; Episcopal Church.

Bibliography

Sykes, Stephen, and John E. Booty, eds. *The Study of Anglicanism.* Philadelphia: SPCK/Fortress Press, 1988.   GEORGE L. CAREY

Anglican ordination, ordination of priests within the Anglican Communion. Although the Catholic Church formally denied the validity of Anglican ordinations in Pope Leo XIII's bull *Apostolicae Curae* (1896), as recently as 1994 the practice of the Catholic Church has been to reordain former Anglican priests conditionally, not absolutely. Absolute ordination, i.e., ordination with no canonical or theological reservations, is predicated on the judgment that any previous ordination was certainly invalid. Conditional ordination, i.e., ordination with canonical and theological reservations, is predicated on the judgment that any previous ordination, while probably invalid, could also possibly have been valid. Therefore, in the event that the previous ordination may not have been valid, the individual is reordained in a certainly valid rite, conditionally.

The historical problem is whether ordinations are valid when they have been performed according to the rite adopted in 1550 (the Ordinal), when the medieval rite (the Pontifical) of the Catholic Church was set aside by the authority of the English king Edward VI (1547–53) and the Ordinal composed by the archbishop of Canterbury, Thomas Cranmer, was imposed by the king.

Queen Mary to Pope Leo XIII: The question arose under Queen Mary (1553–58) when Cardinal Reginald Pole was reconciling with the Holy See the English clergy ordained under Edward VI. It arose again when Pope Leo XIII (1878–1903) created a commission to examine the problem. The instructions of Julius III (1550–1555) to Cardinal Pole did not decide the value of the Ordinal. Their main concern was that those priests who had married when clerical marriage was authorized by Edward VI could not function as priests unless they abandoned their wives, their marriages being illicit in the case of diocesan clergy and invalid in the case of religious orders. The pope stated the principle that ordinations must have been made "according to the accustomed form of the church," but the practical decisions about whether to accept the orders received under Edward VI were left to Cardinal Pole. There is no evidence that reordination was the rule, though there were some reordinations. The further instructions of Pope Paul IV (1555–59) did not discuss the Anglican Ordinal. But the pope would not recognize clergy whose ordination included the acceptance of the king's supremacy over the Church. He therefore specified that bishops and priests could be admitted as bishops or as priests only if the bishop who had ordained them had himself been ordained according to the old ritual from the time of

Henry VIII (before the adoption of the Anglican Ordinal); the old ritual did not affirm the royal supremacy and recognized the authority of the pope.

On two occasions in the seventeenth and eighteenth centuries the Holy See did not admit the value of Anglican ordination. But these cases (an anonymous French Calvinist and the case of John Gordon) were so peculiar that they do not warrant a general conclusion.

In the eighteenth and nineteenth centuries several investigations by French and British scholars reached opposite conclusions on the value of Anglican ordinations. In the late 1880s, however, Pope Leo XIII, who was greatly interested in religious developments in England, created a special commission composed of both partisans and opponents of the validity of Anglican orders. This commission reached no conclusion. Pope Leo's bull, *Apostolicae Curae* (1896), was not its work. It was composed by Cardinal Mazzella on the basis of a draft by the Master of Sacred Palace, the pope's official theologian, by tradition a Dominican. It concluded that lack of proper form and proper intention in the ordinal used at the consecration of Matthew Parker as archbishop of Canterbury in 1559 made Anglican ordinations invalid.

Mid-Twentieth Century to Today: Several more recent events that have thrown new light on the question may be listed: (1) The opening of the relevant archives by Pope John Paul II has made possible a better knowledge of Leo XIII's commission. (2) After the determination of the proper form of ordination by Pope Pius XII in November 1947, and the simplification of rites by Paul VI in June 1968, the Anglican form is much closer to the standard Roman form. (3) Due to the liturgical movement the understanding of intention that was assumed in *Apostolicae Curae* is no longer shared by the generality of theologians. Thus the two main points of the condemnation of Anglican orders, deficiency of form and deficiency of intention, have lost their standing in sacramental theology. (4) Both Paul VI and John Paul II have received Anglican bishops as bishops and have joined with them in prayer and in blessing the people. (5) The concept of the Church as communion, favored by most theologians, allows for more diversity in the expression of the common faith and in the form of the sacraments than was the case in the theology of the Counter-Reformation. (6) It is generally accepted that in a restored communion there will be room for different "types" of the Church, of which Anglicanism is one. (7) The dialogue between Anglicans and Catholics in the United States has determined that the intent of Leo XIII was not to block further relations; the two churches should study together their conception of the Church.

Thus, the possibility that the validity of Anglican ordinations may be recognized is no longer utopian. *See also* Anglicanism; Anglican-Roman Catholic dialogue; England, Catholicism in; ordination; Reformation, the.

GEORGE H. TAVARD

Anglican–Roman Catholic dialogue, a series of official meetings and reports designed to foster closer relations between the Anglican communion and the Roman Catholic Church, beginning with the first Anglican–Roman Catholic International Commission (ARCIC) in 1969 and continuing to this day. Building upon the foundation of the "special place" that the Anglican communion was said to occupy in relation to the Catholic Church in the Decree on Ecumenism of Vatican II, *Unitatis Redintegratio* (n. 13), and as a result of the visit of the archbishop of Canterbury to Pope Paul VI in Rome in 1966, an Anglican–Roman Catholic Joint Preparatory Commission was set up with the task of developing a program for dialogue and cooperation. Its findings were published in the Malta Report of 1968, which spoke of "our quest for the full, organic unity of our two communions." Arising out of this, the Anglican–Roman Catholic International Commission (ARCIC) was established in 1969, with members representing different parts of the English-speaking world and different theological outlooks within both communions.

ARCIC produced three agreed statements, one on the Eucharist (1971), one on ministry and ordination (1973), and one on authority in the Church (1976). While the first two were described by the commission as being "substantial agreements," the third did not go so far as that, but indicated specific problems remaining in the areas of papal primacy, infallibility, and jurisdiction. All three statements were included with some elucidatory notes and comments in the *Final Report* of the commission published in 1982. It should also be noted that a separate Anglican–Roman Catholic International Commission on the theology of marriage reported in 1975.

While the *Final Report* was being referred for discussion to the provinces of the Anglican Communion and to the national episcopal conferences of the Roman Catholic Church, a second commission (known as ARCIC II) was appointed in 1983 to continue the work begun by the first and to explore other areas of theological concern. It has issued two statements, one on salvation and the Church (1987) and one on Church as communion (1991).

In 1991 the Vatican Congregation for the Doctrine of the Faith issued its definitive judgment on the *Final Report.* While welcoming the progress that had been made, the Congregation insisted that from the Catholic point of view certain statements and formulations would need to receive greater clarification.

Alongside ARCIC, regional dialogues have also been taking place in different parts of the world. The Anglican–Roman Catholic Consultation in the United States of America (known as ARC/USA) has met regularly since 1965 and issued joint statements from time to time, many of which were collected in the volume *Called to Full Unity* (1986). ARC/USA has focused mainly on somewhat different issues from those dealt with by ARCIC, including the questions of Anglican orders and of the ordination of women. It is also working on a common eucharistic prayer text for possible use by the two churches in the United States as well as on establishing joint meetings of their bishops. *See also* Anglicanism; Episcopal Church.   PAUL F. BRADSHAW

Anglo-Catholicism, the name given since the Oxford movement in the nineteenth century to the "high church" party within the Anglican communion. Anglo-Catholics emphasize the historic continuity of the Church of England with its medieval predecessor and interpret official Anglican formularies in a way that is consistent with Catholic doctrine. They lay particular stress on the apostolic succession of the episcopate, the priestly character of the ordained ministry, and the Real Presence of Christ in the eucharistic elements. Their liturgical style closely mirrors contemporary Catholic worship, in the past sometimes even going as far as the abandonment of prescribed Anglican forms. *See also* Anglicanism; Episcopal Church; Oxford movement.

Anicetus, St., pope ca. 155–66, when Hegesippus, Justin Martyr, Marcion, and Valentinus were all in Rome. Polycarp of Smyrna (d. ca. 155) also visited Anicetus. Although they disagreed over the celebration of Easter, Polycarp (who favored the celebration on Passover) celebrated the Eucharist while in Rome, and the two parted in peace. At the time the Roman church had no special Easter festival but celebrated the resurrection every Sunday. Feast day: April 17. *See also* Quartodecimans.

Anima Christi (ah'nee-mah krees'tee; Lat., "Soul of Christ"), a prayer from the early 1300s used for private eucharistic devotion after Mass. The prayer's author is not known. Ignatius of Loyola recommended it in his *Spiritual Exercises* (1541).

ANIMA CHRISTI

Soul of Christ, be my sanctification;
Body of Christ, be my salvation;
Blood of Christ, fill all my veins;
Water of Christ's side, wash out my stains;
Passion of Christ, my comfort be;
O good Jesus, listen to me:
In thy wounds I fain would hide,
Ne'er to be parted from thy side;
Guard me, should the foe assail me;
Call me when my life shall fail me;
Bid me come to thee above,
With thy saints to sing thy love.
World without end. Amen.

[Tr. by Cardinal John Henry Newman]

animism (Lat., *anima,* "soul"), the belief of primitive peoples that certain natural objects such as animals, trees, and stones are "animated" by spirits. There is even a suggestion of animism in the OT where Jacob sets up a stone pillar at Bethel (Gen 28:18–22) contrary to the frequent biblical condemnations of stone worship (e.g., Hos 10:1–2; Mic 5:12; Deut 7:5). The Catholic doctrine of creation is opposed to animism. Only human beings, not animals and natural objects, are made in the image and likeness of God (Gen 1:26). Although God is present to all creation, there are no "gods of nature" to be worshiped, including human beings.

annates, tax on a benefice's first year of income. Originally this tax was levied by local bishops, but in 1306 Pope Clement V demanded annates from British benefices for the papacy, and during the fourteenth century payment of annates to the papal

Anne and Joachim, parents of the Virgin Mary, meeting in Jerusalem; fourteenth-century painting by Giotto in the Scrovegni Chapel, Padua, Italy.

treasury became common. In the face of increasing opposition, the Council of Trent (1545–63) severely restriced papal annates. Today, annates are due only from a few Italian benefices. *See also* benefice.

Anne and Joachim, Sts., the legendary parents of the Virgin Mary. According to the second-century *Protevangelium of James,* Joachim is not permitted to offer sacrifice because he has produced no child. Like Hannah in 1 Samuel, Anne has long been barren. Anne and Joachim pray for a child, which Anne vows to dedicate to God's service. When Mary is three years old, they bring her to the Temple where she remains until her betrothal to Joseph at age twelve. The story is repeated in the *Gospel of Pseudo-Matthew,* an eighth-century Latin work influential throughout the Middle Ages. Feast day: July 26. *See also* Mary, Blessed Virgin.

Anno, St., 1010–75, German archbishop. Educated at Bamberg, he was appointed archbishop of Cologne in 1056. Immersed in the politics of his time and often embroiled in scandals, especially nepotism, he spent the last year of his life in rigorous penance at the abbey of Siegburg. Feast day: December 4.

Anno Domini (ah'noh daw'mee-nee). *See* A.D.

Annuario Pontificio (an-yoo-ah'ee-oh pahn-ti-fee'chee-oh; It., "papal yearbook"), official annual publication by the Vatican of a complete list of members of the hierarchy, offices and officials of Roman Curia, and names of dioceses and religious institutes with pertinent statistics. Printed in Italian, it includes historical notes regarding the development of the various departments of the Roman Curia.

annulment, a declaration by a church tribunal system that a marriage was not canonically valid. Perhaps the first thing to be noted about this definition is not so much what it says as what it does not say. It does not, for example, say that an annulment indicates that a relationship, even a loving relationship, never existed between the parties. More importantly, it does not even say that a marriage never existed between the parties, but only that that marriage was not a canonically valid one (in church law, a marriage which is de facto invalid but which was entered with at least one party being in good faith, is known as a "putative" marriage—see can. 1061.3). And finally an annulment does not say that children born of an invalid marriage are illegitimate; the law of the Church (can. 1137) states clearly and unequivocally that all children are to be considered legitimate who are born of either a valid or a putative marriage.

Reasons for Invalidity: A marriage may be invalid according to the Church for one of two reasons: because of a law, or because of a consent that was in some way defective. There are two kinds of laws that render a marriage invalid; the first is called a disqualifying law; the second an invalidating law. The first renders a person ineligible; the second renders the act invalid. A disqualifying law is commonly known, in the field of marriage law, as an "impediment," and the Church recognizes twelve impediments to marriage; that is, twelve situations in which a person, even though naturally capable of marriage, is nevertheless considered disqualified or is rendered ineligible for marriage by Church law. First cousins, for example, are regarded as ineligible for marriage to each other, and if they marry without a dispensation, their marriage is regarded as "invalid." Similarly, a priest or a person who has taken a public perpetual vow of chastity is considered ineligible for marriage by Church law. The twelve impediments (cans. 1083–1094) are nonage, prior bond, disparity of worship, Holy Order, vow, abduction, coniugicide (murder of a spouse), consanguinity, affinity, public propriety, adoption, and impotence. This last, it should be noted, is not an impediment in the strict sense since a truly impotent person (unlike, for example, the first cousins or the priest) lacks a natural capacity for marriage and is not simply rendered ineligible for marriage by a law. Nevertheless, impotence has for centuries been listed as an impediment in Church law and continues to be in the 1983 Code of Canon Law.

The other kind of law that can render a marriage invalid is called an invalidating law. Unlike the disqualifying law, which directly affects the person, an invalidating law directly affects the act and renders that act invalid. A few examples: canon 1108 says that for a Catholic to marry validly, the marriage must be before a priest or deacon; if, therefore, a

Catholic marries "outside the Church," that is, without the presence of a priest or deacon and without a dispensation having been granted, the marriage is invalid. The same canon requires the presence of two witnesses; if therefore a couple exchanged marital consent before a priest alone, with no one else present, or with only one other person present, the marriage would be invalid. Again, that same canon requires that a Catholic marry not just before any priest or deacon but before one who is legitimately empowered to officiate at the wedding. Should the cleric not be so empowered, the marriage would be regarded as invalid. All of these requirements, incidentally, are called the "form" of marriage. Other examples of invalidating laws are canon 1105 (which lists certain requirements when a marriage is entered into by proxy), canon 1116 (which lists requirements for a valid marriage in extraordinary circumstances such as danger of death) and canon 1156 (which lists the special requirements for the convalidation of a marriage).

Besides these two types of laws, disqualifying and invalidating, the other major factor that can render a marriage invalid is a defective consent. It is axiomatic that "consent makes marriage" so when the consent is substantially defective on the part of one or both spouses, the marriage is invalid. Over the centuries canon law has identified several factors that can result in a defective marital consent. The first is a genuine incapacity either for consent itself (as when a mental disorder has deprived a person either of the basic ability to think rationally or at least of the ability to grasp and appreciate what marriage fundamentally entails) or for the "object" of consent. The object of consent is the thing a person consents to; in this case marriage, or more specifically the essential obligations of marriage. If therefore a person is, for some psychological reason, incapable of fulfilling the essential obligations of marriage, then in canon law, that person is considered to enter marriage with defective consent, because one cannot truly consent to do something which he or she is incapable of doing. If, for example, a marriage breaks down because a homosexual partner finds it impossible to function in a heterosexual relationship, then such a marriage could be declared invalid on the ground that the homosexual suffered from a defect of consent insofar as he or she was incapable of fulfilling the essential obligations of that marriage.

Besides these incapacities either for consent itself

or for the object of consent, there are several other consensual defects recognized in law. These are, for example, ignorance about the basic nature of marriage, error about the identity of one's spouse, error caused by fraud regarding some important quality of one's spouse, and error concerning the unity, indissolubility or sacramental dignity of matrimony. There is also simulation, that is the intention to enter either a trial marriage or an open marriage or a childless marriage, or perhaps no marriage at all, as might happen, for example, when the parties go through a marriage ceremony as a mere business arrangement or solely for the purpose of obtaining a citizenship desired by one of the parties. Still another consensual defect that invalidates marriage is the entering into marriage conditionally, that is to say, only if something else, like coming into an inheritance, happens. And a final defect of consent is that caused by entering into a marriage due to force or grave fear. All of these consensual defects are discussed in canons 1095 through 1103 of the Code of Canon Law.

Procedures: Depending on the nature of the invalidity, the Catholic Church uses three different procedures for investigating and declaring invalidity: administrative, informal, and formal.

An administrative procedure is used for a marriage involving a Catholic when the marriage ceremony was "outside the Church," that is before someone other than a priest or deacon and without the Church's having dispensed from that requirement. A Catholic, for example, having no interest in being married in the Church, marries instead before a justice of the peace. This is commonly called a "lack of form" marriage. A ceremony of this kind is considered to be so obviously invalid that it may be declared so without a judicial process but by a simple administrative procedure.

As regards all other marriages, however, the question of their possible invalidity must be investigated by a judicial process, either informal or formal. An informal process, also called a documentary process, may be used in only two situations: (1) when, from a document which is subject to no contradiction or exception, there is certain proof of the existence either of a diriment (invalidating) impediment (one of the twelve mentioned above) or of a defect of legitimate form (as, for example, when the marriage is performed only before the priest and without the two required witnesses), provided it is clear with equal certitude that a dispensation was not granted; and (2) when there is certain proof that, in a proxy marriage, the proxy or procurator was never duly appointed by the spouse to serve as proxy (can. 1686).

Besides these few types of cases, which can be handled by either an administrative or an informal procedure, all other marriage cases are conducted by an ordinary formal procedure. A formal procedure involves extensive testimony from both the petitioner and the respondent, at least where the respondent wishes to participate, as well as from witnesses, and often psychiatric experts as well. A Defender of the Bond, whose duty it is to call to the attention of the court everything that can reasonably be adduced in favor of the validity of the marriage, must also be appointed in every formal trial. And no declaration of invalidity is definitive until a second concordant decision has been given by an appellate court.

Each year United States tribunals give about 36,000 decisions in cases heard in formal trial, about 2,000 decisions following the informal judicial procedure, and about 26,000 administrative decrees of nullity for marriages that were null because of lack of form.

Popular Misconceptions: Cardinal Gasparri (d. 1934), who was probably the most influential canonist of this century, once suggested that the term "null" (on which the term "annulment" is obviously based) be applied only to marriages that are invalid by reason of lack of form. All other marriages that are not valid would be called "invalid" rather than "null." Regrettably, however, this distinction has not been maintained. Had it been, the difference between a declaration of nullity (or annulment) and a declaration of invalidity would be clear, and in general there would be far less confusion regarding this entire matter. When, for example, people hear that a twenty-year marriage of two Catholics, which had taken place in the Catholic Church, is now being declared "null," they imagine that the Church is now saying that that marriage never existed and that the children born of the marriage are therefore illegitimate; which is not at all the case.

Many people seem to be under the impression that when two non-Catholics marry before a rabbi, pastor, minister, or even before a civil magistrate, somehow the Catholic Church does not recognize that marriage as valid. This is false. The Catholic position is that, while a Catholic must marry before an authorized Catholic priest or deacon, all others (except the Orthodox who have a similar regulation) may validly marry before any official recognized by civil law. *See also* Marriage.

Bibliography

Brown, Ralph. *Marriage Annulment in the Catholic Church.* 3d ed. Suffolk, England: Kevin Mayhew, 1990.

Robinson, Geoffrey. *Marriage, Divorce and Nullity.* Victoria, Australia: Dove Communications, 1984.

Wrenn, Lawrence G. *Annulments.* 5th ed. Washington, D.C.: CLSA, 1988.

_____. *Decisions.* 2d ed. Washington, D.C.: CLSA, 1983.

_____. *Procedures.* Washington, D.C.: CLSA, 1987.

LAWRENCE G. WRENN

Annunciation, the proclamation to Mary that she would be the mother of Jesus. The basic account appears in Luke 1:26–38. The angel Gabriel appears in Nazareth to a virgin who is betrothed to Joseph, of the house of David. Gabriel pronounces what has become the first portion of the Hail Mary prayer: "Greetings, favored one! The Lord is with you!" (Luke 1:28). Gabriel then predicts the birth of Jesus and his eternal rule over the "house of Jacob." Mary, incredulous, asks how it may be, and Gabriel responds by promising that the Holy Spirit will cause Mary to conceive (Luke 1:35). The promise grounds the belief in the virginal conception of Jesus. The interchange between Gabriel and Mary provides the opening for the Angelus prayer: "The angel of the Lord declared unto Mary, and she conceived by the Holy Spirit." Mary's response to Gabriel's promise

The archangel Gabriel announcing God's invitation to the Blessed Virgin to become the mother of the Savior; seventeenth-century oil painting by Rubens, located in Vienna.

(Luke 1:38, RSV) expresses her humble submission to God's will: "Behold, I am the handmaid of the Lord; let it be to me according to your word." This response, one of the few direct quotations from Mary in the NT, epitomizes her role as the servant of God.

The Church celebrates the feast of the Annunciation on March 25, nine months before the celebration of the birth of Jesus. *See also* Mary, Blessed Virgin.

anointing, covering the body or an object with oil. The use of oil as a refreshing unguent was common in the ancient Near East (Deut 28:40; 2 Chr 28:15; Mic 6:15; 2 Sam 12:2). It was also used for medicinal purposes (Isa 1:6; Luke 10:34). Its origin as a sacred rite is not clear, but anointing was used in the consecration of priests (Exod 29:1–9), of the tent of meeting, and of the ark (Exod 30:26). It is also a sign of investment with power. The king is called "the Lord's anointed" (Heb., *mashiah*, 1 Sam 24:6), and the first kings of Israel were anointed (Saul, in 1 Sam 10:1–8; David, in 1 Sam 16:13; Solomon, in 1 Kgs 1:39). Though prophets or priests conduct the anointing, the true agent is God (1 Sam 10:1) and the person anointed receives God's spirit (1 Sam 16:13). The promise to David in 2 Sam 7:8–16 gave rise to the hope for an ideal Davidic ruler who in the intertestamental literature is called messiah. The Dead Sea Scrolls testify to an pre-Christian expectation of a priestly and a royal "anointed one" (1QS 9:11; 1QSa 2:14). The Gospels portray Jesus' hesitancy to accept the designation "Messiah" (Gk., *Christos*) without qualification, often by reference to the suffering Son of Man (Mark 8:29–31; 14:61–64). Early creedal formulas (such as Rom 1:1–4, 1 Cor 15:3) and public proclamation (Acts 2:36) call Jesus "the anointed one" (Christ) by virtue of his death and Resurrection. The term quickly becomes virtually a proper name for Jesus (Gal 3:26–27) as the bearer of God's spirit (Luke 4:14–18) and authority. The only NT reference to anointing as a sacred rite is Jas 5:14, where elders of the Church pray over sick people and anoint them "in the name of the Lord." *See also* Anointing of the Sick.   JOHN R. DONAHUE

Anomoeans (a-noh'mee-uhnz; Gk., *anomoios,* "unlike"), the most radical group of fourth-century Arians under the intellectual leadership of Aetius and Eunomius. Their doctrine was that the Son, although the full expression of the Father, is radically unlike the Father in all things because the Son is dependent on the Father. *See also* Arianism.

ANOINTING OF THE SICK

*A*nointing of the Sick is one of the seven sacraments of the Catholic Church. It is one ritual component of a more extensive ensemble of ritual prayer that is part of the Church's pastoral care for the seriously sick and/or the dying. Since the medieval period this sacrament has been called Extreme Unction (Lat., "last anointing") and has been perceived almost exclusively as part of the ensemble of rites celebrated for the dying Christian. In accordance with the Second Vatican Council (Constitution on the Sacred Liturgy, n. 73), the 1972 reformed rite restored the more traditional (premedieval) perspective on this sacrament as the ordinary rite for the strengthening of those whose health is debilitated by physical illness or old age. This change in perspective has been well accepted by the faithful.

THEOLOGY

Sickness, physical decline with age, a person's final journey in death—all of these realities are as much the stuff of mystery as are birth, the full vigor of healthy youth, marriage, and family life. Illness is part of the human condition. Christians are called to the faith-filled acceptance of suffering as a sign of their incorporation into Christ, who took upon himself our human pain (Col 1:22–19). This is no passive act of helpless surrender. Christ's concern for the bodily and spiritual welfare of the sick was a declaration that in his ministry the reign of God was breaking through in a new and definitive manner (Mark 2:1–12).

In inviting all seriously ill Christians to the sacrament of Anointing the Church proclaims its belief in Christ's power over the pain and isolation of grave illness and dying. The Church, in imitation of Christ's example and in obedience to his command, supports and is itself engaged in fighting illness. A holistic vision of the human person, however, calls for medical personnel and Church ministers who look to the comforting of the spirit as well as to the healing of the body. Authentic pastoral care of the sick necessarily comprises both.

Pope Paul VI's apostolic constitution promulgating the reformed rite (1972) stresses a theological dimension of this sacrament far too often neglected, namely, that this holy anointing is not only a ministry to the sick and the dying but also an act of setting those anointed in special state of ministry to the rest of the Church. Like all other sacraments and blessings of persons, Anointing of the Sick institutes the baptized into an *ordo* (Lat.), or college of ministry. In this instance, those anointed are raised up as particular models of faithful and hope-filled association with Christ in his Passion and death.

THE HISTORY OF THE RITE

The use of oil, the laying on of hands, and ritual prayer for the healing of the sick are rooted in Jewish tradition. Jesus and his disciples (Mark 6:13; Jas 5:13–16) did not invent new symbols and rites of healing but employed traditional forms they invested with new meaning. For at least the first eight centuries of the Church's life, the more formal ritual emphasis was upon the bishop's blessing of oil for the anointing of the sick. It seems that just as ordinary Christians brought the Eucharist from the Sunday celebration to their homes for Communion during the week, so they also brought blessed oil home for use as needed. The bishop and/or other members of the local clergy undoubtedly visited the sick and may well have been the ministers of anointing. For the most part, however, baptized members of the local church were the ordinary ministers of this sacrament.

The gradual clericalization of the rite had much to do with the evolution of the sacrament of Penance, or Reconciliation. Because of the rigorous demands made upon those who entered into public penance during the first eight centuries and the fact that it could be received only once in a lifetime, Christians tended to postpone entrance into this state until close to death. Because the sacrament of Anointing was reserved to those in full communion with the Church, it necessarily needed to be delayed until after deathbed Reconciliation. Thus the development of the continuous rite of Penance, Anointing of the Sick, and Viaticum (the final reception of Holy Communion)—all administered by a priest. Lost in this development was the awareness that the anointing is directed to physical as well as to spiritual healing. From about the beginning of the ninth century until the Second Vatican Council (1962–65), this sacrament was associated almost exclusively with death. The reform of the rite mandated by the council has emerged as one of the more successful and most eagerly accepted aspects of contemporary liturgical renewal.

THE CELEBRATION OF THE RITE

Though medieval rituals make it clear that the anointing of the dying was normatively celebrated with the presence and participation of the local community, the usual practice was individual celebration; that is, few if any other members of the faithful participated. This was especially the case when, as frequently happened, the confession of the dying person preceded the sacrament of Anointing and Viaticum.

The reformed rite clearly calls for the participation of members of the family and other members of the community in the celebration of this sacrament. Except in emergency situations, the rite envisions other ongoing acts of pastoral care that precede anointing. In addition to attending to those concerns of the seriously ill that often make illness an experience of isolation and emotional suffering, e.g., concern for the spouse and children of an afflicted parent, the rite presumes that the Church's members have visited with the sick, prayed with them, and regularly brought them Communion. In this perspective Anointing is the culmination of a series of rites and other acts of pastoral care. Except in emergency situations, pastors and other ministers to the sick should prepare the sick, their relatives, and other members of the community for this celebration as they would prepare for all other sacramental rites that are normatively celebrated with the proclamation of the word, song, and symbol.

The rite provides for the celebration of the sacrament of Anointing within a Mass celebrated in the home or hospital room of the sick person. This requires the permission of the ordinary. In many parishes and homes for the elderly it has become the custom to celebrate with some regularity the Anointing of the Sick within the Sunday and/or daily Eucharist.

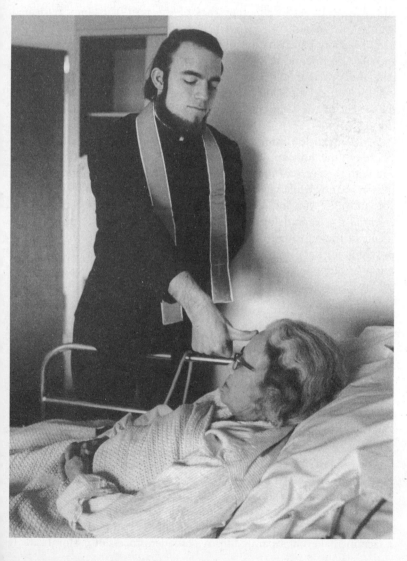

A priest administers the sacrament of Anointing of the Sick, signing the forehead and hands with oil while praying: "Through this holy anointing may the Lord in his love and mercy help you with the grace of the Holy Spirit. May the Lord who frees you from sin save you and raise you up. Amen."

The reformed ritual sees the continuous rite of Penance, Anointing, and Viaticum as exceptional. A rite for emergencies is provided for situations when the danger of death from catastrophic injury or illness is sudden and unanticipated or when the priest has been unable to attend the sick until the point of death. Anointing may be repeated when the sick person recovers after Anointing but later becomes sick again or when, during the same illness, the condition of the sick person becomes more serious.

THE SHAPE OF THE RITE

The texts, ritual directives, and pastoral notes in the 1983 edition of the rite are an expanded and more pastorally adapted version of the original Latin edition of this reformed rite (1972) and the provisional English edition (1973). As in all other rites of the post–Vatican II reformed liturgy this sacrament, even when celebrated outside Mass, always includes some proclamation of the word of God. The ritual elements specific and integral to this sacrament are: the prayer of faith, which takes the form of a litany; the priest's laying on of hands, which indicates that the particular person for whom the sacrament is being celebrated is the object of the Church's prayer; and the anointing with the oil of the sick.

While the priest anoints the forehead of the sick person he says: "Through this holy anointing may the Lord in his love and mercy help you with the grace of the Holy Spirit." Then the priest anoints the sick person's hands while saying: "May the Lord who frees you from sin save you and raise you up." These anointings and sentences comprise the essential matter and form of the sacrament. Particularly positive elements of the reformed rite are the thanksgiving over blessed oil or the provision for the priest to bless a fresh supply of the oil of the sick when it is not otherwise available.

ISSUES OF PASTORAL CARE

Contemporary pastoral theology and the insights of the human sciences make us more aware of the needs of the sick and their families and communities, needs to which the Church must attend if the Anointing of the Sick is to be experienced as an authentic element of Christian healing. Sickness places human beings into a state of isolation. The daily fabric of life is altered and broken. Because of this, relationships change: spouses and children go untended, work commitments suffer, ministries are neglected.

The Church's tradition of pastoral care for the sick sets these experiences within a context of faith. This is necessary because the more serious and disorienting the illness, the more it is experienced by the sick and those close to them as an experience of evil and a test of their faith, hope, and love. Thus Anointing of the Sick has never been envisioned as a sacramental event separated from a broader process of pastoral care. It

A priest administers the sacrament of Anointing of the Sick in a communal ceremony in church. As he anoints the woman's forehead, he says the words, "Through this holy anointing . . ."

must be stressed that the reformed rite presumes that in nonemergency situations the normal order of rites will be visits to the sick, Communion calls, and, only after the community's ministers have also attended to the sick persons' sense of isolation and concern for those most intimately affected by their illness, the full celebration of the rite for the Anointing of the Sick.

The popular acceptance of this reformed rite has raised a more specific question about who may be anointed. The shift from the perception of this sacrament as a rite for those in danger of death to one for people who are seriously ill has given rise to situations in which there come forward for Anointing, especially at communal Anointing rites celebrated in churches, people who are victims of substance addictions, of temporary or long-standing mental disturbance, or in need of "inner healing." Through and in this rite the Church addresses God's healing and forgiving word and sacramental symbols to those whose actual physical affliction is so serious that their lives and the lives of those near to them need consciously and in a very specific way to find new meaning in terms of the paschal suffering of Jesus Christ. Thus one does not anoint a soldier about to undertake a particularly dangerous mission. Anointing is not meant to replace other sacraments and/or forms of pastoral care such as pastoral counseling, the sacrament of Reconciliation or simpler forms of prayer, or the laying on of hands and blessing.

See also anointing; death and dying; healing; holy oils; oil of the sick; sacrament; Viaticum.

Bibliography

Ahlstrom, Michael, Peter Gilmour, and Robert Tuzik. *A Companion to Pastoral Care of the Sick.* Chicago: Liturgy Training Publications, 1990.

Fink, Peter. *Anointing of the Sick. Vol. 7: Alternative Futures for Worship.* Collegeville, MN: Liturgical Press, 1987.

Gusmer, Charles W. *And You Visited Me: Sacramental Ministry to the Sick and the Dying.* Collegeville, MN: Liturgical Press, 1984.
ANDREW D. CIFERNI

anonymous Christianity, a term that describes, from within Christian theology, the positive possibility for the salvation of non-Christians. In general, this term reconciles the Christian claim of the necessity of Christ for salvation with the Christian acknowledgment of God's will for the salvation of all.

As proposed by Karl Rahner (d. 1984), the term is an application of his assertion that humanity has a fundamental transcendental orientation. Any choice for the good, in this view, implies some already operative understanding of, and assent to, the reality of divine revelation. The substance of this term, although not the term itself, appears in the work of Rahner's contemporaries Henri de Lubac (d. 1991) and Hans Urs von Balthasar (d. 1988) and in the documents of Vatican II.

The term "anonymous Christianity" has proven unhelpful in dialogues between Christians and non-Christians, as it is seen by the latter as evidence of a profound paternalism. The term implies that the most significant insights of non-Christian belief systems are, in some *a priori* sense, Christian. The term is of value only in its original context: it asserts the universality of grace while maintaining that, for Christian theology, grace is always the self-gift of the God of Jesus Christ. *See also* salvation outside the Church; universal salvific will of God.

Anselm of Canterbury, St., ca. 1033–1109, monk, theologian, and archbishop of Canterbury. Born in Lombardy, he entered the Norman monastery of Bec, where he studied under Lanfranc, eventually serving as prior and then abbot. He succeeded Lanfranc as archbishop of Canterbury (1093). Disagreement about the rights of investiture made relations with the English king difficult, and Anselm spent much of his tenure on the Continent seeking the support of the pope and others.

Anselm was a prolific author of letters, prayers, and theological treatises, and his theological reflections continue to fascinate Catholic and Protestant alike. In his *Proslogion* (1077–78), for example, he advances what has come to be called the "ontological argument" for the existence of God. The *Cur Deus Homo* (Lat., "Why God Became Man"), written after he became archbishop, describes Christ's death on the cross as an act of satisfaction, returning to God the honor stolen by human sin. His *The Procession of the Holy Spirit* (1102) rehearses arguments on the double procession of the Holy Spirit that he employed at the Council of Bari, called to restore the Eastern churches to unity with the West.

Anselm of Canterbury, famous for his succinct definition of theology as "faith seeking understanding"; a school of Della Robbia ceramic, Museo della Collegiata, Empoli, Italy.

Other treatises written toward the end of his life sought to define free will and to show the compatibility of human freedom with divine grace, providence, and predestination. Anselm characterized his theological work as "faith seeking understanding." Beginning with the affirmation of faith, he sought through argument a firmer grasp and deeper appreciation of truths that at the end of the process continued to be held by faith.

Despite the shared commitment to the principled use of reason in theological inquiry, Anselm is only imperfectly styled the "first of the Scholastics." Anselm concentrated on discrete problems, eschewing the construction of comprehensive statements of Christian faith associated with later Scholastics such as Aquinas. Nor did he attempt to adjudicate among conflicting scriptural, patristic, and ecclesiastical authoritative texts, preferring to offer his theology directly in his own voice. Feast day: April 21. *See also* Canterbury; Scholasticism.

JOSEPH WAWRYKOW

Anselm of Laon, d. 1117, theologian. Perhaps a student of Anselm of Canterbury at Bec, he later established a school at Laon with his brother Randolph that attracted scholars such as William of Champeaux and Peter Abelard. Anselm's writings are known through quotations by his students; these indicate that in his comments on the Bible he summarized the Church Fathers on specific verses and adjudicated their differences. He participated in the development of the *quaestio* (the process of raising theological questions) as part of biblical commentary and contributed by his work on Paul and the Psalter to the medieval textbook of biblical commentary known as the *Glossa Ordinaria*. *See also* *Glossa Ordinaria;* Scripture, interpretation of.

Ansgar, St., 801–65, bishop and missionary. A Benedictine, he labored in both Denmark and Sweden and is regarded as the Apostle of Scandinavia. Feast day: February 3. *See also* Scandinavia, Catholicism in.

Ansovinus, St., d. 840, Italian-born hermit and bishop of Camerino, protector of crops. Feast day: March 13.

Anthony Claret, St., 1801–70, bishop and missionary. A Spaniard, he labored in Cuba until his return to Spain as royal confessor. He founded the Claretians, a religious congregation. Feast day: October 24. *See also* Claretians.

Anthony of Egypt, St., ca. 251–356, often called Anthony the Great or Antony, an early Coptic solitary in Egypt who was considered the prototype of the hermit. Born of prosperous peasant stock, he became a hermit in early adulthood near his home and later retired into the deep desert. Eventually many disciples gathered around him for spiritual guidance. Biographical details rely heavily on the almost contemporary, but stylized, *Life of Antony,* written ca. 357 by the theologian Athanasius of Alexandria. This widely read work turned Anthony into the hero of early monasticism, the "father of monks." He is the classic representative of the solitary version of early monasticism in Lower Egypt. Solitude was moderated, however, as hermits were accessible to each other and to visitors, including pilgrims, and as they exercised an important social role. Anthony seems to have visited Alexandria at least twice in support of the local church.

The inspiration for his life of withdrawal was not extreme asceticism but radical simplicity, poverty, and charity in imitation of Christ. The anecdotes and words of advice of the desert solitaries, women and men, are preserved in collections known as the *Sayings of the Fathers.* About a thousand of these sayings are considered authentic, of which almost

Anthony of Egypt, the first of the Church's hermits and generally regarded as a founder of monasticism; eighteenth-century painting in the Pitti Palace, Florence.

forty probably date back to Anthony himself. Feast day: January 17. *See also* hermit; monasticism.

Anthony of Padua, St., ca. 1191–1231, Franciscan friar, preacher, and Doctor of the Church. Born in Lisbon, probably of a family of Crusader knights, Anthony joined the Augustinian Canons Regular as a young man, receiving an excellent theological education at Coimbra. When the remains of the first missionary martyrs of the new Franciscan order were brought there for burial in 1220, Anthony was inspired to follow their example; he transferred to the Friars Minor and sailed for North Africa. Forced to return to Europe due to ill health, he arrived in Italy in 1221 and was assigned to the province of the Romagna, a region in which heretical groups were very active. Anthony's exceptional skills as a preacher and scholar quickly brought him into prominence and he was granted permission by Francis to teach theology to the friars. From 1224 to 1227 he was engaged in a similar mission in southern France. Returning to northern Italy, for the next four years he enjoyed extraordinary success as a preacher. His sermons, which

Anthony of Padua, regarded as one of the greatest preachers of all time, with the biblical word of God; fifteenth-century painting by Alvise Vivarini, Correr Museum, Venice.

reveal a profound knowledge of Scripture, often focused on social problems.

Anthony died at Padua in 1231, where a great popular devotion to him sprang up; he was canonized less than a year after his death. Numerous miracles were attributed to him, and he enjoys to this day the reputation as a wonder-worker. His concern for the poor is recalled in the practice of St. Anthony's Bread, contributions from which are devoted to the relief of the needy. Feast day: June 13. *See also* Franciscan order.

Anthony Zaccaria, St., 1502–39, priest. A popular preacher from Cremona (Italy), he founded the Barnabites. Feast day: July 5. *See also* Barnabites.

anthropic principle, philosophical idea emanating from contemporary scientific cosmology holding that the universe is peculiarly oriented toward life and consciousness—in the sense that all the conditions for their possibility have been fulfilled. Its apparent triviality is balanced by the recognition that there are thousands of different physical characteristics of the universe and of the laws that describe the processes within it which, if just slightly changed, would render the universe inhospitable to life as we know it. Thus, the laws that describe reality seem to have been "fine tuned" to produce life.

Cosmological models are severely limited by such conditions. From a scientific point of view, however, anthropic constraints do not add to those already given in physical and astronomical observations and measurements. But many scientists and philosophers assert that such fine-tuning demands an explanation, and some have proposed arguments for the existence of God based on these observations and measurements. Others go so far as to suggest that our presence, and the presence of life, *is* the explanation for the universe being the way it is. But this can only be understood in a teleological sense, which is outside the competency of the sciences. From a philosophical point of view it is unclear what can be validly concluded from these tantalizing physical coincidences. A valuable source book is *The Anthropic Cosmological Principle,* by John D. Barrow and Frank J. Tipler (New York: Oxford University Press, 1986). *See also* cosmology; five ways of St. Thomas Aquinas; God; philosophy and theology.

anthropology, theological, critical reflection on the origin, purpose, and destiny of human life in the light of Christian belief. In distinction from cultural and physical anthropology, which, as disciplines of a social science, undertake empirical analyses of specific human societies, theological anthropology employs a variety of methods (e.g., transcendental reflection, historical investigation, phenomenological inquiry) in its study of Scripture, the Jewish-Christian tradition, the findings of the social sciences, contemporary life and thought (e.g., philosophy), and the Church's current experience (e.g., worship, communal life, and service). Its primary questions include the following: In the perspective of Christian faith, what does it mean to be a human being, to be made "in the image and likeness of God" (Gen 1:26–27)? How are we to understand evil and sin, as attested to in the Bible (e.g., Gen 3:1–13; 4:8) and experienced by people today? In what ways does God's grace enter into human life, and how is human existence potentially open to God's love and self-disclosure? What is it about being human that points toward the incarnation and redemption of Jesus Christ? In addressing these kinds of questions theological anthropology treats such topics as creation, grace, personal existence, freedom, sin, redemption, history, and the Beatific Vision. As evident in the writings of Augustine (d. 430), Anselm (d. 1109), and Aquinas (d. 1274), theological anthropology has always been a major area within theology. Nevertheless, many theologians would now say that since the Enlightenment and modernity's emphasis on the knowing subject, theological anthropology must be theology's foundation, as it is in the work of Friedrich Schleiermacher (d. 1834) and Karl Rahner (d. 1984). *See also* grace; human nature; theology.　　　　　　　　　　ROBERT A. KRIEG

anthropomorphism, the practice of attributing human characteristics to the deity. Common in all theistic religions, anthropomorphism was offset in Israel by the prohibition of making an image of Yahweh and thereby seeking to exercise some measure of control over him. Analogous and metaphorical language in speaking about God was, nevertheless, inevitable; hence the frequent allusions to, e.g., God's face, eyes, hands, and to God's seeing, hearing, touching, smelling. Some sources, especially the Yahwist (J), are particularly replete with anthropomorphisms, e.g., God walking in the cool of the day (Gen 3:8) or closing the door of the ark after Noah had entered (Gen 7:16). Human emotions, e.g., pity and anger, are also attributed to God (Hos 1:6–7; 8:5), but these should more properly be called anthropopathisms.

anti-Catholicism, prejudice toward Catholicism as an institutional entity. Such prejudice has taken a number of different forms. Post-Enlightenment Europe saw contempt for the ancient Church spawned by the rise of deism and rationalism and taking the form of anticlericalism and/or laws enforcing secular control over schools and charitable institutions once in the hands of the Church. Such attitudes resulted in restrictive legislation over the Church (e.g., priests were forbidden to wear clerical garb in Mexico after 1929) and expulsion of religious orders (e.g., the Jesuits were expelled from Portugal in 1759 and from Spain and its empire in 1767 and were finally suppressed in 1773). Sometimes anti-Catholic sentiments were based on nationalist sentiments as, for example, in post-Reformation England, where Catholicism was seen as "unpatriotically subversive," or in the nineteenth-century United States (with the torching of the Ursuline convent in Charlestown, Massachusetts, in 1834), where "nativism" identified Catholicism with immigrants who were thought to be "un-American." Strains of this prejudice exist down to the present day among, for example, extremist groups like the Ku Klux Klan. It also manifested itself in the 1928 U.S. presidential election, in which New York's Governor Alfred E. Smith was the first Catholic to run for president, and again in 1960, when another Catholic, John F. Kennedy, was a candidate for president. Kennedy won in spite of public opposition from many Protestant ministers. Another form was distrust of the Catholic Church among some intellectuals either because of its perceived political power or because of its antimodern attitudes on issues like population control and the role of women in the Church. It perdures even in the United States, where anti-Catholicism has sometimes been referred to as the anti-Semitism of the intellectuals. Also, tensions exist because of past sociopolitical struggles (e.g., between Rome and the Byzantine East) or because Catholicism is identified with the West (as in some Muslim countries today, like Saudi Arabia and Iran, which restrict or forbid missionary activities).

Long-standing tensions between Catholics and other Christians provide a long history of anti-Catholic sentiments whose effects are mitigated by the recent emphasis on ecumenical dialogue. Because dialogue works both ways, Catholics have also begun to modify some of their own anti-Protestant and anti-Semitic sentiments, partially rooted in the beliefs that Protestants are heretics and Jews, "Christ-killers." A growing appreciation of the universal salvific will of God and of the Catholic Church's own share of responsibility for the existence of prejudice and intolerance have brought about a major change in attitude on all sides. *See also* anticlericalism.　　　　LAWRENCE CUNNINGHAM

antichrist, a personified opponent of Christians and of the good who appears in the last times in early Christian apocalyptic theology. While usually thought of in connection with the book of Revelation, the name really occurs only in the Johannine Letters, but the idea is common in Jewish intertestamental literature and in the NT under a variety of names, especially Belial or Beliar (Heb., "wickedness," "worthlessness"; 2 Cor 6:15), perhaps Gog and Magog (Rev 20:8) or the beast (Rev 13:11–18), and perhaps the fourth beast in Dan 7. It is not clear in some texts whether the opponent is the devil or a human figure who represents the devil. In 2 Thess 2:8–9, "the lawless one" accompanies the work of the devil as sign of the last times. In the Johannine Letters, a knowledge of the antichrist is presumed and a group of persons is so labeled because they have seceded from the community (1 John 2:18–23; 4:3; 2 John 7–11) and teach false doctrines. The test applied here is whether they confess that Jesus is the

Christ (1 John 2:22) come in the flesh (1 John 4:2; 2 John 7), so the opponents may have held a Gnostic theology of a spiritual Christ who did not really suffer. The number 666, the "number of the beast" (Rev 13:18), may have referred to Nero, but all other attempts to match specific historical figures with this passage, which does not even use the term "antichrist," are pointless. *CAROLYN OSIEK*

anticlericalism, a state of mind and form of social behavior that reflect a negative attitude toward the clergy. Anticlericalism is found both within Catholicism and outside it and has at times been expressed in political movements directed against Catholicism.

Within Catholicism, anticlericalism first appeared during the Middle Ages. Widespread failure on the part of the clergy to bear credible witness to the gospel by their manner of life elicited criticism from Bernard of Clairvaux (d. 1153), as well as from later, more satirical sources like Erasmus (d. 1536).

Today, anticlericalism within Catholicism is coupled with a mistrust of, and hostility toward, perceived abuses within the institutional Church by a clergy who do not hold themselves accountable to those whom they are ordained to serve. Notably, at Vatican II (1962–65), Bishop De Smedt of Belgium protested against clericalism in his objections to the preliminary draft of the Dogmatic Constitution on the Church, which he maintained was too clericalistic, triumphalistic, and juridical in its outlook. Subsequently, much anticlerical sentiment within Catholicism developed as a reaction against intransigent and patriarchal institutional structures and corresponding clerical patterns of behavior.

Anticlericalism outside of Catholicism is part of a larger antireligious impulse that targets highly visible religious structures. It views religion as an error (at best) or a danger (at worst) that must be eliminated for the good of society. The antireligious writings of Voltaire (d. 1778) epitomize perhaps the most vitriolic expressions of anticlerical sentiment.

The French Revolution transformed anticlericalism into a political program. Churches were closed and priests, religious, and lay believers were persecuted. The shifting political tides in nineteenth-century France rendered the position of clergy uncertain. The post-Napoleonic government remained hostile to clergy and, in particular, to Jesuits. In 1879 the French senate formally approved this hostility with a series of anticlerical laws.

Italy also experienced a wave of anticlerical senti-ment in its efforts to unite as a single nation. Francesco Crispi generated much anticlerical sentiment in Italy and in Europe by arguing that the pope was the single greatest threat to European peace.

Portugal, Mexico, Spain (during its civil war), Germany (under the National Socialist, or Nazi, party), and the former Soviet Union also enacted programs of anticlericalism.

In some cases, of course, the anticlericalist reaction was at least partially justified. When the clergy becomes too closely identified with a repressive political regime, it suffers the punishments inflicted on the regime toppled by revolution. For this reason the Church now actively discourages its clergy from partisan political activities, urging them instead to be vigorous advocates of justice, human rights, and peace, regardless of the political regime (see, for example, Vatican II's Pastoral Constitution on the Church in the Modern World, n. 76). *See also* clericalism. *JAMES K. VOISS*

Antide Thouret, St. Joan, also known as Antida, 1765–1826, French-born founder of the Sisters of Charity of St. Joan Antide. She educated children, ministered to the poor and the sick, and hid priests from persecution by the French revolutionaries. Feast day: August 24.

antidoron (ahn-tee' doh-rahn; Gk., "in place of the gift"), unconsecrated blessed bread left over from the prosphoras (eucharistic loaves) prepared during the Prothesis for use at the Byzantine-rite Eucharist. Distributed to the people at the end of the liturgy, for those who do not receive Communion it is "in place of the (consecrated) gifts." *See also* eulogia; Prothesis.

antimension (an-ti-men'shuhn; Gk., "in place of the mensa, or table"), Byzantine-rite portable altar in the form of a cloth corporal with relics sewn into a small pocket. It usually bears the image of the burial of Jesus, with the Holy Week Triduum burial refrain inscribed around its borders. Always consecrated by a bishop, the antimension was originally destined for use only on unconsecrated altars. Now it is used, together with the *eiliton*, or Byzantine-rite corporal, on all altars, consecrated or not. Roman-rite priests sometimes adopt it as a portable altar in place of the cumbersome altar stone.

antinomianism, the claim that Christians have been freed by grace from observing the moral law.

This idea has been advanced at several times in the Church's history beginning with the misinterpretation of Paul (rejected by him, Rom. 3:8; 6:15), which understood his denial of the saving efficacy of Mosaic law and his emphasis on the gratuity of grace through faith in Christ as a rejection of the need to observe the moral commandments. Various Gnostic sects taught that the radical division between spirit and matter renders all bodily actions irrelevant to the life of the spirit, thus permitting all forms of licentiousness. *See also* moral theology.

Antioch, until the rise of Constantinople, the third most important city of the Roman Empire, after Rome and Alexandria. Founded in 300 B.C. by Seleucus I (son of Antiochus, whence its name), Antioch was famous for its magnificent public monuments, buildings, and streets. Its location in the fertile region of the Orontes River in Syria contributed to its prosperity. One of the earliest cities evangelized, with both Jewish and gentile converts (who had an uneasy coexistence according to Gal 1–2), it was the location where the name "Christian" was first used (Acts 11:19–26). Paul's first missionary journey was based there. The Christian community, like the city itself, was divided between Greek speakers and Syriac speakers.

By the time of Ignatius of Antioch, martyred ca. 107, the monoepiscopate seems to have been firmly in place in Antioch. Theophilus, bishop of Antioch, wrote his apology *To Autolycus* ca. 180, but his writings against Marcion and Hermogenes have not survived; nor have the writings of Serapion, bishop 199–ca. 211, apart from fragments. Origen visited the city, perhaps in the 220s, to meet with Julia Mammaea, mother of the emperor Alexander Severus. During the persecution of the Roman emperor Decius (249–51), the bishop Babylas was martyred; later, Paul of Samosata, bishop from 260, was deposed in 268 for heresy.

At the Council of Nicaea (325), Antioch was represented by its bishop, Eustathius. Its supermetropolitan privileges, fourth after Rome, Constantinople, and Alexandria, were confirmed by can. 6, thus ensuring its status as one of the five patriarchates of the imperial Church (with Jerusalem, from 451, as fifth). Shortly thereafter Eustathius was deposed and exiled (ca. 327) and an Arian bishop installed in his place. A party loyal to Eustathius broke off and remained in schism even in 360, when the anti-Arian Melitius was elected. Melitius was immediately exiled by the emperor Constantius after an

openly anti-Arian inaugural homily. When he returned in 362 he found the Eustathians had secured the consecration of a priest, Paulinus, by Lucifer of Cagliari. There were now three rival communities, the Melitian majority and the Eustathian and pro-Arian minorities. Melitius, who presided at the First Council of Constantinople (381) until his death, had the support of the East, while Paulinus and, for a time, his successor Evagrius (388–93) had the support of Egypt and the West, until in 398 the West recognized Flavian, Melitius's successor, as had Theophilus of Alexandria somewhat earlier. The schism persisted until 413 (although no successor to Evagrius was ever appointed); a small group of schismatics would not be reconciled until much later (ca. 482).

Antioch's theological distinction rests on the contributions to scriptural interpretation and preaching by the group of theologians collectively known as the Antiochene "school." Their ardent defense of a "two-nature" Christology was ultimately vindicated at the Council of Chalcedon (451), but Monophysite resistance to Chalcedon spread from Egypt and eventually reached Antioch itself. Severus of Antioch, a moderate Monophysite, was installed as bishop by the emperor Anastasius in 512. He was deposed by Justin I in 518, but due to the efforts of Jacob Baradaeus (ca. 500–78), a strong Monophysite church was established in Asia Minor and Syria. The Persians, who took the city in 540 and again in 611, encouraged the Monophysites; when the Muslims conquered Syria in the seventh century, they found at Antioch a church weakened by division between Jacobite (Syrian Christians who rejected the Council of Chalcedon) and the orthodox, or "Melchite," churches. The city fell to them ca. 637–38. *See also* Antioch, school of; Ignatius of Antioch, St.

JOHN C. CAVADINI

Antioch, school of, designation for an exegetical and theological tradition centered at Antioch (on the Orontes in Syria) that emphasized the literal interpretation of Scripture and the humanity of Christ. The Antiochene tradition received its classical form and mature articulation in the late fourth and early fifth centuries, but its roots are evident earlier. Paul of Samosata, bishop from 260 until deposed for heresy in 268, taught that Mary gave birth not to the "Word" but to a complete human being, Jesus, whom the Spirit indwelt as in a temple from the time of his baptism. There is no preexistent "Son," only the Logos/Spirit, *homoousios* (Gk., "of one substance") with the Father—by this Paul meant to deny hypostatic distinctions within the inner life of God. It is likely that Lucian of Antioch (d. 312), one of whose pupils was Arius, advanced his own teaching, which gave the Logos some hypostatic, if subordinate, independence from the Father, against Paul. Lucian, also an excellent biblical scholar, edited the text of the Greek Bible and emphasized a literalist approach to interpretation, later taken up by Eustathius, bishop ca. 324–27, whose sole surviving work, *On the Witch of Endor,* argues against the allegorizing of Origen. Eustathius, however, was an ardent anti-Arian who returned to a modified Monarchianism related to Paul's and defended the Council of Nicaea on that basis.

In fact, theologically speaking, the Antiochene school received its classical form as a result of its continuing polemic against Arianism. Eustathius had already critiqued Arianism by rejecting the Alexandrian "Word/flesh" Christology it presupposed. The Christ was not simply the Word incarnate or appearing in flesh, but a complete human being indwelt by God's Word (a moderated version of Paul of Samosata's Christology). Diodore of Tarsus (d. ca. 390) and especially his pupil Theodore of Mopsuestia (ca. 350–428) continued to develop this "Word/Man" Christology, countering Arian usage of passages that emphasized Jesus' weakness by arguing that they referred not to the Logos, who was *homoousios* with the Father and therefore equally God, but to the human being Jesus whom the Logos indwelt as in a temple. This man truly grew in wisdom (Luke 2:52), truly did not know the time of the last judgment (Mark 13:32), etc.; he was the true subject of the predicates of weakness and growth made in the Gospels. Perfectly assumed by the Logos, fully anointed by the Holy Spirit, he truly was the Son of God.

As an ambassador for this Christology, Nestorius (d. ca. 451, patriarch of Constantinople, 428–31) overstated his case, seeming to separate the two subjects in Christ altogether. He was condemned (Council of Ephesus, 431), although the more moderate form of the Antiochene tradition was ably represented by John (d. 441), bishop of Antioch from 429, who was able to compromise with Cyril of Alexandria, and Theodoret of Cyrrhus (ca. 393–ca. 466, bishop from 423), a brilliant exegete, apologist, and theologian who ultimately anathematized Nestorius at the Council of Chalcedon (451). All of these theologians and in addition the Antiochene school's most brilliant and beloved preacher, John Chrysostom (ca. 347–407), retained the school's characteristic preference for the literal sense of the text, seeking to solve difficulties in interpretation not on the basis of allegory but by paying close attention to literary style and rhetorical form, to the individual characteristics and peculiarities of the various biblical books, historical circumstance of the writer, and so forth. *See also* Alexandria, school of; Christology; Chrysostom, St. John; Ephesus, Council of; John of Antioch; Logos; Lucian of Antioch, St; Nestorianism; Paul of Samosata.   JOHN C. CAVADINI

Antiochene rite, the liturgical usages that developed around the metropolis of Antioch (Antakiya in southernmost Turkey, near the coast), main center of ecclesiastical culture and liturgical diffusion in the entire prefecture of Orient, which stretched from Syria through Asia Minor to Thrace (present European Turkey). First seen ca. 380 in patristic documents from the environs of Antioch like the *Apostolic Constitutions* and the homilies of John Chrysostom (who was a preacher there before he became bishop of Constantinople in 398), the ancient Antiochene liturgical foundations are still clearly visible in the Antiochene-based Armenian, Byzantine, and West Syrian rites and, for certain elements, in other traditions, too. Today the classical Antiochene anaphoral structure (presanctus, sanctus, postsanctus with institution narrative, command to repeat, anamnesis, oblation, epiclesis, intercessions) is often considered an ideal model, and attempts have been made to revive elements of Antiochene cathedral offices, too. *See also* Eastern rites; rite.

Antipas, St. (an'ti-pahs), an early Christian martyr. According to Rev 2:13, Antipas was a "faithful witness" slain at Pergamum in Asia Minor. Feast day: April 11.

antiphon (an'tih-fahn; Gk., *antiphones,* "responsively"), a short verse, usually from the Bible, sung at the beginning and end of psalms or canticles or as a refrain between verses. Marian antiphons are not associated with the Psalter, but with devotion to Mary, and are sung at the conclusion of Evening Prayer in the Liturgy of the Hours. The best-known Marian antiphons are the *Salve Regina* (Lat., "Hail Holy Queen"), *Alma Redemptoris Mater* ("Loving Mother of the Redeemer"), *Ave Regina Coelorum* ("Hail Queen of Heaven"), and *Regina Coeli* ("Heavenly Queen [Rejoice]"). Several antiphons are tied to liturgical processions on special feast days: *Pueri*

Hebraeorum ("Children of the Hebrews") on Palm Sunday and *Lumen Gentium* ("Light of the nations") on Presentation of the Lord (February 2).

antiphonal, a responsorial style of singing used in the liturgy. Two choirs of equal strength chant alternating verses of a psalm or canticle. Antiphonal, or antiphonary, also refers to the liturgical book that contains all the parts of the Liturgy of the Hours sung in choir. *See also* antiphon.

antipope, an individual whose claim to be pope is rejected by the Church as invalid. Although this definition is relatively straightforward, it is difficult to apply in practice, because guidelines as to what exactly constitutes an invalid claim to the papacy have fluctuated. Correct election is not an unambiguous indicator: the rules for papal elections have changed over time, and in some cases these rules have been bypassed. Innocent II (1130–43), for example, was elected by a minority of cardinals in a clandestine meeting but is considered a pope. Nor is personal sanctity a definitive factor: the martyr and saint Hippolytus (217–ca. 235) is considered the first antipope, while a legitimate pope, John XII (955–64), was excommunicated and deposed by a Roman synod for gross immorality. *See also* pope.

anti-Semitism, although the word "Semite" refers to Arabs as well as Jews, a term that has come to mean opposition to Jews specifically. It can take any form from discrimination to the systematic arrest and extermination associated with the Nazis during the Second World War.

Theories about why anti-Semitism has persisted include the Jewish claim to exclusivity as God's chosen people and Jewish dedication to the Law, which isolated them from the society and culture in which they lived.

In the first century the relationship between Judaism and Christianity broke down with the destruction of the Temple and the expulsion of the Christian community from the synagogue. Jewish Christianity became numerically insignificant while the numbers of gentile Christians increased. Throughout the centuries, the relationship of the Church towards anti-Semitism has been both positive and negative. Two faiths, both of which lay claim to exclusive election by the one true God, may find themselves unavoidably in conflict. After Constantine's conversion in 312 and the subsequent

LIST OF ANTIPOPES

If an antipope shares the same name and number as a legitimate pope, his number is given in parentheses. The dagger symbol following the dates indicates that there is a separate entry on that particular antipope elsewhere in the encyclopedia.

ANTIPOPE	DATES
St. Hippolytus	217–35†
Novatian	251–58
Felix II	355–65
Ursinus	366–67
Eulalius	418–19
Lawrence	498–99, 501–506
Dioscorus	530
Paschal	687
Theodore	687
Constantine	767–68
Philip	768
John	844
Anastasius Bibliothecarius	855†
Christopher	903–904
Boniface VII	974, 984–85
John XVI	997–98
Gregory (VI)	1012
Benedict X	1058–59
Honorius (II)	1061–64
Clement (III)	1080, 1084–1100
Theodoric	1100–101
Albert	1101
Sylvester IV	1105–11
Gregory (VIII)	1118–21
Celestine (II)	1124
Anacletus II	1130–38
Victor IV*	1138
Victor IV*	1159–64
Paschal III	1164–68
Callistus (III)	1168–78
Innocent (III)	1179–80
Nicholas (V)	1328–30
Clement (VII)	1378–94
Benedict (XIII)	1394–1417
Alexander V	1409–10†
John (XXIII)	1410–15†
Clement (VIII)	1423–29
Benedict (XIV)	1425–?
Felix V	1439–49

*Note that there are two Victor IVs among the antipopes. The second Victor IV took no note of the first one because he was "in office" less than two months.

links between Church and state, the Jews were regarded as anti-Christian and, therefore, a threat.

69

More recently, from popes Leo XIII in 1880 to Benedict XV in 1916 to an official statement by the Holy Office in 1928, anti-Semitism as well as racism in every form has been condemned by the Church. At the Second Vatican Council the Declaration on the Relationship of the Church to Non-Christian Religions (*Nostra Aetate,* 1965) stated that "The Church . . . decries hatred, persecution, displays of anti-Semitism, directed against Jews at any time and by anyone" (n. 4). *See also* Jews, Catholicism and.

KATHERINE S. BARRETT

Antonelli, Giacomo (jah'koh-moh an-tuh-nel'ee), 1806–76, cardinal and papal Secretary of State to Pope Pius IX, 1850–76. He exerted conservative, Ultramontane influence on papal policy, although he opposed the summoning of Vatican I (1869) and thought any statement on papal infallibility unwise. Ordained to the diaconate but not the priesthood, he was more a temporal than a religious leader. As temporal ruler of Rome until 1870, he was nicknamed the "Red Pope." *See also* Pius IX; Ultramontanism.

Antonia of Florence, St., ca. 1400–1472, Franciscan tertiary and then superior consecutively of three convents in Italy, including the convent of Corpus Christi from 1447 to 1454. Feast day: February 28.

Antoninus of Florence, St., 1389–1459, Dominican, founder in 1436 of San Marco Convent at Florence, and archbishop of Florence from 1446. He was well known for his aid to the poor and to the victims of plagues and famines; his writings on moral theology and canon law were highly influential. Feast day: May 10.

Antony of Egypt, St. *See* Anthony of Egypt, St.

Antony of Padua, St. *See* Anthony of Padua, St.

Aphraates, St. (ah-fray'teez), d. ca. 345, ascetic and cleric, earliest known Christian writer in Persia, and first of the Syriac Church Fathers. Twenty-three of his sermons, called "Demonstrations," are preserved. They attest to his belief in the triune God, Christ's victory over Satan, the Real Presence, and the value of asceticism, especially celibacy. Feast day: April 7.

apocalypse (uh-pahk'uh-lips; Gk., "revelation," "unveiling"), a type of revelatory literature. As a lit-erary form, it designates ancient works similar to the Apocalypse, or Revelation, the last book in the canonical order of the NT. Such works typically describe the process through which a human visionary receives secret knowledge about the future and the cosmos from a heavenly being. The revealing figure is usually an angel in Jewish apocalypses and the risen Christ in Christian works. The revelation is often given through symbolic visions or journeys to heaven or other places normally inaccessible to humanity.

Symbolic visions are characteristic of the apocalypses that show an interest in history and emphasize its fulfillment. Both of the canonical apocalypses, Daniel in the OT and Revelation in the NT, belong to this group. Daniel was written in response to the persecution of the Jewish people by Antiochus Epiphanes in the second century B.C. and reviews history from the Babylonian captivity until the end. Revelation was written to articulate the Christian vision of reality in opposition to the ethos of the Roman Empire.

Tours of heaven or the hidden regions of the cosmos are typical of apocalypses that emphasize the heavenly destiny of holy human beings, such as the Jewish work known as the Book of the Watchers, preserved in a collection of apocalypses attributed to Enoch (*Ethiopic Enoch* or *1 Enoch*). A Christian example is the *Ascension of Isaiah,* according to which thrones and crowns await the righteous in heaven. *See also* apocalypticism.   ADELA Y. COLLINS

apocalypticism (uh-pahk-ah-lip'ti-si-zuhm), a view of the world that emerged in Judaism during the Hellenistic period and had a formative influence on early Christianity. It takes its name from the literary genre "apocalypse," and more specifically from the Apocalypse, or book of Revelation, in the NT. Apocalypses are revelations and take the form of either symbolic visions or tours of heaven. In either case, the meaning of the revelation is typically explained by an angel. The content of the revelation involves both the secrets of the heavenly world and the eschatological future, especially the judgment of the dead. Some apocalypses incline more to the mystical exploration of the heavenly world, others to the future course of history. The latter type, the historical apocalypses, are the only ones represented in the Bible, in the books of Daniel and Revelation. Other apocalypses are attributed to Enoch, Adam, Moses, Abraham, Ezra, and Baruch. It is typical of these books that they are assigned to famous ancient figures, and that the real authors are not named. The Apocalypse of John is an exception in this regard, but later Christians composed apocalypses in the names of Peter, Paul, Mary, and others. The impact of apocalypticism on Judaism around the turn of the era can be seen in the Dead Sea Scrolls, which anticipate a final battle between the forces of light and darkness. It can also be seen in early Christianity. The expectation that Jesus would come as the Son of Man on the clouds of heaven was prompted directly by Dan 7. Paul's notion that Jesus was risen as the first fruits of a general resurrection (1 Cor 15) presupposes an apocalyptic view of history. The apocalyptic element in Christianity was submerged by philosophical concerns in the works of the Church Fathers, but flourished in some circles throughout the Middle Ages (Joachim of Fiore in the thirteenth century is a famous example). *See also* apocalypse; Joachim of Fiore.   JOHN J. COLLINS

apocatastasis (un-pahk'uh-tuh-stay'sis; Gk., "restoration"), universal salvation. This term comes from late Jewish prophetic and apocalyptic literature, where it expressed the hope for the restored unity and security the Messiah would bring to Israel (e.g., Mal 4.6 [Septuagint: Mal 3.24]; Acts 3.21). In Christian theology, the term is mainly associated with Origen (d. 254), who used it to express his belief that all created spirits, including the demons, will ultimately be restored to the loving unity with God that was their original state. Although this hope was sharply criticized by many of Origen's opponents, it was shared by such later sympathizers as Gregory of Nazianzus, Gregory of Nyssa, and Ambrose of Milan. A synod held in Constantinople in 543, ratified by the Second Council of Constantinople (553), condemned the thesis that the punishment of sinners, angelic or human, is only temporary. The Catholic Church has understood this to mean one must not claim that the salvation of all is dogmatically certain; however, many modern theologians, Catholic and Protestant, hold one may and indeed should hope that all will be saved. *See also* salvation; universal salvific will of God.

Apocrypha (uh-pahk'rif-uh; Gk., "hidden things"), books of the OT that are not found in the Hebrew Bible but are included in the Latin Vulgate. There are fifteen such books, or portions of books: 1–2 Esdras, Tobit, Judith, Additions to Esther, Wisdom of Solomon, Sirach (Ecclesiasticus), Baruch, Letter of Jeremiah, Song of the Three Young Men and Prayer of Azariah, Susanna, Bel and the Dragon (these three are Additions to Daniel), Prayer of Manasseh, and 1–2 Maccabees. The Jewish canon was not closed until the late first century A.D. Prior to that time, a much larger body of writings enjoyed authority, and many of these were taken over by the early Christians. Clement of Alexandria cited Tobit, Sirach, and the Wisdom of Solomon as Scripture and Judith and 2 Maccabees as historical sources. Origen accepted Susanna and Tobit. Tertullian even cited the book of *Enoch* with approval. Jerome advocated the *Hebraica veritas* (Lat., "the Hebrew truth") and so did not regard these books as canonical. Nonetheless, he translated them and included them in the Vulgate. Augustine favored the larger canon, and his view prevailed through the Middle Ages. The Protestant Reformers denied the canonicity of these books, although they granted their value as spiritual reading. They were still included in the King James Version of 1611, but were frequently omitted in later printings. The Council of Trent declared them canonical in 1546, except for 1–2 Esdras and the Prayer of Manasseh, and this decision is still accepted by the Catholic Church. The disputed books are sometimes called "deuterocanonical." In addition to the books accepted by the Catholic Church, the Greek Orthodox Church accepts 1 Esdras, Psalm 151, the Prayer of Manasseh, and 3–4 Maccabees. The Russian Orthodox Church accepts 1–2 Esdras, Psalm 151, and 3 Maccabees. Modern ecumenical translations of the Bible, such as the New Revised Standard Version, regularly include all these books.

The Apocrypha are distinguished from other Jewish religious writings from the turn of the era that did not win canonical status in the Western Church. Some of these writings, such as the books of *Enoch* and *Jubilees*, were regarded as canonical in other churches, notably in Ethiopia. Many of them are classified under the heading pseudepigrapha. *See also* deuterocanonical books; pseudepigrapha

JOHN J. COLLINS

apocryphal Gospels, Christian works that recount the life or sayings of Jesus but are not included in the NT. The production of such popular literature began in the first century but continued throughout the Middle Ages. The *Infancy Gospel of Thomas,* which portrays the child Jesus as a precocious miracle worker, survives in Greek, Syriac, Latin, and Slavonic. The distinct *Gospel of Thomas,* discovered at Nag Hammadi in 1945, contains 114 sayings of

Jesus. Some sayings are familiar from canonical Gospels or patristic traditions; others were previously unknown. The *Gospel of Peter,* discovered in 1886, dramatically recounts the Passion, death, and Resurrection of Jesus. The *Gospel of the Egyptians* survives only in fragments, most in the work of Clement of Alexandria, who complains (*Stromateis* 3.63; 3.91) that the extremely ascetic Encratites used the work.

Patristic sources mention various Jewish-Christian Gospels. Jerome often cites a *Gospel of the Nazareans,* apparently an Aramaic text resembling Matthew. Epiphanius mentions a Gospel used by the Ebionites. Origen notes a *Gospel of the Hebrews.*

Papyrus fragments of unknown Gospels have been discovered in the last two centuries. The most important, Papyrus Egerton 2, contains accounts similar to John.

Some works were formally rejected by the Church, e.g., by the sixth-century Gelasian Decree, which lists Gospels of Matthias, Barnabas, James, Peter, Thomas, Bartholomew, and Andrew, forgeries of Lucian and Hesychius, and books about the childhood of Jesus. *See also Decretum Gelasianum;* gospel; infancy Gospels.   HAROLD W. ATTRIDGE

apodosis (ap-oh'dah-sis; Gk., "return, giving back"; Slav., *otdanie*), Byzantine-rite liturgical "closure" or concluding day of the festive periods (Gk., *metheorta,* "afterfeasts"). Like Western octaves, these periods follow the nine fixed feasts of the cycle of Twelve Great Feasts, solemnized with a forefeast (Gk., *proeortion*) of one day, except for Christmas (five days) and Epiphany (four), a *metheorton* of one to eight days, concluding with an *apodosis.*

Apollinarianism, composite of views based on the works of Apollinarius of Laodicea, emphasizing the unity of the person of Jesus Christ as one incarnate nature of the divine Logos, and thereby denying the existence of a human soul in him. Because of Apollinarius's literal interpretation of the Johannine text, "the Word became flesh," and because of his strong reaction against Arianism, he developed the Logos-flesh (Gk., *sarx*) model for the person of Christ, denying that Jesus had a human intellect or rational soul. Apollinarius held that the divine Logos became embodied in human flesh but that Jesus had only one nature. While Apollinarius's friend, Athanasius of Alexandria, never explicitly resolved in his writings the issue of a human center of life and consciousness in Jesus, Apollinarius flatly de-

nied that Jesus had a human soul and two distinct natures. For this reason Apollinarianism was condemned as heresy in 381 by the Council of Constantinople. *See also* Christology; Incarnation, the; Jesus Christ; Logos.

Apollinaris of Hierapolis, St., apologist and bishop of Hierapolis during the reign of Emperor Marcus Aurelius (161–80), to whom he addressed an apology. All his works are lost. Feast day: January 8.

Apollinarius of Laodicea, ca. 310–ca. 390, theologian and bishop, whose denial of any human center of consciousness (soul) in Christ was condemned as heresy by the first Council of Constantinople (381). Apollinarius was twice excommunicated, once for giving hospitality to Athanasius of Alexandria. Apollinarius was later elected bishop of Laodicea (ca. 361) and became renowned for his opposition to Arianism. His Logos-flesh model of the person of Christ, however, was denounced by Basil of Caesarea and others. Some of Apollinarius's works survive under pseudonyms. *See also* Apollinarianism.

Apollonia, St., d. 249, deaconess martyred at Alexandria. After having teeth pulled out by torturers, she was burned alive. She is the patron saint of dentists. Feast day: February 9.

apologetics (Gk., *apologia,* "justification"), that part of theology which seeks to explain what believers do and think to those who do not share their fundamental commitment of faith. In the second century, Justin Martyr (d. 167) and others were called "Apologists" because of their effort to present Christianity to Greco-Roman culture; using the language and concepts of that culture they sought to explain the divinity of Jesus Christ.

One strategy of the apologist is to find a language common to all those concerned. In that language, one tries to show how the actions and the beliefs of faithful believers make sense. This tactic is not always a promising one, as Paul found out in Athens when he spoke to those assembled of God's "raising [Jesus] from the dead" (Acts 17:31). Their reaction could be called a normal human one to such a claim: derision. Yet one aim of apologetics is to alter the inclinations of unbelievers from a negative to at least an inquiring posture.

The second approach is to write about faith in a language accessible to as many people as possible, yet without hesitating to speak with the specific accents of a believer. The Trappist monk Thomas Merton (d. 1968) excelled in this form of apologetics and so made the life of faith accessible to many persons otherwise sceptical of it. But Merton made no "apologies" for his faith; he simply avoided all technical expressions and used images that could convey the depth of his commitment to those unable to use the language of faith.

A classic example of apologetics is Thomas Aquinas's five ways for the existence of God, offered at the beginning of the *Summa Theologiae*. Thomas clearly does not pretend to begin from a posture of no faith at all, but he does propose arguments accessible to rational persons to show how it is intelligible to believe that God exists. These "five ways" of Aquinas are not proofs that will always convince, but Thomas's intent to show that belief in God was not irrational can be appreciated.

When apologetics is seen as a strategy for persuading others of the reasonableness of one's faith, philosophy is usually considered to be the best tool for executing it. Yet philosophy means different things to different people, so there is no single line of demonstration to show the plausibility of faith. The other approach, that of Thomas Merton, shows that the language of evocative description is as valuable as strict philosophical argument. Apologetics may be more an art than a science, and its best practitioners have always been aware that faith is not the sort of thing that one can talk others into adopting. Human sensibilities can be addressed in a number of ways, any one of which may converge with others to help unbelievers glimpse something of the beauty and veracity of faith. *See also* faith and reason.

DAVID B. BURRELL

Apologists, those second- and third-century Christian writers who first developed whole works to the informed "defense" (Lat., *apologia*) of the faith in refutation of pagan accusations and the persecutions to which they gave rise. Among the Greeks, Quadratus's *Apology* (117–38) to the emperor Hadrian is lost, although fragments are preserved in Eusebius (*Ecclesiastical History* 5.3). Aristides' *Apology* (138–47) is best preserved in a Syriac translation. Justin Martyr, perhaps the most important of all the Apologists for subsequent theology, wrote his two *Apologiae* ca. 153 as well as the *Dialogue with Trypho the Jew*. Tatian, who studied with

Justin, wrote a violently anti-Hellenistic *Oration to the Greeks* ca. 170, and Athenagoras wrote his *Supplication* to Marcus Aurelius ca. 177. From about the same time come the three-volume *To Autolycus* (ca. 180) by Theophilus of Antioch, lost works by Melito of Sardis and Apollinaris of Hierapolis, and, ca. 200, the anonymous *Letter to Diognetus*. Among Latin works, Tertullian's are the most prominent (*Apology, To the Nations, To Scapula,* all ca. 200), but the roughly contemporaneous *Octavius* of Minucius Felix, the seven books of *Against the Nations* of Arnobius (written ca. 303–10), and *On the Deaths of the Persecutors* (ca. 315) and *The Divine Institutions* (ca. 309), both works by Lactantius, are also important. Although some of the Apologists (Tatian, Tertullian, Arnobius, and to a lesser extent Lactantius) reject philosophy and denounce Greco-Roman civilization, most try to show the continuity between the best strands of the pagan philosophical tradition and the proclamation of the gospel, which is held to correct and fulfill them. Often, too, there is an extensive attempt to refute the specific charges (of cannibalism, incest, atheism, and misanthropy) customarily leveled against the Christians. *See also* apologetics; Justin Martyr, St.; Minucius Felix; Tertullian.   *JOHN C. CAVADINI*

apostasy (ah-pahs'tah-see; Lat., "defection"), the complete and public rejection of the faith into which one has been baptized and of all the Church's teaching. Apostasy is distinguished from heresy, by which one rejects a part of the Church's teaching while still claiming membership in the Church. According to Roman Catholic canon law, an unrepentant apostate is excluded from the sacraments.

The issue of apostasy and of the relationship between the apostate and the Christian community arose during the second century when some baptized Christians denied Christianity in the face of imprisonment and death. Their denial was considered both a failure in faith and a scandal to other Christians.

In the second and third centuries, some theologians taught that apostasy was an unforgivable sin, perhaps the sin against the Holy Spirit. According to their understanding, an apostate could not be readmitted to Christian communion. By the fourth century, when Christianity had gained public acceptance, the earlier opinion was no longer popular. Augustine of Hippo (d. 430) was a leader in the fight against the Donatists, who taught that Christians who had apostatized in order to avoid martyrdom needed to be rebaptized in order to return to the sacraments. Donatism was condemned as heretical. *See also* Donatism; heresy.

apostle (Gk., *apostolos,* "one who is sent out," "messenger"), a function or office within early Christianity. "Apostle" is used in the NT to refer to various individuals and groups in the early Church, and its meaning and the extent of its application were matters of dispute. Paul regularly described himself as an apostle (Rom 1:1; 1 Cor 1:1; 2 Cor 1:1; Gal 1:1). By it he meant someone who was specially called by God and sent out to preach the gospel, in his case particularly to the Gentiles (Rom 11:13). From Paul it is clear that other individual Christians and groups of Christians who had been similarly called and sent to preach the gospel were also recognized as apostles (Rom 16:7; 1 Cor 4:9; 9:5; 12:29; 15:7; 1 Thess 2:6). Paul was adamant, however, about denying the title to Christians who claimed to be apostles but who opposed his preaching (2 Cor 11:13), even though these opponents functioned in ways very similar to his. This same broad view of an apostle is also found in *Didache* 11.3–6, a Christian instruction from the late first century A.D. In the Pauline traditions of the late first century A.D., Paul continued to be seen as an apostle (e.g. Eph 1:1; 1 Tim 1:1). Paul also attests to a more restricted use of the term. In Gal 1:17–19 and 1 Cor 15:7 the term seems to be limited to a specific group of prominent Jewish-Christians in Jerusalem, perhaps identical with the Twelve (1 Cor 15:5). This more restricted use prevailed in the development of the synoptic tradition. Mark 6:30 seems to identify the "apostles"

Apparition of the risen Christ to Peter (center) and the other apostles while they were fishing on the Sea of Galilee (John 21:4–8); Byzantine mosaic in the basilica of St. Apollinaris, Ravenna, Italy.

with "the Twelve" whom Jesus called in 3:13–19 and sent out two by two in 6:7–13. This identification is made quite clear in Matt 10:1 and Luke 6:13. All three synoptic Gospels and Acts give lists of the twelve apostles, although the lists are not in complete agreement (Mark 3:16–19; Matt 10:2–4; Luke 6:14–16; Acts 1:13). The symbolism of the twelve apostles emphasized the continuity of the early Church with the twelve tribes of Israel (Matt 19:28; Luke 22:30). Luke, however, in Acts significantly develops this restricted notion of the twelve apostles. According to him, after Jesus' ascension into heaven, the apostles met to cast lots to choose someone who would take the place of Judas and so bring the number of the apostles once again to twelve (Acts 1:15–26). The lot fell to Matthias. For Luke this new apostle had to be someone who had accompanied Jesus from his baptism by John until his Ascension and who would be a witness to his Resurrection (Acts 1:21–22). Because of this viewpoint Luke does not (with the exception of Acts 14:14) refer to Paul or early Christians other than the Twelve as apostles. In Acts the twelve apostles serve primarily as the group that approved of and ensured the continuity between Jesus and the Jerusalem church, on the one hand, and Paul and the gentile Christian churches of which Luke was a part, on the other hand. In the second century the apostles came to be seen as part of the inspired foundational stage of Christianity but no longer as a contemporary reality in the Church. The term was used primarily, although not exclusively, of the twelve apostles and Paul. Because the apostles were those who had had personal contact with Jesus, appeals were made to them and their authority as touchstones of authenticity during the controversies of the next several centuries. Such appeals were made by all sorts of Christian groups, whether considered ultimately "orthodox" or "heretical." Authorship by an apostle or a close associate of an apostle was one criterion for inclusion of a document in the canon of the NT; traditions were traced back to the apostles as a means of legitimation; the validity of the ministry and organization of various Christian communities was claimed on the basis of apostolic succession of the community leaders. *See also* disciple; Twelve, the.

THOMAS H. TOBIN

Apostles' Creed, creed according to legend written by the apostles themselves, but this view has been overturned since the research of Lorenzo Valla

THE APOSTLES' CREED

I believe in God, the Father almighty, Creator of heaven and earth.

And in Jesus Christ, his only Son, our Lord; who was conceived by the Holy Spirit, born of the Virgin Mary, suffered under Pontius Pilate, was crucified, died, and was buried. He descended into hell; the third day he rose again from the dead; he ascended into heaven, sits at the right hand of God, the Father almighty; from thence he shall come to judge the living and the dead.

I believe in the Holy Spirit, the holy Catholic Church, the communion of saints, the forgiveness of sins, the resurrection of the body, and life everlasting. Amen.

(1405–57) and Reginald Pecock (ca. 1393–ca. 1461). Nevertheless, the legend does contain a truth: the creed's basic theological formulations date back to the first decades of the Church. Thus, in a loose sense, one can say that the creed conveys the "mind" or "intention" of the apostles.

Origins: The Apostles' Creed is clearly the fruit of the Christian tradition. The earliest text of the Apostles' Creed, as we know it, appears in a treatise *Scarapus* by the monk Pirminius (or Priminius, d. 753). The creed is, however, mentioned by name in a letter of Ambrose (*Epistle* 42.5) written in approximately 390. What Ambrose is referring to is the creed that developed out of the Old Roman Creed, which had taken shape by the end of the second century. This earlier statement of belief is evidenced within three sources: (1) the interrogatory creed for Baptism found in Hippolytus's *Apostolic Tradition* (ca. 215), (2) the creed given by Marcellus, the bishop of Ancyra, to Emperor Julius I (340), and (3) the commentary on the Apostles' Creed (ca. 404) by the monk Tyrannius Rufinus (345–410). In his commentary Rufinus includes the earliest continuous Latin text of the Apostles' Creed as confessed at the Church of Aquileia, and he also notes its differences from the Old Roman Creed. The emergence and authorization of the Apostles' Creed in the West may have occurred through its adoption by Charlemagne (742–814), who imposed it upon his empire. Its widespread use may then have led to Rome's approval of this creedal form.

Structure and Content: The Apostles' Creed is determined by the trinitarian form of 2 Cor 13:13 and Matt 28:19, the form that shapes, too, the Old Roman Creed, the interrogatory creed, the creed of Marcellus, and Rufinus's creed.

The first article, on God, affirms the OT understanding of God as the only God (Deut 6:4–5), who is appropriately spoken of in personal terms and is both transcendent and immanent in history. The second article, on Jesus Christ, incorporates the Church's earliest Christological confessions: Jesus is the "Christ" (Acts 2:36), the "Lord" (1 Cor 12:3), and the "Son of God" (cf. Acts 9:20). It also recites the narrative of the Christ kerygma (1 Cor 15:3–7; Acts 13:16–41). It goes beyond these early proclamations by specifying that this is God's "only Son," that his conception occurred through the "Holy Spirit," and that he "descended into hell." This last clause is not found in the Nicene-Constantinopolitan Creed.

The third article, on the Holy Spirit, highlights the Spirit's activity in history and in eternity. Unlike the Nicene-Constantinopolitan Creed, it mentions neither the Spirit's personal existence, nor theSpirit's relation to the Father and the Son. But it does include the clause on the communion of saints, which is not found in the Nicene-Constantinopolitan Creed.

The overall structure is, therefore, trinitarian, confessing belief in the Father, Son, and the Holy Spirit. It sets the kerygmatic narrative within confessional statements that are both self-involving (i.e., "I believe") and propositional (i.e., declarative statements about the triune God). The Apostles' Creed is terser than the Nicene-Constantinopolitan Creed but possesses less doctrinal precision.

Function: Since the Old Roman Creed functioned in the baptismal rite beginning in the second century, it is not surprising to learn from Rufinus that the Apostles' Creed was employed at baptisms in the church at Aquileia in the fifth century. It is likely, then, that in the West a version of the Apostles' Creed was being confessed at baptisms and used in catechetical instruction at least by the early 400s. In the Western Church, too, it was recited between the seventh and ninth centuries in the Divine Office, and, since then, it has frequently been recited by the faithful in their daily prayers. By the Middle Ages, the Church in the West was using the full version of the Apostles' Creed at baptisms. Nevertheless, at the Council of Florence (1438–45) Church representatives of the East stated that they had never heard of the Apostles' Creed. Today, the

Catholic Church permits the Apostles' Creed to be recited at Masses for children in place of the Nicene-Constantinopolitan Creed. Moreover, ecumenical discussions have considered the proposal that the Apostles' Creed be regarded as the binding formulation of the Christian faith. *See also* creeds.

ROBERT A. KRIEG

Apostleship of Prayer, an association of Catholics whose purpose is to foster special devotion to the Sacred Heart of Jesus. Founded in Vals, France, in 1844 by Francis Gautrelet, a Jesuit, the organization promotes unity among its members through prayer for special monthly intentions. The apostleship publishes the *Messenger of the Sacred Heart*. *See also* Sacred Heart, devotion to the.

apostolate, the saving mission of Christ in the world and the participation of Christian faithful in that mission through different roles and functions. Members of the Church hierarchy are designated for participation in, and moderation of, the apostolate through ordination. Laity are called to apostolic participation through Baptism and Confirmation and are commissioned to this task by the Lord himself (Dogmatic Constitution on the Church, n.33). Spouses and parents participate through marriage, while members of institutes of consecrated life and societies of apostolic life, as well as other Christian faithful, exercise the apostolate through both charism (charismatic gifts) and specific ecclesiastical mandate. *See also* Church; laity.

Apostolicae Curae (a-poh-stoh'lee-chay koo'ray; Lat., "Of Apostolic Concern"), encyclical of Pope Leo XIII, September 13, 1896, declaring Anglican orders invalid because they were considered defective in both form and intention. The form of ordination employed by the Anglican church beginning with the Ordinal of Edward VI (1550) omitted several necessary elements of the rite (later restored, however, with Archbishop William Laud, d. 1645), and the intention of the ordination as expressed in the Anglican ritual did not include the conferral of the power to offer sacrifice. Those Anglican clergymen, including bishops, who have been received into the Roman Catholic Church in recent years have been conditionally re-ordained (i.e., on the condition that the first ordination may not have been valid). *See also* Anglicanism; Anglican ordination; Holy Orders; ordination.

apostolic age, a term referring roughly to the lifetime of the twelve apostles. The term itself is a modern one, used to refer to the foundational period of Christianity and corresponding to the period between the death of Jesus (ca. A.D. 30) and the end of the first century or the beginning of the second century A.D.

Apostolicam Actuositatem, (ah-poh-stah'lee-kahm ahk-*too*-ah-see-tah'tem). *See* Decree on the Apostolate of the Laity.

apostolic constitution, a papal document that is solemn in form, legal in content, and ordinarily deals with matters of faith, doctrine, or discipline that are of import for the universal Church or are especially significant for a particular diocese. It is usually issued in the form of a bull, so called because it is issued with a "seal" (lat., *bulla*), and may be signed by the pope himself, or may begin by stating the pope's name and the purpose of the document and be signed by the Chancellor of the Roman Church or by some other official of an appropriate department of the Roman Curia, the Church's central administration in Rome and the Vatican. *See also* bull, papal.

Apostolic Constitutions, a sizable collection of Church legislation dating from the late fourth century. Its eight books contain norms pertaining to, among other things, clerical activity and demeanor, Christian moral standards and behavior, early penitential discipline, liturgical celebrations of the Eucharist and other sacraments, ceremonies for feasts, practices regarding fasts, and early Church reactions to heresy and schism. The collection relies on and incorporates portions of other documents, such as the *Didiscalia Apostolorum* (Lat., "teachings of the apostles") and the Apostolic Canons, and is a valuable reference for information on the early development of the Mass. *See also* canon law.

apostolic delegate, a specific category of papal legate, namely, a cleric or layman who acts as emissary of the Bishop of Rome to the Church in a particular area or country with which the Holy See does not have diplomatic relations (Code of Canon Law, can. 363.1), or as a representative of the Apostolic See to international councils or conferences or meetings who has voting status at these gatherings (can. 363.2). *See also* nuncio; papal legate.

Apostolic Fathers, the name given to a group of Greek Christian authors of the late first to mid-second centuries who have been thought to have had historical connections with the apostles. The Apostolic Fathers are our chief source of information about Christianity in the period immediately following the apostolic age. Their writings, which are diverse both in content and in form, include the seven Letters of Ignatius of Antioch, the two Letters of Clement of Rome to the Corinthians (although the second is in fact spurious), a series of visions known as the *Shepherd of Hermas*, the *Letter* of St. Polycarp to the Philippians, the *Martyrdom of St. Polycarp*, the *Letter of Barnabas*, the *Letter to Diognetus*, the *Didache*, or *Teaching of the Twelve Apostles*, and the fragments of Papias.

Though lacking the literary and theological sophistication of the later Church Fathers, the Apostolic Fathers provide a vivid witness to Christianity at a critical stage in its development, when the Church had to establish boundaries between itself and Judaism on the one hand and paganism on the other, while at the same time maintaining cohesion and unity in the face of internal threats of heresy and schism. In meeting these challenges, the Apostolic Fathers reflect significant growth in ecclesiastical authority, and their references to the sayings of Jesus and the Letters of Paul bear crucial testimony to the development of a sense of Scripture and tradition in the first generations after the apostles. *See also* Clement I, St.; *Didache;* Fathers of the Church; Hermas, Shepherd of; Ignatius of Antioch, St.

apostolicity, the fundamental identity of the Church, in faith and ministry, with the Church of the apostles. The faithful continuity of the Church as it develops in space and time with the Church of the NT involves fidelity to what was handed on by the apostles. This, as Vatican II declares, "includes everything which contributes to the holiness of life, and the increase in faith of the people of God, and so the church, in her teaching, life and worship, perpetuates and hands on to all generations all that she herself is and all that she believes" (Dogmatic Constitution on Divine Revelation, n. 8). This fidelity does not exclude, but rather requires, growth and development of the Church's understanding of the apostolic faith and authoritative interpretation as new questions arise about its meaning. The Church's apostolicity in faith therefore demands apostolicity in ministry, which means that the pastoral ministry of the apostles is perpetuated by legitimate successors, to whom is entrusted the task of interpreting the word of God for each generation with the assistance of the Holy Spirit. From the second century, the Christian churches have recognized their bishops as the legitimate successors of the apostles. The Catholic, Orthodox, and Anglican churches believe that the apostolicity of the Church requires that it maintain an unbroken succession of apostolic ministry through episcopal ordination. It is the further conviction of the Catholic Church that full apostolicity requires communion with the Bishop of Rome as successor to the chief of the apostles. *See also* apostolic succession; marks of the Church.

Apostolic Nuncio. *See* nuncio; papal legate.

Apostolic Penitentiary. *See* Penitentiary, Apostolic.

Apostolic Pro-Nuncio. *See* pro-nuncio; papal legate.

Apostolic See, originally, any location in which an apostle was considered to have established a primary center of the early Church. Currently the noun "see" means a diocese or the primary location (seat) of the bishop within a diocese, from which the diocese usually takes its name. In Church law, the term "Apostolic See" or "Holy See" now refers to the See of Rome as a moral entity by divine law and, in practical application, to the pope, Secretariat of State, Council for Public Affairs of the Church, and other departments of the Roman Curia who assist in Church governance and administration (Code of Canon Law, cans. 113; 361). *See also* Holy See; Roman Curia.

Apostolic Signatura. *See* Signatura, Apostolic.

apostolic succession, the perpetuation, in the college of bishops, of the pastoral charge given by Christ to the college of the apostles. The Catholic doctrine of apostolic succession is expressed in the statement of Vatican II: "Just as the office which the Lord confided to Peter alone, as first of the apostles, destined to be transmitted to his successors, is a permanent one, so also endures the office, which the apostles received, of shepherding the Church, a charge destined to be exercised without interruption by the sacred order of bishops. The sacred synod consequently teaches that the bishops have by divine institution taken the place of the apostles as pastors of the Church, in such wise that whoever listens to them is listening to Christ, and whoever despises them despises Christ, and him who sent Christ (cf. Luke 10:16)" (Dogmatic Constitution on the Church, n. 20).

Basis in the New Testament: The four Gospels are unanimous in their witness that Jesus formed a special group of twelve disciples during his public ministry (Matt 10:1–4; Mark 3:13–19; Luke 6:12–16; John 6:70). All four Gospels and Acts bear witness to the belief of the early Church that these men were sent out by the risen Christ, with the mandate to make disciples by witnessing to his Resurrection (Matt 28:19–20; Mark 16:15; Luke 24:48–49; John 20:21–23; Acts 1:8). Others to whom the risen Christ appeared were given a similar mission; foremost among these was the apostle Paul. While the apostles had a foundational role that no one in the following generations could have, the mandate that Christ had given them to teach, baptize, forgive sins, and pastor the flock, was to be passed on, because such ministry was essential to the life of the Church. During their own lifetimes, the apostles shared their ministry with others, meeting the needs of the churches under the guidance of the Holy Spirit. In the NT we see two kinds of such associates of the apostles: the missionary co-workers, who helped to found new churches, and the resident leaders of the local churches. Indications that such people were expected to carry on the work of the apostles in the following generations are found in the NT, e.g., in the speech of Paul to the elders of Ephesus (Acts 20:18–35), and in the pastoral Letters (2 Tim 2:2; 4:1–8).

Development in the Early Church: The NT indicates that the apostles and their co-workers established a collegial form of leadership in the churches that they founded. A number of men called either "elders" (Gk.; *presbyteroi*) or "overseers" (*episkopoi*) had the ministry of presiding and teaching in the local communities. This is the system that the first letter of Clement to the Corinthians indicates was still in force at Corinth in the last decade of the first century. According to Clement, the first generation of such men had been appointed by the apostles, and the second generation by "other eminent men," following the rule that the apostles had laid down to provide for successors in this ministry (*1 Clem.* 44:1–4). Two decades later, the letters of Ignatius of Antioch testify that in Syria and parts of Asia Minor, each church was led by a single bishop, assisted by presbyters and deacons. The development from the earlier collegial form of local leadership to the emergence of the single bishop seems to have taken place gradually during the first half of the second century, somewhat later in the West than in the East.

In the Christian writings of the late-second century we find consistent testimony to the belief that these bishops were the successors of the apostles and were, therefore, the authorized witnesses to the genuine apostolic tradition. This was the chief argument of Irenaeus against the Gnostic heretics (*Adversus Hereses* 2.3.1–3). It was likewise the argument of Tertullian to prove that heretics have no right to interpret the Scriptures (*De Praescriptione Haereticorum* 20–21). In these writings the emphasis is on the teaching role of the bishops, succeeding one another in the leadership of the apostolic churches, as witnesses to the apostolic "rule of faith." The *Apostolic Tradition* of Hippolytus (ca. 215) sheds light on another aspect of apostolic succession by describing how a bishop was ordained for his church by the bishops of neighboring churches. This reflects the conviction that in order to share in the apostolic mandate, one had to be ordained by those who already shared it. The ordination prayer recorded by Hippolytus expresses the belief that bishops participate in the powers given by Christ to his apostles, and that the Holy Spirit equips them with the gifts needed for the fulfillment of their ministry (*Traditio Apostolica* 2–3).

Apostolic Succession by Divine Institution: Vatican II declares that "by divine institution bishops have succeeded to the place of the apostles" (Dogmatic Constitution on the Church, n. 20). Catholic theologians do not take this to mean that Christ explicitly determined the episcopal structure of the local churches. Christ did not leave a blueprint for his disciples to follow in the organization of the Church. What is certain is that within a century after the death of the apostles, each church was led by a single bishop, and that these bishops were recognized by all the orthodox Christian churches as the legitimate successors of the apostles and, thus, as guarantors of the authentic apostolic tradition. The argument for divine institution is based on the belief that this development was guided by the Holy Spirit, as part of God's design for the Church. A sound reason for this belief is the fact that from the second century on, Christians everywhere accepted the teaching of their bishops as normative for their faith. It is a basic article of Christian belief that the Holy Spirit maintains the Church in the true faith. A

Church that is divinely maintained in the true faith could not have been mistaken when it determined the very norms of its faith. Having good reason to be confident that it was the Holy Spirit who guided the Church in its acceptance of bishops as successors of the apostles, Catholics can also be confident that the development of the episcopal succession also was guided by the Holy Spirit and, in that sense, was of divine institution. *See also* apostle; bishops, college of; Petrine succession.

Bibliography

Brown, Raymond. *Priest and Bishop: Biblical Reflections.* New York: Paulist Press, 1970.

Rahner, Karl, and Joseph Ratzinger. *The Episcopate and the Primacy.* New York: Herder and Herder, 1962.   FRANCIS A. SULLIVAN

apostolic visitation, a long-standing Church procedure, now conducted under the auspices of the Congregation for Bishops, which is designed "to correct exercise of the pastoral function of bishops" (*Pastor Bonus* [1988], n. 79) by gathering information and making recommendations to effect reforms deemed necessary or helpful in a particular diocese. Now most commonly conducted by administrative procedure, apostolic visitations can be instituted for various reasons, such as a specific serious problem or widespread pastoral difficulties, and they can result in paternal correction with a view to amendment or in some public form of punishment.

apparitions of the Blessed Virgin Mary, manifestations or appearances of the mother of Jesus centuries after her death. Apparition is the technical term for an inexplicable appearance of someone, usually someone deceased. While there are instances in Church history of claims regarding apparitions of saints or of Jesus Christ, the most frequent claims are those involving the Blessed Virgin Mary. From the Middle Ages on, as devotion to the Blessed Virgin became an ever more integral part of Catholic devotional life, word of apparitions has spread and given the Church hierarchy new challenges regarding the discernment of spirits. In modern times, each claim is checked by the local bishop, who may also appoint a commission to study the situation. While some apparitions have been recognized by the Church as authentic, such recognition does not mean that belief in the appearance of the Blessed Virgin Mary at a particular place and time is binding on all Catholics. It means only that the Church does not regard belief in the apparition to be misguided or harmful to the faithful.

Four of the most famous and widely recognized apparitions are the appearances of Our Lady of Guadalupe, Our Lady of La Salette, Our Lady of Lourdes, and Our Lady of Fátima. Taken together, they demonstrate what an apparition of the Blessed Virgin Mary most frequently involves.

Our Lady of Guadalupe: On December 9, 1531, an Aztec Indian whose indigenous name was Singing Eagle and whose Christian name was Juan Diego set out for the Catholic church near his home, about five miles north of Mexico City. As he neared the hill consecrated to the Mother Goddess of the Aztecs, he heard strange music, then an unnerving silence. Suddenly the silence was broken by a woman's voice calling to him. The maiden identified herself as the "ever virgin, Mary, Mother of the true God who gives life and maintains it in existence." Juan Diego had no difficulty understanding her, for she spoke in her native language. She expressed her desire for a little house to be built in her honor on the spot and sent Juan Diego with this request to the local bishop.

The Lord Bishop, while reportedly courteous, was not prepared to believe word of such an occurrence without proof, and he sent Juan Diego back to get it. The mysterious lady agreed to give the proof on the following morning, but Juan Diego's uncle fell seriously ill. Thinking it more important to get a priest for his uncle, the go-between tried avoiding another meeting with the lady, but she was too alert for him. Promising that she would care for the ailing uncle, the lady sent Juan Diego to the top of a hill to gather flowers on the December morning. Doubtful of finding any, he went and discovered roses growing in the frosty ground. Gathering them in his native cloak, or *tilma,* he came down to receive the lady's blessing and go off to confront the bishop. When he had gained entrance to the bishops's quarters once more, Juan Diego opened his cloak to let fall the roses. At that moment an image of the maiden was revealed on the inside of the *tilma,* an image that is revered to this day as the imprint of the figure of Our Lady of Guadalupe, the name by which she called herself.

It is difficult to overstate the impact of this event: an apparition of the Mother of the Christian God to a native of the new land barely ten years after the conquest of Mexico, with the result that a shrine was built on the spot once dedicated to the Mother Goddess. The report is that within six years, nine million natives were baptized. To this day, the image of Guadalupe is enshrined in her church, surrounded by other paintings depicting the cures believed to have been effected through her intercession. Our Lady of Guadalupe appears as a brown-skinned maiden in a pink robe wearing a turquoise mantle that is covered with stars and outlined in gold. The gown is caught at the waist by a black cincture, symbol of pregnancy for the time. She is surrounded by rays of light and supported by a crescent moon, beneath which is the figure of a small man. The feast of Our Lady of Guadalupe is December 12. She has been proclaimed patron saint of all the Americas.

Our Lady of La Salette: In a similarly out-of-the-way place in France on September 19, 1846, two young cattle herders came home from the fields with the story of seeing a beautiful lady. The two, Melanie Mathieu and Maximin Giraud, reported spotting within a circle of brilliant light the figure of a woman seated and weeping. The lady arose and called them to come near. At first, she spoke to them in French, but then, seeing their confusion, changed to their dialect. She spoke of her son and of his heavy arm that she was worn with holding back. She upbraided their people for working on Sunday and for curses that used the name of her son. She warned of dire consequences that would attend a failure to reform in these matters and admonished the two teenagers to say their prayers faithfully, if only the Our Father and Hail Mary. Then the lady charged them to "make this known to all my people." At that, the lady rose into the air. Such was the account of Melanie and Maximin.

They did not identify the lady as Mary, the Mother of God, though those who heard the story quickly did. As news spread, belief took a variety of forms. People drank from a spring that was discovered at the spot where the lady sat, in the hope that the waters had curative powers. Pieces of the stone on which she reportedly sat were broken off and even ground up to be touched or consumed in the same hope of cures. Cures were claimed. Melanie and Maximin were repeatedly interrogated to test their stories, but they never introduced the slightest variation into the account, according to the reports. Under the direction of Bishop de Brouillard, an intense investigation was launched. It lasted five years and, at times, stirred great controversy. But in November 1851, the bishop authorized what was termed by his proclamation "the cult of Our Lady of La Salette" and he personally laid the cornerstone for the basilica to be built in her honor. Since that time this apparition has passed into the annals of such religious

phenomena. Images of Our Lady of La Salette can be recognized by the unusual crucifix she wears, with a hammer suspended below one side of the crossbar, pincers below the other. She has been given the additional title, "Reconciler of Sinners."

Our Lady of Lourdes: The site now famous worldwide for reports of cures was once a simple grotto in the foothills of the French Pyrenees. There on February 11, 1858, a young girl named Bernadette Soubirous, out with her sister and a friend to gather firewood, saw coming toward her from the mouth of the cave a golden-colored cloud enveloping a beautiful young lady. The lady beckoned for Bernadette to approach and signaled with the rosary that hung on her arm for Bernadette to begin to pray. After the recitation of the Rosary, the lady and the cloud went back into the grotto and disappeared. Thus began a series of appearances, eighteen in all, of the person Bernadette called simply, *aquero,* or "that one," in her native dialect. In the course of these apparitions, the lady gave to Bernadette three secrets, which the young girl was never to reveal. The lady also helped Bernadette to discover a spring nearby and instructed her to drink from it and bathe in it. In one of the later appearances the lady expressed her wish for a chapel on the site to which people would come in procession. Toward the end, she acceded to Bernadette's request to know her name. Though the lady spoke in Bernadette's local dialect, the meaning of her words was not immediately clear to the untutored young girl: "I am the Immaculate Conception," the lady said. As the story spread increasing numbers of pilgrims visited the spot. It became apparent that, in addition to the reconciliation of sinners and the cure of crippled bodies, one of the enduring effects of the story of Lourdes would be an increased commitment to the belief, proclaimed as official teaching just four years before the apparitions began. This was the dogma of the Immaculate Conception, that is, the teaching that Mary the Mother of Jesus was conceived without original sin.

Bernadette Soubirous, also known as Bernadette of Lourdes, has been declared a saint of the Catholic Church. Her feast day is April 16. Representation of Our Lady of Lourdes can be recognized by the white robe girdled by a blue ribbon, white veil and yellow roses on her feet. Over her arm she wears a rosary of white beads with a golden chain. The feast of Our Lady of Lourdes is February 11.

Our Lady of Fátima: In the spring of 1917 three

young Portuguese shepherds had an experience that, when publicized, caught the attention of a world at war. Lucia dos Santos and her cousins, Francisco and Jacinta Marto, were privy to six appearances of the Blessed Virgin Mary between May and October of that year. To them the lady also entrusted "secrets," some of which have not been revealed to the world to this day.

The Fátima story began in the spring of 1916 with the appearance of a young man who identified himself as the angel of peace. The figure taught the children to pray and make sacrifices in a specified way, then left them. For a year, the children followed his directions, praying intensely. Then, in May of 1917, while the three tended their flock near the Cova da Iria, they beheld a lady all dressed in white, who shed rays of brilliant light all round her. She told them not to fear. Then she indicated her wish for the children to return on the thirteenth of every month until October, when she would tell them who she was and what she wanted of them. She also told them to pray the Rosary daily. As family and parish members learned of the reported apparition, the children withstood intense pressure to renounce their story. Few would believe that the Blessed Virgin would appear only to tell children to say the Rosary. The lady promised a sign that would convince the skeptics, and the children continued to go to the Cova da Iria on the thirteenth of each month, during which time they were granted apocalyptic visions and prophetic warnings. The lady asked that Russia be consecrated to her Immaculate Heart and requested a communion of reparation on the first Saturday of each month.

The apparitions culminated in a final revelation and the promised sign on October 13, 1917. To the children, the visitor identified herself as "Our Lady of the Rosary." As she left the children's sight, the assembled crowd experienced what has come to be known as the "Miracle of the Sun." According to reports, the sun "danced" in the heavens, with the result that many people fell to their knees in awe. The children, meanwhile, were granted in their ecstasy visions of the Holy Family, the Sorrowful Mother with her Son, and the glorious Lady of Mount Carmel.

The apparition at Fátima was authenticated by the bishop of Leiria on October 13, 1930. Since that time, interest in the story has increased, especially with the coming of the Second World War and the rise of the Soviet Union. Rumors about the famous "third secret," the one that has only been revealed to the popes, abound. Responsible accounts dismiss the stories of popes fainting or keeping the secret locked in their private quarters or on their person. It does seem that the secret has been entrusted from pope to pope, and that each has made a decision about whether or not to reveal it to the world. That is as much as is known.

Our Lady of the Rosary appears in a garment and mantle of white bordered in blue, hands folded in prayer holding a white rosary, and wearing a jeweled crown. Her feast day is October 7.

Other Apparitions: In the twentieth century, claims of apparitions of the Blessed Virgin Mary proliferate. In Ireland, Belgium, Italy, Canada, and the United States, investigations of supposed apparitions have been undertaken. The apparition that recently claimed great attention, however, is in Medjugorje, in the former Yugoslavia. Since 1981, when six children began reporting appearances of the Blessed Virgin Mary, the site has drawn pilgrims and gained devotees from all over the world, despite the refusal of church authorities to authenticate the appearances. Medjugorje, too, involves secrets, prophecies, and admonitions to prayer and penance.

Significance of the Apparitions: While some believers are frequently drawn to reports of the miraculous and the paranormal, professional theologians customarily hesitate to give credence to such seemingly irrational occurrences. The apparitions have been, for that reason, relegated to the realm of what is called "popular religion," especially by theologians and professional educators. Of late, however, liberation theologians, in particular Third World and/or feminist ones, are looking anew at the claimed apparitions and their revelations. From these studies emerge challenging new questions concerning the nature of personal religious experience and its movement into the Church's public worship; the manifestation of the divine intentions for humanity in images and symbols that reach new ages with new cultural settings; the need for the feminine in a world run-down by the triumph of the masculine; the place of apocalypticism in a civilization of comfort; and the tension between the personal testimony of those outside the power structures and the hierarchical assessment of what is good for the whole Church. The history of the apparitions of the Blessed Virgin Mary, a distinctively Catholic phenomenon, provides matter for reflection on religion, no matter the stand one takes on their possibility or validity. *See also* Fátima; Guadalupe, Our Lady of; La Salette, Our Lady of; Lourdes; Mary, Blessed Virgin; Medjugorje.

Bibliography

Delaney, John J., ed. *A Woman Clothed With The Sun, Eight Great Appearances of Our Lady.* New York: Doubleday, 1961.

Kselman, Thomas. *Miracles and Prophecies in Nineteenth-Century France.* New Brunswick, NJ: Rutgers University, 1983.

Walsh, William T. *Our Lady of Fatima.* New York: Doubleday, 1990.

Zimdars-Swartz, Sandra L. *Encountering Mary.* New York: Avon Books, 1991.   MARY AQUIN O'NEILL

appetites, concupiscible and irascible, technical terms from Scholastic philosophy that describe the movement of the physical senses toward or away from objects. A concupiscible appetite (desire) is a capacity that inclines one to move toward an object that perceived to be good or to move away from an object seen as harmful. This appetite seeks pleasure in something it does not have. An irascible appetite (passion) is a capacity that seeks to resist what stands in the way of the pursuit of a perceived good. This appetite opposes what is seen as a danger. *See also* body and spirituality.

apse, the semicircular or polygonal end of basilica-style churches. The altar and the seats for the ministers are usually located in the center of the apse, which is modeled on the Roman architectural design of official buildings. *See also* basilica.

Aquila (ak'wi-luh), author of a mechanically literal revision of the Greek OT ca. A.D. 130. Originally a Gentile, Aquila converted to Christianity, was later excommunicated, then became a proselyte to Judaism. His revision, which could serve as a basis for Jewish-Christian debate, sought to produce a Greek version as faithful as possible to the form of the rabbinic (proto-Masoretic) Bible current in his day. Thus, his version is not very helpful for determining the original Greek of the Septuagint, but it is a very reliable witness to the second-century Hebrew Bible. *See also* Scripture, versions of.

Aquila and Prisca (Priscilla in Acts), Jewish-Christian converts, with whom Paul first lived in Corinth (Acts 18:1–3). Expelled from Rome under Claudius (A.D. 49), they became important co-workers with Paul, established a house church in Ephesus (1 Cor 16:19) and instructed Apollos (Acts

18:24–26). Paul greets them and their house church in Rom 16:3–5.

Aquileia, Council of, an anti-Arian synod of bishops, convened in 381 by the local bishop of Aquileia, Valerian, and presided over by Ambrose of Milan. Aquileia, located on the Adriatic coast of Italy, was an important city and center of learning during the later Roman Empire (fourth century) and was the seat of a Western patriarchate.

Aramaic, a Semitic language closely related to Hebrew. Imperial Aramaic, the official language of the Persian Empire (550–333 B.C.), is used in the OT in Ezra and Daniel. A later form of the language, related to that of Jewish Targums, was probably the primary spoken language of Jesus.

An apse, or semicircular end of a basilca-style church.

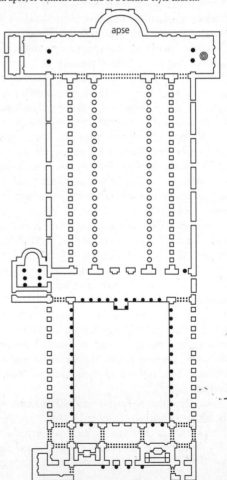

ST. THOMAS AQUINAS

Dominican friar and Doctor of the Church ("Angelic Doctor," "Common Doctor"), St. Thomas Aquinas (uh-kwị'nuhs) lived ca. 1225–74. His theology has acquired a quasi-official status in the Church through repeated formal endorsements by various popes.

LIFE AND WORKS

Offered by his ambitious father as an oblate to the nearby Benedictine monastery of Monte Cassino, Italy, in 1231 or 1232, the young Thomas received his elementary education there until 1239. He then studied at Naples, encountering Aristotle's natural science and metaphysics, until 1244, when he entered the Order of Preachers. Overcoming family opposition, he went to Paris in 1245, first as a novice and then as a student. In 1248 he went to Cologne for studies under Albertus Magnus until 1252. During this time he was ordained a priest. There (or at Paris, 1252–54) he lectured on the Bible "in a cursory way" as a "bachelor of the Bible."

Returning to Paris in 1252 for further theological studies, Thomas lectured on Peter Lombard's *Sentences* as a "bachelor of the *Sentences*," producing his *Scriptum Super Sententiis*. In 1257 he was admitted as a regent master of theology. He then undertook the threefold functions of a master: commenting on the Bible, something he continued throughout his life; conducting disputed questions (*On Truth*) and a first set of quodlibetal questions; and taking his turn among the masters for preaching. At this time he also began his *Summa Contra Gentiles* and defended the mendicant orders against their opponents. From 1259 to 1268 he was at first in Naples; then he taught his Dominican confreres at Orvieto and afterward at their house in Rome, where he began his *Summa Theologiae*. Several disputed questions (*On the Power of God, On Free Choice, On Spiritual Creatures*) date from this period, as does the completion of the *Summa Contra Gentiles* and the *Office for the Feast of Corpus Christi*, composed for Pope Urban IV. For the same pope Thomas also composed the *Golden Chain*, compiling texts on the four Gospels from the Latin Fathers and an even greater number from the Greek Fathers and early councils; this work, widely diffused and influential, was very important for Thomas's own theological development.

The years 1268–72, spent in Paris, marked a period of extraordinary activity: Thomas continued his Scripture commentaries, completed a large part of the *Summa Theologiae*, conducted eight disputed questions and a second series of quodlibetal questions, and wrote again to defend the mendicants. Some scholars have observed a shift in Thomas's thought at this time from a stricter intellectualism to greater attention to affectivity. During this period he also completed a large number of commentaries on Aristotle, written to counteract Averroistic interpretations of Aristotle that were penetrating the university; these were leading some professors to argue by reason to conclusions opposed to faith, even though in such cases they always claimed to adhere to faith as above reason.

From 1272 to 1274 Aquinas was back in Italy, teaching Scripture and theology at the newly founded University of Naples, where he worked to complete the third part of the *Summa Theologiae*. In December 1273, however, he had a mystical experience whose intensity so overpowered him that he could no longer write. Invited to the Second Council of Lyons in 1274, Thomas fell ill en route, perhaps as the result of an accident, and died on March 7, 1274.

Beside the works already mentioned, he left numerous others, including several treatises on politics, as well as sermons, replies to questions, letters, and prayers. Sweeping condemnations—by Bishop Stephen Tempier of Paris and Archbishop Robert Kilwardby of Canterbury—of 219 philosophical and theological propositions at Paris in 1277 included a few of his teachings. Although this, plus attacks from rival theological schools, slowed the influence of his thought outside the Dominican school, his holiness was officially recognized by his canonization in 1323, and in 1325 the Paris condemnation was revoked insofar as it touched his teachings.

SAINT AND THEOLOGIAN

Nurtured by a deep love of Scripture that was fostered by his desire as a mendicant to lead the gospel life and cherishing the Fathers, especially Augustine (d. 430) and Gregory the Great (d. 604) but also the Eastern Fathers whom he sought to know more and more, Thomas was not only an intellectual genius and energetic scholar, but also a kind, warm-hearted friar. His entire existence and ministry of teaching and preaching were fed by a life of deep contemplative prayer. From this prayer came Thomas's great zeal to "give to others what [he] had contemplated"—for him the highest of all activities when done out of charity (*Summa Theologiae* 2–2.188.6; all references are to this work unless otherwise noted).

It was this same love that led Aquinas, despite opposition from those of the Augustinian school, to use extensively, even daringly, any authors who could lead him to truth, whether they were Christian (Origen, Pseudo-Dionysius, John Damascene), Jewish (Avicebron, Maimonides), Muslim (Avicenna, Averroes), or pagan (Aristotle, Proclus, Cicero). Like his teacher, Albertus Magnus, he saw no opposition between nature and grace or between truths discovered by reason and those revealed by God. It cannot be stressed too much, however, that Thomas intended to be and always was primarily a theologian: even his commentaries on Aristotle were done for theological purposes. To treat him as a philosopher and to extract a "Thomistic" philosophy from the theological context in which Aquinas uses philosophy is a disservice too frequently done by many professing to follow him. Divorced from its living theological context, such a desiccated body of doctrines loses the force and vitality of

Aquinas's thought and is at least partly responsible for the current neglect of his teaching in many quarters. Although Thomas Aquinas used Aristotle more than others, his use of so many other sources shows that he was more than an Aristotelian. For example, from Augustine and the Pseudo-Dionysius he received many elements of Neoplatonism, e.g., the doctrines of participation and negative knowledge of God.

THE TRINITARIAN GOD AND CREATURES

For Aquinas, God's very essence is to be Self-subsisting Be-ing (Lat., *ipsum esse per se subsistens*), Pure Act of Be-ing or Existing and, as such, is the transcendent and unique source of all created existents. This very transcendence of God as Self-subsisting Be-ing means that God, existing beyond all created categories, is not really related to creatures as they are to God, for such a relation would enclose God within the created order.

God's concern for creatures is expressed in many ways: the Father, Son, and Holy Spirit eternally and freely choose to create, conserve, and govern creatures in the natural order by being in them through their divine "essence, presence, and power" (1.8.3); they call and elevate intellectual creatures to share divine life through grace, faith, hope, and love (defined by Aquinas as "friendship with God"); they are present to graced creatures by dwelling in them as objects of their intimate experience in this life—a preparation for the fullness of this presence in the Beatific Vision, an immediate knowledge of God that overflows into love and joy.

Thomas's theology of the missions and indwelling of the trinitarian persons links his study of their interior relational life with the creation and elevation of intellectual persons to share this life. In his later *Summa Theologiae* he prefers the Word-Love analogy to the Nature-Love analogy when examining the procession of the Word-Son and Holy Spirit. In this analysis he holds that creatures are "spoken" and "loved" into existence within the very same speaking and loving in which the Word-Son and Holy Spirit proceed. While the Father, Word-Son, and Holy Spirit concur in creating and in all other effects, each person acts according to its way of being God: this teaching, often neglected, provides a basis for a strong emphasis on trinitarian vestiges and images in creation, sanctification, and the creature's return to God.

THE HUMAN PERSON ON THE WAY TO GOD

Sacra doctrina (Lat., "sacred doctrine" or "sacred teaching") includes for Aquinas divine revelation, sacred Scripture, and a mode of teaching that is scientific in that the theologian, receiving assured first principles by sharing God's knowledge through faith, can argue to conclusions, thereby finding an order among the truths of faith or discovering new truths. In all this, however, Thomas insists that negative knowledge about God is more certain. While confident that we can make true positive statements about God by using analogies, he shows his awareness of the ineffability of God by qualifying his analogies with "mental genuflections" such as "as it were," "in a certain way," "to some degree" (e.g., he says Christ's Passion was, "as it were, a kind of price by which we were freed" [3:48.4]).

In every case of divine-human cooperation, Thomas solves the problems involved in two such diverse subjects acting together by analogical use of the notion of instrumental causality: God as principal cause uses a human person as "a kind of instrumental cause." This neither takes away God's glory nor eliminates any true human contribution under God. Aquinas thus differs from the Augustinian theologians of his time by giving full value to the created order. Creatures glorify God by achieving the ends God has inscribed in their natures. Except for faith, the human knower needs no special added illumination to guarantee certitude, since God has provided the light of reason as an intrinsic natural power. The human body is an essential part of the human person, who is an integral whole. The soul is the unique substantial form of the person, whose unity derives from the one act of be-ing or existing that the person has in both soul and body. This means that the sensitive appetites can be well ordered within themselves by virtues such as temperance and fortitude that reside in them rather than by having an order imposed from without by the will. Well-ordered passions or emotions flowing from these appetites add to the moral goodness of human acts, which are better performed with such ordered passions than without them.

While recognizing natural ends, Aquinas holds that the natural finalities of human beings and angels are intermediate, not ultimate, because intellectual creatures have a natural desire to "see" God, that is, to know the Divine Essence and Be-ing in Itself and not only through creatures. God freely calls intellectual creatures, who are "capable of God" (Lat., *capax Dei*, that is, ordered to life with God by more than an obediential potency); the divine graciousness intrinsically heals the defects produced in human beings by original and actual sin and elevates their natures in their essence, powers, and activities so that they can fulfill this otherwise unattainable desire.

Aquinas rejects the Augustinian view that identified original sin with disordered concupiscence. Following Anselm, he maintains that original sin was formally a disorder of the human will through pride, upon which the other disorders followed. Despite these disorders, human nature is not totally corrupted and even one in sin can perform some naturally good acts. By actual sin a person turns away from God and turns toward the creature, which is often the self. Justification is an unmerited gift from God, who by infusing grace intrinsically changes sinners and makes them sharers in the divine nature.

Human persons, both women and men, are created by nature "in the image of God" (Gen 1:27) because, like God, they are intellectual, have free choice, and are the source of their own actions. The person transformed by grace becomes even more fully an image and likeness of the trinitarian God, especially by acts of faith, hope, and love directed toward God (1.93.4–8). In human activity, moral goodness or evil is determined neither by the principle of obligation nor by commandments or obedience; rather, the end of human nature, beatitude, gives us "the reasons of those things [human acts] that are ordered to that end" (1–2.1.intro.). As image of God, the human person is the primary agent of moral choice looking to this end and these reasons, exercising self-counsel and prudence in judging moral goodness and in applying the commandments and laws to individual situations. For Aquinas one is morally bound to follow the final judgment of conscience, even if it is erroneous.

With respect to human persons, when Aquinas discusses whether Eve should have been created at the same time as Adam, he gives opening arguments denying that she should have been. The first of these, quoting a text of Aristotle saying that a woman is a misbegotten male (Lat., *mas occasionatus*), argues from this that Eve should not have been created from the beginning (1.92.1.1m). Summarizing and accepting Aristotle's teaching as his chief authority in biology, Aquinas's frequently ignored reply continues by indicating that the quotation from Aristotle is insufficient to answer the question. He first makes another statement based on Aristotle: "But with respect to nature as a whole, woman is not something misbegotten, but is intended by nature as ordered to the work of generation." He then adds the fundamental theological reason not found in Aristotle: "The intention of nature as a whole depends on God, who is the author of the whole of nature. Therefore, in establishing nature, God produced not only

Thomas Aquinas, surrounded by Jesus, the apostles, the saints, and the holy men and women of West and East alike.

87

the male but also the female." Although Aquinas has some other statements about women that are unacceptable today, they should be seen as deficiencies produced by his historical conditioning.

Thomas's ordering of moral-spiritual life is positively oriented toward beatitude: he begins with virtues having God as their direct object—faith, hope, and charity—and follows them with the cardinal virtues of prudence, justice, temperance, and fortitude, which are concerned with a person's rightly ordering created things on the way to God. Connected with these virtues are the gifts of the Holy Spirit: for Aquinas the New Law or New Covenant is the inner presence and gifts of the Spirit and only secondarily Scripture and laws. The Holy Spirit's presence and gifts are necessary for a person to live on the high plane of supernatural gospel life. The gift of wisdom, for example, gives an experiential knowledge of God that through intense love can blossom into mystical contemplation, even in the simplest person. Other virtues are linked with these seven major virtues. Only then do vices and sins appear, precisely as opposed to these virtues. Finally come the commandments, which for Aquinas are meant for both instruction and discipline.

CHRIST AND THE SACRAMENTS

Thomas has particular reasons for placing the theology of Christ in the last part of the *Summa Theologiae* (which, in any case, should be read as an organic whole, not as a series of sequential tracts). Since he states emphatically that in sinful human history God has willed Christ as the absolutely necessary way to salvation, everything he has said previously about moral-spiritual life must be seen as related to Christ. The Scripture commentaries, since they deal with our concrete history, bring out even more clearly this key mediatorial role of Christ.

Thomas's doctrine of *esse* (Lat., "being"), including its real distinction from essence in created things, enables him to grasp more fully how Christ could have a complete human essence or nature—a full human psychology with all human faculties, powers, knowledge, free will, and passions—without there being a human ontological person. The union is not in essence or nature but in the personal *esse* of the Word, who subsists or exists in a fully perfect human nature belonging so much to the Word that Thomas will speak of the Son of God as a "person of human nature." Christ saves all human beings not precisely by suffering but by meriting, satisfying, and sacrificing through his loving obedience during his life and especially in his Passion and death; his Resurrection is also saving, not only as an exemplary cause of human resurrection but also as an efficient instrumental cause by which God already raises souls (through justification) and will raise bodies in the resurrection. For Western theology, Aquinas integrates the Resurrection into the saving work of Christ in an original way that recaptures both the Pauline teaching and that of the Greek Fathers.

In the *Summa Theologiae* Thomas revises his earlier view of the sacraments as primarily remedies for sin; he now sees them chiefly as specific helps for different stages of personal and social life. Thomas teaches that the sacraments are equally signs and causes, a balanced view lost by later theologians when their disputes about sacramental causality led them to neglect the sign-value of the sacraments. Indeed, for Aquinas the sacraments cause precisely by their signifying, and they are acts of worship of God as much as causes of grace in creatures. His view of the sacramental characters of Baptism, Confirmation, and Holy Orders as ways of sharing in the priesthood of Christ and his development of many aspects of the Eucharist have had lasting influence.

It is unfortunate that Aquinas did not complete the *Summa Theologiae,* since he may well have used his modified view of the sacraments to produce a revised theology of Matrimony; he might also have fashioned a corporate eschatology, which is less fully treated in his other works.

He was canonized by Pope John XXII in 1323, less than fifty years after his death. He was declared a Doctor of the Church by Pope Pius V in 1567. In his encyclical *Aeterni Patris* in 1879, Pope Leo XIII enjoined Aquinas's thought upon all theological students. The following year he was made patron of all Catholic universities. Feast day: January 28.

See also Thomism.

Bibliography

Chenu, Marie-Dominique. *Toward Understanding St. Thomas.* Chicago: Regnery, 1964.

Gilson, Étienne. *The Christian Philosophy of St. Thomas Aquinas.* New York: Random House, 1956.

Principe, Walter. *Thomas Aquinas' Spirituality.* The Gilson Lecture Series 7. Toronto: Pontifical Institute of Mediaeval Studies, 1984.

Weisheipl, James A. *Friar Thomas d'Aquino: His Life, Thought, and Works.* 2d ed. Washington, DC: Catholic University of America Press, 1983.   *WALTER PRINCIPE*

Aramaic, a Semitic language closely related to Hebrew. Imperial Aramaic, the official language of the Persian Empire (550–333 B.C.), is used in the OT in Ezra and Daniel. A later form of the language, related to that of Jewish Targums, was probably the primary spoken language of Jesus.

archaeology, biblical, the branch of archaeology whose object is to enhance understanding of the Bible. Archaeology is the scientific study of the material remains of past human life and activities in their historical and physical context. Since its raw material is universal, clarity demands subdisciplines with limited foci. The theoretical focus of biblical archaeology is the lands and peoples of the Bible, but in practice the term is reserved for excavations on either side of the Jordan River.

Its origins in a fundamentalist concern to prove the OT right have led some to condemn the term "biblical archaeology," but others have correctly argued that it describes a valid field of research, provided that the Bible offers only inspiration and direction. The Bible cannot limit the scope of research, dictate, or even suggest, conclusions, or lead to neglect of postbiblical periods that have to be dug through. The basic tool of all archaeological assessment is the changing style of artifacts which, through correlations, have been given approximate absolute dates, but modern excavation teams also include botanists, geologists, and zoologists.

Archaeology is the unique source of new data and makes its contribution to the understanding of the Bible in a number of different areas. Surface exploration combined with excavation can establish which sites were occupied at different periods, thus highlighting settlement patterns and stimulating questions concerning routes and resources. Very rarely have inscriptions identifying sites been discovered, e.g., Lachish. Occasionally, as in the case of the Church of the Holy Sepulchre, the correspondence of an excavated site to a detailed physical description can make the identification certain.

On the more specific level of material culture, if sufficient data have been assembled, archaeology may permit the recreation of the life-style of a region or period. The volume of water available provides an upper limit for the population of a town or village, whose diet is revealed by agricultural implements and refuse dumps. Imported objects indicate trade connections. Liturgical furniture betrays the type of cultic activity. Construction techniques suggest the level of technology. Variations in decoration

and building illustrate the gap between rich and poor. Room sizes determined the probable number of members of a house-church. Roofing and paving bring to life incidents and parables.

The excavation of written material increases the body of comparative material for both linguists and historians. Libraries of cuneiform tablets (e.g., Mari, Ebla) permit the reconstruction of mythologies and economic systems. Inscriptions furnish names and occupations, detail a method of tunnel construction, or date the tenure of office of a Roman official. Biblical texts from Qumran have pushed back the OT textual tradition by one thousand years. A copy of John's Gospel from Egypt (ca. A.D. 150) destroyed the hypothesis that the Fourth Gospel was a late second-century creation. The sectarian documents of the Essenes furnish inside information on the ethos of an ill-known branch of Judaism. Papyrus letters highlight the unique features of NT Letters. *JEROME MURPHY-O'CONNOR*

archaeology, Christian, properly speaking, the search for and scientific study of material remains of early Christianity. These remains consist of Christian locations, such as burial grounds, inscriptions, and buildings. Such remains can first be identified from about the end of the second century. Until that time, Christians used locations, buildings, symbols, art, and other artifacts that cannot be distinguished from remains of the Greco-Roman world.

The first Christians met in the homes of congregational members (Col 4:15; Rom 16:3). Eventually these house churches were modified for more fre-

Partial view of a second-century cemetery beneath St. Peter's Basilica, Vatican City, excavated in 1939 and a prime example of Christian archaeology; workers uncovered both pagan and Christian symbols, the latter including a depiction of a woman drawing water on a marble slab and various wall markings that some believe may refer to St. Peter himself.

quent use by the congregation. During the siege of Dura-Europos in 256 A.D. a house church was covered by dirt and debris. That house, the earliest house church than can be identified for certain, had been modified to include a large room for worship, a rostrum, and a decorated baptistery. Another probable house church can be seen in Rome. Early Christians met in an apartment complex fronted by a row of shops. Eventually the congregation built the present-day church of Sti. Giovanni e Paulo in the top two floors of the apartment.

When ecclesiastical edifices did begin to appear, for the most part they did so in burial situations. The first Christians ate meals with the significant dead—both within the family (as was the custom in Greco-Roman society) and then with martyrs of the church (a *martyrium*). One of the earliest known *martyria* consists of a table (*mensa*) and ledge as found in Bonn, Germany, under the Münster. The first Christian edifices were built over or adjacent to such *martyria*. This was particularly true in Rome where, under the direction of the emperor Constantine, a number of *martyria* were extended to make "covered cemeteries." Of particular interest are extant buildings like Santa Agnese, built with an apse around the *martyrium* and a colonnade extended into the nave in a manner that creates a clerestory. Most important of these Roman covered cemeteries is San Sebastiano, thought by pilgrims to be the final resting place of St. Paul and St. Peter. Early Christians met at the presumed *martyrium* to eat with St. Peter and St. Paul as well their own significant dead. The actual burial of the apostle Peter occurred near the Vatican Hill in a burial lot for the poor (now called Campo P by archaeologists). In the second century, a niche in honor of Peter was built into a holding wall in Campo P. Eventually a covered cemetery was also built over this burial, except that this building had a double colonnade and an apse constructed like a cross so as to increase access to the burial niche. Archaeological studies have confirmed a presence of Peter's remembrances here, but the remains of Peter have likely disappeared over the centuries. Many of the churches of later Christendom followed the cruciform structure of the original St. Peter's, although most early churches, like San Crisogono of Rome, reflect the structure of those covered cemeteries with a spherical apse.

Thousands of Christian inscriptions from the first four centuries of Christian history have been recovered. The vast majority of these come from grave markers in catacombs, early Christian underground cemeteries. Most of them have been found in the extensive (ninety miles) of catacombs in Rome, though other collections have been assembled from places like Trier, Phrygia, the house church in Dura-Europos, and *martyria* like that under San Sebastiano and St. Peter's. Christian funerary inscriptions can often be identified by the use of *In Pace* (Lat. "in peace [with God and each other]") in the place of the pagan *Dis Manibus* ("to the spirits of the prior dead"). Generally speaking, the inscriptions indicate some aspects of everyday life. According to the names, most early Christians were slaves or had been slaves, yet the inscriptions do not indicate any slave status. Other inscriptions show Christians encouraged a trend toward democratization by dropping the use of noble names.

Early inscriptions also were decorated with symbols. As symbols, the first Christian culture used the lamb, anchor, vase, dove, boat, olive branch, orante or praying figure, palm, bread, good shepherd, fish, and vine and grapes. All of these independent symbols had a pre-Christian history. The first Christians did not offer substitute symbols (they had none!), but they so utilized the ones they borrowed that these images in some way came to represent the nascent Christian faith. Eating together was expressed by bread, fish, vase, vine and grapes, and possibly the good shepherd. Healing was expressed by the community peace symbols: the dove and the olive branch (and eventually the orante). Tension with the dominant culture was expressed by the boat, the anchor, and likely the fish (water symbolized the dominant social matrix). And the hope for good life was expressed by the tree. *See also* archaeology, biblical.

Bibliography

Frend, W. H. C. *History and Archaeology in the Study of Early Christianity.* London: Variorum, 1988.

Krautheimer, Richard. *Early Christian and Byzantine Architecture.* Harmondsworth: Penguin Books, 1975.

O'Conner, Daniel William. *Peter in Rome.* New York: Columbia University Press, 1969.

Snyder, Graydon F. *Ante Pacem: Archaeological Evidence of Church Life Before Constantine.* Macon, GA: Mercer University Press, 1985.

GRAYDON F. SNYDER

Archaeology, Pontifical Commission for Sacred,

an agency instituted by Pope Pius IX in 1852 which superintends the preservation, exploration, study, care, and protection of those Christian cemeteries, monuments, and churches in and around Rome which date from the first centuries of Christianity. *See also* archaeology, Christian.

archangel, chief angel, or angel of a higher order. In the later biblical period, and on into NT times, angels begin to be designated by personal names. Preeminent among these angels of a higher order are Michael, patron angel of Israel (Dan 10:13); Gabriel, whose special role is that of messenger (Dan 8:16; Luke 1:19); and Raphael, whose function is to protect and heal (Tob 3:17; 12:15). These and other similar heavenly beings (e.g., Uriel) are prominent in apocalyptic writings (2 Esdr 4:1; 10:28). *See also* angel.

archbishop, bishop given a higher rank because he heads an archdiocese, has more significant administrative responsibilities in Church affairs, or is being specially honored with the title. *See also* bishop.

archdeacon. 1 The principal deacon of a Byzantine monastery. 2 An honorific title conferred on Byzantine deacons, sometimes including the right to wear a second orarion or diaconal stole. 3 The title of the principal presbyter of the Chaldean or East Syrian tradition, who functions as master of ceremonies for the bishop at pontifical liturgies. *See also* deacon.

archdiocese, the principal diocese, headed by an archbishop, in a regional cluster of dioceses known as a province. An archdiocese is centered in a city of greater importance than others in the province or that played a special role in the history of Christianity in the given area. Most often the pastoral leadership of an archdiocese has some supervisory responsibility for the other dioceses within the province, which are called suffragan sees. The archdiocese is the metropolitan see. *See also* metropolitan; province.

archimandrite (Gk., *archimandrites,* "chief of a *mandra,* or fold"), highest ranking Byzantine abbot, sometimes graded according to the importance of the monastery. Originally restricted to the overseer of a group of monasteries, the title was later applied to abbots of the principal monasteries. Some Byzantine churches confer the title on monastic priests as the highest grade below bishop. The highest ranking Russian archimandrites may use certain pontificalia like the crown (miter) and the two episcopal candelabra (*dikirion, trikirion*) when presiding at the liturgy, and the Melkites confer the title even on nonmonastic and married priests. *See also* abbot.

architecture. *See* Catholicism and architecture.

archpriest, title given in some areas to a dean or priest in charge of overseeing the clergy of a district or deanery, or to the principal presbyter of a major church. In the Byzantine rite it is an honorary title (Gk., *protoiereus;* Slav., *protoierej;* not to be confused with *archiereus, archierej,* "bishop"), like "Monsignor," conferred on nonmonastic priests along with the right to wear certain insignia like the gold pectoral cross. A "mitered archpriest" may also wear the crown or miter. The highest grade, protopresbyter, was a rare title held in Russia by only a handful of the highest secular clergy of the court and of the Kremlin cathedrals. *See also* priest.

Ardo, St., d. 843, monk and biographer of Benedict of Aniane, whom he succeeded as abbot. Feast day: March 7. *See also* Benedict of Aniane, St.

Argentina, Catholicism in. Catholicism first came to Argentina in 1519 with the expedition of Ferdinand Magellan. The organization of dioceses began in the late 1540s. Throughout its history the Church has been shaped by Spanish cultural and institutional traditions. There are 13 archdioceses and 49 dioceses and almost 30 million Catholics, constituting just over 91 percent of the total population (1994). *See also* Latin America, Catholicism in.

Arianism, a fourth-century movement declared heretical by the Church at the Council of Nicaea (325) for denying the true divinity of Christ. Arius, the Alexandrian priest from whom the movement derived its name, taught that the primary characteristic of God is to be "unbegotten" (Gk., *agennesia*). He reasoned that if both the Father and the Son are said to be unbegotten, then it must be said that two separate Gods exist. Such a teaching would be contrary to monotheism, which Arius wanted to uphold in continuity with ancient Jewish belief. He maintained that only the Father is unbegotten, hence truly God, and that the Father created the Son. Hence Arianism's catechetical slogan, "There was once when he [the Son] was not," meaning that the Son came into existence at some point in time, before which the Son did not exist.

Arianism built its arguments upon Scripture passages like Prov 8:22 ("The Lord created me at the beginning of his work") and Col 1:15 ("the firstborn of all creation"). At the same time, Arianism recognized that the Son of God possessed a dignity superior to human dignity. In its view, Jesus Christ was truly Savior through the example he provided.

To counteract the disruptive effects Arianism caused in his empire, Constantine convened a council in Nicaea in 325. The assembled bishops rejected the teaching of Arius, affirming that the Son was begotten, not created, of the Father and "of the same substance" (Gk., *homoousios*) with the Father. The bishops expressed this teaching in the Nicene Creed, which Arius and two Libyan bishops refused to accept; as a result, they were banished to Illyricum.

Opposition to the Nicene supporters and to the word *homoousios* resurfaced along three fronts after the council. (1) Eusebius of Caesarea and Eusebius of Nicomedia, loyal to Arianism, sought to replace bishops loyal to Nicaea with bishops loyal to Arianism. (2) The Eastern bishops were concerned that the Nicaean formula, particularly *homoousios,* repeated an earlier heresy which did not distinguish between the divine Persons. (3) Under the leadership of Aetius and Eunomius of Cyzicus, a radical Arian movement emerged opposing the Nicene party.

Following the death of Constantine (337) and Constans (350), Constantius II, who supported Arianism, ruled the entire empire. During his reign, four reformulations of the formula of faith, known as the Formularies of Sirmium, were proposed. (1) The Eastern bishops promulgated a creed that omitted reference to *homoousios* (351). (2) In 357, under the leadership of the radical Arian movement, a creed was promulgated stressing the "difference" (Gk., *anomoios*) between the Son and the Father. (3) In reaction, Basil of Ancyra and George of Laodicea lead another synod (358) which proposed a formula describing the Son as *homoiousios* (Gk.), "of like substance to the Father". (4) A creed defining the Son as *homoios* (Gk.), like the Father in all things discussed in Scripture, was declared the creed for the entire empire in 359–60. Not until the councils of Constantinople in the East (381) and Aquileia in the West (381), partially through the influential teaching of the Cappadocian Fathers, was the term *homoousios* reestablished as normative for the entire Church. *See also* *homoousios;* Jesus Christ; Nicaea, First Council of.　　　ANTHONY W. KEATY

aridity (Lat., *aridus,* "dry"), a period of spiritual desolation during which a person loses enthusiasm for prayer and meditation. Sometimes considered a test of fidelity initiated by God, aridity may last for only a short time or may extend into months, even years. Spiritual writers counsel patience and persistence during this experience. Above all, one should never discontinue prayer because feelings of joy or other fruits of prayer are temporarily absent. God's grace, though less tangibly evident, is still being lavished. Once aridity passes, people frequently report having an even greater fervor for prayer than before. *See also* prayer.

Aristotle, 384–322 B.C., Greek philosopher. The son of the court physician of the king of Macedon, he studied and worked from 367–47 B.C. with Plato at the Academy in Athens. A sympathetic yet critical assimilation of Plato's philosophy marks all of Aristotle's thought. He generally emphasized more than Plato the role of sense perception in cognition, was less radical in his criticisms of conventional morality and politics, and resisted the Platonic tendency to unify all science, stressing instead the relative autonomy of the principles underlying inquiries into different subject matters.

Aristotle's own philosophical contributions covered an astonishing range of fields. He founded the systematic study of logic; made profound and still relevant inquiries into such fundamental concepts in the study of nature as cause, motion, time, and space; presented a powerful metaphysical doctrine that culminated in an account of God as the prime mover of the cosmos; developed an approach to ethics and politics that balanced the claims of reason and emotion; and carried out a carefully empirical research program into animal biology. The school he founded, the Lyceum, focused mainly on these last two areas. For three centuries after Aristotle's death his logical, physical, and metaphysical treatises seem to have had little influence, and perhaps to have been virtually unknown. These treatises were then edited and published in the middle of the first century B.C. by Andronicus of Rhodes, the eleventh head of the Lyceum. The treatises became the focus of a penetrating series of Greek commentaries, mostly written over a period of some two centuries by pagan Platonists.

This commentary tradition tended to harmonize Aristotle with Plato, assimilating him into an overarching Neoplatonic scheme of thought, and this Platonized Aristotle was to be the main link to the Catholic tradition. Aristotle's treatises and their Greek commentaries were disappearing in the Christian West by the fifth century. The sixth-century Latin translations by Boethius of two short treatises on ontology and logic, the *Categories* and *On Interpretation,* were the only works of Aristotle known in Europe until the middle of the twelfth century. At that time, the treatises and the commentaries began to be rediscovered and translated into Latin, having been preserved and studied (often in Arabic through Syriac) in the Islamic world.

The impact of Aristotle on Catholic thought received new impetus a century later with another round of translations, and culminated in the work of Thomas Aquinas (d. 1274), whose commentaries still represent the pinnacle of Catholic appreciation of Aristotle. Beyond this time, Aristotle's philosophical vocabulary becomes the basic idiom of Scholastic theology and philosophy, so that his independent influence is hard to determine, waxing and waning with Scholasticism. A renewed independent Catholic interest in Aristotle in the twentieth century was fueled by Pope Leo XIII's encyclical of 1879 *Aeterni Patris,* since his encouragement of the study of Aquinas naturally led to further interest in Aristotle, whom Aquinas referred to simply as "The Philoso-

Arius (left), whose name is forever associated with one of the earliest and most divisive heresies of the Church, with the Islamic philosopher Averroës; fourteenth-century painting by Andrea Bonaiuti, Santa Maria Novella, Florence.

pher." *See also* Aquinas, St. Thomas.   DAVID K. O'CONNOR

Arius, ca. 250–336, Libyan theologian whose heretical teachings sparked the fourth-century trinitarian controversies. An ordained presbyter (priest) in Alexandria, Arius taught that the Son was not God as the Father was God, but was created by the Father. This subordinationist teaching resulted in Arius's denunciation to Alexander, the bishop of Alexandria. After Arius was excommunicated by a council of Egyptian and Libyan bishops, he traveled to Palestine and Syria and found support for his teaching among prominent church leaders such as Eusebius of Caesarea and Eusebius of Nicomedia. Arius's teaching, now called Arianism, spread and led to such controversy that the emperor, Constantine, convened an ecumenical council in Nicaea in 325. The council rejected Arius's doctrine and banished him to Illyricum. In 327, Arius accepted a controverted formulation of the faith and presented Constantine with a written statement of his beliefs. Arius died shortly before reinstatement as a presbyter in Alexandria. *See also* Arianism.

ark of the covenant, a sacred box containing the tablets of the law. Moses instructed Bezalel to make

the ark (Exod 25:10–21), which he did (Exod 37:1–9), although Deut 10:1–5 reports that Moses made the ark and put in it the tablets of the law. In early traditions the ark symbolized the presence of Yahweh and was a rallying point for Israel's military endeavors (Num 10:35–36; 1 Sam 4–7). David brought it to Jerusalem, thus giving Yahweh a home (2 Sam 6; Ps 132). In the NT the ark is dismissed as part of the old ritual system in Heb 9:4, but is seen as part of the heavenly temple in Rev 11:19.

Arles, Council of, three different episcopal synods convened in the Greco-Roman city of Arelate, the present-day city of Arles in south central France. The first Synod was convened on August 1, 314, by Constantine, the first ecclesiastical synod convoked by a Roman emperor. It met to resolve a dispute between supporters of the Carthaginian bishop Caecilian, who had been granted communion with Rome and the churches north of the Mediterranean, and supporters of Donatus, whose predecessor had been ordained by the Numidian bishops. The council supported Rome's earlier decision—and the preference of Constantine—to declare the Donatist episcopacy illegitimate. The effect of this council was to exacerbate the Donatist schism in North Africa. A second synod met at Arles in 353 under the Arian emperor Constantius to carry out his intention to condemn Athanasius, bishop of Alexandria. Yet another synod met at Arles around 473 to consider the extreme predestinarian teaching of a Gallic priest, Lucidus, who was compelled to sign a letter of retraction. *See also* Athanasius, St.; Donatism; predestination.

Armageddon (ahr-mah-ged'uhn), a place-name appearing in Rev 16:16. The Greek text actually reads Harmagedon, identified as a Hebrew word. The most likely interpretation of the name would be "Mount Magedon," usually understood as a reference to the biblical city of Megiddo, a site of famous battles (Judg 4–5; 2 Kgs 9:27). A problem with the interpretation is that Megiddo is not on or near a mountain. The emended reading, Armageddon, could be understood as "City of Megiddo."

Whatever the source of the image, Armageddon has come to symbolize both the place of final confrontation between the forces of good and evil and the confrontation itself. This interpretation is rooted in Rev 16, which describes the gathering of the kings of the East and the unclean spirits sent by the forces of evil, the dragon, the beast, and the false prophet, who come to assault the saints.

Interpreters have debated the significance of the imagery of Revelation throughout Christian history. Some understand the text to predict a literal battle in the end time between Christ and the forces of evil. For them Armageddon is a place, either in Israel or elsewhere, where a decisive battle will take place. Others argue that the text uses imagery to symbolize the eternal confrontation of the forces of good and evil. Still others argue that the author himself assumed that an eschatological battle at a specific place was imminent, but that the struggle continues throughout history. Catholic interpreters have tended to favor a symbolic interpretation. For them, Armageddon refers not a specific site of a battle yet to come but is an evocative allusion to a place where the people of God have often confronted their enemies. That confrontation, in fact, goes on in every age and locale.

In the military rivalry of the cold-war period Armageddon came to symbolize the possibility of total destruction of the world in a nuclear holocaust. Those who have favored a literalist reading of Revelation found support for that reading in such a political and military scenario. *See also* apocalypse; apocalypticism; eschatology, universal.   HAROLD W. ATTRIDGE

Armagh, Book of, a collection of texts assembled at Armagh in 807 for its abbot, Torbach. Now at Trinity College, Dublin, the manuscript contains a full NT, the *Life of St. Martin* by Sulpicius Severus, the *Confession* of St. Patrick, and several Patrician documents written during the seventh century, when Armagh claimed ecclesiastical supremacy and actively promoted the cult of its (probable) founder. *See also* Ireland, Catholicism in.

Armenia, Church in.   *See* Armenian Catholic Church.

Armenian Catholic Church, the ecclesiastical community of Armenian-rite Catholics who are in communion with Rome. It is the Catholic counterpart of the Armenian Apostolic Church that was formed after the Council of Chalcedon (451) when the Armenians, for reasons that were as much political as theological, refused to accept the Christological teaching of the council that in Christ there are two natures, one human and one divine, and not only a single divine nature, as the Monophysites held.

Armenian Catholics are descendants of those

Armenian Orthodox Christians of Little Armenia (Cilicia) who, from the end of the twelfth century until 1375, enjoyed political independence. During this same period they came into contact with the Crusaders as they passed through Asia Minor on their way to the Holy Land. As a result, they absorbed from the Crusaders some Latin liturgical usages. An alliance between the Crusaders and the Armenian king contributed to the establishment of a union between the Church of Rome and the Armenian Apostolic Church in 1198. However, the union was not accepted by Armenians outside of Cilicia, and it ended with the conquest of the Armenian kingdom by the Tatars in 1375. The relatively small Armenian Catholic Church is what remains of that union.

At the Council of Florence a decree of reunion with the Armenians was published in 1439. Although it had no immediate results, the document provided the doctrinal basis for the establishment of an Armenian Catholic Church much later.

Catholic missionary activity among the Armenians had begun early, led initially by the Friars of Union, a now-defunct Armenian community related to the Dominicans, founded in 1320. With the passage of time, scattered but growing Armenian Catholic communities began to ask for a proper ecclesial structure and their own patriarch. In 1742 Pope Benedict XIV confirmed a former Armenian Apostolic bishop, Abraham Ardzivian (1679–1749) as patriarch of Cilicia of the Armenians, based in Lebanon, and with religious authority over the Armenian Catholics in the southern provinces of the Ottoman Empire. In the north, they continued to be under the spiritual care of the Latin vicar apostolic in Constantinople. The new patriarch took the name Abraham Pierre I, and all his successors have likewise taken the name Pierre in their ecclesiastical title.

The Ottoman government had placed all Armenian Catholics under the civil jurisdiction of the Armenian Apostolic patriarch in Constantinople. This resulted in serious difficulties for Armenian Catholics and even persecutions until 1829 when, under French pressure, the Ottoman government gave them the right to be organized civilly as a separate group, known as a millet, with an archbishop of their own in Constantinople. In 1846 he was vested with civil authority as well. The anomaly of having an archbishop with both civil and religious authority in the Ottoman capital and an exclusively spiritual patriarch in Lebanon was resolved in 1867 when

Pope Pius IX united the two sees and moved the patriarchal residence to Constantinople.

The vicious persecution of Armenians in Turkey at the end of World War I decimated the Armenian Catholic community in that country: 7 bishops, 130 priests, 47 nuns, and as many as 100,000 faithful died. Since the community in Turkey had been drastically reduced in size, an Armenian Catholic synod in Rome in 1928 decided to transfer the patriarchate back to Lebanon (Beirut), and to make Constantinople (now Istanbul) an archbishopric.

There were also a number of Armenian Catholic communities in the section of historic Armenia that came under Russian control in 1828. Pius IX established the diocese of Artvin for all Armenian Catholics in the Russian empire in 1850. But czarist opposition to Eastern-rite Catholicism resulted in the abandonment of the Artvin diocese within forty years. In 1912 the Armenian Catholics in the empire were placed under the distant Latin bishop of Tiraspol. The Armenian Catholic Church was entirely suppressed under Communism, and it was only with the independence of Armenia in September 1991 that communities of Armenian Catholics began to resurface. In October 1991 the Holy See established an Ordinariat for Armenian Catholics in Eastern Europe based in the new republic.

The oldest Armenian Catholic religious order is now the Mechitarist Fathers, founded in Constantinople in 1701. It transferred to the island of San Lazzaro, Venice, in 1717. In 1811 a second foundation of Mechitarists was set up in Vienna. These two communities have long served the entire Armenian nation through their scholarship both in Europe and the Middle East.

The Armenian Sisters of the Immaculate Conception were founded in Constantinople in 1847. The community, whose motherhouse has been in Rome since 1922, is dedicated to the education of Armenian girls.

A brotherhood of priests at Bzoummar, Lebanon, has an extensive library and a seminary that dates back to 1771. For higher theological studies, an Armenian College was founded in Rome in 1883. In 1992 a proposal to open a seminary in Armenia was being considered.

Today the largest concentrations of Armenian Catholics are in Beirut, Lebanon, and Aleppo, Syria. The church has seven dioceses in the Middle East: two in Syria and one each in Lebanon, Iraq, Iran, Egypt, and Turkey. Dioceses have also been established for the growing diaspora to North America,

France, and Argentina. The total membership in 1992 was about 150,000. *See also* Armenian rite; Chalcedon, Council of; Eastern Catholics and ecumenism; Eastern Catholics and Rome; Eastern churches; Eastern liturgies; Eastern rites.   RONALD G. ROBERSON

Armenian rite, the liturgical tradition of the Armenian Apostolic (Orthodox) and Catholic churches, which developed in Armenia from the native genius via cultural exchanges with its two principal neighboring churches from the fifth century through the Middle Ages.

Early Armenia, centered around Lake Van (eastern Turkey), was a buffer state between the Byzantine and Persian empires, the two superpowers of late antiquity, and later became the prey of Arab and Turkish invaders. Evangelized by two traditions, the first in the southern provinces in perhaps the second and third centuries from Syriac Osrhoene and Adiabene in the south and the second in the fourth and fifth centuries from Greek Cappadocia to the east under the Apostle of Armenia, St. Gregory the Illuminator (ca. 231–325, an Armenian educated in Caesarea in Cappadocia and consecrated bishop there around 302). Early Armenian liturgy and Bible translations show the traces left by both influences, though the Cappadocian and later Byzantine strains would ultimately predominate.

The earliest liturgical celebrations in Armenia were in Syriac and Greek. From the fifth to the seventh centuries the indigenous Armenian Christian tradition was in the golden age of its formation. This period also saw the conversion of Greater Armenia and the formation of an independent Armenian church, which separated from its neighboring Nestorian (East Syrian) and Chalcedonian (Byzantine) churches after the councils of Ephesus (431) and Chalcedon (451). But the Armenians, more ritually tolerant than their Byzantine neighbors, remained open to outside liturgical influences, which can be observed in several phases. The development of the Armenian alphabet in this period permitted the growth of a native Christian literature, including the liturgy in Armenian. During this golden age the influence of the liturgical tradition of Jersualem is preponderant, above all in the development of the Armenian calendar and lectionary system.

A period of byzantinization followed, from the ninth to the thirteenth centuries, when much of Armenia was under Byzantine dominance. This second wave of Greek influence, noticeable especially in the eucharistic liturgy, has misled some to wrongly consider the Armenian rite a branch of the Byzantine. In fact, it is a fully distinct liturgical tradition.

Then, in the twelfth through fourteenth centuries, as the Armenians came into contact with Crusaders passing through Asia Minor en route to the Holy Land, some Latin liturgical usages were absorbed. This was a freely accepted cultural exchange and cannot be stigmatized like the "latinization" that has occurred in modern times among the Armenians united to the Catholic Church, when pefectly legitimate native traditions such as the unmixed chalice, the creed without the *Filioque*, the consecratory epiclesis, and the Theopaschite Trisagion were modified to conform to Latin prejudices and misunderstanding. The restoration of the Armenian Catholic liturgical books presently under way under the guidance of the Vatican Congregation for the Oriental Churches has purged the liturgical books of these latinizations.

The Armenian rite is distinguished by its cross-in-square, triple-apsed churches with their stagelike sanctuary and distinctive conical roof on a high drum; the baroque opulence of its vestments; and the haunting beauty of its chant, often with organ accompaniment, unlike other Eastern traditions where all but percussion instruments are banned. Other distinguishing traits are the complicated system of sanctoral commemorations in the calendar, the use of unleavened bread, and the chalice unmixed with water at the Eucharist, and, in the Divine Office, a different division of the hours. The Armenian Orthodox no longer practice the sacrament of the Anointing of the Sick, though it is found in liturgical manuscripts of the tradition. *See also* Armenian Catholic Church; Eastern rites; rite.

ROBERT F. TAFT

Arnauld, Antoine (ahr-noh'), 1612–94, Janenist theologian. Known as the "great Arnauld," he came under the influence of Abbé St. Cyran, the leader of the Jansenists. With his *De la fréquente communion* (*On Frequent Communion*, 1643) he began a lifelong struggle against the Jesuits. Retiring to Port-Royal in the 1640s, he continued his attacks on the Jesuits and his defense of Jansenism from there for thirty years. In 1655 he argued that the pope had condemned articles not found in Jansen's works, which resulted in his expulsion from the Sorbonne. He died in exile in Brussels after defending the "Gallican Liberties" against Louis XIV (1679). *See also* Jansenism; Port-Royal

Arnauld, Jacqueline Marie Angélique (ahr-noh'), 1591–1661, Mother Angélique, abbess and reformer of Port-Royal. Appointed coadjutor to the abbess of Port-Royal at the age of seven, she succeeded to that post in 1602. In 1608 she experienced a conversion and proceeded to reform that worldly cloister. The community of Port-Royal replaced her as abbess in 1630, but she was still able to effect the appointment of the Jansenist leader Abbé St. Cyran as spiritual director in 1636. In her second term as abbess (1642–55) Port-Royal became the center of the Jansenist movement involving her own brother Antoine Arnauld and the brilliant mathematician Blaise Pascal. *See also* Jansenism; Pascal, Blaise; Port-Royal.

Arnobius, d. ca. 327, North African apologist and rhetorician. An opponent of Christianity before converting late in life, he wrote the seven-volume *Against the Nations* during the Great Persecution (303–11). Although his thought is unsystematic and shows little familiarity with Scripture, he argues that Christianity agrees with the best pagan philosophy and rebuts charges that Christians caused the empire's misfortunes. *See also* Apologists.

Arnold of Brescia, ca. 1100–55, radical Church reformer who argued for the absolute poverty of the clergy and their abandonment of temporal power. Condemned at the Second Lateran Council (1139) and the Council of Sens (1141), he joined forces with the Roman senate and forced Pope Eugenius III from Rome in 1145. Himself driven from Rome in 1154, Arnold was returned, tried, and executed the following year.

Arrowsmith, St. Edmund, 1585–1628, one of the Forty Martyrs of England and Wales canonized in 1970. Ordained at Douai in 1612 and sent on the English mission, he joined the Jesuits in 1624 and was executed in 1628. Feast day: August 28. *See also* Forty Martyrs of England and Wales.

Arrupe, Pedro, 1907–91, Jesuit superior general. Born in the Basque region of Spain, he entered the Society of Jesus in 1927, was ordained in 1936, and served as a missionary in Japan from 1938 to 1965, where he cared for the wounded, sick, and dying after the dropping of the atomic bomb on Hiroshima on August 6, 1945. As superior general of the Society of Jesus (1965–83), he led the Jesuits through the difficult post–Vatican II period of renewal, emphasizing the theme "a faith that does justice." His influence extended beyond the Jesuit order to other religious communities and the Church at large. *See also* Jesuits.

art. *See* Catholicism and the visual arts; liturgical art.

artificial insemination, any treatment to fertilize a woman by a means that is a substitute for natural intercourse. In its broadest sense, therefore, it would include *in vitro* fertilization with embryo transfer (IVF) and gamete intrafallopian transfer (GIFT). These two, however, are generally treated as separate forms of reproductive technology distinct from artificial insemination. In its proper (narrow) sense, artificial insemination refers to the aspiration of semen (obtained either by masturbation, interrupted intercourse, condomistic relations, or various massage techniques, etc.) into the cervical canal. Artificial insemination may occur using the husband's semen (AIH) or that of a donor (AID).

At the level of official Catholic teaching, Pope Pius XII had most to say about the practice of AID. He rejected it utterly. He stated that only the spouses have, by virtue of the matrimonial contract, a reciprocal right to each other's body and generative acts, a right that is, as Pius XII says, "exclusive, nontransferable, inalienable." Pius also appealed to the good of the child in his rejection of AID.

Most Catholic moral theologians have employed these and other supportive arguments to reject AID, though a small minority believe that the procedure is morally acceptable given careful counseling and the fulfillment of other stringent conditions.

Pius XII also rejected AIH in 1949 and 1951. His main reason for rejecting AIH seems to be the dignity of the married partners; he saw AIH as an attack on this dignity.

In 1987 there appeared *Donum Vitae,* Instruction on Respect for Human Life in Its Origin and on the Dignity of Procreation, from the Congregation for the Doctrine of the Faith. The instruction rejected heterologous insemination (AID) as a "violation of the reciprocal commitment of the spouses and a grave lack in regard to that essential property of marriage which is its unity."

As for homologous artificial insemination (AIH), it rejected it also as "procreation ... deprived of its proper perfection" and an attack on spousal dignity. It appealed to the teaching of *Humanae Vitae* (1968) about the "inseparable connection, willed by God and unable to be broken by man on his own initiative, between the two meanings of the conjugal act: the unitive meaning and the procreative meaning." Where contraception separates these two meanings by having the unitive while blocking the procreative, "homologous artificial fertilization, in seeking a procreation which is not the fruit of a specific act of conjugal union, objectively effects an analogous separation between the goods and the meanings of marriage."

While rejection of AIH remains official Catholic teaching, the teaching is not accepted by many Catholic people (theologians, bishops, laypeople), much as the central conclusion of *Humanae Vitae* condemning every act of contraception remains contested by a great majority of the Catholic world. *See also* bioethics; reproductive technologies.

RICHARD A. MCCORMICK

Ascension, the translation of Jesus to heaven. In the Scriptures, many ancient holy figures were said to be taken up to heaven, especially Enoch (Gen 5:24) and Elijah (2 Kgs 2:1–14). Later, other great figures joined them in being raised to heaven, such as Baruch, Ezra, and Moses. In the Greco-Roman world, heroes as well as emperors renowned for their great deeds were taken to the heavens and exalted as deities (Livy *History* 1.16.1–8; see Justin,

The ascension of Christ into heaven, the prelude to his enthronement at the right hand of the Father; twentieth-century painting on linen by Frederick Brown, Metropolitan Museum of Art, New York.

First Apology 1.54; *Dialogue with Trypho* 69). Thus, ascension to the heavens came to be expected of holy and great persons; it indicated divine approval of them as well as their accession to heavenly power.

Jesus was raised not only to life but also to heaven (Luke 24:50–51; Acts 1:2–12). This act by God acclaims his vindication over his enemies as well as his enthronement at the right hand of God (Acts 2:33–36; Heb 1:3–4). Some versions of the story speak both of prior descent and subsequent ascent (John 6:62), thus articulating more clearly Jesus' original heavenly status. Yet his "descent/ascent" might mean simply his descent into death, followed by his vindication and ascent to God (Eph 4:8–10). Jesus' ascension, then, was first interpreted as God's action on his behalf, bestowing honor that cancelled the shame of the cross. Later it indicated Jesus' accession to heavenly rule as Lord, seated at God's right hand. Finally, as understanding of Jesus as a divine figure matured, Jesus was said to ascend of his own power to the glory he originally had. Since the ancients imagined God in the "heavens," seated on a throne, when Jesus is brought into God's presence, he must "ascend" to where God is. *See also* Ascension, Feast of; Jesus Christ.   *JEROME NEYREY*

Ascension, Feast of, the day commemorating Christ's return to heaven forty days after his Resurrection. It is observed on the Thursday before the Seventh Sunday of Easter, and is a holy day of obligation in the universal Church. The Ascension is the final event of Jesus' visible earthly ministry. The Feast of the Ascension may be regarded as the day on which Jesus, in his glorified body, took his seat at the right hand of God. This feast may also be interpreted metaphorically as an expression of the enduring relationship between the transcendent Jesus and the community he left behind. It was through the Ascension that Jesus' supremacy over creation was revealed; it was the Ascension, too, which made possible the sending of the Holy Spirit on Pentecost. Just as the Resurrection expressed the reality of Jesus' triumph over death, revealing Jesus as the Risen Christ, so the Ascension assures believers that Jesus is eternally present with God. After the Ascension, Jesus was no longer present among his followers in a physical sense; paradoxically, the ascended Jesus is forever present in the world. *See also* Ascension.

Ascent of Mount Carmel. *See* John of the Cross, St.

ascetical theology, branch of theology concerned with the spiritual life taught in Catholic seminaries in the nineteenth and first half of the twentieth centuries. Its methodology was neo-Scholastic and covered the nonmystical aspects of what, with mystical theology, was also known as spiritual theology. The same materials, including the mystical aspects, are now studied in a course called spirituality or Christian spirituality. The manual most frequently used in ascetical theology during the first half of the twentieth century was Adolf Tanquerey's *The Spiritual Life: A Treatise on Ascetical and Mystical Theology,* a text used also in novitiates, female and male. *See also* mystical theology; spirituality, Christian; Tanquerey, Adolf Alfred.

asceticism (Gk., *askesis,* "exercise"), the practice of religious discipline with an emphasis on self-control and the fostering of virtue. The notion was taken over by Christians from Greek philosophers. Asceticism has affinity with terms like abnegation, mortification, self-denial, renunciation, and penance. Christian asceticism is rooted in a discipleship that is an imitation of Christ, whose life and death served as a model for the ascetics of the deserts of Egypt and Palestine. Other models were John the Baptist and Paul the Apostle. The latter offered his life as a pattern for others. According to Paul, the baptized through their asceticism participate in the dying and rising of Jesus.

Key themes in the Christian life during its first centuries were martyrdom, virginity, and widowhood. After the end of the persecution, self-denial in various forms was a way of living the commitment of the martyrs. Monasticism in the late third century broadened the scope of Christian asceticism. Anthony of Egypt (d. 356) became the personification of the Christian ascetic. His *Life* written by Athanasius (d. 373) spread word of Anthony throughout the Christian world. This asceticism of the desert sought to restore a fuller humanity through the control of passion and desire. Jerome (d. 420) and John Cassian (d. ca. 435) were also figures whose writings brought the asceticism of the East to the attention of Western Christians. Augustine (d. 430) accented the grace of God but also encouraged self-control. The Rule of St. Benedict taught moderation in asceticism, though in the tradition physical asceticism at times became dominant.

In the twelfth and thirteenth centuries an intense devotion to the humanity of Jesus developed that drew attention to his suffering and death. Fran-

ciscans especially spread this theme. The Devotio Moderna movement in the late Middle Ages brought ascetical practices of monasticism into the life of the laity.

Protestantism reacted against ascetical practices like clerical celibacy, though Protestant Pietism tried to find a balance in this rejection of asceticism. Ignatius of Loyola (d. 1556) taught his followers that asceticism is at the service of ministry, and John of the Cross (d. 1591) emphasized an asceticism of the heart as a means of liberating one from the disordered attachments that keep one from the quest for God.

Vatican II (1962–65) marked a reaction against the formalism of asceticism. Fasting, abstinence from meat, and Lenten self-denial no longer received in the Catholic community the same attention they once did. Yet, there is a new interest in the ascetical confrontation of addictions to food, drugs, alcohol, tobacco, and whatever else holds the heart prisoner. In addition, there is a contemporary concern to develop an asceticism that respects modern psychological insights and that is based on the duties of one's life, e.g., the discipline required in parenting and building community. Moreover, wisdom from the tradition points to liberation as asceticism's fundamental role in the Christian life, a freedom to accept and give love. Therefore, asceticism and mysticism are no longer seen as opposites. *See also* mysticism; spirituality, Christian.   KEITH J. EGAN

ashes, symbols of penance and reconciliation, at present used in the Roman liturgy only on Ash Wednesday and in the rite for the dedication of a church. The ashes come from the burning of the palms used on Passion Sunday of the previous year. The Christian use of ashes is rooted in the Jewish custom of sprinkling ashes on the head as a sign of repentance. *See also* Ash Wednesday.

Ash Wednesday, the first day of Lent. On this day, ashes are blessed and applied to the foreheads of the faithful as a sign of penance. In the fourth century, public penitents dressed in sackcloth and were sprinkled with ashes to show their repentance. The practice of public penance gradually died out. By the eleventh century, it had become customary for the faithful to receive ashes at the beginning of Lent, the season of penance in preparation for the celebration of Easter. On Ash Wednesday, ashes may be distributed during Mass, usually after the homily, or outside of Mass; in the latter case, the distribution takes place as part of a Liturgy of the Word. The traditional formula for the placing of ashes on the forehead is, "Remember you are dust and will return to dust." The formula "Turn from sin and live the gospel" is frequently used today. In the Roman calendar, Ash Wednesday is a day of fast and abstinence. *See also* abstinence; ashes; fasting; Lent.

Asia, spirituality of, an experience of the sacred founded on the Vedic scriptures (1800–500 B.C.) and encompassing several religions—Hinduism, Buddhism, Confucianism, and Taoism. Many Catholics have incorporated elements of Asian spirituality into their own prayer and meditation.

Most spiritual traditions deriving from Hinduism, the major religion of India, are called yogas. Important recent Indian yogas include Ramakrishna's (d. 1886) devotional practices, Ramana Maharsi's yoga of discriminating wisdom, and Sri Aurobindo's (d. 1950) integral yoga which encompasses various schools.

Ramana Maharsi strongly influenced Benedictine monks who established in 1950 a Hindu style Benedictine monastery in southern India. Bede Griffiths (d. 1993) was a member of this community. Their work brought Hindu ideas into both Catholic practice and integrative theoretical work in the United States and Europe. The early yoga of Patanjali (ca. 500 B.C.) also appears in posture, breathing, and *mantra* (Sanskrit, "sacred word") meditation practices used by Catholics.

Theravadan ("school of elders") Buddhism, begun around 500 B.C. and found mainly in southeast Asia, represents early Buddhist thought. Its practice of *vipassana* (Pali, "insight"), or insight meditation, has been perceived as being compatible with the teachings of the mystic John of the Cross.

Mahayana ("great vehicle"), or northern Buddhism, incorporated elements of Taoism and Asian folk religion. Its many forms include Zen Buddhism. The Jesuit tradition has developed zen practices, and some Jesuit priests are also zen masters. Some Mahayana Buddhism, influenced by Christian missionaries, has taken on an ecclesial expression.

Most martial arts, used by some Catholics as part of their spiritual practice, developed from Chinese Taoism and Confucianism. Taoist *tai chi*, meditative posturing, is also popular with some Catholics.

The Trappist monk Thomas Merton (d. 1968) was also strongly influenced by Asian spirituality, but of the Buddhist, not Hindu, variety. *See also* Merton, Thomas; spirituality, Christian.   *MARY JO MEADOW*

Asia Minor, land mass roughly equivalent to modern Turkey, site of some of the earliest Christian communities outside of Palestine and Syria. This is established, e.g., by Paul's Letter to the Galatians, the Letter to the Ephesians, and the account in Acts of Paul's missionary journeys there. 1 Peter was written from Rome to churches in Asia Minor (perhaps ca. 70); the seven churches of the book of Revelation (Ephesus, Smyrna, Pergamum, Thyatira, Sardis, Philadelphia, and Laodicea) are all in Asia Minor; 2 John indicates the presence of a Johannine community at Ephesus. Ignatius of Antioch passed through Asia Minor on his way to martyrdom in Rome, perhaps toward the end of the reign of Trajan (98–117). Stopping at Smyrna, where he met Polycarp, the bishop, he wrote letters to the churches at Ephesus, Magnesia, Tralles (and Rome); from Troas, he wrote, in addition, to Philadelphia and Smyrna, and to Polycarp (whose own letter to the Philippians is also extant). Earlier in Trajan's reign (112), Pliny, the governor of Bithynia, had written to Trajan inquiring about the proper treatment of Christians. Trajan's answer—that Christianity in itself was a capital offense but that Christians were to be freed if they recanted, that they were not to be sought out, and that no anonymous denunciations were to be accepted—indicates the growing prominence of Christianity in Bithynia.

The Church of Asia Minor is connected to the West through Irenaeus, bishop of Lyons from ca. 178, who was born in Smyrna, knew Polycarp, and could recall Polycarp's reminiscences of Papias (bishop of Hierapolis in Phrygia in the early second century) and his stories about "John" (whether "Apostle" or "Elder" is not clear). Irenaeus echoes Papias's millenarianism. While still a presbyter, Irenaeus presented to Pope Eleutherus, on behalf of the church of Lyons, a defense of the Montanists, the ecstatic, apocalyptic movement that had arisen in Phrygia ca. 170 and that ultimately gained Tertullian as an adherent. In a letter (190) to Pope Victor, Irenaeus also defended the cause of the churches of Asia Minor who wished to preserve their Quartodeciman practice regarding the date of Easter (i.e., celebrating it on the day of Passover), the theology of which is reflected in a homily of Melito of Sardis *On the Pasch,* written in the last third of the second century. Polycarp, martyred at Smyrna ca. 156, had himself defended this practice in a mid-century visit to Pope Anicetus.

Also in Rome in the mid-second century was Marcion, a shipowner from Sinope in the Pontus, excommunicated from the Roman church ca. 144 for rejecting the Hebrew Bible and its God. In the third century Gregory Thaumaturgus (ca. 210–70), bishop of Neocaesarea in the Pontus from the 240s, wrote a famous encomium on Origen, with whom he had studied ca. 233–38. He had to flee the persecution of the Roman emperor Decius (249–51); later, he participated in the excommunication of Paul of Samosata at a synod in the 260s. The Great Persecution of the early fourth century began with the demolition of the church at Nicomedia in 304 and the burning of its Scriptures. Christian resistance prompted Diocletian's massacre of 268 Christians at Nicomedia; Bithynia was also subjected to terror.

In the Arian controversy the churches of Asia Minor made crucial contributions to the articulation of orthodox trinitarian teaching, most notably in the work of the Cappadocian theologians Basil the Great, Gregory of Nazianzus, and Gregory of Nyssa. The first ecumenical council was held at Nicaea (325); Eusebius, bishop of Nicomedia ca. 317–342, was one of the foremost champions of Arius, as was Theogonis of Nicaea (d. before 343) and Asterius the Sophist, a layman from Cappadocia (d. ca. 341). Eusebius was one of the most trusted advisers of Constantine; he baptized Constantine on his deathbed (337). Marcellus of Ancyra (ca. 280–ca. 374) was one of the early defenders of the Nicene Creed, but he was suspected of Modalism and finally condemned by the Council of Constantinople (381), which added the line "whose kingdom will have no end" to the creed against his teaching. Basil of Ancyra (d. after 363, bishop of Ancyra from 336, when Marcellus was deposed), who had been a physician, played a major role in reconciling the most moderate of the Arian party, the *homoiousians,* with the orthodox Nicenes. Amphilochius (ca. 340–ca. 395), bishop of Iconium from 373 and cousin of Gregory of Nazianzus, played a role in the defense of the divinity of the Holy Spirit.

After the fourth century the prominence of the Church in Asia Minor was eclipsed by controversies centering on Alexandria, Constantinople, and Antioch. Although the councils that grew out of these controversies (Ephesus, 431; the "Robber Council" of Ephesus, 449; Chalcedon, 451) were held there, the churches of Asia Minor never regained their earlier prominence. *See also* Arianism; Cappadocian Fathers; Constantinople; Eusebius of Caesarea; Gregory Thaumaturgus, St.; Irenaeus of Lyons, St.; Modalism; Montanism; Nicaea, First Council of.   JOHN C. CAVADINI

asperges (ah-spair'juhs; Lat., *aspergere,* "to sprinkle"), the ceremony in which a priest sprinkles the congregation with holy water. The name echoes the words of Ps 51: "Purge me with hyssop, and I shall be clean." Purging with hyssop is a reference to a ceremony of sprinkling mentioned in Exod 12:22 and Lev 14:51. An older translation of "purge" is "sprinkle." This is the ordinary psalm used with the Rite of Sprinkling, as it is now called, except during the Easter Season, when the antiphon *Vidi aquam* (Lat., "I saw water") is sung. *See also* holy water.

aspergillum (ah-spair-jil'uhm; Lat., "sprinkler"), the liturgical instrument used to sprinkle people and objects with holy water. The aspergillum, or aspergill, may consist of a silver, brass, or wooden handle with a long brush or hollow pierced orb through which the water is sprinkled. The handle also may be hollow to hold more water. *See also* holy water.

aspersion, a method of baptism, in which the candidate is sprinkled with baptismal water. In the West, the usual manner of conferring Baptism is through the pouring of water (affusion) on the candidate's head while the baptismal formula is pronounced. Immersion in water is also an approved method of conferring the sacrament. Aspersion is

Aspergillum

aspergillum

permissible only in exceptional circumstances. *See also* Baptism.

aspirant, a title formerly used in some Catholic religious communities for those seeking admission but not yet received formally as postulants or novices. *See also* novice; postulant.

assembly (Fr., *assembler;* Lat., *assimulare,* "to assemble"), liturgical term used to describe the community gathered for worship. The reality expressed by the term is ultimately derived from the Hebrew *kāhāl,* a word signifying both the divine call summoning the faithful to gather and those who respond to that call as a community, and then from the Greek *ekklesia.* Originally used by Christians with reference to the local community of Jerusalem, *ekklesia* soon signified not only the local community but also the universal Church. Vatican II (1962–65) emphasized in its Constitution on the Sacred Liturgy the importance of the assembly by declaring that the liturgical event is, above all else, the place in which the Church's basic reality is manifestly actualized. The liturgical assembly is a community of faith; it is in the prayer of that community that ecclesial faith resides. Christ is present in an active way in the liturgical assembly, presiding at the community's prayer (n. 7). To be complete, liturgical actions must be marked by full participation on the part of all the members, in union with Christ and with one another (n. 14). *See also* worship.

associate pastor. *See* parochial vicar.

Association for the Rights of Catholics in the Church, an organization formed by a group of lay Catholics in 1980 in response to the Vatican's censuring of prominent theologians, such as Hans Küng. Its stated goal is to bring about substantive structural change in the Church. Its headquarters is in Delran, New Jersey. It publishes a regular newsletter called *Light.*

Association of Catholic Trade Unionists (ACTU), a national lay organization of Catholic trade unionists, established to instruct its members in the Church's social and economic teachings and thereby to influence the American labor movement. Begun in 1937 in New York City, its founders were active in the Catholic Worker movement but thought that movement too utopian and not effective in dealing with Communist influence in labor unions. Organized in local chapters in major cities, the ACTU was loosely joined together nationally. The local chapters sponsored schools to provide instruction in papal social encyclicals, public speaking, parliamentary procedure, the ethics of labor, labor history, and industrial relations. The ACTU fought corrupt, racketeering unions and Communist influence in the labor movement. It regularly supported union organizing, striking workers, unions struggling against Communist control, and the spread of the industrial union movement as represented in the Congress of Industrial Organizations (CIO).

Association of Contemplative Sisters (ACS), an organization formed in 1969 to support the contemplative religious orders. In 1986 the ACS opened its membership to all women who pursue a life of prayer.

associations of the Christian faithful, groupings of the faithful, distinct from religious orders and congregations and from institutes of consecrated life and societies of apostolic life, that exist for religious and/or apostolic ends. They may take many forms, some of which have a closer relationship with Church authority than others, e.g., Association for the Rights of Catholics in the Church, National Federation of Priests' Councils. At times such an association is the genesis of a religious institute. *See also* Association for the Rights of Catholics in the Church; Association of Catholic Trade Unionists; National Federation of Priests' Councils.

Assumptionists, a congregation of priests with the title Augustinians of the Assumption (A. A.). Emmanuel d'Alzon (1810–80), a priest of the diocese of Nîmes, France, and an Ultramontanist, founded the Assumptionists in 1845 and remained their superior general until his death. He also founded the Oblate Sisters of the Assumption. Several other congregations of women have, through their origins, a kinship with the Assumptionists: the Ladies of the Assumption, Little Sisters of the Assumption, and the Orantes of the Assumption. The ministry of the congregation has been directed to the Christian education of youth, missionary activities, parishes, social apostolates, the Catholic press, and the sponsorship of pilgrimages. The congregation has been much involved in efforts toward

Christian unity, especially relations with Eastern churches.

The spirituality derived from d'Alzon was trinitarian and Christological with roots in the French spirituality of the seventeenth century. D'Alzon's writings have been published as *Les Cahiers d'Alzon* (Paris). Francis Picard, the next superior general, 1880–1903, had a profound impact on the spirituality of the congregation, especially through his Circular Letters.

The Assumptionists conduct Assumption College in Worcester, Massachusetts, founded in 1904. A tornado almost completely destroyed the campus in 1953. A new campus replaced the old. There are undergraduate and graduate programs at the college. In accord with the intellectual goals of the congregation, this Assumptionist college maintains an affiliation with the congregation's Institute of Augustinian Studies and its Institute of Byzantine Studies, both in Paris, France. The headquarters of the Assumptionists is in Rome.   KEITH J. EGAN

Assumption of the Blessed Virgin Mary, the dogma that at the end of her life Mary was taken body and soul into heaven. Promulgated by Pius XII in the papal bull *Munificentissimus Deus* on Novem-

The Blessed Virgin Mary bodily assumed into heaven; sixteenth-century painting by Titian in the church of Santa Maria dei Frari, Venice.

ber 1, 1950, and celebrated liturgically on August 15, this dogma states that "the Immaculate Mother of God, Mary ever Virgin, when the course of her earthly life was finished, was taken up body and soul into the glory of heaven." In this definition no position is taken on the disputed question of whether Mary actually died, nor are any historical details given. Rather, with the encouragement of 98 percent of the Catholic bishops who affirmed that the doctrine was both possible and opportune, the pope declared the faith of the Church that Mary in the fullness of her historical personality lives now in union with the risen Christ.

History: Scripture holds no clear evidence for this belief, although the woman clothed with the sun (Rev 12) is interpreted as a significant pointer. Patristic writings are likewise silent. Belief in Mary's Assumption first appeared in the sixth century when her feast day, which like the feasts of all the saints and martyrs celebrated the day of her death, coalesced with an apocryphal narrative (*Transitus Mariae*) purporting to give details about her death, funeral, empty tomb, and bodily reception into heaven. Then in various Eastern churches and by the mid-seventh century in Rome, Mary's main feast day became a celebration of her bodily assumption into heaven.

Belief in this doctrine developed mainly through preaching and devotional literature. Sermons explored the suitability of the Assumption: in view of Mary's salvific mission as Mother of God, it was fitting that she taste death but not that she undergo the corruption of the tomb. She gave bodily life to Christ as it was within her maternal power to do; fittingly, he returned the favor and gave life to her body, as it was within his divine power.

In the West during the Middle Ages these arguments were augmented by the appeal to Christ's filial piety toward his mother (he obeyed the Fourth Commandment requiring honor for one's parents) and by recoil at the image that the flesh that gave birth to Christ should be "consumed by worms." From the thirteenth century onward, any vacillation between agnosticism or affirmation on the question ended as, using Scholastic reasoning (*potuit, voluit, fecit,* Lat., "he could [do it], he willed [to do it], he did [it]"), theologians such as Aquinas and Bonaventure validated the belief.

Theology: The papal decree on the Assumption contains an element of interpretation consistently found in subsequent theology. Alluding to the bloody world wars of the twentieth century and the growth of materialism, the document deplores how the destruction of life, the desecration of the human body, and moral corruption threaten to obviate our human sense of our God-given identity. By holding forth the example of Mary, Pope Pius XII intended that "the exalted destiny of both our soul and body may in this striking manner be brought clearly to the notice of all persons," with subsequent growth in virtue and care for others.

The Assumption thus has a universal significance. The religious meaning of this dogma centers on the eschatological victory of God's grace, freely given in Christ, which consecrates and ultimately saves the whole person, both body and soul. God's creation of the new heaven and new earth, inaugurated in the Resurrection of Jesus, comes to further fruition in this woman who embodies the final destiny of all the redeemed in Christ. In her very person she participates in the new life promised to the human race through the word of the Cross. In so doing, she signifies to all persons caught in the struggle of history that the loving power of God will prevail. With this in mind Vatican II writes:

"In the bodily and spiritual glory which she possesses in heaven, the Mother of Jesus continues ... as the image and first flowering of the Church as she is to be perfected in the world to come. Likewise, Mary shines forth on earth, until the day of the Lord shall come, as a sign of sure hope and solace for the pilgrim People of God" (Dogmatic Constitution on the Church, n. 68).

Ecumenical Import: As with the dogma of the Immaculate Conception, the Assumption raises difficulties in ecumenical dialogue. The problem lies not so much with the content of the dogmas, which may be seen as acceptable developments in piety, as with their status as dogma. Insofar as both beliefs are promulgated with the full strength of papal authority (indeed, the Assumption is the only dogma proclaimed since the 1870 decree on papal infallibility), and insofar as both are connected with what amounts to anathemas resulting in excommunication for nonbelief, Protestants in particular object that these dogmas as they stand contradict the gospel by binding consciences with matters that are not in Scripture.

One interim step forward has been proposed by the Lutheran/Catholic Dialogue (U.S.A.): if Lutherans do not brand Catholic belief in these dogmas a violation of the gospel and if, insofar as these dogmas were promulgated during the time of division and are not central in the hierarchy of truths, Catholics do not require belief in them by Lutherans, then these dogmas need not be an obstacle to continuing growth in unity. Then greater church life together could provide the context for fresh interpretations acceptable to both communities.

Meanwhile, for the Catholic imagination, both dogmas take very seriously the ideas that life and death are a struggle, that the forces of sin and evil are enormous, and that only by the power of God can anyone ultimately prevail. Each recognizes the critical distance that history still has to travel before salvation is complete and revitalizes hope in the ongoing power of God operating in human persons to renew the face of the earth. Amid the constant hostility of history, the narrative power of these dogmas reminds the Church of the undaunted power of this woman, free in her love for God and others through the power of grace and finding ultimate victory. These dogmas can be professed as prophecy in the midst of the history of suffering. *See also* Ascension; Mary, Blessed Virgin; resurrection of the body.

Bibliography

Brown, Raymond, et al., eds. *Mary in the New Testament: A Collaborative Assessment by Protestant and Roman Catholic Scholars.* Philadelphia: Fortress Press, 1978.

Graef, Hilda. *Mary: A History of Doctrine and Devotion.* 2 vols. New York: Sheed & Ward, 1963.   ELIZABETH JOHNSON

astrology, the study of the movement of heavenly bodies in order to predict or interpret individual and communal destinies on earth. Astrology appeared in the Hellenistic world in the third century B.C. as a combination of Chaldean and Egyptian astral religion with Greek mathematics and astronomy. It became influential in every area of human life and thought in the ancient world. Its influence can be seen in some of the imagery of the NT, e.g., the star at Jesus' birth (Matt 2:1–10) and the solar eclipse at his death (Matt 27:45; Mark 15:33; Luke 23:44). Christian opposition to astrology began very early, e.g., Paul's criticism of observance of special days (Gal 4:9–10) and devotion to cosmic powers (Rom 8:38; Col 1:16, 2:8, 20). Patristic writers (Tertullian, Lactantius, Augustine) denounced astrological predictions, often ascribing them to demons. Augustine (d. 430) trenchantly criticized astrology (e.g., *City of God* 8.19) as a fatalistic system that denies all human freedom. Medieval Western Christianity encountered astrology through Islamic contacts. Many Catholics during the Middle Ages allowed for some astrological influence on human life, including Thomas Aquinas (d. 1274) and Dante

(d. 1321). Some of the Reformers rejected astrology (e.g., John Calvin, d. 1564) and others accepted it (e.g., Philipp Melanchthon, d. 1560). Some popes acknowledged it (Julius II and Paul III regularly consulted astrologers; Leo X established a university chair for its study); other popes strongly denounced it (e.g., Innocent VIII). The cumulative results of seventeenth- and eighteenth-century astronomy finally discredited astrology's scientific pretensions.　　　　　MICHAEL J. HIMES

Athanasia, St., fifth-century anchoress. She renounced the world after allegedly having a vision of St. Julian. St. Daniel sent her to be an anchoress in the wilderness of Egypt. Feast day: October 9.

Athanasian Creed, creed also known as the *Quicunque Vult* (Lat., "Whoever wishes [to be saved]"), which are its opening words.

Origin: Incorrectly attributed to Athanasius (d. 373) or Ambrose (d. 397), the Athanasian Creed probably originated in southern France, perhaps at the abbey of Lérins, after the Council of Constantinople (381) and before the Council of Chalcedon (451). Originally written in Latin, it was likely formulated by Vincent of Lérins (d. ca. 450), Caesarius of Arles (d. 542), or someone close to one of them. It was fashioned in response to the post-Nicene controversies concerning the person of Jesus Christ, specifically regarding the Incarnation and the relationship between Christ's divine and human na-

THE ATHANASIAN CREED

Whoever wishes to be saved must, first of all, hold the Catholic faith, for, unless he keeps it whole and inviolate, he will undoubtedly perish for ever.

Now this is the Catholic faith: We worship one God in the Trinity and the Trinity in unity, without either confusing the persons or dividing the substance; for the person of the Father is one, the Son's is another, the Holy Spirit's another; but the Godhead of Father, Son and Holy Spirit is one, their glory equal, their majesty equally eternal.

Such as the Father is, such is the Son, such also the Holy Spirit; uncreated is the Father, uncreated the Son, uncreated the Holy Spirit; infinite (*immensus*) is the Father, infinite the Son, infinite the Holy Spirit; eternal is the Father, eternal the Son, eternal the Holy Spirit; yet, they are not three eternal beings but one eternal, just as they are not three uncreated beings or three infinite beings but one uncreated and one infinite. In the same way, almighty is the Father, almighty the Son, almighty the Holy Spirit; yet, they are not three almighty beings but one almighty. Thus, the Father is God, the Son is God, the Holy Spirit is God; yet, they are not three gods but one God. Thus, the Father is Lord, the Son is Lord, the Holy Spirit is Lord; yet, they are not three lords but one Lord. For, as the Christian truth compels us to acknowledge each person distinctly as God and Lord, so too the Catholic religion forbids us to speak of three gods or lords.

The Father has neither been made by anyone, nor is He created or begotten; the Son is from the Father alone, not made nor created but begotten; the Holy Spirit is from the Father and the Son, not made nor created nor begotten, but proceeding. So there is one Father, not three Fathers; one Son, not three Sons; one Holy Spirit, not three Holy Spirits. And in this Trinity there is no before or after, no greater or lesser, but all three persons are equally eternal with each other and fully equal. Thus, in all things, as has already been stated above, both unity in the Trinity and Trinity in the unity must be worshipped. Let him therefore who wishes to be saved think this of the Trinity.

For his eternal salvation it is necessary, however, that he should also faithfully believe in the incarnation of our Lord Jesus Christ. Here then is the right faith: We believe and confess that our Lord Jesus Christ, the Son of God, is both and equally God and man. He is God from the substance of the Father, begotten before the ages, and He is man from the substance of a mother, born in time; perfect God and perfect man, composed of a rational soul and a human body; equal to the Father as to His divinity, less than the Father as to His humanity. Although He is God and man, He is nevertheless one Christ, not two; however, not one because the divinity has been changed into a human body, but because the humanity has been assumed into God; entirely one, not by a confusion of substance but by the unity of personhood. For, as a rational soul and a body are a single man, so God and man are one Christ. He suffered for our salvation, went down to the underworld (*ad infernos*), rose again from the dead on the third day, ascended to the heavens, is seated at the right hand of the Father, wherefrom He shall come to judge the living and the dead. At His coming all men are to rise again with their bodies and to render an account of their own deeds; those who have done good will go to eternal life, but those who have done evil to eternal fire.

This is the Catholic faith. Unless one believes it faithfully and firmly, he cannot be saved.

tures. It addresses Apollinarianism and Nestorianism and perhaps also Eutychianism, which were condemned at the councils of Constantinople (381), Ephesus (431), and Chalcedon (451), respectively.

Structure and Content: Consisting of forty declarations, it is unlike the tripartite creeds (e.g., the Apostles' and Nicene-Constantinopolitan creeds), in that it consists of two major parts, the first on the doctrine of the triune God and the second on the doctrine of the Incarnation and redemption. The word "substance" is employed in speaking of God. The term "person" is used in reference to the Father, the Son, and the Spirit, and the distinction of the three persons is highlighted. The Holy Spirit is said to be "from" the Father "and" the Son, a formulation that was disputed during the *Filioque* controversy in the seventh century.

In the second part the narrative of the Christ kerygma (1 Cor 15:3–7) is set within a series of propositions against Christological errors. This part declares that Jesus Christ is fully divine and fully human. His humanity is constituted with a rational soul and human body. Seemingly addressing Eutychianism as well as Apollinarianism, it denies any confusion of natures in Jesus Christ and affirms that the Son of God assumed a full human nature.

The creed's introduction and conclusion assert that belief in this creed is necessary for salvation, and the body of the text includes condemnations of doctrinal errors. (Anathemas are not found in the Apostles' and Nicene-Constantinopolitan creeds.)

Function: It is likely that at the outset the creed was primarily used for instruction, especially of the clergy. By the ninth century it was being employed within the liturgy in Germany, where it was recited by the congregation after the sermon. Eventually, however, it came to be sung at liturgy in the West, even though it did not lend itself to this usage because of its technical style and condemnatory tone. Beginning in the twelfth century, the Eastern Church recognized the creed, but did not put it to regular use, and it was translated into Greek in the fourteenth century. (Since ca. 1780 it has been included in the Greek *Horologium*, a liturgical book containing portions of the Liturgy of the Hours, though without the *Filioque* clause.) In the thirteenth century theologians in the West gave it the same authority as the Apostles' and Nicene-Constantinopolitan creeds. Beginning in the seventeenth century, the Athanasian Creed was included in the Russian liturgy. Also in the Western Church it came to be recited in the Liturgy of the Hours and in the liturgy for the Solemnity of the Holy Trinity. *See also* Apollinarianism; Christology; Eutyches; Incarnation, the Nestorianism; Trinity, doctrine of the.

ROBERT A. KRIEG

Athanasius, St., d. 373, bishop of Alexandria from 328, and the strongest defender of the Council of Nicaea, convoked by Emperor Constantine in 325. A coalition of Oriental bishops led by Eusebius of Nicomedia had supported the Alexandrian priest Arius in his doctrinal dispute with his local superior, Bishop Alexander, regarding the relation of Christ with God the Father. Defeated at Nicaea, the same Eusebian party soon attacked Alexander's successor, Athanasius, questioning the validity of his election and allying themselves with the schismatic Melitians of Egypt. Constantine sent Athanasius into exile in 335 to Trier, but the emperor died in 337 and the exiled bishop returned home. His episcopal opponents, eager to establish themselves in the eye of the administration, continued to deny the legitimacy of Athanasius's tenure of office. They

Athanasius (lower right), one of the greatest theologians and bishops of the early Church and the principal defender of Catholic orthodoxy against the Arians; painting by Luca Signorelli (d. 1523) also depicting the Trinity, the Blessed Virgin, and Augustine of Hippo (lower left).

rejected the creed of Nicaea itself as an unsound innovation, preferring a more traditional formulation in line with Arius's own ideas about the Christian doctrine of God. Since this party, denounced as "Arians" by Athanasius, had the support of Constantius II (337–361), son of Constantine, Athanasius had to face the wrath of the imperial administration. In 339 he fled to the West, where Pope Julius I and Constans, another son of Constantine who ruled the Western empire, offered him protection until 346. He fled again in 356 and remained in hiding until 362 with the monks of the Egyptian deserts. Constantius's successor, Julian (361–363), disgruntled with the bishop's pastoral success, sent Athanasius into a fourth exile (362–363). The next emperor, Valens (364–378), also exiled the bishop, but recalled him from this fifth exile (365–366) within a few weeks because of popular discontent. Famous for his theological writings, such as *On the Incarnation* and the *Discourses Against the Arians,* Athanasius clarified the notion of Trinity and focused on the central belief in divine Incarnation. He underlined the full divinity of the Holy Spirit, equal to that of the Son, several decades before the First Council of Constantinople (381). Most of his works were addressed to the monks, his friends, whose ideals he exemplified in the *Life of Antony,* enthusiastically received in both East and West. Feast day: May 2. *See also* Arianism; Christology; Constantinople, councils of; Incarnation, the; Trinity, doctrine of the.

PAMELA BRIGHT

atheism, the denial of the reality of God. The term possesses an inherent ambiguity both in meaning and in application. The meaning of "atheism" depends upon the "god" that is denied, and the term has been applied for thousands of years to vastly divergent forms and systems of thought. Analyses and histories of atheism have focused upon acknowledged denials or hidden implications of thought. Distinctions are made between atheism, agnosticism, and antitheism; indifference and postulation; and practical and theoretical atheism. The canonical index of ancient atheism comprises some seven or eight figures, but often their "atheism" has proved to be an unsympathetic reading of their thought. Even the early Christians had to defend themselves against the charge of atheism.

Modern atheism, not as an invective against one's enemies but as a signature, emerged in Western civilization during the Enlightenment with such savants as Denis Diderot (d. 1784). It took from Isaac Newton (d. 1727) the universality of mechanics and from René Descartes (d. 1650) the confinement of mechanics to mechanical principles. Matter was recognized as intrinsically dynamic and as comprehensive of all reality. Georg Hegel (d. 1832) recognized that something religiously unique had entered European thought, a philosophy that "defined matter, nature, etc., as that which is to be taken as the ultimate" (*Lectures on the History of Philosophy* 3.387).

Nineteenth Century: During the nineteenth century, philosophical theism argued its case not so much from nature as from the necessities of human nature; the denials followed suit and fathered an "atheistic humanism." Ludwig Feuerbach (d. 1872) maintained that human consciousness was essentially self-consciousness and argued that God was nothing but the projection of the human species. He was followed and corrected by Karl Marx (d. 1883), who contended that the fundamental human activity was human sensuous activity flowering as revolutionary practice. Religion resulted from contradictions within the social and economic world, which must be revolutionized to destroy the alienation that was God. In the anthropology of Friedrich Nietzsche (d. 1900), the will to power became the central human reality, and God was rejected as a factor limiting the development of the human into the *Übermensch* (the superman). Nietzsche announced the cultural reality of the death of God, i.e., that "belief in the Christian God has become no longer believable" (*The Gay Science* 5.343). Though technically agnostic, Sigmund Freud (d. 1939) also found the providential God a projection, but now it was the oedipal projection, out of human weakness, of the protecting and threatening father figure. By the end of the nineteenth century, atheism had defined God as the antihuman. Massive political and social changes with origins in the French Revolution (1789) contributed to a sense of emancipation that countered religious influences, while the churches during that same period became identified with reaction.

Twentieth Century: Three forms of atheism marked the twentieth century. There were those intellectual currents that achieved ideological domination in the totalitarian regimes that controlled great masses of Europe and Asia. In the United States, John Dewey (d. 1952) spoke for an increasingly alienated intellectual culture, arguing that the ethos of scientific inquiry dated belief in God. Existential philosophies found a frankly advocated atheism in Jean-Paul Sartre (d. 1980), casting God both as an internal contradiction and an intolerable limitation of authentic human freedom. Together with these should be included the many forms of positivism that assert that any statements about God are nonsense. During the twentieth century, atheism and its lesser forms (such as agnosticism) have come to characterize hundreds of millions of the world population, constituting one of the fastest growing religious persuasions of the past two hundred years.

The Teaching of the Church: While the Church has historically condemned atheism as sinful when it entails a deliberate suppression of truth, Jesuit theologian Karl Rahner (d. 1984) has noted that the Church only began to deal seriously with atheism as a new, worldwide phenomenon at the Second Vatican Council (1962–65). The Dogmatic Constitution on the Church (n. 16) allows for an atheism that is inculpable, hence, does not exclude one from salvation. Even more important, the Pastoral Constitution on the Church in the Modern World (nn. 19–21) recognizes the urgency of contemporary atheism, the various forms it assumes, its possibility of being a protest against false gods, the sources of its rise, and the contribution to its growth made by a Christianity unfaithful to itself. Increasingly also the Church has condemned the practical atheism embodied in economic exploitation and social injustice. *See also* agnosticism; Enlightenment, the; Marxism; Nietzsche, Friedrich. MICHAEL J. BUCKLEY

Athenagoras, second-century apologist whose *Presbeia* (Gk., "Supplication"), addressed ca. 177 to Emperor Marcus Aurelius, pleaded ably for toleration toward Christians, claiming agreement between Scripture and established philosophy and refuting charges that Christians practiced cannibalism and incest. Especially concerned to rebut the charge of atheism, Athenagoras provided an early philosophical defense of the doctrine of the Trinity. *See also* Trinity, doctrine of the.

Athos, Mount, a peninsula extending south into the Aegean Sea from Macedonia (the northeast coast of Greece). Athos belongs to the Eastern Orthodox Church and is home to twenty autonomous monasteries. Its monastery libraries house collections of important manuscripts. The settlement dates from 962. Neither women nor female animals are permitted on the peninsula.

atonement, biblical view of, reconciliation, the setting of someone at one with another. Reconciliation is not found in the Hebrew Scriptures. In Judg 19:3 the Septuagint (LXX) introduces the Greek verb *diallaxai,* "reconcile," but the Hebrew says merely "to cause her to return." The notion of reconciliation (Gk., *katallagē*) is borrowed from the Greek world and denotes the restoration of correct relations between individuals, groups, or nations. It is a social idea, expressing the change from hostility to friendship, from alienation to intimacy. It eventually enters the deuterocanonical Greek writings of the OT (2 Macc 1:5; 5:20; 7:33; 8:29).

In the NT *diallassein, katallassein,* "reconcile," is used in a secular sense (Matt 5:23–24; 1 Cor 7:11), as in extrabiblical Greek (Mur 115.5). But it also takes on a distinct religious meaning in the Pauline writings, where it expresses an effect of what God has brought about through Christ Jesus for humanity. Through the life, Passion, death, and Resurrection of Christ Jesus, human beings have been "reconciled" with God: "If while we were enemies, we were reconciled to God through the death of his Son, much more surely, having been reconciled, will we be saved by his life" (Rom 5:10). Paul also describes this restored status as one of peace: "Since we are justified by faith, we have peace with God" (Rom 5:1, which peace is explained in terms of reconciliation in vv. 10–11). The apostle also speaks of his own evangelization as a "ministry of reconciliation" (2 Cor 5:18). Paul sees the effect as having not only an anthropological impact, but also a cosmic impact; it affects not only human beings, but even the "world" (Gk., *kosmos*): "in Christ God was reconciling the world to himself" (2 Cor 5:19; see Rom 11:15). This Pauline notion is extended in the deutero-Pauline writings (Col 1:21; Eph 2:11–18), where it is considered not only vertically (reconciliation between God and human beings), but also horizontally (between Jews and Gentiles).

Though reconciliation or atonement is thus said to be achieved "through the death" or "by the blood" of Christ, such specification should not be understood to give the idea a sacrificial connotation. Pauline and deutero-Pauline writings use such phrases to describe reconciliation as an effect of the Christ-event, but reconciliation does not thereby acquire a sacrificial nuance.

This nuance has often been associated with atonement, because interpreters have mistakenly associated with it *hilasmos* (Gk., expiation), a different idea found in both the OT (Lev 25:9) and the NT

(1 John 2:2), but wrongly translated in the New Revised Standard Version as the "Day of Atonement" or "atoning sacrifice." It should be the "Day of Expiation" (Fr., *Jour de l'Expiation*); or "expiation for our sins" (1 John 2:2, NABRNT). Part of the problem here is the systematic theological heritage, which the *Oxford English Dictionary* describes when it says that atonement means "reconciliation, propitiation, expiation, according to the view taken of its nature" (1. 135). *See also* redemption.   JOSEPH A. FITZMYER

atonement, doctrine of, the forgiveness of sin and expiation of human guilt through Christ's loving fidelity, expressed in his suffering, death, and Resurrection, which reconciled humanity with God.

The fact that the Crucifixion took place at the time of the Jewish Passover encouraged the first Christians to recognize Christ as the Paschal Lamb who had been sacrificed (1 Cor 5:7). Connecting his death with another great Jewish feast, the Day of Atonement (Heb., *Yom Kippur*), they understood Jesus to be the great high priest and victim whose unique self-sacrifice had once and for all expiated sins and brought a new covenant relationship between God and human beings (Heb 4:14-10:39).

The Tradition: In his *The Incarnation of the Word of God (De Incarnatione Verbi)* Athanasius of Alexandria (d. 373) emphasized human weakness and divine initiative. The word of God first created humans and then, after the fall into sin, recreated them through the Incarnation that culminated in the self-offering of his death. In *Cur Deus Homo (Why God Became Man)* Anselm of Canterbury (d. 1109) provided what was to prove the most successful Christian treatise devoted explicitly to the atonement. His theory of "satisfaction" presented Christ's freely accepted death as vicariously making amends for the offense to the divine honor caused by human sin. Because of his divinity, humanity, and sinlessness, Christ (and only Christ) could satisfy on humanity's behalf for the infinite dishonor to God that is sin. Faced with the Reformation controversy over the nature of justification, the Council of Trent (1545–63) echoed the language of Anselm and even more that of Thomas Aquinas (d. 1274) in teaching that the sacrifice of the Cross merited human justification and made satisfaction to God the Father.

A Misunderstanding: For centuries, not only Protestants but also Anglicans and Roman Catholics have at times taken "satisfaction" language to an extreme never intended by Anselm. They have misrepresented Christ's atoning death to depict God condemning Jesus as personally burdened with our sins, punishing him as a substitute for guilty humanity, and so being appeased or propitiated by the blood shed on the cross. This view of the atonement takes very seriously sin and the objective nature of what Jesus accomplished through his suffering, death, and Resurrection. Yet it has misunderstood the scapegoat ceremony from the Jewish Day of Atonement (Lev 16:8–10, 20–22), misapplied the fourth suffering servant song (Isa 52:13–53:12), misinterpreted several classical texts from Paul (Rom 8:3; 2 Cor 5:21; Gal 3:13), and ignored the fact that, while sometimes speaking of the divine anger (e.g., Rom 1:18; 2:5, 8; 12:19; 13:4–5; 1 Thess 1:10), the NT never associates that anger with Christ's suffering and death. Ultimately this view directly attributes Christ's Passion to God's vindictiveness rather than to human cruelty.

In fact, instead of passively accepting punishment in humanity's place, Christ acted "for us" and on human behalf (Rom 5:6; 1 Cor 8:11; Gal 1:4) in representatively carrying through his mission with utter fidelity and freely accepting the execution that the world thrust upon him. So, far from needing to manipulate or persuade an angry deity who was "out for blood," Christ was sent by divine love (Rom 8:3; Gal 4:4–5) to reconcile humans with God and with one another (Eph 2:12–18). Accepting for others the suffering that his goodness faced in the world, Christ purified and repaired a moral order defiled by human sin.

In his *On the Trinity (De Trinitate* 13.11.15) Augustine (d. 430) rightly questioned the view of those Christians who were already misinterpreting atonement as if it meant the Son appeasing the Father's anger and thus winning back divine love for humanity. In contrast, from the outset the Son was sent by the Father to forgive and save fallen human beings. Augustine asked: "Is it necessary to think that being God, the Father was angry with us, saw his Son die for us and thus abated his anger against us? But what then could be the meaning of the words of St. Paul? How shall we respond to his question: if God is for us, will he not give us all things? Unless he had already been 'appeased,' would the Father have given over his only Son for us?"

What then of Christ's blood shed upon the cross? It symbolized and effected not only the expiation of sinful humanity's guilt (Rom 3:25; 1 John 1:7) but also the deliverance from evil (1 Pet 1:18–19) and peace found with God (Col 1:19–20) through a new covenant (Mark 14:24; 1 Cor 11:25). The range of meanings for "blood" in the OT characterizes the full power of Christ's atoning blood. *See also* blood of Christ; crucifixion; expiation; propitiation; redemption; sacrifice; salvation.

Bibliography

Dillistone, F. W. *The Christian Understanding of Atonement.* Philadelphia: Westminster, 1968.

Hengel, Martin. *The Atonement.* Philadelphia: Fortress, 1981.

GERALD O'COLLINS

Atticus, St., d. 425, patriarch of Constantinople from 406. From Sebaste in Armenia, later priest at Constantinople and an opponent of John Chrysostom, he was appointed patriarch by the emperor Arcadius, but after Chrysostom's death Atticus returned his name to the diptychs and restored relations with Rome. He also corresponded with Augustine and expelled the Pelagian Celestius from Constantinople. Feast days: October 11, January 8 (both Eastern). *See also* Chrysostom, St. John.

attrition, a desire for forgiveness based on fear of God rather than on love for God. Attrition is a technical term found in Catholic theology from medieval times on. Attrition and contrition were generally contrasted, so that the definition of one shaped the definition of the other. In medieval theology, the distinction attrition/contrition arose over the way forgiveness of sin outside sacramental confession was theologically related to forgiveness of sin in sacramental confession. Franciscan and Dominican theologians disputed the theological relationship of attrition and contrition. In medieval Scholastic theology, attrition was considered either from its motive or from its effect. The motive in attrition was often presented as fear of eternal punishment or as horror over one's own evil act; in contrition, the motive was presented as perfect love for God. In effect, attrition was often presented as an antecedent step, disposing one for the sacrament of confession. Of itself attrition did not merit sanctifying grace. Contrition had as its effect the infusion of sanctifying grace. The Council of Trent (1545–63), without settling the theological Franciscan and Dominican dispute, used a fairly common theological view for attrition or "imperfect" contrition (D 1678). Canon 5 of Trent (D 1705) focused on the accusation of some Reformers that the Catholic approach to both contrition and attrition was a good work, nullifying God's grace, and was therefore of no Christian value. This canon must be interpreted by the decree on justification that the bishops of Trent had already formulated (D 1520–83). No new approach to attri-

tion has been proposed in post–Vatican II theology, although there has been study on the relationship of a theology of sin to psychological studies on human motivation. *See also* contrition; Reconciliation.

KENAN B. OSBORNE

Aubert, Roger, b. 1914, Belgian-born Church historian. Ordained a priest for Malines in 1938, Canon Aubert of the University of Louvain followed his *Le Problème de l'acte de foi* (Fr., "The Problem of the Act of Faith," 1945) and *Le Pontificat de Pie IX* (Fr., "The Pontificate of Pius IX," 1952) with other studies of nineteenth century European Catholicism. He has also served as editor of the *Nouvelle histoire d'Église* (1963–75) and of the *Revue d'histoire ecclésiastique*.

audience, papal, visits or receptions given by the pope to a person or group of persons who have business with the Holy See or who are pilgrims or visitors to the Vatican. General and public papal audiences are ordinarily held on Wednesdays in the Audience Hall on the south side of St. Peter's Basilica, with semiprivate or private audiences in the papal residence scheduled for other times under the auspices of the Prefecture of the Pontifical Household (*Pastor Bonus* [1988], n. 181.3). During the summer audiences are held at the pope's summer residence at Castel Gandolfo, fifteen miles outside of Rome. Papal audiences often involve Church hierarchy and curial officials and are conducted in solemn fashion when diplomats from various nations or heads of state are received. *See also* Pastor Bonus.

auditor, in canon law judicial appointee who, according to mandate, helps the tribunal collect proofs, including examination of witnesses, but may not adjudicate. Judges may appoint another judge or any qualified person specifically approved by the bishop for this function. Since judges of the Roman Rota were originally auditors for cases the popes judged, they retain the title. *See also* tribunal.

Augsburg Confession (Lat., *Confessio Augustana*), the primary confession of the Lutheran church. Written by Philipp Melanchthon on the basis of earlier Lutheran statements, it was submitted by seven imperial princes and two imperial cities to the Holy Roman emperor Charles V at the Diet of Augsburg (1530) as an official statement of belief and a defense against charges of heresy. The first part of the confession argued that Lutheran doctrine either agreed with Catholic teaching or held to the true primitive doctrine from which the Catholic Church had departed. It was composed of twenty-one articles on God, original sin, the Son of God, justification by faith alone, ministry, new obedience, the Church, Baptism, the Lord's Supper, confession, repentance, use of the sacraments, ecclesiastical order, humanly instituted rules, civil affairs, Christ's return in judgment, free will, the cause of sin, faith and good works, and veneration of the saints. The second part listed seven reforms of abuses in the areas of Communion of the laity with both bread and wine, the marriage of priests, the Mass, confession, human traditions, monastic vows, and the authority of bishops. A group of Catholic theologians led by John Eck presented a confutation (*Confutatio Pontifica*) that approved nine articles without exception, approved six in part or with qualifications, and condemned thirteen. The Lutheran response written by Melancthon, the *Apology,* was accepted by the Lutheran churches in 1537 as the authoritative commentary on the confession and was included in the *Book of Concord* (1580). *See also* Lutheranism; Melanchthon, Philipp.   R. EMMET MCLAUGHLIN

Augsburg Interim, a doctrinal formula imposed on the Protestant estates by Charles V (1548) as a temporary (Lat., *ad interim*) arrangement. Because it essentially expressed Catholic dogma, it was rejected by most Protestants. Because it allowed Communion with both consecrated bread and consecrated wine for the laity and permitted Protestant clergy to retain their wives, it was rejected by most Catholics.

Augustine, Rule of St., rule for religious life attributed in part to Augustine of Hippo (d. 430) outlining a life of love, community, service, and obedience. Though it is cited in some early medieval authors, it was only in the eleventh century that its observance became widespread; at the Fourth Lateran Council (1215) it was accepted as one of the approved rules of the Church, and the new Dominican order adopted it soon thereafter. Promoting a community under the direction of a superior in which property is held in common, it continues to prove attractive to many different religious, to active and contemplative, to male and female alike; over one hundred and fifty communities follow it today. *See also* Augustine of Hippo, St.

Augustine of Canterbury, St., d. ca. 605, apostle of the English and first archbishop of Canterbury. Pope Gregory the Great sent Augustine, a Roman monk, with forty companions as missionaries to the Anglo-Saxon pagans who had overrun Roman Britain. When his reluctant associates refused to follow Augustine any further than southern Gaul, he returned to Rome, and Gregory sent him back with letters appointing him their abbot. It is not clear when or where Augustine was consecrated bishop.

The mission arrived in Kent in 596 or 597. Bertha, queen of Kent, was a Frankish Christian princess, with a bishop in her household, but King Ethelbert remained unconverted, perhaps fearing that a Frankish mission would be followed by Frankish hegemony. Augustine soon baptized the king and many of the people, and Ethelbert gave him some surviving Roman churches in which to worship. Augustine established new sees in London and Rochester but was unable to reach an understanding with the remaining British Christians. Despite a pagan reaction in Kent after the death of Ethelbert in 616, the English church survived. Feast day: May 27. *See also* Canterbury; England, Catholicism in; Gregory I, "the Great," St.

Augustinian Canons, also Austin, Black, or Regular canons, originally cathedral clergy living different forms of the common life, who were reformed and united under the Rule of St. Augustine in the twelfth century. At the same time separate congregations of canons (diocesan priests who embraced community life under a kind of monastic rule) were established, including the Victorines and Premonstratensians, the latter being the largest group of such canons today. By the fifteenth century there were over forty-five hundred houses in Europe, their apostolic works including cathedrals, collegiate churches, parishes, hospitals, and schools. *See also* Augustine, Rule of St.; canons regular.

Augustinian Hermits, or Austin Friars, one of the four great medieval mendicant orders, still active today. Not to be confused with Augustinian Canons, these were groups of hermits brought together under the Rule of St. Augustine in the thirteenth century. Their apostolic rule encouraged a more active and urban involvement; some of their greatest members were scholars such as the theologian Giles of Rome and the canonist James of Viterbo. By the fifteenth century there were perhaps two thousand houses in Europe, though they declined in influence after the Reformation. Martin Luther belonged to the German Reformed Congregation. *See also* Augustine, Rule of St.; mendicant orders.

ST. AUGUSTINE OF HIPPO

Bishop of Hippo (North Africa) from 395 and Doctor of the Church, St. Augustine lived 354–430. No other single theologian has exercised as decisive an influence on the shape and character of Western theology, both Catholic and Protestant, as Augustine.

LIFE

The sources for Augustine's life are abundant. They include his *Confessions, Retractions, Letters,* and autobiographical passages in his early works. Possidius's (d. ca. 440) *Life of St. Augustine* is also important.

Augustine was born November 13, 354, at Tagaste in Numidia, North Africa, to Monica, a Christian, and Patricius, a pagan until just before his death in 372. He had a brother and at least one sister. His parents scraped funds together for his education, first at Tagaste, then at Madaura (where his studies were interrupted for a year due to lack of funds), and finally at Carthage. At the age of eighteen he took a concubine, to whom he was faithful for the next fifteen years. Adeodatus, their son, was born ca. 373.

Augustine of Hippo, author of the classics *Confessions* and *The City of God*; a fifteenth-century painting by Piero della Francesca, National Museum of Ancient Art, Lisbon.

At age nineteen, a reading of Cicero's *Hortensius* occasioned what must be regarded as a kind of religious conversion to wisdom or "philosophy." Augustine turned to Scripture, but finding it stylistically embarrassing and anything but philosophical, he joined the Manichees, who shared his abhorrence of the OT yet, like Augustine, thought of themselves as following Christ. They claimed to rely upon reason, not authority, and their absolute cosmic dualism seemed a satisfying explanation of the problem of evil.

Augustine returned to Tagaste to teach rhetoric ca. 375 but moved back to Carthage after the death of a friend (ca. 376). In 383 he sailed for Rome, seeking advancement; by the next year, through the good offices of his Manichaean connections and the pagan prefect of Rome, Symmachus, he was appointed professor of rhetoric in Milan, where the imperial court resided. Monica followed a year later, arranged a socially advantageous marriage for her son, and insisted on the dismissal of his concubine, who returned to Africa vowing celibacy. Augustine, however, was unable to wait the two years until his marriage and contracted another liaison.

Progressively disenchanted with Manichaeism, he came under the spell of a loosely connected circle of Christian Neoplatonists in Milan, the most prominent one being the bishop, Ambrose, whose sermons captivated Augustine with their eloquence and with their Origenistic style of allegorical exegesis. He became convinced that the OT was not as crude as he once had thought. After a short period of skepticism, his original teenage conversion to philosophy seemed finally to come to fruition when he was introduced to certain texts of Plotinus and/or Porphyry. Against the Manichees, they explained evil not as an eternal substance coexistent with God but as the privation or corruption of the good, in all respects equivalent with being. The highest level of being was immaterial, and the soul could attain to contemplation by ascending from things bodily, in themselves good, to an apophatic vision of the absolute immaterial Good underlying their form.

Further, Augustine heard stories of the monks and nuns in Italy and Egypt. He read Athanasius's *Life of Antony.* He became convinced that Christ had made the ascetic, philosophical life that Plotinus taught for a tiny few attainable for the many, educated and uneducated alike. Augustine decided to renounce marriage and career and seek Baptism. In August 386 he retired from teaching and withdrew to a villa at Cassiciacum, where, with his mother, brother, son, friends, and former students, he began what he thought would be his way of life from then on, a communal existence in leisured philosophical conversation. Here he wrote the dialogues *On the Happy Life, Against the Academics, On Order,* and the *Soliloquies.*

Returning to Milan in early 387, he took the catechetical course of Ambrose and was baptized at Easter. That same year his mother died and was buried at Ostia (her relics were transferred to Rome in 1430). Augustine returned to Tagaste where he established on his family's estates a quasi-monastic community of educated laymen, but visiting the port city of Hippo in 391, he was acclaimed by the congregation at church and forced to agree to ordination; in 395 he was consecrated bishop. There he presided, preaching, adjudicating cases referred to the bishop's tribunal, polemicizing, and living in community with his clergy, until his death during the siege of Hippo by the Vandals.

CONTROVERSIES

Augustine played a crucial role in three major controversies. Even before his ordination as priest he wrote two anti-Manichaean works, *On Genesis Against the Manichees* and *On the Catholic and Manichaean Ways of Life* (388–89), and he continued to produce such works well into his episcopacy, sometimes on the basis of actual public debate or as refutation of a written text (e.g. *Against Faustus,* 397–98). The *Confessions* (397–401) themselves may be regarded, in part, as one of Augustine's last—and greatest—anti-Manichaean works.

To the Manichees, the material world was the creation of the powers of evil, and procreation was therefore to be shunned. Augustine taught, on the contrary, the goodness of the Creator and of creation; that marriage was a positive good; and that even if virginity is a higher ideal,

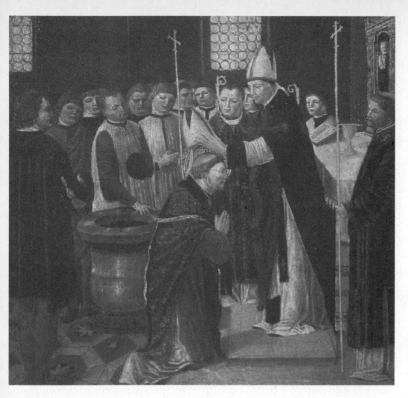

Augustine of Hippo, one of the two most influential theologians in the history of the Church (the other being Thomas Aquinas), being consecrated bishop of Hippo in North Africa in 395; sixteenth-century painting by Bergognone, Sabauda Gallery, Turin, Italy.

married persons may be more virtuous than their celibate counterparts. Further, the origin of evil is not to be located in a mythic realm of eternal darkness but is to be found in the perversity of the individual, created will, which freely turns away from God.

DONATISM

Upon Augustine's ordination to the priesthood he became immediately involved in the Donatist controversy, a dispute of long standing in the African church stemming from charges that the consecration of Caecilian as bishop of Carthage in 312 was invalid because one of the bishops consecrating him had handed over the Scriptures to persecutors. Since then the schismatic Donatist church had acquired majority status in North Africa as a kind of indigenous national church, claiming to be the true heir of the theology of Cyprian of Carthage. The Donatists insisted that the sacraments, and especially Baptism and Ordination, were valid only if the ministers of them were free of serious sin. They rebaptized Catholics who wanted to gain admittance to Communion.

Against this rigorist view of the Church as a society of the pure, Augustine argued that the sacraments belong to Christ and his Church, and that as such their validity does not depend upon the holiness of the minister, who may in any event have secret sins impossible to know, and that the Church is a mixed body of sinners, some progressing toward holiness, some lapsing away. Baptism is valid even if administered by a schismatic and need not be repeated upon entrance into the Catholic Church. Augustine further criticized the Donatists for their self-imposed status as a parochial church, separated not only from Rome but from all the other patriarchal sees. Unfortunately, he also gave his approval to the imperial "Edict of Unity" against the Donatists in 405, which made it impossible for Donatists to make valid wills, engage in litigation, or hold office. After the Council of Carthage in 411, at which the Donatist and Catholic bishops engaged in debate, the imperial commissioners decided in favor of the Catholics, and from January 412 the Donatists were declared heretics. Although Augustine argued against the death penalty, he endorsed the right and responsibility of Christian rulers to recall by civil measures those who err.

PELAGIANISM

The third major controversy of Augustine's career was just beginning in 411. Pelagius, a British monk whose spiritual teachings had attracted a following among the Roman aristocracy, had come to Hippo with other refugees fleeing the sack of Rome by Alaric in 410. When his associate Caelestius applied for ordination to the priesthood at Carthage, he was rejected and condemned for teaching, among other things, that all human beings were born with the same degree of freedom that Adam had enjoyed before his sin; that there were sinless people before Jesus; and that newborns did not need Baptism. Whether or not Pelagius himself had adopted such extreme conclusions, bound to be offensive to any North African, Catholic or Donatist, he did teach that perfection was both possible and imperative for human beings and that sufficient freedom to attain it was available to all. Grace was necessary as an aid to freedom, which had been "rusted over" by bad habit, but by "grace" Pelagius meant for the most part something external, the preaching of the law and the gospel. Pelagius found the *Confessions* wanting, an invitation to mediocrity and even fatalism.

Augustine, informed in 411 by his friend Marcellinus that Pelagius's ideas were spreading in Carthage, responded in 412 with *On the Spirit and the Letter,* perhaps the best statement of his position against Pelagianism. In Augustine's view the sin of Adam had vitiated human nature to such an extent that, although freedom of choice is retained, people are free only to sin, unable to love the good unless God's grace frees them. He observes quite simply that people are unable to force themselves to love anything, least of all the good; it is incoherent to speak of forced delight. And it is only God's grace, the Holy Spirit shedding charity abroad in people's hearts (Rom 5:5), that moves them to take delight in God such that they are freed to love and thus enjoy the good. Nor are they freed in one bold stroke of choice at Baptism; rather, they enter upon a long course of healing, a kind of convalescence of the heart resulting in an ever enlarging degree of charity. The elect are predestined by God's mercy from eternity to receive such grace; others continue on to the damnation incurred by complicity in sin, unable ever to want and love the good which would itself be their eternal reward.

CITY OF GOD

The results of Augustine's reflection on these controversies are integrated into his most comprehensive and mature work, the *City of God,* begun ca. 412 (completed only ca. 427) in response to charges arising from Alaric's sack of Rome in 410. Pagans alleged that Rome had fallen because the pagan imperial religion had been discontinued. Augustine replied that the rise and fall of empires was nothing unusual in the landscape of human history and went on to critique the character and content of the empire's ideals.

In the *City of God,* original sin appears as the sin of pride (Lat. *superbia*), which absolutizes the self as the criterion of value and valuation, assuming for it, in effect, the position of God. This primal sin, Augustine believes, is obsessively reenacted in every particular sin, but it is most clearly glimpsed and most fully realized in social structures of domination such as those of the pagan Roman Empire. Here the primal evil has been transferred from the mythological realm of Manichaean cosmology and the metaphysical realm of Neoplatonic speculation to the realm of time and history. Redemption has been accomplished in the same realm. The Word of God, by assuming the human being Jesus into unity with the Word's person on the basis of no previous merits, becomes incarnate in Jesus, who thus becomes the supreme instance of grace. His death out of love for sinners is his sacrifice, at once a supreme act of worship and God's supreme act of compassion.

In the Eucharist Christians are invited to be formed, by the worship/compassion that is the sacrifice of Christ, into a new communion or *societas.* Thus, in keeping with Augustine's anti-Donatist polemic, the sacrament is not dependent for its efficacy on the holiness of the minister; it is itself the true sacrifice of the Lord who invites persons to be "transformed by the renewing of [the] mind" (Rom 12:2; *City of God* 10.6) away from the world and its ambitions, away from the earthly city and toward the City of God. In its liturgical repetition the Eucharist becomes a locus of the sort of healing the necessity of which Augustine insisted upon, in opposition to the Pelagians.

Augustine of Hippo, one of the greatest Christian teachers and bishops of all time, whose primary theological focus was on the interaction of God's grace and human freedom, and the call to salvation.

AGAINST JULIAN

In other, later works these themes threaten to come unraveled. From ca. 420 Augustine engaged in increasingly bitter controversy with Julian, bishop of Eclanum in Italy, who in 418 refused to subscribe to Pope Zosimus's *Epistula Tractoria* condemning Pelagius. Julian accused Augustine of having elaborated such an exaggerated and physicalist notion of original sin (passed on hereditarily by the concupiscence that Augustine believed to be inevitably involved in intercourse) that he had in effect returned to Manichaeism with its denial of the good of marriage. And, despite Augustine's insistence that there is no salvation apart from Baptism, the objective efficacy of the sacraments seems almost to come undone in the shadow of his massive insistence on the necessity of a mysterious, predestined, and continual inner infusion of grace. He replied that we see so many horrors around us, crippled infants and disfiguring diseases, that, unless Julian is either insensitive or prepared to admit all such evils into paradise and God's original creative intention, we must ascribe them to God's wrath in response to original sin, or God's goodness and omnipotence cannot be defended against the Manichees.

Augustine's theological legacy is thus divided. Theologically, it includes a deep appreciation of the utterly gratuitous yet necessary character of grace; a thoroughgoing (and unprecedented) understanding of the socially mediated character of all aspects of the human being (including sexuality); a consequently thoroughgoing critique of dualistic anthropologies; and a refusal to accept the ugliness of natural and social evil as reflective of God's creative intentions. It includes too *On the Trinity* (ca. 399–ca. 420) and its influence on all subsequent discussions of trinitarian doctrine in the West; *On Christian Doctrine* (ca. 397, finished 426), which gave the Middle Ages an educational vision and mandate; and the immense *Enarrationes on the Psalms* and *Homilies on the Gospel of John,* which served as substrates for exegetes from the Carolingian period to the Renaissance and later. Yet Augustine's legacy also seems to have included a deep pessimism about the goodness of the sexual act as we know it and about the possibilities of human reformation (and *a fortiori,* perfection) in general. Some would claim that this, together with his approval of civil disciplinary measures against the Donastists, provided a blueprint for Christian regimes just as repressive as the pagan Roman Empire.

Perhaps the last word, however, should rest with the *Confessions.* In their psychological realism amounting almost to a phenomenology of subjectivity, they are a foundation stone for Western culture. Yet in their moving evocation of the absolute freedom and benevolence of God's grace, working through but ultimately independent from every cultural form and historical person, they present that grace to each generation as a kind of question mark, challenging all particular cultural forms and projects to resist the idolatry of self-deification. As such, the last word of Augustine's influence has yet to be spoken. Feast day: August 28.

See also Augustine, Rule of St.; Augustinians.

Bibliography

Bonner, G. *St. Augustine of Hippo: Life and Controversies.* Philadelphia: Westminster Press, 1963.
Brown, P. *Augustine of Hippo.* Berkeley, CA: University of California Press, 1967.
Chadwick, H. *Augustine.* Oxford and New York: Oxford University Press, 1986.
Guardini, R. *The Conversion of Augustine.* Chicago: Regnery, 1960.
Markus, R.A. *Saeculum, History and Society in the Theology of St. Augustine.* 2d. ed. Cambridge, Cambridge University Press, 1988.
Van der Meer, F. *Augustine the Bishop.* London: Sheed and Ward, 1961.   JOHN C. CAVADINI

Augustinianism, an approach to theology, rooted in the thought of Augustine of Hippo (d. 430), that gives primacy to the will and to love over the intellect and knowledge, as in Thomism. Augustinianism characterized the Franciscan theology of the twelfth and thirteenth centuries, especially that of Alexander of Hales, Bonaventure, and Duns Scotus. But Augustinianism has a negative meaning as well, also rooted in Augustine's theology, namely, an emphasis on human depravity brought about by the original sin of Adam and Eve and the incapacity of individuals to achieve salvation by their own effort. This type of Augustinianism holds that only because of the undeserved mercy of God will some members of the human community, the *massa damnata* (Lat., "damned mass"), be saved. Babies who die without Baptism are condemned to hell.

Even though these pessimistic elements in Augustine's writings were not fully representative of his outstanding theological achievements, they were incorporated into the theological perspective of the Protestant Reformers, especially Martin Luther and John Calvin, and the seventeenth-century French Jansenists, who placed great emphasis on the depravity of human nature and the moral consequences thereof. *See also* Augustine of Hippo, St.; Thomism.

Augustinians, popular name for the Order of Hermits of St. Augustine (OSA), a mendicant order spiritually linked to Augustine of Hippo (d. 430). Historical linkage with Augustine has never been established, but the order follows his rule, which calls for unity of heart and mind in God and living a common life according to the evangelical counsels.

During the eleventh and twelfth centuries, the Church attempted to regulate religious life and to organize and centralize the large number of groups that existed. Many independent penitential and eremitic communities at the time followed the Rule of St. Augustine. Pope Innocent IV united some of these groups into one order, the Tuscan Order of the Hermits of St. Augustine in 1243. The members of this "little union" were subsequently united with other groups into the Order of Hermits of St. Augustine by Pope Alexander IV in 1256. This "Grand Union" bound the groups under one prior general in Rome with provincial superiors ruling the various provinces.

By the beginning of the fourteenth century, the order had spread throughout Europe and as far as the Holy Land. They, like other mendicants, served in the active apostolate while maintaining community life and prayer. They numbered more than eight thousand, but during the Black Death more than five thousand members died.

The first constitutions directed the study of Scripture, the teachings of the Church, and the writings of Augustine. Augustine's teaching on the primacy of grace marks the theology developed by Augustinian theologians. Education of the members has been a high priority since the Grand Union. Gregor Mendel, the founder of the science of genetics, was an Augustinian.

Devoted to the Holy See, they defended the papacy repeatedly when it was attacked from within and from without. Augustinians held the office of papal chaplain from 1352 to 1991.

Martin Luther, too, was an Augustinian. While an unknown number of friars followed him, some of his staunchest opponents were Augustinians. In the post-Reformation period, monasteries in Protestant areas were confiscated and were forbidden to accept new members. The entire Augustinian province (territorial organization) in England was destroyed.

During the sixteenth century, Augustinians established missions in South America, the Philippines, India, China, Japan, Africa, and Iraq. Suppressions by civil powers in the eighteenth and nineteenth centuries completely destroyed the French province and decimated the order in other countries.

In 1794, the Irish province sent missionaries to the United States, and the new province was approved by Rome in 1796. Since that time other provinces have been established in the United States and Canada. In 1842, Augustinians established a college in Pennsylvania that eventually became Villanova University.

There are more than fifty congregations of sisters that participate in the heritage and tradition of the Augustinian order. Augustinian Cloistered Nuns (OSA) came to the United States from Spain in 1968.

Current apostolates of the Augustinians include secondary and higher education, parish ministry, and retreat work. North American provinces maintain missions in Peru and Japan. *See also* Augustine of Hippo, St.   *REGINA COLL*

Augustinians of the Assumption. *See* Assumptionists.

Augustinus, treatise on grace and human nature based on the most pessimistic writings of Augustine. Written by Cornelius Jansen and published posthumously (1640), *Augustinus* denied the natural ability of humankind to cooperate in its own salvation, providing a theological foundation for Jansenism. The Jesuits opposed its publication, claiming the book violated papal prohibitions on public discussion of these issues. *See also* Jansenism.

aumbry (awm'bree), also known as ambry, in a church, a niche or cupboard recessed into the sanctuary wall reserved for the storage of sacred vessels. Typically the aumbry houses the vessels containing the sacramental oils: chrism, the oil of the sick, and the oil of catechumens. Occasionally, as in the pre-Reformation churches of Scotland, the aumbry was used for the reservation of the Eucharist. Some modern church designs accord the aumbry a visual emphasis equal in comparison to the tabernacle.

aureole (Lat., "golden"), an artistic device consisting of a field of light surrounding the whole of a person (a halo surrounds the head only) used in ancient non-Christian and then in Christian art to symbolize the divinity or special status of the one so decorated. The aureole is also known by its Italian name, the *mandoria,* since it sometimes is in an almond shape. Christian artists have reserved the aureole for representations of the Trinity and Jesus and by extension to Mary, the Mother of Jesus. *See also* halo.

Australia, Catholicism in. The original Australian Catholics were Irish lay people under penal sentence who arrived as early as 1788 on a group of ships known as the First Fleet. In the penal settlement, lay faith survived until the coming of official chaplains in 1820. The first bishop, J.B. Polding, an English Benedictine, arrived in 1835. In the second half of the century, Irish secular clergy came into power. In 1885, an Irishman, Patrick F. Moran, third archbishop of Sydney, became a cardinal. By then, state financial aid to church schools had been withdrawn throughout most of Australia. Catholics decided to construct their own system, paid for and staffed by themselves. They relied on members of religious orders, principally women, to run the schools, which aimed to provide a place in the classroom for every Catholic child. Thus almost every Australian Catholic was influenced by religious sisters in parish schools. Secondary schools came later, often in central locations and, for boys, staffed by religious brothers. As the number of religious vocations declined after Vatican II (1962–65), the schools were administered by lay teachers. The reintroduction of state aid made this possible without the collapse of what had become an overextended system. To date, Catholic higher education has been minimal.

Catholics and Australian Society: The denial of state aid to their schools, often for openly secularist reasons, provided Catholics a continuing sense of grievance. Australian society was dominated by a British Protestant hegemony which held Irish Catholics at a disadvantage. Because Catholics made up about one-quarter of the total population, however, they exerted pressure on the dominant ideology by force of numbers. Their refusal to accept second-class status destabilized the British imperialist ethos, opening the way to a nationalist sentiment and modern multiculturalism. Catholic resistance generated debates about conscription for military service during World War I, the opposition being led by Catholics Thomas J. Ryan, premier of Queensland, and Daniel Mannix, second archbishop of Melbourne.

The size of the Catholic population and its grievances encouraged the development of the Church as an alternative society. Parish clubs offered a full round of social, dramatic, sporting and other activities, which matched the rich varieties of popular religion available in the sodalities and pious societies. Yet parish life did not force Catholics into isolation from Australian society; often it energized them to make a wider contribution. In a similar way, Catholic hospitals were never for Catholics only; sometimes the only hospitals available, they were open to all. They continue to be an important segment of Australian health care. Likewise, social services, such as the strong St. Vincent de Paul Society, were open to everyone. In politics Catholics found their natural home in the Australian Labor party, where they predominated. Most Catholic prime ministers—the first was James Scullin in 1929—have been Labor members. In recent years, as Catholics entered the middle class, they have become more prominent in non-Labor circles.

This involvement outside the Labor party was accelerated by events in church circles, where Catholic Action on Jocist (Young Christian Workers) models had begun in the 1930s. Growing Communist power within the trade union movement during World War II brought appeals to Catholic Action to develop an anti-Communist force. A lay intellectual, Bob A. Santamaria, fashioned a secret organization, known as The Movement, which had rapid success. Because of constitutional links between unions and the Labor party, The Movement's industrial victories gave it access to political power. Misuse of this power led to public recriminations and in 1955 Santamaria's followers formed their own party, the Democratic Labor party, which delivered Catholic votes to the non-Labor coalition. The political split was paralleled by a split in the Church, with only half of the dioceses continuing to officially recognize The Movement.

Developments in the Church: Bitterness over Church involvement in politics eased during the euphoria of Vatican II. In particular, liturgical reforms were quickly welcomed, although they were implemented in an authoritarian way. The rejection of the encyclical on birth control, *Humanae Vitae* (1968), showed that authority's grip on lay consciences was slipping. The growth of non-Irish Catholic traditions due to massive national immigration programs meant that Australian Catholicism was becoming pluralistic. Prayer groups and retreat houses have replaced parish sodalities. Feminism flourishes in the remaining convents, which provide significant nonepiscopal leadership. Intellectual life is predominantly literary (history, novels, poetry, films) rather than theological. Social change attracts individual radicals, such as the Aboriginal Shirley ("Mumshirl") Smith, rather than the mass of Catholics. The Catholic Church and its hierarchy are strongly committed to the education and defense of the rights of the Aboriginal population through such organizational vehicles as the Aboriginal and Islander Catholic Council. Having been evangelized by Catholic missionaries in the late nineteenth and early twentieth centuries, the Aborigines today constitute an important part of Australian Catholicism. Meanwhile, anti-Protestantism, once a social glue, is no more.   *EDMUND CAMPION*

Austria, Catholicism in. The Christianization of the area today known as Austria occurred in phases. It began through Roman soldiers, laborers, and merchants mostly in the cities, while rural population remained pagan. Florian, a Roman army officer serving in Noricum (Austria), was martyred in 304 after protesting the killing of Christians during Diocletian's persecution. He is patron saint today of Upper Austria. The so-called Edict of Milan (313) eased life for Christians throughout the Roman Empire, including Austria, but the ensuing migration of un-Christianized masses (known as the barbarian invasions) plunged the Church once again into darkness. In the eighth century Frankish and Irish-Scottish monks evangelized the area and founded numerous monasteries. The victory of Otto the Great over the Magyars in 955 was the end of Christianization and the beginning of the present-day organization of the Catholic Church. During the Reformation more than 80 percent turned Protestant. The House of Habsburg started its own counter-reformation, which brought spiritual renewal but also persecution, exile, and forced conversions. In 1527 and 1683 the Turks were turned back. Josef II's Decree of Tolerance eased conditions for Protestant and Orthodox Christians and for Jews. In the 1960s complete equality was legally established.

Protestantism, which for two hundred years survived in secret, today constitutes 4.9 percent of the population and is mostly Lutheran. Ten percent of the 7.8 million citizens declare themselves without religious affiliation. Eighty percent of the population is Catholic, divided into two church provinces (Vienna and Salzburg) with nine dioceses. Austria's liturgical and biblical renewal movements, led by Pius Parsch, influenced Vatican II. Cardinal Franz Koenig, archbishop of Vienna, was one of the council's leaders. Today, Catholicism in Austria is involved with ecumenical collaboration in works of charity, pastoral endeavors, and the media. Vienna in particular plays an important role as a bridge to the East.   *JACINTA VAN WINKEL*

authenticity of teaching, the authoritativeness that the Catholic Church attributes to the teaching of the pope and bishops in matters of faith and morals. Vatican II describes bishops as "authentic teachers, that is, teachers endowed with the authority of Christ, who preach to the people committed to them the faith they must believe and put into practice" (Dogmatic Constitution on the Church, n. 25). The phrase "endowed with the authority of Christ" makes it clear that the term "authentic" as used here does not mean "genuine," but "authoritative," and also indicates the source of this authority. This is further spelled out when the council states in the same document: "In matters of faith and morals, the bishops speak in the name of Christ and the faithful are to accept their teaching and adhere to it with a religious assent of soul. This religious submission of will and of mind must be shown in a special way to the authentic teaching authority of the Roman Pontiff, even when he is not speaking *ex cathedra*" (n. 25).

The term "authentic" is often used, as in the text

just cited, to denote the exercise of magisterium that is authoritative but not infallible. Other examples of this use of the term are found in canons 752 and 753 of the 1983 Code of Canon Law, which speak of authentic teaching by the pope or bishops that calls for "religious submission" on the part of the faithful, but not the firm assent that infallible teaching would require. *See also* magisterium.

authority, the power to command, exact obedience, enforce laws, judge conduct, etc. Religious authority, however, is a power to influence belief or conduct, but without coercion or threat of harm. Authority in the Catholic Church is based on the authority of Jesus himself and his commission to his disciples: "All authority in heaven and on earth has been given to me. Go therefore and make disciples of all nations, baptizing them in the name of the Father and of the Son and of the Holy Spirit, and teaching them to obey everything that I have commanded you. And remember, I am with you always, to the end of the age" (Matt 28:18–20) and on belief in the promise of the "Spirit of truth" (John 16:12–15). In the NT this authority is dispersed in a variety of gifts given to different persons—apostles, prophets, teachers, workers of miracles, healers, administrators, and those who speak in tongues—all of which were manifestations of the Spirit for the common good (1 Cor 12:4–31; Eph 4:11; Rom 12:6–8). These were all forms of service for the building up of the Body of Christ. Authority in the NT is service (Gk., *diakonia*). The apostles, among whom Peter and the Twelve (in whom Peter himself is numbered) are singled out, had particular authority as witnesses to the Resurrection and as the missionary founders of Christian communities. Thus, in later developments, apostolicity was a criterion of authority.

Historical Developments: With the death of the apostles, the various local communities organized themselves in diverse ways. The development of the threefold offices of bishop, presbyter, and deacon was gradual but widespread by the end of the second century. The authority of the bishop was emphasized but this was a spiritual authority and closely linked with the whole community, including the laity, who had a voice in selecting the bishop. It was also tied to the bishops' apostolicity, i.e., their continuity with the apostolic teaching.

When Christianity became the official religion of the Roman Empire in 380, bishops became men of public rank, administrators of justice, defenders of the poor, widows, and orphans. The authority of the Church became more secular and juridical and tended to become authority for its own sake, divorced from the spiritual gifts and from the influence of the community. The more charismatic or spiritual elements were kept alive by the growth of monasticism. Spiritual authority became separated from the hierarchical structure and was found in the holy "men of God," although many bishops were monks or men trained in a monastic tradition and lived accordingly.

The great reform movement of the eleventh century led by Pope Gregory VII attempted to free the Church from its identification with secular society and its domination by local rulers. The pope claimed for the Church a completely autonomous and sovereign system of rights proper to a spiritual society, including papal authority over kings and their kingdoms. This gave rise to the development of canon law and a more juridical notion of authority. From this time on, spiritual or charismatic authority was almost completely identified with the institutionalized offices of the Church.

The Middle Ages witnessed a growth of papal authority that has remained significant in Catholicism. Although some form of primacy had been accorded the Bishop of Rome in the early Church, the great popes of the fifth and sixth centuries such as Leo I (440–61), Gelasius I (492–96), and Gregory the Great (590–604), and of later centuries, especially Gregory VII (1073–85), enhanced the papal claims to supremacy and fullness of power over the universal Church. While asserting the rights of the Church and its legitimate autonomy from the secular powers, the medieval papacy also adopted many of the features of the imperial court, including the language, insignia, style and customs.

Although the centralizing and juridicizing of authority in the Church was the dominant trend from the eleventh to the fifteenth centuries, there were antiecclesiastical spiritual protest movements such as the Spiritual Franciscans, the Lollards, and the Hussites. The movement known as conciliarism, occasioned in part by the Avignon papacy and the Great Western Schism when there were two or more claimants to the papal throne (1378–1418), argued that ultimate authority in the Church lay with an ecumenical council rather than the papacy. These protests culminated in the Protestant Reformation of the sixteenth century.

The challenge to authority posed by the Reformers was a very basic one, since it was not just a questioning of authority in the historical form then existing, but a challenge to ecclesiastical authority in principle. The Reformers insisted that ultimate authority in the Christian community was to be found only in Scripture (Lat., *sola Scriptura*), not in hierarchical offices. The Catholic response at the Council of Trent (1545–63) and thereafter was to reemphasize unwritten tradition handed down from the apostles as complementing the canonical Scriptures. Subsequently, however, post-Tridentine theologians moved away from a quantitative conception of tradition as content and deposit handed on from the apostles, to an idea of tradition identified with the transmitting organism and residing above all in the magisterium of the Church. Since the sixteenth century, the Catholic Church has practiced a veritable "mystique" of authority, identifying the will of God with the institutional form of authority. In the latter it is God's voice we supposedly hear.

This mystique of authority reached its highwater mark with the definition of papal infallibility at the First Vatican Council in 1870. Since that council was unable to complete its work due to the outbreak of the Franco-Prussian War, an overemphasis on papal authority remained until the Second Vatican Council (1962–65).

Present Status: Conscious of the unfinished agenda of its predecessor, Vatican II deliberately set out to balance the definition of papal authority with a renewed emphasis on the authority of the bishops, individually and collectively (Dogmatic Constitution on the Church, *Lumen Gentium*, n. 18). It also resituated all authority in the larger context of the whole Church, the People of God. The council stressed that all hierarchical authority is "true service," which in the NT is significantly called *diakonia* (Gk.), or ministry (n. 24). It taught that bishops together with the Roman pontiff are successors to the apostles and as such constitute "one apostolic college," which has been manifested throughout history in synods and ecumenical councils. After repeating the definition of papal infallibility from Vatican I, the council taught that "The infallibility promised to the Church resides also in the body of bishops when that body exercises supreme teaching authority with the successor of Peter," either when gathered in an ecumenical council or dispersed around the world (n. 25). The council urged that the synodal and conciliar tradition "flourish with new vigor" and encouraged the formation of national and regional episcopal conferences (Decree on the Bishops' Pastoral Office in the Church, *Christus Dominus*, nn. 36–38).

Since Vatican II, this has in fact happened as evidenced by the significant meetings of the Conference of Latin American Bishops (CELAM) at Medellín, Colombia, in 1968; Puebla, Mexico, 1979; and Santo Domingo, Dominican Republic, 1992, and the pastoral letters on national issues of the National Conference of Catholic Bishops in the United States. Thus, authority in the Catholic Church today is more widely distributed than in the recent past. There has also been an attempt to recover the evangelical and charismatic character of authority as found in the early Church. *See also* magisterium.

Bibliography
Granfield, Patrick. *The Limits of the Papacy: Authority and Autonomy in the Church.* New York: Crossroad, 1987.
Reese, Thomas J., ed. *Episcopal Conferences: Historical, Canonical and Theological Studies.* Washington, DC: Georgetown University Press, 1989.
Todd, John M., ed. *Problems of Authority.* New York: Seabury, 1962.   T. HOWLAND SANKS

authority of Scripture. *See* Scripture, authority of.

Authorized Version of the Bible. *See* King James Bible.

autocephalous church (Gk., "himself/itself the head"), one of the Eastern Orthodox churches with canonical and administrative independence from any other church, as distinguished from an autonomous or self-governing church jurisdictionally subject to an external hierarch. Autocephalous churches are in theological, spiritual, and liturgical communion with other Orthodox churches but appoint their own primate bishop who may be a patriarch, archbishop, or metropolitan. Granted by a mother church and recognized by the patriarch of Constantinople, autocephaly can be lost through territorial absorption of a conquered nation with subsequent assimilation of autocephalous and autonomous churches in that territory into the conquering nation's Orthodox church.

auto-da-fé (ou-toh-dah-fay'; Port., "act of faith"), a solemn public ceremony of the Inquisition at which judgment was pronounced on heretics and other sinners. The auto-da-fé included a procession of the condemned along with the bones of dead miscreants and pictures of absent ones. A sermon, announcement of sentence, and public confession followed. A full range of penances were imposed. Heretics were handed over to the secular authority to be burned at the end of the ceremony. Heretics who recanted at the last moment were garroted in an act of mercy. The auto-da-fé took place in southern France, Italy, Portugal, Spain, and their colonies but disappeared after the middle of the eighteenth century. *See also* heresy; Inquisition.

auxiliary bishop, bishop appointed by the Holy See at the request of the diocesan bishop to assist him in the performance of his duties. Canon law recommends that he also be appointed vicar general or at least an episcopal vicar. *See also* bishop; diocesan bishop; titular bishop.

avarice, the excessive desire for wealth or possessions; one of the capital sins. The avaricious person regards material riches as ends in themselves rather than means toward a greater good. While wealth or possessions may be considered good things, even gifts from God, attachment to them above all else represents a perversion of values. Avarice is a serious vice because desire for possessions may well lead a person to commit other wrongs in order to gain more money or possessions. Avarice may be indirectly destructive in particular of the development and exercise of the virtues of charity and justice. *See also* capital sins; detachment; poverty.

Ave Maria (ah'vay mah-ree'ah). *See* Hail Mary.

Ave Maris Stella (ah'vay mah'ris stel'ah; Lat., "Hail, Star of the Sea"), anonymous hymn in honor of the Virgin Mary. Earliest copies date from the ninth century. Widely popular in the Middle Ages, it has been ascribed to Paul the Deacon and to Venantius Fortunatus, among others. It is still used in Marian offices. The first stanza reads:

> *Ave maris stella,*
> *dei mater alma*
> *atque Semper Virgo,*
> *felix caeli porta.*

> Praise to Mary, Heaven's Gate,
> Guiding Star of Christians' way,
> Mother of our Lord and King,
> Light and hope to souls astray. *See also* Marian devotions.

Averroism, Christian philosophical trend from thirteenth-century Paris. Named after Averroës, the most Aristotelian Islamic philosopher, Averroists generally defended Aristotle or common interpretations of Aristotle in matters affecting belief in Genesis, heaven and hell, and providence. They argued that the world has always existed in timeless dependence on God, that humans share a common intellect such that immortality is impersonal, and that God knows creatures universally, not particularly. Since they professed orthodox beliefs but judged them false according to philosophical principles, contemporaries accused them of positing a double truth, whereas they claimed to be simply defending the autonomy of distinct sciences. *See also* Aristotle.

Avignon (ahv-een-yohn'), city and archdiocese in southeastern France and the seat of the papacy from 1309 to 1377 (a period known as the "Babylonian Captivity" of the papacy) and of rival popes during the Great Schism (1378–1417). Clement V moved the papal court to Avignon because of the dangerous situation in Rome created by the Italian ambitions of the Holy Roman emperor Henry VII and the need to resolve the continuing enmity of King Philip VI of France toward the papacy after his conflict with Pope Boniface VIII. In 1378, Gregory XI transferred the court back to Rome, but the French cardinals rejected the move and elected a rival pope at Avignon, thus instigating the Great Schism.

Claims by some scholars that papal residence on French soil subjected the Church to French control have not generally been accepted. It was not unusual in medieval Europe for the papal court to reside outside of the persistently dangerous city of Rome. During the Avignon papacy, vastly increased expenditures required an overhaul of the Church's financial and judicial machinery, resulting in the most efficient governmental administration in Europe. *See also* Great Schism.

Ávila, St. Teresa of. *See* Teresa of Ávila, St.

Azor, John, 1535–1603, Jesuit moral theologian. His treatise on moral theology was organized according to the Ten Commandments instead of the virtues, as had been the traditional practice. *See also* Commandments, the Ten.

Azymites, (Gk., *azymos,* "unleavened bread"), name given by Greek Christians to Latin Christians at the time of the schism of 1054 because of the Latin use of unleavened bread in the celebration of the Eucharist, a practice regarded by the Greeks as unscriptural and tending toward heresy. *See also* bread, eucharistic; Communion, Holy.

B

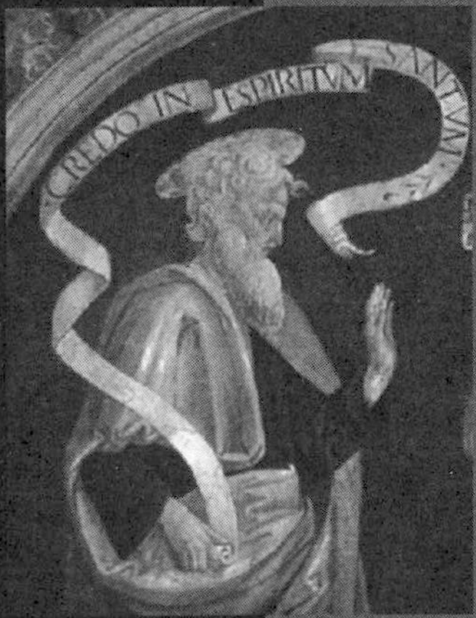

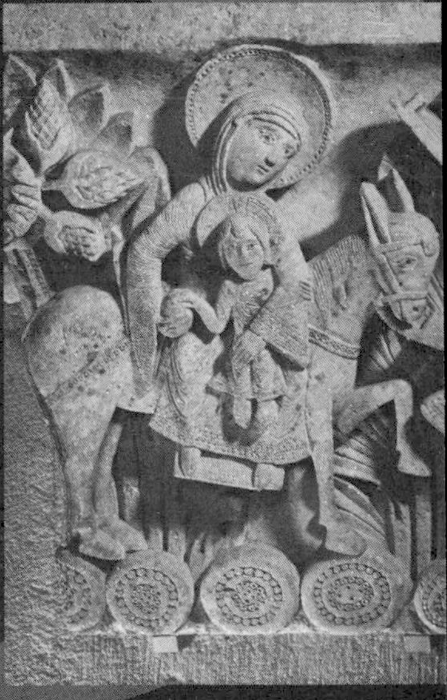

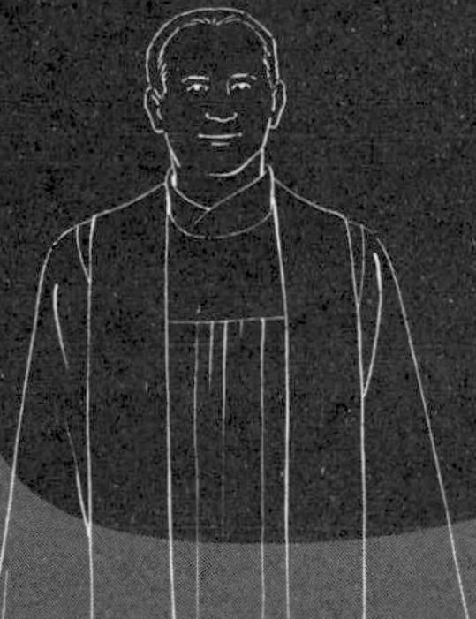

Baader, Franz von, 1765–1841, German philosopher of religion. After careers in engineering and medicine, Baader turned to philosophy. He composed romantic-idealist systems in which a history of humanity and the cosmos could be fashioned from areas as diverse as medieval mysticism, psychology, and chemistry. His thought anticipated cultural upheavals in Europe and served as an early stimulus to ecumenism among Christian churches.

Babel/Babylon (bay'buhl, bab'uh-lahn), a symbol for the oppressive power of Rome (as the center of the ancient Roman Empire) against Christians (1 Pet 5:13; Rev 14:8; 16:19; 17:5). Though the identification is never made directly, references like the "seven mountains" (Rev 17:9) leave little to the imagination. *See also* Rome.

Bacon, Roger, ca. 1213–ca. 1292, English Franciscan and scientist. One of the first to teach Aristotle's works at Paris, Bacon believed that all knowledge was implicit in Scripture and unfolded by philosophy and canon law and that knowledge was for the sake of doing good. To make possible the universal spread of Christianity, he sought to reform Christian learning by rejecting what he considered obsolete science, by using mathematical and experimental methods, and by studying Greek and Semitic tongues. His order condemned his teaching for unspecified novelties (perhaps the influence of the ideas of Joachim of Fiore); he never wrote more than sketches of his proposed synthesis. *See also* Aristotle; Joachim of Fiore.

Badin, Stephen T., 1768–1853, missionary priest, the first Catholic priest ordained in the United States. Born in France, Badin emigrated to the United States during the upheaval of the French Revolution. He continued his seminary studies in Baltimore and was ordained a priest by Bishop John Carroll in 1793. Badin then journeyed to Kentucky where he ministered to numerous Catholics living along the Kentucky, Tennessee, and Indiana frontier. He is regarded as one of the founders of Catholicism in these regions. He was also known for his stern ascetical understanding of Catholicism, which he sought to spread among the Catholic laity. In his later years he worked among Native Americans in the Michigan and Indiana regions. The land he acquired in northern Indiana became the site of the University of Notre Dame and he is buried on campus. *See also* Notre Dame, University of.

Baius, Michael (bi̯'uhs), also known as Michel de Bay, 1513–89, Belgian theologian. Rejecting the Scholastic formulation of doctrine, he preferred to appeal directly to Scripture interpreted in an Augustinian manner. Pope Pius V's condemnation (1567) of seventy-nine articles drawn from Baius's writings along with the later condemnation of Jansenism gave formal expression to Catholic suspicions of Augustine's teachings on sin, grace, and redemption, suspicions that had their origin in the Augustinianism of Luther, Calvin, and other Protestant Reformers. Some of the more important of Baius's condemned positions were: Fallen humans are determined to evil unless filled with God's charity. Charity is a transitory impulse (and not an habitual gift) of God; it is the sole source of good works. Humans are not free even when filled by God's grace. Concupiscence, even when one acts unwittingly, is sin. All the works of unbelievers are sin. Baius recanted his views and died in communion with the Church. *See also* Augustine of Hippo, St.; Jansenism.

Baker, Augustine, 1575–1641, English Benedictine spiritual writer. A lawyer by training, Baker converted to Catholicism in 1603 and shortly thereafter became a Benedictine monk. His treatises, based on the teaching of the fourteenth-century English and Rhenish mystics and the later mystics of France and Spain, were posthumously edited and published under the title *Sancta Sophia* (1657).

baldachino (bahl-duh-kee'noh), a covering or canopy built over an altar. The papal altar in St. Peter's Basilica features a famous baldachino designed by the sculptor Bernini. The term is also used for the ceremonial canopy that was carried over clerics, especially when a priest carried the Blessed Sacrament to the sick, or in procession on a feast day like Corpus Christi. This latter is also called an *ombrellino* (It.). *See also* canopy.

Baldwin of Canterbury, d. 1190, Cistercian, archbishop of Canterbury, canonist, and author of a treatise on the Eucharist. The first archbishop of Canterbury to extend the supremacy of his see over Wales, he preached the Third Crusade, on which he died. *See also* Canterbury; Crusades.

Balthasar, Hans Urs von, 1905–88, Swiss Catholic theologian and cardinal. Having studied at the universities of Vienna, Berlin, and Zurich, he completed his doctorate in Germanistics and philoso-

Bernini's famous baldachino over the high altar in St. Peter's Basilica, Vatican City.

phy in 1928, with a dissertation titled, "The History of the Eschatological Problem in Modern German Literature." In 1929, he entered the Jesuits, with whom he studied philosophy in Pullach near Munich from 1931 to 1933, and theology in Lyons (Fourvière) from 1933 to 1937. At Pullach, Balthasar came into contact with Erich Przywara (d. 1972) and at Lyons with Henri de Lubac (d. 1991), both of whom were to have a decisive impact on his thinking (although neither of them was actually his teacher). Przywara's work on the analogy of being was the focus of a widely publicized discussion between Przywara and the Reformed theologian Karl Barth. Balthasar's *Karl Barth* (1951) is an attempt—"joyfully welcomed and approved" by Barth himself—to bring about a rapprochement between Barth and the Catholic tradition concerning the relation between what is called the "analogy of faith" and the "analogy of being." Barth's Christocentrism exercised a lasting influence on Balthasar, though there remained differences between the two regarding the place of philosophical reflection in Christianity. With de Lubac, Balthasar said, he found his "theological home": here he discovered the spirituality-theology of the Church Fathers; the sense of the paradox of the human, according to which the human person is constitutively oriented to grace (the God of Jesus Christ), even as this grace

remains absolutely undeserved; and the sense of the catholicity of the Church, and of the Church as *communio* (Lat., "community").

In 1940, given the choice of going either to Rome as a professor at the Gregorian University or to Basel as a chaplain to students, Balthasar chose the latter. Here also began Balthasar's activities as an editor of the "European Series" of the Klosterberg collection, for which he prepared anthologies and did translations. Also at this time (1940), Balthasar met the physician Adrienne von Speyr (1902–67), who became a Catholic under his spiritual direction. The association with von Speyr, whose work Balthasar insisted could not be separated from his own, led in 1945 to the founding of the women's branch of the Community of St. John. Balthasar stressed that this "secular institute" was more important to him than his own writing (though he wrote over 100 books!). At the heart of his theology lay an insistence on the Church's intrinsic openness to the world, and on the role of the laity in realizing the presence of the Church in the world. In 1947, he established the Johannes Verlag, a publishing house whose purpose was to make available the writings of von Speyr and of the Catholic tradition more generally. Also in 1947 began the discussions and painful period of discernment that led to Balthasar's decision to leave the Jesuits in 1950 because the order could not assume responsibility for the Community of St. John. In 1972, together with Jean Daniélou, Henri de Lubac, Joseph Ratzinger, and others, Balthasar founded *Communio: International Catholic Review*. Its purpose was to assist with the theological-spiritual renewal called for at the Second Vatican Council, and to provide a more conservative counterpoint to the international journal *Concilium*.

The writings of what may be called Balthasar's "second creative period" find their center in his trilogy, published in fifteen volumes (1961–87): *Herrlichkeit (The Glory of the Lord)*, *Theodramatik (Theo-Drama)*, and *Theologik (Theo-Logic)*. The trilogy is organized in terms of the transcendentals: "A being *appears*, it has an epiphany: in that it is beautiful and makes us marvel. In appearing it *gives* itself, it delivers itself to us: it is good. And in giving itself up, it *speaks* itself, it unveils itself: it is true (in itself, but in the other to which it reveals itself)" ["A Résumé of My Thought," in *Hans Urs von Balthasar: His Life and Work*, edited by David L. Schindler, San Francisco: Ignatius Press, 1991, p. 4]. Balthasar's theology of mission, the centerpiece of his work, is found in *Theodramatik* (II/2). Balthasar insisted that his "theological aesthetics" was not a dispensable theological byroad, but perhaps the one possible way to escape the limitations of the more commonly used cosmological and anthropological methods. At the heart of Balthasar's aesthetics lies the love—the "being permitted to be"—which "cannot be surpassed by any additional insight into the laws and necessities of the world" (*The Glory of the Lord,* p. 633).

Bibliography

Kehl, Medard, and Werner Löser, eds. *Hans Urs von Balthasar: The Von Balthasar Reader.* New York: Crossroad, 1982.

DAVID L. SCHINDLER

Baltic countries, Catholicism in the. Christianity was brought to the Baltic peoples by invasion and domination by German knights. Throughout history the political status of these countries played an important role in their religious development. The Christianization of Latvia and Estonia (formerly Livonia) came at the hands of the Livonian branch of the Teutonic Knights late in the twelfth century. Lithuania, whose religion was rooted in animism (a deification of nature), was the last European country to accept Christianity. The actual date of its conversion is disputed. Mindaugas, the first grand duke, was baptized in 1251 and accepted a royal crown from the pope in 1253. However, after his assassination in 1263, Christianity was tolerated but the native population returned to the pagan customs of its ancestors. Not until 1386 was a deliberate effort made toward the nation's reconversion.

Both Latvia and Estonia had been influenced by northern European Protestantism; Lithuania, by central and eastern European Catholicism. After conquering Slavic territory, Lithuania became a cultural battleground between the Latin rite and the Orthodox traditions of the East Slavs. Resolution favoring the Latin rite came in 1386. Catholicism flourished in Lithuania under a two-hundred-year shared monarchy with Poland, but with it also came the Polish nobility's dominion over Lithuania.

In 1795 Russia conquered all three Baltic countries. By 1865 the Latin rite was curtailed in Lithuania, and a Lithuanian national movement was subsequently formed as part of the struggle for religious freedom. Meanwhile, as a result of successful Russian Orthodox proselytizing and a strong German-dominated Lutheran church, Latvia and Estonia did not suffer as great a persecution as Lithuania. Following World War I Latvia, then 24 percent Catholic, signed a concordat with the Holy

See in 1922, and Lithuania signed one in 1927. Estonia, with only 0.2 percent Catholics, maintained official diplomatic relations.

In June 1940, the Soviets occupied all three countries. The religious life of the people was completely disrupted. Orthodox congregations were created with total allegiance to the patriarch of Moscow. All other ecclesiastical buildings were confiscated, the clergy were persecuted, and all religious instruction was prohibited. Church holidays were abolished, and clergy and congregations were assessed extra taxes, rents, and utility fees.

With the Nazi takeover in June 1941, these countries experienced yet another form of oppression. The churches came under the control of the Nazi commissar. In 1944 the Soviet oppression was reimposed. One-third of all priests in Lithuania and Latvia were deported. In Lithuania Catholic literature was banned (until 1956). Between 1954 and 1968, national cultures reemerged. Atheistic propaganda was toned down. Two bishops were named in Lithuania and 130 priests returned from deportation. However, in 1957 another campaign was waged against religious freedom. Once again churches were closed, and secular holidays replaced Christian feasts.

During the winter of 1989–90, inspired by Soviet President Gorbachev's policy of *glasnost* (Russ., "openness"), the Baltics once again rebelled against Soviet domination. Lithuania, first under Algirdas Brazauskas and then Vytautas Landsbergis, declared its independence from the Soviet Union.

Over these turbulent years, Latvians and Estonians sustained a strong Lutheran tradition. In Latvia in 1994 there were a half-million Catholics, or less than 20 percent of the total population. In Estonia, however, a recent estimate placed the number of Catholics at only three thousand. Although forcibly deprived of priestly leadership and places of worship, the Lithuanians held on to their Catholic faith, with its rituals, processions, lanterns, and incense. Following this history of oppression, Lithuania claimed in 1994 over 2.5 million Catholics, about 80 percent of the total population. There were two archdioceses and four dioceses. Since the Communist regime was ousted, baptisms once again abounded and Catholic life entered a renewed phase of existence.

BEVERLY M. BRAZAUSKAS

Baltimore, councils of, the seven provincial councils of 1829, 1833, 1837, 1840, 1843, 1846, and 1849, and the three plenary councils of 1852, 1866, and 1884, in which the hierarchy of the U.S. Catholic Church addressed various pastoral challenges facing the young Catholic community in America. These councils had their remote origin in the decree of the Council of Trent (1545–63) that provincial councils, the formal meetings of the bishops of an ecclesiastical province, be held every three years.

A plenary council is composed of bishops from more than one ecclesiastical region. Laws promulgated in its sessions bind the dioceses represented in the plenary council, whereas provincial council legislation affects only the territory of that ecclesiastical province. From 1808 until 1846, Baltimore functioned as the only ecclesiastical province in the United States. Therefore, the first seven provincial councils of Baltimore were practically, though not formally, plenary councils of the United States. It was the responsibility of the bishop of Baltimore to convene councils. Though Bishop John Carroll convoked a provincial council in 1812, the meeting was not held and neither of his successors, Leonard Neale nor Ambrose Marechal, called a council. The persistent urging of John England, bishop of Charleston, South Carolina, convinced Archbishop James Whitefield, Marechal's successor, to convene the First Provincial Council of Baltimore (1829). Six bishops and the apostolic administrator of Philadelphia attended, as well as three lawyers, including the future Chief Justice of the Supreme Court, Roger B. Taney. Taney and his colleagues furnished advice concerning questions of legal incorporation. The decrees of the council reflected the concerns of the U.S. church in regard to the sacramental life of the Church, trusteeism, priestly conduct, the need for Catholic publications, a uniform catechism, and the establishment of Catholic schools. The Second Provincial Council (1833) issued decrees that determined boundaries of dioceses, the process for episcopal appointments, and called for the establishment of seminaries. The next five provincial councils (1837, 1840, 1843, 1846, and 1849), presided over by Archbishop Samuel Eccleston, continued to confront the problems of the growing immigrant Church. Many of the decrees reiterated the legislation of the past but also addressed the anti-Catholicism of the era; they warned against the perils of secret societies, the dangers of the public schools and mixed marriages.

The First Plenary Council met in 1852; six archbishops, twenty-seven U.S. bishops, and the Canadian bishop of Toronto attended. Francis P. Kenwick, archbishop of Baltimore, served as apostolic delegate. The council decreed that the legislation from the seven provincial councils extended to all U.S. dioceses. Though the nation grappled with the issue of slavery, the council made no statement about that impending crisis. The intent of the Second Plenary Council (1866) was to show the unity of Catholics in the aftermath of the Civil War and to respond to the needs of emancipated blacks. Once again, the council proclaimed the indispensability of parochial schools and encouraged parish missions and devotional practices. Archbishop James Gibbons convened the Third Plenary Council (1884); seventy-two prelates attended. The council's decrees called for a Catholic university, a uniform catechism (the *Baltimore Catechism*), aid to blacks and Native Americans, and better seminary and clergy education, and mandated the establishment of parochial schools. The councils of Baltimore created a strong diocesan organization, brought uniformity to church discipline and worship, and strengthened ties to Rome. *See also* Baltimore Catechism; parochial school; seminary; trusteeism, lay; United States of America, Catholicism in the.   JANET WELSH

Baltimore Catechism, catechism approved by the archbishop of Baltimore, Cardinal James Gibbons, on April 6, 1885, as the official text for the religious instruction of Catholic children in the United States. It remained the standard catechism in the United States until the Second Vatican Council (1962–65).

Historical Background: Martin Luther introduced to the Western world of the sixteenth century a concise, question-and-answer handbook of Christian doctrine known as a catechism. This new literary genre served as an influential and effective instrument for spreading the teachings of the Protestant Reformation. The Catholic Church emulated this method of instruction, and the catechism became a basic educational tool of Catholics for the next four hundred years. Peter Canisius (d. 1597), a Dutch Jesuit, produced the first major catechism for Catholics, *Summa Doctrinae Christianae* (1555), and later composed two other works designed for children. The Council of Trent (1545–63) mandated the writing of a catechism for clergy to assist their teaching and preaching. At the end of the sixteenth century, Italian Jesuit Robert Bellarmine (d. 1621) composed a catechism that was strongly endorsed by church authorities for the next several centuries. Catechisms were written for the Catholic population of various European nations; Edmund Auger (d.

1591) composed a manual for the Church of France; Jerome Ripalda (d. 1618) and Gaspar Astete (d. 1601) wrote catechisms for the Spanish church. English-speaking Catholics learned from catechisms written by Lawrence Vaux (d. 1585), Henry Turberville (d. 1678), and Richard Challoner (d. 1781). The archbishop of Cashel, James Butler, produced a catechism for the Catholics of Ireland, a manual marked by its apologetic and defensive tone.

John Carroll (d. 1815), the first bishop of the United States, looked to the European catechisms for assistance. The "Carroll Catechism" (1785), used in the United States in the late eighteenth and nineteenth centuries, was not written by Carroll but approved by him. This catechism reveals a dependence upon the English tradition of Vaux, Turberville, and especially Challoner. Like the Challoner manual, the first questions posed in the Carroll Catechism were: "Who made you?" and "Why did God make you?"

The nascent U.S. Catholic Church embraced many catechisms for the religious education of its people; local bishops adapted and edited versions of the European catechisms to meet the needs of their dioceses. In 1827, Ambrose Marechal, archbishop of Baltimore, suggested to John England, bishop of Charleston, South Carolina, that the United States needed a common catechism. He also wrote to Cardinal Cappellari, prefect of the Sacred Congregation de Propaganda Fide (Propagation of the Faith), that he feared the multiplicity of catechisms in the United States. Marechal was critical of England's catechism, as well as the works of Bishop Henry Conwell of Philadelphia and the controversial priest, William Hogan. The First Provincial Council of Baltimore (1829) addressed the catechism issue; it forbade the use of unapproved catechisms and mandated that a catechism for all dioceses be prepared and issued with the approbation of Rome. The Propaganda Fide insisted that the American catechism be based upon the Bellarmine Catechism. However, no uniform catechism appeared and the following six councils of Baltimore gave no attention to the common catechism.

After the First Council of Baltimore, record numbers of Irish and German immigrants swelled the Catholic population of the nation. Many Protestants feared this influx of Catholics; U.S. Catholics worried about the religious life of the newcomers. The First Plenary Council of Baltimore (1852) recommended a uniform catechism for the U.S. Church; *A General Catechism of the Christian Doctrine* was prepared and issued, but it did not satisfy all the bishops, and the episcopal practice of diocesan catechisms continued. The Second Plenary Council (1866) reiterated the importance of the single catechism but the established catechisms prevailed. The push for a standard catechism was not only the concern of the U.S. Church. At the First Vatican Council (1869–70) there was more debate concerning a universal catechism than papal infallibility. The council voted in favor of the universal catechism, but implementation of the proposal never materialized and the question of the universal catechism did not surface again until the late twentieth century.

The Origin of the Baltimore Catechism: Eight months prior to the Third Plenary Council, James Gibbons, archbishop of Baltimore, informed his colleagues that the council's agenda included the question of the uniform catechism. He appointed Joseph S. Alemany, archbishop of San Francisco, to chair a catechism committee composed of six bishops. Gibbons instructed the committee to consider: (1) the expediency of adopting a uniform catechism; (2) its name; and (3) whether the manual should be translated into other languages or other catechisms should be adopted for non-English-speaking Catholics. The Third Plenary Council convened on November 9, 1884; the catechism committee met in special session on November 11. After this meeting the size of the committee was increased and it met again in two special sessions. At this time, Reverend Januarius De Concilio, pastor of St. Michael's Parish in Jersey City and former Seton Hall philosophy and theology professor, accepted the task of writing a catechism. The Italian-born priest spent approximately one week composing the first draft of the manual. Later when the catechism suffered severe criticism, De Concilio minimized his participation in its composition. This hurriedly prepared text was submitted to the plenary session on December 6. The council closed the next day, so the galley proofs of the catechism received little attention. The committee requested that the prelates study the manual and send their suggestions to John L. Spalding, bishop of Peoria. From the end of the council until January 25, 1885, Spalding stayed in New York with the Paulist Fathers. During that time Spalding and De Concilio worked on the catechism; on February 23, Spalding reported to Gibbons that he had received "suggestions from all the archbishops concerning the catechism and have made such changes as seemed desirable." Cardinal John McCloskey of

New York gave his imprimatur to the manual on April 6; on that same day, Archbishop Gibbons issued approval for *A Catechism of Christian Doctrine, Prepared and Enjoined by the Order of the Third Plenary Council of Baltimore*. The catechism, 72 pages in length, consisted of 421 questions and answers in 37 chapters and followed the sequential order of the *Roman Catechism:* creed, sacraments, commandments. Spalding, however, was not satisfied with the catechism, and in September 1885 he revised it. He reduced the text to 208 questions in 33 chapters and rearranged and altered the context of the questions. This abridged edition, known as *Baltimore Catechism No. 1,* was not so widely used as the original text. Like the catechisms utilized prior to the Third Plenary Council, the *Baltimore Catechism* relied upon other manuals. Only 49 questions and answers are unique to the *Baltimore Catechism*.

Evaluation of the Baltimore Catechism: At the last session of the Third Plenary Council, several bishops questioned the quality of the proposed catechism. Archbishop Sebastian G. Messmer of Milwaukee recalled that "To several objections raised at the last meeting that the proposed catechism was very imperfect, in fact inferior, answer was made that uniformity was more important and that quite evidently many improvements were to be made in the course of time as experience would show the present deficiencies." Between September 1885 and October 1886 the German periodical *Pastoral Blatt* published nine articles against the new catechism. The anonymous author criticized the text for both its pedagogical and theological ineptitude. The catechism, according to the author, was unsuitable for children because of its incomprehensible language, the number of yes/no questions (91), the manual's size, and its monotonous style. The author pointed out the theological weaknesses of the text; the catechism considered the Resurrection, the central mystery of faith, in one question—"On what day did Christ rise from the dead?" Divine Providence and the Holy Spirit received scant attention. Although this evaluation of the *Baltimore Catechism* was valid, the other catechisms of the era merited similar assessments. The archbishops met in 1896 and established a committee to revise the *Baltimore Catechism,* but no action was taken. By the turn of the century, fifteen new catechisms had appeared, all approved by local bishops. The Baltimore Catechism endured more than fifty years of criticism before it was finally revised. Archbishop Edwin V. O'Hara, founder of the National Catholic Rural Life Conference and champion of the Confraternity of Christian Doctrine, spearheaded the movement for the catechism's revision. In 1936, O'Hara, representing the episcopal conference, invited theologian Francis J. Connell to organize and synthesize the bishops' recommendations for the revision of the catechism. After four drafts, *The Revised Baltimore Catechism* made its debut in 1941. Three versions went to press; one for young children, a second for first communicants, and a fuller rendition for adults. The revised edition consisted of 515 questions in 38 chapters. It ordered the questions according to creed, commandments, and sacraments. This sequential pattern differed from the original *Baltimore Catechism,* the *Roman Catechism,* and the catechetical practice of the early Church. The *Baltimore Catechism* prevailed as a dominant catechetical tool in the U.S. Catholic Church until the Second Vatican Council (1962–65). *See also* Baltimore, councils of; catechism; Catechism of the Catholic Church; United States of America, Catholicism in the.

Bibliography

Bryce, Mary Charles. *Pride of Place: The Role of the Bishops in the Development of Catechesis in the United States.* Washington, DC: The Catholic University of America Press, 1984.

Ellis, John Tracy. "Episcopal Vision in 1884 and Thereafter." *U.S. Catholic Historian* 4 (1985): 197–222.

Sharp, John K. "How the Baltimore Catechism Originated." *Ecclesiastical Review* 81 (December 1929): 573–586. JANET WELSH

Bañez, Domingo, 1528–1604, Spanish Dominican theologian. One of the most promising proponents of the Spanish revival of Thomism at Salamanca, Bañez was the defender and spiritual director of Teresa of Ávila. As professor of theology in Salamanca after 1581, he continued the tradition set by Francisco de Vitoria of defending the Indians. Bañez's rejection of Luis de Molina's theology of divine grace encountering human free will through a "middle knowledge" led to the famous controversy *De Auxiliis. See also De Auxiliis;* grace.

Banneaux, Our Lady of (bahn-oh'), a title for the mother of Jesus taken from apparitions in 1933 to Mariette Beco, of Banneaux, Belgium. These visions were seen as a verification of the Beauraing apparitions. Banneaux became a popular pilgrimage site. In 1942 the local bishop authorized a cult to Our Lady of Banneaux. *See also* apparitions of the Blessed Virgin Mary; Beauraing, Our Lady of.

banns of marriage, announcement of an intended marriage, made in order to help ascertain that both parties are free to marry. The number and method of such announcements are to be regulated by the national conference of bishops in any given territory (can. 1067). *See also* marriage law.

Bapst, John, 1815–87, Swiss-born Jesuit missionary. He was ordained a priest in 1846. After arrival in America in 1848, he ministered to Native Americans in Maine's Jesuit missions. He was the victim of nativist violence at Ellsworth, Maine, in October 1854, when he was tarred, feathered, and ridden on a rail following a controversy about Bible-reading in local schools. He later served as first president of Boston College and superior of the New York–Canada Jesuit mission. In later years, he was haunted by memories of the Ellsworth incident.

baptismal font, a water receptacle where the sacrament of Baptism is celebrated. According to present Church guidelines fonts should allow for immersion of infants at least, and the pouring of water over the entire body of a child or an adult. The Book of Blessings sees portable fonts as exceptional substitutes for stationary ones, which must be con-

A marble baptismal font in the right aisle of the basilica of Aquileia, Italy.

structed out of a suitable material and be clean and beautiful. The water should be running and heated where climate necessitates. There are three possible locations: a separate baptistery, near the entrance of the church, or in the community's midst. *See also* Baptism; baptistery.

baptism of blood, a substitute for the sacrament of Baptism in the case of unbaptized adults who are martyred for the faith. Thomas Aquinas held that death for Christ produced the same effect as the sacrament of water. All of the person's sins are remitted, and one is given title to eternal life.

Baptism of blood is only a sacrament by analogy (it is "like" the sacrament of Baptism). It reminds us, however, that faith is always more important than a sacramental ritual. The sacrament is a sign of faith. Without faith, the sacrament is without effect. *See also* Baptism; martyr; martyrdom.

baptism of desire, a substitute for the sacrament of Baptism in the case of adults of goodwill who, through no fault of their own, did not receive the sacrament. According to the Council of Trent (1545–63), an unbaptized person can achieve eternal salvation by the *votum* (Lat., "desire") for Baptism. The desire is to lead a good and upright life, even though one does not know the gospel of Christ and of his Church (Vatican II, Dogmatic Constitution on the Church, n. 16). The most obvious example of baptism of desire is the case of a catechumen who dies before receiving the actual sacrament of Baptism. The more general example is that of a morally upright person who is never given the opportunity, or sees the need, for accepting Jesus Christ as savior. *See also* Baptism; universal salvific will of God.

baptistery, "the area where the baptismal font flows or has been placed. It should be reserved for the sacrament of Baptism and should be a place worthy for Christians to be reborn in water and the Holy Spirit. It may be situated in a chapel either inside or outside the church or in some other part of the church easily seen by the faithful; it should be large enough to accommodate a good number of people" (*Christian Initiation: General Introduction,* 1973, n. 2274). The Code of Canon Law says that every parish is to have a baptismal font (can. 848). A study of baptisteries from the third century until the present, along with the accompanying rites of Baptism, provides a thorough understanding of the sacrament. *See also* Baptism.

BAPTISM

Baptism is the sacrament by which one becomes a member of the Christian community. The origin of the word is from the Greek *baptein*, "to dip, to immerse." Classical Greek used it figuratively as "being overwhelmed," e.g., with suffering. This sense is reflected in Mark 10:38–39 where Christ and the apostles are "baptized" with suffering. The NT uses the term in a technical sense to refer to the religious ceremony of baptism.

BAPTISM IN THE BIBLE

2 Kgs 5:14 relates the story of Naaman, commander of the army of the king of Aram, who immersed himself seven times in the Jordan. The Fathers of the Church would later interpret this gesture to be quasi-sacramental.

For Jews the Torah prescribed ritual baths in the context of purification from ritual impurities: e.g., after touching a corpse (Num 19:19) or after being cured of leprosy (Lev 14:8–9). Thus purified, one was fit for worship. An extension of this concept can be seen in the practice of proselyte baptism required of gentile converts to Judaism. Shortly before NT times, such converts were initiated with rituals of circumcision, baptism, and sacrifice. These rituals made them legally pure and bestowed juridical incorporation as full-fledged Israelites.

The Qumran sect practiced many ritual ablutions. The *Manual of Discipline* points out that such baths cannot cleanse a person. Only with personal submission to God can perversity be removed and the Spirit of truth come alive. The ritual bath was a token of the sincere inner disposition of the person. While a connection with the baptism of John the Baptist is not excluded, there are marked differences.

The baptism of John, not conferred primarily on Jews, had a unique moral character to it, although it did not produce anything of and by itself. It was called in the Gospels (Mark 1:4; Luke 3:3; Matt 3:11) a baptism of repentance for the forgiveness of sins. John asked for a confession of sins and a manifest conversion; he sought moral purity. John expected his baptism to be superseded; it was provisional, as Matt 3:11 indicates. John expected someone to surpass him who would baptize with the Holy Spirit and with fire. This messianic baptism would inaugurate a new world.

Acts points out that the baptism of John, in contrast to that of Jesus, did not confer the Spirit (1:5; 11:15–16; 19:1–6). Jesus' submission to John's baptism did not indicate his sinfulness but his union with sinful humanity (John 1:32–34). The synoptic accounts (Matt 3:13–17; Mark 1:9–11; Luke 3:21–22) see this as the inauguration of the messianic mission of Jesus. The voice of the Father and the appearance of the Spirit as

The baptism of Paul by the disciple Ananias in Damascus following Paul's dramatic conversion experience on the way to the city (Acts 9:10–19); mosaic in the Palatine Chapel, Palermo, Sicily.

a dove mark the proclamation of the sonship of Jesus as his investiture with the Spirit, which fulfills the prophecies (Isa 11:2; 42:1; 61:1). Tradition has seen this as the prototype of Christian baptism inasmuch as the believer becomes a child of God through the gift of the Holy Spirit.

Matt 28:19–20 records the postresurrectional mandate of the Lord to preach the gospel to all nations, teaching them to observe all that Jesus commanded, in effect making new disciples. Mark 16:15–16, while more reserved than Matthew, stresses the condition of faith for baptism. Both passages contain the commission to baptize. While the explicit formula in Matthew might come from the liturgy of the Church, the commandment to baptize and the central meaning of baptism come from Jesus. From its earliest days, the Church celebrated baptism.

John 3:1–21 describes baptism in water and the Spirit as a rebirth from above by the work of God the Father. The clearly formulated necessity of baptism in the Fourth Gospel seems rooted in the actual experience and practice of the apostolic Church.

Acts relates the practice of administering baptism to almost every group or individual who believed in the preaching of the apostles (2:37–41; 8:12–38; 9:10–18; 10:44–48). All those who accepted the preaching of the gospel and abandoned their former ways of life then came forward for "baptism in the name of Jesus" (cf. Acts 2:38; 8:16; 10:48; 19:5; 22:16). These instances probably do not deal with a formula used in baptism but the completion of the conversion process by the acceptance of Christ's claims, the unification with the community founded by Christ and the forgiveness of sins.

Several Pauline passages highlight the meaning of the sacrament and its continuing significance in and for the life of the Christian. The classic Pauline passage is Rom 6:3–11, which sees baptism as a burial with

Christ and a rising with him. Three elements characterize Paul's under-standing of baptism: it is in Christ Jesus; it is in the Holy Spirit; it is for-mative of community. Paul proclaims that baptism in Christ establishes a vital union with Christ in the saving events of his history, his dying and rising again. Union with Christ involves the reception of the Spirit of Christ, the Spirit of God (cf. Rom 8:1–17). These two elements meet in Paul's vision of the Church. Baptism for Paul brings into existence and establishes the People of God, formed through union with Christ in his Spirit (cf. 1 Cor 12:12–13; Gal 3:27–29; 4:4–7).

THE LITURGY OF BAPTISM

The NT does not provide us with the exact rite of baptism or the exact formula. It does seem that baptism in the early Church was by immer-sion. Paul's reference in Rom 6:4 to being "buried" with Christ implies immersion. The account of the Ethiopian eunuch also speaks of a going down into the water and a coming up out of the water (Acts 8:36–38).

BAPTISM IN THE HISTORY OF THE CHURCH

The *Didache,* a late first-century Christian manual, prescribes baptism in living water, that is, in streams and rivers. There is a preference for immersion, although the pouring of water on the head (baptism by infu-sion) was also accepted when water for immersion was not available.

The second and third centuries could be seen as the great period of development of the rite of baptism. Justin, Tertullian, and Hippolytus of Rome provide us with descriptions of baptism. At the end of his *First Apology,* Justin remarks that the candidates were instructed to pray and fast. They were then brought to water and their sins washed away. He speaks of a negative effect of baptism, the remission of sins, and a posi-tive effect, an illumination that comes about through faith in Jesus Christ. The baptized were then brought into the midst of the community to partake in the Eucharist.

Tertullian, in *On Baptism,* describes a renunciation of the devil by those to be baptized, followed by a threefold immersion in water. After this, the newly baptized received milk and honey. Indication is given that the baptismal font was consecrated. After the immersion, the baptized were anointed with oil. There followed the imposition of hands during which the gift of the Spirit was given. Before these ritual actions, how-ever, there was a period of catechumenal preparation during which the authenticity of the conversion was ascertained and also another period of preparation consisting of prayers, vigils, and fasting immediately pre-ceding the baptism.

The *Apostolic Tradition* of Hippolytus indicates a three-year period of formation. An initial examination ascertained if the candidate should be admitted to the catechumenate. Another examination was held before the baptism. At cockcrow, the water was blessed. Little children were baptized first, answering for themselves if they could; otherwise parents or family members answered for them. The bishop blessed the oil of thanksgiving and the oil of exorcism, corresponding to today's chrism and oil of catechumens. The candidates renounced Satan and were anointed with the oil of exorcism. Then each candidate descended into the water with the deacon. The candidate made a threefold profession of faith and each time was immersed. The newly baptized was then anointed with the oil of thanksgiving. Thereafter, the candidates joined the assembly and the bishop imposed his hands upon them, anointed them, and sealed them on the forehead. The bishop then offered the Eucharist. The newly baptized were also given a mixture of milk and honey and a chalice of water as well as the consecrated bread and wine.

The period of the fourth to the sixth centuries was one of deterioration of the rite. The title of catechumen lost its significance. Bishops tried to push catechumens into baptism, which began to be postponed. The bishops tried to maintain the principle of conversion, but they faced an increasingly difficult pastoral problem, and entry into the catechumenate lost its character of a step taken in faith. The meaning of baptism also became blurred. Some catechumens saw it as a right; others saw it as a type of insurance one should obtain at the end of life.

From the sixth century on, reforms were attempted, but by the Middle Ages the catechumenate for all practical purposes no longer existed. Some of the elements (e.g., anointings, profession of faith, renunciation of Satan) of the ancient catechumenate were retained, but more and more they were mixed together into one baptismal rite.

Strong reform efforts were made from the sixteenth to the eighteenth centuries to revive some type of catechumenate, but the efforts often lacked a proper liturgical dimension. Successful reform came in the twentieth century with the Second Vatican Council (1962–65). The Constitution on the Sacred Liturgy decreed that the catechumenate be revived. Initiation rites as practiced in mission lands, especially Africa, were offered as a starting point. The result was the Rite of Christian Initiation of Adults (1972). This rite, known as the RCIA, recognizes that people become Christians through a process. It demands both an adherence to Christ and the active participation of the community in the process. In the United States a final edition of the RCIA appeared in 1988. This ritual also contains a number of rites approved specially for the dioceses of the United States.

The council also asked that the rite for infants be reformed. The Rite of Baptism for Children appeared in 1969. It contains a welcoming rite, a questioning of the parents as to their willingness to undertake their responsibilities, and a signing by the priest, parents, and godparents of the child with the sign of the cross. The celebration of the Liturgy of the Word follows. There is an exorcism, with alternate texts provided, and then the anointing with the oil of catechumens. The actual celebration of the sacrament follows: the blessing of the water, the parents' renunciation of sin and promise of faith, the baptism, anointing with chrism, the clothing with the white garment, the giving of the candle, and the *Ephphatha* (Gk., "Be opened" [Mark 7:32], an optional rite of blessing the ears and mouth). All process to the sanctuary for the Lord's Prayer and the blessing.

It is noteworthy that the ritual for the baptism of adults resurrected the old Roman catechumenate. The Rite of Becoming a Catechumen celebrates entrance into this order. Through it, inquirers become members of the household of faith. The second stage admits candidates to an intense forty-day period of Lent (thus refocusing the understanding of Lent). The Rite of Election marks this stage. Through it, the catechumens become the elect, those chosen for Easter initiation. The third stage is initiation by Baptism, Confirmation, and Eucharist. The fourth and final period is the postbaptismal or mystagogical period. Part II of the rite deals with the initiation of children of catechetical age who were not baptized as infants.

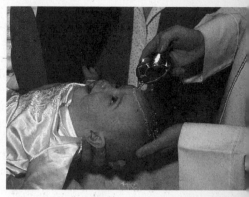

Most baptisms are, as here, of infants; as the priest pours the water, he says, "[Name], I baptize you in the name of the Father, and of the Son, and of the Holy Spirit."

The manner of administration of the sacrament today is either by immersion or the pouring of water, whichever seems to better ensure that the baptism is not a mere purification but the sacrament of being joined to Christ. Specific instructions are given in the Book of Blessings for making the font ready for immersion.

The ordinary minister of Baptism is a bishop, priest, or deacon. If a person is in imminent danger of death or at the moment of death and no ordinary minister is available, any member of the faithful or anyone with the right intention may, and sometimes must, administer the sacrament. In a case of danger of death, there is a special shorter rite designed particularly for use by catechists and laypersons. If a priest or deacon is available, he should use the abbreviated form found in the revised rite, making changes required by circumstances of place and time. In either instance a small community of at least one or two witnesses should be present. The minister, whether ordinary or extraordinary, must use water either by immersion or pouring while repeating the Trinitarian invocation: "I baptize you in the name of the Father, and of the Son, and of the Holy Spirit." This action should be informed by the intention to baptize the person into the Church.

THEOLOGICAL ISSUES

The sacrament of Baptism has various effects. It incorporates the recipient into the Body of Christ and forms one in his likeness (1 Cor 12:13). Catholics and non-Catholic Christians alike see this as a nonrepeatable action that links all of the recipients in a sacramental bond of unity (Dogmatic Constitution on the Church, n. 15). This sacrament pardons all sins, rescues recipients from the power of darkness, and joins them to Christ's suffering, death, and Resurrection (Rom 6:4; Eph 2:6; Col 3:1; 2 Tim 2:11). They become new creations through water and the Holy Spirit and so are then called sons and daughters of God. The baptized are marked with a special character empowering them to share in the priestly function of Christ, especially in the offering of the Eucharist (n. 10).

The institution of the sacrament of Baptism by Jesus Christ cannot be traced to one particular moment. The Church teaches that Christ willed this sacrament to be established and determined its inner meaning. Certainly the early Church believed that the practice of baptism was due to the authoritative command of the Lord.

Regarding the necessity of Baptism, two truths have to be kept in balance: the universality of God's call to salvation in Christ and the apparently unequal response of people to this call. The Church does not know exactly the fate of the unbaptized, but it teaches that baptism of desire (that of one preparing for baptism, or that of a person of goodwill who simply is unaware that God is calling the person to the Church) and baptism of blood (martyrdom) may substitute in the case of water baptism for adults. The salvation of unbelievers remains a matter of theological discussion.

Infant baptism is yet another difficult issue. Normally, in order to receive a sacrament explicit faith and an explicit desire are required. In the case of infants, it is the Church that "supplies" the faith and it is the faith community that nurtures and nourishes that faith as the young child grows into maturity.

Godparents play a significant role in Baptism. This is more of a challenge in today's secular culture. Sometimes parents cannot find godparents who have been fully initiated and are active Catholics.

As a general rule those who have not yet reached the age of reason are to be baptized according to the norms of the Rite of Baptism for Children. Children who have attained the use of reason and are of catechetical age seek initiation either at the direction of their parents or guardians or on their own initiative, with their parents' permission. They are subject to the norms of the Rite of Christian Initiation of Adults. At present, within the same family, individuals may be initiated at different times and in different ways depending upon their age, whether or not they have been baptized already in another church, and the extent to which they have been formed in their Christian life.

As a result of the Church's renewed appreciation of the process of initiation and conversion, a new understanding of evangelization has developed that will have a significant impact on the way initiation will be celebrated in the future.

See also baptismal font; baptism of blood; baptism of desire; baptistery; catechumenate; Confirmation; Rite of Christian Initiation of Adults; sacrament; sacramental character; salvation outside the Church.

Bibliography

Beasley-Murray, G.R. *Baptism in the New Testament.* Grand Rapids, MI: Eerdmans, 1962.
Brown, Kathy, and Frances C. Sokol, eds. *Issues on the Christian Initiation of Children: Catechesis and Liturgy.* Chicago: Liturgy Training Publications, 1989.
Kavanagh, Aidan. *The Shape of Baptism: The Rite of Christian Initiation.* New York: Pueblo, 1978.
Morris, Thomas H. *The RCIA: Transforming the Church.* Mahwah, NJ: Paulist Press, 1989.
Osborne, Kenan. *The Christian Sacraments of Initiation.* New York: Paulist Press, 1987.
Searle, Mark. *Christening: The Making of Christians.* Collegeville, MN: Liturgical Press, 1980.
Yarnold, Edward. *The Awe-inspiring Rites of Initiation.* Middlegreen, England: St. Paul, 1971.

ANTHONY SHERMAN

Barat, St. Madeleine Sophie (ba'rah), 1779–1865, founder of the Society of the Sacred Heart. Guided by Père Varin, a priest recommended by her older brother Louis, Madeleine founded in 1800 in France an institute of women dedicated to the education of girls. Since 1818 the Society has become renowned in the United States for educating daughters of the wealthy. Feast day: May 25. *See also* Society of the Sacred Heart.

Barbara, St., a popular saint of the Middle Ages. Barbara's birth and death dates are unknown; in fact, her existence is doubtful. According to legend, she was martyred by her own father because of her faith. She is the patron saint of architects and builders and protector of those in danger of dying without the sacraments. Feast day: December 4.

Barbarigo, St. Gregory (bahr-bah-ree'goh), 1625–97, Italian cardinal, ecumenist. He was bishop of Bergamo (1657), cardinal (1660), and then bishop of Padua (1664). Famous for his charities and love of learning, he tried to bring about a reunion with the Greek church. In 1960 he was canonized by Pope John XXIII, one of his successors, as bishop of Bergamo. Feast day: June 17.

Barber, Virgil, 1782–1847, Jesuit priest and educator. Born in Simsbury, Connecticut, he was ordained an Episcopal priest, but in 1816, along with his wife and five children, he joined the Catholic Church. He entered the Society of Jesus the following year; his wife, the Georgetown Visitation convent. In 1822, at Claremont, New Hampshire, he began the first Catholic school in New England. He later taught at Georgetown and other Jesuit colleges.

Barberini, an aristocratic Italian family whose members were important in the papacy of the seventeenth century. The family's fortune was made by the election of Maffeo Barberini as Pope Urban VIII in 1623. He showered his family with wealth and offices. Two nephews, Francesco and Antonio, were made cardinals at the ages of twenty-five and twenty. A brother was made a cardinal despite the fact that he was a Capuchin, and two sisters who were Carmelites were also granted benefices. With the wealth they had gathered, the family founded the Barberini Library and built extensively in Rome. *See also* Urban VIII.

Bardesanes (bahr-deh-sah'neez), also known as Bar-Daisan, 154–222, Christian writer whose 150 hymns were the first composed in Syriac. Educated at the court of Edessa and converted to Christianity ca. 179, he impressed contemporaries with dazzling gifts as poet, scientist, archer, and philosopher. Although his *Dialogue of Destiny* argues against Marcionite distinctions between God and the Creator, he was accused by Ephraem the Syrian of Docetism and other Gnostic teachings. The validity of these accusations remains unclear. *See also* Docetism; Gnosticism; Marcion.

Barnabas, Letter of, Christian treatise attributed by Clement of Alexandria to the Barnabas of the Acts of the Apostles, but now ascribed to an anonymous author of the late first or early second century. The Greek text interprets Jewish Scriptures nonliterally in order to attack the Jews for their formalistic legal observance, which rejected God's true covenant and obscured the witness to Christ.

Barnabas, St. (bahr'nuh-buhs), an early Christian missionary, whose name in Hebrew means "son of consolation." A Levite from Cyprus originally named Joseph, he became a follower of Jesus, sold some property, and donated the proceeds to the apostles (Acts 4:36–37). He introduced Paul to the leaders in Jerusalem (Acts 9:27). He and Paul collaborated in Antioch (Acts 11:22–30), and then journeyed together as missionaries (Acts 13–14; 1 Cor 9:6). They attended the apostolic conference in Jerusalem that settled the question of circumcision for Gentiles (Acts 15; Gal 2:1–10). Subsequently they parted ways, disagreeing over the presence of Mark (Acts 15:39) and over the appropriate form of table fellowship between Jewish and gentile Christians (Gal 2:11–14). Yet Paul continued to use Barnabas as an example of apostolic behavior (1 Cor 9:6). Barnabas and Mark sailed to Cyprus (Acts 15:39), where according to tradition he was stoned to death at Salamis after founding the Cypriote church. The fifth-century *Acts of Barnabas* expands on the account in Acts.

No certain writings of Barnabas survive. The *Letter of Barnabas* is the work of an anonymous Christian of the late first or early second century. It offers a lengthy argument about the superiority of Christianity to Judaism and practical moral advice. Tertullian believed, and some modern scholars agree, that Barnabas wrote the NT Letter to the Hebrews,

An example of Baroque art: a ceiling painting in the apse of the church of Santa Maria in Vallicella, Italy, depicting the Blessed Virgin in glory.

but both Hebrews and the *Letter of Barnabas* are more extreme in their rejection of Jewish tradition than is likely for Barnabas. Feast day: June 11.

HAROLD W. ATTRIDGE

Barnabites, Clerics Regular of St. Paul (C.R.S.P.), an order founded in Milan in 1530 by Anthony Zaccaria and others and approved in 1533. Most noted for their work with Charles Borromeo, since the seventeenth century they have concentrated on missions and educating children. *See also* Anthony Zaccaria, St.

Baronius, Caesar, 1538–1607, cardinal and historian of the Church, author of the influential twelve-volume *Annales Ecclesiastici.* Born to a noble family, Baronius earned a doctorate in law at Rome (1561), where he participated in Philip Neri's Roman Oratory (diocesan priests living in community without religious vows), later succeeding Neri as its head (1593). It was in response to Neri's order to reply to the Lutheran Church history *Centuriae Magdeburgenses* that Baronius began his scrupu-

lously detailed, nonpolemical attempt to demonstrate the apostolic foundations for Catholic beliefs and practices. At his death, however, his *Annales Ecclesiastici* had only reached the year 1198. Volume 11, published in 1605, included a note supporting the claims of the papacy against Spain in Sicily. It so angered the Spanish king Philip III that Baronius probably lost his chance to be elected pope. *See also* Oratorians; Oratory of Divine Love.

Baroque Catholicism (Port., *barocco,* "rough pearl"), a renewal of Roman Catholicism that emphasized emotion and displayed action and variety within unity. Traditionally, the Baroque period is dated from 1580 to 1680, but extends, for Catholicism, into the late nineteenth century. Figures of Baroque Catholicism in Spain were Teresa of Ávila and Melchior Cano; in France, Pierre de Bérulle, Margaret Mary Alacoque, Vincent de Paul, and Louise de Marillac. Theology, monastic life, mysticism, and authority, with parallels in art from Mannerism to Rococo (often stimulated by the Church), found new directions and styles: there was an emphasis upon the personal, a desire to explain texts and to arrange the many areas of theology, and an interest in the mystical and the heroic. A new experience of God's vastness, of human potential, and the world's diversity led to a veneration of Christ in his humanity and redemptive love. The Church was a place of grace: there the presence of God inspired and sustained heroic servants of the gospel while the arts depicted a festive Church in heaven. There was a shift toward the individual, as laymen and laywomen pursued intense spiritual lives in society and presented Christianity as a personal life of prayer and service rather than as an institution. Actual grace was a principal theme of the Baroque: grace is a transient force acting in conversion, meditation, and supernatural decisions (this led to "an extrinsicism" of grace, whereby it is regarded as something quantitative and external to the spiritual life of the individual, and a separation of liturgical form from inner intention).

Three focuses of Baroque Catholicism as manifested in spiritual autobiographies, theologies, liturgies, and communities are the self, method, and drama. Spiritual life drew upon the force of actual grace, the stories of the Bible, and the examples of the saints. Methods and exercises of Christian life were central (perhaps mirroring the order of Descartes, Galileo, and Newton) and they would lead to a certain mechanization in prayer and liturgy. Christian thought and life during the Baroque period had a theatrical component as it pondered conversion or heroic ministry. A strong emotional and visual orientation was confirmed by visions, miracles, and conversions. The liturgy became increasingly elaborate, devotions more and more dramatic.

Since the Enlightenment's influence was not extensive in Catholicism, the restoration of Catholicism after 1830 through the religious orders, devotions, and spiritualities continued the Baroque with communities patterned after the Society of Jesus, the Tridentine liturgy of solemn high Mass and Benediction, dramatic devotions to ethnic Baroque saints, prayer as stages of meditation, sharp distinctions between the natural and the supernatural, silent retreats, and miraculous appearances. The metamorphoses of Catholicism in recent decades show that it is Baroque Catholicism (not the Counter-Reformation or Modernity) that is challenged by developments after Vatican II (1962–65). Many of the issues and conflicts within contemporary Catholicism—the balancing of papal absolutism by bishops and their episcopal conferences, the introduction of liturgical forms from early centuries, spiritualities drawn on contemporary psychology and devoid of unhealthy masochism—have challenged Baroque structures and the mentality supporting them. *See also* devotions; grace; saints, devotion to.

THOMAS F. O'MEARA

Barth, Karl, 1886–1968, Swiss Protestant theologian known for his insistence upon God's utter transcendence. As a student at the universities of Bern, Berlin, Tübingen, and Marburg, Barth favored "liberal" theology. But in light of his parochial ministry and World War I, he came to reject the theology of his teachers, Adolf von Harnack and Wilhelm Herrmann. Appealing to the Protestant principle of *sola Scriptura* (Lat., "Scripture alone"), Barth set out to move beyond a reliance on historical-critical methods and to read the Bible on its own terms, so as to discover the God who is "wholly other" than human thought about God.

The first fruit of this endeavor was his commentary entitled *Epistle to the Romans* (1919), in which Barth argues that, according to Paul, God condemns all human undertakings and saves only those people who trust not in themselves but solely in God. This book and Barth's subsequent writings won him academic appointments at the universities of Göttingen (1921–25), Münster (1925–30), and Bonn (1930–35). In 1933, judging that the claims of Adolf Hitler were idolatrous, Barth joined Germany's "Confessing Church" and helped in the drafting of the Barmen Confession (1934). Deprived of his professorship by the Nazi regime, he returned to Switzerland, where he taught at the University of Basel (1935–67).

In his early years, Barth advocated a "dialectical theology," according to which little can be said about God who, as the divine absolute, cannot be known by the human mind (*The Word of God and the Word of Man*, 1924). In his middle years, he sought for a way to speak about God that depended not on a natural theology and the "analogy of being," but solely on divine revelation and the "analogy of faith." This effort produced his four-volume (thirteen-part) *Church Dogmatics* (1932–67), inspired in part by John Calvin's *Institutes*. In his last years, Barth gave greater recognition to theological anthropology (*The Humanity of God*, 1956). Barth's thought has influenced both Protestant theologians such as Hans W. Frei, Eberhard Jüngel, Jürgen Moltmann, and Wolfhart Pannenberg, and also Catholic theologians such as Hans Urs von Balthasar, Hans Küng, and Walter Kasper.

ROBERT A. KRIEG

Bartholomew, St., one of Jesus' twelve disciples,

Bartholomew, one of the original twelve apostles, reputed to have preached the gospel in India; fifteenth-century Pier Matteo d'Amelia mural (with the words, "I believe in the Holy Spirit") in the Borgia apartment in the Vatican.

according to the four lists in the NT (Matt 10:3; Mark 3:18; Luke 6:14; Acts 1:13). His name in Hebrew means "son of Talmai," but nothing certain is known of him. Some scholars identify him with Nathanael of John 1:45–51, because both are closely associated with Philip. Bartholomew's name appears after that of Philip in the synoptic Gospels, and Nathanael is brought to Jesus by Philip in John. An identification is possible, but unproven.

The earliest Church tradition about Bartholomew is a report from the second-century Alexandrian teacher Pantaenus, preserved in Eusebius (*Eccl. Hist.* 5.10.3). Pantaenus had visited India, probably the Malabar Coast, which had trading relations with the Roman Empire. There he found a Christian community that revered Bartholomew as its founder and possessed a Hebrew "Gospel of Matthew" that Bartholomew left them.

Several apocryphal works circulated under the name of Bartholomew. Jerome mentions a *Gospel of Bartholomew,* although he may have simply inferred its existence from Eusebius. The *Questions of Bartholomew* is a fifth-century work with dialogue between Jesus and his disciples after the Resurrection about such matters as the harrowing of hell and the virgin birth. The Coptic *Book of Bartholomew on the Resurrection,* also from the fifth or sixth century,

contains various loosely connected stories about the death and resurrection of Jesus and his harrowing of hell, along with several hymns. Feast day: August 24. *See also* apostle; Twelve, the.   HAROLD W. ATTRIDGE

Bartholomew's Day Massacre, St., a mass slaughter of Huguenots in Paris and elsewhere beginning on August 24, 1572 (St. Bartholomew's Day). After a failed assassination attempt on the Protestant leader Coligny, who was in Paris for the marriage of the Protestant Henry of Navarre (later Henry IV) to the sister of the Catholic Charles IX, the panicked king, at the urging of his mother Catherine de Médici and the Catholic Guises, ordered the murder of the Protestants in Paris. Thousands of men, women, and children were killed all over France.

base communities, small groups led by laity who gather together for Scripture and Communion services in the absence of a priest. The participants reflect upon the relation of the Bible to their daily lives and, on occasion, make social decisions resulting from these discussions.

Three areas of the Catholic Church in the developing world, independently of one another, have experienced an extraordinary growth of base communities: Latin America, Africa, and Asia. Base communities began in Brazil in 1956 (Barra do Piral Diocese) and were known as "Sunday services without a priest." In 1963, they were developed in the San Miguelito Parish of the archdiocese of Panama. These were creative pastoral efforts motivated by laypersons desiring to support their bishops.

Base communities are not mentioned in the documents of the Second Vatican Council, but appear first in Pope Paul VI's 1975 apostolic exhortation "On Evangelization in the Modern World" (*Evangelii Nuntiandi,* n. 58). These communities represent a new way of being Church and provide a means for laypeople to become more active participants in a renewed evangelization.

In the rapid growth of base communities there are now many different names applied to them, implying that they mean many things to various groups. However, in a church context they may be described as "basic ecclesial communities." Basic— in the sense that they are a gathering of active laypersons "at the base" of the Church; ecclesial—insofar as they strive for a unity in faith, and a linkage with the institutional Church; community—as an effort to live out a community life in a modern society that rewards individualism and competitiveness. In 1968, at the Medellín (Columbia) Conference of Latin American bishops, base communities were given official encouragement. In 1979 the bishops at Puebla (Mexico) both reviewed the communities and urged an even closer bond with official pastoral leadership. In 1992 the Latin American bishops renewed this support in their sessions in Santo Domingo (Dominican Republic).

On January 30, 1989, the Vatican released the apostolic exhortation "On the Mission of the Lay Faithful in the Church and in the World," signed by Pope John Paul II. This exhortation provides clear support for building these communities throughout the Catholic world (n. 26). Later in the same document base communities are seen as a "notable" help in the formation of lay leadership (n. 61). These sections are placed in the context of an ecclesiology of community that encourages the development of the gifts of all members of the Church.

Base communities not only help the Third World, but have positive implications for the Church in the First World. In the so-called developed world a rugged individualism often leads to deep alienation and mistrust. The Church, by contrast, is moving toward a kind of ministry in which all are responsible for the spiritual and pastoral life in their own small community. In fact, these communities are now growing gradually in the First World. As this happens, the Church is being reborn, not only as a dynamic response to impersonal times but also as a way of incarnating the vision and spirit of the Second Vatican Council.   ROBERT S. PELTON

Basel, Council of, 1431–49, final of three Church councils (after Pisa and Constance) meeting from 1431 to 1449 to resolve the crisis of papal authority provoked by the Great Schism (1378–1417). The conciliar movement triumphed at Basel, but internal factionalism and the rehabilitation of papal authority made it a short-lived victory. Pope Martin V called the council to complete the reform work of the Council of Constance but died before it began. His successor, Eugenius IV, sought to undermine the assembly by announcing another council, in Bologna. The council members refused to disperse, invoked the conciliar superiority decreed in *Sacrosancta* at Constance, and compelled Eugenius to recognize Basel's validity. The participants also forced papal appointees to sign an oath affirming conciliar supremacy and promulgated reforms against simony.

Those at Basel also negotiated independently with Greek envoys to reunite Latin and Greek Christendom. The rejection of Byzantine demands for a council in Italy split the conciliar ranks. A minority of council members, the Greeks, and the pope agreed to hold the Council of Union in Ferrara (1437), effectively restoring papal prestige. After the council was transferred, some in Basel defiantly stayed on and deposed Eugenius (1438), declared conciliar authority a truth of Catholic faith, and elected an antipope, Felix V (1439). The strengthened papacy, however, forced Felix's resignation (1448), and the proceedings at Basel, invalid after the council's transfer to Ferrara, came to an end. *See also* conciliarism; Constance, Council of; Great Schism.

Basil, Rule of St., term commonly used for two works of Basil the Great (d. 379) that traditionally bear the title, not given them by Basil, of Long Rules (55 in number) and Short Rules (313 in number). Neither is a monastic rule proper, comparable to the Rule of St. Benedict. Instead, they are integral parts of the totality of his ascetical works (*Asceticon*, Gk., "Ascetical [Teachings]") and arose out of questions posed to him by monastic communities that had arisen already earlier in Cappadocia. Basil continued to respond to similar questions and to edit his responses to the end of his life. His Rules were never understood by Eastern monastics as canonically binding documents, but due to their intrinsic spiritual merit and to the ecclesial authority of their author, they had a profound influence on monasticism in the East and also in the West. An early edition of the Long Rules was translated into Latin in Basil's lifetime.

Basilians, name given since the twelfth century to Greek monks in southern Italy, later to other Eastern Christian monastics. The term refers to Basil the Great (d. 379) and was intended to designate him as the founder and legislator of monasticism in the East as Benedict was in the West. Eastern monks and nuns in their own milieu use no such designation; they are simply monastics. Only when groups of monasteries within various Eastern Catholic churches in the seventeenth century began to be organized into orders did the term Basilians, as part of the official name of such newly centralized monastic groups, come into wide use. In the 1990s there are various orders of Basilians in the Italo-Greek, Ukrainian, and Melkite Catholic churches; to distinguish them, the Congregation for the Oriental

Churches introduced additional designations in their official names (such as "of St. Josaphat" for the Ukrainian Basilians). *See also* Order of St. Basil the Great.

basilica, term used to designate certain official buildings in the time of the Roman Empire, later adapted, as was the architectural style of such buildings, for Christian use. The word itself has Greek origins and means "king's hall"; Christian use refers to Christ as the king of kings. Currently the term is used to designate a certain church of historical significance that continues to play an important part in the religious life of at least a particular region. In addition to the major basilicas, all of which are located in Rome, the Holy See honors other significant churches with this title. The insignia of these minor basilicas include a red and yellow striped umbrella (It., *ombrellino*) reminiscent of those carried over imperial and papal authorities, the papal coat-of-arms over the door, and a bell (*tintinabellum*) recalling those once used to warn people of the approach of a papal procession.

Basilicas are expected to celebrate with greater solemnity than other churches certain feast days related to the Petrine ministry and to commemorate certain historical days in the life of the current pope. In addition they are to be models for liturgical celebration and places of pilgrimage for the faithful. Particular indulgences, unavailable in other churches, may be gained at basilicas.

Minor basilicas in North America include Mission Dolores in San Francisco, California; the Cathedral of St. Augustine in St. Augustine, Florida; Sacred Heart Basilica on the campus of the University of Notre Dame in Notre Dame, Indiana; the Basilica

The basilica of St. Apollinaris in Ravenna, Italy; Apollinaris was the first bishop of Ravenna.

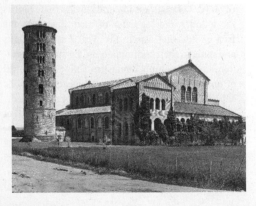

of Notre Dame in Ottawa, Canada; and the Basilica of Notre Dame in Quebec, Canada. *See also* basilica, major; basilica, minor; basilica, patriarchal.

JOHN LAHEY

basilica, major, a principal papal church in Rome. Major basilicas are of ancient origin and have served as places of pilgrimage. Four of them are considered patriarchal basilicas (basilicas traditionally assigned to Eastern patriarchs in union with Rome) as well: St. John Lateran, St. Peter's, St. Paul's Outside the Walls, and St. Mary Major. *See also* basilica; basilica, patriarchal.

basilica, minor, a church of particular historic, artistic, or devotional importance honored by the pope. The church so honored must be a center for a vibrant faith community where the sacraments are properly celebrated. *See also* basilica.

basilica, patriarchal, a church known for its antiquity, dignity, and historical importance that has been assigned as a titular church to an Eastern patriarch in union with the see of Rome. The four major basilicas of Rome (St. John Lateran, St. Peter's, St. Paul's Outside the Walls, and St. Mary Major) are also patriarchal, as is the Church of St. Lawrence in Rome, a minor basilica. The churches of St. Francis and of St. Mary of the Angels in Assisi, Italy, are also major patriarchal basilicas. *See also* basilica.

Basilides (baz-uh-lee'deez), ca. 120–45, Christian Gnostic who taught in Alexandria ca. 132–35 and earlier. He wrote his own Gospel, a biblical commentary (*Exegetica*), and a book of *Odes*. Irenaeus, Hippolytus, Clement of Alexandria, Origen, and Eusebius responded to his teachings, which stressed the living Jesus and denied that the Christ, as the word of God, had been crucified. *See also* Gnosticism.

Basil, "the Great," St., ca. 330–79, bishop of Caesarea in Cappadocia (370–79) and one of the Cappadocian theologians whose work brought the Arian controversy to a close. One of nine children (including Macrina the Younger and Gregory of Nyssa) born to Basil the Elder, a teacher of rhetoric, and the wealthy aristocratic Emmelia, Basil was educated first by his father and grandmother (Macrina the Elder), then at Caesarea, Constantinople, and finally Athens. Upon his return in 355 he taught rhetoric, but after a tour of the ascetic settlements in the Middle East and Egypt and after his father's

Basil of Caesarea, one of the three Cappadocian theologians, shown dictating his doctrine about the divinity of the Holy Spirit and of the Trinity; seventeenth-century painting by Francisco Herrara the Elder, Louvre, Paris.

death (358), he renounced his career, was baptized, and joined the ascetic community his sister and mother had founded on a family estate. Basil's monastic rules and the *Philocalia* date from this period. Ordained presbyter (ca. 362), he came to Caesarea in 364 when his bishop Eusebius required his support against the Arian emperor Valens (364–78). In 368 Basil was acclaimed for his relief efforts during a famine in Cappadocia. Succeeding Eusebius as bishop at his death, Basil's episcopacy was marked by building projects for the relief of the poor and by continuing controversy with the Arians and with the Pneumatomachians, who denied the divinity of the Holy Spirit. His *On the Holy Spirit* and *Against Eunomius* substantially advanced the articulation of Nicene orthodoxy; the *Hexameron* commentary (on the six days of creation) offered a brilliant, moderated critique of allegorical approaches. The *Address to Young Men* acquired a second life among the Renaissance humanists, who admired its openness to secular education. Basil is a Doctor of the Church. Feast day: January 2 (West, formerly June 14); January 1 (East). *See also* Arianism; Cappadocian Fathers; Holy Spirit; Pneumatomachians; Trinity, doctrine of the.

JOHN C. CAVADINI

Battifol, Pierre (pee-air' bah'ti-fol), 1861–1929,

Church historian. Rector of the Institut Catholique at Toulouse, 1898–1908, he worked especially on early Christian doctrine and liturgy but was suspected of Modernist tendencies. He was forced to resign his rectorship at Toulouse and his book on the Eucharist was placed on the Index of Forbidden Books in 1911. His work encouraged the growth of critical studies in France.

Baum, Gregory, b. 1923, Canadian Catholic theologian. As a Jewish youth, Baum escaped Nazi Germany and was educated in Canada. He converted to Catholicism and taught for many years at St. Michael's College of the University of Toronto. At McGill University of Montreal, Baum's work can be described as the theological study of human society. He is author of many works, including *Man Becoming* (1970).

Baumstark, Anton, 1872–1948, German Catholic orientalist, philologist, and liturgiologist famous especially for his pioneering history of Syriac literature (1922) and the "laws" of liturgical evolution outlined in *Vom geschichtlichen Werden der Liturgie (On the Historical Evolution of the Liturgy,* 1923) and *Comparative Liturgy* (1940, 1958). His contribution remains seminal in spite of the inadequacies of some of his theories. A man of boundless energy, he taught at several German and Dutch universities, published 546 works, founded and edited the renowned scholarly journal *Oriens Christianus (The Christian East)* from 1901 to 1938, and cofounded with O. Casel the *Jahrbuch für Liturgiewissenschaft (Yearbook of Liturgical Science).* The mark left on modern oriental liturgiology by his writings and those of his students, like H. Engberding, is still felt. Baumstark's involvement with Nazism tarnished his later years.

Bavo, St. (bay'voh), 589–654, Belgian monk. Converted as a widower by Amandus, he founded an abbey on his estate in Ghent. He is patron saint of the dioceses of Ghent (Belgium) and Haarlem (Netherlands). Feast day: October 1.

Bayley, James Roosevelt, 1814–77, American prelate. A nephew of Elizabeth Bayley Seton, he was ordained an Episcopalian priest in 1841. The following year he became a Roman Catholic and in 1844 he was ordained a Roman Catholic priest by John Hughes, the bishop of New York. He was appointed the first bishop of Newark, New Jersey, in 1853. He founded Seton Hall College in 1856 and promoted parochial schools. In 1872 he became the archbishop of Baltimore. He was an advocate of temperance and a promoter of Gregorian chant. *See also* Seton, St. Elizabeth Ann Bayley.

Baylon, St. Paschal. *See* Paschal Baylon, St.

B.C./B.C.E., before Christ/before the common era. The neutral designation B.C.E., often preferred to B.C. out of deference to other faiths' different calculations of time, reflects the more ecumenical approach to the study of the OT. Correspondingly, and for the same reasons, C.E. (common era) is used by many in preference to A.D. (Lat., *Anno Domini,* "in the year of the Lord"). The alternative Jewish calculation is from the (putative) date of the creation of the world, and that of Islam from the *hegira* (Med. Lat., from Arabic *hijrah,* "flight") of Muhammed from Mecca to Medina in the year 622. *See also* A.D.

Bea, Augustine (bay'ah), 1881–1968, Scripture scholar, ecumenist, and leading figure at Vatican II (1962–65). Born in Riedböhringen, Baden, Germany, he entered the Society of Jesus in 1902. From 1928 to 1959 he was professor at the Pontifical Biblical Institute, serving as rector from 1930 to 1949. He was an influential consultant for policy and documents of the Holy See, including the epoch-making papal encyclical *Divino Afflante Spiritu* (1943). Created cardinal in 1959, he played a significant role at the Second Vatican Council, especially with regard to the documents on revelation, ecumenism, and non-Christian religions (esp. Declaration on the Relationship of the Church to Non-Christian Religions, n. 4). A pioneer Catholic ecumenist, he organized and headed the Secretariate for Promoting Christian Unity (1960–68). *See also* ecumenism.

beast of the Apocalypse, a complex image of evil found in the book of Revelation. The beast first appears in Rev 11:7, arising from the abyss. In 13:1 the beast, which now arises from the sea, combines features of a leopard, a bear, and a lion and receives its power from Satan, the great dragon, described in Rev 12:3–4. The beast enforces worship of the dragon and it battles the saints (Rev 13:3–8). The great beast from the sea is followed by a beast from the land, which leads inhabitants of the earth astray (Rev 13:11–18). The pair of beasts is also referred to as the beast and the false prophet (Rev 16:13; 19:20).

The imagery of the beast has been applied to various forces, secular and religious, that have been felt to be oppressive throughout the history of the Church. The immediate referent of the image in the historical context of Revelation was apparently the Roman Empire. This identification is particularly clear in Rev 17:3–14, the vision of the harlot riding on the beast, whose seven heads are identified with seven hills. Similarly the number of the beast, 666, mentioned in Rev 13:18, is best understood as a cryptic reference to the name Nero Caesar. *See also* apocalypse; apocalypticism; Roman Empire.

beatification (bee-a-ti-fi-kay'shuhn), the second step in the process of proclaiming a person a saint. After the Congregation for the Causes of the Saints in Rome has accepted the documents about a holy person from a local church or religious group and has declared that person "venerable," a rigorous investigation of the person's life and writings is made to determine whether he or she demonstrates a heroic level of love and of all other virtues. The Congregation discusses the merits of the case. Evidence for one uncontested miracle wrought through prayers to the holy person must be presented. A thorough examination of the theological and scientific evidence for the miracle is needed if it is to be accepted as proof of divine approval. When all the evidence is gathered, it is presented to the pope in a formal meeting. If the pope is convinced of the candidate's holiness, he issues a decree that it is appropriate to venerate the person as truly holy or blessed.

The ceremony of beatification includes a public declaration of the person's holiness, a papal mass, and the authorization of a prayer to the person beatified. The blessed one is presented to the faithful as an example to be imitated, but the person is not enrolled on the universal calendar of the Church.

A simpler process, called equivalent beatification, involves a thorough historical investigation to determine the validity of the honor paid to a person from a remote historical period. *See also* canonization; saints.

Beatific Vision, the direct knowing and loving of God after death. Also called the intuitive vision of God, it refers to the unsurpassable and perfect fulfillment of the human person in this union with God. The visual metaphor stresses the absolute, unmediated character of this knowing and loving. However, this unmediated directness, seeing God "face to face" (1 Cor 13:12) or knowing God as God is, does not imply a comprehensive knowledge of God, for, as theologian Karl Rahner (d. 1984) has underscored, God remains ineffable Mystery.

The foundations for this doctrine are present in the NT. Matt 5:8 ("Blessed are the pure in heart, for they shall see God") is classically invoked, along with 1 Cor 13:12. Other texts that contribute to the development of this doctrine include 1 John 3:2; 2 Cor 3:18; and 2 Cor 5:7. The "eternal life" texts of the NT (e.g., Rom 2:7; 6:23; 1 Tim 1:16; John 3:16; 20:31) tie the doctrine to faith in Jesus Christ. Church teaching reached its normative articulation in *Benedictus Deus* (1336), which describes the Beatific Vision, and the *Decree for the Greeks* (Council of Florence, 1439), which speaks of seeing God as God truly is. These teachings were restated in later doctrine.

As a particular way of speaking about heaven, the Beatific Vision is the perfect fulfillment of God's gracious self-communication to those who freely accept it, resulting in the most intimate possible union with God. It is thus an individual's final participation in the redemption accomplished by Christ, a redemption of all the "elect" who constitute the communion of saints. As participation in the redemption of the fullness of personal existence, it begins before death, in a gradual assimilation to Christ through love of God and neighbor, with the help of God's grace mediated through faith in Jesus Christ.

The development of the doctrine of the Beatific Vision is closely tied to an understanding of the relationship between grace and nature. Two classic questions are whether the Beatific Vision is the result of a natural desire and whether it is attainable by natural means alone. Thomas Aquinas (d. 1274) argued that although the human person possesses a natural desire to know and possess God, this natural desire cannot reach its fulfillment by natural powers alone; it is impossible for a human person to attain such knowledge of God on one's own (*Summa Theologiae* II–I.5.5). Nor does the existence of such a natural desire require that it be satisfied by God. The Beatific Vision is, therefore, an utterly gratuitous gift of God, offered to a free human person whose nature has already been disposed by God toward such a union by grace. The "nature" involved here is that of a spiritual personhood, the fulfillment of which is human apprehension of God by knowledge and love. Knowing has its finality in a direct intuition of God, an end that coincides with loving God, who is both the "object" and giver of this knowledge.

Beatific Vision thus draws together elements of eschatology, grace, and theological anthropology. These elements find their cohesion in the triune Mystery who is giver of the gift of the Beatific Vision, the gift itself, and the giving of the gift. As the fulfillment of faith in Jesus Christ, who as Son is the actual expression of the Father and the giver of the Spirit with the Father in the life of grace, Beatific Vision therefore implies full personal participation in the trinitarian life of God. Beatific Vision is also essentially a Christological doctrine, in that the union implied, that between a graced human nature that finds its finality in God and a God who is self-communicating love, is already established as a possibility for human persons in the union of human and divine natures in Jesus Christ. The resurrection of Jesus definitively reveals the fulfillment of this union and stands as the central symbol of the Christian hope of being perfectly united with God, seeing God face to face. *See also* eschatology, individual; eschatology, universal; eternal life; heaven; *lumen gloriae;* nature and grace.   *PAUL CROWLEY*

beatitude, the achievement of the final good that is the fulfillment of spiritual beings in grace. Catholic doctrine holds that this final good is God, who is the end of the natural human operations of knowing and loving. But God is not simply an objective goal of these operations; God is the connatural end of these operations. The promise of the gospel is that people shall participate in the very life of God, so that by human knowing and loving people shall share in the relationship of knowing and loving among the Father, Son, and Spirit that constitutes the life of the Trinity. Though the attainment of this beatitude is beyond the capacities of unassisted human powers, human nature is intrinsically oriented toward God as its ultimate end. Even those who do not explicitly desire God may, through their normal human patterns of life, seek that beatitude which is essentially transcendent. The transcendent beatitude of knowing God is, however, itself a gift of God: God's grace working in and through a human nature already oriented by God toward the final happiness of knowing and loving God. The notion of beatitude thus opens up the panorama of issues involving nature and grace, as well as the finality of human personhood (eschatology). *See also* Beatific Vision; eternal life; heaven.

beatitudes, declarations of praise or congratulations for a condition or virtue. In the OT the literary form appears primarily in Psalms and in wisdom literature. It may comment on a desirable state, such as living with an intelligent or good wife (Sir 25:8; 26:1) or being chosen by God (Pss 65:4; 84:4). It may also praise virtues, either such generic qualities as fear of the Lord (Pss 1:1; 112:1) and doing justice (Ps 106:3), or more specific acts such as considering the poor (Ps 41:1) and keeping the Sabbath (Isa 56:2). Beatitudes often indicate, as grounds for the congratulations, the rewards that come from the state or virtue being extolled.

Beatitudes introduce Jesus' great sermon in both Matt 5:3–12 and Luke 6:20–23. The different emphases of the two accounts reflect the possibilities inherent in the form. In Luke, Jesus congratulates people for conditions of real poverty, hunger, and desolation by promising them future recompense. The four consolatory Beatitudes are balanced by an equally concrete set of four threatening woes.

In Matthew, Jesus' nine Beatitudes generally praise people for virtues to be cultivated, e.g., poverty of the spirit, meekness, hunger for righteousness. The final two (Matt 5:10–12) praise people for being persecuted. Future rewards still ground the praise, but the dominant function of the passage is to instruct. Matthew's version seems to have undergone more editing than Luke's, although Jesus may have used beatitudes in both ways.

Beatitudes appear elsewhere in the NT (John 13:17; Jas 1:12; 1 Pet 3:14; Rev 16:15) primarily as words of praise for virtues.   HAROLD W. ATTRIDGE

Beauduin, Lambert, 1873–1960, pioneer of the liturgical movement in Europe. A Benedictine of the Abbey of Mont-César in Louvain, Beauduin is considered by many to be the founder of the modern liturgical movement. In *Manifesto,* given at the Malines Catholic Congress in Belgium in 1909, Beauduin called for a greater understanding of the liturgical texts, and for active participation in the liturgy by the faithful. *See also* liturgical movement.

Beauraing, Our Lady of (boh-rang'), a title for the mother of Jesus taken from apparitions in 1932–33 of Mary to children at Beauraing, Belgium. In 1943 the bishop of Namur authorized a cult to Mary under this title. Many pilgrims have come to this site where the children were believed to have heard secrets never to be revealed. *See also* apparitions of the Blessed Virgin Mary; Banneaux, Our Lady of.

Bec, Abbey of, Benedictine monastery in Nor-

mandy, France. Founded by Hirluin in 1034, Bec prospered under the patronage of the dukes of Normandy (later the kings of England). Its prior, Lanfranc, was friend and counselor of William the Conqueror, who made him archbishop of Canterbury. Lanfranc's successor as prior, Anselm, became abbot of Bec in 1078 and then followed Lanfranc as archbishop.

Bec's wealth made it a target for taxation and occupation from the thirteenth century on, but the community survived. In 1626 the abbey was reformed along Maurist lines; dissolved during the French Revolution, it was reestablished in 1948. *See also* Anselm of Canterbury, St.; monasticism.

Becket, St. Thomas, ca. 1118–70, archbishop of Canterbury and martyr. After studying in Paris, he returned to England in service to the archbishop of Canterbury as clerk. By 1155 he was the king's chancellor and in 1162 Henry II had him made archbishop of Canterbury, a position he accepted only reluctantly. After a religious conversion, Thomas adopted an austere life, resigned his post as chancellor, and was soon in open conflict with the king, especially over the matter of secular and spiritual jurisdic-

Thomas Becket being murdered by knights of King Henry II in Canterbury Cathedral in 1170; from the Playfair Book of Hours, Victoria & Albert Museum, London.

tions. Charged with treason, Thomas fled England for refuge at the French and papal courts. In spite of negotiations, the rift grew wider in 1170 when Henry disregarded Canterbury's prerogatives and had his son crowned king by the archbishop of York. A reconciliation was arranged but Thomas refused to lift the excommunication of episcopal supporters of Henry during the dispute. Convinced it was their king's will, four of Henry's knights assassinated Thomas in Canterbury Cathedral on December 29, 1170. Canonized in 1173, Thomas was the most popular saint in medieval England. Feast day: December 29. *See also* Canterbury.

Bede, St. (beed), styled "The Venerable," ca. 673–735, monk and Doctor of the Church. According to the autobiographical note appended to his *Ecclesiastical History of the English People,* Bede was born in Northumbria on land that later became part of Benedict Biscop's monastery of Wearmouth-Jarrow and was sent to the monastery for his education when he was seven. Educated by Benedict and Ceolfrid, Bede was ordained deacon at nineteen and priest at thirty. Having spent his life at the monastery, he died on the eve of the feast of the Ascension in 735; we have a description of his last days written by his student Cuthbert.

He is best known for the *Ecclesiastical History,* which surveys events in Britain from the Roman period down to 731. He himself attached greater importance to the exposition of the Scriptures, and his commentaries and homilies were widely read in the Middle Ages. Other works include grammatical and rhetorical studies, scientific and hagiographical treatises, and hymns.

A council at Aachen in 835 referred to Bede as a contemporary doctor; in 1899 Pope Leo XIII pronounced him Doctor of the Church. Feast day: May 25. *See also* England, Catholicism in.

Beelzebub (bee-el'zay-buhb), a Philistine deity. King Ahaziah sent to "Beelzebub, the god of Ekron" for an oracle (2 Kgs 1:2–16). In a polemic against this "god of the heavenly abode," his name was changed to "Lord of the flies" or "Lord of dung" (Josephus *Antiquities* 9.19). In the *Testament of Solomon* the king summons this "ruler of the demons," the highest ranking evil angel still in heaven. Beelzebub confesses that he binds humans, causes destruction, arouses passion, and instigates jealousies (*T. Sol.* 6:4). In two traditions Jesus is accused of acting in league with this "prince of demons" (Mark 3:22–30 and Matt 12:24–30; Luke 11:15–23). But he argues for liberating victory over this prince of evil powers.

Beghards/Beguines (beg-ahrds'/bay-geens'), lay groups who led lives of prayer, communal living, sharing of goods, and Christian service, especially in times of plague and epidemics. They were named after Lambert le Bégue ("the stammerer"). Founded in the twelfth century in the Low Countries (the Netherlands, Belgium, and Luxembourg), these men (Beghards) and women (Beguines) took no vows, but lived in small groups and earned a living through weaving, dying, and other skilled labor.

In the fourteenth century they aroused ecclesiastical suspicion because of their putative connection with radical groups, and they were condemned by the Council of Vienne in 1311. After a period of reformation they continued their commitments with varying degrees of success. The Beghards did not survive into the modern period, but a few Beguinages (communal dwellings) still exist.

Modern scholarship has shown a keen interest in the Beguines because of their lay character and their focus on the religious experience of women.

Belarusian Byzantine Catholics, a group of Orthodox Belarusians converted at the Union of Brest (1595–96) and received into full communion with the Catholic Church. Although Brest is usually associated with Ukrainians, at first the majority of those adhering to the union were Belarusians.

The union was gradually suppressed, however, with the expansion of Orthodox Russia into the area. In 1839 the czar formally abolished the Byzantine Catholic Church throughout Belarus. When Nicholas II granted more religious freedom in his empire in 1905, about 230,000 Belarusian Catholics came forward. But, not being allowed to form a Byzantine community, they passed to the Latin rite.

After World War I, a community of about thirty thousand Byzantine Catholics emerged in areas of Belarusia that were now part of Poland. An apostolic visitator was appointed for them in 1931, and an exarch in 1940. But after World War II, when the area was absorbed by the Soviet Union, the church was again suppressed and integrated into the Russian Orthodox Church.

Following the granting of religious freedom in the Soviet Union and the subsequent independence of Belarus, Belarusian Byzantine Catholics have emerged once again and have been making efforts to resume a normal ecclesial life. By early 1992, three priests and two deacons were at work and, unlike most of their Roman Catholic and Orthodox colleagues, were celebrating the liturgy in Belarusian. Although gaining legal recognition was proving difficult, at least ten parishes had applied for registration in the newly independent republic.

In 1992 there were about five thousand Belarusian Byzantine Catholics outside their homeland. They have a parish in Chicago and a religious and cultural center in London. *See also* Brest, Union of; Byzantine rite; Eastern Catholics and ecumenism; Eastern Catholics and Rome; Eastern churches; Eastern liturgies; Eastern rites.   *RONALD G. ROBERSON*

Belgium, Catholicism in. In the early 300s Christians began to settle in what is today Belgium. In eastern Belgium, Servatius (Sarbatios) became the bishop of Tongeren (Tongres), and in the western region (now in France), Superior was bishop of Bavai (Cambrai). All of Belgium was evangelized by the eighth century, in part due to the efforts of Amandus (d. ca. 675). Charlemagne (ca. 742–814) strengthened the Church and Christian culture, as is evident today in the church at St. Trond and the palace chapel at Aachen (Aix-la-Chapelle). In the Middle Ages, Lutgardis fostered the veneration of the Sacred Heart; Juliana of Liège promoted the Feast of Corpus Christi; and Jan van Ruysbroeck (1293–1381) made lasting contributions to the mystical life. After the Reformation, Archduke Albert and Archduchess Isabella (1598–1633) were such effective leaders of the Catholic restoration that, since the seventeenth century, Belgium has been one of the most Catholic countries in the world.

Belgian Catholics have a strong tradition of vigorous participation in educational, social, and political activities. In 1893 Désiré Joseph Mercier (1851–1926) established the Institut Supérieur de Philosophie at the University of Louvain, the institute whose work in transcendental Thomism influenced many theologians, including Bernard Lonergan and Karl Rahner. As the cardinal-archbishop of Malines, Mercier courageously asserted the independence of Belgium during the First World War. Furthermore, the liturgical renewal in the Catholic Church came about in large part because of the work done beginning in the late 1800s at Belgium's Benedictine monasteries of Maredsous, Mont-César, and Saint-André-lez-Bruges. In 1914 Lambert Beauduin's paper at the liturgical congress at Mechelen came to be regarded as the keynote ad-

dress of the worldwide liturgical movement. Moreover, in 1925 Canon Joseph Cardijn (named a cardinal in 1965) founded the "Jeunesse ouvrière chretienne" (JOC, or Jocism), the "young Christian workers," which promoted "Catholic Action." This movement prepared the way for today's unfolding of lay leadership and lay ministries in the Church. Although Cardinal Cardijn was influential at the Second Vatican Council (1962–65), no bishop played a more prominent role than Cardinal Leo Josef Suenens, archbishop of Mechelen-Brussels.

As of 1993, out of Belgium's total population of approximately 10 million, over 85 percent are Catholic. There are one archdiocese, the metropolitan see of Mechelen-Brussels, and seven dioceses. *See also* Beauduin, Lambert; Cardijn, Joseph; Mercier, Désiré Joseph; Ruysbroeck, Bl. Jan van; Suenens, Leo Josef.

ROBERT A. KRIEG

bell, metallic instrument used to call the faithful to worship. In Christian worship, the use of bells, which filled a practical need before clocks became common, dates to the sixth century. From the eighth century on, bells increased in size, eventually requiring campaniles or bell towers. Bells may be blessed in a rite resembling Baptism.

Bellarmine, St. Robert, 1542–1621, Italian cardinal and Doctor of the Church. The first Jesuit professor of theology at Louvain, he defended Catholic doctrine against the Reformation, in part by revitalizing Catholic biblical and patristic studies. His work, although polemical, was more systematic than that of many of his contemporaries. This is evident in his three-volume *Controversies,* which examines the teachings of the Reformers and gives arguments supporting Catholic theology. This was in contrast to others, who fought Protestantism with dogmatic assertions and polemics. He is perhaps best known for his theory of the indirect temporal power of the papacy. Innovative at that time, his theory asserted that the proper and primary power of the pope is spiritual and justified papal use of temporal power only in matters of spiritual concern. The teaching was considered suspect for limiting papal power. Only the sudden death of Pope Sixtus V in 1590 saved Bellarmine's work from being placed on the Index of Forbidden Books. Bellarmine, however, utilized his theory in defense of papal power in several disputes with civil authorities and played a significant role in the development of the doctrine of papal infallibility. Other works of his include cat-

St. Robert Bellarmine, sixteenth-century cardinal, theologian, and defender of the Catholic faith against Protestantism.

echisms and spiritual writings. Although the process of his canonization was begun in 1627, for various reasons (including his teachings on papal power) it was not completed until 1930. He was declared a Doctor of the Church in 1931 by Pope Pius XI. Feast day: May 17. *See also* Counter-Reformation/ Catholic Reformation; infallibility; primacy, papal.

Belloc, Hilaire, 1870–1953, English writer and critic. After a brief political career (member of Parliament, 1906–10), he wrote political commentary with G. K. Chesterton, defenses of his idiosyncratic understanding of Catholic economic and social teaching, and popular history, as well as essays and light verse.

Beloved Disciple, a designation for the unnamed follower of Jesus who figures prominently in the Fourth Gospel. He is singled out in the account of the Last Supper (John 13:23), the Crucifixion (John 19:26), and the Resurrection (John 20:2; 21:7, 20). This figure has been traditionally identified as John, the son of Zebedee, understood to be the author of the work. Yet an explicit identification is lacking. The figure may simply symbolize the ideal disciple. Or he may have been an important figure in the Johannine community, but not one of the Twelve. *See also* John the Evangelist, St.

bema (bee' mah; Gk., "platform"), the sanctuary of a Byzantine-rite church, usually an elevated platform at the east end of the building, separated from the nave by the iconostasis, or altar screen. The term is also used for the raised platform formerly in the center of the nave in ancient East Syrian and some West Syrian churches, surrounded by a low wall enclosing seats for the clergy and pulpits for the lectionaries. It was there that the Liturgy of the Word and other services were celebrated. The enclosed sanctuary with the altar was reserved for the strictly eucharistic part of the Mass. *See also* sanctuary.

Benedicamus Domino (bay'nay-dee-kah'moos doh'mee-noh; Lat., "Let us praise the Lord"), an acclamation to conclude the Liturgy of the Hours. The proper response is *"Deo gratias,"* "Thanks be to God." Sometimes the "Benedicamus Domino" is substituted for the dismissal at Mass. Before the reform of the liturgy following Vatican II (1962–65), during some penitential seasons this acclamation and its response signaled the transition from the end of Mass to one of the hours of prayer, Morning or Evening Prayer, when one of those services immediately followed the Mass. Following the Midnight Mass for Christmas, for example, this dismissal was used since the Office of Morning Prayer could immediately follow that Mass. The acclamation is no longer used as a transition.

Benedicite (bay'nay-dee'chee-tay; Lat., "Bless"), Latin title for the Canticle of the Three Young Men, Dan 3:52–90. Sung by Shadrach, Meshach, and Abednego, who endured Nebuchadnazzar's furnace, the stars, moon, birds, and even dolphins are encouraged to join the three in praise of God. Nebuchadnezzar II was a Mesopotamian king who threw three of the prophet Daniel's companions into a fiery furnace when they were accused of not serving his gods or worshiping the golden statue he had set up. The canticle is part of the Easter liturgy and Sunday Morning Prayer.

Benedict, Rule of St., the sixth-century monastic code attributed to Benedict of Nursia, patriarch of monasticism in the Latin West. In his *Life* of Benedict (*Dialogues* 2.36), Gregory the Great (d. 604) attributes to Benedict a monastic rule "remarkable for its discretion and its clarity of language." The consensus of scholarly opinion continues to support the traditional view that the rule referred to by Gregory is indeed the Rule of St. Benedict. Consisting of a prologue and seventy-three chapters, this relatively brief monastic code draws creatively from multiple sources, chief of which was a version of a somewhat earlier anonymous sixth-century monastic rule, probably from central or southern Italy, known as the Rule of the Master (Lat., *Regula Magistri*). The arguments in favor of the priority of the Rule of the Master are based on a comparative study of the vocabulary and of the sources utilized by the authors of the two rules, the institutions and practices they describe, and the structure of the two rules and the arrangement of their subject matter.

The Rule of St. Benedict combines both spiritual doctrine and practical norms governing daily life in the monastery. The spiritual doctrine is concentrated in a prologue and the first seven chapters, which concern the nature of cenobitic (communal) life (ch. 1); the role of the abbot or superior of the community and his consultation of the brethren (chs. 2–3); the tools of the monastic craft (ch. 4); and the essential monastic virtues: obedience, restraint of speech, and humility (chs. 5–7). The remaining chapters deal chiefly, but not exclusively, with the practical organization of the life: a liturgical code (chs. 8–20), a penitential code (chs. 23–30 and 43–46), and norms for the structure of the community (chs. 58–63). Other chapters deal with matters such as deans, the dormitory, food and clothing, sleep, work, prayer, and relationships within the monastery and outside; there are also further directives for abbot, prior, and porter, and a final appendix of an exhortatory nature. The rule thus sets up the framework for the living out of the integral Christian life within a form of cenobitic life in unbroken continuity with earlier monastic practice, both Eastern and Western.

Until the early ninth century, diffusion of the rule was generally slow; and in many places its norms were combined with those of other rules. With the Carolingian monastic reforms enacted under the direction of Benedict of Aniane (d. 821), pride of place was accorded throughout Western Europe to the Rule of St. Benedict, which became the chief basis for monastic practice to the present time. The astonishing success of this monastic code is amply demonstrated by the many forms of monastic life to which, according to regional circumstances and historical contexts, it has given rise. Whether within a monastic enclosure in a life characterized chiefly by prayer, work, and the celebration of the liturgy, or in a more active apostolate of Christian charity, such as

education and missionary work, these various forms of Benedictine life continue to draw their vitality and inspiration from the Rule of St. Benedict. *See also* Benedictine order; Benedict of Nursia, St.; monasticism.   CHRYSOGONUS WADDELL

Benedict II, St., pope from June 684 to May 685. Known for his knowledge of Scripture and love for the poor, he tried, unsuccessfully, to get Macarius, patriarch of Antioch, to recant Monothelitism, a Christological heresy. During his reign, the emperor Constantine IV remitted the mandate that papal elections had to be ratified by the emperor. Feast day: July 2.

Benedict XII [Jacques Fournier], ca. 1280–1342, the third of the Avignon popes, from 1334 to 1342. A French Cistercian monk, learned doctor of theology, and confidant of his predecessor John XXII, he distinguished himself as a tireless and effective inquisitor. Though politically weak, Benedict's pontificate was marked by large-scale attempts at Church reform, which included the reorganization of the Curia and more stringent regulation of the mendicant orders. His bull *Benedictus Deus* (1336) settled the disputed theological question of what knowledge the souls of the blessed possess prior to the Last Judgment by ruling that such knowledge is a direct, face-to-face vision (known as the Beatific Vision) of the divine essence. *See also* Avignon; Beatific Vision.

Benedict XIV [Prospero Lorenzo Lambertini], 1675–1758, pope from 1740 to 1758. Educated in theology and law, he was appointed Promoter of the Faith by Pope Clement XI in 1708, and in that capacity published a multivolume work on the canonization of saints (*De Servorum Dei Beatificatione et Beatorum Canonizatione*), which remains to this day an influential study of the subject. As pope, Benedict pursued a conciliatory policy with the aggressive and belligerent absolutist European nation states. Concordats signed with Naples (1741), Spain (1753), and others conceded papal authority in ecclesiastical appointments, while enabling the Church to maintain a measure of influence in these lands. *See also* canonization.

Benedict XV [Giacomo della Chiesa], 1854–1922, pope from 1914 to 1922. After earning his doctorate in civil law (1875) and his ordination (1878), della Chiesa was trained as a papal diplomat, joining the secretariat of state as aide to Archbishop Rampolla (1883). He accompanied the papal

Pope Benedict XV, perhaps the most underrated of the modern popes, who, in his first encyclical, *Ad Beatissimi,* called a halt to the anti-Modernist crusade conducted by ultraconservative Catholics against progressive Catholics.

ambassador first to Spain, where he helped to organize the relief of a particularly violent cholera epidemic. He returned to Rome after Rampolla was named papal secretary of state and cardinal (1887). In 1901 he became undersecretary himself. From 1907 until 1914, he served as archbishop of Bologna. Benedict's pontificate was characterized by the attempt to bring peace both to a war-ravaged Europe and to a Church recently torn by the Modernist crisis, a hope signaled by the first of his twelve encyclicals, *Ad Beatissimi Apostolorum* (1914), in which he called a halt to the virtual civil war between traditionalists and progressives in the Catholic Church. Though insisting upon his neutrality during World War I, Benedict was perceived by both the Central and Allied powers as complicit with the other. He repeatedly called for an end to the "useless slaughter," but his seven-point peace plan, proposed in 1917, was rejected by both sides. After the war, his encyclical plea for international reconciliation, *Pacem Dei Munus* (1920), preceded a growth of diplomatic relations between the Holy See and European states. His canonization of Joan of Arc (1920) proved especially helpful in healing relations with France. Benedict also oversaw the promulgation of the 1917 Code of Canon Law, the establishment of the Pontifical Oriental Institute in Rome (1917), and, in *Maximum Illud* (1919), he called for more adequate training of missionaries and the formation of native clergies.　　　PAUL J. WOJDA

Benedict Biscop, St. [Biscop Baducing], ca. 628–ca. 690, abbot and patron saint of English Benedictines. Biscop left the court of Northumbria at age fifteen to become a monk. After visits to Rome, two years in the monastery of Lérins (where he took the name Benedict), and two years as prior at Canterbury, he returned to Northumbria, where King Ecgfrith gave him lands for monastic foundations at Wearmouth and Jarrow. His further pilgrimages (he made six to Rome) enriched those houses with books and paintings. Feast day: January 12. *See also* Benedictine order.

Benedictine order, the confederation of monasteries adhering to the Rule of St. Benedict and presided over by an abbot primate who resides in Rome.

History: Benedict of Nursia (d. ca. 550) was not the founder of a religious order in the sense of later founders like Francis of Assisi (d. 1226) or Ignatius of Loyola (d. 1556). There is considerable evidence in the rule itself that Benedict was simply intent on transmitting the monastic wisdom of earlier centuries and adapting it to the conditions of the sixth century. Although he clearly expected his rule to be followed in some monasteries other than his own at Monte Cassino, Benedict almost certainly did not foresee the extent to which the rule would eventually spread throughout the entire Christian world. In fact, for the first several centuries after its composition, the rule was often only one of several rules (e.g., the Rule of St. Columban or the Rule of Ferreolus) that would be followed in a given monastery. In that era of the *regula mixta* (Lat., "mixed rule"), the abbot or abbess would determine just which regulations would obtain on a given issue.

Gradually, however, the Rule of St. Benedict superseded all others, both because of its intrinsic excellence and moderation and because the emperor Charlemagne (d. 814) wished all the monasteries of his empire to be characterized by uniformity of observance under the "Roman rule" of St. Benedict. A decisive step in this direction occurred shortly after Charlemagne's death when his son and successor Louis authorized the monk Benedict of Aniane (d. 821) to enforce a standard observance throughout the northern part of the empire. A key element in this program was the exclusive use of the Rule of St. Benedict, supplemented by "customaries" or "statutes" that specified details of liturgical and disciplinary practice. In fact, this reform was short-lived, falling into disuse with the dissolution of the empire under Louis's quarrelsome sons and the invasions of the Norsemen and Saracens.

Nevertheless, the work of Benedict of Aniane provided a norm to which future generations could and did return. Thus, the tenth century saw the founding of a number of new centers of reform, the most influential of which was the abbey of Cluny, south of Dijon in Burgundy. Under a succession of five particularly capable abbots between the years 927 and 1157, this monastery became the center of an "order" that, by the middle of the twelfth century, had more than three hundred other monasteries under allegiance to the abbot of Cluny. This highly centralized system clearly diverged from the assumption of the rule that each monastery would be independent, headed by its own abbot, but the Cluniac program did have the distinct advantage of keeping its affiliated houses exempt from interference by local feudal lords, whether secular or ecclesiastical.

The liturgical splendor of Cluny, its growing wealth, and the practical disappearance of manual labor as a normal part of the monastic day contributed to the rise of reform orders in the eleventh century, preeminently the Cistercian. The evident success of the Cistercian institutions of visitation (according to which the abbot of a founding monastery would visit each daughter house yearly for the purpose of maintaining discipline) and general chapter (at which all the abbots would meet regularly as a legislative and judicial body responsible for the direction of the order) led the Fourth Lateran Council in 1215 to impose these and some other administrative reforms on the independent houses that were following the Rule of St. Benedict. Thus, in each ecclesiastical province the leaders of all monasteries were to meet in general chapter every fourth year under an elected president, this chapter having powers and duties similar to those of the Cistercians. This directive met with some resistance on the part of monasteries accustomed to the autonomy presumed by the rule, but the reform did take hold with notable success in England, where general chapters regularly formulated and revised statutes for all Benedictine monasteries within that realm.

In countries directly affected by the Protestant Reformation some three centuries later, a majority of the monasteries disappeared. Those that survived were often grouped into national congregations, some of which became centers of European scholarship (especially the Congregation of St. Maur in France), but in the decades following the French Revolution most European monasteries were again closed or even destroyed; scarcely thirty remained in Europe by the end of the Napoleonic era. Revival occurred under the guidance of nineteenth-century abbots like Prosper Guéranger (d. 1875) in France and Maurus Wolter (d. 1890) in Germany, and from these and other European countries foundations were soon made in other parts of the world.

In the late nineteenth century, the desire of Pope Leo XIII (d. 1903) to bring the whole body of Benedictines into some sort of union led to the foundation of the international college of Sant'Anselmo in Rome and the establishment of the office of abbot primate, headquartered there. While the primate does not enjoy ordinary jurisdiction over any of the various Benedictine congregations, he does have some powers of supervision and (depending on the individual elected to fill this office) considerable moral authority.

Present Status of the Order: The Benedictine order is not highly centralized. In fact, to emphasize the note of local autonomy and thereby distinguish the Benedictine from such orders as the Franciscan or Jesuit, it is probably more helpful to speak of it as a confederation than as an order. At the present time, the Benedictine Confederation embraces twenty-one congregations of monks in more than two hundred and fifty monasteries, plus twenty-four major congregations or "federations" of nuns (*moniales,* Lat., "who take solemn vows") in more than three hundred and fifty monasteries, and thirty-four congregations or federations of Benedictine sisters (*sorores,* Lat., "women in simple vows") in more than six hundred houses. A congress of abbots is held every four years at Sant'Anselmo in Rome, attended by abbots from throughout the world; the purpose of this gathering is more learning and sharing of ideas than the passage of definitive legislation, a function more characteristic of the congregational general chapters. Benedictine women have no similar assembly on a worldwide basis but regularly have regional or national assemblies of superiors and elected delegates from the houses of each congregation. According to the *Catalogus Monasteriorum O.S.B.,* in 1990 the total number of professed Benedictine monks was 9,096, of nuns 7,428, and of sisters 10,979.

More important than such statistics, however, is a sense of what characterizes the life of these men and women. While the constitutions of the various congregations may exhibit significant differences one from another, all Benedictines profess allegiance to the Rule of St. Benedict and consequently place great weight on the essential attitudes and practices enshrined in that document: life in community, with each member "supporting with the greatest patience one another's weaknesses of body or behavior" (72:5); ownership of all goods in common; communal praying of the Liturgy of the Hours; prayerful reflection on the scriptures and related literature (*lectio divina*); and "preferring nothing whatever to Christ" (72:11). On the basis of this spiritual foundation, Benedictines perform a great variety of works, including agriculture, hospitality, education, skilled craftwork, scholarship, counseling, and parochial ministry. Almost all of the monasteries of nuns and some men's monasteries observe strict enclosure, whereas Benedictine sisters and many monks can often be found working at some remove from the monastery itself. Whatever their worksite, they all ideally strive to carry out Benedict's well-known exhortation "that in all things God may be glorified" (57:9). *See also* Benedict, Rule of St.; Benedictine Sisters; Benedict of Nursia, St.; Cluny; monasticism.

Bibliography

Fry, Timothy, ed. *RB 1980: The Rule of St. Benedict in Latin and English with Notes.* Collegeville, MN: The Liturgical Press, 1981.

Kardong, Terrence. *The Benedictines.* Wilmington, DE: Michael Glazier, 1988.

Rees, Daniel, and Other Members of the English Benedictine Congregation. *Consider Your Call: A Theology of Monastic Life Today.* Kalamazoo, MI: Cistercian Publications, 1980.   JAMES WISEMAN

Benedictine Sisters, women's branch of the Order of St. Benedict (O.S.B.). Benedict of Nursia founded his first monastery in 529 in Italy. He named his sister Scholastica the superior of the women's monastery nearby. His rule served as the norm for women religious until the twelfth century. According to Benedict, the monastic life required only the rule and an abbot, that is, a living interpretation of the rule. Central to the life are community, daily liturgical prayer, meditative reading of Scripture, silent reflection, and some type of productive labor. Because they profess vows that allow them to be less strict than Benedictine nuns, the sisters are not bound to remain in the enclosure nor to chant the entire Divine Office. They profess vows of stability to remain in one priory, of conversion of life, and of obedience according to the rule. The first Benedictine women came to the United States in 1846 from Eichstätt, Germany, and settled in Latrobe, Pennsylvania. Most Benedictine sisters in the United States are involved in education or justice and service ministries. *See also* Benedict, Rule of St.; Benedictine order; religious orders and congregations; Scholastica, St.

Benedictine spirituality. *See* Benedictine order.

Benediction (Lat., *benedictio,* "blessing"), a service of exposition and adoration of the Blessed Sacrament, concluding with a blessing of the people with the Sacrament. Peculiar to the Western Catholic tradition, Benediction originated together with the practice of elevating the consecrated elements for adoration at Mass, the reservation of the Sacrament in public view, and the celebration of the Feast of Corpus Christi. These practices reflect the shift from a symbolic to a realistic understanding of the Eucharist, which began with the eucharistic controversies of the ninth century and reached its apogee in the oath Berengar of Tours (d. 1088), a French scholastic theologian, was required to sign in 1059. Such theological developments were manifestations of a change of mentality that also displayed itself in ritual and devotional changes and the proliferation of legends concerning miraculous hosts. Benediction itself may well have grown out of the older practice of blessing people at the end of a rite with a cross or relic or, in the case of Communion of the Sick, with the Eucharist itself. In the early fourteenth century, this practice was extended to blessing with the Sacrament (exposed in pyx or monstrance) those who gathered at the place of reservation to sing an anthem after Compline. Similarly, a pause for adoration of the Sacrament, introduced into the newly established Corpus Christi processions, concluded with the priest blessing the people with the Sacrament. After the Council of Trent (1545–63) had reaffirmed Catholic belief in the Real Presence, churches tended to be built whose interior lines focused the eye upon the tabernacle (placed directly on the altar), and upon the throne provided at the heart of the reredos for the monstrance. With such developments, Benediction became a regular part of Catholic life from Trent to Vatican II (1962–65). Although not as common a devotion as it once was, a revised "Rite of Eucharistic Exposition and Benediction" is included in the Roman document *Holy Communion and Worship of the Eucharist Outside Mass* (1973). *See also* eucharistic devotions; Real Presence.   MARK SEARLE

Benedict of Aniane, St., ca. 750–821, official in the government of Pepin III and Charlemagne who became a monk, first at St. Seine and then at Aniane, Languedoc, France. From the latter monastery Benedict's reform spread to other French monasteries. He is known for his opposition to Adoptionism, a Christological heresy, and for his asceticism. Feast day: February 11. *See also* Adoptionism.

Benedict of Canfield, 1562–1611, English spiritual leader. Born William Fitch, Benedict converted to Catholicism in 1585. Two years later, he became a Capuchin. He is best known for his teaching that the spiritual life consists in discerning and following the will of God.

Benedict of Nursia, St., ca. 480–ca. 547, abbot, founder of Western monasticism, and patron saint of Europe. Our only source for the life of Benedict is the *Dialogues* of Pope Gregory the Great (d. 604). Gregory's own sources included men who had known Benedict, but it was not his purpose to prepare a detailed biography, and as a result so little is known about Benedict that there has even been debate as to whether the rule that bears his name today is the same one Gregory credits him with writing.

Benedict was born at Nursia, near Spoleto. He studied at Rome, then took up life as a hermit at Subiaco. He left the hermitage briefly to serve as abbot of a nearby cenobitic community. Finding the monks there hostile, he returned to Subiaco to found twelve small monasteries federated on a Greek model. After some years, he abandoned this experiment and founded a single large monastery at Monte Cassino, near Naples. A daughterhouse was later founded at Terracino. Gregory describes Benedict's many miracles and his contacts with notable figures of his day, including the Gothic king Totila, whom he met around 546.

He was buried at Monte Cassino in the same grave as his sister, Scholastica. The monastery was destroyed ca. 577 and rebuilt ca. 720: in the interim, the relics may have been translated to Fleury (Saint-Benoît-sur-Loire). Feast day: July 11. *See also* Benedict, Rule of St.; Benedictine order; Monte Cassino.

JOHN W. HOUGHTON

Benedict the Moor, St., 1526–89, Franciscan brother and patron saint of African-Americans. Born of black African slaves in Sicily, he was freed at age eighteen and eventually became part of a group of hermits, later becoming their superior. In 1562 the group was ordered by the pope to join an established community, and Benedict chose the Friars Minor of the Observance. Benedict entered as a lay brother, originally serving as cook. He was later chosen to be guardian of the friary and novice master and was sought out by many for his gifts of prayer and counsel. He chose to spend his final days as a cook. Feast day: April 4.

Benedictus (be-nay-dik'tuhs; Lat., "blessed"), the psalm uttered by Zechariah, father of John the Baptist, in Luke 1:68–79. The title derives from the first word of the psalm, which praises God in traditional scriptural language. The Benedictus serves as a canticle Morning Prayer in the Liturgy of the Hours.

benefice, an ecclesiastical office that carries the right of the incumbent to collect revenue for his support. From its earliest days the Church has promoted the ideal of a clergy freed from everyday activities and able to devote its time entirely to spiritual duties. During late antiquity rich landlords were exhorted to support the clergy, and in the Middle Ages feudal lords set aside lands for the incumbents of specific ecclesiastical offices. During the revolutions of the eighteenth and nineteenth centuries, most of these lands were seized by secular governments, and benefices are rare today. Indeed, the Second Vatican Council (1962–65) and the 1983 code of canon law urged their suppression.

The 1917 code of canon law defined a benefice as "a juridic entity perpetually constituted or erected by the competent ecclesiastical authority, consisting of a sacred office and the right to receive the income from the endowment connected with the office" (can. 1409).

benefit of clergy, legal exemptions and privileges granted to clergy and other religious because of their office. Roman law beginning in the fourth century and then the secular law of many countries in the Middle Ages granted such privileges as clerical immunity from the judgments of lay courts and the exemption of clergy from certain civil duties such as military service and taxation; Church law confirmed and expanded these privileges. Benefit of clergy has vanished from the legal codes of most countries. *See also* clergy.

Benno of Meissen, St., 1010–ca. 1106, bishop of Meissen and missionary to the Wends. Although he had served as chaplain to Emperor Henry IV, Benno supported Pope Gregory VII against Henry on the question of lay interference in Church appointments and in 1085 was deposed from his bishopric by pro-imperial German bishops. He was reinstated in 1088 by Clement III, an antipope known also as Guibert. In 1097 Benno changed his allegiance from Clement to Pope Urban II and spent his last years as a missionary. His canonization in 1523 evoked a strong denunciation from Martin Luther. Feast day: June 16.

Benoit, Pierre Maurice (ben-wah'), 1906–87, French Dominican biblical scholar. From 1933 he taught at the École Biblique in Jerusalem. He made contributions to form criticism, the theology of inspiration, hermeneutics, and the study of the Septuagint. He was NT editor for the Jerusalem Bible (1956), of the *Revue Biblique* (1953–68), and of the Dead Sea Scrolls (1971–86). At the Second Vatican Council (1962–65) he played an important role as expert for the documents on divine revelation, religious freedom, ecumenism, and non-Christian religions. *See also* École Biblique.

Benson, Robert Hugh, 1871–1914, English writer, son of Edward White Benson, archbishop of Canterbury. He was ordained an Anglican priest in 1894, entered an Anglican religious community in 1898, became a Roman Catholic in 1903, and was ordained a Catholic priest in 1904. He published sermons and popular novels on religious themes.

berakah (be-rah-kah'; Heb., "blessing"), the action both of God in endowing human beings with abundant gifts and of human beings in praising God for these gifts and seeking their extension for themselves and for others. God's blessing is both a sign and a means of the divine salvific presence and intervention, by which human beings are invited and brought into communion with God. The human response of praising God through the formula of blessing is a recognition and remembrance of divine gifts in order to further communion with God through the persons or objects included in the blessing. The North American Academy of Liturgy (NAAL) annually confers a Berakah Award on an American liturgical scholar whose writings and teachings have advanced the liturgical movement. *See also* blessing.

Berchmans, St. John (buhrk'mahns), 1599–1621, Belgian Jesuit scholastic. Born in Diest, he entered the Jesuit order in Mechlin. Excelling in philo-sophical studies in Rome, he died there shortly after completing his studies. Much loved by his confrères, he is revered today for the simplicity and fidelity of his life. Feast day: November 26.

Berengar of Tours (bair'en-gahr uhv toor), ca. 1000–1088, French theologian. He studied with Fulbert of Chartres and by 1030 was a canon of St. Martin's at Tours, where he began his teaching. About 1040 he found employment with the powerful counts of Anjou at Angers and became archdeacon there (1040–60) and treasurer of the cathedral (1047–53). He achieved a considerable reputation as a teacher and returned to Tours, retiring to Saint-Côme ca. 1080. Berengar became notorious for his eucharistic theology. Although his teaching can be reconstructed from only a few sources, his study of the Eucharist employed the dialectical tools of his age, logic and grammar, thereby preparing the way for Scholasticism. He apparently concluded that the attitudes of the participants are changed in the celebration of the Mass, not the eucharistic species. His doctrine evoked much theological debate and was condemned by synods in 1050, 1051, 1059, and 1079. He accepted the condemnations and died in communion with the Church. *See also* Eucharist; Real Presence.

Bergson, Henri, 1859–1941, French philosopher. Influenced by empiricism and evolutionism but frustrated with their shortcomings, he sought to defend spirit, intuition, and freedom against materialism, rationalism, and determinism. He contrasted intelligence (the basis of scientific knowledge) with intuition and advocated an integral empiricism combining the two. He described evolution as the creative thrust of an *élan vital* (Fr., "life force") through history, rather than mere conflict and determinism. He contrasted moralities and religions concerned with group survival with those that sought human unity. He influenced twentieth-century French Catholic thinkers such as Maurice Blondel. *See also* philosophy and theology.

Bernadette of Lourdes, St. [Marie Bernarde Soubirous], 1844–79, French peasant girl to whom the Blessed Virgin appeared. Bernadette saw visions of Mary at Lourdes beginning February 11, 1858, at age fourteen. Although she grew up weak with asthma and other ailments, and although it was most difficult for her to receive the countless visitors who came to her in search of cures and information

Bernadette of Lourdes, known also as Marie Bernarde Soubirous. Her visions of the Blessed Virgin Mary (who proclaimed, "I am the Immaculate Conception") established the small French town of Lourdes as one of the world's most popular pilgrimage sites; canonized in 1933, she is depicted here in a rare photograph.

about the Blessed Virgin, Bernadette never turned away anyone and never accepted any form of payment. At twenty-two she entered the convent at Nevers and remained there until her death at thirty-five. Her constant humility is characterized by her prayerful cry from Nevers: "Oh! if only I could see without being seen!" Feast day: April 16. *See also* apparitions of the Blessed Virgin Mary; Lourdes.

Bernanos, Georges (buhr-nah'-nohs), 1888–1948, French novelist, dramatist, essayist. Born in Paris, his early Jesuit education was followed by studies in law and literature at the University of Paris and the Institut Catholique. Bernanos was a staunch Catholic and royalist, joining the right-wing *Action Française,* and spending much of his almost nomadic life supporting monarchist movements in France and abroad. As a Catholic intellectual, his influence was primarily through numerous novels and short stories that captured the moral struggles and achievements of men and women, e.g., *The Diary of a Country Priest* (1938), *The Open Mind* (1943) and the Carmelite *Dialogues* (1949). *See also* Action Française.

Bernardino of Siena, St., 1380–1444, the most influential and popular Franciscan preacher of fifteenth-century Italy. He was canonized in 1450, only six years after his death. Vicar General of the Friars of Strict Observance (1438), he participated in the Council of Florence (1439). His greatest im-

pact came as an itinerant preacher of moral reform. He also promoted devotion to the Holy Name of Jesus. Feast day: May 20. *See also* Holy Name of Jesus.

Bernard of Clairvaux, St., 1090–1153, French Cistercian abbot and spiritual writer. Born the third son of a noble family near Dijon, Bernard decided at the age of twenty-one to enter the new and struggling reform monastery of Cîteaux, located a few miles south of his family's estate. Bernard's powers of leadership were already evident at this time, for he persuaded some thirty of his relatives and friends to join him in this venture. Three years later he was sent out as the founding abbot of a new monastery at Clairvaux, which in turn made sixty-eight foundations of its own during the thirty-eight years of Bernard's abbacy.

As abbot, one of Bernard's main responsibilities was the instruction of his monks. The fervor with which he addressed them in his sermons and the inherent excellence of his monastic theology soon led to requests to put his doctrine into writing. His first written work, *The Steps of Humility and Pride,* was composed at the behest of his own monks, while the Carthusians at the Grande Chartreuse requested his *Letter on Love,* which he later appended to his short masterpiece *On Loving God.* Perhaps the best known of all Bernard's works, his eighty-six sermons on the Canticle of Canticles were undertaken at the suggestion of still another Carthusian monk. This unfinished series of sermons is based much more on his own experience than on the text of that

Bernard of Clairvaux, one of the greatest monastic leaders and theologians in the history of the Church, exorcising an evil spirit from a possessed person; sixteenth-century painting by Jorg Breu, from the collection of the Sammlunger des Stifles abbey, Zwettl, Austria.

book of the Bible. The sermons contain his reflections on such diverse subjects as the reform of the clergy, the death of his brother Gerard, and the errors of Rhenish heretics of his day.

Bernard's many talents brought numerous other kinds of requests his way. Between 1130 and 1138 he traveled throughout Europe, championing the cause of Pope Innocent II (d. 1143) against a schismatic rival for the papal throne. Two years after the end of the schism, and at the request of his close friend William of St.-Thierry (d. 1148), he wrote a lengthy letter to the pope "Against the Errors of Abelard," that bold Parisian master who, in Bernard's opinion, was guilty of a destructive rationalism in matters of faith. Still later, the first Cistercian pope, Eugenius III (d. 1153), asked Bernard to preach the Second Crusade, whereupon he traveled throughout northern Europe promoting the idea of the crusade among monarchs, the nobility, and the general population; when the crusade failed at the end of 1149, Bernard was widely held responsible and accepted the personal humiliation that ensued.

His final years were largely taken up with the writing of his long work *On Consideration*, another request of Pope Eugenius III, who desired a comprehensive treatise on papal spirituality. By the spring of 1153 all these labors left Bernard physically exhausted. After acting as mediator of an ecclesiastical dispute at Metz, he returned to Clairvaux a sick man and died there in late summer. He was canonized twenty-one years later and was declared a Doctor of the Church in 1830. Feast day: August 20. *See also* Cistercian order; Cîteaux; Crusades; monasticism.

JAMES WISEMAN

Bernard of Montjoux, St., ca. 996–1081, patron saint of mountain climbers. He established two Alpine hospices to aid lost travelers in the mountain passes that were named after him: Great Bernard and Little Bernard. Feast day: May 28.

Bernardo Gui (gwee), 1261–1331, inquisitor vilified in Umberto Eco's *The Name of the Rose*. A Dominican, he was inquisitor of Toulouse from 1307 to 1324, when he was made a bishop. Author of numerous works, his most famous is a handbook for the inquisitor. *See also* Inquisition.

Bertram, St. Louis. *See* Bertrand, St. Louis.

Bertrand, St. Louis, 1526–81, a Spanish Dominican recognized for his preaching, missionary zeal

in South America (1562–69), and gift of prophecy. He was canonized in 1671, but his feast day, October 9, is no longer observed.

Bérulle, Pierre de (bay-rool'), 1575–1629, cardinal, theologian, and spiritual writer. Of a distinguished family, Bérulle was the leading spiritual director of his time in France, with particular influence at the royal court. He helped introduce the Teresan Carmelites into France. He also established the French Congregation of the Oratory in imitation of Philip Neri in order to help meet the need for clerical education. By his death the Oratory had seventeen colleges. He was also involved in French foreign policy seeking to form a Catholic grand alliance against the Protestants. The process for his beatification was interrupted by the Jansenist controversy and never resumed. *See also* Oratorians.

Bessarion, John (bes-sair'ee-uhn), 1403–1472, Greek cardinal, theologian, and humanist. As archbishop of Nicaea, Bessarion was instrumental in convincing his fellow Orthodox bishops to accept a short-lived union with Rome at the Council of Florence (1439). Made cardinal (1440), he was a generous patron of humanism in Italy. *See also* Florence, Council of.

Bethany (beth'uh-nee), a small village on the eastern side of the Mount of Olives, approximately a mile and a half from Jerusalem. The Gospels report that Martha, Mary, and Lazarus lived there (John 11:1–44), that Jesus lodged there at the time of Passover (Matt 21:17; Mark 11:11), and that he dined there at the house of Simon the leper where he was anointed (Mark 14:3; Matt 26:6). The village, now named El-'Aziriyeh, has been a pilgrimage site since the fourth century.

Another Bethany, east of the Jordan River, is mentioned in John 1:28 as the locale of John the Baptist's ministry, but the site has not been identified.

Beza, Theodore, 1519–1605, Calvin's successor as moderator of the Company of Pastors in Geneva (1564–80). Converting to Protestantism, he moved to Geneva in 1548. A prolific author, he had a profound influence on Calvinist theology. *See also* Calvinism.

Bibiana, St., also known as Viviana, virgin and martyr of unknown location and date. A church in Rome has honored her since the fifth century. Feast day: December 2.

BIBLE

The Bible (Gk., neut. pl., *ta biblia*, "short writings") is a collection of writings held to be of divine and human origin and accepted by Jews or Christians as authoritative for belief and practice. A Latin derivative, *biblia* (fem. sing.), appeared in the early Middle Ages and the English, "Bible," was first used in the fourteenth century. Synonymous terms are "Scripture" and "Holy Scripture." The Christian Bible is divided into the Old Testament (OT), or the collection of thirty-nine books from the Jewish tradition, and the New Testament (NT), comprising twenty-seven early Christian works. Jewish scholars often prefer the acronym "Tanakh" to "Old Testament" for the collection of the Torah (the Law), the Nebi'im (the Prophets), and Kethubim (Writings). Christians frequently use "Tanakh," "the Hebrew Bible," or "the Jewish Scriptures" in place of "Old Testament."

CONTENT OF THE BIBLE

Jews and Christians have different views on the content and order of the OT. The traditional names of the books derive usually from their content (e.g., Judges) or from their purported authors (e.g., Amos). In the Jewish canon, which numbers twenty-four books, the five books of the Torah are Genesis, Exodus, Leviticus, Numbers, and Deuteronomy. In the Prophets, the Former Prophets include Joshua, Judges, 1–2 Samuel, 1–2 Kings (double books are counted as one) and the Latter Prophets include the three major prophets Isaiah, Jeremiah, and Ezekiel and "the twelve" (counted as a single book; Hosea, Joel, Amos, Obadiah, Jonah, Micah, Nahum, Habakkuk, Zephaniah, Haggai, Zechariah, Malachi). These are followed by the eleven books of the Writings: Psalms, Proverbs, Job, Canticle of Canticles, Ruth, Lamentations, Ecclesiastes (or Qoheleth), Esther, Daniel, Ezra-Nehemiah, and 1–2 Chronicles.

The Roman Catholic OT canon numbers forty-six books in the following order (books marked * are often called "deuterocanonical" by Catholics, but "apocryphal" by Protestants, who do not accept them as canonical). The Pentateuch (Gk., "five scrolls"), which consists of Genesis through Deuteronomy, is followed by the historical books: Joshua, Judges, Ruth, 1–2 Samuel, 1–2 Kings, 1–2 Chronicles, Ezra, Nehemiah, Tobit*, Judith*, Esther (with the Additions*), and 1–2 Maccabees. These are followed by the wisdom books: Job, Psalms, Proverbs, Ecclesiastes, Canticle of Canticles, Wisdom of Solomon* (or simply Wisdom*), and Sirach* (Ecclesiastes*). Next come the prophets: Isaiah, Jeremiah, Lamentations, Baruch* (with the Letter of Jeremiah*), Ezekiel, and Daniel (with the addition of the Prayer of Azariah*, Susanna*, and Bel and the Dragon*), followed by the "minor prophets" in the Jewish order.

The traditional Protestant OT follows the Jewish tradition in content but varies in order. Ruth is inserted after Judges before 1–2 Samuel while

1–2 Chronicles, Ezra, Nehemiah, and Esther are added after 1–2 Kings. These historical books are followed by Job, Psalms, Proverbs, Ecclesiastes, Canticle of Canticles (as in the Catholic list but with the omission of Wisdom and Sirach). The listing concludes with the prophets again in the same order as the Catholic canon, but omitting the additions to Jeremiah and Daniel as well as 1–2 Maccabees.

Some Eastern Orthodox Christian groups count as canonical books such as 1 Esdras (2 Esdras in Slavonic and 3 Esdras in the appendix to the Vulgate), the Prayer of Manasseh, Psalm 151, and 3 Maccabees.

Among Christians there is a virtual consensus on the order and content of the twenty-seven books of the NT. Beginning it are the four Gospels: Matthew, Mark, Luke, and John (though the order in the early Church is often Matthew, John, Mark, Luke, i.e., giving precedence to Gospels attributed to apostles). These are followed by the thirteen letters attributed to Paul (or fourteen if Hebrews is considered Pauline): Romans, 1–2 Corinthians, Galatians, Ephesians, Philippians, Colossians, 1–2 Thessalonians, 1–2 Timothy, Titus (these three, known as "the Pastorals," contain pastoral directives to individuals), Philemon, and Hebrews. Then come the "catholic Letters" (so called because they are not written to particular churches): James, 1–2 Peter, 1–3 John, and Jude. The last book is Revelation (also called the Apocalypse).

THE FORMATION OF THE BIBLE

The Bible itself evolved over eleven hundred years and virtually every book includes earlier oral and/or written traditions. Often it is impossible to describe exactly the elements or process of composition. With the flowering of historical criticism of the Bible in the nineteenth century, attention focused on the formation of the Pentateuch. Its present form combines narrative, law, and poetry and its content narrates the primeval history (Gen 1–12), the stories of the ancestors (Gen 12–50), the liberation from Egypt (Exod 1:1–15:21), the wilderness wanderings and sojourn at Sinai (running from Exod 15:22 through Exodus, Leviticus, and Numbers), and Moses' farewell (Deuteronomy).

The Documentary Hypothesis, associated principally with Julius Wellhausen (1844–1918), postulated four major traditions for Genesis through Deuteronomy. The Yahwist (J), so called because it uses the name YHWH (Ger., JHWH) for God (see Exod 3:14), begins at Gen 2:1. An anthropomorphic view of God, emphasis on the saving acts of God in history, and vivid realistic narrative style characterize the Yahwist source. Some scholars claim that it was composed at the court of Solomon (ca. 930 B.C.). The other major tradition, the existence of which as an independent source is strongly questioned today, is "the Elohist" (E) (because it uses principally the Hebrew term *Elohim* for God). It supplements the J narrative and is thought to derive from the Northern Kingdom (Israel) in the eighth century B.C.

In the classical Documentary Hypothesis this national epic, a combination of J and E, underwent a radical transformation by the addition of "D," which is a term for both a source and a movement. The source is often identified with the book of the law found in the eighteenth year of the reign of Josiah (640–609 B.C.; see 2 Kgs 23:2), the substance of which may be Deut 12–26. The "D" editor, who wrote during or shortly after the Babylonian exile (587–539 B.C.), is thought to be responsible for supplanting the original ending of the Pentateuch by the addition of the book of Deuteronomy with its continued warnings about the perils of infidelity to the law in the promised land. This editor or movement also recasts the historical books Joshua through 2 Kings and creates the "Deuteronomistic History," which evaluates the kings of Israel and Judah according to their fidelity to the law. "P" also designates both a tradition (the Priestly tradition) and a editor or group of editors who are responsible for final form of the Pentateuch.

The initial creation story (Gen 1:1–2:4^a), with its stress on the powerful word of God, is from the P tradition. P is best seen in the whole book of Leviticus and in Exod 25–31. Concern for holiness (see the integration of the Holiness Code, Lev 17–26, into the P narrative), sacrifice, the priesthood, and the cult characterize P. The final composition of the Pentateuch is due to P and is dated by most scholars during the Persian period (522–333 B.C.). Though the Documentary Hypothesis has been modified since the time of Wellhausen, it remains a good working hypothesis for the significant traditions and movements behind the Pentateuch.

The prophetic books underwent similar complex development. Narrative cycles of prophetic figures such as Elijah (1 Kgs 17:1–19:21; 2 Kgs 1:1–2:18) and Elisha (2 Kgs 2:19–8:15) are found in the historical books, but no writings are attributed to them. Prophetic literature begins with the "writing prophets" in the eighth century B.C. The prophetic works are composed mainly of prophetic oracles, collections of sayings from God to the prophet often containing judgment on foreign nations and warnings to Israel or Judah. Though many of the prophetic oracles go back to the named figures (e.g., Amos, Isaiah, and Jeremiah), the existing books are compilations by disciples or prophetic schools often extending for centuries after the original prophet (see Jer 31). For example, "Deutero-Isaiah," Isa 40–55, reflects the Babylonian exile, and "Trito-Isaiah," chs. 56–66, was composed after the return from exile. The collection of the prophetic writings remained somewhat fluid. Sir 49:10 (ca. 190 B.C.) speaks of Isaiah, Jeremiah, Ezekiel, and "the twelve." The phrase "the law and the Prophets" appears in the prologue to the Greek translation of Sirach (ca. 132 B.C.). The NT usages (Matt 5:17; 22:40; Luke 24:44, "the law of Moses, the prophets, and the psalms") suggest that the prophetic books formed a distinct collection in the last two centuries before Christ.

Most difficult to describe is the formation of the collection known as the Writings, which comprises mainly Psalms and the wisdom books. Since the psalms are clearly collected into five books in imitation of the Pentateuch, their final edition is postexilic, though many of the individual psalms reflect the preexilic Temple worship. Because of their nature, the collection of wisdom books is almost impossible to characterize. Prov 22:17–24:22, for example, integrates material from Egyptian wisdom traditions dating back a millennium. Wisdom shows clear influence of Hellenistic culture, and emerges therefore after the conquest of Palestine by Alexander the Great in 333 B.C.

Though it is often asserted that the Jewish canon was fixed at the so-called synod of Jamnia (Jabneel on the Mediterranean coast) ca. A.D. 100, debates among Jews continued into the Christian era over books such as the Canticle of Canticles and Ecclesiastes.

Though less complex, the NT went through a lengthy process of formation. Behind the Gospels stand collections of oral traditions about Jesus including sayings (e.g., parables) and narratives (miracle stories and passion narratives). Around the mid-50s of the first century emerged a document scholars call Q, which consisted primarily of a collection of sayings of Jesus. Mark, composed between A.D. 68 and 71, was the earliest written Gospel. Matthew and Luke, composed a decade later, incorporated virtually all of Mark as well as Q. John's Gospel, which emerged around A.D. 100, incorporated earlier traditions that are often different from those in the synoptic Gospels. The Letters of Paul, which occasionally take over earlier materials such as hymns (Phil 2:6–11), words of Jesus (1 Cor 11:23–25), or confessional formulas (1 Cor 15:3–7), were written to specific churches and were not collected as a group until the mid to late second century. Marcion's (d. ca. 160) rejection of the OT and much of the NT and the threat of Gnosticism in the second century were stimuli for the early Church to define its sacred and canonical texts. Though disputes continued in the West about whether Hebrews was canonical and in the East over the book of Revelation, Athanasius in his *Easter Letter* (A.D. 367) lists as authoritative and canonical the twenty-seven books that form the present NT. For Roman Catholics the decision of the Council of Trent (1545–63), followed explicitly by Vatican I (1869–70) and implicitly by Vatican II (1962–65), defined as canonical the forty-six books of the OT mentioned above and the twenty-seven books of the NT.

LANGUAGES, TEXTS, AND TRANSLATIONS

The Bible was handed down in two principal languages: Hebrew for the OT, except for Ezra 4:8–6:18; 7:12–26; Dan 2:4–7:28; and Jer 10:11, which are in Aramaic, and Greek for the NT. The earliest translations of the OT were into Greek and Aramaic. The Greek version, the Septuagint (Lat., *septuaginta*, "seventy"), so called because of the legend that it was translated by seventy-two scribes, was completed in Alexandria between 250 and 150 B.C. It was later revised in a literal translation by Aquila (ca. A.D. 128) and more freely by Symmachus (end of second century A.D.). The vast majority of citations and allusions to the OT in both the NT and early Church writings are to the Septuagint. The Hebrew Scriptures were also translated into Aramaic, which gradually became the ordinary language of Palestine after the return from exile. These are called Targums (Aram., "translations"). The oldest of these is a Targum on Job, fragments of which have been found at Qumran.

Though there are more manuscripts for the Bible (about five thousand for the NT alone) than for any ancient classical text, there is no manuscript of any biblical book that dates to the time of its named author. Text criticism is the aspect of biblical studies that seeks to determine among the different readings those that are earliest and closest to the lost original text. Until the discovery of the Dead Sea Scrolls at Qumran, the earliest OT manuscript was the ninth-century Aleppo codex. At Qumran, however, manuscripts or fragments of virtually every biblical book were discovered. Though different in some respects from the later manuscripts, the Dead Sea Scrolls confirm the great fidelity with which the Hebrew text was handed on.

Though often erroneously asserted, there is no evidence that any NT book ever existed in either Hebrew or Aramaic. Since the language of both ordinary and educated people in the Roman Empire was Greek, the earliest NT manuscripts are Greek papyrus fragments from the early second century. By the late fourth century and throughout the fifth there appear elegant Greek manuscripts of the complete Bible, principally Codex Vaticanus, Codex Sinaiticus, and Codex Alexandrinus. Latin translations begin to appear in the late second century, since the North African writer Tertullian (160–ca. 225) cites the Bible in Latin. This version, called the "Old Latin," which was also used by Cyprian of Carthage (d. 258), was supplanted by the monumental translation of the whole Bible into Latin, the Vulgate (principally by Jerome, 347–420), which became the official version of the Bible for over a thousand years. Other ancient translations were into Syriac, Coptic, and Ethiopic.

Though the early biblical manuscripts often contain lectionary divisions, they appear without division into chapters and verses. The chapters derive from Stephen Langton, archbishop of Paris (d. 1228). Verse numbers were first added to Christian Bibles by Sanctes Pagnini in 1528 and fixed in place by Robert Étienne (Stephanus) in 1555.

Though in the West there were sporadic translations into the vernacular before the Reformation, the return to the Bible advocated by the Reformers and the invention of printing evoked an explosion of translations. Two seventeenth-century translations, the King James Version for Protestants and the Douay-Rheims version for Catholics, achieved virtual canonical status for almost three hundred years. The first Roman Catholic version from original languages was the New American Bible, first issued in 1970, with revision of the NT in 1987 and of the Psalms in 1991. A complete revision of the OT is projected.

THE AUTHORITY OF THE BIBLE

The basis of biblical authority is a conviction formulated differently at different periods that the Bible contains revelation from and about God and God's design for humanity: "All Scripture is inspired by God and is useful for teaching, for reproof, for correction, and for training in righteousness" (2 Tim 3:16). For centuries inspiration was understood as virtual dictation from God to the biblical author. With the rise of historical criticism, more sophisticated theories have been proposed, such as a prophetic or poetic theory of inspiration. The 1965 Dogmatic Constitution on Divine Revelation of Vatican II (n. 7) simply states that the books were composed "through the prompting of the Holy Spirit," leaving open the precise manner of the prompting. Recent theories have suggested that inspiration is a communal or ecclesial charism rather than an individual one. An author or authors hand on those traditions that embody the faith of the community.

A correlate to inspiration is the doctrine of inerrancy. As God's word, the Bible was considered free of all error. Prompted by scientific discoveries about the age of the universe and of humanity and the disclosure of innumerable factual mistakes in the Bible with the rise of historical criticism, the struggle over inerrancy became acute and often bitter. The document on revelation of Vatican II, following Pope Pius XII's encyclical *Divino Afflante Spiritu* (1943), provided a significant breakthrough by teaching that, prior to any judgment of the truth of a biblical text, due consideration must be given to the literary form (e.g., whether a text is history or poetry) and to the customary modes of speaking in the culture that produced it in order to determine what the sacred writers intended to say and what God wanted to communicate through their words. The council also rejected a fundamentalist interpretation of inerrancy by stating that "the books of Scripture must be acknowledged as teaching firmly, faithfully and without error, *that truth which God wanted put into the sacred writings for the sake of our salvation*" (n. 11, italics added). History, archaeology, and culturally conditioned worldviews are not the subject of inerrancy.

The major achievement of Vatican II was in the larger area of restoring the authority of the Bible to the Church as a whole. In reaction to the sixteenth-century Reformers (esp. Luther and Calvin) who returned to the Bible as a critical principle against Church doctrine and practice, post-Tridentine Catholicism stressed tradition and magisterium (understood as the official teaching of the pope and the hierarchy) rather than the Bible. A misconception of the Tridentine decrees was that the council taught two sources of revelation, "tradition" and "Scripture." Vatican II avoided the two-source language and gave a definite priority to Scripture. Though sacred Scripture and sacred tradition "flow from the same divine wellspring," sacred Scripture is "the word of God," and the function of tradition is to hand it on in its purity (Dogmatic Constitution on Divine Revelation, n. 11). The magisterium is not above the word of God; it is its servant. The liturgical reforms mandated by the council stressed the authority of the Bible by introducing a three-year lectionary cycle, including especially the OT, which was rarely used in the post-Tridentine liturgy. Also, Scripture readings are to accompany the administration of sacraments other than the Eucharist. In the council decrees, the first ministry listed for both bishops and priests is the ministry of the word (Decree on the Bishops' Pastoral Office in the Church, n. 12; Decree on the Ministry and Life of Priests, n. 4), and biblical studies are to be the "soul" of seminary education (Decree on Priestly Formation, n. 16). Laypeople are encouraged to read and study the Bible (Dogmatic Constitution on Divine Revelation, n. 22), and the post–Vatican II period was characterized not only by the growth of Catholic biblical scholarship, but by a vast explosion of biblical institutes for religious, clergy, and laity.

INTERPRETATION OF THE BIBLE

As a text from a different culture and in an original language unknown to most readers, the Bible must be interpeted. Hermeneutics (from the Gk., "to translate" or "explain") is the general term for the theory and practice of interpetation. Exegesis (a loanword from the Gk., "drawing out," or "explanation") is the most basic form of interpretation, involving the exposition of a biblical text in its original literary, historical, and religious context, with an array of methods used for reading any ancient text: attention to the grammar, syntax, and style of the ancient languages, concern for literary forms and structure, and study of the historical conditions reflected in the text. Biblical texts, however, like other "classic texts," possess an excess of meanings not intended by their original authors. Also, since the Bible points to the mystery of God and of the divine-human relationship, it makes claims not simply on its original audience but on subsequent generations. The early Church distinguished between the "literal" sense and "spiritual" sense of Scripture, the latter being the divine message behind the letter of the text. This gave rise to the medieval theory of the four senses of Scripture: the literal or plain meaning of the text; the allegorical or theological meaning; the anagogical or eschatological meaning; and the moral or ethical meaning.

While very few contemporary biblical scholars or theologians hold the doctrine of the four senses, the major task of post–Vatican II theology has been to evolve hermeneutical theories that explain how the Bible remains a resource for theology and Church life. Often these involve the search for a central principle within the Bible itself (e.g., covenant, liberation, the option for the poor). More recent theories stress the role of the reader in creating meaning (reader-response criticism), along with awareness of the social context of different readers (e.g., feminist hermeneutics). There is growing admission that biblical texts admit multiple interpretations and that the hermeneutical task demands dialogue between the magisterium and biblical scholars and between biblical scholars, literary critics, and theologians, as well as attention to the lived religious experience of believers and the pastoral practice of the Church (see Dogmatic Constitution on Divine Revelation, nn. 8, 11).

See also Bible, Church teachings on the; biblical theology; canon of the Scriptures; inerrancy of Scripture; inspiration of Scripture; Scripture, authority of; Scripture, interpretation of; Scripture and tradition.

Bibliography

Ackroyd, P. R., et al., eds. *The Cambridge History of the Bible*. 3 vols. Cambridge: Cambridge University Press, 1963–70.

Brown, Raymond E. *Responses to 101 Questions on the Bible*. Mahwah, NJ: Paulist Press, 1990.

Campenhausen, Hans von. *The Formation of the Christian Bible*. Philadelphia: Fortress Press, 1972.

Megivern, James J., ed. *Official Catholic Teachings: Bible Interpretation*. Wilmington, NC: McGrath, 1978.

Schneiders, Sandra. *The Revelatory Text: Interpreting the New Testament as Sacred Scripture*. San Francisco: HarperCollins, 1991.

JOHN R. DONAHUE

Bible, Church teachings on the. A recent official summary of Church teachings on the Bible is to be found in *The Catechism of the Catholic Church* (1992). The summary contains eight points: (1) All of Sacred Scripture is but a single book, which ultimately speaks about Christ. (2) The Scriptures are inspired and contain the word of God. Hence, they can be called the Word of God. (3) God is the author of the Scriptures, whose human authors have been inspired by God and given special assistance in order that their writings teach truth, without error, for the sake of our salvation. (4) The interpretation of Scripture must be especially attentive to what God intends to reveal for the sake of our salvation. (5) The Church receives and respects as inspired forty-six books of the OT and twenty-seven books of the NT. (6) Within the Scriptures the four Gospels hold a central place because Jesus Christ is their center. (7) The unity of the OT and NT derives from God's single plan of salvation and revelation. (8) As the Church venerates the body of the Lord, so it venerates the Scriptures.

Tradition: The catechism's summary affirms that the canon, the complete and authoritative list, of inspired Scriptures includes seventy-two books. This reiterates a teaching expressed in the Decree of Damasus of the Roman synod of 382 and reaffirmed by the Council of Trent in 1546.

The unity of the Scriptures is a very ancient teaching of the Church. Of major significance in the development of the canon was a contention by Marcion, a mid-second century Roman heretic, that there was absolute incompatibility between the OT's God of wrath and the God of Jesus, a loving Father. Marcion accepted as authoritative only a small collection of the writings of Paul and a heavily edited version of the Gospel according to Luke. In reaction to Marcion, defenders of Christian orthodoxy, such as Irenaeus, proclaimed the unity of the fourfold Gospel and asserted the divine origin of the Scriptures of the OT.

In the fourth and fifth centuries, the Manichees denied that God was the author of the OT. In reaction, a number of local church councils in North Africa affirmed that God is the single author (Lat., *unus auctor*) of the books of the OT and NT. This formula became an important part of the Church's tradition. It was included in the decrees of the councils of Florence, Trent, and Vatican II (Dogmatic Constitution on Divine Revelation, n. 11).

Augustine (d. 430) highlighted the unity of the OT and NT when he wrote that "the New Testament lies hidden in the Old; the Old Testament is made manifest in the New." Augustine's teaching was reiterated by Vatican II (1962–65), which explained that the purpose of the Old Covenant was to prepare for the coming of Christ and the kingdom, to announce it and to clarify its meaning (Dogmatic Constitution on Divine Revelation, nn. 15–16).

The idea that all of the Scriptures point to Christ has its roots in the NT. Matthew, for example, repeatedly uses a fulfillment formula to express this conviction (Matt 1:22–23). Reflecting the tradition of the manna given to Israel during the Exodus, the Gospel according to John portrays Jesus as the bread of life (John 6). Paul recalls that Adam is a type of the one to come (Rom 5:14). The Letter to the Hebrews portrays Jesus as a high priest according to the order of Melchizedek (Heb 5:6; Ps 110:4). Subsequently, by means of an allegorical reading of the OT, the Fathers of the Church were able to find Christ in virtually every line of the text.

Vatican Council II: Vatican II proclaimed the preeminence of the fourfold Gospel among the Scriptures as a matter of "common knowledge." It explained that the Gospels are "the principal witness to the life and teaching of the incarnate Word, our Savior" (Dogmatic Constitution on Divine Revelation, n. 18). Jesus is the incarnate Word and the fullness of revelation.

God's plan of revelation has as its purpose the salvation of humankind. This plan, the council teaches, is realized by deeds and words. The words proclaim the deeds and clarify the mystery contained in them (Dogmatic Constitution on Divine Revelation, n. 2). At first transmitted orally, the words were put into writing under the inspiration of the Holy Spirit. With God as their origin and testifying to revelation as they do, the Scriptures are received and venerated by the Church as the word of God.

Because of this understanding, the Scriptures enjoy an importance in the life of the Church that the council has described in this way: "the Church has always venerated the divine Scriptures just as it venerates the body of the Lord, since from the table of both the word of God and of the body of Christ it unceasingly receives and offers to the faithful the bread of life, especially in the sacred liturgy. It has always regarded the Scriptures together with sacred tradition as the supreme rule of faith, and will ever do so" (Dogmatic Constitution on Divine Revelation, n. 21).

Vatican II's Dogmatic Constitution on Divine

Revelation, promulgated on November 18, 1965, represents the Church's most extensive and most authoritative teaching on the Scriptures. By formulating this teaching in one of its two dogmatic constitutions, the council expressed the importance of the Scriptures in the life of the Church. By calling the constitution *Dei Verbum* (Lat., "the Word of God"), it indicates how the Scriptures are to be understood, namely, as the message of salvation.

In addition to those aspects of its teaching recalled in the eight-point summary of *The Catechism of the Catholic Church,* the council highlighted Scripture's relationship with tradition. Commenting on the inspired nature of the Scriptures, the council declared that "the books of Scripture must be acknowledged as teaching firmly, faithfully, and without error that truth which God wanted put into the sacred writings for the sake of our salvation" (Dogmatic Constitution on Divine Revelation, n. 11).

Along with its significant teaching on the nature of Scripture, the council had much to say about the members of the Church and the Scriptures. It affirmed that the task of authentic interpretation of Scripture has been entrusted to the teaching office of the Church and that this office is not above the word of God, rather it serves it. Its decree encouraged biblical scholarship, noted the importance of studying the biblical text in its original languages, and highlighted the significance of the Bible's use of different literary forms.

The council urged that all the faithful be provided with easy access to the Scriptures. It drew attention to the Church's multiform ministry of the Word, especially as it is exercised by priests, deacons, and catechists, and it repeatedly underscored the importance of the reading and preaching of the Scriptures in the Church's liturgy. The Scriptures are also, it noted, to serve as the soul of theology.

Before the Council: Vatican II's comprehensive teaching on the Scriptures was the result of a century-long interaction between the Church and modern biblical criticism. A number of encyclicals and various pronouncements by the Pontifical Biblical Commission had expressed the developing teaching of the Church on the Bible during that period.

Leo XIII's encyclical *Providentissimus Deus* (1893) taught that the Bible was not formally intended to teach natural science, but that it used language as it was commonly spoken at the time of the composition of the various books. The encyclical also taught that the entire Bible was inspired and without error.

Pius X's *Pascendi Dominici Gregis* (1907) represented a reaction to errors presumed to have come from the Modernists. The encyclical appealed to a doctrine of inspiration it did not otherwise explain. Papal caution continued to be reflected in Benedict XV's *Spiritus Paraclitus* (1920), which praised the memory of Jerome and commended the efforts of those scholars who used modern methods of interpretation, but issued stern warning against some of the modern interpretive techniques. The pope emphasized that spiritual perfection, the defense of the faith, and effective preaching of the Word were the goals of biblical scholarship.

On the occasion of the golden jubilee of Leo XIII's encyclical, Pius XII issued the encyclical *Divino Afflante Spiritu* (1943). The pope noted that the Scriptures were relevant even in most difficult times and he taught Catholics that the literal sense of the Scriptures, which is their proper sense, can only be understood within the context of the literary forms and expressions in use at the time that the Scriptures were written.

In 1902 Leo XIII established the Pontifical Biblical Commission. Its early decrees affirmed the general historicity of the biblical texts and the traditional authorship of many of the biblical books. *Sancta Mater Ecclesia* (1964) was the final decree of this commission, in its pre–Vatican II configuration. The instruction asserted the general historicity of the four Gospels, but demonstrated a far more sophisticated view of history than had been present in earlier commission texts. Since Vatican II the commission has been reorganized and given the task of serving as adviser to the Congregation for the Doctrine of the Faith. *See also* Bible; Bible and doctrine; inerrancy of Scripture; inspiration of Scripture; Scripture, authority of; Scripture, interpretation of; Scripture and tradition.

Bibliography

Brown, Raymond E., and Thomas Aquinas Collins. "Church Pronouncements." In *The New Jerome Biblical Commentary.* Englewood Cliffs, NJ: Prentice Hall, 1990. Pp. 1166–74.

Collins, Raymond F. *Introduction to the New Testament.* Garden City, NY: Doubleday, 1983. Ch. 10, "Rome and the Critical Study of the New Testament." Pp. 356–84.

Megivern, James J., ed. *Bible Interpretation. Official Catholic Teachings.* Wilmington, DE: McGrath, 1968.   RAYMOND COLLINS

Bible, English translations of the. Since most people do not have access to the Bible in its original languages (Hebrew, Aramaic, Greek), the task of producing an exact and readable version in the vernacular languages has always assumed the greatest importance. This task must be undertaken anew at various intervals because of changes in the receptor language and because our knowledge of the original languages and access to new textual material is increasing all the time. Thus, the discovery of the cuneiform texts from Ugarit, beginning in 1929, has greatly increased our knowledge of Hebrew, and the biblical texts from Qumran, including an entire scroll of Isaiah (1QIs[a]), have greatly enlarged our understanding of the early stages of the transmission of the Hebrew text.

English Versions Before Printing: Until the sixteenth century all translations of the Bible into English were made on the basis of the Latin Vulgate version produced by Jerome at the bidding of Pope Damasus (383–84). We do not know how and to what extent the Bible was read during the Roman occupation of England, but within a century of the mission of Augustine biblical paraphrases were being made by the Anglo-Saxon poet Caedmon. The Venerable Bede (d. 735) produced a translation of the Gospel of John, and a century later Alfred the Great, first king of the English nation, himself translated some psalms into the native tongue. The beautiful Lindisfarne codex of the Gospels in Latin contains an interlinear Anglo-Saxon translation written by the scribe Aldred, and other early interlinear Psalters have survived. Aelfric, writing shortly before the Norman Conquest (1066), produced an abridged version of several OT books and, in his homilies, a good cross-section of biblical passages were translated literally from the Vulgate. After the conquest, translations of different parts of the Bible into Anglo-Norman were produced, generally for aristocratic lords and ladies or for religious houses, but until the thirteenth century little enthusiasm was shown for the vernacular. Latin was firmly established as the language of the educated classes, which, unfortunately, did not include most of the clergy.

The fourteenth century, the century of Chaucer, witnessed a revival of the English language (Middle English) and, from the middle of the century, translations of different parts of the Bible, especially Psalms and the NT. The first complete version of the Vulgate was the work of John Wycliffe (ca. 1330–84) and his associates, of whom the most important was Nicholas Hereford. A first draft, completed in 1384, was unduly literal and was therefore revised in the last years of the century by John Purvey, Wycliffe's secretary. Ecclesiastical opposition to this version was triggered by Wycliffe's protest against papal corruption and espousal of Lollard doctrines, as well as suspicion that the production of a vernacular version was motivated by the desire to find scriptural support for Wycliffe's theological opinions. In any case, Wycliffe's Bible was widely used and retained its popularity into the early sixteenth century.

From the Sixteenth Century to the Present: The invention, or perfection, of the printing press by Johann Gutenberg of Mainz and the printing of the first surviving book in 1457 (a Latin Psalter) radically changed the situation with respect to the use of the Bible in the vernacular. In 1526 William Tyndale translated into English the NT, and in the following years the Pentateuch and Jonah. His Lutheran views, which found their way into the notes and the translation of certain passages, made his work suspect in England, and he died a martyr at the stake in 1536. The previous year saw the appearance of the first complete version from the Vulgate, that of Miles Coverdale, who incorporated much of Tyndale's work. In 1537 John Rogers (alias Thomas Matthew) produced a new version based on the work of Tyndale and Coverdale, which was ordered to be placed in every church in England and thus became the authorized version until it was replaced by a revision commissioned by Archbishop Matthew Parker in 1568. After Mary Tudor ascended the throne in 1553 and reimposed Catholicism, refugees from religious persecution gathered in Geneva and produced a revision of the "Great Bible" of John Rogers, known as the Geneva Bible. It was this version that achieved the greatest popularity for private reading and accompanied the pilgrim fathers to the New World.

The culmination of all these efforts came with the publication of the King James Version (KJV) in 1611, the work of committees including the best scholars in the land. In due course it established itself as the classical version of the Scriptures and was recognized as one of the great masterpieces of English writing. It served unchanged until a Revised Version (RV) was called for in the late nineteenth century, beginning with the NT in 1881. This was followed by an American version in 1901. Important discoveries and advances in knowledge of the textual transmission of the Bible during the following half-century, however, necessitated a revision, resulting in the Revised Standard Version (RSV) commissioned by the National Council of Churches in America and published between 1946 and 1957. More recently (1990) the RSV was again revised, special attention being paid to the elimination where possible of gender-exclusive language. In the form of the Oxford Annotated Bible, the RSV was approved for Catholic use in 1966. The last few decades have seen an abundance of new translations. The most notable of these are the New English Bible (NEB), the work of British biblical scholars, the revised edition of which appeared in 1989; the New American Bible (NAB), produced by members of the American Catholic Biblical Association (1970; revised NT 1987); the Jerusalem Bible (JB) based on the French translation by the faculty of the École Biblique in Jerusalem (1966, rev. ed. 1985); the Jewish Publication Society Bible, completed in 1982; and the New Revised Standard Version (NRSV), completed in 1990, under the direction of the Division of Christian Education of the National Council of the Churches of Christ in the U.S.A.

The papal encyclical *Divino Afflante Spiritu* (On promoting biblical studies, 1943) encouraged the study of the Bible in the original languages or in translation and promoted the use of English in the liturgy. The encyclical makes clear the distance traversed since the appearance of the Douay-Rheims version from the Vulgate, the first in English made expressly for Catholics and the work of exiles from religious persecution under Elizabeth I and James I (1582–1609). *See also* Douay-Rheims Version of the Bible; King James Bible; Lollards; Vulgate.

Bibliography

Bailey, Lloyd R., ed. *The Word of God: A Guide to English Versions of the Bible.* Atlanta: John Knox Press, 1982.

Meeks, Wayne A., ed. *The HarperCollins Study Bible: New Revised Standard Version.* San Francisco: HarperCollins, 1993.

JOSEPH BLENKINSOPP

Bible, versions of. *See* Scripture, versions of.

Bible and art. The use of biblically inspired imagery (including biblical references) has been part of the Catholic tradition since the second century, despite the iconoclastic controversies of the eighth and ninth centuries. Biblical imagery traditionally has been related to the role of Christ in salvation history and has included scenes from Christ's life and OT subjects, the latter seen as the reasons for Christ's mission (Adam and Eve) or as the prototypes of his priesthood and sacrifice (Melchizedek, Abel, Abraham) and Resurrection (Jonah, Daniel).

Biblical art has had no single "best" style or medium. Styles have changed to reflect differing theological understandings and cultural conditions. Many early Christian images were painted on catacomb and house-church walls (e.g., Dura-Europos

The flight of Mary, Joseph, and the child Jesus into Egypt; Cathedral St. Lazare, Autuo, France.

baptistery) and were often sketchy and unnaturalistic. Late-fourth-century sarcophagi and sculpture reflected Greco-Roman naturalism (e.g., the Cleveland Museum *Jonah* sculptures). Byzantine-influenced mosaics and icons were hieratic, flattened, and dematerialized. German Gothic images were exuberant and emotional. Netherlandish art was noted for its combination of photographic realism and hidden symbolism, while the Italian Renaissance placed idealized and graceful figures in an ideal and balanced world. The Baroque took the Renaissance forms and introduced passionate drama. Twentieth-century biblical art has employed many styles, with some of the finest modern work belonging to the Expressionists (Rouault, Nolde, Schmidt-Rottluff).

Biblical imagery relies on many influences; clothing, architecture, and landscape from different periods and locations were often intermingled. Furthermore, biblical narratives were frequently combined with stories from other sources such as the *Golden Legend,* the apocryphal Gospels, and mystical writings.

TERRENCE E. DEMPSEY

Bible and doctrine, the relationship between Sacred Scripture and the official teachings of the Church. During the first centuries of the Church, the Fathers of the Church used the Scriptures as the principal source for the instruction of the faithful. In the Middle Ages, the Bible was revered as the "sacred page" (Lat., *sacra pagina*). As such, it was the basis on which theology was developed. When an apologetic approach to the teaching of the Church became popular after the Council of Trent (1545–63), texts from Scripture were used as "proof texts" to support the teaching of the Church. With the development of modern biblical criticism, various papal encyclicals and pronouncements urged Catholic biblical scholars to clarify those passages of the Scriptures that had doctrinal significance.

In these various ways the Church has given expression to its constant conviction that there is a close connection between the Bible and Church teaching. Vatican II (1962–65) stated that "the sacred page [the Bible] is, as it were, the soul of theology" (Dogmatic Constitution on Divine Revelation, n. 24; Decree on Priestly Formation, n. 16). Theology rests on the written word of God, together with tradition, because it bears witness to that which God has revealed for the sake of humankind. Vatican II reaffirmed the often repeated dictum of Jerome that "ignorance of the Scriptures is ignorance of Christ" (Dogmatic Constitution on Divine Revelation, n. 25; cf. Decree on the Bishops' Pastoral Office in the Church, n. 12). The Church, it said, "has always regarded the Scriptures together with sacred tradition as the supreme rule of faith [*suprema fidei suae regula*], and will ever do so" (Dogmatic Constitution on Divine Revelation, n. 21).

The Scriptures are the "unnormed norm" (Lat., *norma non normata*) of the experience and expression of Christian faith. The canon of the Scriptures is the context within which Christian doctrine is developed and its critical point of reference. Although it is the entirety of the scriptural canon that is normative for Christian doctrine, and the texts are not to be isolated from their biblical contexts, some biblical texts are more significant for doctrine than others. Texts whose religious value is apparent and that contribute significantly to the Church's process of pedagogy are more important than those whose religious value is not as manifest. A preeminent place is to be accorded to the four canonical Gospels.

Not all of Church doctrine is contained within the Scriptures, nor is Church doctrine to be construed merely as the exposition of the meaning of the Scriptures. Together with tradition, Scripture provides a primary and perpetual foundation for doctrine. Doctrine develops within a context of Scripture and the tradition of the Church's experiences.

As the soul of Christian theology, the Scriptures vivify and give unity to the doctrine of the Church. Consistency within the biblical witness is a major factor in the normative function of the Scriptures.

Rather, the Scriptures have a function that is at once constitutive and critical with regard to the doctrine of the Church.

In their constitutive function the Scriptures continue to serve as a principal source of the Church's teaching. Its doctrine develops by means of a continual interfacing between the Church's contemporary situation and its foundational texts. The development of doctrine is to be consistent with the scriptural witness.

Church doctrine is renewed and revivified by means of a return to the Scriptures. Vatican II affirmed, for example, that biblical themes are to be presented first in the exposition of dogmatic theology. It called for a more thorough nourishing of the scientific exposition of moral theology by scriptural teaching (Decree on Priestly Formation, n. 16).

In their critical function, the Scriptures move the Church ever to renew its teaching. Recourse to the Scriptures prevents the Church from developing its teaching in a too narrow or otherwise skewed fashion. Teaching that is inconsistent with the Scriptures must be regarded as an unauthentic expression of the Church's faith. *See also* doctrine; dogma; magisterium; Scripture and tradition. RAYMOND COLLINS

Bible and ecumenism. Attempts to surmount denominational differences by a return to the Bible as the sole source of belief and practice have characterized Protestantism since the early part of the nineteenth century. Prior to Vatican II (1962–65), Catholics were forbidden to engage in common Bible study with Protestants, or to read translations of the Bible prepared by non-Catholics. Yet, Catholic scholars could not ignore the research of non-Catholic scholars in fields such as archaeology, philology, text criticism, and literary criticism. The biblical scholar Augustine Bea, a major influence on *Divino Afflante Spiritu* (1943), was a leader in ecumenism prior to and during Vatican II, and became first head of the Secretariat for Promoting Christian Unity. Vatican II called the Bible the soul of theology (Decree on Priestly Formation, n. 16) and mandated greater use of the Bible in the liturgy and pastoral practice. Today study and use of the Bible bring Catholics and non-Catholics together on all levels. Both critical editions and contemporary translations of the Bible (e.g., New Revised Standard Version and the Revised New American Bible) are the work of Catholic, Jewish, and Protestant scholars. Catholics and Protestants work together and have been presidents of the major scholarly organizations, i.e., the Catholic Biblical Association and the (originally Protestant) Society of Biblical Literature. Church-sponsored ecumenical dialogues have returned to the Bible, only to discover fundamental agreements on issues that had been obscured by centuries of controversy. Most Catholics and mainline Protestant denominations follow the same biblical lectionary cycle, the order of Scripture readings used in the Sunday and daily liturgy. Common prayer centers on the Bible, and Catholic and non-Catholic laypeople participate in group Bible study. *See also* ecumenical movement; ecumenism.

JOHN R. DONAHUE

Bible and liturgy. Many books of the Bible are the result of setting oral traditions in writing, and they often contain elements drawn from public worship, e.g., Israel's confessions of faith (Deut 6:4–9; 26:3–10). A number of psalms originally accompanied worship in the Temple (e.g., Pss 95–100; 121). In the NT, 1 Peter, Revelation, and even the bulk of Philippians may have originally been liturgies. Prebiblical hymns are employed in the NT, e.g., Phil 2:6–11; Col 1:15–20; Luke 1:46–55. The various traditions of the institution of the Eucharist (1 Cor 11:23–26; Mark 14:22–25; Matt 26:26–29; Luke 22:15–20) show signs of having been used liturgically before they were incorporated into liturgical texts. Theories claiming that the Gospels themselves originated as liturgical readings that were spread out over the year have not met with general acceptance. It is fair to say that public worship influenced the creation of a number of biblical texts.

Jewish Liturgy: The Bible has traditionally played a major role in both Jewish and Christian liturgy. The OT provides the basis for the celebration of major Jewish festivals (Passover, Weeks, Tabernacles, Day of Atonement; see, e.g., Deut 16) as well as the observance of the Sabbath. While it is difficult to date the origins of the synagogue (in either the exile or the postexilic period), it is fairly certain that Scripture played a major role in the Sabbath morning service with readings from the law (Torah) in a fixed cycle of either one or three years and with readings freely chosen from the prophets to accompany them. The synagogue readings were done in descending order. Three passages from Scripture (Deut 6:4–9; 11:13–21; Num 15:37–41) were included in the daily morning and evening recitation of the Shema ("Hear, O Israel").

Christian Liturgy: The first full description of the Sunday Eucharist in Justin Martyr's *First Apolo-*

gy (67) reveals that the writings of the prophets and the memoirs of the apostles were read from at least the middle of the second century. In some of the early liturgies (e.g., *Apostolic Constitutions* 8) four or more readings from Scripture were employed, always ending with the Gospel. Up to the fourth century, books of the Bible were probably read in continuous fashion (Lat., *lectio continua*), but from the fourth century on the developing calendar of feasts and fast days required a new method of selecting passages to correspond to the celebration of the day. In addition, a number of OT passages were read in conjunction with the NT to show how the old covenant foreshadowed the new. This procedure is called typology. The requirements of the liturgy itself provided an interpretation of the Bible depending on the setting of readings in the liturgical calendar.

A number of elements in Catholic liturgy in addition to liturgical readings have traditionally been biblical (the entrance chant, greeting, responsorial psalm, verse for the Gospel acclamation, Holy, Holy, Lord's Prayer, Lamb of God [indirectly], and Communion chant). Scripture by way of psalms, canticles, readings, and responsories forms the bulk of the Liturgy of the Hours. In the post–Vatican II liturgy every liturgical service, including individual celebration of Penance and Anointing, contains at least some proclamation of Scripture.

In many ways the post–Vatican II liturgy has fulfilled the desire of the sixteenth-century Protestant Reformers for a greater attention to the Bible in public worship. The Constitution on the Sacred Liturgy (n. 35) mandated greater variety and content of Scripture; this mandate has been put into practice with the current three-year cycle of Sunday readings and two-year cycle of daily readings. *See also* liturgy, theology of; worship; worship [in the Bible].

JOHN F. BALDOVIN

Bible and theology. *See* biblical theology.

Bible service, Bible paraliturgies consisting of the public reading of and meditation on Sacred Scripture, along with intervals of prayer and song. To provide for more ample and varied scriptural readings and to highlight the connection of word and rite, the Constitution on the Sacred Liturgy of Vatican II (1962–65) encouraged Bible services on solemn feast vigils, Sundays and holidays, and some Advent and Lenten weekdays, especially when a priest is not available; deacons or deputed laity may preside (n. 35). *See also* biblical spirituality.

Biblia Pauperum (Lat., "Bible of the poor"), a genre popular in the later Middle Ages and into the age of printing, offering a series of illustrations of the life and activity of Christ, as well as of the after-life. The book was composed of forty sets of illustrations, one set per page. Each set includes two scenes drawn from the OT that anticipate some episode, portrayed between them, from the NT. Brief texts accompany each set of illustrations, providing the appropriate OT prophecies, as well as some material explaining the typological relations between the OT and NT scenes. The precise function of this "Bible" remains debated. Rather than a "picture book" for illiterates, who in any case would have been unable to read the accompanying texts, or an aid for preachers, it seems more likely that the work was developed to stimulate the meditation of a literate and devout audience.

biblical chronology, the historical dating of biblical books, persons, and events. The many chronological markers that punctuate the biblical narrative, especially in Genesis (the birth of patriarchs, the succession of events in the Flood) are undoubtedly fictive and arranged in accordance with a pre-conceived schema, perhaps based on a 4000-year cycle or world epoch. The 430 years in Egypt (Exod 12:40–41) match exactly the period of the monarchy from the building of Solomon's Temple (1 Kgs 6:1) to its destruction by the Babylonians. The relative chronology of Israelite and Judean rulers, and of events during their reigns, can now be checked against the absolute chronology established for Mesopotamia and Egypt and bolstered by relevant archaeological data.

Apocalyptic writings occasionally calculate the time of the final drama of history (e.g., Dan 12:11–13; Rev 20:1–3), but the figures are often interpreted symbolically; hence attempts to predict the course of the future based on them are misguided.

In the NT, Luke-Acts provides the most chronological data, but much remains uncertain, e.g., the length of the ministry of Jesus and the date of the census under Quirinius, governor of Syria (Luke 2:2). The chronology of the life of Jesus can be established only approximately: he was born before Herod the Great died in 4 B.C. and he died while Pilate was prefect of Judea (A.D. 26–36). Since Paul's Letters rarely refer to events in the Roman world of that time, their dating and chronological sequence have to be determined almost exclusively on internal evidence. *See also* Bible.   JOSEPH BLENKINSOPP

biblical commission. *See* Pontifical Biblical Commission.

biblical criticism (Gk., *krisis*, "judgment," "decision"), the process of making judgments about the nature of biblical literature, including dating, authorship, historical background, sources, literary form, transmission, and meaning of biblical texts. Though the term is neutral, it often carries a connotation of negative judgments that challenge traditional understandings, e.g., about the Mosaic authorship of the Pentateuch or whether certain sayings attributed to Jesus were actually uttered by him. A number of specific disciplines come under the umbrella of biblical criticism. Textual criticism seeks to produce a text with the greatest claim to antiquity, i.e., it seeks to establish the original wording or form of the biblical text; source criticism identifies the traditions or written documents an author may have employed; literary criticism is concerned with the style, structure, and distinctive language of a given text; form criticism identifies the formal elements of a text (e.g., is the creation account in Genesis a myth?) and postulates preliterary settings for given forms; redaction and composition criticism focuses on the final product and the activity of the author in editing a previous text (e.g., Matthew's retelling of Mark's Passion narrative), or in composing new material (e.g., the Johannine farewell discourses). The present state of biblical studies witnesses the rise of many new forms of criticism, e.g., rhetorical criticism, which seeks to understand how a text moves its hearers to action or decision, and canonical criticism, which describes the formation of the canon and the function of the canon in the believing community.   JOHN R. DONAHUE

biblical exegesis, thirteenth-century. The century of Bonaventure, Aquinas, and Henry of Ghent saw great advances in theological science, stimulated by the struggle to meet the challenge posed by the newly translated philosophical writings of Aristotle. Yet, in their approach to the Bible, theologians were quite conservative: the Bible retained its privileged place at the heart of theological inquiry; it was seen as expressing God's truth at many levels of meaning, the literal as well as the various spiritual senses; knowledge of the original biblical languages remained the exception, with theologians preferring to encounter God's word in the Vulgate Latin and its variants.

The Bible was central to the training and teaching of the Scholastic theologian. The advanced student of theology, the "biblical bachelor," was required to lecture on the Bible before being permitted to pass to the final stage of training, lecturing on the *Sentences* of Peter Lombard. Lectures on the Bible ran quickly over the biblical text, primarily to give the novice theologian better acquaintance with Scripture. Once the requirements of the theological degree were met, the Bible was the sole subject for the lectures of the regent master. At Paris and elsewhere, in these lectures, which explored difficult questions emerging from the biblical text, the custom was to alternate between books of the OT and the NT. Numerous commentaries, many of which are rooted in these classroom exercises, are extant. All the biblical books found their commentators, with the Scholastics showing a special fondness for the sapiential books. The commentaries of the Scholastics display their dialectical skills, knowledge of the readings of earlier commentators, and a concern to highlight the organizational and literary features of the biblical text.

The Bible was also prominent in their more systematic writings, which can be characterized as comprehensive restatements in modern terms of the truths of God found in Scripture. While the Bible was acknowledged to have many levels of meaning, in Scholastic argument the literal level, the meaning conveyed by the words of the text, was preferred.

The century also saw in Scholastic circles some technical advances. Early in the century at Paris, the Latin text was divided into chapters, for ease of reference (the division of chapters into verses came much later); these chapter divisions have been retained in all twentieth-century versions of the Bible. Similarly, especially due to the work of Parisian Dominicans under the leadership of Hugh of Saint Cher, repeated attempts were made at constructing concordances of the Bible, listing all instances of individual words and suggesting their differing applications. Again, the goal was ease of reference, indicative of the perceived need to be adept in handling the biblical text.

Other religious authors shared the Scholastic enthusiasm for the Bible. Indeed, its continued emotional appeal is even more apparent in the works of spiritual authors such as Mechthild of Magdeburg and the nuns of Helfta. The century saw an explosion of spiritual writings. Male and female authors were especially taken by the Gospel depictions of the Passion, and employed biblical language to express their experience of God through the crucified Christ. As in such twelfth-century authors as Bernard of Clairvaux, spiritual authors also saw the religious potential of the rich imagery of the Canticle of Canticles. Especially in Franciscan circles, the hermeneutical theories of Joachim of Fiore (d. 1202) enjoyed a wide following. Joachim had divided human history into three main stages, each of which was under the guidance of a person of the Trinity. Reading the Bible typologically, Joachim foretold the imminent arrival of the age of the Holy Spirit, in which history would attain its perfection. In the course of the continuing debates about spiritual poverty, Franciscan writers employed Joachimite ideas to enhance the position of their order, which, they thought, would play a key role in inaugurating the new age. *See also* biblical criticism; biblical theology; exegesis; Scripture, interpretation of.

JOSEPH WAWRYKOW

biblical exegesis, twelfth-century. During the twelfth century, the Bible was the most influential book in Europe. Its language, worldview, and doctrine formed the foundation of medieval culture. The developments in biblical exegesis (textual interpretation) that took place during that century transformed not only the practice of exegesis itself but also the nature of the theological enterprise. Interpreting Scripture, once practiced almost exclusively within a monastic culture with its contemplative ambiance, became increasingly open to the ideas and methods of a new breed of scholars, the teachers and students at the cathedral centers of northern France.

At the onset of the twelfth century, biblical exegesis flourished at the Cathedral School of Laon under the leadership of Anselm, who began the process that created a standardized biblical text (Latin Vulgate) and surrounded each passage with selected patristic commentary. In this way the teachers at Laon continued to incorporate traditional exegesis by following the four senses of Scripture: the literal or historical, allegorical or typological, moral, and anagogical. In its final form, this format of the *sacra pagina* (Lat., "sacred page") was known as the *Glossa Ordinaria* ("Ordinary Gloss").

However, new methods for exegesis developed as scholars brought a more scientific approach to bear upon the sacred page. For example, techniques used for introducing secular literature to the reader were now extended to the biblical books; the *quaestio* or "question," with arguments given for and against, gradually developed a formal structure, becoming a distinct genre itself. Hugh of St. Victor was a leader in this movement. His introductory notes *On Sacred Scriptures and Writers* consciously raised questions of biblical content and exegetical method and, along with his major study of doctrine, the *Didascalion,* influenced future generations. Hugh placed a great emphasis on the literal, historical meaning of texts, believing this to be the foundation of spiritual exegesis. The next generation at St. Victor continued to promote these ideas. Andrew of St. Victor's work is perhaps the most notable because of his careful integration of Jewish and rabbinic exegesis into his own commentaries on the OT.

That scholars were increasingly self-conscious about exegetical method is nowhere more apparent than with Peter Abelard, Hugh's contemporary. Abelard's perception of the sacred page as a text to be scrutinized, and his vigorous insistence on the primacy of dialectic and inquiry itself as the way to discern the meaning of texts brought a new élan to biblical exegesis. In the prologue to *Sic et Non,* Abelard presented rules for intepretation, and in his own commentaries on the Hexaemeron (the Genesis account of the six days of creation) and on the Letter to the Romans, he introduced provocative questions, some with equally provocative responses. With Héloïse, Abelard collaborated on a major work of textual analysis dealing only with problematic scriptures (*Problemata Heloissae*). Abelard's pupil Robert of Melun employed this approach in a collection of questions on the Pauline Letters.

By the end of the twelfth century, the new methods were in place and, although the monastic approach to exegesis continued, its influence was limited. Biblical exegesis in the following centuries belonged to the university scholars, especially the friars who refined and advanced the achievements of twelfth-century theologians. *See also* biblical exegesis, thirteenth-century; biblical theology; exegesis; Scripture, interpretation of.　　　*EILEEN KEARNEY*

biblical institute. *See* Pontifical Biblical Institute.

biblical spirituality, the lived experience of Christian faith as it is expressed in, or characterized by, the religious content and perspective(s) of the Bible. Although no generally accepted definition of the term exists, it is used in at least two different ways. First, the Bible as a whole presents a unique faith experience. For the Christian this experience develops throughout the OT into the NT. It is essentially a historically mediated, covenantal relationship between the one creator God and a community who have been saved by God, first from human slavery through Moses and then from sin by Jesus Christ, and who respond to God's saving love by a life of faith, praise, love, and justice. This basic biblical spirituality is diversely realized and expressed in different OT and NT traditions, e.g., with an emphasis on justice in the OT prophets, on missionary zeal in the Letters of Paul, and on contemplative interiority in John's Gospel.

Second, while all authentically Christian spirituality is rooted in, and shaped by, biblical revelation, some historical forms of Christian spirituality are more characterized by explicit reference to the Bible while the biblical rootedness of other traditions is more implicit. The former, e.g., the Benedictine tradition, are sometimes called "biblical spiritualities" in contrast to those that are more ascetical, apostolic, or contemplative. *See also* spirituality, Christian.

biblical theology, statements about God and God's relation to humanity as found in the Bible, with a secondary sense of a postbiblical theology based on the Bible and using biblical categories and expressions. From the second century until the end of the high Middle Ages, theology (language about God) was primarily dialogue with the Bible. A theologian was a *magister sacrae paginae* (Lat.), literally an expert in the sacred text (the Bible). With the development of Scholasticism, and especially with the polemics of the post-Tridentine period, theology became increasingly divorced from the Bible among both Catholics and Protestants. The Bible served as an archive of proof-texts for doctrine. Biblical theology as an independent discipline dates to a lecture in 1787 by Johann Gabler calling for an historical and descriptive biblical theology. "Theology" here becomes virtually synonymous with description of religious beliefs and practices. In the 1950s Protestantism, and later Catholicism, were influenced by the "biblical theology movement," which opposed doctrinal synthesis, stressed the distinctiveness of the biblical worldview (over both its environment and later developments) and understood theology in terms of "salvation history" (Ger., *heilsgeschichte*), i.e., the revelation of God in the history of the people of Israel and the early Church. Pius XII's encyclical on biblical studies, *Divino Afflante Spiritu* (1943), and Vatican II (1962–65) were a stimulus to a renewal of biblical theology within Catholicism. *See also* New Testament theology.   JOHN R. DONAHUE

bidding prayers. *See* Prayer of the Faithful.

Biel, Gabriel, 1410–95, German scholastic theologian. A member of the Brethren of the Common Life (ca. 1468), he became provost of houses in Butzbach, Hesse (1470), and Urach, Württemberg (1479). He accepted the chair of theology at Tübingen (1484), serving twice as rector, and there completed his influential *Commentary on the Four Books of Sentences* and *Lectures on the Canon of the Mass.*

Biel represented the late medieval *Via Moderna,* a theological movement influenced by William of Ockham's nominalism and opposed to the *Via Antiqua* associated with Thomas Aquinas (d. 1274). Generally, nominalism rejected Thomistic realism, and the *Via Moderna* emphasized God's absolute freedom. On justification, Biel believed that God owed salvation to no person but freely agreed to provide grace to those "who do the best that lies within them" (Lat., "*facere quod in se est*"), thus requiring some human effort as a prerequisite for salvation. Similarly, in sacramental penance Biel demanded some contrition (sorrow grounded in pure love of God as opposed to fear of punishment) as a prelude to absolution. Martin Luther (d. 1546) received his theological training through Biel's tradition but ultimately rejected his tenets in the Protestant Reformation. *See also* nature and grace; nominalism; Via Antiqua, Via Moderna.

Big Bang, the explosive beginning or origin of the universe as it is modeled in standard twentieth-century cosmological theory. It is pertinent to the question of God's creation of the universe. The universe has been expanding and cooling for about fifteen billion years. We know this from the systematic redshifting of distant galaxies, the presence and equilibrium character of the cosmic microwave background radiation, and the high abundance of helium, as well as the significant abundance of deuterium. That is, as we go back farther and farther into the past, we encounter a succession of ever hotter and denser phases. The past limit to these hotter, denser phases, which is a singularity (where temperature, density, and spatial curvature are infinite), is called "the Big Bang." It is conventionally designated by time $t = 0$. It is not just one point, but is a spacelike manifold of points with these properties. Some have regarded the Big Bang as "the cre-

ation event," in the theological sense. But there are strong scientific and philosophical reasons for resisting this identification. Its singular character probably signals a breakdown in the cosmological model itself, particularly in the underlying manifold model of space-time itself; at these extremely high energies, a cosmological model based on a quantized theory of gravity is needed. This would strongly alter key categories, including those of space, time, and event at and near the Big Bang. *See also* creation; evolution; God; philosophy and theology.

Billiart, St. Julie, 1751–1816, founder of the Sisters of Notre Dame of Namur. Gifted with prayerfulness, skill in teaching religion, and a profound sense of God's goodness, after the French Revolution, Julia trained women to teach poor children. Since its foundation in France in 1804, Julia's institute has produced two independent branches and has spread throughout the world. Feast day: May 13. *See also* Sisters of Notre Dame de Namur.

Billot, Louis (loo'ee bee-yoh'), 1846–1931, Jesuit philosopher and theologian. He taught at the Gregorian University in Rome for much of his career and was one of the principal figures in the neo-Thomistic revival sponsored by Pope Leo XIII. He became an influential consultant for the Holy Office under Pius X and in 1911 was created cardinal, a dignity he later agreed to renounce as a result of his association with *Action Française,* a politically reactionary movement that favored monarchy over democracy. A brilliant metaphysician with an extensive knowledge of the work of Thomas Aquinas, Billot wrote numerous theological treatises that represented a movement away from the more historical and philosophical Scholasticism of the nineteenth century and toward a more speculative and deductive approach to theological questions.

bilocation, the capacity to be in two places at one time. Certain saints and other holy persons are reported to have appeared to someone in one location while, in fact, the saint has been in another location hundreds of miles away. Such stories need not be taken at face value. Even traditional theology admits that there can be no true bilocation, because to be in one place by definition means not to be elsewhere. All bilocation is, in fact, seeming bilocation. Explanations of seeming bilocation among the saints range from dismissal as pious imagination, to an appeal to unknown physical forces, to a belief in an authentic miracle where a person appears in a vision while located somewhere else.

While bilocation is discussed in some traditional manuals of spirituality, it is best treated with a healthy attitude of skepticism.

bination, the practice of having a priest preside at the celebration of the Eucharist twice on the same day. Ordinarily a priest may preside at the Eucharist only once a day, but if there is a pastoral need and too few priests, a priest may be given permission to celebrate twice a day or even three times a day (trination) on Sundays and feasts of obligation (can. 905).

binitarianism, the twentieth-century name for the belief that in God there are only two divine Persons, not three. In the NT, a binitarian understanding of God (1 Tim 2:5–6; Rom 4:24; 2 Cor 4:14) stands beside trinitarian statements (Matt 28:19; 2 Cor 13:13). While the former specify God as Father and Son, the latter profess belief in God as Father, Son, and Holy Spirit. The Pneumatomachians ("Spirit-fighters") of the second through fourth centuries confessed belief in God as Father and Son, but refused to recognize the full divinity of the Holy Spirit. Their binitarianism was opposed by the First Council of Constantinople (381). In contemporary theology the term is applied to theological positions that deny either the divinity of the Holy Spirit or the divinity of Jesus Christ. *See also* Trinity, doctrine of the.

bioethics, an interdisciplinary field that probes the ethical dimensions of technological developments in the life sciences. It emerged as a distinct area of inquiry in the United States in the late 1960s and early 1970s. At that time, developments such as heart transplantation, withdrawal of life-sustaining treatment, genetic counseling, the definition of death, experimentation on human subjects, and allocation of scarce resources (especially dialysis) posed moral dilemmas at both individual and public policy levels. Individuals from a variety of disciplines—philosophy, theology, law, the social and biological sciences, and medicine—began to address these and other issues. Of the early players, theologians were among the most prominent (e.g., Joseph Fletcher, James Gustafson, Paul Ramsey, Seymour Siegel, Charles Curran, and Richard McCormick). Their involvement was natural because many of the questions raised by new biotechnologi-

cal developments were of a religious nature. In addition, both the Catholic and Jewish traditions had long histories of attending to medical-moral matters. Within a relatively brief time, however, as the need arose for public discussion of the issues and for development of public policy, the disciplines of philosophy and law came to dominate the field. This shift greatly influenced the shape of bioethics in the United States. The field has been characterized by a preoccupation with individual rights, the application of universal principles to cases—particularly autonomy, beneficence, and justice—the development of procedures, rationalism, and a focus on problem solving. Since the late 1980s, however, bioethics has been undergoing a gradual transformation in its self-understanding, scope, and methodology.

While bioethics is a relatively new field of inquiry, reflection on moral issues related to the medical realm is not new to Catholicism. Patristic writers of the first centuries and authors of the penitential books of the sixth through eleventh centuries referred to actions having to do with sex and reproduction, particularly those considered sinful. With the development of manuals for confessors in the twelfth century and the increasing professionalization of medicine in the fifteenth and sixteenth centuries, particular attention was given to the moral obligations of physicians. By the seventeenth century, moral theology had become a discipline in its own right and developed its own textbooks. Within these, topics related to medicine were grouped under discussions of some of the commandments and virtues, the sacrament of Matrimony, and duties of various states of life. A new discipline evolved in the eighteenth and nineteenth centuries, generally referred to as "pastoral medicine." It included both medical treatises to assist rural pastors and theologians in their work, as well as theological treatises to assist physicians in understanding their ethical responsibilities and the spiritual dimensions of patient care. From the 1940s until the 1960s, throughout Western Europe and North America, the latter type of treatise evolved into a distinct subdiscipline of moral theology, medical ethics. This new discipline focused on an ethical analysis of routine medical procedures encountered by medical professionals. A. Bonnar, J. Healy, G. Kelly, J. P. Kenny, A. Niedermeyer, T. J. O'Donnell, and J. Paquin were among the many noteworthy authors of the time. Pope Pius XII also spoke and wrote extensively on medical moral topics during the 1940s and 1950s.

Prior to Vatican II (1962–65), Catholic medical ethics was characterized by a natural law approach that frequently considered natural biological processes as determinative of what is morally right and by the authoritative teaching of the Church on specific issues. Several principles generally guided moral reflection: sanctity of life, stewardship, the inseparability of the unitive and procreative aspects of intercourse, totality, cooperation, and double effect. Catholic medical ethics since Vatican II has been influenced by developments in the broader realm of moral theology resulting in a variety of methodologies in addition to the natural law approach. *See also* medical ethics; moral theology.   RON P. HAMEL

biretta (bir-ret'tah; Lat., *birrus*, "hooded cloak"), a black square cap worn by clerics. The biretta is four-cornered and topped by a tassel. Birettas coordinate with the color and style of cassock a cleric wears. They vary in color according to the rank of the priest. Cardinals may wear red birettas; bishops, purple; and priests, black. Together with the Roman collar, cassock, and surplice, the biretta traditionally completed the clerical uniform that is worn out of doors, or on pastoral calls. Birettas are no longer commonly worn by priests in the United States.

biritualism, the use of more than one liturgical tradition or rite in the celebration of liturgical services. In late antiquity, before the unification of liturgical usages into clearly distinct rites, there were biritual monasteries, especially in the Holy Land. Today the term generally refers to the practice of Catholic clergy who have received an indult from the Holy See to celebrate the liturgy in a rite other than

Biretta

biretta

their own, a practice open to abuse and ritual superficiality and often frowned upon by members of Eastern traditions, though the permission is granted only for pastoral reasons, not for personal gratification. *See also* Eastern rites; rite.

birth control, the attempt to regulate and limit the procreative potential of human sexuality. "Birth control" is often used synonymously with "contraception," which in the Catholic tradition has been understood to mean an interference with the sexual act so that conception does not occur. Sterilization interferes with the sexual power or faculty to produce conception, as in vasectomy. However, in more popular usage contraception often includes sterilization, as illustrated in the often used term "contraceptive sterilization" to indicate the purpose of the sterilization or by the fact that the contraceptive or anovulant pill really constitutes a temporary sterilization, since it suppresses the procreative potential. This article speaks about contraception primarily in the narrow sense, but also logically includes contraceptive sterilization.

Contraception, or birth control, concerns the means to achieve family planning or responsible parenthood. Contraception is also employed in sexuality outside marriage, but this article concentrates on marital sexuality. The hierarchical magisterium teaches that Catholic couples should practice responsible parenthood, but artificial contraception is always wrong. However, the use of the sterile period (the rhythm method, natural family planning, the Billings method) is morally acceptable. Within the Catholic Church not all agree with this official hierarchical teaching.

Historical Development of the Teaching: The writings of John T. Noonan constitute the best source for understanding the historical development of Catholic teaching on contraception. No explicit condemnation of contraception exists in the Scriptures. Most scholars agree that the sin of Onan (Gen 38:8–10) consisted in disobeying his father and not in spilling his seed, even though the word "onanism" came to mean contraception. However, the Christian condemnation of artificial contraception arose quite early. Contraception in the form of *coitus interruptus* was known in the ancient world, as was the custom of taking some potions to prevent birth. In early Christian times contraception was often associated with prostitution and extramarital sexuality. Potions to prevent birth could also be used to induce abortion and sometimes were perceived to have some connection with magic or superstition. In this context the early Church, as illustrated in Clement of Alexandria (d. ca. 215), accepted the Stoic rule that the procreative purpose of marital sexuality opposed the wasting or damaging of the seed. The teaching arose as a middle position between two Gnostic extremes, one that opposed all use of sex, in imitation of Jesus, and the other that extolled the freedom to use sexuality in any manner. In the fourth century the very influential Augustine of Hippo supported the understanding of sexuality in marriage as justified only by the procreative purpose. Augustine himself, however, and many of the early Church writers held a rather negative view of human sexuality because, in their minds, original sin was transmitted through the sexual act itself, as illustrated by the power of concupiscence in sexuality. Developments in the understanding of marriage and of the meaning of human sexuality occurred among theologians and canonists in medieval and later times with a recognition that procreation was not the exclusive lawful purpose for initiating marital intercourse. Many values such as pleasure and health were mentioned; love was increased through sexual acts, although marital love was not directly related to coitus; procreation included the educational and economic welfare of existing children. Such reasons could justify continence. But the condemnation of contraception remained, with emphasis on contraception's violating the order of nature, which called for the depositing of male semen in the vas of the female. This condemnation also served as the basis for the condemnation of other sexual acts, such as masturbation, and any other type of intercourse, such as anal or oral. The Catholic condemnation of contraception was shared by the Orthodox Church in the East and by Protestants in the West as well as by society at large.

Developments Outside Catholicism: In 1798 Thomas Malthus published his influential *An Essay on the Principle of Population,* which proposed to check population growth by moral restraints, such as postponing the age for marriage, but did not recommend or consider contraception. Others soon recommended contraception. Proponents of birth control (e.g., Margaret Sanger) ran into strong opposition well into the twentieth century. In the 1950s and 1960s most families in the United States used birth control. The global population explosion gave greater urgency to the use of contraception throughout the world. Truly by the present time a contraceptive revolution has occurred.

The Church of England, at the Lambeth Conference in 1930, became the first church in the West to accept officially the morality of artificial contraception. Soon Protestant churches in the United States and throughout the world strongly supported family planning and birth control. The Eastern Orthodox Church today also accepts contraception as a means of responsible parenthood within marriage.

Many factors help to explain the widespread acceptance of contraception by the 1960s. Developments in medicine and especially public health care of mothers and children dramatically increased the life expectancy of all human beings and especially of young children. The industrial revolution and urban growth created an environment unlike the earlier rural environment in which children tended to be an economic asset. Problems of poverty abounded in the new urban cultures. The role of women changed, with women having more say in family matters and also entering into the workforce in large numbers. Demography pointed out the growing problem of overpopulation in many parts of the world. The introduction of better and more efficient means of contraception significantly influenced the entire development. In the 1950s drug companies introduced progesterone or anovulant pills, which prevent conception by preventing ovulation in women. Later the IUD (intrauterine device) was introduced.

Catholic Reaction to These Developments: Many Catholic couples, especially in France in the early nineteenth century, apparently used contraception. Official Catholic teaching condemned such use, but Pope Leo XIII in his major encyclical on marriage (*Arcanum Divinae Sapientiae,* 1880) did not even mention contraception. Pope Pius XI in 1930 issued his encyclical *Casti Connubii,* implicitly responding to the Lambeth Conference, and strongly condemned artificial contraception as intrinsically against nature, since the spouses deliberately deprive the act of its natural ordering to the generation of offspring. Some influential theologians maintain that the pope here proclaimed infallible Church teaching, but the majority refuse to see the teaching as infallible. Pope Pius XII (1939–58) continued to reaffirm strongly the teaching of his predecessor, but his 1951 Address to Midwives sanctioned the use of rhythm or the use of the infertile period when serious medical, eugenic, economic, or social reasons indicate that births should be regulated or avoided. In 1958 he condemned the anovulant pill when used for contraceptive purposes.

The 1960s and *Humanae Vitae:* Before 1963 no Catholic theologian had ever publicly questioned the magisterium's teaching on artificial contraception. But developments were occurring in the 1960s on many fronts. In 1963 Dr. John Rock, the Catholic physician who helped develop the anovulant pill, wrote a book advocating that the Church accept the pill. In late 1963 and early 1964, Louis Janssens in Belgium, William van der Mark in Holland, Bishop Joseph Mary Reuss in Germany, and Louis Dupré in the United States all called for some change in Church teaching. More theologians and laity joined the growing call for change; some bishops, especially in Holland, seemed very open to change.

On June 23, 1964, Pope Paul VI publicly called attention to the existence of a special commission, originally appointed by John XXIII, that was studying the question of birth control with a mandate to report back to him. During the debates of the Second Vatican Council some council fathers spoke in an open way about change on this issue. Pope Paul VI took the matter of contraception out of the council in the light of the existence of his special commission, but some intense jockeying for position took place in the drafting of the council documents on the family. The long fifth session of the commission meeting in the spring of 1966 produced two theological working papers, one representing the conservative minority and the other the liberal majority. A third document favoring change apparently constituted the official report from the commission to the pope. The bishops on the final commission voted nine in favor, three against, and three doubtful about this document. *The National Catholic Reporter* obtained the three documents mentioned above and published them in April 1967.

On July 29, 1968, Pope Paul VI released his encyclical *Humanae Vitae,* which reiterated the condemnation of artificial contraception. The encyclical calls for responsible parenthood and again approves the use of the sterile or infertile period. "[The] Church, calling men back to the observance of the norms of the natural law as interpreted by her constant doctrine, teaches that each and every marriage act must remain open to the transmission of life." The document rejects the positions defended by advocates for a change in the teaching. Evil consequences from contraception would lead to moral laxity and harm the ideal of Christian marriage. The encyclical gives pastoral directives, which among other aspects recognize the pressures faced by married couples and imply that the failure to live up to the teaching might not always be gravely sinful.

Pope Paul VI himself spoke of the lively discussion touched off by *Humanae Vitae.* Others have spoken of a crisis. Immediately after the encyclical, national conferences of bishops issued statements supporting the papal teaching, but commentators point out three generic approaches found in these different statements. On the right, some bishops' conferences asserted without any qualification that disobedience to the teaching of the encyclical is seriously wrong for Catholics. The U.S. Catholic bishops in their letter "Human Life in Our Day" illustrated the center position. The U.S. bishops recognized the pressures and circumstances that might reduce the moral guilt of those who use contraception. The U.S. pastoral letter affirmed a presumption in favor of noninfallible teaching but also recognized the legitimacy of public theological dissent from such teaching under certain conditions. However, the U.S. bishops did not explicitly endorse the legitimacy of dissent in this case. On the left, some bishops' conferences maintained that after serious study and reflection a Catholic could dissent from the encyclical's teaching on contraception.

The majority of Catholic moral theologians writing and speaking on the topic in the United States and throughout the world have expressed some dissent from the teaching of *Humanae Vitae.* The dissenting theologians disagreed with the neo-Scholastic natural law theory employed by the encyclical, especially its physicalism whereby the human moral act is identified with the physical structure of the act. For the good of the person or the marriage itself couples should be able to interfere with the sexual act. Many dissenting theologians point out that this teaching belongs in the category of noninfallible teaching and sufficient reasons exist to justify dissent both in theory and in practice. The issue of natural law and of the role of authoritative hierarchical teaching have since come to the fore in the discussion of many other moral and social issues.

A smaller number of theologians have strongly defended the encyclical's reasoning and its conclusions. Germain Grisez, an American Catholic philosopher, and others have adopted a new understanding of natural law to see the malice of contraception as directly going against the basic human good of procreation. Grisez and some others also claim that the teaching of the encyclical is infallible, not based on the encyclical itself but on the fact that its teaching has been taught infallibly by all the bishops of the world.

Catholic laity have increasingly disagreed in practice with the teaching. According to the studies of the National Opinion Research Center in 1963, 45 percent of U.S. Catholics approved of artificial contraception for married couples; in 1974 the figure rose to 83 percent. In practice most confessors do not seem to regard contraception as a major issue. Some sociologists (e.g., Andrew M. Greeley) claim that the encyclical was the reason for massive apostasy and for a notable decline in Catholic religious devotion and belief. On the other hand, natural family planning (NFP), especially with the Billings method, has many adherents who praise it as an effective way of regulating birth that requires the cooperation of husband and wife and does not put the woman at unnecessary risk. Pope John Paul II continued into the 1990s to stress the condemnation of artificial contraception. Dissent by many in practice seems to be somewhat tolerated, but no official acceptance of such dissent has ever been made and some theological dissenters have been censured. Most lay Catholics today seem to have made their conscientious decision for contraception and are at peace with it. However, the credibility of the Church remains at stake because of the gap between hierarchical teaching and pastoral practice.

Additional Issues: Birth control, or contraception, involves many other moral issues. The Catholic tradition has recognized that the condemnation applied to voluntary sexual relations does not apply to involuntary relations, as illustrated by the fact that after rape a woman may attempt to prevent conception.

All recognize that contraception has given human beings more power to control their lives, but power can be abused. Historically, women have borne a disproportionate share of the burden of contraception and of the medical risk connected with it (e.g., the anovulant pill, the IUD, tubal ligation). The strong and the wealthy can often use the power of contraception against the weak and the poor. Some population programs have suffered because of this fact. Even advocates of birth control today generally see voluntary use as the ideal, but government programs of education, incentives, and at times even some limited coercion have been accepted.

The ready availability of contraception has undoubtedly aided the so-called sexual revolution, the growing acceptance of sexual relationships outside marriage, and more irresponsible sexual relations. Proponents of birth control respond that such abuse does not justify doing away with the proper and good use of contraception.

The moral issue of contraceptive use arises very acutely in nonmarital sexuality. Catholic teaching sees sexual relationships in the context of marriage and does not accept any form of nonmarital sexuality. Many blame the ready accessibility of contraception for encouraging nonmarital sexuality and oppose efforts to provide contraceptive information and devices to young people to prevent both pregnancy and diseases such as AIDS. Other Catholics apply the accepted principle of counseling the lesser of two evils to this question. Young people are probably going to be sexually active anyway, and it is a lesser evil to use means to make sure pregnancy and/or sexually transmitted diseases do not occur. The issue of birth control thus has many aspects and continues to spark a lively debate within Catholicism. *See also* Humanae Vitae; infallibility; magisterium; sexual morality.

Bibliography

Hoyt, Robert G., ed. *The Birth Control Debate*. Kansas City, MO: National Catholic Reporter, 1968.

Kaiser, Robert Blair. *The Politics of Sex and Religion: A Case History in the Development of Doctrine*. Kansas City, MO: Leaven Press, 1985.

Noonan, John T., Jr. *Contraception: A History of Its Treatment by the Catholic Theologians and Canonists*. Enlarged ed. Cambridge: Harvard University Press, Belknap Press, 1986.

Shannon, William H. *The Lively Debate: Response to Humanae Vitae*. New York: Sheed and Ward, 1970.   CHARLES E. CURRAN

bishop, a priest who enjoys "the fullness of the sacrament of orders" (Decree on the Bishops' Pastoral Office in the Church, n. 15), usually the pastoral leader of a diocese. There are diocesan bishops (also known as ordinaries), who exercise the ministry of "supervision" or "oversight" (Gk., *episkopos*); and titular bishops, who are either auxiliary bishops, that is, assistants to the diocesan bishop, or coadjutor bishops, that is, assistants to the diocesan bishop but with special faculties and the right of succession (see cans. 376; 381; 403).

Bishops have no clear identity or function in the NT. The word *episkopos* (pl., *episkopoi*) occurs only five times (Acts 20:28; Phil 1:1; 1 Tim 3:2; Titus 1:7; 1 Pet 2:25) and seems interchangeable with the title of elder (*presbyteros*) as in Acts 20:17, 28; 1 Tim 3:2, 5:17; Titus 1:5; and 1 Pet 5:1–3. In some local churches the elders seemed to have formed ruling councils, as in Judaism, and designated one of their own as council president, with specific supervisory responsibilities. Although the task of supervision touched matters of administration, it was primarily concerned with the spiritual realm, namely, with

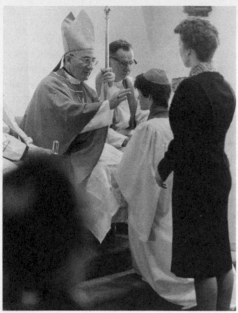

A bishop administers the sacrament of Confirmation.

er the pastor of the local church for which they had been ordained. The creation of titular bishops was another major change from the practice of the early centuries when only one bishop at a time served in a local church.

Moreover, bishops were never regarded as bishops unto themselves, so to speak. By ordination a bishop becomes a member of the college of bishops, whose head is the Bishop of Rome (the pope). The bishops, however, are not vicars of the Bishop of Rome; they are vicars of Jesus Christ himself (Dogmatic Constitution on the Church, n. 27). *See also* Decree on the Bishops' Pastoral Office in the Church; episcopacy. RICHARD P. MCBRIEN

Bishop, Edmund, 1846–1917, liberal English Catholic liturgical scholar, originally Anglican. A civil servant with no university education, Bishop was a self-taught historian and liturgiologist who spent all his free time in the British Museum and other libraries in Europe, becoming an unequaled connoisseur of liturgical sources. A brilliant writer of considerable acumen and originality, Bishop favored hard-nosed Cambridge scholarship, disdained the Oxford liturgiologists, and did not hesitate to take on accepted theories or their prestigious promoters. His judgment was usually as sure as it was sober. His essays appended to R. H. Connolly's *The Liturgical Homilies of Narsai* (1909) and the posthumous anthology *Liturgica Historica* (1918) contain the best of Bishop's writings. A promoter of the English Benedictine revival at Downside, where he is buried, and antagonistic to the Jesuits, Bishop sympathized with many aspects of the Modernist movement and deplored the obscurantism and exaggerated Ultramontanism of its generally far less capable opponents.

the unity of the local church within itself and with the wider community of churches, and with the transmission of the faith received from the apostles.

The bishop's role as presider over the Eucharist was so important during the first centuries that when the Sunday Eucharist was presided over by one of the presbyters, a piece of the eucharistic bread consecrated by the bishop in his cathedral was placed into the chalice. As the Church grew numerically and geographically, it became impossible for the bishop to preside over every Eucharist in his local community, so the presbyters (priests) increasingly assumed this function. Today in the Western Church the only function specifically reserved to the bishop is that of ordination to the priesthood and the diaconate.

The rite of ordination notes that the "title of bishop is not one of honor but of function." Since the end of the second century diocesan bishops have exercised three principal functions: teaching (through preaching and explanation of the faith); leading, or shepherding (maintaining the unity of the local church); and sanctifying (through priestly and sacramental ministry). Among these duties, "the preaching of the gospel occupies an eminent place" (Dogmatic Constitution on the Church, n. 25).

In the earliest centuries bishops were never transferred to other dioceses. They remained forev-

bishops, appointment of, the process by which an individual is selected to be ordained a bishop. The process is governed by special norms for the Latin church, and by special laws for the Eastern Catholic churches.

For the Latin church the bishops in a province regularly discuss potential candidates for bishop and draw up a list, which they forward to the Apostolic See through the papal representative (apostolic delegate or papal nuncio).

For the naming of a diocesan bishop or a coadjutor (a bishop who assists the diocesan bishop and has the right to succeed him in office), the papal representative conducts an investigation into the needs of the diocese, the qualifications needed in a new bishop, and the suggestions of bishops in the province for candidates. He does a background check on names under consideration. In addition to the bishops of the province, selected priests and laypersons may also be consulted—all in secret and through individual contacts, not by consulting with groups of people.

The resulting list of three names, called the *terna,* is forwarded by the papal representative to the Congregation for Bishops, together with a profile of the diocese, background information on each individual, and the papal representative's recommendation. The congregation reviews the candidates, consults with other departments of the Roman Curia, and makes a final recommendation to the pope. The pope makes the final selection.

The papal representative contacts the candidate to ask his acceptance of the appointment. If the candidate consents, he must keep the matter secret until the appointment is announced at the Vatican and by the papal representative. The new bishop has three months to be consecrated, and four months to take charge (possession) of the diocese.

In some countries civil authorities have a voice in the process, either to veto potential candidates or to propose their own *terna.* The Holy See is gradually rescinding these arrangements. Some European dioceses retain the centuries-old process of selection in which the chapter of canons (similar to the college of consultors) selects the *terna,* or selects one individual from a *terna* submitted to them by the Holy See.

The naming of auxiliary bishops is less complicated. The diocesan bishop requesting an auxiliary draws up the list of three names. The Congregation for Bishops reviews the list, and the pope makes the final selection.

In Eastern Catholic churches a similar process is followed for dioceses that are outside the traditional patriarchal territories (e.g., outside Egypt and the Middle East), although if the church has a patriarch, a suggested *terna* is developed by the patriarch with the Patriarchal Synod.

Patriarchs themselves are selected by the Patriarchal Synod and enthroned (installed) by the synod. Patriarchs must exchange letters of communion with the Apostolic See before they can exercise their office fully.

In Eastern churches headed by a major archbishop the Archiepiscopal Synod elects the archbishop. To be enthroned, he needs letters of communion from the Apostolic See. *See also* bishop.

JAMES H. PROVOST

bishops, college of, the body of bishops headed by the pope who succeed the college of the apostles in teaching authority and pastoral governance in the Church.

One becomes a member of the college by ordination as a bishop and hierarchical communion with the college's head (the pope) and members. This applies to bishops in charge of dioceses (diocesan bishops), titular bishops (who usually assist diocesan bishops or exercise some office in service to the Church, such as in the Roman Curia), and retired bishops (emeritus bishops).

The college exercises supreme authority in the Church when it acts in an ecumenical council or by collegial action of the bishops scattered around the world acting together with the pope. Usually the pope, as head of the college, determines how it will act, although historically others have taken the initiative, and the action is considered collegial once it is accepted or received by the pope.

Members of the college are expected to show solicitude or mutual concern for all the other members of the college, to assist each other in their pastoral charge in the Church, and to foster the missionary work of the Church everywhere. At times members of the college gather in organized groups to promote this work; for example, in episcopal conferences, particular councils, etc. While these are not actions of the whole college, they do express the collegial bond among bishops and their shared responsibilities as college members. *See also* bishop; collegiality; communion, Church as.

JAMES H. PROVOST

Bismarck, Otto von, 1815–98, the first chancellor of Germany. A Prussian conservative, he was able to bypass south German Catholic particularism by appealing to nationalism in a war against France in 1870; this led to the creation of modern Germany in 1871. The particularism did not die, however, and the Catholic Center party emerged as the single most powerful political bloc, partly as a result of Bismarck's attack on the Church known as the *Kulturkampf* (Ger., "culture struggle"). *See also Kulturkampf.*

black Catholics, Catholics of African descent, also known as African-American Catholics. It would be inaccurate to limit the history of black Catholics to the twentieth century. To do so would disregard the African origins of Sts. Augustine, Benedict the Moor, Moses the Black, and Felicitas, and three popes—Victor I, Militiades, and Gelasius I. It would also overlook the mid-sixteenth-century reappearance of the Church in Africa with the Portuguese, in what is now known as Angola, during the rule of King Alfonso. In the New World, the presence and sacramental lives of hundreds of black Catholics are recorded in the parochial registers in the oldest Spanish colonial settlement in the United States, St. Augustine, Florida, from 1565 to 1763.

Nineteenth Century: The roots of the contemporary movement among black Catholics in the United States lay in the nineteenth century. From 1889 until 1894, under the leadership of Daniel Rudd, black Catholic laity created and sustained a national intellectual and social movement to urge their Church to address the spiritual and temporal needs of black Catholics.

A survey conducted by the 1889 congress of American black Catholics revealed the Church's participation in national customs of segregation, discrimination, and benign neglect. Black Catholic membership in the United States stood at approximately two hundred thousand out of a black population of roughly seven million. There were twenty churches, each with its own primary school; sixty-five other schools providing instruction for approximately five thousand children; and nine orphanages. There were about 150 sisters in two institutes. An early effort to begin a religious congregation of black women, the Sisters of Loretto, failed in 1824. The first successful foundation of a group of black religious women, in 1829, was the Oblate Sisters of Providence in Baltimore, Maryland; it was led by Elizabeth Lange. Henriette Delille and Juliette Gaudin were the founding members of the Sisters of the Holy Family in New Orleans, Louisiana, in 1842. The third community of black sisters, the Franciscan Handmaids of Mary, was founded in 1916 in Savannah, Georgia. Seven young black men were enrolled in Catholic seminaries—a marked improvement over the treatment given Father Augustus Tolton (1854–97), who is generally recognized as the first black American Catholic priest. Since no American seminary would admit him, Tolton prepared for ordination in Rome (1882–86).

Matters discussed by the congresses included civil rights for blacks; the end of racial discrimination in housing, the trades, unions, and professions; the study of African history; cultural development; industrial training and all types of education; ongoing religious instruction for the laity; recruitment of vocations to the religious life and priesthood; and just and equal treatment in the Church.

Twentieth Century: The first renewal of a movement among black Catholics dates from the work of Dr. Thomas Wyatt Turner, who in 1924 established the Federated Colored Catholics (FCC)—an action-oriented lay group, dedicated to ending racial discrimination within Church and society. This period also witnessed the founding, in 1925 by Katherine Drexel, of Xavier University of New Orleans, the only black Catholic university in the United States, and the organization of the fraternal and benevolent society, the Knights of Peter Claver.

The second renewal arose in 1968 in response to the frustration and anger that swept the country at the assassination of Martin Luther King, Jr. Meeting in Detroit in April 1968, a group of black Catholic priests charged that their Church was racist. They called upon the Church to abandon its silence and seize an active moral role in eradicating discrimination and racism. The National Black Catholic Clergy Caucus (NBCCC) and the National Black Sisters' Conference (NBSC) were formed as a result of this meeting. Within two years, the National Office for Black Catholics (NOBC), the National Black Seminarians Association (NBSA), and the National Black Lay Catholic Caucus (NBLCC) were also formed.

Contemporary black Catholics continue to express concerns similar to those of their nineteenth century counterparts. Since the late 1960s some positive changes can be reported, due to the establishment and staffing of national offices of various black organizations, especially those of the NOBC and NBSC, and the gradual emergence of a small cadre of black Catholic scholars in the ecclesiastical disciplines. The NBSC, NOBC, and NBLCC developed and directed workshops and institutes (1) to introduce insights of black culture and black theology; (2) to support ministry to black parishes and social programs; (3) to foster lay leadership and spiritual formation, and (4) to combat racism in the Church. The creative genius of the Reverend Clarence Joseph Rivers led the NOBC to conduct workshops on liturgical adaptation. Such efforts laid the groundwork for the 1987 publication of *Lead Me, Guide Me: The African American Catholic Hymnal.* In 1979, encouraged by its black members, the

Catholic bishops issued a pastoral letter on racism, "Brothers and Sisters to Us." And in 1984 the black bishops themselves issued a pastoral letter on evangelization, "What We Have Seen and Heard." In 1987, the first black Catholic congress in the twentieth century was held in Washington, D.C., and in that same year the NCCB created the Secretariat for African American Catholics.

As of 1993 black Catholics in the United States numbered about 2.5 million, including twelve members of the episcopacy; five hundred sisters; and six hundred priests, permanent deacons, vowed religious brothers, and seminarians. *See also* Africa, Catholicism in.   M. SHAWN COPELAND

black fast, penitential practice involving abstinence from all food and drink except bread and water. Such a fast was either a voluntary act of devotion, a religious practice in a particular monastery or convent on certain days, or, in the early Church, an imposed penance for a determined period and for specific faults. *See also* abstinence; fasting.

Black Friars. *See* Dominican order.

black Mass, traditional term for the Mass for the Dead (so named because of the black vestments worn by the priest); also a parody of the Eucharist that developed with the rise of Satanism after the twelfth century. Before Vatican II (1962–65), all funerals were celebrated in black vestments. In the 1990s, white is used to remind us of the joy of the Resurrection. *See also* Mass.

Black Monks. *See* Benedictine order.

Blaise, St. (blayz), early-fourth-century martyr. He is counted as one of the "Fourteen Holy Helpers," a group of saints who were popular objects of devotion in Germany in the fourteenth and fifteenth centuries. The list included Barbara, Christopher, and Erasmus. He is thought to have been from Armenia, but events in his life are considered legendary. One story that has him helping a person with a bone caught in the throat is the origin of the custom of having throats blessed on his feast day. In art he is often depicted with a wool-comb, which is thought to have been the instrument of his torture before his beheading. Feast day: February 3. *See also* throats, blessing of.

Blanchet, François N. (blahn-shay'), 1795–1883,

priest and missionary to the Pacific Northwest. After several years as a missionary in the Oregon Territory, he was chosen to be the first archbishop of Oregon City in 1846. He worked tirelessly to promote the spread of Catholicism in the Pacific Northwest by securing personnel and resources from Europe. To facilitate work with Native Americans, he founded the Bureau of Catholic Indian Missions and copyrighted the "Catholic Ladder," an important catechetical tool for Native Americans.

Blase, St. *See* Blaise, St.

blasphemy, contemptuous language to or about God. In the OT it is punishable by stoning (Lev 24:16). In the NT it is one of the evils that defile a person (Mark 7:21–23; Matt 15:19–20). Jesus' claim to be the Messiah (Matt 26:64–65) and Son of God (John 10:31–36) was considered blasphemous. The attribution of Jesus' authority over demons to Beelzebub is regarded as blasphemy "against the Holy Spirit" (Mark 3:28–29; Luke 12:10), an unforgivable sin. Paul's pre-Christian activity is characterized as blasphemous (1 Tim 1:13); after his conversion his opponents attack and punish him (Acts 13:45; 18:6). The beast will utter blasphemy against God and his saints (Rev 13:1–6). The NT warns against blasphemy (2 Tim 3:2; 2 Pet 2:2) and promises divine judgment upon it (Rev 16:9, 11). Thomas Aquinas regarded blasphemy as a sin against faith by which one attributes to God that which does not belong to God or denies God that which is God's due. In moral theology it is a sin against the virtue of religion.

blessed. *See* beatification.

Blessed Sacrament, the term used to refer to the Eucharist as preeminent among the seven sacraments. It often more narrowly refers to the consecrated bread as it is reserved outside the celebration of the Eucharist.

Before the twelfth century, the sacred species was reserved privately to be administered to the sick in emergencies. During that century there was significant development of the doctrine of the Real Presence. Accompanying this development was the desire on the part of the faithful to see and worship Christ present in the sacrament.

The liturgical renewal following the Second Vatican Council emphasizes the Eucharist as an action. This has had a number of implications for the

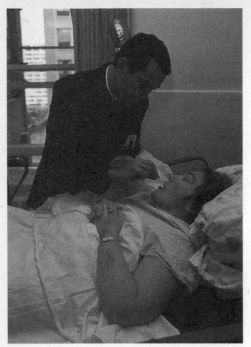

A hospitalized Catholic receives the Blessed Sacrament from a priest.

reservation of the Blessed Sacrament. The first of these is the stress that is placed on the primary and original reason for reserving the sacred species, that is, the administration of Communion to the sick and dying. Distribution of Communion outside of Mass and the adoration of Jesus Christ as really present under the appearance of bread are secondary reasons.

Another implication is that the relationship of the Blessed Sacrament to the action of the Mass is always to be made clear. For example, exposition should not occur during the celebration of Mass, and when it occurs after the Mass, the host should be one consecrated at that Mass.

Congregations are also encouraged to place the tabernacle formerly located on the main altar in some appropriate place apart from that altar. These changes notwithstanding, adoration of the Blessed Sacrament is still an approved form of eucharistic devotion. *See also* Eucharist; eucharistic devotions; Real Presence.

Blessed Sacrament, exposition of the. *See* exposition of the Blessed Sacrament.

Blessed Virgin Mary. *See* Mary, Blessed Virgin.

blessing, a liturgical expression of God's generosity and love. Blessings are sacramental signs used by the Church to make holy various objects and occasions in human life. In the Bible, blessings have two aspects: they call down God's gifts on the people and in turn express the people's thanks for the gifts thus bestowed. These two aspects of blessing are found most perfectly in the Eucharist, and the Church's action in other sanctifying prayers is an extension of that central action. A prayer of blessing is accompanied by the raising of the right hand, and the sign of the cross is usually made over the congregation, an individual, or the object being blessed. *See also* sign of the cross.

Blondel, Maurice (blahn-del'), 1861–1949, French Catholic philosopher. He sought to overcome the division between philosophy and theology without denying philosophy its proper autonomy. *L'Action,* his doctoral thesis, traced the workings of the human will and its inability to find a natural object equal to its striving. This implied an openness in the human person to the supernatural destiny ascribed to it by Christianity. His work was important to twentieth-century Catholic theology, apologetics, and social action because it challenged conceptions of the supernatural that separated grace from the everyday world and made Christianity seem detached from life, art, and politics. *See also* philosophy and theology; supernatural.

blood of Christ, the blood that Jesus shed on the cross in atonement for the sins of humankind, and that which is received sacramentally in Holy Communion. In the Bible, blood is identified with the whole living person, not just what flows through the body's veins and arteries. By shedding his blood for the human race, Jesus purchased its eternal redemption (Heb 9:12), for "without the shedding of blood there is no forgiveness of sins" (9:22). By his blood Jesus made expiation for our sins (Rom 3:25), cleansed us (Heb 9:14; 1 John 1:7), purified and delivered us (1 Pet 1:2), sanctified us (Heb 13:12), and justified us (Rom 5:9). The Church has given a eucharistic meaning to the words Jesus said at the Last Supper, "This cup that is poured out for you is the new covenant in my blood" (Luke 22:20). We share in the blood of Christ, and therefore in his life, through the eucharistic cup of blessing (1 Cor 10:16). *See also* atonement, biblical view of; atonement, doctrine of; Body of Christ; Communion, Holy; crucifixion; expiation; mixed chalice; Precious Blood, devotion to the; propitiation; redemption; sacrifice; unmixed chalice.

boat, incense, the small liturgical vessel used for holding incense. The boat has long been used in art and literature as a symbol of the Church, because several of the first disciples were fishermen. The Church of Rome has often been referred to as the Bark (or Boat) of Peter. *See also* incense.

Bobbio, monastery in northern Italy. It was founded by the Irish abbot and missionary Columbanus after his expulsion from Gaul in 610 for his criticisms of the royal court and about a year before his death in 615. Guided by able and scholarly abbots, it became an important center of learning with a remarkable library. *See also* Columbanus, St.

Bobola, St. Andrew (boh'boh-lah), 1591–1657, Polish Jesuit priest. Preacher and director of sodalities (church organizations that promote personal piety and charitable acts), he dedicated himself to pastoral ministries in war-filled Poland. When he was captured by Cossacks and refused to repudiate the Apostolic See (i.e., the papacy), he was tortured and beheaded. Feast day: May 16.

Böckle, Franz, 1921–91, German moral theologian noted for his emphasis on the contingent nature of ethical norms due to the complexities of the human condition.

body. *See* mind/body.

Incense boat

body, resurrection of the. *See* resurrection of the body.

body and spirituality. Fundamental to a Catholic understanding of the relationship between human bodiliness and spirituality is the conviction that the bodily and the spiritual belong together. They are not separate realms. The human person is one being in reality. To be holy is to be whole, an integrated person or self. The desire for wholeness is a deep longing of the human heart.

Catholic spirituality affirms the sacramentality of the human body, recognizing it as a sacrament of God's presence and grace. The body receives and expresses the life and love of God. Lived creatively and compassionately, human bodiliness manifests God through feeling, gesture, movement, song, sexuality, speech, stillness of being, and loving action.

A spirituality that proclaims the sacramentality of the body has a strong component of justice. It rejects discrimination against persons who are different. It espouses basic bodily rights for all: the right to adequate food, shelter, clothing, health care, and an environment free from domestic, institutional, or military violence. Recognizing the human body as part of the created order, it promotes ecological awareness to oppose exploitation of the earth and its resources.

A spirituality that values the human body honors the intrinsic relationship between the sensual and the spiritual. It regards sexuality as an expression of God's love in life, a gift to be lived responsibly and sensitively. The integration of sexuality and spirituality is an essential aspect of Christian life.

Catholic and Christian spirituality begins with the mystery of God-made-flesh. From this central tenet, one derives affirmation of the sacredness of the human body, care for one's own physicality, and concern for the well-being of the bodies of others. The God who assumed humanity in the person of Jesus continues to do so in the People of God. The Risen Christ is manifest in and through human bodies. *See also* sacramentality, principle of; spirituality, Christian.   COLLEEN M. GRIFFITH

Body of Christ, term referring to the ways that Christ is present to humanity and to the world. It has a spectrum of interrelated meanings derived from the human body of the historical Jesus. That human body has not been destroyed by death; the risen and glorified Jesus still possesses it at the right hand of God. The mystery of the Father's raising of Jesus means that Jesus will always be one with humankind, but now in a glorified or transformed humanity, i.e., one completely receptive to, and permeated by, the Spirit.

The post-Resurrection appearance narratives of the NT, particularly those of Luke and John, highlight the physical features of Christ's resurrected body, the corporeal reality of the risen Christ. The continuity between the crucified body and the risen body means that Jesus has moved into a divine dimension of existence and yet at the same time, in a very real sense, he remains entirely in this world, though in a new way given him by God. Paul speaks of the risen body as *soma pneumatikon* (Gk.), "spiritual body" (1 Cor 15:44), by which he does not mean some sort of spiritualized matter or ephemeral substance, but a body existing in the domain of the Spirit. Christ's body, now suffused with the light of God's glory, is the foundation for a new creation. Thus it can be said that the Eucharist is truly the body of Christ; and so, too, is the Church, the place where Christ dwells in the midst of his people, the Body of Christ.

The notion of the body of Christ as present both in the Church and in the Eucharist is developed in the Pauline writings, particularly in 1 Corinthians, Romans, Ephesians, and Colossians. For Paul, Christians constitute one body of Christ, for there is one bread and one body (1 Cor 10:16). As the body is one, so members of the body are one in Christ (Rom 12:5). The Eucharist is a participation in the body of Christ; partaking reinforces union with the Lord Jesus (1 Cor 10:17).

The concept of sharing life with the Lord and with other participants is not a metaphor for Paul; it is real, verging on the physical. Christ and the Church are one person in a real unity so close that it can only be called his Body.

The later Letters (Ephesians and Colossians) expand these ideas and stress the notion of the Church as the fullness of the Body of Christ. Christ is now called the head from whom the whole Body is nourished.

As eucharistic practice changed in the history of the Church, the link between the Church as the Body of Christ and the Eucharist as body of Christ became weaker. But Vatican II (1962–65) retrieved these biblical images and gathered them together once again in the Dogmatic Constitution on the Church, n. 7. *See also* blood of Christ; Church; Eucharist.

KATHLEEN CANNON

Boethius, St. Severinus, ca. 480–524, translator (from Greek into Latin), philosopher, theologian, and Roman statesman. Anicius Manlius Severinus Boethius planned to translate and comment on all of Plato and Aristotle and to show, in Neoplatonic fashion, that their teachings were in harmony (though he preferred Plato's); however, he did not get past Aristotle's treatises on logic, which remained the only Aristotelian texts the Middle Ages knew until the twelfth century. His translation of Porphyry's *Isagoge* transmitted the problem of universals to medieval thinkers. His theological tractates have enjoyed almost unrivaled authority in matters pertaining to the Trinity and the Incarnation; especially significant was his defining "person" as an individual substance of a rational nature. He composed his best-known work, *The Consolation of Philosophy,* in a prison near Pavia while awaiting execution, allegedly for treason; this purely philosophical discussion of the problem of evil has had an enormous influence on speculation about God's eternity and about divine foreknowledge and human freedom. Because religious differences among the Eastern empire, Italians, and the Arian king Theodoric seem to have played some part in Boethius's downfall, Pavians have long venerated him as a martyr. Feast day: October 23. *See also* Aristotle; evil; Incarnation, the; Person, divine; Trinity, doctrine of the.

Boff, Leonardo, b. 1938, a leading exponent of Latin American liberation theology. A native of Brazil and a former Franciscan priest, he has long been concerned with developing an ecclesiology and a Christology for the Latin American church. Boff's theology is permeated by a sacramental view of creation. The 1981 publication *Church, Charism and Power,* in which he outlined an ecclesiology based on gifts rather than hierarchical structures, led to his being silenced by Rome for a year. Exasperated by the Vatican's persistent efforts to restrict his work, Boff left the Franciscan order and the priesthood in 1992. *See also* liberation theology.

Bogomils, heretical dualist sect despising matter and its creator as evil and extolling spirit as good. Founded by Bogomil (Bulgarian, "beloved of God") in Bulgaria in the tenth century, they influenced the Cathari. Once widespread in the Balkans, most eventually converted either to Catholicism or Islam. *See also* dualism.

Bohachevsky, Constantine, 1884–1961, U.S.

Ukrainian Catholic bishop. He was born in Ukraine, ordained priest in 1909, and became bishop in 1924, named apostolic exarch for Ukrainian Catholics in the United States. In 1959, when the exarchate was raised to a metropolitan province, he became the first metropolitan of Philadelphia for the Ukrainians.

Bollandists, group of Jesuit editors of the *Acta Sanctorum,* a collection of saints' lives. Organized by Jean Bolland (1596–1665) in Antwerp, Belgium, they sought to prepare accurate lives of the saints without legendary or apocryphal material and were influential in the development of modern manuscript studies because of their diligence. Their most famous scholar was Daniel von Papenbrock (d. 1714). Disbanded with the suppression of the Jesuits in 1773, they resumed work in 1837 and continue to publish *Acta Bollandiana,* a journal of hagiographical information. *See also* saints.

Bonaventure, St., ca. 1217–74, Franciscan friar, theologian, and Doctor of the Church, known as the "Seraphic Doctor."

Life and Writings: Bonaventure was born at Bagnoregio in the Papal States and christened Giovanni di Fidanza. He studied in the faculty of arts at the University of Paris, where he entered the Franciscan order about 1243. His precocious talent was immediately apparent, and he began to teach publicly in the Franciscan school in 1248, becoming regent master in 1254–55, a time when the university

Bonaventure, the greatest Franciscan theologian in the history of the Church, at his own funeral in 1274, the same year Thomas Aquinas died; painting by Zurbaran, Louvre, Paris.

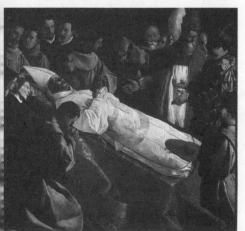

was torn by the bitter quarrel between the secular masters and the mendicants. His writings from this period include his *Commentary on the Sentences* of Peter Lombard, three biblical commentaries, a series of sophisticated disputed questions, and a theological handbook, the *Breviloquium.*

Bonaventure's academic tenure was brief, for in 1257 he was elected minister general of an increasingly divided Franciscan order. In this capacity he provided both intelligent and conciliatory leadership for seventeen years, his work shaping the fundamental directions of the order for generations. He systematically codified the general constitutions governing the fractious brotherhood and composed a *Life of St. Francis,* which became the official biography of the founder in 1266. Most of the writings of his generalate are defenses of the mendicant way of life or spiritual treatises, including the celebrated *Journey of the Soul into God.* Still, Bonaventure continued to make his primary residence in Paris and so remained active in the intellectual developments there, chiefly through a series of university sermons. His advice was much in demand by the popes of the period, eventually leading to his appointment as cardinal-bishop of Albano in 1273. He took a prominent part in organizing the Second Council of Lyons in 1274, dying while it was in session. Bonaventure's exemplary Franciscan life and the abiding influence of his thought in the Western Church were recognized by his canonization in 1482 and his being declared a Doctor of the Church in 1588.

Thought: Bonaventure's thought is a highly original if eclectic synthesis of historical sources— chiefly Augustine, Denys the Areopagite (Pseudo-Dionysius), and Aristotle—and his own Franciscan interpretation of human experience. Its foundational structure is the classic Neoplatonic circle of emanation, exemplarity, and return. His theological metaphysics is based on the doctrine of the Trinity as the absolute mystery of self-diffusive Good. For Bonaventure the "first person" is the fecund "womb of being," an overflowing fountain of goodness. Out of a boundless desire to communicate self, the Father generates the Word, or perfect expression of his eternal Art; the Spirit is their eminently personal mutual love, completing the circle of giving and return.

Bonaventure views creation as a further overflow and expression of this divine self-communication; in the absolute self-expression of the Word the Father also produces the archetypes of everything he can possibly create. The further decision of God to communicate being to that which is exterior to the inner divine life is thus grounded in the Word. The son who became incarnate in the person of Christ is "the hidden center" of the universe; all of created reality is somehow contained in him as primal expression of God and in its very being points back to him. Following Francis, Bonaventure's universe is symbolic: "Every creature, because it speaks God, is a divine word." Like a stained-glass window, creation is translucent; its significance can be read only because of the divine light that permeates it, making it reflect a source beyond itself. This is the basis of Bonaventure's strong reaction to the radical Aristotelianism increasingly in vogue at Paris in the 1260s; for him, all things are theonomous in their very being. Nothing created can really be autonomous, as if it could somehow be considered in itself; nothing makes sense apart from God.

This fundamentally dynamic structure is especially evident in human beings, because in them creation is reflexively self-conscious. Rational creatures reflect God's being in a heightened manner because their spiritual faculties of memory, intellect, and will are images of the divine Trinity itself. God is thus present within their very being as the ultimate object of all their concrete acts of knowledge and love. However, a sinful humanity has lost sight of its true nature; "curved in on themselves," people were unconscious of their divine source and goal. But by himself assuming human nature, the Word incarnate in Christ has exemplified humanity's true vocation; his self-emptying life has overcome the human tendency toward nonbeing; by uniting themselves to him in his response of love other people can also attain their fulfillment through a process of divinization that is imaged by Bonaventure as a journey of the soul into God.

The self-communication of God to the soul through grace rectifies its faculties through the theological virtues of faith, hope, and love, so that God may be experienced and chosen for God's own sake in all concrete human knowing and willing. In this way, in conformity to the pattern revealed in Christ, the human soul is gradually refashioned into its primal image, finally attaining a total resemblance to its divine source. The theological task cannot be considered apart from this dynamism; its goal is not so much to know facts about God, but, in achieving affective union with God, the wisdom that experiences the realities of which it speaks. Thus all theology is ultimately mystical: the objective knowing characteristic of the intellect must lead to and be transcended by the subjective knowing of love, an experience that is ultimately ineffable, when God is all in all.

There has been a great revival of interest in Bonaventure's theology in the twentieth century; many of its elements have been creatively retrieved by such contemporary thinkers such as Karl Rahner (d. 1984). Its popularity today may be especially due to its holistic character: for Bonaventure nature cannot be divorced from grace, abstract thought from symbolic modes of apprehension, or theology from spirituality. Feast day: July 15. *See also* Franciscan order; mystical theology; mysticism; Scholasticism.

Bibliography

Bougerol, J. Guy. *Introduction to the Works of Bonaventure.* Paterson, NJ: St. Anthony's Guild Press, 1964.

Cousins, Ewart. *Bonaventure and the Coincidence of Opposites.* Chicago: Franciscan Herald Press, 1978.

Hayes, Zachary. *The Hidden Center.* New York: Paulist Press, 1981.

DOMINIC MONTI

Boniface VIII [Benedict Caetani], ca. 1235–1303, pope from 1294 to 1303. An ambitious and talented administrator, he was a papal diplomat to France and England in the 1270s before being made cardinal in 1281. The architect of the resignation of Celestine V (1294), Boniface set out, after his own election as pope, to restore papal strength, which had faltered under the easily influenced Celestine; he also worked for peace in Europe and revived crusading efforts in the Holy Land.

The assertion of papal power meant inevitable conflicts with secular authorities, mainly with the French king Philip IV. In 1296 Boniface ordered the kings of England and France to cease taxing their clergy without papal authorization. Philip responded by stopping the flow of church contributions from France to Rome, an action that prompted Boniface to temper his formerly belligerent position. During this conflict Boniface managed to make other enemies including the powerful Colonna family and their two cardinals, whose enmity would add to the pope's difficulties. The tenuous peace with Philip was broken in 1301 when the king disregarded Church law and tried a French bishop in a royal court. Boniface's reaction was swift and uncompromising: without reviewing the case the pope warned the king that his unrepented actions would bring dire consequences. These were defined in the famous bull *Unam Sanctam* (1302), in which Boniface laid out in bold terms the manner in which kings related to spiritual and papal authority. He invoked

Pope Boniface VIII, the quintessential medieval pope who vigorously asserted the primacy of the pope, even over temporal rulers, and who permitted so many statues of himself that his enemies accused him of encouraging idolatry; he is depicted here between two pilgrims in a fresco by the Florentine artist Giotto (d. ca. 1337) in the Lateran Basilica, Rome.

traditional views of papal power but in an extreme and unbending manner: papal authority extended over all creatures in the world, and while the Church wielded the spiritual sword for salvation, the secular power was to wield the temporal sword but in service to the spiritual. Philip, with the support of the Colonna cardinals, called for a general council to try the pope on charges that ranged from heresy to usurpation of the papal throne and the murder of Celestine V. Boniface stood firm and threatened to

dismiss the king "like a servant" if need be. Philip boldly sent a contingent of soldiers to Anagni to seize Boniface and bring him to France. The pope was held for three days before the townspeople expelled the French force. Badly shaken by the incident, he returned to Rome where he died a month later.

A strong and determined champion of traditional papal rights, Boniface was also out of step with the times and blind to the powerful nationalism that was rising in Europe and that eventually brought him low. Still, his pontificate was important in other respects: among his many accomplishments were the inauguration of the first Holy Year in 1300, papal legislation for the education of parish clergy, and the expansion of canon law. A patron of art and education, Boniface gave Giotto work in Rome, reestablished the Vatican Library, and founded Rome's university, the Sapienza. *See also* Celestine V, St.; Holy Year; papacy, the; *Unam Sanctam;* Vatican Library.

WILLIAM J. DOHAR

Boniface, St. [Wynfrith], ca. 675–754, Anglo-Saxon missionary to the Germans and martyr. A monk from childhood, Wynfrith at the age of forty left his English abbey in 716 to become a missionary in Frisia. Returning in failure, he refused election as abbot and traveled to Rome, where in 719 Pope Gregory II commissioned him as a missionary and named him Boniface.

Boniface preached in Thuringia, Frisia, and Hesse, corresponding frequently with the pope, who consecrated him bishop in 722. In 732, Gregory III raised him to the rank of archbishop; in 738, he became papal legate to Germany. Boniface founded several sees and monasteries, including the abbey of Fulda, and took an active part in Frankish church reform in the 740s.

In 753, Boniface and his companions undertook another mission to Frisia, where they were massacred at Dokkum in 754. Boniface's tomb is at Fulda. Feast day: June 5. *See also* Germany, Catholicism in.

Book of Hours, liturgical book containing the prescribed prayers for the canonical hours of the day. Such books were often lavishly illuminated in the medieval Church and were considered works of art in their own right. Such a book is also called a breviary or the Liturgy of the Hours. *See also* breviary; Liturgy of the Hours.

Book of Kells. *See* Kells, Book of.

Borgia, St. Francis, 1510–72, Spanish Jesuit, friend of Ignatius of Loyola, and third general of the Society of Jesus. He demonstrated an orientation toward religious life from his earliest years. However, his father, the duke of Gandia, prevailed upon him to join the court of Charles V. There he received a royal appointment, eventually becoming Viceroy of Catalonia. After his wife's death in 1565, Francis contributed to the establishment of several schools including the Collegium Romanum. Feast day: October 10, observed regionally.

Borromeo, St. Charles (baw-roh-may'oh) 1538–

84, Italian cardinal-archbishop of Milan, reformer, and founder of seminaries. He was born into the wealthy and aristocratic Medici family and was educated in the humanities at Milan and Pavia. When he was twenty-two, his uncle Gian Angelo Medici was elected pope (Pius IV) and within a week Charles, still a layperson, was named a cardinal and appointed archbishop of Milan. Though expected to emulate the luxurious life-style of his family, Charles chose a more moderate way of life, refusing to succumb to the quest for personal power and prestige. During the final session of the Council of Trent, he made significant contributions to the Tridentine Catechism. The death of his older brother in 1562 had a profound impact on him. It is said that,

Charles Borromeo, one of the greatest of the sixteenth-century Catholic reformers, shown here at the right of the enthroned Blessed Virgin (with another great reformer, Ignatius of Loyola, founder of the Jesuits, at her left); a Carlo Maratta (d. 1713) painting in the Chiesa Nuova ("New Church"), Rome.

despite the advice of his family to abandon his ecclesiastical career and raise a family, he was moved rather to live an even holier life. Not long after his brother died, Charles was ordained, and when Pius IV died in 1565, he went back to Milan as the city's archbishop and voice of reform. Until his death in 1584, Charles implemented the directives of Trent by opening seminaries, challenging clergy to live more moral lives, establishing a confraternity of Christian doctrine for children and, often with his own funds, attending to the poor and sick, particularly during the plague in 1576. Charles was canonized in 1610. Feast day: November 4.

Bosco, St. John, also known as Don Bosco, 1815–88, founder of the Pious Society of St. Francis de Sales (the Salesians), priest, and patron saint of youth and of Catholic publishers. Born in Turin, Italy, he is remembered especially for his work with homeless boys, whom he served by establishing hospices where they could live, learn trades, and receive spiritual guidance. This ministry prompted two other pastoral accomplishments in his career: the publication of catechetical materials for the instruction of youth under his care and the foundation of a religious community, the Salesians (1859), to assist in the work of training youth. The Salesians were approved by Rome in 1868. Don Bosco was a deeply spiritual person who is said to have had many visions throughout his life. He was particularly devoted to the Blessed Mother. He was canonized in 1934. Feast day: January 31. *See also* Salesians.

Bossuet, Jacques Bénigne (bah'sway), 1627–1704, preacher, bishop, and Catholic apologist. Born in Dijon, France, he displayed a talent for preaching when he was still a teenager. Educated by Jesuits at Dijon and prepared for the priesthood by Vincent de Paul in Metz, he quickly gained a reputation for his oratorical skills and his defense of Catholicism against Protestants. By all accounts, he was a passionate and articulate preacher whose funeral sermons were particularly popular. He became a bishop in 1669, and throughout his episcopal career he dedicated himself to a variety of apologetic activities, including the publication of several works on Catholic doctrine. Among these, his two-volume work, *Histoire des variations des Églises protestantes* (1688), is the best known. During this period, he also devoted himself to spiritual writing. Though he vigorously opposed Protestantism, he never gave up hope for reconciliation with the reformers.

Botte, Bernard, 1893–1980, Benedictine monk of Mont César, Belgium, and influential liturgical scholar and teacher. Dom Botte promoted the liturgical movement by his scholarly research and critical editions of early liturgies and by founding a graduate school of liturgical studies at the Catholic University of Paris (1956).

Botticelli, Sandro, ca. 1444–1510, Florentine painter, born Alessandro di Mariano Filipepi. His early paintings were based on secular themes, e.g., *Spring* and *Birth of Venus,* which pointed to the triumph of love and reason over brutality. His paintings became religious in his later years, including some frescoes in the Sistine Chapel, depictions of the Madonna, the *Nativity,* the *Last Communion of St. Jerome,* and various altar panels. The popularity of his work declined after his death, but was revived in the nineteenth century.

Botulph, St., seventh-century Anglo-Saxon monk. Virtually all that is known of Botulph is the notice in the *Anglo-Saxon Chronicle* for 654 that he built a monastery at Icanhoe: this is often identified as Boston (derived from "Botulph's town"). A popular saint in medieval England, he had, according to legend, a brother named Adulph. Feast day: June 17.

Bourget, Ignace (boor zhay'), 1799–1885, second bishop of Montreal (1840–78). He was the strongest voice for Ultramontanism (an extreme pro-papal movement) and the neo-Thomistic revival in the Canadian church. He actively recruited religious communities for the diocese and made Montreal a center for Ultramontanism. A major religious revival followed in the wake of his policies and Bourget acquired a reputation as a forceful publicist for papal primacy and centralized jurisdiction. *See also* Canada, Catholicism in; Thomism; Ultramontanism.

Bouyer, Louis Jean (loo'ee zhahn boo-yay'), b. 1913, French theologian. Born into a Lutheran family in Paris and educated at the universities of Paris and Strasbourg, he renewed his profession of Christian faith in the Catholic Church and was ordained a priest of the Oratorians. A professor in the faculty of theology at the Institut Catholique of Paris and author of numerous books and articles in ecclesiology, liturgy, and spirituality, he initially rendered theological support to Vatican II and its renewal, but in later years his writings became theologically cautious.

bowing, an inclination of the head, or of the head and the body. Liturgically, bowing is a mark of supplication and adoration toward God; bowing can also denote respect or reverence toward persons or things, or express a greeting. Through the years, the use of bows multiplied, but the practice has been greatly simplified in recent Church legislation. The bow of the head is made at the doxology, at the name of Jesus, Mary, or the saint of the day, and at the consecration of the Eucharist. Bowing of the body is made before the altar and at specified times during the Mass.

Boys' Town, a residential program for troubled boys founded near Omaha, Nebraska, in 1917 by Edward J. Flanagan (d. 1948). The nonsectarian institution serves 550 youth on a 1300-acre home campus to which young women were admitted in 1979. Boys' Town gained national fame from the 1938 motion picture *Boys' Town,* starring Spencer Tracy. Expansion in later years included a research hospital for hearing impairments (1975), an inner-city alternative high school (1983), a nationwide family-home program (1983), a short-term shelter program (1989), training and counseling services, and a $469 million endowment (1991).

Bradwardine, Thomas, ca. 1290–1349, English theologian, mathematician, and confessor to King Edward III. Consecrated archbishop of Canterbury (1349), he died the same year from the Black Plague. Bradwardine's theological writings stressed the irresistible power of divine will and predestination as necessary for salvation, opposing the views of contemporary "Pelagians." *See also* Pelagianism.

Braig, Karl, 1853–1923, German Catholic theologian. Influenced by the liberal Catholic faculties of Tübingen and Freiburg, Braig's works on Leibniz and Kant were followed by studies on Christ and then by considerations of the nature of Christianity and the dialectic between freedom and modern theology in the Church.

Brazil, Catholicism in. Brazilian Catholics constitute the largest body of Catholics in the world. Catholicism first came to Brazil in 1500. The first diocese was established in 1551. During the colonial period, ending in 1822 when the country gained its independence from Portugal, Catholic missionaries devoted themselves to the protection of the Amazon Indians against exploitation and slavery by govern-mental and economic interests. The Jesuits were suppressed and expelled in 1782 and other missionaries were expelled as well. Even after the country gained its independence, the Church was subjected to severe anticlericalism and a general decline in religious life. Church and state were constitutionally separated in 1891. The Franciscan order has had an active presence in Brazil since the sixteenth century. Two of the world's best known cardinals are Brazilian Franciscans, Paul Evaristo Arns, archbishop of São Paulo (created cardinal in 1973), and Aloisio Lorscheider, archbishop of Fortaleza (created cardinal in 1976). There are 37 archdioceses and 199 dioceses and over 135 million Catholics, or about 88 percent of the total population (1994). *See also* Latin America, Catholicism in.

bread, eucharistic, unleavened bread that is consecrated during the Eucharistic Prayer and distributed during the Communion rite at Mass. Unleavened bread recalls the Jewish exile, when bread was made in haste without leavening. New meaning was given to this unleavened bread at the Last Supper, when Jesus blessed, broke, and gave the Passover bread to his disciples. Eucharistic bread recalls this meaning as "the body of Christ," the sacrifice of Jesus offering himself to others by blessing, breaking, and sharing both the bread and himself. The Eucharistic Prayer and the sharing during Communion are the ritual enactments of this meaning. *See also* Communion, Holy.

bread, the breaking of, an ancient name for the eucharistic celebration. At the Last Supper, Jesus took bread, blessed it, and broke it as he gave it to his disciples (Matt 26:26). Acts 2:42 describes the earliest Christians as devoting themselves to the apostles' teaching, fellowship, the breaking of the bread, and prayers. *See also* Eucharist.

Brébeuf, St. Jean de (bray-burf'), 1593–1649, French-born Jesuit missionary and martyr of New France who arrived in America in 1625 to evangelize Native Americans. He lived among the Huron for over fifteen years under difficult and challenging circumstances. In 1648 the Iroquois launched a war of extermination against the Huron, their traditional enemies. Refusing to flee when their Huron village was attacked, Brébeuf and his assistant, Gabriel Lalemant, were captured the following year and tortured to death by the Iroquois. Brébeuf was canonized in 1930 with seven other missionaries who are collectively called the North American Martyrs. He is the patron saint of Canada. Feast day: October 19. *See also* North American Martyrs.

Bremond, Henri, 1865–1933, French priest, spiritual writer, and member of the French Academy. Influenced by Blondel and Newman, friend of Tyrrel and Loisy, Bremond shared in the nineteenth-century revival of Catholic thought. Editor of *Etudes* before leaving the Jesuits in 1904, Bremond's writings drew upon nontraditional resources such as literature and psychology to describe religious experience, e.g., *Poetry and Prayer* or the eleven volumes of *Literary History of Religious Sentiment in France.*

Brendan, St., ca. 486–575, abbot of Clonfert and other monasteries in western Ireland. The eighth-century *Navigatio Sancti Brendani* describes his marvelous travels over the sea in search of paradise. Brought by the Irish missionaries to Germany and the Low Countries, this work became very popular in medieval Europe, with several vernacular translations, and is suggestive of the ideals of early medieval monasticism. It was later claimed that Brendan had reached North America. Feast day: May 16.

Brest, Union of, an agreement, ratified in 1596, that brought the Orthodox metropolitan province of Kiev into full communion with the Catholic Church.

This union involved the Slavic "Ruthenian" Orthodox Church located within the Catholic Polish-Lithuanian Commonwealth. The Orthodox bishops who agreed to it were concerned chiefly with stopping the spread of Protestantism among their faithful, raising the standards of their clergy, and preserving their Byzantine heritage in the face of an expanding Polish Roman Catholicism.

With this in mind, the Orthodox bishops met in Brest in June 1595 and decided to seek union with Rome on the basis of a draft "Articles of Union." Here the bishops called for the preservation of traditional rites and discipline, such as married clergy and Communion under both kinds (consecrated bread and wine), and stipulated that they would not be obliged to observe Latin customs. They claimed the right to choose and ordain their own bishops and requested the implementation of strict regulations to preserve the integrity of their church. They also enumerated a number of measures that should be taken to enhance the status of their faithful within the civil sphere. The hope was that the union would spark a general revitalization of this church

by instituting reforms and establishing its status as an equal partner with the Latin Church in the Commonwealth.

After insisting on certain conditions, Rome accepted the proposal and asked that another synod be held to ratify the agreement. But, although the union was supported by the Polish king, opposition arose among certain Orthodox groups. The result was that six of the eight Orthodox bishops attended the second synod at Brest in October 1596 to ratify the agreement, but the other two participated in a simultaneous counter-synod, also in Brest, presided over by a representative of the patriarch of Constantinople. The two synods excommunicated each other, and a violent struggle between the two groups began.

Although not all the envisaged improvements materialized, in the end this new Byzantine Catholic Church gained the allegiance of about two-thirds of the Orthodox in the area and may have had as many as twelve million faithful at its height. But this situation lasted only as long as Catholic governments held sway: with the expansion of Orthodox Russia into the area following the partitions and ultimate absorption of large areas of eastern Poland into the Russian Empire in the eighteenth and nineteenth centuries, the union was forcibly suppressed and Orthodoxy restored.

Today only a small segment of the original Byzantine Catholic Church established at Brest survives: the Ukrainian and much smaller Belarusian Catholic churches plus a significant number of their faithful outside the homeland. *See also* Belarusian Byzantine Catholics; Poland, Catholicism in; Ruthenian Catholic Church; Ukrainian Catholic Church.

RONALD G. ROBERSON

Brethren and Sisters of the Common Life, religious communities, promoters of the Devotio Moderna, that flourished from the late fourteenth century until the Reformation. Inspired by Geert de Groote (1340–84), communities of women and men first sprang up at Deventer and Zwolle in the Netherlands under the leadership of Groote's disciple Florens Radewijns (ca. 1350–1400) and later spread into Germany along the Rhine. The communities evolved into two branches: one lived a common life without solemn vows, the other, called the Windesheim Congregation, adopted the rule of the Augustinian Canons Regular. By the mid-fifteenth century there were about one hundred houses of Brethren and Sisters, most with less than a dozen members, and about eighty monasteries of the congregation. Their common life revolved around the reading of Scripture, meditative prayer, and work as copyists of devotional literature.

Their distinctive spirituality came to be known as the New Devotion (Lat., *Devotio Moderna*), emphasizing interior fervor and simple faith. They encouraged lay spirituality and supported the distribution of vernacular translations of Scripture and devotional works, including the popular *Imitation of Christ*, attributed to Thomas à Kempis (ca. 1380–1471), a Windesheim canon and novitiate master at St. Agnietenberg, near Zwolle. Although their devotional life anticipated in many ways Protestant concerns, the communities of the Common Life were unable to survive the dismantling of the religious orders during the Reformation. *See also* Augustinian Canons; Devotio Moderna; *Imitation of Christ;* Windesheim Congregation.   MICHAEL WOODWARD

Brethren of Czech Unity, also known as Bohemian Brethren, a movement that arose among Hussites in Prague in the mid-fifteenth century. Advocating a return to primitive Christianity and strict adherence to Scripture, the Brethren shunned political involvement, the taking of oaths, and the bearing of arms. *See also* Hus, John.

Brethren of the Free Spirit, the name variously attributed to Waldensians, Beghards, Beguines, and others in the later Middle Ages who claimed independent inspiration and freedom from ecclesiastical authority. They were often charged by inquisitors with teaching a form of Pantheism and a union with God that bypassed the sacramental system. *See also* Beghards/Beguines; Waldensians.

breviary (breev'ee-air-ee), the liturgical book containing the Liturgy of the Hours, formerly called the Divine Office. The breviary represents a late medieval compilation of several books: the antiphonary or book of short verses (antiphons), psalter or book of psalms, lectionary or book of lessons, martyrology or book of martyrs, and hymnary or book of hymns. It was first fashioned during the eleventh and twelfth centuries to assist the daily prayer of the mendicant orders, whose members could not have been expected to carry such a library on their travels. The breviary contributed to the privatization and clericalization of the Church's daily prayer. It came to be regarded as a prayer book for priests, with the Liturgy of the Hours only for clerics. *See also* Liturgy of the Hours.

Briant, St. Alexander, d. 1581, priest canonized in 1970 as one of the Forty Martyrs of England and Wales. He was admitted to the Society of Jesus while under arrest and unwilling, despite torture, to reveal the whereabouts of his associate, Robert Parsons. Feast day: December 1. *See also* Forty Martyrs of England and Wales.

Bridget of Sweden, St., 1302/3–73, a mystic from a noble family and major religious figure of the late Middle Ages. As a widow with eight children, she founded the Brigittines, an order of women and men who lived in double monasteries with the abbess as superior. Like Catherine of Siena, Bridget worked for the return of the popes at Avignon to Rome. Her *Revelations,* in which there is a renewed interest, record her visions, spiritual experiences, and life. Her daughter was St. Katherine of Sweden. She died in Rome and was canonized in 1391. Feast day: July 23.

Brigid of Ireland, St., d. ca. 525, also known as Brigit, Bridget, Bride, with Patrick and Columba a patron saint of Ireland. What little is known of Brigid's life is associated with myth, folklore, miracle stories, and later cultic elements difficult to disentangle. Born near Kildare, Ireland, and said to have been baptized by Patrick, she established a monastery at Kildare, which later became a double monastery of women and men. Irish missionaries carried the cult of Brigid to the Continent and elsewhere. Attempts to identify Brigid with a pagan goddess have not been credible. Feast day: February 1. *See also* Patrick, St.

Brigittines, the Order of the Most Holy Savior (O.SS.S), an order founded in 1344 by St. Bridget of Sweden (d. 1373). A contemplative order devoted to liturgical worship, it had approximately eighty houses at the beginning of the Reformation. *See also* Bridget of Sweden, St.

Britto, St. John de, 1647–93, Portuguese martyr. After ordination to the priesthood, he sailed to India with sixteen other Jesuits as the superior of the Madura (India) mission. He was beheaded for trying to evangelize a prince of Malabar. Feast day: February 4. *See also* India, Catholicism in.

Broadstole

broadstole

broadstole, a purple or black sash worn by deacons during Lent and Advent. The broadstole is not a true stole, originally having been a chasuble, i.e., the outer vestment worn by the priest at Mass, rolled up lengthwise. It is draped over the left shoulder and clasped beneath the right arm. The broadstole is not commonly in use in the 1990s. *See also* stole.

brothers, religious, male members of clerical orders or congregations of lay religious communities who take vows of poverty, chastity, and obedience. From the very beginning brothers have been an integral part of religious life and often the majority of members in early monastic communities. Members of monastic and religious communities were ordained only when the community had a need for priestly services.

The brother is a consecrated layperson who professes the evangelical counsels of poverty, chastity, and obedience. The cleric is an ordained person who may share the brother's consecration as a member of a religious community. The brother is distinguished from the secular layperson by his consecration, his participation in a particular community, and his participation in a ministry of the Church.

Rather than presenting himself for ordination, the brother freely elects this lay religious state as his way of participating in the Church's faith community. This is the brother's way of responding to a call to live the gospel deeply, radically, publicly, and in community. Women religious choose this same commitment but do not currently have the option to choose the clerical state. Religious life is not a middle way between the clerical and lay conditions of life; rather it is recognized and is considered as a form of life to which some Christians, both clerical and lay, are called by God so that they may enjoy a unique gift of grace in the life of the Church (Dogmatic Constitution on the Church, 1964, n. 43). The brother's life is identified, therefore, with following Christ, on the basis of a deliberate choice of the lay state.

The fundamental characteristics of the religious life are three: religious consecration as a complete expression of one's baptismal consecration expressed by vows to live a life of poverty, chastity, and obedience; community life as a manifestation of fraternal community existing in the Church; and specific ecclesiastical missions, participating in the Church's ministry of evangelization, with a variety of apostolates.

Since the Second Vatican Council (1962–65), many brothers have moved from more traditional ministries to a wide variety of other ministries, especially in meeting peace and justice needs. The traditional ministries such as education and health care have not been abandoned but expanded to better meet the needs of the day. Brothers, consecrated and living in community, actively engage in mission and create a unique path among the People of God.

Brothers, like other religious, have opened their communities, in spiritual life-style and in mission, to associate members and to short-term volunteers. This is a natural development as the Church becomes more aware of itself as the People of God, with all its members actively participating. The brothers share their rich traditions and works by including other believers as their associates.

The constituent elements of the life of the brother are the public profession of vows within a community and the apostolic service rendered according to the special vocation and gifts of the community. "Monks," "friars," and "little brothers" are terms used to describe brothers who are members of older orders.

Brothers in the older monastic orders, such as Benedictines, Trappists, and canons regular, and in the more active clerical orders that evolved beginning in the thirteenth century (Franciscans, Dominicans, Jesuits, Redemptorists, Passionists), were termed lay brothers. They were professed community members serving in auxiliary works, assisting the priests of the particular order. Often these lay brothers were uneducated, pious men who performed the menial tasks in the religious community. These brothers did not participate in choir or office but had their own simple common prayer.

Equal membership for brothers in clerical communities has historically been difficult. Some orders such as the Brothers of St. John of God were established for a special apostolic work and included ordained members only as needed for community sacramental purposes. The original Franciscans were termed "friars" with few ordained, the founder himself resisting ordination. Since the sixteenth century, the majority of members in the Franciscan order have been ordained; less educated members serve as domestic lay brothers. St. Francis did not have such a system in mind when he founded the friars to give radical Christian witness.

As religious orders developed, emphasis on ordination precluded equal membership for the brothers, who then became auxiliary, adjunct, or coadjutor members of the community. These classifications or levels of membership in religious communities found definition in the constitutions or rules for the different orders and eventually were written into canon law. This discrimination of community membership of clerics and lay brothers often created a caste system comparable to that of the feudal nobles and peasants.

Since Vatican II, brothers in clerical communities have become better educated and have moved toward equal standing with ordained members. Equal membership for brothers continues to be limited by the Church's prohibition of brothers holding the office of superior in clerical communities. *See also* religious orders and congregations.   BONAVENTURE SCULLY

Brothers of Holy Cross, a society of laymen of the Congregation of Holy Cross, a religious institute founded by Basil Anthony Moreau in 1837 in Le Mans, France. The brothers were founded as the Brothers of St. Joseph by Canon Jacques-François Dujarie in 1820 at Ruille-sur-Loir; later they united with Moreau's association of priests. At the request of the bishop of Vincennes, Indiana, Holy Cross Brothers accompanied Edward Sorin, Holy Cross priest, to the first foundation of the Congregation in North America at Black Oak Ridge, Washington, Indiana, in 1841 and then to Notre Dame du Lac in 1842.

In 1946, the Congregation of Holy Cross split into two societies, brothers and priests. In 1992, there were 848 brothers in countries throughout the world, including Canada, the United States, Chile, Peru, Brazil, Kenya, Uganda, India, Bangladesh, Italy, and France. They serve the Church in a number of ministries, e.g., as teachers (St. Edward's University in Austin, Texas, and many secondary schools), pastoral associates, hospital chaplains, and missionaries.

Holy Cross Brother André Bessette (1846–1937), a porter at the Oratory of St. Joseph in Montreal who cared for the poor and provided spiritual guidance to many, was declared Blessed André Bessette by Pope John Paul II on May 23, 1982. *See also* Congregation of Holy Cross; Sisters of Holy Cross.

brothers of Jesus, siblings of Jesus, mentioned in the Gospels and in Paul's Letters. Mark records that the villagers of Nazareth remarked: "Is not this the carpenter, the son of Mary and brother of James and Joses and Judas and Simon, and are not his sisters here with us?" (6:3). Matthew's version is identical (13:55). All the Synoptics record "his mother and brothers" standing outside his house (Mark 3:31; Matt 12:46; Luke 8:19). John tells of his brothers who do not believe in him (7:3–5; but cf. 2:12). Paul speaks about the support afforded "the brothers of the Lord" (1 Cor 9:5); he mentions seeing once "James the Lord's brother" (Gal 1:19). Scholarship has tended to interpret these references in three ways: "brother" means stepbrother, i.e., children of Joseph by a previous marriage; "brother" means cousin; and "brother" means true brother, subsequent children of Joseph and Mary. The evidence for "stepbrother" is merely legendary (*Infancy Gospel of James* 9:2; 17:1). The linguistic evidence for "brother" meaning "cousin" is very thin. We have but one example where a cousin might be called a "brother" (1 Chr 23:22). Moreover, Hegesippus calls a certain Symeon, the second bishop of Jerusalem, "another cousin of the Lord" (Eusebius *Ecclesiastical History* 4.22.4), distinguishing him from "James the Just," brother of the Lord. No linguistic evidence warrants our interpreting Gospel passages about Jesus' brothers and sisters as his cousins. "Cousins" of Jesus, when noted, were called just that, "cousins," not "brothers." Therefore NT authors apparently understood Jesus' "brothers" as blood brothers, not as "cousins" or "stepbrothers." *See also* Jesus Christ; virginity of Mary.   *JEROME NEYREY*

Brothers of St. Patrick (F.S.P.), an Irish religious community whose main apostolic work is teaching and counseling. There are very few members currently in the United States.

Brothers of the Christian Schools, also known as De La Salle Christian Brothers, *Fratres Scholarum Christianarum* (F.S.C.), an order founded in 1680 by Jean Baptiste de La Salle in Rheims, France, for the education of poor children. De La Salle revolutionized the existing system of education.

Christian Brothers are members of a religious congregation of laymen who do not aspire to become priests (de La Salle excluded priests in 1690) but who devote their lives to serving God's people through education. The brothers profess the vows of poverty, chastity, and obedience and live a communal life of service to others through education.

These brothers are the largest group of lay religious men in the Church dedicated exclusively to education. In the United States, as of 1993, 1,500 brothers serve in eight provinces. Brothers are also located in eighty countries throughout the world.

As lay religious men, the brothers freely choose in their profession to deepen their baptismal consecration, committing themselves to celibacy, to simplicity of life-style, to discernment of God's revelation in a community setting, to service to the poor through education, and to fidelity to their religious congregation.

The Christian Brothers continue their three hundred years of tradition of teaching youth, especially the poor, also serving in allied ministries including family counseling, refugee work, parish, diocesan, and educational professional work, writing and publishing, retreats, and campus ministry.

The brothers sponsor and staff the following colleges and universities in the United States: Christian Brothers University, Memphis; Manhattan College, Bronx, New York; La Salle University, Philadelphia; St. Mary's College of Minnesota, Winona, Minnesota; Lewis University, Romeoville, Illinois; St. Mary's College, Moraga, California; and the College of Santa Fe, Santa Fe, New Mexico. Their national center is located in Romeoville, Illinois. *BONAVENTURE SCULLY*

Brown, Raymond E., b. 1928, internationally renowned Scripture scholar and leader of biblical renewal in the United States. Ordained a priest of the diocese of St. Augustine, Florida (1953), he is a member of the Society of St. Sulpice, S.S. He received the S.T.D. from St. Mary's Seminary and University, Baltimore (1955), a Ph.D. in Semitic languages from the Johns Hopkins University (1958), the S.S.L. from the Pontifical Biblical Commission (1963), and over twenty honorary doctorates from U.S. universities and from Edinburgh (1972), Glasgow (1978), Uppsala (1974), and Louvain (1976). A professor of New Testament at St. Mary's Seminary (1959–71), and at Union Theological Seminary, New York (1971–90), he retired as Auburn Distinguished Professor Emeritus of Biblical Studies. Active in national and international ecumenical dialogues, he was a member of the Pontifical Biblical Commission (1972–78), and was President of the Catholic Biblical Association (1971–72), the Society of Biblical Literature (1976–77), and the international *Studiorum Novi Testamenti Societas* (1986–87). In 1983 he was elected to the American Academy of Arts and Sciences. Author of more than twenty-five books on the Bible, most notably major commentaries on the Gospel and Letters of John (Anchor Bible, vols. 29, 29a, 30) and on the birth and death of the Messiah, he is editor, with J. A. Fitzmyer and R. E. Murphy, of *The Jerome Biblical Commentary* (1968) and *The New Jerome Biblical Commentary* (1990).

Brownson, Orestes Augustus, 1803–76, the leading American Catholic thinker of his time. Obsessed by religious questions even in his boyhood, he practiced Presbyterianism, Universalism, Unitarianism, and Transcendentalism before becoming a Catholic in 1844. *Brownson's Quarterly Review* (est. 1844), most of which he wrote himself, was the main channel of his influence. At first, Brownson took a combative line as a Catholic controversialist. But like his friend and fellow convert, Isaac T. Hecker, he believed that Catholicism and Americanism were ideally suited to each other, and in the mid-1850s he adopted a more irenic tone. This liberal phase lasted until 1864, when he stopped publishing his *Review*. Brownson was a strong Unionist, and the Civil War prompted his major constitutional treatise, *The American Republic* (1866). After the war, he was overwhelmed by personal grief and discouraged by changes in the religious climate, and the *Review*, which he revived briefly in the 1870s, reflected his renewed conservatism.

Bruno Hartenfaust, St., ca. 1030–1101, priest, chancellor of Rheims, and founder of a monastery at La Grande Chartreuse near Grenoble that began the Carthusian order. Called to Rome against his wishes in 1090 as adviser to Pope Urban II on matters pertaining to the reform of the clergy, Bruno soon persuaded the pope to allow him to resume his eremitical life. He founded another monastery at La Torre in Calabria, and declined an offer from the pope to become archbishop of Reggio. Feast day: October 6. *See also* Cistercian order.

Buckley, William F., Jr., b. 1925, a conservative Catholic opinion leader in the United States. One of the founders of the modern American conservative movement, he established America's leading conservative journal of opinion, *National Review,* in 1955.

bugia (boo'juh), a low candlestick consisting of a small plate and a metal or porcelain socket for the candle. The name comes from Bougie, Algeria, a source of wax. The bugia, which could be carried without the candle dripping on the hand or floor, was used as an additional light for the reading of the Missal at a bishop's Mass. Its liturgical use was abolished in 1968.

Bulgarian Byzantine Catholic Church, the Catholic counterpart to the Bulgarian Orthodox Church, which united with Rome in 1861 to preserve its regional autonomy. Its liturgical language is Old Slavonic. Under Ottoman rule, Bulgarian Orthodox Christians, who twice before had had their own patriarchate, were gradually brought under the control of ethnic Greek bishops as part of a systematic hellenization of their ecclesial life. In 1767 they were placed directly under the jurisdiction of the Greek patriarchate of Constantinople.

In the nineteenth century, when a struggle to obtain ecclesiastical independence from the ecumenical patriarchate was gaining momentum, some influential Bulgarian Orthodox in Constantinople began to consider union with Rome as a solution to their problem. They thought that as Catholics they would be able to retrieve their national ecclesiastical traditions, which they felt Constantinople had denied them.

In 1861 they sent a delegation, headed by the elderly archimandrite Joseph Sokolsky, to Rome to negotiate with the Holy See. These talks were successful: Pope Pius IX himself ordained Sokolsky a bishop on April 8, 1861, and named him archbishop for Bulgarian Catholics of the Byzantine rite. The following June he was recognized as such by the Ottoman government.

But in June 1861, almost immediately after his return to Constantinople, Sokolsky disappeared under mysterious circumstances, was taken to Odessa on a Russian ship, and spent the remaining eighteen years of his life in the Monastery of the Caves at Kiev. It has never been established whether he returned to Orthodoxy and fled or was abducted.

Nevertheless, having successfully identified itself with the Bulgarian nationalist movement, the Bulgarian Byzantine Catholic Church initially gained about sixty thousand members. The Russian government, meanwhile, began to support attempts to establish a separate Bulgarian Orthodox Church within the Ottoman Empire. This effort bore fruit in 1870 when a distinct Bulgarian Orthodox exarchate was set up. This effectively put an end to the movement toward Catholicism, and before the turn of the century, three-quarters of the Bulgarian Byzantine Catholics had returned to Orthodoxy.

Most of those who remained Byzantine Catholic lived in villages in Macedonia and Thrace. Therefore in 1883 the Holy See created a new ecclesiastical organization for them. Apostolic vicariates were established in Thessalonica for Macedonia and in Adrianople for Thrace, while an apostolic administrator with the title of archbishop remained in Constantinople. But the community suffered grievously during the Balkan Wars of 1912–13, and the few surviving members fled to the new Bulgarian kingdom for safety.

Given this new situation, Byzantine Catholics within Bulgaria were reorganized in 1926: the previous ecclesiastical entities were abolished, and a new apostolic exarchate was established in Sofia. This was accomplished on the advice of the apostolic visitator (1925–31) and later apostolic delegate (1931–34) to Bulgaria, Archbishop Angelo Roncalli, subsequently Pope John XXIII. He also supported the opening of an interritual minor seminary in Sofia in 1934, which was directed by the Jesuits until it was closed in 1945.

Unlike most other Byzantine Catholic churches in Eastern Europe, this church was allowed to function openly during the Communist regime in Bulgaria, although it was subjected to many restrictions. In 1991 the membership of the apostolic exarchate was estimated at 15,000. *See also* Byzantine rite; Eastern

Catholics and ecumenism; Eastern Catholics and Rome; Eastern churches; Eastern liturgies; Eastern rites.

RONALD G. ROBERSON

bull, papal (Lat., *bulla,* "lead seal"), since the thirteenth century, the common term applied to documents stamped with a lead seal, and currently referring to a form of papal document that affects matters of import for a substantial portion of the Church. The lead seal is embossed with the facial imprints of the apostles Peter and Paul on one side and the signature of the pope on the other. Along with silken cords it holds the document together and is used to authenticate it. *See also* apostolic constitution.

Bullinger, Johann Heinrich, 1504–75, successor to Ulrich Zwingli as pastor of the Great Minster in Zurich. Converted from Catholicism by Zwingli in 1528, he helped compose the First Helvetic Confession (1536) and the Second Helvetic Confession (1566), which were widely influential in the Reformed churches. *See also* Zwingli, Ulrich.

Bultmann, Rudolf, 1884–1976, NT scholar, founder of NT form criticism. Early in his studies, Bultmann became convinced of the collapse of traditional Lutheran orthodoxy. In search of a solution, he developed two interrelated lines of thought. Following nineteenth-century liberal Protestant scholars, he worked out a historical-critical reading of the NT. He argued that distinct literary forms in the Gospels were shaped by the social situation and experiences of the early communities (*History of the Synoptic Tradition,* 1921) and that canonical texts should be seen as part of the religious life of late antiquity (*Theology of the New Testament,* 1951). As a critical historian, Bultmann assumed the world was a closed causal system in which God had no influence; no miracles were possible, no Incarnation, atonement, or Resurrection. All these were myths no longer believable in the modern age.

Bultmann's second line of thought, in this case opposed to nineteenth-century liberal Protestantism, argued that the true function of NT myths was to challenge human beings to an authentic self-understanding under God's redeeming Word, Jesus Christ. From this perspective, "demythologizing" the NT was a mode of interpreting myth, not a simple rejection of it. Bultmann understood these two lines of thought as an application of the principle "simultaneously justified and sinner" (*simul iustus et peccator*) to knowledge. In this application historians remain bound to the sinful construction of a closed objective world while, at the same time, being freed from this sin by the existential encounter with Jesus, the Word of God preached by the Church. The content of faith could not be formulated because dogmatics would remythologize God's Word and deprive it of its absolute lordship.

Bultmann is the single most influential NT scholar of the twentieth century. Many prominent professors at German universities are his students. His writings, translated into many languages, still have a great impact. Catholic scholars have been working for some decades with insights of Bultmann's historical-critical work (see Vatican II, Dogmatic Constitution on Divine Revelation, n. 19, for a positive evaluation of form-criticism). They tend, however, to be skeptical of Bultmann's sharp disjunction between faith and historical reason and of his refusal to formulate the content of faith. *See also* biblical criticism; form criticism. MICHAEL WALDSTEIN

Burchard of Worms, ca. 965–1025, canonist who made an extensive collection of Church law in twenty books called *Decretum Collectarium* (or *Decretum Burchardus*). Appointed bishop of Worms by Emperor Otto III in the year 1000, his *Decretum* brought greater order to the study of canon law and was a source for later canonists, including Gratian. The last two books of the *Decretum* also circulated as separate treatises because of their practical nature: Book 19 provides a guide to the sacrament of Penance and Book 20 is a summary of doctrine with particular attention given to eschatology, or last things: judgment, heaven, hell, purgatory. *See also* canon law.

Burghardt, Walter J., b. 1914, American theologian, editor, and homilist. Ordained a priest in the Society of Jesus (1941); Ph.D., The Catholic University of America (1957); professor of patristics, Woodstock College, Maryland (1946–74) and The Catholic University of America (1974–78), he served as managing editor of *Theological Studies* (1946–67) and then as editor in chief (1967–90). Senior Fellow of Woodstock Theological Center, he is the author of nine volumes of homilies.

burial, Christian, the rituals and prayers that accompany the interment of a Christian and express the Christian belief in eternal life with God.

The cultures of the ancient world, as a rule, had a

profound respect for the dead, and their burial rituals supported this belief. In the Hebrew Scriptures there is a concern for decent burial of Jews and non-Jews (e.g., Gen 23; 2 Sam 21:13–14). Early Christian funerary art showed a firm conviction that the deceased had the prospect of a place of refreshment, light, and peace with Christ. The sacraments of Baptism and Eucharist, in particular, focused on the death and Resurrection of Jesus as the model for Christian belief about life after death, and the Eucharist was called "the medicine of immortality." Unlike their pagan contemporaries, Christians were encouraged to rejoice and give thanks for their dead in the belief that they were with God. The bodies and burial sites of early Christian martyrs, in particular, were the source of great reverence and celebration.

Aside from the common customs of sharing a funeral meal at the tomb of martyrs and the washing and clothing of the corpse, early Christians seem to have initially had no particular burial rituals. There is a Roman ritual of the seventh century (*Ordo* 49) that directs that the Eucharist be given to a dying person and the narrative of Christ's death read; after death, the body was to be brought to the church, where psalms were prayed, and then carried in procession to the cemetery. But even by the ninth century, there was no universal Christian ritual of burial; local churches still followed their own customs in the matter. There was a shift, in the medieval period, from the joyful thanksgiving for the life of a Christian to a deepening concern about the judgment of God. The prayers of the burial Mass reflect this view of death as an ordeal, especially in the sequence *Dies Irae* (Lat., "Day of Wrath"), a highly imaginative and apocalyptic account of the last judgment.

Although an initial reform of the rites of burial was authorized in 1969, a definitive revision was issued in the United States in 1989. The new rituals deal with the three specific moments involved in the death of a Christian: the time before the funeral Mass, the Mass itself, and the committal rituals after the Mass. In the United States, the "wake" of a deceased Christian has retained its importance even though it is now usually held in a funeral parlor rather than at home. The basic structure of the vigil rituals follows the Liturgy of the Word: a gathering song and opening prayer, reading, psalm of response, the Gospel, and homily, followed by prayers of intercession and the Lord's Prayer.

Two possible rituals are offered for the funeral itself, one with and one without a Eucharist. The funeral Mass takes its specific character from the reception of the body at the door of the church with its reminders of Baptism (the sprinkling with holy water, the lighting of the Easter candle, etc.), the suggested readings from Scripture, and the final commendation, which emphasizes the shared hope of all Christians because of the death and Resurrection of Christ. The committal rituals likewise insist on this hope in Christ while recognizing the sorrow of family and friends for the death of a loved one. *See also* funeral Mass; wake service.   REGIS A. DUFFY

Burke, John Joseph, 1875–1936, American Paulist priest, a founder and first general secretary of the National Catholic Welfare Council from 1919 to 1936. As general secretary, he promoted the participation of the laity in the public life of the Church and won particular praise for his efforts to regularize relations between the Vatican and the Mexican government. *See also* National Catholic Welfare Conference.

burse (Lat., *bursa,* "purse"), most commonly, the container used to convey the corporal—a square piece of linen on which the bread and wine are placed—to and from the altar. The burse, which came into use during the eleventh century, is used infrequently in the 1990s. "Burse" can also refer to the leather case used to carry the host to the sick or elderly, or to a fund providing for the education of seminarians. *See also* corporal.

buskin (bus'kin; Old Fr., *bouzequin,* "half-boot"), silk stockings worn by a bishop during solemn or pontifical liturgies. The buskin covers the foot, reaching up and over the calf. Buskins vary in color according to the liturgical season. They are never black, because buskins are not worn during Lent or at funeral Masses. Their use is optional today.

Butler, Alban, 1710–73, English Catholic priest, best known for his scholarly interest in the saints. His book *The Lives of the Saints* required thirty years of research. He also taught philosophy and theology at English College in Douai, France. *See also* saints.

Butzer, Martin, also known as Martin Bucer, 1491–1551, German Protestant Reformer. A member of the Dominican order, Butzer became an early follower of Luther after seeing him at the Heidelberg Disputation (1518). Called to Strassburg in 1523 to

help lead the Reform movement there, he was instrumental in establishing a Reformed church. John
Calvin, who lived in Strassburg from 1538 to 1540,
learned much from Butzer. Concerned by the eucharistic controversy that divided the Lutherans and
the followers of Zwingli, Butzer negotiated a compromise, the Wittenberg Concord (1536), that allowed some southern German states to enter the
Lutheran military alliance. Butzer has been accused
of theological superficiality and lack of principle as
a result. Despite his irenic efforts abroad, he was
committed to suppressing dissent in Strassburg. In
1549, after the military defeat of the Protestants in
the Schmalkaldic War, he fled to England where he
died. *See also* Reformation, the.

Byzantine Catholic Church of the Diocese of Krizhevci

(kreez'chev-see), formerly known
as the Yugoslavian Byzantine Catholic Church, the
ecclesiastical community of Byzantine-rite Catholics who are in communion with Rome and whose
principal concentration is in Croatia. It is the Catholic counterpart of the Serbian Orthodox Church in
the former Yugoslav federation.

The first Byzantine Catholics in Yugoslavia were
Serbians living in Croatian territory under Hungarian control in the early seventeenth century. In 1611
they were given a bishop who functioned as Byzantine vicar of the Latin bishop of Zagreb. His headquarters were at Marcha monastery, which became
a center of efforts to bring Serbian Orthodox faithful
into full communion with Rome.

After a period of tension with the local Latin
bishops, the Serbs in Croatia were given their own
diocesan bishop by Pope Pius VI on June 17, 1777,
with his see at Krizhevci. He was made suffragan at
first to the primate of Hungary and later (1853) to
the Latin archbishop of Zagreb.

The diocese of Krizhevci was extended to embrace all the Byzantine Catholics in Yugoslavia when
the country was founded after World War I. The diocese then included five distinct groups: ethnic Serbs
in Croatia, Ruthenians who had emigrated from
Slovakia around 1750, Ukrainians who emigrated
from Galicia in about 1900, Macedonians in the
south of the country who became Catholic because
of nineteenth-century missionary activity (they
now have their own apostolic visitator), and a few
Romanians in the Yugoslavian Banat.

In 1992 it was estimated that the diocese of
Krizhevci had a total membership of just under fifty
thousand. However, given the fact that Yugoslavia

has broken up into a number of independent republics, a new arrangement for Byzantine Catholics in
the various successor states may be required. *See
also* Byzantine rite; Eastern Catholics and ecumenism;
Eastern Catholics and Rome; Eastern churches; Eastern
liturgies; Eastern rites.   RONALD G. ROBERSON

Byzantine chant. *See* chant, Byzantine.

Byzantine Italy, historically the area controlled
by the exarchate of Ravenna (roughly northern Italy
east of the Apennine watershed from Ravenna to
Ancona) plus southern Italy (the toe and heel of the
peninsula plus Sicily) from the Byzantine conquest
(535–53) until the fall of Bari to the Normans in
1027. In classical times southern Italy, known as
Magna Graecia, had a flourishing Greek culture in
cities like Syracuse in Sicily.

In the Byzantine period, Byzantine Orthodoxy
predominated there, and Byzantine monasticism
flourished. The overthrow of Romulus Augustulus,
last Roman emperor in the West, in 476, left Constantinople as the only imperial authority. In 488
the Ostrogoths invaded Italy, establishing the center
of their kingdom in Ravenna in 493. Under Emperor
Justinian I (527–65) the Byzantines restored imperial power in a war that caused much suffering to
the local population. In the north the Lombard invasion of 568 left only the area under Ravenna to the
Byzantines, though they retained Magna Graecia as
both the Lombards and the papacy inexorably
moved south. Ravenna was lost to the Lombards in
751, but the Byzantines consolidated their hold on
Sicily, confiscating papal estates there and transferring it to the ecclesiastical control of the patriarchate of Constantinople.

Arab control of Sicily in the tenth century gave
way to the Normans, who established their kingdom
in southern Italy and Sicily in the eleventh. Meanwhile the Byzantine church, reinvigorated by an influx of Greek-speaking Christian refugees from the
Arab takeover of the Middle East, many of them
monks, continued to flourish in Magna Graecia
throughout the Norman period, with hundreds of
Byzantine monasteries, some of them major foundations like St. Salvatore at Messina, Sicily, and Patir
of Rossano in Calabria on the mainland. The copyists in monastic scriptoria have left behind numerous invaluable Italo-Greek liturgical manuscripts in
which scholars identify distinct Italo-Byzantine liturgical usages in Otranto and the Siculo-Calabrian
region. The Latin conquest of Constantinople in

1204 put an end to Byzantium as a world power, but in Norman Italy cultural and ecclesial contacts with Constantinople continued and even intensified in the fourteenth and fifteenth centuries.

Though Greek-based dialects are still spoken in some isolated rural areas of the peninsula, the decline of the Normans brought decadence to the Byzantine monasteries, cradle of Italo-Byzantine ecclesiastical culture, and by the fifteenth century the Byzantine churches and monasteries in southern Italy had succumbed to latinization.

Soon, however, the Byzantine rite would revive in Magna Graecia as a result of an influx of Orthodox Albanians fleeing the Turkish domination of their country in the fifteenth century. In 1596 they received papal recognition within the Catholic communion, where they have preserved their Byzantine rite until today.　　　*ROBERT F. TAFT*

Byzantine rite, sometimes called the "Greek rite," the liturgical system of the Orthodox and Byzantine Catholic churches, called "Byzantine" because it originated in the Orthodox patriarchate of Constantinople (Byzantium). In the Middle Ages the other Chalcedonian Orthodox patriarchates of Alexandria, Antioch, and Jerusalem, weakened by schism and conquests and no longer able to maintain their own traditions, adopted the Byzantine rite, making it the sole liturgical tradition of Eastern Orthodoxy. Like the Roman rite, this liturgical synthesis is a hybrid, created when Constantinopolitan and Palestinian monastic elements synthesized during the ninth through fourteenth centuries in the monasteries of the Orthodox world. A unique symbolic matrix renowned for the sumptuousness of its ceremonial and liturgical symbolism and heritage of the imperial splendors of Constantinople before the eighth century, the Byzantine rite is by far the most widely used Eastern liturgical tradition. Its history went through seven stages: (1) Paleo-Byzantine origins (third–fourth centuries), (2) the "Imperial Age" or "Golden Age" (fifth–sixth centuries); (3) the "Dark Ages" and iconoclasm (610–ca. 850); (4) the Studite era (ca. 800–1204); (5) the neo-Sabaitic synthesis following the Latin occupation of Constantinople in 1204–61; (6) the period of uniatism and latinization from the end of the sixteenth century; and (7) the modern renewal.

Origins and Golden Age: We know little of the origins of the rite of Byzantium, a suffragan see in the prefecture of Orient before it became the new capital of Constantinople in 330. But Antioch was the major see in the prefecture, and the earliest extant Constantinopolitan liturgical sources bear unmistakable Antiochene traits.

In the sixth through seventh centuries, especially under Justinian I (527–65), the Byzantine rite became "imperial," acquiring ever more ritual splendor and theological explicitation, especially as a result of the Christological controversies, via the addition of new feasts, the creed, and several new immortal chants (Trisagion, Cherubicon, etc.). Its evolution was especially marked by the stational processions (i.e., from church to church) of the capital: entrances, processions, and accessions have come to characterize all Byzantine liturgy.

Iconoclasm and the Studite Reform: With the seventh century began a period of decline, as the "Dark Ages" and then iconoclasm (726–843) forced the Church to turn inward and consolidate its tradition. Liturgical creativity was limited to liturgical interpretation, as a more representational, narrative vision of the liturgical rites was integrated into Byzantine liturgical theology by Patriarch St. Germanus I (ca. 730).

The victory of Orthodoxy over iconoclasm in 843 stimulated a veritable liturgical reform: changes in the Euchologion (Sacramentary) under Patriarch St. Methodius I (843–47); new Holy Week and Easter services from the same symbiosis with Palestinian usages that would create the new monastic offices; new church music; and a new church architecture and iconography. Most important, the defeat of iconoclasm, basically a monastic victory, inaugurated the period of monastic dominance in the Orthodox church. This was largely due to the leadership of St. Theodore of Stoudios (d. 826) and his followers, who in 799 took over and revivified the dying Monastery of Stoudios, inaugurating the Studite era from about 800 until the Latin conquest of Constantinople in 1204–61.

The monks of Stoudios gradually synthesized the *Horologion (Book of Hours)* of the imported Palestinian office of the Monastery of St. Sabas with the Euchologion of Constantinople to create the hybrid "Studite" office: Palestinian monastic psalmody and hymns grafted onto the skeleton of litanies and prayers from the Cathedral Office of Constantinople. This period is characterized by the creation of the canon of *orthros* (Matins) via a massive infusion of new liturgical poetry into the offices. Gathered into new anthologies, the *Oktoechos, Triodion, Pentekos-*

tarion, and *Menaion,* these monastic compositions from Palestine and Constantinople constitute the backbone of the new liturgical books still in use today. It is in this same period that the first Studite Typika or custom books appear to regulate the use of this new synthesis, which represents the victory of monastic popular devotion over a more spiritualist and symbolic approach to liturgy.

This popular spirituality was communicated to the masses through the ritual celebration of the liturgy and its setting, the Middle Byzantine church building and its representational art programs that developed at the turn of the tenth century. These had unitary decorative schemes, which were feasible only in churches so small that the whole decorated interior could be seen at one glance.

This reduction in church size, caused by the economic crisis of the period, also affected the liturgy. As churches became smaller, liturgical life became more compressed, more private. The splendors of the urban stational and basilical rites destined for the thoroughfares, public squares, and great basilicas of the metropolis were now played out in a greatly reduced arena. Monasticization played its part in this too: monastic liturgy is a stay-at-home rite, confined to the buildings of the monastic complex. This compression of liturgical activity was accompanied by a shift toward greater symbolization as rites lost their original purpose and survived only as symbolic relics. The classic example is the once-great public entrance procession of the liturgy, which was reduced to ritual turns within the interior of a now tiny nave and in which the appearances of the sacred ministers were symbolically reinterpreted as epiphanies of Christ.

By the end of this period there were new liturgical books, a new Divine Office, new liturgical music, new iconography, new architecture and liturgical arrangement of the church, and new mystagogy to interpret it all: the Middle Byzantine synthesis was complete.

The Neo-Sabaitic Ascendancy: With the early breakdown of Studite cenobitism after the Fourth Crusade (1204) and the rise of hesychast monasticism on Mount Athos begins the final phase of the history of the rite, characterized by the abandonment of the Studite offices in favor of the more austere neo-Sabaitic usages of Palestinian monasticism as restored in the twelfth century.

The Studite office, adopted throughout the Byzantine monastic world, had undergone a second wave of Sabaitic influence in Palestine. The result, codified in the Sabaitic Typika, was adopted on Mount Athos, where it received its final form under Philotheos Kokkinos, hegumen of the Great Lavra and later patriarch of Constantinople (1353–55, 1364–76). This neo-Sabaitic rite spread in the wake of the reform movement propagated by the Athonite hesychasts under Philotheos's leadership. By the end of Byzantium with the fall of Constantinople to the Turks in 1453, this rite was in use throughout the Orthodox world except southern Italy and Rus', which retained Studite usages longer.

Latinization and Modern Renewal: Later changes in the Byzantine rite are minor and do not modify the substance of this neo-Sabaitic tradition except among Byzantine-rite Catholics, who underwent a dolorous period of liturgical and spiritual latinization, a true erosion of their religious heritage, as a consequence of their union with the Catholic Church. In modern times a renewed sense of the necessity of preserving and restoring this Eastern patrimony has led to numerous calls for renewal from the Holy See and Vatican II, calls often ignored by the Byzantine Catholics themselves, long comfortable with their hybrid traditions, ignorant or even distrustful of their true historic heritage, and often eager to distinguish themselves from their Orthodox counterparts. Nevertheless, slow but real progress toward renewal has been made since the 1940s with the excellent new Vatican editions of the liturgical books. *See also* Eastern rites; rite.

Bibliography

Taft, Robert F. *The Byzantine Rite: A Short History.* Collegeville, MN: Liturgical Press, 1991.

Schulz, H.-J. *The Byzantine Liturgy.* New York: Pueblo, 1986.

ROBERT F. TAFT

Byzantine style, a type of architecture characterized by roofing a square area with a dome on pendentives or vaults springing upward toward one another from four piers to join in a circle or drum on which the dome rests. Perfected in Justinian's Hagia Sophia (537), the system was developed on a greatly reduced scale thereafter in much smaller middle and late Byzantine "cross-in-square" churches in which the central square, roofed by a dome raised on a drum over four supporting piers, is extended out by wings on all four sides, often similarly roofed with domes on drums. Medieval churches of this type are still found all over Greece and the Balkans. *See also* Catholicism and architecture.

Frances Xavier Cabrini, first American citizen to be canonized a saint.

Cabrini, St. Frances Xavier, 1850–1917, patron saint of immigrants and first U.S. citizen to be canonized. Born in Lombardy, Italy, Maria Francesca Cabrini desired to be a sister but was refused entrance into two religious communities due to her delicate health. In 1880, Bishop Domenico Galmini encouraged her to establish a new congregation. The Institute of the Missionary Sisters of the Sacred Heart won papal approval (1887) and grew rapidly. In 1889, Archbishop Michael Corrigan of New York invited Mother Cabrini and five of her sisters to his diocese, but when they arrived Corrigan rescinded his invitation and suggested that they return to Italy. The sisters remained and Cabrini established numerous hospitals, schools, orphanages, and convents throughout the United States, as well as foundations in Central and South America. Mother Cabrini was canonized in 1946. Feast day: November 13.

Cabrol, Fernand, 1855–1937, French liturgical scholar, Benedictine monk of Solesmes, France. Appointed prior of Farnborough, England, in 1890, he became abbot in 1896. He is chiefly remembered for the impetus he gave to liturgical scholarship. Together with M. Ferotin and H. Leclercq, he launched the *Monumenta ecclesiae liturgica* (Lat., "liturgical monuments of the Church") and the *Dictionnaire d'archéologie chrétienne et de liturgie* (Fr., "Dictionary of Christian archaeology and liturgy"), begun in 1903 and completed in 1953.

Caesarea (sez-uh-ree'uh; called Caesarea Maritima to distinguish it from Caesarea Philippi), a major city on the eastern coast of the Mediterranean built by Herod the Great (37–4 B.C.) and named after his patron, Augustus Caesar; it was the only major seaport between Egypt and Syria. In NT times, it was the site of Peter's preaching (Acts 10:24–48) and the residence of the Roman governor, thus the place of Paul's two-year imprisonment and trial (Acts 24–26) before his being sent to Rome. Later it was a major Christian Byzantine city and center of learning where the famous biblical scholar Origen lived for many years. Its massive remains are only partially excavated; work will continue for many years.

Caesarea Philippi (sez-uh-ree'uh fil-ip'pi), city rebuilt by Herod Philip, son of Herod the Great, named after himself and his patron, Caesar Augustus, on the site of an older Greek city sacred to the god Pan, near the sources of the Jordan River on the south side of Mount Hermon, at the northern edge of his kingdom, Gaulanitis (present Golan). Little is known of the city, since systematic excavations are just beginning. Matt 16:13–20 and Mark 8:27–30 place Peter's confession of faith in the surrounding countryside. The location continued as an early Christian city under the name Paneas, whence its present name, Banias.

Caesarius of Arles, St., ca. 470–542, archbishop of Arles from ca. 500. He presided over the Council of Orange (529), at which semi-Pelagianism (which held that the first step toward salvation is taken without grace) was condemned. He composed works on grace and on the Trinity but is most remembered as a pastor and preacher whose sermons skillfully adapted the teaching of Augustine for his congregations of new and uneducated converts. Feast day: August 27. *See also* Orange, Council of; semi-Pelagianism.

Caesarius of Heisterbach, ca. 1180–ca. 1240, Cistercian monk and writer. His many writings include sermons and homilies, narrative accounts of miracles, and histories, including lives of Cistercian saints. *See also* Cistercian order.

Caesaro-papism, a political system whereby a lay ruler is given complete sovereignty over royal and sacerdotal (priestly) powers within a designated realm. The lay ruler exercises authority over doctrine and ecclesiastical polity traditionally reserved for ecclesiastical authorities. The historical precedent for this arrangement was set during the Roman Empire, when the emperor, as the divinely appointed vicegerent of God, was given complete responsibility for ensuring the peace and stability of the empire. Given the importance of theological disputes and ecclesiastical politics following the Peace of Constantine in 313, Roman emperors began to assert their authority over the faith of the Church and the right to control ecclesiastical appointments beginning in the fourth century.

Caesaro-papism became a practical reality in the fifth century when Emperor Zeno, in an effort to unify the empire, made concessions to the Monophysites against the Orthodox beginning in 482. Caesaro-papism reached its zenith in the policies of Justinian I (527–65) and remained a governing principle of Byzantine rulers for a millennium. Due to countervailing developments in Western ecclesiology, Caesaro-papism contributed to the tensions between Rome and Constantinople that eventually resulted in schism.

Although traditionally associated with the authority of the Byzantine emperor over Eastern patriarchates, elements of Caesaro-papism are apparent in the policies of the Russian czars, in the post-Reformation claim that the religion of the king determines the religion of a people (Lat., *cuius regio, eius religio*), and in some forms of Josephinism, Febronianism, and Gallicanism. *See also* Church and state.   MICHAEL O'KEEFFE

Cafasso, St. Joseph, 1811–60, Italian moral theologian, diocesan priest, patron saint of prisoners. An opponent of Jansenism, he encouraged and supported John Bosco in his ministry to young boys and came to be known as the second founder of the Salesians. He won renown for his work with prisoners and those awaiting execution. Feast day: June 23. *See also* Bosco, St. John; Salesians.

Cahensly, Peter Paul, 1838–1923, German Catholic layman. He helped to establish a Catholic Society for German Immigrant Passage, the St.

Raphaelsverein. In 1891, representatives of European St. Raphael societies met in Lucerne, Switzerland; they petitioned the Vatican to ensure the spiritual welfare of immigrants by establishing national parishes in the new homelands. Cahensly presented the Lucerne Memorial to Pope Leo XIII; it fueled a controversy in the United States between advocates of the national parish and the Americanist clergy. The Americanists judged the memorial as foreign interference in American ecclesiastical affairs and labeled this action "Cahenslyism." *See also* Americanism; national parish.

Cajetan, St., 1480–1547, Italian cofounder of the Theatine order. A diocesan priest who was concerned about the devotional life of the clergy as well as the general state of the Church, he founded in 1524, with Pietro Caraffa (later Pope Paul IV) and two other priests (Paul Consiglieri and Boniface da Colle), a congregation of clerics living under vows in community, but still engaged in pastoral work, especially ministry to the poor and the sick. Such congregations are known as clerks regular. Feast day: August 7. *See also* clerks regular; Theatines.

Cajetan [Thomas de Vio], 1469–1534, Dominican Thomist theologian. Born Giacomo de Vio of Gaeta and called Gaetamo, or Cajetan, from his birthplace, he took the name Thomas upon entering the Dominican order in 1484. After studying in Naples and Bologna and teaching at Padua (1493) and Pavia (1497), he was made procurator general of the Dominicans (1501) in Rome, where he began his magisterial commentary on Aquinas's *Summa Theologiae* (1507–22). Master general of the Dominicans from 1508 to 1518, seeking to reform the theological and community life of the order, he was made cardinal by Leo X in 1517, partly in recognition of his support for the full authority of the pope over councils. While serving as papal legate to the Diet of Augsburg (1518) to gain German support for a crusade against the Turks, he met with Luther but failed to change his mind about the sacraments or indulgences. Cajetan reached the height of his ecclesiastical influence with the election in 1522 of Hadrian of Utrecht as pope, under whom he hoped for reform of bishops, clergy, and religious orders. After the election of Clement VII (1523), he devoted himself to three years of scriptural study (1524–27), convinced that the Reformers could only be answered effectively on the basis of the literal meaning of Scripture alone, checked against the Hebrew and

Greek. Cajetan produced a series of biblical commentaries on the Psalms (1527), the Gospels (1527–28), Acts and the Letters (1528–29), the Pentateuch (1531), the historical books (1532), the wisdom literature (1533–34), and Isa 1–3 (1534). His writings against Zwingli (1525), the remarriage of Henry VIII (1530), and the Augsburg Confession (1531–32) are marked by their empathy for the concerns of the Reformers and their arguments based on Scripture alone, earning the respect of Erasmus and even Luther (who said, "Cajetan, in his later days, has become Lutheran") and the deep suspicion of his more conservative contemporaries. He died on August 10, 1534, while preparing his commentary on the prophets. *See also* Dominican order; Reformation, the; Scripture and tradition.   RANDALL C. ZACHMAN

Calasanz, St. Joseph, 1556–1648, Spanish founder of the Clerks Regular of Religious Schools in 1621. After renouncing family property and ecclesiastical status, Joseph went to Rome and began teaching poor children. Because of internal dissension, the new order was dissolved in 1646 by Pope Innocent X and made into a society of diocesan priests subject to bishops. The order is known today as the Order of the Pious Schools (Sch.P.), or Piarists. In 1993 there were less than one hundred Piarist priests in the United States. Feast day: August 15.

calced. *See* discalced.

Calixtus [name of pope]. *See* Callistus.

Callahan, Patrick Henry, 1865–1940, American Catholic business executive. President of the Louisville Varnish Company for thirty years, Callahan became known for his policy of sharing profits with employees. After chairing the Knights of Columbus Committee on War Activities, he cofounded the Catholic Association for International Peace in 1926. A prohibitionist, he opposed Al Smith in his campaign for the presidency of the United States in 1928. Callahan served on various national boards during Franklin D. Roosevelt's first two terms.

Callistus I, St., d. 222, pope from ca. 217 to 222. Originally a slave, Callistus was sent to the mines for being Christian (although Hippolytus, his enemy, hints at suspicious circumstances). Victor I granted him a pension upon his release. Callistus had charge of the present Catacomb of St. Callistus as Pope

Zephyrinus's deacon. Elected his successor, Callistus was tolerant toward clergy who were twice married or who had sinned, which earned him the ire of Tertullian and Hippolytus, who accused him also of too readily readmitting sinners to communion. Hippolytus charged Callistus with Patripassianism (the belief that God the Father also suffered on Calvary), although Callistus excommunicated Sabellius. He was probably martyred. Feast day: October 14. *See also* Patripassianism.

calumny, the communication of falsehoods about another person, with a consequent injury to the other's reputation and good name. It is a sin against justice, charity, and truthfulness that demands a retraction of the falsehood and a sincere effort to restore the good name of the injured party. Calumny differs from detraction in that detraction injures another by telling truths about the other. On the other hand, calumny is practically indistinguishable from slander. *See also* detraction; justice; slander; truthfulness.

Calvary, Mount (kal'vuh-ree), Latin translation of Golgotha (Aram., "place of the skull," probably a place of execution), the site of Jesus' crucifixion (Matt 27:33; Mark 15:22; John 19:17; Luke 23:33 gives only a Greek translation). Outside the walls at the time (John 19:20), it was incorporated into the city about thirty years later. After A.D. 134 the emperor Hadrian built there a temple of Venus, which was torn down by Constantine to make way for his monumental Church of the Resurrection, whose courtyard enclosed the site, today part of the Crusader Church of the Holy Sepulchre.

Calvert, Cecil, 1605–75, second Lord Baltimore, founder of Maryland. Educated at Oxford and a convert to Catholicism, he carried out the plans of his father, George Calvert, to found a colony where religious toleration and separation of Church and state would prevail. Because of the Puritan upheaval in England, he was obliged to remain at home to protect the interests of a colony he never saw. Under his instructions, Maryland in 1649 passed the first act of religious toleration in the English-speaking world.

Calvert, Charles, 1637–1715, third Lord Baltimore, governor of Maryland. He was sent in 1661 by his father, Cecil Calvert, to Maryland as governor. After his father's death in 1675, his authoritarian policies and favoritism toward relatives and Catholics provoked a rebellion in 1689 that occasioned the loss of the colony by the Calverts, thereby ending toleration for Catholics,

Calvert, George, ca. 1579–1632, first Lord Baltimore, founder of Maryland. Born in Yorkshire, educated at Oxford, he rose in British politics through the influence of Robert Cecil. In 1525 he resigned as secretary of state upon his conversion to Catholicism. Though awarded the title "baron of Baltimore" in the Irish peerage, he sought his fortune in the New World. When his attempt to found a colony in Newfoundland failed, he asked the king for a land grant on the Potomac River, where Catholics and Protestants might live together peacefully. Though he died before the Maryland charter passed, his plans were carried out by his sons. He was a man of great integrity, imagination, and political skill.

Calvert, Leonard, 1610–47, first governor of Maryland. He was sent by his brother Cecil, second Lord Baltimore, to plant the colony of Maryland, where the first settlers landed on March 25, 1634. Though attacked by Puritans and other enemies, he succeeded in establishing the colony of Maryland, where there was tolerance for Catholics and Protestants alike.

Calvin, John, 1509–64, French/Swiss Protestant Reformer. Born to a lay official of the Catholic Church in Noyon, France, Calvin began to study for the priesthood at Paris in 1523. In 1528 his father ordered Calvin to turn to the study of law, which he did at Orléans and Bourges. He was introduced to humanism by Melchior Wolmar, who was also favorable to Lutheranism. With the death of his father in 1531 Calvin returned to Paris to pursue classical studies and Hebrew. At the same time he was undergoing a slow conversion to Protestantism, a process that was completed by 1533. Feeling increasingly threatened in Paris, he left in 1534, resigned the benefices that had financed his education, and proceeded to wander through France, Germany, and Italy.

In 1536 he published the first edition of his *Institutes of the Christian Religion* in Basel, a work that would grow with each republication during his lifetime and that became the classic statement of Reformed Protestant theology. Passing through Geneva in 1536, he was threatened by the local reformer Guillaume Farel with divine punishment should he

not remain and take up the task of reform in the city. He accepted the mission but was forced to leave the city in 1538 by opposition to his rigorous religious policies. He moved to Strassburg, where he was influenced by Martin Butzer. In 1540 Calvin married Idelette de Bure, the widow of an Anabaptist whom Calvin had converted. Recalled to Geneva in 1541 after his supporters got the political upper hand, Calvin started to put into practice his vision of the Church. Though facing opposition throughout most of his remaining years and though holding no political office, Calvin came to exercise remarkable influence in Geneva. As a result it became a model of the godly city to reformed Protestants.

Through his writing and extensive correspondence Calvin's influence extended throughout Europe, but particularly in his native France. Calvin was perhaps the greatest biblical commentator of his age and he held Christians to a strict biblical standard. In worship, discipline, and doctrine, nothing commanded in Scripture was to be ignored; nothing beyond what Scripture expressly ordained was to be accepted. As a result the simplified form of worship introduced in 1542 was a radical departure from the Catholic Mass, which Calvin considered idolatry. Since Calvin could not find the Catholic hierarchy in the NT, he replaced it (1541) with four biblically attested offices—deacon, elder/presbyter, teacher, and pastor. The lay elders/presbyters remain a distinctive element in Calvinism and give their name to the Presbyterian churches. Geneva's church was governed by a consistory composed of clergy and lay elders who maintained strict moral and religious control over the entire population. This discipline found its most prominent victim in Michael Servetus, who was burned at the stake for blasphemy in 1553. Calvin is best known, however, for his unyielding espousal of full double predestination, that is, that God in eternity has infallibly decreed who will be saved and who will be damned. *See also* Calvinism; Reformation, the.

R. EMMET MCLAUGHLIN

Calvinism, a religious and theological orientation (also called the Reformed movement) within Protestantism that originated with the French Reformer and theologian John Calvin (1509–64), developed in the work of subsequent theologians, and is manifest today in the life of many Reformed (non-Lutheran) churches. Trained in theology and law, Calvin became convinced in 1533 that he was called by God to renew the Church. After fleeing from Noyon, France, to Basel, Switzerland, in 1535, he wrote the first edition of his *Institutes of the Christian Tradition* in 1536 and thereafter continued to revise and expand it until its last edition in 1559. This systematic exposition of Christian belief articulates the principles essential to Calvinism. These include the following: (1) Scripture, consisting of the unity of the OT and NT, is the necessary and sufficient source for understanding the Christian faith. (2) God is absolutely sovereign; his will determines both the ends and the means of all that occurs in human salvation. (3) As a result of the Fall, humankind is totally depraved. It lacks free will, and human actions in themselves are always sinful. (4) Faith brings the gifts of justification and sanctification. (5) God predestines the elect to heaven and the reprobate to hell. (6) God's grace is irresistible, and hence those who are elected necessarily do God's will. (7) The Church is supreme over the state. (8) The sacraments, namely, Baptism and the Eucharist, are external signs of an inner reality, but they do not bring about this reality.

The rigidity of Calvin's teachings led in the late 1600s to a theological controversy in Holland over the doctrine of predestination. Theodore Beza (1519–1605) argued for "supralapsarianism" (i.e., that God intended the Fall). Dirck Coornhert (1522–90) maintained "infralapsarianism" (i.e., that God's election came after the Fall). Jacob Arminius (1560–1609) softened Calvin's teachings on predestination, human freedom, and the irresistible character of grace. In response to Arminius's thought, the Synod of Dort (1618–19) upheld the stricter position in its "five points of Calvinism" concerning God's unconditional election, Christ's atonement only for the elect, humankind's complete depravity, the irresistibility of grace, and the saint's final perseverance. Arminius's views were, however, eventually accepted by the Methodist and Baptist churches.

In the eighteenth century, Jonathan Edwards (1703–58) taught Calvinism in New England. Though he preached a rigid view of predestination, he moderated this doctrine by the fact that he encouraged all people to dispose themselves to personal religious experiences (e.g., at religious revivals). In the twentieth century, Karl Barth (1886–1968) renewed Calvin's teachings, especially emphasizing Scripture as the source for theology, the sovereignty of God, and the depravity of the human condition apart from grace.

Along with being a set of theological principles, Calvinism is also a Protestant form of life. In the 1500s Calvin's community of Geneva not only flourished but also inspired the growth of other Calvinist or Reformed churches. Giving direction to Calvinism, or the Reformed movement, were the First Helvetic Confession (1536) and the Second Helvetic Confession (1566), which reiterated the central doctrines of Calvinism. Calvinism spread throughout Switzerland, Germany, France (i.e., the Huguenots), the Netherlands, Scotland (led by John Knox), England (i.e., the Presbyterians and Congregationalists), and eventually North America. *See also* Protestantism; Reformation, the; Reformed churches.

ROBERT A. KRIEG

Camaldolese, Congregation of Monk Hermits of Camaldoli, religious order founded by Romuald in the eleventh century as a reformed Benedictine community. Primarily a contemplative order, the Camaldolese emphasize fasting, silence, and solitude, along with manual labor. The order is unique in combining the communal monastic life-style with the independent life of the hermit, so that monks or nuns have the opportunity for solitary silent prayer and the hermits the advantages of fellowship and obedience to a superior. Though each house is placed under the rule of a superior, Camaldolese houses are generally independent of one another. St. Romuald never wrote a rule; the Camaldolese customs were drawn up in the eleventh century by Peter Damian and Rudolf and important reforms were introduced in the fourteenth and fifteenth centuries by Ambrose Traversari and Paul Giustiniani. *See also* Romuald, St.

Camara, Dom Helder, b. 1909, retired archbishop of Recife in northeastern Brazil. A relentless advocate for social reform in this impoverished area, he often created tensions among government and Church officials because of his solidarity with the poor. He is known worldwide for his efforts to bring the plight of Third World peoples to the attention of affluent nations. An outspoken proponent of nonviolent social change, he emerged in the second half of the twentieth century as a renowned symbol of the Catholic Church's commitment to social justice and peace.

Camerlengo (kah-mair-lehn' goh; It., "chamberlain"), a title held by the cardinals who hold offices with specific financial duties. The two offices are the Camerlengo of the Holy Roman Church and the Camerlengo of the College of Cardinals.

The Camerlengo of the Holy Roman Church is the cardinal who presides over the Camera Apostolica, the Vatican office that takes charge of the property and financial administration of the Holy See during a vacancy in the papacy. He is assisted by a vice-camerlengo who is an archbishop.

The Camerlengo of the College of Cardinals is the cardinal who oversees the financial assets of the College of Cardinals and records the business of consistories, i.e., official meetings of the College of Cardinals, called by the pope and conducted in his presence. *See also* Cardinals, College of.

Camillus of Lellis, St., 1550–1614, founder of the Order of Camillians and patron saint of hospitals, nurses, and the sick. After having spent his youth as a soldier, Camillus entered the Capuchins as a novice in 1575. But because the coarse clothing of the order continually reopened his war wounds, he was rejected. He returned to the hospital where he had earlier been treated (San Giacomo in Rome), becoming influenced by Philip Neri, its head. He gathered followers into an order around 1582 and was ordained in 1584. The order had 330 members in fifteen cities at his death. He was canonized in 1746. Feast day: July 14.

Campaign for Human Development, a national education-action program of the Catholic Church in the United States. In 1969 the National Conference of Catholic Bishops (NCCB) established the campaign, whose funding derives from annual collections in Catholic churches. Some funds from the collection are distributed in communities where they are raised. Remaining funds are forwarded to the national office for distribution. Two types of grants are available: education programs to spread awareness of poverty and the need for its elimination and action programs for direct assistance. Organizations receiving grants must demonstrate a firm commitment to participation of the poor in planning and operating programs. In 1988 the bishops made the campaign a permanent annual national collection.

Campion, St. Edmund, 1540–81, the most famous of the Jesuit martyrs of England and Wales. A graduate of Oxford, in 1553 Edmund had taken both the Oath of Supremacy acknowledging the queen as head of the Church in England and deacon's orders according to the Anglican Ordinal. He subsequently converted to Catholicism and in 1569 left England

Edmund Campion, Jesuit martyr executed in 1581 for his defense of the pope against the English crown.

for Dublin. In 1573 he entered the Jesuit novitiate in Prague and was ordained in 1578. Campion left Prague in 1580 to open a Jesuit mission in England, where he ministered to many underground Catholic families before being captured in 1581. He was imprisoned in the Tower of London and was tortured on the rack several times. Before being executed for high treason, Campion declared his loyalty to the queen in temporal matters and his gratitude to God for his martyrdom. Feast day: December 1.

Campus Crusade for Christ, a Protestant evangelistic organization. Founded by former businessman William "Bill" Bright in Los Angeles in 1951, Campus Crusade aggressively encourages college and high school students and teachers to convert to a nondenominational, evangelical, "born again" form of Christianity. The organization's best-known evangelistic tool is its "Four Spiritual Laws" pamphlet, a simplified explanation of sin, atonement, and justification by faith. Campus Crusade has influenced young people from all backgrounds and denominations. Because Campus Crusade has turned some Catholics toward Protestant churches, it is regarded with caution on Catholic college and university campuses. As of the early 1990s, Campus Crusade has forty thousand paid and volunteer staff at work in 152 countries around the world, with 4,500 in the United States alone.

Cana Conference, a marriage enrichment program that urged the preservation of Catholic marital and family values through a program of education. Cana began in New York in 1943 with a retreat given to eleven couples by Jesuit John P. Delaney. Delaney's description of the retreat in an article in *America* popularized the idea of a special program for the married. The name Cana was conferred on the budding program when Father Edward Dowling hosted similar gatherings in St. Louis. Whatever uniformity was imposed on the Cana program came from the efforts mounted in the archdiocese of Chicago under Father (later Msgr.) John Egan. Although Egan did not begin the program in Chicago, he was selected to head it by Cardinal Samuel Stritch in 1946. The sheer size of the Chicago see, coupled with Egan's own personal dynamism, made the archdiocese the unofficial Cana leader in the nation. Egan and his co-workers soon were in demand in other dioceses seeking to emulate Chicago's success with the program. Out of Cana eventually emerged a premarital course of instruction called Pre-Cana.

Cana's format was a single day of conferences consisting of three talks, a roundtable discussion based on queries from a question box, and the renewal of the couple's wedding vows. The primary focus of the conferences was husband-wife relationships, but later sessions were devoted to parent-child relationships and parent-teenager relationships. Cana reached its peak in the 1950s. However, it declined in the 1960s, and its chief remnant is the Pre-Cana program, which developed into a marriage preparation program for engaged couples. *See also* Marriage Encounter; Marriage.

Canada, Catholicism in. Catholics have played an active role in Canadian history from its beginning, from the first European explorations of the northern half of the North American continent in the sixteenth century, through the founding of the first permanent settlements by Europeans in the seventeenth century and the establishment of Canada as a sovereign nation in the nineteenth century (1867), to the present. These earliest explorers and settlers were French Catholics; subsequent waves of immigration brought other Catholics from England and Ireland, Germany, Italy, Ukraine, Poland, the Philippines, and elsewhere. While Canada does not have an official state religion, Catholics by far form the largest single religious group. As of the 1991 census, about twelve and a half million Canadians describe themselves as Catholic (about 46 percent of a total population of approximately twenty-seven million Canadians). Of these, just over six million are French-speaking Catholics. For comparative purposes, just under ten million Canadians are

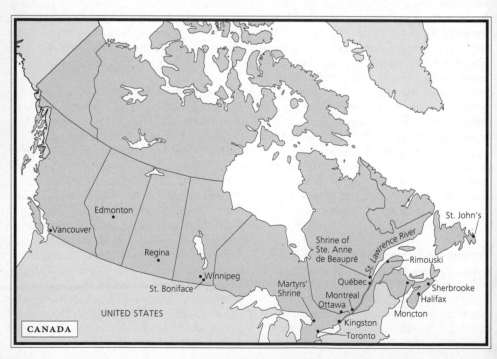

Protestant; of these, the largest group is formed by members of the United Church (just over three million), followed closely by the Anglicans (just over two million).

Canada has two sets of Catholic bishops. There are fourteen metropolitan sees serving the Latin church: Edmonton, Halifax, Kingston, Moncton, Montreal, Ottawa, Quebec (primate), Regina, Rimouski, St. Boniface, St. John's, Sherbrooke, Toronto, and Vancouver; there is also an archdiocese of Winnipeg. The small but thriving Ukrainian Catholic community (approximately one hundred thousand in number), which began its migration in earnest at the end of the nineteenth century, has a separate episcopal hierarchy; its Metropolitan See is located in Winnipeg.

For most of Canadian history, the legal rights of Catholics to practice their religion have been well-protected. Under French rule in the seventeenth and eighteenth centuries, the rights of Catholics were firmly entrenched. In 1763, with the Treaty of Paris that terminated the Seven Years' War, the last of France's mainland North American territories passed into British control, and the situation of Catholics became more tenuous. The passage of the Quebec Act (1774), however, brought relief: on the condition that they take an oath of loyalty to the Crown, Catholics were now free to participate fully in civil life and to practice their religion without restraint. Catholics have thrived indeed in Canadian political life. Catholics have served as prime minister, the highest office in the Canadian federal parliamentary system, and as premier, the highest office in the provincial governments. A signal honor was the appointment in 1959 of a Catholic as governor general, the Queen's official representative in Canada; Georges Vanier, whose son Jean founded the l'Arche communities for the mentally handicapped, was only the second Canadian to hold the position.

In Canada, education falls under the purview of the provincial governments (in the Canadian Confederation, there are ten provinces, Newfoundland, Nova Scotia, Prince Edward Island, New Brunswick, Quebec, Ontario, Manitoba, Saskatchewan, Alberta, and British Columbia, and two territories, the Yukon and the Northwest Territories). Educational prospects for Catholics in their own schools have been mixed. In some provinces, those with healthy Catholic populations, the provincial governments have supported parochial schools with tax relief; hence, in Quebec and Ontario, for example, there are vigorous Catholic school systems catering to the needs of many thousands of elementary and high school students. Elsewhere, as in Manitoba, the provincial governments have offered little in the way of financial and other support, and Catholic schools have been forced to rely wholly on the generosity of parents and local parishes.

There are some Catholic colleges and institutions of higher learning. The founding of colleges mirrors immigration patterns; hence, some colleges in Quebec were established quite early in the history of what would become Canada. Again, university education falls under provincial control, and Catholic colleges are often attached to the provincially-funded universities. For example, in Western Canada, St. Paul's College, a Jesuit institution, is affiliated with the University of Manitoba in Winnipeg.

In significant ways, Catholicism in Canada in the waning years of the twentieth century is similar to that in the United States. Vocations to the priesthood, and even more precipitously for nuns, are declining. The laity continues to follow its own counsel in sexual and moral matters. Attendance at Sunday Mass has declined. The Canadian church has also been buffeted by revelations of sexual abuse of minors by priests, and the bishops are trying to become more responsive to the needs of the victims. Perhaps because of the Canadian penchant for moderation and civility, the "liberal-conservative" disputes that have marked the U.S. Catholic Church have, however, been more muted in Canada.

Catholicism and the Search for Canadian Identity: Canadian Catholic history, however, does differ profoundly from that of the United States in one crucial respect. The debate over language and culture that has coursed throughout Canadian history has left its mark on the Church as well. The search for a distinctive Canadian identity has been much complicated by the historical rivalry between France and England, with its North American repercussions. Canadians have tended to be divided by their founding cultures. One novelist has described French and English Canada as "two solitudes," a phrase that aptly conveys the insularity and, at times, mutual incomprehension of the founding peoples. In present-day Canada, the search for identity has been further complicated by nationalist stirrings in the province of Quebec: the call for Quebec's separation from the rest of Canada, which has been made off and on in recent decades, has stimulated increased reflection by all Canadians about the future shape of the country. Similarly, the many other ethnic groups that have contributed to the development of the nation, and who while now English-speaking are only imperfectly described as "English," also seek recognition of their role. To maintain unity, Canada is now officially a bilingual country, reflecting the historical contribution of French and English settlers. Government services are now available throughout the country in English and French. In recognition of all its peoples, Canada is also an avowedly multicultural country, cherishing the many distinctive cultures that have constituted the Canadian mosaic. It remains to be seen whether the government's recent championing of a bilingual, multicultural policy will sufficiently meet the concerns and aspirations of different Canadians.

The role of religion in Canadian history has been complex. The Church undoubtedly facilitated the maintenance of the distinctive French Canadian culture after the establishment of British rule over the former French North American territories in the eighteenth century. For many in Quebec until quite recently, being French Canadian and being Catholic were synonymous. By the same token, the Catholicism of Quebec proved a lightning rod for anti-French sentiments elsewhere in Canada. Especially in the late nineteenth and early twentieth centuries, some in the ruling elites in English Canada tended to closely associate Anglo-Saxon "virtue" with Protestantism and, correspondingly, to despise Catholicism (and the French) as backward and superstitious. Fortunately, in a more ecumenical age, such notions have disappeared, or at least find less frequent public expression.

Yet, the history of the Catholics in Canada is more than the history of the French Canadians; about half of Canada's Catholics are of non-French descent. Perhaps surprisingly, although subject to the same misapprehension and bigotry, these Catholics, who settled in English Canada, did not as a rule identify with their French co-religionists. Rather, while all the while proudly maintaining their own Catholic identity, in their search for acceptance these Catholic immigrants to English Canada more usually assimilated the anti-French sentiments of the dominant culture.

It is often observed that Canada can boast the only city in the world, Winnipeg, in the western province of Manitoba, with three separate Catholic archdioceses: a French-speaking archdiocese in St. Boniface, a suburb of Winnipeg that is the largest French-Canadian settlement in the Western provinces; the English-speaking archdiocese of Winnipeg; and the Ukrainian Catholic archeparchy and metropolitan see. The situation in Winnipeg is, perhaps, a microcosm of the Canadian Catholic experience. In itself it recalls the waves of Catholic migration to Western Canada, first of French Canadians and then of Catholics from the British Isles, Ukraine, and elsewhere. The establishment of a separate archeparchy for the Ukrainians recognized the distinctiveness of their Eastern-rite church and has done much to preserve Ukrainian culture in the new world. But, the situation in Winnipeg also reflects the more ambiguous, perhaps less hopeful, side of Canadian cultural and religious life. The archdiocese of St. Boniface was the first of the three, established in the nineteenth century to foster the work of French Catholics in developing the West; it produced an impressive string of talented leaders. The heavy influx of non-French Latin-rite Catholics led to the creation early in the twentieth century of the separate archdiocese of Winnipeg. While again demonstrating a sensitivity to their different cultural past and aspirations, this also suggests the unwillingness of these Catholics to remain under the supervision of a French-speaking archbishop. Catholics constitute, in 1994, 45 percent of the total population of over 26 million. The largest concentration of Catholics is in Quebec. *See also* England, Catholicism in.

Bibliography

Murphy, Terrence, and Gerald Stortz, eds. *Creed and Culture: The Place of English-Speaking Catholics in Canadian Society, 1750–1930.* Montreal and Kingston: McGill-Queen's University Press, 1993.

JOSEPH WAWRYKOW

candle, symbol of divine light, purity, and holiness. Though originally candles were functional, providing light in the dark catacombs, their principal use was symbolic. Burning votive candles honored graves of martyrs and images of saints, who were thought to be in some way present there, themselves sharing divine life and light. Lighted candles are held by Christians renewing their baptismal promises, carried before bishops and clergy in processions, carried before the Gospel, and placed at the altar to designate Christ's presence. Finally, the paschal candle stands as a striking symbol of the Risen Christ, Light of the world. *See also* paschal candle; votive candle.

Candlemas, a feast, originally commemorating the purification of the Blessed Virgin and now called the Presentation of Our Lord, celebrated on February 2 with the blessing of candles. Both Christological and Marian themes are reflected in the texts of the day's office and eucharistic liturgy. The feast, which is first mentioned in Egeria's fourth-century descriptions of worship in Jerusalem, apparently spread to Rome at an early date. The use of candles was introduced in Jerusalem in the mid-fifth century by a Roman matron. Although the Christmas season officially ends after the Epiphany (January 6) with the feast of Our Lord's Baptism, Candlemas is sometimes identified as the formal ending of the Christmas cycle. *See also* Presentation.

Canisius, St. Peter (kah-nee'shuhs), 1521–97, Jesuit catechist and missionary, canonized a saint and declared a Doctor of the Church (1925) for defending and reestablishing Catholicism in Reformation Germany. Born in the Netherlands, Peter studied theology in Cologne (1536–46), joined the devout circle of priests surrounding the Carthusian Lanspergius, and entered the Society of Jesus (1543). After working in Italy, he returned to Germany, where his deep piety and inexhaustible energy earned him the title "Second Apostle of Germany after Boniface." Despite his conflicts with Catholics and Jesuit superiors, Canisius organized the German Jesuit province (1556–69) and established a network of Jesuit colleges which anchored the revival of German Catholic piety and learning. Most important, Canisius's popular and enduring catechism, *Institutiones Christianae Pietatis* (1558–59), defined an effective method of German lay religious education by outlining Catholic doctrine in a concise question and answer format. Feast day: December 21. *See also* Germany, Catholicism in.

Cano, Melchior, 1509–60, Spanish Dominican theologian. After studying under Francis de Vittoria in Salamanca (1527–31), he taught at Valladolid (1533–42) before moving on to Alcalá, succeeding de Vittoria at Salamanca in 1546. A zealous supporter of the Inquisition in its attacks on heresy and Erasmian humanists, he was also a determined critic of the Jesuits. At the Council of Trent, he opposed concessions to the Protestants on the Eucharist. Orthodoxy and personal antipathy involved him in long clash with Bartholomew Carranza, archbishop of Toledo. Cano's theology was marked by an unscholastic literary style and extensive use of early Christian authors. His *De Locis Theologicis* categorized and ranked the sources of doctrine for succeeding generations of Catholic theologians: Scripture, oral tradition, the Catholic Church, Church councils, the Roman Church, early Christian authors, theologians, reason, philosophers, and human history. *See also* theology.

canon [liturgical], characteristic liturgical unit of Byzantine-rite *orthros* (Matins), which is comprised of nine odes, each one a series of poetic stanzas or refrains on the theme of one of the nine biblical canticles once distributed throughout the week at *orthros,* with all nine chanted only at the Saturday All-Night Vigil. In the eighth century, the poetic canons began to replace the scriptural canticles. Today ode 2 is always omitted except in Lent. *See also* eucharistic prayer.

canon [title], an ecclesiastical title that refers to a diocesan priest attached to a cathedral and to a member of certain religious orders. A cathedral canon is a member of the college of priests whose duty it is to celebrate solemn liturgical functions in a cathedral or collegial church. A canon regular is a member of a specific kind of religious order. *See also* canoness; canons regular.

canoness, in the early Middle Ages, the designation for a woman living in religious community under a rule, but without taking perpetual vows. Abbeys of secular canonesses were valued by princes who used them as safe haven for their daughters. After the sixteenth century, these abbeys generally functioned as residences for noblewomen. In the wake of the eleventh-century renewal effort of Pope Gregory VII, some communities of secular canonesses adopted the Rule of St. Augustine. These groups, and others formed in tandem with congregations of canons regular, became regular canonesses. Regular canonesses are nuns, living a life of prayer and taking perpetual vows. *See also* abbey; canon [title]; canons regular; religious life.

canonical defect. *See* defect, canonical.

canonical doubt. *See* doubt [canon law].

canonical election. *See* election, canonical.

canonical faculties. *See* faculties, canonical.

canonical form, the requirement that all Catholics be married before a properly authorized Catholic minister and two witnesses. Usually the minister is a priest or deacon who is authorized to perform marriages by virtue of his office or by delegation from the pastor or bishop. Church law allows a lay minister to officiate if the bishops of a country request authorization from the Holy See. In interfaith marriages; i.e., between a Catholic and a non-Christian, Catholics may receive a dispensation from this obligation and marry in any public forum. *See also* marriage law.

canonical hours. *See* Liturgy of the Hours.

canonical mandate. *See* mandate to teach.

canonical mission, authorization to exercise governing power in the Church; used in some instances for other formal authorizations, such as to preach or teach.

The pope receives his mission upon acceptance of election as pope; others receive their missions from competent authority. Prior to Vatican II, canonical mission was seen as the source of power for bishops. Since the council, bishops are understood to receive the functions of teaching, sanctifying, and governing with ordination to the episcopate; canonical mission specifies the persons on behalf of whom bishops exercise these functions with binding force.

Similarly, others receive a share in governing power through canonical mission, either in the conferral of an ecclesiastical office (such as pastor, diocesan official, etc.) or by delegation for a specific task.

Catechists in missionary areas can also receive a canonical mission. This places them in charge of a community, with responsibilities that go beyond catechizing.

Canonical mission is sometimes used for the authorization to preach or teach. Until Vatican II, teaching was considered a dimension of the Church's power of jurisdiction. Teachers in government schools in Germany and other countries bound by treaty (concordat) with the Holy See need a canonical mission to teach Catholic religion. Since 1932, a canonical mission is required to teach theology or related fields on ecclesiastical faculties (which grant degrees on authorization of the Vatican). The proposal to extend this to teachers in other institutions resulted in the 1983 code's requirement of a "canonical mandate." *See also* mandate to teach; theologian.

JAMES H. PROVOST

canonical penance, an elaborate form of sacramental reconciliation in the early centuries of the Church intended for serious, public sinners. It required public acts of penance by an order of penitents. The whole community was involved in the process of reconciliation by its prayers of intercession. In the West, penitents were reconciled to the Church after a period of penitence on Holy Thursday, and in the East on Good Friday. Since canonical penance was offered to the individual only once in a lifetime, many people put it off until the time of death. In the early Middle Ages this form of public penance was gradually replaced by the individual, private confession introduced to Europe by Irish monks. *See also* Reconciliation.

canonicity. *See* canon of the Scriptures.

canonist, a practitioner or scholar of canon law, holding the degree of license (J.C.L.) or doctor (J.C.D.) of canon law, or doctor of both canon law and civil law (J.U.D.). The degree of license confers the right to teach canon law in seminaries and comparable faculties. It is comparable to a master's degree in the United States. Canonists work in marriage tribunals and other Church offices, or they teach canon law in seminaries and universities.

canonization, the process whereby the Church declares a person to be a saint and worthy of veneration by the faithful.

History: The early Church believed that martyrs who gave their lives for Christ attained eternal life. The Church commemorated the anniversary date of their death not in mourning but in joy. Confessors, those who suffered for the faith during the persecutions but were spared death, were also venerated. In time, Christians who lived an exemplary life, especially those who practiced great austerity and penance (in the spirit of the martyrs), were added to the list of those honored.

Eventually, the Church venerated others: e.g., holy bishops, missionaries, virgins, and Doctors of the Church. There was as yet no formal process whereby a person was declared a saint. Popular opinion added innumerable names to the list (Gk., *kanōn*) of those honored as saints. Each locality had its own patron saints. Abuses arose and the Church began to regulate the process. While the devotion of the people still initiated the process, bishops assumed the responsibility for making the official declaration of sainthood. The life of the holy person and a record of alleged miracles were studied, and upon the bishop's affirmation a feast day was assigned to be celebrated within the diocese.

The pope, in his role as chief pastor, became involved in canonizations because it was perceived as adding prestige to the process. According to one source, the first saint for whom records of canonization exist is St. Udalricus, canonized in 973. However, it is generally agreed that the first formal papal canonization was of Ulric, bishop of Augsburg, who died in 973 and was canonized by John XV in 993 at the Lateran Basilica in Rome.

Since that time, the process has become more formalized. In 1234, Gregory IX decreed that papal canonization was the only legitimate one. Sixtus V in 1588 entrusted the Sacred Congregation of Rites with the responsibility of processing candidacies for canonization. In 1983, Pope John Paul II issued the apostolic constitution *Divinus Perfectionis Magister* ("Divine Teacher and Model of Perfection"), which revised and simplified the norms and procedures. The Congregation for the Causes of Saints is responsible for the process.

Process: A preliminary step in the process is the introduction of the cause by a petitioner who writes to the bishop. The bishop then assigns a postulator who investigates the life and writings of the person. The postulator is a person, ordained or lay, who is expert in theological, canonical, and historical matters as well as familiar with the workings of the Congregation. The results of this investigation, a biography, and all published writings are presented to the bishop. Alleged miracles are investigated by experts.

The bishop or his delegate then oversees the questioning of witnesses and the investigation of writings. The bishop is responsible for consulting regional bishops, the faithful, experts called to testify, and the pope. All of the documents, *The Acts of the Cause,* are sent to Rome where they are reviewed by the Congregation for the Causes of Saints.

The juridical process involves beatification and canonization. If, after a person has been beatified, additional miracles are alleged, a further process of investigation and verification is undertaken. Upon a positive completion of this process, the pope issues a bull of canonization declaring the blessed to be a saint and extending veneration of the saint to the whole Church. An elaborate and solemn ceremony celebrates the canonization. *See also* beatification; saints; saints, devotion to. REGINA COLL

canon law, the law of the Church. The word "can-on" is from the Greek word for "rule" and refers to a given ecclesiastical law. Canon law is concerned with matters that touch upon the mission of the Church and upon the relationships within the Catholic communion. These subjects include such matters as norms for the celebration of the sacraments and public worship, for the preaching of the gospel, for the organization of clerical and religious life, for Catholic education, for the use and administration of Church property, for procedures in the adjudication of conflicts, for the allocation of penalties, and for the rights and obligations of the Christian faithful.

The laws of the Church are related to, but not commensurate with, either moral law or Catholic doctrinal teaching. Some of the matters canon law touches upon are purely disciplinary and are subject to change on the part of the Church; indeed many of these have changed in the course of the Church's history. Some of these laws might also be dispensed from, i.e., suspended by proper authority for due cause in a given instance. Other laws are considered to reiterate natural law (discoverable by reason in the created order) or divine positive law (given by revelation) and are considered to be unchangeable. Although canon law itself asserts that the ultimate source of certain canons is natural or divine law, it is helpful to refer to commentators in order to ascertain the origin and force of a given law.

Universal and Particular Laws: Canon law includes both laws that are universal and those that are particular. The universal laws are laid down for everyone everywhere while the particular hold force only for a given territory (e.g., a diocese) or for a given group of the faithful (e.g., members of a religious order). The supreme authority of the Church (i.e., the college of bishops in union with the head of that college, the pope, or the pope as the head of that college) is the ecclesiastical source of universal laws.

The universal laws for the Catholic Church are found first of all in two codes of canon law, both recently promulgated. The first is the *Code of Canon Law* (1983), which holds legislation for the Western Catholic Church. The second is the *Code of Canons of the Eastern Churches* (1990), established for those Eastern churches in full communion with Rome.

In addition to the universal law found in these codes, universal laws are found in the liturgical books of each rite. Liturgical laws, for the most part, are not included in either Eastern or Western codifications. There are as well universal laws that are agreements with civil governments.

Universal laws are also found in other legislative texts dealing with various matters, e.g., the election of the pope or the organization of the Roman Curia. Universal laws are usually promulgated in the official Vatican journal, *Acta Apostolicae Sedis (The Acts of the Apostolic See)*, and usually take effect two months after the date of the issue in which they are printed; at times other methods of promulgation and a shorter or longer hiatus (Lat., *vacatio legis*) between promulgation and effective date are employed.

Particular laws are those enacted for a certain territory or given group of the faithful, e.g., for a given diocese or religious institute. These are legislated by the authority competent to do so and must be promulgated in accord with the laws governing the group.

Historical Development: Canon law has developed historically from a number of sources. Writers from the post-NT era (ca. 95) produced "church orders" treating of such matters as the organization of the early Church and the manner in which the sacraments should be celebrated. The writings of early Church Fathers added to Church laws as well. Church councils, both local and worldwide, have dealt not only with doctrinal issues, but also with concerns touching disciplinary matters; these added to the body of canon law and continued to do so even into the twentieth century. Responses from the Roman see to questions raised by unforeseen situations also augment the law. In the history of the Church a growing degree of sophistication accompanied the collecting of, and commenting upon, Church laws. Of particular note is the canonist Gratian (d. 1140), whose collection was not only the most complete but also the most scientifically organized of the Middle Ages and was used as a common text until the first codification of canon law in 1917.

Although there had been a procedure put into place for the continuous updating of the 1917 code of canon law at the time of its promulgation, that procedure was never used and many modifications of the code made the status of numerous laws confused. More importantly, it was necessary to rethink the very role of law in the life of the Church. Consequently, when Pope John XXIII announced in 1959 his intention to call an ecumenical council (Vatican II), he also announced the revision of the code of canon law. The later task was not, and could not be, thoroughly addressed until the council had deliberated. Pope Paul VI gave the revising commission its charge, and ten principles that were to guide the revision were approved by the Synod of Bishops in October 1967. Among these principles can be found a concern for the necessity for law in the life of the Church so long as the law is used in a pastoral manner, a concern that the law be implemented in accordance with the principle of subsidiarity, and a concern for protecting the rights of the faithful. The revision itself was completed under Pope John Paul II, who promulgated the new code on January 25, 1983, the anniversary of John XXIII's announcement of the revision. The new code went into effect on the first Sunday of Advent, November 27, 1983. Although the Eastern Catholic churches had never had a complete codification of their laws, a commission was established to revise those that had been codified and to complete the process of codification. The Eastern code was promulgated on October 18, 1990, and went into effect on October 1, 1991. Although the Latin text remains normative in both codes, there are approved English translations for the United States done by the Canon Law Society of America. *See also* canon law, interpretation of; Code of Canons of the Eastern Churches.

Bibliography

Code of Canon Law. Latin-English ed. Washington, DC: Canon Law Society of America, 1983.

Code of Canons of the Eastern Churches. Latin-English ed. Canon Law Society of America, 1991.

Coriden, James, Thomas Green, and Donald Heintschel, eds. *The Code of Canon Law: A Text and Commentary.* Commissioned by the Canon Law Society of America. New York and Mahwah, NJ: Paulist Press, 1985.   JOHN LAHEY

canon law, interpretation of, the understanding and application of the rules and regulations of the Church. It is used in two distinct senses: (1) Official and authoritative interpretation is given by the lawmaker or someone empowered by the lawmaker (can. 16). Such authoritative interpretations have the force of law. Judicial and administrative decisions do not have the same power of precedent in interpreting canon law as they do in civil law. In other words, there is no doctrine of *stare decisis* (Lat., "let the decision stand") in canon law. (2) All other persons who attempt to understand the meaning of the Church's canons or rules and their application to individual situations do so in accord with a set of principles or guidelines. Some of these are expressly stated in the code of canon law, while others are drawn from the Church's canonical tradition.

The first step in interpretation is to discern the authority of the source of the rule and the force of its obligation. Then one searches out the accepted canonical meaning of the terms used in the particular setting and in this area of the law. "Ecclesiastical laws are to be understood in accord with the proper meaning of the words considered in their text and context" (can. 17). It is of fundamental importance to determine the literary genre being employed, e.g., doctrinal declaration, exhortation, recommendation, or command. If the meaning is still doubtful or obscure, one looks for parallels, i.e., other places in the canons where the same topic is treated or the same language used. The circumstances in which the law was made (its legislative history and pastoral context) and the purpose for which it was made are of vital importance in understanding the law; canonists say "the purpose of the law is the soul of the law." Closely associated with the purpose of the law is another interpretive source: "the mind of the legislator," i.e., the intention of the Church in proposing the rule.

The Code of Canon law also asserts a principle of strict or narrow interpretation. Laws that include a penalty or restrict the free exercise of rights or that are exceptions to more general norms are subject to strict interpretation (can. 18). That is, they are narrowly construed and applied in as limited a manner and scope as reasonably possible.

In canon law the actions of the community affect the force of the law. "Custom is the best interpreter of laws" (can. 27). This means that the practice of the community of believers confirms and clarifies the meaning of the law. The way that a rule is actually applied by the faithful over time is the best indicator of its meaning. This "sense of the faithful" has another side: the doctrine of reception. When the community accepts a new rule and abides by it, the rule is confirmed by the people's actions in conformity with it. When the community does not recognize or receive the rule in practice, then the rule is without effect.

The overarching principle of canonical interpretation is that stated in the final canon of the code (can. 1752): the salvation of souls is always the supreme law of the Church. The law is to be understood and applied to the spiritual benefit of the people, and never to their detriment.

The principles of *epikeia* (Gk., "act of justice"), canonical equity, pastoral discretion, and *oikonomia* (Gk., "economy") must also be brought to bear in the interpretation of canon law. *See also* canon law; economy, principle of; *epikeia;* reception of law.

JAMES CORIDEN

canon law, rights and obligations in. *See* rights and obligations in canon law.

Canon Law Society of America, a professional association of canon lawyers and persons interested in canon law. Founded in 1939, it is dedicated to promoting pastoral ministry, cooperates in the renewal of church law, encourages canonical research and study, responds to practical needs, and facilitates cooperation and dialogue.

The society holds annual national conventions, publishes books and a newsletter, sponsors workshops and symposia, and provides referral services through its executive coordinator. It is governed by a board of governors formed of elected officers and consultors.

Since 1965 it has worked to implement Vatican II reforms and collaborated in the critique of drafts for the new Code of Canon Law. The society has developed a "due process" plan for protecting and vindicating rights in the Church. The society works to educate Catholics about the new Code of Canon Law (1983). It has published English translations of the 1983 Latin code and 1990 Eastern code and sponsored a major commentary on the 1983 code. *See also* canon law.

Canon of the Mass, the central prayer of the Eucharistic Liturgy, more commonly referred to as the Eucharistic Prayer since Vatican II (1962–65). The word "canon" is Greek in origin and means "measuring rod" or "rule." It thus conveys the sense of an established norm. "Canon of the Mass" was the phrase used to describe the single Eucharistic Prayer that prevailed in the Western Church from the Middle Ages until the introduction of new eucharistic prayers after Vatican II. It has its roots in the fourth century and underwent minor modifications throughout later centuries. Traditionally known as the Roman Canon, it is referred to now as Eucharistic Prayer I. *See also* Eucharist; eucharistic prayer.

canon of the Scriptures (Gk., *kanōn,* "norm," "standard"), an authoritative corpus of writings considered normative for faith. In this sense the word appears to have been first used by Athanasius in his *Decrees of the Synod of Nicaea* (ca. 350). The traditional view is that the Pentateuch, or Torah, was "canonized" by Ezra and the "men of the Great Assembly" after the Babylonian exile, and that the other two parts of the tripartite Hebrew Bible were given final form at the Council of Jamnia (Yavneh) after the fall of Jerusalem in A.D. 70. It is now acknowledged that this view is greatly oversimplified.

The first text claiming an authority that can retrospectively be called canonical is Deuteronomy, the first edition of which is generally dated to the reign of Josiah (640–609 B.C.) and the final version to the Babylonian exile some seventy years later. The book of the law administered by Ezra in the mid-fifth century B.C. (Ezra 7:14, 21, 25–26) was probably not the entire Pentateuch, though the Pentateuch must have achieved its more or less final form not much later in the Persian period. This compilation enjoyed the highest authority as the word of God communicated to Israel through Moses, its human author. Indeed, Sirach, or Ecclesiasticus (24:23), identifies the Torah with personified wisdom, the firstborn of creation.

The designation of the historical books (Joshua through 2 Kings) as Former Prophets is explained by the conviction of later compilers that the writing of the national history was a prophetic prerogative. Additions to the Latter Prophets (Isaiah through Malachi) continued to be made as late as the second century B.C., while the third part, or Writings, was not fixed at least until early Christian times. The propriety of including certain books (Ecclesiastes, or Qoheleth, and Canticle of Canticles) was debated during the Yavnean period following the fall of Jerusalem (A.D. 70), but there was nothing resembling a council at which the biblical canon was fixed. The threefold division of the Hebrew Bible is first attested in the prologue to the Greek translation of Sirach (Ecclesiasticus) which speaks of the law, the prophets, and the other writings. About two centuries later, the Jewish historian Josephus lists the five books of Moses, thirteen prophetic books, and four books containing hymns and precepts (presumably Psalms, Proverbs, Canticle of Canticles, and Job) as the authoritative writings of his people (*Against Apion* 1:37–41). The first complete Jewish list of biblical books with their putative authors appears in the Babylonian Talmud (*b. B. Bat.* 14b–15a).

During the apostolic and subapostolic periods Christians appropriated the Jewish Scriptures and added writings of their own. Most Christian churches, however, read the Scriptures in the Old Greek translation known as the Septuagint, which contained additional books and arranged the contents in a different order. Disregarding the division between Prophets (*Nebi'im*) and Writings (*Ketubim*), the translators set out the books according to literary genre, i.e., historical, poetic and didactic, prophetic. The term Septuagint (LXX) reflects the legendary account of the origins of this version

in Aristeas (ca. 100 B.C.), according to which the translation was made at one time over a period of seventy-two days by seventy or seventy-two translators brought to Alexandria at the instance of Ptolemy II Philadelphus. In point of fact, the translation was made over a long period of time, beginning with the Pentateuch in the third century B.C. It should be added that the understanding of the Septuagint as a distinct Alexandrian canon is no longer widely accepted.

Defining the Canon: In the early days of Christianity there was no fixed and closed canon; witness the fact that NT authors refer to apocryphal (deuterocanonical) writings in much the same way as to other biblical books. The need to define more precisely which books were to be accepted as scriptural arose from the requirements of controversy with Jews, as in the polemical writings of Justin in the mid-second century. The process was hastened by the reaction to the Gnostic Marcion, expelled from the Church about the same time, who rejected the OT and all early Christian writings with the exception of Luke (minus the infancy Gospel) and ten Pauline Letters. Controversy over acceptance of a shorter or longer (Alexandrian) list of biblical books continued throughout the first four centuries and, residually, later. Origen, Athanasius, and Jerome argued for the shorter list, Augustine for the longer. The Council of Trent (1545–63) decided for inclusion of the deuterocanonical books, partly on the basis of Church usage, and partly in response to the Reformers' rejection of them. (One reason was appeal to 2 Macc 12:46 in support of the doctrine of purgatory.) This is no longer a burning issue; some recent versions (e.g., the NRSV) include the deuterocanonical books.

The Canon of the New Testament: The NT as we have it, comprising twenty-seven books, did not win general acceptance until the fourth century, and in fact the term "New Testament" referring to a corpus of early Christian writings is not attested until well into the second century. One of the main reasons for the acceptance of certain books and the rejection of others was apostolic authorship; hence the status of Hebrews was uncertain due to doubts about its Pauline authorship. Equally important, however, were ecclesiastical, and especially liturgical, usage and an assessment of the book's conformity with the rule of faith. Hence several Gospels attributed to apostles, e.g., the *Gospel of Thomas* and the *Gospel of Peter*, were rejected; in some quarters the Gospel of John was suspect due to its popularity with Gnostic groups; and eventually consensus coalesced around four Gospels and four Gospels alone that were thought to be composed either by apostles or their associates. For similar reasons many Acts of apostles (e.g., *Acts of Paul and Thecla, Acts of Peter*) were excluded from canonicity and thirteen Pauline Letters were accepted. Due to its popularity among millenarian groups, Revelation was for a long time treated with suspicion. It can be said, finally, that canonicity is no longer a divisive issue among the churches, and questions of authorship of NT books is a matter of free discussion among Catholic scholars. *See also* extracanonical writings.

Bibliography

Beckwith, Roger T. *The Old Testament Canon of the New Testament Church and Its Background in Early Judaism.* Grand Rapids, MI: Eerdmans, 1985.

Blenkinsopp, Joseph. *Prophecy and Canon: A Contribution to the Study of Jewish Origins.* Notre Dame, IN: University of Notre Dame Press, 1977.

Metzger, Bruce. *The Canon of the New Testament: Its Origin, Development, and Significance.* Oxford: Clarendon Press; New York: Oxford University Press, 1987.　　　JOSEPH BLENKINSOPP

canon penitentiary, diocesan priest, appointed by the bishop, with the power to absolve from automatic censures (Lat., *latae sententiae*) that are not reserved to the Holy See, e.g., the procuring of an abortion (can. 508). *See also* cathedral chapter; Penitentiary, Apostolic.

canons regular, members of a clerical religious institute, as distinct from monastic, mendicant, and apostolic institutes. Most of them adopted the Rule of St. Augustine. Originating in the Middle Ages, at first the canons regular did not generally engage in the care of souls. They came together for prayer and life in community. Today they are active in many kinds of apostolic work, including parishes, missions,teaching,andtheliturgicalapostolate.Fewer than a dozen orders of canons exist today. Chief among them are the Premonstratensians (Norbertines), the Canons Regular of St. Augustine, and the Canons Regular of the Holy Cross (Crosiers). *See also* Augustinian Canons; Crosier Fathers and Brothers; Norbertines.

Canons Regular of Premontré. *See* Norbertines.

canopy, a large covering. In Christian usage, the term may refer to a covering over the altar area (also called a *baldachino;* It.) or the portable covering (also called a *baldachino* or *ombrellino;* It.) carried over a priest who processes with the Eucharist; the latter use is rapidly becoming obsolete. *See also* baldachino.

Canossa, northern Italian fortress and site of a temporary reconciliation between Pope Gregory VII and the excommunicated emperor Henry IV. In 1076, while en route to a council in Germany to depose the emperor, Gregory was intercepted by Henry who, simulating penitence, asked for and received papal absolution. *See also* Gregory VII.

cantata, musical term describing a composition written to be sung (usually by solo voices and a choir), as opposed to one written to be played (a sonata). The composition, usually inspired by biblical material, is more common in the Reformed tradition (especially in Lutheran circles) than in the Catholic tradition.

Canterbury, cathedral city in Kent, England; mother church of Anglicanism and seat of the archbishop of Canterbury. In 597 St. Augustine (d. 605) established a Benedictine mission in England. The mission was successful and a monastery established. The present Cathedral of Christ Church, built by Archbishop Lanfranc (d. 1189), is the third building on the site. Excavations in 1993 revealed the remains of a Saxon church, proving an unbroken continuity of worship on the site since the time of Augustine of Canterbury.

As spiritual leaders of the mother church of England, the archbishops of Canterbury have played significant roles not only in the affairs of the Church but in affairs of state. The formidable men who have sat in the seat of Augustine include Anselm (d. 1109), whose contribution to philosophy, theology, spirituality, and secular life may be unrivaled. In medieval history and spirituality, the impact of Thomas Becket (d. 1170) added to the luster of Canterbury. His bold defiance of the power of the state led to his murder at the hands of four knights sent by King Henry II (December 29, 1170). Such was the sanctity and devotion that Becket inspired that the interior of the Cathedral was adapted to make the building more suitable as a place of pilgrimage. Geoffrey Chaucer's (d. 1400) masterpiece, *The Canterbury Tales,* is evidence of the enthusiasm that Becket's martyrdom produced.

In the sixteenth century, Archbishop Thomas Cranmer (d. 1556) was the compiler of the Book of Common Prayer, widely regarded as one of the greatest liturgical treasures of the Anglican Communion. Although at the Reformation the Holy Catholic Church in England became the Anglican Church of England, an unbroken line of 103 archbishops has served the people of England. The Cathedral attracts more than two million visitors a year. The archbishop of Canterbury resides in Canterbury and London (Lambeth Palace) and, since the growth of the Anglican Communion, is spiritual head of more than seventy million Anglicans in thirty-five provinces. Anglican links with the Catholic Church in England are strong and growing stronger. *See also* Anglicanism; England, Catholicism in.

GEORGE L. CAREY

canticle, a biblical poem apart from the Psalms, often used in liturgical services, especially in the Liturgy of the Hours. Canticles, especially frequent in the OT (e.g., Exod 15:1–19; Deut 32:1–43) but also found in the NT (e.g., Luke 1:46–55; 68–79; 2:29–32), are usually appended to the biblical Psalms in Eastern-rite liturgical Psalters, a practice seen even in some manuscripts of the Septuagint, the Greek OT.

Canticle of Canticles. *See* Song of Songs.

Cantius, St. John, 1390–1473, preacher, Scripture scholar, patron saint of Poland and Lithuania. Born in Kanti, Poland, he was noted for his scholarship (he held the chair of theology at Cracow), preaching, and concern for the poor. Feast day: December 23.

cantor, the person who intones the first note(s) of a musical composition or who serves as the musical leader for congregational singing. Cantors are common both in the performance of the monastic office and in parish liturgies, especially since the reforms of the Second Vatican Council (1962–65).

Canute, St., d. 1086, king and patron saint of Denmark. Having unsuccessfully employed military force to press his claim to the English throne (his uncle, King Canute, had reigned there), he was killed by Danish rebels, including his brother Olaf, who opposed his policy of taxation and tithes. Feast day: January 19.

Capistrano, St. John, 1386–1456, preacher, monastic reformer, and associate of Bernardino of Siena. Of noble background, Capistrano studied law and served as a magistrate before joining the Obser-

vant Franciscans in 1415. For the rest of his career he promoted monastic reform in the Franciscan order and elsewhere. A remarkable preacher, Capistrano spoke against the Fraticelli in Italy and the Hussites in central Europe. At the end of his life he preached and helped lead a crusade against the Turks, during which he died. He was canonized in 1690. Feast day: October 23.

capitalism, one of the two major economic systems—the other being socialism—addressed in modern Catholic social teaching, which extends from Pope Leo XIII's encyclical *Rerum Novarum* (1891) through Pope John Paul II's *Centesimus Annus* (1991). The identifying characteristics of capitalism are the private ownership of the means of production and a free market where the goods of production may be sold for profit. Modern Catholic social teaching is unequivocal in insisting that a market economy, properly ordered by concern for the common good, is a positive phenomenon because it contributes to the material well-being of persons and recognizes their dignity as free moral agents. Whether a particular economic system designated as capitalist is acceptable or not depends on whether concern for the common good is adequately structured into the society as a whole through juridical measures that limit the market.

John Paul II is clear on this point in *Centesimus Annus*, when he raises the question of whether the collapse of socialism means that capitalism is "victorious." The answer, he says, depends on what one means by capitalism. If one means "a system which recognizes the fundamental and positive role of business, the market, private property and the resulting responsibility for the means of production," the answer is yes. If one means "a system in which freedom in the economic sector is not circumscribed within a strong juridical framework which places it at the service of human freedom in its totality," then the answer is no (*Centesimus Annus,* n. 42). The latter constitutes "consumer society," which attempts to defeat Marxism through pure materialism by showing that a free market can fulfill a greater satisfaction of material needs than communism, while still excluding spiritual values (n. 19). *See also* Catholic social teachings.

TODD D. WHITMORE

capital punishment, infliction of the death penalty on persons convicted of serious crimes. It has been part of legal systems from antiquity on. It is called for in the Hebrew Bible as a punishment for murder, for striking or cursing one's parents, and for kidnapping (Exod 21:12–17) as well as for bestiality, for sorcery, and for sacrificing to alien gods (Exod 22:18–20). Reliance on the death penalty virtually disappeared from the Jewish tradition, both as a result of the loss of political autonomy and as result of heightened procedural barriers in the rabbinic period. Christians experienced the death penalty as an element of religious persecutions, but the major theologians (Augustine of Hippo, Thomas Aquinas, the Reformers) did not attack its legitimacy as such. However, capital punishment became a target for social critics in the aftermath of the Enlightenment. In the period since 1945 most Western societies have either completely abolished it or have drastically restricted its application. It often serves as an instrument of coercion in the hands of regimes that violate human rights on a large scale (Iran, South Africa, the former Soviet Union). Catholic teaching has been reluctant to condemn capital punishment in principle; but most recent popes and bishops have favored abolition and have appealed for clemency in particular cases. The major difficulties with justifying capital punishment as a contemporary practice are: (1) doubts about its necessity or usefulness as a means of preserving public order; (2) the possibility of error in the judicial process; (3) the repellent and inhumane character of the act; (4) its incompatibility with the teaching of Jesus on forgiveness; (5) inconclusive evidence on its effectiveness as a deterrent. For these and similar reasons, capital punishment has been rejected by the U.S. (1980) and Philippine (1992) bishops, even though there was strong public support in both societies for imposing the death penalty as a response to greatly increased crime. *See also* consistent ethic of life.

JOHN P. LANGAN

capital sins, those vices (pride, envy, anger, sloth, avarice, gluttony, and lust) that are the wellsprings from which sinful thoughts, behavior, and omissions arise. They are also called the "seven deadly sins." It is more precise to think of the capital sins as dispositions toward sinning rather than as sins properly speaking; that is, they are tendencies in our character that threaten moral goodness by predisposing us to sin. Pope Gregory the Great (d. 604) first used the designation "capital" to describe certain sins as being major, while Thomas Aquinas (d. 1274) employed "capital" as a metaphor to designate those sins that were the source or fountainhead for

other sins, from the Latin *caput*, "head." Over the centuries there have been differences about which sins should be included in the list of capital sins, the proper number of such sins, and the order in which they should be listed.

The enumeration of capital sins had its origin in the first centuries of Eastern monasticism, where lists were drawn up of vices harmful to monastic life. The Egyptian monk Evagrius Ponticus (d. 399) gave some precision to the various lists by defining eight malicious attitudes that engendered sin. John Cassian (d. 435) introduced the practices of Eastern monasticism to the West and with that knowledge came the roster of capital or deadly sins. The list of John Cassian was modified by Gregory the Great and this version is very close to the list as we know it. Gregory, however, specified eight, not seven, sins by distinguishing pride from vainglory. He also sought to make the list applicable to the lives of all Christians and not just those who lived in monasteries. It was Gregory's influence and prestige that ensured the popularity of listing the capital sins, although variations on the number and ordering of the sins continued. Peter Lombard (d. 1160) used Gregory's list and his was the source for Thomas Aquinas, who merged pride and vainglory to establish the seven capital sins we know today. A decision of the Fourth Lateran Council in 1215 to make annual confession of all mortal sin obligatory gave further prominence to the seven capital sins. To assist the worthy reception and administration of the sacrament, the list of capital sins, along with the Ten Commandments, became a common device for the penitent's examination of conscience and the confessor's inquiry into a person's life. Thus, the capital sins became a part of the ordinary experience of popular piety within Catholicism.

Notable in the long history of artistic acknowledgment of the seven deadly sins are Chaucer's inclusion of a long sermon on the capital sins in "The Parson's Tale" in his *Canterbury Tales* and Dante's utilization of the capital sins in his description of the terraces of purgatory in the *Divine Comedy*. Giotto and Lorenzetti created frescoes portraying the capital sins, while Bosch and Brueghel the Elder illustrated the seven deadly sins on canvas. *See also* avarice; gluttony; pride; vice.   *KENNETH R. HIMES*

Capitania, St. Bartolomea, also known as Capitanio, 1807–33, Italian-born cofounder of the Sisters of Charity of Lovere, an order devoted to the care of the poor and the sick, and to the education of children. Feast day: July 26.

cappa magna (Lat., "great cape"), a flowing cloaklike vestment with a train and hooded shoulder cape worn by bishops and cardinals. With the liturgical reforms mandated by the Second Vatican Council (1962–65), its form has been simplified (the cardinal's cappa is no longer made of watered silk and the train has been shortened) and its use has been restricted. Cardinals may wear it on solemn occasions, but only outside Rome. Bishops may also wear it on solemn occasions, but the pope no longer wears it.

Cappadocian Fathers, a designation taken from the name of the Roman province in east-central Asia Minor to apply to the remarkable group of theologians produced by the vigorous church there in the fourth century. Traditionally, the Cappadocian Fathers are Basil the Great, who became bishop of the capital Caesarea in 370, along with two persons he appointed to help him control the Church in the province: his brother Gregory, as bishop of Nyssa, and his friend Gregory of Nazianzus, as bishop of Sasima. All participated in the theological refutation of Arianism in the form developed by Eunomius, who was born in Cappadocia but, as a heretic, was usually not counted as one of this group. Sometimes the controversialist Amphilochius of Iconium is praised as "the fourth Cappadocian," but increasingly that term is reserved for Macrina, sister of Basil and Gregory of Nyssa. *See also* Basil, "the Great," St.; Gregory of Nazianzus, St.; Gregory of Nyssa, St.; Macrina, St.

Capreolus, John, ca. 1380–1444, Dominican theologian and noted interpreter of Thomas Aquinas. A native of Languedoc, he received the licentiate in theology from the University of Paris in 1411. His most famous work is the *Defensiones,* in which he defends the thought of Aquinas from the attacks of other prominent theologians such as Duns Scotus and Durandus of Saint-Pourçain and promotes the view that the *Summa Theologiae* offers the definitive statement of Thomas's thought. *See also* Aquinas, St. Thomas.

Capuchins (It., *cappuccino,* a pointed monastic hood), an independent reform branch (O.F.M. Cap.) of the Order of Friars Minor (Franciscans). The Capuchin reform began in 1525 in the Marches, Italy.

The friars of this area had maintained resistance against what they considered the watering down of the Rule of St. Francis of Assisi, which dates from the early thirteenth century. By the sixteenth century, the Friars Minor, or Franciscans, consisted of the so-called Observants, who refused a fixed revenue but allowed secular agents to accept and use money for them, and the Conventuals, who accepted money without such intermediaries. The leader of the reform was Matteo di Bassi, who obtained verbal authorization from Pope Clement VII (d. 1534) to observe the rule literally by a strict interpretation of the vow of poverty, to depend on daily alms, to wear a habit with a pointed hood (which they considered the original habit of Francis), and to lead an evangelical life of both preaching and hermetical solitude. This reform movement quickly became detached from the Observants, who strongly opposed the reformers. After a somewhat complicated history of papal approval and disapproval, Pope Paul III (d. 1549) solemnly approved the Capuchins in 1536. Today, the Capuchins still form one of the three families of First Order Franciscans. *See also* Franciscan order.

Cardijn, Joseph, 1882–1967, Belgian cardinal, founder of the Young Christian Workers (known popularly as the Jocists). Imprisoned by the Nazis during the Second World War, he played a prominent role at the Second Vatican Council (1962–65), where his writings and pastoral example helped shape the council's teachings on the role of the laity in the Church and in the world. *See also* Jocists.

cardinal, title given to a member of the group, known as the College of Cardinals, that act as the pope's closest advisers in governance of the universal Church and serve as papal electors. The title may have originated from *cardo* (Lat., "hinge"), indicating a significant, permanent administrative official of a church, parish, or diocese, or it may have developed from *incardinare* (Lat., "to hang on a hinge") and the functioning of bishops and priests outside their own parishes or sees, specifically, in certain Roman basilicas and related parish churches during the latter part of the first millennium. *See also* Cardinals, College of.

Cardinals, College of, the juridic collegial body, composed of cardinals, that provides for election of the pope and that assists the pope in governing the universal Church on matters of great import, by participation in consistories, formal meetings of cardinals in the presence of the pope (Code of Canon Law, can. 349).

As part of the ecclesiastical reforms of the eleventh century, the bishops and priests who were cardinals of the church of Rome gained increased significance, became a collegial body, and in 1059, were deputed by Pope Nicholas II (d. 1061) as electors of the pope. The order of cardinal deacon, those deacons who had care of the poor in the seven districts of Rome, was also added to the College of Cardinals during that era. In 1586, Pope Sixtus V set the maximum number of cardinals at seventy, representing the seventy elders of Moses, but this limit was abrogated by Pope John XXIII in 1958. Though not previously required by legislation, with the promulgation of the 1917 Code of Canon Law the dignity of cardinal could be conferred only on a priest or bishop, and in 1962 John XXIII determined that all cardinals then and henceforth would be ordained as bishops. In 1965, Pope Paul VI formulated special norms for oriental patriarchs, bishops of major Eastern sees and heads of their rites, who were elevated to the College of Cardinals. In 1970, he determined that cardinals who had reached the age of eighty would remain members of the College but would cease to hold positions in the Roman Curia and would lose the right to elect the pope, concomitantly losing the right to enter the conclave for such an election. In 1973, Pope Paul VI set a limit of 120 on the number of cardinals who were eligible to elect the pope.

The pope alone appoints cardinals by publishing a decree of their names in the presence of the College of Cardinals. From the time of publication of this decree, those created cardinals are bound to the duties and possess the rights of cardinals, unless for some reason such as danger to the created cardinal the pope reserves the person's name *in pectore* (Lat., "in the breast") or *in petto* (It.), that is, "in secret" (can. 351).

The College of Cardinals has three orders—cardinal-bishop, cardinal-priest, and cardinal-deacon. Cardinal-bishops are those to whom the pope assigns the title of one of six neighboring dioceses of Rome and oriental patriarchs who have been named to the college but retain title to their own patriarchal see. Cardinal-priests are assigned titles to churches in the city of Rome, and cardinal-deacons are assigned title to what were formerly aid stations attached to churches in Rome and staffed by deacons during the late Middle Ages. Cardinal-bishops and cardinal-priests have no jurisdiction over their titular dioceses and churches but are expected to promote their welfare insofar as possible (can. 357).

As a collegial body, the College of Cardinals has a dean and an assistant dean, both of whom are elected by and from the cardinal-bishops and who must be approved by the pope and are required, thereafter, to reside in Rome. The dean presides over the college; the assistant dean presides when the dean is impeded. In either case, the presider acts as the first among equals and possesses no jurisdiction over the other cardinals (can. 352). By long-standing tradition, as well as by law, the dean of the College of Cardinals holds title to the diocese of Ostia, the seventh of the neighboring sees of Rome, in addition to his other titular church (can. 350.4). The dean, or, if impeded, the assistant dean, ordains to the episcopate the person elected pope if he is not already a bishop. The oldest cardinal-bishop may do so if both the dean and assistant dean are impeded. The first cardinal-deacon announces the name of the newly elected pope and, likewise, invests metropolitan bishops with the pallium, a symbol of authority worn about the neck, on behalf of the pope (c. 355).

Cardinals primarily assist in governance of the universal Church by their direct and close relationship to the pope as well as through various meetings with him and the other cardinals (can. 353). They are sometimes commissioned by the pope to represent him at solemn celebrations in the role of *legatus a latere* (Lat., "representative from the side"), or alter ego, and they also function as special envoys with competence over those matters entrusted to them by the pope (can. 357.2–3). *See also* cardinal; conclave; consistory; papal election; papal legate; Roman Curia.   ELIZABETH MCDONOUGH

cardinal virtues   (Lat., *cardo,* "hinge"), prudence, justice, fortitude, and temperance, called "cardinal" because they are hinges on which many lesser virtues turn. In *Nicomachean Ethics,* the Greek philosopher Aristotle (d. 322 B.C.) organizes his discussion of the virtues around four broad traits of character that, in his view, are necessary to living a fully virtuous life. Prudence, or practical wisdom, the most important of all the cardinal virtues, enables its subject to discern the specific course of action that will best fulfill the requirements of a virtuous life in a particular situation; justice disposes to render the fairness due to each person; fortitude enables its subject to pursue the good in the face of contrary fears; temperance enables an individual to maintain a correct balance, and to observe appropriate limits, in the pursuit of sensual pleasures. This fourfold division proved to be of central significance for subsequent reflection on the virtues, becoming the classical form for organizing accounts of the virtuous life. As such, it appears in the writings of the Roman statesman and philosopher Cicero, as well as in the writings of early Christian theologians such as Gregory the Great and Augustine.

In his *Summa Theologiae,* Thomas Aquinas (d. 1274) analyzes the cardinal virtues from two perspectives. In one way, they represent qualities of character that must all be present if someone's actions are to be virtuous in the fullest sense, so that, for example, an action must embody fairness and firmness of soul, as well as moderation, in order to be a fully virtuous action. In another way, they are distinctive virtues having to do with specific areas of human life; when he considers them from this perspective, Aquinas generally follows the analysis of Aristotle. Aquinas follows the classical and Christian authors in asserting that the cardinal virtues are necessary to living a good life, whether that is seen from a purely natural or a distinctively Christian point of view. Hence, the four cardinal virtues, together with the three theological virtues of faith, hope, and charity, form the integrating framework by which Aquinas organizes the detailed moral analysis of the second part of the second volume of the *Summa Theologiae.*

Subsequent Catholic moral theology followed the lead of Aquinas in taking the framework of the cardinal and theological virtues as the basis for organizing the ideals and duties of the Christian life. However, these virtues were increasingly seen as organizing principles for moral laws, and their function as ideals of character was increasingly lost. The movement away from Scholastic moral theology towards a more scriptural and theological understanding of the moral life since the Second Vatican Council (1962–65) had as one of its consequences a loss of interest in the framework of the cardinal and theological virtues. However, the renewed interest in virtue as a category of the moral life has led to a revival of interest in the cardinal virtues among philosophers as well as among moral theologians. *See also* fortitude; justice; prudence; temperance; virtue.

JEAN PORTER

Caritas International, a worldwide conglomerate of national Catholic charity-relief organizations that provide money and other kinds of assistance to those in need. The American branch of Caritas International is Catholic Relief Services (CRS), based in New York, which provides aid to victims of earthquakes, floods, droughts, and other natural disasters. Through CRS, American Catholics give aid to more than 18 million needy people in over eighty countries.

Carmel, Mount, a mountain range in Israel that extends from above Haifa for about fifteen miles southeast to the Samaritan hill country. From the days of the Phoenicians Mount Carmel has been regarded as a holy place. Isa 35:2 speaks of the "majesty of Carmel." Mount Carmel was the site of the confrontation between Elijah and the four hundred and fifty prophets of Baal (1 Kgs 18). Prehistoric caves are along the modern Wadi el-Mugharah above the Plain of Sharon. The Carmelite order had its origins ca. 1200 in a ravine at the Wadi-'ain-es-shiah on the western slope of Mount Carmel. *See also* Carmelite order; Elijah.

Carmelite order, an order of religious whose origins go back to ca. 1200, when penitent lay hermits formed a community at the Wadi-'ain-es-shiah, a ravine on a western slope of Mount Carmel about three miles south of Haifa. Between 1206 and 1214 these hermits received from Albert, patriarch of Jerusalem, a formula of life. Its themes were a following of Jesus in a solitude supported by community (individual cells surrounding an oratory), silence, daily Eucharist when possible, continual prayer, especially the psalms, manual labor, and the usual eremitic asceticism, with no mention of pastoral ministry. The formula initiated the basic tension in Carmelite life: solitude and community. Entry into the ranks of the friars later added ministerial community to that tension. Pope Gregory IX imposed corporate poverty on the hermits. Conditions in the Latin Kingdom forced some Carmelite hermits ca. 1238 to migrate to Cyprus, Sicily, England, and southern France.

In Europe the hermits confronted a dominant religious movement, the friars. In 1247 Pope Innocent IV approved a revision of the formula (now a rule) that allowed the hermits to settle in towns, effectively enrolling the Carmelites among the mendicants. Despite internal opposition to the abandonment of the eremitic life by the prior general Nicholas the Frenchman and others, the Carmelite friars spread rapidly to the towns of Europe. By the end of the thirteenth century the Carmelites were on their way toward becoming a student order like the Dominicans and the Franciscans. The Second Council of Lyons (1274) had put the future of the Carmelites and the Augustinian Friars on hold, but both orders received approval from Pope Boniface VIII in 1298.

Mary and Elijah: The Carmelites identified themselves with the Virgin Mary from their beginnings. The oratory on Mount Carmel was dedicated to her, and the Carmelites became known as the Brothers of Our Lady of Mount Carmel, whom they saw as their patroness. Eventually July 16, the feast of Our Lady of Mount Carmel, became the patronal feast of the order. The brown scapular, worn in honor of Mary, was not part of a literary tradition till late in the Middle Ages. Without a known founder, the Carmelites learned to look to Elijah as their "father"; Mount Carmel is a location sacred to the memory of this prophet. The fourteenth century saw the elaboration of a literary tradition in which Elijah is the inspiration and "founder" of the order. Later much energy was wasted on defending a literalist interpretation of this Elijan mythology, but Teresa of Ávila and John of the Cross had a profound respect for Elijah, and the Carmelite liturgy still celebrates July 20 as his feast day. Carl Jung called Elijah a "living archetype." Modern Carmelites are exploring further this archetype of Carmelite life.

After the rule, the most crucial text in medieval Carmelite spirituality was the *Institution of the First Monks,* composed about 1370 by Philip Ribot, the provincial of Catalonia. This text describes Carmelite life as a withdrawal from ordinary activities, a purification of the heart, and union with God in love, all this seen a journey in the spirit of Elijah. These are the roots of the Carmelite mystical tradition that would flourish in the sixteenth century with Teresa of Ávila and John of the Cross and in the seventeenth century with the Touraine reform. It is likely that Teresa and John had access to the *Institution.*

Reform and the Origin of the Carmelite Nuns: During the late Middle Ages the Carmelites, like other religious orders, attempted reform. In northern Italy they banded together as the Mantuan Congregation, which affirmed the solitude of the rule, poverty, and community life and forsook Pope Eugene IV's mitigation of the rule. The Carmelites' most important reformer prior to Teresa was John Soreth (d. 1471). Under Soreth the Carmelite nuns got their start. Since the thirteenth century women

had associated themselves in various ways with the Carmelite friars, but the Carmelites did not establish a second order, of women, until 1452. With Teresa of Ávila Carmelite women became a primary manifestation of Carmelite life.

Genuine and lasting reform of Carmelite life was due to the genius of Doña Teresa de Ahumada— Teresa of Ávila (d. 1582). From an appreciation of Carmelite lore during the thirteenth century and out of her own religious experience, Teresa initiated in 1562 a series of foundations for women, small enough to ensure the solitude necessary for Carmelite contemplative life. Teresa then enlisted John of the Cross (d. 1591) as a collaborator in the reform of Carmelite women and men. However, the Discalced Carmelites became a separate order only in 1593 (O.C.D.). The original branch of the order, known as the Ancient Observance (O. Carm.), underwent a renewal in the seventeenth century called the Touraine reform, which like the Teresian reform influenced Carmelite life down to the twentieth century.

Modern Carmelites: The Carmelites underwent the same tribulations that other religious orders endured during the nineteenth century. However, two young nuns signaled with their holiness a new day for Carmelite women and men, Thérèse of Lisieux (d. 1897) and Elizabeth of the Trinity (d. 1906). In the middle of the twentieth century, Edith Stein and Titus Brandsma, both killed in Nazi concentration camps in 1942 and later beatified, manifested the vibrancy of the Carmelite charism and its call to foster a more contemplative Church. Today Carmelites of the Ancient Observance and the Discalced Carmelites have friars, nuns (Second Order), and Third Order Regular congregations of women as well as laity affiliated with their orders. The laity were known in the past as Third Order Secular Carmelites, now as lay or secular Carmelites. Most cloistered Carmelite women are under the governance of the local bishop. There is a congregation of men known as the Carmelites of the Blessed Virgin Mary the Immaculate situated in India (C.M.I.). *See also* Elizabeth of the Trinity, Bl.; hermit; John of the Cross, St.; mendicant orders; Simon Stock, St.; Stein, Bl. Edith; Teresa of Ávila, St.; Thérèse of Lisieux, St.

Bibliography

Egan, Keith J. "The Spirituality of the Carmelites." In *Christian Spirituality,* vol 2, edited by Jill Raitt. New York: Crossroad, 1987. Pp. 50–62.

————. "Carmelite Spirituality." In *The New Dictionary of Catholic Spirituality,* edited by Michael Downey. Collegeville, MN: Liturgical Press, 1993. Pp. 117–25.

Smet, Joachim. *The Carmelites: A History of the Brothers of Our Lady of Mount Carmel.* 4 vols. Darien, IL: Carmelite Spiritual Center, 1975–85. Vol. 1 revised 1988.   KEITH J. EGAN

Carmelite Sisters, an order founded by St. Berthold in about 1154 in Palestine. Permission for Carmelites to accept women into the Carmelite Second Order was granted in 1452, and the monastery of Our Lady of the Angels was founded in Florence, Italy.

The Carmelite rule demands strict poverty, a vegetarian diet, and solitude. In the sixteenth century, the demands of the Carmelite rule had become somewhat relaxed, and Teresa of Ávila, Anne of Jesus, and John of the Cross returned some of the Carmelites, then known as the Discalced, to their original severity. The Discalced Carmelites are among the best known cloistered women religious and follow a life of prayer and penance. They meditate for two hours daily and pray for priests and for the work of the Church.

The first Discalced Carmelites in the United States founded a convent at Port Tobacco, Maryland, in 1790. This convent was also the first foundation of women religious in the thirteen colonies. In addition to convents in the United States, the Discalced Carmelites have foundations around the world.

The Calced Carmelite nuns follow a "mitigated rule," less severe than that of the Discalced. They are still a cloistered order and dedicated to a contemplative life. They make altar breads and do needlework in order to support themselves, and pray in particular for priests, religious, and all in church ministries. The first United States Calced Carmelite community was founded in Allentown, Pennsylvania, in 1930. *See also* Carmelite order.

Carmelites of Mary Immaculate (C.M.I.), a Syro-Malabar Catholic religious congregation of men founded in India in 1831 by three diocesan priests, including Kuriakose Elias Chavara, under the protection of the Discalced Carmelite vicar apostolic of Verapoli (a diocese in Kerala, India), and Bernardino Baccinelli, who gave them their name and constitutions. Membership in 1994 is over one thousand men. Only about fifty serve in the United States and Canada. *See also* Carmelite order; Eastern Catholic religious.

Carmelite spirituality. *See* Carmelite order.

carnival (Lat., *carnem levare,* "put away meat"), the period of festivity prior to the beginning of Lent.

It is a custom in many Catholic countries to observe the days before Lent as a period of dancing, parties, and public parades before the penitential season begins. Carnival ends with Mardi Gras (Fr., "Fat Tuesday"), and Lent begins with Ash Wednesday.

Carolingian reform, reform of society and Church carried out in Frankish lands by Charlemagne (d. 814) and his successors. The territories Charlemagne inherited and conquered had a patchwork of laws and traditions. To provide some structure to hold these realms together, he and his successors and their supporters reshaped the institutions of government and reformed the life of the Church. In the reign of Charlemagne's father, Chrodegang had already provided a rule for diocesan clergy. Later ecclesiastical reforms included a monastic revival, displacement of the Gallican liturgy by the Roman, establishment of a new provincial and diocesan structure (accompanied by development of the parish), provision of an educated clergy, and legislation for collection of the tithe. *See also* Charlemagne.

Carpatho-Russian Catholics. *See* Ruthenian Catholic Church.

Carroll, Charles, 1737–1832, American Catholic statesman. Born in Annapolis, Maryland, and educated in Europe, he was probably the richest man in the colonies. He induced Maryland Catholics, through his debate with the Tory Daniel Dulany in 1773, to espouse the patriot cause. As a representative of Maryland, he was the only Catholic to sign the Declaration of Independence. He helped frame the state constitution guaranteeing religious freedom and, as a Federalist, was one of the two senators sent by Maryland to the first Congress in 1789. Active in industry and agriculture, an original director of the Baltimore & Ohio Railroad, he died at the age of ninety-five.

Carroll, Daniel, 1730–96, American Catholic statesman. The older brother of Archbishop John Carroll, he was educated by the Jesuits in Maryland and France. A wealthy planter and merchant, he was elected frequently to the state senate and twice to the Continental Congress. He was (with Thomas FitzSimons) one of two Catholics to help frame and sign the United States Constitution and was one of the original six members elected to the House of Representatives from Maryland. Appointed by President George Washington, he was the most active commissioner in planning the national capital.

Carroll, John, 1736–1815, first Catholic bishop in the United States. Born in Upper Marlboro, Maryland, educated at Jesuit academies in Maryland and France, he entered the Society of Jesus in 1753 and was ordained a priest in 1761. With the suppression of the Jesuits in 1773 he returned to Maryland to serve as a missionary. In 1776 he was chosen by the Continental Congress to accompany a mission to Canada. In 1783 Carroll took the lead in organizing the Catholic clergy in the United States and in 1784 was chosen by Rome as superior of the American mission. When the Holy See allowed the clergy to elect a bishop, the lot fell to Carroll and Baltimore was named in the pontifical brief *Ex Hac Apostolicae* of November 6, 1789, the first Catholic see in the United States. Carroll was ordained bishop at Lulworth Castle in England on August 15, 1790.

In 1791 Carroll held the only synod of his twenty-five year episcopacy. He played a leading role in the founding of Georgetown College and St. Mary's Seminary in 1791, the first Catholic university and seminary in the new nation. Under him were also established the Carmelite and Visitation nuns and the Sisters of Charity. In 1805 he negotiated the restoration of the Society of Jesus in the United States. He was also active in the creation of many secular institutions and organizations devoted to education

John Carroll, first bishop of the U.S. Catholic Church, appointed to the see of Baltimore in 1789; undated engraving.

and philanthropy, the Library Company of Baltimore being the one of which he was proudest.

Carroll published frequently in his early years when he was concerned about presenting Catholics and Catholic belief in a favorable light to Protestant Americans. His most ambitious literary effort was *An Address to the Roman Catholics in the United States* (1784).

Carroll encouraged lay trustees to build churches, and despite the problems visited upon him by several bodies of trustees who sought to usurp the bishop's authority over the temporal affairs of the Church—in New York, Philadelphia, Charleston, and even Baltimore—he never repudiated the system.

To Carroll had fallen the awesome task of adjusting an ancient faith to a new political order, which he accomplished with remarkable serenity and skill. He was architect of the Maryland tradition in American Catholicism: in his devotion to American principles, such as religious freedom and separation of Church and state, his broad ecumenism, his strong sense of public service, and the measure of independence he exercised in his relations with the Holy See while manifesting a strong attachment to the person of the pope as a symbol of unity. He was esteemed by Catholics and Protestants alike. *See also* United States of America, Catholicism in the.   THOMAS SPALDING

Carta Caritatis (kahr'tah kahr-ee-tah'tis; Lat., "Charter of Charity"), constitution of the Cistercian order presented to Pope Callistus II in 1119 and finalized ca. 1155. Often attributed to Stephen Harding (d. 1134), abbot of Cîteaux, it is probably the result of his work as well as years of practice within the order itself. *See also* Cistercian order.

Carthage, former Phoenician colony in North Africa destroyed and then rebuilt by Rome, influential center of early Latin Christianity. Renowned for its martyrs, Perpetua and companions in 203 and Cyprian, martyr bishop in 258, Carthage experienced a lively and sophisticated church life reflected in the works of Tertullian in the first decades of the third century. It also hosted many Church councils of the mid-third century and was the locale of the disputed election of Caelician (311) in the aftermath of the Diocletian persecution. The resulting schism between Donatists and Catholics was not resolved for more than a century, even after the Council of Carthage (411) under the leadership of Augustine. Carthage fell to the Vandal invaders (439) under their king, Genseric. The Catholics were restored when the Arian Vandals were conquered by the Byzantine general, Belisarius (534), but the virtual end of Christianity in Carthage was signalled by the destruction of the city (698) by Islamic forces under the Arab general, Hassan ibn Al-Numan. *See also* Africa, the Church in Roman; Cyprian of Carthage, St., Donatism.

Carthusian order (O. Cart.), an order of men and women that emphasizes solitude and silence in the search of God in the context of monastic community. Fidelity to its eremitic ideals has led to this Carthusian boast: "They have never been reformed because they have never been deformed." Through the centuries this life of solitude elicited profound respect from deeply religious figures like William of Saint-Thierry, who, after a visit to the Charterhouse of Mont-Dieu, admiringly dedicated to them his enormously popular *Golden Letter;* Thomas More, who lived at the London Charterhouse for four years; John of the Cross, who wanted to leave the Carmelites for the Carthusians until Teresa of Ávila persuaded him otherwise; David Knowles, who composed some of his finest prose in honor of the London Carthusians martyred under Henry VIII; and Thomas Merton, who pondered departure from the Trappists so that he could become a Carthusian monk.

Origins: In 1084 Bruno (1030–1101), born at Cologne and dean of the cathedral school at Rheims, founded the Carthusians at a deserted and remote place in the Chartreuse mountain area in the French Alps about thirty miles from Grenoble. This monastery has been known as La Grande Chartreuse and is to this day the motherhouse of the Carthusians. Bruno, who founded another monastery in Calabria, wrote no rule since he wished his followers to follow the Benedictine rule. Bruno's writings and those of Guigo I (1109–36), the fifth prior of La Grande Chartreuse, are the foundational documents of the Carthusians and orient the order to a solitude that is for the sake of being alone with God. Guigo's *Customs*, a description of practice rather than proposed ideals, has served since its composition as the basic legislation governing Carthusian life. Guigo was a friend of Bernard of Clairvaux and Peter the Venerable. The order reached its peak of expansion at the time of the Reformation.

Women became Carthusians about 1145, when an ancient monastery of nuns at Prebayon, near Orange, France, impressed by the holiness of the

Carthusian life, requested that they be affiliated with the order. Carthusian women lead an austere, simple, eremitic life of prayer within community structures like those of the men. Once she is finally professed and has completed her twenty-fifth year, a Carthusian nun may receive the rite of Virginal Consecration, which makes her a witness to the spousal relationship of Christ with the Church.

The supreme authority in the Carthusian order is the general chapter held at La Grande Chartreuse, whose prior is the minister general of the order. In the local charterhouses, the name for Carthusian monasteries, the officers are prior, vicar, procurator, and novice master with feminine variants for the nuns.

Setting and Life-style: The buildings at charterhouses are arranged to ensure a contemplative solitude. The cloister monks live in individual hermitages along a cloister that leads to the communal areas of the monastery. A hermitage of a cloister monk has an enclosed garden and is usually a two-story structure with four rooms where the monk spends most of his day. On the first story there is a workshop and an area for the storage of wood. On the second floor is a small Hail Mary room, so called because the monk pauses here to recite this prayer. The next room is where the cloister monk prays alone at an oratory, studies alone at a desk with bookshelf, and eats alone at a dining table. A large window in this room invites the monk to contemplate God's creation. Cloister monks are ordained to the priesthood but do not engage in ministry outside the monastery. Brothers, who are full members of this contemplative community, spend more time in manual labor than do the cloister monks. The brothers live in cells with workshops nearby. Besides these two categories of Carthusian life there are donate brothers, who have fewer obligations than the others and make a promise rather than take vows. The Carthusian nuns have the following forms of membership: choir religious, lay religious, and donate sisters.

The genius of Carthusian life lies in its unique and happy combination of communal gatherings and solitude. The community activities prevent solitude from degenerating into individualism and harmful isolation. Common areas of the monastery include the church, chapterhouse, refectory, and library. Community is further fostered by walks together through the countryside. The cloister monks take a long walk once a week. The brothers, who in their work share more of a common life, do so once a month. Twice each year the walk lasts a whole day.

Liturgy: The Carthusians have a distinctive rite that originated with the liturgy of Lyons used in the twelfth century in the diocese of Grenoble. The Carthusian liturgy is simple and sober, as befits an order committed to solitude and silence. The Carthusians recite much of the Divine Office in their hermitages but gather in the middle of the night to chant Matins and Lauds. On Sundays and special feast days more of the Office is recited in common. Carthusians have special devotion to Mary. Each day they recite the Office of the Blessed Virgin.

Despite the anonymity of their life, a number of Carthusians have become well-known authors. Besides Bruno and Guigo I, there were Guigo II (d. 1188), who composed the widely read *Ladder of Monks;* Ludolph of Saxony (d. 1378), author of a very influential *Life of Christ;* and Denis the Carthusian (d. 1471), prolific author whose mystical writings became very popular. The Carthusian libraries have been unique depositories of spiritual writings that have enriched both the monks and those for whom Carthusians have written.

The Charterhouse of the Transfiguration, Arlington, Vermont, is the only Carthusian monastery of men in North America. A handful of Carthusian monasteries of women exist in Italy, France, and Spain. *See also* Bruno Hartenfaust, St.; John of the Cross, St.; Knowles, David; Merton, Thomas; More, St. Thomas; William of Saint-Thierry.   *KEITH J. EGAN*

Carthusian spirituality. *See* Carthusian order.

Casanova, St. Leonard, also known as Leonard of Port Maurice, 1676–1751, patron saint of parish missions. An Italian Franciscan, he preached missions and retreats throughout Italy and was an ardent promoter of the Stations of the Cross devotion. Feast day: November 26.

Casel, Odo (oh'doh cas'uhl), 1886–1948, liturgical scholar and theologian. A Benedictine monk of Maria Laach and a major theologian of the twentieth-century liturgical movement, he elaborated a "theology of mystery" that understood the liturgy, especially the Mass, as the Church's representation of the Paschal Mystery. *See also* mystery; Paschal Mystery.

Casimir, St., 1458–84, patron saint of Poland and Lithuania. A member of the Polish royal family, he led a life of prayer, devotion to charity, and penance, resisting his family's desire that he marry. He died in Lithuania while on a royal visit and was buried in Vilna, where his tomb was much venerated. He was canonized in 1522. Feast day: March 4. *See also* Baltic Countries, Catholicism in the; Poland, Catholicism in.

Cassian, St. John, ca. 365–ca. 435, one of the most important early monastic figures in the West. Formerly a monk in Bethlehem and Egypt and deacon in Constantinople, he established two monasteries near Marseilles ca. 415. His *Institutes* and *Conferences,* expositions of Egyptian monasticism, strongly influenced the Rule of St. Benedict. Feast day: July 23. *See also* Benedict, Rule of St.

Cassiodorus, Flavius Magnus Aurelius (cas-ee-oh-dohr'uhs), ca. 485–ca. 580, statesman, scholar, and monastic founder. Cassiodorus served several Ostrogothic kings of Italy; after the collapse of their kingdom, he founded a monastery called Vivarium. His many translations and commentaries, along with the community library and scriptorium, were meant to preserve classical and Christian learning.

cassock, straight, ankle-length robe with long

Cassock

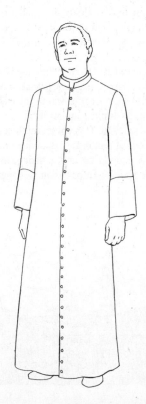

sleeves traditionally worn by clergy as ordinary dress and under their liturgical vestments. Color and trim indicate rank. The pope wears white; cardinals wear black with scarlet trim; bishops wear black with red trim; and priests wear solid black. Priests who belong to a religious community wear the habit proper to their community, instead of the cassock. The use of the cassock has declined since the Second Vatican Council (1962–65).

Castel Gandolfo, hill town on the shore of Lake Albano eighteen miles southeast of Rome. Named for an early medieval family (Gandulfi) who had a fortress (It., *castello*) there, the town is now best known for a villa commissioned by Pope Urban VIII and designed by Carlo Maderno (ca. 1629–30) that is the summer residence of the pope.

In 1930 the Vatican Observatory moved its telescope from the Vatican to the summer villa where the astronomical observatory still remains under the supervision of the Jesuits.

The entire estate, together with the papal villa, belongs to the Vatican City State and, hence, is considered by the Italian government to enjoy extra territorial status. *See also* Vatican City State.

Casti Connubii (kah'stee kah-noo'bee-ee; Lat., "pure marriage"), "On Christian Marriage," encyclical letter of Pope Pius XI issued in 1930 affirming the Christian doctrine of marriage as chaste, monogamous, and faithful, emulating the Church's relationship to Christ. The encyclical's strong condemnation of contraception was the official Catholic response to its limited approval by the Lambeth Conference of 1930. This encyclical, together with the 1917 Code of Canon Law, is credited with introducing as a secondary end of marriage the mutual help of the spouses (procreation was the primary

A papal audience at Castel Gandolfo, the pope's summer residence in the hills just outside of Rome.

end). *Casti Connubii* inspired moral theologians to begin reflecting on the significance of marital love in assessing the morality of sexual acts, particularly contraception, which was then generally considered to be violative of both the primary and secondary ends of marriage. *See also* birth control.

casuistry (Lat., *casus,* "a case"), the method of bringing general moral principles or norms to bear on particular cases for the purposes of informing conscience and guiding conduct. Such attention to the circumstantial features of moral action has long been a part of Christian moral inquiry, a natural consequence of the ongoing attempt to apply the broad scriptural imperatives of love and forgiveness, and the abstract precepts of natural and divine law, to the specific situations of everyday life. Early examples of casuistry may be found in the NT (cf. Mark 2:23–28; Luke 20:20–26; 1 Cor 7–8), and among early Christian writers (cf. Tertullian, *On Spectacles;* Augustine, *On Lying*); however, casuistry as a formal system developed only after the emergence and subsequent ecclesiastical regulation of universal private penance from the seventh to tenth centuries. Following the mandates of the Fourth Lateran Council (1215), making annual confession obligatory, and the Council of Trent (1551), requiring penitents to confess sins with respect to kind, number, and circumstance, specific courses in and manuals of "cases of conscience" were developed to train clerics charged with the pastoral duty of hearing confessions. With only slight modification this approach characterized Catholic moral theology until the Second Vatican Council (1962–65). Historically, casuistry has been criticized for, on the one hand, its tendency to moral laxism, and, on the other hand, a hairsplitting scrupulosity, Pascal's *Provincial Letters* (1656–57) giving voice most famously to the former. Recent moral theology has stressed the importance of biblical, systematic, and spiritual theology as the indispensible contexts for a casuistic approach. *See also* moral theology.

catacomb art, decoration, mainly painting and incising on marble, found in the underground Christian cemeteries of antiquity. Of uneven artistic quality, the painting, epigraphy, and artifacts are valuable clues to early Christian beliefs. The scientific study of catacomb art began in the nineteenth century when Christian archaeology gained prominence. *See also* archaeology, Christian.

Mural depicting Christ's multiplication of the loaves; Catacomb of St. Callistus, Rome.

The Catacomb of Pope St. Callistus I, on the Appian Way outside of Rome; the oldest surviving catacomb.

catacombs, subterranean cemeteries constructed by Christians from about the late second to the early fifth centuries. Although there were catacombs elsewhere, the majority are in Italy, and especially Rome, where several hundred miles of catacombs survive. Cemeteries were required by law to be outside city living quarters, and thus the catacombs were constructed along the roads leading to the city, especially in the north and southeast, in layers of soft clay rock called *tufa.* Since all burial places were protected by law, the catacombs were free from molestation and developed into an elaborate system of galleries, rooms, and corridors, dug and maintained at Church expense. Niches for tombs were cut into, and parallel to, the walls. Occasionally there were burials in the floors or, for prominent Christians, in tombs placed in recesses carved out of the walls. Many of the catacombs were adorned with frescos. Shafts admitted light and air, an especially important feature as the popularity of eucharistic celebrations at the tombs of the martyrs grew (fourth century).

The oldest surviving catacomb is that of St. Callistus on the Appian Way, part of which, including the Crypt of the Popes, dates from the late second and early third centuries. Use of the catacombs for burial stopped after the Gothic invasions of the fifth century began to make burial outside the walls impractical. By the ninth century, most of the relics of the martyrs had been translated to churches, and the existence of the catacombs was forgotten until 1578. They remain a remarkable testimony to the determination of the early Church to afford all of its members a decent burial, wealthy and indigent alike. *See also* burial, Christian.   *JOHN C. CAVADINI*

catafalque (kah-tah-fawlk'; Lat., *catafalicum,* "siege-tower"), the stand or framework supporting the coffin at funerals. It is another name of the *castrumdoloris,* the middle coffin (of three) in which the pope is buried. The catafalque is placed outside the sanctuary of the church, and the coffin is covered with a white pall symbolizing the white robe of baptism. *See also* funeral mass.

catechesis (Gk., *katechein,* "to echo"), a ministry of the word (Dogmatic Constitution on Divine Revelation, n. 24). Originally the term applied to the oral instruction given adults and children before Baptism (Acts 18:25; Rom 2:18; Gal. 6:6). *Sharing the Light of Faith: The National Catechetical Directory* (1979) refers to catechesis as "the efforts which help individuals and communities acquire and deepen Christian faith and identity through initiation rites, instruction, and formation of conscience. It includes both the message presented and the way in which it is presented" (n. 5). More than the acquisition of knowledge, catechesis involves awakening, nourishing, and developing faith. Although this ministry is normally exercised by specially designated and trained individuals, it is ultimately the responsibility of the whole faith community. *See also* religious education.

catechetics (Gk., *katechein,* "to echo"), a systematic study of catechesis. The words "catechesis" and "catechetics" are often used interchangeably.

However, catechesis refers to the process of forming one in a faith community, while catechetics is the study of how to do catechesis. Catechesis can be found in the NT; catechetics emerged only in the twentieth century. With Vatican II's richer understanding of revelation (Dogmatic Constitution on Divine Revelation), the catechist's responsibility broadened. No longer is catechesis simply involved with a deductive passing on of the deposit of faith. Catechists need to be trained in the human as well as the ecclesiastical sciences.

Progress in interdisciplinary fields during the twentieth century had a tremendous effect on catechetics. The works of Joseph Jungmann, Johannes Hofinger, D. S. Amalorpavadass, Pierre-André Liégé, and Francis H. Drinkwater helped reclaim the centrality of the liturgy for catechesis. The developmental theories of Jean Piaget, Erik Erikson, Lawrence Kohlberg, and James Fowler helped to determine the appropriate ages for the distribution of doctrinal material. A praxis method of education, based on experiential and inductive learning, forms the basis of mainline catechetical texts. The acknowledgment that the goal of catechesis goes beyond the mere acquisition of knowledge to a living, conscious, and active faith (*Sharing the Light of Faith: The National Catechical Directory,* n. 32) demands an awareness of and involvement in the social, moral, and public life of the faith community.

During the second half of the twentieth century graduate programs in religious studies at Catholic universities and colleges began to offer professional degrees to people preparing for catechetical ministry. Diocesan offices were established for the sole purpose of directing catechetical ministries, and parishes made commitments to the ongoing formation of its catechists as well as of adults in general. *See also* religious education.   BEVERLY M. BRAZAUSKAS

catechism (Gk., *katechein,* "to echo"), a manual of religious instruction using simple language and a question-and-answer format. According to the *General Catechetical Directory,* its object is "to convey in summary and practical form the documents of revelation and of Christian tradition, as well as the main elements which must be of service for catechetical activity, that is, for personal education in the faith" (n. 119). After the Reformation and with the invention of the printing press, catechisms became the primary tool and method of religious instruction until recent times. Emphasis was placed on the role of the intellect and on memorization. The material was sequentially organized by creed, commandments, and sacraments. The best-known example in the United States is the *Baltimore Catechism,* originally commissioned by the bishops in 1885. A *Catechism of the Catholic Church* was released by the Vatican in 1992. *See also* Baltimore Catechism.

Catechism of the Catholic Church, also known as the Universal Catechism, a compendium of Catholic teaching originally published in French, with the approval of Pope John Paul II, on October 11, 1992. It was prepared by a papal commission of twelve cardinals and bishops, under the direction of Cardinal Joseph Ratzinger, head of the Congregation for the Doctrine of the Faith. The Catechism is intended to guide bishops in formulating local catechetical programs. It is divided into four parts: Profession of Faith, the Celebration of the Christian Mystery, Life in Christ, and Christian Prayer. Emphasis is placed respectively on the Apostles' Creed, the seven sacraments, the Ten Commandments, and the Lord's Prayer.

The document originated after the 1971 publication of the General Catechetical Directory, which some cardinals considered too vague. In 1986, Pope John Paul II appointed the commission, which submitted a provisional text to the world's bishops in 1989. The draft met with considerable criticism during the review period because its content seemed not to reflect recent developments in theology and biblical studies. Various revisions were initiated in response to these criticisms. The official English translation, originally scheduled for publication in 1993, was delayed until 1994 largely because of objections from some conservative Catholics that the translation reflected too much sensitivity to feminist concerns.

catechist (Gk., *katechein,* "to echo"), someone commissioned by the Church "to hand down" its faith tradition. Although parents, parish priests, and the faith community at large are to be engaged in catechesis, the term "catechist" usually refers to the designated and specially trained person who introduces catechumens, candidates, and/or young people to the faith.

catechumen (Gk., *katechein,* "to echo"), an unbaptized person undergoing instruction and formation in preparation for Baptism. An inquirer, after hearing the mystery of Christ proclaimed (evangelization), embraces a process of conversion leading to Christian initiation (catechumenate). A catechumen enters into a formation period with other catechumens and members of a faith community. This period provides the catechumen with time to experience and learn about the Christian life. Among those related to the catechumen during this period are a godparent, sponsor, catechist, pastor, and, most importantly, the faith community itself. The term "catechumen" is strictly reserved for those who are unbaptized; those already baptized and seeking full communion are called "candidates." *See also* Rite of Christian Initiation of Adults.

catechumenate (Gk., *katechein*, "to echo"), the second period in the process of Christian initiation. After a period of initial inquiry about the faith, interested persons publicly state their intention before the Church and become catechumens. It is at this time that they are "joined to the Church and are part of the household of Christ" (*Rite of Christian Initiation of Adults*, n. 18) and enter the catechumenate. This rite, also known as the RCIA, was restored in 1972, in accordance with the mandate of the Second Vatican Council (Constitution on the Sacred Liturgy, n. 64) and by decree of Pope Paul VI.

During the catechumenate catechumens not only study the doctrines of the faith but are introduced to the prayer life and apostolic works of the community. It is formation in the whole of Christian life. Catechumens are assigned sponsors who assist them in the process of initiation by praying with and for them, accompanying them to various activities, as well as answering their many questions. At their regular sessions they are introduced to the person of Jesus Christ and to conversion to a Gospel life-style through scriptural studies and prayer. In addition to the lectionary, the Creed and the Lord's Prayer constitute the content of catechesis during this period.

Since they are as yet unable to share fully in the eucharistic banquet, catechumens are usually dismissed from the Sunday assembly after the Liturgy of the Word and prior to the Liturgy of the Eucharist. They depart to continue their study of the lectionary.

There is no determined length for the catechumenate. The process continues until the catechumens are ready to request Baptism and the Church is willing to accept them. At that point they celebrate the rite of election and enter the period of election, usually coinciding with the season of Lent. *See also* Rite of Christian Initiation of Adults.

BEVERLY M. BRAZAUSKAS

Cathari (Gk., *katharos*, "pure, clean"), general definition for various sects, including Novatianists, Manichaeans, and especially dualist heretics in southern France and northern Italy active between the twelfth and fourteenth centuries, known also in France as Albigensians. Cathar dualism expressed itself in two forms: "absolute" dualism, which claimed the existence of two rival and eternal powers of Good/Spirit and Evil/Matter, and "mitigated" dualism, which claimed that Evil/Matter was inferior to and would be overcome by the Good/Spirit. Critical of the Church, which it viewed as corrupt, the medieval Cathari were eventually overcome by preaching, a crusade against them, and the Inquisition. *See also* Albigensians; dualism.

Catharinus, Ambrosius [Lancelot of Politi], ca. 1484–1553, Italian Dominican theologian and bishop active at the Council of Trent from 1545–1547. One of the earliest and most prolific Catholic opponents of Martin Luther, he emphasized the teaching authority of the Church and a reliance on Scripture and early Christian authors.

cathedra (kath-ay'drah; Lat., "chair"), technical term for an episcopal throne and, by extension, episcopal authority. It is also used, less frequently, to refer to the academic chair held by a professor. A diocesan bishop's church is called a cathedral because it houses his episcopal chair. *See also* cathedral.

cathedral (Lat., *cathedra*, "chair") the church where the bishop presides over the liturgy and, by symbolic extension, over his diocese. So named for the chair where the bishop exercises his authority, the cathedral in time became the locus of episcopal administration. His supporting clergy became part of the cathedral staff as canons who had certain responsibilities for divine worship. The position of canon never became customary in the United States.

With the reemergence of cities in the Middle Ages, cathedrals became great centers of urban life (e.g., the Gothic cathedrals of the Ile de France) and the place where schools were erected and maintained. Today, cathedrals are usually conspicuous for their size and central locations, although in some places other churches overshadow cathedrals; in Rome St. Peter's Basilica is far better known than the cathedral of St. John Lateran. *See also* basilica.

cathedral chapter, the body of diocesan priests, known as canons, responsible for the spiritual and temporal concerns of the diocesan cathedral. The cathedral chapter was for the most part a European institution with origins in the Merovingian period (ca. eighth century); its authority, not only over the cathedral but over the diocese itself, was considerable by the time of the Council of Trent (1545–63). The members of the chapter, for example, governed the diocese during a vacancy of the see and served as electors of the diocesan bishop. One member of the chapter has always had an important spiritual function, namely, the canon penitentiary, with the power to absolve from automatic censures (Lat., *latae sententiae*) that are not reserved to the Holy See, e.g., the procuring of an abortion. In dioceses where there is no cathedral chapter, the bishop is required by canon law to appoint a diocesan priest to fulfill this function (can. 508.2). Even in dioceses that have a cathedral chapter, a college of consultors is to be established (can. 502). *See also* chapter; consultors, college of.

cathedraticum, the tax that was to be paid by parishes to the bishop under the 1917 code of canon law. According to that code, it was to be a sign of submission to the authority of the bishop, and as such was mainly a symbolic gesture. In some dioceses, however, it developed into a larger financial payment. The 1983 code allows bishops to impose a moderate tax for diocesan needs, but "only after hearing the diocesan finance council and the presbyteral council" (can. 1263).

Catherine Labouré, St. *See* Labouré, St. Catherine.

Catherine of Alexandria, St., d. ca. 310, patron saint of philosophers, young unmarried women, preachers, nurses, and craftsmen, and one of the Fourteen Holy Helpers, a group of saints notable for their answering of prayers, especially for cures from disease and at the hour of death. Venerated in the East since the ninth century, Catherine's life is largely a matter of legend. Joan of Arc was thought to have heard Catherine's voice. Upon Catherine's death by beheading, after a wheel of torture (known as Catherine's wheel) broke, her body was supposedly carried by angels to Mount Sinai. She is widely depicted in painting, stained glass windows, literature, and other art forms. Feast day: November 25 (dropped from the liturgical calender in 1969).

Catherine of Bologna, St., also known as Catherine de'Vigri, 1413–63, patron saint of artists. A member of the Poor Clares, she is said to have experienced visions of Christ and Satan. Her vision of Mary with the infant Jesus in her arms has been reproduced often in art. Feast day: March 9.

Catherine of Genoa, St., 1447–1510, Italian mystic. Born Caterinetta Fieschi, she underwent a spiritual conversion as a married laywoman in 1473. Henceforth, she devoted her life to serving the poor and sick in a Genovese hospital. Her spiritual teachings concern the purification of the soul. Feast day: September 15.

Catherine of Siena, St., 1347–80, mystical writer and Doctor of the Church. Born in Siena, Italy, she

Catherine of Siena, one of the few women to have been named a Doctor of the Church and who played an important role in resolving the Great Schism of the fourteenth century, depicted here receiving the stigmata; sixteenth-century painting by Domenico Beccafumi, National Gallery, Siena, Italy.

experienced her first mystical vision at the age of seven and soon after pledged virginity to Jesus. Young Catherine spent many hours in prayer at home and frequently attended morning Mass in the neighboring church of St. Dominic. As Catherine reached adolescence, her family arranged suitors for her. When she declined marriage, her family discharged the domestic help and assigned Catherine excessive household duties that curtailed her prayer. One day, while Catherine stole away from chores to pray in her room, her father reported seeing a dove hover over her head. Taking this as a sign from heaven, her father permitted Catherine to live the life of prayer and fasting which she desired. In 1365 she received the Dominican habit and continued to live a life of seclusion in the family home. In 1368, during a mystical vision, she became espoused to Christ and received a mandate to undertake an apostolic life. Catherine cared for the sick at La Scala Hospital and visited prisoners on death row, accompanying them to the gallows. She trained a growing company of disciples, some of whom were priests. Around 1370 she began a cycle of letters of spiritual instruction, which gradually evolved into a critique of political and ecclesial conditions. She favored a crusade against the Turks and lamented the clergy's low standard of morality. The Dominicans summoned her to a general chapter in 1374 to defend her public profile. Having proved her position, the chapter appointed Raymond of Capua as her director. With Raymond she preached a crusade of repentance throughout Italy. While preaching at Pisa in 1375 Catherine stopped to pray in the Church of St. Christina. There, while she knelt before the crucifix, Christ spoke to Catherine and she received the stigmata, bleeding wounds similar to those of the crucified Christ. Between 1376 and 1378 she mediated a treaty between Florence and the papacy. In June of 1376 she also met with Pope Gregory XI at Avignon, France, to convince him to return the papal court to Rome. For seven generations French popes ruled the Church from the royal palaces of Avignon. Although Gregory reinstated the Curia at Rome, he died before he could return.

Between 1377 and 1378, amid much unrest, Catherine composed *The Dialogue*, a book describing her understanding of the Church and the sacraments. The basic theme of her spirituality was the creative and saving love of God, symbolized by the Blood of Jesus.

During the reign of Gregory's successor, Urban VI, there was a dual papacy in Rome and Avignon. In November 1378, Urban VI summoned Catherine to Rome to negotiate an end to the Great Schism. Catherine traveled with her companions to Rome and lodged next to the Church of the Minerva, but the arduous journey so weakened her health that she spent her last months in great suffering. In imitation of Jesus she offered her pain as an immolation for others. She was declared a Doctor of the Church in 1970. Feast day: April 29. *See also* Avignon; Dominican spirituality.   PATRICIA M. VINJE

Catherine Tekakwitha, Bl. *See* Tekakwitha, Bl. Kateri.

Catholic (Gk., *katholikos,* "universal"; adverbial phrase, *kath' holou,* "on the whole"), member of the Catholic Church. The term, first used in Christian literature by Ignatius of Antioch (d. ca. 107) in his *Letter to the Smyrnaeans* (n. 8.2), refers also to the Catholic Church itself as well as to the orthodox faith that is embraced and proclaimed by Catholics. The word is commonly used in opposition to "Protestant," but is, in fact, more directly opposed to "sectarian," which pertains to a part of the Church that has separated itself from the worldwide Church and from the world itself.

Thus, Augustine of Hippo (d. 430) contrasted the separatist and sectarian movements of his time, especially Donatism, with the Catholic Church that is both universal and orthodox in its faith. In his letter to Honoratus, a Donatist bishop, he wrote: "Do you happen to know why it should be that Christ should lose his inheritance, which is spread over the whole world, and should suddenly be found surviving only in the Africans, and not in all of them? The Catholic Church exists indeed in Africa, since God willed and ordained that it should exist throughout the whole world. Whereas your party, which is called the party of Donatus, does not exist in all those places in which the writings of the apostles, their discourse, and their actions have been current" (*Epistle 49,* n. 3).

Cyril of Jerusalem (d. 386) was even more explicit: "The Church is called 'Catholic' because it extends through all the world . . . because it teaches universally and without omission all the doctrines which ought to come to man's knowledge . . . because it brings under the sway of true religion all classes of men, rulers, and subjects, learned and ignorant;

and because it universally treats and cures every type of sin . . . and possesses in itself every kind of virtue which can be named . . . and spiritual gifts of every kind" (*Catechetical Lectures* 18. 23).

The word "Catholic" was incorporated into the creeds along with the other notes of the Church: one, holy, and apostolic. It appears in the Creed of Cyril of Jerusalem, the Creed of Epiphanius, and, of course, in the Nicene-Constantinopolitan Creed that is still recited in the liturgy today.

However, the use of the word "Catholic" became divisive after the East-West Schism of the eleventh century and the Protestant Reformation of the sixteenth. The West claimed for itself the title Catholic Church, while the East, which broke the bonds of unity with Rome, appropriated the name Holy Orthodox Church. After the Reformation split, those in communion with Rome retained the adjective Catholic, while the churches that broke with the papacy were called Protestant. Some of them now insist that the adjective "Catholic" applies also to many other Christians who regard themselves as evangelical, reformed, and Catholic alike.

The Second Vatican Council (1962–65) broadened the notion of catholicity to include churches outside the Catholic Church (Dogmatic Constitution on the Church, n. 8), and spoke of them as possessing varying "degrees" of catholicity (Decree on Ecumenism, n. 3). *See also* Catholic Church; Catholicism.

RICHARD P. MCBRIEN

Catholic, life of a, how an ordinary Catholic experiences the reality of Catholicism from Baptism to death. Since Catholicism is essentially a sacramental religion, the ordinary Catholic's life is shaped and framed in large measure, but not exclusively, by the reception of the sacraments.

Most Catholics are baptized in infancy, usually a few weeks or months after birth. In their early childhood years they receive rudimentary instruction in their faith from their parents, usually through teachings of, and about, familiar rituals (the sign of the cross), symbols (crucifixes, medals, holy cards), and prayers (Lord's Prayer, Hail Mary), through attendance at Mass, and through explanations and stories evoked by holy pictures and books portraying Jesus, the saints, and various Bible stories. Around the age of seven, also known as the "age of reason," a young Catholic begins a year-long instruction in preparation for the reception of First Holy Communion. In most cases, the parents are also involved, or should be, in the process of preparing their children for First Penance, or Confession, and Confirmation. The children continue their religious instruction and formation in parish religious education classes or in parochial school. Between the ages of twelve and sixteen most receive the sacrament of Confirmation, after which many tend to disengage from formal religious education. Others continue through parish programs for high-school students and in Catholic high schools. At varying ages a Catholic will enter into marriage, receiving the sacrament of Matrimony after a period of formal preparation. A few will enter a religious community of women or men, and others will enter a seminary to study for the ordained priesthood. In the normal course of events, a young Catholic seminarian will receive the sacrament of Holy Orders around age twenty-five. As the young married couple begins to raise a family, they reenter the process of preparing for Baptism, Reconciliation, First Eucharist, and Confirmation by participating in their own children's process of instruction and formation. Throughout the years the ordinary Catholic will have the Eucharist at the center of his or her religious life. The Eucharist is, according to the Second Vatican Council (1962–65), the summit and the fountain of the whole Christian life (Constitution on the Sacred Liturgy, n. 10).

When serious sickness enters individuals' lives, the Church offers them yet another sacrament, the Sacrament of the Anointing of the Sick, formerly known as Extreme Unction (Lat., "last anointing"). The last sacrament in actuality, however, is Viaticum (Lat., lit., "on the way with you," "[food] for a journey"), the final reception of the Eucharist, or Holy Communion, before death.

Many other Catholics enter the Church at a later age. They are traditionally called "converts." Oftentimes, a non-Catholic decides to become a Catholic because of his or her marriage to a Catholic and the desire to share fully in the religious experience of the spouse and children. Those who enter the Catholic Church later in life do so through the Rite of Christian Initiation of Adults (RCIA), restored by Pope Paul VI in 1972 under mandate from the Second Vatican Council.

Many Catholics serve in various ministerial roles throughout their lives: as young altar servers at Mass, as lectors (readers of Scripture at Mass), ministers of the Eucharist (distributors of Holy Communion under the species of both bread and wine), directors of religious education (DRE's), catechists, youth ministers, ministers to the elderly, permanent deacons, and the like. Whether one is ordained, religiously professed, or lay makes no difference. "Everything" that the Second Vatican Council said about the nature and responsibilities of the People of God "applies equally to the laity, religious, and clergy" (Dogmatic Constitution on the Church, n. 30).

In the final analyis, however, Catholic life isn't just about sacramental and ministerial life within the Church. It is about life in the world beyond the Church, and especially about fidelity to the gospel as it applies to our relationships with one another. Catholics are called to a life of justice and compassion, honesty and courage, peacemaking and forgiveness. The ordinary Catholic finds enough guidance for a lifetime not only in the gospel but in the social teachings of the Church as well. *See also* Catholic social teachings; religious education; Rite of Christian Initiation of Adults; sacrament; sacramentals.

RICHARD P. MCBRIEN

Catholic Action, a movement of Catholic laity first suggested by Pope Pius X and actively encouraged by Pope Pius XI in his 1931 encyclical *Quadragesimo Anno.* This pope sought "the participation of the laity in the apostolate of the hierarchy" in order to turn society back to its Christian foundations. Pius XI envisioned nonpolitical organized lay works directed toward the reform of society through legislation and institutional reconstruction.

In the United States there were many organizations that participated in this movement and that were distinguished by their reliance upon the hierarchy. Closely associated with clerical control were organizations such as the National Councils of Catholic Men and Women and the Confraternity of Christian Doctrine, which bishops mandated for their respective dioceses. The Legion of Decency (1934) evaluated the moral content of motion pictures and recommended what was suitable for Catholic viewing. The Sodality of the Blessed Virgin, the Catholic Interracial Councils, and Serra International existed with hierarchical approval, but without direct charter from the local ordinary.

Often inspired by European movements, more autonomous associations also emerged and were promoted by priests such as Raymond A. McGowan, Donald Kanaly, and others. These included the Grail movement (1921); Young Christian Students (1925); Young Christian Workers (1925); the Catholic Worker, founded by Peter Maurin and Dorothy Day (1933); the Christian Family Movement (men's group in 1943, couples in 1947); and Friendship House (Toronto in 1930, New York City in 1938). Led by Pat and Patricia Crowley, the Christian Family Movement proved particularly wide-reaching and popular. *See also* Christian Family Movement.

MICHAEL E. ENGH

Catholic Biblical Association of America (CBA), a scholarly society for the service of the faith through the promotion of biblical scholarship. Its beginning was occasioned by a meeting of Catholic Scripture scholars called by Bishop Edwin V. O'Hara in 1936 to plan a revision of the Challoner-Rheims NT; the group quickly moved toward formation of a permanent association, which came into existence on October 3, 1936, at a meeting of about fifty scholars. Edward P. Arbez was elected its first president. A constitution and by-laws were adopted in 1937. It was incorporated in the District of Columbia in 1941 and reincorporated in 1958. Initially the CBA was under the patronage of the Confraternity of Christian Doctrine (CCD). O'Hara's aim of revising the Challoner-Rheims NT, based on the Vulgate, was realized by the publication, in 1941, of the CCD NT; in the meantime work had begun on revising the OT, again based on the Vulgate. But in 1943 the publication of *Divino Afflante Spiritu* encouraged a switch to a totally new translation of both OT and NT from the original languages; the result was the New American Bible, published in 1970; a further revision of the NT was published in 1987 and a revision of the Psalter in 1991.

The CBA publishes the *Catholic Biblical Quarterly* (begun in 1939), the Catholic Biblical Quarterly Monograph Series (first volume in 1971), and *Old Testament Abstracts* (since 1978). General and regional meetings are held. Qualifications for membership are scholarly rather than creedal and many non-Catholics are numbered among the CBA members.

Catholic Biblical Quarterly (*CBQ*), the official scholarly publication of the Catholic Biblical Association of America. Publication was begun in 1939 and has been continuous ever since. *CBQ* contains articles designed to provide scholarly exchange on biblical and related matters; it also provides an extensive book review section in the same areas.

CATHOLIC CHURCH

*T*he Catholic Church (Gk., *katholikos,* "universal"; *kyriakon,* "belonging to the Lord"; *ekklesia,* "assembly") is the world-wide Church that recognizes the Bishop of Rome, the pope, as "the perpetual and visible source and foundation of the unity of the bishops and of the multitude of the faithful" (Dogmatic Constitution on the Church, n. 23). There are approximately one billion Catholics in the world, by far the largest body of Christians and the largest single religious community on the earth.

THE SCOPE OF THE CATHOLIC CHURCH

The universal Catholic Church is in principle (if not always in reality) a college of local churches (parishes, dioceses, regional churches, patriarchates, and national churches), whose unity is rooted in the presence of the Holy Spirit, a common faith in Jesus Christ, the celebration of the Eucharist and the other sacraments, and the visible unifying ministry of the Bishop of Rome. The Catholic communion encompasses eight distinct Catholic traditions: Armenian, Byzantine, Coptic, Ethiopian, East Syrian (Chaldean), Maronite, Roman, and West Syrian. Some of these have more than one local expression. For example, the Chaldean and Syro-Malabar churches are both expressions of the East Syrian tradition, and the Ukrainian and Melkite churches are expressions of the Byzantine tradition.

Before the sixteenth century this worldwide church was simply the Catholic Church. The adjective "Catholic" had its origin in Ignatius of Antioch (early second century) and was found also in the writings of the early Fathers of the Church and in the creeds. When the authority of the Bishop of Rome became a source of contention between West and East in the eleventh century and between Catholics and Protestants in the sixteenth, the adjective "Roman" served to distinguish those Christians who remained in union with Rome from those who did not.

However, the adjective "Roman" tends to confuse rather than define the reality of Catholicism since it is not the Roman primacy that gives Catholicism its distinctive identity within the family of Christian churches, but the Petrine primacy. Indeed, it was in Jerusalem, not Rome, that the Petrine primacy was first conferred and exercised. The adjective "Roman" applies more properly to the diocese of Rome than to the worldwide Church that is in union with the Bishop of Rome.

According to the Second Vatican Council's Decree on Ecumenism, the Catholic Church includes more than Catholics alone. Those other Christians "who believe in Christ and have been properly baptized are brought into a certain, though imperfect, communion with the Catholic Church" (n. 3). Consequently, the worldwide, or universal, Church is at once identical with the Catholic Church and larger than the Catholic Church. However, even as it recognizes this wider dimension of the universal Church, the Catholic Church continues to teach that the Catholic Church and its traditions are normative for other Christian churches and traditions. Only those who "accept her entire system and all the means of salvation given to her" are "fully incorporated into the society of the Church" (Dogmatic Constitution on the Church, n. 14).

NEW TESTAMENT BEGINNINGS

One must always remember that the history of the Catholic Church is a history not only of leaders and major institutional events, but a history of the Catholic people. What follows, therefore, is only a framework for identifying, describing, and interpreting persons and events that have shaped and influenced the development of the Catholic people.

Since the Catholic Church does not see itself as simply one Christian denomination among many in the universal Church or as merely a product of the Counter-Reformation of the sixteenth century, it situates its beginnings in the NT itself, with Jesus' gathering of his disciples and, following the Resurrection, his commissioning of Peter to be the chief shepherd and foundation of the Church (Matt 16:13–19; Luke 22:31–32; John 21:15–19). Given the symbolism of keys as instruments for opening and closing the gates of the kingdom of heaven, the conferral of the power of the keys upon Peter clearly suggests that he was given an imposing measure of authority by the Lord. On the other hand, special authority over others is not clearly attested. Indeed, Peter is presented elsewhere as consulting with the other apostles and even being sent by them (Acts 8:14), while he and John act almost as a team (3:1–11; 4:1–22). Nevertheless, there seems to be what biblical scholars call a trajectory of images relating to Peter and his ministry that sets him apart within the original company of disciples and explains his ascendancy and that of his successors throughout the early history of the Church. He is portrayed as the fisherman (Luke 5:10; John 21:1–14), as the shepherd of the sheep of Christ (John 21:15–17), as an elder who addresses other elders (1 Pet 5:1), as proclaimer of faith in Jesus, the Son of God (Matt 16:16–17), as receiver of a special revelation (Acts 1:9–16), as one who can correct others' doctrinal misunderstandings (2 Pet 3:15–16), and as the rock on which the Church is to be built (Matt 16:18). These biblical images were later enriched by others: missionary preacher, great visionary, destroyer of heretics, receiver of the new law, gatekeeper of heaven, helmsman of the ship of the Church, coteacher and comartyr with Paul.

Although founded on the rock of Peter, the Church of the NT was diverse and pluralistic in character. Despite many differences from place to place, however, certain common elements of belief and practice existed: faith in Jesus as Messiah and Lord, the practice of baptism and the celebration of the Eucharist, the apostolic preaching and instruction, the practice of communal love, and the expectation of the coming reign of God. There was freedom in all other matters.

CHRISTIAN COMMUNITIES AT THE END OF THE FIRST CENTURY

By the end of the first century the Church had begun to establish itself throughout the eastern and northeastern Mediterranean. Beginning in Jerusalem it moved north and west through the missionary journeys of St. Paul and others to modern-day Syria (Damascus, Antioch), modern-day Turkey (Ephesus, Colossae), Greece (Corinth, Philippi, Thessalonia), and Rome, where a large Christian community existed from at least the middle of the century.

As the Church spread through the Greco-Roman world, it adapted itself to contemporary social, political, and cultural forms and structures, particularly the organizational and administrative patterns that prevailed in the areas of missionary activity. It adopted the organizational divisions of the Roman Empire (dioceses, provinces) and identified its own center with the empire's (Rome). This decision was supported by the tradition that Peter had founded the Church in Rome and that he and Paul were martyred and buried there. By the latter half of the second century there were synods and councils and the emergence of the monarchical episcopate (one bishop governing each diocese).

FROM CONSTANTINIANISM TO MONASTICISM

The Church continued to change and develop in response to various crises and heresies. In the controversy with Gnosticism, defenders of Catholic orthodoxy like Irenaeus (d. ca. 200) appealed to the faith of local churches founded by the apostles (apostolic succession), and especially the faith of the Roman church, which was by now clearly associated with Peter and Paul. During the first five centuries, the church of Rome gradually assumed preeminence among all the local churches. It intervened in the life of distant churches, took sides in theological controversies, was consulted by other bishops on doctrinal and moral questions, and sent delegates to distant councils. The local church of Rome came to be regarded as a kind of final court of appeal as well as the focus of unity for the worldwide communion of churches. The correlation between Peter and the Bishop of Rome became fully explicit in the pontificate of Leo I (440–61), who claimed that Peter continued to speak to the whole Church through the Bishop of Rome.

One of the defining events in these early centuries of the Church's history was the conversion of the emperor Constantine I (306–37) in the year 312. Thereafter, pagan practices were suppressed and the Church and its clergy received privileged status. Some sectarian Protestants have pointed to this development as the beginning of "Constantinian Catholicism," a pejorative term. Christian commitment would no longer be tested by persecution and martyrdom, and the Church itself was now vulnerable to the negative influences of the secular culture.

The strongest protest against Constantinianism, however, came not from the sectarians but from monks. The quintessential countercultural movement, monasticism took hold almost immediately within the Church. Bishops were recruited from among those who had some monastic training. Not surprisingly, the new-style bishops brought with them some traits of their monastic background: celibacy and a certain antiworldly asceticism. Already separated from the laity by legal status and privilege, some of the hierarchy drew even further away by reason of divergent spiritualities.

Monasticism reached its high point in the West in the middle of the sixth century with the founding of Monte Cassino by Benedict of Nursia (d. 547). Although devoted primarily to work and prayer (Lat., *ora et labora*), monks were also directly involved in the missionary expansion of the Church into England, Ireland, Scotland, and Gaul (France) between the fifth and seventh centuries, and by the eighth century former mission countries, like England, were sending missionaries to the still-pagan regions of Europe. By the middle of the eleventh century, following the restoration of political stability in Europe, monks had largely withdrawn from temporal and ecclesiastical affairs and returned to their monasteries. Under the impact of this monastic renewal, new religious orders were founded (e.g., Franciscans, Dominicans, Cistercians, Jesuits).

THE DOCTRINAL CONTROVERSIES OF THE EARLY CHURCH

As the new monastic movement was taking root, the Church was racked with doctrinal controversies over some of the most basic elements of its faith: the nature of God, the divinity of Christ, the meaning of the redemption, and the divinity of the Holy Spirit. Arianism held that the Son of God was only the greatest of creatures. The Council of Nicaea condemned this belief in 325, declaring that the Son and the Father are of the same divine substance (Gk., *homoousios*). The First Council of Constantinople (381) condemned Apollinarianism, which held that Christ had no human soul, and Macedonianism, which denied the divinity of the Holy Spirit. The Council of Ephesus (431) condemned Nestorianism, which held that in Christ there is only one nature, a human nature, and that the human Jesus is separate from the divine Word, or Logos. At the opposite end of the doctrinal spectrum, Monophysitism (Gk., "one nature") held that Christ's human nature was completely absorbed by the divine person, so that in Christ there is only one nature, a divine nature. This elicited the Christological definition of the Council of Chalcedon (451): Jesus Christ has two natures, the one divine and the other human, united in one divine person "without confusion or change, without division or separation." This stress on balance (both/and rather than either/or) has been a hallmark of Catholic teaching from its beginning.

The same balance was maintained in the great debates about nature and grace. Against Pelagianism, which held that salvation can be achieved through human effort alone, Augustine of Hippo (d. 430) insisted on the primacy of grace without denying human responsibility. In the seventeenth century, the Church would also condemn Quietism, which held that we can do nothing on our own spiritual behalf. The Scholastics argued that grace and nature are not opposed, but that grace builds on nature.

CRISES AND REFORMS

Around the same time as these doctrinal controversies were being resolved, German tribes began migrating through Europe with no effective control. These "barbarian invasions" lasted some six hundred years and changed the face of Catholicism from a largely Greco-Roman religion to a broader European religion. Catholic devotion, spirituality, and organizational structure were reshaped by the militaristic and feudal character of the Germanic culture. Christ was portrayed as the most powerful of kings; the place of worship was described as God's fortress; monks were regarded as warriors of Christ; the profession of faith became an oath of fidelity to a kind of feudal lord; and Church officials, wearing the trappings of temporal authority (e.g., ring, staff, headgear), were seen more as political than pastoral leaders. The line between the sacred and the temporal became so blurred, in fact, that emperors, kings, and princes began arrogating to themselves the right to appoint bishops. This led to the investiture controversy, eventually resolved in favor of the Church through the persistent efforts of Pope Gregory VII (d. 1085).

At the beginning of the eighth century, with the eastern emperor no longer able to aid the papacy against the aggressive Lombards in northern Italy, the pope turned to the Franks for help. The new alliance led to the creation of the Holy Roman Empire, culminating in the crowning of Charlemagne (d. 814) in 800. After the empire's eventual collapse, however, the papacy fell into the hands of the corrupt Roman nobility and the Church entered what historians have called the "dark ages" of the tenth and eleventh centuries. The papacy regained its footing under the reformer Gregory VII, who dealt decisively with three major abuses: simony (the selling of spiritual goods), the alienation of Church property (allowing ownership to pass from the Church to private hands), and lay investiture. Papal prestige reached its highest point in the Middle Ages during the pontificate of Innocent II (1198–1216), who fully exploited the Gregorian claim that the pope has supreme, even absolute, power over the whole Church. Boniface VIII (1294–1303) took that claim one step further and asserted dominion over the temporal order as well in the famous papal bull *Unam Sanctam* (Lat., "One Holy") of 1302.

Canon law was codified to support the new claims. The Church became increasingly legalistic in its theology, moral life, spirituality, and sacramental administration, especially with regard to marriage, viewed more as a contract than as a covenant. By the middle of the thirteenth century the papal-hierarchical model of the Church was securely in place, and it would dominate Catholicism until the Second Vatican Council some six centuries later. Newly elected popes were crowned like emperors—a practice discontinued by Pope John Paul I in 1978.

Meanwhile, through a series of unfortunate and complicated political and diplomatic developments in the eleventh century, a major breach occurred between the church of Rome and the church of Constantinople. The excommunication of the patriarch of Constantinople, Michael Cerularius (d. 1058), by papal legates in 1054, and the Fourth Crusade (1202–1204) and the sack of Constantinople by Western knights dealt the crucial blows to East-West unity.

Catholicism in medieval Europe (eighth through fifteenth centuries) represented by major Christian centers (e.g., Rome, Paris), universities (e.g., Paris, Oxford, Bologna), and monastic foundations (e.g., Monte Cassino, Cluny, Cîteaux, Clairvaux, Fulda, St. Gall, Bec).

EUROPE IN THE MIDDLE AGES

THE REFORMATION AND COUNTER-REFORMATION

The process of disintegration continued within the West as well. First, there was the confrontation between Boniface VIII and Philip the Fair (d. 1314) over the latter's power to tax the Church. After asserting his jurisdiction over the emperor in the bull *Unam Sanctam,* the pope was arrested and died a prisoner. Then there were the financial abuses during the subsequent "Babylonian Captivity" of the papacy at Avignon, France (1309–78), the rise of anticlericalism in reaction to papal taxes and of conciliarism in opposition to the new claims of papal power, and, finally, the Great Schism of 1378–1417 in which there were three different claimants to the papacy at one time.

But there were other, more immediate causes of the Reformation that followed: the corruption of the Renaissance papacy of the fifteenth century, the divorce of popular piety from sound theology and of theology from its biblical and historical roots, the debilitating effects of the Great Schism, the rise of the nation-state, the too-close connection between Western Catholicism and Western civilization and culture, and the powerful personalities of the Reformers themselves, especially Luther, Calvin, and Zwingli.

The Catholic Church's official response to the challenge of the Reformation was vigorous, if belated. The centerpiece of the Counter-Reformation was the Council of Trent (1545–63), conducted largely under the leadership of Pope Paul III (1534–49). The council reaffirmed those traditional Catholic teachings that had been rejected or attacked by the Protestants: the importance of human effort in salvation, the place of tradition alongside Sacred Scripture, the seven sacraments, including the ordained priesthood, the authority of the hierarchy, and so forth. The council also instituted the Index of Forbidden Books and it established seminaries for the education and formation of future priests. The post-Tridentine Church continued to emphasize those doctrines, institutions, and devotions that the Reformers had most directly challenged: veneration of the saints, devotion to Mary, eucharistic adoration, and the hierarchy and the priesthood. Catholic missionary activity was reduced in countries where Protestantism flourished, but the Catholic faith was carried abroad by the two Catholic sea powers, Spain and Portugal. The Dominicans, Franciscans, and the newly established Jesuits brought Catholicism to India, China, Japan, Africa, and the Americas. The Congregation for the Propagation of the Faith was founded in 1622 to oversee these new missionary enterprises.

POST-REFORMATION MOVEMENTS

Tensions between Rome and France were exacerbated by the rise of Jansenism in France at the beginning of the seventeenth century. Drawing much of their inspiration from Augustine but taking his theology to an extreme, the Jansenists tended to view human nature as totally corrupt and developed a spirituality that was excessively rigorous and puritanical. When Rome finally moved against Jansenism, many in France took it as an affront to the independence and integrity of French Catholicism. Gallicanism (from the original Latin word for France, "Gaul") surfaced as an essentially nationalistic movement, but with clear theological overtones. It asserted that only a general council has supreme authority in the Church and that all papal decrees are subject to the consent of the whole Church as represented in such a council. Gallicanism was condemned by the First Vatican Council (1869–70), which taught that infallible teachings of the pope are irreformable, that is, not subject to the consent of any higher ecclesiastical body or authority.

The Catholic Church in northern Europe, especially in the Catholic states of Germany, was also severely challenged by an eighteenth-century movement known as the Enlightenment. The movement was characterized by a sometimes uncritical confidence in the powers of human reason, an optimistic view of human nature, and a passion for human freedom. At the same time, it displayed an often hostile attitude toward religion and the supernatural and against all authority other than that based on reason. Although it influenced Protestantism far more than it did Catholicism, the Enlightenment stimulated advances in theological and biblical scholarship, in the education of the clergy, in the promotion of popular education, and in the struggle against religious superstition.

If the Enlightenment marked the beginning of the end of an unhistorical Catholic theology, the French Revolution of 1789 marked the end of medieval Catholicism. The feudal, hierarchical society on which medieval Catholicism had been based abruptly disappeared. In uprooting the clerical system, the French Revolution forced the French clergy to look to Rome and the papacy for support. Since Rome was "beyond the mountains," the new dependence of French Catholics on the papacy gave rise to an ultraconservative movement known as Ultramontanism. Perhaps the greatest hidden benefit of the French Revolution was what some have called the "grace of destitution." By stripping the French church of most of its wealth and power, the Church was free once again to pursue its basic mission of preaching the gospel and serving people in fidelity to its central teachings.

Not only in France but also in Germany, the French Revolution provoked a counterreaction among many intellectuals who returned enthusiastically to the values of the past, including those of Catholicism, which they extolled now as the mother of art and the guardian of patriotism. This countermovement was known as Romanticism. There emerged from it a rigid traditionalism that was distrustful of all critical thinking and speculation in theology and that looked to Rome for authoritative answers to all questions.

THE WINDS OF MODERNITY

The popes of this time—Gregory XVI (1831–46) and Pius IX (1846–78)—condemned the winds of change and modernity, nowhere more forcefully than in the latter's *Syllabus of Errors* (1864). Although Pius IX persuaded the bishops of the First Vatican Council to define papal primacy and papal infallibility, he lost the Papal States (September 1870) and the papacy's last bit of political power. It was only with the Lateran Treaty of 1929 (renegotiated in 1983) that the pope's temporal rights to the Vatican territory were legally recognized.

The nineteenth century also witnessed the rapid development of industrialization and the rise of many new social problems, including the worsening condition of workers. Too long wedded to, and identified with, traditional social, political, and economic powers, the Church began to lose the loyalty of the working classes. Partly to attract them back to the Church and partly to restore stability to the social order, Pope Leo XIII (1878–1903) issued a major encyclical, *Rerum Novarum* (Lat., "Of New Things") in 1891, defending the rights of workers to form unions, to earn a just wage, and to work under humane conditions. Catholic social teachings were developed in subsequent decades by popes Pius XI, Pius XII, John XXIII, Paul VI, and John Paul II, as well as by the Second Vatican Council (1962–65) and individual conferences of bishops. John Paul II marked the hundredth anniversary of *Rerum Novarum* with an encyclical of his own, *Centesimus Annus* ("The Hundredth Year") in 1991.

Just as the Catholic Church was buffeted by "new things" on the economic front, so, too, was it challenged anew intellectually. Although not really a single movement but a cluster of movements, Modernism emerged at the beginning of the twentieth century as a major threat to traditional Catholic orthodoxy, as formulated and interpreted by neo-Scholasticism. Modernism was condemned in 1907 by Pope Pius X (1903–14) through a decree of the Holy Office, *Lamentabili,* and an encyclical, *Pascendi,* and in 1910 bishops, pastors, and theologians were required for many years thereafter to swear to an oath against Modernism. Theologians and biblical scholars were forbidden to use the resources of modern scholarship in their research, writing, and teaching, and if they did, they were reported ("delated") to Rome through a spy network the pope himself encouraged. Many were silenced, removed from their positions, suspended from the priesthood, or even excommunicated. Because of the virulence of the anti-Modernist campaign, Catholic scholarship sunk into decline for fifty years, not recovering until just before the Second Vatican Council. Ironically, several of the Modernists' principal positions were later reflected in the teachings of that council and in some contemporary Roman decrees; namely, that the truths of Scripture and the dogmas of the Church are affected by history and must be interpreted in light of historical circumstances and that there is a development of dogma.

With the election of Pope Benedict XV (1914–22) the anti-Modernist era came to an end, and the First World War began. In these turbulent years the Catholic Church continued to move into the modern world. The liturgical movement, later endorsed by Pope Pius XII's encyclical *Mediator Dei* in 1947, began to close the gap between altar and congregation. Catholic biblical scholarship received crucial support from the same pope in his encyclical *Divino Afflante Spiritu* in 1943. The social apostolate was given impetus by a series of papal pronouncements, including Pius XI's *Quadragesimo Anno* (1931). The lay apostolate was promoted by popes Pius XI and Pius XII. The ecumenical movement had a more difficult time, especially in light of Pius XI's negative encyclical *Mortalium Animos* in 1929, but pioneers like Yves Congar were preparing the way for Vatican II. Finally, the missionary movement, which had experienced a major revival in the nineteenth century with as many as eight million converts, became increasingly independent of colonial and European influence. Both Pius XI and Pius XII stressed the importance of establishing native clergies and native hierarchies in mission lands.

THE SECOND VATICAN COUNCIL AND THE POSTCONCILIAR CHURCH

No event in the twentieth century, or indeed in the modern era, has shaped and influenced the Catholic Church more substantially than the Second Vatican Council (1962–65). Convened by Pope John XXIII (1958–63) for the sake of updating the Church (It., *aggiornamento*), the council effectively brought the era of Tridentine Catholicism to an end.

Among the council's distinctive teachings, in contrast to beliefs prevalent before Vatican II: (1) The Church is, first and foremost, a mystery, or sacrament, and not primarily an organization or institution. (2) The Church is the whole People of God, not just the hierarchy, clergy, and religious. (3) The Church's mission includes action on behalf of justice and peace and is not limited to the preaching of the word and the celebration of the sacraments. (4) The Church includes all Christians and is not limited exclusively to the Catholic Church. (5) The Church is a communion, or college, of local churches, which are not simply administrative subdivisions of the Church universal. (6) The Church is an eschatological community; it is not yet the kingdom of God. (7) The lay apostolate is a direct participation in the mission of the Church, and not simply a sharing in the mission of the hierarchy. (8) There is a hierarchy of truths; not all official teachings of the Church are equally binding or essential to the integrity of Catholic faith. (9) God uses other Christian churches and non-Christian religions in offering salvation to all humankind; the Catholic Church is not the only means of salvation. (10) The dignity of the human person and the freedom of the act of faith are the foundation of religious liberty for all, over against the view that "error has no rights."

The history of the Catholic Church since Vatican II has been shaped largely by the Church's efforts to come to terms with the various challenges and opportunities that council presented and at the same time to remain faithful to its distinctive Catholic identity. These efforts have not been without great difficulty. Although the majority of Catholics, especially those who have had the advantage of an education, have been generally responsive to the council's teachings, a vocal minority continued to resist and oppose them, at least implicitly. Pope Paul VI agonized over the divisions in the postconciliar Church. To some extent, Pope John Paul II (elected in 1978) unwittingly exacerbated them by seeming to encourage the discontented minority to believe that elements of pre–Vatican II Catholicism could somehow be restored. The long and still-evolving history of the Catholic Church clearly suggests that it cannot.

WHAT CATHOLICS BELIEVE

There are individual entries throughout this volume on various aspects of Catholic doctrine, theology, and spirituality. There is also a substantial entry on "Catholicism" that elaborates three of the principal characteristics of the Catholic tradition: sacramentality, mediation, and communion. What follows here are some highly abbreviated expressions of Catholic teachings.

1. Jesus Christ is the fullest revelation of God. That revelation is available in Scripture and tradition alike, not as two separate and distinct sources, but as rooted in a single source, which is the word of God. The response to this revelation is what we mean by faith. Catholicism rejects fideism (the belief that faith has no rational component) as well as rationalism (the view that we can believe only what can be rationally demonstrated to be true).

2. God created the world, so it is good. There is no question of an ongoing battle between two coequal (or nearly coequal) forces: God and Satan. The forces of evil have been overcome once and for all in Jesus Christ. The created order, although fallen and wounded by original sin and the actual sins of humankind, is nevertheless redeemed by Christ and renewed by the Holy Spirit.

3. Although God alone saves us, we cannot be saved without our own cooperation. This teaching is encapsulated in a formula attributed to Ignatius of Loyola (d. 1556); namely, that we should pray as if everything depended upon God, and work as if everything depended upon ourselves.

4. Grace really transforms and sanctifies us. Our sins are not simply covered over. We have become new creatures in Christ and temples of the Holy Spirit.

5. Jesus Christ is our Redeemer, who is truly divine and human. Because he is divine, his suffering, death, and Resurrection on our behalf are of infinite value. And because he is human, we are taken up with him into the mystery of redemption.

LARGEST CONCENTRATIONS OF CATHOLICS BY COUNTRY
OVER 10 MILLION

Brazil	135,160,000	Germany	28,599,000
Mexico	83,815,000	Peru	20,380,000
United States	56,399,000	Venezuela	18,638,000
Italy	55,728,000	Zaire	18,583,000
Philippines	52,325,000	India	14,585,000
France	47,625,000	Canada	11,972,000
Spain	37,039,000	Chile	10,761,000
Poland	36,616,000	Nigeria	10,587,000
Colombia	31,298,000	Ecuador	10,081,000
Argentina	29,965,000		

SOURCE: *1994 Catholic Almanac* (Huntington, IN: Our Sunday Visitor Publishing Division, 1993).

6. The God who created us and who redeemed us is a triune God: creator, redeemer, and sanctifier; Father, Son, and Holy Spirit. Each person is God, and yet there is only one God.

7. Mary is the Mother of God and the Mother of the Church. She is the firstborn of those who have been redeemed and is a type, or symbol, of the Church through her faith in, and readiness to abide by, the word of God. The Church does not place Mary on a coequal basis with her Son, nor does it require its members to believe in any of the apparitions attributed to her by others.

8. The Church is necessary for salvation because it is the Body of Christ, continuing his mission for the sake of the coming reign of God. Although it will not come about until the end of history, God's reign is already present in mystery, in the Church and in the world. God wills the salvation of all.

9. The Church is essentially sacramental, signifying and celebrating the presence and activity of God through the seven sacraments, especially the Eucharist.

10. We are called to live in accordance with the gospel in our own individual lives and also to contribute to the common good in the world around us. The sources of morality are to be found not only in the Bible and the official teachings of the Church, but also in every human heart (natural law).

11. We are all destined for eternal happiness in heaven, but it is at least conceivable that some few may totally and with full deliberation reject the gift of salvation. Hell is for them the state of eternal absence from God. For others a period of purification, called purgatory, may be necessary to prepare them for the vision of God. The once-popular belief that infants who die without Baptism enter a state of natural happiness known as limbo is not an official teaching of the Church, and no Catholic is bound to hold to it.

12. The Catholic Church has assumed many different organizational forms throughout its history. Although there is a fundamental equality of members by reason of Baptism, some are given special ministerial responsibilities. For Catholics the Bishop of Rome has a unique ministerial function: to stand in Peter's place as the proclaimer of faith to the universal Church and as an instrument of unity.

The story of the Catholic Church is ongoing. Its destiny is the reign of God in all its fullness. Its present is that of a pilgrim's existence, "at the same time holy and always in need of being purified, and incessantly [pursuing] the path of penance and renewal." Its abiding mission is "to show forth in the world the mystery of the Lord . . . until at the last it will be revealed in total splendor" (Dogmatic Constitution on the Church, n. 8).

See also Catholicism; Church.

Bibliography

Bokenkotter, Thomas. *A Concise History of the Catholic Church.* Rev. ed. Garden City, NY: Image Books, 1990.

Congar, Yves. *Divided Christendom: A Catholic Study of the Problem of Reunion.* Trans. by M. A. Bousfield. London: Geoffrey Bles, 1939.

Congar, Yves. *After Nine Hundred Years: The Background of the Schism Between the Eastern and Western Churches.* Trans. by the Russian Center of Fordham University. New York: Fordham University Press, 1959.

McBrien, Richard P. *Catholicism.* Rev. ed. San Francisco: HarperCollins, 1994.

Rogier, Louis J., ed. *The Christian Centuries: A New History of the Catholic Church.* 3 vols. New York: McGraw-Hill, 1964, 1968; Paulist Press, 1978.

RICHARD P. MCBRIEN

Catholic Church Extension Society, U.S. missionary society. At the turn of the century, Father Francis Clement Kelly traveled the United States in search of funds for his poor parish in rural Lapeer, Michigan. On this journey he discovered the dire state of the Church in the West and South. On October 18, 1905, Kelly and a group of bishops and laypersons established the Catholic Church Extension Society to meet the Church's needs in rural and impoverished areas. Since its foundation, the society has built more than ten thousand churches; it offers emergency relief, contributes to the salaries of church personnel, and subsidizes campus ministry, seminarian education, and evangelization programs in the United States, Puerto Rico, American Samoa and Guam. The society publishes a magazine, *Extension Magazine,* and presents the annual Lumen Christi Award for outstanding missionary service.

Catholic colleges and universities—statistics. While there has been no systematic statistical worldwide study of Catholic colleges and universities, it is estimated that there are approximately 450 postsecondary Catholic educational institutions that would answer to the description of "college" or "university" as the terms are applied in the United States. For the purposes of a recent study by the Vatican Congregation for Catholic Education, the estimate was 900 such institutions, but these included such things as seminaries, vocational schools, and finishing schools.

United States—History: The first Catholic college in the United States was Georgetown University in Washington, D.C., founded in 1789 and chartered by Congress in 1815. Its 1993 enrollment was 11,985 students.

Between 1789 and 1849, 42 Catholic colleges were founded in the United States, 18 by bishops of dioceses, 18 by religious communities, 5 by diocesan priests as private ventures, and 1 college that folded soon after its founding. Between 1850 and 1900, 152 colleges for men were founded, with the vast majority of them (98) started by religious communities. From 1901 to 1955, another 73 were founded. From 1956 on, the rate slowed dramatically to only 3 colleges founded by religious communities and 1 by the bishop of a diocese. For the schools founded between 1850 and 1899, just under 30 percent survived; for those begun between 1900 and 1955 about 36 percent survived, compared to a 20-percent survival rate for non-Catholic institutions.

FOUNDING DATES AND ENROLLMENT OF TWELVE LEADING AMERICAN CATHOLIC COLLEGES AND UNIVERSITIES

Name	Founded	1993 Enrollment
Georgetown	1789	11,985
St. Louis	1818	11,747
Fordham	1841	14,500
Notre Dame	1842	10,000
Villanova	1842	11,100
Holy Cross	1843	2,712
Dayton	1850	10,658
Santa Clara	1851	7,750
Seton Hall	1856	9,700
Boston College	1863	14,455
St. John's/N.Y.	1870	19,105
Catholic University	1887	6,749

Most Catholic colleges for women had their roots in secondary educational academies. A significant number of such academies were begun between 1829 and 1852, all but three by women's religious communities. The first Catholic college for women, College of Notre Dame of Maryland, was founded in 1895.

The first Catholic college to admit women was St. John's College in New York, which opened extension classes in "pedagogy" for men and women in 1908. Marquette began the popular tradition of summer school for women religious in 1909. Marquette also broke the gender barrier for Catholic professional education for women when it granted a law degree to a woman in 1909.

Because one of the significant missions of the early Catholic colleges was the education of clerics, the curriculum was centered on the classics. Later, the curriculum expanded to include studies in commerce and the professions. In 1869, Notre Dame became the first Catholic college to open a law school; Georgetown and Catholic University followed suit in 1870 and 1895, respectively. St. Louis University opened the first Catholic medical school in 1842; Georgetown opened its medical school in 1851.

Contemporary Statistics: *The Official Catholic Directory, 1992,* reports that there were 659,155 students enrolled in 235 Catholic colleges and universities in the United States in 1992, up from 650,314 in 1991 and compared to 533,086 students in 237 institutions in 1981. The largest Catholic university is St. John's in New York, with 19,105 students. New York is the state with the greatest number, with 28 Catholic colleges and universities enrolling 107,490 students; Pennsylvania has 26 with 71,878; Illinois has 17 with 51,630.

The 1991 report of the Association of Catholic Colleges and Universities (ACCU) is a wide-ranging study of U.S. Catholic colleges, universities, and in-stitutions it classifies as "professional/specialized" or "corporate," such as seminaries. The ACCU study reports that there are 229 Catholic colleges and uni-versities with 609,350 students, in relation to 1,656 other independent institutions that enroll a total of 2,758,660 students. Findings of interest about Cath-olic colleges and universities in relation to other in-dependent institutions of higher education are in-cluded in the accompanying tables.

GEOGRAPHY OF U.S. HIGHER EDUCATION

	North-east	Mid-west	South	West
All higher education	23%	25%	29%	22%
Catholic higher education	45	34	12	9
All independents	41	24	23	12

LEVEL AND ATTENDANCE

	Catholic	Other
UNDERGRADUATE		
Full-time	55.2%	61.5%
Part-time	22.4	15.4
GRADUATE		
Full-time	6.9	11.6
Part-time	15.5	11.5

RACE, ETHNICITY, AND CITIZENSHIP STATUS

	Catholic	Other
Black, non-Hispanic	6.0%	8.5%
American Indian/ Alaskan Native	0.3	0.4
Asian/Pacific Islander	2.4	3.4
Hispanic	7.7	5.7
White, non-Hispanic	81.3	77.1
Non-resident alien	2.4	5.0

GROWTH IN ENROLLMENT: 1982–88

	Catholic	Other
Full-time	0.6%	3.9%
Part-time	9.3	5.7
TOTAL	3.8	4.4

FULL-TIME SHARE OF TOTAL ENROLLMENT

Catholic	Other
62.1%	73.1%

CLASSIFICATION OF CATHOLIC INSTITUTIONS (ACCORDING TO CARNEGIE REPORT)

	No. of Institutions	% Dist.	Total Enrollment	% Dist.	Average Enrollment
Research/Doctoral	11	5%	127,072	21%	11,552
Comprehensive	100	44	366,561	60	3,666
Liberal Arts	91	40	103,007	17	1,132
Two-year	24	10	12,023	2	501
Prof./Spec./Corp.	3	1	687	0	229
TOTAL	229	100	609,350	100	2,661

	Catholic	Independents	Public
Native American	11.6%	10.0%	5.2%
Asian/Pacific Islander	47.3	65.5	37.2
Black, non-Hispanic	0.1	8.8	0.9
Hispanic	5.3	25.7	31.6
Non-Resident Alien	10.4	8.8	8.7
TOTAL CHANGE IN MINORITIES	8.0	20.7	15.5

WOMEN'S SHARE OF
TOTAL ENROLLMENT

Catholic	Other
59.0%	51.9%

AVERAGE EDUCATIONAL &
GENERAL EXPENDITURES &
TRANSFERS FOR FISCAL YEAR 1989

	Number	Avg. E&G
Catholic		
Institutions	208	$22,057
Other		
Independents	1129	23,291

Bibliography

Leahy, William P. *Adapting to America: Catholics, Jesuits, and Higher Education in the Twentieth Century.* Washington, DC: Georgetown University Press, 1991.

Petit, Joseph. *Enrollment for Fall, 1988 and Finances and Student Aid Year Ending June 30, 1989 at U.S. Catholic Colleges and Universities.* Washington, DC: American Catholic Colleges and Universities, 1991.

Power, Edward J. *Catholic Higher Education in America: A History.* New York: Appleton-Century-Crofts, 1972.

MARK POORMAN

Catholic Daughters of the Americas, charitable organization for women founded by the Knights of Columbus in 1903. Its aims are the preservation of the Catholic faith, the intensification of patriotism, the spiritual and intellectual development of Catholic women, and the promotion of charitable projects. Membership in 1991 numbered about 150,000. *See also* Knights of Columbus.

Catholic education. *See* Catholicism and education.

Catholic Foreign Mission Society of America. *See* Maryknoll.

Catholicism, a Christian tradition, community, and way of life that emphasizes the universality of the Church and of its faith and at the same time recognizes the Bishop of Rome, the pope, as "the perpetual and visible source and foundation of the unity of the bishops and of the multitude of the faithful" (Dogmatic Constitution on the Church, n. 23).

There are Anglican, Protestant, Orthodox, and Oriental Christians who also identify themselves with Catholicism. By way of contrast they insist on the use of the adjective "Roman" to describe those Catholics who acknowledge the primacy of the Bishop of Rome. For such Catholics, however, the adjective "Roman" tends to confuse rather than define the reality of Catholicism. The history of the Church begins with Jesus' gathering of his disciples and with the post-Resurrection commissioning of Peter to be the chief shepherd and foundation of the Church—in Jerusalem, not in Rome. Therefore, it is not the Roman primacy that gives Catholicism its distinctive identity within the family of Christian churches, but the Petrine primacy. The adjective "Roman" applies more properly to the diocese, or see, of Rome than to the worldwide Church that is in union with the Bishop of Rome.

The Catholic Reality: Catholicism, so defined, is not a reality that stands by itself. The word "Catholic" is a qualification of Christian, and Christian is a qualification of religious, and religious is a qualification of human. Thus, Catholicism refers to a community of persons (the human dimension) who believe in God and shape their lives according to that belief (the religious dimension) and who believe

God to be triune and Jesus Christ to be the Son of God and the redeemer of humankind (the Christian dimension).

As the name itself suggests, Catholicism is characterized by a radical openness to all truth and to every value. It is comprehensive and all-embracing toward the totality of human, religious, and Christian experience. Its direct opposite is not Protestantism but sectarianism, a way of being Christian that separates itself from the worldwide Church and from the world itself lest the purity of its faith and moral witness be compromised or sullied. Catholicism, therefore, is not limited to any one culture, national or ethnic group, school of theology, or spirituality. It is a way of being Christian that is characterized by a both/and rather than an either/or approach: nature *and* grace, faith *and* reason, Scripture *and* tradition, faith *and* works, authority *and* freedom, unity *and* diversity. Thus, Catholicism is a moral universe of laws but also of dispensations, of rules but also of exceptions, of respect for authority but also of respect for freedom of conscience, of high ideals but also of minimal requirements, of censures and excommunications but also of absolution and reconciliation.

Sacramentality, Mediation, and Communion: Catholicism is marked by other characteristics, but none so central or so distinctive as its commitment to the theological principles of sacramentality, mediation, and communion. None of these theological principles is more characteristic of Catholicism or more central to its identity than the principle of sacramentality. The Catholic vision sees God in all things: persons, communities, movements, events, places, objects, the world at large, the whole cosmos. The visible, the tangible, the fleshly, the finite, and the historical are actual or potential carriers of the divine presence. Indeed, Catholicism holds that it is only in and through these material realities that we can encounter the invisible and spiritual God. No fleshly reality is more central or crucial to this process of encounter than the Word made flesh himself. Jesus Christ is the great sacrament of our encounter with God, and the Church, in turn, is the sacrament of our encounter with Christ. At the opening of the second session of the Second Vatican Council (1962–65) Pope Paul VI referred to the Church, in fact, as "a reality imbued with the hidden presence of God." The seven sacraments, furthermore, are the signs and means by which that ecclesial encounter with Christ is effected and celebrated. But it is in our encounter with one another—the sacrament of the neighbor—that we most frequently encounter Christ within his Body, the Church.

Catholicism, therefore, insists that grace (the presence of God within us) actually enters into, transforms, and elevates our human nature in its fullest sense. We are sinners, to be sure, but more fundamentally we are temples of the Holy Spirit, new creatures in Christ. We are not simply justified by a declarative act of God; we are interiorly sanctified by grace.

For Catholicism, the world, too, is essentially good, though fallen, because God is present to it. Although fractured and fragmented, the world has the capacity for ultimate unity because of the gift and abiding presence of the Holy Spirit who is the source of all unity.

A corollary of the principle of sacramentality is the principle of mediation. A sacrament not only signifies the invisible presence of God, but it also causes what it signifies. Thus, God is not only present in material realities; God also works through these realities instrumentally, as means of the divine plan of salvation. Jesus Christ is God's first and most fundamental instrument or means of salvation. He is the one Mediator between God and humans. The Church, which is the Body of Christ, participates in the same work of mediation through the sacraments, the priesthood, the intercession of the saints, especially the Blessed Virgin Mary, the services of all kinds of ministers, and the use of sacred objects and rituals.

Finally, there is the principle of communion, which affirms that our way to God and God's way to us is not only mediated but also essentially and necessarily communal. Catholicism's sense of sin is corporate, and so, too, is its understanding of redemption. Nowhere is this communal vision more strikingly expressed than in the official social teachings of the Catholic Church: in papal encyclicals, conciliar documents, episcopal pronouncements, and the like. For Catholicism, the encounter with God is mediated through a community of faith. And that is why for Catholicism the mystery of the Church has always had so significant a place in its theology, doctrine, pastoral practice, moral vision, and devotional life. It is here, at the point of Catholicism's understanding of itself as Church, as a community of faith, that we come to the heart of the distinctively Catholic understanding, expression, and practice of Christian faith. For here, in Catholic ecclesiology, we find the convergence of these three theological principles of sacramentality, mediation, and communion. The Church is the sacrament of Christ, mediating salvation within a worldwide community of faith. *See also* Catholic, life of a; Catholic Church; sacramentality, principle of.

Bibliography

Cunningham, Lawrence. *The Catholic Faith: An Introduction.* New York: Paulist Press, 1987.

Happel, Stephen, and David Tracy. *A Catholic Vision.* Philadelphia: Fortress Press, 1984.

Lubac, Henri de. *Catholicism: A Study of the Corporate Destiny of Mankind.* Translated by Lancelot Sheppard. New York: Sheed & Ward, 1958.

McBrien, Richard P. *Catholicism.* Rev. ed. San Francisco: Harper-Collins, 1994.   RICHARD P. MCBRIEN

Catholicism and architecture. Throughout its history Catholicism has shaped church architecture, and, in turn, architecture has shaped worship experience. The house church at Dura-Europos, Syria (231), represents the earliest type of structure dedicated to Christian worship, an ordinary domestic residence renovated by removing a wall to enlarge an assembly room and by the addition of a canopied baptismal font in a separate room. The practical simplicity of house churches for small neighbor-

The floorplan of the famous Gothic Chartres Cathedral, about 40 miles southwest of Paris, begun in 1194 and completed in 1240. Renowned for its spires, its stained-glass windows, and the sculptures on the portals, the cathedral was the site of the preaching of the Second Crusade (1146) and the crowning of Henry IV as king of France (1594).

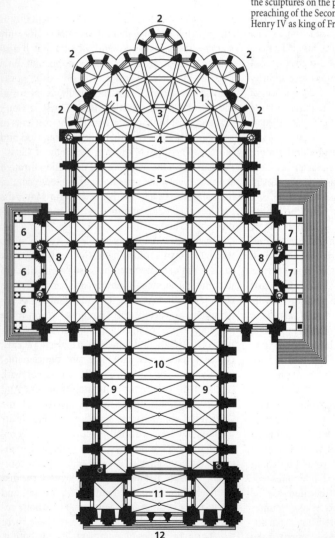

1 ambulatory
2 radiating chapels
3 apse
4 altar
5 choir
6 north portals
7 south portals
8 transept
9 aisle
10 nave
11 narthex (entrance hall)
12 main portal

0   50   100 feet

hood communities gave way in the fourth century under the patronage of Emperor Constantine to grandiose public buildings, adopting the scale and opulence of imperial architecture such as basilicas, public baths, and imperial tombs. Sanctioned as the state religion, Christianity appropriated a courtly processional ritual well served by the longitudinal imperial basilica and enthroned images of Christ as emperor in the apse at the altar end of the building.

At least four distinctively different types of Christian basilicas emerged, responding to specific community needs: (1) cemetery churches in covered cemeteries filled with tombs and used for banquets to celebrate anniversaries of deaths; (2) martyrial basilicas built above the tomb of a martyr with a transept (a tall transverse hall) distinguishing the commemorated tomb site from the nave and apse, such as at Old St. Peter's in Rome; (3) shrine churches incorporating rotundas to emphasize sites significant in the life of Christ, such as the church of the Nativity in Bethlehem or the Holy Sepulchre in Jerusalem; and (4) episcopal or congregational churches, large gathering places for the celebration of the Eucharist such as St. John of the Lateran in Rome, which had no burials, no martyrium, and no commemoration of any site. Baptisteries, such as at the Lateran in Rome (ca. 315) or the Baptistery of the Orthodox in Ravenna (ca. 451), in which catechumens descended into the cleansing waters of death with Christ, derived from central plan imperial tomb architecture and possibly the Roman baths.

Yearning for the prestige and splendor of fourth-century Constantinian Rome, Charlemagne (d. 814) revived early Christian architectural styles throughout the Frankish kingdom and imposed Roman liturgical norms. The introduction of Roman stational liturgies (liturgies associated with specific churches in Rome, known as "stational churches," the most famous of which are the basilicas of St. Mary Major and St. John Lateran), the ordination of large numbers of monks, and the development of a tariff penance system among Irish monks, by which uniform penances were assigned, led to a multiplication of altars to meet requirements of stational liturgies, daily Mass celebration, and the increase of Masses offered for expiation of sin. As the plan of the monastery church of St. Riquier at Centula (790–799) or the Monastic Plan of St. Gall (ca. 820) demonstrate, previously uncluttered spaces became filled with numerous altars, each with separate dedications, often screened off from each other.

Religious pilgrimages, especially to Santiago de

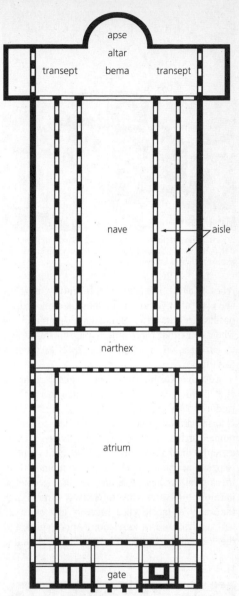

The floorplan of a basilica. The bema is the platform and sanctuary area on which the altar is situated. The narthex is the antichamber to the nave.

Compostela in Spain in the eleventh and twelfth centuries, encouraged on an even more extensive scale the building of the immense solid "romanizing" churches, which would accommodate large numbers of pilgrims coming to venerate relics collected by the churches precisely to attract visitors. Again, unencumbered spaces were made more complex, now by the addition of auxiliary chapels flanking the transept and apse for the exposition of

A view of the exterior of the basilica of St. Vitalis in Ravenna, Italy; Vitalis was a third-century Italian martyr about whom almost nothing is known.

relics on altars. The late eleventh-century "pilgrimage plan" of St. Sernin in Toulouse, a cross-shaped basilica with its new continuous aisle around the whole church for more orderly pilgrim traffic, and its proliferation of additional chapels exemplifies this type.

Advent of Gothic Style: The royal abbey church at St.-Denis, north of Paris (dedicated in 1144) introduced a new architectural vision. Using structural forms already known in the Romanesque period, pointed arches, ribbed groin vaults, flying buttresses, and stained glass, Abbot Suger sought to express Neoplatonic philosophical ideas combined with theological notions of luminosity and geometric harmony. His aim was to convey symbolically the beauty of the jewelled heavenly city of Jerusalem, as described in Revelation (Apocalypse), and the Johannine image of Christ as light. A Gothic

The interior of the church of St. Ignatius in Rome.

"dematerialized" or "spiritual" architecture resulted, light and airy, in which the walls seemed to disappear, lifting the heart and spirit to the transcendent. The cathedrals at Chartres (begun 1145) and Amiens (begun 1220) became the models for churches throughout Europe.

The contemplative and mystical role of Gothic architecture as quiet revelation of God's order and perfection began to give way by the fifteenth century in Italy to political needs of the papacy to reassert its authority and power. In the sixteenth and seventeenth centuries, church architecture, in particular St. Peter's, became a means of proclaiming papal and Roman preeminence in the face of challenges from Protestant opposition. Renaissance architects Bramante (d. 1514) and Michelangelo (d. 1564) began rebuilding Old St. Peter's, work continued by Carlo Maderno (d. 1629) with additional architectural and sculptural projects under the direction of Gian Lorenzo Bernini (d. 1680). Bernini's canopy over the tomb of St. Peter (1624–1633) and his sculpture of the Chair of St. Peter triumphantly celebrate the supremacy of the Bishop of Rome and the Roman Catholic Church. This Baroque visual language of unrestrained energy and pageantry, triumph and superiority, provided a legacy of ecclesiastical architectural vocabulary that persisted through the mid-twentieth century.

St. Paul's Church, Esslingen, Germany; the stark interior of this thirteenth-century Gothic church is said to be typical of the churches of the Dominican order.

The liturgical movement in the mid-nineteenth century, emerging in monastic centers in France, Belgium, and Germany, led to a systematic study of the Church's liturgy, laying the groundwork for Pope Pius XII's encyclical on the liturgy, *Mediator Dei* in 1947, and the reforms initiated by Vatican II. Principles and guidelines outlined in the Constitution on the Sacred Liturgy (1963), the U.S. Bishop's 1978 document "Environment and Art in Catholic Worship," and the ongoing revisions of the liturgy of the sacraments, particularly the catechumenate in the Rite of Christian Initiation of Adults, have shifted the role of church architecture from Catholic Counter-Reformation polemical theater to the original idea of the building as the "house for the church."

Contemporary church design reclaims preeminence for spaces designed to assist the liturgy celebrated by the assembly. Prominent baptismal fonts invite descent into the earth and lavish bathing. The altar is relocated among the people. Chapels for individual reconciliation and eucharistic reservation take secondary place, clarifying a distinction between devotional piety and the assembly's corporate

Church of Our Lady of Loretto, Saint Mary's College, Notre Dame, Indiana; the floorplan reflects the liturgical renewal of the Second Vatican Council (1962–65). The community (seated on both sides of the altar) and the altar ministers are clearly visible to one another; the altar is in the central place of prominence, separated from the ambo from which the word of God is proclaimed; the baptismal font is at the entrance, underscoring the connection between Baptism and Eucharist.

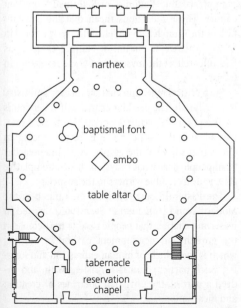

narthex

baptismal font

ambo

table altar

tabernacle
reservation
chapel

worship as reflection of a eucharistic theology of active celebration by the assembly. *See also* Baroque Catholicism; basilica; Gothic style liturgical architecture; liturgical art.
                              MARCHITA B. MAUCK

Catholicism and culture. Culture is a complex human symbolic system, rooted fundamentally in language, reflecting the broadest social values and political worldview of a given people at a given period in time. The explicit use of the term "culture" became current in theological discussion only with the rise of the social sciences. The word "culture," for example, never appears in conciliar documents before Vatican II (1962–65). The relationship of the Catholic faith to such symbolic systems has both historical and theoretical components.

Historical Considerations: Viewed historically, as Christianity emerged and developed in the Roman Empire it related to the predominant culture of classical antiquity in a number of ways. Because from its beginnings it was an outcast and persecuted religious movement, Christianity was forced into an antagonistic or countercultural position: to choose the Church was, in essence, to choose against many values, especially the sociopolitical values of the predominant society. Nonetheless, many within the Church (e.g., the second-century apologists) argued that this did not have to be the case. Some, like Justin Martyr, argued that the pagan culture of antiquity carried intimations of God's revelation and, further, that Christians could be—if allowed—valuable citizens of the empire. Other writers borrowed freely from pagan philosophical ideas and vocabulary to express the meaning of the gospel in a culturally intelligible language. Early Christianity had to define itself both in terms of, and in contrast to, its parent religion, Judaism. The NT itself overtly reflects the attempts to come to grips with its Jewish past and Jewish culture.

In his own day, Augustine of Hippo (d. 430) argued (in *On Christian Doctrine*) that Christians had the right to use pagan learning for the good of the gospel, just as in the *Confessions* he stated baldly that in the writings of the Neoplatonists he found every true thing except "the name of Christ." After the birth of Christ, however, Christianity had a particular right to the inheritance of pagan culture, which it had come to replace at the end of time, as *The City of God* also so eloquently argues. Augustine's attitudes prevailed over earlier attempts to place Christianity in an antagonistic position toward pagan culture.

This tension between the Church as countercultural and as culture-dependent has marked Christianity from its beginnings. After the Peace of Constantine in the early fourth century, the Church borrowed heavily from the classical world in everything from law and administration to language and philosophy. In both the West and the East there developed a close relationship between Church and state—a relationship known as Caesaro-papism in the East. In the West, medieval popes claimed parity with, and eventually superiority over, secular rulers. Even such countercultural movements as monasticism did not escape the interpenetration of civil culture and religious ideas.

In the High Middle Ages a poet such as Dante Aligheri (d. 1321) well illustrates the complexity of the relationship of culture and Catholicism. Dante's *Divine Comedy* marries Christian revelation to pagan learning in a fashion already made acceptable by the theological tradition of Thomas Aquinas (d. 1274) and, in a different manner, Bonaventure (d. 1274) from whom Dante borrowed freely. Nonetheless, Dante's great poem is also a plea for the papacy to remove itself from civil governance in favor of the Holy Roman Emperor so that the Church could be free from the power entanglements that had shamed and harmed it in the previous centuries. Dante, in short, both appreciated and was worried about the interpenetration of culture and religion.

The increased centralization of Church life after the Council of Trent in the sixteenth century as well as the resistance of the Church both to the rise of the Enlightenment and to newer, more revolutionary, ideals produced a Catholicism that was both unflinchingly Roman in tone and reactionary in its politics. The notion that "Europe is the Faith and the Faith is Europe" reflected a wildly romantic view of earlier European history as well as a rather simpleminded correlation between a particular culture ("Europe") and the gospel message (the "Faith"). But this view gripped the imagination of many Catholics even to our own day. The anti-Modernist position of Catholicism before the Second Vatican Council can be well understood as an attempt of the Church to resist the Modernist culture that flowed from the Enlightenment.

Early modern attempts to express the faith in different cultural forms for different cultural situations did not meet with easy acceptance in the sixteenth and seventeenth centuries. Jesuit missionaries like Matteo Ricci in China and Roberto DeNobili in India attempted to provide both a vernacular worship and a diverse expression of Christian doctrine, but they met both incomprehension and resistance in Rome.

It was only in the colonial period of the nineteenth century that scholars began to reflect on the necessity of expressing the Christian faith in forms culturally appropriate for non-European Christians. These early attempts at "missionary accommodation" were timid enough (e.g., utilizing indigeneous forms of architecture or art), but they were the first steps that would lead to detailed attempts, in our time, to inculturate the gospel.

After Vatican II, as Karl Rahner noted, Catholicism entered the era of the World Church (Ger., *Weltkirche*) which not only marked the end of the European-centered Catholic Church, but raised (and continues to raise) the issue of what an African or Indian or Chinese Catholicism would look like.

Theoretical Considerations: It only takes a moment's reflection to realize that Christian doctrine itself is culturally conditioned in the sense that it is expressed in language, itself a product of culture. We need not identify the faith with culture but, as Pope Paul VI made abundantly clear in his 1975 exhortation *On Evangelization in the Modern World (Evangelii Nuntiandi),* "the building up of the Kingdom cannot avoid borrowing the elements of human culture or cultures" (n. 20).

One could look at the larger phenomenon of Catholicism itself and say that it is a culture that can be described in its own right and as different from, for example, Islamic, Buddhist, or Reformed Protestant culture. Those reflections mean that the constant task of the Church is to be self-reflectively critical in asking whether its culture or cultural expressions faithfully reflect the mysteries of God's revelation in Christ.

Such critical reflection cuts across every ministry in the Church. The need for critical self-reflection is as urgent for the pastoral worker (Do these strategies advance the gospel?) as it is for the theologian (Does that say what the gospel says?), the preacher (Can people hear what I say?), or the contemplative (Is my life a credible witness to the gospel?).

The Pastoral Constitution on the Church in the Modern World (*Gaudium et Spes,* 1965) insisted in its second chapter that people need to participate in the growth and development of human culture, which is the vehicle of human expression and longing. Such participation is consistent with, and indeed a part of, the Christian doctrines of creation and incarnation.

The council also recognized that culture, as a human construct, can carry within it forces and ideas that are dehumanizing and prone to sin and degradation. For that reason, the Church, bearer of the gospel tradition, must also be ready to critique, to transform, and, when necessary, to reject those aspects of human culture that are in conflict with the gospel.

More difficult to assess is the relationship of Catholicism to "high" culture: the world of the arts, ideas, philosophy, social studies, technology, and the hard sciences. In the past (e.g., in the High Middle Ages) there was a close correlation between high culture and the Catholic faith. That is certainly not the case today. Modern and postmodern culture is autonomous (it possesses its own claims and criteria of credibility) and secularized (it does not appeal to the perspective of transcendence). Ignorance of, or hostility toward, this culture would make the Church sectarian, while acquiesence to its worldview would produce a theological sentimentalism that could not endure.

The third strategy, vigorously pursued by most Catholic thinkers of the modern period, has argued for a sustained dialogue between the world of faith and secular culture; an acknowledgment that profane culture also is a bearer of insight and constructive human advances; a willingness to cooperate in what human good the high culture of our time points to or has achieved. The worst mistake would be for the Church to think that culture can only learn from it; it must have the humility and clarity to recognize that culture also teaches. That is why *Gaudium et Spes* (n. 62) argued that theological inquiry should not be divorced from a "close contact with its own era."

Well over a generation ago, the Protestant theologian H. Richard Niebuhr, in *Christ and Culture* (1951), set out five ways in which culture and Christianity interact. They were ideal types and do not always hold up under close scrutiny. What is clear, however, is that Church and culture have a complex relationship: Church expresses itself in culture, but also critiques culture and attempts to transform it. Precisely because the Church expresses itself in cultural forms, it must be alert to the hidden presuppositions of a culture (i.e., the ideology of a given culture) it may assume but that are not always openly recognized or articulated. Contemporary debates over the "Roman" character of Catholic authority, for example, are really arguments over the degree to which an ideology of power is operative in Church governance.

Since the Second Vatican Council (1962–65), the Church has taken a much more consciously explicit attitude toward the need for Catholics to work for the increased humanization of culture. This attitude derives from the incarnational and sacramental character of Catholicism. The writings of Pope John Paul II, in particular, have focused on human dignity and Christian personalism as expressions of human culture in essential harmony with the Christian message.

Future Prospects: As the Catholic Church moves toward a new millennium, it faces a number of challenges and opportunities brought to the fore by new cultural upheavals. At the level of science and technology, there is a range of issues ranging from moral questions about biotechnologies to evangelization issues raised by new information technologies. Politically, there is the prospect of an entirely new concept of Europe, which could range as far east as the Urals. The tensions between developed and underdeveloped countries is, as it has been for a generation or more, a central concern of the Church. To that concern one must also be sensitive to the rise of militant forms of fundamentalist religion, like Islam, which do not share the values of postmodern culture.

In the last analysis, however, the great problematic for theology and culture is to understand how the gospel lives in, and is transformative of, human culture. In that sense, the whole history of the Church and of theology can be seen as a continuing effort to bring the gospel into critical dialogue with culture. What Pope Paul VI wrote in 1975 is true today and will be true tomorrow: "Evangelization loses much of its force and effectiveness if it does not take into consideration the actual people to whom it is addressed, if it does not use their language, their signs and symbols, if it does not answer the questions they ask, and if it does not have an impact on their concrete life" (*Evangelii Nuntiandi*, n. 64). *See also* acculturation; inculturation.

Bibliography

Niebuhr, H. Richard. *Christ and Culture.* New York: Harper & Row 1951.

Shorter, A. *Towards a Theology of Inculturation.* Maryknoll, N.Y.: Orbis Books, 1988.

Tillich, Paul. *Theology of Culture.* New York and London: Oxford University Press, 1959.   *LAWRENCE S. CUNNINGHAM*

Catholicism and economics. *See* capitalism; Catholic social teachings; Marxism.

Catholicism and education. An abiding commitment to scholarship and learning has always marked the history of Catholicism; the partnership between Catholicism and education is as old as Christianity itself. The most frequent title for Jesus in the NT is "teacher"; it portrays him as "the truth" (John 14:7), as "the wisdom of God" (1 Cor 1:24), and as giving disciples the mandate to "go . . . make disciples of all nations, . . . teaching them . . ." (Matt 28:19–20). Since NT times, the Church has been involved in education, teaching and learning within each context of time and place.

Grounds for the Partnership: The Jewish context of Christianity provided deep roots for a commitment to education and scholarship. As the canonical corpus of Jewish sacred writings emerged during the Second Temple period (ca. 400 B.C.), Jews became "people of the book." The synagogues were centers for systematic study of the sacred texts, and rabbis taught that such scholarship was akin to prayer and worship; its purpose was wisdom and holiness of life.

Christianity inherited this Jewish appreciation for scholarship, and Catholicism came with at least three theological warrants of its own for commitment to education: (1) an optimistic but realistic anthropology that recognizes both the brokenness and inherent goodness of human existence, and thus encourages holistic education that promotes people's potential to be the glory of God as fully alive (Irenaeus, d. ca. 200); (2) a this-worldly as well as an otherworldly understanding of salvation that recognizes God's saving action in Jesus Christ as improving the quality and promise of life both here and hereafter, thus recommending humanizing education as an aspect of fulfilling this saving work; and (3) the conviction that reason and revelation are essential partners in the life of Christian faith. This third and perhaps central warrant for the partnership has prompted Catholicism throughout its history to pick a careful path between the extremes of fideism and rationalism. Instead of favoring either "blind faith" or the sufficiency of reason alone, it has been convinced that understanding and faith, reason and revelation need and enhance each other. Though there has always been support for Tertullian's defiant stance that "Jerusalem has no need of Athens" (*The Prescription of Heretics* 7), Catholicism has favored a more balanced view, well summarized in a classic statement of Thomas Aquinas (d. 1274): "Just as grace does not destroy nature but perfects it, so sacred doctrine presupposes, uses, and perfects natural knowledge" (*Summa Theologiae* 1a. 1.8.–2).

A Christian Paideia: The early Apologists (ca. 120–220) used their classical education to present Christian faith in a compelling way to the learned; they posed Christianity as the true and ultimate philosophy. At Alexandria, a group of scholars began to forge a "Christian *paideia*" (Gk., "pedagogy"), a synthesis of "the gospel" and secular learning into a Christian humanism. Under the leadership of Clement (ca. 150–ca. 215) and then Origen (ca. 185–ca. 254), this "school" educated people in both Christian faith and the best of classical culture, convinced that the latter could be "stirrups to reach the sky" of spiritual wisdom (Origen). Some two centuries later, Augustine (354–430) reiterated and deepened this appreciation of secular scholarship, arguing that as the Israelites had taken booty from Egypt, so Christians should take as their own the best of pagan learning.

As Augustine lay on his deathbed, the Vandals were already at the gates of Hippo; thereafter uncultured tribes swept over the empire and the rich tradition of Greek and Roman scholarship was severely threatened. But the vestiges of education and enlightenment were kept alive and then revived by the Church.

The Celtic monasteries remained beacons of learning during those "dark ages." Irish monasticism had a particular commitment to scholarship and especially to copying manuscripts in order to preserve the classic texts of Western culture. The great monasteries of Clonard, Durrow, and Clonmacnoise were like modern-day universities with as many as three thousand students, and the abbey of Kildare under Brigid (d. ca. 523) was a center of learning, culture, and peacemaking. Columba (Columkille, ca. 521–97), educated at Clonard, founded the great monastic center of learning at Iona (an island off Scotland) that became a seedbed for the revival of education throughout Europe.

Carolingian Renaissance and the Universities: Charlemagne (ca. 742–814) became king of the Franks in 771 and sole emperor of the West in 800; during his reign he pacified and extended the empire to include most of western Europe, with its palace at Aachen. A brilliant politician and military leader, he was also committed to Church reform; his rule epitomized "Christendom," the unified worldview that saw the religious and secular as aspects of the same reality of God's reign in history. But Charlemagne recognized that military might alone could not pacify his huge empire and reform the Church; education was essential if his civilizing and Christianizing legacy was to survive. In this he was assisted by the Anglo-Saxon scholar Alcuin of York.

Alcuin (735–804) was educated at the cathedral school of York and in 778 became its master. (York was founded from Lindisfarne, which had been founded from Iona.) He met Charlemagne at Parma in 781; thereafter began one of the most significant partnerships in Western history. Together they were the moving forces behind the Carolingian Renaissance, which revived education and marked the end of the "dark ages."

Alcuin moved from York to Aachen and established a very effective palace school. It educated many of the future leaders of Church and state, and its curriculum became the model for all schools in the Carolingian Renaissance. Before Charlemagne, many Benedictine monasteries were centers of learning (e.g., Tours in France, Monte Cassino in Italy, Jarrow in England, and Fulda in Germany), but such monastic schooling was for future monks. Likewise some great cathedral schools predated Charlemagne (Canterbury, Seville, Liege, Utrecht, Cologne, Paris, and Orléans) but they were only to educate future priests. Now with his famous decree of "universal education" of 787 (likely written by Alcuin), Charlemagne ordered all monasteries and cathedrals to sponsor schools open to everyone in the empire who desired education.

The Carolingian schools favored a Socratic method for teaching the seven liberal arts as revived by Alcuin at the palace school. The liberal arts were divided into the trivium, a study of classical texts through grammar, rhetoric, and dialectic, and the more advanced quadrivium of music, arithmetic, geometry, and astronomy. All these arts were cumulatively to prepare students to study Sacred Scripture and the patristic literature of the Church; thus, the ultimate purpose of the whole curriculum was spiritual wisdom. Through the monastic and cathedral schools of the Carolingian Renaissance the Church became the primary educator of the Western world; many of them were precursors for the universities of the High Middle Ages.

Around 1150, the first of the great universities began to emerge at Salerno and Bologna, dedicated to the study of medicine and law, respectively. The University of Paris followed shortly thereafter, and then Oxford, Cambridge, Padua, Pisa, Salamanca, Lisbon, and many other great universities that continue to this day.

The universities began as loose-knit guilds of teachers and students. They were called "general schools" because they welcomed all who wished to study, they prepared people to teach the knowledge they acquired, and they were to serve all of Christendom. Gradually they organized themselves as juridical corporations with "faculties" of teachers and "nations" of students. The great universities came to have four faculties—theology, law, medicine, and arts, the last seen as essential preparation for studying the other three.

Though the emperor or a local ruler often gave a university official recognition and guaranteed protection and safe passage to its teachers and students, the whole university movement was extensively the work of the Church. Most universities had a rector or chancellor who was ecclesially appointed; their power to grant degrees was by papal charter; most of the professors were clerics, especially Dominicans, Franciscans, and Augustinians, and likewise many of the students; and Catholicism lent the common faith and language that enabled faculty and students from diverse cultures to work together.

The Church could sponsor the university movement because of the new synthesis of faith and reason being forged by its own theologians of the time. The rediscovery of Aristotle, especially at the beginning of the second millennium, encouraged a more scientific and systematic theology. From Anselm (d. 1109) onward, such Scholastic theology took its place at the very heart of the university as the "queen" of the sciences and provided the "sacred canopy" for the investigation of a unified universe in the others.

An Uneasy Alliance: Though the Church's schools and universities of the late Middle Ages spawned the great Renaissance of the next era, the Church's relationship with this movement of cultural retrieval and growth was an uneasy one. The Renaissance revived the classical learning of Greece and Rome and championed a humanism centered on the dignity and value of the individual person. This encouraged freedom of intellect and will unfettered by creeds of faith or by Church directives. Though threatened at first, the Church's own traditions of a positive anthropology and appreciation of reason enabled it to appropriate the Renaissance spirit in its educational ministry. The *Ratio Studiorum* (Lat., "method of studies") of Ignatius of Loyola, for example, was suffused with Renaissance humanism and rationality. The work, issued in 1599, divided the program of studies into three divisions: letters (Latin and Greek), philosophy, and theology.

The Protestant Reformation was launched by Martin Luther (1483–1546) when he published his Ninety-five Theses on October 31, 1517. Though the Reformers favored revelation over reason as the source of truth (*sola Scriptura*, Lat., "Scripture alone"), the Renaissance challenge to Church authority encouraged emphasis on individual interpretation of Scripture. This in turn became a major impetus for universal literacy in the Western world.

The Reformation also encouraged the replacement by the state of the Church as primary educator. For his reform movement to succeed, Luther recognized the need to wrest control of education from the Church of Rome. Condemning the cathedral and monastery schools as "unchristian" and "tools of the devil," he wrote his famous educational manifesto of 1524, urging civil rulers to establish government-funded and -sponsored schools for the welfare of both state and Church. This encouraged what later became the "national school system" throughout Europe, though the separation between "public" and Church education was not widely effected until well into the nineteenth century.

Education in the Catholic Counter-Reformation: Prior to the Reformation, the Dominicans, Franciscans, and Augustinians had papal approval to be involved in education as a function of their ministry, and Geert de Groote (1340–84) had founded the Brethren of the Common Life in 1376, likely the first order of vowed religious brothers dedicated to educating the common people. In the post-Reformation period, however, the Church approved a great number of new teaching orders of men and women, beginning with the Ursulines, founded in 1535 by Angela de Merici (1474–1540), and the Jesuits of Ignatius of Loyola (1491–1556), which received papal approval in 1540.

The Council of Trent (1545–63), in fact, discouraged women's religious orders from participating in the educational ministry of the Church. However, the faith and persistence of many great women, who often knowingly functioned contrary to the expressed directives of the Church, prevailed over papal opposition and led gradually to approval.

Some of the notable women's orders dedicated to teaching that emerged in this era were: the Congregation of Notre Dame, cofounded in 1598 by Alix le Clerc with her pastor Peter Fourier; the Visitation Sisters, cofounded in 1610 by Jane Frances de Chantal (1572–1641) and Francis de Sales; the Institute of the Blessed Virgin Mary (Loretto Sisters), founded ca. 1615 by Mary Ward (1585–1645); the Daughters of Charity, cofounded ca. 1633 by Louise de Marillac (1591–1660) and Vincent de Paul; the Sisters of St. Joseph founded in 1650 by John Peter Medaille. Likewise, many new teaching orders of religious men emerged, most notably: the Oratorians (1575), the Vincentians (1625), the Sulpicians (1642), and the Brothers of the Christian Schools founded by Jean-Baptiste de La Salle in 1684.

The Modern Era: Through these and many other religious orders, the Church continued to be a major influence on education down to the present. From the seventeenth to the nineteenth centuries they helped to forge many of the "national school systems" of Europe. With the revival of the missionary movement in the nineteenth century (from the pontificate of Gregory XVI, 1831–46, onward), these orders brought their commitment to education throughout the world and particularly to the developing countries. Their pedagogy, especially of the women's orders, was an enlightened one that anticipated or reflected the personalist and humanizing pedagogies of great educational reformers like John Amos Comenius (1592–1670), Johann Heinrich Pestalozzi (1746–1827), and Friedrich Wilhelm Froebel (1782–1852).

The Enlightenment era of the eighteenth and nineteenth centuries brought a deeper and more critical rationalism than ever before. Its driving conviction was that the triumph of critical reason and free thinking over "common sense" and authority would solve, with ever evolving progress, most human problems and bring true happiness. The Enlightenment's skepticism and "deism" (natural religion based on reason) challenged the whole fabric of Christianity, and its battle cry of "dare to think" (Immanuel Kant) challenged the authority of Scripture and of the Church's magisterial role. As with its predecessor, the Renaissance, the Church was defensive at first and has ever remained a bit cautious toward the Enlightenment; but it came to recognize that its own traditions enabled it to appropriate the asset of critical reason to its faith life and education. At Vatican I (1869–70) Catholicism reiterated its age-old conviction that "Faith and reason . . . are . . . mutually advantageous. . . . Right reason demonstrates the foundations of faith . . . and faith . . . sets reason free" (Dogmatic Constitution on the Catholic Faith). Much of the scriptural, historical, theological, and pastoral scholarship that encouraged the *aggiornamento* (It., "updating") of the Second Vatican Council (1962–65) reflected the critical methods and canons of the Enlightenment period. And

Vatican II in its introduction to the Declaration on Christian Education reiterated Catholicism's ancient partnership with education, insisting that because of "the mandate she has received from her divine Founder to proclaim the mystery of salvation to all," the Church always has a "role to play in the progress of education" and in seeing to it that every person's "inalienable right to an education" is duly honored.

Catholicism and Education in the United States: Throughout history, there is likely no more compelling instance of Catholic commitment to education than the school system created by the U.S. Catholic community. The story of American Catholic education goes back to the very first Catholic settlers in the New World.

Outside of the original colonies, Spanish missionaries from the sixteenth to nineteenth centuries created a system of mission centers whose purpose included the education of the native peoples. As early as 1606, Spanish Franciscans opened a formal school in St. Augustine, Florida, with the stated purpose "to teach children Christian doctrine, reading, and writing."

Likewise, the first French missionaries and explorers who came into the Great Lakes region and Mississippi Basin from Montreal and Quebec understood their mission work to include education. The first French-sponsored Catholic formal school for boys was opened by Franciscans in New Orleans in 1718, and the Ursulines opened a school there for girls in 1727.

In the thirteen original colonies, the English settlers vigorously opposed education for and by Catholics, who constituted a small minority (ca. twenty-five thousand in 1776), largely of indentured laborers and servants. In 1642 the Massachusetts Bay Colony enacted a law that required a school in every settlement lest, through inability to read the Bible, "Ye Olde Deluder Satan" led people astray. Thereafter and throughout the colonial period of a century and a half, each colony had a common school system, but one controlled by the Protestant churches and clergy. A Protestant ethos and an overt anti-Catholic bias permeated the whole curriculum (e.g., the McGuffey readers). Even into the late 1700s, the few Catholic schools run by Jesuits, Franciscans, and Ursuline sisters received no public support and much opposition, while the Protestant denominational schools had full freedom and public funding.

Independence (1776) and the Bill of Rights (1791), with its guarantee of religious liberty, coupled with a major influx of Catholic immigrants from Europe (the Catholic population rose to six million by 1850), brought new opportunity and need for Catholic education. Catholics in the colonies began to challenge the Protestant control and curriculum of the common school, which they saw as a serious threat to the faith of their children.

At first many Catholic bishops favored a truly "public" school system, free of undue Protestant influence. This was also the intent of such educational leaders as Horace Mann (1796–1859)—a nonsectarian school system supported by the public. However, this "secularization" of the schools met with stiff opposition from the Protestant establishment. Spearheaded by such bishops as John Hughes (1797–1864) of New York, Catholics began to establish their own schools and petitioned the states for the same funding already enjoyed by other denominational schools and academies. The predictable outcome was that one state after another prohibited state funds to all denominational schools. This refusal of public funds, coupled with the presence of organized anti-Catholic sentiment in "nativist" groups like the Know-Nothing Society of the 1850s (founded to eradicate "foreign influence, Popery, Jesuitism and Catholicism"), prompted U.S. Catholics and the episcopacy to establish their own independent school system.

U.S. Catholic education was made possible by the generosity of Catholic parents and parishioners and especially by the religious orders of women and men who emerged to staff the schools for a minimum living allowance. Between 1840 and 1900 more than sixty European religious orders of women and men came to teach in the United States. Likewise the emergence of the first American sisterhoods gave major impetus to the parochial school system. The Sisters of Charity of St. Joseph were founded by Elizabeth Ann Seton (1774–1821) ca. 1809; the Dominican sisters of St. Catherine were founded in Kentucky in 1822; the Oblate Sisters of Providence were founded in Baltimore in 1829, the first congregation of African-American sisters to take vows in the United States; the Servants of the Immaculate Heart of Mary were founded in 1845 at Monroe, Michigan.

The Catholic bishops of the United States assembled at the First Plenary Council of Baltimore (1852) urged that every parish build a parochial school, a plea reiterated by the Second Plenary Council (1866). But the Third Plenary Council (1884), of *Baltimore Catechism* fame, was even more legislative and decreed that "near each church, where it does not exist, a parochial school is to be erected within two years.... All Catholic parents are bound to send their children to the parochial school."

Though this mandate of Baltimore III was never fully realized because of financial and other constraints, it lent new impetus to the founding of parochial schools. By 1900 there were as many as 3,500 Catholic elementary schools in the country (about 45 percent of the 8,000 parishes). By 1920 this number had doubled to 6,551 schools with 41,581 teachers and 1,759,673 pupils. Catholic elementary school enrollment doubled twice again until it reached an all-time high in the mid-1960s with 4.5 million children enrolled. Similarly, the secondary schools grew from approximately 100 in 1900 to 1,552 by 1920, to 2,119 in 1940, and 2,392 in 1960 with an enrollment of almost 1 million students.

In 1789 the great John Carroll (1735–1815) of Baltimore, first bishop of the United States, founded the first Catholic institution of higher education at Georgetown, later confided to the Jesuits. During the nineteenth century religious orders opened some 200 Catholic colleges for men in the United States. Among the early ones that have survived and grown into renowned colleges and universities were St. Louis University (1818), Fordham (1841), Notre Dame (1842), Villanova (1842), Holy Cross (1843), Santa Clara (1851), and Boston College (1863). Colleges for women were slower to emerge, but among the first were Notre Dame of Maryland (1873), St. Mary's, Indiana (1894), Trinity College, Washington, D.C. (1897), and the College of New Rochelle (1904).

Present and Future: In 1991–92 there were 8,508 Catholic elementary and secondary schools in the United States, with a combined enrollment of 2.5 million students. The decline from the high of 5.5 million students in the 1960s is due, at least in part, to the decrease in numbers of vowed religious to staff the schools, thus requiring higher tuition. (The United States is the only Western democracy to refuse public funding to such schools.) In 1964, 85 percent of faculty and staff were vowed religious; in 1992, 87 percent of full-time faculty were lay women and men, 11 percent sisters, and 3 percent brothers and priests.

In spite of cutbacks in enrollment and ever-rising costs, contemporary research indicates that U.S. Catholic schools continue to be very successful educational ventures. In their 1987 study, *Public and Private Schools,* James S. Coleman and Thomas Hoffer found that Catholic-school students do better than their public-school peers in reading, mathematics, and verbal skills. Likewise, minority and other disadvantaged students at Catholic high schools have higher achievement levels and lower drop-out rates than in public schools, and a greater percentage go on to college. Coleman and Hoffer propose that the greater success of Catholic schools over public ones (with far more budget) is due to the "social capital" of the religious community that surrounds the school. After twenty-five years of chronicling the life of American Catholic education, Andrew Greeley offers a similar thesis, that it is the "community-forming" component of Catholic schools that explains their effectiveness. *See also* academic freedom; Catholic colleges and universities—statistics; parochial school; religious education.

Bibliography

Buetow, Harold A. *A History of Catholic Schooling in the United States.* Washington, DC: National Catholic Education Association, 1986.

Power, Edward J. *Main Currents in the History of Education.* New York: McGraw-Hill, 1970.

Sawicki, Marianne. *The Gospel in History: Portrait of a Teaching Church.* New York: Paulist Press, 1988.

Ulich, Robert. *Three Thousand Years of Educational Wisdom.* Cambridge, MA: Harvard University Press, 1971.   THOMAS GROOME

Catholicism and journalism. Catholic weekly and daily publications are a result of the nineteenth-century expansion of journalism. England's weekly *The Tablet* began publication in 1840; Holland's Catholic daily *De Tijd* in 1845; the Vatican's *L'Osservatore Romano* in 1861; and France's *La Croix* in 1883.

Catholic Journalism in the United States: In the United States, the earliest efforts in Catholic journalism were affected by the immigrant communities they served. An interesting exception was a short-lived bilingual (English and French) newspaper, Michigan's first, called the *Michigan Essay,* or. *Impartial Observer.* Established in 1809 by Father Gabriel Richard, pastor of St. Anne's parish in Detroit, the four-page publication relieved his sacristan of extra duty as town crier. Welcoming contributions from all "gentlemen of talent," regardless of creed, the newspaper's columns consisted largely of reprints of stories from secular periodicals, an advertisement for St. Anne's school, and a promise that a future issue would include an essay on "Nine Days' Devotion to the Sacred Heart of Jesus."

Bishop John England of Charleston, South Carolina, founded the first advertently Catholic newspaper in the nation, the weekly *United States Catholic Miscellany* (1822), and this publication continued, closely supervised by England's successors, into the final days of the Civil War. Nevertheless, during its nearly half-century history, the *Miscellany* was sufficiently influential and challenging to spawn numerous imitations, most of them edited by laypersons. While the American bishops of this era applauded the growth of a Catholic press, they were disconcerted by the independence of these lay editors. This ambivalence, lasting well into the next century, found its way into a pastoral letter issued from the bishops' 1837 meeting in Baltimore. "We feel disposed," they wrote, "to exhort you to sustain with better efforts those journals, which, though not officially sanctioned by us, still are most useful to explain our tenets, to defend our rights and to vindicate our conduct." By the end of the nineteenth century, Catholics in America were reading more than two hundred and fifty such journals.

The establishment of the Catholic Press Association (CPA) in 1911 made possible numerous improvements in Catholic journalism, not the least of which was the formation of a news service for Catholic newspapers. Independent of ecclesiastical control, the CPA included priests and members of religious orders, but for the first three decades of its existence, laypeople presided. After World War I, the American bishops reorganized their first corporate institution, the National Catholic War Council into the National Catholic Welfare Council (NCWC), which included a press department. In 1919, by mutual agreement, the CPA's news service joined the NCWC press department, simultaneously expanding its subscriptions and ceding editorial control to the national hierarchy. The CPA remains an indispensable organization for Catholic journalists today, providing a variety of services and professional education programs to a network of more than three hundred publications in the United States and Canada.

Catholic colleges and universities played a significant role in the expansion of the Catholic press. Marquette University established a department of journalism in 1910, and the University of Notre Dame established a chair in journalism in 1912. An educated Catholic readership was increasingly stimulated by the emergence of national magazines providing distinctive commentary on politics, culture, and the faith. Salient among these were *America,* a Jesuit magazine founded in 1909, and *Commonweal,* founded by laypeople in 1924, both of which survive today. *The Catholic World,* a monthly begun in 1865, still publishes under the name *The New Catholic World.* By the 1950s, the total circulation of Catholic periodicals in North America had reached 15 million, a figure that would nearly double by the closing of Vatican Council II in 1965.

Postconciliar Developments: The Second Vatican Council had remarkably little of interest to say about journalism. Cardinal John Heenan, archbishop of Westminster, went so far as to pronounce its Decree on the Instruments of Social Communication (*Inter Mirifica*) the council's "greatest failure." Nevertheless, the excitement surrounding the council itself and its firm commitment to the free flow of information as later expressed in *Communio et Progressio* (the 1971 pastoral instruction on the application of *Inter Mirifica*) deeply affected the operations of America's Catholic newspapers and magazines. "For many editors," wrote A. E. P. Wall, formerly of the *Catholic Review* in Baltimore, "the council was a signal to broaden the scope of their coverage of the news and to publish articles exploring such controversial subjects as the role of authority, homosexuality, [and] the ordination of women to priesthood." These subjects and, since the U.S. Supreme Court decisions of the early 1970s, abortion continue to fascinate postconciliar editors, reporters, and columnists. One effect of this absorption, whether intended or not, is a discourse that strikingly relies on conventional American political categories, so that, for example, the "liberal" *National Catholic Reporter* (a national weekly based in Kansas City, Missouri) is arrayed against the "conservative" *Wanderer* (a national weekly based in St. Paul, Minnesota).

Whatever these postconciliar developments in Catholic journalism have done or failed to do for the Church in the United States, they have not increased readership. In 1965 the CPA reported that the combined circulation of Catholic newspapers, magazines, and newsletters in North America had reached 28,944,724. Three decades later, and despite a remarkable growth in the Catholic population, that figure stood at 27,348,517. *See also America; Catholic Press Association; Catholic World, The; Commonweal; Decree on the Instruments of Social Communication, National Catholic Reporter; Osservatore Romano; Tablet, The; Wanderer, The.*   MICHAEL GARVEY

Catholicism and mass media. Catholicism interacts with mass media through official church statements concerning mass media, Catholic media activity, and media coverage of the Catholic Church. Throughout its history the Catholic Church has utilized various modes of communication—oral tradition, medieval manuscripts, and the printed word. In the twentieth century modern modes of social communication (newspapers, film, radio, and television) have become major components of popular culture throughout the world. As early as 1896 a film projector was demonstrated at the Vatican. In 1931 a radio station was established there and Pius XI was the first pope to use the medium. The first papal encyclical, *Vigilanti Cura,* wholly devoted to the motion picture appeared in 1936. In 1957 Pope Pius XII's encyclical *Miranda Prorsus,* concerned with radio and television, spoke of the pastoral problems posed by modern communications media.

In 1963 the Vatican II Decree on the Instruments of Social Communication (*Inter Mirifica*) called modern means of social communication "marvelous technical inventions from creation." This document noted that an interdependent world had a need for, and a right to, information. Bishops were called to oversee media activities in their dioceses. The council directed a Vatican commission to initiate international consultation and to publish a pastoral instruction to "ensure that all the principles and rules of the council on the means of social communication be put into effect."

The pastoral instruction *Communio et Progressio,* published in 1971, and the document *Aetatis Novae,* issued by the Pontifical Council for Social Communications in 1992, reflected on the revolution in human communications that had occurred in the two decades since the earlier instruction. Both documents pointed out that communications media are powerful instruments for progress. The role of media is noted in the formation of public opinion— agenda-setting, as media experts call it. These church documents stressed the justice of equal access for all to information and media channels. Also noted were the need for special training in media techniques and the special affirmation necessary for media professionals of good will.

Communio et Progressio sees the Church maintaining lines of communication with the whole human race and building closer communion within the Church itself. *Aetatis Novae* cites newer mass media technologies (satellites, cable television, videocassettes, compact discs, computerized image-making) as "new languages." *Communio et Progressio* is "rooted in a vision of communication as a way toward communion" and holds that media should be at the service of dialogue with the world. "The dialogue also involves support for media artists; it requires the development of an anthropology and a theology of communication. . . ." *Aetatis Novae* concludes: "It is not enough to use the media simply to spread the Christian message and the church's authentic teaching. It is also necessary to integrate that message into the new culture created by modern communications . . . with new languages, new techniques and a new psychology."

The 1992 document cited a need for a pastoral plan of social communications. "Catholic media work is not simply one more program alongside all the rest of the church's activities; social communications have a role to play in every aspect of the church's mission." An appendix to the document offers guidelines for designing such a pastoral plan and a process for implementing it.

Catholic Media Activity: Global mass media content is heavily influenced by media activities in the United States: Hollywood film techniques, Cable News Network's on-the-spot coverage, and American advertising and marketing. The economics of mass media are also moving to the American model as many nations alter their media from government-sponsored to commercially-based systems.

Communications scholars have long debated the realities of "media effects" or the precise way media influence audience choices and values. Of special concern has been the impact of violence in media programming and its effect on culture. Music has been a significant aspect of programming, with the advent of rock music and the combination of sound and sight in music videos. Minorities, senior citizens, and women are often under-represented in media.

It has become obvious that mass media reflect popular culture and that the dynamics of myth, ritual, and storytelling are at work within media viewers as they interact around the world with dramas, situation comedies, and soap operas. Theologians have discussed this in terms of the religious imagination. Indeed, media scholars and theologians have begun a systematic dialogue on these topics under the guidance of the Gregorian University in Rome and the Jesuit Center for the Study of Communication and Culture in London. Joint conferences have been held with subsequent book publications.

Many religious communities have had members trained in mass media techniques, and a communications office exists in most dioceses. Catholic universities and colleges have programs of study in communications with many summer programs available.

Organizations exist to unite Catholic media personnel: the International Organization for the Press (UCIP); for cinema (OCIC); and for radio and television (UNDA). An annual World Communications Day often elicits an address by the Holy Father on the significance of media.

After regional hearings in the United States, an annual national communications collection was established, with a portion of the proceeds remaining in the local diocese for its own communication efforts. This funding has been used to sponsor the production of selected materials for international broadcast and cassette distribution. Some of this national funding helped establish the Catholic Television Network of America (CTNA), a satellite system linking many dioceses for program delivery and teleconference meetings. In addition, a number of dioceses operate closed circuit television systems for extensive educational and pastoral tasks.

Media Coverage of the Catholic Church: In 1991 the Knights of Columbus and the Catholic League for Religious and Civil Rights, two conservative organizations, commissioned a study of U.S. news coverage of the Catholic Church to be undertaken by the Center for Media and Public Affairs. The study examined a sample of nationally influential media outlets during three five-year time blocs. The study used content analysis, with the final sample numbering 1,876 news items. Subject categories included sexual morality, church authority and dissent, ecumenism and church-state relations, and the use of descriptive language.

The study found that opinions in the media "were tilted against the church's teaching on issues involving sexual morality and authority relations within the church and its involvement in secular politics (aside from support for church statements opposing war). Only on the relatively noncontroversial issue of ecumenical outreach did the church receive support from a majority of sources."

The Catholic Church is sensitive to the influence of mass media in society—as information shared, as storytelling, and as news source. The continuing challenge is to utilize media creatively and honestly to build a faith community and to advance its mission in the world. *See also* Catholicism and culture; Catholicism and journalism.

Bibliography

Coleman, John, and Miklos Tomka, eds. "Mass Media." *Concilium: International Review of Theology,* Winter 1993.

Communication Research Trends, A Quarterly Information Service from the Centre for the Study of Communication and Culture, St. Louis.

Soukup, Paul A. *Communication and Theology: Introduction and Review of the Literature.* London: World Association for Christian Communication, 1983.   FRANCES F. PLUDE

Catholicism and music. This entry examines the Roman Catholic tradition of liturgical music specifically, but also refers to music of the Byzantine church and Reformed churches.

The history of church music is a chronology of musical developments, but it also includes liturgical dimensions, such as the shape of worship and the interplay of rite and music. Music ministries shed light on specific musical developments.

Jewish Worship: Ancient Near Eastern language usage employed the same verb for speaking and singing, indicating "to execute vocally." Because no clear distinction between speech and song existed, it is difficult to speak of "music" as a separate category. The heightened speech of proclamation of the Scriptures and prayers in Jewish worship bore the stamp of rhythm and incipient melody.

The Jerusalem Temple, local synagogues, and homes of believers were the loci of Jewish worship in Jesus' time. Temple singers and musicians, a large professional staff, rendered psalms and other poetic texts musically, the congregation responding with refrains.

Synagogue worship, centered on scriptural study and proclamation and the offering of prayers, had two focal worship elements: the proclamation of the *Shema* (Heb., "hear") and the chanting of the *Amidah* (Heb., "standing"; Eighteen Benedictions) with responses from the congregation. These texts, like readings from the Law and Prophets, were cantillated. After the Temple was destroyed in A.D. 70, professionals took a larger role in the synagogue, where the cantor's art music developed. Synagogal musical elements, like domestic ritual song, initially were of a folk style.

Early Christianity: Early Christians continued Temple worship (Acts 3:1) and synagogue prayer (Acts 13:14), but gradually developed a distinctive Christian domestically centered cult. Obviously familiar with Jewish lyrical expression, they could have continued similar "musical" expression. The NT itself gives an indication of Christian worship's lyrical quality by reference to hymn fragments (1 Pet 1:3–5; Phil 2:6–11), acclamations ("Hosanna," "Marana tha") and song (Rev. 4). Early Christian vocal "music," clearly nonprofessional, supported and elaborated the word proclaimed in a flexible service.

From the second to the third centuries vocal lyricism characterized the proclamation of readings, improvisation of prayers and communal responses in the domestic churches. Vocal music predominated; the use of instruments in pagan cults and the association of instruments with immorality led to their gradual banning in Christian worship.

During this period Christians began to develop distinctive musical texts and forms. Despite Pauline references to psalms (Col 3:16; Eph 5:19), the first irrefutable evidence we have showing psalm usage in worship, perhaps to counteract heterodox hymns, is from the late second and third centuries. Original compositions, nonbiblical psalms called *psalmi idiotici* (Lat., "idiotic psalms"), also emerge, as well as the hymn form.

Fourth to Seventh Centuries: The legalization and imperialization of Christianity, after Constantine's victory, dramatically transformed worship. The locus of Christian worship shifted from home to basilica, a public gathering space. Professional clerics emerged as leaders of the now public prayer of Roman society. Music, too, underwent considerable changes.

Specially designated cantors appeared, first mentioned in Canon 15 of the Canons of Laodicea (343–381), an early collection of ecclesiastical law. A forerunner of a *schola cantorum* (Lat.), a school for liturgical singers, developed in Rome. *The Pilgrimage of Egeria* (end of fourth century) attests to choirs of boys in Jerusalem, and Ephraem the Syrian (d. 373) notes the worship role of choirs of women.

From the beginning, music specialists engaged the assembly in sung prayer and added artistic embellishment. With the gradual distancing of formal worship from the people, spatially and linguistically, music personnel became performers rather than leaders of song. In the West, monasteries cultivated boy choirs, professionally trained, which later took over the assembly's song. In some localities and for various reasons—nighttime dangers and association with pagan cults are two—women choirs were forbidden and disappeared altogether when communal singing ceased in the early Middle Ages.

Christian hymnody as a specific musical genre received impetus from Hilary of Poitiers (d. 367), Ambrose (d. 397), and Prudentius (d. ca. 410) in the West and Ephraem in the East. Despite some prohibitions against using nonbiblical texts, hymnody became an important element in worship, especially in the Divine Office. Ambrose, the "Hammer of the Arians," used hymnody to combat heretical catechetical hymns.

In the Byzantine church, a rigid structure determined its musical shape. The *Apostolic Constitutions* (380) witnesses to psalmic congregational refrains and a sung *Kyrie eleison* (Gk., "Lord, have mercy") response to prayers. As the liturgy developed, sung formulas increased and were frequently repeated during the service, creating a dialogue among celebrant, clergy, and congregation.

Early on, the Byzantine Mass admitted a certain number of hymns, such as the *Trisagion* (a refrain, "Holy God, holy and mighty, holy and immortal, have mercy on us") and the Cherubic hymn. Byzantine hymnography flourished from the fifth to eleventh centuries, when ecclesiastical authority forbade including new compositions in worship. The mid-fifth century saw a new poetic form develop, the *Kontakion*, a hymn that resembled a poetic sermon, setting forth the narrative of the feast with rhetorical flourish. In the seventh century, the *Kanon* (a series of nine odes or canticles) all but replaced the *Kontakion*. This new poetic hymn form was structurally more diverse and often linked verbally to liturgical texts.

From ecclesiastical centers in Constantinople, Toledo, Milan, Metz, and Rome styles of plainsong emerged: Greco-Byzantine, Mozarabic, Ambrosian, Gallican, and Old Roman. An expanding body of specific Christian music developed, complex in nature, requiring special training for its execution.

The emergent distinction between word and music, previously unknown, allowed for music-less worship; prayer and song texts could be recited silently by the prayer leader. Music became a separable element of the rite.

Eighth to Eleventh Centuries: Pepin III (d. 768) and Charlemagne (d. 814) orchestrated the importation of Roman chants and liturgy in Frankish lands. The mandated Roman liturgy did not displace Gallican music and texts; rather Roman and Gallican music and texts fused together, resulting in so-called Gregorian chant. Musical elaborations of the chant, the sequence and the trope, can be credited to ninth and tenth-century professionals. These Latin hymnic chants never achieved the prominence of Byzantine hymnography.

Though early "popular" musical styles were easily admitted into a fluid liturgy, standardization of music, in a language generally unavailable to the people, created the need for music for the people. The new nonliturgical vernacular song appeared as an occasional addition to the liturgical rite, but more often in popular devotions. What Bede (d.

735) called "devotional and religious songs" developed and flourished.

Polyphony was born during this era, originating as *organum* (Lat., "ornamentation"), a second musical line matched note for note with the chant, usually a musical fourth or fifth higher. Creative musicians developed more complex polyphonic forms, obscuring the liturgical texts themselves. Music was triumphing over the liturgy.

An opposite movement paralleled musical elaboration—the total disappearance of song in worship. Published books included chants in appendices and the thirteenth-century full missal presumed the possibility of the presiding minister's taking all liturgical roles, reducing sung texts to silent recitation.

Twelfth to Fifteenth Centuries: Once the possibility of simultaneously singing two musical (though parallel) lines was realized, it was a short step to two-, three- and four-part singing, involving different melodies. Simple ornamentation (*organum*) led to florid elaboration, and rhythmic advances supplanted plainsong's nonmetered rhythm. This musical verticality and rhythm found an ally in the Gothic architecture of the period. Concomitantly, musical leadership shifted from monasteries to urban cathedrals. For example, the Notre Dame School in Paris developed a novel style of *organum* in which the tenor part in shorter, metered notes moved in contrary motion to the parallel parts. Again, the motet, a thirteenth-century development, consisted of a rhythmically-modified plainsong in the lowest part, to which were added two higher original melodies in faster moving rhythm. Gradually, vernacular texts were added in the upper voices, making textual comprehension impossible. Motets sometimes replaced the chant gradual (the psalm sung after the Lesson, or Pauline Letter) and alleluia, but became more popular in Office responsories.

In the fourteenth-century Byzantine church, whose chant is more formulaic than Western plainsong, a new florid style also developed. Called "kalophonic," the style affected all chant genres. Although the codified Byzantine liturgy remained almost unchanged from the eleventh century to the present day, musical ornamentation continued. Often ornamented style led to the shortening of texts, and the unchecked embellishment eliminated textual intelligibility.

Though professionals shaped the choral tradition of the cathedrals, ordinary people continued a flourishing vernacular devotional hymn and song tradition. Popular music was confined to nonliturgical settings; the official chant, Latin language, and professionalism of ministries moved the assembly to become spectators at worship.

Sixteenth to Nineteenth Centuries: Though the Protestant reforms of the sixteenth century were theologically rooted, they created musical transformations. Martin Luther's (d. 1546) strong belief in the universal priesthood shifted musical ministry especially to the congregation by introducing vernacular hymns and chants. Popularly styled religious hymns, often textually nonliturgical, found a significant place in worship. Luther himself was responsible for many metered psalm translations. In contrast, Ulrich Zwingli (d. 1531), a trained musician, eliminated music from the Zurich churches, considering it a secular invasion. John Calvin (d. 1564) banned textually unintelligible polyphony and distracting instruments, but, like Luther, encouraged monophonic singing, especially of the psalms, which led to prayer and served God's word.

The Council of Trent (1545–63), seeking to correct musical abuses, emphasized the need for intelligibility (apparently on the part of the clergy who could understand Latin) and musical restraint. It banned nonchurchly vernacular songs and worldly and lengthy organ compositions. Trent implicitly affirmed a style of composition wherein music serves the text.

Spurred by the Reformers' example, vernacular hymnals began to appear. The mainly devotional and catechetical hymns of German diocesan hymnals were used at Mass (e.g., a postsermon hymn). The 1605 Mainz Cantual permitted substituting hymns for the proper texts of the liturgy. Within two centuries, hymns replaced the ordinary chants, giving rise to what is called the *Singmesse* (Ger., "sung Mass"). Though this development restored congregational sung participation, it was not an integration of music and rite; it signaled singing *at* Mass, rather than a sung liturgy.

Baroque styles influenced the Latin compositions that found a place in some of the reform movements. English polyphonic settings of Morning and Evening Prayer and Holy Communion were composed. Lutheran chorale motets appeared, and chorale cantatas reached a zenith with the works of J.S. Bach (d. 1750). Despite Tridentine decrees, restraint was abandoned, as evidenced by operatic vocal works and massive compositions that overshadowed the liturgy itself.

Churches had lost preeminence in musical leadership by the mid-eighteenth century. Art-music, e.g., Mass settings composed for the concert hall, held its ground as a new Catholic reform emerged, urging the return to Gregorian chant and Palestrina-styled polyphony. The Society of St. Caecilia was a chief proponent of this restoration.

In the United States, while New England pilgrims relied initially on English hymnals, the Bay Psalm Book gained ascendency in the late seventeenth century and retained primacy. Camp meetings were another center of musical activity, where secular folk tunes joined with religious texts and replaced the staid Puritan psalter with heartier group song. This style had a gradual influence on some Protestant worship. Catholic immigrants brought their own hymnals, stamped with European influence of the post-Baroque concerto style and Viennese classical form.

The Caecilian movement, seeking objectivity of expression, challenged lush romantic composition. It found strong support in midwest German communities, where it fostered revival of older German hymns, though they were still relegated to devotional services.

The Twentieth Century: Pope Pius X issued various instructions that, in principle, held to music as an integral part of worship and urged the participation of the people in the liturgy. At the same time he reiterated the ban against the use of the vernacular song.

The Vatican II Constitution on the Sacred Liturgy restated the position of Pius X that congregational participation is desirable and that music, integral to worship, should serve the text, but it also underscored the connection between rite and music.

The 1972 publication "Music in Catholic Worship" by the U.S. Catholic Bishops' Committee on the Liturgy was a watershed document that gave impetus to restoring the tradition of musical participation of the assembly, especially through singing liturgical texts. Universa Laus, an international group researching liturgical music and singing, published guidelines in 1980 under the title "The Music of Christian Ritual." The document strongly supported the subordination of music not just to liturgical text, but to ritual action. Ritual music embraces distinct categories: music alone, music wedded to text, music joined with ritual action, music wedded to a text accompanying a rite. This ritual approach, currently under much discussion, requires an understanding of both the macro- and micro-structures of worship

to determine which music can be genuinely integral to, and servant of, worship. *See also* chant, Byzantine; chant, Gregorian; liturgical music.

Bibliography

Foley, Edward. "Liturgical Music." In *The New Dictionary of Sacramental Worship.* Ed. Peter E. Fink. Collegeville, MN: Liturgical Press, 1990. Pp. 854–70.

Gelineau, Joseph. *Voices and Instruments in Christian Worship: Principles, Laws, Applications.* Trans. Clifford Howell. Collegeville, MN: Liturgical Press, 1964.

Quasten, Johannes. *Music and Worship in Pagan and Christian Antiquity.* Trans. Boniface Ramsey. Washington, DC: National Association of Pastoral Musicians, 1983.

Routley, Erik. *The Music of Christian Hymns.* Chicago: GIA Publications, 1981.

Wellesz, Egon. *A History of Byzantine Music and Hymnography,* 2d ed. Oxford: Clarendon Press, 1961.

Werner, Eric. *The Sacred Bridge II: The Interdependence of Liturgy and Music in Synagogue and Church During the First Millennium.* New York: Ktav Publishing, 1984.   JOHN A. MELLOH

Catholicism and politics. *See* Church and state.

Catholicism and psychology/psychiatry. The history of the relationship between Catholicism and the scientific disciplines of psychiatry and psychology parallels and reflects that of these clinical disciplines themselves. The latter, insofar as they have generated research-based theories and humane therapies for mental illness, are an outgrowth of the efforts of pioneers such as Phillipe Pinel (1745–1826) in France and William Tuke (1732–1822) in England, to "loosen the chains," that is, to remove the restraints from institutionalized patients and to pioneer "moral" treatment modes.

History of Psychiatry and Psychology: The early history of American psychiatry, begun through its acknowledged founder, Benjamin Rush (1745–90), a signer of the Declaration of Independence, and later spurred by the efforts of such figures as Dorothea Dix (1802–87), was, like the country itself, largely a Protestant enterprise. It emphasized the construction of small, private "asylums," such as the Friends Hospital in Philadelphia (1817) and Connecticut's Hartford Retreat (1822).

Later in the century, larger public institutions were erected to meet the demands of the increasing numbers of mentally ill. These included many immigrants beset with the stress of adapting themselves to a new and at times difficult, if not hostile, social environment, especially for Catholics. "Moral" treatment, with its gentle attention to the care and rehabilitation of the individual, deteriorated and a more impersonal style of "custodial" care became the norm.

In tandem with this, a better understanding of mental functioning and mental illness began to develop, especially in Germany, in which experimental psychology began to separate itself from philosophical psychology under such figures as Wilhelm Wundt (1832–1920), and the systematic classification of the manifestations of mental illness was begun by Emil Kraepelin (1856–1926). The latter work enabled the identification of basic symptoms, modes of onset, and the course of mental illness.

At the same time, Sigmund Freud (1856–1939) began to publish his seminal works on the unconscious and its relationship to the conscious manifestations of mental illness. In the United States, Swiss psychiatrist Adolph Meyer (1866–1950) initiated his work at Johns Hopkins Hospital in Baltimore, Maryland. The latter focused on the patient's life history and the origin of mental illness as a function of the individual's interaction with specific life stressors. Drawing on Freud's insights, Meyer and other psychiatrists and psychologists oversaw a convergence of both disciplines on a more dynamic understanding of the meaning and treatment of mental illness.

Catholic Attitudes Toward Psychiatry and Psychology: Psychiatry emerged as a new speciality in medicine just as psychology embraced the experimental method of physics. The former, strongly influenced by the work of Freud, seemed a threat to the Catholic views of the human person, the nature of sin, moral responsibility, and sexual morality. The latter, attempting to quantify and measure behavior as hard science did other phenomena, was thought to have by-passed traditional Catholic views on the soul. It is not surprising that the Church, still reeling from the challenges of the Enlightenment a century earlier, viewed both of these movements as further evidences of a "modern" world that had lost its vision and faith.

Nonetheless, as Catholics settled into American society, they began to produce a new generation, some of whose members, although few in numbers, would make their way into these growing professions. For example, Father Edward Pace studied under Wundt and established an experimentally oriented psychology department at the American bishops' fledgling Catholic University of America in 1892. Two years later, in an example of an altogether too typical reaction, a priest-philosopher wrote that anybody who wished to have anything to do with this new psychology "must commit a formal dogmatic error in his Christian faith."

Psychiatry, and especially psychoanalysis, were similarly condemned by Church leaders, largely on the basis of misunderstanding Freudian therapy as sprung from a corrupt, pansexual interpretation of personality that obliterated sin. As late as 1953, Monsignor, later Cardinal, Pericle Felici, a highly placed curial official, wrote a widely disseminated article suggesting that any Catholic who voluntarily undertook psychoanalytic treatment committed a mortal sin. Popular pamphlets heaped scorn on psychiatry as if it were the enemy of Catholic life and practice.

Catholic laypersons, including Leo Bartemeier, M.D. (1895–1982), Francis Braceland, M.D. (1900–85), and John Cavanagh, M.D. (1904–82) were among those who entered and became leaders in psychiatry and proved instrumental in helping the Church to revisit and to revise its harsh *a priori* rejection of the field. Bartemeier, for example, already president of the International Psychoanalytic Association, became at mid-century president of the American Psychiatric Association, as did Braceland a few years later.

Their example and success, along with the emergence of a new literature written by Catholic professionals for a better educated generation of American Catholics, contributed to the Church's new respect for, and acceptance of, psychiatry. In 1953, Pope Pius XII authored an address for the Fifth International Congress on Psychotherapy and Clinical Psychology in which, with certain cautions about the reality of sin, he gave what amounted to his blessing to the once roundly condemned dynamic psychotherapies.

It was several years, however, before the American Catholic Psychological Association, established largely through the influence of Father William C. Bier, as a parallel professional companion organization to the American Psychological Association, transformed itself into an ecumenical Psychologists Interested in Religious Issues (1936) and later under that title, into Division 36 of the national association.

In similar fashion, the Guild of Catholic Psychiatrists (1950) had been founded to allow a forum for Catholics to explore and discuss issues relating to psychiatry and religion. These structures were at first embattled against ecclesiastical skepticism and disapproval. As Catholics matured in American culture, as Church attitudes, accelerated by the work of Vatican Council II (1962–65), were transformed, and as professional psychiatry and psychology became more receptive and responsive to religion as a significant factor in human life, the role of these separate organizations has diminished significantly.

As the last decade of the twentieth century began, Catholics were extensively involved in the professions of psychology and psychiatry. The Church itself, aided by such pioneering developments as the summer institutes on psychiatry and religion begun in 1953 at St. John's University in Collegeville, Minnesota, and the burgeoning interest by the clergy in counseling, had dropped most of its straw-man criticism, and it accepted and widely employed the professions' techniques of assessment and treatment in its own internal life as well as its pastoral work. *See also* Jung, Carl Gustav; psychology and spirituality.

Bibliography

Myers, D. C., and M. A. Jeeves. *Psychology Through the Eyes of Faith.* Washington, DC: Christian College Coalition, 1987.

Wulff, D. M. *Psychology of Religion: Classic and Contemporary Views.* New York: Wiley, 1991.

EUGENE C. KENNEDY AND SARA C. CHARLES

Catholicism and the social sciences. Until the second half of the twentieth century, Catholic authorities tended to regard the social sciences with mixed emotions. Respect for the obvious utility of social analysis in performing the mundane tasks of a worldwide organization was combined with suspicion that such learning relied heavily on non-Christian conceptions of human nature and experience. Some imagined that the social sciences could prove useful in arriving at the technical knowledge necessary to implement the social doctrine of the Church. The more discernible feeling, however, was one of trepidation. Religious belief presumably would erode when confronted by models for science that confined inquiry to empirical observation of the material world.

Distinctively Catholic Approaches: More optimistic Catholics saw potential gains in the social sciences, even if the precise contributions varied by discipline. The Catholic study of politics, for example, would shun treatment of issues like state power and elite domination. In their places, Catholic theorists were charged with examining how governments could be shaped to promote the common good while cultivating in individual citizens a habit of virtue. A Catholic economics, for its part, would abandon familiar expectations of market competition and class conflict. Instead, Catholic students of the economy in the first half of the twentieth century were to follow the lessons of the social encyclicals, *Rerum Novarum* (1891) and *Quadragesimo Anno* (1931). Catholic societies could then plan how

workers, managers, and owners together might cooperate in the interests of greater human welfare. Yet, practical value notwithstanding, these ideals largely muted the scientific element of each discipline and in the end subordinated its results to the official teachings of the Church.

A Sociography of Religious Practice: In Western Europe, and particularly in France and Belgium, harnessing social science to the temporal work of the Catholic Church took a somewhat different turn. Eventually the steady labors of scholars like Gabriel Le Bras (1891–1970) and Fernand Boulard (1898–1977) produced a unique style of research, one that came to be known as *sociologie religieuse* (Fr., "religious sociology"). More the practice of geography than of sociology, research in the mode of *sociologie religieuse* was typified by the meticulous tabulation of statistics on ecclesiastical activities such as baptisms and church marriages across decades and sometimes centuries. When painstakingly mapped over parishes, localities, and departments, the figures revealed a historical portrait of whole regions moving through a process of religious declension that was dubbed "dechristianization."

Minutely detailed and relentlessly descriptive, the findings of these European researchers ordinarily were not arranged into a general theory of cultural change. Rather, *sociologie religieuse* was social investigation with a pastoral mission. An American Jesuit, Joseph H. Fichter (1908–94), beginning in the 1950s extended and improved this style of research through his comprehensive studies of parish life. As moderate as Fichter's publications appear four decades later, in their day they were controversial enough to provoke at least one bishop to request suppression of his writings.

Attitudes of the Church Toward Sociology: The official Church long approached sociology with special skepticism. The bulk of the Church's concerns apparently were associated with objections to the "positive philosophy" of Auguste Comte (1798–1857), the French theorist who gave the discipline its name. Comte, a true disciplinary imperialist, had predicted that his fledgling study of society would one day stand at the head of the sciences. By synthesizing human knowledge, sociology would force religion from its privileged social position. Moreover, the practitioners of this new and final science, according to Comte, would come to occupy the status of priests in a renewed secular rite. All things considered, there was a lot in the excesses of Comte's theory to make the traditionally faithful nervous.

So one finds in a textbook recommended to undergraduate students in Catholic colleges during the 1930s (Paul J. Glenn, *Sociology: A Class Manual in the Philosophy of Human Society* [St. Louis: B. Herder, 1935]), a condemnation of the legacy of Comte and Herbert Spencer (1820–1903) as "an evil thing," for it "rules out God, makes humanity divine, and establishes the 'service of humanity' (*humanitarianism*) as the only religion" (p. 6; emphasis in the original). Modern sociology "is wrong," the author insists, "is evil, is an affront to the mind and a damage to the soul ..." (p. 8).

In the period before the Second World War, while Catholic scholars were reacting to the antireligious allergens in sociology's intellectual heritage, the discipline's own establishment veered in a militantly secular direction, endorsing the conviction that a commitment to science precluded belief in the supernatural. This trend left it to priests like Paul Hanly Furfey (1896–1992) of The Catholic University of America and Raymond W. Murray (1893–1973) of the University of Notre Dame to champion a "sacred sociology." Friction between the religious and secular camps peaked with the 1938 founding of an autonomous American Catholic Sociological Society (ACSS).

Within twenty years, the increasingly rapid assimilation of Catholics into the American mainstream eased tensions, while a softening of positivism among American social scientists undermined the felt need to continue with an identifiably Catholic sociology and its attendant parallel structures. Indeed, the ACSS survives today as the Association for the Sociology of Religion, an ecumenical affiliation devoted to the social scientific study of religion.

The distance separating Catholicism and the social sciences has certainly diminished with time. The United States Catholic Conference today maintains its own research office, and a number of the larger dioceses in the United States now assign permanent staffs of social scientists to "pastoral research and planning." Nevertheless, most large-scale social research on the Catholic Church and its members around the world is conducted by researchers based in academic settings, without the sponsorship of the national hierarchy. Despite important efforts by the priest-sociologist Andrew M. Greeley (b. 1928), it is still not common for the Catholic Church expressly to commission professional survey research through universities or academic research centers. *See also* Catholic social teachings.

Bibliography

Fichter, Joseph H. *One-Man Research: Reminiscences of a Catholic Sociologist.* New York: Wiley, 1973.

Greeley, Andrew M. *The Catholic Myth: The Behavior and Beliefs of American Catholics.* New York: Scribner, 1990.

Salvaterra, David L. *American Catholicism and the Intellectual Life: 1880–1950.* New York: Garland, 1988.   KEVIN J. CHRISTIANO

Catholicism and the visual arts. Catholicism's impact on the visual arts pervades the Christian tradition from the late second and early third centuries to modern times. Its range embraces everything from grassroots populism to imperial patronage to high points of episcopal and papal court patronage during the Renaissance and Baroque periods.

Contrary perhaps to modern presumptions, early Christian imagery did not illustrate Scripture. Using a visual shorthand, simple austere catacomb images such as Moses striking the rock, Noah and the ark, or the three youths in the fiery furnace served to remind viewers of God's fidelity to God's people. Christological images of Christ as the Good Shepherd or the miracles (in which Christ is often not represented) recalled Christ's saving power rather than illustrated his life. There are no catacomb images of the Passion or Crucifixion.

A shift in perception from pastoral representations of Christ as the Good Shepherd to Christ as an imperial king occurs beginning with the reign of Constantine in the fourth century. Imperial patronage produced monumental churches with apse paintings and mosaics of Christ enthroned in Rome, Jerusalem, Constantinople, Milan, and by the sixth century, in Ravenna. This was conceptual art that pointed toward theological dogma and affirmed conciliar pronouncements. Roman examples

Twentieth-century depiction of the crucifixion by the English painter Graham Sutherland (d. 1980); part of the Vatican collection of modern religious art.

include the fifth-century mosaic of Christ enthroned and flanked by the apostles in Santa Pudenziana and the fifth-century Marian mosaic program at St. Mary Major following the Council of Ephesus of 431 that affirmed Mary as *Theotokos*, Mother of God.

A need for liturgical books by Irish missionaries of the seventh and eighth centuries led to the establishment of monastic artistic centers in Ireland and England for book production. The Lindisfarne Gospels and the Book of Kells with their pages alive with the writhing dragons and complex interlace patterns of the Hiberno-Saxon style, attest to the sophistication of these scriptoria.

Lavishly illustrated Bibles appeared in the ninth century. The Alcuin Bible, the Moutier-Grandval Bible, and the San Callisto Bible, produced for the Carolingian court, continued the early Christian practice of selecting themes that allude to theological truths rather than illustration. OT scenes prefigure NT events. Apocalyptic images of Christ as the Lamb emphasize the redemptive act of Christ's Passion, death and Resurrection, Christ's final triumph.

Religious imagery appealing directly to the laity emerged in the eleventh century in the sculptural decoration of churches along the French pilgrimage routes to Santiago de Compostela in northwest Spain. Here popular religiosity, steeped in miracle and marvel, found expression in the great portal programs that are theophanies of salvation, exemplified by the Last Judgment at Autun (1130–35) or the Mission of the Apostles at Vezelay (1120–32).

Throughout the twelfth and thirteenth centuries popular piety focused on the Virgin, to whom all Gothic cathedrals were dedicated and about whom

Tympanum depicting the enthronement of the Blessed Virgin; west facade, south entrance (St. Anne Gate), Notre Dame Cathedral, Paris.

countless sculptures, stained glass windows, manuscript illuminations, tapestries, and goldsmith work were produced. Mary became the vehicle of access to the Lord whose divinity rendered Christ remote, both theologically and literally. A pervasive sense of unworthiness and penitential discipline excluded the laity from Communion, except on rare occasions. Popular meditations on the Passion of Christ emphasizing his suffering humanity, attributed to the Rhineland Dominican mystic Henry Suso (1295–1366), underlie the emergence of a new Marian iconographic theme, the *Pietà* (It., "pity"), Mary seated with the dead Christ in her lap.

Michelangelo to the Present: The majestic pontificate of Julius II (1503–13) swept up in its militant reform juggernaut artists and architects who, with Julius, defined the High Renaissance and whose works undergirded his imperial ambitions and spiritual fervor. Julius's vision of a magnificent new St. Peter's began with the demolition of the early Christian basilica and new plans by the architect Bramante for a project that would extend through twelve architects, including Michelangelo, and twenty-two popes. The first major monument for the new church was to be Julius's own tomb designed by Michelangelo. Of this grandiose project, occupying forty years of Michelangelo's career, only the sculptures of two slaves and Moses were completed.

Michelangelo's Sistine Chapel ceiling (1508–12), commissioned by Pope Julius, exuberantly celebrates the creation, fall of humanity, and redemption, including the renowned *Creation of Adam* scene. As Michelangelo worked in the Sistine Chapel, Raphael (1483–1520) began a series of frescoes in the Vatican Palace, the most famous of which is the *School of Athens*. Michelangelo completed the chapel decoration twenty years later with his brooding *Last Judgment* (1534–41) painted in the midst of the Reformation crisis.

The Catholic Counter-Reformation swiftly appropriated a visual language of both architectural grandiosity and spiritual intensity. Gian Lorenzo Bernini's (1598–1680) projects at St. Peter's Basilica, the canopy over the tomb of St. Peter (1624–33), the piazza and colonnade (1657) whose arms, Bernini said, reach out like Mother Church, and the immense sculpture of the Chair of St. Peter (1657–52) all proclaim the primacy of Peter, celebrating the supremacy of the Bishop of Rome and the Roman Catholic Church. Painter Domenikos Theotocopulos (1541–1614), called El Greco, captured the spiritual ecstacy of the Catholic Reformation in a flame-like agitated style, plumbing the depths of the soul's search for union with God. El Greco introduced new themes of the *Tears of St. Peter* and the *Repentant Magdalen,* reflecting Catholic insistence on the grace of repentance in the face of sin, a theological polemic of the time.

The Counter-Reformation marks the last great burst of artistic energy and vibrancy by Catholicism. Within the Catholic milieu, a hiatus of some three hundred fifty years settles in until post-World War II, when several remarkable church commissions occurred in France. These included the church at Assy, which commissioned works by Roualt, Lipchitz, Lurçat, and Richier; the Dominican chapel at Vence designed by Matisse; and the church of Notre Dame du Haut at Ronchamp by Le Corbusier.

The renewed but still tentative dialogue between the Church and artists, begun in the 1940s, continues at a cautious pace as new churches are built and older ones renovated in response to new guidelines from liturgical deliberations at the Second Vatican Council (1962–65) and subsequent revisions of the rites calling for ritual spaces and art that engage the assembly in active participation. *See also* Bible and art; Counter-Reformation/Catholic Reformation; liturgical art. *MARCHITA B. MAUCK*

catholicity, the Church's attribute of being universal, destined for all of humanity, and endowed with the fullness of the means of grace. The word "catholic" is derived from the Greek term meaning "according to the whole." Catholicity refers both to the inner completeness of the Church, and thus to the rich variety of its components, and also to its openness to all of humanity and its extension throughout the world as one Church consisting of many particular churches in communion with one another.

Vatican II describes catholicity as the gift of universality by virtue of which the Church strives energetically and constantly to bring all of humanity with all its riches back to Christ its head in the unity of his Spirit (cf. Dogmatic Constitution on the Church, n. 13). As other aspects of catholicity it mentions the variety of gifts with which the Spirit endows members of the Church, as well as the distinctive traditions that characterize the particular churches. The council insists that such legitimate differences are to be protected by the central authority, which promotes the communion by which these different traditions enrich the catholicity of the Church without diminishing its unity. A further claim to universality is made when the council declares that every human person either belongs to the Church or is related to it (Dogmatic Constitution on the Church, n. 13). This relatedness is based on the universal offer of grace by which all are called to salvation. This call involves an objective orientation toward the Church, of which the person may not be aware. *See also* Catholic; Catholicism; marks of the Church. *FRANCIS A. SULLIVAN*

Catholic League for Religious and Civil Rights, Catholic civil rights organization founded by the Jesuit Virgil Blum of Marquette University in 1973. Convinced that adverse Supreme Court rulings on education issues were the result of anti-Catholicism, Blum formed the organization as the first independent civil rights organization in American history intended specifically to defend the religious freedom and rights of Catholics. Headquartered in Milwaukee, the league exposed and re-butted Catholic defamation in print or in the electronic media, vigorously promoted pro-life activities, and pressed for freedom of choice in education. One commentator referred to the league as a "Catholic B'nai B'rith." *See also* anti-Catholicism.

catholic Letters, a term used to refer to seven NT Letters: James, 1–2 Peter, 1–3 John, and Jude. They are called "catholic" (Gk., *katholikos,* "universal," "general") because they were addressed to a general audience or to an otherwise unidentifiable community (2 John) or individual (3 John). 1–3 John reflect the disputes dividing the Johannine tradition at the end of the first century A.D. about the humanity of Jesus and the obligations of love. The Letter of James, purportedly written by James, "the Lord's brother" (Gal 1:19), is a series of moral exhortations steeped in Jewish wisdom traditions and probably written in the last quarter of the first century A.D. 1 Peter, while claiming to have been written by the Apostle Peter, dates more likely from the late first century A.D. and is a general exhortation to newly baptized Christians about how they should lead their new lives. 2 Peter and Jude have so much in common that there must be a literary relationship between them. Most think that 2 Peter depends on Jude. Although the author describes himself as "Jude, . . . brother of James" (Jude 1:1), the Letter probably comes from the end of the first century A.D. and is a general exhortation meant to serve as a warning against ungodly Christians. 2 Peter is primarily concerned with the question of theodicy and defends God's providence and the certainty of God's final judgment. Because it depends on Jude, it probably comes from the early second century A.D. *See also* pastoral Letters.   THOMAS H. TOBIN

catholicos, originally the chief bishop of a local church, subordinate to and dependent on a patriarch. The title is now practically interchangeable with patriarch. Among Catholic patriarchs the title "catholicos" is held by the Chaldean and Armenian patriarchs. The Armenian Orthodox Church has two catholicosates (Etchmiadzin, Cilicia) and two patriarchates (Jerusalem, Constantinople), both dependent on the catholicos of Etchmiadzin. *See also* patriarch [ecclesiastical].

Catholic press. *See* Catholicism and journalism.

Catholic Press Association, the association of Catholic newspapers, magazines, and general publishers and their staff members in the United States and Canada. Founded in Columbus, Ohio, in 1911, the Catholic Press Association seeks to assist its members in publishing works of high quality. With over three hundred members, it holds an annual convention and several annual regional conferences, and sponsors special awards programs. *The Catholic Press Directory,* its annual publication, provides a complete listing of Catholic newspapers, magazines, and newsletters in the United States and Canada. *See also* Catholicism and journalism.

Catholic social teachings, papal, conciliar, and synodal teachings on the political, social, economic, and international order. To analyze Catholic social teachings it is first necessary to distinguish them from the Catholic social tradition. The distinction is necessary for two reasons. First, the social teachings are a relatively late development in Catholic theology, dating from the nineteenth century. Second, the social teachings themselves do not include major figures in the Catholic tradition, some of whom are responsible for the basic ideas developed in the social teachings.

The Catholic social tradition is rooted in the Hebrew and Christian Scriptures as well as in the patristic writings, notably those of Augustine (d. 430). The tradition finds unique expression in the Middle Ages, particularly in the work of Thomas Aquinas (d. 1274). The Spanish Scholastics Francisco de Vitoria (d. 1546) and Francisco Suarez (d. 1617) adapted it to the rise of the nation-state and the collapse of the medieval Christian commonwealth. In the nineteenth century Luigi Taparelli d'Azeglio (d. 1862) prepared the way for the papal teachings that are today recognized as Catholic social teachings.

The social tradition, therefore, is broader and older than the social teachings. It provides a framework and an intellectual legacy from which the more recent social teachings draw. The tradition is a point of reference against which the social teachings are tested, even as the latter develop beyond the tradition by applying it to new issues and questions.

Catholic social teachings are composed of papal statements and conciliar or synodal documents. The social teachings originated with Pope Leo XIII (d. 1903) and continue through the teaching of John Paul II (elected 1978). While there may be some dispute about exactly which documents constitute the social teachings, an overwhelming consensus would support the following order: Leo XIII's *Rerum Novarum* (1891), Pius XI's *Quadragesimo Anno* (1931), Pius XII's *Pentecost* Address (1941) and *Christmas Messages* (1939–57), John XXIII's *Mater et Magistra* (1961), and *Pacem in Terris* (1963), Vatican II's *Dignitatis Humanae* (Declaration on Religious Freedom, 1965) and *Gaudium et Spes* (Pastoral Constitution on the Church in the Modern World, 1965), Paul VI's *Populorum Progressio* (1967) and *Octogesima Adveniens* (1971), the World Synod of Bishops' *Justitia in Mundo* (1971), Paul VI's *Evangelii Nuntiandi* (1975) and John Paul II's *Laborem Exercens* (1981), *Sollicitudo Rei Socialis* (1987), and *Centesimus Annus* (1991). Particularly in the teaching of John Paul II there are documents that have distinctive social themes but that are not usually classified under the social teachings.

While the social tradition has an extensive biblical foundation, the social teachings from 1891 through 1963 were principally structured in philosophical terms, drawing heavily upon a natural law philosophy of the person and society. Beginning with the documents of Vatican II and continuing in the social teachings of John Paul II, there is a greater reliance upon biblical categories joined with social philosophy. The strong philosophical tenor of the social teachings had a dual purpose: first, philosophical categories were used as mediating language, designed to explicate the broadly defined social vision of the Scriptures and relate them to the complexity of contemporary social issues; second, the philosophical language provided a method of addressing the wider civil society in categories that do not presuppose the perspective of Catholic faith.

Both the principal analytical categories of the social teachings and their historical development can be sketched as a means of understanding the content of the teachings and their role in the life of the Church and society. Nine basic ideas provide an insight into the structure of the social teachings.

Concepts and Principles: First, the foundational concept of the social teachings is the sacredness or dignity of the human person. The social ministry of the Church exists to protect and promote human dignity. The dignity of the person can be expressed in philosophical terms based on the spiritual nature of the person, rooted in the capacity for knowledge and love; it can also be expressed in theological terms: the person as the image of God. The dignity of persons sets them apart from the rest of the created order. Creation exists to be of service to the person—to every person, because all share the same intrinsic dignity. This strong emphasis on the uniqueness of the person has come under some criticism recently, because its anthropocentric focus seems to some to omit sufficient regard for the cosmos, particularly the care of the environment. Environmental issues are now reflected in Catholic social thought, but they do not displace the singular status given to the human person.

Second, the social teachings draw a direct line from human dignity to human rights and duties. Human rights are moral claims to goods of the spiritual and material order that are necessary to protect and promote human dignity. Duties are responsibilities that flow from the person's status as a creature (duties toward God) and from the social bonds one has in the human community (duties toward others). The use of human rights language in Catholic social teachings has grown steadily from the time of Pius XII through that of John Paul II. A complex history lies behind the Church's relationship to human rights categories. The natural law tradition has a strong conception of the social nature of the person and a primary emphasis on the duties each person must fulfill to God and others. The natural rights tradition, rooted in the major social philosophers of the seventeenth and eighteenth centuries, has at its foundation an individualistic conception of the person and a view of rights as the means of protecting individual freedom and autonomy. The encyclical *Pacem in Terris* of Pope John XXIII provided an expansive view of human rights that did not resolve the philosophical differences of the two traditions, but did offer a way to find some common ground on the importance of human

rights as a way to support human dignity. John Paul II's address to the United Nations (1979) built upon and enriched the teachings of *Pacem in Terris*. In his teachings, John Paul II accords particular emphasis to the link between the right of religious freedom and the spiritual nature of the person.

Third, a central dimension of Catholic social philosophy is its stress on the social nature of the person. Society and state are natural extensions of the social nature of the person. This perspective, along with the different view of rights already indicated, distinguishes Catholic social thought from the social contract conception of society. In the latter position the stress on the autonomy of the individual in full possession of his or her rights leads to a view of society in which obligations to others are only those freely undertaken. The more organic conception in Catholic thought conceives of the person as a member of multiple social communities: the family, civil society, and the human community. Society is the product of the full range of relationships—political, economic, cultural, and legal—that shape the social fabric of life at the local, national, and international level. The state is one dimension of society; it is the center of political authority in society. Among the institutions that arise from the social nature of the person, the state holds a unique role. A fundamental issue in Catholic thought, as in political philosophy generally, is that of the moral responsibilities entrusted to the state and the moral restraints placed upon it. Determining the right relationship of society and state is the burden of the next two pairs of concepts in Catholic social thought.

Fourth, the society-state distinction is a complement to the distinction of the common good and public order. The common good, a central idea in Catholic thought, is the complex of spiritual, temporal, and material conditions needed in society if each person is to have the opportunity to develop his or her human potential. These conditions encompass goods as different as religious freedom, economic growth, security, education, and cultural values. The concept of the common good is rooted in the social nature of the person and in the rights of the person. Because the person is a social being, there is need of a social context—the common good—if the person is to be supported and provided with the means to pursue his or her individual good. Each person needs the support of the common good, and each person and group should test his or her specific goals and objectives in light of the wider needs of the common good. Finally, the common good is intrinsically tied to the rights of the person in the sense that the fulfillment of the common good entails the satisfaction of basic rights for each person in society.

The concept of public order is of more recent vintage in Catholic teaching, finding its authoritative expression in the conciliar Declaration on Religious Freedom, *Dignitatis Humanae*. The public order is that part of the common good that properly belongs to the state. It is constituted by the goods of public peace, public morality, and the enforcement of basic standards of justice. The guarantee of these three goods can require the use of coercive force; hence it belongs properly to the political authority in society. The effect of distinguishing the terms common good and public order is to limit the role of the state, to make clear that the achievement of the common good is a responsibility of the whole society—individuals, groups, and social institutions—not simply the role of the state.

Fifth, the society-state relationship is evaluated in Catholic thought by the principle of subsidiarity and the concept of socialization. Subsidiarity finds its authoritative definition in Pius XI's encyclical *Quadragesimo Anno*. The principle seeks to preserve as much freedom in society as possible, by contending that responsibility for addressing social questions should begin with the local or smallest institutional authority and be referred to the state only when it becomes clear that other institutions cannot fulfill the need. There is a presumption, therefore, not to appeal to the state first in addressing the problems of society. At the same time, the purpose of the principle is not to prevent the state from exercising responsibility in society. The state has positive moral responsibilities and is the ultimate guarantor of the rights of the person in society.

This responsibility is made clear by the way Pope John XXIII complemented the principle of subsidiarity by the idea of socialization in the encyclical *Mater et Magistra*. Socialization is the product of increasing complexity in society, generated by the growing involvement of the state in the socioeconomic order. The pope saw this enhanced role of the state as a method of satisfying human rights. He judged this growth of state activity to be compatible with subsidiarity. Since *Mater et Magistra*, subsidiarity and socialization are used in tandem to determine what the appropriate role and function of the state should be in society.

Sixth, in the social space beyond the control of the state in society Catholic teaching locates the role of intermediate associations, often termed voluntary associations in Western society. These groups come together by the choice of citizens; while not under the auspices or control of the state, they exist for public purposes. Examples include labor unions, professional societies, political parties, and cultural or ethnic associations. They exercise a public role beyond the capacity of any individual, and they contain the power of the state, often acting as a buffer between the citizen and the state.

In summary, therefore, the crucial society-state relationship is governed in Catholic thought by three elements: the common good–public order distinction, the subsidiarity-socialization relationship, and the role of intermediary associations.

Seventh, permeating the entire structure of Catholic social teachings is their theory of justice. The ideas are rooted in Aristotle but have been reshaped by Aquinas and by Pius XI's *Quadragesimo Anno*. The theory of justice distinguishes commutative, distributive, and social justice, with the latter category providing the dominant framework for the social teaching.

Eighth, a postconciliar addition to the social teachings is the "option for the poor." The theme arose from the Church in Latin America, particularly from the theology of liberation. Since the early 1970s it has made its way into the vocabulary of papal teaching. John Paul II speaks of "a preferential but not exclusive option for the poor." The phrase, in either of its formulations, conveys the idea that special attention to the needs of the poor is a moral obligation for individuals, for the Church, and for society as a whole. Within a concern for the welfare of all in society (the common good) there should be systematically weighted concern to respond to the voice and the needs of the poor.

Ninth, John Paul II uses the concept of solidarity as a central theme in his social teaching. The idea found expression in the social teachings of Pius XII, but the development of it in *Sollicitudo Rei Socialis* and in *Centesimus Annus* goes extensively beyond the earlier teaching. John Paul II sees solidarity as analogous to charity; it assumes in his teaching the status of virtue. The principal role solidarity has is to direct the dynamic of interdependence, which is reshaping the socioeconomic life of societies and the international community. In a world of increasing interdependence, a vision of solidarity is needed as the foundation for just relationships.

Historical Development: The historical evolution of the social teachings can be divided into the papal encyclicals, on the one hand, and the contribution of the Second Vatican Council and subsequent international synods of bishops, on the other.

Papal social teachings can be divided into four periods: (1) the response to the Industrial Revolution; (2) the response to the nuclear age and international interdependence; (3) the response to postindustrial societies; and (4) the social teachings of John Paul II. The responsive nature of the teachings highlights the fact that in most instances the social teachings have emerged from the pastoral experience of the Church, seeking to direct the ecclesial community in light of major social challenges.

The response to the Industrial Revolution is the theme joining *Rerum Novarum, Quadragesimo Anno,* and the *Pentecost Address* of 1941. The papal teachings focused on the dignity of human work and the rights of the working person. The papal teachings defended the intrinsic dignity of each person, articulated a body of rights that protected the person in the workplace (including the right to a just wage and the right to form unions), and affirmed a duty of the state to protect workers. Themes set forth in *Rerum Novarum* were repeated and extended in John Paul II's *Laborem Exercens* and *Centesimus Annus.* In responding to the Industrial Revolution, the popes consistently sought to distinguish Catholic social teachings from Marxism, on the one hand, and liberal capitalism, on the other.

The consequences of the Second World War established the setting for the second stage of the social teachings. The onset of the nuclear age and the emergence of global interdependence set the context for the social teachings of Pius XII, John XXIII, and Paul VI. The social teachings of this period are built on the *Christmas Messages* of Pius XII, particularly his teachings on human dignity, on democracy, and on the ethic of war. Both John XXIII and Paul VI develop this foundation in new ways. Both placed more stringent restraints on the use of force, and both emphasized the moral problem of the condition of the developing countries in the global economy. In this second stage of development the papal teachings shift their basic focus from the nation to the international community. In Paul VI's phrase, the social question had become a worldwide issue. As the scope of the problem expanded, so did the concepts of the moral teachings: they spoke of an international common good and international social justice. Both concepts were designed to test the relationship between the traditional notion of national interest and the rapidly developing international interest.

In the third stage of development the social teachings focused upon the problems of postindustrial society. The apostolic letter *Octogesima Adveniens* of Paul VI and *Centesimus Annus* of John Paul II both distinguished between the kinds of social questions facing the developing countries and those facing the industrialized democracies. Paul VI spoke of the new social questions rooted in advanced technology, mass communications, and an increasingly bureaucratized society. In these societies the dominant moral issues were not primarily the absence of material goods, but questions that were spiritual and cultural, bearing upon the quality of human life in highly organized, secular, technocratic societies.

The fourth stage of the social encyclical tradition is the teachings of John Paul II. The scope of his concerns and the amount of attention he has given to "the social question" makes independent treatment of his writings necessary. John Paul II has authored clearly identifiable social encyclicals, e.g., *Laborem Exercens, Sollicitudo Rei Socialis,* and *Centesimus Annus.* He also makes extensive use of social categories in documents that are not contained neatly in the social tradition, e.g., *Redemptor Hominis* (1979) and *Veritatis Splendor* (1994). John Paul II's social teachings exhibit both continuity and change in relationship to his predecessors. He addresses many of the same topics of the earlier tradition and relies on the teachings of earlier encyclicals. But his work is distinctive in the way he blends the dominant philosophical arguments with a much greater reliance on the Scriptures. He also extends the style of *Gaudium et Spes,* making extensive use of Christological and ecclesiological categories; his teachings are distinguished by their emphasis on human rights, religious freedom, and the imperative of addressing the international dimensions of "the social question."

In addition to this progressive development within the framework of the social encyclicals, the other dimension of the social teachings in the twentieth century has been the contribution of the Second Vatican Council and the Third and Fourth International Synods (1971–74). The principal text, *Gaudium et Spes* of Vatican II, provided an ecclesiological foundation for the social teachings, which had never been specifically articulated in the social encyclicals. In its stress (n. 76) on the Church's obligation to defend the dignity of the person, *Gaudium et Spes* tied Catholic ecclesiology to the full range of moral issues addressed in the papal social teachings. The Synod of 1971, in its document *Justitia in Mundo* ("Justice in the World"), intensified the link of ecclesiology and social teachings, describing the social ministry as a constitutive dimension of the Church's work.

In summary, the past century of Catholic social teachings has remarkably enhanced the Catholic social tradition, addressing "the social question" on a consistent basis in its local, national, and international dimensions. *See also* Church; Church and state; social justice.

Bibliography

Calvez, J. Y., and Perrin, J. *The Church and Social Justice: The Social Teaching of the Popes from Leo XIII to Pius XII (1878–1958).* Chicago: Henry Regnery, 1961.

Coleman, J. A., ed. *One Hundred Years of Catholic Social Thought: Celebration and Challenge.* Maryknoll, NY: Orbis Books, 1991.

Dorr, D. *Option for the Poor: A Hundred Years of Catholic Social Teaching.* Rev. ed. Maryknoll, NY: Orbis Books, 1992.

Hollenbach, D. *Claims in Conflict: Retrieving and Renewing the Catholic Human Rights Tradition.* New York: Paulist Press, 1979.

O'Brien, D. J., and Shannon, T. A. *Catholic Social Thought: The Documentary Heritage.* Maryknoll, NY: Orbis Books, 1992.

J. BRYAN HEHIR

Catholics, statistics on. The statistics in this article are for the year 1990 and have been taken from the *Statistical Yearbook of the Church* (Vatican City, 1992). The information is taken from reports from 2,588 out of 2,761 patriarchal or metropolitan sees, archdioceses, and prelatures that are known as ecclesiastical jurisdictions.

NUMBER OF PARISHES

Parishes are listed as administered by a priest, entrusted to a nonpriest, or vacant, i.e., with no appointed administrator.

Area	Priest	Nonpriest	Vacant
Africa	8,485	354	128
Asia	16,265	131	338
Europe	134,812	920	446
Central America	7,627	81	11
North America	24,954	467	63
South America	17,574	525	241
Oceania	2,302	57	24
Worldwide	212,019	2,535	1,251

CLERGY

Since the Second Vatican Council, the number of lay ministers has dramatically increased. While the *Statistical Yearbook* does list the number of permanent deacons, it does not list the number of laypeople who serve in parishes, hospitals, and schools. The table is therefore incomplete.

Area	Bishops	Priests	Deacons
Africa	494	20,392	275
Asia	584	33,855	92
Europe	1,435	224,606	4,505
Central America	254	16,929	775
North America	538	65,510	10,410
South America	799	36,443	1,377
Oceania	106	3,431	91
Worldwide	4,210	403,173	17,525

Area	Diocesan Priests	Religious Priests
Africa	10,287	10,112
Asia	18,799	15,056
Europe	156,312	68,294
North America (including Central America)	51,234	31,205
South America	18,274	18,169
Oceania	2,790	2,641
Worldwide	257,696	145,477

MINISTRIES OF HELP

Hospitals, dispensaries, and leprosaria are among the ministries of the Church. The Church also conducts institutions such as orphanages and nursing homes for the elderly and disabled.

Area	Hospitals	Dispensaries	Homes for the Aged/ Disabled
Africa	898	3,591	402
Asia	1,005	3,117	835
Europe	1,565	2,564	6,812
Central America	288	1,658	377
North America	745	149	942
South America	1,022	3,056	1,411
Oceania	152	165	239
Worldwide	5,675	14,300	11,018

BAPTISMS AND MARRIAGES

This list provides statistics on baptisms, marriages, and mixed marriages (between a Catholic and a non-Catholic).

Area	Baptisms	Mixed Marriages	Marriages
Africa	2,799,470	203,546	40,901
Asia	2,463,222	442,187	56,789
Europe	3,067,784	1,188,190	92,313
Central America	2,943,133	501,827	3,381
North America	1,245,918	261,235	120,110
South America	5,471,800	1,014,560	15,799
Oceania	140,142	21,310	17,913
Worldwide	18,131,469	3,980,061	347,206

NUMBER OF CATHOLICS BY CONTINENT

The fourth column indicates the percentage of Catholics in the total population of a given area. In this table, unlike in others, Central, North, and South America are listed together.

Area	Population	Catholics	Percentage
Africa	638,121,000	88,899,000	13.9
Asia	3,149,064,000	86,012,000	2.7
Europe	713,908,000	285,294,000	40.0
The Americas	723,648,000	461,264,000	63.7
Oceania	26,497,000	7,031,000	26.6
Worldwide	5,251,238,000	928,500,000	17.7

ORDINATIONS TO THE PRIESTHOOD

A comparison of statistics for 1985 and 1990 indicates that the number of ordinations to the priesthood has risen in all areas except North America and Oceania.

Area	1985	1990
Africa	492	716
Asia	645	959
Europe	2,097	2,456
Central America	271	426
North America	612	517
South America	640	820
Oceania	65	44
Worldwide	4,822	5,938

NUMBER OF CATHOLICS PER PRIEST

The number of Catholics per priest varies widely on each continent. The average figures for different regions as a whole are given in this table.

Area	Catholics per Priest
Africa	4,358
Asia	2,541
Europe	1,270
Central America	7,748
North America	1,023
South America	7,276
Oceania	1,294
Worldwide	2,303

PASTORAL CENTERS

Pastoral centers include parishes, quasi-parishes, missions, and occasionally a section of a parish. This table gives the number of such centers and the average number of members in each.

Area	Centers	Catholics
Africa	80,841	1,100
Asia	54,274	1,585
Europe	153,731	1,856
Central America	22,388	5,391
North America	28,824	2,325
South America	59,677	4,443
Oceania	4,906	1,436
Worldwide	404,641	2,295

RELIGIOUS CONGREGATIONS AND SECULAR INSTITUTES

All who are not ordained are lay members of the Church. Some of these belong to religious congregations or secular institutes. The overwhelming majority of members of secular institutes are women; there are only 538 male members worldwide.

Area	Male Religious	Female Religious	Members of Secular Institutes
Africa	5,963	42,429	423
Asia	6,637	112,127	861
Europe	28,525	448,348	24,834
Central America	2,416	36,333	505
North America	10,279	136,222	1,129
South America	6,246	93,098	3,082
Oceania	2,460	13,554	46
Worldwide	62,526	882,111	30,880

NUMBER OF CATHOLIC ELEMENTARY AND SECONDARY SCHOOLS

The Catholic Church has a long history of educational ministry. Worldwide there are more than 24 million elementary-school students, 12 million secondary-school students, and 2.8 million college and university students in Catholic educational institutions.

Area	Elementary	Secondary
Africa	23,650	4,449
Asia	12,608	7,572
Europe	18,422	9,933
Central America	4,194	1,857
North America	8,668	1,658
South America	8,578	5,070
Oceania	2,428	661
Worldwide	78,548	31,200

Catholics United for the Faith (CUF), ultra-conservative lay Catholic association. It was founded by H. Lyman Stebbins in 1968, following the controversy over Pope Paul VI's encyclical on birth control. CUF encourages loyalty to the pope and the magisterium. By 1986, the by-then international association had 15,000 members, with headquarters in New Rochelle, New York. CUF publishes reviews of Catholic literature and actively opposes Catholic individuals and movements with whom it disagrees.

Catholic Theological Society of America (CTSA), professional organization of U.S. and Canadian Catholic theologians, founded in 1945. It has as its purpose, "within the context of the Roman Catholic tradition, to promote studies and research in theology, to relate theological science to current problems, and to foster a more effective theological education, by providing a forum for an exchange of views among theologians and with scholars in other disciplines." (CTSA *Constitution*, a. 1).

Active membership is open to all who possess doctoral degrees in theology or related studies, and who are or have been actively engaged in teaching or research in various religious disciplines. Exceptional cases can be considered for active membership. Associate membership is open to those who have completed at least the course requirements for a doctorate. Honorary membership can be given to recognize special service to the society. Total membership in 1992 was about 1,450, including nearly 25 percent women. The CTSA annually confers the John Courtney Murray Award (formerly the Cardinal Spellman Award) for "distinguished achievement in Theology." The *Proceedings* of the annual convention appear toward the end of each year.

Catholic Truth Society, an organization for the dissemination of information about, and defense of, Catholicism. It was founded in England in 1884 by Bishop Herbert Vaughn and layman James Britten; its stated aims were to provide devotional and educational works to Catholics and to provide non-Catholics with reliable information about Catholicism. Branches were later started in most of the English-speaking world.

Catholic University of America, The, national Catholic university in Washington, D.C. After John Lancaster Spalding, bishop of Peoria, and others inculcated the need for a university on a higher level than the existing Catholic institutions, and after Mary Gwendoline Caldwell offered a substantial sum of money, the Third Plenary Council of Baltimore (1884) decreed that a "principal" or advanced seminary be established under the control of the American hierarchy as the kernel of a complete university and a distinguished center of learning. In spite of some episcopal opposition, Pope Leo XIII approved the project in 1887 and two years later sanctioned the statutes and conferred pontifical status. The bishop of Richmond, John J. Keane, was appointed the first rector, and Washington, D.C., was selected as the site. Incorporated in 1887 under the laws of the District of Columbia, the university opened on November 13, 1889, with ten professors (half of them recruited in Europe) and forty-six clerical students. Subsequently, fifty-six religious congregations of men built houses of study in the vicinity. Besides the original school of theology, two more schools, embracing philosophy, letters, the mathematical, physical, biological, and social sciences, and law, were organized in 1895, when laymen were first admitted.

At first intended exclusively for graduate studies, the university admitted undergraduate men to every school except theology in 1905. Administrators and professors helped the Sisters of Notre Dame de Namur to found Trinity College for women nearby. Catholic Sisters College was established on a separate but neighboring campus in 1911 for the training of teachers, and eventually more than thirty houses of study were opened by congregations of women religious. Women were first admitted to graduate studies in 1928, to undergraduate study in education in 1950 (when Sisters College was discontinued), and to the other undergraduate departments shortly thereafter. In 1993 the university consisted of ten schools: architecture and planning, arts and sciences, engineering, law, library and information science, music, nursing, philosophy, religious studies, and social service. It grants pontifical degrees in three disciplines: sacred theology, canon law, and philosophy; it has the only departments of biblical studies, canon law, and church history among Catholic universities in the United States. It houses the national offices of the American Catholic Historical Association, the American Catholic Philosophical Association, the Canon Law Society of America, the Catholic Biblical Association, and others.

As the capstone of the American Catholic educational system, the university set up programs of affiliation for seminaries in 1907 and for colleges and high schools in 1912, in order to improve and standardize instruction. As a research institution the university itself became a charter member of the Association of American Universities in 1900. Its third rector, Denis J. O'Connell, was elected the first president of the [National] Catholic Educational Association in 1904, and his successor, Thomas J. Shahan, was president of the National Conference of Catholic Charities from its founding until his retirement. Bishop Shahan, who had the longest tenure (1909–28) as rector (or president), also began building on the campus the National Shrine of the Immaculate Conception, the foundation stone of which was laid in 1920. Several learned journals were established by or at the university; those still being published there are the *Catholic Historical Review* (since 1915), *Primitive Man,* now the *Anthropological Quarterly* (since 1928), *The Jurist* (since 1941), *The Americas,* the *Review of Metaphysics,* and the *Living Light.*

Never adequately endowed, the university has suffered from financial stringency since its earliest years. Conservative and German-American Catholics were long reluctant to support it. In 1903 Pope Pius X authorized the first national collection to be taken up in all the parishes of the United States; it has since been an annual source of income.

The chancellor of the University *ex officio* was the archbishop of Baltimore until 1947 and since then has been the archbishop of Washington. The Board of Trustees now consists of equal numbers of clerical and lay members. All the nine rectors up to 1967 were or became bishops; in 1969 the first lay president was appointed. *See also* United States of America, Catholicism in the.   ROBERT TRISCO

Catholic Worker movement, lay apostolate in service of the poor founded in 1933 by Dorothy Day and Peter Maurin in New York City. Although Day credited Maurin with the idea of the movement, it was Day who managed to find ways of embodying his ideals. She began a newspaper, *Catholic Worker,* that sold for a penny a copy. She also opened a "house of hospitality" on Mott Street in New York City where not only were a soup kitchen and beds provided for the poor, but where workers and intellectuals could meet and hold "round-table discussions." Later, she began a farm commune. As the Catholic Worker movement spread across America, the concept of a newspaper, a house of hospitality, and support for rural life continued to define the movement.

The Catholic Worker movement was a gathering of diverse people. Those who joined were cosmopolitan scholars and reformers who identified themselves with the disinherited. They embraced a life-style of voluntary poverty and focused their attention on economic and social changes that were consistent with the goals of Christian personalism, a philosophical orientation that stresses the value and dignity of each individual human person.

The Catholic Worker movement was never dependent on the institutional Church for financial support. It also rejected the institutional power of the state. Catholic Workers did not participate in government nor depend on it to correct social injustice. Rather, the Catholic Worker movement viewed itself as a leaven for the creation of a new social order and professed Christian personalism as the solution to economic, social, and political injustice. Catholic Workers under the leadership of Dorothy Day also consistently opposed the United States' war efforts from World War II through the Vietnam War. *See also* Day, Dorothy M.; Maurin, Peter; pacifism; personalism, Christian.   PATRICIA MCNEAL

Catholic World, The, a U.S. Catholic periodical. Founded by the Paulist Fathers in 1865, it was one of the first journals to consider the wider context of the Catholic Church in America and to engage progressively culture and society. It has been published as *New Catholic World* since 1972.

Catholic Youth Organization (CYO), the umbrella organization that oversees youth activities in most dioceses in the United States. Founded in 1930 in Chicago by the auxiliary bishop Bernard J. Sheil, the CYO sought to solve the "youth problem" of the 1930s by offering young people worthwhile activities. It incorporated existing programs such as scouting, day camps, and vocational training with a heavy emphasis on athletics, including track meets, swim meets, golf tournaments, and parish-based sports leagues for basketball and baseball. In April 1931, the CYO gained much notoriety by hosting a citywide boxing tournament. In 1932, a CYO center was built in downtown Chicago to provide a Catholic alternative to the YMCA. In 1934, an attempt was made to create a national CYO, but only the archdioceses of Chicago, Los Angeles, and San Francisco cooperated. The Chicago CYO held national tournaments, which succeeded in publicizing the CYO throughout the country. In May 1938 the first annual national conference was held in Chicago. Since that time CYO has expanded to most dioceses, where the CYO name has become synonymous with parish sports. But the CYO also continues to oversee homes for children, summer camps, and other youth work.

Caussade, Jean-Pierre de, 1675–1751, French Jesuit spiritual writer and spiritual director in the mystical tradition. He is celebrated for defending mysticism (knowledge of God through personal prayer experience) in the wake of Quietism, a doctrine of passivity in prayer and action, condemned in 1687. He preached acceptance of God's will. *See also* mysticism; Quietism.

C.E., common era. Together with B.C.E. (before the common era), C.E. is used by many in preference to A.D. (Lat., *anno Domini,* "in the year of the Lord") out of deference to other faiths and their different periodizations of history. This more neutral designation is, however, based on the same calculation of the date of the birth of Jesus as is A.D. *See also* A.D.

Cecilia, St., second- or third-century martyr who died in Rome during a time of religious persecution. As a young girl, Cecilia fasted, prayed, and pledged her life to God. However, her father arranged a marriage to the patrician Valerian. On their wedding night Cecilia informed Valerian about her pledge, and he allowed Cecilia to remain a virgin. She opened her house for prayer and spiritual direction, and hundreds were converted through her influence. Cecilia is honored as patron saint of music because of the song for God in her heart. Feast day: November 22.

CELAM (Sp., Consejo Episcopal Latino-Americano), Conference of Latin American Bishops. Established in 1956 with statutes approved in 1974, CELAM represents twenty-two Latin-American national bishops' conferences. Its aim is to coordinate the work of church activities in Central and South America, focusing on the adaptation of the teachings of Vatican Council II (1962–65) to the spiritual, social, and economic needs of the people. General conferences at Medellín, Colombia (1968), and in Puebla, Mexico (1979) resulted in affirming Christian base communities, in protesting the oppression of the poor, and in promoting creative strategies for spreading the faith. A general conference in Santo Domingo, Dominican Republic, in 1992 addressed the challenge of the evangelization of the Americas. *See also* Latin America, Catholicism in.

celebrant. *See* presider.

celebret (sel'ah-bret; Lat., "let him celebrate"), a commendatory letter certifying that a priest is in good standing so that he can be permitted to celebrate the Eucharist in churches where he is unknown. The letter must be written by the priest's bishop or religious superior and dated within a year of presentation. The presentation of the celebret by a visiting, unknown priest is not strictly required. Canon law says he may be permitted to celebrate the Eucharist without a celebret if it can be prudently judged that he is in good standing with the Church.

Celestine V, St. [Peter of Marrone], 1215–96, the only pope to resign his office, having served only five months, July 5 to December 13, 1294. At the time of his election, Peter of Marrone had been a Benedictine hermit for almost sixty years. By his holy life, he attracted many followers and inspired a movement of reformed Benedictines with thirty-six priories by 1294. After two years of deadlock over the election of a successor to Pope Nicholas IV, the cardinals turned in desperation to the devout Peter. He accepted his election as a divine call, taking the name Celestine V. But lacking formal training in law and administration, the eighty-year-old pope became the pawn of the French crown and other factions. Attempting to prevent further mayhem, Celestine issued a bull on December 10 declaring the legality of papal resignation and then resigned three days later. Feast day: May 19.

Celestius, fifth century, associate of Pelagius and condemned by councils from 411 (Carthage) to 431 (Ephesus). He denied that infant baptism was for forgiveness of sins, rejecting the doctrine of original sin altogether. *See also* Pelagianism.

celibacy, clerical, a way of life characterized by a priest's perpetual renunciation of marriage for the sake of the reign of God. The development of clerical celibacy as a discipline in the Western Church is related to, but distinct from, the emergence of vows in monastic and other religious communities. The history of this development is complex and has been shaped by diverse values and concerns.

Historical Development: Prior to Christianity,

perpetual celibacy was generally not valued. In gentile cultures virginity was required of women who consecrated themselves to the service of female deities, but this consecration was not perpetual. For men, perpetual celibacy was not customary and in some cases was censured with civil penalties. Although among Jews virginity was highly valued for unmarried women, it was not seen as a way of life. To be unmarried and childless was considered a matter of shame. An exception to this norm was the ascetical Essene community at Qumran.

Christianity introduced a new perspective. The Gospels indicate that the unmarried state is a reflection of the heavenly kingdom (Luke 20:36), where there is no marriage. Coupled with the imminent expectation of the Second Coming of Christ, this teaching contributed to a positive evaluation of perpetual celibacy as a witness to and preparation for the coming reign of God. Celibacy as a way of life appeared in the first century in the Church; however, it was recognized as a distinctive option because, "not all can accept this teaching" (Matt 19:11–12). Paul recognized the tension surrounding this teaching. Although he advocated celibacy for those who could embrace it, he also acknowledged that the grace of celibacy was not given to all. Those who could not live such a life were to marry to avoid sin (1 Cor 7:1–9, 27–28, 36).

Celibacy as a perpetual life-style option may have achieved the status of a movement in the late third century when hermits retreated to the desert to devote themselves to prayer. The subsequent development of community life in support of prayer and asceticism provided the foundations of monasticism. The rise of a celibate monastic life-style spurred discussion about requiring celibacy of all clergy.

During the first three centuries of the Church there was no universal law or common consensus governing celibacy for bishops, priests, and deacons. All were permitted to contract marriage, and many did. There were tensions over the issue of married clergy, however. The Synod of Gangra (ca. 345) condemned a false asceticism whereby worshipers boycotted celebrations presided over by married clergy. Bishops who abandoned their wives for the sake of their own piety were censured with excommunication. On the other hand, there were also early movements directed toward the imposition of celibacy as a discipline upon the clergy. At the Council of Nicaea (325), Bishop Hosius of Cordoba advocated celibacy as a requirement for all clergy. In this he was promoting as a universal rule the conclusions of the Council of Elvira (300), which he had attended. But Nicaea rejected Hosius's position.

Legislation on celibacy did begin to surface in local councils, however, in part as a response to disagreements in the Church about the requirement that all clergy be celibate. A preliminary development was the exclusion of marriage after ordination (councils of Ancyra, 314, and Neocaesarea, ca. 320). A second restriction resulted from an interpretation of the requirement of monogamy. A cleric could not remarry following the death of his spouse.

The legislation on celibacy took different turns in the Eastern and Western churches. The Eastern churches, under the burgeoning monastic influence of the fourth century, promoted celibacy. In the face of a subsequent backlash against this trend, the Eastern churches moderated their legislation, allowing priests, deacons, and other clerics to live in marriage if contracted prior to ordination. Bishops, however, were forbidden to marry. This legislation was confirmed at the Trullan Synod (692) and has remained operative in the East and for Eastern churches in union with Rome. Today priests and deacons of the Melkite, Maronite, Armenian, Ruthenian, and Romanian churches may marry prior to ordination.

The requirement of celibacy for clergy in the West was effected by a series of local councils, as well as by a growing body of papal teachings. Following the Council of Elvira's decree requiring celibate clergy, various popes from Damasus I (366–384) to Leo I (440–461), as well as European and African councils, issued similar directives.

Despite what developed as a fairly consistent body of teaching, the contemporary practice of the clergy was less than uniform. In the period of social instability following the decline of Charlemagne's empire in the tenth century, church discipline, and with it the observance of celibacy, flagged. This precipitated both a moral and an economic crisis for the Church. A clergy known to be in violation of church discipline gave scandal to the faithful and undermined the ability of the Church to promote social order. At the same time, clergy with children could erode the financial base of the Church by the secularization of church lands through inheritance. Pope Benedict VIII (1012–24) enacted legislation to protect the lands of the Church from this process, but disorder in the observance of celibacy continued. Subsequent popes acted against these trends. However, it was Gregory VII (1073–85), and his program of reform, who is credited with bringing about a more consistent observance of the obligation.

The period of the Reformation posed renewed challenges to the discipline of celibacy. Although at first Martin Luther did not support a married clergy, his views eventually changed. In 1522 he condemned celibacy. Calvin's views were more moderate. While holding that celibacy is an acceptable means of serving God, he argued that it is of no greater value than married life.

These developments generated much discussion at the Council of Trent (1545–63). On the subject of the relative merits of the married and celibate ways of life, Trent distinguished between the objective superiority of celibacy as a way of life that witnesses to beatitude for those who are called to it, and the subjective detriment of attempting to live such a life if not called to it. With respect to clerical celibacy, however, the council upheld the value of retaining the obligation to celibacy for the sake of the service of the Gospel. Significantly, however, Trent recognized that the laws governing celibacy for clergy were church laws rather than divine laws. Consequently, it conceded that these laws could be changed should the Church ever decide to do so. Trent's retention of the law was an affirmation of the value of celibacy, not a rejection of the value of marriage.

Contemporary Issues: Discussion of celibacy has always been deeply influenced by the cultural norms and religious and philosophical perspectives of those engaged in the discussion. This is no less true today. Three perspectives in particular have shaped the discussion of clerical celibacy from Vatican II to the present. First, historical consciousness had led to the awareness that principles of church order are shaped by historical circumstances and are subject to change. Second, greater understanding of human psychology has led to questions regarding the impact of celibacy on the human development of the clergy. Thirdly, the realization that many non-European cultures in which the Church is establishing itself view celibacy negatively has prompted questions concerning the value of retaining celibacy as an absolute and universal requirement for ordained ministry in the Roman Catholic Church.

The second of these influences can be felt in the Vatican II (1962–65) decrees "On the Appropriate Renewal of the Religious Life," "On Priestly Formation," and "On the Ministry and Life of Priests." Pope Paul VI (1963–78) adverted to historical conscious-

ness and questions of cultural diversity as the occasions for writing his encyclical on clerical celibacy, *Sacerdotalis Caelibatus* (Lat., "Priestly Celibacy," 1967). One significant point in this document is the provision for the possibility of married ministers in other denominations entering into full communion with Rome and continuing the practice of priestly ministry as priests in the Catholic Church, even though married. The World Synod of Bishops in 1971 reaffirmed Paul VI's insistence on the requirement of celibacy while also affirming the legitimacy of the papal granting of exceptions in extraordinary circumstances. Pope John Paul II has repeatedly declared his support for Paul VI's position and in 1980 the Vatican authorized "pastoral provisions" granting dispensation from the obligation of celibacy for a limited number of Episcopal priests who entered into communion with Rome.

The consistent teaching that celibacy will remain a requirement for clergy in the Western Church has not diminished the discussion by clergy and laity over the possibility of change. Indeed, the declining number of priests in active ministry, the exemption from the requirement of celibacy for married clergy who enter the Catholic Church after having been ordained in the Episcopal Church, and reported instances of *de facto* nonobservance of the requirement by clergy in various parts of the world, especially in Africa and Latin America, suggest that the discussion will continue. *See also* counsels, evangelical; priesthood; vows; vows, private; vows, public.

Bibliography
Bassett, William, and Peter Huizing, eds. *Celibacy in the Church.* New York: Herder and Herder, 1972.
Schillebeeckx, Edward. *The Church with a Human Face: A New and Expanded Theology of Ministry.* New York: Crossroad, 1985.
Vogels, Heinz-Jürgen. *Celibacy: Gift or Law?: A Critical Investigation.* Kansas City, MO.: Sheed & Ward, 1993. JAMES K. VOISS

Celsus, Platonist, author of the oldest extant pagan polemic against Christianity, *True Doctrine* (ca. 178). It survives only as citations in Origen's *Against Celsus* (248). Celsus ridiculed Christianity as novel, parochial, irrational, and quarrelsome, a subversive movement founded by a sorcerer and proselytizing the uneducated. He provides important evidence for the diversity of second-century Christianity, but also for the growing prominence of the Great Church, i.e., the major Christian centers of the Mediterranean world. *See also* Origen; Plato.

Celtic cross. *See* cross, forms of the.

Celtic spirituality, a Christian tradition that valued monasticism, nature, aceticism and solitude. It flourished in Ireland (the most significant and best documented center), parts of the British Isles, and Brittany from approximately the fifth century to, in Ireland, as late as the twelfth century, when traditional structures gave place to Rome-inspired reforms. From Ireland, monastic colonies spread to Scotland, Northumbria, and across much of Western Europe. Church organization was monastic rather than diocesan. A distinctive feature, therefore, of Celtic spirituality was the social as well as religious importance of monasticism, possibly influenced by the flexibility of the Egyptian tradition. Monastic "towns" were mixed settlements of men, women, celibates and married people, that fulfilled political, social, economic, educational, as well as religious, functions. The closeness of religion to the life of the people was also reflected in a profound sense of the presence of God all around them. Celts were a rural people, close to the land and the sea. Even after the coming of Christianity, the wealth of Celtic prayers and poetry is marked by powerful natural imagery. Celtic spirituality also valued solitude, often accompanied by a vigorous asceticism, pursued on lonely headlands and islands. There was also voluntary exile far from home and familiar landscapes. This wandering of individual ascetics and groups led many Celts, albeit reluctantly at times, to evangelize the people among whom they settled. Celtic spirituality paid close attention to the spiritual needs of the individual, whether monastic or lay. Hence, the widespread practice of spiritual guidance known literally as "soul friendship." *See also* Ireland, Catholicism in; spirituality, Christian.

PHILIP SHELDRAKE

cemetery. *See* burial, Christian.

cenobite (sen'oh-bit). *See* monk.

censer. *See* thurible.

censorship, the prohibition of publications, speeches, or activities thought to be offensive to, or violative of, morality. It is the nature of human law to ensure stability and to promote the common good. Where the public expression of certain ideas was thought to threaten public order, legitimate authority acted to suppress such expression. The Catholic Church has sometimes exercised its teaching authority in matters of faith and morals by an effort to suppress objectionable materials or at least to warn Catholics of the immoral or disruptive content of these materials. Historically the Church has exercised its pastoral role in several ways: proactively, by requiring that Catholics seek ecclesiastical approval of material to be published; negatively, by publishing its Index of Forbidden Books or of movie ratings in diocesan newspapers.

The Catholic Church's position on censorship has been softened considerably since Vatican II (1962-65). The Index was abandoned in 1966. Much of what is commonly called censorship today is actually persuasion, as the individuals or groups involved do not have the authority to enforce the standards they advocate, for example, in nonviolent picket lines, boycotts, and letters to the editor. *See also* Index of Forbidden Books; Legion of Decency.

censure, in canon law a medicinal penalty, i.e., one that seeks the correction of the wrongdoer rather than the repair of damage done the community. Although some censures may result automatically (Lat., *latae sententiae*) from the commission of an ecclesiastical crime, the 1983 code has greatly reduced the number of automatic penalties, so that most censures will be imposed by sentence (Lat., *ferendae sententiae*), and even automatic ones will frequently be announced so that those affected will be aware of them. An individual must be warned before censure is imposed so that there may be time for a change of heart. Because a censure seeks this change of heart, there is no time limit on a censure, but it should be lifted when there has been demonstration of reform. Depending upon given circumstances, the censure may be one of excommunication, suspension, or interdict. *See also* penal law.

centering prayer, nondiscursive meditation technique, considered to be the practice of the Desert Fathers. It has two major forms: Benedictine, taught by John Main, and Cistercian, popularized by Thomas Keating and Basil Pennington. Cistercian teachers consider it a method for the prayer called *The Cloud of Unknowing*, a loving attentiveness to God, which *The Cloud*'s author, whose name has been lost, said is "by invitation only."

As Cistercians teach centering prayer, one sits comfortably to calm oneself and then begins to repeat a sacred word silently. When one feels grounded in a loving attitude toward God, one drops the word and waits in silence. Whenever the mind wanders, one returns to the sacred word to center again.

At the end of practice, one might say a prayer slowly and attentively. Two daily practice periods of about twenty minutes each are recommended.

Two major problems have been reported with this form of prayer. First, voluntary emptying of the mind can lead to fuzziness if one is not attentive. Secondly, subconscious thoughts sometimes surge into the mental emptiness created in centering prayer, and meditators have no techniques for managing them.

As John Main taught centering, one keeps attention on a sacred word, preferably not an English one that can more easily produce thought. The word is silently repeated until one can no longer say it. This maintains a solidly focused meditation, and helps prevent the difficulties encountered in the Cistercian method. *See also* prayer.

Centesimus Annus (Lat., "The Hundredth Year"), social encyclical issued in 1991 by Pope John Paul II to commemorate the one hundredth anniversary of Pope Leo XIII's encyclical *Rerum Novarum* (Lat., "Of New Things"). *Centesimus Annus* reaffirms previous papal pronouncements that the social teachings pertain to the Church's evangelizing mission and are "an essential part of the Christian message" (n. 5; see also n. 54). But, again, the Church has no specific programs to propose. Instead, it offers its social teachings as "an indispensable and ideal orientation" (n. 43). The social message of the Gospel "must not be considered a theory, but above all else a basis and motivation for action" (n. 57). At the center of the message is always the dignity of the human person (n. 53; also nn. 47, 54–56), a point the pope had made already in his first encyclical, *Redemptor Hominis* (Lat., "Redeemer of humankind"). It also reaffirmed the Church's preferential option for the poor (nn. 11; 57) and the importance of the Church's own witness to its social teachings (n. 57). In addition, the encyclical is significant for the positive assessment it makes of democracy: "The church values the democratic system inasmuch as it ensures the participation of citizens in making political choices, guarantees to the governed the possibility both of electing and holding accountable those who govern them and of replacing them through peaceful means when appropriate" (n. 46). *See also* Catholic social teachings; democracy; *Rerum Novarum.*

certitude, moral, the quality of a person's knowledge of something to the extent that all reasonable fear of error is excluded. It is the teaching of the Church that truth can be known while also recognizing that there are different kinds of truth claims and different degrees of confidence with which people can hold a claim regarding the knowledge they have. Put positively, moral certitude allows an individual to give firm assent to what is known. It can be distinguished both from doubt (the inability to either confirm or deny something to be true) and from probability (something is likely to be true but an alternative is plausible). Moral certitude requires that any alternative conviction be less than plausible, otherwise it would not be reasonable for a person to exclude the danger of error. While moral certitude does not eliminate all possibility of error, it is so unlikely that fear of error can be put to rest. Moral certitude thus stands between a probable judgment and the certitude called absolute or metaphysical, wherein error is not only excluded as unlikely but is impossible.

While the area of fundamental principles may admit of absolute certitude, the knowledge striven for in the formation of conscience at the practical level is either moral certitude or, more commonly, probable judgment. In matters of canon law judges are ordinarily held to the standard of moral certitude in their pronouncements.

Cerularius, Michael (ser-*oo*-lahr'ee-uhs), ca. 1005/10–1059, Byzantine Orthodox patriarch of Constantinople (1043–58). In the 1050s, a period of tension between Constantinople and Rome, Emperor Constantine IX sought an alliance with Rome against the Norman penetration into southern Italy. When talks with the papal legate Humbert broke down, mutual excommunications resulted on July 16, 1054. Though some date the East-West schism from this rupture, the break was not finalized until the Crusades. Exceptionally powerful and popular with the common people, Michael was perceived as a threat and removed from office by Emperor Isaac I Comnenus.

Chad, St., d. ca. 672, Anglo-Saxon monk and bishop. Disciple of Aidan, Chad followed his brother Cedd as abbot of Lastingham. Appointed bishop of York by King Oswy (665), he was removed by Theodore of Tarsus (669), who restored Wilfrid to York, reconsecrating Chad to be bishop of Lichfield. Feast day: March 2.

chair, presidential. *See* presidential chair.

Chalcedon, Council of (451), the greatest of the first four general councils of the Church, it expressed in clear terms the Church's scriptural and traditional faith in the unity (one person) and distinction (two natures) of Christ. In the fourth century and, in particular, at the first two councils (Nicaea I in 325 and Constantinople I in 381), the central challenge was to maintain the full divine and the full human reality in Christ. Toward the end of the century, however, some heretical movements were helping to bring up the question of Christ's unity. This question of the unity as well as the distinction of natures in Christ was also raised by those who explored the basis for believing that the eternal Word or Son of God was born, as man, from Mary and died on the cross. How could one justify, for example, the popular Marian title of *Theotokos* (Gk., "God-bearer," "Mother of God"), which is dated at least as early as Origen (ca. d. 254), and which affirmed that Mary conceived and gave birth to the Son of God and not just to Christ's humanity? The new challenge was to legitimate the Christological intuition embodied in this Marian title: the preexistent Word of God was and is the one final subject in Christ.

Nestorius (d. 451), a monk from Antioch who became patriarch of Constantinople, stressed the distinction at the level of Christ's human and divine natures (Gk., *physeis*), while allowing for some "conjunction" (Gk., *synapheia*) at the level of Christ's "person" (Gk., *prosōpon* or *hypostasis*). Initially he preferred to call Mary "Christ-bearer" but eventually agreed to use the title of *Theotokos*. He repudiated the view (attributed to him by his critics) of a separation between the two natures in Christ and hence a double sonship (the Son of God and the son of Mary existing independently yet linked together by a merely moral or accidental unity of mutual love). Nestorius's great opponent, Cyril of Alexandria (d. 444), emphasized Christ's unity (Gk., *henōsis*) and championed the Marian title of *Theotokos*, but was not really able to interpret satisfactorily the distinction between Christ's divinity and humanity. The difference between the two patriarchs' views was also made problematic by the fact that the key terms of *physis, hypostasis,* and the term preferred by the Antiochenes, *prosōpon*, were not clearly defined.

The Council of Ephesus: The debate came to a head in 431 when Cyril opened the Council of Ephesus. It declared Mary to be *Theotokos,* recognized Cyril's teaching in his second letter to Nestorius as being consonant with the creed from the Council of Nicaea, and excommunicated Nestorius. Shortly thereafter the bishops who were gathered around the patriarch of Antioch produced the Formula of Reunion (accepted by Cyril in 433) which called Christ "of one substance (consubstantial) with the Father as regards his divinity and of one substance with us as regards his humanity," and spoke of Christ's one person (*prosōpon*) and two natures (*physeis*).

The Council of Ephesus helped move toward a fuller appreciation of the Nicene Creed. In the context of the early fourth century that creed had been important for the doctrine of the Trinity: the Son is of one being or substance (Gk., *homoousios*) with the Father. Now its significance for the doctrine of Christ and his incarnation could be seen: a double (divine and human) set of attributes (on the one hand, "true God from true God," "consubstantial with the Father" and, on the other hand, "who became incarnate, was made man, suffered and rose again on the third day") was confessed as belonging to one and the same subject ("We believe in the one Lord Jesus Christ, the only begotten Son of God"). The way was prepared for the teaching of the Council of Chalcedon.

Chalcedon: The immediate occasion for this council came from Eutyches (d. ca. 454), a leading monk of Constantinople who apparently taught that the unity in Christ was such that only one nature or *physis* remained in Christ after the incarnation, the human nature being absorbed or swallowed up by the divinity. Drawing on the Scriptures, the earlier Church councils, Cyril's second letter to Nestorius, the Formula of Reunion, Cyril's letter accepting it and, in particular, a letter written in 449 by Pope Leo the Great (d. 461) to the patriarch of Constantinople, the council affirmed the one person (*prosōpon* or *hypostasis*) of Christ in his two natures (*physeis*), human and divine. It specified that "the one and the same Christ, Son, Lord and Only begotten" had been made known in these two natures which, without detriment to their full characteristics, continue to exist "without confusion or change, and without division or separation," while belonging to only one person. In other words, the unity of Christ exists on the level of person, the duality on that of natures. Through the unity of subject in Jesus Christ, the eternally preexistent Son of the Father is also the Son of the Blessed Virgin Mary. "Without confusion or change" was aimed to exclude the current error of Eutyches in merging Christ's two natures; "without division or separation" was intended to exclude the error which had been attributed to Nestorius of separating the two natures.

Subsequent councils would add footnotes to Chalcedon by using the term "hypostatic union" to interpret the personal unity of Christ and by insisting on the integrity of his humanity entailing a human (as well as a divine) will. In regulating language about Christ, Chalcedon had lasting success. Its terminology of "one person in two natures" became normative even into the twentieth century. Its teaching effected a brilliant synthesis between the Alexandrians, who highlighted Christ's unity, and the Antiochenes, who defended the duality of Christ's distinct natures. The subject who acts is one (divine) person; what he does reveals the two natures through which he acts. *See also* Christology; ecumenical council; Ephesus, Council of; Monophysitism; Nestorianism.

Bibliography

Grillmeier, Aloys. *Christ in Christian Tradition*. Vol. 1. Rev. ed. London: Mowbrays, 1975.

Kelly, J. N. D. *Early Christian Doctrines*. 5th ed. London: A. & C. Black, 1977.   GERALD O'COLLINS

Chaldean Catholic Church, the ecclesiastical community of Chaldean rite (also called East Syrian rite) Catholics who are in communion with Rome and whose largest concentration of members is in Baghdad, Iraq. It is the Catholic counterpart of the Assyrian Church of the East, which broke with Rome after rejecting the teaching of the Council of Ephesus (431) that in Christ there is only one divine person, not two persons, human and divine, as the Nestorians held.

As early as the thirteenth century, Catholic missionaries—primarily Dominicans and Franciscans—had been active among Assyrian Christians. This missionary effort led to a series of individual conversions of bishops and brief unions, but no permanent community was formed.

In the mid-fifteenth century a tradition of hereditary patriarchal succession (passing from uncle to nephew) took effect in the Assyrian Church. As a result, one family dominated the church and untrained minors were being elected to the patriarchal throne.

When such a patriarch was elected in 1552, a group of Assyrian bishops refused to accept him and decided to seek union with Rome. They elected the reluctant abbot of a monastery, Yuhannan Sulaka, as their own patriarch and sent him to Rome to arrange for a union with the Catholic Church. In early 1553 Pope Julius III proclaimed him Patriarch Simon VIII "of the Chaldeans" and ordained him a bishop in St. Peter's Basilica on April 9, 1553.

The new patriarch returned to his homeland in late 1553 and began to initiate a series of reforms. But opposition, led by the rival Assyrian patriarch, was strong. Simon was soon captured by the pasha of Amadya, tortured, and executed in January 1555. This initiated a long struggle between Chaldeans and Assyrians in which the Chaldeans eventually got the upper hand. It is now estimated that the Chaldean Catholic Church is three times as large as the Assyrian Church of the East.

The Chaldean Catholics suffered heavily from massacres during World War I (1918) when four bishops, many priests, and about seventy thousand faithful died.

The location of the patriarchate shifted back and forth among several places over the centuries but gained a measure of stability after it was set up at Mossul in 1830. In 1950 it moved to its present location in Baghdad after substantial migration of Chaldean Catholics from northern Iraq to the capital city. Since the nineteenth century the patriarch has had the title "of Babylon of the Chaldeans."

Chaldean candidates for the priesthood study at St. Peter's Patriarchal Seminary in Baghdad. It no longer grants advanced degrees.

Two religious orders are unique to the Chaldean Catholic Church. The Antonine Monks of St. Hormisdas (founded 1830) combine a monastic community life with pastoral ministry. The Chaldean Daughters of Mary Immaculate (founded 1922) work mostly in schools and orphanages.

As of 1992 the largest concentration of these Catholics is in Baghdad, Iraq. There are ten Chaldean dioceses in Iraq, four in Iran, and seven others in the Middle East, as well as a diocese in the United States. Altogether the church has about 500,000 faithful. *See also* Chaldean rite; Eastern Catholics and ecumenism; Eastern Catholics and Rome; Eastern churches; Eastern liturgies; Eastern rites; East Syrian rite; Ephesus, Council of.   RONALD G. ROBERSON

Chaldean rite, also called East Syrian or Assyro-Chaldean rite, the liturgical tradition of the Chaldean and Syro-Malabar Catholic churches and their Orthodox counterpart, the Assyrian "Church of the East." This rite is the descendant of the ancient liturgical heritage of the Church of Mesopotamia in the Persian Empire. *See also* Eastern rites; East Syrian rite; rite.

chalice, the cup used for wine and Precious Blood at Mass. The chalice recalls various scriptural passages in which Jesus associates the use of a cup with himself in a new way: the disciples will "drink the cup" that Jesus drinks from (Mark 10:38); at the Last Supper, the cup contains the wine that is "my blood," and when he is to be crucified, he prays that "this cup" be taken from him. These various meanings are gathered together at Eucharist, and both religious and liturgical significance is attached to a cup or goblet when it is referred to as a chalice. *See also* mixed chalice; unmixed chalice.

Challenge of Peace, The, the U.S. Catholic bishops' 1983 pastoral letter on war and peace, with a particular focus on the problem of the possession and use of nuclear weapons. The letter addresses the problem of nuclear warfare within the context of a biblically-based understanding of peace as right relationship with God, neighbor, and, ultimately, all of creation. The bishops draw upon the just-war tradition to help specify how the United States can help bring about that right relationship in a world disordered by superpower rivalry. On the question of the use of nuclear weapons, the bishops assess three possibilities: counterpopulation bombing, first use

Chalice

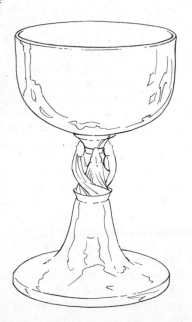

(against military targets), and limited nuclear war. They reject counterpopulation bombing because it would directly take the lives of noncombatants. They reject first use and limited nuclear war out of a concern that any use of nuclear weapons will escalate and therefore be disproportionate to the end of a just peace. On the question of deterrence, they outline a "strictly conditioned moral acceptance" of the practice. Not all deterrence policies are to be condemned, but they must meet certain strict conditions. Deterrence is legitimate only in the context of negotiations and progress towards disarmament. This is the only way that a deterrent policy can be said to be moving in the direction of true peace.

The other noteworthy contribution of the pastoral letter is its recognition—even though the document's own reasoning uses just-war theory—of pacifism as a complement to the just-war tradition. *See also* Catholic social teachings; just-war doctrine; peace.

Challoner, Richard, 1691–1781, bishop, vicar apostolic of the London district (1758–81), and leader of English Catholics. Born of Presbyterian parents in Lewes (Sussex), Challoner was converted to Catholicism in youth, studied and taught at Douai (1705–30), and revised the Douay-Rheims Bible translation, which remained the standard for Catholics until the Confraternity Version (begun 1936). The latter is the predecessor of the New American Bible. *See also* Scripture, versions of.

chamberlain. *See* papal chamberlain.

chancel (Lat., *cancellus,* "balustrade"), often synonymous with "sanctuary," it is that portion of the church building immediately surrounding the altar and the pulpit. The chancel can extend from the space in front of the altar to include also the choir. It can be set off from the congregational space by a rise of several steps. *See also* sanctuary.

chancellor, diocesan, principal archivist of a diocesan curia, a notary by law. Every diocesan bishop is expected to appoint one. The chancellor primarily systematizes, safeguards, and authenticates curial acts though particular law may determine otherwise. In the United States, broad governance faculties are personally allotted many ordained chancellors by delegation. Because such governance powers belong to vicars general by office, and because not only a priest but anyone of good character in full

Church communion may be chancellor, the practice of granting broad governance faculties is now less common. Particular law may adapt or modify tasks of chancellors and distribute work volume among vice-chancellors and other notaries, freely appointable and removable. *See also* diocesan curia.

chancery, diocesan office wherein records called acts of the curia are to be collected, systematized, and safeguarded.

The broad scope of curial operations recorded and sometimes administered through the chancery in many dioceses invites its colloquial designation as the "bishop's office." Functions may include, for example, executing policies and procedures regarding personnel, finances, education, and construction; coordinating special diocesan projects and ministries; and corresponding with Church and secular authorities.

Diocesan bishops frequently rely on their chancery for canonical advice, communications, statistical data, public relations assistance, and disciplinary matters. Chancery personnel always include the chancellor and, if needed, vice-chancellors, other notaries, and secretaries. *See also* diocesan curia.

Chanel, St. Peter, 1803–41, priest and first martyr in Oceania. Born, educated, and ordained a Marist priest in France, he went as a missionary to the New Hebrides in Oceania in 1936. He was murdered by a chieftain on the island of Futuma when the latter heard that his son was to be baptized. Feast day: April 28.

chant. *See* Catholicism and music.

chant, Ambrosian, the repertory of liturgical chant associated with the Ambrosian rite, or the liturgy of the Church of Milan. Distinct from the corpus of Gregorian chant, the Ambrosian chants exhibit a recognizably more ancient musical style than their Roman counterparts. The chant, like the liturgical rites it served, both conserves a local tradition distinct from Rome's and embraces foreign elements and idioms, some from Oriental sources. Transmitted orally until the twelfth century, the melodies range from spartan simplicity (psalm antiphons) to extreme prolixity (Mass alleluias with melismas, i.e., passages sung to one syllable of text, of some three hundred notes). *See also* Ambrosian rite; Catholicism and music.

chant, Byzantine, traditional Greek liturgical chant of the Byzantine rite, a monophonic vocal music unaccompanied by musical instruments, preserved in manuscripts with a musical notation called "ekphonetic." Byzantine hymnody flourished in the fifth and sixth centuries with the development of the *kontakion* (poetic refrains), especially under St. Romanos the Melodist at Constantinople in the first half of the sixth century, and with the development of the canon of *orthros* (Matins, Lauds) in the seventh. Later composers like John Koukouzeles continued the tradition up to the fourteenth century. The old chant has been largely replaced by modern compositions. The Byzantine-rite Slavs also had a form of Byzantine chant called *znamennyj*, now often neglected in favor of modern polyphony outside monastic and peasant usage, where the old *prostopenie* or "plainchant" can still be heard. *See also* Byzantine rite; Catholicism and music.

chant, Gregorian, the plain chant of the Roman rite, named after Pope Gregory the Great (d. 604), although he probably had little or nothing to do with its composition. The present form of Gregorian chant is based on the older chant of Rome, with subsequent pruning of long florid passages and the incorporation of other elements from the eighth- and ninth-century Gallican liturgy of Carolingian France. Gregorian chant was diffused throughout the Frankish Empire at this time as part of the romanizing policy of the imperial court. It eventually supplanted most other forms of local or regional plain chant, but was itself influenced by the traditions it supplanted. Keeping pace with the evolution of the Roman-rite Mass and Divine Office, the ancient repertory of texts and melodies has been progressively enriched up to modern times.

Gregorian chant is monodic, i.e., one vocal part or melodic line predominates, needs no instrumental accompaniment, and its scales or modes run from D, E, F, and G, rather than from C or A, as in modern music. The form in which it is known in the 1990s is traceable only to ca. 900, when its various kinds of musical notation began to emerge. Since the fourteenth century, it is printed in square notes on a staff of four lines. With the rise of polyphony (music with two or more independent melodic parts sounded together) and measured music (music using metric units between two bars on the staff), the Gregorian chant tradition entered upon a serious decline compounded, after the Council of Trent (1545–63), by the publication of the Medicean edition (so called because it was published by a press owned by the famous Medici family of Rome) of the Mass and Divine Office chants (1614 and 1615). The editors recast the ancient melodies of Gregorian chant with a view to making them conform to Renaissance ideas of Latin prosody. Neumes (two or more notes sung to a single syllable) assigned to weak syllables and word-endings were simplified or else shifted to accented syllables; compound neumes and melismas (passages sung to one syllable of text) suffered major amputations; the various shapes of the notes were taken to imply differences of length in the rhythm; tropes and sequences, which abounded from the ninth century onward, were, with few exceptions, abolished; and a multitude of ancient antiphons and responsories were eliminated from the newly edited repertory. This defective edition was used well into the early twentieth century and served as a model for regional editions of liturgical choral books. Meanwhile, nineteenth-century scholarship was making significant progress in the recovery of the tradition, particularly at the French Abbey of Solesmes.

With the encouragement of the abbot, Dom Prosper Guéranger (d. 1875), and in the context of the liturgical revival initiated at Solesmes, monks of the abbey, under the direction particularly of Dom Pothier and Dom Mocquereau, began editing chant books based on a careful study of ancient manuscripts. Of particular importance was the facsimile reproduction of a number of these manuscripts in the series *Paléographie musicale grégorienne* (begun in 1889), as well as numerous books and monographs that served everywhere to stimulate further research. However, the establishment of a musical text is one thing, its interpretation another; and scholars have frequently challenged Solesmes theories concerning the rhythmic interpretation of the chant—theories that have continued to evolve up to the present. Since the turn of the century, Solesmes has played the principal role in the editing of the official Roman rite chant books; and post-Vatican II (1962–65) chant books continue to reflect the advances made at Solesmes in the study and interpretation of the ancient manuscripts. *See also* Catholicism and music; Solesmes.   CHRYSOGONUS WADDELL

chant, Mozarabic (mohts-ah'rah-bik), the body of liturgical chant sung by churches of the Iberian peninsula and associated with the Mozarabic rites. Scholars suggest that these chants, like the liturgical rites for which they were composed, date from the

eighth century. Extant manuscripts date from the tenth and eleventh centuries, just prior to the rite's suppression in 1085. Comparatively more melismatic (singing many notes for one syllable) than their Roman counterparts, the Mozarabic chants exhibit a unique Oriental flavor. Of more than twenty surviving ancient manuscript sources, only five exhibit decipherable notation. *See also* Catholicism and music; Mozarabic rite.

chant, plain, or plainsong, a form of monophonic and rhythmically free melody, generally of ecclesiastical origin. The Latin term, *cantus planus,* served in the thirteenth century to distinguish Gregorian chant from music that was polyphonic and measured. The term has been used since in a wider sense to include the unison nonmetrical melodies proper to churches of both West and East: in the West, Ambrosian, Old Roman, Gregorian, Mozarabic, Gallican, and Beneventan chant; in the East, Byzantine, Armenian, and Syrian chant. By extension, the term also covers liturgical melodies with vernacular texts but based on classical plain chant models, as, for example, Anglican plain chant.

Chantal, St. Jane Frances de, 1572–1641, French spiritual leader. Born Jane Frances Fremyót, she married Baron Rabutin-Chantal when she was twenty. As a young widow she formed a spiritual friendship with Frances de Sales. In 1610 they cofounded the Visitation Sisters. Jane's spiritual writings are primarily in the form of letters. Her spirituality centers on the dual aspects of charitable love—devotion to God and neighbor. Her teachings urge that the practice of simple contemplative prayer fosters the virtues that allow one to serve others. Feast day: August 21. *See also* Francis de Sales, St.; Visitation order.

chantry. 1 The endowed office or duty of a priest to celebrate Masses for a deceased person or persons. 2 The chapel (often attached to a church, but sometimes free-standing) where such Masses were said. Officiants who held such offices were often called "chantry priests." Such benefices and places were common in the late Middle Ages. *See also* benefice.

chapel, place of worship with a separate altar in a cathedral, a large church, an institution (school, convent, prison, hospital, etc.), a private home, or an airport. The principal difference between a church and a chapel is that a church is for the use of all the faithful, whereas a chapel, or oratory, is, according to canon law, "for the benefit of some community or assembly of the faithful" (can. 1223).

chapel of ease, place of worship with a separate altar, for the sake of parishioners who live too far away from their parish church, or to absorb an overflow from the parish church.

chaplain, a priest who is responsible for the spiritual and pastoral welfare of a particular group. Chaplains serve institutions that are not connected with a local congregation. Chaplains originally were appointed to provide spiritual guidance and perform religious services in the chapels of leading families and royalty.

In the United States, chaplains serve a variety of institutions. The army chaplaincy began during the American Revolution, and the first Roman Catholic military chaplain was appointed in 1824. Chaplains are also appointed for service in hospitals, schools, prisons, convents, and lay religious institutes (see cans. 564–72).

chaplet (Fr., *chapeau*, "hat"). **1** A garland of flowers used as a crown. **2** A string of beads, often used of the beads of a rosary. A chaplet was five decades (50 beads), while the complete rosary was fifteen decades (150 beads). Smaller strings of ten beads of a rosary are also known as chaplets. *See also* Rosary.

chapter, an assembly of women or men from a religious institute. The word originated with the monastic practice of assembling daily to listen to a reading of a chapter from a monastic rule. A superior also transacted business at these sessions; hence the legal character of chapters. This assembly took place in the chapterhouse. There are various kinds of chapters. A general chapter represents the entire, perhaps worldwide, religious institute. A provincial chapter consists of representatives of a province, while a local chapter is a meeting of an individual monastery or house. Canons 631–33 of the Code of Canon Law contain the Church's general legislation on chapters. The constitutions of a religious institute specify the character of the chapters in that institute. Chapters promote the active participation of members of a religious institute in the life and welfare of an institute. The chapter of faults is not one of these canonically established meetings. *See also* chapter of faults; general chapter.

chapter, cathedral. *See* cathedral chapter.

chapter of faults, an ancient monastic custom that called for a meeting of religious, often in the chapter room or house, to manifest their failings to the superior in the presence of the community. The accusation of one monk's faults by another was also part of the tradition. The modern form of the chapter first appeared in the ninth and tenth centuries. Most orders except the Jesuits had some form of this exercise. Jansenism gave a punitive cast to this manifestation of conscience. Since the Second Vatican Council (1962–65), most religious orders and congregations have omitted this exercise from their constitutions. *See also* chapter; monasticism.

character, moral, the collection of the ways of acting, responding, and construing situations that bestows a pattern of strengths and weaknesses on an individual's moral life. Moral character is understood as the individual's enduring personality, a way to evaluate the individual as a moral agent with characteristic virtues and faults.

One's moral character is distinguished from the sacramental character bestowed by certain sacraments (Baptism, Orders), by virtue of which individuals gain a certain standing within the Church community. Sacramental character need not be grounded in, or expressed by, any particular qualities of the personality of the individual who possesses it, although ideally it will be. Because it is bestowed in a particular sacramental act, sacramental character is received once by the individual receiving the sacrament, even though it may develop and unfold throughout life. Hence, it is to be understood in a quasijuridical way. Moral character, on the other hand, is essentially equivalent to one's personality, and, as such, it emerges over the course of a lifetime in a way that is best understood in psychodynamic developmental terms. *See also* sacramental character.

character, sacramental. *See* sacramental character.

charism (kair'iz-uhm; Gk., "gift"), divine spiritual gift to individuals or groups for the good of the community. The word was introduced with this meaning by Paul. "To each is given the manifestation of the Spirit for the common good. . . . All these [gifts] are activated by one and the same Spirit, who allots to each one individually just as the Spirit chooses" (1 Cor 12:7, 11). Although some charisms are extraordinary, such as prophecy or healing, most are powers for the ordered growth of the Christian community. Preaching, teaching, administration, and generosity are important charisms; love is the greatest of all.

Having received charisms from the Holy Spirit, each Christian has the power and the responsibility to exercise some office or render some service in the Church. Charisms originate with the Spirit working directly in the baptized, so they can challenge the institutional Church and call it to renewal. Some see charismatic movements as essentially opposed to institutional ordering, but such is not the case. The Catholic Church considers the ecumenical movement the fruit of a charism working among many Christian churches.

Charisms given to one person can become embodied in a large group, such as a religious institute. The unique gift of the founder or foundress is given to every member from one generation to the next. Through these unmerited gifts, the Spirit continues to call the Church to dynamic growth and to renewed fidelity to Christ. *See also* gifts of the Holy Spirit; grace; Holy Spirit.

Charismatic Renewal movement, contemporary spiritual movement that claims to be inspired by the charisms (gifts) present in some of the early Christian communities and associated with the feast of Pentecost. These charisms include words of wisdom, words of knowledge, healings, prophecy, speech in new languages ("tongues"), and interpretation of such speech (1 Cor 12:4-11). Since the late 1960s the claim to, and emphasis upon, charisms has become increasingly common among Catholics and is more generally accepted by the leadership of the Church.

In varying degrees charisms have been present throughout Christian history. Some theologians, including Augustine (d. 430), thought that speaking in tongues had ceased. However, the gifts of spiritual knowledge, miracles, and prophecy continued to be attested in lives of the saints and chronicles of ecclesiastical and monastic renewal movements.

Emphasis upon charisms, including the gift of tongues, has been especially strong among Protestant groups such as the Moravians of the eighteenth century (who influenced John Wesley, the founder of Methodism) and during the Second Great Awakening of the nineteenth century in the United States. The first decades of the twentieth century witnessed the formation of distinct Pentecostal denominations within Protestantism.

At the Second Vatican Council in 1963 the bishops discussed a draft paragraph "on the charisms of the faithful" proposed for the Dogmatic Constitution on the Church (*Lumen Gentium*). Sicily's Cardinal Ruffini, among others, argued that charisms mentioned in the NT were a bridal present to the early Church and had ceased playing a significant role in the ordinary life of Christians. Others, especially Belgium's Cardinal Leo-Josef Suenens, argued that these gifts were vitally important for the building up of the ecclesial body. The council eventually adopted the latter view (*Lumen Gentium,* n. 12).

Charismatic renewal within the Catholic Church followed closely upon the council. In 1967 groups of Roman Catholics at the University of Duquesne in Pittsburgh, Pennsylvania, and later at the University of Michigan at Ann Arbor and at the University of Notre Dame in Indiana spoke of experiencing the broad spectrum of charisms. The experience quickly extended itself in prayer groups and, in some cases, lay-led charismatic communities. Catholics participated in organizing regional, national, and international offices and conferences. From its beginning, charismatic renewal among Catholics has had an ecumenical orientation, but its alliances have been with the most conservative Protestant groups. The Charismatic Renewal movement grew rapidly among Catholics through the 1970s, remained steady in the 1980s, but in recent years has declined. In some cases, it has been the victim of internal conflicts over the exercise of authority.

Twelve major charismatic communities from various parts of the world formed the Catholic Fraternity of Charismatic Covenant Communities and Fellowships (canonically recognized in 1990), which has since been joined by other communities. *See also* charism.　　　　　MICHAEL WALDSTEIN

charity, a theological virtue (along with faith and hope), the highest form of Christian love, whose originating source and ultimate end is God. Although charity in its principal sense is the love we direct towards God—a whole-hearted love awakened, sustained, and fortified by God's own prevenient love for us—it stands as well for the love of neighbor as ourselves, continuously informed and nourished by that love. It is additionally the proper name for the third and most important of the theological virtues. The Latin root of charity, *caritas,* is the term employed most consistently by the Vulgate to render the Greek *agapē*, the dominant word for love in the NT, where it comprises in its most fundamental sense the love of God bestowed through Christ and the Holy Spirit upon humankind, as well as the love required of human beings for both God and one another (cf. 1 John 4:7–21). Among early Christian writers charity functions in a broad sense as the summary principle and metaphor of the Christian life as a whole; it is to be the wellspring of all religious and moral motivation. Only with Augustine (d. 430), to whom tradition gives the title *Doctor Caritatis* (Doctor of Charity), do the first signs of a systematic account of the concept appear. Charity is the complete love of God, which both unifies and perfects the other virtues (cf. *Morals of the Catholic Church* 1.2).

Consequently, all sin is in some sense or degree an offense against and corruption of charity. Still the most influential treatment of charity remains that of Thomas Aquinas (d. 1274), whose reflections blend scriptural and early Christian theological sources with the philosophical insights of Aristotle. In the sections of his monumental *Summa Theologiae* expressly devoted to the three theological virtues (faith, hope, and charity), Aquinas describes charity as our friendship with God, citing the words of Jesus recorded in John's Gospel, "I do not call you servants any longer, ... but I have called you friends" (John 15:15; *Summa Theologiae* 2–2.23.1). As a genuine friendship (cf. Aristotle *Nicomachean Ethics*, Book 8), charity is our love of God for God's own sake, based on the common fellowship in God's eternal happiness extended to us in Jesus (cf. 1 Cor 1:9). It is a love whose motive force is the Holy Spirit, working within us in full cooperation with our own voluntary capacities (*Summa Theologiae* 2–2.23.2). Thus, it is through charity that we are made participants, however imperfectly in our present state, in the trinitarian life of God. Though its formal object and final end is God, charity reaches out to the neighbor as well, including even the enemy and the sinner, who are loved for God's sake (23.1). Indeed, all the more particular and immediate goods of life, and hence the moral and intellectual virtues that direct and order the pursuit of those goods, may be brought under the activity of charity, which completes and perfects them by referring them to the greatest good, which is God (1 Cor 13:1–3; *Summa Theologiae*, 2–2.23.7–8). Charity is therefore the greatest of the virtues, because it both conjoins us to

God and directs all our activity toward the eternal happiness promised us (23.5–6). While it may grow by intensity within us (24.4–8; cf. Council of Trent, Session VI), charity does not render us free from all sinfulness and may, as a consequence of gravely sinful acts, be seriously weakened, if not lost (24.10–12). *See also* agape; love.   PAUL J. WOJDA

Charlemagne (shar'luh-mayn; Fr., "Charles the Great"), ca. 742–814, Frankish king and, from 800 to 814 first emperor of what was later called the "Holy Roman Empire." Son of Pepin III ("the Short") and Bertrada, he inherited, with his brother Carloman, a share of his father's kingdom, and on Carloman's death in 771 became its sole ruler. By 774 he had subdued the Lombards and was thenceforth known as "King of the Franks and Lombards," and as such he exercised enormous influence over the Holy See. His dominion was enlarged by his extensive military campaigns against the Saxons (772–85, with sporadic revolts thereafter until 797); his conquest of the Spanish March, a territory in northern Spain (801); his wars against the Avars (796); and his victories over the Danes and the

Charlemagne, the first Holy Roman emperor, who exerted a profound influence on the Church, appointing bishops and mandating reforms of the liturgy, monasteries, and the clergy; ninth-century statue in the church of St. John the Baptist, Muestaire, Switzerland.

Slavs. In recognition of these victories and of his role in protecting the Holy See, and partly in opposition to the claims of the Byzantine emperor that he was the true temporal ruler of Christendom, Charlemagne was crowned "Emperor of the Romans" by Pope Leo III on Christmas Day, 800.

Charlemagne's importance in the life of the Western Church was immense. His ideal for a united and prosperous commonwealth based on a vision of renewed learning and of religious unity succeeded because he was, in effect if not in title, virtually the head of the Church in his domain (which encompassed the Holy See), controlling all episcopal appointments, promulgating liturgical and monastic reforms as well as disciplinary reforms for clerics, and summoning and presiding at Church councils. The most important of these was the Council of Frankfurt (794), which condemned Adoptionism, a Christological heresy, and attacked the Second Council of Nicaea (787) for supposedly sanctioning image worship. Already surnamed "Great" (*magne*) by 840, the Middle Ages looked back on Charlemagne as an ideal ruler and in some circles he was venerated as a saint (on January 28). *See also* Holy Roman Empire.

Charles II, 1630–85, king of Great Britain and Ireland. He was declared king while in exile in Scotland in 1649, but his invasion of England was rebuffed by Cromwell's army in 1651, after which he fled to the Continent. Upon his restoration in 1660, Charles attempted to establish toleration for dissenting Puritans and recusant Catholics in Declarations of Indulgence (1662, 1672) but was defeated by Parliament, which established Anglicanism in the Act of Uniformity (1662) and excluded Catholicism by the Test Act (1673). Charles professed the Catholic faith on his deathbed. *See also* England, Catholicism in; Puritanism.

Charles V, 1500–58, Holy Roman emperor from 1520 until his abdication in 1556. Ruler of one of the largest empires in history, including Germany, Italy, the Low Countries, Spain, and the Spanish colonies around the world, he combated Protestantism and pushed for reform of the Catholic Church. *See also* Holy Roman Empire.

Charles Borromeo, St. *See* Borromeo, St. Charles.

Charles Lwanga, St. *See* Lwanga, St. Charles.

Charles Martel, ca. 690–741, Frankish "Mayor of the Palace" and grandfather of Charlemagne. The real ruler of the Frankish realm after 718, Charles supported the work of St. Boniface. His victory at Poitiers (732) helped halt Muslim advances and earned him the name "Martel" (Fr.), "Hammer." Charles left the throne vacant when the last of his puppet kings died. *See also* Boniface, St.; Charlemagne; Franks.

Chartres, cathedral of, Gothic-style cathedral in Chartres, a city southeast of Paris. Rebuilt after a fire in 1194, the church is known both for the grandeur of its architecture and the beauty of its exterior sculpture. The stained-glass windows are justly famous. Chartres was both an important trade center and pilgrimage site in the medieval period.

chastity, the virtue by which human sexuality is ordered to its proper purpose. In the past, chastity often was identified with continence and with abstinence from immoral sexual desire and pleasures. It

Chartres, the quintessential Gothic cathedral, famous for its stained-glass windows and exterior sculpture.

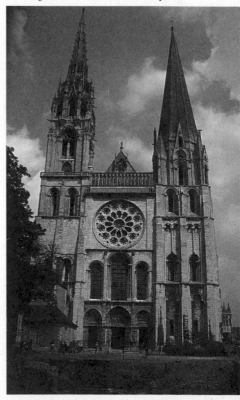

was understood to involve renunciation or control. With the renewal of moral theology called for by the Second Vatican Council (1962–65), chastity has come to be seen in a more positive light. More than continence, it is the virtue that pursues the integration of the true meaning of human sexuality and intimacy, whether one is married or not. Chastity involves an attitude of reverence for the mystery of human sexuality, for one's body, and for one's sexual partner. Chastity never separates sexuality from love. The pursuit of solitary sexual pleasure or treating one's spouse as nothing more than a sex object are both violations of chastity. The pursuit of chastity, whether in thought or deed, is not always easy. It is a fundamental attitude that directs and orders human sexuality whether one is married, single, or celibate. *See also* purity; sexual morality; temperance; vows.

chasuble (chaz'uh-buhl; Lat., "little house," "hooded cloak"), the outer liturgical vestment worn by the presider at Mass. In the Greco-Roman world, the chasuble was a large cone-shaped cloth with a hole for the head worn as the outer garment. Because it completely covered the person, it was called *casula* (Lat., "little house"). When men's fashions

Chasuble

chasuble

changed after the barbarian invasions of the fifth and sixth centuries, the clergy retained the older style, and the chasuble became associated with clerical use. By the ninth century, the presentation of the chasuble to newly ordained priests had become part of the ordination ritual. Chasubles may be made of any suitable material. Traditionally, the chasuble is a symbol of charity. *See also* vestments.

Chateaubriand, François René (sha-toh-bree-ahnd'), 1768–1848, French Romantic writer and diplomat. His first book, *Essay on the Revolutions* (1797), included an account of his religious struggles and a rationalist attack on Christianity. Later, reconciled to the Church, he wrote *The Genius of Christianity* (1802), an apologetic work that defended Christianity on intellectual, aesthetic, and ethical grounds.

Chavez, Cesar, 1927–93, union organizer. Born in Arizona, he moved with his family to California where he picked crops as a migrant worker. In 1958 he formed the National Farm Workers Association. He led a two-year boycott of table grapes (1968–70), after which the growers agreed to collective bargaining. Throughout these years Chavez was openly supported by many Catholics who identified with his cause (Sp., *La Causa*) on religious grounds, including nuns, brothers, priests, and bishops. At the time of his death, many called him a saint.

cheirotonia (ki-rah-toh-nee'uh; Gk., "extending the hand"), ancient term for appointment to an office, used by Christians for the rites of ordination. In later usage the term was usually restricted to ordination to major orders. The Greek synonym *cherothesia* ("imposition of hands") was used for other ordinations and blessings. *See also* ordination.

Chenu, M.-D. [Marie-Dominique], 1895–1990, French Dominican theologian. He entered the Order of Preachers of the French province in 1913. After receiving a doctorate at the Angelicum (Rome, 1920), he taught history of doctrines and introduction to theology at Le Saulchoir in Belgium, which moved to Étiolles (southeast of Paris) in 1937–39. He served as rector of Le Saulchoir from 1932 to 1942, where he led a talented group of Dominican scholars applying historical method to the study of Thomas Aquinas (d. 1274) and to all theology. Much of their work appeared in two journals he edited, the more comprehensive *Revue des sciences* *philosophiques et théologiques* (Review of the philosophical and theological sciences) and the more specialized *Bulletin thomiste* (Thomist bulletin). His privately circulated book, *Une école de théologie: Le Saulchoir* (A school of theology: the Saulchoir, 1937), described their approach in his trenchant, sometimes witty style. At that time, in part from fear of Modernism, historical studies in theology were viewed with suspicion, especially by the speculatively oriented Thomists who dominated the field and whose antihistorical fixations Chenu criticized. They influenced the Vatican to place the unpublished work on the Index of Forbidden Books (1942), and Chenu was deposed as rector of Le Saulchoir.

Undaunted by criticism or injustice from Church authorities and always loyal to the Church as the People of God, Chenu continued his research and publishing in medieval and contemporary theology, including several editions of *La théologie comme science aux XIIIème siècle* (Theology as science in the thirteenth century), *Introduction à l'étude de s. Thomas d'Aquin* (Introduction to the study of St. Thomas Aquinas, 1950), and *La théologie au douzième siècle* (Theology in the twelfth century, 1957, only partly translated into English), a book widely used by medievalists in every field, written during a period when, together with Yves Congar and Henri de Lubac, he was forbidden by Church authorities to teach.

One reason for this action was Chenu's involvement in new theologies and apostolic movements. His historical studies had led him to see the importance of contemporary events and movements for theology, leading him from 1934 on to link theology, sociology, spirituality, and mission in his writing and teaching, and to encourage movements such as Catholic Action and the priest-worker movement. Important works in this area included *Spiritualité du travail* (Spirituality of work, 1941) and *Pour une théologie du travail* (Toward a theology of work, 1955). Historical studies and contemporary concerns constantly fed each other.

Invited by a French missionary bishop to be his theological adviser at the Second Vatican Council (1962–65), Chenu exercised significant influence, especially on the Pastoral Constitution on the Church in the Modern World (*Gaudium et Spes,* 1965), whose emphasis on "the signs of the times" and whose openness to the values of creation and the constantly developing world were consonant with his thought.

After the council he continued to write and speak in the same vein, becoming increasingly critical of what he saw as attempts to blunt the cutting edge of the council's advances and as a retreat from the confidence it had shown that the Church and its theologians must remain in vital contact with the events of history. In his latter years he remained intellectually vigorous, warmly encouraging others by personal interviews and letters. WALTER PRINCIPE

Cherubicon, Byzantine-rite Great Entrance refrain, opening hymn of the eucharistic half of the liturgy, sung during the transfer of gifts to the altar. Strictly speaking, Cherubicon is the proper name of the ordinary refrain used on most days ("We who mystically represent the Cherubim and sing the thrice-holy hymn to the life-giving Trinity, let us now lay aside all worldly care to receive the King of All invisibly escorted by the angelic hosts! Alleluia!"), but the name has come to be used for the other refrains that replace the Cherubicon on Holy Thursday, Holy Saturday, and in the Presanctified Liturgy. Emperor Justin II introduced the Cherubicon into the liturgy of Constantinople in 573–74. *See also* Great Entrance.

cherubim. *See* angel.

Chesterton, Gilbert Keith, 1874–1936, English novelist, poet, essayist, dramatist, biographer, journalist, and apologist. Educated in London, Chesterton is considered the ultimate Edwardian man of letters. Although much remembered for his Father Brown detective stories, begun in 1911, Chesterton was a prolific writer—witty, urbane, and a master of paradox. Writings such as *The Man Who Was Thursday* and his biographies of Thomas Aquinas and Francis of Assisi were immediately successful and reflected his growing commitment to Christianity. Chesterton was formally received into the Catholic Church in 1922. He received several honorary degrees, Fellowship in the Royal Society of Literature, and became Knight Commander with Star, Order of St. Gregory the Great. *See also* apologetics.

Chevetogne (shev'tohn), Benedictine Monastery of the Holy Cross in the Ardennes, Belgium, where the liturgical offices are celebrated in both the Roman and Byzantine rites. Founded in 1925 at Amaysur-Meuse, Belgium, by Dom Lambert Beauduin (1873–1960), noted pioneer of the ecumenical and liturgical movements, the monastery moved to its present site in 1939. The monastery houses an international community dedicated to fostering Christian unity and ecumenical dialogue. Since 1926 its quarterly *Irénikon,* the first Catholic review devoted to ecumenism, has played a seminal role in the formation of an ecumenical spirit among Christians.

Children of Mary, a broad term indicating membership in one of many sodalities or confraternities dedicated to the Blessed Virgin Mary. These sodalities generally have the intention of combining personal piety with a social apostolate. Probably the first such group was the Children of Mary sodality founded in the thirteenth century by Peter de Honestis. In the sixteenth century, the Jesuits also formed various sodalities dedicated to Mary whose mission was the spiritual formation of children and young adults. These Jesuit-led Sodalities of Our Lady continue to this day, with the goal of fostering allegiance to the pope and service to the Church. In 1847 the Daughters of Charity and the Vincentian Fathers revived the Children of Mary movement with the approval of Pius IX. This revival had the purpose of promoting devotion to the Miraculous Medal, whose design was revealed in 1830 by the Blessed Virgin to Catherine Labouré, a Daughter of Charity of St. Vincent de Paul. *See also* confraternities; sodality.

Children's Crusade, mostly legendary account of French and German children who in 1212, after the failure of the Fourth Crusade, journeyed to Italy hoping to be led dry-shod across the Mediterranean to the Holy Land, like another Exodus.

Chile, Catholicism in. Catholicism first came to Chile in the early sixteenth century and the first diocese was established in 1561. Early missionary efforts were more successful with the Indian population in the northern and central regions of the country than in the south, where the Church was hindered by the campaign to secure independence from Spain. Church and state were constitutionally separated in 1925. There are five archdioceses and seventeen dioceses and over 10.7 million Catholics in Chile, comprising approximately 80 percent of the total population (1994). *See also* Latin America, Catholicism in.

chiliasm. *See* millenarianism.

China, Catholicism in. With the largest popula-

Portrait of a Chinese convert to Christianity by Sir Godfrey Kneller, Kensington Palace, London.

tion and longest uninterrupted history, China continues to represent the greatest challenge offered to Christianity by any country. Nestorian monks from Persia, the first Christian presence history records in the Middle Kingdom, entered China in the seventh century. After some growth in succeeding centuries, the communities they had established gradually disappeared. Franciscan missionaries founded Catholic communities in the thirteenth and fourteenth centuries, but these also did not survive. The intense efforts of Jesuit missionaries from the late sixteenth to the end of the eighteenth century to engage in dialogue with Confucian literati, as well as with simpler folk, achieved some notable successes. This dialogue ended with the Chinese rites controversy and the suppression of the Society of Jesus (1773). Hostility toward and persecution of Christians, both native and foreign, by some segments of the Chinese population have continued almost without interruption. The dedication of Catholic missionaries of other religious communities during the seventeenth and eighteenth centuries, joined to the Catholic and Protestant efforts of the nineteenth and twentieth centuries, represents the most concentrated evangelizing effort in the history of Christianity. The results achieved by 1949, the year of the Communist domination of all of China, included the

Procession of Chinese priests at the Sheshan Basilica Cathedral near Shanghai, China.

establishment of Christian educational, health, and other social institutions throughout the country. At that time only some four million Catholics and fewer than a million Protestants, who together comprised less than one percent of the population, embraced the Christian faith.

In the 1950s the Communist government created the Three-Self movement for Protestants (self-administration, self-financing, self-propagation), the Catholic Patriotic Association, and analogous associations for Taoists, Buddhists, and Muslims in order to maintain strict control over believers in the five officially recognized religions. As a consequence, underground movements of both Catholics and Protestants continue to resist government control over Christian life. The Christian churches are thus interiorly divided by circumstances created by government control. The tension between publicly sanctioned Catholics and underground Catholics is particularly strong because of the government's prohibition of any official contact between Chinese Catholics and the Holy See. Many Catholics strongly criticize and bitterly reject those who, in order to conduct worship and other religious activities openly, reluctantly submit to government restriction.

Yet in spite of such tensions, including the expulsion of thousands of missionaries between 1949 and

1954 and violent persecutions during the Cultural Revolution (1966–76), Protestants and Catholics, in both the public and underground sectors, have experienced unprecedented membership growth. It is estimated that the Catholic faithful currently number some ten million and the Protestant faithful number probably forty million. The Catholic Church in the 1990s includes 113 dioceses with 64 China-appointed bishops, 30 unofficial bishops whose names have been made known through public reports of arrests, and probably some 20 other unofficial bishops; 900 priests, half of whom have been ordained during the past twelve years; 740 candidates in government-approved seminaries; 200 students in twelve preparatory seminaries; 1,000 sisters in some forty government-approved convents; and almost four thousand public churches and chapels. Growth continues in spite of the harassment of the official and nonofficial communities, the church's material poverty, and paucity of intellectual resources.

During the past fifty years, Christians in China have persevered in their faith. Those who have opposed government religious policy endure the loss of freedom, possessions, social position, and often health and life itself. Their suffering has attracted others to respect and often embrace Christianity.

The Church in China has begun to have a Chinese

character. For the first time after centuries of Christian life, all church leaders are Chinese. Foreign Christian friends, including Chinese living outside mainland China, when invited to do so, are sharing their material, intellectual, spiritual, and pastoral resources to assist Chinese Christian communities to develop. The development of the church in China is, as it ought to be, in Chinese hands. Perhaps future generations of Chinese Christians will be able to undertake a serious dialogue with Confucianism, Taoism, and Buddhism, the triple root of traditional Han Chinese culture. It is to be hoped that Catholics and Protestants will cooperate to create genuinely Chinese expressions of Christian faith, liturgy, and spirituality.

Because of the persistent repression of religion in China under the Communist regime, there are no statistics available beyond the fact that there are in the 1990s twenty archdioceses, ninety-two dioceses, and twenty-nine prefectures apostolic (missionary territories that have not yet been made dioceses with their own bishops). In 1949, the year of the Communist takeover, there were between 3.5 million and 4 million Catholics, mostly in major cities such as Shanghai, or only about 0.7 percent of the total population of just over one billion. *See also* Chinese rites controversy; Ricci, Matteo.

Bibliography

Latourette, Kenneth Scott. *A History of Christian Missions in China.* New York: Russell and Russell, 1967.

Myers, James T. *Enemies Without Guns: The Catholic Church in the People's Republic of China.* New York: Paragon House, 1991.

———. *Forces for Change in Contemporary China.* Columbia, SC: University of South Carolina Press, 1993.

Tang, Edmond, and Jean-Paul Wiest, eds. *The Catholic Church in Modern China.* Maryknoll, NY: Orbis Books, 1993.

EDWARD J. MALATESTA

Chinese rites controversy, a bitterly fought argument in the seventeenth and eighteenth centuries over the legitimacy of several accommodations of Catholic teaching to Chinese culture. In the sixteenth century Western missionaries operating under Portuguese patronage arrived in the open port of Macao, but it was not until 1583 that the Ming dynasty reversed its long-standing ban on foreign clergy, allowing some Jesuits to enter the country. The leader of this mission, the humanist Matteo Ricci, finally managed to establish himself in Beijing in 1601.

The policies Ricci established for his fellow Jesuits allowed new converts to continue practicing certain Confucian and ancestral rites that pervaded the major sectors of Chinese society: the family, the schools, and the government. The basic Confucian virtue of filial piety dictated that all serve their ancestors "in death as they did in life"; at regular intervals a family performed a ritual reverence (kowtow) and offered sacrifices before the home shrines commemorating their deceased. The periodic rites of the scholarly class in honor of Confucius were similar in nature, but the canonical status of his writings in the Chinese schools and government bureaucracy had gradually elevated these ceremonies to the level of a state cult. Ricci's position was based on the judgment that these rituals were not idolatrous, but essentially civil and social in nature. Related to the issue of rites was a terminological question: Ricci believed it legitimate to use the terms of the Chinese sacred writings, Tien (heaven) and Shangti (Supreme Lord), to convey the Christian concept of God.

Problems arose when Spanish missionaries, chiefly Dominicans and Franciscans, arrived from the Philippines in the 1630s. They were appalled by what they saw as religious syncretism and made clear to their own converts their opposition to these accommodations. The result was a prolonged and acrimonious controversy that eventually involved two congregations of the Roman Curia, the major religious orders, and the courts of China and the European powers.

An initial denunciation of the Jesuit methods to Rome resulted in a largely negative verdict on the rites by the Holy Office in 1645, but a Jesuit appeal clarifying the rationale of their practices led to a more nuanced decision in 1656. Furthermore, an instruction from the Vatican bureau *Propaganda Fidei* (Propagation of the Faith) three years later seemed to be quite open to accommodations. Divergent reactions to these decrees by missionaries led to papal clarifications in 1704 and 1715 that were largely negative regarding the legitimacy of the rites because of their alleged "superstitious character." Because missionaries continued to circumvent these restrictions, a definitive statement proscribing the rites was issued by Benedict XIV in 1742; all missionaries would have to take an oath to observe it.

Some historians attribute the decline of the Chinese mission in the eighteenth century to these negative decisions, although the reasons for this were certainly more complex. The issue was finally reopened in the twentieth century; in 1939 Pius XII declared that the Confucian and ancestral rituals were essentially social in nature and therefore "licit and commendable" practices. *See also* China, Catholicism in; Ricci, Matteo.   DOMINIC MONTI

chirotony (kee-rah'toh-nee). *See* cheirotonia.

choice, moral, that component of a complete human act bearing on the election of a possible means to a desired end. In the concrete pursuit of any end perceived and judged by the acting person to be both good and attainable (e.g., health), a plurality of means to that end naturally presents itself (e.g., diet, exercise, medicine), upon and between which a person must deliberate and eventually choose. Catholic moral philosophy, deeply influenced by Thomas Aquinas (cf. *Summa Theologiae* 1–2.13), has traditionally held the act of choice to be both free and responsible. Morally right choice is ultimately dependent upon the knowledge of those ends that are truly good for the human person.

choir, a group within the liturgical assembly especially entrusted with the ministry of song. The choir emerges out of the *schola cantorum* (Lat., "school of singers") of the Middle Ages. Modern choirs owe their existence both to nineteenth-century English Protestant efforts to reinvigorate sung liturgy and, in Catholic circles, to the efforts of the Solesmes movement, a revival of liturgical music centered in a French Benedictine monastery during the same period. The term also refers to that portion of the church where clergy are seated during liturgical rites. To be seated "in choir" is to be arranged in two groups that face each other across the central aisle of a church.

chorbishop (Gk., *chorepiskopos*, "country bishop"), known in the East after the second century and in the West from the sixth, a bishop who assisted the local bishop by ministering to the needs of communities in the countryside surrounding the diocesan seat. Though chorbishops had faculties and privileges not shared by ordinary presbyters and could vote in synods, they could not ordain presbyters or deacons, and it does not seem that they had formal episcopal jurisdictions. The order died out in the twelfth century except as an honorific title but is still conferred today on leading presbyters in the West Syrian and Maronite churches. *See also* bishop.

Chorniak, Orestes, 1883–1977, Hungarian-born Ruthenian Catholic priest and early supporter of the Ruthenian Catholic hierarchy in the United States. He left the Catholic Church in 1937 in protest at the Vatican-decreed compulsory celibacy for the Ruthenian American clergy. He joined the newly formed Carpatho-Russian Greek Catholic Diocese of the Eastern Rite of the U.S.A. and was consecrated its first bishop by the patriarch of Constantinople.

chrism (kriz'uhm; Gk., *chrisma*, "anointing"), the oil of olives mixed with perfume. Chrism is blessed by the bishop every year at the Chrism Mass, which usually takes place on Holy Thursday, although it may be celebrated at some other convenient time during Holy Week. Chrism is used in the postbaptismal anointing, Confirmation, priestly and episcopal ordinations, and during the dedication of churches and altars. Long treated with great reverence by the Church, chrism is often reserved in a special place in the church sanctuary with the oil of the sick and the oil of catechumens. The strengthening effect and fragrance of the oil reflect the presence of the Holy Spirit when one is anointed with it. Chrism has also been associated with the coronation of kings. Its symbolism is both royal and priestly. Chrism traditionally was made from the oil of the olive, but in the 1990s vegetable, seed, or coconut oil may be used. *See also* holy oils.

Chrism Mass. *See* chrism.

chrismal (kriz'muhl; Gk., *chrisma*, "anointing"), the small cylindrical metal jar in which holy oils are kept. These oils, which are used in the conferring of sacraments, are the oil of catechumens, oil of the sick, and chrism. Formerly, the term "chrismal" was used variously to designate a cloth wrapped around relics, the wax-soaked linen cloth used on a newly consecrated altar, a type of pyx (a receptacle for carrying Holy Communion to the sick), and the white robe of the newly baptized. *See also* chrism; holy oils.

chrismation (kriz-may'shuhn; Gk., *chrisma*, "anointing"), anointing with the holy oil of chrism. Although "chrismation" can be used to mean any anointing, the term is used liturgically to refer to the Eastern church rite that is related to the Western sacrament of Confirmation. *See also* chrism; Confirmation; holy oils.

Christ (Gk., *christos*, "the anointed one"), equivalent of the Hebrew title "messiah." Upon ascending the throne, an Israelite king was anointed with oil by a high priest or prophet (1 Sam 10:1; 16:13; 3 Kgs 1:39), and afterward he was called the anointed one, the messiah (1 Sam 24:7, 11; 26:9, 11, 16, 23). After the Babylonian exile, priests, too, were anointed (Exod 29:7; Lev 8:12). During the two centuries before Jesus of Nazareth, at least some Jews began to expect the imminent arrival of a divine kingly figure (Dan 7:13; *1 Enoch* 37–71). According to the Gospels, Jesus' disciples acknowledged him as "the Christ," "the anointed one" (Mark 8:29; Acts 5:42; 9:22). Among Jesus' followers, this use of "Christ" as a title soon shifted, however, so that "Christ" became a proper name for Jesus (Gal 1:6; Heb 9:11). Jesus was then referred to as "the Christ" (Rom 5:6), "Christ Jesus" (Acts 24:24), and "Jesus Christ" (Mark 1:1). In the years after the death and Resurrection of Jesus of Nazareth, some Jews acknowledged other individuals as the messiah (e.g., Bar Kochba, who led an insurrection and died in 135). *See also* Christology; Jesus Christ.

christening, term used for the rite of baptism. It emphasizes the fact that, by the rite of baptism, one becomes a Christian and is given a name that is publicly proclaimed to the community. In adult initiation, the giving of the name takes place at the Rite of Acceptance into the Order of Catechumens. *See also* Baptism.

Christian (Gk., *christos,* "the anointed one"; Lat., *-ianus,* "belonging to"), follower of Christ. Initially, after Jesus' death and Resurrection, his followers called themselves the "brethren" (Acts 1:16), "disciples" (Acts 11:26), "believers" (Acts 2:44), and "those of the Way." But within ten years or so, the name "Christian" was applied to the disciples by people who did not belong to their communities. The use of this name apparently began at Antioch of Syria in approximately A.D. 40 (Acts 11:26; cf. 26:28). Having heard the disciples speak about Christ, nonbelievers may have mistaken the title "Christ" for a name. Adding the hellenized Latin suffix *-ianus* to "Christ," outsiders spoke of the "Christians," a name parallel to such names as the "Caesarians," i.e., those loyal to Caesar, and the "Herodians," i.e., the supporters of Herod (cf. Mark 12:13). By the time of Nero's persecutions (A.D. 64), this name was Rome's official name for Jesus' followers (Tacitus *Annals* 15.44). In the situation of martyrdom, believers took pride in being seen as followers of Jesus (Luke 21:12). 1 Peter (late first century) encourages the community to be ready to suffer "as a Christian" (1 Pet 4:16). Also, in his letter to the emperor Trajan regarding the Christians (A.D. 112), Pliny the Younger asks whether Jesus' followers should be punished "for the name," that is, simply because they refuse to deny that they are Christians. Prior to his martyrdom, Ignatius of Antioch (d. ca. 107) wrote that he wanted not only to be called "Christian" but also found to be one (Ign. *Rom.* 3.2). As the use of the name "Christian" became more widespread, non-Christians became confused about its origin, mistaking its root for the Greek word for "good," *chrestos,* and, as a result, they referred to Jesus' followers as *Chrestiani,* "those belonging to the good one." ROBERT A. KRIEG

Christian Brothers. *See* Brothers of the Christian Schools.

Christian Democratic parties, a worldwide political movement with representation in sixty-six countries on five continents. These parties stem from the revolutionary upheavals of the nineteenth and early twentieth centuries and have deep roots in Catholic social teaching. Born in an effort to defend believers' social and political rights, to combat secularism, and to give Catholics a political voice, Christian Democratic parties today have all but severed their formal relations with the Vatican. West Germany's Christian Democratic Union, for example, is nondenominational with a sizeable Protestant membership. Although most numerous in Europe and Latin America, Christian Democratic parties exist in Africa and Asia as well. *See also* Church and state.

Christian Family Movement (CFM), a lay couples' social action movement that uses Belgian cardinal Joseph Cardijn's (d. 1967) "observe-judge-act" method of Catholic Action, which he incorporated into the Young Christian Workers organization he founded in 1925. CFM attempts to transform the family environment, thereby making family life easier. The basic unit of CFM is the cell, which is made up of six couples who meet regularly to observe their environment, judge whether or not what they observed is in accordance with the Gospel message of Jesus, and act to lessen the distance between reality and the Gospel ideal. Special emphasis is placed on action; groups are not mere study clubs. Like other Cardijn-inspired groups, CFM is a "like to like" apostolate, which in CFM's case means family ministering to family.

CFM grew out of a number of Catholic Action groups operating in the mid-1940s in Chicago, New York, South Bend, and Milwaukee. In 1949, a national organization was formed, with Chicago chosen as CFM headquarters. The first executive couple was Pat and Patty Crowley, whose charismatic leadership so dominated the movement that they came to be known as Mr. and Mrs. CFM. The same year, CFM published its basic guide for establishing a CFM cell, *For Happier Families*. Each year the national office published an inquiry booklet which examined a specific topic that local groups were to adapt to their own needs. An annual convention was held at the University of Notre Dame. The movement enjoyed remarkable success during the 1950s, peaking in 1963. CFM declined during the 1960s, but continues to exist, enjoying renewed success among Spanish-speaking groups in the *Movimiento Familiar Cristiano* (MFC). CFM has been very influential in promoting other family movements, most notably Cana Conferences and Marriage Encounter. *See also* family.   JEFFREY M. BURNS

Christian initiation, the various stages and periods that constitute the full and paradigmatic form for becoming a member of the Christian community. This communal process has a twofold goal: personal commitment to Christ in a way of life based on the gospel, and integration into the ecclesial community.

The process consists of four periods of formation: the precatechumenate, the catechumenate, the period of enlightenment and purification, and mystagogia. Movement from one period to the next is marked by a liturgical rite. These rites are Acceptance into the Order of Catechumens, Enrollment of Names, and Celebration of Initiation, respectively. *See also* Rite of Christian Initiation of Adults.

Christian Life Communities. *See* sodality.

Christmas, solemnity of the liturgical year celebrated on December 25 to commemorate the incarnation of the divine Word at the birth of Jesus Christ. Christmas is second in importance only to the annual celebration of Easter. Christmas has three proper Masses: at midnight, dawn, and during the day. The single-day solemnity spills over to an octave, which extends eight days after Christmas to

January 1, the Solemnity of Mary, Mother of God. The Sunday within the octave is the Feast of the Holy Family. The Christmas season or cycle begins with Evening Prayer I or First Vespers of December 24 and the evening vigil Mass and concludes on the Sunday after Epiphany, the Feast of the Baptism of the Lord. The Christmas season is preceded by a four-week period of vigil and preparation known as Advent, which begins on the fourth Sunday before December 25.

Although the actual day of Christ's birth is not known, the date for its celebration was designated as December 25 by the early fourth century in Rome and celebrated liturgically as such. One hypothesis for the introduction of a Roman feast of Christ's birth on that date suggests that December 25 was celebrated as the birthday of the invincible or unconquered sun god (Lat., *dies natalis Solis Invicti*), which Emperor Aurelian established in 274 in honor of the Syrian sun god. To counter worship of the pagan god in favor of Christ, the true "sun of justice," the church of Rome located the feast of Christ's birth on that same day.

Another hypothesis locates the origin of Christmas at a time when the cult of the sun was particularly strong in Rome and Christ-as-sun symbolism was deeply rooted in the Christian consciousness. Third-century theologians who were trying to calculate the date of Christ's birth, with no help from Scripture, turned their attention to the equinoxes and solstices. Popular opinion held that John the Baptist was conceived on the autumn equinox and born on the summer solstice on June 24. Since Luke 1:26 states that Christ was conceived six months after John, he must have been conceived at the spring equinox on March 25 and born nine months later on December 25. Whatever the historical inspiration, the old pagan feast provided a convenient day to celebrate the birth of Christ. December 25 was in place in the West by the fourth century for the Solemnity of the Incarnation. In the East, January 6 was celebrated as the Solemnity of the Epiphany (manifestation) and focused on both the nativity and baptism of the Lord. The focus of this feast in the West was the visit of the Magi. *See also* Incarnation, the.

DANIEL P. GRIGASSY

Christocentric ("Christ-centered"), the tendency to direct one's faith, prayer, and theology primarily toward the person and work of Jesus Christ, in distinction from a theocentric tendency (e.g., focused on the triune God) or an anthropocentric tendency (e.g., centered on the presence and action of grace in human life). *See also* Christology.

Christology (Gk., *christos,* "anointed one"; *logos,* "word about"), critical theological reflection upon the Christian confession that Jesus of Nazareth is the Christ (Mark 8:29; Acts 2:26; 10:36; Col 2:6). It answers the questions: Who was/is Jesus? Why was/is he believed to be the anointed one, the Messiah? What did/does he bring about for the eternal well-being, the salvation, of human beings? In what sense can he be said to be the savior of all people?

Christology has developed in the Church as a result of both internal factors (e.g., the demands of intellectual integrity, confessional disagreements, heretical movements) and also external factors (e.g., dialogue with Jewish belief and exchanges with other religions). These factors have challenged Christians to articulate for themselves and for others an understanding of their belief in Jesus Christ, especially as this belief is conveyed in Scripture, creeds, and conciliar formulations.

In the first centuries of the Church, this endeavor was taken up by such individuals as Athanasius, Cyril of Alexandria, and Pope Leo the Great, as well as by the councils of Constantinople (381), Ephesus (431), and Chalcedon (451). In the Middle Ages, questions about the identity and mission of Jesus Christ were treated by such scholars as Anselm, Abelard, and Thomas Aquinas within a systematic or ordered form. As these considerations were refined within Scholasticism, a distinction was made between questions about the "person" of Jesus Christ and questions about the "work" of Jesus Christ. The former topic was called Christology in the narrow sense, and the latter was termed soteriology. Within this framework, it can be said that the great Protestant Reformers (e.g., Martin Luther and John Calvin) contributed primarily to soteriology, for they provided new interpretations of what Jesus Christ has done for humankind.

Since the Enlightenment the conceptual framework in which Christians critically reflect on their belief in Jesus Christ is no longer that of Scholasticism (or neo-Scholasticism) but a mode of thought influenced by the turn to the knowing subject and the rise of historical consciousness (with the fashioning of historical-critical methods of investigation). Within this perspective, one no longer draws a sharp distinction between Christology and soteriology, since this division is seen as artificially separating who Christ was/is from what he did/does.

A distinction is, however, drawn today between functional Christology and ontological (or classical) Christology. The former concentrates on Jesus' aims and message and also what he brought about through his life, death, and Resurrection, and the latter focuses on Jesus' identity in ontological or metaphysical terms, especially as seen in the light of his Resurrection.

Other current distinctions should be noted. One occurs between "high" Christology and "low" Christology, that is, between a Christology that stresses the divinity of Jesus Christ and a Christology that highlights his humanity. Moreover, another distinction is made between two approaches to reflecting upon the mystery of Jesus Christ. A Christology "from below," or an "ascending" Christology, begins with the humanity of Jesus Christ and/or a historical reconstruction of Jesus' message, ministry, and destiny and then proceeds to consider Jesus' Resurrection and relationship with God. A Christology "from above," or a "descending" Christology, starts with an understanding of the triune God and the mystery of God's self-disclosure within creation and history and then moves to reflection upon God's entering into history in Jesus Christ (the Incarnation), his ministry, and his suffering, death, and Resurrection.

To explore the mystery of Jesus Christ from various vantage points, there has recently emerged an interest, especially among feminist theologians, in recovering Spirit Christology, which had a place in the reflections of the early Church. The Spirit of the risen Christ was poured out on all who believe, women as well as men, thereby breaking down all artificial divisions between people. This type of Christology is meant to complement the Logos Christology that has predominated in the West since Augustine. This Christology emphasized the divinity of Christ (the pre-existent Word of God who became flesh). *See also* Jesus Christ.   ROBERT A. KRIEG

Christopher, St., patron saint of travelers. His birth and death dates are unknown. According to the Roman martyrology, while sent to bear travelers across a river, he nearly drowned carrying a child who turned out to be Jesus Christ. Christopher then went to Lycia to convert unbelievers and comfort those facing martyrdom for the faith. A Roman emperor, Decius (d. 251), tried to burn Christopher at the stake, but Christopher survived the flames unscathed, which perhaps led to the popular belief that looking upon an image of Christopher would protect one from harm that day. Christopher was eventually martyred by beheading. He is invoked against water, tempests, and plagues. Given the dubiousness of his existence, his feast day is no longer observed.

Christophers, apostolic movement founded by Father James Keller in 1945. Their motto, "Be not overcome by evil, but overcome evil with good," expresses their desire to encourage each person, through daily activities, to bring Christ's love and truth to the world. One does not become a "member," and there are no meetings or dues. Instead, followers take on personal responsibility at a practical level to bring the message of Christ to all areas of literature, government, entertainment, and business. The Christophers use many forms of media, including print, radio, and television, to bring their message to the world. Prestigious Christopher Awards are conferred annually on authors, film and television producers, and others who further sound moral principles through various communications media.

Christ the King, Feast of, celebration of Christ's kingship on the last Sunday of Ordinary Time. Instituted in 1925 by Pope Pius XI to counteract atheism and secularism, this feast may be termed an "idea feast" because it celebrates no specific event in salvation history, but rather honors Christ's sovereignty over all persons, families, nations, and the whole universe. In particular, the feast affirms the messianic kingship of Christ, who redeemed humanity by the blood of the Cross. This feast duplicates the original kingship feast, the Ascension, which celebrates Jesus' exaltation and crowning with heavenly glory. The last Sunday of Ordinary Time was chosen to highlight the feast's eschatological thrust. *See also* kingship of Christ.

Christus Dominus (krees'*too*s doh'mee-nuhs). *See* Decree on the Bishops' Pastoral Office in the Church.

Chrodegang, St., ca. 715–66, archbishop of Metz. Chief minister of Charles Martel, Chrodegang continued St. Boniface's reforms of the Frankish church after his appointment as bishop of Metz (742). Promoted to archbishop, he wrote a rule for the common life of the diocesan clergy that was influential in the later reforms of the pastoral life of diocesan priests. Feast day: March 6. *See also* Boniface, St.; Charles Martel.

Chromatius, St. (kroh-may'ztee-uhs), d. 407, bishop of the north Italian city of Aquileia from 387 to 407. As a member of an ascetic community that included his mother, brother, and sisters, Chromatius lived in Aquileia as a presbyter (priest) when Rufinus and then Jerome lived there (368–73). While still a presbyter, Chromatius participated in the anti-Arian Council of Aquileia (381). Feast day: December 2. *See also* Aquileia, Council of.

chronology, biblical. *See* biblical chronology.

Chrysologus, St. Peter (kris-ahl'loh-guhs), ca. 406–50, bishop of Ravenna and Doctor of the Church. He was a famous preacher; his extant sermons are the basis for his title of Doctor of the Church. Feast day: July 30.

Chrysostom, St. John, ca. 349–407, patriarch of Constantinople, and Father and Doctor of the Church. The surname "Chrysostom" (Gk., "golden mouth") was given to him in the sixth century, and has largely supplanted his given name.

His early life combined classical learning and Christian asceticism: a student of philosophy and

John Chrysostom, the most prolific of the Fathers of the Church and patron saint of preachers; giving money to the poor; painting by Mattia Preti, National Museum, Valletta, Malta.

rhetoric, he also spent six ascetic years upon the mountains. Ill health brought him back to Antioch where he assumed pastoral duties. Ordained deacon in 381 and priest in 386, he served as preacher in the principal church of the city until 397. Most of his surviving literary work dates from this period.

In 397 John was chosen to succeed Nectarius as bishop of Constantinople. Although initially popular, his sweeping program of reforms quickly antagonized his episcopal colleagues, local monastic leaders, the new aristocracy, and the imperial family. After 399, he was swept up into the Origenist controversy, which allowed his enemies to attack him. In June 403, Theophilus of Alexandria convened the Synod of the Oak, which condemned Chrysostom on twenty-nine charges. The emperor Arcadius ratified the decision and exiled him to Bithynia, but popular riots caused his immediate recall. Two months later, however, he was again exiled, first to Cucusus in Lesser Armenia and then to the remote village of Pityus. Compelled by his guards to march in ill health under the hot sun, John Chrysostom died on September 14, 407.

In 438, Theodosius II brought Chrysostom's body back to Constantinople, where it remained until 1204 when the Venetians sacked the city and sent his relics to Rome. The choir chapel of Saint Peter's now houses his grave.

The most prolific of the Fathers, Chrysostom has left us ascetical, apologetic, and polemical treatises as well as letters. His place as Doctor of the Church is owed not to works of speculative theology but to explication of Scripture, which followed the historico-grammatical method of the school of Antioch. An admired stylist, he wrote homilies that often stirred his congregation to tears and applause. He is the patron saint of preachers. Feast day: January 27.   BLAKE LEYERLE

Church (Gk., *kyriakon*, "belonging to the Lord"; *ekklesia*, "assembly"), the Christian community, also known as the Body of Christ, the People of God, and the Temple of the Holy Spirit. In its earliest phase the young Christian community did not view itself as distinct from Judaism. Upon the admission of Gentiles to the company of disciples, however, a sharp distinction between Church and Judaism did emerge.

The Church and the Churches in the New Testament: The Church of the NT was diverse and pluralistic in character. Indeed, the word "church" applied to the great Church, or Church universal, and

to local churches alike. Thus, there were at least three kinds of post-Pauline communities: those reflected in the pastoral letters (1 Timothy, 2 Timothy, and Titus), with their emphasis on teaching, structures, pastoral care, and apostolic succession; those reflected in Ephesians and Colossians, with their emphasis on the Church as the body and bride of Christ as well as his fullness (Gk., *pleroma*); and those reflected in Luke-Acts, which stresses both the institutional and the charismatic aspects of the Church, but with particular emphasis on the role of the Holy Spirit. There were also two forms of Johannine communities, both emphasizing the equality of disciples living in community under the guidance of the Holy Spirit. There was also a community related to 1 Peter, heavily influenced by Jewish symbolism, which perceived itself as the new Israel and the new People of God. The community of Matthew, a mixture of Jews and Gentiles, revered both Mosaic law and Peter. A strongly Jewish community associated with the Letter of James practiced works of piety on behalf of widows and orphans. And there were still other communities identified with Mark, Hebrews, and Revelation, as well as those connected with non-NT writings, such as the *Didache, 1 Clement,* and the letters of Ignatius of Antioch.

There were differences also by reason of place. Thus, the mother church in Jerusalem was marked by vigorous apostolic activity, supported by healings and miracles, the sharing of goods among the members, and a rich liturgical and prayer life, both in the Temple and in the private homes. This community maintained its close links with Judaism, especially through its strong attachment to the Temple and its continuation of Jewish practices. There were disputes between Jewish and Greek members over the care of widows (Acts 6:1–6) and there was the great debate over the need for circumcision and the observance of Jewish dietary laws (15:1–31).

The church at Antioch was a mixed group of people: former Jews and former pagans ("Greeks") alike. It was a model of harmony between them (Gal 2:1–14). Here for the first time the followers of Jesus Christ were called Christians. They held regular meetings at which large congregations were "instructed" (Acts 11:26). Prophets and teachers were active (13:1–3) and the gifts of the Spirit were evident (11:27; 15:32).

The church at Corinth was predominantly pagan in origin, charismatic in structure (1 Cor 1:5–7; 12:8–11), and marked by human weaknesses, particularly of a sexual kind (1 Cor 5; 6:12–20). The charismatics often created confusion (1 Cor 14), serious disorders erupted at the Eucharist because of the behavior of the rich (11:20–34), and partisan groups attached themselves to individual missionaries (1:11; 3:4–5, 22). On the other hand, there was vigorous apostolic preaching and instruction (2 Cor 3:4–4:6), and worship was at the center of its life (1 Cor 11:17–34), especially Baptism and Eucharist (1:13–16; 6:11; 10:1–11, 16–22). It was a church conscious of its communal bond with other local churches and in particular with the church of Jerusalem, for which the great collection was taken up (1:2; 7:17; 11:16; 16:1, 19; 2 Cor 1:1; 8:24; 12:13; 13:12).

Despite these local differences, certain common elements existed: faith in Jesus as Messiah and Lord, the practice of Baptism and the celebration of the Eucharist, the apostolic preaching and instruction, the practice of communal love, and the expectation of the coming reign of God. There was freedom in all other matters.

The Church located itself between the coming of the kingdom, or reign, of God in Jesus Christ and its full realization at the end of history. Its mission "between the times" is to proclaim, celebrate, signify, and serve the coming reign of God: *kerygma* (Gk., "message"), *leitourgia* ("liturgy," "public work"), *marturia* ("witness"), and *diakonia* ("service").

The Postbiblical Church: As the Church spread through the Roman Empire, it adapted itself to contemporary social and political structures. By the latter half of the second century there were synods and councils and the emergence of the monarchical episcopate (one bishop governing each diocese). The self-understanding of the Church (ecclesiology) was developed in response to various crises and heresies. Over against Gnosticism, Novatianism, and Donatism, the Fathers taught that the Church is the unique sphere of the Holy Spirit and that the truth of its faith and preaching is guaranteed by apostolic succession centered on the Church of Rome (Irenaeus); that orthodoxy alone is an insufficient basis of unity with the one Church and that true unity requires unity with the bishops (Cyprian); that the holiness of the Church is derived from God, not from the members, that schism is diametrically opposed to the reality of the Church as a community of love, that the Church is a mixed community of good and bad alike, and that there is a distinction between the invisible Church, those who truly belong to Christ, and the visible Church, those who belong outwardly to Christ (Augustine).

From the Middle Ages through the nineteenth century the emphasis shifted to the Church's governing structures and jurisdiction. The Church's self-understanding in this period was shaped in large part by its reaction against the challenges to papal authority raised by lay investiture, conciliarism, the Reformation, and Gallicanism and other national movements. An exaggerated notion of papal authority bordering on absolutism emerged.

A new ecclesiology appeared in the twentieth century under the impact of the liturgical, biblical, and ecumenical movements, culminating in the Second Vatican Council (1962–65). For the council the Church is a mystery, or sacrament ("a reality imbued with the hidden presence of God" [Pope Paul VI]), the People of God, a servant community, an ecumenical community, a collegial community, an eschatological community. And it has but a single intention: that the reign of God may come (Pastoral Constitution on the Church in the Modern World, n. 45)—a reign of justice and peace as well as of holiness and grace (n. 39). *See also* Catholic Church.

Bibliography

Cwiekowski, Frederick J. *The Beginnings of the Church.* New York: Paulist Press, 1988.

Dulles, Avery. *Models of the Church.* New York: Doubleday, Image Books, 1978, revised edition, 1987.

Küng, Hans. *The Church.* Translated by Ray and Rosaleen Ockenden. New York: Sheed & Ward, 1967.   RICHARD P. MCBRIEN

church, domestic. *See* domestic church.

Church and state. The need for the Catholic Church to develop a body of principles to order its relationship with civil political authority arose in the earliest days of its history. NT texts testify to the fact that the leadership of the ecclesial community and its members felt the need for guidance in determining how to evaluate the role of the civil power and how to direct Christian life in relationship to the demands of political authorities. In broad outline it is possible to distinguish the following major stages of development of Church-state teaching: the Church and the Roman Empire; the Church in the medieval Christian republic (*Respublica Christiana*); the Church confronting the post-Reformation nation-state; the Church and nineteenth-century liberalism; and twentieth-century Catholic teaching before and after Vatican II (1962–65).

The end product of this evolutionary development is the teaching of Vatican II on Church-state relations, found principally in *Dignitatis Humanae* (the Declaration on Religious Freedom). The conciliar text both draws from the history and constitutes a development beyond the history.

Historical Development: The Church's encounter with the Roman Empire produced a basic principle that has sustained the Catholic tradition since then. The principle affirms that all human authority is rooted in God, but that God has entrusted temporal authority to the state and spiritual authority to the Church. The classical formulation of the principle is found in Pope Gelasius I's letter to the emperor Anastasius in 492. From the fifth century on "the Gelasian dyarchy" is central to Catholic political thought.

While the structure of the Gelasian principle is clear—two kinds of authority, each distinct in its own realm but expected to collaborate for the human and spiritual welfare of people—the history of Church-state relations manifests a continuing struggle for primacy by one power or the other. The medieval contribution to this normative doctrine is found in two sources. Pope Gregory VII (d. 1085), a reforming pope often in conflict with temporal rulers, affirmed the principle of the freedom of the Church as the basic guideline for Church-state relations. John of Paris, a thirteenth-century theologian (d. 1306), played a crucial role in the development of Catholic theory. On one hand, he resisted some of the canon lawyers who argued that all authority was entrusted to the Church, which then granted temporal authority to the state. On the other hand, John affirmed the primacy of the spiritual power in cases of conflict between Church and state. By the end of the Middle Ages, the Gelasian dyarchy, the freedom of the Church, and the primacy of the spiritual principle were the three lasting ideas in Catholic teaching.

The collapse of the *Respublica Christiana* (the medieval Christian republic), the rise of the nation-state, and the consequences of the Reformation shattered the framework within which Church-state theology had been articulated for a thousand years. In addition, the Peace of Augsburg (1555) established the principle *cuius regio, eius religio,* i.e., the religion of the prince is the religion of the place. The Treaty of Westphalia (1648) ending the Thirty Years' War accepted the principle in formulating the terms of peace. From this principle of the unitary religious state, territorial settlements based on Catholic or Protestant states took shape in Europe. Although the principle was secular in origin, Catholic theology developed along parallel lines; in states where Cath-

olics were the majority, it called for the legal establishment of the Catholic Church and legal restraints on the public manifestation of other religious communities. In this situation of legal establishment and legal intolerance, non-Catholics were not to be coerced to accept the faith and they were permitted to profess and follow their faith privately; what was prohibited were public manifestations of faith and any effort to spread a faith other than Catholicism. Undergirding the entire structure of state religion was the concept that "error has no rights," i.e., wrong doctrine has no right to be publicly acknowledged or legally protected.

The post-Reformation position found expression at Vatican I (1869–70) in the "thesis/hypothesis" formula. The thesis, i.e., that which should prevail, was the institution of legal establishment and legal intolerance. The hypothesis designated situations that the Church would "tolerate" because the achievement of the thesis was either impossible or disruptive of public life in society. The thesis/ hypothesis approach was in possession in Catholic teaching until the Second Vatican Council displaced it. The persistence of this conclusion was remarkable because the premises of the teaching were being recast, beginning with Pope Leo XIII (d. 1903) and continuing through the pontificate of John XXIII (d. 1963). Vatican II confirmed the change and promulgated it as Catholic teaching on Church and state. The development of the teaching was effected at two levels: first, through incremental changes made in papal teaching by Leo XIII and Pius XII; second, through the broader and deeper critique of Catholic teaching carried forward by theologians, principally the American Jesuit John Courtney Murray (d. 1967), but also including European theologians like Yves Congar, Pietro Pavan, and Jacques Leclercq. The following survey relies heavily on Murray's work.

Leo XIII opened the Church-state question to development even though he held fast to the thesis/ hypothesis conclusion. His contribution was to restore the Gelasian perspective even while recasting its content. In the medieval framework the spiritual and temporal powers were both part of a single society. Leo XIII recognized that the collapse of medieval society meant that the contemporary formulation of the Gelasian principle had to be made in terms of two societies, each with its own authority and law. This move then led to Leo XIII's second contribution: he placed the citizen at the intersection of the two societies, spiritual and temporal, and argued that the authorities of Church and state had a duty to collaborate lest the citizen be confronted by conflicting claims on his or her conscience.

Leo XIII opened a path for change in the teaching, but did not change it. Pius XII came closer to changing both the premises and the thesis/hypothesis conclusion, but stopped just short of the latter. He did, however, move the argument beyond Leo XIII's formulation in three ways. First, in his Christmas addresses, Pius XII shaped a more expansive theory of human rights than one could find in Leo XIII's pronouncements; particularly as he specified rights of the political-civil order, he opened the way for a right to religious liberty. Second, Pius XII had a more activist conception of the citizen's role in society; the citizen was not only the reason for Church-state cooperation, the citizen was to be the architect of the collaborative relationship. Third, in a distinct departure from Leo XIII, Pius XII set limits to the role of the state in society; a century of experience with various forms of totalitarian rule brought Catholic teaching to a greater appreciation of the need for constitutional restraint on the modern state. The cumulative effect of these three changes was sufficient to produce a change in the thesis/hypothesis conclusion. Pius XII advanced to the threshold of such a change in a 1953 address *Ci Riese*, but he never took the final step.

John XXIII made the change; without extensive argument or even acknowledgment of the significance of his statement he simply affirmed in *Pacem in Terris* (1963) the right of the person "to practice his religion privately and publicly."

Vatican II: It remained for the Second Vatican Council, in the Declaration on Religious Freedom and the Pastoral Constitution on the Church in the Modern World, to set forth the new state of the question in Catholic teaching on Church and state. The elements of the position are the following: (1) the role of the Church in the political order is to defend the dignity of the human person; (2) every person has the right to religious freedom: no one is to be coerced to believe and no one is to be prohibited from expressing his or her belief personally or socially, as long as the demands of just public order are met; (3) the Church endorses the idea of a constitutional state, one limited by law; (4) the state is responsible for public order in society; the whole society is responsible for the common good; (5) the basic principle that should govern Church-state relations is the freedom of the Church. The combined effect of these principles is that the thesis/

hypothesis formula has been displaced, the Gelasian dyarchy has been reaffirmed, and the Church has made a clear, unequivocal statement in principle affirming the right of every person to religious liberty.

The Teaching of John Paul II: John Paul II has made extensive use of and built upon the two Church-state texts of Vatican II. He has developed his teaching in tandem with a vigorous pastoral-diplomatic style of leadership. This double impact on Church-state relations, as a teacher and a diplomatic actor, is the background in light of which three themes can be summarized. First, the pope's repeated support for the right to religious liberty; John Paul II describes religious freedom as "the source and synthesis" of other human rights (*Centesimus Annus*, n. 47). From Pius XII to John Paul II there has been a profound shift in Catholic teaching: Pius XII never clearly affirmed the right at all, but it has become a hallmark of John Paul II's social teaching.

A second theme is the pope's vigorous support for democracy. On this subject John Paul II is building upon the work of Pius XII's Christmas addresses and John XXIII's *Pacem in Terris*. On one hand, he places the Church solidly behind the political institutions of democracy. On the other hand, John Paul II fears that some believe democracy must be founded on "agnosticism and skeptical relativism" (*Centesimus Annus*, n. 46). In his support for democracy, he ties it directly to the need for an objective order of moral truth.

Finally, John Paul II's support for democracy and the constitutional state does not mean he endorses a minimalist role for the state in society. Particularly in the economic order, he seeks to balance the principle of subsidiarity—which restrains state initiatives—with specific responsibilities the state retains in the service of human rights.

Catholic teaching on Church and state undoubtedly will continue to develop; as it does so the remarkable advances made in the period from Leo XIII through John Paul II will be seen as a time of profound change and rich insight. *See also* Americanism; Declaration on Religious Freedom; Gelasius I, St; Gregory VII, St.; John of Paris; Murray, John Courtney; Pastoral Constitution on the Church in the Modern World.

Bibliography

Keogh, D. "Church and State." In *Modern Catholicism: Vatican II and After*, edited by A. Hastings. New York: Oxford University Press, 199 Pp. 289–302.

Murray, J. C. "The Problem of Religious Freedom." *Theological Studies* 25 (1964): 503–75.

———. "The Issue of Church and State at Vatican II." *Theological Studies* 27 (1966): 580–606.

Tierney, B. *The Crisis of Church and State 1050–1300.* Englewood Cliffs, NJ: Prentice-Hall, 1964.

Williams, G. H. *The Contours of Church and State in the Thought of John Paul II.* Waco, TX: Baylor University Press, 1983.

J. BRYAN HEHIR

Church councils. *See* ecumenical council.

churching of women, devotional practice of blessing women following childbirth. Known from the Middle Ages to the nineteenth century as the purification of women, it has roots in the OT practice of ritualistic purification after childbirth (Lev 12:1–8). The modern rite, found in the Book of Blessings, is not mandatory and contains no reference to childbirth as unclean. The blessing after childbirth, as it is now called, is not given, however, when the child is illegitimate. The rite includes a reading from Scripture, a psalm, a prayer of thanksgiving, and a prayer of blessing. *See also* women in the Church.

CHURCHING OF WOMEN
PRAYER OF BLESSING

"O God, author and sustainer of human life, from your goodness your servant [name] has received the joy of becoming a mother. Graciously accept our thanks and give ear to our prayers: defend this mother and child from every evil, be their companion along their pathway through life, and welcome them one day into the joys of your eternal home."

Church Militant, in the doctrine of the communion of saints the spiritual union that Christians have with one another on earth, as distinct from the spiritual union of Christians in purgatory (Church Suffering) and in heaven (Church Triumphant). The modern term, employed by the Second Vatican Council (1962–65), is pilgrim Church. *See also* communion of saints.

Church Suffering, in the doctrine of the communion of saints the spiritual union that Christians have with one another in purgatory, as distinct from the spiritual union of Christians on earth (Church Militant) and in heaven (Church Triumphant). The modern emphasis is less on the suffering of those in purgatory than on their sure hope of salvation. *See also* communion of saints; purgatory.

Church Triumphant, in the doctrine of the communion of saints the spiritual union that the Christian saints have with one another in heaven, as distinct from the spiritual union of Christians on earth (Church Militant) and in purgatory (Church Suffering). The union of the Church on earth with the Church in heaven is most fully realized in the Eucharist. *See also* communion of saints; heaven.

Church Unity Octave, eight days of prayer for the religious unity of all Christians and all people, celebrated annually from January 18, the Feast of St. Peter's Chair, to January 25, the Conversion of St. Paul. The observance originated in 1908 in the Anglican Communion under Paul J. Francis of the Protestant Episcopal Church in the United States. In 1909, seventeen members of the Society of the Atonement, led by Francis, were received into the Catholic Church. The octave was blessed by Pope Pius X in 1909. Subsequent popes have also encouraged observation of the octave, notably Pope Benedict XV, who in 1916 extended the observance to the universal Church. In 1921, Cardinal Dougherty of Philadelphia presented a resolution to the U.S. hierarchy that the octave be observed in all dioceses throughout the United States. It is observed today especially in the Catholic, Anglican, and Orthodox churches. *See also* ecumenism.

ciborium (si-bohr'ee-*oom*; Lat., *cibus,* "food," or Gk., *kiborion,* "cup"), a covered metal cup holding hosts for Communion of the faithful. The interior

Ciborium

Cincture

cincture

groups and Egyptian priests in the third millennium B.C. In the Bible, Israel is commanded to circumcise males on the eighth day after birth (Lev 12:3) as a sign of the covenant between God and Israel (Gen 17:9–14) and as a boundary between Israel and uncircumcised nations (Judg 14:3; 1 Sam 14:6). Circumcision was frowned upon in Greco-Roman culture and suppressed during persecutions (1 Macc 1:60–61). Thus it became an important indicator of Jewishness. Metaphorically circumcised hearts and ears are obedient to God (Deut 10:16; 1QH 18.20; Rom 2:29). In the NT Paul argues against the necessity of circumcision for gentile followers of Jesus (Gal 5:2–12; Rom 2:25–29).

circumincession (Lat., *circumincedere*, "to move around," or *circuminsedere*, "to sit around," Gk., *perichoresis*), mutual interdependence of natures or persons. First used in Christological controversies to signify the relationship between divine and human natures in Christ, circumincession came into prominence in trinitarian theology to explain the interdependence among the three divine Persons. Although the term is not used in Scripture, the idea is found in John 17:21; 10:38; and 14:11.

In Latin trinitarian theology, circumincession means that the three divine Persons, by virtue of their interdependence and essential unity, share intellect, will, and freedom; they act entirely in concert as one God. In the more dynamic Greek theology, the Godhead originates with God the Father and is passed to Son and Spirit, yet the divine unity is shared by the three Persons in the ceaseless exchange of love and life. In both theologies, each divine Person must be thought of in relation to the other divine Persons. *See also* Trinity, doctrine of the.

circumstances, moral, aspects of an action that are distinguishable from its object. In Catholic moral theology the morality of an action—whether it is morally right or wrong—has been derived from the so-called fonts of morality. These fonts were seen as three: the object of the act, the end, and the circumstances. Seven circumstances are usually listed: status of the agent, quality or quantity of object (e.g., grave or slight theft), place, means, motive, manner, and time. Sometimes circumstances alter the very meaning of the action, hence its morality. For instance, traditional theology has not viewed taking another's property when one is in extreme need (circumstance) as theft. At other times circumstances do not affect the morality of the action at all,

must be gold-plated. The cup, similar to the chalice, developed from the pyx. Earlier, the term "ciborium" referred to a stone, wooden, or metal canopy over the altar. *See also* Communion, Holy; pyx.

cincture (sink'chuhr; Lat., *cingulum,* "girdle"), a rope-like cord tied around the waist to hold the priest's or deacon's alb in place. It may be decorated with tassels at each end. It is usually white, but may follow the liturgical color of the day. It has symbolized priestly chastity. A new fitted-style alb has rendered the cincture unnecessary. *See also* vestments.

Circumcellions (Lat., *circum cellas,* "around [the] shrines"), members of a violent North African religious and social protest movement of the fourth century. Donatist in allegiance but feared by many Donatists as well as Catholics, they gathered around the martyrs' shrines, often appropriating supplies stored there. Styling themselves *Agonistici* ("Fighters") and crying "*laudes Deo*" ("praises to God"), they ambushed creditors, landowners, imperial agents, and Catholic prelates, sometimes kidnapping them, sometimes demanding martyrdom at their hands. *See also* Donatism.

circumcision, a religious or cultural practice in which the foreskin of the penis is cut off or incised. It was practiced among some Northwest Semitic

for example, whether one uses a gun or a knife in a murder.

Cistercian order, an order of monks in the Benedictine monastic tradition. In 1098 twenty-one monks and Robert, their abbot, left the Benedictine abbey of Molesmes in Burgundy to follow the Rule of St. Benedict to the letter, to sacrifice centuries of customs and devotional accretions for the sake of evangelical simplicity. At Cîteaux (Lat., *Cistercium*), near Dijon, in Burgundy, they established a "school of charity" that balanced solitude and community, prayer and manual labor. Simplicity governed everything from their undyed woolen habits and their diet to their liturgy and their architecture. The Cistercian Eucharist and Divine Office took about half the time of the elaborate contemporary Benedictine liturgy. When the Cistercians replaced the original wooden buildings with stone, the Burgundian Romanesque abbeys were unpainted and devoid of representational carvings. They accepted no child oblates, had no schools or parishes, and tried to avoid direct involvement in feudal society.

When, in 1113, Cîteaux founded a second monastery, the new autonomous abbey did not sever all ties with the motherhouse, as had been the previous custom. Instead, a system of "filiation" required the abbot of the motherhouse to visit annually each of the daughterhouses. The first foundation outside France was made in Italy (1120), and abbeys soon appeared in Germany (1123), England (1129), Slovenia (1135), Scotland (1136), Spain and Wales (1140), Ireland (1142), Denmark, Sweden, and Bohemia (1143), Norway (1146), Portugal (1153), and Poland and Hungary (1179). By 1151 there were 333 Cistercian men's abbeys; a century later, 647.

Uniformity of custom and discipline—juridical, liturgical, and even architectural—was maintained by annual visitations and by an annual general chapter of all Cistercian abbots, a system that later served as a model for other religious groups. The founders' ideals found expression in brief accounts of the early monks' experiences, especially in the frequently revised *Charter of Charity*, and in the decrees of the general chapter.

"Bearded laymen" were early admitted as lay brothers. These usually illiterate *conversi* (Lat., "converted") lived in quarters separate from the monks, recited a simple office consisting mostly of repetitions of the Lord's Prayer, and worked and managed monastic farms (granges) located at a distance from the abbeys. The lay brotherhood allowed uneducated men to share a way of life much admired by twelfth-century people. Houses of nuns and lay sisters soon followed. A few were founded by Cistercian abbots; some were officially incorporated by the order on condition of enclosure, but most simply adopted the Cistercian habit and usages without being juridically affiliated with the order.

Spirituality and Theology: Much of the Cistercians' spectacular diffusion can be attributed to Bernard of Clairvaux (1090–1153). The dominant figure of the early-twelfth-century Church, Bernard articulated in sermons, letters, and treatises a theology of reformed monasticism that expressed the ideals of the Cistercian founders—as did the works of William of Saint-Thierry (d. 1147/48), Aelred of Rievaulx (d. 1166/67), Guerric of Igny (d. 1157), and a host of Cistercians whose treatises, scriptural commentaries, letters, biographies, and edifying tales carried Cistercian ideals to contemporaries and subsequent generations. Using the resources, vocabulary, and methods common to their day, they created a distinctively Cistercian spirituality marked by a thorough knowledge of Scripture, heard at liturgy and read and pondered privately in *lectio divina* (spiritual reading); familiarity with patristic works; a clear concept of the human person, made in the image and likeness of God but deformed through sin, and a pattern of return through conversion (turning away from absorption with self and things); physical, mental, and spiritual asceticism; and, through grace, loss of self-centeredness in an experience of God. Through participation in Christ by the action of the Holy Spirit, they believed, the divine likeness and, therefore, full humanity may be restored to the human person. Thus, the person can become by grace what God is by nature.

As early as Isaac of Stella (d. ca. 1167) some Cistercians attempted to reconcile the theology of the cloister with the theology of the schools, using terminology new to monastic life. As universities became the focus of European intellectual life, Cistercian houses of studies were founded in 1245 at Paris, and later at Montpellier (1260), Toulouse (1280), and Oxford (1281), and then Würzburg, Cologne, Prague, Leipzig, Vienna, Heidelberg, Cracow, and Louvain. Pope Benedict XII, a Cistercian monk, made university training a keystone in his plan for Cistercian reform in the bull *Fulgens sicut stella* (1335).

After the Middle Ages: After the Reformation's suppression of monasticism in Britain, Scandinavia, and Protestant areas of northern Germany and the

Low Countries, Cistercians in Catholic countries regrouped into congregations by language, nation, or province. Regional variations led, especially in France, to a "war of observances" between "ancients," who defended the evolution of the order, and "abstinents," who sought to restore what they considered the primitive "strict" observance. Of the houses within the strict observance, the most influential was the abbey of La Trappe under its once commendatory abbot, Armand-Jean Bouthillier de Rancé (d. 1700), whose monastic reform was noted for its rigorous asceticism. Other reformers fostered the collection of early Cistercian literature.

The Enlightenment and the revolutionary fervor unleashed in France led to the suppression of monastic life in France (1791), Austria-Hungary (1782), Spain and Portugal (1835), Switzerland (1846), and Italy (1870), although some communities of nuns survived by moving inconspicuously into towns. A band of monks from La Trappe took temporary refuge in Switzerland, and from there colonies of refugees made their way to Russia, Germany, Belgium, England, Spain, Canada, and the United States. In the nineteenth century the revival of congregations maintained a distinction between "original" and "strict" observances. At papal insistence, three of the strict observance congregations were united in 1892 as the Order of Cistercians of the Strict Observance (popularly called "Trappists"). These monks and nuns were strictly cloistered, observed almost perpetual silence, and abstained from meat, fish, eggs, and dairy products.

Early-twentieth-century French Trappist writers emphasized prayer, simplicity of life, and fraternal love in community more than heroic austerity. The American Trappist Thomas Merton (d. 1968) brought Cistercian spirituality to the attention of a wide readership. Postwar vocations and post–Vatican II renewal resulted in a rapid expansion in the Americas and the Third World. Trappists reclaimed the early Cistercian ideals, adopted vernacular liturgy, and set about translating the works of Bernard of Clairvaux and other Cistercians into modern languages. New constitutions allowed diversity of observances in an order now at home in Europe, North and South America, Asia, Africa, and Oceania and have given Cistercian nuns a greater voice in the governance of the order.

There are now two orders of Cistercians: the Cistercians of the Strict Observance (O.C.S.O. or O.C.R.), and the Cistercians of the Common Observance, known simply as the Order of Cistercians

(O. Cist.). Strict Observance houses were first founded in Canada and the United States in the mid-nineteenth century: Petit Clairvaux in Nova Scotia (1825); Gethsemani Abbey in Kentucky (1848); and New Melleray Abbey in Iowa (1849). In the United States there are seventeen Strict Observance houses (five of them for women). Canadian and American houses of the order of Cistercians followed in 1928, and there are now five American monasteries of this observance (one for women). In Canada there are seven Strict Observance houses (two for women) and one men's monastery of the order of Cistercians. Worldwide there are one hundred Trappist houses of monks and sixty-nine monasteries of nuns. In the Common Observance there are sixty-nine houses of monks and ninety-one houses of nuns. *See also* Trappists.

Bibliography

Bouyer, Louis. *The Cistercian Way*. London: Mowbray, 1958.

Lekai, Louis J. *The Cistercians: Ideals and Realities*. Kent, OH: Kent State University, 1977.

Louf, Andre. *The Cistercian Way*. Kalamazoo, MI: Cistercian Publications, 1989.

Pennington, M. Basil. *The Cistercian Spirit*. Spencer, MA: Cistercian Publications, 1970.   E. ROZANNE ELDER

Cistercian spirituality. *See* Cistercian order.

Cîteaux (Lat., *Cistercium*), the motherhouse of the Cistercian order in Burgundy, France. Founded in 1098 by Robert of Molesmes (d. 1111), Alberic of Molesmes (d. 1109), and Stephen Harding (d. 1134) in order to provide a stricter and more primitive form of monastic life based on the Rule of St. Benedict, Cîteaux gained ecclesiastical credibility through its connection with Bernard of Clairvaux (d. 1153), who entered the monastery as a novice in 1112 with thirty other young noblemen of Burgundy, including his own brothers. The monastery of Cîteaux was lost to the order in 1791 at the time of the French Revolution, but was restored to it in 1898. *See also* Cistercian order.

City of God, book of Augustine of Hippo. Augustine began this work after the sack of Rome by the Vandals in A.D. 410, and continued writing from 413 to 427. The massive treatise is divided into twenty-two books. The first ten treat the polytheism of the Romans and the ancient philosophers of Greece. The final twelve books deal with the biblical doctrines of creation, the unfolding of the Christian dispensation, and the return of all things to God.

Augustine's work may be the first great philosophy/theology of history of the West. It has been enormously influential in its insistence on a direction to history and for its theme that all of human culture was a preparation for, and an anticipation of, God's revelation in Christ. *See also* Augustine of Hippo, St.

civil disobedience, a practice rooted in the idea that, under certain circumstances, it is morally legitimate and even mandatory to disobey the law of the state. The presumption is that there are obligations that transcend one's loyalty to the state. In cases where loyalty to the state and fidelity to the transcendent source of one's moral obligations conflict, civil disobedience may be required.

In Catholic thought, there are two dominant theological approaches to the idea of civil disobedience. The first is that of natural law theory. According to this theory, the natural law is God's eternal law inscribed in the heart of the human person and discerned by reason. The role of civil law is to reflect, as best as possible, the natural law. Civil laws that contradict natural law are illegitimate. In such cases, it is legitimate to disobey the civil law. The key resource for this approach to civil disobedience is Thomas Aquinas's "Treatise on Law" in the *Summa Theologiae.*

The second theological approach to civil disobedience emphasizes the eschatological kingdom of God. The task of the Christian is to live in accordance with Jesus' claim that the reign of God is already among us. This requires not only the rare case of civil disobedience, but a way of life that sets itself at odds with any earthly government. It is a more countercultural approach than that of the natural law theory, and is expressed in the Catholic Worker movement and the writings of Dorothy Day (d. 1980). *See also* Church and state; civil law and morality; conscience.

civil law and morality. The relationship of these two constitutes one of the most contentious and least understood aspects of American democratic life. On the one hand, some people believe that public policy (law) ought to be completely neutral where morality is concerned. The rallying cry of this group, often stamped by a strongly libertarian philosophical set of assumptions, is "You cannot and should not legislate morality." At the other extreme is a group that would immediately translate their moral convictions into law. Their rallying cry is "There ought to be a law."

It seems clear that there is some relationship between morality and legality. For example, if fetal life is to be regarded as disposable tissue, clearly abortion ought not be on the penal code, except to protect women against irresponsible tissue-scrapers. If, however, fetal life is to be regarded as human life, then there is the possibility that taking such life should be on the penal code and prohibited. The word "possibility" is used because in pluralistic democracies moral tenets must pass yet other tests.

It is generally admitted that when individual actions or policies have ascertainable consequences on the maintenance and stability of society (some would say "the public order," others more broadly "the common good"), they are the proper concern of society. But when should this concern take the form of public policy?

Many contemporary Catholic philosophers and theologians argue that the practical relationship of morality and law is best understood in terms of feasibility. In *We Hold These Truths* (1960), John Courtney Murray describes the notion of feasibility: "A moral condemnation regards only the evil itself, in itself. A legal ban on an evil must consider what St. Thomas calls its own 'possibility.' That is, will the ban be obeyed, at least by the generality? Is it enforceable against the disobedient? Is it prudent to undertake the enforcement of this or that ban, in view of the possibility of harmful effects in other areas of social life? Is the instrumentality of coercive law a good means for the eradication of this or that social vice? And, since a means is not a good means if it fails to work in most cases, what are the lessons of experience in this matter?" (pp. 166–67).

Conscientious public servants must constantly reassess the circumstances in which judgments of feasibility are made. What was not feasible in the past may gradually have become so at a different time. Furthermore, in matters of basic moral concern, a judgment of present nonfeasibility does not justify public passivity on the part of the public servant. There remains the duty of public leadership via persuasion. Furthermore, the law itself may have a pedagogical effect and change hearts and minds. *See also* Church and state.   RICHARD A. MCCORMICK

Civiltà Cattolica, journal of Catholic thought published by Italian Jesuits. Founded at Naples, Italy, in 1850, it is unique among Catholic journals for its close but autonomous relationship to the Holy See. Edited by a consortium of Jesuits, it provides a

Clare of Assisi, founder of the Poor Clares and a close associate of Francis of Assisi (also depicted here); mural in the church of St. Clare, Assisi, Italy.

Catholic viewpoint on contemporary social, religious, political, and cultural issues.

Clare of Assisi, St., ca. 1193–1253, founder of the Poor Clares, a religious community of women. Clare was born in Assisi, Italy, and learned of Francis and his group of friars, who were traveling from town to town, begging and preaching the gospel. She refused an arranged marriage and sought advice from Francis. In 1212 he received her commitment to follow the gospel and promised to care for her as he did his own friars. After a short stay with Benedictine nuns, Clare settled at a house attached to San Damiano, a church that had been recently rebuilt by Francis. There she served as superior until her death. Among those who joined her were her sisters, Agnes and Beatris, and her mother, Ortolana. Throughout her life she fought to maintain the Franciscan ideal of rigorous poverty for the Poor Clares while the friars were accepting modifications of their original rule. Clare was canonized in 1255. Feast day: August 11. *See also* Francis of Assisi, St.

Claretians, Missionary Sons of the Immaculate Heart of Mary (CMF), founded in 1849 by Anthony Mary Claret. They received papal approval in 1924. When the Dominicans and Franciscans were suppressed in Spain, Claret gathered diocesan clergy to continue the work of catechizing and preaching. At first they took no vows; since 1862 they have taken simple vows of poverty, celibacy, and obedience. They also take an oath to persevere and not to accept any honor without permission. There are two provinces in the United States. The U.S. Claretians publish *U.S. Catholic* and *SALT* magazines. *See also* Anthony Claret, St.

Claudel, Paul, 1868–1955, French poet and playwright. After a powerful religious experience in 1886, he embraced the Catholic faith, an event that would have a profound influence on his writing. Active in the diplomatic service of France, he was elected to the French Academy in 1946 and was much honored as a preeminent voice of French literature.

Claver, St. Peter. *See* Peter Claver, St.

Clemens, Franz Jakob, 1815–62, a leader of the neo-Scholastic revival in Germany. His works written in Latin in the 1850s argued for an exclusive role for Scholasticism in explaining revelation. He began the controversy over nature and grace (a struggle over idealist and Scholastic theologies) with J. E. Kuhn of the Tübingen school. After political activity in Germany and professorships at Bonn and Munster, he assumed a position in Rome, where he taught Matthias J. Scheeben.

Clement I, St., also known as Clement of Rome, d. ca. 101, traditionally regarded as the fourth bishop of Rome, from ca. 91 to 101, and likely author of the letter known as *1 Clement*. Sent ca. 96 from the Roman church to the church at Corinth, it instructs the Corinthians to reinstate elders improperly deposed. In Clement's view, the apostles had established "bishops" (Gk., *episcopoi,* used interchangeably with *presbyteroi,* "elders") and "deacons" in all places, and neither they nor their successors were to be deprived of office. Clement offers no defense for intervening in the Corinthians' affairs and expects the letter carriers to report on the outcome, but neither does he appeal to Roman privilege. Clement adduces the holy persons of the Hebrew Bible as examples for Christian virtues, emphasizing hospitality, faith, and humility, and makes use of many Christian writings (especially 1 Corinthians) later regarded as Scripture. Clement's second "letter" (*2 Clement,* actually a homily) is spurious. Feast day: November 23 (West); November 24 or 25 (East). *See* *also* apostolic age; Apostolic Fathers; apostolic succession; bishop.

Clement V [Bertrand de Got], ca. 1260–1314, pope from 1305 to 1314. Born in France, he became archbishop of Bordeaux in 1299 and was elected pope following the turbulent reign of Boniface VIII. Avoiding strife-ridden Rome, in 1309 Clement moved the papal court to Avignon, inaugurating the "Babylonian Captivity" of the papacy, which lasted until 1378. Easily influenced, he was no match for Philip IV of France, and in 1311 when he suppressed the Knights Templar for alleged sodomy, blasphemy, and heresy, he turned their French properties over to Philip. Among his positive accomplishments are the convening of the Council of Vienne (1311), the strengthening of canon law, and the founding of the universities of Orléans and Perugia. *See also* Avignon; Knights Templar; Vienne, Council of.

Clement VII [Giulio de Medici], 1478–1534, pope from 1523 to 1534. An illegitimate son of the dominant family of Florence, the Medici, he was named cardinal-archbishop of Florence in 1513 by Pope Leo X, also a Medici. In 1523 he was elected to succeed Hadrian VI. A typical Renaissance pope, more political than theological, Clement proved ineffective in dealing with the Protestant Reformation. He resisted calling a council to reform the Church and to respond to the Protestants. Clement's refusal to grant Henry VIII a divorce provided the occasion for the English Reformation.

Clement of Alexandria, ca. 150–ca. 215, theologian and head of the Alexandrian catechetical school. Born Titus Flavius Clemens, he studied in several philosophical schools before settling in Alexandria. In 202, he was forced to flee the city under persecution. Little is known of the remainder of his life, although his presence was noted in Caesarea and Antioch. Clement tried to reconcile Greek philosophy and the Christian faith. He considered philosophy as preparatory for the Christian revelation. His principal writings include *Protrepticus,* "An Exhortation to the Greeks"; *Paedagogus,* "The Instructor"; and *Stromateis,* "Miscellanies." In the first, he encourages pagans to accept the Christian faith. The second contains ethical instructions for Christians whose tutor is the Logos. The third book is made up of loosely woven threads of contemplation for the more enlightened Christian. His name was assigned to December 4 (feast day) in some early martyrologies but was excised in 1586 by Pope Sixtus V because he questioned the orthodoxy of certain of Clement's writings. *See also* Alexandria, school of; Logos; philosophy and theology.

Clementines, formally known as the Constitutions of Clementine, the decrees enacted by Pope Clement V (1305–14) and the Council of Vienne (1312), promulgated as an authentic collection of laws by Pope John XXII in 1317. Their historical importance lies in their forming a part of the *Corpus Iuris Canonici,* the chief collection of canon law in force before the first Code of Canon Law of 1917. *See also* canon law.

Cleophas, St. (klee'uh-fuhs), or Cleopas, a disciple who met Jesus on the Emmaus road (Luke 24:18). He is sometimes identified with Clopas, husband of one of the women at the Cross (John 19:25). Feast day: September 25.

clergy, an ecclesiastical state, or status, distinguished from that of the laity. The clergy consists of persons who are deputized for the sacred ministry by the sacrament of Holy Orders. There are three ranks of the clergy: deacons, presbyters (priests), and bishops. A person becomes a cleric by diaconal ordination when he is incardinated into a diocese or other particular church, or into an institute of consecrated life or other society of clerics. Ordination confers a sacramental character that can never be lost, but the clerical state can be lost by the declaration of the invalidity of sacred ordination, by the penalty of dismissal from the clerical state, or by a rescript from the Apostolic See, given to deacons only for serious reasons and to presbyters only for very serious reasons.

Clerics are bound by canon law to observe special disciplinary requirements, among them to pray the Liturgy of the Hours daily, to make an annual retreat, and to show reverence to, and obey, the Bishop of Rome and their own ordinary (diocesan bishop). They are also obliged to observe celibacy unless, in the case of permanent deacons (and also presbyters and deacons in the Eastern churches), they are already married when they are ordained. Clerics are prohibited from exercising certain functions and professions, including the holding of public offices that entail the exercise of civil power. Permanent deacons are exempt from many of the clerical obligations. *See also* bishop; deacon; presbyter; priest.

clergy, regular, clergy who are members of religious orders. They are so called because they are obligated to follow the rule (Lat., *regula*) of their religious order. The term is contrasted with "diocesan clergy" and "secular clergy," i.e., clergy who are attached to a diocese and are not members of a religious institute.

clergy, secular, clergy attached solely to a diocese. Secular clergy are not members of a religious institute or society of apostolic life, so they are not considered "regular," i.e., obliged to follow a rule (Lat., *regula*) of religious life. Because they do not withdraw from the world (Lat., *saeculum*) in the same way religious vow to do, they are called "secular." Almost all secular clergy are diocesan clergy.

cleric. *See* clergy.

clericalism, a term coined ca. 1865 in Italy to describe a supposed system employed by clergy to oppose Italian unity. It also refers to attitudes and behaviors of clergy designed to underscore the privileged status of priests and bishops. The term enjoyed some currency in both France and Italy in the nineteenth century because it provided a convenient label by which those who mistrusted religion in general, and the Catholic Church in particular, could advance an antireligious agenda. The supposed aim of the clericalist system was the subjugation of civil government to the control of the pope through the influence of local bishops and priests. The term later expanded in meaning to include any perceived incursion of religion into public affairs, particularly those involving attempts to gain power over the state.

Since Vatican II (1962–65), the term has taken on another, more common meaning. Less an accusation leveled at the Church by hostile outsiders, the term is now most often employed by Catholics themselves to designate a vision of church that emphasizes its institutional, patriarchal structures and the privileged position of clergy over the laity, and especially over women. *See also* anticlericalism; clergy.

Clericis Laicos (clair'i-chees lay'i-kohs; Lat.), bull promulgated February 1296 by Pope Boniface VIII. The title comes from the opening words: "In the past laymen (*laicos*) were extremely violent toward the clergy (*clericis*)." At the time, contrary to canon law, the kings of England and France had resorted to taxing the clergy to raise funds for military

ventures. In this bull, Boniface threatened to excommunicate any lay lord who taxed the clergy without the pope's consent and to depose any clergy who payed such taxes. In the face of economic pressure, Boniface later granted both monarchs permission to tax their clergy. *See also* Boniface VIII.

clerks regular, groups of Catholic clergy who take religious vows and are committed to a variety of pastoral ministries. The concept of clerks regular arose within the sixteenth-century reform movements, especially in Italy, through the creation of a series of men's religious orders like the Barnabites, the Camillians, the Caracciolini, Clerks Regular of the Mother of God, the Piarists, the Somaschi, the Theatines, and the largest and best known of the clerks regular, the Company of Jesus (the Jesuits). This list is taken from the *Annuario Pontificio,* but some other congregations have identified themselves with the clerks regular. *See also* Barnabites; Cajetan, St.; Calasanz, St. Joseph; Camillus of Lellis, St.; Jerome Emiliani, St.; Jesuits; Theatines.

Clermont, Council of (1095), reform council called by Pope Urban II at which he inaugurated the First Crusade. The council also confirmed the Truce of God for all Christendom and clarified other issues such as lay investiture of bishops, Lenten fasting, and the reception of Communion under both kinds, that is, the consecrated bread and consecrated wine. *See also* Urban II, Bl.

Cletus. *See* Anacletus, St.

Climacus, St. John, 570–649, monk, hermit, and, later, abbot of Sinai monastery. He practiced a spiritual discipline of self-denial and wrote that perfection requires mastery over feelings and emotions. His best-known work is *Ladder of Paradise,* which deals with monastic life. His feast day, March 30, is no longer observed universally.

Clitherow, St. Margaret, 1556–86, one of the Forty Martyrs of England and Wales canonized in 1970. Converting to Catholicism after her marriage in 1571, she was arrested in 1586 for hiding priests and was put to death. Feast day: October 21. *See also* Forty Martyrs of England and Wales.

cloister, the areas of a convent or monastery reserved exclusively for religious; also the body of laws governing entering and leaving these areas. Cloister

The Renaissance cloisters of La Badia Benedictine monastery in Fiesole, Italy, just outside of Florence.

Cluny, located in Burgundy, France, one of the most important monasteries in the history of the Church; it became the center of widespread monastic reform in the tenth, eleventh, and twelfth centuries.

law is obligatory in established houses of men and women religious. Entrance of persons of the opposite sex is prohibited except for spouses of heads of state. In women's convents, Church dignitaries and men whose professional services are needed may be admitted. Members of cloistered orders are usually not permitted to live outside the cloister. *See also* convent; monastery.

Cloud of Unknowing, The, English contemplative work by an anonymous monk, possibly Carthusian, of the fourteenth century. Conversant with the mystical tradition of Pseudo-Dionysius and incorporating anecdotes from everyday life, the *Cloud* outlines the need to withdraw from the world of sensation and to enter the cloud of forgetting, or unknowing, in order to reach God in love. Other works of the same author include *The Book of Privy Counsel* and free translations of Pseudo-Dionysius and Richard of St. Victor. *See also* Denys the Areopagite.

Clovis, ca. 466–511, king of the Franks. Succeeding his father Childeric I ca. 481 as ruler of a small barbarian tribe, by his death he was master of most of France. Clovis was converted to Christianity by his wife, Clotilde; he and thousands of his followers were baptized by St. Remigius. *See also* Franks; Remigius, St.

Cluny, French Benedictine monastery founded near Mâcon in Burgundy in 909 by William the Pious, Duke of Aquitaine. Cluny was the center of monastic reform during the tenth and eleventh centuries and was known for its concentration on communal prayer and the expansion and elaboration of the liturgy. Technically the property of Sts. Peter and

Paul, Cluny emphasized the choral Office and the singing of psalms (the monks sang the whole Psalter every week and read the whole Bible every year), with little concern for manual labor. By the mid-twelfth century there were over one thousand Cluniac monasteries, including both new establishments and reformed Benedictine houses. Eventually eclipsed by newer orders, Cluny was suppressed in 1790 by the French Revolution. *See also* Benedictine order.

coadjutor bishop, special bishop-assistant to a diocesan bishop. Distinguished from an auxiliary by appointment at the initiative of the Holy See, the right of immediate succession, and the manner of taking office (comparable to a diocesan bishop), he is normally appointed for circumstances that are personal to the diocesan bishop, like age, health, or special responsibilities.

By law the coadjutor is to be appointed a vicar general and is a prime policy consultant and administrative collaborator to the diocesan bishop. Like the auxiliaries, he performs pontifical and other uniquely episcopal functions that are not habitually to be entrusted by the diocesan bishop to any except bishops. *See also* bishop; diocesan bishop.

coat-of-arms, an artistic representation consisting of shield, headgear, motto, and various liturgical ornaments and insignia to designate the person and rank of an ecclesiastical personage. First used by secular nobles, the Church's hierarchy adopted coats-of-arms in the late Middle Ages and have used them ever since. Distinguishing features on the papal coat-of-arms are the tiara and keys; for cardinals, the red hat; for patriarchs, archbishops, and bishops a green hat, but with differing numbers of

Coat-of-arms

tassels. Lesser prelates, major superiors, priests, and religious may also have their own coats-of-arms, but this is rare.

Code of Canon Law, a codification of canons, or laws, of the Latin-rite Roman Catholic Church. Until the twentieth century, Church law, called canon law, was assembled in large, cumbersome collections. This made knowledge and interpretation of the law difficult, especially in pastoral practice. To remedy this, Pope Pius X in 1904 acceded to the wishes of many bishops and established a pontifical commission to codify Church law, akin to the modern civil law codes in Europe. The first Code of Canon Law was promulgated by Pope Benedict XV on Pentecost Sunday, May 27, 1917, and it took effect the following Pentecost, May 19, 1918.

The second Code of Canon Law was promulgated by Pope John Paul II on January 25, 1983, exactly twenty-four years after Pope John XXIII had called for the revision of the first code; it took effect on November 27, 1983.

The 1917 code consisted of 2,414 canons organized in five parts, called "books": general norms, persons, things, processes, and delicts (ecclesiastical crimes) and penalties. The second code of 1983 was revised considerably, both in content and structure, in light of the theological renewal and disciplinary reforms begun at Vatican II (1962–65) and carried out chiefly under the papacy of Pope Paul VI. Consisting of 1,752 canons, the 1983 code is organized in seven books: general norms, the People of God, the teaching office of the Church, the office

of sanctifying in the Church, the temporal goods of the Church, sanctions in the Church, and processes.

The code is universal law, binding all Latin-rite Catholics who are at least seven years old and who are mentally competent. The Eastern-rite Catholic churches collectively have their own code, known as the Code of Canons of the Eastern Churches. It was promulgated by Pope John Paul II on October 18, 1990, and took effect October 1, 1991. Unlike the Latin code, the Eastern code is not divided into "books"; the 1,546 canons are gathered into thirty "titles." *See also* canon law; Code of Canons of the Eastern Churches.

JOHN M. HUELS

Code of Canons of the Eastern Churches, the codification of the ecclesiastical laws that are common to all twenty-one of the Eastern Catholic churches. The word "Eastern" is to be understood historically rather than geographically; it refers to those churches that originated in the Eastern part of the Roman Empire. Members of these churches have since emigrated in large numbers to the West, so that in the 1990s "Eastern" churches are to be found worldwide. The code directly concerns only those Eastern churches that are in full communion with Rome. It is not binding on other Eastern Christians, nor does it affect the Latin Church except in a number of specific instances.

With the promulgation of this code in October 1990, the Catholic Church completed the revision of its law that had been in process since the Second Vatican Council (1962–65). The Code of Canon Law, promulgated for the Latin Church in 1983, the apostolic constitution, *Pastor Bonus* (1988), with its revised legislation on the Roman Curia, and finally the Code of Canons of the Eastern Churches now constitute a new and complete collection of law for the whole of the Catholic Church. Pope John Paul II expressed the desire that this body of legislation be studied as a whole by all the Catholic churches.

The Code of Canons of the Eastern Churches contains only those laws that are common to all the Eastern Catholic churches. Other matters are left to be decided by the particular law of each individual church. The common Eastern canons are based on the ancient disciplinary patrimony of those churches that have their origin in Alexandria, Antioch, Armenia, Chaldea, and Constantinople. The "sacred canons" that came out of these ancient traditions constitute the common foundation for the canonical discipline of all the Eastern churches.

The codification of the canon law of the Eastern

churches dates to 1929, when Pope Pius XI constituted a commission of cardinals to examine the question under the presidency of Cardinal Pietro Gasparri, who had organized the first Latin Code of Canon Law, promulgated in 1917. The work of codification was begun in 1935 and continued until the Second Vatican Council (1962). Between 1949 and 1957 Pope Pius XII promulgated part of this revised law, for example, the law on marriage, on procedure, on monastic institutes, and on the hierarchical structure of these churches. When Pope John XXIII called the Second Vatican Council, work on the revision of Eastern law was suspended. In 1972 Pope Paul VI set up a new commission to revise and complete the work. This commission was composed of the patriarchs and other heads of the Eastern Catholic churches plus a number of cardinals from the Roman Curia. A college of seventy consultors was appointed, consisting largely of bishops and priests of the Eastern churches. Some Orthodox observers were also invited to cooperate in the revision. The president of the commission was Cardinal Joseph Parecattil, archbishop of Ernakulam, of the Syro-Malabar Church in Kerala, India.

At the inauguration of the work of this commission, Pope Paul VI established two guiding principles to direct the process of codification: the canon law of the Eastern Catholic churches was to be revised according to the principles of the Second Vatican Council, and in complete fidelity to the ancient patrimony of Eastern church discipline. The commission completed its work in 1988, and on October 18, 1990, Pope John Paul II, for the first time in history, promulgated a code of canon law for all the Eastern Catholic churches. It came into force on October 1, 1991.

The new Code of Canons of the Eastern Churches is systematically arranged, not in seven books like the Latin Code, but in thirty titles, which is more in harmony with the structure of traditional Eastern canonical collections.

Characteristics of the Code: The Second Vatican Council, in its Decree on Eastern Catholic Churches, prescribed that the ancient discipline concerning the sacraments of the Eastern churches should be restored where necessary. The sacramental legislation of the Code of Canons of the Eastern Churches differs considerably from that of the Latin Code. This is particularly clear where the sacraments of Christian initiation are concerned.

The Eastern code preserves the ancient ecclesial tradition of ministry by both celibate and married clergy. It also has its own way of dealing with missionary activity and with ecumenism. In penal law, too, there are many important differences between the two codes. For example, in accordance with Eastern tradition, all penal sanctions have to be imposed directly by Church authorities.

Another important feature is that the ancient synodal structure of Church government has been revived. The Second Vatican Council prescribed that the powers of the Eastern patriarchs should be restored and that the patriarch with his synod should be the highest authority within the patriarchal church. The new Eastern code has legislated this change. Legislative power now resides in the episcopal synod of the patriarchal church, and all the bishops of the patriarchal church are members of this synod. Judicial power also resides in the episcopal synod, though recourse to the primatial See of Rome remains possible. The patriarch possesses extensive administrative power, which he exercises with the consent or counsel of his permanent synod—a council of five bishops with the patriarch as president. Similar concern for synodal structure can be seen in the legislation on Major Archiepiscopal and Metropolitan Churches. *See also* canon law; Eastern churches; Eastern rites.   *CLARENCE GALLAGHER*

codex, the forerunner of the modern book, in which sheets of papyrus or vellum (animal skin scraped to produce a smooth writing surface) are sewn together so that they open into pages. First appearing in the second century A.D., the codex is superior to scrolls in its durability, ease of storage, and the ease with which it may be opened and read. Both sides of the writing material may be used. It was employed early in Christian history for copies of Scripture.

Codex Iuris Canonici (koh'deks yoo'rees kah-nahn'ee-chee). *See* Code of Canon Law.

Codex Sinaiticus, a fourth-century manuscript of the Greek Bible, discovered by Constantin von Tischendorf at the monastery of St. Catherine on Mount Sinai (Egypt). He found some leaves of the OT in 1844, and the NT in 1859. Though the codex includes the whole NT, much of the OT is missing. Three hundred forty-seven of its leaves (199 OT and 148 NT) are in the British Museum, forty-three are in the University Library at Leipzig, and fragments of three leaves are said to be in the Library of the Society of Ancient Literature in St. Petersburg. In 1975 twelve more leaves were reported to be among the more than four thousand new manuscripts found after a fire at St. Catherine's monastery.

Codex Vaticanus, a fourth-century manuscript of the Greek Bible, probably of Egyptian origin now in the Vatican Library. Codex Vaticanus is missing Gen 1:1–46:8; 2 Sam 2:5–7, 10–13; Pss 105(Septuagint; Hebrew 106):27–137(138):6. It apparently never included 1–2 Maccabees. All NT Scripture after Heb 9:14 is missing.

Cody, John Patrick, 1907–82, bishop of Kansas City (1956–61), archbishop of New Orleans (1964–65), then Chicago (1965–82). In New Orleans he played an active role in the excommunication of prominent Catholics who supported racial segregation. In June 1965 he succeeded Cardinal Albert Meyer as archbishop of Chicago and in 1967 was made a cardinal by Pope Paul VI. His style of governing the large and very active archdiocese met with a great deal of criticism, especially from priests who enjoyed greater latitude under his predecessors. The last years of his life were mired in controversy about his financial stewardship, and there were persistent rumors that the Vatican wanted to remove him from office. However, he died in office.

Colet, John, ca. 1466–1519, English humanist and reformer. Beginning with his lectures on St. Paul (1497), Colet advocated a return to primitive Christian discipline, influencing Thomas More and Erasmus's Christian humanism. As dean of St. Paul's Cathedral (1504–19) he combined humanist studies and piety in an influential educational curriculum. *See also* humanism, Catholic.

Colette, St., 1381–1447, reformer of Poor Clare nuns, a Franciscan order. Born Nicolette Boilet, the daughter of a carpenter at Corbie abbey in France, she was inspired by a vision of St. Francis to restore the Poor Clares to their original austerity. She founded and restored convents in northern Europe. One branch of the Poor Clares is called Colettines. Feast day: March 6. *See also* Colettines; Poor Clares.

Colettines, Poor Clare nuns who embrace the reforms of St. Colette. In the early fifteenth century, Colette of Corbie began the restoration of the Second Order of St. Francis to its original rigor of poverty and prayer. Colettines came to Cleveland, Ohio,

in 1877 and spread across the United States. *See also* Colette, St.; Poor Clares.

collateral line, the manner in which one person is related to another by blood relationship. It describes all blood relationships except those of descendants and ancestors. Canon law prohibits marriages up to and including the fourth degree (of closeness) of the collateral line. *See also* consanguinity; marriage law.

Collect, the opening prayer of the Mass. The Collect, now called in English the Opening Prayer, takes place at the end of the introductory rites of the Mass, just before the Liturgy of the Word. The name "collect" derived from the concept of the priest collecting the prayer of those assembled and offering it to God in the name of the congregation. The Opening Prayer is usually addressed to the First Person of the Trinity and concludes, as do all Christian prayers, through the Son in the unity of the Holy Spirit.

collection, the offering of money for the support of the Church and its ministers, given by the faithful during the liturgy. The collection usually takes place at the time of the offertory or Preparation of the Gifts. In ancient times, the wealthy gave money while the others brought what they could contribute to the life of the Church, such as animals, cheese or bread, other kinds of produce, or cloth. Regardless of what is offered, the collection fulfills the biblical mandate to return thanks to God by offering part of what we have. The collection also reflects the responsibility of all members to contribute to the support of the Church and to provide for needy members of the community. This tradition is rooted in the OT and in first-century Judaism. The NT speaks of a great collection gathered from the gentile churches to relieve the distress of fellow Christians in Jerusalem (Acts 4:37; 11:27–30; Gal 2:10). *See also* offertory.

college of bishops. *See* bishops, college of.

College of Cardinals. *See* Cardinals, College of.

college of consultors. *See* consultors, college of.

College Theology Society (CTS), a professional organization of primarily North American theology and religious studies teachers of college or university undergraduates, founded in 1954 as the Society of Catholic College Teachers of Sacred Doctrine. The organization's original purpose was to provide mutual support among Catholic undergraduate religion teachers. Through the early 1960s, the society concerned itself with professional training for teachers of sacred doctrine and the undergraduate religion curriculum. The Second Vatican Council (1962–65) precipitated the society's reorientation to a less narrowly defined "Catholic" focus, reflected in the 1967 change of name to College Theology Society (CTS). In 1969, the CTS joined with six other professional organizations, including the American Academy of Religions (AAR) and the Catholic Theological Society of America, to form the Council of Societies for the Study of Religion. The CTS declined a 1971 invitation to merge with the AAR; its unique focus on undergraduate pedagogy as well as certain Catholic concerns with academic freedom and ecclesial loyalty motivated its decision to remain a separate organization. The CTS has produced a variety of publications. *Proceedings* (1954–) publishes articles that reflect annual meeting themes. *Magister* (1957–65), *Sacred Doctrine Notes* (1966–67), and *College Theology Notes* (1968) were newsletters that addressed the members' teaching and professional interests. From 1969 to 1970 the CTS sponsored the *Journal of Ecumenical Studies*. Its current journal *Horizons* began publication in 1974. The articles reflect the CTS's two major interests: the academic study of religion and the translation of scholarship for the undergraduate classroom. *See also* Catholic Theological Society of America.

SANDRA Y. MIZE

collegiality, a doctrine that asserts that the worldwide episcopate, together with and under the pope as its head, has supreme authority and bears pastoral responsibility for the Church as a whole. By virtue of their receiving the episcopal office by sacramental means and in hierarchical communion with the pope, bishops become members of a college and thereby assume responsibility for the care not only of their own particular churches but for the whole Church (Dogmatic Constitution on the Church, nn. 22, 23). Two documents of Vatican II, the Dogmatic Constitution on the Church (*Lumen Gentium*) and the Decree on the Bishops' Pastoral Office in the Church (*Christus Dominus*), while not using the noun "collegiality," describe episcopal governance in the Church as "collegial" (fifteen times) and see the hierarchy unified into a "collegium" (thirty-seven times). The reality of *collegialitas* is also described by Vatican II in the words *ordo, corpus,* and *fraternitas* (Lat., "order," "body," and "fraternity").

As the order of the initial chapters of *Lumen Gentium* indicates, one cannot understand episcopal collegiality (ch. 3) without situating this function in light of the Church's origin in the triune God (ch. 1) and in light of the fact that it is the entire People of God who constitute the Church (ch. 2). The Church is not primarily hierarchy; it is the People of God chosen by the Blessed Trinity. Furthermore, because of the nature of their pastoral care bishops cannot reach decisions apart from the dynamic process of listening and responding to the people. The Church is a sacrament of the unity of God with human beings.

Collegiality is one expression of the communion that exists in the Church; it is closely related to the catholicity of the Church. Teaching about collegiality was stressed at Vatican II to complement the doctrine never completed at Vatican I about the role of bishops. Vatican II states in *Lumen Gentium,* "Together with its head, the Roman Pontiff, and never without this head, the episcopal order is the subject of supreme and full power over the universal Church" (n. 22). It also notes, "One is constituted a member of the episcopal body by virtue of sacramental consecration and by hierarchical communion with the head and members of the body." Episcopacy is not a "jurisdictional creation of the papacy" but an outgrowth of the communion of the Church and the nature of ordination.

Strictly speaking, the term "collegiality" should be restricted to the collegiality of bishops. However, in popular usage, it is sometimes used loosely to describe the fact that in the Church the laity too should be consulted and have a role in decision making. It would be better to describe that fact by the term co-responsibility.

The final report of the Extraordinary Synod of Bishops (December 7, 1985) adds further comments about the nature of episcopal collegiality. It notes, "The ecclesiology of communion provides the sacramental foundation of collegiality. Therefore the theology of collegiality is much more extensive than its mere juridical aspect. The collegial spirit is broader than effective collegiality understood in an exclusively juridical way" (2.C.4). The text notes that there are partial realizations of collegiality that are authentically sign and instrument of the collegial spirit such as the synod of bishops, the episcopal conferences, the Roman Curia, and visits by bishops to the see of Rome.

How collegiality is concretely expressed in the Church has been the topic of some concern among those who feel papal centralism occasionally hampers the free and effective exercise of episcopal collegiality. It is not always clear that collegiality has received a full "reception" by the Church. Another question about collegiality is how those bishops not in full communion with the Church of Rome share in this ministry. *See also* bishops, college of; communion, Church as; conciliarity; ecumenical council; episcopal conference; primacy, papal.   MICHAEL A. FAHEY

Colman of Lindisfarne, St., ca. 670, bishop and abbot of Lindisfarne who defended the Irish eighty-four-year Easter cycle at the Synod of Whitby. Rather than submit to the Roman system, he retired first to Iona, then to the island of Inishboffin off the west coast of Ireland, from which he founded the monastery of Mayo. Feast day: February 18. *See also* Lindisfarne; Whitby, Synod of.

Colman of Stockerau, St., d. 1012, Irish or Scottish pilgrim executed as a spy in Stockerau, near Vienna. He is one of the patron saints of Austria. Feast day: October 13.

Colombière, St. Claude La, 1641–82, French Jesuit priest best known for promoting the popular devotion to the Sacred Heart of Jesus, with Margaret Mary Alacoque. Later sent as Catholic chaplain to the Duchess of York, he was charged with treason in 1678 and contracted tuberculosis while imprisoned in London. He was canonized in 1992. Feast day: February 15. *See also* Sacred Heart, devotion to the.

Colonna, Vittoria, 1490–1547, Renaissance poet who inspired a circle of pious reformers and artists, including Gasparo Contarini and Michelangelo.

colors, liturgical, a sequence of colors for vestments and liturgical objects during church seasons and feasts. The association of particular colors with seasons and feasts developed for varied historical and psychological reasons. It seems natural to associate red with blood, green with growth, white with purity, etc., but the color usage in Christian worship shows historical variance. Vestment color in the first millennium was not significant. A preference for white developed and perdured. Twelfth-century Jerusalem Augustinian canons prepared the first sequence of colors, proposing black at Christmas and Marian feasts and blue for Epiphany and Ascension.

Color sequences, however, developed locally; wearing magnificent vesture for festivals, irrespective of color, was common. A generally accepted pattern gradually developed in the medieval West, and Pope Innocent III (1198–1216) set white for feasts, red for martyrs, black for penitential seasons, and green otherwise. In 1570 the missal of Pope Pius V mandated a color sequence similar to what is in use today. Though more noble vestments may be used on special occasions irrespective of color, the major norms are white for Easter and Christmas seasons and non-Passion feasts of the Lord and for feasts of Mary, angels, and nonmartyred saints; red for Passion Sunday, Good Friday, and Pentecost and for celebrations of the Passion and feasts of apostles, evangelists, and martyrs; green during Ordinary Time; violet during Lent and Advent; rose for Gaudete and Laetare Sundays; and white for funeral services. *See also* liturgical year; vestments.   JOHN A. MELLOH

Columba, St., 521–97, also known as Colm, Columcille, and Colum, Irish monk, abbot, and missionary. After forming a monastery in his native Ireland, he and twelve companions embarked on a mission to the island of Iona off the coast of Scotland in 563. An aggressive missionary to the Picts and deeply involved in the social life of both Scotland and Ireland, he was also a poet and a scribe. Three of his Latin poems survive. His *Vita*, written by Adamann, was widely read in the medieval period. Feast day: June 9.

Columban Fathers and Brothers, also known as St. Columban's Foreign Mission Society (SSC), a religious community founded in Ireland in 1917 to establish a seminary to train secular priests for missionary work in China. It became a pontifical society in 1924. Members were sent to China, where they worked until they were expelled in 1952. The Columbans have missions in the United States, Australia, the Philippines, Korea, and South America. The general headquarters are in Dublin, Ireland. The American headquarters are in St. Columbans, Nebraska. The procurator general is in Rome.

Columbanus, St., ca. 543–615, Irish monk, traveler, and founder of monasteries. In his travels he founded such monasteries as Luxeuil and Bobbio. He also wrote a monastic rule, a penitential, and numerous letters. Feast day: November 23. *See also* Bobbio; Luxeuil.

Columbus, Christopher, 1451–1506, Italian-born European explorer whose voyages were primarily responsible for the establishment of permanent contact between the Eastern and Western hemispheres. The son of a weaver, Columbus became a sailor at age fourteen and eventually entered the service of Portugal, becoming familiar with its Atlantic explorations. He became convinced that the Indies could be reached by sailing westward, and after his plans were rejected in Portugal, convinced Queen Isabella of Castile to underwrite the voyage that led to his landing in the New World on October 12, 1492. He engaged in three further voyages of exploration and was named governor of the territories he had explored, but his poor administration and ill treatment of the natives led to his recall, and he died in poverty. In spite of his flaws, Columbus seemed sincerely impelled by a desire to spread the Christian faith, as shaped and influenced by Franciscan apocalyptic mysticism. The five-hundredth anniversary of his "discovery of America" generated much controversy, however. Some view him today as an instrument of colonialism and exploitation. Others, especially in the Italian community, continue to regard him as an international hero. The Knights of Columbus take their name from him.

Columkille, St. *See* Columba, St.

Commandments, the Ten, also known as the Decalogue, a collection of ten short guidelines for human conduct presented in Exod 20:2–17 and Deut 5:6–21 as God's direct revelation on Mount Sinai/Horeb to Moses and Israel. Unlike any other part of the revealed law in the Hebrew Scriptures, the Decalogue is described as spoken directly by God to the people of Israel and written directly by God's own hand on two stone tablets. Most commentators have held that the first tablet contained the commandments directly referring to God while the second tablet contained those governing the social order. A few have recently postulated that both tablets were identical, the second tablet functioning as a second copy of a contract.

The requirements of the Decalogue are not unique to Israel. As concrete commandments, the entire second tablet can be found in other sacred texts from the ancient Near East. Besides the uniqueness of the commandments on the first tablet, what distinguishes the Decalogue is that these commandments are nowhere else so concisely and forcefully expressed, and never in a context of being revealed directly by God. Neither does any other ancient code focus on the exclusive claims of a god upon a particular people.

The most distinguishing characteristic of the Ten Commandments is their consistent use of the apodictic form: they are brief, unconditional imperatives, usually prohibitions, complete in themselves without any explanation. They contrast sharply with the more typical casuistic form of law characterized by an elaboration of conditions that distinguish cases.

Though some differences in the two versions of the Decalogue may be attributed to accidents in transmission, most variants appear deliberate. Because the community seems to have allowed such amendments, it appears that the original and authoritative form of the commandment can still be found in the common elements of the different forms. The divergent material is comprised of amplifications, implications, and exhortations. Details in the Decalogue that presuppose settled conditions may thus be expansions of the original commandment.

That there are "ten" commandments is expressed in Deut 4:13, 10:4, and Exod 34:28. The text leaves some room for flexibility in numbering. The debate is centered on what is included in the first and tenth commandments. Does the first commandment contain prohibitions of worshiping other gods and a prohibition of images? Does the tenth commandment include a prohibition of coveting one's neighbor's wife along with a prohibition of coveting his property? There are legitimate arguments for seeing both as comprising two distinct commandments, which would yield eleven or even twelve, not ten commandments. Catholics and Lutherans combine what the Greek Orthodox, Calvinists, and Anglicans divide in the first commandment. Reverse positions are held on the tenth. Orthodox Judaism counts what Christians consider to be the preface as the first commandment, while holding combined versions of both the first (their second) and the tenth commandments. Most Catholic Scripture scholars today agree that the division of the first commandment is most appropriate, but since the other enumeration was used by Augustine (d. 430), followed by Aquinas (d. 1274), adopted by the Council of Trent (1543–65), and used for centuries in catechisms, it is difficult to foresee a change on this matter.

The Commandments as Understood by Ancient Israel: Prologue: "I am the Lord your God, who brought you out of the land of Egypt, out of the house of slavery." This preface to the commandments sets the law within the context of God's redemptive action. By putting proper emphasis on the prologue and the surrounding covenant framework, one avoids the mistake of treating the Decalogue as separable from the covenant instead of as an integral part of it. The Decalogue was important to ancient Israel as an expression of its relationship with Yahweh. It was not treated as an expression of an abstract moral order.

(1a) "You shall have no other gods before me." The first commandment is a claim for Yahweh's exclusiveness. It is a call to monolatry, not monotheism. Only later would Israel claim that Yahweh alone has existence.

(1b) "You shall not make for yourself an idol...." Concerning the extent of the first commandment, the question turns upon whether the prohibition of idols, or images, is distinct from the first commandment or whether it is merely an elaboration of its implications. If it is a separate commandment, then it would serve a function distinct from the prohibition of worshiping other gods and forbid images of Yahweh himself. If it only prohibits idols of other gods, then it is not regulating any matter distinct from the initial prohibition and thus serves simply as a negative complement designed to bolster Yahweh's preeminence over all other gods.

Most Scripture scholars see the prohibition of idols as originally forbidding images of Yahweh. In contrast to numerous archaeological findings of idols of neighboring gods, the absence of images of Yahweh, especially in the Temple, indicates that this is how ancient Israel understood it. No people in such an environment would have naturally worshiped an imageless God unless they were commanded not to make a representation. However, the present form of the commandment with its reference to jealousy appears to ban only idols of other gods. Most scholars attribute this confusion to the work of an editor who, by inserting the reference to a jealous God, incorporated this distinct prohibition within the framework of the first commandment.

What could be the purpose of such a command? Among other things, it underscores the difference between God and every part of God's creation. It implies that Yahweh is a transcendent God who is revealed when and where God wills. It guards against false and inadequate images of God. Furthermore, Yahweh could not be identified or tied with any particular object or place, not even the ark or the Tem-

ple. It was because of this that faith in God could survive the exile and true worship could be restored.

(2) "You shall not make wrongful use of the name of the Lord your God." The original purpose of this commandment is not clear. There is no textual reason to believe that it was an injunction against profanity, as it is popularly viewed today. Others ascribe to it the prohibition of a variety of sinful uses of Yahweh's name such as divination, blasphemy, imprecation, and magic. The seriousness of the accompanying threat, that God will not hold innocent the one who commits this wrong, possibly explains why the Hebrew people developed circumlocutions to avoid using the divine name. The Hebrews held seriously the obligation to carry out a vow made in God's name. It was the misuse of this command that Jesus sought to correct in Matt 5:33 and 23:16. Jesus teaches that a person's personal word should be as strong an obligation as any oath.

(3) "Remember the Sabbath day and keep it holy." This is the first of two commandments expressed in positive form. It could just as easily be expressed, "Do not work on the Sabbath." The core of this commandment is identical in both versions. Similarly, both versions make it clear that work must be balanced by rest and relaxation. However, different doctrinal bases are supplied for observing the Sabbath. In Genesis, God set the example of resting on the seventh day of creation. In Deuteronomy, the Sabbath is in remembrance that before the Exodus the Israelites lived a life of forced labor. These two explanations, highlighting the doctrines of creation and redemption, vividly expose the two theological foundations on which the whole Decalogue is built.

(4) "Honor your father and your mother." Since most parallels to this commandment in the Hebrew Scriptures have a negative form, many have argued for an original negative form in the Decalogue. Modern catechists, following Paul's admonition to children to obey their parents in Eph 6:1–3, have tended to view this commandment as though it were addressed to children. The commandment, however, concerns the responsibilities of adult Israelites. It charges them to look after their aged parents in their need and weakness.

Jesus upheld this responsibility when he criticized the legalistic practice of dedicating one's resources to God in a way that removed one's responsibility to parents (Mark 7:10–12). In protecting the aged, this commandment indicates that human value lies in something other than productivity. The principle underlying this rejection of function-based worth would later be extended to apply, not only to one's parents, but all the aged, the weak, the ill, and orphans, widows, aliens, and the poor. In the NT, Paul writes that whoever does not provide for relatives and especially for members of the immediate family has denied the faith and is worse than an unbeliever (1 Tim 5:8).

(5) "You shall not murder." The scope of this commandment is difficult to capture. Clearly the Hebrews did not take "murder" as applying to all killing, because they participated in holy wars and practiced capital punishment. Ancient Israel clearly saw the commandment as applying to both accidental homicide and self-defense. Israel later developed an elaborate plan of cities of refuge to help overcome the obvious moral difficulties of holding someone legally responsible for either of these two acts. It appears that what the commandment initially forbade was any unauthorized claim to the right of life or death over a fellow Israelite. In the Sermon on the Mount, Jesus extended the scope of this commandment to include hatred (Matt 5:22).

(6) "You shall not commit adultery." In ancient Israel, this commandment only forbade sexual intercourse with a married woman. It did not seek to impose sexual fidelity on the husband. Its concern was probably with paternity: protecting the husband's name by assuring him that his children would be his own. That is why the crime of adultery is extended to include the lack of proof of virginity at marriage (Deut 22:21). As with the ban on killing, Jesus made this commandment much more radical by expanding it to include lustful thoughts (Matt 5:28).

(7) "You shall not steal." The prohibition of more traditional theft would be taken care of by the tenth commandment. The Hebrews understood this commandment as a prohibition of kidnapping (Exod 21:16). This understanding keeps the commandment consistent in seriousness with the commandments that surround it because the breaking of those three warranted the death penalty at this stage of Israel's history. Stealing in general, however, was punished by means of fines and restitutions.

(8) "You shall not bear false witness against your neighbor." The original aim of this commandment was to ensure truthful witness in the law courts (Exod 23:1; Deut 19:16–19). The trial of the accused was conducted at the town's gates by drawing upon whatever male Israelites were present. Because the accused was presumed guilty upon the testimony of two witnesses, and since the sentence was executed immediately with no chance for appeal, guaranteeing the truthfulness of testimony was essential. The scope of this commandment naturally expanded to demand integrity in all types of relationships.

(9) "You shall not covet your neighbor's wife." (10) "You shall not desire your neighbor's house...." What drives the argument to divide this final commandment into two is the repetition of the prohibition. In both versions the verb is repeated with different objects following. Deuteronomy also uses two distinct verbs: "covet" and "desire." In Exodus a man's wife ranks with his servants and animals as forming part of his "house." In Deuteronomy she is listed first and separately from the prohibition of desiring his house.

Most significant about this prohibition, however, is its emphasis on a subjective element. One must not only not steal another's house or wife, one must not even desire or covet them.

New Testament: There are more explicit references to the commandments in the NT than in the entire Hebrew Scriptures, but all ten are never listed together. When a rich man asked Jesus what he must do to inherit eternal life, Jesus cited five commandments from the second table, but not in the usual order. Jesus also inserts "do not defraud" from Deut 24:14 into the traditional list (Mark 10:19). In general, the lack of complete citation of the Decalogue and conflations of it with other sources of law make it clear that the Decalogue had not yet acquired either the set form or the overarching significance that it would acquire in later Christianity.

While the Sermon on the Mount cites and reinterprets the prohibitions of murder and adultery, it does this in a context not of reinterpreting the Decalogue alone, but of Jewish law in general. Those two commandments are not given any more authority than the marriage laws cited from Deut 24:1 (Matt 5:31) or the conflation of Num 30:3 and Deut 23:22 concerning oaths (Matt 5:33). Jesus' famous twofold summary of the law, to love God and neighbor, is a compilation of the Shema and the Holiness Code, though it functions well as a summary of the Decalogue.

Paul consistently rejects the law as a means of salvation. Instead, it is what convicts sinfulness and highlights the need for grace. Once that point is established, however, Paul does see some positive role for the law. In Rom 13:8–10, four commandments from the second table, as well as an all-inclusive reference to "whatever other commandments there may be," are seen as being summed up by the imperative to love one's neighbor as oneself. However, nowhere in Paul is there an explicit directive to follow the law in order to live the obedient life, as was the case in later Reformed dogmatic theology.

Church History: The Decalogue played a significant role in Judaism at the beginning of the common, or Christian, era. Scrolls discovered at Qumran contained the Decalogue, along with other traditional biblical passages. The Decalogue was read in synagogue services until the second century. The early connection of the Decalogue with the natural law, inherited from Jewish dialogue with Gentiles, loosened the commandments' original integral connection to the covenant. The Church's emphasis shifted from speaking of the Decalogue's relevancy in terms of discipleship to its relation to the natural law. Debate often centered on why they were revealed if they could be known by reason. For Aquinas, all the precepts of the Decalogue are capable of being known by the exercise of natural human reason with the exception of the Sabbath commandment's designation of a specific day.

The significant role of the Decalogue in the Christian Church began in second-century catechesis. Augustine established the format used in Catholic catechisms to this day when he saw the theological virtue of faith as summarized by the creed and sacraments, hope by the Lord's Prayer, and charity by fulfillment of the Decalogue. In the *Roman Catechism* adopted at the Council of Trent in 1563, as in almost all Catholic catechisms, the Decalogue serves as the foundation for presenting Christian morality. The Decalogue is treated as a fairly comprehensive code in which it is possible to find a niche for almost every kind of offense. The new Universal Catechism (*Catechism of the Catholic Church*) published in 1992 continues this use of the Decalogue as the framework within which it conveys its modern moral teaching.

Though much of the justification for this catechetical dependence on the Decalogue is rooted in Augustine and confirmed by citations of Aquinas, it is not the heart of either of their understandings of Christian ethics. They saw the twofold law of the gospel as fulfilling the Decalogue, not vice versa. In Augustine's noting that the Decalogue is summarized in the two precepts of charity, his point was that the commandments require a new mode of observance: that what distinguishes Christian observance of the Decalogue is love, not fear. Catechesis must stress this internalization. Specification of sins must be subordinated to the practice of virtue. Similarly for Aquinas, the law does not take the primary place in Christian ethics, certainly not in any extrinsic sense.

The breakthrough book that has enabled modern Catholic moral theology to escape the legalistic understanding of the Decalogue was Bernard Häring's *The Law of Christ* (1954). It marked the beginning of a shift away from the Decalogue's emphasis on "boundary-defining" moral norms that establish minimum requirements in the form of prohibitions and a shift to "goal commandments" consistent with the Sermon on the Mount and the Great Commandment (John 13:34).

Häring does not reject the value of the Decalogue, but rejects it as the basis for structuring and developing the Christian life. He does not say that the Decalogue does not apply to the Christian. He sees it as an enduring expression of the natural law and as a part of NT law. The goal commandment of loving others as Jesus loves us includes the boundary-defining norms of the Decalogue. *See also* moral theology; natural law.

Bibliography

Collins, Raymond F. *Christian Morality: Biblical Foundations.* Notre Dame, IN: University of Notre Dame Press, 1986.

THOMAS POUNDSTONE

Commandments of the Church, also known as Precepts of the Church, moral and ecclesiastical precepts enjoined on all Catholics by the Church. While any law that the Church issues for its members may be referred to as a commandment, this term refers to a set of precepts spelling out specific behaviors enjoined on Catholics that have been accepted, in some form, since the Middle Ages and that were explicitly mentioned by Peter Canisius in 1555 and Robert Bellarmine in 1589. These precepts are intended to preserve good order in the Church, to maintain discipline, and to offer a distinct character to its members. Since they are moral and ecclesial in nature, they do not require internal motivation. The Commandments are fulfilled when the actions are performed, regardless of the motivation. Although they are concerned with external behaviors, these behaviors are also meant to foster the spiritual development of the faithful.

Form and Number: While there are minimal behaviors expected of members of the Church, the form or the number of the Commandments has never officially been defined.

Scripture and the early history of the Church give no evidence of a formal body of commandments for

Christians beyond the Ten Commandments and the Two Great Commandments preached by Jesus. In the fourth century, however, documents indicate that the Church began to insist on certain behaviors expected of members: attendance at Mass on Sundays and special feasts, receiving the sacraments of Penance and Communion, and not celebrating marriage during certain seasons. Ninth-century prayerbooks provide lists of obligations imposed by ecclesiastical law to be used in preparation for confession.

Throughout history, the three practices already mentioned were linked together and proposed as minimal obligations for Church members. Eventually other obligations were added. The number varied from five to ten. Antoninus of Florence listed ten Commandments, spelling out the three mentioned in greater detail and adding: to abstain from acts prohibited under pain of excommunication; to avoid excommunicated persons; and not to assist at Mass celebrated by clerics who publicly lived in concubinage.

Peter Canisius listed five and Robert Bellarmine, six. Canisius wrote so often and so strongly on the Commandments of the Church in the sixteenth century that it was thought that he had formulated them. Canisius's list includes observance of feast days appointed by the Church; reverent attendance at Mass on Sundays and holy days of obligation; observance of obligatory days of fasting and abstinence; and annual confession and reception of Communion at Easter. Bellarmine combined the first two of Canisius into one Commandment and added two others: contribute to the support of the Church, and do not solemnize marriage during prohibited times. Germany follows Canisius in listing five Commandments of the Church, as does most of Latin America. France and Italy follow Bellarmine. Other lists have included the obligation of parents to provide a Catholic education for their children.

The Council of Trent (1545–63) says nothing regarding the Commandments of the Church as a body of laws, but it does recommend them in a general way. They are not mentioned in the catechism published by order of that council. Neither does the Second Vatican Council (1962–65) make any mention of the Commandments of the Church.

The six Commandments accepted for the United States by the Third Plenary Council of Baltimore in 1886 were those published in England in the nineteenth century. *The Catechism of Christian Doctrine* lists the Commandments of the Church as: (1) to keep holy Sunday and holy days of obligation by hearing Mass and refraining from servile work; (2) to keep the days of fast and abstinence appointed by the Church; (3) to go to confession at least once a year; (4) to receive Communion at least once a year at Easter time; (5) to contribute to the support of one's pastor; and (6) not to marry within the third degree of kindred or to solemnize marriage during forbidden times. The *Catechism of the Catholic Church* (1992) lists five precepts of the Church, making no mention of marriage (nn. 2041–43).

Regarding Individual Commandments: The first Commandment of the Church is the only one that is related to the Ten Commandments. It specifies how Catholics are to keep the third Commandment of God, to keep holy the Sabbath day. The Commandment regarding fast (one full meal per day; no eating between meals) and abstinence (no meat all day) has been modified in recent years. In the past, Catholics were forbidden to eat flesh-meat on Fridays and were required to fast on Fridays during Advent, the weekdays during Lent, and on the vigils of great feasts. Now only Ash Wednesday and Good Friday are days of fast and abstinence, and only Fridays during Lent are days of abstinence. Catholics are encouraged, however, to abstain from meat every Friday. The third Commandment of the Church requiring confession once a year refers only to persons guilty of serious sin. It is meant to reconcile the serious sinner with the community. Venial sins need never be confessed. The sixth Commandment concerning forbidden times to celebrate marriage refers to a law that banned the celebration of marriage during the seasons of Advent and Lent. This law was repealed in 1964. Since 1965, nuptial Masses may be celebrated during those seasons and the nuptial blessing may be given. *See also* abstinence; confession, auricular; Easter duty; fast days; fasting; Sunday observance. *REGINA COLL*

commentator, a "special minister" who exercises a genuine liturgical function by providing "meticulously prepared," brief "explanations and commentaries with the purpose of introducing the faithful to the celebration and preparing them to understand it better" (General Instruction on the Roman Missal, 68). Critical for introducing Vatican II reforms, this ministry is no longer much in evidence.

Commission for Latin America. *See* Pontifical Commission for Latin America.

commissioning, the public act of installing lay-men and laywomen into ministries that do not re-quire ordination. These ministers may be commis-sioned for a single occasion or for a longer duration of service. Extraordinary ministers of the Eucharist, lectors, and catechists are among those commonly designated for service by commissioning. *See also* ministry.

common error, theory in canon law that address-es an incorrect judgment by a given community of faithful concerning the presence of proper authori-zation for a given minister. Under certain specified circumstances, the Church "supplies" for the lack of authorization, thus protecting the faithful from im-proper ministrations. Thus, if a validly ordained priest visiting from another diocese lacks faculties (i.e., authorization from the local bishop) to hear confessions yet announces to people assembled for Mass that he will hear confession before or after Mass, the community is led to the erroneous judg-ment that the priest does have the authority to hear confessions. The Church supplies it in this case, for the good of the people (can. 144.1). This theory has roots in Roman law.

common good, "the sum of those conditions of social life by which individuals, families, and groups can achieve their own fulfillment in a rela-tively thorough and ready way" (Pastoral Constitu-tion on the Church in the Modern World, n. 74). The concept underscores the basic claim in Catholic teaching that the person is fundamentally social. This is as opposed to certain modern understand-ings of the person as fundamentally autonomous and separate from society, entering into society by contract only because it is to the individual's advan-tage. The concept of the common good, in contrast, forms the basis for both societal claims on the indi-vidual and individual claims on society. If society is to provide the conditions for fulfillment for individ-uals, families, and groups, then all persons must contribute to society. However, since society does have the obligation to provide support for persons, individuals have a claim on society to provide that support. Therefore, the concept of the common good regulates the reciprocal relationship between person and society in Catholic social teaching. It is important to note that ultimate fulfillment for the person is union with God. Society provides only the concrete conditions for that fulfillment.

What constitutes more precisely the conditions for fulfillment will vary from society to society de-pending on what is possible culturally, politically, and economically. This is why Catholic social teach-ing does not endorse any one political or economic system, but critiques each system in terms of whether it provides the conditions for a human ful-fillment that is ultimately theological. *See also* Catho-lic social teachings.   TODD D. WHITMORE

common life, the sharing of life together as broth-ers or sisters in religious communities. This in-volves residing under the same roof, taking meals together, recreating together, sharing goods and property, and, of course, praying together. Common life as such also exists in families and is an option even for diocesan priests, who do not take religious vows (can. 280). Common life is both a right and an obligation for members of a religious community, but religious can be excused from it under certain circumstances. Under special circumstances a com-petent Church authority might prohibit a religious from full participation in the common life.

Commonweal, a biweekly journal published by the Commonweal Foundation of New York. Founded in 1924 by Michael Williams to create space for Catholic views in American culture, the periodical solicits reviews of public affairs, religion, literature, and the arts from lay and religious, Catholic and non-Catholic contributors.

communal penance service. *See* penance service, communal.

communicatio idiomatum   (kah-moo-nee-kah'tzee-oh id-ee-oh'mah-toom; Lat., "the exchange of attributes"), the teaching that those properties proper to God and also those properties proper to a human being may both be predicated of Jesus Christ in such a way that what is human can be attributed to the divine nature and what is divine can be at-tributed to the human nature. This exchange of properties is possible because Jesus Christ is one person possessing both a divine nature and a hu-man nature, which, though remaining distinct, are united in the one person. For example, one can say that the Son of God died on the cross, and also that the son of Mary rose from the dead. However, in making statements like these, it must be kept in mind that since the two natures remained distinct, the divine nature itself did not die and that the human nature itself did not have the power to overcome death. This paradoxical teaching was initially developed by such fourth- and fifth-century theologians as Origen, Athanasius, and Cyril of Alexandria. It was included by Pope Leo the Great in his *Tome* and was reiterated by the Council of Chalcedon (451). *See also* Jesus Christ.

communicatio in sacris (kah-moo-nee-kah'tzee-oh in sah'krees). *See* intercommunion.

communion, Church as, the nature of the Church as a community rooted in, and expressive of, the communal life of the triune God. The Christian word "communion" is a translation from the Greek term *koinonia* used by Paul to indicate sharing, fellowship, or close association. Paul frequently combines the word communion with a modifier, "by the Holy Spirit." His conviction is that Christians, through the Holy Spirit, enjoy communion with the triune God and are also "in communion" with other baptized Christians. Communion therefore has a vertical dimension (contact with God) and a horizontal dimension (bonding with other Christians). Basically communion is the effect of God's mercy and faithfulness shown toward those to whom the gift of faith is bestowed. This closest union of humans with God and with one's neighbors is accomplished through the Holy Spirit.

Sharing in the body and blood of Christ in Eucharist at the celebration of the Lord's Supper is regarded as a special moment in the Church's celebration of its life. Eventually the word "communion" came to be used by Christians principally to refer to reception of the Eucharist seen as a high point in sharing the gifts from God. But Paul's original usage was far more inclusive. The early Latin translations of the Greek Bible rendered that NT term as *communio, societas, participatio,* or *communicatio.* The last Latin term is used in *ex-communicatio,* the state in which one is outside the full fellowship of the Church, or the practice of *communicatio in sacris,* ecumenical sharing in the sacramental life of another church.

The communion that Christians experience within the Church was expressed in a variety of ways from earliest times, such as letter writing, offering of money to needy Christians, bishops' participating at regional gatherings, their laying on of hands at the consecration of bishops in neighboring churches, mutual consultation about disciplinary and doctrinal issues, and shared eucharistic fellowship with other Christians in distant churches. The custom of breaking off a piece of the eucharistic bread before the communion rite (the *fractio panis*) and sending it to neighboring churches was intended to express visibly the communion that exists among churches.

The term "communion" later appears in creeds such as Jerome's *Confession* (378) regarding belief in the *communio sanctorum,* originally meaning belief that Christians share in the communion of "holy things" (especially Baptism, Eucharist, Scripture) but eventually coming to refer mainly to the communion of saints, the vibrant relationship by which living Christians remain in prayerful and affective contact with those who have entered eternal life.

More recently, especially by theologians working to restore visible unity to the Church, ecumenical dialogue has stressed the notion of "communion" ecclesiology. This "communion" ecclesiology (in contrast to ecclesiologies stressing the Mystical Body of Christ, the Church as a perfect society, or the People of God) places special emphasis on the local, particular church and tries to understand its relationship with the churches scattered throughout the world, some of which are not in "full communion" with them. Communion ecclesiology is sensitive to the fact that, despite the divisions within the Church, there is a fundamental unity or communion through Baptism, but not necessarily full, visible communion. *See also* Church; collegiality; communion of saints; ecclesiology; excommunication; *koinonia.*   MICHAEL A. FAHEY

Communion, Holy, phrase describing the culmination of the Eucharistic Liturgy, that is, the reception of the body and blood of the Lord under the forms of bread and wine. In some circumstances, Holy Communion can also be received outside of the Eucharistic Liturgy (e.g., when no priest is available to celebrate the Eucharist on a Sunday or when someone is ill or dying.)

The concept of communion can be traced to the NT where it describes the intimate bond of unity that Christians have among themselves because of their common life in the Lord through Baptism. Christians share in the same spiritual realities because of their membership in the one Body of the Lord. Thus communion describes the very life of the Church itself. But as St. Paul makes clear, to share in

Distribution of Holy Communion (by Bishop Moses Anderson, S.S.E., auxiliary bishop of the archdiocese of Detroit).

the bread and the cup of the Lord's Supper is to share in his body and blood (cf. 1 Cor 10:16–22). Thus, through the Eucharist, Christians have communion with the Lord and with one another.

This concept of the Eucharist as the source of communion with the Lord and the Church was part of Christian consciousness until the Middle Ages. All those present at the Eucharist participated in the action of taking Communion. Only public sinners, who were doing penance before reconciliation, did not partake. Excommunication was part of their public penance and continued until reconciliation by the bishop.

Theological controversies in the early Middle Ages led to increasing concentration on the presence of the body and blood of the Lord under the forms of bread and wine. This was accompanied at times by an attitude of extreme realism regarding the elements of bread and wine. The consequence was intensified reverence for the consecrated bread and wine, causing a growing sense of unworthiness to receive the Eucharist and an actual decline in re-

ception. The Fourth Lateran Council (1215) had to insist that the faithful receive the Eucharist at least once a year at Easter. But the concentration on communion with the Lord in the Eucharist also led to obscuring communion with the Church as a consequence of reception.

Despite attempts throughout the centuries to encourage more frequent reception of Holy Communion, only since Vatican II (1962–65) has this become the case. Liturgical and theological studies before and after the council recovered the ancient notion of the Eucharist as a meal at which the Lord presides and nourishes his people with his body and blood, furthering communion with himself and among themselves. Participation in the eucharistic liturgy is incomplete without the reception of Holy Communion. The ancient principle of the Eucharist as the source of the Church's unity has been rediscovered and is emphasized in official documents and catechesis.

The 1983 Code of Canon Law reiterates the discipline of Lateran IV regarding reception of the Eucharist once a year at Easter, though it allows for the fulfillment of the obligation at some other time for a just cause. The code also permits a second reception of Holy Communion on the same day, but only at a celebration of the Eucharist. *See also* Eucharist; Real Presence.   JOHN J. STRYNKOWSKI

communion of saints, the faithful on earth, in purgatory, and in heaven. The communion of saints is formed by the Holy Spirit into one body participating in Christ's life by Baptism. It is mentioned in the third article of the Apostles' Creed and probably dates from the late fourth century.

All who share the one spirit through the one baptism become one body in Christ (1 Cor 12:12–13), also called "the Mystical Body of Christ" (Pius XII, *Mystici Corporis* [1943]). All the faithful on earth, in purgatory, and in heaven share the common life of the body (Vatican II, Dogmatic Constitution on the Church, nn. 49–51).

Manifestations of the common life of the communion of saints on earth are union with the ecclesiastical community (i.e., one is joined to a local community in union with its bishop, and so in union with the Church universal, built on Peter and his successors); participation in the sacraments, particularly the Eucharist; other forms of common prayer, including prayer for one another; common service to others; and the love produced and urged by the Spirit, who animates the ecclesiastical community in its sacramental participation, prayer, and service.

Prayer for the dead is an ancient custom (2 Macc 12:43–46) by which the faithful on earth and in heaven care for those in purgatory. Tertullian speaks of suffering after death (*On the Resurrection of the Body* 43), which he understood might be relieved by the intercession of the living, and mentions the practice of offering the Eucharist for the dead (*On Monogamy* 10), as does Augustine (*Confessions* 9.12.32). In systematizing earlier teaching on purgatory, Gregory I (d. 604) teaches clearly that the prayers of the faithful on earth and of the saints in heaven could aid in obtaining the release of those in purgatory (*Dialogues* 4.40).

In the medieval period, prayers for the dead, while retaining their intercessory character, also became strongly associated with the notion of satisfying the penalty for forgiven sin. At this time the system of indulgences developed as a method of applying one's suffrages to the dead to hasten their release. The Council of Florence (1439) explained suffrages as "the sacrifice of the Mass, prayers, alms and other religious activities which, according to the laws and customs of the Church, the faithful normally offer" (DS 1304). The Council of Trent (1563) affirmed that "a purgatory exists and the souls detained in it can be assisted by the suffrages of the faithful" (DS 1820).

Those in heaven are in a position to assist not only those in purgatory but also the faithful on earth, who have honored the saints in heaven and sought their intercession from the earliest days of Christianity. Honor of the saints includes imitation of them, prayers addressed to them, reverence given to their relics, and the right use of images. Prayer asks the intercession of the saints with God, and honors God's holy creatures, so giving honor to the Creator, the source of all holiness. Reverence to relics and images is paid not to these material realities but to whom or what they represent, and so to the faithful in glory (Council of Trent, DS 1821–25). *See also* Church; eschatology, individual; eschatology, universal; indulgences; prayers for the dead.   MARY A. DONOVAN

Communion Service, the practice, new to Catholicism (apart from Good Friday), of communal distribution of Communion outside the context of the Mass. The liturgy of the Communion Service is governed by the Roman *Rite of Distributing Holy Communion Outside Mass. 1: The Long Rite with the Celebration of the Word* (1973), and was originally intended as an exceptional usage "when Mass is not celebrated or when Communion is not distributed at scheduled times" (n. 26). However, with the shortage of priests, it has become the usual form of Sunday celebration in an increasing number of parishes. To meet the new situation, the Congregation for Divine Worship issued a *Directory for Sunday Celebrations in the Absence of a Priest* (1988). In 1991, the U.S. Catholic bishops approved an *Order for Sunday Celebrations in the Absence of a Priest* for use at Sunday Communion services in the United States. *See also* Communion, Holy.

Communion under both kinds, the practice of receiving the body and blood of the Lord under the forms of bread and wine. Jesus himself at the Last Supper gave bread and wine to his disciples after declaring the former to be his body and the latter his blood. Christians continued this practice, though with adaptations according to circumstances (e.g., it was simpler to bring the Eucharist to the sick in their homes only under the form of bread). But in the West, theological controversies in the twelfth and thirteenth centuries led to the reception of the Eucharist under the form of bread alone. Controversialists insisted that one had to receive the Eucharist under both forms in order to be saved. Other theologians responded that the Lord was present under either form in the entirety of his being, both body and blood (the doctrine of concomitance). Thus while the practice of Communion under both kinds continued in the East, in the medieval West it gradually disappeared.

Reformers in the sixteenth century declared Communion under one form to be contrary to the scriptural norm. The Council of Trent (1545–63) reaffirmed the doctrine of concomitance and the Church's authority to restrict reception of the Eucharist to one form, that of bread. However, Vatican II (1962–65) called for the reestablishment of Communion under both kinds. The restoration of this practice enables participants in the eucharistic liturgy to experience the abundance of the Lord's self-gift in his body and blood through both sacramental signs of bread and wine. *See also* Communion, Holy. JOHN J. STRYNKOWSKI

Communism, the system of social organization based on the common ownership of property. The term is associated with the social, political, and economic doctrines of Karl Marx (d. 1883) and Vladimir Lenin (d. 1924) and the international political movement based on those doctrines. For Marx, Communism was the inevitable culmination of the historical process of class conflict, a process moving forward in stages through a series of revolutions, each stage successively eliminating the prior characteristic forms of domination. The final revolution, from capitalism to Communism, would occur when the increasingly disenfranchised working class (the proletariat) organized to seize the ownership of industry. A brief period of socialism (dictatorship of the proletariat) would be followed by the definitive end of all domination in a classless, propertyless, and stateless society of equals. Lenin subsequently shaped Communism as an international political movement by emphasizing the central role of the Communist party as the instigator of revolution, and the export of Communist doctrine to developing nations. Because of its explicit denigration of spiritual and religious values as illusory ideologies, which in practice has often led to the persecution of

the Church and the abuse of basic human rights, Communism as both a social theory and political movement has been repeatedly condemned in Catholic social teaching.

With the collapse of the Berlin Wall in November 1989, Communism as a coherent, global political movement began to unravel. The Soviet Union itself went out of existence. The Church and many former Communist countries found themselves faced with a new threat: nationalism and ethnic rivalries. *See also* Marxism. PAUL J. WOJDA

community Mass, the public Mass celebrated by religious or canons, bound to the Divine Office in choir. While no special form for the Mass exists, it is proper to celebrate with singing and full participation of all community members, exercising the functions proper to their order or ministry. *See also* conventual Mass.

commutation, the changing of certain obligations imposed upon either a physical person or a juridical person (legal entity). Obligations may have been imposed due to conditions of a benefaction or by way of penance or reparation. The impossibility of or serious inconvenience in fulfilling the obligations or any other just reason allows proper Church authority to change obligations to more suitable ones in canon law. *See also* rights and obligations in canon law.

Compline (Lat., *complere*, "to complete"), the official night office that concludes the Liturgy of the Hours and signals the end of day. The pre–Vatican II office was invariable, the chief elements being a short lesson, *Confiteor* (Lat., "I confess"), three psalms and responsory, hymn, canticle, and Marian antiphon. The present brief office, intended to be prayed before retiring, begins with an examination of conscience, a variable hymn and psalm, a short lesson, invariable response, and the Canticle of Simeon. The Sunday options may be used daily. *See also* Liturgy of the Hours.

Complutensian Polyglot Bible, an edition of the Bible with accompanying translations sponsored by Cardinal Ximenes and produced at Alcalá (Lat., *Complutum*) in Spain (1521–22) in six folio volumes. The first four volumes contained the Hebrew OT, the Greek Septuagint, and the Latin Vulgate in parallel columns, and the Aramaic Targum Onqe-los at the bottom of the page. The NT (volume 5) contained the Greek text and the Latin Vulgate, and volume 6, a Hebrew grammar and a Hebrew-Aramaic dictionary. *See also* Scripture, versions of.

Comunione e Liberazione (kah-m*oo*-nee-oh'nay ay lee-bavr-ah-tsee-oh'nay; It., "Communion and Liberation"), Catholic renewal movement founded and led by Father Luigi Giussani (b. 1922). In 1993 the movement claimed 90,000 members in Italy and 10,000 in other countries. In 1954, Giussani, then professor of Protestant and Orthodox theology at the Milan seminary (Venegono), decided to become a high school religion teacher, convinced that Christian life among young people was suffocating under moralism. When a group of students formed around him, he first organized them within Catholic Action, an international lay movement, but in 1956 founded Gioventù Studentesca (It., "Student Youth") on different principles: Christian life was to take place where students lived and worked; female and male students were to pray and work together; lay mission was to be seen as flowing from Baptism, not from the bishops' call for helpers.

In the early 1970s the phrase "Communion and Liberation" came to express the group's guiding intuition. In the student unrest of 1968 the majority of Gioventù Studentesca left to embrace Marxist liberation movements. The manifesto "Communion and Liberation" proposed that true liberation flows from communion with Christ, from a visible ecclesial communion that can transform daily life.

Comunione e Liberazione is a loosely organized movement without formal membership. Two communities sprang from it and have been canonically recognized: the Fraternità di Comunione e Liberazione ("Fraternity of Communion and Liberation"), recognized in 1982, with 25,000 members as of 1993, is designed for adults who want to make a life-long commitment to the movement; Memores Domini ("Those Who Remember the Lord"), recognized in 1988 (with 800 members in 1993; 600 novices), live lay lives in celibacy, poverty, and obedience. Rooted in the theology of de Lubac, Guardini, and von Balthasar, Comunione e Liberazione has aligned itself closely with the pastoral vision of John Paul II. It has become a sometimes controversial presence in Italy and elsewhere. *See also* Balthasar, Hans Urs von; Catholic Action; Lubac, Henri de.

MICHAEL WALDSTEIN

concelebration, term commonly used to designate the participation of more than one ordained minister in a liturgical celebration, though in fact any liturgical service is a concelebration of all the baptized participants in the celebration of their common mystery of faith. Ministerial concelebration originally meant the participation of presbyters in the liturgy of their bishop. The Greek term to concelebrate (*sylleitourgein*) is also commonly used for the Church's liturgy as a concelebration with heavenly service of the angelic powers. Today the narrower, technical sense of the term "concelebration" usually refers to several priests acting together in the administration of the same sacrament, most commonly in the consecration of the Eucharist, an ancient practice restored in the Roman rite following Vatican II. Authors distinguish between this "real" concelebration, consisting in the coconsecration of the sacrament, and "ceremonial" concelebration, in which more than one minister actively participates wearing priestly vestments, but only one recites the sacramental formulas. Such distinctions, based on a rationalistic Western view of ritual in which only words express symbolic meaning, are foreign to the early sources.

Historically, one can distinguish three kinds of eucharistic concelebration: (1) sacramental, verbal coconsecration, as in the Roman, Byzantine, Coptic Catholic, and Maronite rites. Since Vatican II this form has been growing among the Armenian and Syro-Malabar Catholics, too; (2) distributive concelebration, as in the Armenian, Coptic, East and West Syrian, and Ethiopian traditions, in which the ministers share the prayers and actions but do not recite the same prayers together, not even the consecration; and (3) coordinated celebration, in which each priest consecrates his own bread and wine at a separate altar. This custom, admitted in the West Syrian and Ethiopian rites, is actually a form of synchronized multiple Eucharists, not a concelebration.

Sacramental forms of concelebration are also practiced for the Anointing of the Sick in the Byzantine rite and are provided for in Armenian and Coptic sources, too. In addition to the bishop's Eucharist, concelebration is common at other pontifical celebrations (vespers, vigils, Presanctified Liturgy, etc.) in the East. *See also* Eucharist.   ROBERT F. TAFT

conciliarism, also known as "conciliar theory," a view emanating from canonists of the twelfth and thirteenth centuries according to which an ecumenical council is regarded as being the highest authority in the Church, superior even to the pope. Earliest forms of conciliarism considered a general council as a representation of the whole Church, not as an assembly of autonomous bishops. The word "conciliarism" encompasses the history and theology surrounding the debates among those canonists and later controversies associated with the Great Schism of 1378–1417 when more than one pope claimed to be the legitimate authority.

Historically conciliarism was an attempt to limit papal immunity and to require greater accountability on the part of the pope. It also was haunted by the theoretical possibility of the pope being in error, even in heresy or schism. Marsilius of Padua (ca. 1278–1342/3) is regarded as the founder of conciliarism. He argued for a kind of "democratic" Church in which the people would exercise a kind of sovereignty.

The Great Schism gave practical importance to the theoretical discussion about conciliarism since it offered a means of solving the uncertainties about who was the legitimate pope. Other theologians associated with conciliarism were Jean Gerson, John of Paris, Pierre d'Ailly, and others at the University of Paris.

The decree *Haec Sancta,* promulgated at the fifth session, April 6, 1415, of the Council of Constance (1414–18) taught that "this synod holds its power directly from Christ; all persons, of whatever rank or dignity, even a pope, are bound to obey it in matters relating to faith and to the end of the schism as well as to the reform of the Church in its head and in its members." As such this assertion was not novel or unheard of in the canonical tradition. It was an attempt to describe certain limitations of papal powers. The exact canonical status of this decree is disputed, some holding that it was not ecumenical, others claiming that it had only a temporary pertinence.

Conciliarism reached a high point at the Council of Basel (1431–38), which asserted the supremacy of a council over a pope. Catholic theologians generally do not consider this a truly ecumenical council because it did not represent the Church universal (only fourteen bishops and abbots were present) and did not receive papal approbation. (The council moved subsequently to Ferrara and then to Florence—both in Italy.)

What differentiates conciliarism from collegiality or from current teaching about the role of an ecumenical council is that it fostered independence from the pope, whereas collegiality views the collective episcopacy as acting in union with the pope, and ecumenical councils are convoked and presided over now by a pope. Gallicanism, whose influence especially in France was strong even at the time of Vatican I (1869–70), is correctly seen as an ecclesiological attitude akin to conciliarism. *See also* Church; communion, Church as; conciliarity; Constance, Council of; democracy in the Church; ecumenical council.

MICHAEL A. FAHEY

conciliarity, or synodality, the ongoing process by which the Church comes together through its representatives in synods or meetings to pray, seek advice, and reach practical decisions. Conciliarity describes the synodal character of the Church; the term should not be confused with conciliarism and it refers to an ecclesial reality far more comprehensive than collegiality.

The term in recent usage seems to have entered English through French (*conciliarité* or *synodalité*), which in turn was an attempt to express what Russian Orthodox calls *sobornost* (from the Slavonic word *sobor,* meaning "council"), whose adjectival form *sobornaja* translates the word "catholic" in the Nicene Creed. For the Russian Orthodox writer A. Khomiakov, *sobornost* unites the faithful, assists them in the reception of doctrine, and undergirds the infallibility of the Church.

In modern times, since the establishment of the World Council of Churches (Amsterdam, 1948) and the sessions of Vatican II (1962–65), interest in the conciliar structure of the Church has come to the fore. Since 1965, there have been numerous ecumenical discussions about the nature and demands of "conciliar fellowship." The Louvain meeting of Faith and Order (1971) began to study conciliarity described as "the coming together of Christians—locally, regionally or globally—for common prayer, counsel and decision, in the belief that the Holy Spirit can use such meetings for its own purpose by reconciling, renewing and reforming the Church by guiding it towards the fullness of truth and love." Faith and Order's meeting in Salamanca (1973) stated: "The one Church is to be envisioned as a conciliar fellowship of local churches which are themselves truly united. In this conciliar fellowship, each local church possesses, in communion with the others, the fullness of catholicity, witnesses to the same apostolic faith, and, therefore, recognizes the others as belonging to the same Church of Christ and guided by the same Spirit." *See also* Church; collegiality; com-

munion, Church as; conciliarism; ecumenism; *sobornost*; synods.
MICHAEL A. FAHEY

conclave (Lat., *cum clavis*, "with key"), the meeting of cardinals held to elect a pope. It also refers to the separate, locked portion of the Vatican where the election occurs, in which the cardinals remain day and night until the election is completed. The conclave originated in 1271 when local authorities at Viterbo, Italy, wearied by a delay of two years and nine months, confined the cardinals in limited quarters with minimal resources and services until a new pope was chosen. The right to elect the pope belongs solely to those cardinals who are less than eighty years old, but a limited number of specifically designated persons, called conclavists, may enter and remain in the conclave. These include, for example, the secretary of the College of Cardinals, the master of pontifical ceremonies, some priest-religious as confessors, two doctors, and one or several assistants as sacristans, who prepare the altar and vestments for liturgical celebrations. Cardinals may not be accompanied by private ministers except by reason of special health needs. All officials and ministers of the conclave take an oath of secrecy for, during, and after the conclave regarding each and all things directly or indirectly related to it. Cardinals who leave the conclave due to illness, as affirmed by doctors and a majority of the electors, may be readmitted upon recovery, but the election continues in their absence. The conclave concludes after announcement of the name of the new pope to the people by the senior cardinal-deacon. *See also* Cardinals, College of; papal election.

ELIZABETH MCDONOUGH

concomitance, the teaching that Christ is present in the entirety of his being under each form of the Eucharist, either the bread or the wine. Thus, under the form of the bread Christ is present in his body and blood and the same is true for his presence under the form of wine. Since body and blood are constitutive elements of human nature together with the soul, the Church teaches that Christ is present in the fullness of his human nature, including his soul, and since as person he is divine, the Church teaches that he is present in his divine nature as well. This doctrine was given its definitive formulation by the Council of Trent in 1551. *See also* Communion under both kinds; Real Presence.

Concord, Book / Formula of, foundational Lutheran confessional statement. The Formula of Concord (1577) resolved the theological differences that divided Lutherans after Luther's death. Composed of twelve articles (on original sin, free will, righteousness of faith, good works, law and gospel, third use of the law, Holy Communion, Christ, the descent into hell, ceremonies, predestination, and condemnation of sectarians), the formula formed part of the *Book of Concord* (1580), which contained the Augsburg Confession and other statements of belief. In some ways the counterpart of the decrees of the Council of Trent, the *Book of Concord* became legally binding in most Lutheran states. *See also* Lutheranism.

concordance, alphabetical listing of all words in a given book, with a phrase identifying the context. For concordances to the original texts of the Bible, see J. A. Fitzmyer, *An Introductory Bibliography for the Study of Scripture* (Rome: Biblical Institute, 1990). B. Metzger, *New Revised Standard Version Exhaustive Concordance* (Nashville: Nelson, 1990), is an example of a concordance to a version of the Bible in English.

concordat, an agreement between the Holy See and a political body made to safeguard certain rights of the Church. There is nothing in the code of canon law that negates any existing agreements. The study of these matters constitutes part of the *ius publicum externum* (external public law) of canon law as contrasted with the study of the more extensive *ius publicum internum* (internal public law). An example of a concordat is the Lateran Treaty of 1929. *See also* Lateran Treaty.

concupiscence, desire. The term "concupiscence" has been used in two senses throughout most of the history of the Catholic moral tradition. In one sense, concupiscence is identified with desire in a morally problematic sense, and more particularly, with morally problematic forms of sexual desire. But Scholastic moral theology, following the analysis of Thomas Aquinas (d. 1274), also defined concupiscence in a more general and morally neutral sense, i.e., as equivalent to any desire grounded in an organism's responses to its own needs and its environment. So understood, concupiscence is the passion of desire for the good, and is immediately linked with the passions of love, joy or delight, and sadness. Concupiscence is understood in this context to be the soul's passionate movement toward whatever is perceived to be lovable; joy or sadness follows, depending on whether the desired object is attained or not. Concupiscence is contrasted with the will, which is understood as the faculty by which the individual desires and moves toward the good because of the judgment of the intellect. This contrast did not imply that concupiscence was contrary to the will in the concrete operations of the psyche. Indeed, Aquinas held that all human action is necessarily grounded in the will, which can be influenced by concupiscence and the other passions only through the medium of the intellect. *See also* free will; sexual morality; temperance.

concupiscible appetites. *See* appetites, concupiscible and irascible.

condign merit (kahn'din; Lat., [*con*]-*dignus*, "worthy"), a human entitlement to a divine reward, based upon God's acceptance of human actions that are performed with the aid of grace. This merit, grounded in the value of Christian activity, stands in contrast to merit *de congruo* (Lat.), which is a reward (of grace or heaven) given out of "fittingness," solely out of divine generosity, and with less reference to human activity. Merit *de condigno* makes no human claim in strict justice upon divine gifts or rewards but does suggest a human claim upon further grace and heaven by graced human activity. Condign merit flows from the free, graced actions of an individual who is citizen and heir of the reign of God.

Although some of the late-medieval theologians claimed that the first arrival of grace to an individual, i.e., justification, might be merited by good actions, graced or not, after the Council of Trent (1545–63) Catholic theologians have taught clearly that human beings in no way merit God's free gift of initial grace. While the concept of merit calls attention to the real contribution of our human freedom and activity, it also holds that the Christian life and its activities are gifts of God. *See also* merit.

conditional baptism, the celebration of Baptism with the condition "If you are not already baptized...." This may occur in two instances: (1) there exists a doubt about the fact of one's baptism that cannot be resolved even after serious investigation, e.g., no record or witness can be found; and (2) after

serious investigation, a doubt exists whether the baptism, which can be determined to have occurred, was valid in view of a defect regarding the use of water (matter) or the required words (form). *See also* Baptism.

condonation, the acceptance of an act without necessarily indicating approval. The code of canon law, for example, speaks of the condonation by one spouse of another's adultery (can. 1152). This indicates a willingness not to separate (as the law would allow), but it certainly does not indicate approval.

conference of bishops. *See* episcopal conference.

Conference of Major Superiors of Men, official organization of the major superiors of men in the United States, founded in 1956. It includes all major superiors of priests' and brothers' religious communities. The statutes of the conference are approved by Rome. The purpose of the conference is primarily to promote the spiritual and apostolic life of the religious communities. It also provides opportunities for cooperation among religious communities and with the hierarchy and serves as a national voice for religious superiors. In 1994 there were 269 major superiors representing communities with a combined membership of about 30,000. *See also* Council of Major Religious Superiors of Women Religious; Leadership Conference of Women Religious; major moderator in religious institute.

confession, auricular, the private confessing of one's sins to a priest. There is no clear evidence of private or auricular confession either in Scripture or during the early Church period, when the ritual of Penance itself was public and the sins of a penitent were publicly known. Only in the late sixth century, when the Celtic form of sacramental Reconciliation became popular, did the issue of private confession to a priest become an integral part of the sacrament. As this Celtic form became both widespread throughout the Church and eventually adopted officially by the Lateran Council of 1215, theologians and canonists began to formulate their teaching on the basic components of auricular confession. In their teaching, the most important element of one's confession, whether public or private, is this: a baptized Christian who has sinned must acknowledge, i.e., confess, sinfulness. A person must candidly accept responsibility for personal sin; one must admit that one is a sinner. This is the starting point for every aspect of "confession of sin." Such an admission of sin must be "integral," i.e., it must include all serious sins. A person cannot select only certain sins for Penance and reject others. This is the basic meaning of an "integral" confession of sins.

At the time of the Reformation, the leadership of the Catholic Church was accused of "inventing" private confession of sin. At the Council of Trent, the bishops responded by stressing first of all the "integral" element in one's confession of sin (D 1679). They clearly allowed that such a confession of sin could be public, although this form was not required by divine law (D 1683). In the corresponding canon, they stressed that private confession of sin to a priest was neither a human invention nor alien to the command of Christ (D 1706). At the time of Trent, theologians and canonists taught that the private confession in an act of perfect contrition of itself took away all sin. The theological relationship between such an internal private confession and contrition of sin, on the one hand, and the sacramental confession of sin to a priest, on the other, was disputed by theologians and canonists. The bishops at Trent did not attempt to resolve this relational issue, leaving it open to further investigation. However, the bishops maintained the necessity of confessing one's mortal sins annually to a priest, as prescribed by the Fourth Lateran Council (1215).

In the post–Vatican II (1962–65) sacramental rite of Penance the stress on the social nature of all sin helps one understand theologically the need for confession of sin to a priest. Sin is presented as an offense against both God and the community. Consequently, Reconciliation is reconciliation with both God and the community. Since every sin has a social dimension, every confession of sin or act of Reconciliation must also have a social dimension. The Christian community, therefore, must play a role in the reconciliation of sinners, and this is done, generally, through an official Church leader, i.e., a bishop or priest. In the early Church, when the procedure was public, it was the bishop or priest who, in the name of God and of the community, accepted a sinner back into the community. In a later period of Church history, when the procedure had become private, it was once again an official of the Church community who accepted a sinner back into a community. With the renewal of Vatican II, the communal or public nature of the priest's role in Reconciliation is more apparent, particularly in the communal forms of celebrating this sacrament. Form II involves the reconciliation of several penitents with individual confession and absolution, while form III allows for general confession and absolution of several penitents. However, even in the more private form (form I) the priest does not act alone, but in the name of the Church community.

There remains, however, a serious theologically unresolved issue regarding auricular confession. In the case of general absolution, although all sins are forgiven, a penitent is required to confess serious sins to a priest at the next private confession. Theologians currently have not presented a clear reason for this canonical regulation. *See also* general confession; Reconciliation; seal of confession.

KENAN B. OSBORNE

confessional, a place where priest and penitent celebrate the sacrament of Reconciliation. In the patristic period, the final rites of sacramental Reconciliation took place in a church, except in case of death. The beginnings of the Celtic form of Penance give no clear indication of place. Eventually, the church became the ordinary place for the sacrament. Confessionals, as we know them today, began in Milan in the sixteenth century with Charles Borromeo. The confessional was mandated by the Council of Trent (1545–63). In current canon law, a confessional room is the proper location. A place for anonymous confession must always be provided (can. 964). *See also* confession; auricular; Reconciliation.

confessor (Lat., *confiteri*, "to declare openly"), in the early Church a name for those who had suffered imprisonment or torture for the faith without actually being killed. Later it came to refer more generally to any saint who was not a martyr. *See also* martyr.

Confiteor (kahn-fee'tay-ohr; Lat., "I confess"), an optional part of the introductory rites at Mass in the Roman rite. The *Confiteor,* which was once part of the prayers recited at the foot of the altar at the beginning of Mass, grew out of the medieval *apologiae,* prayers of unworthiness said by the clergy during the procession to the altar.

CONFIRMATION

onfirmation is a sacrament in the Christian initiation process. At present it may be celebrated as part of the Rite of Christian Initiation of Adults or as a sacrament separate from Baptism, in the case of those baptized as infants. The difference in these two experiences raises questions as to the meaning of the sacrament when celebrated apart from Baptism and the Eucharist. A brief survey of its historical development followed by a discussion of the present reforms sheds some light on the problem and points to possible future directions.

PRIMITIVE CHURCH

While Scripture shows the importance of the act of Christian initiation and its relationship to the gift of the Holy Spirit, it provides no evidence for a specific rite of Confirmation. The *Apostolic Tradition* of Hippolytus (third century) indicates that initiation took place within one celebration consisting of several ritual moments: (1) a water bath; (2) an anointing by a presbyter with consecrated oil; (3) laying on of hands by the bishop, accompanied by a prayer; (4) an anointing on the head by the bishop with the same oil used for the anointing by the presbyter; and (5) the kiss of peace. Scholars differ as to the meaning of the anointing by the bishop, but the fact that the bishop had a significant role in the initiatory process affected future developments.

By the fifth century, the anointing by the bishop had become associated with the coming of the Holy Spirit. This may have been connected to fourth- and fifth-century controversies concerning the Holy Spirit. It is also during this period that the word "confirmation" appears, stressing the bishop's role in an initiation process over which he has not presided. While there is evidence that some Western bishops were "confirming" those baptisms presided over by a presbyter, the practice was not universal. The East continued to hold for the unity of the sacraments of initiation by permitting presbyters to complete the process.

MEDIEVAL PRACTICE

Throughout the Middle Ages, changes in local church structure affected the initiation process. Lack of sufficient bishops in outlying areas raised the question of how initiation should be completed. Unlike in the East, the majority of churches in the West opted to retain the final anointing by the bishop. Thus, the practice of delaying full initiation until such time as a bishop was available became common outside Rome. But at no time in the early medieval period can it be said that initiation practices were uniform throughout the Western Church. By the ninth century, however, theological reflection on the practice of delayed anointing by a bishop had already led to the interpretation that the Spirit was conferred by the imposition of hands and chrismation (anointing with oil).

SCHOLASTIC THEOLOGY

Medieval theologians had both a rite independent of Baptism, celebrated by a bishop, and a theological tradition associating this rite with the gift of the Holy Spirit as a background for their debates concerning the number of sacraments. They focused on the anointing with chrism, consecrated oil, and its accompanying prayer as the most important element in the rite. Convinced that the Spirit was given in Baptism, they sought to distinguish these separate conferrals of the Spirit. Thomas Aquinas (d. 1274) clearly articulated the unique gift of the Spirit in the sacrament of Confirmation in his *Summa Theologiae.* Baptism was the sacrament of Christian birth, Confirmation the sacrament of Christian growth or maturity. The matter for the sacrament according to Thomas was the chrism. The form of the sacrament was the words: "I sign you with the sign of the cross and confirm you with the chrism of salvation in the name of the Father, Son, and Holy Spirit."

FROM TRENT TO THE MODERN PERIOD

Tridentine discussions of the sacrament of Confirmation accepted the Scholastic position stated by Thomas Aquinas and yielded one change in the ritual, namely, the bishop's placing his hand upon the head of the candidate as he anointed the forehead with chrism. The Tridentine rite of Confirmation consisted of (1) a collective imposition of hands by the bishop, accompanied by a prayer for the sevenfold gifts of the Holy Spirit; (2) an anointing with chrism by the bishop, whose hand rested on the head of the individual as he anointed the forehead with oil and spoke the formula "I sign you . . . "; (3) a slight blow on the cheek accompanied by the words "Peace be with you"; and (4) a prayer for the indwelling of the Holy Spirit.

Throughout this period, the practice of receiving Confirmation prior to the reception of First Eucharist continued. It was with the call by Pius X in the 1910 decree from the Congregation of Rites *Quam Singulari* that a radical change in practice was set in motion. In this decree, First Confession was placed prior to the reception of First Eucharist and both were received at the age of reason (approximately seven years).

Thus, at the time of the Second Vatican Council (1962–65), the practice was to baptize infants and provide First Confession along with First Eucharist at the age of seven and Confirmation at a later age (about ten). The delay in the reception of Confirmation until an age of ten or more coupled with a theology that stressed Confirmation as a sacrament of maturity set the stage for a catechesis that stressed growth in the faith as synonymous with making a mature, adult commitment. One became a "soldier in Christ's army," ready to profess and defend the faith. The sacrament of Confirmation took on the aspect of a puberty rite or a graduation exercise.

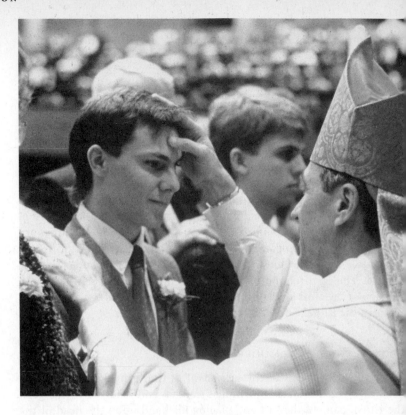

The sacrament of Confirmation (conferred by Bishop Joseph Charron, C.PP.S., former auxiliary bishop of the archdiocese of St. Paul and Minneapolis, now bishop of Des Moines, at St. Stephen's Church, Anoka, Minnesota).

REFORMS OF THE SECOND VATICAN COUNCIL

The Constitution on the Sacred Liturgy (*Sancrosanctum Concilium*) called for the revision of the sacraments of initiation (nn. 64–71), specifically the restoration of the ancient process of initiation of adults (nn. 64–66). This revision resulted in the promulgation in 1972 of the Rite of Christian Initiation of Adults (*RCIA*). The constitution also called for the revision of the rite of Confirmation so that it might be seen within the context of an initiation process (n. 71). A revised Rite of Confirmation was promulgated in 1971.

RITE OF CHRISTIAN INITIATION OF ADULTS

The sacrament of Confirmation as celebrated in the adult rite of initiation (which includes children of catechetical age [*RCIA*, n. 3]) is one moment in a unified celebration of initiation. This initiation liturgy is to be "celebrated by parish priests . . . at the Easter Vigil" (*RCIA*, n. 17). While other times may be chosen due to need, they should fall within the octave of Easter or at least in the season prior to Pentecost. Confirmation may be delayed but only for "serious reason" (*RCIA*, n. 24). When such delay occurs, the priest who baptized may confirm if the bishop is not available. Again, the time for such celebration should be in keeping with the paschal character of the sacrament. If a Sunday in the Easter season is not available, then preference is to be given to a Sunday in Ordinary Time.

The parish priest who presides at the Easter Vigil celebrates the sacraments of initiation. If the numbers to be initiated are large, he may be assisted by other priests in the ritual of confirming the candidates. It is presumed that the local bishop will preside at the Easter Vigil in the cathedral and therefore will also preside over the sacraments of initiation celebrated that evening.

The celebration of Confirmation follows the presentation of the lighted candle in the baptismal component of the rite. The presider addresses the newly baptized, reminding them that they are to "share in the outpouring of the Holy Spirit" (*RCIA*, n. 233). He then "holds his hands outstretched over . . . those to be confirmed" and says a prayer for the sevenfold gift of the Holy Spirit. Each candidate goes to the presider (accompanied by the godparents, who place a right hand on the candidate's shoulder), who anoints the forehead of the candidate with chrism in the sign of the cross saying, "Be sealed with the Gift of the Holy Spirit" (*RCIA*, n. 235). The presider then says, "Peace be with you," to which the newly confirmed answers, "And also with you."

The introduction to the act of Confirmation and the prayer during the laying on of hands both speak of the coming of the Spirit, permitting an interpretation that the Spirit does not come until Confirmation. Yet, the rhythm of the entire body of ritual moments in this one liturgical event overpowers any such interpretation of a "moment" of Baptism or a "moment" of Confirmation. One is initiated during the course of an evening of celebration that culminates as the newly initiated take their place around the eucharistic table and offer the Eucharist for the first time as members of the faith community.

RITE OF CONFIRMATION

The Rite of Confirmation (RC) as celebrated with children baptized as infants is a sacrament seeking a theology, for several significant problems result from its separation from the unity of the original initiation process. To understand fully the problems raised by the present practice of the rite of Confirmation as received by children or young adults, it is necessary to view it in light of the norms set by the *RCIA*. Here, in the introduction to the collection of rituals, the ancient order of Baptism, Confirmation, Eucharist is the norm (*RCIA*, n. 2). The introduction further indicates that initiation is a process or a "spiritual journey" (*RCIA*, n. 5) that takes place "within the community of the faithful" (*RCIA*, n. 4). An individual begins the process as a catechumen journeying through the various stages with others in the catechumenate. The journey climaxes in the celebration of the sacraments of Baptism, Confirmation, and the Eucharist at the Easter Vigil. However, if pastoral necessity demands, the sacraments may be celebrated at another time but must be celebrated in a single liturgical event (*RCIA*, n. 8).

The revised sacrament of Confirmation for children baptized as infants was promulgated in August 1971 by Paul VI's *Apostolic Constitution on the Sacrament of Confirmation*. This text along with the introduction to the ritual provide a direction for present theological reflection on the state of the sacrament. Paul VI stresses the ancient sequence of the sacraments of initiation: "The faithful are born anew by baptism, strengthened by the sacrament of confirmation, and finally are sustained by the food of eternal life in the Eucharist." The introduction to the Rite of Confirmation speaks of those to be confirmed as either "adult catechumens who are to be confirmed immediately after baptism" or as "children" who are to be prepared "for the fruitful reception of the sacraments of confirmation and Eucharist" by parents "with the help of catechetical institutions" (n. 3). It is evident from the above that the revised rite considers as normative the reception of First Eucharist prior to Confirmation and the confirmation of children at the age of reason. However, exceptions are permitted: "For pastoral reasons, however, especially to strengthen the faithful in complete obedience to Christ the Lord and in loyal testimony to him, episcopal conferences may choose an age which seems more appropriate, so that the sacrament is given at a more mature age after appropriate formation" (n. 11).

In addition to continuing to stress the need to adhere to the ancient order of the sacraments of initiation, the Rite of Confirmation offers further connections to infant baptism by suggesting that the godparent at Baptism be the sponsor at Confirmation, candidates renew their baptismal promises, and the sacrament be celebrated within Mass. Unlike the adult rite, which speaks first of the local priest as the minister of the sacraments of initiation at the Easter Vigil, the Rite of Confirmation speaks of the bishop as the ordinary minister (*RC*, n. 7). The rite does introduce the possibility of associating other priests with the bishop in the administration of the sacrament (*RC*, n. 8).

The revised Rite of Confirmation attempts to clear up the confusion between the imposition of hands and the anointing with chrism. Paul VI definitively states the following in his apostolic constitution: "The sacrament of confirmation is conferred through the anointing with chrism on the forehead, which is done by the laying on of the hand, and through the words: Be sealed with the gift of the Holy Spirit." This anointing with chrism follows the collective laying on of hands with prayer for the coming of the Spirit. The hand of the bishop no longer rests on the head of the candidate, thus eliminating one confusing element found in the Tridentine rite. The rite concludes with the bishop saying, "Peace be with you," to which the newly confirmed responds. Eliminated is the confusing "blow on the cheek" from former rites.

See also Baptism; catechumenate; chrism; Holy Spirit; Rite of Christian Initiation of Adults; sacrament; sacramental character.

Bibliography

Austin, Gerald. *The Rite of Confirmation: Anointing with the Spirit.* Collegeville, MN: Liturgical Press, 1985.

Kavanagh, Aidan. *Confirmation: Origins and Reform.* Collegeville, MN: Liturgical Press, 1988.

MARY A. PIIL

confraternities, associations, almost exclusively lay, dedicated to acts of public worship and/or Christian doctrine. While such groups had canonical prescriptions under the old Code of Canon Law, the present code deals with groups under the general rubric of "Associations of the Christian faithful" (can. 298). Such groups, many with a long history going back into the late Middle Ages, are distinguished from religious orders by their absence of vows. Historic confraternities did everything from caring for condemned prisoners and assisting the poor to teaching catechism and burying the dead. Typically, they had their own chapels, patronal feast days, and extra-liturgical ceremonies.

In the contemporary Church those associations that derive from a private impulse should be reviewed by competent authorities in order to gain recognition (can. 299.3) and none may assume the adjective "Catholic" without such authority (can. 300). Only competent ecclesiastical authority may establish associations for the teaching of doctrine in the name of the Church or for the end of public worship; only such associations may be recognized as "public associations" in canon law. *See also* associations of the Christian faithful.

Confraternity of Christian Doctrine (CCD), official organ for the catechetical instruction of the Catholic laity. First proposed in the period of Catholic Reform in the late sixteenth century, it was reborn through the efforts of Pope Pius X, whose encyclical *Acerbo Nimis* (1905) called for a renewed approach to religious instruction and the establishment of the CCD in every Catholic parish.

In the modern U.S. Church the CCD was established as an independent apostolate in 1935 with a national director and a publishing arm. CCD was seen as the means of instructing youth (and their parents) who did not have the advantage of Catholic schooling. This catechetical effort was (and is) closely tied to the administrative structure of the office of the U.S. bishops, which still coordinates such educational efforts.

Today, the CCD is practically synonymous with parish catechetical and religious education programs. Most are headed by professionally trained directors of religious education (DRES) who are responsible for the selection, formation, and supervision of lay catechists. *See also* catechesis; catechetics; religious education.

Congar, Yves, 1904–95, French Dominican theologian, cardinal, and ecumenist. Perhaps the most influential Catholic theologian of this century prior to Vatican II (1962–65), Congar broke new ground in Catholic theology regarding the Church (ecclesiology), specifically concerning the episcopacy, tradition, ministry, laity, and ecumenism (all of which constituted, in addition to liturgy, the agenda of the Second Vatican Council). Early in his life he met pioneers of the ecumenical movement, important historians of medieval theology, Russian Orthodox refugees, advocates of new Protestant thinking, and French intellectuals who were seeking a contemporary Catholic theology. At the time of his ordination as a Dominican priest in 1930, he decided to devote himself to the renewal of the history of ecclesiology. He was convinced that meticulous historical research into the cultural forms of Church life could help to revitalize the Church itself. Historical contextualization would disclose the underlying, perduring reality of the Church but, at the same time, show what could and should be discarded for the sake of renewal. In 1937, Congar began a series of reports on ecumenism, and for decades he published surveys of books and articles on the Church.

He spoke at countless meetings, large and small, on the ecumenical movement and he preached a moving series of sermons on ecumenism at Sacré-Cœur in Paris in January 1936. That week was seen

Yves Congar, French Dominican theologian generally regarded as the greatest ecclesiologist of the twentieth century.

as a watershed for Catholic involvement in the ecumenical movement, which until then was a Protestant movement. Congar attended the great ecumenical conferences of 1937 at Oxford and Edinburgh, and a year later *Chrétiens Désunis* (Divided Christendom) appeared—the first major expression of Catholic ecumenical theology. He preached the Week of Christian Unity every year from 1936 to 1964 in France and elsewhere. He served in World War II as a medical orderly and was a prisoner of war. His first major book after the war was *True and False Reform in the Church* (1950), a markedly ecumenical treatment of church renewal and of Martin Luther. The book was withdrawn from circulation upon orders from the Vatican. Three years later he produced his large study, *Lay People in the Church*.

In 1954 growing threats from the Vatican led to his removal from teaching, lecturing, and publishing. While in exile at the École Biblique in Jerusalem, he wrote *The Mystery of the Temple*, a study of the biblical sources of the Christian community.

Congar's work expresses both theological and historical gifts. He emphasized the essential sacramentality of Catholicism exemplified in his theology of Mary, the Church, and the Eucharist. Drawing on Eastern theologians and on Catholic thinkers in conversation with German Idealism, he offered in *Tradition and Traditions* (1966) a history of the doctrine of tradition and a theology of tradition viewed as the organic life of the Church as it continually reflects on revelation, both past and present. *L'Eglise de S. Augustin a l'epoque moderne* (1970, The Church from St. Augustine to the Modern Era) sums up Congar's basic vocation as it traces through fifteen centuries dozens of forms of Church life that range from the liturgical role of abbesses to the expansion of Roman curial congregations. An incapacitating nervous disease that developed in 1965 has not hindered him from publishing studies on Vatican II (including his diaries), an insightful revision of his earlier work on lay ministry, and a multivolume study on the Holy Spirit, *I Believe in the Holy Spirit* (1979). He was named a cardinal in 1994.

Bibliography

Jossua, Jean Pierre. *Yves Congar*. Chicago: The Priory Press, 1968 [with a bibliography of Congar's writings up to 1968].

Lauret, Bernard, ed. *Fifty Years of Catholic Theology: Conversations with Yves Congar*. Philadelphia: Fortress Press, 1988.

Nichols, Aidan. *Yves Congar*. Wilton, CT: Morehouse Publishers, 1989.   THOMAS F. O'MEARA

congregation, one of several categories of juridically equivalent departments, or dicasteries, of the Roman Curia. Each congregation is composed of cardinals and bishops only, is headed by a cardinal prefect or an archbishop president, and is assisted by a secretary, subsecretaries, administrative staff, and consultors. According to *Pastor Bonus* (1988), there are nine congregations: For the Doctrine of the Faith; For the Eastern (Oriental) Churches; For Divine Worship and the Discipline of the Sacraments; For the Causes of Saints; For Bishops; For the Evangelization of Peoples (Propagation of the Faith); For the Clergy; For Institutes of Consecrated Life and Societies of Apostolic Life; On Seminaries and Institutes of Studies (Catholic Education). *See also Pastor Bonus;* Roman Curia.

Congregationalism, a movement, originally within Puritanism, founded on the conviction that the primary ecclesial polity should be the local assembly of Christians, whose faithfulness to Jesus Christ spiritually manifests the universal Church. In this view institutional structures, especially hierarchical ones, are incompatible with the Gospels. It appeals to the biblical account of Jesus exclaiming that where two or three are gathered in his name, he is there among them (Matt 18:20). Interpreting this text in the light of the modern idea of democracy, Congregationalism maintains that all members of the Church should have the opportunity for an equal voice in the life and worship of the Church. In this regard, it emphasizes the priesthood of all those who are baptized (1 Pet 2:5, 9).

This movement arose in England in the sixteenth century, in large part through the efforts of Robert Browne (1550–1633), whose views were shared by the separatists Henry Barrow (1550–93), John Greenwood (d. 1593), and John Penry (1559–93). In North America, Congregationalism initially assumed two forms. The "Pilgrims" of the Plymouth Bay Colony separated from the Church of England and the Puritans of Massachusetts Bay remained in communion with the Church of England. Today, Congregationalism stresses each person's experience of God, the life of the assembly, and the preaching of the word of God. It is reluctant to make creedal or doctrinal statements. It recognizes two sacraments, Baptism and the Lord's Supper, though it does not require Baptism for membership.

In 1957 many Congregational churches in the U.S. merged with other Protestant bodies to form the United Church of Christ. In England and Wales the greater part of the Congregational Church united in 1972 with the Presbyterian Church of England to form the United Reformed Church. *See also* Protestantism; Reformation, the. *ROBERT A. KRIEG*

Congregation for Bishops, a department of the Roman Curia originally established by Pope Sixtus V in 1588 and known as the Sacred Consistorial Congregation. It became the Sacred Congregation for Bishops when the Roman Curia was reorganized by Pope Paul VI in 1967 and retained that title (without Sacred) in the 1988 reorganization of the Curia by Pope John Paul II. It has oversight in all matters pertaining to the constitution, division, union, and suppression of particular churches (i.e., dioceses), except for missionary areas subject to the Congregation for the Evangelization of Peoples, and it also establishes military ordinariates. Its wide range of responsibilities includes moderating all aspects of episcopal appointments; assisting bishops in the correct exercise of their pastoral functions; conducting apostolic visitations; handling ad limina visits; establishing episcopal conferences and reviewing their decrees as required by law; dealing with personal prelatures; and relating specifically to the Pontifical Commission for Latin America (*Pastor Bonus,* 1988, nn. 75–84). *See also* bishop; *Pastor Bonus;* Roman Curia.

Congregation for Catholic Education, also known as the Congregation for Seminaries and Institutes of Studies, a department of the Roman Curia founded in 1588 by Pope Sixtus V with oversight of universities in Rome, Bologna, Paris, Salamanca, and Louvain. After 1870 its competence was restricted specifically to Catholic universities and this role was confirmed in the curial reorganization of Pope Pius X in 1908. In 1915, Pope Benedict XV renamed it the Congregation for Seminaries and Universities, and Pope Paul VI renamed it again in 1967 as the Congregation for Catholic Education. Its current title was given by Pope John Paul II in 1988. This congregation has responsibility for formation of all clergy, especially regarding the program of study for seminarians (*Pastor Bonus,* 1988, nn. 112–13). It is also responsible for promotion and organization of Catholic education, including establishing norms for governance of Catholic schools. In addition, it has concern for Catholic universities, and it erects, approves, and ratifies the statutes of ecclesiastical universities and institutes. *See also* Catholic colleges and universities—statistics; Catholicism and education; *Pastor Bonus;* pontifical universities; Roman Curia; seminary.

Congregation for Divine Worship and the Discipline of the Sacraments, a department of the Roman Curia that moderates sacred liturgy, safeguards valid and licit celebration of sacraments, furthers effective liturgical action (especially concerning the Eucharist), revises liturgical texts and reviews translations thereof, establishes commissions for liturgical music, chant, and art, and regulates sacred relics. It also examines nonconsummatum (unconsummated) marriage cases and cases of nullity of sacred orders (*Pastor Bonus,* 1988, nn. 62–69). This congregation evolved from divisions and combinations of formerly autonomous congregations. The Congregation for Divine Worship and the Congregation for the Discipline of the Sacraments were united by Pope Paul VI in 1975 as the Congregation for the Sacraments and Divine Worship. In 1984 Pope John Paul II reestablished them as separate congregations, but four years later, in his apostolic constitution *Pastor Bonus,* he reunited them again as the Congregation for Divine Worship and the Discipline of the Sacraments. *See also* Roman Curia; sacrament; worship.

Congregation for Institutes of Consecrated Life and Societies of Apostolic Life, a department of the Roman Curia founded in 1586 by Pope Sixtus V with oversight of pontifical institutes both of men and of women whether religious institutes (Code of Canon Law, cans. 607–709), secular institutes (cans. 710–30), or societies of apostolic life (cans. 731–46) in the areas of government, discipline, studies, property, and legislation. It establishes pontifical institutes (can. 589) and judges the suitability of establishment of diocesan institutes by bishops (can. 579). In addition, it can establish conferences of major superiors (cans. 708–9) and has competence over both the eremitical life, i.e., that of monks living by themselves (can. 603), and the order of virgins (can. 604), as well as those associations of the faithful (cans. 298–329) that have been founded with the intent of becoming institutes of consecrated life or societies of apostolic life (*Pastor Bonus,* 1988, n. 111). *See also* apostolate; consecrated life; religious institute; Roman Curia; secular institute.

Congregation for Seminaries and Institutes of Studies. *See* Congregation for Catholic Education.

Congregation for the Causes of the Saints, originally the Sacred Congregation of Rites, a congregation of the Roman Curia established by Pope

Sixtus V in 1588 to regulate both divine worship and the beatification and canonization of saints. In 1969 Pope Paul VI divided the Congregation of Rites into the Congregation for Divine Worship and the Congregation for Causes of Saints, giving the latter a new structure with three offices (judicial, Promotor General of the Faith, and historical-judicial). In 1983 this congregation was again internally reordered and, simultaneously, the norms for conducting investigations for canonizations were entirely reformed. In addition to making recommendations to the pope on specific canonizations subsequent to completion of required procedures, it decides on conferral of the title "doctor" on a given saint and is responsible for the authentication and preservation of sacred relics (*Pastor Bonus*, 1988, nn. 72–74). *See also* beatification; canonization; relics; Roman Curia; saints.

Congregation for the Clergy, a congregation of the Roman Curia instituted by Pope Pius IV in 1564 as the Sacred Congregation for Interpretation of the Council of Trent (1545–63), commonly referred to as the Congregation of the Council until given its present title by Pope Paul VI in his reorganization of the Roman Curia in 1967. In 1988 Pope John Paul II expanded its oversight duties and added to it a Pontifical Commission on the Preservation of Artistic and Historic Patrimony (*Pastor Bonus*, nn. 99–104). The congregation has three offices. One is responsible for matters concerning the holiness of life, the intellectual and pastoral renewal, and the equitable distribution, or assignment, of the clergy around the world, including the obligations of Masses and pious foundations for use in the charitable, missionary, and other works of the Church (nn. 93, 95–97). Another has competence over preaching and the organization and promotion of religious instruction, including catechisms (n. 94). Yet another is responsible for all matters pertaining to ecclesiastical goods and property as well as their administration (n. 96). *See also* catechism; clergy; pious foundation; Roman Curia.

Congregation for the Doctrine of the Faith, a congregation of the Roman Curia originally established by Pope Paul III in 1542 as the Sacred Congregation of the Universal Inquisition (not to be confused with the Spanish Inquisition). Its purpose was to safeguard the faith, proscribe false doctrines, and defend the Church from heresy. The pope endowed the cardinals assigned to it with unlimited competency in matters of faith and morals for all Christians. In 1588, Pope Sixtus V changed its name to the Sacred Congregation of the Holy Inquisition, gave it first rank in the Roman Curia, and located it in its current headquarters near the Basilica of St. Peter. In 1908, Pope Pius X changed the name to Sacred Congregation of the Holy Office and united it with what was then the curial Section on Indulgences, but in 1917 Pope Benedict IV transferred the Section on Indulgences to the Sacred Penitentiary. He simultaneously suppressed the Congregation for the Index as a separate curial department and made it a subsection of the Holy Office. In the reorganization of the Roman Curia by Pope Paul VI in 1967, this congregation was renamed the Sacred Congregation for the Doctrine of the Faith and, since the mid-1980s, it, along with the other congregations of the Roman Curia, has no longer been referred to as "sacred." The 1988 reorganization of the Curia by Pope John Paul II did not change the name of this congregation, and its proper function continues to be the promotion and safeguarding of faith and morals (*Pastor Bonus*, n. 48).

The Congregation for the Doctrine of the Faith is charged with fostering scholarship with a view to a deepened understanding of the faith and an ability to respond to new initiatives in science and culture. It also assists bishops in their roles as authentic teachers and doctors of the faith (nn. 49–50). It has oversight of publications that deal with faith and morals, including oversight of documents touching on these matters that are published by other departments of the Roman Curia (n. 54). It investigates and reproves writings that seem contrary or dangerous to the faith, after affording authors the opportunity of an explanation and after appropriate warning to the competent ordinary, i.e., diocesan bishop or other religious superior (n. 51). It also handles ecclesiastical offenses against the faith and against morals and violations related to celebrations of the sacraments, and can provide for canonical sanctions if necessary (n. 52). Finally, it has the authority to grant privilege-of-the-faith dispensations (dissolving of marriage between a baptized and an unbaptized person) from the natural bond of marriage. The Pontifical Biblical Commission and International Theological Commission are subentities of this congregation (nn. 53, 55). In its functioning, the Congregation for the Doctrine of the Faith proceeds either administratively or judicially according to its own special norms. It is assisted by consultors representing the entire Catholic world, though not always reflecting its rich diversity, and its final decisions are underscored by the approval of the pope himself. *See also* faith; heresy; Inquisition; International Theological Commission; Pontifical Biblical Commission; Privilege of the Faith; Roman Curia.

ELIZABETH MCDONOUGH

Congregation for the Evangelization of Peoples,

also known as Congregation for the Propagation of the Faith, a commission of cardinals established by Popes Pius V and Gregory XIII for the Orient, with its range of responsibility later expanded to include Protestants in Europe. It was given the title Propagation of the Faith by Pope Clement VIII in 1599, and Pope Paul VI gave it the present name when he reorganized the Roman Curia in 1967. This congregation directs and coordinates the evangelization of all peoples and missionary cooperation throughout the world, fosters missionary vocations, cares for the education of catechists and clergy, supervises the establishment of churches as well as the delineation of territorial boundaries for future dioceses, and organizes distribution of subsidies for missionary works. In several of these areas of responsibility it works with the Congregation for the Oriental Churches, the Congregation for Catholic Education (on seminaries and institutes of studies), and the Congregation for Bishops. *See also* evangelization; Roman Curia.

Congregation for the Oriental Churches,

Vatican congregation of the Roman Curia with responsibility for all Eastern-rite Catholics and churches everywhere and over all Catholics of whatever rite in traditionally Eastern Christian countries. Apart from matters that are the responsibility of the Congregation for the Doctrine of the Faith and the Sacred Apostolic Penitentiary, this jurisdiction is almost all-inclusive, extending even to mixed cases involving both Eastern and Latin Catholics. So the Oriental Congregation, as it is usually called, is for the Catholic East the Roman Curia in microcosm. The congregation was established by Pope Benedict XV on May 1, 1917, but its origins go back to 1573, when Gregory XIII set up a Congregation for Greek Affairs, later absorbed into the new Congregation for the Propagation of the Faith in 1622. From time to time this congregation established special commissions for Eastern questions, among them the important Commission for the Correction of the Greek Euchologion (1636–45), expanded by Clement XI in 1719 into the Congregation for the Correction of the Books of the Oriental Church. From these commissions and their successor, the Special Commission for Liturgy, have come the universally acclaimed Roman editions of the Eastern liturgical books, used by Catholics and Orthodox alike. The congregation, comprising all Eastern Catholic patriarchs and major archbishops, the cardinal prefect of the Pontifical Council for Christian Unity ex officio, and other cardinals and hierarchs appointed by the pope, is presided over by a cardinal prefect assisted by the secretary, always an archbishop. But the day-to-day work of the congregation is carried out by those latter two full-time officials and their assistants, aided, for particular questions, by consultants and special commissions appointed by the pope. The congregation offices occupy the second floor of the Congregation Palace on the Via della Conciliazione leading from the Tiber to St. Peter's. *See also* Eastern Catholics and Rome; Eastern Catholics and Vatican II.

ROBERT F. TAFT

Congregation for the Propagation of Faith.

See Congregation for the Evangelization of Peoples.

Congregation of Holy Cross

(C.S.C), a religious institute of priests and brothers founded by Father Basil Anthony Moreau in 1837 in Le Mans, France. The congregation was formed when the Brothers of St. Joseph, founded by Canon Jacques-François Dujarie in 1820 to provide primary education, joined with the auxiliary priests of Le Mans, founded by Moreau in 1833 to assist diocesan clergy. The congregation took its name from its first community center at Sainte Croix, a suburb of Le Mans, and not the holy Cross. Edward F. Sorin and six other congregation members established the first foundation in North America at Notre Dame, Indiana, where the school was granted a charter as the University of Notre Dame du Lac in 1842.

After a split in 1946, the congregation consists of a society of priests (known historically as the Salvatorists) and a society of brothers (Josephites). As of 1992, there were 1,842 members, 998 priests, and 844 brothers in the United States, Canada, Kenya, Uganda, India, Bangladesh, Chile, Peru, Brazil, Haiti, France, and Italy, with the majority in the United States and Canada. Members currently work in universities (University of Notre Dame, University of Portland, St. Edward's University, King's College, Stonehill College), schools, parishes, foreign missions, and various individual apostolates. Outstanding members of the congregation have included

Father Julius Nieuwland, discoverer of synthetic rubber; Father Theodore M. Hesburgh, president of Notre Dame from 1952 to 1987; and Father Patrick Peyton, founder of the family Rosary movement.

In 1841, Moreau also founded a religious institute of women known as the Marianite Sisters of Holy Cross, but Rome would not grant approval for their incorporation, so they became an autonomous community in 1857. *See also* Brothers of Holy Cross; Sisters of Holy Cross.

Congregation of the Holy Ghost. *See* Holy Ghost Fathers.

Congregation of the Priests of the Sacred Heart. *See* Sacred Heart, Congregation of the Priests of the.

congregations. *See* sisters, congregations of.

Congress, Eucharistic. *See* Eucharistic Congress.

congruism. *See* Suarez, Francisco de.

Conrad of Constance, St., d. 975, bishop of Constance from 934, remarkable among medieval bishops for his aversion to secular politics. Feast day: November 26.

consanguinity, blood relationship between two persons described by lines (the type of relationship) and degrees (the closeness of relationship). Type and closeness of blood relationship constitute impediments to marriage in canon law (can. 1091). All relationships in the direct line (ancestors and descendants) are prohibited; in the collateral line (common ancestor, but no direct descendency) the fourth degree and closer (e.g., uncle-niece, first cousins, brother-sister) cannot marry. Each degree represents one generation. Thus, a great-grandmother is related to her great-grandson in the third degree. There are three persons involved, excluding the root. It is possible to receive a dispensation from this impediment in the collateral line up to, but not including, the second degree (brother-sister or half brother–half sister). *See also* marriage law.

conscience, the whole self trying to make judgments about who one ought to be and what one ought to do or not do. It is a person's "most secret core and sanctuary" where one is "alone with God" (Pastoral Constitution on the Church in the Modern World, 1965, n. 16). Traditionally, conscience has been spoken of as the subjective norm of morality. This means that conscience is the person's final, or supreme, arbiter of right and wrong. Its judgments must be followed because they reflect convictions and internalized values that set the boundaries within which one acts with integrity. To say, "My conscience tells me" means, "I hold this conviction as true and must live by it lest I betray my truest self."

With conscience, our moral strength is inside us. The moral awareness of the obligation to be good and to do what is right is not imposed from without, but it arises from within our being. To transgress internalized boundaries of value and conviction would be to act contrary to a God-given guide and thereby to lose integrity. Moral conscience, then, is not a feeling or a special faculty; nor is it the unconscious superego.

The judgment of conscience has its roots in the innate human inclination to know and to do the good. This innate capacity gives rise to the lifelong task of discovering and appropriating moral value through the process of forming conscience. The formation of conscience is a community achievement. While the judgment of conscience is always made *for* oneself (what *I* must do), it is never formed *by* oneself. Convictions are shaped, and obligations are learned, within the communities that influence us.

The freedom to follow one's judgment of conscience presupposes that one has sincerely searched for the moral truth pertaining to the issue one is facing. Therefore, Catholics have the duty to inform conscience by consulting sources of moral wisdom: human sources, such as corporate and personal counsel; Christian sources, such as Scripture, especially the words and deeds of Jesus, and the tradition of theological reflection; and Catholic sources, especially the teaching of the magisterium to which Catholics are to give the presumption of truth. The goal of forming conscience is to commit one's freedom to what is right and good so that, in judging and acting, one identifies with what one does. The moral decision becomes a commitment of the self to value.

Since people are not always sensitive to the many personal and social factors that influence judgments, the conscience that is formed can err. Even when one sincerely searches for truth, one may still miss the objective moral order that leads to human fulfillment. Yet the traditional teaching on the sanctity and dignity of conscience is not only that conscience can go astray without losing its dignity, but also that one must follow even an erring conscience that one has taken reasonable care to inform. The judgment of conscience, then, does not guarantee that one is doing the objectively right thing. It only assures that one acts with integrity and according to what one understands to be right.

A mature conscience takes responsibility before God for its judgments. It does not pin one's soul on another, and so abdicate responsibility. The teaching of conscientious objection (associated with military service) applies when one does not obey an order, if obeying the order would violate conscience and damage integrity.

Following conscience requires that one searches for truth, discerns what is right and good, and then acts according to what one understands that truth to be. In this way, following conscience is being true to the call from the "core and sanctuary" of one's heart where one is "alone with God." *See also* authority; civil law and morality; moral theology; prudence.

RICHARD M. GULA

conscience, examination of, the act of calling to mind one's sins, usually in preparation for the sacrament of Reconciliation. Sometimes referred to as examen when done apart from private confession, this practice requires an honest evaluation of one's spiritual and moral faults. An examen may and should be made frequently, focusing either on particular problems with living a virtuous life or on general tendencies toward failure in responding to God's grace. An examination of conscience before confession is a special kind of examen in that it disposes penitents to express sorrow for their sins and to resolve not to repeat their failings. It is also a time to remember particular sins committed since one's last confession so that they can be related accurately to the confessor. In making an examination of conscience, it is helpful to review prayerfully the commandments of God and the precepts of the Church. Once a pattern of failings in one's sinfulness is identified, the penitent can continue examining his or her conscience by turning to Scripture passages that encourage conversion from repeated sins. When the sacrament of Reconciliation is celebrated in large groups with an opportunity for individual private confession, the examination of conscience can be made in the context of a proclamation of the Word, a homily, and, often, a guided reflection on specific aspects of Christian holiness. In these cases, penitents should take additional time to personalize this exercise. *See also* conscience; Reconciliation.

conscientious objection, the claim that a citizen should be exempted from obligatory military service on the grounds of moral conviction. It may arise in two forms.

Since the First World War Western democracies have come to recognize that for citizens morally opposed to all participation in war (the position usually called "pacifist"), respect for their religious liberty calls for government to dispense them from obligatory military service, usually while demanding from them some other form of service to the nation. Such "humane provision" for the objector is approved in Vatican II's Pastoral Constitution on the Church in the Modern World (n. 79). In the United States, Selective Service regulations since 1940 have provided for such persons to be assigned to nonmilitary service "of national importance" once the authenticity of the person's convictions has been validated. The U.S. Catholic bishops' pastoral letter "The Challenge of Peace" (1983) recognized (nn. 73–79, 119–21) that such pacifism may be a valid Christian calling; this was a new development, because Pope Pius XII had rejected conscientious objection in 1956.

Within the majority just-war tradition, on the other hand, all participation in war cannot be condemned. Yet it may be morally imperative in a particular case to refuse to serve in an unjust war, or to use an illegitimate weapon, or to obey an unjust order. The term "selective conscientious objection" has come to be used to label this possibility. Logically it should be more congenial to Catholics. In principle this possibility was always implied by the just-war tradition, but practically it only came alive for numbers of American draftees during the Vietnam War. No government has given this position legal status.

In "Human Life in Our Day" (1968) and in "The Challenge of Peace" (n. 118), the National Conference of Catholic Bishops called for the recognition of both kinds of objection. *See also* conscience; just-war doctrine; pacifism.

JOHN H. YODER

consecrated life, a form of Christian existence undertaken by sacred ministers and laypersons who have made a public profession, recognized and sanctioned by the Church, of the evangelical counsels of poverty, chastity, and obedience. For members of religious institutes the consecration takes the form of public vows (can. 607.2). Sometimes vows are also taken by members of secular institutes (can. 712) and some societies of apostolic life (can. 731.2). It is important to note that those who do make a special consecration of their lives do not form a third state between clergy and laity (see Vatican II, Dogmatic Constitution on the Church, n. 43), although they do have a distinct place in the Church as a community of holiness and mission (n. 44). *See also* counsels, evangelical; religious institute; secular institute; society of apostolic life; vows; vows, public.

consecrated virgin, a form of religious life rooted in the sacraments and contemplative prayer and lived under the scrutiny of a spiritual director chosen by the candidate and a canonical director selected by the diocese. Espousal with Christ is the foundation and charism (gift) of this vocation.

The diocesan bishop admits a candidate into the ecclesial order of virgin and consecrates her according to the rite of the Church after approving her rule of life. The rite of consecration used to be a sacrament. In the first centuries of the Church the virgins chanted the Letters and Gospels at liturgy. *See also* consecrated life; consecration; virginity.

consecration, the term traditionally used to describe the moment of the Eucharistic Prayer at which the presider recites the words of the Lord over the bread and wine so that they become his body and blood. The priest who presides at the Eucharist acts in the person of Christ and so it is Christ himself who, through the power of the Holy Spirit, transforms the bread and wine into his body and blood as the gift of himself to his people. Although the entire Eucharistic Prayer is consecratory, the bread and wine are traditionally understood to be changed into the body and blood of Christ at the recitation of the Lord's words of institution. *See also* eucharistic prayer; Real Presence.

consent, marital, the free and irrevocable giving of self by one person to another for the purpose of establishing the marital covenant. In canon law it is consent that constitutes marriage. The consent can be placed only by those capable of so doing, e.g., someone without the ability to live out the marital covenant is not capable. In addition, canon law regulates certain conditions under which Catholics must exchange this consent, e.g., the necessary offi-

ciant, and prohibits some from placing consent, e.g., those in Holy Orders. *See also* Marriage; marriage law.

consequentialism, a view of moral reasoning and a way of justifying actions that are apparently forbidden or wrong. It has affinities with, but is distinct from, utilitarianism and proportionalism. Like utilitarianism, it regards the consequences of an action as constitutive of the rightness or wrongness of the action; but it is not committed to the utilitarian claim that nonmoral consequences are the sole determining factor. Thus it can build on Aquinas's position that consequences are among the circumstances that determine the morality of an action and the commonsense view that consequences have moral as well as nonmoral aspects. Consequentialism is narrower in focus than proportionalism, which holds that an action is to be justified by "a proportionate reason," of which consideration of consequences is only one. Consequentialism directs our attention to one of the most fundamental concerns of our practical thinking, namely, the results of our actions. This is a major source of its appeal. Also, it avoids the maximizing and hedonistic aspects of utilitarianism, even while it gives up the utilitarian effort to provide one decision-procedure for ethics and to reduce all normative principles to the Principle of Utility.

Consequentialism has elements that are clearly part of the Catholic tradition; but when it is taken as a unique basis for ethical reasoning, it strikes most observers as a dangerous oversimplification. It is perhaps best seen as the statement of a needed corrective to the excessive ridigity and complexity of older forms of moral theology. *See also* proportionalism; utilitarianism. JOHN P. LANGAN

consignatorium (kon-seen'nuh-tor'ee-uhm; Lat., *consignare*, "to seal"), also known as chrismarium, a container for holding holy oils. During the first Christian millennium it was a room or building used for the conferral of Confirmation. The latest reference to it is in a twelfth-century Roman Pontifical. *See also* chrism.

consistent ethic of life, a moral framework to protect human life. The idea of a "consistent ethic of life" is usually associated with a proposal first made by Cardinal Joseph L. Bernardin of Chicago in 1983. In a series of addresses Cardinal Bernardin set forth a framework drawn from Catholic moral theology that was designed to relate several issues of concern to the Church in a single moral perspective.

The consistent ethic had two different sources. First, societal conditions, particularly technological changes and increasing interdependence within and among states, create a range of threats to human life. The issues of abortion, capital punishment, modern warfare, euthanasia, and socioeconomic issues of justice all pose distinct challenges to protecting human life and promoting human dignity. While each question along the spectrum of life is in itself a distinct problem, the premise of the consistent ethic is that a relationship exists among these issues.

Second, in analyzing the nature of these threats to life, the consistent ethic proposal draws upon the structure and key concepts of Catholic moral theology. A principal purpose of the consistent ethic has been the effort to provide an explicit, systematic connection between the Church's positions on abortion and euthanasia (pro-life issues) and its positions on social ethics (human rights, peace, social justice). The consistent ethic is designed to test the Catholic moral vision in terms of two questions: which issues are defined as moral concerns, and how moral principles are used across a spectrum of issues. It is also designed to provide a means for the Catholic community to engage the broader civil society on these same issues. *See also* abortion; capital punishment; just-war doctrine; social justice.

Bibliography

Bernardin, J. *Consistent Ethic of Life.* Kansas City, MO: Sheed and Ward, 1988.   J. BRYAN HEHIR

consistory (Lat., *consistere*, "to stand together"), from Roman times, the antechamber of the imperial palace; also, a term designating meetings with the emperor; now refers to a formal gathering of cardinals convoked and presided over by the pope (Code of Canon Law, can. 353.1). Consistories may be ordinary or extraordinary, as well as private or public. Ordinary consistories, which include at least all the cardinals present in Rome, involve consultation on serious matters or the carrying out of solemn acts that, nevertheless, occur with some frequency or regularity. Extraordinary consistories, to which all the cardinals are summoned from around the world, are convened when special needs of the Church warrant it. Ordinary consistories are usually secret but are often opened or closed with a papal allocution, which is later published and outlines the substantive matters treated. Such is the case when new cardinals are created in consistory and subsequently made known to the public. Ordinary consistories are public when related to the canonization of saints or the reception of foreign dignitaries, in which case other prelates, legates, and invited guests are admitted to the ceremonial formalities surrounding their celebration (can. 353.1). *See also* Cardinals, College of.

Consortium Perfectae Caritatis (kahn-sawr' tzee-uhm pair-fek'tay kah-ree-tah'tihs; Lat., "Association of Perfect Charity"), a support organization for the development of religious life according to Vatican Council II (1962–65) guidelines. Established in 1971, it is committed to gospel values, fidelity to the Holy See, community life centered in the Eucharist, corporate apostolates, and common religious garb. *See also* Decree on the Appropriate Renewal of the Religious Life.

Constance, Council of, 1414–18, sixteenth ecumenical council of the Church and second of three reform councils (with Pisa and Basel) called to deal with the crisis of papal authority provoked by the Great Schism (1378–1417). Pisa had worsened the schism by creating a third pope (Alexander V and his successor, the notorious John XXIII, who are not recognized as legitimate popes by the Catholic Church because of doubts about Pisa's validity) to rival Gregory XII and the Avignon claimant, Benedict XIII. Reluctantly convoked by John XXIII through Emperor Sigismund's pressure and led by Pierre d'Ailly and Jean Gerson, Constance sought the abdication of all three claimants to the papacy, but John XXIII, supported by the numerically superior Italians, refused. The council then changed the voting procedure from individuals to national blocs, with England, Germany, France, Italy, and later Spain each having one vote. John fled, but the participants pronounced themselves (in the decree *Sacrosancta*) a general council receiving authority from Christ directly, without papal approval, and binding on all Christians, even the pope. John XXIII was imprisoned and deposed for simony (1415), upon which Gregory XII resigned (1415). After deposing Benedict XIII (1417), the council elected Pope Martin V (November 11, 1417).

Only the decree *Frequens,* which demanded new councils at regular intervals, represented a significant effort at reform. As to heresy, Constance condemned 267 teachings of the Englishman John Wycliffe (ca. 1329–84). Wycliffe's Bohemian follower

John Hus (1369–1415) consented to attend, but despite the emperor's guarantee of safe conduct, Hus was imprisoned, condemned for heresy, and burned at the stake (July 6, 1415). *See also* conciliarism; Great Schism.

W. DAVID MYERS

Constantine, Edict of (313), sometimes called the "Edict of Milan," a document that granted toleration to all religions, including Christianity. On the basis of agreements reached at a meeting in Milan between Constantine and his coemperor Licinius, a letter, not technically an edict and not issued from Milan, was written to all provincial governors ordering religious toleration, including freedom of worship for Christians. The letter also mandated the return of all confiscated Church property, thus recognizing the Church as a legal entity, able to own and dispose of property. The text is preserved, in two variant forms, by Lactantius (*On the Deaths of the Persecutors* 48) and Eusebius of Caesarea (*Ecclesiastical History* 10.5). *See also* Constantine the Great.

Constantine the Great, ca. 288–337, Roman emperor from 306 to 337. Son of Constantius Chlorus

Constantine the Great, the first temporal ruler to grant official status to the Church in the famous Edict of Constantine in 313; marble sculpture in the Palazzo dei Conservatori, Rome.

and Helena, at his father's death he was acclaimed emperor at York (in present-day England) by the troops, perhaps after being appointed by his father. He rapidly consolidated power over the West, taking Rome in 312 after defeating his brother-in-law Maxentius at the Milvian Bridge. In 313 he and his coemperor in the East, Licinius, granted religious toleration to all and restored confiscated property to Christians. From 314 his relationship with Licinius deteriorated, until in 324, when Licinius attempted renewed persecution of the Christians, he was defeated and Constantine became sole ruler of the empire.

Constantine was not baptized until just before his death, yet he regarded himself as a Christian, perhaps even from the time of his battle against Maxentius, when both Lactantius and Eusebius report he adopted a Christian standard (incorporating the Chi-Rho monogram in some form) for his army after instruction from a dream or heavenly vision. He rebuilt Byzantium and established it as his capital, Constantinople, dedicated in 330. His legislation was consistently pro-Christian, including immunization of the clergy from certain taxes, observance of Sunday as a public holiday, establishment of episcopal tribunals, and establishment of the right of the Church to manumit slaves. His conviction that the well-being of the empire was connected to the unity of the Church prompted him in 316 to hear the appeal of the Donatists personally (and to enforce his verdict against them when violence erupted) and also to summon and attend the Council of Nicaea (325) in an effort to resolve the burgeoning controversy in the East over Arius. Although at first he enforced its decrees, toward the end of his life he veered closer to the Arian position, pardoning Arius and his ally Eusebius of Nicomedia and in 336 even exiling Athanasius. But for his decisive patronage of the Church, for his humanitarian projects for debtors and the poor (especially children), and for his subvention of projects of church building among other things, he is venerated in the East as a saint. Feast day: May 21. *See also* Arianism; Constantine, Edict of; Constantinople; Helena, St.

JOHN C. CAVADINI

Constantinople, the traditional seat of Eastern Christianity. The emperor Constantine the Great (d. 337) transferred the capital of the Roman Empire from Rome to Constantinople in 330, building it on the site of the Greek city of Byzantium. Located on both sides of the Bosporus (linking the Black Sea and the Mediterranean Sea) in modern northwest

Turkey, Constantinople eventually became the largest and most splendid medieval European city. It remained the capital of the Eastern empire until 1453, when it fell to the Turks. However, it was the capital of the Latin empire from 1204 until 1261 following its capture by Crusaders. From 1453 until 1923 it was the capital of Turkey, under the name Istanbul. (In 1923 the Turkish capital was transferred to Ankara.)

Byzantium had a Christian community beginning probably in the second century. At first its bishop was subject to the see of Heraclea, but after the imperial capital was moved there and it became "New Rome," the bishop of Constantinople took his place of honor alongside the bishops of Alexandria, Antioch, and Rome. At the First Council of Constantinople (381), the local bishop was second only to the Bishop of Rome, and in 451, against the objections of Pope Leo the Great, the Council of Chalcedon's canon 28 granted Constantinople patriarchal status equivalent to Rome's, since both were imperial cities. Because of the council's action, the pope withheld his endorsement of the council's proceedings until March 21, 453, but even then he declared canon 28 invalid on the ground that it contravened the canons of the Council of Nicaea (325). Since the sixth century the patriarch of Constantinople has been recognized as the Ecumenical Patriarch of the East.

Tensions between Rome and Constantinople continued after the Council of Chalcedon, with the final breach traditionally linked with the year 1054 when Michael Cerularius, the patriarch of Constantinople, and his supporters were excommunicated by Pope Leo IX. The patriarch had shut down the Latin churches in Constantinople and launched an attack on the Western use of unleavened bread in the Eucharist. The bull of excommunication was dramatically laid on the altar of the Church of Santa Sophia (Hagia Sophia) in full view of the congregation. A week later the patriarch responded with counter-anathemas. On December 7, 1965, at the conclusion of the Second Vatican Council (1962–65), a joint declaration by Pope Paul VI and Ecumenical Patriarch Athenagoras I was read out deploring the mutual anathemas of 1054 and the schism that followed them. *See also* Asia Minor; Byzantine Italy; Byzantine rite; Byzantine style; Constantine the Great; Constantinople, councils of; Crusades; Great Schism; Hagia Sophia; primacy, papal; Rome.   *RICHARD P. MCBRIEN*

Constantinople, councils of, four church councils held in Constantinople between 381 and 870. The First Council of Constantinople (May to July 381), also called the Second Ecumenical Council, reiterated the Council of Nicaea's teaching on Christ's equality with God (against Arianism), recognized the full humanity of Jesus Christ (against Apollinarianism), and declared the divinity of the Holy Spirit (against the Pneumatomachians). The council was convoked by Emperor Theodosius I, who wanted to unite the Church on the basis of the Nicene faith, thereby ending the controversy over Arianism. In attendance were 186 bishops from the East (of whom 36 were considered "heretical"), but there were no bishops from the West and no representatives of Pope Damasus I. It was presided over by Meletius, bishop of Antioch (who died during the council), and then by Gregory of Nazianzus. It granted Constantinople honorary precedence over all churches except Rome. This council is usually credited with the Nicene-Constantinopolitan Creed (a longer version of the original creed of Nicaea), which was, in fact, formulated a few decades later.

The Second Council of Constantinople (May 5 to June 2, 553), the Fifth Ecumenical Council, posthumously condemned the "Three Chapters," i.e., Theodore of Mopsuestia (d. 428), Ibas of Edessa (d. 457), and Theodoret of Cyrrhus (d. ca. 458), on the grounds of Nestorianism. Motivated by the desire to reach a reconciliation with the Monophysites (who had been alienated by the Council of Chalcedon), Emperor Justinian I had issued an edict (543–44) condemning the three Antiochene theologians. Pope Vigilius disapproved of this edict, since it undermined the teaching of Chalcedon, which had not condemned Theodore of Mopsuestia. To resolve the ensuing controversy, Justinian I convened the council, which was attended by 165 bishops, almost entirely from the East. Vigilius did not attend, and afterward he was coerced into accepting the council's condemnation of the Three Chapters. The churches of Milan and Aquileia were so displeased with the pope's acceptance of the condemnation that each temporarily severed its ties with Rome.

The Third Council of Constantinople (November 7, 680, to September 6, 681), the Sixth Ecumenical Council, declared that Jesus Christ possessed both a human will and a divine will. Faced with the continuing adherence to Monothelitism (that Christ had only a divine will) in the East, Pope Agatho held a synod at Rome early in 680 and received confirmation of the teaching that Jesus Christ had two wills. In light of this decision, Emperor Constantine

IV immediately convoked a council of the bishops from Constantinople and Antioch. Agreeing with Agatho and the synod, the council reiterated the doctrine of the Council of Chalcedon and specified that the doctrine of the two natures implicitly affirms Christ's two wills, which function together in perfect moral harmony. The council also condemned the leaders of Monothelitism, including Macarius, the patriarch of Antioch, and the former pope Honorius I (d. 638).

The Fourth Council of Constantinople (October 5, 869, to February 28, 870), the Eighth Ecumenical Council in the view of the Catholic Church, condemned Photius, the former patriarch of Constantinople, in part because of his opposition to the inclusion of the *Filioque* clause in the Nicene-Constantinopolitan Creed. The council was convoked by Emperor Basil I to resolve the controversy surrounding Photius. It was attended by 103 bishops, most of whom were aligned with Rome. This council is not regarded as authoritative by the Orthodox Church, which instead recognizes the council of 879–80 in Constantinople, which approved of Photius and annulled the decision of the council of 869–70. *See also* Apollinarianism; Arianism; Holy Spirit; Monophysitism; Monothelitism; Nicene Creed; Pneumatomachians.   ROBERT A. KRIEG

constitution, apostolic. *See* apostolic constitution.

constitution, conciliar, the most solemn and formal type of document issued by an ecumenical council (Code of Canon Law, cans. 337–41). For the most part they deal with doctrinal matters, but they also treat matters of discipline or of other great significance. Vatican Council II (1962–65) promulgated a Constitution on the Sacred Liturgy (*Sacrosanctum Concilium*), a Dogmatic Constitution on the Church (*Lumen Gentium*), a Dogmatic Constitution on Divine Revelation (*Dei Verbum*), and a Pastoral Constitution on the Church in the Modern World (*Gaudium et Spes*). *See also* ecumenical council; Vatican Council II.

Constitution on the Sacred Liturgy (Lat., *Sacrosanctum Concilium,* "This holy council"), the first major official document of the Second Vatican Council, issued on December 4, 1963. It is a preamble for the entire work of the council that followed. Four themes govern the document: a renewed pastoral concern, an emphasis upon missionary adaptation, the first expression since Trent (1545–63) of

a clear desire for liturgy in the vernacular and the desire for clarified and simplified rites. Additionally, two significant principles emerged within the document. These principles indelibly marked the character of subsequent liturgical reform. The first is the statement that "the liturgy is the summit toward which the activity of the Church is directed; it is also the fountain from which all her power flows" (n. 10). With this statement, the council fathers clearly located the liturgical life of the Church within the Church's entire apostolate. A Church without prayer would be but another social service organization; a Church without commitments to the circumstances of people's lives could not be worshiping in the true spirit of Christ. The second principle is stated: "Pastors of souls must ... realize that, when the liturgy is celebrated, something more is required than the laws governing valid and lawful celebration. It is their duty also to ensure that the faithful take part fully aware of what they are doing, actively engaged in the rite and enriched by it" (n. 11). This principle, "full and active participation," is the single most cited norm governing the revision of rites following the council. Its importance lies in the fact that, for the first time, the Church has officially described the importance of the entire celebratory event of the liturgy.

Questions of validity had once dominated theological discussions of the liturgy. Were sacramental rites conducted according to the will of Christ and the Church? If they were minimally in accord with that norm, they were deemed effective, if not always licit. This new principle indicates the Church's desire that sacramental events must be celebrated in such a manner as not to hinder their reception by individuals, no matter what their cultural, physical, or mental conditions. The affective or subjective dimension of sacramental celebration cannot be ignored. Because God desires to save all people, so must the Church. And, because God desires to meet people in and through the sacraments and other liturgical rites of the Church, the Church must not hinder, even as it must regulate, the circumstances of that meeting.

Among the specific reforms recommended by the Constitution on the Sacred Liturgy are the promotion of liturgical studies in seminaries, religious houses, universities, and among the faithful (nn. 15–19); the establishment of diocesan liturgical commissions (n. 45); the inclusion of more Scripture in the liturgy (nn. 24, 35); the exercise of different ministerial roles by the laity (n. 29); the active participation of the congregation in word and song, preferably in the vernacular language (nn. 30, 54); the restoration of the biblically and liturgically based homily at most Masses (nn. 35, 52) and of the prayers of the faithful (n. 53); and the reception of Communion under both kinds, body and blood, for all the faithful (n. 55).

The Constitution also restored the catechumenate (n. 64) and called for a revision of the rites of all the sacraments and sacramentals (nn. 66–79), as well as that of the consecration of virgins (n. 80) and the rite of burial, which is to express more clearly the paschal character of death, and particularly the hope of resurrection (n. 81). The sacrament known as Extreme Unction, for example, is no longer to be administered exclusively for those at the point of death and may fittingly be called the sacrament of the Anointing of the Sick (n. 73).

The Constitution simplified the Divine Office, or Liturgy of the Hours, making Morning and Evening Prayer the two "hinges" upon which the prayer of the day is to turn (nn. 83–101). It also restored Sunday and feasts of the Lord to their central importance, while leaving the feasts of saints to local churches except in those cases where the individual saints have a universal significance (nn. 102–11).

Finally, the constitution recommended that singing should no longer be limited to the choir and clergy (nn. 112–21) and that sacred art and sacred furnishings should always "worthily and beautifully serve the dignity of worship" (n. 122). *See also* liturgy, theology of; worship.

Bibliography

Braza, L., and A. Bugnini, eds. *The Commentary on the Constitution and on the Instruction on the Sacred Liturgy.* New York: Benziger Brothers, 1982.

Flannery, Austin, ed. *Vatican Council II: The Conciliar and Post-Conciliar Documents.* Northport, NY: Costello, 1984. Vol. 1, pp. 1–36.

Jungmann, J. A. "Constitution on the Sacred Liturgy." In *Commentary on the Documents of Vatican II,* edited by H. Vorgrimler. New York: Herder and Herder, 1967. Vol 1, pp. 1–88. *JEFFREY T. VANDERWILT*

constitutions, religious, the stable, proper law of a religious institute. In addition to being regulated by the common or universal canon law of the Church, each religious institute has its own law, proper to itself. This law articulates the purposes for which a given institute exists and the general and particular means it uses to achieve its ends. As the theology of religious life regards each institute as having a particular charism or gift given to the Church, canon law sees that different institutes must have leeway within the general laws to express different particular gifts and often refers certain matters to a given institute's proper law. These proper laws and any changes thereto must receive approval from Church authority. They should articulate elements that remain stable in the life of the given institute. *See also* religious institute.

consubstantiation, the theory that the substance of bread and wine remain together with the body and blood of Christ in the eucharistic sacrament. From the earliest times, the liturgy, preaching, and theology had taught that the bread and wine are changed into the body and blood of Christ. Medieval theologians explained this as a change in the substance of the bread and wine into the body and blood of Christ (transubstantiation). Some writers, including Duns Scotus and the nominalists, did not consider consubstantiation to be contrary to the Scriptures or God's omnipotence but rejected it because of Church teaching affirming transubstantiation (Lateran IV, 1215).

Martin Luther favored the theory of consubstantiation, using as an analogy the Incarnation in which the divine and human natures coexist unchanged. He maintained that the bread and wine form a sacramental unity with the body and blood of Christ. In 1551 the Council of Trent rejected the theory of consubstantiation and reaffirmed the doctrine of transubstantiation. *See also* Real Presence; transubstantiation.

consultor. 1 Generally, an authority whose advice and sometimes consent is solicited or required, individually or as a member of a college. Roman curial offices frequently rely on consultors. Roman Congregations consult experts in their respective fields, individually and in council. The Apostolic Signatura calls upon its consultors for clarifications on the law and opinions in specific cases.

2 A member of an official papal study commission (Lat., *coetus*), such as the Pontifical Commission for the Revision of the Code of Canon Law.

3 In diocesan contexts, a member of the college of consultors. *See also* consultors, college of; *peritus*.

consultors, college of, mandatory diocesan consultative body of six to twelve priests (or bishops) selected by the diocesan bishop from among presbyteral council members for a five-year term. It is principally a transitional or temporary governing board when a see is vacant or impeded and its functions are strictly stated in canon law. As a board of financial trustees, it advises the bishop on naming and removing the finance officer. With the finance council, its consent is required for acts of extraordinary administration and for the alienation of Church property. *See also* consultor.

consummated marriage, marriage in which sexual intercourse, freely engaged in by both parties, has taken place. This intercourse, an act open to procreation, is a sign of that communion of the whole of life between spouses that marriage is, and in a sacramental marriage it is also a sign of the union of Christ and the Church (Eph 5:32). The medieval argument about whether consent or consummation made the marriage resulted in the theory that, although consent made the marriage, intercourse established the marriage in a more stable manner. *See also* Marriage; marriage law.

Contarini, Gasparo, 1483–1542, lay reformer and cardinal. A Venetian noble made cardinal in 1535, he is best known for his efforts at administrative reform within the Catholic Church and his mediating efforts between Catholics and Protestants at Regensburg (1541). His compromise theological formulations were rejected by both sides.

contemplation, prayer in which reasoning and structure give way to a simple focus on God's presence. It is traditionally distinguished from active meditation. In the West, such distinctions derive from the monastic *lectio divina* (Lat.), prayerful reflection on Scripture. Later medieval writers distinguished four stages in this process. Reading led to meditation, a ruminative repetition of a word or phrase until mind and heart were filled with it. Prayer, as conversation with God, followed naturally. Sometimes this led into contemplation, or simply "being present" to God. In practice, contemplation takes different forms. Some writers, such as Ignatius of Loyola, use "contemplation" both in the traditional sense and to describe the use of imagination in praying with Scripture.

Classical expressions, such as that of John of the Cross or *The Cloud of Unknowing,* may appear narrow by assuming the necessity of a monastic or solitary context for contemplation. However, they suggest important features of the experience that do remain valid. First, contemplation is not a method of prayer to be chosen at will. Contemplation is a gift into which one is drawn. Second, contemplation is associated with questions of life-style and attitude;

it is a way of being, not merely of praying. Third, contemplation involves the deepest levels of one's desire where hopes, needs, and personal identity fuse, as it were, with the all-embracing presence of God's love. Fourth, familiar methods of prayer cease to satisfy. The experience is one of relative stillness and receptivity rather than activity.

Contemplation does not bypass Scripture or Jesus but is fed by them. Contemplation is not totally passive, for desire still operates and choice is still possible. Often there are few or no words in prayer, yet it is simplistic to say that contemplation is totally "wordless" or "imageless" in all circumstances. *See also* meditation; prayer. PHILIP SHELDRAKE

contemplative life, a life characterized by solitude and prayer, which dispose one toward contemplation. Ancient and especially medieval monasticism perceived its way of life as contemplative; nuns and monks were called contemplatives. Medieval interest in the mystical life perceived the contemplative life as mystical in orientation. For some men and usually for women the enclosure was seen as a necessary safeguard of the contemplative life. Post–Vatican II developments have shown an interest in a broader conception of the contemplative life for laity and religious yet one that retains the solitude necessary for living in the presence of God. *See also* contemplation; mysticism.

continence, a term that pertains to partial or complete abstention from sexual activity, but whose usage is not uniform. Sometimes the word is meant to signify mere material abstinence from sexual acts. In this sense, the term is entirely different from chastity, which is a virtue inclining one to moderate sexual expression according to right reason illumined by faith. At other times continence is taken to mean the persevering will to maintain chastity amid difficulties. Continence in this second sense lacks the perfection of chastity, which connotes facility. But goodwill is present, leading some theologians to call it "the diminished virtue of chastity." *See also* sexual morality.

contraception. *See* birth control.

contract, canonical, a contract recognized by Church law. As a general principle, canon law follows the secular laws of the applicable jurisdiction with respect to contracts. In a Church court, therefore, judgments concerning contracts would be made on the basis of the secular law in question. Exceptions to this rule are instances where the secular law violates natural or divine law, e.g., if the secular law would not permit ecclesiastical institutions to make contracts.

contrition, a desire for forgiveness of sins. Since medieval times, contrition has often been divided into two types: perfect contrition, based on the love of God; and imperfect contrition, sometimes called "attrition," based on fear of hell and the horror of one's own evil. Medieval discussion focused on a process for justification with Peter of Poitiers's form finally becoming standard: contrition, confession, absolution, and satisfaction. Franciscan theologians considered contrition only as an integral part of the sacrament of Penance; Dominican theologians considered it an essential part of the sacrament. In the Reformation the relationship of contrition to good works became a major source of dispute. In current Catholic theology, God's gift of grace is the basis for all contrition, which is considered an ever-present aspect of one's Christian life. Therefore, contrition is not simply an individual act but a lifelong process. *See also* attrition; confession, auricular; imperfect contrition; perfect contrition; Reconciliation.

contumacy, in canon law contempt for the law, the defiant disposition of one who knowingly persists in crime or delinquency in contempt of Church authority. Inexcusable delay in answering a summons or following an order of the court could result in a declaration of contumacy. In penal law, contumacy may be inferred from repeated offenses.

By its obstruction of the institutes of justice through recidivism or dilatory subterfuge, contumacy wounds both the offender and the Church community. Penalties aim at reconciliation and restitution and are not imposed without warning. Even if the offender should cease from contumacy, compensation may be required for any detriment to individuals or the community.

convalidation, ratification of a canonically invalid marriage. In simple convalidation this is done by means of a new act of consent. Convalidation always presupposes that the parties once attempted and still intend marital commitment. The attempted marriage, nevertheless, was invalid due to a defect of consent, certain impediments, or, if at least one party was Catholic, failure to comply with canonical form.

Before convalidation, invalidating factors must have ceased or been dispensed from. Then at least the Catholic parties must renew their consent in some manner, depending upon the invalidating factor: its nature, public or private character, and apparentness to each party. *See also* marriage law.

convent (Lat., *conventus,* "assembly," "meeting"), an association of religious; also, the building in which they reside. The term originally applied to congregations of twelve or more professed men or women. The Council of Trent (1545–63) included smaller houses in its definition by distinguishing between major convents (twelve or more professed members) and minor convents (fewer than twelve). The term is not found in the 1983 Code of Canon Law, which prefers to speak of institutes, houses, or monasteries of nuns (cans. 573–709). The word is used in the constitutions of some male and female mendicant orders. In its most common contemporary usage, it refers to residences of religious women who are bound together by vows to a religious life under a superior. In a less precise usage, it refers to the parochial residence of the teaching sisters of a parish school.

conventual Mass, the celebration of the Eucharist to which women and men in religious orders and congregations are obliged by their rule or constitutions. This is usually a daily obligation. This daily celebration of the Eucharist is meant to be the source and summit of the common search for holiness in religious communities. *See also* Eucharist; eucharistic spirituality; Mass.

Conventuals, a branch of the Franciscan order taking its name from the large urban friaries or convents that were increasingly characteristic of Franciscan life after the mid-thirteenth century. As the order settled down from its earlier itinerant lifestyle, friars increasingly adopted a life-style characteristic of regular canons, with a daily routine centered on the Liturgy of the Hours; friars generally spent most of the day in their convents, with the faithful gathering for services in their churches. The needs of these larger communities led to certain modifications in the original practice of strict poverty legislated in the Rule of St. Francis; after 1322, the Franciscans accepted papal privileges to own and administer their property and handle money like the other mendicant orders. As the Observant reform began in the later part of the century, there was increasing pressure to return to a more primitive tradition. The term "Conventual" was actually first applied during the resulting controversies in the early fifteenth century to those friars whose communities wished to remain with the more mitigated style of life rejected by the reform party. Finally, the Conventual and Observant friars were separated into two independent congregations in 1517. The Conventuals have continued to favor adaptation of the Franciscan way of life in order to serve the current pastoral needs of the Church. *See also* Francis, Rule of St.; Franciscan order.

conversi (Lat., "the changed"), old term for monks, known as lay brothers, not obliged to attend choir services, i.e., not bound to the chanting of the Divine Office. The vocation of the *conversi* was attractive to the illiterate because they were not obliged to participate in the celebration of the Liturgical Hours. Their work usually involved some form of manual labor. *See also* choir; lay brother; monk.

conversion, the profound transformation of mind, will, and heart toward God. Although conversion is often associated with entry into a particular religion or denomination, its fundamental meaning rests in that personal transformation whereby a person lives by a profoundly new assessment of what is important and valuable. Conversion generally is associated with religious acknowledgment of God. In the Christian understanding, religious conversion is a response to the awesome presence of God's grace and self-revelation. Beside religious conversion, however, one may also distinguish several other types. Intellectual conversion occurs, for example, when a thinker no longer limits the "real" only to what can be seen or empirically verified. Moral conversion involves the transformation of one's behavior, for one chooses what is truly valuable rather than satisfies spontaneous, unreflected desires. And affective, or psychic, conversion is the ongoing process of taking responsibility for the state of one's feelings, including those urges and drives in one's subconscious that lead to compulsive, addictive, or other harmful behavior. Each of these conversions, as transforming, enables individuals to begin to become the kind of persons that God intends but that sin prevents humans from being—self-constituting, responsible, good, and holy. Conversion opens up the horizon out of which we think and act by challenging the slavery due to sin (Rom 6:6), which darkens the mind, distorts the will, and

suffocates the heart. Religious conversion, a gift of grace, opens a person to the ultimate horizon, the promise of union or friendship with God. *See also* discipleship.   MARK MILLER

convert (Lat., *convertere,* "to turn around"), one who has turned to belief in Christ or to religious faith. In popular, though inaccurate, Catholic usage, a convert is a former non-Catholic Christian now practicing Christian faith as a Catholic. *See also* conversion; discipleship.

Conway, Katherine, 1853–1927, journalist and educator. She served as managing editor for the *Boston Pilot* (1905–8), managing editor for Boston's *The Republic,* adjunct professor at St. Mary's College, Notre Dame, Indiana, and recipient of the University of Notre Dame's Laetare Medal (1907). Conway's numerous essays and novels emphasized the traditional role of Catholic women. *See also* Laetare Medal.

Cooke, Terence J., 1921–83, cardinal-archbishop of New York. Ordained in 1945, Cooke became secretary to Cardinal Francis Spellman (1958), and advanced from chancellor to auxiliary bishop and vicar general, succeeding Spellman as archbishop of New York in 1968. Credited with great administrative and financial skills, he was especially revered for his personal spirituality.

cooperation in evil, concurrence with another in a sinful external act. Such concurrence may be either moral or physical in character.

Cooperation was traditionally divided into formal and material. Formal cooperation is that wherein the cooperator consents to the evil action of the other and thus directly intends it. Therefore, there is concurrence with not only the evil act but with the evil intent.

Material cooperation is that whereby one provides a certain aid for another without either explicitly or implicitly sharing the evil intent. For instance, one steadies the ladder for the robbers entering another's house to rob it. Material cooperation can be immediate (in the act itself, e.g., one helps the robbers carry the stolen safe) or mediate (one sells a gun to a suspicious individual). Furthermore, material cooperation may be proximate or remote depending on whether the cooperator's action is causally proximate or remote to the wrongful act. It may be necessary or unnecessary depending on whether the evil effect can be produced without the cooperation or not.

All theologians condemn formal cooperation since it involves one in approval of another's wrongdoing and therefore immediately activates one's own attitudes toward good and evil. Material cooperation is ordinarily wrong because one is bound not to fortify a neighbor in wrongdoing by becoming a partner to the externalization of his or her evil designs. Under certain conditions, however, it becomes morally permissible. First, one's own contribution must not be the evil act itself (one must not, e.g., join a killing stab-fest). Second, there must be a proportionate reason for contributing to the wrongdoing. Whether the reason is morally justified will depend on many factors: the nature of the evil, the proximity and necessity of the cooperation, etc. These concrete considerations are often very complex and mean that, while the general principles are clear, in practice this is the most difficult question in all of moral theology.   RICHARD A. MCCORMICK

cope (Lat., *cappa* or *capa,* "cape"), an ankle-length cloak worn by a bishop or priest at ceremonies other than Mass. Usually made of silk, it is draped over

Cope

cope

the shoulders and fastened, chest-high, with a clasp. The remnant of a hood, shaped like a shield, adorns the back. *See also* vestments.

Copleston, Frederick C., 1907–94, historian of philosophy. After studying at Oxford, he joined the Society of Jesus in 1930 and was ordained in 1937. Professor of the history of philosophy at Heythrop College (where he also served as principal, 1970–74), the Gregorian University in Rome, and the University of London, he authored the highly praised, multivolume *History of Philosophy,* covering the full scope of philosophical development from the pre-Socratics (sixth and fifth centuries B.C.) to Jean-Paul Sartre (d. 1980).

Copt, Coptic (Arab., *gupt,* from *gypt* in *Aigyptos;* Gk., "Egyptian"), terms for the original Egyptians, the remnant of those who successfully resisted the Islamization of that land. Coptic was the native language of Egypt before the Arab conquest of 640 and the consequent Arabization led to its disappearance as a living tongue. Coptic existed in several dialects, one of which, Bohairic, has survived as the liturgical language of Coptic Christians. Coptic literature, which flourished from the third century until the Arab conquest, mostly in the Sahidic dialect, was largely a monastic and popular literature or translations from the Greek. Greek was the language of the upper strata of Egyptian society, the intellectuals of Alexandria and the coast, some of whom, like Athanasius (d. 373), wrote in Coptic as well. Anthony of Egypt (d. 355) and Pachomius (d. 347) wrote in Coptic, but the greatest Coptic writer was Shenute of Atripe (d. ca. 457), abbot of the White Monastery at Atripe near modern Sohag. *See also* Coptic Catholic Church; Coptic rite.

Coptic Catholic Church, the ecclesiastical community of Coptic-rite Catholics who are in communion with Rome. Coptic Catholics are based in Egypt (the Arabic derivation of the word "Copt" means Egyptian). The Coptic Catholic Church is the Catholic counterpart to the Coptic Orthodox Church, which has never accepted the teaching of the Council of Chalcedon (451) that in Christ there are two natures, human and divine, and not only one divine nature, as the Monophysites held.

A formal reconciliation between the Catholic and Coptic Orthodox churches took place with the signing of the document *Cantate Domino* by a Coptic delegation at the Council of Florence on February 4,

1442. But because this act was not supported in Egypt, it had no practical results.

Catholic missionaries began to work more intensely among the Copts in the seventeenth century, with the Franciscans in the lead. A Capuchin mission was founded in Cairo in 1630, and in 1675 the Jesuits began missionary activity in Egypt. During the same century a number of lengthy but fruitless theological exchanges took place between Rome and the Coptic Church.

In 1741 a Coptic bishop in Jerusalem, Amba Athanasius, became Catholic. Pope Benedict XIV appointed him vicar apostolic of the small community of Egyptian Coptic Catholics, which at that time numbered no more than two thousand. Although Athanasius eventually returned to communion with the Coptic Orthodox Church, a line of Catholic vicars apostolic continued after him.

In 1824, under the mistaken impression that the Ottoman viceroy wished it to do so, the Holy See erected a patriarchate for Coptic Catholics, but for now it only existed on paper. The Ottoman authorities permitted the Coptic Catholics to begin building their own churches in 1829.

In 1895 Leo XIII reestablished the patriarchate, and in 1899 he appointed Cyril Makarios as Patriarch Cyril II "of Alexandria of the Copts." Cyril had presided over a Catholic Coptic synod in 1898 that introduced a number of Latin practices, but he became embroiled in controversy and felt compelled to resign in 1908. The office remained vacant until 1947, when a new patriarch was finally elected, and the line that continues today began.

While the offices of the patriarchate are located in Cairo, the largest concentration of Coptic Catholics has always been in Upper Egypt. In more recent times, however, there has been some migration to other parts of the country.

Most candidates for the priesthood are trained at St. Leo's Patriarchal Seminary in Maadi, a suburb of Cairo. There are also minor seminaries at Tahta and Alexandria. More than one hundred Coptic Catholic parishes administer primary schools, and some have secondary schools as well. The church maintains a hospital in Assuit, a number of medical dispensaries and clinics, and several orphanages.

There are no Coptic Catholic monasteries that would rival the Coptic Orthodox monastic tradition, but there are religious orders modeled on Western apostolic communities involved in educational, medical, and charitable activities. The Coptic Congregation of the Preaching of Saint Mark was founded in 1959, and there are also Coptic branches of the Franciscans, Jesuits, and Lazarists. There are also two Coptic Catholic orders of sisters, the Egyptian Religious of the Sacred Heart and the Coptic Sisters of Jesus and Mary. In 1992 the church had six dioceses with about 200 priests and 180,000 faithful, making it by far the largest Catholic church in Egypt. *See also* Chalcedon, Council of; Copt, Coptic; Coptic rite; Eastern Catholics and ecumenism; Eastern Catholics and Rome; Eastern churches; Eastern liturgies; Eastern rites.   RONALD G. ROBERSON

Coptic rite, the liturgical traditions of the Coptic Orthodox and Catholic churches of Egypt, the modern form of the ancient Alexandrian rite as it developed among the Coptic-speaking Christians of Egypt in the period following the division of the Egyptian church after the Council of Chalcedon in 451. Egyptian Christianity began in Hellenic Alexandria, but by the third century there were numerous Coptic-speaking converts, and the Scriptures and liturgy had been translated into the native tongue. But it was monasticism that solidified Coptic Christianity as a native counterbalance to the cosmopolitan, theologically sophisticated Hellenic church of Alexandria, whose speculative, spiritualizing intellectualism stood in marked contrast to the popular, traditionalistic piety of the peasant and monastic Upper Egypt south of the Delta, a largely oral culture transmitted through sayings, proverbs, and ritual, rather than theological treatises. This monastic culture, concrete and ascetic, created the liturgy, offices, and spirituality of the Coptic rite. In the aftermath of the Council of Chalcedon those who had rejected its decisions suffered fierce persecution by the orthodox Chalcedonians until the Arab conquest of 640. This period sealed the separation of the two traditions and put an end to Greek dominance of Egyptian Christianity forever. The Coptic patriarchate, forced to flee Alexandria, took refuge in the Monastery of St. Macarius in the desert of Scetis, the present Wadi an-Natrun halfway between Cairo and Alexandria. Today's Coptic rite is basically the monastic usage of Scetis somewhat modified by later reforms. Coptic Orthodox patriarch Gabriel II Ibn Turayk (1131–45) reduced the number of anaphoras (the central prayer of the Eucharist, including the consecration, anamnesis, and Communion) to the present three (St. Mark/Cyril, St. Basil, St. Gregory), and Gabriel V (1409–27) composed a *Liturgical Order* to unify divergent usages. These regulations still govern the Coptic rite.

The present Coptic rite has been strongly marked by this history. Its liturgical language is Bohairic, the Coptic dialect of Lower Egypt. Its spirituality and offices are strongly monastic, popular, ascetic; its liturgy and offices highly penitential, contemplative, long, solemn, even monotonous, with much less speculative poetry, symbolic splendor, and sumptuous ceremonial than, for example, the Byzantine rite. *See also* Coptic Catholic Church.   ROBERT F. TAFT

Corbie, daughterhouse of Luxeuil founded in 657 and richly endowed by Bathild, the Anglo-Saxon wife of Clovis II. With an extensive library and an important scriptorium, it remained a strong cultural center under the Carolingians. *See also* Luxeuil.

Corcoran, James A., 1820–89, priest, theologian, educator, and editor. A native of Charleston, South Carolina, and trained in Rome, Corcoran taught theology at seminaries in Charleston (1844–61) and Philadelphia (1870–89). He was editor of the *United States Catholic Miscellany* (1848–61) and a founding editor of the *American Catholic Quarterly Review* (1876). The outstanding American expert on conciliar legislation, he was the U.S. representative in preparing for the First Vatican Council (1869–70) and a *peritus* (Lat., adviser) to Archbishop Martin Spalding of Baltimore. *See also* Vatican Council I.

Coredemptrix, title describing the Blessed Virgin Mary's role in the world's salvation. The title is rare today because of its pastoral and ecumenical difficulties. A three-stage progression marked the growth of this view of Mary: (1) By her consent at the Annunciation and by her actual maternity, Mary gives life to Christ and, therefore, brings redemption into the world (from the patristic era). (2) By offering Christ in the sacrifice on the cross and by suffering in her heart the wounds he receives in his flesh, she actively shares in the redemptive work of her Son at its most critical moment (early medieval era). (3) By her maternal mercy and intercession in heaven, she continues to distribute the fruits of Christ's redemption to unworthy sinners (late medieval era). Given the misunderstanding that this title occasions, seeming to reduce Christ to being one-half of a team of redeemers, Vatican II deliberately omitted it from its Marian teaching. *See also* Mary, Blessed Virgin; redemption.

Cornelius, St., pope and martyr. A Roman priest elected as Bishop of Rome in 251 after the Decian persecution of 250, he held out the right of forgiveness (against the rigorists) to those who renounced their faith in time of persecution. He died in exile in 253. Feast day: September 16.

coronation, papal, the crowning of a pope with the tiara at the beginning of his term of office. The tiara is a beehive-shaped headdress with a triple crown, formerly used for certain nonliturgical papal ceremonies. The bishops of Rome began wearing the tiara in the third century. At first the tiaras were simple in design, but by the time of the Renaissance they were made of precious metals and ornamented with costly jewels. The coronation of the pope was modeled after the coronation of secular royalty. This was not unfitting since the pope was a temporal as well as a spiritual ruler. Pope Paul VI (1963–78) sold his tiara and gave the proceeds to the poor. Since then, the popes have chosen to be installed rather than crowned in order to emphasize the essentially spiritual role of the papacy today.

corporal (Lat., *corpus,* "body"), an approximately twenty-inch-square white linen cloth placed on the altar under the chalice, paten, and host. Together with the pall, the corporal derives from the uppermost of two earlier full-length altar cloths. Its name indicates its role of holding the eucharistic body of Christ.

corporal works of mercy. *See* mercy, corporal works of.

Corpus Christi, Feast of, Solemnity of the Body and Blood of Christ on the Sunday following Trinity Sunday. This feast originated in the diocese of Liège, France (1246), based on revelations of the French nun Juliana of Mont-Cornillon (1192–1258). Enthusiastic acceptance in Europe led to universal promulgation by Pope Urban IV in 1264. From its inception, the feast celebrated both the body and blood of Jesus Christ. In a sense, it duplicates the eucharistic focus of Holy Thursday, highlighting the redemptive effects of the sacrament. A prominent feature of the feast since the fourteenth century has been a eucharistic procession. Current legislation allows a procession immediately after Mass in which the host to be carried has been consecrated, or after a lengthy period of public adoration. The procession may take place on or near the feast day itself. *See also* blood of Christ; Body of Christ.

Corpus Iuris Canonici (kohr'puhs yoor'is kuh-nahn'ee-chee; Lat., "Body of Canon Law"), collection of Church laws firmly established by the sixteenth century and used as a text and primary reference until the 1917 code of canon law. It includes Gratian's Decree followed by various collections of papal decretals. *See also* canon law; Code of Canon Law.

Corrigan, Michael Augustine, 1839–1902, American prelate. Born in Newark, New Jersey, educated at Mount St. Mary's College in Emmitsburg, Maryland, and the Roman Urban College, he served first as director of the seminary at Seton Hall College in South Orange, New Jersey (1864–69), and then as president of the institution. From 1873 to 1880 he was bishop of Newark, then was coadjutor to Cardinal John McCloskey of New York for five years before succeeding him as archbishop. During his long administration of the archdiocese (1885–1902) he developed and consolidated many charitable institutions, schools, a seminary, and ethnic parishes to meet the growing needs of the pluralistic Catholic population. He also became the leader of the conservative forces in opposition to the "Americanists," especially in his disciplining of Edward McGlynn and in his promotion of parochial education. *See also* Americanism.

Cor Unum (Lat., "one heart"), an international organization founded by Pope Paul VI in 1971 to co-ordinate Catholic relief services and to disseminate necessary information worldwide.

Cosmas and Damian, Sts., martyrs. Nothing certain is known of these men. According to legend they were twin brothers who left their native Arabia in order to practice medicine. Exemplary Christians, they died in the persecution of Diocletian in 303. With St. Luke, they are the patron saints of physicians. Feast day: September 26.

cosmology, the empirical science that seeks to understand the origin, evolution, and large-scale structure of the universe. The reigning cosmological theory is the "Big Bang" model, which proposes that the entire universe—space itself—is expanding out of a "singularity," an initial state of infinite density. Based on the observed rate of expansion (measured by how fast galaxies appear to be receding from one another), the model estimates the visible universe is from ten to twenty billion years old. As cosmologists continue to debate the validity of the model in light of new data, scientific evidence that the visible universe had an origin in time should not be seen as evidence for creation. Moreover, science is in principle incapable of detecting an absolute beginning for all that exists. For example, cosmologists cannot rule out the possibility that the universe endlessly expands and contracts. *See also* Big Bang; creation.

Couderc, St. Teresa, 1805–85, French-born founder of the Congregation of Our Lady of the Retreat in the Cenacle (R.C.), devoted to giving retreats for laywomen. Feast day: September 26.

Coughlin, Charles Edward, 1891–1979, priest and political activist. Born in Hamilton, Ontario, Coughlin became a member of the Basilian Fathers and was educated at St. Michael's College (Toronto). He was ordained in 1916. In 1923, he became a diocesan priest, subject to the authority of the bishop of Detroit. In 1926 Coughlin established a parish in Royal Oak, Michigan, a suburb of Detroit and a center of Ku Klux Klan activity. After a cross burning at his church, The Shrine of the Little Flower, Coughlin convinced a Detroit radio station, WRJ, of the necessity for a program to offset religious bigotry. Coughlin's melodic and authoritative voice soon captured the attention of the nation. By 1932, Coughlin's weekly audience numbered an estimated forty million listeners and he became known as "the Radio Priest." His broadcasts shifted from religious themes to political and economic issues. Though initially an enthusiastic supporter of President Franklin D. Roosevelt, by 1934 Coughlin was railing against Roosevelt's policies. Coughlin believed that the Roosevelt administration was infiltrated by Communists and controlled by international bankers. He organized the National Union for Social Justice (1934), which provided the foundation for the Union Party (1936), and he established the weekly newspaper, *Social Justice* (1936). When Coughlin's broadcasts became saturated with anti-Semitic and pro-Nazi and fascist rhetoric, his credibility was destroyed. After Pearl Harbor, Coughlin, pressured by his bishop and the U.S. government, withdrew from public life and returned to parish work in Royal Oak. *See also* Church and state.   *JANET WELSH*

council, official gathering of Church leaders and representatives that assists in the process of decision making within the Church. Councils of bishops have a particular role in the governance of the Church. Ecumenical councils are supreme exercises of the collegial authority of bishops. Current canon law allows only the pope as head of the episcopal college to call an ecumenical council, though not all ecumenical councils have, in the past, been called by the pope. The pope has, as well, the sole responsibility to set the council's agenda and to approve the decisions of the council.

In addition to the worldwide gathering of bishops in an ecumenical council, gatherings of bishops and ecclesiastical superiors may occur on a national (plenary) level or regional (provincial) level. Examples of nonecumenical councils of the Church are those held at Arles in France (314), Milan in Italy (355), Pisa in Italy (1409), and the three plenary councils of Baltimore (1852, 1866, 1884). The word "council" is also applied to other groups of clergy, religious, and laity that offer advice on financial and pastoral matters. *See also* ecumenical council.

council, finance. *See* finance council.

council, provincial. *See* provincial council.

Council for Promoting Christian Unity. *See* Pontifical Council for Promoting Christian Unity.

Council for the Family. *See* Pontifical Council for the Family.

Council for the Interpretation of Legislative Texts. *See* Pontifical Council for the Interpretation of Legislative Texts.

Council for the Laity. *See* Pontifical Council for the Laity.

Council of Major Religious Superiors of Women Religious, an organization of superiors of active apostolic women's congregations in the United States, it is parallel in canonical status with the Leadership Conference of Women Religious (LCWR). Approved by the Holy See in 1992 and representing about 10 percent of active congregations, it is a more traditional grouping of religious that works closely with the Church hierarchy in fostering communally lived profession of vows and community-based ministries. *See also* Consortium Perfectae Caritatis; Leadership Conference of Women Religious.

councils of Baltimore. *See* Baltimore, councils of.

counseling, pastoral. a specialized aspect of the practical face-to-face response of the Church's ministers to the human problems and possibilities of its members. This discipline is rooted in the traditional "cure [or care] of souls." These roughly synonymous words imply not only modes of dealing with the troubled individuals but a generalized and, to some degree, institutionally committed attitude of concern and responsibility for the spiritual well-being of believers.

Care of the Soul: Soul, in this formulation, was considered to mean the spiritual principle that identifies the individual and, while essentially eternal, is conditioned by and tested through the field of time. Pastoral counseling is a manner of dealing with the person, that unity of soul and body to which "soul" refers in an extended sense. Pastoral counseling aims, then, not only at leading the soul to holiness but to integrating the disordered and compromising emotional conflicts that characterize men and women in what is commonly referred to as "the human condition."

This mission has been associated, in traditions as different in orientation and practice as those of philosophers and tribal medicine men, with "healing," that is, with restoring tranquillity to and making whole again the spirits of those seeking assistance. Socrates sought to be *iatros tes psuches* (Gk.), a healer of the soul, the words that, reformulated, are recognized in the title "psychiatrist."

While figures such as Socrates and, later, Cicero in his *De Consolatione* offered what might be termed natural wisdom about the gains and losses of life, strong dogmatic and moral theological notes were introduced in the practice of the great religious traditions, which viewed the "care of souls" as one of their primary obligations. The wedding of the insights and styles of psychological and psychiatric therapy for emotional disturbance with traditional pastoral responses occurred in the latter third of the twentieth century. These dimensions defined pastoral counseling as a distinctively modern phenomenon.

Modern pastoral counseling descends, in the Catholic as well as other traditions, through, and has been modified by, complex interactions of history and culture as well as steadily unfolding theological exploration and debate. The latter have centered on human nature as well as the meaning and implication of various doctrinal positions and practices, such as those concerning Penance, for the ultimate healing of the soul, which is salvation.

Spiritual Direction: The art of "spiritual direction," as it has been known, was a true precursor of pastoral counseling. This practice reflects, in its fashions and traditions, a history of Catholic spirituality, including, for example, the evolutionary and shifting perceptions of institutional Catholicism's authority over the souls of individual Catholics.

Spiritual direction was at one time linked closely with the sacrament of Penance (now Reconciliation) and ordered almost exclusively to the sanctification of "souls," as individual Catholics have commonly been described in the vocabulary of pastoral practice. Tension arose as this personal pursuit of holiness came to be measured by the individual's "obedience" or "docility" to the authority of the institutional Church as expressed through the latter's ecclesiastical leaders, structures, and regulations.

Pastoral counseling developed an identity separate from spiritual direction as a result of the gradual and hesitant acceptance within Catholicism of the legitimacy of psychiatric and psychological theories and therapies in identifying and treating what were once classified as "spiritual" problems. For example, "scrupulosity," once considered and dealt with as a torment of souls excessively sensitive to religious obligations, came to be recognized as fundamentally a problem of obsessive-compulsive behavior requiring treatment by psychological methods.

Such an understanding does not, in the richest meaning of pastoral counseling, eliminate or preclude the spiritual impact or significance of such an experience. Indeed, it is essential for an understanding of pastoral counseling to recall that every spiritual experience has psychological effects, just as every psychological state has spiritual effects.

Catholic and Protestant Approaches: The American Protestant tradition pioneered the use of scientific counseling as a psychologically based adjunct in pastoral work. Influenced by Carl Rogers, and such students of his as Seward Hiltner at Princeton, client-centered or nondirective counseling became its dominant methodology. This approach implemented a democratized, American emphasis on the inborn capacity of individuals to identify and deal with their emotional problems, setting them against more traditional advice giving from experts or the expectations of institutional authority.

In Roman Catholicism, counseling for Catholics and its use by parish priests was successfully introduced through a series of books that carefully demonstrated its compatibility with Church teaching and organizational practices. Thus Father Charles

A. Curran (not to be confused with the theologian of the same first and last names), a student of Rogers, employed Thomistic philosophical categories to explain client-centered therapy in his *Counseling in Catholic Life and Education* (1952). This became the text in the pastoral counseling program for its priests that was initiated and underwritten by the archdiocese of Chicago in 1956. This was soon replicated at The Catholic University of America (1959) as well as in seminaries, institutes, and in other institutions of higher learning.

In American Protestantism, pastoral counseling rapidly developed into a specialty that distinguished itself from traditional pastoral work, provoking intense conflict about ministers who, in effect, became professional, fee-compensated therapists dealing almost exclusively with psychological problems. While such a distinction has not occurred on any large scale within Catholicism, which has continued to associate most counseling with pastoral settings, the influence of such Protestant-originated programs as clinical pastoral education in seminary training has been extensive.

Pastoral counseling had, by the last decade of the twentieth century, become an accepted aspect of Catholic life. Some of its techniques were joined again to the sacrament of Reconciliation when the practice of the latter was reformed in the mid-1970s, with debatable results, to incorporate counseling-like settings as an alternative to the traditional confessional box.

Pastoral counseling remains closely related to formal parish and educational settings in the Catholic tradition. Significant issues, such as those concerning its focus, professional standards, govern-ing theories, and capacities for adequate self-monitoring and supervision demand ongoing review and exploration. *See also* Catholicism and psychology/psychiatry; soul; spiritual direction.

Bibliography
Kennedy, Eugene C., and Sara Charles. *On Becoming a Counselor: A Basic Guide for Non-Professional Counselors.* New York: Continuum, 1990.   EUGENE C. KENNEDY AND SARA C. CHARLES

counsels, evangelical, ideals, known as poverty, chastity, and obedience, given by Jesus to those who would live perfect Christian lives. In their efforts to appropriate the austere and sometimes obscure ethical sayings of Jesus as presented by the NT and read in the context of the Hebrew Scriptures, the early churches adopted two complementary strategies for translating these texts into practical moral codes.

They tended to equate the minimal moral demands of the Christian life, which were seen as absolutely necessary for salvation, with the basic requirements of natural law; these latter were in turn equated with the Ten Commandments. Seen in this context, Jesus' more austere demands could be interpreted as ideals rather than as absolute commands. At the same time, the early churches created institutional structures within which individuals who wished to put the ideals of Jesus' morality into practice could attempt to do so. These structures gave rise to monasticism and other forms of organized religious life. The teachings of Jesus by which these communities tried to live came to be summarized as the evangelical counsels of poverty, chastity (which in this context is equivalent to celibacy), and obedience, so called because they were seen as Jesus' invitations to a more perfect imitation of him rather than as commands placed on all Christians. The exact meaning of these counsels has of course varied considerably, in correspondence with the different forms of religious life that have flourished within the Church. *See also* chastity; obedience; poverty.

Counter-Reformation/Catholic Reformation, European Catholic spiritual, intellectual, and institutional renewal of the late fifteenth and sixteenth centuries enabling the Catholic Church to recover from the Protestant Reformation and establishing Catholic practice and theology until the Second Vatican Council (1962–65). Historians debate whether this renewal was primarily a reaction to nascent Protestantism (Counter-Reformation), an independent inner renewal of Catholic Christianity (Catholic Reformation), or whether both the Protestant and Catholic Reformations developed from a single reforming impulse. The emerging modern consensus is that the inner renewal of fifteenth- and sixteenth-century Christian life produced both Protestantism and the Catholic Reformation and that the impulse to renewal was employed successfully by the Catholic Church to thwart Protestant advances in sixteenth- and seventeenth-century Europe (Counter-Reformation).

The demand for "reformation of head and members" that also brought about the Protestant Reformation attacked clerical immorality, especially concubinage, and fiscal and moral abuses throughout Western Christendom, but particularly in Rome. The Counter-Reformation ultimately intertwined separate strands of reform. Spontaneous lay and clerical spiritual renewals forced reluctant ecclesiastical institutions to recognize and incorporate them into the structure of Catholicism, which managed to moderate and tame the most extreme and independent elements. Finally, Catholic princes in Spain, France, Italy, and Germany, seeking to bolster their own realms by championing papal authority, provided the political and military force to implement reforms over wide territories. Despite the religious impulses of the Catholic Reformation, its success, like that of the Protestant Reformation, depended on the support of secular rulers.

Catholic Reformation: Spiritually, reform impulses can be traced as far back as the founding of the influential Brethren of the Common Life by Geert de Groote (d. 1384) and they gradually spread throughout Europe. In the fifteenth century, new devotional tracts appeared, notably the *Imitation of Christ*. In sixteenth-century Italy, the Roman Oratory of Divine Love (diocesan priests living in community without vows) inspired influential churchmen such as Giovanni Pietro Carafa (later Pope Paul IV) and saints such as Philip Neri to distinguish themselves by their charity and holiness. Indeed, the Catholic Reformation was also distinguished by the numerous saints it produced. At the same time, the new Christian humanism, associated particularly with Desiderius Erasmus (d. 1536), Gasparo Contarini (d. 1542), and Jacopo Sadoleto (d. 1547), and laymen such as Thomas More (d. 1535), provided an accessible and pious alternative to the technical complexity of Scholastic theology, culminating in the work of the French bishop Francis de Sales (d. 1622) at the end of the century. In Spain, John of the Cross (d. 1591) and Teresa of Ávila (d. 1582) spurred a renewed interest in mysticism.

Religious orders such as the Benedictines, Augustinians, Franciscans, Dominicans, and Carthusians experienced reforming movements, and new orders arose. The Theatines (1524) grew out of the Roman Oratory, the Capuchins (1528) emerged from the Franciscans, while the Somaschi (1532), the Barnabites (1530), and the Ursulines (1535) distinguished themselves in charity, missionary work, and teaching. Among the most significant of the new orders was the Society of Jesus (1540), founded by Ignatius of Loyola (d. 1556) to propagate Catholicism; the order soon moved to the forefront of its defense.

Reforming prelates emerged to support individual efforts. In Spain, the humanist Cardinal Francisco Jiménez de Cisneros (d. 1517) institutionalized Catholic renewal by vigorously reforming religious orders, furthering clerical education, and also employing the Inquisition extensively to combat heresy and persecute Jews and Moors.

Counter-Reformation: In Rome, only decisive papal initiative could eliminate corruption and clerical immorality. Pope Paul III (1534–49) appointed reforming cardinals and convened the Council of Trent (1545). Paul IV (1555–59) severely curtailed fiscal abuses and brought the Curia and the hierarchy under strict control, forcing bishops to reside in their dioceses and using the Roman Inquisition to investigate moral and doctrinal corruption. He also combated Protestantism and heresy through the Index of Forbidden Books. Pope Pius IV (1559–65) concluded the Council of Trent and began to implement its measures. Pope Pius V (1566–72) continued the Tridentine reforms, made monastic austerity the model for episcopal life, issued a uniform missal and breviary, and strengthened the Roman Inquisition. In a direct challenge to Protestant Reformers, the pope championed Thomas Aquinas (d. 1274) as a Doctor of the Church and a model for Catholic theology. These popes also established the future direction of Catholicism by elevating eminent reformers to the hierarchy, such as the humanist Sadoleto and the future saints Charles Borromeo (d. 1584, the model of a Counter-Reformation bishop), Francis de Sales, and Robert Bellarmine (d. 1621).

Corruption in the fifteenth century and theological challenges in the sixteenth had led to demands by Protestants (especially Martin Luther) and Catholics alike for a new ecumenical council, a goal fitfully but finally fulfilled without the Protestants at the Council of Trent (1545–63). Meeting in three separate sessions (1545–47, 1551–52, and 1562–63), Trent undertook both moral reform and doctrinal clarification, defining the central tenets of contemporary Catholicism. Against Protestantism, the council upheld papal primacy and proclaimed Scripture and tradition to be equal fonts of revealed truth. Trent also clarified the Catholic doctrine of the seven sacraments and of justification, refuting Protestantism by reaffirming the Scholastic theologies of the Middle Ages. The council attacked abuses by requiring bishops to reside in their dioceses and strengthening their authority, establishing seminaries to provide clerical education, curbing concubinage, and by reforming prayer books and catechisms. Finally, the council advocated censorship to limit the influence of suspect ideas.

Catholic reforms ultimately required the support of European princes. Royal enforcement in Spain and governmental sponsorship or acquiescence in Italian lands guaranteed success. In France, religious war and near disintegration of the kingdom resulted, but Catholicism finally triumphed when Henry IV agreed to become Catholic in return for the French crown (1593). The military power and staunch Catholicism of the Habsburg emperors enabled the Counter-Reformation to stem the Protestant tide and reconvert (often forcibly) much of Germany and central Europe, especially Bohemia, Austria, and Hungary.

The age of the Catholic Reformation and the Counter-Reformation also included the conquest and conversion of the New World and missions to India, China, and Japan, making Catholicism a worldwide religion. Internal European missions along with literary and artistic revivals created a distinctive but sometimes insular Catholic culture and ethos that would endure until the mid-twentieth century. *See also* Brethren and Sisters of the Common Life; Erasmus, Desiderius; Inquisition; Jesuits; missions; Oratorians; Oratory of Divine Love; Protestantism; Reformation, the; religious orders and congregations; Trent, Council of.

Bibliography

Delumeau, Jean. *Catholicism Between Luther and Voltaire: A New View of the Counter-Reformation.* Philadelphia: Westminster, 1977.

Evennett, H. Outram. *The Spirit of the Counter-Reformation.* Notre Dame, IN: University of Notre Dame Press, 1968.

Iserloh, Erwin, Joseph Glazik, and Hubert Jedin. *Reformation and Catholic Reformation.* In H. Jedin, *History of the Church,* vol. 5. New York: Seabury Press, 1980.

Jedin, Hubert. *A History of the Council of Trent.* 2 vols. St. Louis: Herder, 1957–61.

O'Malley, John W. *The First Jesuits.* Cambridge, MA: Harvard University Press, 1993.   W. DAVID MYERS

court, ecclesiastical. *See* tribunal.

covenant, an agreement between two parties. In the OT there are two kinds. The first is unconditional; that is, an outright grant is made by one party to the other as a reward for faithfulness. Examples are the agreement between the Lord and Abram in Gen 15, Phinehas in Num 25, and David in 2 Sam 7. The second kind is conditional; that is, continuation of the agreement depends on fulfilling its requirements, as in the Sinai covenant between the Lord and Israel. Jeremiah anticipated a new covenant (Jer 31:31) after the old one failed. The NT presents the gospel as this new covenant or testament, as indicated by Jesus' words at the Last Supper (e.g., Luke 22:20), Paul's message to the Corinthians (2 Cor 3:6–18), and the Letter to the Hebrews (Heb 8:7–13; 9:15–16).

A cowl, worn over the head by a Trappist monk at work in the fields.

cowl, traditionally, a hood on a monk's habit. It originated from the large hooded work-cloak of laborers in late imperial times (fifth century), gradually acquiring the spiritual function of creating an atmosphere of solitude for each monk. *See also* monk.

Cranmer, Thomas, 1489–1556, archbishop of Canterbury and English Reformer. Made archbishop of Canterbury in 1532, he sought under Henry VIII to reform the Church of England in a decidedly Lutheran direction, culminating in the Ten Articles (1536), the Bishop's Book (1537), the English Bible (various editions appearing after 1535), the English litany (1544), and the *Homilies* (published in 1547). Under Edward VI, Cranmer came to be influenced by Calvin's theology, especially his understanding of the Eucharist and critique of images, as reflected in the *Book of Common Prayer* (1549), *The True and Catholic Doctrine of the Lord's Supper* (1549), and especially the *Book of Common Prayer* of 1552 and the Forty-two Articles of 1553. He was executed by Mary Tudor on March 21, 1556, publicly recanting his recantations concerning transubstantiation and papal supremacy. *See also* Anglicanism; England, Ca-

tholicism in; papacy, the; Reformation, the; transubstantiation.

creatio ex nihilo (kray-ah'tzee-oh eks nee'hih-loh, or, frequently, nik'uh-loh; Lat., "creation from nothing"), a phrase indicating creation's dependence upon God. "From nothing" signifies that God's action alone brings the created order into existence. *See also* creation.

creation, the divine causality by which God made the entire universe out of nothing and continuously sustains it. Without being wedded to any scientific explanation of how this was accomplished, belief in creation affirms the radical gift character of existence, for all things receive their being from God.

Christian belief in creation stems from Israel's faith. The one living God who had brought the Jews out of the land of Egypt was also, upon reflection, the maker of heaven and earth. Freely adapting the cosmogonic myths of surrounding peoples, Israel expressed this in the great dramatic narrative of Gen 1. "In the beginning," by the power of the divine word, God created earth, sky, and sea with all their creatures, culminating on the sixth day in the human male and female made in God's image. And everything was good. The rest of the OT sees the world as belonging to God and telling of God's glory; the resulting religious response of admiration and praise is given voice in the Psalms (8, 19, 24, 104) and wisdom literature.

The NT links creation with Jesus Christ, the Word of God through whom all things were made (John 1:3) and himself the firstborn of all creation (Col 1:15). This enables Christians to interpret salvation as renewal of the original creation rather than a separate enterprise.

Patristic theology emphasized that God creates the world out of nothing (Lat., *ex nihilo*) to counteract the Greek idea that God was simply a world architect who created by rearranging preexisting matter. That would make matter independent of divinity and compromise the radical dependence of the world upon God. Properly speaking, *ex nihilo* undermines the analogy of making, for "nothing" is not something that already exists from which something else can be made. Use of this term points to the fundamental difference between God's creative act and the making activity of creatures and underscores divine transcendence.

By the time the Nicene-Constantinopolitan Creed took shape in the fifth century, the fundamentals of

Michelangelo's sixteenth-century masterpiece depicting the creation of Adam; ceiling of the Sistine Chapel, Vatican City.

the Christian doctrine of creation had become clear. Against dualism, which posited good and evil principles for the universe and considered matter to be evil and unworthy of being God's creature, the doctrine of creation holds that one triune God is the "Maker of heaven and earth, of all that is seen and unseen." Against Pantheism, which blurred the distinction between God and the world, the doctrine of creation declares that God is Maker, Creator, Originator of the world out of nothing. Against the view that the world was a necessarily occurring emanation, the creation doctrine holds that God creates in the sheer exuberance of freedom. Finally, against absenteeism, the doctrine of creation affirms that the Holy Spirit, "Lord and Giver of life," remains actively and intimately present to the world, connecting, renewing, and drawing all things to their goal.

The doctrine of creation is part of a cosmic vision that sees the world as ultimately reliant on the transcendent God, who fashions it in the freedom of divine love and dwells within it, energizing all existence. God is the ultimate source, ground, and goal of the world and humanity, while in their own autonomy creatures are endowed with the power to collaborate in the ongoing course of history.

As Israel drew on the cosmology of the ancient Near East to express its creation faith, and as patristic and medieval theology used the cosmology of the Greeks, the challenge today is to express this truth in ways coherent with the cosmology of contemporary science. *See also* cosmology; creationism; evolution.   *ELIZABETH JOHNSON*

creation-centered spirituality, a view of Christian life as a celebration of the divine creative will in the universe. The believer is called to cooperate in this divine activity in all areas of life. While the reality of sin is acknowledged, it is not conquered by withdrawal from the world. Rather the believer is called to embrace the world and its creative process by active engagement with it. Redemption is seen as an integral part of divine creation, rather than as a separate divine activity necessitated by the reality of sin.

Proponents of creation-centered spirituality find its origins in ancient spiritual traditions, especially in the cultures of matriarchal societies and indigenous peoples. These cultures model a way of life lived in solidarity with both nature and humankind. Within Catholicism men and women such as Thomas Aquinas (d. 1274), Pierre Teilhard de Chardin (d. 1955), Rosemary Ruether, Thomas Berry, and especially Matthew Fox have contributed to the development of creation-centered spirituality, which challenges the body/spirit dualism prevalent in much of Western spirituality. This spirituality is distinctively incarnational as it proclaims the divine presence in the material as well as the spiritual realm. Holiness is sought in the lives of ordinary people as they embrace the world by their labor and their relationships with others and with the planet.

Creation-centered spirituality also rejects the sexist dualism found in Western culture. According to creation-centered spirituality, women's immediacy to the life process reveals the life-affirming values characteristic of a healthy spirituality: harmony with nature, nonviolence, and cooperation.

Creation-centered spirituality is not without its critics. Some theologians note its diminishment of the sense of divine transcendence; others object to its rigid dichotomy between sin and grace, and claim that both poles are always present in the fabric of life. Defenders of creation-centered spirituality, on the other hand, point to the Christian humanism of Thomas Aquinas and the incarnational theology of the Second Vatican Council (1962–65) in support of it.   *DANIEL DI DOMIZIO*

creationism, based on a fundamentalist reading of Genesis, the doctrine, in opposition to the biological theory of evolution, that living organisms are the products of "special" divine creation. The most radical form asserts a "young" earth (less than ten thousand years old), six twenty-four-hour days of creation, and a worldwide flood responsible for the fossil record. Less radical forms accept evidence for an "ancient" earth: the "gap" theory proposes that millions of years separate the creation "in the beginning" from a second creation that occurred over a six-day period; the "day-age" theory (or "progressive creation") identifies the days of creation with geological eras. All forms assert the special creation of an original human pair.

Creationism as a political-religious movement (primarily American and Protestant) has gone through two stages. Key figures in the first stage (roughly the 1920s) were William Jennings Bryan (1860–1925), who spearheaded the fight to halt the

Traditional crèche with the figures of St. Joseph, the child Jesus, and the Blessed Virgin Mary; fifteenth-century Florentine sculpture by Antonio Rossellino, Metropolitan Museum, New York.

teaching of evolution in public schools, and George McCready Price (1870–1963), whose book denying the antiquity of the fossil record, *The New Geology* (1923, rev. ed. 1926), made Price the most prominent scientific voice among creationists despite his lack of formal scientific training. The second stage, or "scientific creationism," is associated with Henry M. Morris (b. 1918), an engineer who coauthored with John C. Whitcomb, Jr., *The Genesis Flood* (1961), updating Price's work. In 1970, Morris established the Institute for Creation Research, which since 1981 has offered graduate degrees in science, indicative of recent efforts to cast creationism as a scientific alternative to evolutionary theory. *See also* creation; evolution.   *STEVEN D. CRAIN*

crèche (kresh; Fr., "manger," "crib"), popular name for a Nativity set displayed in homes and churches during the Christmas season. The custom derives from the early practice (1223) of Francis of Assisi celebrating Christmas in a barn with animals and straw. Such representations of Christ's birth are now almost universal in Catholicism. *See also* Christmas.

credence table (Lat., *credere*, "to believe"), a small table, or shelf in the wall, near the altar. It holds the paten, chalice, small basin, and finger towel for the celebration of the Eucharistic Liturgy. It may hold cruets and unconsecrated bread if these are not presented by the faithful.

Credo of the People of God, profession of faith pronounced by Paul VI at St. Peter's Basilica, June 30, 1968, at the close of the "Year of Faith," the nineteenth centenary anniversary of the martyrdom of Sts. Peter and Paul. The Credo reaffirms the fundamental truths of the Catholic faith, especially those truths most questioned by modernity. It reiterates the articles of the Nicene-Constantinopolitan Creed by stating them in traditional pre-Vatican II (1962–65) theological language and elaborating on them in relation to Christian life today. For the text, see *The Pope Speaks* 13 (1968).

creeds (Lat., *credo,* "I believe"), also called "symbols of faith," concise, authorized statements of the essential tenets of religious belief that a believing community employs primarily in its worship and initiation rites. One meaning of the Greek term *symbolon* ("sign") in the expression "symbol of faith" is "token," in the sense of "name." This meaning indicates the basic purpose of creeds: they serve as tokens, names, that identify God, the believer, and the community of belief.

The use of the term "symbol" may have also come about because *symbolon* may mean "sign" in the sense that for Christians the threefold interrogatory creed for Baptism, by its very form, symbolizes the triune God. It is possible, moreover, that "symbol" originated because the Greek word *symbole* ("collation") refers to a creed as a collection of a community's articles of religious belief.

Creeds are highly developed within Christianity, and yet they also exist within other religious beliefs as well. Judaism has the confession of the one God in the Shema (Deut 6:4) and the confession of God's saving work in the profession regarding the "wandering Aramaean" (Deut 26:1–11). Islam possesses the Shahada, which declares that only God is God and that Muhammad is the messenger of God. Hinduism employs the Gayatri Mantra (*Rigveda* 3.62.10), which professes "the resplendent glory of Savitr." Buddhism relies on the Triple Refuge (in the Buddha, the doctrine, and the community of believers).

Christianity possesses many kinds of creeds, if "creed" be understood as a broad category encompassing NT confessions, creeds in a narrow sense, doctrines, and (denominational) confessions of belief. The NT evinces simple confessions, for example, "Jesus is the Christ" (Acts 2:26), binitary confessions (Rom 1:3–4), trinitarian confessions (Matt 28:19), and the Christ kerygma (1 Cor 15:3–7). Along with these formulations, the early Church gradually fashioned fuller articulations of the faith. These include the "rules of faith" (e.g., of Ignatius, Irenaeus, and Tertullian), the trinitarian interrogatory creeds (e.g., of Hippolytus), the Old Roman Creed, and the "ecumenical creeds," namely, the Apostles' Creed, the Nicene Creed, and the Nicene-

Constantinopolitan Creed, the doctrine of Chalcedon, the Athanasian Creed, and the Creed of the Third Council of Constantinople.

Beginning with the Reformation, the Christian churches fashioned even more precise (denominational) confessions of belief. The Lutheran church upholds the Augsburg Confession (1530) and the Formula of Concord (1577). The Reformed (Calvinist) church is defined by the First Helvetic Confession (1536), the Second Helvetic Confession (1566), and the Canons of the Synod of Dort (1619). The Catholic Church identifies itself with the dogmatic decrees of the Council of Trent (1563) and the constitution *Ineffabilis Deus,* on the Immaculate Conception of the Blessed Virgin Mary (1854). The Greek and Russian churches attest to the Orthodox Confession (1643) and the Longer Catechism of the Russian Church (1839). In the twentieth century, the formulating of creeds has continued with the Barmen Confession (1934), Pope Paul VI's Credo of the People of God (1968), and the World Council of Church's Lima Document on Baptism, Eucharist, and Ministry (1982).

In Christianity, the creeds function in a variety of specific contexts, including at liturgy as a communal confession of belief (e.g., the Nicene-Constantinopolitan Creed), at Baptism as a declaration of an individual's new identity within the community (e.g., Hippolytus's interrogatory creed), in private prayer as confession (e.g., Acts 2:36), during catechetical instruction (e.g., the Apostles' Creed), as the norm for theological inquiry (e.g., the doctrine of Chalcedon), within ecumenical dialogue (e.g., the Augsburg Confession), and amid political-social opposition to the Church (e.g., the Barmen Confession).

For the texts of the creeds, see J. Neuner and J. Dupuis, *The Christian Faith,* rev. ed. (1992); J. Leith, *Creeds of the Churches* (1982); J.N.D. Kelly, *Early Christian Creeds* (1972); P. Schaff, *The Creeds of Christendom,* 3 vols. (1919). *See also* Apostles' Creed; Athanasian Creed; Nicene Creed.   ROBERT A. KRIEG

cremation, the reduction of a dead body to ashes by burning. A common form of disposal of bodies after death in many cultures, it was traditionally shunned by Christians and actually forbidden to Catholics during the modern period, except in case of public necessity.

The traditional resistance to cremation was largely based on a resistance to the pagan or anti-Christian ideology associated with cremation and not to the practice itself. The new Code of Canon Law (can. 1176.3) has substantially modified the older restriction, stating that cremation is not forbidden "unless it has been chosen for reasons which are contrary to Christian teaching."

crib, Christmas. *See* crèche.

crime, impediment of, in canon law the invalidating obstacle to a marriage where one of the parties has murdered a spouse in order to be free to marry or where both parties have cooperated in the murder of a spouse (can. 1090). These actions are considered so heinous that the dispensation that would allow such a marriage must be given by the Holy See. The older form of the impediment included the prohibition of marriage after an adulterous relationship. Although this is still morally unacceptable, the impediment is removed in the current code. *See also* marriage law.

Crispin and Crispinian, Sts., d. third century, patron saints of shoemakers and leatherworkers, a trade they practiced by night while preaching, teaching, and baptizing converts by day in Gaul (France). Beheaded by order of the emperor Maximian. Feast day: October 25.

criticism, biblical. *See* biblical criticism.

Cromwell, Oliver, 1599–1658, lord protector of England. In the English Civil War he led the "New Model Army" successfully against the Royalists (1645) and the Scots (1648), after which Charles I was executed, with Cromwell's approval (1649). Eventually coming into conflict with Parliament, which attempted to establish intolerant Presbyterianism, Cromwell dismissed it in April 1653. Made "Lord Protector" by the army on December 16, 1643, he ruled the Commonwealth with a combination of Puritan zeal for godliness, religious toleration, and often ruthless determination. *See also* Protestantism; Puritanism; Reformation, the.

Cromwell, Thomas, ca. 1485–1540, Earl of Essex. First rising to prominence under Cardinal Wolsey, he transferred his allegiance to Henry VIII after Wolsey's fall in 1529 and strongly advocated royal supremacy over the Church. Named vicar general in 1535, he became the chief counselor to the king in all ecclesiastical matters, consistently advising Henry toward a Lutheran reform of the Church

crosier

Crosier

and a political alliance with the Protestant German princes. He arranged for the visitation and dissolution of the lesser and greater monasteries (1536, 1539). His arrangement for the marriage of Henry VIII to Anne of Cleves (1540) proved less successful and led to his downfall. In spite of being named Earl of Essex by Henry on April 7, 1540, he was arrested and beheaded for treason on July 28, 1540. *See also* dissolution of the monasteries; Reformation, the.

crosier (kroh'zhur), the crook-shaped staff carried in procession by archbishops and bishops and some abbots and abbesses. Its original significance is unknown, but it is often taken as a symbol of the bishop's pastoral or shepherding role.

Crosier Fathers and Brothers (O.S.C.), also known as Canons Regular of the Order of the Holy Cross, a community of canons regular (clergy who adopted a monastic rule of life) founded in Belgium in 1210 by Theodore De Celles to serve the spiritual and pastoral needs of the People of God while living in community and praying the Liturgy of the Church together. The Crosiers in the twentieth century live in small communities of priests and brothers as equal members sharing communal prayer and ministries. They retain in their rule the spirit of Augustine (d. 430) with a tradition of devotion to the Cross.

Crosiers arrived in the United States in 1910. They conduct missions in Irian Jaya, Indonesia. Their ministries include parishes, campus ministry, and education. *See also* canons regular.

cross, an instrument of execution and symbol of redemption. The Roman cross, consisting of a stake to which was affixed a horizontal beam, was carried by the victim to the site of execution. Crosses could appear in either a T-shape or in the more familiar Christian form, with the crossbeam slightly below the top of the upright.

As a penalty reserved for lower-class criminals, the cross connoted shame and disgrace (Gal 5:11; Phil 2:8; Heb 12:2) that scandalized pagans (1 Cor 1:18). Paul, however, boasts of Christ's Cross (Gal 6:14), in which God's salvific power was present (1 Cor 1:17) and through which God effected reconciliation with all (Col 1:20). Hence the heart of Paul's preaching is Christ crucified (1 Cor 1:23; 2:2).

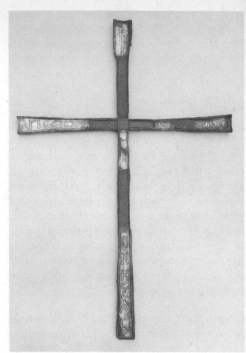

Sixth-century Eastern Christian wooden cross with mounted silver found near Antioch, Syria; Metropolitan Museum of Art, New York.

Twelfth-century English cross of walrus ivory; Cloisters Collection, Metropolitan Museum of Art, New York.

The gold reliquary cross of Pope Urban V (d. 1370); in St. Vitus Cathedral, Prague, Czech Republic.

Crosses

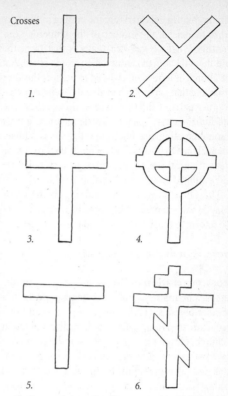

1. Greek cross. 2. St. Andrew's cross. 3. Latin cross (the most common shape of the cross in Catholicism). 4. Celtic cross. 5. Tau (Gk., "t") cross. 6. Byzantine cross.

Celtic cross; the Muirdeachs Cross, Monasterboice, County Louth, Ireland.

In the NT the Cross symbolizes both the act of redemption and the imitation of Christ, whose followers are to take up their own crosses daily (Matt 10:38; Mark 8:34; Luke 9:23; 14:27).

The practice of signing oneself with the cross is mentioned by Tertullian in the second century. Feasts associated with the Cross are the Exaltation of the Cross on September 14 and the feast of the Finding of the Cross, commemorating its discovery around 326 by Helena, mother of the emperor Constantine, until 1960 celebrated on May 3. *See also* crucifixion; sign of the cross.

cross, forms of the. Christian iconography knows various forms of the cross. An ancient usage, based on the Greek *tau*, looks like the letter T; the form of the cross with the vertical extending above the horizontal arm (†) is the more common. Other forms include such shapes as the St. Andrew's cross, which looks like the letter X, as well as shapes that have been ornamented in one fashion or another,

including the Maltese cross, the Crusader's cross, the Celtic cross, or the ancient Chi/Rho cross. *See also* cross.

cross, pectoral. *See* pectoral cross.

cross, processional, an image of the cross mounted upon a pole, carried at the head of liturgical processions. The processional cross may or may not bear a *corpus* (Lat.), an image of the crucified Jesus. Sometimes fashioned of precious metals, some processional crosses are among the most precious works of art possessed by the Church. The cross is borne aloft by a liturgical minister called a crucifer, or crossbearer. Protocol for liturgical processions demands that there be only one processional cross and that it be carried in front of all else, save an incense bearer when there is one. On the most formal occasions the processional cross is accompanied by two candlebearers.

cross, relics of the, objects of devotion connected with the Passion of Christ. Various, not always

381

compatible, legends attribute the finding of the True Cross to Helena, the mother of the emperor Constantine. What we know factually is that from the middle of the fourth century, the records relate that the church of Jerusalem claimed to possess the True Cross and that parts of it had already been dispersed to other parts of the Christian world as relics. The late-fourth-century pilgrim Egeria mentions a feast commemorating the finding of the Cross. Subsequent claims to possess fragments of the Cross have met with great skepticism, although such relics are still exhibited around the Christian world.

The Church's feast of the Finding of the Cross (May 3) was suppressed by Rome in 1960 as part of the reform of the liturgical calendar. *See also* relics.

cross, sign of the. *See* sign of the cross.

cross, veneration of the, homage paid to the central Christian symbol. Such homage exists at a number of levels: (1) the common practice of bowing before the cross, which is ordinarily exhibited in a church; (2) the kissing of a cross or the corpus on the cross in various ceremonies or as an act of devotion; and (3) as part of the liturgical service of Good Friday, where there is a presentation of the cross, which is then kissed as part of the liturgical celebration of the death of the Lord. This last liturgical practice was known in the fourth century in Jerusalem and was part of Roman usage by the eighth century. *See also* cross.

Crowley, Patricia (Patty), b. 1913, and **Patrick F.,** 1911–74, Catholic activists. Instrumental with others in founding the Christian Family Movement in 1943, they served on the Papal Birth Control Commission, 1965–66. Patty received her A.B. degree in French and history at Trinity College, Washington, D.C. (1936); Patrick received his A.B. from the University of Notre Dame (1934) and a law degree from Loyola University of Chicago (1937). They were married in 1937. *See also* birth control; Christian Family Movement.

crown, episcopal, Byzantine-rite liturgical mitre, an imitation of the Byzantine imperial crown. Once worn only by the pope of Alexandria, its use became more general from the Middle Ages and is now conceded to the highest ranks of presbyters, both secular (mitred archpriests, protopresbyters) and monastic (archimandrites). Other rites (Coptic, Ethiopian) use a similar crown or have adopted a

Christ crowned with thorns; fifteenth-century oil painting by Antonello da Messina, Metropolitan Museum of Art, New York.

Western-style mitre (Armenian, East and West Syrian, Maronite). *See also* mitre.

crowning, liturgical (Gk., *stephanoma*, from *stephanos*, "crown"), Byzantine-rite marriage ritual in two parts, the betrothal and the crowning of the spouses with ritual crowns, often of precious metal. A traditional element of pre-Christian weddings, the crowning was reinterpreted by John Chrysostom (d. 407) as a sign of the victory over concupiscence and had become a customary part of the Byzantine marriage ritual by the end of the sixth century. *See also* Marriage, liturgy of.

crown of thorns, an element of the Passion of Jesus. Before his crucifixion, Jesus was mocked and scourged by Roman soldiers. Deriding his claims to be king of the Jews, they clothed him in purple and placed on his head a crown woven of thorns or briers (Matt 27:29; Mark 15:17; John 19:2). *See also* Passion, the.

crucifix, a cross that bears the image of the crucified Christ; a common devotional object in Catholic churches (usually over the altar) and households.

Late-twelfth-century French copper and enamel crucifix; Metropolitan Museum of Art, New York.

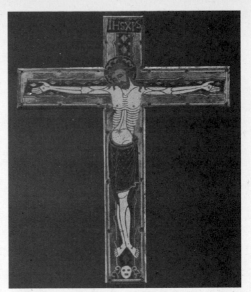

Medieval crucifix; twelfth- or early-thirteenth-century northern Italian sculptured crucifix inspired by the "Volto Santo" of Lucca and located in a monastery near Treviso, Italy.

The portrayal of Christ on the cross was absent in the first centuries of Christian art. During the time of Constantine (early fourth century), the cross was presented as a sign of Christ's triumph over death at Easter. It was in the thirteenth century that sculpted figures of Christ on crosses attained greater realism

in depicting the physical details of his Passion and became common fixtures on the altar table. Contemporary renderings have recovered the theological emphasis of the early crucifixes, sometimes showing a risen Christ on the cross. *See also* cross.

crucifixion, a method of execution of criminals. Crucifixion was used by Phoenicians and Persians and adopted by Romans, who regarded it as the most shameful form of execution, reserved for slaves and aliens. In a crucifixion the victim carried

Thirteenth-century crucifix by Cimabue; in the church of St. Dominic, Arezzo, Italy.

Panel from the *Isenheim Altarpiece*, Matthias Grünewald's sixteenth-century masterpiece; Unterlinden Museum, Colmar, France.

a beam to the site of execution, where it would be affixed as a crossbeam to an upright stake. The victim, stripped of all clothing, would normally be nailed or bound to the crossbeam at his wrists, his feet nailed to the upright through the ankles. His buttocks would rest on a small stake or board to prolong his agony. Death came slowly, often after several days, usually by exhaustion and asphyxiation, as the weight of the body prevented breathing. Death could be hastened by breaking the knees (as in John 19:31–32), preventing the victim from raising himself to relieve pressure on the diaphragm.

Jesus' Crucifixion took place on a Friday at the beginning of (Matthew, Mark, Luke) or just before (John) Passover. Jesus was first scourged by Roman soldiers (Matt 27:27–31; Mark 15:16–20; John 19:1–2), then led to the place of execution, Golgotha. Since Jesus was too weak to carry his own cross, Simon of Cyrene was pressed into service (Matt 27:32; Mark 15:20; Luke 23:26). Jesus was crucified between two criminals (Luke 23:33; John 19:18), more specifically, brigands (Matt 27:38; Mark 15:27). An inscription on the cross indicated that Jesus' crime was political, involving a claim to be king of the Jews (Matt 27:37; Mark 15:26; Luke 23:38; John 19:19–22). *See also* cross. HAROLD W. ATTRIDGE

cruets (Medieval Fr., *cruette,* "little jug"), small flasks made of glass, metal, ceramic, or clay, holding water and wine for the celebration of the Eucharistic Liturgy. Together with unconsecrated bread, they may be presented to the priest by two of the faithful before the Preparation of the Gifts (formerly the Offertory).

Crusades, a series of wars fought under the banner of Christ either for the recovery of or in defense

Cruets

of Christian lands. As pious as it was military in its origins, crusading began in the eleventh century with Christian campaigns against Muslim expansion in Spain and Sicily. In late 1095 Pope Urban II (d. 1099) summoned the nobles of the West to the First Crusade in partial response to the Byzantine emperor's plea for defense against the Seljuk Turks. But the impelling force of this and other early crusades was the liberation of Jerusalem and the Holy Land from Muslim rule. To attract crusaders the popes offered indulgences, assurances that those who carried the cross merited the remission of temporal punishment due to sin. The First Crusade (1096–99) was a military success, as Western armies moved from victories in the East to Jerusalem in 1099. Christian states were established in the conquered territories to secure the victories, but these were troubled with divisiveness from the start. The Second Crusade (1146–48) was summoned by the pope and preached by Bernard of Clairvaux to recapture the fallen kingdom of Edessa, though without much effect. Jerusalem had held its own for years until 1187 when it fell to Saladin and prompted the Third Crusade (1189–92) under the leadership of the formidable Emperor Frederick I. He died en route to the Holy Land and left the campaign in the hands of Richard the Lion-Hearted, whose hard-fought battles resulted only in a diplomatic victory promising safe passage to Christian pilgrims from Jaffa to Jerusalem. The Fourth Crusade (1202–4) signaled a portentous turn in the movement from Christian warfare aimed at the recovery of the Holy Land for spiritual motives to sheer economic enterprise. Its only successful battles were fought in Christian Constantinople and its victory saw the establishment of a Latin empire there, only widening the rift between Christian East and West. The Fifth Crusade (1217–21) was a bizarre affair as well, when Emperor Frederick II, while excommunicated, carried the cross to impressive victories. From that point on Western princes fought lesser campaigns against Muslim strongholds in Jerusalem and Egypt.

The idea of the crusade never really disappeared but during the later Middle Ages political and economic developments in the West made the prospect of distant and costly crusades less popular in spite of repeated papal efforts to rouse Western princes. Similarly, the Western states were increasingly unable to resolve their own differences sufficiently to liberate and defend the Holy Land. The redirection of Christian campaigns against Western heretical sects (as in the Albigensian Crusade, 1209–19) and enemies of the papacy under the name of crusade inevitably weakened the movement's original ideals. On the positive side, they promoted cultural, technological, and economic exchanges and fostered the growth of the great military orders, including the Hospitallers and the Knights Templar. *See also* Albigensians; Constantinople; Holy Land; Hospitallers; Islam; Jerusalem; latinization. WILLIAM J. DOHAR

crypt (Lat., *crypta,* "vault," "cave"), an underground area excavated directly beneath a sanctuary or choir. In the Middle Ages crypts were formed when larger cathedrals were erected over the vestiges of earlier church buildings. In the early centuries of the church they were also used as burial places and for worship.

Cuba, Catholicism in. Evangelization of Cuba began in the early sixteenth century. Cuba became independent of Spain in 1902 following the Spanish-American War. In 1961, after Fidel Castro brought the country under Communist rule, the University of Villanueva was closed, 350 Catholic schools were brought under government control, and more than 130 priests were expelled. There are two archdioceses and five dioceses in Cuba with over 4.4 million Catholics, comprising about 40 percent of the total population (1994). After Castro came to power, many Cuban Catholics fled to the United States, with the highest concentration in Florida. *See also* Latin America, Catholicism in.

Cuius regio, eius religio (koo-yuhs ray'jee-oh, ay'uhs rel-ij'ee-oh; Lat., "whose region, his religion"), political formulation from the Peace of Augsburg (1555) legalizing secular control of religion in both Catholic and Protestant areas. Under its terms the current political ruler of any given city or principality in the empire had the right to determine the religion of all its subjects, though the choice was limited to Catholicism or adherence to the Augsburg Confession. Individuals who refused to accept the religion of their rulers were allowed to emigrate upon paying a fee. Prince-bishops who converted to Protestantism, however, could not change the religion of their territories. *See also* Reformation, the.

cult (Lat., *cultus,* "tilling," "cultivation," "worship," "reverence"), a system or community of religious worship and ritual. Catholic teaching has tradition-

ally distinguished between public and private cult. Public cultic acts are referable only to God, the saints, or the beatified, according to the 1983 Code of Canon Law (can. 1187), and are performed in the name of the Church by persons legitimately designated (can. 834). Private cultic acts are rituals that do not meet one or more of the above characteristics. Since the time of Pope Urban VIII (1623–44), the Church has prohibited public cultic recognition of figures prior to their beatification.

The anthropological, sociological, and psychological study of religious phenomena expands the contemporary definition of cult. "Cult" may refer to the public existence or behavior of any group, religious or non-religious, that exhibits some of the following characteristics: focus on individual concerns; indifference to the world; privatized or ecstatic religious experience; syncretistic doctrines of a mystical, esoteric, or psychic nature; a charismatic leader; lack of formal criteria for membership; weak organizational structure; a preference against rigorous ethical demands; tolerant stance toward other religious groups; transient existence. Cults may exhibit less formal organization and allow for more spontaneous individual expression (audience cults) or may be formally structured to provide services related to self-mastery (client cults).

Social scientists have further identified certain factors that contribute to the emergence of cults: breakdown in traditional social structures, social alienation, and weak institutional churches. *See also* liturgy; worship. CATHERINE MURPHY

culture. *See* Catholicism and culture.

Cunegund, St., also known as Cunegunda, ca. 978–1033, empress, patron saint of Lithuania and Poland. After the death of her husband Henry II, emperor of Germany, she became a Benedictine nun and devoted the rest of her life to prayer and care of the sick. Feast day: March 3.

Cuomo, Mario Matthew (qwoh'moh), b. 1932, governor of New York State 1983–94. Cuomo received his B.A. *summa cum laude* from St. John's College in 1953, received an LL.B. *cum laude* from St. John's University in 1956, and was a member of its law school faculty from 1963 to 1973. He was New York secretary of state from 1975 to 1979 and lieutenant governor from 1979 to 1983. Cuomo delivered a major address on religion and politics at the University of Notre Dame on September 13, 1984, considered by some the most important and influential address on the subject ever given by a U.S. Catholic layperson.

Cupertino, St. Joseph of. *See* Joseph of Cupertino, St.

Cur Deus Homo (Lat., "Why God Became Man"), an extended treatise of the last decade of the eleventh century on the work of Christ, cast in the form of a dialogue between its author, Anselm of Canterbury, and his disciple and fellow monk, Boso. Seeking to overcome doubts about the compatibility of the Incarnation and affirmations about the love, justice, mercy, and wisdom of God, Anselm argues that only the voluntary acceptance of the penalty owed for human sin by an agent who is both God and human can fully satisfy for sin. Criticisms of Anselm's account of satisfaction as too legalistic are thought to be overstated, because they neglect the love that motivates God's initial ordination of people to eternal life and Christ's death on the cross. *See also* Anselm of Canterbury, St.

curate (Lat., *cura,* "care"), older title for parochial vicar; the office involved in the care of souls. *See also* parochial vicar.

Curé d'Ars [Jean-Baptiste Marie Vianney], 1786–1859, French priest, confessor, patron saint of parish priests. He was born and grew up during the Napoleonic era. Because of religious persecution at that time, he had to make his First Communion secretly. He was drafted into Napoleon's army but, because of ill health, he found himself absent without leave and branded a deserter. In 1815, he was ordained even though he had been dismissed from the seminary for failing his examinations and for his inability to learn Latin. After serving as an associate for three years in the parish at Ars, he became pastor (Fr., *curé*) in 1818. He soon became famous as a spiritual counselor and confessor. It is said that he spent up to eighteen hours a day hearing confessions. He was canonized in 1925. Feast day: August 4.

curia, collective papal or diocesan governing agency. The term includes both persons and offices assisting the pope or diocesan bishop in their respective pastoral, governing, and administrative responsibilities. "Curia" alone often implies the Ro-

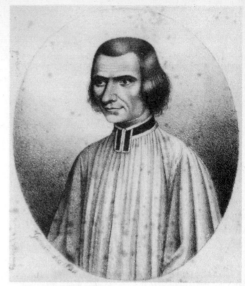

Jean-Baptiste Vianney, the Curé d'Ars, a model of the parish priest totally devoted to his congregation without regard for personal recognition or reward.

man Curia, which assists the pope in matters of service and governance beyond the diocese of Rome. Each diocesan curia comparably assists the diocesan bishop in local affairs.

The Latin word probably meant a Roman tribal subdivision or its meeting place, the Roman senate house itself, or simply assembly. From medieval times, Church usage has evolved to include persons and offices within Roman Congregations, chanceries, tribunals, and other agencies. *See also* diocesan curia; Roman Curia.

Curia, Roman. *See* Roman Curia.

Curran, Charles E., b. 1934, Catholic moral theologian. Since 1958, a priest of the diocese of Rochester, New York, and a former seminary professor in that diocese, he was for many years professor at The Catholic University of America (1965–91). In 1968 he led the public dissent against *Humanae Vitae* (the encyclical prohibiting birth control by artificial means) in the United States, an incident that many believe played a role in the decision by the Congregation for the Doctrine of the Faith (July 25, 1986) that Curran could "no longer be considered suitable or eligible to exercise the function of a professor of Catholic theology." Author of many books, including *The Living Tradition of Moral Theology* (1992) and *Faithful Dissent* (1986), he was elected president of the Catholic Theological Society of America (CTSA), the Society of Christian Ethics, and the American Theological Society. In 1972 he won CTSA's annual John Courtney Murray Award for "distinguished achievement in theology." Since 1991 he has been Elizabeth Scurlock University Professor of Human Values at Southern Methodist University.

Cursillo movement (Sp., *cursillo*, "little course"), a renewal program, originating in Spain in 1949. It focuses on Christ as the center of the spiritual life and all human activity. The movement grew out of an idea, first advanced at the monastery of San Honorato, to teach local Catholics the importance of Christ in their lives. Since then, Cursillo has grown into an international movement, introduced into countries all over the world. The point of Cursillo is to help Catholic Christians network with one another in the context of shared prayer, spiritual reading, and discussion. One becomes part of the movement by attending a "little course," a structured program of three courses, each taking three days. During this time the method of the movement is learned. After completing this exercise, *cursillistas* (those having made their Cursillo) are encouraged to gather from time to time (if convenient, every week) to pray, hear a teaching, and discuss Scripture. These gatherings are called *ultreyas* or "fourth day" to suggest the ongoing nature of renewal in Christ. The community emphasis of the movement conveys a strong sense of Church: people gathered in Christ's name as members of the universal Body of Christ.

Cushing, Richard James, 1895–1970, archbishop of Boston, 1944–70; cardinal, 1958. A man with an outgoing personality, Cushing superintended the growth of the Church in the Boston area in the post–World War II period. A prodigious fund-raiser, he built new parishes and Church institutions at a frenetic pace. He also supported foreign missionary work, especially in Latin America. He was influential in local and national politics, particularly through his friendship with the Kennedy family. He played a minor role at the Second Vatican Council (1962–65), helping draft the council's statement on Catholic-Jewish relations (the Declaration on the Relationship of the Church to Non-Christian Religions) and lending crucial support to the Declaration on Religious Freedom.

custody of the eyes, the practice of lowering or diverting one's gaze to protect the imagination and the memory from sights that might tempt one to greed, lust, or idle curiosity.

custom, term in canon law used in connection with certain limited, specified circumstances where the actions of a community can become the source of law for that community. It is also a principle of interpreting canon law that articulates that the best way to understand a law is to see how it is observed by the community (can. 27).

Cuthbert, St., ca. 634–87, Anglo-Saxon monk and bishop. After an active monastic ministry, Cuthbert retired to a hermitage on the island of Farne (676). Elected bishop of Hexham (684), he exchanged sees with the bishop of Lindisfarne and resumed pastoral work until his death. His relics were moved from Lindisfarne to Durham to protect them from Viking raids. Feast day: March 20.

Cyprian of Carthage, St., d. 258, bishop of Carthage, martyred under the Roman emperor Valerian, and a founder of Latin theology. Born in

Cardinal Richard Cushing, archbishop of Boston (1944–70), one of the most ecumenical and mission-minded bishops in U.S. Catholic history and a strong supporter of religious liberty at the Second Vatican Council.

Carthage and converted to Christianity in middle life (ca. 245), Cyprian devoted the early years of his conversion to the study of Scripture and Christian writers like Tertullian. Cyprian was ordained presbyter and soon after elected bishop of Carthage (249) just before the edicts against the Christian Church by the Roman emperors Decius (250–51) and Valerian (257–60). In a community often divided between "rigorist" and "laxist" attitudes to those who apostatized, Cyprian authored a voluminous correspondence and twelve theological treatises and presided over seven Church councils from 251 to 256. His works provide invaluable information about theological and institutional developments in the African church in the mid-third century, particularly on Baptism, the Holy Spirit in the Church, and ascetical theology. *On the Unity of the Church*, written in 251, argues for the unity and the universality of the Church against local factionalism on one side and against schisms provoked by the rigorist teaching of Novatian. The fourth chapter of the treatise has been transmitted in two versions, one insisting on the primacy of the see of Peter, while the other version is silent on this issue. The problem

of the two versions reflects not only the dispute between Cyprian and Pope Stephen I on the question of the rebaptism of heretics and schismatics, but also it is a witness to the close ties between the Roman see and the African churches. A constant referent for both Donatists and Catholics in the fourth and fifth centuries, Cyprian was included in the Roman festal calendar on September 16 by Pope Damasus I. *See also* Africa, the Church in Roman; Carthage; Donatism; *lapsi;* persecutions; primacy, papal; Stephen I, St. *PAMELA BRIGHT*

Cyril and Methodius, Sts., 826–69 and ca. 815–85, "Apostles of the Slavs" and patron saints of Europe. Constantine (only later, from 868, was he called "Cyril") was the youngest of seven children born to a senatorial family in Thessalonica. Methodius, his brother, is known only by his religious name. Constantine was educated in Constantinople at the imperial university, acquired a reputation as a philosopher, and was ordained priest, appointed librarian at Hagia Sophia, and in his mid-twenties made professor of philosophy at the imperial university. Ca. 855 he joined his brother, who after a government career had become a monk at a monastery in Bithynia.

At the request of Ratislav, Duke of Greater Moravia, the emperor Michael III commissioned the brothers as missionaries (862). Constantine invented a Slavonic alphabet (Glagolithic, not, as formerly thought, Cyrillic), and the brothers translated not only the Gospels, the Psalter, and Pauline Letters, but also the liturgy. Traveling to Rome in 868, they obtained the approval of Pope Hadrian II for the Slavonic liturgy and had three of their disciples ordained priests. At Rome Constantine became a monk and, named "Cyril," died shortly thereafter. Methodius, continuing the work alone, was consecrated bishop by Hadrian II in 869, although opposition to him caused his exile for three years. Pope John VIII was able to gain his release (873). In 880 he reauthorized the Slavonic liturgy, restricted or prohibited in 873. Near the end of his life, Methodius translated the remainder of the Bible, except for Maccabees. Feast day: May 11 (East); February 14, formerly March 9 and then July 7 (West). *See also* Old Church Slavonic. *JOHN C. CAVADINI*

Cyprian, third-century bishop of Carthage in North Africa, known for his writings on the unity of the Church, including the oft-quoted statement, "One cannot have God for a father who does not have the Church for a mother"; early-fourteenth-century detail from the Sant Cebria de Cabanyes Church, Museo Episcopal de Vic, Osana, Catalonia, Spain.

Cyril of Alexandria, St., ca. 375–444, patriarch of Alexandria and Doctor of the Church. Best known as a Christological thinker, he was honored by both Chalcedonian and Monophysite traditions, by those who accepted the teaching of the Council of Chalcedon (451) that Jesus Christ has both a human and a divine nature, and by those who affirmed only one nature, namely, the divine.

He succeeded his uncle Theophilus as patriarch of Alexandria in 412. His early rule was marked by serious violence toward Jews and pagans, including the fatal attack on the philosopher Hypatia, probably by supporters of Cyril. Both theologically and temperamentally inclined toward ascetic views, Cyril supported the growth of Egyptian monasticism.

Though he was a trinitarian thinker in the tradition of Athanasius and the Cappadocians, Cyril's principal contribution was to Christology. He was a vigorous opponent of Nestorius, who held that there were two persons in Christ, one human and one divine, and that Mary was only the Mother of the human Jesus, not the Mother of God (Gk., *Theotokos*). With Cyril's strong support, the Council of Ephesus deposed Nestorius from the patriarchate of Constantinople in 431. Thereafter, Cyril was sometimes willing to compromise in theological formulas, but his own focus remained constant: on the initiative of God's action in Jesus Christ, in whom the divine Word had humbled itself (see Phil 2) and so divinized the humanity of Jesus that death's hold was broken. Indeed, the Council of Chalcedon in 451 appealed to Cyril's authority in its own teaching on the Incarnation. In later centuries both orthodox and Monophysite theologians in the East continued to find good reason to claim his inheritance. Feast day: June 2 (West); June 9 (East). *See also* Chalcedon, Council of; Christology; Ephesus, Council of.

KATHRYN L. JOHNSON

Cyril of Jerusalem, St., ca. 315–ca. 386, bishop of Jerusalem from 348 to 386. He was banished three times (357–59; 360–62; ca. 367–78) over jurisdictional and property disputes at the hands of pro-Arian authorities (Acacius, bishop of Caesarea, and later the emperor Valens), although he was not himself a strict Nicene until sometime after the Council of Antioch (363), when he moved from the *homoiousion* (Gk., the Son is of a similar substance with the Father) position to acceptance of the *homoousion* (Gk., the Son is of the same substance with the Father). Gregory of Nyssa, traveling to Jerusalem to question Cyril, found him orthodox in 379, and he was regarded as such at the Council of Constantinople (381). But he is principally remembered for his brilliant catechesis, preserved in a series of twenty-three homilies addressed to baptismal candidates (homilies 2–19) and to those just baptized (homilies 20–24; some scholars attribute these to Cyril's successor, John). The homilies explain the meaning of the Christian mysteries using a typological exegesis of Scripture, and they are important evidence for Palestinian liturgical practice in the fourth century. Cyril was made a Doctor of the Church in 1882. Feast day: March 18. *See also* Arianism; Nicaea, First Council of.

Czestochowa, Our Lady of (ches-tah-koh'vah), a famous icon in Czestochowa, Poland. The icon was brought to Czestochowa from Ukraine in 1382 by Prince Ladislaus Opolszyk, who built a chapel and founded a monastery of Pauline monks to care for it. After the monastery withstood an attack of antipapal Swedes in 1655, Our Lady of Czestochowa was proclaimed the Queen of Poland in 1656. Since then the icon has served as a symbol of Polish nationalism and religious liberty.

According to tradition, the three cuts on the cheek of the image of Mary were caused by Hussite bandits in 1430. Tradition also claims that St. Joseph built the tablet and St. Luke painted the icon, although historians consider the icon to be a ninth-century Greek or Greek-Italian work that was restored in the thirteenth century in Angevin, Naples. Over a million pilgrims visit the site each year. *See also* Poland, Catholicism in.

The icon of Our Lady of Czestochowa, religious and national symbol of Poland, located in the monastery of Jasna Gora ("Hill of Light"), above the city of Czestochowa in south-central Poland (during the celebration of the Eucharist by Pope John Paul II, June 1991).

d'Ailly, Pierre (dī-yee'), 1350–1420, French Scholastic theologian and cardinal. As a professor and chancellor of the University of Paris, he championed the calling of a Church council to overcome the Great Schism. He believed that Church councils were superior to popes and denied the infallibility of both popes and councils. *See also* conciliarism; Great Schism.

dalmatic, the outer vestment worn by the deacon at Mass or in processions. It derives from a white tunic worn in second-century Dalmatia. Since the twelfth century, it has followed the day's liturgical colors. Variations have included closed or open sides; ample or cut sleeves; ankle or knee length. *See also* vestments.

Damasus I, St., ca. 304–84, pope from 366 to 384. He was appointed deacon by his predecessor Liberius, but his election as Bishop of Rome was contested and subsequently marred by violence because he had served the antipope Felix II while Pope Liberius was still alive but in exile. Damasus promoted the organization of the cult of the martyrs, restoring and decorating their tombs with his own marble inscriptions. He secured from the emperor Gratian the right of Western bishops to appeal directly to the pope (378), customarily designated Rome the "Apostolic See," and rebutted the claims of the see of Constantinople (381), relegating it to a rank second to Rome and applying Matt 16:18 to Roman primacy. In 383 he appointed St. Jerome his secretary and commissioned him to revise the Latin Bible, thus inaugurating the translation later known as the Vulgate. Some of Damasus's letters survive, including the *Tome of Damasus,* but the medieval attribution of the *Liber Pontificalis* to Damasus is incorrect. Feast day: December 4. *See also* Constantinople; primacy, papal; Rome; Vulgate.

Damian, St. *See* Cosmas and Damian, Sts.

Damian, St. Peter. *See* Peter Damian, St.

Damien, Father [Bl. Joseph de Veuster], 1840–89, Belgian-born missionary to Hawaii. The son of prosperous peasants, he was professed a member of the Congregation of the Sacred Hearts of Jesus and Mary (the Picpus Fathers) in 1860. Three years later, he left Belgium for the Sandwich Islands (now Hawaii), where he was ordained in 1864. Initially responsible for several districts on the islands of Ha

Father Damien, nineteenth-century Belgian missionary to lepers on the island of Molokai in Hawaii.

waii and Molokai, he volunteered to serve lepers in the Kalaupapa colony on Molokai in 1873 and worked there for sixteen years as pastor, physician, counselor, sheriff, and undertaker. Damien also founded two orphanages at the colony. He contracted leprosy in 1884, worked until March of 1889, and died one month later. A posthumous investigation exonerated him of charges of moral wrongdoing rumored during his life. In 1936, his remains were removed to Louvain. Beatified, 1995.

damnation, eternal banishment from the face of God resulting from a definitive and final rejection of divine grace. Damnation, understood as the subjection of those who die in sin to eternal punishment, is well attested in Scripture, especially in the NT (e.g., Matt 3:12; 5:22; 13:42; Mark 9:43; Luke 13:28; 2 Thess 1:9). Theologians agree that damnation is essentially the loss of the Beatific Vision, that is, exclusion from the presence of God, but there has been some debate as to whether or not additional punishment is entailed. Such figures as Origen, Jerome, and Gregory of Nyssa thought that the "fires of hell" should be understood symbolically for the psychological suffering entailed by the alienation from God. Others, such as Augustine and Aquinas, maintained the imposition of additional torments derived from the created order, the "positive punishments of hell." The official magisterium has never authorized one of these options over the other, nor has the Church ever affirmed the actual damnation of any individual. Nevertheless, damnation has consistently been regarded by the Church as a distinct and real possibility following from the principles of retributive justice and personal freedom. If human freedom is taken seriously, and the proper end of humanity is understood as union with God in love, there must exist the possibility of a free rejection of God's self-offer, as well as the responsibility for such an action once it has been taken. *See also* hell; reprobation.   *GERARD JACOBITZ*

dance, liturgical. *See* liturgical dance.

danger of death, a canonical factor that allows for the suspension of an ecclesiastical law. For example, any priest, even one under censure, can administer the sacrament of Reconciliation to a dying person. The authority to dispense from marriage impediments is also considerably expanded. Such provisions allow the fullest possibility for those in danger of death to receive the Church's ministry. A person need not be actually dying; it is sufficient that a person be in danger of dying.

Daniel the Stylite, St. *See* Simeon Stylites, St.

Daniélou, Jean (zhohn dahn-yeh-loo'), 1905–74, bishop, cardinal, and French Jesuit patristics scholar. A professor at the Institut Catholique in Paris, he was a key figure in the movement reintroducing the resources of the early Church known as the "New Theology." His translation of Gregory of Nyssa's *Life of Moses* opened the important series *Sources Chrétiennes,* which he edited with Henri de Lubac, his mentor.

Daniélou's life mirrored his scholarly engagement with the question of Christianity and culture. As a *peritus* (Lat., "expert") at Vatican II, he was consulted on the Pastoral Constitution on the Church in the Modern World (*Gaudium et Spes*). In his later years he often spoke polemically against what he saw as the secularism of the post–Vatican II Church.

Dante Alighieri, 1265–1321, Italy's greatest poet and a major figure in world literature. His best-known poem is *La commedia,* later called *The Divine Comedy* when Dante became known as the "divine poet." *The Divine Comedy* has three divisions: the *Inferno* (Hell), *Purgatorio* (Purgatory), and *Paradiso* (Paradise). It explores life as journey using symbols of the next life. The *Inferno* confronts evil; the *Purgatorio* is a journey of liberation until Dante becomes "free, upright, whole" (canto 27); *Paradiso* culminates in the contemplation of the divine. Classical stories and symbols abound, but the journey is Christian to the core. The composition of this poem in Italian had a definitive and immediate effect on European literature and on literature since, e.g., on the poetry of T. S. Eliot. This poem is filled with wide-ranging erudition—ancient classics, history, philosophy, theology, and contemporary politics. Dante's use of imagery and story is powerful and compelling. Dante was born in Florence, a city of expanding horizons during his youth. In his writings he honored his teacher, Brunetto Latini, and his friend, Guido Cavalcanti. Dante credited Beatrice, whom he first saw when both were nine years old, with being the inspiration of his life and work. He celebrated Beatrice in *The New Life, The Banquet,* and in *The Divine Comedy,* where Beatrice takes the place of Virgil as Dante's guide through *Paradiso.* Dante wrote an immense amount of poetry and prose, yet readers worldwide think of Dante as the poet of *The Divine Comedy.*

Dark Ages, obsolete term for the era in western Europe from the fall of Rome (fifth century) to the Renaissance; now sometimes used for the first six centuries of that period. The phrase reflects the Renaissance attitude that these centuries lacked the light of classical culture. In fact, though the barbarian invasions destroyed most of Roman civilization, the Church preserved much classical learning, especially in the monasteries, and even Roman government in the episcopal sees. By A.D. 800, Charlemagne, a descendant of barbarian Franks, was crowned by the pope and proclaimed a renewed empire based in northern Europe.

dark night, the, a symbol in the mystical tradition. Remembering Moses' experience of darkness (Exod 20:21), writers like Gregory of Nyssa developed a symbolism of darkness for the divine encounter. Denys the Areopagite (Pseudo-Dionysius) through his *Mystical Theology* became the major resource for darkness as the symbol of encounter with divine incomprehensibility. The most compelling use of dark night in the tradition has been by John of the Cross (d. 1591) in his poem "Dark Night" and in his commentaries on this poem, *The Ascent of Mount Carmel* and *The Dark Night.* In these commentaries John enumerates his signs for the transition from meditation to contemplation (*Ascent* 2.13; *Dark Night* 1.9). This experience is of the impotence of human effort and of the wholly gifted character of contemplation. This liberation of the human person takes place on the level of sense (dark night of) and the spirit (dark night of), a division of the human person according to Scholastic philosophy in the sixteenth century. John of the Cross considers the entire human journey to God as night: the purification of attachments, night as a journey of faith, and night as encounter with God as mystery (*Ascent* 1.2.1). Today some apply John's symbolism of dark night to corporate experiences. *See also* John of the Cross, St.

Darwinism, the theory of evolution by natural selection proposed by Charles Darwin (1809–82) in *The Origin of Species* (1859). According to the theory, the various species of plant and animal life have arisen through a gradual process of natural selection spanning eons and beginning with the simplest forms of life. The immediate challenge of Darwinism was to the literal interpretation of the biblical account of creation. Therefore, the public battle against Darwinism was fought by fundamentalist Protestants in the famous Scopes trial (1925) in Dayton, Tennessee. Their antievolutionary views today are known as "scientific creationism."

In his encyclical *Humani Generis* (1950) Pope Pius XII rejected polygenism, descent of the human race from more than one couple, in favor of monogenism, descent of the human race from a single couple. At the same time, he allowed for the development of a so-called moderate evolutionism. The Church's official position, therefore, is that any scientific explanation of the origin and development of the human species is acceptable so long as it does not exclude God from the creative process and, in particular, God's role in the creation of the human soul. *See also* creation; creationism; evolution.

Daughters of Charity of St. Vincent de Paul (D.C.), religious community of women founded in France in 1633 by Vincent de Paul and Louise de Marillac. It began as a group of women devoted to assisting the poor. Because they were not originally founded as a consecrated religious community, they avoided the confines of the cloister and were able to work actively among the poor. The community was given papal approval in 1668. They quickly expanded their mission to include other European countries. In 1809 they were established at Emmitsburg,

Maryland, by Elizabeth Ann Seton. Unlike other religious communities, the Daughters of Charity profess their vows for only a year at a time. Today the community is present throughout Europe, Asia, Africa, and North and South America. In 1994 there were nearly fifteen hundred Daughters of Charity in the United States engaged in teaching; hospital work; day care; social services; justice and peace apostolates; ministry to unwed mothers, the elderly, and the dying; and parish work. *See also* Seton, St. Elizabeth Ann Bayley; Vincent de Paul, St.

Daughters of Isabella, a Catholic women's organization. Originating as a ladies' auxiliary of the Knights of Columbus, Russell Council No. 65 of New Haven, Connecticut, the Daughters of Isabella (DI), Circle No. 1, was incorporated in the state of Connecticut on March 7, 1904. Like the Knights it is a Columbian society, but its ceremonials depict the role of Queen Isabella of Spain in the voyages of Christopher Columbus. The society has expanded throughout the United States, Canada, Mexico, and the Philippines. Another DI Circle originated in Utica, New York, but because the New Haven group had been incorporated, the Utica Circle ultimately became the Catholic Daughters of the Americas (CDA). In 1992 the DI numbered nearly 100,000 while the CDA membership was almost 150,000. *See also* Knights of Columbus.

Daughters of Wisdom (D.W.), a congregation of religious women begun by Louis Grignion de Montfort and Marie Louise Trichet in France in 1703, with the intention of caring for the sick among the poor. In the early twentieth century, following the institution of anticlerical laws in France, they founded communities in New York, Maine, Connecticut, and Virginia. The Daughters of Wisdom, today a pontifical institute, run hospitals and clinics as well as institutions for abandoned and retarded children. They also serve in parishes and retreat centers, where they continue to live their founders' vision, the insight that Jesus is the Wisdom of God. *See also* Montfort, St. Louis Grignion de.

David, the most important king of Israel. Of the tribe of Judah and the city of Bethlehem, David rose to prominence under Saul, Israel's first king. David became king around 1010 B.C. and ruled the united tribes from Hebron for seven years. He made Jerusalem his religious and political capital until his death around 970 B.C. Known as a poet, he is credited with a dirge in 2 Sam 1, as well as many psalms. The promise of the prophet Nathan that God would maintain David's line forever (2 Sam 7:5–16) grounded later messianic hopes. According to the NT, those hopes were fulfilled in Jesus, who was descended from David (Matt 1:6–17; Luke 1:27; Acts 2:22–36; Rom 1:3; Rev 5:4).

David, St., or Dewi, sixth-century abbot and bishop of Menevia, Wales. Little but legend is known of this patron saint of Wales. He was apparently bishop and abbot of a monastery at the place now called St. David's in Pembrokeshire. Many ancient Welsh churches were dedicated to him. Feast day: March 1.

Dawson, Christopher, 1889–1970, English historian. A convert to the Catholic Church in 1914, he spent his life as both an academic and independent scholar. He was the first holder of the Stillman Chair of Roman Catholic Studies at Harvard University in 1958. His strong conviction that European civilization was dependent on the Christian faith and the influence of the Catholic Church was best expressed in his work *The Making of Europe* (1932).

Day, Dorothy M., 1897–1980, journalist, pacifist, and cofounder of the Catholic Worker movement.

Dorothy Day, cofounder of the Catholic Worker movement and one of the leading Catholic laywomen of the twentieth century.

After the birth of her only child, Tamara, she abandoned her Bohemian lifestyle in Greenwich Village and converted to Catholicism in 1927. Five years later, Day met the French peasant philosopher and teacher Peter Maurin, and her life changed forever. Maurin provided her with an understanding of the meaning of the Church and her position in it. Together they founded the Catholic Worker movement, a community of laypeople from all walks of life.

Day's belief centered on Christian personalism, a philosophical orientation that stresses the value and dignity of each individual human person. Attempting to make this Worker ideal available to every individual who desired it, she started a newspaper. She entitled it *Catholic Worker,* to announce a Catholic presence and concern for the poor and the oppressed. Day witnessed daily to this concern by embracing voluntary poverty and establishing a house of hospitality and a farming commune.

Day's unique contribution was her proclamation of Catholic pacifism as the ideal response to war. The Catholic Worker was the first Catholic group in American history to claim such a position. Through the influence of Robert Ludlow, who edited the *Catholic Worker,* and Ammon Hennacy, who brought an activist dimension to the movement, nonviolence was integrated into the pacifist position and encouraged lay initiative in changing the social order by performing direct actions on behalf of peace and social justice. Day and the Catholic Worker movement were committed to pacifism and nonviolence and were the heart of the American Catholic peace movement during the Vietnam War, assisting in the formation of other groups such as the American Pax Association, the Catholic Peace Fellowship, and Pax Christi USA. *See also* Catholic Worker movement; Maurin, Peter; pacifism; personalism, Christian. PATRICIA MCNEAL

day of recollection, a day spent in a quiet space to collect one's thoughts and feelings about life. Many parishes and retreat centers have designed thematic programs that span all or part of a day. Unlike retreat programs, days of recollection are not residential, nor do they require overnight accommodation. They are conducted for groups of all sizes and have minimal housing and meal requirements. The experience provides an opportunity for prayerful reflection and the social environment for faith-sharing among participants. Topics can cover, among others, Sacred Scripture, family life, devotion to Mary, Lent and Advent, Eucharist, marriage, reconciliation, and prayer.

day of the Lord, an expression for a time of judgment in the prophets. Isa 24:17–23 describes terror, the pit, and the snare; Joel 2:30–32, a day of portents with the sun darkened and the moon turned into blood. Mal 4:5–6 predicts that Elijah will precede the day. Such predictions inspired the imagery of judgment day in the NT (Matt 24; Mark 13; Luke 21; Rev 19–20).

d'Azeglio, Luigi Taparelli (dah-zayl'-yoh), 1793–1862, Jesuit philosopher and social thinker. Ordained in 1820, six years after the Society of Jesus was restored, he became the first rector of the reopened Roman College (1824) and served as editor of *Civiltà Cattolica* (1850–62). His major five-volume study of the natural law (1840–43) was a forerunner of modern sociology. He is credited with anticipating the move toward internationalism in the mid-twentieth century and with having influenced Pope Leo XIII's social encyclical *Rerum Novarum* ("On the Condition of the Working Person," 1891). *See also Civiltà Cattolica; Rerum Novarum.*

d'Azeglio, Massimo Taparelli (dah-zayl'yoh), 1798–1866, Italian writer, painter, and statesman. Under Pope Pius IX, d'Azeglio espoused a progressive political program supportive of social morality and the supremacy of law. He served as diplomat, premier of Sardinia, envoy to Rome, and governor of Milan.

D.D., Doctor of Divinity, degree, usually honorary, given to bishops in the United States.

deacon, a member of the diaconate, one of the three forms of the sacrament of Holy Orders. The diaconate recently was restored in Latin-rite Catholicism as a permanent and distinct ministry with its own proper function.

The origins of the diaconate are found in the NT period. A reference to what developed into the office of deacon may be found in the reference to "ministers" (Gk., *diakonoi*) associated with the "overseers" (*episkopoi*) in Phil 1:1. Another reference is found in Rom 16:1, where Phoebe is named as a "minister" (*diakonos*) of the church at Cenchreae. 1 Tim 3:8–10; 12–13 describe the qualities of those who would fulfill this office. The reference to "women" in v. 11 of the same passage seems to refer to women deacons, though it is possible that wives of deacons are meant. In none of these passages do we find a clear description of the precise role of the deacon. Earlier interpreters sometimes saw the institution of the diaconate in Acts 6:1–6. Recent critical studies see rather an indication of the early Church's creating new structures in response to the needs of a growing community, not the specific institution of the diaconate. The post-apostolic letters of Ignatius of Antioch (d. ca. 107) have several references to the offices of bishop, presbyters, and deacons in local churches of Asia Minor.

History: The diaconate flourished in the second and third centuries. While diaconal functions varied in different places, ministries of charity, liturgy, and diverse forms of ministry of the Word were common. In some areas deacons were the principal administrative agents of the bishops; their importance in this capacity often exceeded that of the presbyters. In the third and fourth centuries the diaconate in the West began to decline for several reasons: tensions arose between deacons and presbyters because bishops were often chosen from the ranks of deacons; as the Eucharist became more the focus of ministry, the role of presbyters, who presided at Eucharist, became more important than the role of the deacon; and monastic centers took over some of the deacon's charitable responsibilities. Increasing emphasis on celibacy and lack of support for full-time deacons also contributed to the decline of the diaconate. Fourth-century councils emphasized the inferior status of deacons vis-à-vis presbyters and insisted on prior reception of the diaconate before ordination to the priesthood or episcopate. By the seventh century the diaconate in the West became a transitional step for candidates for priesthood. The deacon's role was almost exclusively liturgical. So it remained until the sixteenth century.

The Council of Trent (1545–63) reaffirmed the place of the diaconate in Church order, though its call for a restoration of the diaconate was never implemented. Vatican Council II (1962–65) sought the restoration of the diaconate as a permanent and distinct ministry in the Church. The council not only desired to restore a ministry that was present in apostolic times, but also to grant the grace of the office to those doing diaconal work and to provide ministers for basic functions of Church life. Vatican II's Decree on Eastern Catholic Churches (1964) called for a reintroduction of the diaconate as a permanent office in those churches where it had fallen into disuse.

Vatican II: The texts of Vatican II and the decrees of Pope Paul VI, which implemented the call for a restored diaconate, point to three areas of diaconal ministry. Reflecting early Church tradition, the ordained deacon's basic ministry is to represent and promote the Church's call to service and to be a sign of Christ's own serving mission. The deacon is to function as minister of the word in preaching and in such ministries as catechetical instruction, retreat ministry, or counseling. The deacon's liturgical ministry is to be a visible reminder of the link between the Church's liturgy and its service of others in the name of Christ. The relationship between the various aspects of the deacon's ministry will vary according to local needs. A deacon may be authorized to exercise a limited leadership role in designated pastoral responsibilities in the absence of a priest. Deacons may also serve in the development of small Christian communities. The ministry of the deacon is not to replace the call of all the baptized to share in the serving mission of the Church; rather, it should promote the service role of the entire community.

The order of diaconate in the Catholic Church is at present restricted to men, though women engage in many of the pastoral activities associated with diaconal ministry. The transitional diaconate continues to exist in the Latin rite for candidates for priesthood. *See also* bishop; deacon, woman; Holy Orders; ordination; priesthood.   *FREDERICK J. CWIEKOWSKI*

deacon, permanent, one ordained to the diaconate for life. Although considered for many centuries in the West a separate order within the ancient threefold ministry of the Church, the diaconate was used almost solely as a step on the way to ordination to the presbyterate or priesthood. The Eastern churches, both Catholic and Orthodox, retained the practice of ordaining someone a deacon with the intention that the person would continue in the ministry of a deacon as a lifelong mission and not proceed to ordination as a priest.

Vatican II (1962–65) restored the permanent diaconate in the West. Sometimes incorrectly called a "lay deacon," a permanent deacon is understood in canon law to be a cleric and hence is required to be attached (incardinated) to a diocese and subject to the laws governing clerics, though with some exceptions. The most visible of these is that a married man may be ordained to the permanent diaconate. However, no one ordained to the diaconate can marry subsequently (or remarry upon the death of his wife). In addition, a permanent deacon is neither obliged to wear clerical clothing nor restricted as to occupations. He should ordinarily derive his own financial support from his secular occupation. *See also* deacon; deacon, transitional.

deacon, transitional, one ordained to the diaconate with the expectation of being ordained to the priesthood after a limited period of time. While a transitional diaconate had existed in the West since the seventh century, the present term came into use after the restoration of the permanent diaconate at the Second Vatican Council (1962–65). *See also* celibacy, clerical; deacon; deacon, permanent; Holy Orders; ordination.

deacon, woman, one group of ministers in the early Church. Rom 16:1 refers to Phoebe as the *diakonos* (Gk., "deacon") of the church at Cenchreae, though her role is not specified. A second reference to women deacons may occur in 1 Tim 3:8–13. In the context of a description of qualifications of deacons, one sentence (v. 11) concerns qualifications of women. The meaning of the verse is debated; more probably it refers to women deacons; less likely does it refer to wives of deacons. Pliny the Younger, writing in the early second century, refers to women deacons (Lat., *ministrae*).

Evidence from the patristic period is difficult to summarize. Ministry of women deacons, sometimes called deaconesses in patristic documents, varied from place to place. The ministry of women deacons flourished in the early Church, more so in the East than in the West. The Council of Chalcedon (451) speaks of their ordination. In the early centuries of the Church, women deacons were prominently engaged in liturgical ministry to women and children in the community. Singularly important was their preparation of women catechumens and their role in baptismal anointing of women. As infant baptism replaced adult baptism, the role of women deacons diminished. In Western Christianity their role ceased to exist around the sixth century; in Eastern Christianity women deacons continued to function until the eleventh century.

In contemporary Catholicism, women engage in a variety of pastoral ministries historically associated with the diaconate. The 1976 Vatican declaration against ordination of women to priesthood did not extend to women in the diaconate. *See also* deacon; Holy Orders; ordination; ordination of women.

FREDERICK J. CWIEKOWSKI

deaconess. *See* deacon, woman.

dead, prayers for the. *See* prayers for the dead.

Dead Sea Scrolls, a collection of fragmentary manuscripts in Hebrew, Aramaic, and Greek, copied ca. 225 B.C.–A.D. 135 and belonging to Jewish groups at Qumran and other sites near the Dead Sea. The majority of scrolls, about 800, were discovered in eleven caves immediately west and north of the Qumran settlement, while others were found at Masada, Murabbaat, and Nahal Hever. Cave 1, discovered by an Arab Bedouin in 1947, yielded complete scrolls of the book of Isaiah and the *Rule of the Community,* plus large fragments of five other manuscripts. Formal excavations in the cave unearthed small fragments of some seventy more manuscripts. The main cave (Cave 4) containing 575 manuscripts was discovered in 1952, and the last (Cave 11) in 1956. The dating of the manuscripts is secured independently by archaeological, paleographical, and radiocarbon analysis, as well as by literary similarity with other Jewish works of this period (from *Jubilees* and Daniel to the NT and Mishnah).

Many of the scrolls contain works common to the wide spectrum of late Second Temple Judaism (biblical, liturgical, apocryphal, pseudepigraphical texts), while some reflect the beliefs and perspectives particular to a devout, ascetic, priestly, Torah-centered (the *Rule of the Community,* the *Zadokite Document, Some Works of the Torah*) and apocalyptic (the *Rule,* the *War of the Sons of Light Against the Sons of Darkness*) community. Most scholars, with some exceptions, identify the community with the little-known Essenes. With proper qualifications this is the most cogent hypothesis developed over the past generation. There is no mention of Jesus Christ nor any specific link with Christianity in the scrolls, though Christianity, along with rabbinic Judaism, emerged from the rich spectrum of Judaism illuminated by the scrolls. *See also* Essenes; Masoretic Text; Qumran. *EUGENE ULRICH*

dean. *See* vicar forane.

deanery, or vicariate forane, optional supraparochial grouping, usually of neighboring parishes, to promote more effective pastoral care. Organized under a priest (or bishop) called a vicar forane (or dean, or archpriest) named or approved by the diocesan bishop after appropriate consultation, the deanery is adaptable to personal, geographical, and demographical exigencies. As historically conceived, it may help extend episcopal solicitude to outlying areas or, as often today, where isolation more likely results from urban, sociocultural, or health-related conditions. More than a supervisor, the dean may have broad faculties, for example, to encourage clerical development and morale, promote interparochial cooperation, and allay intraparochial conflicts.

Dearden, John F., 1907–88, cardinal-archbishop, leader at Vatican II and in the postconciliar U.S. Church. After seminary studies in Cleveland, Ohio, and Rome, he was ordained in 1932 and earned a doctorate in theology from the Gregorian University in 1934. He served as instructor and rector at St. Mary's Seminary, Cleveland. Ordained bishop in 1948, he served as coadjutor bishop and, after 1950, as bishop of Pittsburgh before promotion to archbishop of Detroit in 1959. He participated in Vatican Council II (1962–65), was elected first president in 1966 of the National Conference of Catholic Bishops, and was created cardinal in 1969. He was a strong supporter of the Vatican Council II reforms. *See also* National Conference of Catholic Bishops.

death and dying, the irreversible process of decline and termination of human life. The theological understanding of death and dying has been shaped by the biblical record and the philosophical traditions of Western Civilization. In the OT, death is most often portrayed as the passage of the person from the land of the living to *sheol* (Heb.), the dark, cheerless realm of the dead where there can be no happiness and no praise of God (Ps 6:5; Isa 38:18). The later books come closer to the Greek philosophical notion of death as the separation of soul and body (Wis 3:1–5; 4:15), though eternal life came to be understood, not in terms of the immortality of the soul but in terms of the resurrection of the body (Dan 12:2). NT perspectives incorporate these views, understanding death as the enslaving consequence of sin (Rom 5:12; 6:23), yet additionally as that power decisively overcome by the death and resurrection of Jesus (Heb 2:14; 2 Tim 1:10). Drawing on these sources, Catholic theology has traditionally viewed death as a consequence of original sin (Council of Trent, D 788, 793). More recent reflections, influenced by contemporary philosophy, have also emphasized death, and correlatively one's lifelong preparation for it, as a definitional event in the life of the Christian. In the face of death, one's essential disposition toward the mystery of God is disclosed as either an obedient and humble acknowledgment of one's finitude and dependence, or as a rebellious and ultimately self-defeating assertion of one's autonomy. *See also* Anointing of the Sick; eternal life; resurrection of the body.

De Auxiliis (day awg-zil'ee-ees; Lat., "concerning the helps" [toward salvation]), a sixteenth-century theological controversy over grace and free will. The controversy began in Spain with a debate started by the Dominican Domingo Bañez, in response to the Jesuit Luis de Molina's theology of God's grace and its influence, when encountering human freedom, on the individual. The Dominicans saw themselves as true followers of Thomas Aquinas (d. 1274), holding for an efficacy of divine grace that moves free will freely; the Jesuits also understood themselves as Thomists even as they focused upon human freedom. The controversy was held in a series of meetings attended by Clement VIII (d. 1605) and Paul V (d. 1621); it ended in 1607 with papal permission for both sides to teach their theologies. *See also* free will; grace.

decade. *See* Rosary.

Decalogue. *See* Commandments, the Ten.

declaration, conciliar, a statement of less weight than a conciliar constitution indicating the current position of the Church concerning topics of contemporary interest, which may be developed and revised with the passage of time. Vatican Council II (1962–65) issued the declarations On Christian Education (*Gravissimum Educationis*), On Religious Freedom (*Dignitatis Humanae*), and On the Relationship of the Church to Non-Christian Religions (*Nostrae Aetate*). *See also* ecumenical council; Vatican Council II.

Declaration on Christian Education (Lat., *Gravissimum Educationis*, "The most serious [importance] of education"), one of the sixteen documents of Vatican II. Promulgated on October 28, 1965, the declaration focuses on the education of the young in the home, the school (including colleges, universities, and seminaries), and the Church (through catechesis and liturgy), but the greatest emphasis is on schooling. The declaration, original-

ly conceived as a constitution on Catholic schools, insists that education must be broadly humane, open to scientific advances, and concerned with nurturing personal maturity and social responsibility. It is different from other conciliar documents in that it deals only with a few basic principles and leaves their development to the postconciliar process. The pertinent documents of implementation are the *General Catechetical Directory*, issued by the Sacred Congregation for the Clergy in 1971; *Catholic Schools; Lay Catholics in Schools: Witness to Faith;* and *The Religious Dimension of Education in a Catholic School*, issued by the Sacred Congregation for Catholic Education in 1977, 1982, and 1988, respectively; and the *Catechism of the Catholic Church*, issued by the Sacred Congregation for the Doctrine of the Faith in 1992.

Declaration on Religious Freedom (Lat., *Dignitatis Humanae*, "Of the dignity of the human [person]"), one of the sixteen documents of Vatican II. Promulgated on December 7, 1965, the document was first intended as a chapter on Church-state relations in the Dogmatic Constitution on the Church (*Lumen Gentium*), as a chapter on religious freedom in the Decree on Ecumenism, and later as an appendix of that decree. At the council's third session (1964) it was given independent status as a separate schema (proposal), to be revised by the Secretariat for Promoting Christian Unity. A key drafter was the American Jesuit theologian John Courtney Murray, who had previously been silenced by the Vatican for his views on Church and state and religious liberty.

This was the most controversial document produced by the council because it raised the question of doctrinal development. In light of so many strong condemnations of the principle of religious freedom in previous papal teachings from the Middle Ages and the nineteenth century (esp. Pope Pius IX's "Syllabus of Errors," 1864), it seemed theologically impossible for the council to take a new doctrinal stance on this issue. The schema elicited intense opposition from conservative forces at the council, led by Cardinal Alfredo Ottaviani, prefect of the Holy Office.

The declaration is a landmark document because it explicitly intended "to develop the doctrine of recent popes on the inviolable rights of the human person and on the constitutional order of society" (n. 1); it acknowledged for the first time in official Catholic teaching the fact of religious pluralism without condemning or bemoaning it; it defined the role of government as constitutional and limited in function, namely, the protection and promotion of human rights and duties, and disavowed any sacral function for it; and it affirmed the freedom of the Church, rather than its privileged legal status, as "the fundamental principle in what concerns the relations between the Church and governments and the whole civil order" (n. 13).

The declaration grounded its teaching not only on the dignity of the human person but also on revelation. The act of faith is, of its very essence, a free act. Jesus Christ himself never compelled anyone to believe in him. His manner was always meek, humble, and patient. His miracles were intended to rouse faith in his hearers and to confirm them in faith, not to coerce them. Taught by Christ's example, the apostles followed the same way (nn. 9–12).

Religious freedom, rooted in freedom of conscience, demands personal immunity from all manner of compulsion and restraint in everything pertaining to the making or rejecting of an act of religious faith (n. 9). But such freedom also demands autonomy for religious bodies in matters concerning their own organization, governance, and spiritual mission and immunity from coercion in the public expression of their religious faith, that is, in what concerns worship, religious observances and practices, the proclamation of religious faith, and the declaration of the social, economic, and political implications of religious faith (n. 13). This freedom can only be limited when it interferes with public order, that is, when the public peace, commonly accepted standards of public morality, or the rights of other citizens are threatened (n. 7). *See also* Murray, John Courtney; religious liberty.

RICHARD P. MCBRIEN

Declaration on the Relationship of the Church to Non-Christian Religions (Lat., *Nostra Aetate,* "In our age"),

one of the sixteen documents of Vatican II. Promulgated on October 28, 1965, the declaration was originally intended as a chapter in the Decree on Ecumenism. It was also to have been concerned principally with the Jews because this was a matter of personal concern to Pope John XXIII. However, that idea proved unworkable not only because of the political situation of Christian Arabs in the Middle East, but also because of the Church's own broader vision of the religious world beyond it, reflected, for example, in Pope Paul VI's encyclical *Ecclesiam Suam* (1964).

The declaration acknowledges that the human community is one because it comes from the creative hand of the one God (n. 1) and that variations in religious faith and practice are simply a reflection of the rich diversity that characterizes humankind itself: "The Catholic Church rejects nothing which is true and holy in these religions.... [They] often reflect a ray of that truth which enlightens all persons" (n. 2). Consequently, the declaration encourages "dialogue and collaboration" with the followers of other religions in order to promote common spiritual, moral, social, and cultural values.

The declaration praises Hinduism's emphasis on contemplation, asceticism, meditation, and trust in God (n. 2), Buddhism's recognition of the insufficiency of the material world (n. 2), and Islam's belief in the one God, its reverence for Jesus as a great prophet, its honoring of Mary, his mother, its high moral standards, and its commitment to prayer, almsgiving, and fasting (n. 3).

But the greatest emphasis is placed on Christianity's relationship to Judaism, in which the beginnings of the Church's faith and election are to be found. Thus, "the Jews still remain most dear to God because of their fathers, for he does not repent of the gifts he makes nor of the calls he issues" (n. 4).

The declaration directly challenges the prejudice that all Jews are somehow responsible for the death of Christ and, therefore, are to be reviled throughout history as "Christ-killers." What happened to Jesus, the council declares, "cannot be blamed upon all the Jews then living, without distinction, nor upon the Jews of today. Although the Church is the new people of God, the Jews should not be presented as repudiated or cursed by God, as if such views followed from the holy Scriptures" (n. 4). This principle should always be reflected in the Church's catechetical instruction and preaching.

The Church "deplores the hatred, persecutions, and displays of anti-Semitism directed against the Jews of any time and from any source" (n. 4). Indeed, we cannot pretend to love God if we reject our brothers and sisters who are created in God's image (n. 5). "As a consequence, the Church rejects, as foreign to the mind of Christ, any discrimination against persons or harassment of them because of their race, color, condition of life, or religion" (n. 5).

The declaration has had a decidedly positive impact on Catholic-Jewish relations since Vatican II, promoting theological dialogue, joint prayer, and collaboration in social ministry. *See also* Jews, Catholicism and; salvation outside the Church.

RICHARD P. MCBRIEN

decree, one of any number of types of official proclamations issued by a competent authority, most often by papal or episcopal authority. The decree of an ecumenical council is its most solemn form. *See also* constitution, conciliar; declaration, conciliar.

decree, conciliar, a doctrinal or pastoral statement concerning a specific group of people or Church matter and sometimes containing directives for renewal or reform. Vatican Council II (1962–65) issued nine decrees, including On Ecumenism (*Unitatis Redintegratio*), On the Apostolate of the Laity (*Apostolicam Actuositatem*), and On the Appropriate Renewal of the Religious Life (*Perfectae Caritatis*). *See also* ecumenical council; Vatican Council II.

Decree on Eastern Catholic Churches (Lat., *Orientalium Ecclesiarum*), Second Vatican Council document on Eastern-rite Catholic communities and one of the shortest conciliar decrees. Debated at Vatican II in October 1964 and approved on November 20, it deals with particular churches, preservation of the spiritual heritage of the Eastern Churches, Eastern patriarchs, sacraments, divine worship, and relations with the separated brethren.

The document insists on equality of rites, avoidance of latinization, and the fostering and restoration of the Eastern heritage, all of which must be understood against the background of centuries of Latin ecclesiastical and cultural imperialism against Eastern Catholics throughout the world, a discrimination that was especially prejudicial in North America. The text reflects the actual state of the Catholic Church as a basically Western Church with several minority satellite communities enjoying a special status and special rites, rather than a communion of several sister churches, each one an equally particular church. Noteworthy in this context is the provisional nature of the decree: it applies only to Eastern Catholic churches (title and n. 30), thus abandoning any pretense that Eastern Catholicism represents the whole of Eastern Christendom.

Though silent on Eastern traditions threatening to entrenched Latin prejudices such as married clergy, the decree is in many ways a notable document containing several progressive elements. Most remarkable, with implications hardly appreciated at the time, is the affirmation that Eastern Catholic communities are distinct churches (not just "rites") enjoying the same rights and obligations, including the right and obligation to spread by preaching the gospel (n. 3). Therefore, Eastern hierarchies should be established where needed (n. 4), and these churches have the right and duty "to govern themselves" according to their own traditions (n. 5). Astonishingly, the decree specifies these as follows: "The rights and privileges . . . which existed in the time of union between East and West" (n. 9). Where necessary, new patriarchates should be established (n. 11).

Several statements on liturgy are also noteworthy: the Eastern liturgical heritage is to be preserved, but also modernized (nn. 6, 12), an invitation that contained the seeds of future friction between local churches and Rome. There are unexpected advances, too, such as the explicit recognition of the Eastern practice that the Sunday or holy day precept can be fulfilled by attendance at the cathedral offices (n. 15), of the fact that the Divine Office is not a prayerbook but liturgy (n. 22), and of the age-old custom of vernacular liturgy (n. 23) under the control of the local church authorities (and, therefore, not of Rome).

Failure to implement some of the positive elements of this decree in the aftermath of Vatican II remains a major source of friction between Rome and, especially, the Ukrainian, Melkite, and Syro-Malabar Catholic churches. *See also* Eastern Catholics and Rome; Eastern Catholics and Vatican II.

ROBERT F. TAFT

Decree on Ecumenism (Lat., *Unitatis Redintegratio*), one of the sixteen documents of the Second Vatican Council (1962–65), and the most authoritative charter of the Catholic Church's active participation in the one ecumenical movement. Promulgated on November 21, 1964, its ecclesiological positions shifted the Catholic understanding of the one Church of Christ, of the relationship between the Catholic Church and the other churches, and of attitudes and methods in "the restoration of unity." The shift is from a former ecclesiology of Catholic self-sufficiency and the unification model of "return" (to the Catholic Church) to that of an ecclesiology that acknowledges the incompleteness of the Church and the need for one another in the one, but still divided, fellowship or Church. Ecumenism is not a return to the past but a common search for future reconciliation.

The decree describes the understanding of the fundamental invisible and visible unity of the Lord's "one Church and one Church only" as the expression of the undivided Trinity. This Church "subsists in" the Catholic Church but is not coextensive with it, because "outside its visible borders," i.e., in other Christians and their communions, exist "elements and endowments which together build up and give life to the Church itself" (n. 3).

Division among Christians "openly contradicts the will of Christ, scandalizes the world, and damages ... the proclamation of the gospel" (n. 1). Nevertheless, there already is a real communion between Christians because of what God has done and does to and through them; this communion is imperfect because of what they have done and continue to do to each other—"a real but imperfect communion" among all Christian communions (n. 3).

Ecumenism in practice demands the "continual reformation" of the pilgrim Church and the continual conversion—"change of heart and holiness of life"—of each Catholic (nn. 6, 7). A loving understanding of each other's communion through dialogue, an ecumenically oriented formation and education, and a common search into the word of God foster mutual understanding and esteem. And common witness to the Servant Lord is strongly encouraged through cooperative action, especially in social matters (n. 12).

The decree describes the principal historical divisions in the Christian family—in East and West. The Eastern churches have the right to govern themselves according to their own traditions and historical developments. The Eastern liturgical and monastic traditions, spiritualities, and church disciplines, and "complementary rather than conflicting" theological formulations should be respected, for they contribute to the comeliness of the one Church and to its witness (n. 17).

For the Christian communions of the West, the decree proposes a program for dialogue. The commitment to Christ as Lord and Savior, the reverence for Holy Scripture, the baptismal liturgy and celebration of the Lord's Supper, or Eucharist, the apostolic witness to the gospel in social action—all provide points of agreement among Catholics and their Anglican and Protestant sisters and brothers in Christ.

The basic theological and pastoral positions of the decree motivated and guided the post–Vatican II Church. The experience is officially expressed in the 1983 Code of Canon Law, and in the 1993 Ecumenical Directory, issued by the Pontifical Council for Christian Unity. "The will of Christ binds the Church to promote the restoration of unity" (can. 755). Ecumenism, in the words of the 1985 Synod of Bishops, "inscribes itself deeply and indelibly in the consciousness of the Church." *See also* Church; ecumenical movement; ecumenism; unity of the Church.

THOMAS F. STRANSKY

Decree on Priestly Formation (*Optatum Totius*, Lat., "the wish of the whole [Church]"), 1965 document of Vatican Council II. The decree contains directives and counsels concerning the formation of candidates for priesthood in light of the council's teaching and pastoral concerns. The document is meant to be read in conjunction with the council's Dogmatic Constitution on the Church, the Pastoral Constitution on the Church in the Modern World, and the Decree on the Ministry and Life of Priests. The Decree on Priestly Formation was intended to do for Vatican II what the Council of Trent's Decree on Seminaries (1563) did for the needs of the Church four hundred years earlier. This decree of Vatican II holds to proven norms but adapts according to the orientations of the council and the pastoral needs of the present. The text treats, at different lengths, seven topics: the need for each nation or rite to have its own "Program for Priestly Formation" drawn up by the episcopal conference and revised at regular intervals; suggestions on fostering priestly vocations; the necessity of major seminaries in preparing candidates for the basic responsibilities of pastoral ministry; directives for spiritual formation of priestly candidates; the revision of ecclesiastical studies in the light of Catholic teaching and contemporary pastoral needs; the incorporation of pastoral concerns into all aspects of priestly training; and the need for continuing education beyond the seminary program. The decree begins and ends with a reminder of the role of the priest in the renewal of the Church, a concern of the council. *See also* priesthood. FREDERICK J. CWIEKOWSKI

Decree on the Apostolate of the Laity (Lat., *Apostolicam Actuositatem,* "The apostolic activity"), one of the sixteen documents of Vatican II. Promulgated on November 18, 1965, the decree was originally a much longer document, comprehensively examining all aspects of the lay apostolate. Some of that material was transferred to the Pastoral Constitution on the Church in the Modern World, the Dogmatic Constitution on the Church, the Decree on the Church's Missionary Activity, and other documents.

Like the Dogmatic Constitution on the Church (n. 33), the decree rejects the notion that the lay apostolate is simply a participation in the apostolate of the hierarchy (Catholic Action). Rather it "derives from [the laity's] Christian vocation" (n. 1) and from their sacramental incorporation into the Body of Christ. They are "assigned to the apostolate by the Lord himself" (n. 3). Indeed, the laity "share in the priestly, prophetic, and royal office of Christ and therefore have their own role to play in the mission of the whole People of God in the Church and in the world" (n. 2).

Although the decree situates the lay apostolate firmly in the temporal sphere, namely, the family, culture, economics, the arts and professions, politics, and international relations (n. 7), it does not exclude the laity from direct participation in the internal life of the Church (ch. 3). They "exercise their apostolate both in the Church and in the world, in both the spiritual and temporal orders" (n. 5). They do this either as individuals or as members of organizations and associations (ch. 4) and in cooperation with the hierarchy and clergy (ch. 5). *See also* laity.　　　　　　　　　*RICHARD P. MCBRIEN*

Decree on the Appropriate Renewal of the Religious Life

(Lat., *Perfectae Caritatis*, "Of perfect charity"), one of the sixteen documents of the Second Vatican Council. Promulgated on October 28, 1965, the decree called for the renewal of religious orders and congregations that involved two processes: "(1) a continuous return to the sources of all Christian life and to the original inspiration behind a given community and (2) an adjustment of the community to the changed conditions of the times" (n. 2).

The document calls on congregations and orders to study Scripture and the spirit of the founders for guidance as they adapt to the current demands of society and the Church. In accord with the Dogmatic Constitution on the Church (*Lumen Gentium*, 1964) this decree deals with the way that members of religious congregations and orders follow the universal call to holiness preached by Jesus.

Among the adaptations called for were modifying the papal cloister according to the conditions of time and place; doing away with outdated customs; and revising constitutions, directories, custom books, books of prayers, and ceremonies to bring them into harmony with the documents of the council. The decree states that religious habits should correspond to requirements of health and be suited to the conditions of time and place and to the services required by those who wear them.

The most significant change recommended did not concern exterior adaptations but demanded a renewal of spirit that could enliven exterior changes. This document marked the beginning of dramatic changes in the style of living and ministries of the members of religious congregations and orders. *See also* religious life; religious orders and congregations.

　　　　　　　　　REGINA COLL

Decree on the Bishops' Pastoral Office in the Church

(*Christus Dominus*, Lat., "Christ, the Lord"), 1965 document of Vatican Council II. It focuses on practical applications of the council's teaching on the office of bishops. The decree is to be read in conjunction with the Dogmatic Constitution on the Church, ch. 3. The decree focuses on three basic areas of episcopal responsibility. The first chapter deals with the bishops' collegial responsibility for the universal Church and their relationship with the pope. Special mention is given to the synod of bishops. The decree calls for a reorganization of the departments of the Roman Curia, with membership representative of the universal Church and more frequent recourse to the advice of laypersons.

The second chapter looks to the bishop's responsibilities in the local diocese. His teaching role, one of his principal duties, is to take account of contemporary needs and opportunities. In describing the bishop as pastor, the decree looks to the role of diocesan councils and the bishop's relations with priests, with special attention to religious.

The third chapter deals with the cooperation of bishops responsible for the Church in a particular region and calls for the use of synods and councils to serve that purpose. Specific attention is given to the nature and authority of the episcopal conference.

The decree emphasizes bishops' responsibilities and duties, with minimal attention to prerogatives and rights. This reflects the council's teaching that service is at the heart of episcopal ministry. *See also* bishop.　　　*FREDERICK J. CWIEKOWSKI*

Decree on the Church's Missionary Activity

(Lat., *Ad Gentes Divinitus*, "To the nations"), one of the sixteen documents of Vatican II. Promulgated on December 7, 1965, this decree was promoted especially by missionary bishops in an effort to draw attention to the challenge of evangelizing the Third World and to attract financial and personnel support from the bishops of Europe and America. The document presupposes the Dogmatic Constitution on the Church and the Pastoral Constitution on the Church in the Modern World, but it differs from both in that they speak of the "mission" of the Church in its comprehensive sense of preaching the gospel in word, sacrament, witness, and service to the whole human community, Christian and non-Christian alike, while this decree is concerned with one important aspect of that total mission, namely, "preaching the gospel and planting the Church among peoples or groups who do not yet believe in Christ" (n. 6). The distinction is between the "mission of the Church" and "the missions." In both senses, "the whole Church is missionary" in its very nature (n. 35). The immediate purpose of missionary activity in the latter sense is the establishment of a local church with its own native hierarchy (n. 6; ch. 3).

Wherever missionaries go, however, they are not to impose an alien cultural reality from outside, but to recognize and preserve "whatever truth and grace are to be found among the nations, as a sort of secret presence of God" (n. 9). This pastoral principle is rooted in the theological principle of the incarnation (n. 10). *See also* missions.   RICHARD P. MCBRIEN

Decree on the Instruments of Social Communication

Decree on the Instruments of Social Communication (Lat., *Inter Mirifica,* "Among astonishing [inventions]"), one of the sixteen documents of Vatican II. Promulgated on December 4, 1963, before the council's theology had fully developed, the decree tended to adopt a moralistic and maternalistic tone (nn. 1–2). The first chapter insists on the primacy of the moral order in the world of communications and art and on the competence of Church authorities in making pertinent moral judgments. The second and final chapter exhorts the faithful to establish and support a Catholic press and to promote good films, radio, and television.

A much lengthier, less narrow Pastoral Instruction on the Means of Social Communication, *Communio et Progressio,* was issued in 1971. It noted that it would be "impossible" to lay complete blame on the media for declining moral standards (n. 22) and that the development of public opinion requires the free flow of information not only in society (nn. 24–47), but also in the Church (nn. 114–21).

Decree on the Ministry and Life of Priests

Decree on the Ministry and Life of Priests (*Presbyterorum Ordinis,* Lat., "the order of priests"), 1965 document of Vatican Council II. The decree concerns the ministry of priests in light of the council's teaching and the pastoral circumstances of the day. Even though presented in the juridical form of a decree, the statement also contains an elaboration of the council's teaching on priests given in article 28 of the Dogmatic Constitution on the Church (1964). The decree reflects the council's intent to expand the notion of priestly ministry from one focused largely on ministry of the sacraments to a broader threefold ministry of God's Word, sacraments, and community leadership.

The decree develops the notion of priestly ministry in terms of four relationships of priests discussed in the Dogmatic Constitution on the Church. By sacramental ordination, the priest is said to act "in the person of Christ the head" in the exercise of the threefold ministry. The ministry of the priest is to be understood also in terms of his relationship to the body of bishops, with which he shares the one priesthood of Christ; to other priests, with whom the priest is united by a sacramental bond; and to the laity for whom the priest functions as pastor, even though he is one with the faithful by virtue of a common baptism and with whom he shares a common call to discipleship. The decree teaches that the priest's holiness is achieved precisely through the ministry he exercises. *See also* priesthood.

decretal, a letter of precept issued by a pope in response to a doubt or question. Decretal letters had the binding force of law and were gathered in collections of canon law. First issued by popes in the late fourth century, papal decretals were a major source of canon law in the Middle Ages. *See also* canon law.

Decretum Gelasianum (day-kray'toom gelahs-ee-ah'noom), Latin ecclesiastical text from possibly the sixth century. The name of the last section, *De Libris Recipiendis et Non Recipiendis* (Lat., "On Books to Be Received and Not to Be Received"), is sometimes used for the whole; this part includes an early biblical canon. It was erroneously ascribed to Pope Gelasius (492–96) among others. *See also* canon of the Scriptures.

Decretum Gratianum (day-kray'toom grahtzee-ah'noom; Lat., "Gratian's Decree") a private, unofficial collection of canon law and related canonical sources, with commentaries, compiled ca. 1140 by the monk John Gratian. Comprising the first part of the *Corpus Iuris Canonici* (Lat., "Body of Canon Law"), it remained an important source of canon law until the Code of Canon Law of 1917. *See also* canon law; Gratian.

dedication of churches, a solemn form of blessing of new churches performed by the diocesan bishop or a bishop or presbyter (priest) delegated by him. The Rite of Dedication of a Church and an Altar is found in the Roman Pontifical, a book of ceremonies performed by a bishop.

The rite begins before the church is built, with the blessing of the site of the new church and the blessing and laying of the foundation stone. After the building is completed, the dedication itself consists of four parts: (1) the entrance into the church; the handing over of the church to the bishop by those involved in building it; the sprinkling of holy water on the people, the walls of the church, and the altar; (2) the Liturgy of the Word; (3) the prayer of dedication, the anointing of the church walls and altar with sacred chrism, the incensation of the altar and church, the covering of the altar with the altar linens, and the lighting of the candles on the altar; and (4) the celebration of the Eucharist.

A dedication, like a blessing, is a sacramental. Churches, especially cathedral and parish churches, should be dedicated and not merely blessed since they are set aside permanently for divine worship.

defect, canonical, some aspect of a person, a thing, or a legal act that indicates some legal deficiency. A defect of form with respect to marriage, for example, indicates that the required manner of entering into marriage was not followed; a defect with respect to Holy Orders was spoken of in the 1917 code and indicated some characteristic of an individual that made him unsuitable for ordination or for the exercise of ordained ministry.

defender of the bond, qualified canonist whom the diocesan bishop must appoint and whose presence is mandatory in cases of nullity or dissolution of marriage or of nullity of sacred orders.

The acts of such cases are invalid without the participation of the defender of the bond. He or she must ensure that all arguments that reasonably can be adduced against the nullity or dissolution are proposed and clarified. Required for the office is at least a licentiate in canon law. *See also* Holy Orders; marriage law.

Defender of the Faith, a title conferred by the pope on individuals who distinguish themselves as exponents of the Catholic faith. The title was first conferred by Pope Leo X on King Henry VII of En-

gland in 1521 in recognition of his treatise in defense of the doctrine of the seven sacraments against Martin Luther. In 1544 Parliament authorized the title for Henry and all of his successors in the British monarchy.

de fide (day fee'day; Lat., "[a matter] of faith"), a theological note describing a doctrinal proposition's relationship to divine revelation. Doctrines of the Church that are held to be *de fide* are doctrines the Catholic Church teaches are contained in divine revelation. These doctrines are taught infallibly by the magisterium and as such should elicit from the faithful an assent of faith. Doctrinal propositions that are solemnly defined by the pope or an ecumenical council are taught as *de fide definita*, "of defined faith." Some theologians assert that teachings can be taught as *de fide ecclesiastica*, "of ecclesiastical faith." These are doctrinal propositions that may not be found directly in divine revelation but that are necessary for the preservation of revelation and are, therefore, also taught infallibly. *See also* doctrine; dogma.

deification, a theological theme also known as divinization. Judaism emphasized the transcendence of God, but the Incarnation gave Christians an intimation of accessibility to the divine. Paul said: "For in him we live and move and have our being" (Acts 17:28). Elsewhere in the NT it is said: "You . . . may become participants of the divine nature" (2 Pet 1:4). Clement of Alexandria's words became a commonplace: "The Word of God became man that you may learn from man how man may become God." Eastern theology has been very much at home with this theme. Not so in the West, where theologians have striven to avoid any hint of pantheism or affirmation of the preexistence of souls. Theologians have, therefore, been careful to speak of participation in the divine through grace. Yet, contemporary theologians Karl Rahner and Hans Urs von Balthasar have come closer to the Eastern language of deification. *See also* grace.

Deipara (day-ee-pahr'ah; Lat. translation of Gk., *Theotokos,* "God-bearer"), title applied to Mary at the Council of Ephesus in 431 to attest that she is truly the Mother of God, and not of the human Jesus alone. Although the intent of Ephesus was Christological, the claim that Mary was *Deipara* hastened the development of Mariology and encouraged the proliferation of Marian feasts. It is now regarded as the fundamental principle of Mariology. *See also* Ephesus, Council of; *Theotokos.*

deism, a view of God that maintains the concept of an intelligent creator-deity while rejecting any notion of divine revelation. Deism takes many forms, from views that include the idea of divine providence to those that negate any concern on God's part for human beings.

The combination of the discoveries of Galileo and Newton with the Enlightenment's exaltation of rationality prepared the ground for deism's postulation of a deity who merely set the universe in motion (the divine clock-maker). Deism holds that human reason alone leads to the principles of natural religion and morality without needing recourse to divine revelation. This view, therefore, rejects as unnecessary and untenable Christian doctrines on the Trinity, the Incarnation, and grace.

Deism first appeared in seventeenth-century Britain and France. In America, Ethan Allen and Thomas Paine produced deistic works in the eighteenth century, and the writings of Benjamin Franklin and Thomas Jefferson indicate an affinity for deism. *See also* God; revelation.

Dei Verbum (day'ee vair'boom). *See* Dogmatic Constitution on Divine Revelation.

Delanoue, St. Jeanne, also known as Joan Delanoue, 1666–1736, founder of the Sisters of St. Anne of Providence of Saumur. A French businesswoman, she had a conversion experience at the age of thirty, closed her shop, and began to minister to orphans. She later entered religious life and in 1704 founded her own community to carry on her ministry to those in need. She was canonized in 1982. Feast day: August 16.

delegation of jurisdiction. *See* jurisdiction.

Delp, Alfred, 1907–45, German Jesuit theologian, sociologist, and martyr. A student of Karl Rahner, he was ordained a priest in 1938. While pursuing a degree in sociology at the University of Munich, he served as a consultant for the journal *Stimmen der Zeit* ("Voices of the Time"). In his parochial ministry, he boldly preached against Nazism and clandestinely assisted Jews to flee Germany. In 1942, at the request of his Jesuit superior, he joined the German Resistance group, the Kreisau Circle, and collaborated in drafting plans for a new German democracy founded on principles of social justice. Arrested along with the Circle's other members on July 28, 1944, he was convicted of treason by a People's Court and hanged in Berlin-Plötzensee. Delp's writings include his doctoral dissertation on Martin Heidegger, *Tragic Existence* (1935).

de Maistre, Joseph (duh-may'strah), 1754–1821, French diplomat, apologist, advocate of traditionalism and Ultramontanism. A fervent royalist, he opposed the French Revolution and Enlightenment philosophy. Arguing that reason was incapable of discerning the moral and religious truths upon which society rests, he asserted that these had been revealed divinely and were handed on through tradition. Society lacks stability without the support of revealed religion, he argued. In *Du Pape* (1819), the charter document of Ultramontanism, he argued that society requires a unifying principle: the king for civil society and the pope for the Church. Social harmony requires the alliance of the two. *See also* traditionalism, Catholic; Ultramontanism.

democracy (Gk., "rule by the people"), a system of government in which all the people share in the activities of governance. Basic to democracy, especially as practiced in the United States, are certain inalienable rights: freedom of speech, freedom of the press, freedom of religion, freedom of assembly, freedom of election, due process of law, and so forth. "The protection and promotion of the inviolable rights of persons ranks among the essential duties of government," the Second Vatican Council declared (Declaration on Religious Freedom, n. 6). "At the same time," the council pointed out elsewhere, "the choice of government and the method of selecting leaders is left to the free will of citizens" (Pastoral Constitution on the Church in the Modern World, n. 74).

Although the Catholic Church has never officially expressed a preference for one form of government over another, Pope John Paul II came close to making such an endorsement in his encyclical marking the one hundredth anniversary of Pope Leo XIII's *Rerum Novarum:* "The church values the democratic system inasmuch as it ensures the participation of citizens in making political choices, guarantees to the governed the possibility both of electing and holding accountable those who govern them, and of replacing them through peaceful means when appropriate" (*Centesimus Annus* [1991], n. 46).

democracy in the Church, the full participation by members in governing the Church either directly or through representatives. This idea remains somewhat controversial.

The Catholic Church is not a democracy, but neither is it a monarchy, a continuation of the Roman Empire, or a multinational corporation. It is a church, and as such has a unique constitution as the People of God and Body of Christ, in which Christ alone is the head and power derives from him.

There are many democratic elements in Catholic Church tradition. Some religious orders such as the Dominicans most closely resemble democratic practices, where decisions are made by the members, frequently through a search for consensus.

On a more fundamental level, the understanding of the Church as communion, which requires participation and shared responsibility, provides an important foundation for the application of certain democratic practices within general church life. Church law already provides for some of this by attention to rights, structures for participation, and concern for accountability.

The fundamental equality of all the baptized, affirmed by Vatican II (Dogmatic Constitution on the Church, n. 30), is expressed in the canons for the Latin church (can. 208) and for Eastern Catholic churches. So, too, are lists of the rights and obligations of all the faithful (cans. 208–31). This attention to rights, even though still only in a beginning stage and without well-developed structures for their protection and vindication, is a characteristic of democratic concerns today.

Structures of the Church: Structures for participation in the inner life of the Church are organized around the practice of consultation. Parish and diocesan pastoral councils and diocesan synods, while not mandatory, are gaining greater acceptance and carry the potential for improved involvement in mission. Presbyteral councils, parish and diocesan finance councils, and colleges of consultors are required structures that participate in the governance of the Church. The law provides improved potential for representative participation in provincial and plenary councils.

In one sense the college of bishops is a democratic expression insofar as bishops are considered to "represent" their dioceses. The bishops, together with the pope, share responsibility for the pastoral governance of the Church, even exercising supreme power within the Church when they act as a college.

The principle of accountability of officeholders is also accepted in church law, although procedures to assure this accountability remain primarily hierarchical. That is, officeholders are accountable to their superiors, not to the members of the Church.

The hierarchical structure of the Church, founded in divine law, limits the practice of democracy within the Catholic Church. Although the pope is elected by the college of cardinals, who theoretically represent the clergy of the diocese of Rome, the selection of other church leaders is not democratic. Power in the Church does not derive from the consent of the governed but, ultimately, from Christ; Christ's presence, however, is assured through sacraments and charisms, as well as office. In the Church, mission has priority over individual interests, but all share a common responsibility for that mission, though with various particular responsibilities. *See also* Church. JAMES H. PROVOST

demon (Gk., *daimon,* "spirit"), a spirit, either good or bad, especially one associated with cosmic forces. The concept of malevolent spirits arose in the ancient world from a dualist cosmology, the polarity of good and evil, light and darkness, God and Satan. In the Jewish-Christian tradition this belief is well illustrated by the *Testament of Solomon.* Here we find different physical, psychological, social, and cosmic disorders attributed to an amazing number and variety of spirits. Archaeologists have discovered numerous artifacts that were used as prophylactics against demons, e.g., amulets, also bowls with protective spells and incantations inscribed on the inside of the vessels. The Hebrew Scriptures give little emphasis to evil spirits until the postexilic period. The NT bears witness to them, especially in Mark. They are noticeably absent from John. In Revelation we see the activity of both good and malevolent spirits (e.g., Rev 5:6; 16:14). Although the existence of demons has been presupposed by the Catholic Church, there is no dogmatic teaching on the subject. Many modern theologians attribute demonic activity to psychiatric disorders. *See also* demonic possession.

demonic possession, a phenomenon where the psychic power of a demon takes over the personality of a human recipient so that she or he is incapable of voluntary action (in contrast to demonic obsession, where the person can still exercise volition). Possession frequently manifests bizarre symptoms, such as histrionic behavior, incoherent speech, uncontrollable physical movements, and extraordinary feats of physical strength. The patient may be self-destructive or destructive to others or to material objects. Demonic possession is a common cultural phenomenon among less sophisticated religious groups. It is often attributed to mass hypnosis or experimentation with the occult. The OT records only one explicit case of demonic possession (Tob 3:7–9), but the NT portrays Jesus ministering to many who are purported to be possessed by demons; while the synoptic Gospels, especially Mark, portray many cases of demonic possession, no cases are specifically recorded in the Pauline corpus or in the Gospel of John. The two cases in Acts 16:16 and 19:13–19 relate to non-Christians. Modern biblical research, studying the pertinent texts from an anthropological point of view, often interprets the phenomenon as the manifestation of repressed feelings of oppression, both personal and social. *See also* exorcism [in the Bible].

demythologization, the theory that biblical myths can be interpreted according to the understanding of existence that they enshrine (i.e., their anthropology). A literal translation of the German term *entmythologizierung,* demythologization is associated with the theology of Rudolf Bultmann (d. 1976). Bultmann began with the dilemma of how post-Enlightenment men and women could relate to a biblical picture of a prescientific "three-storied universe" (i.e., God in heaven above, humans on earth, demons below the earth). Myth for Bultmann is not "untruth" but language about the divine, explaining the divine in human terms. For example, God's transcendence is thought of in spatial terms, "up there." Resurrection appearances, narratives of the transfiguration and ascension, and statements about Jesus returning on the clouds of heaven are mythic. When demythologized, such statements speak of human existence in relation to God, for example, that one must live through grace rather than through achievement or that one must always be open to the transcendent or future action of God, even when that future is threatening.

Bultmann's project was linked to the existentialist philosophy of Martin Heidegger (d. 1976). Bultmann believed that one achieves "authentic" existence only through a radical faith based on the proclamation of the reality of the Cross, which challenges us to complete trust in a self-sacrificing God, so that knowledge of specific events of Jesus' life is not essential to faith. Though Bultmann highlighted the historical and cultural distance between the biblical text and subsequent history, and underscored the need for a consistent theory of interpretation, both his existentialist philosophy and his ahistorical approach to Jesus have been largely superseded in recent years. *See also* myth.   JOHN R. DONAHUE

Denifle, Heinrich S. (hinʹrik denʹih-flay), 1844–1905, Dominican medievalist. Born in the Tyrol (Austria), he preached and taught philosophy and theology in Graz, Austria, from 1870 to 1880. In 1880 he was called to Rome to collaborate on a new edition of the works of Thomas Aquinas commissioned by Pope Leo XIII. He served as one of three assistant papal archivists, where he promoted access to Vatican source materials. He wrote in the areas of mysticism, Scholasticism, and the history of the universities in the Middle Ages and on Martin Luther.

Denis, St., also known as Denys and Dionysius, d. ca. 250, bishop associated with the founding of Paris. Denis was confused with Dionysius the Areopagite (see Acts 17:13–14) in medieval France. His cult was centered in the abbey of St.-Denis, the burial place of French kings. He is patron saint of France. Feast day: October 9.

de Nobili, Robert, 1577–1656, Jesuit missionary in South India. In the adaptation controversy he opposed the prevalent method of conversion that required converts to assume European customs, arguing that missionaries should adapt to the customs of the land as far as possible. Pope Gregory XV approved this approach in 1623. *See also* India, Catholicism in.

denunciation, the reporting to the proper ecclesiastical superior of some scandal or offense occurring in the exercise of ministry, the handling of church finances, or the personal lives of clerics and religious. The concern of canon law is that such reporting is to receive a hearing that is fair to all parties concerned, including the accused. On the one hand, no one is to be deprived of his or her good name without a proper and fair process and, on the other hand, it is the responsibility of authorities to deal with abuses for the common good.

Denys the Areopagite, also known as Dionysius or Pseudo-Dionysius, pseudonymous writer of the late fifth or early sixth century who adopted the name of the famous Pauline convert (Acts 17:34). His identity and details of his life are unknown. His writings, originally in Greek, influenced major figures in the development of medieval Western mystical theology, such as John Scotus Eriugena (d. ca. 877), Richard of St. Victor (d. 1173), Thomas Aquinas (d. 1274), Bonaventure (d. 1274), Meister Eckhart (d. 1327), and the author of *The Cloud of Unknowing*. Arguably, Western theologians took some Neoplatonic aspects of Denys's thought out of context. Denys was not concerned with the technicalities of subjective mystical experience but summed up the patristic tradition of mystical theology. All believers are "mystics" because they are plunged into the mystery of Christ through baptism, exposure to Scripture, and participation in liturgy. The soul eventually passes beyond sign and concept to be grasped by the divine mystery of love and is thus transformed.

Of Denys's five known works, *The Divine Names, The Mystical Theology,* and *The Celestial Hierarchy* were particularly influential in the West. Denys is associated primarily with the so-called negative or apophatic theology, which emphasizes that one must ultimately pass beyond definitions and images of God into silence and darkness because God is beyond all names. However, Denys also wrote about what is called positive or kataphatic theology, which emphasizes what can be affirmed about God and concerns God's self-disclosure in creation, Scripture, and liturgy. There is no justification for understanding these theologies as alternative ways; for Denys, they are inextricably linked. *See also* mystical theology; mysticism; Neoplatonism.   PHILIP SHELDRAKE

Denzinger, Heinrich Joseph, 1819–83, Catholic theologian and teacher at Würzburg, Germany. He is best known as compiler of the *Enchiridion Symbolorum* (1854), a comprehensive collection of official ecclesiastical statements. *See also* Enchiridion Symbolorum.

Deo gratias (day'oh grah'tsee-ahs; Lat., "Thanks be to God"), a liturgical acclamation sung or recited by the assembly in response to blessings or dismissals. The *Deo gratias* is thus sung at the conclusion of Mass, at the Liturgy of the Hours, and at other occasional rites or blessings. During the Easter season an Alleluia is appended.

deontology (Gk., *deon,* "duty"), the study of moral obligation, commonly known as duty or obligation ethics. The term is not consistently defined and used in contemporary discourse.

In contrast to teleology, deontology is a way of thinking about right and wrong on the basis of an action's conforming to a moral principle or duty independently of the consequences. Principles play a major role because, as products of natural law, they express and measure obligations, duties, prized values, basic goods, or rights.

This theory holds that certain actions are right or wrong in themselves by virtue of intrinsic features. For example, telling the truth and keeping promises are always right, and killing the innocent is always wrong. When intrinsically evil acts are the major moral term in a principle, that principle functions as a moral absolute so that no set of intentions, circumstances, or consequences could alter the objective morality of those acts.

Immanuel Kant (d. 1804), with his categorical imperative (respect persons as ends in themselves), is the major philosopher associated with deontology. Even though Catholic morality has strong teleological elements in some areas, its conclusions have been understood deontologically.

The strength of this theory is that it preserves consistency in the moral life and holds a pluralistic society together by giving a common point of reference for shared expectations and duties. A weakness is that it gives no guidance on what to do when moral principles appear to be in conflict. Also, it does not take into account the numerous contextual factors that influence the meaning and value of actions. Deontology needs to be complemented by considerations from teleology and an ethics of virtue. *See also* moral theology; teleology.   RICHARD GULA

deposit of faith, generally understood to be the teaching of Jesus Christ as found in Scripture and in the apostolic tradition. The precise import of this term for Catholic theology is best understood when the "deposit" is seen as an inexhaustible treasure of which the Church is the trustee. This treasure comes to expression in the Scriptures, in written tradition (council documents, encyclicals, etc.), and in the sacramental life of the Church.

The content of this deposit is not primarily a complex of religious truths or propositions. Rather, the content is the person of Jesus Christ; Jesus Christ *is* the "treasure" of Christian faith, a living resource in which revelation and salvation are coextensive. According to the tradition of the Church, revelation came to an end with the death of the last apostle and, therefore, nothing can be added to or subtracted from this deposit. This is so because the fullness of the revelation of God is given only in the person of Jesus Christ.

History: "Deposit of faith" appears as a technical term at the close of the sixteenth century, in the language of the Council of Trent (1545–63), and was formally included in the vocabulary of the magisterium in the documents of Vatican I in the late nineteenth century (D 1800, 1836). Its use at Vatican I (1869–70) reflects a battle between the culture of the time and the Church's self-understanding. The seventeenth-century Enlightenment had already given birth to revolutions against the monarchical rule exemplified by the Roman Catholic Church's governing structure. Furthermore, the notion of a fixed body of truth that had always and everywhere been infallibly put forth began to crumble under the rise of historical consciousness. In the polemical atmosphere of the late nineteenth century, the Church's response was to explicate the term in a restrictive sense, denoting an atemporal and propositional understanding of the tenets of a faith under siege.

By the time of Vatican II (1962–65), the impact of resulting theological movements such as the French "New Theology," which refocused attention on Scripture and the patristic period as primary theological resources, was inescapable. Drawing on a historical understanding of tradition, Vatican II returned to the NT notion of the deposit (Gk., *parathēkē*) of faith as a sacred trust ("guard what has been entrusted to you," 1 Tim 6:20; also 2 Tim 1:12, 14). While the Dogmatic Constitution on the Church (n. 25) speaks of bishops drawing upon the "treasury of revelation," this treasury is not the "property" of the magisterium. Under the guidance of the Holy Spirit, this sacred deposit (Dogmatic Constitution on Divine Revelation, n. 10) is entrusted to the Church as a whole. Setting aside an earlier positivistic understanding of infallibility, Vatican II views the Church as the trustee of an inexhaustible treasure, and its authentic expositor. This exposition takes many forms, from study of the Scriptures, to the rearticulation of doctrine, to the faithful celebration of the Eucharist. The sacred trust that is the Incarnation of God is a truly immeasurable deposit, preserved by the Church only by its continuous witness to the life, death, and Resurrection of Jesus Christ. *See also* doctrine; dogma; faith; revelation; tradition.   NANCY DALLAVALLE

De profundis (day proh-*foon*'dees; Lat., "out of the depths"), title for Psalm 130: "Out of the depths I cry to you, O Lord. Lord, hear my voice!" In Christian use the psalm is closely associated with occasions of death, mourning, and penitence. This psalm is sung at funerals and during the Office for the Dead, with its typical antiphon: "Grant them eternal rest O Lord, and may light perpetual shine upon them."

derogation, in canon law the partial abolition of a law. Although not to be presumed (can. 21), derogation takes place when a new law expressly says it abolishes the old, entirely reorders the subject matter of the law, or is contrary to the old law (can. 20).

Descartes, René (day-kahrt'), 1596–1650, French philosopher. Educated by Jesuits, he eventually moved to Holland, where he wrote his most important works: *Discourse on Method* (1637), *Meditations on First Philosophy* (1641), *Principles of Philosophy* (1644), and *The Passion of the Soul* (1649). Descartes inaugurated modern critical thinking by doubting everything he had received from tradition or sense experience, seeking to establish true and certain knowledge only by means of that which could not be doubted. Because he could doubt everything except the fact that he doubted, he was certain that he existed as a thinking substance: "I think, therefore I am." Because he could not doubt without an idea of perfection, then the perfect substance, God, must exist, otherwise neither the thinking substance nor its idea of God would exist. And since God is not a deceiver, all clear and distinct ideas must be certainly true, while what our senses tell us about extended substance (our bodies and nature) must be reliable, if not certain. *See also* philosophy and theology.

descent of Christ into hell, the sojourn of Jesus Christ among the dead after his death. To understand the meanings of this expression, one must distinguish between its use in Scripture and its use in tradition.

In the NT this motif conveys the conviction that Jesus truly died prior to going beyond death to new life. In the OT "hell" (Heb., *Sheol*) is a realm not of punishment but simply of all the deceased. In general, to say that "one descended into hell" is simply to say that one died. The purpose of this motif in the NT, then, is to declare that Jesus really did die and yet was not ultimately overcome by death (Matt 27:52, 63; Luke 23:43; Acts 2:24–31; Rom 10:6–9; Eph 4:9–10; Col 1:18). When 1 Pet 3:18–20 states that "in the spirit" Jesus Christ "went and made a proclamation to the spirits in prison," it is attesting to Jesus' victory over sin and death. 1 Pet 4:6 does not specify the bearer of the good news to those who have died.

In tradition, the motif of Christ's descent into hell grew in meaning. In the second and third centuries, its soteriological significance was discussed by Ignatius of Antioch, Justin Martyr, Hermas, Irenaeus, Clement of Alexandria, and Origen. It was basically interpreted to mean that Christ visited hell in order to free from Satan's grasp the souls of the righteous who had died prior to the Resurrection. Although the motif was not part of the Old Roman Creed (second century), it is contained in the Apostles' Creed (A.D. 400) and the Athanasian Creed (early fifth century). It is not, however, contained within the Nicene Creed (325) and the Nicene-Constantinopolitan Creed (early fifth century). Thomas Aquinas (d. 1274) understood the expression to mean that Christ brought salvation to the dead who were united with him by their faith that had expressed itself in love. John Calvin interpreted Christ's "descent into hell" to mean the culminating point of his suffering, his complete abandonment by God. In sum, Christ's descent into hell is an article of faith whose minimal meaning is that Jesus Christ truly died but whose full meaning is not agreed upon in the Church. *See also* Jesus Christ.   ROBERT A. KRIEG

desecration, an act that violates the sacred character of a place or object. Churches, oratories, private chapels, and cemeteries that have been dedicated or blessed are desecrated by actions performed in them that are seriously harmful and scandalous. After the local ordinary (diocesan bishop) determines that desecration has occurred, a special rite of reparation must be performed there before other acts of worship may be resumed.

The Blessed Sacrament is desecrated by discarding it or using it for a sacrilegious purpose. The penalty for willful desecration of the consecrated bread or wine is automatic excommunication reserved to the Apostolic See (can. 1367).

desert, a physical reality and a symbol of the human encounter with evil and grace. The Exodus of Israel was a journey from slavery in Egypt to the promised land. This journey in the desert became a model for God's liberation of the person and community. Elijah's journey to Horeb/Sinai was another model for life's spiritual journey. John the Baptist and Jesus in the desert are examples of the liberation from illusion and the encounter with the divine that can occur in the desert. Origen saw Israel's journey through the desert as a type of the journey to God. From the late third century women and men went out to the desert in Egypt and Palestine. They faced the demons of the desert and discovered also the presence of God. The personification of this experience was Anthony of Egypt, whose biography composed by Athanasius stirred the hearts of countless God-seekers including Augustine of Hippo. John Cassian's *Conferences* and *Institutes* made the wisdom of the desert available to the West and had a special impact on the Benedictine rule. The desert is a place where solitude and community confront each other, where the solitude necessary for human life, in the imagery of theologian Henri Nouwen, renders compulsion into compassion. Desert and solitude, symbols for the encounter between the human and the divine, have a special place in the modern quest for God through the example of Charles de Foucauld in the Sahara and Thomas Merton in his hermitage. *See also* Foucauld, Charles de; hermit; Merton, Thomas; monasticism.

Desert Fathers and Mothers, spiritual leaders in the Christian monastic movement during the late third and fourth centuries in Egypt and Palestine. These spiritual leaders included Anthony of Egypt, Macarius of Egypt, Abba ("father") Moses, Abba Poemen, Ama ("mother") Sarah, and Ama Syneletia. Male and female ascetics of the time sought wisdom about the spiritual life from these experienced women and men. Their wisdom has been preserved in collections of pithy sayings and stories known as the *Sayings of the Elders. See also* desert; hermit; monasticism.

design, argument from, attempts to demonstrate the existence of God from the order found in nature. The first premise observes that natural objects that lack intelligence accomplish specific goals regularly. Acorns invariably become oak trees. Accomplishing these goals often requires the complex cooperation of many different elements, as does the human eye when it sees. The second premise states that order implies the existence of a designer. The order in a watch implies the existence of a watchmaker. The conclusion, then, claims that the order in nature implies the existence of its designer, God. *See also* five ways of St. Thomas Aquinas.

desire(s), the willing of a particular good represented to imagination and not yet possessed. The morality of a desire depends on the morality of the imagined act and whether the desire is absolute or conditional. If the imagined act is wrong, so is the desire. If the desire were fulfilled as soon as the opportunity presented itself (absolute), then the desire would be of the same moral gravity as the act itself; if conditional, then the desire is not sinful if the condition removes the evil of the external object, e.g., the desire to eat meat if it were not a day of abstinence.

Desmaisières, St. Mary Michael, 1809–65, born in Spain, founder of the Institute of the Handmaids of the Blessed Sacrament and of Charity, a community devoted to the care of unchaste women. Feast day: August 24.

De Smet, Pierre Jean, 1801–73, Belgian-born Jesuit missionary and writer who evangelized Native American tribes in the Midwest and Pacific Northwest and served often as an agent of the U.S. federal government.

despair, the abandonment of hope. Depending upon the reason for one's despair and the degree of one's responsibility, despair may be legitimate, sinful, or pathological. Theologically, despair is the abandonment of one's supernatural objective. Among the possible motives for such despair is the belief that one's sins are too heinous for God's mercy or that one's weaknesses are so great that one will not have sufficient grace to sustain one's conversion. Sins against hope are simultaneously sins against faith, demonstrating the interrelatedness of the theological virtues. Temptations to despair are not uncommon in the spiritual life and are vividly described by St. John of the Cross's metaphor of the "dark night."

detachment, a theme in Christian spirituality that has at times been expressed in negative terms like self-denial and mortification, too often communicating a rejection of the goodness of creation. More correctly, detachment is a process of liberation from or a prevention of a disordered relationship to a person or a thing. In modern society twelve-step movements have discovered the need for detachment from that to which one is addicted, since addiction is an enslavement to something or someone. Total abstinence from some substances like drugs and alcohol are necessary so that one may attain the freedom needed to lead a fully human life. All religions require of their adherents self-discipline attained through detachment from whatever keeps one from a proper relationship with the divine. Detachment is freedom from things that prevent spiritual growth. In the Christian tradition detachment is rooted in the life and death of Jesus of Nazareth and in what Jesus taught his disciples about a God and neighbor-centered life. One needs to be detached from whatever impedes love of God and love of neighbor. Monasticism emphasized detachment from wealth, one's will, and sexual expression through the vows of poverty, obedience, and chastity. In this tradition the practice of detachment is meant to make one available for prayer, service, and/or ministry. Christian tradition at its best demands not extraordinary physical asceticism but, according to John of the Cross, a detachment that is a freedom of the heart. *See also* asceticism.

detraction, an act of taking away something from the good name or reputation of another with the intention of lessening that person's standing in the view of others. Detraction may involve envy or malice and may be the result of representing another's worth or merit as less than it actually is. Modern usage reserves detraction for the unnecessary revelation of true but hidden details of another's life that harm the victim's reputation, while deliberate lies that have a damaging effect are called calumny. Detraction is a sin against both charity and justice because revealing the truth is not only damaging but unnecessary. The degree of the sinfulness of detraction is determined by the level of damage done to the victim's reputation. Others participate in the sinfulness of detraction by listening eagerly or questioning the detractor to initiate or prolong harmful conversation. *See also* calumny; slander; truthfulness.

deuterocanonical books, books in the Greek translation of the OT but not in the Hebrew Scriptures. Jews and Protestants designate them (and three other works: 1–2 Esdras and the Prayer of Manasseh) Apocrypha and do not include them in their Bibles. In the Catholic Bible, the deuterocanonical books are Tobit, Judith, Wisdom of Solomon, Sirach, Baruch (of which the Letter of Jeremiah is ch. 6), and 1–2 Maccabees. Also included are passages in Esther and Daniel additional to what is found in the Hebrew or Aramaic original: 107 verses spread over six additions in Esther, and in Daniel the Prayer of Azariah and the Song of the Three Young Men (3:24–90); Susanna (ch. 13); and Bel and the Dragon (ch. 14). Some of these books were written in Hebrew (Sirach, 1 Maccabees, and perhaps others) or Aramaic (Tobit), but their originals were lost until modern discoveries of parts of them among the Dead Sea Scrolls and other finds. These books were written at different times between about 300 B.C. (Tobit) and perhaps the first century A.D. (Wisdom of Solomon). In reaction to Protestant doubts about them, the Council of Trent (1545–63) declared them sacred and canonical. *See also* Apocrypha.

The devil depicted as a fallen angel with wings, tail, and monstrous-looking head; portion of a fifteenth-century Fouquet painting, Condé Museum, Chantilly, France.

Deutinger, Martin, 1815–64, German philosopher. A disciple of Franz von Baader and influenced by Friedrich Schelling, as a professor in Munich he developed a philosophical system of God and being, a critique of Schelling, and an original aesthetics. He was disappointed by the rise of neo-Scholasticism.

De Vaux, Roland, 1903–71, French Dominican biblical scholar and archaeologist. From 1933 he taught at the École Biblique in Jerusalem. He excavated at Tell el-Far'ah (biblical Tirza), and then became a figure of international renown as excavator and editor of the Dead Sea Scrolls (1949–71). He was the general and OT editor of the Jerusalem Bible (1956) and author of over thirteen books, including *Ancient Israel: Its Life and Institutions* (1958–60, Eng. 1961) and *History of Israel* (1971–73, Eng. 1978), as well as works on OT sacrifice and Qumran. He was the leading Catholic OT scholar and archaeologist of his day. *See also* École Biblique.

development of doctrine. *See* doctrine, development of.

devil, a personified spiritual creature who freely sinned and is eternally damned. The Catholic Church teaches the following about the devil: devils are spiritual creatures, subordinate to God and created good by God; they freely sinned and are responsible for their own eternal damnation; they have limited power in the world, but Christ's death and Resurrection are victorious over that power;

humans do experience their evil influence, but cannot distinguish it from the corruption that has resulted from human sins through the ages.

The devil is not an important figure in the OT. The word appears in only five books, and is mentioned only once in four of them. The snake in the account of the temptation of Adam and Eve in Genesis was not meant to symbolize the devil. Most likely it was introduced as a trickster to awaken Eve's curiosity. God cursed it because, to the Hebrews of the writer's time, serpents were used in pagan worship. Later Jewish and Christian writers applied the figure of the snake to the devil. In the story of Job, the character called Satan (Heb., "adversary") acts as a court-appointed prosecutor empowered by God to present human failings before the heavenly judge's bench. Satan is not equal to God, nor is he a malevolent power.

The devil is much more active in the NT. Besides the terms for devil and demon, Gospel writers also used terms such as Evil One, Father of Lies, or Murderer from the Beginning. The devil has limited power to cause some sicknesses, to take possession of persons' bodies, and to tempt to sin. However, it cannot cause moral wrongs or corruption, does not know Christ's true identity, and must obey the word of Christ and his disciples. The lessons from the NT about the devil are these: it is not a figment of Jesus' imagination or a personification of human sins; there is not a clear distinction between a single principle demon and other devils; it is difficult to separate the corruption that results from devils and that which results from human sin; the coming of Jesus has overcome all forms of evil, even though the demons continue to exercise limited power in the world.

Christian theologians in the first centuries reflected on the devil's activities and often personified human evil as if it were the devil because they wanted to communicate the seriousness of a particular heresy or pagan cult.

Reference to the devil appears very seldom in official Catholic statements of faith. In the first document of the Fourth Lateran Council in 1215, the opening words refer to Christian faith in God as Creator of all things, visible and invisible, including the devils, who made themselves evil by their own power. The crucial statement refers to God, and the implication is that the devils are not the source of evil nor are they equal to God. The devil is not mentioned in any official Christian creed. *See also* Satan.   LOUISE PROCHASKA

Devil's Advocate. *See* Promoter of the Faith.

devolution, in canon law the passing on of certain unperformed responsibilities to higher authorities. The word also refers to a type of appeal that does not suspend an original decision.

Devotio Moderna (Lat., "Modern Devotion," "New Devotion"), a spiritual-renewal movement with origins in fourteenth-century Holland that laid great stress on the inner life of the individual. The name "Devotio Moderna" was probably first used in the early fifteenth century by Henry Pomerius. The movement looked for inspiration to Geert de Groote (1340–84), with beginnings in the Lowlands but spreading to Germany and elsewhere. Its most characteristic text was *The Imitation of Christ.* Sisters and brothers, not members of religious orders except some groups of canons, lived in small communities, women and men separately. Their spirituality was Christocentric, with an emphasis on Scripture, meditation, and a strong, nonmystical interior life. *See also* Groote, Geert de; *Imitation of Christ;* Thomas à Kempis.

devotions, nonliturgical prayer forms that promote affective (and sometimes individualistic) attitudes of faith. They may also suggest a more effective response to personal religious needs than liturgical prayer. Familiar devotions in the pre–Vatican II period (before 1962) were, for example, the Miraculous Medal novena, devotions to the Sacred Heart and the Sorrowful Mother, Stations of the Cross, and the Rosary. (The singular form of the term "devotion" usually refers to the affective dimension of faith. Devotions [plural] are often thought to foster devotion.)

As a general rule, when liturgical prayer and ritual are less accessible to people's understanding and participation, there is usually an increase in devotions. In the early Middle Ages, when understanding and participation in the Eucharist had begun to decline sharply, popular devotions to the Eucharist began to develop. Scholars point, for example, to the medieval desire "to see the Host." People would run from church to church in order to look at the elevated consecrated host and cup during Mass in the belief that this would prolong youthfulness and provide other benefits. A more balanced devotion was prayer before the Eucharist reserved in the tabernacle (receptacle holding the Host). Such devotions arose from praiseworthy sentiments of adoration for the eucharistic presence of Christ, but they sometimes tended to become highly privatized exercises of piety that had little connection with the meaning and celebration of the Eucharist.

Devotions and Popular Religion: Devotions might best be understood as a form of popular religion or of personal piety. Popular religion is a bridge between, on one hand, the more formal celebrations and the intellectual teaching of the faith and, on the other, the appropriation and expression of that faith in the ordinary culture of a particular historical period. Pilgrimages, for example, are a form of popular religion that makes sense even to illiterate Christians because they concretize some of the basic tenets of the faith (repentance, conversion, etc.) and stimulate popular expressions of prayer (e.g., recitation of certain prayers, making part of the journey barefoot or on one's knees). Devotional piety emphasizes the affective aspects of redemption (e.g., the incarnation of Christ becomes more accessible to some people under the form of the Christmas crib). Liturgical worship may, in fact, encourage popular expressions of devotion (e.g., the use of holy water as derived from the blessed waters of Baptism, devotion to the reserved Eucharist as an extension of its celebration). Some scholars note that liturgical developments such as those of Holy Week in the church of Jerusalem in the fourth century would have been regarded as devotions by modern standards.

As liturgy became increasingly removed from the

comprehension and participation of most people, popular devotions took their place. The U.S. Catholic bishops, for example, faced with the problem of ministering to vast numbers of nineteenth-century Catholic immigrants, strongly fostered the devotional life of parishes as one way of helping these displaced Christians maintain contact with their faith. Thus, it was common to see many people reciting the Rosary during Mass in the pre–Vatican II period. People who might not regularly participate in the Eucharist would often take part in novenas. Even before the reforms of Vatican II, the liturgical movement in the United States sought to bring Catholics into a more active participation in worship and to connect it with the mission of the Church to the larger world. To counteract the pervasive influence of devotions, attempts were made in more liturgically minded parishes to reintroduce Sunday evening prayer and to encourage families to celebrate the anniversary of important sacramental events such as Baptism.

Current Teaching: Vatican II reaffirmed the legitimacy of devotions approved by the Church but laid down the principle that devotions should be in harmony with the worship of the Church and should derive from and lead back to that worship since liturgy "by its very nature far surpasses any of them" (Constitution on the Sacred Liturgy, n. 13). Some years later, Pope Paul VI noted that conciliar directives had been difficult to implement, especially in regard to devotion to Mary. The problem was twofold, he argued: some parishes have suppressed popular devotions while others have simply inserted them into the liturgy (e.g., the novena within the Mass). The pope also insisted on the connection between the historical and cultural context of a particular church as a key to its development of appropriate devotions. Finally, Paul VI maintained that authentic devotions should lead to a more committed gospel life. A historical example of this might be the devotion of the early Church, and the North African church in particular, to the cult of martyrs. This devotion was usually celebrated in the liturgy on the anniversary of the martyr's death and served to encourage other Christians to witness to their faith even to the death, if need be. *See also* eucharistic devotions; Marian devotion; novena; pilgrimage; Rosary; Sacred Heart, devotion to the.

Bibliography

Duffy, Regis. "Devotio Futura: The Need for Post-Conciliar Devotions." In *A Promise of Glory,* edited by M. Downey and R. Fragomeni. Washington, DC: Pastoral Press, 1992. Pp. 163–83.

REGIS A. DUFFY

Devout Life, Introduction to the. *See Introduction to the Devout Life.*

d'Herbigny, Michel (dair-been-yee'), 1880–1957, French Jesuit ecumenist and Vatican expert on Russia. After the publication of his book on Vladimir Solov'ev entitled *Michael Soloviev: Russian Newman,* he became the first Jesuit rector of the Pontifical Oriental Institute. He was consecrated bishop by the nuncio in Berlin (the later Pope Pius XII) in semi-secrecy because of the anti-Catholic regime in the Soviet Union. He made three trips to Soviet Russia where he ordained four other bishops secretly. For reasons still unknown, he fell into disgrace in 1937 and died in obscurity.

diabolical possession. *See* demonic possession.

diaconate. *See* deacon.

dialogue Mass, a pre–Vatican II (1962–65) low Mass in which the congregation responded vocally to the presider, taking the parts that normally were recited quietly by the altar servers. In the 1950s dialogue Masses were introduced in many parishes as a way of fostering congregational participation. After the publication of Vatican II's Constitution on the Sacred Liturgy, as the new missal was being prepared, reformed ritual elements gradually were introduced. These included the vocal recitation of parts of the Proper and Ordinary, acclamations, responses to dialogical formularies, and prayers, such as the Amen at the eucharistic doxology. Although not termed dialogue Mass, the interim Mass had similar characteristics. The term "dialogue Mass" is no longer in use.

Diaspora (di-as'pohr-ah), also called the Dispersion, the scattering of the Israelite/Jewish people from their homeland. The process began with the exiles of Israelites in the 730s and 720s B.C. and continued with the dispersion of Judeans in the 590s and 580s B.C. Major settlements in the Diaspora were in Babylon and Egypt, but eventually there were Jewish centers throughout the Mediterranean lands and farther east in Mesopotamia. Jews in the Diaspora often maintained contact with the motherland through pilgrimages for festivals (see Acts 2:5–11) and payment of the Temple tax. The Letter of James (1:1) is addressed to the "twelve tribes in the Dispersion."

Diatessaron (dī-ah-tes'sah-ron; Gk., "through four"), a second-century harmony of the Gospels, i.e., a continuous narrative drawn from all four Gospels. The Syrian apologist Tatian, who was for some time a pupil of Justin Martyr in Rome, composed this account of the life and teachings of Jesus as a conflation of the four Gospels known to him. The original text of the Diatessaron, written in either Greek or Syriac around A.D. 170, does not survive. The work is known from a few fragments as well as a commentary on it by the Syrian father Ephraem (d. 373). Its influence extended to the many Gospel harmonies and popular lives of Jesus written in late antiquity and in the Middle Ages. *See also* gospel; synoptic Gospels, problem of.

dicastery (Gk., *dikastēs*, "judge," "law court"), generic term for an agency of Church government, especially a bureaucratic subdivision of the Roman Curia. At present the dicasteries of the Roman Curia include the Secretariat of State, Congregations, tribunals, councils, offices, commissions, and committees. *See also* Roman Curia.

Dictatus Papae (dik-tah'tuhs pah'pay; Lat., "Pronouncement of the Pope"), a series of statements placed in the register of Gregory VII, dated March 1075, describing a papacy with vast powers in both the religious and secular spheres. Included are such claims as: "The Roman pontiff alone is rightly called universal"; "That he [the pope] may depose emperors"; and "That he himself may be judged by no one." The *Dictatus Papae* is generally considered a collection of chapter titles for an unfinished canon law compilation. *See also* Gregory VII.

Didache (dih'dah-kay; Gk., "the teaching"; *The Teaching of the Lord to the Gentiles Through the Twelve Apostles*), an ancient book of basic instructions for Christians that drew upon very early traditions and combined material from a number of different sources. The subject matter and the variegated style and source material of the *Didache* make it very hard to determine either a date or a point of origin. Estimates run from mid-first century to (less probably) late second century, and from Egypt to (more probably) Syria.

The structure of the *Didache* includes: the teaching of the "Two Ways" (chs. 1–6), liturgical instructions (chs. 7–10), disciplinary matters related to prophets, bishops, deacons, divisions in the community, and the Eucharist (chs. 11–15), and a concluding warning against the antichrist and encouragement to remain faithful until the Second Advent (ch. 16).

The "Two Ways" incorporates Matthean material from the Sermon on the Mount but has a strong literary relationship with the Qumran *Manual of Discipline*. In this it is joined by the *Letter of Barnabas* and the *Doctrina Apostolorum* ("The Teaching of the Apostles"). These connections have raised the issue of the interrelatedness of this literature and have drawn scholars to reexamine the strong influence of its Jewish heritage upon earliest Christianity.

The liturgical instructions have also generated much interest. Baptism is to be by immersion when possible and threefold affusion when necessary. Fasting is undertaken on Wednesdays and Fridays. There are two very ancient eucharistic prayers, perhaps modeled upon Jewish meal prayers, thus raising the possibility that the Last Supper was not the only pattern for this ritual. *See also* apostolic age.

Didascalia Apostolorum (dee-duh-scal'ee-uh uh-pahs-toh-lohr'um; Lat., "The Teaching of the Apostles"), a document on Church order composed in Greek (first half of third century) but preserved in its entirety only in Syriac. It focuses on bishops, but includes instruction on such things as deacons, deaconesses, widows, spouses, children, Easter, the abrogation of the ceremonial Law, and retention of the Decalogue. Regarding forgiveness of sins, it is remarkably lenient for its time. *See also* apostle.

Didymus the Blind, ca. 313–98, theologian appointed head of the Alexandrian catechetical school by Athanasius. His students included Gregory of Nazianzus, Jerome, and Rufinus. Blind from age five but a prolific writer, his staunch anti-Arianism is evident in his *On the Holy Spirit*. His surviving exegesis, strongly Origenistic, includes commentaries on Genesis, Job, and Zechariah, while many other works survive only in fragments due to a posthumous condemnation for Origenism (Constantinople II, 553). *See also* Alexandria, school of.

Diekmann, Godfrey, b. 1908, American Benedictine monk and liturgical scholar. For more than twenty-five years, beginning in 1938, he edited the influential periodical *Worship* (then called *Orate Fratres*). A *peritus* (Lat., "expert") at Vatican Council II (1962–65), he also served on the postconciliar commission responsible for the reform of Roman Catholic worship.

Dies irae (dee'ez ee'ray; Lat., "Day of Wrath"), title for the sequence hymn, "Day of Wrath, O day of mourning." Attributed to Thomas of Celano (d. 1260), the chant was synonymous with funeral liturgies until the reform of the funeral rite following Vatican II (1962–65). The text is based upon Zeph 1:14–16 and presents a vivid picture of the apocalypse and last judgment. One of the most renowned melodies of the Gregorian chant repertoire, it was adapted by many composers and occurs in more than one symphony, e.g., Berlioz's *Symphonie fantastique*. An English translation of this hymn with its traditional melody can be found in the *Episcopal Hymnal* (1928).

Dignitatis Humanae (deen-yee-tah'tees hoo-mah'nay). *See* Declaration on Religious Freedom.

dignity. *See* human dignity.

dikirion, trikirion (di-keer'ee-ahn, tri-keer'ee-ahn; Gk.), the two- and three-branch episcopal candelabras used by Byzantine-rite bishops to impart solemn blessings during liturgical services. The *trikirion,* with three (*tri*) candles (*kerion*) in honor of the Trinity is held in the right hand, the *dikirion* with two (*di*) for the divine and human natures of Christ in the left. There is evidence that the liturgical use of candles in imparting blessings dates back to at least the tenth century.

dimissorial letters, the documents presented to the ordaining bishop attesting to the fact that a

Dikirion   Trikirion

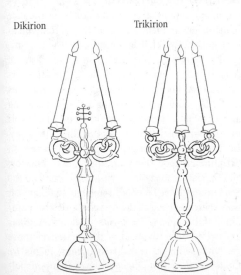

candidate for Holy Orders has received the necessary preparation and has those qualities required for ordination. The letters must be issued by the bishop of the diocese to which a diocesan candidate is attached or incardinated or by the major superior of the institute in which the religious-community candidate is ascribed. These letters are not necessary when a diocesan candidate is ordained by his own bishop.

diocesan bishop, pastoral and legal head and representative of a diocese. Although law and papal decree reserve certain powers, the diocesan bishop possesses all legislative, administrative, and judicial authority required for his office by divine right and not as a delegate of the pope. Through such authority, he exercises within his diocese the threefold pastoral office of teaching, sanctifying, and governing.

The diocesan bishop must form a unique bond with his priests and foster vocations. His strong relationship to the diocese through stable residence, pastoral visitation, liturgical presence, teaching, and preaching also embraces specific administrative and disciplinary responsibilities. He must also foster ecumenism. *See also* bishop; Decree on the Bishops' Pastoral Office in the Church.

diocesan curia, a collective body of persons and agencies assisting the diocesan bishop in governing the diocese. The bishop appoints all officeholders, who are bound to fidelity and confidentiality. Their assistance is administrative or judicial in nature, legislation belonging to the bishop. Included are vicars general, episcopal vicars, chancery and tribunal officials, and a finance officer, but the notion is more expansive. Any agency involved in diocesan administration might be considered part of the curia, typically, departments of religious education, liturgy, finance, and social action. Coordination of the curia may be entrusted to a moderator who must at least be a priest and most appropriately a vicar general. *See also* curia; diocese.

diocesan pastoral council, representative and consultative pastoral planning organization of Christian faithful under the authority of the diocesan bishop. The pastoral council is to be established wherever circumstances recommend it. As a permanent institution, it should represent the sociocultural, professional, and occupational breadth and diversity of the diocese, especially the laity. Members themselves serve fixed terms determined by the statutes. While not a decision-making body, it investigates, evaluates, and offers practical advice on the pastoral activity of the diocese. The bishop presides over, and should convoke, the council at least once a year. The council ceases when the see is vacant. *See also* council; diocese; pastoral council.

diocesan right, status of a religious institute for which a diocesan bishop has responsibility. Although every religious institute has the pope as its first superior, a diocesan community looks primarily to the authority of its bishop rather than to that of the Holy See. *See also* religious institute.

diocesan synod, group of Christian faithful (laity, religious, and priests) to be convoked, when warranted, by the diocesan bishop to collaborate with him for the good of the entire diocese. Implicit is the aim of prudent lawmaking through the bishop, as sole legislator, presiding over a responsible and articulate consultative body (see cans. 460–68). Extensive participatory representation is especially ensured by those obliged or permitted in law to be convoked as voting consultants. Others are invited as observers, even if non-Catholic. Free, active, and frank discussion is expected prior to any legislative promulgation by episcopal decree. Suspension or dissolution of the synod is a matter for the bishop's prudent judgment. *See also* synods.

diocese, a Catholic community, usually circumscribed territorially, established by the supreme Church authority, entrusted to the pastoral care of a bishop, and possessing all the constitutive marks of the Church. Among several types of particular churches, in and from which the universal Catholic Church exists, the diocese is the most typical. More than an administrative subdivision of the universal Church, it is a fully constituted church in communion with other particular churches.

The diocesan bishop, collaborating with his priests, forms a pastoral bond with the Catholic community through shared sacramental life. From this communion, eucharistically centered, flows the apostolic mission of the diocese. To foster communion and further its mission, the diocese is subdivided into parishes, usually territorial, and other configurations.

Governing the diocese as its head, the diocesan bishop also represents it in the communion of particular churches and in juridical affairs. Legitimate-

ly erected, a diocese is a juridical person under the law itself. *See also* diocesan bishop; eparchy.

Diodore of Tarsus (di'uh-dohr), d. ca. 390, bishop of Tarsus (378–90) and founder of the Antiochene school of exegesis, which eschewed allegory in favor of history and typology. His pupils included Theodore of Mopsuestia and John Chrysostom. Diodore was a fervent anti-Arian recognized by Theodosius I as a standard of orthodoxy, but his writings have mostly perished because Theodore, who taught Nestorius, was posthumously condemned (Constantinople II, 553). *See also* Antioch, school of.

Diognetus, Letter to (di-ahg-nee'tuhs), early Christian apologetic writing, perhaps from the second century, that tersely refutes pagan religion as idolatrous and Jewish practice as ritualistic. In contrast, it elegantly commends the faith of Christians, the "third race" and soul of the world who accept God's revelation in Christ and return God's love.

Dionysius Exiguus (eks-ig'yoo-uhs), ca. 500–550, monk. "Little Dennis"—the adjective indicates his humility rather than his stature—came to Rome from Scythia. A friend of Roman monk Cassiodorus, he prepared a collection of canons, revised the system for calculating the date of Easter, and introduced the A.D. system of dating, later popularized by Bede.

Dionysius of Paris, St. *See* Denis, St.

Dionysius the Carthusian, ca. 1402–71, theologian and mystic called Doctor Ecstaticus because of his visions and renown as a teacher of contemplation. Born at Ryckel, Belgium, he studied at the University of Cologne, receiving the degree of Master of Arts in 1424. He then entered the Carthusian charterhouse at Roermond, where he lived until his death. Dionysius was a theologian of vast reading and a prolific writer whose works fill over forty volumes, a virtual encyclopedia of medieval theology. He wrote commentaries, his preferred genre, on Scripture, Pseudo-Dionysius, Boethius, Climacus, and Cassian, among others. His commentary on the *Sentences* of Peter Lombard is intriguing because it was written outside of the university. He also paraphrased the *Summa Theologiae* of Thomas Aquinas and wrote many treatises at the request of those consulting him on religious questions. In his *De Contemplatione (On Contemplation),* Dionysius follows the apophatic tradition that strips away conceptual apprehension of God so that one might reach God through love. Nevertheless, his teaching on contemplation was highly speculative, in contrast to the anti-intellectual mysticism of much of late medieval spirituality. He accompanied Nicholas of Cusa on his mission in 1451 aimed at the reform of the Church in Germany. *See also* contemplation.

Dionysius the Great, d. 264/5, bishop of Alexandria from 247 to 264/5, succeeding Heraclas as head of the catechetical school and then as bishop. A pupil of Origen, he was accused, but later exonerated, of tritheism by Pope Dionysius (260–68). He readmitted lapsed Christians, did not require rebaptism of those baptized by heretics or schismatics, and denied John's authorship of Revelation. Feast day: November 17. *See also* Alexandria, school of; *lapsi;* Origen.

Dioscorus (di-ahs'kuh-ruhs), d. 454, patriarch of Alexandria from 444 to 451. Supporting the one-nature (Monophysite) Christology of Eutyches, he presided at the "Robber Synod" at Ephesus (449), which deposed Flavian, bishop of Constantinople. When Eutyches was condemned by the Council of Chalcedon (451), Dioscorus was himself deposed, excommunicated, and exiled. He is venerated in the Monophysite churches. *See also* Ephesus, Robber Council of; Eutyches; Monophysitism.

diptychs (dip'tiks; Gk., *diptychon,* "folded together"), a hinged folder formed from two panels of wood or metal upon which were inscribed the names of Christians both living and dead to be included in the Eucharistic Prayer. The word now refers not to a physical object but to that portion of eucharistic prayers where intercessions for the ill, the dying, Church leaders, political authorities, saints, and the deceased are said.

direction, spiritual. *See* spiritual direction.

diriment impediment, term used in the 1917 code of canon law to refer to a class of marriage impediments that render the celebration of marriage illicit (i.e., against the law) but not invalid (i.e., not recognized by the law as existing). The present code (1983) does not use the term, though it requires a bishop to give permission for the licit celebration of a marriage in some situations similar to those formerly called diriment impediments. *See also* marriage law.

discalced (Lat., "unshod"), term applied to religious orders or branches of orders whose members do not wear shoes. The custom of going without sandals had roots in Matt 10:10. This injunction by Jesus was followed by early Eastern monks, Francis of Assisi, and the Spanish Discalced Franciscans founded by Peter of Alcantara. The name Discalced was used of those Carmelites who became a new order in 1593 after the deaths of Teresa of Ávila and John of the Cross. Calced, meaning shod, was used of the original Carmelite order, now known as Carmelites of the Ancient Observance. The distinction between calced and discalced was also used of branches of the Trinitarians and Passionists. Discalced religious, especially in intemperate climates, have worn sandals.

discernment of spirits, the prudent evaluation of the presence or absence of God, or the presence of an evil spirit, in making decisions and carrying them out. It was initially described in Gal 5, 1 Corinthians, 1 Thess 5 and 12. John Cassian (d. 435), John Climacus (d. 649), Ignatius of Loyola (d. 1556) and others further developed the notion. The term "spirits" refers to the movements of the human will. Whether the source of movement is God or some evil spirit, it is filtered through the complicated morass of past and present human experiences. The interior movements convey feelings of consolation or desolation, and usually some training is necessary to help a person learn how to decipher whether or not a consolation or desolation is from God. A spiritual director can teach a person to assess how temporary emotional distress that ends in an enduring sense of peace is "good," whereas spiritual favors that initially delight the soul but then end in confusion are not positive. The spiritual director can also teach how turning away from deeply ingrained bad habits may cause long-term desolation even though this inner movement has been initiated by "good" spirits.

Discernment is an ongoing process, but is particularly necessary at peak moments when one is beginning a serious attempt at prayer, experiencing extraordinary or mystical phenomena, or making vocational and career decisions. Even though God's movements in the soul are a mystery, the gift of prudence, along with practical experience, helps the believer to cooperate with the inspirations of grace. *See also* prudence.

disciple (Lat., "one who learns"), pupil who follows, shares the life of, and imitates a master, the normal way in ancient times to learn anything from a trade to a philosophy. Prophets sometimes had disciples (Isa 8:16; 50:4). In the NT, John the Baptist and the Pharisees have disciples (Matt 9:14; Mark 2:18), but disciple is the name most frequently given to those around Jesus who accept him as master, both the wider circle (Matt 5:1; Luke 6:17; 19:37) and the smaller, inner circle (Mark 3:7; 4:34; Matt 10:10), sometimes explicitly the Twelve (Matt 10:1). In general, Matthew tends to call the Twelve "the disciples" (Matt 5:1 is an exception), while Mark, Luke, and John use it often for an indeterminate group, Luke generally reserving the name "apostles" for the Twelve. Even where the word does not occur, persons who travel with Jesus (Luke 8:1–3) or listen to his teaching in faith (Luke 10:39) are disciples. The Christians of Jerusalem are disciples (Acts 6:1–7). Though women are included elsewhere, the feminine form occurs only for Tabitha (Acts 9:36). Though sometimes the same persons act in both roles, the role of disciple (learner) and that of apostle (representative) are distinct. *See also* apostle; discipleship.

discipleship, the following of Jesus by women and men of faith. They were called disciples and apostles in the NT and in Christian tradition. The NT frequently calls Jesus Rabbi or Teacher. One who learned from a teacher was a disciple. In a general sense the Scriptures refer to disciples as those who believe the teaching of Jesus (Acts 9:1, 20). In a more specialized sense the disciples are those who followed Jesus, like the seventy (or seventy-two) sent on mission by Jesus (Luke 10:1, 17). Jesus called the disciples to follow him, to become a new family, a family of service, to pray with him as at Gethsemane, to die and to rise with him, and Jesus commissioned his followers to make disciples "of all nations" (Matt 28:19). Discipleship is the whole matrix of activities and values that derive from close association with Jesus. At core, discipleship is identification with the dying and rising of Jesus and issues in the imitation of Christ that is initiated at Baptism and nourished at the eucharistic table.

Throughout the Christian tradition discipleship has again and again been affirmed as the primary paradigm for being a dedicated Christian. Martyrdom quickly was perceived as committed discipleship. Ignatius of Antioch (d. ca. 107) saw his impending death as making him a true disciple of Jesus. Virginity became another way to follow Christ. Toward the end of the third century the monastic movement got under way when women and men withdrew to the deserts of Palestine and Egypt as followers of Jesus. Monasticism called this following of Jesus *vita apostolica* (Lat.), "the apostolic life," a discipleship that looked to the earliest followers of Jesus for inspiration. Francis of Assisi (d. 1226) and other friars saw their life and ministry as a response to the invitation of Jesus to "Come, follow me." Eventually in the tradition, a popular notion of discipleship restricted this model for Christian life to religious and clergy.

With the Reformation, Protestantism restored the notion of discipleship to the whole Christian community; however, the more narrow sense of discipleship continued to predominate in Catholic thinking until the Second Vatican Council (1962–65). The modern classic exposition on discipleship is Dietrich Bonhoeffer's *The Cost of Discipleship* (Eng. trans., 1949). *See also* disciple; imitation of Christ; *Imitation of Christ.*   KEITH J. EGAN

Disciples of Christ, an American religious body that originated in 1811 through the work of Alexander Campbell (d. 1866), a former Presbyterian who emigrated from Scotland. Originally a group within Presbyterianism, the Disciples of Christ were organized as a separate religious communion in 1827. The doctrine and practice of its members were largely influenced by John Glas, who seceded from the Church of Scotland in 1728, and Robert Sandeman, who spread Glas's views in New England. The Scriptures are the sole basis of faith; all credal statements are rejected. The churches are congregationally organized, believer's baptism is practiced, and the Lord's Supper is the chief act of worship every Sunday. The Disciples of Christ are dedicated to the causes of Christian education and Christian unity. In Great Britain, Australia, New Zealand, and South Africa, they are known as the Churches of Christ. Their membership, as of 1993, is reputed to be over two million people. In addition to Disciples of Christ and Churches of Christ, they are sometimes referred to as Campbellites.

Dismas, St., d. first century, traditionally known as the good thief crucified with Christ on Good Friday and to whom Jesus promised salvation (Luke 23:39–43). He is the patron saint of prisoners. Feast day: March 25 (observed on the second Sunday of October in U.S. prison chapels).

disobedience, civil. *See* civil disobedience.

disparity of cult, impediment of, in canon law invalidating obstacle to a marriage of a Catholic with an unbaptized person. This is often dispensed by diocesan authorities, provided that the Catholic party promises to remain Catholic and to raise the children as Catholics; the non-Catholic party must be informed of the promise. *See also* marriage law.

dispensation, the relaxation of a law in a particular instance. Canon law foresees the possibility that in a given instance the observance of the law might not bring about those values the law seeks to serve. While maintaining the permanence of the law itself, the canonical system offers the possibility of exemption from its application. A dispensation requires a reason sufficient to the seriousness of the given law, together with permission given by the authority competent to make a dispensation from that law.

Vatican II taught that diocesan bishops, because of their responsibility for the universal Church, are able to dispense from universal law. The Code of Canon Law acknowledges this. The law in question, however, must not be procedural or penal or reserved to another authority (can. 85). In circumstances where communication with the Holy See is impossible, the dispensing power of bishops is even broader. A bishop may also delegate another to perform some of his duties in this regard. Other officials in a diocese or in a religious institute also have power to dispense from some of their respective laws. *See also* economy, principle of.

dissent, a judgment of disagreement with an official Church teaching or practice. An understanding of dissent and its place in the life of the Catholic Church requires an understanding of the various levels of authoritative Church teaching and the appropriate response to them. When the Church, through the pope or the bishops with the pope, uses its fullest authority to propose a matter of revealed faith or morals, it acts infallibly. The proper response to such teaching is an act of faith. Such pronouncements are relatively rare.

Noninfallible Teaching: Declarations that do not use the fullest authority of the Church are known as authoritative but noninfallible acts of the magisterium. Such acts constitute the ordinary, day-to-day teaching of the Church. This teaching is said to enjoy the presumption of truth rooted in the fact that the pope and bishops have been commissioned to teach and enjoy the guidance of the Holy Spirit in fulfilling this commission. The strength of this presumption can vary considerably since there is a broad range of subjects that can be proposed authoritatively and their status can vary. Some enjoy greater certainty than others. For instance, universal moral principles are proposed more authoritatively than their applications.

The proper response to authoritative noninfallible teaching is said to be "religious submission of mind and will" (Lat., *obsequium religiosum*). The exact meaning of this phrase is disputed. In the first half of the twentieth century it was understood as a true internal assent, closely akin to intellectual obedience. After Vatican II (1962–65), in which past errors were both implicitly (in the rehabilitation and use of condemned theologians) and explicitly admitted, many theologians began to understand the proper response to authoritative but noninfallible teaching as a kind of docility of mind and will that did not exclude a critical component and the possibility of dissent. This possibility became even clearer as a result of a number of ecclesiological emphases introduced by Vatican II. Some of these are: the notion of Church as the People of God, the ecclesial reality of other non-Catholic Christian churches, the historical nature of the Church, the place of laypeople in the Church, and collegiality.

Humanae Vitae: The question of dissent became highly visible and practical with the publication of the encyclical *Humanae Vitae* in 1968. Many Catholics—including theologians and priests—could not accept the central assertion of that document (the intrinsic immorality of every contraceptive act). Such dissent was viewed by some authorities as illegitimate and, if public, punishable. Others viewed it as a dimension of the critical responsibility of Catholics and as an indispensable part of the teaching-learning process of the Church. The U.S. bishops in their pastoral letter "Human Life in Our Day" (1968) viewed dissent as legitimate under three conditions: (1) it is based on serious reasons; (2) it is respectful of teaching authority; and (3) it does not cause scandal.

Dissent is usually individual; but it can be, and has been, public and organized. Where dissent is both public and organized, it carries with it special risks and hence demands special warrants. They are that other forms of dissent are ineffective and/or an unopposed error would cause grave harm. Restorationist attitudes prevalent since 1980 in the Vatican have tended to view any dissent as unacceptable. *See also* doctrine; dogma; magisterium; theologian; theology.   RICHARD A. MCCORMICK

dissolution of marriage, termination by the pope of certain marriages between a baptized and a nonbaptized person (the so-called Petrine Privilege), of certain marriages between two nonbaptized persons (the so-called Pauline Privilege), or of nonconsummated marriages, even of two baptized persons, for just cause on request. *See also* marriage law; Privilege of the Faith.

dissolution of the monasteries, the suppression of monasticism in England in 1535–40. Henry VIII, pressed for money, ordered the confiscation of the over three hundred English monasteries in order to acquire their immense wealth. The money was primarily used to pay off war debts, but some was applied to education and other reform measures.

divine law, God's governance of the universe. More narrowly, divine law refers to divine positive law, God's ordinances known through revelation.

According to Thomas Aquinas (d. 1274), such divine law is necessary for four reasons: (1) human beings are directed to a fulfillment that exceeds their natural capacity, hence they are in need of a law above natural and human law; (2) human judgment is uncertain and, therefore, the laws proceeding from it are inadequate for guidance; (3) human laws can regulate only outward conduct, whereas the perfection of virtue requires regulation of interior acts; and (4) human legislation cannot forbid or punish all wrongdoing but reaches only to criminal acts (*Summa Theologiae* 1–2.91.4).

Divine law has two main divisions, corresponding to the two Testaments of the Bible: the Mosaic Law, given to Moses on Mount Sinai for the Jewish people, and the evangelical law promulgated by Jesus, above all in his Sermon on the Mount. The evangelical differs from the Mosaic in that it directs persons to eternal life, guides the interior acts of the mind as well as outward acts, and motivates observance through love rather than through fear.

Divine law comprises moral, ceremonial, and judicial precepts. The evangelical law has abrogated the ceremonial precepts pertaining to the forms of Jewish worship through the institution of the Church and its sacraments. And it has replaced the judicial precepts, the detailed civil laws of Israel, with a love of justice animated by the love revealed in Christ and given through grace.   ROBERT P. KENNEDY

Divine Liturgy, Byzantine-rite eucharistic service and its formularies, two of which, from Constantinople, are in common use: the Liturgy of St. John Chrysostom and the Liturgy of St. Basil. The Jerusalem Liturgy of St. James is also used on occasion. Though the name "Divine Liturgy" is sometimes borrowed by other Eastern traditions, it is proper only to the Byzantine Eucharist. *See also* Eucharist.

Divine Office. *See* breviary; Liturgy of the Hours.

Divine Praises, a series of praises beginning with "Blessed be God" commonly used at Benediction before reposition of the Host. They are usually recited in the vernacular with the assembly repeating the phrases of the presider. Probably compiled by Louis Felici ca. 1779 as prayer to atone for blasphemy and profanity, Pope Pius VII attached indulgences to them in 1801. Additions to the original series include: Immaculate Conception in 1856, Sacred Heart in 1897, St. Joseph in 1921, the Assumption in 1950, the Precious Blood in 1960, and the Holy Ghost in 1964. *See also* Benediction.

DIVINE PRAISES

Blessed be God.
Blessed be his Holy Name.
Blessed be Jesus Christ, true God and true man.
Blessed be the Name of Jesus.
Blessed be his Most Sacred Heart.
Blessed be his Most Precious Blood.
Blessed be Jesus in the Most Holy Sacrament of
   the Altar.
Blessed be the Holy Spirit, the Paraclete.
Blessed be the great Mother of God, Mary most holy.
Blessed be her holy and Immaculate Conception.
Blessed be her glorious Assumption.
Blessed be the name of Mary, Virgin and Mother.
Blessed be St. Joseph, her most chaste spouse.
Blessed be God in his angels and in his saints.

Divine Word, Society of the. *See* Society of the Divine Word.

divinization. *See* deification.

Divino Afflante Spiritu (Lat., "Inspired by the Holy Spirit"), encyclical of Pope Pius XII of September 30, 1943, on the promotion of biblical studies. It was described as the Magna Carta of biblical renewal, and followed the anti-Modernist opposition to Leo XIII's cautious approval of biblical research. The encyclical directs exegetes to describe the literal sense of Scripture, i.e., "what the writer intended to express." They are to use historical-critical methods to study the sources and forms of expression used by the sacred writers, along with their cultural and historical contexts. When describing the theology of each book of the Bible, exegetes and preachers should avoid the unrestrained use of "figurative" senses (e.g., allegory and typology). Despite sustained conservative opposition, the directives of *Divino Afflante Spiritu* were incorporated by Vatican II (1962–65) into the Dogmatic Constitution on Divine Revelation (*Dei Verbum,* 1965). *See also* Bible, Church teachings on the.

divorce, termination of a marriage in civil law by court decree or judgment. While the Church has no dispute with legitimate state interest in the marital status of parties, the canonical effects, i.e., the legal consequences in Church law, do not automatically follow from any civil divorce proceeding. As far as the Church is concerned, the presumption that the parties are married continues. (The same presumption remains after a civil annulment.) In practice, the Church usually accepts a civil authority's disposition of the incidents of a marriage, such as the continuing obligations to the spouse or to children. The Church, however, finds the termination of a marriage to be, in most circumstances, impossible because it is against the dominical command (found in Matt 19:6; Mark 10:9): "what God has joined together let no one separate." This teaching does not, however, forbid the faithful from obtaining a civil divorce or living apart from a spouse, especially in those instances when continuing conjugal life would bring harm to one of the parties or to children.

The most common way for a divorced person to be able to marry again in the Church while the former spouse is still living is to obtain an annulment from a Church tribunal. Such an action follows an examination of the union and a declaration that it is not considered to be a marriage in Church law. An annulment does not attempt to affix blame or affect the legitimacy of any offspring. Virtually all dioceses in the United States expend considerable resources for this ministry. In some cases the Church sees itself capable of dissolving a marriage by a process called the Privilege of the Faith, which arose from an understanding of certain scriptural passages.

Those who have divorced and remarried without Church approval should not, as a general rule, receive Communion. However, a former law that excommunicated people in such circumstances (established in the nineteenth century by American bishops solely for Catholics in the United States) has been abolished. The pastoral leaders of the Church, especially Pope John Paul II, have emphasized the Church's obligation to relate in a pastoral and understanding way to those who have suffered the trauma of divorce. At the same time there is concern among Church leaders to improve both marriage preparation and support for the married in order to lessen the frequency of divorce. *See also* annulment; dissolution of marriage; marriage law; Privilege of the Faith.   JOHN LAHEY, EDWARD SCHARFENBERGER

Docetism, theological doctrine claiming that Christ had merely the appearance (Gk., *dokein,* "to seem") of a physical body, without corporeal reality. It was explicitly condemned by Ignatius of Antioch early in the second century. The roots of Docetism seem to be linked to a belief that materiality, including human flesh, is evil. The doctrine thus found many allies among Gnostics of the second and third centuries and among Pelagianists of the fifth century. Among the strongest adversaries of Docetism were those early Christians who defended the orthodox view of the full humanity of Jesus Christ: Polycarp of Smyrna, Irenaeus, and Tertullian. *See also* Christology; Incarnation, the; Jesus Christ.

Doctors of the Church, canonized saints officially recognized by the pope or an ecumenical council as eminent teachers of the faith. Of the eight original Doctors, four were from the West (proclaimed in 1298)—Ambrose, Jerome, Augustine of Hippo, and Gregory the Great—and four were from the East (1568)—Athanasius, John Chrysostom, Basil the Great, and Gregory of Nazianzus. The following have been added: Thomas Aquinas (1567); Bonaventure (1588); Anselm of Canterbury (1720); Isidore of Seville (1722); Peter Chrysologus (1729); Leo the Great (1754); Peter Damian (1828); Bernard of Clairvaux (1830); Hilary of Poitiers (1851); Alphonsus Liguori (1871); Francis de Sales (1877); Cyril of Alexandria, Cyril of Jerusalem (1882); John of Damascus (1890); the Venerable Bede (1899); Ephraem the Syrian (1920); Peter Canisius (1925); John of the Cross (1926); Robert Bellarmine (1931); Albertus Magnus (1932); Anthony of Padua (1946); Lawrence of Brindisi (1959); Teresa of Ávila, Catherine of Siena (1970). *See also* theologian; theology.

doctrine (Lat., *doctrina*, "teaching"), an official teaching of the Church. A doctrine that is taught definitively, that is, infallibly, is called a dogma. Every dogma is a doctrine, but not every doctrine is a dogma. Official teachings are promulgated by official teachers and teaching bodies, that is, by the magisterium: ecumenical councils, popes, and regional or national bodies of bishops, including local, regional, and international synods.

One finds official teachings already in the NT, usually identified with the *kerygma* (Gk., "message"), that is, the core of Christian faith that is proclaimed. Paul speaks, for example, of handing on what he himself received concerning the death and Resurrection of Christ (1 Cor 15:3–5; see also Acts 2:36). The word of God is the norm of every official teaching. Therefore, the "teaching office is not above the word of God, but serves it, teaching only what has been handed on, listening to it devoutly, guarding it scrupulously, and explaining it faithfully" (Dogmatic Constitution on Divine Revelation, n. 10).

Since doctrines normally are not protected by the charism of infallibility, they are subject to error as well as other linguistic and conceptual deficiencies deriving from the limitations of the culture and circumstances in which they were initially formulated. As such, doctrines are subject to critical evaluation by those competent to offer it. The process by which doctrines are modified or supplanted is called doctrinal development. The evolution of the official teachings of the Church on religious liberty, culminating in Vatican II's Declaration on Religious Freedom, is a classic example of such development. *See also* doctrine, development of; dogma; magisterium.

RICHARD P. MCBRIEN

doctrine, development of, the progressive de-

velopment in the Church's understanding of its faith. The problem raised by the development of doctrine (and especially of defined doctrine, known as dogma) is to explain how it is possible for the Church later to define a truth that was not always expressly taught as divinely revealed in the original apostolic teaching. Catholic doctrine teaches that public revelation concluded with the death of the last apostle (D 1502, 3421), so this postapostolic teaching cannot constitute new revelation. Moreover, it is necessary to demonstrate the actual identity between later expositions and the apostolic exposition even when the terminology of the teaching did not exist during the apostolic age.

The reason revelation is closed at the end of the apostolic period is that revelation culminates in Christ, and the apostolic generation coincides with the life of those who were eyewitnesses to Christ's life, death, and Resurrection. After this period the Church cannot teach new truth, but only bear witness to what was received from Christ.

The Church cannot only continue to repeat what it has received, but must strive to understand what it has received and teach it in ever-changing cultural contexts. This growth in understanding becomes dogmatic development when it is infallibly defined by the Church's magisterium as a revealed truth (D 1792). What is defined must be objectively and demonstrably contained in the deposit of faith.

Theories of Development: There is no uniform Catholic theory of how, exactly, this new teaching is contained in the original revelation. Two theories have received acceptance within the Church. First, within a propositional view of revelation, one which sees revelation as consisting of a series of statements, new propositions are a logical development and are implicitly contained in the verbal expressions of primitive faith.

Another theory traceable to the work of J. S. von Drey, J. A. Moehler, John Henry Newman, and M. Blondel, sees development as a supernaturally guided continuity in doctrine. This view is particularly adaptable to the view of revelation in Vatican II (1962–65), where revelation is no longer identified with propositions, but with the mystery of Christ himself. Propositions are only imperfect, partial, and often culturally circumscribed expressions of this mystery. Faith is assent, not only to propositions, but to the mystery they intend. From this perspective, doctrinal development is the coming to consciousness of that which was implicitly contained within that mystery. What was formerly not explicitly believed is declared as belonging to the original revelation even though it may be difficult to demonstrate this historically or through logical syllogistic reasoning. There are definite connections between earlier teaching and more recent development, but the manner of asserting this connection is no longer a demonstration of logical development.

Rather than a process of logical deduction, the process is one of seeing how the new teaching fits in with the totality of what is believed by an analogy of faith. The final determination that the development forms a part of the totality of faith is the authentic teaching authority of the magisterium, which defines it as such.

The development of doctrine is acknowledged as a reality by the Congregation for the Doctrine of the Faith's *Mysterium Ecclesiae* (1973). *See also* doctrine; revelation. SUSAN K. WOOD

dogma (Gk., "what seems right"), a definitive, or infallible, teaching of the Church. The promulgation of a dogma is the prerogative of an ecumenical council, including the pope, or of the pope acting as earthly head of the Church, apart from a council.

It was not until the eighteenth century that the term "dogma" acquired its present meaning. The notion was formally adopted by the First Vatican Council (1869–70) and in the 1917 Code of Canon Law (cans. 1323.2; 1325.2; 2314.1). According to Vatican I, a dogma must meet the following conditions: (1) it must be contained in Sacred Scripture or in the postbiblical tradition of the Church and as such considered part of divine revelation; (2) it must be explicitly proposed by the Church as a divinely revealed object of belief; and (3) this must be done either in a solemn decree or in the Church's ordinary, universal teaching.

Every dogma is a doctrine, but not every doctrine is a dogma. It is no easy matter to determine the difference between the two, and there is no list of dogmas to which all Catholics would agree, bishops and theologians included.

The formal and deliberate rejection of a dogma is an act of heresy. This is not to say, however, that dogmas are beyond critical evaluation or immune from development. Not every dogma was originally expressed in the best form. A dogma can reflect "the changeable conceptions of a given epoch" (*Mysterium Ecclesiae*, 1973) and as such is open to improvement and development. *See also* doctrine; infallibility; magisterium. RICHARD P. MCBRIEN

Dogmatic Constitution on Divine Revelation (Lat., *Dei Verbum,* "Word of God"), one of the sixteen documents of Vatican II and one of two such dogmatic constitutions (the other being the Dogmatic Constitution on the Church, *Lumen Gentium*), promulgated on November 18, 1965. The schema (draft document) prepared for the first council session (October–December 1962) reflected the conservative theology of the Holy Office (under Cardinal Ottaviani). Through the direct intervention of Pope John XXIII this schema was tabled and the preparation of a new draft was assigned to a mixed commission of conservatives and progressives. Prior to final approval, the schema was discussed in the third and fourth sessions of the council.

Dei Verbum made several important statements: (1) it characterized revelation as a personal communication between God and humans, manifest in deed as well as in word (n. 6); (2) it rejected the popularly understood "two source" theory of revelation (Scripture and tradition) in favor of a more nuanced position holding that, though they both "flow from the same divine wellspring," Scripture is the word of God, while tradition faithfully hands it on (n. 9); (3) it understood inerrancy not as the guarantee of literal historicity but as the truth that God "wanted put into the sacred writings for the sake of our salvation" (n. 11); (4) it approved of historical critical methods of exegesis (n. 12); (5) it stated that the Church is nourished from the table of both the word of God and of the body of Christ (n. 21). *See also* Bible, Church teachings on the.

JOHN R. DONAHUE

Dogmatic Constitution on the Church (Lat., *Lumen Gentium,* "the light of nations"), one of the sixteen documents of Vatican II (1962–65). Never before has the Church presented its self-understanding and its mission so comprehensively in a dogmatic document. Together with the Pastoral Constitution on the Church in the Modern World (*Gaudium et Spes*), the Dogmatic Constitution on the Church characterizes Vatican II as the council of the Church about the Church.

The History of the Constitution: Vatican Council I (1869–70) had already prepared a schema, or proposed decree, about the Church; however, it was not able to act upon all of this document. In the dogmatic constitution *Pastor Aeternus*, it did, however, decide on those parts of the schema that concern the papacy's juridical primacy and the infallibility of its teaching office. But this isolated definition of papal authority expressed a one-sided juridical and centralist ecclesiology.

In the twentieth century, theology sought a more balanced ecclesiology. It discovered the essence of the Church as mystery and community, and it also gained a new appreciation for the mission of the laity, whose apostolate in Catholic Action had attained worldwide significance. From 1960 through 1962 the Preparatory Theological Commission drafted the schema *De Ecclesia,* which was discussed by the council in December 1962. Because of the council Fathers' criticism of *De Ecclesia,* the doctrinal commission drafted the schema *Lumen Gentium,* which was discussed by the council in the autumn of 1963. Then the council decided to integrate a revised schema about Mary into *Lumen Gentium.* Amended proposals generated a further draft, which was voted upon in detail in the autumn of 1964. The most important result of the conciliar debate was that the document's first chapter about the mystery of the Church was no longer followed by the chapter about the hierarchical structure of the Church, but by a new chapter about the People of God.

In November 1964 Pope Paul VI sent a "preliminary explanatory note" to the council intended to eliminate the objections of the minority who held that the document's expressions about the college of bishops stood in opposition to the teaching of Vatican I about the juridical primacy of the pope. On November 21, 1964, the council decreed the Dogmatic Constitution on the Church (*Lumen Gentium*) with a vote of 2,151 to 5.

The Composition of the Constitution: The constitution consists of sixty-nine articles arranged in eight chapters: "The Mystery of the Church," "The People of God," "The Hierarchical Structure of the Church and the Episcopate in Particular," "The Laity," "The Universal Call of Holiness in the Church," "Religious," "The Eschatological Nature of the Pilgrim Church and Its Union with the Church in Heaven," and "The Blessed Virgin Mary, Mother of God, in the Mystery of Christ and of the Church."

The Teaching of the Constitution: The first chapter, on the Church as mystery, is foundational. At the outset is the definition of the Church that unites *Lumen Gentium* with the Pastoral Constitution on the Church in the Modern World (*Gaudium et Spes*): "The Church, in Christ, is in the nature of the sacrament, a sign and instrument, that is, of communion with God and of unity among all people" (Dogmatic Constitution on the Church, n. 1). Thus the Church is not a goal in itself, but stands in the service of the universal and reconciling mission of Jesus Christ.

The mission of the Church is determined accordingly in God's universal plan of salvation, and this mission is linked, as Paul said, with "mystery" and "sacrament." Since the first judgment of Abel, God gathers together all people, in particular through the calling of the people of Israel, through Jesus Christ and through the descent of the Holy Spirit. The Church is the seed and the beginning of the reign of God on earth (nn. 2–5).

In place of an abstract or juridical definition of the Church, the council describes the essence of the Church in biblical images and metaphors as the work of the triune God: as a field, a building, a family, and the temple of God in the Holy Spirit, as well as flock, spouse, and Body of Christ (nn. 6–7).

While many people today see the Church only as an external organization, the council underlined the unity in tension that characterizes the Church both as the work of God and also as the community of human beings. "The visible society and the spiritual community, the earthly Church and the Church endowed with heavenly riches, are not to be thought of as two realities. On the contrary, they form one complex reality which comes together from a human and a divine element." Thus a realization is possible that is important for the reform of the Church. "The Church, clasping sinners to her bosom, at once holy and always in need of purification, follows constantly the path of penance and renewal" (n. 8).

The polarity of external form and divine activity in the Church also makes it possible to overcome confessional narrowness. The sole Church of Christ, "constituted and organized as a society in the present world, subsists in the Catholic Church. . . . Nevertheless, many elements of sanctification and of truth are found outside its visible confines" (n. 8). Finally the council declares the option of the Church for the poor.

The second chapter, on the Church as the People of God, has brought about a new awareness that we are all the Church. This chapter presents the common calling and mission of every member of the Church before consideration is given to any differentiation of office. All baptized persons participate in the common priesthood and in the priestly, prophetic, and kingly office of Christ. The whole body of the faithful cannot err in matters of belief. The Holy Spirit distributes special graces among the faithful of all social strata in the Church, and through their use of these gifts the faithful share in the building up of the Church. The Church is the community of the faithful. The diversity in the local churches contributes to the catholicity of the Church.

The third and fourth chapters specify the roles of the pastors and the laity. In complementing Vatican I, the council teaches that the responsibility for the whole Church is entrusted to the college of bishops, whose visible head is the pope. It underlines the specific responsibility of the bishops in their own particular churches. The Church is a community of particular churches; "it is in these and formed out of them that the one and unique Catholic Church exists" (n. 23). The council restores the diaconate as a proper and permanent rank of the hierarchy.

The specific role of the laity arises from the laity's place in the family, in the work place, and in society. Since the Church is sent to witness to the gospel in the world, the Christian witness of the laity in society is essential for the Church. As members of the Church, laypersons also assume responsibility for the Church and in their parish.

The fifth and sixth chapters, on the call to holiness, belong together. All members of the Church are called to give witness by means of their holy lives to the liberating power of the reign of God. Those in religious communities can give this witness in an especially clear manner through their living of the evangelical counsels.

The seventh and eighth chapters, on the pilgrim Church, Mary, and the saints, also form a unity. The Church is still on the way to its completion. It is both gift and challenge. To the Church belong also its deceased members. The deceased who are still en route to their final perfection need our solidarity, and those who have already reached perfection, the saints, join in solidarity with us. This solidarity is especially evident in Mary's motherly care for us. *See also* Church; Vatican Council II.

Bibliography
Hastings, Adrian, ed. *Modern Catholicism: Vatican II and After.* New York: Oxford University Press, 1991.

Vorgrimler, Herbert, ed. *Commentary on the Documents of Vatican II.* Vol. 1. New York: Herder and Herder, 1967.

HERMAN J. POTTMEYER

Doherty, Catherine de Hueck, 1900–1985, social reformer. A child of Russian nobility, and driven by her experiences of the Communist Revolution of 1917, she dedicated her life to following the "gospel without compromise." Emigrating to Canada, she founded two social apostolates: Friendship House, located in Toronto and several U.S. cities to promote interracial justice, and Madonna House, a rural community in Combermere, Ontario.

Döllinger, Johann J. I. von (der'lin-ger), 1799–1890, German-born Church historian and theologian. A critic of Protestant and liberal historiography, Döllinger wrote a history of Martin Luther and the Lutheran Reformation. He defended theologians' freedom of inquiry and their vocation to lead by influencing public opinion. He became increasingly critical of what he considered growing papal absolutism and the revival of Scholastic theology. His book on papal and conciliar authority, written under the pseudonym Janus, was placed on the Index of Forbidden Books (1869). For his outspoken rejection of the First Vatican Council's decree on papal infallibility, he was excommunicated by the archbishop of Munich (1871) and lost his professorship (1872) but not his support from the Bavarian kingdom. *See also* infallibility.

dolus, a quality partaking of maliciousness and deceit. The presence of *dolus* is a factor in judging actions. The differing translations of the Latin word *dolus* between the two major English translations of the code of canon law (namely, maliciousness and deceit) are indicative of the complex meaning of the term.

Dom, abbreviation of *Dominus* (Lat., "Master"), a title given to professed monks of the Benedictine and some other monastic orders. Among the Trappists it is used only of abbots. *See also* abbot; monk.

dome, large hemispherical ceiling or roof of a building, especially of a church. Dome interiors are often decorated to represent the cosmos or heaven.

domestic church, the family as the most basic unit of the Church. The family has been called the domestic church by the Second Vatican Council's Dogmatic Constitution on the Church (1964, n. 11), Pope Paul VI's apostolic exhortation *Evangelii Nuntiandi* (On Evangelization in the Modern World, 1975, n. 71), and in Pope John Paul II's apostolic exhortation *Consortium Socialis* (On the Family, 1981, n. 21). The term suggests that the community of faith begins in the home, in the family unit. It is the family unit that begets new members of the Church. It is in the family unit that the faith is first transmitted by word and by example, both within and beyond the home. Accordingly, "there should be found in every Christian family the various aspects of the entire Church" (Pope Paul VI). *See also* family.

domestic prelate. *See* Honorary Prelate of His Holiness.

domicile (Old Fr., "dwelling-place"), canonical residency, or the diocese or parish one belongs to for the purposes of canon law. It is the usual place in which a Catholic receives the ministrations of the Church. It is acquired by moving to a given place with the intention of remaining there permanently or actually living in a given place for five years. *See also* quasi-domicile.

Dominican order, officially known as the Order of Preachers (O.P.), a religious order of priests and brothers founded in 1216 by Dominic de Guzman for the purpose of the ministry of the Word, to teach and preach the gospel. It is part of a larger association, the "Dominican Family," which includes cloistered nuns, sisters in active ministry,

Dominican friars in the Convento de Santo Domingo, Lima, Peru. The order is devoted especially to preaching (hence its name, Order of Preachers), as well as to teaching, missions, research, and parish ministry.

secular institutes, the Dominican Laity, and various confraternities; these groups are autonomous but united under the Master of the Order.

Dominic believed that for preachers of the gospel to be credible they must return to the "apostolic life," in which the preachers were freed by their poverty from the care of property to travel and preach, as described in the Bible. At the same time he was convinced that priests must be men of profound, contemplative prayer and charity, who would support one another as brothers (friars) in their difficult work.

To offer the gospel to others effectively, the local communities of this brotherhood share a way of living devoted to the contemplation of God in liturgical worship, private prayer, and study of God's Word. They are freed for this devotion by the practice of poverty and asceticism. Study as a means of sanctification as well as of ministry was a special contribution of Dominic to religious life.

Government of the Order: The order is governed according to the Rule of St. Augustine and constitutions, which can be modified in all respects except the fundamental elements just mentioned, namely, the commitment to poverty, prayer, and study. The basic unit of the order is the priory, headed by a chapter of the brethren, who elect a first brother or prior. Periodically, the priors of communities along with elected delegates meet in a provincial chapter that elects a prior provincial and his council, who then govern the province for a term. Again at intervals, the provincials and elected delegates from the provinces meet in a general chapter that periodically elects a Master of the Order, who with his council governs the order for a term.

The government of Dominican friars differs from that of monks who are vowed to a local monastery ruled by an abbot or Father, and from that of more modern orders, like the Jesuits, whose government is vertical, with assigned rather than elected offices.

History: The Dominican order has never been divided into branches but has undergone four major historical phases. The first period (1216–1347) was marked by a rapid expansion to about twenty thousand members, and featured brilliant successes in the medieval universities, with theologians and philosophers like Albertus Magnus (ca. 1200–1280) and his pupil Thomas Aquinas (ca. 1225–74) (both now Doctors of the Church), Peter of Tarantaise (Pope Innocent V, d. 1276), and the biblical scholar Hugh of St. Cher (ca. 1200–1263). These thinkers did much to show how the findings of science and philosophy could be used to present the gospel in a systematic and coherent way. The plague of 1347, called "The Black Death," brought an end to this period.

The second period lasted until the Protestant Reformation (1347–1517). It began with a decline in membership and religious discipline but took a positive turn in the successful reform movement, which returned the order to its original commitment to poverty, prayer, and study, inspired by Catherine of Siena (ca. 1347–80) and led by Raymond of Capua (1330–99), who established houses of discipline in many provinces. This reform polarized provinces into observants, who followed a stricter rule, especially with regard to poverty, and conventuals, who allowed for the holding and use of property. Observant congregations outside the provincial structure were erected because of the reform. The period was characterized, however, by a great increase in the numbers of nuns, and produced mystics such as Catherine of Siena, Meister Eckhart (ca. 1260–1327), John Tauler (ca. 1300–1361), and Henry Suso (ca. 1295–1366). Thus, the order had fostered two lasting spiritualities: an apostolic and reform-oriented spirituality (Catherine of Siena and Girolamo Savonarola, d. 1498), and an inward-oriented "negative" spirituality, such as that of Meister Eckhart.

The third period began with the loss of the provinces of Northern Europe to the Reformation (ca. 1530) and lasted until the French Revolution (1789). It was a time of the expansion of missions to the New World and the Far East. It saw a revival of Thomism, especially in Spain, with the development of a teaching on human rights and social justice by theologians such as Francis de Vitoria (ca. 1485–1546) and Bartolomé de las Casas (1474–1566). During this time Dominicans played a major role at the Council of Trent (1545–63), and debated with the Jesuits over the nature of predestination, grace, and free will.

The fourth period lasted until Vatican II (1962–65). It began with a decline of membership from about thirty thousand to three thousand Dominicans as a result of the French Revolution and Napoleonic wars, but then witnessed the revival of the order by Henri Lacordaire (1802–61), the expansion of the order in the United States and Canada, the tremendous growth of the active sisters, and the revival of Thomism by Pope Leo XIII in 1879. The order furthered countless schools and centers in Thomism but also pioneered theologies of ecu-

menism, liturgy, and pastoral life as well as biblical studies. Dominican theologians such as Yves Congar (b. 1904) greatly contributed to Vatican II.

After Vatican II, the order revised its constitutions in 1968. This renewed the fundamentals of the spirit of its founder, especially by fully restoring the order's democratic, elective form of government. As of 1993, the Dominicans had about 7,500 members, and, despite a decline in vocations in the decade after 1968, it has expanded throughout the world so that it now carries out its mission in forty-eight provinces and in eighty-six countries.

The Dominicans in the United States were founded by Dominic Fenwick in 1805, and in the 1990s have four provinces (there are also provinces in Canada and Mexico) with headquarters in New York, Oakland (CA), Chicago, and New Orleans. They publish a number of periodicals, conduct schools of theology in Berkeley, California, Washington, D.C., and St. Louis, Missouri, direct Providence College in Providence, Rhode Island, and work in dozens of parishes, hospitals, and university centers. *See also* Aquinas, St. Thomas; Augustine, Rule of St.; Catherine of Siena, St.; Dominican spirituality; Dominic de Guzman, St.; religious orders and congregations.

Bibliography

Hinnebusch, William A. *The History of the Dominican Order.* 2 vols. Staten Island, NY: Alba House, 1966, 1973.

Tugwell, Simon, ed. *Early Dominicans: Selected Writings.* Classics of Western Spirituality. New York: Paulist Press, 1982.

BENEDICT M. ASHLEY

Dominican Sisters. *See* Sisters of St. Dominic.

Dominican spirituality, the mode of Christian prayer and life developed in the Order of Preachers, founded by Dominic de Guzman (d. 1221). Dominic's concern was to revive the apostolic life portrayed in the Gospel of Matthew and directed to preaching. This could best be supported by a fraternal community living a contemplative life of liturgical and private prayer, by asceticism, especially poverty, and by devotion to the study of the word of God. Dominic was devoted to Christ in his Passion, to the Eucharist, and to Christ's mother, Mary.

History: The tradition was further shaped by Albertus Magnus (ca. 1200–1280) and his pupil Thomas Aquinas (ca. 1225–74). Aquinas emphasized our dependence on God even as he understood "grace as perfecting nature." Christian holiness consists in union with God through the Incarnate Word by the grace of the Holy Spirit realized in the actions of the theological virtues of faith, hope, and love, which inform and unite the Christian journey. Growth in faith, hope, and love demands a balanced development of the moral virtues. The heights of sanctity and mystical life are open to all the baptized, and can be achieved through the guidance and empowerment of the Holy Spirit acting through seven "gifts" urging Christians to prayer's union with God and to the service of one's neighbors. Aquinas summed up this ideal in the maxim, *"Contemplare, et contemplata aliis tradere"* (Lat.), which means "To gaze with love on God, and then to share what has been seen with others."

From Catherine of Siena's (ca. 1347–80) and Girolomo Savonarola's (1452–98) concern for ecclesiastical reform, this spirituality also took on a social dimension; this characteristic sparked the concern for human rights of Francisco de Vitoria (ca. 1485–1546) and Bartolomé de las Casas (1474–1566) and influences theology of social justice and liberation in the 1990s. This balanced and outgoing spirituality has dominated the Dominican tradition, but it has been complemented by an inward-looking spirituality that stems from the Neoplatonism of

the Pseudo-Dionysius (ca. 500) through Albertus Magnus (ca. 1200–1280) and Meister Eckhart (ca. 1260–1327). This "negative theology" of detachment from created reality empties the soul for the interior birth of the Word. Through Eckhart's Dominican disciples John Tauler (ca. 1300–1361) and Henry Suso (ca. 1295–1366), it influenced the Lowland (Netherlands, Belgium, and Luxembourg), Spanish, and French schools of mysticism, as well as Protestantism through Martin Luther (d. 1546) and German idealism.

In the twentieth century, the Dominicans Juan Arintero (1860–1928) and Reginald Garrigou-Lagrange (1877–1964) have been notable for their defense of the universal vocation of all Christians to mystical contemplation through the gifts of the Holy Spirit.

A sometimes overlooked aspect of this spirituality is that it has found expression also in the fine arts through painters like Fra Angelico (1387–1455) and Fra Bartolomeo de la Porta (1472–1516), and in the twentieth century the pioneer of the encounter between modern and Christian art, Pierre M.-A. Couturier (1897–1954). *See also* Dominican order; spirituality, Christian.   BENEDICT M. ASHLEY

Dominic, founder of the Dominicans, beholding an apparition of Sts. Peter and Paul; early-fifteenth-century painting by Fra Angelico, Louvre, Paris.

Dominic de Guzman, St., ca. 1170–1221, founder of the Order of Preachers (Dominicans). Born in Caleruega, Spain, and educated at Palencia, he became a canon of the newly reformed cathedral chapter of Osma. While accompanying Bishop Diego of Azevedo to Denmark and Rome in 1203 and 1205, he was motivated to oppose the advance of the Albigensian heresy in southern France, founding a community of nuns at Prouille (1206) and a community of mendicant, itinerant preachers in Toulouse (1215) under the Rule of St. Augustine. The latter community received full papal approbation as the Order of Preachers in 1216.

Dominic, traveling on foot, founded communities of his brethren and nuns in France, Italy, and Spain. After undertaking another preaching mission in northern Italy, he died in Bologna in 1221, unable to fulfill his lifelong dream of becoming a foreign missionary. Gregory IX, who knew him personally, canonized him in 1234. Contemporaries testified to his fidelity to the apostolic life of poverty and chastity, to his compassionate love for sinners, and to his joyful fraternal leadership. His special love for Mary is demonstrated in the legend that he initiated devotion to the Rosary. The constitutions of his order, written under his presidency by the organizational chapters (assemblies) of 1220 and 1221 at Bologna, gave Dominicans an elective, fraternal form of community life, fostered by contemplation of divine truth in liturgy and study, all directed to evangelical preaching. Emphasis on sanctification by study and elective government are Dominic's special contributions to religious life. Feast day: August 8.   *BENEDICT M. ASHLEY*

Dominus vobiscum (doh'mee-nuhs voh-bees' koom; Lat., "The Lord [be] with you"), a liturgical greeting. Said by a presider to a liturgical assembly, the common response is *"Et cum spiritu tuo"* (Lat., "And with your spirit"). The current English version of the Mass translates the phrase "And also with you."

Domitilla, Flavia, niece of the emperor Domitian (81–96). She and her husband, Flavius Clemens (consul in 95 and cousin of Domitian), were probably Christians; charged with atheism and adoption of Jewish ways, they were punished (95) with death (Clemens) and exile (Domitilla). It is disputed whether the Catacomb of Domitilla, a Christian burial place from the second century, was land originally owned by Flavia, or by another Flavia, niece of the emperor Titus, also exiled as a Christian. Feast day (until 1969): May 12. *See also* catacombs.

Donation of Constantine, the emperor Constantine's supposed bequest to Pope Sylvester (314–35) of temporal dominion over Italy and other Western regions. Included in the *False Decretals* and Gratian's *Decretals*, it enjoyed widespread authority until the mid-1400s when its authenticity was questioned by Aeneas Sylvius (later Pius II) and refuted by Nicholas Cusanus, Reginald Pecock, and Lorenzo Valla. *See also* Constantine the Great; *Decretum Gratianum; False Decretals.*

Donatism (doh'nuh-tizm), North African schismatic sect of the fourth and fifth centuries tending to moral rigorism; it is named for Donatus, the movement's institutional organizer. The schism arose from the contested election of Caecilian as bishop of Carthage in 311, on the grounds that his consecrator had been a *traditor,* one who "handed over" the Scriptures during the time of the Diocletian persecution. In 313 a commission appointed by Miltiades, Bishop of Rome, decided against the Donatists, who then appealed unsuccessfully to a synod at Arles in 314 and to the emperor Constantine in 316. Fueled by anti-imperial sentiment and social unrest in North Africa, the schismatic church prospered despite persecution, Tyconius (d. ca. 400) being its only notable theologian. Despite the work of opponents such as Optatus of Milevis (d. ca. 370) and Augustine of Hippo (354–430), the schism lingered until the Moslem conquest of North Africa in the seventh century.

Theologically, the sect held the Church to a rigid standard of holiness, insisted that sacraments conferred by *traditores* were invalid, and that those who communicated with *traditores* were also infected with sin. In effect, the Donatists formed their own church and rebaptized converts to it. *See also* schism.

Donne, John, 1572–1631, English metaphysical poet, Anglican preacher, Dean of St. Paul's Cathedral, London. Born in London of a Roman Catholic family, Donne studied at Oxford and Cambridge Universities as well as at the Inns of Court in London. He accepted a secretarial post to Sir Thomas Egerton that lasted until the discovery of his secret marriage to Egerton's niece, which led to his dismissal and imprisonment in 1601.

A few years earlier, Donne had abandoned Catholicism for Anglicanism. Ultimately, he was ordained, and became Dean of St. Paul's. Donne's sermons and poetry are remarkable achievements, combining deep passion with brilliant wit and intellectual rigor, e.g., the *Holy Sonnets* and the *Divine Poems.*

Dooley, Thomas A., III, 1927–61, Catholic physician known for his heroic medical work in Southeast Asia. Born in St. Louis, Missouri, he attended the University of Notre Dame (1943–44, 1946–48) and St. Louis University School of Medicine (1948–53). Having served as a medical corpsman in the U.S. Navy (1944–46), he was commissioned into the Navy Medical Corps as a physician in April 1953. From August 1954 to May 1955, he assisted the Navy's evacuation of refugees in North Vietnam by tirelessly working in the camps that aided hundreds of thousands of Vietnamese fleeing from the North to the South. In 1956, Dooley resigned from the Navy, assembled a small medical staff, and opened a privately funded medical clinic in a remote area of Laos. In 1958, he established an independent organization, Medico, Inc., which eventually founded nineteen clinics in thirteen nations in need of medical assistance. Diagnosed with cancer in August 1959, he continued to work vigorously in Laos while making fund-raising trips to the United States. After a brief hospitalization, he died in St. Louis.

Dormition of Mary, literally the falling asleep of Mary, or Mary's death. Although a fifth-century feast is still celebrated in the East, contemporary theology, particularly in the West, accents the glorification of Mary's body in the Assumption rather than the circumstances surrounding her death. *See also* Assumption of the Blessed Virgin Mary.

Dorothy, St., d. ca. 303, virgin and martyr of questionable historicity. She is said to have died during the reign of Diocletian. Her feast, formerly on February 6, is no longer observed.

Douay-Rheims Version of the Bible, an English translation of the Latin Vulgate prepared by Gregory Martin. The NT translation was published at Rheims (1582) and the OT in Douay (1609). Bishop Richard Challoner revised it several times (NT: 1749, 1752; OT: 1750, 1763), modernizing the English and providing explanatory notes. This version was used by English-speaking Roman Catholics for two centuries. *See also* Scripture, versions of.

double effect, principle of, a traditional guideline for determining the morality of an action based on the distinction between what is directly willed or only indirectly willed. This distinction has been used to help resolve many practical conflict situations where an evil can be avoided or where a more or less necessary good can be achieved only when another evil is reluctantly caused. In such situations the evil caused in the course of doing good has been viewed as justified under four conditions: (1) The action from which evil results is good or indifferent in itself; it is not morally evil. (2) The intention of the agent is upright, that is, the evil effect is sincerely not intended. (3) The evil effect must be equally immediate causally with the good effect, for otherwise it would be a means to the good effect and would be intended. (4) There must be a proportionately grave reason for allowing the evil to occur. When these four conditions are fulfilled, the resultant evil would be an unintended by-product of the action, that is, only indirectly willed, and it would be justified by the presence of a proportionately grave reason.

The so-called double-effect principle has been taken over and used extensively in official documents of the magisterium. For instance, Paul VI states in *Humanae Vitae:* "Equally to be excluded, as the teaching authority of the Church has frequently declared, is direct sterilization, whether perpetual or temporary, whether of the man or of the woman." The term "direct" refers to a sterilization intended as a means or an end. If it was caused as an unintended effect of a therapeutic procedure, it is said to be indirect. Some contemporary theologians question the decisive character of the distinction.

RICHARD A. MCCORMICK

double monasteries, monastic foundations comprised of both women and men that enjoyed some popularity, especially in the West, from the rise of cenobitic (communal) monasticism in the fourth century to the end of the twelfth century. Notable early medieval monasteries were in Gaul (France) and in England; the Order of Sempringham established by St. Gilbert in the twelfth century also favored the double monastery. While strictly segregated in their living quarters, men and women did share common liturgical facilities and were normally under the rule of a woman superior. Frequently prey to the suspicions of the Church hierarchy, their eventual suppression may have been due as much to the uneasiness ecclesiastical and lay authorities felt about powerful women superiors as to doubts concerning the ethical propriety of religious women and men living in such close proximity. *See also* monasticism.

doubt [canon law]**,** in canon law the inability of an individual to make a judgment between two probable opinions. Doubt is not the same thing as error, i.e., a mistaken judgment, and so canonical theory requires that the opinions formed have some basis for probability. When the doubt concerns the meaning of a given law or the very existence of the law, it is called doubt of law. Between 1983, when the revised code of canon law was promulgated, and 1994, there was a doubt of law whether women and girls could be altar servers. That doubt was resolved by the Holy See in the affirmative in 1994. In such a case, the Code of Canon Law (can. 14) holds that the law does not bind, which explains why so many parishes legitimately allowed girls to serve at the altar before 1994. When the doubt concerns some fact, i.e., when the individual lacks sufficient information to fulfill the law, canon 14 allows ordinaries, i.e., certain authorities within a diocese or religious order, to dispense from any associated requirements. For example, a man must be at least sixteen and a woman fourteen in order to marry. But in an individual case, the age of one or both of the parties might not be clear. If a particular dispensation is reserved to higher authority, ordinaries may still dispense as long as they are in the habit of granting such dispensations. *See also* error [canon law]; ignorance [canon law].

doubt, moral, mental uncertainty regarding the morality of a contemplated action or lack of action. An individual possessing certain knowledge of the moral law may still have practical uncertainty about its specific application. Moral theologians disagree about the degree of certainty required for moral action. *See also* certitude, moral.

Dougherty, Dennis, 1865–1951, American cardinal-archbishop. Educated in Philadelphia and Rome, he was ordained (1890) and assigned to St. Charles Seminary, Philadelphia. After episcopal ordination (1903), he served as bishop of Nueva Segovia, Philippines; bishop of Buffalo (1915); arch-

bishop of Philadelphia (1918); and was created cardinal (1921). Known as "God's bricklayer," he greatly expanded the institutional church in Philadelphia.

dove (Gk., *peristera*), a Byzantine-rite tabernacle, in the form of a dove, for reserving the eucharistic species, often suspended by chains from a ciborium or baldachino above the altar. *See also* tabernacle.

doxology (dahks-ah'luh-jee; Gk., *doxa-logia*, "praise-words"), any ascription of praise to God. Doxologies conclude liturgical prayers, the most solemn of which is the concluding doxology of the Eucharistic Prayer: "Through him [Christ], with him, in him, in the unity of the Holy Spirit, all glory and power is yours almighty Father, for ever and ever. Amen." The following doxology concludes psalms during the Liturgy of the Hours: "Glory be to the Father, and to the Son, and to the Holy Spirit: As it was in the beginning, is now and ever shall be, world without end. Amen." Doxologies also form the final verse of many hymns, following the example of the Roman office hymns.

dread, an emotional state that arises when a person encounters freedom. The concept was developed by the existentialist thinker Søren Kierkegaard in his book *The Concept of Dread* (1844). Dread must be distinguished from fear. Fear is an emotion concerning a particular object, like an illness. Unlike fear, dread concerns no particular thing. Dread arises in the face of a profound awareness of freedom that promises both new possibilities as well as the uncertainty of the unknown. Theologically, the concept of dread can be used to explain the sinner's attraction and resistance to the freedom promised by God's grace. *See also* freedom; free will; grace.

Drexel, Bl. Katherine, 1858–1955, American Missionary. She was the daughter of a wealthy, Philadelphia banker. Pope Leo XIII encouraged the young heiress to devote both her fortune and her life to the poor. She entered the Sisters of Mercy but felt called to do missionary work among black and Native Americans. In 1891, she founded the Sisters of the Blessed Sacrament for Indians and Colored People (S.B.S.); the congregation's mission concerns the education of African and Native Americans. Drexel established many schools on Indian reservations and instituted the first and only Catholic University designed for African-Americans, Xavier University,

New Orleans (1925). She was beatified in 1988. Feast day: March 3.

Drey, Johann Sebastian (drī), 1777–1853, German theologian. Ordained in 1801, he was professor of theology at the University of Tübingen from 1817 to 1846. Founder of the *Tübinger theologische Quartalschrift* in 1819, Drey wrote articles on such issues as revision in theology, the nature of Catholicism, revelation, and mysticism. His *Kurze Einleitung in das Studium der Theologie* ("Brief Introduction to the Study of Theology," 1819) emphasized the ecclesial context, mystical roots, and practical orientation of all theology. His three-volume work on apologetics (1838–47) established him as one of the founders of the modern discipline of fundamental theology. *See also* apologetics.

dry Mass, a rehearsal of the Mass, its prayers and actions, without the Eucharistic Prayer or the use of bread, wine, or their vessels. In the Middle Ages, the *missa secca* (Lat., "dry Mass") or *memoria* ("memorial") was sometimes regarded as "quasisacramental." It was viewed as a substitute for the Mass when the Mass was not allowed, e.g., when no priest who had fasted was available or in territories under interdict or edicts of excommunication.

dualism, term with multiple meanings referring to diverse doctrines that posit some form of coexisting, opposing principles, entities, forces, or distinctions as basic components of the world or of human life. The term has been applied ontologically, and has also been used to define or describe epistemological and moral categories and distinctions. For example, a central feature in Platonic thought is the radical separation of the eternal world of forms from the temporal world of particulars or individual things. In Platonism, the world of ideas is known by the mind whereas the particulars appear to the senses.

In the history of the Christian religion, the prevalence of dualism is often ensconced in questions dealing with the origin or coexistence of good and evil. On one level, doctrine reflects a radical dualism when two irreducible and opposing principles—one good, the other evil—are believed to be coequal and coeternal. Some Manichaean groups from the third century held this view, envisioning a primeval conflict between two ultimate forces—Light and Darkness. On the moral level, this struggle between good and evil is understood as taking place within each individual.

A more prevalent and influential understanding of dualism holds that there is only one primordial principle, cause, or creator, namely, the good. Evil, a second principle, is inferior and at some point in history, usually the end of time, will be conquered by good. Various groups followed this view, for example, the Gnostics, Cathars, and Bogomils.

Contemporary dualistic doctrines generally refer to the problem of knowledge, for example, Descartes's teaching on the opposition between mind and matter, or Kant's distinction between the noumenal and the phenomenal world. *See also* Manichaeism; mind/body.   *EILEEN KEARNEY*

Dubourg, Louis Guillaume Valentine, 1766–1833, bishop of New Orleans. Born in Santo Domingo (Haiti), raised in Bordeaux, and educated at the seminary of St. Sulpice in Paris, he was ordained a priest in 1788. Fleeing the French Revolution, he lived in Spain before coming to Baltimore in December 1794; DuBourg soon thereafter joined the Society of St. Sulpice. He founded St. Mary's College, was president of Georgetown College, and was a close confidant of Elizabeth Ann Seton. He was bishop of New Orleans from 1815 to 1825, when he resigned his see and returned to France.

Duchesne, Louis (doo-shayn'), 1843–1922, priest and historian. Born in France, Duchesne developed an interest in Christian antiquity from his archaeological studies in Rome. In 1877 he assumed the chair of Church History at the Institut Catholique in Paris where one of his students was the famous Modernist Alfred Loisy. In 1885 he resigned his post when his lectures on the development of pre-Nicene doctrine and his questioning of the apostolic foundation of French dioceses drew criticism. His historical investigations into the nature of early Christianity favored the notion of development and continued to be unsettling to ecclesiastical authorities, who placed his three-volume *Histoire ancienne de l'église chrétienne* (Fr., "Ancient History of the Christian Church") on the Index of Forbidden Books during the Modernist crisis. *See also* Index of Forbidden Books; Modernism.

Duchesne, St. Rose Philippine, 1769–1852, French missionary and educator. She entered the Visitation order in 1788, but religious persecution spawned by the French Revolution forced the order o exile. After the Concordat of 1801, she joined e Congregation of the Religious of the Sacred Heart (called in the 1990s the Society of the Sacred Heart). As a missionary to the United States, she established at St. Charles, Missouri, the first convent of the Religious of the Sacred Heart in America (1818) and founded many schools and orphanages. She labored among the Potawatomi tribe at Sugar Creek, Kansas (1841); they called her "Woman Who Prays Always." Duchesne, known for her holiness and sacrificial life, was canonized in 1988. Feast day: November 18. *See also* Society of the Sacred Heart.

due process, canonical processes appropriate to protect rights and obtain justice. The major concerns regarding due process in canon law are twofold. The first is that there be established processes for the protection of the rights of those involved. The second is that those processes be, in fact, available and followed. Concern for the rights of individuals should be accompanied by concern for the good of the community. The community is, of course, strengthened when individual rights are respected and justice is obtained in any given instance. In cases where there appears to be a conflict of rights, due process should protect the rights of all concerned.

Canon law has complex and well-developed norms for protecting the rights of those involved in judicial proceedings and in many administrative processes as well. In addition, canonical equity (the virtue that seeks justice) should be part of any application of the law. Often, however, administrative proceedings do not have as many clear formal safeguards for the protection of rights as judicial processes do. Because of this, there has been concern for the development of norms and appeal processes so that the justice the law seeks may be obtained. *See also* rights and obligations in canon law.

Duffy, Francis P., 1871–1932, military chaplain. Ordained in 1896, Duffy taught philosophy at St. Joseph's Seminary (Dunwoodie, NY) and edited the *New York Review* (1905–8). Serving in the New York National Guard—"Fighting 69th Regiment"—he was decorated by the American, Canadian, and French governments. He became famous as America's best-known chaplain, recording his experiences in *Father Duffy's Story* (1919). As pastor of Holy Cross Church, he helped prepare New York Governor Alfred E. Smith's reply to questions about Catholic loyalty to American ideals during the presidential election campaign of 1928. A memorial to Father Duffy, erected in New York's Times Square in 1937, was the first statue of a Catholic priest built on public property in New York State.

dulia (Gk., "service"), the honor that is given to those who deserve respect. In Catholic theology it is traditionally associated with the honor given to the saints, who manifest in a unique way the activity of God in their lives. *Dulia,* therefore, honors God by recognizing the presence of God manifest in the lives of the saints. It is distinguished from *latria* (Gk.), which is the worship that Christians render to God alone, and *hyperdulia,* which is the special honor given to the Blessed Virgin Mary because of her unique role as the Mother of God. *See also hyperdulia; latria.*

Dulles, Avery Robert, b. 1918, U.S. Jesuit theologian specializing in ecclesiology and the theology of revelation. He has taught at Woodstock College in Maryland, The Catholic University of America, and Fordham University. He served as president of the Catholic Theological Society of America (1974–75) and received its Cardinal Spellman Award for Theology (1970).

Dulles pioneered the use of models in Catholic theology in his *Models of the Church* (1974) and later in *Models of Revelation* (1983). His ability to describe the characteristics of different groups of theologians sympathetically and to discover new avenues of dialogue are hallmarks of his work.

Duns Scotus, John. *See* Scotus, John Duns.

Dunstan, St., ca. 908–88, Anglo-Saxon abbot and archbishop. A cousin of the kings of Wessex and an accomplished artisan, he was active at court and in the reform of English monasticism. Around 943, King Edmund made Dunstan abbot of Glastonbury; ca. 959, King Edgar appointed him archbishop of Canterbury. Feast day: May 19. *See also* Canterbury; monasticism.

Dupanloup, Félix Antoine Philibert (doo-pahn-loo'), 1802–78, bishop and educator. As a priest in Paris from 1825 to 1837, he developed new catechetical methods, which he applied successfully to higher education as rector of the seminary of Saint-Nicolas du Chardonnet from 1837 to 1845. As bishop of Orléans (1849–78), he defended Catholic interests in public policy, securing in 1850 the right of the Church to operate private schools in France. Although a proponent of the independence of the Papal States, he was the leader of the "inopportunists" at the First Vatican Council (1869–70) and absented himself rather than vote for the doctrine of papal infallibility. Subsequently, he did accept it. *See also* infallibility; Vatican Council I.

Durandus of Saint-Pourçain, ca. 1275–1334, Dominican, bishop, and Scholastic theologian called Doctor Modernus and Doctor Resolutissimus. A critic of Thomas Aquinas, he was censured by his order and Pope John XXII, but vindicated by Benedict XII after his death. His teachings remained popular into the sixteenth century. *See also* Scholasticism.

Durocher, St. Marie-Rose, 1811–49, founder of the Sisters of the Holy Names of Jesus and Mary, an order dedicated to Christian education. She was born near Montreal, Quebec. Feast day: October 6. *See also* Sisters of the Holy Names of Jesus and Mary.

Dymphna, St., ca. seventh-century Irish maiden, patron saint of the mentally ill. Legend has it that she escaped from her father by running to Belgium. Her relics were found in the thirteenth century at Gheel. An asylum stands at this site. Feast day: May 15.

Dyophysites (Gk., *dyo,* "two,"; *physeis,* "natures"), the name used by Monophysites to refer to Christians (i.e., Catholics, Protestants, and Orthodox) who accept the doctrine of Chalcedon (451), namely, that Jesus Christ has both a divine and a human nature, existing in one divine person. *See also* Chalcedon, Council of; Monophysitism.

Eadmer, ca. 1060–ca. 1130, monk at Canterbury. Secretary to Anselm, Eadmer wrote a biography of him as well as a chronicle of contemporary events. *See also* Anselm of Canterbury, St.; Canterbury.

Ea Semper, papal bull of 1907 that severely restricted the rights of the Greek Catholic Church in the United States. The Ruthenian bishop was not granted jurisdiction but was made dependent on the local Latin hierarchy. Priests were to remain celibate and were forbidden to administer Confirmation. Preference was given to the Latin rite in mixed marriages. The Ruthenian community expressed outrage and more moderate legislation was introduced in 1914 with the decree *Cum Episcopo*.

Easter, the feast of the Resurrection of Christ, the oldest and most important Christian celebration, also called Pascha (Gk., "Passover").

Since the Council of Nicaea (325) Easter has been celebrated on the Sunday following the full moon after the vernal equinox (between March 22 and April 25). Catholics and many Eastern Christians celebrate Easter on different days because each follows a different calendar: the Gregorian in the West, and the Julian in the East. The date of Easter determines the dates of other movable feasts, such as the Ascension and Pentecost, as well as the number of weeks before Lent and after Pentecost.

The Easter season begins on Easter Sunday and extends until Pentecost, fifty days later. The first eight days after Easter are known as the Octave of Easter. The paschal candle, which is blessed at the Easter Vigil, is lighted at Mass during the entire Easter season, and the water that is also blessed at the Easter Vigil is used for Baptism throughout the Easter season. The Easter season is also the time for the newly baptized (neophytes) to continue their catechetical formation, known as *mystagogia* (Gk., "mystagogy").

The Jewish Passover represents the fusion of two originally separate festivals: a spring sacrifice of nomadic shepherds (Passover) and a Canaanite agricultural festival (Unleavened Bread), adopted after the Hebrew settlement in Canaan. In the first century, as today, the developed Passover feast remembered Israel's redemption from slavery; rabbinic tradition also saw the feast as one of hope for final redemption. This Passover celebration provided the context for the Last Supper of Jesus with his disciples and the events leading to his Crucifixion and Resurrection.

By the second century, the Church began to celebrate a Christian Passover (Pascha), a modulation of Jewish themes. Celebrating in memory and hope a unitive feast of both the Cross and the Resurrection, the Church identified Jesus as the Paschal Lamb of the New Covenant, gave thanks for deliverance from sin and final death, and awaited ultimate redemption. The primitive Pascha was not focused exclusively on the Resurrection, but on the totality of redemption in Christ.

There is second-century evidence from Asia Minor, whose churches followed the Johannine chronology celebrating Pascha on 14 Nisan regardless of the day, indicating that the feast primarily celebrated more than the death of Jesus as an isolated moment. Incarnation, Passion, death, Resurrection, and glorification, i.e., the total work of redemption, were celebrated, symbolically epitomized in the Cross as the locus of victory.

Divergent Practices: Churches celebrating Pascha on 14 Nisan, known as Quartodecimans (Lat., "fourteen"), were a minority. Other churches opted for a dominical (Sunday) celebration, because of the strong linkage of Sunday with eucharistic celebration; the weekly Sunday Eucharist is the earliest liturgical celebration. Heated disputes concerning the observance of Easter and the pre-Easter fast erupted in the late second century. Differences in the calendars used (e.g., solar, lunar, Jewish, Babylonian, etc.), as well as computation methods for dating Easter, along with scanty and at times historically inaccurate textual evidence make it impossible to draw definitive conclusions about the day on which Easter was celebrated in the first two centuries of the Church. What is clear is that churches in Palestine and Alexandria celebrated the dominical Pascha without reference to the practice in Rome. There is evidence that both the Quartodecimans and dominical adherents agreed that the celebration of completed redemption in Christ was the content of the feast.

During the fourth century in Jerusalem, a major center for pilgrims, the celebration of Easter included a three-day (Triduum) period of preparation. On what is called Holy Thursday, the Last Supper account was read at the Eucharist. The events of the Passion of Jesus were liturgically commemorated in the city at the various places (known as stations) that were associated with those events. On what is called Good Friday, there was a veneration of the cross and a "three hours" service to commemorate Jesus' three hours on the cross. New members were

...ated into the Church through the sacraments of ...ptism, Confirmation, and Eucharist on the eve, or ...igil, of Easter. This has set the pattern for the observance of Holy Week to the present.

Easter, as a living symbol rather than a commemoration, is not a series of gospel representations, but rather the passage of God's people in Christ through death to new life. The full and proper recovery of the unity of the feast remains pastorally challenging. *See also* Easter Vigil; liturgical year; Quartodecimans; Resurrection of Christ.   *JOHN A. MELLOH*

Easter duty, also called the "Eucharistic Precept," the obligation of Catholics to receive Holy Communion at least once each year, usually during the Easter season. From the sixth century onward, various Church councils enacted legislation requiring reception of Communion at Easter time. This developed as a safeguard against neglect of the Sacrament. The Fourth Lateran Council (1215) promulgated this as law for the Latin church. The Council of Trent (1545–63) and the 1917 and 1983 codes of canon law preserve this obligation with some minor variations. The requirement to receive Communion "in the Easter season" has been variously interpreted. The 1983 code specifies the period from Palm Sunday to Pentecost Sunday. In the United States, this has been extended to include the period from the first Sunday of Lent until Trinity Sunday, which is the first Sunday after Pentecost. *See also* Communion, Holy; Easter; Paschal season.

Eastern Catholic cardinals, members of the College of Cardinals who belong to one of the Eastern Catholic churches. Originally a dignity, or honor, conferred on priests of the local church of Rome and the bishops of its surrounding dioceses, the cardinalate was only gradually extended to Latin bishops outside Rome, who received the title of a Roman church. The merely honorary assignment to a Roman church was designed to maintain an historical link with the original practice of naming pastors of these churches as cardinals. Except for the two Greek bishops who remained faithful to the Union of Florence (1439), Bessarion of Nicaea and Isidore of Kiev, no other Eastern Catholic cardinals were named until the second half of the nineteenth century. In the twentieth century some Eastern Catholic patriarchs have resisted accepting the cardinalate, maintaining rightly that it was a Latin church dignity of the patriarchate of the West, and hence lower than the dignity they already possessed as patri-

archs and heads of their Eastern churches. At Vatican II (1962–65) the issue of precedence between cardinals and patriarchs was avoided by giving the patriarchs separate seating, and the newly reformed Catholic canon law is silent on the issue. In the history of the Church there have been only eighteen Eastern Catholic cardinals, the most recent appointment in 1994. *See also* Cardinals, College of.

Eastern Catholic liturgical languages, the official languages in which Eastern-rite liturgies are celebrated. These are dead languages except for Arabic, Romanian, Hungarian, and Albanian. Each rite has one "official," traditional liturgical tongue (Grabar for the Armenian rite; Syriac for the Chaldean, West Syrian, Maronite rites; Coptic for the Coptic rite; Ge'ez for the Ethiopian rite) except the Byzantine, which is supranational and plurilingual (Greek, Old Slavonic, Romanian, Hungarian, Arabic, Albanian). But in the twentieth century the vernacular has been introduced almost everywhere except among the Russians and the Greeks, who celebrate in Old Slavonic and the Greek of Christian antiquity. *See also* liturgical language.

Eastern Catholic patriarchates, Eastern Catholic churches with a patriarchal form of government, an autonomous, self-governing federation of dioceses under the jurisdiction of a chief bishop, called "patriarch," and his synod. There are six such patriarchates: Alexandria of the Copts (residence in Cairo), Alexandria-Antioch-Jerusalem of the Melkites (one titulary, resident in Damascus), Antioch of the Maronites (Bkerké, Lebanon), Antioch of the Syrians (Beirut), Babylon of the Chaldean (Baghdad), Cilicia of the Armenian (Beirut). The two largest Eastern Catholic churches, the Ukrainian and Syro-Malabar, have requested the Holy See to grant them patriarchal status. In 1994 the request had not yet been granted. *See also* Latin patriarchates; patriarch [ecclesiastical]; patriarchate.

Eastern Catholic religious, men and women belonging to religious orders or congregations of the Eastern Catholic churches. Such nonmonastic religious are a relatively modern development. Even today in the non-Catholic Eastern churches, the only form of religious life is the monastic. From the early seventeenth century onward in many Eastern Catholic churches the need was felt for religious personnel dedicated to preaching, religious instruction, and other pastoral and charitable works; these concerns and the example of apostolic work carried out by Western religious led to the foundation of new religious congregations. The first such institutes, based on native traditions, attempted to retain as many elements of monastic life as could be combined with a centralized structure and an active mission. Examples are the Ukrainian Basilians and the Lebanese Maronite order (Maronite Antonians), founded in 1695 and in 1770 divided into Baladites and Aleppites. Similar to these are the Chouerite and Salvatorian Basilians (Basilian Order of St. John the Baptist) among the Melkites, founded respectively in 1697 and 1707; the Chouerites since 1829 are divided like the Antonians into Baladites and Aleppites.

The object of these institutes was to serve their churches in parishes and otherwise. A Chouerite monk founded the first Arabic printing press in the Ottoman empire. These Maronite and Melkite religious have retained a strong imprint of Eastern monastic spirituality; eremitism is prominent among the Antonians. These congregations were long considered monastic, but after the publication in 1952 of the *motu proprio* of Pius XII, *Postquam Apostolicis Litteris,* promulgating canon law for religious in the Eastern churches, they were declared to be "nonmonastic religious orders" (December 16, 1955).

Recent Developments: Since the nineteenth century new congregations have arisen in all the Eastern Catholic churches, often closely influenced by Latin-rite congregations and devoted to similar works, active or contemplative. Numerous institutes exist, especially in the Syro-Malabar Church, such as the Congregations of Carmelite Brothers of the Immaculate Virgin Mary (founded 1855), the Sisters of Adoration of the Blessed Sacrament (founded 1908), the Franciscan Clarist Congregation of Kerala (founded 1888), and the Sisters of the Sacred Heart (founded 1976 through the fusion of three local institutes). Congregations in other Eastern Churches include the Bethany Sisters of the Syro-Malankar Church (founded 1925); the Sisters, Servants of the Immaculate Virgin, in the Ukrainian Catholic Church (founded 1892); the Society of Missionaries of St. Paul, founded in the nineteenth century on the model of the White Fathers, and the Congregation of Our Lady of Perpetual Help, founded in 1936, in the Melkite Church; in Romania the Sisters of the Holy Mother of God, founded in 1921, carried on an apostolate clandestinely under the Communist regime.

A number of Western congregations have Eastern-rite branches. Such are the Redemptorists and Salesians, both of whom have branches serving the Ukrainian Catholic Church. Before 1948 the Assumptionists, the Brothers of the Christian Schools, the Conventual Franciscans, and the Jesuits had houses for their members of the Romanian Catholic Church. *See also* hermit; monasticism; religious; religious life; religious orders and congregations; religious profession.

SOPHIA SENYK

Eastern Catholic sanctoral, the calendar of saints commemorated liturgically in the Catholic Eastern rites. Some Eastern sanctorals still bear the traces of early liturgical calendars, when the cycle of celebrations was centered on the week, and not on fixed dates. The Chaldean calendar, for instance, traditionally has favored Fridays for the commemoration of saints, whereas the Armenian calendar excludes saints' feasts on Sundays, Wednesdays, and Fridays, which are dedicated to other commemorations. Such calendars now have a mixed system, with commemorations also on set dates. Though Eastern Catholics have generally accepted Western saints into their sanctoral—some, like the Maronites, on a massive scale—they did not immediately venerate those Eastern saints who had lived outside of the Roman communion after the separation of the churches that occurred gradually after 1054 and accelerated in the thirteenth century. The traditional cutoff point for the veneration of Orthodox saints was the rejection by the Orthodox of the Decree of Union at the Council of Florence (1439). The Decree had held that, although Latin and Greek saints expressed their faith differently, because they were saints they were always in substantial agreement with one another. Catholics in communion with Rome were thereby permitted to venerate such popular Orthodox saints as Sergius of Radonezh (d. 1392) because he had lived before the Orthodox rejection of the Decree of Union. Some Eastern Catholics, however, venerate Orthodox saints who lived long after the Florence date. *See also* Eastern churches; saints, devotion to.

ROBERT F. TAFT

Eastern Catholics and ecumenism, primarily the relationship between Eastern Catholics (groups of Orthodox Christians who have entered into union with the see of Rome beginning at the end of the sixteenth century) and their Orthodox counterparts in Eastern and Western Europe, the Middle East, and the Americas.

The Eastern Catholic churches originated in

‚hly diverse circumstances. Except for the Mar-
ﬁites, they resulted from a split within an Eastern
ﬁr Oriental Orthodox Church where one part became Catholic but retained most of its original liturgical, canonical, and theological tradition. In most
cases this split was partially due to Catholic missionary activity among the Orthodox (sometimes
with the support of Catholic governments controlling Orthodox populations), which gained momentum after the failure of the reunion Council of Florence (1438–45).

Although this policy, now known as uniatism,
was intended to foster unity between Eastern and
Western Christians, in fact it weakened the Orthodox churches and created new divisions within
them. Thus the policy intensified a feeling among
the Orthodox of being innocent victims of Catholic
aggression.

For centuries most Eastern Catholics and Orthodox shared the isolation and mutual hostility that
existed generally between the Catholic and Orthodox churches. It was only in the 1960s that Catholic-
Orthodox relations began to improve.

Vatican II and Beyond: One of the documents
of Vatican II, the Decree on Eastern Catholic
Churches (*Orientalium Ecclesiarum*, 1964), said that
Eastern Catholics have a special duty to promote
unity among Eastern Christians by observing the
principles set forth in the Decree on Ecumenism
(*Unitatis Redintegratio*) and by remaining faithful
to their authentic Eastern heritage.

Relations between Orthodox and Eastern Catholics improved after the council, particularly in parts
of the Middle East and the diaspora (Western Europe and the Americas). However, many Orthodox
continued to view the existence of the Catholic
churches as a negation of their ecclesial reality and
as instruments of Catholic proselytism. Some still
called for the abolition of these churches as a precondition for any fruitful dialogue.

The collapse of Communism created new problems. Some of the largest Eastern Catholic churches,
especially in Ukraine and Romania, had been suppressed and forced to become Orthodox by the
Communists in the late 1940s. Consequently they
were absent at Vatican II, and none of its documents
was published in those countries. This, along with
the perception that the Orthodox had collaborated
with the Communists in their destruction, explains
why, when Eastern Catholics emerged from the catacombs at the end of the 1980s, it was difficult for
them to assume a positive attitude toward the Or-

thodox. Confrontations with Orthodox over repossessing the churches that had been taken from them
at the time of the suppressions complicated the situation. Although Pope John Paul II has encouraged
Eastern Catholics to adopt the conciliar ecumenical
teachings, most agree that it will take time for such
changes in attitude to take root.

All this has prompted the international Catholic-
Orthodox theological dialogue, which had been in
progress since 1980, to focus on the question of uniatism and the existence of the Byzantine Catholic
churches. It has been elaborating a common position that rejects uniatism as a contemporary model
for unity, while affirming the right of Eastern Catholic churches to exist in freedom. *See also* Decree on
Eastern Catholic Churches; Eastern Catholics in the diaspora; Orthodox Christianity; uniatism.

RONALD G. ROBERSON

Eastern Catholics and Rome, the relationship
between the papacy and those Eastern-rite Christians, pejoratively called "uniates," who entered into
or renewed their union with Rome beginning with
the Crusades (1095–1291), during the period of
missionary expansion at the end of the fifteenth
century, and during the period of Tridentine Catholicism (1563–1962).

History: Tensions between center and periphery, endemic to any large centralized system, have
been especially acute between Rome and the Eastern Catholic churches. This history began with the
Maronites during the Crusades and peaked with Jesuit attempts to enforce latinization of liturgy, ecclesiastical law, and structure on the Syro-Malabarians
and Ethiopians in the sixteenth century. Ethiopia
was closed to the Catholic Church for centuries, and
large numbers of Syro-Malabar Catholics went into
schism in 1653 to escape Jesuit domination. Roman
policy toward the Catholic East was dominated, implicitly, by a sense of Latin superiority and tutelage
mixed with support and help. The Roman approach
to Eastern liturgical customs, canon law, and hierarchical structures and autonomy gradually evolved
from latinization with tolerance of what could not
be latinized, while safeguarding the "superiority" of
the Latin rite, to, in the eighteenth century, genuine
esteem and nurturing of the Eastern traditions,
though still in a context of paternalism and control.

Such attitudes were not limited to the Latins. In
fact, the Latins were more interested in submission
than uniformity, and tolerated ritual diversity,
which they considered secondary to submission.

The Byzantines, on the other hand, impugned Armenian and Latin uses at the Council in Trullo (692). During the azyme controversy, when the East regarded the Latin use of unleavened bread in the Eucharist as invalidating the rite, Patriarch Michael I Cerularius (1043–58) tried to impose Greek usages on the Latins in Constantinople, as he had done with the Armenians, and closed their churches when they refused.

Shift of Attitudes: A new era dawned with the bulls of Pope Benedict XIV, *Etsi pastoralis* (1742) and *Demandatum caelitus* (1743). Since that time there has been slow but consistent progress, despite setbacks encountered by Eastern Catholic hierarchs at Vatican Council I (1869–70) under Pope Pius IX.

In 1894 Benedict XIV's norms were restated and reinforced by Pope Leo XIII's Apostolic Constitution *Orientalium dignitas,* considered the Magna Carta of Eastern Catholicism. It shows great solicitude for the conservation and nurturing of the Eastern heritage, forbids all forms of latinization, and sets strict limits on the activities of Latins in the East. Since that time, this has been the official, if often ignored, teaching of the Holy See.

Vatican II (1962–65) opened another new chapter. Council Fathers spoke out in defense of an unambiguous affirmation of the autonomous patriarchal structure of the Eastern Catholic churches, of their right to rule their own affairs and to expand through missionary activity. Certain Eastern ideas advanced at the council remain unrealized in the post–Vatican II Church: a truly effective synodality, the provision of adequate hierarchical structures for the Eastern Catholic churches throughout the world, and the proposal that the Roman Curia assume its proper place within a healthy ecclesiology. *See also* Eastern churches. ROBERT F. TAFT

Eastern Catholics and Vatican II. A new chapter in modern Catholic history was written when for the first time dissenting non-Latin voices were heard and heeded at a Church council, and when several council Fathers, Western and Eastern, spoke to defend the autonomous patriarchal structure of the Eastern Catholic churches and their right to rule their own affairs, and called for a more open approach to Orthodoxy as the "missing partner" at the council. The most electrifying interventions were those of the Melkite bishops, especially Patriarch Maximus IV. Maximus played a key role at Vatican II (1962–65). Speaking always with dignity and courtesy, but with great firmness and unambiguous clarity, he defended the Eastern heritage and argued f[or] a Church that is catholic in reality and not just i[n] name.

The Melkite bishops proposed many important items on the Vatican II and postconciliar agenda: liturgy in the vernacular, eucharistic concelebration, and Communion under both species (consecrated bread and consecrated wine); the permanent diaconate; the establishment of what ultimately became the Synod of Bishops held periodically in Rome, as well as the Secretariat (now Pontifical Council) for Christian Unity; new attitudes and a more ecumenical vocabulary for dealing with other Christians, especially with the Orthodox churches; the recognition of Eastern Catholic communities as "churches," rather than "rites." In the case of other Eastern Catholic churches, factors such as Communist persecution, insignificant numbers, or a latinized mentality rendered such changes unlikely, though individual bishops such as Ignatius Ziade, Maronite archbishop of Beirut, and Isaac Ghattas, Coptic Catholic bishop of Luxor-Thebes, gave voice at Vatican II to the aspirations of these churches. Their Eastern heritage enabled these bishops to distinguish what is essential (i.e., Catholic) from what is contingent (i.e., Latin) in Catholicism, and to witness to another, complementary way of seeing things as a counterbalance to Latin Catholic unilateralism.

Certain Eastern ideas advanced at the council remain unrealized in the post–Vatican II Church: that collegiality should be operative not just among bishops, but on the diocesan level, between the bishop and his presbyterate; that the laity, especially women, should be given their proper dignity and role in Church life; that adequate hierarchical structures be provided for Eastern Catholics worldwide; that a more compassionate approach, like the Orthodox "principle of economy," be taken regarding the remarriage of unjustly abandoned spouses; that the date of Easter be resolved in ecumenical agreement with other churches; that the Roman Curia assume its proper place within a healthy ecclesiology, no longer operating as a substitute for the College of Bishops or assuming the incommunicable powers that belong by divine right to the Bishop of Rome alone. *See also* Decree on Eastern Catholic Churches; Eastern churches; Maximus IV Sayegh; Vatican Council II. ROBERT F. TAFT

Eastern Catholics in North America, two groups: Catholics of Slavic origin and those of non-Slavic descent. Of the latter, there exist groups of

⌐nites, Melkites, Chaldeans, Romanians, Arme-
⌐s, and Italo-Albanians.

Non-Slavic Eastern Catholics: The Maronites
⌐nd Melkites emigrated from formerly Syrian Lebanon and today's Syria (hence the misleading term
Syrian Greek Catholics, previously used for the Melkites in the United States). The Chaldeans mostly
originate from Iraq. While the Melkites and Maronites speak Arabic, the Chaldeans speak Soureth,
an Aramaic dialect. The first Middle Eastern emigrants arrived toward the end of the nineteenth century. They settled at first in the northeastern industrial centers and around Detroit and Chicago,
although today they also live in other areas.

The Maronites are the most numerous after the
Slavs, and constitute the only Eastern church that
has no Orthodox counterpart. In 1993 they numbered about 53,000 with some fifty-four parishes.
Originally under the jurisdiction of the local Latin
bishops, they received a bishop of their own in 1962.
Later in 1971, the diocese of St. Maron was created
for them with its see first in Detroit and later in
Brooklyn.

The Chaldeans are the Catholic counterpart of
the Assyrian Church of the East. Their union dates
from the sixteenth century when this church of the
Nestorian Christological tradition split over the
question of the rights of succession to the patriarchate. Some emigrated at the end of the last century;
others more recently were forced to leave as a result
of the Kurdo-Iraqi war of the 1960s and 1970s. In
1985 the diocese of St. Thomas the Apostle of Detroit of the Chaldeans was created for them. In 1993
they numbered about 52,000 in some fourteen parishes.

Unlike other Middle Eastern Christians, the Melkites, like the Slavs, are of the Byzantine rite. As a
church with its own particular customs and jurisdictional structure, they have been in communion
with Rome since the eighteenth century. Their Orthodox counterpart is the patriarchate of Antioch.
Mostly prosperous merchants in the Middle East,
where they still form the largest Catholic community, they founded their first church in Brooklyn. One
time heavily latinized and under the control of the
local Latin hierarchy, they began to rapidly redis-
cover their ecclesiastical identity during Vatican II.
They have made great strides. In 1966 they received
their own bishop. In 1976 the separate diocese of
Newton, Massachusetts, was created for their faithful who in 1993 numbered 26,500 in forty-four parishes.

In the United States in 1993, there were about
38,500 Armenian Catholics divided among six parishes. Since 1972 they are under the jurisdiction of
an apostolic visitor. In 1981, an apostolic exarchate
was created for them and they received their own
bishop. The Romanian Catholics are non-Slavic
Byzantines, who mostly emigrated from what was
Hungarian Transylvania before the First World War.
Their first parish in the United States dates from
1916; their first fraternal organization from 1919. As
of 1993 they numbered only about 5,000 faithful in
sixteen parishes. After repeated requests, they were
granted an apostolic visitor in 1975, who resigned
two years later. In 1987 the diocese of St George of
Canton of the Romanians was established for them
in Ohio. Many third-generation Romanian Americans have become members of Roman Catholic parishes.

Although Latin-rite Albanians have a few ethnic
parishes in the United States, the Italo-Albanians,
or Arberesh of the Byzantine rite, were assimilated
into the Italo-American community and have no
parish of their own.

Slavic Eastern Catholics: Eastern-rite Catholics
of Slavic descent in the United States derive mainly
from the mass emigration of eastern Slavs from
both sides of the Carpathian mountains, within the
Austro-Hungarian Empire. This began at the end of
the 1870s and continued until the First World War.
They settled mostly in the industrial centers on the
East Coast and in the mining areas of Pennsylvania.
Known collectively at first as Ruthenians, some of
them retained this name; others eventually identified themselves as Russians, Ukrainians, Carpatho-
Russians, Slovaks, and Carpatho-Rusyns.

From the beginning, church affairs among them
were troubled. Internal difficulties included lay control of the parishes, disciplinary problems among
the clergy, and growing disputes regarding ethnic
identity. External problems stemmed from the lack
of comprehension with which they and their clergy
were met by otherwise capable members of the local
Roman Catholic hierarchy. Particularly irksome to
the American bishops, many of whom wished to integrate their faithful into American society, was the
married status of the Ruthenian clergymen. Likewise, most of the Ruthenian clergymen did not willingly sever jurisdictional ties with bishops of their
rite in Europe.

In 1891, Alexis Toth, a Ruthenian Catholic priest
from Hungary, was refused permission to function
as a priest in the archdiocese of St. Paul, Minnesota,

by Archbishop John Ireland and entered the Russian Orthodox Church, which eagerly accepted the new convert together with his parish. His example was followed by 25,000 Ruthenian Catholics and later by more than 200,000 others. This caused the Orthodox Church in America to grow at the expense of Eastern Catholicism. In 1907, Soter Ortynsky, a Basilian monk, was appointed the first bishop for the Ruthenian Greek Catholics in America. The appointment of Ortynsky, a Galician, exacerbated ethnic sensibilities between the Ruthenians from Hungary who rejected him as a foreigner and those from Polish culturally dominated Galicia, who began to consider themselves Ukrainians. In 1916 two administrators were appointed. In 1924 two exarchates were created, with separate bishops for Ukrainians and Ruthenians. Property disputes caused a second wave of difficulties, while in 1929 many more left the Catholic Church when the decree of the Holy See *Cum Data Fuerit* was promulgated, obliging celibacy for the Ruthenian clergy in the United States.

In 1993 the Ukrainians numbered about 145,400. They have a metropolitan in Philadelphia, four dioceses, and 206 parishes. They are less Americanized than the Ruthenian group because a new wave of emigration after the Second World War added to their numbers and increased their ethnic consciousness. In 1993 the Ruthenians were estimated at about 243,800 faithful in four dioceses and 258 parishes, headed by a metropolitan with his see near Pittsburgh, Pennsylvania. Among them are groups of ethnic Hungarians, Slovaks, and Croatians.

Russian Catholics have three parishes under the jurisdiction of the local American hierarchy in New York, San Francisco, and Los Angeles. There is also a Belorussian parish in Chicago.

Eastern Catholics in Canada: In Canada the Ukrainians are strongest, with about 202,000 faithful (as of 1993), followed by the Maronites and Melkites. The Ukrainians settled mostly in the Western provinces and in Toronto. There is no Ruthenian counterpart in Canada, but there does exist a more ethnically conscious group of Slovak Catholics of the Byzantine rite who (in 1993) numbered about 30,000 and have their own diocese. *See also* Armenian Catholic Church; Chaldean Catholic Church; Italo-Albanian Catholic Church; Maronite Catholic Church; Melkite Catholic Church; Ruthenian Catholic Church; Slovak Byzantine Catholic Church; Ukrainian Catholic Church.

Bibliography

Attwater, Donald. *The Christian Churches of the East.* Milwa WI: Bruce Publishing, 1961.

Magocsi, Paul Robert. *Our People; Carpatho-Rusyns and their scendants in North America.* Toronto: Multicultural History Society Ontario, 1984.

Procko, Bohdan P. *Ukrainian Catholics in America.* Washington, DC: University Press of America, 1982.

Roberson, Ronald G. *The Eastern Christian Churches.* Rome: Pontificium Institutum Studiorum Orientalium, 1990.

CONSTANTINE SIMON

Eastern Catholics in the diaspora, Eastern Catholics who have emigrated from their historic homelands in eastern Europe and the Middle East. Virtually all of the Eastern Catholic churches have experienced emigration of their faithful, especially to the Americas. Where these new communities are small, Catholics of the various Eastern traditions remain under the pastoral care of local Latin bishops. However, where numbers warrant, the Holy See through the Congregation for the Oriental Churches has erected special ecclesiastical jurisdictions for Eastern Catholics so that they may be able to preserve their own heritage.

As of 1993, eight Eastern Catholic churches had dioceses outside the region of their historic homeland. The Maronites had dioceses in Argentina, Brazil, the United States, Australia, and Canada for 1,400,000 diaspora faithful. Melkite jurisdictions had been set up in Brazil, the United States, Canada, Mexico, Australia, and Venezuela to cover almost 500,000 members. The Ukrainian diaspora numbering over 700,000 had eparchies in the United States, Canada, Great Britain, Australia, Germany, France, Brazil, and Argentina. For the approximately 110,000 Armenians there were jurisdictions in France, Greece, Argentina, the rest of Latin America, Romania, and the United States. The Romanians (5,000), Ruthenians (243,000), and Chaldeans (52,000) had diaspora dioceses only in the United States, and the Slovaks only in Canada (30,000).

Eastern churches, those Christian churches of Eastern rite that had their origins in the eastern half of the Roman Empire, or beyond the Empire's eastern frontiers in Armenia, Mesopotamia within the Persian Empire, Ethiopia, and the Malabar Coast of southwest India. In the course of history, theological and jurisdictional controversies led these churches into separation from the Western or Latin Catholic Church: the East Syrian Church of Mesopotamia after the Council of Ephesus in 431; the Armenian, Syrian, Coptic, and Ethiopian churches following

. Council of Chalcedon in 451, and the Byzantine ꞏrthodox Church via a process of gradual estrangeꞏnent that was consummated during the Crusades.

Several unsuccessful attempts were made to heal this breach, most notably at the councils of Lyons II (1274) and Florence (1439). The Maronite Church—it is the only Eastern church that is exclusively Catholic, with no Orthodox counterpart—reaffirmed its communion with Rome in the Middle Ages, after coming into contact with the Crusaders, and since the end of the sixteenth century small groups of faithful from all the other churches have entered, in some cases under political duress, into union with Rome to constitute the Eastern Catholic churches, sometimes called "uniates," a term now considered pejorative. *See also* uniatism.

Eastern Code of Canon Law. *See* Code of Canons of the Eastern Churches.

Eastern liturgies, the seven liturgical traditions or "Eastern rites" in use in the Orthodox and Eastern Catholic churches: Armenian, Byzantine, Coptic, Ethiopian, East (Assyro-Chaldean) and West (Antiochene) Syrian, and Maronite. Eastern liturgies are notable because of their length; because of their frequent use of incense; because they are always sung; and because parts of the service are hidden from view within a sanctuary enclosed by a curtain or barrier. The sumptuousness of their symbolism, vestments, and ceremonial—the beauty of their chant, and the rich iconography of their churches—combine to make an almost overwhelming sensible impact on the worshiper. On a deeper, interior level, these rites are characterized by their transcendental, eschatological spirit and profound sense of mystery and awe; by the richly developed trinitarian, Christological, and Marian theology of their prayers and hymns; and by their strong monastic stamp.

In the first seven centuries of Christianity, before the Islamic conquests, Eastern liturgies underwent notable growth and development, paralleling the growth of the Church and the need to respond to the theological problems of the time. Western Christianity was much less dynamic in this early period, and its liturgies more conservative. The widespread notion that Eastern liturgies almost always reflect an older, apostolic form of Christian worship is unfounded. *See also* Eastern rites; liturgy; rite.

Eastern rites, the distinct liturgical families or traditions of the Eastern Christian churches and the spiritual heritage of which these liturgical traditions are the supreme—but not the only—ecclesial expression. Like the Roman rite, most Eastern rites are composite traditions that synthesize various strains of influence. In the first seven centuries of Christianity, before the Islamic conquests, Eastern Christianity was preeminent intellectually and culturally, developing a rich and theologically sophisticated patristic literature especially in Greek, Syriac, and Armenian. The liturgies of these churches still reflect the trinitarian, Christological, and Marian theological controversies and subtleties of that epoch, as well as the later influence of medieval monasticism. As intermediate church structures developed after the fourth century, uniting scattered local churches in one geographical area into ecclesial federations usually called patriarchates or catholicosates, the diverse liturgical usages within these zones of jurisdiction were gradually consolidated to form the present Eastern rites. The principal church centers of the Eastern Empire that were most influential in the process of unifying local usages into the seven extant rites were Constantinople for the Byzantine rite, Alexandria and later the desert monasteries in Egypt for the Coptic rite, Antioch and Jerusalem for the West Syrian and Maronite rites, and Edessa for the Chaldean, Maronite, and Armenian rites. Other rites, formed outside the limits of the empire but influenced by the great imperial sees combined with native elements, include the Armenian rite, which originated in usages from Syriac Mesopotamia and Greek Cappadocia; the Ethiopian rite from Alexandria and Syria; and the East Syrian rite from Edessa, a Mesopotamian metropolis within the Empire, and Nisibis and Seleucia-Ctesiphon in Persian Mesopotamia.

Before Vatican II (1962–65) the term "rite" was used by Catholics as a synecdoche for the ecclesial communion to which one belongs canonically. Thus, one spoke of "changing rites," or of "belonging to" a rite. This gave the false impression that Eastern ecclesial traditions differ from the Latin only in ritual; since Vatican II the term *Ecclesia sui iuris* (Lat.), i.e., a distinct church with its own ecclesial heritage and self-government, is used to denote all churches of the Catholic communion, including the Latin. *See also* Eastern churches; rite.

ROBERT F. TAFT

Eastern Schism, the common, if inaccurate, term used to denote the interruption of ecclesial communion between the Eastern and Western churches, especially the separation between the Eastern, i.e., Byzantine Orthodox, and Western, i.e., Latin Catholic churches. The first divisions were provoked by the Christological disputes of the fifth century. The Assyrian Church of the East was separated following the condemnation of Nestorianism at the Council of Ephesus in 431, and the Oriental Orthodox churches (Armenian, Coptic, Ethiopian, Syrian Orthodox) in the aftermath of the condemnation of Monophysitism by the Council of Chalcedon in 451. The division between the two great churches of the Eastern and Western Empire, the Byzantine and Latin, was a process of slow estrangement with several periods of tension (such as the so-called Photian Schism in the mid-ninth century and the Schism of Michael Cerularius in 1054), but was not consummated until the Crusades (1095–1291) and the Orthodox rejection of the Decree of Union of the Council of Florence (1439).

Though generally called "the Eastern Schism" in Western writings, responsibilities for the breach were shared. The West's share consisted mainly in confronting the East in the eighth and ninth centuries with an expanding concept of papal authority, the establishment during the Crusades of Latin hierarchies in traditionally Eastern Christian territories in competition with already existing Eastern churches, and the Latin conquest and occupation of Constantinople in the Fourth Crusade (1204–61). The Orthodox were responsible for similar aggressions, such as the Byzantine conquest of Italy (535–53) and the annexing of Sicily to the patriarchate of Constantinople, the incorporation of Illyricum into the patriarchate of Constantinople in the ninth century, and pogroms against the Latins at Constantinople shortly before the Fourth Crusade.

In the centuries following the failure of Florence these divisions were exacerbated by Catholic proselytism, especially during the era of missionary expansion from the sixteenth century, and by the creation, sometimes with the help of the secular arm, of "uniate" churches via the incorporation of sections of Eastern churches into the Roman communion. On the Orthodox side there was the persecution of the Catholic Church in areas, like Poland, that fell under Russian domination in the partitions of 1772–1815. Since Vatican II (1962–65) the Catholic and Orthodox churches are coming once again, gradually and with many setbacks along the way, to recognize one another as "sister churches" already in partial, if imperfect, communion. *See also*
Crusades; Florence, Council of; schism; unity of Church.

ROBERT F. TAFT

Easter Vigil, a nocturnal vigil or watch, the third part of the Easter Triduum of the Passion and Resurrection, celebrating Christ's victory over death, held on Holy Saturday night. Dating from at least mid-second century, this is one of the oldest Christian celebrations. This "mother of all vigils" (Augustine, *Sermon* 219) is a culmination of the entire Church year, an encapsulation of the Paschal Mystery and a rehearsal of salvation history in word and song.

By the third century, and especially in the fourth, the vigil was the primary time for initiation in many churches; the newly baptized stood as living icons of the resurrected Christ. Gradually the lighting and blessing of the new fire and paschal candle were introduced.

The Easter Vigil today consists of a brief light service, a service of the word, solemn Baptism and Confirmation, and Eucharist. The Roman Missal directs that the vigil take place after nightfall and end before dawn. The light service, derived from the ancient practice of evening lamplighting, proclaims that Christ is Light through the lighting and blessing of the new fire, paschal candle, and the Easter proclamation, the *Exsultet*. Seven readings from the Hebrew Scriptures (two are required, one of which is

Easter Vigil Mass, during the light service when all hold a lighted candle to proclaim that Christ is the Light of the World.

d 14), with psalmic responses and collects, form
e service of the word. The Gloria follows the last
eading, and the Eucharist begins with the normal
Liturgy of the Word. The 1969 *ordo* changed Pope
Pius XII's 1955 revision, in which the vigil including
Baptism preceded the Eucharist. The 1955 rites better emphasized the vigil aspect of the service. The
baptismal rites include the litany of saints, blessing
of the water, renunciation of Satan and profession of
faith, water baptism, clothing with a white garment,
giving of the Christ-light, and Confirmation. The
congregation renews their baptismal promises in
solidarity with the newly initiated. The Eucharist
proceeds as usual with proper texts for the day. *See
also* Easter; Holy Week; Rite of Christian Initiation of
Adults.   JOHN A. MELLOH

East Syrian rite, liturgical tradition of the
Chaldean and Syro-Malabar Catholic churches, and
of the corresponding Orthodox church, the Holy Apostolic Catholic Assyrian Church of the East, from
which the rite derives. This church, sometimes
called "Nestorian," separated from the other churches over the condemnation of Nestorianism at the
Council of Ephesus in 431. The rite, which originated among Syriac-speaking Christians in the Mesopotamian church under the Persian Empire, is celebrated in the Eastern variant of classical Syriac.

The Mesopotamian church was centered in the
catholicosate of Seleucia-Ctesiphon on the Tigris
River, about thirty miles south of Baghdad, Iraq. A
synod held there in 410 unified the liturgical usages
of Mesopotamia to form the basis for this rite. Rich
in ecclesiastical poetry by famous Syriac Fathers
like Ephraem (d. 373), Marutha of Maipharkat (d.
ca. 420), Narsai (d. 502), Babai the Great (d. 628),
this rite is noted for the pure spirit of adoration expressed in prayers that ask for nothing but the privilege of glorifying God. The rite underwent several
adjustments throughout history, most notably the
reform under Catholicos Isho Yahb III at the Upper
Monastery of Mar Gabriel on the Tigris, in Mosul, in
650–51. The Liturgy of the Hours has preserved the
combination of cathedral and monastic usages synthesized in this monastery, and the chief eucharistic
prayer, the Liturgy of Addai and Mari, is one of the
most ancient Christian liturgical texts still in use.

Medieval liturgical commentaries enrich our understanding of this tradition and its history, and notable liturgical compositions continued through the
thirteenth century. The liturgical disposition of the
church building was distinguished by an enclosed
sanctuary reserved to the eucharistic anaphora (the
central eucharistic prayer), and a bema, or large
platform, in the center of the church where the Liturgy of the Word and other offices were celebrated.
See also Chaldean Catholic Church; Syro-Malabar Catholic
Church.   ROBERT F. TAFT

Ebionites (Heb., "poor men"), an ascetic sect of
Jewish Christians, who took their name from the
beatitude on "the poor in spirit" (Matt 5:3; Luke
4:18; 7:22). In their view, Jesus was a human being
who lived the Jewish law to perfection because of
the descent of the Holy Spirit upon him at his baptism. He was, therefore, the Messiah, the new
Moses, who showed the real meaning of the law. Because the Ebionites believed in the permanent validity of the Mosaic law, they opposed Paul's ministry to the uncircumcised. They discredited Paul by
denying that he had a vision of the risen Christ. Living a simple, communal life east of the Jordan for
two hundred years after Jesus, they practiced ritual
ablutions and baptism. Their relationship to other
sects (e.g., the Nazarenes and the Essenes) remains
unclear. *See also* Adoptionism.

Ecclesia discens (e-klay'zee-ah di'shenz; Lat.,
"the learning Church"), a term traditionally used by
Roman Catholic authors for the laity and sometimes
the lower clergy, contrasted with the *Ecclesia docens,*
"the teaching Church," which applied exclusively to
the hierarchy, and sometimes to the clergy as well.
The division, which in large measure can be explained historically, was often approached polemically, artificially elevating the hierarchy and the clergy and downgrading the laity. The Second Vatican
Council (1962–65) effectively set aside the distinction by claiming that the Church is the whole People
of God, by insisting that every person has a responsibility to proclaim the gospel, and by accenting the
importance of consultation and reception. *See also
Ecclesia docens;* magisterium; reception of doctrine.

Ecclesia docens (e-klay'zee-ah doh'chenz; Lat.,
"the teaching Church"), a term traditionally used by
Roman Catholic authors for the hierarchy and
sometimes all the clergy, contrasted with the *Ecclesia discens,* "the learning Church," which applied exclusively to the laity, and sometimes to the lower
clergy as well. The distinction was often interpreted
in an artificial sense, as if the clergy was never in a
position to learn and the laity was never in a position to teach. The Second Vatican Council (1962–

65) supplanted the distinction by identifying the Church as the whole People of God, by giving the laity a constitutive role in the spreading of the gospel, and by recognizing the importance of reception and consultation. *See also Ecclesia discens;* magisterium.

Ecclesiam Suam (ek-klay'zee-am *soo*'am; Lat., "His Church"), first encyclical of Pope Paul VI, issued on August 6, 1964. The document proposes "three thoughts" about the Church: that it "should deepen its consciousness of itself," that it should be ready to correct its own defects through reform, and that it should be marked by the spirit and practice of dialogue. The encyclical outlines the terms of the dialogue by situating the Church of Rome at the center of a series of concentric circles: the first and widest comprises the whole human community; the second circle embraces all religious people; the third, all Christians; and the fourth, all Catholics.

ecclesiastical person, a person subject to canon law. There are two types of ecclesiastical person: the first is a physical person, i.e., a human person baptized into the Catholic Church or received into it after Baptism. The second is a juridical person, i.e., some aggregate of being or of things that, by the law or by special act of competent authority, is recognized as an ecclesiastical person and so can be the subject of rights and obligations, e.g., a parish, diocese, or religious institute.

ecclesiastical province. *See* province.

ecclesiology, the theological study of the Church. Although it did not formally begin as a coherent subdiscipline in theology until the conciliarist controversies of the early thirteenth century, there are ecclesiologies already in the NT. For example, Ephesians and Colossians present the Church as the body and the bride of Christ; Luke-Acts, as the community of the Holy Spirit; and the Johannine books, as a community of equal disciples. Matthew emphasizes the role of Peter.

In the fourth and fifth centuries the theologians of the East stressed the Church's oneness in Christ achieved through the power of the Holy Spirit as well as its eschatological, or otherworldly, dimension, expressed in the Eucharist; the West, confronting heresies like Donatism, had to focus more on juridical questions such as the validity of the sacraments. The Western emphasis on papal authority and the hierarchical structure of the Church intensified in the Middle Ages, especially during the concil-

iarist controversies, the Reformation, and Counter-Reformation. Robert Bellarmine (154.–1621) exercised the dominant influence over Catholic ecclesiology from this period until Vatican II (1962–65).

The council brought about a convergence of Western and Eastern ecclesiologies by emphasizing, for example, the sacramentality of the Church and the role of the bishops within a collegial rather than a monarchical structure of governance. The council also served as a corrective to Bellarmine with its teaching on the Church as mystery and as People of God. By the mid-twentieth century Yves Congar had replaced Bellarmine as the Church's premier ecclesiologist. *See also* Bellarmine, St. Robert; Church; Congar, Yves.
RICHARD P. MCBRIEN

Eck, John, 1486–1543, theologian and Martin Luther's principal Catholic opponent. Eck debated Luther at Leipzig (1519) and helped confute the Augsburg Confession (1530). His defense of Catholicism, the *Enchiridion,* had ninety editions. *See also* Luther, Martin.

Eckhart, Meister, ca. 1260–ca. 1328, Dominican theologian and spiritual writer. Born in Thuringia, Eckhart entered the Dominican order ca. 1275, studied in Paris and Cologne, held various administrative positions within his order, and on two separate occasions occupied a magisterial chair of theology at the University of Paris. He later spent about ten years in Strasbourg and in 1323 was named spiritual director and professor at the Dominican *Studium Generale* in Cologne. The bold phrasing of many of his sermons and treatises led the archbishop of that city to begin inquisitorial proceedings against him early in 1326. A year later Eckhart denounced that investigation and appealed to the pope at Avignon but died sometime before the publication of the papal bull *In Agro Dominico* (1329), which condemned a number of his statements as heretical or suspect of heresy.

A key distinction for understanding Eckhart's thought is one between our "formal being" (Lat., *esse formale*) and our "virtual being" (*esse virtuale*). The former refers to our existence as creatures in space and time; from this perspective Eckhart regularly draws the sharpest possible contrast between creatures and God. However, we also have a virtual being, which has been (or rather "is") in God from all eternity; in virtue of it we are utterly one with God, without distinction. In large measure, Eckhart ght to defend himself against his opponents by ᴊisting that they were interpreting from the stand-ᴏint of creaturehood and time what he had meant from the standpoint of eternity. Not surprisingly, diverse interpretations of and judgments about his work continue to this day. *See also* Dominican spirituality.

JAMES WISEMAN

École Biblique (Fr., "Biblical School"), French Dominican biblical and archaeological graduate school in Jerusalem. It was founded in 1890 by Father Marie-Joseph Lagrange and was recognized by the French government in 1920 as its archaeological school in Jerusalem. In 1982 the school was accredited by the Vatican to grant the doctorate in Sacred Scripture. Since 1892 it has published the *Revue Biblique* (Fr., "Biblical Review"), a series of longer works called *Études Bibliques* (Fr., "Biblical Studies"), and a series of shorter works called *Cahiers de la Revue Biblique* (Fr., "Studies of the Biblical Review"). Early on it acquired a good reputation for its decipherment of Semitic and Greek inscriptions and for its series of archaeological publications on the major sites of the Holy Land, especially Jerusalem. Later it undertook excavations at Tirza, Qumran, Keisan, and in Jordan. For its pioneering of a moderately critical approach to the Bible, it has won worldwide respect, but had to suffer a period of ecclesiastical suspicion (1907–43). It was the first resident archaeological school in Jerusalem, but was soon imitated by others. It was also the first Catholic school of modern higher biblical studies and was thus influential throughout the Catholic world. *See also Revue Biblique.*

ecology, moral aspects of, ethical concerns related to the interrelationship of organisms and their environment. The moral aspects of ecology are seen in the context of a larger moral crisis concerning the order and unity of creation and humanity's place within it. The relationship of humanity to the rest of creation is a long-standing concern of the Catholic tradition as seen in the thought of figures like Augustine of Hippo (d. 430), Hildegard of Bingen (d. 1179), and Francis of Assisi (d. 1226). Today our increased knowledge of ecosystems and our growing awareness of humanity's role in environmental change have also increased our moral reflection on the topic of ecology.

The moral problems related to ecology are several: (1) the indiscriminate use of advances in science and technology; (2) pollution resulting from the dominance of economic interests over other values; (3) a lack of ecological balance due to the imbalance among rich and poor in use of resources; (4) biological research that may lead to unforeseen harms; (5) war's significant ecological damages; and (6) the connection between the environment and development. This last point is characteristic of Catholic social teaching with its insistence that ecological concerns cannot be treated independently of the topic of economic development (see, e.g., Pope John Paul II's *Centesimus Annus,* nn. 30–43).

Catholicism relies upon several axioms when addressing these challenges: (1) the goods of the earth are to be shared by all; (2) there is a human right to live in a safe environment; (3) the diversity of life has inherent value, for it exhibits the grandeur and glory of the Creator; (4) aesthetic appreciation of the beauty of the universe is a classic path to knowledge and love of God; (5) any attempt at resolving environmental abuses must not ignore the poor, who have a right to authentic development; and (6) a new spirit of solidarity among nations is necessary to resolve issues that are global in scope.

KENNETH R. HIMES

ecology, theological aspects of, the systematic delineation of specifically religious reasons for caring about the welfare of nonhuman nature. Concern for nature's integrity has not been a special area of concern throughout most of Christian history. Several prominent environmentalists have chastised Christianity and other faiths not only for failing to address the ecological crisis but also for some complicity in bringing it about. Ecological theology seeks to retrieve from tradition those resources relevant to the alleviation of contemporary threats to the earth's ecosystems.

Only recently have Catholic leaders, following the example of the World Council of Churches, begun to address the ecological crisis. Noteworthy are the 1988 pastoral letter by the Philippine bishops, *What Is Happening to Our Beautiful Land?,* the World Day of Peace message by Pope John Paul II entitled *The Ecological Crisis: A Common Responsibility* (1990), and the U.S. Catholic bishops' statement *Renewing the Earth* (1992).

Ecology is becoming a major issue in theology. Some suspicion about theology's focusing so explicitly on the state of the natural world came initially from economically impoverished countries, where some Christians voiced their fear that too much attention to ecological problems could distract theology from its task of promoting the liberation of socially and economically oppressed peoples. Now, churches and theologians are acknowledging the inseparable connection between poverty and ecological degradation. Issues of justice can no longer be treated separately from concern for the survival of the many complex and interdependent layers of life on our planet.

Ecology and Creation: Catholicism shares with the wider Christian world a sense of obedience to the biblical charge that we remain faithful stewards of God's creation. Likewise it bases its ecological outlook on the Psalms' exaltation of God's handiwork, the biblical theologies of creation, the wisdom literature, John's incarnational theology, and Paul's cosmic Christology, all of which entail a holistic vision of nature and its goodness. The Catholic tradition also has conspicuous ecological authority in the practices of Francis of Assisi (d. 1226), Benedict of Nursia (d. ca. 550), and many others who have encouraged a moderate, nonexploitive attitude toward nature. However, many critics still wonder whether, in spite of these positive features, Catholic Christianity has a sufficiently deep interest in the cause of conservation. At times the faith has been interpreted in such otherworldly terms that the present natural order seems insignificant except perhaps as a stage for the drama of salvation to be consummated elsewhere. The Christian sense of exile here has been unfortunately misinterpreted as an excuse for not caring for the earth as our home. In modern times, a one-sided preoccupation with salvation history and with God-human relationships has drawn theology's attention away from the earth-human connection.

On the other hand, Catholicism has always emphasized the sacramentality of creation, a feature that implicitly affirms nature's intrinsic value. All sacramental religions hold that the sacred mystery is disclosed primarily through symbols or "sacraments." In many religious traditions aspects of nature such as clean water, bright light, fertile soil, fresh air, and the fertility of living beings have given humans symbolic access to a sacred presence. In its worship and theology Catholicism enthusiastically embraces not only the revelatory word of God, but also this sacramental character of religion with its implied obligation of respect for the wholeness of nature. God is made known through the mediation of components of nature (such as water, life, and light) or elements close to nature (e.g., bread and wine) that have been shaped by the "work of human

hands." Consequently, at least in principle, Cath faith has a very special interest in the conservati of nature. As the American theologian Thomas Ber ry has observed, if we lose the environment we will lose our sense of God as well.

Thomas Aquinas (d. 1274) also illustrates this sacramental vision when he states that the goodness of God cannot be manifested in any one creature; thus God created a multiplicity of beings so that in the manifestation of the divine goodness what was lacking in one could be supplied by another (*Summa Theologiae* 1.48.2). In the 1990s, ecologically sensitive theologians emphasize that preserving natural diversity contributes to the coming of God's reign which is partially shaped not only through the practice of social justice and love, but also through the maintenance of nature's richness and integrity.

Theology's gradual appropriation of evolutionary ideas also contributes to the conviction that human life shares a common ancestry with plants and animals and that the destiny of the cosmos is inseparable from our own. Awareness of evolution can foster an ecologically positive sense of kinship, interdependency, and communion and at the same time give a more cosmic scope to biblical and traditional images of hope. *See also* creation; creation-centered spirituality.

Bibliography

Berry, Thomas. *The Dream of the Earth*. San Francisco: Sierra Club Books, 1988.

Birch, Charles, William Eakin, and Jay McDaniel, eds. *Liberating Life: Contemporary Approaches to Ecological Theology*. Maryknoll, NY: Orbis Books, 1990.

McDonagh, Sean. *The Greening of the Church*. Maryknoll, NY: Orbis Books, 1990.   JOHN F. HAUGHT

Economic Justice for All, the U.S. Catholic bishops' 1986 pastoral letter on the U.S. economy. The letter consists of five chapters. The first describes the economic setting of the United States as including both failures—for instance, the persistence of the problem of homelessness—and signs of hope— for example, the number of parents who balance work and family life. The second chapter sets out a Christian vision of economic life within which to address the realities described. Such a vision accents the dignity of persons, which is grounded in the fact that all persons are created in the image of God. Such dignity is fostered wherever persons actively participate in the life of the community. Human rights, on this account, are the minimum conditions for life in community. A society fails when it marginalizes persons from the life of the community. In the third chapter, the bishops bring this emasis on participation to bear on the specific issues ~~of~~ employment, poverty, agriculture, and the global economy. The fourth chapter makes a broad proposal for a "new American experiment" where the bishops call for expanding the participatory ethos that marks American political life to include economic life as well: we best carry forward the bold experiment in democracy of the American founders by extending it to the economy. The fifth chapter returns to explicitly confessional language in urging Christians to a holiness in the modern world that reflects their commitment to the eschatological community of God's kingdom, where love and justice unite. Specifically, it reminds the Church that it must practice what it preaches about justice: *"All the moral principles that govern the just operation of any economic endeavor apply to the church and its agencies and institutions; indeed the church should be exemplary"* (n. 347; italics in original). *See also* Catholic social teachings; social justice.   TODD D. WHITMORE

economics. *See* capitalism; Catholic social teachings; Marxism.

economy, divine (Gk., *oikonomia,* Lat., *dispensatio*), the mystery of salvation and God's providential plan. *Oikonomia* means the law or management (*nomos*) of the household (*oikos*), thus the salvific economy is God's providential management of the household of creation, redemption, and consummation.

According to the Pauline writings, the divine economy has been hidden in the mind of God from all eternity (Eph 3:9; 1 Cor 2:7) but was revealed in Christ for the first time. The great plan of salvation described in Eph 1:3–14 begins with our election before the creation of the world, adoption as daughters and sons in Jesus Christ, redemption through the blood of the cross, forgiveness of sins, and the final consummation of all things in Christ. This mystery of the economy is a plan set out for the fullness of time, and all who believe in Christ are sealed with the Holy Spirit.

Economy has the related meaning of stewardship; Paul refers to himself as a steward (*oikonomos*) of the mysteries of God (1 Cor 4:1; Col 1:25); he has a commission to preach the gospel (1 Cor 9:17). In the pastoral Letters the bishop is called God's steward (*oikonomos;* Titus 1:7).

In the pre-Nicene period of the Church, economy generally meant the saving dispensation by which God redeems all things through Christ. Gradually economy took on the restricted meaning of the Incarnation of Christ, in contrast to "theology" (*theologia*), meaning the hidden mystery of God. In connection with early trinitarian theology, economy meant the "distribution" of the Godhead among the divine Persons. *See also* creation; redemption; salvation.   CATHERINE M. LACUGNA

economy, principle of, a term used by Orthodox churches for the basis on which the Church's authority grants a departure from strict conformity with a canonical norm in particular cases. It closely resembles the use of dispensation in the Catholic Church, which is the relaxation of an ecclesiastical law granted in a particular case when the spiritual good of the faithful requires it.

The principle of economy is invoked to resolve a number of difficult situations. For example, it is in virtue of economy that the Orthodox Church may recognize the validity of sacraments administered by non-Orthodox Christians. It is economy that permits church authorities to show leniency toward second and third marriages and allows people to have a second chance even after divorce. The principle also allows Church authorities to declare that certain laws are no longer binding even though they may not have been formally abrogated. *See also* dispensation.

ecstasy (Gk., *ekstasis,* "to stand outside oneself"), in the Christian mystical tradition, the suspension of internal and/or external sense activity as a result of being in the presence of or in union with the divine. The physical phenomena associated with mystical ecstasy are the result of the weakness of the human person coming under the influence of the Holy Spirit and are not an indication in themselves of holiness, since these phenomena can have many causes. These experiences are transient and cease when the spiritual life has become strong enough to host the divine presence. Teresa of Ávila (d. 1582) offers the traditional Christian discernment of mystical experience and phenomena: love of God revealed through love of neighbor. Teresa of Ávila, in the fourth mansions (introduction) and sixth mansions of *The Interior Castle,* her *Life* (20.1), and *Spiritual Testimony* (59), sorts out the various ways that ecstatic mystical prayer manifests itself, e.g., rapture, wound of love, flight of the spirit, sleep of faculties, etc. Teresa sees these and other ecstatic experiences as essentially the same and only perceptually distinct. *See also* mysticism; Teresa of Ávila, St.

There have been twenty-one ecumenical councils recognized by the Catholic Church. Each council is listed in this table with the year or years in which it was held and a brief summary of its most important teachings or decrees. Separate entries on all twenty-one councils (e.g., "Nicaea, First Council of") appear elsewhere in the encyclopedia, although some individual councils are included in clustered entries, i.e., the five Lateran councils and the four councils of Constantinople.

1. FIRST COUNCIL OF NICAEA
325

The council taught against Arianism that the Son is of the same divine substance (Gk., *homoousios*) as the Father. Arianism held that the Son is the greatest of creatures, but not himself divine.

2. FIRST COUNCIL OF CONSTANTINOPLE
381

The council ratified the teaching of the First Council of Nicaea and condemned Apollinarianism, which held that Christ was fully divine but not fully human, since he lacked a human spirit. The Nicene-Constantinopolitan Creed recited today at the Eucharist is traditionally associated with this council.

3. COUNCIL OF EPHESUS
431

The council condemned Nestorianism, which held that there are two persons in Christ, one divine and one human. As such, Mary is the mother of Christ, but not the Mother of God. The council affirmed that she is also the Mother of God (Gk., *Theotokos*), because in Christ there is only one divine Person.

4. COUNCIL OF CHALCEDON
451

The council condemned Monophysitism, which held that in Christ there is only one divine nature. The Chalcedonian definition taught that in Christ there are two natures, one divine and one human, hypostatically united in one divine Person. The definition remains the doctrinal framework for Christology today.

5. SECOND COUNCIL OF CONSTANTINOPLE
553

In order to placate the Monophysites, the council, at the instigation of the emperor Justinian, condemned the Three Chapters of Theodore of Mopsuestia, Theodoret of Cyrrhus, and Ibas of Edessa, on the grounds that they were Nestorian in tone.

6. THIRD COUNCIL OF CONSTANTINOPLE
680–81

The council condemned Monothelitism, which held that in Christ there is only one divine will rather than two wills, one divine and one human. It also censured Pope Honorius as a Monothelite.

7. SECOND COUNCIL OF NICAEA
787

The council condemned iconoclasm, a movement that opposed the use of icons and other images for liturgical and devotional purposes. The council distinguished between the veneration that is appropriate for such images and the worship (Gk., *latria*) that belongs to God alone.

. FOURTH COUNCIL OF CONSTANTINOPLE
869–70

This council and those following it are not recognized by the Eastern Orthodox churches. Constantinople IV upheld the Roman synod's condemnation of Photius, patriarch of Constantinople, and also established the order of precedence among patriarchates: Rome, Constantinople, Alexandria, Antioch, and Jerusalem.

9. FIRST LATERAN COUNCIL
1123

The first ecumenical council held in the West. It confirmed the Concordat of Worms, which ended the controversy regarding lay investiture, i.e., the practice of lay rulers' determining appointments to ecclesiastical offices.

10. SECOND LATERAN COUNCIL
1139

The council met following an eight-year schism that had taken place at the time of Pope Innocent II's election. An antipope, Anacletus II, was elected at the same time. Upon Anacletus's death, the council annulled all of his and his followers' decisions, acts, and ordinations.

11. THIRD LATERAN COUNCIL
1179

The council ended a schism created by the election of an antipope, supported by the emperor. To avoid future problems of this sort, it decreed that a two-thirds majority of cardinals was necessary for the election of a pope, a rule that still applies today.

12. FOURTH LATERAN COUNCIL
1215

The most important of the Lateran councils, it decreed that all Catholics must receive the sacrament of Penance at least once a year, defined the Eucharist in terms of transubstantiation, prohibited the foundation of new religious orders, and required Jews and Muslims to wear distinctive dress.

13. FIRST COUNCIL OF LYONS
1245

The council was called by Pope Innocent IV to deal with the "five wounds of the Church": the immoral lives of the clergy and faithful, the danger posed by the Saracens, the Greek schism, the invasion of Hungary by the Tartars, and the break between the Church and Emperor Frederick II, whom the council formally deposed.

14. SECOND COUNCIL OF LYONS
1274

Attended by some of the greatest figures in medieval Christendom (e.g., Albertus Magnus, Bonaventure), the council defined the double-procession of the Holy Spirit from the Father and the Son (Lat., *Filioque*) and forged a short-lived union between Rome and the Greek Church. Thomas Aquinas died en route to the council.

15. COUNCIL OF VIENNE
1311–12

Under pressure from the French king, Philip IV, the council condemned the Knights Templar, who were being accused of heresy and immorality by those, including Philip, who coveted their wealth. The council also decided in favor of the stricter Franciscan observance of poverty.

16. COUNCIL OF CONSTANCE
1414–18

The council was called to end the Great Western Schism, involving three separate claimants to the papal throne. It deposed John XXIII and Benedict XIII, received the abdication of Gregory XII, and conducted a conclave in which Martin V was elected.

17. COUNCIL-OF-BASEL-FERRARA-FLORENCE-ROME
1431–45

This council met in four different cities (some official lists do not include Basel). The chief object of the council was reunion with the Greek Church. The Greeks, eager for Western help against the Turks, accepted the Latin formulations on the *Filioque*, the Eucharist, purgatory, and papal primacy. When the Turks captured Constantinople in 1453, the union fell apart.

18. FIFTH LATERAN COUNCIL
1512–17

The council declared invalid the decrees of the Council of Pisa (1409), which deposed two claimants to the papal throne during the Great Western Schism and elected the antipope Alexander V, and the council also repudiated the Pragmatic Sanction of Bourges, issued by the French clergy in 1438, asserting the independence of the French church from papal control.

19. COUNCIL OF TRENT
1545–47, 1551–52, 1562–63

The council was held to address the challenges posed by the Protestant Reformation. It touched upon almost every major aspect of Catholic doctrine: Scripture and tradition, the Church's teaching authority, original sin, justification, and the sacraments, especially the Eucharist. Its most important disciplinary decree established seminaries for the training of clergy.

20. FIRST VATICAN COUNCIL
1869–70

The council taught papal primacy (the pope's authority over all other bishops and over the whole Church) and papal infallibility (the pope's immunity from error in defining matters of faith and morals). It also taught that faith is consistent with reason and that reason is illumined by faith, thereby condemning both rationalism (only reason can establish truth) and fideism (only faith can establish truth).

21. SECOND VATICAN COUNCIL
1962–65

An exception in the history of ecumenical councils, this council was not called to combat error or to deal with disciplinary problems. It was convoked by Pope John XXIII to update the Church and to open it up to the modern world. Its main emphases were on renewal and reform of the liturgy, the role of the laity, ecumenism, the role of the Church in the temporal order, the collegiality of bishops and the pope, religious freedom, and the saving activity of God outside the Church.

umenical council, an assembly (Gk., *synodos;* at., *concilium*) of representatives from the whole Church or from specific churches for consultation and decision making regarding ecclesial matters. The ecumenical councils, which represent the whole Church, are distinguished from the different types of particular councils (often called synods): general, patriarchal, plenary, primatial, regional, and provincial.

Theological Basis: The meaning of councils can be understood correctly only within the framework of a comprehensive theology of the Church. In this perspective, the Church itself (Gk., *ekklesia,* from *kaleo,* "to call together") is the comprehensive "assembly" (*concilium,* from Lat., *concalare,* "to call together") of the believing people, called together by God. For this reason, the Church itself can be called in a profound theological sense the "ecumenical council formed in response to the divine convoking." It follows that the whole Church as the community of believing people has a completely conciliar, synodal (collegial) structure, a fact that should shape the life and structures of local churches (parishes and dioceses), national churches, and the whole Church.

In light of this consideration, an ecumenical council in the ordinary sense, i.e., one formed in response to a "human convoking," can be defined as a representation of the ecumenical council that is formed in response to the divine convoking, i.e., the whole Church. Thus a council is not the only, or even the most concentrated, representation of the Church (other practices, e.g., the liturgy, especially the Eucharist, represent the Church in other ways); but it is a comprehensive representation, comprehensive in both concerns and constituency, designed for, but not limited to, consultation and decision making regarding the governance and formation of the whole Church. Representation means not merely the use of delegates to "take the place of" members of the Church; the council also represents the Church by serving as an expression of it. The first Christian report about Christian councils expresses this fundamental theological understanding of the council as the locus of representation: "There were held in the Greek lands at definite places those councils of all churches, at which important matters are communally treated and also the representation of all Christianity is expressed in a reverential manner" (Tertullian *De Paen* [*Concerning Repentance*] 13.6–7). Since the early Church, the idea of representation, though in different forms, has been fun-

damental for understanding the ecumenical councils.

Historical Forms: The concrete forms of an ecumenical council are also very different. According to contemporary canon law, there can be no ecumenical council that is not convoked by the pope. Among the rights of the pope also belong the leadership of the council (by himself or another), the determination of the topics for consideration and their order, and the composition, adjournments, and dissolution of the council as well as the juridically binding confirmation of the definite resolutions (cans. 338, 341). Only the bishops, who are members of the college of bishops, have the right and the obligation to participate in a council with a deliberative vote. Other persons can be called to the council by the "supreme authority of the Church" (the pope), who will also determine the degree of their participation (can. 339). The college of bishops exercises with the pope the "highest and most perfect form of oversight over the whole Church" (can. 336), which occurs "in celebratory manner" in an ecumenical council (can. 337). If the papacy should become vacant, the council is interrupted until a new pope orders its resumption or has it dissolved.

These specifications codify the governance observed by the councils of Trent (1545–63) and Vatican I (1869–70). Nevertheless, many of these specifications are innovations of the past thousand years, postdating the establishment of the specifically Roman Catholic paradigm with the Gregorian reform in the eleventh century. In particular, it cannot be historically maintained that the ecumenical councils of roughly the first one thousand years of the Church were called, led, and confirmed by the pope. Thus, all the rules and regulations governing ecumenical councils are simply specifications of ecclesial, not divine, law (Lat., *ius humanum*). They are not required by the Church's essential constitution as given in the Gospels. Because the Petrine office (i.e., the papacy), however, belongs to the essential constitution of the Church, it must be canonically represented (in the ancient councils legates sufficed) at an ecumenical council so that the council may be a genuine representation of the whole Church (can. 338).

The forms of this representation have nevertheless differed greatly in the various councils in the history of the Church. In several instances there was only subsequent approval by the pope. Also, cases of conflict between the Church and the pope (e.g., a heretical or schismatic pope, the removal of such a pope) have actually happened historically and cannot be foreclosed as a possibility for the future. Moreover, direct representation of the laity—men and women—in councils is not only dogmatically possible but also theologically desirable and in some situations unconditionally necessary in light of the universal priesthood of all believers. It is also of practical value given the laity's direct knowledge of the world and responsibility in the world.

On the other hand, a council held in opposition to those in ecclesiastical office would be contrary to church governance and the essence of an ecumenical council, which is meant to represent the whole Church. Thus, without the participation of those in Church offices, an ecumenical council is not possible. From every point of view, observable differentiations are evident among the provincial councils of the second and third centuries (out of which the ecumenical councils proceeded), the eight ancient ecumenical councils of the Byzantine East that were called by the emperor, the general synods of the Latin High Middle Ages, the late medieval Fifth Lateran Council on the eve of the Reformation, the purely ecclesial Council of Trent for Catholic reform, the First Vatican Council, which was controlled by the pope, and the Second Vatican Council, which stressed collegiality.

A Theological Viewpoint: In the spirit of Vatican II, a theology of the council that opposes papalist restriction and resists the centralist tendencies of the Curia must be promoted anew. The ecumenical council should be a credible manifestation of the Church—one, holy, catholic, and apostolic. This concretely means that the resolutions of a council should be decided in unanimity and with a spiritual consensus. The external framework, conduct, and resolutions of a council should be shaped by the gospel. The apostolic spirit, the apostolic witness, and—in a subordinate capacity—the apostolic office should be decisive for the council. Insofar as, according to the promise of Jesus, the Holy Spirit operates in the Church itself, the Spirit is also at work in the special event of its representation, namely, in an ecumenical council in response to human convoking. On this basis, an ecumenical council may claim a special binding authority, even though its decrees and definitions are incomplete, fragmentary human words (cf. 1 Cor 13:9–12). The acts of a council—different from decrees on doctrine and discipline—have only the binding character that the meeting council wants to give to them.

Every council and every decree of a council is to be understood historically and to be interpreted in relation to its period in time. *See also* council.

Bibliography

Küng, Hans. *Structures of the Church.* New York: Thomas Nelson and Sons, 1964.

Tanner, Norman P., ed. *Decrees of the Ecumenical Councils.* 2 vols. Washington, DC: Georgetown University Press, 1990.

HANS KÜNG

ecumenical movement, the process by which Christian churches that had been separated by doctrinal, social, ethnic, political, and institutional factors move toward cooperation and unity, by mutual understanding and respect through dialogue; by cooperation or common witness to whatever divine gifts and gospel values they already share and experience; and by a common search for that unity which the Lord wills for his one and only Church, "so that the world may believe" (John 17:21).

History: Church historians describe the 1800s as the "great century" of prolific Catholic, Protestant, and Orthodox missions; they label the 1900s as the decades of the ecumenical movement. The two movements relate in their origins, and fuse in intent.

In the 1800s Protestants across denominational lines formed associations, notably Bible and tract societies. Some mission agencies agreed to policies of collaboration in health and education. Various Protestant groups divided mission territories into spheres of activities, a "denominationalism by geography" that kept distant those variant forms of teaching, worship, and policy that could scandalize non-Christians and hinder witness to the basic gospel message.

In 1910 at Edinburgh, a world missionary conference gathered 414 delegates from 122 denominations and 43 countries. They discussed Christian education and national life, the missionary message in relation to non-Christian religions, the preparation of missionaries, missions, and governments, and cooperation between mission agencies and their denominations. The delegates confessed that "our divisions were contrary to the will of Christ," and professed that "a unity in Christ and fellowship in the Spirit is deeper than our divisions."

The modern ecumenical movement was born at this Edinburgh conference, from which issued, after the First World War, the International Missionary Council (1921, a forum of Protestant national councils of mission agencies in Europe and North Amer-

, and local councils of churches in Africa, Asia, ..d Latin America); the Life and Work movement 1925, social ethics and "practical collaboration in the secular order"); and the Faith and Order movement (1927, church teaching, sacraments, and governance).

In 1920 the Orthodox patriarchate in Constantinople had appealed publicly for a permanent institution of fellowship and cooperation of "all the churches," similar to the proposed League of Nations. Other leaders later supported this appeal. In 1948, shocked by the scandal of a second world war among Christian nations, 147 Protestant, Anglican, and Orthodox churches formed the World Council of Churches.

The official Catholic response to these developments was a suspicious wariness, typified by Pope Pius XI's *Mortalium Animos* on "fostering religious union" (1928). The pope judged that Catholic participation at non-Catholic assemblies would easily confirm that one religion or church is as good as another, and would "countenance a false Christian religion quite alien to the one true Church of Christ." The model of reunion is the return of non-Catholics to the Catholic Church, because it believes itself to be coextensive with the One Church. Catholics would compromise that witness by mixing with others who were not clear on what the ecumenical movement was, or where it was to move.

Vatican II and Beyond: But Vatican Council II (1962–65) reversed this ecclesial understanding and chartered the Catholic Church's active participation in the one movement "fostered by the grace of the Holy Spirit, for the restoration of unity among all Christians" (Decree on Ecumenism, n. 1).

The ecumenical movement is wider and deeper than any or all of its local, national, regional, or world expressions. It continues to mirror the interplay of different forces that are affecting both converging and diverging understandings of ecumenism.

Since the rapid decolonization of the world after the Second World War, the traditional Christian heartland, which in 1948 had embraced the local churches of the North Atlantic, Eastern Europe, and Mediterranean areas, is fading in its dominant influence over the southern hemisphere. The local churches in Africa, Asia, the Caribbean, Latin America, and Oceania are becoming their own subjects of theological articulations, personal and social ethical stances, spiritualities, church disci-

plines, and interchurch cooperation in common witness. These new centers do not accept without question the ecumenical priorities of renewal, mission, and unity that are based on the historical experience of church divisions: East and West, and later in the West, the Roman Catholic Church and the churches that issued from the Reformation.

Ecumenical experience no longer supports the oversimplified dictum of a few decades ago, that doctrine divides, action unites. For just as formal bilateral and multilateral dialogues are leading to convergences on those doctrinal affirmations that helped to cause and perpetuate classical church separations, personal and social ethical issues are emerging that are more divisive in the public arena than they were in the 1960s: among others, abortion and euthanasia; active homosexuality and premarital sex; justice, peace, and economic issues and prudential decisions based on them; women's rights in society and the churches.

Even with recent Catholic participation, the ecumenical movement remained sectarian because of the absence of conservative evangelical Christians and most Pentecostal and Holiness churches. Once intentionally "antiecumenical," an increasing number of Evangelicals are becoming active allies to the ecumenical movement, bringing new energies and nuances to old ecumenical agendas. Forming at the same time is a new coalition of Protestant and Catholic fundamentalists who, with often opposing reasons and judgments, reject the ecumenical movement. For them it is too accommodating to the modern world, too compromising with biblical fundamentals and/or Church traditions, and too eager to cover a multitude of sins by downplaying theological barriers in favor of organizational unity based on cooperative social action.

Indeed, the ecumenical movement is a relatively young movement with its deepest hopes for unity still to be fulfilled. *See also* Church; Decree on Ecumenism; ecumenism; unity of the Church; World Council of Churches. *THOMAS F. STRANSKY*

ecumenism, a process that is directed toward the achievement of unity among all Christian churches, and ultimately among all religious communities. The term is derived biblically from both "the household of God" (Gk., *oikodome*) of the whole Church (cf. 1 Cor 3:9; Eph 2:19; 1 Tim 3:15; Heb 3:6) and "the whole inhabited earth" (Gk., *oikoumene*, Luke 2:1). The still developing understanding of ecumenism tries to hold relational tensions between the unity and the mission of the Church in the context of the whole world, and between the present era and the expected reign of God, "the *oikoumene* to come" (Heb 2:5).

Ecumenism, therefore, is the unceasing search to draw all Christians together through the renewal of the churches in order to manifest the unity that Christ wills for his one and only Church, and the obligation of the Church to proclaim the whole gospel to the world, as the servant to both that gospel and that world.

There may be general Christian consensus on this paradigm of unity-in-mission, mission-in-unity, but there is not the same consensus on the nature of this unity, on the Church, or on the full communion (*koinonia*). Fundamental orientations are emerging.

First, the unity confessed in the Nicene-Constantinopolitan Creed of ca. 381 ("one, holy, catholic, and apostolic") is not only a spiritual, invisible reality, but also the visible expression of one apostolic faith by the preaching of one gospel and the breaking of one bread in a corporate life that reaches out in witness to all peoples.

Second, unity with the whole Christian fellowship in all places and all ages needs the visible, full, and unqualified acceptance of all members and ministries.

Third, unity is not uniformity but a diversity of theological expressions and forms of ecclesiastical life, rooted in different traditions and various cultural, ethnic, or historical contexts.

Fourth, emerging from the above convergences are the unavoidable questions that find the least consensus today: What and for what is the Christ-given authority in and of his one Church? Where is that authority, and how should it be exercised?

Fifth, all forms of unity are provisional, the first fruits of that ultimate fulfillment when God will unite and complete all things in the perfect communion of the divine heavenly banquet.

Official Catholic teaching stresses "full visible communion" in the confession of one faith, the common celebration of divine worship, and the fraternal harmony through the ecclesiastical governance of collegiality (Decree on Ecumenism, 1964, n. 3), without sacrificing "the rich diversity of spirituality, discipline, liturgical rites, and elaborations of revealed truth that has grown up among the churches" (1993 Ecumenical Directory, n. 17). *See*

also Decree on Ecumenism; ecumenical movement; u. of the Church.　　　　　THOMAS F. STRANSKY

Edessa, present-day Urfa (Turkey), ancient capital of the kingdom of Osrhoene and early center of Syriac Christianity. Associated with Edessa are such works as the *Odes of Solomon,* the *Gospel of Thomas,* and the *Acts of Thomas* and such figures as Bardesanes, Tatian, and St. Ephraem. Edessa fell to the Arabs in 639.

Edict of Constantine/Milan. *See* Constantine, Edict of.

editio typica (ed-ee'tsee-oh teep'ee-kah, Lat., "official edition"), the official, usually Latin, edition of a document, often a liturgical rite. All other editions and translations are to be in agreement with it.

Edmundites, Society of St. Edmund (S.S.E.), a religious community of priests and brothers founded in Pontigny, France, by Fathers Jean-Baptiste Muard and Pierre Bouyer in 1843. The motherhouse of the Edmundites is located in Vermont, and the approximately seventy members of the community serve in the United States and Venezuela. Dedicated to evangelizing the materially and spiritually poor, the Edmundites engage in pastoral and educational work. In the United States, they have concentrated on ministry to African-Americans in the southern states, on higher education (notably St. Michael's College in Vermont), and on retreat ministry.

education, Catholic. *See* Catholicism and education.

education, moral, education for the purpose of the development of character and formation of conscience. Character is developed through the cultivation of virtues by habit. Conscience gives the virtuous life rational direction by applying general principles to particular cases. Acting according to conscience, each individual expresses divinely given freedom and dignity. The primacy of conscience does not, however, entail moral relativism, which denies the existence of unchanging, universal principles of moral behavior. Conscience must be formed through moral education. Such education fosters the ability to make free and responsible decisions in dialogue with others, and imparts information about particular values, rules of behavior, and official teachings of the Church. In recent years, research in psychology and sociology has deepened the understanding of moral development, influencing Catholic as well as secular approaches to moral education. This research has underscored traditional teaching that family, Church, school, and society all play a significant role in the lifelong process of moral education. These communities foster moral growth by providing a context for sharing norms, values, and ideals, discussing moral issues, and encouraging the practice of the virtues. Moreover, family, Church, and Catholic education nourish a specifically Christian moral life of service based on the Gospels. *See also* moral theology; religious education.

Edward the Confessor, St., 1003–66, king of England from 1042 to 1066. Son of King Aethelred, he returned in 1042 to England as king, after spending most of his youth in Normandy. He died childless in 1066 and the crown passed to Harold of Wessex, igniting a contest with Edward's cousin Duke William of Normandy. A pious man known as a friend to the poor and the clergy, Edward was buried at Westminster, the abbey he built. Feast day: October 13.

Egan, John J., b. 1916, priest and social activist. A priest of the archdiocese of Chicago, he was named head of the Cana Conference in Chicago in 1947 where his work gained him a national reputation. In the 1950s he became involved in urban affairs and, with the assistance of Saul Alinsky, noted community organizer, he placed the Church's financial and moral strength behind many community organizations in Chicago. In 1967, together with other social activists, he founded the Catholic Committee on Urban Ministry, which sought to promote social and racial justice. For thirteen years (1970–83) he worked at the University of Notre Dame as a special assistant to the president, Father Theodore Hesburgh, and as director of the Institute for Pastoral and Social Ministry, which he founded. In 1987 he became an assistant to the president of DePaul University in Chicago, after having served the archdiocese of Chicago in the areas of ecumenical and community relations since 1983. *See also* Cana Conference.

Egbert, St., 639–729, abbot, bishop, and supporter of the evangelization of Germany. An Englishman studying in Ireland during a plague, Egbert made a vow never to return home if he survived. He was a principal organizer of the mission to Germany, especially that of Willibrord in 690. After serving as bishop in Ireland, he became abbot of Iona (716), which adopted the Roman observance of Easter under his influence. Feast day: April 24. *See also* Iona; Willibrord, St.

Egbert of York, d. 766, bishop and teacher of Alcuin. Bishop of York from 732, Egbert was brother of King Edbert and a student of Bede, who wrote a letter offering him pastoral advice and recommending that York should be an archdiocese (734), a promotion granted by Pope Gregory III in 735. *See also* Bede, St.

Egeria, Pilgrimage of (eh-jehr'ee-ah), early-fifth-century travel diary in Latin dialect, also known as Pilgrimage of Aetheria. Valued especially for descriptions of ceremonies in Jerusalem during Epiphany, Holy Week, Easter, and Pentecost, this account of visits to OT and NT holy sites was discovered in 1884 in an eleventh-century manuscript. In addition to the Holy Land, Egeria visited Egypt, Syria, and Constantinople. Nothing is known of the author beyond what can be inferred from the text—that she was a wealthy woman who could spend years on pilgrimage, enjoyed considerable social standing, knew the Bible well, and belonged to a devout sisterhood, to whom the report is addressed. *See also* Jerusalem.

Egypt, one of the most illustrious centers of Christianity in the ancient world. The origins of Christianity in Egypt are obscure, although they certainly date at least to the latter part of the first century and are to be located among the strong Jewish populations of Alexandria, who were evangelized by groups from Jerusalem. With the savage destruction of the Jews by Trajan (98–117), Christianity at Alexandria acquired a more thoroughly gentile and Greek character, and the first Egyptian Christians we know by name are the speculative and philosophical heterodox teachers of the early second century, including the Gnostics Valentinus and Basilides. Their style of theology was continued in a more orthodox vein by Pantaenus (late second century), his student Clement (ca. 150–215), and the great Origen (ca. 185–ca. 254), whose thought set the intellectual agenda for the influential

Alexandrian catechetical school until the end of the fourth century. From the time of Demetrius (190–232), the first bishop about whom we have substantial information, the see of Alexandria grew in power and prestige until it became one of the three most influential sees in the empire, after Rome and (later) Constantinople.

But no less important are the achievements of the non-Alexandrian, native Egyptian population, Coptic rather than Greek speaking. The celebrated history of monasticism in the Egyptian desert belongs to the Coptic church, from Anthony of Egypt (251–356), who inspired a movement of anchorites, or hermit ascetics; to Pachomius (292–347), who founded cenobitic, or communal, monasticism; to Shenoute (ca. 350–ca. 450), abbot of the White Monastery in Upper Egypt, whose prose is the flowering of Coptic literature. Strictly speaking, the Coptic or Coptic Orthodox church dates from the time of the Council of Chalcedon (451), which was rejected by the great majority of the Egyptian church. It subsequently developed a hierarchy of its own, separate from both Rome and Constantinople, and this has continued to the present despite conquest by the Arabs (641) and their intermittent persecution and repression of Christians. The Coptic church reckons as its first era, the "Era of the Martyrs," the time from the accession of the emperor Diocletian (284) to the end of the Great Persecution (311), particularly savage in Egypt, and claims as its heritage, through Dioscorus, the whole succession of Alexandrian bishops from Demetrius and Dionysius, to Peter, Athanasius, Theophilus, and especially Cyril. *See also* Alexandria, school of; Anthony of Egypt, St.; Copt, Coptic; Coptic Catholic Church; Coptic rite; Pachomius.

JOHN C. CAVADINI

Einhard, or Eginhard, ca. 770–840, abbot, courtier, and scholar. According to a biographical sketch by Walafrid Strabo, Einhard, educated at Fulda, was sent to Aachen as a youth. There he became a friend of Alcuin (whom he succeeded as head of the palace school), Charlemagne (whose biography he wrote), and Charlemagne's son, Louis the Pious.

Einsiedeln (in'tseed-uhln; Ger., "Hermitages"), Abbey of Our Lady of the Hermits, near Schwyz, Switzerland. The site of the martyrdom of the hermit St. Meinrad attracted other hermits, then (937) a Benedictine monastery. A popular pilgrimage site, the abbey founded houses in the United States and Argentina. *See also* Meinrad, St.

ejaculation (Lat., *ex*, "from"; *iacere*, "to throw"), short prayer usually expressing love or praise of God. These prayers are also called aspirations since they are so brief they can be said in a single breath. It is not necessary, however, to vocalize ejaculations. They may be offered mentally. Examples of popular ejaculations include: "Jesus Christ, I love and honor you"; "Sacred heart of Jesus, I trust in you"; "Jesus, Mary, and Joseph, I give you my heart and soul"; "Lord, have mercy." *See also* prayer.

elder, a respected leader of a community. The elders of Israel are specifically named by Moses at the Exodus (Exod 12:21); they served as candidates for special appointments (Num 11:16). They are mentioned frequently from Joshua through 2 Kings and continued to function in Jewish society in Jesus' time (e.g., Matt 15:2; 21:23).

Christian elders or (in Gk.) presbyters emerge as the Church organizes. Paul does not mention them, but they are portrayed in Acts in Jerusalem (Acts 15:2–6; 16:4) and elsewhere (Acts 13:1–3; 20:17). By the late first century, distinct presbyters (1 Pet 5:1; 1 Tim 5:1) received compensation (1 Tim 5:17) and had defined functions, including ordination (1 Tim 4:14). By A.D. 200 a hierarchical order was in place (Hippolytus *Apostolic Tradition*). *See also* presbyter; priesthood.

election, canonical, one of the means of filling some ecclesiastical offices. Canon law has strict general norms regulating elections: the convening of the electors, the process of voting, the qualities necessary for a valid vote, the majority required on a given ballot, and the obligation of having the election confirmed by higher authority. There are other norms as well for particular elections. The election of the pope is currently governed by an apostolic constitution, *Romano Pontifici Eligendo*, issued by Pope Paul VI in 1975. Religious institutes and other organizations can have election laws particular to them. *See also* papal election.

election, divine, God's decree that certain individuals or peoples receive grace sufficient and efficacious for salvation. In Catholic theology, divine election refers first and foremost to the general intention and action of God that orders created beings to a happy end; it is applied only secondarily to individuals as subjects of redemption. The chief means by which God accomplishes this end in a world tainted by sin is the calling forth of an elect group,

People of God, which then becomes the locus and effective sign of God's salvific activity in the world. Such election is only realized in community; the retelling of God's deeds both establishes this chosen people and initiates salvation history.

Divine election is first manifested with the foundation of Israel whom God calls "his treasured people" (Deut 26:18). This election is the fulfillment of God's promise to Abraham that his descendants should become more numerous than the stars in the sky (Gen 15:5). Such election is completely gratuitous and not a function of merit: "It was not because you were more numerous than any other people that the Lord set his heart on you and chose you—for you were the fewest of all peoples. It was because the Lord loved you and kept the oath that he swore to your ancestors" (Deut 7:7–8). The instrumental nature of God's special election in effecting the redemption of all people cannot be overemphasized. In the figure of the Suffering Servant in Deutero-Isaiah, Israel is chosen by God as "a light to the nations" (Isa 42:6). The sufferings borne by Israel are undertaken for the benefit of all (Isa 52:13–53:12). This election and service to the entire human race foreshadows that of the Church in the NT, "a chosen race, a royal priesthood, a holy nation, God's own people" (1 Pet 2:9; cf. Exod 19:5–6), and is reaffirmed by the Second Vatican Council in the Dogmatic Constitution on the Church, *Lumen Gentium* (1964). *See also* predestination; salvation.

GERARD JACOBITZ

election, papal. *See* papal election.

electronic church, a term that refers collectively to the creators and consumers of religious programs on radio and television. The expression originated as a variant of "the electric church," a phrase coined in 1976 by Ben Armstrong, executive director of National Religious Broadcasters, and later used as the title of his 1979 book.

Few religious broadcasters in North America are affiliated directly with any denomination. Rather, media ministries function more like independent enterprises lodged alongside the existing churches, with their own staffs, policies, and budgets. The majority are Protestant in orientation, with the evangelical and fundamentalist traditions predominating.

Several pioneers of the electronic church in America, such as Bishop Fulton J. Sheen (1895–1979), were Catholic clergymen. Nevertheless, the Catholic influence in this sphere is less pronounced. An exception, however, is the Eternal Word Television Network of Mother M. Angelica (b. 1923). Based near Birmingham, Alabama, EWTN offers inspirational programs with a decidedly traditionalist orientation to cable operators across the country via satellite. In addition, Catholic producers collaborate in programming VISN, the Vision Interfaith Satellite Network. *See also* Catholicism and mass media.

elevation, the moment in the Roman Mass when first the consecrated bread and then the cup are raised for the adoration of the faithful following the words of consecration. An older elevation is actually that which accompanies the concluding doxology. This elevation was overshadowed by the one at the consecration, which was introduced in the thirteenth century as part of the wave of "Eucharistic realism" that swept Europe in the High Middle Ages. *See also* Eucharist.

Elias of Cortona, ca. 1180–1253, vicar general under Francis of Assisi and, later, third general of the Franciscan order. Elected general in 1232, he was deposed and excommunicated by Pope Gregory IX in 1239 because of his self-indulgence and despotism.

Eligius, St., ca. 588–660, patron saint of metalworkers. He was a skilled metalsmith who was master of the mint for King Clotaire II and, after being ordained in 640, was made bishop of Noyon the following year. He founded a monastery at Solignae and convents in Paris and Noyon. Feast day: December 1.

Elijah (ee-li'juh), a ninth-century B.C. Jewish prophet. He battled with priests of Baal (1 Kgs 16:29–19:18), condemned a royal murder (1 Kgs 21; 2 Kgs 9), prophesied Ahaziah's death (2 Kgs 1–2), and instructed his successor, Elisha (1 Kgs 19:19–21; 2 Kgs 2). Mal 4:5 predicted his return. Hence, some thought of Jesus as Elijah (Matt 16:14; Mark 6:15; 8:28; Luke 9:8), but Jesus identified John the Baptist as Elijah (Matt 17:9–13; Mark 9:9–13). *See also* prophecy; prophet.

Elipandus, ca. 718–ca. 802, archbishop of Toledo (ca. 753–ca. 802) and leader of the Spanish Adoptionists, who taught that Jesus in his humanity was God's adoptive Son. To Pope Hadrian I and Carolingian theologians such as Alcuin this was tantamount to Nestorianism. Elipandus was condemned by four councils (Regensburg, 792; Frankfurt, 794; Rome, 798; Aachen, 799) but was never removed from his see, since Toledo was under Muslim rule. *See also* Adoptionism.

Elizabeth I, 1533–1603, queen of England. Daughter of Henry VIII and Anne Boleyn, she was placed in line for the throne after Edward VI and Mary Tudor by the Act of Succession (1544). Upon succeeding to the throne in 1558, she addressed the religious controversy created by Mary's reign. The Acts of Supremacy and Uniformity (1559) restored the ecclesiology and liturgy of 1552. With Matthew Parker as archbishop of Canterbury, Elizabeth sought to stabilize the reform of the Church of England by means of monarchical episcopal polity and moderate Lutheran and Reformed doctrine, rendered as inoffensive as possible to Catholics, culminating in the Thirty-nine Articles of 1563 and Parker's "Advertisements" of 1566. Elizabeth's policy took a decidedly anti-Catholic direction after her excommunication by Pius V in 1570, but she never acceded to Puritan demands to abandon episcopacy for a presbyterian polity and to purify the worship of the Church of all remnants of Catholic ritual. *See also* England, Catholicism in; Protestantism; Reformation, the; Thirty-nine Articles.

Elizabeth, St., wife of Zechariah and mother of John the Baptist. Luke 1 recounts how, aged and barren, she miraculously conceived. At her cousin Mary's visit she pronounced the Hail Mary's second verse, "Blessed are you among women and blessed is the fruit of your womb" (Luke 1:42), eliciting Mary's Magnificat. Feast day: November 5. *See also* John the Baptist, St; Magnificat.

Elizabeth Ann Seton, St. *See* Seton, St. Elizabeth Ann Bayley.

Elizabeth of Hungary, St., also known as Elizabeth of Thuringia, 1207–31, queen. After an extraordinarily happy marriage and three children, she was widowed in 1227. Exiled from court, she lived in Marburg (Germany) as a Franciscan tertiary devoted to her children, a life of prayer, and charity to the sick and the poor. Her spiritual director, Conrad of Marburg (d. 1233), a papal inquisitor, was a very severe man who may have helped shorten her already overburdened life. Feast day: November 17.

Elizabeth of Portugal, St., 1271–1336, queen of Portugal, known for her charitable works and as a peacemaker. She retired, in her last years, to a convent near Coimbra. Feast day: July 4.

Elizabeth of Schönau, ca. 1129–64, Benedictine prioress of a double monastery (in which men and women live in separate but neighboring houses) near Bonn, Germany. She authored three books describing her mystical experiences of the Passion and Resurrection of Jesus and conversations with many saints. Some of her revelations were once attributed to Elizabeth of Hungary. Although she was never formally beatified or canonized, she was referred to as St. Elizabeth in the Roman Martyrology. *See also* double monasteries.

Elizabeth of the Trinity, Bl., 1880–1906, Carmelite nun of Dijon. Born Elizabeth Catez near Bourges, France, she was influenced by John of the Cross, Thérèse of Lisieux, and Jan van Ruysbroeck. Her spirituality, which leads through deepening silence to the indwelling Trinity, is strongly Christocentric. She sees transformation into the image of God taking place on earth as individuals relive the mysteries of the Incarnate Word in their personal humanity. In the Letter of Paul to the Ephesians, she found her "new name," Praise of Glory (1:12). Her writings emphasize heaven and eternity permeating every temporal moment. She died of Addison's disease. Feast day: November 8.

Elkesaites, a Judeo-Christian sect originating east of the Jordan ca. 100 and centered around the "Book of Elkesai." Sometimes considered Gnostic, their actual beliefs are poorly attested. Mani (ca. 216–76), the founder of Manichaeism, grew up in an Elkesaite community. *See also* Manichaeism.

Ellard, Gerald, 1894–1963, American Jesuit priest and liturgical scholar. A founding co-editor (in 1926) of the influential journal *Orate Fratres* (now *Worship*), he worked for almost forty years to promote liturgical instruction at the popular level. His book *Christian Life and Worship* (1933) was long a standard college text.

Ellis, John Tracy, 1905–92, priest and Church historian. Regarded as the "dean of American Catholic historians," he spent most of his career at The Catholic University of America (1938–63, 1978–89). Of more than twelve books and hundreds of articles, most famous work is a two-volume biography (1952) of Cardinal Gibbons. In 1955, he gained wider influence with his critique of the lack of American Catholic intellectual life. In 1968, he received the Laetare Medal from the University of Notre Dame.

Elmo, St. 1 Also called Erasmus, d. ca. 300, bishop of Formiae and legendary patron saint of sailors. His emblem is the discharge of light often appearing near masts of ships after a storm. He was one of the Fourteen Holy Helpers of the later Middle Ages. Feast day: June 2. **2** Peter Gonzalez, ca. 1190–1246, Spanish Dominican, not to be confused with the first St. Elmo. Feast day: April 14.

Elvira, Council of (ca. 300–310), first known Spanish council famous for its harsh disciplinary canons and its insistence that bishops and other clergy not marry or, if already married, not live with their wives. Other canons penalize such things as usury, idol possession, fornication, adultery, and abortion (or perhaps infanticide). *See also* celibacy, clerical.

ember days, four sets of three days each (Wednesdays, Fridays, Saturdays) in each of the seasons of the year, until 1969 set aside for special liturgical and penitential observance. The ember days were, in winter, the week after the third Sunday of Advent; in spring, the week after the first Sunday of Lent; in summer, in the octave of Pentecost; in autumn, after the feast of the Holy Cross on September 14. On these days there were proper liturgical texts, and fast and abstinence were required.

The origins of the ember days can be traced at least to the third century. A product of the church of Rome, the observance was widespread in the West by the middle of the ninth century. In 1966 Pope Paul VI removed the obligation of fast and abstinence on ember days, allowing this and most other penitential discipline to be regulated by the national conferences of bishops. The bishops of the United States decided that each bishop could determine the practice for ember days in his own diocese. Subsequently, the ember days became obsolete despite isolated attempts to revive them.

Since the revision of the Roman Calendar in 1969, ember days are no longer considered penitential days but as times to pray for the needs of people, for the productivity of the earth and human labor, and to give public thanks to God. The precise nature

of, and times for, their observance is left to the conference of bishops.

embolism, an insertion into the "Our Father" prayer asking for the deliverance from the power of evil for the entire community, part of the rites introducing the reception of Communion in the Roman tradition. The embolism derives from the "Our Father" and develops that prayer. The use of an embolism dates to the time of Gregory the Great (590–604), when the *Libera* prayer of the Tridentine Mass called on the intercession of Mary, Andrew, Peter, and Paul to bring peace to the faithful through the Eucharist. According to the General Instruction of the Roman Missal, the embolism is said by the presider alone, with the faithful participating in the concluding doxology, "For the kingdom, the power and the glory are yours. . . ." *See also* Lord's Prayer.

embryo, the term used to refer to the human organism in the early stages (first six weeks) of development. Biological science distinguishes the successive stages of development as follows: zygote, blastocyst, embryo, fetus. The term "preembryo" is often used to designate the period prior to implantation (zygote, blastocyst), because the earliest stages of mammalian development primarily involve the development of the nonembryonic trophoblast (feeding layer), which is the precursor of the later placenta and is discarded at birth.

The central question surrounding the embryo is its status and the moral claims it generates. For centuries there was vigorous debate among Catholic theologians about when the developing organism was ensouled or animated. Most theologians argued for delayed animation, a position still held by some contemporary authors. The distinction between the ensouled and nonensouled fetus was largely concerned with the nature of canonical penalties that would be incurred for abortion, since all interruptions of the reproductive process were condemned as immoral. In 1869 Pope Pius IX dropped the reference to "the ensouled fetus" and since that time official formulations are very similar to what is found in the work of Vatican II (1962–65): "From the moment of conception, life must be guarded with the greatest of care" (Pastoral Constitution on the Church in the Modern World, n. 51).

Modern Developments: With the advent of modern reproductive technologies such as *in vitro* fertilization with embryo transfer, the status of the preembryo (the preimplantation period) has assumed new significance and urgency. At stake are issues such as: what may be done to preembryos before transfer; whether all preembryos must be transferred; what may be done to preembryos that are not transferred.

In 1982 Pope John Paul II, in an address to a group of scientists, stated the traditional Catholic evaluation as follows: "I condemn, in the most explicit and formal way, experimental manipulations of the human embryo, since the human being, from conception to death, cannot be exploited for any purpose whatsoever." The Congregation for the Doctrine of the Faith, in its 1987 Instruction on Respect for Human Life in Its Origin and on the Dignity of Procreation (*Donum Vitae*), attributes great importance to genetic uniqueness. On that basis it makes two quite different statements about the embryo: (1) It *is* a person ("How could a human individual not be a human person?"); and (2) It must be treated as a person ("The human being is to be respected and treated as a person from the moment of conception").

Some contemporary theologians argue that, before personhood can be attributed, there is required beyond genetic individuality developmental individuality (developmental singleness). Such individuality is not present prior to the appearance of the primitive streak around the fourteenth day. Before that time the possibility of twinning and recombination of two preembryos indicates that developmental singleness has not been achieved. Authors proposing such a view still may argue for strong protection of the preembryo. *See also* abortion; bioethics; in vitro fertilization; reproductive technologies.

RICHARD A. MCCORMICK

Eminence, the title of honor given to a cardinal, first bestowed by Pope Urban VIII in 1630 and in use to the present day. It is preceded by the words "Your" or "His," and in formal address is conjoined with "Most Reverend," as in "His Eminence the Most Reverend [first name] Cardinal [last name]." *See also* cardinal.

Emmanuel (Heb., *Immanuel,* "God is with us"), name given to the child mentioned in Isaiah's prophecy (Isa 7:14; 8:8) as a sign of God's presence and protection. Matt 1:23 cites Isa 7:14 as a prophecy of Jesus' miraculous conception.

emotions, moral aspects of. Over the past century, Catholic moral theologians, attempting in their reflections to take account of the findings the human sciences, have increasingly turned from the Scholastic language of the passions to a more contemporary and developmentally oriented language of the emotions. Although there are many definitions of emotion within the literatures of psychology and philosophy, most would agree that the emotions are affective responses to real or imagined aspects of individuals and the external world, which typically incorporate sensual and even physiological components in their origin and response. There is wide disagreement as to the moral significance of the emotions, ranging from arguments that the emotions are irrelevant to the moral life, to arguments that there can be no fully moral life if one's emotions are stunted or deformed. Within traditional Catholic moral theology, certain emotions have been seen as being morally problematic, e.g., envy and hatred, and others have been seen as potentially praiseworthy but also subject to corruption, e.g., anger and sexual longing.

enarxis (en'arks-is; Gk., "introduction"), the part of the Byzantine eucharistic liturgy that precedes the Introit (entrance song). The enarxis comprises an opening blessing followed by three litanies, collects, and antiphons, the third of which is the primitive Introit antiphon during which the Minor Introit (Lat., "Little Entrance") procession with the Gospel takes place. This is a relic of the original Introit into the church, before the enarxis began to develop from the stational rites of Constantinople between the fifth and eighth centuries. *See also* Introit.

enchiridion (en-ki-ri'dee-uhn; Gk., *en,* "in"; *cheir,* "hand"), a handbook or manual; in modern usage, any of several books containing selections of documents for theological study. The most famous is Heinrich Denzinger's *Enchiridion Symbolorum* (1854; many subsequent editions) with its anthology of Church councils and papal pronouncements; it was widely used in theological education, especially in seminaries, before Vatican II (1962–65). *See also* Denzinger, Heinrich Joseph; *Enchiridion Symbolorum.*

Enchiridion Symbolorum, also known as "Denzinger," the name of the original editor, a handbook of articles of faith and morals that contains a collection of Latin and Greek theological or historical texts used in ecclesiastical studies. Each entry is coded with a number for referencing in bibliographic citations. This handbook contains the Eastern

Western creeds, documents of the popes from ~ement I through Paul VI's *Instruction to the Pon-~ fical Biblical Commission* (1964), and conciliar de-crees through Vatican I. The material is indexed ac-cording to scriptural references, initial phrases, systematic themes, and alphabetical names and terms.

Originally edited by Heinrich Joseph Denzinger (d. 1883) and published at Wurzburg in 1854, the handbook has passed through thirty-three editions. The most recent was edited by A. Schönmetzer in 1965. The most recent English version is *The Sources of Catholic Dogma,* translated by Roy J. Deferrari from the thirtieth edition (Herder, 1957). *See also* Denzinger, Heinrich Joseph.

enclosure, the separation of members of a con-templative religious order from nonmembers. The 1983 Code of Canon Law stipulates that strict enclo-sure is to be observed by monasteries of nuns totally dedicated to the contemplative life; that is, such nuns may not leave their cloister, nor may others en-ter it, except under very limited circumstances. Monasteries of monks totally dedicated to the con-templative life are not bound by canon law to ob-serve the strict enclosure. Contemplative orders (both monks and nuns) that also engage in some apostolic work may regulate for themselves a modi-fied observance of enclosure. A papal enclosure is a section of a religious house of contemplatives re-stricted to members of the contemplative commu-nity. *See also* cloister; contemplative life; monastery.

Encratites (ehn'krah'tits; Gk., "self-control" or "continence"), a name that Hippolytus (d. ca. 235), Irenaeus (d. ca. 200), and Clement of Alexandria (d. ca. 215) applied loosely to a variety of ascetic groups that were probably distinct. The practices said to characterize them—including renunciation of meat and of wine (even in the Eucharist) and condemna-tion of all sexual relations—were incorporated into a cohesive body of teachings by Tatian, whom Euse-bius and Jerome call the founder of the Encratite sect. *See also* Tatian.

encyclical, a formal pastoral letter (lit., a circular letter) written by, or under the authority of, the pope concerning moral, doctrinal, or disciplinary issues and addressed to the universal Church. With Pope John XXIII (d. 1963) such letters have also been addressed to all persons of goodwill. The mod-ern use of papal encyclicals began with Benedict XIV's *Ubi Primum* (1740) and since the pontificate of Pius IX (1846–78) has become the standard means for exercising the pope's ordinary teaching authority.

Although Catholics are normally obliged to give assent to the moral and doctrinal content of papal encyclicals, three issues are important for reception. First, papal encyclicals possess less authority than dogmatic pronouncements made by the extraordi-nary infallible magisterium, whether by the pope acting in the name of the whole Church or by an ec-umenical council. Second, because encyclicals do not normally contain definitive, or infallible, teach-ing, a Catholic assent remains conditional and some forms of dissent are permitted. Finally, the publica-tion of an encyclical does not imply that the theolog-ical issues examined in the encyclical are now "closed." An encyclical necessarily expresses a par-ticular theological point of view, but it is usually not a definitive assessment.

Although an encyclical may be written by the pope, it is usually the product of a collaborative ef-fort. Ideally, encyclicals should reflect the collegial nature of the Church, respect legitimate theological diversity, uphold the importance of local theology and pastoral practice, and embody the principle that ecclesial authority is always in service to the community for the common good. *See also* doctrine; magisterium.   MICHAEL O'KEEFFE

encyclicals, social, papal letters circulated to the whole world concerning matters of social justice, human rights, and peace. Each of the encyclicals listed hereafter has a separate entry in the encyclo-pedia:

Rerum Novarum (1891), Leo XIII

Quadragesimo Anno (1931), Pius XI

Mater et Magistra (1961), John XXIII

Pacem in Terris (1963), John XXIII

Populorum Progressio (1967), Paul VI

Laborem Exercens (1981), John Paul II

Sollicitudo Rei Socialis (1987), John Paul II

Centesimus Annus (1991), John Paul II.

See also Catholic social teachings.

ends, morality of, the moral status of conse-quences in the determination of rightness or wrong-ness of actions. In Catholic theology the ends or consequences of an action are the good or evil results that follow from the performance of an action. Persons are held morally responsible for all the consequences that are directly intended. In general, ends that are foreseen but unintended are not morally imputed to the agent. However, in some cases evil consequences may be attributed to the agent even if they were not the object of a direct rational choice, e.g., if the agent had a moral obligation to avoid the action in the first place. Other moral theories, e.g., consequentialism and Joseph Fletcher's situation ethics, have proposed that actions are right or wrong only according to the consequences that they produce. Thus, actions are judged to be right or wrong according to whether they do or do not bring about the desired consequences. Because there are factors other than consequences that must be included in judgments of moral rightness or wrongness, e.g., how the ends of actions are brought about, Catholic moral theology denies that the ends in themselves can justify the means.

Engel, Howard R., b. 1930, physician. Having obtained his undergraduate and medical degrees from the University of Chicago (M.D., 1955), he has practiced internal medicine in South Bend, Indiana, since 1960. His patients have included theologians and biblical scholars on the faculty of the University of Notre Dame, including the general editor, several of the associate editors, and various other contributors to this volume. He has been married to Sondra Friend since 1958.

England, Catholicism in. The Church in England, with its primate the archbishop of Canterbury, had a continuous history within the Latin Church from the sixth century, with Augustine of Canterbury's mission from Rome, until Crown and parliament rejected papal authority in the sixteenth century. A small minority of English people, led by Thomas More (d. 1535) and John Fisher (d. 1535), firmly refused to share in this rejection. Centuries of intermittent persecution followed. English Catholicism survived chiefly in more remote areas of the north, especially in Lancashire, Yorkshire, and Durham, but it did so only through the establishment in continental Europe of a remarkable network of seminaries, monasteries, and convents, fed generation after generation by English youth. It was for a long time a poorly organized community, subject to much party strife, but by the eighteenth century, with vicars apostolic ruling four districts, it had become a stable, viable, but almost insignifi-

cant minority. When the French Revolution dro[ve] most of the seminaries and monasteries of the Con[ti]tinent back to England, they were able to settle quietly into country villages. They were no longer a threat to the nation's Protestantism.

Nineteenth-Century Developments: The nineteenth century brought three major developments. The first, Catholic Emancipation in 1829, removed all legal disabilities and was granted chiefly to pacify Ireland, still part of the United Kingdom. This was followed by the reestablishment of dioceses and a hierarchy in 1850, with Nicholas Wiseman as first cardinal-archbishop of Westminster. The second development was Irish immigration produced by overpopulation, underdevelopment, and famine. By the second half of the century, four-fifths of Catholics in England were Irish, mostly gathered in the poorest areas of Liverpool and other cities. The third development was a wave of distinguished converts from Anglicanism brought by the Oxford movement and led by John Henry Newman (d. 1890) and Henry Edward Manning (d. 1892). Newman was unquestionably the greatest English theologian of the century, Manning probably its greatest ecclesiastical statesman. Manning, like most of the converts, emphatically repudiated earlier Anglican attitudes and became a leading Ultramontane whose forcefulness was much felt at the First Vatican Council (1869–70). Newman's theological position remained more ambiguous. Never an Ultramontane and in some ways remarkably liberal and ecumenical, he came under official suspicion for years. A tension between the influence of the two was added to tensions between "Old Catholics" and converts, between English and Irish. While there had always been a sturdy working-class English Catholicism in the north, the strain between English and Irish was often a class one between gentry (whether the squires of old families or Oxford converts) and an urban underclass. Manning's Ultramontanism, however, combined with social radicalism and sympathy for Irish grievances, enabled him as second archbishop of Westminster to contribute to the development of a Church that united the various strands.

The Twentieth Century: In the twentieth century Irish Catholics were increasingly integrated into English society as they moved up the social scale and out of the ghettos. Only in Liverpool did an Irish character to English Catholicism dominate until after the Second World War. Nevertheless, parochial ministry remained heavily dependent upon a flow of priests from Irish seminaries to English dioιes. Against this Irish clerical influence is set the ιensely English character of both the *Venerabile*, ιhe English College in Rome (dating from the sixteenth century) where many of the bishops were trained, and the principal schools run by Benedictines and Jesuits. John Heenan, eighth cardinal-archbishop of Westminster (1963–75), typified the new mix. Born in London of working-class Irish parents, educated by the Jesuits and at the *Venerabile*, he was wholly English in outlook and Ultramontane in theology—Manning's natural heir.

While the Church in England struggled hard to develop a network of schools, it has had no university. Manning tried unsuccessfully to create one in Kensington. After his death Catholics studied increasingly at Oxford, Cambridge, and the modern universities. This has greatly helped to integrate them into the national community not only socially and politically but intellectually as well. Only theology had to be studied at university level abroad until after the Second Vatican Council (1962–65). Catholic journals (especially the influential weekly *The Tablet*) and publishing houses have also been controlled mostly by laypeople. In few countries has intellectual and political control of the Church by the hierarchy been so limited.

The lay character of English Catholicism, its close links with the national universities, and the continued reception of distinguished converts all helped to give it an exceptionally impressive cultural and intellectual character. G. K. Chesterton, Christopher Dawson, Ronald Knox, E. Evans-Pritchard, Christopher Butler, Graham Greene, and Evelyn Waugh are just a few of the outstanding converts received between the First World War and the Second Vatican Council. They and other English Catholics, like Barbara Ward, have had a wide influence both upon the country as a whole and upon the English-speaking world outside Britain. Where they had least influence was upon the Catholic Church in England, at least upon its clergy. After the Modernist crisis of the early years of the twentieth century, particularly affecting English Catholics like George Tyrrell and Baron Von Hügel, the clergy avoided theology and held to a marked pastoral and liturgical conservatism. Only the English Dominicans, centered upon Blackfriars at Oxford, were exceptions.

The 1950s may appear to be the golden age of an English Catholic Church, numerically and institutionally growing, endowed with an array of famous literary names yet theologically conservative. The Second Vatican Council (1962–65) took it almost wholly by surprise and Cardinal Heenan was increasingly bewildered by postconciliar developments.

No church has been more affected by the issues of *Humanae Vitae* (1968) and clerical celibacy. Considerable statistical decline has been experienced since the late 1960s despite the widely respected leadership of Cardinal Basil Hume from 1976. The 1992 election of the first English Master General of the Dominicans in seven hundred years, Timothy Radcliffe, former prior of Blackfriars, like Hume an upper-class Oxford graduate, suggests that English Catholicism may still have unexpected contributions to make, but in the 1990s it is closer in its predicament and problems to other churches of Western Europe than in the past, and its future must depend increasingly upon the way in which wider issues facing Catholicism as a whole are tackled internationally. *See also* Canterbury; Chesterton, Gilbert Keith; Greene, Graham; Manning, Henry Edward; Modernism; Newman, John Henry; Oxford movement; Ultramontanism; Waugh, Evelyn.

Bibliography

Bossy, John. *The English Catholic Community 1570–1850*. London: Darton, Longman and Todd, 1975.

Hastings, Adrian. *A History of English Christianity 1920–1990*. London: SCM Press, and Philadelphia: Trinity Press International, 1991.

Norman, Edward. *Roman Catholicism in England*. Oxford and New York: Oxford University Press, 1986.   *ADRIAN HASTINGS*

England, John, 1786–1842, Irish-born bishop of Charleston, South Carolina (1820–42). Considered liberal by his French ecclesiastical colleagues, England believed that the success of Catholicism in the United States depended upon the Church's ability to adapt to the political and cultural milieu of the people. His accomplishments were numerous: he established a newspaper, *The United States Miscellany* (1823); founded a seminary for native-born clergy (1825); addressed the U.S. Congress (1826); organized a diocesan religious community, the Sisters of Our Lady of Mercy (1829); and created a diocesan constitution that called for lay participation in annual diocesan conventions. England's insistence on episcopal cooperation initiated the councils of Baltimore. *See also* Baltimore, councils of; United States of America, Catholicism in the.

English Martyrs, those executed for their profession of faith from the time of Henry VIII to that of Charles II. For Catholics, the English Martyrs are the approximately 360 people executed for their allegiance to the faith and the pope (and, after 1570, for seeking the overthrow of the English monarch) from 1535 to 1680. The Holy See approved 316 as martyrs in 1886, of whom 42 were canonized as saints (1935, 1970), including John Fisher, Thomas More, and Edmund Campion. Of the martyrs, the overwhelming majority were clerics; 93 were laypeople, including 4 women. The feast day of the Forty Martyrs, canonized in 1970, is October 25; for Fisher and More, June 22. For Anglicans and Protestants, the English Martyrs are the approximately 280 people executed under Henry VIII and Mary Tudor for advocating reform of the Church of England, including William Tyndale and Thomas Cranmer. Many of these martyrs are memorialized in the *Acts and Monuments* of John Foxe (1563), also known as "Foxe's Book of Martyrs." *See also* Forty Martyrs of England and Wales; martyr; martyrdom.

English Mystics, a group of fourteenth-century English spiritual writers known for their wisdom and originality. They were somewhat protected from academic controversy because they wrote in English, whereas most academics of the time wrote in Latin. Each of them was influenced by the eremitical spirit in England and a literary tradition of English spiritual writings. They based their spiritual teaching on personal mystical experience, and most of the time they directed their advice to individuals living outside religious communities. Richard Rolle, a hermit, addressed his poetry and scriptural commentaries to lay devotees or other hermits. Walter Hilton wrote his well-known *Scale of Perfection* for an anchoress. The anchoress Julian of Norwich described the compassion of God for individuals in her *Book of Showings*. The anonymous author of the *Cloud of Unknowing,* who also wrote *The Book of Privy Counselling, The Epistle of Discretion,* and translations of Denis's *Hid Divinity* and *Benjamin Minor,* directed his original works to a young solitary; his description of the true spirit of prayer and the way to progress toward union with God anticipate the teachings of John of the Cross. *See also Cloud of Unknowing, The;* Hilton, Walter; Julian of Norwich, Bl.; Rolle, Richard.

English translations of the Bible. *See* Bible, English translations of the.

enhypostasia (en-hi̲p-ah-stah-see'uh; Gk., "in the person"), an interpretation of the doctrine of Chalcedon regarding the full humanity of Jesus Christ originally proposed by Leontius of Byzantium (d. ca. 543) and later reaffirmed by John Damascus (d. ca. 749). In this view, Jesus' human nature remained personal to himself, although it subsisted in, or was taken up by, the divine *hypostasis* (person) of the Logos. In other words, although rooted in the divine personhood of the Son of God, the personal humanity of Christ was not lost. This teaching stands in opposition to the theory of *anhypostasis* (Gk., "without a hypostasis") associated with Cyril of Alexandria (d. 444), which affirms the full humanity of Jesus but denies Jesus' human *hypostasis,* or personal humanity. Today, advocates of the *enhypostasis* theory maintain that it ensures the full humanity of Jesus better than the *anhypostasis* theory, while its critics claim that the *enhypostasis* theory compromises the unity of the one divine person, Jesus Christ. *See also* Chalcedon, Council of; Christology; hypostatic union; Incarnation, the.

enlightenment, period of, the final period of the catechumenal preparation before the reception of the sacraments of initiation. This final period usually takes place during Lent and through rituals and teaching concentrates on the question of conversion in the lives of the candidates. Conversion is presented as a profound reevaluation of the purpose and goals of life as prompted by the death and Resurrection of Christ (the Paschal Mystery). This process of prayer and reflection is celebrated in rituals that purify and enlighten—the scrutinies and the presentations.

The scrutinies consist of intercessions for the catechumens and prayers of exorcism after the readings and homily of the Mass, celebrated on the third, fourth, and fifth Sundays of Lent. Their aim is gradually to enlighten the conscience of the candidate. The so-called presentations are the handing over of the texts of two prayers central to Christian faith, the creed and the Lord's Prayer. These prayers are also a means of enlightenment. The creed (the Apostles' or the Nicene) is given during the week following the first scrutiny, preferably in the presence of a community, after the homily of the Mass. The prayer is recited by the presider and the assembly. The candidates may give back this prayer during the preparation rites of Holy Saturday. The Lord's Prayer is usually presented during the week following the third scrutiny. The candidates recite this prayer after their Baptism during the celebration of their first Eucharist. *See also* Rite of Christian Initiation of Adults; scrutinies.

ightenment, the, philosophical, political, d scientific movement of eighteenth-century Europe in which the ideas of the great seventeenth-century thinkers—Newton, Bacon, Hobbes, Locke, Descartes, and Spinoza—were carried forward by thinkers such as Diderot, Rousseau, Hume, and Kant, as well as popularized and disseminated in an effort to reform society. Enlightenment thinkers rejected tradition and authority, whether philosophical, political, or religious, and relied instead on human reason. Kant enjoined: "Have courage to use your own reason!" They had great confidence in the capacity of human reason, an optimism generated from the progress of the natural sciences, and hoped to extend this progress by applying reason to all problems of human life. The Enlightenment fostered important advances in science and technology and promoted humanitarian ideals of tolerance, equality, and freedom in social reforms.

Enlightenment figures derived a narrow conception of reason from the natural sciences. This promoted a tendency to view society and the human person in mechanistic and materialistic terms and to deny the validity of any knowledge that is not empirically verifiable, whether metaphysical or religious. This mechanistic and materialistic outlook and skepticism are reflected in Enlightenment thought in a strongly individualistic conception of society in which the state, considered the creation of sovereign individuals, exists to provide only for the minimal material conditions for human existence, that is, protecting one's person and one's property. Similarly, these thinkers accepted religion only as reduced to practical moral guidance, dismissing as groundless affirmations based on revelation and rejecting subservience to any authority other than reason.

For several generations the Catholic Church reacted negatively against Enlightenment values, but a greater openness came with the Second Vatican Council (1962–65). Many now speak of our time as the post-Enlightenment period, in which an uncritical reliance on reason is no longer accepted without question. *See also* faith and reason; philosophy and theology.   JAMES LE GRYS

enneagram (en'nee-uh-gram; Gk., "graph of nine"), a popular method of personality assessment. There are different versions regarding the origins of the system. The two major figures in its modern development are George Ivanovitch Gurdjieff (d. 1949), a Russian spiritual teacher, and Oscar Ichazo (b. 1931), a Bolivian mystic who is said to have brought it to the United States in 1970. American Jesuits played a key role in spreading its use for spiritual direction.

The system posits nine basic personality types with three centers of intelligence: affective, theoretical, and effective. Each personality type is defined by one compulsion: resentment, flattery, vanity, melancholy, stinginess, cowardice, escapism, vengeance, or indolence. Every person has one of these basic patterns and is ruled by its compulsion, defenses, and false self-image until redemption occurs. This brings corresponding virtues, which are the person's strong points.

There are different listings of these virtues in the various presentations of the enneagram system. One rendering includes: the reformer, the helper, the motivator, the artist, the thinker, the loyalist, the generalist, the leader, and the peacemaker.

Some consider the enneagram's focus to be negative, but many of its proponents strongly emphasize its positive characteristics, namely, its capacity to help individuals to understand and transform themselves and to improve and enrich their relationships with others.

Entrance, Great. *See* Great Entrance.

envy. *See* capital sins.

eparch (ep'ahrk; Gk., "ruler"), in Eastern canon law, the bishop who governs an eparchy (diocese) in his own name. He exercises this authority in full communion with the Apostolic See of Rome. Within a patriarchate he is elected by the synod of bishops. The equivalent in the Latin Church is the diocesan bishop. *See also* bishop.

eparchy (ep'ahr-kee; Gk., "territory under rule"), in Eastern canon law, a portion of the People of God under the pastoral care of a particular bishop (eparch). An eparchy constitutes a particular church in which the Church of Christ is present and active in a particular place. It is the equivalent of the diocese in the Latin Church. *See also* diocese.

Ephesus (ef'uh-suhs), a major Greek city on the western coast of Asia Minor and a center of early Christianity. It had a magnificent temple to the Greek goddess Artemis. The Apostle Paul used Ephesus as the center for his activities on his third missionary journey (Acts 19:10; 20:31) and wrote some of his Letters from there. It was the first church addressed in Revelation (1:11; 2:1–7). Ephesus was also traditionally associated with John the Apostle. Ignatius of Antioch (early second century A.D.) addressed one of his letters to the Ephesian church. In A.D. 431 Ephesus was the site of the third ecumenical council that condemned Nestorius, who held that there are two separate persons in Christ, one divine and one human, rather than one divine person. *See also* Ephesus, Council of; Nestorianism.

Ephesus, Council of, the third ecumenical council of the Church (431), summoned to settle a complex controversy between Nestorius and Cyril of Alexandria, but acknowledged today principally as the council that declared Mary the Mother of God (Gk., *Theotokos*). The Council of Ephesus was convoked by the Emperor Theodosius II at the request of Nestorius, whose preaching against use of the title *Theotokos* for Mary had ignited great controversy between Oriental bishops led by John of Antioch in support of Nestorius and the Alexandrian partisans of Cyril. Cyril actually opened the council prior to the arrival of John of Antioch and his adherents and managed to secure the condemnation of the absent Nestorius and his teachings that in Christ there are two persons and that Mary is mother of the human person, not the Mother of God. Upon their arrival at Ephesus, the Antiochian prelates convened their own council and excommunicated and deposed both Cyril and Memnon, the bishop of Ephesus. Of the two rival councils of Ephesus, however, the larger Cyrillian assembly won the approval of the Apostolic See and met again for a total of seven sessions, during which Nestorianism was officially condemned, John of Antioch was excommunicated, and the Nicene-Constantinopolitan Creed was established as the only acceptable formula of faith. Two years after the council's stormy inception, Cyril and John of Antioch forged an agreement whereby the Antiochians confessed that Mary is *Theotokos* and that two natures are distinguished in Christ but are united in one person. Cyril, on his part, agreed to refrain from further use of his contested formula about "the one nature of the Incarnate Word," and made no further mention of the anathemas against Nestorius. Ultimately, the Council of Chalcedon (451) affirmed adherence to the ordinances and the doctrinal declarations of that Council of Ephesus that had been under the guidance of Pope Celestine and Cyril of Alexandria.

Precisely what declarations were made by the Cyrillian council is still debated, as is the corresponding doctrinal significance of the Council of Ephesus. But as a result of the later agreements between John and Cyril, and since Cyril had expressly claimed to have formulated the faith of Nicaea at the first session of Ephesus, historians and theologians have tended to settle upon the following as the most noteworthy formulations of the Council of Ephesus: The council affirmed that within the one Christ, both Son of God and Son of Man two natures are conjoined without the suppression of either the divinity or humanity of Christ. Moreover, because Christians affirm not that the Word is united to a human nature but rather that the Word has become flesh, they rightly declare that the one Christ was born of Mary, suffered and died for us, and is worshiped as Lord. Consequently, the divine maternity of Mary is understood as concomitant to the mystery of the hypostatic union. Because the Council of Chalcedon (451) went further to clarify Christological terminology for this union, the Council of Ephesus is traditionally associated almost exclusively with the definition of Mary as Mother of God. *See also* Christology; Incarnation, the; Jesus Christ; Nestorianism; *Theotokos*.   JANICE POORMAN

Ephesus, Robber Council of, also known as Latrocinium, a council held in Ephesus in 449 to deal with difficulties related to the condemnation of Eutyches, head of a large monastery in Constantinople. Eutyches' sharp denunciation of Nestorianism, a heresy that held that there are two persons in Jesus Christ, one human and one divine, was perceived by many to be equally, but oppositely, heretical. He was accused of Monophysitism, a heresy that denied that Jesus had a human nature, and was condemned by Flavian, archbishop of Constantinople, at the Synod of Constantinople in November 448 and was also deposed from the headship of his monastery. In response, he and his supporters called for a Council at Ephesus in August 449. Pope Leo I was present by virtue of his *Tome* to Flavian, as were the bishops who had condemned Eutyches the year before, but both were suppressed by the conciliar president, Dioscorus. When Flavian and the bishops protested, they were forcibly removed by soldiers. The first session thus ended with Eutyches' reinstatement. A second session later in the month dismissed other Nestorian bishops and condemned the doctrinal compromise struck by Cyril of Alexandria and John of Antioch in 433. In September, Pope Leo condemned the decisions of this *latrocinium* (Lat.),

...ber council." *See also* Ephesus, Council of; Mono-...sitism; Nestorianism.

Ephraem the Syrian, St., ca. 306–73, poet, theologian, and Doctor of the Church. A lay Christian, he founded a theological school at Nisibis under the auspices of Jacob. Here he taught until the city was ceded to the Sassanids in 363. He continued his composition and instruction in Edessa until his death.

Ephraem draws heavily from Jewish exegetical traditions in developing a complex matrix of symbols centering upon Christ. The Cross and paradise are intertwined in a manner distinct from Western concepts of "the Fall." Eve is counterbalanced by Mary, Adam by Christ, and the expulsion from paradise by a future readmission. Current feast day: June 18 (historically July 9 or February 1).

epiclesis (ep-ik'lay'sis; Gk., "calling down upon," "invocation"), in the liturgy, the prayer to God the Father for the coming of the Holy Spirit (or, rarely, the Word), especially the prayer in the anaphora (the central eucharistic prayer) for the Spirit to be sent (or to come) to sanctify the gifts of bread and wine, or the similar invocation for the blessing of the waters of Baptism. The eucharistic epiclesis became a source of dispute between Greeks and Latins in the fourteenth century when the Latin Scholastic theory of instantaneous transubstantiation of the substance of the bread and wine into the body and blood of Christ at the moment of consecration led to determining a specific "moment of consecration" in the liturgy. In the 1990s, ecumenical theologians avoid attempts to locate a "moment of consecration" at either the epiclesis or Words of Institution ("This is my body.... This ... is ... my blood" from 1 Cor 11:24–25), preferring to consider the entire Prayer over the Gifts, and not one of its isolated moments, as the consecratory prayer. *See also* Eucharistic Prayer.

epigonation (eh-pig-uh-nah'tee-awn; Gk., "on the knee"), a lozenge-shaped Byzantine liturgical insignia of stiffened vestment cloth, decorated with a cross, and measuring about one foot. It is worn on the right side of the body at knee-level, hanging from a tape around the neck or from the cincture, the rope worn around the midriff like a belt. Restricted to bishops at least until the fourteenth century, it is now also worn by the higher ranks of presbyters (priests) such as hegumens, archpriests, and archimandrites.

epigonation

Epigonation

epikeia (ep-ee-ki̯'ah; Gk., *epieikes*, "act of justice"; Lat., *aequitas*, "equity"), also rendered as *epicheia* and *epieikeia*, an act of justice whereby, for the sake of the common good and the good of individuals, the intention of a law in a given instance is recognized as a higher norm of moral reasoning and interpretation than the letter of the law. A moral concept taken over from Aristotle (d. 322 B.C.), especially by Thomas Aquinas (d. 1274) and Francisco de Suarez (d. 1617), *epikeia* means that a law need not be obeyed when its observance would be detrimental to the common good or the good of individuals. Its use does not imply that the law itself is invalid or that it can be disregarded at will. *Epikeia* is a principle of moral reasoning that is only applicable in specific instances under circumstances of necessity or urgency. *Epikeia* is opposed to legalism, which makes the observance of the letter of the law always primary, even over the demands of justice. *See also* canon law, interpretation of; justice; legalism; moral theology.

epimanikia (ep-ee-mahn-ih'kee-ah; Gk., "cuff," lit., "on the sleeves"), Byzantine liturgical vestment, a set of detachable cuffs of stiffened vestment material. Now worn by deacons, priests, and bishops, their use was restricted to bishops at least until the late twelfth century.

Epiphanius of Salamis, St. (ep-i-fay'nee-uhs), ca. 315–403, bishop of Salamis (365–403), known mainly for his *Panarion,* an attempt to refute all known heresies, which remains an important historical source. He figured prominently in the fourth-century campaign against Origenism, although he was not sympathetic to Theophilus's attempt to depose John Chrysostom. Feast day: May 12. *See also* heresy; Origenism.

Epiphany (Gk., "the manifestation"), a feast, probably of Eastern origin, celebrated on January 6. Where it is not observed as a holy day of obligation, it has been assigned to the Sunday occurring between January 2 and January 8. This feast, which was designed to supplant the pagan celebration of the winter solstice, celebrated in the East on January 6, may be an older celebration of the birth of Christ than that of December 25. When the feast of Christmas was adopted by the Eastern churches in the fourth century with an emphasis on the birth of Christ, their celebration of Epiphany then changed its focus to the baptism of Christ with a commemoration of the adoration of the three wise men. The Western Church seems to have accepted the feast of Epiphany from the church in Gaul by the fifth century, and the three themes of the adoration of the wise men, the baptism of Christ, and his first miracle at Cana seem to have been adopted in whole or in part by the various local churches. In the current liturgical calendar, the churches of the East and West celebrate the birth of Christ on December 25, with the East also commemorating the adoration of the three wise men. The theme of Epiphany in the East is the baptism of Christ, and in the West, the adoration of the newborn Jesus by the wise men.

episcopacy (Gk., *episkopos,* "overseer"), the highest level, or fullness, of the sacrament of Holy Orders, also known as the episcopate. Those ordained to the episcopacy are called bishops. The term denotes the body of bishops as well as the ecclesiastical system of governance in which bishops exercise pastoral authority over their own dioceses and over the whole Church in union with the Bishop of Rome.

"The order of bishops is the successor to the college of the apostles in teaching authority and pastoral rule. . . . Together with its head, . . . the episcopal order is the subject of supreme and full power over the universal Church" (Dogmatic Constitution the Church, n. 22). *See also* bishop.

Episcopal Church, formerly known as the Protestant Episcopal Church in the U.S.A.; part of the worldwide Anglican communion. It currently has about two and a half million baptized members. The first Anglican church was built at Jamestown, Virginia, in 1607, and other congregations were gradually established on the American continent, but it was only after the American Revolution that the Episcopal Church became a fully autonomous body within the Anglican communion. Its first bishop, Samuel Seabury, received his consecration from bishops of the Episcopal Church in Scotland in 1784, and other bishops were consecrated in England in 1787 and 1790. The first General Convention of the Church was held in 1789, at which a constitution and canons were drawn up and a prayer book issued. General Convention, held every three years, continues to be the supreme governing body of the Church. It consists of a House of Bishops, in which all the bishops of the Church sit, and a House of Deputies, composed of elected representatives of the clergy and laity from each diocese. Either house may initiate legislation, and all acts of the convention require adoption in both houses.

All the varieties of theological positions and ecclesiastical parties that exist in the Church of England are also found in the Episcopal Church: there are "high church" or Anglo-Catholic Episcopalians whose doctrinal stance and liturgical style closely mirror those of the Roman Catholic Church; there are "low church" or evangelical Episcopalians who have a close affinity with the Protestant churches; there are those who are very conservative theologically (among them the group known as the Episcopal Synod of America); and there are those so radical that severe strains develop within the church over theological and ethical issues from time to time. There are, however, also some notable differences from the Church of England. Partly because of the freedom from state control and partly because of the absence of a resident episcopate in its early history, local congregations have much greater autonomy and power in the Episcopal Church; and because there are proportionately fewer Episcopalians at the Protestant end of the theological spectrum, they exercise much less influence on the church's life than is the case in England. Above all, the American context has encouraged the Episcopal Church to be less bound by tradition and more open to change and

...iovation than other parts of the Anglican com-...union. Thus, it is not surprising that practices ...uch as the ordination of women and the communion of infants first gained firm hold within Anglicanism in the United States. Beside its involvement in the worldwide Anglican ecumenical dialogues with other churches (Lutheran, Orthodox, Reformed, and Roman Catholic), the Episcopal Church has entered into an agreement of "interim eucharistic sharing" with the Evangelical Lutheran Church in America. *See also* Anglicanism.　PAUL F. BRADSHAW

episcopal college. *See* bishops, college of.

episcopal conference, the periodic assembly of the bishops of a nation or a region for the purpose of addressing pastoral issues affecting those nations or regions. National conferences of bishops originated in Europe after 1848 when Pope Pius IX fled Rome in disguise, under pressure from the forces of Italian nationalism. They were in some cases hindered; they were not taken into consideration in canon law (1917). The conference of bishops as an important institution for the Church first gained formal recognition at Vatican II, where their establishment was recommended for the entire Church (Dogmatic Constitution on the Church, n. 22; Decree on the Bishops' Pastoral Office in the Church, nn. 37, 38). In the *motu proprio* (papal document) *Ecclesiae Sanctae* (1966) of Paul VI and in the new code of canon law (1983) they are placed in the hierarchy between the individual bishops of dioceses and the Apostolic See.

Nevertheless, the council and the postconciliar codification did not adopt the proposal of respected conciliar theologians to give to the conference of bishops general jurisdiction for all questions that pertain to a region with a unified ecclesial structure. These theologians argue that the conference of bishops will become an effective balancing mechanism between tendencies toward overcentralizing the Church on the one side and extreme particularizing of pastoral activity on the other. Theologically speaking, based on the principle of collegiality, an individual bishop could be bound by the resolutions of the majority of bishops in a region. Objections to this proposal were raised at the Second Vatican Council. It was feared that the binding resolutions of a conference of bishops would limit both the authority of a bishop in his diocese—an authority the council wanted to strengthen—and also the rights of the pope. Above the bishop stands *iure divino*

(Lat., "according to divine decree") only the highest authority, the pope. Talk about collegial acts in the strict sense could not be applied to a conference of bishops, since such acts can be undertaken only by the college of bishops as a whole.

Pastoral Implications: Practical considerations addressed these basic objections. Regional legislation, which is seldom necessary, is better left to the episcopal conferences. Therefore, the current custom that any decisions taken by the bishops should come about only through a consensus will continue. The council has left open the fundamental question of the theological status of a conference of bishops. The codification follows the middle course. Instead of being granted general authority over pastoral and doctrinal matters, the conference of bishops was assigned various specific areas of authority. Binding resolutions in these areas of authority require a two-thirds majority of the bishops of a conference. Outside of these areas of authority, a joint action requires the agreement of all bishops.

According to the 1983 Code of Canon Law (cans. 447–59) a conference of bishops is an association of the bishops of a nation or of a definite region. Thus, alongside national conferences of bishops are also continental conferences of bishops, whose members include the bishops of dioceses and also all bishops who exercise an ecclesiastical office in the territory. A permanent board and a general secretariat are authorized to handle the conference's ongoing work; the conference elects a president.

After Vatican II: Since Vatican II, it has become clear that the general recognition of the conference of bishops by the council has proven to be a farsighted reform. Conferences of bishops have undeniably displayed their value in the areas of pastoral coordination and the presence of the Church in society. The pastoral letters of some conferences of bishops have received worldwide respect. Synods of bishops have repeatedly recommended that the theological status of the conference of bishops now be clarified. A working paper on this topic by the Roman Curia of 1988 met criticism from bishops and theologians. It repeated the objections presented at the council and denied that the conference of bishops has teaching authority.

More recent theological discussion has recovered the original intention of the council, which wanted to make connections between the conference of bishops and the institution of the patriarchs (Dogmatic Constitution on the Church, n. 22). The ancient Church developed a threefold ecclesial structure: the local churches, the regional community of the local churches, and the whole Church. Only in this form can the basic structure of the Church realize itself as the community of churches (Lat., *communio ecclesiarum*). The particular church needs the community of the neighboring dioceses of a nation or of a region in order to assume its mission in its social context. The whole Church needs the regional community of the Church in order to make possible catholic diversity. *See also* bishop; collegiality; Decree on the Bishops' Pastoral Office in the Church; National Conference of Catholic Bishops.

HERMAN J. POTTMEYER

episcopal vicar, office within a diocese held by a priest who functions as the bishop's vicar for people within a geographical segment of a diocese or for a specified group of the faithful, e.g., Hispanics. The episcopal vicar has, for such a group, authority comparable to that of a vicar general, i.e., he may perform certain acts of executive power in the diocesan bishop's name. He is considered a local ordinary. Vatican II called for the establishment of this office (Decree on the Bishops' Pastoral Office in the Church, n. 27). *See also* vicar general.

epistle. *See* letter.

epitaphios (ep-ee-tah'fee-aws; Gk., "funerary," lit., "on the tomb"), a large, rectangular Byzantine liturgical cloth bearing an image that depicts the scene of the deposition from the Cross and burial of the dead body of Jesus. The epitaphios is carried in solemn procession during Good Friday Matins and Vespers, and placed on a "tomb" in the center of the church for veneration until Holy Saturday Compline. Both the epitaphios and its Good Friday processional use originate in the "aer" or great veil carried in the Great Entrance procession and used to cover the eucharistic gifts after their deposition on the altar.

epitrachelion (ep-ee-trah-kay'lee-awn; Gk., "on the neck"), Byzantine-rite liturgical stole worn by priests and bishops. Like the Western stole, it consists of a long band of cloth worn around the neck; the two bands that come down over the breast of the minister do not hang free but are sewn or buttoned together. *See also* stole.

equality, in moral theology, the condition of parity between persons or groups. Natural equality is based on inherent qualities of the human and is presumed in the use of "human nature" in moral argument. Political and social equality are terms that usually include a prescriptive content requiring, e.g., equal treatment under the law or mutual acceptance among members of society. The concern of Christian social ethics for the common good and supportive reciprocal relationships among persons assumes the equality of persons and leads to the development of principles of distributive and commutative justice that regulate relations among persons and things. *See also* common good.

equiprobabilism, an approach to moral decision making employed by Alphonsus Liguori (d. 1787) whereby an opinion favoring freedom from obligation had to be "equally probable" before it could be followed in practice. Catholic moral theology in the eighteenth century struggled with two extremes. On the one hand, there were certain laxist interpretations of moral laws that allowed applications without any genuine support in sound moral reasoning. On the other hand, a seventeenth-century reaction, particularly among the Jansenists, held to a rigorist position known as probabiliorism, whereby only the more probable opinion on a controverted issue could legitimately be followed. In confronting the extremes of rigorist legalism and laxist permissiveness, Alphonsus Liguori sought to protect the freedom of conscience as a moral certainty where a specific law proved doubtful. Alphonsus's equiprobabilism, by allowing a person to avoid the seeming obligation of a law only on condition that the contrary position was at least as probable, did not then succumb to permissive interpretations of the law. *See also* probabiliorism; probabilism.

Erasmus, Desiderius, also known as Erasmus of Rotterdam, 1466–1536, Dutch scholar, author, and critic central to the emergence of Christian Humanism and to both Protestant and Catholic Reformations. Educated in humanist fashion by the Brethren of the Common Life at Deventer and steeped in the Devotio Moderna, Erasmus developed a lifelong love of classical Latin and Greek language and literature. He adopted and then abandoned monasticism after six years (1492). He attended the Collège de Montaigu in Paris, but left in 1494, disenchanted with Scholastic theology and the lack of intellectual challenge.

While visiting England in 1499, Erasmus underwent a spiritual and intellectual transformation

Desiderius Erasmus, sixteenth-century Christian humanist and scholar, who, in spite of his own criticisms of the Catholic Church, remained faithful to it to the end; sixteenth-century painting by Hans Holbein the Elder.

influenced by Thomas More and John Colet. They convinced him of the possibilities for employing his literary gifts in the service of Christian piety and reform, which could be furthered more through humanist study of the Bible and early Church Fathers than by Scholastic debates. He wrote several books after his return to the Continent, including the *Enchiridion Militis Christiani* (*Handbook of the Christian Soldier,* 1503, on Christian virtues). On a subsequent trip to England (1509), Erasmus produced his most famous work, *The Praise of Folly.* While appearing frivolous and ambiguous, this book was in fact an eloquent testimony to reason, humaneness, and Christian love.

In 1514 Erasmus returned to Basel, Switzerland, from Cambridge and produced critical editions of St. Jerome, Seneca, and Plutarch. He also published a Greek and Latin version of the NT, *Novum Instrumentum Omne* (1516), translating critical Greek terms differently from the standard medieval Vulgate. Along with the *Enchiridion,* Erasmus's biblical edition proved influential with early Protestant Reformers, especially Ulrich Zwingli and Martin Butzer, who were also struck by his attacks on formalism and Scholasticism and his appeal to an ancient biblical piety.

Despite influencing the early Reformers, Eras-

mus himself remained a devout Catholic, opposed the Reformation, and challenged Luther on free will and predestination in *On the Freedom of the Will* (*De Libero Arbitrio,* 1524). He attempted unsuccessfully to urge toleration in an atmosphere of growing religious violence, which led both Protestants and Catholics to accuse him of cowardice. Counter-reformers especially viewed Erasmus as a cause of the Protestant revolt, eventually placing his work on the Index of Forbidden Books.

Forced to leave Basel in 1529 because of the Reformation there, Erasmus settled in Catholic Freiburg, where he continued to work, editing the Church Fathers. He returned to Basel in 1535 and died there in 1536.

A renowned literary figure of the sixteenth century, Erasmus greatly influenced humanists and religious reformers alike in three different areas. First, his satires and colloquies combined with his great works the *Enchiridion* and *Praise of Folly* to call for a constructive, pious reform of life and Church, effective among both Protestants and Catholics. Second, his editions of early Christian writings and especially the NT laid the groundwork for exegesis and theology based on historically authentic texts. Finally, Erasmus used the new printing press more creatively than most of his contemporaries to establish a wide audience. *See also* Counter-Reformation/Catholic Reformation; Devotio Moderna; humanism, Catholic; Reformation, the.   *W. DAVID MYERS*

Erastianism, the authority of the state over all ecclesiastical jurisdiction, named after Thomas Erastus (1524–83), a Swiss professor of medicine at the University of Heidelberg from 1558 who was made the elector Frederick's personal physician and a member of his council. Opposing efforts to institute Calvin's polity in the Palatinate, he argued instead for the polity of Zwinglian Zurich, in which the civil authority had ultimate jurisdiction over civil and ecclesiastical discipline and punishment. His work in defense of this position, the *Explicatio Gravissimae Quaestionis* (*An Explication of a Most Serious Question*) was published in London in 1589, influencing Richard Hooker's *Treatise on the Laws of Ecclesiastical Polity* (1594–97) and the Westminster Confession. *See also* Church and state.

eremitic life. *See* hermit.

Eric IX, St., d. 1160, king and, by tradition, patron saint of Sweden. He supported Christian evangelization in his realm, but was killed by rebelling Swedish nobles in league with Danish invaders. He was never formally canonized.

Eriugena, John Scotus (air-ee-yoo'jah-nuh), ca. 810–ca. 877, Carolingian theologian. Arriving at the court of Emperor Charles the Bald ca. 845, Eriugena—the word means "Irish born"—taught in the palace school, writing a commentary on the liberal arts and a treatise on single predestination directed against Gottschalk of Orbais. About 860, the emperor asked Eriugena to prepare a translation of the works of Pseudo-Dionysius, replacing that made earlier by Abbot Hilduin of St. Denis. Eriugena followed this with other translations from the Greek.

Eriugena's greatest work is the dialogue *Periphyseon* or *De Divisione Naturae* ("On the Division of Nature"), composed ca. 862–64. *Periphyseon* stresses God's transcendence of all categories of being but also pictures God as the essence of all created beings. Condemned as pantheistic, the book was ordered burned in 1225 and placed on the Index of Forbidden Books when printed in 1681.

error [canon law], in canon law an individual's incorrect judgment regarding the meaning of the law or a mistake concerning the facts of the matter. In cases of error the law does not lose its force, and it is possible that such a mistake may result in an act that is canonically invalid (can. 15.1). For example, a priest thinks he does not need to obtain faculties to witness a marriage when, in fact, he does. The priest's acting on his error may result in a marriage considered canonically invalid. If the Church's legal system—or any legal system—were ordinarily to depend on the knowledge or beliefs of persons under the law, there would be no end to uncertainties and litigation, and the whole Church would suffer. Error must be distinguished, however, from cases of doubt in which the law does not bind, and from ignorance, which is a lack of knowledge altogether. *See also* doubt [canon law]; ignorance [canon law].

Error has no rights, a formula widely in use during the pre–Vatican II and conciliar debates over religious liberty and Church and state to indicate that, where there is a sufficient Catholic majority (as in Spain during the Franco regime), the state has the obligation of suppressing all forms of non-Catholic worship and religious practice. This is so, it was argued, because the rights of an erroneous conscience, even if sincere, cannot be considered equal to the rights of a conscience that is both sincere correct. The Second Vatican Council (1962–65) jected this thinking in its Declaration on Religio Freedom (n. 3). *See also* religious liberty.

eschatology, individual (Gk., *eschatos,* "last," "farthest"), the study of the final condition of individual human beings. Eschatology means literally the study of last things. Eschatological statements at first glance seem to be direct affirmations about the absolute future, whether of individual human beings or of the human race and the whole world. Traditionally, one speaks about death, divine judgment, purgatory, the resurrection of the body, eternal life, the Second Coming of Christ, the heavenly Jerusalem, the end of the world, the new heavens and the new earth, and hell.

However, Karl Rahner (d. 1984), in *Foundations of Christian Faith,* has suggested that eschatological statements are really about the present as it tends toward the future. Rahner's view stands in contrast to the approach, sustained by Jürgen Moltmann in *Theology of Hope,* that sees the eschaton breaking into time from the future, contradicting all temporal achievement, and bearing no relation to events that transpire in history, except to the Cross and Resurrection of Jesus.

Rahner contends that the dynamism of grace operating within the individual points ahead to death, judgment, purgatory, resurrection, and eternal life. Hell is the contradiction of this dynamism.

Dynamism of Grace: Death, of course, in itself is a natural event. But grace is working within human beings now to transform this natural event into a supernatural event wherein human beings ratify the meaning of their whole lives by committing themselves irrevocably to God. However, it is possible for an individual to resist grace throughout life and at death to turn oneself irrevocably away from God. It is not known whether anyone ever does this.

This irrevocable commitment for or against God coincides with a divine judgment that makes real what the individual has definitively chosen. This is the particular judgment.

Present within the dynamism of grace is the call to repentance and purification. As it operates within the decisive moment of death it brings about perfect repentance and purification from every sinful tie. Residual selfishness causes the person to experience this purification as a kind of suffering that is joyfully embraced. This is purgatory.

The grace of the Spirit now dwelling in our mor-

bodies is already the seed of the resurrection. It a participation in divine life, whose full effect is to transform the mortality of our flesh into the immortality of a glorified body after the model of the Risen Christ (1 Cor 15:49, 53).

Finally, the eternal life of Beatific Vision, unfailing love, and unselfish joy is the final and unending fruit of the present participation in divine life through grace.

There is no dynamism toward hell or eternal punishment. But human self-centeredness can lead one to resist the dynamism of grace and to so center one's life in oneself that one is cut off from God as the last end. Such a person would be lost and would experience the frustration of the fundamental orientation toward God as radical and unending suffering. *See also* Beatific Vision; eternal life; heaven; hell; judgment, particular; last things; purgatory.

JOHN H. WRIGHT

eschatology, universal (Gk., *eschatos,* "last," "farthest"), the study of the final state of the universe, the goal toward which God is moving all creation. Like individual eschatology, universal eschatology does not make statements directly about the future, but about the power now at work in the world to bring about God's intended goal.

This power is found in the Risen Christ, who himself has passed to the end state. Underlying the consummating activity of Christ is the evolutionary movement of the universe. This is the natural foundation that his grace elevates and brings to perfection. Matter possesses the inherent tendency to bring forth life, sentience, intelligence, and freedom under the personalizing presence of God. God intends this development in order to bring creatures into personal relationship with God. This movement is summed up in Christ, through whom God "created the worlds" and who "sustains all things by his powerful word" (Heb 1:2, 3). The Risen Christ, by acting within the universe and communicating the Holy Spirit, shares with the world, especially with intelligent creatures, his access to the Father. This is God's "plan for the fullness of time, to gather up all things in him, things in heaven and things on earth" (Eph 1:10).

The present activity of Christ is to "reign until he has put all his enemies under his feet" (1 Cor 15:25). He looks forward to the time of his Parousia or Second Coming, when he will fully exercise "the power that also enables him to make all things subject to himself" (Phil 3:21).

The Final Events: This final exercise of power will manifest itself first in the resurrection of the dead. This is not simply restoration to life, but an act conforming us to Christ who "will transform the body of our humiliation that it may be conformed to the body of his glory" (Phil 3:21).

Sinners also will be raised, "to shame and everlasting contempt" (Dan 12:2; see also John 5:29). For the action of Christ in raising the dead is also the act of general judgment (Matt 25:31–46). This judgment is not just a way of letting everyone know how everyone else has done. It is an effective divine action exercised by the Son of God to realize in the world what God has intended from the beginning. While it is essentially a faithful and effective response to the love of those who have done good, it is also a response ratifying the self-chosen separation from God of those who have done evil.

The transformation of the present world into the new heaven and the new earth (Rev 21:1) could conceivably take place when the physical universe collapses in upon itself in a reversal of the Big Bang. The whole nature of matter could be transformed to become fully subject to spirit. At this moment Christ "hands over the kingdom to God the Father . . . so that God may be all in all" (1 Cor 15:24, 28). *See also* heaven; hell; judgment, general; kingdom of God [in the Bible]; kingdom of God [theology of]; last things; purgatory.

JOHN H. WRIGHT

espousals, spiritual. *See* marriage, spiritual.

essence (Lat., *essentia,* Gk., *ousia,* "what something is"), that which makes something the kind of thing it is. The term came into Christian theological usage (in its Greek form) in the attempt to understand how Jesus could have a human and a divine essence, yet not be two distinct persons. *See also* homoousios; Incarnation, the.

Essenes (es-seens'), a Jewish party, like the Pharisees and Sadducees, that flourished in Palestine from about the mid-second century B.C. to the defeat by the Romans, ca. A.D. 70. Descriptions of the group are found in first-century authors, both Jewish (Philo, Josephus) and Roman (Pliny), but not in the NT, the Mishnah, or the Talmud. The Essenes are described as devoted to the Torah, ascetic, highly organized in structure, holding property in common, and believing in providence and the immortality of the soul (but not necessarily bodily resurrection). They lived in towns throughout Judea.

Pliny narrates that on the northwest shore of the Dead Sea there was a settlement of Essenes, which many scholars think included the scribes of the Qumran scrolls. *See also* Dead Sea Scrolls; Qumran.

Estonia, Catholicism in. *See* Baltic countries, Catholicism in the.

Eternal City, a title for the city of Rome reflecting the widespread belief that the end of Rome would mean the end of the world. Because the pope is the Bishop of Rome, the term appears frequently in Church prose, since it is believed that the Church will last until the end of time. *See also* Rome.

eternal life, a participation in the life of God, which begins in the present and comes to fullness beyond death. It is not just unending existence, which even the damned would have. The expression "eternal life" first appears in late OT literature. The prophecy of Daniel says of the final consummation: "Many of those who sleep in the dust of the earth shall awake, some to everlasting life, and some to shame and everlasting contempt" (Dan 12:2; see also Wis 5:15; 2 Macc 7:9).

At the time of Christ, the idea of eternal life was current in Jewish religious thought. A young man asked Jesus: "Good Teacher, what must I do to inherit eternal life?" (Mark 10:17). Jesus himself used the expression in his own teaching, e.g., "the righteous [will go away] into eternal life" (Matt 25:46). In Johannine literature eternal life is a central theme: "For God so loved the world that he gave his only Son, so that everyone who believes in him may not perish but may have eternal life" (John 3:16).

It is not enough to say that in eternal life the mind finally sees all truth and the will possesses all good. Eternal life essentially is living in personal relationship with God through the work of Jesus Christ and the gift of the Holy Spirit. This relationship begins in the graced activity of the present life and unfolds hereafter. Faith, hope, and love become intuitive vision, unselfish joy, and unfailing love.

The face-to-face vision of God in eternal life (1 Cor 13:12; Rev 22:4; 1 John 3:2) is the future perfection of the personal knowledge of God that has begun in faith. In John's Gospel, Jesus likens the union of knowledge between him and his followers to the union between him and the Father: "I know my own and my own know me, just as the Father knows me and I know the Father" (John 10:14b–15a). Indeed,

Jesus in prayer describes eternal life as knowing Father, "the only true God, and Jesus Christ who you have sent" (John 17:3).

The unselfish joy of the future (Matt 25:23; John 17:13; Rom 8:18) is the transformation of our present hope and joyful confidence of one day possessing God. Already human beings may taste the peace that "surpasses all understanding" (Phil 4:7) and know the joy that no one can take from them (John 16:22).

The unfailing love of heaven (1 Cor 13:8; Rom 8:39; John 17:23) is the eternal realization of a present loving union with God. Paul sees the special excellence of love in this, that whereas other charismatic gifts, like prophecy, speaking in tongues, and knowledge, pass away, "love never ends" (1 Cor 13:8). Such persons are already grasped and transformed by the love of God that will bring them into the fullness of eternal life (Eph 2:4–7). *See also* Beatific Vision; heaven; immortality.   JOHN H. WRIGHT

eternity, an attribute of God, denoting God's timelessness. Time is defined in relation to change (Aristotle, *Physics* 4.12). Words that depend on the notion of time, like "before" and "after," have meaning only in relation to a being that has changed. Simply removing a beginning and an end from time does not alter the essence of time since unending change is still change (sempiternity). Eternity, then, does not mean a time with no beginning and no end. Eternity as timelessness must involve no change, i.e., immutability.

Immutability refers to God's perfection. God neither grows nor deteriorates in knowledge and goodness. God enjoys the fullness of life "always." Since God is unchanging in perfection, God is eternal. The human hope for eternity is the hope to share in God's fullness of life. *See also* God.

Ethelbert, St., d. 616, king of Kent from ca. 560 to 616 and first Christian king in England, converted by his Frankish wife, Bertha, and baptized ca. 601. Through her influence he had also received the mission of Augustine of Canterbury, sent to England by Pope Gregory the Great in 597. Feast day: February 25. *See also* England, Catholicism in.

Etheria (eth-ee'ree-ah). *See* Egeria, Pilgrimage of.

ethics, Christian, those moral norms that are thought to be distinctive of Christianity; the aca-nic discipline that reflects on morality from the erspective of Christian belief. Some scholars draw a distinction between Christian ethics, which they associate with Protestant traditions, and moral theology, which is related to the Catholic and Anglican traditions. This distinction reflects the historical lack of contact among Protestant, Catholic, and Anglican scholars, which led in the past to the discussion of quite different problematics among scholars who were concerned with the moral life from a Christian perspective. It also reflects the distinctive influence of the practice of the sacrament of Penance (now Reconciliation) on Catholic, and to a lesser extent Anglican, moral thought. But the influence of the ecumenical movement, and the decline of the practice of individual confession, have led to a convergence of the concerns and approaches of Christian ethicists and moral theologians today. *See also* moral theology.

Ethiopian Catholic Church, the ecclesiastical community of Ethiopian-rite Catholics who are in communion with Rome. It is the Catholic counterpart to the Ethiopian Orthodox Church, which separated itself from full communion with Rome when it rejected the teaching of the Council of Chalcedon (451) that in Christ there are two natures, human and divine, and not only a single divine nature, as the Monophysites held.

After some early unsuccessful missionary activity by Dominican friars, in the sixteenth century the Portuguese Jesuits became involved in a major effort to bring the Ethiopian Church into union with Rome.

Largely through the efforts of Father Peter Paez, the Ethiopian negus (king) Susenyos became Catholic and declared his new faith the state religion in 1622. In 1623, Pope Gregory XV appointed another Portuguese Jesuit, Affonso Mendez, as Ethiopian patriarch. Formal union of the two churches was proclaimed when Mendez arrived in Ethiopia in 1626.

However, Mendez imposed a series of latinizations on the Ethiopian liturgy, customs, and discipline, which Susenyos then tried to enforce with cruelty and bloodshed. Susenyos died in 1632, and his successor was hostile to the union. In 1636 Mendez was expelled, the union was dissolved, and many Catholic missionaries were put to death. The country was closed to Catholic missionary activity for two hundred years.

In 1839 limited activity was resumed by the La-

zarists and Capuchins, but public hostility was still very strong. It was only with the accession of King Menelik II to the throne in 1889 that Catholic missionaries could again work freely in the country. Their activity expanded in Ethiopia during the Italian occupation from 1935 to 1941, as it had earlier in Eritrea, which had been under Italian control since 1889.

The present ecclesiastical structure of the Ethiopian Catholic Church dates from 1961, when a metropolitan see was established at Addis Ababa, with suffragan dioceses in Asmara and Adigrat. Most Ethiopian Catholics, numbering in 1992 about 125,000, live in Addis Ababa and Asmara.

The church maintains minor and major seminaries in each of the three dioceses. An Ethiopian College was founded in Rome within the Vatican walls in 1919. *See also* Africa, Catholicism in; Chalcedon, Council of; Eastern Catholics and ecumenism; Eastern Catholics and Rome; Eastern churches; Eastern liturgies; Eastern rites; Ethiopian rite.   RONALD G. ROBERSON

Ethiopian rite, the liturgical and ecclesial tradition of the Ethiopian Orthodox and Ethiopian Eastern Catholic churches. In the second half of the fourth century a bishop for the Kingdom of Axum was consecrated in Alexandria and began the conversion of Ethiopia. Egyptian influence was strengthened by the presence in Ethiopia from 480 of monks who had received their monastic initiation in Egypt. At the same time, monks from Syria were also active in the region. From these beginnings until 1270, when the predominance in Ethiopia of the Coptic Church and its rite were reaffirmed, little is known about the history of the Ethiopian rite. But its Alexandrian origins are still visible, especially in the eucharistic liturgy, monastic hours, liturgical vestments, and liturgical year, which, like the Coptic, has a large number of fast days.

The Ethiopian rite is also distinguished by a number of Jewish usages. Some scholars trace this to the Jewish origins of the original Christian community, others to the large Jewish community in Ethiopia, and still others to later Judaizing tendencies (keeping the Sabbath, circumcision, dietary rules) and the influence of apocryphal literature, such as the books of *Enoch* and the *Ascension of Isaiah*. In addition to the customary services common to all traditional Eastern churches, the popular Ethiopian folk tradition includes a large body of legendary and folkloristic material and practices. It is a church culture based more on popular and monastic traditions and ritual practices than on speculative theology or religious instruction. The traditional liturgical language, Ge'ez, is a dead language, but in the twentieth century Amharic, now the official tongue of Ethiopia, has been used in the liturgy.

Peculiar to this rite is the presence of not one but three distinct Divine Offices, only one of which is derived from the Coptic monastic Horologion. The other two are independent, native offices. The Ethiopian rite is thus a synthesis of Egyptian and indigenous Ethiopian elements, and cannot be labeled simply a branch of the Alexandrian tradition. *See also* Eastern churches; Ethiopian Catholic Church.

ROBERT F. TAFT

Études (ay-tood'; Fr., "studies"), French Jesuit journal of religious and cultural thought. Founded in 1856 in Paris, it has chronicled and confronted the French dialogue between Catholicism and society. Since World War II and Vatican II (1962–65) its horizons have become global and its emphases frequently on ethical issues.

eucharistic adoration, a devotion centered on worshiping Christ as Divine Lord and Savior in the consecrated bread (and wine). Though such adoration is expressed in the liturgy itself, this term has come to designate nonliturgical worship, usually involving exposition of the Blessed Sacrament. Many persons also have engaged in such adoration privately through visits to the Blessed Sacrament.

Though special reverence and adoration were offered the eucharistic Christ in the early Church, eucharistic adoration outside of Mass rose to prominence only in the thirteenth century. Often in the popular mind, it replaced the Mass and reception of Communion as the most significant Christian experience of worship. Current ecclesiastical legislation governing worship seeks to reintegrate eucharistic worship outside of Mass with the Mass itself. Devotions are seen as prolongations of thanksgiving, of interior communion with one's saving Lord, of prayer for the Church and world, all of which are celebrated and actualized in the Eucharistic Liturgy. *See also* Benediction; Blessed Sacrament; Real Presence.

Eucharistic Congress, a series of over forty-five major meetings or assemblies held since 1881 for the purpose of deepening understanding of, and devotion to, the Eucharist. The term may refer to local, regional, or international meetings.

Marie Marthe Emilia Tamisier (1834–1910) conceived the idea of the Eucharistic Congress both foster eucharistic devotion and to respond to the antireligious policies of the French government. Her first efforts were not successful, but in 1881 she obtained the approval of Pope Leo XIII. The first Congress was held at the University of Lille, in France.

The success of the international meetings has also spurred the development of national congresses. Several have been held in the United States since 1895 when the first American Eucharistic Congress convened in Washington, D.C.

eucharistic devotions, nonliturgical religious practices centered on Christ's presence to the Church in the reserved Sacrament. Public or private, they include exposition of the Blessed Sacrament (for long or short periods), usually followed by Benediction, holy hours of adoration, and eucharistic processions and visits.

Eucharistic devotions developed from the thirteenth century, inspired by the desire of the faithful to look at and to contemplate Christ in the sacred species (the consecrated bread and wine) in order to foster interior communion with him. Emphasis on the divinity of Jesus, convictions of personal unworthiness to receive Communion, and the coldness and distance of the Latin Mass created a need for such devotions. Their simplicity, their use of local languages, and the warmth of their hymns and prayers filled that need, engaging persons not only in mind but also in heart.

Because of the value of eucharistic devotions, the Congregation of Rites, in a 1967 instruction, *Eucharisticum Mysterium,* sought to promote them. The congregation called for their reintegration with the Mass, the "source and summit" of Christian life. It stipulated that Scripture readings and suitable hymns and prayers should accompany eucharistic devotions, particularly exposition, for such devotions should be seen as prolongations of the Eucharistic Liturgy itself. Thus, they provide Christians with additional inspiration and time to contemplate the mysteries celebrated in the Eucharist. Eucharistic devotions offer believers further opportunities to give thanks to God for God's redemptive love, to enter into personal communion with Christ, to seek from him strength for the journey of discipleship, and to pray with Christ for the Church and the world. *See also* Blessed Sacrament; devotions; Eucharist.

GERARD H. LUTTENBERGER

EUCHARIST

*T*he Eucharist (Gk., "thanksgiving") is the sacramental celebration of the Paschal Mystery (i.e., Christ's dying and rising for humankind) in a context of praise and thanks for all that God has done and continues to do. During the Eucharist the Holy Spirit is called down on the assembly that it might become the Body of Christ, the People of God.

THE NEW TESTAMENT CHURCH

The Christian Scriptures give four accounts of the Last Supper (Mark 14:22–25; Matt 26:26–29; Luke 2:15–20; 1 Cor 11:23–26), in which Christ took the bread and cup of a sacred meal and transformed them by his action and words. John's Gospel also has a Last Supper scene, but in place of the bread and cup actions, the writer recounts Christ's washing the feet of his disciples. Some Scripture scholars point out, however, that there is a strong eucharistic element in John's narration of the multiplication of the loaves and fishes and the "bread of life" discourse of ch. 6. The four accounts can be reduced to two traditions (Mark/Matthew and Luke/Paul) by looking at the words spoken over the bread and cup and the theological ideas that are emphasized. As an example, in the words over the cup, Mark and Matthew speak of the "covenant," referring to the Sinai covenant that Moses and the people made with God (Exod 24:5–8). Paul and Luke prefer to speak of the "new covenant in my blood," echoing a phrase of the prophet Jeremiah (Jer 31:31–34).

These discrepancies do not change the essential meaning of Jesus' words and actions at the Last Supper. Among the possible reasons for these differences is the fact that twenty to fifty years elapsed before these accounts were actually written down. These accounts also bear marks of liturgical use over the years by Christian communities. What is common to all the accounts is that a religious meal was celebrated by Christ and his disciples on the night before his death during the course of which Christ gave a new and transforming meaning to the bread ("This is my body") and to the wine ("This is my blood"). These words prophetically predict and enact Christ's self-gift on the cross for all people.

THE JEWISH CONTEXT

As a Jew, Christ was formed in and influenced by the prayer and worship traditions of his people. The Last Supper is described as a Passover meal, which traditionally celebrates God's liberation of the Jewish people and the continuing covenant with them. Such a celebration offers a model for understanding Christ's liberation of the world from sin through his death. The ways in which Jews prayed to God in the Temple and in synagogue were also a rich heritage that influenced Jesus' prayer at t. Last Supper. The bread and cup in the religious meals of Jews wer accompanied by a *berakah* (Heb.), a blessing and thanksgiving to God for all the benefits received. Some scholars detect this type of prayer in Jesus' actions (he took the bread and cup and blessed and thanked God). Other scholars point to another form of prayer, the *todah* (a "sacrifice of praise"), in which a thank offering of leavened bread and prayers of praise were offered. This meal sacrifice with prayer was another way to celebrate and renew the covenant with God. This type of meal could have provided a way of interpreting Jesus' death as a new covenant with God. Although these scholarly discussions continue, all agree that the Last Supper is a religious meal that theologically interprets and explains Christ's death on the cross.

The meals of Jesus with sinners, as frequently described in the Gospels, also have a profound meaning within the Jewish tradition. In the Hebrew Scriptures the reign of God at the end of time is depicted as a festive meal. This image is continued by Jesus in his parables and his actions. A frequent criticism by Jesus' enemies is that he eats with sinners, an action a pious Jew would avoid. Yet Luke's Gospel in particular emphasizes these meals with social outcasts (e.g., tax collectors, prostitutes) as a prophetic action showing that God's mercy and reign were open to anyone who would repent. The Last Supper should be understood within the important context of meals with sinners in Christ's public life and reconciling meals in eating scenes with his disciples after his Resurrection.

THE POST–NEW TESTAMENT CHURCH

The first Christians continued to celebrate the Last Supper in their gatherings. Although Christ's actions and words are described as taking place during the course of a ritual meal, by the time Paul writes to the Christians at Corinth in the mid-first century, the celebration of the Eucharist occurs at the end of a meal shared together. Since the first Christians were Jews, they initially continued their prayer in the Temple and celebrated their Eucharist domestically. As Jews in other parts of the Roman Empire became converts, they too adapted their Eucharist to the style of prayer with which they were familiar. (Some scholars, for example, believe that chs. 9–10 of the *Didache*, an early East Syrian Christian manual, may be such an adaptation.)

As Gentiles became converts, the eucharistic celebrations continued to be adapted to the culture and practical situations of the converts. Eventually "families" of such prayers, reflecting different geographical areas of the Roman Empire, developed (e.g., Western eucharistic prayers including Roman, Mozarabic, Gallic, Ambrosian, and North African examples). Justin Martyr, writing in the mid-second century, describes the Eucharist at Rome to non-Christians as offering bread and wine to a presider who then gives praise and glory to God through the name of the Son and the

ly Spirit, followed by a lengthy thanksgiving. Such prayers were usu-
ly improvised by the presider.

In the first three centuries of the Christian era, the local churches were
periodically persecuted. These persecutions had two practical effects on
the types of eucharistic teaching that were presented. Against frequent
pagan distortions of the meaning and practice of the Eucharist, apologists like Justin Martyr at Rome and Tertullian at Carthage in North
Africa gave limited descriptions and explanations of the Eucharist to
pagan readers. As the persecutions continued, local churches saw the
need for preparing candidates more extensively for their initiation in the
Christian life.

This preparation was called the catechumenate and could extend several years. When these candidates were finally initiated, they were
baptized and anointed and received the Eucharist as part of the one initiation rite. In many local churches it seems that these sacraments were
explained to the newly initiated only after they had been received. In the
fourth century, with the end of the persecutions, catechumenal leaders'
instructions were written down. Thus, the eucharistic teachings of Eastern (e.g., of Cyril of Jerusalem and Theodore of Mopsuestia) and of

The celebration of the
Eucharist in Mali, West
Africa, with the active participation of the congregation gathered around the
altar. Although Catholicism
was introduced in Mali in
the second half of the nineteenth century, Catholics
comprise only 1 percent of
the total population of
almost 10 million.

Western churches (e.g., of Ambrose of Milan and Augustine of Hippo North Africa) have survived. These teachings on the Eucharist emphasi. Christ's death for humankind and its practical moral applications to the lives of the converts, as well as repeat Paul's teaching that the one bread of the Eucharist makes Christians the one Body of Christ.

THE MEDIEVAL CHURCH

The transition from the eucharistic preaching of Augustine and Ambrose in the fifth century to the early medieval eucharistic teaching and practice is best understood as a movement away from symbolic thinking about the Eucharist (i.e., why Christ gave the Eucharist to the Church) to an instrumental thinking (i.e., a practical "how" the bread becomes the body of Christ). There were two immediate effects of this change to instrumental thinking: the proliferation of miracle stories and devotional practices about the Eucharist and the types of theological discussions about the Eucharist that eventually led to heresy.

These changes must be seen against the historical and social background of the barbarian invasions that devastated the religious, cultural, and sociopolitical world of Augustine and his contemporaries. The practical result was an impoverishment of religious and ethnic culture from which people drew their symbolic resources and inspiration. Religious education also suffered, with the result that most people no longer understood the highly developed rituals of the medieval Mass or the Latin language in which it was now celebrated.

The early medieval period witnessed a decrease in reception of Communion by eucharistic participants. Also, stories about miraculous hosts or wine that emphasized the presence of Christ in the Eucharist in a way that caught ordinary people's imagination were widely disseminated. These miracle stories frequently replaced people's religious understanding about the Eucharist and often misled them by their one-sided emphasis on the purported sensational aspects of the Eucharist and by encouraging a passive eucharistic piety rather than an active participation in the Eucharist.

In a similar way, some theologians described the parts of the Mass in fanciful and metaphorical ways (e.g., the priest washing his hands at the altar refers to Pontius Pilate washing his hands of the judgment of Christ). These problems are best exemplified in the growing medieval practice of people running from church to church in order to be present only at the moment in the Mass after the consecration when the host and cup were elevated, because of a popular belief that looking at the Eucharist helped preserve youthfulness.

Other examples of eucharistic practice divorced from the larger purposes of the sacraments were the proliferation of private Masses because of a privatized piety and especially a preoccupation with Masses for the dead. The ancient custom of reserving some of the consecrated hosts for the Communion of the sick resulted in the construction of elaborate tabernacles, which eventually were moved to the main altar (except in

⎯hedrals) and promoted a eucharistic piety frequently unconnected to ⎯ie celebration and purposes of the Mass.

The theological discussions about the Eucharist also reflected concerns different from those of Augustine or Ambrose. As theologians emphasized the presence of Christ in the Eucharist rather than the Paschal Mystery, they searched for language that might help them. Until the ninth century, theologians did not have the sophisticated terminology of later medieval philosophy with which to discuss the Eucharist. As a result, in the debate about how Christ was present after the consecration of the bread and wine, their language tended to be vague, if not ambiguous. Theologians cited the texts of earlier writers like Augustine but without their contexts of church and eucharistic celebration.

These weaknesses finally coalesced into the first heresy about the Eucharist, that of Berengar of Tours in the eleventh century. In the oath that Berengar took at the Synod of Rome in 1079, he acknowledged that there was a substantial change from bread and wine to the body and blood of Christ. The term "substance" is a technical term that refers to the essence of a particular reality. Although this term would become more nuanced and developed in later medieval writing, it provided a way of affirming that Christ was really present in the Eucharist, once the earlier symbolic language of Augustine and others was no longer fully understood.

When Thomas Aquinas in the thirteenth century writes of the Eucharist, he retains the classical understanding of Augustinian symbol but also brilliantly employs the insights of Aristotle to discuss how bread and wine can be changed substantially into the Real Presence of Christ while the "accidents" (e.g., color, taste, shape) of bread and wine remain. This explanation, known as transubstantiation, had already been used at the Fourth Lateran Council in 1215.

Even with such an explanation, Thomas ultimately still insists that the Eucharist is a mystery no theological explanation can hope to master. Thomas also teaches that the priest acts "in the person of Christ" in consecrating the bread and wine with the words of Christ, for it is Christ who is acting.

But these sophisticated explanations did not touch the ordinary pastoral life of the European church. Ignorance and superstition were constant pastoral problems in the teaching and practice of the Eucharist among mostly illiterate Christians. By the sixteenth century there were major problems (e.g., rare reception of the Eucharist) and abuses (e.g., money was given so that the Mass would be offered for one's intention) that provoked some of the strongest attacks of Reformation theologians such as Martin Luther and John Calvin.

The Council of Trent (1545–63), while acknowledging in its pastoral sessions the rampant abuses of the sixteenth-century Church, reaffirmed the real, true, and substantial presence of Christ under the appearance of bread and wine after the consecration of the Mass. A new and reformed celebration of the Eucharist resulted from this reform council. Trent also encouraged a catechetical renewal with a more responsible preparation for the reception of the Eucharist. The Reformed churches attempted return to a more biblical and less frequent celebration of the Lord's Supper and to a theology of ministry that did not privilege the role of the eucharistic presider as a consecrator of the bread and wine.

THE LITURGICAL RENEWAL

The contemporary renewal of eucharistic understanding and participation has its roots in the late-nineteenth- and early-twentieth-century liturgical movement, which sought to reconnect worship and sacraments of the Church more intimately with the lives of Christians. Liturgi-

cal scholars studied the development of the eucharistic celebrations in the Eastern and Western churches and rediscovered a rich heritage of celebrating and understanding the Mass. Biblical scholars uncovered many illuminating connections between Jewish prayer and worship that further enriched the contemporary appreciation of how the Last Supper was connected to the death of Jesus on the cross.

Pope Pius X (d. 1914) in the early part of the twentieth century strongly encouraged a more frequent reception of the Eucharist and the earlier first reception by young children. Pius XII (d. 1958) introduced some limited liturgical reforms

A priest elevates the consecrated blood of Christ at a Eucharist celebrated at St. Ann's Church, Cassopolis, Michigan.

dealing with the Mass (e.g., eucharistic fasting) that facilitated participation, and his encyclicals on the Mystical Body and on liturgy signaled a more contemporary theological appreciation of the Eucharist in the daily life of the Church.

The discussions of Vatican II on worship and sacraments in the contemporary Church resulted in one of the most important documents of that council, the Constitution on the Sacred Liturgy, in 1963. In it the council members called for a full, conscious, and active participation in the liturgy that would preclude Christians' being strangers or silent spectators at its celebration. To facilitate participation, the council called for a reform of the eucharistic ritual and the use of the vernacular. The ancient practice of Communion under the species of bread and wine was stored in certain situations and concelebration of Mass by several priests was again permitted.

The postconciliar commissions that implemented the mandated liturgical reforms provided the Church with a renewed version of the "Roman" Canon (the only eucharistic prayer in use in the Western Church at the time of Vatican II) as well as several other eucharistic prayers, eventually including ones for Reconciliation and for children. Since the council acknowledged the need for adaptation of the liturgy to the cultural contexts of each local church and even allowed for a more radical adaptation in some situations, other eucharistic prayers were eventually approved (e.g., for the church of Switzerland and that of Zaire).

As a result of Vatican II's insistence on the importance of the celebration of the Eucharist in the life of the Church, postconciliar theologians have re-studied the Eucharist within its larger context, the worshiping Church. In other words, the Eucharist is always connected to the way in which Christians are the Body of Christ (Paul's teaching that because we eat the one bread, we are one body [1 Cor 10]). The teaching that the Eucharist is the sacrifice of the Cross has also been enriched by the scholarly insights of Scripture scholars so that an ecumenical consensus on this teaching now seems possible. Finally, the eucharistic presence of Christ has been better appreciated within the council's teaching on the other presences of Christ in his word, in the sacramental ministries, in the liturgical prayer of the Church, and in the worshiping assembly itself (Constitution on the Sacred Liturgy, n. 7).

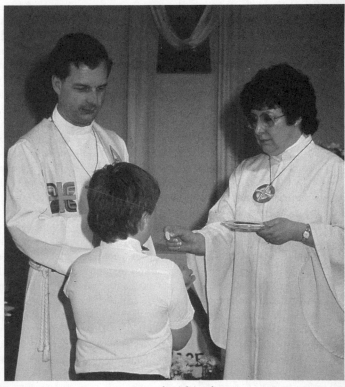

A eucharistic minister distributes Holy Communion to a young boy, while a priest waits to offer the chalice containing the Precious Blood.

See also Last Supper; Mass; Real Presence; Rite of Christian Initiation of Adults; sacrament; worship.

Bibliography

Hay, Leo. *Eucharist: A Thanksgiving Celebration.* Wilmington, DE: Michael Glazier, 1989.

Mazza, Enrico. *The Eucharistic Prayers of the Roman Rite.* New York: Pueblo, 1986.

Power, David. *The Sacrifice We Offer.* New York: Crossroad, 1989.

_____. *The Eucharistic Mystery.* New York: Crossroad, 1992.

REGIS A. DUFFY

eucharistic fast, the practice of abstaining from food and drink before receiving Communion. Current canon law stipulates that (1) water never breaks the fast; (2) one must abstain from solid food and liquids for one hour before communicating; (3) sick persons may take nonalcoholic liquid and medicine without restriction; (4) sick persons, elderly persons, and persons accompanying them may take food and alcoholic beverages until one-quarter hour before Communion.

Originally, Christians celebrated the Eucharist during a commemorative meal. Early abuses (see 1 Cor. 11:17–34), however, brought about the separation of the eucharistic memorial from the meal. Reverence for Christ, the desire to foster devotion, and the desire to forestall further abuses led to the practice of abstaining from all food and drink from midnight on before receiving Communion. This practice, documented in the third century, became universal by the fourth century. The current law originated with Pope Pius XII (1953, and again in 1957), Pope Paul VI (1964) and the Congregation for Divine Worship and the Discipline of the Sacraments (1973). *See also* Eucharist; fasting.

eucharistic minister, a person who distributes the Eucharist either within or outside of the celebration of Mass. The ordinary minister of the distribution of the Eucharist is the priest who presides at the celebration. However, when there are large numbers of people receiving Communion, various assisting ministers are employed. When present, the deacon distributes the cup and may also distribute the host. Special ministers of the Eucharist, both men and women, are permitted to function in the distribution during Mass when deacons and acolytes are not available and in the bringing of Communion to the sick (*Immensae Caritatis,* 1973). *See also* extraordinary minister of Eucharist.

eucharistic prayer, the liturgical expression of praise and thanksgiving for all that God has done in creation and in the Paschal Mystery (i.e., Christ's dying and rising for humankind) in and through the Holy Spirit. In the NT, the four accounts of the Last Supper (Mark 14:22–25; Matt 26:26–29; Luke 22:15–20; 1 Cor 11:22–26) narrate, with some variations, the last meal that Christ shared with his disciples on the night before he died. The tradition represented by Luke's and Paul's account (often called the Antiochene account) contains explanatory phrases in the words over the bread ("body [given]

for you") and cup ("new covenant in my blood"). the Marcan account there is an emphasis on the cov enant ("my blood of the covenant which is poured out for many"). Although it is debated whether the Last Supper was a Passover meal or simply a farewell religious meal, this meal setting and its interpretation of the death of Christ provided a model for the early Christian communities in fulfilling Christ's command, "Do this in memory of me."

Early Christian Eucharists: The earliest Christian communities were composed of Jewish converts whose worship was modeled on that of the Temple and synagogue. There is still disagreement among scholars as to the particular Jewish prayer forms that influenced the eucharistic prayers of these communities. (The *berakah,* or "blessing," models, for example, are favored by some, while others point to the *todah,* or "sacrifice of praise," as the chief source of inspiration.) What is more certain is that the Eucharist of these first Christians continued to be celebrated within a meal, though by Paul's time, a decade or so after the Last Supper, the Eucharist followed the meal in the Christian community at Corinth. There are no extant eucharistic prayers from this earliest period because improvised or extemporaneous prayers were the normal style of worship, a practice that continued until at least the fourth century.

Texts of Early Eucharistic Prayers: In the *Didache* (Gk., "The Teaching," a late-first-century document on church practice) we find the first example of Jewish prayers, transformed by belief in Christ, that served either as table prayers or as a very early example of a eucharistic prayer (possibly the end of the first century). In ch. 9 the meal begins with a prayer of thanksgiving over the cup followed by a similar prayer over the bread and then a petition for the Church. In ch. 10, at the end of the meal, the prayers follow the order of the Jewish blessings for this portion of the meal (*Birkat ha-Mazon*) with three sections: God's name is blessed for the work of creation and redemption; there is a blessing of spiritual food and drink given to those who believe in Christ; and finally, there is a prayer for the Church, whose gathered members are a promise of God's final banquet at the end of time. Since the Lord's words over the bread and cup are lacking, some scholars believe this could not have been a eucharistic prayer. Others believe that it still might have been.

When the earliest known texts of eucharistic prayers are examined, the influence of Jewish prayer till seen. In the *Apostolic Tradition* of Hippolytus om Rome (the text dates from 215, but the prayer self may be much older) and in the prayer of *Addai and Mari* from Syria, there is either praise or thanksgiving for creation, followed by thanksgiving for redemption (a Last Supper narrative in the *Apostolic Tradition*), and then intercessions, a calling down of the Holy Spirit, and a final praise of God. The themes of these prayers generally centered on Christ (who is called God's servant-child), who has restored creation, revealed God's life, and destroyed evil.

Later Eucharistic Prayers: Eucharistic prayers from the fourth and fifth centuries in the Eastern and Western churches show that improvisation is no longer common and that there is a wide borrowing of texts from one another. (Some scholars believe that the eucharistic prayer in the West was already fixed by the first half of the fourth century.) The prayers usually are longer than earlier prayers, are more developed in their theology, and have acquired certain characteristics and order that permit us to divide them into families (East Syrian, West Syrian, Western, etc.). In the Western Church, the so-called Roman Canon gradually became the only text used.

On April 3, 1969, Pope Paul VI approved the new Roman Missal, which had been called for by Vatican II. It contained three new eucharistic prayers, in addition to the so-called Roman Canon. (The words of institution over the bread and wine were, however, to be identical for all forms of the Eucharistic Prayer.) In 1974, three eucharistic prayers for children and two for Masses of Reconciliation were also approved for experimental use. Subsequently, eucharistic prayers for some local churches (e.g., that of Switzerland and Zaire) have also been approved. *See also* anaphora; Canon of the Mass; Eucharist.

Bibliography

Mazza, E. *The Eucharistic Prayers of the Roman Rite.* New York: Pueblo, 1986.

Power, D. *The Eucharistic Mystery.* New York: Crossroad, 1992.

REGIS A. DUFFY

eucharistic presence. *See* Real Presence.

eucharistic spirituality, devotions and religious attitudes centered on the Eucharist. The Eucharist has served as a focus for Christian devotion since the earliest centuries, although the form that devotion has taken has varied. In the first through fifth centuries, devotion to the Eucharist was understood to effect a close identification of one's own life with that of Christ. Thus Ignatius of Antioch (d. ca. 107) could speak of his martyrdom as a eucharistic celebration of Christ's own sacrifice (*Letter to the Romans*). This identification of a Christian life of sacrifice with the sacrifice of Christ celebrated in the Eucharist continued well into the Middle Ages, when theologians, following the example of Augustine (d. 430) would most commonly identify a life of active faith and love as that which the Eucharist produced and that which it celebrated.

Starting in the twelfth century, a growing devotion to the Real Presence of the Risen Lord in the Eucharist added a new dimension to this earlier active form of spirituality. The Feast of Corpus Christi, the elevation of the host, the practice of the exposition of the Sacrament and other extraliturgical devotions gave rise, in the early modern period, to a number of new religious orders whose prayer life centered on meditation and contemplation on the eucharistic presence outside of the liturgy. Emphasis was placed on communing with Christ rather than imitation of Him. Lay devotions also followed this trend.

Liturgical renewal in the twentieth century revived the more active spirituality of the early Church. Both forms of spirituality now exist within the Catholic community. GARY MACY

Euchologion (ev-koh-loh'gee-awn; Gk., "prayerbook"), principal Byzantine liturgical book, equivalent to the old Roman Sacramentary, containing those prayers and formulas priests and deacons need to fulfill their roles in the liturgical services. Printed liturgical books distinguish between the "great euchology" and extracts thereof, such as the Hieratikon or Leitourgikon containing Eucharist, Vespers, and orthros (Matins); and the ritual, called the "small euchologion" or hagiasmaterion (book of blessings), containing the other sacraments, blessings, funerals, and occasional services.

Eudes, St. John, 1601–80, priest and founder of the Congregation of Jesus and Mary (the Eudists). Born in Normandy, France, and educated by the Jesuits at Caen, he was ordained in 1625 and served in the Oratory of Paris. For many years, he preached missions throughout France. In 1643 he left the oratory to found the congregation that bears his name. The principal work of the Eudists was the training of seminarians, though now Eudists are mostly involved in secondary education. He was canonized in 1925. Feast day: August 19.

Eugene [names of popes]. *See* Eugenius III, Bl.; IV.

Eugenius III, Bl. [Bernardo Paganelli], d. 1153, pope from 1145 to 1153. Elected pope after being a Cistercian monk at Clairvaux and then abbot of Sts. Vincent and Anastasius, he was forced to flee Rome due to opposition from the senate and Arnold of Brescia, returning for good only in 1153 with the aid of Frederick I Barbarossa. Eugenius issued the first formal Crusade bull and authorized Bernard of Clairvaux to preach the Crusade. During his pontificate, he also sought to reform clerical and monastic life; Bernard addressed his famous treatise *On Consideration* to him. *See also* Bernard of Clairvaux, St.; Crusades.

Eugenius IV [Gabriel Condulmaro], ca. 1383–1447, pope from 1431 to 1447. He was made cardinal in 1408 by his uncle, Pope Gregory XII. He remained in papal service after his uncle was forced to abdicate at the Council of Constance (1415). As pope he resisted calling the Council of Basel (1431–38) and eventually tried to dissolve it as a threat to papal power. He yielded and recognized its validity in 1433. At the Council of Florence (1439–45), he negotiated a short-lived union with the Greek church that served as a model for all further unions based upon agreement in faith with diversity in rite. *See also* Basel, Council of; Florence, Council of.

Eulalia, St., d. ca. 304, virgin and martyr. She was burned at the stake in Mérida, Spain, at age twelve for allegedly denouncing a judge for attempting to induce Christians to renounce their faith. Feast day: December 10.

eulogia (ev-loh-gee'ah; Gk., "blessing"), term used for a blessing, also a holy place or object through which a blessing or other benefit was thought to be conferred. More specifically, the term *eulogia* is used for the consecrated eucharistic species (bread and wine) as well as for the unconsecrated bread offered by the faithful for use at the Eucharist, and distributed to them at the end of the liturgy. This blessed bread is now more commonly called *antidoron*. *See also* antidoron.

eulogy (yoo'luh-jee; Gk., "blessing" or "praise"), a sermon delivered at a funeral. Current regulations for funeral liturgies forbid the practice of delivering eulogies or such "verbal obituaries." Good words spoken in regard to the faithful deceased during a funeral liturgy ought instead be subordinated to t proclamation of God's saving work performed i them through Christ. Hence, in place of a eulogy, the practice of expressing gratitude to God for specific aspects of a person's life and their persistence in faith during the funeral homily is now regarded as pastorally appropriate. *Eulogia* also refers to the blessed bread that is distributed in Orthodox and Oriental Catholic churches following the Eucharist. *See also* eulogia; homily.

Eunomius, d. 394, bishop of Cyzicus and theologian. His views are known mainly from his opponents, the Cappadocians, although some fragments of his writings survive. An extreme Arian, Eunomius believed in the subordination of the Son to the Father and also that God's essence could be named as "Unbegottenness." *See also* Arianism; Cappadocian Fathers; subordinationism.

Eusebius of Caesarea, ca. 260–ca. 339, bishop of Caesarea in Palestine and often called the "Father of Church History." As a young man Eusebius studied at Caesarea under the martyr Pamphilius, inheritor of the library of Origen, and began to write his *History of the Church*. He became bishop of Caesarea ca. 313. In the Arian controversy regarding the divinity of Jesus, Eusebius initially offered qualified support to Arius, who held that Jesus was only the greatest of creatures, but later recanted and gave assent to the Nicene Creed, which taught that Jesus was "of the same (divine) substance" as God the Father. At the time of his death he was a respected scholar-bishop. Eusebius was a prolific writer in diverse fields such as biblical interpretation and Christian apologetics, and he also wrote on the idea of a Christian empire—an idea that had been realized in his lifetime in the emperor Constantine. But his fame rests principally on his *History*, the first major account of the rise of Christianity in which are preserved long excerpts of important earlier works that otherwise would have been lost.

Eusebius of Vercelli, St., fourth-century bishop noted for his stand against the Arians. Some of his writings were previously attributed to Athanasius. He is thought to have translated the Gospels before Jerome. Feast day: August 2.

Eustace, St., also known as Eustachius, d. ca. 118, patron saint of hunters. His life is legendary, including his conversion as a Roman general to Christian-

while hunting. He is said to have seen a stag with the figure of Christ on the cross between its antlers. Feast day: September 20.

Eustochium, St. Julia, ca. 368–418/419, virgin and close associate of Jerome. The third daughter of St. Paula, Eustochium was the recipient of Jerome's famous Letter on virginity (*Epistle* 22). As a child she vowed herself to virginity before settling with her mother near Jerome in Bethlehem. There Paula founded three convents, which Eustochium directed after 404. Feast day: September 28.

euthanasia (*yoo*-thin-ay'zhuh; Gk., "easy death"), according to the Vatican Declaration on Euthanasia (1980), "an action or an omission which of itself or by intention causes death, in order that all suffering may in this way be eliminated."

"Mercy killing" is another name for euthanasia. It emphasizes killing out of compassion to relieve suffering. "Assisted suicide" is a related concept that emphasizes helping someone to take their own life by providing the means and the knowledge to do so. "Aid-in-dying" is a concept now being used to include either assisted suicide or active euthanasia.

Types of Euthanasia: Euthanasia is often distinguished as voluntary or involuntary, direct or indirect, active or passive. It is voluntary when the person whose life is at stake explicitly requests help to die. It is involuntary when the person killed has expressed no desire to die, as in the case of infants or the comatose. Direct euthanasia means death is the primary goal of the intervention. By contrast, it is indirect when the action is primarily intended to relieve pain but has the side effect of hastening death, such as in giving narcotics to comfort the patient, even though they also hasten death by repressing respiration. Active euthanasia refers to death intentionally brought on by intervention, such as a lethal injection. Legal endorsement is being sought for direct, voluntary, active euthanasia—none of which is morally acceptable according to Catholic teaching.

Passive euthanasia is more complicated. It entails a moral difference between ordinary and extraordinary treatment and between killing and allowing to die. These distinctions are common in Catholic medical ethics, and a solid base of support for the traditional Catholic position on these matters can be found among many who debate the issue of euthanasia.

Moral Issues: The common misunderstanding of the ordinary/extraordinary distinction relates these terms to the state of the medical art for treating the pathological condition in question. The vagueness and confusion of these terms has led the Vatican declaration to suggest that "proportionate/disproportionate" may better express the substance of this distinction. According to the traditional Catholic use of this distinction, treatments are "ordinary" (required or proportionate) or "extraordinary" (optional or disproportionate) relative to the benefits their effects will bring over the burdens they entail physically, emotionally, or economically for the patient and the patient's family. "Ordinary" means bring reasonable hope of benefit and tolerable burdens. "Extraordinary" means are futile and/or overly burdensome. This distinction is always patient-specific and a moral assessment of treatment must be made on a case-by-case basis.

The other moral difference that distinguishes active and passive euthanasia is that between killing and allowing to die. "Killing" refers to a human agent being morally responsible for causing death. "Allowing to die" refers to withholding or withdrawing extraordinary treatment so that the underlying pathology can run its course and cause the patient's death. It follows from the moral conviction that no one is morally obliged to receive treatment when treatment is judged to be futile or overly burdensome. Withholding and withdrawing useless or burdensome treatment is not a question of euthanasia, murder, suicide, or assisted suicide, since the physical cause of death is ultimately the underlying pathology that first required the medical treatment. No one is morally responsible for the death since the fatal pathology causes it. All those involved should be considered as humbly accepting the inherent limitations of the human condition.

Moral Arguments: Before one can endorse euthanasia or not, one must determine whether there is a moral difference between killing and allowing to die. If they are not morally different, then whether one kills or allows to die makes no difference. Advocates of euthanasia regard this distinction as indicating a descriptive difference in the way a patient dies. What matters to them is not how the patient dies but what the patient chooses. The Catholic moral tradition and other opponents of killing patients, however, maintain a moral difference in the distinction. They see it validly separating those deaths for which people are morally responsible from those for which they are not. It protects the overall respect for life because it recognizes that people are limited in their ability to control the ultimate progression of a fatal disease. It also has social validity by preserving the role of health-care providers as ones committed to curing and caring rather than to killing. It supports the bonds of trust in the doctor-patient relationship and does not introduce suspicion or insecurity into the hospital room.

Advocates of active euthanasia, such as the Hemlock Society, defend it on the libertarian principle of patient autonomy. For them, what gives humans their dignity and worth is free choice. They put the burden of proof on anyone who would deprive persons of freedom over their bodies and their lives. They advocate active euthanasia as the ultimate civil liberty, and claim that anyone should be allowed aid-in-dying who chooses it freely without violating another's freedom, or when no overriding duty prevails. Their goal is to allow the person to retain control over one's own dying, to avoid the prolonged agony of dying, and to assure that no one's life will be artificially prolonged by technological means when quality-of-life is gone.

Opponents of killing patients argue on religious and philosophical grounds. They invoke not only the divine prohibition against killing but also the principles of sanctity of life and of God's dominion and human stewardship. Sanctity of life entails the positive obligation to nurture and support life, and the negative obligation not to harm or destroy life. It creates a presumption in favor of sustaining life and so places the burden of proof on those who would take life or fail to forestall death.

The principle of God's dominion and human stewardship tells us that human freedom is limited, especially when it comes to having absolute control over life. Life is entrusted to humankind to use and make fruitful, but it is not a possession that an individual can end when one chooses. Since people are made in the image of God—a community of loving persons—we are social by nature. Because individuals live in community as interdependent persons, no one person's freedom is absolute. An individual's action must be weighed in light of its impact on the social good, and not just whether it satisfies self-interest. To give someone else power over one's freedom and life, as active euthanasia does, also gives away too much of what it means to be human. Euthanasia actually contradicts the very freedom and life it claims to respect.

Moral arguments such as these are necessary but not sufficient by themselves as a moral response to the euthanasia movement. Action is also required that witnesses to convictions. Healing communities that strive to carry on the mission of Jesus mu. bear convincing witness in personal and corporate ways to the care of the dying. Hospice care is one such response. Hospice creates an environment in which one maintains the best quality of life possible while dying without actively prolonging dying or hastening death. The great challenge of the euthanasia movement is for the Catholic health-care community to incorporate the hospice concept of care throughout its delivery system in caring for the dying. The standards of care embodied in hospice make killing patients mistaken and unnecessary. *See also* death and dying; hospice movement.

Bibliography

Callahan, Daniel. *The Troubled Dream of Life: Living with Mortality.* New York: Simon and Schuster, 1993.

Congregation for the Doctrine of the Faith. "Declaration on Euthanasia" (May 5, 1980). In Gula, *What Are They Saying About Euthanasia?*

Gula, Richard M. *What Are They Saying About Euthanasia?* Mahwah, NJ: Paulist Press, 1986.

Veath, Robert M. *Death, Dying, and the Biological Revolution: Our Last Quest for Responsibility.* New Haven, CT: Yale University Press, 1989.   RICHARD M. GULA

Eutyches (yoo'tee-keez), ca. 378–454, abbot of a monastery near Constantinople during the mid-fifth century and a vigorous opponent of Nestorianism. His alternative, Monophysitism, insists that after the Incarnation Christ had but one nature, the divine, into which the human was fully absorbed. The effect of this view was to eliminate the reality of the human nature of Christ, thus negating the possibility of humanity being saved through Christ's death. Eutyches' Christology was condemned by the Synod of Constantinople in 448, reauthorized by the "Robber Council" of Ephesus, also known as Latrocinium, in 449, but condemned again by the Council of Chalcedon in 451, after which Eutyches was exiled. *See also* Chalcedon, Council of; Monophysitism.

Evagrios of Pontus, ca. 344–99, Greek mystic and theologian. A noted preacher who attended the Council of Constantinople (381), he retired to the Nitrian Desert in 382 and remained there for the rest of his life. His numerous writings, especially on prayer, influenced Christian spirituality via John Cassian, Denys the Areopagite, Maximus the Confessor, and, through them, John Scotus Eriugena and Bernard of Clairvaux.

evangelical counsels. *See* counsels, evangelical.

evangelicalism, an interdenominational Protestant movement dedicated to spreading the gospel to n-Christians and revitalizing faith among Christ-ans. Evangelicalism emphasizes individual conversion (the "new birth") to a personal, experienced faith in Christ; Christ's atoning sacrifice for individual sin; the Bible's authority in matters of faith and life; holy living; and the obligation of laity and clergy to propagate the gospel through preaching and missionary effort. Evangelicals tend to deemphasize denominational differences and fine points of theology in favor of the shared experience of salvation through faith.

Evangelicalism originated in the Protestant Reformation of the sixteenth century. The doctrines of salvation by faith, authority of the Scriptures, and the priesthood of all believers were central to the Reformers' understanding of Christianity. The evangelical revivals of the early eighteenth century gave the movement definitive shape through two related impulses. First, Pietism in Europe generated new denominations, notably the Moravians, and renewal movements in Lutheran, Reformed, and Anabaptist churches. Second, Methodism in England brought forth a host of new Wesleyan denominations and renewal within the Anglican church.

Since the eighteenth century, evangelicalism has produced new denominations, revitalization movements within existing traditions, and new transdenominational religious movements (such as fundamentalism and Pentecostalism). Twentieth-century evangelicalism has influenced many Roman Catholics, especially Hispanics in the United States and Latin America, at the grassroots level through missionary and evangelistic work, publications, radio and television, and informal contacts. Because this has turned many Catholics toward Protestant churches, evangelicalism is regarded with some caution in Catholic circles.

Evangelicals are found in every denomination, as well as outside organized churches. It has been estimated that one of every four adults in the United States is an evangelical, but that figure cannot be verified statistically. *MICHAEL S. HAMILTON*

Evangelii Nuntiandi (ay-vahn-jay'lee-ee noon-tsee-ahn'dee; Lat., "Of proclaiming the gospel"), "On Evangelization in the Modern World," apostolic exhortation issued by Pope Paul VI on December 8, 1975. The document was occasioned by three events: the end of a Holy Year, the tenth anniversary of the closing of the Second Vatican Council, and the anniversary of the Third General Assembly of the Synod of Bishops, which had focused on evangeliza-

tion. Many commentators regard this as Paul VI's best and most important pronouncement.

The document links the process of evangelization with the Church's abiding concern for the social question. Evangelization proclaims the coming of the reign of God as a form of liberation "from sin and the Evil One," but also from every form of economic, social, and political oppression (nn. 9, 29). While it is of the essence of the Church's mission to evangelize, it must begin "by being evangelized itself" (n. 15). *See also* evangelization.

evangelism. *See* evangelization.

evangelist (Gk., "proclaimer of the good news"), anyone engaged in spreading the gospel; also an itinerant preacher with no fixed pastoral charge. In Isa 52:7 the herald brings good news of salvation (see Luke 4:18). Eph 4:11 lists evangelists after apostles and prophets among God's gifts to the Church. Philip (Acts 21:8) and Timothy (2 Tim 4:5) are called evangelists. The term "evangelists" is first

Tenth-century ivory plaque depicting the four Evangelists as a man (Matthew), a lion (Mark), an ox (Luke), and an eagle (John), figures drawn from Rev 4:7.

used of the canonical Gospel writers in the third century by Hippolytus and Tertullian. Under the influence of Ezek 1:10, the symbol of the human being came to represent Matthew; the lion, Mark; the calf, Luke; and the eagle, John. *See also* gospel; John the Evangelist, St.; Luke, St.; Mark, St.; Matthew, St.

evangelization, the proclamation of the gospel. Jesus understood this to be at the center of his own ministry: "I must proclaim the good news of the kingdom of God to the other cities also; for I was sent for this purpose" (Luke 4:43). He conferred the same mandate upon his apostles: "Go into all the world and proclaim the good news to the whole creation" (Mark 16:15). The Church, in turn, receives the mandate from the apostles and makes its own the words of the Apostle Paul, "Woe to me if I do not proclaim the gospel" (1 Cor 9:16). Thus, it sends missionaries "until such time as the infant churches are fully established and can themselves carry on the work of evangelizing" (Dogmatic Constitution on the Church, n. 17).

Through the proclamation of the gospel, the Church "prepares the hearers to receive and profess the faith, disposes them for baptism, snatches them from the slavery of error, and incorporates them into Christ so that through charity they may grow up into full maturity in Christ" (ibid.). The "specific purpose" of missionary activity, therefore, is "evangelization and the planting of the Church among those peoples and groups where it has not yet taken root" (Decree on the Church's Missionary Activity, n. 6). The former, evangelization, is the "chief means" of achieving the latter, implantation.

Evangelization is not only the responsibility of the bishops and the clergy, but of "every disciple of Christ, according to his or her ability" (Dogmatic Constitution on the Church, n. 17). Indeed, "the whole Church is missionary, and the work of evangelization is a basic duty of the People of God" (Decree on the Church's Missionary Activity, n. 35).

Because the kingdom of God that Jesus, the apostles, and the Church proclaim is a kingdom of justice and peace as well as of holiness and grace (Pastoral Constitution on the Church in the Modern World, n. 39), evangelization is about liberation from every form of sin and oppression (*Evangelii Nuntiandi*, 1975, n. 29). Jesus himself evangelized in more than word. He cured the sick, fed the hungry, raised the dead, and gave hope to the poor (n. 12). For the Church, therefore, "evangelizing means bringing the Good News into all the strata of hu-

manity, and through its influence transforming h manity from within and making it new" (n. 18).

The "first means" of evangelizing is "the witness of an authentically Christian life." And that applies to the Church as well as to its individual members. The Church "will evangelize the world . . . by its living witness of fidelity to the Lord Jesus—the witness of poverty and detachment, of freedom in the face of the powers of this world, in short, the witness of sanctity" (n. 41). Evangelization also occurs through preaching, that is, the verbal proclamation of the message. It occurs in the liturgy and sacramental life of the Church; through catechesis; through the use of the mass media; and through various forms of popular piety (nn. 40–48). In effect, evangelization encompasses the entire mission of the Church. *See also* Catholic social teachings; gospel; missions; sacramentality, principle of.

RICHARD P. MCBRIEN

Evans, St. Philip, 1645–79, a Jesuit martyr of Wales. For fourteen years he ministered to Catholics in southern Wales until he was arrested for being a Catholic priest and sentenced to death for high treason. Feast day: December 1.

Eve (Heb., *hawwah*, "life"), the first woman. Her Hebrew name can be from a word for "life" and also from one for "snake." According to Gen 2–4, she was made from the rib of her husband, Adam. Though she was an appropriate helper for him, she surrendered to the serpent's temptation, ate the forbidden fruit, and persuaded her husband to do likewise, who then shared fully in the sin. Both were expelled from the garden of Eden and were subjected to various afflictions, including, in Eve's case, the pain of childbirth. She was the mother of Cain, Abel, Seth, and other unnamed children. In 1 Tim 2:11–15 the author argues that since Adam preceded Eve who, moreover, was deceived first (see also 2 Cor 11:3), women should be silent, should not teach, and should have no authority over a man. Nevertheless, women in the Pauline churches held responsible positions: Phoebe (Rom 16:1–2); Prisca (Rom 16:3; 1 Cor 16:9) and Junia (Rom 16:7) are depicted as preaching (1 Cor 11:5) and teaching (Acts 18:26). *See also* Adam; Adam and Eve; original justice; original sin.

Evening Prayer. *See* Vespers.

Evensong. *See* Vespers.

l, in classical terms, the privation of the good, :., the absence of the being or perfection that is proper to a creature. Evil may refer to the absence in itself, to the subject in whom the evil exists, or to the effects of evil in human subjects, such as the injustice suffered by one or many persons at the hands of evildoers. As privation or absence, however, evil lacks any inherent intelligibility. As such an ontological surd and an existential scandal, it resists systematic understanding.

The prevalent Catholic approach to understanding evil is influenced by Thomas Aquinas's interpretation of Aristotle and Augustine. This approach avoids the radical dualism of Manichaeism, in which the goodness of God is opposed by evil as a second, independent principle; Pelagianism, in which evil can be effectively countered by that self-effort that effects a growth in virtue; Stoicism, which identified the effects of evil with fate; and Pantheism, which so fuses creation with God that evil can be rendered a mere human interpretation of reality, but not real (Spinoza). Catholic moral theology and social ethics have noted the intersubjective, social, and political dimensions of moral evil.

In this approach, evil is a privation of being. For example, blindness is an evil because it is the absence of a function that is part of human completeness; calumny is an evil because it deprives a person of his or her due reputation. To say that evil is a privation is not to deny it any reality. It is to deny that there is an "essence" of evil, that is, that evil subsists on its own or could exist apart from created reality or from human subjects who are essentially good because they are God's creation. Evil can only exist in another; it is parasitic on the good.

Physical Evil: A distinction is usually made between physical and moral evil. Physical evil is that privation of good experienced as disorder within the perceived order of creation. This includes both physical pain and mental anguish. While hurricanes, earthquakes, and various "acts of God" are typically given as examples of physical evil, the evil in question here is to be seen essentially in the suffering these events cause, for in themselves they are natural. (Indeed, the very notion of disorder as an exception to an orderly state has been placed in doubt by some contemporary physics, which has proposed entropy tending toward chaos as a normative state.)

Still, physical evil is a reality and is a source of real suffering and death. The Christian recognizes that suffering and death are experienced as evils, but they are only experienced as ultimate evils when this earthly life is placed above other ends and transcendent meaning is excluded from suffering and death. Death is the natural end of the physical organism, an organism created as good; in this view, death is not understood only as an evil in itself. On the other hand, death and other forms of physical evil cannot be adequately understood simply as the necessary by-products of finite processes. While physical evil may be a statistical necessity, the Catholic tradition has drawn an ultimate linkage between the disorder that characterizes physical evil, especially death, and the ontological disorder of moral evil symbolized by the fall of Adam and Eve.

Moral Evil: One must distinguish moral evil from premoral evil. Premoral evil (also called ontic or nonmoral evil) refers to a lack or absence in reality that conditions the moral situation before any moral actions occur. Moral evil is of personal origin, a disorder of the will, which has been created in freedom to affirm or to deny the intelligent and loving intentions of God. When human beings exercise their freedom in such a way as to introduce destruction into their lives, lives that impinge upon the lives of others, one may speak of moral fault or ontological guilt. Because such moral fault or ontological guilt constitutes an offense against God, one can speak of sin. Sin entails an understanding of human persons as ontologically free, i.e., as ultimately responsible for themselves in relation to other free subjects. The freedom of the human subject is presupposed by the very possibility of sin.

The trajectory of a human life can be understood as the result of the exercise of the will in freedom, in greater or lesser degrees of correspondence with God's intelligent and loving intention (Gk., *telos*). It is possible to choose a denial of God with such a consistent resoluteness that one in effect has chosen eternal loss, or hell. Hell is the state of perpetual decision against God, the utter loss of God.

Sin or moral evil is intimately related to suffering because it can directly or indirectly cause suffering—spiritual, psychological, and physical; it is related to death (Rom 5:12–14) because the free decision to deny God's intelligent and loving intention is the decision, however germinal, to destroy the possibility for life. Moral evil filters the experience of natural death such that natural death is seen and experienced as an unrelieved evil, often as a tragedy. Sin or moral evil can, therefore, be understood as a kind of death (in reality, a spiritual death); it cannot be considered in any sense good.

Moral evil is also related to the various forms of social evil that afflict humankind, from war and famine to racism, sexism, and poverty. These kinds of evil, which wreak havoc at the heart of human existence, constitute injustices because their ultimate cause is a deprivation of the goodness of God and of the original justice in which humans were created in the sight of God.

Freedom, Radical Guilt, and Providence: Though Catholic theology speaks of the ontological freedom of the moral subject, the extent of this freedom can be questioned. It could seem, in fact, that people are "doomed" to an existence riddled with moral evil. The mysterious conjunction of ontological freedom with the existential fact of evil is the focus of the biblical story of the Fall (Gen 2–3), which was extrapolated by Augustine and later theologians into the doctrine of original sin. This doctrine holds that the exercise of human freedom has, from the very origins of its exercise, initiated a rejection of God's directive influence and thus lost the sanctifying presence of God. The effect of original sin is the real human and historical situation wherein the exercise of human freedom is in fact compromised by any number of personal and historical factors that give distorted contour to the moral playing field. Theologian Karl Rahner (d. 1984) describes it as the radical codetermination of the situation of human freedom by guilt. Thus, evil can seem inescapable, and humans can seem trapped in a morass of evil of overwhelming proportions. However, human beings are not predestined toward evil; any such predestination would compromise both human freedom and the goodness of God.

Catholic moral theology has largely focused on the evil possible in individual acts. But the last third of the twentieth century has seen a retrieval of the understanding of sin as a fundamental and pervasive distortion of one's relationship to God. This period has also seen a renewed perception of the social dimensions of evil, not only by moral and systematic theologians, but also by the social teaching of the Church's magisterium. Sin itself is seen not simply as an objective personal act or omission, but also as an intersubjective reality, extending beyond discrete evil acts or omissions to the infection of entire social structures. In liberation theology, evil is described in a comprehensive fashion, after the manner of the prophets. The horror and banality of evil typified in the twentieth century by the Holocaust have raised in Catholic circles (and beyond) timeless questions about the mystery of iniquity Thess 2:7).

The perennial question is how evil can exist when God is infinitely good. Part of the answer lies in the freedom with which the Creator endowed human beings. This freedom is part of the perfection of the human creature, and should God have withheld this freedom, the dignity of the human person as a rational being capable of love would also have been denied. However, the freedom of the human person is played out within the ambit of God's providence, the ultimate context for all moral action. The doctrine of providence holds that God's designs are most perfectly realized through the freedom of God's creatures, that God's intelligence and loving will pervade all of creation and act victoriously in concert with it, and that ultimately in all things God works for the "good for those who love God" (Rom 8:28). Thus, God is the One for whom all things are possible, including the possibility of the intrusion of evil, sin, and death into creation; but God, in God's infinite goodness, is also the One who can draw good out of all eventualities in and through the freedom and autonomy of creation, especially of the human person who is the image of God. God does not remain aloof from creation and human history (the position of deism), but is actively involved in it, acting through created freedom.

Christian Hope: The doctrine of providence is a source of Christian hope not that all forms of evil will ultimately be expunged from earthly human existence, but that ultimately the goodness of God works toward the good of all things. More somberly, Karl Rahner invoked a "Christian pessimism," a posture toward reality that sees the situation of human freedom as inescapably codetermined by the objectification of evil, but one that finds its transcendent meaning in the Cross of Jesus Christ. It is in the Cross that the mystery of moral evil, that meeting of God's goodness with the human repudiation of it, comes to its emblematic focus. But it is also in the Cross that the love of God condescends to meet and suffer that evil, and ultimately to supersede it, not through a denial of suffering and death, but in a passage through the reality of suffering and death to the definitive reality of the Resurrection. The Resurrection is the reclaiming by God of the life that has been robbed by the invasion of evil and the reestablishment of all creation in the ambit of God's life. *See also* dualism; Fall, the; free will; guilt, moral; Manichaeism; original sin; providence; sin.

liography

Gula, Richard. *Reason Informed by Faith: Foundations of Catholic Morality.* New York: Paulist Press, 1989.

Maritain, Jacques. *God and the Permission of Evil.* Milwaukee, WI: Bruce Publishing, 1966.

Ricoeur, Paul. *The Symbolism of Evil.* Boston: Beacon Press, 1967.

PAUL CROWLEY

evil, intrinsic, that which is absolutely opposed to the will of God and the laws of nature. This term refers primarily to a type of action that is evil because of its object, meaning that some types of action are wrong no matter what the circumstances or the motives of the agent may be. The prohibition of these types of action, such as the killing of an innocent nonaggressor, is absolute, i.e., allowing of no exceptions. One may, therefore, never directly will an action of this kind.

The term "intrinsic evil" has been variously understood. For instance, medieval theologians classified stealing as an intrinsically evil act, yet they also taught that to take what someone considers as personal property is not stealing when taking it is necessary for one's survival. Thus, for medieval writers, the prohibition of what normally would be stealing allows of exceptions in abnormal circumstances. Contemporary theologians generally restrict the meaning of the term to types of action that are never permissible.

Many prominent theologians question whether there are intrinsically evil acts in the second sense, that is, apart from qualifying circumstances. For this group, the morality of any act cannot be determined apart from consideration of motivation and circumstances. *See also* evil, moral.

evil, moral, a lack of integrity resulting from a disordered will, i.e., one oriented away from God's own will. A physical evil, such as blindness or illness, is experienced as a real lack or privation but its presence or absence does not make the person bad or good. A moral evil involves voluntary activity and the transgression of a norm or law. Moral evil pertains to a disorder or defect in human action and affects one's moral integrity. Other organisms suffer physical evil, but only a rational creature with free will can be a subject of moral evil. A human action is morally evil (i.e., sinful) when someone is sufficiently free in its performance. Such freedom includes adequate knowledge and absence of significant obstacles.

The existence of moral evil is the central enigma of human life. The possibility of moral evil or sin is a corollary of free will. God's bestowal of the capacity to be in control of one's actions enables humankind to attain a kind of goodness not available to nonrational beings. The realization of moral evil, however, is essentially mysterious, so that theologians refer to "the mystery of iniquity." The question is, Why would a creature spurn God's goodness and deform itself? Although the doctrine of original sin provides clues about the origins of moral evil and how it affects all people, the doctrine's assertion that human nature remains basically good serves rather to emphasize the mysteriousness of moral evil than to explain it. *See also* evil, intrinsic; good, moral.

ROBERT P. KENNEDY

evolution, the descent of all forms of life, with modification, from earlier forms. According to standard Darwinian theory, the natural selection and reproduction of favorably adapted organisms accounts for the origin and diversity of all living species. Some drastic revisions of Darwin's theory are being proposed today, but most scientists still accept the "modern synthesis" of molecular biology, genetics, and Darwinian principles. In an extended usage, however, the term "evolution" refers not only to the transformations of life on earth, but also to the unfolding of the entire cosmic story.

Catholicism and Evolution: In spite of some initial misgivings, Catholic teaching and theology have been comparatively hospitable to the theory. Pope Pius XII's encyclical *Humani Generis* (1950) acknowledged its plausibility, insisting however on the immediate creation of the human soul by God. The documents of Vatican II (1962–65) give evidence of Catholic thought's having assimilated some evolutionary motifs (Pastoral Constitution on the Church in the Modern World, 1965, n. 5).

Catholic theology strives for a formulation consistent with contemporary evolutionary science. Much of this effort is influenced by the synthesis of Christianity and evolution undertaken by the Jesuit paleontologist Pierre Teilhard de Chardin (1881–1955). At the same time, some Catholic theologies of evolution owe much to non-Catholic religious thought, including some aspects of "process theology" inspired by philosophers Alfred North Whitehead (d. 1947) and Charles Hartshorne (b. 1897).

Catholic theology is comfortable with the view that God "creates" through evolution. It has distanced itself, therefore, from "creationism," which, on the basis of a literalist reading of Genesis, insists that evolution is completely incompatible with the doctrine of divine creation. Likewise it dismisses the version of creationism known as "creation science" or "scientific creationism," which considers the Bible a more reliable source of scientific information concerning the origins of life than modern evolutionary biology. Scientific creationism not only fails to give science its own legitimate authority, but it also trivializes biblical teachings by implicitly placing them in the same genre as scientific discourse.

Biblical revelation is debased whenever it is considered another source of information that science is capable of discovering on its own. Following the principle that truth is one, Catholic teaching has consistently maintained that there can be no contradiction between authentic science and an integral faith in revelation. Respect for this principle places the expressions of theology not in a competitive but a complementary relation to evolutionary thinking. Thus, in keeping with the traditional doctrine that God's creativity works continuously and not just "in the beginnings," Catholic theology generously allows for the possibility that evolution is a medium of divine creativity.

Evolution and Contemporary Theology: Nevertheless, much Catholic thought today shares with Christian theology in general the characteristic of not being deeply affected by evolutionary ideas. Perhaps because of theology's understandable preoccupation with human freedom and social justice, nature's evolution has not been a central theme in modern Catholic theology. Though Catholicism has a strong tradition of natural theology that relates divine activity closely to the cosmos, its recent theology has portrayed God as acting almost exclusively in the area of human history rather than in nature and its evolution.

Nevertheless, a growing number of Catholic theologians now object to this one-sided emphasis on salvation history. By relating God only to humanity and its history, theology runs the risk of dualism, of separating human beings from the natural world in which they are rooted. An evolutionary accent in theology, on the other hand, brings out the intimacy of the Christian story of creation with the themes of revelation, incarnation, and redemption. Likewise it allows us to see more clearly the ecological connections between our species and the plants and animals that constitute with humans a single "earth community." It is unwise for theology to tie itself too intimately to the always revisable science of any particular historical period, but many Catholic theologians are grateful nonetheless that evolutionary thinking has deepened our understanding of God's and humanity's relationship to the natural world.

Questions: While fundamentalists find Darwin's theory incompatible with faith, many prominent scientific thinkers consider Christianity to be hostile to the notion of evolution. This supposition is not alleviated when some Christian groups insist that the creation stories of the Bible should become mandatory reading in science classes in the public schools. Media coverage of court cases surrounding this issue also inflames the controversy at times, leaving the impression that Christianity and the idea of evolution are irreconcilable.

This impasse can be overcome only if, on the one hand, Christians allow for a wider understanding of God's creativity than they have accepted in the past and, on the other hand, if scientific thinkers are willing to abandon the unnecessarily materialistic and pessimistic philosophical assumptions that have tainted many of their portraits of the evolutionary process. Scientific skeptics interpret the prominent role of chance in organic variations, for example, as evidence of a universe unguided by providence. And they consider evolution's requirement that countless individuals and species die out in the struggle for existence to be a refutation of God's power and care. Moreover, they often situate evolution only within the restrictive framework of a now outdated mechanistic philosophy of nature.

Contemporary theologies of evolution, on the other hand, interpret the data of evolutionary science as consistent with a God of compassionate love and persuasive power. They underscore the compatibility of nature's randomness (and other manifestations of indeterminacy) with a God who loves freedom and who "lets the world be." And they assimilate the suffering in evolution to the theme of the "kenotic," self-emptying God revealed in the cross of Christ. This God does not stand aloof from evolution, but enters into it, takes its suffering and struggle into the divine life and, consistent with the way God is presented in the Bible, continually offers possibilities of renewal to the cosmos at every stage of its unfolding. Many Catholic theologians now embrace Teilhard de Chardin's vision, according to which the human species carries the world's evolution toward its ultimate destiny by virtue of "a great hope held in common," centered on the incarnate and coming Christ. *See also* creation; creationism.

bliography

Barbour, Ian. *Religion in the Age of Science.* San Francisco: Harper-Collins, 1992.

McMullin, Ernan, ed. *Evolution and Creation.* Notre Dame: University of Notre Dame Press, 1985.

Rahner, Karl. *Hominization: The Evolutionary Origin of Man as a Theological Problem.* Tr. W. T. O'Hara. New York: Herder & Herder, 1965.

Teilhard de Chardin, Pierre. *The Phenomenon of Man.* Tr. B. Wall. New York: Harper & Row, 1959.   JOHN F. HAUGHT

exaltation, elevation to heavenly glory. The affirmation that the resurrected Christ was brought to a position of honor with God is common in the NT (Acts 5:31; 7:55; Rom 1:3; 8:34; Phil 2:9; Eph 1:20; Heb 1:3; 8:1; 12:2; 1 Pet 3:22; Rev 3:21). Such texts frequently use the language of Ps 110, which describes the enthronement of an Israelite king. The Fourth Gospel, trading on the physical and spiritual meanings of certain terms, insists on the intimate association of the exaltation with the Passion, when Jesus is "lifted up" on the Cross (John 3:14; 12:32). *See also* Ascension.

Exaltation of the Cross, currently known as Triumph of the Cross, a liturgical feast celebrated on September 14. The origin of the feast dates to the finding of the True Cross of Christ by Constantine's mother, St. Helena, and the subsequent dedication of a basilica on the site at Golgotha in 335. In the Eastern Church, the feast is marked by veneration of the cross through elevation and blessings in the directions of the four compass points. In Rome, a procession from St. Mary Major to the Lateran preceded a veneration of the cross before Mass. The exalted cross, prefigured in Moses' lifting up the serpent staff in the desert, is glorified on this feast as the instrument of Christ's victory over death. *See also* cross; Helena, St.

examination of conscience, a prayerful review of one's own life on the basis of gospel values. In the history of the Church, an examination of conscience has been part of spirituality from the earliest centuries. Egyptian monasticism included a form of this examination. Celtic monasticism made it a central part of its spiritual program. When the Celtic monks began in the late sixth century to popularize a private form of sacramental confession, the examination of conscience became structured even more into Christian life. In the Middle Ages, popular piety was focused on the confession of sins, and this required a preliminary examination of conscience. Medieval Scholastic theologians formulated moral theology in a more technical way, with a distinction of sins according to number, species, and circumstances. This led to the development of set forms for the examination of conscience. Medieval monasticism emphasized daily or weekly examination of faults, and this custom contributed to the development of a set form for such an examination, based either on the Ten Commandments or a list of virtues. In the post-Tridentine period, Catholic pastors strongly encouraged detailed confession of sin. Under the influence of Jansenism, a seventeenth-century French movement that stressed human sinfulness and the need for severe forms of penance, many of the confessional books of the eighteenth and nineteenth centuries were unnecessarily rigorous but influenced the way many priests viewed the examination of conscience. After Vatican II (1962–65), the examination of conscience, in the renewed rite of Penance, is presented as a prayerful consideration of one's past, but with a major focus on the future, i.e., conversion of one's life. *See also* confession, auricular; Reconciliation, Sacrament of.

KENAN B. OSBORNE

exarch (eks'ahrk; Gk., "leader"), in Eastern canon law, the person who governs an exarchy. He does not govern the exarchy in his own name but in the name of the authority that appointed him. This can be the patriarch, in a patriarchal church, or the Apostolic See of Rome outside patriarchates. The exarch may or may not be a bishop. The term "exarch" is used in a different sense by the Orthodox churches. Here it may be applied to metropolitans (bishops who exercise authority over several dioceses in a province) or to a bishop who has authority over metropolitans.

exarchate. *See* exarchy.

exarchy (eks'ahr-kee), in Eastern canon law, the portion of the People of God that because of particular circumstances has not been canonically erected or established into a fully constituted eparchy (diocese). The Latin equivalent is the apostolic vicariate or prefecture. *See also* prefect apostolic; vicar apostolic.

excardination, the process in which a cleric loses canonical attachment to a particular diocese. This can only occur when a cleric definitively joins a religious institute or is permanently attached to a different diocese. Certain specific circumstances must be verified before either of these actions is effected. For example, if a cleric asks to move to a diocese with a warmer climate for the sake of his health, some medical verification is required. If, however, there is evidence of mere restlessness or instability, the request may be denied. Among the concerns of canon law here are a more equitable geographical distribution of priests, the possibility for a priest to discern and follow a vocation to religious life, and the necessity of a cleric's never being without a proper ecclesiastical superior. *See also* clergy; incardination.

ex cathedra (eks kah-tay'drah; Lat., "from the chair"), the highest level of papal teaching. The expression originated in the early Church, where it was customary for a bishop to preside, preach, and give instructions from his chair near the altar; eventually *ex cathedra* came to designate "authoritative teaching." The First Vatican Council (1869–70) used *ex cathedra* to describe the highest level of papal teaching: "when the Roman Pontiff speaks *ex cathedra*..., he is empowered with that infallibility with which the Divine Redeemer willed to endow his Church." This statement was intended to reject the Gallican claim that the See (Lat., *Sedes*) of Rome is empowered with infallibility, but an individual pope (*Sedens*) is not. Following Vatican I, theologians have emphasized that for a papal teaching to be *ex cathedra*, it must be (1) universal, i.e., enunciated by the pope as teacher of all Christians, (2) supreme, i.e., expressing the highest level of papal teaching authority, (3) definitive, i.e., defining a doctrine concerned with faith and morals, and (4) mandatory, i.e., requiring acceptance by all Christians. Given these requirements, *ex cathedra* teaching is infrequent. *See also* infallibility.

exclaustration, permission for a religious to live apart from the common life (outside the cloister). Although a religious may be assigned to live outside a religious community for reasons of work, health, or study, a religious may not otherwise leave the common life without the special permission of the highest authority of the religious institute. This permission may only be given for a period of up to three years. A frequent reason for this permission is to assist the religious in vocational discernment. The Holy See might require a religious to live outside the common life at the request of the superiors of the religious if he or she is judged harmful to community life. Such an exclaustration is without time limit; it is *ad nutum Sanctae Sedis* (Lat., "at the pleasure of the Holy See").

exclusive language, words or phrases used for class or group that are not applicable to all its members. Such terms are commonly called "false generics." The English word "man" is an example. Though originally (like the Latin *homo*) a generic term for "human being" applicable to either sex, "man" has acquired, historically, a narrower, gender-specific meaning ("man" means "male"). Thus, a phrase like "the future of man (or mankind)" appears to exclude women, even though it purports to designate everyone. In 1990 the U.S. Catholic bishops addressed this problem as it concerns biblical texts in the liturgy by issuing "Criteria for the Evaluation of Inclusive Language." These criteria note that words like "men," "sons," or "brothers," which were once considered inclusive terms, are often understood today as excluding women. Hence, the bishops conclude, such terms should not be used in Scripture texts intended for liturgical usage.

excommunication, the penalty in canon law that partially excludes a Catholic from the life of the Church. Excommunication does not expel a person from the Church, but it does distance one from the Christian community. Excommunication is considered a very serious penalty in canon law, one used for very serious canonical offenses. These offenses are of such a nature that they must be strongly repudiated by the Christian community. Because of their seriousness, an unrepentant perpetrator is to be, to a certain degree, repudiated by the Christian community and disbarred from full communion therein. Of itself excommunication says nothing concerning the moral standing of a given person before God; rather, it addresses the person's relationship with the Christian community.

Reasons for Excommunication: The penalty of excommunication is ancient and references are made to it in early Church councils (see, e.g., the First Ecumenical Council, Nicaea [325], can. 5). In some instances it is incurred automatically (Lat., *latae sententiae*) after the commission of a given offense; if the offense is notorious, this automatic excommunication might also be formally declared by proper Church authority. In other cases excommunication is the result of a formal process (*ferendae sententiae*) and is imposed after such a process. The penalty is incurred automatically in cases of apostasy, heresy, schism, and the absolution by a priest of an accomplice in a sin against the sixth commandment. Automatic excommunication is also the punishment in cases where a bishop consecrates another bishop without permission from Rome or a priest violates confessional secrecy. Incidents of successful abortion, profanation of the Eucharist, or physical force against the pope are also punished by automatic excommunication. The penalty of excommunication is not limited to the above cases and may be given in other cases after a canonical hearing. For the most part, this penalty is used for cases judged under universal Church law established by Rome, though proper ecclesiastical authority might establish the penalty for particular territories. A notable example is the former law in the United States excommunicating anyone who was divorced and remarried. This law was established in the nineteenth century by the American bishops for the United States and has been subsequently abolished.

Effects: Excommunicated persons are not allowed to receive or administer the sacraments. In addition, they may not discharge any ecclesiastical office or function. If the excommunication has been declared or imposed publicly, any attempted discharge of duties of an ecclesiastical office or function is considered invalid in Church law, and even the mere presence of the excommunicate at a church service is proscribed.

It is important to note that canon law is hesitant about the infliction of all penalties, even automatic ones, and that there are a number of factors that might legitimately block the incurrence of a prescribed penalty. In general, anything that diminishes responsibility on the part of the perpetrator might also diminish the penalty. In addition to allowance of such excusing factors that can lessen guilt and hence punishment and penalties, ecclesiastical penal law itself must always be so construed that the number of cases that fall under its purview is limited rather than expanded.

Excommunication is lifted when suitable penance has been performed. Often the penalty is lifted within the private context of sacramental confession. In some cases, especially those in which the excommunication was publicly imposed or declared, the lifting of the penalty can be more public. A few of the most serious offenses (e.g., profaning the Eucharist) require permission from Rome in order to rectify the person's relationship with the Christian community.

Public excommunication is not often used as a penalty. Some of the more notable cases in recent times have involved ultraconservative dissidents, e.g., Father Leonard Feeney, S.J. (d. 1978), who preached that one must be Catholic to be saved (he was later reconciled with the Church), and Archbishop Marcel Lefebvre (d. 1991), who started a schismatic church by consecrating bishops without permission from the pope. *See also* Church; penal law.

JOHN F. LAHEY

exegesis (eks-e-jee'sis; Gk., *exēgeisthai*, "to draw out or explain"), explanation of a biblical text. In principle the methods of biblical exegesis are no different from those used for the study of any ancient text. It is employed with units as small as verses or as large as whole books, e.g., a biblical commentary. The goal of exegesis is to offer enough information to make an ancient text intelligible to contemporary readers. The methods of exegesis comprise textual criticism, i.e., determining among variant readings in the manuscript tradition those that have the greatest claim to originality and antiquity; lexical study of the meaning of words in the original language along with attention to grammar and syntax; translation from one of the biblical languages into an accurate and idiomatic modern language; study of the literary integrity of a text, i.e., are there interpolations by authors later than the original author?; attention to the form and structure of a text, and to the relation of a given text to its proximate and larger literary context (e.g., the Lord's Prayer in the context of Matthew's Sermon on the Mount, and in the context of the Gospel); investigation of the historical, social, and religious contexts of a given text or body of texts; and descriptions of the religious or theological content of a text.

Biblical exegesis is an integral part of historical criticism, which has developed since the Enlightenment as an attempt to use all the available historical sciences to arrive at the original meaning of a text. In its initial phases historical-critical exegesis served to counter encrusted doctrinal interpretations and met with great opposition in both Protestantism and Catholicism. The encyclical *Divino Afflante Spiritu* (On the promotion of biblical studies) of Pius XII (September 30, 1943) and the Dogmatic Constitution on Divine Revelation of Vatican II (November 18, 1965) sanctioned the use of historical-critical exegesis by Catholic scholars. It has become a positive tool for opening the riches of the Bible to the other theological disciples, and to clergy and laypeople.

Often exegesis is contrasted to "eisegesis" (Gk., a "reading into" the text) and is seen as a caution against subjective interpretation. The ideal of a purely objective interpretation or exegesis without presuppositions, which is a legacy of the Enlightenment, has been challenged by recent theories of interpretation. They stress that the biblical texts as religious and often poetic literature do not offer a single clear meaning and that different readers in different historical and social circumstances, though guided by the text, can find meanings not "intended" by the original author, and that extend the meaning of the text beyond its original context (e.g., the use of the Exodus as a paradigm for liberation from oppressive social and political structures). Exegesis can describe well the framework and guidelines that preclude misinterpretation of a text, but can never exhaust the potential for fruitful interpretation. *See also* biblical criticism; biblical exegesis, thirteenth-century; biblical exegesis, twelfth-century; Scripture, interpretation of. JOHN R. DONAHUE

exemplarism, a theory of atonement, also called the "moral" or "subjective" theory, according to which Jesus Christ effects our salvation by being the perfect embodiment of love within history. His witness of selflessness, especially in his suffering, death, and Resurrection, can transform human hearts and minds so that people are inspired to give themselves completely to God and one another. A form of this theory was advocated by Peter Abelard (d. 1142); recast in sacramental terms, it operates in the theology of Karl Rahner (d. 1984). *See also* atonement, doctrine of.

exemption of religious, removal of a religious institute from the immediate authority of the local bishop. Such an institute is then under the direct authority of the Holy See. Religious communities of pontifical right all enjoy such exemption with respect to their internal affairs. This exemption prohibits a local bishop from interfering in the internal life of a religious community.

Institutes are responsible to the local bishop with regard to the external works of the apostolate. Preaching, teaching, and the celebration of the liturgy are under the bishop's supervision. Canon law allows the possibility for further exemption on the part of the Holy See, but does not specify the meaning or degree of that exemption. *See also* religious institute.

Exercises, Spiritual. *See Spiritual Exercises.*

existentialism, a philosophy that emphasizes the radical singularity of individual existence and the encounter between such individual "existents" or between an individual and a moment of the prevailing culture. The mood of existentialism can be one of alienation, as with Jean-Paul Sartre's (1905–80) anguished individual facing an absurd world, or reconciliation, as with Martin Buber's (1878–1965) insistence that the "I" is realized only in the encounter with a "Thou." The most important existentialist thinker for Christian theology is Martin Heidegger (1889–1976), whose writings focus on the encounter, even the confrontation, between humanity and the question of its own existence.

Pius XII rejected existentialism in his 1950 encyclical *Humani Generis,* finding existentialism's vocabulary of radical temporality, situation, and encounter at odds with Scholastic theology's emphasis on eternal truths and immutable essences. Nonetheless, existentialist motifs are widespread in contemporary Catholic theology, primarily due to the influence of Karl Rahner (d. 1984), whose fundamental theology utilizes elements from Heidegger in a Thomistic framework. Heideggerian existentialism has also influenced the work of the twentieth-century Protestant theologians Rudolf Bultmann and Paul Tillich. *See also* philosophy and theology.

Exodus, Israel's departure from Egypt, probably ca. 1200 B.C. Jacob's descendants who had moved to Egypt (Gen 46) were enslaved after several generations. The Lord then commissioned Moses to lead these Israelites from Egypt, but he succeeded only after the ten plagues had weakened the pharaoh's resolve. The Passover meal, which the Israelites ate while the tenth plague was occurring, was followed by a hasty exit from Egypt and crossing of the Reed Sea into the wilderness. The importance of these events to the biblical narrative caused the second book of the Bible to be named Exodus in the Greek and subsequent translations.

ex opere operantis (eks oh'pair-ay oh-pair-ahn'tis; Lat., "from the work of the doer"), expression used in sacramental theology to refer to the actions or merits of the minister or recipients of the sacraments, in contrast to God's own action in and through the sacraments. This phrase does not deny that the validity of a sacrament depends ultimately on God's saving will as expressed in the promises of Christ, but it emphasizes the importance of the interior disposition of human beings. Although the subjective disposition of a person receiving or celebrating a sacrament has no bearing on its validity, a sacrament's spiritual effects or fruitfulness can be blocked by lack of faith or attentiveness, or by sin. The phrase *ex opere operantis* is especially applicable to the reception of sacramentals, whose celebration does not carry the same guarantee of grace as the seven sacraments. *See also* ex opere operato; fruitfulness of the sacrament; sacrament; sacramentals.

ex opere operato (eks oh'pair-ay oh-pair-ah' toh; Lat., "from the work done"), expression used in the theology of the sacraments to emphasize that, since God is the chief agent of the sacrament, the sacrament can never fail to celebrate the salvation promised in Christ provided that it is celebrated under proper conditions. This assertion underscores the traditional Christian conviction that God's salvific will is not ultimately dependent upon human action or attitudes, but is expressed publicly in the Church's sacraments, which are objectively valid pledges of God's grace. This teaching also emphasizes that sacraments are not discrete, magically effective signs, but are the self-expressions and actualizations of the Church, which itself is Christ's continuing saving presence in the world. It is the intrinsic connection of the sacraments with the Church as the fundamental sacrament that guarantees that those who approach the sacraments in faith will unfailingly receive grace from God. *See also* ex opere operantis; sacrament.

exorcism, the act of liberating persons, places, or things from the power of evil through prayer and symbolic deeds. Such acts of liberation characterized the ministry of Jesus (see, e.g., Luke 11:14–23) and that of his disciples (see, e.g., Acts 16:18). Historically, two basic types of exorcism developed in the Church. The first of these ("major" or "solemn" exorcism) involved freeing persons from obsessive spiritual conditions thought to derive from evil powers or diabolical spirits. Such solemn exorcisms came to be restricted, in time, to bishops or to priests with explicit episcopal permission. More common are exorcisms of the second type: ritual prayers for adult catechumens, associated with the process of Christian initiation. Such exorcisms already are found in early Christian documents like the *Apostolic Tradition* of Hippolytus (ca. 215), which directs the bishop to exorcise the catechumens on the day before their baptism. Similar prayers of exorcism were retained, even when (increasingly, after the fourth century) the majority of candidates for baptism were infants. The Rite of Baptism for Children, reformed following Vatican Council II, contains only one exorcism (which may be omitted). The 1972 Rite of Christian Initiation of Adults, however, restores exorcisms at several points in the process of initiation: when candidates are enrolled in the order of catechumens; during the period of the catechumenate itself; and, more elaborately, during the three "scrutinies," which take place on the third, fourth, and fifth Sundays of Lent, prior to the catechumens' Baptism at the Easter Vigil. *See also* demonic possession; Rite of Christian Initiation of Adults.   NATHAN MITCHELL

exorcism [in the Bible], a rite performed to expel an evil spirit from a person or from a habitation. In the Greco-Roman world the practice was widespread and varied greatly in form. The exorcist might invoke a sacred name or a particular angel who had power over that spirit or use incantations, spells, or physical objects, such as herbs or the entrails of animals. One particular technique involved ascertaining the name of the demon and commanding it to leave the victim. Sometimes the demon was directed to go into the sea or another ill-omened place. These ceremonies involved explicit use of magic and were condemned by Jews and Christians. There is only one clear reference to exorcism in the OT, namely, Tob 6:7–18 and 8:1–3, where Raphael frees the victim by the use of the heart and liver of a fish. Paul (1 Cor 12:1–10) does not list exorcism as a ministry of the Spirit. The two cases of exorcism in Acts involve pagan persons (Acts 16:16; 19:13–19). The synoptic Gospels, especially Mark, portray Jesus as an exorcist, but he does not use any of the magical rites or physically touch a possessed person. Only in one case does he ask the demons' names and cast them into the abyss (Mark 5:1–20; Matt 8:28–34; Luke 8:26–39). There are no exorcisms in John.

The Catholic Church has always proceeded with extreme care in dealing with cases of supposed possession. The Church requires that the patient undergo both physical and psychological examinations before it will consider exorcism. In rare cases it chooses a minister of exceptional talent and stable character to perform the rite, which is found in the Roman Ritual. Most cases of purported demonic possession should be appropriated to and handled by a professional psychiatrist. *See also* demonic possession.   J. MASSYNGBAERDE FORD

exorcist, formerly the third minor order. This office was based on the belief that malign spiritual forces exist and have influence on human affairs. It emerged as an ecclesiastical institution in the third century. The task of the exorcist is to drive out evil spirits. The early Church incorporated exorcism into the preparation of a catechumen for Baptism. The exorcist later acquired other liturgical responsibilities as well. Although Pope Paul VI (1963–78) eliminated this minor order in 1972, bishops may still appoint priests to perform the rite of exorcism when a person has been determined to be possessed by a demon. It is, however, something to be rarely, if ever, invoked. *See also* minor orders.

experience and moral theology, the relationship between human experience and theological reflection on it. Attention to human experience has long been a part of Catholic moral theology, implicit in its consideration of how particular circumstances may contribute to the meaning of a moral act. However, influenced by contemporary philosophical and theological personalism, and in reaction to overly deductive and law-centered approaches to morality, moral theology after the Second Vatican Council (1962–65) has increasingly turned to experience as an explicit source and criterion of moral judgment. The appeal to experience, which involves the attempt to delimit more precisely its nature and scope within moral reflection, and its relation to moral theory, has had the most far-reaching effects in the areas of biomedical and sexual ethics.

experimentation, medical, procedures performed on human beings for the purpose of gaining knowledge beneficial to others. Differentiation is often made between therapeutic experimentation, where benefit to the individual patient is anticipated, and nontherapeutic, or research, experimentation, where the only benefit is knowledge gained for others.

Catholic tradition bases its approval of proper human medical experimentation on the inherently social character of the human person as created by God and saved by Jesus Christ, and supports two sets of requirements generally mandated in this context: informed consent and criteria assuring the proper balance of risk and benefit.

Patients and research subjects must be adequately informed about the experiment, including its risks and benefits and any alternative therapies, about the odds of receiving a placebo if applicable, and about the right to withdraw at any time. Voluntariness must be assured by reducing pressure to consent; particular care should be taken regarding institutionalized persons and others who might experience psychological or material need. Disagreement persists about the validity of proxy consent for children, and some reject it for all nontherapeutic experiments.

No experiment is permitted that entails unjustified risk, regardless of consent. Thus needless experiments, including those done to benefit the researcher or to provide knowledge of dubious value, are illicit. Prior computer and animal testing are usually mandatory. Therapeutic experiments may entail more risk than nontherapeutic research, since a balanced benefit to the patient is anticipated. Children may be subjected only to minimal risk in nontherapeutic research. Placebos must be discontinued if it becomes clear that the subject will benefit from the investigated therapy. *See also* medical ethics.

DAVID F. KELLY

expiation, to make satisfaction, or to cleanse from guilt or pollution by religious ceremonies (2 Sam 21:3; Num 35:33). In Leviticus it refers to the "mercy seat" (Heb., *kapporet*) on the ark, where God appears on a cloud (Lev 16:2), and where expiation was made by the sprinkling of blood on the day of atonement (Lev 16:14–16). In Rom 3:25, "Christ Jesus, whom God set forth as an expiation," in the Revised Standard Version and the New American Bible Revised New Testament, "expiation" translates the Greek, *hilasterion,* where Christ is the new "mercy seat" (see also 1 John 2:2, 4:10). The New Revised Standard Version's "put forward as a sacrifice of atonement" is inaccurate. Though often used synonymously with propitiation, the terms have different nuances. Propitiation is a more legal, forensic term and suggests warding off divine punishment. Expiation refers to the sin or guilt itself and looks to the restoration of the covenant relationship with God. *See also* atonement, biblical view of; atonement, doctrine of; propitiation; satisfaction.

exposition of the Blessed Sacrament, a religious devotion in which the consecrated host is displayed for the worship of the faithful. The host is usually in a monstrance placed upon the altar or above the tabernacle. The devotion arose from the desire of the faithful to focus their eyes and attention upon the host as a means of fostering interior communion with the Lord and of contemplating the mystery of Christ's presence. As such, this practice is an extension of the custom, originating in the thirteenth century, of the priest's elevating the bread, then the cup, after reciting the words of consecration during the Mass.

Exposition has been part of Forty Hours devotion, First Friday devotions, holy hours of adoration, perpetual adoration, Benediction, and Corpus Christi processions. The liturgical renewal of Vatican Council II, however, promoted an active lay participation in Mass, including Communion. The result has been a decreased need and desire for exposition. *See also* adoration; Benediction; Blessed Sacrament; Real Presence.

Exsurge Domine (ek-suhr'jay dohm'ee-nay; Lat., "Rise up, Lord"), bull excommunicating Martin Luther. Promulgated June 15, 1520, by Pope Leo X, it gave Luther sixty days to submit. Luther refused and appealed to a future Church council. Although excommunication made Luther liable to civil prosecution, the bull was ineffective, simply marking Luther's final break with Rome. *See also* Luther, Martin.

Extension Society. *See* Catholic Church Extension Society.

external forum, process of judgment in canon law that deals with matters publicly known or provable. Matters dealt with in the external forum are not issues that are confined solely to the confidence of the seal of confession or to a strictly confidential pastoral conversation (internal forum). While knowledge of such matters may be held within a certain degree of confidence, they may also be shared with appropriate individuals and may be the basis for making decisions effective in the public realm, e.g., a decision concerning the nullity of a marriage. *See also* internal forum.

extracanonical writings, several books that, for one reason or another, did not find their way into the Hebrew Bible but were included in the Old Greek (Septuagint) translation and enjoyed considerable popularity and authority in NT times. These were 1–2 Esdras, Judith, Tobit, Wisdom of Solomon, Sirach (Ecclesiasticus), Baruch with the Letter of Jeremiah, 1–2 Maccabees, and Additions to Esther and Daniel. In Protestant usage these are known as Apocrypha (esoteric, to be excluded), while Catholics refer to them as deuterocanonical, though the distinction is now considered to be less important. Most if not all of these books were written between the second century B.C. and the first century A.D. *See also* Apocrypha; apocryphal Gospels; canon of the Scriptures; pseudepigrapha.

extraliturgical service, a public form of worship that may make use of liturgical elements (e.g., Scripture readings), but which is technically not part of the Church's official liturgy. Examples include popular devotions such as the Rosary or the Stations of the Cross. Neither of these devotions— though frequently celebrated in parishes (especially during seasons like Lent)—has ever been considered part of the Church's official liturgical rites. They are optional practices that play a legitimate role in Christian life but whose contents (so Vatican II insisted in its Constitution on the Sacred Liturgy, n. 13) must be in harmony with the Church's liturgy. *See also* devotions; paraliturgy.

extraordinary means. *See* ordinary/extraordinary means.

extraordinary minister of the Eucharist, a nonordained (hence "extraordinary") person who distributes Holy Communion to the faithful. Since 1973, diocesan bishops (or their delegates) have been authorized to appoint nonordained Catholics to administer Communion at Mass and to take the Eucharist to the sick or dying. This appointment (for which a rite of commissioning exists) may be either permanent or limited to a specified period. The principle supporting this "extraordinary ministry" is outlined in the 1983 Code of Canon Law (can. 230. 3), which states that laypeople can exercise the ministry of the word, preside over liturgical prayers, confer Baptism and distribute Holy Communion whenever the needs of the Church require it, or whenever sufficient ordained ministers are not available. Thus, extraordinary eucharistic ministers may be appointed whenever the lack of ordained clergy would unduly lengthen a service or whenever the spiritual needs of the infirm in homes or hospitals require it. *See also* eucharistic minister.

Extreme Unction. *See* Anointing of the Sick.

Eymard, St. Peter Julien, 1811–68, founder of two religious communities. Born in Grenoble, France, he was ordained a Marist in 1834. He founded the Blessed Sacrament Fathers (1856) and helped establish a contemplative women's community, the Servants of the Blessed Sacrament (1858). He was canonized in 1962. Feast day: August 1.

1 "Give to the emperor the things that are the emperor's," he said, "and to God the things that are God's" (Luke 20:25); Jesus speaks with the priests, scribes, and elders; painting by Rubens (ca. 1612), Fine Arts Museums of San Francisco. **2** *The Face of Jesus,* a contemporary depiction of Jesus by American artist Norman LaLiberté; plaster plate. **3** "And the soldiers wove a crown of thorns and put it on his head, and they dressed him in a purple robe. They kept coming up to him, saying, 'Hail, King of the Jews!' and striking him on the face" (John 19:2–3); Christ with the crown of thorns; twentieth-century African wood sculpture.
4 "He went out to what is called The Place of the Skull, which in Hebrew is called Golgotha. There they crucified him . . . " (John 19: 17–18); seventeenth-century painting of the crucifixion by Diego Velásquez, Prado, Madrid.

5

6

7

5 The Nativity, depicting the Blessed Virgin Mary, the infant Jesus, Joseph, an angel, and God the Father; medieval painting on oakwood by Melchior Broederlam (d. 1409); Mayer van den Bergh Museum, Antwerp. **6** The baptism of Jesus by John the Baptist, with the Holy Spirit in the form of a dove hovering overhead; fifteenth-century Renaissance painting by Piero della Francesca, National Gallery, London. **7** "So they went with haste and found Mary and Joseph, and the child lying in the manger" (Luke 2:16); the adoration of the newborn Savior by the shepherds, with angels overhead; seventeenth-century painting by G. B. Castiglione, Louvre, Paris. **8** Jesus and the apostles at the Last Supper (Peter is to Jesus' left, and John is to his right); fourteenth-century Pietro Lorenzetti painting, in the Church of St. Francis, Assisi, Italy.

8

9

10

9 "This Jesus God raised up, and of that all of us are witnesses" (Acts 2:32); Peter preaches in Jerusalem; detail of a fresco by Tommaso Masolino (d. 1447), in the Brancacci Chapel, Santa Maria del Carmine, Florence. **10** The stoning of Stephen, the first martyr, depicted anachronistically in a deacon's dalmatic, or outer liturgical vestment; fifteenth-century illustration by Jean Fouquet, Condé Museum, Chantilly, France. **11** The meeting of Pope Silvester I (on the horse) and the first Christian emperor, Constantine the Great (d. 337), who granted a privileged status to the Church in 313 and who called the Council of Nicaea in 325; thirteenth-century painting, in the Church of the Four Crowned Saints (Quattro Santi Coronati), Rome. **12** St. Patrick, fifth-century British missionary bishop known as the Apostle to the Irish; stained-glass window in St. Patrick's Cathedral, New York. **13** Augustine of Hippo (354–430), one of the greatest saints, bishops, and theologians in all of Church history; fifteenth-century painting by Sandro Botticelli, in the Church of All Saints, Florence.

11

12

13

14

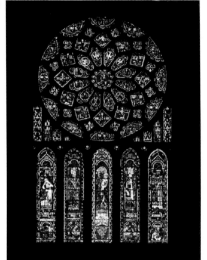

15

16

17

18

14 Rose window, on the north side of Chartres Cathedral in France. Along with its magnificent spires, this Gothic church is most renowned for its stained-glass windows. **15** Benedict of Nursia (ca. 480–ca. 550), a founder of Western monasticism and author of the Rule of St. Benedict; fourteenth-century fresco in Sacro Speco, Subiaco, Italy. **16** Thomas Aquinas (ca. 1225–74), one of the most important theologians in the history of the Church; fourteenth-century Traini painting, in the Church of St. Catherine, Pisa, Italy. **17** Pope Gregory VII, whose pontificate (1073–85) marked a major turning point in the history of the Church because of his exercise of temporal as well as spiritual authority; portion of a Federico Zuccari (d. 1609) fresco, Scala Regia, Vatican City. **18** Christ's coronation of the Blessed Virgin Mary as Queen of Heaven; fourteenth-century illustration for the *Book of Hours of François de Guise,* Condé Museum, Chantilly, France.

19 Robert Bellarmine (1542–1621), cardinal, Jesuit theologian, and fair-minded defender of the Catholic position against Protestants during the Counter-Reformation; painting by Andrea Pozzo (d. 1709), in the Church of St. Ignatius, Rome. **20** Pope Paul III (1534–49), a leading figure in the sixteenth-century Catholic Reformation, who called the Council of Trent, an ecumenical council that would shape Catholicism for centuries thereafter; sixteenth-century Titian portrait, Kunsthistorisches Museum, Vienna. **21** The Council of Trent (1545–63), in northern Italy, the Catholic Church's belated but doctrinally and pastorally forceful response to the Protestant Reformation; constituted the single greatest influence on the shape of Catholicism until the Second Vatican Council in 1962; painting by Titian, Louvre, Paris. **22** Michelangelo's classic depiction of the last judgment, in the Sistine Chapel, Vatican City. He worked on the painting from 1534 until 1541. **23** Ignatius of Loyola (1491–1556), Spanish founder of the Jesuits, one of the most influential religious orders in the history of the Church; seventeenth-century Rubens painting, Kunsthistorisches Museum, Vienna.

19

20

21

22

23

24 25

26

24 Interior of the early eighteenth-century Wieskirche, in Steingaden (Bavaria), Germany, a church in the ornate Baroque style by Domenikus Zimmermann. **25** The young Wolfgang Amadeus Mozart, eighteenth-century Austrian Catholic composer who began his artistic career at the age of five and who, by the time of his death at age thirty-five, had produced some of the world's greatest operas, symphonies, concertos, and sonatas; Mozart Museum, Salzburg, Austria. **26** The gilded interior of a Baroque church in Morelia, Mexico. In this church, the Mexican flag stands alongside the depiction of Our Lady of Guadalupe above the tabernacle. **27** Pius IX, the longest reigning pope (1846–78) and one of the strongest opponents of modern democratic movements in the mid-nineteenth century, particularly through his *Syllabus of Errors* (1864). This portrait hangs, ironically, in the Museo del Risorgimento (the name for the Italian reform movement he opposed), Milan. **28** Pope Leo XIII (1878-1903), who adopted a more realistic posture toward modern developments than his predecessor, Pius IX, is celebrated for *Rerum Novarum* (1891), the first major papal encyclical on social justice; portrait by Benjamin Costant (1900), Historical Museum of the Lateran Palace, Vatican City.

27 28

29

30

29 Pope John XXIII (1958-63), who called the Second Vatican Council and presided over its first session in 1962; one of the most beloved popes in the history of the Church. **30** The Second Vatican Council (1962–65), the most important Catholic event in modern times, with the bishops of the world gathered in St. Peter's Basilica, Vatican City, and Pope Paul VI presiding at the altar at the second of the council's four sessions (October 1963). **31** A view from St. Peter's Basilica of the Vatican Gardens and other portions of Vatican City, which became an autonomous territorial state in 1929 with the signing of the Lateran Treaty between Italy and the Holy See. **32** Pope Paul VI (1963-78), one of the leading bishops of the Second Vatican Council during its first session (1962) and pope during its three remaining sessions (1963–65); although he was devoted to the implementation of the council, the latter part of his pontificate was marred by the debate about birth control and the decline of priestly and religious vocations.

32

31

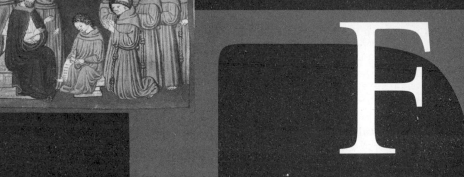

Faber, Frederick W., 1814–63, author, priest, composer. Born into a Calvinist family and educated at Oxford, Faber first converted to Anglicanism and then in 1845 to Catholicism. He was ordained a Catholic priest in 1847 and soon earned a reputation as a composer of popular hymns and a writer of spiritual books.

Faber, Jacobus, also known as Jacques Lefèvre d'Étaples, ca. 1450–1536, French priest, humanist reformer, and translator of the NT into French. Though condemned by the French government for his Lutheran sympathies, he never fully sympathized and remained personally committed to Catholicism.

Fabian, St., pope (from 236 to 250) and martyr. He was executed during the Decian persecution; his tomb is still extant in the catacombs of Callistus. Feast day (with St. Sebastian): January 20.

Fabiola, St., d. 399, Roman matron who, having divorced a dissolute husband, remarried. Upon her second husband's death she did public penance, distributing her wealth to the poor and caring for the sick. From 394 she lived in Bethlehem with Paula and Eustochium and studied Scripture with Jerome, but eventually she returned to Rome to continue her work with the poor. Feast day: December 27. *See also* Jerome, St.

faculties, canonical, the authorization, given either by canon law itself or by delegation from competent authority, to perform certain acts of ministry or of governance. Most common are the faculty of hearing confessions and the faculty of officiating at marriages. In these cases, as well as many others, the Church does not recognize the validity of acts performed without the requisite faculties. In order to assure adequately prepared and properly disposed ministers, delegated faculties may be withdrawn or refused under certain specified circumstances.

Faith, Defender of. *See* Defender of the Faith.

faith and morals (Lat., *fides et mores*), a phrase used by theologians to identify those areas where the Church is competent to teach. The inner reality of faith is expressed in the revealed truth given in Jesus Christ and the Scriptures and preserved in tradition. The term "morals" has a more ambiguous history. *Mores* originally referred to the religious and devotional customs and practices of Church life. The ambiguity arose in modern times as "morals" connoted ethical behavior. At the Council of Trent (1545–63) *mores* clearly meant "customs," although the ethical conduct, particularly of the clergy, was an underlying concern. The shift in meaning can be recognized at the First Vatican Council (1869–70), where a question was raised whether "morals" should be rendered as "the general precepts of morals." Since the definition of papal infallibility concerns the pope's competence to proclaim on "matters of faith and morals," the question of exact meaning becomes crucial. Many moral theologians argue that only the most general precepts of morality are found in revelation, even though the life of faith entails certain moral behavior. Here the power of infallible declarations would include only these most general moral precepts. Others argue that the teaching of the Church aims towards salvation, which requires both living faith and good moral conduct. Hence, infallible papal teaching could provide safeguards for specific moral principles along with truths of faith. That no pope has explicitly declared any moral precept infallibly suggests that the understanding of the phrase "faith and morals" remains unsettled. *See also* infallibility.

MARK MILLER

Faith and Order, a study commission of the World Council of Churches (WCC) that focuses on the ecumenical call to the churches to pursue "the goal of visible unity in one faith and in one eucharistic fellowship, expressed in worship and in the common life of Christ, and to advance toward that unity in order that the world may believe."

The commission is composed of 120 men and women theologians of various disciplines, from church traditions across all six continents. They include full participants from WCC nonmember churches; for example, there are twelve Roman Catholics (since 1968).

History: In 1921, over four hundred Anglican, Protestant, and Orthodox theologians held the first Faith and Order world conference in 1927 (Lausanne). At its second conference in 1937 (Edinburgh) the theologians decided to fuse their movement into what would become the WCC (1948). The new commission at Lund (1952) moved from the "comparative ecclesiology" method of registering points of agreement and disagreement on church-dividing issues to the method of facing them from that common biblical and Christological basis uncovered in a common history.

Over four decades, Faith and Order had dealt with a broad spectrum of theological issues: the one Church, the churches, and the nature of Church unity; Scripture and tradition; the role of creeds and confessions; so-called nontheological factors on efforts for Church unity; Christian hope today; ordination of women; worship and spirituality; inter-communion.

Since 1982 Faith and Order work has become widely known for its broad discussion and reception process of the Baptism, Eucharist and Ministry (BEM) document, which revealed a formulated agreement on teaching and practice related to the three historically divisive issues mentioned in the title of the document. BEM complements two other ongoing major studies: on the common understanding and common expression of the apostolic faith today, and on the inseparability of the search for Church unity from the quest for renewed human community, for the formulation of doctrinal agreements "cannot be divorced from the redemptive and liberating mission of Christ in the modern world."

The commission prepared jointly with the Pontifical Council for Christian Unity the materials for the annual Week of Prayer for Christian Unity in January. *See also* World Council of Churches.

THOMAS F. STRANSKY

faith and reason, the relationship between the gift of divine faith and the role of human reason in understanding and explaining it. The Catholic Church avoids two extreme positions regarding the relationship between faith and reason: fideism and rationalism. Fideism denies the possibility of arriving at certain knowledge of the existence of God and the facts of revelation by natural powers. In fideism the sources of religious and moral knowledge lie exclusively in divine revelation. Rationalism subjects the objects of religious faith and the data of revelation to the judgment of unaided human reason.

Vatican I: Vatican I's Dogmatic Constitution on the Catholic Faith (1870) declared that unaided natural reason could acquire certain knowledge of God's existence and nature. The guarantee of the proof of the true religion is not to be found in interior experiences, but in the exterior signs given by God. These signs are the miracles performed by Christ. These objective and external criteria offer rational proof of the existence and authority of God, according to the preambles of faith. They also permit one to hold that one religion is more believable than another.

Vatican II: The Dogmatic Constitution on Divine Revelation (1965) promulgated by Vatican II does not negate the previous council's pronouncements on faith and reason, but casts them in a different light. Where Vatican I begins with the natural knowledge of God and states that it pleased God to reveal "the eternal decree of his will," Vatican II states that God reveals the sacrament of the divine will. Thus, rather than a legalistic and propositional notion of revelation, we have a sacramental view that encompasses the mystery of Christ.

In Vatican II, all the individual miracles are set within the one miracle, which is Christ. The word uttered is the Word, the Son of God. The sixth paragraph of chapter 1 on the nature of divine revelation reiterates that not only is God self-manifested and communicated, but also "the eternal decrees of [the divine] will." It further states that "God, the first principle and last end of all things, can be known with certainty from the created world, by the natural light of human reason." However, the position of these statements gives priority to the revelatory action of God. We are able to come to knowledge of God's existence through reason only because those created realities grounding the basis of rational proof are themselves manifestations of God. This negates the possibility that reason operates independently of grace, for in addition to the subjective assistance that grace provides the person who seeks the preamble of faith, the fact that all created reality is founded in Christ because it proceeds from God's creative word places both faith and reason in a dependence on the revelation of God. Thus, even though reason may precede faith, revelation supplies the criteria of reason. Rather than setting faith and reason against each other, it is more correct to examine their mutual interdependence.

Vatican I teaches that there can be no true contradiction between faith and reason because the source of both is God and God cannot engage in self-denial nor can truth contradict truth. The council attributes any apparent contradiction to the misinterpretation of faith or an error of reason. *See also* faith; fideism; rationalism; Vatican Council I.

SUSAN K. WOOD

FAITH

Faith is the graced but free human acceptance of God's self-communication in Christ as mediated by the Christian community. Grace and freedom, God's free initiative and the free human response of acceptance, comprise the mystery of faith. Christian faith assumes and transforms the universal experience of human faith and the diverse and varied experience of religious faith. Human faith is the simple capacity to trust another person. As such, it is not peripheral to, but constitutes, the human condition. It assumes that there are reasonable grounds for such trust. When two people meet, they go through a process of getting to know one another by sharing names, background, interests, and so forth. But if the relationship is to move beyond mere acquaintance to a deeper level of friendship, there comes a moment of self-transcendence, which carries with it the risk of deception or betrayal. This is the moment when each person entrusts him- or herself to the other. There are reasonable grounds for such trust in that each knows the other through a shared history, but there is no way to prove with absolute certainty that the other is fully trustworthy. There is always risk, but the risk is credible, not foolish. Without the capacity for self-transcendence in trust and the actual experience of trust in a particular relationship, people cannot grow as mature human beings. Faith in this sense is what makes people human. This human experience is analogous to religious and Christian faith but is the experiential ground that must be subsumed into, and transformed by, a human relationship of friendship with God.

The religious understanding of faith is central to the Judeo-Christian experience as well as to Islam. All three religions claim Abraham as their common father in faith. Faith is central to these religions because they have a historical understanding of world process. Abraham had a personal experience of God who called him forth from the comfort of his ancestral home and promised him a new future for countless generations to come. Faith is precisely trust in the one who promises this future and who is understood to accompany the people on their journey. In this personal and historical sense faith is unique to the Judeo-Christian heritage. It is the appropriate and indeed necessary stance in a world that has not yet arrived at its final consummation. Other religious traditions that have a more cyclical notion of world process and a more impersonal understanding of the divine do not use faith in this sense. However, all religions, insofar as they seek knowledge of the divine and some sort of relationship with the divine that affects human life, can be said to be religious "faiths" or "beliefs." What follows is a further explanation of Christian faith.

A GRACED ACCEPTANCE

Christian tradition has always recognized that faith is a gift of God that depends totally on God's initiative. Individuals cannot enter into a personal, trusting relationship with God unless God invites them into the divine life. While God seeks human friendship, the mutuality that friendship implies can never be that of equals. Jesus said, "I have called you friends, because I have made known to you everything I have heard from my Father" (John 15:15), yet the initiative for such self-revelation is completely from the bosom of the Father (John 1:18). John gives a particularly rich description of the life of faith, which he equates with eternal life, as consisting primarily of the triune God (Father, Son, and Spirit) dwelling in the one who believes and the believer dwelling within the triune God. At its most fundamental, faith is an invitation from God to live the divine life. It is the firm conviction of Christian and Catholic faith that God wills the salvation of all people (1 Tim 2:3–7). Therefore, all people receive this invitation from God (Vatican II, Dogmatic Constitution on the Church, nn. 2, 13–16) but experience it differently within the concrete conditions that constitute their particular life situation. The invitation offered through creation and covenant comes to its deepest and fullest expression in the incarnation of God's only Son (John 1:14–18). One can understand this as the progressive deepening of God's personal self-involvement in the creative process. It is God's own breath (Spirit) that humans breathe to become living creatures (Gen 2:7). It is God's compassionate love for the children of Abraham that frees them from slavery, makes them a people, and brings them to the land of promise (Exod 2:23–4:17). It is God's continuing fidelity in love that has given the world the ultimate gift of grace, his only Son (John 1:17; 3:16; Rom 5:1–11; 8:1–4). Thus, the whole of creation is the expression in ever-deepening ways of God's gracious love.

The certainty of faith, as a gift from God, can be called absolute because it comes from God, who can neither deceive nor be deceived. The inward illumination of grace enables one to entrust oneself to God who is worthy of absolute and total trust. This excludes doubt with regard to the object of faith, because the object of belief is God. But, since faith is neither self-evident nor based on apodictic or empirical "proof" (in a scientific sense), the certainty of faith cannot exclude the possibility of serious questioning and even doubt from the perspective of one's personal, subjective apprehension of the gift. This is normally where the question of certitude arises. As in the case of Abraham, faith gives persons the kind of certainty that allows them to trust in a promised future and to act on that trust. Were apodictic or empirical proof possible, talk would no longer be of faith but of vision (1 Cor 13:12; 1 John 3:2; Heb 11:1).

A FREE HUMAN ACCEPTANCE

Faith in the fullest and deepest sense is not just the intellectual assent of the mind to the truths that God reveals, although that dimension is integral. It is not a question of the mind's grasping something so much as it is of the whole self's being "grasped" by the presence and power of God's Spirit who illumines the mind and draws a person into a life of intimacy and friendship with God. Thus, faith is not reducible to a particular act; it is a whole way of life, a basic orientation of the whole person that includes intellect, will, emotions—in a word, one's deepest desires. Faith is a kind of knowledge, but knowledge in the biblical sense of an intimate and personal involvement of oneself in the life of another. Its primary exemplification in human experience is the total gift of two persons one to another in sexual union. God as portrayed in the Bible is repeatedly characterized as "faithful love" (through the joining of the terms for "merciful love" and "fidelity in truth" in the Hebrew Scriptures, which is then translated as "grace and truth" in John 1:14, 17). One believes God and trusts God because God is faithful to the divine promises (Gen 15:1–6; Rom 4:1–3, 13–25; Heb 11:1–3, 8–12, 17–19) which are fulfilled in Jesus who is "the pioneer and perfecter of our faith" (Heb 12:2).

Faith, then, is a call from God to be faithful in love as God is faithful. In this sense, as with Martin Luther's view of faith, faith is something to be lived and so includes the virtues of love and hope, the experience of union with God, and the desire to live forever in that union. Faith and hope will be subsumed into and transformed by love when we see God "face to face" (1 Cor 13:12–13). Faith and hope are appropriate and necessary in this life, but faith without works is dead. For Paul, "works" mean "works of the law" (Gal 3:2–5, 10–12), so he prefers to speak of "the fruit of the Spirit" (Gal 5:22–23, 25). What is finally effective is a faith that works through love (Gal 5:6). The Letter of James, on the other hand, which Luther called an "epistle of straw," exhorts believers to be "doers of the word, and not merely hearers" (Jas 1:22). The reason is that "faith by itself, if it has no works, is dead" (2:17). For Luther, one is justified by "faith alone," but he understood faith in the full Pauline sense to include the effective power of love and hope. When James says "a person is justified by works and not by faith alone" (2:24), he is distinguishing faith and works but he is also saying that justification requires their inseparable unity. The distinction allowed the Council of Trent (1545–63) to maintain, against Luther, that faith can coexist with sin. However, all Christians—Lutherans and Catholics alike—agree that the faith necessary for justification and salvation must include endurance, character, hope, and love (Rom 5:1–5).

GOD'S SELF-COMMUNICATION IN CHRIST

The term "mystery" in the Christian Scriptures refers to the eternal plan or intention of God, i.e., God's will, hidden in God through the centuries, fully and finally revealed in Christ, and proclaimed by the Christian community (Rom 16:25–26; Col 1:24–28; 2:2–3; Eph 1:9–10; 3:2–12). Christian faith is centered in Christ, but to speak of God's self-communication in Christ is to speak of Jesus' personal relation to the Father in the power of the Spirit, i.e., the inner triune life of God. Equally important is the Christian community, which is the sacramental embodiment of God's own inner life to the degree that humans are enabled to receive and express visibly the mystery. The only and unique mediator between God and humans who makes this possible is the fully human Christ Jesus (1 Tim 2:4–6). Cardinal John Henry Newman (d. 1890) said that no people has been denied a revelation from God. It is true that God reveals the divine Self through experiences of nature, of consciousness and conscience (moral exigence), of self-transcending relationships with other persons, especially in love, and of personal and communal histories. Vatican II affirms the constant tradition that God can be known with certainty from created reality by using human reason and reflection (Vatican II, Dogmatic Constitution on Divine Revelation, nn. 3, 6), but the council is more concerned to emphasize that in Christ is the fullness of revelation (nn. 2, 4, 6). This revelation is final in that humanity awaits no new public revelation before the final coming and it is full because it communicates the divine mystery, which totally transcends the capacities of the human mind. The mystery hidden in God and revealed in Christ is the fullness of the triune life of God.

It is helpful to distinquish two ways in which this revelation is received in faith. First, *fides qua* (Lat., "faith by which") refers to the self-involving act of trust in the personal God who reveals the inner divine life to individuals and calls them into a promised future. The Hebrew Scriptures understand faith primarily in these concrete and personal terms as fidelity (or obedience) to God's word. The Hebrew word *'emet* refers to something solid or firm, something that can be relied upon to be true in the sense of trustworthy or faithful. Faith, in effect, says "I believe you." Signs, e.g., miracles that might provide motives for belief, are secondary to the personal relationship as such. The Christian Scriptures continue this understanding, but the Greek word *pisteuein* means not only to trust or show confidence, but also to accept as true. Thus, Paul speaks of "the obedience of faith" (Rom 1:5; 16:26), which includes not only fidelity but also acceptance of "the word of faith that we proclaim" (Rom 10:8). This involves both believing in the heart that God raised Jesus from the dead and confessing with the lips that Jesus is Lord (Rom 10:9–10; 4:24–25). In other words, the experience of faith also includes doctrinal content. This is the second way in which the revelation is received in faith, *fides quae* (Lat., "faith which"). This refers to the knowledge and acceptance of revealed truth, the content of teaching (doctrine). Concern for this becomes more evident in the Christian Scriptures as Church structure and organization develop. For example, the term "mystery" takes on a clear doctrinal meaning in 1 Timothy, where the emphasis is on correct teaching and right Church order (1:3–7; 3:9, 16; 4:1–3, 6; 6:20–21). Likewise, the Gospel of John, with its strong emphasis on personal relationship with God, concludes with the affirmation that these things were written "so that you may come to believe that Jesus is the Messiah, the Son of God, and that through believing you may have life in his name" (20:31). It should be emphasized, however, that the ecclesial concern for correct doctrine, which involves intellectual assent to propositions

("I believe that something is true"), while integral and necessary for a complete understanding of faith, is secondary and subordinate. It can never displace the primary and essential commitment of one person to another ("I believe you").

MEDIATED BY THE CHRISTIAN COMMUNITY

Faith is personal not only in an individual sense but also in a social sense. Through Baptism persons are incorporated into a community of believers/disciples that is the matrix of growth into mature faith. Each individual, through his or her particular gifts of the Spirit, builds up the whole body into an integrated and harmonious unity. "For as in one body we have many members, and not all the members have the same function, so we, who are many, are one body in Christ, and individually we are members one of another" (Rom 12:4–5; cf. 1 Cor 12:4–11, 12–31; Col 3:14–15; Eph 4:11–16). As Ephesians so beautifully puts it: "Speaking the truth in love, we must grow up in every way into him who is the head, into Christ" (4:15). However, communal faith must not be confined to the building up and maintenance of the Church as such (which is the concern of Vatican II's Dogmatic Constitution on the Church). Such faith must serve the primary mission of the Church by going outside it, by proclaiming the gospel to all nations and building the kingdom of God on earth as in heaven (which is the concern of Vatican II's Pastoral Constitution on the Church in the Modern World). It is increasingly recognized today that the service of faith includes the promotion of justice as an absolute requirement. Thus, Christian faith as the following of Jesus can never be adequately understood as an asocial, individualistic reality. A true believer is one who reaches out to all of God's children, both within and outside the Church, and indeed to the whole of creation, which is to be cared for as the expression of God's creative love (Gen 2:15; 1:26–27). In a word, living faith includes not only the love of God whom one does not see, but inseparably the love of all those whom one does see (1 John 4:20).

OFFICIAL CATHOLIC TEACHINGS

The Second Council of Orange (529), following the teaching of Augustine of Hippo (d. 430), condemned all forms of Pelagianism or semi-Pelagianism, which sought to displace the priority and continuance of divine grace with purely human efforts. The Council of Trent (1545–63), following the teaching of Thomas Aquinas (d. 1274), maintained the distinction between faith, hope, and love. Faith is caused by the internal movement of the Holy Spirit, to which the intellect assents by a movement of the will. Thus, the process is one of graced, but free human acceptance. Faith is not simply a matter of trust (as Luther was understood at the council), but includes assent to revealed truths. As distinct from love and hope, faith can coexist with sin, but as the free gift of God that involves the whole person it is necessary for salvation. The First Vatican Council (1869–70), against the excesses of both rationalism (which displaces faith with reason alone) and fideism (which exalts faith at the expense of reason), emphasized both the authority of God who reveals, and so the need for the enlightenment of the Holy Spirit, and the coherence of reason with the obedience of faith. Finally, the Second Vatican Council (1962–65) remained in continuity with the traditional understanding of faith while recognizing in the Decree on Ecumenism that true faith, which justifies and sanctifies, exists in all Christian churches, not just in the Catholic Church. Likewise, in the Declaration on Religious Freedom the council recognized the priority of conscience in matters of faith. Faith as the graced but free human acceptance of God's self-communication cannot be forced, and so a certain legitimacy is accorded religious pluralism.

See also faith and reason; grace; revelation.

Bibliography

Haight, Roger. *Dynamics of Theology.* Mahwah, NJ: Paulist Press, 1990.
Hellwig, Monika K. *Understanding Catholicism.* New York: Paulist Press, 1981.
McBrien, Richard P. *Catholicism.* Rev. ed. San Francisco: HarperCollins, 1994.

MICHAEL L. COOK

Faithful, Mass of the. *See* Mass of the Faithful.

faith healing, health cures brought about by prayer or the laying on of hands. The NT gives abundant indications of healings performed in the name of God. The healing of the sick is alluded to in the sacramental practice of the Anointing of the Sick. Some denominational movements (e.g., Christian Science) substitute such healing for conventional medicine.

Today faith healing tends to be identified with certain practices and services connected with charismatic Christians, both Protestant and Catholic, in which healings are sought through ecstatic prayer, the laying on of hands, and, infrequently, anointings with oil. Such healings often invoke the notion of the exorcism of evil spirits or malign powers. Catholics are not required to believe in such healings. *See also* healing.

Falconieri, St. Alexis, 1200–ca. 1310, one of seven Florentine nobles who founded the Servite order. This group withdrew from society to live in prayer and austerity. Unlike the others, Alexis refused ordination and remained a lay brother until his death at age 110. Alexis was canonized with the other founders in 1888. Feast day: February 17. *See also* Servites.

Falconieri, St. Juliana, 1270–1341, niece of Alexis Falconieri. Refusing an arranged marriage, she became a Third Order Servite. After her mother's death, Juliana lived in a group with other pious women. The order of life which she composed for this group eventually became the rule for Servite nuns. Feast day: June 19. *See also* Servites.

faldstool (fawld'stool; Old Eng., "movable stool"), a small, backless, folding stool with arms; used as a seat for bishops. Auxiliary and coadjutor bishops, who may not occupy the bishop's cathedra (chair), always use the faldstool instead of the throne. In conjunction with a cushion it is used as a support for kneeling. The faldstool may substitute for the *prie-dieu* (Fr., "pray God"), a prayer desk with kneeler.

Fall, the, term referring to the early Christian interpretation of Gen 3. According to the narrative, a serpent tempts the woman to eat fruit from the tree in the middle of the garden, the tree God had forbidden to the man and woman. God had warned that eating from it would cause death, but the serpent enticed the woman to eat, promising that eating the fruit would make the man and woman like God, knowing good and evil. The woman, persuaded by the fruit's attractiveness and the serpent's ploy, ate of the fruit and gave some to the man, who also ate.

When God questioned the man and woman, the man blamed the woman for giving him the fruit, and the woman blamed the serpent. God proceeded to punish them for their action: the serpent would crawl on his belly, eat dust, and have an adverse relationship with humankind; the woman, in spite of increased pain in childbearing, would still be sexually attracted to the man, and he would dominate her; the earth would yield food for humankind only after very hard work on the part of the man until his death.

This narrative, because it tells the story of the first man and woman's disobedience to God's directive and its consequences, has been described theologically as "the Fall." The term affirms that the harmonic relationship God intended at creation was ruptured when humankind disobeyed God and "fell" from grace. The action has been understood as the "original sin" that began a history of humankind's unfaithfulness to God. Only Jesus and Mary were preserved from the effects of this first sin.

Historical criticism has provided another interpretation of Gen 3. The chapter is understood as an etiological narrative, that is, a story intended to explain why certain things are the way they are, in this case why, in spite of God's love and goodness, humankind suffers. God should not be blamed for the harsh realities the ancient Israelites experienced—for the threat poisonous snakes represented, for the physical pain endured by women at childbirth, for male domination over females, and for the hard work essential to the production of food. The narrative explains that humans, not God, are responsible for these difficult experiences.

If one understands the text in this way, it no longer narrates "the Fall." The sufferings are not punishments sent by God to be borne bravely. On the contrary, humankind should—and has—set about diminishing them. The domination of women by men is the one curse named in Gen 3 that, often unrecognized as an evil, continues to prevail.

"The Fall" remains a theological term but it has been generalized to refer to the recognized fact that human beings have been, and continue to be, unfaithful to God. *See also* Adam and Eve; original sin.

ALICE L. LAFFEY

False Decretals, a series of papal letters and canonical documents supposedly originating in early Christianity that were forged ca. 850 in France, perhaps at Rheims. Part of a collection falsely attributed to Isidore of Seville (d. 636), the forgeries as a whole seek to buttress the episcopal office and secure bishops from legal attack. Influential in later medieval canon law and ecclesiology, they were used by the Gregorian reformers to support their claims for episcopal independence from lay control. *See also* Gregorian reform; Gregory VII.

family, the most basic unit of the Church. Echoing John Chrysostom's late fourth-century commentary on the book of Genesis in which he called the family *ekklesia* (Gk., "church"), Pope Leo XIII (d. 1903) wrote, "The family was ordained of God. . . . It was before the Church, or rather the first form of the Church on earth" (*Arcanum Divine Sapientiae,* "On Christian Marriage," 1880). The Second Vatican Council (1962–65) revived this ancient but neglected aspect of the Church's self-understanding. In the Dogmatic Constitution on the Church the council declared that the family is "the domestic Church" (n. 11), and in the Pastoral Constitution on the Church in the Modern World it said, "The Christian family . . . will show forth to all . . . the authentic nature of the Church" (n. 48). The Decree on the Apostolate of the Laity called the family "a domestic sanctuary of the Church" (n. 11).

Teachings on the Family: Since Vatican II, popes Paul VI, John Paul I, and John Paul II have all restated the importance of understanding the family as "the domestic Church." Paul VI, in his 1975 apostolic exhortation on evangelization, *Evangelii Nuntiandi,* wrote, "At different moments in the Church's history and also in the Second Vatican Council, the family has well deserved the beautiful name of 'domestic Church.'" In an address to the bishops of the United States, John Paul I said, "The Christian family is so important, and its role is so basic in the kingdom of God, that the council called it a 'domestic Church'." In his 1981 apostolic exhortation on the family, John Paul II repeated, "The Christian family . . . can and should be called 'the domestic Church'" (n. 21). He continued, "The family, called together by word and sacrament as the Church of the home, is both teacher and mother, the same as the worldwide Church" (n. 38). "No plan of organized pastoral work at any level," the pope wrote, "must ever fail to take into consideration the pastoral area of the family" (n. 70).

During the course of his 1987 visit to the United States, John Paul II declared that family life is central to the life of the parish. He said that "every parish is a family of families. The vitality of a parish greatly depends on the spiritual vigor, commitment and involvement of its families. The family in fact is the basic unit of society and of the Church." The pope pointed out that families "are those living cells which come together to form the very substance of parish life." At the same time, the pope expressed realism: "Some [families] are healthy and filled with the love of God. . . . In some there is little energy for the life of the Spirit. Some have broken down altogether."

For John Paul II, families are a major source of pastoral concern: "The priests and their collaborators in a parish must try to be very close to all families in their need for pastoral care, and to provide the support and spiritual nourishment they require." He continued, "Each parish must be fully committed to [the pastoral care of families], especially in the face of so much breakdown and undermining of family life in society. I appeal to all priests—pastors, associates and all concerned . . . to do everything possible, working together, to serve the family as effectively as possible."

The 1983 Code of Canon Law states that "pastors of souls are obliged to ensure that their own church community provides for Christ's faithful the assistance by which the married state is preserved in its Christian character and develops in perfection." Among the ways "pastors of souls" are to do this is "by the help given to those who have entered marriage, so that by faithfully observing and protecting their conjugal covenant, they may day by day achieve a holier and a fuller family life" (can. 1063).

Family Rights and a Family Perspective: At the request of the 1980 Synod of Bishops, in 1983 the Vatican issued a "Charter of the Rights of the Family." This charter states that "the rights of the person, even though they are expressed as rights of the individual, have a fundamental social dimension which finds an innate and vital expression in the family." The family "exists prior to the state or any other community, and possesses rights which are inalienable."

In 1988, the ad hoc committee on Marriage and Family Life of the National Conference of Catholic Bishops in the United States issued "A Family Perspective in Church and Society." This document defined the family as "an intimate community of persons bound together by blood, marriage, or adoption, for the whole of life." In the Catholic tradition, "the family proceeds from marriage—an intimate, exclusive, permanent, and faithful partnership of husband and wife." According to this document, "the Church needs to support positive developments, to look for new ways to help families, and to unearth the resources that enable families to move from crisis to growth, from stress to strength. This can be done by incorporating a family perspective, as a pastoral strategy, in all its policies, programs, ministries, and services." The Church needs to do this, not so much because family life is in trouble today, but because family life "is fundamental to the healthy life of the Church and society."

Family Life and the Future of the Church: There is an interdependent relationship between the parish and the families, or home churches, that constitute the parish. Each must nourish and support the other if the Church as a whole is to carry out faithfully the mission entrusted to it by Christ.

The family—including two-parent families, single-parent families, childless married couples, couples whose children are grown and gone, single and widowed persons in the context of their extended family network, and blended families—is meant to "constitute the Church in its fundamental dimension" (John Paul II). Therefore, as family life goes, so goes the future of the Church. Any complete theology of the Church, and any effective pastoral ministry, must take this strand of tradition seriously. *See also* domestic church; Marriage.

Bibliography

Finley, Mitch, and Kathy Finley. *Christian Families in the Real World: Reflections on a Spirituality for the Domestic Church.* Chicago: Thomas More Press, 1984.

Finley, Mitch. *Your Family in Focus: Appreciating What You Have, Making It Even Better.* Notre Dame, IN: Ave Maria Press, 1993.

Kehrwald, Leif. *Caring That Enables: A Manual for Developing Parish Family Ministry.* Mahwah, NJ: Paulist Press, 1991.

Papal Committee for the Family. *The Family in the Pastoral Activity of the Church.* Washington, DC: United States Catholic Conference, 1978. MITCH FINLEY

Farley, John M., 1842–1918, cardinal-archbishop of New York. An Irish immigrant educated at Fordham University and the North American College (Rome), he was ordained a priest in 1870. He became secretary to Cardinal John McCloskey (1872), advanced to vicar general (1891) and auxiliary bishop (1895), and succeeded McCloskey to become the fourth archbishop of New York (1902) and was later made a cardinal (1911). His career was dedicated to education and pastoral care, especially of immigrants. He doubled the number of archdioc-

esan parochial schools, and opened Cathedral College and Seminary in 1903. A patron of the original *Catholic Encyclopedia,* he published two books: *The History of St. Patrick's Cathedral* (1908), and *The Life of John Cardinal McCloskey* (1918).

Farley, Margaret, b. 1935, Catholic moral theologian. She is currently the Gilbert L. Stark Professor of Christian Ethics at Yale Divinity School. She received a Ph.D. from Yale University in 1973. Her works include *Personal Commitments: Making, Keeping, Breaking* (San Francisco: Harper & Row, 1986). She is a member of the Religious Sisters of Mercy.

Fascism, one of the most important and successful extreme right-wing movements in post–World War I Europe. Its creator was the Italian politician Benito Mussolini (1883–1945). Mixing together nationalism, the philosophy of Friedrich Nietzsche, and the political theory of Karl Marx, Mussolini emerged after World War I at the head of a political party called the *Fasci di Combattimento* (It., "combat groups") from which the name *Fascism* derives. The Fascist party called for an end to the power of capitalist elites, increased state control over the economy through state/labor corporative councils, and for Italy's return to the imperial greatness of its Roman past. Mussolini rapidly rose to power, helped greatly by the instability of Italy's postwar democracy. In 1922, faced with a Fascist army marching on Rome, King Victor Emmanuel III asked Mussolini to form a new government.

In 1929, Pope Pius XI and Mussolini signed the Lateran Treaty. The treaty recognized papal control over Vatican City and its political independence. It also made Catholicism the official religion of the Italian state and allowed Catholic religious education in public schools.

However, the following year the pope criticized the Fascists, claiming that the party trained the young to worship the state. A papal encyclical in 1937, *Mit Brennender Sorge,* similarly denounced Nazism for promoting racism and paganism. *See also* Lateran Treaty.

fast, eucharistic. *See* eucharistic fast.

fast days, days on which solid food may not be taken between meals, meals are meatless, and the smaller meals combined are not to equal in size the main meal of the day. Prior to the reforms of the

Second Vatican Council (1962–65), fast days were far more numerous, but the current discipline of the Western Church prescribes only two fast days in universal law: Ash Wednesday and Good Friday. Fasting on these days is required for those who have reached canonical majority (eighteen years of age) and have not yet celebrated their fifty-ninth birthday. It is important to note that the purpose of the fast, indeed of any penitential practice, is to give the faithful the opportunity to reflect on their lives, to express sorrow for sins, and to resolve to lead a more fervent Christian life. *See also* abstinence; fasting.

fasting, a spiritual discipline by which food is voluntarily given up for a defined period. With clear warrant in the Bible, especially the example of Jesus who fasted in the desert, fasting has had a long history in the Catholic tradition.

Various religious communities have institutionalized full or partial fasts as part of their weekly regime. It was common in the Catholic tradition to fast on the evening before the reception of Holy Communion as the word breakfast indicates. Today, however, only a partial fast (for one hour before communion) is demanded.

In the contemporary Church, fasting (with the meaning of only one full meal in a day) is enjoined on adult Catholics on Ash Wednesday and Good Friday by the Code of Canon Law (can. 1251), although the practice is encouraged as a private devotion whenever appropriate (can. 1249). The practice of a daylong fast in solidarity with the poor of the world has been an informal custom in many areas of the Catholic world. *See also* abstinence; penance.

fate (Lat., *fatum,* "that which has been spoken"), an ancient concept denoting a force that moves all human affairs toward a predetermined end.

Within Christianity, fate is acknowledged to the extent that an individual's life finds definition within contexts where not all factors may be controlled. Although individuals may shape their own reactions to the world, the world itself often seems uncontrollable. In this sense, one's life is determined not only by personal actions, plans, and dreams, but also by what happens outside oneself. All people ultimately share death as a common fate. While an individual may either temporarily postpone or hasten death, each person must finally surrender to death as a universal given.

For Christians, fate is not an impersonal force.

Rather, God remains as the essential mystery that grounds the world and all its conditionings in love. Indeed, Jesus' Resurrection even deprives death, the most common and perhaps most feared fate, of its lasting power. Events and situations will remain to which people can only resign themselves in an acceptance founded in faith. In contrast, deterministic notions of fate as the basic condition of life severely weaken human responsibility and freedom. *See also* providence.

Father, title generally given to a priest, denoting a spiritual relationship between the priest and his congregation or with anyone else to whom he ministers. In the early Church, the bishop was often viewed as a spiritual father, as one who had teaching authority over the local church. The title "Father" was extended to priests who were sacramental confessors and during the medieval period to all mendicant friars. However, it was not until the nineteenth century that the title was extended to all priests in the English-speaking world. Today, the title is sometimes used by priests and ministers of the Anglican (especially Anglo-Catholic) and Lutheran churches. *See also* priest.

Fatherhood of God, the role of father commonly, though now controversially, attributed to God. In the OT God is called Father only rarely, but in the NT this is a relatively common name for God. In the Gospels God is called the Father (Lat., *pater*) of Jesus Christ 170 times: 4 times in Mark, 15 in Luke, 42 in Matthew, and 109 in John. In the Greek Gospels Jesus uses the Aramaic term for Father, "Abba," only once (Mark 14:36). "Abba" is used only two other times in the Scriptures, by Paul in Rom 8:15 and Gal 4:6. In twelve places Jesus addresses himself in prayer to God as Father (Matt 11:25–6; Luke 10:21; John 11:41; Mark 14:36; Matt 26:39; Matt 26:42; Luke 22:42; Luke 23:34; Luke 23:46; John 17:1, 5, 11, 21, 24, 25), leading most exegetes to conclude that God's fatherhood is a clear and consistent hallmark of Jesus' prayer. The distinction Jesus makes between "my Father" and "your Father" is post-Easter but is based on Jesus' distinction between "my Father" and "the Father in heaven"; the latter term is used to talk to others about their God. By addressing God as "Abba" or Father, one uses a term of intimacy that was a characteristic feature of Jesus' own prayer. However, just as the early Christian community did not infer the uniqueness of Jesus' sonship directly from his prayers to "Abba" but from other data about Jesus, so also one cannot deduce an ontological fatherhood of God directly from the fact that God was called "Father" by Jesus.

Despite the fact that God is so often called Father (and not Mother) in the NT, it would be improper to draw a strict correlation between divine and human fatherhood, for example, by concluding that God is male. First, God is beyond all names and, second, God's being is not marked by sexuality. Fatherhood is clearly an analogous or metaphorical term and cannot be applied literally to God's being. God is as much like as unlike human fathers.

Doctrine of the Trinity: The biblical metaphor of God's fatherhood came into even greater prominence through the doctrine of the Trinity. Prior to the fourth century, "God" and "Father" were synonyms; there was not yet an "intratrinitarian" meaning to fatherhood. In time, the Father-Son relationship, well attested especially in John's Gospel, became the cornerstone of speculation on God's Trinity. Divine fatherhood came to be understood as indicating more than God's relationship to creation, specifically, God the Father's eternal relationship to God the Son.

These doctrinal developments took place within a patriarchal society, which assumed that fathers (not mothers) were the active, life-giving principle. The great temptation was to use the biblical witness to legitimate the social arrangements of patriarchy. Recently, feminist criticism has unmasked the extent to which the Christian tradition has literalized the image of God's fatherhood, thereby failing to observe the cardinal theological principle of God's incomprehensibility. Further, feminism has criticized the tendency of the tradition to project the supposed dominance of male over female onto God's being, thereby eclipsing women as equal carriers of the divine image. Feminism preserves the authentic Christian insight into the incomprehensibility and unnameability of God's essence, as well as the doctrine that each individual woman and man is created *imago Dei* (Lat., "in the image of God"). *See also* God; Trinity, doctrine of the.

CATHERINE MOWRY LACUGNA

Fathers, Apostolic. *See* Apostolic Fathers.

Fathers of the Church, in contemporary usage an informal designation generally reserved for those early figures whose teaching, collectively regarded, is considered the foundation of orthodox Christian doctrine. The age of the Fathers is gener-

ally held to close in the East with John of Damascus (d. 749) and in the West with Gregory the Great (d. 604), although some extend the latter to Isidore of Seville (d. 636) or even Bede (d. 735). The term is not restricted to bishops (Jerome and Anthony of Egypt are included) or even to persons of unquestionable orthodoxy (Origen, Tertullian, John Cassian, and even Theodore of Mopsuestia are generally included) and is almost always used in the plural.

Contemporary usage has its roots in mid-fourth century usage by Basil and Gregory of Nazianzus, among others, who use the term "fathers" to describe earlier authorities, especially the bishops gathered at Nicaea (325). At the Council of Ephesus (431) Cyril had a dossier of earlier authorities, and the formula of the Council of Chalcedon (451) refers to the bishops of the councils of Nicaea and of Constantinople (381) as the "fathers." By the fifth century it was common in polemical situations to invoke among the "fathers" any earlier orthodox teacher whose authority was generally recognized, whether bishop or not (and Augustine so refers to Jerome in polemic against Julian of Eclanum). By the time of the Carolingians the word is used collectively not only to designate authority, but with a sense of closure and distance, so that, for example, Alcuin (d. 804) can speak of wandering through the "cellars" or "storehouses" of the "fathers," who are thus collectively imaged as a respository of authority that cannot be duplicated. *See also* Apostolic Fathers; patristics.

JOHN C. CAVADINI

Fátima (fa'ti-muh), a small town in Portugal associated with one of the most important Marian shrines. On May 13, 1917, three illiterate children, Lucia dos Santos and her two cousins, Francisco and Jacinta, claimed to have seen a vision of a woman standing on a cloud in an evergreen tree near the Cova de Iria. In a conversation heard only by Lucia and Jacinta, the woman asked the children to return to the site on the thirteenth of each month until October. Despite local resistance and an effort to refute the testimony of the children, the popularity of the apparitions grew, so that by October fifty thousand pilgrims assembled with the children at the Cova de Iria. Although many claimed to have witnessed a "miracle of the sun," the woman was visible only to the children. She identified herself as "Our Lady of the Rosary," and asked the children to recite the Rosary daily, proclaim the need for moral conversion, and erect a chapel in her honor.

In 1930, after a seven-year study, the bishop of

Leiria proclaimed the legitimacy of the apparitions and authorized the cult of Our Lady of Fátima. Subsequently, Jacinta provided two important accounts of the apparitions in 1936–37 and 1941–42, from which the "Threefold Message of Fátima," namely, the practice of penance, the recitation of the Rosary, and devotion to the Immaculate Heart of Mary was made known.

Although approved by the Church, the events surrounding Fátima are private revelations. Catholics are not required to give assent to the apparitions themselves or to the revelations disclosed at Fátima. *See also* apparitions of the Blessed Virgin Mary.

MICHAEL O'KEEFFE

Faulhaber, Michael von, 1869–1952, cardinal-archbishop of Munich, Germany, and a leader against the Nazis. He forcefully condemned totalitarianism and racism, especially anti-Semitism. After World War II, he worked with American occupation forces in reconstructing Munich. He received the Grand Cross of the Order of Merit, the highest award from the then West German Republic.

Faustus of Riez, ca. 410–ca. 490, preacher, writer, abbot of Lérins beginning in 433 and bishop of Riez in Gaul (now France) beginning in 457. He produced two treatises, *De Gratia* (Lat., "On Grace") and *De Spiritu Sancto* (Lat., "On the Holy Spirit"), and a large correspondence. His views on grace, written against predestinarianism, align him with what is generally termed the "semi-Pelagian" position, which held that the beginning of faith is an act made independently of the grace of God. *See also* predestination; semi-Pelagianism.

favor of law, in canon law a device establishing legal presumptions and indicating what facts or ways of proceeding are to be followed to overturn presumptions. The fact, for example, that marriage enjoys the favor of the law (can. 1060) indicates that a marriage is presumed to be valid; only proper juridical procedure can overturn this presumption. An annulment proceeding must, therefore, establish the invalidity of a given marriage with moral certitude and, if it does not, the marriage is still considered valid.

Fawkes, Guy, 1570–1606, born in Yorkshire, England, a member of the Gunpowder Plot conspiracy, an apparent attempt by Roman Catholic conspirators to blow up the English Parliament during the state opening on November 5, 1605. A former Protestant, Fawkes was recruited into the plot by Robert Catesby. Discovered with the explosives, Fawkes was executed with coconspirators. *See also* England, Catholicism in.

fear of God, the attitude of respect and awe that humans are to have toward God. The Hebrew word *yir'âh,* though it literally means "fear," is best translated as "awe" or "respect." As an attitude toward God, it acknowledges the greatness and power of God. Faithfulness and obedience are appropriate responses to the awesome God.

Many passages in the OT specify behavior appropriate to those who fear the Lord. For example, they will not obstruct the path of the blind (Lev 19:14) or cheat others (25:17). The NT records the awe/fear toward God that was experienced, for example, at the birth and naming of John the Baptizer (Luke 1:65); at Jesus' marvelous calming of the storm (Luke 8:25); and at the wonders the apostles performed after the Ascension (Acts 2:43).

Because believers are to fear God, no one and nothing else need be feared. Abram is counseled not to fear, for God is his shield (Gen 15:1); Isaac, because God is with him (Gen 26:24); Joseph's brothers, because God had intended their actions for good (Gen 50:19); and the Hebrews, because God would accomplish their deliverance (Exod 14:13). God is in charge; there is no need to be anxious. Similarly, the NT counsels not to fear. Joseph should not fear because Mary's child is from the Holy Spirit (Matt 1:20); Mary, because she has found favor with God (Luke 1:30); and the shepherds, because the Anointed One, the Lord, had been born (Luke 2:10).

Like wisdom, knowledge, and understanding, fear of God is a gift of God whose attainment is to be ardently sought. *See also* gifts of the Holy Spirit.

ALICE L. LAFFEY

feasts, liturgical, days in the Church calendar that commemorate significant events in the life of Christ, the saints, or the Christian people. Sunday, the weekly commemoration of Christ's Resurrection, is the original feast and, since Constantine's Edict of Toleration (313), has been considered a Christian "day of rest." At an early period, however, two principal categories of feasts developed: "movable" (with no fixed date) and "immovable" (fixed date). The most important movable feast is Easter, always celebrated (following a decree of the Council of Nicaea in 325) on the first Sunday following the first full moon after the vernal equinox (hence, between March 22 and April 25). Easter's variable date also determines the dates of other major feasts such as Ascension (forty days after Easter) and Pentecost (fifty days after Easter). Similarly, Ash Wednesday and the beginning of Lent are computed by working backward from the date of Easter for that year. (If Easter falls on April 25, for example, Ash Wednesday is March 10.) Among the immovable feasts are the anniversaries of martyrs' deaths (celebrated in Rome by at least the third century); saints' birthdays (e.g., John the Baptist on June 24, the Virgin Mary on September 8); and, most prominently, the feast of Christ's Nativity (December 25). In the Roman Catholic calendar, reformed after Vatican Council II, "feast" is a technical term for days that are of less importance than "solemnities" (like Easter), but of more importance than "memorials" (most saints' days). *See also* liturgical year.

Febronianism, an eighteenth-century movement in Germany that subordinated the Church to national interests. Under the penname of Justinus Febronius, Johann Nikolaus von Hontheim (1701–90), auxiliary bishop of Trier, proposed this popular theory in 1763. In 1778, after Pope Pius VI condemned the view, Hontheim recanted, but Febronianism continued into the nineteenth century.

Febronianism restricted papal authority to supervising Church unity and promulgating decrees of general councils. If the pope did not regularly convene a general council, bishops or the emperor should do so. Papal pronouncements would bind only with the bishops' consent. To promote Church unity, Hontheim would have divided the Church into state-controlled national churches. The movement collapsed after the French Revolution and for lack of support from other German bishops. *See also* ecumenical council; Germany, Catholicism in; primacy, papal.

Federation of Diocesan Liturgical Commissions (FDLC), an organization of diocesan liturgical commissions. A 1968 suggestion from the U.S. Bishops' Committee on the Liturgy (BCL) resulted in a BCL-sponsored meeting of twenty-four representatives from the twelve episcopal regions of the United States. A second meeting in El Paso, Texas, in 1969 established FDLC. Its main purpose is the promotion of the liturgy as the heart and center of Christian life, especially in parishes. The FDLC is directed by an executive secretary and its headquarters are in Washington, D.C.

Feehan, Patrick Augustine, 1829–1902, archbishop of Chicago (1880–1902). Born in Ireland, he emigrated to the United States in 1850 and was ordained in 1852. He was made bishop of Nashville in 1865 and in 1880 was chosen to head the archdiocese of Chicago. At this time Chicago witnessed a major influx of southern and eastern European Catholics. Feehan graciously welcomed the newcomers and allowed a proliferation of ethnic churches and social welfare institutions to blossom in his diocese. He also established the archdiocesan newspaper *New World.*

Feeney, Leonard, 1897–1978, Jesuit priest, poet, founder of "The Slaves of the Immaculate Heart of Mary." He was dismissed from the Jesuits and was excommunicated in 1953 for refusing to recant his strict interpretation of Boniface VIII's axiom, "Outside the Church, no salvation." According to Feeney, only Catholics could be saved. The Vatican's Holy Office rejected his view by distinguishing between those who "really" (Lat., *in re*) belong to the Church by explicit faith and Baptism and those who belong to the Church "by desire" (*in voto*). The desire would be explicit in the case of catechumens and implicit in the case of those people of good will who would join the Church if they knew it to be the one, true Church of Christ. In his earlier years, Feeney was known for his work as spiritual director for Catholic students at Harvard University, for his books and poetry, and for his controversial street-preaching in Boston, with its disturbingly anti-Semitic overtones. Pope Paul VI lifted the excommunication prior to Feeney's death, without requiring him to make a public retraction of his views. *See also* salvation outside the Church.

Felician Sisters, the Congregation of the Sisters of St. Felix of Cantalice of the Third Order of St. Francis (C.S.S.F), a congregation dedicated to prayer and works of mercy. It was founded in Warsaw, Poland, in 1855 by Sophia Truszkowska under the direction of a Capuchin priest, Honorat Kozminski. They adopted the Third Order Regular Franciscan rule and the patronage of St. Felix, an Italian Capuchin brother. In the late nineteenth century a group came to the United States, originally to serve Polish immigrants and eventually the broader population. In 1993 there were just over three hundred sisters, the largest number being in the United States. There are also Felicians in Poland, Canada, and South America. *See also* Franciscan Sisters.

Felicity, St. 1 Roman widow and martyr. Felicity, also known as Felicitas, suffered death in A.D. 165 with her sons in Rome. Feast day: November 23. **2** Slave of St. Perpetua, martyred in Carthage in A.D. 203. Feast day: March 7.

Felix III (II), St., d. 492, pope from 483 to 492, formerly Felix III until the removal of Felix II (papal claimant during the reign of Liberius) from the list of popes. He is famous for his rejection of the *Henoticon* (favoring Monophysitism) and his excommunication of the patriarch Acacius of Constantinople (471–89) for supporting it. The ensuing Acacian Schism lasted until 519. Feast day: March 1. *See also* Acacianism.

Felix of Urgel, d. 817, supporter of the Spanish Adoptionist Elipandus, and principal exponent of Spanish Adoptionism in the border areas of Charlemagne's realm. Charlemagne's anxiety prompted Felix's condemnation in 792 (Regensburg), 794 (Frankfurt) and, after a debate with Alcuin in which Felix declared himself convinced, 799 (Aachen). He died under house arrest in Lyons, reformulating his teaching for a salon of admirers. *See also* Adoptionism.

Felix of Valois, St., 1126–1212, cofounder of the Order of the Most Holy Trinity (Trinitarians). Born in France, he lived as a hermit until he and one of his disciples, John of Matha, secured papal approval for a new religious order to ransom Crusaders who were taken captive by the Moors in Spain and by Muslims in the Holy Land and elsewhere. Felix administered the French province from his hermitage in Cerfroid. Feast day: November 20. *See also* Trinitarians.

feminism, the belief that women and men should have equal economic, political, and social opportunity and should be accorded the same dignity and rights. Feminists strive to create social attitudes, policies, and structures to attain those goals. Feminism maintains that both women and men are dehumanized by androcentric and patriarchal structures that subordinate women. The aim, therefore, is for the transformation of systems and structures that are oppressive. Feminism may be liberal, radical, romantic, or socialist. Liberal feminism emphasizes legal and political equality for women; radical feminism analyzes patriarchal structures for the purpose of liberating women from them. Romantic feminism aspires to bring so-called feminine values to bear on the public order, while socialist feminism focuses on the sexual division of labor, production, and reproduction and the connection between class, race, and gender in oppressive systems.

The feminist movement that has grown since the publication of *The Feminine Mystique* by Betty Friedan in 1963 is not a new phenomenon. In 1792, Mary Wollstonecraft published *A Vindication of the Rights of Women,* in which she proposed that women deserve the same opportunities as men in education, employment, and politics and that they be judged by the same moral standards. The Declaration of Sentiments and Resolutions issued by the First Women's Rights Convention at Seneca Falls, New York, in 1848 declared that "all men and women are created equal."

Christian Feminism: The modern feminist movement has given rise within the Church to feminist theology that is rooted in the experience of women. Christian feminists, both male and female, continue to develop a liberation theology from the perspective of the experience of women. Social, political, and economic equality, while important, is not their primary concern. Feminist theologians put the Christian message and feminist thought in conversation, mutually critiquing one another. They investigate to what extent theology may have contributed to the oppression of women even as they acknowledge the contributions theology has made to women.

Feminist theology holds that all theology is culturally and historically conditioned, that traditional theology is rooted in an androcentric and patriarchal culture, and that the prejudices and biases of that culture have served to oppress women and dehumanize men. Therefore, feminist theologians consciously and deliberately write from the perspective of women's experience. Like other liberation theologies, feminist theology insists that theology is not a purely academic and intellectual pursuit. It demands praxis—action and reflection together. Theology, then, is understood not just as faith seeking understanding but faith seeking understanding and the transformation of life. This transformation includes both personal and systemic conversion.

Feminist Theologies: Feminist theology is a multifaceted rather than a one-dimensional endeavor. Its various manifestations are affected by liberal, radical, romantic, and socialist thought as well as by the gospel. Feminist theologians have been broadly described as reformist, revolutionary, and separatist.

Reformist theologians bring a feminist paradigm to bear on the symbol systems, language, myths, rituals, and traditions that have been used to support an androcentric view of humanity and a patriarchal view of the Church. They critique Scripture and tradition for elements that have oppressed women, search for women whose contributions may have been ignored, and interpret foundational doctrines from the perspective of women's experience. In their work, they are not attempting to destroy or replace the rich tradition but to enrich the enterprise by bringing the talents, experiences, scholarship, and reflections of women to bear on it. Reformist theologians have a strong commitment to the sacramental, incarnational, and communal aspects of Catholicism.

Revolutionary or reconstructive feminists perceive the Christian tradition itself to be irredeemably patriarchal. They call for a total redefinition of Christian symbols and traditions. Among their priorities are the creation of egalitarian and nonhierarchical communities.

Separatist theologians define salvation for women as freedom from the misogynous chains of Christianity. They, therefore, withdraw from institutions that are male-centered and create supportive communities of women. While defined as post-Christian, their work has a profound effect on mainstream Christian feminism.

Recent feminist theology, like socialist feminism, addresses the connection between sexism, racism, and classism. It also focuses on the attendant breakdown of relationships among persons and between persons and God. African-American and Third World feminists argue that white feminists may be guilty of another form of cultural imperialism in defining their experience as "women's experience." A process of self-critique on the part of European and North American feminist theologians has resulted.

Feminists have also begun to focus on the destruction of the earth's resources, pollution, militarism, and poverty. What is emerging from this new focus is an ecofeminist theology. *See also* feminist interpretation of Scripture; women in the Church.

Bibliography

Carmody, Denise Lardner. *Responses to 101 Questions About Feminism.* New York: Paulist Press, 1993.

Coll, Regina. *Christianity and Feminism in Conversation.* Mystic, CT: Twenty-Third Publications, 1994.

Loades, Ann, ed. *Feminist Theology: A Reader.* Louisville, KY: Westminster/John Knox Press, 1990.

Ruether, Rosemary Radford. *Sexism and God-Talk: Toward a Feminist Theology.* Boston: Beacon Press, 1983, 1993.   REGINA COLL

feminist interpretation of Scripture, a way of reading Scripture based on feminist theology. There is no one single feminist way to read Scripture; rather there is a range of approaches generally based on the assumption that the biblical texts and the cultures that produced them and have continued to interpret them through the centuries are androcentric (male-centered) and patriarchal (paternalistic). The four principal forms of feminist interpretation might be characterized as: revisionist, deconstructionist, symbolic, and liberation.

Forms of Interpretation: Revisionist feminist interpretation seeks to retell the biblical stories with better use of historical methods to highlight the roles and contributions of women that have been obscured by androcentric interpretation. For example, the story of Martha and Mary with Jesus (Luke 10:38–42) portrays Mary not as contemplative, a traditional and safe characterization, but as a disciple who learns Jesus' teaching in the same way the male disciples did.

Deconstructionist interpretation aims to expose more directly the androcentric and patriarchal bias behind the texts themselves and their ongoing interpretation. For example, the stories of the sacrificed daughter of Jephthah and the gang-raped and murdered concubine (Judg 11:30–40; 19:1–30) reflect not only situations of violence and abuse, but a world in which women are expendable to save male honor. Abraham's hand was stayed from sacrificing his only son (Gen 22), while Jephthah was not so divinely prevented from sacrificing his only daughter.

Symbolic feminist interpretation develops the positive significance of female figures, for example, Eve as mother of all the living (Gen 3:20); daughter Zion (Isa 52:2); the woman clothed with the sun (Rev 12:1–6); and the Church and the new Jerusalem as bride (Eph 5:25–27; Rev 21:2).

Liberation feminist interpretation emphasizes the biblical call for everyone to work for the liberation of the poor and oppressed, not only in heaven, but for the establishment of the reign of God in history as well. It calls attention to the strong female figures of Scripture who were empowered by God and who empowered others, for example, Deborah (Judg 4–5), Judith, and Esther as saviors of the people and the Samaritan woman and Mary Magdalene as apostles (John 4:39–42; 20:17–18). It brands oppressive texts (e.g., 1 Tim 2:11–16) as nonrevelatory, not only in the abusive ways that they have been used throughout history to exploit and control women, but in the intentions of the biblical authors themselves.

No biblical interpreters who incorporate feminist insights use only one of the above approaches, but a combination of them, depending on each one's basic assumptions. Modern interpretive theory has made us aware that there is no such thing as a completely "objective" interpretation, for every interpreter comes with given assumptions based on his or her worldview, more or less explicit. Feminist interpretation aims to expose the biases that have lessened the full equality of women. Many of the most prominent feminist biblical interpreters, female or male, are Roman Catholics, and the Church's continuing stance on justice and the elimination of discrimination compel ongoing reassessment of biblical interpretation in this regard. *See also* feminism; hermeneutics; Scripture; interpretation of.   CAROLYN OSIEK

Fénelon, François, 1651–1715, French archbishop and spiritual writer. Ordained a Sulpician in 1675, he was appointed tutor to the prince in the royal court in 1689. During this time, Fénelon wrote the fictional *Telemachus*. Intended as an aid to educating the prince, the book contained a veiled satire of the absolutism characteristic of the reigning king, Louis XIV. Fénelon was named archbishop of Cambrai in 1695. About this time he became engaged in a famous controversy with Jacques Bossuet. After the writings of Jeanne-Marie Guyon were condemned for their Quietist tendencies, Fénelon wrote his *Maxims of the Saints*. The book revealed his continued support for much of Guyon's spiritual teaching. In response, Bossuet, one of the judges in Guyon's case, sought the condemnation of the *Maxims*. In 1699, Innocent XII condemned the *Maxims* as dangerous but refused to categorize the book as heretical. *See also* Quietism.

Fenwick, Benedict Joseph, 1782–1846, U.S. bishop. An American Jesuit, he administered the diocese of New York (1815–17) and for one year served as president of Georgetown College (1818). In 1819 he went to the diocese of Charleston, South Carolina, as Bishop John England's vicar-general, and then returned to Georgetown as president and procurator general of the Jesuits (1811–25). In 1825 he was appointed the second bishop of Boston, founded a newspaper, the *Jesuit* (1829), dispelled tensions after the burning of the Charlestown Convent (1834), and established Holy Cross College in Worcester, Massachusetts (1843). Fenwick's leadership transformed the Boston diocese into a powerful influence in the U.S. church. *See also* Georgetown University.

Feodorov, Leonid, 1879–1934, first exarch of the Russian Catholic Church. Of partially Greek origin and of an Orthodox family, he became a Catholic through study of the early church Fathers and Vladimir Solov'ev. He entered the Studite order in Bosnia and was chosen as exarch of the Russian Catholics by Metropolitan Sheptyckyj of Galicia. In spite of innumerable obstacles put in his way by the Bolshevik Revolution, Feodorov was able to organize the Russian Catholics and open a short-lived chapel at St. Petersburg. For his time, Feodorov was ecumenical in his approach, enjoyed rather good relations with several Orthodox clergymen, and stood staunchly for liturgical purity. After serving a long sentence in prison and the concentration camps, Feodorov died in exile, a victim of the general persecution.

Ferdinand II, 1578–1637, Holy Roman emperor from 1619 to 1637. Influenced by the Jesuits and the example of the Bavarian dukes, Ferdinand devoted his reign to forcibly recatholicizing his lands. Although he was most successful in Austria, Protestant resistance ignited the Thirty Years' War (1618–48).

Ferdinand III, St., 1199–1252, king of Castile and Leon, founder of the University of Salamanca, and patron saint of engineers. A warrior-king, he drove the Muslims (Moors) from portions of present-day Spain. Feast day: May 30.

Ferdinand of Aragon, 1452–1516, king of Aragon from 1479 and, with his wife Isabella of Castile, sponsor of the Spanish Inquisition (1478) and of Columbus's discovery of America. Forcibly reforming the Church by placing it under royal control, he and his wife united most of the Iberian Peninsula into Catholic Spain and conquered the last Spanish Muslim state (Granada, 1492). *See also* Inquisition; Spain, Catholicism in.

ferendae sententiae (fair-en'day sen-ten'tsee-ay; Lat., "imposed sentence"), a penalty that has been imposed by order of a tribunal or by the action of another competent authority. Canon law lays down certain necessary procedures for such imposition. This type of penalty is contrasted to an automatic penalty (*latae sententiae*), which occurs without any direct involvement of authority when a given action has been performed under specified circumstances. *See also latae sententiae;* penal law.

feria (Lat., "holiday"), weekday. The classical Latin term referred to a holiday or feast day; the ecclesiastical term refers to days on which no feast falls. Days of the week were designated numerically; *feria prima,* Latin for "first day" of the week, Sunday, which was also called *dies dominica,* Latin for "the Lord's day" (Rev 1:7).

fermentum (Lat., "leaven"), in fifth–century Rome, the fragment of eucharistic bread consecrated at the pope's Sunday Mass and sent to parish priests who were celebrating with their people in the suburbs and could not attend the papal liturgy. The fragment signified the unity of all the faithful in Christ. *See also* Communion, Holy.

Ferrer, St. Vincent. *See* Vincent Ferrer, St.

Ferrini, Bl. Contardo, 1859–1902, legal scholar, patron saint of universities. Italian-born expert in Roman law and author of some two hundred monographs, he combined a commitment to the intellectual life with a deep spirituality.

fetal research, experimental procedures on human fetuses, often including procedures with fetal tissue taken from fetal cadavers, especially for transplant purposes. Recent Vatican documents judge that even the earliest human embryos are, or at least must be considered as if they are, human persons. Thus experimental procedures on living fetuses within the womb (Lat., *in vivo*) are judged morally right only if they offer hope of benefit for the individual fetus. Informed consent must be given by the mother and the potential benefit to the fetus must be proportional to the risk to woman and fetus.

Theoretically, nontherapeutic procedures, which offer no potential benefit to the individual fetus, might also be permitted if the risk to the fetus is minimal and the potential benefit to future fetuses substantial. This is similar to experiments performed on children, whose membership in society entails certain obligations to others. Proxy consent by the parents is said to suffice. But this position is rejected by those who argue that proxy consent is always invalid for nontherapeutic research. And almost all nontherapeutic fetal research now conducted or proposed implicitly or explicitly denies the personhood of the fetus and thus discounts fetal risk, anticipating death as a result of the research or of elective abortion. This is not acceptable to those who consider the fetus a human person.

The Instruction on Respect for Human Life, published by the Vatican in 1987, rejects all *in vitro* (Lat.) fertilization, where the sperm and egg are mixed outside the woman's body. But many Catholic moral theologians accept it in some cases of infertility when the husband's sperm and the wife's egg are used. Those who maintain this position allow experimental procedures *in vitro* with the same criteria that apply *in vivo*.

Fetal Tissue Research: Fetal tissue research, including transplantation research, is different since the fetus has died before the tissue is taken. Here it seems proper for the same principles to apply as apply to any cadaver transplant. Some allow cadaver transplantation from fetuses spontaneously aborted (miscarriages) or indirectly aborted as in ectopic pregnancies, but reject transplantation from directly aborted fetuses, arguing that this practice cooperates in immoral abortions and that it lends support to abortion or to laws permitting it. This effectively eliminates fetal tissue transplantation altogether since tissue from miscarried or ectopic fetuses is rarely fit for transplant. Other Catholic moralists accept these procedures under the usual criteria for cadaver transplantation. They deny the implication of proximate cooperation with abortion and insist that there is little or no reason to anticipate that abortions will be chosen specifically to provide tissue as long as legal safeguards separate the abortion and donation decisions.

Recent theological argument, returning to earlier Catholic tradition, has questioned the judgment that all fetuses are human persons. Some Catholic scholars maintain that the very early embryo, or "pre-embryo," cannot be a person. Strong theological, philosophical, and biological arguments support this position. Many who hold it, however, continue to reject risky nontherapeutic research, arguing that even the pre-embryo, which cannot be a person, must not be made the object of research that does not respect its intrinsic claim to life. *See also* abortion; bioethics; in vitro fertilization; medical ethics.

DAVID F. KELLY

fetishism, undue and exaggerated devotion to, or belief in, an object, practice, or idea. The term embraces several overlapping definitions and may now be so vague as to be useless in moral theology. Historically, fetishism described the belief that supernatural power resided in objects such as magic charms or carved figures. Fetishism is also used by twentieth-century psychologists to describe pathological erotic fascination with particular objects or rituals. Fetishism is morally significant because each of its definitions describes a disordered attachment to created goods rather than to their Creator. As such, it violates the principles of Catholic morality.

feudalism (Lat., *feudum,* "land"), a social form of interlocking relationships based on the use of land in payment for military services. Flourishing in ninth-century France after the collapse of Charlemagne's empire, it endured, with its conventions of homage and tenure, through most of the medieval period and into early modern times. In the early medieval economy land was the only real means of payment for necessary military service. But rather than alienate land permanently, lords gave up its use to vassals in exchange for specified military assistance, an arrangement that was sealed with promises of mutual loyalty (homage). The medieval Church, also needing military protection, entered into feudal relationships, interweaving the religious with the secular. This association and its attendant compromises, including the right of secular leaders to appoint bishops, were of central concern to the Gregorian reformers. *See also* Gregorian reform.

Feuerbach, Ludwig Andreas (foy'uhr bahk), 1804–72, German philosopher. He studied theology at Heidelberg and was then drawn to Berlin by Hegel's reputation. Leaving Berlin in 1826 because of insufficient financial support, he completed his doctorate in philosophy at Erlangen in 1828. Until 1835 he lectured on modern philosophy at Erlangen. But all hopes of a permanent academic position faded after he published in 1830 *Thoughts on Death and Immortality,* in which he criticized fundamental Christian tenets and denounced the conservative alliance between the churches and the reactionary regimes of the day. His marriage to a woman of wealth in 1835 allowed him to continue his scholarly and literary work without an academic appointment. His most famous book, *The Essence of Christianity,* appeared in 1841 and was followed by *Preliminary Theses for the Reform of Philosophy* (1842), *Foundations for the Philosophy of the Future* (1846), and *Lectures on the Essence of Religion* (1851). During these years he became the leader of the "left-wing" Hegelians and greatly influenced Karl Marx's critique of religion.

Feuerbach turned religion in general and Christianity in particular into anthropology. Religion, he taught, is the projection of qualities inherent in the human species outward into "God." Statements about God are really statements about humanity. Religion has served a useful purpose in humanity's development and culminated in Christianity which, with its doctrine of the God-man, is the fullest religious statement of the disguised anthropological truth. But now that humanity has attained its maturity in modernity, religion has been outgrown and must be discarded. Thus, he sought "to turn the lovers of God into the lovers of humanity." Feuerbach is a major figure in the development of modern atheism and was a prime source for the "death of God" theology of the mid-twentieth century. Modern Catholic apologetics has had to take the Feuerbachian anthropological critique with great seriousness. *See also* apologetics; faith and reason; philosophy and theology.

MICHAEL J. HIMES

Fiacre, St. (fee-ah'kruh), also known as Fiachra, d. ca. 670, patron saint of gardeners and the cabdrivers of Paris, whose vehicles are called "fiacres" because the first cab for hire in Paris was located near the Hotel Saint-Fiacre. An Irish hermit, Fiacre moved to France to live a solitary life there on land given to him by St. Faro, bishop of Meaux. Fiacre built a hospice for travelers and established a reputation for charity and spiritual wisdom. Feast day: September 1.

Fichter, Joseph H., 1908–94, sociologist. He entered the Society of Jesus in 1930, was ordained in 1942, received his doctorate in sociology from Harvard University, and served on the faculty of Loyola University in New Orleans for almost his entire academic career, beginning in 1947. From 1965 to 1970 he held the Charles Chauncey Stillman professorship of Roman Catholic Theological Studies at Harvard Divinity School. A past president of the Society for the Scientific Study of Religion, he was the author of more than thirty books and reports, including his classic, *Southern Parish* (1951).

Ficino, Marsiglio (mahr-seel'yoh fee-chee'noh,), 1433–99, Italian humanist, theologian, and leader of the influential Florentine Platonic academy. Rejecting Scholasticism, he became a champion of Christian Platonism through his study of Augustine, insisting that philosophy and religion are parallel means to truth based on contemplation of God, the final end of human nature. In *Theologica Platonica* (1469–74) and *De Christiana Religione* (1474), Ficino conceived the universe Neoplatonically, as a hierarchical structure flowing from God, with humankind providing the crucial link between spirit and matter. Among those influenced by Ficino were the Italian scholar Pico della Mirandola (d. 1694), the dean of St. Paul's in London John Colet (d. 1519), and the French humanist Jacobus Faber (d. 1536). *See also* Neoplatonism.

fideism (fee' day-iz-uhm), the view that religious knowledge is an act of faith (Lat., *fides*) alone and not at all an act of the human intellect (*ratio*). In general, fideism refers to any view that rejects reason as the basis for truth and insists that such grounds are found only in acquiescence to some other authority, be it that of instinct (Charles S. Pierce) or feeling (Friedrich Schleiermacher) or an empirical sensibility (William James) or practical reason (Immanuel Kant).

A narrower understanding of fideism restricts human knowledge of God to divine revelation. This is the position of the fourteenth-century William of Ockham, whose influence is seen in the sixteenth-century Martin Luther. In the nineteenth century, Catholic traditionalists commonly responded to the rationalism of the day by insisting that a spark or germ of faith was necessary for an intellectual grasp of speculative truth.

Vatican I's Dogmatic Constitution on the Catholic Faith (*Dei Filius*) opposed both fideism (and its Catholic variant, traditionalism) and rationalism. Unaided natural reason, the document states, is sufficient for knowledge of the existence of God. Faith in itself is possible only by grace and results in a different kind of knowledge, supernatural knowledge. For believers, both natural reason and supernatural

knowledge are operative in the human response to divine revelation. Vatican I, therefore, steers a middle ground. The act of faith is both reasonable and marked by a supernatural character. In other words, it retains the integrity of the human intellect while remaining subject to the freedom and gratuity characteristic of divine revelation. *See also* faith; faith and reason; revelation.　　　*NANCY DALLAVALLE*

Fidelis of Sigmaringen, St. (fee-day'lis uhv sigmahr-eeng'en), 1577–1622, priest and martyr. After a legal career, he joined the Capuchin order. He was murdered while on a mission in Calvinist Switzerland. Feast day: April 24.

fidelity, oath of. *See* oath of fidelity.

fidelity of God, God's commitment to the divine promises. In the OT, God remains faithful to the chosen people even when Israel strays from the covenantal relationship (e.g., Exod 34:6–7; Deut 7:9–11). The NT reaffirms God's covenant of salvific love with Israel and through Jesus, and institutes a new relationship with all humanity (e.g., Gal 4:24–31; 2 Tim 2:12–13; Eph 2:11–22). This new partnership fully acknowledges the dignity of the promises made to Israel while broadening its scope to include the entire human community (Heb 7–10).

The course of human lives, however, sometimes appears arbitrary and chaotic. Attempts to impose meaning or coherence onto one's life through personal plans and actions are sometimes dashed by factors outside one's control. God's fidelity, however, provides humanity with the certain assurance that God loved humankind first, and thus life itself has an ultimate goal. Although the meaning of God's pledge may only become apparent through the course of history, God's promise of faithfulness provides the assurance that human redemption stands as an irrevocable offer.

fides fiducialis (fee'dez fee-doo-chee-ah'lis; Lat., "trusting faith"), an understanding of faith, associated especially with Martin Luther, that stresses the operation of the will (trust) over the intellect. The Council of Trent (1545–63) taught that sins are not forgiven to anyone who boasts of confidence and certainty of the forgiveness of sins and rests on that alone (ch. 9). It also condemned the proposition that justifying faith is nothing other than "confidence in the divine mercy which remits sins for Christ's sake, or that it is this confidence alone by which we are justified" (can. 12). Sacramental grace is "conferred from the work which has been worked" rather than by faith alone in the divine promise (can. 9 on *The Sacraments in General.*) *See also* faith; Luther, Martin.

fides quarens intellectum (fee'days kwair'renz in-tel-lek'toom; Lat., "faith seeking understanding"), the classic definition of theology provided by Anselm of Canterbury (d. 1109). Theology begins from the standpoint of faith and, by unique methods and use of sources, attempts to understand the God who is the object of theological understanding. *See also* theology.

Filioque (fee-lee-oh'kway; Lat., "and the Son"), Latin term added to the Nicene-Constantinopolitan Creed (381) after the phrase "the Holy Spirit who proceeds from the Father." Both its theological meaning and the way in which it was added to the creed have been and continue to be sources of controversy between Eastern and Western Christians.

Early History: The doctrine of the double procession of the Holy Spirit, that is, the idea that the Holy Spirit proceeds from the Father and the Son (Lat., *a patre filioque*), was a subject of disagreement between Christian theologians as early as the fourth century and of division by the ninth century. In the fourth century, Theodoret of Cyrus (d. ca. 460) accused Cyril of Alexandria (d. 444) of teaching erroneously that the Son has a role in the origin of the Holy Spirit. It is unlikely that Cyril intended to teach such a doctrine. The differences between Theodoret and Cyril do, however, demonstrate the differences between two approaches to theology: the school of Antioch whose theologians leaned toward literal interpretation of Scripture and emphasized the distinction of divine persons, and the Alexandrian school that favored analogical interpretation of Scripture and emphasized the oneness of the divine essence. From within these two approaches would develop the two sides of the *Filioque* controversy.

The first clear statement of the doctrine of the *Filioque* is found in the *On the Trinity* of Augustine of Hippo (d. 430), who stated that the Holy Spirit proceeds from the Father and the Son, though principally from the Father. Although it was not a major tenet of his theology, the *Filioque* fit naturally within Augustine's approach to the doctrine of the Trinity, in which the Holy Spirit is pictured as the bond of love between the Father and the Son.

During the same century, three Eastern Fathers of the Church, Basil of Caesarea (d. 379), Gregory of Nazianzus (d. 390), and Gregory of Nyssa (d. 395), often called "the Cappadocian Fathers," developed their teaching on the Trinity along the lines of the Antiochene tradition mentioned above. They stressed the real distinction of the divine Persons and defined the distinguishing characteristic of the Father as Unoriginate Origin. They also emphasized the distinction between the incomprehensible divine essence and the divine energies through which we know God. Within their system, Filioquist thought is radically out of place because it obscures what is unique to the person of the Father. Furthermore, biblical references to Christ's sending of the Spirit show the relationship between the missions of the Son and the Spirit, but do not explain the essential relationship of the Son and Spirit to each other within the inner life of God.

The East-West Conflict: The term *"Filioque* controversy" is sometimes applied specifically to the argument among Eastern and Western theologians of the ninth century. In 810, theologians of Charlemagne's court, where the creed including the *Filioque* was already in use, petitioned Pope Leo III (d. 816) for official approval of their practice. Leo refused, although he declared his theological agreement with the *Filioque*. The Carolingian theologians composed an extensive defense of the *Filioque*, now called the *Libri Carolini*. In the East, the patriarch Photius (d. ca. 893) responded to the practice of certain Frankish monks in Jerusalem who attempted to impose the Western practice on their Eastern brothers. Photius's *Mystagogy of the Holy Spirit* introduced the formula that became the Eastern motif during the controversy and was eventually defined as dogmatic for Orthodox Christians: the Holy Spirit proceeds "from the Father alone." According to Photius, the *Filioque* is not only an illegitimate addition to the creed but a grave theological error.

The dispute was heated and complicated by political events including the deposition and reinstatement of Photius as patriarch. The issue of the *Filioque* remained alive. It was listed among the complaints against Rome by Michael Cerularius and his followers when the relationship between Western and some Eastern Christians was officially broken in the eleventh century (1054).

At a council in Lyons in 1274 and again at Florence in 1439, Western Christians sought to impose acceptance of the *Filioque*, though not its recitation, on Eastern Christians. Popular Eastern response to the proclamations of those councils demonstrates the growing importance of the underlying issues of trinitarian theology, as well as the ecclesiological issue regarding the authority to change the creed. At a council in Constantinople in 1351, the distinction between divine essence and divine energies, which had begun with the Cappadocians and developed especially in the writings of the Byzantine theologian Gregory Palamas (d. 1359), was defined as dogmatic. On the basis of that distinction, as well as the conviction that it is the Father's personal property to be the source of divine life, Eastern theologians continue to insist that the *Filioque* is irreconcilable with Orthodox trinitarian faith.

The Filioque and the Creed: The Nicene-Constantinopolitan Creed, because of its antiquity, is almost universally recognized among Christian denominations as a true expression of Christian faith. That creed states simply belief in "the Holy Spirit who proceeds from the Father, who together with the Father and Son is worshiped and glorified." The first official proclamation of a creed with the addition of the *Filioque* is found in the documents of the Third Council of Toledo (589), which strongly affirmed the divinity of the Son against a growing Arian heresy in the West. Eastern monks, on hearing the altered creed, accused Westerners of defying the orders of the Council of Ephesus (431) that no addition should be made to the creed approved at Constantinople (381). Western response indicated that the phrase was considered a clarification of the faith already expressed in the creed and not a true addition.

Pope Leo III's rejection in 810 of the amended creed as an official element of the liturgy also stood in the West until the eleventh century (1014), when Pope Benedict VIII (d. 1024) gave his approval. Even the Council of Lyons (1274), which required Eastern churches wishing to be reunited with Rome to accept the *Filioque* as a legitimate expression of the faith, did not require those Christians to change the recitation of the creed in their liturgy.

The *Filioque* is currently a matter of concern among theologians interested in ecumenical discussion, especially those connected with the work of the World Council of Churches. The vast majority of Western theologians propose that the *Filioque* be dropped from the creed when it is recited in the liturgy for two reasons: the process by which it was added was questionable at best, and it remains a barrier to the profession of a common Christian faith. Pope Paul VI (d. 1978), meeting with Ortho-

dox Catholics, not only recited the creed in its earlier form but referred to the meeting at Lyons as a "Western synod" rather than as an ecumenical council. Further discussion centers on the likeness and differences between Eastern and Western trinitarian theology, and the ecclesiological implications of the two approaches. *See also* Eastern Schism; Holy Spirit; Nicene Creed; Trinity, doctrine of the.

Bibliography

Congar, Yves. *I Believe in the Holy Spirit.* 3 vols. New York: Seabury Press, 1983.

Kelly, J. N. D. *Early Christian Creeds.* 3d ed. New York: Longman, 1972.

LaCugna, Catherine Mowry. *God for Us: The Trinity and Christian Life.* San Francisco: HarperCollins, 1991.   CORINNE WINTER

Filippini, St. Lucy, 1672–1732, founder of the Pontifical Institute of Religious Teachers, popularly called the Filippini Sisters, in Italy in 1704. The purpose of the congregation was for the education of young poor girls. The Filippini Sisters came to the United States in 1910. She was canonized in 1930. Feast day: March 25.

final perseverance. *See* perseverance, final.

finance council, group mandated by canon law to give advice and, under specified conditions, required consent to administrators of Church property. Every ecclesiastical juridical person (e.g., diocese, parish, religious community) is obliged to have a finance council.

Finbar, St., seventh-century Irish hermit and bishop (and patron saint) of Cork. Feast day: September 25.

finding of the cross. *See* invention of the cross.

Fiorenza, Elisabeth Schüssler, b. 1938, biblical scholar and Krister Stendahl Professor at Harvard Divinity School. Known for her work in feminist biblical interpretation, especially her 1983 study *In Memory of Her: A Feminist Theological Reconstruction of Early Christian Origins,* she is founding coeditor (with Judith Plaskow) of the *Journal of Feminist Studies in Religion* and active in the women church movement. *See also* feminist interpretation of Scripture.

First Fridays, a nonobligatory, devotional custom of receiving the Eucharist on the first Friday of nine consecutive months. The custom originated in a promise that Christ is alleged to have made to Margaret Mary Alacoque (1647–90), a nun of the Visitation order. She claimed that over a period of eighteen months, beginning in December 1673, Christ revealed to her a new devotion centered on his Sacred Heart, afire with love for humanity. Practitioners of the devotion were expected to receive Communion on the first Friday of each month, to spend a holy hour in the presence of the Blessed Sacrament each Thursday, and to celebrate, annually, the Feast of the Sacred Heart (authorized in 1765 by Pope Clement XIII). According to Margaret Mary, those keeping the First Fridays will not die in sin or without the sacraments, and Christ will be their refuge at the moment of death. *See also* Alacoque, St. Margaret Mary.

First Saturdays, a set of devotional customs in honor of the Immaculate Heart of Mary performed on the first Saturday of five consecutive months. These devotions (which no Catholic is obliged to practice) consist of participating in the sacrament of Penance ("confession"), receiving Communion, and reciting five decades of the rosary while meditating on its mysteries for fifteen minutes. In some parishes, a special votive Mass in honor of Mary is celebrated on first Saturdays. This devotion appears to have originated in the alleged Marian apparitions at Fátima, Portugal, in 1917. The link between Saturday and devotion to Mary, however, is far more ancient; it surfaced in the West as early as the eighth century. Eventually, it assumed liturgical form in the recitation of the "Office of the Blessed Virgin Mary" on Saturday, a practice supposedly introduced by Pope Urban II at the Council of Clermont in 1096. *See also* Immaculate Heart of Mary.

fish, ancient Christian symbol. Found among catacomb graffiti as well as wall frescos and sarcopha-

The fish, an early Christian symbol for Christ.

gus sculpture, stylized drawings of a fish were common symbols of Christ. Such stylized drawings are still found today among Christians as medallions and automobile bumper stickers.

The first letters of the Greek phrase "Jesus Christ, Son of God, Savior" spell out the Greek word for fish (*ichtys*). There is no scholarly consensus as to whether this acrostic led to the iconographic symbol or vice versa.

Fisher, St. John, 1469–1535, chancellor of Cambridge University, bishop of Rochester (from 1504), and cardinal (1535). Seeking to reinvigorate Scholasticism with humanist criticism, he became renowned both for his preaching and for his educational reforms. From 1519 to 1527, Fisher wrote polemical defenses of Church tradition against Martin Luther, John Oecolampadius, and others, making a decisive contribution to Counter-Reformation theology. After 1527, Fisher led the ecclesiastical opposition to Henry VIII's divorce and claims to supremacy over the Church. Arrested in 1534 and executed for treason on June 22, 1535, he was canonized in 1935. Feast day: June 22. *See also* England, Catholicism in; English Martyrs; Forty Martyrs of England and Wales.

fistula (fis'tchoo-lah; Lat., "pipe"), a silver straw used to sip Communion wine from the chalice. Communicants sip a small amount of wine through the fistula. They then drink a sip of water from another chalice to purify it. This was the most common method for Communion from the chalice in Rome from the late classical period until the early Middle Ages. Though permitted, the fistula is not commonly used in the United States today. *See also* chalice; Communion, Holy.

Fitzmyer, Joseph A., b. 1920, internationally renowned NT and Aramaic scholar. Ordained a Jesuit priest (1951), he received a Ph.D. from the Johns Hopkins University (1956), the S.S.L. from Pontifical Biblical Institute (1957), honorary doctorates from various U.S. universities and from Lunds Universitet (Sweden) and the University of St. Andrews (Scotland). He taught at Woodstock College, Maryland (1958–69), the University of Chicago (1969–71), Fordham University (1971–74), Weston School of Theology, Cambridge, Massachusetts (1974–76) and The Catholic University of America (1976–86). He was president of the Catholic Biblical Association

(1969–70), the Society of Biblical Literature (1979–80), and *Studiorum Novi Testamenti Societas* (1992–93), and a member of the Pontifical Biblical Commission since 1984. Author of more than thirty books, most notably *The Gospel According to Luke* (Anchor Bible, vols. 28, 28a), he is editor, with R. E. Brown and R. E. Murphy, of *The Jerome Biblical Commentary* (1968) and *The New Jerome Biblical Commentary* (1990).

five ways of St. Thomas Aquinas,

five proofs for the existence of God found in the *Summa Theologiae* of Thomas Aquinas (d. 1274). Thomas's second question of the *Summa Theologiae* asks, "Does God exist?" After dispensing with claims that God's existence is self-evident, he goes on to show that human ways of explaining the universe cannot be made complete on their own terms. Human reason itself leaves a space for the God whom Jews, Christians, and Muslims believe freely created the world. The source for the faith of Jews and of Christians is not human reason alone, but the Scriptures. Yet the God whom those Scriptures reveal is not foreign to human beings who use reason to explain how it is that things are as they are. God's role as Creator cannot be offered as a scientific explanation because science cannot totally explain the world as it is; there must be room for an account such as that given by the Bible.

Drawing from Aristotle, Aquinas's "five ways" are based on explanatory schemes considered sufficient in his time for accounts of what happens in the world, specifically, (1) what makes things change, (2) how causality works, (3) what is always the way it is or what happens contingently, (4) degrees of excellence in things, and (5) the goal of natural things. He shows how each of these schemes cannot suffice when speaking of the universe itself, where one must move to another level. That very opening in human discourse, then, offers him a way of connecting the rest of his monumental theological treatise to the widest range of human intellectual concerns. And that is precisely how these "five ways" should be considered. They connect theology with the human enterprise of explaining without claiming that theology is that sort of an explanation.

Finally, these arguments of Aquinas ought not to be considered to be "proofs" (in any acceptable modern sense of that word) of God's existence. Their role is essentially as an introduction to a theological inquiry grounded in faith. What the "five ways" do show is that the inquiry into God's existence connects with wider human inquiries, without being itself a part of them. The premises for Thomas's arguments come from revelation, yet that revelation addresses the concerns of both intellect and heart. Aquinas's "five ways" show that human inquiry leaves space for a transcendent God. *See also* God.

DAVID B. BURRELL

flagellants, organized groups in the Middle Ages who scourged themselves in public processions in penance for their sins and those of the whole world. First organized in Italy in 1260 and revived in the fourteenth century after the Black Death, they were condemned by the popes for their excesses.

flagellation, scourging of oneself or another. The practice of scourging as a punishment was known in the ancient world. In early and medieval Christianity clerics, monks, and laity were punished by scourging for some crimes. Voluntary flagellation became common in the Middle Ages as expiation for one's sins or those of others. An incentive was the scourging of Christ. Flagellation of oneself or taking the discipline became customary in religious communities but has largely been abandoned since Vatican II (1962–65). The Church has frowned on the public processions of flagellation, a few of which have lasted to modern times.

Flaget, Benedict Joseph, 1763–1851, French-born bishop and missionary. A French Sulpician, he served as bishop of Bardstown, Kentucky (1810–51), a diocese extending from the Allegheny Mountains to the Mississippi River. An insightful bishop, he was often consulted in the selection of bishops for U.S. sees. He established schools, colleges, and a seminary, and welcomed the foundation of the Trappist (Cistercian) Monastery of Gethsemani, south of Bardstown.

Flavian, St., d. 449, the patriarch of Constantinople beginning in 446. An opponent of Monophysitism, he excommunicated Eutyches at the synod in Constantinople in 448. His decision was supported by Pope Leo I, but it was reversed at the Council of Ephesus in 449, the "Robber Synod," which also condemned and exiled Flavian. He was posthumously exonerated at the Council of Chalcedon (451). Feast day: February 18. *See also* Chalcedon, Council of.

Fleury, abbey at Saint-Benoît-sur-Loire, in central

France. Fleury acquired the (alleged) relics of Benedict of Nursia in the seventh century and was noted for its learning and wealth throughout the Middle Ages. Reformed according to Cluniac and Maurist patterns, the abbey was suppressed in 1790 but revived in 1944. *See also* Cluny; Maurists.

flight from the world (Lat., *fuga mundi*), a Christian attitude of rejection toward earthly things. This theme in Christian spirituality has largely been rejected since Vatican II (1962–65) as being dualistic and unappreciative of the goodness and beauty of creation. However, an authentic understanding of this tradition sees flight from the world as a rejection of sin, e.g., in modern times a rejection of greed and consumerism. It is a flight to conversion and to God. Monks and nuns in the desert sought to live together in love so as to live separated from the sin of the world. *See also* asceticism; detachment; world, responsibility for.

Flood, the, a destruction of the inhabited world by water narrated in Gen 6–9. The story reflects traditions about a flood recorded in Mesopotamian literature. The best known example is the *Epic of Gilgamesh,* published in 1873 from tablets discovered in the library of the seventh-century B.C. Assyrian king Ashurbanipal. There the surviving hero, equivalent to Noah, is named Utnapishtim. In an earlier Sumerian version he is Ziusudra. Berossus, a Babylonian priest writing in Greek in the third century B.C., recorded the Mesopotamian stories in a form cited by the *Chronicle* of the fourth-century bishop Eusebius. The Mesopotamian traditions build local catastrophies into events of worldwide significance. The biblical story in turn typified the coming judgment (Matt 24:27–28; Luke 17:26–27; Heb 11:7; 1 Pet 3:20; 2 Pet 2:5).

Florence, Council of, a council held between 1438 and 1445 for the purpose of reuniting the Roman Catholic Church and the Greek church, which was seeking Western aid against the Turks. It was convened in Ferrara in 1438, moved to Florence in 1439 due to economic problems, and concluded in Rome after the Greek participants had signed the Decree of Union and departed. The theological issues discussed included the double procession of the Holy Spirit, the use of unleavened bread for the Eucharist, the doctrine of purgatory, and papal primacy.

The chief obstacle to agreement proved to be the *Filioque* (Lat., "and the Son") clause, an expression of the doctrine of the double procession of the Holy Spirit from the Father "and the Son," which the Roman church had added to the creed. The Greeks argued that the addition had been made in violation of the decision of the Council of Ephesus (431) that nothing should be added to the creed approved at the Council of Constantinople (381). Furthermore, the *Filioque* was not attested in Scripture and had been denied by important Greek Fathers of the Church. After protracted discussion, the Greek participants themselves became divided on the issue. Unionists among them urged the acceptance of the formula on the grounds that because it was found among some of the saints or Fathers of the early Church, it must be consistent with the faith expressed by the Greek Fathers. The Decree of Union, *Laetentur Coeli,* signed on July 5, 1439, included the acceptance by some of the Greeks of the *Filioque* as a legitimate expression of the universal faith. The patriarch Mark of Ephesus refused to sign the agreement. On his return to Constantinople, Mark garnered considerable popular support, and some of the bishops repented of having signed the decree.

In addition to the acceptance of the *Filioque,* the decree included decisions on the other major issues. Both the eucharistic rite that used leavened bread and the one that used unleavened bread were valid. Also, after death some souls are cleansed by undergoing punishment while others receive immediately either eternal reward or eternal punishment. Further, the pope is the successor of Peter, head and teacher of the whole Church. After him come the patriarchs in a specified order.

The conquest of Constantinople by the Turks in 1453 cut short whatever union was achieved between Rome and the Greek church. After Florence, decrees of union were issued with other Eastern churches on similar terms. Many of those were also short-lived. *See also* Azymites; Eastern Schism; *Filioque;* primacy, papal; purgatory.   CORINNE WINTER

Florian, St., d. 304, martyr, patron saint of Poland. His conversion to Christianity while a Roman officer led to his execution by drowning. Feast day: May 4.

florilegia (floh-rih-lay'gee-ah; Lat., "flower collections"), collections of excerpts, whether sacred, secular, or both, especially important in antiquity and the Middle Ages, when books were costly. A sacred florilegium may include biblical, patristic, liturgical, or legal texts and serve purposes ranging from apologetics to inspiration.

Focolare (foh-kuh-lahr'ay; It., "fireplace"), modern religious movement within the Roman Catholic Church. Founded in 1943 by Chiara Lubich (who won the Templeton Prize in 1977) in Trent, Italy, and approved by Rome in 1962, Focolare has a number of different branches within a larger movement. There are celibate communities of men and women who observe the evangelical counsels (poverty, chastity, and obedience) but do secular work; married people who identify with the ideals of the movement; and a young people's movement and priestly fraternities who do the same. The general purpose is to change the world through the observance of gospel ideals. Annual meetings called Mariapolis ("City of Mary") are held to intesify the zeal of the movement, which is found in Europe, North and South America, and Africa. *See also* counsels, evangelical.

following Christ. *See* imitation of Christ.

font, baptismal, the receptacle, containing water, in which baptisms are performed. Fonts vary in size from small holy water stoups (basins) to installations of sufficient size and shape for the immersion of adults. Fonts may be found in one of three locations in a church: at or near the door to the church; in a baptistery, which is a small room off to the side of the nave or in the vestibule; or in or near the sanctuary or pulpit. Fonts are sometimes octagonal in shape or may include a three-step entrance and exit from the basin. Thus, by their shape, size, or other visual features, they depict symbolic aspects of the sacrament, e.g., death and resurrection, water and new life. Among furnishings recognized as vital to the appointment of a church building, the baptismal font ranks as high as the altar in its importance. *See also* baptismal font; baptistery.

font, holy water, the vessel for holy water set near the entrances to churches and chapels. Sometimes called stoups, such water vessels may have derived from the fountains often found in the forecourts of Roman basilicas, in which worshippers could wash their face and hands before services. In modern times, holy water is collected on the fingers of the right hand and, with the sign of the cross, applied to one's self as a blessing and reminder of Baptism. *See also* holy water.

Holy water font

Fontevrault, Order of (fohn-tev-roh'), double order of nuns and monks ruled over by an abbess, derived from a community of Benedictine nuns founded by Robert d'Abrissel ca. 1101 and centered in the convent of Fontevrault, France. Suppressed in 1790, it was revived as a women's order without lasting success in the nineteenth century. *See also* double monasteries.

Fools, Feast of, mock religious festival celebrated in the Middle Ages, generally held on New Year's Day and noted for its burlesque and unseemly behavior. Opposed and later forbidden by the Church, remnants of it existed into the sixteenth century.

Ford, John, 1902–89, prominent American Jesuit moral theologian with teaching assignments at Weston School of Theology and The Catholic University of America. Author of many articles, including the famous "The Morality of Obliteration Bombing" (*Theological Studies,* 1944), he coauthored with Gerald Kelly *Contemporary Moral Theology: Questions in Fundamental Moral Theology* (1958), and *Contemporary Moral Theology: Marriage Questions* (1963). A member of the papal commission on birth control, he supported the traditional ban on all forms of contraception and vigorously opposed critics of *Humanae Vitae.*

forgiveness, the act of being restored to a good relationship with God, others, and self following a period or incident of sin or alienation. In the Christian tradition, forgiveness is the sinner's transforming acceptance of the unconditional mercy of God through Jesus Christ and the subsequent extending of that experience to other persons by accepting them. The practice of forgiveness is central to the Christian identity as described in the Lord's Prayer (Luke 11:1–4; Matt 6:9–15), and it is to be offered as often as it is requested (Matt 18: 21–35).

Historically, the Christian community has required of the individual sinner penance, almsgiving, and even separation from the community as means of conversion and reconciliation. Forgiveness is celebrated ecclesially in Baptism and Eucharist, as well as the sacrament of Reconciliation, in which there is to be confession of sin, contrition, and absolution by the Church's minister. Since Vatican II (1962–65), the celebration of the sacrament of Reconciliation has stressed the social dimensions and structures of sin and forgiveness. *See also* Reconciliation.

form criticism, the study of a text according to its generic, structural, and formal characteristics, and the attempt to locate its form in the oral stage of the lived experience of a people (the "setting in life"). OT material is divided into prose forms (e.g., myths, legends, sagas, historical narrative) and poetic forms (e.g., prophetic oracles, and in the Psalms, hymns, laments, thanksgivings, and wisdom psalms). The more frequent distinction in the NT (esp. in the Gospels) is between narrative and discourse material, the former involving legends (e.g., Mark 6:14–29) and miracle stories, while the latter include proverbs, parables, apocalyptic sayings, and apophthegms (Gk., "utter forth"), which consist of narratives used to illustrate sayings (e.g., Mark 2:15–17). Since it challenged the literal historicity of traditional material, form criticism was strongly resisted within Catholicism until Pope Pius XII's *Divino Afflante Spiritu* (1943), and was approved by the Dogmatic Constitution on Divine Revelation (1965) of Vatican II (see n. 12). *See also* biblical criticism.

form of a sacrament. *See* sacrament, form of a.

form of marriage. *See* marriage, form of.

fornication, heterosexual intercourse between two unmarried persons. From the NT writings of Paul to the present, fornication has been understood to be a moral evil. This is because the only proper context for intercourse is marriage. Various

reasons are given for this teaching. The Genesis vision of "two becoming one flesh" in marriage is one reason. Another, emerging in the Middle Ages, was concern for the well-being and education of a child that might result from such a union. *See also* chastity; Marriage; temperance.

Fortescue, Adrian, 1874–1923, priest and liturgist. He was a linguist and an expert in Eastern liturgies. His book *The Mass: A Study of the Roman Liturgy* (1907) was a pioneering work in English on the subject, though he is more widely known for his book *Ceremonies of the Roman Rite Described* (1918).

fortitude, a cardinal virtue that is equivalent to courage. Within the framework of traditional moral theology, fortitude is one of the four cardinal virtues necessary to living a completely moral life. It is traditionally associated with the other cardinal virtues of temperance, justice, and prudence. Fortitude is equivalent to courage, although within the Catholic moral tradition it has come to have a broader meaning than is usually given to courage. Fortitude may be defined as that quality of character through which its possessor is enabled to endure hardships and to overcome fears that would tend to deflect an individual from the pursuit of the aims of a humanly and Christian good life. Fortitude is expressed not only in the physical courage that is exhibited by soldiers on a battlefield, but also through the moral courage that enables a person to endure social disapproval for one's efforts to attain social justice, and through the patience that enables another to pursue a vocation as an artist in spite of obstacles. The vices contrary to fortitude would include a tendency to shrink from danger and tendency to take unnecessary or unjustified risks.

Within the Catholic tradition, fortitude, like all the other virtues, can only be understood within the context of the overall goods of human life, and the kinds of risks and hardships that a person can be expected to undergo in pursuit of those goods. As our understanding of the aims of life and the obligations that result from those aims has developed and changed, our understanding of what can be called fortitude has also developed and changed. *See also* cardinal virtues.   *JEAN PORTER*

fortune-telling, the prediction of the future or reading of one's personality by means of cards, tea leaves, palm-reading, crystal balls, and astrology.

Fortune-telling, or divination, is generally considered to be a sin against religion, specifically the First Commandment, because it involves a claim to know what only God can know and is a false form of prophecy. Many forms of fortune-telling, which describe events of the future as fixed and inescapable, are sinful because such predictions and their acceptance neglect human moral agency. In addition, many fortune-telling operations involve fraudulent practices. Nevertheless, the culpability of some adherents of fortune-telling may be reduced because of their ignorance or naiveté.

Forty Hours devotion, a form of prayer before the Blessed Sacrament as it is solemnly exposed during an uninterrupted period of forty hours. The practice is in continuity with late medieval eucharistic devotions connected with the Sacred Triduum. After the Holy Thursday evening procession with the Blessed Sacrament, the faithful took turns praying at the altar of reservation until midday of Holy Saturday, a period of forty hours. According to Augustine (*On the Trinity* 4.6), Jesus would have lain in his tomb precisely forty hours, and it is this symbolism that lies behind the origin of the devotion. At Milan, in 1527, the priest Antonio Bellotti imposed on members of his confraternity, founded in the Church of the Holy Sepulcher, the obligation of celebrating Forty Hours not only during the Sacred Triduum, but also in connection with the feasts of Pentecost, Assumption, and Christmas. The practice soon spread to other churches, often with a eucharistic procession from one church to another. Frequently celebrated during times of calamity and public need, the devotion took on an increasingly penitential character and, in the context of the revelry of carnival time, a spirit of reparation. The devotion quickly spread throughout Europe. Until modern times, the complex ceremonial followed was based on the *Clementine Instruction* published in 1731 by Pope Clement XII. Since Vatican II (1962–65), the aspect of penance and reparation is less in evidence, and the much simplified ceremonial is governed by the general norms for the prolonged exposition of the Blessed Sacrament. *See also* Blessed Sacrament; devotions; eucharistic devotions.

CHRYSOGONUS WADDELL

Forty Martyrs of England and Wales, English and Welsh Catholics who were put to death by the English state between 1535 and 1680 for refusing to take the Oath of Supremacy that acknowledged the English's sovereign's leadership of the Church of England, or simply for being priests or for sheltering priests. The forty are representative of a larger group of 357 martyrs whose causes of beatification and eventual canonization are still under consideration. The forty were canonized by Pope Paul VI in 1970. Thirteen were diocesan seminary professors, ten were Jesuits (including Edmund Campion and Robert Southwell), three were Benedictines, three were Carthusian monks, one was a Brigettine nun, two were Franciscans, one was an Austin Friar, and the remaining seven were laypersons—four men and three women (including Margaret Clitherow). The names of the forty martyrs (the dagger symbol indicates a separate entry under that name in this encyclopedia) are: John Almond, Edmund Arrowsmith†, Ambrose Barlow, John Boste, Alexander Briant†, Edmund Campion†, Margaret Clitherow†, Philip Evans†, Thomas Garnet, Edmund Gennings, Richard Gwyn, John Houghton, Philip Howard†, John Jones, John Kemble†, Luke Kirby†, Robert Lawrence, David Lewis, Anne Line, John Lloyd, Cuthbert Mayne†, Henry Morse†, Nicholas Owen, John Payne†, Polydore Plasden, John Plessington†, Richard Reynolds†, John Rigby†, John Roberts†, Alban Roe, Ralph Sherwin, Robert Southwell†, John Southworth†, John Stone†, John Wall, Henry Walpole†, Margaret Ward†, Augustine Webster, Swithun Wells†, Eustace White. Feast day: October 25. *See also* England, Catholicism in; English Martyrs; martyr; martyrdom.

forum, tribunal or judicial situs. The appropriate forum or tribunal in which to hold a canonical trial is one wherein an ecclesiastical judge may legally declare himself or herself competent by reason of subject matter and place as provided in canon law. Forums are also distinguished as extraordinary or ordinary, external or internal. *See also* external forum; internal forum; tribunal.

Foucauld, Charles de, 1858–1916, priest, hermit, and inspiration for the founding of the Little Brothers (and Sisters) of Jesus. He spent several years in the military and served in North Africa. As an adolescent, he abandoned the practice of his faith, but in 1886 he was drawn back to God. For a time, he was a Trappist. In 1901, his deepening conversion and devotion to the Blessed Sacrament led him to ordination, after which he returned to the Sahara and built a hermitage. He was unsuccessful in his efforts to convert Muslims to Christianity and he attracted no disciples to his hermitage. It was only after his death that de Foucauld's private papers inspired those who founded the Little Brothers of Jesus in 1933 and the Little Sisters of Jesus in 1936. *See also* Little Brothers of Jesus.

foundations, called pious foundations in canon law, resources established either as a juridical person or dependent upon another juridical person that are destined to fulfill the purposes of religion or charity. There are specific regulations concerning their establishment and administration. *See also* juridical person.

Four Crowned Martyrs, d. early fourth century, patrons saints of sculptors. They were either four Persian stonemasons (named Claudius, Nicostratus, Simpronian, and Castorius) executed by the Romans under Emperor Diocletian for not sacrificing to the gods, or four Roman soldiers also executed under Diocletian for the same reason. Venerable Bede records that an early seventh-century church in Canterbury was dedicated to them and contained their relics. Feast day: November 8.

Fourier, St. Peter, 1565–1640, French-born cofounder of the Augustinian Canonesses of Our Lady, an order devoted to the education of poor children. Feast day: December 9.

Fourteen Holy Helpers, a group of saints known for their response to prayers of petition, especially for recovery from diseases and for spiritual strength at the hour of death. Popular in the Rhineland from the fourteenth century, the devotion was strongly criticized by the reformers for its superstitious overtones and was eventually discouraged by the Council of Trent in the sixteenth century. The names of the fourteen saints are: Acacius, Barbara, Blaise, Catherine of Alexandria, Christopher, Cyricus, Denis, Erasmus, Eustace, George, Giles, Margaret of Antioch, Pantaleon, and Vitus.

Fox, Matthew, b. 1940, spiritual writer. Since the publication of his book *On Becoming a Musical, Mystical Bear* (1972), Fox has become the most articulate and best-known proponent of creation-centered spirituality in Catholic circles. He is the

founder of the Institute for Creation-Centered Spirituality, located at Holy Names College in Oakland, California. He is the author of numerous other books and articles. In 1992 he left the Dominican order after a dispute with his superiors regarding his relationship to his province, and in 1994 he left the Roman Catholic Church to become an Episcopalian. *See also* creation-centered spirituality.

fraction, the breaking of bread. At the Eucharist this action repeats the most ancient of Christian liturgical gestures, the recognition of Christ "in the breaking of bread" (Luke 24:3). After the fraction, the presider drops a part of the host into the chalice (commingling). During the Agnus Dei litany, presider and assistants solemnly divide the consecrated breads into portions suitable to the Communion that will follow. *See also* Communion, Holy; host.

France, Catholicism in. It is not known when Christianity came to Roman Gaul, although probably the Church there traced its roots to Asia Minor. A flourishing community existed at Lyons by 150; the reputation of the bishop of that city, Irenaeus (d. ca. 200) and the fact that the first great Western synod was held at Arles in 314 attest to the importance of Christian Gaul. During the fourth century, the number of bishoprics grew from about twenty to seventy; major figures were Hilary of Poitiers (d. 367) and Martin of Tours (d. 397), generally acclaimed as the greatest ascetic figure of the West. This Gallo-Roman church was just beginning to penetrate the rural districts when the country was overrun by Germanic tribes; the conversion of the Frankish king, Clovis, in 496 marked the beginning of the assimilation of these Germanic peoples to Catholic

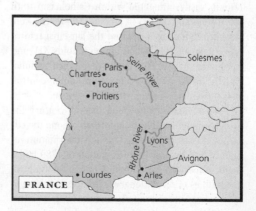

Christianity, an event that gave France its title "the eldest daughter of the Church."

Under Frankish rule, there was a good deal of political unrest; the condition of the Church reflected the prevailing lack of order. Celtic monks were active in evangelization efforts, and the English missionary bishop Boniface, as papal legate, helped reorganize the Frankish church in 747–751, bringing closer assimilation to Roman practices.

By the eleventh century, France had disintegrated into over fifty virtually independent feudal states; with Church support, Hugh Capet was installed as king in 987. The new dynasty had a very close working relationship with the Church: the monarchs gave enthusiastic support to monastic reform movements and were a reliable source of backing to the popes in their Crusading efforts and in their continual political struggles with the Holy Roman emperors. A high point of this relationship was the reign of St. Louis IX (1226–70). However, the later Middle Ages were marked by growing tensions between the French kings seeking to consolidate power over their domains and the papacy.

Post-Reformation: The Reformation quickly made an impact in France. The most important Protestant leader was John Calvin, who directed his efforts from French-speaking Switzerland and gained many adherents. By 1560 about 10 percent of the country was Protestant. From 1562 to 1593 the country was torn by bloody religious wars; an equilibrium was reached with the Edict of Nantes in 1598, which guaranteed a good measure of toleration to the Protestants.

The seventeenth century witnessed a great Catholic revival with such figures as Francis de Sales (d. 1622) and Vincent de Paul (d. 1660); a distinctive French school of spirituality blossomed that would remain vastly influential within Catholicism until the twentieth century. Catholics, however, were strongly divided as a result of the Jansenist reform movement, and the policies of both Louis XIV and the hierarchy sought to make the French national church virtually autonomous from Roman control. This movement was known as Gallicanism.

Post-Revolution: In the eighteenth century the Enlightenment made strong inroads among the educated classes, weakening Counter-Reformation religious conformism. The Revolution of 1789 had a major impact on the Catholic Church; the Gallican sympathies of revolutionary legislators led them to nationalize Church property, and the Civil Constitution of the Clergy (1791), which put the choice of bishops and pastors into the hands of the voters, was condemned by the pope. The result was a schism in the French church that was finally healed by Napoleon's concordat with Rome in 1801.

Although the Catholic Church retained its legal establishment and enjoyed a remarkable renaissance throughout the nineteenth century, there was a growing polarization within French society. The majority of Church leaders, allied with conservative aristocratic and rural elements, were intransigently opposed to the "liberties" of the Revolution; working-class people, drawn to the cities as a result of the Industrial Revolution, increasingly desired those liberties for themselves and thus perceived the Church as the enemy. The broadening of the suffrage in the later part of the century brought anticlerical forces to power; the result was a gradual weakening of Church influence; education was secularized in 1882, and complete separation of Church and state was decreed in 1905.

Although French Catholics continued to be at the forefront of the theological and liturgical movements that led up to Vatican II, at the same time a far-reaching transformation of French society was taking place caused by the great exodus of the population from rural areas, long the bastion of the Church. Today France is one of the most secularized countries of Western Europe; over 20 percent of the population no longer claims any religious affiliation, and only about 10–15 percent of professing Catholics practice the faith on a regular basis. *See also* Avignon; Francis de Sales, St.; Gallicanism; Holy Roman Empire; Jansenism; Paris; Protestantism; Vincent de Paul, St.   *DOMINIC MONTI*

Frances of Rome, St., 1384–1440, founder of the Oblates of Tor de'Specchi. Her husband was still living when Frances founded a community of women without vows to serve the poor. After she was widowed, she became a member and superior of this community. Frances is a patron saint of motorists. Feast day: March 9.

Frances Xavier Cabrini, St. *See* Cabrini, St. Frances Xavier.

Francis, Prayer of St., also known as the Peace Prayer of St. Francis, one of the most popular Christian prayers. Though probably not written by Francis of Assisi himself, it is at least Franciscan in spirit and tone.

PRAYER OF ST. FRANCIS

Lord, make me an instrument of your peace;
where there is hatred, let me sow love;
where there is injury, pardon;
where there is doubt, faith;
where there is despair, hope;
where there is darkness, light;
and where there is sadness, joy.
Grant that I may not so much seek
    to be consoled as to console;
to be understood as to understand;
to be loved as to love;
for it is in giving that we receive;
it is in pardoning that we are pardoned;
and it is in dying that we are born to eternal life.

Francis, Rule of St., the rule of life drawn up by Francis of Assisi (d. 1226) for himself and his associates, rooted in the evangelical call to a life of poverty and to the peaceful and gentle love of all people, especially the poor, and of the whole of God's creation. The first rule, now lost, was known as the *Regula Primitiva* (Lat., "primitive rule"). It was based on sayings from the Gospels and was approved by Pope Innocent III during Francis's visit to Rome in 1209–10. A second, recast form of the rule, known as the *Regula Prima* ("first rule"), was drawn up in 1221 and, after still further revision, received formal papal approval by Pope Honorius III in 1223. The approved version was known as the *Regula Bullata* ("[papally] sealed rule"). It enjoins complete poverty not only on individual members of the Franciscan order (friars) but on the whole order. Beginning about 1245, there were often bitter disputes within the order about the implications of the requirement of poverty. The Spiritual Franciscans insisted on a literal interpretation, while the majority adopted a more moderate and pragmatic interpretation in accordance with changing historical circumstances and pastoral needs. *See also* Conventuals; Franciscan order; Franciscan spirituality; Francis of Assisi, St.; Spiritual Franciscans.

Franciscan Friars of the Atonement (S.A.), a branch of the Third Order Regular of St. Francis of Assisi founded in 1898 by Lewis Thomas Wattson (Father Paul) at Garrison, New York; they are also known as Graymoor Frairs or Atonement Friars.

Wattson, an Episcopalian clergyman, wished to begin a preaching order modeled on the religious poverty of Francis of Assisi. Early efforts were hampered by low numbers, poverty, and the lack of support from fellow Anglicans. In 1909, Father Paul was received into the Catholic Church. Today the society is most known for its missionary and charitable endeavors and its promotion of Christian unity.

Franciscan order, the common designation of the Order of Friars Minor ("Lesser Brothers"), who follow the rule of life written by Francis of Assisi and approved by Pope Honorius III in 1223. In a broader sense the term is also used in reference to two other orders descended from Francis's original followers: the contemplative nuns known as the Poor Clares and the lay penitential movement later known as the Third Order. Today, the latter has evolved into two distinct ways of life: the Secular Franciscans for the laity and a large number of religious congregations of both men and women following the Third Order Regular Rule.

Early History: The Friars Minor arose as one of the many movements of devout laity in the late twelfth and thirteenth century who sought to return to life of the primitive Church, following the example of Jesus and his first disciples. When Francis and his little brotherhood received initial papal approval in 1209, they were laymen who had rejected the desire for wealth and status characteristic of the emerging commercial towns of central Italy to become an itinerant evangelical brotherhood living on the margins of society. After their annual chapter the friars would disperse in small groups, supporting themselves by whatever trade they knew, devoting themselves to lives of simple gospel witness and

Pope Honorius III approving the definitive rule of the Franciscan order in 1223 in the presence of Francis of Assisi and other friars; fifteenth-century manuscript illustration.

popular penitential preaching. At the chapter of 1217, the friars decided to spread north of the Alps and to the Crusader states in the Middle East; within two years friars brought their evangelical witness even among Muslim "unbelievers."

However, during these same years Francis's "Lesser Brothers" began undergoing a rapid and thoroughgoing transformation whose effects have divided the order to the present day. The phenomenal growth of the brotherhood, which by 1221 numbered between three thousand and five thousand friars, demanded that more complex internal structures be instituted; the Friars Minor quickly began to conform to more recognizable patterns of religious life. At the same time, the papacy recognized in the Franciscan movement a potent instrument to implement the pastoral reform vision of the Fourth Lateran Council of 1215 and increasingly intervened to oversee and channel its growth toward this end. The attitude of Francis himself toward these changes has long been debated by historians. In any event, whether this development is viewed as a betrayal or a natural evolution, by mid-century the life of the Friars Minor was increasingly focused on the organized pastoral ministry of the Church, especially formal preaching and the hearing of confessions. A predominantly lay brotherhood had become an order of educated clerics; the friars largely abandoned their rural hermitages, settling down in urban friaries and following a traditional conventual routine with churches attached to accommodate their growing clientele. To support these apostolic tasks, the original rigorous observance of poverty was relaxed by several papal interventions. The training schools of the order in such centers as Paris and Oxford produced some of the greatest masters of Scholastic theology, such as Bonaventure (d. 1274), John Duns Scotus (d. 1308), and William of Ockham (d. 1347).

Later Developments: Within the order, however, there was a vocal minority that resisted these changes. Toward the end of the thirteenth century, this faction, known as the Spirituals, grew increasingly restive, refusing to submit to the modifications of absolute poverty increasingly accepted by the majority of friars. The increasingly acrimonious debate eventually led to outright schism on the part of the Spirituals and their eventual condemnation in a series of decisions by Pope John XXII between 1317 and 1323. With the theoretical underpinnings of their distinctive observance thus undercut, the Friars Minor gradually conformed to the pattern of common ownership of property customary among other religious orders.

During the latter part of the fourteenth century however, a certain reaction set in, with small groups of friars receiving permission to retire to remote houses to live a more primitive form of Franciscan life while accenting the ministry of itinerant popular preaching. This movement, known as the Observant reform, gained momentum during the next century under such leaders as Bernardino of Siena (d. 1444) and John Capistrano (d. 1456). Relations between the friars who accepted this reform and those who did not, known as the Conventuals, grew increasingly tense, until Pope Leo X finally split them into two separate congregations in 1517. But the zeal for primitive patterns of life refused to be contained; finding that the Observance itself had become too lukewarm, in the course of the sixteenth century, new reform movements arose within the friars. The largest of these, the Capuchins, achieved a large measure of autonomy almost immediately. Pope Clement VII gave canonical approval to the Capuchin reform in 1528, and in 1536 Pope Paul III solemnly approved the order as a reform branch of the Franciscan order. The Capuchins were immensely successful as popular preachers among the lower classes during the Counter-Reformation, finally becoming a third independent congregation (with their own Minister General) in 1619. A number of other reform groups—the Reformed, the Recollects, and the Discalced—attained a large degree of autonomy, living under their own statutes within the Observant branch. However, these latter observances were ended with the Leonine Union of 1897. Thus today, the Franciscan order is actually divided into three independent congregations: the Friars Minor, the former Observant groups, generally simply referred to as Franciscans in English-speaking countries; the Conventual Franciscans; and the Capuchin Franciscans. As of the early 1990s there were about 19,000 Friars Minor, 11,300 Capuchins, and 4,300 Conventuals.

Although the Franciscans lost some of their intellectual preeminence in Catholicism after the sixteenth century, the order has remained in the forefront of the Church's preaching ministry and mission activity. Franciscans played a notable role in the evangelization of the Americas, and since Vatican II (1962–65) have recaptured a focus on living among and ministering to the poor. Although Franciscans have remained committed to the pastoral ministry and as such are still considered by Rome to be a clerical order, there has been much more emphasis on the fundamental equality of all friars and their contribution to the mission of the order as heralds of the gospel in the world. In the nineteenth and twentieth centuries the friars have worked very closely in their ministries with the numerous congregations of Third Order Franciscan women devoted to teaching, nursing, and other charitable activities that were founded during these years. *See also* Capuchins; Conventuals; Franciscan spirituality; Francis of Assisi, St.

Bibliography

Iriarte, Lazaro. *Franciscan History.* Chicago: Franciscan Herald Press, 1982.

Short, William. *The Franciscans.* Wilmington, DE: Michael Glazier, 1989. DOMINIC MONTI

Franciscan Sisters, members of any religious congregation of women governed by a rule of life and constitution reflecting their affiliation with the Third Order Regular of St. Francis of Assisi. Franciscan Sisters have traditionally professed simple vows of poverty, chastity, and obedience and have demonstrated in various ways their dedication to the spirituality of Francis, a spirituality characterized by peacefulness, compassion, poverty of spirit, and a deep love for all of God's creation. Many historically have worn the brown or black habit associated with Francis himself, with both male and female congregations dating back to the thirteenth century. Most of the Third Order Franciscan congregations of women, of which there are many, were founded in the nineteenth century and continue to exercise ministerial apostolates with either papal or episcopal approbation. *See also* Franciscan spirituality; Francis of Assisi, St.

Franciscan spirituality, the approach to the Christian life characteristic of the followers of Francis of Assisi. There has never really been a systematic Franciscan spirituality. Francis himself was keenly aware of the uniqueness of his own and each individual's experience of God; nevertheless, his life and writings and their appropriation in the spiritual experience of countless men and women across the centuries have shaped a distinctively Franciscan approach to the experience of God and the Christian life.

Its starting point is the profound awareness of God as the "Most High," totally transcendent mystery manifest especially in God's goodness. Francis experiences God's absolute otherness as total self-gift, evident in all of creation, but especially in God's special concern for the poor, little ones. For God pours out all that is within, holding nothing back, a mystery that has taken human flesh in the person of Jesus Christ. Franciscan spirituality is therefore Christocentric. Christ is the incarnation of God's eternal self-gift, a light who reveals the world to itself, as existing from and for God, stamped with God's beauty and goodness. The Incarnation completes the world by recapitulating all that is.

But it is precisely in his own self-emptying that Christ redeems the world; he reestablishes the primacy of God's gift by accepting the poverty of being human and sharing the goodness of God. For the root of human sinfulness, that alienation from God and one another that all people experience, is ultimately due to self-appropriation, taking to oneself what only belongs to God. Human beings have refused to live within the experience of God's gift, but have attempted to make themselves like God. Through his entry into the poverty of the human condition, through his own self-emptying in loving service, Christ redeems the world, showing all people how they too can truly experience God and creation.

Elements of the Spirituality: Thus, for the Franciscan the privileged symbolic moments have always been Bethlehem, Calvary, and the Eucharist: the child Jesus, the suffering Christ, and the littleness of broken bread and poured out wine are the most compelling images of the fact that in Christ God has chosen to become "poor for us in this world." This also explains the centrality of poverty and thanksgiving in Franciscan spirituality: humble thanks recognizes that all has been given to us, and poverty imitates God by giving it all away. By choosing to be among the poor of this world, Francis sees himself as sharing in a truly divine activity, accepting his true identity as fashioned in the image of a self-giving God.

Franciscan spirituality has always been at the same time deeply contemplative and essentially mission-oriented. The Franciscan needs to step back to savor God's goodness, creating "a dwelling place for God" within where "his holy working" in each one might be recognized. But it is precisely this awareness that impels Franciscans to imitate Christ by becoming heralds of the gospel, proclaiming God's goodness by demonstrating it through their peaceful and gentle love of all people, especially the little ones of this world. *See also* Francis, Rule of St.; Franciscan order; Francis of Assisi, St. DOMINIC MONTI

Francis de Sales, St., 1567–1622, bishop of Geneva, best known for the spiritual direction he provided for the laity and clergy through conversations, sermons, letters, and treatises. His writings, such as *The Introduction to the Devout Life,* reveal a thorough understanding of the spiritual tradition of the Church and an ability to make it relevant for people in various circumstances. Born to a noble family in Savoy, he studied theology and law at the University of Padua and was consecrated bishop in 1602. He was declared a saint in 1665 and a Doctor of the Church in 1877. Feast day: January 24. *See also Introduction to the Devout Life.*

Francis of Assisi, St., 1181/82–1226, founder of the Franciscans. The son of Pietro di Bernardone, a wealthy cloth merchant of Assisi, Italy, and his wife, Pica, Francis became a junior partner in the family business. His youth was marked by high living and a concern for social status. In 1202, in a war between Assisi and neighboring Perugia, Francis was taken prisoner. Released after a year's confinement, he returned home, but began questioning his former values. He found himself increasingly drawn to a life of penance marked by intense periods of prayer, pilgrimages, and almsgiving. Confirmed in these new directions by an encounter with a leper, he began to spend much of his time working among these social outcasts. All this provoked a prolonged conflict with his father, which finally reached a climax in 1206. Responding to what he felt was a divine call to rebuild the ruined chapel of San Damiano, Francis sold some valuable cloth from the family store to raise money for the project. Brought to trial by his father, he renounced his patrimony in a dramatic scene before the bishop of Assisi. Living as a penitent hermit, Francis spent several years caring for lepers and repairing small chapels in the neighborhood.

Founding of the Franciscans: In the spring of 1208, his life took a new turn: responding to what he felt was a personal call to implement Jesus' mission to his apostles (Matt 10), Francis began to preach publicly; he also attracted his first followers. A new movement was born. By early 1209 there were twelve brothers; writing down a brief statement of their way of life based on a few Gospel texts, Francis journeyed to Rome and secured tentative approval from Innocent III for the group. Returning to Assisi, these "Lesser Brothers" (Friars Minor) settled at the rural chapel of the Portiuncula; from there they

Francis of Assisi, founder of the Franciscans, in the desert, where he manifested his love of nature and his simplicity of life; late-fifteenth-century painting by Bellini, Frick Collection, New York.

would spread out in small bands through central Italy, devoting themselves to contemplative prayer, working as day laborers and preaching, calling all to conversion by their word and example. In 1212, Clare, a young aristocratic woman of Assisi, joined Francis's movement; with several other women she founded a community of "Poor Ladies" at San Damiano. About the same time, Francis also began to guide groups of devout laypeople, who were called the Brothers and Sisters of Penance or, later, the "Third Order." The preaching ministry of the Friars Minor soon spread beyond Italy, for Francis was convinced that God had sent his brothers to bring their lives of Gospel witness to the whole world. At the chapter of 1217, he sent missions beyond the Alps and even to the Crusader states in the Near East. Francis himself had long possessed the desire to preach Christ to the Muslims and, by doing so, win a martyr's death. He finally was able to get to Egypt in 1219, where Crusaders were mounting an attack on the forces of Sultan al-Kamil. He somehow managed to pass through the lines and meet the sultan, who was deeply impressed by his transparent sincerity (although remaining unconverted). However, Francis was forced to return to Italy by growing tensions among his friars, now about three thousand strong. There were strict divisions in the ranks about the directions the order should take; furthermore, there were many in the hierarchy opposed to this novel religious community. Realizing that he was unequal to the situation, Francis resigned the administration of the order and also sought the appointment of Cardinal Hugolino da Segni as protector of his movement. However, he was always viewed as the spiritual head of the brotherhood; in this capacity he prepared a revision of his rule, which won definitive papal approval in 1223. During these years Francis was plagued by serious illness, and he increasingly withdrew for long periods of prayer. While on one of these retreats on Mount La Verna in the fall of 1224, he underwent a profound mystical experience, returning with the scars of Christ's Passion, or stigmata, imprinted in his body. He died at the Portiuncula on October 3, 1226, and was canonized two years later by his old friend, Hugolino, now Pope Gregory IX.

Francis has always enjoyed a widespread cult as "another Christ," but the twentieth century has witnessed a remarkable revival of devotion to him, even among nonbelievers. His charismatic personality, deep compassion for all people, and love for God's creation are features that have made him one of the best-loved saints. He is the patron saint of Italy and of the environment. Feast day: October 4. *See also* Francis, Rule of St.; Franciscan order.

DOMINIC MONTI

Francis of Paola, St., 1416–1507, a Calabrian Franciscan who, after a life of solitude and penance, founded a branch of Franciscans known as Minims, which received papal approval in 1474. Famous as a prophet and miracle worker, he spent the last years of his life in France. Feast day: April 2. *See also* Minims.

Francis Xavier, St., 1506–52, French Jesuit missionary, known as the "Apostle of the Indies" and "Apostle of Japan." While a student in Paris, he met Ignatius of Loyola, whom he eventually joined as a companion in what would become the Society of Jesus. In 1534, Xavier, Ignatius, and five other companions vowed themselves at Montmartre to the service of God.

In 1536 the group left Paris. When plans to work as missionaries in the Holy Land failed, they gathered in Rome to deliberate about their future. While still awaiting formal approval of their new institute (the Society of Jesus), the king of Portugal, John III, requested a Jesuit for missionary work among the Christians in the East. Xavier was given the mission when the first candidate, Bobadilla, became ill. Xavier arrived in Goa, India, in 1542. There he baptized many among the lower caste of India, but he was unsuccessful at gaining a hearing among the higher caste Brahmin.

At Malacca in Malaya Xavier met a Japanese nobleman and decided to undertake a mission to Japan. After returning to Goa for a period to oversee the growing missionary effort in the east, Xavier left for Japan in 1549. He spent two successful years in Japan before returning to Malacca. While in Japan he learned of the influence of China on Japanese culture. In 1552, while trying to arrange entry into China, Xavier fell ill and died on the island of Sancian off the coast of China. He was canonized on March 12, 1622. Feast day: December 3. *See also* China, Catholicism in; India, Catholicism in; Japan, Catholicism in; missions.

JAMES K. VOISS

Frankfurt, Council of (794), Frankish synod. When the condemnation of Adoptionism and of Felix of Urgel at the synod of Regensburg in 792 failed to quell the Spanish heresy, Charlemagne summoned a new council at Frankfurt, presiding over its sessions and arranging for Alcuin, though only a deacon, to present the orthodox position to the assembled bishops. *See also* Adoptionism; Alcuin; Charlemagne.

Franks, a Germanic people who settled along the right bank of the Rhine and, from the late third century, invaded Gaul, most of which they eventually (by 511) occupied. Clovis (ca. 481–511) united all the Franks under his own rule with his capital at Paris. Baptized in the late 490s, he was the only Catholic king in the West, in the eyes of many the protector of the orthodox. In his kingdom Franks and Romans, united under a single episcopacy, mingled more freely. From 639 the Merovingian dynasty began to be supplanted by the Carolingians, the two most notable of whom were Charles Martel, who checked Arab ambitions on Europe east of Spain at the battle of Poitiers (732), and Charlemagne, crowned emperor of the West by the pope on Christmas Day, 800. *See also* Charlemagne; Charles Martel; Clovis.

Fransen, Piet, 1913–83, Flemish Jesuit theologian. He served on the faculty at the University of Louvain and is known for his work in the theology of grace, ecumenism, and ecclesiology.

Franzelin, Johann Baptist (yoh'hahn bahp-teest' frahnz'eh-lin), 1816–86, Jesuit theologian, cardinal, and professor at the Gregorian University in Rome. Franzelin shared with his colleagues in Rome, G. Perrone, C. Passaglia, and K. Schrader, an interest in the integration of biblical and patristic sources into Scholastic theological treatises, which separated him from the proponents of the budding neo-Thomistic revival. A consultant for several Roman congregations, he wrote the first draft of Vatican I's constitution on reason and faith. His ecclesiology reflected the influence of the German Tübingen theologians in viewing the Church as the Mystical Body, the exemplar of the Incarnate Word. He wrote theological manuals on the sacraments, the Trinity, and fundamental theology. In his theology of tradition Franzelin recognized that while the hierarchy had a principal role in preserving and articulating the deposit of faith, the laity, too, participated in the transmission of tradition. The hierarchy possessed an "active infallibility" in teaching, but the whole faithful possessed a "passive infallibility" in believing.

Frassinetti, St. Paola, also known as Paula, 1809–82, Italian-born founder of the Sisters of St. Dorothy, an order dedicated to the education of poor children. Feast day: June 11.

fraternal correction, a spiritual work of mercy patterned after Jesus' words: "If another member of the church sins against you, go and point out the fault when the two of you are alone. If the member listens to you, you have regained that one. But if you are not listened to, take one or two others along with you. . . . If the member refuses to listen to them, tell it to the church. And if the offender refuses to listen even to the church, let such a one be to you as a Gentile and a tax collector" (Matt 18:15–17). The words "against you" are not in some texts, so that sin may be interpreted less narrowly. Paul advises, "Brothers, if anyone is caught in a transgression, you who have received the Spirit should restore such a one in a spirit of gentleness" (Gal 6:1). Fraternal correction is an act of love. Jesus offers a process for the loving confrontation of evil. There may be an obligation to confront a neighbor's evil, just as one may be obliged to aid a hungry or homeless neighbor. *See also* mercy; spiritual works of.

Fraternity of St. Peter, Priestly, a society of apostolic life (see can. 731) with a special mission to active and former members of the Society of St. Pius X. The Fraternity was founded in Switzerland in 1988 by members of the society who did not wish to follow Archbishop Marcel Lefebvre into schism; it was canonically erected (i.e., established) by the Holy See on October 18, 1988. Its priests celebrate the Eucharist according to the old Tridentine rite. *See also* Lefebvre, Marcel; traditionalism, Catholic; Tridentine Mass.

Fraticelli, a name given to the Spiritual Franciscans of Italy and Provence in the early fourteenth century. Inspired by the teachings on poverty and apocalypticism of Petrus Joannis Olivi, Angelo Clareno, and Ubertino of Casale, the Fraticelli separated from the Franciscan order and were condemned by Pope John XXII in 1317. *See also* Spiritual Franciscans.

Frederick I, "Barbarossa," ca. 1123–90, king of Germany (1152) and Holy Roman emperor from 1155. He attempted to subdue Italy but was opposed successfully by the allied forces of the Lombard League and the Papal States. He died in Turkey while en route to the Third Crusade. *See also* Holy Roman Empire.

Frederick II, 1194–1250, Holy Roman emperor who wore the crowns of Sicily, Germany, Jerusalem, and the empire. He was a patron of translators and scientists, although his intellectual and military accomplishments were overshadowed by his headstrong ambitions and bitter opposition to the papacy. *See also* Holy Roman Empire.

Frederick III, 1415–93, Holy Roman emperor and king of Germany from 1440. His support of the papacy against the conciliarist Council of Basel (1431–38) earned him the imperial crown; he was the last emperor to be crowned in Rome. *See also* Basel, Council of; Holy Roman Empire.

Free churches, certain Protestant churches in England and Wales that, although agreeing with the Church of England in doctrinal areas, refused to conform (thus, the term "nonconformist") to its discipline and liturgical practices in the seventeenth century. Eventually, the Free churches rejected the principle of establishment and fought for the separation of Church and state. The Act of Uniformity (1662) marks the formal beginnings of separatism, and the formation of Free Church councils began in the late nineteenth century. The term is usually associated with Methodists, English Presbyterians, Congregationalists, Baptists, Quakers, Unitarians,

Churches of Christ, Plymouth Brethren, and various Pentecostal sects. *See also* Protestantism.

freedom, the absence of compulsion and determination from anything within or outside of a person or persons. In positive terms, it is the ability to weigh possibilities, choose among them, and act on this choice. Insofar as human beings possess this self-agency for thinking, deciding, and acting, they can truly act and engage in activity of a moral and religious character. According to Catholic teaching, human freedom was not completely destroyed by Adam's sin but was damaged and has been restored by Jesus Christ (Gal 5:1, 13; Council of Trent, 1545–63). In other words, human freedom needs to be set free by someone other than ourselves, namely, by Christ, and full freedom is a gift from God. *See also* free will; grace, actual; nature and grace; religious liberty.

Freemasonry, fraternal organization founded in eighteenth-century England on the basis of an earlier tradition of a guild of masons. The organization spread to the continent of Europe (and later to the Americas) as a social organization with strong ties to deist religion in northern Europe and with an unremitting hostility to organized Christianity in Latin countries. Membership was forbidden to Catholics under pain of excommunication and papal documents frequently condemned the movement.

The new Code of Canon Law (1983) does not forbid membership in the Masons by name but does forbid membership in societies that plot against the Church (can. 1374). Decrees of the Congregation for the Doctrine of the Faith have said, however, that membership is forbidden and violations of the prohibition are gravely sinful.

free will, the human faculty to choose among courses of action. Common sense and moral theology agree that free will is required for moral responsibility. People do, in fact, hold one another accountable for their actions, though like St. Paul (Rom 7:15–24) they sometimes feel powerless to do what they know is right.

Catholic moral theology affirms that limited human responsibility is sufficient for deciding among alternative courses of action insofar as a person understands them. Since the time of Pelagius (third century), the Catholic Church has formally taught that God's grace does not take away free will. The Council of Trent (1545–63) affirmed that original sin does not destroy human free will. Trent's "Decree on Justification" (can. 5) formally proclaims that rejection of the doctrine of free will is grounds for expulsion from membership in the Catholic Church.

Debate about both the nature and the level of freedom of the human will continues to engage philosophers and theologians. In the twentieth century, psychology and other sciences have pointed out that a person's ability to determine a course of action is limited in ways that elude awareness. Some theories of human personality go so far as to claim that freedom is an illusion and that all human actions are determined by external influences upon our human psyche. Catholic moral theology, like civil law, has traditionally noted that human responsibility can be reduced or destroyed by a variety of factors—fear, ignorance, emotional disturbance, passion, drugs, habits, etc. *DANIEL KROGER*

freewill offerings, charitable donations. As opposed to a tithe or some other bequest to the Church due by law or custom, freewill offerings are those gifts, usually of a monetary nature, that are given to the Church for any of a number of charitable or religious purposes, purely as acts of generosity.

Frequens (fray'kwenz; Lat., "Frequent"), reform decree of the Council of Constance, promulgated October 1417, calling for frequent general councils to reform the Church, one to meet five years after Constance, the next seven years later, and then every ten years thereafter. This scheme was abandoned by Pope Eugenius IV (1431–47). *See also* Constance, Council of.

fresco (It., "fresh"), artistic technique of painting on wet plaster. Typically done on a wall or ceiling,

Eleventh-century fresco depicting the burials of Sts. Peter and Paul, in the basilica of San Piero a Grado, Tuscany, Italy.

it is, historically, a favored form of church decoration.

friar (Fr., Mid. Eng., *frere,* "brother"), the distinctive title of the members of the mendicant orders which arose in thirteenth-century Europe. The major orders of friars were the Dominicans, Franciscans, Augustinians, and Carmelites. The mendicants were distinguished from the traditional monastic orders by three chief characteristics: friars pursued an ideal of corporate poverty, refusing landed endowments and being supported instead by the freewill offerings of the faithful; they united their common life with active involvement in pastoral ministry; and they belonged to a centralized international brotherhood, thus enabling them to move about according to need. *See also* mendicant orders.

Friday (Old Eng., *frigedaeg,* "day of Frig," a goddess), the sixth day of the week. The Jewish Sabbath begins at sundown on this day, and it is the special day of prayer for Muslims. Christians remember the Passion and Crucifixion of Jesus, which occurred on that day. Until recently, it was a day of abstinence from meat. *See also* abstinence; First Fridays; Good Friday.

friendship, in the spiritual tradition, an affectionate relationship between and among Christians that serves to increase their love of God and others. John Cassian (d. 435), Augustine (d. 430), Aelred of Rievaulx (d. 1167), and Francis de Sales (d. 1622) are among those who sought to define the nature of true spiritual friendships. Traditionally, such friendships are said to include mutual affection and service, combined with conversations that reveal what is in the depth of each one's heart. The love that friends have for each other is a gift from God and the support, encouragement, and correction provided through the relationship allows friends to grow toward spiritual perfection.

Fries, Heinrich (freez), b. 1911, German Catholic theologian. As professor at Tübingen and Munich, and through writings ranging from an original survey of modern philosophies of religion (1949) to a system of fundamental theology (1985) and an overview of church unity (written with Karl Rahner

[1983]), Fries has been an important figure in the development of the Catholic theology of revelation and ecumenism.

Frohschammer, Jakob, 1821–93, German theologian and philosopher of nature. Two years after he became professor at Munich in 1857, his study on the generation of the soul was placed on the Index of Forbidden Books. Because of his writings on the history of philosophy, natural science, and Thomas Aquinas, he was embroiled in controversies with the Vatican that ended in suspension from the priesthood and papal condemnation.

fruitfulness of the sacraments, expression that describes whether the sacrament has indeed bestowed the grace it contains. This concept emphasizes the need for human beings to cooperate with the grace God offers in the sacraments in order for the sacraments to have any spiritual effect. The sacraments are not simply automatic mechanisms of grace, but require cooperation on the part of those receiving them to be fruitful. An individual can receive a valid sacrament but frustrate the sacrament's ultimate purpose, which is conversion in love to God and to neighbor. For example, if one receives the Eucharist in an unrepentant state of sin that persists after Communion, and experiences absolutely no increase in love for others or for God, then it is said that the reception of the Eucharist in this instance did the individual no spiritual good—the Communion was not fruitful. *See also* grace, sacramental; sacrament.

fruits of the Mass, the theory originating with Duns Scotus (d. 1308) that the Eucharist is the source of blessing to the celebrant, the whole Church, and those for whose intention the Eucharist is offered and who thus were considered to be the recipients of "special fruits." This terminology is little used today because no one can measure either the abundance of God's blessings or the receptivity of the human heart to them. The 1983 Code of Canon Law states that those who make an offering for the celebration of the Eucharist support the Church's ministers and works (can. 946). Because of this special involvement in a particular celebration they might, if properly disposed, derive greater spiritual benefit from it. *See also* Eucharist.

fruits of the Spirit, more properly designated the fruit of the Spirit, that is, the effect(s) of the Holy Spirit active in human life. The term is based on qualities listed in Gal 5—love, joy, peace, patience, kindness, generosity, faithfulness, gentleness, and self-control. The Latin Vulgate translation adds modesty, continence, and chastity to the list. The fruit of the Spirit acts as a counterpart to the works of the flesh or the seven capital sins.

Generosity fosters a sense of values and is willing to do that which may be unpopular, such as disciplining a child. Generosity also considers the ultimate welfare of one's enemies. Faithfulness abides by the decision to follow what is good and is willing to endure suffering in order to overcome evil. Love entails surrendering oneself to God and to the important people in one's life. Love flows from a profound experience of God's love and mercy, and joy follows upon that experience. Peace, patience, and gentleness address emotional states, whereas self-control, continence, and chastity counterbalance human desires. Peace fears no external forces of evil and patience bears wrongs without anger or vengeance. A gentle person has no need for power over others, for the power and authority of Jesus enables a person to submit even to death with equanimity. The fruit of the Spirit is not the habit of virtue but the strengthened condition of those possessed by God's Spirit. *See also* gifts of the Holy Spirit; Holy Spirit; love.

Frumentius, St., d. ca. 380, patron saint of Ethiopia. A native of Tyre, he landed in Ethiopia after surviving a shipwreck and became secretary to the king. Upon the king's death he remained and helped rule the country, introducing Christianity. When the king's sons came of age, he left Ethiopia but was sent back later as a missionary bishop by Athanasius. He was called Abbuna ("Our Father") in Ethiopia, and that remains the title of the primate of the Ethiopian church. Feast day: October 27.

Fuchs, Josef, b. 1912, prominent German Jesuit moral theologian. He taught moral theology at St. George Hochschule, Frankfurt, from 1947 to 1954, then at the Pontifical Gregorian University, Rome, beginning in 1954. Author of many articles and books, the latter including *Natural Law: A Theological Investigation* (1965), *Human Values and Christian Morality* (1967), and *Personal Responsibility and Christian Morality* (1983).

Fulbert of Chartres, St., ca. 970–1028, bishop. A student of Gerbert of Aurillac (Pope Sylvester II), Fulbert was a master in the school of Chartres and chancellor when elected bishop (1006). Among his students was Berengar of Tours. Many of his letters, poems, and sermons survive. He began rebuilding Chartres after the fire of 1020. Feast day: April 10 (in Chartres and Poitiers). *See also* Chartres.

Fulda, German monastery founded by Boniface and Sturmi ca. 744; Boniface's relics rest there. Among students at Fulda's school and library were Gottschalk of Orbais, Lupus of Ferrières, and Walafrid Strabo. The ninth-century chapel is still in use, though the abbey was suppressed in 1802. *See also* Boniface, St.

Fulgentius of Ruspe, St., ca. 467–ca. 532, monk, bishop, and theologian. Born in Vandal North Africa, he became Catholic bishop of Ruspe ca. 507. Exiled, recalled, and exiled again by the Arian king Thrasimund, he was finally recalled (523) by the Catholic king Hilderich. His writings against Arians and semi-Pelagians reproduce Augustine's thought. Feast day: January 1. *See also* Arianism; semi-Pelagianism.

functional Christology, critical inquiry into the mission of Jesus Christ. Its focal questions are: What was Jesus' aim and message? What did/does Jesus Christ bring about by his life, death, and Resurrection? Also, what did/does God accomplish in and through Jesus Christ? Functional Christology points beyond itself to ontological (or classical) Christology, which treats who and what Jesus Christ was/is. *See also* Christology.

fundamentalism, biblical, an approach to the Bible, associated mainly with conservative movements within Protestantism, that asserts that what the Bible says is always literally true (literalism). Fundamentalism developed among Protestants out of a series of Bible conferences first held in Niagara Falls in 1895 in reaction to the rise of historical criticism in the late nineteenth century. Its name derives from a series of publications (1905–15) that defined five "fundamentals" of the Christian faith (the verbal inerrancy of Scripture, the divinity of Jesus Christ, the Virgin Birth, a substitutionary theory of the atonement that views Jesus as a substitute for humanity in enduring divine punishment for sin, and the physical Resurrection and bodily return of Christ). Fundamentalists generally do not recognize literary forms other than history; thus, Gen 1–2:4a describes six actual days of creation and Jonah was really in the belly of the whale. Concomitant with fundamentalism is a dictation theory of inspiration where the biblical author is held to be simply a scribe of divine revelation. Biblical fundamentalists assert absolute inerrancy of Scripture and argue that Scripture provides an adequate guide for all areas of Christian life (biblicism).

Fundamentalism is less a method of biblical exegesis than a religious disposition. Fundamentalists operate out of a distorted understanding of the "literal" (which should instead be understood as the "literary") sense of Scripture. When the Bible uses literary forms that are not historical to present its message (e.g., the book of Jonah as an edifying religious tale), the "literal" or literary sense is not historical. Fundamentalists themselves often ignore or interpret in nonliteral ways texts such as turning the other cheek or giving one's cloak to the poor (Matt 5:38–42). Catholics who are challenged by fundamentalists should realize that fundamentalists are offering interpretations, not literal meanings, of biblical texts. The appeal of biblical fundamentalism is simplicity of belief and security in a world that often seems threatening. Though biblical fundamentalism has historically not been strong within Catholicism, it has been gaining ground since Vatican II (1962–65), partially as a reaction to the council's liberalizing initiatives and partially under the impulse of the council's strong emphasis on the Bible. On November 5, 1987, the U.S. Catholic bishops issued a pastoral statement on biblical fundamentalism in which they urged greater knowledge and study of the Bible as the best Catholic response to fundamentalism (see *Origins* 17/21). *See also* fundamentalism, Catholic; Scripture, intepretation of.

JOHN R. DONAHUE

fundamentalism, Catholic, the Catholic forms of religious fundamentalism, including especially an unhistorical and literal reading not only of the Bible but also of the official teachings of the Church. In general, fundamentalism tends to isolate and control the divine in objects, to claim special and direct access to God, to encourage the miraculous, and to hold an apocalyptic and elitist stance toward

humanity. Catholic forms of fundamentalism often focus upon things and authorities: regarding things, exaggerated attention is given to dramatic powers vested in medals, water, clothes, visions, oils, and photographs; regarding authorities, claims are made that a few church members (officials or visionaries) are instructed by the Holy Spirit on many topics and are given immediate and certain information apart from research and consultation. This fundamentalist spirit is manifested in the attention given to unapproved visions or to pictures with paranatural activities (e.g., weeping). There are also fundamentalist communities ranging from the Lefebvre schism within the Catholic Church to movements of a dubious spirituality or to unapproved religious communities. Authoritarian fundamentalism may work to discredit theology, to replace the discussion of issues with shallow piety, to censure divergent views not on matters of dogma but on theological issues, and to locate the gospel solely in one vision or activity.

The rise of Catholic fundamentalism includes typical characteristics of anger, anxiety, self-doubt, and revenge. Best seen as a reaction against movements in the Church that seek to introduce maturity and diversity, it is threatened by the underlying drive of the present-day Catholic Church to become a worldwide, diverse, but united Church. The fundamentalist personality is usually ignorant of Catholicism's diverse, rich, and complex traditions. Fundamentalism of any sort is opposed to basic facets of the Catholic understanding of Christianity: a variety of traditions in theology, liturgy, and the spiritual life; a theology of grace that focuses on the presence and image of God in each human being; the absence of an angry God or an apocalyptic future; the importance of the local church; and Church authority. To some Catholics, fundamentalism appears to be more a psychological problem than a theology; pastorally it is often a search for real personal and communal experiences of God. *See also* fundamentalism, biblical.

Bibliography

Marty, Martin, and Scott Appleby. *Fundamentalisms Observed.* Chicago: University of Chicago Press, 1991.

O'Meara, Thomas. *Fundamentalism: A Catholic Perspective.* New York: Paulist Press, 1990.   THOMAS F. O'MEARA

fundamental moral theology, that part of moral theology that deals with basic questions such as human acts, the law of Christ, the vocation of the

Christian, the theological virtues of faith, hope, and love, moral norms, and the imputability of effects. Fundamental moral theology is usually contrasted with special moral theology, that part of the discipline that treats various concrete problems such as war and peace, poverty, sexuality and marriage, the beginning and end of life, race relations, justice problems, and sexism. For many decades, under the influence of the moral manuals, fundamental moral theology was one-sidedly confession-oriented, magisterium-dominated, canon-law related, sin-centered, and seminary-controlled. For this reason, Vatican II stated: "Special attention needs to be given to the development of moral theology. Its scientific exposition should be more thoroughly nourished by scriptural teaching. It should show the nobility of the Christian vocation of the faithful, and their obligation to bring forth fruit in charity for the life of the world" (Decree on Priestly Formation, n. 16). *See also* moral theology.

fundamental option, a technical and even misleading term that refers to a dimension of freedom in human action deeper than mere freedom of object choice. This dimension is not the freedom of choice to do a particular thing or not, that is, a choice of specific objects. It is rather the free determination of oneself with regard to the totality of existence. It is a fundamental choice between love and selfishness, between self and God, who is our destiny.

Theologians, following above all the anthropology of Karl Rahner (d. 1984), assert that in the moral act there are two distinguishable aspects. First, there is a particular object of choice (an act of obedience, a lie). This is the explicit and reflexively conscious concern of the agent. Second, there is the disposition or commitment of the agent as a person with relation to God, the person's ultimate end. This anthropology sees the constitutive core of the person as a capacity or freedom to accept or deny the divine self-communication known as grace. This acceptance or rejection is not a thematic datum of human experience that is immediately and empirically observable. The reason for this is that the human person is conscious of the self as a subject without necessarily reflecting on the self as an object.

This self-disposition of the person reflects the fact that human persons cannot be indifferent to their ultimate end. They cannot not opt for or

against the God of their lives. Persons must say yes or no in the depths of their being. This answer is said to be a use of basic or fundamental freedom. It is fundamental for several reasons. First, it is not an activity like the many daily activities that occupy people's lives. It underlies all other choices. Second, since it underlies other, more superficial choices and manifests itself in them, there is a continual interplay between this basic freedom and particular acts. Acting according to this option, one deepens it. Acting contrary to it, one undermines its stability. Finally, actions derive their moral seriousness from the presence or absence in them of this basic freedom. Thus, many theologians understand both mortal sin and conversion from it as necessarily being fundamental options. *See also* free will; mortal sin; sin.   RICHARD A. MCCORMICK

fundamental theology, a discipline that establishes the basic intelligibility of theology, using the tools of philosophy, linguistics, and historical-critical methods. The task of fundamental theology may be understood analytically, for example, to establish the facticity of an event or the truth of a doctrine solely on historical or metaphysical grounds. Or, in an approach now called foundational theology, this task can be understood synthetically, acknowledging that the claim of faith is integral to its intelligibility. Both these approaches are generally considered to be distinct from apologetics, which attempts to establish the credibility of faith claims for nonbelievers.

The need for fundamental theology dates, for Christians, from the NT exhortation to "always be ready to make a defense to anyone who demands from you an accounting for the hope that is in you" (1 Pet 3:15). In the history of Christian thought, an implicit fundamental theology has always functioned, arising in response to the intellectual exigencies of various times and places.

History: The term "fundamental theology" first appears in the work of Pierre Annat (in 1700) as another term for positive theology, the theology of Protestant writers that based itself on the texts of Scripture and the early Church (i.e., that which was "posited"). It was opposed to the Catholic Scholastic theology of the time, which employed metaphysical categories to systematize its treatment of faith and doctrine.

To adequately address the rationalism of the seventeenth century, and in particular, to counter deism's rejection of the possibility of divine revelation, fundamental theology had to present the Christian faith as both logically necessary and empirically verifiable. To this end it saw its task as the demonstration of the possibility of revelation and the verifiability of the miraculous.

Fundamental theology took two different forms in the nineteenth century. Fideism, the position that religious knowledge is not an act of the intellect but rather resides in a "leap of faith," called for new scientific approaches to ground the intelligibility of belief. German writers, responding to the rise of historical consciousness and the corresponding development of the idea of human subjectivity, cast theology as a properly scientific discipline by examining the structures of human knowing, as exemplified in Johann Nepomunk Ehrlich's 1859 *Fundamentaltheologie*. This approach continues in the work of the twentieth-century theologian Karl Rahner (d. 1984), and is especially evident in the structure of his *Foundations of Christian Faith* (1978).

By contrast, the Catholic neo-Scholastic theology of the nineteenth and early-twentieth centuries saw its task as the defense of the Catholic faith. Such works would begin by grounding the idea of religion, then defending the notion of God's revelation, particularly the revelation of God in Christ, and finally demonstrating the authority of the Catholic hierarchical magisterium, and its continuity with the tradition of the apostles.

In the contemporary context, new questions in philosophy and linguistics recast the nature of fundamental theology's focus on the intelligibility of the claim that God is definitively revealed to humanity in Jesus Christ. For example, fundamental theology now must begin by defending the very possibility of theological statements, and even the assumption that language refers to anything outside of itself. In this milieu, both the German and Roman approaches appear with a new focus. The epistemological starting point of the heirs of German idealism now poses the question of the difference, if any, between fundamental theology and theological method. And the Roman approach now must defend the very possibility of metaphysics, if it is credibly to propose a fundamental theology that is independent of the faith-claims of systematic theology. *See also* theology.　　　　NANCY DALLAVALLE

funeral Mass, or the Mass of Christian Burial, second part of the three-part complex of rites by which the Church bids farewell to the dead: prayers following the time of death, the Mass of Christian Burial, and the rite of committal. The funeral Mass reflects the paschal character of the death of Christians. Hence, the funeral Mass employs the following themes: the Christian's union with Christ in Baptism, the communion of saints into whose community the deceased will be welcomed, the Second Coming of Christ, and the longed-for reunion with all the faithful at the end of time. The funeral follows the order of Mass with two major revisions: the body of the deceased is greeted at the door of the church at the beginning of Mass, and a rite of final commendation follows the Communion. Although funeral Masses are not permitted during the Triduum (Holy Thursday, Good Friday, and the Easter Vigil), on holy days of obligation, or on the Sundays of Advent, Lent, or Easter, simple burial is permitted. *See also* burial, Christian.

future, the, a perennial theme in Christian theology. St. Paul and other early Christians were preoccupied with the resurrection of the body and the Second Coming of Christ. Medieval and early modern Christians developed extensive treatises on the four last things (death, judgment, heaven, and hell). In the twentieth century, the theology of the future has exhibited new characteristics. Among contemporary Christians there is growing concern about the future of humankind and about the grounds for Christian hope. Teilhard de Chardin's *The Phenomenon of Man* (Eng. trans., 1959), for example, focused on Christ as the Omega Point of cosmic evolution. Likewise, Jürgen Moltmann's *Theology of Hope* (Eng. trans., 1967) accented the Resurrection as the promise of a future greater than present reality. Moltmann's thought also reflects the tension in contemporary theology about responsibility for the future: is it God's or ours? Obviously, it must be both God's and ours; but classically and process-oriented theologians differ in their explanations. Classically oriented thinkers believe that God is the primary cause of everything in the world, ordering the free actions of humans and the spontaneous activity of other creatures to the divine purposes. Process-oriented thinkers argue that God works through hidden persuasion, luring creatures to the good that God has in mind for them. In both cases, however, the mystery of God's action in the world remains so that Christians must ultimately trust in God's enduring love for them. *See also* eschatology, universal.

JOSEPH A. BRACKEN

Gabriel (Heb., "man of God"), archangel. In the later biblical and postbiblical period Gabriel is preeminently revealer (e.g., to Daniel, 8:15–26; 9:20–27) and heavenly intercessor (e.g., *1 Enoch* 9:1). He is one of those who stand in the presence of God (Rev 8:2) and is sent to announce the births of John the Baptist (Luke 1:11–20) and Jesus (Luke 1:26–38). *See also* angel; archangel.

Gabriel of the Sorrowful Mother, St., 1838–62, Passionist priest, patron saint of clerics and youth. Born Gabriel Possenti in Assisi, Italy, he took the name Brother Gabriel of the Sorrowful Mother upon entering the Passionists. Having lived an exemplary religious life marked not only by penance but also cheerfulness, he died of tuberculosis at the age of twenty-four. Feast day: February 27. *See also* Passionists.

Gaetano da Tiene (gi-tah'noh dah tee-ay'nay). *See* Cajetan [Thomas de Vio].

Galilee, a region in the north of the land of Israel. It extended from the rugged hills in the north around Safed, through the lower hills around the plain of Gennesaret and the valley of Jezreel (or Esdraelon), ending in the northern reaches of the central hill country of Palestine. In the distribution of land among the tribes of Israel it fell to Asher, Zebulun, Naphtali, and Issachar. Annexed by the Assyrians in 734 B.C., it remained under foreign domination until 80 B.C., when it was conquered by Alexander Jannaeus. At the death of Herod the Great (4 B.C.), it became a separate district under Herod Antipas who reigned until A.D. 39. Galilee then became part of the kingdom of Herod Agrippa I (A.D. 41–44) and thereafter part of a Roman province. Between A.D. 27 and 30 it was the location of most of Jesus' ministry.

Galileo [Galilei] 1564–1642, Italian scientist and philosopher. Galileo began studying medicine in 1581 at the University of Pisa, but his mathematical and philosophical abilities soon became apparent and he gave up medicine in 1585 to begin lecturing at the Florentine Academy. In 1586 he published his invention of the hydrostatic balance. In 1588 he published on the center of gravity in solid bodies. He was appointed professor of mathematics in 1592 at Padua, where he published his study of the motion of falling bodies (*De Motu*). With the newly invented telescope Galileo began to explore the heavens. His *Sidereus Nuncius* (*Starry Messenger,* 1610) made him famous. In it he announced that the moon was not a perfectly smooth object, that the Milky Way was composed of countless stars, and that Jupiter had four moons.

Galileo was attacked for his views by representatives of the dominant, primarily Aristotelian, scientific community. The prevailing Ptolemaic/Aristotelian theory of the cosmos placed an immovable earth at the center of the universe and encased by spheres in which the sun, stars, planets, and other celestial bodies revolved in perfect circles. These spheres, beginning with that of the moon, were perfect and unchanging. Galileo's observations placed these theories in doubt. In fact, Galileo was an adherent of Nicholas Copernicus (1473–1543), who placed the sun at the center of the universe. In 1613 Galileo published his *Letter on Sunspots* in which he openly advocated the Copernican theory (though he had admitted his private acceptance as early as 1597).

The resulting philosophical controversy eventually drew in the Church. It is important to realize that Galileo could not prove the Copernican theory. For some aspects of it, it would only be in the nineteenth century that proof would be found. The Ptolemaic/Aristotelian system explained phenomena as well as did the Copernican, it had wide and long-lived acceptance by scientists and philosophers, and, very importantly, it was more easily accommodated to the text of Scripture, which in a number of passages (Josh 10:12–13; Ps 104:5; Eccl 1:5) describes the earth as motionless and the sun as moving. For these reasons the Congregation of the Index suspended republication of Copernicus's *De Revolutionibus Orbium* until it was rendered more hypothetical. (It was republished four years later with the necessary corrections.) Galileo argued that Scripture was not designed to teach science. Cardinal Robert Bellarmine warned Galileo that without convincing scientific proof it was not permissible to teach on this issue against Scripture as interpreted by Church tradition. Galileo was ordered by the Inquisition not to teach or seek to prove the Copernican theory. Obeying the letter but not the spirit of the injunction, Galileo published *A Dialogue on the Two Great World Systems* (1632). He was brought before the Inquisition again (1633), was forced to abjure, and lived the rest of his life under house arrest, where he proceeded to publish perhaps his greatest work, *Discourses Concerning Two New Sciences* (1638). The *Dialogue,* however, remain banned until 1822. In 1979 Pope John Paul II conceded that the

Church had erred in its treatment of Galileo. In 1984 all of the documents on the case in the Vatican archives were made public. *See also* Inquisition.

R. EMMET MCLAUGHLIN

Gall, St., ca. 560–after 615, one of St. Columbanus's twelve companions and exiled with him from Gaul. Settling in Switzerland, he spent the rest of his life converting the Alamani. The Benedictine Abbey of St. Gallen was established on the site of his hermitage a century after his death. Feast day: October 16. *See also* Columbanus, St.

Gallicanism (Lat., *Gallus* [Gaul], the ancient name of France), an ecclesiology, with roots already in the thirteenth century, that claimed for France the right to resist all but very restricted forms of papal intervention within its jurisdiction. The French kings had controlled the papacy in Avignon from 1303 to 1377. The subsequent Great Western Schism (1378–1417) was concluded only when the Council of Constance (1414–17) declared the supremacy of general councils over popes (conciliarism) and removed the three papal claimants. These events encouraged the French church to resist papal interventions. The state courts (*parlements*), basing themselves on the royal ordinance, the "Pragmatic Sanction of Bourges" (1438), interpreted this right of resistance rigorously.

The faculty of the University of Paris defended a more moderate version of Gallicanism even after the Council of Trent (1545–63), and under Louis XIV this version was formulated in the four articles of the "Declaration of 1682" of the Assembly of the Clergy of France: (1) rejection of the extreme parliamentary position that denied any papal intervention in temporal matters; (2) admission of papal authority but only subject to conciliar supremacy; (3) demand that popes respect the ancient canons and customs of the French church; (4) admission of papal primacy in matters of faith but denial of papal infallibility apart from the consent of the universal Church.

Gallicanism never proposed schism from the Roman see. Gallicanism became obsolete with the French Revolution, but the restoration of the monarchy in France in the nineteenth century revived its influence until secular democracy and the conciliar definition of papal infallibility at Vatican I (1870) removed its influence. *See also* ecumenical council; France, Catholicism in; primacy, papal; Vatican Council I.

BENEDICT M. ASHLEY

Gallican rite, a collective name for several non-Roman forms of liturgy found in Western Europe between the fourth and eighth centuries. Despite Rome's early importance as an ecclesiastical center, its liturgy was not immediately adopted by all other churches. Northern Italy, Gaul, Spain, and the British Isles developed indigenous liturgical traditions that differed markedly from those of Rome. Differences were especially evident in three areas: Eucharist, Baptism, and ordination. In Gallican Masses, for instance, the kiss of peace occurred before the eucharistic prayer (not after it, as at Rome) and the eucharistic prayer itself was largely variable (not invariable, as at Rome). Some Gallican baptismal rites included the ceremony of foot washing (unknown at Rome). Gallican ordinations included anointings (e.g., of the priest's hands) that were adopted only later at Rome. Although Charlemagne tried to abolish it, the Gallican rite survived as an important element in—and influence on—the Roman liturgy. *See also* rite.

gambling, the staking of money or other valuables on outcomes that are the product of chance. Gambling is in general morally permissible provided that the parties to this type of contract are reasonably equal, indulgence is moderate, there is no fraud involved, and the activity is legal. Gambling involves personal property, which may morally be disposed of as the individual wishes unless requirements of justice or charity should conflict with such disposition. Therefore, a person may not gamble if this endangers his or her family or prevents the person from discharging obligations. In no case may a person gamble with money or property that does not belong to her or him. Gambling may be sinful when no proportion exists between the amount wagered and the possibility of return. Disproportion is permissible, however, in cases where loss of the property may be considered an act of charity, as in fundraising raffles or lotteries contributing to state revenue. Gambling, however, can be addictive. In that case, all forms, including even the latter, are to be discouraged.

Garabandal, Our Lady of (gah-rah-bahn-dahl'), a Marian title associated with a reported apparition in a mountain village in northwest Spain. On June 18, 1961, four young girls, led by twelve-year-old Conchita González, reported a vision of the archangel Michael, who announced that the Blessed Virgin Mary would appear to them beginning on July 2.

During the more than two thousand alleged apparitions, which lasted until 1965, the actions of the four children were filmed by Spanish, Italian, and British networks. Although no official judgment has been made regarding the authenticity of the apparitions, the Vatican did not accept the negative conclusions reached by a diocesan investigation conducted between 1962 and 1967. *See also* apparitions of the Blessed Virgin Mary.

Gardeil, Ambrose, 1859–1931, French Dominican theologian. He brought Thomism into modern French religious life. His work in apologetics and spiritual theology can be found in his book *The Structure of the Soul and the Mystical Experience.* In 1893 he cofounded the *Revue Thomiste. See also* Thomism.

Garrigou-Lagrange, Reginald (gahr-ee-goo'-lah-grahnj'), 1877–1964, French Dominican theologian and philosopher. After studying medicine in Bordeaux, he joined the Dominicans and studied under Ambrose Gardeil. From 1909 to 1960 he taught fundamental, dogmatic, and spiritual theology at the University of St. Thomas Aquinas in Rome ("Angelicum"), publishing over five hundred articles and books and often serving as a consultor to the Holy See. His thought centered on two issues he believed especially timely: (1) the need to ground theology in a realistic metaphysics rather than in idealistic and anti-intellectualist trends; and (2) the defense of the universal call of all Christians to the mystical life as the ordinary way of holiness.

Gaspar del Bufalo, St., 1786–1836, Italian priest, founder of the Society of the Precious Blood, an order dedicated to parish ministry, chaplaincies, and missionary work. He was canonized in 1954. Feast day: January 2. *See also* Precious Blood Fathers.

Gasparri, Pietro, 1852–1934, professor of canon law at the University of Paris and author of canonical treatises, including *Treatise on Matrimony.* He was cardinal, papal secretary of state (1914–30), and chair of the commission responsible for compiling 1917 Code of Canon Law. He negotiated the Lateran Treaty (1929) with the Italian government. *See also* Lateran Treaty.

Gasser, Vinzenz Ferrer (gahs'sair), 1809–79, Austrian prince-bishop of Brixen (Germany), influential theologian at Vatican I. A professor at the seminary in Brixen, Gasser was nominated prince-bishop by Franz Joseph I and approved by Pope Pius IX in 1856. As bishop, he established the Vincentinum seminary in Brixen and sought recognition of Catholicism as the exclusive religion in Tirol. A member of the Commission on Faith at Vatican I, he composed the first draft of the decree on papal infallibility, the first part of the second schema *De Fide* (Lat., "On Faith"), and proposed language in the decree on papal primacy defending the authority of local bishops. *See also* Vatican Council I.

Gaudete Sunday (Lat., *gaudete,* "rejoice"), the Third Sunday of Advent, so-called from the opening word of the Introit (the antiphon of the Roman Gradual). *Gaudete,* taken from the Latin translation of Phil 4:4, sets a tone of joyful expectation for the Lord's birth and Second Coming, as do the permitted rose-colored vestments. *See also* Laetare Sunday.

Gaudium et Spes (gou'dee-oom et spez). *See* Pastoral Constitution on the Church in the Modern World.

Ge'ez (gayz), an ancient south Semitic language, the classical tongue of Ethiopian Christian literature and the official liturgical language of the Ethiopian Orthodox and Catholic churches. Ge'ez, observable in written form by the fourth century, is now a dead language, replaced as the Ethiopian vernacular by Amharic, another Semitic tongue, by the year 1000. Though Amharic has been the Ethiopian literary language since the sixteenth century, Christian works continued to be written in Ge'ez until more recent times. In the 1990s, Amharic is being gradually introduced into the Ethiopian liturgy. *See also* Ethiopian rite.

Gehenna (ge-hen'nah; Heb., *ge'hinnom,* "valley of Hinnom"), ravine south of Jerusalem that was the site of a cult of Moloch during the Israelite monarchy (2 Kgs 23:10; Jer 7:31–32). By the first century Gehenna came to symbolize a place of fiery torment for the wicked (Matt 5:22–30; 10:28; 23:33; Mark 9:43–47; Jas 3:6). *See also* hell.

Geiler von Kaisersberg, Johann, 1445–1510, greatest Catholic reform preacher in late medieval Germany, holding an endowed preachership in Strassburg from 1478 until his death. His sermons catalogue the vices, abuses, and crimes of both Church and society.

Geiselmann, Josef Rupert (gi'zehl-mahn), 1890–1970, German theologian. He followed the early Tübingen school approach to tradition and revelation as a constructive alternative to dominant Thomistic models of theology. On the basis of his careful historical studies of the Council of Trent (1545–63), he challenged the prevailing Catholic assumption that revelation is partly in Scripture and partly in revelation. In this regard he anticipated the teaching of Vatican II's Constitution on Divine Revelation (n. 10). *See also* Scripture and tradition.

Gelasian Sacramentary, a liturgical book containing presider's prayers for Eucharist, Baptism, ordination, and other services. The name "Gelasian" derives from L. Muratori, who in 1748 incorrectly attributed the book's contents to Pope Gelasius I (492–496). Several sacramentaries fall into the "Gelasian" category. The oldest of them (the "Old Gelasian") is preserved in a single manuscript produced in a convent near Paris ca. 750. Other manuscripts of the Gelasian category (so-called "Gelasians of the eighth century") were copied in Gaul later in that century. The Gelasian books follow the Church (not the civil) calendar, and most contain the text of the eucharistic prayer. *See also* sacramentary.

Gelasius I, St., d. 496, pope from 492 to 496. He is remembered for his strong stand against emperor and patriarch in the Acacian Schism (484–519) and for his defense of papal primacy in this context, which included the theory of the "two powers" or "two swords," so influential in the Middle Ages. Over a hundred letters or fragments and six theological treatises of his survive, including one against Pelagianism and four against Christological heresies. Neither the Gelasian Sacramentary, however, nor the *Decretum Gelasianum* are his. Gelasius was the first pope to be titled "Vicar of Christ," although the title was not exclusively attached to the pope until the pontificate of Eugenius III (1145–53). Feast day: November 21. *See also* Acacianism; primacy, papal.

Gelineau, Joseph, b. 1920, French Jesuit liturgist and composer, well-known for his translation and musical settings of the Psalter. Closely associated with the *Centre de Pastorale Liturgique,* he is professor of liturgy and musicology at the *Institute Catholique* in Paris.

general, a title for the highest superior of a religious institute, called in the Code of Canon Law (can. 622) the supreme moderator. There is a variety of combinations in which this title is used, e.g., among the Franciscans, minister general, for the Dominicans, master general, and for Augustinians and Carmelites, prior general. *See also* superior general.

general absolution, the sacramental forgiveness of sins within a ritual that does not require individualized confession of sins to a priest. This form of sacramental absolution became common in the Middle Ages. As Scholastic theologians focused more on individual confession of sin to a priest, general absolution was viewed alternatively as a sacrament, not a sacrament, or reserved only for instances in which a large number of people were in danger of death, e.g., during a plague or prior to a battle. In 1972 the Sacred Congregation for the Doctrine of the Faith issued norms for general absolution which were incorporated into the revised rite of the sacrament of Penance (1973), and provide conferences of bishops with guidelines for the use of general absolution. *See also* absolution; confession, auricular; Reconciliation.

general chapter, the gathering of a religious institute that has ultimate authority within the institute or order. Canon 631 of the Code of Canon Law describes the scope and responsibilities of the general chapter. It "should be a true sign of . . . unity in love" and is to protect the institute's patrimony, promote renewal, elect superiors general, and publish norms for observance by the institute. Papally approved constitutions of the institute determine the composition of the chapter and its powers. General chapters are a remarkable instance of the collegial process in which all delegates to the chapter have equal voice in the chapter's affairs. *See also* chapter; superior general.

general confession, the confession of one's sins in a generic rather than a detailed way, e.g., all of one's sins of anger. The general acknowledgment that one is a sinner is found in the NT (cf. the "Our Father"; Rom 2:9–20; 1 John 1:8). A general confession of one's sinfulness and a desire for conversion played a major role in the origins of monasticism. The medieval addition of a *confiteor* (Lat.) to the Mass became a form of general confession. When frequent private confession was emphasized in the late medieval and post-Tridentine Church, general sacramental confession became part of Christian spirituality. The practice of confessing previously forgiven sins in a generic way was more common before Vatican II (1962–65), especially for those making a retreat or entering a new state in life. Vatican II's theology is ambiguous on general confession, due to the reevaluation of the nature of sin and of the sacrament. *See also* confession, auricular; Reconciliation.

General Instruction of the Roman Missal, a document on eucharistic celebration published in 1969 by the Sacred Congregation of Divine Worship and accompanying the Order of Mass. The 1975 edition contains minor changes. In eight chapters plus an appendix for the United States, the document treats eucharistic celebration under headings of structural elements and choices, offices and ministries, forms of celebration, arrangement of churches, and requisites for celebrating Mass. Rubrical material is presented in relation to theological and pastoral considerations. *See also* Roman Missal.

general intercessions. *See* Prayer of the Faithful.

general judgment. *See* judgment, general.

Genesius of Arles, St., d. ca. 303, martyr, patron saint of actors, lawyers, printers, secretaries, and stenographers. Although there is no doubt of his existence, what is known about him is probably legendary. He is said to have been a court reporter who left his profession in disgust over a sentence and was later beheaded. He was also thought to have been a comedian who, in the midst of an anti-Christian satire, converted to Christ and was beheaded. Feast day: August 25.

Geneviève, St., d.ca. 500, virginal patron saint of the city of Paris. Renowned for her charitable deeds, she is said to have averted Attila II and the Huns from sacking Paris in 451. Feast day: January 3. *See also* Paris.

genocide, the deliberate and methodical extermination of a particular human group. Strictly speaking, the term applies to the killing (Lat., *cidium*) of members of a race, nation, or ethnic minority (Gk., *genos*) only because they happen to belong to that group. However, the Convention on Genocide, ratified by the General Assembly of the United Nations, includes in its definition the violation of basic human rights of members of a group.

Among the unprincipled acts committed in a situation of total war and condemned as inexcusable,

the Second Vatican Council (1962–65) singled out genocidal acts as "horrendous crimes" (Pastoral Constitution on the Church in the Modern World, 1965, n. 79).

genuflection, the gesture of lowering oneself momentarily on the right knee, acknowledging divine presence. This gesture is made as one enters or leaves a church where Christ is present in the Blessed Sacrament.

George, St., d. ca. 303, legendary knight and martyr. Martyred probably under Diocletian, according to legend he was a Christian knight who killed a dragon that had been terrorizing the town of Sylene, Libya. As an exemplary knight he was very popular in the Middle Ages, especially among the Crusaders, and was included in the *Golden Legend*. He is the patron saint of England and of soldiers. Feast day: April 23.

Georgetown University, oldest Catholic institution of higher education in the United States. Founded in 1786 by a group of ex-Jesuits led by John Carroll, Georgetown began classes in 1792 as an academy to provide candidates for the ministry. Within its first decade, however, it became a college, offering a full range of courses to a student body that was national and even international in its character and pluralistic in its religious affiliation. In 1805, with the partial restoration of the Society of Jesus, the order was given the direction of the school. A decade later the college secured a federal charter.

In 1849 and 1870 the institution sponsored its first professional schools, in medicine and law re-

The Healy Building at Georgetown University, Washington, D.C., the oldest Catholic university in the United States. It has been under the direction of Jesuits since 1805.

spectively. Two presidents in the last three decades of the century, the Reverends Patrick Healy (1873–82) and Joseph Havens Richards (1888–98) attempted to convert these loosely connected schools into a university, with limited success. Healy reformed the curriculum and standards in all three schools and constructed a major facility to provide adequate housing for library, classrooms, laboratories, and undergraduates. Richards began graduate courses in the arts and sciences and built new facilities for the law and medical schools, including a hospital. A dental school and a nursing school were also established. In 1919 the newly founded School of Foreign Service offered the first program in the nation to prepare students for careers in diplomacy or international business. Ultimately two additional schools, Languages and Linguistics (1949) and Business Administration (1955), developed from the School of Foreign Service. Finally the School for Summer and continuing Education was organized in the 1950s.

In the decade after World War II enrollment doubled to more than five thousand. Under the leadership of Reverends Edward Bunn (1952–64), Gerard Campbell (1964–69), and Robert Henle (1969–76), the university entered the modern world of higher education with the restructuring of schools and the introduction of professional standards. By the mid-1970s, enrollment had doubled again, to nearly twelve thousand, including women in all schools by 1969. The student body, which during the first half of the twentieth century had become overwhelmingly Catholic and regional (Northeast) in its composition was again truly national, international, and pluralistic (ethnically and religiously). During the administration of Timothy S. Healy (1976–89), the university achieved national prominence for the quality of its undergraduates, law school, certain medical research programs (e.g., the Lombardi Cancer Center), and special institutes (e.g., Kennedy Institute of Ethics). *See also* Catholicism and education; Healy, Timothy Stafford.   R. EMMETT CURRAN

Georgian Byzantine Catholics, a group adhering to the Byzantine rite that was formed by Catholic missionaries working in Georgia, a traditionally Orthodox former Soviet republic on the eastern shore of the Black Sea.

In about 1230, Franciscan missionaries began to work among the remaining pagans in the Georgian kingdom. They were joined a few years later by the Dominicans. In 1329 Pope John XXII created a Latin diocese in Tbilisi, but no bishops were appointed to it after 1507, and the Catholic missions ended. In 1626 the Theatines were sent to work as missionaries among the Orthodox Georgians. They were replaced by the Capuchins in 1661.

In 1845, the Russian government, which had controlled Georgia since 1801, expelled the Capuchin missionaries. But in 1848, Czar Nicholas I agreed to the creation of a Latin diocese at Tiraspol with jurisdiction over Catholics in the vast southern regions of the empire, including Georgia.

A small community of Armenian Catholics existed in Georgia since the eighteenth century. But because the czars forbade Catholics to use the Byzantine rite and the Holy See did not promote its use among Georgians, no organized Georgian Byzantine Catholic Church ever existed. In 1920 it was estimated that of 40,000 Catholics in Georgia, 32,000 were Latins and the remainder of the Armenian rite.

A small Georgian Catholic parish has long existed in Constantinople (Istanbul). Twin male and female religious orders "of the Immaculate Conception" were founded there in 1861, but have since died out. *See also* Byzantine rite; Eastern Catholics and ecumenism; Eastern Catholics and Rome; Eastern churches; Eastern liturgies; Eastern rites.

Gerald of Aurillac, St.   (aw'ree-yak), 855–909, count known for his personal piety, chastity, and gift of healing, as well as his defense of the poor. Feast day: October 13.

Gerard Majella, St., 1726–55, patron saint of mothers in childbirth. A tailor by trade, he joined the Redemptorists as a lay brother and became known for his extraordinary charity and spiritual gifts. Feast day: October 16.

Gerard of Brogne, St. (brohn' yuh), ca. 880–959, abbot of Brogne and monastic reformer. After rebuilding the oratory in Brogne and establishing it as a monastery, Gerard was commissioned to reform monasteries throughout France, following the ideals of Benedict of Aniane (d. 821), an abbot who reformed Benedictine life by making it more austere. Feast day: October 3. *See also* Benedict of Aniane, St.

Gerhoh of Reichersberg (gair'hoh uhv rīk' uhrs-bairg), 1093–1169, German historian and ecclesiastical writer. A prolific polemicist for the papal side during the investiture controversy, he also began the *Chronicle of Reichersberg* and wrote moral and theological treatises. Highly symbolic, his writings on the antichrist influenced later medieval apocalyptic thinkers. *See also* investiture controversy.

Germain-des-Prés, St. *See* Saint-Germain-des-Prés.

Germany, Catholicism in. The Catholic Church in Germany has been shaped by its history of close ties to German rulers and to principalities divided by religious confessions.

Early History: The Christian evangelization of the German tribes began in the second century in the regions conquered by the Romans. The great migrations of Germans, Goths, Vandals, and others after the third century into Gaul, Spain, and Italy largely eradicated this Christianity. Some Germanic tribes, notably the Visigoths, adopted Christianity in the form of Arianism, which held that Christ was not equal to God but was only the greatest of creatures. The conversion of the king of the Franks, Clovis I, to Catholic Christianity (A.D. 500) was of decisive importance. Franks along with the Alamannen, Bavarians, and Saxons formed the basis of an emerging empire. Influenced by Frankish and Irish missionaries, the Alamannen and Bavarians became Catholic.

A characteristic of Germanic Christianity was the system of proprietary churches. The dioceses,

GERMANY

churches, and cloisters belonged to the king and the landlords, who also appointed the clergy. Later this system led to conflicts with Rome. The situation in which independence and influence were tied to the ownership of land led to the existence of ecclesiastical territories owned by the pope and the bishops. Boniface (d. 754) came from England as the "apostle to the Germans," and Charlemagne completed the Church's missionary activity and institutional organization. Boniface secured a close tie with Rome; Charlemagne accomplished the conversion of the Saxons and created the *Reichskirche* (Ger.), the church of the empire. His coronation as Holy Roman emperor (A.D. 800) established the continuity between the Roman Empire and the empire of the Franks, and created a newly integrated social and religious world of Europe and the West overseen by the emperor and the pope. The status of emperor gave the German kings the responsibility for the well-being of the papacy. The ties between the empire and the Church became even closer when Otto I (d. 973) named bishops to important imperial offices. These imperial bishops evolved over time into prince-bishops who ruled over a specific territories, an institutional practice that continued until 1803.

The German kings' claim that they had the right to appoint bishops to their offices led to the investiture controversy between Pope Gregory VII and Henry IV, which ended with the compromise of the Concordat of Worms (1122). Since then, the German church developed amid often hostile interaction between popes and emperors concerning the governance of Christianity. This process caused the gradual separation of the spiritual and secular authorities, something characteristic of the West in contrast to the East.

After the Reformation: The Reformation and its effects meant the end of the unity of Western Christianity that was attained during the Middle Ages. Ruling families and free states in Germany became Protestant. The Peace of Augsburg in 1555 resulted in the recognition of Catholic and Protestant regions, which determined the confessional map of Germany's states until the Second World War. The Counter-Reformation deepened the chasm between the Catholic and Protestant churches. In the Catholic regions the imperial-ecclesial structure was maintained until secularization in 1803, a structure that limited the influence of Rome upon German affairs.

After the dissolution of the Holy Roman Empire in 1806, Rome attempted a new ecclesiastical organization through concordats with the newly formed states. Romanticism and the Restoration of the nineteenth century led to renewal in Catholic theology, education, monasticism, and other areas and to the mobilization of the laity and the formation of lay associations. The new founding of the empire in 1871 by Bismarck, with the exclusion of Austria and the establishment of a Protestant realm, made Catholics a minority. Rome's efforts toward restoration and centralization, as well as measures of the First Vatican Council (1869–70), led to splitting off of the Old Catholics from Rome and also to the *Kulturkampf* (Ger., "culture struggle" [against the Church]), in which Bismarck was eventually defeated. The political party of the Catholics, the Center party, played an important parliamentary role, especially during the Weimar Republic (begun in 1918). The Vatican's concordats with Bavaria (1924), Prussia (1929), and Baden (1932) and with the Third Reich (1933) still determine the relationship between Church and state in Germany and influence features of Catholic organizations. The Third Reich of Adolf Hitler dissolved the Center party and all Catholic associations and planned the annihilation of the Church after "the final victory." The institutional Church's opposition to the Third Reich unfortunately remained weak.

World War II to the Present: With the end of the Second World War, Church life in West Germany flourished once again. This vitality manifested itself in many ways: the rebuilding of destroyed churches and church buildings, the construction of many new churches, the establishment of new educational institutions, the emergence of lay associations, the increase of vocations to the priesthood and religious life, and the development of an internationally respected theology. Collection of the church tax by the state and governmental agencies provided the financial resources for theological faculties at universities, religious education at public schools, and church hospitals, schools, and preschools. Given the political-geographical configuration of West Germany, the Federal Republic of Germany, Catholics played an important role, not the least through the Christian Democratic party, which united Catholic and Protestant Christians in one party. In East Germany, the former German Democratic Republic, Catholics formed for historical reasons a small minority, 5 percent of the population, living under Communist rule.

After the Second Vatican Council (1962–65) a series of synods were held in Germany. The council awakened lay interest in the study of theology. Disillusionment regarding the stalled reform of the Church and social uncertainties mirrored in the student revolution of 1968 have generated opposition groups within the Church, the "church from below." Furthermore, general developments in Western society and Rome's perceived program of restoration have led to a drastic decline in participation in the Church, a decline of vocations to the priesthood and religious life, and an increasing number of departures from the Church.

The 27 million Catholics of West Germany live in twenty-three dioceses. In light of the recent unification of Germany some new dioceses are being planned. In 1990, in former West Germany, 22 percent of the Catholics attended Mass weekly, but in the same year over 90,000 Catholics left the Church. Reliable studies of Catholic belief and Church life in the former East Germany are not yet available. *See also* Boniface, St., *Kulturkampf;* Nazism; Reformation, the.   HERMAN J. POTTMEYER

Gerosa, St. Vincentia, 1784–1847, Italian-born cofounder of the Sisters of Charity of Lovere, an institute devoted to the poor and the sick, and to the education of children. Feast day: June 28.

Gerson, Jean, 1363–1429, theologian, chancellor of the University of Paris and conciliarist during the Great Schism, and spiritual author. Succeeding his teacher Pierre d'Ailly as chancellor of the University in 1395, Gerson was an important figure among the conciliarists who strove to heal the Great Schism in the West (1378–1417). Arguing for the authority of council over pope in numerous writings, he advocated the resignation or deposing of the rival popes and conciliar election of a new pope. This strategy failed at the Council of Pisa (1409), resulting only in three papal claimants, but succeeded at the Council of Constance (1414–18), where Gerson headed the French delegation and made a stirring defense of the council's right to act without a pope presiding. Gerson spent his remaining years at Lyons concentrating on spiritual and pastoral writings. Writing both in Latin and French, Gerson adapted speculative theology for a more general audience. *See also* conciliarism; Constance, Council of; Great Schism; Pisa, Council of.

Gertrude the Great, St., ca. 1256–ca. 1302, German nun and mystic. From age five, Gertrude lived at the convent of Helfta in Thuringia, which also housed a kindred mystic, Mechtilde of Hackeborn. Gertrude's mystical revelations are related in *Revelations* and her *Spiritual Exercises*. Feast day: November 16.

Gethsemani, Abbey of Our Lady of, monastery of Cistercians of the Strict Observance (Trappists), founded in 1848 from the Breton Abbey of Melleray, and located near Bardstown, Kentucky. With six foundations in the United States and South America since 1944, Gethsemani Abbey is known chiefly as a retreat center and as the home and burial place of the influential spiritual writer, Thomas Merton (d. 1968). *See also* Merton, Thomas; Trappists.

Gibbons, James, 1834–1921, American cardinal-archbishop. Born in Baltimore but raised in Ireland, he returned to New Orleans in 1853. Educated by the Sulpicians in Baltimore, he was ordained in 1861. As secretary of Archbishop Martin John Spalding of Baltimore, he was named vicar apostolic of North Carolina in 1868. In 1872 he was appointed bishop of Richmond, and in 1878 coadjutor to Archbishop James Roosevelt Bayley of Baltimore, whom he succeeded that year.

In 1884 Gibbons was appointed to preside over the Third Plenary Council of Baltimore and in 1886 was named a cardinal, the second in the United States. At that time he formed a warm friendship with Archbishop John Ireland of St. Paul, John J. Keane, rector of The Catholic University of America, and Denis O'Connell, rector of the American College in Rome. Together they led the "liberal" party against a formidable coalition of conservative bishops, such as Archbishop Michael Corrigan of New York, Germans generally, and the Jesuits in particular, in a series of controversies involving the Knights of Labor, demands for German autonomy, the school controversy, the Catholic University, and "Americanism," the last condemned by Rome as a heresy in 1899.

Gibbons survived the fall of the liberal party to continue as the recognized leader and spokesman of the Catholic Church in the United States until his death in 1921. He was a friend of presidents and perhaps the most admired American Catholic churchman of his time. He was also a noted author; his *Faith of Our Fathers* (1877) proved the most popular apologetical work in the English-speaking world. *See also* Americanism; Baltimore, councils of; United States of America, Catholicism in the.

THOMAS SPALDING

Giberti, Gian Matteo, 1495–1543, bishop, reformer, and member of the Oratory of Divine Love. After his appointment as bishop of Verona, he was one of the model bishops who reformed the Catholic Church in the sixteenth century. At Worms (1540) he sought to heal the breach with the Protestants. *See also* Oratory of Divine Love.

gifts of the Holy Spirit, unmerited spiritual favors or benefits bestowed by the Spirit. They are seven in number according to the Catholic tradition that is based on the numbering in the Septuagint version of Isa 11:1–3, which added piety to the list of six gifts in the Hebrew version: wisdom, understanding, counsel, fortitude, knowledge, and fear of the Lord.

Catholic tradition recognizes the full manifestation of these gifts in Jesus at his baptism and a subsequent bestowal of the gifts of the Holy Spirit on the disciples of Jesus at Pentecost. The Second Vatican Council (1963–65) has spoken of these gifts as bestowed on the members of the Church for the sake of the Church's vitality.

In the early Church it was understood that a Christian was called to grow beyond a minimal observance of the commandments of God and the Church to a life lived more fully under the influence of the Holy Spirit. Greek Fathers of the Church wrote about the gifts of the Holy Spirit without concern for their number. However, the Latin Fathers were specific about these gifts as seven. Pope Gregory the Great (d. 604), influenced by the writings of Augustine of Hippo (d. 430), laid the foundations for a theology of the gifts of the Holy Spirit that was more fully articulated in the Middle Ages by Thomas Aquinas (d. 1274). Aquinas saw the seven gifts of the Holy Spirit as distinct from virtues. Moreover, he described the gifts as the way the Christian can be habitually open to the influence of the Holy Spirit.

Mystical theologians have written of the gifts of the Holy Spirit as disposing a person to be responsive and docile to the work of the Holy Spirit, who is the agent of mystical contemplation in the human person. *See also* charism; fear of God; fortitude; fruits of the Spirit; Holy Spirit; wisdom.   PATRICIA M. VINJE

Gilbert of Poitiers, also known as Gilbert Poretta, ca. 1075–1154, theologian, bishop of Poitiers from 1142 to 1154. After studies with Bernard of Chartres, Anselm of Laon, and Peter Abelard, Gilbert taught at Chartres for about twenty years, serving as chancellor from 1126 to 1137. Gilbert was a leader in the struggle to establish theology as a distinct science within the school curriculum. His teaching and writings, especially his commentaries on Boethius's theological works (*Opuscula sacra*), were widely read even in the thirteenth century and influenced the development of ideas about Christology and the Trinity. Accused of tritheism, Gilbert was cleared of all charges both at a papal consistory (1147) and at the Council of Reims (1148).

Gilbert of Sempringham, St.,   1083–1189, founder of the (now extinct) Gilbertine order, the only medieval religious order originating from England. Gilbert's order, while starting with only seven women, grew to include men and lay brothers and sisters. Feast day: February 4.

Giles, St. (Lat., "Aegidius"), hermit of perhaps the eighth century. Known only by legend, he was patron saint of the poor and of the physically disabled; his shrine at Saint-Gilles near Arles was a pilgrimage center throughout the Middle Ages. Feast day: September 1.

Giles of Rome, ca. 1243–1316, Augustinian Hermit, theologian, and bishop. A student of Thomas Aquinas at Paris, he was elected Augustinian prior general in 1292 and in 1295 was appointed archbishop of Bourges. He wrote numerous philosophical and theological works; his most famous is *On the Rule of Princes* (1285), which he wrote for his precocious pupil the future King Philip IV of France. In another work influential for the developing papal response to regal claims, *On the Power of the Supreme Pontiff,* he ardently defended papal dominion over all things, spiritual and temporal. Members of his order were urged to follow his teaching. *See also* Augustinian Hermits.

Gillespie, Eliza, also known as Mother Mary of St. Angela, 1824–87, American educator. Founder of the Sisters of Holy Cross, she administered St. Mary's College, Notre Dame, Indiana (1855–70, 1878–87). During the Civil War she organized the sisters into a nursing corps and established military hospitals. Gillespie was the principal founder of the publication *Ave Maria* (1865). *See also* Sisters of Holy Cross.

Gillis, James M., 1876–1957, Paulist priest and journalist. Born in Boston, he studied for the dioce-

san priesthood before joining the Paulist Fathers, for whom he was ordained in 1901. After teaching for several years in the Paulist seminary, Gillis served as a missionary before becoming editor of *The Catholic World* in 1922. He wrote a widely circulated newspaper column, "*Sursum Corda:* What's Right with the World," lectured regularly on NBC's "The Catholic Hour," and wrote numerous books and pamphlets on religious and controversial questions. Gillis was an acute critic of modern literature and a strong political conservative. He resigned as editor of *The Catholic World* in 1948.

Gilson, Etienne, 1884–1978, French philosopher and leading scholar of medieval thought. A professor at various European and North American universities, he founded the Institute of Mediaeval Studies in Toronto (1929) that achieved pontifical status in 1939 and remains important for the study of medieval culture. Born in Paris and trained at the Sorbonne, he came to the study of the Middle Ages through his graduate work on the medieval antecedents of Cartesian philosophy. Although he wrote important accounts of the thought of Augustine and of the mystical theology of Bernard of Clairvaux, his great love was for the study of the thirteenth century, specifically the thought of Thomas Aquinas. Because of the centrality of the act of existence (Lat., *esse*) for Aquinas, Gilson provocatively characterized Thomist thought as "existentialist," in contrast to the alleged "essentialism" of other medieval philosophers. Such works as *The Christian Philosophy of Saint Thomas Aquinas* remain essential reading for students of the Middle Ages. An overarching notion in Gilson's scholarship is "Christian philosophy," which emphasizes the harmony of reason and revelation. Christian philosophy is a sapiential endeavour; reason's search for the highest truth, which will fufill the deepest aspirations of the human person, can be successful only under the guidance of faith. *See also* Thomism.

Glenmary Home Missioners, society of diocesan priests (Glmy.). In 1936, Father William Howard Bishop proposed a plan for a society of priests, brothers and sisters to work in counties of the United States that had no resident priests. The Home Missioners of America, as the society of priests is formally called, was established in 1939. With headquarters and a major seminary at Glendale, Ohio, and a research center in Atlanta, Georgia, the society establishes parishes and works to bring them to the point of being able to support a resident priest. Then the parish is returned to the diocese and the Glenmary member moves on.

Gloria in Excelsis (gloh'ree-ah in eks-chel'sees; Lat., "glory in the highest"), words beginning the brief hymn of the angels to the shepherds after the birth of Jesus (Luke 2:14). They also serve as the opening verse of the Gloria in the Mass.

Glorious Mysteries of the Rosary. *See* Mysteries of the Rosary.

glory of God, an expression that can be understood in two senses: as the reality of God and as creation's appropriate acknowledgment of God. In the OT, God is depicted as majestic and filled with power, frequently conveyed in the images of fire and light, for example, in the burning bush, on Mount Sinai, and in Moses's tent (Exod 3:1–6; 24:17; 33:18–23). The NT sustains this imagery, for example, in the infancy narrative (Luke 1:35, 79; 2:9) and the accounts of Jesus' Transfiguration (Mark 9:2–8). Also, Jesus speaks of revealing the Father's glory (John 17:1, 4–5). This understanding of glory as the divine reality is complemented by the sense of giving glory as the fitting act of creation before God. At Jesus' birth, the angels declare "Glory to God in the highest" (Luke 2:14). All people should give glory and praise to God (Luke 17:18; Acts 12:23; Rev 4:9–11). In sum, "the glory of God" expresses the wondrous mystery of God as well as God's will to draw all of creation into this mystery. *See also* creation; God.

gloss, a word or words inserted between the lines or in the margin of a text to explain difficult or foreign words; also used more broadly of commentary, especially the medieval *glossa ordinaria* (Lat.), consisting principally of comments on Scripture from patristic authors. These developed into full-scale compilations and were called "the bible of Scholasticism." Gloss is also used to mean comments on canon law.

Glossa Ordinaria, (glah'sah ohr-dee-nah'ree-ah; Lat., "ordinary interpretation"), the standard gloss or commentary on the Latin Vulgate and an important medieval reference tool for the interpretation of the Bible. Drawn from the writings of important Latin patristic and Carolingian authors, glosses are both interlinear and marginal, and of varying lengths. Typically, the layout of the manuscript page would distinguish clearly between the biblical text itself and interpretive comment: the biblical text might be larger in size, centered, even marked off in different ink, thus showing its greater authority.

Details of the evolution of the *Glossa* remain shrouded in mystery; the wrongful ascription of the marginal gloss to Walafrid Strabo (d. 849), a German abbot, is a late medieval theory. The *Glossa* took shape over the course of the first half of the twelfth century, due to the efforts of scholars in northern France; the exact contribution of individual scholars is obscure. The fact that the *Glossa* had its origin in the leading region of theological inquiry in the High Middle Ages ensured its subsequent prominence. More than three thousand manuscripts of the *Glossa* are extant. *See also* Scripture, interpretation of.

glossolalia (Gk., *glossa*, "tongue," "language"; *lalein*, "speak"), the phenomenon of speaking in a "language" not learned in a human way. It is found in almost all religious traditions, particularly in primitive forms of worship and especially as a group phenomenon. It does not specifically occur in the OT, but in the NT it is mentioned in Acts 2:1–13; 8:9–25 (implicitly); 10:11–18; and 19:1–7. In Acts glossolalia is always a group phenomenon; it is temporary and it takes place as a symbol of God's approval of the Christian community taking a new step in its missionary activity. Paul discusses glossolalia at length in 1 Cor 12–14. Here, in contrast to Acts, it is an individual prayer/prophecy gift that is under the control of the recipient and is permitted to be used with care at prayer meetings (1 Cor 14:28–40). Paul prefers an interpreter to be present. Glossolalia is also mentioned in the longer ending of Mark (16:15–18), which is not considered authentic. Here the term "new tongues" is used and the gift appears to enable the missionary to communicate with persons whose language he or she does not know. Glossolalia has been attributed to a number of saints in the Catholic Church, e.g., Teresa of Ávila and Alphonsus Liguori. It has occurred as a group phenomenon in a number of revivalist movements, Catholic and other Christian, throughout the Church's history. Whereas there may be a genuine gift consequent upon a private or communal spiritual experience, synthetic glossolalia occurs frequently with negative results, such as regression of the ego, dependence on the authority figure who introduced the recipient to "tongues," elitism, histrionic behavior, and uninhibited euphoria. Linguistic researchers (using numerous tape recordings) conclude that glossolalia is not a true language but rather "play words" or partially formed speech. Considerable anthropological research has been conducted on this subject and its findings suggest that it may be a type of induced ecstasy. Scholars differ in their appraisal of personalities prone to glossolalia. Some find that they are balanced, but others find that they often exhibit hostility toward authority, tendencies toward dependency, suggestibility, inferiority, and a desire to compensate for feelings of isolation. Those who have a more positive approach to glossolalia see it as a prayer speech that opens up new realms of spiritual joy and redemptive experience.

Bibliography

Mills, Watson E. *Speaking in Tongues: A Guide to Research on Glossolalia.* Grand Rapids, MI: Eerdmans, 1986.

J. MASSYNGBAERDE FORD

gluttony, inordinate indulgence in food or drink. Desire for food and drink, essential to human beings, must be moderated by the virtue of temperance. Gluttony, the vice opposed to temperance, consists in the habitual, inordinate enjoyment of food and drink, including eating or drinking too often, too much, too voraciously, or too fastidiously. Gluttony does not indicate a serious moral disorder unless it becomes an obstacle to one's fulfillment of serious obligations, health, or love of God. Gluttony is the source of other faults, such as mental torpidity, excessive speech, loud behavior, and the like. *See also* capital sins.

Gnosticism (Gk., *gnosis,* "knowledge"), a system of religious belief according to which salvation depends upon a singular knowledge or inner enlightenment about God, which liberates a person from the ignorance and evil that characterize the created order. While the historical origins of Gnosticism remain unclear, it is evident that Gnosticism was present almost at the very beginning of Christianity itself. Its teachers (e.g., Basilides, Marcion, and Valentinus) denied the full humanity of Jesus Christ, refused to acknowledge the validity of the entire OT and the NT, and rejected the authority of the Church and its tradition. Our knowledge of Gnosticism at the time of the early Church comes from the writings of the Church Fathers (e.g., Irenaeus) and the discovery in 1945 of fourth-century Gnostic texts at Nag Hammadi, Egypt.

Though Gnosticism has assumed different specific forms and has been embraced by a variety of distinct religious groups, it possesses basic traits. It is dualistic, regarding human life as imprisoned in a creation controlled by sinister forces, especially a semidivine being (the demiurge), and yet possessing a yearning for a truth and goodness outside of space and time. It is soteriological, maintaining that there exists an utterly transcendent God who has willed to send a bearer of divine enlightenment into the (fallen) created order, so that those human beings who choose to receive this special knowledge or revelation can be led out of the evil material reality and into the kingdom of truth and goodness. It is sectarian, distinguishing between the saved, those people who have received divine illumination, and the damned, those who continue to live in ignorance. It is syncretistic, including ideas and practices from various, even divergent, philosophical and religious traditions (e.g., Hellenistic mystery cults, Jewish cabalism, Iranian dualism, Babylonian and Egyptian mythology, and Christian scriptures and rituals). *See also* Docetism. ROBERT A. KRIEG

godparent, a fully initiated Catholic Christian who represents the faith community and assists the catechumen throughout the initiation process. In the case of infant baptism, godparents pledge to support the parents or guardians in their role of Christian formation. Godparents are chosen by the catechumens or by the parents or guardians of the child to be baptized. The godparents should be mature (at least sixteen years old, unless another age is determined by the diocese and/or pastor). A baptized and believing Christian not belonging to the Catholic Church may be chosen as one of the godparents, but the Catholic godparent must meet the above requirements. It is the responsibility of the godparents to show the candidates how to practice the gospel in personal and social life, to sustain the candidates in moments of hesitancy and anxiety, to bear witness, and to guide the candidates' progress in the baptismal life (Rite of Christian Initiation of Adults, n. 11). *See also* catechumen; catechumenate; sponsor.

Gog and Magog, distant enemies of the people of God. In Ezek 38–39 Gog is chief prince of the land of Magog. Both are otherwise unidentified. The land lies situated to the north of Israel. In Rev 20:8 Gog and Magog are two nations at the end of the earth mustered by Satan after Christ's millennial reign.

GOD

God is the supreme and supremely personal Source and Creator of the universe, revealed in creation and in the events of salvation history (covenant, prophecy, the Incarnation of Jesus Christ, and the ongoing presence of the Holy Spirit), and object of religious devotion and subject matter of theology. The specifically Christian way of speaking of God is by means of the doctrine of the Trinity. The doctrine of the Trinity is not one doctrine among others but lies at the center of Christian faith. It affirms and summarizes the most profound convictions of Christian believers and also determines the systematic structure of the whole of Christian dogmatics. At its root, the doctrine of the Trinity expresses what Christians believe about who God is, namely, the eternal, loving, personal source of all of reality, who created the world and all in it for loving union with God through the person of Jesus Christ. In this respect the doctrine of the Trinity also expresses what Christians believe about the nature of the world and of the human person and so comprises a comprehensive theological perspective on all of reality. In short, the doctrine of the Trinity affirms, first, that it belongs to the nature of God to be in communion with all persons and all creatures of the earth, a communion that is brought about by redemption through Jesus Christ and the ongoing power and presence of the Holy Spirit; second, that all of reality is deeply personal since it is created by a personal God and that it is the destiny of human persons to live in authentic communion with God, with other human beings, and with all the creatures and goods of the earth.

Despite its centrality and indispensability, once the doctrine of the Trinity was formulated in the late fourth century and refined in the Middle Ages in both Eastern and Western Christianity, it largely passed to the margins of Christian consciousness, particularly in Latin Christianity. There are many reasons for this, explored below, but Catholic theologian Karl Rahner (d. 1984) has pointed out that for many Christians, were the doctrine of the Trinity to be removed or even proved false, little or nothing of their faith or piety would change. In effect, Rahner argued, many Christians are, practically speaking, unitarians, even though Christian faith is irreducibly trinitarian.

ORIGINS OF THE DOCTRINE OF THE TRINITY

It was common in neo-Scholastic manuals of dogmatic theology to cite texts such as Gen 1:26, "Let us make humankind in our image, according to our likeness" (see also Gen 3:22; 11:7; Isa 6:2–3), as proof of a plurality in God. Today, however, scholars generally agree that there is no doctrine of the Trinity as such in either the OT or the NT. However, the foundations for what later became this doctrine are indeed found in Scripture.

The OT depicts God as the Father of Israel and personifies God with terms such as Word (Heb., *dabar*), Spirit (*ruah*), Wisdom (*hokmah*), and Presence (*shekinah*). While it would go far beyond the intention and thought-forms of the OT to suppose that a late-fourth-century or thirteenth-century Christian doctrine can be found there, still it is consistent with the general tradition of Christian interpretation of Scripture to see in the ancient texts of the OT precedents and foreshadowings of the revelation of God in Jesus Christ.

Likewise, the NT does not contain an explicit doctrine of the Trinity; however, later doctrinal formulations owe a more obvious debt to NT texts. In antiquity, God and Father were synonyms; God the Father is source of all of creation (Gk., *Pantokrator*). Early liturgical and creedal fragments refer to God as the "Father of our Lord Jesus Christ," and Paul instructs his readers to offer all praise to God through Jesus Christ and indeed to do all things in the name of Jesus Christ. Some texts mention the names of both Father and Son, or God and Christ (Rom 4:24; 8:11; 2 Cor 4:14; Col 2:12; 1 Tim 2:5–6; 6:13; 2 Tim 4:1) and a few link the names of Father, Son, and Spirit (or God, Christ, and Spirit). The Roman Catholic eucharistic liturgy uses the text from 2 Cor 13:14 to open the celebration of the Mass: "May the grace of our Lord Jesus Christ, the love of God, and the communion of the Holy Spirit be with you." The baptismal formula of Matt 28:19 ("Baptizing them in the name of the Father and of the Son and of the Holy Spirit") is an obvious trinitarian text, though many exegetes today suppose that this text did not originate with Jesus but was a later interpolation. There is the description of Jesus' baptism in Matt 3:16–17, during which God speaks from the heavens and the Spirit rests on Jesus. There are what appear to be prayer fragments in Gal 4:6 and Rom 8:15 (the Spirit praying in us calls God *Abba*). Other trinitarian texts include 1 Cor 6:11; 12:4–6; 2 Cor 1:21–22; 1 Thess 5:18–19; and Gal 3:11–14. The text from Eph 1:3–14 deserves special mention; it summarizes the basic providential plan of salvation initiated by God, fulfilled in Jesus Christ, and consummated in the Holy Spirit. It describes this plan as an "economy" (Gk., *oikonomia*, providential plan or management) foreordained by God through which God destines all creatures for ultimate and eternal union with God. Jesus Christ is the revelation of God's economy, and the Spirit is the active power bringing God's providential plan to fruition and completion. Finally, the high-priestly prayer of Jesus in John 17 contains important ingredients of what later theology will develop as God the Father's special relationship with Jesus Christ.

In sum, a number of NT texts bear witness to Jesus Christ and the Spirit as essential to our salvation. The pattern of these texts is mediatory; God's salvation and revelation are made known through Jesus Christ and in or by the power of God's Holy Spirit. Moreover, it is important to keep in mind that what the later doctrine of the Trinity attempts to express is the whole mystery of salvation through Christ. Thus, in order to avoid a "proof-text" approach, biblical texts regarded as authentically trinitarian should not be limited solely to those that contain three divine names. Every shred of testimony to the saving power of God realized through Christ belongs to the fount of biblical witness to the mystery of the triune God.

It would be anachronistic to say that the NT necessarily implies what will later be expressed with metaphysical refinement as a Trinity of three coequal divine Persons who share the same substance. While it is entirely legitimate to see later dogmatic development as springing forth from the witness of the Scriptures, the language of the Bible remains economic, that is, rooted in the concrete history and stories of salvation and redemption. The vocabulary of metaphysics cannot be found in Scripture. Because of this, there are theologians who regard all postbiblical doctrinal developments as arbitrary or even aberrant. For them, one cannot go beyond the language and concepts of the Bible. The Catholic approach, however, has always been to see doctrinal developments as legitimate provided one can show the connection between the Scripture, which is normative, and doctrine, which is derivative. Doctrine can never replace Scripture; the Bible remains the authoritative witness to God's providential plan of salvation.

The early liturgical practice of Christians is another important source for the origins of trinitarian doctrine. Although Christian prayer is largely an adaptation of Jewish prayer, it was new to offer prayer to God through Jesus Christ, in his name, by the power of the Holy Spirit. The mediatory pattern of the new doxologies is well attested in the Letters of Paul and in those attributed to Paul (see Eph 5:20; 1 Cor 15:57; Col 3:17; Rom 1:8; 16:27; 7:25: 2 Cor 1:20; Heb 13:15; 1 Pet 4:11). The earliest liturgical texts do not refer to the Holy Spirit; however, the early Church was very much aware that the power for prayer came from the Spirit. Rom 8:15 and Gal 4:6 are evidence that Christians understood themselves to be called "in the Spirit" to new relationship to the God of Jesus Christ: "And because you are children, God has sent the Spirit of his Son into our hearts, crying, 'Abba! Father!'" The eucharistic prayers (anaphorae) duplicate the mediatory pattern of prayer; all praise and thanksgiving were offered to God through Jesus Christ.

Christian Baptism was an exception. The text of Matt 28:19b to baptize in the name of the Father, and of the Son, and of the Holy Spirit is unusual because of the prepositions ("and . . . and"). Even if the command to baptize cannot be traced back to Jesus himself, it undoubtedly reflects the Church's early baptismal practice. The candidate was asked a triple set of questions: "Do you believe in God the Father the Almighty? Do you believe in Jesus Christ? Do you believe in the Holy Spirit?" The candidate "handed back" (Lat., *redditio*) what had been "handed over" (*traditio*) by affirming each portion of the creed. The interrogation was followed by a triple immersion in water. Early Christian creeds were not the full-blown, antiheretical summaries of faith and doctrine that emerged in the fourth century and thereafter, but collections of biblical and apostolic teaching that were fashioned for baptismal practice. The creed was a "symbol" (*symbolum*), a sign of the God into whose name one was initiated.

DEVELOPMENT OF TRINITARIAN DOCTRINE

In the immediate post-NT period of the Apostolic Fathers, there were no attempts to speculate about the relationship between God and Christ, Father and Son. The second-century Apologists, however, identified the preexistent Christ mentioned in the prologue of John's Gospel with the Logos (Word) of Greek philosophy. Justin Martyr (d. ca. 165) used the Stoic distinction between the immanent word (Gk., *logos endiathetos*) and expressed word (*logos prophorikos*) to explain a two-stage theory of the Incarnate Word. In the third century, Monarchianism (*monē archē*, "one principle"), which upheld the absolute unity of God and the sole divinity of God the Father, arose in reaction to Logos Christology. Sabellius, whose name is linked with "Modalism," believed that God's being could manifest itself in different modalities in history, such as the person of Jesus Christ, but that these historical modes of existence did not affect God's being as such. The great Eastern theologian Origen (d. 254) was responsible for the idea of an eternal generation of the Son within the being of God; for him, the Son is a distinct *hypostasis* (person) who always resided with God. In the West, the lawyer and theologian Tertullian (d. ca. 225) conceived of the three divine Persons as a kind of plurality in God's being.

It was Arius, the priest from Alexandria, around whom the greatest controversies over the status of Christ took place. Around 320 Arius wrote a public letter claiming that Jesus Christ was not divine in the same sense that God (Father) was divine; Jesus Christ was the highest of creatures, but still a creature who had a beginning. Arius's argument was stunningly simple: God (Father) is absolutely transcendent; God's essence (Gk., *ousia*) cannot be shared by another; therefore, God and Christ cannot be "of the same substance." If they were of the same substance, there would be two gods. Therefore, Christ is subordinate to God. The slogan of Arianism, "there was when he [the Son] was not [in existence]," meant that Jesus Christ was begotten of God in time, not from all eternity. One of the factors that allowed Arianism to evolve into such a vital movement was the fact that the Church's mediatory prayer at this time, along with numerous biblical texts (e.g., Prov 8:22: "The Lord created me at the beginning . . . ") seemed, at least on the face of it, to support Arius's position. Arius's views provoked Christian theologians to ask new questions about the status of Jesus Christ with respect to God. If Christ was God's mediator, was he then "less than" God? If he was less than God, could he be the Savior?

To refute Arius, the Council of Nicaea (325) taught that Christ is not created but is *homoousios* (Gk., "of the same substance") with God. Although from one perspective this word settled an immediate problem, few in the Church were happy with it. Greek theologians protested that the term *homoousios* was illegitimate because it was not biblical, and, moreover, it could be interpreted to mean that God and Christ are numerically identical (thus blurring any distinction between them). Some suggested that the word *homoiousios* ("of similar substance") be used instead, but this could be interpreted as subordinating Christ to God. In any case, Arius had pushed Christian theology in the direction of ontology: what would it mean to say that Christ is "same in being" with God?

Athanasius (d. 373), who is considered the great defender of Nicene orthodoxy, wrote several tracts against Arius basically arguing that since Christ is essential to our salvation, he must be divine. Athanasius had a limited philosophical vocabulary and made his arguments primarily on the basis of his reading of the Scriptures. Late in the fourth century the Cappadocians Basil of Caesarea (d. 379), Gregory of Nyssa (d. 394), and Gregory of Nazianzus (d. 390) formulated the classic expression of orthodox trinitarian doctrine: the one God exists in three equal persons. Their teaching made it possible for the Council of Constantinople (381) to affirm the divinity of the Holy Spirit, which up to that point had nowhere been clearly stated, not even in Scripture. The Cappadocians regularized the philosophical vocabulary of trinitarian doctrine by distinguishing clearly between *hypostasis* (Gk., "particular person") and *ousia* ("common substance or nature"). Further, they distinguished between being begotten (*gennesia*) and being created (*genesia*). Jesus Christ the Son was begotten, not created, which placed him on the side of God, not of creatures. The Cappadocians also maintained the biblical and liturgical sense of God (Father) as the monarch, the sole originating principle and source of all that is, including source of Son and Spirit. Godhood is the same as God's fatherhood; everything originates with God the Father, is brought into being through the Son, and is perfected by the Holy Spirit.

The Arianism of the early fourth century had evolved into various forms by the time of Cappadocians, most notably, Eunomianism. Eunomius believed that he knew the definition of God's essence to be "Unbegottenness." Eunomius's argument about the inferiority of the Son was simple to state but enormously difficult to refute: The Father is Unbegotten; the Son is Begotten; therefore they do not share the same substance of divinity; and therefore the Son is less than God. Unlike Eunomius, who claimed to know the name of God's essence, the Cappadocians were filled with respect for the absolute unknowability of the inaccessible divine essence. In order to refute Eunomius, Gregory of Nazianzus argued that "Unbegottenness" cannot be the name of the divine essence. No one knows the definition of the divine essence. Not even the word "Father" names God's hidden essence. Indeed, Gregory argued, "Father" is the name of a relation, namely, the relation of God to Christ. In effect, the two Gregories and Basil argued (against Eunomius) that God and Christ, Father and Son, do share the same divine substance because what makes God to be God is not to be Unbegotten, but to be uniquely personal as Father, Son, and Spirit. This brilliant move made the first full-fledged trinitarian doctrine possible. The closest we can get to defining the divine Persons is indirect and oblique, depicting their origin: God the Father comes from no one; God the Son comes from the Father; God the Spirit comes from the Father through the Son.

The emergence of a trinitarian doctrine of God's fatherhood altered what it had meant up to that point. In the Bible and in early creeds and liturgical prayers, God and Father were synonyms. The Cappadocian teaching added the meaning that God is the eternal Father (Begetter) of the eternal Son. God the Father could still be thought of as the monarch, however, now that three persons shared the monarchy of divinity. The unity of God resided in part in the Father as the source of Godhood, but also in the "perichoretic" (Gk., *perichōrēsis,* "interdependence") relationship among the three persons. This "intratrinitarian" sense of God's fatherhood and of Christ's sonship set Christian theology on a course toward further refinement of the intradivine relations among the divine Persons.

Western trinitarian theology followed a different course with Augustine (d. 430). He, too, was influenced by Neoplatonism, but instead of seeing the Father as the source of divinity, Augustine began with the unity of the divine substance common to all three Persons. Believing that the soul was a mirror of its Creator, Augustine held that contemplating the soul was a means of contemplating God. He sought images for the Trinity within the human soul and formulated several so-called psychological analogies (such as lover-beloved-love; memory-understanding-will) to explain how one substance could be internally differentiated without dividing the substance. Knowing and loving are distinct operations of the soul, but one would not say that there are two souls.

In the more philosophical part of Augustine's *On the Trinity,* he argued against Arian subordinationism by emphasizing that the three divine Persons are fully coequal sharers in the one divine substance. Each Person *is* the divine substance. While this approach was an effective way to circumvent Arianism, it also meant that the distinctiveness of each Person—whatever makes the Son or Spirit unique—became less pronounced. Augustine's idea that "all works of the Trinity *ad extra* are indivisible" highlighted the equality of the divine Persons, but made it difficult to see the unique roles of Son and Spirit in human salvation. This tension gave rise to the "doctrine of appropriations," according to which various roles and acts within salvation history, such as creation, redemption, and sanctification, are "appropriated" to one of the divine Persons.

The Cappadocians and Augustine followed fundamentally different routes in their trinitarian theologies. Although all generalizations have their exceptions, in general, Greek theology emphasizes the divine Persons, whereas Latin theology emphasizes the divine nature. In the Greek approach, all of reality emanates from its one source in God the Father, passes through the Son and to the Spirit who is the bridge to the world, whereas Latin theology tends to depict God as a self-enclosed Trinity of Persons. The Greek scheme can be represented as a point on a line moving outward; the Latin scheme can be represented by a circle or triangle. The danger in the Greek approach is subordinationism, in the Latin it is tritheism.

After Nicaea, and with the advent of trinitarian doctrine per se, both traditions, Eastern and Western, shifted from the earlier concern with soteriological questions (how Christ saves; what salvation means) to ontological questions (how Christ and God are of the same substance). This shift is sometimes described as the shift from the perspective of the "economic Trinity" to the "immanent Trinity," that is, from the works of God in the economy of redemption to the intradivine relations among the divine Persons. In recent Catholic theology Karl Rahner formulated the axiom that "the economic Trinity is the immanent Trinity, and vice versa" to indicate that there is a fundamental unity between what we know of God in God's self-revelation through Christ and the Spirit, and God's eternal, invisible being. While the essence of God can never be known as it is in itself, however, it is truly and fully given in the course of salvation history.

The Cappadocian and Augustinian approaches were refined throughout the medieval period in both traditions. In the East, John of Damascus (d. 749) summarized all patristic developments up to that point. Gregory Palamas (d. 1359), who stands at the summit of Orthodox theology, was embroiled in a controversy over hesychasm (Gk., *hesychia*, "silence"). The Hesychasts practiced a form of contemplation that they believed led to an inner vision of God's uncreated light, just like the light revealed on Mount Tabor during the Transfiguration of Christ. Palamas defended the Hesychast doctrine by distinguishing three aspects of God's being: the imparticipable and unknowable divine essence; the three divine hypostases, Father, Son, and Spirit; and the uncreated divine "energies" (self-expressions). Although God's essence remains beyond the reach of the creature, even in Hesychastic prayer, the contemplative does enter into real union with God through the divine energies which are "God as such." Thus in prayer and mystical union one participates in the divine energies, not the divine essence. Although Palamism amounts to a very strong theology of grace, there is some concern that the divine essence and indeed the divine Persons are too distant from the creature. If this critique made by Western theologians is true (and the Orthodox deny it), then Palamas's doctrine of God would contribute to the sense that the Trinity is remote from Christian life.

In the West, Augustine's thought was extremely influential. Boethius (d. 524) formulated the classic definition of person, "individual substance of a rational nature." The main lines of Augustine's theology were given further elaboration in the medieval period by Anselm (d. 1109) and Thomas Aquinas (d. 1274). Thomas provided a sophisticated philosophical treatment of all of the themes of Christian faith using the principles of Aristotelian science and metaphysics. Thomas's theology in the *Summa Theologiae* is rich and profound and has served as a wellspring for Catholic theology ever since. Like Augustine, Thomas saw the human acts of knowing and loving as images of the divine acts of knowledge (through the Son) and love (through the Spirit). Thomas also greatly clarified the metaphysical vocabulary appropriate to this new science of the Trinity; he defined divine personhood as a "subsistent relation" (that is, a relation that is its own substance). He was original in writing two distinct tracts on God: *On the One God (De Deo Uno)* and *On the Triune*

God (De Deo Trino). This arrangement has been severely criticized in contemporary theology because it gives the impression (surely at odds with Thomas's own intention) that the philosophical unity of God is prior to God's Trinity. In its own way, perhaps, this structural arrangement contributed to the general irrelevance of the doctrine of the Trinity within Western theology. Insofar as personhood was seen as secondary to substance or nature, the Christian doctrine of God appeared to be unitarian rather than trinitarian. Trinitarian theology became abstract and speculative, divorced from other theological tracts (such as grace and the sacraments), from liturgy, and from the ordinary concerns of Christian life. Through Thomas's influence as mediated by the neo-Scholastic manuals of theology, most people today associate "Trinity" with the self-relatedness of God, rather than God's relationship to humans through the mysteries of creation, redemption, and sanctification. As Karl Rahner notes, "The treatise on the Trinity locks itself in even more splendid isolation, with the ensuing danger that the religious mind finds it devoid of interest" (*The Trinity* [New York: Herder & Herder, 1970], p. 17). In contemporary theology there are efforts to rehabilitate the positive aspects of Thomas's theology of God without adopting the whole of his method and procedure.

Also influenced by Augustine but focusing on person rather than nature, Richard of St. Victor (d. 1173) and Bonaventure (d. 1274) used a more "social" than "psychological" analogy for the Trinity. Richard taught that God is the supreme instance of charity. Perfect charity requires not just two, a lover and beloved, but a third who is loved without jealousy or competition. Bonaventure, much like the Cappadocians, emphasized the monarchy of the Father who is self-diffusive and fecund and who created the whole world full of trinitarian vestiges.

After the medieval period there was very little development concerning the Trinity. Although the Reformers, especially John Calvin, were keen on the trinitarian creedal structure of Christian faith, they had no interest in furthering the medieval metaphysical project. In the nineteenth century, Friedrich Schleiermacher relegated the doctrine of the Trinity to an appendix in his work *The Christian Faith*. Palamism was discovered by the West and reinvigorated by the East in the twentieth century. In the last thirty years, the *Church Dogmatics* of Reformed theologian Karl Barth (d. 1968) and the monograph by Karl Rahner entitled *The Trinity* inaugurated the current renewal of trinitarian theology.

FUTURE DIRECTIONS AND REMAINING PROBLEMS

As of this writing the renaissance of interest in trinitarian theology is only in its beginning stages. In several denominations, but particularly within Catholic theology, the doctrine of the Trinity is being used as the foundation to explore issues in diverse areas such as spirituality, ethics, and ecclesiology. Since the concept of personhood lies at the heart of every trinitarian theology of God, this teaching forms the basis for reflection on the nature of the human person, especially the relationship between individual persons and communities or societies. For example, liberation and feminist theologians appeal to the trinitarian emphasis on the equality of persons to base their vision of egalitarian society. The "tract" approach to theology, according to which theological themes were treated separately as discrete topics with little bearing on each other, is gradually being overcome by a more unified vision of the theological enterprise. Amid these new developments, the following issues and questions will continue to require attention.

First, the classical approach to trinitarian doctrine was to treat the internal workings of the Trinity—how many divine Persons, how they were related to each other, how they were produced, what analogies might be found in the created order, and so forth. It has been amply shown in many current theological writings why this preoccupation with the so-called immanent Trinity is unsatisfactory. We live in an age that thinks in historical, personalist, and existential, rather than metaphysical and speculative terms. Thus the force of the doctrine of the Trinity must concern God's relationship with humankind not merely God's relationship with God. Questions of salvation are at the heart of every religion, and Christians believe that God is involved with humanity in a saving relationship that is transforming the face of the world. Contemporary theologians favor the "economic" approach to theological questions, which is a way of saying that because theological questions are inherently existential, they must be also treated in their practical and pastoral dimensions. This has required a fundamental reevaluation of the traditional framework of trinitarian theology, specifically, the relationship between "immanent" and "economic" Trinity, in such a way that the practical implications of the doctrine of the Trinity can be realized.

Second, the development of feminist theology over the last few decades has meant the reassessment of both the method and content of all areas of theology. The Christian tradition has presented God nearly exclusively in masculine concepts, images, metaphors, and stereotypes, even though it is one of the cardinal rules of theology that God exceeds all such depictions and can never be fully expressed in any one manner. The doctrine of the Trinity is particularly subject to the feminist critique because of the centrality of the metaphors of Father and Son. To meet feminist objections, contemporary theologians typically focus on the nonpatriarchal dimensions of these names for God or substitute nonsexual and/or feminine names for God (e.g., Eternal Source, Savior, Advocate), or emphasize the deeply egalitarian vision of human persons and human society implied by the doctrine of the Trinity. Liturgical experimentation is increasingly common, as the churches seek to overcome the oppressively patriarchal and one-sided image of God. In this instance the vast Christian tradition is both a rich resource and yet in other respect also needs to be overcome.

Third, some have called the modern period "the age of the Spirit," meaning a deemphasis on institutional religion and the crossing-over between and among disparate religious traditions. The Christian doctrine of God must be developed in light of the truth-claims of other world religions. This is not to compromise the uniqueness of the Christian tradition, but only to say that trinitarian doctrine need not be narrowly Christomonistic, in the sense that Jesus Christ is essential to every person's salvation, including the pious Hindu and Jew. Other paths to salvation cannot be denigrated but must be seen as part of God's universal plan of salvation. While Christians see this plan fully realized in Jesus Christ and must hold to this faith, it would be unrealistic to yearn for the days of a narrow-minded apologetics that saw all non-Christians as heathen.

Finally, theologians must continue to reflect on God within the context of the God-question of a particular age or race or nation. In an age where we are more aware of the global dimensions of human suffering, the classical depiction of God as immutable and passionless needs to be rethought from the perspective of trinitarian theology. Secular society brings its own unique questions and doubts about the God presented by traditional religion and classical theism. These challenges must be faced openly and honestly, bringing to bear the riches of the Christian tradition, where possible. Further, the current ecological crisis has generated fresh reflection on God's intent in making human beings stewards of creation. Science and religion must be seen as partners in search of the ultimate truth about the universe and all creatures in it.

Among the many resources that can enable trinitarian doctrine to once again stand at the center of Christian faith and to be a vital expression of that faith are: the voices and experience of those who have been on the margins of Christianity or of society but who testify nonetheless to the saving power of God; the insights of modern cultures, especially to the extent that cultural insights call the Church back to a more faithful witness to God's presence and mercy; the doubts and questions of unbelievers who continually press the Church toward greater truthfulness; the wisdom of other religious traditions; the collective wisdom of prayer and mystical experience, across religious traditions; and the liturgical and sacramental life of the churches.

See also creation; eternity; fatherhood of God; five ways of St. Thomas Aquinas; monotheism; providence; salvation; Trinity, doctrine of the.

Bibliography

Congar, Yves. *I Believe in the Holy Spirit.* 3 vols. New York: Seabury, 1983.
Hill, William J. *The Three-Personed God.* Washington, DC: University Press of America, 1983.
Kasper, Walter. *The God of Jesus Christ.* New York: Crossroad, 1985.
LaCugna, Catherine Mowry. *God for Us: The Trinity and Christian Life.* San Francisco: HarperCollins, 1991.
Rahner, Karl. *The Trinity.* New York: Herder & Herder, 1970.   *CATHERINE MOWRY LACUGNA*

Goldbrunner, Josef, b. 1910, German priest, educator, and author. Ordained in 1936, he is known for his spiritual writings, which emphasize the relationship between personal holiness and psychological health. His best known work is *Holiness is Wholeness* (Eng. trans., 1964).

Golden Legend, The, a popular collection of saints' lives compiled by the mid-1260s by the Dominican Jacobus de Voragine, providing concise readings for feast days according to the ecclesiastical calendar. The *Legend* draws upon earlier collections and was meant to be used by the clergy for sermon illustration and devotional reading. Originally in Latin, the *Legenda Aurea* or *Legenda Sanctorum* was soon translated into the vernacular languages of Europe, with William Caxton's translation (1483) being the most popular in English. Phenomenally successful in the later Middle Ages, it was criticized by humanists as catering to the crassest kind of credulity and superstition. Recent years have seen a renewed interest among historians, who see the *Legend* as reflective of late medieval piety and culture.

Golden Rose, a rose-shaped ornament blessed by the pope on the fourth Sunday of Lent. The custom of giving the Rose as an honor (usually to a royal recipient) originated in the early eleventh century.

Golden Rule, designation coined in the sixteenth century for the proverb "In everything do to others as you would have them do to you" (Matt 7:12; see also Luke 6:31). Taking the proverb from the sayings gospel, Q, Matthew added "for this is the law and the prophets," making it a summary principle; Luke set it among sayings on love stressing more than reciprocity (6:27–36). Early Christians cited it in both positive and negative ("silver rule") forms (e.g., "And what you hate, do not do to anyone," Job 4:15). The proverb was widely known before Christianity: Confucians, Greeks, Romans, and Jews all knew it.

Golgotha (gahl'guh-thuh). *See* Calvary, Mount.

Gonzaga, St. Aloysius. *See* Aloysius Gonzaga, St.

good, moral, the orientation of a person toward the fulfillment of human potential as manifested by habitual dispositions and human acts. Although the ultimate human fulfillment occurs through God's grace, a moral agent must also cooperate by developing dispositions and habits that dispose a person to perform right actions (the virtues). Such dispositions and habits make oneself and one's actions good, because they nourish one's ability to choose good under the proper circumstances and for the right reasons. Thus, a morally good choice differs from one that is morally right in that it not only observes the objectively correct order of values but also subserves the human fulfillment of the agent. *See also* evil, moral; virtue.

Good Friday, the first full day of the Easter Triduum, or the Friday in Holy Week, the day on which the Passion and death of Jesus are commemorated. The liturgy for the day is the most simple of all days during the liturgical year. The Liturgy of the Passion and Death of Our Lord consists of three parts: the Liturgy of the Word, the Veneration of the Cross, and the Service of Communion. The Liturgy of the Word begins in profound silence followed by an opening prayer. Readings are from Isa 52:13–53:12, Ps 31, and Heb 4:14–16, 5:7–9. The Passion from the Gospel of John (John 18:1–19:42) is proclaimed, sometimes by several lectors. An extended form of the intercessions concludes this part of the liturgy. A large cross is either unveiled or processed into the front of the church. During this unveiling or procession, the acclamation, "This is the Wood of the Cross on which hung the Savior of the World," is sung with its congregational response, "Come, let us worship." The acclamation is sung three times, after which members of the assembly approach the cross and venerate it. The Communion Service on Good Friday does not make this liturgy a Mass. The eucharistic bread consumed on Good Friday was consecrated on Holy Thursday evening, was solemnly adored through the evening until midnight, and was reserved in some other location through the night. After the Lord's Prayer, the Communion rite, and a short prayer, the ministers and assembly depart in silence. Good Friday is a day of fast and abstinence for Catholics. *See also* crucifixion; Holy Week; triduum.

JEFFREY T. VANDERWILT

Good Shepherd, the, one of the most ancient representations of Jesus Christ, based especially on John 10:1–42; Luke 15:3–7; Matt 18:12–14; Heb 13:20; 1 Pet 2:25; and 5:4. In early Christian art, Jesus Christ is frequently depicted as a young, beardless man either with a lamb on his shoulders or with a flute in his hand and protecting the sheep that gather around him. The image itself of the

Christ, the Good Shepherd, surrounded by his sheep, whom he loves and cares for (Luke 15:3-7; John 10:7-18); mosaic, in the Galla Placidia Mausoleum, Ravenna, Italy.

shepherd has pre-Christian origins. *See also* Jesus Christ.

Goretti, St. Maria, 1890–1902, virgin and martyr. An Italian child murdered while defending her chastity, she was canonized in the presence of her killer in 1950. Feast day: July 6.

Görres, Johann Joseph von (ger'rez), 1776–1848, German lay theologian and political philosopher. He defended a free Church independent of the state, without promoting Ultramontanism. The culmination of his research into mysticism can be found in his four-volume work *Christliche Mystik* (1836–42), but also significant were his contributions with the Catholic circle in Munich to the review *Eos* (1828–32) and the *Historisch-politische Blätter* (1838). *See also* mysticism.

gospel (Old Eng., *godspel,* "good news"), the message of God's salvific action in Christ and the accounts of Jesus' activity produced by the early Church. The simple sense is regularly found in Paul's Letters (e.g., Rom 1:1, 9; 1 Cor 9:12–14; Gal 1:11; 2:2; 1 Thess 1:5). The literary sense stems from the word's use in the opening of the Gospel of Mark (1:1).

Transmission of the gospel in the first sense was facilitated by brief formulations of the proclamation (Gk., *kerygma*) of essential events of Christ's Passion, death, and Resurrection, as in 1 Cor 15:1–5. Development of the literary genre is more complex.

The four Gospels (Matthew, Mark, Luke, and John) of the NT were built on oral and written traditions that probably included collections of sayings, miracle stories, and a passion narrative. The first three Gospels have much in common and are termed "synoptic" because they can be, for the most part, "viewed together." Most scholars believe that

Mark, written around A.D. 70, was the first of the Synoptics. Matthew and Luke, written in the 80s and 90s, independently used Mark alongside a collection of sayings of Jesus. Some scholars, however, still defend the priority of Matthew. The relationship of John to the Synoptics is uncertain. Although there are parallels in both sayings and deeds of Jesus, John, written in final form around A.D. 100, seems to have drawn on independent traditions for much of his story of Jesus.

In addition to the four canonical Gospels, early Christians produced numerous other works that reported the sayings or deeds of Jesus. These works, which did not win formal approbation by the Church, are usually termed "apocryphal" Gospels. *See also* apocryphal Gospels; evangelist; evangelization; infancy Gospels; synoptic Gospels.   HAROLD W. ATTRIDGE

Gospel book, the liturgical book containing the readings from the Gospels used during Mass. Ornately embroidered or jewel-encrusted bindings were common from the eighteenth century onward. The Gospel book is accorded all the honors due a symbol of Christ's presence. When carried in procession it may be flanked by candles and preceded by incense. *See also* gospel.

Gothic. *See* Catholicism and architecture.

Gothic spirituality, a form of asceticism and style of art that emphasized the humanity of Jesus, especially his suffering and Crucifixion, in increasingly realistic ways. An urban intellectual world of theologians and university scholars preoccupied with the meaning of symbols established the foundations of Gothic spirituality in the early twelfth century. Major influences included the mathematical and cosmological speculations of scholars at Chartres, such as William of Conches (ca. 1080–1154), who described the hierarchy of the universe in terms of a golden chain, and the legacy of the mystical theology of Pseudo-Dionysius the Areopagite, a fifth-century Syrian writer confused with St. Denis, patron saint of France. A commentary on the Pseudo-Dionysian *Celestial Hierarchy* by Hugh (d. 1142), of the Parisian abbey of St. Victor, led to a more nuanced understanding of the Neoplatonic idea that the material world leads beyond itself to God. Hugh of St. Victor redefined the notion to mean that only through the humanity of the suffering and ascended Christ can one understand the created world as a source of God's self-revelation.

The translucency of glass and jewels, the weightlessness, harmony, and unity of Gothic architecture symbolically expressed the ineffable presence of God, the immaterial True Light to which the believer aspired to ascend. Theological emphasis on the humanity of Christ encouraged the emerging realism of the sculptural tradition, presenting in an increasingly more naturalistic style images affirming a popular perception of the presence of God in everyday life. Out of this climate arose theological and artistic interest in new themes of popular religiosity, including the cult of the Virgin, the *Pietà* (It., "pity"), the Man of Sorrows, and the Crucifixion. *See also* Gothic style.　　　MARCHITA MAUCK

Gothic style, French architectural development. Gothic style originates at the royal abbey church of St.-Denis near Paris, rebuilt by Abbot Suger between 1137–44. It represents a new spirit, combining pointed arches and ribbed groin vaults with harmonious mathematical proportions, and a quest for luminosity, expressed by translucent walls of stained glass invisibly supported by exterior buttresses. Derived from cosmological speculations and interpretations of the mystical treatises of Pseudo-Dionysius the Areopagite (a fifth-century Neoplatonic writer confused with St. Denis, patron saint of France), Gothic style symbolically expresses both the rationality of divine creation and the ineffable presence of the Divine. *See also* Catholicism and architecture; Gothic spirituality.

The interior of the basilica of St.-Denis, a Gothic church located in Paris and the burial place of many French kings.

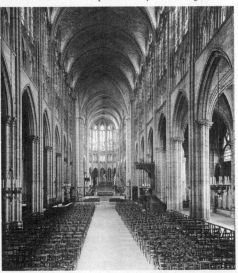

Gothic vestments, a style of chasuble, the sleeveless outer garment worn by priests and bishops presiding at the Eucharist. The Gothic style of chasuble extends from the collar to the midportion of the forearm. It drapes from the shoulders to the knees or midcalf in both front and rear panels. The Gothic style contrasts with the baroque, "fiddle-back" chasuble which covered the shoulders and upper torso only. The Gothic style found its champions in the Cambridge movement of the nineteenth century and has since become the standard style of chasuble for the Roman Catholic and many Protestant churches. *See also* Gothic style; vestments.

Gottschalk of Orbais, ca. 808–ca. 867, Carolingian theologian. A child oblate at Fulda, Gottschalk as an adult attempted to escape the childhood vows but was frustrated in these attempts by his abbot, Rabanus Maurus. Gottschalk's teaching of double predestination (to eternal life and eternal death) sparked widespread controversy and led archbishop Hincmar of Reims to imprison him at Hautvilliers, where he died. *See also* predestination.

Goupil, St. René, 1606–42, missionary, North American martyr, patron saint of anesthetists. Born in France and trained as a surgeon, he went to Quebec as a lay assistant to Jesuit missionaries among the Hurons. He was captured and killed by the Iroquois, along with Isaac Jogues and others. Feast day: October 19. *See also* North American martyrs.

Grabar (grah-bahr'), classical Armenian, an Indo-European language and the liturgical language of the Armenian Orthodox and Catholic churches. The invention of the Armenian alphabet ca. 400 inaugurated the Golden Age of Armenian literature. Grabar is the language in which Armenian Christian literature of late antiquity and the Middle Ages is written. Now a dead language, Grabar—and hence the liturgy—is not understood by speakers of modern East and West Armenian. *See also* Armenian rite.

Grabmann, Martin, 1875–1949, theologian and historian of medieval Scholastic theology and philosophy. By 1918 professor of theology at Munich, Grabmann made great contributions in manuscript research, discovering lost works of important theologians, and in charting the evolution of Scholastic thought. *See also* Scholasticism.

GRACE

Grace is God's free and forgiving self-communication that enables humans to share in the trinitarian relationship of love. A search for the biblical roots of the term cannot be limited to Hebrew and Greek words translated as "grace," since the mystery of God's saving love is central throughout the Scriptures. In the Hebrew Scriptures God's favor is the liberating power behind the Exodus event, the creative energy that is the source of all that is, the faithful covenant relationship that God constantly extends to Israel in spite of betrayal, and the firm and reliable promise of God to provide future salvation for all creation.

In the Christian Scriptures Jesus embodies God's covenant love and offer of salvation. In the life, death, and Resurrection of Jesus the early Christians experienced the power and presence of God's love. The risen Jesus bestows the gift of the Holy Spirit on the Christian community; through Baptism, Christians are granted an unmerited share in the relationship between Jesus and the Father. Paul explicitly identifies Jesus Christ as the *charis* (Gk., "grace") of God and describes this Christian experience of God's mercy and favor with such diverse terms as salvation, redemption, sanctification, freedom, transformation, new creation, reconciliation, and justification. Paul emphasizes that grace is freely given as a gift to the baptized; it is totally unmerited and cannot be earned through any works of the law. Paul also uses the term "grace" (*charisma*) to refer to the variety of gifts bestowed on individuals in the Christian community "for building up the body of Christ" (Eph 4:12). A complete theology of grace in the Christian Scriptures would include not only the Pauline emphasis on forgiving love, but also the notions of divine indwelling (John 14:23) and of God's freely bestowed favor that planned and destined humankind in love before the foundation of the world (Eph 1:3–14).

EARLY CHRISTIAN PERSPECTIVES: EAST AND WEST

In general, the emphasis among the early Christian writers in the Eastern (Greek-speaking) tradition was on divinization or participation in divine life, while the emphasis in the (Latin-speaking) West was on the healing aspect of grace as salvation from sin.

The Eastern tradition developed the mystical and sacramental symbolism of the Johannine writings and the passage from 2 Peter that proclaims Christians to be "participants of the divine nature" (2 Pet 1:4). The accent on divinization (or deification) was connected with reflection on the incarnation ("He became human that we might become divine"; Irenaeus *Against Heresies* 4.28.1) and the indwelling of the Holy Spirit ("If the Spirit is not divine, how are we divinized?"—a motif popularized by the Cappadocian Fathers). Manifest in the many texts and rites of the liturgy, the Eastern tradition emphasized that Christians come to share the divine life through participation in the sacraments, preeminently Baptism and the Eucharist. Eastern theologies of the incarnation included with the divinizing effects of the incarnation the healing grace of redemption, since in Christ all humanity is reunited with God. Because death, rather than guilt, was viewed as the major consequence of sin in the East, many writers stressed that a special effect of grace is immortality; we become, like God, incorruptible, immortal. The Eastern doctrine of divine "energies," uncreated forces or powers distinct from the divine essence by which God creates and divinizes the world, provided a way of speaking of God's immanence while respecting the transcendence and inaccessibility of the divine.

The Western approach to a theology of grace is influenced markedly by Augustine of Hippo (d. 430), whose language and categories for grace, sin, and psychology set the stage for centuries of theological disputes. The mystery of grace is at the heart of Augustine's writings, which include a sacramental view of reality that sees the "vestiges of the Trinity" present throughout creation, an inner desire for God at the core of every human heart, and Baptism as a share in the inner divine life of love. However, the controversy between Augustine and Pelagius determined Augustine's strong emphasis on grace as a divine force liberating the human will from the bondage of sin.

Pelagius, a British spiritual director in Rome at the beginning of the fifth century, emphasized the moral responsibility of the baptized to live a "new life in Christ." He reasoned that if we are responsible to keep God's law, we must be able to do so; the God-given ability to choose between good and evil is itself a grace of God. In response, Augustine stressed the damage done to human nature by original sin, interpreted as the bondage of the human will that results from sin. The ability to live the Christian life is sheer gift: "Command what you wish, but give what you command" (*Confessions* 10.29).

Augustine argued that grace is necessary to heal and liberate the freedom (Lat., *libertas*) that is at the core of the human person. Grace is the internal assistance of the Holy Spirit that releases one from the bondage of sin, illuminates the mind, and provides a new delight in the good. Augustine's view on the necessity and gratuity of grace became the teaching of the Church and received lasting recommendation with the condemnation of Pelagianism at the Council of Carthage (418) and the later condemnation of semi-Pelagianism at the Council of Orange (529). Due to ecclesial approval and the depth and breadth of his thought, Augustine gained extraordinary authority in subsequent centuries.

THE MEDIEVAL SYNTHESIS OF THOMAS AQUINAS

Both the Eastern and Western Christian traditions on grace were integrated into a systematic approach to the mystery of the relationship between the trinitarian God and human persons in the medieval synthesis of Thomas Aquinas (d. 1274). Aquinas's theology of grace cannot be limited to the tract on grace in the *Summa Theologiae* but rather pervades his systematic writings as well as his biblical commentaries. The very structure of the *Summa Theologiae* suggests that everything comes from God and is meant to return to God. While incorporating Augustine's emphasis on grace as healing, Aquinas developed the Eastern tradition on divinization through the notion of participation in the divine life of love.

In the medieval textbook the *Sentences,* Peter Lombard had identified grace, charity, and the Holy Spirit with one another. Aquinas, on the other hand, made a distinction between "uncreated grace"—the very inner life of the Trinity—and "created grace"—the effects that being drawn into that life of love have on humans. Aquinas described grace not only as healing human nature that had been wounded by sin, but also as elevating human nature to what is beyond merely human capacity—participation in the divine nature through friendship with the Trinity. To preserve the integrity and autonomy of the human yet account for the profound transformation of the person by grace, Aquinas drew on Aristotle's natural philosophy and psychology.

According to Aristotle, reality can be understood as a system of natures with capacities and operations proportioned to their final goal (Gk., *telos*). Because the final goal of human beings is life in union with God, a goal that remains beyond human capacity, Aquinas concluded that an "elevation" of human nature is necessary if humans are to reach their goal. This inner transformation of the human soul through the indwelling of the Holy Spirit expands fundamental human capacities and operations through the theological virtues of faith, hope, and charity. Grace enables persons to share in the relationship of mutual friendship with the trinitarian mystery of God. What is "natural" to the Trinity is extended to humans "by adoption." Finally Aquinas's theology of grace as a special kind of "habit" or "quality" emphasized the perduring presence of the Spirit in Christians.

TRENT'S RESPONSE TO THE REFORMERS

Throughout the fifteenth through the twentieth centuries, Thomas's subtle distinctions were often misunderstood. To emphasize that grace was a free gift, theologians began to speak of "pure nature" with its own "natural end" as separate from a higher "supernatural" destiny. Many considered grace a transient impulse necessary for salvation that could be increased by good works and prayer, but that remained elusive, temporary, fragile. Teachings from the Augustinian and Franciscan schools, about predestination and the sovereignty and freedom of God, prompted fear of God's arbitrary will and absolute power. Disturbed by both the arbitrary power of God and the rampant "works righteousness" of the devotional practices of the time, the Augustinian monk Martin

Luther turned to the Pauline doctrine of justification by faith and by grace alone. According to Luther's interpretation, the "justice" or "righteousness" of God (Rom 1:17) imputes the redemptive works of Christ to believers without any work or merit on their part. Those who have been "acquitted" or "declared righteous" remain at the same time both justified and sinners (Lat., *simul justus et peccator*). The Reformers argued that "righteousness" refers to God's righteousness or justice; the grace of Christ is an "alien righteousness."

The Council of Trent (1545–63) in its Decree on Justification gave an official Catholic response to the Reformers' theologies. Trent argued that justification is not only a remission of sins, but the radical transformation of the baptized. This renovation of the human soul by habitual (sanctifying) grace is such that the unjust person moves from "being an enemy" to friendship with God. This inner transformation (grace inheres in the just) fashions the human being as capable of meritorious actions that are totally God's initiative but that are also fully actions of the person. While Trent talks about good works done in Christ meriting a reward, the document on justification reaffirms the primacy, gratuity, and necessity of grace and underscores that merit is really God's crowning of God's gifts (an expression taken from Augustine).

After the Council of Trent, the Catholic theology of grace focused on a variety of disputes over the nature of created grace, distinctions between sanctifying and "actual" (assisting) grace, the relationship of grace and human freedom, questions of predestination and God's universal salvific will, and the relationship of nature and grace. Various positions were represented by different schools (Salamanca, Paris, Louvain) or orders (Jesuits, Franciscans, Augustinians, Dominicans). Dominicans and Jesuits debated the relationship between grace and human freedom (*De Auxiliis* controversy, 1597–1607), a question that remains open even to this day. With the censures of the forty propositions of Baius (1567) and the teachings of Cornelius Jansen (1653), both God's universal salvific will and the possibility of human rejection of God's grace were reaffirmed.

TWENTIETH-CENTURY PERSPECTIVES

By the twentieth century, the post-Tridentine focus on diverse kinds of "actual" graces and the sharp separation of a human "natural finality" as distinct from a supernatural goal known only from revelation resulted in a major problem. Many Catholics did not see how the doctrine of grace had any connection with a lasting, sovereign love of God or with their human experience. Rooted in the biblical, patristic, and liturgical renewal of the early twentieth century, a variety of theologians attempted to restore the central focus of the theology of grace to the mystery of God's self-communication in love.

Retrieving Augustine's experiential approach to grace and Aquinas's more nuanced view of the relationship of nature and grace, Henri de

Lubac (1991), Karl Rahner (1984), Pierre Teilhard de Chardin (1955), Edward Schillebeeckx, and others proposed ways of preserving not only the transcendence and gratuity of God's self-offer, but also the immanent desire for grace rooted in the human heart. De Lubac insisted that grace is both a truly "natural desire" of human beings and an utterly free offer on God's part, since friendship is never "deserved" or "owed" even between human beings. Rahner agreed that a desire for God (whether conscious or not) is a fundamental orientation of every human being. Rahner insisted that this real and concrete, if silent and unexpressed, orientation of human existence should be called a "supernatural existential" to indicate that it is an utterly gratuitous gift of God that need not have been.

Rahner restored the Catholic theology of grace by reemphasizing the trinitarian presence of God's self-communication ("uncreated grace") and by drawing together human nature and divine grace. He advanced the discussion on both the universality of grace outside of Christian Baptism and the ways people experience grace. Emphasizing God's universal salvific will and yet maintaining the Christian conviction that Jesus Christ is the unique mediator of grace/salvation, Rahner explained that when people live their ordinary lives in fidelity to the truth discovered in the depths of their hearts, they are responding to God's self-offer in Christ whether they are aware of that or not. Grace encompasses all persons and seeks to touch or heal their lives at a depth.

The Belgian theologian Piet Fransen (1983) described grace in psychological categories. How did grace touch consciousness? He emphasized that God's grace promotes an interior harmony by transforming, deepening, and healing freedom with all of its powers, hopes, and impulses.

Emphasizing the social and political dimensions of grace, the Flemish Dominican Edward Schillebeeckx maintains that the Christian experience of God's saving presence has to be rethought in a world of secularization and excessive, senseless human suffering. Grace and salvation are to be found in fragmentary experiences where the flourishing of humanity is encouraged and nurtured and in human efforts to protest and resist evil as well as to stand in solidarity with those who suffer ("God's cause is the human cause").

Liberation theologians criticize an overly individualistic approach to grace and translate the traditional Catholic emphasis on grace as mediated and the importance of human cooperation into social and structural terms. Gustavo Gutiérrez, Leonardo Boff, Juan Luis Segundo, and others probe the meaning of grace as the liberating power and presence of God in the context of the social and political "disgrace" of Central and South America.

Feminist liberation theologians have begun to reflect on grace both in psychological categories more descriptive of the experience of conversion for women and in social terms of critiquing patriarchal systems and structures. In many varied contexts, liberation theologians insist that the conversion that grace empowers is both a gift and a task that has been entrusted to human beings and specifically to Christian communities.

Recent theological reflection is beginning to grapple with the mystery of God's presence throughout the cosmos as the broader context for a theology of grace. In dialogue with the natural sciences and the growing ecological movement, theologians are extending their reflections on grace to include God's relationship with all forms of life in this universe and beyond. The mystery of God's love and presence extends beyond human experience or the history of salvation (no matter how broadly defined) to the mystery of God's creation.

See also deification; free will; Holy Spirit; justification; nature and grace; Pelagianism; predestination; sanctification.

Bibliography

Boff, Leonardo. *Liberating Grace*. Maryknoll, NY: Orbis Books, 1979.
Fransen, Piet. *The New Life of Grace*. New York: Seabury, 1969.
Haight, Roger. *The Experience and Language of Grace*. New York: Paulist Press, 1979.
Rondet, Henri. *The Grace of Christ*. Philadelphia: Westminster, 1966.
Schillebeeckx, Edward. *Christ: The Experience of Jesus as Lord*. New York: Crossroad, 1980.

MARY C. HILKERT

grace, actual, divine assistance given for a particular need or action. Following the Council of Trent (1545–63), treatises on grace were divided into two parts: sanctifying or habitual grace (the inner, permanent transformation of the human person or soul), and actual grace (the divine assistance that moves the person to do good). Disputes ensued (lasting until Vatican II [1962–65]) regarding the existence, necessity, and gratuity of actual grace, its further subdivisions, its compatibility with human freedom, and the notion of merit.

The theology of actual grace attempted to preserve the twofold teaching of the Church that grace is absolutely necessary for every salutary human act (against Pelagianism and semi-Pelagianism) and yet that grace can be resisted (against Jansenism). The danger was that grace gradually came to be viewed as a quantity through which God moves or elevates the human soul, rather than as the relationship between God and human persons. Contemporary theologians note that the mystery of grace comprises both God's self-gift and God's enabling human beings to be open to, and faithful to, that relationship. *See also* grace; Jansenism; merit; Pelagianism; semi-Pelagianism.

grace, cooperating, the action of the Holy Spirit that enables the human response to God's initial action in the divine-human relationship. Totally dependent on the prior initiative of God (operating grace), cooperating grace empowers the human response in both initial conversion and the ongoing living of the Christian life. *See also* grace.

grace, habitual, another term for sanctifying grace, or the abiding presence of God in the soul. Drawing on the Aristotelian term "habit," Thomas Aquinas (d. 1274) identified sanctifying grace as "habitual" to explain the profound effect that God's friendship has on the human person. Being drawn into participation in the divine life of love, human persons are transformed at the core of their being—recreated in love. In classic terminology, grace elevates and heals human nature, vivifying the personality in a new way, giving it new capacities (virtues, gifts, charisms) that enable the human person to enter into relationship with God and Christian discipleship. This "state of grace" or "habitual grace" (terms popular from the seventeenth to the twentieth centuries) is a dynamic life-principle given to the person, an orientation to act in accord with the love with which God has first loved us and with the Spirit of the Risen Christ dwelling within us. *See also* grace; grace, sanctifying.

grace, operating, a term used to emphasize the priority of God's free initiative in the divine-human relationship, as distinct from the subsequent gift that enables and elicits human response (cooperating grace). Operating grace can refer either to a principle of life (God's love effects justification and sanctification) or an activity (God moves the human person to act). *See also* grace.

grace, sacramental, the self-communication of God that takes place through the celebration and reception of the sacraments. The sacraments are more than signs bereft of content. They are effective signs or announcements of God's power and love and God's desire to confer a particular kind of help and presence based on the way God communicated to humankind in Christ. Thus, in the sacrament of Anointing, Christ's continuing work is seen of healing the sick through the ministry of the Church; in Reconciliation, the grace of God's forgiveness is conferred and celebrated; and in the Eucharist, the grace of the presence of Christ is received in the context of the worshiping community. *See also* grace; sacrament.

grace, sanctifying, the effect of the self-communication of God by which we are made holy, transformed into "participants of the divine nature" (2 Pet 1:4). To speak of grace as sanctifying is to focus not only on the forgiveness of sins, but also on other aspects of the mystery of the divine-human relationship: becoming adopted children of God, incorporation into Christ, friendship with God, participation in the divine life, and the indwelling of the Trinity.

The Protestant Reformers claimed that sins, personal and original, are forgiven in Christ but with a righteousness that remains an "alien righteousness." The Council of Trent (1545–63) insisted that the essence of justification consists not only in the forgiveness of sins, but in the sanctification and renovation of the inner person by God's love. The person ceases to be a sinner and "becomes just" (DS 1528).

Using Scholastic categories, Catholics spoke of sanctifying grace as "infused" or "inherent" in the human person. Thomas Aquinas (d. 1274) had described the transformation of the human person in love as "habitual grace"—the radical vitalization of the human soul in such a way that human persons are truly drawn into friendship with God and can be said to be in the "state of grace." One can grow in grace through a life of virtue; God's gifts become our merit. According to Trent, it is possible to lose sanctifying grace by grave (mortal) personal sin. The relationship with God can be restored through the sacrament of Penance (now called Reconciliation). *See also* grace; Holy Spirit; sanctification.

MARY C. HILKERT

grace at meals (Lat., *gratia,* "thanks"), the practice of prayer before the sharing of food. The grace acknowledges God as the source of all blessings, especially of food and of other forms of material and psychological sustenance. Graces express the desire that Christ will be present in the communion of meal-sharing, that he will bless both the food and the sharers of food.

A simple, yet common, Catholic grace is used before meals: "Bless us, O Lord, and these your gifts which we are about to receive from your goodness. Through Christ our Lord. Amen."

grace, efficacious, grace that always produces its effect. From the sixteenth to the twentieth centuries grace was viewed largely in mechanical categories expressing modes of moving the human will. In terms of this "actual grace" an extensive dispute arose over predestination and the relationship between grace and human freedom (*De Auxiliis* controversy, 1597–1607). If God's grace were infallibly efficacious, i.e., if it always achieved its effect, how could the freedom of the human person be preserved? Emphasizing human freedom and responsibility, Luis de Molina (d. 1600) maintained that God's grace is sufficient for salvation, but only becomes efficacious upon its acceptance by the human person. God's decree of predestination to salvation logically follows upon a divine foreknowledge of a person's merits. Domingo Báñez (d. 1604) stressed in his theology of grace a divine movement and argued that those who are predestined receive "efficacious" grace to respond freely to the offer of salvation, a grace in time prior to the decisions or actions of the human person. A Vatican examination permitted both positions. The relationship between grace and human freedom remains an open theological question to this day. *See also De Auxiliis;* grace.

grace of happy death, dying in the state of grace. Prayer for the "grace of final perseverance"

recognizes that our relationship with God is utterly dependent on God's initiative and fidelity. While noting that we cannot have absolute certitude about final salvation, the Council of Trent (1545–63) exhorts "a most secure hope" that God will bring to perfection what God has begun. *See also* death and dying.

grace of office, one of the diverse charisms or gifts that the Holy Spirit bestows on church ministers to be used for the sake of the common good (1 Cor 12:7). The charism for leadership in the Christian community, publicly recognized and commissioned through ordination, enables the ordained to exercise the ministry to which they have been called. *See also* ordination.

Gradual (Lat., *gradus,* "step"), the psalm verse(s) sung between the first lesson (scriptural reading) and the Alleluia or Tract (a psalm sung "straight through" without a responsory) in the Mass prior to its revision following Vatican II (1962–65). Originally sung "on the steps" of the chancel, the Gradual has been replaced by the responsorial psalm. Gradual also refers to the liturgical books in which one finds the chants for Mass.

Graham, Aelred, 1907–84, English Benedictine, ecumenist, and spiritual writer. He advanced a spirituality that bridges both Western (Catholic) and Eastern (Buddhist) traditions.

Grail, international women's movement. Founded by Dutch Jesuit Jacques van Ginneken in 1921, it is dedicated to the development of laywomen's leadership in the Church. Lydwine van Kersbergen and Joan Overboss established Grail in the Chicago archdiocese in 1940. Its headquarters moved later to Loveland, Ohio.

Granada, Luis de, 1504–88, Spanish Dominican preacher and spiritual author. He pioneered methods of interior mental prayer adapted to the needs of laypeople. His treatises *On Prayer* (1544) and *Sinner's Guide* (1567) were popular throughout Europe, influencing Francis de Sales and Vincent de Paul.

Gratian (gray'shen), twelfth-century Italian jurist who taught canon law at Bologna during the 1130s and 1140s and died sometime before 1160. Around 1140, Gratian completed his *Concordia Discordantium Canonum* (Lat., "Concordance of Discordant

Canons"), also known as the *Decretum*. This massive compilation of nearly 4000 canonical rulings, gathered into 101 *distinctiones* ("distinctions") and 36 *causae* ("cases"), quickly became the standard canon law textbook and continued in use until the Church's legal reforms of 1917. *See also* canon law; *Decretum Gratianum*.

Gravissimum Educationis (grah-vi'see-moom ed-joo-kah-tsee-oh'nees). *See* Declaration on Christian Education.

gravitas materiae (grahv'i-tahs mah-teer'ee-ay; Lat., "gravity of matter"), the gravity or importance of the basic meaning of an action. For a sin to qualify as a serious sin, three requirements were ordinarily demanded: grave matter, sufficiently full knowledge, and full consent. Only those violations that caused serious harm to persons or to the social order were viewed as grave matters and were likely to involve serious sin. *See also* mortal sin; sin.

Great Church, a term used in late antiquity and modern Greek for the principal church of an area, the cathedral or church of the bishop. It was used without further specification for the first cathedral of Constantinople, and for the two later churches, also called Hagia Sophia, on the same site. By extension, it was also used to refer to the Church of Constantinople. Some theologians use the term to designate the Church Catholic, the universal Church and its orthodox traditions. *See also* cathedral; Church; Hagia Sophia.

Great Doxology, a fourth-century liturgical hymn that opens with the words "Glory to God in the highest heaven, and on earth peace among those whom he favors" of Luke 2:14. The chant is used liturgically in the Western Mass, and, in the East, in Matins (except among the Maronites), as well as in Compline in some traditions. It is called "great" to distinguish it from the "lesser" doxology or "Glory be to the Father. . . ." Later Byzantine nomenclature, which distinguishes between the "great" Gloria (Lat., "Glory [to God]") chanted at festive Matins celebrated on feasts and the "lesser" one at ferial Matins and Compline celebrated on weekdays, without a special feast, is erroneous. The Great Doxology is substantially the same in both cases. The Gloria at ferial Matins is a late development. *See also* doxology; *Gloria in Excelsis*.

Great Entrance, or "Major Introit," the transfer of gifts or offertory procession of the Byzantine and Armenian Eucharists, formerly found in the West Syrian rite. One of the principal symbolic rites of the Byzantine liturgy, the Great Entrance comprises the opening ritual act of the second, eucharistic half of the service. In this solemn procession, performed during the chant of the Byzantine Cherubicon hymn, the clergy carry the gifts of bread and wine from the prothesis, or altar of preparation, to the main altar. The ritual prefigures Christ's coming to us in the sacrament of his body and blood, and is called "great" to distinguish it from the first or "Little Entrance," which opens the Liturgy of the Word. *See also* introit; Little Entrance.

Great Lent, Byzantine-rite term for Lent, to distinguish from the other three Byzantine "Lents" or penitential periods before the feasts of Christmas, Sts. Peter and Paul (June 29), and Dormition (Assumption, August 15). Great Lent, as in other Eastern traditions, begins on the Monday before Western Ash Wednesday and ends before Holy Week, which is not considered a part of Lent. *See also* Lent.

Great Schism, 1378–1417, also known as the Great Western Schism, period of crisis in the Church in which two and then three rival popes claimed papal authority. (The term "Great Schism" is also sometimes used to refer to the division between Eastern and Western Christendom after 1054, when papal legates and the patriarch of Constantinople mutually excommunicated each other.)

After the death of Pope Gregory XI in 1378, who had returned the papacy to Rome from Avignon in 1377, his successor's election was interrupted by violence among the citizenry, who demanded an Italian pope. Panic-stricken, the cardinals elected Bartolomeo Prignano as Pope Urban VI (April 8, 1378). Despite his piety and administrative skills, Urban's unstable behavior and determination to increase papal authority alienated many cardinals, who then raised doubts about his election's validity. Abandoning Rome, virtually the same college that elected Urban now rejected him and chose Cardinal Robert of Geneva as Pope Clement VII (September 10, 1378). England, the Holy Roman Empire, and most of Italy sided with Urban VI, while France, Sicily, Scotland, Naples, and Spain championed Clement in Avignon. Among monasteries, religious orders, bishoprics, and even parishes, confusion reigned as appointees from each camp contended for the same authority.

The spirit of conciliarism, a movement with roots in the early thirteenth century, resurfaced with new force in response to the crisis. Adherents argued that since a general council had supreme authority in Christendom, even over the pope, a general council should be convened at once to resolve the problem. In 1409 cardinals from both obediences (the Roman, Gregory XII, and the Avignon, Benedict XIII) called the Council of Pisa, which deposed both Benedict XIII (Clement's successor) and Gregory XII (Urban's successor, following Boniface IX and Innocent VII), and elected Alexander V (1409). Neither Benedict nor Gregory accepted the council's decision, leaving the Church now with three popes instead of two. Finally, with the help of the Emperor Sigismund, the Council of Constance (1414–18) was convened and it deposed Alexander's successor, John XXIII. Gregory resigned, Benedict fled, and Martin V was elected. *See also* conciliarism; Constance, Council of; Eastern Schism; papacy, the. w. DAVID MYERS

Great Week, traditional name for Holy Week in the Christian East since the fourth century. It is still the common term for Holy Week in the Byzantine rite. *See also* Holy Week.

greca (grek'ah; It., "Greek"; perhaps a corruption of Eng., "great coat"), a long overcoat worn by European clergy over the cassock. It is suggested that because the coat resembled one worn by Greek or Byzantine clergy it assumed the name greca.

Greek Catholic Church, the Catholic counterpart to the Greek Orthodox Church in Greece and Turkey. The creation of such communities became possible after 1829 when Ottoman sultan Mohammed II removed his non-Latin Catholic subjects from the civil authority of the Orthodox patriarchs.

A Latin priest, John Marangos, began missionary work among the Greek Orthodox in Constantinople in 1856 and eventually formed a very small group of Byzantine Catholics. In 1878 Marangos died and was succeeded by Polycarp Anastasiadis, a former student at the Orthodox Theological School at Halki. In the 1880s Byzantine Catholic communities were also formed in two villages in Thrace.

In 1895 the French Assumptionist Fathers began work in Constantinople, where they founded a seminary and two small Greek Byzantine parishes. These Assumptionists were distinguished above all for the valuable scholarly studies they produced on the Eastern churches.

In 1911 Pope Pius X created an apostolic exarchate for the Byzantine Catholics in Turkey and named Isaias Papadopoulos as first bishop. He was succeeded in 1920 by Bishop George Calavassy (d. 1957). It was his task to oversee the immigration of virtually the entire Byzantine Catholic community of Constantinople to Athens and those of the two villages in Thrace to a town in Macedonia. This was part of a general exchange of populations that took place between Greece and Turkey in the 1920s. In view of this new situation, the Holy See erected a separate apostolic exarchate in Athens for Byzantine Catholics in Greece in 1923.

Although their appearance in Greece caused tension with the local Orthodox hierarchy, these Greek Catholics were determined to serve their neighbors by works of charity and social assistance. In 1944 they founded Pammakaristos hospital in Athens, which became known as one of the best in the nation.

The Greek Orthodox Church continues to oppose the existence of this church, which it views as a gratuitous creation of the Catholic Church in Orthodox territory. It is still illegal in Greece for Catholic priests to dress in a way typical of Orthodox clergy. In 1975 a new bishop was appointed for the Byzantine Catholics in Greece over the strong objections of the Orthodox archbishop of Athens.

The community remains very small, numbering in total about 2,350. In Greece, most of the faithful live in Athens, while in Turkey there is still one small parish in Istanbul. Currently eleven priests serve in Greece and one in Istanbul. All of them are celibate and originally of the Latin rite. *See also* Byzantine rite; Eastern churches; Eastern rites; Greek Catholics; Greek rite. RONALD G. ROBERSON

Greek Catholics, term used, especially in the Austro-Hungarian Empire, for Ruthenian and Romanian Byzantine or "Greek-rite" Catholics, to distinguish them from "Latin-rite Catholics." After Greece became an independent country in 1830 the term "Greek Catholics," which could also refer to Catholic citizens of Greece regardless of rite, became a source of confusion. In the twentieth century the term "Byzantine Catholics" largely replaced "Greek Catholics," but the latter name has become current again in the 1990s, especially in areas where Byzantine Catholic churches, suppressed by the Communists after World War II, have recovered their freedom. *See also* Ruthenian Catholic Church; uniatism.

Greek College, the Pontifical Greek College of St. Athanasius, oldest of the Roman colleges for Eastern Catholic seminarians, located in Rome. Erected by Pope Gregory XIII in 1576, the college has been administered by various groups of clergy, most notably the Jesuits (1591–1602, 1621–1773, 1890–97). Closed for lack of funds in 1803, the college was reopened in 1835, then reformed and assigned by Pope Leo XIII, in 1897, to the Belgian Benedictines, who are still in charge of it. Its early alumni, not just ethnic Greeks but other "Greek (i.e., non-Latin) Catholics," included Albanians, Melkites, Romanians, and Slavic Ruthenians. The college has produced many notable alumni, including such Greeks as Leo Allatius (1586–1669), versatile scholar and Vatican librarian, and Peter Arcudius (ca. 1562–1633), controversialist and defender of the union of the Orthodox with Rome. Later, separate colleges were opened for such "Greek Catholic" nations as the Ruthenians (1897), Russians (1929), and Romanians (1936). Today the Greek College serves both Latin and Byzantine Catholic seminarians from Greece, as well as the Melkites and Italo-Albanians.

Greek rite, older synonym for the Byzantine rite. The earlier name dates back to the pre–Vatican II period (before 1962) when "Greek rite (or Mass)" and "Latin rite (or Mass)," common if inaccurate names for the Byzantine and Roman rites, were correlative contrasting terms in Latin ecclesiastical nomenclature. *See also* Byzantine rite.

Greeley, Andrew Moran, b. 1928, priest, sociologist, novelist, and columnist. Ordained priest in the archdiocese of Chicago in 1954, Greeley earned a Ph.D. in sociology from the University of Chicago in 1961 and served as director of the National Opinion Research Center in Chicago from 1961 to 1973. Since 1978 he has been professor of sociology at the University of Arizona and since 1991 professor of social science at the University of Chicago. He is the author of many works of nonfiction and fiction, including *Unsecular Man* (1974), *The Communal Catholic* (1976), and *The Cardinal Sins* (1981), and is one of the most widely quoted Catholics in America.

Greene, Graham, 1904–91, English novelist, critic, and playwright. One of the premier English men of letters in the twentieth century, he converted to the Catholic faith in 1926. His struggles with religious faith in a bleak world are best reflected in a trilogy of "Catholic" novels: *The Power and the Glo-*

ry (1940), *The Heart of the Matter* (1948), and *The End of the Affair* (1951), although there had been hints of these interests in his 1938 novel, *Brighton Rock*. Similar religious themes occur in two of his plays: *The Living Room* (1953) and *The Potting Shed* (1958).

In his later career, he was increasingly a religious skeptic, once describing himself as a "Catholic atheist." His later fiction reflected his restless travels, his commitment to left-wing politics (as well as a persistent antipathy toward the United States), and his continuing interest in issues of heroism as a form of saintliness and the ambiguity of human existence. He published the first volume of his autobiography in 1971 (*A Sort of Life*), with a second volume in 1989, *Ways of Escape*.

Gregorian calendar, the modern calendar. By the thirteenth century mathematicians had become aware that the Julian calendar (introduced by Julius Caesar) with its 365 1/4 days, made the year eleven minutes too long, producing a growing inconsistency between the real vernal equinox and the calendar. Since Easter and the moveable feasts of the Christian calendar were based upon the vernal equinox, the liturgical calendar was becoming increasingly inaccurate. Efforts were made at the councils of Constance (1414–1417) and Basel (1431–38) to reform the calendar, but it was only during the reign of Pope Gregory XIII (1572–85; hence the name) that a resolution of the Council of Trent on the calendar was finally put into effect. In 1582 the ten days between October 4 and 14 were dropped. This system was quickly accepted by Catholic countries, but Protestant and Orthodox lands resisted. Russia only adopted the Gregorian calendar after the Revolution of 1917.

Gregorian chant. *See* chant, Gregorian.

Gregorian Masses, the custom of celebrating Mass for thirty consecutive days at the request of a donor who makes an offering for a deceased person. The purpose is to seek God's deliverance of the deceased from purgatory. The custom derives from the Church's belief that the celebration of the Eucharist is efficacious for the living and the dead.

Gregorian reform, the movement of Church renewal beginning in the tenth century but associated with its most ardent champion, Pope Gregory VII (1073–85). Invigorated by the monastic reforms of houses like Cluny and Gorze in the tenth century and the wide religious revival of Europe at the time, the reformers turned their attentions to freeing the Church from compromising secular entanglements. Lay investiture was a general concern of these reformers as they sought to end this ritualization of secular involvement in religious affairs. Two specific issues, however, were at the heart of the reform agenda: simony, the buying or selling of Church offices, and clerical marriage. Celibacy was urged on all religious and clerics as a worthy aim for all consecrated in service to God; it was also designed to prevent the troublesome inheritance of Church properties by clerical offspring.

History: The reform was given new impetus and real direction by Leo IX (1049–54), who sought to eradicate widespread abuses in the Church by beginning with the papacy itself. He reformed election procedures, defined the role of cardinals, appointed reformers to key positions in the Church, and summoned provincial councils for the implementation of reforms. A successor, Nicholas II (1058–61), continued in a similar vein, but it was Gregory VII's pontificate that determined the course of ecclesiastical reform for the next half century.

A determined reformer and single-minded in his views regarding secular encroachments, Gregory insisted that all religious offices were under the dominion of the Church, over which he ruled as St. Peter's successor. As Gregory's recorded statements on the papacy, the *Dictatus Papae,* suggest, the ecclesial principles of Gregory's program were traditional but couched in strong and sometimes unyielding terms. His personality contributed more than his statements to his long and bitter feud over lay investiture with the headstrong Emperor Henry IV (1056–1106). Unused to compromise, Gregory ended his campaign in flight from Rome and an apparent failure.

The movement was given new life by Urban II (1088–99), a man every bit as determined as Gregory but abler as a politician. In the course of his campaign against lay investiture and other abuses, he excommunicated the kings of France and England. The struggle that was at the heart of the reform officially ended when a compromise was reached between the two sides and formalized in the Concordat of Worms (1122). There it was agreed that ecclesiastical elections would be free and canonical and that investiture would come from a spiritual lord. Secular rulers retained certain rights of presentation to vacancies and participated to a degree in elections. Other important results of the reform period included collections of laws and treaties generated by both sides of the debate leading up to Gratian's *Decretum* in the twelfth century and new developments in royal administration and theories of power. The papacy was a stronger institution after the reform period and the boundaries of authority between Church and state were articulated in ways that would influence political history for the rest of the Middle Ages. *See also* canon law; *Dictatus Papae;* Gregory VII; investiture controversy; papacy, the; simony; Urban II, Bl.   WILLIAM J. DOHAR

Gregorian Sacramentary, a collection of prayers, prefaces, and some rubrical material of the Roman Church originally collected at the time of Gregory I (seventh century). In its original form it presented the liturgy celebrated at the Lateran, i.e., the papal liturgy. Various attempts during the sixth and seventh centuries to produce a sacramentary which would combine both the papal liturgy and the less formal presbyteral liturgy (represented by the Gelasian Sacramentary) had failed to bring about unity. Charlemagne, in his attempt at unifying the empire, saw a single liturgy as a possible aid. The Gregorian Sacramentary was not popular outside Rome. Gradually, a sacramentary comprised of elements from both the ancient Gregorian Sacramentary and an edition of the Gelasian Sacramentary was adopted in northern Italy and France. This hybrid sacramentary is evident in Roman usage by the tenth century and is the forerunner of our present sacramentary. *See also* sacramentary.

Gregorian University, formally known as Pontifical Gregorian University, Jesuit university in Rome. Founded as the Roman College by Ignatius of Loyola and Francis Borgia in 1551 and constituted by Pope Julius III in 1553, it was confirmed and established as a university by Pope Gregory XIII in 1582. Closely associated with the university, yet autonomous, are the Pontifical Biblical Institute, a center for biblical studies in Rome, and the Pontifical Oriental Institute, also in Rome, which deals with the history, traditions, and theology of the Eastern churches.

The university has faculties of theology, canon law, philosophy, ecclesiastical history, missiology (dealing with evangelization), and social sciences. There are institutes of psychology, religious sciences, and spirituality (concerned with Christian life and practice), a center of social communications, a center of Marxist studies, and a school of advanced

Latin letters. The departments are all at postgraduate level.

The university is under the direction of the Society of Jesus (Jesuits). The Grand Chancellor of the Gregorian and associated institutes is the cardinal-prefect for the Sacred Congregation for Catholic Education. The Vice–Grand Chancellor is the general of the Jesuit order. The rector is the equivalent of university president.

In 1992, of the 294 faculty members, 162 were Jesuits, 104 were diocesan priests or members of other religious orders, 6 were nuns, 11 were laymen, and 11 were laywomen. The student body of 3,000 students from more than 100 countries included 615 women, of whom 287 were laywomen. Most of the men were either seminarians in training for the priesthood or priests and religious seeking advanced degrees, but their members also included 147 laymen.

Some of the Gregorian's publications include: *Gregorianum, Studia Missionalia, Periodica de re morali canonica liturgica, Archivum Historiae Pontificiae, Analecta Gregoriana,* and *Miscellanea Historiae Pontificiae.*   JOHN NAVONE

Gregory I, "the Great," St., ca. 540–604, pope from 590 to 604.

Gregory was born into an aristocratic Roman family related to the Anicii. His ancestors included popes Felix III (II) (483–92) and Agapitus I (535–36), and his father, Gordianus, was a senator. Ca. 572 Gregory was appointed Prefect of the City of Rome, but in 574–75, after his father's death and the retirement of his mother, Silvia, into religious life as a widow, he disbursed his fortune, converted the family home in Rome into a monastery (St. Andrew's), and retired there as a monk (not as abbot). Subsequently, Pope Pelagius II ordained him deacon and sent him as *apocrisarius* (Lat., official representative) to Constantinople, where he stayed from 579 to 586, debating the patriarch Eutyches on the resurrection of the body, attempting to secure the support of the emperor Maurice for the beleaguered populace of Italy, and living in a circle of conversation with other Latin clerics such as Leander of Seville (ca. 540–ca. 600) also resident in the capital. Recalled to Rome, Gregory returned to St. Andrew's, but at Pelagius II's death (590, of plague) was elected pope. He set about encouraging the people, preaching, and organizing penitential processions to pray for advertence of the plague. To Maurice's dismay, he negotiated independently with the Lombards, arranging settlements that restored

Pope Gregory the Great, one of the most influential popes in the history of the Church, known for the guidelines he set down for the pastoral ministry of bishops, his liturgical reforms, and the development of Gregorian chant; tenth-century ivory panel.

peace to a ravaged countryside (on terms, however, that refused to destroy the Lombards by taking advantage of their own internal feuds).

Gregory's writings were enormously influential in the Middle Ages and later. Most influential among his exegetical writings is the great *Moralia* on Job, a compendium of Gregory's spiritual teaching, begun in Constantinople. The *Forty Homilies on the Gospels* (590–91) are examples of his popular preaching; the *Homilies on Ezekiel* (593–94) are examples of more learned exegetical discourse addressed to an audience of clerics and monks. Homilies on the Canticle of Canticles and a *Commentary on the First Book of Kings* also survive. But Gregory's most famous works may be the nonexegetical ones, the *Dialogues* and the *Pastoral Rule.* The latter, addressed to bishops, was widely read in all subsequent ages, including the Reformation. It sets out a vision of pastoral care that is adapted to the individual needs of the people, rooted in personal example and preaching, and characterized by the blend of contemplative renewal and social service so peculiarly Gregory's. The *Dialogues* describe the miracles and deeds of Italian saints, most notably St. Benedict (Book II). The letters of Gregory's papacy are preserved in the *Registrum Epistolarum;* the degree of his involvement in the Gregorian Sacramentary is disputed. He is a Doctor of the Church. Feast day: September 3 (formerly March 12). *See also* bishop.

JOHN C. CAVADINI

Gregory II, St., 669–731, pope from 715 to 731. A supporter of the Benedictine order and of the missions of St. Boniface, Gregory rebuked Emperor Leo III the Isaurian for his iconoclasm (727). Feast day: February 13.

Gregory VII, St. [Hildebrand], ca. 1020–85, pope from 1073 to 1085, one of the most influential popes of the Middle Ages. Born in Tuscany, Hildebrand came to Rome at an early age, took minor orders, and became chaplain to Pope Gregory VI. After Gregory VI's death, he entered a Cluniac monastery, possibly even Cluny itself, but was soon called back to Rome, becoming an important figure in reformist circles.

Pope Gregory VII, whose pontificate is the great turning point between first- and second-millennial Catholicism; in increasing the temporal as well as the spiritual power of the papacy, he transformed the Church itself into a legal institution with a monarchical form of government.

As pope, Gregory was an ardent reformer and stubborn idealist, concentrating on clerical reform. At synods in 1074 and 1075, Gregory reaffirmed his predecessors' rulings against simony and clerical marriage, dispatching special legates throughout Europe to ensure that these rulings were enforced. At the synod of 1075, Gregory also issued a general ban on lay investiture. This ban brought Gregory into conflict with the German emperor Henry IV, during which Henry attempted to depose Gregory, and Gregory in turn excommunicated Henry, leading to the dramatic temporary reconciliation at Canossa. In 1084, Henry seized Rome and placed a candidate of his own on the papal throne. Gregory escaped through Norman intervention but remained a captive of the Normans and died in exile.

During his pontificate, Gregory expanded the authority of the Roman see. Through his influence, the Spanish church abandoned its own liturgy for the Roman. His emphasis on the purity of the clergy increased the moral standing of the papacy. Feast day: May 25. *See also* celibacy, clerical; investiture controversy; simony.

Gregory IX [Ugolino da Segni], ca. 1148–1241, pope from 1227 to 1241. Gregory, nephew of Innocent III, spent much of his reign in conflict over

Pope Gregory IX, although a strong supporter of the young Dominican and Franciscan orders and of the new universities in Paris and Toulouse, was distracted by political conflicts with the emperor Frederick II. Here he approves the first collection of papal decretals; painting by Raphael, in the Raphael Rooms, Vatican City.

papal rights with Emperor Frederick II. An ardent reformer, he oversaw as patron of Raymond of Peñafort important developments in canon law, championed the cause of the early Franciscans, and entrusted the Inquisition to the Dominicans. *See also* Inquisition.

Gregory X, Bl. [Tedaldo Visconti], 1210–76, pope from 1271 to 1276. While on pilgrimage in the Holy Land and not yet a priest or cardinal, Tedaldo Visconti was elected pope in 1271 after a lengthy vacancy. Though papal-imperial tensions marked much of his reign, his real interests lay in the liberation of Jerusalem, reunion with the Eastern Church, and continued ecclesiastical reform. Some reforms were achieved at the Second Council of Lyons, which he convened in 1274, but the pope's designs for a successful crusade and reunion with Constantinople were not realized. Feast day: January 9. *See also* Constantinople; Crusades; Jerusalem; Lyons II, Council of.

Gregory XI [Pierre-Roger de Beaufort], 1329–78, pope from 1370 to 1378. The last French pope, he was also the last of the Avignon popes before the Great Schism of 1378. Despite his personal will and Catherine of Siena's entreaties, he hesitated to return the papacy to a politically turbulent Rome. However, in 1376, after two failed attempts, he left Avignon and reached Rome in January 1377. His untimely death in 1378, the predominance of French cardinals, and Roman demands for an Italian pope led to the controversial election of 1378 and the following schism. *See also* Avignon; Catherine of Siena, St.

Gregory XIII [Ugo Buoncompagni], 1502–85, pope from 1572 to 1585. As pope Gregory pushed a militant Counter-Reformation with great success in Poland, the Low Countries, and Germany. He celebrated a *Te Deum,* the traditional way for celebrating a great victory, for the St. Bartholomew's Day Massacre, but victory in France came only after his death. Within the Catholic Church he implemented the decisions of the Council of Trent (1545–63), supported reforming efforts by the Jesuits, Capuchins, and Philip Neri, and founded a number of colleges to educate the clergy. In 1582 he promulgated the modern Gregorian calendar. *See also* Bartholomew's Day Massacre, St.; Counter-Reformation/Catholic Reformation; Gregorian calendar; Trent, Council of.

Gregory XVI [Bartolomeo Alberto Cappellari], 1765–1846, pope from 1831 to 1846. A Camaldolese monk, he wrote a defense of papal sovereignty and infallibility in 1799, became a cardinal in 1826, and was prefect of the Propagation of the Faith. He centralized much Church activity in the Holy See, especially missionary activity. An opponent of political and theological liberalism, he condemned F. R. de Lamennais, L. Bautain, and G. Hermes. He was a determined reactionary who resisted attempts at reform of papal government and insisted that the independence of the Church required maintenance of the Papal States, twice calling on Austrian troops to suppress revolts. He is remembered for having banned railways in his domain, denouncing them as a dangerous modern invention.

Gregory of Nazianzus, St., also known as Gregory Nazianzen, ca. 329–90, one of the Cappadocian Fathers, bishop, and Doctor of the Church. Son of the bishop of Nazianzus in Cappadocia, Gregory was educated broadly in Christian writings, including Origen's, and in Greek philosophy. His career in the Church was politically uneven and personally painful, but his clarity of theological exposition won him the epithet "the Theologian," a celebration specifi-

Gregory Nazianzus, one of the most influential defenders of Catholic orthodoxy at the Council of Constantinople in 381; during the council he was appointed bishop of Constantinople, but he resigned before the end of the year and returned home to Nazianzus.

cally of his teaching about God, which he shares with John the Evangelist.

Gregory's intense but troubled friendship with Basil of Caesarea (Basil the Great) shaped much of his life. He accompanied Basil to Pontus on his ascetic retreat but found it uncongenial, despite their progress on the *Philocalia,* a digest of Origen's works. When Basil as bishop pressured Gregory to help him resist Arianism in Cappadocia by becoming bishop of insignificant Sasima, Gregory felt a betrayal still evident even through the eloquence of his funeral oration for his friend. His brief time (379–81) as bishop of the beleaguered orthodox community at Constantinople, including the time of the meeting of the second ecumenical council there, also ended in acrimony, ecclesiastical confusion, and his withdrawal again to Nazianzus. Finally, he departed even from that responsibility to a life of seclusion. From his letters and from his voluminous poetry, Gregory's responses to the events of his life are known with unusual fullness for the fourth century.

It was in his theological orations, particularly the *Five Orations on the Divinity of the Word,* that he most clearly displayed his ability to bring resources from his classical education together with his incisive presentation of Christian doctrines. His refutation of Eunomian claims to know God's essence developed a view of God's incomprehensibility crucial for Orthodox theology. On the Trinity, he was clearer than Basil about the deity and procession of the Holy Spirit—clearer, by his own account, than was the NT—and he took the lead in providing arguments against Apollinarianism. Feast day: January 2 (West); January 25 and 30 (East). *See also* Cappadocian Fathers; Christology; Trinity, doctrine of the.

KATHRYN L. JOHNSON

Gregory of Nyssa, St., ca. 335–ca. 395, bishop and theologian. The youngest and the least prominent of the three Cappadocian Fathers, neither "doctor" nor "theologian" of the Church, he lacked Basil the Great's eminence as a monastic legislator or Gregory of Nazianzus's crispness of orthodox expression; on topics like the possibility of universal salvation, he remained close enough to the Origenist heritage to arouse concern among some theologians. Twentieth-century theology, however, has been increasingly interested in the individual subtlety of his positions and the evocative power of his spiritual writings.

The younger brother of Macrina and Basil, Gre-

Gregory of Nyssa, younger brother of Basil the Great and one of the Cappadocian theologians, who championed the teaching of the Council of Nicaea (325) on the divinity of Jesus Christ and that of the Council of Constantinople (381) on the divinity of the Holy Spirit.

gory received his wide-ranging education from them and his own efforts, rather than in the secular schools as did Basil. After a foray into marriage and work as a rhetor, he accepted his brother's appeal for help with anti-Arian resistance in Cappadocia and so was ordained bishop of Nyssa in 372. Although disappointing to Basil as an administrator and providing at least a pretext of mismanagement to allow Arians temporarily to depose him, Gregory was effective in Church politics. Active in synods and local elections, he played a role at the Council of Constantinople in 381 and emerged into his greatest productivity after Basil's death.

In addition to sharing with Basil and Gregory of Nazianzus in the theological refutation of Eunomius, he wrote an important brief catechism and an explanation of God's unity which grounds the Christian affirmation in the oneness of divine operation. His explication of the creation of humanity, with an intricate treatment of the *imago Dei,* was meant to supplement Basil's *Hexaemeron.* Especially intriguing is his *Life of Moses,* which treats the ascent of

Mount Sinai both as narrative and as mystical experience in order to suggest never-ending growth in enjoyment of God: here both Gregory's indebtedness to Origen and his creative transformation of that heritage are clearly evident. Finally, it is in Gregory's works that the otherwise-silent theological voice of Macrina can be heard. Feast day: March 9. *See also* Cappadocian Fathers; Christology; *imago Dei*; Trinity, doctrine of the. KATHRYN L. JOHNSON

Gregory of Palamas, St. *See* Palamas, St. Gregory.

Gregory of Rimini, d. 1358, Augustinian Hermit, philosopher, and theologian. Philosophically a nominalist and thoroughly steeped in the writings of Augustine of Hippo, he emphasized the corruption of human nature, the incapacity of free will, the need for grace, and predestination. *See also* Augustine of Hippo, St.; nominalism.

Gregory of Tours, St., 538–94, bishop of Tours (573–94) famous for his *History of the Franks* covering events from creation to 591, but especially focusing on the rise of Frankish power, the years 580–91 in particular. Gregory's other surviving works, mostly hagiographical, are considered much less reliable than the *History*. Feast day: November 17. *See also* Franks.

Gregory Thaumaturgus, St. (thaw-muh-tuhr' guhs; Gk., "wonder-worker"), ca. 210–ca. 270, bishop of Neocaesarea (ca. 240–70). A pupil of Origen (to whom Gregory addressed his famous *Thanksgiving*) and later teacher of Macrina the Elder (grandmother of Basil and Gregory of Nyssa), he is an important link between Origen's generation and the flowering of Cappadocian theology. Later lives, including one by Nyssa, credit him with miracles, hence his name. Feast day: November 17. *See also* Cappadocian Fathers; Origen.

Gregory the Illuminator, St., also known as the Enlightener, ca. 231–ca. 325, apostle and patron saint of Armenia. As bishop of Ashtishat, he organized the Church in Armenia, established a native clergy, and evangelized the people. Feast day: September 30.

gremial (greh'mee-uhl; Lat., "lap"), a small, silk apron or lapcloth. The gremial was laid upon a bishop's lap during liturgical rites to protect the bishop's garments from stains during anointings and the distribution of ashes, palms, or candles.

Gremillion, Joseph, 1919–94, pastor, Vatican official. A priest of the diocese of Shreveport, Louisiana, ordained in 1943, he served as the first secretary of the Pontifical Commission (now Council) for Justice and Peace, 1967–74. He also served as director of the Institute for Pastoral and Social Ministry at the University of Notre Dame, 1983–86, and remained at Notre Dame engaged in research and writing until his death. He was author or editor of more than a dozen books, including *Journal of a Southern Pastor* (1957).

Grey Friars, the popular name of the Franciscan order in England, so called from the color of their habit, which distinguished them from the members of other mendicant orders. In 1224 the first Franciscans arrived in England, immediately establishing themselves in the ecclesiastical, commercial, and intellectual centers of the country: Canterbury, London, and Oxford. Their evangelical way of life and preaching soon made them immensely popular, and by 1250 there were some fifty houses with over twelve hundred friars in the country. Franciscan theologians, such as John Duns Scotus (d. 1308), were prominent at Oxford, and John Peckham eventually became archbishop of Canterbury (1279–92). The English province was dissolved by Henry VIII during the Reformation, when a number of friars suffered martyrdom. A second province was established in the seventeenth century, which survived despite penal laws for two hundred years; new foundations of Observants and Capuchins were established in the mid-nineteenth century. The medieval name survives in Greyfriars College, Oxford. *See also* Franciscan order.

Grey Nuns, officially known as the Sisters of Charity, a pontifical congregation of religious women, founded in Montreal in 1738 by Marie Marguerite d'Youville. When Madame d'Youville and three companions rented a house to care for the poor and ill, Montreal scoffed at the efforts of the widow of the disgraced François d'Youville. In derision, the group was called *les soeurs grises* (Fr., "the drunken nuns"), a title they embraced and transformed by adopting a grey (Fr., *gris*) habit in 1755. The Grey Nuns formally became a religious community under King Louis XV in 1753 and received papal approval in 1865.

The Sisters of Charity comprise six autonomous congregations: the original foundation in Montreal (S.G.M.); the Grey Nuns of St. Hyacinthe, near Montreal (S.G.S.H.); the Grey Nuns of Quebec (S.C.Q.); the Grey Nuns of the Cross, Ottawa (S.G.C.); the Grey Nuns of the Sacred Heart, Philadelphia (G.N.S.H.); and a separate group based in Pembroke, Ontario, the Grey Sisters of the Immaculate Conception. The Grey Nuns are known for their work among the poor, the orphaned, the aged, and the mentally ill (especially the Quebec congregation) and for their schools and hospitals.

Griffiths, Bede, 1906–93, English Benedictine priest, missionary, and ecumenist. His ministry took him to India (1955), where he attempted to adapt Eastern spiritual practices to Christianity.

Grignion, St. Louis Mary (green'yohn). *See* Montfort, St. Louis Grignion de.

Groote, Geert de, 1340–84, Dutch reformer and spiritual writer. Influenced by the Carthusians, he sought to counteract the moral laxity of the clergy in the diocese of Utrecht. His followers gathered into communities of Brethren and Sisters of the Common Life. *See also* Brethren and Sisters of the Common Life.

Grosseteste, Robert, ca. 1170–1253, scientist, theologian at Oxford, and bishop of Lincoln from 1235. Of poor origin, he was in his early career deeply interested in scientific endeavors, augmenting traditional accounts of the sciences by personal observation. After mid-life, his interests shifted to theology; he lectured at Oxford and had a special concern for the Franciscans such as Adam of Marsh attached to the university. Rare among medieval theologians for a knowledge of Greek, he translated anew Pseudo-Dionysius, and his translation of the complete *Nicomachean Ethics* of Aristotle was highly valued. As bishop of Lincoln, he demonstrated a genuine concern for pastoral care and reform.

Grotius, Hugo, 1583–1645, Dutch jurist and statesman, known as "the father of international law." A child prodigy, Grotius served as attorney general of Holland before being exiled as a result of conflict between conservative and liberal Calvinists. An intellectual disciple of the Spanish Jesuit theologian Francisco de Suarez (d. 1617), Grotius was noted for his recognition of a natural law conforming to divine law but recognizable without the assistance of revelation because of its self-evidence or a consensus about its requirements. In addition to natural law, nations are governed by volitional laws dependent upon the consent of the governed. Grotius's notion of volitional law formed the basis for later developments in positive international law. *See also* just-war doctrine; natural law.

Grottaferrata, Abbey of, Byzantine Catholic monastery in the Alban Hills eleven miles southeast of Rome. Founded by the Italo-Byzantine monk Nilus of Rossano in 1004, before the Eastern Schism which broke communion between the Catholic and Orthodox churches, this abbey is notable for being the only Byzantine monastery in unbroken communion with Rome since before the schism. The last surviving institution of the numerous medieval Greek monasteries that once dotted southern Italy and Sicily, Grottaferrata was reformed under Pope Leo XIII in 1881, after a period of latinization and decline. The famous collection of Greek manuscripts in its library includes some of the oldest extant Byzantine liturgical codices. Most of the abbey's vocations come from the Italo-Albanian Catholic Church of Calabria and Sicily, and the monks run a minor seminary for this church.

grotto (It., "cavern"), an artifical structure made to look like a cave or a natural recess. Caves and other natural recesses are often associated with religious sites. The cave at Lourdes (France) where the Virgin is believed to have appeared to Bernadette Soubirous in the last century has been frequently reproduced at churches and retreat centers as devotion to Our Lady of Lourdes spreads.

Guadalupe, Our Lady of, apparition and icon of

The famous grotto of Our Lady at the University of Notre Dame in Indiana, where throughout the day and night students and others come to pray.

the Blessed Virgin Mary, considered as the empress, patron saint, and mother of the Americas. The first apparitions were reported to have taken place between December 9 and 12 of 1531 in Tepeyac, a poor area on the periphery of Mexico City. She appeared first to the Amerindian Juan Diego, then to his dying uncle Juan Bernardino (whom she healed), and finally, miraculously painted on the mantle of Juan Diego, to the bishop and others present. The icon remains in the Basilica of Our Lady of Guadalupe at Tepeyac, where millions from the Americas and around the world go on pilgrimage every year. Scientific investigations have attested to the authenticity of the cloth and to the unexplainable nature of the painting. Many miracles continue to be attributed to her, yet the greatest is the ongoing response of the people. In order to appreciate the full religious impact of Guadalupe, it is necessary to situate it historically and anthropologically.

Historical Background: The devastating and unequal encounter in the early sixteenth century between the European and the Amerindian worlds was a clash between the two cruel and violent empires: the Iberian Christians of Europe and the Aztec Nahuatls of the Americas. The culture of the former was based on the anthropology of reason, individual struggle, and conquest while that of the latter was based on the anthropology of ritual, cosmic communion, and submission to the gods. Both killed: the Spanish slaughtered natives to conquer land and reap profits from gold; the Aztecs performed human sacrifice for the sake of cosmic harmony.

Militarily, the Iberians proved to be more powerful than the Amerindians and no compromise between the two worlds seemed possible or desirable. With the bloody defeat of the Aztec Empire in 1521, the entire Amerindian world was defeated. The conquered had no option but to submit or die and their numbers were decreasing drastically. At this moment of collective death the totally unsuspected event of Guadalupe took place at Tepeyac. For the defeated peoples of the Americas, it functioned as a resurrection event—no longer victory or defeat but the birth of a new people. Some may argue about what really happened at Tepeyac in 1531, but there is no doubt about its phenomenal effects: the Mestizo Church of the Americas was born.

The Apparition: Our Lady of Guadalupe spoke to Juan Diego in Nahuatl, with its rich religious imagery, but her message was new both to the Amerindians and Iberians alike. The Aztecs had demanded human sacrifice and the missioners had spoken of judgment, punishment, and eternal damnation, but she spoke to Juan Diego of love, compassion, and hospitality.

At a festival of Our Lady of Guadalupe in Mexico, reproductions of the image of Our Lady visible on the cloak of the peasant Juan Diego after she appeared to him in 1531.

She presented herself to Juan Diego as the Mother of God, but Juan Diego in turn presented her to the bishop as the mother of Our Savior, Jesus Christ.

In the depiction of Our Lady of Guadalupe, based on Juan Diego's report of the apparition, she is neither a native goddess nor a European Madonna, but combines both in a new way. Her dress is European while the decorations on the dress are indigenous and her face is Mestizo. She appears very human, but her whole self radiates divinity. She appears pregnant and over her womb appears the Nahuatl symbol for the new center of the universe: Christ, who through her will be profoundly incarnated in the soil that is the collective consciousness of the new humanity.

Theological Meaning: In her, the two anthropologies come together so as to produce something totally different than either of the two had been able to achieve independently: the change is from the absolute exclusion of the other as other for the sake of ethnic/religious unity to the inclusion of otherness for the sake of new life. In the Mestizo Mother of the Americas, irreconcilable differences are not only reconciled but a new "beyond exclusion existence" is introduced, one that will destroy the very basis of cruel violence produced by any exclusion-based existence. She does not demand sacrifice or victims, but only confidence and acceptance of her universal motherhood. She says to Juan Diego: "Do not be afraid, you have nothing to fear. Am I not here, your compassionate mother?" Through the apparition at Guadalupe, the most original aspect of the kingdom of God as lived and proclaimed by Jesus of Nazareth was effectively introduced into the New World. It marked the profound anthropological birth of the truly new Christian humanity of the Americas. In Latin American Catholicism today she is both the feminine aspect of the face and heart of God, which was absent from the Christianity of that period, and the Mother of Jesus in the Americas: the mother of the new man or woman of the Americas. Feast day: December 12. *See also* apparitions of the Blessed Virgin Mary; Latin America, Catholicism in.

Bibliography

Elizondo, Virgilio. *La Morenita: Evangelizer of the Americas.* San Antonio, TX: MACC Publications, 1974.

Lafaye, J. *Quetzalcoatl and Guadalupe.* Chicago: University of Chicago Press, 1976.

Rodriguez, J. *Our Lady of Guadalupe: Faith and Empowerment Among Mexican American Women.* Austin: University of Texas Press, 1993.

Sylvest, Edwin. *Nuestra Señora de Guadalupe: Mother of God, Mother of the Americas.* Dallas, TX: Bridwell Library (Southern Methodist University), 1992.   VIRGILIO ELIZONDO

guardian angel, spiritual being who protects a person. Pious Catholic belief assigns to each person a special angel who watches over the bodily and spiritual health of that person. Based on affirmations in the NT (e.g., Matt 18:10; Acts 12:15), the belief has been widespread but never a part of Church dogma. The Matthean text has led to a close association of guardian angels and the protection of children in both prayer and art. There is a liturgical observance in honor of such angelic guardians on October 2 in the Roman calendar of feasts. *See also* angel.

Guardini, Romano, 1885–1968, German Catholic theologian and leader of the liturgical renewal. Born in Verona, Italy, he grew up in Mainz, Germany, was ordained a priest (1910) and received a Ph.D. from the University of Freiburg im Breisgau (1915). After further studies at the University of Bonn, he was appointed the first professor of Catholic theology at the University of Berlin (1923) and simultaneously assumed leadership of the influential Catholic youth association "Quickborn." He was removed from his professorship by the Nazi regime in 1939, but after the war was awarded academic positions at the University of Tübingen (1945–48) and the University of Munich (1948–63).

Guardini is recognized as one of the great theologians of the twentieth century, one who anticipated the changes begun at the Second Vatican Council

A guardian angel; seventeenth-century Domenichino painting, Gallerie Nazionali di Capodimonte, Naples, Italy.

(1962–65). He was the author of more than sixty books and over one hundred articles, including *The Spirit of the Liturgy* (1918), *The Lord* (1937), and *The End of the Modern Age* (1950). He received numerous awards, among them the Peace Prize of the German Publishers (1952), the Great Cross of Service of the Bundes Republic of Germany (1959), and the Erasmus Award (1962). Shortly before his death he was offered the cardinal's hat by Pope Paul VI, but he respectfully declined.

Guéranger, Prosper (gay-rahn-zhay'), 1805–75, restorer of the Benedictine order at the abbey of Solesmes (1837) in France. His multivolume *Liturgical Year* renewed interest in the spirituality of worship. *See also* liturgical movement; Solesmes.

Guibert, Joseph de, 1877–1942, French Jesuit priest and theologian. De Guibert is known for contributions to mystical and ascetical theology, and founded *Revue d'ascétique et de mystique* (currently *Revue d'histoire de la spiritualité*). From 1922 until his death, he taught mystical theology at the Gregorian University in Rome. *See also* mystical theology.

guilds, professional associations. In the medieval period each of the skilled crafts (e.g., masons, blacksmiths, apothecaries) formed associations to maintain standards of work and to oversee the training of apprentices. These associations had their own patron saints, their own forms of charity, and, frequently, their own chapels and meeting halls. In some ways they were precursors of modern labor unions. Beyond mutual benefits, the guilds often contributed to the larger needs of society, as attested by their donations to the decoration of medieval cathedrals like Chartres.

More recently the term has been taken to mean any church organization dedicated to a special skill, service, or devotion.

guilt, moral, the condition of accountability or culpability that is incurred by committing sin. Guilt in moral theology results from a deliberate violation of the moral law. It involves both the state of being at fault, or guilty, and the state of just liability to punishment. Guilt as a moral concept should be distinguished from guilt feelings of distress that follow a transgression, although they may be experienced by people who have committed no transgression. Guilt feelings may be healthy or pathological. *See also* sin.

Günther, Anton, (guhn'tair), 1783–1863, Austrian philosopher and theologian. Ordained in 1820, he developed a form of ontological argument that deduced the existence of God from an analysis of self-consciousness. He viewed the threefold creation of the human person as spirit, nature, and human person, an image of the Trinity. His books were placed on the Index of Forbidden Books in 1857 for being semi-rationalist, i.e., reducing supernatural truths to truths of reason. Günther founded an influential theological school in the mid-nineteenth century, one interested in the modernization of theology and opposed to the ascendant neo-Scholastic model of theology. After the First Vatican Council, some of his followers joined the Old Catholics. *See also* Old Catholics; rationalism.

Gutiérrez, Gustavo, (goos-tahv'oh goo-tee-air'-ehz), b. 1928, Peruvian Catholic theologian often credited with the founding of Latin American liberation theology. After receiving a diploma in medicine, Gutiérrez studied philosophy, psychology, and theology at the Catholic University of Lima, the University of Louvain, and the University of Lyons, which awarded him a Ph.D. in theology (1959). During studies at Rome's Gregorian University, he was ordained a priest for the diocese of Lima in 1959. Returning to Lima in 1960, Gutiérrez served as a pastor and simultaneously taught theology at the Catholic University of Lima. In 1968 he was a theological adviser at the Second General Conference of Latin American Bishops (CELAM II) in Medellín, Colombia. Author of numerous books and articles on Christian faith and the plight of the poor, his book *A Theology of Liberation* (1971) inaugurated the development of the liberation theologies of Latin America. *See also* Latin America, Catholicism in; liberation theology.

Guyon, Madame Jeanne Marie, 1648–1717, French mystic. As a young widow, she became a controversial spiritual guide. Her teaching and writing stressed that the love of God requires great detachment and passivity. She greatly influenced Jean de Caussade and François Fénelon. *See also* Quietism.

gyrovagi (gi-roh-vah'gee; Gk, *gyros,* "circle"; Lat., *vagari,* "to wander"), wandering monks. Mentioned in the Rule of St. Benedict (ca. 540) as the "worst kind" of monk, the term refers to those who do not maintain stability in a single monastery. *See also* wanderer.

Haas, Francis Joseph, 1889–1953, educator, bishop, and government official. A priest of the archdiocese of Milwaukee, Haas received a doctorate in sociology from The Catholic University of America in 1922. He served on the faculty of St. Francis Seminary in Milwaukee, was director of the National Catholic School of Social Service in Washington (1931–35), and was dean of the School of Social Science at Catholic University (1937–43). Appointed to numerous government positions, he was a member of President Franklin Roosevelt's National Labor Board and President Truman's Committee on Civil Rights and chair of the Fair Employment Practices Committee in 1943. Named bishop of Grand Rapids, Michigan, in 1943, he served until his death in 1953.

habit, the distinctive clothing worn by members of religious orders. "Religious are to wear the habit of the institute made according to the norm of proper law [their respective constitutions] as a sign of their consecration and as a testimony of poverty" (Code of Canon Law, can. 669). As religious orders and congregations were established, their founders usually required the members to wear some simple uniform garb. Often it reflected the contemporary dress of the period. In the case of women's congregations, the habit was frequently an adaptation of what widows were wearing at the time.

Vatican II (1962–65) reiterated the need for simplicity in the choice of a habit. It further stipulated that habits "should meet the requirements of health and be suited to the circumstances of time and place as well as to the services required by those who wear them" (Decree on the Appropriate Renewal of the Religious Life, n. 17). In many cases this has been interpreted as requiring only that some sign of religious commitment be visible.

Religious orders that still require a habit have adopted a simple street-length black dress and short black veil. Religious orders of men, on the other hand, have long been required to wear the dress of secular clergy (a black suit and Roman collar) outside their residence or place of ministry. Members of those congregations who still wear a habit at home or at work continue to wear the traditionally distinctive habit of their order. *See also* religious life; religious orders and congregations.

habit, moral, a disposition toward certain virtuous or sinful acts. To understand the significance of the concept of habit in traditional moral theology, as it developed from the writings of Thomas Aquinas (d. 1274) in particular, one must be familiar with the main lines of Scholastic philosophical psychology. According to this theory, the rational capacities of intellect and will, as well as the passions, are indeterminate in that they must be given some definite content and form in order to function properly. For example, communication presupposes the possession of certain rational capacities by every human being, but in order to communicate with others, one must develop these capacities so that one acquires habitual knowledge of a language, together with an ability to use this knowledge in the proper way. This knowledge may be more or less accurate, and one's skill in using it may be more or less complete; some habitual knowledge and facility in the use of language is necessary to communication, but the relevant habits may be badly formed, even though they are sufficient to enable some degree of communication.

If they are well formed, the habits that qualify the human capacities for knowledge, passionate response, and action are known as virtues. In this sense, the concept of virtue expands the usual definition of a morally good quality to include such purely intellectual qualities as wisdom and understanding. In the more properly moral sense, a virtue is a habit qualifying those powers of the human soul that result directly in action, namely, the passions, will, and the practical intellect. At the same time, these powers can be qualified in ways that are ultimately destructive and deforming, rather than perfecting; in that case, the habits in question are vices rather than virtues. *See also* vice; virtue. JEAN PORTER

Trappist monks in habit, eating a meal in silence.

Hadewijch of Antwerp (hayd'wich), a thirteenth-century Flemish Beguine (a semimonastic) and mystic. Her *Poems in Stanzas, Poems in Couplets, Visions,* and *Letters* display a familiarity with Scripture, Christological and trinitarian theology, courtly love literature, music, astronomy, and numerology. Hadewijch's mysticism of love is characterized by theological precision, poetic genius, and human experience. *See also* Beghards/Beguines; mysticism.

Hadrian I, or Adrian, d. 795, pope from 772 to 795. A deacon before being elected pope, Hadrian faced various assaults by the Lombard king Desiderius; the pope's appeals to Charlemagne for help resulted in Charlemagne's conquest of the Lombards in 774. Charlemagne's subsequent gifts of lands helped complete the Papal States. Hadrian supported the iconophile Second Council of Nicaea (787) and helped end the Adoptionist heresy in Spain. In support of Frankish church reforms, he gave Charlemagne in 774 a collection of canons and decrees, the "Dionysio-Hadriana," based on earlier work of Dionysius Exiguus. *See also* Adoptionism; Charlemagne; iconoclasm; Nicaea, Second Council of; Papal States.

Hadrian VI [Adrian Florensz Dedal], 1459–1523, pope from 1522 to 1523. Born in Utrecht, Holland, Hadrian was the last non-Italian pope before John Paul II, elected in 1978, and the first reforming pope of the sixteenth century. The election to the papacy of this student of the Brethren of the Common Life, professor of theology at Louvain, and tutor to the future emperor Charles V raised the hopes of reformers among both Catholics and Protestants. In his twenty months as pope his efforts to reform the Church were thwarted by the Roman Curia and his overtures to the Protestants were rebuffed.

Haec Sancta (hayk sahnk'tah; Lat., "This Holy"), decree of the Council of Constance, promulgated April 1415, declaring the council legitimately assembled with authority directly from Christ. Authorized to end the Great Schism and reform the Church, it could thus demand obedience from all Christians, including the pope. *See also* Constance, Council of; Great Schism.

haggadah, also spelled ag(g)adah (Heb., *nagad,* "to tell, show"), refers to the nonlegal material in rabbinic literature. It includes various narratives and folktales, biblical interpretations, moral and wisdom teachings, sermonic materials, and rab-

binic stories. *Haggadah* is usually treated as less authoritative than *halakah,* the rabbinic system of laws.

Hagia Sophia (hah-gee'ah saw-fi'ah; Gk., "Holy Wisdom"), also called Sancta Sophia or Saint Sophia, the name of several Greek Orthodox church buildings, especially the two cathedral churches built on the same site in Constantinople (today Istanbul, Turkey). The name, Hagia Sophia, originally only Sophia (Gk., "wisdom"), is attested ca. 430 for the earlier Constantinople cathedral of that name. The term Sophia, from the second century used for the second Person of the Trinity, refers to Christ as "Wisdom of God" (cf. Luke 12:49; 7:35). The first Hagia Sophia—actually the second church built on the site—burned down in the Nika Revolt of 532. The new Hagia Sophia, which is still standing, was commissioned by Emperor Justinian I and inaugurated in 537. The largest surviving church of antiquity and, at the time, one of the largest structures ever built, it is considered one of the greatest buildings in the history of architecture. Its dome-on-pendentives solution for roofing the large, unobstructed space of the nave established what is known as the "Byzantine style." Justinian's Hagia Sophia played a central role in Byzantine imperial and church ceremonial, and had a determinative influence on the formation of the ritual and symbol-

View of the cupola and interior of the sixth-century Hagia Sophia basilica in Constantinople (now Istanbul).

ism of the Byzantine rite. The alterations demanded by later strengthening and repairs of the building have not substantially altered its original design. Four minarets were added when the building was turned into a mosque of the same name (*Ayasofya Camii*) after the fall of Constantinople to the Turks in 1453. Hagia Sophia, secularized since 1934, is now a museum. *See also* Constantinople.

ROBERT F. TAFT

hagiography (hay-gee-ah' gruh-fee; Gk., *hagios,* "holy"; *graphein,* "writing"), biographical narratives, largely of the saints. Beginning with the records (Lat., *acta*) of early judicial processes of martyrs, through stories of the actual martyrdom (Lat., *passiones*), to later narratives of the virtues and miracles of the saints, there has been an enormous body of literature over the millennia devoted to the lives of the saints. The most characteristic form of this literature is the *legendum* (Lat., pl. *legenda*), a story written to be read (Lat., *legere,* "to read") at liturgical services on the saint's feast day.

The historical evolution of these texts has led to an entire field of study to establish their historical core, the different genres of writing, and the evidence they give of different spiritualities. *See also* saints.

Hagiology (hah-gee-ah'-loh-jee; Gk., *hagios,* "holy"), also called Hagiody, the Armenian *Srbasac'at'iwn* (*sorb,* "holy") or liturgical chant sung during the Great Entrance of the Armenian Patarag or Eucharist, so-called because the chant normally concludes with the hymn, "Holy, holy, holy is the Lord of hosts" of Isa 6:3.

Hail, Holy Queen. *See Salve, Regina.*

Hail Mary, a popular Catholic prayer based on the angel's greeting spoken to the Virgin Mary at the Annunciation (Luke 1:28), and on Elizabeth's greeting when Mary visited her (Luke 1:42). "Hail Mary" translates the original Latin title of the prayer, *Ave Maria.* Sometimes referred to as the Angelic Salutation, forms of this prayer date from the eleventh century in the West and perhaps from as early as the sixth century in the East. The Hail Mary said today was not popular until the sixteenth century. During the Crusades, Mary was invoked with this prayer for success in efforts to recapture the Holy Land. From 1568 until 1955, this prayer was part of the Divine Office (Liturgy of the Hours) offered daily by monks

and clergy. Most Catholics are familiar with the Hail Mary from its use in praying the Rosary. In the five-decade Rosary, the Hail Mary is recited ten times in each of the decades as one meditates on the mysteries of Jesus' ministry and redeeming activity. The Hail Mary is still found in the Little Office of the Blessed Virgin Mary, and its inclusion there can be dated from the eleventh century. *See also* Annunciation; Marian devotion.

THE HAIL MARY

Hail Mary, full of grace:
The Lord is with thee.
Blessed art thou among women,
and blessed is the fruit of thy womb, Jesus.
Holy Mary, Mother of God,
pray for us sinners,
now and at the hour of our death.
Amen.

Haiti, Catholicism in. Catholicism first came to this Caribbean republic with the expedition from Spain led by Christopher Columbus in 1492. Capuchins and Jesuits were the principal missionaries to Haiti in the eighteenth century. Catholicism has faced many problems in Haiti, including the abject poverty of its people, the lack of an adequate native clergy, oppressive governments, and the persistence of superstition among the people, including the practice of voodoo. It is the only country in modern times, however, where a priest (of the Salesian order) has been elected president, Jean-Bertrand Aristide, in 1991. He was driven from the country the same year by a military coup, but was restored to power in 1994. Under pressure from the Vatican, he resigned from the priesthood the same year. There are 2 archdioceses and 7 dioceses and almost 6 million Catholics in Haiti, comprising approximately 90 percent of the total population (1994). *See also* Latin America, Catholicism in; voodoo.

halakah (Heb., *halak,* "to walk"), denotes a rabbinic legal ruling or statement and also the system of laws that make up the rabbinic way of life. *Halakah* derives from biblical interpretation, Jewish custom, and rabbinic reasoning and is usually contrasted with *haggadah,* the nonlegal material in rabbinic literature.

Hallinan, Paul J., 1911–68, archbishop and progressive leader at Vatican II. Born in Painesville, Ohio, he attended the University of Notre Dame and was ordained a priest for the diocese of Cleveland in 1937. He did parish work before serving as an Army chaplain and winning a Purple Heart for service in World War II. After the war, he held a number of diocesan posts and served as national chaplain for the Newman apostolate on non-Catholic university campuses. In 1958 he was named bishop of Charleston, South Carolina, and, in 1962, he became the first archbishop of Atlanta. He won national recognition during the Second Vatican Council (1962–65) as an advocate of liturgical renewal and ecumenical dialogue and as a spokesman for civil rights and international peace. Regarded as an emerging leader of the Church in the United States, he died at the age of 57.

halo, a ring or circle of light surrounding the head of a holy person and various artistic representations of Christ. The use of the halo is not original to Christianity. The Greeks and later the Romans employed it to signify deity or close association with the gods. Drawing upon the liturgical symbolism of light, Christians began to associate this image with God's grace mediated through Jesus Christ as early as the third century. At first, only Jesus was depicted with a halo, but, by the fifth century, this honor was extended to angels and saints, particularly the Blessed Virgin Mary.

hands, imposition of, a liturgical gesture found in the OT, continued in the NT, and still used by the Church today. It expresses identity and solidarity between the one imposing hands and the one receiving the imposition. It is employed for blessing, healing, invocation of the Holy Spirit, and conferral of office and authority. It is the principal gesture in the rite for ordination of deacons, presbyters and bishops. Evidence for the use of this gesture for appointment to office in the Church is found in the NT (cf. 1 Tim 4:14). It symbolizes and effects communion among ordained ministers. *See also* blessing; healing; ordination.

happiness, the complete fulfillment of all one's desires. All persons seek happiness but differ in their conceptions of what will lead to it. The Catholic Church teaches that happiness consists in being united with God, the ultimate goal of human existence. Unity with God is achieved through knowledge and contemplation of God as God is. We come at least to partial knowledge of God by acting in accord with the virtues and by conforming our will to the will of God. Complete knowledge of God, and thus complete happiness, is not attainable in this life.

Harding, St. Stephen. *See* Stephen Harding, St.

Häring, Bernard, b. 1912, German Redemptorist priest and moral theologian. He taught moral theology at the Alfonsian Academy in Rome before his retirement in 1988. Häring has written extensively, lectured throughout the world in many different languages, and is reputed by many to be the most significant Catholic moral theologian of the time. His three-volume *Law of Christ,* published originally in German in 1954 and translated into more than fifteen languages, signaled a new approach to Catholic moral theology. Häring has called for a biblically based, liturgically celebrated, pastorally sensitive, dynamic morality stressing conversion and responsibility. He has disagreed with some hierarchical teachings on sexual and medical morality.

hatred, the hostility or malevolence aroused by and directed against those persons, things, or events perceived to be evil, harmful, or in some other way repugnant. Hatred of God, neighbor, or oneself is directly contrary to the love required of Christians by Jesus (Matt 22:37–40), a love that is to encompass even one's enemies (Matt 5:43). Hatred is condemned as gravely sinful both for the evil actions that characteristically flow from it and for its debilitating effects on the sinner, hatred in the latter sense understood as the corruption of charity, the highest of the Christian virtues. While hatred of sin has been held permissible, hatred of the sinner has not.

healing, restoration to health. In antiquity healing had two aspects: professional medicine and faith healing. Some of the most prominent medical figures were Hippocrates (469–399 B.C.), Erasistratus (third century B.C.), Herophilus (third century B.C.), Galen (129–99 B.C.), and Celsus (A.D. 14–37). Medical schools were founded, e.g., by Asclepides of Bithynia in Rome (ca. 40 B.C.). However, nonprofessional medical practices also prevailed. Patients interceded with the gods and goddesses of healing; healing sanctuaries were abundant. Methods of healing included exorcism, the use of herbs, incubation in a temple, dedication of models of the affected parts in the sanctuaries, and the use of amulets, prayers, charms and incantations. In the OT the priests are the custodians of public health, adjudicating, for example, cases of leprosy. Many of the Levitical laws with reference to diet, health, sexual practices, quarantine, and Sabbath rest were seen as God's concern for physical health. But professional doctors and pharmacists were also respected (Sir 38:1–15). The Talmud contains a long line of rabbi-physicians. In the NT, especially in Mark, Jesus is represented as a healer of multiple physical diseases and also psychiatric conditions, but he does not use magical practices. He heals by voice command and he often touches a physically ill patient but not a demoniac. The early Church continued Jesus' healing ministry, and the structure of the Gospel of Luke parallels closely the structure of Acts so that this ministry is thrown into high relief. Oil was often used in healing (Mark 6:13; Jas 5:14). The Christian Church was one of the first communities to found hospitals, and its religious sisters have been foremost in devoting their lives to the ministry of healing. *See also* faith healing.   J. MASSYNGBAERDE FORD

Healy, Timothy Stafford, 1923–92, Jesuit priest, educator, and president of the New York Public Library (1989–92). As professor of English with a doctorate from Oxford, Father Healy taught at Fordham University, City University of New York (where he was also vice chancellor), and Georgetown University. He also served as president of Georgetown University (1976–89). *See also* Georgetown University.

heart (Heb., *lēb, lêbab*), the locus of emotion, passion and appetite; also, and primarily, the seat of intellection and interior dialogue (e.g., "the fool has said in his heart, 'there is no God,'" Ps 14:1). In this sense, therefore, it corresponds more to our idea of mind than of heart (e.g., Prov 16:9). While ancient Israel did not develop a distinct concept of the soul as the core of personality analogous to the Greek *psychē*, the idea comes to expression in other ways, including frequent allusions to the heart. The heart is the center of the moral life; one can therefore have a deceitful (Isa 44:20) or a clean and upright heart (Pss 32:11; 51:10). The "hardening of the heart" (e.g., Pharaoh, Exod 7:3.) denotes a condition of religious and moral insensitivity. *See also* Immaculate Heart of Mary; Sacred Heart, devotion to the.

heaven, the perfect and final completion of human life in union with God. The Christian doctrine of heaven is dependent upon the Church's faith in the Resurrection of Jesus Christ. As the personal participation in the Resurrection of Christ, heaven is the result of acceptance of God's grace in one's life. (Hell, by contrast, is the utter loss of God through a definitive repudiation of that same grace).

Scriptural Basis: The Christian tradition of speaking of final union with God as "heaven" finds its roots in Semitic cosmology. The OT represents heaven as a celestial sphere that is the home of God (Gen 1:1; 1:8; Isa 66:1; Pss 2:4; 11:4; 139:8), although this cosmology is not unique to the biblical tradition. God is surrounded by a heavenly court with whom he takes counsel (1 Kgs 22:19; Isa 6:3–8; Ps 82). This Hebraic image of heaven is implied in the NT, especially at Jesus' baptism (Mark 1:9–11, Matt 3:13–17, Luke 3:21–22, John 1:29–34). More precisely, heaven is the place where the Father of Jesus dwells (Matt 3:17; 6:9; 10:32). Heaven is eventually understood to be the finality of salvation, a salvation that includes the history of the cosmos (Rev 21:1). Jesus' preaching of the "kingdom of heaven" (Matt 3:2) evokes not only the transcendent dimension of God's glory, but the essentially interpersonal, social, and historical dimensions of human personhood that find their ultimate fulfillment in union with God. Heaven is thus not a radical interruption of these dimensions of human personhood; rather, the entirety of human personhood is taken up into God in the glory of risen life which bears the name heaven. Biblical anthropology stresses the unity of spiritual personhood represented in the integral relationship between body and soul. The biblical doctrine of resurrection speaks of the resurrection of the dead (Acts 4:2; 1 Cor 15:42; Rev. 20:5), i.e., of the entire spiritual person, not simply the resurrection of the material body or the immortality of the spiritual soul. At the same time, there is foundation in Scripture for the view that the soul, separated from the body, enjoys the presence of God and is thus in heaven (Wis 3:1–3; Matt 10:28; 2 Cor 5:1–10).

Church Teaching: The Church's teaching concerning heaven has generally, though not always, construed heaven as a spiritual "place" or state of being. It is construed as a place because the intrinsic relationship between soul and body, even a glorified body, implies some notion of location. It is construed as a state of being because the spiritual person is said truly to exist beyond death in life with God. In ordinary Church teaching, then, heaven is the place or state of being in which the just enjoy the direct intuitive knowledge of God in company with the elect, the communion of saints. This knowledge has also been called the Beatific Vision, the direct spiritual apprehension and delight in God without any material mediation, a state that, apart from the experience of Jesus, can only be attained beyond death. Pope Benedict XII (*Benedictus Deus*, 1336) declared that the souls of the just could attain such a state immediately upon death and before the final general judgment and the resurrection of the body.

Although there is no definitive teaching of the magisterium that would give us a "proper picture" of heaven, the Council of Lyons (1274) refers to souls being received in heaven, and the Council of Florence (1439) refers to a state of the elect where God will be seen as God truly is. The Church has clearly distinguished its conception of heavenly glory from Gnostic and certain Greek philosophical notions of a state of immortal bliss enjoyed by a disembodied soul by affirming that the entire human person, body and soul, ultimately participates in eternal beatitude in heaven. At the same time, ordinary Church teaching has made regular use of some Greek notions, including the distinction between body and soul, when making statements about personal salvation.

As a doctrine dependent upon the Resurrection of Christ, heaven can also be understood as a consequence of the "hypostatic" union of the divine and human natures in Jesus Christ, a doctrine that implies that human nature is created for union with God. Jesus' own resurrection is thus seen as the human acceptance and divine pledge of this union. According to theologian Karl Rahner (d. 1984), Jesus' entry into glory was not, therefore, entry into a pre-existing place called heaven, but in fact the establishment of "heaven" in its most radical sense, as the fulfillment of the human possibility for union with God. *See also* Beatific Vision; beatitude; eschatology; individual; eternal life; immortality; *lumen gloriae*; salvation. PAUL CROWLEY

Hebblethwaite, Peter, 1930–94, English Catholic journalist and Vaticanologist. Ordained a Jesuit in 1963, he left the Society of Jesus to marry in 1974. A former editor of the Jesuit periodical *The Month,* he served as Vatican Affairs correspondent for the *National Catholic Reporter* in the United States

(1979–94) and was a regular contributor to *The Tablet* in London. He was author of several books on the Catholic Church, including biographies of Popes John XXIII (1984) and Paul VI (1993).

Hebrews, according to the Table of Nations in Genesis (10:21), descendants from Eber, son of Shem. The ethnic term "Hebrew" is more often used by foreigners than by Israelites (e.g., Gen 39:14; Exod 1:16; 1 Sam 4:6), and in some instances it may denote a social category more inclusive than the ethnic term "Israelite." In the early Christian context it refers to Hebrew- or Aramaic-speaking Christians (e.g., Acts 6:1), and later still simply to Jews.

Hecker, Isaac Thomas, 1819–88, founder of the Missionary Society of St. Paul the Apostle, the Paulists. Born in New York of German immigrant parents, he left school at an early age. He worked in the family business until a profound religious experience led him to search for a more committed life at Brook Farm and Fruitlands, New England utopian communities, before joining the Catholic Church in 1844. A short time later, he entered a European seminary to study for the priesthood with the Redemptorist order. He returned to the United States in 1851, where he joined a band of English-speaking priests offering parish missions. Anxious to convert Americans to Catholicism, he authored two original works of apologetics, *Questions of the Soul* and *Aspirations of Nature.* In 1857, he went to Rome to seek support for a more energetic apostolate among English-speaking Americans. After a painful conflict with his Redemptorist superiors, Hecker and his associates were permitted the freedom to establish a new religious community, the Missionary Society of St. Paul the Apostle, the Paulists.

A leader of the new community until his death, Hecker presented public lectures, initiated a monthly review, *The Catholic World,* and launched a publishing company, while his priests staffed a parish in New York and continued parish missions. Hecker, anxious to arouse enthusiasm for the non-Catholic apostolate, was disappointed by the internal preoccupations of Church policy, especially at the First Vatican Council (1869–70), which he observed in Rome. Soon after, he became ill, traveled extensively in Europe and the Near East, then returned to resume leadership of the Paulists. In his later years he developed his uniquely American spirituality, ideas that led to controversy after his death in 1888. In

1899 Pope Leo XIII condemned "Americanism," a body of ideas associated with Hecker through a controversial biography written by his Paulist protégé, Walter Elliott. Hecker's emphasis on evangelization, together with his affirmation of freedom, reason, and democracy, made him the premier witness to a distinctively American Catholicism. *See also* Americanism; Paulists.   DAVID O'BRIEN

Hedwig, St., ca. 1174–1243, aristocrat and religious. After a tumultuous life as wife of the Duke of Silesia (and mother of his seven children), she retired to a Cistercian convent to lead a life of prayer and solitude. Her reputation as peacemaker and prophet led to an early canonization (1267). Feast day: October 16.

Hefele, Karl Joseph, (hef'uh-lay), 1809–93, German bishop and Church historian. He was ordained in 1833 and in 1836 he began teaching Church history at the University of Tübingen, succeeding J. A. Möhler. He served as rector from 1852 to 1853. His seven-volume *Konziliengeschichte* (1855–74) treats regional and ecumenical synods in their historical settings down to the mid-fifteenth century. He was appointed bishop of Rottenburg in 1869. At the First Vatican Council he was one of the leading opponents of the effort to define the doctrine of papal infallibility. Nevertheless, he resisted pressure by the Old Catholics to join their ranks. Although he was the last German bishop to do so, he promulgated the conciliar decrees in his diocese. *See also* infallibility; Vatican Council I.

Hegel, Georg Wilhelm Friedrich, 1770–1831, German philosopher. He studied philosophy and theology at Tübingen and was greatly influenced by Immanuel Kant and Johann Gottlieb Fichte. He taught at Jena (1800–06), initially with Friedrich Wilhelm Schelling as a colleague, but developed his philosophical system of dialectical idealism in opposition to the latter's "philosophy of identity." After directing the *Gymnasium* in Nuremberg (1807–16) and teaching at the University of Heidelberg (1816–18), he settled at the University of Berlin (1818–31). Hegel's philosophy has had enormous impact on Western thought in almost all areas, not least religion. He attempted to overcome all oppositions in thought and reality, even that between subject and object, not by positing identity, as Schelling had, but by recognizing nonidentity as an inherent element of final or absolute identity. He traced this dialecti-cal unfolding of thought and being through all its manifestations by empirical observation in his *Phenomenology of the Mind* (1807) and then, reversing the procedure, sought in the *Science of Logic* (1812–16) and *Encyclopedia of Philosophical Science* (1817, 1827, 1830) to deduce, in an *a priori* (Lat., "from the former") way, all existing realities from initial indeterminate identity culminating in absolute knowledge by absolute spirit. Absolute knowledge finds expression in three forms: sensually, in art; representationally, in religion; and in its full conceptual form, in philosophy. Thus revelation finds no real place within Hegel's system. Although in his early writings he sought to reconcile oppositions through love, his mature system sees the reconciliation of opposites as the dialectical work of reason. Thus it is a fully rationalistic philosophical replacement of religion.

Hegel's influence has been especially pronounced on Protestant theology, particularly the Tübingen school (Ferdinand Christian Bauer, David Friedrich Strauss), but he has also had an impact on German Catholic theology, especially that of Karl Rahner (d. 1984).   MICHAEL J. HIMES

Hegesippus, St. (hej-uh-sip'puhs), ca. 110–ca. 180, early Church historian. His five books of "Memoirs," written in Greek, defended the Church against Gnosticism. Feast day: April 7.

hegumen (hey-goo'men; Gk., *hegoumenos,* "leader"), the abbot or superior of a Byzantine monastery, generally one of lesser rank than a monastery governed by a superior with the title "archimandrite." Some Byzantine churches confer the title "hegumen" on monastic priests as a purely honorific rank. *See also* abbot.

Hehir, J. Bryan (hay'uhr), b. 1940, social ethicist and counselor to the U.S. Catholic bishops. Hehir was ordained a priest for the archdiocese of Boston in 1966 and received a Th.D. from Harvard University in 1977. He has served as counselor for the United States Catholic Conference since 1973, and was staff director for the bishops' pastoral letter "The Challenge of Peace" in 1983. A MacArthur Fellow (1984–89), he has been Kennedy Professor of Christian Ethics (1988–92), associate vice president (1991–92), and senior research scholar (1984–92) at Georgetown University. He is the author of many articles on the Church in international relations. Since 1992 he has been pastor of St. Paul's Church, Cambridge,

Massachusetts, and Professor of the Practice in Religion and Society at Harvard Divinity School.

Heidegger, Martin, 1889–1976, a major German philosopher and innovator in art, psychology, theater, and theology. Heidegger grew up in a Catholic world of parish church, Jesuit novitiate, and seminary. His university studies in neo-Kantianism and Husserlian phenomenology were complemented by an acquaintance with medieval mystics and Tübingen Catholic theologians. Beyond influencing the development of existentialism, he was in fact "a thinker of Being" much indebted to idealist, medieval, and Greek philosophers and theologians. Hostile to Catholicism in the Nazi decades (1933–45), after the war he turned toward meditation on Being in landscape, culture, art, and poetry. He influenced, among Protestant thinkers, Rudolf Bultmann, Paul Tillich, and Heinrich Ott. Catholics influenced by him include Erich Przywara, Alfred Delp, Karl Rahner, Hans Urs von Balthasar, Johannes Baptist Lotz, Gustav Siewerth, and Max Müller, all of whom drew Heideggerian motifs into dialogue with the thought of Thomas Aquinas and/or with the work of theologians who were preparing for Vatican II (1962–65). Heidegger's thinking assisted theology in understanding the personal nature of grace, the disclosing manner of revelation, the historicity of salvation, and the historical pluralism of theology and dogma.

Heiler, Friedrich, 1892–1967, German Protestant theologian and ecumenist. As a student at the University of Munich, Heiler converted from Catholicism to Lutheranism as he was completing his doctoral studies (1918). He was appointed a professor of the history of religions at the University of Marburg (1920), where he remained until his retirement (1960). Committed to ecumenical and interreligious dialogue, he advocated the reunion of Catholics and Protestants in an "evangelical Catholicism," and he was active in the International Congress for the History of Religions.

Heilsgeschichte (hilz'ge-shik-tah; Ger., "salvation history"). *See* salvation history.

Helena, St., ca. 250–ca. 330, mother of the emperor Constantine. Of low social origin, she was dismissed by Constantine's father, Constantius Chlorus, in 292, when he married for political reasons the stepdaughter of Augustus Maximian. On Con-

stantine's accession in 306, however, she regained a position of honor, as Augusta. She is venerated for her foundation of churches, her service to the poor, and her journey (326) to Palestine, where she discovered, as she believed, Christ's cross. Feast day: August 18. *See also* Constantine the Great; invention of the cross.

Heliand, ninth-century Old Saxon poem retelling the gospel story in alliterative verse for pastoral purposes.

hell, the eternal loss of God. God has created the world in order to bestow divine life upon it in a personal relationship of love. This relationship begins here and now in the life of grace and reaches its perfection in the kingdom of heaven, the life of glory. Because humans are free, they can turn away from God, refusing to enter into a relationship of love, and live accordingly. This denial is the heart of sin and the ultimate reason why hell is a possibility, for hell is simply the final state of one who has utterly and deliberately refused to live one's life with God. Church teaching says that the soul of a person who dies in a state of mortal sin goes directly to hell (*Benedictus Deus,* 1336; Council of Florence, 1439). While moral theologians have perhaps been careless over the centuries in designating certain actions as mortally sinful, the Church has never taught that anyone has, in fact, died in such a state.

Biblical Images: In the context of the gospel of God's universal saving love (1 Tim 2:4), hell can be understood as a self-chosen state of alienation from God and not simply as a subsequent punishment inflicted by God. Indeed, Christ is the revelation that God's justice and judgment are precisely merciful love. It is not God who rejects the sinner, but the sinner who rejects God. God does not torture the sinner or seek retribution. The biblical images about the torments of hell are not to be interpreted literally. Symbolically they refer to the suffering that is inherent in the state of sin itself. To turn away finally and completely from God, who alone can give peace, healing, and life, inevitably means suffering and death. Hell, therefore, does not refer to a place created by God, into which God will cast sinners. Hell is a creation, or better, a kind of "anticreation" of the sinner. As the opposite of heaven, an eternal communion of love with God and all the saints in the new creation, hell is best conceived as the state of being utterly alone in self-chosen isolation. Hell is

Thirteenth-century mosaic of hell with Satan, demons, and other fallen creatures; baptistery, Florence, Italy.

the state of a person who definitively rejects God. Heaven means to be finally and completely drawn out of oneself in love; hell means to be utterly absorbed and trapped in oneself.

Heaven and Hell: While the possibility of hell is a proper part of the gospel, it should not be viewed as an equal alternative to heaven. The possibility of hell stands in sharp contrast to the reality of heaven. NT texts that deal with judgment, heaven, and hell are not to be interpreted fundamentalistically. They must be understood according to the dynamics of the eschatological and apocalyptic genres that they exemplify. They are not eyewitness reports of the final judgment. They express the ultimate seriousness and eternal significance of choices made here and now. With theologians such as Rahner (d. 1984) and von Balthasar (d. 1988), it is appropriate to speak of a fundamental asymmetry between human sin and God's abundant grace, a theme central to Pauline theology as well. Because of the power of God's love, as revealed in Christ's victory over sin and death, the Church's hope is that all humanity will be saved. This hope, which can not be stated as a foregone conclusion in a theory of universal salvation (apocatastasis), is expressed in the liturgy of the Eucharist: "Remember our brothers and sisters who have gone to their rest in the hope of rising again. Bring them and all the departed into the light of your presence." Likewise, while the Church has

canonized many saints, affirming that there are human beings in heaven, it has never affirmed that there is, in fact, a single human being in hell. *See also* damnation; last things; reprobation; Satan.   JOHN R. SACHS

Hellenism, the language and categories of ancient Greek culture. Alexander the Great (d. 323) aimed to make Greek culture universal, and although his empire did not survive his death, his project of hellenization was continued by the states that were its heirs. By the first century the Romans in turn had inherited a world in which, at least in the East, Greek was the *koiné*, or common language, and an eclectic blend of Platonism and Stoicism the common philosophical denominator. The Jews, especially in the Diaspora but also in Palestine itself, were no less affected than other peoples. Although resisting polytheism and its cult and generally living in separate communities, they used the Greek language, had a Greek translation of the Scriptures (Septuagint), and developed philosophical articulations of biblical teaching (Aristobulus, third to second century B.C.; Philo of Alexandria, ca. 20 B.C. to A.D. 50). Thus the alleged opposition between "Jewish thought" and "Hellenism" underlying eighteenth- and nineteenth-century debates about the contamination of the "gospel" with Greek thought is a category mistake. The Gospels themselves were written in Greek, and if the doctrine of the "Word" in the Prologue to John's Gospel has Hellenic resonances, this does not make it any less Jewish in provenance.

Doctrinal Development: The charge of contamination of the gospel with Hellenism refers largely, however, to doctrinal developments of the fourth and fifth centuries, which presuppose a kind of Stoicized Platonist natural theology based on God's incorporeality, immutability, infinity, and impassibility, attributes that at times seem to be only indirectly related, and perhaps even opposed, to the picture of God in the Scriptures. This development began in an apologetic context, with teachers like Justin Martyr (d. ca. 165) whose aim was to demonstrate the compatibility of Christian doctrine with the best of Greek thought, and was furthered in a polemical context, in which teachers like Origen (d. 254) attempted to articulate a philosophical Christianity over against the spiritualized systems of the Gnostics. These philosophical commitments were then carried over into the doctrinal formulations of the next two centuries, and it is to these formulations that the charge of contamination of the gospel with Hellenism is most often leveled. Were the controversies about the Trinity and Christ actually controversies about points of philosophical teaching essentially unrelated to the gospel? And thus the formulations themselves based on irrelevant, but canonized, philosophical distinctions?

In evaluating this charge, which has been directed especially against Catholicism because of its continued commitment to "natural" theology, it must be remembered that the gospel cannot exist apart from a cultural matrix and that, as already noted, there was no feature of Greco-Roman culture that was not to some degree "hellenized." It would be odd, therefore, if Greco-Roman Christianity were not hellenized to some extent; if it had existed in thought forms and categories unintelligible to the culture at large, it could hardly have laid claim to proclamation of the gospel. From this perspective, the blanket charge of "hellenization" is tautological.

The question is better put to individual figures within their own individual contexts: in each case, how did they use the categories and language they inherited? Was there any way in which, by their very use of these categories, the categories were transformed or even critiqued? Did the recontextualization of metaphysical language into uniquely Judeo-Christian genera, such as the homily, transform that language? Questions such as these, which one must ask of any particular enculturation of the gospel, are much more likely to lead to useful assessments of the Christianity of Greco-Roman antiquity and of the doctrinal formulations that come from it. *See also* Catholicism and culture; philosophy and theology.

JOHN C. CAVADINI

Héloïse, ca. 1100–ca. 1163, wife of Peter Abelard and abbess of the Paraclete, a community of nuns in Troyes, France. One of the most intriguing people of the twelfth century, Heloise was famous for both her passionate relationship with Abelard and her learning. She is widely recognized for her distinctive teaching on the ethics of pure love, and for her singular influence on the formation of Paraclete literature (e.g., the rule). *See also* Abelard, Peter; Paraclete, the.

henotheism (he-noh'thee-iz-uhm), a belief that recognizes the existence of several gods but regards one particular god as the god of one's family or tribe, leaving the other gods without practical significance.

Henoticon, formula of union between Orthodox and Monophysites drawn up in 482 between Acacius and Peter Mongus, patriarchs of Constantinople and Alexandria, an initiative of the emperor Zeno. It condemned Eutyches and Nestorius, but sidestepped the question of the number of natures in Christ and failed to mention Leo's *Tome*. Pope Felix III (II) excommunicated Acacius for concessions to Monophysitism. *See also* Acacianism; Monophysitism.

Henry II, St., 973–1024, German king and Holy Roman emperor (crowned 1014). A pious, energetic monarch much concerned with the reform and expansion of the Church, he founded the see of Bamberg as a center for missions to Slavic lands. Feast day: July 13.

Henry IV [emperor], 1050–1106, Holy Roman emperor from 1056 to 1106. The opponent of Pope Gregory VII, Henry desired to maintain imperial authority and clashed with the Gregorian reform's efforts to free the Church from lay control. Excommunicated by Gregory (1076), Henry humbled himself at Canossa and was absolved (1077). His struggle with the papacy continued until his death. *See also* Gregory VII; Holy Roman Empire.

Henry IV [king], 1553–1610, king of France from 1589 to 1610. Despite his being Protestant, Henry succeeded to the throne of France. Having converted to Catholicism in 1593, he issued the Edict of Nantes (1598) granting Protestants toleration and ending the wars of religion. He was assassinated in 1610 by a Catholic.

Henry VIII, 1491–1547, king of England from 1509. Second son of Henry VII, he was educated in the Renaissance humanist tradition, displaying skills in languages, music, and theology. His treatise on the seven sacraments (1521) against Luther won for him the title of "Defender of the Faith" from Pope Leo X. He later came into conflict with Clement VII over his attempt to dissolve his marriage with Catherine of Aragon, who had failed to bear him a son. Upon revocation of the case to Rome in 1529, Henry took the advice of Thomas Cranmer to appeal the case to the universities of Europe. Ultimately, he was declared the "supreme head on earth of the Church of England" in 1534, for which he was excommunicated by Clement VII. With Cranmer as archbishop of Canterbury and Thomas Cromwell as vice-regent, Henry pursued an antipapal, moderately Lutheran course of reform, culminating in the dissolution of the monasteries (1536, 1539), the Ten Articles (1536), the Bishop's Book (1537), and the English Bible (1535) with various other editions following); during his reign, such Catholics as Thomas More and John Fisher were executed. His personal

Henry VIII, king of England from 1509 to 1547, whose divorce of Catherine of Aragon and marriage to Anne Boleyn in 1533 precipitated the break between the Church of England and the papacy.

Catholic piety, however, emerged in the Six Articles (1539) and the King's Book (1543). His reign ended in the direction of reform with the English Litany (1544), the suppression of chantries and foundations (1545), and the entrusting of the education of his son Edward VI to Protestants. *See also* Anglicanism; England, Catholicism in; Reformation, the.

Henry of Ghent, d. 1293, the leading secular theologian at the University of Paris in the final quarter of the thirteenth century, regent master from 1276–92; the "solemn doctor," author of a large *Summa* of established questions as well as many quodlibetal (Lat., "whatever one pleases") questions, i.e., those that were raised spontaneously by students and other teachers. Thorough in his approach to important theological problems, he usually considers a wide range of biblical, patristic, and philosophical authorities, quoted at length, in the presentation of his own position. Important on his own right for the attempt to uphold an "Augustinian" epistemology and metaphysics in the face of the newly-translated Aristotle, he also sheds considerable light on Duns Scotus (d. 1308), who used Henry as a foil in developing his own teaching. A new critical edition of Henry's *Summa,* in preparation in 1994 will doubtless restore him to his rightful prominence in the history of Christian thought. *See also* Paris; Scholasticism.

Henry Suso, Bl., ca. 1295–1366, Dominican preacher and mystic. Having entered the Dominican order in Constance at the age of thirteen, he experienced a conversion at age twenty-eight, perhaps under the influence of Meister Eckhart. His later defense of Eckhart would cause him much trouble. His own mystical theology was more cautious, making clear (as Eckhart's did not) that mystical union with God did not entail the loss of personal identity. His most important works are the *Little Book of Eternal Wisdom, Horologium Sapientiae,* and his autobiographical *Life of the Servant.* He was beatified in 1831. Feast day: March 15. *See also* mysticism.

heresy, the obstinate denial or doubt, on the part of a baptized person, of a truth that must be believed by divine and catholic faith. The First Vatican Council (1869–70) declared that by divine and catholic faith all those things must be believed that are contained in the word of God, whether written or handed down, and have been proposed by the Church, whether by solemn judgment or by its ordinary universal magisterium, as divinely revealed and to be believed as such (DS 3011). This faith is called "divine" because it embraces truth that is divinely revealed and is, thus, a response to God as revealer. It is called "catholic" because it is the assent to what has been definitively proposed for belief by the supreme teaching authority of the Catholic Church. This authority pronounces a solemn judgment when the pope or an ecumenical council defines a truth as a "dogma of faith." The assent of faith is also given to revealed truths that have never been defined but which Catholic bishops throughout the world, together with the pope, consistently teach as definitively to be held with divine faith.

In Catholic canon law, heresy is a crime of which only baptized Christians can be guilty. The "obstinacy" that is an essential component of heresy distinguishes it from inculpable error in belief. In the modern Catholic Church, other Christians are not considered guilty of heresy because it is presumed that they err in good faith in rejecting certain truths that the Catholic Church holds as dogmas of faith. However, in the past, the terms "heresy" and "heretics" were used more widely, of beliefs at variance with the orthodox faith and of those holding such beliefs.

Heresy has played a providential role, in the course of Church history, by obliging the Church to clarify its understanding of revealed truth in order to identify and reject erroneous interpretations of the faith. Thus, the Arian heresy of the fourth century led to the definition of the true divinity of the word of God. The Nestorian and Monophysite heresies of the fifth century led to the clarification of Church teaching concerning the unity of person and distinction of natures in Christ. Similarly, the errors of Pelagius obliged the Church to clarify its teaching about original sin and the necessity of divine grace for the keeping of the divine law.

It is axiomatic that there is no heresy that does not contain some element of truth. In its negative reaction to what it recognized as erroneous in a heretical position, the Church has sometimes so insisted on the contrary of that error as to neglect an aspect of the truth that the heresy actually upheld. Subsequent reflection has sometimes led to a more objective appreciation of the elements of truth contained in doctrines that the Church had condemned as heretical. *See also* dogma.   FRANCIS A. SULLIVAN

heresy [canon law], the obstinate post-baptismal denial or doubt of a truth that must be believed with catholic and divine faith (can. 751). Such truths, known as dogmas, are spoken of in canon 750 as those contained in Scripture or tradition that have been proposed as divinely revealed either by the Church's solemn magisterium (teaching office) or by its ordinary and universal magisterium. *See also* dogma; magisterium.

Hergenröther, Joseph, 1824–90, German canonist and Church historian. A professor at the University of Würzburg and a consultor for Vatican I (1896–70), he was made cardinal in 1879 and first prefect of the Vatican Archives. Noted for his three-volume manual of Church history (1869) and extensive Byzantine studies, he opposed the views of Johann Döllinger, a Church historian who rejected the dogma of papal infallibility as taught by Vatican I and was subsequently excommunicated. *See also* Vatican Council I.

Hermas, Shepherd of, a second-century apocryphal apocalypse. The *Shepherd* consists of five visions, twelve commands, and ten parables. Traditional scholarship has argued for a very early (ca. 100) provenance for the first four visions written by Hermas, while the fifth vision and the commands and parables are believed to have been provided by an anonymous author in the mid-second century (ca. 140–50). Both authors employ apocalyptic allegory throughout and drew heavily from Jewish literary traditions.

Testimony by the Muratorian Canon suggests that some Christians sought its inclusion in the NT. Its prominence was certainly enhanced by its close association with Rome; however, its lack of widespread acceptance precluded such a development.

The *Shepherd* has a strong ethical emphasis underlying its allegorical stylistic conventions. Repentance is a major theme, particularly for sins committed after Baptism. The conclusion that these sins could only be pardoned once had an impact upon Catholic theology for centuries.

In the first four visions, the Church, which appears in the form of an old woman who develops into a young maiden, calls Hermas to repentance. Her appeals are punctuated by warnings of imminent persecution and danger. The fifth vision introduces the moral instruction of the second portion of the *Shepherd*. An angel of penance disguised as a shepherd first provides commands, or precepts, on faith, charity, chastity, prayer, good works, prophets, and desires and then concludes with the parables. The first five stress the avoidance of pride and the need to provide for the poor. The last five renew the call for penance on a communitywide and individual basis. *See also* apostolic age; Muratorian fragment.   MIKE R. BEGGS

hermeneutics (huhr-muh-noo'tiks), the theory and/or practice of interpretation, particularly of biblical texts. The problem of interpretation arises from the fact that the meanings of certain classical, even normative, ancient texts of the Christian tradition, especially the Bible, are obscured for modern readers. Interpretation is the process of overcoming the obstacles created by linguistic, cultural, and intellectual distance so that the ancient text can become meaningful in the contemporary believing community. The process of interpretation involves three moments that are distinct but interactive. *Exegesis* is the process of establishing the meaning of the text in the context in which it was written. This involves the use of various methods for establishing an authentic text, translation, historical investigation, and literary and theological analysis. The reader is able to base interpretation on a valid understanding of the text's own intentionality. *Criticism* is the process of determining how the text invites and guides the reader's interaction with it. Thus, historical criticism investigates how, and how well, the text conveys data about the past to the reader. Literary criticism investigates how the text engages the reader through narrative or other genres and how effectively it does so. Ideological criticism unmasks how a text carries and reinforces certain worldviews and power agendas and how this affects readers. *Appropriation* is the actual experience of understanding, of achieving transformative meaning, in and through engagement with the text.

Hermeneutical theory proposes an understanding of texts and how they function and of the interaction of reader with text through exegesis, criticism, and appropriation. Hermeneutical practice is the art and science of interpreting ancient texts, i.e., of rendering them meaningful in the present in a way that is faithful to, but does not imprison them in, their original settings. *See also* Scripture, interpretation of.   SANDRA M. SCHNEIDERS

Hermes, Georg (hair'meez), 1775–1831, German philosopher and theologian. Ordained in 1799, he was appointed professor of dogmatic theology at

Münster in 1807. He accepted a position at the newly founded University of Bonn shortly after the publication of the first part of *Einleitung in die christkatholische Theologie* (1819), which treated the philosophical presuppositions of knowing the truth, God, and revelation. After Hermes's death, his writings were condemned and placed on the Index of Forbidden Books by Pope Gregory XVI for being semi-rationalist, i.e., reducing supernatural truths to truths of reason. *See also* rationalism.

hermit (Gk. *erēmia*, "desert"), one who embraces a solitary life. Christian hermits appeared in the deserts of Egypt and Palestine at the end of the third century. The dangers, physical and spiritual, associated with living alone, however, prompted a move within monasticism toward a cenobitic (communal) life. Yet, a great variety of eremitic life thrived among early Christians and again from the tenth to the twelfth centuries. These hermits developed an intense devotion to Jesus, a deep life of prayer, and great austerity. The best known of the hermits of the early Church was Anthony of Egypt (d. 356), about whom Athanasius (d. 373) wrote an influential biography. *See also* anchorite, anchoress; Anthony of Egypt, St.; desert; monasticism.

Hermits of St. Augustine, Order of. *See* Augustinians; Augustinian Hermits.

heroic virtue, the exemplary practice of Christian virtues so that one becomes a model and ideal of Christian discipleship. All Christians are called to live virtuously. They should cultivate habits that demonstrate the power of God's grace in their lives. Virtue (Lat., *virtus*, "strength") becomes heroic when the cardinal and theological virtues exceed the demands of simple compliance. The cardinal virtues are prudence, justice, fortitude, and temperance. The three theological virtues are faith, hope, and love. Before someone is canonized, heroic virtue must be proved. *See also* virtue.

Hesburgh, Theodore Martin, b. 1917, Holy Cross priest, president of the University of Notre Dame for thirty-five years (1952–87), and perhaps the most admired American Catholic of his generation. Born in Syracuse, New York, he studied for the priesthood at the University of Notre Dame, the Gregorian University in Rome, and at Catholic Univer-

Theodore M. Hesburgh, C.S.C., for thirty-five years president of the University of Notre Dame (1952-87) and one of the most influential Catholic leaders in U.S. history.

sity in Washington, D.C. He was ordained a priest of the Congregation of Holy Cross (C.S.C.) in 1943 and earned a Ph.D in theology from The Catholic University of America in 1945. Seasoned by service as chaplain to returning World War II veterans at Notre Dame's "Vetville," as classroom teacher and theology department chairman, and as vice president for three years, Hesburgh took over as president of Notre Dame in 1952 and led the university through a period of unprecedented growth. By the time he retired in 1987, student enrollment had almost doubled; some three dozen new buildings had been erected; the annual operating budget increased from $9 million to $200 million, and the endowment from $10 million to $450 million. Qualitative improvement matched quantitative growth, as reflected in rising academic credentials among entering freshmen, enhanced scholarly productivity by faculty members, and the development of new graduate programs. Hesburgh's leadership quickly attracted attention beyond the Notre Dame campus. He has served on scores of national and international bodies, including fourteen presidential commissions. As a charter member of the Civil Rights Commission, and its chairman for three years, Hesburgh established himself as a leading champion of racial justice. He has received over one hundred honorary

degrees, and countless other awards, including the nation's highest civilian honor, the Medal of Freedom. At Notre Dame, the main library and a center for international and peace studies are named for him. In 1994, at the age of 77, he was elected head of Harvard University's Board of Overseers. *See also* Notre Dame, University of.   PHILIP GLEASON

Hesychasm (Gk., *hesychia,* "quiet," "stillness," "peace"), a general name for the contemplative tradition of Eastern Orthodox Christianity but one with a number of specific meanings. It can mean a hermit as distinguished from a cenobitic monk; interior prayer as found among the monks in the East from the fourth century onward and passed on orally for many centuries; prayer of the heart; wordless and imageless prayer; use of the Jesus Prayer along with rhythmic breathing; and interior prayer that makes use of the Jesus Prayer and that leads to vision of divine light as described in the theology of Gregory of Palamas (d. 1359). The *Philocalia,* compiled by Macarius of Corinth (d. 1805) and Nicodemus (d. 1809), is an early modern collection of Hesychast texts that has had a wide influence, e.g., on the Russian *The Way of a Pilgrim* and even on Western Christian spirituality. The Hesychast tradition seeks not mystical phenomena or even ecstasy but, like the best of Western mysticism, divine love that inflames the human heart with love of God and neighbor and brings humanity to its fullness. *See also* mysticism.

Hexapla, a compilation by Origen (d. ca. 254) of the available Hebrew and Greek OT text and translations. Surviving only in fragments, the *Hexapla* contained the Hebrew consonantal text, a transcription into Greek letters, and four Greek translations (Aquila, Symmachus, the Septuagint, and Theodotion) of the OT. *See also* Origen; Septuagint.

hierarchy (Gk., "rule by priests") the ordered body of clergy (bishops, priests, deacons), or more usually, of bishops alone. The term is generally employed only by those who adopt the "Catholic principle" of ecclesial order, namely, by Catholics, Anglicans/Episcopalians, and Eastern Catholic and Orthodox Christians, who regard the threefold hierarchical order of bishop, priest (presbyter), and deacon as divinely instituted by Christ and, therefore, a permanent structural feature of ecclesial life. Contemporary theologians interpret the hierarchical constitution of the Church in light of the principles of legitimate diversity, collegiality, authority as service, and the Church as the whole People of God. *See also* bishop.

hierarchy of truths, a principle that recognizes the relative importance assigned to various Christian doctrines. While the phrase has become popular since Vatican II (1962–65), the principle has functioned throughout the Church's history. The specific phrase originated from a speech delivered by Italian archbishop Andrea Pangrazio of Gorizia-Gradisca and is found in the Decree on Ecumenism (1964) of the Second Vatican Council. "When comparing doctrines with one another, [Catholic theologians] should remember that in Catholic doctrine there exists an order or 'hierarchy' of truths, since they vary in their relation to the foundation of the Christian faith" (n. 11). The text concerns ecumenical relations. While acknowledging that all truths must be believed with the same faith and kept with equal fidelity, the council concedes that all truths are not equally important. To enhance ecumenical dialogue and assist the churches in their mutual quest for truth, the council acknowledges the importance of weighing the truths of the faith. This action ensures that what is peripheral does not obscure what is essential, and conversely, what is constitutive is not judged as fleeting. The affirmation of a hierarchy of truths offers a framework that promotes legitimate diversity while ensuring essential unity. *See also* doctrine; dogma.

Hieratikon (hi-uhr-ah-tee-kawn'; Gk., *hieratikos,* "priestly"), Byzantine "Sacerdotal," or liturgical book used by the priest and deacon, containing the prayers and litanies needed for the celebration of the Eucharist, Vespers, and Matins. The contents of the Hieratikon are excerpted from the larger Euchologion or complete Byzantine Sacramentary. The Hieratikon is also also called Hierotelestikon (*hierotelestia,* "sacred service") or Liturgikon ("liturgical [book]"). *See also* Euchologion; sacramentary.

hierodeacon (hi'uhr-oh-dee-kahn; Gk., *hieros diakonos,* "holy deacon"), Byzantine term for a deacon who is also a monk. *See also* deacon; monk.

hieromonk (hi'uhr-oh-muhnk; Gk., *hiereus,* "priest"), Byzantine term for a monastic priest. *See also* monk; priest.

High Church, originally those in the Church of England who refused to switch their loyalties from James II to William III (1688) and who held Catholic-leaning views of Church, sacraments, and priesthood. The term was later applied to the Oxford movement of the nineteenth century and especially to Catholicizing tendencies in Anglican worship. Now used of liturgies marked by ritual solemnity. *See also* Anglicanism; Anglo-Catholicism; Oxford movement.

High Mass, one of three modes formerly used to celebrate the Tridentine Mass. The High Mass was sung, unlike the Low Mass, which was spoken in a quiet voice. High Mass was celebrated without additional assisting ministers, unlike the Solemn High Mass, which was sung and required the presence of a deacon and a subdeacon. The distinction among Low, High, and Solemn High Mass was dropped after the Second Vatican Council. However, the underlying principle of progressive solemnization, reserving more elaborate ceremonies for higher festivals and occasions, remains as valid in the 1990s as formerly. *See also* Low Mass; Mass; Solemn High Mass.

high priest, the head of the priests at the Temple in Jerusalem. After the Babylonian exile the high priest was the head of the Jewish nation within a foreign empire; in the second and first centuries B.C., the Jewish king was also the high priest. The office became a political appointment in 37 B.C., and it ceased altogether with the Roman destruction of the Temple in A.D. 70. In Heb 3:1 and 9:1–28, Christ's saving work is portrayed metaphorically as that of a high priest on the Day of Atonement. After the early second century A.D. the epithet "high priest" is occasionally applied to a bishop, as it is to the pre-Israelite priest Melchizedek (Gen 14:18–20) in the Canon of the Roman Mass. *See also* priesthood.

Hilarion, St., ca. 291–ca. 371, early Christian monastic figure. Born in Palestine, Hilarion converted to Christianity at Alexandria. From Anthony he learned the ways of the eremitic life. He tried to escape fame by moving to distant places. From Epiphanius, who knew Hilarion, Jerome took information for a biography of Hilarion. *See also* Anthony of Egypt, St.; Jerome, St.

Hilary of Poitiers, St., ca. 315–ca. 367, bishop of Poitiers, expounder of the doctrine of the Trinity against Arianism and, since 1851, a Doctor of the

Church. His exile from modern France to the eastern Mediterranean exposed him to the resources of biblical interpretation in the Origenist tradition, which he used especially in his Christological reading of the Psalms, and to the intricacies of Greek theology in the battles following Nicaea. While Hilary's devotion to anti-Arian defense of the deity of Christ and the Holy Spirit has given him the sobriquet "Athanasius of the West," his positions were marked by flexibility of terminology, openness to multiple ways of resisting Arian conclusions (including some homoiousian positions), and a distinctive perspective on the Trinity and the person of Christ. Feast day: January 13. *See also* Arianism; Christology; Trinity, doctrine of the.

Hilda, St., 614–80, Anglo-Saxon abbess. A Northumbrian princess baptized by Paulinus (627), Hilda later founded and presided over the double monastery at Whitby. Feast day: November 17. *See also* double monasteries.

Hildebrand. *See* Gregory VII, St.

Hildegard of Bingen, St., 1098–1179, German nun, mystic, and scholar. Having entered religious life as a child, Hildegard founded the Benedictine convent of Rupertberg near Bingen in 1147. Renowned for her visions, related in the *Scivias,* Hildegard was a theologian, physician, and composer as well as an energetic reformer. Feast day: September 17.

Hillenbrand, Reynold Henry, 1909–79, priest, social activist, and liturgical pioneer. His priestly career in the archdiocese of Chicago was devoted to making the principles of social justice embodied in the papal encyclicals a reality among U.S. Catholics. This was at the heart of his endeavors in liturgical reform, Catholic Action, and the Christian Family Movement. A dynamic and charismatic figure, Hillenbrand had a profound impact on a generation of Chicago's priests and laypersons. *See also* Catholic Action; Christian Family Movement; liturgical movement.

Hilton, Walter, d. 1396, one of the English Mystics. He lived as a hermit before becoming an Augustinian canon at Thurgarton Priory. His most famous work in English is *Scale of Perfection,* which describes the stages of conversion in the soul. His other writings include *Epistle to a Devout Man in Temporal Estate, The Song of Angels* and various writings in Latin. *See also* English Mystics.

Hincmar of Reims, ca. 806–82, archbishop, canonist, and theologian. Appointed archbishop of Reims (845) by King Charles the Bald, Hincmar was the implacable opponent of Gottschalk of Orbais. Chaotic Carolingian politics involved Hincmar in a number of other controversies, including attacks on various members of the royal family and several disagreements with Pope Nicholas I. *See also* Gottschalk of Orbais.

Hippolytus, St. (hip-pahl'i-tuhs), ca. 170–ca. 236, ecclesiastical writer and martyr. Photius asserted that Hippolytus was a disciple of Irenaeus. As a presbyter at Rome, he fiercely opposed Sabellianism. He attacked Pope Zephyrinus (198/9–217) and Pope Callistus (217–22) and is thought to have established himself as an antipope to the latter. He diverged from the Roman bishops in both doctrine and practice: he promoted a Logos doctrine that involved a change in the relations between the Father and the Word and refused forgiveness to those who sinned after Baptism. During his joint exile with Pope Pontian (230–35) under Emperor Maximinus, he was reconciled to Rome. His body was brought back to Rome by Pope Fabian (236–50) in 236 and given a martyr's burial. His *Refutation of All Heresies* (attribution disputed by some) blames Greek philosophy as the origin of Christian heresies. His *Apostolic Tradition* is a valuable source for the liturgical practice of the Roman church in the second and third centuries. Feast day: August 13. *See also* Irenaeus of Lyons, St.; Sabellianism.

Hirscher, Johann Baptist (heer'shuhr), 1788–1865, German theologian. Ordained in 1810, he began teaching moral and pastoral theology at the University of Tübingen in 1817; in 1837, he accepted a position at the University of Freiburg. Hirscher called for extensive changes in the liturgy of the Eucharist: use of the vernacular, Communion under both species, and suppression of private Masses. He also urged that mandatory celibacy for priests be rescinded. He published a three-volume work on moral theology, discussing the moral life in terms of the realization of the kingdom of God, and two popular catechisms. His advocacy of church reform and his conciliatory posture to the German state led authorities to put his works on these matters on the Index of Forbidden Books in 1849. *See also* moral theology.

history, theology of, interpretation of history from the perspective of faith in the triune God. History is the medium through which the people come to understand and appropriate themselves through interaction and self-giving and rising above the self; history is thus the arena of persons' self-transcending encounters with one another and with God. For the Christian, this encounter with God has taken place preeminently in the life, death, and Resurrection of Jesus of Nazareth and continues in the community through the power of the Spirit. Human history becomes the ongoing story of the self-donating love of the triune God and the response in freedom of the human community. The response finds expression within the personal and structured relationships that bind human beings together in a matrix of meaning and values we call culture. A theology of history includes critical discernment of culture in the light of the gospel, a reading of the "signs of the times."

Sacred and Secular History: The Christian tradition understands God as active in human history: Yahweh parted the sea and entered into covenantal relationship with Israel; Jesus of Nazareth incarnated the revelation of God in his life, death, and Resurrection; the Holy Spirit gathers the community to become the presence of God in the world and leads it toward fulfillment. The Pauline tradition saw Jesus as the new Adam, inaugurating a "new creation"; early apologists, reflecting on Jesus Christ as incarnate Logos present in Jewish prophecy and pagan wisdom, identified Christianity as the necessary continuation and fulfillment of human history; Augustine (d. 430) especially in the *City of God,* underscored the dialectic between the history of salvation and profane political history; medieval disagreement about the motive of the Incarnation (Was the Incarnation motivated by the sin of Adam? Aquinas answered yes, Bonaventure no) revealed differences in the tradition about the integral unity of profane and sacred history.

Secularization accelerated the distinction of general history from salvation history; the collapse of the medieval worldview, the turn to the subject, and the discovery of history as inner element of all created reality mean that today a theology of history has all history—human activity, events, and cultures— as its object.

Pierre Teilhard de Chardin (d. 1955) proposed a teleological, evolutionary approach, grounded in the Incarnation; Karl Rahner's (d. 1984) transcendental framework saw history as the medium of human self-realization through freedom that finds its fulfillment in the radical openness of Jesus of Nazareth to God's self-communication; political and liberation theologians, drawing on eschatology, focus on the God of the future to awaken creativity in transforming cultural and political structures as components in the fulfillment of history.

An explicit appreciation of history as integral component of all created reality, not merely as a chronology of divine or human events, is a modern presupposition with consequences for theology: Christianity can be understood only in relationship to history; theology and dogma are historical realities and are subject to critical and contextual interpretation. *See also City of God;* Joachim of Fiore; salvation history; Teilhard de Chardin, Pierre.

GEORGE GRIENER

Hochland (hohk'lahnd; Ger., "highland"), a German Catholic journal of culture and religion. Around 1900, German Catholicism underwent a literary revival, a reaction to both Prussian and Vatican repressive measures. Carl Muth founded *Hochland* in 1903 as a journal that would focus on areas ranging from religion to the arts; it reported widely on topics such as neo-Scholasticism, Ralph Waldo Emerson, Rembrandt, and Richard Strauss. It became *Neues Hochland* in 1972.

Hofbauer, St. Clement Mary, 1751–1820, Redemptorist priest and Apostle of Vienna. Born in Moravia, Hofbauer studied for the priesthood at the University of Vienna. After ordination in 1784, he joined the Redemptorist order, which he served in various capacities throughout Europe for twenty-four years. Expelled from Warsaw in 1808 by Napoleon I, he returned to Vienna where he worked for the spiritual renewal of the city. Feast day (no longer observed universally): March 15.

Hogan Schism, a conflict between lay trustees and their bishop, which took place at St. Mary's Cathedral, Philadelphia. In 1820 the trustees of St. Mary's corporation appointed an Irish priest, William Hogan, as rector. Late in 1820, when the new bishop, Henry Conwell, arrived, Hogan resisted the bishop's authority and prevented his use of the cathedral. The bishop first suspended and then excommunicated Hogan. During the dispute Hogan proposed establishing a self-governing American Catholic Church. In response to the schism, Pope Pius VII issued the apostolic brief *Non Sine Magno* in 1822 forbidding trustees the power to appoint and remove pastors. *See also* trusteeism, lay.

Holcot, Robert, ca. 1290–1349, English Dominican and theology master at Oxford. He displayed a broad erudition, both classical and Christian, in his most popular works, including an important commentary on Wisdom. Holcot tended to favor the theological opinions of William of Ockham, although bound by his order to follow Aquinas. *See also* William of Ockham.

holiness, a spiritual quality derived from participation in the life of God who is the source of all holiness. God's creatures sense the existence of this holiness by its effects. Holiness is experienced as empowerment that is accompanied by feelings of awe and attraction. In sensing a holy presence one is struck by the realization, "I am not like this." God's greatness is overpowering, but even more importantly, God is incomprehensible. The sense that the holiness of God is a different kind of goodness than human goodness is the foundation of the doctrine of holiness. The immensity of God's goodness triggers a sense of unworthiness in the perceiver who realizes any previous conceptions of goodness pale in the face of "radical holiness."

Simultaneously, the presence of God instigates positive feelings, such as love and beatitude or mercy and peace. The experience of this facet of holiness counterbalances the experience of unworthiness, inspiring an individual to praise or thank God, or perhaps ask for mercy. It is important to note that such actions of praise or expiation do not make a person holy. The response of the creature to God is the result of holiness, not the cause of holiness. In the Christian revelation, the power and presence of God is revealed as love. The Christian is asked to respond to the revelation of God's love, but the ability to respond to this invitation is not automatic. God infuses the virtues of faith, hope, and love that enable believers to turn their whole lives toward God.

The believer's response to God's love can take many forms, such as gratitude and humility, love of neighbor, or the promotion of a just social order. These virtuous acts may be performed with varying degrees of love. The more these actions are informed by love, the more perfect is the holiness. The emphasis is not on the actions performed but on the love with which they are performed. This love, in turn, depends on the degree to which the individual is open to the love of God.

Although there must be concern for overcoming personal sins and imperfections that thwart one's complete response to God, or hamper service towards one's neighbor, the Church's sense of holiness discourages a selfish preoccupation with the perfection of one's soul.

All Christians are called to holiness (see Vatican II's Dogmatic Constitution on the Church, 1964, ch. 5). The Church on earth fosters holiness through the celebration of the sacraments, the teachings of Jesus, and the fellowship of believers. *See also* grace; sanctification. PATRICIA M. VINJE

Holiness, His, a title now restricted in Catholic practice to the pope. For the first several centuries it was used of all bishops, but after the beginning of the seventh century it was restricted to patriarchs. Since the fourteenth century it has been used only of the pope. *See also* pope.

holiness of the Church, the attribute that qualifies the Church as a people consecrated to the worship and service of God and endowed with gifts of divine grace. Vatican II declared it to be a matter of faith that the Church is indefectibly holy. The council based this belief on the biblical teaching that Christ united the Church to himself as his body and bride and endowed it with the abiding gift of the Holy Spirit (Dogmatic Constitution on the Church, n. 39). The council also described the church as "marked with a genuine though imperfect holiness" (n. 48). Thus, one must say that while the Church has a genuine holiness that it cannot lose, this holiness will always be imperfect during the Church's earthly pilgrimage.

There are three aspects of the Church's holiness: first, the objective holiness of its formal elements; second, its consecration as a priestly people; and third, the personal holiness of its members. The Church is structured by such formal elements as the word of God, sacraments, and ministry. These elements enable the Church to be an effective instrument for the holiness of its members. This holiness "is constantly shown forth in the fruits of grace which the Spirit produces in the faithful" (n. 39). On the other hand, "the Church, embracing sinners in her bosom, is at the same time holy and always in need of being purified, and incessantly pursues the path of penance and renewal" (n. 8). Though the pilgrim Church will always consist of saints and sinners, sin will never so prevail as to deprive the Church of its gift of holiness. *See also* marks of the Church.

Holland, Catholicism in. *See* Netherlands, Catholicism in the.

holy cards, small printed cards containing pious sentiments or depicting popular religious figures. Widely distributed after the advent of printing, the cards are used as mementos of religious events, to foster a particular devotion, or as a means of remembrance, e.g., for a deceased person. The subject matter is diverse but some tend toward the sentimental.

Holy cards, depicting (from top to bottom) the Sacred Heart of Jesus, the Holy Spirit descending upon the Blessed Virgin Mary to conceive the child Jesus, a guardian angel protecting a young child, and a traditional prayer to one's guardian angel.

Angel of God, my
guardian dear,
To whom his love
commits me here;
Ever this day be
at my side,
To light and guard,
to rule and guide.

Holy Communion. *See* Communion, Holy.

Holy Cross Fathers. *See* Congregation of Holy Cross.

holy days of obligation, certain days throughout the liturgical year that are dedicated to recalling important events connected with the life of Jesus Christ or persons linked to him. On these days Catholics "are bound to participate in the Mass . . . [and] . . .abstain from those labors and business concerns which impede the worship to be rendered to God, the joy which is proper to the Lord's Day, or the proper relaxation of mind and body" (can. 1247).

Although Sunday is the primary "holy day of obligation" for Catholics, the term is generally used for the particular days to which the canonical obligation is attached. Already in the second century local churches dedicated certain days to the remembrance of their martyrs. The fourth century saw the beginnings of feasts dedicated to the birth of the Lord: in the East the Epiphany and in the West Christmas. By the fifth century these feasts had become universal.

Other feasts developed as well to commemorate other mysteries of the Lord, his Mother and saints of particular importance (e.g., John the Baptist, Peter, and Paul). As these feasts multiplied through the centuries, popes and synods of bishops attempted to bring order among them to distinguish the most important and clarify the obligations attached to them. The multiplication of holy days also demanded their reduction in number, first attempted in the fifteenth century. Only after 1642, however, when Pope Urban VIII discouraged bishops from establishing new obligatory feasts, were genuine attempts at reduction made.

The 1917 Code of Canon Law recognized ten holy days of obligation, which are also listed in the 1983 code: Christmas (December 25), Epiphany (January 6), Ascension (Thursday of the sixth week of Easter), Corpus Christi (Thursday after Trinity Sunday), Holy Mary Mother of God (formerly the Feast of the Circumcision of the Lord, January 1), Immaculate Conception (December 8), Assumption (August 15), St. Joseph (March 19), Sts. Peter and Paul (June 29), All Saints (November 1). Conferences of bishops have authority to abolish or transfer certain holy days of obligation with the approval of the Holy See. Consequently, there is considerable diversity throughout the Catholic Church regarding the number of holy days of obligation actually retained in a particular nation.

In the United States, the National Conference of Catholic Bishops has removed the obligation from the feasts of St. Joseph and Sts. Peter and Paul and has transferred Epiphany and Corpus Christi to the nearest Sunday. In accord with canon 86, a local bishop can also dispense the members of his diocese from the obligation attached to a holy day if he judges that the dispensation "will contribute to the spiritual good of the faithful." A pastor can also do so in individual cases "for a just reason and in accord with the prescriptions of the diocesan bishop" (can. 1245). *See also* feasts, liturgical; Sunday.

JOHN J. STRYNKOWSKI

Holy Door (Lat., *Porta Sancta*), a door in St. Peter's Basilica in Rome that is ceremoniously opened only at the beginning of each Holy Year. Holy doors in the basilicas of St. Paul's Outside the Walls, St. John Lateran, and St. Mary Major are opened simultaneously. *See also* Saint Peter's Basilica.

Holy Family, the family consisting of Jesus, his mother, Mary, and Joseph, regarded as the model for all Catholic families. The feast of the Holy Family is celebrated on the Sunday after Christmas or, if there is no Sunday within the octave, on December 30.

Holy Father, a title of the pope. The Latin equivalent, *Beatissimus Pater,* means "The Most Holy Father," but the title, first used in English in the 1830s, is usually employed in the shorter form. *See also* pope.

Holy Ghost Fathers, the Congregation of the Holy Ghost under the Protection of the Immaculate Heart of Mary (C.S.Sp.), popularly called the Spiritans. Originally founded in France by Claude Francois Poullart des Places in 1703, they were almost eliminated during the French Revolution but were refounded in 1848 when the Congregation of the Immaculate Heart of Mary merged with the Congregation of the Holy Ghost. Francis Mary Libermann was the first superior of the united congregation. They came to the United States in 1873 to work with Catholic immigrants. There are five provinces in France, Ireland, Portugal, Germany, and the United States.

Holy Ghost. *See* Holy Spirit.

Holy Grail, legendary vessel of medieval romances, variously associated with the eucharistic cup of the Last Supper or the dish of the Paschal lamb, which provided spiritual benefits to those who beheld it.

holy hour, a paraliturgical eucharistic devotion involving adoration of the exposed Blessed Sacrament for a one-hour period. Holy hours include time for silent reflection, communal prayer, and sometimes a homily. Benediction of the Blessed Sacrament concludes the devotion. A partial or full indulgence may be received for this pious practice. An individual can also make a holy hour on his or her own. It involves time spent before the Blessed Sacrament, meditating on Scripture, reading a spiritual book, and praying, silently or according to some prescribed form. *See also* Blessed Sacrament; eucharistic devotions.

Holy Innocents, the children massacred in Bethlehem by Herod the Great in an attempt to destroy the child Jesus (Matt 2:16–18). Since the sixth century, the link between these children's fate and the birth of Christ (December 25) has been stressed through their liturgical commemoration as martyrs on December 28.

Holy Land, a designation for Israel. The Bible documents the special character of the land by revealing that the Lord promised it to Abraham and his offspring and that they later gained it through conquest (Numbers, Joshua). There the temples were built, God was worshiped, and the events of the OT transpired. The facts that Jesus lived, died, and rose in it and the earliest events of Christian history took place there led to its being called the Holy Land in the Middle Ages. From the fourth century Christians made the sacred sites in the land the goal of pilgrimages.

Holy Name of Jesus, popular devotion, vigorously preached by the fifteenth-century Franciscan Bernardino of Siena as a way of combatting blasphemy. The devotion became a staple of Catholic piety among, e.g., the Jesuits, and later fostered pious groups like the Holy Name Society founded precisely to honor the name of God. *See also* Holy Name Society.

HOLY ORDERS

*H*oly Orders is the sacrament by which one is received into the ministry of the diaconate, priesthood, or episcopacy in the Church. According to Catholic teaching, the sacrament of Holy Orders is a divinely instituted structure of the Church of Christ. Reception of the sacrament signals the Church's belief that the candidate is united with the ministry of Jesus and the apostolic Church and empowered to minister in the name and power of Christ in the Church and in the world. The ordained is also commissioned to represent the Church to itself and to the world. In practice and in understanding, Holy Orders has undergone profound changes from its origins in the NT period to the developments of the Second Vatican Council (1962–65).

NEW TESTAMENT ORIGINS

It is a tenet of Catholic belief that the origins of what has come to be called the sacrament of Holy Orders are to be found in the ministry of Jesus and in the developments of the early Church described in the NT. Contemporary biblical scholarship confirms the idea that Jesus called disciples to follow him and that among them a group of twelve served as a symbolic representation of the twelve tribes of Israel and of the fulfillment of God's promises dawning in Jesus and his ministry. After Jesus' death and Resurrection the Twelve exercised a collective leadership among the first believers and a key role in the founding decisions of the early Church.

Alongside the Twelve are many other examples of ministerial leadership in the early Church: the Hellenist leaders of Acts 6; James and the presbyters (Gk., *presbyteroi*, "elders") in Jerusalem; Paul and local leaders of the Pauline communities; the second-generation apostolic delegates Timothy and Titus and local church leaders, presbyters, and "overseers" (Gk., *episkopoi*) to be set up under their direction; and presbyters in the communities of the Letters of John. Paul's Letters indicate the presence of yet other types of ministers in the early Church: apostles, prophets, and teachers have a special prominence, but there are other ministers as well (1 Cor 12; Rom 12; 16). The clearest indications of attempts to set up a deliberate structure of ministry are present in the Pastorals (1–2 Timothy and Titus).

NT evidence suggests there were different ways in which Church leaders emerged or were appointed. In light of subsequent developments some indications are especially significant. In Acts 6 seven Hellenists are chosen by the community and presented to the apostles, who pray and lay hands on them. While the exact meaning of this gesture is not evident, texts from the Pastorals (1 Tim 4:14; 2 Tim 1:6) may provide clearer antecedents for later ordination rites.

THE PATRISTIC CHURCH

Between the end of the first century and the early third century the notion of an ordered ministry in the Church came more clearly into focus. Clement of Rome, writing ca. A.D. 96 to promote church order at Corinth, refers to a deliberate provision for a succession of ministers from the apostles. While historical scholarship fails to find evidence for so precise an ordering, it is important to recognize the early Church conviction that later ministers stand in continuity with the ministry of Jesus and the apostles.

Letters of Ignatius of Antioch (d. ca. 107) make a distinction between the offices of overseer and presbyter and promote a threefold Church order of overseer (forerunner of the later bishop), presbyter (forerunner of the later priest), and deacon. It is Tertullian (d. ca. 220) who first uses the terms "ecclesiastical order" or "priestly order" to differentiate overseers, presbyters, and deacons from the body of the laity. Tertullian's understanding of orders and ordination is influenced by the notion of a juridical charge for a function in a Church structured according to responsibilities and powers.

A different approach to orders is present in the *Apostolic Tradition* of Hippolytus (d. ca. 236), written in Rome about 215. Ordination rites described in this document refer to the imposition of hands and prayer for the gift of the Spirit empowering the overseer, presbyter, or deacon for the ministry to be received. Hippolytus also recognizes the role of the whole community in the selection of the overseer, if not the other offices as well. Though the influence of Hippolytus was widespread, the Latin-speaking churches tended to view orders more as an institutional structure rather than, as in Greek-speaking churches, a Spirit-guided ministry for the Church.

Two other developments in these early centuries are important. The gradual application of the OT typology of priesthood, first to the overseer and later to the presbyter, served as a prism through which these orders would be understood. Second, changing Church needs served to alter the roles of the two offices. The overseer/bishop was the focal point of ministry in the earliest centuries, both in his leadership in the local community and in his ministry in the wider community of churches. Presbyters functioned as a council of advisers to the bishop, and deacons assisted the bishop both in administrative tasks and in the liturgy. As the Christian population grew, the presbyter, identified increasingly as priest, came to assume many of the responsibilities of the bishop in the local community, in leadership and in liturgy, with a corresponding lessening of his role as adviser to the bishop. Bishops, for their part, became more involved with administrative and judicial responsibilities both in the Church and in society and less immediately identified with the normal liturgical life of the community. Further, with the increased importance of presbyters, the role of the deacons was reduced to liturgical functions and the order came to be seen as a transition to priesthood.

THE MEDIEVAL PERIOD

These practical developments and the increased numbers of monks and priests whose principal ministry centered on church worship influenced the medieval understanding of orders. Three developments are especially important. The first came in the tendency to understand Holy Orders largely in terms of the power of the priest to consecrate the body and blood of Christ in the sacrifice of the Mass and to administer the other sacraments. The sacramental character associated with ordination was seen as a configuration to Christ, the priest, with power to act in Christ's name when pronouncing the consecratory words. Theologians found support for this theological view in the writings of Jerome (d. 420), who, thinking there was no clear distinction between presbyters and overseers in the NT, taught that the two were equally priests. As the essence of priesthood was thought to consist in power over the Eucharist, the distinction between bishop and priest was regarded as a disposition of Church authority. This touches a second development.

Only in the twelfth century was the notion of sacrament clarified and Holy Orders recognized as one of the seven sacraments of the Church. Discussion continued, however, on what was included in the sacrament of Holy Orders. The common, though not unanimous, opinion held that there were seven orders: porter, exorcist, lector, acolyte, subdeacon, deacon, and priest. It was widely recognized that the first four of these, the minor orders, and the subdiaconate were ecclesiastical institutions and not strictly sacraments. A majority view held that episcopacy was also not a part of the sacrament of Holy Orders but rather a position conferred by ecclesiastical jurisdiction. A minority view, held by canonists and some theologians, affirmed that episcopacy did belong to the sacrament of Holy Orders; some pointed to the power the bishop held in the Body of Christ, the Church.

A third significant development came in the influence of the sixth-century Neoplatonic Syrian author who wrote under the pseudonym of Dionysius (Denys) the Areopagite, the Athenian convert of Paul (Acts 17:34). His writings, thought from the pseudonym to be from the first century and therefore accorded great authority, espoused a hierarchical view of the Church as participating in and reflecting the divinely ordered structure of the entire universe. As there were three orders in the angelic hierarchy, so there were three orders in the clerical hierarchy—bishops, priests, and deacons—and three orders in the lay hierarchy—religious, laity, and catechumens. In this schema of understanding, higher orders influenced lower. And when the catechumenate dissolved, laity were perceived as passively receiving grace from the clergy.

These developments contributed to an understanding and practice of orders that was emphatically cultic, clerical, and hierarchical. This approach was challenged by the Reformation.

THE COUNCIL OF TRENT

The Reformers took issue with several of these developments, most especially in the emphasis on the Mass as an unbloody sacrifice to the neglect of ministry of the word, on the distinction between clergy and laity, and on the teaching of a divinely ordered hierarchy within Church ministry. These complaints reflected Reformers' concern to preserve the gratuity of divine grace, the priority of the Word, and ministry of the word. Trent's teaching, both in its doctrinal statements and in its reform measures, was largely a defense of existing practices as a response to the challenges of the Reformers and not a complete theology of orders.

The principal teachings of the council may be summarized as follows. First, the council defended the existence of a visible and external priesthood with the power of consecrating the body and blood of the Lord and forgiving sins in Christ's name. Neither the responsibility of preaching nor that of community leadership is emphasized in the dogmatic teaching of the council. Second, the council taught that Holy Orders, as one of the seven sacraments instituted by Christ, confers grace on those who receive it. Third, the council defended the hierarchical structure of major and minor orders in the Church and taught that bishops are superior to priests. The council did not settle the question as to whether the episcopacy shares in the sacrament of Holy Orders. Fourth, the council upheld the distinction between the baptized and ordained in the Church. It did not deny, but made no mention of the priesthood of all believers so insisted upon in the writings of the Reformers.

The dogmatic teaching of the council was accompanied by disciplinary decrees that included such matters as directives on preaching and pastoral care. But it was the dogmatic teaching of Trent that guided Catholic perception of orders until the mid-twentieth century.

VATICAN II

The Second Vatican Council (1962–65), drawing upon Church tradition and recent biblical, liturgical, and historical studies, marks a major development in Catholic thought and practice with regard to the sacrament of Holy Orders. Fundamental to its teaching on Holy Orders is the council's basic teaching on the Church and the Christological basis for that understanding. By Baptism all the faithful are called to be a priestly people who, by the Spirit of Christ, continue the threefold mission of Christ as prophet, priest, and servant of the kingdom of God (Dogmatic Constitution on the Church, chap. 1). All the faithful have a share in the mission of the Church and in the worship of the Church. The notion of the priesthood of the faithful is invoked specifically as the basis for the faithful's participation in the offering of the Eucharist (n. 10). The reassertion of the priesthood of all believers is a major element in conciliar teaching on the sacrament of Holy Orders. The post-Tridentine tendency to see the laity as passive recipients of the ministry of the ordained has been corrected. Vatican II does teach that, though there exists an essential difference between the priesthood of the ordained and the priesthood of all the faithful, the two are nonetheless related one to the other and both share in the one priesthood of Christ. The relationship between the priesthood of the faithful and the ordained priesthood, however, is not fully developed.

Conciliar teaching on Holy Orders looks to all three forms of the sacrament. The council teaches that the fullness of priesthood and so of the sacrament of Holy Orders resides in the episcopacy (n. 21). This represents a shift from the previous tendency to see orders in terms of priesthood and signals a retrieval of the patristic view of the bishop's role over the medieval view that episcopacy was not a sacrament but a role of jurisdictional authority within the Church. Further, by sacramental ordination the bishop receives the threefold ministry of preaching and teaching, of sanctifying, and of governing (n. 27). This latter teaching constitutes another change from the medieval view that, while sacramental ordination provided the basis for the sanctifying ministry, the responsibilites of preaching, teaching, and governing were matters of jurisdiction. All three roles, grounded in sacramental ordination, are seen as a ministry of service exercised in hierarchical communion with the episcopal college of which the pope is head.

Priest and deacon share in the one sacrament of Holy Orders, though each in its own way. The priest, by virtue of sacramental ordination, shares in the threefold ministry of Christ as minister of God's word, as minister of sacraments, and as pastoral guide of the community (n. 28). This more comprehensive understanding of priestly ministry contrasts with Trent's linking priesthood so closely with Christ's sacrifice on the cross. While the priest is truly such by ordination, the priest exercises ministry in dependence on the bishop and in union with the entire presbyterate of the diocese.

The deacon receives the sacrament of Holy Orders as one who ministers in conjunction with the bishop and the body of priests. The areas of the deacon's ministry are three: ministry of liturgy, ministry of the word, and ministry of charity. Vatican II provided for the restoration of the diaconate as a permanent order in the ministry of the Church (n. 29).

In 1972 Paul VI abrogated minor orders and the subdiaconate in the Latin Church and replaced the latter with the lay ministries of lector and acolyte.

CONCLUSION

The sacrament of Holy Orders, like the Church itself, is a complex reality, both human and divine, which shows in its history both continuity and dramatic developments in response to different needs and changing understandings.

The principal line of continuity comes in the Catholic conviction that apostolic ministry is a divinely constituted element of Church. The sacrament of Holy Orders, in its different forms, reminds the Church in each age that Christ, present through the Spirit, is the ultimate authority and source of Church order. The ordained minister is a sacramental representation of the Christ, in whom the Church is founded and in whose Spirit the Church continues to maintain its core identity. The ordained minister is also a representative of the Church to itself, a community of people worshiping the Father through Christ in the Spirit, a community that, in the Spirit, continues the mission of Christ to be sign and instrument of God's unity with humankind and, in that unity, of humankind's being one in a reconciliation and peace that last unto eternity. Theological understandings of Christ in his humanity as sacrament of God and of the Church as sacrament of Christ are basic to recent understanding of Holy Orders as a sacrament of Christ to the Church and, always within the body of the faithful, as sacrament of the Church to the world.

The sacrament of Holy Orders is also a historical reality and, as such, influenced by developments in practice and in theological understanding. Both factors will no doubt continue to affect the sacrament of Holy Orders in decades and centuries to come.

See also bishop; clergy; deacon; episcopacy; hierarchy; major orders; ministry; minor orders; ordination; presbyter; priesthood; sacrament; sacramental character.

Bibliography

Cooke, Bernard. *Ministry to Word and Sacraments: History and Theology.* Philadelphia: Fortress Press, 1976.

O'Meara, Thomas Franklin. *Theology of Ministry.* New York: Paulist Press, 1983.

Osborne, Kenan B. *Priesthood: A History of Ordained Ministry in the Roman Catholic Church.* New York: Paulist Press, 1989.

Power, David N. *Ministers of Christ and His Church: Theology of Priesthood.* London: Geoffrey Chapman, 1969.

FREDERICK J. CWIEKOWSKI

Holy Name Society, lay Catholic men's association established to promote devotion to the name of Jesus and the sanctification of its members. A Spanish Dominican friar, Diego of Victoria, founded the society in the fifteenth century, calling it the "Confraternity of the Name of God." Much of the society's growth in the United States resulted from the efforts of another Dominican, Father Charles H. McKenna.

During the late nineteenth century, the society functioned as an important association for promoting the Catholic faith among immigrants to the United States. Only men were allowed to join. In 1896, the U.S. Catholic bishops received permission from the Vatican to establish a Holy Name association in every parish. By 1910 the society had about 500,000 members. It organized parades and rallies not only to spread public devotion to Jesus' name but also to demonstrate Catholic strength, indicative of the Catholic triumphalism of the period.

Many such societies organized events to nurture their members' piety. They would receive Communion once a month as a group, followed by a "Communion breakfast," to which a guest speaker usually was invited. By 1963, the society claimed a worldwide membership of about five million. With many of the changes brought about by the Second Vatican Council (1962–65), interest in the Holy Name Society waned. In many parishes other associations of parishioners have replaced it.

Holy Names, Sisters of. *See* Sisters of the Holy Names of Jesus and Mary.

Holy Office, originally a tribunal for final appeals and papal causes established by Pope Paul III in 1542 and reorganized by Pope Sixtus V in 1587. It became the Sacred Congregation for the Doctrine of the Faith under Pope Paul VI in 1967 and retained that title when Pope John Paul II reorganized the Roman Curia in 1988. *See also* Congregation for the Doctrine of the Faith; Inquisition.

holy oils, oils consecrated by a bishop or priest to be used in the sacraments of initiation, (Baptism, Confirmation, and Eucharist), ordination, or the Anointing of the Sick. Ordinarily the oils are consecrated by the bishop at the Chrism Mass celebrated on Holy Thursday morning.

Holy Places, sites in the Holy Land (modern Israel) reputed to be associated with Jesus. Among the most popular objects of pilgrimage: the Cenacle (Upper Room), the Via Dolorosa (Way of the Cross), the Church of the Holy Sepulchre, and the Mount of Olives. *See also* Holy Land.

Holy Roman Empire, European state founded by the German king Otto I in 962 as a successor to Charlemagne's empire. The borders of the empire underwent many changes, but its core was the German principalities, Austria, and Bohemia, with parts of Italy and the Netherlands incorporated into the empire at various times. Emperors were elected by the more powerful princes and were originally crowned by the pope in Rome, a practice discontinued in 1562. After the fifteenth century, the emperor was almost always a member of the Austrian Hapsburg dynasty. Emperor Francis II dissolved the empire in 1806. *See also* Charlemagne.

Holy Saturday, the day before Easter Sunday. In the ancient Church, Christians marked this Saturday by fasting in preparation for the Easter festival to follow. Then, after sundown, they commenced a vigil that lasted all night and concluded with Baptism and Eucharist at dawn. In the Middle Ages, however, many of the services attached to the Easter Vigil were transferred to Holy Saturday morning. In 1951, Pope Pius XII restored the ancient Easter Vigil, paving the way for Holy Saturday to return (after the Holy Week reforms of 1956) to its ancient character as a day of preparation. *See also* Easter Vigil; Holy Week.

Holy See (Lat., *sancta sedes,* "holy chair"), a term apparently related to ceremonies for installing the bishop of Rome, it now refers only to the Apostolic See, namely, the pope and those persons and departments of the Roman Curia which assist in governance and administration of the universal Church (Code of Canon Law, can. 361). It also refers to the visible and moral position of the pope as pastor of the universal Church and to the Church as a moral entity which exists by divine law and possesses certain juridical rights and obligations (can. 113). *See also* Apostolic See; papacy, the; Roman Curia; Vatican City State.

Holy Sepulchre, Church of the, Jerusalem basilica built over the site traditionally regarded as the tomb of Christ. Originally erected by the emperor Constantine early in the fourth century, the church was destroyed and rebuilt several times. The present church, which dates from the early nineteenth cen-

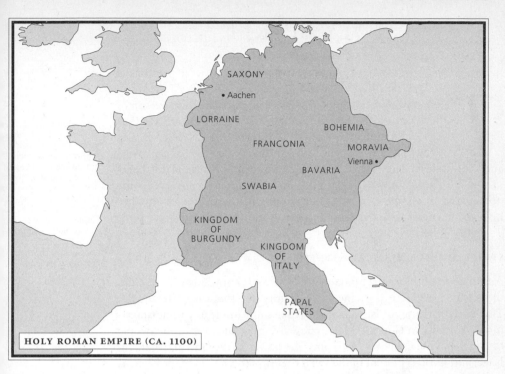

HOLY ROMAN EMPIRE (CA. 1100)

tury, is administered, not always harmoniously, by various Christian denominations.

Holy Shroud, ancient burial cloth, also known as the "Shroud of Turin" because it has been kept in the cathedral of Turin, Italy, since 1578. It became the center of much controversy and speculation that the cloth might be the burial garment of Jesus of Nazareth. Dated to the fourteenth century by carbon-14 testing in 1988, the shroud nevertheless remains the object of scientific study and religious sentiment. The linen wrap, measuring 14 feet 3 inches by 3 feet 7 inches, survived a fire in the 1500s with burn marks and apparent drippings of molten silver. The shroud bears the distinct imprint of the body of a man crucified according to procedures remarkably like those used for the execution of Jesus as recorded in biblical testimony. Forensic pathologists have confirmed that the injuries sustained by this man include scourging, puncture wounds around the head, facial bruises, a stabbing in the chest, and the piercing of wrist areas just below the palms. The crux of current controversy involves the cause of the mysterious imprint, which remains unexplained. Theories of the imprint's origin include a bright flash of scorching light emanating from the shroud victim's body. For some Christians who are intrigued by the shroud, recent scientific study has failed to resolve the issue of whether this cloth should be regarded as authentic or a forgery. *See also* crucifixion.

The Holy Shroud, venerated since the mid-fourteenth century as the burial cloth of Jesus and bearing the imprint of his body; preserved in the Cathedral of St. John the Baptist in Turin, Italy, since 1578.

HOLY SPIRIT

*T*he Holy Spirit (Heb., *ruah;* Gk., *pneuma*) is the third Person of the Trinity. The Christian understanding of God affirms that God's unity is tripersonal. The God whom Jesus called Father is revealed and present to us in the incarnation of the Word and the gift of the Holy Spirit. To say that the Holy Spirit is the third person of the Trinity, however, does not satisfy the desire for greater comprehension; if anything, it brings awareness of the degree of mystery involved in efforts to understand the person and work of the Holy Spirit.

SPIRIT OF JESUS/BIBLICAL WITNESS

Although the Bible is the fundamental source of knowledge about God, there is no systematic doctrine of the Trinity in either the OT or the NT. The sacred writings of Israel neither express nor imply any understanding of plurality in God. God does many things in the lives of the people of Israel, but the God of Israel is one. The power of the God of Abraham, Isaac, and Jacob is present in the spirit that stirs the waters of creation, as well as in the strength and courage of the priests, prophets, and kings who guide, reproach, and inspire the people of Israel; but this power cannot rightly be equated with the third Person of the Trinity. Efforts to isolate passages where the spirit of Yahweh is mentioned so that one might come to an understanding of the third Person of the Trinity are misleading at best.

Nevertheless, one of the factors in Jesus' understanding of God was the OT metaphor of God's Spirit. According to the Jewish tradition, the spirit of Yahweh functions as the creative and life-giving energy of God, as well as the power of Yahweh that comes to rest on the judges, kings, and prophets anointed to guide and challenge God's people. The spirit of Yahweh is thus God's presence at work in the lives of God's people, especially in those called to lead the community to live according to God's will.

Among the thematic links between the OT and the NT was the expectation of an ideal leader who would be anointed with God's Spirit and thus be able to definitively establish God's rule in Israel (Isa 42:1–4; 61:1–2). The NT reveals that Jesus is not only conceived by the power of the Holy Spirit (Luke 1:35), but that he is the one anointed by the Spirit of God (Matt 3:13–17; Mark 1:9–13; Luke 3:21–22) to proclaim in his person the presence of God's reign. The biblical affirmation that Jesus is the Christ, that is, that Jesus is the anointed one of Yahweh, is one of the most significant pneumatological affirmations (affirmations concerning the Holy Spirit) in the Bible.

God anoints Jesus of Nazareth with the Spirit. The resultant identification of Jesus with God brings the Christian understanding of God to a new and decisively different level. God is preeminently present in Jesus of Nazareth. In the context of Jesus' death and Resurrection, this divine presence is sent to dwell within and to empower the small band of disciples who experienced the Risen Lord. This Spirit of Jesus becomes at Pentecost (Acts 2:1–4) the unity of the otherwise disparate believers and

the pneumatic presence of the Risen Lord enabling all who believe to remain faithful until the Lord Jesus comes again (Rev 22:17–21). It is the power of the Spirit of the resurrected Lord Jesus that unites and animates the Christian community even today.

Thus the biblical witness concerning God's Spirit points to the elusive, energizing, and universal presence or activity that the Christian community has come to affirm as that of the divine Person who (together with the Son) is sent by the Father as the means of human union with God.

SPIRIT OF GOD/DOCTRINAL DEVELOPMENTS

Belief in the one God who is Father, Son, and Spirit is the central truth of all Christian theology and the core reality of Christian living. In an attempt to name the specific personal identity and unique role of the Holy Spirit one encounters the most basic and foundational questions of theology: Who is God? How do persons experience God? The Christian community maintains that it is Jesus of Nazareth, born of Mary by the power of the Spirit, who is the revelation of God. In the life, death, and Resurrection of Jesus is found the specifically Christian answer to the question of God's identity. The Christian community also maintains that it is God's gift of the Holy Spirit that enables human relationship with God. Persons are one with the triune God insofar as they accept the gift of divine grace, that is, the sanctifying presence of the Holy Spirit. Thus, Jesus reveals God's identity, and the Holy Spirit makes human relationship with God possible.

Knowledge of God's reality and experience of God's presence are inseparable. Although there is a logical and necessary distinction between who God is and how people experience God, there is no real separation between the two. There is no knowledge of the triune God apart from oneness with that Holy Mystery. In like manner there is no awareness of the lordship of Jesus without a corresponding intimacy with the Holy Spirit. Thus, whatever is said of Jesus has an impact on an understanding of the Spirit, just as whatever is understood of the Spirit influences what can be said of Jesus. The Spirit is the transcendent power given by God within whom believers recognize the historical person who is God's self-revelation. The Spirit is the intangible presence that enables believers to touch God in the humanity of Jesus.

In like manner, pneumatology (the theology of the Holy Spirit) is distinct (but inseparable) from both trinitarian theology and Christology. There is no pure or isolated doctrine of the Spirit that develops independently from the other central doctrines of the Church. Since all theology of the Holy Spirit is intrinsically related to Christology and trinitarian theology, extreme caution must be taken in making any definitive claims about the manner of the Spirit's being and activity. The theological model that a community of believers chooses to make central in an explication of the Holy Spirit will need to be correlated with the analogies that particular community (or individual) uses in Christology and trinitarian theology.

The existence of models or metaphors for talking about the reality of God made manifest and present in the person of Jesus and the power of the Spirit need not suggest that nothing true can be said about the mystery of God. The need for analogical language in theology does require, however, a degree of pluralism in theology; otherwise a metaphorical explanation can be mistaken for the reality itself. Although no one conceptual model of God or of the Holy Spirit can hope to be sufficient, it is nonetheless true that not all theological efforts are equally satisfactory. Selectivity is needed about any proposed models for understanding the Holy Spirit.

Christian theology in the West, however, has not tended to err on the side of saying too much about the Holy Spirit. Unfortunately, the greater danger seems to be the absence of serious theological reflection on the uniqueness of the Spirit's person and role. Both the nature of theology and the particular manner of being of the Spirit make the task difficult. Efforts to focus theological inquiry on the Spirit's person and function are hampered by the fact that the Spirit is less an object of interest or a focus of inquiry than the focusing power of all theological speculation as well as the source of all prayerful commitment. There is a kind of self-effacing quality to the Spirit's manner of being within and among persons that often leads to a benign neglect of the Spirit's unique role in the knowledge of and union with the God of Jesus. The Spirit is God's gift enabling recognition and acceptance of the lordship of Jesus. Thus, both knowledge of Jesus and commitment to God can be enriched insofar as one becomes more explicitly attentive to the unique role of the Holy Spirit in one's life as a Christian.

The most succinct statement of the Christian community's understanding of the Holy Spirit is found in the third article of the Nicene Creed (the Nicene-Constantinopolitan Creed, or creed of the Council of Constantinople, 381). In the first article of the creed the Christian community asserts its faith in the Father who is creator; in the second article the community affirms its belief in the Incarnate Word who redeems; in the third article the Church proclaims its commitment to the Spirit in whom the unity of God as well as the unity of the community with God rests.

In 325 the creed of the Council of Nicaea stated that orthodox faith included belief "in the Holy Spirit," but it did not further specify who the Spirit is or how the Spirit works in the lives of the faithful. During the decades that followed Nicaea the question of the Spirit's divinity came to the fore in a series of theological debates between those who followed the Pneumatomachians in denying the divinity of the Spirit and those who

"When the day of Pentecost had come, they were all together in one place. . . . All of them were filled with the Holy Spirit and began to speak in other languages, as the Spirit gave them the ability" (Acts 2:1, 4); *The Coming of the Holy Spirit* by the Master of Osma (ca. 1460), in the Osma-Soria Chapter House, Soria, Spain.

followed the Cappadocians (Basil, Gregory of Nazianzus, and Gregory of Nyssa) in affirming that the Spirit is God. Thus, the Council of Constantinople added a series of affirmations about the Spirit's full lordship as well as the Spirit's role in the mystery of salvation. The Catholic Church thus prays in its Sunday eucharistic celebration: "We believe in the Holy Spirit, the Lord, the giver of life, who proceeds from the Father and the Son. With the Father and the Son he is worshiped and glorified. He has spoken through the Prophets. We believe in one, holy, catholic and apostolic Church. We acknowledge one baptism for the forgiveness of sins. We look for the resurrection of the dead, and the life of the world to come."

The Council of Constantinople and all subsequent theological reflection link the Spirit to the formation of the Christian community, the experience of salvation through Baptism, and the hope for future glory. The creed suggests that the Spirit works within believers as the source of their union with one another, as a means of their oneness with God through the baptismal initiation commitment, and as the promise and impetus of their glorious transformation in the resurrection of the dead.

The Holy Spirit descending as a dove upon the Blessed Virgin Mary and the apostles, early fifteenth-century illustration in the *Missale Romanorum*, Tarazona Cathedral archives, Zaragoza, Spain.

SPIRIT OF COMMUNION/ECCLESIOLOGY AND GRACE

Most of what could be said about the Holy Spirit usually remains implicit in ecclesiology (the study of the Church) and theological anthropology (the doctrine of grace). Since the Spirit has been given to humanity as the source of unity with God and among God's people, the theology of grace and the theology of the Church are implicitly theologies of the Holy Spirit. Pneumatology seeks to make explicit God's role in the experience of communion—with one another and with God.

The Holy Spirit is the animating principle of the Church of God which has the Lord Jesus as its head. The Nicene Creed's statement of Christian belief in (that is, commitment to) the "one, holy, catholic and apostolic Church" summarizes the Catholic Church's understanding of the role of the Spirit in the community of the baptized; it summarizes the pneumatology implicit in Catholic ecclesiology. The characteristics delineated in the phrase "one, holy, catholic and apostolic" are known as the marks of the Church. The Holy Spirit's function is to endow the community with these qualities and to enable the members of the Church to cooperate with one another in making these essential aspects more fully realized in the community.

The oneness or unity of the Church is a way of asserting that the baptized are united in the Spirit so that they can be one with each other and with Jesus in their common commitment to proclaim God's reign. The Pauline image of Church as the Body of Christ (1 Cor 12:12–31) reminds believers that they are one in Christ because they have been anointed by the one Spirit who is manifested differently according to the various gifts and ministries received (1 Cor 12:1–11). Diversity is not a detriment to unity insofar as the Spirit is its source. The Spirit of God makes people one in Christ, but not at the cost of personal uniqueness with regard to distinct roles in the community. It is particularly important to remember that the unity occasioned by the presence of the Holy Spirit is the unity of the diverse. Thus the Spirit of Jesus is as much the cause of appropriate diversity as the cause of unity. Divisiveness among members of the Catholic Church as well as the division among the various denominations of Christian communities are signs of the lack of the fullness of God's Spirit.

The holiness that characterizes the Church is also the gift of the Spirit. The Church is the temple of God because God's Spirit dwells in it (1 Cor 3:16–17). The sacramental life of the Church celebrates and intensifies the experience of being called to this intimacy with the triune God. The Catholic Church identifies seven paradigmatic moments of Christian life to celebrate sacramentally: Baptism, Confirmation, Eucharist, Reconciliation, Anointing of the Sick, Holy Orders, and Matrimony. Each of the seven is an occasion for experiencing the ongoing presence of the Holy Spirit.

The link between the Catholic celebration of Confirmation and the Holy Spirit is particularly rich in symbolism. Confirmation (originally part of the baptismal initiation rite itself) celebrates the presence of the Spirit and raises the community's consciousness of God's power at work in the lives of the baptized. Confirmation is not, as is sometimes erroneously thought, the first moment of a Christian's experience of the Spirit. If there is a "first" sacramental experience of the Spirit, that moment occurs at Baptism. The baptismal commitment itself, however, is a celebration and confirmation of God's prior presence in the baptized and the Church's means of welcoming that person into the life of the Christian community.

Reflection on the implications of the holiness of the Church is the focus of theological discussion on the mystery of grace. The Christian's participation in the life of God (the grace of holiness) is the effect of the presence of the gift of God who is the Spirit of union. One of the principal themes in the doctrine of grace concerns the manner in which the efficacious grace of God works with the inalienable freedom of the individual person. Efforts to articulate the mystery of the life of faith often stumble on the presumed conflict that must exist between the grace of God and the exercise of human freedom. Although numerous texts have been written to address the dynamic of God's gracious activity in the lives of free persons, all theological speculation eventually must acknowledge that the unity of the divine and the human in the experience of grace is the effect of the gift of the Holy Spirit. The Spirit makes individuals one with God without diminishing God or destroying persons.

The third mark of the Church, catholicity, is perhaps the most easily misunderstood of the four. The term "catholic" does not refer to the Catholic Church in its difference from other Christian churches, but to the wholeness or oneness of the Church. It is a reiteration of the mark of unity but draws attention to the need for the Church to be inclusive—racially, culturally, and sexually. In addition, the catholicity of the Church serves as a reminder that the particularity of this or that local Christian community is not a threat to the universal Church. The Spirit is the divine presence who enables the particular to have universal significance.

The fourth characteristic of the Church, apostolicity, says that the Church is a missionary body called to fidelity to the fundamental mission of Christ, that is, to proclaim the presence of God's reign. Church members share the task of the apostles; they are called and enabled to pass on the faith of the apostolic community and to continue the proclamation of the Good News until the Risen Lord comes in glory. The Holy Spirit is the bond of union not only with the Church of the apostles, but also with the Church of the last days.

SPIRIT OF ALL CHRISTIANS/ECUMENICAL REFLECTIONS

Although there are numerous theological nuances that distinguish the efforts of theology to name the person and work of the Holy Spirit, Christians of all denominations generally understand the Holy Spirit as the personal gift of the Father of Jesus, the gift who enables relationship with God. There are, however, a few significant differences that require some comment.

Catholics and Protestants can be distinguished from the Eastern Orthodox tradition in their inclusion of the phrase "and the Son" in the Nicene Creed to identify the manner in which Western Christian theology has tended to explain the Spirit's procession from the Father. The theological debate around this issue (the *Filioque* controversy) has been an aspect of the ecumenical efforts of the Eastern Orthodox and the Catholic churches.

Although less sharply defined, Catholic understanding of the doctrine of grace also notably differs from the usual Protestant understanding. In the Catholic tradition great emphasis has been placed on the real change that occurs in graced persons as a result of God's salvific activity on their behalf. The traditional distinction between uncreated grace (God) and created grace (God's effect in the lives of the justified) has sometimes led Catholics to so stress the latter that they appear to reify and quantify grace rather than affirm its fundamental reality, namely, the actual presence of God in persons.

A related matter concerns the question of whether uncreated grace can best be understood as the presence of the Holy Spirit or as the indwelling of the triune God. Is the experience of grace the experience of the Spirit's unique (or proper) work in salvation or is grace only attributed to the Spirit? In other words, does the Spirit function in one's life in a specific manner that communicates the Spirit's unique personal identity in the triune God?

All Christian theology struggles with the desire to say something meaningful about God and God's relationship with humans in Jesus and the Spirit. Sometimes the limits of the language distract searchers from the truth. There are two common affirmations about the Holy Spirit that may easily be misinterpreted.

First, to say that the Spirit is the source of union with God and with one another in Christ is not to say that the Spirit is not also the source of plurality. As noted above, the Spirit unites without destroying or diminishing real difference. The personal distinctiveness of the divine Persons is not denied by their communion; the infinite difference between God and humans is never obliterated; the diversity of gifts within the Christian (and broader human) community is a blessing.

Second, to say that the Spirit is the third Person of the Trinity is not to say that the Spirit is in any sense subordinate to the first and the second divine Persons—unless one is willing to also affirm a similar dependence of the others on the Spirit. Too often Christian theology speaks of God and Jesus and presumes that all has been said. The difficulty in being definitive about the elusive, energizing, and universal presence of God's Spirit is no reason for silence. The silence to which believers are called is the silence of prayerful adoration of the Mystery who envelops their being.

See also Confirmation; *Filioque;* God; pneumatology; spirituality, Christian; Trinity, doctrine of the.

Bibliography

Congar, Yves M. J. *I Believe in the Holy Spirit.* 3 vols. Trans. by David Power. New York: Seabury, 1983.
Heron, Adasdair I. C. *The Holy Spirit.* Philadelphia: Westminister, 1983.   BARBARA A. FINAN

holy souls, the just persons in purgatory. The term is a popular designation for those who are still in purgatory being cleansed of the last remains of sin before entering heaven. It is a pious designation often associated with All Souls' Day, November 2. *See also* purgatory; soul.

Holy Spirit, sin against the. *See* sin against the Holy Spirit.

Holy Thursday, the day before Good Friday. Its traditional English name, "Maundy Thursday," comes from a Latin phrase linked to the ceremony of foot washing (*Mandatum novum*, "a new command"; see John 13:34). Foot washing appeared in the Holy Thursday liturgy at Rome during the thirteenth century. The Holy Thursday services resulted from a complex historical evolution to which three distinct liturgies contributed: the public reconciliation of penitents (no longer used, but attested in seventh-century sources); the blessing of holy oils (the "Chrism Mass," which appears in eighth-century sources and is still celebrated today); and the commemoration of the Last Supper (attested already in the late fourth century). The Missal of Paul VI (1970) restores the evening Mass of the Lord's Supper as the principal liturgy of Holy Thursday, the

Christ washing the feet of his disciples on Holy Thursday to set an example of ministry for them (John 13:3-20); sixteenth-century French painted enamel, Metropolitan Museum of Art, New York.

solemn beginning of the Easter Triduum. During the Chrism Mass (now celebrated earlier in Holy Week) priests renew their commitment to service and celibacy. *See also* Holy Week.

holy water, water blessed and used for prayer, both private and liturgical. Recalling the water of Baptism, holy water is placed in fonts and in small containers at entrances to churches. Holy water is sprinkled in blessing of both people and objects. *See also* font, holy water.

Holy Week, the last week in Lent, immediately preceding Easter. It is marked by solemn liturgical celebration of Christ's Passion. In spite of the elaborate passion chronologies found in the Gospels, Christians of the first three centuries made no attempt to imitate in their liturgies the literal details of Jesus' last days (entry into Jerusalem, the Last Supper, arrest and trial, crucifixion). Each year, instead, they remembered Christ's suffering, death, and Resurrection in a single unified liturgical celebration known as *Pascha* (Gk., Christian "Passover," or Easter). This yearly paschal observance occurred either, according to Jewish reckoning, on a fixed day of the lunar month (14 Nisan) or on the following Sunday. Eventually, the ancient Jewish date (14 Nisan) was rejected, so that "Christian Passover" (Easter) would always fall on Sunday, the Lord's Day.

Historical Development: During the fourth century, decisive changes occurred in the way Christians celebrated Easter. The earlier, unified celebration of *Pascha* (preceded by a short period of preparatory fasting) was split into a series of liturgies that imitated or reenacted the events of Jesus' final week. This development occurred, quite naturally, in Jerusalem, where Jesus was believed to have spent that week and where numerous shrines had grown up "on the very sites" where the holy events had happened. A travel diary kept in 383 by a European woman named Egeria during a pilgrimage to Jerusalem provides many details about these Holy Week liturgies. According to Egeria, the ceremonies for Palm Sunday, Holy Thursday, Good Friday, and Holy Saturday were especially noteworthy. On Palm Sunday afternoon, an elaborate procession began outside Jerusalem at the Mount of Olives. The bishop "reenacted" the role of Christ, while children waved palm fronds and the procession wound through the entire city. On Holy Thursday night, after the Eucharist had been celebrated in the afternoon, the events of Jesus' agony were reenacted: the prayer in Gethsemane, the arrest, the appearance before Pilate. Further representational liturgies occured on Good Friday, beginning with veneration of the cross for four hours before noon and followed by a solemn afternoon Liturgy of the Word that concluded with a reading of the Passion according to John. The Easter Vigil—which focused on the celebration of Baptism—began in midafternoon on Holy Saturday, with the final preparation of the adult catechumens. That night, while the catechumens were being baptized, the rest of the faithful kept vigil. Then, when the neophytes were led into church, everyone joined in the celebration of Eucharist.

This shrine-centered pattern of "representational" services soon caught on everywhere, even among communities that could claim no immediate historical connection with the sites where the original events had occurred. By the fifth and sixth centuries, the influential churches of Constantinople and Rome had imported these services, which then spread to other ecclesial communities within their jurisdictions. In the medieval West, the links between the liturgies of Holy Week and their "original times and places" were obscured. In 1956, Pope Pius XII sought to remedy this situation, and further reforms followed at Vatican Council II (1962–65). See also Easter; Easter Vigil; Egeria, Pilgrimage of; Good Friday; Holy Thursday; Palm Sunday.

NATHAN D. MITCHELL

Holy Year, proclaimed by the pope as a propitious time for pilgrimage and other observances by those who wish to grow in holiness of life and to obtain a solemn plenary indulgence. Originally celebrated every one hundred years, as was its precursor in Judaic tradition, the Jubilee year, the Holy Year gradually came to be observed every twenty-five years unless special occasions warranted additional celebrations. An ordinary Holy Year now begins the evening of December 24 with the opening of the Holy Door at St. Peter's in Rome and the doors of three other basilicas that were traditional cites for pilgrimage: St. Paul's Outside the Walls, St. John Lateran, and St. Mary Major. Local ordinaries now designate cites for pilgrimage outside Rome and dispense those observing the jubilee from conditions, decreed by papal proclamation, which they are unable to fulfill. The focus of Holy Years in recent times has been upon the celebration of God's forgiveness and mercy. See also indulgences.

homily, formerly called a "sermon." Vatican II's Constitution on the Sacred Liturgy gives pride of place to the liturgical homily, esteemed as a part of the liturgy itself (n. 52). The content of the homily may be drawn from the Scriptures or the liturgical texts of the day, taking into account the mystery celebrated and the needs of the hearers. The homily is directed toward entering more deeply into mystery so that the assembly, nourished for Christian living, is formed for witness in the world.

Homobonus, St. (Lat., "good man"), d. 1197, patron saint of tailors and clothworkers. Italian-born merchant known for his charity and concern for the poor. He was one of the few lay saints canonized in the Middle Ages who was neither a martyr nor a king. Feast day: November 13.

homoousios (Gk., "the same substance," "consubstantial"), a term meaning that Christ is equal in status with the Father and, thus, is truly God, used at the Council of Nicaea (325) to define the proper understanding of the divinity of Christ. A nonbiblical term, homoousios had been used in controversial and even heretical ways previous to 325. Nevertheless, the Council of Nicaea used homoousios against the Arians, who denied that the Son was equal in status to the Father. Opponents of the council later said that Christ was homoiousios, that is, "similar in substance" to the Father. See also Arianism; Nicaea, First Council of.

homosexuality, sexual attraction to persons of the same gender. There is no scientific agreement about the exact percentage of the human population who are homosexual in orientation. Estimates suggest that 5 to 10 percent of the population are gay (male homosexual) or lesbian (female homosexual). Similarly, there is no agreement as to the source or cause of homosexuality. Recent studies suggest that its origin may be genetic in nature. Other studies have focused on psychological or environmental causes. It is generally agreed that homosexuality is not a condition that is freely chosen. (Homosexual activity that occurs in isolated settings, such as prison, and is transitory in nature, should not be equated with true homosexuality.) While the Christian tradition has rejected homosexual activity as immoral, it is only in recent years that science and Church teaching have accepted the distinction between a homosexual orientation and overt homosexual activity. Though there is some debate as to how to describe the moral significance of a homosexual orientation, it is clear that a gay or lesbian person has the same human dignity as a heterosexual person. There is no moral guilt associated with being homosexual.

The reason homosexual activity is objectively immoral is that it lacks the finality that is proper to human sexuality. Traditionally Catholic teaching has grounded its understanding of human sexuality in the Genesis vision of man and woman coming together to be "as one body." In other words, heterosexual genital expression is normative. And while homosexual activity could be an expression of a certain type of love, it excludes the possibility of transmitting life. In recent years the pastoral application of this teaching has been marked by a greater sensitivity to the individual homosexual and by a less judgmental and censorious approach. An individual's subjective culpability is judged with prudence, while the objective norm is maintained.

As in other areas of moral discourse, there are some who disagree with this teaching. Some argue that homosexuality is another way of being human; therefore, homosexual activity is natural and good. Another position affirms that heterosexual relationships are the normative ideal. In the love of man and woman human sexuality finds its fulfillment. This ideal is not possible for all persons. For that reason homosexual activity can be accepted as a lesser evil. While morally permissible, it would be lacking in fullness. A third position would reject heterosexuality as normative and would evaluate homosexual activity in the same manner as it would heterosexual activity, by using relational criteria. If these criteria are met, then such activity would be morally acceptable. On several occasions the Church's hierarchical magisterium has rejected all three of these positions and reaffirmed previous teaching. At the same time it has called on the pastors of the Church to provide effective pastoral care for those who are homosexual. *See also* sexual morality.

MICHAEL D. PLACE

Honorary Prelate of His Holiness, until 1968 known as Domestic Prelate, a title of honor given to a priest by the pope to recognize his distinguished service to the Church or because of an important office he holds, such as vicar general. He has the title of Monsignor or Reverend Monsignor. He belongs to the pontifical family and the pontifical chapel group. For ceremonial purposes he wears a purple cassock and purple silk sash with fringes, unpleated surplice, black biretta with black tuft; on solemn but nonliturgical occasions, he wears a black cassock with red piping and other ornaments, purple sash and fringes of silk at both ends of the sash. The honor and its customs have largely fallen out of favor since the Second Vatican Council (1962–65). *See also* monsignor.

Honorius I, d. 638, pope from 625 to 638. Born in Campagna, son of the consul Petronius, he was an able pastor and administrator but is most remembered for his role in the Monothelite controversy, which debated whether there was one will or two in Christ. Replying (634) to Sergius, patriarch of Constantinople, Honorius injudiciously referred to "one will" in Christ; in a second letter, he rejected the formula "two wills" although strongly defending the Council of Chalcedon's (451) doctrine of two natures. For this he was condemned at Constantinople III (680–81), a condemnation affirmed by Pope Leo II. He has come to serve as one of the principal arguments against papal infallibility, although his teaching was clearly orthodox in intent and used language condemned only subsequently. Furthermore, he was not teaching in a solemn or definitive manner for the universal Church. *See also* Constantinople, councils of; Monothelitism.

Honorius III [Cencio Savelli], d. 1227, pope from 1216 to 1227. Old and frail when elected pope, he was determined to continue the reform program of his predecessor, Innocent III, and supported evangelical missions in Spain and the Baltics. He approved the Dominican, Franciscan, and Carmelite rules and mobilized the friars for preaching and Church reform. An accomplished administrator, Honorius added to the corpus of canon law and reorganized papal finances. He was perhaps too trusting of his former pupil Frederick II and crowned him emperor despite his unfulfilled promises to go on crusade.

Honorius Augustodunensis, or Honorius of Autun, ca. 1080/90–ca. 1156, theologian. A prolific writer, he wrote a handbook on Christian doctrine, an interpretation of the liturgy, and a work on cosmology and geography. He taught that the cause of the Incarnation was the predestination of humanity to deification, not the Fall. *See also* predestination.

hope, one of the three theological virtues that direct the human person toward union with God. In traditional Catholic theology, hope is identified as one of the virtues, together with faith and charity, by which the human person is oriented toward personal union with God in the Beatific Vision. It cannot be acquired by human efforts, but like the other theological virtues, must be bestowed directly by God. Specifically, hope is the enduring orientation of the human will toward final union with God, considered as a goal that can be attained with God's help, but without divine help impossible to attain. Hope was traditionally said to presuppose faith, since it is impossible to hope for the attainment of a goal unless one is aware of its existence and believes in it as a real possibility. At the same time, hope was said to be both prior to, and less perfect than, charity (the love of God for God's own sake) apart from whatever benefits God bestows on us. The theological virtue of hope was contrasted with two opposing vices, despair and presumption; despair leads the individual to conclude that one cannot attain salvation, even with God's help, or else to assume that God will not offer help, whereas presumption leads the individual to believe that one is sure of salvation, or can attain it readily through one's own efforts.

Developments in contemporary theology have called the presuppositions of this conception of hope into question at a number of points. Nonetheless, almost all Catholic moral theologians would agree that an attitude of hopefulness in God, or at least in some form of goodness that transcends the individual, is an integral component of a good human life. *See also* faith; theological virtues.

JEAN PORTER

Hopkins, Gerard Manley, 1844–89, English Jesuit priest and poet. Hopkins studied with Walter Pater at Oxford and was converted from Anglicanism to Catholicism by John Henry Newman in 1866. Ordained in 1877, he served as parish priest in Liverpool and later as professor of classics at University College, Dublin. He had forsworn poetry and burned his early verse upon entering the novitiate, but in 1875 he resumed with "The Wreck of the Deutschland," pondering God's role in the drowning death of five Franciscan nuns. Hopkins was characteristically influenced by Ignatian spirituality and Duns Scotus (d. 1308). His work stresses the Incarnation and its implications for the Mystical Body, individuality, the grandeur of creation, and Ignatian imagery; late poems ponder the dark night of the soul. His poetry contains innovative rhythms but remained unpublished until 1918.

Hormisdas, St., d. 523, pope from 514 to 523. He ended the thirty-five-year-old Acacian Schism in 519. His formula for union, the *Libellus Hormisdae,* signed by the patriarch of Constantinople (John II) and approximately 250 Eastern bishops, reaffirmed the teachings of the Chalcedonian formula and of Leo's *Tome* and condemned Acacius. Feast day: August 6. *See also* Acacianism.

Horologion (haw-roh-loh'gee-ahn; Gk., "timepiece," "Book of Hours"), Byzantine-rite Book of Hours. Unlike the Western breviary, an anthology with all the elements needed for the Divine Office, the Horologion contains only the "ordinary" or invariable parts of the Byzantine Divine Office, the celebration of which requires the employment of other liturgical books such as the Psalter and the propers of the temporal cycle (Oktoichos) and of the fixed (Menaion) and movable (Triodion, Pentecostarion) feasts. The native Office of Constantinople had no separate Book of Hours, and the Horologion derives from the Sabaitic Office of Jerusalem, of which there are manuscripts extant from the ninth century. The present Byzantine Horologion contains a composite office formed from the fusion of the old Palestinian monastic Horologion with the prayers and litanies of the Constantinopolitan Office in the Euchologion or Sacramentary of that church. The synthesis, a central process in the formation of the Byzantine rite, began in the Studite monasteries of Constantinople at the end of the ninth century, but was not completed until the fourteenth century. *See also* Liturgy of the Hours.

Hosanna (hoh-zahn'uh; Heb., "May God save"), word that concludes the final portion of the Sanctus ("Holy, holy, holy") during the Eucharistic Prayer. First found in Psalms (see Ps 118:25–26), "Hosanna" is said to have been a word with which the crowd acclaimed Christ's last entry into Jerusalem (Matt 21:9, Mark 11:9, John 12:13). Hosanna entered Christian liturgical use from at least the second century (see *Didache* 10:6).

Hosius, Stanislaus, 1504–79, cardinal and leader of the Polish Counter-Reformation. First as bishop of Culm (1549) and then as bishop of Ermland (1551), Hosius had great success in suppressing Polish Protestantism. His *Confessio Fidei Catholicae* became the standard of orthodoxy; thirty-two editions were published during his lifetime. *See also* Counter-Reformation/Catholic Reformation.

hospice movement, the development of physical and emotional resources for the compassionate care of the terminally ill and their families. The modern movement began in 1967 when Dame Cicely Saunders opened St. Christopher's Hospice, London. Earlier precedents took place in the nineteenth century at Saint Mary's Hospital, Dublin, and in 1905 when the Sisters of Charity inaugurated St. James Hospice, London. The first hospice in the United States opened in 1974 at New Haven, Connecticut. In two decades the North American Hospice movement has grown rapidly with nearly two thousand hospices serving almost a third of a million patients in the United States. In the Middle Ages hospices were small institutions that served the ill, the elderly, and travelers. Some modern hospices provide care in the home while others serve patients and their families in residential centers. Hospice is a celebration of life in the face of death offering medicinal, emotional, and spiritual support for the terminally ill and their families. *See also* death and dying.

hospitality, minister of, one charged with overseeing and enhancing the Church's ministry of hospitality. Greeters, ushers, parish administrators, musicians, deacons, pastors, and presiders, are all, in some sense, ministers of hospitality. Their respective roles include ensuring, at every gathering of the church, that no one is hindered from worshiping God because of external obstacles. The ministry of hospitality is a biblical value, originating in the ancient Semitic ethic of "welcoming the stranger." It continued in monastic communities, which were, by rule, required to maintain lodgings for guests, travelers, and pilgrims. In many contemporary Christian communities, the ministry of hospitality is interpreted in broad and inclusive terms by maintaining facilities that are accessible to the physically disabled, by interpreting printed materials for the sightless and spoken portions of the liturgy for the hearing-impaired, and by providing food for the hungry and clothes and housing for the poor.

Hospitallers, or Knights of St. John, a military order of crusading monks. Originating around 1070 in Jerusalem for the management and defense of a hospital for Christian pilgrims, they received papal recognition in 1113 as a separate order. Along with the Knights Templar, Hospitallers formed the army of the Crusader states, at the same time continuing to build hospitals and serve the sick and wounded. After the fall of Acre in 1291, the Hospitallers trans-formed themselves into a powerful navy based at Rhodes and then Malta that fought pirates and Turks in the Mediterranean. Present Knights continue to supervise hospitals. *See also* Crusades; Knights Templar.

host, the eucharistic bread. The term derives from the Latin *hostia,* "victim," thus recalling Christ as the Paschal Lamb sacrificed for all. *Hostia* was used as one of several names for the eucharistic bread in the Middle Ages and remains untranslated in most languages today. *See also* Communion, Holy.

Hours [Canonical], the obligatory times of daily liturgical prayer, also known as the Liturgy of the Hours. According to ancient tradition, there were seven Canonical Hours: Matins and Lauds, Prime, Terce, Sext, None, Vespers, and Compline. In 1971, following Vatican Council II, the number of hours was reduced and their contents simplified. *See also* breviary; Liturgy of the Hours.

house church, the gathering of Christians in NT times for worship in a fellow member's house (Acts 2:46; 12:12; Rom 16:5; 1 Cor 16:19; Col 4:15). There may have been a connection between the role of householder and that of presbyter (Titus 1:6; 1 Tim 3:4). Since some of the houses were owned by women (1 Cor 1:11; Acts 12:12), questions arise regarding the ministerial role of women in the NT.

Howard, St. Philip, 1557–95, Earl of Arundel, one of the Forty Martyrs of England and Wales canonized in 1970. Under the inspiration of Edmund Campion, he began in mid-life to take his Catholicism more seriously. Arrested for his beliefs and condemned to death as a traitor in 1589, he died in prison in 1595. Feast day: October 19. *See also* Forty Martyrs of England and Wales.

Hrosvit (rohz-veet'), ca. 935–1001/3, poet and nun. She was well read in Scripture, the Church Fathers, and Latin poetry, Christian and classical, especially Terence, on whose style she modeled her own plays. The first Christian dramatist to follow classical forms, she invented the form of plays in rhymed prose.

Hubert, St., d. 727, patron saint of hunters. He turned to religious life after his wife died, and he became a priest in Maastricht and a bishop of Liège. It is alleged that he did so because, while hunting one day, he had a vision of a crucifix between the horns of a stag. Feast day: November 3.

Hügel, Friedrich von, 1852–1925, baron, biblical critic, theologian, and philosopher. Born in Italy of an Austrian diplomat and a Scottish aristocrat, he was educated privately in several European cities, settling in England in 1867. Of frail health and deaf, he traveled widely throughout his life, becoming the friend of many distinguished religious thinkers, Catholic (e.g., Maurice Blondel) and Protestant (e.g., Ernst Troeltsch). In 1905, he founded the London Society for the Study of Religion. He championed the need for the Church to come to terms with critical biblical and historical scholarship and with modern science; he was himself a noted biblical exegete. He was closely associated with most of the principal "Modernists," including Alfred Loisy and George Tyrrell, but escaped condemnation because of his lay status and prominent social position. Esteemed for his character and as a spiritual director, he was an influential figure in English religious life. His principal works are *The Mystical Element of Religion* (2 vols., 1908), *Essays and Addresses on the Philosophy of Religion* (first series: 1921; second series: 1926), and *The Reality of God* (his undelivered Gifford Lectures, 1931). *See also* Modernism.

Hugh of Cluny, St., also Hugh of Semur, 1024–1109, abbot. Son of the Count of Semur and Arenberge, Hugh entered the monastery of Cluny in 1038 and became abbot in 1049. Active in ecclesiastical affairs, Hugh also began construction of a new abbey church at Cluny and founded the first convent of Cluniac nuns. Feast day: April 29. *See also* Cluny.

Hugh of Lincoln, St., ca. 1140–1200, Carthusian and bishop of Lincoln. At the request of King Henry II, he established the first Carthusian house in England. A defender of Church liberties, he also was known for his charity. His tomb became an important pilgrimage site. Feast day: November 17.

Hugh of St. Victor, ca. 1090–1141, theologian, biblical exegete, and founder of the Victorine tradition of thought and spirituality, which influenced such later Scholastics as Peter Lombard and Bonaventure. Hugh brought the ascetic, contemplative life of the monastery together with the new dialectical discoveries in the schools. In his writings he provided a program for theological studies based on Scripture. *Didascalicon: On the Love of Reading,* fol-

lowing the *De Doctrina Christiana (On Christian Doctrine)* of Augustine, provided a guide to the use of philosophy and liberal and practical arts as preparation for reading the Bible. Books 4–6 introduce Hugh's exegetical theory. History, allegory, and tropology are three successive disciplines of study as well as senses of Scripture. Each has distinct methods and a specific order for reading the appropriate books of Scripture. History is the foundation, not only as literal sense of Scripture but also as the historical narrative of the divine interaction with humanity. Hugh's program for reading Scripture is expanded in *On the Sacraments of the Christian Faith,* which was among the first major comprehensive statements of theology in the Middle Ages. Structured according to a historical framework, it records the works of creation in six days and the works of restoration commencing with the Incarnation. Therefore, Hugh's sacramental theology, understanding "sacrament" in a broad sense as a "visible sign of invisible grace," develops within a biblical narrative framework. Complementing his dialectical works are the works about mystical contemplation such as *On the Ark of Noah* and *The Contemplation of the Soul;* Hugh based these works on his study of the *Celestial Hierarchies* of Pseudo-Dionysius the Areopagite, on which he also commented. *See also* sacrament; Scripture, interpretation of; Scripture, senses of; Victorines.   MICHAEL A. SIGNER

Hughes, John Joseph, 1779–1864, archbishop of New York. Born in Ireland, Hughes emigrated to the United States in 1817. After ordination to the priesthood in 1826 he served as pastor in Philadelphia and earned a reputation as a forceful apologist for Catholicism. He was named coadjutor-bishop to John Dubois of New York in 1838. In 1842 he succeeded Dubois as bishop of New York and was named its archbishop in 1850. Hughes gained a national reputation as a fighter for the rights of immigrant Catholics. He was a strong advocate of Catholic schools. An autocratic prelate, he opposed the lay trustee system and promoted the clerical control of the Church. His most visible legacy is St. Patrick's Cathedral, whose construction began under Hughes in 1858. *See also* Saint Patrick's Cathedral; trusteeism, lay.

Hughes, Philip, 1895–1967, Church historian. Born in Manchester, England, he was educated at Ushaw College and the University of Louvain. After his ordination for Salford (Manchester) in 1920 and a period of research in the Vatican Archives, he served as parish priest in his diocese and then as archivist of Westminster Cathedral (London). He emigrated to the United States in 1955 to become professor of history at the University of Notre Dame. The most celebrated of his many historical works is *The Reformation in England* (1950–54), and he is known to a wider public through his *A Popular History of the Catholic Church* (1947).

Huguenots (hy*oo'* geh-nots), a term for French Protestants, perhaps derived from *Eidgenossen* (Ger., "confederates, conspirators"), which in French-speaking Geneva became *eiguenotz*. The term was in common use after the conspiracy of Amboise (1560) in which Protestant nobles sought to kidnap the French king Francis II. The Edict of Nantes (1598) gave them freedom of worship, but this was revoked under Louis XIV (1685). Final legal recognition came only in the nineteenth century.

human act. *See* acts, human.

Humanae Vitae (h*oo*-mahn'ay vee'tay; Lat., "Of human life), the 1968 encyclical of Pope Paul VI that reaffirmed the condemnation of artificial contraception for Catholics. The first part mentions new aspects of the question and reaffirms the competency of the Church and its hierarchical magisterium to teach on these matters. The pope infers that a majority of the papally appointed commission to study contraception came out in favor of a change in Catholic teaching, but after prayer and discussion the pope now gives his reply. The second part recognizes the importance of conjugal love and calls for responsible parenthood but condemns artificial contraception. Natural law shows the inseparable connection, willed by God and unable to be broken by human beings on their own initiative, between the unitive and the procreative meaning of the sexual act. The rhythm method, or natural family planning, is acceptable because it makes legitimate use of a natural disposition and does not impede the development of natural processes. The pope also mentions some grave consequences of artificial birth control. The third part gives practical directives recognizing that the teaching is somewhat difficult and requires encouragement and effort by individuals, families, and society at large. Pope Paul VI referred to the "lively discussion" sparked by his encyclical; others have called it a crisis for the Church. In any case, Paul VI was so distressed by the negative reac-

tion that he issued no more encyclicals during the remainder of his pontificate, which ended with his death some ten years later. *See also* birth control.

human dignity, the idea that the human person has an intrinsic worth. In Catholic teaching, this idea is grounded in the claim that all persons are created in the image of God. A person's dignity, therefore, transcends any social order. Such dignity forms the basis of the claim that persons have inherent rights that society cannot grant and must not violate. Because the person is both a political and an economic being, human dignity grounds both political rights—for instance, the freedom of speech—and economic rights—for example, the right to a living wage. The insistence on human dignity as the foundation of Catholic social teaching is especially strong in the writings of Pope John Paul II, beginning with his first encyclical, *Redemptor Hominis* (1979). *See also* Catholic social teachings.

Humani Generis (h*oo*-mah'nee jayn'-air-uhs; Lat., "Of the human race"), an encyclical issued by Pope Pius XII in 1950. It attempted to halt new theological and pastoral trends (particularly among French theologians writing on nature and grace, original sin, ecumenism, and liturgical renewal), to show errors in contemporary philosophy and science (existentialism, historicism, evolutionism), and again to propose Thomism as the true Christian philosophy. Although some of its concerns were valid, the encyclical too readily condemned approaches that proved to be important preparations for Vatican II (1962–65), where they found some measure of vindication. The encyclical is also important for the claims it made in behalf of the teaching authority of papal encyclicals. It asserted that when a pope carefully pronounces on a controverted theological subject, it "can no longer be regarded as a matter of free debate among theologians." This statement later was included in the first draft of the Dogmatic Constitution on the Church at Vatican II and was rejected. *See also* encyclical; supernatural.

humanism, Catholic, sixteenth-century movement, largely inspired by Erasmus of Rotterdam (ca. 1469–1536), to utilize the results of humanistic scholarship in philology and text criticism as an instrument of Church reform. The work of these humanists concentrated on biblical studies, patristic scholarship, and ethical studies as a counterforce to what they saw as the decadence of Scholastic learning. Catholic humanists (and those connected with the Reform; Calvin was a trained humanist) had an enormous influence both on the Catholic reform of the sixteenth century and on those connected with the Reformation (e.g., the production of the King James Bible would not have been possible without the efforts of the humanists).

In the modern period there was an attempt to fuse human learning and revelation into a Christian humanism that would paint a broad picture of human existence and destiny. This effort was an attempt to rethink nontheistic views of humanism reflected in the work of such thinkers as Jean-Paul Sartre. Such works as Louis Bouyer's *Christian Humanism* (1959) and the earlier work of Jacques Maritain's *True Humanism* (1938) are representative. The sort of "cosmic" humanism of Teilhard de Chardin (d. 1955) has had a limited but persistent appeal. The thought and teachings of Pope John Paul II, elected to the papacy in 1978, have been characterized by a view of humanism derived from a blend of philosophical personalism and Thomism.

The somewhat cautious use of "humanism" in the Pastoral Constitution on the Church in the Modern World (*Gaudium et Spes,* 1965) at Vatican II reflects the cooption of the word by "secular" humanists and by Marxists (n. 7). Vatican II, however, did want to enter into dialogue with those currents of thought (n. 55). *See also* Erasmus, Desiderius; humanism, secular.   LAWRENCE CUNNINGHAM

humanism, secular, modern philosophical world-view marked by some or all of the following characteristics: ethical relativism, denial of the transcendent, evolutionary view of humankind, cultural pluralism, optimistic view of human nature, and emphasis on the post-Enlightenment virtues of rationality, equality, and freedom.

Critics argue that such a philosophy is an ersatz religious ideology that governs much of the thinking of our intellectual elites to the detriment of more traditional views, especially those expressed in Judaism and Christianity. *See also* humanism, Catholic.

human nature, the comprehensive term for the characteristic principles, properties, and ends that in their totality define the human being. Catholic thought has traditionally relied upon Sacred Scripture and human experience as explored in the theological and philosophical traditions of Western Civilization as the primary sources for reflection on human nature. At the heart of this reflection is the conviction that human nature can be fully understood only in the revelation of divine grace. Human nature, as chosen and created by God, is fundamentally ordered toward God as its final end and highest good.

However, human nature is also wounded nature; it bears the marks of sin, understood as both the absence and rejection of God's grace. The rejection of God's grace obscures both the signs and the knowledge of our relationship with God. The capacity for either accepting or spurning God's gracious gift of self manifests a freedom of choice, as does the capacity for moral deliberation and responsibility in the face of both God and neighbor.

Human nature may also be comprehended in terms of a range of inclinations or desires, some of which are shared by other animals (e.g., for food and procreation). Human nature is distinguished, however, by the person's possession of both intelligence (the capacity to know the truth), and love, which unifies and perfects desire in our movement toward God and neighbor. Human nature is, finally, social. The variety of goods that perfect it, preeminently justice and friendship, are achievable only within participation in the life of a community. *See also* nature; nature and grace.   PAUL J. WOJDA

human rights, claims that persons have on society simply on the basis of their being human. The force of the idea of human rights is that no social institution can, with legitimacy, fail to recognize and respect those rights. In Catholic teaching, such rights are grounded philosophically in the concept of the dignity of the human person. All persons have an inherent dignity that transcends social structures. This idea of human dignity is further backed by the theological doctrine of *imago Dei* (Lat.): all persons are born in the image of God. It is this theological grounding that gives force to the claim that persons have transcendent worth.

The idea of human dignity grounded in the *imago Dei* doctrine supports both civil rights and economic rights. Civil rights are those rights that make up the core of the liberal democratic state, for instance, freedom of speech, freedom of assembly, and the right to a fair trial. These are often termed "negative rights" because they constitute protections against infringement on individual freedom. Economic rights are often termed "positive rights" because they require constructive action, and not mere protection, on the part of the state. Included are the rights to employment, a just wage, housing, and other basic material needs. According to Catholic teaching, human dignity requires both protection from an overextended state and the support of governmental institutions. The principle of subsidiarity (that nothing should be done by a higher agency that can be done as well, if not better, by a lower agency) regulates when the state is intruding and when it is providing necessary support for persons.

Under criticism that the idea of human dignity grounded in the *imago Dei* doctrine stressed the individual at the expense of the community, recent U.S. Catholic documents have offered the more inclusive idea that human rights are the "minimum conditions for life in community" (U.S. bishops' pastoral letter, "Economic Justice for All," 1986, nn. 79–84). *See also* Catholic social teachings.

TODD D. WHITMORE

Humbert of Silva Candida, ca. 1000–1061, cardinal and reformer. As a representative of the pope, he formally excommunicated Patriarch Keroularious (Cerularius) in Constantinople in 1054, an act which many regard as the beginning of the split between East and West. He also drafted the oath on the Eucharist that Berengar of Tours was required to swear in 1059. His several treatises against simony proved influential in the investiture controversy. *See also* Berengar of Tours; Great Schism; investiture controversy; simony.

humeral veil, a rectangular silk or brocade shawl worn around the shoulders and used to cover the hands. Its liturgical use was confined to the Solemn High Mass in which the subdeacon held the paten with it from the offertory to the Lord's Prayer. In eucharistic processions and devotions, it is used for holding the sacramental container, e.g., ciborium, monstrance.

Humiliati (hoo-mil-ee-ah'tee; Lat., *humiliatus,* "humbled"), twelfth-century lay movement that promoted poverty as a way of life in imitation of Christ, as well as service to the poor. Having grown rich and lax itself, it was suppressed in 1571 after one of its members assaulted Charles Borromeo, who was trying to reform the group.

humility (Lat., *humus,* "earth," *humilis,* "low"), the Christian virtue that may be popularly defined as knowing one's place and taking it. Considered a

humeral veil

Humeral veil

moral virtue by Thomas Aquinas, humility avoids inflation of one's worth or talents on the one hand, and avoids excessive devaluation of oneself on the other. Humility requires a dispassionate and honest appreciation of the self in relationship to others and to God. In effect, humble people recognize the limitations as well as the possibilities of the lives God has given them and they are willing to work within these personal parameters in order to be the unique creatures God has created them to be. In this, they praise God and demonstrate obedience to the divine will. Arrogance and false pride are the opposites of humility. The finest examples of humility are Jesus and Mary. Jesus did not consider his divinity something to grasp at. Instead, he "emptied himself and took the form of a slave" (Phil 2:6–8). Mary, the Mother of God, displayed humility when, at the Annunciation, she proclaimed that she was God's servant, and, even though she could not understand the angel's message, she joyfully accepted God's will (Luke 1:34–38).

Hungarian Byzantine Catholic Church, Catholics in Hungary who adhere to the Byzantine liturgical, canonical, theological, and spiritual tradition.

Most of these Catholics are not ethnic Hungarians but are descended from the many Byzantine

Christians of other nationalities who settled in Hungary over the centuries and eventually became Hungarian-speaking. Nevertheless, many maintain that there is at least a partial link between this community and the significant Byzantine Church that existed in Hungary in the Middle Ages. Indeed, there were several Byzantine monasteries in Hungary in the eleventh and twelfth centuries, but all of them were destroyed during the thirteenth-century Tatar invasions.

It was in the fifteenth and sixteenth centuries, due to the widespread population shifts caused by the Turkish invasions, that communities of Byzantine Serbs, Ruthenians, Slovaks, and Greeks moved into the area. Most of them eventually became Catholics but retained their Byzantine heritage. In the eighteenth century a number of Hungarian Protestants became Catholic and chose the Byzantine rite, again adding to the number of Byzantine Catholics in the country. They were placed under the jurisdiction of non-Hungarian Byzantine bishops.

Because a significant community of Byzantine Catholics otherwise entirely integrated into Hungarian society now existed, the question of the use of Hungarian in the liturgy became pressing. But such a proposal was resisted by Church authorities. For this reason, the first Hungarian translation of the liturgy of John Chrysostom had to be published privately in 1795. Through the nineteenth century several other liturgical books were published in Hungarian, still without the approval of the ecclesiastical authorities.

In 1900 a large group of Hungarian Byzantine Catholic pilgrims in Rome presented Pope Leo XIII with a petition requesting that a separate Byzantine diocese be established in the country with the right to use Hungarian in the liturgy. Finally, in 1912 Pope Pius X erected the diocese of Hajdúdorog for Hungarian Byzantine Catholics. But he made Greek the obligatory liturgical language and gave the priests three years to learn it. World War I intervened, however, and the requirement to use Greek was never enforced. The use of Hungarian gained ground and gradually by the 1930s all the main liturgical texts had been translated.

In 1923 an apostolic exarchate was set up at Miskolc for twenty-one Ruthenian parishes formerly in the diocese of Presov that remained in Hungarian territory after Czechoslovakia was created. They were provided with a distinct identity because they used Slavonic in the liturgy. By the 1940s, however,

they had all begun to use Hungarian, and consequently the apostolic exarchate since that time has been administered by the bishop of Hajdúdorog.

Originally, the diocese of Hajdúdorog included only areas of the country in which Byzantine Catholics were concentrated. But in 1968 its jurisdiction was extended to include all Byzantine Catholics in Hungary, who now number about 250,000. There is a seminary at Nyiregyháza.

The rather small number of Byzantine Hungarians who emigrated to North America have a few parishes. They are included in the Ruthenian dioceses in the United States and in the Ukrainian dioceses in Canada. *See also* Byzantine rite; Eastern churches; Eastern rites.   *RONALD G. ROBERSON*

Hungary, Catholicism in. The Christian faith was accepted by the Magyars in what is now Hungary at the end of the tenth century, and it was institutionalized by St. Stephen I (d. 1038), who promoted the formation of dioceses. Throughout the Middle Ages, Church and state were closely connected as the archbishops of Esztergom crowned the kings, who, in turn, had the authority to name bishops, create dioceses, and control Church property. During this time, the Franciscans and Dominicans had a strong influence on Church life, and Elizabeth of Hungary and Thuringia (1207–31) gained recognition for her work with the poor and the sick. In the sixteenth century the Jesuits played a key role in the Catholic restoration. In the 1700s the domination of the Church by Maria Theresa and Joseph II (Josephinism) created tensions between the Church and the state that existed into the twentieth century. After the Second World War, the Church suffered under Communist rule. Catholic organizations were disbanded beginning in 1946, and on December 26, 1948, Cardinal József Mindszenty (1892–1975) was arrested and eventually sentenced to life imprisonment. (During the uprising of 1956, Mindszenty moved to the U.S. embassy, where he remained until September 1971, when he was allowed to leave Hungary. He died in Vienna four years later.) In 1950 the government suppressed the religious orders, imprisoning approximately ten thousand brothers, priests, and sisters, and it authorized a national "Progressive Catholic" church. The government's opposition to the Vatican's appointment of bishops was formally resolved in 1964 in an agreement with the Holy See. Sharp tensions between the state and the Church continued until a new accord was signed on February 9, 1990. The Catholic Church has three archdioceses and eight dioceses in Hungary. It is estimated as of 1993, that Catholics constitute more than 60 percent of the nation's almost 11 million people. *See also* Mindszenty, József.　ROBERT A. KRIEG

Hus, John, ca. 1369–1415, Czech priest, theologian, preacher, and rector of the University of Prague (1409). Influenced by John Wycliffe's ideas about Church reform, Hus led the reform movement that ultimately expelled German influence from the University of Prague. Hus (and his followers) rejected transubstantiation, demanded Communion in both kinds, and claimed that reprobate priests (including popes) forfeited their authority within the Church. Excommunicated in 1410, Hus was summoned to the Council of Constance (1414) where, despite an imperial guarantee of safe conduct, he was arrested and burned as a heretic (July 6, 1415). His execution helped ignite a revolution against the medieval Church in Bohemia. *See also* Communion under both kinds; transubstantiation.

Huvelin, Henri, 1838–1910, French pastor and acclaimed spiritual director. Among his penitents were Charles de Foucauld and Friedrich von Hügel. This saintly, learned priest influenced many. *See also* Foucauld, Charles de; Hügel, Friedrich von.

Hyacinth, St., 1185–1257, Dominican missionary to the Slavs and patron saint of Poland. Born into a noble family, Hyacinth became a Dominican about 1220. Though the details of his life are unknown, he is remembered for his extensive missionary work from Poland to possibly as far east as Tibet. Feast day: August 17. *See also* Poland, Catholicism in.

hylomorphism (Gk., *hule,* "matter"; *morphe,* "form"), an Aristotelian philosophical theory regarding all material being made up of two coprinciples: prime matter (the principle of indetermination) and substantial form (the principle of determination). Catholic theology, from the thirteenth century, utilized this theory to explain the constitution of human beings as a composite of body (matter) and soul (form). Theology has also applied the theory to the sacraments: Each sacrament is constituted by a basic element, the "matter" (e.g., water for Baptism, bread and wine for the Eucharist) and a clarifying word, the "form" (e.g., "I baptize you....;" "This is my Body...."). *See also* sacrament.

hymnal, the liturgical book containing hymns and other music for worship. Hymnals contain psalms (strophic or nonstrophic), versified nonbiblical texts with tunes (hymns), musical settings of liturgical acclamations, or other liturgical texts accompanied by music for various rites and ceremonies of the Church.

hymns (Gk., *hymnos,* "song in praise of gods or heroes"), nonbiblical religious texts set to music. Used both in the liturgy (Mass and Divine Office) and in popular devotions, sacred songs have a long history in the Catholic tradition. Their general use dates back at least to the fourth century. Some of the most famous theologians of the Church (Thomas Aquinas, d. 1274; John Henry Newman, d. 1890) have contributed to the hymnic tradition. *See also* liturgical music.

Hypapante (hee-puh-pahn-tee'; Gk., "meeting"), Byzantine feast of the Meeting of Our Lord, celebrated on February 2; one of the Twelve Great Feasts of the Byzantine rite. Hypapante corresponds to the Western feast of the Presentation, and though the Byzantine Church lists it as a festivity of Mary, it celebrates the meeting of Jesus with God's people represented by Simeon and Anna in Luke 2:22–38. A Presentation feast is first seen in Jerusalem, ca. 384, on February 14, the fortieth day after Epiphany (January 6), which was the original Nativity feast in the East. The Hypapante feast gradually spread to other Eastern churches, and with the Eastern adoption of Western Christmas on December 25, its celebration was moved to February 2. Emperor Justinian I (527–65) decreed its celebration throughout the empire. *See also* Presentation.

hyperdulia (Gk., *huper,* "more than,"; *dulia,* "service"), the special honor Catholics render to the Blessed Virgin Mary. It is distinguished from *latria* (Gk.), which is the worship that Christians render to God alone, and *dulia,* which is the honor given to the saints. Mary is uniquely honored because of her role as the Mother of God. *See also dulia; latria.*

hypostasis (Gk., *hypo,* "under"; *stasis,* "standing"; hence "substructure," "substance"), the objective essence of something, according to Aristotle and the Neoplatonists. The term functions in this way in the NT (e.g., "the exact imprint of God's very being," Heb 1:3). Elsewhere the word was also used for "confidence" or "assurance" (Heb 3:14; 11:1; 2 Cor 11:17).

In the theological discussions of the third and fourth centuries *hypostasis* was used at times in distinction from *ousia*, "being," in order to speak of the three *hypostaseis* ("persons") of God in one being. This language was accepted by the Church at the Council of Nicaea (325). In the Christological discussions of the fourth and fifth centuries the term had a variety of meanings until Pope Leo the Great distinguished between Christ's *hypostasis*, "unity of person," and his *physeis*, "natures." Accepting this distinction, the Council of Chalcedon (451) declared that Christ is "one person and one *hypostasis* possessing two natures, *physeis*." Hence, for the council "person" and *hypostasis* are almost synonymous. They differ in that "person" accentuates the relational character of personal existence, and *hypostasis* stresses the unifying principle of individuation. *See also* hypostatic union; Incarnation, the; person of Christ.

hypostatic union, the uniting of the divine nature and the human nature of Jesus Christ in one person, or *hypostasis* (Gk.). This notion is meant to illumine the mystery of Christ's personal unity, while at the same time safeguarding the Church's insight regarding the mystery of Jesus Christ's two natures, his full divinity and full humanity.

The early Church could not remain silent regarding the personal unity or individuation of Jesus Christ. If it were to acknowledge the two natures of Christ without affirming their union in a single, integrated person, this silence could be interpreted to mean: that Jesus Christ was some kind of dualistic being similar to a split or psychotic personality (Adoptionism and Nestorianism); that Christ's human nature was subsumed into his divine nature (Monophysitism, Apollinarianism, Eutychianism); or that in Jesus Christ some essential aspect of human nature was missing and replaced by an attribute of the divine nature (Monothelitism). Faced with one-sided ("heretical") solutions to the complex issue of the individuation of Jesus Christ, the Church gradually developed the notion of the hypostatic union.

As presented in the NT, Jesus Christ is clearly a single subject, one self-agent. This apostolic witness attests to the mysterious reality of the unifying point, the hypostatic union, that is constitutive of the person of Jesus Christ. This insight was elaborated into the theory of the hypostatic union by Cyril of Alexandria (d. 444), who built on the work of Athanasius and the Cappadocian Fathers (Basil the Great, Gregory of Nazianzus, and Gregory of Nyssa). This teaching was accepted by the Council of Chalcedon (451). In recent years the theologian Karl Rahner (d. 1984) shed new light on the hypostatic union in his reflections on the direct proportionality between grace and freedom. *See also* Chalcedon, Council of; Incarnation, the; Jesus Christ; person of Christ.

ROBERT A. KRIEG

ichthys (ik'thuhs). *See* fish.

icon (Gk., *ikona,* "image"), a painted panel with representations of Christ, the Blessed Virgin Mary, or a saint used mainly in the official liturgy of the Eastern Christian tradition and in the decoration of its churches. After a period of reaction against the use of such images (iconoclasm), the Second Council of Nicaea (787) affirmed the legitimacy of icons and their veneration.

The theological view of such images is that they are windows into the eternal world of revelation and that they capture, albeit imperfectly, the realities of which the gospel speaks, including the NT affirmation that Christ is the icon (image) of God.

In the Eastern tradition the painting of icons is seen as a ministry within the Church.

Perhaps the most famous icon of modern times is that of Our Lady of Perpetual Help in Rome. *See also* Catholicism and the visual arts; iconoclasm; iconography.

iconoclasm, in general, destruction of religious images, but especially that sponsored by iconoclast Byzantine emperors extending from the reign of Leo III (717–41) to the restoration of images in 843. For reasons not entirely clear, Leo ordered the

The head of Christ; detail from a seventeenth-century Byzantine icon by Emanuel Lambardos, Paul Canellopoulos Collection, Athens.

destruction of images, including that of Christ over the Chalke palace gate (726). By 730, the iconophile patriarch Germanus was forced to resign. Persecution began. Popes Gregory II and III protested, as did John of Damascus, but Leo's son Constantine V (741–75) confirmed and extended the policy, attempting to provide a theological and ecclesial basis for it at the Council of Hiereia (754). Against arguments urging the incarnational basis for representation of Christ, the council insisted that such representation was either Nestorian (since it divided the two natures in Christ, only one of which could be represented) or Eutychian (since, if it claimed to include and so circumscribe the divine, it was guilty of confusing the natures). Only the Eucharist was an adequate representation of Christ.

Persecution grew brutal. Iconophile monks faced the choice of marrying or being exiled and blinded. Constantine's son Leo IV (775–80), however, relaxed the persecution, and subsequently the empress Irene arranged a complete reversal of imperial policy. She convened Nicaea II (787, the last council to be regarded as ecumenical by both East and West), restoring images and defining their veneration. Due to a faulty translation of its acts, the Frankish bishops argued against the council, although Pope Hadrian I supported it. In the East, with the accession of Leo V (813–20), Nicaea II was annulled (815). Persecution was renewed, especially under Emperor Theophilus (829–42), yet the iconophiles, led in part by Theodore the Studite, had a stronger political basis and a more articulate theoretical foundation this time. In 843 the empress Theodora restored the icons, celebrating on the first Sunday of Lent a feast still kept in the Eastern churches as the "Feast of Orthodoxy."

Theologically, the controversy is a sequel to the Christological controversies of the fifth through the seventh centuries. Iconoclasm is related to the Monophysitism increasingly popular in imperial circles since the Council of Chalcedon (451). At one point its proponents argued that Christ's flesh, even after the Incarnation, was not subject to normal human limitations. The triumph of iconoclasm would thus have been the triumph of Docetism, a denial of the reality of redemption and of the foundation for any explicitly Christian art. *See also* icon; *Libri Carolini;* Monophysitism; Nicaea, Second Council of.

JOHN C. CAVADINI

iconography, a system or collection of religious symbols. Art history has demonstrated that large-scale religious art (cathedral sculpture, paintings in church) usually reflects a symbolic language, the elements of which are often thematically linked. The study of such symbolism is important for the history of theology. *See also* Catholicism and the visual arts; icon; iconoclasm.

iconostasis (i̲-kahn-ah'stuh-sis; Gk., "icon stand"), Byzantine-rite sanctuary screen, covered with icons, which separates the sanctuary from the rest of the church. Access to the sanctuary is provided by three doors, the central or "Royal Doors," used only during services and only by those in major orders, and the "deacon's doors" on either side of the Royal Doors. The Royal Doors are decorated with icons of the Annunciation and the four evangelists, symbols of the Incarnation of Christ and his Word, mysteries of Word and sacrament communicated through those doors during the liturgical celebrations. The deacon's doors bear images of the protodeacon and martyr St. Stephen, and of the archangels Michael or Gabriel wearing Byzantine diaconal vestments, since deacons are considered to represent the angels of the heavenly liturgy. On the iconostasis, to the right of the Royal Doors there is always an icon of Christ; and to the left, one of the Mother of God

Iconostasis separating choir and apse from the central nave of St. Mark's Basilica, Venice; depicted are four apostles, John the Baptist, and the Blessed Virgin Mary (on the far side of the cross).

bearing the Christ Child. Over the doors is usually depicted the Last Supper or the communion of the apostles. Other images, depending on the space available, might include the feast of the patron saint of the church, the Twelve Great Feasts, or the Twelve Apostles, all arranged according to a prescribed order and symbolism. Now the most characteristic element of the liturgical disposition of the Byzantine church, the iconostasis evolved from the custom of hanging icons on the original Byzantine sanctuary chancel, a structure similar to the Western sanctuary enclosures of the epoch. It usually consisted of a low marble barrier about four feet high, surmounted by a row of small columns topped by an architrave or marble beam. It impeded access to the sanctuary, but not visibility. The fully developed opaque iconostasis barrier did not replace the earlier templon or open chancel until after the fourteenth century. *See also* icon; sanctuary.   ROBERT F. TAFT

idealism, a central direction of modern philosophy, emphasizing abstract, universal ideas over material, particular reality. Expanding on the philosophies of Descartes, Kant, and Johann Fichte, idealism places all things within a process where the abstract, universal ideal is becoming present in the real. Intellectual and cultural ideas appear in philosophy, science, politics, art, and religion. Philosophy provides insight into the structures of consciousness that mirror the unfolding of divine and human life in one history. First appearing in Friedrich Schelling's writings after 1800 and prominent in Hegel (d. 1831), idealism influenced Catholic theologians at Tübingen and Munich in the nineteenth century. Attacked by the anti-Modernist measures of the Vatican and discredited by World War I, its influence survived in the works of German and French philosophers of the twentieth century, among thinkers like Pierre Teilhard de Chardin (d. 1955), Paul Tillich (d. 1965), and Karl Rahner (d. 1984), and in some motifs of Vatican II (1962–65) such as sacramentality and the Church as People of God. *See also* philosophy and theology.

idolatry (Heb., *'abōdāh zārāh*, "alien cult"), in the OT, the worship of a deity other than Yahweh represented in some visible form—usually a sculpture in the round or in relief; the use of such representations in the worship of Yahweh. The prohibition in the Decalogue against making images is explained by the function of such representations, which was to make the deity present and available. Throughout most of the biblical period, however, the use of images in worship was a normal part of popular religion, as may be deduced from the historical narrative, the denunciations of prophets (esp. Hosea, Jeremiah, Ezekiel), and the recurrent reforms aimed at eliminating them (e.g., 2 Kgs 23:4–14). The strongest polemic against idolatry so understood is found in Deuteronomy and is summarized in the Shema ("Hear, O Israel." Deut 6:4–9), the central confession of faith in Judaism. In early Christian times idolatry only became problematic in those cases where Christians occupied a public office requiring them to take part in civic or imperial practices of worship, or partaking of meat offered to alien deities (1 Cor 8:1–13; 10:14–22). The term is more often used figuratively, meaning excessive concern with created things, e.g., food, sex, or wealth (e.g., Eph 5:5; Col 3:5). *See also* images.

Ignatian spirituality. *See* Jesuit spirituality.

Ignatius of Antioch, St., ca. 35–ca. 107, bishop and martyr, one of the Apostolic Fathers. He became bishop of Antioch ca. 69. During Trajan's persecution he was condemned as a Christian and then taken to Rome to be executed. On his journey he

St. Ignatius of Antioch, Apostolic Father, second-century bishop and martyr whose letters to various churches in the ancient Christian world serve as a major source of information regarding the faith, life, and structure of the early Church.

wrote seven Letters, which are a major source for early Church doctrine and organization. The first four Letters were written at Smyrna and sent to the churches of Ephesus, Magnesia, Tralles, and Rome. The last three were written at Troas and sent to the churches of Philadelphia and Smyrna, and to Polycarp, bishop of Smyrna.

Against Docetism, which held that Jesus Christ only "seemed" (Gk., *dokein*) to be human, Ignatius stressed the reality of both the divinity and the humanity of Christ: the Eucharist is "the flesh of our Savior Jesus Christ," and the eucharistic sacrifice has as its locus the Church. The bishop represents Christ and is both the high priest of the liturgy and the authorized teacher of the community. Ignatius attested to the primacy of the church of Rome and to the roles of Peter and Paul in its founding. He was the first writer to use the term "Catholic Church" as a collective designation for Christians, and among the first to attest to the monoepiscopacy, i.e., the rule by one bishop over each diocese.

Ignatius was resolved to bear ultimate witness to Christ by suffering martyrdom. When brought to Rome, he was taken to the Colosseum and thrown to the lions. Feast day: October 17 (Roman Catholic and Antioch); December 17 (Anglican); December 20 (Greek). *See also* Apostolic Fathers.

Ignatius of Loyola, St., 1491–1556, founder of the Jesuits. Ignatius was born at the family castle of Loyola in the Basque province of Guipuzcoa. Originally intended for a career in the Church, he was placed in his late teens in the household of the royal treasurer and there entered the service of the viceroy of Navarre. Until 1521 his personal ideals and values were those of one committed to a career at court and in the military. In that year, while recovering from wounds sustained in the defense of Pamplona in Navarre (May 20, 1520), he underwent a radical religious conversion.

Long months of painful convalescence were followed by almost a year as a beggar at Manresa near the Benedictine monastery of Montserrat. It was here that he first experienced and then began to write his *Spiritual Exercises,* a manual for spiritual growth based on the gifts and graces given to him by God over the course of a year. This culminated in a series of mystical experiences that developed in Ignatius an ever-deepening gift of spiritual discernment.

After a brief sojourn in the Holy Land (1523), where he hoped to spend the rest of his life as a pil-

Ignatius of Loyola, founder of the Jesuits, portrayed in his soldier's armor; during a period of forced inactivity because of a wound, he read the lives of Christ and the saints and decided to become a soldier of Christ.

grim, Ignatius returned to his native Spain to begin formal education with young schoolboys. Educationally he moved from Barcelona to Alcala and Salamanca and finally to Paris where he completed his studies in philosophy and theology (1528–35). In 1534 Ignatius and his companions pronounced vows of chastity and poverty along with promises to work in the Holy Land. In 1537, while awaiting passage to the Holy Land, he and several of his companions were ordained priests. Because war between Venice and the Ottoman Empire prevented their passage to the Holy Land, Ignatius and the group committed themselves to the service of the Church in the person of Pope Paul III (November 1538). After a lengthy period of prayer and deliberation at Venice, the group, led by Ignatius, petitioned the pope to establish a new religious order, the Society of Jesus. Subsequently, on September 27, 1540, Pope Paul III issued the papal bull *Regimini Militantis Ecclesiae,* which formally established the Society of Jesus.

Despite strenuous objections on his part, Ignatius was unanimously elected first general of the Jesuits. The last fifteen years of his life were devoted to composing the *Constitutions* of this new order. Though failing in health, he remained a steadfast administrator of the burgeoning order. He died quietly and unexpectedly at Rome in the early morning of July 31, 1556. He was canonized by Gregory XV on May 22, 1622.

His major works, the *Spiritual Exercises,* the *Constitutions of the Society of Jesus,* the *Autobiography,* and a collection of almost six thousand letters are characterized by a Christocentric apostolic fervor and by a notable quality of spiritual discernment. In his spiritual doctrine he emphasizes the integration of contemplation and action, affect and rationality, prayer and service. His constant injunction to his followers, one he followed in his own life (*Autobiography* 98) was to "find God in all things." Feast day: July 31. *See also* Jesuits; Jesuit spirituality; *Spiritual Exercises.*   FRANK J. HOUDEK

ignorance, a lack of knowledge in someone who is capable of having such knowledge. Discussions of ignorance are concerned with whether and to what degree blame can be attributed to agents who lack knowledge but perform morally wrong actions. Aristotle's and Thomas Aquinas's treatises are the origins of the Catholic position. One can be ignorant of a law or be ignorant of a fact. In ignorance of law, one lacks knowledge about the existence of a law or its meaning; in ignorance of fact, one is ignorant of some condition of an action that would bring it under a law that one knows to exist. *See also* invincible ignorance; vincible ignorance.

ignorance [canon law], a person's or a community's lack of knowledge about either a law or certain facts pertaining to a given situation covered by a law. Canon law presumes that persons and communities know the law, as well as facts pertinent to the law (can. 15). Although ignorance of the law does not excuse one from it, such ignorance may mitigate certain effects with respect to canonical penalties. *See also* error [canon law].

IHS, Christian inscription found frequently in art. The initials are the first three letters of the Greek word for Jesus.

Ildephonsus, St., ca. 610–67, archbishop of Toledo from 657 to 667. Four treatises of his survive, including *On the Perpetual Virginity of Blessed Mary* and *De Viris Illustribus (On Famous Men),* his most important work, which focuses entirely on Hispanic bishops. Feast day: January 23.

illegitimacy, the status of someone born outside a valid marital union. Canon law specifically exempts those born in a putative marriage; thus, those who obtain marriage annulments do not thereby declare their children illegitimate in canon law. Canon law formerly barred illegitimate children from certain offices, e.g., the priesthood; universal law no longer retains any such prohibitions, although certain particular laws (e.g., of a given religious order) might retain some such restraints. *See also* marriage law.

illiceity [canon law], the quality of being contrary to canon law. If an action contrary to law is deliberate, it may also be also sinful. Such an action, whether deliberate or not, does not necessarily render the act invalid. An action can be at the same time valid and illicit. Thus, a suspended priest, forbidden by his bishop to preside at Mass, nevertheless celebrates a valid Mass if he chooses to disobey the bishop's order. It is a "real" (valid) Mass, but the priest may commit a sin in celebrating it. *See also* liceity [canon law]; validity [canon law].

illuminative way. *See* ways of the spiritual life.

images, material representations of a deity fashioned to be objects of worship. The prohibition of images in the Decalogue (Exod 20:4–6; Deut 5:8–10) includes anything in the cosmos that could be the object of worship. Though not stated explicitly, it also implies the prohibition of making an image of Yahweh, analogous to the prohibition of using the divine name for improper purposes. Since antiquity the function of the image in the religious sphere is to make the deity present, and therefore available; the implication is that Yahweh is not a deity who can be controlled for the worshiper's own purposes. The command was not always observed, as the biblical texts (e.g., Judg 17:1–6; 1 Kgs 12:28–29) and archaeological data abundantly attest. According to the Priestly view (the narrative and legal portions of the Pentateuch composed by priests), the human being alone serves as the divine image and therefore as God's representative on earth (Gen 1:26–27). In all three monotheistic religions (Judaism, Christianity, Islam) iconoclastic movements attest to the importance that continued to be attributed to the prohibition. *See also* idolatry.

images, miraculous, devotional pieces of art that pious tradition insists possess supernatural powers of healing or of performing prodigies (e.g., icons that weep). *See also* icon.

imago Dei (Lat., "image of God"), theological concept that denotes the likeness of the human creature to God. According to Gen 1:26, humanity was created "in [God's] image, according to [God's] likeness." Found sparsely in the Hebrew Scriptures, the word "image" was used often in Pauline writings in the NT to interpret Christ's work and became central to early Christian reflections on the human condition, the meaning of redemption in Christ, and hope for humankind. This usage resonates the language of likeness and imaging for Christian readers shaped by Platonic schemes of the relation between levels of being.

Early theologians did not consistently separate "image" from "likeness" in interpreting human existence, and they saw the image of God variously in the human intellect, the capacity for moral decision, and the ability to rule over creation; but these theologians usually agreed it implied a kinship between God and humankind and a call for the imitation of God. Christ, as the one who is the image according to which humanity was made, was seen to meditate the likeness to God both in creation and redemption.

imitation of Christ, a central theme in the Christian life by which all Christians are called to conform their whole lives to Christ's. Although connected with discipleship, the imitation of Christ had a distinctive development. Discipleship emphasizes following Jesus; imitation speaks to conformity with Jesus. Imitation of Christ became explicit with the Apostle Paul, who often wrote of life in Christ. Baptism for Paul was the initiation of the Christian's imitation of the dying and rising of Jesus. The early Church honored martyrs as imitators of Christ.

Imitation of Christ, begun in Baptism and nourished at the Eucharist, is always in the context of community (Church). It is never mere reproduction of actions from the life of Christ. Imitation of Christ is, in fact, a graced activity, the work of the Holy Spirit. Reacting to a literalist notion of imitation, Martin Luther emphasized Christ as gift more than as object of imitation. All forms of the Christian life—single, married, priestly, religious—are a call to imitate Christ, to be conformed to Jesus, the way, the truth, and the life (John 14:6). Paul expresses the profound nature of the imitation of Christ with these words: "I have been crucified with Christ; and it is no longer I who live, but it is Christ who lives in me" (Gal 2:19–20). *See also* discipleship; *Imitation of Christ.*

Imitation of Christ, a book attributed to Thomas à Kempis (d. 1471) and thought to be the widest-read religious text, second only to the Bible. Published in 1472, its first two sections offer compact and proverb-like advice for the spiritual life. The third portrays conversations between a devout person and Christ. The fourth section offers meditations to increase devotion toward the Eucharist. The work continually emphasizes the difference between the glories and pleasures of the world and the humility and suffering proper to those following Christ. Instead of discussing the higher experiences of prayer in the contemplative life, *Imitation* is directed toward those still struggling with ordinary obstacles to the spiritual life. It helps beginners develop an interior life and offers practical methods for overcoming vices and growing in virtues. Love alone makes burdens light, freeing people from worldly affection so that they can find both God and themselves. *See also* Thomas à Kempis.

Immaculate Conception, the dogma that the Blessed Virgin Mary was free from original sin from the first instant of her existence. Officially taught by Pope Pius IX after consultation with the world's

The Blessed Virgin Mary was immaculately conceived, that is, without sin, because she was destined to be the Mother of God; *The Immaculate Conception* by Guido Reni (d. 1642), Metropolitan Museum of Art, New York.

bishops, it was promulgated in the papal bull *Ineffabilis Deus* on December 8, 1854, the day that remains its liturgical feast. This dogma holds that the Blessed Virgin Mary "was, from the first moment of her conception, by the singular grace and privilege of almighty God and in view of the merits of Jesus Christ the Savior of the human race, preserved free from all stain of original sin." This is not to be confused with the virginal conception, which refers to Jesus' being conceived by Mary without male intervention. Nor does it mean that Mary was conceived virginally. Rather, it is a belief about her original sinlessness in union with God.

History: The Immaculate Conception is not found explicitly in Scripture, although the dogmatic definition appeals to certain biblical texts that by extension can support it: promised victory over the serpent (Gen 3:15); the angel's greeting Mary as "favored" or "full of grace" (Luke 1:28); Elizabeth's tribute, "blessed are you among women" (Luke 1:42). The doctrine is also unknown throughout the patristic era, although the Eve-Mary antithesis with its death-life, sin-grace polarity sets the stage.

In the East, tradition about Mary's special holiness developed slowly. There, too, starting in the seventh century, a feast of her Conception was celebrated. These two traditions coalesced in the West in eleventh-century England where a feast of Mary's Immaculate Conception was introduced. Opposition to this feast brought the doctrine under critical discussion for the first time.

The main objection stated by theologians such as Anselm (d. 1109), Bernard (d. 1153), Aquinas (d. 1274), and Bonaventure (d. 1274) was that it removes Mary from the company of those needing salvation, thus detracting from the universality of Christ's redemptive work. These theologians were willing to grant that Mary was sanctified in the womb, but argued that she had to be touched by original sin for at least one instant in order to be redeemed by Christ's grace.

Duns Scotus (d. 1308) resolved these objections with his insight that Christ can save in two ways. In one, he rescues from sin those already fallen. In the other, he preserves someone from being touched by sin even for an instant. This is uniquely the case with Mary, whose being conceived without original sin demonstrates Christ's redemptive power. Given this reasoning the Council of Trent (1545–63) deliberately excluded Mary from its decree on original sin and taught in its decree on justification that she was free from all sins throughout her entire life.

Subsequently, the doctrine developed in liturgy, art, and piety. In the spirit of the age the U.S. bishops (1846) chose Mary under the title of her Immaculate Conception to be patroness of their relatively new country. Marian apparitions also encouraged belief. In Paris (1830) Catherine Labouré had a vision of Mary standing on a globe with rays of light streaming from her hands, surrounded by the words, "O Mary conceived without sin, pray for us who have recourse to thee." Crafted to show this vision, a medal known as "miraculous" became a widely used devotional object. Following the dogmatic definition, Bernadette Soubirous in Lourdes, France (1858), also saw a vision of a lady, who named herself, "I am the Immaculate Conception." The place of this encounter became and remains a center of pilgrimage where the sick in particular are welcomed, some allegedly being cured in waters welling up from a natural spring.

Theology: The religious meaning of this dogma centers on the victory of God's grace, freely given in Christ. Sin is universal, and the whole human race is in need of salvation. This is offered because of God's love and mercy poured out in the life, death, and Resurrection of Jesus Christ, prior to any merits or deserving works on the part of human beings. The dogma of Mary's original sinlessness celebrates God's victory over the powers and principalities of this world as this woman comes into existence. In her very being, through the mercy of God, the grip of evil is broken. To the Catholic imagination it is fitting that grace be freely given to her from the first moment of her existence because of her role in being the faith-filled mother of Jesus. Her yes to God brought Christ into the world, through whom the ancient sin of Adam and Eve is overturned. That God generously graces Mary, enabling her living union with God from her beginning even while not removing her from the sufferings of history, is congruent with divine mercy. It also signifies the good news that for the Church and for every human being, grace is more original than sin. *See also* Mary, Blessed Virgin; original sin.   ELIZABETH JOHNSON

Immaculate Heart of Mary, a Marian devotion promoted in the seventeenth century by John Eudes, who linked it with devotion to the Sacred Heart of Jesus. It was particularly strong during the pontificates of Pius VII (1800–23) and Pius XII (1939–58), who consecrated the world to the Immaculate Heart of Mary in 1942. *See also* Sacred Heart, devotion to the.

Traditional depiction of the Immaculate Heart of Mary, a devotion to the Blessed Virgin fostered by John Eudes in seventeenth-century France and popularized by the apparition of Mary at Lourdes in 1858 and later by Pope Pius XII (d. 1958).

Immaculate Heart of Mary, Servants of the. *See* Sisters, Servants of the Immaculate Heart of Mary.

immersion, first ritually indicated manner of baptism, whereby the individual is lowered bodily into a pool of water. Today's ritual allows for either total or partial immersion, i.e., submersion of the whole body or, in the case of adults, immersion of the head only. *See also* Baptism.

imminence of the end, in eschatological thought, the idea that the time of the promised return of Jesus Christ is fast approaching. The Gospels speak variously of Jesus' Second Coming, which will initiate a period of final judgment and culminate in the coming of the kingdom of God in its fullness, as heralded by calamitous human and natural events such as wars, famines, and earthquakes (Matt 24:1–25:46; Mark 13:1–37; Luke 21:5–36). Certain passages indicate that these things will be witnessed by the generation of Jesus' first disciples (Matt 16:28; 24:34; Mark 13:30; Luke 9:27; 21:32). The expectation is qualified, however, by statements that the time of the Second Coming is known by God alone (cf. Matt 24:32–44). *See also* apocalypticism; eschatology, universal; Second Coming.

immolation, theory developed during the Middle Ages that the sacrifice of Christ must be represented in some visible way during the eucharistic celebration. Various moments of the Mass were discussed as possible points for the immolation, e.g., the breaking of the consecrated bread or Communion. The theory was developed at a time when Christians saw the Mass as a dramatic replication of Christ's Passion. *See also* Eucharist; Mass; sacrifice of the Mass.

immortality, immunity from death. By excluding death, immortality points to endless life, but it does not indicate in what that life consists. Hence, it is not the same as "eternal life," the life of God shared with men and women who have been saved by the death and Resurrection of Jesus Christ. For even the damned would have immortality, but not eternal life.

The NT describes God as "he alone who has immortality" (1 Tim 6:16), for God alone by God's own nature excludes all possibility of death. Through the power of the risen Christ, "those who belong to Christ" (1 Cor 15:23) will share his triumph over death even in their bodies. Paul, speaking of the Resurrection, says: "The dead will be raised imperishable, and we will be changed. For this perishable body must put on imperishability, and this mortal body must put on immortality" (1 Cor 15:52b–53).

The late OT book the Wisdom of Solomon speaks of the final lot of the just in terms of immortality: "The souls of the righteous are in the hand of God, and no torment will ever touch them. In the eyes of the foolish they seemed to have died, and their departure was thought to be a disaster, and their going from us to be their destruction; but they are at peace. For though in the sight of others they were punished, their hope is full of immortality" (Wis 3:1–4).

The teaching that immortality belongs to the nature of the human soul, which for this reason survives separation from the body, was common among Greek philosophers (e.g., Plato, *Phaedo* 105–7) and maintained by Christian thinkers after them (e.g., Aquinas, *Summa Theologiae* 1.75.6). They understood the soul to be the intrinsic principle of human life, vivifying the body and thus making it capable of vital activity like sensation and movement. In addition, the soul was the basic principle of intellectual and volitional activity, which manifested a radical independence of matter in abstract thinking and free choice. It was this that led them to see the soul as capable of existing in itself, apart from a ma-

terial counterpart. Furthermore, as a spiritual principle, the soul is not made up of parts into which it could be dissolved. Thus, being able to exist in itself and not being subject to corruption or dissolution, it is by nature immortal.

Philosophical reasoning, however, is not the basis for the Christian hope of immortality. This rests on Christ's victory over death. Nevertheless, the natural immortality of the soul is not unrelated to eternal life. Grace presupposes and builds on nature. Therefore, it is reasonable that God would create something not naturally subject to death to be the immediate recipient of eternal life. At the resurrection of the body, the immortal soul communicates eternal life to the whole person, so that both body and soul share in it, and the whole person becomes immortal. *See also* eternal life; soul.   JOHN H. WRIGHT

impanation, word first used in the late eleventh century to describe the opinion of those who held that the body of Christ was present, but hidden, in the eucharistic bread, as his divinity was hidden in his human flesh. It was later used to describe theories of consubstantiation. *See also* Real Presence.

impassibility of God, one of the metaphysical attributes of God, derived from Greek philosophy and appropriated by classical theology, which holds that God is not subject to metaphysical change. In Christology, impassibility was ascribed to Christ's divine nature, while passibility was ascribed to Christ's human nature. Some contemporary theologians have rejected the idea of God's impassibility, claiming that a God who is unaffected by God's relationship to creation is incompatible with the biblical presentation of God. *See also* God.

impeccability. *See* sinlessness of Christ.

impediment, in canon law an obstacle to the licit and/or valid performance of an act. Some impediments are grounded merely in Church laws and can, in theory, be dispensed, e.g., marriage between a Catholic and a non-Christian. Some of these are, in fact, seldom dispensed, e.g., marriage between first cousins. Other impediments are based in divine or natural law and cannot be dispensed, e.g., marriage involving one or both parties who are already validly married to a third or fourth party.

imperfect contrition, sorrow for sin that is motivated by fear of punishment or by the horror of evil, rather than by love for God. Augustine (d. 430) used the phrase, "faith perfected by charity," and in medieval Scholasticism this idea was transferred to contrition: grace [charity] "perfects" contrition. In this view, whenever contrition was motivated by love for God and included an aversion toward sin, sanctifying grace was infused into the soul. If contrition did not include the infusion of sanctifying grace, it was "imperfect." Therefore, "imperfect contrition" is understandable in Scholastic theology on the basis of "perfect contrition," not vice versa. In contemporary theology, the issue of motive as regards sin and conversion is considered on the basis of psychological studies on human motivation. Given these studies, contrition cannot be understood as a single act, but only as an ongoing process in the life of a Christian. *See also* attrition; confession, auricular; perfect contrition; Reconciliation.

imperfections, human acts that are neither sinful nor meritorious in and of themselves. Moral theology identifies three types of imperfections: 1) a good act performed without a wholehearted love of God, according to the capacity of the human agent; 2) an objectively sinful act performed without sufficient deliberation; or 3) a deliberate choice to act in a way that is less than perfect but not against the law of God, such as relaxing at home instead of visiting the sick. One's concern to correct imperfections must not foster perfectionism. *See also* perfection; venial sin.

imposition of hands. *See* hands, imposition of.

impotence, impediment of, in canon law marital impediment based on the physical or psychological inability to have sexual relations. This inability is an impediment grounded in the traditionally Catholic understanding of the purpose of marriage and cannot, therefore, be dispensed. To qualify as an impediment, however, the inability must be perpetual, i.e., incurable by ordinary means, and must antedate the marriage. If there is any doubt about the perpetuity of impotence in a given case, the marriage is to be allowed. Impotence may be absolute, i.e., toward any person of the opposite sex, or relative, i.e., toward only one particular person. *See also* Marriage; marriage law.

imprimatur (im-pree-mah'toor; Lat., "it may be printed"), the approval given by the competent ordinary (usually the diocesan bishop of the author or of the place of publication) to publish certain specified types of books. In addition to catechetical works, textbooks dealing with theology, canon law, Sacred Scripture, Church history, and other sacred sciences are to have an imprimatur. Canon law recommends that all books covering these subjects be given this approval, but only requires it of textbooks (strictly understood) and books sold or distributed in a church. The competent ordinary is the local ordinary (cf. can. 134.2) of the author or of the place where the books are published. A local ordinary is to consult with a censor learned in the matters covered by the book for assurance that the book conforms to Church teaching before granting or refusing this approval, and the censor is to give his or her opinion in writing. *See also imprimi potest; nihil obstat.*

imprimi potest (im-pree'mee poh'test; Lat., "it can be printed"), the permission required for a religious to publish writings dealing with faith and morals. This permission does not preclude the possible requirement for approval of a given text by the local ordinary (diocesan bishop). The particular law of a religious institute determines which major superior is competent to give this permission. *See also* imprimatur; *nihil obstat.*

imputation (Lat., *imputare*, "to ascribe"), the soteriological view that God ascribes to those human beings who have faith in Jesus Christ the obedience and righteousness possessed by Jesus Christ himself, even though these human beings are themselves disobedient and alienated from God. This idea was adopted by Martin Luther in his teaching on justification. In its extreme form, the theory of imputation maintains that God simply declares sinners to be just and that no change occurs within human beings. In its moderate form, it holds that God declares sinners to be just and simultaneously gives them the grace to become holy. *See also* grace; justification; nature and grace.

incardination, the canonical bond that exists between a cleric and a given diocese or institute of consecrated life. Canon law allows no cleric to be without this bond and the supervision of a bishop or other ecclesiastical superior that is joined to it. The bond arises at the time of ordination to the diaconate, when a person becomes a cleric. It is possible to transfer subsequently to a different diocese or institute of consecrated life and thus be excardinated, i.e., sever the former bond and be incardinated in the second diocese or institute, i.e., establish a new bond. *See also* excardination.

Incarnation, the (Lat., *caro*, "flesh"; hence, "enfleshing"), the assuming of a human nature by God, specifically by the Logos, the divine Word. This notion can be understood to refer to the moment when God became a human being at the conception of Jesus in his mother, Mary. It can also refer to the abiding reality of the hypostatic union of the divine nature and the human nature in Jesus Christ. In both cases the notion is meant to exclude misinterpretations of the mystery of Jesus Christ, for example, that, on the one extreme, Jesus Christ was simply God in the appearance or guise of a human being (Docetism) or that, on the other extreme, Jesus Christ was simply a human being who was so filled with the Holy Spirit as to seem divine (Adoptionism). The doctrine of the Incarnation upholds the paradoxical mystery that Jesus Christ is one divine person (Gk., *hypostasis*) possessing both a divine nature and a human nature.

New Testament: The NT attests to the mystery of the Incarnation. Key texts include: "the Word became flesh" (John 1:14); "Christ Jesus, who . . . emptied himself, taking the form of a servant, being born in human likeness" (Phil 2:5–8); "God sent his Son, born of a woman" (Gal 4:4–5); and "He was revealed in flesh, vindicated in spirit" (1 Tim 3:16).

Just what the NT means by "flesh" has been the source of long-standing controversy. The Alexandrian school in the early Church, influenced by Platonic thought, at times put forth the view that the Son of God assumed some human attributes but not the whole reality of a human being. However, this interpretation has no basis in the NT, since "flesh" in the texts cited above is synonymous with "human nature." Moreover, the entire testimony of the Gospels regarding Jesus' person and activities leaves no doubt that his followers knew him as a full human being.

Doctrinal Development: As the early Church reflected on the reality of the Incarnation, it found itself having to defend this mystery from reductionistic or simplistic explanations. Along with Docetism and Adoptionism, there were the theories that Jesus Christ possessed only one nature (Monophysitism), lacked a human soul (Apollinarianism), possessed two distinct natures without being one person (Nestorianism), became one nature after the Incarnation (Eutychianism), and possessed only a divine will (Monothelitism). The Church rejected each of these views and upheld the doctrine of the Incarnation in the series of councils that began with the Council of Nicaea (325) and ended with the Third Council of Constantinople (680–81). Another theory that threatened the doctrine, especially in the nineteenth century, was kenoticism, which maintains that in the Incarnation the Son of God emptied himself of his divinity so completely that Jesus lacked a divine nature. This radical view is incompatible with the Christian understanding of the mystery of redemption.

While the Incarnation pertains specifically to Jesus Christ, it does shed light both on the mystery of God and also on the mystery of human life. In the Incarnation God is shown to be so devoted to creation and humankind as to enter completely into the human situation, knowing firsthand its joys, limitations, and burdens. Simultaneously, the Incarnation discloses the essence of being human, namely, openness to God and the longing to enter into relationship with God. This orientation discloses the potential goodness that is inherent in human nature, fallen but redeemed.

Unresolved Questions: Over the centuries, theologians have debated a number of unresolved issues regarding the Incarnation, including the following. Would the Incarnation have occurred if Adam and Eve had not sinned? Are creation and redemption wholly separate acts of God, or are they two distinct, yet connected, acts of God? Further, could any one of the three divine Persons become flesh, or was it most appropriate that the Second Person of the Trinity be born of the Virgin Mary? Also, is there a sense in which it is permissible to say that the Incarnation occurred not just at the moment of Jesus' conception but also in the course of his entire life? Moreover, what is the relationship between the Incarnation and Jesus' suffering, death, and Resurrection? Questions of this sort can be helpful for the Christian faith because they can stimulate prayer, reflection, and insight into the fathomless mystery of God's becoming a human being in Jesus Christ. *See also* Adoptionism; Apollinarianism; Docetism; hypostatic union; Jesus Christ; kenosis; kenotic theories; Monophysitism; Monothelitism; Nestorianism.

ROBERT A. KRIEG

incense (Lat., *incendere*, "to burn"), the aromatic gums of resinous trees that are burned upon coals in a brazier or thurible. Incense is used during processions and to honor sacred objects such as the altar, the Gospel book, the eucharistic bread and wine, and the bodies of Christians, both living and dead. At the Liturgy of the Hours, incense is burned as a sign of prayer, the sacrifice of praise. The first attested Christian use of incense appears in the account of the funeral of Peter of Alexandria (d. 311). *See also* thurible; thurifer.

inclusive language, words and phrases that designate all members of a group by avoiding "false generics" such as "man" when both males and females are intended. Controversy about inclusive language in liturgical and biblical texts has arisen in English-speaking churches because present English usage is androcentric (i.e., understands the male to be the normative human person). Androcentrism is reflected in the use of "man" to denote both human being and male—and in the use of male pronouns only, whenever generic ones are required. This pattern of male-centered language arises from a patriarchal social order that views males as dominant and "superior," while treating women as lesser, inferior beings. It is increasingly seen as incompatible with the equal dignity of men and women as human persons. In 1990 the U.S. Catholic bishops issued criteria opposing liturgical language that seems to exclude the equality and dignity of each person.

inculturation, the process by which individuals learn their group's culture through experience, observation and instruction; and also the process by which the gospel is adapted to a particular culture. The Second Vatican Council (1962–65) made the first detailed statement about the relationship of the Church to diverse cultures in the Pastoral Constitution on the Church in the Modern World (n. 58). In order to evangelize, pastoral initiatives need to be carried on from *within* the cultures of humankind (Pope Paul VI, "On Evangelization in the Modern World," [*Evangelii Nuntiandi*] 1975).

Through inculturation the Church endeavors to reformulate Christian life and doctrine within the thought-patterns of each people. Efforts to achieve such integration have not been easy. There have been both successes and failures. The Vatican was not supportive of Father Matteo Ricci (1552–1610), as he developed the Chinese rites. However, in 1982, Pope John Paul II praised Ricci for "building between the Church and the Chinese culture a bridge that seems still solidly anchored and secure" (address at the Gregorian University on the occasion of the 400th anniversary of the arrival of Father Ricci in China). Also, in spite of earlier hesitations, Pope

John Paul II named Sts. Cyril and Methodius the co-patrons of Europe in 1980.

Although the Second Vatican Council initiated serious efforts toward inculturation, much work remains to be done to achieve what is implied in Acts 10:34–36: "Then Peter began to speak to them: 'I truly understand that God shows no partiality, but in every nation anyone who fears him and does what is right is acceptable to him.'" *See also* Catholicism and culture.   ROBERT S. PELTON

inculturation, liturgical, the process of adaptation in which worship creatively employs the cultural heritage of a particular people. Their local ritual and symbolic forms and systems are invested with Christian meaning. Inculturation, therefore, differs from acculturation in that the latter only incorporates those native rituals and symbols which are seen as compatible with the Roman liturgical tradition. Acculturation purifies and reorientates, while inculturation is more confident about the congruence between the native culture and Christian worship. Vatican II (1962–65) called for this process to be done under the competent authority (the national conference of bishops) and with the assistance of experts (Constitution on the Sacred Liturgy, n. 40). This marked a significant change from the historical imposition of the sober Roman liturgy in countries like Spain and Gaul or in countries later evangelized by the Western Church. In the post-Vatican II Church, there has been notable success in inculturating the liturgy in certain areas of Africa and elsewhere. *See also* acculturation; Catholicism and culture.

indefectibility, the Church's "inability to fail" in its mission of teaching the authentic message of the gospel. The basis for this belief is found in the NT: the Church is built upon a rock (Matt 16:18); the Holy Spirit has been sent to the apostles to lead them to all truth (John 14:16); Christ will be with his apostles even to the end of the world (Matt 28:30). Such texts do not mean that individual Christians will not fail in their commitment to Christ; as long as people are sinful, reform will be needed in the Church. Nor do such texts mean that theological and doctrinal changes will not be needed in the Church; as new questions emerge, the gospel will have to be expressed in new thought-forms. In this regard, indefectibility means that the Church will always be faithful to teaching the essential message of the gospel. Closely related to, but different from, indefectibility is the concept of infallibility, which means that, when teaching definitively on a matter of faith or morals, the Church will never fall into error about the fundamental meaning of the gospel. *See also* infallibility.

indeterminism, the philosophical and scientific doctrine denying determinism, according to which a given cause or set of causes necessarily brings about the same effect. For each theory of determinism there is a contradictory species of indeterminism. Controversy exists over how much human choices are determined by physical and psychological factors. Less controversial is the physical theory that subatomic processes are indeterministic; the theological implications of microphysical indeterminism are unclear.

Index of Forbidden Books (Lat., *Index Librorum Prohibitorum,* abbreviated ILP), list of books Catholics were forbidden to read or even possess except under specified circumstances. Penalty for noncompliance was excommunication. Books on the Index were forbidden because they were thought to contain materials contrary to faith and/or morals. The Index was established in 1557 by Pope Paul IV and was later overseen by a special curial office (Congregation of the Index) founded by Pope Pius V in 1571. In 1917 supervision passed to the Holy Office. The Index was abolished by Pope Paul VI in 1966 because it was by then regarded as inconsistent with the freedom of inquiry encouraged by the Second Vatican Council (1962–65), especially in its Pastoral Constitution on the Church in the Modern World (n. 62).

India, Catholicism in. Catholicism in India employs a complex, multiritual worship with diverse origins. A significant community of Christians has lived on the southwest Malabar coast of India since the fourth century. They trace their roots, according to a strong but unprovable tradition, to the extensive Indian missionary activity of the Apostle Thomas, whose presumed tomb is venerated near Madras. These "Thomas Christians" existed for many centuries as a self-contained and fully inculturated church with strong ties to the (Nestorian) Assyrian Church of the East in what is now Iraq and Iran.

The Portuguese arrived in India at the end of the fifteenth century and soon initiated a process not only of integrating the Thomas Christians into the Catholic Church, but also of compelling them to give up many of their own traditions and conform to Latin practices. This triggered a schism between those who accepted these changes (now the Syro-Malabar Catholic Church) and those who broke with Rome and formed what would become the Malankara Orthodox Syrian Church.

The coming of the Portuguese also marked the beginning of extensive Catholic missionary activity in India and the formation of a parallel Latin Catholic Church based in areas under Portuguese control. The Jesuit Francis Xavier arrived in Goa in 1542 and with his companions gave strong impetus to the Catholic mission, especially through publishing and educational activity. Several other Catholic missionary communities began work in the subcontinent before 1600, when the rate of conversions peaked. Largely unsuccessful missions were also sent to the empire of the Great Mogul in the north and to other regions as far away as Tibet. The mission declined sharply, however, as the Portuguese presence waned and after the Jesuits were expelled from Portugal and its possessions in 1759.

Aware of Portuguese weakness, the Holy See began to set up vicariates apostolic in other parts of India under the Congregation for the Propagation of the Faith. Tensions soon arose between these new mostly Italian jurisdictions and the regular Portuguese hierarchy. This led to the long-standing practice of double jurisdictions in some areas, and even to a virtual schism between the two groups in the mid-nineteenth century. The problem was finally resolved in 1886 when a new concordat provided for the establishment of a regular hierarchy throughout India.

A second Eastern Catholic Church came into being in Kerala in 1930 when two bishops of the Malankara Orthodox Syrian Church were received into full communion with Rome, forming the Syro-Malankar Catholic Church. In the following decades it experienced rapid growth.

In recent times, there have been some difficulties in the relationship between the Eastern and Latin churches in India because of the limitations imposed on the Eastern Catholics concerning the establishment of pastoral structures for their faithful outside Kerala and the ability to engage in missionary activity in other parts of India. These limitations were removed by Pope John Paul II in 1987.

In 1993 in India there were 150 dioceses and over 14,000 priests serving just under 14 million Catholics. *See also* Syro-Malabar Catholic Church; Syro-Malankara Catholic Church; Thomas Christians.

RONALD G. ROBERSON

indifferentism, the belief that the differences that separate Christian denominations or Christianity itself from other religions are of no real significance. All religions are understood as being equally capable or incapable of displaying divine truths.

Indifferentism became an important issue in the nineteenth century when it was perceived to characterize theological liberalism. Indifferentism was explicitly condemned by a series of popes in the nineteenth century.

Current Church doctrine holds that Christianity most fully embodies the saving grace of God, with Catholicism as the norm for the interpretation and realization of the Christian tradition (Vatican II, Dogmatic Constitution on the Church, 1964, nn. 13–16). Other religions can mediate salvation through what is true and holy within them (Declaration on the Relationship of the Church to Non-Christian Religions, 1965, n. 2). *See also* salvation outside the Church.

indissolubility of marriage, an essential property of marriage that excludes any potential for its dissolution either by the mutual consent of the spouses (intrinsic indissolubility), or by an ecclesiastical or civil authority (extrinsic indissolubility).

Catholic belief and practice uphold both types of indissolubility in all sacramental and consummated marriages, i.e., marriages lawfully celebrated between two baptized persons and consummated "in a human manner" (knowingly and willingly) through sexual union. If at least one of the partners is Catholic, lawful celebration means "according to Catholic canon law"; if both are from another Christian community, a demonstrable manifestation of consent is enough. The scriptural foundation for this indissolubility is in Jesus' sayings against divorce (e.g., Mark 10:2–9) and in Paul's assertions of marriage as the symbol of Christ's union with his Church (Eph 5:21–33).

In the case of marriages sacramentally celebrated (both spouses were baptized) but not consummated (e.g., because of impotency), and of marriages non-sacramentally but lawfully contracted (at least one of the spouses was not baptized), the Catholic Church still honors an intrinsic indissolubility, but is willing to lend its authority, in rather restrictive circumstances, to bring about the termination of the marital bond, always for the sake of some benefit accruing to an individual believer (freedom, peace of conscience, practice of faith). A specific precedent can be found in the Scriptures: Paul freed believers from unbelieving spouses who wished to separate or kept disturbing the peace (1 Cor 7:12–15). *See also* annulment; Marriage.　　LADISLAS M. ORSY

individualism, the term generally given to the wide variety of attitudes, theories, and doctrines associated with a belief in the underived and absolute value of the individual. The rise of modern individualism owes something to the historical Christian emphasis on the sanctity and dignity of the person (cf. Matt 10:30), though the often exaggerated distinction drawn by modern individualism between the individual and community—particularly in the moral, social, and economic spheres—is inconsistent with the traditional Christian belief in the inherently social nature of the person, the unity of humankind, and the ultimate dependence of the individual upon God.

indulgences, the remission of temporal punishment for sin, in response to certain prayers or good works (cans. 992–97). In this canonical description, indulgences are neither the remission of sin itself nor the remission of eternal punishment due to sin. Indulgences remit only temporal punishments, also called "remnants" or "vestiges" of sin. It is God, through the Church, who remits the temporal punishment. Both the history and the theology of indulgences are complicated. In the NT baptism is described as a new birth, a new creation, a burial and resurrection with Jesus. In Baptism all sin is removed. That Christians who committed certain serious sins after Baptism should undergo a ritual of Reconciliation gradually became normative. After Baptism and Reconciliation, Christians continued to experience both temptation and sin. To resist this call to sin, they prayed and performed penitential works. They also prayed and fasted for each other. These prayers and fastings were seen as helpful because of their connection to Christ. The Christian belief in the abundance of God's forgiving love through Jesus and the unity of all Christians in a communion of saints forms the major foundation of the theology of indulgences. When tariff penance began to establish itself in the Western Church from the ninth century onward, various penances that a person would find difficult to fulfill were commuted, e.g., into a specified number of prayers or a specified amount of alms. This gave rise to a mathematizing of Penance: e.g., a set number of fast days equalled a pilgrimage to Jerusalem. With the beginning of the Crusades under Urban II (1088–99), indulgences became both popular and monetary. Christians, unable to take part in the Crusades personally, could share in the merits of the Crusades by almsgiving. Those who personally took part in the Crusades received a plenary indulgence at the moment of death, i.e., all the temporal punishment still due to their forgiven sins was declared remitted. The bull of Clement VI (1343) mentions a "treasury of merits," which Church authority dispenses. Luther strongly objected to the connection of indulgences to the merits of saints and to the merits of Jesus Christ. In Luther's view, indulgences were good works, denying two fundamental theological issues: the absolute gratuity of God's grace and the full efficacy of Jesus' redemptive act. In its response to Luther, the Council of Trent (1545–63) defended indulgences on the basis of Church tradition (D 1835). Theologically, Trent used Matt 16:19 and 18:18 as the scriptural proof. At Vatican II (1962–65) a reformulation of both the theology and practice of indulgences was requested. Paul VI wrote a response, *Indulgentiarum Doctrina* (*AAS* 59, 1967, nn. 5–24), in which he tried to avoid any commercial overtones, substituted the term "treasury of satisfactions" for "treasury of merits," marginalized indulgences as they relate to Christian spirituality, stated that plenary indulgences are connected with one's deliberate rejection of all sin, even venial, and made the use or nonuse of indulgences completely voluntary. *See also* merit; purgatory; sin.   KENAN B. OSBORNE

indult, permission given by the Holy See for nonobservance of a requirement of canon law. Such a permission might be by way of dispensation (relaxation of the law in a given instance), privilege (a favor granted to certain a person, physical or juridical), or faculty (capacity to perform certain acts). An indult may be given for a specified period of time or in perpetuity. *See also* dispensation; faculties, canonical.

Ineffabilis Deus (in-ef-ahb'i-lis day'oos; Lat., "The Ineffable God"), the constitution of Pope Pius IX, issued on December 8, 1854, defining the dogma of the Immaculate Conception. *See also* Immaculate Conception.

inerrancy of Scripture, the common teaching of the Church that the Scripture teaches truth, without error, for the sake of salvation. This doctrine is a corollary of the doctrine of inspiration: "Since ev-

erything asserted by the inspired authors or sacred writers must be held to be asserted by the Holy Spirit, it follows that the books of Scripture must be acknowledged as teaching firmly, faithfully and without error that truth [*veritatem . . . sine errore*] which God wanted put into the sacred writings for the sake of our salvation" (Vatican II, Dogmatic Constitution on Divine Revelation, n. 11).

The conciliar teaching, explicitly cited in the *Catechism of the Catholic Church* (1992), reflects the earlier teaching of Popes Leo XIII (*Providentissimus Deus,* 1893) and Pius XII (*Divino Afflante Spiritu,* 1943). Moreover, it identifies the inerrancy of Scripture as a function of the fact that Scripture is the word of God and that by means of the Scriptures truth is taught for the sake of salvation.

Understanding what is meant by "truth put into the sacred writings for the sake of our salvation" is the key to understanding what is meant by the inerrancy of Scripture. Leo XIII had affirmed that "the sacred writers or more truly the Spirit of God, who spoke through them, do not offer a scientific explanation of nature but sometimes describe and treat the facts either in a figurative manner or in the common language of the times" and added that this principle is also applicable to the biblical authors' way of dealing with history.

Echoing his predecessor, Pius XII declared that "no error exists" when the sacred writer "followed sensible appearances" (as Thomas Aquinas put it), or spoke either metaphorically or in the common manner of the day, or when the true sense of a particular passage remains uncertain.

During the Second Vatican Council (1962–65), the Pontifical Biblical Commission's instruction "The Historical Truth of the Gospels" (1964) put the truth and authority of the Gospels in their proper light. The instruction noted that the truth of the Gospels must be understood according to the norms for rational and Catholic hermeneutics and reiterated the fact that "the sacred writers employed the way of thinking and writing which was in vogue among their contemporaries." With regard to the reliability of these Scriptures, the instruction underscored the importance of the various stages of tradition and the fact that the sacred authors occasionally synthesized and/or adapted the traditions within which they were writing.

According to the council fathers, the truth of the Scriptures, which witnesses to the truth of God, is an expression of the "condescension" (as Chrysostom put it) of divine wisdom. The language of

Scripture is adapted to "our weak human nature," that is, to our human situation (Dogmatic Constitution on Divine Revelation, n. 13). The truth of the Scriptures is consonant with God's truth, that is, with divine fidelity and self-revelation for the sake of the salvation of humankind. *See also* inspiration of Scripture.   RAYMOND COLLINS

infallibility, a charism (or gift of the Spirit) that ensures "immunity from error" in the Church's definitive teachings on matters of faith and morals. In its fullest sense, infallibility is a divine attribute: only God is infallible, totally immune from error. If infallibility is to be predicated of anyone else, it can only be in a very restricted sense.

Teaching of the First Vatican Council: The constitution *Pastor Aeternus* of the First Vatican Council (1869–70) described the "infallible magisterium of the Roman Pontiff" in the following words: "when the Roman Pontiff speaks *ex cathedra,* that is, when ... as the pastor and teacher of all Christians in virtue of his highest apostolic authority he defines a doctrine of faith and morals that must be held by the Universal Church, he is empowered, through the divine assistance promised him in blessed Peter, with that infallibility with which the Divine Redeemer willed to endow his Church."

The first thing to be noted about this definition is that it does not say that "the pope is infallible"; rather, it states that the pope is "empowered" with the infallibility that Christ conferred on his Church. Thus, in teaching with infallibility, the pope exercises a power that essentially belongs to the Church and that he utilizes on behalf of the Church. Second, the council did not define what "infallibility" is, but only the way in which the pope is to exercise it. Third, while the council states that the pope can exercise infallibility, it does not exclude the possibility that others can also use this power along with the pope (see below). Fourth, an exercise of infallibility is a use of the highest authority the pope possesses; thus, he is speaking in his official capacity as "the pastor and teacher of all Christians," not as an individual theologian. Fifth, "a doctrine of faith and morals that must be held by the Universal Church" is not simply a matter of ecclesiastical governance or canonical discipline, but a matter directly connected with revelation (though theologians still debate about the nature of this connection). Sixth, the pope is able to exercise infallibility not because of his personal intellectual abilities or theological knowledge, but because of the "divine assistance"

promised by Christ to Peter and his Church. Finally, the council stated that such "definitions of the Roman Pontiff are irreformable of themselves and not from the consent of the Church." This statement was directed against the proponents of Gallicanism, who maintained that papal decisions did not go into effect unless and until they were ratified by the Church.

Teaching of the Second Vatican Council: *Lumen Gentium,* the Dogmatic Constitution on the Church approved by the Second Vatican Council (1962–65), clarified Vatican I's teaching on infallibility in several important ways. First, Vatican II indicated that the college of bishops, either assembled in council or dispersed throughout the world, could teach infallibly in communion with the pope. In this regard, it is important to note that bishops do not individually exercise infallibility, but only corporately as members of the college of bishops in communion with the pope. Second, Vatican II described the object of infallibility as "co-extensive with the deposit of revelation." Third, while Vatican II indicated that the pope and the bishops must take "every suitable means" to give expression to the message of revelation, "they do not admit any new public revelation as pertaining to the divine deposit of faith." Finally, the council insisted that Catholics should give a "loyal submission of intellect and will" not only to teachings given under the aegis of infallibility, but also to "the authentic teaching authority of the Roman Pontiff, even when he does not speak *ex cathedra*" (n.25).

Infallibility Debates: Few doctrines have given rise to as much debate as infallibility. At the time of Vatican I, at least one-fifth of the bishops in attendance had misgivings about promulgating the proposed teaching on infallibility. Many of these bishops felt that a definition was unnecessary and would only cause difficulty for Catholics and strain ecumenical relations with other Christians; other bishops felt that a definition was premature, insofar as a clearer theological explanation of the doctrine was needed; a few bishops had serious reservations about the truth of the proposed definition. Although the definition of Vatican I was generally accepted by Roman Catholics (with the exception of a small group that left to form the "Old Catholic Church"), some of the problems about infallibility voiced at Vatican I are still being debated today.

Some aspects of this debate could be resolved by a more careful use of terms. For example, "infallibility," immunity from error, must not be confused with "impeccability," immunity from sin. Thus, "infallibility" does not imply that popes cannot sin. Similarly, infallibility is not "omniscience," knowledge about everything. Thus, the pope and the college of bishops can teach with infallibility only in the very restricted area of revelation. Moreover, the exercise of infallibility is rare; the only generally acknowledged use since the time of Vatican I is the declaration of Mary's Assumption by Pope Pius XII in 1950.

Other aspects of infallibility continue to be the subject of theological debate. For example, since Vatican II, the biblical basis for the pope's exercise of infallibility (in Matt 16:18 and parallel texts) has been widely debated. Theologians also disagree about the "extent" of infallibility. Some feel that many of the Catholic Church's teachings should be considered as definable under infallibility. Many others have warned of the danger of "creeping infallibility" and point to the fact that Vatican II did not exercise infallibility. Still others have questioned how doctrine can develop if the Catholic Church's teaching is considered "irreformable." Such debates are likely to continue in the future. In any case, the doctrine of infallibility is much too complicated to be summarized in the simple sentence "The pope is infallible." *See also* magisterium.

Bibliography

Cwiekowski, Frederick J. *The English Bishops and the First Vatican Council.* Louvain: Publications Universitaires, 1971.

Empie, Paul C., T. Austin Murphy, and Joseph A. Burgess, eds. *Teaching Authority and Infallibility in the Church.* Lutherans and Catholics in Dialogue VI. Minneapolis, MN: Augsburg, 1978.

Hennesey, James. *The First Council of the Vatican: The American Experience.* New York: Herder and Herder, 1963.

O'Gara, Margaret. *Triumph in Defeat: Infallibility, Vatican I, and the French Minority Bishops.* Washington, DC: The Catholic University of America Press, 1988.

Sullivan, Francis A. *Magisterium: Teaching Authority in the Catholic Church.* New York and Ramsey, NJ: Paulist Press, 1983.

JOHN T. FORD

infancy Gospels, popular accounts of the "hidden years" of Jesus and his family. The most important of this popular Christian genre are the *Infancy Gospel of Thomas* and the *Infancy Gospel of James.* The first dates from the second century and survives in numerous languages. It portrays Jesus as a precocious miracle worker from ages two through twelve. The *Infancy Gospel of James,* or *Protevangelium Jacobi,* also composed in the second century, tells of the childhood of Mary and of Jesus' miraculous birth. These two works served as the basis for the eighth-century *Gospel of Pseudo-Matthew,* a Latin work influential throughout the Middle Ages. An Arabic infancy Gospel, dependent on the *Infancy Gospel of Thomas,* was known to Muhammed. An Armenian infancy Gospel expands on the *Protevangelium Jacobi.* Numerous other derivatives were composed during the Middle Ages and afterward. *See also* gospel.

infant baptism, the baptism of children before the age of reason. In both the East and the West this practice is traditional. *The Apostolic Tradition* (ca. 220) directs that children should be baptized before the adults. Those who can speak should do so for themselves, otherwise the parents or someone else should speak for them. Cyprian of Carthage (ca. 250) insisted that no one born should be deprived of God's grace.

Historical Development: During the fourth century the practice of baptising infants declined. Baptism of both adults and children was postponed because of apprehension about future sins and the fear of public penance. At that time the sacrament of Penance was received only once in a lifetime. Since Baptism forgives all sins, some delayed it for as long as possible. The Church Fathers expressed concern about this practice because Baptism is necessary for salvation.

The baptism of an infant with water and the words, "I baptize you in the name of the Father, and of the Son, and of the Holy Spirit."

In response to Pelagianism, which was understood as denying original sin and making Baptism unnecessary, the Council of Carthage (418) emphatically stated that newborn infants should be baptized. The council taught that babies who are unable to commit any sin personally are nonetheless to be baptized for the forgiveness of sins.

The Council of Vienne (1312) taught that Baptism granted to infants both grace and the virtues. The Council of Florence (1442) wanted infants to be baptized *quam primum commode* (Lat., "as soon as is convenient").

The Reformation surfaced conflicting views on the practice. The Anabaptists denounced Luther's retention of infant baptism and rebaptized adults who had been baptized in infancy. Calvin's predestinatinarian view made the question of infant baptism moot. The Council of Trent (1545–63) reiterated the teaching of the Council of Carthage.

Vatican II to Today: Vatican II (Constitution on the Sacred Liturgy) requested a revision of the rite, resulting in the Rite of Baptism for Children (1969). An instruction issued by the Congregation for the Doctrine of the Faith (1980) provided two principles: (1) Baptism, which is necessary for salvation, is the sign and means of God's prevenient love, which frees us from original sin and communicates to us a share in the divine life. The gift of these blessings to infants must not be delayed. (2) Assurances must be given that the gift thus granted can grow by an authentic education in the faith and Christian life in order to fulfill the meaning of the sacrament. As a rule, these assurances are to be given by the parents or close relatives, although various substitutes are possible within the Christian community. But if these assurances are not really serious, there can be grounds for delaying the sacrament; if they are nonexistent, the sacrament should be refused.

Infant baptism presumes continued sharing of the experience of faith and ongoing religious education. Aware that the infant believes through the faith of the Church, the Rite of Baptism highlights the role of parents and godparents. The local community is challenged to hand on and nourish the faith it has received from the apostles.

In the Rite of Baptism for Children, a ritual is provided in case of danger of death. It is sufficient in the absence of the ordinary minister to baptize with water: "[Name] I baptize you in the name of the Father, and of the Son, and of the Holy Spirit." The parish priest should be notified and, if the infant sur-

vives, the Rite of Bringing a Baptized Child to the Church should be celebrated. *See also* Baptism.

ANTHONY SHERMAN

infidel (Lat., *infidelis*, "unfaithful"), in the literal sense, a person who does not have faith in God's revelation. Traditionally, a distinction is made between positive infidels, those who have formally refused the Christian faith when it was sufficiently presented to them, and negative infidels, those who have never been introduced to or adequately taught about God's revelation and, therefore, do not have explicit Christian faith because of ignorance. It is possible, therefore, that negative infidels possess implicit belief in divine revelation. Strictly speaking, infidels are not atheists, since atheists deliberately deny all forms of belief in God. In the Middle Ages the term was used in a broader sense, applying at times to Jews, Muslims, and "pagans." *See also* salvation outside the Church.

infinity of God, one of the metaphysical attributes of God, signifying that God is without end, limit, termination, or determinant. It means that God is superior to all created, finite things. The idea of God's infinity first became important during the thirteenth century with Thomas Aquinas and Bonaventure. In addition to describing the divine essence, infinity is a property that applies to all other attributes. For example, divine knowledge is omniscient; divine power is omnipotent. The attribute of infinity has also been used as a basis for God's incomprehensibility, which has meant that theological discourse about God is incapable of circumscribing God. *See also* God.

infused knowledge, a knowledge given to a human or angelic consciousness directly and immediately by God. This knowledge may include ideas, concepts, words, feelings, or intuitions that do not come from empirical experience or intellectual deduction from sense data.

The topic arises in relation to the knowledge of Jesus Christ. Passages in the Gospels implied that Jesus had a special inner knowledge (e.g., Luke 2:46–52). Medieval theology (Alexander of Hales) posited three kinds of knowledge in Jesus: (1) human empirical knowledge acquired through the senses; (2) a beatific knowledge which overflowed from the incarnate presence of the Logos in the human mind of Jesus of Nazareth; (3) infused knowledge, that is, intelligible forms impressed directly upon Jesus' consciousness by God. Whether others, such as the prophets, inspired biblical writers, Mary, Joseph, visionaries, or saints, also had infused knowledge has been a matter of speculation over the centuries. The Church has not taught definitively on the subject, and Catholics are free to take whatever position they find persuasive. *See also* angel; Jesus Christ.

infused virtue. *See* virtue, infused.

infusion. *See* affusion.

In Hoc Signo Vinces (ihn hawk seen'yoh vihn' chez; Lat., "You will conquer in this sign"), a message to the Emperor Constantine from Christ and the reported cause of his conversion to Christianity in 312. Christ told him in a dream to paint the Chi-Rho symbol (the first two letters in Greek of "Christ") on his soldiers' shields to ensure victory in battle. After winning the Battle at the Milvian Bridge, the emperor is thought to have converted. *See also* Constantine the Great.

initiation. *See* Rite of Christian Initiation of Adults.

Innocent I, St., d. 417, pope from 401 to 417 and staunch defender of the prerogatives of the Apostolic See in matters of doctrine and Church discipline. When John Chrysostom appealed for Innocent's intervention against Theophilus, patriarch of Alexandria, Innocent supported him, breaking communion with Alexandria and Antioch. He also supported the African bishops' condemnation of Pelagianism (417), succeeded in separating eastern Illyricum from the ecclesiastical jurisdiction of Constantinople, and played an important role in securing an imperial decree against Donatism in 404. His letters provide evidence for the sacrament of Anointing and for the separation of Confirmation from Baptism. Feast day: July 28. *See also* Anointing of the Sick; Chrysostom, St. John; Confirmation; Donatism; Pelagianism.

Innocent III [Lotario di Segni], 1160–1216, pope from 1198 to 1216. Lotario studied theology and law under the greatest scholars of his day. In 1190 his uncle, Clement III, made him a cardinal and in 1198 at age thirty-seven he was elected pope. His reign is considered the summit of the medieval papacy. By dint of his personality, intellect, and diplomatic skill, Innocent was able to match theories of papal

Pope Innocent III, one of the greatest of the medieval popes, depicted here (with Francis of Assisi, whose new order he approved) asleep and dreaming; fourteenth-century painting by Giotto, Basilica of St. Francis, Assisi, Italy.

power with concrete and extensive application. For him the papacy was based on moral, not temporal, authority and his pastoral office required him to champion the cause of Christ whenever required. Insisting on the title Vicar of Christ, Innocent unhesitatingly intervened in the affairs of sovereigns for moral reasons. He forced Philip of France to take back his wife and put England under interdict when King John refused to accept the papal appointment to the archbishopric of Canterbury. Innocent extended papal authority to Scandinavia, Spain, the Balkans, Cyprus, and Armenia, but his highest achievements were in Church reform. He summoned the greatest reform council of the Middle Ages, Lateran IV (1215). Innocent endorsed the early constitutions of Dominicans and Franciscans and supported Cistercian evangelization in Russia. He strengthened papal authority over episcopal in the extensive use of legates and reserved certain cases for his own tribunal. He attempted to use means such as these to combat heresy but reluctantly summoned a crusade against the Albigensians in southern France in 1209. *See also* Albigensians; Crusades; Lateran councils; papacy, the; Vicar of Christ.

Innocent IV [Sinibaldo Fieschi], d. 1254, pope from 1243 to 1254. A Genoan nobleman and a brilliant canonist, he was elected pope following an eighteen-month vacancy. The major challenges of his pontificate include the continued reform of the

Church, the Crusades, the Mongol invasion of Hungary, and especially the conflict with the Hohenstaufen emperor Frederick II. Innocent formally deposed Frederick at the First Council of Lyons (1245), which he convoked to reform the Church and which finally resolved the conflict with the empire. Even after Frederick's death in 1250 the papacy struggled haplessly for political stability in Italy. In 1252 Innocent approved the use of torture by the Inquisition. *See also* Inquisition; Lyons I, Council of.

Innocent V, Bl. [Peter of Tarentaise], ca. 1224–76, pope from January 21 to June 22, 1276. As a Dominican professor of theology, he published a widely used commentary on the *Sentences* of Peter Lombard dependent on that of his teacher Thomas Aquinas. As cardinal-bishop of Ostia (1273), he took part in negotiations to end the schism with the Eastern Church at the Second Council of Lyons (1274). Feast day: June 22. *See also* Lyons II, Council of; *Sentences*.

Innocent X [Giovanni Battista Pamphili], 1572–1655, pope from 1644 to 1655. He opposed the religious toleration provided in the Treaty of Westphalia (1648), sought to unite the Catholics of Ireland against the English, and in 1653 condemned five articles drawn from Cornelius Jansen's *Augustinus. See also* Jansenism.

Innocent XI, Bl. [Benedetto Odescalchi], 1611–89, pope from 1676 to 1689. He condemned the four Gallican Articles (1682), approved by the French clergy asserting their rights and privileges while limiting those of the pope, and the doctrines of Miguel de Molines (1687), urged frequent Communion and confession (1679), and devoted himself to resisting the Turkish advance into Europe. He was beatified in 1956. Feast day: August 12. *See also* Gallicanism.

inopportunists, the party at Vatican Council I (1869–70) who regarded the definition of papal infallibility unwise, not because they disbelieved the doctrine but because they regarded its timing as "inopportune." The term describes the position of most of the bishops who opposed the definition, with Bishop Dupanloup of Orléans as their head. Rather than vote against the doctrine when it was brought to a final vote, most of the inopportunists absented themselves. *See also* infallibility; Vatican Council I.

Inquisition, a now defunct institution in Catholicism for the eradication and punishment of heresy. The Fourth Lateran Council (1215) called for secular authorities to help in the eradication of heresy. In 1231 Pope Gregory IX issued a papal bull, *Excommunicamus,* establishing procedures for identifying heretics in various parts of Europe. At first, largely under the direction of Franciscans and Dominicans, traveling tribunals went into Germany, France, and Italy to examine those suspected of formal heresy. Punishment for such crimes ranged from public penances to imprisonment and, for those who were obdurate, the death penalty carried out by secular authorities. In 1252 Pope Innocent IV permitted torture to be used in the seeking out of the truth. These traveling tribunals met everything from compliance to resistance as they carried out their investigations. By the fourteenth century, the tribunals had lost most of their vigor.

The so-called Spanish Inquisition was a creation of the Spanish monarchs Ferdinand and Isabella in 1479. The aim of this highly centralized office was to seek out heretics and to ferret out converted Jews (Sp., *Marranos*) and Muslims (*Moriscos*) who still covertly practiced their own religion. The Spanish Inquisition was most vigorous in the late sixteenth century but as an institution it lasted in Spain until 1834, when it was abolished by monarchical decree.

The Roman Inquisition was established as a papal congregation by Pope Paul III in 1542 as part of the Church's response to the Protestant Reformation. It was the final tribunal of the Church dealing with matters of heresy. It also examined and proscribed heretical books through a list (the Index of Forbidden Books) of books that Catholics could not read without special permission.

The record of imprisonment, torture, and execution connected with the Inquisition has been a blot on the history of the Church. Its most famous victim was the Italian astronomer and mathematician Galileo (d. 1642). Despite attempts by some historians to put the phenomenon into larger historical perspective, the popular picture of the Inquisition as despotic, narrow, and cruel has persisted in the popular imagination to the extent that the very word "inquisitorial" has an ominous ring to it.

The Roman Congregation of the Inquisition was active until modern times. In 1966, after the Second Vatican Council, the Index of Forbidden Books was abolished (it is no longer stipulated in the new Code of Canon Law promulgated in 1983), and the congregation was renamed by Pope Paul VI in 1965 the

Congregation for the Doctrine of the Faith (CDF) as part of the papal reorganization of the Roman Curia. *See also* Congregation for the Doctrine of the Faith; Galileo; heresy.   *LAWRENCE CUNNINGHAM*

I.N.R.I., Christian inscription, often found on crucifixes, that stands for the Latin phrase, "Jesus of Nazareth, King of the Jews" (*Iesus Nazarenus Rex Iudaeorum*). According to John's Gospel this was the phrase Pilate had written on Jesus' cross (19:19).

inscriptions, early Christian, writings, carvings, engravings, etc., usually in cemeteries or churches, that were very common from the fourth century on but are also well attested in the third century and perhaps as early as the first. Mostly in Latin or Greek, they are important evidence for the character and spread of early Christianity. Inscriptions are considered Christian if their content is obviously Christian or if they use symbols typically Christian, such as the anchor, Alpha and Omega, Chi-Rho monogram, palm branches, victor's crown,

The Chi Rho, the first two letters (x, p) in the Greek word for "Christ," remains a common Christian inscription, especially after the emperor Constantine the Great claimed to have had a vision of the two letters in the sky during his victorious battle against his rival Maxentius at the Milvian Bridge in 312; on a Christian sarcophagus, in the Lateran Museum, Rome.

etc. Christian epitaphs commonly evince hope in the resurrection, but the occupation of the deceased and date of death are rarely mentioned until well into the fourth century. *See also* anchor-cross.

inspiration of Scripture, the doctrine that ultimately affirms that the Scriptures are "the word of God." The terminology derives from 2 Tim 3:16–17: "All scripture is inspired by God [Gk., *theopneustos*] and is useful for teaching, for reproof, for correction, and for training in righteousness, so that everyone who belongs to God may be proficient, equipped for every good work." Elsewhere in the NT, Jesus is described as proclaiming that David uttered the psalms (Ps 110:1) by the power of the Holy Spirit (Matt 22:43; Mark 10:36), and 2 Pet 1:21 affirms that "men and women moved by the Holy Spirit spoke from God."

Although the passage from 2 Timothy made explicit reference only to the Scriptures of the OT, the Fathers of the Church, convinced of the unity between the NT and the OT, used similar language to describe the Scriptures of the NT and OT. Clement of Alexandria (d. 215), for example, wrote about the inspired writings (Gk., *hai theopneustoi graphai*). Some Fathers of the Church spoke about God as the "one author" of Scripture. Their teaching was that God was the source of the writings of both the OT and the NT.

Doctrinal Development: The dogmatic tradition of the Church has been reaffirmed in all the papal encyclicals that deal with the Bible. The tradition was authoritatively summed up in Vatican II's assertion that, "Holy Mother Church, relying on the belief of the apostles, holds that the books of both the Old and New Testaments in their entirety, with all their parts, are sacred and canonical because, having been written under the inspiration of the Holy Spirit, they have God as they author and have been handed on as such to the Church herself" (Dogmatic Constitution on Divine Revelation, n. 11).

According to the dogmatic tradition, it is the Scriptures themselves that are inspired. Scholastic theology, and especially Thomas Aquinas (d. 1274), interpreted the traditional doctrine of the inspiration of the scriptural text by means of an analogy with the divine inspiration of prophets. Thus Catholic theology, and its expression in various magisterial and conciliar pronouncements, commonly spoke about the "inspired authors" as a way to explain how the scriptural text was inspired.

Under pressure from the Enlightenment and various tendencies to interpret the Scriptures in a merely human fashion, nineteenth-century theologians began to examine the doctrine of inspiration in a more systematic fashion. A common explanation was that God is the principal efficient cause of the Scriptures and that its human authors are the instrumental cause. In some circles, Catholic as well as Protestant, a notion of plenary verbal inspiration seemed compelling, but the theory as generally presented is all too simple, almost implying that God virtually dictated the words of Scripture. The insights provided by modern biblical scholarship as to how the various books of the Bible came to be written demands a far more sophisticated notion of inspiration.

The doctrine implies (1) that the entirety of the canonical Scriptures comes from God in a way distinct from the way that all things have been created by God or that gifted poets can be said to be inspired; (2) that those who actually wrote the Scriptures did so in a truly human fashion; (3) that the Scriptures of the OT and NT are foundational with regard to Israel and the Church; (4) that the Scriptures are inspired in their origin and inspiring in their effect; and (5) that the truth to which the Scriptures attest is given for the salvation of humankind. *See also* inerrancy of Scripture; Scripture, authority of; Scripture, senses of; *sensus plenior.*   RAYMOND COLLINS

installation, the formal initiation into Church office. Canon law specifies that a diocesan bishop show the papal letter of appointment to the diocesan College of Consultors. In a new diocese that lacks consultors, the candidate must present such a letter to the clergy and people present in the cathedral. This action, called in canon law "taking possession of the see," must take place within a specified period of time from the date of appointment. It is fitting that the celebration of the Eucharist be joined to it. Inauguration into other offices is governed by the letter of appointment or by particular law.

Institut Catholique (Fr., "Catholic Institute"), a Catholic institution of higher studies that replaced the theology faculty of the University of Paris abolished in the French Revolution of 1789. The institute, legally established in 1875, was a center of critical historical and theological scholarship that was characterized by some conservative Catholics as Modernist. Its faculty included the Church historian Louis Duchesne (d. 1922) and the biblical scholar Alfred Loisy (d. 1940). More recent faculty members have included Louis Bouyer and Jean Daniélou (d. 1974). In the 1990s the Institut is also a center for liturgical studies. *See also* Paris.

institute, religious. *See* religious institute.

institute, secular. *See* secular institute.

institution, words of, the words of Jesus at the Last Supper over the bread and wine as used in the celebration of the Eucharist. These words are given with some variations in Matt 16:26–29; Mark 14:22–25; Luke 22:15–20; and 1 Cor 11:23–24 and are understood as Jesus' interpretation of his death. In most of the earliest eucharistic prayers some form of these words are used in the central prayer of blessing and praising God. The actual text of these words in the Mass combines elements from these four sources. *See also* Eucharist.

instruction, an official explanation concerning the proper implementation of a Church law. Given by the authority competent to oversee matters concerning the law in question, it can neither add to, nor delete from, the law in question; its purpose is explanatory.

instructor, in canon law the tribunal official whose responsibility it is to collect the proofs of a case and present them to the judge. *See also* tribunal.

instruments, tradition of the, the rite in ordinations during which the bishop hands to the newly ordained some symbol of the office he will exercise. In 1947 Pope Pius XII settled the centuries-old controversy as to whether the handing over of the instruments was essential for the validity of the ordination by determining that the imposition of hands and the prayer that follows alone are necessary. *See also* ordination.

insufflation, ritual gesture of breathing into or upon an individual or object, often associated either with an exorcism or the coming of the Holy Spirit. Used frequently in the early Church, this practice has all but disappeared in modern times except in the blessing of the water at the font during the Easter Vigil and in the consecration of chrism on Holy Thursday. *See also* blessing; exorcism.

Integralism, a nineteenth- and early-twentieth-century ultraconservative movement in France that opposed ecumenism and modern biblical studies and theology. More broadly, it refers to the attitudes of the Integralists. Pope Leo XIII's encyclical *Aeterni Patris* (1879) encouraged a more critical form of Catholic scholarship. In response, *Integrisme* (Fr., "Integralism") developed in France to protect against the possibility of doctrinal deviations in Catholic teaching. This movement secretly investigated and censured scholars whose work it disapproved. After the condemnation of Modernism by Pope Pius X in 1907, *Integrisme* achieved some organizational permanence as the *Sodalitium Pianum* (1909), essentially a spy network to monitor and then to discredit theologians, biblical scholars, and even bishops whom it considered dangerous to the faith.

Pope Pius X's successor, Benedict XV, denounced the practices of the Integralists in his first encyclical *Ad Beatissimi* (1914) and in 1921 suppressed the *Sodalitium Pianum* permanently.

Although the organized form of Integralism no longer exists, its spirit lives on in those movements that seek to discourage theological inquiry and to suppress and punish those who propose ideas about Catholicism different from their own. *See also* Pius X, St.; traditionalism, Catholic; Ultramontanism.

intention, moral, act of the will in regard to the end of a moral action. For an act to be moral, and not merely an action that a human does, it must proceed freely from the will. The good, which is the proper object of the will, can be striven for in itself and for the sake of itself or as the reason of the choice of the means. When the will is moved to an end as acquired by the means, it is called the intention of the agent. For Thomas Aquinas (d. 1274), the movement of the will to the end (intention) and its movement to the means (choice) are one and the same thing (*Summa Theologiae* 1–2.12.4). In the handbooks of moral theology, intention is considered one of the three sources of morality, along with the object and the circumstances of an action, though these terms are understood differently by different authors. If the object or the end of the action considered in itself does not already possess morality, then the intention of the agent can confer morality on the action. However, if the action is viewed as intrinsically evil, no intention can make the action morally right. Thus, one may not do moral evil in order that the good end of the agent result.

intention, sacramental, the desire or will to receive or administer a sacrament that affects the validity of the sacrament. The desire not to receive a sacrament, for example, always makes the latter invalid. The validity of the sacraments of Matrimony, Reconciliation, and Anointing of the Sick depends on the positive intention of the subject to celebrate the sacrament and receive the particular grace it offers. However, this is not the case with infant Baptism and Confirmation. Since faith and incorporation in the Church are understood as pure gifts of God, these sacraments can be validly received before the age of reason and without a specific positive intention. Ministers, provided that they are able to celebrate the sacrament, must at least have a minimal desire of doing what the Church intends in order to celebrate it validly; that is, they must intend to celebrate the religious rite as prescribed by the Church. *See also* sacrament.

Inter Mirifica (in'tair meer-ee'fee-kah). *See* Decree on the Instruments of Social Communication.

intercession, an act of prayer in which one seeks the help of God for a special favor. Intercessory prayer relies on the power of God to whom one prays through Jesus Christ to give what one truly needs (Rom 8:34). Intercession also may be made through Mary and the other saints. *See also* prayer.

intercommunion, sharing in liturgical worship, especially the Eucharist, between Catholic and non-Catholic Christians. Before Vatican II (1962–65), intercommunion was expressly forbidden. The council's Decree on Ecumenism, however, made possible a change in attitude and practice by recognizing first of all that the Catholic Church is in communion, though imperfect, with non-Catholic churches and ecclesial communities and that the liturgical actions of these bodies can be used by the Holy Spirit as sources of grace.

More particularly the decree (cf. n. 8), while cautioning against using intercommunion indiscriminately as a means for reestablishing unity, takes note of two principles. The first is that common worship presupposes unity in faith. The second is that the sacraments are sources of grace. While common worship cannot ordinarily be practiced because of division in doctrine, in some circumstances it is possible and even necessary because it is a means of salvation.

Since Vatican II numerous dialogues on the local,

national and international levels between the Catholic Church and other churches and ecclesial communities have revealed much common understanding on a variety of doctrines and issues. This has led to proposals from theologians and ecumenists for the establishment of intercommunion in order to foster the movement toward unity. Some non-Catholic churches and communities have embarked upon intercommunion among themselves.

The Holy See, while recognizing increasing convergence in doctrinal understanding, considers the agreement achieved thus far as insufficient to warrant full intercommunion. However, the 1983 Code of Canon Law does establish some norms for its practice in particular circumstances. Canon 844 permits Catholics who do not have access to a Catholic priest to receive Penance, Eucharist, and Anointing of the Sick "from non-Catholic ministers in whose churches these sacraments are valid." This can be done "whenever necessity requires or genuine spiritual advantage suggests." This permission can most obviously be utilized in relation to the Eastern churches not in union with Rome since the Catholic Church recognizes all of their sacraments to be valid. Occasions for the exercise of this permission could be illness, danger of death, or residence in a region where there are no Catholic priests.

Catholic ministers may also administer Penance, Eucharist, and Anointing of the Sick to members of non-Catholic Eastern churches "if they ask on their own accord . . . and are properly disposed." These sacraments can also be administered to members of other churches who uphold the validity of these sacraments. The Holy See, however, has not identified those churches. But the canon does state that Catholic ministers may administer the sacraments to Christians who do not belong to the Eastern churches or churches similar to them if "they cannot approach a minister of their own community and on their own ask for it." However, they have to share in the Catholic faith regarding these sacraments and be properly disposed.

The canon urges that no general norms be established by a bishop or a bishop's conference without consultation with the non-Catholic church or community affected by the norms. *See also* ecumenism; Eucharist; sacrament.   JOHN J. STRYNKOWSKI

interdict, ecclesiastical penalty that prohibits a person from ministerial participation in public worship and from reception of the sacraments and sacramentals. Although the current law views interdict as a penalty to be imposed on persons, the previous law saw it as a penalty that might be inflicted within the boundaries of a place, e.g., a parish. If the interdict has been officially declared or imposed as the result of a juridical proceeding, the interdicted person is to be prevented from engaging in ministerial acts at the celebration of the Eucharist. If this is not possible, the celebration is to cease.

intermediate state, the condition of the human person between death and resurrection of the body. In 1336 Pope Benedict XII solemnly declared (*Benedictus Deus*) that purified souls during this interval enjoy the Beatific Vision, that those needing purification are purified, and that any dying in mortal sin suffer in hell. *See also* Beatific Vision; soul.

internal forum, the realm of conscience where God's grace, forgiveness, and peace are experienced. Communications in the internal forum are characterized by complete confidence. Canonists distinguish the internal forum from the "external forum," which is the arena of the Church's public governance, and wherein communications are official and a matter of record.

"Internal forum solutions to irregular marriages" refers to the pastoral reconciliation of those who have experienced the tragedy of divorce and have remarried. The ordinary process of reconciliation of the divorced and remarried is in the external forum. One of the parties to the original marriage petitions for an annulment of the marriage in a Church court. After careful investigation and weighing of evidence, the ecclesiastical judges decide whether or not the first marriage was valid or invalid, and, consequently, whether the petitioner can enter a second union.

When it seems that the original marriage was canonically valid or when it is not possible to obtain a judicial decision on its validity, reconciliation to the sacraments of Penance and Eucharist can be achieved through the internal forum. This is essentially a moral discernment, usually involving a pastoral advisor, based on the state of conscience of those in the second marriage. It is not a canonical process, and it represents an exception to the Code of Canon Law (can. 1085.2).

Internal forum solutions to otherwise insoluble marriage situations are very widely accepted in pastoral practice.

For background and bibliography confer *The Jurist* 30 (1970) pp. 1–74; 40 (1980) pp. 128–196; and 50 (1990) pp. 573–612. *See also* conscience; external forum. JAMES CORIDEN

International Commission on English in the Liturgy (ICEL), a body established by the English-speaking hierarchies of the world to supervise translation of Latin liturgical texts into English and to propose English adaptations in accordance with conciliar and postconciliar directives. The initiative was taken by archbishops Grimshaw of Birmingham, England; Hurley of Durban, South Africa; Young of Hobart, Australia; and Hallinan of Atlanta, Georgia, in 1963. ICEL consists of an episcopal board, with representatives from each of the eleven member conferences, which directs and reviews the commission's work; an advisory committee, whose members represent a range of pertinent competencies and national origins, and which supervises and reviews the work of the various working subcommittees; and the subcommittees, which in turn do the actual work of translation, prepare new texts, and plan the layout of liturgical books. Since 1965, ICEL's executive secretariat has been located in Washington, D.C. *See also* liturgical language.

International Theological Commission, an organization of theologians established by Pope Paul VI in 1969. The First World Synod of Bishops (1967) had suggested the formation of a body "composed of theologians of diverse schools . . . whose duty it will be, acting with all lawful academic freedom, to assist the Holy See, and especially the Sacred Congregation for the Doctrine of Faith, in connection with questions of greater importance." Other goals specified by Paul VI included contributions to "ecumenical dialogue" and to "the art of teaching, which is termed kerygmatic, and our ability to proclaim the message of Divine Revelation and human salvation."

The commission is composed of thirty theologians, with statutes definitively approved by Pope John Paul II in 1982. It is not part of the Congregation for the Doctrine of the Faith, although its cardinal-prefect presides, appoints the influential general secretary, and influences the choice of topics and the appointment of members. Nearly every year since 1969 its annual week-long meetings and subsequent implementation of decisions reached there have produced documents giving substantive but cautious theses or essays on topics suggested by the pope, the Curia, bishops' synods, or the members themselves.

The commission has been subject to significant criticism: its limited meetings and restricted topics mean that "questions of greater importance" are usually settled by the pope or Curia without the commission's help; appointed members—exclusively male, practically all Western, mostly clerics, two-thirds European, mainly from ecclesiastical institutions—are hardly "theologians of diverse schools"; consensus statements, usually reflecting official Vatican opinions, fail to represent the vitality or richness of the legitimate theological pluralism Paul VI "willingly allowed" in his inaugural address to the commission; the commission has not seriously addressed the ecumenical and pastoral teaching issues Paul VI set as its goals. *See also* theologian; theology. WALTER PRINCIPE

interpretation of canon law. *See* canon law, interpretation of.

interpretation of Scripture. *See* Scripture, interpretation of.

interstices, an interval or period of time that must elapse between reception into the diaconate and reception into the presbyterate (six months), and between reception into the ministry of acolyte and reception into the diaconate (six months). The reason for such an interval is to provide the candidate with a suitable period of time in which to exercise the responsibilities given before receiving new responsibilities. *See also* Holy Orders.

intinction, the practice of dipping consecrated eucharistic bread (leavened or unleavened) into consecrated wine in order to provide the faithful with Communion under both species (bread and wine). The practice, first noted in seventh-century Spain, has been common in the East since the ninth century. It was abandoned in the West when Communion under the species of wine was discontinued. In accord with the liturgical renewal of Vatican Council II, the Sacred Congregation of Rites, on March 7, 1965, restored intinction as one of four methods of providing the faithful with Communion under both forms. *See also* Communion, Holy; Communion under both kinds.

intrinsic evil. *See* evil, intrinsic.

Introduction to the Devout Life, a popular guide to the spiritual life by Francis de Sales (d. 1622). The text was developed from letters of spiritual direction given in 1607 to Mme. de Charmoisy, wife of the Duke of Savoy, when she returned to court after a leave of several months. She was anxious not to fall away from the spiritual life recently begun under Francis's direction. The text's ninety-five short chapters provide balanced instructions and meditations to help those living secular lives grow in love of God and others. The *Introduction* focuses on the purification of motives and the gradual development of virtuous habits. It uses examples from Scripture, the Christian spiritual tradition, and everyday life. Among the topics covered are the need for a guide, reception of the sacraments, annual retreats, spiritual dryness and consolations, poverty of spirit amid wealth, proper behavior at parties, friendship, and instructions for married persons. *See also* Francis de Sales, St.

introductory rites, those actions and words that initiate a particular liturgical celebration. Thus, the gathering of candidates, sponsors, participants, and liturgical ministers at the church door for the sacraments of initiation (Baptism, Confirmation, Eucharist) and the opening words of greeting and of explaining the purpose of the celebration constitute an introductory rite.

Introit (in'troyt; Lat., "entrance"), entrance prayer consisting of a short antiphon (verse that is said before and after the prayer), a verse from the Psalms, the simple doxology ("Glory be to the Father"), and the repetition of the antiphon. As the first element in the Roman Mass before the Second Vatican Council (1962–65), it was sung as the ministers entered the church. Since the Introit is no longer a part of the Roman Catholic Mass, its place is usually taken by an entrance hymn sung by the entire congregation. *See also* Great Entrance.

invalidity [canon law], the quality of not being legally recognized. In canon law it is presumed that acts are valid until the contrary is proven; thus, a marriage is presumed valid until proven otherwise. Canon law attaches to certain acts the pain of invalidity if they are not done in a specified manner. *See also* illiceity [canon law]; liceity [canon law]; validity [canon law].

invention of the cross (Lat., *invenire,* "to find"), the finding of the True Cross. According to a legend, Helena (d. ca. 330), the mother of Emperor Constantine, found the True Cross of Christ while on pilgrimage in Jerusalem. In 350, Cyril of Jerusalem assured catechumens that the church in Jerusalem possessed the cross. Today, the Church of the Holy Sepulchre in Jerusalem contains a relic of the cross. From the seventh century until 1960 a liturgical commemoration known as the Invention of the Cross was observed on May 3. *See also* cross, relics of the; Helena, St.

investiture controversy, late-eleventh- and early-twelfth-century debate concerning relations between Church and state. In the early Middle Ages, lay lords frequently chose candidates to fill vacant bishoprics. During the consecration ceremony, the bishop-elect would pay homage to the lay lord and was invested by him with both the lands attached to the bishopric and the episcopal crosier and ring. What lay rulers viewed as a method of ensuring the loyalty of their bishops, Church reformers saw as an undesirable intrusion of secular leaders in religious matters.

In 1075, Pope Gregory VII issued a decree forbidding such lay investitures. This decree was opposed by the German emperor Henry IV, and in the ensuing conflict, Gregory excommunicated Henry and Henry called a council of German bishops to depose Gregory. The excommunication was lifted in 1077 and reinstated in 1080. In 1084, Henry drove Gregory from Rome and placed his own candidate on the papal throne.

The early decades of the twelfth century saw many attempts to end the quarrel between pope and emperor. A compromise was finally reached in 1122 at the Council (or Diet) of Worms between Pope Callistus II and Emperor Henry V: the emperor gave up the power to appoint bishops and to invest with the ring and crosier, while retaining the right to receive the homage of the bishop in exchange for the lands of the bishopric. *See also* Gregory VII, St.

invincible ignorance, a type of ignorance that cannot be removed even with diligence. Discussions of invincible ignorance are concerned with excusing a person from moral responsibility for performing an action that is objectively morally wrong. Ignorance of this kind does not imply subjective fault because the agent is either not aware of a moral obligation that applies in the situation or is unaware of the circumstances or conditions of the action. If ignorance remains after making every reasonable and prudent effort to discover the moral obligations and circumstances that apply to the action, then the person is inculpably ignorant. Several factors determine if a reasonable effort was made, e.g., the seriousness of the action, the availability of resources to consult, and the ability of the person to understand the circumstances of the act. Because a person cannot will what is unknown, the action that results from invincible ignorance is involuntary and, therefore, sinless. *See also* ignorance; vincible ignorance.

invitatory, in the Latin breviary, Psalm 95 ("*Venite*"), used to open the first Canonical Hour of the day (Matins). The Liturgy of the Hours, as reformed by Vatican II, uses the invitatory to open either Lauds or the Office of Readings and permits the use of alternative psalms (24, 67, 100). *See also* breviary; Liturgy of the Hours; Matins.

in vitro fertilization (IVF), the extracorporeal fertilization of an ovum and its subsequent transfer to the uterus. The first birth of an IVF baby occurred in 1978. Since that time techniques and success rates have improved and many thousands of babies have been born via IVF. Success rates vary, but they have been reported up to 25 percent per cycle of treatment.

Most centers doing IVF stimulate the ovaries with clomiphene citrate, human menopausal gonadotropin, or combinations of these so that multiple eggs are produced. Pregnancy rates rise when more than one preembryo is transferred. IVF involves co-incubating sperm and eggs for twelve to eighteen hours to allow fertilization to occur. After an additional forty-eight to seventy-two hours, the preembryo(s) is transferred to the uterine cavity. Implantation should begin in the next two to three days and verification of pregnancy is possible within two weeks after transfer.

There are several medical indications for IVF. A very common one is tubal damage or destruction. Another is pelvic endometriosis that has failed conservative therapy. Anomalies of the uterus or of the reproductive tract are also accepted indications. IVF can be performed with the husband's sperm (homologous IVF) or that of a donor (heterologous IVF).

Church Teaching: The Church's official response to the new reproductive technologies is found in the Congregation for the Doctrine of the Faith's Instruction on Respect for Human Life in Its Origin and on the Dignity of Procreation (*Donum Vitae,* 1987). The instruction rejects heterologous IVF as a violation of the unity of marriage and an infringement of the rights of the child by depriving the child of a filial relationship with parental origins. By disrupting familial relationships, it can be a "source of dissension, disorder and injustice in the whole of social life."

The instruction also rejects homologous IVF. It returns to the analysis of *Humanae Vitae* on contraception, specifically to the "inseparable connection, willed by God and unable to be broken by man on his own initiative, between the two meanings of the conjugal act: the unitive meaning and the procreative meaning." Just as contraception separates these two meanings (pursuing the unitive while blocking the procreative), so in an analogous way IVF separates them (pursuing the procreative without the unitive). The instruction sees this as procreation "deprived of its proper perfection" and not in conformity with the dignity of the spouses.

Many theologians have expressed reservations about the use of third parties in procreative procedures and would very likely support the instruction's rejection of heterologous IVF. The same is not true of homologous IVF. Many would judge this so-called simple case to be morally justifiable as a last resort. They would view procreation "deprived of its proper perfection" as a departure from the ideal, but not as morally wrong. Even more radically, many would question the inseparability of the unitive and procreative as applied to every act.

IVF should not be viewed as an isolated technique. It is part of a multifaceted technology that is constantly evolving and brings into play some basic human values. For that reason it deserves constant public oversight. *See also* bioethics; reproductive technologies.
RICHARD A. MCCORMICK

Iona, important monastery founded ca. 565 by Columba, Irish abbot and missionary, on the island of Hy, off the west coast of Scotland. It soon became the center for Irish missionary activity in Scotland and northern England, as well as a channel for cultural contacts between Ireland and these areas. *See also* Columba, St.

irascible appetites. *See* appetites, concupiscible and irascible.

Ireland, Catholicism in. St. Patrick, a Roman missionary, is traditionally believed to have con-

IRELAND

"Strongbow," came to the chieftain's aid. In 1171 Henry went to Ireland to assert his authority. He confirmed Strongbow and other nobles in their titles in return for their recognition of his lordship over Ireland. The Normans were never able to control the whole island; much of the north and west remained under the control of Gaelic chieftains. The Church developed very differently in the two regions. In the Pale—the Norman-dominated region around Dublin—the reforms that had begun in the previous decades continued. Parishes were established and tithing was encouraged. In the Gaelic areas, the monasteries remained formidable.

In the fourteenth and fifteenth centuries the Church's fortunes declined. Bishops and priests became more worldly; monks became more lax; and the laity followed the clergy's lead. There were some signs of renewal as well. The Franciscans reformed themselves in the fifteenth century and established dozens of Observant houses across the island. Observants argued for a return to the spirit of poverty, in opposition to the Conventualists, whom they regarded as lax.

In 1534 Henry VIII broke with Rome and declared himself head of the Church of England. In 1536 the Dublin Parliament recognized Henry as the head of the Church of Ireland. Henry's viceroy persuaded some bishops and noblemen within the Pale to accept the change. Henry's successor, Edward VI, appointed Calvinists to key bishoprics in Ireland, a policy that antagonized many of the Irish. When Mary I took power in 1553, most Irish supported her efforts to reestablish Catholicism. Five years later, Elizabeth I revived the Church of Ireland. For much of her reign Elizabeth contended with rebellions by Irish chieftains such as Hugh O'Neill, who battled the English for nine years before surrendering in 1603.

In 1607 O'Neill and ninety other Ulster nobles fled to the continent fearing imprisonment. James I expropriated their lands and invited thousands of Scottish Presbyterians and English Anglicans to settle there. In 1641 Catholic forces capitalized on the civil war ravaging England and launched another uprising. Much of the fighting occurred in Ulster where angry peasants killed hundreds of Protestant planters. Oliver Cromwell came to Ireland in 1649, laying waste to Drogheda and Wexford. In 1652 he decreed that Catholics would only be allowed to own land in Connaught, the westernmost and least fertile region of Ireland. All priests were ordered to leave Ireland and the Mass was proscribed.

verted the Irish people to Christianity in the early fifth century (ca. 432). Although Patrick baptized thousands, paganism persisted in parts of Ireland for at least one hundred and fifty years after his death.

Early History: Patrick organized the Church around an episcopal structure, but monasteries became dominant in the decades after his death. Among Ireland's most noteworthy monks were St. Columkille (d. 597) and St. Columbanus (d. 615). From his monastery on the island of Iona, Columkille evangelized the peoples of Scotland and northern England. Columbanus traversed continental Europe, founding houses that became renowned as centers of scholarship.

Monasteries were often under the control of laymen who were descendants of the house's founder. Periodically, efforts were undertaken to reorganize the Irish Church around dioceses and parishes. In response to pressure from Rome and from domestic reformers, a synod was convened in 1111 that divided the island into provinces and dioceses. The naming of St. Malachy as archbishop of Armagh in 1132 and papal legate in 1140 bolstered the reform movement further. In 1152 the Synod of Kells redrew diocesan boundaries: the island was divided into four provinces—Armagh, Dublin, Cashel, and Tuam.

Beginnings of English Authority: In 1155 Pope Adrian IV, an Englishman, issued *Laudabiliter,* a bull encouraging the English king to subdue Ireland and reform the Church there. The king, Henry II, ignored the pope's recommendation. Twelve years later, an Irish chieftain asked Henry to come to Ireland to help him defeat his rival. Henry refused, but Richard de Clare, a Norman knight nicknamed

With the Restoration of 1660, persecution of Catholics eased but Cromwell's land settlement was not modified. Irish Catholics' hopes rose when James II, a Catholic convert, succeeded to the throne in 1685. James called for religious toleration and appointed a Catholic viceroy. In 1688 a Protestant coalition invited James' son-in-law, William of Orange, to depose him. James fled to France but then landed in Ireland in a bid to regain the throne. James was routed in the Battle of the Boyne in 1690, and fled again to France.

Oppression and Revival: In the years following, a series of penal laws were enacted against Catholics. Under these statutes, bishops and regular clergy were banished; Catholic laymen were not allowed to vote, hold political office, purchase land, or serve as lawyers or military officers. In the last quarter of the eighteenth century these laws gradually were dismantled. By 1793 all restrictions on Catholics—except the ban on holding office—had been lifted. In 1829 the government dropped that barrier in response to lobbying by Daniel O'Connell's Catholic Association.

In the early years of the nineteenth century the Church experienced a great revival. New churches were erected throughout the island. The number of priests and religious increased dramatically. Maynooth College, established in 1795, offered high caliber training to hundreds of seminarians. Newly established religious communities—the Christian Brothers, the Sisters of Mercy, the Sisters of Charity and others—expanded rapidly and staffed a network of Catholic schools, orphanages, and hospitals.

While the Potato Famine of 1845–49 wrought destruction throughout Ireland, the Church emerged even stronger in its aftermath. After the famine Ireland had a considerably smaller and more affluent population that was more manageable for the Church. The Church was also strengthened by the appointment of Paul Cullen as archbishop of Armagh in 1849. Roman trained, Cullen was an able administrator who improved discipline at all levels of the Church during his thirty-year tenure.

In the 1880s the bishops backed the home rule campaign of Charles Stewart Parnell, a Protestant landlord. The hierarchy withdrew its support from him in 1890 when his affair with Catherine O'Shea became public. Nationalists continued to press for home rule legislation for the next twenty-five years. In 1916 Patrick Pearse led the Easter Rising in Dublin, which failed but paved the way for Irish auto-

nomy. In 1921 the British divided Ireland into two semi-independent states: the six Protestant-dominated counties in Ulster became Northern Ireland, and the twenty-six southern counties became the Irish Free State (the Republic of Ireland after 1948).

Church and State: Because the Free State was overwhelmingly Catholic, its leaders decided to frame much of the state's public policy around Catholic teaching. In 1925 divorce was outlawed and in 1930 a censorship board was established. In 1937 Eamon de Valera drafted a new constitution that was heavily influenced by Catholic moral and social teaching. Although Catholicism was not declared the established religion, the constitution recognized Catholicism's "special position" in Irish society.

Through the 1970s the Church remained a very powerful force in Irish society. Surveys taken in 1971 indicated that 96 percent of Catholics were regular churchgoers. By the 1980s, however, the Church's influence was waning. Mass attendance rates were dropping—especially in the urban areas. In 1985 the government enacted a liberal contraceptive law over the strenuous objections of the bishops. In 1986 it tried unsuccessfully to legalize divorce. While an anti-abortion amendment was added to the constitution in 1983, pressure increased on the government to liberalize the law. *See also* Celtic spirituality; Maynooth College; Patrick, St.

JOHN F. QUINN

Ireland, John, 1838–1918, archbishop of St. Paul. Born in Ireland, settled in St. Paul, Minnesota Territory, seminary trained in France, he was ordained in 1861. Brief service as chaplain in the Union Army was followed by parochial work in St. Paul, where he was renowned for his eloquence and his civic leadership, especially as a temperance advocate and a sponsor of agricultural colonies for indigent immigrants. First as coadjutor, then bishop, and finally, from 1888, first archbishop of St. Paul, he presided over the vast expansion of Catholicism across the Upper Midwest. Deeply committed to the rapid assimilation of immigrant Catholics into American culture, he was the leader of the "Americanist" party within the hierarchy, favoring a greater spirit of accommodation between Catholic faith and American culture, which involved him in many bitter controversies. The collection of his major addresses, *The Church and Modern Society* (1904), is the best introduction to his thought. *See also* Americanism.

Armenian). Irenaeus teaches that there is no secret doctrine apart from the rule of faith, publicly handed down and guaranteed by the continuous succession of bishops. Against Gnostic depreciation of the material order, he teaches that Christ, as the Incarnation of God's Word and in the Resurrection as the perfection of the Spirit's work, "recapitulates" God's loving intentions in creating the world, revealing its destiny and providing the "first fruits" of that destiny. Against Gnostic separation of the (evil) Creator God of the Jews from the Father of Jesus, Irenaeus teaches a doctrine of growth and development, of God's progressive teaching in a plan desired to bring humanity to its fullest maturity and freedom in Christ, the Second Adam. Feast day: June 28. *See also* apostolic succession; Gnosticism; recapitulation.

JOHN C. CAVADINI

Irenaeus of Lyons, one of the greatest bishops and theologians of the early Church, best known for his defense of the faith against the Gnostics and his development of the notion of apostolic succession.

Irenaeus of Lyons, St., ca. 130–ca. 200, bishop of Lyons from ca. 178 to ca. 200. A native of Smyrna who as a youth knew Polycarp, he moved west, probably to Rome, where he may have studied with Justin Martyr. Later at Lyons, he served as official representative of that church to Pope Eleutherius, presenting the *Letter of the Martyrs of Lyons* and urging toleration of the Montanists in Asia Minor (177). He may already have been bishop at this point; if not, he was elected upon his return, successor to the martyred Pothinus. The last historical act attributable to Irenaeus is his correspondence with Pope Victor objecting to his treatment of the Quartodecimans of Asia Minor (190). The tradition that he was martyred is late (Gregory of Tours, d. 594).

Irenaeus is a great watershed in the history of theology, the first to provide a coherent rationale for a Christian Bible including both OT and NT and the first to offer a comprehensive account of Christian belief in God's universal providential and redemptive economy. He is the first great spokesman of the Great Church, the emerging orthodox consensus among churches as far away as Nisibis and Rome, Carthage and Alexandria. His most famous work, *Against Heresies,* is an anti-Gnostic treatise in five books, fully preserved apart from Greek fragments only in a Latin translation (Books 4 and 5 are also in

irenicism (i̱-ren'i-siz-uhm; Gk., *irene,* "peace"), conciliatory methods of healing Church differences as opposed to polemics or argument. Pope Pius XII, in the encyclical *Humani Generis* (1950), warned against a "false irenicism" that would smooth over doctrinal differences among churches as a means of achieving unity or harmony. *See also* ecumenism.

Irish spirituality. *See* Celtic spirituality.

Irish tariff penance, a form of forgiveness of sin, originating in Irish monasticism probably in the sixth century, in which a specific penance was assigned for each sin and its frequency, probably followed by absolution. It is not certain that absolution followed, because this form of penance differed from canonical penance, i.e., the penance conferred within the sacrament of Penance (Reconciliation). The Irish tariff penance was based on contemporary Irish monastic practice in which monks would discuss their spiritual life and its failings with another monk or with the abbot, who would in turn suggest a penance and then pray that God might forgive the sins. The practice was extended to laypeople through the monks who offered them spiritual direction. Many scholars conclude that the modern practice of auricular confession (confession of sins to a priest in private) derives from this development.

The term "tariff" is derived from the schedule of penances applied to each sin that was listed in the penitential books developed to assist the monks in assigning appropriate penances. *See also* confession, auricular.

irregularity, in canon law a permanent impediment or legal obstacle either to the reception of Holy Orders or to the exercise of Holy Orders already received. The dispensation from many irregularities is reserved to the Holy See, although some can be dispensed by the person's bishop or religious superior.

Isaac, Israelite patriarch, son of Abraham and Sarah. The name in Hebrew means "he laughs." Gen 21–27 tells of his birth, his brother Ishmael, God's demand that he be sacrificed, his wife Rebekah, and his sons Jacob and Esau. The NT highlights his special birth (Gal 4:28) and his binding for sacrifice (Heb 11:17–20). *See also* patriarch [biblical].

Isaac Jogues, St. *See* Jogues, St. Isaac.

Isabella of Castile, 1451–1504, queen of Spain from 1474 who, with her husband Ferdinand of Aragon, created a unified Catholic Spain. The last Muslim state fell in 1492. In that same year all Jews were required to convert or emigrate. The Muslims were placed under the same requirement in 1502. Isabella was deeply religious and drove the reform of the Spanish church under Ximénez de Cisneros, employing the Spanish Inquisition as an important weapon for political and religious unity. Isabella personally commissioned Columbus and was committed to the conquest and evangelization of the New World. Her zeal and accompanying intolerance have made attempts at canonization in the 1990s controversial. *See also* Inquisition; Spain, Catholicism in.

Isidore of Kiev, ca. 1385–1464, Greek-born Orthodox metropolitan of Kiev and All Rus' and an active proponent of the Union of the Orthodox and Catholic churches at the Council of Florence. Born in Monemvasia in the Peloponnesus, Isidore became a monk there, then abbot, and in 1434 was sent by Byzantine emperor John VIII to the Council of Basel to arrange for a union council. In 1436 he was ordained Metropolitan of Kiev and All Rus', and thus head of the Orthodox Church in Kievan Rus' and Muscovy (the Moscow patriarchate was created in 1589). He arrived in Moscow in 1437, only to leave for the Council of Ferrara-Florence, where he arrived in 1438 and became one of the six official Greek Orthodox spokesmen at the council. He signed the Decree of Union in 1439 and never retracted. Created a cardinal that same year, he returned to Kiev and Moscow, where he proclaimed

the Union in 1441. But the Union was ultimately rejected in Rus' and Muscovy, and Isidore was imprisoned. He escaped and returned to Italy, where he subsequently held many high offices in the Catholic Church. Sent as papal legate to Constantinople, Isidore proclaimed the union there on December 12, 1452, fought and was wounded in the siege of the city, and was taken prisoner at its fall on May 29, 1453. He escaped to Rome where he died, still faithful to the Union of Florence, in 1464. *See also* Florence, Council of.

Isidore of Seville, St., ca. 560–636, encyclopedist, historian, archbishop of Seville (ca. 600–36), and Doctor of the Church. His life spans the transition of the Visigothic kingdom of Spain from an Arian to a Catholic kingdom (589), and his life and work were dedicated to the diffusion of a uniform and literate Catholicism throughout the realm. His presidency over the Fourth Council of Toledo (633) enabled it to serve as the basis for the characteristic and uniquely Visigothic symbiosis between episcopacy and monarchy. Isidore was the most learned person of his age, a crucial link between the learning of antiquity and the Middle Ages. His *Etymologies* is an encyclopedia of received knowledge on all subjects, including theology. His *Chronica Majora* and *History of the Kings of the Goths, Vandals, and Sueves* are indispensable sources for the history of Spain, and his *Three Books of Sentences* are an influential synthesis of Augustinian and Gregorian teaching. The *De Ecclesiasticis Officiis* is a crucial source for the Mozarabic liturgy and the customs of the Visigothic church. Feast day: April 4. *See also* Fathers of the Church; Spain, Catholicism in.

Isidore the Farmer, St., 1070–1130, Spanish saint. A simple married peasant who worked his entire life for a wealthy landowner, he was known for his piety, love of the poor, and the care of animals. Feast day: May 15.

Islam, one of the three great religions of the West, with historical connections both to Judaism and Christianity. Founded in the Arabian peninsula by the Prophet Muhammad (A.D. 570–632), who received direct revelations from God over a period of twenty years and codified these revelations in the *Qur'an,* the holy scriptures of the religion, Islam is unremittingly monotheistic. The word "Islam" means "submission" to God.

Elements of Islamic Faith: Islam rests on five

"pillars": (1) The confession of faith: "There is no God but God and Muhammad is the messenger of God"; (2) The obligation to pray five times a day (Friday noon prayers are communal); (3) A tithe of wealth for the poor; (4) A rigorous fast (from food and drink and abstinence from sex from sunup to sundown) once a year during the ninth month of the calendar (Arab., *Ramadan*); (5) A pilgrimage (called the *Hajj*) to Mecca once in the lifetime of a pious Muslim.

Although there is no formally established clergy in Islam, there is a class (the *ulama*) of religious scholars and recognized leaders in a given community (the *mullahs*). The main task of the religious scholar is to comment on and interpret the legal tradition (*Shariah*) of Islam for the faithful.

Disputes over the succession to the Prophet caused a split in Islam, which resulted in two main groups of Muslims: Sunni (who in the 1990s account for over 80 percent of Muslims) and Shi'ites. There is also a lively, but relatively small, mystical tradition whose followers are known as Sufis.

The rise of Islam in the seventh century, fueled by its assertive missionary attitude, saw its ascendency both into the Middle East and into Europe and the Far East. In the 1990s it is the second largest religion in the world (after Christianity), with more than 900 million adherents. Current demographics tend to show Islam as overtaking Jews numerically in the United States early in the twenty-first century. Muslims also make up significant minorities in some Western countries (largely through immigration), such as France and Italy.

Islam's largest struggle is to reconcile Islamic thought with the rise of modernity. Sharp divisions exist between those who wish for a total Islamic society and those who try to accommodate their faith with the rise of modern industrial and capitalistic societies.

Catholic-Islamic Relations Today: Until the Second Vatican Council (1962–65) relations between Islam and the Catholic Church were marked by mutual hostility. From Islam's origin in the sixth century and lasting in various places until the fifteenth century (with the capture of Constantinople by the Turks in 1453), there were Muslim invasions of the Holy Land (including the Holy Sepulchre), Central Europe, Italy, Spain, and North Africa. These provoked various Christian efforts at resistance and expulsion, principally through the Crusades (1095–1291), which, in turn, generated pro-

found anti-Western and anti-Christian sentiments in the East.

Vatican II, however, acknowledged that Muslims "are related in various ways to the People of God." Indeed, Muslims hold "first place" among those who "acknowledge the Creator." They profess "the faith of Abraham" and along with Catholics "adore the one and merciful God" (Dogmatic Constitution on the Church, 1964, n. 16). Moreover, God looks upon Muslims "with esteem." Although they do not recognize Jesus as divine, they revere him as a prophet and they honor Mary, his mother, as well. Muslims are also people who "prize the moral life, and give worship to God especially through prayer, almsgiving, and fasting." The council urged both sides to forget the past and to "strive sincerely for mutual understanding," making "common cause for safeguarding and fostering social justice, moral values, peace and freedom" (Declaration on the Relationship of the Church to Non-Christian Religions, 1965, n. 3).

Since the council the Catholic Church has established the Pontifical Council for Inter-Religious Dialogue (originally called the Secretariat for Non-Christians when established in 1964 by Pope Paul VI). Attached to the Pontifical Council is the Commission on Religious Relations with Muslims, established in 1974. A Vatican-sponsored meeting of Christians and Muslims was held in Tripoli, Libya, in 1976, and another interfaith assembly involving Catholics and Muslims met in Assisi, Italy, in 1988 with Pope John Paul II in attendance. Various religious orders such as the Franciscans and Missionaries of Africa have also fostered contacts with Muslims in Africa and other parts of the Muslim world. *See also* Crusades; Declaration on the Relationship of the Church to Non-Christian Religions.

LAWRENCE CUNNINGHAM

Israel, collective name of twelve tribes, descendants of Jacob. The first datable occurrence of the name "Israel" occurs on a stele erected by Pharaoh Merneptah in the late thirteenth century B.C. that commemorates the defeat of several cities and a people called Israel ("Israel is laid waste, his seed is not"). This has been taken as proof that Israelites had begun to settle in the land by that time. The biblical name for this people is "sons of Israel," i.e., Israelites, members of a group claiming descent from an ancestor called Israel. This is the name bestowed on Jacob after his struggle with a supernatural being at the Jabbok ford (Gen 32:22–32; cf. 35:9–10). The name is here connected with the idea of struggle or strife (Gen 32:28), but the real etymology remains obscure. The original settlement area of the Israelites was the central hill country around Bethel and Shechem. After the death of Solomon the name was used of the Northern Kingdom, distinct from the Davidic kingdom of Judah. The ideal of a united people organized as a twelve-tribal entity persisted, and the term is often used in this sense, e.g., in Psalms and Ezra–Nehemiah. The land itself is rarely called Israel, the more common appellation being the land of Canaan; but in the State of Israel today the designation "land of Israel" (*'eres yiśra'ēl*) is preferred to Palestine, a name that reflects the Philistine presence from the eleventh century B.C. and was in common use from Roman times. In the NT, "Israel" refers to the Jewish people as a whole (e.g., Luke 1:54; John 1:31; Acts 1:6) or the chosen people inclusive of Christians (e.g., Rom 9:6).

JOSEPH BLENKINSOPP

Italo-Albanian Catholic Church, Catholics of the Byzantine tradition in Calabria and Sicily, Italy.

Southern Italy and Sicily had a strong connection with Greece in antiquity and for many centuries there was a large Greek-speaking population there. In the early centuries of the Christian era, although most of the Christians were of the Byzantine tradition, the area was included in the Roman patriarchate, and a gradual but incomplete process of latinization took place.

During the eighth century, the Byzantine emperor Leo III removed this region from papal jurisdiction and placed it within the patriarchate of Constantinople. There followed a strong revival of the Byzantine tradition in the area. But the Norman conquest of the region in the early eleventh century resulted in its return to the Latin patriarchate. By this time the local Byzantine church was flourishing, and there were hundreds of monasteries along the coasts of southern Italy. The Normans, however, discouraged Byzantine usages in their lands, and the Greek bishops were replaced by Latin ones. This marked the beginning of a process that led to the almost total absorption of the Byzantine faithful into the Latin Church.

This decline was reversed in the fifteenth century with the arrival of two large groups of Albanian immigrants who had fled their country following its conquest by the Turks. Those from the northern part of Albania, where the Latin rite was prevalent, were quickly absorbed into the local population. But those from the Orthodox south of the country remained loyal to their Byzantine traditions. At first they met with little understanding from the local Latin bishops. Although in the sixteenth century popes intervened in favor of the Byzantines—in 1595 an ordaining bishop was appointed for them—the community continued to decline.

The situation began to improve in the eighteenth century. In 1742 Pope Benedict XIV published the bull *Etsi Pastoralis,* which was intended to buttress the position of the Italo-Albanians in relation to the Latins. It paved the way for more progressive legislation—and recognition of the equality of the Byzantine rite with the Latin—in the next century.

Italo-Albanian seminaries were founded in 1732 in Calabria and in 1734 in Palermo. Seminarians in advanced theological studies in Rome reside at the Greek College.

Today there are two dioceses for the Italo-Albanians of equal rank: the diocese of Lungro (in Calabria) was founded in 1919, has twenty-seven parishes, and has jurisdiction over continental Italy. The diocese of Piana degli Albanesi, founded in 1937, covers all of Sicily and has fifteen parishes. Alongside these two dioceses is the monastery of Santa Maria di Grottaferrata, just a few miles from Rome, which, having been founded in the eleventh century, is the only remnant of the once-flourishing Italo-Greek monastic tradition. Since 1937 the abbot has been a bishop with jurisdiction over the monks of the monastery and local faithful. Total membership of these three jurisdictions in 1993 came to about 62,000. *See also* Byzantine Italy; Byzantine rite; Eastern churches; Eastern rites.

RONALD G. ROBERSON

Italo-Greek Catholics. *See* Italo-Albanian Catholic Church.

Italy, Catholicism in. The Catholic religion has profoundly affected Italian culture. The area that comprises the modern state of Italy did not form a political unit until 1870. Nevertheless, the historical development of Catholicism in the Italian peninsula has influenced the direction of the Church while the Church has helped to shape many aspects of modern Italian society, culture, and politics. The overwhelming majority of popes have been Italian and

ITALY

Rome and with taking back from the Lombards the exarchate of Ravenna. After defeating the Lombards, Pepin gave the territory of Ravenna to the Church thus creating the Papal States, whose control by Rome also stems from the forged Donation of Constantine. Pepin's son Charlemagne conquered the Lombards and was crowned Roman emperor by Pope Leo III in 800. While this move liberated the papacy from Byzantine control, for the next five centuries Italy would be marked by conflict between the papacy and the emperors who succeeded Charlemagne as heirs to what later became known as the Holy Roman Empire.

The eleventh and twelfth centuries witnessed the growth of various heresies in Italy along with numerous evangelical movements. Francis of Assisi (1182–1226) led a spiritual revolution that was to have profound effects on the development of Christianity and on Italian culture. New mendicant, or preaching, orders such as the Franciscans and the Dominicans ministered to the urban communities and combated heretical teachings. Dante Alighieri (1265–1321) wrote the *Divine Comedy*, which expresses the truths, sentiments, and beauty of Catholicism along with presenting a scathing attack on ecclesiastical abuses. Due to the anarchical conditions prevailing in Italy, the popes took up residence at Avignon in France from 1309 to 1378.

From the Renaissance to the Unification of Italy. From the mid-fourteenth until the mid-sixteenth centuries, the Middle Ages gave way to the Italian Renaissance. In the mid-fourteenth century, the fear caused by the Black Death sparked a revival of religious feeling that is reflected in the art and literature of the period. The Florentine humanists of the fifteenth century centered at the court of the Medicis developed Neoplatonism, a philosophy indebted to Christianity. The Renaissance popes were active patrons of the great artists of the period (Michelangelo, Raphael) and exercised temporal power over much of central Italy. The French invasion in 1494 took advantage of Italian political disunity and led to several centuries of warfare among the French, Austrian, and Spanish monarchies for control of the Italian peninsula. The Council of Trent (1545–63), called to respond to the challenge of the Protestant Reformation, stifled the development of Italian art, science, and philosophy and marked the end of the Renaissance in Italy.

In the following centuries Italy remained disunited with large areas under the control of France,

so, too, those who make up the central administration of the Church in the Roman Curia.

From the Origins of Christianity to the Later Middle Ages: Although a small Christian community existed in Rome before the middle of the first century, it was only after the Edict of Constantine in 313, which put an end to the persecution of Christians, that the Church began to grow in Italy. Organized into regional dioceses, the Church assumed a position of leadership among the local populations during the decay of the Roman Empire and the so-called barbarian invasions. Benedict of Nursia founded monasteries at Subiaco and Monte Cassino and developed the Benedictine rule (ca. 529–34) as a guide not only to the spiritual life but also to the economic organization of the monastic communities that proved invaluable in the preservation of learning.

The early Middle Ages in Italy (500–1000) witnessed political struggles between the newly arrived immigrant peoples, especially from Germany, and the Church, which sought to incorporate them within existing structures of governance. Germanic kingdoms in Italy (the Lombards) gave rise to a heretical Arian church alongside the older Catholic organization. Tensions between Rome and the Byzantine emperors came to a head in the eighth century. After the collapse of Byzantine military power in central Italy, the papacy turned to the Franks for protection against the Lombards. In 754 Pope Stephen II solicited the aid of the Frankish King Pepin III, entrusting him with the task of defending

Spain, and Austria. The eighteenth century was a difficult period in the life of the Church, which had come under attack for its complicity with the European monarchies and aristocracies. The spirit of the French Enlightenment and eventually the French Revolution spread to Italy and led to the abolition of clerical privileges, the suppression of monasteries, and the seizure of Church property.

The nineteenth century in Italy was marked by the movement for liberty, independence, and national unification known as the *Risorgimento*. The series of wars that freed the peninsula from foreign domination, together with the political movement toward unity, culminated in the declaration of the unified kingdom of Italy in 1861. Rome became the capital of the new Italian state after it was acquired by the new republic of Italy in 1870. The First Vatican Council (1869–70) asserted papal infallibility in spiritual matters while the loss of Rome and of the Papal States terminated the temporal power of the papacy. The ensuing struggle between the Church and the new Italian state was intense. The popes refused to recognize the legitimacy of the state and urged all Catholics not to participate in Italy's nascent parliamentary democracy. For their part, successive Italian governments worked to further reduce the influence of the Church and tolerated widespread anticlericalism. Despite these difficulties, the period of the *Risorgimento* also saw the growth of some three hundred new religious congregations in Italy and the birth of the modern Catholic movement.

The Twentieth Century: Fascism (1922–43) suppressed all democratic freedoms but made a historical agreement with the Church and the papacy. The Lateran Treaty of 1929 conceded privileges to the Church in return for its support of the Fascist regime led by Benito Mussolini, whose imperialistic, dictatorial, and racist policies created dissension among the Catholic clergy and laity. After Mussolini's downfall (1943) many Catholics took part in the Resistance movement and after the war joined the Italian Christian Democratic Party, which dominated Italian politics from 1948 until 1993, when widespread corruption undermined its political influence. Italy became a Republic in 1946 and its new constitution stipulated that Church-state relations would continue to be regulated by the Lateran Treaty—although this was later redefined in 1985. Catholicism was no longer to be the official religion of Italy, there was to be no more mandatory reli-

gious instruction in government schools, and the clergy were no longer to be paid by the Italian government.

Pope John XXIII revitalized the Church through the Second Vatican Council (1962–65) and brought it into line with the momentous changes affecting modern life. His encyclicals *Mater et Magistra* ("Mother and Teacher," 1961) and *Pacem in Terris* ("Peace on Earth," 1963) address social justice, global interdependence, and the scourge of modern warfare. Despite a decline in participation in Catholic religious life, Catholicism remains a vital force in Italy today. Its contributions to Italian society can be seen in the development of Christian base communities, in the popularity of Catholic youth groups, in the health of the Catholic press and media, in Catholic education, and in the continuing, although increasingly critical, respect for the moral authority of the pope and for Catholic social teaching.

There are 1 patriarchate (in Venice), 58 archdioceses, and 158 dioceses in Italy. Catholics constitute almost 98 percent of a population of nearly 58 million. *See also* Byzantine Italy; Lateran Treaty; Papal States; Renaissance; Rome; Vatican City State.

JOHN P. WELLE

Ite, missa est (ee'teh, mee'sah est; Lat., "Go, this is the dismissal"), the formula that concluded the Roman Mass for centuries. It took its name from the Latin *missa* (variant of *missio*, "dismissal"). English translations of the Roman Missal (1970) provide several dismissal formulas. The most commonly used is, "The Mass is ended, go in peace." *See also* Mass.

Ives, Levi Silliman, 1797–1867, prominent Catholic convert. Episcopal bishop of North Carolina, 1831–52, he converted to Catholicism under the influence of the Oxford movement. Unable to continue in the ministry, he founded an orphanage in New York City and served as president of the Society of Saint Vincent de Paul.

Ivo of Chartres, St., ca. 1040–1115, bishop of Chartres whose canon law compilation was the standard text of Church law in northern Europe until it was surpassed by Gratian's. Ivo's writings on the episcopal office contributed to resolving the investiture controversy. Feast day: May 20 or 23. *See also* investiture controversy.

Jacob, Israelite patriarch, son of Isaac and Rebekah. The name in Hebrew means "he overreaches." Gen 25–33 tells of Jacob's birth, his winning of his brother Esau's birthright, his vision at Bethel, his wives Leah, Rachel, Zilpah, and Bilhah, his twelve sons, his wrestling with God, and his change of name to Israel. *See also* patriarch [biblical].

Jacob of Nisibis, St., early fourth century, first bishop of Nisibis, present at the Council of Nicaea (325). Revered by Armenian and Syrian Christians as a theologian, his works, if any, have not survived. Feast day: July 15. *See also* Nicaea, First Council of.

Jacob of Voragine. *See* Golden Legend, The.

Jacopone da Todi (yahk-oh-poh'nay dah toh' dee), ca. 1230–ca. 1306, Franciscan brother and poet. Jacopone became a Franciscan after the death of his wife. He lived austerely and composed *laudi* (Lat., religious poems or songs), but his authorship of the Marian hymn *Stabat Mater* has been questioned. He sympathized with Franciscan Spirituals and was imprisoned for doing so.

James I, 1566–1625, king of England. Succeeding his mother, Mary, Queen of Scots, as king of Scotland in 1567, in 1603 he succeeded Elizabeth I as the first Stuart king of England and was greeted on his arrival by the Millenary Petition of the Puritans. At the Hampton Court Conference (1604), James responded to the mention of Presbyterianism by pronouncing, "No bishops, no king." His failure to bring promised relief to the Catholics led to the Gunpowder Plot (1605), bringing about stricter laws against Catholics who refused to attend the services of the Church of England (recusants). He reestablished the episcopacy in Scotland in 1610 and issued the Book of Sports, allowing sports on Sunday, in 1618, earning the strong resentment of Puritans and Presbyterians, which, combined with his refusal to compromise with Parliament, set the stage for the Civil Wars under Charles I. *See also* Presbyterianism; Puritanism.

James, St. [brother of Jesus], a prominent figure in the early Church. Mark 6:3 records Jesus' villagers acknowledging that he has four brothers (James, Joses, Judas, and Simon) and sisters (see Matt 13:55). Although John 7:3–5 and Mark 3:31 indicate that Jesus' brothers did not believe in him, Acts and Paul's Letters indicate that James, at least, became a disciple and a high-ranking person in the early Church. Luke records that after the death of James (son of Zebedee), another James becomes prominent, who is James the brother of the Lord. In the lists of Jerusalem's bishops, he is regularly named first (Eusebius *Ecclesiastical History* 4.5.3–4). Hence he is presumably the figure in Acts 12:17 and 15:14. This is the "James, the Lord's brother" whom Paul visited in Jerusalem (Gal 1:19) and of whom Paul testifies that the Lord appeared to him (1 Cor 15:7). He is sometimes called "James the Less" for his shortness, but also "James the Just" for his piety: "The charge of the church passed to James the brother of the Lord . . . called the 'Just' by all men from the Lord's time to ours, since many were called James, but he was holy from his mother's womb" (Eusebius *Eccl. Hist.* 2.23.4–7). He is credited with authorizing the mission to the Gentiles and thus became Paul's patron. And he is the alleged author of the Letter to James. Ananias the high priest had James arrested and executed: "He convened the Sanhedrin and brought before them a man named James, the brother of Jesus who is called Christ . . . and delivered them up to be stoned" (Josephus *Antiquities* 20.200; Eusebius *Eccl. Hist.* 2.23.22). Feast day: May 3. *See also* apostle; brothers of Jesus; Twelve, the.　　　*JEROME NEYREY*

James of Nisibis, St. *See* Jacob of Nisibis, St.

James the Great, St. [son of Zebedee], one of the twelve apostles. With his brother John, he was a fisherman whom Jesus called among his first disciples (Matt 4:21; Mark 1:19; Luke 5:10). The list of apostles in Mark 3:17 reports that Jesus gave James and John the nickname "sons of thunder." According to the synoptic Gospels, James, along with his brother and Simon Peter, was among Jesus' closest followers. Jesus brought these three with him into the home of Jairus, whose daughter he raised (Mark 5:37; Luke 8:51). The same three accompany Jesus at his Transfiguration (Matt 17:1; Mark 9:2; Luke 9:28), ask him about the end time (Mark 13:3), and fail him in Gethsemane (Matt 26:37; Mark 14:33). James and John ask Jesus whether to call down fire on Samaritans who reject him (Luke 9:53), and they request seats of honor on his right and left when he sits in royal glory (Mark 10:35–37; but Matt 20:20–21 attributes the request to their mother).

James died a martyr under the persecution of Jesus' followers launched by King Herod Agrippa I between A.D. 42 and 44 (Acts 12:1–3). An expanded version of James's miracles and martyrdom appears in the sixth-century *Apostolic History of Abdias*. Later traditions report that James preached in Spain or that his body was transferred from Jerusalem to Compostela in Spain, which became a major pilgrimage site in the Middle Ages.

James is the patron saint of pilgrims, Spain, Guatemala, and Nicaragua. Feast day: July 25. *See also* apostle; Twelve, the.

James the Less, St. [son of Alphaeus], one of the twelve apostles. The son of Alphaeus (Matt 10:3; Mark 3:18; Luke 6:15) is sometimes identified with James "the Less," whose mother, Mary, was present at the Cross (Mark 15:40). Feast day: May 3. *See also* apostle; Twelve, the.

Jane Frances de Chantal, St. *See* Chantal, St. Jane Frances de.

Jansen, Cornelius, also known as Jansenius, 1585–1638, Flemish theologian, author of the *Augustinus*. After an exhaustive study of all of Augustine of Hippo's writings and especially of his anti-Pelagian writings, Jansen began to write the *Augustinus* in 1628. It was not published until 1640, two years after his death. (In 1636 Jansen had been ordained bishop of Ypres.) The work became very controversial because it seemed to contain ideas on grace and free will that were closer to Protestantism than to the Catholic tradition. Protestants had insisted on the principle of *sola gratia* (Lat., "grace alone"), while Catholics taught that human beings must cooperate with God's grace through good works. Five propositions were extracted from the *Augustinus* (two that were actually there and three that were compressions of material). The propositions emphasized the absolute necessity and irresistible character of grace, leading critics to conclude that the book was denying free will, promoting moral rigorism, and generating pessimism about the possibility of salvation. The propositions were condemned by Pope Innocent X in 1653. They became the basis of a movement, centered principally in France, known as Jansenism. *See also* *Augustinus;* Jansenism; nature and grace; salvation.

Jansenism, a seventeenth-century Catholic reform movement originating in the Low Countries and France, which expanded into Habsburg lands and Italy during the eighteenth century. Basically Augustinian in theological orientation, Jansenism was pessimistic about human nature without God's grace, demanded strict asceticism, fought the centralizing tendencies of Tridentine Catholicism, and rallied opponents of French absolutism, whose proponents from Richelieu to Louis XIV assisted ecclesiastical authorities in suppressing Jansenism. Regarded as an extreme but legitimate branch of the Catholic Reformation, Jansenism raised important questions about Catholic theology, papal authority in theological matters, and the relation of individual conscience to that authority.

History: Jansenism originated in Bishop Cornelius Jansen's Augustinian treatise, *Augustinus*, affirming God's absolute predestination based on human nature's incapacity to perform good works without grace. Accused by Jesuits of violating the papal ban on discussion of such topics and of Calvinist leanings, the *Augustinus* was published posthumously in 1640 and condemned by the Inquisition in 1641. Jansen's thought became a basis for piety through the Abbé de Saint-Cyran, an opponent of Cardinal Richelieu's absolutism and principal spiritual guide to the Cistercian convent of Port-Royal and its patrons the Arnauld family, including the convent's abbess Angelique Arnauld. Antoine Arnauld defended Saint-Cyran's rigorism in his *Fréquente Communion* (1642) and launched an attack on Jesuit moral theology.

Richelieu's successor, Mazarin, sought to destroy Port-Royal, now the center of the movement, and along with the Jesuits persuaded Pope Innocent X to condemn the five propositions on grace and human nature attributed to Jansen (*Cum Occasione*, 1653). Antoine Arnauld countered that Jansen's *Augustinus* itself did not contain the condemned ideas, while Blaise Pascal attacked Jesuit moral theology in his *Provincial Letters* (1656). Pope Alexander VII then issued *Ad Sanctam Beati Petri Sedem* (1656), specifically condemning Jansen. Arnauld responded, distinguishing between *droit* (admitting the papal "right" to condemn the propositions) and *fait* (silence on the "factual" issue of whether the ideas were really Jansen's). Alexander finally forced all French ecclesiastical personnel to sign a formulary admitting both *droit* and *fait* (*Regiminis Apostolici,* 1665) and exiled the Port-Royal nuns or deprived them of the sacraments.

Port-Royal's supporters later sought compromise with Pope Clement IX to permit signing the formulary while leaving open the question of *droit* and *fait*. Recurring controversy forced Antoine Arnauld into exile in the Low Countries. Arnauld's ally Pasquier Quesnel published his highly Augustinian *Nouveau Testament avec des réflexions morales* (Fr., "New Testament with Moral Reflections," 1694), leading to arrest in 1703. Jansenist resurgence led to renewed pressure by Louis XVI on Pope Clement XI, who issued *Unigenitus Dei Filius* (1713), condemning 101 propositions taken specifically from Quesnel, eliminating the question of *fait* and concentrating on papal rights (*droit*). French Jansenist bishops effectively rejected the papacy on the issue of *droit* by appealing to a general council. Forced by the king to accept the bull in 1714, the French Jansenist party gradually withered after the death of sympathetic archbishop Noailles of Paris in 1729, but at Utrecht, a schism produced the Jansenist Church of Holland (1723), which still survives in the twentieth century as a branch of the Old Catholic Church. *See also* Arnauld, Antoine; Arnauld, Jacqueline Marie Angélique; Augustinianism; Jansen, Cornelius; nature and grace; Old Catholics; Port-Royal; predestination; Saint-Cyran, Abbé de.   W. DAVID MYERS

Catholics at prayer in Japan, a country with more than 124 million people, of whom less than 500,000 are Catholics, or .35 percent of the total population.

Janssens, Louis, b. 1908, professor emeritus of moral theology at the Catholic University of Louvain, Belgium. He is known for his contributions to a personalist approach to morality.

Januarius, St., d. ca. 305, bishop of Benevento, Italy, and patron saint of Naples. Almost nothing else is known of him. The frequent liquefaction of his blood, preserved in a vial as a relic, each year draws large crowds to the cathedral of Naples, where it is kept. Feast day: April 21 (East); September 19 (West).

Japan, Catholicism in. Catholicism in Japan dates from the landing of Francis Xavier in Kagoshima in southern Japan on August 15, 1549. The Jesuits were the first to preach the gospel in Japan. Some feudal lords accepted the faith with an eye toward foreign trade, since the Jesuits were closely aligned with the Portuguese merchants from Macao. Many subjects followed the lords into the Church. The number of missionaries was never large, but the number of converts is reported to have reached to 300,000.

Early History: In 1587, Toyotomi Hideyoshi, the powerful lord who fought to unify the country, at first favorable to the missionaries, turned against them. He issued an edict ordering them to leave Japan, but it was not enforced for some time. In 1597,

twenty-six Christians, including four Spanish missionaries, one Mexican, and one Portuguese, were crucified on a hill in Nagasaki (they were canonized in 1862). Meantime, the Dominicans and Franciscans arrived from the Philippines. In 1614, the Tokugawa regime issued an edict banishing Christianity. Thousands died for the faith, and only a small number of Christians survived. They went underground and kept their faith without any priests.

From this period until the opening of Japan by Commodore Matthew Perry in 1853, Japan was closed to Christianity. Members of the Paris Foreign Mission Society were the first to reenter the country. On March 17, 1865, at Nagasaki Father Bernard Petitjean discovered a group of "hidden Christians," who were descendants of the early Christians and had kept the faith through the early persecutions. Eventually, an estimated 20,000 Christians were found. The government again ferreted out the Christians and persecuted them. This action stopped at the insistence of the Iwakura mission, sent by the new Meiji government to seek amicable relations with the Western countries.

When the edicts against Christianity were abolished by the government, other missionary orders entered the country. Many French-speaking religious congregations of women followed and started schools for girls. New vicariates and dioceses were established.

Modern Developments: At the turn of the twentieth century, there were an estimated 55,000 Catholics. The Church grew slowly and the number of native priests and sisters increased. During the 1930s, nationalism put great stress upon the Church. A crisis of conscience arose when the government forced all nationals to bow in front of state Shinto shrines. After repeated objections from the Church, the government declared that worship at the shrines was civil and not religious in character. The government continued to curtail the activities of all religious personnel. In 1941, the foreign ordinaries resigned and were replaced by Japanese bishops. At the time, the number of Catholics was about 120,000, more than half of whom lived in Nagasaki, where the second atom bomb was dropped toward the end of the Second World War (1945).

After the war, diplomatic relations were established in 1952 between Japan and the Vatican; in 1958, the Apostolic Delegate (personal representative of the pope) was elevated to the rank of Internuncio (special legate of the pope, lower than a nuncio, or regular ambassador, but higher than an Apostolic Delegate). Converts, especially from the upper middle class, entered the Church. In this era, many Christian writers arose, notably Endo Shusaku and Sono Ayako among the Catholic writers. The number of Catholics grew gradually and around 1960 it neared the number of Catholics before the outbreak of the persecution in the seventeenth century. In 1990, there were 428,830 Catholics out of a population of 123,642,000.

Bibliography

Jennes, Joseph. *A History of the Catholic Church in Japan.* Rev. enl. ed. Tokyo: Oriens Institute for Religious Research, 1973.

Laures, Johannes. *The Catholic Church in Japan: A Short History.* Tokyo and Rutland, VT: Tuttle, 1954.   GEORGE MINAMIKI

J.C.D., *Juris Canonici Doctor* (Lat.), Doctor of Canon Law, pontifical academic degree that attests to one's knowledge of canon law.

J.C.L., *Juris Canonici Licentia* (Lat.), Licentiate in Canon Law, academic degree (roughly equivalent to a master's degree) given in the subject of canon law.

Jean-Baptiste de La Salle, St. *See* La Salle, St. Jean-Baptiste de.

Jedin, Hubert, 1900–80, Church historian. Edu-cated at Breslau, Munich, Freiburg, and Rome, he was ordained in 1924 and began a teaching career that culminated with his appointment as professor of medieval and Church history at the University of Bonn in 1949. His unparalleled knowledge of sixteenth-century sources resulted in many scholarly works, most notably the monumental *Geschichte des Konzils von Trient (History of the Council of Trent,* 1951–57).

Jehovah's Witnesses, members of a millennialist Protestant sect formally known as the Watchtower Bible and Tract Society. Organized by Charles Taze Russell in New York in the 1870s, the group was originally known as Russellites, Millennial Dawnists, or International Bible Students. Russell taught that Christ's return was imminent, at one time setting the date at 1914, and his writings acquired prophetic status among his followers. When Russell died in 1916, Joseph "Judge" Rutherford became president, modifying Russell's doctrines and instituting a tightly controlled central bureaucracy.

Jehovah's Witnesses regard the Bible as a body of literal instructions to believers, and their distinctive interpretations support a unique pattern of practices and beliefs. All Witnesses are expected to spend substantial time preaching door-to-door, and they circulate millions of copies of their publications each year. They reject the doctrines of the Trinity and Christ's divinity. They refuse blood transfusions, based on the OT proscription against eating blood (Lev 3:17). Witnesses also reject nationalistic activities such as military service, standing for anthems, and flag salutes. Coupled with their aggressive proselytizing, marked by a virulent anti-Catholicism, Jehovah's Witnesses have experienced a great deal of persecution worldwide. In the United States and Canada, Witnesses have fought and won a number of important court victories on religious liberty issues.

In the early 1990s there were 4.3 million Jehovah's Witnesses (890,000 in the United States). Their greatest growth in recent decades has been in traditionally Catholic nations, and perhaps half of their membership worldwide consists of former Catholics. Witnesses tend to attract members from the working and lower-middle classes. In the United States this has included large numbers of African-Americans. *See also* millenarianism.

MICHAEL S. HAMILTON

Jerome, St., also known as Eusebius Hieronymus,

Jerome, not only the most famous biblical scholar in the history of the Church but also a devoted monk and ascetic, with the traditional lion at his feet; fifteenth-century Pietro Perugino painting, Kunsthistorisches Museum, Vienna.

ca. 340–ca. 420, Church Father, the greatest biblical scholar of his age. Jerome was born at Stridon, in Dalmatia, and, after a splendid education at Rome, traveled widely. In 374 following a dream in which a heavenly judge accused him of being a Ciceronian rather than a Christian, he devoted himself to biblical studies and a severe asceticism. In 379 Jerome was ordained a priest and in 382 became secretary to Pope Damasus, who encouraged him to revise the Old Latin Bible. Following Damasus's death in 384 he left Rome, eventually establishing a monastery at Bethlehem with the support of a wealthy follower, Paula. Here he completed his work on the Bible, which included a translation of the OT directly from the Hebrew that superseded the Old Latin Version, which had been based upon the Greek Septuagint. The resultant Bible, the Vulgate, became the standard of the Roman Catholic Church and Jerome's most influential achievement. He also wrote commentaries on biblical books (most notably those of the prophets), translated works of various Greek Fathers (e.g., Eusebius), and compiled a catalog of Christian authors. As a controversialist he fiercely opposed Pelagianism, Arianism, and Origenism and staunchly defended clerical celibacy, the cult of the saints, and the doctrine of Mary's perpetual virginity. His correspondence, especially with Augustine, is of profound historical interest. Since the eighth century he has been honored as one of the four great Doctors of the Western Church. Feast day: September 30. *See also* Vulgate.

Jerome Emiliani, St. (em-eel-ee-ahn'ee), 1483–1537, Venetian saint. After a soldier's career, he was ordained a priest and devoted his life to the sick and especially to abandoned children. He founded the Somaschi Fathers. Feast day: February 8.

Jerusalem (Heb., "the foundation of [the god] Shalem"), capital of the modern state of Israel, a city sacred to Judaism, Christianity, and Islam. In ca. 1000 B.C. it was taken by David, who made it the center of Jewish life by bringing into it the ark of the covenant, which Solomon enshrined in a temple. Restored many times, this Temple was completely rebuilt by Herod the Great (37–4 B.C.). Here Jesus was presented as a child; to it he came on pilgrimage; and from it he expelled the money changers. In ca. A.D. 30 he was crucified and buried outside the walls in an abandoned quarry; the site is now covered by the Church of the Holy Sepulchre. The Romans destroyed the Temple in A.D. 70, and Jews

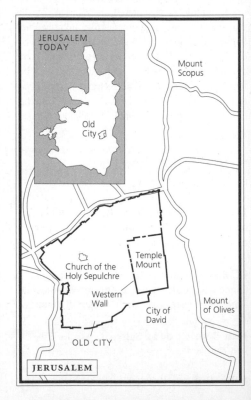

were forbidden to live in the city beginning in A.D. 135, when its name was changed to Aelia Capitolina. Monasteries and churches proliferated in the fourth century when Jerusalem became a center of pilgrimage for all Europe. A specifically Catholic presence is first attested in the ninth century when Charlemagne built a hospice for Latin-speaking pilgrims. In the eleventh century it was staffed by Benedictines. During the Latin Kingdom (1099–1187) this hospice developed into the great hospital of the Knights of St. John. The Crusaders established a Latin patriarchate, which disappeared with the Latin rite when Saladin captured Jerusalem in 1187. The Franciscan Custody of the Holy Land was set up in 1335 and gradually secured Catholic access to the holy places through unceasing negotiation and persistance to the point of martyrdom. In the second half of the nineteenth century the Latin patriarchate was reestablished, the Sisters of St. Joseph of the Apparition founded schools and hospitals, and the Dominicans founded the École Biblique, the first Catholic institution to specialize in biblical studies. *See also* École Biblique; Jerusalem rite. JEROME MURPHY-O'CONNOR

Jerusalem Eucharistic Congress, the first International Eucharistic Congress (1893) to be held outside Europe and a major turning point in Catholic policy toward the Christian East. Carefully prepared by Assumptionist experts on the Christian East and by the papal legate Cardinal Langénieux of Rheims, the congress led directly to Pope Leo XIII's two historic documents of 1894, *Praeclara Gratulationis* and *Orientalium Dignitas;* the latter has been considered the Magna Carta of Eastern Catholicism. These papal documents used a new language in speaking of the distinct patrimony and ecclesial autonomy of the Christian East, and in resolutely opposing latinization. In intellectual Catholic circles in the West this new openness gave rise to new scholarly journals and other initiatives dealing with the Christian East. *See also* Eucharistic Congress.

Jerusalem rite, the Greek liturgical traditions of the patriarchate of Jerusalem before they were supplanted by the Byzantine rite through a gradual process completed by the end of the thirteenth century. Though no longer extant as an independent liturgical tradition, the Jerusalem rite influenced almost every other rite in Christendom, and elements such as its Horologion or Book of Hours and its eucharistic Liturgy of St. James are still in use in other churches. The destruction of Jerusalem in the revolt of Bar Kochba in 135 brought an end to Aramaic Judeo-Christianity in the Holy Land. Thereafter, the bishops and liturgy of the rebuilt city were Greek. With the Peace of Constantine in 313 and the rediscovery of the Holy Places, Jerusalem became a magnet for pilgrims from every corner of the Christian world, who brought home with them the memory of the dramatically impressive liturgical services they had participated in there. These services are described in such fourth-century sources as the travel diary of the Spanish nun Egeria (384) and the contemporary catechetical homilies attributed to Jerusalem bishops Cyril or his successor John II. These sources not only provide early evidence of Holy Week services and stational (processional) liturgy. They also reveal a new view of liturgy, strongly anamnetic, focused on the memorial of Jesus' saving activity in his incarnate life on earth—e.g., Baptism as a ritual reenactment of Jesus' baptism rather than as rebirth in the Spirit (John 3:3–7) or dying and rising in Christ (Rom 6:3–5)—and a topographical resurrectional symbolism centered on the Church of the Anastasis or Holy Sepulchre in the Jerusalem cathedral basilica. This symbolism would later be transferred to other Eastern traditions, whose churches would be interpreted as Jerusalem writ small, their sanctuary the Holy Sepulchre in microcosm, its altar the tomb where Jesus' body lay. This mimetic and historicizing salvation-history vision of the liturgical services has remained an integral aspect of Eastern liturgical interpretation. From Jerusalem comes Holy Week at Easter and the feast of the Mother of God on August 15. Jerusalem developed the first lectionary system, which by the fifth century had already been translated into Armenian, then into Syriac, Georgian, and Arabic. Jerusalem liturgical usages became a major component in the formation of the West Syrian rite, and its Liturgy of St. James provided the framework of the West Syrian and Armenian Eucharists. From the ninth century the Byzantine Liturgy of the Hours and Holy Week lectionary undergo strong Jerusalem influence, while at the same time the byzantinization of Jerusalem usages had already begun. Indeed, much of the liturgical poetry so characteristic of the Byzantine rite was composed in the Monastery of St. Sabas in the Judean desert beyond Jerusalem, in the revival that followed the Persian depredations of 614. The Byzantines ultimately adopted the Palestinian Horologion or Book of Hours, and the present Byzantine Divine Office is a composite of Constanti-

Ignatius of Loyola receiving Holy Communion in Paris (left), where he founded the Jesuits in 1534, and shown with five of his Jesuit companions (right).

nopolitan and Jerusalem usages. The destruction of the Holy Sepulchre by Caliph al-Hakim in 1010, followed by the fall of Jerusalem to the Seljuks in 1072 and the resulting Crusades, which established a Latin Patriarchate of Jerusalem in place of the Greek one from 1099–1291, gradually confirmed the Jerusalem rite as an independent tradition. *See also* Byzantine rite; Jerusalem.   ROBERT F. TAFT

Jesuits, popular name for members of the Society of Jesus (S.J.), a religious order founded by Ignatius of Loyola (1491–1556) and canonically established by Pope Paul III on September 27, 1540, with the bull *Regimini Militantis Ecclesiae.* The Jesuits' unofficial motto is "For the Greater Glory of God" (*Ad majorem Dei gloriam*), a phrase or idea found over one hundred times in their *Constitutions.*

The purpose of the order stated in the bull was to engage in active ministry for "the progress of souls in Christian life and doctrine and the propagation of the faith." The Jesuits were not founded to oppose the Reformation, as is often said, but in 1550 they explicitly adopted opposition to the Reformation as a major objective, especially in northern Europe. Jesuits such as Peter Canisius (d. 1597) in Germany and Piotr Skarga (d. 1612) in Poland were outstanding in revitalizing Catholicism in those areas.

In some ways similar to older orders, the Jesuits from the beginning had features that were quite distinctive, e.g., the greater authority vested in the su-

perior general, the private rather than communal recitation of the liturgical hours, wearing street clothes rather than a distinguishing religious habit, the elimination of regular and frequent chapters (deliberative meetings of membership), a special vow "concerning missions" to go anywhere in the world when sent by the pope on pastoral assignment. Such features were the structural articulation of the Jesuits' intense dedication to ministry, which helped inaugurate in Catholicism a new era of the so-called apostolic orders of both women and men.

Two other factors gave the Society a special character. The *Spiritual Exercises* of Ignatius of Loyola provided the Jesuits with a unique handbook of spiritual principles and methods useful in all their ministries and activities. When after 1548 the Jesuits undertook on a large scale the running and staffing of schools, they created a ministry no other order had ever professedly undertaken, which soon became their foremost pastoral instrument. Within the Society, teaching consolidated the commitment to learning insisted upon by the first members and made it systemic.

History: Ignatius, while studying at the University of Paris (1528–35), attracted nine other students to form the nucleus of the future Society. In 1541 Ignatius was elected superior and soon thereafter set about writing the *Constitutions,* which were substantially completed by 1552 and officially ratified by the first General Congregation in 1558.

The Society grew rapidly, with about one thousand members by the death of Ignatius in 1556, about 16,000 by 1615, and about 22,600 in 1773. Aside from its other ministries, by 1615 it ran 450 high schools and universities and 55 seminaries, and by 1773 about 670 schools and 175 seminaries.

Jesuits became confessors to monarchs, and they entered into theological controversy with other Catholics, most notably in the seventeenth century against the Jansenists, who stressed moral austerity in contrast with the more realistic approach of the Jesuits. Their success made them easy targets for their enemies, culminating in the suppression of the order by Pope Clement XIV in 1773. A clause in the papal decree allowed a tenuous survival in parts of Poland and Lithuania. Pope Pius VII fully restored the order on August 7, 1814.

The Jesuits tried to begin where they had stopped in 1773, even though they had only a few documents like the *Exercises* and *Constitutions* to guide them. They again grew rapidly, to about fifteen thousand members by 1900. The Society currently numbers about twenty-four thousand, of which some four thousand are preparing for ordination and about three thousand are "temporal coadjutors," full members who will not be ordained. There are over four thousand Jesuits in the United States.

Missions: The missionary character of the order manifested itself almost immediately when Francis Xavier was sent to India, where he arrived in 1542 and was joined by some fifty others by 1555. In 1549 a few Jesuits arrived in Brazil. In a few years the number of Jesuits in Brazil grew to twenty-five, and that same year Xavier laid the foundations for a flourishing mission in Japan that lasted until persecutions in the seventeenth century.

In time the Jesuits surpassed the other orders in the number of men serving outside Europe, about 3,300 by 1750. Their "reductions" (supervised colonies) for the Guaraní Indians in present-day Paraguay and their adaptation to Chinese culture and religious customs were their two most innovative missionary ventures, both of which they were forced to abandon by 1750. In the 1990s, there are about 1,170 Jesuits in Africa, 1,900 in East Asia, 1,500 in Eastern Europe, 3,500 in Latin America.

Jesuits landed on the southeastern coast of present-day United States in 1566 but left in 1572. In the immense territories of New France and Louisiana, the French Jesuits began to work in 1611, and Jacques Marquette accompanied Louis Joliet in 1673 in the exploration of the Mississippi River. In 1634 Andrew White arrived from England with the first settlers of Maryland, where by 1770 there were twenty-three Jesuits, including John Carroll, who in 1789 became, in Baltimore, the first bishop of the United States. Eusebio Kino (d. 1711) established missions in present-day Arizona.

Spirituality, Theology, Learning: Jesuit spirituality is fundamentally derived from the *Spiritual Exercises,* the *Constitutions,* and other writings by Ignatius and his closest collaborators, especially Jerónimo (Jerome) Nadal (d. 1580). An expression of the message of the Gospels, framed in the belief and practice of the Catholic Church, it has some special characteristics.

Among these is a movement inward, constituted especially by growing sensitivity to one's relationship to God as manifested in the soul through "consolation" and "desolation," as explained in the *Exercises*. This aspect of the Jesuits' spirituality accounts for their commitment to retreats, spiritual direction, and other "ministries of interiority."

Another is a movement outward, in service to the world and to other human beings. The writings of Ignatius and his colleagues defined the purpose of the Jesuits as "the help of souls." Although especially intent upon helping people to a better relationship with God through preaching, hearing confessions, and teaching contemplation and other forms of prayer, the Jesuits were also much concerned with improving the physical situation of those to whom they ministered by establishing orphanages, women's asylums, and other works of social assistance. This tradition grounded a new commitment to "the service of the faith and the promotion of justice" adopted by the Jesuits in 1974–75 as central to their mission today and an essential aspect of their spirituality.

The Society has produced a large number of important theologians, beginning with Peter Canisius, Robert Bellarmine (d. 1621), and Francisco Suárez (d. 1617), and continuing to the present. Among recent Jesuits, the best known are Pierre Teilhard de Chardin (d. 1955), Bernard Lonergan (d. 1984), and Karl Rahner (d. 1984). Consistently characteristic of Jesuit theologians has been a notably positive understanding of the relationship between grace and human endeavors.

Jesuits have been outstanding scientists and mathematicians, and Jesuit schools gave to Calderon, Moliére, and other great dramatists their first training in theater. Robert Southwell (d. 1595) and Gerard Manley Hopkins (d. 1889) were Jesuit poets. In the 1990s in the United States the Jesuits sponsor twenty-eight colleges and universities, as well as forty-five high schools. Around the world they publish hundreds of popular and scientific journals, including in English *Theological Studies, New Testament Abstracts, The Heythrop Journal, The Way, America,* and *Thought. See also* Francis Xavier, St.; Ignatius of Loyola, St.; Jesuit spirituality; *Spiritual Exercises.*

Bibliography

Bangert, William V. *A History of the Society of Jesus.* St. Louis: The Institute of Jesuit Sources, 1972.

Ignatius of Loyola. *The Constitutions of the Society of Jesus.* Translated with introduction and commentary by George E. Ganss. St. Louis: The Institute of Jesuit Sources, 1970.

———. *Ignatius of Loyola: Spiritual Exercises and Selected Works.* Ed. George E. Ganss. New York: Paulist Press, 1991.

O'Malley, John W. *The First Jesuits.* Cambridge, MA: Harvard University Press, 1993.

O'Malley, John W., John W. Padberg, and Vincent T. O'Keefe. *Jesuit Spirituality: A Now and Future Resource.* Chicago: Loyola University Press, 1990.   JOHN O'MALLEY

Jesuit spirituality, the spiritual vision and values communicated by Ignatius of Loyola (d. 1556) to the Society of Jesus and elaborated by the Society of Jesus over the 450 years of its life. This vision and these values shape the apostolic priorities, the choice of ministry and mission, the community life and prayer, and the decision-making processes of the entire Society of Jesus and its individual members. This spirituality is grounded in the *Spiritual Exercises* of Ignatius of Loyola, a manual of spiritual growth and development drawn from the actual experience of Ignatius himself.

Elements of the Spirituality: Jesuit spirituality, as grounded in the *Spiritual Exercises* and articulated in the *Constitutions* of the Society of Jesus, displays the following facets: (1) A high degree of Christocentrism: The Christ of the Gospels is preeminent in Jesuit spirituality. The *Spiritual Exercises* are structured to generate and nurture a deepening and affective bond with the living Christ. (2) A sense of collaboration with the action of God in the world: The *Spiritual Exercises* communicate a belief that God is vigorously at work in the world for the well-being of the human family and that God needs human collaboration to accomplish this work. Jesuit spirituality, therefore, has a major focus on service in collaboration with God for the well-being of others. (3) Spiritual discernment in decision making: The *Spiritual Exercises* presume that the action of God in the world is discernible from subjective experience and objective criteria. Jesuit spirituality inculcates principles and practices of spiritual discernment to ascertain the origin, rhythm, patterns, and direction of individual and communal experi-

ence and to choose options that support and collaborate with God's action in the world. (4) Magnanimity and generosity of response: The *Spiritual Exercises* were developed in medieval Spain in an environment of chivalry and romance, an environment that expected great and courageous deeds simply for their own sake. Jesuit spirituality embodies this in the *Ignatian magis* (Lat., "more"), a generous and magnanimous service of God and the human family. (5) Fraternity and companionship in service: The Society of Jesus was formed out of a desire to maintain the fraternity and fellowship that Ignatius and the first companions enjoyed. This was a fraternity based on shared experience of Jesus Christ in the *Spiritual Exercises.* The early Jesuits called themselves "friends in the Lord" and viewed themselves as a fraternity whose bond of union was a shared affective commitment to Christ in apostolic service. This is a central facet of Jesuit spirituality. (6) Finding God in all things: Spiritual integration is a constant theme of the *Spiritual Exercises* and the *Constitutions* of the Society of Jesus. Therefore, the integration of prayer and service, contemplation and action, affect and reason is a hallmark of Jesuit spirituality. This characteristic of Jesuit spirituality is best stated by Ignatius's famous dictum, "to find God in all things." It is further articulated by Jerome Nadal (d. 1580), one of Ignatius's first companions, who styled the Jesuit as "a contemplative in action." In short, Jesuit spirituality is Christocentric, apostolic, discerning, generous, and fraternal. It is an integrated spirituality that allows and encourages the whole Society of Jesus and the individual Jesuit to seek God in the entire fabric of life, prayer, and ministry. *See also* Ignatius of Loyola, St.; Jesuits; *Spiritual Exercises;* spirituality, Christian.   FRANK J. HOUDEK

Jesus [name], name derived from the Greek rendering of the Hebrew *Yĕhôšûaʿ.* It means "Yahweh saves" or "Yahweh is salvation." Its popular etymology comes from *Yēšûāʿ,* meaning "salvation," which is alluded to in Matt 1:21. It was a common Jewish name in the pre-Christian era and it was the name given to Jesus of Nazareth by his parents. The name carries the promise of salvation for humanity. In the NT it is used as a synonym for the person of Jesus and it is in his name (i.e., in the power of his name) that the disciples baptize and work miracles. Peter's speech as recorded in Acts proclaims that salvation is given only in Jesus, "for there is no other name under heaven . . . by which we must be saved" (Acts 4:10, 12). *See also* Christ; Jesus Christ.

JESUS CHRIST

*J*esus Christ is the person called Jesus of Nazareth, recognized by Christians as the Christ, who was crucified on a cross, rose from the dead, and is proclaimed as the Son of God incarnate. He is perceived to be personally active as embodied Spirit in the visible community called the Church and in the world. The purpose of Christian doctrine, morality, spirituality, and Scripture is knowledge and experience of the living person of Jesus Christ.

The renewal of Catholicism that took place at the Second Vatican Council (1962–65) initiated a recovery of the centrality of Christ to the Church. Though the council was principally an ecclesiological event, the renewal that took place at Vatican II was animated in part at least by a refocusing of the primacy of Christ in the life, mission, and ministry of the Church.

The great documents of the Second Vatican Council are held together by strong Christological statements. For example, the Dogmatic Constitution on the Church points out that Christ is "the one mediator" between God and humanity and "the head of that body which is the church" (nn. 8, 7). The Pastoral Constitution on the Church in the Modern World describes Christ as "the goal of human history, the focal point of the longings of history and of civilization, the center of the human race, the joy of every heart, and the answer to all its yearnings" (n. 45; see also nn. 10, 22). The Constitution on the Sacred Liturgy highlights the Paschal Mystery of Christ as the norm guiding the revision of the liturgy (n. 107). The Dogmatic Constitution on Divine Revelation says that "Jesus perfected revelation by fulfilling it" through his life, death, Resurrection, and sending of the Spirit of truth (n. 4).

"They spat on him, and took the reed and struck him on the head. After mocking him, they stripped him of the robe and put his own clothes on him. Then they led him away to crucify him" (Matt 27:30–31); the Passion of Christ; twentieth-century French expressionist painting by Georges Rouault.

This Christocentric focus, however, was not developed in any detail at the Second Vatican Council. Because of this lacuna, the post–Vatican II period has witnessed a veritable springtime of Christological reflection and practice in the life of the Church at all levels: encyclicals, synods, commissions, the theological community, and pastoral practice. For instance, Pope John Paul II in his first encyclical, *Redemptor Hominis* ("Redeemer of Humankind," 1979), points out that "Jesus Christ is the chief way for the Church" (n. 13). The 1985 Extraordinary Synod, commemorating the twentieth anniversary of Vatican II, suggests with striking candor that "The Church becomes more credible if it speaks less about itself and more and more preaches Christ crucified (1 Cor 2:2) and witnesses to him by its life." The International Theological Commission and the Pontifical Biblical Commission have published a variety of documents on Christology since Vatican II. The theological community has turned out more monographs on the person of Jesus Christ in the three postconciliar decades than in the previous three hundred years.

THE PARAMETERS OF CHRISTOLOGY

Clearly the person of Jesus Christ stands at the center of Christian faith and theology. The parameters of the mystery of Christ, however, need to be mapped out. Christology, the study of the person of Jesus Christ, is the part of theology that seeks to answer the question of who Jesus of Nazareth is, past and present. The sources of Christology are the Scriptures, the Christian tradition, and contemporary human experience.

Broadly speaking, the mystery of Jesus Christ embraces two distinct but closely related elements: the Christ event and the universal significance of the Christ event. The Christ event came into being at that particular time in history when Jesus of Nazareth became known as the Christ, that is, the Messiah, the anointed one of Yahweh whom the Jewish world foretold and awaited. When a small group of women and men came together to confess that Jesus as Christ, Christianity was born. The Fourth Gospel concludes its reflection on Jesus by telling us: "these are written so that you may come to believe that Jesus is the Christ" (20:31; see also Acts 9:22). This earliest expression of the Christ event is expanded into other equally important creedal statements such as: Jesus is Lord (Rom 10:9; see also 1 Cor 12:3; 8:6; Acts 2:36; Phil 2:11), Jesus is the wisdom of God (1 Cor 1:24; Col 1:15–16; Heb 1:3), Jesus is the Son of Man (Mark 2:28; 8:31; 13:26), Jesus is the Son of God in power (Rom 1:3–4), and Jesus is the Word of God made flesh (Rev 19:13; 1 John 1:1; John 1:1, 14).

These early confessional statements in turn are developed into elaborate theological narratives concerning the universal significance of the Christ event (e.g., Col 1:15–20; Eph 1:3–10). The particularity of the Christ event, rooted in the history of Jesus, therefore gives way to a new awareness of the universality of the significance of Jesus of Nazareth. Indeed, it is precisely the particularity of the Christ event that mediates the universal significance of Christ for the world.

The universal significance of the Christ event lights up understanding of God, the self, and the world. This universal significance of the Christ event is loosely present in the NT and is spelled out in greater detail in the Christian tradition through reflection on Christian practice.

The interplay between history and interpretation, between human experience and theological understanding, between the practice of discipleship and contemplation is at the heart of Christology. A crucial and critical influence bringing about the transition from the experience to the interpretation is the ongoing presence of the Spirit of Christ in the Christian community, a presence released by the Resurrection of Jesus, which effected the movement in the first place from the Jesus of history to the Christ of faith. The proper object of Christology, therefore, is not simply the historical Jesus or the Gospels but rather the crucified and risen Christ who is present as Spirit in the Christian community and in the world through word, sacrament, Christian practice, and human experience.

A study of the NT data, especially the Gospels, presents its own problems. There is no single portrait of Jesus in the NT. Indeed the Gospels display a variety of perspectives on the life, death, and Resurrection of Jesus. Further, the Gospels, written some thirty to sixty years after the death of Jesus, do not give a strictly historical account of the life of Jesus; instead, they contain theological portraits written by a community of faith to foster faith. In addition, there is no agreed approach among Scripture scholars to the study of Christ in the Gospels. The 1983 document from the Pontifical Biblical Commission entitled "Scripture and Christology" outlines eleven different approaches to the Gospels and indicates that these approaches have both strengths and weaknesses.

The development of the universal significance of the Christ event begins in the NT period, especially after the destruction of the Temple in Jerusalem in the year 70, and continues into the patristic era through the Middle Ages right up to the present moment in the life of the Christian community. If Jesus Christ is the Lord, the Son of God, the Word made flesh, then this has important theological consequences for the way people see God, other persons, and the world around them.

"He is the image of the invisible God, the firstborn of all creation; for in him all things in heaven and on earth were created, things visible and invisible" (Col 1:15–16); the glorified Christ; twelfth-century Byzantine mosaic in the south gallery of the Hagia Sophia, Istanbul (Constantinople), Turkey.

The broad terms of reference of the universal significance of the Christ event have been laid down in the NT and the great Christological councils of the first five centuries. The import of these Christological councils, especially their technical language, is in continual need of historical retrieval and theological transposition. This need arises out of the ongoing desire to understand God, the human person, and the world.

THE GENESIS OF THE CHRIST EVENT

The Christ event is grounded in the historical life of Jesus as given in the NT. The problems associated with tracking down the historical life of Jesus, such as the distance between the time when the Gospels were written and the actual events they describe as well as the explicitly theological nature of the Gospels, should not lead to a position of historical skepticism. On the other hand, one cannot simply read the Gospels as if they give a blow-by-blow account of the life of Jesus. A middle way can be found between historical skepticism and fundamentalism that recognizes that some reliable historical data can be gleaned from the Gospels by means of the historical-critical method.

A helpful guide, though by no means an exhaustive one, is the 1964 instruction from the Pontifical Biblical Commission "The Historical Truth of the Gospels." This instruction indicates the presence of at least "three stages of tradition" within the Gospels that must be taken into account in any search for the historical foundations of the Christ event. These are the original words and deeds of Jesus, the oral proclamation of the words and deeds of Jesus in the light of his death and Resurrection by the Church, and the gathering together of the preaching of Jesus and

"And when they had crucified him, they divided his clothes among themselves by casting lots; then they sat down there and kept watch over him. Over his head they put the charge against him, which read, 'This is Jesus, the King of the Jews'" (Matt 27:35–37); Christ on Calvary, Jean Fouquet illustration in the *Book of Hours* of Etienne Chevalier, Condé Museum, Chantilly, France.

the Church into the written form of the Gospels as we have them today.

The early life of Jesus was lived in relative obscurity in Nazareth for a period of about thirty years, with the exception of a brief appearance at the age of twelve in the Temple in Jerusalem at the feast of Passover (Luke 2:41–52). Jesus first emerges in Galilee in association with John the Baptist and submits to John's baptism. This event marks the beginning of his public ministry. He appears as a prophet within the long line of prophets, declaring "the time is fulfilled, and the kingdom of God is at hand; repent and believe in the gospel" (Mark 1:14).

The announcement of the reign of God is central to the mission and ministry of Jesus. It locates the life of Jesus within a Jewish matrix and an apocalyptic context. The reign of God is a special kind of symbol representing the dynamic action of God within creation and history, giving life a purpose and goal, namely, the restoration of right relationships between God and humanity and the world.

The parables of Jesus, a form of wisdom discourse, are ways of introducing his audience to the meaning and implications of the coming reign of God. Some parables describe the sudden discovery of the reign of God (Matt 13:44–46); others focus on the reversal of values that the reign of God brings (Matt 10:39; 20:25–26); and still others are an injunction to a new kind of practice (Matt 25:31–46).

The miracles of Jesus, especially the healing miracles, which are prominent in the ministry of Jesus, are expressions of the triumph of the reign of God in the present, pointing to the promise of a new order coming through the preaching and practice of Jesus.

A call to faith and conversion are key elements in the preaching and practice of Jesus concerning the coming reign of God. Also central to the coming reign of God was the setting up by Jesus of a new table fellowship among the socially and religiously marginalized people of Palestine, like tax collectors and sinners. This new table fellowship symbolized the inclusive character of the coming reign of God.

Alongside this announcement of the reign of God, Jesus issued an invitation to discipleship, forming new communities of equality among women and men, rich and poor, religious and nonreligious people alike. Within this call to discipleship he gathered a small group whom he describes as "the Twelve," representing the twelve tribes of Israel as part of the eschatological end time of the reign of God.

This kingdom-centered mission of Jesus is animated in particular by his personal experience of God as *Abba* ("Father"), described by some as the source and ground of Jesus' message, practice, and ministry as a whole. The *Abba* experience in turn provides a strong sense of sonship in Jesus' life.

These words and deeds of Jesus gradually brought him into conflict with the religious and political leaders of the day. Jesus, for example, is criticized for breaking the Sabbath, for claiming to forgive sins, for calling God his father, for eating and drinking with sinners, for setting himself above the authority of Moses, for casting out demons with the help of Beelzebul (Matt 12:24), and for promising salvation.

Inevitably the possibility of death begins to emerge, just as it had for previous prophets within Judaism. The fate of other prophets was a reminder to Jesus of what could happen to him (see Luke 13:34).

The journey from Galilee up to Jerusalem at the time of the Passover is a significant turning point in the ministry of Jesus. The growing conflict with the religious and political leaders of the day comes to a head in Jerusalem with the incident of Jesus casting out those who are buying and selling in the Temple (Mark 11:15–17).

After this incident, the pace and significance of events gather momentum, making it difficult to gauge with any degree of accuracy the precise historical details. There is the Last Supper which, it must be emphasized, comes as a final meal in a series of suppers celebrated within the public ministry of Jesus. Jesus, aware of the mounting tension, associates the Last Supper with his imminent death, the restoration of the covenant with Israel, and the coming eschatological banquet of the reign of God. Following the Last Supper there is a period of prayer in Gethsemane, the betrayal by Judas, the arrest by an armed band, the trial before Pontius Pilate, and finally his death on the cross.

For his disciples Jesus' crucifixion comes as a serious moment of crisis: their hopes are dashed, their faith is shattered, and many return to their previous occupations. On "the third day," however, Jesus is experienced in a new way as personally present to his disciples, restoring and transforming their faith, empowering and sending them forth to preach the good news. The Resurrection of Jesus "by its very nature cannot be proved in an empirical way" (Pontifical Biblical Commission, "Scripture and Christology," [1983]). Yet there is strong evidence for the reality of the Resurrection in terms of the new postcrucifixion experiences, the change (more than psychological) effected in his disciples, a new confidence and sense of mission in his disciples, the existence of different resurrection *kerygmata* (Gk., "proclamations") and resurrection narratives in all four Gospels, and the empty tomb tradition. The language of the Resurrection, not to be confused with the language of resuscitation, is metaphorical, embracing elements of change within continuity, identity within personal transformation, newness within sameness. The elements of transformation are captured consistently by the eschatological language of exaltation, glorification, living again, ascension, and pentecost.

This historical and corporate experience by the disciples of Jesus' life, death, and Resurrection is the basis of the Christ event. The resurrection experience in particular is the catalyst effecting the recognition of Jesus as the Christ who is the Lord, the Son of God, the Word made flesh. The application and transformation of titles from the Hebrew Scriptures to Jesus provide the initial concepts for articulating the disciples' experience of the personal messiahship and divinity of Jesus.

What is most influential throughout the NT period is the underlying presence of the paradoxical but creative unity of the death and Resurrection of Jesus. The words and deeds of Jesus take on a new meaning in the light of his death and Resurrection. The personal Resurrection of Jesus stands out as the fulfillment of Jewish hopes and the dawning of a new age. The meaning of the close relationship between God as Father and Jesus as Son gradually unfolds through the impact of the Resurrection.

THE UNIVERSAL SIGNIFICANCE OF THE CHRIST EVENT

As the early Church moved out into the world of Hellenistic culture, it was forced to move from functional accounts of the Christ event (emphasizing the redemptive activities of Christ) to ontological descriptions (emphasizing the "being" of Christ). These ontological descriptions are a further step in defining the universal significance of the Christ event. While this was happening implicitly in the biblical accounts of the messiahship and divinity of Jesus, it became quite explicit from the second century onward.

The challenge of translating the doctrinal implications of Jewish-Christian categories into Hellenistic categories became pressing in the second century. The process of transposition was guided by a variety of factors such as fidelity to the NT data, the preservation of ecclesial unity, liturgical experience, and theological reflection on Christian practice and human experience.

The key category facilitating this cultural adaptation in the second century was that of the Logos (Gk., "the word," or "the truth"), a concept common to both Judaism and Hellenistic philosophy. Jesus is now understood as the Logos, that is, the key to the meaning of both Jewish history and the philosophical world of Hellenistic thought. This breakthrough enabled Christianity to hold its own in the second-century world of Hellenistic culture. Jesus was proclaimed as the answer to the philosopher's search for truth.

At the same time the relationship between Jesus as the Logos and God the Father began to become an issue. Adherence to the absolute oneness of God gave rise to a subordination of Jesus the Logos. Finding suitable language to describe Jesus became a major problem. Questions about the the bodily humanity of Jesus surfaced in some circles. These complex issues continued in the third century and were only fully resolved in the fourth century with the challenge made by Arius.

Arius, a priest in Alexandria, struggled with the identity of Jesus and ended up describing Jesus as half God and half human. In effect, Jesus as the Logos was like one of the hero gods of the ancient world, an emanation from the one true God. The Logos in Jesus, therefore, was not truly God, not really equal to God the Father; there was a time when the Logos did not exist; the Logos was created in time by God out of nothing. The full divinity of Jesus now appeared to be compromised. A council was convened by the emperor Constantine in the year 325 at Nicaea.

The Council of Nicaea condemned Arius, rejected the subordination of the Logos to the Father, and stated as part of its creed that the Son "is true God from true God, begotten not made, of one substance/being [Gk., *homoousios*] with the Father." Although Nicaea provided a point of departure for future discussions, the actual issues raised by Arius did not go away.

Some, mainly from Alexandria (e.g., Athanasius), stressed the union in Jesus between the Logos and flesh (Gk., *sarx*), giving rise to what became known as *Logos-sarx* (Word-flesh) Christology, with the main focus on the divinity of Jesus. Others, largely from Antioch (e.g., Theodore of Mopsuestia), highlighted the distinction between the human and the divine in Jesus, giving rise to what was known as *Logos-anthropos* (Word-human) Christology, which concentrated on the humanity of Jesus. This tension between the humanity and divinity of Jesus came to a head in a controversy between representatives from these schools.

Nestorius, an Antiochene monk, refused to call Mary "bearer of God," *Theotokos*, insisting instead on the title "bearer of Christ," *Christotokos*. Though the context is Mariological, the underlying issue is Christological. Nestorius's position implies a dualism of person in Jesus.

Cyril of Alexandria disagreed with Nestorius. Both appealed to Rome. A council was held at Ephesus in 431. Nestorius was condemned and Cyril's position was affirmed; namely, that there is a real union, a "hypostatic union" between the eternal Logos in Jesus and the human nature of Jesus. Ephesus did not produce a creed; instead it sought to settle a dispute, with little success. Increasing concern was expressed about the humanity of Jesus.

Another council was convened at Chalcedon in 451. This well-attended council gathered the threads from previous discussions and councils, especially Nicaea, and knitted them together into a new synthesis that affirmed the full divinity and full humanity existing as a unity in the person of Jesus Christ. Chalcedon stated that "our Lord Jesus Christ is one and the same Son . . . perfect in Godhead . . . perfect in humanity, truly God (Lat., *vere Deus*), truly a human being (*vere homo*), of one being (Gk., *homoousios*) with the Father . . . of one being (*homoousios*) with us as to his being human . . . made known in two natures, without confusion, without change, without division, without separation . . . concurring in one Person (*Prosopon*) and one independence (*hypostasis*)."

Chalcedon was a council of checks and balances. By far the most influential council in the history of Christology, Chalcedon provided the framework for subsequent discussion and debate, becoming the touchstone of orthodoxy right up to the present. The language of Chalcedon, namely, one Person, hypostasis, two natures, divine and human, continued to need refinement and this took place in subsequent centuries. At the same time Chalcedon was careful to use the inclusive Latin term *homo* ("human being") and not the male term *vir* ("man")—a matter of no small importance for twentieth-century feminist theology.

In spite of the balance of Chalcedon, not everybody accepted its teachings. Although it remains the norm, traces of Monophysitism in one form or another have persisted down through the centuries. Monophysitism denied the existence of a human nature in Christ, thereby exaggerating his divinity at the expense of his humanity.

The dogma of the Incarnation became the focus of Christological discussion in the Middle Ages. For example, Anselm (d. 1109) and Aquinas (d. 1274) argued that God became human in order to repay the debt to God created by human sin. In contrast Duns Scotus (d. 1308) suggested that the Incarnation was built into creation and that, therefore, it would have taken place irrespective of the reality of sin, a view that has become popular in twentieth-century Christology.

Another area receiving attention in the Middle Ages concerned the knowledge that Christ possessed. According to Aquinas, Christ enjoyed the direct vision, or experience, of God (Beatific Vision) during his earthly life as well as having infused knowledge (independent of sense experience) and experiential knowledge (strictly sense experience). This view of Aquinas has prevailed by and large down through the centuries right up to the middle of the twentieth century in Catholic theology.

In broad terms, classical Christology continued to hold a center-stage position through the Reformation and Counter-Reformation periods right up to the twentieth century in Catholic circles. In the middle of the twentieth century, from 1951 onward, classical Christology was challenged. The major influences were the delayed impact of the Enlightenment, Enlightenment, whose insights had been rejected by the Church and excluded from its theology, and the rise of historical consciousness, the retrieval of Chalcedon through studies commemorating its fifteen-hundredth anniversary in 1951 and, above all, the renewal of biblical studies.

CONTEMPORARY CHRISTOLOGY

By far the most significant development in contemporary Christology has been a recovery of the full humanity of Jesus in a manner that respects at the same time his divinity. The humanity of Jesus is seen as the key to a proper understanding of his divinity.

A major voice in the renewal of Catholic Christology was that of Karl Rahner (d. 1984), who argued that the Council of Chalcedon should be read as a beginning and not as an end. Rahner also critiqued the presence of Monophysitism in so much Christological thinking over the centuries. In particular Rahner showed how the Incarnation can be understood as the unique point of contact within history between God's gracious descending self-communication to the world and humanity's dynamic movement of ascending self-transcendence toward the divine. In the person of Jesus Christ, God and humanity come together in perfect unity.

At the same time Rahner was rethinking classical Christology, the new quest for the historical Jesus came to the fore in 1953. This search for the historical Jesus of the Gospels complemented the renewal of interest in the humanity of Jesus.

Two very distinct Christological streams emerged in Catholic theology in the 1960s and 1970s, namely, incarnational and paschal Christologies.

"For fear of him the guards shook and became like dead men. But the angel said to the women, 'Do not be afraid; I know that you are looking for Jesus who was crucified. He is not here; for he has been raised, as he said'" (Matt 28:4–6); Piero della Francesca's fifteenth-century painting of the Resurrection, in the Pinacoteca Comunale, Sansepolcro, Italy.

It is no mere coincidence that the language of these streams is quite evident in the final documents of the Second Vatican Council. Though Vatican II did not develop in any detail a systematic Christology, it did make significant Christological statements. Indeed the Second Vatican Council is not as Christologically deficient as some have suggested.

While it has always been part of the Christian tradition to say that Jesus reveals God to the world, the Second Vatican Council went a step further, pointing out that the same Jesus "fully reveals man to man himself and makes his supreme calling clear" (Pastoral Constitution on the Church in the Modern World, n. 22). In the same document the council also highlights the humanity of Jesus, noting that the "human nature as He assumed it was not annulled. . . . He worked with human hands, He thought with a human mind, He acted by human choices, and loved with a human heart" (n. 22). Further, Vatican II reunited the lost links between Christology and eschatology by emphasizing that Christ is the ground and goal of humanity, history, and creation (nn. 45, 10, 25, 2) and that the Paschal Mystery is the key to the future of the world (n. 25; see also the Constitution on the Sacred Liturgy, nn. 6, 18; Dogmatic Constitution on the Church, nn. 49, 51). Perhaps even more significant, Vatican II effects a shift from an exclusivist Christology to an inclusivist Christology by acknowledging the spiritual and moral values of the other world religions (Declaration on the Relationship of the Church to Non-Christian Religions, nn. 2–4).

In the post–Vatican II period Christology has moved to the center of the stage in Catholic theology. At least three particular developments should be noted briefly. The first of these is the existence of liberation Christologies in Latin America. The point of departure for liberation Christology is the widespread presence of so much poverty and injustice in the Third World. Against this background it points out that Jesus came "to bring good news to the poor . . . to proclaim release to the captives and recovery of sight to the blind, to let the oppressed go free" (Luke 4:18). From this perspective liberation Christology proceeds to focus on the primacy of practice, especially the practice of liberation, within the life of Jesus. The cross of Christ is perceived to symbolize the solidarity of God with the suffering of humanity and the Resurrection reveals the triumph of that divine solidarity.

Closely related to liberation Christology is the rise of feminist Christology. Certain forms of feminism have been able to reread the NT in a way that is liberating for women and men alike. Feminist Christology retrieves the neglected presence of women in the ministry of Jesus and exposes the existence of a critique of patriarchy implicit in the preaching and practice of Jesus. The appearances of the risen Christ to women is stressed and the commissioning of the two Marys to go and tell the disciples that Christ has risen from the dead is also highlighted (Matt 28:1–10). Above all, the early baptismal formula, "There is no longer Jew or Greek, there is no longer slave or free, there is no longer male or female; for all of you are one in Christ Jesus" (Gal 3:28), is singled out as an ongoing challenge to the Christian community today.

A third development is the ever increasing focus on the possibility of an ecological Christology. A new conversation has been initiated between Christology and contemporary cosmologies. Such a dialogue can be found to be present in the NT, especially in the wisdom Christologies of the Pauline corpus (Phil 2:6–11; Rom 8:19–23; Eph 1:3–14; Col 1:15–10) and the synoptic Gospels, and the Logos Christology of John and early Hellenistic theology. This conversation has released a new appreciation of the cosmic Christ in the world. Within this perspective the intrinsic unity of creation and incarnation stressed by Irenaeus (d. ca. 200), Duns Scotus (d. 1308), and Teilhard de Chardin (d. 1955) takes on new meaning and provides a foundation for an ecological Christology in the future.

By way of conclusion it must be stressed that Christology is ultimately about a new awareness of the mystery of the hidden God revealed in the person of Jesus. In the end Christology must be judged by its ability to light up the incomprehensible reality of God's presence and action in the world. Christology does this in at least two ways. First of all, the mystery of Christ reminds one that God has drawn near to humankind in the shape and form of the humanity of Jesus. The human being as other is the Logos of God's self-revelation, especially the *humanum* of the crucified and risen Christ. Because the eternal Word of God was made flesh in Jesus, the apparent gulf between heaven and earth, between God and humanity, between the sacred and the secular has once and for all been overcome, so that now in the light of the mystery of Christ people are able to glimpse heaven on earth, find God in humanity, and discover the sacred within the secular.

Second, Christology also lights up the mystery of God by disclosing God as Father, Son, and Spirit. The *Abba* experience of Jesus, the drama of the cross, the outpouring of the Spirit, and the unique Christian insight that God is love (1 John 4:16) are stepping stones to the trinitarian consciousness of the early Church. The present renaissance of trinitarian theology taking place in the works of European scholars like Walter Kasper and U.S. scholars like Catherine Mowry LaCugna and Elizabeth A. Johnson is indicative of the theocentric character of Christology and represents the flowering of the renewal of Christology since Vatican II.

See also Arianism; Ascension; Chalcedon, Council of; Christology; crucifixion; God; hypostatic union; Incarnation, the kingdom of God [in the Bible]; Logos; Monophysitism; Monothelitism; Nestorianism; preexistence of Christ; redemption; Resurrection of Christ.

Bibliography

Fitzmyer, Joseph A. *A Christological Catechism.* 2d ed. New York: Paulist Press, 1991.
Johnson, Elizabeth A. *Consider Jesus.* New York: Crossroad, 1990.
Krieg, Robert A. *Story-Shaped Christology.* New York: Paulist Press, 1988.
Lane, Dermot A. *Christ at the Centre.* New York: Paulist Press, 1991.
_____. *The Reality of Jesus.* New York: Paulist Press, 1975.
Meier, John P. *A Marginal Jew.* 2 vols. New York: Doubleday, 1991, 1994.
Senior, Donald. *Jesus: A Gospel Portrait.* Rev. ed. New York: Paulist Press, 1992.
Thompson, William M. *The Jesus Debate.* New York: Paulist Press, 1985.   DERMOT A. LANE

Jesus Prayer, the name of a prayer addressed to Jesus, sometimes also linked to a special method of prayer involving physical techniques. The text of the Jesus prayer is: "Lord Jesus Christ, have mercy on me, a sinner." The prayer itself, used extensively in contemporary Orthodox Christianity, dates from around the sixth or seventh centuries. Its origin is probably Greek and it served as a salutory invocation of the Holy Name and a petition for divine pardon. The development of the prayer's association with a specialized praying technique is more difficult to trace. Some believe that this use of the prayer did not occur until the fourteenth century. The method involves controlled breathing, bowed head and concentration upon one's heart, not unlike meditation techniques common in raja yoga, an Indian meditation tradition. These physical aspects of the Jesus Prayer, however, are not practiced today by the Orthodox. *See also* prayer.

Jewish Christianity, a term somewhat fluid in reference partly because the earliest Christians were all Jews and partly because, even in the case of gentile converts, early debates about the terms of admission were debates not about admitting Gentiles to a new religion but to a form of Judaism. The question in both cases, until ca. 100, was which form of Judaism represented the true Israel. Between ca. 70 and ca. 90, Christians began to be expelled from synagogues as heretics (somewhat later, a curse against them was included in the synagogue liturgy). With the expansion of gentile churches, most Christians differentiated themselves from "the Jews," arguing that Christians, not the Jews, were the heirs of the promises made to the patriarchs and that observance of the Sabbath, circumcision, ceremonial laws, etc., was never meant literally or was meant as a punishment for the incident of the golden calf (Exod 32).

This left in an awkward position Jewish Christians who still observed the law, as the earliest Christians had done, but who were heretics to orthodox Judaism. They soon diminished in prominence, sometimes merging with Gnostic or other heretical sects, sometimes regarded as heretical simply because of their increasingly unfamiliar, but ancient, practice. Their groups are given various names (Ebionites, the most significant group; Cerinthians, Elkesaites, Hemerobaptists, Nazareans, Symmachians), and fragments of Jewish-Christian literature survive (*Gospel According to the Hebrews*, perhaps a revision and translation of Matthew; *Gos-pel of the Ebionites; Gospel of the Nazareans*). The Pseudo-Clementine literature incorporates the *Acts of Peter* and the *Preaching of Peter*. Most Jewish Christians were located in the Transjordan, where, according to Eusebius, they fled from Jerusalem at the beginning of the Jewish War (66). *See also* Judaism.

JOHN C. CAVADINI

Jews, Catholicism and. The history of Catholic-Jewish relations is coterminous with the history of the Church itself. Jesus and the apostles were Jewish, acknowledged the Bible of Israel as Sacred Scripture, and adhered to Jewish practice in worship and religious life. The attitude of Christians toward Jews who continued to observe their ancestral faith tradition of Judaism became increasingly ambiguous over the centuries.

On the one hand, Church law and patristic theology insisted that the Jewish people be protected, since they witnessed to the authenticity of the Bible of Israel (which came to be known as the Old Testament). On the other hand, the people of Israel, albeit God's chosen, had missed their moment, "blind" as they were to Christian claims concerning Jesus as their Messiah. Although medieval canon law made it an excommunicable offense for Christians to disrupt Jewish prayer, it legislated restrictions on the Jewish community economically, politically, socially, and religiously.

Negative Developments: Large-scale violence by Christians against Jews first occurred throughout Europe with the Crusades, beginning in 1096. Along with it came an escalation of anti-Jewish rhetoric and theologizing, so that, beginning in the twelfth century, Talmuds were burned, and Passion plays and the blood libel (the notion that Jews ritually murder Christians) proliferated in the fourteenth century. This same period saw the expulsion of the Jewish communities of most of western Europe (with some exceptions, such as Italy and Poland), culminating in the exile of the ancient Jewish communities of Spain in 1492. Most of the lies against, and stereotypes of, Jews and Judaism developed and spread in societies, such as England, that were largely lacking in Jewish populations.

The Protestant Reformation did not attempt to reform these ancient Christian animosities toward Jews. Nor did the Enlightenment succeed in shedding light on the dark images of Jews that were harbored by vast numbers of Europeans. The pseudo-scientific racial theories of the late eighteenth and nineteenth centuries found widespread acceptance, perhaps because the protective pole of the Church's traditional theological stance was effectively neutralized as a moral force in society at large.

In the twentieth century the Nazi Holocaust (Heb., *Shoah*) saw an attempt to muster the full resources of a modern, highly technical state to the goal (Ger., *Endlosung*) of murdering an entire people. When the death camps were liberated, a new vocabulary, with such words as "genocide," had to be invented to describe this new reality.

Vatican II: In 1965 the Second Vatican Council's Declaration on the Relationship of the Church to Non-Christian Religions (*Nostra Aetate*) implicitly took up the Holocaust's challenge to Catholic teaching by mandating strict guidelines for Catholic biblical interpretation and catechesis. "The Jews must not be presented as rejected by God or accursed as if this followed from Sacred Scripture.... Now, as before, God holds the Jews most dear for the sake of their fathers: God does not repent of gifts made nor calls issued" (n. 4). As Pope John Paul II summarized the council, the Jews remain "the people of God of the Old Covenant never revoked by God."

Official Catholic teaching today boldly affirms God's continuing covenantal love for the Jewish people, and calls on all Catholics to respect the integrity and spiritual fecundity of the Jewish faith. The Catholic Church approaches the Jewish people today in a spirit of repentance and dialogue, not triumphalism. *See also* Judaism.   EUGENE J. FISHER

Joachim, St. *See* Anne and Joachim, Sts.

Joachim of Fiore, ca. 1135–1202, Italian monk and exegete. Joachim, who had been a Cistercian monk and abbot in southern Italy, founded at Fiore his own order, the Florensians, which received papal approval in 1196. He is most famous for his original exposition of Scripture in which he divides salvation history into three ages: (1) the age of the Father, characterized by the married state; (2) the age of the Son, characterized by the clerical state; and (3) the age of the Spirit, by the monastic state. Although Joachim gave no exact dating for these stages, his work was used by later writers, notably the Franciscan Gerard of Borgo San Donnino in his *Introduction to the Eternal Gospel* (1254), to argue that the age of the Spirit was imminent. Joachim's schema has since often been used to read current political events as signs of the end times.

Joan, "Pope," medieval fable. According to one version of this legend, which seems to date from the thirteenth century, Pope Leo IV (d. 855) was succeeded by a Pope Joan, rather than by the historical Benedict III. This Joan, the story goes, was actually a learned woman who, traveling in men's clothing, came from Athens to Rome and began an ecclesiastical career. When she eventually gave birth during a papal procession, her secret was revealed, and she was removed from office and punished. The story was generally accepted as fact until the sixteenth century.

Joan of Arc, St., 1412–31, a patron saint of France. A peasant girl, in the midst of the Hundred Years' War she began to experience a series of supernatural visions that convinced her that she had a divine mission to save France from the English. By 1429 she had convinced the dauphin Charles VII to allow her to lead an expedition to relieve the siege of the city of Orléans and persuaded Charles that same year to receive formal coronation as king of France. Taken prisoner in a campaign against the Burgundians, French allies of the English, she was burned at the stake by the English for witchcraft. Pope Callistus III declared her innocence in 1456, and she was canonized in 1920. Feast day: May 30. *See also* France, Catholicism in.

Joan of Arc, fifteenth-century French national heroine who is credited with saving France at the battle of Orléans; depicted here in her suit of white armor and bearing a banner with a symbol of the Trinity and the words, "Jesus, Maria."

Joaquina de Vedruna de Mas, St., 1783–1854, founder of the Carmelite Sisters of Charity. Born of a noble Spanish family, she married, was widowed, and founded a religious community to teach the young and care for the sick. Feast day: August 28.

Jocists (Fr., Jeunesse Ouvrière Chrétienne, "Young Christian Workers"), a post–World War I Belgian Catholic Action movement that became popular in France and the United States in the late 1920s and 1930s. Established by Cardinal Cardijn (d. 1967), the Jocists encouraged their lay members to see the workplace as an opportunity for evangelization. By the way they conducted themselves, Jocists believed that they could be living examples of Catholic faith in action, thereby spreading the gospel and encouraging non-Catholics to consider conversion to the Church. In effect, Jocists attempted to create an apostolate of their employment and to do their best to incorporate Christian values into the work environment. *See also* Cardijn, Joseph.

Jogues, St. Isaac (zhog), 1607–46, Jesuit missionary. Born in France, Jogues entered the Jesuits in 1624 and arrived in New France in 1636, where he worked in missions among the Hurons along Lake Superior. Rather than escape the attacking Mohawks in 1642, Jogues and his lay associate, René Goupil, chose captivity with their Huron companions. Goupil was quickly killed, but Jogues was tortured until adopted as a slave by a Mohawk woman.

With the aid of the Dutch, one year later he escaped to New Amsterdam. Feted upon his return to France, Jogues again volunteered for missionary work among the Mohawks in 1646. On the day after his arrival at the village of Ossernenon near present-day Auriesville, New York, he was felled by a hatchet blow from an Iroquois warrior who feared Jogues as a sorcerer causing the ruin of the corn crop. Jogues and seven companions were canonized in 1930 and proclaimed the patron saints of Canada in 1940. Feast day: October 19. *See also* North American Martyrs.

Johannine Comma, the words "in heaven, the Father, the Word, and the Holy Spirit, and these three are one. And there are three who testify on earth" (1 John 5:7–8). They are found in some Latin manuscripts dating before A.D. 1000 and were adopted into the Sixto-Clementine version of the Vulgate. Their authenticity is repudiated by modern textual critics, especially as the context speaks of the

Isaac Jogues, seventeenth-century Jesuit missionary to the New World (Canada and northern New York) and one of the North American Martyrs; the Latin inscription on the New York State memorial reads: "To the greater glory of God."

three witnesses as "the Spirit, the water and the blood" (1 John 5:8).

John I, St., d. 526, pope from 523 to 526. The Gothic king Theodoric, an Arian, forced John to travel to Constantinople to persuade the emperor Justin to annul his anti-Arian decrees. Only partially successful, John was imprisoned by Theodoric upon his return. He died in prison. Feast day: May 18. *See also* Arianism.

John XII [Octavian], ca. 936–64, pope from 955 to 964. Known for his corrupt life-style, John gained control of much of Italy at the price of imperial interference in papal elections. Forced from Rome because of a conflict with Emperor Otto I, he returned in 964 but died soon after deposing Leo VIII, who had been elected in his absence.

John XXII [Jacques Duèse], 1244–1334, the second Avignon pope, from 1316 to 1334, and the one who authorized the canonization of Thomas Aquinas. When he assumed the papacy, after teaching law and serving as bishop of Avignon, John furthered the centralization of Church administration and reformed papal finances. His papacy was contentious, marked by continual battles with the emperor, Louis of Bavaria, and with the Franciscans over the poverty question. During his last three years of life John preached that the saints will not enjoy the Beatific Vision until after final judgment, a view condemned by his successor. *See also* Avignon.

John XXIII [**Angelo Giuseppe Roncalli**], 1881–1963, pope from 1958 to 1963. He is perhaps the greatest, certainly the most beloved, pope of modern times; convener of the Second Vatican Council. After twenty-five years as a papal diplomat in Bulgaria, Turkey, and France, and six as patriarch of Venice, Angelo Roncalli was elected pope just before his seventy-seventh birthday. He was not expected to do more than keep the papal chair warm for Giovanni Battista Montini, then archbishop of Milan and later Pope Paul VI. Yet within six months John XXIII astonished the world by calling an ecumenical council.

Even more astonishing was the kind of council he envisaged. It was not called to condemn errors—though he did not deny they were numerous enough. "Nowadays men are condemning them of their own accord," he said, noting that these errors vanished like mist in the morning sun. The Church today needed the medicine of mercy more than severity. So his council would be pastoral and would try to express the substance of the faith in new language. The project was ecumenical from the outset because it concentrated minds on the gospel.

John's own outgoing personality gave vast resonance to these themes. He was accessible and friendly, seeing no reason to emulate the formal aloofness of his predecessor, Pius XII. John strolled in the Vatican Gardens. He visited the Regina Coeli prison for Christmas and recalled the arrest of one of his numerous relatives. He disarmed traditional enemies like the Communists. He made grace seem natural. Above all, he was open to the Holy Spirit,

Pope John XXIII (d. 1963), one of the greatest and most beloved popes in the entire history of the Church, best known for calling the Second Vatican Council (1962–65) and for initiating a period of major renewal and reform of the Catholic Church; this official Vatican photo was taken in 1958, just after his election to the papacy.

his only "superior." His alertness to the Holy Spirit in the modern world led him to speak of the "signs of the times." He saw the Spirit at work in the end of colonialism, the emancipation of the working class, and the promotion of women in society. This provided the method of *Gaudium et Spes,* the council's Pastoral Constitution on the Church in the Modern World.

The Pope and the Council: John thought in images. We are not born to be "museum-keepers, but to cultivate a flourishing garden of life," he said. He expressed this sense of burgeoning new life in the Church by calling the council "a new Pentecost." This implied far more than the juridical observation that the Holy Spirit would "assist" the ecumenical council. In John's mind, the council was an event of the Holy Spirit in which the whole Church was involved. Everyone was urged to say his "prayer for the council": "Renew thy wonders in this day, as by a New Pentecost."

This, though it aroused enthusiasm, could not set the agenda. For him the purpose of the council was the *aggiornamento* (It., "updating") of the Catholic Church. This would, of itself, set off ecumenical vibrations leading toward what he called "the re-composition of the whole mystical flock of Christ." He knew this would involve "a change in mentalities, ways of thinking and prejudices." The council's language should "shed light on and remove misunderstandings, and it should dissipate error by the force of truth."

However, John appeared to approve of the texts prepared by the Curia for the council. Cardinal Joseph Ratzinger declared later that the pope "had not envisaged the possibility of rejection and expected a rapid and painless vote in favor of projects that he had read through and welcomed with full approval." The implication is that Pope John sided with the minority at the first session and was upset by the rejection of such excellent draft documents. But this view cannot be sustained. Although Pope John approved in general of the prepared texts, he was not deeply attached to them and was prepared to see them dropped without any deep sense of personal loss. They would do—until something better came along. In any case, the council was sovereign.

On September 11, 1962, John broadcast to the world and asked: "Has there ever been an ecumenical council which was not a way of self-renewal through an encounter with the Risen Jesus, the glorious and immortal King, whose light illumines the whole Church for the salvation, joy and glory of all peoples?" The question was rhetorical. There was also a new note. It would be illuminating and helpful to present the Church "in the underdeveloped countries as the Church of all, and especially of the poor." This provided the impetus for the opening chord of the pastoral constitution *Gaudium et Spes*.

One last idea was slotted into place in this broadcast. From Cardinal Leo-Josef Suenens of Belgium Pope John had learned to distinguish between the Church *ad intra* and the Church *ad extra*. It helped to clarify two sets of problems the council would have to deal with: internal questions (the nature of the Church, worship, ecumenism, etc.), and external questions (war, peace, birth control, hunger, etc.).

The Last Months: Just over a week later, on September 23, 1962, X-ray examinations revealed that Pope John was suffering from stomach cancer. Nothing was said publicly, but he realized that if the council lasted more than one session, he would not be able to see it through. He said to a friend: "At least I have launched this big ship—others will have to bring it into port."

But he still had time to overcome the theory, de-fended by Cardinal Alfredo Ottaviani (d. 1979), head of the Holy Office, that "error has no rights." The abandonment of this thesis was a precondition of the council's treatment of ecumenism, religious liberty, and non-Christian religions. This issue dominated the first session of the council, the only one Pope John knew. He intervened rarely, but always decisively, to ensure joint commissions so that the minority (mostly from the Curia) would be able to accept the council's verdict without being humiliated.

During this autumn of 1962 the Cuban missile crisis brought the United States and the Soviet Union close to war. Pope John's message to heads of state—broadcast on Vatican Radio on October 25—made the front page of the Soviet newspaper *Pravda* the next day under the banner headline: "We beg all rulers not to be deaf to the cry of humanity." This was unheard of. John's appeal enabled Nikita Krushchev, the Soviet leader, to back down without losing face. It encouraged Pope John to compose his last will and testament, the encyclical *Pacem in Terris* on universal peace. Then he could die, before the gaze of the whole world, offering his life for the success of the council, whose outline and spirit he had so clearly laid down. *See also* aggiornamento; Mater et Magistra; Pacem in Terris; Vatican Council II.

Bibliography

Hebblethwaite, Peter. *Pope John XXIII: Shepherd of the Modern World.* Garden City, NJ: Doubleday, 1985.

Zizola, Giancarlo. *The Utopia of Pope John XXIII.* Maryknoll, NY: Orbis Books, 1978.   PETER HEBBLETHWAITE

John XXIII [Baldassarre Cossa], ca. 1370–1419, antipope from 1410 to 1415, second pope of the Pisan line, who ruled a large part of the Church during the last years of the Great Western Schism. He was elevated to cardinal in 1402 and was instrumental at the Council of Pisa (1409) in the election of Alexander V, whom he succeeded the following year. He convened the Council of Constance in 1414, but withdrew when he realized it would call for his own resignation. For years canonists disagreed about the legitimacy of his papacy. As an antipope, he is to be distinguished from the better-known modern pope, John XXIII (d. 1963), who convened the Second Vatican Council. *See also* antipope; Constance, Council of; Great Schism; Pisa, Council of.

John Bosco, St. *See* Bosco, St. John.

John Cantius, St. *See* Cantius, St. John.

John Capistrano, St. *See* Capistrano, St. John.

John Cassian, St. *See* Cassian, St. John.

John Chrysostom, St. *See* Chrysostom, St. John.

John Climacus, St. *See* Climacus, St. John.

John de Brébeuf, St. *See* Brébeuf, St. Jean de.

John Eudes, St. *See* Eudes, St. John.

John Fisher, St. *See* Fisher, St. John.

John Gualbert, St., ca. 995–1073, abbot and founder of the Vallumbrosan congregation. A Florentine knight who adopted the monastic life, John became a hermit in the forest of Vallumbrosa, near Florence (ca. 1030). Here he founded a monastery under the Rule of St. Benedict, with additional provisions to emphasize poverty. Feast day: July 12. *See also* Benedict, Rule of St.; Vallumbrosan order.

John Moschus. *See* Moschus, John.

John Nepomucen, St. (nep-uhm'oo-sen), 1350–93, martyr and patron saint of the Czechs. As vicar general of Prague, he disputed with King Wenceslaus IV of Bohemia over the administration of the abbey of Kladruby. Seized by royal troops, he was tortured and drowned. Feast day: May 16.

John of Antioch, d. ca. 441, bishop of Antioch and supporter of his friend Nestorius. Ordered to the Council of Ephesus (431) to explain that support, he arrived after Nestorius's condemnation for teaching that Jesus Christ was a human person as well as a divine person. In response, he called a rival council vindicating Nestorius and condemning Cyril of Alexandria, who had championed the condemnation of Nestorius. A later reconciliation with Cyril in 433 caused a schism with many Eastern Nestorian churches.

John of Ávila, St., 1499–1569, spiritual adviser of Teresa of Ávila, John of the Cross, Francis Borgia, and Peter of Alcántara, among others. A Spanish priest devoted to a life of austerity, he preached so strongly against the rich that he was imprisoned for a time by the Inquisition at Seville. After his release he continued preaching all over Spain and was immensely popular. Feast day: May 10.

John of Damascus, St., ca. 675–ca. 749, Greek theologian and Doctor of the Church. An Arab Christian, he succeeded his father and grandfather as a minister to the caliphs, but after 700 retired to the monastery of St. Sabas near Jerusalem, where he was ordained a priest. John is known principally for his extensive theological works, especially *On the Orthodox Faith,* a brilliant compilation and synthesis of Greek theology that became enormously influential in the medieval West, being used by Peter Lombard, Thomas Aquinas, and others. John's other works include homilies, ascetic writings, polemical and dogmatic treatises, as well as poetry, some of which is incorporated into the Greek liturgy. His defense of the veneration of images against iconoclasm developed into a highly original spiritual teaching centered on the Incarnation and on the imaging of Jesus by the saints. John teaches the Real Presence, and also Mary's exemption from sin and her Assumption. Feast day: December 4. *See also* Fathers of the Church; iconoclasm.

John of God, St., 1495–1550, patron saint of the sick and of hospitals. Portuguese soldier, slave overseer, shepherd, and finally peddler of religious books in Gibraltar, he was spiritually overcome while hearing a sermon by John of Ávila in 1538. Filled with such guilt over his life, he appeared to everyone to have gone mad. By 1540 he began to devote himself more calmly to helping the sick and poor and opened a hospital in Grenada that was the beginning of the Brothers Hospitallers (Brothers of St. John of God). Feast day: March 8. *See also* Hospitallers.

John of Kanti, St. *See* Cantius, St. John.

John of Matha, St., 1578–1618, cofounder with Felix of Valois of the Order of the Most Holy Trinity (Trinitarians). Born in France, he lived for a time as a hermit under the spiritual direction of Felix, to whom he confided his desire of founding a religious order to recover Christian captives from the Muslims by nonviolent means. Upon papal approval of the order, John became its first superior. Feast day: February 8. *See also* Trinitarians.

John of Paris [Jean Quidort], d. 1306, Dominican theologian. Trained in theology at the University of Paris, he wrote over twenty works, including an important defense of Thomas Aquinas against Franciscan attack. He is undoubtedly best known for his

Tractate on Regal and Papal Power (1302–3). This work shuns the extremism of much contemporary political theory, refusing to make either the spiritual or the temporal authority subservient to the other. Rather, following Aquinas, John insists that when functioning properly, each should operate autonomously. As the Vicar of Christ, the pope is the source of spiritual authority on earth; the ecclesiastical hierarchy is commissioned by Christ to promote the attainment, in the next life, of the human person's supernatural end, i.e., life with God in heaven. Temporal authority, on the other hand, is in origin and justification independent of the pope: rooted in natural law, it is designed to facilitate the realization in this life of ends natural to being human. Only if there is a breakdown in one sphere of activity, John adds, should the other authority intervene. The tone, as well as the content, of the treatise is moderate: it offers little indication that its composition coincided with the struggle for supremacy between the French king, Philip the Fair, and Pope Boniface VIII. *See also* Church and state.

John of Parma, ca. 1208–89, Franciscan friar and minister general of the order from 1247 to 1257. A famous reformer, theologian, and preacher, John was forced to resign as minister general in 1257 because of his Joachimite (Joachim of Fiore) sympathies. *See also* Joachim of Fiore.

John of Salisbury, 1115–80, bishop and philosopher. Educated at Paris, John served as secretary to Thomas Becket. He was later elected bishop of Chartres (1176). His *Metalogicon* is one of the first medieval commentaries on Aristotelian logic; he also wrote the *Policraticus*, or *Statesman's Book,* and lives of Anselm of Canterbury and Becket. *See also* Becket, St. Thomas.

John of St. Thomas, 1589–1644, Dominican philosopher and theologian, champion of the thought of Thomas Aquinas. Of noble descent, John Poinsot had a varied career, as university professor (at Alcalá), advisor to the Spanish Inquisition, and confessor of King Philip IV of Spain. His major works, which proved highly influential in later Thomism, include a large philosophical study covering formal and material logic and natural philosophy and a similar theological work broadly patterned on Aquinas's *Summa Theologiae.* Although his reading of Aquinas has its detractors, the teaching on signs in the first part of John's great philosophical work has brought him renewed interest from semioticians. *See also* Thomism.

John of the Cross, St., 1542–91, Doctor of the Church, reformer of the Carmelite order, and one of the greatest of Catholic mystics and Spanish poets. He entered the Carmelite order in 1563, taking the name of John of St. Matthias. He studied in Salamanca (1554–68) and was ordained in 1567. That same year, John met Teresa of Ávila, who persuaded him to collaborate in the reform of the order. On November 11, 1568, his name changed to John of the Cross, he assumed the Primitive Rule and helped to found the first monastery of the reform. He was subsequently rector of the college at Alcalá and then confessor of the Carmelite nuns at Incarnation in Ávila, where Teresa was prioress. Kidnapped by Carmelites hostile to the reform, he was harshly imprisoned in Toledo where he began to write his greatest poetry. He escaped from this prison and continued to write mystical poems and to compose lengthy commentaries upon a few of them, his Scholastic theology becoming a hermeneutic of the religious experience contained in these art objects.

John of the Cross, sixteenth-century mystic, cofounder of the Discalced Carmelites, and author of such spiritual classics as the *Ascent of Mount Carmel* and *Dark Night of the Soul.*

John held various positions within the reformed ("Discalced") Carmelites and underwent significant persecution at the end of his life.

Writings and Teachings: Besides his poetry, various compilations of maxims and counsels, and letters, John wrote three (or four) major treatises: *The Ascent of Mount Carmel–The Dark Night of the Soul, The Spiritual Canticle,* and *The Living Flame of Love,* describing with profound insight the movement of the person into contemplation and union with God, of becoming "God by participation" (*Ascent of Mount Carmel* 11.5.7). The "dark night" provides the metaphor for the purification through which the person journeys, night distinguished by that which is being purified (senses and spirit), the agency predominating (active and passive), the formal purification (privation of appetite, faith, communication of God), and the finality achieved (contemplation and union with God).

The night of the senses brings about the purification of motivation from the dominance of pleasure and satisfaction, either actively, through the choices made under the guidance and motivation of Christ, or passively, when satisfaction is gone and one continues to follow the movements of grace even through there seems to be no recompense. Gradually out of this night emerges a contemplative prayer that is peaceful and without images.

The night of the spirit, the night of faith, is far more demanding than the night of the senses. The issue here is not so much a question of motivation as of support systems: the concepts, the systems of meaning, the symbols and structures by which reassurance is forthcoming. Faith alone becomes the ultimate guide. This night is a purification of all other sources of security and guidance, either actively, as a person takes faith increasingly as the guide of his or her life, or passively, when the supports drop away from one's consciousness and there is only the experience of emptiness, impurity, weakness, abandonment, and death. If the night of the senses is the experience of the desert, the night of the spirit is the experience of the Cross.

The night of the senses terminates in contemplation; the night of the spirit terminates in transformation or union with God. Within this state of habitual union, the soul will occasionally experience the acts of love that are the activity of the Holy Spirit with which the soul is now united and "made one with it, loves most sublimely" (*Living Flame* 1.2).

John of the Cross was canonized in 1726 and declared a Doctor of the Church in 1926. Feast day: December 14. *See also* Carmelite order; dark night, the; Primitive Rule; Teresa of Ávila, St.

MICHAEL J. BUCKLEY

John Paul I [Albino Luciani], 1912–78, pope from August 26 to September 28, 1978. He left his mark on the papacy first by his choice of a double-barreled name as a debt of gratitude to his two predecessors, John XXIII and Paul VI. He admitted that he did not have the wisdom of heart of Pope John nor the culture of Pope Paul. He knew that popes John and Paul were popularly contrasted, with John symbolizing openness to all people of good will while Paul was perceived as a hesitant worrier. John Paul's choice of name meant a refusal to separate them.

The second achievement of his brief reign was to simplify the papal style. John Paul banished the tiara and the *sedia gestatoria* (Lat., portable chair) and simply inaugurated his pastoral ministry as supreme pastor.

His thirty-three-day pontificate did not provide enough evidence to show how he would have

Pope John Paul I, who served only thirty-three days in the papacy, dispensed with the centuries-old tradition of being crowned like a temporal sovereign and instead was invested with the simple pallium, worn around the neck as a symbol of an archbishop's pastoral office, and the miter; he is shown here being carried on the traditional *sedia gestatoria* as he prepared to enter the Lateran Basilica, his cathedral church as Bishop of Rome.

developed. He was himself a skilled catechist with a talent for communication. But on his only sortie from the Vatican he revived the *sedia gestatoria* (in response to popular demand) and denounced false notions of creativity that led to liturgical excesses.

His death, probably late on the night of September 28, 1978, was made needlessly mysterious by the Vatican claim that he was found by his Irish priest-secretary. This was false. He was found by Sister Vincenza, his housekeeper. Nor was his last reading *The Imitation of Christ.* The Vatican manipulated the story for public relations purposes, thus giving rise to extravagant theories about the "real" cause of death. The truth is, John Paul died prematurely because he needed treatment for serious health problems and did not seek or receive it.

Ordained in 1935, appointed bishop of Vittorio Veneto in 1958, then patriarch of Venice in 1969, he was the author of *Illustrissimi,* a series of letters to historical and fictional characters. He was the first pope born of working-class parents.

PETER HEBBLETHWAITE

John Paul II [Karol Wojtyla], b. 1920, pope since 1978. He is the first non-Italian pope since the Dutchman Hadrian VI in 1523, the first ever Polish pope, and at fifty-eight the youngest pope since Pius IX in 1846. He considered the name Stanislaus, after the patron saint of Cracow, where he had been archbishop since 1963. In the end, he followed the example of his predecessor and chose John Paul II.

The Pope and History: For John Paul II, his election to the papacy was providential, a compensation for Polish sufferings in the nineteenth century, and then under Nazism and Communism. His mission would be to bring the insights and values of the suffering Church of the East to the comfortable churches of the West and to put a stop to postconciliar drift.

He made saints Cyril and Methodius coequal patron saints of Europe alongside St. Benedict. He meant that the Church needed to, in his words, "breathe with two lungs," combining the Latin tradition of order and law with the more mystical Greek tradition. These ideas were expressed in the encyclical *Slavorum Apostolorum* (1985, the first encyclical on Europe).

On his first visit home in 1979 he prayed that the Holy Spirit might renew the face of the earth, of "this earth" (Pol., *ziemen*) he added, meaning Poland. Soviet President Mikhail Gorbachev's visit to the Vatican on December 1, 1989, just as the Berlin

Wall was torn down, seemed like the answer to the pope's prayer.

The Ukrainian Catholic Church, brutally suppressed by Stalin in 1946, emerged from the underground after 1989 with four million adherents and recovered more than three thousand churches and other properties. Gorbachev's successor, Boris Yeltsin, was able to overcome the coup of August 1991 thanks in part to the shortwave transmitter of Radio Blagovest, a Moscow-based Catholic radio station.

These dramatic events confirmed John Paul's sense of providential purpose. The failed assassination attempt on May 13, 1981, seemed to be further evidence that he was right. John Paul forgave his assailant, Mehemet Ali Agca, in prison.

In December 1991 John Paul held a Roman synod to celebrate the Church's victory over what he called "the greatest attempt to destroy Christianity since the Roman Emperor Diocletian." Monstrous tyranny had been overcome by nonviolent means. The Soviet empire was the first in history to fall to spiritual power.

But to pursue this grandiose vision, the rest of the Church had to be in disciplined good order. John Paul had a different agenda from that of the Western Church. Debates about the ordination of married men or of women or about contraception and sexual

Pope John Paul II, the first Slav ever elected to the papacy and the most widely traveled pope in history.

morality seemed to him trivial compared with the great cosmic struggle in which he was engaged.

The Pope and the World: The next problem came from Islam, the only other religious force capable of rivaling Christianity. But John Paul II sought cooperation rather than confrontation— hence, his relative indulgence toward Iraq's President Saddam Hussein during the Persian Gulf War of 1991. John Paul refused to see it either as a Muslim *jihad* (Arabic, "holy war") or a Christian crusade. After it was over, he was thanked by the Organization of Muslim States for his evenhandedness.

If John Paul's grand design was to succeed, the place of Israel would have to be assured and the Palestinian problem resolved. John Paul was the first pope to visit the chief synagogue in Rome, where he talked about "Abraham, our father in faith." In 1992 he took the first steps toward the diplomatic recognition of Israel.

After Vatican II many Catholics believed that the papacy would be less monarchical and more collegial in style. John Paul II disappointed this expectation. The Church in his pontificate has become more centralized, not less so. The appointment of bishops has been tightly controlled. In Austria, Switzerland, Brazil, and elsewhere, "unpopular" bishops have been appointed. Right-wing movements like Opus Dei and Communion and Liberation (*Comunione e Liberazione*) have been encouraged.

These moves have been based on an analysis of the state of the postconciliar Church, which John Paul believed was undergoing a crisis of identity. Ecumenism had blunted the edges of Catholic identity: the remedy was to stress those things that divided Catholics from other Christians—papal infallibility, Mariology, defense of Paul VI's encyclical on birth control (*Humanae Vitae*), and the presentation of homosexuality as a "disorder." Priestly identity was also reasserted: the Catholic priest was to be celibate for life, dressed in clericals, spiritual, and "above" or at any rate "out of" politics. Nuns were to resume wearing their habits. Theologians were to be docile and not raise awkward questions.

John Paul has carried these policies around the world in the more than one hundred twenty countries to which he has gone "on pilgrimage." This wholly unprecedented papal jet-travel has been the most striking external feature of his papacy, and the sight of him kissing the tarmac at airports has become familiar on television. The effects of the papal visits has depended entirely on the local situation.

On his travels, John Paul has shown his mistrust of liberation theology. Two documents in 1984 and 1985 from Cardinal Joseph Ratzinger, prefect of the Congregation for the Doctrine of the Faith, the Vatican doctrinal watchdog, left no doubt that the pope believed liberation theology was tainted with Marxism. Yet John Paul admitted, in a 1986 letter to the Brazilian bishops, that once purified of Marxism, it could be "legitimate and necessary."

The general public was overawed by the pope's superstar quality. His visit to Britain in May-June 1982 was a triumph. John Paul walked up the aisle of Canterbury Cathedral alongside Dr. Robert Runcie, the Anglican archbishop. It seemed that a new era was dawning in Catholic-Anglican relations, underpinned by the solid theological agreements reached by ARCIC (the Anglican/Roman Catholic International Commission). Yet in December 1991 Cardinal Ratzinger, the head of the powerful Vatican Congregation for the Doctrine of the Faith, gave a negative verdict on the ARCIC agreements and showed no understanding of their method.

On July 15, 1992, Pope John Paul had an operation to remove a benign intestinal tumor. It reduced the intensity of his activity, but he was still able to go to Santo Domingo for the fifth centenary of Columbus' explorations. The question of resignation briefly resurfaced, as it did again in 1994 when he twice fell and broke bones in his arm and leg. But resignation will only happen if John Paul is incapacitated. Otherwise, he is fascinated by the year 2000, when, if he lives, he will be 80. He had declared the 1990s the decade of evangelization. John Paul fulfilled his mission when he said in New York in October 1979: "We are an Easter people, and alleluia is our song."

His major encyclicals include *Laborem Exercens* (1981), *Sollicitudo Rei Socialis* (1988), and *Centesimus Annus* (1991), all on social justice. *See also Centesimus Annus; Laborem Exercens;* Poland, Catholicism in; Ratzinger, Joseph; restorationism; Sollicitudo Rei Socialis.

Bibliography

John Paul II. *Sources of Renewal: The Implementation of Vatican II.* San Francisco: Harper & Row, 1980.

————. *Crossing the Threshold of Hope.* Ed. Vittorio Messori. New York: Knopf, 1994.

Williams, George Huntston. *The Mind of John Paul II: Origins of His Thought and Action.* New York: Seabury Press, 1981.

PETER HEBBLETHWAITE

John the Baptist, St., an eschatological preacher and precursor of Jesus. According to Luke 1:5–80, John, a cousin of Jesus, was of priestly descent, son of Zechariah and Elizabeth. Luke 3:1 reports that in the fifteenth year of Tiberius (A.D. 28), John

John the Baptist, wearing "clothing of camel's hair with a leather belt around his waist," prepared "the way of Lord" and made "his paths straight" (Matt 3:3–4); painting by Luca Signorelli (d. 1523).

emerged preaching repentance and practicing baptism. Matt 3:7–10 and Luke 3:7–9 record John's diatribes against sinners. All the Gospels (Matt 3:11–12; Mark 1:7–8; Luke 3:15–18; John 1:24–28) report John's proclamation of a stronger one to come. The synoptic Gospels report that Jesus was baptized by John. John was executed by Herod Antipas, ruler of Galilee, because of his prophetic denunciation of the ruler's morals (Matt 14:3–12; Mark 6:17–29; Luke 3:19–20). The Jewish historian Josephus (*Antiquities* 18.5.2) generally confirms the data about John's message and martyrdom.

Traditions in the Gospels contrast the ministries of John and Jesus. John insisted on ascetical practice (Matt 3:4; Mark 1:6), while Jesus was more lenient (Mark 2:18; Matt 11:16–19). Jesus apparently respected John (Matt 11:11; Luke 7:28), applied Mal 3:1 to him (Matt 11:10; Luke 7:27), and explicitly identified him as Elijah (Matt 11:14; Mark 9:11–13).

Followers of John constituted a community after his death that in some areas rivaled early Christians (Acts 18:25; 19:1–7). John is the patron saint of monks. Feast day: June 24.

John the Evangelist, St. [son of Zebedee], one of the twelve apostles and traditional author of the Fourth Gospel. With his brother James he was a fisherman who was among Jesus' first disciples (Matt 4:21; Mark 1:19; Luke 5:10). According to Mark 3:17, Jesus gave John and James the nickname "sons of thunder." In the synoptic Gospels John, along with his brother and Simon Peter, are among Jesus' closest followers. They accompanied Jesus at the raising of the daughter of Jairus (Mark 5:37; Luke 8:51) and at the Transfiguration (Matt 17:1; Mark 9:2; Luke 9:28). They questioned Jesus about the end time (Mark 13:3) and failed him in Gethsemane (Matt 26:37; Mark 14:33). John and James asked Jesus whether to call down fire on Samaritans who rejected him (Luke 9:53), and requested seats of honor on his right and left when he would come in royal glory (Mark 10:35–37; but Matt 20:20–21 attributes the request to their mother). John reported to Jesus the disciples' rebuke of an exorcist who used Jesus' name (Mark 9:38; Luke 9:49). In Luke 22:8 he went with Peter to prepare the Passover supper.

John played a leading role in the first Christian community in Jerusalem, as Paul attests (Gal 2:9). He is listed in Acts as second to Peter among the disciples in the upper room (Acts 1:13). He accompanied Peter to preach in the Temple, where the two were arrested (Acts 3–4). John traveled with Peter to Samaria to examine the new converts there (Acts 8:14–25).

Writings: John is traditionally associated with five books of the NT. He is often identified as the Beloved Disciple of the Fourth Gospel (John 13:23; 19:26; 20:2; 21:7, 20), but the identification is not explicit and remains uncertain. A John wrote the book of Revelation from the island of Patmos (Rev 1:4, 9). He is identified with John the Apostle as early as Justin Martyr (*Dialogue with Trypho* 81), but he seems to view the twelve apostles as a distinct group of the past (Rev 21:14). 1 John 1:1–5 implies that its author was an eyewitness of Jesus, but the author remains anonymous. 2–3 John were written by an "elder" who enjoyed some status, but he is also anonymous.

These attributions were debated even in the early Church. A Roman presbyter named Gaius and a group called the Alogoi denied the authorship of the Fourth Gospel by John (Irenaeus *Against Heresies* 3.11.9). Dionysius of Alexandria in the third century disputed the authorship of Revelation (Eusebius *Ecclesiastical History* 7.25.1–27).

Activities: The NT reports the martyrdom of James (Acts 12:2), but says nothing of John's death, (unless one accepts the identification with the Beloved Disciple, whose death is implied in John

John the Evangelist, traditionally regarded as the author of the Fourth Gospel, holds his Gospel showing its opening words (in Latin), "In the beginning was the Word"; above his head is his symbol, the eagle; ninth-century Carolingian ivory plaque, Metropolitan Museum of Art, New York.

21:23). Two sources of the eighth and ninth centuries (George Hamartolos; the epitome of the *Chronicle* of Philip of Side) report that both James and John died as martyrs, but this may be an inference from Mark 10:39.

Second-century traditions record activity of John at Ephesus in Asia Minor. Irenaeus, writing around 185 (*Against Heresies* 3.3.4; 5.33.4; also in Eusebius, *Eccl. Hist.* 5.20.5), reports the testimony of Polycarp and Papias, elders prominent in the early second century. Polycrates of Ephesus (in Eusebius *Eccl. Hist.* 5.24.3) also reports that John was there as "a priest, wearing the sacerdotal plate." Eusebius records other traditions to the same effect (*Eccl. Hist.* 3.18.1; 3.20.9; 3.23.4; 5.18.14). It is possible that some traditions may have confused John the

Apostle with an "elder John" active in Asia Minor in the late first or early second century according to Papias (Eusebius *Eccl. Hist.* 3.39.4).

Tertullian (*On the Proscription of Heretics* 36), at the end of the second century, reports that John went to Rome in the time of Domitian (A.D. 81–96) where he was dipped unscathed into boiling oil.

Several groups later declared to be heretical claimed the legacy of John. Christians with extreme ascetical or "encratite" tendencies composed the *Acts of John* around A.D. 200. These reported on John's activity in Ephesus and his peaceful death. Gnostics and Manichaeans appropriated and modified this work. Gnostics also composed the *Apocryphon of John,* a dialogue of the risen Jesus with his disciples in which he reveals cosmic mysteries.

John is often represented with an eagle, symbolizing the etherial quality of his Gospel. Feast day: December 27. *See also* apostle; evangelist; Twelve, the.

HAROLD W. ATTRIDGE

John Vianney, St. *See* Curé d'Ars.

Jordan River, a river that runs from the Hermon range, north of the Sea of Galilee, down the Rift Valley and into the Dead Sea. It traverses a length of more than two hundred miles. It formed the eastern boundary of the promised land and features prominently in the story of the conquest of the land by Joshua and many other incidents in the OT. For Christians its primary association is with the preaching of John the Baptist and the baptism of Jesus.

Josaphat Kuncevych, St. (joh-sah-faht' koon-say'vich), 1580–1623, bishop-martyr, the first Eastern saint to be formally canonized by the Catholic Church. Born in Volodymyr Volyns'kyj in Ukraine, in 1604 he entered the Holy Trinity monastery in Vilnius, where he led a life of deep prayer and asceticism. Named archbishop of Polock (Polotsk) in 1617, he was tireless in preaching and in promoting adherence to the Union of Brest, which concluded in 1596 when some of the Ruthenian hierarchy and faithful entered into union with Rome. He was killed by opponents of the Union of the Ukrainian-Belorussian Church with Rome. He was beatified in 1643 and canonized in 1867. Feast day: November 12.

Joseph, St., husband of Mary, the mother of Jesus. In the NT Joseph is mentioned as the father of Jesus

Joseph, the husband of the Blessed Virgin Mary and the foster father of Jesus, shown here in his carpenter's workshop surrounded by the tools of his trade; fifteenth-century Flemish painting by Robert Campin, Metropolitan Museum of Art, New York.

in John 1:45 and 6:42, in Luke 4:22, and in Luke's genealogy of Jesus (Luke 3:23). Otherwise he appears only in the infancy narratives of Matt 1–2 and Luke 1–2. Both (Matt 1:2–16, 20; Luke 1:27; 3:23–38) report that he was of Davidic descent. Luke indicates that, although his native town was Bethlehem, he and Mary lived in Nazareth. They returned to Bethelem to register for a census (Luke 2:1). Matthew suggests that they lived in Bethlehem and only moved to Nazareth after return from their flight to

Egypt (Matt 2:22–23). Joseph was a carpenter (Matt 13:55), a trade followed by Jesus (Mark 6:3). Joseph disappears from the NT after the holy family's pilgrimage to Jerusalem (Luke 2:42–52), and it is likely that he died before Jesus' public ministry.

Apocryphal works embellish the scriptural details. The second-century *Protevangelium of James* claims that Joseph was an aged widower with children when he married Mary, thus resolving the problem that Jesus' siblings presented for belief in Mary's perpetual virginity. It also relates the miraculous sign by which Joseph was chosen to be Mary's husband. The *Infancy Gospel of Thomas* describes Joseph's difficulties with his precocious son. The fourth-century *History of Joseph the Carpenter* tells of Joseph's death.

Joseph was declared patron saint of the Universal Church by Pope Pius IX. Feast day: March 19; feast of Joseph the Worker: May 1.   *HAROLD W. ATTRIDGE*

Josephinism, an eighteenth-century effort of the Austrian emperors to subordinate the Church to national interests. The name is derived from Joseph II, Holy Roman emperor (1765–90). Under Enlightenment influences that were more extreme than Gallicanism, the Austrian government, beginning with Prince Kauntiz, minister under Maria Theresa (the wife of Emperor Francis I and mother of Joseph II) and becoming more rigorous under Joseph II (d. 1790), instituted a policy of state control of all Church affairs. This policy was in force until 1850, when it was rescinded by Francis Joseph I. Josephinism tolerated other religions, refused to recognize the corporate nature of the clergy, and abrogated the contemplative religious orders. Under this policy, the state effected certain reforms of ecclesiastical abuses and bettered the support of the clergy, but many spiritual and pastoral goals of the Church were frustrated. *See also* Austria, Catholicism in; Church and state; Gallicanism.

Josephite Fathers and Brothers, St. Joseph's Society of the Sacred Heart (S.S.J.), an American religious congregation of priests and brothers dedicated to developing leadership in the African-American community. Founded in England in 1866 by Cardinal Herbert Vaughan (d. 1903), the Josephites were established in Baltimore in 1893 by five men who had belonged to an English missionary group. Joseph R. Slattery is credited as the founder. The original group included Charles R. Uncles (1859–1933), the first African-American man

trained and ordained in the United States (ordained in 1891). They work primarily in the southern states of the United States, in rural and inner city parishes and other specialized ministries. In 1992 the membership included 160 priests and 12 brothers.

Joseph of Arimathea (air-uh-muh-thee'uh), a wealthy councillor responsible for Jesus' burial. In all four Gospels (Matt 27:57; Mark 15:43; Luke 23:50–51; John 19:38), Joseph asks Pilate for Jesus' body, which he places in a new rock tomb. Matthew and John make him a disciple. Mark and Luke simply say that he awaited the kingdom of God.

Joseph of Cupertino, St., 1603–63, Franciscan known as the "Flying Friar." An ecstatic, Joseph was famous for levitating during Mass or at other times of great devotion, once in front of Pope Urban VIII. An embarrassment during his lifetime, he was canonized in 1767. Feast day: September 18 (no longer observed).

journal, spiritual, a daily record or timely account of important events in one's spiritual life, especially experiences that mark progress in one's quest for deeper union with God. Journal writing is practically as old as Christianity itself. Augustine's *Confessions* exemplifies this practice. In modern times, some secular writers like Ira Progoff, who developed the "intensive journal method" in 1966, have explored new approaches to keeping spiritual journals. The value of a journal lies in the prayerful and disciplined self-reflection required for its composition and its use for those under spiritual direction.

journalism. *See* Catholicism and journalism.

Journet, Charles (shahr zhoor-nay'), 1891–1975, Swiss theologian and cardinal. His greatest contribution to theology was a massive four-volume study in ecclesiology, *The Church of the Word Incarnate*, a theological consideration of the Church analyzed according to the categories of Aristotelian causality: material, formal, efficient, and final.

Journet Ibars, St. Teresa [of Jesus], 1843–97, Spanish-born founder of the Little Sisters of the Abandoned Aged, a community devoted to the service of the elderly poor. Feast day: August 26.

Jovinian, d. ca. 406, Milanese monk and antiascetic teacher condemned by Jerome, Pelagius, Augustine, Ambrose, Pope Siricius, and the emperor Honorius, who exiled him in 398. Deferring to the grace of baptism, equal in all, he denied that virginity was a state intrinsically higher than marriage and that eschatological rewards were arranged hierarchically according to states in life (e.g., virgin, widow, wife); and he denied Mary's perpetual virginity. *See also* virginity; virginity of Mary.

Joyful Mysteries of the Rosary. *See* Mysteries of the Rosary.

Jubilee, a Catholic journal that emphasized aesthetics and spirituality. From 1953 to 1968 its pages introduced U.S. Catholics to progressive movements in Europe, brought access to modern tastes in liturgical art, and emphasized monastic and lay movements. It prepared many readers for the changes of Vatican II (1962–65) and furthered the liberal inclinations of Catholics after World War II.

Jubilee, Year of, every fiftieth year, in which, according to Jewish law, the land was to lie fallow, mortgage debts remitted, and slaves freed. The theological meaning of the jubilee was that all life and land belongs to God. The term "jubilee" has been used in Catholicism since 1300 in connection with the Holy Year, a year in which the pope grants special spiritual benefits (indulgences) for those who make a pilgrimage to Rome and perform other religious acts. *See also* Holy Year.

J.U.D., *Juris Utrius Doctor* (Lat.), Doctor of Both Laws, academic degree that attests to knowledge of both canon and civil law.

Judaism, the religious perspectives, practices, and way of life of the Jewish people over the centuries. It is not a biblical or Talmudic term, but appears first as a Greek term, *Judaismes,* in 2 Macc 2:21, 8:1; 14:38, where it represents that which Jews "remained faithful to" as opposed to adopting Hellenistic practices and beliefs. Similarly, Paul uses it to speak of his "former way of life in Judaism" (in which he felt he excelled) before he joined the Church (Gal. 1:13–14).

Biblical and Rabbinic Traditions: The Greek term, *Judaismes,* finds no Hebrew equivalent in either biblical or rabbinic literature. It was not until the medieval period (e.g., Ibn Ezra's twelfth-century commentary on Deut 21:13) that the Hebrew term,

Yahadut, appeared. It is this term that is most frequently used today in Hebrew. Perhaps the most correct Jewish term to describe the body of Jewish teachings is *Torah* ("teaching"), derived from the term for the Pentateuch but extended over time to include later commentaries and rulings as well.

While "Judaism" has a philosophical nuance, "Torah" carries the divine, revelatory connotations of Jewish tradition. Jewish sacred history, according to the Torah, begins with God's call to Abram (Gen 12) and covenant with Abraham and Sarah's descendants (Gen 17). The beginnings of this sacred history and the terms of God's subsequent covenants with God's people, Israel, are contained in the Hebrew Bible, which Christians call Old Testament but which Jews call *Tanakh,* after its major portions: *Torah* (the Pentateuch), *Nebi'im* (Prophets), and *Kethubim* (Writings). Jews read the entire Pentateuch plus selections from the Prophets each year during synagogue services.

For Jews, the biblical period closed with the last of the minor prophets, and the ancient sacrificial rites ceased with the destruction of the Jerusalem Temple by the Romans in A.D. 70. In place of the latter, there arose the practice of prayer, study and *mitzvoth,* obligatory religious deeds based upon interpretations of biblical commandments, such as the observance of food purity or *kashruth* laws, or deeds of charity.

After the Jews were driven by Roman armies from the land of Israel, Jewish teachers ("rabbis") continued to debate the application of the *mitzvoth* to the daily life of the Jewish people, in the process infusing even the most commonplace activities (such as eating and resting) with sacred significance. In this way, Judaism developed as a tradition in which the home became the Temple on the Sabbath, and the dinner table the Holy of Holies of the Temple. The literature of the rabbinic debates, set down over some six hundred years beginning with the *Mishnah* at the end of the second century, came to be known as the *Talmud,* which exists in two major forms, that of Babylon (the *Bavli*) and that of Jerusalem (*Yerushalmi*).

Over the centuries many attempts have been made to define the essence of Judaism. Talmud *Bavli* (*Šabb.* 31a) recounts the response of the Pharisee Hillel to the challenge of a heathen to teach him the Torah while standing on one leg. "What is hateful to you do not do unto your neighbor," Hillel replied. "That is the whole of the Torah. The rest is commentary: Go and study" (see Tob 4:15; Matt 7:12; Luke

6:31). Jesus' answer (Mark 12:29–31) to the same question first evokes a central Jewish prayer, the Shema (Deut 6), and adds to it the climactic verse of the covenant laws of Lev 19, thus linking love of God to love of neighbor in classically Jewish fashion.

While rabbinic tradition is much more concerned (as is Sacred Scripture) with meaningful narrative (*haggadah,* Heb., stories and sayings) and prescriptive practice derived from covenantal law (*halakah,* Heb., "the Way") than with attempts to develop systematic doctrine, there exists a rich literature of philosophical theology in response to Greek, Roman, Christian, Persian, Muslim, and other intellectual challenges as well. Writing in the twelfth century in a Muslim-dominated environment but with Christianity also evidently in mind, Moses Maimonides drew up thirteen basic principles of Jewish faith, a listing recited by Orthodox Jews to this day. Consideration of this list provides insights into the commonalities of the Jewish and Catholic traditions and into the difference between the deepest beliefs of the two ancient faith communities.

Maimonides's thirteen principles can be abbreviated as belief in God's (1) existence, (2) unity, (3) incorporeality, and (4) eternality; (5) belief that God alone is to be worshiped; (6) belief in prophecy and (7) that Moses is the greatest of the prophets; belief that the Torah is (8) divine and (9) unchanging; belief that God (10) knows the thoughts and deeds of every person and (11) will reward goodness and punish evil; and belief (faith, trust) in (12) the coming of the Messiah and (13) the resurrection of the dead.

Again, Maimonides's awareness of the looming presence of Judaism's sibling Abrahamic faiths, Christianity and Islam, historically if not religiously, is close to the surface here. One does not know how much emphasis Maimonides would have placed on God's incorporeality or Moses' greatness as a prophet, without the Christian claim of Incarnation, on the one hand, or the Muslim claim about Muhammad as the "seal of the prophets," on the other. But it is a question worth pursuing.

Communal and Prayer Life: Communal and prayer life in Judaism, as indicated above, have developed around two major Jewish institutions. One is the home and the other is the synagogue (gathering place for joint worship, Torah study, and community services such as burial societies). Indeed, so important is the study of the *mitzvoth* that popular alternate names for synagogues have been such terms as the Hebrew *beth ha midrash*

(house of study) and the Yiddish *schul* (Old German, "school"). Synagogue worship features elements quite familiar to Catholics: readings from Scripture alternating with prayers (often psalms), commentaries on Scripture, prescribed gestures, and a hymnody similar to Gregorian chant.

There is, however, no festival meal in the synagogue service (though some congregations do one as a matter of convenience for their members today) or altar table there. The table at which the Sabbath meal is celebrated weekly and the Passover (Heb., *pesach*) meal is celebrated annually is in the Jewish home, which for this sacred time becomes a renewal site of the Exodus and a foretaste of the *olam ha ba* (Heb., "the world to come"). Jewish ritual celebrates God in song and word as Lord of creation and of sacred history. Over the centuries it has adapted itself to the particular needs of the people. While maintaining a sense of continuity with the ritual of biblical Israel, Jewish ritual has been able to interpret and reinterpret Jewish historical circumstances, whether joyful or tragic, always coming back to praise of the sanctity of God's Name (Heb., *Qadosh/Kiddush ha Shem*). The Christian liturgical cycle is based upon that of the Jewish people, with Easter/*Pesach* and Pentecost/*Shavuoth* the most obvious examples of the historical linkage.

Just as Christian liturgy has developed over the centuries, so has Jewish liturgy. The Jewish liturgical cycle of feasts praises God at once for God's gracious deeds of salvation in history (e.g., freedom from slavery in Egypt, the free gift of God's Torah) and for the passage of the seasons. The autumn, for example, sees the High Holy Days of *Rosh Hashana* and *Yom Kippur,* respectively, New Year and Day of Atonement. Marked by fasting and a sense of penitence, these feasts focus on the final judgment and require reconciliation. They are followed by the lesser, but liturgically rich feasts of *Sukkoth* (Tabernacles, Booths—an agricultural celebration of the harvest and a time of covenant-renewal for Jews) and *Simchat Torah* ("Rejoicing of the Torah," which celebrates the conclusion of reading the entire Pentateuch and beginning again with Genesis). The latter festival is marked by dancing with the Torah scrolls in joyful celebration—hardly the "burden of the law" image that Christianity has had of Judaism over the centuries. Also joyful is *Purim,* which comes in February or March. Like *Hanukkah,* which celebrates the victory of the Maccabees and rededication of the Jerusalem Temple in 165 B.C., *Purim* joyfully celebrates the deliverance of the Jewish people, this time from a threatened massacre by the Persians through the intervention of Esther. On the other hand, "The Ninth of Av" commemorates the destruction of the Temple and subsequent Jewish tragedies, such as the expulsion from Spain in 1492, while the more recent holy day *Yom Hashoah* memorializes the victims of the Nazi Holocaust.

Over the centuries, Judaism has developed rich mystical and spiritual traditions alongside its more philosophical and *halakic* traditions. These are embodied in such medieval classics as the *Zohar* (Heb., "book of splendor") and popular religious movements such as that of the *Hasidim* (Heb., "the pious ones"), which originated in Eastern Europe in the sixteenth century.

Twentieth-Century Judaism: Modern Judaism, like modern Christianity, reflects a range of responses to the challenges of the Enlightenment and of its own internal reforming movements. In the United States today, the major branches are Reform, which, put simply, translated the liturgy into the vernacular and relativized many of the ancient *halakah* of Israel to the options of the individual; Conservative, which represents a movement away from Reform and back toward traditional Orthodox practice. It has been argued that modern Orthodoxy, developing in reaction to the former two movements, may be more strict than its medieval counterpart. Each grouping, of course, has subgroups, so that some Conservative congregations are virtually Orthodox in practice while others tend toward the Reform. None of these three major movements are by any means static. Many Reform Jewish congregations today use more Hebrew in their worship than earlier Reform congregations would have allowed, while among the Orthodox there are those who are varyingly open to considering "modern" or contemporary ideas, such as dialogue with Christians and non-Orthodox Jews.

Likewise, there are various other distinct groups, ranging from those who have little or no synagogue affiliation of any sort ("secular" Jews) but who do identify closely with the Jewish community and base their lives on Jewish moral values, to those such as some of the contemporary Hasidim who have little to do with any other Jews, including the Orthodox. A very influential subgroup in the larger community may be found among Reconstructionist Jews, an offshoot of Conservative Judaism which has few congregations, but whose thinking has influenced many rabbis within both Reform and Conservative Judaism.

Critical to any understanding of contemporary Judaism must be an awareness of the influence on Jewish identity and spirituality of the Holocaust (*Shoah*) and the rebirth of a Jewish State in the land of Israel after a hiatus of almost two millennia. With the possible exception of the writing of the Talmud and the expulsion of the Jews from Spain in 1492, no historical events of Jewish history since the close of the biblical period have ever had as profound an impact on Jewish beliefs and practice as these two events of the twentieth century.

It is far too early to predict how the Judaism(s) of the twenty-first century and beyond will incorporate these new realities into the sacred history of the people Israel. But that incorporation will be of more than academic interest to the development of Catholicism, which has, by definition, always been interwoven with the fate of God's people Israel, with whom Christians are adopted heirs (Rom 8:12–17; Gal 4:1–7) and with whom, in the words of the Second Vatican Council (1962–65), Catholics share an unbreakable "spiritual bond" (Declaration on the Relationship of the Church to Non-Christian Religions, n. 4). *See also* Jews, Catholicism and.

Bibliography

Fisher, Eugene, ed. *The Jewish Roots of Christian Liturgy.* Mahwah, NJ: Paulist Press, 1990.

Flannery, Edward. *The Anguish of the Jews.* Mahwah, NJ: Paulist Press, 1985.

Greenberg, Irving. *The Jewish Way: Living the Holidays.* New York: Summit Books, 1988.

Heschel, Abraham Joshua. *Israel: An Echo of Eternity.* New York: Farrar, Straus & Giroux, 1969.

Strack, H. L., and G. Stemberger. *Introduction to the Talmud and Midrash.* Edinburgh, Scotland: T. & T. Clark, 1991.

Wylen, Stephen M. *Settings of Silver: An Introduction to Judaism.* Mahwah, NJ: Paulist Press, 1989.   EUGENE J. FISHER

Judas Iscariot, treasurer of the twelve apostles (John 13:29), the one who betrayed Jesus. His name in Hebrew probably means "man from Kerioth." For unclear motives, he betrayed Jesus for thirty pieces of silver (Matt 26:14–16; Mark 14:10–11; Luke 22:3–6; John 13:2, 27). His death has been described either as a suicide (Matt 27:5) or an accident (Acts 1:18). *See also* Twelve, the.

Judas Maccabeus (joo'duhs mak-uh-beh'uhs), leader of the second-century Jewish revolt against Greek domination. 1–2 Maccabees depict the struggle for religious freedom against King Antiochus. Hanukkah commemorates its success.

Jude, St., one of the twelve apostles. There are only

three brief mentions of an apostle named Jude in the NT. Luke 6:16 and Acts 1:13 speak of "Jude, son of James," and John 14:22 notes that "Judas, not the Iscariot" asked Jesus a question. Curiously two lists of apostles do not contain Jude but mention a certain Thaddaeus (Mark 3:16–17; Matt 10:2–4). These few texts imply that Jude was an obscure figure who is mentioned eleventh in the list of apostles and easily confused with a host of better-known persons also named Jude. Hence, Jude the apostle is often twinned in legends with one or another of these Judes. There is a Jude, an ancestor of Jesus (Luke 3:30), a Galilean revolutionary (Acts 5:37), the owner of a house where Paul stayed (Acts 9:11), an emissary to Antioch (Acts 15:22), the brother of Jesus (Mark 6:3), and finally the apostle. Sometimes Jude the apostle is thought to have a double name, Jude Thaddaeus, because Thaddaeus replaces Jude in the apostolic lists in Mark and Matthew. Sometimes he is confused with Jude, brother of the Lord, and stories about that Jude attach themselves to the apostle. But we have no reliable information about this obscure figure. Ancient legends mention his work in Mesopotamia and Persia; in the liturgy he is paired with Simon. Only in this century has Jude become the object of a popular devotion as a patron and helper of hopeless causes. Feast day (with Simon): October 28. *See also* apostle; Twelve, the.

JEROME NEYREY

Jude [brother of Jesus], name included in Mark's list of the four brothers of Jesus (6:3; see Matt 13:55). He is presumably included among the "the brothers of the Lord" who gathered with the eleven apostles and Mary after the Lord's Ascension (Acts 1:14). Thus he is presented not as an unbeliever (Mark 3:31; John 7:3–5), but as a disciple of his brother Jesus. The Letter of Jude is written by a certain "Jude, servant of Jesus and brother of James" (v. 1). Scholars identify the author as Jude, brother of Jesus. Nevertheless, this seems to be a pseudonymous attribution, for the author of that document is considered a scribe with considerable Greek language skills and wide knowledge of esoteric Jewish writings, skills unthinkable for an artisan in a peasant village. But the early Church thought highly enough of Jesus' two brothers, Jude and James, to consider them proper and likely authors of authoritative letters. Some traditions from eastern Syria near Edessa (the *Gospel of Thomas,* the *Acts of Thomas*) identify Jude with the apostle Thomas, also known as Judas Thomas. Since Thomas is a twin

("Didymus," John 14:22), he would presumably be Jesus' twin brother. But this late and quite local tradition is improbable for the historical identity of Jude. Finally, Eusebius records an account about Jude's grandsons, who were taken before the emperor Domitian: "There still survived of the family of the Lord grandsons of Jude, who was said to have been his brother according to the flesh, and they were delated as being of the family of David.... But when they were released they were the leaders of the churches, both for their testimony and for their relation to the Lord" (*Ecclesiastical History* 3.20.1, 6). *See also* brothers of Jesus. JEROME NEYREY

judge, canonical, qualified cleric or, if permitted by the conference of bishops, a layperson appointed by the diocesan bishop to serve for a definite time period adjudicating trials in the Church's judicial system. Judges must have an unimpaired reputation and at least a canonical licentiate (J.C.L.). Laypersons may only serve, when necessary, on a collegiate (three- or five-judge) tribunal. *See also* tribunal.

judgment, general, the doctrine that God, in the person of Jesus Christ, will pronounce a definitive judgment upon the moral quality of each person's life at the Second Coming (Gk., *Parousia*). In Christian eschatology, this doctrine of a general judgment has an important place because of its relationship to the Second Coming and the general resurrection of all the dead.

The background for the Christian doctrine of a general judgment developed from antecedent ideas in the OT (e.g., 4 Ezra) and the NT (e.g., Rom 2:5–13; 1 Cor 3:11–15). Both Greek anthropology, with its insistence upon the immortality of the human soul, and the Jewish theology of eschatological judgment have contributed to the historical development of the doctrine. Thus the tension between the Jewish interest in a collective judgment and the Greek concern for the fate of the individual soul led to the later Christian doctrine of a dual judgment, a general and a particular judgment.

The notion of a collective judgment pronounced by Jesus Christ at the end of time is found from the second century A.D. onward in all versions of the earliest creeds. In such creedal statements the concept of a final judgment is exclusively related to the idea of a collective or general judgment. The idea of a particular judgment, while implicit in many Scriptural texts and early conciliar teachings, did not have the character of an explicit Christian teaching until quite late in the medieval period (*Benedictus Deus*, 1336). *See also* eschatology universal; judgment, particular; last things.   DONAL LEADER

judgment, particular, divine judgment of the moral character of a person's life rendered immediately following death. According to Christian eschatology, God assigns the person to heaven, hell, or purgatory on the basis of this judgment.

Though the notion of a general judgment reflects an OT eschatology that looks to a future divine judgment of peoples and nations, the Christian theological concept of a particular judgment reflects the interest in the fate of the individual soul after death found in Greek anthropology. Both Justin (d. ca. 165) and Irenaeus (d. ca. 200) argued for some kind of judgment occuring immediately after death. Yet for much of the Church's history, the notion of a particular judgment remained vague. Disputes between the Latin and Greek churches, however, gave impetus to the theological discussion of the question. In the Second Council of Lyons (1274), the doctrine of a particular judgment is implied, though not stated. Pope Benedict XII in the decree *Benedictus Deus* (1336) affirmed that persons who die are immediately assigned to heaven, hell, or purgatory. This traditional teaching concerning the particular judgment has been affirmed by Vatican II (Pastoral Constitution on the Church in the Modern World, n. 17). Contemporary theologians stress the anthropological character of the notion of a particular judgment so that it is understood as the final realization of the fundamental ethical option of a person made during life on earth. Thus, the notions of a general and a particular judgment together show the relationship between moral action on earth and the finality of human existence beyond death. *See also* eschatology universal; judgment, general; last things.

judicial vicar, qualified priest appointed by the diocesan bishop to judge cases in his name. Introduced in the 1983 code of canon law as a title interchangeable with the traditional Latin *officialis*, it illustrates the vicarious nature of the ordinary (nondelegated) judicial power through which his vicar constitutes one tribunal with the bishop.

Jugan, Bl. Jeanne, 1792–1879, founder of the Little Sisters of the Poor. In 1845 she received an award from the French Academy for her work in ministering to the poor. Feast day: August 30. *See also* Little Sisters of the Poor.

Julian of Norwich, Bl., ca. 1342–ca. 1420, English mystic. She lived a life of solitude as an anchoress in a cell attached to the Church of St. Edmund and St. Julian in Norwich, East Anglia. At the age of thirty, and seemingly near death due to illness, she received sixteen mystical visions on the Passion of Christ and the Trinity (described in her *Book of Showings,* also known as the *Revelations of Divine Love*), on the love of God, the Incarnation, redemption, sin, penance, and divine consolation.

Through the development of images of the Creator as father and mother, of Jesus as brother, savior, and mother, and of the Spirit as spouse, Julian faced the reality of sin, the struggle between good and evil, and the mercy of God, particularly experienced in the Church's sacramental celebrations. Julian created a unique language combining special words and images to develop her mystical doctrines. Her work was influenced by the English mystic Walter Hilton (d. 1396) and the anonymously written *The Cloud of Unknowing*.

At the time of her death her reputation for sanctity was already widespread. Visitors from all over Europe were attracted to her monastic cell. Although she is popularly called "Blessed," there has never been any formal ecclesiastical confirmation of this title. However, those devoted to her memory and example observe May 13 as her feast day. *See also* anchorite, anchoress; *Cloud of Unknowing, The;* English Mystics; Hilton, Walter.

Julian the Apostate, ca. 331–63, emperor. With his family eliminated by internecine quarrels, this nephew of Constantine was raised under Christian influence but repudiated it in favor of a Neoplatonic paganism of sacrifice and austerity. In his two-year reign he rescinded laws supporting the Church or taking sides in Christian quarrels, restricted teaching of classical literature to those believing in its gods, and planned the rebuilding of the Jerusalem Temple, whose destruction some Christians had seen as a sign of their supersession of Judaism.

Julius I, St., d. 352, pope from 337 to 352 and defender of Nicene orthodoxy. Julius sheltered Athanasius (339) and convened a council of over fifty bishops at Rome that declared Athanasius the rightful bishop of Alexandria (341). The Council of Sardica (343) approved the right of bishops condemned by local councils to appeal to Julius as Bishop of Rome. Feast day: April 12. *See also* Athanasius, St.; Nicaea, First Council of.

Julius II [Giuliano della Rovere], 1443–1513, pope from 1503 to 1513. He benefited from the nepotism of his uncle, Pope Sixtus IV, and later acquired the papacy through diplomatic skill and bribery. Notorious for extending papal temporal authority through warfare, he also liberated Italy from foreign domination, for which subsequent generations of Italians were grateful. He was a renowned Renaissance patron of Michelangelo, Raphael, and Bramante, and commissioned Bramante to prepare plans for the new St. Peter's and assisted at the laying of the cornerstone in 1506. He decided to finance the building through the "sale" of indulgences, which Martin Luther challenged.

Jung, Carl Gustav, 1875–1961, Swiss psychologist. Concerned with religious questions from youth, Jung chose medicine over the ministry and pursued psychological studies under E. Bleuler and Sigmund Freud. Eschewing Freud's foundation of neurosis solely in sexuality, Jung emphasized the symbolic, clusters of (complex) associations, psychological types, forms of the subconscious, and archetypes. All of this made him sympathetic to religion. In the liturgy, symbols, and saints (particularly Mary) and the demonic, he found forms of the collective (religious) unconscious of humanity; there, too, the Trinity was complemented by Mary or the Devil (a quaternity), and the shadow competed for attention in the formation of identity. In contrast to Freud's dismissal of religion, Jung found sympathetic interest among Catholics whose basic view of nature and grace was receptive to the role of psychology in theology. The English Dominican Victor White (d. 1960) pioneered the work of relating the psychological dimension to Catholic life, and this direction has continued in the work of Ira Progoff (a proponent of journal-writing) and in studies of Jung and mystics like Meister Eckhart and Teresa of Ávila.

Jungmann, Joseph Andrew (yoong' mahn), 1889–1975, Austrian Jesuit priest and liturgical and catechetical scholar. Ordained in 1913, he served as professor of pastoral theology at Innsbruck University, Austria, 1925–75, where he edited the theological journal *Zeitschrift für Katholische Theologie*. Author of many books and articles on the history of liturgy and catechetics, he is best known for his two-volume *The Mass of the Roman Rite: Its Origins and Development* (1949).

Junipero Serra, Bl. *See* Serra, Bl. Junipero.

juridical person, an artificial entity distinct from the human persons who form it, manage its affairs, or benefit from its activity. Created by ecclesiastical authority, a juridical person is the equivalent in canon law to a corporation. It is established for an apostolic purpose, with the capacity for continuous existence, and with rights of its own to acquire property, enter into contracts, and sue or be sued in Church courts. Some entities (e.g., diocese, parish, religious institute), once formed, are juridical persons as a matter of law; others (e.g., a Catholic hospital or university) may be constituted juridical persons by a decree of ecclesiastical authority (e.g., diocesan bishop, Holy See). Public juridical persons are closely supervised by, and act in the name of, ecclesiastical authority; private juridical persons enjoy considerable autonomy in the management of their affairs.

jurisdiction, the power of governance in the Church. Authority within the Church is exercised in many ways and not all acts that concern the exercise of authority require jurisdiction in the proper sense. Jurisdiction is a technical term describing a particular type of authority necessary for the governance of the Church.

Although there is some current debate whether or not jurisdiction and the power of governance are the same, both the current (1983) and former (1917) codes of canon law equate them (can. 129, 1983; can. 196, 1917). While older canonical theory saw two sources of power in the Church, one stemming from Holy Orders, the other from jurisdiction, current theory, since Vatican II, sees the power of jurisdiction as based in sacramental ordination and activated by being properly chosen for a given office. Laypersons are allowed by present canon law to participate in the exercise of jurisdiction, e.g., one may sit as judge on a three-judge court (the other two judges must be clerics).

Currently the power of governance is classified under the headings of executive, legislative, and judicial. The pope, as successor to Peter and head of the college of bishops, has full jurisdiction in the universal Church, although those who assist him in this governance exercise jurisdiction on a day-to-day basis. Each diocesan bishop has that jurisdiction needed to govern the local church and is assisted by those who exercise that power on a day-to-day basis. Major superiors in pontifical clerical institutes also exercise the power of governance.

Jurisdiction for some acts may be delegated to another priest but there are special rules governing such delegation. Some faculties given, e.g., for the hearing of confessions, were in former law called jurisdiction, but are currently called simply "faculties." *See also* authority.   JOHN F. LAHEY

jus gentium (Lat., "law of nations"), that part of international law that has its basis in the customary behavior of nations rather than written agreement. For instance, many nations recognized the immunity of noncombatants from warfare well before its adoption by the Geneva conventions.

justice ministry. *See* social ministry.

justice, the regulative principle and key, or cardinal, virtue of the social order, directing persons to render each person his or her due. More specifically, justice requires that equals be treated equally and unequals unequally, but in proportion to their relevant differences. Most debates about justice are disagreements about what are the relevant differences between persons.

Christian understandings of justice include this philosophical understanding, but they approach it from within the broader context of one's relationship with the God who frees humankind from sin and then forms a covenant with all people. The U.S. Catholic bishops write, "The quest for justice arises from loving gratitude for the saving acts of God and manifests itself in the wholehearted love of God and neighbor" ("Economic Justice for All," 1986, n. 39). From a Christian perspective, love of God and neighbor enlivens the just community. This is because the acts that God has performed for humankind can never be reciprocated. The only appropriate response on the part of the Christian community is thankfulness. Because the gap between God's acts and human efforts can never be closed, the responsive gratitude is unending, continually revitalizing the just community.

The covenant with God does require specific patterns of behavior between persons in community and between communities. It is at this point that a Christian perspective intersects with a more strictly philosophical approach to justice—Thomas Aquinas understands justice to be "the strong and firm will to give each his due" (*Summa Theologiae*

2–2.58.1)—but without losing the broader context of love of God and neighbor. The necessity of specifying more precisely what constitutes each person's due has led to the elaboration of three primary types of justice: commutative, distributive, and social.

Commutative Justice: Commutative justice requires fairness in agreements and exchanges between persons or groups. Such agreements and exchanges can take place either between owners of capital or between owners and employees. In the first case, commutative justice might lead, for example, to laws against monopolies, which lead to unfair advantages between businesses. In another example, commutative justice is behind requirements for adequate food labeling, so that the consumer knows what she or he is receiving when buying the product.

In the case of relationships between employers and employees the focus of commutative justice is first of all on the just wage. Employers are required to pay their workers a wage sufficient for a life of dignity for the family of the wage earner. Secondly, the employer must provide working conditions adequate to the human dignity of the workers. This includes reasonable safety in the workplace and working hours that allow time for rest and time with family. In return, employees owe their employers diligent and productive work.

Distributive Justice: Distributive justice focuses on the question of the allocation of social resources, wealth, and power. Debates over which persons should receive how much of society's resources are grounded in the problem of justice itself. Equal persons are to be treated equally and unequal persons unequally, but in proportion to their relevant differences. Who is equal, and in what way? In what way are they different that is relevant to differential treatment by society? Three main bases for differential treatment dominate the philosophical literature: arithmetical equality, merit, and need. Different social theories combine these considerations in different ways. Modern Catholic teaching has drawn on all three.

Arithmetical equality, which Aristotle emphasizes, suggests that each person should receive goods from society in arithmetical proportion to what she or he contributes. This concept of distributive justice backs an understanding of the social order as stratified. It is reflected in the encyclical *Rerum Novarum* (1891): "it is not to be supposed that all can contribute in the same way" (n. 27), neither is it supposed that all are to receive from the social order in the same way. Persons receive in proportion to their social station.

Consideration of merit enters into Catholic social teaching in its emphasis that both owners of the means of production and workers contribute to the social order. The key means of recognizing merit in Catholic teaching is the affirmation of the right to private property. Such affirmation allows persons to retain the fruits of their labor.

There has always been an emphasis on human need in Catholic consideration of distributive justice. This is strongly reflected in modern teaching. Even *Rerum Novarum,* with its understanding of society as stratified, states, "Justice demands that the interests of the poorer populations be carefully watched over by the administration" (n. 27). In more recent documents, particularly the social encyclicals of Pope John Paul II, and through the influence of liberation theology, the emphasis on human need has been crystallized in the concept of the "option for the poor."

Social Justice: Modern Catholic social teaching has shifted in the relative weight it gives to each of the considerations of arithmetical equality, merit, and need. In brief, an increased emphasis on need, a developing stress on the right of workers to private property and ownership of the means of production, and more definite criteria for limiting how much property one may own, have led to the virtual disappearance of any emphasis on arithmetical equality. The result is a more egalitarian view of society.

This trend toward egalitarianism coincides with the emergence of the concept of social justice in Catholic teaching. The concept is first mentioned in Pope Pius XI's encyclical, *Quadragesimo Anno* (1931). It accents the point that in a just arrangement all persons are active participants in the institutions that constitute society. As a result, social justice requires recognition of the mutual obligation of individual and society: the individual has an obligation to contribute to society through participation and society has the obligation to order its institutions so that such participation is possible. The primary form of social injustice is the exclusion or marginalization of persons from participation in the life of the society. *See also* Catholic social teachings; social justice.　　　　*TODD D. WHITMORE*

justification, God's gracious act of rendering a sinful human being holy and endowed with grace

(in Catholic and Orthodox doctrines) or as acceptable to God (Lutheran). Justification appears as a central theological theme in Paul's Letters, particularly in Romans and Galatians. Various writings in the NT describe it not only as a favorable juridical declaration by God regarding men and women, but also as an inner presence of the Spirit of Jesus in people following upon their conversion to him (John 14; Rom 8). In the Gospels and the Pauline Letters, the citizen of the reign of God is a member of the household of God, a new creation, one who has passed from death to life. In Catholic doctrine, justification is an event where God in freedom and love brings an individual person into a new relationship and a new form of life that can and will flourish in the present and future reign of God. There is a certain pluralism and complexity in the Catholic understanding of justification because it concerns God's presence and action on earth amid the lives of individuals, and this active presence of God not only brings faith and love but healing and forgiveness for sin.

In medieval theology God's justification concludes with sanctification, the gift of a new life principle, "grace." Against the Reformers' theologies of external imputation, the Council of Trent (1545–63) held that justification is not simply a judicial declaration about someone who remains evil in God's eyes but that, through the merits of Christ, a person is transformed and made holy even as their personal sins and original sin alike are forgiven and removed (although the effects of sin, such as illness, death, and proneness to further sin, remain).

Justification by faith or by works, as well as justification conditioned by finite freedom and by the cooperation of human activity and freedom—these were from the sixteenth through the twentieth centuries dominant topics of theological systems and of arguments between Protestants and Catholics; they were also frequently and bitterly debated between schools and churches within the two groups. Theological discussions within the ecumenical movement since World War I have brought surprising agreement in the theology of justification. We know now that neither Aquinas nor the Council of Trent held for justification initially or mainly by human works, and that Luther himself spoke of an inner change and of a life fruitful in the love of neighbor. Catholicism has in recent decades reemphasized the sovereign plan and activity of God in Church, sacraments, and Christian life; Protestant churches more frequently develop the idea of grace as a principle of

Christian life in individuals, Church, and society. Because this topic ponders the mystery of how God is present in fallen human life, justification remains a fundamental theological issue and is still the central issue underlying differences in the Christian churches. *See also* faith; grace; sanctification.

THOMAS F. O'MEARA

Justin Martyr, St., d. ca. 165., Apologist and martyr. Born at Flavia Neapolis in Palestine, Justin studied with Stoics, Peripatetics (Aristotelians), Pythagoreans, and Platonists, but finally, moved in part by the courage of the martyrs, he embraced Christianity, "the only safe and worthy philosophy." He taught at Ephesus, where ca. 135 he debated Trypho, a Jew (recorded later in *Dialogue with Trypho the Jew*). Moving to Rome, he continued to teach wearing the philosopher's cloak, writing a *First Apology* addressed to Emperor Antoninus Pius (138–61) and a briefer *Second Apology* protesting recent executions. Other writings, now lost, are known by title. Justin was the first Christian to consistently use philosophical categories in elaborating an orthodox doctrine of revelation, admirably balancing the primacy of revelation in Christ with an articulation of a revelation universally present. He understood human reason as a seedlike participation in God's reason or Logos, fully manifest only in Christ. Junius Rusticus (prefect 162–68) had Justin beaten, then beheaded. Feast day: June 1. *See also* Apologists; philosophy and theology.

Justinian, Code of, revision of Roman law published by the emperor Justinian I (483–565) in 529. Together with the *Novellae* (new laws), the *Digest*, and the *Institutes* (passages from classical jurists), it forms the *Corpus Juris Civilis* (Lat., "Body of Civil Law"), which was highly influential in the later development and understanding of canon law. *See also* canon law.

Justinian I, 483–565, Byzantine emperor from 527 to 565, famous for his brilliant achievements on a variety of fronts. He recaptured enough of the Western empire to ensure Roman domination of the Mediterranean. His legal reforms produced codes of legislation (together known as the *Corpus Juris Civilis*) that served the empire until its fall in 1453 and thereafter continued to influence both civil and canon law in the West. Justinian's famous building projects included the rebuilding of the basilica of

Hagia Sophia at Constantinople (still standing). He was also personally accomplished as a theologian and hymn writer. He called the fifth ecumenical council (Constantinople II, 553) as part of an ongoing, but finally unsuccessful, attempt to reconcile the Monophysites. *See also* canon law; Constantinople, councils of; Hagia Sophia.

just-war doctrine, the approach that claims that war, despite its coercive and destructive character, is morally justifiable in certain circumstances and under certain limitations. The just-war doctrine thus differs from pacifism, which denies that war is ever morally justifiable; from a holy war or crusade, in which war is seen as divinely authorized and required and in which usually there is little concern about limiting the means and the scope of warfare; and from *Realpolitik,* in which war is primarily a means to advance national interest. In the just-war approach, moral justification is needed (because of the enormous harms and risks inflicted on others) and is possible (because of the weighty public values of justice, peace, and order that are at stake). Contemporary application of the theory will not be credible for those who hold very negative moral evaluations of either the international order as a whole or of the particular nation-states that are invoking the theory.

Conditions for a Just War: The just-war doctrine lays down the conditions that must be met if a particular war is to be justified and if the prima facie presumption against the use of force is to be overridden. These conditions fall into two main groups: (1) *jus ad bellum* (Lat., "right to [go to] war") criteria, which state the conditions that must be met before hostilities can be rightly begun; (2) *jus in bello* (Lat., "[what is] right in a war") criteria, which are to be observed in the way war is conducted. The major *jus ad bellum* criteria (which are formulated in somewhat different ways in different sources) are (a) just cause, which traditionally included the undoing of injustices and the recovery of things unjustly taken but which is now effectively restricted to defense against aggression; (b) competent authority, which has usually meant national governments but which in the twentieth century has come to include international bodies maintaining collective security; (c) right intention, which excludes revenge and hatred of the enemy; (d) last resort, which requires that it be clearly established that nonviolent methods of dispute resolution will not resolve the conflict without grave damage to moral-political values of fundamental importance; (e) proportionality, which requires that the values being defended and the goals that are achievable are sufficiently important to outweigh the harms that can reasonably be foreseen; (f) a reasonable hope of success, which excludes a resort to force in which defeat is highly likely and so in which there is little prospect of actually defending the values that are at stake; (g) comparative justice, which broadens criterion (a) above so that, in the uncertainties and complexities of a specific dispute, judgment considers the whole range of issues between the contending parties. The major *jus in bello* criteria are (a) discrimination and (b) proportionality. The principle of discrimination or noncombatant immunity is an application of the general prohibition against killing the innocent; it forbids the direct killing of civilians and persons not actually engaged in combat. Both proponents and critics of "total war" have argued that the practice of total war in modern societies makes the distinction between combatants and noncombatants useless. Applying the principle of discrimination in combat situations, where civilians are also present and are likely to be harmed, involves using the principle of double effect. The principle clearly forbids attacks aimed at the destruction of population centers, as Vatican II affirmed (Pastoral Constitution on the Church in the Modern World, 1965, n.80). The principle of proportionality forbids practices within warfare that would inflict harm on either military participants or civilians that would be unnecessary or excessive. It is generally held that the principle of proportionality rules out the use of weapons of mass destruction, whether these be conventional or nuclear, biological, or chemical.

This body of principles or criteria constitutes the applicable or working part of the just-war doctrine. It has been developed from military and diplomatic practice, and most of it has been incorporated in international law. It can be applied without reliance on theological premises or on religious practices and attitudes.

Understandings of the Just-War Doctrine: The just-war doctrine should be seen as both a specific response to the political and military history of the West and a work of practical reason restraining the use of force. The elaboration of non-Western analogues to the just-war doctrine is still in its early stages. The just-war doctrine, which has roots in the classical world and in the Hebrew Scriptures, was given its most influential formulation by Augustine,

who saw warfare justified as love's response to the plight of the neighbor threatened by force. Thomas Aquinas accepted the legitimacy of war waged in self-defense. Just-war teaching, or an equivalent set of attitudes and norms, was the dominant view of the churches both in the East and in the West, with the exception of some groups shaped by the radical Reformation (Mennonites, Moravian Brethren, Quakers), who drew directly on the pacifist teachings in the NT. The major theological expositions of just-war theory (Augustine, Aquinas, Francisco de Vitoria, Francisco de Suarez) antedate the rise of modern democratic and participatory political systems and were intended to guide rulers and their advisors rather than social critics, citizens, and soldiers. As a result, they do not clearly address the issue of selective conscientious objection, which is now seen to be a clear implication of the theory in a democratic society. Selective conscientious objection, rejected by Pope Pius XII (1939–58) and not recognized in U.S. law, was clearly affirmed by Vatican II (1962–65). The just-war doctrine is acceptable to those theological traditions that combine respect for reason and for established social institutions (Catholicism, Anglicanism) and to those that employ a sharp contrast between a world in which the power of human sinfulness needs to be restrained and a realm of divine grace and peace (Orthodoxy, Lutheranism, Calvinism). It is less acceptable to more perfectionist and individualistic traditions that stem from the radical Reformation or the Enlightenment. Challenges to just-war teaching have arisen within the older churches, including Catholicism, as a result of the increased destructiveness of warfare in the twentieth century and as a result of religious and theological forms of renewal that aim at an unmediated conformity to early Christian teaching and practice, in which neither the norms of the just-war doctrine nor military institutions are to be found. *See also* conscientious objection; double effect, principle of; pacifism; peace; peace movement, Catholic.

Bibliography

Childress, James. "Just War Theories." *Theological Studies* 39 (1978): 427–45.

Johnson, James T. *Just War Tradition and the Limitation of War.* Princeton, NJ: Princeton University Press, 1981.

———. *Can Modern War Be Just?* New Haven, CT: Yale University Press, 1984.

Russell, F. H. *The Just War in the Middle Ages.* London: Cambridge University Press, 1977.

U.S. Catholic Bishops. *The Challenge of Peace: God's Promise and Our Response.* Washington, DC: United States Catholic Conference, 1983.

JOHN P. LANGAN

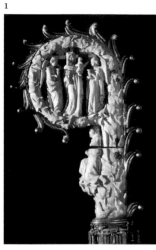

1

2

3

1 The top of a crosier, one of the bishop's symbols of authority, decorated in ivory and gold with an image of the Blessed Virgin Mary, the Christ Child, and angels; Museum of the Middle Ages (Cluny), Paris. 2 The Tassilo Chalice, a medieval gold chalice that was a gift from Duke Tassilo III of Bavaria and his wife to the abbey of Kremsmuenster, Austria; the chalice is decorated with silver medallions of Christ and the four Evangelists. 3 Fourteenth-century gilded silver paten, a flat dish used at Mass to hold the Host; in the monastery of the Sisters of Notre-Dame, Namur, Belgium. 4 Gothic-style monstrance with images of the baptism and crucifixion of Christ, the Blessed Virgin in glory, and saints; late fifteenth- or early sixteenth-century metalwork in silver, Metropolitan Museum of Art, New York. 5 Fourteenth-century gilded copper and enamel ciborium, a container for the consecrated hosts distributed to the faithful in Holy Communion; Stiftus Collection, Klosterneuburg, Austria.

4

5

6

7

8

6 The Blessed Virgin Mary portrayed as Our Lady of Mercy, with the donors of the painting kneeling under her wide mantle; fifteenth-century painting by Piero della Francesca, Civic Museum, Sansepolero, Italy. **7** Detail from a fifteenth-century Renaissance painting of the Madonna and Child with five angels by Sandro Botticelli; Uffizi Gallery, Florence. **8** The angel Gabriel announces the coming birth of the Messiah to the Blessed Virgin Mary (Luke 1:26–38); fifteenth-century painting by Beato Angelico, Museum of St. Mark, Florence. **9** The Blessed Virgin Mary being laid to rest after her death and before her bodily Assumption into heaven; fifteenth-century Gothic oil-on-wood painting by Konrad von Boest, in the Marien-kirche, Dortmund, Germany.

9

10

10 Francis of Assisi (ca. 1181–1226), founder of the Franciscans (depicted here on either side of him) and a classical embodiment of the Christian life marked by simplicity and concern for the poor. **11** Clare of Assisi (1194–1253), founder of the Poor Clares and close associate of Francis of Assisi, with several of her nuns; seventeenth-century painting, Louvre, Paris. **12** Teresa of Ávila (1515–82), Spanish Carmelite nun and mystic who taught that mystical contemplation is not incompatible with practical Christian action; Bernini's seventeenth-century sculpture *The Ecstacy of St. Teresa,* in the Church of Santa Maria della Vittoria, Rome. **13** Francis Xavier (1506–52), Jesuit missionary to India and Japan to whom have been attributed some seven hundred thousand conversions to the faith; oil painting on wood by Rubens (d. 1640), Kunsthistorisches Museum, Vienna.

11

12

13

14

15

14 St. Patrick's Cathedral, on Fifth Avenue in New York City, one of the most recognizable symbols of American Catholicism. Dedicated in 1879 and solemnly consecrated in 1910, it exhibits the clearly visible cross form typical of Gothic churches. 15 The famous Golden Dome above the Main Building of the University of Notre Dame, Notre Dame, Indiana, founded by the Congregation of Holy Cross in 1842. A statue of the Sacred Heart stands in front with arms outstretched, and a statue of Mary (Our Lady, Notre Dame) stands atop the dome. 16 The Spanish Mission in Santa Barbara, California, one of many monuments to the pastoral labors of Spanish missionaries from the sixteenth century in the American Southwest and West. 17 The abbey of Our Lady of Gethsemani, a Trappist monastery near Bardstown, Kentucky, well known as a retreat center for U.S. Catholics and as the home and burial place of Thomas Merton (d. 1968).

16

17

18

18 Mother Elizabeth Ann Bayley Seton (1774–1821), the first American-born saint and founder of the Sisters of Charity, a religious community devoted to the poor and the sick. **19** Archbishop John Carroll of Baltimore (1735–1815), the first priest to be ordained a bishop in the United States and one of the most forward-looking pastoral leaders in the history of American Catholicism. **20** A priest presides at Sunday Mass in San Jose Church, Austin, Texas. The cross with the risen Christ, the plain, free-standing altar, the presidential chair to the rear left, the tabernacle set against the back wall, the priest facing the congregation—all are indicative of the liturgical renewal brought about by the Second Vatican Council (1962–65). **21** Thomas Merton (1915–68), Trappist monk, peace activist, and writer, whose books and personal witness significantly influenced the intellectual and spiritual life of American Catholicism in the second half of the twentieth century. **22** Father Theodore M. Hesburgh, C.S.C., President Emeritus of the University of Notre Dame (after a record thirty-five years in office), the leading Catholic educator in the twentieth century, and one of the most important figures in the history of U.S. Catholicism.

19

20

21

22

23 The celebration of the sacrament of Baptism in Riobamba, Ecuador, on the west coast of South America. First Christianized in the sixteenth century, Ecuador is more than 93 percent Catholic. **24** A First Communion procession in La Elvira, in the Cauca Valley, Colombia. Ninety-three percent of the country's population is Catholic. **25** The celebration of the Day of the Dead, a blend of pre-Christian and Christian imagery and tradition, in Mexico, where over 95 percent of the population is Catholic. **26** A shrine of Our Lady of Guadalupe, in Baja California, Mexico, which reproduces the life-sized image of the Blessed Virgin Mary that appeared on the mantle of the Indian Juan Diego in 1531. Both a national and religious symbol of unity, Our Lady of Guadalupe was declared patron saint of Latin America in 1910 and of the Americas in 1945. **27** An Easter Sunday procession in Guatemala, where over 80 percent of the population is Catholic. **28** Palm Sunday procession of Otavalo Indians, in Cotocachi, Ecuador.

23

24

25

26

27

28

29

30

32

31

33

29 Catholics at worship in Sudan, in northeastern Africa. Although it is the largest country on the continent, Catholics comprise only about 7.5 percent of the total population of 26 million and live mostly in the south. **30** Easter Sunday procession at St. Matthew Church in Khartum, Sudan. **31** Cardinal Jaime Sin sprinkles the congregation with holy water at the beginning of Mass at the Church of Jesus and Mary in Manila. There are over 52 million Catholics in the Philippines. **32** A Catholic church in Xining, China. Although Christianity first came to China in the seventh century, Catholics constitute less than 1 percent of the total population of over 1 billion. **33** Catholic worshipers at prayer in Beijing, China. Because of the country's political isolation until the early 1970s, Catholics there have been largely unaffected by the reforms of the Second Vatican Council.

34

35

36

34 Tens of thousands gather in the square in front of St. Peter's Basilica, Vatican City, during the fourth and final session of the Second Vatican Council in 1965. **35** The nave of St. Peter's Basilica looking toward the main altar, with Bernini's famous baldachino overhead. Built between 1506 and 1626, it is now the second largest church in Christendom (after the Basilica of Our Lady Queen of Peace in Ivory Coast). **36** Pope John Paul II, elected in 1978, the first Slavic pope in the history of the Church and also the most widely traveled of popes. **37** Young African-American at prayer. There are about 2.5 million African-American Catholics in the United States, including at least a dozen bishops, five hundred sisters, and six hundred priests, permanent deacons, brothers, and seminarians. **38** Mother Teresa, founder of the Missionaries of Charity, a community dedicated to the service of the poor and the dying. She is generally regarded as a modern-day embodiment of the meaning of Christianity.

37

38

K

Kaam, Adrian van, b. 1920, Dutch-born priest (Congregation of the Spiritans), psychologist, and founder/director of the Institute of Formative Spirituality at Duquesne University in Pittsburgh, Pennsylvania. He is the author of many books, including *Religion and Personality* (1964).

kamilaukion (kah-mee-lahv'kee-ahn; Gk., "covering the neck"), also called kalymaukion, the cylindrical hat, called *kamilavka* in Slavic usage, worn by Byzantine-rite clergy in major orders. Monks wear the same hat with a veil over it (Russ., *klobuk*).

Kane, Theresa, b. 1936, American Sister of Mercy. As president of the Leadership Conference of Women Religious, she addressed Pope John Paul II at the National Shrine of the Immaculate Conception in Washington, D.C., on his first pastoral visit to the United States (1979), requesting that all Catholic ministries be open to women.

Kant, Immanuel, 1724–1803, Prussian (German) philosopher. In moral theology, Kant's insistence that freedom is central to ethical discourse and that moral questions are independent of metaphysics and religion has affected the course of discussion in many ways.

Kamilaukion, Klobuk

kamilaukion

klobuk

For Kant, morality is independent of the empirical conditions that attend human action. These conditions yield only hypothetical imperatives, i.e., contingent demands that spring from directing oneself to goals. Although all action occurs because of desires for goals, the only basis of morality is the goodness of the will legislating to itself the intrinsic demands of freedom; hence, an act is moral only insofar as it is done for the sake of duty or, in Kant's words, fulfills the categorical imperative. Consequences, therefore, have no moral weight in Kantian ethics.

Those who agree with Kant that actions are right or wrong regardless of consequences belong to a school of thought often called deontology, from the Greek *deon*, "duty." Among the most notable Catholic deontologists are German Grisez and John Finnis, who have combined Kant's methodology with elements of Thomas Aquinas's (d. 1274) ethical system to arrive at a comprehensive list of basic goods (e.g., life, truth, friendship) that one must respect as absolutely inviolable in order to respect one's own freedom and thus make progress as an authentic human being.

Kant's teaching that knowledge of moral norms is independent of metaphysical or religious beliefs has generated considerable debate, especially in Europe, about whether Christian faith contributes anything distinctive to ethical thought and, if so, whether this contribution concerns only the motivation of the agent. *See also* moral theology.   ROBERT P. KENNEDY

Kanti, St. John of. *See* Cantius, St. John.

Kasper, Walter, b. 1933, German Catholic theologian and bishop. Ordained a priest for the diocese of Rottenburg-Stuttgart (1957), he received his doctorate in theology from the University of Tübingen (1961). He was professor of theology in Münster (1964–70) and in Tübingen (1970–89), a member of the Vatican's International Theological Commission, and theological secretary for the Extraordinary Synod of Bishops in Rome (1985). He was ordained the bishop of Rottenburg-Stuttgart on June 17, 1989. His writings include *Jesus the Christ* (1974) and *The God of Jesus Christ* (1982).

Kateri Tekakwitha, Bl. *See* Tekakwitha, Bl. Kateri.

Katherine Drexel, Bl. *See* Drexel, Bl. Katherine.

kathisma (kah'thiz-mah; Gk., "seat," "session"),

Byzantine-rite liturgical poetry attached to the psalmody of the liturgical hours, once recited while the monks sat for a brief respite from the long psalmody. By extension, the term is also used for the sections of psalmody which this poetry accompanies. The Byzantine psalter is divided into twenty kathismata, each comprising about nine psalms subdivided into three antiphons, also called *doxai* or "glorias," because each antiphon ends with the "Glory be to the Father...." *See also* psalmody; Psalter.

Keane, John Joseph, 1839–1918, Irish-born American prelate and educator. Ordained in 1866, he was appointed bishop of Richmond and administrator of the vicariate apostolic of North Carolina in 1878. In 1886 he was chosen to be the first rector of the not-yet-opened Catholic University of America; in 1887 he was formally appointed by the Board of Trustees. He assembled the first faculty, drafted the statutes, and planned the first two buildings. He was untiring in soliciting funds and students, and by the lectures and sermons he delivered across the country, he drew widespread attention to the new institution. Like his friend Archbishop John Ireland of St. Paul, Keane was an "Americanizer" in the hierarchy and upheld the liberal or progressive side in the numerous controversies dividing the Catholic Church in the United States and the university faculty. He was widely criticized by conservatives for his active participation in the World Parliament of Religions in Chicago in 1893. He was also opposed by German professors and journalists but was supported by the chancellor of the university and archbishop of Baltimore, Cardinal James Gibbons. Having lost the confidence of the apostolic delegate, Archbishop Francesco Satolli, however, Keane was dismissed from the rectorship by Pope Leo XIII on September 15, 1896, though he remained a trustee of the university.

After a period of two and a half years in Rome in various positions, he returned to the United States in 1899. On August 18, 1900, he was appointed archbishop of Dubuque, where he promoted Catholic education, especially St. Joseph's (now Loras) College, held four synods, and tried to safeguard his people against socialism and anarchism. He also carried on a vigorous campaign against alcohol and its attendant evils and personally criticized the mayor of Dubuque and the saloonkeepers. He was elected president of the Catholic Total Abstinence Union of America in 1907. From 1908 on, his physical health and mental faculties deteriorated, and in 1911 he resigned his see. He continued to reside in Dubuque until his death seven years later. *See also* Americanism.

ROBERT TRISCO

Kells, Book of, a magnificently illustrated manuscript of the Gospels dating from around the year 800; it is now in the library of Trinity College, Dublin (most recently bound in four volumes corresponding roughly to the separate Gospels). It was probably copied and illustrated in the monastery of Kells (County Meath), although some say it was produced in Iona and brought to Kells when the Vikings raided Iona. The text is of the Irish mixed-Vulgate type. The lavish ornamentation and several full-page illustrations reveal a wide range of artistic influences. *See also* Ireland, Catholicism in.

Kemble, St. John, 1599–1679, one of the Forty Martyrs of England and Wales canonized in 1970. Ordained at Douai in 1625, he worked on the English mission for over fifty years until his execution. Feast day: August 22. *See also* Forty Martyrs of England and Wales.

Kempe, Margery, ca. 1373–d. after 1433, author

The cover of the *Book of Kells*, a highly ornamented manuscript of the Gospels, named after the monastery of Kells in Ireland, where they were copied ca. 800; the four Evangelists are represented by the biblical figures, drawn from Rev 4:7, of the man (Matthew), the lion (Mark), the ox (Luke), and the eagle (John); located in Trinity College, Dublin, Ireland.

of *The Book of Margery Kempe.* She described in unusual mystical language her pilgrimages to holy places, including Canterbury and the Holy Land, and summarized her discourses with several spiritual directors. Under the direction of the Carmelite William of Southfield, Margery sought spiritual advice from the anchoress Julian of Norwich.

Kempis, Thomas à. *See* Thomas à Kempis.

Kennedy, Eugene Cullen, b. 1928, psychologist and writer. Kennedy received his B.A. from Maryknoll College in 1950, an S.T.B. from Maryknoll Seminary in 1953, and a Ph.D. from The Catholic University of America in 1962. Professor of psychology at Maryknoll College, Glen Ellyn, Illinois, from 1960 to 1969 and at Loyola University in Chicago from 1969 to 1991, he married Sara Connor Charles, M.D., in 1977. He is the author of more than forty books and many articles and columns on the Church, human behavior, and politics, including *The Pain of Being Human* (1972), *Tomorrow's Catholics, Yesterday's Church* (1988), and a television play about Pope John XXIII, *I Would Be Called John* (PBS, 1987). He received the Thomas More medal in 1972.

Kennedy, John Fitzgerald, 1917–63, first Catholic president of the United States. Of Irish ancestry, Kennedy graduated from Harvard University in 1940. He was elected as a Democrat from Massachusetts to the U.S. House of Representatives in 1946 and to the U.S. Senate in 1952.

In 1960 Kennedy ran for the presidency and faced concerted opposition because of his religion. He partly defused the issue by insisting that his reli-

John Fitzgerald Kennedy, first Catholic president of the United States, shown here with his wife, Jacqueline, during the 1960 election campaign.

gion was a private matter and that his constitutional duties would always come first. His election seemed to shatter the last political barrier to America's acceptance of Catholics.

Kennedy's "New Frontier" administration, while full of promise, had accomplished relatively little by the time of his assassination in Dallas, Texas, in 1963. His administration did establish the Peace Corps and the Alliance for Progress to provide economic aid to Latin America. Kennedy also worked for racial integration in the South, a goal carried through by his successor, Lyndon Johnson.

kenosis (ken-oh'sis; Gk., "emptying"), a term referring to the "emptying" of Jesus' divinity through the Incarnation. Although the Greek noun is not found in the NT, the verb translated "he emptied himself, taking the form of a slave" is used in the Christ hymn of Phil 2:5–11. Recent interpreters, both Catholic and Protestant, propose an "Adamic" interpretation. Unlike Adam, who disobeyed God by seeking equality with God (Phil 2:6; see Gen 3:4), Jesus (the "last Adam," see 1 Cor 15:45) took the form of a slave by submitting to God's will. Kenotic theology stresses the radical humanity of Jesus, often, according to its critics, to the detriment of the creedal affimation "true God and true man." *See also* Incarnation, the.

kenotic theories, various interpretations of the Incarnation as the condescension or self-emptying (Gk., *kenosis*) of the divine Logos. The term is taken from Phil 2:5–11. The two most important advocates of kenotic Christology in the nineteenth century were Gottfried Thomasius (d. 1875) and Charles Gore (d. 1932). Assuming that the full humanity of Jesus Christ required a limited human consciousness, they claimed that the incarnation of the Logos resulted in the temporary cessation of the Logos's divine attributes such as omniscience, omnipresence, and omnipotence. Although these radical views were abandoned in the early twentieth century, moderate forms of kenotic Christology were presented by Karl Barth (d. 1968) and Karl Rahner (d. 1984). *See also* Christology; Incarnation, the; Logos.

kerygma (key-rig'muh; Gk. "proclamation," "public notice"), term used in the NT for both the act and the content of the proclamation of the good news of God's saving activity manifest in the life, teaching, death, and Resurrection of Jesus (see 1 Cor 1:21; 2:4; 15:14; Rom 16:25; 2 Tim 4:17). The preaching of

Peter and Paul in Acts has been called "kerygmatic sermons" (Acts 2:14–39; 3:13–26; 4:10–12; 5:30–32; 10:36–43; 13:17–41). Faith and conversion are the proper response to the kerygma. Kerygma is contrasted to *didache* (Gk., "teaching") or instruction about the implications of the Christ event, and to *parenesis* (Gk.), ethical admonitions. The term "kerygmatic theology" is used of the work of Karl Barth (d. 1968), Rudolf Bultmann (d. 1976), and Emil Brunner (d. 1966), major Protestant scholars who sought to restore the Pauline and Reformation stress on the proclaimed word.

Ketteler, Wilhelm Emmanuel (ket'ler), 1811–77, German bishop and pioneer in Catholic social teaching. He studied law, was a member of the Catholic circle in Munich, was ordained in 1844, and appointed bishop of Mainz in 1850. Outspoken on social questions, he opposed the emerging *Kulturkampf* (Ger., "culture struggle") against the Church and the effects of secularization. He criticized liberalism and socialism in light of the teachings of social Catholicism. His argument on labor, which he drew from the natural law ethics of Thomas Aquinas (d. 1274), provided the basic framework for the papal encyclical *Rerum Novarum* (1891). At the First Vatican Council (1869–70) he opposed the definition of papal infallibility. *See also Rerum Novarum.*

Kevin, St., d. ca. 618, Irish abbot and monastic founder. Apart from his association with the monastery of Glendalough (Wicklow) and his cult there, little is known of him. Feast day (in Ireland): June 3.

keys, power of the, a reference to Jesus' commission of Peter and the authority thereby granted. Matt 16:13–20 reports Peter's declaration of Jesus as the Messiah, and Jesus' response, granting to Peter the keys of the kingdom, an image of stewardship. Jesus builds the metaphor using the language of Jewish legal interpretation of Scripture. Whatever Peter "binds" as a legal obligation on earth is bound in heaven; whatever he looses is loosed in heaven. Peter is thus chief interpreter of God's law. *See also* papacy, the; Peter, St.

Kierkegaard, Søren, 1813–55, Danish philosopher and religious thinker, generally considered the father of modern existentialism. Born in Copenhagen, the son of a devout Lutheran businessman, Kierkegaard studied at the university and in 1840 received his diploma in theology. Beginning in 1843, Kierkegaard wrote numerous books in which, in opposition to the widespread Hegelian philosophy of his day, he emphasized personal decision as determinative of individual existence. For Kierkegaard, the most profound personal decision is that of faith. His influence has been more pronounced on Protestant theologians than on Catholics. *See also* Existentialism.

Kilian, St., d. 689, bishop and martyr. An Irish monk who went to the Continent, he became bishop of Würzburg (Germany), where he was murdered after a dispute with the king. Feast day: July 8.

Kilwardby, Robert, ca. 1215–79, Dominican theologian at Oxford, archbishop of Canterbury (from 1273), and cardinal in Italy (1278). Famed for his knowledge of the Church Fathers, he wrote, among other works, an important commentary on the *Sentences* of Peter Lombard and a treatise on the classification of the sciences. *See also* Canterbury; *Sentences.*

King, Philip J., b. 1925, Catholic biblical scholar. A priest of the archdiocese of Boston (ordained, 1949), he was professor of Biblical Studies at St. John Seminary, Brighton, Massachusetts (1958–74), and is currently professor of Biblical Studies at Boston College (since 1974). He was director of the W. F. Albright Institute of Archaeological Research in Jerusalem (1972–76) and is the only scholar to have been president of the three major learned societies in the fields of Bible and archaeology: American Schools of Oriental Research (1976–82), the Catholic Biblical Association of America (1982), and the Society of Biblical Literature (1988). He is the author of *American Archaeology in the Mideast* (1983), *Amos, Hosea, Micah: An Archaeological Commentary* (1988), and *Jeremiah: An Archaeological Companion* (1993).

kingdom of God [in the Bible], an image of God's sovereign authority and its consequences. The emphasis in the image is on the activity of God's rule, not the realm over which it is exercised.

Old Testament: Although the only explicit use of the phrase "kingdom of the Lord" in the OT appears in Chronicles (1 Chr 28:5; 2 Chr 13:8; see also 1 Chr 17:14), the image of God as king is widespread. The image rests on ancient Israelite tradition. Yahweh was envisioned as the royal master of his territory and, eventually, of the whole world. Hymnic language frequently celebrates his reign (1 Kgs 22:19; Pss 22:28; 47:2; 93:1; 97:1; 99:4; Isa 6:5; Zeph 3:15). God's sovereignty has already been manifested in the establishment or reestablishment of Israel (Exod 15:18; Deut 33:5; Obad 20–21). Some texts emphasize the perpetuity of God's reign (Exod 15:18; Pss 145:13; 146:10); others speak of its future coming (Isa 24:23; Obad 21; Zech 14:9). God's reign can connote various things, including the establishment of justice (Ps 99:4), defense of the helpless (Ps 146:5–10), and liberation of the oppressed (Ps 97:10). The full implementation of this reign of justice and peace is viewed by some of the prophets to be a reality of an ideal future (Zech 14:16–9).

The eschatological orientation of the book of Zechariah is intensified in the book of Daniel, which makes a sharp distinction between the empires of Persia and Seleucid Syria that have oppressed Israel and the final, eternal kingdom of the saints. Dan 7 symbolically portrays this hope with its image of the "son of man" who receives royal authority from God as a representative of God's people (Dan 7:27).

Daniel's expectation is shared by other Jewish apocalyptic works (e.g., *As. Mos.* 10:1), which may occasionally envision God's future reign as a restored Davidic kingdom (*Pss. Sol.* 17:23). The Kaddish prayer, which probably originated in the period of the Second Temple, contains a petition that God establish his kingdom. Such hopes, with their obvious political implications, continue alongside affirmations of God's universal and eternal sovereignty (*Pss. Sol.* 5:18; 17:1–4; *1 Enoch* 84:2). Jewish Targums, as well as wisdom texts (Wis 10:10), emphasize the cosmic reality and ethical implications of God's rule.

New Testament: The richness of the image found in the OT and Jewish tradition is reflected in the synoptic Gospels, where God's kingdom or reign is the central theme of Jesus' message. Expressions vary; Matthew uses the reverential "kingdom of the heavens," while Mark and Luke use "kingdom of God," but the content is the same.

The theme of God's imminent reign characterizes the proclamation of John the Baptist (Matt 3:2), who emphasized the need to repent in the face of the coming judgment (Matt 3:10; Luke 3:9). Jesus followed in John's footsteps (Matt 4:17; Mark 1:15), but developed the image of the kingdom in his own way. God's reign remained a reality still to come in its fullness (Matt 16:28; Mark 9:1; Luke 9:27), and Jesus taught his disciples to pray for its arrival (Matt 6:10; Luke 11:2). Upon its arrival God's reign would

vindicate the poor (Luke 6:20; Matt 5:3 moralizes the beatitude) and the persecuted (Matt 5:10). It would be a festive time in the company of Israel's patriarchs (Matt 8:11–12; Luke 13:28–29). Yet God's reign was already in the midst of the disciples (Luke 17:20). It was being manifested in Jesus' exorcisms (Matt 12:28; Luke 11:20) and his disciples' healings (Matt 10:7–8; Luke 9:2; 10:9).

To enter the service of God's rule in the company of Jesus required sacrifice. Money could be an impediment (Matt 19:23–24; Mark 10:23–24; Luke 18:24–25), as could family (Matt 10:37–38; Luke 14:25–33), and adult pride (Matt 18:3–4). That some have "made themselves eunuchs," presumably by voluntary celibacy, is proposed as an acceptable sacrifice for the kingdom (Matt 19:12).

Jesus taught of the gracious yet demanding reign of God in his complex, evocative, and challenging parables. God's reign was like a hopeful sower, a lowly mustard bush acting like a cedar of Lebanon, insidious leaven, an unscrupulous treasure hunter, a fishnet (Matt 13:24–48). It can be imaged in the decisions of an employer (Matt 20:1–16) or a banqueter (Matt 22:2–14; Luke 14:15–24). In such images Jesus described God's often surprising presence in human affairs and invited a response to it.

Outside the synoptic Gospels, the kingdom of God forms part of the apostles' preaching (Acts 8:12; 14:22; 19:8; 20:25; 28:23). Paul emphasizes the future reality of the kingdom (1 Cor 15:24) to which Christians have been called (1 Thess 2:12) and which they will inherit if they avoid sin (1 Cor 6:9–10; Gal 5:21). Christ's followers will inherit not in "flesh and blood" but when transformed by resurrection (1 Cor 15:50). Yet Paul can occasionally refer to God's reign as present, manifested not in word but in power (1 Cor 4:20), consisting not of dietary observances but of justice, peace, and joy (Rom 14:17). Jas 2:5 recalls the Beatitudes' promise of the kingdom to the poor.

Later works of the NT emphasize the present reality of God's kingdom, often identifying it with the Church. Matthew's version of Peter's commission (Matt 16:18–19) makes the connection explicit. Col 1:13 celebrates Christians' incorporation into the kingdom of God's Son and Heb 12:28 affirms that they have received a "kingdom that cannot be shaken." The Fourth Gospel mentions the kingdom of God as something to be entered through the rebirth of Baptism (3:3–5). Jesus also refers to his kingdom as distinct from those of this world (John 18:36). The book of Revelation celebrates the establishment of God's kingdom (Rev 11:15; 12:10) in the form of a priestly community (Rev 1:6; 5:10).

Bibliography

Chilton, Bruce. *The Kingdom of God in the Teaching of Jesus.* Philadelphia: Fortress Press, 1984.

Perrin, Norman. *The Kingdom of God in the Teaching of Jesus.* Philadelphia: Westminster Press, 1963.

Schnackenburg, Rudolf. *God's Rule and Kingdom.* New York: Herder and Herder, 1963.

HAROLD W. ATTRIDGE

kingdom of God [theology of], a scriptural metaphor describing God's redemptive and life-giving rule over creation and over human history in particular. In the OT, God is the King who rules over Israel (Deut 33:5), the nations (Ps 22:28), and the entire created order (Ps 103:19), and whose sovereign direction of history is manifest in the history of Israel, from the Exodus and conquest of Canaan to the Babylonian exile and return. Israel recognized the reign of God in the early part of its history as the absence of war, material prosperity, and freedom from oppression by other nations. This understanding was deepened and extended by the prophets, who looked forward to the day when God would assert divine sovereignty not only by delivering Israel from bondage and establishing it as a nation, but also by effecting a new relationship between God and the people of Israel, pouring the spirit of the Lord upon them and transforming their hearts (Jer 31:31–34; Ezek 36:24–31). After the exile and subsequent national misfortunes, the apocalyptic writers came to recognize that the full establishment of God's kingdom would come only with the completion of the course of history, when God would destroy all the powers of evil and resurrect the just, granting them everlasting life (Dan 7:27; 12:2).

Present and Future Kingdoms: This apocalyptic expectation appears in the NT when Jesus proclaims the urgent necessity for conversion, since "the time is fulfilled and the kingdom of God has come near" (Mark 1:15). On the one hand, the kingdom is already present with Jesus' appearance, though in a hidden, mysterious way (Mark 4:30–32), as indicated by his overthrowing of the reign of Satan through healings and exorcisms (Mark 3:27; Luke 11:20). On the other hand, the full realization of the kingdom will come only with the future return of Christ (Mark 13:26–27), as the present age is still engaged in a struggle with the power of Satan (Luke 4:5–6; John 12:31). The advent of the kingdom is good news for sinners, offering forgiveness for the repentant (Luke 15:11–32). For the poor, it brings an end to suffering (Luke 6:20–21). The

Christian community experiences the kingdom in the new life in Christ granted through the infusion of the Spirit (Rom 14:17), though this new life will be perfected only at the Second Coming of Christ, when the just will reign with Christ forever (Rev 22:5).

Christian life and theology are marked by this tension between the present kingdom and the future kingdom. The pilgrim Church is not identical to the kingdom of God, though it is the sacramental sign of God's presence and activity in history. The Church is called to continue Jesus' mission, to proclaim the kingdom and to work toward its establishment. There is another tension in that the kingdom is God's creation, yet it depends also on the Church's activity. The kingdom of God is not identifiable with any political program or social utopia of human making, but the faithful are not permitted to be passive or indifferent to situations not in accord with God's reign. They are called upon to cooperate with the work of the Spirit by striving to bring about the kingdom of God in all its dimensions, personal and social (Vatican II, Pastoral Constitution on the Church in the Modern World, n. 39). *See also* apocalypticism; eschatology individual; eschatology universal; kingdom of God [in the Bible]; salvation history.

JAMES LE GRYS

King James Bible, also called the Authorized Version, the first complete printed Bible in English, so called because it was mandated by King James I of England in 1604. Translated by a committee of English scholars, it was begun in 1607 and published in 1611. The basis for the new translation was the Bishops' Bible (1568), which was itself a revision of the Great Bible (1539). The lineage of the King James Bible can ultimately be traced back to the first English translation of the NT in 1526 (and about half of the OT in 1530–31) by William Tyndale. Along with the Book of Common Prayer, the King James Bible has shaped the piety of Anglican and Protestant English-speaking Christians for three centuries. *See also* Bible, English translations of the; Scripture, versions of.

kingship of Christ, a designation that celebrates the absolute and supreme authority of Jesus Christ affirmed by the NT (Mark 11:9–10; 13:26; 15:29–39; John 19:1–22; Col 1:12–20). The title became important for Catholics in 1925, when Pius XI, in the face of rising nationalism and Fascism, instituted the feast of Christ the King to reassert Christ's sovereignty over all forms of political governance. The feast is now celebrated by Catholics on the last Sunday of the liturgical year, or the Sunday before Advent.

Christ is celebrated as king in two ways. First, Christ is the messianic king, the redeemer who has obtained salvation for all human persons by his life, death, and Resurrection. Through Christ and in the Spirit, we enter into the kingdom of God. Second, the title affirms that all persons and all human institutions are subordinate to Christ. Primary allegiance must be given to Christ and the kingdom of God.

Although intended to challenge the absolutism of political sovereigns, recent scholarship has stressed the ecclesiological implications of the title. For example, because the Church is not the kingdom of God, but the initial budding forth of the kingdom (Dogmatic Constitution on the Church, n. 5), the Church must remain the servant of the kingdom. The task of the Church is not to draw all persons into itself, but to usher in the kingdom by serving its sovereign Lord whenever and wherever God is actively present. *See also* Christ the King, Feast of.

Kino, Eusebio Francisco (kee'noh), 1645–1711, Tyrolian-born Jesuit missionary priest and explorer in Spain's service. After an unsuccessful colonizing and missionary venture in Baja California, he founded numerous Spanish missions among the Pima Indians of Pimería Alta (northern Sonora, Mexico, and southern Arizona) that resulted in the conversion and hispanization of thousands of native peoples.

Kirby, St. Luke, d. 1582, one of the Forty Martyrs of England and Wales canonized in 1970. Ordained in 1577 and sent on the English mission in 1580, he was tried along with Edmund Campion and Alexander Briant for conspiracy against the queen and executed in 1582 after extensive torture. Feast day: May 30. *See also* Forty Martyrs of England and Wales.

kiss of peace, the mutual greeting of baptized Christians during the eucharistic liturgy, as a sign of their love and unity. As a liturgical greeting, the kiss of peace is mentioned by Justin Martyr (second century), although the NT Letters may also allude to its use (see Rom 16:16; 1 Pet. 5:14). In the East (and in some ancient Western rites), the kiss is exchanged when the gifts of bread and wine are brought to the altar (see Matt. 5:23). In the Roman and Ambrosian (Milanese/north Italian) rites, the kiss occurs shortly before the Agnus Dei and Communion.

Kleist-Lilly version. *See* Bible, English translations of the.

Kleutgen, Joseph (kloyt'gen), 1811–83, German philosopher and theologian. A Jesuit, he taught ethics at the University of Freiburg beginning in 1837. In *Die Theologie der Vorzeit* (3 vols., 1853–60) and *Die Philosophie der Vorzeit* (2 vols., 1860–63) he commended the Scholastic method and criticized the teachings of G. Hermes, A. Günther, and J. B. Hirscher and the German philosophical tradition of I. Kant, F. Schelling, and G. W. F. Hegel. At the First Vatican Council (1869–70) he contributed to the dogmatic constitution on revelation, *De Fide Catholica*. In 1878 he became professor of dogmatic theology at the Gregorian University in Rome. Kleutgen is often credited with influencing the composition of the first draft of Pope Leo XIII's encyclical commending the teachings of Thomas Aquinas, *Aeterni Patris* (1879). *See also Aeterni Patris;* Vatican Council I.

kneeling, the posture of praying on one's knees. Particularly during private and devotional prayer, kneeling emphasizes adoration of God and the presence of Christ in the Eucharist. The attitudes of penitence, adoration, and humility are associated with kneeling.

Knights of Columbus, a Catholic fraternal society. Incorporated in Connecticut on March 29, 1882, the Knights of Columbus (K of C) was founded by Father Michael J. McGivney at St. Mary's Church in New Haven. The young priest, concerned with the plight of widows and their families, emphasized the insurance feature. Because Christopher Columbus symbolized the Catholic foundations of the New

Although primarily an international fraternal insurance society with over 1.5 million members, the Knights of Columbus also provide a kind of honor guard at ecclesiastical ceremonies, as shown here processing into a church in full regalia of plumed hats, capes, and swords.

World, the Knights proudly proclaimed him their patron as a way of grounding their legitimacy in an atmosphere frequently charged with anti-Catholicism.

The Columbian ceremonials were intended to attract young Catholic men who may have drifted into the Masons, a society prohibited by the Catholic Church. By 1910 the order had expanded into every state, all the provinces of Canada, and into Mexico, the Philippines, and Puerto Rico. Over the years it has established its character as a Catholic antidefamation society eager to assert its loyalty to Church and country.

Among its cultural interests are such projects as the Vatican Film Library at St. Louis University and its Catholic advertising program. It has established a strong presence in Rome: K of C playgrounds, Vatican radio and television projects, and programs associated with the renovation and renewal of St. Peter's Basilica. The order's Vicarius Christi Foundation yields more than $2 million annually for the pope's private charities.

With over 1.5 million members and over $20 billion of insurance in force in 1992, the order contributes nearly $100 million annually to charitable projects and almost 200 million hours of volunteer work.

A blend of faith and fraternalism, the K of C represents a distinctively conservative rendering of what it means to be Catholic and American.

CHRISTOPHER J. KAUFFMAN

Knights of Labor, a nineteenth-century labor union that included many Catholics. Founded in 1869, this union stressed organizations of the crafts until it shifted to an industrial union in the 1880s. Its agenda included an eight-hour working day, occupational-safety regulations, the abolition of child labor, and equal pay for women. It was originally a secret fraternal society, but Terence V. Powderly, a Catholic machinist and mayor of Scranton, Pennsylvania (1878–84), became grand master worker of the union in 1879 and reformed its ritualistic character. Powderly was eager to dispel prejudice against the union among episcopal leaders who condemned it as a secret society. In contrast to the archbishop of Quebec, who had prompted a Vatican condemnation of the union in 1884, Archbishop James Gibbons of Baltimore defended the Knights in a strong letter of protest to the Congregation for Propagation of Faith (*Propaganda Fide*) in Rome, urging that the condemnation not be extended to

the United States. The letter emphasized that a condemnation would be considered a blow to social justice and religious liberty as well as impair Catholic workers' loyalty to the Church. Not only did James Gibbons's letter prevent a Vatican condemnation of the Knights, but it was also one of the influential factors that prompted Pope Leo XIII to issue the social encyclical *Rerum Novarum* (1891), a defense of the rights of labor to form associations.

The Knights of Labor were eventually eclipsed by the rise of trade unionism and officially terminated in 1917.

Knights of Malta, a military religious order, known officially as the Military Hospitaler Order of St. John of Jerusalem, of Rhodes, and of Malta. After a long history of hospice work and military efforts on behalf of pilgrims in the Holy Land dating at least to the twelfth century, the organization today is both a religious order (with a core of vowed members from whom the master general is chosen) and a symbolic sovereign state accredited to the Holy See and a few other countries. The Malta Palace in Rome is the order's headquarters. It enjoys extraterritoriality along with a few other properties. Both laypeople (chosen for their power and wealth as a general rule) and clerics have affiliated with the organization in order to support its charitable works, which focus on hospital work and the maintenance of ambulance services in various parts of the world.

Knights of the Holy Sepulchre, fraternal organization, also known as the Equestrian Order of the Holy Sepulchre of Jerusalem. While the historical origins are cloudy, there is evidence of honorary knights connected to the Franciscans and to Jerusalem's Church of the Holy Sepulchre since the fifteenth century. Until 1847 the Latin patriarch received knights into the confraternity, but that privilege has now passed to Roman control. Currently, the confraternity is under the leadership of a curial cardinal. The order admits both men and women into various ranks. Membership is bestowed as an honor on influential Catholics who aid in the work of the Church. The standard regalia of the confraternity includes a white cape and a red crusader cross of Jerusalem. *See also* Holy Sepulchre, Church of the.

Knights Templar, monastic military order that was founded in the twelfth century; also known as the Poor Knights of Christ and of the Temple of Solomon. Their rule may well have been developed by

Bernard of Clairvaux (d. 1153). For over one hundred years they had a presence in the Holy Land and fought bravely in the various Crusades. They engaged in a building program and were seen as the protectors of pilgrims. Their great accumulated wealth was held in Parisian and London "temples." The order was suppressed in 1312 after an inquisitorial process, managed by Pope Clement V and Philip the Fair of France, that involved torture and forced confessions. The charges of sodomy, atheism, and blasphemous behavior leveled against the Templars have been vigorously debated by historians, but the innocence of the Templars is now generally recognized.

Knock, Our Lady of (Gaelic, *Cnoc Mhuire,* "Hill of Mary"), a Marian title associated with a reported apparition of the Virgin Mary in the small village of Knock in the region of Connemara, County Mayo, Ireland. In 1879 Mary allegedly appeared to fifteen villagers on the gable end of the local parish church. Thereafter, the place became a center of Marian devotion and pilgrimage, and an important symbol of Irish Catholicism. Knock now has an airport to facilitate international pilgrimages.

Knowles, David, 1896–1974, Benedictine Regius Professor of Modern History, University of Cambridge. His writings on English monastic history received much acclaim for content and style.

Knox, John, ca. 1513–72, Scottish Reformer. After the execution of George Wishart by Cardinal Beaton in 1546, Knox worked to bring reform to Scotland through his own preaching. Exiled in France, England, Frankfurt, and Geneva, he returned to Scotland in 1559 at the invitation of the nobility and preached throughout the country for reform, culminating in the reforming Parliament of 1560, which approved the Scots Confession drafted by Knox with six fellow pastors. Other important works are *The Book of Discipline* (1560), the *Treatise of Predestination* (1560), the *Book of Common Order* (1556–64), and the *History of the Reformation of Religion Within in the Realm of Scotland* (1584). *See also* Presbyterianism; Reformation, the

Knox, Ronald Arbuthnott, 1888–1957, English writer and biblical translator. The son of an Anglican bishop, he was ordained an Anglican priest in 1910, became a Roman Catholic in 1917, and was ordained a Catholic priest in 1919. Catholic chaplain at Oxford from 1926 to 1939, he translated the Latin Vulgate into English.

Knox Bible. *See* Bible, English translations of the.

koinonia (Gk., "fellowship," "communion"), the communion experienced by Christians. In the NT it refers to communion with God (1 John 1:3,6), the Son (1 Cor 1:9), and the Holy Spirit (2 Cor 13:14) as well as the committed communion among believers (Acts 2:42–47). *See also* communion, Church as.

Kolbe, St. Maximilian, 1894–1941, Polish Franciscan, founder of the Militia of Mary Immaculate. Imprisoned at the Nazi concentration camp in Auschwitz (1936), he volunteered to take the place of a young father condemned to execution (1941). Feast day: August 14.

kontakion (kahn-tah'kee-ahn; Gk., "scroll"), Byzantine-rite liturgical refrain. Formerly, kontakion was the name for a series of poetic religious refrains, e.g., the Akathistos Hymn. Now it more commonly refers to the refrain that follows the sixth ode of the canon of Matins, the first of the liturgical hours, prayed during the middle of the night, or to

Maximilian Kolbe, Polish priest who exchanged his life for another's in Auschwitz during the Second World War.

the last in a series of refrains proper to a day or feast.

Koran (also spelled Qur'ān; Arab., "recitation"), the scripture of Islam, dating to the prophet Muhammad (570–632), who is said to have transcribed these teachings over twenty years as they were dictated to him by an angel. This sacred book is said to be a perfect copy of the original tablet preserved in heaven. As a result, Muslims regard the Koran as the infallible Word of God, which must not be interpreted but taken literally, as expressed in Arabic. The authoritative text is the one compiled by the prophet's third caliph (successor), Uthman (644–56). It consists of 114 chapters (*sūras*), which include verses from the OT, *haggadah,* NT, and NT Apocrypha. The Koran teaches an absolute monotheism, from which springs belief in the unity of all people who believe in God and which rejects all gods other than Allah. According to Muslim belief, God is also revealed to Jews and Christians, who fail, however, to acknowledge him. The Koran requires complete obedience (*islām*) to God and his teachings. *See also* Islam.

Korea, Catholicism in. Although some Catholics may have been on the Korean peninsula (divided after 1948 into the nations of North Korea and South Korea) before it was closed to foreigners in the sixteenth century, the real introduction of Catholicism to Korea came in 1784 through lay converts. A priest who arrived ten years later found four thousand Catholics who had never had the ministry of a priest. By the middle of the nineteenth century there were fifteen thousand Catholics in Korea, but four separate persecutions later in the century reduced that number drastically. One hundred and three martyrs of those persecutions were canonized by Pope John Paul II during his pastoral visit to South Korea in 1984.

In 1883, when Korea's borders were opened once again to foreigners, its government granted freedom of religion. The Catholic hierarchy in Korea was established in 1962, but since the Korean War of 1950–53 there have been no reports of Catholic life in Communist North Korea. The Forty-fourth International Eucharistic Congress was held in Seoul, South Korea, October 5–8, 1989. In the 1990s there are two dioceses in North Korea, and three archdioceses and eleven dioceses in South Korea. Catholics in South Korea comprise a little more than 6 percent of the total population of some 43 million.

Kostka, St. Stanislaus, 1550–68, Polish youth who died as a Jesuit novice. He studied at the Jesuit college in Vienna and was known for his piety. He walked 350 miles to Dillengen, Germany, to enter the order there despite intense family opposition. Peter Canisius, provincial of Upper Germany, sent him to Rome where he was received into the Jesuits in 1567. He died nine months later. He is one of the patron saints of Poland. Feast day: November 13.

Kraus, Francis Xavier (krows), 1840–1901, German historian of the Church and art. Ordained in 1894, he became professor of the history of Christian art in Strasbourg in 1872 and of Church history in Freiburg in 1878. He wrote extensively on the history of the Church and of Christian art. His diaries are an important source for the history of the Church in the nineteenth century. *See also* Catholicism and the visual arts.

Krizhanich, Jurij (yoo'ree krih'sahn-itch), 1618–83, Croatian-born linguist, missionary, and early precursor of the Slavophiles, mid-nineteenth-century Russian intellectuals who preferred Slavic culture to Western culture. He entered Russia in 1659, planning to convert it to Catholicism. He advocated a common Slavic language and the political union of all Slavs.

Kuhn, Johann Evangelist (koon), 1806–87, German theologian. Ordained in 1831, he became a professor of NT exegesis at Giessen in 1837 and at Tübingen in 1839. In 1838 he published *Das Leben Jesu* ("The Life of Jesus"), which offered a critique of Protestant D. F. Strauss. The next year he became professor of dogmatic theology at Tübingen until 1882. He wrote the four-volume *Katholische Dogmatik* (1846–68).

Kulturkampf (kool'tuhr-kahmpf; Ger., "culture struggle"), a Church-state dispute in Germany during the 1870s. A major episode in modern German history, the *Kulturkampf* erupted between 1874 and 1878 as a "battle of cultures." Anti-Church liberals in the Prussian parliament attacked the influence of the Catholic Church in matters such as education, marriage, and papal authority. Although conservative, the German chancellor Otto von Bismarck joined in the attack. German Catholics rallied around their bishops and priests, many of whom had been banned from parish service, forcing Bismarck to seek ways to reconcile the Church with the state after the death of Pope Pius IX in 1878. *See also* Germany, Catholicism in; Pius IX.

Küng, Hans, b. 1928, Swiss Catholic theologian and ecumenist. Küng was ordained a priest in 1954 and received his doctorate from the Institut Catholique at the Sorbonne (Paris) in 1957. He has been professor of theology at the University of Tübingen since 1960 and director of the Institute for Ecumenical Research at Tübingen.

Küng is the author of some twenty-five books on ecclesiology, Christology, interreligious dialogue, and other pastoral questions, including *Justification: The Doctrine of Karl Barth and a Catholic Reflection* (1964); *The Council, Reform and Reunion* (1961); *Structures of the Church* (1964); *The Church* (1967); *Infallible? An Inquiry* (1971); *On Being A Christian* (1976); *Does God Exist?* (1980); *Christianity and the World Religions: Paths of Dialogue with Islam, Hinduism, and Buddhism* (1986); *Global Responsibility: In Search of a New World Ethic* (1991).

From the beginning of Küng's scholarly career, a Vatican dossier was compiled on him. Despite this, Küng was invited by Pope John XXIII to be a *peritus* (Lat., "expert") at Vatican II. In 1967 the Vatican's Sacred Congregation for the Doctrine of the Faith

Professor Dr. Hans Küng, a Swiss diocesan priest who, in spite of his censure by the Vatican in 1979, remains one of the Catholic Church's leading theologians and ecumenists.

initiated official proceedings against Küng and forbade *The Church* to be translated or discussed. Around the same time Küng published *Infallible? An Inquiry,* which generated a worldwide debate and prompted condemnations by several national groups of bishops. After a series of other investigations and censures, on December 18, 1979, the Sacred Congregation issued a declaration against Küng's teaching and, judging that he no longer could be considered a Catholic theologian, withdrew his canonical mission to teach Catholic theology.   *CATHERINE MOWRY LACUGNA*

Kurisumala Ashram, a Syro-Malankara Catholic monastery in Kerala, India. The ashram was founded in 1958 by Belgian Trappist Father Francis Maheiu, called Francis "Acharya" (spiritual guide), aided by the English Benedictine Bede Griffiths (d. 1993). Their ideal was to create a monastic life at once authentically Indian and faithful to the Eastern Christian traditions of South India. The ashram, a popular spiritual center for Christians and Hindus alike, has successfully integrated Indian elements into the West Syrian liturgy, and adopted traditional Indian forms of dress, asceticism, and simplicity of life. *See also* monastery; Syro-Malankara Catholic Church.

Kyr (keer; Gk., *kyrios,* "Lord"), title for a bishop in Old Slavonic and some modern Slavic languages, especially common among Ruthenians and Ukrainians. *Vladyko* ("Master") is the corresponding title in Russian usage. *See also* bishop.

Kyrie eleison (kee'ree-ay ay-lay'ee-suhn; Gk., "Lord, have mercy"), an early brief prayer for divine mercy, used as a response to diaconal prayers in the Eastern churches. In the Western churches, it was used as an independent rite: three Kyrie eleisons, three Christe eleisons ("Christ, have mercy"), three Kyrie eleisons. Today it is part of the introductory penitential rite used in various ways.

Kyrios (kih'ree-aws). *See* Lord.

Laberthonnière, Lucien (loo-see-en' lah-bair-tohn-yair'), 1860–1932, French Catholic philosopher and theologian. An ordained priest of the Oratorians (1886) and professor of philosophy from 1887, he sought to reconcile philosophy and theology through his personalist thought and was accused of Modernism. Many of his writings were placed on the Index of Forbidden Books. *See also* Modernism.

Laborem Exercens (lah-bohr'em eks-air'chenz; Lat., "Doing work"), "On Human Work," third encyclical letter of Pope John Paul II. Issued on September 14, 1981, to commemorate the ninetieth anniversary of Leo XIII's *Rerum Novarum,* the encyclical sought "to call attention to the dignity and rights of those who work, to condemn situations in which that dignity and those rights are violated, and to help guide the [contemporary] changes so as to ensure authentic progress by man and society" (n. 1). It sees human work as an act of cocreation with God (n. 4) and as an expression of self-realization (n. 6). This is the basis for a spirituality of work (n. 25). Insisting on the priority of labor over capital (n. 12), the pope condemns a "rigid" capitalism that sees private ownership as an "untouchable 'dogma' of economic life" (n. 14). On the contrary, "the first principle of the whole ethical and social order [is] the principle of the common use of goods" (n. 19). *See also* work, theology of.

Labouré, St. Catherine, 1806–76, French mystic

Catherine Labouré, French Sister of Charity whose visions of the Blessed Virgin Mary gave rise to devotion to the Miraculous Medal, which depicts Mary standing on a globe with shafts of light coming from her hands.

and initiator of devotion to the Miraculous Medal. An uneducated peasant girl, Zoé Labouré entered the Sisters of Charity of St. Vincent de Paul in 1830. Within months she took the name Catherine and moved to Paris. On July 18, the Blessed Virgin Mary is said to have appeared to her for several hours in the convent chapel. On November 27 Mary again appeared and asked her to have the vision before her struck as the Miraculous Medal. Several other visions followed until September 1831. Her confessor, M. Aladel, promoted devotion to the Miraculous Medal while Catherine's identity remained virtually unknown until her death. She was canonized in 1947. Feast day: December 30. *See also* Miraculous Medal.

Labre, St. Benedict Joseph, 1748–83, ascetic and beggar. After trying unsuccessfully to join various religious orders, he devoted his life to making pilgrimages to Europe's many religious shrines, sustaining himself by begging alms. He was particularly devoted to the Blessed Sacrament. His feast, no longer observed universally, is April 16.

Lacordaire, Henri (on-ree' lah-kohr-dair') 1802–61, French Dominican preacher. Trained in law, he was ordained a priest for the archdiocese of Paris (1827), where he gained national recognition for his preaching in the cathedral of Notre-Dame (1835–36). After making a retreat with Dom P. Guéranger in Rome, he joined the Order of Preachers and subsequently restored the Dominican order in France, suppressed since 1790. His preaching in apologetics resulted in his widely read *Conférences de Notre-Dame de Paris* (4 vols., 1844–51).

Lactantius, ca. 250–ca. 325, Latin Apologist and teacher of rhetoric under Diocletian. His conversion to Christianity compelled him to leave the court when persecution began (303). His works include *The Divine Institutions,* the first Latin attempt at a systematic, philosophical theology. Although Lactantius was not a profoundly consistent thinker, his style gained the admiration of Jerome who (followed by the Renaissance humanists) compared him to Cicero. *See also* Apologists; philosophy and theology.

ladder, spiritual, a symbol in Christian spirituality derived chiefly, though not exclusively, from Gen 28:12. Jesus connected himself to Jacob's ladder (John 1:51). This ladder now symbolizes God's descent into human life through revelation and self-communication and also the human ascent to God as a spiritual journey.

Ladislaus of Hungary, St., 1040–95, king of Hungary from 1077 to 1095. In 1083, he successfully promoted the canonization of King Stephen I of Hungary. Working tirelessly to spread the faith among his subjects in Croatia and Dalmatia, in 1091 he founded the bishopric of Zagreb. In the investiture struggle in which lay princes claimed the right to invest bishops with the ring and staff and to receive homage from them, he sided with the papacy, Gregory VII and Victor III. He died while preparing for the First Crusade. Feast day: June 27. *See also* Hungary, Catholicism in.

Lady, Our, a common title used by Catholics for the Blessed Virgin Mary. It is traditionally employed when speaking about the importance of Mary as model, advocate, and protectress, in contrast, for example, to the title "Mother of God," which pertains to her divine maternity, and the "Blessed Virgin," which is often associated with important Marian events. *See also* Mary, Blessed Virgin.

lady chapel, a separate chapel in a cathedral or large church, devoted to the Blessed Virgin Mary in which her sculpted or painted figure over an altar is conspicuous. Such devotional chapels were especially prominent in English cathedrals. *See also* cathedral; chapel.

Laetare Medal (lay-tahr'ay), medal awarded annually by the University of Notre Dame to an outstanding American Catholic and announced on *Laetare* (Lat., "Rejoice") Sunday, the fourth Sunday of Lent. Established in 1883, the medal, a solid gold disk inscribed with the words, "Truth is great and will prevail," has honored men and women in many fields, including John Gilmary Shea (1883), John Fitzgerald Kennedy (1961), and Dorothy Day (1972). *See also* Notre Dame, University of.

Laetare Sunday (Lat., *laetare*, "rejoice"), the fourth Sunday of Lent, so-called from the first word of the Introit (the antiphon of the Roman Gradual). *Laetare,* taken from the Latin translation of Isa 66:10, sets a tone of joyful anticipation of the Easter mystery, as do the permitted rose-colored vestments. *See also* Gaudete Sunday.

Laetare Medal, the award given annually to an American Catholic by the University of Notre Dame in recognition of distinguished service to the gospel and the Church.

Laetentur Coeli (lay-ten'tuhr chay'lee; Lat., "The heavens rejoice"), decree of union between Latin and Byzantine communions (July 6, 1439). The Council of Florence, occasioned by the desire of the embattled Greek church to secure aid against the Turks, who were advancing against Constantinople, promulgated *Laetentur Coeli* to reunite Latins and Byzantines. The decree cautiously proclaimed the spiritual supremacy of the pope and carefully stipulated that the Latin insertion of *Filioque* (the Holy Spirit proceeds from the Father *and* the Son) in the Nicene Creed implied no subordination of the Holy Spirit, as the Byzantine church contended. Despite the decree's cautious attempt at union, the Byzantine church in Constantinople almost immediately rejected it. John Bessarion (d. 1472), archbishop of Nicaea, and some of the younger Greek bishops continued to favor the union, but it ceased entirely with the capture of Constantinople by the Turks in 1453. *See also* Florence, Council of.

LaFarge, John, 1880–1963, American Jesuit priest, journalist, and promoter of interracial justice. He worked for fifteen years as a pastor in rural Maryland and then as writer for *America* magazine and other journals. A popular public lecturer, he wrote many books on the Catholic position on civil rights and race relations.

Lagrange, Marie-Joseph Albert, 1855–1938, French Dominican biblical scholar. Born in Bourg-en-Bresse, he completed a law degree before entering the Dominicans in 1879. After ordination in 1883, and graduate study in Vienna, he founded in 1890 the École Biblique, the first modern Catholic school of biblical and archaeological research. The approach was moderately critical, supporting, e.g., source criticism of the Pentateuch with evidence from archaeology. Its historical method was the union of document and monument. At first Lagrange focused on the OT, and received encouragement from Pope Leo XIII. But under Pope Pius X he fell into disfavor. To avoid controversy he switched to NT studies. In 1892 he founded the *Revue Biblique;* in 1900 the monograph and commentary series Études Bibliques. Both continue publication in the 1990s. A prolific author, he produced over 30 books, 248 articles, and more than 1,500 reviews. In addition to full-scale commentaries on Judges (1903), Mark (1911), Romans (1916), Galatians (1918), Luke (1921), Matthew (1923), and John (1925), he produced works on the NT canon and textual criticism, messianism, intertestamental Judaism,patristics,historicalmethod,apologetics, and a widely translated life of Christ. In 1935 he returned to France, where he died in 1938. He has been reburied in Jerusalem. He received posthumous vindication in 1943, in the encyclical of Pius XII on biblical studies, *Divino Afflante Spiritu.* The story of his struggle and triumph is the paradigmatic heroic model of Catholic intellectual life in the twentieth century, a pattern for pioneers who came after. The cause of his beatification is in active process. *See also* École Biblique; *Revue Biblique.*

BENEDICT T. VIVIANO

laicization, the process used in legally returning a cleric to the status of a layperson. Although the Catholic understanding of Holy Orders includes the notion that the sacrament is unrepeatable, thus "once a priest always a priest," the ordained may be released from the rights and obligations of the clerical state and be treated as a layperson. The validity of the ordination might not be at question here, but there are other considerations that render such a release appropriate.

The most common process used for laicization is initiated by the cleric himself. In the years immediately following Vatican II (1962–65) large numbers of priests discerned a necessity for leaving the ordained ministry and continuing their Christian lives as laypersons. Their decisions were facilitated by a process, approved by Pope Paul VI, that required that their reflections on their original decision to seek ordination and reasons for the requested change be submitted to the Congregation for the Doctrine of the Faith. Large numbers of priests took advantage of this process. From the beginning of the pontificate of Pope John Paul II in 1978, however, the number of such laicizations has decreased considerably. New norms were issued in 1980 and in 1988 the matter was placed in the hands of the Congregation for Divine Worship and the Discipline of the Sacraments. Recently there has been a modest increase of such permissions.

Laicization may also be used as a penalty when a cleric has abused his responsibilities. This usage results from a formal ecclesiastical trial or from an administrative decree of the Holy See. *See also* clergy.

JOHN F. LAHEY

laity (Gk., *laos,* "people"), the Christian faithful. The word originally referred to the early Christian community as the new "chosen people." Eventually it was used for the nonclergy, distinguishing them as the common, uneducated dependents of the clerical, governing elite. In modern usage "laity" is a term that refers to over 98 percent of the Catholic Church, the faithful who are consecrated to the Lord by the sacraments of initiation. In that sense, however, the term "laity" applies to every member of the Church, clergy and religious included.

Laity in the Early Church: All early Christians referred to themselves as the newly chosen people of God. Jesus called most of his disciples and all of the apostles from the Jewish laity. Many famous missionaries in the NT were laity—Aquila and his wife Priscilla, Junia, Nereus and his sister, and a host of others. Early communities were organized in the homes of lay leaders like Mary and Nympha. In fact, Christianity was from the beginning a lay movement, and as it developed, laity held key leadership roles, presiding over communities, preaching, teaching, and celebrating rituals of prayer and worship. While there were always dedicated Christians who served the community and others who consecrated themselves as ascetics, almost two hundred years passed before some of the faithful began to be called "priests" and three hundred and fifty years before others would organize themselves as monks or religious.

The positive description of the faithful as the people of God (Gk., *laos theou*) lasted about two hundred years. However, some early Christian writers, like Clement of Rome, Origen, and Clement of Alexandria, used the pejorative word *laikos* in a way that suggested incompetent masses of the common people, in contrast to their leaders.

Laity in History: Three developments in the early Church had negative effects on laity: the development of clergy, the growth of monasticism, and the disdain for the material world. Like any other organization, as Christianity expanded and developed, it became more structured, and some members took on specific roles for the community. First, there were teachers and prophets, then elders and overseers (or bishops), and later priests and monks. Under the influence of the Roman emperors who made Christianity the state religion, the leadership of the Church became hierarchical and separated itself from the ordinary people. By the third to fourth centuries the Church was divided into three groups: clergy, religious, and laity; the clergy were considered the most important, and laity the least.

In the persecutions of the early centuries, those who gave their lives for the Lord in martyrdom were respected as saints. After the persecutions, the saintly gave their lives to the Lord in monasticism and through consecrated virginity and asceticism. Thus, monks and religious came to be as greatly respected as the clergy, while the laity remained at the lowest spiritual level.

Laity were not only considered the lowest rung on the ladder of Church membership, but, under the influence of philosophical movements (e.g., Neoplatonism), many in the Church began to think that anything material was bad and only the spiritual was good. Since laity spent every day of their lives dealing with the material aspects of life—work, politics, family, sex—they were seen to be at a disadvantage for spiritual growth. The subordination of laity in the Church continued for over eighteen hundred years.

Laity in Vatican Council II: Although laity did not play a very active role at the Second Vatican Council (1962–65), they were perhaps its prime beneficiary. Conciliar emphases on community, service, holiness of all the baptized, new understandings of vocation, openness to the world, participatory government, broader views of ministry, and the need for world transformation all stressed the increased importance of lay life in the Church.

Since the council's conclusion in 1965, and as a result of its teachings, laity have found new opportunities to be involved in the life of the Church by collaborating in parish and pastoral councils and local, regional, and national task forces; by ministering as directors of religious education, youth ministry, social service, and in leadership roles in spiritual movements; by appreciating the religious dimensions of their ordinary daily efforts in work, family life, civic and social involvement. Local church life now looks different, as the faithful become accustomed to a more highly visible role for the laity.

Although the council's call to upgrade the role of laity in the Church was clear, the faithful, whether laity, religious, or clergy, still tend to interpret the teaching in different ways: as a call to the laity to increase their help to the pastor in his work, to be a "leavening" influence in the contemporary world, to dedicate themselves to social justice, to minister to the needs of Church communities, or to courageously discover new ways of serving the Lord in changing times.

Laity in the Contemporary Church: In 1987 the Catholic Church held a World Synod on the Laity. Many laity were invited as observers; others came as personal advisers or experts for bishops. The synod and its final document stressed the laity's equality with clergy and religious in the Church's life of communion and mission. It saw the specific vocational role of the laity as one of ministry to the world in the ordinary circumstances of daily life. Subsequently, emphasis has been given to the importance of baptismal vocation, the universal call to holiness, the charisms given to every person, the common call to build community, the common priesthood of all the faithful, and a lay-centered Church. Thus, the synod led the Church full circle, recalling the essential contribution the laity made to the growth of the early Church and summoning all to participation in the mission and ministries of the Church today. *See also* Decree on the Apostolate of the Laity; lay ministries; lay spirituality.

Bibliography

Doohan, Leonard. *The Lay Centered Church.* San Francisco: Harper & Row, 1984.

Finn, Virginia Sullivan. *Pilgrims in this World.* New York: Paulist Press, 1990.

John Paul II. "Apostolic Exhortation on the Laity" *(Christifideles Laici). Origins* 18 (1989): 561–95.

Osborne, Kenan B. *Ministry: Lay Ministry in the Roman Catholic Church.* New York: Paulist Press, 1993.

Parent, Remi. *A Church of the Baptized.* New York: Paulist Press, 1987.

Rademacher, William J. *Lay Ministry.* New York: Crossroad, 1991.

LEONARD DOOHAN

Lalement, St. Gabriel, 1610–49, Jesuit missionary and martyr. Born in France, he volunteered for missionary work among the Hurons in Canada, serving as assistant to Jean de Brébeuf. Both priests were tortured and killed by the Iroquois. They were canonized as two of the Martyrs of North America in 1930. Feast day: October 19.

Lallemant, Louis, 1587–1635, French Jesuit spiritual authority. Although he himself did not write, his students' notes were preserved and published sixty years after his death and had a great influence on the spiritual formation of Jesuits. He emphasized docility to the Holy Spirit as well as the close union between prayer and action. Isaac Jogues (d. 1646), one of the North American Martyrs, was one of his disciples.

Lalor, Teresa, 1769–1846, founder of the American branch of the Visitation order. Born in Ireland, she emigrated to Philadelphia, Pennsylvania, in 1794. In 1797 she cofounded, with Father Leonard Neale, a religious community. After Neale became president of Georgetown in 1798, Lalor established an academy near the college. In 1816 Pius VII formally recognized Lalor's community. *See also* Visitation order.

lamb, paschal. *See* paschal lamb.

Lambeth, London palace of archbishops of Canterbury since the thirteenth century. Across the Thames from Parliament, Lambeth has been the site of many meetings of English bishops. Since 1867, it has given its name to the decennial worldwide synod of Anglican bishops—though the "Lambeth Conference" now meets in Canterbury. *See also* Canterbury.

Lamb of God, a symbolic designation for Jesus. The use of the epithet probably arose from its application to Jesus of Isa 53:7, cited in Acts 8:32 and alluded to in 1 Pet 1:19. The testimony of John the Baptist, according to John 1:29, 36, highlights the phrase. A similar image, using a different Greek term, appears in Revelation (e.g., Rev 5:6–13; 7:9–17). All these uses portray Jesus as a sacrificial victim, whose death effects expiation for sin. This phrase (Lat., *Agnus Dei*) is used during the Mass just before the Communion, with precisely these connotations.

Lamennais, Félicité Robert de (lah-men-nay'), 1782–1854, French priest, advocate of Catholic liberalism, traditionalism, and Ultramontanism. Anticipating Modernism, he insisted that reliance on individual reason leads to skepticism and that the common consent of all humanity, which he believed was informed by primordial revelation, was the norm of truth. Convinced that union with civil power hinders religion, he opposed Gallicanism, advocated Ultramontanism, religious liberty, and separation of Church and state. This engendered antipathy among Gallican bishops who sought his condemnation. His political liberalism and theory of common consent were condemned in 1834 by Pope Gregory XVI. The excesses of his opponents embittered him, and he left the Church. *See also* Gallicanism; Ultramontanism.

Lamentabili, a decree issued by the Holy Office under the authority of Pope Pius X on July 3, 1907, condemning sixty-five propositions associated with "Modernism" concerning the nature of the Church, revelation, biblical exegesis, the sacraments, and the divinity of Jesus Christ. Its full Latin title is *Lamentabili sane exitu* ("A lamentable departure indeed"). Although not mentioned by name, the propositions reflected the views of several Catholic theologians, particularly Alfred Loisy (d. 1940), George Tyrrell (d. 1909), Éduoard Le Roy (d. 1954), and Albert Houtin (d. 1926). *Lamentabili* was preceded by the apostolic letter *Testem Benevolentiae*, which condemned Americanism on January 22, 1899, and was followed by the encyclical *Pascendi Dominici Gregis* on September 8, 1907, which characterized "Modernism" as the "synthesis of all the heresies." In 1910 a widespread effort to root out "Modernism" was initiated with the Pontifical letter, known as a *motu proprio,* entitled *Sacrorum Antistitum,* which contained the oath against Modernism. *See also* Modernism; oath against Modernism; Pius X, St.

Lamy, Jean Baptiste, 1814–88, bishop (1853–75) and archbishop (1875–85) of Santa Fe, New Mexico. The French-born Lamy was the founding missionary of the Catholic Church throughout the southwestern United States and was later memorialized in Willa Cather's novel *Death Comes for the Archbishop* (1927).

Lanfranc of Bec, ca. 1010–89, monk and archbishop of Canterbury. Italian by birth, Lanfranc was a recognized expert in law and theology and prior of the monastery of Bec in Normandy, when William the Conqueror appointed him archbishop of Canterbury (1070). Lanfranc supported the doctrine of Christ's eucharistic Presence against the attacks of Berengar of Tours. *See also* Bec, Abbey of; transubstantiation.

Langton, Stephen, d. 1228, theologian and archbishop of Canterbury. He studied at Paris, where he lectured on Scripture and the *Sentences* of Peter Lombard. He supported papal authority and ecclesiastical privilege in England, promulgating the reforms of Lateran Council IV (1215). *See also* Canterbury; Lateran councils.

language, liturgical. *See* liturgical language.

language, religious, language designed to describe God. God's transcendent nature makes speaking about God in human language exceedingly difficult. Religious language attempts to meet this challenge.

One form of religious language is mythological, portraying God as a particular character in a narrative. In the book of Exodus (6–14), for example, God is described as a powerful agent who inflicts disasters on the Egyptians, parts the waters of the Red Sea, and instructs Moses on what he should say and do.

Another form of religious language is metaphor, a nonliteral figure of speech that describes the unfamiliar in terms of the familiar. The Bible frequently uses metaphors to describe God. God is called "my rock" (Ps 28), a "light" (Ps 27), and a "shepherd" (Ps 23). In a literal sense God is not a rock, a light, or a shepherd. Rather, these words describe something unfamiliar, namely God, with characteristics that are familiar. Closely associated with metaphor is another figure of speech, the simile. The parables of the NT make use of similes to describe God. God's kingdom is like a mustard seed (Mark 4:31), like leaven (Matt 13:33), or like a treasure buried in a field (Matt 13:44).

Analogy, a third form of religious language closely analyzed by Thomas Aquinas (d. 1274), involves stretching the use of a word to describe a unique situation. To say that "God knows" describes the unique activity of God by comparing God's activity with a human activity. However, God's knowledge is both like and unlike human knowledge. Like human knowing, God truly understands. Unlike human knowing, God does not depend upon experience

and reason for knowledge. Thus, the verb "to know" is used analogously, not literally, to describe God's activity. *See also* analogy; myth; theology.

ANTHONY W. KEATY

Laodicea, Canons of, rules derived from a fourth-century local council in the Roman province of Asia that are part of the basis for canon law. The council is of uncertain date (most likely the later part of the fourth century), but its canons form part of the earliest collections of canon law.

Lapide, Cornelius à (lah'pi-day), also known as Cornelius Cornelissen van den Steen, 1567–1637, Flemish author of commentaries on all canonical books except Job and Psalms. After studies at Douay and Louvain, he entered the Jesuits, was ordained (1595), and taught Scripture at Louvain (1596–1616) and at the Roman College (1616–36). His commentaries were characterized by allegorical and mystical exegesis, with extensive quotations from the Church Fathers and medieval theologians.

lappets (lap'its; Mid Eng., "flap"), decorative folds or flaps on a garment or hat. In ecclesiastical vesture, lappets are the two linen strips that extend from the bottom of the rear panel of the bishop's mitre. Lappets are often decorated with Christian symbols and end in decorative tassels.

lapsi (Lat., pl. of *lapsus,* "fallen"), in a technical sense, those Christians who denied their faith during the Decian persecution (249–51) by offering sacrifice to pagan gods, burning incense during pagan rites, or by obtaining certificates that witnessed to their doing so. In general, it refers to persons who have fallen from the practice of their faith. *See also* Libellatici.

L'Arche (lahrsh; Fr., "ark"), communities of physically and mentally disabled persons and those who live, work, and pray with them. Founded in France in 1964 by Canadian philosopher Jean Vanier, the movement attempts to lead people to appreciate and be enriched by the human dignity and spiritual gifts of disabled persons. The name of the movement derived from the house used by members of the first community, called "Noah's Ark." Catholic in its origins, the movement is now ecumenical and interfaith in character and is without any canonical links with the Church.

La Salette, Our Lady of, a Marian title associated with a reported apparition in a small village in southeastern France. On September 19, 1846, two children, Melanie Mathieu-Calvat and Maximin Giraud, claimed they had a vision, while tending cattle, of the Blessed Virgin Mary. Mary, who was weeping, told the children to deliver a message: unless there was repentance from widespread religious apathy, Mary would allow the judgment of her Son against a sinful world to take place. The children were then given a secret and told to pray. In the valley where the apparition allegedly occurred, a spring began to flow and miraculous cures associated with its waters were reported.

In 1851, after a five-year investigation, the bishop of Grenoble proclaimed the legitimacy of the apparition and authorized the cult of Our Lady of La Salette. Although approved by the Church, the events surrounding La Salette are private revelations. Catholics are not required to give assent to the apparition itself or to the revelations allegedly disclosed at La Salette. *See also* apparitions of the Blessed Virgin Mary; La Salette Fathers.

La Salette Fathers, the Missionaries of Our Lady of La Salette (M.S.), founded in 1852 for the numerous pilgrims to the Shrine of Our Lady of La Salette in France. The institute was approved by Rome in 1890. Since their founding, the La Salette Fathers have established foundations in the United States and Canada, as well as in Belgium, Poland, and Brazil. The spirit of the congregation, which is one of prayer and sacrifice, is intimately connected with Our Lady's appearance on the Mountain of La Salette. La Salette Fathers are trained to lead people away from evil and toward repentance and divine mercy. *See also* La Salette, Our Lady of.

La Salle, St. Jean-Baptiste de, 1651–1719, founder of the Brothers of the Christian Schools, an order composed of laymen devoted to education, and patron saint of all teachers. Devoting himself at first to the education of the poor in charity schools, he later established normal schools to train teachers, boarding schools for the middle classes, and special schools for delinquents. La Salle insisted upon the combination of religious and secular instruction. His *Duties of a Christian* (1703) has gone through more than two hundred and fifty editions. La Salle was canonized in 1900. Feast day: May 15. *See also* Brothers of the Christian Schools.

Las Casas, Bartolomé de, 1474–1566, Spanish Dominican author and missionary. Traveling to the New World in 1502 and appalled by the treatment of the native population, he sought to reform the early Spanish colonial practice. In 1515 he was named Protector of the Indians by the king of Spain. Thwarted in his efforts, he went to Spain and joined the Dominican order (1523). He returned to the New World bringing the new laws of 1542–43 that were designed to alleviate the exploitation of the Indians. Meeting with meager success, he was back in Spain after 1547, where he wrote extensively. His most famous work was the *Brevísima relación de la destrucción de las Indias* (1552), which was a response to the justification of the conquest of the New World by the historian Sepulveda in *De Justis Belli Causis*. Las Casas argued for the humanity of the conquered peoples against those who viewed them as children or not fully human.

Last Adam, Paul's Christological model according to which Christ is seen as the last (heavenly) Adam (1 Cor 15:45), both undoing and salvifically redoing the sinful actions of the first (earthly) Adam (see Rom 5:12–21). *See also* Adam; Adam and Eve.

last days, the calamitous time heralding the imminent return of the victorious Christ, described in the NT with traditional apocalyptic imagery as a period of cataclysmic and destructive events of the human and natural orders: wars, famines, widespread immorality and lawlessness, earthquakes, plagues, the appearance of false prophets and messiahs, and the persecution of the faithful (e.g., Matt 24:3–28; 2 Tim 3:1–9). Through these tribulations the fidelity of the people of God will be tested and then reach its fulfillment in the realization of the kingdom of God. *See also* apocalypticism; kingdom of God [in the Bible].

Last Gospel, John 1:1–14, read at the conclusion of the Tridentine Mass, the Latin Mass rite in use before the Second Vatican Council (1962–65). The Last Gospel was omitted during Lent, at vigils, on the Sundays of major feasts, and on Christmas at the Mass of the Day, where it had already been read as the Gospel. With the termination of the Tridentine Mass by the council, the Last Gospel disappeared from the liturgy of the Mass.

last judgment. *See* judgment, general; judgment, particular.

Last Rites, the sacramental rites and other prayers that may, in whole or part, be employed in pastoral care for the dying. In exceptional circumstances, such as emergency, Last Rites may be one continuous rite of Penance, Anointing, and Viaticum. In ordinary circumstances, Viaticum is the sacrament for those close to death. The commendation of the dying person to God through prayer has traditionally been an element of these rites. Prayers for the dead can be said by a minister attending to the family and friends of the person who has died. Sacraments are never administered to the dead. *See also* Anointing of the Sick.

Last Supper, a term describing the final meal Jesus celebrated with his disciples on the evening before his death (1 Cor 11:23–25; Mark 14:22–25; Matt 26:26–29; Luke 22:15–20; see John 13–17 and *Didache,* 9:1–5), which Paul calls "the Lord's supper" (1 Cor 11:20) or the partaking of the table of the Lord (1 Cor 10:21). The term "Last Supper," however, is never used in the NT. Though there is no verbatim unanimity in the accounts of the Last Supper, all contain words spoken over the bread and over the cup, with clear statements indicating that the bread is the body of Jesus (to which Luke and

Jesus, the twelve apostles, and attendants at the Last Supper on the night before Jesus' crucifixion; fifteenth-century oil painting by the Dutch artist Dieric Bouts, in St. Peter's College, Louvain, Belgium.

Paul add "for you") and that the wine is the blood of the covenant (Mark, Matthew) or the new covenant "in my blood" (Luke, Paul).

Though the synoptic Gospels describe a Passover meal, Paul does not say this explicitly (but see 1 Cor 5:7), and in the Johannine chronology Jesus eats the meal before the feast of Passover (13:1–2) and dies on the "day of preparation" for the Passover (John 19:14). One proposal to resolve this discrepancy holds that John follows the older, lunar priestly calendar (found also at Qumran) while the synoptic Gospels follow the official calendar. Other proposals suggest that the meal was not really a formal Passover meal, but a celebratory meal in anticipation of the feast. Despite uncertainty about the precise event, the meal continues Jesus' practice of announcing God's reign by celebratory meals, especially with sinners. In all traditions the meal anticipates or prophetically enacts the death of Jesus for others and points to the future reign of God. *See also* Eucharist.   *JOHN R. DONAHUE*

last things, the "four last things": death, judgment, heaven, and hell. In Catholic theology, the doctrine of the "last things" brings theological reflection to bear on the ultimate finality of the human person. This kind of reflection defines the theological category of eschatology. Christian eschatology asserts and defends the notion of personal survival after death. Hence, the theological consideration of the "last things" addresses the questions of death, the judgment of the person at the moment of death (particular judgment), the collective judgment of the human community at the Second Coming (general judgment), the Resurrection of the body, and the Second Coming of Christ (Gk., *Parousia*).

Traditional Catholic teachings concerning the last things were not fully elaborated until the work of the medieval theologian Hugh of St. Victor (d. 1141) and Pope Benedict XII's decree *Benedictus Deus* (1336), which affirmed that the particular judgment and its consequences follow immediately the moment of death. The Council of Florence (1439) and the Council of Trent (1563) approved these doctrines as official teachings of the Church.

In 1979 the Congregation for the Doctrine of the Faith and in 1992 the *Catechism of the Catholic Church* reaffirmed traditional Catholic teachings concerning the resurrection of the body and the immediate judgment of the human person following death. Modern Catholic theology stresses the continuity between the end of human life and human action in the present. A key element in the reorientation of traditional eschatology was German theologian Karl Rahner's (d. 1984) highlighting of the relationship between a person's fundamental option during life and the character of his or her death as a climactic realization of the profoundly personal and inalienable responsibility for the self. *See also* eschatology individual; eschatology universal; heaven; hell; judgment, general; judgment, particular.

latae sententiae (lat'tay sen-ten'tsee-ay; Lat., "concealed sentence"), an automatic penalty attached to a given ecclesiastical crime. In the recent revision of the code of canon law (1983) the number of such penalties has been greatly reduced, because of concern that each individual case, with its own particular circumstances, be examined before any kind of censure be imposed. Certain actions, however, are considered so reprehensible that it is deemed appropriate that particular penalties be attached to their commission (e.g., apostasy, heresy, schism, profanation of the Eucharist). In addition, although these penalties are said to be automatic, certain conditions, mostly relating to the culpability of the delinquent, must also be verified before their application. *See also ferendae sententiae;* penal law.

Lateran Basilica, part of the Lateran complex on Mount Celio in Rome, the episcopal seat of the pope as Bishop of Rome, and the highest-ranking Catholic church. The basilica, originally known as the Church of the Savior, was first built in the early fourth century on a site formerly occupied by the palace of the Laterani, a noble Roman family. The property was donated to the Church by Constantine.

The Lateran Basilica, formerly Constantine's imperial palace and now one of the four major basilicas of Rome and the pope's cathedral as Bishop of Rome; its full title is the Patriarchal Basilica of the Most Holy Savior and St. John the Baptist at the Lateran.

The basilica and papal dwelling served as the official residence (Lat., *patriarchum*) of the popes from the fourth century until the removal to Avignon in 1309. During that time, the basilica suffered from earthquakes (443, 896) and barbarian attacks (455, 700s). It was rebuilt regularly and rededicated to St. John the Baptist in 905. Fires destroyed the building in 1308 and 1360, after which the basilica remained largely in a state of disrepair until the late 1500s, when Pope Clement VIII commissioned a baroque renovation. The façade dates to 1735. *See also* basilica; Rome.

Lateran councils, five ecumenical councils held at the Lateran Palace in Rome between 1123 and 1517. Lateran I (1123), the ninth ecumenical council, was convened by Pope Callistus II to ratify the settlement on lay investiture achieved in the Concordat of Worms (1122). Over three hundred bishops and six hundred religious heads issued twenty-two disciplinary canons representing major aspects of the Gregorian reform, including prohibitions against simony and clerical marriage.

Lateran II, the tenth ecumenical council, was convoked in 1139 by Innocent II to heal the Church of the schism of 1138. Championed by Bernard of Clairvaux, Innocent found wide support for his claim to the papacy and ratified it by convening the council. Lateran II reaffirmed the traditional reform agenda of the Gregorian period but added its own disciplinary canons reflecting the changing world of the twelfth century: condemned were usury, tournaments, and the monastic study of medicine and civil law. Heretical followers of Arnold of Brescia were likewise condemned.

Forty years later the papacy emerged from another schism and Lateran III, the eleventh ecumenical council, was convened by Alexander III to promote unity in the Church and deal with abuses. Among its reforms were the requirement of a two-thirds majority among the cardinals for papal elections and the establishment of grammar teachers in cathedral schools for the education of poor scholars.

Lateran IV (1215), convoked by Innocent III as the twelfth ecumenical council, was the greatest of the Lateran councils and the most important ecclesiastical assembly of the Middle Ages; it was often referred to by medieval writers as "The Great Council." The council achieved an impressive representation of Christendom with bishops and religious superiors from all parts of the Church, East and West; great nobles represented the sovereigns of Christian kingdoms. The council sat for only three sessions in two weeks during which seventy canons representing major concerns of doctrine and discipline were approved. A profession of faith headed the canons in order to clarify orthodox belief and condemn the opinions of Joachim of Fiore, the Cathars, and Waldensians. The council affirmed transubstantiation and made mandatory for all Christians annual confession and Communion. Bishops were to add theology masters to the grammarians in their cathedrals stipulated by Lateran III for the enhancement of clerical education. They were also obliged to hold annual provincial councils in order to implement the council's decrees. The council also dealt with the place of nonbelievers in Christian society and ordered identifiable clothing for Muslims and Jews.

Lateran V (1512–17) was convoked by Julius II but was attended mainly by Italian bishops to deal with an antipapal council recently held in Pisa. Julius died shortly after the council was opened and the assembly was continued under his successor, Leo X. The council was in many ways a missed opportunity for the major reforms needed in the Church; the fathers contented themselves mainly with minor but useful changes in ecclesiastical administration. Ominously, the assembly closed only a few months before Martin Luther posted his theses at Wittenburg. *See also* ecumenical council; Gregorian reform; Innocent III; investiture controversy; Reformation, the.   WILLIAM J. DOHAR

Lateran Treaty, agreement signed on February 11, 1929, between the Holy See and the Italian government settling the "Roman Question," which had resulted from the fall of the city of Rome as the last territory of the Papal States. The Holy See was financially compensated for the loss of property, the Vatican City State was established as a political entity, or sovereign state, independent of Italy, and a concordat was agreed upon that guaranteed and regulated the role of the Church in the life of Italy, making it the official religion of the country. The concordat was renegotiated and formally ratified on June 3, 1985. Catholic instruction is no longer mandatory in government schools, and the clergy are no longer paid salaries by the government. *See also* Papal States; Vatican City State.

Latin America, Catholicism in. After Christopher Columbus reached the West Indies in 1492, the Catholic kings of Spain and Portugal asked the pope to grant them title to the lands of the New World. This request included a desire to extend the dominion of the Catholic faith. On May 4, 1493, Pope Alexander VI granted these petitions in his bull *Inter Caetera* and consequently missionary work became a priority for the kings. In the bull *Universalis Ecclesiae* (July 28, 1508) Pope Julius II gave universal patronage to the Spanish crown. In 1569 King Philip II established inquisitorial tribunals in Spanish America in order to assure purity of faith and doctrine. The Church became thereby one of the principal agents of civil power in the Americas.

Early Missionary Efforts: As soon as the news of Christopher Columbus's voyage to America had spread throughout Europe, the other European countries outside of Spain—Portugal, England, France, Italy, Belgium—responded to the fresh opportunities for missionary and economic expansion (the two interests unfortunately were not always to be separated). Religious orders like the Franciscans, Dominicans, and Jesuits committed themselves almost immediately to bring the gospel to these newly discovered shores. The Franciscans focused their efforts on Mexico, Ecuador, and Bolivia; the Dominicans, on Peru and Colombia; the Jesuits, on Paraguay and Brazil. In many instances, the missionaries functioned as rulers of the Indians, often without regard for royal officials or bishops.

But this initial phase of missionary work came to an end in 1530 when King Charles I of Spain forbade foreign priests from going to his American territories without special royal permission. That prohibition marked the beginning of the Hispanicization of Latin America and of the Latin American Catholic Church for centuries to come. The new dioceses were erected in accordance with the ritual and customs of the cathedrals of either Toledo or Seville and their liturgical and sacramental practices were patterned after those of Seville.

A period of stagnation and conflict within and between the religious orders, between the orders and the bishops, and between the bishops and the royal officers followed the initial period of missionary enthusiasm and achievement. After 1640 the missionary efforts of both Jesuits and Franciscans lagged, either for lack of missionaries or for lack of training centers. In 1673, however, the Jesuits were granted royal permission to enlist missionaries from Germany, with Hispanicized names.

In 1752 and 1754 a new set of royal decrees removed the religious from most of their Indian parishes and in 1767 the Jesuits themselves were

LATIN AMERICA

suppressed. As time passed, people began wondering why the religious were there at all, so little did they have to do any longer. That situation changed, however, with the struggle for independence and the emergence of new states.

With the independence of Spanish America beginning in 1808, the politico-ecclesiastical balance was changed. Although religion was not the cause of the revolutions, shortcomings in the Church, such as its vast wealth, contributed to them. The great leader for Latin American independence, Simón Bolívar, was in favor of separating Church and state; however, the basis of the early opposition to the Catholic Church was largely political and not religious. By the mid-nineteenth century the position of the Catholic Church in Latin America had become very unstable. Since 1950 there has been a strong tendency toward a "free Church–free state" relationship. As the Second Vatican Council began in 1962 the Catholic Church was in a weakened position in Latin America. However, after the council the Church began to renew itself. Whereas the majority still identify themselves as Catholics, in recent years other religious denominations, especially the Pentecostal and evangelical churches, have grown substantially through proselytism.

Inculturation: Although the Catholic faith was introduced in Latin America near the end of the fifteenth century, it did not take root in the native cultures until near the end of the twentieth century.

A Palm Sunday procession of Otavalo Indians portraying Christ riding the donkey into Jerusalem; in Cotacachi, Ecuador, a South American country with some 10 million Catholics.

However, almost from the beginning there has been a type of popular religiosity that has reflected indigenous culture in varying ways. A much closer look at the relations between such popular religiosity and official teaching and pastoral practice was pursued in greater depth after the Second Vatican Council.

With some exceptions, the pastoral practices during these hundreds of years have largely reflected those of the European missioners. The Latin American countries were looked upon as colonies. Among the striking exceptions to this attitude was that of Fray Antonio de Montesinos, who was sent by the Spanish crown to the Americas in 1510. He accused his Spanish congregation of mortal sin because of their mistreatment of the Indians. Another missioner, Fray Bartolomé de las Casas (1474–1566), after initially agreeing with the Spanish plan of conquest and forcible conversion, radically changed his thinking in view of his own pastoral experience. He eventually was named "Protector of the Indians" and said that wars of conquest against Indians were "unjust, perverse and tyrannical." The sixteenth century had many such clergymen who committed themselves to the cause of the Indians. A number of these were Dominican and Franciscan missionaries. However, toward the end of the sixteenth century the clergy, both religious and diocesan, became lax in their defense of the natives. Many Jesuits remained faithful to the cause of the indigenous, but in 1767 they were expelled from Latin America. Thus, until the mid-twentieth century the Church in many ways collaborated with the elite power structure. It accepted the principle of Church-state cooperation and social inequality, which included a type of fatalism preached to the poor.

It was with the close of World War II that significant changes were initiated in the Latin American Church. The so-called cold war, which pitted Marxist-Leninism against Christianity, forced Church leaders to reevaluate both their ideas and pastoral practices. Papal teachings on social justice, lay movements such as Catholic Action, and the *Cursillos de Cristiandad* assumed great importance. The Latin American Church was being prepared for important changes.

CELAM: Although the Latin American bishops met in Rome in 1899, it was not until 1955 when they came together in Rio de Janeiro to form CELAM (the Conference of Latin American Bishops) that they established a permanent transnational structure. From this point on they were to have regular meetings every ten years. However, it was not until the Second Vatican Council (1962–65) that CELAM assumed real strength. A key motivator was Bishop Manuel Larrain of Chile. He did everything possible to bring the Latin American Church together and to integrate the pastoral theology of Vatican II with the cultures of the continent. In 1963 he was elected president of CELAM. Pope Paul VI supported these efforts and this support continued under Pope John Paul II. The Vatican representative who consistently collaborated in this process was Cardinal Antonio Samore (d. 1983).

Vatican II brought the first clear effort by the Church to become a "World Church," i.e., one that seriously integrates its values within the various cultures. CELAM followed the methodology in the council's Pastoral Constitution on the Church in the Modern World by studying the facts, reflecting upon them, and then making recommendations. This was a bottom-up rather than a top-down approach. Unfortunately, Bishop Larrain died in an auto accident in 1966. Nonetheless, CELAM's momentum could not be stopped as it prepared for an extraordinary session at Medellín, Colombia, in 1968.

During these same years other developments affected the emerging identity of Latin American Catholicism. One was the influx of missionaries, both clerical and lay, from other countries. A specific example was the papal request in 1961 that religious orders of the United States send 10 percent of their members to Latin America. These were joined by many from other countries.

Within CELAM itself there were established departments, publications, and training centers. A parallel organization of religious, CLAR (Latin American Conference of Religious), was also initiated. Research centers and intellectual networking became common.

Medellín: In 1966 the officials of CELAM decided that at the 1968 extraordinary conference at Medellín there would be pastoral representatives from apostolic sectors rather than merely canonical representatives from ecclesiastical regions. This meant that the Church would be judged primarily in terms of its pastoral experience. This would have a great impact on the methodology and outcome of the Medellín conference. Part of this methodology included an ever-increasing social analysis throughout the continent. This led to a much sharper awareness of the "realities" of Latin America. The bishops realized that there was widespread "institutionalized injustice." The Church itself was part of this and was now being called to make the option for the poor. Evangelization and lay participation were to be emphasized, especially through grass-roots communities. Finally, the statements on justice, peace, and poverty were the strongest ones of the sixteen

sections of the *Conclusions*. Gradually the Church was becoming "Latin American."

Puebla: Eleven years later, in 1979 in Puebla, Mexico, it was judged important to review the process of pastoral integration since Medellín. Some leaders were concerned that the basic commitments of Medellín were in danger of being weakened. Others felt that there were misunderstandings of the Medellín agreements. In the end, however, the delegation reconfirmed Medellín and moved it modestly forward. Pope John Paul II, who was present in the first days of Puebla, expressed ecclesiological and pastoral concerns, particularly as they related to the role of the magisterium. However, the theme at Puebla, "Evangelization Today and Tomorrow in Latin America," had its roots not only in the Second Vatican Council but also in the document *Evangelii Nuntiandi* of Paul VI (1975). Consequently Pope John Paul II drew heavily upon this document, and the conference proved to be a unifying force. It accepted the assumptions of Medellín and reiterated the preferential option for the poor. It challenged both official leadership and the grass roots to collaborate in facing the monumental tasks of Latin America. This was a positive step ahead.

From the time of Medellín an inductive pastoral analysis assumed greater prominence. In pastoral circles this was known as liberation theology. There were to be many discussions and reviews of this kind of theologizing, which culminated in two instructions from the Vatican, in 1984 and 1986.

A religious festival in Brazil, the Latin American country with the largest Catholic population in the world (over 135 million); the people are carrying pictures of Jesus, Mary, Joseph, and the pope.

Finally, in 1986 John Paul II wrote to the Brazilian bishops saying that liberation theology is "not only opportune, but also it is useful and necessary." Still, some tension would continue between the deductive and inductive approaches to theology.

Santo Domingo and Beyond: The year 1992 marked the Quincentenary of the introduction of the Catholic faith into Latin America. It was also the occasion for CELAM IV—the assembly of the Latin American bishops during October, in Santo Domingo, Dominican Republic. The theme of the assembly was "A New Evangelization for a New Culture." As the conference began there were differences between those who were committed to the present authority structures as a significant factor in improving the social order and those who strongly supported more grass-roots input in seeking an alternative plan of society. How these differences are negotiated over the long term will determine the ultimate effect of a "new" evangelization and inculturation. In the latter part of the twentieth century the Catholic Church in Latin America moved strongly in the direction of a deeper inculturation. This will have a significant influence on the future of the Church on that continent.

The latter part of the twentieth century has proved to be a time of great suffering for the Latin America Church. As pastoral leaders, both clerical and lay, became conscious of great injustice in their societies, they spoke out. In doing this many of these leaders were aware that they were risking their lives. The best known of these pastors was Archbishop Oscar Romero of El Salvador, who was assassinated as he celebrated Mass on March 24, 1980. Other examples include the six Jesuit priests and two laywomen killed in El Salvador in 1989 and the four U.S. women (three religious, one a laywoman) murdered in that same country in December 1980. However, there were many other deaths of deeply Christian *campesinos* (people of the land) who served as catechists and proclaimers of the word. There is some dispute as to the political influence in such religious sacrifices. However, many believe that this suffering has purified the Latin American Church and brought it to a new level of maturity. *See also* base communities; Guadalupe, Our Lady of; liberation theology; Spain, Catholicism in.

Bibliography

Eagleson, John, and Philip Scharper, eds. *Puebla and Beyond: Documentation and Commentary.* Maryknoll, NY: Orbis Books, 1979.

Keough, Dermot. *Church and Politics in Latin America.* New York: St. Martin's Press, 1990.

Richard, Pablo. *Death of Christendoms, Birth of the Church: Historical Analysis and Theological Interpretation of the Church in Latin America.* Maryknoll, NY: Orbis Books, 1987.   ROBERT S. PELTON

latinization, the imposition or imitation of Latin-rite liturgical customs and principles and the resulting erosion or dilution of the Eastern Catholic liturgical traditions. Liturgical rites have always influenced one another. "Latinization" has been considered a contaminating influence because it has been seen as forced or unnatural, and therefore destructive of the liturgical ethos and spirit of the Eastern rite in question—e.g., the introduction of exposition of the Blessed Sacrament in a rite that traditionally elicits devotion by concealment of the mysteries. The issue is not which spirit is better, but which is native to a people that deserves to be left in peace with its own heritage. During the Crusades (1095–1291) and the Portuguese colonization of India (after 1498, when Vasco da Gama arrived), this latinization was imposed on Eastern Catholics who were in communion with Rome. In the twentieth century, it was more often the result of Eastern Catholics uncritically imitating Latin ways out of a sense of inferiority or inadequate knowledge and appreciation of their own heritage. This practice was induced by the expressed Catholic policy of the *praestantia ritus Latini* (Lat., "superiority of the Latin rite").

The term "latinization" is also used to describe the way in which Latin missionaries and schools in the East have served, deliberately or unwittingly, to move Eastern Christians, Catholic or Orthodox, away from their native churches to the Latin rite. These practices did not begin to change until condemned by the 1743 constitution *Demandatam* of Pope Benedict XIV. *Orientalium Dignitas* of Pope Leo XIII in 1894 set strict guidelines to control the activities of Latin clergy in the East, and both these forms of latinization have been forbidden by the explicit and often repeated—though widely ignored—policy of the Holy See. *See also* Crusades; Latin rite; Roman Catholic; Roman rite.   ROBERT F. TAFT

Latin Mass. *See* Tridentine Mass.

Latin Patriarchate of Jerusalem, a Roman Catholic ecclesiastical circumscription (limited area) with jurisdiction over Latin Catholics, their institutions, and the Catholic-controlled Holy Places, in Israel, Jordan, Cyprus, and the Gaza strip. It was established during the Crusader occupation of the Holy Land (1099–1187). When the Holy City fell to

Saladin in 1187, the patriarchs resided in what was left of the Latin Kingdom of Jerusalem until 1291. Thereafter the patriarchate survived as the purely honorific title of absentee patriarchs resident in Rome. The patriarchate was reestablished at Jerusalem in 1847, and the present patriarch Michel Sabbah (since 1987), a native Palestinian, is the first non-Italian incumbent. The Orthodox and Catholic Melkites (Byzantine-rite Catholics) have traditionally viewed the patriarchate as a Western intrusion responsible for weaning away their faithful.

Latin patriarchates, Western Catholic ecclesiastical jurisdictions, under the pastoral authority of a patriarch. In the West, between the ninth century and modern times the purely honorific title "patriarchate" was assigned to Latin sees like Aquileia (later transferred to Venice) and Lisbon. The title was also held by Latin bishops imposed on Eastern patriarchal sees during the Crusader occupation (1099–1187). After the Latin occupation these titles were maintained for a time as Catholic titular sees but were later suppressed. Missionary jurisdictions like the patriarchates of the West Indies (1524) and East Indies (1886) were also established. Although the Latin Patriarchate of Jerusalem was reestablished in 1847, the only real Western patriarch is the pope. *See also* patriarch [ecclesiastical]; patriarchate.

Latin rite, popular though inaccurate name for the religious usages (liturgical, canonical, monastic) of the Church in the Roman Catholic West. Apart from North Africa, the West became "Latin" only when the gradual shift from Greek to Latin in the liturgy was completed in Rome in the fourth century.

The Latin Rites: The Latin Church leaders were more interested in submission than ritual uniformity, and were relatively more tolerant of ritual diversity, than were the Byzantines. Liturgically, the West maintained a pluralistic polity, and historically there were several non-Roman Latin rites: African, Ambrosian (Milanese), Aquileian, Celtic, Gallican, Iberian (Mozarabic of Toledo and Braga of Portugal), some of which are still in limited use in the 1990s. Originally, Roman liturgical usages prevailed only in the area around Rome and in "Suburbican Italy," i.e., southern Italy and the islands of Sicily, Sardinia, and Corsica. The rest of Italy had distinct local uses not only in metropolitan sees like Milan and Aquileia but in over forty other centers. Local usages in southern Gaul and the Iberian peninsula under the Visigoths evolved into the Gallican rites.

North Africa was also Latin but not Roman in rite; Norway followed the rite of Nidaros; Ireland had its Celtic rituals.

Geographical Extension of Latin Rites: Latin usages extended throughout the West and into North Africa west of Egypt, as well as in Pannonia, Illyricum, and Thrace. In the latter three areas, ruled in the seventh and eighth centuries by vassals of Byzantium, the Latin bishoprics had all but disappeared except along the Dalmatian and Albanian coastline. There were also numerous Latin-rite colonies in the East, chiefly merchants from the Italian mercantile cities and mercenaries in the Byzantine imperial service, but the churches serving them were under the jurisdiction of the local Byzantine hierarchy until the Crusaders implanted Latin ecclesiastical jurisdictions in the East.

Later Predominance of the Roman Rite: Roman uses gradually came to predominate throughout Europe in the eighth and ninth centuries under the Carolingian and Ottonian emperors. In the seventh century, Roman missionaries under Augustine of Canterbury had implanted the Roman rite in the British Isles, where it evolved local uses such as those of Sarum, Hereford, York, Bangor. In the eighth century, Rome-oriented missionaries from Britain returned to the Continent to reform the Gallican Church and evangelize the Germans. They brought with them a Roman liturgy, fostering the further amalgamation of Roman usages with local Gallican and Visigothic customs to form the Franco-Germanic-Roman synthesis that was reintroduced to Rome in the late tenth century and is the immediate ancestor of the Roman rite. *See also* rite; Roman Catholic; Roman rite.

Bibliography

Klauser, T. *A Short History of the Western Liturgy.* London, New York, Toronto: Oxford University Press, 1969.

Vogel, C. *Medieval Liturgy.* Trans. and rev. by W. Storey and N. Rasmussen. Washington, DC: The Pastoral Press, 1986. ROBERT F. TAFT

latria (la'tree-uh; Gk., *latreia,* "worship"), the worship or adoration owed to God alone. It is commonly contrasted with *dulia* (Gk.), which is the honor given to the saints, and *hyperdulia* (Gk.), which is the special honor given to the Blessed Virgin Mary because of her unique role as the Mother of God. *See also dulia; hyperdulia.*

Latrocinium (lah-troh-chee'nee-uhm). *See* Ephesus, Robber Council of.

Latter-day Saints. *See* Mormons.

Latvia, Catholicism in. *See* Baltic countries, Catholicism in the.

Lauds (Lat., "praise"), Morning Prayer, the official morning office of the Liturgy of the Hours, signaling the beginning of the day. Lauds and Vespers are the chief, or hinge, hours of each day. The office, prayed as the new day dawns, recalls the Resurrection of Jesus, the True Light enlightening all (see John 1:9), the Sun of Justice (Mal 4:2), arising on high (Luke 1:78). Chief elements of Lauds are a hymn, two psalms and an OT canticle, a short reading and responsory, the Canticle of Zechariah, intercessions, and the Lord's Prayer. *See also* Liturgy of the Hours; Morning Prayer.

lavabo (lah-vah'boh; Lat., "I will wash"), an ablution, or ritual washing. During the preparation rite, after the bread and wine have been placed on the altar, the presider washes his hands in a small basin. He may pray silently while doing so: "Lord, wash away my iniquity, cleanse me from my sin."

lavra (lahv'rah; Gk., *laura*, "city lane," "monastery"), originally a community of semi-reclusive monks under the direction of one spiritual father or superior. The monks lived as solitaries in scattered cells, usually in a wilderness or desert area, within walking distance of common monastic buildings. These included a church where the monks would gather for services on weekends and feasts. In later times the term "lavra" came to mean any large Greek Orthodox monastery, even one following a cenobitic (community) rule. *See also* monastery.

law. *See* canon law; natural law.

law, favor of. *See* favor of law.

law, penal. *See* penal law.

Lawrence, St., d. 258, deacon of Pope Sixtus II and martyr mentioned in the Canon (Eucharistic Prayer) of the Roman Mass. He was admired by Ambrose, Prudentius, Augustine, and others. They repeat the story that, when asked by the Roman prefect to surrender the Church's riches, Lawrence assembled the poor, to whom he had distributed the Church's possessions, and said that they (the poor) were the Church's real treasure. For this, according to tradition, he was roasted alive on a gridiron. Most scholars believe he was beheaded. In Rome the

Lawrence, third-century deacon known for his kindness to the poor and the most famous of Rome's postapostolic martyrs, enthroned with saints and donors; fifteenth-century Florentine painting on wood by Fra Filippo Lippi, Metropolitan Museum of Art, New York.

basilica of St. Lawrence-Outside-the-Walls is dedicated to him. Feast day: August 10.

Lawrence of Brindisi, St. (brin'duh-zee), 1559–1619, Capuchin Franciscan. Scholar, papal emissary, missionary preacher, religious reformer, and writer, he retired from active life in 1618 only to be sent by papal authority to Lisbon, where he died. He was named a Doctor of the Church in 1959. Feast day: July 21.

Lawrence of the Resurrection, 1614–91, religious name of Nicholas Herman, a Discalced Carmelite brother in Paris. Previously a soldier, he became a cook as a Carmelite. Abbé de Beaufort posthumously published a collection of Lawrence's sayings and letters which in English is known as *The Practice of the Presence of God.*

Lawrence O'Toole, St., 1128–80, archbishop of Dublin. After a monastic formation, he assumed the see of Dublin in 1162. Active in clerical reform and as an intermediary between the Irish and English, he was conspicuous not only for his reforming spirit, but also for his personal austerity and charity. Feast day: November 14.

Lawrence Ruiz, St. (roo-eez'), ca. 1600–1637, martyr. A married Filipino of Chinese extraction, he accompanied Dominican friars on a mission to

Japan. He was martyred in Nagasaki with his companions. Feast day: September 28.

laxism, a moral system that permits an individual experiencing moral doubt to take the options representing more liberty, provided some degree of probability about its moral rectitude exists. It is considered a perversion of the contemporary moral system of probabilism, which held that one can safely follow a moral opinion only if it is proposed by someone having sufficient theological authority and standing. Laxism and several conclusions following from it were condemned by Pope Alexander VII in 1665 and 1666 and Pope Innocent XI in 1679. It was also strongly opposed by Jansenism, a seventeenth-century French movement that favored a strict and rigorous approach to the moral law. *See also* Jansenism; probabilism.

lay (Gk., *laos,* "people"), adjective denoting the nonclerical or nonordained members of the Church. Canon law recognizes that the lay members of Christ's faithful have certain rights and obligations (cans. 208–31). *See also* laity.

lay apostolate, the ministry provided by those members of the Church who are not ordained. In virtue of their baptism, lay Christians share the vocation of the original apostles of Jesus, that is, to witness to Jesus Christ and to promote the salvation of all people. They accomplish this apostolate primarily by living according to Christian principles and also by speaking for those principles. The lay apostolate can be exercised within the family, within Church communities, and in the context of professional and social relationships. Its goal is the sanctification of individuals and the renewal of the temporal order. According to Vatican II (1962–65), "The lay apostolate . . . is a participation in the saving mission of the Church itself" (Dogmatic Constitution on the Church, n. 33), and not simply a participation in the work of the hierarchy, known as Catholic Action. *See also* apostolate; laity.

lay brother, a member of a male religious community who is fully incorporated in the religious institute and is not ordained. This phrase has two connotations. In many instances, the adjective "lay" intensifies "brother," emphasizing only that a brother is a nonclerical religious. In traditional usage, lay brothers were members with less education who were destined to the service of manual labor. The lay

brotherhood originated in monastic orders; the brothers were to relieve the clerical monks of any tasks that would hinder their study and ministry. This monastic model was adopted in various ways by other religious communities. *See also* brothers, religious.

lay ministries, official and unofficial roles of service or leadership carried out by nonordained persons in the Church. Although laypeople have been closely linked to the Church's mission and service from earliest times (see, e.g., Rom 16:1–16), their properly ministerial role was recognized anew by Vatican Council II, especially in its Constitution on the Sacred Liturgy (1963, n. 14), its Dogmatic Constitution on the Church (1964, nn. 30–38), and its Decree on the Apostolate of the Laity (1965, esp. nn. 2–3). As the council repeatedly emphasized, lay participation in roles of leadership and service is rooted in Baptism, a sacrament that gives all believers a share in the priestly, prophetic, and royal ministry of Christ. Lay ministries are often, though not exclusively, liturgical in nature. (Nonliturgical roles of service and leadership are performed, for instance, by lay teachers and catechists, by hospital administrators or members of a pastoral-care team, by campus ministers, by directors of diocesan offices, by pastoral associates, etc.). Since Vatican Council II, laypersons have become increasingly visible in liturgical roles such as reader, acolyte (altar-server), cantor, and extraordinary minister of Communion. In some places, laypeople are also entrusted with the ministry of preaching. The basis for this is found in the 1983 Code of Canon Law (can. 766), which says that laypeople may be allowed to preach in church if it is necessary or (in particular cases) advantageous. Decisions about preaching by laypersons are in the hands of the various national episcopal conferences. *See also* laity; ministry.

Laynez, James, 1512–65, Spanish Jesuit theologian, one of the original seven members of what became the Society of Jesus, and general of the order in 1558. He was active at the Council of Trent (1545–63) and his contribution was decisive in establishing the council's position on the key doctrine of justification against Protestantism. *See also* Jesuits.

lay spirituality, the practice of life in the Spirit by the Christian people (Gk., *laos*). In early Christianity, *laos* included all the baptized, with their different gifts for building up the community. Soon, the adjective *laikos* designated the people in contrast to their leaders. By the Middle Ages, those desirous of a radical Christian life had recourse to rich institutional models of holiness developed by clerical-monastic or mystical elites. Ordinary Christians tended to eucharistic devotion, veneration of relics and sacred places, and participation in popular feasts that often mixed religious fervor and superstitious ancestral customs. After the Reformation, doctrine, sacrament, and tradition set the norms for Catholic personal piety. In modern times, the Church used Marian devotions, pilgrimages, and Catholic Action to foster corporate lay presence as it defended Western ecclesial interests amid secularization and industrialization. Twentieth-century biblical, liturgical, and patristic revivals, supported by Vatican II (1962–65), have encouraged Catholic laity to develop their own diverse mystical, prophetic, and creation-centered spiritualities.

Whether traced through influential figures, religious movements, or the daily reality of ordinary believers, Christian life involves a dialectical relation of opposition and participation in the world and in history. Any study of contemporary lay spiritualities in Catholicism involves this tension as well as the role of the universal Church with its various cultural manifestations, including the evolution of base communities, new religious groups, prophetic forms of political witness, ethical questions of sexuality, power, and justice, the women's movement, and openness to ecumenism and interreligious dialogue. *See also* laity; spirituality, Christian.

PHYLLIS H. KAMINSKY

lay trusteeism. *See* trusteeism, lay.

Lazarists, also called Vincentians, Congregation of the Mission (C.M.), an order founded by St. Vincent de Paul (1625) of diocesan priests devoted to preaching missions to the poor, foreign missions, training clergy, and Catholic education. They have been joined with the Daughters of Charity under one superior general since St. Vincent founded both orders. *See also* Vincentians.

Lazarus, a friend of Jesus' from Bethany. According to John 11:1–44, Lazarus, the brother of Martha and Mary, died in Jesus' absence. Jesus came to Bethany and after discussion with Lazarus's sisters raised him from the dead. Lazarus is also the name of the poor beggar in a parable recounted in Luke 16:19–31.

Lazarus Saturday, the Saturday before Palm Sunday, commemorating Jesus' raising Lazarus from the dead (John 11:11–44). Noted in the Jerusalem calendar in the fourth century, it is still celebrated in several Eastern-rite Lenten calendars in the 1990s, where it comprises the final day of Lent before Holy Week begins. *See also* Lazarus.

Leadership Conference of Women Religious, one of two official organizations of the major superiors of women in the United States. The conference was founded in 1956, and its statues were approved by Rome in 1959. The purpose of the conference is primarily to promote the spiritual and apostolic life of the religious communities, and also to promote collaboration among the communities and with the hierarchy, and to serve as a national voice for the major superiors. In 1994 there were approximately 800 members. The other conference is called the Council of Major Superiors of Women Religious, established in 1992. *See also* Conference of Major Superiors of Men; Council of Major Superiors of Women Religious.

leave of absence [from religious life], unofficial term used to indicate a period of vocational discernment spent away from one's religious community. A religious on such a leave might request and receive an indult of exclaustration, which would alter his or her official status. The term also applies to diocesan priests who leave the active ministry for a time.

Le Brun, Pierre, 1661–1729, French liturgist and Oratorian priest. He taught at Saint-Magloire Seminary in Paris. His commentaries on the Mass aroused controversy. In them he defended the proposition that an epiclesis, the prayer that calls down the Holy Spirit, is necessary for the eucharistic consecration. *See also* epiclesis.

lectern, or ambo, the place from which the word of God is proclaimed. A focal point for the assembly during the Liturgy of the Word, the lectern is a stationary reading stand reserved for the scriptural readings, responsorial psalm, and the Easter Proclamation (*Exsultet*); it may be used for the homily and general intercessions.

lectio continua (lek'zee-oh cohn-tin'*oo*-uh; Lat., "continuous reading"), a reference to the liturgical practice of sequential reading of the books of Scripture. Collections of patristic homilies following the order of the biblical books constitute the principal evidence for early Church practice. The liturgical reforms that followed Vatican II (1962–65) restored *lectio continua* in both the Sunday and weekday lectionaries. *See also* lectionary.

lectio divina, (Lat., "divine reading"), a meditative reading of Sacred Scripture leading to prayer. Such reading enjoyed an important place in Christian and monastic practice well into the Middle Ages. Monastic codes, such as the Rule of St. Benedict, assign to *lectio* daily periods as long as two to three hours. In time this meditative reading came to include, in addition to the Bible, biblical commentaries, patristic writings, and treatises dealing with the spiritual life, often of a moralizing nature. In current usage the term is often applied loosely to any meditative reading done with a view to the enrichment of one's spiritual life. *See also* meditation.

lectionary, the book containing the scriptural lessons appointed for public reading at Mass according to the liturgical calendar.

The concept of the lectionary dates to the synagogue, which had readings appointed for feasts and Sabbaths. The extent to which the Church borrowed from Jewish lectionaries is unclear; the Exodus reading for Passover is, however, used for Pascha (the Christian Passover). Early methods of identifying appointed lessons, or pericopes, included marginal notations of the beginning and ending in the Scriptures, a separate list of scriptural references (capitulary), a book of lessons, or written texts, included with Mass prayers (Lat., *missale plenum,* "full missal").

Before the Council of Nicaea (325) a lectionary existed only for feasts; Sunday readings followed *lectio continua,* i.e., continuous reading from a chosen book, read in portions until the book was finished. Several lessons from both testaments with interspersed psalms were used; gradually, three lessons became standard in the Mozarabic, Gallican, Milanese, and Armenian rites. At Constantinople (fifth century) and Rome (sixth century) the lessons were reduced to two.

The revised lectionary of 1969 provides for three lessons on Sundays and feasts. Three annual Sunday cycles apportion the synoptic Gospels semi-continuously; John's Gospel, generally reserved for feasts and seasons, also fills in when the Marcan readings end. The first lesson, usually from the Hebrew Scriptures, is paired with the Gospel and is followed by a responsorial psalm. The second, a lesson taken from one of the Pauline Letters, follows a semicontinuous pattern of readings without reference to the Sunday or feast. Feast day and seasonal readings are often discrete, rather than continuous, readings. The Roman lectionary has been widely adopted by other Christian traditions, with minor adjustments. *See also* liturgical year.   JOHN A. MELLOH

lector, or reader, one who proclaims at Mass the first or second reading from Scripture, other than the Gospel. In the absence of a deacon, the reader may carry the Gospel book in procession and lead the general intercessions. Previously, lector was a "minor order," preparatory to the ordained priesthood; today it is termed a "ministry," and may be committed to the laity. *See also* ministry; minor orders.

Leen, Edward, 1885–1944, Irish priest and spiritual author. A member of the Congregation of the Holy Ghost, his career included administrative service to Blackrock College and to his own community. He was best known for his many popular books on the spiritual life, including *In the Likeness of Christ* (1936).

Lefebvre, Marcel (mahr-sel' luh-fev'), 1905–91, French prelate and schismatic. Ordained a Holy Ghost priest (1929), he did missionary work in France and Africa. Named bishop in 1947, he served as vicar apostolic of Dakar (Senegal) and later as apostolic delegate of all of French-speaking Africa. He attended the Second Vatican Council (1962–65) but refused to sign some of the conciliar documents. Disenchanted with postconciliar directions, he opened a traditionalist seminary in Switzerland in 1970. His vehement rejection of the council led, finally, to his suspension *a divinis* (Lat., "from all priestly and episcopal powers") in 1976. After a period of reconciliation and negotiation with the Vatican, he again split with Rome over the questions of his right to ordain bishops and the autonomy of his movement within the Church. After his excommunication in 1988 for ordaining bishops without papal authority, his movement split into those who returned to Roman obedience (including the Society of St. Peter) and those who remain committed to his schismatic course. *See also* Fraternity of St. Peter, Priestly.

Lefèvre d'Étaples, Jacques (luhr-fev' day-tahl'). *See* Faber, Jacobus.

legalism, a moral attitude that identifies Christian morality with the observance of laws. Legalism has its origin in nominalism, a fourteenth-century philosophical theory that denied the existence of universal concepts, such as human nature. If morality is not rooted in universal human nature (as nominalists hold), then morality can only be based on divine commands as expressed in rules and laws. Legalism was dominant in Catholic moral theology and practice until the Second Vatican Council (1962–65), which emphasized Scripture, the mystery of Christ, and salvation history as a more appropriate basis for making moral decisions. *See also* laxism; moral theology.

legate, papal. *See* papal legate.

Léger, Paul-Emile (lay-zhay'), 1904–91, cardinal-archbishop of Montreal. He resigned from that post in 1967 to work for twelve years among lepers and impoverished and disabled children in Africa. Léger was ordained priest in 1929 and archbishop in 1950 and created a cardinal in 1953. Founder of the Fame Pereo Institute for Lepers and the Center for the Rehabilitation of the Handicapped in Cameroon, he was widely regarded as one of the most saintly members of the Church's hierarchy in his day.

Legion of Decency, an organization established in 1934 by the U.S. Catholic bishops to promote quality motion pictures. As a guide for parents who were selecting films for their children, the National Legion of Decency in 1936 established a classification system for motion pictures, based upon their moral suitability. Since 1968, the United States Catholic Conference Department of Communications' Office of Film and Broadcasting has provided ratings and reviews of motion picture, television, and video releases for Catholic newspapers and has published weekly guides. It also maintains Preview Line, a telephone information service. Ratings include: A-I (general patronage); A-II (adults and adolescents); A-III (adults); A-IV (adults, with reservations); and O (morally offensive). *See also* Catholicism and the visual arts.

Legion of Mary, lay Catholic association founded in Dublin, Ireland, in 1921 by Frank Duff (1889–1980) and others. Duff had been inspired by his long association with the St. Vincent de Paul Society, of which he had been an active member.

Organized along strict hierarchical lines, the Legion borrows the language of ancient Rome: an individual group is a presidium; a district is a curia; the next level is the comitatus, which is organized into a senatus, which answers to the general headquarters in Dublin known as the concilium. *The Official Handbook of the Legion of Mary* (many editions translated into various languages) is the guiding text of the group.

Found in most parts of the Catholic world, the Legion stresses a Marian spirituality inspired largely by the writings of Louis Grignion de Montfort (d. 1716). Weekly attendance at meetings and regular time spent in a variety of apostolic activities shape the spiritual discipline of the group. Active in religious work in all parts of the world, especially in Third World countries, the Legion's delegate to Africa in the 1950s, Edel Quinn, has had her cause for canonization introduced in Rome. *See also* Marian devotion; Montfort, St. Louis Grignion de.

Lellis, St. Camillus de. *See* Camillus of Lellis, St.

Lent (Mid. Eng., *lenten,* "springtime"), the forty days (not including Sundays) of fasting, prayer, and penitence before Easter. The origins—and duration—of Lent are related to the development of Easter. During the first three centuries most Christians prepared for Easter by fasting for only two or three days. In some places, this "paschal fast" was extended to the entire week before Easter (the period now known as "Holy Week"). In Rome this paschal fast originally may have lasted three weeks, but by the fourth century it had developed into a "Lent" of forty days.

This Roman Lent (in its earlier three-week form) was linked to the pastoral and liturgical preparation of catechumens for baptism at the Easter Vigil. Until recently this baptismal motif was thought to explain, fully, the origins of Lent—and also to show why the paschal fast was calculated "backward" from Easter Sunday (first, two days; then a week; then three weeks [at Rome]; then forty days, the length of Jesus' fast in the desert [Luke 4:1–13] and the length of the modern Lent). But recent research has shown that the development of Lent was also influenced by another forty-day fasting tradition, an ascetical one based on imitation of Jesus' life, which began immediately after the feast of Epiphany

(January 6, and on other dates where it is not observed as a holy day of obligation). This post-Epiphany fast (popular among monks) emphasized prayer and penance, themes that made sense especially after infant baptism began to prevail in the fifth and sixth centuries. Following Vatican II (1962–65), the renewal of the Rite of Christian Initiation of Adults helped restore the ancient Lenten baptismal motif. *See also* Baptism; Easter; Rite of Christian Initiation of Adults. NATHAN D. MITCHELL

Leo I, "the Great," St., d. 461, pope from 440 to 461. Little is known of his life before his election, although he was a highly placed deacon during the tenure of his two immediate predecessors. A vigorous and articulate advocate of papal prerogative, he rejected the canon of the Council of Chalcedon (451) that declared Constantinople and Rome equal in dignity, and he advanced papal claims over all Western provinces. But it was not only his theory that fostered the prestige of the papacy, but his own pastoral courage and genius. He personally met the Vandals as they approached to take the city in 455, pleading on behalf of the populace. His homilies, on matters both doctrinal and disciplinary, were elegant and clear. He is perhaps best remembered, however, for his intervention in the Christological controversies of the East. Both parties, the Monophysites associated with Eutyches and the Dyophysites headed by Flavian, patriarch of Constantinople, actively sought his judgment. His *Tome* to Flavian, which condemned Eutyches and affirmed a doctrine of two natures, one person in Christ was accepted by Chalcedon as a standard of Christological orthodoxy. He was made a Doctor of the Church in 1754. Feast day: November 10 (formerly April 11, West); February 18 (East). *See also* Chalcedon, Council of; Christology; Constantinople; Dyophysites; Eutyches; Monophysitism; *Tome* of Leo.

Pope Leo the Great, fifth-century pope who substantially increased the ecclesiastical and political prestige of the papacy, rooting its supreme and universal authority in the unbroken succession of popes from the time of St. Peter.

Leo II, St., d. 683, pope from 682 to 683. He is remembered principally for his ratification of the acts of Constantinople III (680–81), which condemned Pope Honorius I (d. 638). Leo's statement, however, did not accuse Honorius of heresy, but only of permissiveness with regard to a heresy regarding the will of Christ (Monothelitism). Feast day: July 3. *See also* Honorious I; Monothelitism.

Leo III, St., d. 816, pope from 795 to 816. Forced from Rome by relatives of his predecessor Hadrian I, he returned with Charlemagne in 800 and crowned him emperor of the West on Christmas Day. He worked with Charlemagne against the Spanish Adoptionists but resisted the addition of the *Filioque* (Lat., "and from the Son") to the Nicene Creed. He was active in building and renovating churches in Rome. Feast day: June 12. *See also* Adoptionism; Charlemagne; *Filioque;* Holy Roman Empire.

Leo IV, St., d. 855, pope from 847 to 855. Leo IV did much to repair the city of Rome after the Muslim attacks of 846, including the erection of a forty-foot wall surrounding St. Peter's and much of Vatican Hill, creating the "Leonine City." The *Asperges* (sprinkling of holy water at Mass) and the Octave of the Assumption have been attributed to him. Feast day: July 17.

Leo IX, St. [Bruno of Egisheim], ca. 1002–54, reformer and pope from 1049 to 1054. Having studied at Toul where he was bishop in 1026, Bruno was a supporter of Cluny's monastic renewal; he subsequently devoted himself to the reform of the entire Church. His chief concerns were secular interference with Church appointments and clerical marriage. Called the "Apostolic Pilgrim," Leo implemented his reforms by traveling extensively and appointing some of the greatest reformers of his day, including the future Gregory VII, to positions of authority. His final years as pope were troubled by schism with the Eastern Church. Feast day: April 19. *See also* celibacy, clerical; Eastern Schism; investiture controversy.

Leo X [Giovanni de Medici], 1475–1521, son of Lorenzo the Magnificent and pope from 1513 to 1521. Leo's patronage of the arts, his entanglements in the wars between France and Spain, a planned crusade against the Turks, as well as extensive building (including St. Peter's) strained papal finances and led to the indulgences against which

Martin Luther complained. Leo's attempts to suppress Luther were futile, including the issuing of *Exsurge Domine,* as were his half-hearted efforts to reform the Church at Lateran V (1512–17), an ecumenical council originally convened by his predecessor, Pope Julius II (d. 1513). *See also* Lateran councils; Luther, Martin.

Leo XIII [Gioacchino Pecci], 1810–1903, pope from 1878 to 1903. He is best known for his social encyclical *Rerum Novarum* (1891), generally regarded as the first major document of modern Catholic social teachings. Pius IX's Syllabus of Errors (1864) had declared war on the contemporary world and democracy, but Leo sought pragmatic reconciliation with his time. As nuncio to Belgium, he had witnessed the start of the industrial revolution; as bishop of Perugia (1846–78; cardinal, 1853), he had encouraged scholars. As pope, he defused the *Kulturkampf* ("culture struggle" with the Church) in Germany and Switzerland, secured the withdrawal of anticlerical legislation in Chile, Mexico, and Spain, and restored diplomatic relations with Brazil, Colombia, and Russia. Despite, perhaps because of, the loss of temporal power in 1870, heads of state began to visit the Vatican and invite it to arbitrate international disputes. Leo called on French Catholics, traditionally monarchist, to rally to the Republic. He attempted in *Rerum Novarum* to speak for downtrodden workers, condemning impartially socialist collectivism and *laissez-faire* capitalism and asserting strongly the right to private property.

A Reinvigorated Papacy: Leo dreamed of restoring Christian unity under the leadership of a reinvigorated papacy. His vision was welcomed by Russian Orthodox thinkers like Vladimir Soloviev. But the condemnation of Anglican orders, pronounced "absolutely null and utterly void" by *Apostolicae Curae* (1896), was a setback to his ecumenical hopes.

Leo saw the need to revive Catholic scholarship. The Vatican Observatory for astronomical study was modernized. Thomism was made the basis of seminary teaching in *Aeterni Patris* (1879). Though an improvement on previous eclecticism, the motives of some neo-Thomists were suspect. Leo half-opened the Vatican archives to *bona fide* scholars and famously declared that "the Church has nothing to fear from the truth." His encyclical intended to encourage biblical studies, *Providentissimus Deus* (1893), used a narrow concept of inspiration, but he created the Biblical Commission and assigned it relatively liberal members.

The Pope and America: Leo's weaknesses became apparent in his handling of U.S. Affairs. American Catholics were divided over the Knights of Labor, some denouncing it as a secret society while Archbishop John Ireland defended it on the grounds that the Church should be allied with the workers rather than with kings or princes. Cardinal James Gibbons took part in the World Parliament of Religions in Chicago in 1893, intended to illustrate the basic unity of belief shared by all the great world religions. But Leo condemned a similar attempt at the Paris exhibition of 1900. Denunciations and quarrels led to *Longinqua Oceani* (1895), which praised some aspects of the Church in the United States but warned against idealizing the separation of Church and state.

More misunderstandings about the life of Father Thomas Hecker, founder of the Paulists, led to *Testem Benevolentiae* (1898), which condemned the notion of adapting doctrines to the modern world and criticized "activism" and the peril of "indifferentism." A case could be made for saying that Leo had France in view rather than the United States.

Sixty-eight years old when he was elected pope in 1878, Leo lived to be ninety-two. "We elected a Holy Father," said one rueful cardinal, "not an Eternal Father." His pontificate showed that the papacy could be effective without temporal power, but his liberal impulses were not deeply rooted and were easily reversed by his saintly, but very conservative, successor, Pius X. *See also Aeterni Patris;* Americanism; Anglican ordination; *Rerum Novarum;* Thomism.

PETER HEBBLETHWAITE

Pope Leo XIII, the first pope in modern times to show an openness to scientific and scholarly progress and best known for his pioneering social encyclical *Rerum Novarum* (1891), on the condition of workers in the new industrial age.

Leonardi, St. John (lee-uh-nard'ee), 1542–1609, Italian religious founder. After ordination (1572), he started a catechetical confraternity as well as a small congregation of clerks regular devoted to the reform of priestly life. He helped found the Roman College (now the Pontifical Gregorian University) and the *Propaganda Fide,* the Vatican Congregation in charge of missionary activity (today called the Congregation for the Evangelization of Peoples or for the Propagation of the Faith). He died nursing plague victims in Rome. Feast day: October 9.

Leonardo da Vinci, 1452–1519, Italian Renaissance artist. Leonardo studied in Florence with Verrocchio, from 1481–99 was court painter and engineer for the duke of Milan, and in 1517 retired to France where he died in 1519 as court artist to Francis I. In addition to remarkable scientific contributions in anatomy, biology, physics, and hydrology, Leonardo introduced into Renaissance painting figures emerging from darkness into light (It., *chiaroscuro*); a mysterious misty atmosphere (*sfumato*) in the *Virgin of the Rocks* and the *Mona Lisa;* and was the first to visually explore the psychology of the inner life as seen in the apostles thrown into confusion in the *Last Supper.*

Leonine Prayers, vernacular prayers ordered by Pope Leo XIII (d. 1903) in 1886 to be recited by priests and people after Mass, consisting of three Hail Marys, the *Salve Regina,* a collect, and a prayer to St. Michael the Archangel. Pope Pius XI (d. 1939) ordered their continued recitation for the conversion of Russia. The practice of reciting the prayers after Mass was discontinued in 1964.

Leonine Sacramentary, the earliest surviving book of prayers for use in the liturgy of the Roman rite. It is also known as the Verona Sacramentary. Called "Leonine" because its author was long thought to be Pope Leo I (440–461), the book's manuscript actually dates from the seventh century. The Leonine Sacramentary was not an official liturgical book but a private collection of material possibly intended for use in parishes. It contains texts needed by those presiding at Eucharist (e.g., Opening Prayer; Prayer over the Gifts; Prayer After Communion; but no text of the Eucharistic Prayer), as well as formulas for "occasional services" such as ordinations. The book follows the civil calendar. *See also* sacramentary.

Leontius of Byzantium (lee-ahn'shee-uhs uhv bi-zan'tsee-uhm), ca. 500–43, Byzantine monk and theologian of the New Laura monastery (Palestine). He supported the doctrine of Chalcedon against Monophysitism, defended Origenism (which was condemned by Emperor Justinian I in 543), and took issue with the theology of Theodore of Mopsuestia. He introduced the notion of *enhypostasia* (Gk., "in person") into Christology. According to this view, the divine Person of Christ included all the attributes of perfect humanity. *See also enhypostasia; hypostatic union;* Incarnation, the.

Lepanto, Battle of, Mediterranean sea battle in October 1571 in which the combined military forces of Spain, Venice, and the papacy defeated the Turks. The victors credited the Virgin Mary as patroness of their success and celebrated a feast in her honor on October 7.

Lérins (Lerinum, Île de St.-Honorat), an island monastery off the Gallic (French) coast between Antibes and Fréjus. Founded in the first decade of the fifth century by Honoratus, a Gallic aristocrat, it produced several of southern Gaul's leading bishops and writers. A monastic community exists there to the present day. *See also* Vincent of Lérins, St.

Le Saulchoir. *See* Saulchoir, Le.

Lessius, Leonhard, 1554–1623, Jesuit theologian. Born near Antwerp, he studied at Louvain (1567) and taught philosophy at Douai (1574–81) and at Louvain (1585–1600). He became embroiled in the debate between the Dominicans and the Jesuits over the efficacy of grace, defending the Molinist position that grace is given in light of God's foreknowledge of the predisposition of free will. His position was condemned in 1587 by the Louvain theological faculty, led by Michael Baius, but supported by other universities, until Pope Sixtus V silenced the dispute. *See also De Auxiliis;* grace; Molinism.

Lestonnac, St. Jeanne de, also known as Joan de Lestonnac, 1556–1640, founder of the Religious of Notre Dame of Bordeaux. Born in France, she entered religious life after the death of her husband. The Cistercian life, however, proved too arduous and she left and formed her own community, devoted first to plague victims and then to the teaching of young girls. Feast day: February 2.

letter, a form of written communication, also called an epistle. Letters were widely used in the ancient world as a means of communication. Although no OT document is written in letter form, the use of letters is mentioned a number of times in the OT, and several OT documents contain letters embedded in them (e.g., 2 Chr 2:3–10, 11–16; Ezra 4:11–16; Jer 29:4–23). Of the twenty-seven documents in the NT, twenty-one are basically in letter form. Paul used letters extensively to supervise the communities he had founded. The letter was also used by other early Christian writers (*1 Clement,* Ignatius of Antioch, Polycarp).

Levite, a descendant of Levi, one of the twelve sons of Jacob (i.e., Israel; Gen 29:34; 35:23). It is often assumed that, after losing title to land, the tribe of Levi took over priestly duties, but the origins of the Levites as a priestly caste remain obscure. Moses was born of Levitical parents (Exod 2:1) and Aaron, his brother according to genealogical tradition, became the ancestor of the principal priestly family. As a second and subordinate order of clergy, Levites are not unambiguously attested before the Babylonian exile in the sixth century B.C. Their functions were to assist the priests in the sacrificial rituals (e.g., Num 1:50), take care of the sanctuary (1 Chr 23:28), and instruct the people in the law (e.g., Neh 8). In the course of time the Temple guilds (Asaph, Heman, Jeduthun) responsible for the composition and rendition of liturgical music were also classed as Levites (e.g., 1 Chr 25). *See also* priesthood.

Lex Ecclesiae Fundamentalis (Lat., "The Fundamental Law of the Church"), a proposal submitted as part of the post-Vatican II reform of canon law to provide the Church with a legal constitution. Although the proposal was not accepted, many of its laws dealing with the rights and obligations of individual Christians and of various groups of Christians were later incorporated into the revised code of canon law (1983).

Lex orandi, lex credendi (leks ohr-ahn'dee, leks kray-den'dee; Lat., "the law of worship is the law of belief"), a fifth-century axiom of Prosper of Aquitaine. Prosper, in writing against certain Pelagian heretics who did not believe in the need for God's grace, pointed out that the Church throughout the world prayed for people's needs in the prayers of the faithful in the liturgy (e.g., in the Good Friday liturgy, for unbelievers and heretics). Such authentic worship always points to true doctrine. Against these same heretics Augustine had earlier taught that in the worship of the Church one sees Christ in the Holy Spirit at work.

But there are certain criteria for applying this rule: first, this worship must be connected to the presider's role in worship; second, it must be connected to the apostolic tradition; and third, it must be universally used. An example that is frequently given is the opening greeting in the liturgy, "The Lord be with you." This greeting of the presider is found in the Scriptures and is used in the worship of the Eastern and Western churches. Therefore, this prayer is not simply a wish on the presider's part. It is an assurance that the risen Christ is one with his people. Another example would be the liturgy of initiation into the Church, i.e., Baptism, Confirmation, Eucharist. This liturgy clearly teaches among other things that everyone needs to benefit from Christ's sacrifice on the cross and that the Church is a community gathered by Christ through the Holy Spirit. *See also* doctrine; worship.

Libellatici (lee-bel-aht'i-chee; Lat.), those Christians during the Decian persecution (249–51) who avoided both martyrdom and outright sacrifice to the gods by purchasing the required certificate (*libellus*) testifying that sacrifice had been accomplished. They were readmitted to communion only after penance, but a penance less severe than that assigned to the *sacrificati* (those who had actually sacrificed).

liberalism, a general philosophical perspective which places emphasis on preserving and promoting the freedom of the individual person as the highest value in human life. Liberalism has influenced political, economic, personal, and religious aspects of the modern world. Rooted in the Enlightenment's belief in the free and scientific inquiry of individual persons, it has customarily provided a significant challenge to political and ecclesiastical authority. In the area of economics, liberals in the United States have generally supported government regulation of business, while conservatives have favored the limiting of government involvement.

Liberalism often employs the concept of rights to affirm the prerogatives of the individual within society. John XXIII affirmed the existence of the "natural rights" of persons in his 1963 encyclical *Pacem in Terris.*

liberation spirituality, a style of Christian life and prayer that is founded on the awareness of God's liberating activity in human history, especially on behalf of oppressed peoples. The context of liberation spirituality is sociopolitical. God's liberating concern for the Hebrew slaves in Egypt (Exod 3–12) is viewed as the paradigm of the spiritual life of the Christian community. The believer undergoes conversion to a new way of seeing and responding to the divine presence. The Scriptures are interpreted as the story of God's option for the lowly. Even the traditional staples of the spiritual life—prayer, piety, and discernment—find their meaning within this sociopolitical setting.

Since the 1960s Latin American theologians such as Gustavo Gutiérrez, Jon Sobrino, and Leonardo Boff have been widely recognized proponents of liberation spirituality. Similar visions of spirituality have been proposed by Native Americans, African-Americans, and feminists. *See also* liberation theology.

liberation theology, the form of theological inquiry that takes as its first principle and ordering idea the emancipation of oppressed peoples from unjust political, economic, or social subjection. "Liberation theology" currently describes a diverse array of practical theologies—feminist, black, and Hispanic, among many others—each of which attempts to understand and articulate the Christian faith from the perspective of its own group's particular experience of the struggle to overcome oppression. However, the term's original referent is the politically and socially conscious theology that first emerged in Latin America during the 1960s and 70s, and which received its perduring and most exemplary presentation in Peruvian theologian Gustavo Gutiérrez's *Theology of Liberation* (Eng. trans., 1973).

Origins: Liberation theology arose in its Latin American context principally as a moral reaction to the widespread and collective suffering of that area's poor, a suffering whose proportions and consequences were decried as unjustifiable assaults on human dignity. Politically, liberation theologians rejected the idea that such large-scale impoverishment was a tragically necessary stage in the economic development of the region. Relying on the insights of social and political theorists, often Marxists, they pointed instead to the debilitating dependence of Latin American countries on the industrialized and essentially self-interested nations

of the north as the primary explanation for the region's chronic underdevelopment. Theologically, liberation theologians rejected the notion that such suffering was God's will and dismissed purely charitable initiatives as inadequate responses to the cries of the poor for justice. Emphasizing the politically charged character of the biblical witness, they challenged both individual Christians and the established Church order to adopt a more critical stance toward oppressive regimes, and to take up the cause of the poor, thereby working for the transformation of unjust social structures.

Growth: Among other important factors contributing to the emergence of liberation theology in Latin America is the Second Vatican Council (1962–65), which challenged the worldwide Church to make its own the "joys, hopes, griefs and aspirations of humanity, and especially the poor" (Pastoral Constitution on the Church in the Modern World, n. 1) and to draw more deeply from the font of Scripture in its earthly mission of transforming the world (Decree on Priestly Formation, n. 16). The encyclical letters of Popes John XXIII and Paul VI on the social questions of the day (*Mater et Magistra,* 1961; *Pacem in Terris,* 1963; *Populorum Progressio,* 1967) reinforced the general direction of the council, and lent further weight to the possibility of a theologically informed socio-economic critique. On another level, the "political theologies" then emerging in Europe were introducing to Catholic theology the analytic techniques of contemporary social sciences (economics, sociology, political theory) in ways that would prove highly beneficial in the development of liberation theological method. Of special significance in the rise of liberation theology is the 1968 meeting of the Second General Conference of Latin American Bishops (CELAM) in Medellín, Colombia, where the teachings of Vatican II were applied to the Latin American church in a manner that deeply reflected the influence of liberation theologians.

Themes: (a) Preferential option for the poor. Solidarity with the victims of unjust oppression—in the form of a concrete commitment to or actual involvement in their emancipatory struggles for justice—remains the fundamental starting point of liberation theology. This identification with the oppressed has been expressed, in the Latin American context, as a "preferential option for the poor," what Gutiérrez describes as the "first act" of liberation theology, the necessary prelude to the more theoretical "second act" of systematic reflection.

Active concern for the poor and marginalized is of ancient vintage within the Christian tradition; what is new in liberation theology is the privileged role given to the experience and perspective of the oppressed themselves in articulating the theological ground and ethical entailments of that concern. As part of an overall recasting of traditional theological method, liberation thinkers insist that the central claims of the Christian faith (e.g., about the existence and nature of God, the identity of Jesus Christ, the work of the Holy Spirit, and the nature of the Church) be tested "from below," against the experience of the powerless and the oppressed, and that ultimately such claims cannot be ratified apart from that standpoint.

(b) Unity of theory and practice. Committed methodologically to transforming as well as better understanding the reality of the oppressed, liberation theologians seek continually to relate perception to action. Critical reflection on the intersections of theory and practice (*praxis*, Gk.) in the light of faith underscores the importance of "doing" as well as "seeing" the truth. Consequently, liberation theologians favor the concepts and insights of political and social thinkers over the tools of philosophical speculation to describe and interpret reality.

(c) Ideology critique. The critical, or "prophetic," task of liberation theology is to unmask the false ideologies concealing oppressive systems of economic and social privilege, and in their place to construct alternative liberating ideologies informed by the vision of a social order free of such inequities. Forms of church order and theological analysis indifferent to the just claims of the oppressed, or overtly hostile to their concrete liberation, are sharply criticized as complicit in such oppressive systems.

(d) Use of Scripture. At the theological center of liberation thought is an interpretation of the biblical drama of creation and redemption as disclosing a God who, in the people of Israel and the person of Jesus Christ, liberates; who takes the side of the poor and vulnerable; who is intimately involved in their historical struggle for justice. Israel's release from bondage in Egypt (Exod. 1–20), the prophetic denunciation of oppression (cf. Amos); and the Gospel portrayals of Jesus' ministry among the outcast (cf. Matt 25:31–46), figure prominently in liberation readings of the Bible. Of more than simply historical interest, the biblical texts, read "from below," constitute the theological basis for present hope—and action.

Critical Reaction: Liberation theology has provoked a great deal of controversy. Two official Vatican documents on liberation theology, in 1984 and 1986, note an "insufficiently critical" borrowing of Marxist concepts (e.g., class struggle), and warn of the danger of reducing faith to politics. While recognizing the legitimacy of liberation as a theological theme, the documents criticize liberation theology for its single-minded focus on the institutional dimension of sin, to the virtual exclusion of the individual; and for undermining church authority by identifying the hierarchy as members of the privileged class. Despite such criticisms Pope John Paul II affirmed, in a 1986 letter to the Brazilian bishops, the "useful and necessary" character of liberation theology. *See also* base communities; Latin America, Catholicism in; theology.

Bibliography

Gutiérrez, Gustavo. *A Theology of Liberation.* Maryknoll, NY: Orbis Books, 1973.

Hennelly, Alfred T. *Liberation Theology: A Documentary History.* Maryknoll, NY: Orbis Books, 1990.

McGovern, Arthur. *Liberation Theology and Its Critics.* Maryknoll, NY: Orbis Books, 1989.　　　　PAUL J. WOJDA

Liberatore, Matteo (mah-tay'oh lee-bair-uh-tohr'-ay), 1810–92, Jesuit philosopher and theologian. In 1850 he became a member of the neo-Thomistic revival spearheaded by the coeditors of the newly founded journal *La Civiltà Cattolica.* His writings systematized nineteenth-century Thomism, which, he contended, was the only philosophical system capable of resolving the problems being raised by modern philosophy.

Liber de Causis (lee'bair day kow'zees; Lat., "Book of Causes"), twelfth-century Latin translation of an anonymous, probably ninth-century Arabic text. A monotheistic reworking of parts of Proclus's *Elements of Theology,* it influenced speculation about angelic cognition and about the relation between divine and created causality. *See also* angel; five ways of St. Thomas Aquinas.

Liberius, d. 366, pope from 352 to 366. The Arian emperor Constantius deposed Liberius (355) for refusing to endorse the condemnation of Athanasius. His health progressively harmed by a harsh exile in Thrace, Liberius eventually submitted and was then readmitted to his see. He was forced to sign a formulary, either the Arianizing formula of Sirmium of 357 or (more probably) the essentially orthodox formula of Sirmium of 351. His acts and correspondence after the death of Constantius (361) evince an unqualified support for the Nicene Creed. He was listed in the fifth-century Hieronymian Martyrology (Martyrology of St. Jerome), with a feast day of September 23, but his name does not occur in any later calendars. *See also* Athanasius, St.; Nicene Creed.

Liber Usualis (Lat., "book for general use"), a Roman-rite book containing chiefly Mass and Divine Office chants of the principal liturgical days. First published in 1896 (revised editions in 1903, 1934), this compilation also includes Mass and Divine Office texts, the whole being excerpted from the Roman gradual, antiphonal, missal, and breviary. *See also* chant, Gregorian.

Libri Carolini (lee'bree kair-oh-leen'ee; Lat., "Caroline Books," i.e., the books of Charlemagne), Carolingian retort, written between 790 and 793, to the iconophile teachings of the Second Council of Nicaea (the Seventh Ecumenical Council, 787). The Franks took little interest in the early phases of the iconoclastic controversy, which dominated Byzantine life from 725. The Italians, however, were violently iconophile, and a papal synod condemned iconoclasm in 731, provoking retaliation by the iconoclastic Eastern emperor Leo III, who removed four provinces from the papal jurisdiction. This action, in turn, contributed to the papacy's increasing dependence upon the Frankish king rather than the Byzantine emperor as its protector. Thus when the Empress Irene called for an ecumenical council to reject iconoclasm, Pope Hadrian I was happy to send legates and endorse the results.

When the Greek decrees of the council were translated into Latin, however, the pope's Frankish protectors were aghast. Part of their reaction stemmed from the fact that the Latin translation was faulty, obscuring the careful Greek distinctions between veneration and worship, between saint and image. But the Franks had historically been less exuberant than the Greeks in their use of holy images (other than the Cross), and they also saw the political gain to be won by questioning the orthodoxy of the Byzantines.

The four books of the *Libri* attack the council on every conceivable front, beginning with a condemnation of the imperial styles used by Irene and her son as sacrilegious. Later chapters discuss what makes a council universal and offer a biblical and logical refutation of the actual Nicene teachings. An embarrassment to the pope, the *Libri* were ignored by the Byzantines.

Scholarly opinion as to the authorship of the *Libri* is divided. There is almost universal agreement that Charlemagne himself was not the real writer, though manuscript evidence indicates that the final draft may have been read aloud to him for his comments. Alcuin of York is known to have written a letter on the subject of iconoclasm, but he was in Northumbria for most of the period during which the *Libri* were composed. Certain Visigothic characteristics of the text have made Theodulf of Orléans the leading candidate. *See also* Charlemagne; iconoclasm; Nicaea, Second Council of.   JOHN W. HOUGHTON

liceity [canon law], canonical term describing the status of a sacrament vis-à-vis the law of the Church. It is often used with another juridical term, "valid," or efficacious. A sacrament is licit or legal if the provisions of the law regulating its celebration have been followed; it is illicit if the opposite is true. For example, it is the law in the Roman rite to celebrate the Eucharist using unleavened wheat bread. If leavened wheat bread is used, the eucharistic matter is considered illicit, although the validity of the sacrament in this case cannot be questioned. *See also* sacrament; validity of sacraments.

licentiate (Lat., *licentia*, "permission"). **1** Medieval academic degree allowing the recipient to lecture from approved books (a *doctor* could write and publish his own works). **2** Modern ecclesiastical academic degree granted between the bachelor's degree and the doctorate. *See also* J.C.L.; S.S.L.; S.T.L.

Liebermann, Bruno (lee'bair-mahn), 1759–1844, an important figure in the renewal of German pastoral life in the nineteenth century. Ordained in 1783, he was a pastor, lecturer in dogmatic theology, and cathedral preacher. As regent and professor for the new seminary in Mainz, he developed innovative pastoral approaches for the formation of priests and furthered an ecclesial piety among the laity. He also worked to retain biblical and contemporary philosophical ideas within a neo-Scholastic framework.

life, origins of. The first organisms are thought to have arisen from inorganic compounds more than four billion years ago. There is no direct evidence for the origins of life because the first forms of life were too small and too easily degenerated to be preserved in the fossil record. Neither is there evidence of spontaneous generation in the present that could corroborate a theoretical explanation of the origins of life. Experimenters have duplicated the atmospheric conditions at the time of the origins of life and have shown that the spontaneous production of amino acids can result from a spark of electricity or a ray of ultraviolet light. Accepted theory holds that amino acids thus formed eventually accumulated to form an organic broth from which self-replicating life arose. However, the origins of the genetic code remain unknown. From this most primitive form of life, the divinely-guided process of evolution by natural selection brought about the higher life forms. Pope Pius XII, in *Humani Generis* (1950), taught that the theory of evolution is to be viewed with caution outside the proper scope of biology. In particular, he reaffirmed the doctrine of creation and the immediate creation of the human soul by God. "The teaching of the Church," he wrote, "does not forbid that the doctrine of evolutionism, insofar as it inquires into the origin of the human body from already existing and living matter, be, according to the present state of human disciplines and sacred theology, treated in research and discussion by experts on both sides." *See also* creation; creationism; evolution.

ligamen, impediment of (Lat., "a binding"), invalidating obstacles to a new marriage by someone currently married. A person is bound by an existing marriage. Because the prohibition is based upon the understanding that an essential property of marriage is indissolubility, the impediment cannot be dispensed from. *See also* indissolubility of marriage; marriage law.

Liguori, St. Alphonsus. *See* Alphonsus Liguori, St.

limbo (Lat., *limbus,* "hem," "edge"), place or state of natural happiness for the nonbaptized dead. At issue is the reality of original sin and the necessity of Baptism for salvation. In response to Pelagius (d. ca. 425), who taught that Baptism was not necessary for salvation, Augustine (d. 430) contended that unbaptized children who die are condemned to hell, though they do not suffer all its pains because they are not guilty of personal sin. Medieval theologians, wishing to mitigate the harshness of Augustine's po-

sition, postulated the existence of limbo. Limbo, they held, is a place or state where unbaptized persons enjoy a natural happiness, though they remain excluded from the Beatific Vision. Some incorrectly identify this limbo with the hell of the Apostles' Creed where, according to tradition, Christ spent the interval between Good Friday and Easter Sunday.

Modern theology, when it does not reject the notion outright, questions the theological premises upon which limbo is based. It is difficult, if not impossible, to reconcile the concept of limbo with the Christian affirmation of God's universal salvific will and the fundamental solidarity of redeemed humanity. Besides, the notion generates obvious pastoral difficulties where the death of infants is concerned.

Neither officially defined nor abrogated by the Church, this theological postulate plays no role in contemporary Catholic theology. Instead, contemporary theology and church practice stress the fundamental solidarity of redeemed humanity and the universal salvific will of God. *See also* universal salvific will of God.

Linacre, Thomas, ca. 1460–1524, English physician and humanist. Influential friend of John Colet, Desiderius Erasmus, and Thomas More, he was physician to Henry VII and Henry VIII and founder of the Royal College of Physicians in 1518. The *Linacre Quarterly,* the official journal of the National Federation of Catholic Physicians' Guilds, published continuously since 1932, is named in his honor.

Lindisfarne, island off the east coast of Northumbria, where Aidan in 635 established a monastery and his bishopric. Enjoying a succession of saintly bishops, it remained an important religious and cultural center until Viking raids forced the transfer of the see to the mainland, eventually to Durham. *See also* Aidan of Iona, St.

Linus, St., d. ca. 78, traditionally regarded as the immediate successor to Peter as Bishop of Rome in all early episcopal lists; sometimes identified with the Linus of 2 Tim 4:21. Feast day: September 23.

lion, biblical symbol of courage and strength. It represents Mark the Evangelist in Christian iconography. *See also* Mark, St.

litany (Gk., *litanea*, "supplication"), a form of prayer made up of a series of petitions or invocations to which the faithful respond. Litanies, which can be found in Jewish worship, have been part of the Christian tradition from its earliest days. Pope Gregory the Great (590–604) restricted the use of litanies to feast days; only the Kyrie (Gk., "Lord, [have mercy]") was retained for use at every Mass. The most widely used litany apart from the regular liturgy of the Eucharist is the Litany of the Saints, recited, for example, at the Easter Vigil and at ordination ceremonies. *See also* Litany of the Saints.

Litany of the Saints, a prayer invoking many holy people. The Litany of the Saints is actually composed of two parts. In the first, a series of holy people is named by the leader; the second part consists of a series of petitions. The faithful participate by making appropriate responses. The Litany of the Saints, which has traditionally been used as part of the Forty Hours devotion and to accompany various processions, is most commonly heard at the Easter Vigil and at ordination ceremonies in the Roman Catholic Church. Though the Christian practice of calling upon the saints for assistance also dates to the days of the martyrs, a lengthy catalog of saints, such as is found in the first part of the litany, is a later development. One of the most ancient examples of a litany of saints dates from the seventh century in Rome. From Rome, the use of the litany spread to England, Ireland, and other countries.

literal sense of Scripture, the meaning that emerges from the biblical words themselves in their literary and historical context. Pius XII's encyclical on biblical studies, *Divino Afflante Spiritu* (1943), further describes it as that sense that the author intended (n. 34). Attention to the literal (or literary sense) has nothing to do with the literalism of fundamentalists, since the literal sense can be metaphorical or mythic, and proper attention to literary form is one of the prime criteria for finding the literal sense. In church tradition it is often contrasted to the spiritual sense, but according to Thomas Aquinas (d. 1274) "nothing necessary to faith is contained in the spiritual sense that scripture does not put forward elsewhere in the literal sense" (*Summa Theologiae* 1.1.10). *See also* Scripture, senses of.

Lithuania, Catholicism in. *See* Baltic countries, Catholicism in the.

Little Brothers of Jesus, a congregation of mostly lay brothers founded in Algeria by René Voillaume in 1933 and inspired by the example of Charles de Foucauld (1858–1916). Although de Foucauld wrote the rule for the Little Brothers, the ascetic contemplative never saw the creation of his community. The ideal, realized by Voillaume and other priests who were attracted to the rule, incorporates contemplative spirituality into a ministry of simple living and manual labor, largely in the blue-collar work force. The brothers live in small communities and their goal is to proclaim the gospel on the job by the way they live and work. *See also* Foucauld, Charles de.

Little Entrance, or "Minor Introit," in the Byzantine Eucharist, a ritual procession in which the Gospel book is carried from the altar through the church and back to the altar again. Today a purely ceremonial procession that introduces the Liturgy of the Word and symbolizes Christ's coming as Logos (Word), it is a ritual remnant of the original introit (entrance) of clergy and people into the church at what was once the beginning of the liturgy, before the addition of the three antiphons (refrains) that now precede it. The Armenian Eucharist has a similar procession with the Gospel book. The entrance is called "little" to distinguish it from the "Great Entrance," or transfer of gifts before the anaphora, the central prayer of the eucharistic liturgy. *See also* Great Entrance.

Little Flower of Jesus, the. *See* Thérèse of Lisieux, St.

Little Office of the Blessed Virgin Mary, an abridged version of the common office of the Blessed Virgin Mary that may have developed in conjunction with a Saturday Mass in honor of Mary, composed by Alcuin (d. 804). By the tenth century, the office was recited daily, and after it was reorganized by Peter Damian (d. 1072), its use became common during the twelfth century. Once binding on religious and diocesan clergy, the office became a matter of private devotion only under Pope Pius X (1903–14). It is currently recited by certain nonclerical religious institutes and by individual members of the laity. The new Liturgy of the Hours (formerly the Divine Office) provides for a Saturday memorial of the Blessed Virgin during Ordinary Time, and the texts for it are drawn almost entirely from the Little Office. *See also* breviary; Liturgy of the Hours.

Little Sisters of the Poor (L.S.P), a religious community for women founded in 1839 at St. Servan, France, by Jeanne Jugan (d. 1879) and two women companions. Other women joined them and they formally organized themselved into a congregation dedicated to caring for the infirm and indigent elderly. By 1854 the original group had grown to five hundred sisters and had spread beyond the borders of France into England and Belgium. In the 1990s this international community specializes in geriatrics and gerontology, and includes almost four thousand members worldwide, with more than five hundred in the United States.

liturgical architecture, the study and practice of designing and building structures worthy to house the Church and to serve its rites. The church must first be understood as an assembled community, and secondarily as the building in which that community gathers. While liturgical architecture is primarily concerned with the second notion, it must also be interested in the first insofar as houses for the Church's worship shape and influence gathered communities, their self-understanding, and intentions for the worship of God. Those changes in liturgical architecture that have occurred from age to age correlate with changes in Christian self-understanding.

The Early Christian Period: During the first to fourth centuries Christians met in the homes of wealthy Church members. The Eucharist was observed in the dining room, the largest room of the *domus* (Lat., "house"). Despite the notion that early Christians baptised in lakes or rivers, baptismal pools were more often built in the siderooms of the Christian *domus,* and have been found to exist in the early Christian synagogue of Dura-Europos. At this time Christian worship and its architecture centered around the domestic table, the water-bath of baptism, and the funeral meals, *refrigeria* (Lat., "cold meals"), of the cemeteries.

The Post-Constantinian Basilica: Following Constantine's conversion to Christianity (312), public buildings, or basilicas, were given over to the Christian communities. The basilical design was virtually a wholesale importation of the architecture of the courthouses of Roman magistrates. The basilicas were built on a longitudinal axis with a wide central nave surrounded by clerestory windows in the upper gallery. On either side of the nave, there was a narrower, columned aisle. At the head of the nave, an apse, a round extension of the nave, provided a place for the seating of the bishop and lesser clergy. The altar was generally placed in the center of the nave. A waist-high wall came to be built around the altar to discourage the crowd from disrupting the liturgy. In the same general area, an ambo or pulpit was erected several feet above the floor. The basilical style represents the aspiration of the Church to rise from its marginal status into the mainstream of Roman civic life as a uniquely powerful political and religious institution.

The Monastic Churches of the Middle Ages in the West: Monastic styles of worship, with their emphasis on the Liturgy of the Hours and the attendant frequency of Masses in monastic communities, indelibly marked the development of Romanesque and Gothic styles. Both architectural styles are essentially elaborations upon the basilical style. Four characteristics stand out: (1) the exaggeration of the seating for the clergy in the expansion of the choir space, (2) the increase in number of altars and side chapels to accommodate the many priests of the abbey who desired to celebrate a private daily Mass, (3) the vaulted arches of the Gothic churches and (4) the invention of the flying buttress, which enabled churches to become the skyscrapers of the late

The nave and apse of Notre-Dame Cathedral in Paris, originally built in the twelfth century and restored in the nineteenth, one of the world's most celebrated examples of Gothic architecture.

An example of modern liturgical architecture; the Church of Notre Dame du Haut in Ronchamp, France (a view from the southeast).

Middle Ages, extending skyward and admitting an unprecedented amount of natural light. The church buildings of the Middle Ages were built to support a clericalized liturgy and to project a hierarchical understanding of the cosmos and the place of human beings within it.

The Modern Period: The best church buildings of the modern period represent a renewal in the understanding of liturgical architecture. Buildings must serve and not hinder the gathering of the Church into a single, unified body. They ought not themselves distract from the activity of that ecclesial body, but should enhance it. Modern building materials such as reinforced concrete expand the possible shapes of buildings, their floor plans, and their sight lines. Modern Catholic churches are supposed to be designed around the sacramental centers for worship: ambo, altar, font, assembly, and the presidential chair used by the presiding priest, corresponding with the fundamental symbols by which the modern Catholic assembly is said to experience the presence of Christ. Architects and architectural consultants who desire to serve the modern Catholic Church will incorporate these values into their designs. *See also* Catholicism and architecture.

Bibliography

Bishops' Committee on the Liturgy. *Environment and Art in Catholic Worship.* Washington, DC: NCCB, 1978.

Macauley, David. *Cathedral: The Story of Its Construction.* Boston: Houghton Mifflin, 1973.

White, James F. *Protestant Worship and Church Architecture.* New York: Oxford, 1964.   JEFFREY T. VANDERWILT

liturgical art, the study, design, and creation of images in service to Christian revelation, the human expression of encounter with God or the holy.

Early History: In the first Christian century there were reservations about the use of images be-cause of the Hebraic injunction against "graven images" and the constant concern about idolatry. One of the earliest purposes of Christian artistic imagery, in addition to human and faith development, was religious education. Artistic images visually portrayed persons and narrated events from salvation history in order to edify and instruct the viewer. However, with the Christological controversies of the fourth through the eighth centuries regarding the humanity and divinity of Christ, it became more difficult for artists to visually portray and narrate these saving persons and events in a manner that would satisfy the various parties to the theological debates.

The iconoclastic controversies of the eighth and ninth centuries were especially critical in the development of Christian art, and of liturgical art in particular. On the one side were those who shared the historic Hebraic skepticism about imagery; on the other were those who shared the Greco-Hellenistic appreciation for beauty. The emerging influence of Islam in Europe added pressures against the use of imagery, since Islam also opposed the veneration of images. It was the Second Council of Nicaea (787) that officially resolved the controversy in favor of the use of images (icons), although iconoclastic tendencies did not disappear and would reemerge with new intensity at the time of the Protestant Reformation in the sixteenth century.

Christian Art as Liturgical: To call Christian art "liturgical" suggests that such works of art are not ends in themselves, but represent liturgical acts, that is, acts of corporate public worship (which is liturgy) and of personal prayer and devotion linked with the public worship of the Church. Early Christian art of the first three centuries includes murals, mosaics, and "graffiti," short prayers inscribed on the walls of tombs. There were representations of Noah's ark and simple symbolic figures such as loaves and fishes. An especially popular image was that of the Good Shepherd, depicting Christ as a youth supporting a lamb across his shoulders. He becomes a model for pastors. Elsewhere Christ is depicted as a teacher, instructing the apostles about the mission they are about to embark upon. He becomes thereby a model for bishops. Following the conversion of Constantine in the fourth century, the figure of Christ came more closely to resemble that of the emperor. Christ is depicted enthroned, scepter in hand, crowned, and enrobed in imperial garb. He became thereby a model for medieval popes.

Such images of Christ the King, rooted in an imperial culture, persist to the present day. This points up an important facet of liturgical art, as for Christian art in general: its materials and media, its use of symbols and conceptual metaphors convey the particularities of Christian peoples in various individual cultures, historical periods, and regions even as the art strives to embody the more universal truths of God's redemption wrought by Christ for all humanity.

One can consider the liturgical arts by media: (1) icons and paintings, (2) statuary, (3) furnishings and appointments, and (4) vesture and textiles. To be sure, music is also a liturgical art, but that is the subject of another entry.

Icons and Paintings: The two-dimensional arts—iconography, painting, and mosaic—are among the oldest of Christian arts. Works in these media tend to be figures of Christ, the Mother of God, the apostles, and saints. They are presented as manifestations (epiphanies) of the divine in the human, the eternal in the temporal. In the East, the icon in particular draws one into a higher, heavenly order of being. Human figures are presented in static tableaux. Events are presented as interventions of the divine into the human order. In the West, the best preserved works of art of the eighth and ninth centuries are small objects such as illuminated manuscripts, splendid book covers, ivory carving, and metalwork. From the tenth until the fifteenth centuries the use of images supported the catechetical mission of the Church to a largely illiterate population. Paintings and icons appeared on the walls of cathedrals, churches, chapels, refectories, and chapterhouses, and were incorporated onto the enameled cases which preserved valued relics and into liturgical furnishings such as the reredos (a decorative wall, screen, hanging, or metalwork behind and above the altar). Great theologians like Thomas Aquinas (d. 1274) viewed art, like philosophy, as a handmaiden of theology.

From the late Middle Ages into the Renaissance (fourteenth to mid-seventeenth centuries), human figures were presented in movement, on pilgrimage, or as manifestations of the sacred. Saints were superimposed upon landscapes, medieval fortresses, or city squares replete with city halls and Gothic cathedrals—scenes that would be familiar to the audiences. Other art-forms like dance and drama served similar educational and spiritually formational purposes.

With the Renaissance, however, there was a shift away from the sacramental (the experience of the infinite in and through the finite) to a celebration of the beauty of nature and of the human body. Although some of history's most magnificent artistic works were produced during this period, and under papal patronage (for example, Michelangelo's Sistine ceiling, 1508–13, supported by Pope Julius II, d. 1513), much of the contemporary art was regarded as secular, even pagan. Thus, the Reformers cleansed the walls of churches, removed all images and statues, and shifted the focus from visual expression to the written and spoken word of God.

In 1563 the Council of Trent (1545–63) decreed that images were to be produced by Christian artists and placed in churches for teaching purposes. Distortions of this central purpose, e.g., the display of human nudity, were to be avoided. Art, therefore, was not "for its own sake" (*ars gratia artis*, Lat.), but for the sacred meaning that lay beyond it. It was a means to a higher end. At the same time, the council's guidelines did inspire other forms of art, even if apologetical and even polemical in character. Doctrines and practices condemned by the Reformers were depicted with renewed emphasis: the Sacrifice of the Mass, the sacrament of Penance, the holy souls in purgatory, the corporal works of mercy, and in particular the Blessed Virgin Mary.

Statuary: The Eastern churches do not use statuary in their vocabulary of aesthetic expression. In the West, since the Carolingian period (eighth and ninth centuries) the carving of holy figures, saints, or angels in wood or in stone (presently also in plastics) has found acceptance. Some have suggested that liturgical statuary ought not limit itself only to the presentation of historical pageants or the saints, but might also express common human experiences that impart an understanding of the divine regard for human beings, e.g., a mother embracing her child, or a figure leaping loose from its chains. A vivid example of such art is Giovanni Bernini's carving of Teresa of Ávila in ecstasy (St. Peter's in Rome). There the mystic is depicted almost completely enthralled by a rapture that borders on the sexual. Many Catholics maintain small private shrines for the display and veneration of saints or holy men and women. Such practices extend the presence of the entire Christian community, especially its important historical figures, into the community and everyday life of the contemporary Christian household. They may also be signs or

The risen and triumphant Christ, enthroned in heavenly majesty with the saints (the Latin inscription reads, "The Lord preserves the Church from shame"); fresco in the Church of Santa Pudenziana, Rome.

tangible reminders of God's protective presence over the family and its belongings.

Furnishing and Appointments: Liturgical arts also include the skills and crafts with which liturgical furnishings are created and adorned. For centuries chairs and pulpits, altars and rood screens have been the stages upon which the biblical dramas have been enacted. Ironworking and stonecarving or masonry have played a role. Metal work has wrought beautiful chalices, patens, and thuribles (used for incensing sacred persons and objects, including the altar). Contemporary sensibilities and liturgical guidelines prefer an aesthetic simplicity in instruments of worship.

The guiding liturgical principle is that the worshipping assembly's attention should be centered on what is most important, namely, the celebration of the Eucharist and everything that leads up to, and flows from, it. Accordingly, the focal points are the altar table, the baptismal font, the ambo (lectern), and the presider's chair. Statues and other images of the saints, stations of the cross, or other images of popular devotion (e.g., banners, vigil lights, the Communion rail) are not to distract one's attention from the main worship space.

The altar is accorded the primary place. It is that around which the community gathers for the Eucharist. The altar symbolizes Christ who is simultaneously altar, priest, and victim. It is a place of both sacrifice and celebratory feasting.

The baptismal font is rich in the symbolism of flowing water, the source of new life in Christ. It is to be large enough to accommodate the baptism of adults, the immersion of infants, and the celebration of the Easter Vigil, and at the same time visu-

ally linked with the altar, so that the journey from font to altar may become an image of the Christian journey itself.

The ambo is the place from which the word of God is proclaimed and interpreted. As such, it is dignified in appearance, but never distractingly ornate. The positioning and the appearance of the presider's chair reflects the presider's function as the one who calls the community to worship and leads it in prayer and who represents Christ's presence to the assembly.

The holiness of the assembly itself is also acknowledged in the plants and flowers, the special lighting, and the festive colors that reflect the season and the occasion.

Vesture and Textiles: The primary vesture (coverings) for both altar and ministers is made of white linen. The baptismal alb, or white robe, represents the putting on of Christ and the sharing in his Easter glory. Chasubles (the presider's outer vestment) and other vestments fulfill their function by their color, design, and enveloping form. Hanging banners communicate primarily through patterned embroidery, abstract images, or simple variations in texture of color rather than through verbal messages.

Twentieth Century: In his encyclical *Mediator Dei* ("On the sacred liturgy," 1947), Pope Pius XII (d. 1958) urged Christian artists to steer a middle course between modernism and traditionalism. But in 1952 an *Instruction on Sacred Art* from the Holy Office (in the 1990s called the Congregation for the Doctrine of the Faith) reaffirmed the more restrictive guidelines of the Council of Trent.

During the Second Vatican Council (1962–65) Pope Paul VI (d. 1978) celebrated a special Mass for artists (May 4, 1964) and called for a revival of the close bond between artists and the Church. Perhaps the strongest affirmation of the use of contemporary art for liturgical purposes came from the U.S. Catholic Bishops' Committee on the Liturgy in its instruction on *Environment and Art in Catholic Worship* (1978).

The discussion about liturgical art since the Second Vatican Council has centered on the relative merits of the traditional (i.e., Trent to Vatican II) and of the contemporary (Vatican II and beyond). Should new churches have stained-glass windows or clear windows? Should there be a Communion rail? Where should the tabernacle be located? Should there be statues in and around the sanctuary? Should there be side-altar chapels? Where should the baptismal font be located and how should it be constructed? How should the various ministers, including altar servers, be vested?

But at least the fundamental question faced by the Church in the first eight or nine centuries seems to have been settled. It is not whether the Church should employ various forms of art in its liturgy, but rather what kind of art should it employ. "Christians have not hesitated to use every human art in their celebration of the saving work of God in Jesus Christ," the U.S. Catholic Bishops' document on *Environment and Art in Catholic Worship* (1978) points out, "although in every historical period they have been influenced, at times inhibited, by cultural circumstances. In the resurrection of the Lord, all things are made new. Wholeness and healthiness are restored, because the reign of sin and death is conquered" (n. 4). *See also* altar; ambo; baptismal font; Byzantine style; Catholicism and music; Catholicism and the visual arts; Gothic style; liturgical music; presidential chair; vestments.

Bibliography

Lowrie, Walter. *Art in the Early Church.* New York: Norton, 1969.

Regamey, Pie-Raymond. *Religious Arts in the Twentieth Century.* New York: Herder and Herder, 1963.

U.S. Catholic Bishops' Committee on the Liturgy. *Environment and Art in Catholic Worship.* Washington, DC: United States Catholic Conference, 1978. (Reprinted in *The Liturgy Documents: A Parish Resource,* edited by Mary Ann Simcoe, pp. 265–92. Chicago: Liturgy Training Publications, 1985.)   *JEFFREY T. VANDERWILT*

liturgical books, collections of officially approved liturgical texts (prayers, songs, readings). They sometimes include directions written in red (rubrics) for specific liturgical ministers. The Eastern churches and Western churches with a strong liturgical tradition (Roman, Anglican, some Protestant) have well-developed liturgical books. Liturgical books can be grouped according to services, e.g., eucharistic celebration or initiation. Eucharist and daily prayer (Divine Office) books can also be classified with reference to ministries: books for presiders (usually prayer texts), for deacons and other readers (usually scriptural texts), for cantors and psalmists (various song collections).

Historical Development: The earliest liturgical accounts seem to indicate that the Bible, from which the lessons were read, was the only book employed. As a system for readings developed over time, beginnings and endings of readings were listed in a book called the *Comes,* the forerunner of the lectionary. The evangeliary containing only Gospel pericopes (passages) developed later. As the Divine Office took on a fixed form, collections of biblical lessons, patristic sermons, and acts of the martyrs read at prayer gave rise to separate books: Office lectionary, homilary, and *legenda* (Lat., "material to be read"). Other Office books included the Psalter, ordered and arranged for singing; the *Liber responsorialis,* a responsory collection; and the *Antiphionale,* containing psalmic antiphons.

Prayer texts, originally improvised, became stereotypical over time and were written down. Little books (*libelli*), employed as memory aids for prayer leaders of domestic Eucharists, grew into sacramentaries, prayer collections used at various sacramental celebrations. Early sacramentaries had few, if any, ceremonial directions. Elaborate papal rites brought ordinals, collections of ceremonial directions, into existence.

The early ninth century saw the beginnings of the pontifical, employed at services where the bishop's ministry was required. More significant, however, was the development of the missal, a compilation of the presider's sacramentary, the readers' book(s), and the musicians' song books. This book, convenient for private celebrations in which the priest took all but the server's part, was detrimental to worship as a truly corporate act, for eventually the presider was expected to read *sotto voce* (It., "in a low voice") all the parts assigned to other ministers, even while enacted by others.

Vatican II's Constitution on the Sacred Liturgy (1963) mandated the wholesale revision of all Roman books "as soon as possible" (n. 25). By 1973 the Latin editions of major books were introduced, categorized under missal, Office (Liturgy of the Hours), ritual, and pontifical. The Roman Ritual's sacramental celebrations appeared in separate volumes.

The work of conciliar commissions resulted in published revisions of the following rites: (1) missal—Order of Mass and Lectionary (1969), Sacramentary (1970); (2) ritual—Baptism of Children, and Marriage (1969), Funerals (1969, revised 1985), Religious Profession (1970), Adult Initiation (1971), Pastoral Care of the Sick (1972), Eucharistic Cult (1973), Penance (1973), Blessings (1984); (3) pontifical—Ordinations (1968), Consecration of Virgins and Abbatial Blessings (1970), Blessing of Oils (1970), Confirmation (1971), Institution of Readers and Acolytes (1972), Church Dedication (1972); (4) Liturgy of the Hours (1971).

The revised books are marked by extensive introductions of a theological, liturgical, and pastoral nature. *See also* liturgical reform.   *JOHN A. MELLOH*

LITURGICAL CALENDAR

TEMPORAL CYCLE (PROPER OF TIME)

CHRISTMAS CYCLE

First Sunday of Advent	(the Sunday falling on or closest to November 30)
Second Sunday of Advent	
Third Sunday of Advent	(also popularly known as *Gaudete* Sunday, from the first word of the old Latin Introit prayer for this day)
Fourth Sunday of Advent	
Holy Family	(the Sunday after Christmas; celebrated on December 30 if Christmas and its octave fall on a Sunday)
Epiphany	(the Sunday falling between January 2 and January 8)

ORDINARY TIME-I

Sundays in Ordinary Time	(Ordinary Time, thirty-three or thirty-four weeks in duration, begins on Monday after the Sunday following January 6 and continues until Tuesday before Ash Wednesday inclusive, resumes on the Monday after Pentecost, and ends before Evening Prayer of the First Sunday of Advent.)
Baptism of the Lord	(the Sunday following Epiphany)

EASTER CYCLE

First Sunday of Lent	(the Sunday following Ash Wednesday)
Second Sunday of Lent	
Third Sunday of Lent	
Fourth Sunday of Lent	(also popularly known as *Laetare* Sunday, from the first word of the old Latin Introit prayer for this day)
Fifth Sunday of Lent	(formerly known as Passion Sunday)
Passion Sunday	(also known as Palm Sunday)
Easter Triduum	(Holy Thursday, Good Friday, Easter Vigil)
Easter Sunday	
Second Sunday of Easter	
Third Sunday of Easter	
Fourth Sunday of Easter	
Fifth Sunday of Easter	
Sixth Sunday of Easter	
Seventh Sunday of Easter	
Pentecost Sunday	

ORDINARY TIME-II

Trinity Sunday	(Solemnity of the Holy Trinity)
Body and Blood of Christ	(Solemnity of Corpus Christi)
Christ the King	(the thirty-fourth and last Sunday in Ordinary Time)

SANCTORAL CYCLE (PROPER OF SAINTS)

SOLEMNITIES, FEASTS, AND MEMORIALS [S,F,M]

January 1	Octave of Christmas; Solemnity of Mary, Mother of God [S]
January 2	Sts. Basil the Great and Gregory of Nazianzus [M]
January 4	St. Elizabeth Ann Seton (United States) [M]
January 5	St. John Neumann (United States) [M]
January 17	St. Anthony, abbot [M]
January 21	St. Agnes [M]
January 24	St. Francis de Sales [M]
January 25	Conversion of Paul, Apostle [F]
January 26	Sts. Timothy and Titus [M]
January 28	St. Thomas Aquinas [M]
January 31	St. John Bosco [M]
February 2	Presentation of the Lord (also known as Candlemas Day) [F]
February 5	St. Agatha [M]
February 6	St. Paul Miki and companions [M]
February 10	St. Scholastica [M]
February 14	Sts. Cyril and Methodius [M]
February 22	Chair of Peter, Apostle [F]
February 23	St. Polycarp [M]
March 7	Sts. Perpetua and Felicity [M]
March 19	St. Joseph, Husband of Mary [S]
March 25	Annunciation [S]
April 7	St. Jean-Baptiste de La Salle [M]
April 25	St. Mark, Evangelist [F]
April 29	St. Catherine of Siena [M]
May 2	St. Athanasius [M]
May 3	Sts. Philip and James, Apostles [F]
May 14	St. Matthias, Apostle [F]
May 26	St. Philip Neri [M]
May 31	Visitation [F]
(Thursday before the Seventh Sunday of Easter)	Ascension
June 1	St. Justin [M]
June 3	St. Charles Lwanga and companions [M]
June 5	St. Boniface [M]
June 11	St. Barnabas, Apostle [M]
June 13	St. Anthony of Padua [M]
June 21	St. Aloysius Gonzaga [M]
June 24	Birth of John the Baptist [S]
June 28	St. Irenaeus [M]
June 29	Sts. Peter and Paul, Apostles [S]
(Friday after Corpus Christi)	Sacred Heart [S]

July 3	St. Thomas, Apostle [F}
July 11	St. Benedict [M]
July 15	St. Bonaventure [M]
July 22	St. Mary Magdalene [M]
July 25	St. James, Apostle [F]
July 26	Sts. Joachim and Anne, parents of Mary [M]
July 29	St. Martha [M]
July 31	St. Ignatius of Loyola [M]
August 1	St. Alphonsus Liguori [M]
August 4	St. John Vianney [M]
August 6	Transfiguration [F]
August 8	St. Dominic [M]
August 10	St. Lawrence, Deacon and Martyr [F]
August 11	St. Clare [M]
August 15	Assumption [S]
August 20	St. Bernard [M]
August 21	St. Pius X [M]
August 22	Queenship of Mary [M]
August 24	St. Bartholomew, Apostle [F]
August 27	St. Monica [M]
August 28	St. Augustine [M]
August 29	Beheading of John the Baptist [M]
September 3	St. Gregory the Great [M]
September 8	Birth of Mary [F]
September 9	St. Peter Claver (United States) [M]
September 13	St. John Chrysostom [M]
September 14	Triumph of the Cross [F]
September 15	Our Lady of Sorrows [M]
September 16	Sts. Cornelius and Cyprian [M]
September 21	St. Matthew, Apostle and Evangelist [F]
September 27	St. Vincent de Paul [M]
September 29	Michael, Gabriel, and Raphael, Archangels (also known as Michaelmas Day) [F]
September 30	St. Jerome [M]
October 1	St. Theresa of the Child Jesus (the Little Flower) [M]
October 2	Guardian Angels [M]
October 4	St. Francis of Assisi [M]
October 7	Our Lady of the Rosary [M]
October 15	St. Teresa of Ávila [M]
October 17	St. Ignatius of Antioch [M]
October 18	St. Luke, Evangelist [F]
October 19	Sts. Isaac Jogues and Jean de Brébeuf, and companions [M]
October 28	Sts. Simon and Jude, Apostles [F]
November 1	All Saints [S]
November 2	All Souls
November 4	St. Charles Borromeo [M]

November 9	Dedication of St. John Lateran [F]
November 10	St. Leo the Great [M]
November 11	St. Martin of Tours [M]
November 12	St. Josephat [M]
November 13	St. Frances Cabrini (United States) [M]
November 17	St. Elizabeth of Hungary [M]
November 21	Presentation of Mary [M]
November 22	St. Cecilia [M]
November 30	St. Andrew, Apostle [F]
December 3	St. Francis Xavier [M]
December 7	St. Ambrose [M]
December 8	Immaculate Conception [S]
December 12	Our Lady of Guadalupe (United States) [M]
December 13	St. Lucy [M]
December 14	St. John of the Cross [M]
December 25	Christmas [S]
December 26	St. Stephen, First Martyr [F]
December 27	St. John, Apostle and Evangelist [F]
December 28	Holy Innocents [F]

See also liturgical year.

liturgical commission, a diocesan body charged with assisting and advising the local bishop on liturgical matters. In the United States, the Federation of Diocesan Liturgical Commissions meets periodically to coordinate the research and activities of the local commissions. These liturgical commissions were mandated by the Second Vatican Council's Constitution on the Sacred Liturgy (1963, nn. 44–46).

liturgical dance, rhythmical movements and steps set to dance forms to express embodied prayer in public worship. While gesture and movement have always been a part of the Roman liturgy, dance movement is of recent development, rooted in the desire to incorporate into the liturgy cultural elements that can validly express faith. Little has been done on the official level, except in *The Missal for the Diocese of Zaire,* which incorporates rhythmic movements and dance in the rite. Dance, like any other liturgical art form, has a ministerial function, i.e., the visible expression of the prayer of the assembly. If genuinely liturgical, it engages and expresses the entire human person and leads the assembly into the mystery celebrated; it should avoid the merely ostentatious, theatrical, and the purely entertaining.

liturgical language, a comprehensive term for both the verbal and nonverbal components of ritual acts or liturgical events. Broadly considered, liturgical language includes both words and deeds, metaphoric speech, and symbolic gesture. It is thus communicative, performative, and metaphorical.

The basic qualities of liturgical language are derived, first, from the fact that rituals are acts of communication (acts by which someone "says" something "to" someone "about" something; acts that transmit meanings and values through verbal and nonverbal codes). As communication, liturgical language should be intelligible and inclusive, capable of using human speech and gesture to put believers in touch with divine realities. (The sublimely sacred aspect of liturgical language derives not from some esoteric source, but from the conviction that ordinary human language can, through the power of metaphoric word and deed, disclose ultimate mystery.)

Secondly, liturgical language is performative. The words and deeds used in worship do not merely "describe," they do, perform, and enact. To borrow the traditional language of Catholic theology, liturgical language "accomplishes what it symbolizes" ("effects what it signifies"). When spouses vow love and fidelity to each other in the ritual of marriage, they really enact the nuptial covenant—they do not merely describe it. Pronouncing the vows actually marries the couple.

Thirdly, liturgical language is metaphorical. Following the strategy of all metaphor, liturgical speech creates conflict between two apparently irreconcilable fields of meaning (one literal, the other poetic), and so opens up fresh horizons of meaning and possibility that exceed the limits of literal or conceptual discourse. *See also* exclusive language; inclusive language. NATHAN D. MITCHELL

liturgical law, the provisions of canon law pertaining to the structure and ordering of the liturgical life of the Church. Liturgical law strives for the harmonious unity of Christian worship within the churches. Not to be confused with rubricism (a slavish fidelity to the rules, or rubrics, of liturgical celebration), adherence to liturgical norms signals a concern to maintain the quality of liturgical rites as they express the faith of the entire Christian community. The sources for liturgical law are similar to those for canon law, though somewhat broader in scope and application. There are five sources for the liturgical ordinances: (1) the dogmatic decrees of Vatican Council II (1962–65), (2) the liturgical books themselves, (3) the Code of Canon Law, revised in 1983, (4) the Roman Curia, and (5) local custom and the regulations of the diocesan bishop.

The Decrees of Vatican II: The fundamental document currently directing and shaping the liturgical lives of Catholics today is the Constitution on the Sacred Liturgy, *Sacrosanctum Concilium,* promulgated on December 4, 1963. The norms and standards established by the council in this document, such as the ones regarding full and active participation or the adaptation of liturgical forms to bear the Christian message more clearly to a modern world, govern and color the interpretation of all subsequent norms and liturgical revision.

The Liturgical Books: The typical editions of liturgical rites and their authorized translations carry in themselves the force of law. Most liturgical rites begin with lengthy introductions called "praenotanda." The praenotanda outline the rite, its significance within Christian worship, who may celebrate it and under what circumstances. The praenotanda then describe the normative performance of the rite as well as any optional portions. Within the texts of rites themselves are found "rubrics," descriptions of gestures or actions which may or must accompany the rite.

The Code of Canon Law: Book Four of the Code of Canon Law (1983), "The Office of Sanctifying," covers the sacraments, other acts of divine worship, and "sacred times and places." Part One, on the sacraments, reiterates norms issued in the various liturgical books, but emphasizes the administrative aspects of the sacramental disciplines: e.g., who may or may not be married in the Church, how sacramental acts are to be recorded. Part Two covers remaining acts of public worship: sacramentals, the Liturgy of the Hours, funerals, veneration of saints, images, relics, and sacred vows. Part Three, regarding sacred times and places, establishes norms for ecclesiastical architecture, the ranking of churches, cathedrals, shrines, and basilicas, the regulation of cemeteries, feast days, and days of penance.

The Roman Curia: Although the supreme authority for the regulation of rites belongs to the pope and the college of bishops, the pope alone or through his curia can issue liturgical directives and official interpretations of liturgical norms. The Roman Curia publishes editions of the liturgical books and approves the translations of rites for local churches. Two Vatican congregations now regulate the liturgical life of the Catholic Church: the Congregation for the Oriental Churches regulates the liturgical life of the churches of the Eastern rites while the Congregation for Divine Worship and the Discipline of the Sacraments regulates the liturgy for the remainder of the Church.

Local Custom and the Episcopal Ordinary: The local ordinary (the bishop, apostolic vicar, or abbot) is the primary liturgist in any local church. To the ordinary is given the authority to oversee the liturgical life of the diocese. The ordinaries are the "custodians of the whole liturgical life of the church entrusted to them" (can. 835.1). Local custom and the ordinary determine when local observances take precedence over the calendar of the universal Church. Along with the liturgical commission of the diocese, the bishop may regulate such matters as liturgical music, liturgical art and architecture, the liturgical ministries of lector, ministers of the Eucharist, and servers. The local bishops in the United States have formed a conference of bishops, the National Conference of Catholic Bishops, which has its own Bishops' Committee on the Liturgy (BCL). The BCL assists the U.S. bishops in maintaining the unity of U.S. churches through studies of the liturgical life of parishes, the publication of periodical literature, and the preparation of U.S. editions of the liturgical books. Local parishes and religious communities may, within the limits allowed to them, observe liturgical events or prepare local calendars that reflect the genius and gifts of the particular community. Such events might include the anniversary of the dedication of a church, the observance of the patronal feasts, or the maintenance of a parish necrology. *See also* Congregation for Divine Worship and the Discipline of the Sacraments; Congregation for the Oriental Churches; Constitution on the Sacred Liturgy.

JEFFREY T. VANDERWILT

liturgical movement, the period of growing interest in liturgy and liturgical reform that led up to the promulgation of the Constitution on the Sacred Liturgy (1963) at Vatican II. Though considerable research into the history of liturgy was done in the seventeenth and eighteenth centuries, and though a number of interesting reform initiatives were undertaken under the influence of the Jansenists and of the Enlightenment, the history of the liturgical movement is usually related in three phases, beginning in the first half of the nineteenth century.

Monastic Phase (1833–1903): The origins of the liturgical movement may be traced to the phenomenon known as "New Catholicism," which arose spontaneously in a number of European countries in response to the destruction wrought by the French Revolution, the Napoleonic wars, and the rise of secular states. In England, it was manifest in the Oxford movement and is associated especially with the name of E. B. Pusey (1800–82); in Denmark with N. S. F. Grundtvig (1783–1872); in Germany, with the Catholic theologian J. B. Möhler (1796–1838) and the Lutheran pastor Wilhelm Loehe (1837–72); and in France with the Benedictine Prosper Guéranger (1805–75). What all these figures had in common, and what inspired the beginnings of the liturgical movement, was the twofold conviction that, first, the source of all evils in the modern world was the eclipse of community by the rise of individualism; and that, second, the balance between individual and community could be restored by a return to past models.

Guéranger refounded the abbey of Solesmes in 1833 with the intention of countering the secularist spirit of the age with a living model (albeit monastic) of a community of believers devoted to worshiping God in the liturgy of the Church. It would edify visitors by the beauty and dignity of the services, and by the stability, regularity, and discipline of the offices. A wider public was reached by Guéranger through his publications, especially *l'Année liturgi-que* (Fr., "The Liturgical Year"), fifteen volumes of commentary on the feasts and seasons of the year, begun in 1841.

Guéranger's ideas found a fertile reception in Germany, where the abbey of Beuron was founded in 1867. From Beuron sprang the abbeys of Maredsous (1872) and Mont-César (1899) in Belgium and Maria Laach (1892) in Germany, which served not only to exemplify the splendors of the liturgy, but as centers of historical research and popular promotion of the liturgy. The historical scholarship of these abbeys succeeded in pushing past the medievalism of Guéranger's restoration to establish the patristic period as the model for liturgical renewal.

Pastoral and Theological Phase (1903–47): Although Pius X is generally credited with launching the twentieth-century liturgical movement, his motivations were more closely connected with the nineteenth century and with the desire to restore ecclesial and social life to the (idealized) medieval model in the face of the secularizing and anticlerical spirit of the age. It was precisely to rally the faithful against the spirit of the age that his initiatives regarding Gregorian chant (1903), frequent Communion (1905), earlier First Communion (1910), and a relaxed Eucharistic fast for the sick (1911) were taken. For Pius X, "active participation" in the liturgy, which he described as "the indispensable source of the authentic Christian spirit," had a social and political goal: the rallying of the Catholic faithful as a step toward an eventual restoration of a Catholic state.

For Lambert Beauduin (1873–1960), however, the goal of liturgical renewal was a recovery of the sense of the mystery of the Church. In 1909 he gave a famous address to the Eucharistic Congress at Malines and in the same year began a series of "liturgical weeks" for clergy. He also founded a periodical, *La vie liturgique* (Fr., "liturgical life"), known since 1911 as *Quéstions liturgiques et paroissiales* (Fr., "liturgical and parochical questions"), a title expressing the new constituency—the parish—to which the liturgical movement was turning.

Thus the Belgian abbeys began to promote a popular liturgical apostolate, a task in which they were joined, in Germany, by the Oratory at Leipzig and by the monks of Beuron and Maria Laach, and in Austria by Pius Parsch and the canons regular of Klosterneuberg, to mention only the best known.

At Maria Laach, particularly, the work of serious liturgical scholarship proceeded apace. Alongside historical studies, Maria Laach, under Abbot

Herwegen, fostered a new development of liturgical theology. The way for this had already been prepared by J. B. Möhler's writings on patristic ecclesiology in the nineteenth century, but a new beginning was made with Odo Casel's patristic studies, focusing on the *Kultmysterium,* or the Paschal Mystery as realized in the sacramental liturgies of the Church. Casel's "mystery theology," together with the writings of Herwegen and Romano Guardini, a German diocesan priest-scholar, came to bring a new and deeper appreciation of the centrality of liturgy in the life of the Church.

In the United States, the liturgical movement was initiated by the German-speaking Benedictines of St. John's Abbey in Collegeville, Minnesota, most notably Virgil Michel. The American movement was more popular than scholarly, but its particular contribution, made under Michel's leadership, was to combine the liturgical movement with the social justice movement. While he did not share the reactionary social and political views of Guéranger and Pope Pius X, Michel very much shared their conviction that the liturgical movement was a means to awaken the baptized to a sense of their solidarity in Christ and to their responsibilities towards society at large.

The Reform Phase (1939–63): Under National Socialism, when the Church in Germany was largely confined to its sacramental ministry, many considered the liturgy to play an indispensable role in awakening and fostering a sense of Christian identity. The German bishops approved the liturgical movement as an apostolate to German Catholic youth, but not as a parochial apostolate. As a result, there were growing pressures for changes that would make the liturgy more effective, such as the restoration of the Easter Vigil and a wider use of the vernacular. At the same time many German bishops and clergy were suspicious of the movement and attempted to have it suppressed. Because the hierarchy of Greater Germany was divided, appeal was made to the new pope, Pius XII, to intervene. The result was the encyclicals *Mystici Corporis* (1943) and *Mediator Dei* (1947), which took the image of the Church as the Body of Christ as their starting point and offered a first formal endorsement (along with a series of warnings about excesses in theology and practice) of the liturgical developments since Pius X.

But while Pius XII's encyclicals ratified the work of the previous phase, a new phase had already begun. Previously the aim of the liturgical movement had been to bring the people to the liturgy. With the German pastoral-liturgical proposals for change and the growing sense in postwar Europe of the need for a new approach to pastoral work based on the liturgy, the aim now became to bring the liturgy to the people. Increasingly, the work of teaching people about the liturgy was accompanied by a list of desirable changes that would bring the liturgy closer to the people: reform of the calendar, and especially of Holy Week; breviary reform for the clergy; wider use of the vernacular; simplification of rubrics; a fuller presentation of liturgical symbols; Mass facing the people.

In 1943, the *Centre de pastorale liturgique* (Fr., "center for pastoral liturgy") was set up in Paris to coordinate efforts in France, while a German equivalent was established at Trier in 1947. These centers provided coordination not only for their own countries, but across national boundaries. International congresses brought liturgical scholars and promoters together annually from 1951 onward. With encouragement from Rome, where Pius XII had set up a secret commission in 1948 to advise him on the feasibility of a general reform of the liturgy, the agenda of liturgical reform, based on historical and theological research into the liturgy, gradually grew. Pius XII had himself begun to implement some of these changes with a series of reforms, including a new Latin psalter, permission for evening Mass, general relaxation of the eucharistic fast, bilingual rituals, and restoration of the Easter Vigil and of the Order of Holy Week.

With this third phase of the liturgical movement, the original goal of reanimating the faithful for reconstruction of the social order tended to be forgotten. The aims became those of deepening Christian life in the increasingly unchurched world of Catholic Europe and fostering ecumenism. Such, at least, were the goals set at the beginning of Vatican II's liturgy constitution (n.1) to guide the reforms that it would launch. Since these reforms had been thoroughly researched and discussed since World War II, the Constitution on the Sacred Liturgy was the first document to be debated by the council. It was promulgated on December 4, 1963. *See also* Beauduin, Lambert; Benedictine order; Constitution on the Sacred Liturgy; Maria Laach; *Mediator Dei;* Michel, Virgil; Solesmes; worship.

Bibliography

Botte, Bernard. *From Silence to Participation: An Insider's View of Liturgical Renewal.* Washington, DC: Pastoral Press, 1988.

Franklin, R. W., and Robert Spaeth. *Virgil Michel: American Catholic*. Collegeville, MN: Liturgical Press, 1988.

Koenker, Ernest B. *The Liturgical Renaissance in the Roman Catholic Church*. Chicago: University of Chicago Press, 1954. MARK SEARLE

liturgical music, term now frequently used to designate the usually sung music integral to the Roman rites reformed by Vatican II (1962–65). Prior to the council, the generic term "sacred music," designating music that, by its inspiration, function, or use expresses a connection to faith, was the preferred phrase in universal Roman documents. Other designations include the term "church music," that is, music employed in worship by various Christian churches throughout history, and "religious music," referring to any music with a religious theme (e.g., popular "Christian rock," spirituals, Buddhist chants, etc.)

  Church Teachings: Pope Pius X's 1903 *motu proprio* document entitled *Tra le Sollicitudini* called for the assembly's participation in worship's song (then, Gregorian chant), viewing music as an integral part of the liturgy. Asserting that music's primary role was to clothe the words of the liturgy, the document assigned the role of "handmaid of the liturgy" to sacred music.

  Vatican II's Constitution on the Sacred Liturgy speaks of the "ministerial," rather than ancillary, function of music, which, intimately connected with liturgical action, can make prayer more pleasing or rites more solemn and promote unity among the congregants (n. 112). In keeping with the conciliar insistence on true participation in liturgical rites, the constitution encourages new compositions with "qualities proper to genuine sacred music" (n. 121) and musical indiginization (n. 119), while still encouraging the use of Gregorian chant, "specially suited to the Roman liturgy" (n. 116).

  Musicam Sacram, the 1967 instruction, written to clarify previous documents and eliminate various perceived problems, defines music as sacred "insofar as it is composed for the celebration of divine worship and possesses integrity of form" (n. 4a). Sacred music embraces Gregorian chant, ancient and modern polyphony of various styles, instrumental music, and the "sacred, i.e., liturgical or religious, music of the people" (n. 4b). The instruction advocates singing at public eucharistic celebrations, especially on Sunday, and specifies "degrees of solemnity" for sung Masses. The first degree includes presider's prayers and greetings with their responses; the second degree adds the Kyrie, Gloria and Agnus Dei, Creed, and intercessions; the third

enumerates entrance and Communion processionals, responsorial chant and alleluia, songs at the preparation of gifts, and the scriptural readings themselves (n. 28–30). The thrust of the document's directives can be described as "singing the liturgy," similar to the sung liturgies of many Eastern churches, where the liturgical texts themselves are sung or chanted.

  By way of contrast, the 1972 document, "Music in Catholic Worship," a statement on music prepared by the U.S. Bishops' Committee on the Liturgy, offers guidelines to "foster interest with regard to music in the liturgy" (Intro.). Beginning with a "theology of celebration," the document then treats liturgical planning and the place of music in celebration, offering criteria for musical, liturgical, and pastoral judgments. The document considers the structure of the eucharistic rite and then applies stated principles. Avoiding specificity regarding "degrees of solemnity," it speaks of the importance of singing acclamations (Alleluia, Sanctus, Memorial Acclamation, Great Amen, Lord's Prayer, Doxology), processional songs (entrance and Communion), responsorial psalms, and chants of the ordinary, "now treated as individual choices" either spoken or sung (Kyrie, Gloria, Lord's Prayer, Lamb of God, Creed). Other songs for which there are no specified texts nor any requirement for a spoken or sung text are treated under "supplementary songs." The pastoral orientation and goal of establishing musical participation moves in the direction of highlighting congregational song, rather than the chants of the presider. *See also* Catholicism and music.

JOHN A. MELLOH

liturgical reform, the process of altering liturgical laws, customs, texts, and ceremonies, usually as a result of conciliar, papal, or local (episcopal) legislation. Prior to the fourth century, Christian liturgy was characterized by creativity, improvisation, and local variation. Since Church unity was not thought to depend upon rigid "uniformity," local customs—especially in the choice of liturgical prayers, Scripture readings, hymns and music—varied widely. Even an important text like the Eucharistic Prayer could be improvised according to the individual presider's abilities. Ministerial competence, shared faith, and respect for cultural diversity established the parameters within which early liturgies developed. Textual and ritual rigidity were not required.

  History: From the fourth century on, this spirit of liturgical freedom led to a veritable revolution, during which the forms of Christian worship were creatively adapted to the cultural and religious traditions of the Greco-Roman world. Elements of secular court ceremonial were imported into the liturgy (e.g., the vesting of liturgical ministers; the use of lights and incense to honor persons or objects); the venue of worship shifted from homes or small buildings to large, public spaces like basilicas; secular festivals were "baptized" for Christian purposes (e.g., the winter feast of *Sol Invictus* [Lat., "Unconquered Sun"] was absorbed into the festival of Christmas). In short, Christian liturgy was routinely reformed by a process of creative cultural adaptation through which both liturgy and culture were enriched and infused with fresh ideas.

In time, this process took on a more "official" character, as popes like Gregory I (d. 604) worked to reorganize the liturgy of the Roman church following the collapse of the empire and the expansion of Christianity into northern and central Europe. Reformers like Gregory, however, respected local custom and permitted liturgical variation in jurisdictions outside their own, so long as no essential matters of faith were jeopardized.

Historically, however, liturgical reform has not been a one-way street. The Roman liturgy has not only been a source of reform, it has also been an object of reform, as it was in the eighth to the tenth centuries, when Franco-Germanic adaptations reshaped the Roman rite (which Charlemagne had imported into his empire). Indeed, these inculturated Franco-Germanic elements (evident especially in the liturgies of Holy Week, baptism, and ordination) eventually made their way back to Rome, where they influenced the liturgy of the papal court and helped shape the "modern" Roman rite.

The Roman liturgy of today is itself the result of four major reform movements: those of Pope Gregory VII (1073–85); Pope Innocent III (1198–1216); the Council of Trent (1545–63); and Vatican Council II (1962–65). All these movements shared a common goal: to renew worship by returning to its ancient biblical and patristic sources. Gregory, Innocent, and Trent sought to accomplish this renewal by eliminating cultural or ethnic diversity and by bringing worship in European churches under strictly centralized Roman control. By contrast, Vatican II's Constitution on the Sacred Liturgy (1963, nn. 37–40) recognizes that worship must be adapted to the varying temperaments and traditions of peoples. *See also* inculturation; liturgical movement.

NATHAN D. MITCHELL

liturgical seasons. *See* liturgical year.

liturgical year, the annual cycle of seasons and feasts that celebrates the Paschal Mystery (Christ's life, death, Resurrection and Ascension). The unfolding of the entire Christian story makes its power available once again in each retelling.

The smallest unit of the liturgical year is the liturgical day, made holy through the Eucharist and the Liturgy of the Hours. Liturgical days are divided into four degrees of celebration: solemnities, feasts, obligatory memorials, and optional memorials. The source and center of the liturgical year is the Paschal Mystery, which the Church celebrates every day but most especially on the first day of the week known as the Lord's Day or Sunday, the first of all holy days.

Easter Cycle: Easter Sunday is the first of all Sundays and has its own octave. The Easter season extends fifty days beyond Easter Sunday to Pentecost Sunday, the "fiftieth day," when the Church remembers the sending of the Holy Spirit and the commission to preach and evangelize all nations. To prepare for the Easter Vigil and Easter Sunday, the Easter Triduum is a sacred period of three days beginning with the evening Mass of the Lord's Supper on Holy Thursday, climaxing at the Easter Vigil and closing with Evening Prayer on Easter Sunday. It is considered the culmination of the entire liturgical year. The Easter fast is observed everywhere on Good Friday and on Holy Saturday, if possible, until the Easter Vigil, the mother of vigils in which the Church celebrates Christ's life, death, and Resurrection in the sacraments of initiation: Baptism, Confirmation, and Eucharist. A forty-day period of preparation for the celebration of the sacred Triduum and the Easter cycle, known as the season of Lent, begins on Ash Wednesday and ends on Holy Thursday. Baptismal and penitential themes are woven through the lectionary, the presidential prayers at Eucharist, and the Liturgy of the Hours.

Christmas Cycle: In a similar way, the annual commemoration of Christ's birth on December 25, second only to Easter, has its own octave and cycle of feasts following that date, as well as a time of preparation before it. The Christmas cycle runs from Christmas Eve to the Sunday after Epiphany or after January 6 if Epiphany is transferred to a Sunday (as in the United States). To prepare for Christmas and its cycle, the season of Advent, beginning on the fourth Sunday before December 25, is observed primarily in a spirit of joyful expectancy and hope with its penitential character remaining secondary. The first weeks of Advent look to Christ's second coming in glory on the last day; December 17–24 focus on the immediate preparation for his birth in Bethlehem.

Ordinary Time: The Easter and Christmas cycles of feasts, with their times of preparation and their festal endings, are the two supporting pillars of the liturgical year. Outside the limits of these two cycles of feasts are thirty-three or thirty-four neutral weeks known as Ordinary Time or Time of the Year, which extends from the Monday after the feast of the Baptism of the Lord to and including the Tuesday before Ash Wednesday. Ordinary Time resumes on Monday after Pentecost and ends before Evening Prayer on the Saturday before the first Sunday of Advent. During Ordinary Time, the fullness of Christ's mystery is celebrated in all its aspects. Two cycles of feasts (Easter and Christmas), together with Ordinary Time and other solemnities and feasts of the Lord, are also known as the Temporal Cycle or Proper of Time, which is always privileged over other solemnities, feasts, and memorials. The last Sunday of the year escalates to the Solemnity of Christ the King, which anticipates the fulfillment of all time when Christ will be all in all.

As the yearly cycle unfolds the Paschal Mystery of Christ, it also attends to the anniversaries of the saints, holy men and women who continue to serve as models for gospel living. The Sanctoral Cycle, or Proper of Saints, honors the memory of Mary, the martyrs, and other saints while always reaffirming the centrality of the mysteries of Christ in the celebration of their lives. *See also* liturgical calendar; Paschal Mystery; worship. *DANIEL P. GRIGASSY*

Liturgikon (Gk., "liturgical [book]"), a Hieratikon or Byzantine-rite liturgical book containing the deacon's and priest's parts for Eucharist, Vespers, and Matins. *See also* sacramentary.

liturgy (li'tur-jee; Gk., *leitourgia*, "work of the public"), the public and official prayers and rites of the Church. The term signifies that worship is an activity of the whole Church, laity and clergy alike. Liturgical worship is a corporate gesture of praise, neither originating in nor directed toward any one individual person or group. Instead, it finds its source and goal in the common glorification of God whose saving works are accorded universal significance. *See also* worship.

liturgy, theology of, a systematic reflection on the process and components of worship given to God by a community gathered in Christ's name and by the power of the Holy Spirit. A theology of liturgy is distinguished from the theology of sacraments by its larger concerns, that is, not only about sacraments but also about any worship offered in the Church's name (e.g., the office of psalms, readings and prayers that individuals and communities pray).

Elements: The theology of liturgy begins with an examination of the celebrations of worship (praxis) rather than theories about these celebrations. This follows the actual history of worship in the first Christian communities: they prayed, baptized, and celebrated the Eucharist together before they reflected on the meaning of what they were doing. This preference for praxis is also a reminder that it is God's action in the community through the Holy Spirit that enables the community to have honest worship. Furthermore, authentic worship always leads to true doctrine. A second point is the contribution of the human sciences to this theology. Since worship is done by human beings who are shaped and affected by their familial and educational background and their cultural and historical heritage, the theology of liturgy must take into account the research and findings of such disciplines as anthropology, sociology, and psychology. These disciplines continue to probe, for example, the honest and dishonest use of rituals by communities and individuals, the ways in which communities renew themselves through ritual, and the cultural forces in a society that can aid or obstruct worship.

Theology and Worship: A Catholic theology of liturgy gives great importance to the connections between the gathered church community and its worship. The human sciences reinforce this concern by pointing to the ways in which community is shaped by cultural and societal rituals. The Church discovers its essential doctrine and its mission to the world in the actions and prayers of worship. Liturgy also speaks of God's nature, which is revealed, above all, in the ways in which God has freely chosen to save humankind. Liturgy is a grateful response for God's saving work in Christ's death on the cross and much more. A theology of liturgy learns about this redeeming God especially on the feasts of the Holy Trinity, of Christ, and of the Holy Spirit and in the celebration of the sacraments. Liturgical theology also acknowledges that worship is only possible because God is present. This theology studies the ways in which Christ is present in the

Eucharist, in the person of the presiding minister, in the prayers and songs, in the readings of Scripture, and in the worshiping assembly itself.

The liturgical year also provides a rich source of reflection on God's gift of time, and its purposes. Liturgical theology studies how worship helps Christians to be aware of how God saves in time and to understand the meaning of the end of time. Finally, liturgical theology examines the nature of a full, conscious, and active participation by the whole community in God's praise and how this can be facilitated in particular cultures and situations. *See also* liturgy; worship. REGIS A. DUFFY

Liturgy of Addai and Mari (ah-di'; mah'ree), the earliest Syriac anaphora (central prayer of the eucharistic liturgy), which is one of the oldest and most studied eucharistic prayers. Its clear Semitic stamp reflects the ethos of early Judeo-Christianity uninfluenced by the Hellenic Christian culture of the Roman Empire. It follows the East Syrian anaphoral structure, which orders the components thus: divine praise, Sanctus, intercessions, epiclesis (the prayer calling down the Holy Spirit)—with no Words of Institution ("This is my body, this is my blood"). This presumed lacuna has provoked an enormous literature with as yet no universally accepted solution to the ongoing debate. *See also* anaphora.

Liturgy of St. Basil, one of the two eucharistic formularies of the Byzantine rite, along with the Liturgy of St. John Chrysostom. Once used frequently, it is now celebrated only on Sundays in Lent, the feast of St. Basil (January 1), Holy Thursday, Holy Saturday, and the vigils of some major feasts. Its long and beautiful anaphora (eucharistic prayer), which served as the model for the Roman Fourth Eucharistic Prayer (there are four Eucharistic Prayers available as options for the presider in the Mass of the Roman rite), is characterized by its lengthy narration of salvation history and by a highly developed trinitarian theology. In addition to the Byzantine edition of the Basil anaphora there is also a more ancient and shorter Egyptian edition, often called "Egyptian Basil," extant in both Greek and Sahidic. But the Basil anaphora is an Antiochene, not an Egyptian-type prayer, so the Egyptians probably borrowed it from the churches in Cappadocia, modern-day Turkey. Though scholarly opinion varies, it is agreed that the longer edition of the Basil anaphora is an expansion of the shorter, that the prayer mirrors the ideas and style of Basil the Great (d. 279), and that he wrote one, or the other, or both redactions. At any rate, scholars long ago disproved the popular legend that Basil composed his liturgy by abbreviating the Liturgy of St. James. There are variant versions of the Basil anaphora in several Oriental languages. *See also* anaphora; Liturgy of St. John Chrysostom.

Liturgy of St. James, the ancient Greek eucharistic liturgy of the no-longer extant Jerusalem rite, a fragment of which is cited by Eusebius of Caesarea ca. 317–25. Contrary to popular legend, the extant Greek edition of James, heavily byzantinized even in its earliest ninth-century manuscript, is in no way one of the most ancient representatives of the apostolic liturgy. The liturgy is still used occasionally in the Byzantine rite. There are widely variant editions of the James liturgy in several Oriental languages. The Syriac edition forms the basis for the West Syrian eucharistic structure. *See also* Jerusalem rite.

Liturgy of St. John Chrysostom, main Eucharist formulary of the Byzantine rite and the most widely used Eastern eucharistic liturgy. It follows the same structure as the Byzantine Liturgy of St. Basil, though the text differs. The Chrysostom anaphora (central eucharistic prayer) has primitive traits that are certainly older than the saint of that name, and computer analysis of the text has demonstrated with a high degree of probability that John Chrysostom, a priest at Antioch until he became bishop of Constantinople (398–404), took the Antiochene Anaphora of the Apostles and expanded its text via the addition of certain theological elaborations to create the anaphora that now bears his name. But there is no basis for attributing the other prayers of this liturgy him. Though the Chrysostom anaphora is a relatively short, even austere prayer of great antiquity, without the exaggerated rhetorical devices of some later Greek prayers, it is a text of great beauty and symmetry, replete with features characteristic of classical prose style. Its anaphoral structure follows the Antiochene order of praise, Sanctus ("Holy, holy, holy"), narration of salvation with the Words of Institution ("This is my body . . . This is my blood"), anamnesis (prayer commemorative of the Passion, death, and Resurrection of Jesus), oblation (prayer of offering), epiclesis (prayer calling down the Holy Spirit), intercessions. Notable is the absence of the "command to repeat" ("Do this in memory of me") before the anamnesis.

There is also a variant Armenian edition of the Chrysostom liturgy. *See also* anaphora; Liturgy of St. Basil.

Liturgy of St. Mark, the native Egyptian anaphora, or eucharistic prayer, attributed in Greek to St. Mark, in Coptic to St. Cyril of Alexandria. It has the traditional characteristics of the fully developed Egyptian anaphora, with double epiclesis, intercessions before the Sanctus ("Holy, holy, holy"), Sanctus without Benedictus ("Blessed is He who comes in the name of the Lord"), with the components ordered as follows: praise, intercessions, Sanctus, epiclesis I (prayer calling down the Holy Spirit), narration and Words of Institution, ("This is my body . . . This is my blood"), epiclesis II. Greek fragments of the text are extant from the fourth and fifth centuries. *See also* anaphora.

Liturgy of the Eucharist, name for the whole Mass, i.e., the celebration of praise and thanksgiving for God's gift of salvation achieved through the death and Resurrection of Christ, as well as for the second main part of the Mass, including the people's offering, the Eucharistic Prayer, and the Communion rite. In the early Church the Eucharist took place within a meal, as at the Last Supper. By Paul's time, a meal preceded the Eucharist in some places. Second-century descriptions of this liturgy note the reading of Scripture and the offering of bread and wine by the people, followed by an improvised prayer of thanksgiving (Gk., *eucharistia*) to God for Christ's self-gift on the cross. The structure of the Roman Catholic Eucharist today is: introductory rite (including the penitential rite), readings and prayers, homily, intercessory prayers, Creed (on Sundays and major feasts), presentation of the gifts, Eucharistic Prayer, Communion rite, dismissal. *See also* Eucharist; Mass.

Liturgy of the Hours, the public prayer of the Church for praising God and sanctifying the day. It is also known as the Divine Office. It consists of an Office of Readings, Morning and Evening Prayer, Daytime Prayer, and Night Prayer.

Daily Prayer in the NT and Early Church: The daily gatherings of Christians for public prayer has a rich historical foundation in the NT. Jesus was said to attend to the communal prayer of the synagogue (Luke 4:16). He commanded prayer to the disciples (Matt 5:44, Mark 13:33, Luke 6:28, 18:1) and gave them a model from which to fulfill that command (Matt 6:9–13, Luke 11:2–4). According to the Acts, the apostles gathered in daily and in "constant" prayer (Acts 2:46, 20:36–38, 21:5). Until persecution prevented them, they attended the daily worship of the Jerusalem Temple (Acts 3:1). Paul exhorted fellow Christians to "pray without ceasing" (1 Thess 5:16–18, Eph 6:18). From the third century, evidence suggests that Christians gathered regularly in the morning and evening for daily services. According to Tertullian (North Africa, early third century) these daily gatherings were supplemented by prayers made in private to mark the passage of the day: at rising, at the third, sixth, and ninth hours, upon retiring and, interrupting sleep, during the night. These various hours of prayer came to signify events within the life of Christ.

Therefore, according to the *Apostolic Tradition,* the third, sixth, and ninth hours signified the hours of Christ's Passion. According to Tertullian, prayer at night (the vigil) disciplined Christians for the Second Coming of Christ, who, it was said, would come "as a thief in the night." Morning and evening prayer also presented Christ to the believer. He who is "Light of World" was seen to rise with the sun and to illumine the darkness of the night of sin with "the splendor of his radiant face."

Daily Prayer in the West: The history of Christian prayer from the fourth century is a history of conflicting tendencies: the pious attempt to honor the injunction to pray duly circumscribed by the demands of the anatomical and social bodies, their needs for commerce and material sustenance. This conflict is evident in the divergence between two historical types of daily prayer, conveniently called "cathedral" and "monastic."

Monastic styles of daily prayer are marked by the following characteristics: a relatively larger number of offices prayed in common, an increase in the number of different psalms sung during any given office, all-night vigils and a greater variety in the texts sung during the weekly cycle. For example, the Office of St. Benedict included the entire Psalter in each weekly round of prayer. In some Egyptian communities of the fourth century, the anchorites (monks) were said to recite 150 psalms each day from memory.

By contrast, the majority of Christians, even during the "Golden Age" of monasticism (the fourth and fifth centuries), lived in cities and attended to daily commercial pursuits. For these Christians, the cathedral forms of prayer were more suitable.

Cathedral offices were shorter, included fewer, if any, psalms, and the psalms that were included varied little from day to day. The chief hours were Morning and Evening Prayer. Night vigils preceded major feasts and Sundays. Nonbiblical songs (such as the Roman office hymns attributed to Ambrose) became quite popular. The cathedral offices concluded with litanies and the benediction of the bishop.

The history of daily prayer in the West is finally a history of the conflation of these two types. During the Middle Ages the number of hours became set at the following: Vespers, Compline, Matins, Lauds, Prime, Terce, Sext, and None. The central act of each hour was the chanting of psalmody (as many as twelve psalms during Lauds). Vespers, Compline and Lauds each came to be associated with a proper gospel canticle: the Magnificat, Nunc Dimittis, and Benedictus respectively. The Te Deum was sung at Matins on high feast days. Most hours were preceded by a hymn. Between the psalms and the reading from Scripture (or hagiographic writings), some of the most elaborate and difficult of the Gregorian chants, the responsories, were sung. The Office in the West, because of its length and difficulty and because of its enactment in Latin (even while the vernacular languages were emerging), came less and less to interest the laity. The Hours came to be seen as the preserve of clerical professionals, the typifying activity of either the monks and nuns or the canons and choirs, i.e., clergy attached to the cathedral specifically for the purpose of maintaining the daily prayer.

Two developments further fortified the clerical nature of the Office. The twelfth-century invention by the mendicant friars of the breviary as a distinct liturgical book permitted the Office to be recited in private and according to the convenience of the priest, who rarely observed the hours at their given times. The French prelate, Cardinal Richelieu (1585–1642), prime minister of the court of King Louis XIII, boasted that he could dispose of the Office in one sitting every other day. He read the first day's office from eleven at night until midnight; the second day's from midnight until retiring. The laity preferred not to leave prayer in the hands of clergy alone. Such as they could, and with the assistance of concerned pastors, various devotions, including condensed versions of the breviary, were offered to the laity. For example, the most popular Catholic devotion, the Rosary with its fifteen decades of prayers, was at origin a self-conscious abbreviation of the Psalter with its 150 psalms.

Daily Prayer since Vatican II: The Constitution on the Sacred Liturgy (*Sacrosanctum Concilium*) addressed the reform of the Liturgy of the Hours. The council (1962–65) decreed: (1) The Hours were to be observed at their proper times. (2) Vespers (Evening Prayer) and Lauds (Morning Prayer) "are the two hinges on which the daily Office turns." Despite the mixed metaphor, they are to be seen as the "chief hours of prayer." (3) Compline is to "mark the close of the day." (4) Matins is to become a "floating hour." Renamed the Office of Readings, it may be observed at any time of day. (5) The hour of Prime is no longer to be observed. (6) Of the three minor hours, Terce, Sext, and None, "outside of choir" only one need be observed (as Daytime Prayer). (7) Pastors are to see that at least some portion of the Hours is observed in their parishes. The council suggested that Sunday Vespers might be celebrated in parishes. Since the reform of the breviary, the Liturgy of the Hours now also exhibits the following features: (1) The Psalter is distributed over three weeks instead of just one; (2) the lectionary has been expanded; (3) the Liturgies of the Hours may be officially observed by any gathering of Christians, whether or not a priest or deacon is present; and (4) the Offices generally follow this structure: hymn, two psalms, and a canticle (OT at Morning Prayer; NT at Evening Prayer); each psalm may be concluded with a prayer. A proper responsory follows the Scripture lesson. The Gospel canticle is sung (Benedictus or Magnificat). The Office concludes with intercessions, the Lord's Prayer, concluding collect and benediction. Morning Prayer may begin with the Invitatory Psalm, Ps 95, should it be the first liturgical service of the day. Compline (Night Prayer) consists of a hymn, one psalm, a short reading, response, Nunc Dimittis, prayer, and blessing. The remaining hours were similarly streamlined.

The Liturgy of the Hours, when properly prayed and celebrated, nurtures the deeper intuitions that the value of incessant prayer instills: the sacramentality of time and the joyful expectation of the establishment of God's dominion among humankind. The Liturgy of the Hours also inspire among Christians the performance of daily deeds of charity and justice. Finally, the practice of daily prayer in the company of others delivers Christians from the need to devise ways to express their own needs and desires to God. Alternatively and at its best, the public prayer of the Church delivers humanity to a God who calls people out of themselves and into the mystery of infinite love. *See also* breviary; liturgy; prayer; worship.

Bibliography

Campbell, S. "Liturgy of the Hours." In Peter Fink, *New Dictionary of Sacramental Worship.* Collegeville, MN: Glazier, 1987.

Jones, C., G. Wainwright, E. Yarnold, and P. Bradshaw. "The Divine Office." In *The Study of Liturgy.* 2d ed. London: Oxford, 1992.

JEFFREY T. VANDERWILT

Liturgy of the Word, that part of the Mass from the first reading until the Prayer of the Faithful. Liturgies of the Word, even when abbreviated, typically precede the celebration of all sacraments and sacramental blessings, e.g., weddings, funerals, baptisms, blessings of objects or persons. Not merely the public reading of ancient texts, the Liturgy of the Word is described as one of four focal points for the presence of Christ to the Church (Constitution on the Sacred Liturgy, n. 7). Along with his presence in the Eucharist, in the worshiping assembly, and in the person of the priest, Christ is understood by Catholics to be present also through the proclamation of God's word. That word is understood to be preeminently, but not entirely limited to, the Scriptures. God's word is also discerned in the words preached to and received by the assembly and in the Prayers of the Faithful, a proclamation and rehearsal of the Church's concern for others. The Liturgy of the Word during the Mass on Sundays and solemnities includes a reading from the OT, the singing of a portion of a psalm, a reading from one of the Letters of Paul or the book of Revelation, a Gospel acclamation and the Gospel lesson. The lessons, so-called, are followed by the homily, the Creed, and the Prayer of the Faithful. On weekdays there are two readings, first from either the OT or NT, and a psalm is sung. The Gospel acclamation and the Gospel follow. On weekdays the homily may be shortened, and the Creed is omitted, though the Prayer of the Faithful is retained. The readings for Mass are found in the lectionary, the published compendium of Scripture texts assigned to each day and feast of the liturgical year. The Entrance rite is often considered part of the Liturgy of the Word. The Liturgy of the Word is separable from the Liturgy of the Eucharist and may be observed independently. *See also* Eucharist; Liturgy of the Eucharist.   *JEFFREY T. VANDERWILT*

local church, the Body of Christ in a particular place, that is, a parish, a diocese, a region, or a nation, also known in canon law as a particular church. Before Vatican II (1962–65) local churches were viewed as administrative divisions (dioceses) and subdivisions (parishes) of the Church universal. The council corrected this overemphasis on the Church universal at the expense of the local church: "This Church of Christ is truly present in all legitimate local congregations of the faithful which, united with their pastors, are themselves called churches in the New Testament. For in their own locality these are the new people called by God, in the Holy Spirit and in much fullness" (Dogmatic Constitution on the Church, n. 26).

In the beginning the church of Jerusalem was the whole Church. The notion of local church developed as the Church moved to other communities (1 Cor 1:2; 16:1, 19) and to smaller communities within these urban centers. One example was the so-called house church (Acts 2:46; 12:12; 1 Cor 16:19; Col 4:15), in which the local Christian community gathered for the Eucharist (1 Cor 11:18–21). Eventually the Church adopted the political framework employed by the Roman Empire, dividing itself into dioceses, provinces, and the like.

In the Code of Canon Law particular churches are "first of all" dioceses (can. 368). Other examples include a territorial prelature or abbacy (can. 370) and an apostolic vicariate or prefecture (can. 371). Particular churches are also grouped into provinces and regions (cans. 431–59). The code refers to a parish as "a definite community of the Christian faithful established on a stable basis within a particular church" (can. 515). *See also* diocese; parish; prelature, territorial.   *RICHARD P. MCBRIEN*

local ordinary, title for an individual who holds one of a certain class of offices within the Church. Although in common parlance the term often refers to the bishop of a diocese, canon law includes a greater number of officeholders under this title. Canon 134 gives a taxative list. The term includes the pope, diocesan bishops, vicars general and episcopal vicars of a diocese, and those in charge of groups legally equivalent to a diocese (e.g., a vicariate apostolic).

The law frequently uses the term "local ordinary" and reserves certain powers to those who hold an office so designated. All of these officeholders have executive power of governance. *See also* ordinary.

logia (sing., *logion,* Gk., "short sayings"), a term used to describe brief statements of Jesus, proverbs, or pronouncements (e.g., Mark 2:17, 27; Luke 19:10), in contrast to longer parables and discourses.

Logos (Gk., "word," "speech," "reason"), according to Heraclitus, the rational principle that governs the universe and, according to Plato, the transcendent source (also called the *nous*) of the rational principles that shape creation. In the OT, the Logos is personified wisdom who is manifest in creation (Prov 8:1–36; Wis 7:22–30; 9:1–2). The Platonists of Alexandria conceived of the Logos as the divine intermediary between God and the world. Integrating these views, Philo (20 B.C.–A.D. 50) spoke of the Logos as the divine intention operating at the heart of creation. It is the power of creation and the means through which we know God. In John's Gospel, the Logos is neither a rational principle nor an intermediary agent, but God's preexisting Word who formed creation and became flesh in Jesus Christ (John 1:1–14). The early Church writers Ignatius of Antioch, Justin Martyr, Clement of Alexandria, and Athanasius employed the notion of Logos to shed light on the mystery of God's self-revelation in Jesus Christ. But, as Irenaeus warned, logos-language can be pushed into Gnosticism. *See also* Christology; Incarnation, the.

Loisy, Alfred (lwah-see'), 1857–1940, French biblical scholar and Modernist. He attempted to construct an apologetic response to the concerns of his time. Making a sharp distinction between the material and supernatural worlds, he denied that dogmas have any correspondence with the realities that they attempt to express. Advocating critical biblical exegesis, he proposed that the Bible be interpreted as any other historical document rather than as a privileged expression of faith. His teachings seemed to be the object of condemnation in Pope Pius X's encyclical *Pascendi* in 1907; he was excommunicated in 1908. If his positions were extreme, they anticipated later theological developments concerning revelation, Scripture, and the development of doctrine. *See also* Modernism.

Lollards, adherents of a medieval English heresy (Lollardy) initiated by John Wycliffe (d. 1384). The derivation of the name is unclear. It may have come from Middle Dutch, *lollen* or *lullen,* "to mumble." In any case, it was intended as a term of opprobrium, to mean, for example, "mumblers of prayers." After the execution of Sir John Oldcastle (1417), it became a lower-class movement. The Lollards criticized the corruption of the clergy, rejected Catholic sacraments and the cult of the saints, and emphasized preaching and reading Scripture, which they translated into English. *See also* Wycliffe, John.

Lombard, Peter, ca. 1100–60, theologian, also known as the Lombard, and as the Master of the *Sentences.* Born in Lombardy (northern Italy), Peter studied theology in France, at Reims, St. Victor, and Notre Dame in Paris (ca. 1134). He remained in Paris teaching theology at Notre Dame, and in 1144 or 1145 he became canon of the cathedral. By 1156, Peter was archdeacon of Paris, and was elected bishop of the city in 1159.

The Lombard's historical significance is due to the extraordinary influence he exerted on the development of theology as a science. He wrote many sermons, an early gloss on the Psalms (ca. 1138), and a Pauline commentary (1134–41). In 1147 and 1148, he participated in two ecclesial investigations of Gilbert of Poitiers. By 1157–58, Peter completed the final draft of a four-volume collection of *Sentences,* a text that provided students and teachers of theology with a systematic and comprehensive overview of Christian doctrine that was brief, timely, and accessible. The format, method, and questions or distinctions of the *Sentences* shaped theological discussion for centuries: book 1 examines the Trinity; book 2 considers creation, grace, and sin; book 3 presents the Incarnation, redemption, and virtue; and book 4 covers the sacraments and eschatology. From the early thirteenth century to the middle of the seventeenth century, students of theology were required to comment on all or part of this text. Once integrated into the curriculum, the *Sentences* soon became a primary focus of theological study, second only to the Bible. *See also* Scholasticism; theology.

Lombards, Germanic tribe that invaded northern Italy in 568, establishing a kingdom centered around Pavia. Expanding southward, the kingdom reached its peak in the eighth century. When the Lombards threatened Rome in 772, Charlemagne intervened and seized the Lombard crown. A Lombard state survived in Benevento until the eleventh century.

Lonergan, Bernard J. F., 1904–84, Jesuit philosopher and theologian. Canadian born, he entered the Society of Jesus in 1922 and was ordained in 1936. He received his doctorate in theology at the Gregorian University in Rome in 1936 and taught there from 1953 until 1965 when he returned to

Regis College, Toronto. He was Chauncey Stillman Professor of Roman Catholic Studies at Harvard Divinity School, 1971–72, and taught at Boston College from 1975 until 1983. He returned to Canada and died the next year.

Influence of Augustine and Aquinas: His work was dedicated to an ever more adequate understanding of both human intelligence and the mysteries of Christian faith. His *Grace and Freedom: Operative Grace in the Thought of St. Thomas Aquinas* (1971) traced the developments of speculative theology on grace from Augustine to Aquinas, set out the terms and relations in the notion of operative and cooperative grace, and presented an as yet unsurpassed analysis of Aquinas's theories of causation, operation, divine transcendence, and human liberty.

From Augustine, Lonergan learned that Christian conversion to Jesus Christ as Lord involves intellectual and moral dimensions, as well as the religious dimension. He reflected on Augustine's narratives of his intellectual conversion to the truth, moral conversion to goodness, and religious conversion to God revealed in Christ Jesus (*Confessions* 8–9). For Lonergan this threefold conversion process of Augustine becomes in Aquinas the basis for the intellectual, moral, and theological virtues (*Summa Theologiae* 1–2. 55–67; 2–2. 1–170). To understand the systematic breakthrough in the theology of Aquinas, Lonergan realized that he had to reach up to the mind of Aquinas by undergoing himself what he would later term "intellectual conversion."

Lonergan's *Verbum: Word and Idea in Aquinas* (1967) sets out the basic terms and relations operative in the cognitional theory of Aquinas and also shows how those terms and relations are derived from the human experiences of questioning, understanding, and judging. Insight into images generates understanding and this understanding expresses itself in concepts. Human understanding is not content with mere thinking. People want to know what is really true, so questions of truth emerge, and only when they grasp the sufficiency of the evidence do they reach judgment of truth or falsity. Lonergan shows that what Aquinas terms "the light of active intellect as a created participation in divine light" is, in fact, the human capacity to raise even more questions. As Augustine saw that human hearts are restless until they rest in God, so for Aquinas human minds are restless until they rest in God.

Insight and Method: *Insight: A Study of Human Understanding* (1957) transposes the cognitional theory Lonergan learned from Aquinas into contemporary contexts. The book is an invitation to the reader to appropriate his or her own conscious acts of experiencing, understanding, judging, and deciding. The first part sets out insight as activity, showing how attention to acts of understanding enables the reader with Lonergan to correlate methods of the natural and human sciences in such a way as to arrive at an understanding of a coherent and open worldview designated as "emergent probability." The second part builds on the reader's own self-appropriation as a knower, showing how genetic and dialectical methods operate in a cognitionally grounded metaphysics, ethics, and natural theology. *Insight* demonstrates how human understanding does, in fact, consist in related and recurrent operations, and that failure to attend to and understand those operations has led to the dialectical contradictions in modern cultures, philosophies, and theologies. The program of the book is succinctly stated by Lonergan: "Thoroughly understand what it is to understand, and not only will you understand the broad lines of all there is to be understood, but also you will possess a fixed base, an invariant pattern, opening upon all further developments of understanding" (*Insight*, p. xxviii).

Reason and faith, as Lonergan learned from Aquinas, are intrinsically related. From his discoveries in *Insight* Lonergan advanced to *Method in Theology* (1972), in which he shows that his notion of transcendental method can restructure how theology is done. Transcendental method is neither Cartesian nor Kantian but involves sets of related and recurrent operations of understanding and acting yielding cumulative and progressive results. After treating the human good, meaning, and religion, the book develops the notion of functional specialties in theology. There are three types of specialties: (1) Field specialties continually divide and subdivide the fields of data to be investigated, as when biblical, patristic, medieval, and Reformation fields become *genera* to be ever further subdivided. (2) Subject specialties classify the results of the investigations in order to teach those results, as when departments are separated into areas such as Hebrew history, early Christian antiquities, Christian theology, ethics, etc. (3) Functional specialties differentiate the successive stages in the process from data to results.

Lonergan's writings in whole or in part have been translated into all the European languages as well as several Asian ones. There are ten Lonergan research centers in North America, South America, Europe, Australia, and the Philippines. The Lonergan Research Institute in Toronto publishes a regular newsletter and directs the publication of his *Collected Works* by the University of Toronto Press in twenty-two volumes. Almost three hundred dissertations have been written on Lonergan's thought and methods, with more than a third published in whole or in part. Two journals are devoted to advancing Lonergan's method: *Method: A Journal of Lonergan Studies* and *Lonergan Workshop,* published by the Lonergan Institute at Boston College. *See also* philosophy and theology; theology

Bibliography

Crowe, Frederick E. *Lonergan.* Collegeville, MN.: Liturgical Press, 1992.

Lonergan, Bernard J. F. *Insight: A Study of Human Understanding.* 5th rev. ed. Toronto: University of Toronto Press, 1992.

———. *Method in Theology* New York: Herder and Herder, 1972.

MATTHEW L. LAMB

Longinqua Oceani (lawn-jink'kwuh oh-shee-ahn'ee), Pope Leo XIII's apostolic letter of January 6, 1895, to the U.S. Catholic Church. The pope said he completed the work of the Third Plenary Council (1884) by appointing an apostolic delegate in 1893. Acknowledging the growth of the Church in the United States, he regretted its lack of public patronage and warned against idealizing the U.S. separation of Church and state. *See also* Americanism; Church and state; United States of America, Catholicism in the.

Lopez, Gregory, 1611–91, first native Chinese Catholic bishop. A Dominican, he was ordained a priest in 1656 and consecrated a bishop in 1685; he was promoted to the new diocese of Nanking but died before taking office.

Lopez y Vicuña, St. Vicenta Maria, 1847–96, Spanish-born founder of the Daughters of Mary Immaculate for Domestic Service, a congregation dedicated to helping young working women. Feast day: December 26.

Lord, English translation of several Hebrew, Aramaic, and Greek terms denoting a human or deity with power or authority. The most important term in Hebrew is *'ādôn,* "lord, master, owner." In the OT it most frequently denotes a human master except for the specific form *'ǎdōnāi,* which is almost exclusively reserved for divine lordship. The meaning of

'ǎdōnāi is disputed: some think it means "my Lord" while others contend for "Lord of all." It is frequently juxtaposed with the much more common Tetragrammaton (*yhwh*), the four consonants conventionally vocalized as "Yahweh" and translated as "LORD." In tandem the two terms are rendered as "Lord GOD," "Lord" for *'ǎdōnāi* and "GOD" for *yhwh.* In the postexilic period, *'ǎdōnāi* began to displace the Tetragrammaton, especially in speaking. When Jews translated their Scriptures into Greek, they left the Tetragrammaton in Hebrew or paleo-Hebrew characters, even though they vocalized a surrogate word, e.g., *'ǎdōnāi.* Later Christian scribes replaced the Hebrew consonants with the Greek word *kyrios,* "Lord."

NT authors, especially in the Pauline corpus and Luke-Acts, use the Greek *kyrios,* which was common in the Hellenistic world. The most important development is the application of the absolute use of *kyrios* ("the Lord" or "Lord" rather than "my lord") to Christ. While the historical Jesus may have been called "lord" as a title of respect (Aram., *mārā'î* or *mārî,* "my lord"), it was the early Aramaic-speaking Christian community that first used "Lord" confessionally. The initial usage was probably tied to his Parousia (1 Cor 16:22 [Aramaic phrase preserved]; Rev 22:20 [same Aramaic phrase translated into Greek]) and then applied retroactively to his Resurrection and exaltation (Phil 2:6–11; Acts 2:36) and finally to his earthly ministry (Luke). NT texts use it to affirm the transcendent status of Jesus Christ without claiming full equality with God—that awaits the councils of Nicaea (325) and Chalcedon (451). *See also* Jesus Christ.   *GREGORY E. STERLING*

Lord, Daniel A., 1888–1955, Jesuit priest, editor, and pamphleteer. As director of the Sodality of the Blessed Virgin, the largest Catholic youth organization in the United States, he revitalized the group and edited its journal, the *Queen's Work. See also* sodality.

Lord of Hosts, an ancient title of God in the OT, especially in the prophetic books (e.g., Isa 1:9). God leads the Israelite armies, the "hosts," to victory (e.g., Exod 7:4). Since the ark of the covenant was regarded as God's place of earthly enthronement, it was brought into battle by the Israelites (1 Sam 4:4). God also commands all of the forces of creation (Ps 89:6–8). In the NT, the title occurs in Rom 9:29 and Jas 5:4.

Lord's Prayer, a prayer, also known as the "Our Father" or "Pater Noster," that Jesus taught his disciples. Two forms of the prayer survive in the NT. Luke 11:2–4 has a shorter form, omitting the words "who art in heaven," the petition that God's will be done, and the request for deliverance from evil. Matt 6:9–13, part of the Sermon on the Mount, preserves a longer version, on which most modern forms are based. Some manuscripts of Matthew also contain a doxology ("for thine is the kingdom and the power and the glory forever"), common as the conclusion of the Lord's Prayer in Reformed traditions and now used as a separate communal prayer after the Lord's Prayer in the Roman Mass.

That early Christians prayed in imitation of Jesus is clear from Paul, who notes the use of an address to God as Father at Rom 8:15 and Gal 4:6. This Christian practice may indicate the use of the Lord's Prayer or one of its petitions. Early Christian use of the prayer in the Matthean form is attested at the end of the first century in the *Didache,* which stipulates that it be used three times a day (*Did.* 8.2.3).

The heart of the prayer is a petition that God make the kingdom, or divine sovereign authority over humankind, a present reality. In the interim, the petitioner asks for physical sustenance, reconciliation with God and neighbor, and preservation from temptation and evil.

The prayer is an important part of the Mass, the Rosary, and other forms of Catholic devotion.

Lord's Supper. *See* Eucharist.

Loreto, House of, a stone structure located in the Italian city of Loreto on the Adriatic coast, purported to be the house of the Blessed Virgin Mary. Now incorporated into a basilica, the original 403-square-foot building was said to have been transported by angels from Nazareth to three other sites before finally arriving at Loreto. Since then, it has attracted countless pilgrims, including Pope John XXIII. Though the tradition of the house's Palestinian origin and miraculous translocation is regarded today as unhistorical, visitors still may gain the indulgences granted for pilgrimages to Lourdes or to the Holy Land.

Loretto, Sisters of. *See* Sisters of Loretto at the Foot of the Cross.

Lough Derg (lahg darg). *See* Saint Patrick's Purgatory.

Louis I, "the Pious," 778–840, Holy Roman emperor. The last surviving legitimate son of Charlemagne, Louis, crowned in 813, became sole emperor at Charlemagne's death in 814. He furthered Church reform and sponsored Slavic missions. The latter part of his reign was overshadowed by struggles among his sons. With papal support, Lothair, the eldest, briefly (833–34) dethroned Louis. *See also* Holy Roman Empire.

Louis IX, St., 1214–70, king of France from 1226 to 1270. As king, Louis showed integrity and justice in his royal administration, dealing firmly with unruly vassals and reforming France's judicial system. His success on crusade in 1249 was short-lived, though he turned to crusading again in 1270, dying in Tunisia. A devout Catholic, Louis built Sainte-Chapelle in Paris as a worthy reliquary for the Crown of Thorns, which he acquired in 1239. He was canonized in 1297; feast day: August 25. *See also* Sainte-Chapelle.

Louis XIV, 1638–1715, king of France from 1643 to 1715. Known as the "Sun King," Louis devoted himself to establishing an absolute monarchy over a united and uniform France. This led him to support the Gallican Articles (1682), which asserted the rights of the French church against Rome, to revoke the Edict of Nantes (1685), which granted toleration to Protestants, and to suppress the Jansenists, a morally rigorist group at odds with the leadership of the French church. *See also* Gallicanism; Jansenism.

Louis de Granada. *See* Granada, Luis de.

Lourdes (loordz), a town in the southwest of France associated with an important Marian shrine. Between February 11, 1858, and July 16, 1858, the Blessed Virgin Mary is said to have appeared to Bernadette Soubirous eighteen times at the grotto of Massabielle. Although by March twenty thousand pilgrims had gathered to witness the apparition, Mary was visible only to Bernadette.

On February 24 Bernadette was instructed to bathe and drink from a spring that began to flow on the following day. Since then, the bath at Lourdes has been associated with miraculous healings. On March 24 Bernadette was instructed to have a chapel built in honor of the Blessed Virgin, and on the following day Mary identified herself as the Immaculate Conception, confirming for many Pius IX's

The physically disabled are wheeled to the grotto at Lourdes, France, in the hope of receiving a cure from its sacred waters or at least some measure of spiritual strength and comfort from the Blessed Virgin Mary, who appeared there to Bernadette Soubirous in 1858.

declaration of the dogma of the Immaculate Conception that had taken place on December 8, 1854.

After extensive review, the bishop of Tarbes proclaimed the legitimacy of the apparitions and authorized the cult of Our Lady of Lourdes in 1862. Bernadette entered the Sisters of Charity and Christian Instruction at Nevers in 1865 and died in 1879. She was beatified in 1925 and canonized in 1933.

Lourdes continues to serve as one of the most important pilgrimage sites in the world, attracting over two million visitors each year. Of the reported five thousand cures, fifty-eight have been declared miraculous by Church officials. Although clearly an important shrine for many, and the subject of papal encyclicals by Pius XI, Pius XII, and John XXIII, the events surrounding Lourdes remain private revelations. Catholics are not required to give assent to the apparitions themselves or to the healings associated with Lourdes. *See also* apparitions of the Blessed Virgin Mary; Bernadette of Lourdes, St. MICHAEL O'KEEFFE

Louvain, University of, the oldest continuously operating Catholic university in the world. Located in Louvain, Belgium, it was founded by Pope Martin V in 1425 through the efforts of John IV, duke of Brabant. Adrian of Utrecht (1459–1523) studied at the university, became a professor of theology and also rector of the university, and then was eventually elected Pope Hadrian VI in 1522. Erasmus of Rotterdam also studied there for a time (1517–21), refusing a professorship. The university subsequently flourished under Archduke Albert and Archduchess Isabelle (early seventeenth century). In 1857 the American College was established for the training of priests for North America, and in 1893 Désiré Mercier founded the Institut Supérieur de Philosophie at the university. The university's extensive library, dating to the eighteenth century, was tragically destroyed by the German military in World War I and again in World War II. It has been in part restored and is again internationally renowned. In 1968 the university separated into two autonomous units: the Flemish-speaking Katholieke Universiteit te Leuven (the largest university in Belgium) remained in Louvain (Leuven), and the French-speaking Université Catholique de Louvain was established at Ottignies (Louvain-la-Neuve).

love, in its most general sense, the experience and expression of the strong desire for those persons or things in which one takes a particular joy or delight. The roots of the specifically Christian concept of love are to be found in the interplay between the traditions of Greek philosophical speculation on human nature and the paradigmatic theological meditations on the drama of creation and redemption recorded in both Hebrew and Christian Scriptures. In its most characteristic OT usage, love (Heb., '*ahabah*) signifies a quality or state of personal attachment marked by unwavering fidelity, such as that between a husband and wife, or, importantly, the "steadfast love" both expressed by God and required of Israel under the terms of their covenant relationship (Deut 6:5; cf. Isa 54:5). The concept is generally translated in the Septuagint by the Greek *agapē*, which more accurately conveys the notion of preferential love than either of the more common Greek words for love, *eros* (connoting sexual love), and *philia* (friendly affection). Subsequently adopted by the NT, *agapē* is used there, fundamentally, to describe the boundless love of God (John 3:16), who is proclaimed as love itself (1 John 4:16), the source and model for the love enjoined by Jesus upon his disciples (Matt 5:48). *Agapē* is the love that is to bind and distinguish the Christian community (1 Cor 12–13) and against which individual behavior will ultimately be judged (Matt 25:31–46). Love as the human longing for God, and as the disinterested seeking of the neighbor's good, were incorporated by later tradition, influenced by Neoplatonic philosophy, under the concept of *caritas* (Lat., "charity"). *See also* agape; charity. PAUL J. WOJDA

Low Church, originally those in the Church of England who accepted the 1688 settlement of William of Orange. They favored the inclusion of Puritans and dissenters within the Church, but not the inclusion of Catholics (recusants). In the nineteenth century, the term came to designate the more "evangelical" or Protestant wing of the Church of England. Today it is used more broadly to refer to those who prefer informality and immediacy in liturgical celebrations. *See also* Anglicanism; Reformation, the.

Low Mass (Lat., *Missa lecta*), the simplest of three forms of the Tridentine Mass, the Latin Mass rite in use before the Second Vatican Council (1962–65). Unlike both the High and Solemn High Mass, the Low Mass was celebrated by a single priest, *sotto voce* (It., "in a low voice"), assisted by a single server. During the middle part of the twentieth century, permission was given for the singing of suitable hymns by the assembly during the celebration of a Low Mass. Otherwise, the people's silent prayers could have been accompanied by quiet organ music. The Low Mass could be said in the presence of a congregation or semiprivately, with the presence of a single server. With the liturgical reforms of Vatican II, there is no longer a distinction among Low Mass, High Mass, and Solemn High Mass. The term Low Mass is no longer used. *See also* High Mass; Mass; Solemn High Mass.

Low Sunday, the Sunday after Easter. It is called "low" in contrast to the "high" feast of Easter the preceding Sunday. Also called *Dominica in albis depositis* (Lat., "Sunday [when] the white clothes are put aside"), because it was on this Sunday that newly baptized Christians were to put away their white baptismal albs (tunics) for more ordinary attire. Since the Second Vatican Council (1962–65) this Sunday is called the Second Sunday of Easter.

Loyola, St. Ignatius of. *See* Ignatius of Loyola, St.

Lubac, Henri de (loo'bahk), 1896–1991, French Jesuit theologian and cardinal. Educated in the renewed Thomism of Maurice Blondel, Pierre Rousselot, and Joseph Maréchal, de Lubac sought to revitalize and expand Catholic theology by studying patristic theology, where he found the diversity he considered essential to Catholicism. He cofounded *Sources chrétiennes,* an important series of patristic texts with translations. During the Second World War he combatted Nazi attempts to encourage anti-Semitism among French Catholics. One of his important theological contributions was his attack on narrow neo-Scholastic theologies of the supernatu-

ral, which, misinterpreting patristic and Scholastic thought, separated Christianity from secular concerns. Despite postwar conflicts with the Vatican, he produced important studies on atheism, Buddhism, medieval biblical exegesis, and the sacramental nature of Catholicism. He defended Teilhard de Chardin from condemnation and participated in Vatican II as *peritus* (Lat., "expert"). After 1970, he found some post-conciliar developments unsettling and became increasingly critical of them.

Among his many scholarly works translated into English are *Catholicism: A Study of the Corporate Destiny of Mankind* (1950); *The Mystery of the Supernatural* (1967); *Augustinianism and Modern Theology* (1969); and *The Sources of Revelation* (1968). Some of his most important works, however, were not translated, for example, *Corpus Mysticum* (1944) and *Exégèse Médiévale* (1959). *See also Nouvelle Théologie;* supernatural.   VINCENT MILLER

Lubachivskyj, Myroslav Ivan (mee'roh-slahv ee-vahn' loo-bah-chiv'skee), b. 1914, metropolitan of Halych, archbishop of Lviv. Ordained a priest in 1938, in 1979 he became metropolitan of Philadelphia for the Ukrainians and in 1980 was elected coadjutor with right of succession to the metropolitan of Halych, Joseph Slipyj. He was created a cardinal on May 25, 1985.

Lucernarium (loo-chen-ah'ree-uhm; Lat., "lamplighting service"), ancient term for cathedral Vespers, the sundown office at the lamplighting hour, corresponding to the ancient Greek name *lychnikon.* It comprised, with Matins, one of the two major cathedral services that opened and closed the day (the notion that Vespers begins the liturgical day and Compline closes is a later monastic development). The purpose of the service was to thank God for the day's graces and seek divine pardon for its sins. Its basic symbol was light, the evening lamp symbolizing Christ, the Light of the World, so the service opened with a light ritual. This was followed by other elements, such as the vesperal psalm 140/141 plus an offering of incense. The service concluded with litanies, a blessing, and dismissals. *See also* Vespers.

Lucerne Memorial, a document presented to Pope Leo XIII by Peter Paul Cahensly in 1891, expressing European concern for the spiritual welfare of immigrants (especially Germans) in the United States and calling for the establishment of national parishes for German-speaking Catholics. *See also* Cahensly, Peter Paul; national parish.

Lucian of Antioch, St., d. 312, priest at Antioch and martyr whose revisions of the Septuagint (Gk. OT) and NT became standard. Allegedly a disciple of Paul of Samosata, he was more likely his opponent, elaborating against him an anti-Monarchian subordinationist Christology that probably influenced Arius. He was tortured and martyred January 7, 312. Feast day: January 7 (West); October 15 (East). *See also* Arianism; Monarchianism; subordinationism.

Lucifer (Lat., *lux,* "light," *ferre,* "carry," literally "light-bearer"), alternate name for Satan, the leader of the rebellious angels (see Rev. 12:7–9). The Vulgate and King James Version translation of the Hebrew *hll* ("to flash forth light" in Isa 14:12) describe the king of Babylon's fall from power and glory. Christians applied it to Luke 10:18, where Jesus speaks about Satan falling like lightening from heaven. *See also* Satan.

Lucy, St., d. 304, virgin and martyr. Martyred during the persecution of Diocletian, she is the patron saint of persons suffering from eye disorders and is portrayed carrying a tray containing two eyes. Her name was introduced into the Canon of the Mass by Pope Gregory I (d. 604). Feast day: December 13.

Ludolph of Saxony, ca. 1300–78, Carthusian author whose *Life of Christ* was widely read and studied in the late Middle Ages and sixteenth century, influencing Ignatius of Loyola and Teresa of Ávila. First a Dominican and master in theology, Ludolph became a Carthusian in 1340.

Lugo, John de (loo'goh), 1583–1660, Spanish Jesuit theologian and cardinal. He taught at Valladolid in Spain from 1616 to 1621, then at Rome, where he achieved international recognition as a theologian; he was created a cardinal in 1643. Although influential as a moral theologian, he also wrote on the Eucharist and the act of faith, maintaining that saving faith is possible for all, including non-Christians.

Luke, St., a companion of Paul and traditional author of the Third Gospel. Paul mentions Luke as his "fellow worker" in Phlm 24. He is called the "beloved physician" in Col 4:14 and Paul's sole companion in 2 Tim 4:11. The Pauline authorship of the latter two works has been disputed, but even if inauthentic they probably contain reliable information about Paul's entourage. Some have also identified Luke with the Lucius mentioned in Acts 13:1 and Rom 16:21, but that is unlikely.

The tradition of the early Church adds biographical details and attributes to Luke both the Third Gospel and Acts. A prologue to the Third Gospel dating to the late second century (often labeled the anti-Marcionite prologue) notes that Luke was a Syrian physician from Antioch who wrote his Gospel in Achaea (Greece) and lived as a celibate to the age of eighty-four, when he died in Boeotia. The Muratorian Canon, a list of NT books probably from the late second century, names Luke as author of the Third Gospel. Irenaeus (*Against Heresies* 3.1.1; 3.14.1) attributes both Gospel and Acts to Luke and argues that Luke is the person intended by the first-person references in Acts.

The so-called we-sections of Acts (Acts 16:10–17; 20:5–15; 21:1–18; 27:1–28:16; and 11:28 in one manuscript) have occasioned considerable debate. They are probably parts of a travel diary, written by a companion of Paul who assisted in his second and third missionary journeys to Macedonia and Greece, who accompanied Paul on his final trip to Jerusalem, and, after the apostle's arrest, accompanied him to Rome.

Luke, author of the Third Gospel and the Acts of the Apostles, in the act of writing, with his biblical symbol, the ox, overhead (Rev 4:7); illustration from the early-eighth-century *Lindisfarne Gospels*, British Museum, London.

The relationship between the author of the travel diary and the author of Acts is debated. Some doubt the natural inference that they are identical, because of the ignorance or lack of clarity displayed by Acts about several aspects of Paul's life and teaching, surprising in a close companion of the apostle. Yet the recollections of the author of Acts, probably written in the late first century, could well have been colored by time and the contemporary concerns of the Church.

The author of Acts, whether or not the diarist, was clearly the author of the Third Gospel. The opening of Acts refers to the Gospel and is dedicated to the same person. Both share stylistic similarities and thematic concerns. Their author was clearly a man of considerable literary talent, who obviously had Hellenistic rhetorical training. He was probably born to a Greek family and may have been among the "God-fearing" Gentiles (Acts 10:2, 35; 13:6, 26) who were attracted to Paul's preaching. There is no significant literary evidence of his having had medical training.

Luke, whose emblem is the ox, is the patron saint of doctors, artists, and butchers. Feast day: October 18. *See also* evangelist. HAROLD W. ATTRIDGE

Lull, Bl. Ramón, also known as Raymond Lull, ca. 1232–1316, Franciscan tertiary and lay missionary to Muslims. He learned Arabic, adopted Sufic elements, argued in the style of Muslim theologians, promoted the study of Semitic languages, and wrote numerous books (including theological treatises in his Catalan vernacular). He also wrote mystical poetry and is considered the forerunner of Teresa of Ávila (d. 1582) and John of the Cross (d. 1591). Feast day: September 5. *See also* Islam; mysticism.

Lumen Gentium (loo'men jen'tzee-oom). *See* Dogmatic Constitution on the Church.

lumen gloriae (Lat., "light of glory"), Scholastic term for the supernatural perfecting of the human power of knowing through which the intellect is made capable of the immediate vision of the divine essence (the Beatific Vision). The expression, which originates in the theology of Bonaventure and Thomas Aquinas (see especially *Summa Theologiae,* 1.12.5–2) has biblical antecedents in Ps 36:9, "For with you is the fountain of life; in your light we see light," and Rev 22:5, "They need no light of lamp or sun, for the Lord God will be their light, and they will reign forever." Because human beings, accord-

ing to the state of nature, are infinitely removed from the divine essence, the light of glory must be regarded as a divine gift that elevates human reason beyond its natural state to the state of glory. As such, the light of glory represents the culmination of a threefold process beginning with the light of reason (*lumen rationis*) and progressing through the light of faith (*lumen fidei*), which elevates reason and makes it capable of supernatural faith. *See also* Beatific Vision; heaven.

lunette (Fr., "little moon"), a small circular glass receptacle in which a consecrated Host may be exposed in a monstrance for the purposes of eucharistic devotions. It is also called a *lunula,* or a *luna. See also* Benediction.

lust. *See* capital sins.

Luther, Martin, 1483–1546, leader of the German Reformation, a movement that ultimately led to a break between Protestantism and Catholicism in the Western Church. He remains a source of controversy insofar as his life and work continue to generate both reform and division.

Luther in Catholic Context: Born at Eisleben, Germany, Luther was educated at Erfurt and Magdeburg in preparation for a career in law. Following a near-death experience he vowed to become a monk. He entered the Augustinian order in July 1505 and was ordained to the priesthood on April 3, 1507, by Erfurt's suffragan bishop. On the advice of

Martin Luther, the leading figure in the Protestant Reformation, began as an Augustinian monk troubled by the corruption he saw in the Church, especially in Rome itself; oil-on-wood painting by Lucas Cranach the Younger (d. 1586), Uffizi Gallery, Florence, Italy.

the vicar of the Augustinian order, Luther went to Wittenberg in 1511. He received his Doctor of Theology on October 19, 1512, and began to teach Bible at the university.

The move from Erfurt to Wittenberg was crucial in Luther's formation as a teaching theologian. His lectures on Psalms, Romans, Galatians, and Hebrews (1513–17) led to insights that became the foundation for his career as a Reformer and established many of the issues to which Catholic scholars continue to respond. Luther's arguments against indulgences and his understanding of grace and faith posed a threat to the theological underpinnings of the Church's sacramental system and to the economic and ecclesiastical links between Germany and Rome.

In July 1518, the first official Catholic response to Luther's teaching was made by the Dominican Sylvester Prierias, commissioned by Pope Leo X to refute Luther. Prierias summarized the issue between Luther and Rome: "Whoever does not rest on the doctrine of the Roman Church and of the Roman Pontiff as the infallible rule of faith from which even Sacred Scripture draws its strength and authority is a heretic." The indulgence dispute thus led to the more basic problem of authority which has continued to characterize Lutheran and Catholic division.

In a series of ecclesiastical and political moves between 1518 and 1521 Luther was ordered to explain and finally to renounce his teaching. Three critical treatises written in 1520 crystallized his theological positions. The *Address to the Christian Nobility* invited civil rulers to undertake reforms in the Church as "emergency bishops." *The Babylonian Captivity* attacked sacramental teaching, reducing the number of sacraments and denying the doctrine of the Sacrifice of the Mass. *The Freedom of the Christian Man* challenged ecclesiastical authority.

A papal bull in 1521 excommunicated Luther. On May 26, 1521, he was condemned as an outlaw by the German emperor. While confined for safety at Wartburg castle, he translated the NT into German. It was a decisive contribution to the evangelical movement. The availability of the Bible in the vernacular rooted Protestant theology in Scripture. Catholic response to Luther did not address the relationship between biblical interpretation and doctrinal tradition until the twentieth century.

Political developments allowed Luther to return to public life and teaching. He married the former nun Katherine von Bora in 1525, symbolizing his repudiation of monasticism and the obligation of celibacy for clergy. Luther continued to function as pastor, preacher, teacher, and leader of the Reformation until his death.

Luther as Source of Division and Reform: Luther was clearer than many of his followers about his desire to reform, not split, the Church. He hoped for a general council to resolve issues, but by the time the Council of Trent began in 1545, the opportunity for constructive change had passed. The negative response at Trent precluded any sympathetic Catholic assessment of Luther or the reform movement.

Catholic scholarship thus moved slowly from an early, uncritical condemnation of Luther to renewed interest in his life and work and recently to appreciation of his contributions in theology. Research in the twentieth century can be summarized in three phases. The first began with Henrich Denifle's 1904 work condemning Luther as a person and accusing him of being a pseudoreformer who made no contributions to theology. A few years later Hartmann Grisar reinforced this approach by portraying Luther as mentally ill. English-speaking Catholic scholars were strongly influenced by Denifle and Grisar.

Joseph Lortz's history of the Reformation, which appeared in 1939–40, and a study of Catholic interpretation of Luther by Adolf Herte in 1943 signaled a decisive shift to a second phase in Luther research. These works took Luther's life and work seriously in the context of Church history and biography. Their efforts opened the door for Catholics to see Luther as a religious figure and to hold the late medieval Church accountable for its role in the schism. At the same time appreciation for Luther's theology emerged, especially in relationship to late Scholastic theology. The underlying assumption in this phase was that Luther could be affirmed only to the extent that he was Catholic.

The third phase, ecumenical reassessment, is characterized by the systematic study of Luther without apologetic intentions, the desire to discern points of agreement or consensus, and the willingness to learn from Luther as a theologian. Earlier revisionist research excused the divisive consequences of his life and work but did not admit to any essential contribution by Luther to Catholic tradition. Catholic theology today has moved to consideration of Luther as a resource for the faith and life of the whole Church. His teaching is explored in the context of a new understanding of the sixteenth century. Reevaluation of the Council of Trent in light of the Second Vatican Council has also fueled renewed interest in Luther as a Reformer.

The clearest example of changing perspectives is the treatment of Luther and Lutheran theology in official international and U.S. Roman Catholic–Lutheran dialogues. Key areas of historical divergence such as Eucharist and ministry, teaching authority and papal infallibility, Mary and the saints, as well as the role of justification in salvation, have been reopened. As long as such reassessment is in progress, the prospect for further convergence remains. *See also* Lutheranism; Protestantism; Reformation, the.

Bibliography

Kittelson, James. *Luther The Reformer.* Minneapolis, MN: Augsburg, 1986.

Obermann, Heiko A. *Luther: Man Between God and the Devil.* New Haven, CT: Yale University Press, 1989.

Todd, John M. *Luther: A Life.* New York: Crossroad, 1982.

RALPH F. SMITH

Lutheran–Catholic dialogue,

theological conversations between official representatives of the Lutheran churches and the Catholic Church. Dialogue began in 1965 based on contacts made at the Second Vatican Council. International-level dialogue has addressed mutually agreed upon topics: "The Gospel and the Church" (1972); "The Eucharist" (1978); "Ways to Community" (1980); "All Under One Christ: Statement on the Augsburg Confession" (1980); and "The Ministry in the Church" (1981).

Dialogues in the United States between theologians appointed by the Bishops' Committee for Ecumenical Affairs and the U.S.A. National Committee of the Lutheran World Federation also began in 1965. Ground-breaking papers and agreed statements have been issued on: "Status of the Nicene Creed as Dogma of the Church" (1965); "One Baptism for the Remission of Sins" (1966); "Eucharist as Sacrifice" (1967); "Eucharist and Ministry" (1970); "Papal Primacy and the Universal Church" (1974); "Teaching Authority and Infallibility in the Church" (1978); "Justification by Faith" (1985); and "The One Mediator, the Saints, and Mary" (1992). Dialogue on Scripture and tradition began in 1992.

While dialogue team members at both the international and U.S. levels have been able to arrive at agreed statements and recommendations, the results of the dialogues have not been received by Vatican and Lutheran church authorities in such a way that concrete ecclesiastical actions have thus far resulted. *See also* Lutheranism.

Lutheranism,

evangelical reform movement inspired by Martin Luther (1483–1546). Its central theological principle is justification by grace through faith. It also affirms: grace alone (Lat., *sola gratia*), faith alone (*sola fide*), and Scripture alone (*sola Scriptura*). Lutheranism is defined by formal acceptance of the confessional teachings in the *Book of Concord* (1580), especially the Augsburg Confession (1530). The term distinguishes it from other forms of Protestantism (e.g., Reformed, Calvinist, Anabaptist). Under the authority of lay rulers, which replaced papal authority in sixteenth-century Germany and Scandinavia, Lutheranism undertook ecclesiastical reform. Today Lutheranism refers to a body of doctrine, a worldwide communion of churches, and forms of piety.

Liturgy: In liturgy Lutheranism retains many traditional Catholic forms (e.g., order of the liturgy, liturgical year, observance of saints' days, vestments, use of the crucifix). Sacraments are defined as means of grace instituted by Christ, with Christ's promise of grace, employing a physical element. Under this definition two sacraments were affirmed: Baptism and Eucharist. The practice of infant baptism was continued. In the Eucharist, medieval understandings of sacrifice were rejected and replaced by emphasis on fruitful reception of grace in the Communion of the faithful, under both kinds, i.e., consecrated bread and wine. Against Reformers such as Ulrich Zwingli, Lutheranism affirmed the Real Presence of Christ in the sacrament, "in, with, and under" the forms of bread and wine, by the power of God's word. Absolution was also affirmed as sacramental in both private and public forms. Ordination was affirmed as sacramental in a limited sense. The celebration of marriage and confirmation continued and anointing of the sick has been recovered in some places as important rites of the Church, not as sacraments.

Lutheranism is characterized by a strong emphasis on preaching as the proclamation of God's word through both law and Gospel. It is also known for its vigorous musical tradition in hymns and liturgical music (e.g., J. S. Bach). Commitment to education, primary, secondary, college, and seminary, is characteristic. The ongoing use of Luther's *Small Catechism* and *Large Catechism* characterizes its catechetical instruction. Lutheranism has been a major contributor to modern scientific biblical scholarship.

Piety: The piety of Lutheranism is focused on the atoning work of Christ for sinners and the faith of believers. Lutheran orthodoxy (seventeenth century) concentrated on correct doctrine. Lutheran Pietism (eighteenth and nineteenth centuries) rebelled against this intellectual emphasis and stressed personal conversion and holiness of life (sanctification) among believers. Pietism fostered active mission movements that spread Lutheranism to Africa, India, and Asia in the nineteenth century. Pietism also exerted strong influence among European Lutherans who immigrated to North and South America and Australia in the eighteenth and nineteenth centuries.

With some 60 million adherents in 1994, Lutheranism constitutes the largest form of Protestant Christianity. It is organized in state churches in Germany and Scandinavia. Elsewhere it follows various patterns. The Lutheran World Federation facilitates cooperation among 105 of its independent churches. Once separatist in its outlook, Lutheranism in the twentieth century has become an active ecumenical partner with the Catholic and other Christian churches. *See also* Luther, Martin; Protestantism; Reformation, the. PAUL R. NELSON

Luxeuil, important monastery founded ca. 590 by the Irish abbot and missionary Columbanus in the Vosges; it became the motherhouse for a series of reformed monasteries in Gaul. *See also* Columbanus, St.

Lwanga, St. Charles (lah-wahng'ah), martyr. One of twenty-two Christians (both Catholic and Protestant) martyred in Uganda in 1885–86. Canonized as a group in 1964, they are honored as the "proto-martyrs" of black Africa in the Roman calendar. Feast day: June 3.

Lydwina, Bl., 1380–1433, patron saint of skaters. Born in Holland, she was injured as a young girl while ice-skating and remained an invalid for life, enduring great suffering and eventual blindness. She is said to have experienced visions and to have required little food or sleep. Feast day: April 14.

lying, communicating something other than what one believes (speech contrary to the mind's thought). The essence of lying is the misrepresentation to an audience of one's judgment, not of the state of affairs. Someone who states a truth, believing it false, is lying.

Until recently most theologians taught that lying is an intrinsically evil act. Today, many distinguish between false speaking and lying, such that lying would include only those intentional falsehoods that tend to disrupt the trust necessary for good human relations. *See also* mental reservation.

Lyons, Rite of, the liturgical rite of the archdiocese of Lyons in France. This rite dates from Charlemagne's imposition of the Roman rite upon his empire in the 800s. Distinctive features include a rite for testing the wine between the reading of the Letter (Epistle) and the Gospel, ash-colored vestments in Lent, and special blessings on farmland each Sunday from May 3 to September 14.

Lyons I, Council of (1245), thirteenth ecumenical council of the Church. Convoked by Innocent IV after fleeing Rome before the advancing armies of the emperor Frederick II, the assembly sat for three sessions from June through July and addressed the major issues of the day: clerical abuses, the liberation of Jerusalem, the Latin Empire of Constantinople, and the Mongol threat to eastern Europe. The most urgent business was Frederick II's persecution of the papacy and seizure of papal lands. After issuing a warning and receiving no response from the emperor, Innocent excommunicated and deposed Frederick, the first deposition of an emperor in nearly two centuries. *See also* Constantinople; Jerusalem; Papal States.

Lyons II, Council of (1274), fourteenth ecumenical council of the Church, summoned by Gregory X to accomplish reunion with the Greek Church, the liberation of the Holy Land, and reform of the Church. Over five hundred bishops, sixty abbots, and a thousand other clerics and lay representatives attended, including Albertus Magnus and Bonaventure. The political backdrop of the council was the end of the Hohenstaufen dynasty, so troublesome to the papacy, and the ascendancy of Charles of Anjou as king of Sicily, who had ambitions to restore the Latin Empire of Constantinople. In hopes of receiving military and political support, the Greek emperor and delegates gave their full assent to the Roman faith, including the *Filioque*. Unaccepted in Byzantium, the reunion lasted only as long as the emperor lived, and crusading efforts similarly proved ineffectual. *See also* Constantinople; Eastern Schism; *Filioque;* Holy Land.

Mabillon, Jean (mah-bee-yohn´), 1632–1707, Maurist scholar. Mabillon's most famous work is his *De Re Diplomatica* (1681), which has served as a basis for the scientific method of documentary criticism. Other works include critical editions of the works of St. Bernard, lives of Benedictine saints, and a study of Gallican liturgy. *See also* Maurists.

Macarius of Egypt, St., ca. 300–ca. 390, saintly monk who knew Anthony of Egypt, a founder of monasticism. He is to be distinguished from Macarius of Alexandria (fourth century) and Macarius, bishop of Jerusalem (d. ca. 334). He went into the desert at about age forty and lived near Anthony. He was considered a miracle worker by many.

Macedonianism, one name for the doctrine that denies the full divinity of the Holy Spirit on the grounds that Scripture does not provide sufficient basis for believing that the Holy Spirit is a divine Person. The title refers to Macedonius, bishop of Constantinople in the mid-fourth century. He was mistakenly credited with leadership in a sect that viewed the Holy Spirit as a creature or as an intermediate being between God and creatures. The teaching was condemned at the Council of Constantinople (381). *See also* Holy Spirit.

Machiavelli, Niccolò, 1469–1527, Florentine humanist and writer. Machiavelli served the restored Florentine republic from 1498 to 1512, when the Medici family returned to power. To regain their favor, he dedicated *The Prince* to the unofficial Florentine ruler, Lorenzo de Medici. Often considered on the basis of *The Prince* a champion of amoral, unscrupulous government, his *Discourses on the Ten Books of Livy* reveals a man of strong republican convictions who distinguished between the goals of private and public good and the means to achieve them. Although conventional in his personal beliefs, Machiavelli blamed Catholicism and the pope for Italy's disunity and chaos.

MacRae, George Winsor, 1928–85, Jesuit, American NT scholar. Educated at Boston College, Louvain, Johns Hopkins, and Cambridge, his scholarship focused on the Fourth Gospel and on editing Coptic Gnostic texts from Nag Hammadi (Egypt). Committed to ecumenism, he was the first tenured Stillman Professor of Roman Catholic Studies at Harvard Divinity School, where he served as acting dean at his death.

Macrina, St., ca. 327–79, older sister of Basil the Great (Basil of Caesarea) and Gregory of Nyssa. Gregory's *Vita* attests to the holiness of Macrina's "philosophical life" and her influence on the family. After persuading Basil, attracted to secular pursuits by his education in Athens, to serve the Church instead, she convinced their widowed mother to form, with the family's servants, an ascetic community in which Macrina assumed leadership. While no writing of hers is known, she appears plausibly as the theological teacher in Gregory's *On the Soul and the Resurrection.* Feast day: July 19.

Madonna, the (It., "My Lady"), a designation for the Blessed Virgin Mary. It is commonly used with reference to statues and pictures of her, particularly in the West, where she is portrayed holding the Christ Child. *See also* Mary, Blessed Virgin.

Magdalene, St. Mary. *See* Mary Magdalene, St.

Magdeburg Centuriators, the author of the first Protestant history of the Church. Under the direction of Matthias Flacius, Protestant historians published the *Historia Ecclesiae Christi* (Lat., "History of the Church of Christ"; 1559–74) to prove the errors of Catholicism. Although it was tendentious and filled with errors, its critical use of original documents (with which it took many liberties, however) was a milestone in Church history. Caesar Baronius's *Annales Ecclesiastici* (1588–1607) was the Catholic response. *See also* Baronius, Caesar.

Magi (Gk., *magos,* "wise person," "interpreter of dreams"; pl. *magi*), the astrologers who, led by a star, visited Jesus in Bethlehem (Matt 2:1–12). They came from the East, most probably Arabia, Mesopotamia, or Babylon, and symbolize the manifestation of Christ to the Gentiles. People assumed that they were three in number because they brought three gifts—gold, frankincense, and myrrh. Tertullian is the first to call them kings (see Isa 60:3–6; Ps 72:10) and in later tradition they are given names Melchior, Balthasar, and Gaspar. Their purported relics are in the Cologne Cathedral.

magic, the belief that certain forms of ritualized human behavior can produce effects that are beyond the power of natural causes. This occurs usually by "forcing" supernatural powers to behave in accordance with the will of the person who possesses the required esoteric knowledge. Magic is usually

The Magi, traditionally known as the Wise Men from the East, pay homage to the newborn Savior with gifts of gold, frankincense, and myrrh; fifteenth-century Gothic painting by Stefan Lochner, Altar of the Patron Saints, Cologne Cathedral, Germany.

perceived as good ("white" magic) or evil ("black" magic) according to the helpful or harmful ends pursued by the practitioner, but in the Catholic moral tradition reliance upon magic is considered a sin against the First Commandment. This is to be distinguished, of course, from the use of "magic" as a form of entertainment in which there is no recourse to supernatural forces.

magisterium (mahg-i-stair'ee-oom), teaching office and authority of the Catholic Church; also the hierarchy as holding this office. In classical Latin, *magisterium* meant the role and authority of one who was a "master" in various senses of the term. In medieval usage, it generally referred to the role of the teacher; thus, Thomas Aquinas uses the term *magisterium* to refer to the teaching role both of the university professor and of the bishop. However, in modern Catholic usage the term has become identified with the office and authority to teach that is proper to the pope and bishops. Even more recently, the hierarchy itself is spoken of as "the magisterium." When their teaching is described as "authentic," this term does not mean "genuine," but "authoritative."

Theologians have a teaching authority based on their mastery of their subject, but only those ordained to the episcopate share in the authority Christ gave to the apostles to teach in his name. In the NT one already finds the principle of succession in a teaching office entrusted to those with pastoral care for the faith of the Christian community (see Acts 20:17–35; 2 Tim 2:2).

Since it belongs to the nature of the Christian Church to be a people united in the profession of the apostolic faith, it has to have a common creed and a common understanding of its faith. When conflicts arise as to the terms of its creed or when new questions are raised that demand authoritative answers, it is part of God's design that in every age there should be successors of the apostles with pastoral authority to act as judges in matters of faith (Dogmatic Constitution on the Church, n. 25). As Vatican II insists, this does not mean that bishops are above the word of God, but that they listen to it, guard it, and explain it faithfully, by divine commission and with the help of the Holy Spirit (Dogmatic Constitution on Divine Revelation, n. 10).

Bearers of Magisterium: Each bishop with pastoral responsibility has authority regarding the teaching of Christian doctrine in his diocese. The bishops of a nation or region can exercise their teaching function collegially in episcopal conferences or in regional synods. The whole episcopal college is the bearer of supreme magisterium, which it exercises both when dispersed throughout the world and when gathered in an ecumenical council. The pope, as head of the episcopal college, can exercise the supreme teaching authority that resides in this college.

The Object of Magisterium: Both Vatican councils have described the object of magisterium as "matters of faith and morals." This means that pastoral teaching authority is limited to what pertains to Christian faith or to the practice of the Christian way of life. There are two ways in which something can belong to this object: either as contained in revelation (whether explicitly or implicitly) or as so connected with revelation as to be necessary for the defense or explanation of some revealed truth. The latter kind of matter is described as the "secondary object" of magisterium.

The Exercise of Magisterium: The major distinction here is between the definitive and the non-definitive exercise of pastoral teaching authority. Only the supreme teaching authority (the episcopal college or the pope as its head) can settle a question of faith definitively, that is, in such a way that the judgment thus rendered can never be rescinded. Ecumenical councils or popes are said to "define" a

The teaching authority, or magisterium, of the Church is but a limited, error-prone participation in the teaching authority of Jesus Christ himself; seventeenth-century Rembrandt etching of Christ in the role of a teacher.

doctrine when the manner in which they express their judgment leaves no doubt about their intention to oblige the universal Church to an irrevocable assent to the doctrine thus taught. The consensus of the whole episcopal college, in its ordinary teaching throughout the world, proposing a point of doctrine as definitively to be held, is also a definitive exercise of magisterium.

It is only the definitive exercise of magisterium that is understood to be infallible, that is, to enjoy a special assistance of the Holy Spirit that prevents such teaching from being erroneous and thus leading the whole Church into error in its faith. Propositions taught in a definitive way as expressing revealed truth are termed "dogmas of faith." It is such a dogma, defined by the First Vatican Council, that when the pope speaking *ex cathedra* (Lat., "from the chair") defines a dogma of faith for the universal Church, he enjoys in that act the same infallibility that ecumenical councils have in dogmatic definitions. It is a matter of ordinary Catholic teaching, but not a dogma of faith, that the whole episcopal college, and the pope as its head, speak infallibly

also when they express definitive judgments about matters that are necessarily connected with revelation. However, at the present time there is no clear consensus among Catholic theologians as to what is included in the secondary object of infallible teaching. This is the case especially with regard to matters of the natural moral law.

All the subjects of magisterium, including ecumenical councils and popes, can also exercise their teaching function in a nondefinitive way. The most obvious examples of such teaching are found in papal encyclicals. While these letters often contain much that has already been definitively taught, they have not been used by the popes to define new dogmas, but rather to teach in a nondefinitive way. The same is true of the documents of Vatican II, since this council chose not to define any new dogma.

While this nondefinitive "ordinary" teaching does not enjoy infallibility, it is authoritative and calls for a response described in official documents as religious *obsequium,* a Latin term that has been translated both as "submission" and as "respect." This is best understood as an attitude of willingness to accept the teaching and to do one's best to convince oneself of its truth. It is called "religious," since it is based on belief in the divine origin of the teaching authority. However, despite genuine willingness and sustained effort, a person might be unable to give sincere mental assent to some point of nondefinitive teaching. In such a case, an individual's nonassent does not signify a failure to give religious *obsequium* to the authority of the magisterium. *See also* doctrine; dogma; hierarchy; infallibility; magisterium and morality.

Bibliography

Örsy, Ladislas. *The Church: Learning and Teaching.* Wilmington, DE: Michael Glazier, 1987.

Sullivan, Francis A. *Magisterium: Teaching Authority in the Catholic Church.* Mahwah, NJ: Paulist Press; Dublin: Gill and Macmillan, 1983.   FRANCIS A. SULLIVAN

magisterium and morality, a reference to the official teaching function of the Church in the area of morality. Before the relationship can be clarified, the very notion of magisterium must be put in historical perspective. Until the nineteenth century the term did not mean what is now called *the* magisterium.

History: In the early Church, there were *didaskaloi* (Gk., "teachers") whose activity was more catechetical than speculative. In the second and third centuries the schools began to appear and with them a certain element of theological speculation. But from this period that which characterized the bishop was the *cathedra* (Lat.), or chair. This episcopal authority, symbolized by the bishop's chair, was the guarantor of the transmission of the apostolic message. This was not conceived as a juridical authority. The tradition or transmitted truth was the true authority.

The Middle Ages witnessed the full development of the schools. At this time a distinction was formulated between teaching that is pastoral and teaching that is scientific. Thus, Thomas Aquinas (d. 1274) distinguished two magisteria, the pastoral and the scientific. The latter rested on scientific competence, whereas the former was tied to public office (prelature). Theological faculties judged doctrinal theses. In the nineteenth century a growing unilateralism began to occur with the teaching function centered more and more on the Bishop of Rome, the pope. This development reached its zenith in the encyclical *Humani Generis* (1950), when Pius XII stated that once the Supreme Pontiff expressed a judgment about a matter hitherto controverted, "that matter ... can no longer be held to be a question of free debate among theologians." Unquestioning obedience became the norm. While the Church has always taught morality, the teaching function has been in different hands at different stages of history. At the present time the term "magisterium" refers, for all practical purposes, to the hierarchical magisterium alone, especially that of the pope.

Popes, at least from the time of Gregory XVI (1831–46) and Pius IX (1846–78), have been conscious of their teaching authority in the area of morals. Pius X states in *Singulari Quadam* (1912) that all human actions "in so far as they are morally good or evil, that is, agree with, or are in opposition to, divine and natural law, are subject to the judgment and authority of the Church." It is clear that "authority of the Church" refers to the pope. Similar statements are found in the pronouncements of Pius XI, Pius XII, John XXIII, and Paul VI. For instance, Pius XII states in *Magnificate Dominum* (1954) that the power of the Church extends to "the whole matter of the natural law, its foundation, its interpretation, its application."

Current Teaching: Vatican II (1962–65), with its keen historical sensitivity and the ecclesiological shifts in emphasis it introduced, was not so sweeping. It stated in the second part of the Pastoral Constitution on the Church in the Modern World (where urgent moral problems are treated) that interpreters had to be aware of "the changeable circumstances which the subject matter, by its very nature, involves" (Abbott-Gallagher, *Documents of Vatican II*, footnote 2). The council further noted that "it happens rather frequently, and legitimately so, that with equal sincerity some of the faithful will disagree with others on a given matter" (n. 43). This legitimate pluralism is to be expected if even official teachers do not have all the answers, a point explicitly made by the council when it stated: "The Church, as guardian of the deposit of God's word, draws religious and moral principles from it, but it does not always have ready answers to particular questions" (n. 33).

This appropriate modesty was clearly stated in the pastoral letter of the U.S. bishops "The Challenge of Peace" (1983). The bishops note that when they deal with applications of more general moral principles "prudential judgments are involved based on specific circumstances which can change or which can be interpreted differently by people of good will." They conclude that their judgments of application are "not binding in conscience."

It can be said, therefore, that in the contemporary Church there is a much greater awareness of the need to take account of all the experience and wisdom in the Church before formulating official teaching. Failure to do so means that the presumption of truth that accompanies official teaching is weakened, and the teaching office rendered less credible.

Moral Teachings: The Church's teaching function roots in the Catholic conviction that the apostles and their successors were commissioned to transmit the deposit of faith. In the Council of Trent (1545–63) the formulation "in matters of faith and morals" was used to describe the Church's competence. The term "morals" is a tricky phrase and clearly did not mean what it is taken to mean now. Rather it most likely referred to the practices and customs of the apostolic Church, some of which were doctrinal in character, others disciplinary and ceremonial. A similar phrase reappears in a document of Vatican II. It reads as follows. "Although the individual bishops do not enjoy the prerogative of infallibility, they can nevertheless proclaim Christ's doctrine infallibly. This is so, even when they are dispersed around the world, provided that while maintaining the bond of unity among themselves and with Peter's successor, and while teaching authentically on a matter of faith or morals, they concur in a single viewpoint as the one which must be held conclusively" (Dogmatic Constitution on the Church, n. 25).

This text raises many problems of interest. One is whether the Church can propose moral positions infallibly. The question may be raised as follows. On the one hand, the magisterium claims competence with regard to questions of the natural moral law. On the other, Vatican II states that the charism of infallibility is coextensive with the "deposit of divine revelation" (n. 25). This would seem to exclude from infallibility those moral positions that are not revealed. If that is the case, the magisterium can be competent in concrete moral questions without being infallibly competent.

This question remains a disputed one, but it is hardly very practical since, in the view of most theologians, the magisterium has never taught infallibly on the level of concrete morals, nor would such authority be required for the Church to fulfill its mandate to provide moral guidance. *See also* infallibility; magisterium.

Bibliography

Curran, Charles, and Richard A. McCormick. *Readings in Moral Theology No. 3: The Magisterium and Morality.* New York: Paulist Press, 1983.   RICHARD A. MCCORMICK

magnanimity (Lat, *magnanimitas,* "greatness of soul"), the virtue that disposes one to accomplish great and even heroic deeds for honorable and just causes, though never for personal honor or reward. In the Catholic perspective magnanimity includes the recognition that one's achievements have been made possible by the grace of God.

Magnificat (mahg-ni'fee-caht; Lat., "it praises"), the hymn of Mary in Luke 1:46–55. The Latin title derives from the opening word of the hymn in the Vulgate. Delivered by Mary at her visit to Elizabeth, the Magnificat lauds God's salvific power manifested in the overthrow of the mighty, the vindication of the lowly, and the divine mercy perpetually shown to Israel.

The hymn imitates the content and style of the Song of Hannah in 1 Sam 2:1–10, another exultant prayer by a woman to whom God had shown special favor. Some manuscripts and patristic sources attribute the hymn to Elizabeth, whose situation as an aged and barren woman miraculously allowed to conceive closely paralleled that of Hannah. Yet the preponderance of the manuscript evidence favors the traditional attribution to Mary. The phrase in Luke 1:48b, "From now on all generations will call me blessed," is particularly appropriate for her.

The hymn has long played a major role in the Liturgy of the Hours. In the East it is sung in the morning as part of the office of Lauds. In Western liturgies it is used at Vespers, or Evening Prayer.

Maimonides, Moses (mi̱-mahn'i-deez), 1135–1204, Jewish philosopher and theologian. Having learned the Peripateticism (Aristotelianism) of his native Spain, Maimonides settled near Cairo and became a physician and head of the Jewish community there. His *Guide of the Perplexed,* translated into Latin ca. 1240, explained to young scholars the interpretation of unphilosophical biblical terms. Showing that philosophical arguments contrary to Scripture were inconclusive and that biblical teachings could not be disproved, he underscored the dangers of using invalid arguments merely because their conclusions happen to agree with Scripture. Such Christians as Albertus Magnus (d. 1280), Thomas Aquinas (d. 1274), and John Duns Scotus (d. 1308) imitated his procedures. *See also* Albertus Magnus, St.; Aquinas, St. Thomas; Aristotle; Scotus, John Duns.

Maistre, Joseph de. *See* de Maistre, Joseph.

major basilica. *See* basilica, major.

major moderator in a religious institute, superior of an entire religious institute or of a significant part of an institute. These superiors are called by different names depending upon the particular law of a religious community, e.g., superior general, abbot, mother general, father general, master general, president, provincial superior, regional superior.

major orders, the orders of subdiaconate, diaconate, and priesthood. The term was used in the Latin rite from medieval to recent times to distinguish these orders from minor orders. In response to Reform critiques, the Council of Trent (1545–63) defended the role of major orders, though subdiaconate and diaconate then functioned only as stages toward priesthood. Since Vatican Council II (1962–65) the diaconate has been restored as a permanent order in the Church, with a transitional diaconate maintained for candidates for priesthood. The order of subdeacon has been eliminated, its basic functions being given to the lay ministries of reader and acolyte. *See also* Holy Orders; minor orders.

major superior. *See* major moderator in a religious institute.

Malabar Catholics. *See* Syro-Malabar Catholic Church.

Malachy, Prophecies of, a sixteenth-century forgery attributed to St. Malachy (d. twelfth century) concerning the popes beginning with Celestine II (1143–44). Each pope is given a short Latin epithet. The epithets of popes up to 1590 are formulated on the basis of a family, baptismal, or place name, but those of popes after 1590 become distinctly vague. The final prophecy concerns "Petrus Romanus," saying that in the final persecution of the Holy Roman Church there will reign Peter the Roman, who will feed his flock among many tribulations, after which the seven-hilled city will be destroyed and the dreadful Judge will judge the people. The prophecies have generated many commentaries and defenses of their authenticity, continuing into this century. *See also* Malachy of Armagh, St.

Malachy of Armagh, St., ca. 1094–1148, archbishop of Armagh active in reforming the Irish church according to Roman practices. Friend of Bernard of Clairvaux (who later wrote his *Life*), he introduced the Cistercians to Ireland with the foundation of Mellifont Abbey in 1142. Feast day: November 3. *See also* Cistercian order; Ireland, Catholicism in.

Malta. *See* Knights of Malta.

Maltese cross. *See* cross, forms of the.

Mandaeans, a Gnostic sect. In the second century it was present east of the Jordan River, and today is found in southern Iraq and Iran. It believes that the redeemer, the "Manda da Hayyê," enlightens human beings, thereby freeing their souls from the imprisonment of their bodies and leading them into the heavenly realm. Though this sect opposes Christianity, it may have Christian origins. Its writings speak with respect of the John the Baptist. Its holy book is the *Ginza Rba* ("treasure") from the seventh century. *See also* Gnosticism.

mandate to teach, a requirement for those who teach theological disciplines in institutes of higher studies. The mandate is required by canon 812 of the 1983 Code of Canon Law.

A teacher with a mandate teaches with the authorization of the Church but does not teach "in the name of the Church," which is restricted to pastoral leaders (bishops, and priests and deacons when they give a homily, etc.).

The mandate is not a grant of governing power, such as the canonical mission, nor does it delegate a teacher to act on behalf of a church official or the Church itself. Some consider the mandate to be similar to the "mandate" in Catholic action, whereby an apostolic activity by laypersons participates in the apostolate of the hierarchy. Others consider the mandate a type of certification by competent church authority that the teacher is acceptable to church officials.

The mandate applies to teachers of theological disciplines but not to teachers of other subjects, and to teaching in institutions of higher studies subject to church authorities, or concerning which there is an agreement (concordat) with the secular government.

Some episcopal conference norms (e.g., in Germany) specify the procedures for granting and withdrawing the mandate. Where no such legislation is in effect, the determination of what authority is competent to grant or remove the mandate, the procedure to be followed, and the institutions for which it is required, are resolved on a case-by-case basis. *See also* canonical mission; theologian.

JAMES H. PROVOST

Mandatum (mahn-dah'toom; Lat., *mandatum*, "commandment"), optional foot-washing rite of the Evening Mass of the Lord's Supper on Holy Thursday. The term is derived from John 13:34 ("I give you a new commandment [Lat., *mandatum novum*], love one another as I have loved you") when Jesus washed his disciples' feet on the night before he died. Not a pantomime of a past event for its own sake, the rite embodies Jesus' call to service. The presiding priest approaches the designated people, pours water over each one's feet, and dries them with a towel. An unspecified number of people representative of the assembly sit for the rite. Conflicts regarding the gender of those designated to have their feet washed strain the rite and threaten its future. *See also* Holy Thursday.

mandyas (mahn-dee'ahs; Gk., "mantle"), black monastic mantle, corresponding to the Western cappa, worn by Byzantine-rite monks. A Byzantine bishop's "choir dress" also includes a more elaborate mandyas of blue or purple cloth decorated with

Mandyas

mandyas

lateral stripes called "rivers" (Gk., *potamoi*) and, at its four corners, with rectangles of stiff ornamented cloth. The black mandyas of a Byzantine abbot (archimandrite) is distinguished from an ordinary monk's by these four ornaments. The mandyas is worn with its four corners joined at the wearer's throat and feet. *See also* cappa magna.

Mani. *See* Manichaeism.

Manichaeism, a dualistic religion, essentially Gnostic in character, founded explicitly as a world religion by Mani in Mesopotamia in the third century A.D.

History: In 240/41, at the age of 24, Mani claimed to have received his apostolate from the angel al-Taum to preach the final divine revelation of Zoroaster, Buddha, and Jesus. He took his message first to India. Returning to Persia, he was summoned to the court of Shapur I. Shapur's war on Rome in 241 spread Manichaeism to the West. But under Bahram, Shapur's successor, Zoroastrianism assumed dominance. Mani was accused of heresy, and at 60, thrown into jail; he died twenty-six days later (March 276/77).

His message, however, spread: "I have come from the land of Babel to make my cry heard throughout the whole world" (Turfan Fragment M4). It spread along the silk-trade routes far into China; at the beginning of this century, Manichaean literature was discovered in Turfan (in northwest China). In the West, Manichaeism spread through Syria and came to Egypt in the third century. From Egypt, it spread into Africa Proconsularis, where Augustine was an auditor from 373 to 383, and thence into Spain.

In 302, Diocletian issued the first Western anti-Manichaean edict; its sanctions were extreme. Despite persecution, three thousand leaves of Manichaean text, found in 1930 in Egypt's Fayyūm (a basin located south of the Delta on the west side of the Nile), prove the movement's resilience. A letter of Pope Leo I (444) tells us that Manichaeans numbered among the clergy. In the Middle Ages, types of Manichaean belief were still current among the Paulicians, Bogomils, and Cathars.

Elements: Like other Gnostic systems, Manichaeism rests on a dualistic concept of the world's structure. A radical duality between Light and Darkness, Good and Evil, existed from the beginning. An initial time of complete separation of the two kingdoms ended when Darkness attacked Light and brought about the middle time of mixture, which now reigns. A third, end time will restore the initial separation.

The Manichaean myth of this struggle involves a Primal Human, who emanated from the Father of Greatness. Sent to battle against Darkness, he is defeated. While he is unconscious, Darkness swallows his soul, the five luminous elements (i.e., light, wind, fire, water, and air). With this soul, Darkness gives birth to matter. When Primal Human awakes, he cries out for deliverance. It is to this cry that all Manichaeans must respond until the end of the age. The Living Spirit leads the Primal Human back to the Paradise of Light, but the soul, the five luminous elements, remain engulfed in matter; it is the work of the elect to free them. Light particles reside particularly in vine-growing fruits and vegetables and in semen. Humans were formed by the rulers of Darkness; procreation is of demonic origin.

Manichaean morality rests on this theoretical foundation. Believers are to abstain from contact with matter. They renounce property, work, rest, war, hunting, business, and agriculture. They must show zeal in spreading knowledge of salvation. This ethic was enabled by a two-tiered church membership. The elect lived these precepts strictly. Traveling and preaching, they observed the three symbols: of the mouth, abstention from blasphemy, meat, and wine; of the hands, abstention from work and the destruction of plants and animals; and of the lap/breast, abstention from sexual contact. While practicing extensive fasting, they partook of ritual meals: in an atmosphere of prayer and hymnody, they liberated light particles through reverential eating of vine-growing fruits, especially melons.

Auditors, in turn, lived a laxer life. They might farm, butcher animals, and even marry, but were to avoid procreation and to fast on Sundays. By the auditors' bringing the elect their food, the elect could eat in ritual purity. In return, the elect prayed for the auditors, that they would become incarnate in the soul of an elect, who, at death, would enter immediately into the Kingdom of Light.

Unlike other religious founders, Mani not only wrote at least seven works, but also translated them into the languages of those he evangelized. Of these, fragments exist or can be extracted from authors such as Augustine. *See also* Albigensians; Cathari; dualism; Gnosticism.　　　*BLAKE LEYERLE*

maniple, a short, colored, silk vestment formerly worn by priests over the left forearm. Originally

maniple

Maniple

used as a handkerchief, the maniple came to be worn solely as an ornament. Its use was officially discontinued in 1967, as part of the liturgical reforms mandated by the Second Vatican Council (1962–65).

manna, the food providentially made available to the Israelites in the wilderness (Exod 16:4 36; Num 11:4–9), generally identified with the waferlike excretions of insects that feed on the sap of the tamarisk tree. In the NT it becomes a type, or foreshadowing, of Christ as the living bread from heaven (John 6:31–65) and of the Eucharist (1 Cor 10:3). *See also* Eucharist.

Manning, Henry Edward, 1808–92, English cardinal, archbishop of Westminster, and prominent Anglican archdeacon. Talented in administration and a champion of workers, Manning was a reformer both as an Anglican and, after his conversion in 1851, as a Catholic. Influenced by the Oxford movement, variably friend and foe of John Henry Newman, he founded the Oblates of St. Charles and made major contributions to Catholic elementary education and social reform in England and Ireland. He served with royal commissions on housing and education and was a consultant of Pope Leo XIII for the encyclical *Rerum Novarum* (On the Condition of the Working Person). Defender of diocesan clergy and advocate of papal infallibility and temporal power, Manning was a leading figure at the First Vatican Council (1869–70). *Eternal Priesthood* is his best-known book. *See also* Newman, John Henry; Vatican Council I.

Mansi, Giovanni Domenico, 1692–1769, Italian theologian and Church historian who founded an academy for Church history and liturgy in Lucca, where he was archbishop from 1765. His collection of the acts of the councils up to 1440, *Sacrorum Conciliorum Nova et Amplissima Collectio* (thirty-one volumes, 1759–98), remains unmatched in its completeness.

manualists, name given to the authors of the theological manuals, or textbooks, written primarily for seminary instruction that came to constitute a unique theological genre in the nineteenth and early twentieth centuries. This genre had important antecedents in the penitential manuals and *Summae Confessorum* of the Middle Ages, which were basic handbooks for confessors. The development of this genre was furthered by the reforms of the Council of Trent (1545–63) regarding the training and education of the clergy. The late seventeenth and eighteenth centuries saw the rise of the dogmatic method and of theological texts that avoided convoluted Scholastic questions in favor of systematizing and explaining Catholic doctrine. The manuals of the nineteenth and twentieth centuries were characterized by a remarkable uniformity in organization in which speculative concerns and creative inquiries gave way to pedagogical clarity. The following structure of a topic was typical: thesis, state of the question, historical proofs, rational proofs, solution of difficulties (response to adversaries), official teachings of the Church, corollaries (Lat., *scholia*), and practical applications. A great value was placed on massive, encyclopedic systematizations of the entire Catholic doctrinal tradition. This approach was exemplified in the nine-volume manual of the Roman theologian Giovanni Perrone, *Praelectiones Theologicae* (1835–42). This theological genre received its most developed expression under the inspiration of the neo-Thomistic revival of the late nineteenth century. The manuals of this period had two goals: first, to offer a defense of the Catholic faith against the rationalism inspired by the Enlightenment, and, second, to offer a systematic, internally coherent presentation of Catholic doctrine that could be seen as an alternative to the problematic systems inspired by philosophical idealism. In dogmatic theol-

ogy the prominent manualists included D. Palmieri, C. Pesch, H. Dieckmann, J. M. Hervé, and J. Salaverri. The more significant manualists in moral theology included A. Sabetti, J. McHugh, D. Prümmer, E. Genicot, H. Davis, and M. Zalba. *See also* manuals, moral; moral theology; theology.   RICHARD R. GAILLARDETZ

manuals, moral, textbooks on moral theology distinct from those in systematic theology. They originated in the sixteenth century. Thereafter special treatises, e.g., on justice, began to appear by authors such as Domingo Báñez, Dominic de Soto, Leonhard Lessius, Luis de Molina, and John de Lugo. The most famous moral textbook of the seventeenth century was H. Busenbaum's *Medulla Theologiae Moralis*. It went through several hundred editions between 1645 and 1770 and became the basis for pastoral practice nearly everywhere. Alphonsus Liguori's moral tomes were commentaries on Busenbaum, and his work was succeeded by authors such as Gury-Ballerini, Gury-Sabetti, Gury-Ferreres, *et al.*

Such works were the predecessors of the modern manuals of moral theology used throughout the world, chiefly in seminaries. Some better-known manuals include those of the following: A. Lehmkuhl, T. Aertnys, A. Ballerini, H. Noldin, E. Genicot, A. Vermeersch, B. H. Merkelbach, D. Prümmer, F. Hurth, H. Jone.

Since Vatican II (1962–65) there has been a concerted attempt to link moral theology with its scriptural and systematic sources. As a result, the older manuals have largely been replaced, notwithstanding their compassionate prudence and practical wisdom. *See also* manualists; moral theology.

Mar (mahr; Syr., "Lord, sir"), ecclesiastical title for a saint or bishop in the Syriac and derived traditions.

Maranatha (mah-rah-nah-thah'; Aram., "Our Lord has come," "Our Lord, Come"), prayer. The prayer in Greek in Rev 22:20, "Come, Lord Jesus!" strongly supports the second rendering. Such prayers (1 Cor 16:22; *Did.* 10:6) attest the intense expectation among early Christians of Jesus' imminent return. *See also* Mary, Blessed Virgin.

Marcellinus, St. (mahr-sel-een'uhs), d. ca. 304, pope (296–304) and martyr. Although mentioned in the Roman eucharistic canon, little reliable information is known about him. He is said to have complied with an order from the emperor Diocletian to hand over copies of the Scriptures and also to have offered incense to the gods, for which acts he was dropped for a time from the official list of popes. He may have abdicated or been deposed before his death. Feast day (with Peter, exorcist and martyr): June 2.

Marcellus I, St., d. 309, pope from 306 to 308, elected four years after the death of his predecessor Marcellinus due to confusion resulting from Diocletian's persecution. Marcellus reorganized Rome's parishes. Exiled by Maxentius (Western emperor, 300–12), he died in exile on January 16 and is buried in the cemetery of Priscilla on the Via Salaria. He is sometimes confused with another Marcellus who died on October 4 or 7 and is buried in the cemetery of Balbina on the Via Ardeatina. Feast day: January 16.

Marcellus of Ancyra, ca. 280–ca. 374, bishop of Ancyra who attended the Council of Nicaea (325). He defended the Son as *homoousios* (Gk., "of one substance") with the Father but interpreted this to mean that Son and Spirit were temporary distinctions that would not subsist after God was "all in all" (1 Cor 15:24–28). He was condemned by the Council of Constantinople (381), and the clause "his kingdom will have no end" was added to the creed against him. *See also* Constantinople, councils of; *homoousios;* Nicaea, First Council of.

Mar Charbel, 1828–98, also known as St. Charbel (or Sharbel) Makhlouf, priest-monk of the Lebanese Maronite order. A hermit and mystic renowned for holiness, from 1875 until his death he lived as a solitary in a hermitage dependent on the Monastery of St. Maron at Annaya, Lebanon. He was canonized in 1977.

Marcion, ca. 85–ca. 160, one of the most formidable heretics ever faced by the Church. He was opposed by virtually all the Church Fathers. Born in Asia Minor, Marcion came to Rome ca. 140 and joined the Church there, perhaps also at this time coming under the influence of the Gnostic teacher Cerdo. In 144 he was excommunicated by the Roman Church for heresy. Undaunted, he established his own church, similar in organization and rites to the Catholic Church, to which it soon became a serious rival, spreading throughout the empire.

Marcion's central belief was that the God of love revealed in Jesus Christ was utterly different from the God of law revealed in the OT. Christianity was thus not the fulfillment of Judaism, but its replacement. In place of "the Law and the Prophets," Marcion offered "the Gospel and the Apostle," a radically edited version of Luke's Gospel and ten of Paul's Letters. Marcion's proposed canon accelerated the Catholic Church's efforts to establish its own. In rejecting the creator of the OT, Marcion rejected creation itself as well, regarding matter and the body as evil. Consequently, he affirmed a Docetic Christology that denied the reality of Jesus' human body and practiced a rigorous asceticism. *See also* canon of the Scriptures; creation; Docetism.

Maréchal, Joseph (mah-ray-shahl'), 1878–1944, Belgian Jesuit philosopher and a founder of Transcendental Thomism. His major work is the five-volume *Le Point de depart de la metaphysique,* which traced problems in modern thought to the breakdown of Scholasticism and attempted to develop a new synthesis between modern and medieval thought. Influenced by Maurice Blondel (d. 1949) and phenomenology, he asserted that Kant's critical philosophy could be reconciled with Thomism if the intellect was conceived as a dynamic, rather than static, faculty. His other important work includes a study on the psychology of mysticism. He significantly influenced twentieth-century Catholic theology through the work of fellow Jesuits Bernard Lonergan (d. 1984) and Karl Rahner (d. 1984). *See also* philosophy and theology; transcendental Thomism.

Maredsous, Benedictine monastery in Belgium. Its abbots have included Placidus Wolter and Columba Marmion. Among its monk scholars were Germain Morin, Ursmer Berlière, and Cyril Lambot. *See also* Marmion, Joseph Columba.

Margaret Mary Alacoque, St. *See* Alacoque, St. Margaret Mary.

Margaret of Scotland, St., ca. 1050–93, queen of Malcolm III of Scotland. Raised in the court of England's Edward the Confessor, she was celebrated for her pious and charitable life and for her support of church reform. Feast day: November 16.

Maria Goretti, St. *See* Goretti, St. Maria.

Maria Laach, an ancient Benedictine abbey in Germany founded in 1093. Under Abbot Herwegen it became a center of liturgical scholarship with such scholars as Odo Casel (d. 1948) and K. Mohlberg, and it was a major center of the liturgical movement.

Marialis Cultus (mahr-ee-ahl'is kool'-tuhs; Lat., "Marian Cult"), "For the Right Ordering and Development of Devotion to the Blessed Virgin Mary," apostolic exhortation of Pope Paul VI issued on February 2, 1974. It seeks to shape and guide devotion to the Blessed Virgin in light of the theological, liturgical, and spiritual renewal promoted by the Second Vatican Council. For example, while the encyclical encourages devotion to the Rosary, it points out that the Rosary is not to be recited during Mass (n. 48). The encyclical also underscores the ecumenical dimension of Marian devotion as well as its necessary connection with the struggle for social justice, so eloquently expressed in Mary's prayer, the Magnificat. *See also* Marian devotion.

Maria Monk, alleged author of a nineteenth-century book (*The Awful Disclosures*) purporting to reveal the secrets of convent life. Her lurid story, a best-seller of anti-Catholic propaganda, had little factual basis but has been reprinted many times and is still quoted on occasion in anti-Catholic literature.

Mariana, Juan de, 1536–1624, Spanish Jesuit theologian and historian whose *De Rege et Regis Institutione* (*On the King and the Institution of the King*) argued for regicide. Opponents ascribed this view to the Jesuits as a whole.

Marian Academy. *See* Pontifical Marian Academy.

Marian devotion, an attitude of piety or veneration toward Mary, often expressed in acts of devotion. Vatican II's Dogmatic Constitution on the Church (*Lumen Gentium*) views Mary not only as Mother of God, but also as a type and mother of the Church, exemplar of faith, sign of hope, and preeminent member of the communion of saints. Because of her privileged position, the Church accords her special veneration both within the liturgy and without.

The liturgical cult and Marian devotional exercises are to be generously fostered, never losing sight of the unique and sole mediation of Christ (nn. 67, 60). Pope Paul VI's 1974 apostolic exhortation *Marialis Cultus* elaborates the seminal notions of

Lumen Gentium, setting out "certain principles designed to give Marian devotion new vitality" (n. 40). After considering Marian liturgical feasts, the exhortation stresses the intrinsic trinitarian and Christological character of Marian devotion, makes special mention of the Person and action of the Holy Spirit, urges an explanation of Mary's place in the Church, underscores the importance of biblical themes, signals genuine ecumenical concern, and encourages openness to the findings of the social sciences. Explicitly treated are two Marian devotions, the Angelus and the Rosary.

Marialis Cultus seeks to ground Marian devotion within an orthodox faith and practice, avoiding the extremes of Marian minimalism or maximalism. The minimalist approach exaggerates divine initiative toward Mary and devalues the human response; thus, Mary is not venerable, for that detracts from God's work in Jesus. The maximalist approach overplays Mary's human response at the expense of the divine, resulting in a deemphasis of Christ's salvific mediation. *See also Marialis Cultus;* Marian feasts; Mary, Blessed Virgin. JOHN A. MELLOH

Marian feasts, liturgical celebrations honoring Mary in both Eastern and Western traditions. Marian feasts have always enjoyed distinctive importance, above the commemorations of other saints.

While early liturgical history evidences no specific Marian feasts, celebrations of the birth and infancy of Jesus showed Marian dimensions. The Council of Ephesus (431), in formally approving Mary's title of *Theotokos* (Gk., "bearer of God"), gave impetus to the rise of Marian feasts. The Jerusalem church celebrated "Mary, Mother of God" outside Bethlehem on August 15; the feast was later transferred and became a feast of Mary's death or dormition. Sixth-century Roman churches celebrated Mary on January 1 and Syrian and Byzantine churches honored the Mother of God on December 26. From about the same time Spanish churches honored her on December 18, a week prior to Christmas. The Jerusalem church originated in the sixth century the feasts of Mary's birth (September 8) and the Presentation in the Temple (November 21) and probably the Annunciation (March 25). By the seventh century, the Jerusalem feasts were celebrated not only in the Byzantine empire, but also in Rome.

The fifteen Marian feasts of the revised Roman calendar honor Mary's role in the birth and life of Jesus, celebrate grace in her own life, or hail her as the model of Christian living and an instrument of grace. Among these feasts are four solemnities (Mary, Mother of God, January 1; Annunciation, March 25; Assumption, August 15; Immaculate Conception, December 8), three feasts (Presentation of the Lord, February 2; Visitation, May 31; Birth of Mary, September 8), four memorials (Queenship of Mary, August 22; Our Lady of Sorrows, September 15; Our Lady of the Rosary, October 7; Presentation of Mary, November 21), and four optional memorials (Our Lady of Lourdes, February 11; Immaculate Heart of Mary, Saturday after the Second Sunday of Pentecost; Our Lady of Mount Carmel, July 16; Dedication of the Basilica of St. Mary Major, August 5). In the United States, the memorial of Our Lady of Guadalupe, December 12, is a feast day. *See also* Marian devotion; Mary, Blessed Virgin.　　　　　　　　*JOHN A. MELLOH*

Marianists, the name commonly used for the religious congregation of priests known as the Society of Mary (S.M.) and brothers, known as Brothers of Mary, founded in Bordeaux, France, in 1816 by Father William Chaminade, and for the congregation of sisters founded in 1816 by Adele de Batz de Trenquelleon, known as the Congregation of the Daughters of Mary Immaculate (F.M.I.), in cooperation with Father Chaminade. Both communities evolved from sodalities, organizations devoted to prayer and good works, dedicated to the Virgin Mary. To counteract certain effects of the French Revolution, they committed themselves to a strong community life and the education of youth. In 1993 the women's group numbered 400 worldwide and men's group 1,700. The Marianists sponsor the University of Dayton (Ohio), St. Mary's University in San Antonio, Texas, and Chaminade University in Honolulu, Hawaii.

Marian maximalism, an exaggeration of the role and spiritual powers of Mary in the work of redemption and salvation. Also known as Mariocentricism, it places Mary at the center of the mystery of redemption on a coequal basis with Jesus Christ. Consequently, there is no limit to the veneration given her.

Marian minimalism, a disparagement of the role and spiritual powers of Mary in the work of redemption and salvation. Also known as Mariophobia, it fears that veneration of Mary would detract from the central role of Jesus Christ in redemption and from the glory owed to God alone.

Marian Year, a period of twelve months set aside by papal proclamation as a time of renewed devotion to Mary as Mother of God. From the time of the Council of Ephesus (431), when Mary was affirmed as *Theotokos* (Gk. "God-bearer"), the Church has encouraged honoring Mary as contributing to the adoration of the triune God. Most recently (1987), Pope John Paul II proclaimed a Marian Year and issued an encyclical, *Redemptoris Mater,* calling for renewal of Marian spirituality. The National Conference of Catholic Bishops in the United States responded by publishing new prayers and rites for the celebration of Marian devotions in the form of litanies, invocations, hymns, and processions, as well as Liturgies of the Hours and Rosary celebrations. *See also* Marian devotion.

Marie-Rose Durocher, St. *See* Durocher, St. Marie-Rose.

Marillac, St. Louise de, 1591–1660, founder, with Vincent de Paul, of the Sisters of Charity. After being widowed, she aided Vincent by taking young women into her home to train them to work with the poor. When this group took vows as the Sisters of Charity, Louise became their first superior. Feast day: March 15. *See also* Daughters of Charity of St. Vincent de Paul; Vincent de Paul, St.

Mariolatry, the worship (Lat., *latria*) of Mary. Because God alone deserves worship, divine honors given to creatures, even one so elevated as Mary, would be objectively sinful. According to Catholic theology the angels and saints may be given *dulia* (veneration) only, while Mary, greatest of the saints, may receive *hyperdulia* (special veneration). *See also* Marian devotion.

Mariology, a branch of theology that focuses on the person and role of the Blessed Virgin Mary in the Church and in the work of redemption. There is an incipient Mariology already in the NT and in the writings of the early Fathers of the Church, but for Thomas Aquinas and other medieval authors it was simply an appendix to Christology. Beginning in the seventeenth century, however, Mariology became a separate theological treatise, a trend that intensified in the nineteenth century with the definition of the dogma of the Immaculate Conception (1854) and especially during the pontificate of Pius XII, who defined the dogma of the Assumption (1950). The Second Vatican Council (1962–65) rejected the separate-treatise approach and situated the schema on Mary within the document on the Church (Dogmatic Constitution on the Church, ch. 8), viewing her as a type of the Church, a model of faith, and the preeminent member of the communion of saints. *See also* Mary, Blessed Virgin.

Marists, a family of religious congregations dedicated to missionary work and education. In 1816 Jean-Claude Colin founded at Lyon, France, the Society of Mary (S.M.), a community of priests and brothers. An original member of that group, Marcellin Champagnat, founded the Marist Brothers of the Schools (F.M.S.) in 1817. Jeanne-Marie Chavoin organized a group of women in 1824 that became the Marist Sisters, or the Congregation of Mary (S.M.). These three Marist congregations include about three thousand members worldwide. Father Colin and his brother established a third order for lay people, from which later sprang the Marist Missionary Sisters.

Maritain, Jacques, 1882–1973, French Thomist philosopher. Reared a liberal Protestant, he studied under the philosopher Henri Bergson (d. 1941). Maritain and his wife, Raïssa (1883–1960), a Russian Jewish poet, became Catholics in 1906 and ardent disciples of Thomas Aquinas (d. 1274). After teaching in Paris at the Institute Catholique (1914–33), he taught at the Institute of Mediaeval Studies in Toronto (1933–45) and at Princeton University (1948–56). He also taught briefly at Columbia University, the University of Chicago, and at Notre Dame. He was French ambassador to the Vatican, 1945–48. From 1961 he lived with the Little Brothers of Jesus in Toulouse and joined their congregation in 1970.

Among Maritain's more than sixty books, *The Degrees of Knowledge* and *Creative Intuition in Art and Poetry* are characteristic. His democratic political philosophy influenced Catholic social thought after World War II. *The Peasant of the Garonne* bemoaned the aftermath of Vatican II (1962–65). *See also* neo-Thomism; Thomism.

Maritain, Raïssa, 1883–1960, poet and philosopher. A Jew born in Russia, she converted, with her husband, Jacques Maritain, to Catholicism. She collaborated extensively in his scholarly endeavors. *See also* Maritain, Jacques.

Marius Victorinus, ca. 283–after 362, rhetorician whose conversion to Christianity ca. 355 influenced Augustine. Marius gave up his chair after the emperor Julian forbade Christians to teach (362). His commentaries on Paul are the first written in Latin. His brilliant but heavily Neoplatonic trinitarian works were not widely influential after his death. *See also* Augustine of Hippo, St.; Neoplatonism.

Mar Ivanios (mahr ee-vahn'yohs), 1882–1953, Syro-Malankara archbishop who initiated the union of the Syro-Malankara Catholics with Rome in 1930. A leading bishop (1925) and metropolitan (1928) of the independent Syro-Jacobite church of India under the catholicos (Eastern patriarch), he initiated contacts with Rome with the approval of other Jacobite leaders. The only ones ultimately to join him in uniting to Rome were the men and women religious of the Order of the Imitation of Christ, which he founded as a Jacobite, and his suffragan bishop Mar Theophilos and a few other followers. *See also* Syro-Malankara Catholic Church.

Mark, St., the author of the Second Gospel. According to Catholic tradition, the author of the Second Gospel was John Mark. According to the Acts of the Apostles, his mother, Mary, owned a house in Jerusalem in which the earliest Christian community gathered (Acts 12:12). Barnabas and Saul (Paul) visited Jerusalem in order to bring a contribution to the poor of the community, who were suffering because of a famine (Acts 11:27–30). When they returned to Antioch, they took John Mark with them (Acts 12:25). He assisted them as they proclaimed the gospel in Cyprus (Acts 13:1–12). But when they arrived by ship in the city of Perga on the southern coast of Asia Minor (modern Turkey), John Mark left them and returned to Jerusalem (Acts 13:13). Later, after returning to Antioch, Paul and Barnabas decided to make a journey to visit the communities that they had founded. Barnabas wanted to take John Mark with them, but Paul objected since he had not persevered during the first journey. This led to a split between Barnabas and Paul; Barnabas traveled to Cyprus with John Mark, and Paul set out for Syria and Cilicia with Silas (Acts 15:36–41).

In the Letter of Paul to Philemon, Mark is mentioned among the fellow workers of Paul who send greetings (Phlm 24). In the Letter to the Colossians,

Mark, the Evangelist known as the interpreter of Peter, shown with the first page of Mark's Gospel, in an illustration from the ninth-century *Gospel Book of Bishop Ebo of Reims.*

whose Pauline authorship is disputed, Mark is mentioned as the cousin of Barnabas. The Christians of Colossae are urged to receive him hospitably, if he comes to them (Col 4:10). In 2 Timothy, which is attributed to Paul, but probably not actually written by him, Timothy is asked to bring Mark to Paul, since he is useful for the apostle's ministry (2 Tim 4:11).

The first letter attributed to Peter presents itself as written in "Babylon," i.e., Rome (1 Pet 5:13). "Babylon" is a nickname for Rome, since Rome destroyed Jerusalem, as did the Babylonian Empire. In the same verse, Mark is mentioned as the "son" of Peter. The term is either an expression of affection or an indication that Peter was Mark's father in the faith. This indication that Mark was in Rome with Peter is probably connected with the tradition that Mark took notes that recorded Peter's reminiscences of the teaching and deeds of Jesus. This tradition was written down by Papias of Hierapolis, according to Eusebius, who also said that Mark was Peter's "interpreter" (*Ecclesiastical History* 3.39.15).

Eusebius also recorded the tradition that Mark was the first to bring the Christian faith to Egypt, that he made known there the gospel that he had written, and established churches in Alexandria (*Eccl. Hist.* 2.16.1–2). Eusebius portrays Mark as the first bishop of Alexandria (*Eccl. Hist.* 2.24). In later tradition, Mark is also associated with Venice. Feast day: April 25. *See also* evangelist.   ADELA Y. COLLINS

marks of the Church, the four "notes" that the Creed of Constantinople (more popularly known as the Nicene Creed) attributes to the Church, describing it as one, holy, catholic, and apostolic. The term "marks," or "notes," of the Church reflects the apologetic argument developed in confessional controversy, whereby Christians attempted to prove their Church to be the "one true Church" on the grounds that it alone possessed all the properties that the Church of Christ must have. The supposition of such an argument was that the marks or notes would be visible to all, easily verified, found in the true Church alone, and hence apt to demonstrate which of the various churches was the true one. It also involved the necessity of showing that the other churches did not manifest these marks, at least in the degree that would be required of the true Church.

Apologetics: Louvain theologian Gustave Thils has written the history of this apologetic argument, focusing on the problems that have led to its being largely discarded. The most serious of these was that the description of the notes that must be verified in the true Church tended to be modeled on the qualities that the apologist's own church possessed. Thus the premises of the argument would be established in function of the conclusion to be demonstrated. To give an obvious example: a Catholic controversialist would include in his definition of the unity of the Church, the requirement that the universal Church must be united under one supreme pastor. In fact, in some Catholic manuals, the four notes were practically reduced to the requirement that the true Church must be the one governed by the Bishop of Rome.

Another problem with the apologetic use of the marks of the Church was that it restricted the consideration of the four creedal properties of the Church to their visible or empirical aspects, because it was only in this respect that they could serve to identify the true Church. However, there is much more to the oneness, holiness, catholicity, and apostolicity of the Church than what can be seen of them.

In view of the problems inherent in the apologetic argument, theologians now more commonly discuss the four notes of the creed as properties of the Church, taking into account all their aspects, whether they are empirically verifiable or knowable only by faith. These theologians insist that as the Church itself is a mystery of faith, so also each of its properties shares in its nature as mystery. Theological discussion begins, therefore, with what we believe about the Church and seeks a deeper understanding of the Church precisely as one, holy, catholic, and apostolic.

One approach is to show how each of these properties is rooted in the nature of the Church as People of God and Body of Christ animated by the Holy Spirit. The oneness of the People of God is called for by the oneness of God whose people it is; its holiness by God's holiness; its catholicity by the universal salvific will of God; and its apostolicity by the fact that its mission comes ultimately from the Father who sent his Son into the world. The Church, as the Body of Christ, must likewise be one and holy in order to resemble its head; its catholicity is founded in the role of Christ as the one mediator of salvation for all of humanity; its apostolicity in its sending by the Risen Christ. Finally, it is the Holy Spirit who effectively brings about and maintains the Church's unity, holiness, catholicity, and apostolicity. The abiding gift of the Holy Spirit provides the guarantee that the Church is indefectibly one, holy, catholic, and apostolic.

The Marks of the Church as Challenges to the Church: While the gifts that Christ has bestowed on his Church cannot be lost, they can be obscured, diminished, imperfectly realized. Each of these properties is a gift definitively given, but is also a task to be achieved. Because the Church is one, it must work to overcome divisions and to achieve full communion. Because it is holy, it can never give up the struggle against its own sinfulness or give up the practice of penance and purification. Because it is catholic, it must strive to become present in every place where the gospel is still unknown. Because it is apostolic, it has to examine itself constantly to see whether it is being wholly faithful to the message and mission it has received from the apostles.

It follows that during its earthly pilgrimage, each of the Church's properties is both an object of faith and a test of faith. While Catholics believe that the Church is one, they see how divided it is and how slow is the progress being made toward reunion. While Catholics believe the Church is holy, they experience the sinfulness of God's people in ourselves. While Catholics believe the Church is catholic, statistics tell them that Christians are a diminishing minority of the world's people. While Catholics believe the Church is apostolic, they cannot help remarking on the many contrasts between the Church of today and the Church of the apostles.

However, Catholics cannot reconcile the Church of their profession of faith with the Church of their experience by imagining that there are two churches: one the ideal church of the creed and the other the real church of everyday life. Nor can Catholics settle for the idea that it is only when the Church has arrived at the kingdom of God that it will really be one, holy, catholic, or apostolic.

What Catholics say about the Church in the creed is an expression of Christian hope, grounded in the promises of the Lord, that the Church will enter into the kingdom as the one, holy, universal People of God. What Catholics say is also a profession of faith about the Church as it is now, during its earthly pilgrimage. Finally, it is a call to Catholics to take their part in the task laid upon the Church, to strive to be ever more fully the one, holy, catholic, and apostolic Church that they believe it already to be. *See also* apostolicity; catholicity; Church; holiness of the Church; unity of the Church.

Bibliography

Sullivan, Francis A. *The Church We Believe In: One, Holy, Catholic and Apostolic.* Mahwah, NJ: Paulist Press, 1988.

FRANCIS A. SULLIVAN

Marmion, Joseph Columba, 1858–1923, abbot of Maredsous and influential spiritual author. Marmion was a spiritual guide to many, including the Belgium philosopher and bishop Cardinal Désiré Joseph Mercier (d. 1926). A Christ-centered spirituality is evident in his books *Christ the Life of the Soul* and *Christ in His Mysteries.* Marmion's reputation for holiness grew much after his death. *See also* Maredsous; Mercier, Désiré Joseph.

Maronite Catholic Church, an Eastern-rite Catholic community of Antiochene origin that has no Orthodox counterpart.

History: The history of the Maronites of Lebanon began in the late fourth century when a group of disciples gathered around the charismatic figure St. Maron. They later founded a monastery located midway between Aleppo and Antioch. In the fifth century the monastery was noted for its defense of the Christological doctrine of the Council of Chalcedon (451) espousing the two natures of Christ, one human and one divine.

Due to the Muslim invasions of the seventh century, the monks were compelled to move with their band of followers into the remote mountains of Lebanon, where they lived in relative isolation for centuries. It was during this period that they began to develop a distinct identity as a church and to elect their own head, who took the title of Patriarch of Antioch and All the East.

The Maronites came into contact with the Latin Church in the twelfth century, when the Crusader Kingdom of Antioch was founded. In 1182 the entire Maronite nation formally affirmed its union with Rome. But there is a strong tradition among the Maronites that their church never lacked communion with the Holy See.

Patriarch Jeremias II became the first Maronite patriarch to visit Rome when he attended the Fourth Lateran Council in 1215. This marked the beginning of close relations with the Holy See and a strong latinizing tendency.

The Maronite homeland was conquered by the Turks in the sixteenth century, and a long period of Ottoman domination began. By the nineteenth century the Western powers, especially France, began to offer protection to the Maronites. A massacre of thousands of them in 1860 provoked intervention by French military forces. The French formally took control of Lebanon after World War I.

When France granted Lebanon independence in 1944, it attempted to provide for the safety of the Maronite community by leaving behind a constitution guaranteeing that there would always be a Maronite president. The civil war that erupted in Lebanon in 1975 revealed, however, that the community's future remains precarious. Indeed, many thousands of Maronites have been leaving Lebanon for the West.

Structures: There is a Maronite patriarchal seminary at Ghazir and a diocesan seminary at Karm Sadde, near Tripoli. Advanced theological education is provided at the University of the Holy Spirit in Kaslik. A Maronite College was founded in Rome in 1584.

There are three Maronite monastic orders: the Lebanese Maronite Order, the Maronite Order of the Blessed Virgin Mary, and the Antonine Maronite Order. There is also an apostolic community, the Maronite-Lebanese Missionaries (Kreimists). Maronite women's orders include the Antonine Sisters, the Religious of the Lebanese Maronite Order, the Sisters of the Holy Family, the Sisters of Saint Thérèse of the Child Jesus, and the Sisters of the Blessed Sacrament of the Eucharist.

The Maronite patriarchs have resided at Bkerke, near Beirut, since 1790. In 1994 there were ten dioceses in Lebanon and six other jurisdictions in the Middle East. There are also Maronite dioceses in Argentina, Brazil, the United States, Australia, and Canada. In total, the Maronite Church has almost three million members. *See also* Antioch; Eastern churches; Eastern rites; Maronite monks; Maronite rite.

RONALD G. ROBERSON

Maronite College, one of the oldest of the pontifical Roman colleges for Eastern Catholic seminarians. Founded as a hospice by Pope Gregory XIII in 1581, it was converted into a seminary under the direction of the Jesuits from 1584 until their suppression in 1773. Since then it has had a precarious existence, having been closed, reopened, and closed again several times. The building remains in use in 1994. In the Jesuit period it produced brilliant scholars like the orientalists and liturgiologists Joseph Simon Assemani (1687–1768) and his nephew Joseph Aloysius Assemani (1710–82), whose works are still used today.

Maronite monks, Lebanese monks of the Maronite Catholic Church. The Maronite church was monastic in its roots, and its monks, following the Eastern model, resided in independent monasteries. Often called "Antonines" after Anthony of Egypt, a founder of monasticism, the Maronite monks are organized into religious congregations on the Western model: the Lebanese Maronite order (O.L.M.); the Mariamites or Maronite Order of the Blessed Virgin Mary (O.M.M.), an offshoot from the former; and the Maronite Antonine Order of Mar Isaya (O.A.M.). Though no longer strictly monastic orders, the Maronites have in the twentieth century seen a revival of traditional anchoritic (secluded monastic) life among some of their members, and they have given the Church a new hermit-saint in Mar Charbel. *See also* Mar Charbel; monk.

Maronite rite, the liturgical usages of the Maronite Catholic Church native to Lebanon. Often viewed as a latinized variant of the West Syrian rite, the Maronite rite is in fact an independent liturgical tradition related to but not identified with either the West Syrian or Chaldean rites. The Greek cities of Jerusalem and Antioch within the Eastern Empire, and Edessa, the cradle of Syriac Christian culture, were the three chief centers of liturgical creativity contributing to the formation of the Syriac liturgies. The Maronite rite originated as a monastic liturgy in Syria. It seems to have been an independent branch of the Edessene tradition developed by the Chalcedonian Syriac-speaking communities which established themselves independently of the Greek-speaking Mediterranean coastal region and preserved their ancient Syriac usages. Most of these Syriac-speaking Chalcedonian Orthodox ultimately adopted the Byzantine rite. The ancient Syriac usages were preserved by the monks who had taken refuge in the mountains of Lebanon at the beginning of the eighth century, laying the foundation for the Maronite church and rite. Living together with the Monophysites who developed the West Syrian tradition, the Maronites were heavily influenced by their usages. The Maronite calendar and Liturgy of the Hours are very closely related to the West Syrian. After coming into contact with Latin Catholics during the Crusades (1095–1291), the Maronite rite underwent progressive latinization, especially in the sanctoral (feasts of saints) and in the vestments and other externals of the eucharistic liturgy. But this latinization did not affect the Divine Office and the temporal cycle of the liturgical year, which retained their traditional shape. In the twentieth century the Maronite liturgy was restored, and Syriac has been gradually abandoned as the liturgical language in favor of Arabic or, in lands outside the homeland, other vernaculars. *See also* Maronite Catholic Church.

ROBERT F. TAFT

Marquette, Jacques, 1637–75, French Jesuit missionary and explorer. After his priestly ordination in 1666, he sailed from France to become a missionary to Native Americans. He spent several years evangelizing numerous tribes around the Great Lakes and helped found missions at Sault Ste. Marie and at St. Ignace (both in present-day Michigan). In 1673 Marquette accompanied Louis Jolliet on his exploration of the Mississippi River as far south as the mouth of the Arkansas River; he also founded a mission at Kaskaskia in Illinois. After falling ill, he decided to return to New France, but died enroute to Sault Ste. Marie.

marriage, form of, the manner of entering into a marriage. Until the sixteenth century Catholics in the West could marry simply by exchanging consent. In view of the abuses caused by clandestine, or secret, marriage and to protect spouses from desertion, the Council of Trent (1545–63) required a certain public procedure for Catholics entering into marriage. Though particulars have changed over the years, present legislation is substantially the same as then. Catholics are to marry in the presence of a properly authorized minister and two witnesses. *See also* Marriage; marriage law; Tametsi.

Marriage, liturgy of, the rite that celebrates and consecrates the union of a man and a woman in the sacrament of Matrimony. The 1969 reformed Rite of Marriage provides three ritual options: a rite for celebrating marriage during Mass, a rite for celebrating marriage outside of Mass, and a rite for celebrating marriage between a Catholic and an unbaptized person. A fourth entry offers optional texts for use in the wedding Mass or in the Marriage rite when celebrated outside of Mass. Common features of the three ritual options include the entrance rite, the Liturgy of the Word, the rite of Marriage, general intercessions, and the concluding rite.

The entrance rite is described in general terms, suggesting a flexible and adaptable approach to the action of entry and gathering of the assembly. The bride and groom are free to determine the pattern of entry in their preparation of the liturgy, based on local custom and aesthetic sensibility. After the entrance procession, the presider extends a word of welcome and then prays an opening prayer. The assembly then sits for the Liturgy of the Word, during which assigned readers proclaim two or three Scripture readings. The first is from the OT and the second from a NT Letter or the book of Revelation. The third reading is taken from one of the four Gospels and read by a priest or deacon, who then gives a homily drawn from the sacred texts. After the homily, the actual rite of Marriage begins with the presider's invitation to the bride and groom to state their intentions. Three questions are posed concerning freedom of choice, fidelity, and perpetuity, and the acceptance of children and their Christian formation. The declaration of consent and exchange of vows is followed with the blessing and exchange of rings.

Whether the rite of Marriage is celebrated during or outside of Mass determines what follows. Within the context of Mass, general intercessions and the liturgy of Eucharist—with the nuptial blessing after the Lord's Prayer—lead into the Communion rite, concluding rite, and dismissal. When the rite of Marriage is celebrated outside of Mass, general intercessions follow upon the blessing and exchange of rings. The nuptial blessing, the Lord's Prayer, general blessing, and dismissal conclude the rite. *See also* Marriage.

DANIEL P. GRIGASSY

MARRIAGE

Since the thirteenth century marriage has been recognized officially as one of the seven sacraments of the Catholic Church. Marriage is described in the revised Code of Canon Law as a "covenant by which a man and a woman establish between themselves a partnership of their whole life and which of its own very nature is ordered to the well-being of the spouses and to the procreation and upbringing of children" (can. 1055). This description, which follows the Second Vatican Council's Pastoral Constitution on the Church in the Modern World (n. 48), provides headings to examine both marriage and the sacrament of marriage.

MARRIAGE

Everyone has probably been to and been moved by a wedding. For a valid marriage, however, only one wedding moment truly counts, the solemn moment of giving consent. After each partner has declared the willingness to take the other as husband or wife ("to have and to hold, from this day forward, for better, for worse, for richer, for poorer, in sickness and in health, until death do us part"), they are pronounced husband and wife. If their free consent is missing or is seriously flawed, there is no marriage, for free consent establishes marriage (can. 1057). An apparent marriage is null or invalid from the moment a seriously flawed consent is given. A later declaration of nullity, called an annulment, does not make such a marriage invalid; it merely declares that it was always invalid, despite appearances to the contrary.

Since the consent of the spouses establishes a marriage, in common with the other Western churches the Catholic Church teaches that the spouses, not the witnessing priest or deacon, are the ministers of the sacrament. The Orthodox churches of the East, on the other hand, teach that the presiding priest is the minister. Though in the Catholic Church he may not be the minister of the sacrament, the presiding priest plays a central liturgical role in the wedding ceremony, accepting and blessing the marriage on behalf of the Church.

What is the marriage that free consent establishes? An ancient Roman definition, found in the *Digesta* of the emperor Justinian, has dominated the answer to this question in the West. "Marriage is a union of a man and a woman, and a communion of the whole of life" (23.2.1). Marriage is a union of, and a communion between, a man and a woman by which they establish, as the canon law asserts, "a partnership of their whole life." The phrase "whole life" is ambiguous. It can mean as long as life lasts, and then it implies that marriage is a lifelong commitment. It can mean everything that the spouses have, and then it implies that nothing is left unshared between them. Over the years, both meanings have been so interwoven that marriage is looked upon as the union of a man and a woman sharing throughout the whole of their lives all their goods (see the concluding section).

Marriage, then, is a partnership of the whole of life between a man and a woman. But what is the partnership for? Again, in both the other Western and the Catholic traditions, there is no doubt. Marriage has two ends, the well-being of the spouses and the procreation and upbringing of children. For many years in the Catholic tradition, these two ends of marriage were categorized as secondary and primary, respectively. Where a conflict between the ends arose, the personal and marital well-being of the spouses, the secondary end, had to yield to the primary end of the procreation of children. The Second Vatican Council (1962–65) significantly altered that tradition.

The council taught, in the Pastoral Constitution on the Church in the Modern World, that both marriage and the marital love of the spouses "are ordained for the procreation and education of children, and find in them their ultimate crown" (n. 48). It refused, however, to employ the traditional primary/secondary end terminology. It taught that procreation "does not make the other ends of marriage of less account" and that marriage "is not instituted solely for procreation" (n. 50). That the omission of the traditional terminology was the result of deliberated choice was demonstrated beyond doubt when revised canon 1055, cited above, repeated the council's nonhierarchical formulation.

Marriage, therefore, is a loving partnership of the whole of life, established by the free consent of the spouses, and ordered equally to the mutual well-being of the spouses and to the procreation and nurture of children. When such a marriage is between two believers, the Catholic Church teaches, it is also both covenant and sacrament.

MARRIAGE AS COVENANT AND SACRAMENT

Since marriage is established by the consent of the spouses, it was traditionally considered under the legal heading of contract. Since the Second Vatican Council, however, it has come to be considered more under the religious heading of covenant. For Christians of all denominations, "covenant" echoes both the covenant between God and God's people and the covenant between Christ and his people, the Church. "Covenant," however, is not merely a biblical word; it is also a personal word. Covenants engage people and the mutual services of people; they are forever; they are religious realities, witnessed by God; they can be made only by adults who are mentally, emotionally, and spiritually mature. The designation of a marriage between Christians as a covenant, a common designation today in all the Christian churches, is intended to imply the religious fact that it is not only an echo of the two biblical covenants, but also an extension and a participation in both. It is precisely this idea that situates it also as sacrament.

Religions are always striving to find ways to image God and God's relationship to the human world. Since the ancient Israelites' idea of their special relationship to God, arising out of the covenant, was absolutely central to their self-understanding, it is not difficult to understand that they would search out a human reality to symbolize the covenant relationship. Neither is it difficult to understand why the reality they chose was the human covenant of marriage. The prophet Hosea was

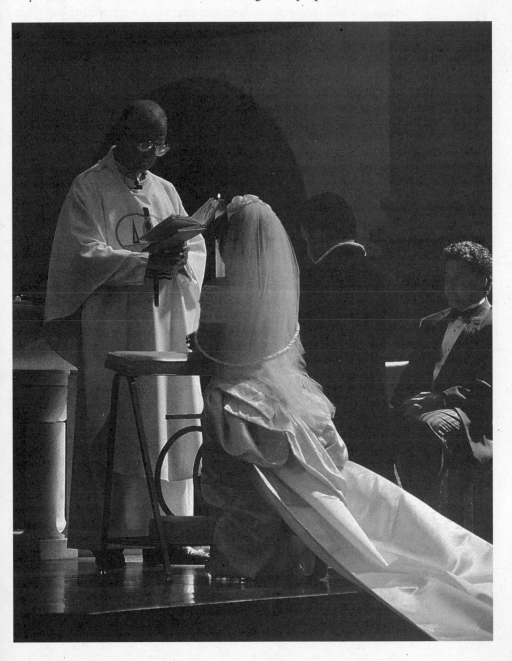

The sacrament of Marriage being performed by a Catholic couple in the presence of a priest and two witnesses in San Juan Capistrano, California.

the first to speak of marriage as the image and symbol of the covenant between God and God's people.

Hosea interprets his marriage to his wife, Gomer, a marriage superficially like any other marriage, as a prophetic symbol, announcing and making explicit in representation the covenant union between God and Israel. As Gomer left Hosea for other lovers, so also did Israel leave its God for other gods. As Hosea waits faithfully for Gomer's return and takes her back without recrimination, so, too, God waits for and takes back Israel. The marriage of Hosea and Gomer is dealt with as symbol and image of the relationship between God and Israel. In both covenants, the relationship has been damaged, even violated. But Hosea's human action images and reveals God's divine action of abiding and steadfast love. His action announces and makes explicit not only Hosea's faithfulness to his marriage, but also God's faithfulness to the covenant with Israel.

Hosea's prophecy introduces into religious history a clear, if mysterious, meaning about marriage. Beside being a secular institution, it is also a religious and prophetic symbol, announcing and making explicit in representation the abiding and steadfast love between God and Israel. Lived into from this perspective, lived into in faith, as Christians say today, marriage is a two-storied reality. On a first story, it signifies the mutual covenant love of this man and this woman; on a second story, it signifies in representation the mutual covenant love of God and God's people. This two-storied view of marriage becomes the Christian view. Jewish prophetic symbol becomes Catholic sacrament.

The classical Catholic definition of a sacrament, an outward sign instituted by Christ to give grace, can now be more fully explicated with respect to marriage. To say that a marriage between Christians is a sacrament is to say that it is a two-storied reality. On a first story, the ordinary human story, it announces and makes explicit the communion of life and love between a Christian man and woman. On a second story, the religious and symbolic story, it announces and makes explicit in representation the communion of life and love between Christ and Christ's people, the Church.

The partners entering into any marriage say to one another before witnesses: "I love you and I give myself to you." Christian partners entering into the sacrament of marriage say that too, but they also say more. They say: "I love you as Christ loves the Church, and I give myself to and for you as Christ gives himself to and for the Church." A sacramental marriage is, therefore, more than the civil marriage of a man and a woman; it is more than human covenant. It is also a religious marriage and covenant. God and God's Christ are present in it, theologically third partners in it, from its beginning.

This presence of grace in its most ancient Catholic sense, namely, the presence of the gracious God, is not something extrinsic to the covenant of sacramental marriage. It is something essential to it; without it the marriage is neither Christian or sacramental. Of course, Christian marriage announces and makes explicit the mutual love of a Christian man and woman. It also announces and makes explicit in representation their love for Christ, as well as their covenant to make their marriage an image and a symbol of Christ's steadfast covenant with his Church. It is in this sense that it is a sacrament, an outward sign in the human world of the presence of the God who is Grace. This two-storied meaning is what the Catholic Church intends when it teaches that the marriage covenant has been raised by Christ the Lord to the dignity of a sacrament.

MARRIAGE FOR THE WHOLE OF LIFE

In the contemporary world, it has become fashionable to be cynical about the marital promise "until death do us part," because, it is said, unconditional promises covering a period of some fifty years are just not possible. To promise to do something next week is one thing; to promise to do it fifty years from now, when so much will have changed, is another. Only conditional promises, made on the condition that nothing substantially changes in either spouse, can be made with any binding weight. At least, so runs the argument. The Catholic Church does not accept that argument, responding that marriage, especially sacramental marriage, is indissoluble (can. 1056).

Following its interpretation of Jesus' Gospel words (Mark 10:11–12; Matt 5:32; 19:19; Luke 16:18), the Catholic Church teaches that a man

The bride and groom receive the Eucharist under both species, consecrated bread and wine, in Cali, Colombia.

and a woman marry for as long as life lasts. The Catholic Church regards it as self-evident that loving covenant creates a moral obligation to be faithful to one's covenant word. This is what both covenant and love mean. Covenant creates a relationship in which one binds oneself to keep one's word; love, by its very nature, tends to be lifelong.

The claim that the marriage vow "until death do us part" is impossible to make is false. It is perfectly possible for a man and a woman to commit themselves unconditionally, for commitment is a statement of present intention, not of future circumstance. It is false that they are helpless when and if one or the other wavers in marital commitment, even if one or the other or both have changed. It is entirely possible that principles freely chosen and lovingly embraced can continue to be freely chosen and lovingly embraced fifty years hence, even in substantially changed circumstances.

An example is the soldier going off to war. Like all other men and women, soldiers value life, liberty, and happiness. They do not value, however, just any life; they value the life of honor. They have freely chosen the principle of honor and, at any cost, they remain faithful to that principle.

That same choice has been made and continues to be made by those men and women who have freely committed themselves in marriage, not only to one another but also to love and honor, and who have willed to be faithful "until death do us part." For spouses in a sacramental marriage, their love of, and covenant with, one another is enhanced by their mutual love of, and their faithful commitment to, God in Christ.

The love that is at the root of sacramental marriage is the same love that is at the root of covenant, "steadfast love and faithfulness" (Exod 34:6). It is with such love that God loves Israel and Christ loves the Church. It is such love that is enjoined upon Christian husbands, who are to love their wives "as Christ loved the church and gave himself up for her" (Eph 5:25). We can be sure that the same love is also required from Christian wives. Christian spouses are to love one another steadfastly and faithfully.

This steadfast love, traditionally called fidelity, makes sacramental marriage exclusive and permanent (can. 1056). Christian marriage is indissoluble because Christian love is steadfast and faithful and indissoluble. Indissolubility is a quality of Christian marriage because it is, first and foremost, a quality of Christian love. If marital love exists only in germ on a wedding day, and it surely does, then so also does indissolubility exist only in germ. Marital love, the mainspring of indissoluble partnership of the whole of life, is not a given in a Christian marriage. It is an ongoing challenge, an eschatological challenge theologians call it, to which the spouses are called to respond as followers of the Christ who is for them the sacrament and the Incarnation of God.

Though the Catholic Church teaches that all marriages are indissoluble, in practice it does dissolve valid marriages. It dissolves nonsacramental marriages in the ancient procedure known as the Pauline Privilege, first enunciated by the Apostle Paul (1 Cor 7:15). It also dissolves valid marriages that have not been consummated (can. 1142). It never dissolves marriages that are both sacramental and consummated (can. 1141). These marriages are held to be absolutely indissoluble; only these marriages, in practice, are held to be for the whole of life.

See also annulment; indissolubility of marriage; Marriage, liturgy of; marriage, spiritual; marriage law; Privilege of the Faith; sacrament.

Bibliography

Fischer, Kathleen R., and Thomas N. Hart. *Promises to Keep: Developing the Skills of Marriage.* New York: Paulist Press, 1991.

Kasper, Walter. *Theology of Christian Marriage.* New York: Crossroad, 1981.

Lawler, Michael G. *Secular Marriage: Christian Sacrament.* Mystic, CT: Twenty Third Publications, 1985.

Schillebeeckx, Edward. *Marriage: Secular Reality and Saving Mystery.* New York: Sheed and Ward, 1965.

Tetlow, Elizabeth M. and Louis M. *Partners in Service: Towards a Biblical Theology of Christian Marriage.* Lanham, MD: University Press of America, 1983.

MICHAEL G. LAWLER

marriage, spiritual, symbolism from Christian mysticism expressing the highest union with God. This imagery for union with God appeared in early Greek and Jewish sources. In the latter the Lord took Israel as bride (Hos 2:19). Jesus referred to himself as bridegroom (Matt 9:15). In the early Jewish tradition commentators on the Song of Songs saw the young woman and man as symbolic of union between the Lord and Israel. Christian commentators extended that symbolism to the union of Christ with the Church and then to the individual. The Incarnation is the paradigm and source of a theology of this nuptial symbolism. Origen (d. 254), Gregory of Nyssa (d. 395), and Bernard of Clairvaux (d. 1153) were key articulators of this symbolism. Classical expression of this mystical symbolism awaited Teresa of Ávila (d. 1582) and John of the Cross (d. 1591). The former described this marriage symbolism in *The Interior Castle* with the spiritual espousals or betrothals taking place in the sixth mansion and spiritual marriage as transforming union in the seventh mansion. The latter is habitual, deeper loving union. For John of the Cross's comparison of spiritual espousals and spiritual marriage, see *The Spiritual Canticle* (22) and *The Living Flame of Love* (3. 24–7). *See also* Bernard of Clairvaux, St.; Carmelite order; Gregory of Nyssa, St.; Incarnation, the; John of the Cross, St.; Origen; Teresa of Ávila, St.

Marriage Encounter, a marriage enrichment program developed by Father Gabriel Calvo in Barcelona, Spain, in the early 1960s. The encounter consists of a married couples' retreat weekend in which the couple seeks to deepen their relationship with one another and with God through personal reflection, dialogue with each other, and dialogue with other couples. The encounter employs various techniques such as journal writing, structured dialogue, group discussion, and "love letters," in which each partner in the couple reveals his or her deepest self to the other in the light of God's grace. The goal of the encounter is to deepen the marital bond and to encourage more open communication between the couple.

From Spain the encounter quickly spread to Latin America, Mexico, and in 1966 to the United States, where it was first introduced in Miami, Florida. The first English-speaking encounter took place at the 1967 annual convention of the Christian Family Movement at the University of Notre Dame. Since then, thousands of couples have experienced the encounter. Two groups promote Marriage Encounter: Worldwide Marriage Encounter, which is predominantly Catholic, and National Marriage Encounter, which is ecumenical. *See also* Christian Family Movement; Marriage.

marriage law, norms and legal reasoning related to marriage. The Catholic Church justifies its legislating with respect to marriage because of its theological understanding of the sacredness of marriage. The Church's laws regarding marriage deal only with the marriages of Catholics and those who are married to, or seek to marry, Catholics. The laws are, in some cases, based on aspects of marriage that are, in Catholic teaching, considered of divine institution and hence unchangeable by the Church (e.g., marriage's indissolubility); in other cases, the laws are based on considerations that admit to change and are of solely human origin (e.g., the requirement that the marriage take place before the parish priest).

The norms cover such matters as preparation for marriage, capacity to enter into marriage, the proper manner of celebrating marriage, record keeping of marriages celebrated within the Church, and certain rights and obligations of the spouses. The norms also consider the circumstances under which marital rights might be modified and the proper procedures to be used in seeking a dissolution or annulment of a marriage.

Matrimonial jurisprudence is the legal reasoning that considers how the theological and legal understanding of marriage is to be applied in a given instance or in cases similar to it. Such jurisprudence is used in the solution of cases within the ecclesiastical courts.

Post–Vatican II Developments: Marriage law has developed considerably ever since Vatican II (1962–65) in the Pastoral Constitution on the Church in the Modern World (n. 48) asserted the personalist end of marriage as well as the procreative end. This development is reflected especially in the jurisprudence used in cases dealing with annulments of marriage. In particular, the capacity to fulfill the personalist end together with adequate decision making prior to entering into this personalist relationship became matters of greater concern in the review of a marriage done by marriage tribunals. These concerns have led to changes within the code of canon law itself, specifically with regard to the capacity for marriage. Canon 1095 considers marital capacity and the proper discretion to be taken in making a decision to marry. The understanding of capacity to wed found in this canon developed directly from cases in which tribunals considered the meaning of the obligations of marriage in light of the teaching of the Pastoral Constitution on the Church in the Modern World.

These newer avenues of investigation have given rise to a greater number of successful applications for annulment. The larger number of successful annulments has led, in turn, to a larger number of applicants. The consequently larger number of annulments granted has also caused some to criticize marriage tribunals for laxity, although the causes of increased annulments are more likely to be found in developing theology and canonical jurisprudence, together with the willingness of more people to apply.

Another significant development in marriage law has arisen from increased ecumenical contacts and activities in the postconciliar age. Although Catholics in a mixed or interfaith marriage must still promise to do all they can to raise the children Catholic, non-Catholics are no longer required to make such a promise. In addition, the bishop may allow the marriage ceremony to take place in the rite of the non-Catholic's religion. *See also* annulment; indissolubility of marriage; Marriage.   JOHN F. LAHEY

Marsilius of Padua, ca. 1275–1342, political theorist who attacked monarchical papal ecclesiology in his famous work *The Defender of the Peace* (1324). Rejecting centuries of claims about the divine origin of the Church, he insisted that whatever rights it possesses are granted the Church at the will of the state. He also undercut the authority of popes within the Church, giving the primacy to general councils in ecclesial affairs. When his teachings were condemned by John XXII in 1327, he was protected by the pope's enemy, Emperor Louis of Bavaria. *See also* conciliarism.

Martha, St., NT figure who, with her sister Mary, received Christ into her home (Luke 10:38) and witnessed the raising of Lazarus from the dead (John 11:1–46). Later hagiographical tradition links her, her sister (identified with Mary Magdalene), and Lazarus with the evangelization of Provence in France. Feast day: July 29.

Martha/Mary story, a story that appears only in Luke's Gospel (10:38–42). It has been commented upon extensively in the contemplative tradition affirming the primacy of prayer and contemplation.

Both women were disciples who offered hospitality to Jesus—Martha provided food and other courtesies, but Mary, who chose the "better part" of hospitality, "sat at the Lord's feet and listened to what he was saying." The story is remarkable as a revelation of women as disciples and as an affirmation of listening to Jesus. *See also* discipleship.

Martin de Porres, St. (mahr'tin deh pohr'ez), 1579–1639, Dominican lay brother. From his convent in Lima, Peru, he cared for the sick, ministered to the poor, and had a special ministry to African slaves. Of mixed blood himself, he is the patron saint of interracial justice. Feast day: November 3.

Martin I, St., d. 655, pope from 649 to 653 and martyr. After being elected pope Martin convoked a council that condemned Monothelitism (649), a Christological heresy. Emperor Constans II, a Monothelite, had Martin arrested and brought to Constantinople. Already ill, Martin was first imprisoned, then exiled to the Crimea, where he died. Feast day: April 13 (formerly November 12). *See also* Monothelitism.

Martin de Porres, patron of interracial justice, a Dominican lay brother who was devoted to the poor and to slaves brought to Peru from Africa; he was canonized by Pope John XXIII in 1962.

Martin IV [Simon de Brie], 1210–85, pope from 1281 to 1285. An ambitious servant of the Church and crown, his election was assured by the king of Sicily. Martin spent much of his pontificate promoting Sicily's interests in Constantinople at the expense of peace with the Eastern Church.

Martin V [Oddo Colonna], 1368–1431, pope from 1417 to 1431. Elected at the Council of Constance to replace the three rival claimants deposed by the council, he provided strong leadership to rebuild Church unity, consolidating power at Rome and reestablishing his authority in the Papal States. A moderate conciliarist, Martin undertook to implement many of the reforms issued at Constance, opposing those limiting papal power. His hopes of ending the schism with the East went unfulfilled. *See also* Constance, Council of; Great Schism.

Martini, Carlo Maria, b. 1927, Italian cardinal. He entered the Society of Jesus in 1944 and was ordained a priest in 1952. After receiving his doctorate in theology at the Pontifical Gregorian University, Rome, and then a doctorate in Sacred Scripture at the Pontifical Biblical Institute, also in Rome, he became professor and then rector of the Pontifical Biblical Institute (1969–78) and rector of the Pontifical Gregorian University (1978–79). In 1980 he was appointed archbishop of Milan and was made a cardinal in 1983. Since 1987 he has been president of the Council of Episcopal Conferences of Europe. A biblical scholar and spiritual writer, he is the author of over forty books, including *Ignatian Exercises in the Light of St. John* (1981), *Reflections on the Church: Meditations on Vatican II* (1987), *Through Moses to Jesus: The Way of the Paschal Mystery* (1988), *Women in the Gospels* (1990), and *Perseverance in Trials: Reflections on Job* (1992). In the 1990s he is frequently mentioned as a likely successor to Pope John Paul II. If Martini were elected, he would be the first Jesuit pope in history.

Martin of Braga, St., ca. 515–80, bishop. Having introduced monasticism to Galicia, in the northwest of Spain, Martin was ordained bishop of Dumium (556), then became archbishop of Braga (before 572). He presided over the Second Council of Braga (572) and wrote (among other works) a treatise against pagan superstitions. Feast day: March 20.

Martin of Tours, St., ca. 316/17–97, patron saint of France and a founder of Western monasticism. Martin's life is known primarily from the biography written by Sulpicius Severus, who shared the account with Martin before the saint's death on November 8, 397. Martin was born to pagan parents, became a catechuman at age twelve, took a military oath at fifteen, and was baptized at eighteen. The emperor Julian granted him a discharge from military service at Worms in 356. Martin took up the monastic life in Milan. Later, after Hilary of Poitiers returned from exile, Martin moved to Gaul and established the first French monastic community south of Poitiers in 360–61. He became the bishop of Tours on July 4, 371, lived at the cathedral for a time, and then resumed his monastic existence outside the town. He protested the execution of Priscillian, ca. 386. A huge crowd attended his burial in Tours, and many miracles were reported at the site. Feast day: November 11. *See also* monasticism.

martyr (Gk., *martys,* "witness"), a person who has given up his or her life for the Christian faith. Many martyrs died in the persecutions before Constantine's edict of toleration (313). The shedding of one's blood in the face of persecution was seen as a kind of second baptism in which one's sins were forgiven and salvation assured. The custom of the celebration of the martyr's "birthday," usually on the date of death, began in the second century. Later theologians established three criteria for proclaiming a person a martyr: (1) physical death occurred; (2) the death was the result of malice toward Christian life and truth; and (3) it was undergone voluntarily in defense of Christian life and truth. *See also* martyrdom; martyrology.

martyrdom, death as a result of refusal to renounce or compromise one's faith and thus the "witness" *par excellence* to one's faith. In the book of Revelation (ca. 95) the word "martyr" (Gk., "witness") is used of those who have shed their blood for Jesus (2:13; 17:6), and the word is used in this sense in the earliest extant account of a Christian martyr, *The Martyrdom of Polycarp* (ca. 157). Like the slightly later *Letter of the Churches of Lyons and Vienne* (ca. 177) describing the sufferings of Christians there, it is a letter meant to be read publicly, probably liturgically, and circulated to other churches. The veneration of the martyrs often included celebration of the Eucharist at the martyr's tomb on his or her "birthday," i.e., anniversary of death; already

The martyrdom of Stephen, the first martyr; he was despised perhaps as much by Jewish Christians, who were opposed to his bringing the gospel to non-Jews in the Greek-speaking world, as by non-Christian Jews, who opposed his preaching of Christ as the Messiah; painting in the Church of St. Mary of the Purification, Bologna, Italy.

Cyprian of Carthage (d. 258) regards this practice as ancient. In many places a funerary banquet accompanied the celebration.

Martyrs were inspired by the story in 2 Macc 6:18–7:41 (cf. 4 Macc) of Eleazar and the woman with seven sons, whose heroic refusal to comply with anti-Jewish laws resulted in torture and death. The martyrs regarded their passion as a share in the Passion of Christ, who suffered with the martyr and enabled him or her as an "athlete of Christ" to endure and triumph in combat with the devil. Those confessing the faith in defiance of the authorities were regarded as Spirit-filled and thus as able to forgive sins in the name of Christ, both in their life on earth and subsequently in heaven. Unbaptized persons who died for the faith were regarded as baptized by the shedding of their own blood.

Accounts of martyrs' deaths are preserved in two basic types, the "passion" or narrative account, such as that of Polycarp or the *Passion of Perpetua and Felicitas* (ca. 203), and the "acts" of the martyr, an account of the trial, sentence, and execution, e.g., the *Acts* of Justin Martyr (ca. 165), of the Scillitan martyrs (ca. 180), of Cyprian of Carthage (ca. 258).

Cult of Martyrs: In the fourth century the cult of the martyrs was greatly expanded. The funerary banquets were gradually suppressed but the commemorative liturgies were amplified with vigils, readings, chants, and panegyrics; churches were built on the site of the martyrs' tombs, and these became frequented by pilgrims; the relics of the martyrs were themselves honored and sometimes translated from their original burial site to a repository in a church or basilica (the first remains to be so translated were those of the martyr Babylas of Antioch, ca. 351). The martyr's body was (and is still) venerated as a temple of God. As persecutions ceased in the Roman Empire (although they continued in Persia), ideals of virtue or asceticism as spiritual equivalents of martyrdom were developed, and persons who were not martyrs came to be venerated as saints. But the refusal of the martyrs to apostasize in the face of physical death continued to be regarded as the witness to faith *par excellence* and was one of the primary reasons for the survival, spread, and eventual triumph of the Church. *See also* martyr; martyrology; Passion, the; Roman Martyrology.

JOHN C. CAVADINI

martyrology, a list of the feast days of saints with all applicable names for any given date, unlike a church calendar, which usually gives only one name per day. A martyrology gives some biographical data with each name, such as place of origin, death, or burial. Other important dates are sometimes noted, e.g., dates of discoveries and translations of relics, of episcopal consecrations, of birth, of the dedications of churches to the saint. The most influential martyrologies in Western history were the *Martyrologium Hieronymianum,* attributed to Jerome and the source of all medieval martyrologies, and the Roman Martyrology, which emerged at the end of the Middle Ages. Monastic reading from the martyrology at daily chapter (community assembly) led to an increase in the number and kinds of lists. *See also* martyr; martyrdom; Roman Martyrology.

Marxism, the philosophy and political system proposed by Karl Marx (1818–83). Rejecting idealism and skepticism, Marx held that nothing exists except matter that develops dialectically by a conflict of forces producing higher syntheses through violent revolutions. Hence, human history is a struggle between social classes that arise from technological progress in the mode of economic production. The mode of "industrial capitalism," based on private property and advanced technology, inevitably develops an organized labor force conscious that it is being exploited by nonproductive capitalists, who raise profits by reducing wages, or seizing colonies for cheap labor. This internal "contradiction" of capitalism will generate wars and finally revolution. The workers will control the means of production in a socialist state, but will be forced to defend themselves through rule by a vanguard Communist party ("dictatorship of the proletariat"). Once these counterforces have been liquidated, communism will arise as a classless, anarchistic (cooperative), nonviolent, democratic society based on economic abundance and a materialist education free of religious ideology.

Marxism has received many interpretations, ranging from emphasis on democratic and humanistic gradualism (i.e., an incremental movement toward democracy and respect for human rights) to apologies for the necessity of violence and dictatorship, as in the Marxist Leninism of the former Soviet Union, now largely discredited, and Maoist China. From Pope Leo XIII's time (d. 1903), the Church has condemned Marxist atheism, materialism, violence, and violation of human rights, but has also agreed with much of Marx's criticism of unregulated capitalism. Liberation theology has been influenced by Marxism's advocacy of the rights of the poor and its critique of systemic economic injustices. *See also* Catholic social teachings; communism; liberation theology.　　　　BENEDICT M. ASHLEY

Mary, Gospel of, a second-century apocryphal account of Mary (Magdalene) comforting the other grieving disciples and her report of secret teachings she had received, including an account of the soul's journey past hostile powers. The male disciples challenge her words as being strange and deny that the Savior would confide in a woman. *See also* apocryphal Gospels; Mary Magdalene, St.

Mary Clopas, St., one of the women at the Cross, wife of Clopas, (John 19:25). She may be the mother of James "the Less" and Joseph (Matt 27:56; Mark 15:40). If Clopas is Joseph's brother, mentioned in Eusebius (*Ecclesiastical History* 3.11; 4.22), this Mary would be the Blessed Virgin's sister-in-law. Feast day: April 9.

Maryknoll, Catholic Foreign Mission Society of America (M.M.), foreign missionary society based in the United States. Concern among American Catholics for the foreign missions began to intensify in the early twentieth century. At this time two diocesan priests, James A. Walsh of Boston, Massachusetts, and Thomas F. Price of Raleigh, North Carolina, promoted the idea of an American Catholic foreign mission society among prominent members of the American hierarchy. The hierarchy officially approved the concept at their annual meeting in 1911, and with the authorization of Pope Pius X, Maryknoll was established that year with Walsh and Price as its cofounders. Its name is derived from the hill, or knoll, on the property in New York State where Fathers Walsh and Price first purchased land. Both had a special devotion to the Blessed Virgin Mary.

Modeled on the French organization the Foreign Missionaries of Paris, Maryknoll priests are secular priests who do not take religious vows. The first Maryknoll mission was in China in 1918, and by the time of World War II there were missions scattered throughout the Far East. Maryknoll established missions in South America in 1942 and in Africa four years later. Maryknoll attracted many young men, and by 1965 there were 1,240 members in the society. Included in the society were brothers, laymen who wished to devote their lives to the foreign missions. A parallel society of women religious, officially known as the Maryknoll Sisters of St. Dominic, was also founded in 1912 by Mother Mary Joseph (Molly Rogers, Bishop Walsh's secretary). Maryknoll has been active in mission education since its founding, and most laypeople first hear about Maryknoll through the society's magazine, *Maryknoll* (formerly *Field Afar*).

In 1994 there were 602 priests and 49 brothers serving in twenty-four countries in Asia, Africa, and Latin America. There were 774 sisters serving in twenty-nine countries worldwide. Four hundred lay missioners (men, women, and families) have also served since 1975, when the Maryknoll Lay Mission Program was established. In 1994 there were 148 lay missioners serving in seventeen countries. The Lay Mission Program was founded as a coequal Maryknoll group in August, 1994. *See also* clergy, secular; Maryknoll Sisters; missions.　　　JAY P. DOLAN

BLESSED VIRGIN MARY

The Blessed Virgin Mary is the first-century Jewish woman who was the mother of Jesus; now a preeminent member of the communion of saints. The image of Mary in its many forms is woven throughout the life of the Church and her importance is expressed in doctrine, liturgy, piety, and theology.

BIBLICAL PICTURE

The NT depicts Mary in various ways. Mark's Gospel casts her along with Jesus' brothers in a negative light, placing them outside the crowded circle of those who form his eschatological family which is based on faith (3:20–35). In Matthew's Gospel this negative connotation is removed. His infancy narrative depicts Mary fulfilling the ancient promise that a virgin would conceive and bear a son who would be Emmanuel (Heb.), "God with us." While the annunciation of this news is given to Joseph, Mary's husband, Mary is the one with child from the Holy Spirit (1:18–25).

The Madonna and Child with John the Baptist; sixteenth-century Renaissance painting on wood by Raphael, Louvre, Paris.

Luke presents a highly positive portrait of Mary. In the scene parallel to Mark's, with the brothers and the crowded house, she is now included in the eschatological family of those who hear the word of God and do it (8:19–21). His infancy narrative depicts her story in scenes of literary artistry: the angel Gabriel's annunciation along with her willing response; the encounter with the pregnant Elizabeth; her canticle, the Magnificat, praising God for the great things done for her and for those who are poor and lowly; the birth scene in a stable in Bethlehem because there was no room in the inn; the visit of the shepherds; the presentation of Jesus in the Temple where she hears the prophecy of her own future suffering (chs. 1–2). Luke concludes his portrait of Mary by placing her in the upper room in Jerusalem after the Ascension of Jesus, where with the rest of the post-Easter community she prays and awaits the coming of the Holy Spirit (Acts 1:14). She is thus a woman of faith and member of the earliest Christian community.

John's Gospel depicts "the mother of Jesus" (he never uses her name) in two highly symbolic scenes. At the beginning of Jesus' ministry she attends the wedding feast at Cana, bringing the lack of wine to Jesus' attention and instructing the servants to obey his word (2:1–11). At the end, she, along with Mary Magdalene, some other women, and "the disciple whom Jesus loved," stands by the cross of Jesus. His mother and beloved disciple are entrusted into each other's care, the nucleus of the new community of believing disciples (19:25–27).

HISTORICAL DEVELOPMENT

Biblical depictions of Mary were conflated in the following centuries, so that various images of the woman of faith, the virgin who gave birth to the Messiah, and the woman at the cross reinforced each other. Additional material was added from the book of Revelation's parable of a woman clothed with the sun giving birth to a son of destiny amid apocalyptic agonies (ch. 12, originally intended to depict collectively the People of God); and from apocryphal writings, most notably the *Protevangelium of James,* which gives a legendary account of her parentage, youth, and marriage. The Marian symbol as it grew through history is an amalgam of various sources.

Patristic theology contains relatively little about Mary, but three themes steadily emerged. She is the new Eve who, by her obedience, overturns the ancient mother's disobedience, bringing into the world not death but the life that is Christ. Her virginity in conceiving Christ, which is biblically attested, remains when she gives birth to Christ and forever after. And her maternity of the Word-made-flesh makes it legitimate to address her as *Theotokos* (Gk.), "God-bearer," or Mother of God.

This last belief came under scrutiny in the fifth century in a dispute over the unity of Christ. Nestorius, the patriarch of Constantinople, argued that since Christ had two distinct natures, human and divine, the latter indwelling the former, Mary could be called the Mother of Christ but not the Mother of God. Against this the Council of Ephesus (431) ruled that since there was only one divine person in Jesus Christ, it could truly be said that Mary was the Mother of God. Although the focus of this decision was on Christology, it gave a major impetus to Marian devotion.

In Western medieval piety and theology, the image of Mary as mediatrix of God's grace to unworthy sinners came to the fore. The idea that Mary had a maternal influence over God, that she could turn away Christ's just anger and obtain mercy for sinners had already been accepted in the East, as seen in the popularity of the Theophilus legend. In this story a man bargains his soul away to the devil to gain a lucrative job. Near death he implores Mary to get back the contract, which she does after contending with the devil. Theophilus dies forgiven and avoids eternal hell. Translated into Latin in the eighth century, this story exercised great influence on the West's notion of Mary's power to save.

The Blessed Virgin Mary, Mother of the Lord, shown here with a choir of angels, all bejeweled with white harts, the personal symbol of King Richard II; late fourteenth-century Flemish-school painting on wood, National Gallery, London.

Her privileges grew in a way commensurate with her powers. The principle that God could gift Mary in a certain way, should do so, and therefore did (Lat., *potuit, decuit, fecit*) shaped theological reflection. She was called the aqueduct along which divine grace flows to earth, the neck between the Head and the Body of Christ, "mediator with the Mediator," Mother of mercy, and refuge of sinners; she was approachable because of her maternal love. The doctrines of her Immaculate Conception and Assumption gained ground. People showed their devotion through pilgrimages, veneration of her images, dramatizing stories of her miracles and apparitions, and a wealth of new prayers. Prayers such as the Hail Mary and the Rosary, still in use, date from this period.

The Protestant Reformers criticized the luxuriant growth of this devotion, deploring the lack of trust in God's graciousness communicated through Christ alone. The response of the Council of Trent (1545–63) was muted. It simply taught that it was good and useful to invoke the saints and called upon each local bishop to correct abuses. Subsequent centuries saw renewed growth of the Marian tradition in the Catholic Church. The Immaculate Conception (1854) and the Assumption (1950) were declared dogmas by papal decrees, which elicited strong criticism from Protestants. A new series of reported apparitions (at La Salette, Lourdes, Fátima, and many more), pious books such as *The Glories of Mary* by Alphonsus Liguori (d. 1787), papal encyclicals, customs such as wearing the miraculous medal and scapular, Marian years, Marian congresses, and new feasts (the Queenship of Mary) all kept Mary paramount in the Catholic mind.

On the eve of Vatican II theologians were divided into at least two factions: those who wished to use the occasion of the council to define yet another Marian dogma and those who, in accord with twentieth-century theological renewal and ecumenical dialogue, wished to realign the Marian tradition more in accord with Scripture, liturgy, and the patristic tradition.

VATICAN II

The council decided in its closest vote to incorporate its teaching on Mary into the Dogmatic Constitution on the Church (*Lumen Gentium*), thus ending Marian theology's isolation and rooting it firmly in the mainstream of the truths of faith. Entitled "The Role of the Blessed Virgin Mary, Mother of God, in the Mystery of Christ and the Church," ch. 8 of this constitution situates Mary in the midst of the communion of saints, those whose example and prayer in heaven give courage and consolation to the pilgrim Church on earth (ch. 7) and all of whom live in the light of Christ (ch. 1).

A preface to this chapter connects Mary to Christ and the Church by noting that Mary is "one with all human beings in their need for salvation" at the same time that she is a "preeminent and altogether singular member of the Church" (n. 53). In relation to Christ, her life was lived as a "pilgrimage of faith" from his birth to his death as she actively cooperated with the work of salvation through free faith and obedience (n. 58). In relation to the Church, she is a member who stands as a model and excellent exemplar of faith, charity, and union with Christ. Taking up the thorny matter of her mediation, the chapter notes that calling upon her within a rightly ordered faith as Advocate or Mediatrix does not detract from the sole mediation of Christ but rather shows forth his power, since his mediatión gives rise among creatures "to manifold cooperation which is but a sharing in this unique source" (n. 62). The chapter closes with teaching about the proper devotion directed toward Mary. It differs essentially from the adoration given to God alone but shows reverence to her as the God-bearer. In preaching and practice two extremes are to be avoided: narrow-mindedness, on the one hand, and exaggeration or vain credulity, on the other (n. 67). In the end the Church looks to Mary in hope, for she is the first flowering of what the pilgrim People of God are destined to become.

On balance this chapter steered a judicious middle course between opposing views. Its structure, which places Mary in relation to Christ and the Church, and its insights into her faith continue to shape the Marian tradition, being utilized in every postconciliar magisterial instruction about Mary, such as Paul VI's apostolic exhortation *Marialis Cultus* (On Marian Devotion, 1974) and John Paul II's encyclical *Redemptoris Mater* ("Mother of the Redeemer," 1987).

DOCTRINE

The Church teaches four major doctrines about Mary, two ancient and two modern. Stemming from the patristic period are beliefs in her virginity (before, during, and after the birth of Christ) and divine maternity, the latter summed up in the title Mother of God. The Immaculate Conception (Mary was conceived without original sin) and Assumption (she was taken into heaven body and soul at the end of her life) were officially declared dogmas in the nineteenth and twentieth centuries, respectively.

LITURGY

In every celebration of the Eucharist there is a remembrance of Mary along with the apostles, martyrs, and all the saints. The pilgrim Church joins them in praising God and hopes one day to share their joy before the face of God. Throughout the liturgical year, which begins with the first Sunday of Advent, the Church also honors Mary in differently ranked liturgical celebrations comprised of four solemnities, three feasts, and a number of memorials. The solemnities are Immaculate Conception (December 8), Mary Mother of God (January 1), Annunciation of the Lord (March 25), and Assumption (August 15). The feasts are Presentation of the Lord (February 2), Visitation (May 31), and Birth of Mary (September 8). Memorials include Our Lady of Guadalupe (December 12), Queenship of Mary (August 22), Our Lady of Sorrows (September 15), Our Lady of the Rosary (October 7), Presentation of Mary (November 21), and other optional memorials.

DEVOTION

In addition to liturgical remembrance Catholics honor Mary by prayers and practices, both private and public, such as the rosary, pilgrimages, and veneration of icons. Developing the teaching of Vatican II, Paul VI wrote the apostolic exhortation *Marialis Cultus* in 1974. In it he lays down theological principles and practical guidelines by which the legitimacy of any aspect of Marian devotion may be judged.

The principles stem from basic creedal truths. Honoring Mary should occur within the bounds of a rightly ordered faith and thus not overshadow the one triune God: Father, Son, and Spirit. It should keep clearly in view that Christ alone is the merciful Savior and one Mediator between God and human beings. It should give due recognition to the working of the Holy Spirit in the gift of grace. And it should give expression to the newly recognized connection between Mary and the Church.

The guidelines are drawn from the biblical, liturgical, ecumenical, and anthropological developments endorsed by the council. Honoring Mary should be imbued with the Scriptures, not just a text or symbol here or there but the great biblical themes of salvation history. Since the liturgy is the golden norm of Christian piety, devotion to Mary should harmonize with its spirit, themes, and seasons. Ecumenically, care should be taken lest a wrong impression be given to other Christian churches, even unintentionally, especially with regard to Christ's unique role in salvation. Culturally, practices should cohere with the mores of a people, such as the emergence of women today into all fields of public life. All of these principles and guidelines should be used to judge the adequacy of traditional devotional practices or the formation of new ones.

THEOLOGY

The amount of attention given to the theology of Mary (Mariology) by itself has waned since the council, with Marian themes now integrated into the theologies of Christ and the Church. The central theological image is that of Mary as a woman of faith, preeminent among the disciples, the first of the redeemed in Christ. While not significant on the world stage, her simple human life shows forth the victory of God's grace. Her historical role as the mother of Jesus, while unique, is interpreted through the lens of graced existence, which she shares in solidarity with all the people of God. Only in this way can she be a model, or symbolic embodiment, of the Church.

From the vantage point of systemic poverty, liberation theology builds on this image to interpret Mary as a peasant, village woman, a woman of the people who has particular care for the poor, a point emphasized by John Paul II in *Redemptoris Mater*. In her Magnificat she sang of the liberation coming from God, who puts down the mighty from their thrones and exalts the lowly, fills the hungry with good things but sends the rich away empty (Luke 1:52–53). And she paid the price in suffering: giving birth while homeless, fleeing from a murderous ruler, becoming a refugee in a strange land, being the mother of an unjustly executed son. Criticizing the passivity of the traditional image of Mary held out as a model for women, feminist theology interprets the biblical scenes to highlight her as a free woman, active, courageous, and intelligent, a point emphasized by Paul VI in *Marialis Cultus*. In this view the dogmas of the

Immaculate Conception and Assumption also attest to the goodness of women's human nature, capable of grace and glory.

Ecumenically, in addition to these two Marian dogmas, a main point of contention is the Catholic practice of invoking Mary as well as other saints and asking her to "pray for us." This seems to overshadow Christ as the sole Mediator and historically, in fact, such was the case. Catholics respond that within a rightly ordered faith this is an expression of our solidarity in the communion of saints, analogous to asking other living persons to pray for us. But it persists as an issue where the churches diverge.

For all the cultural, class, gender, and theological differences that are evident in the interpretation of Mary, it remains the case that remembering her, thanking God for her, drawing on her example, and asking for her prayers is an abiding and deeply rooted characteristic of the Catholic community.

See also apparitions of the Blessed Virgin Mary; Assumption of the Blessed Virgin Mary; communion of saints; Immaculate Conception; infancy Gospels; Magnificat; *Marialis Cultus*; Marian devotion; Marian feasts; Mariology; Mediatrix; Mother of God; *Theotokos*.

Bibliography

Anderson, H. George, J. Francis Stafford, and Joseph Burgess, eds. *The One Mediator, the Saints, and Mary.* Minneapolis, MN: Augsburg, 1992.

Brown Raymond, Karl Donfried, Joseph Fitzmyer, and John Reumann, eds. *Mary in the New Testament.* New York: Paulist Press; Philadelphia: Fortress Press, 1978.

Donnelly, Doris, ed. *Mary, Woman of Nazareth.* New York: Paulist Press, 1989.

Gebara, Ivone, and Maria Clara Bingemer. *Mary, Mother of God, Mother of the Poor.* Maryknoll, New York: Orbis Books, 1989.

Graef, Hilda. *Mary, A History of Doctrine and Devotion.* Combined ed. Westminster, MD: Christian Classics, 1985.

ELIZABETH A. JOHNSON

The Blessed Virgin Mary hands a pomegranate to the child Jesus; Renaissance painting by Hans Holbein the Elder (d. 1524), Kunsthistorisches Museum, Vienna.

Maryknoll Sisters (M.M.), a religious order for women founded at Ossining, New York, by Mary Josephine Rogers in 1912. Inspired by the missionary zeal of her Protestant friends at Smith College, Rogers associated herself closely with the work of Father James A. Walsh, a leader in the emerging missionary movement among American Catholics. Father Walsh gathered the first women who would be the nucleus of the Maryknoll Sisters. By 1920 they were officially established as the Foreign Mission Sisters of St. Dominic. Today they are known as the Maryknoll Sisters of St. Dominic. The following year the first group of sisters went to China. In the 1990s they serve in missions in over twenty countries and include over eight hundred members. *See also* Maryknoll.

Mary Magdalene, St. (Magdalene, "of Magdala"), a follower of Jesus. According to Luke 8:2 she was healed of demon possession by Jesus, then was among the women who accompanied and supported Jesus and the twelve apostles. She was present at the Crucifixion (Matt 27:56; Mark 15:40; John 19:25) and was among the women who came to Jesus' tomb on Easter morning (Matt 28:1; Mark 16:1; John 20:1). Matt 28:9–10 and John 20:14–18 record Jesus' appearance to her.

Mary Magdalene, close friend and disciple of Jesus and one of the first and most important witnesses of his Resurrection; painting by Caravaggio (d. 1610), Doria Pamphili Gallery, Rome.

Later traditions erroneously equated Mary with the sinful woman of Luke 7:36–50 who anointed Jesus, and with Mary of Bethany, who also anointed Jesus (John 11:1–12:8; Luke 10:38–42).

Mary Tudor, 1516–58, daughter of Henry VIII and Catherine of Aragon and queen of England from 1553. A devout Catholic, Mary became queen in 1553 after quelling the Protestant plot to place Lady Jane Grey on the throne. Her initial leniency toward Protestants hardened after the Thomas Wyatt plot of 1554. Marrying the Catholic Philip of Spain in 1554, she invited Cardinal Reginald Pole to England to reconcile the country with the papacy. After reinstating heresy laws, executions immediately followed, including those of Thomas Cranmer, Nicholas Ridley, and Hugh Latimer, earning for her the name of "Bloody Mary." The persecutions, along with her inability to have children, her marriage to Philip, and the failure of his campaign against France in 1558 all combined to alienate her from the English people. *See also* England, Catholicism in; Pole, Reginald.

Mas de Vedruna, St. Joaquina de. *See* Joaquina de Vedruna de Mas, St.

Masons. *See* Freemasonry.

Masoretic Text, the received text of the Hebrew Bible used in synagogues, in scholarship, and for most modern translations. The term derives from the Masorah (Heb., *msr*, "hand over, transmit") or notes written in the margins by the Masoretes (medieval Jewish Bible scholars). Through their Masorah and their vocalization and punctuation, they sought to ensure special care in the transmission of the biblical text. The Dead Sea Scrolls from a millennium earlier show both that the biblical text existed in several forms in antiquity and that the consonantal form of the Masoretic Text faithfully preserves one of those forms for each book.

Mass (from the old Lat. dismissal rite, *ite, missa est,* "Go, the Mass is [ended]"), the traditional name for the Eucharist, that is, the celebration of the death and Resurrection of Christ in praise and thanksgiving for all that God has done to save humankind. As early as the second century, there is evidence of a basic structure for this celebration of the Eucharist:

The celebration of Mass at St. Stephen's Church, Anoka, Minnesota; unlike the Gothic churches of the pre–Vatican II era, the architectural layout of this church invites people to worship as a community, with the priest and altar facing everyone in clear view and with the baptismal font and Paschal candle within the sanctuary to underscore the connection between Baptism and the Eucharist.

a service of Scripture readings, psalm prayer and preaching, the people's offering of bread and wine with an improvised prayer of praise and thanksgiving for God's work of salvation, followed by a Communion rite. Each section became more elaborated with the passage of time.

The basic elements of the Mass of the Roman rite today are introductory rite (including the penitential rite), readings and prayers, homily, intercessory prayers, creed (on Sundays and major feasts), presentation of the gifts, Eucharistic Prayer, Communion rite, and dismissal. *See also* Eucharist; Tridentine Mass.

Mass, conventual. *See* conventual Mass.

Mass for the People (Lat., *Missa pro Populo*), Eucharist offered for the intentions of the faithful. Diocesan bishops, pastors, and others with similar responsibilities are obliged to offer Mass for the intentions of the people entrusted to their pastoral care on Sundays and holy days of obligation (cf. cans. 381, 388, 534). *See also* Mass.

Massillon, Jean-Baptiste, 1663–1718, French bishop and renowned preacher. In 1681, he joined the Oratory of St. Philip Neri and quickly earned a reputation for his eloquent and spiritually moving sermons, especially during Lent and at funerals. He became bishop of Clermont in 1718.

Mass of the Catechumens, that part of the Mass that includes the introductory rites and the Liturgy of the Word. After the Liturgy of the Word, the catechumens, those preparing for Baptism, are kindly dismissed from the assembly and go to another place for instruction on the word of God. The baptized remain in the main worship space for the Liturgy of the Eucharist (preparation of the altar and the gifts, Eucharistic Prayer, Communion rite, and closing rite). The catechumens leave the church to physically express their separateness from the body of the baptized and their vigilance and anticipation of baptism at the Easter Vigil, when they will be fully incorporated into the Body of Christ by sharing in the Eucharist for the first time. *See also* Eucharist; Liturgy of the Word.

Mass of the Faithful, the part of the Mass that follows the Liturgy of the Word (Scripture readings, homily, and general intercessions). It extends from the "preparation of the gifts" (bringing of bread and wine to the altar) to the dismissal of the assembly after Communion. Known since Vatican Council II as the Liturgy of the Eucharist, the Mass of the Faithful derived its name from the fact that catechumens were excluded from the most sacred parts of the ritual. Only the baptized (called "the faithful") could be present for the consecration of the bread and wine and for Communion. *See also* Eucharist.

Mass of the Presanctified, the rite used on days when the Mass is not celebrated, but eucharistic bread is distributed. The term itself has not been used in the Roman rite since 1955. Good Friday is the only day in the year when the assembly partakes of the Eucharist reserved from the Mass of the Lord's Supper on Holy Thursday. A similar practice in communities without a priest is called for in the Directory for Sunday Celebrations in the Absence of a Priest (1988), which is open to ongoing theological debate. *See also* Good Friday; Presanctified Liturgy.

Mass stipend, offering given for the celebration of the Eucharist. Canon law has strict regulations controlling every aspect of this custom in order to avoid even the appearance of "trafficking in Masses." The custom has been viewed as one way of providing financial support for ordained ministers. *See also* stipend.

master/mistress of novices, director of formation in men's and women's novitiates. The director is responsible for the spiritual formation of those preparing to profess vows in religious communities (novices). New styles of novitiates have developed since Vatican II (1962–65), but directors remain key to the spiritual vitality of these communities. *See also* novice; novitiate.

master of ceremonies, the liturgical minister charged to assure the reverence and dignity of liturgical rites. The master of ceremonies assists the presider and other ministers prior to and during liturgical rites, particularly the more complex or solemn liturgies.

Master of the Sacred Palace, title given to the priest who functions as personal theologian to the pope. Traditionally, that person is a member of the Dominican order since, it is believed, St. Dominic himself was the first to hold the post. A member of the papal household, the Master also serves as theo-logian to the papal Secretariat of State and other offices in the Roman Curia.

masturbation, self-manipulation of sexual organs for erotic pleasure or to achieve orgasm. Long a taboo topic in Western culture, masturbation was described as the cause of various maladies such as insanity and eye disease. Beginning in the 1940s scientific studies demonstrated the prevalence of incidents of masturbation among men and women. In the 1990s, with certain caveats, masturbation is viewed benignly by the human sciences.

Until recently the Church's hierarchical magisterium and theologians agreed that masturbation is an objective moral evil. To pursue sexual pleasure or orgasm in a manner not associated with marital intercourse that is love-giving and open to the creation of new life violates the will of God and is immoral. Though factors such as the existence of a compulsive habit might mitigate subjective or personal guilt, the act itself is always regarded as wrong. Many Catholics have questioned this understanding. While agreeing that masturbatory activity lacks the interpersonal and procreative dimensions of male-female sexuality, they would propose that there could be circumstances in which masturbation would not be an objectively evil action, for example, for semen testing or in procedures to overcome sterility. Furthermore, they do not view every masturbatory act as a serious matter at all stages of development.

The Church's hierarchical magisterium, in particular the Congregation for the Doctrine of the Faith, has generally responded negatively to such proposals. *See also* chastity; sexual morality.   MICHAEL D. PLACE

Mater et Magistra (mah'tair et mahg-is'trah; Lat., "Mother and Teacher"), "Christianity and Social Progress," encyclical of Pope John XXIII. Issued on May 15, 1961, the seventieth anniversary of Leo XIII's *Rerum Novarum,* the encyclical moved the discussion of state intervention in the economic order to a new level of clarity and development. The pope argued that the role of the state needs to be understood in light of three contemporary factors: the impact of technological change, the rise of the welfare state, and the growing aspirations of people to participate in the political process (nn. 46–50). From the confluence of these elements, John XXIII pointed to the notion of socialization, that is, "the growing interdependence of citizens in society giving rise to various patterns of group life and activity and in many instances to social institutions established on a juridical basis" (n. 59).

The principle of socialization complements the principle of subsidiarity, first articulated in Pope Pius XI's *Quadragesimo Anno* (1931). The latter holds that nothing should be done by a higher agency that can be done as well, if not better, by a lower, subordinate agency (*Mater et Magistra*, n. 53). In U.S. political terms, the principle of subsidiarity supports a policy of leaving to state and local governments and voluntary agencies what otherwise might be taken up by the federal government. The principle of socialization, on the other hand, views state and local governments and voluntary agencies as often incapable by themselves of addressing increasingly complex problems, e.g., health care, that transcend state and local boundaries.

materialism, scientific, a philosophical position asserting that all phenomena (including consciousness) can be explained adequately solely in terms of matter. It denies or is agnostic concerning the existence of spirit and excludes teleology (purpose) from the universe, explaining all reality in terms of deterministic, efficient causality. Although indebted to classical materialism and sixteenth-century philosophy, it gained popularity with eighteenth-century advances in science, especially chemistry, which was able to explain phenomena solely in terms of matter. The assumptions of scientific materialism have become problematic for modern physics. Scientific materialism is incompatible with Catholicism because it denies human freedom and the existence of the supernatural. *See also* grace; supernatural.

Matilda, St., d. 968, widow of German king Henry the Fowler and founder of several Benedictine abbeys. Matilda was known for her liberality during her twenty-three years as wife of the king and during her widowhood. When her son Otto became emperor, he accused his mother of giving state revenues to the poor. Before her death she was vindicated and reconciled with her son. Feast day: March 14.

Matins (ma'tins; Lat., *matutinus,* "morning"), formerly the predawn or night hour of the Liturgy of the Hours. Matins was chanted or recited in choir around midnight, in the first half of the night, or at the end of the night before dawn. The 1971 reform of the Liturgy of the Hours changed the term to the Office of Readings, which may be prayed at any time of the day. The rite begins with an invitation to prayer, followed by a hymn, three psalms with antiphons, a verse, a biblical reading with a responsory, then a reading from the Church Fathers or the lives of the saints, and a responsory. A closing prayer and dismissal conclude the rite. *See also* Liturgy of the Hours.

matrimony. *See* Marriage.

matter, that which is, apart from form. It is the reality underlying all visible things before they are determined to be this kind of thing or that. Although some forms of Christian spirituality have been ambiguous in affirming the value of matter, often overstating the dichotomy between matter and spirit and undervaluing material, fleshly existence, the Church consistently has insisted that God created matter and has excluded movements that attributed a negative value to matter. Such movements include Manichaeism, Gnosticism, Docetism, and Albigensianism (e.g., Lateran IV; Florence). The opposite tendency—materialism—has also been condemned. Although the material world is flawed by sin, it is not intrinsically corrupted. Its initial state was paradisaical, and it will be perfected again in the end (Rev 21:1). Many central Catholic doctrines affirm the goodness of matter: creation *ex nihilo;* the Incarnation; Catholicism's sacramental view of reality, which asserts that God touches human lives through created things; the Resurrection and Ascension of Christ; the resurrection of the body. The history of the Catholic theology of matter reveals syntheses with different schools of thought: from the Neoplatonic influence in the patristic period, to Thomas Aquinas's adaptation of Aristotle's doctrine of hylomorphism. Such syntheses continue today, with ongoing efforts to incorporate the insights of evolutionary thought and modern physics into a theology of matter. *See also* creation; hylomorphism.

matter of a sacrament. *See* sacrament, matter of a.

Matthew, St., traditional author of the Gospel bearing his name, probably because the call of the tax collector Levi in Mark 2:14 and Luke 5:27–28 becomes the call of Matthew in Matt 9:9, who is also referred to as "the tax collector" in Matt 10:3. Also in the account of the dinner that follows, Mark 2:15 and Luke 5:29 specify its location in "his" (Levi's) house, while Matt 9:10 seems to presuppose knowl-

Matthew, one of the twelve apostles and the Evangelist traditionally regarded as the author of the First Gospel, whose message is that in Jesus Christ the reign, or kingdom, of God has drawn near and will remain with the Church until the end of time; illustration in the early ninth-century *Evangelarium* (Gospel book) *of Charlemagne.*

edge of the story by simply saying "in the house." The name occurs in all lists of the Twelve (Matt 10:3; Mark 3:18; Luke 6:15; Acts 1:13), while Levi does not, but only Matthew's Gospel associates the name with the call of a tax collector. Matthew and Levi may be two names for the same person, in which case Matthew is son of Alphaeus and brother of the other James (not the son of Zebedee), or two different people confused in the traditions. The second-century scholar Papias first mentions Matthew as a collector of sayings of the Lord written in Hebrew and translated by others into Greek. This has given rise to the modern search for a Hebrew original of Matthew's Gospel. However, it is highly unlikely that the present Gospel of Matthew is either such a translation or the product of a Galilean tax collector; it is more probably the work of an educated Hellenistic Jew well versed in rabbinic scholarship. *See also* apostle; evangelist; gospel.

Matthew of Aquasparta, ca. 1238–1302, regent master of theology at the University of Paris (1277–79), minister general of the Franciscan order (1287–79), adviser to popes, and cardinal (beginning in 1288). A prolific author, his works include a commentary on the *Sentences* of Peter Lombard, numerous sermons, and a number of disputed questions on a wide range of topics.

Matthew Paris, ca. 1199–1259, Benedictine monk, historian, chronicler, hagiographer, poet, and ecclesiastical critic. His major work, the *Chronica Maiora,* is a history in Latin of the world from creation to 1259; he also wrote several saints' lives in French verse.

Matthias, St., the apostle chosen to replace Judas. Acts 1:15–26 recounts the selection process. Peter addressed the brethren assembled in Jerusalem. He stipulated that Judas's replacement should be an eyewitness of Jesus from the time of the baptism by John. Two candidates were put forward, Joseph Barsabbas, also called Justus, and Matthias. After the disciples prayed, they cast lots and the choice fell to Matthias.

Nothing certain is known of the apostolic activity of Matthias. Eusebius (*Ecclesiastical History* 1.12.3) reports that he was one of the seventy disciples (Luke 10:1), but this is probably an inference from the NT. The apocryphal *Acts of Andrew and Matthias* tells an imaginative tale of Matthias's mission to a nation of cannibals where he was taken prisoner and then rescued by Andrew. The story is preserved in Latin by Gregory of Tours as a preface to his version of the *Acts of Andrew* and in an Anglo-Saxon poem "Andreas" attributed to Cynewulf. Whether it belonged to the original *Acts of Andrew* is disputed.

A *Gospel According to Matthias* is mentioned by Origen (*Homily in Luke* 1) and Eusebius (*Eccl. Hist.* 3.25.6) and condemned in the sixth-century Gelasian Decree (3.1). Clement of Alexandria (*Stromata* 2.9.45.4; 3.4.26.3; 7.13.82.1) cites the *Traditions of Matthias,* which is probably a separate work. According to Hippolytus (*Refutation* 7.20.1), the Basilidian Gnostics appealed to secret traditions handed down from Matthias to support their doctrine.

Matthias supposedly suffered martyrdom either at Colchis or in Jerusalem. His relics are venerated in St. Matthias's Abbey in Trier. Feast day: May 14. *See also* apostle; *Decretum Gelasianum;* Twelve, the.

HAROLD W. ATTRIDGE

Maundy Thursday. *See* Holy Thursday.

Maurice, St., 1114–91, French Benedictine abbot of Carnoet. He joined the Cistercian monks and was elected abbot soon after his profession. Feast day: October 13. There is an Armenian martyr of the fourth century with the same name.

Maurin, Peter [Pierre Aristide], 1877–1949, philosopher, teacher, and cofounder of the Catholic Worker movement. Maurin, a French peasant, left the Christian Brothers, a religious community of men, and joined Le Sillon, a lay movement whose goal was to Christianize modern democracy. To escape the draft in France, he emigrated to Canada in 1909. These experiences helped Maurin to form his philosophy of Christian personalism, a philosophical orientation that stresses the value and dignity of each individual human person. He proclaimed this philosophy in his "easy essays." In 1932 he sought out Dorothy Day (d. 1980) and together they founded the Catholic Worker movement. *See also* Catholic Worker movement; Day, Dorothy M.; pacifism; personalism, Christian.

Maurists, Benedictine monks of the Congregation of St. Maur, founded in 1621 and part of a French reform movement dedicated to strict observance of the rule, education, preaching, and historical scholarship. Maurist scholars such as Jean Mabillon (d. 1707) and Edmond Martène (d. 1739) studied the history of the Benedictines as well as works of the Fathers, monuments of the Church, and asceticism, making great advances in the field of manuscript studies and the related sciences of paleography and numismatics. Suppressed by the French Revolution in 1790, the Congregation was formally dissolved by Pope Pius VII in 1818. *See also* Mabillon, Jean.

Maurus, St., sixth-century monk and patron saint of coppersmiths. A member of the monastic community at Monte Cassino under Benedict of Nursia, Maurus is said to have rescued a boy named Placid from drowning by walking on the water. The Benedictines celebrate the feast of Maurus and Placid on October 5 (formerly January 15).

Maximus IV Sayegh, 1878–1967, Melkite Catholic patriarch (1947–67) and cardinal (1965), one of the most quoted council fathers of Vatican II (1962–65). From the start of the council the content and élan of his interventions gave import to the Eastern Catholic minority at the council. At the first session, Maximus's opening speech on October 23, 1962, set the tone for the Melkite criticism of the restricted Latin vision of the Church. He refused to speak in Latin, which was, he insisted, the language of the Latin church, but not of his church nor of the Catholic Church. He refused to follow protocol and ad-

Maximus IV Sayegh, the leader of the Eastern Catholic minority at the Second Vatican Council (1962-65), who reminded the Latin-rite majority that the Catholic Church is larger than the Roman Catholic Church.

dress "their Eminences," the cardinals, before "their Beatitudes," the Eastern patriarchs. In his ecclesiology, patriarchs, the heads of local churches, did not rank behind cardinals, whom he considered to be second-rank dignitaries of one "local church," the Latin church. He also urged the West to allow the vernacular in the liturgy, following the lead of the East, "where," he said, "every language is, in effect, liturgical." He concluded that the matter of the use of the vernacular should be left to the local churches to decide. *See also* Eastern Catholics and Rome; Eastern Catholics and Vatican II.

Maximus, "the Confessor," St., ca. 580–662, Byzantine theologian. During a peripatetic life divided between Palestine (perhaps), Constantinople, Carthage, Rome and sites of exile, he became a defender and developer of the Chalcedonian tradition against Monenergism and Monothelitism, two Christological heresies that effectively denied the full humanity of Christ but were imperially favored compromises with the powerful Monophysite community that continued to hold that in Christ there is only one divine nature.

Maximus was critically and creatively appreciative of controversial expressions of Christian theology. In his hands, the legacies of Origen, Evagrius of Pontus, the Cappadocian Fathers, and Denys the Areopagite had their *ambigua* (Lat., "ambiguities") addressed, their difficulties eased or corrected, and their theological contributions anchored within the Church's developing doctrinal heritage. His own vision was at once cosmic and Christocentric, with God's purpose the unification of all creation in loving communion. For fallen humanity this goal required the incarnation of the Word of God, so that in Christ the human will could act freely and fully in harmony with the divine. The Christian's participation in the reunification thus begun had, in Maximus's view, ascetic consequences and an ecstatic character. His work was honored especially in Eastern monastic circles, which favored his preferred literary device: the "century," a hundred terse paragraphs written as much to invite the reader's contemplation as to develop a sustained argument. Despite their elusiveness, his works have been increasingly recognized in recent decades in the West for the power and range of their synthesis. Feast day: August 13 (West), January 21 and August 13 (East). *See also* Christology; Monenergism; Monothelitism.   KATHRYN JOHNSON

Mayne, St. Cuthbert, 1544–77, one of the Forty Martyrs of England and Wales canonized in 1970. Raised a Protestant, he was ordained at Douai in 1575 and sent as a missionary to Cornwall; he was executed in 1577. Feast day: November 29. *See also* Forty Martyrs of England and Wales.

Maynooth College, also known as St. Patrick's College, the principal Catholic seminary in Ireland, located at Maynooth, County Kildare, fifteen miles northwest of Dublin. Maynooth was established in 1795 by the Irish Parliament at the urging of the Catholic bishops and English prime minister William Pitt. Although funded by the government, it quickly became a center for Irish nationalism. Maynooth professors were also known as rigorists in theological matters. The college remained financially insecure until 1845 when Prime Minister Robert Peel arranged for its annual grant to be trebled. While most Maynooth graduates have worked in Ireland, a considerable number have served in England, the United States, and Third World countries. In 1966 a college for lay students was established.

Mazarin, Jules, 1602–61, cardinal and prime minister of France (1643–61). An Italian, he continued the work of Richelieu in building the French state, putting France's interests before those of the Church or the papacy. He was tolerant of Protestants for political reasons, but agreed to measures against the Jansenists, moral rigorists at odds with the French hierarchy.

Mazzarello, St. Maria, 1832–81, Italian nun. As a girl, Maria belonged to the Pious Union of Daughters of Mary Immaculate. With the help of John Bosco, Maria became the first superior general of the Daughters of Our Lady Help of Christians (Salesian Sisters), a congregation devoted to the education of poor girls. Feast day: May 14.

Mazzuchelli, Samuel, 1806–64, Dominican missionary. A native of Milan, Italy, he came to the United States as a missionary in 1828. The young Dominican completed his studies for the priesthood and was ordained in Cincinnati, Ohio, in 1830. His first mission covered the territory of the Upper Peninsula of Michigan and northeastern Wisconsin. He built the first Catholic church in Wisconsin (Green Bay), established a school for the Memoninee Indians, and compiled for the Winnebago people a prayer book in their own dialect. From 1835 until his death, he labored in the lead-mining region of the Upper Mississippi Valley. He served as chaplain for Wisconsin's first territorial legislature, designed and directed the construction of numerous churches and public buildings, established Sinsinawa Mound College (1846), and founded the Sinsinawa Dominican Sisters (1847). Mazzuchelli wrote an account of his missionary activities, *Memoirs* (1844). He died in Benton, Wisconsin, while ministering to the sick. *See also* Sisters of St. Dominic.

McAuley, Catherine, 1778–1841, founder of the Sisters of Mercy. Born in Dublin, she established a House of Mercy for the poor in Dublin in 1827, and, with encouragement from the local archbishop, founded a religious community in 1831 to serve the poor, the sick, and the distressed. She was declared Venerable by Pope John Paul II in 1990. *See also* Sisters of Mercy; Warde, Frances.

McAvoy, Thomas Timothy, 1903–69, priest of

the Congregation of Holy Cross, historian, and archivist. A professor at the University of Notre Dame and a prolific author, McAvoy made the study of American Catholic history a viable and respected scholarly field. His major work, *The Great Crisis in American Catholic History, 1895–1900*, examined the issue of Americanism. *See also* Americanism.

McBrien, Richard P., b. 1936, ecclesiologist. Ordained for the archdiocese of Hartford, Connecticut (1962), he received a doctorate in theology from Gregorian University, Rome (1967). He has been professor at Pope John XXIII National Seminary, Weston, Massachusetts (1965–70), professor of theology (1970–80) and director of the Institute of Religious Education and Pastoral Ministry at Boston College (1975–80), and chair of the department of theology at the University of Notre Dame (1980–91). Since 1980 he has been Crowley-O'Brien-Walter Professor at Notre Dame. He is the author of fifteen books, including *Catholicism* (1980, 1994), and general editor of this volume. Past president of the Catholic Theological Society of America (1973–74), he received its John Courtney Murray award in 1976.

McCloskey, John, 1810–85, cardinal-archbishop, the first U.S. cardinal. He attended Mount St. Mary's Seminary, Emmitsburg, Maryland, and was ordained in 1834. After studies in Rome (1835–37), he was assigned to ministry in and around New York City. He was appointed coadjutor bishop of New York (1844), bishop of Albany (1847), and archbishop of New York (1864). His years as archbishop were marked by institutional growth of the Catholic community as symbolized by the construction of St. Patrick's Cathedral, dedicated in 1879. He was promoted to cardinal (1875), the first American so honored. *See also* Saint Patrick's Cathedral.

McCormick, Richard Arthur, b. 1922, Jesuit priest and one of the Church's leading moral theologians. McCormick entered the Society of Jesus in 1940, was ordained in 1953, and received his S.T.D. in 1957 from the Gregorian University in Rome. Since 1986 he has been John A. O'Brien Professor of Christian Ethics at the University of Notre Dame. He is the author of many books and articles on moral theology and medical ethics, including the award-winning *The Critical Calling: Moral Dilemmas Since Vatican II* (1989) and the widely read "Notes on Moral Theology," which appeared for twenty-two years in *Theological Studies*. Past president of the

Catholic Theological Society of America (1969–70), he received its Cardinal Spellman Award in 1969.

McGlynn, Edward, 1837–1900, priest and social reformer. Born in New York City and trained in Rome, McGlynn became an activist and renowned advocate for social and economic reform, ultimately as a proponent of Henry George's tax theory as a means of achieving economic democracy. In 1886 he was suspended by his archbishop, Michael A. Corrigan, for his ideological support of George. Ultimately excommunicated by Rome, McGlynn continued his national influence through the Anti-Poverty Society, which he cofounded in 1887. In 1892 he was restored to the priesthood by the pope's special delegate, who found nothing in McGlynn's teaching contrary to Church doctrine. He served his last years in Newburgh, New York.

McKenzie, John L., 1910–91, OT scholar and one of the most significant figures in the biblical renewal both before and after Vatican II (1962–65), especially through *The Two Edged Sword: An Interpretation of the Old Testament* (1956). He entered the Jesuits in 1928, was ordained in 1939, and left the Jesuits and was incardinated in the diocese of Madison, Wisconsin in 1974. He taught at West Baden College, a Jesuit theologate in Indiana, (1942–60), Loyola University, Chicago (1960–65), the University of Notre Dame (1966–70), and De Paul University (1970–78).

McManus, Frederick R., b. 1923, liturgical scholar and priest of the archdiocese of Boston. Ordained in 1947, he has been professor of canon law at The Catholic University of America since 1958 and a major contributor to the field of liturgical law. A member of the Liturgy Commission at Vatican II, he was a founding member of the Advisory Committee of the International Commission on English in the Liturgy (ICEL). He has served as editor and contributor to scholarly journals and has received several honorory degrees, awards, and appointments.

McQuaid, Bernard John, 1823–1909, bishop. Raised by the Sisters of Charity at St. Patrick's Orphanage and ordained in 1848, he became rector (1853) of the cathedral in the diocese of Newark, New Jersey. He founded the state's first parochial school and Seton Hall College and Seminary, where he served as president (1856–68). As the first bishop of Rochester, New York, he created an extensive parochial school system and established St. Andrew's Preparatory Seminary (1870) and St. Bernard's Seminary (1893). During the Americanist crisis he led, along with Archbishop Michael Corrigan, the conservative faction of U.S. bishops who were opposed to the accommodation of Christian faith to American culture. *See also* Americanism.

Mechthild of Hackeborn, St., 1241–ca. 1299, German nun and mystic. As teacher, choir director, and assistant to her sister Gertrude, abbess of Helfta, Mechtilde contributed to the monastery's development as a center of spirituality. Mechtilde's spiritual vision, including devotion to the Sacred Heart, spread beyond Helfta through the dispersion of Gertrude the Great's account of her life in *The Book of Special Grace (Liber Specialis Gratiae).* Feast day: November 16.

Mechthild of Magdeburg, St., 1212–ca. 1282, Beguine and later nun at the great convent of Helfta. Her *Flowing Light of the Divinity,* which describes her many visions and religious experience, is important as one of the earliest treatises on the spiritual life in the vernacular (low German, subsequently translated into high German and Latin). Feast day: November 19. *See also* Beghards/Beguines.

medals, small disks of various shapes, usually made of metal, worn on a neck chain either under or outside the clothing or as a lapel pin. Such medals can depict either a figure of divinity (most commonly Christ or the dove of the Holy Spirit), Mary, or one of the saints, usually including either a pious phrase or Christian symbols.

Medellín (med-ay-een'), a city in Colombia, location of the Second General Conference of Latin American Bishops (CELAM, the acronym for *Conferencia Episcopal Latinoamericana*) in September 1968. Medellín has become almost synonymous with that conference and its documents. CELAM II sought to relate the teachings of the Second Vatican Council to the Church's life and mission in Latin America. It adopted the notion of liberation in its discussion of injustice and criticized both the inequality among Latin America's social classes and the economic policies of "First World" nations. While urging that the poor not become violent in their struggle for justice, it also recognized the "institutional violence" of political-economic systems. CELAM II called for the Church to stand in solidari-

ty with the poor. The documents are available in *The Church in the Present-Day Transformation of Latin America in the Light of the Council* (Washington, DC: United States Catholic Conference, 1973). *See also* Latin America, Catholicism in; liberation theology.

media. *See* Catholicism and mass media.

mediator (Lat., *medius,* "in the middle"), one who acts as a liaison between different parties or who attempts to reconcile contending groups. Though there is no corresponding Hebrew term, the idea is strong in the OT. Priests are mediators between the holy God and profane human life, and bring offerings before God (Deut 26:1–4). Moses acts as mediator when he speaks on behalf of God (Exod 4:21–23), delivers the law from Sinai (Exod 19:16–25), or intercedes for the sinful people (Exod 32:30–34). The prophets are mediators of God's word (Isa 6:6–13; Jer 1:6–9; Ezek 3:1–11). The term appears six times in the NT, twice in the context of the Jewish law delivered through a mediator (Gal 3:19–20), and in the important creedal statement of 1 Tim 2:5, "For there is one God; there is also one mediator between God and humankind, Christ Jesus, himself human, who gave himself a ransom for all." In Heb 12:24 (see 8:6; 9:15), Jesus as priest and victim is "the mediator of a new covenant."

Mediator Dei (Lat., "Mediator of God"), an encyclical letter on the liturgy issued by Pope Pius XII on November 20, 1947. This encyclical was the third in a remarkable series of documents through which Pius XII laid the groundwork for the eventual reform and renewal of church life in the areas of ecclesiology (*Mystici Corporis,* 1943), biblical studies (*Divino Afflante Spiritu,* 1943), and worship. *Mediator Dei* contains four principal parts. Part I deals with the nature, sources, and evolution of the liturgy. Part II includes a detailed discussion of the Eucharist and encourages fuller participation by the faithful in its celebration. Part III focuses on the Liturgy of the Hours (Divine Office) and the church year, while Part IV contains a series of pastoral directives. In spite of its sometimes cautious tone, *Mediator Dei* gave, in effect, papal approval to the liturgical movement that had begun in Europe a century earlier, especially in the pioneering work of liturgists like Prosper Guéranger (1805–75) of the Benedictine abbey of Solesmes. As the first papal encyclical ever devoted entirely to the topic of worship, *Mediator Dei* inaugurated a new period of liturgical history in the Catholic Church. Prior to this time, papal documents focused primarily on educating people about the liturgy's rites and symbols. But *Mediator Dei* established a pastoral and theological basis for reforming the liturgy. Indeed, such reforms began appearing just four years later, when Pope Pius XII restored the Easter Vigil (February 9, 1951). *See also* liturgical movement.

Mediatrix (mee-dee-ay'triks; Lat., *medius,* "in the middle"), a title popularly applied to Mary in recognition of her role in salvation. First used in the eighth century, it became a more common designation for Mary by Catholics by the seventeenth century. In traditional Mariology, Mary was regarded as the Mediatrix for three reasons. First, because of the specific holy acts she performed during her life, Mary was regarded as the Coredemptrix (Lat.) who cooperated with the plan of God. Second, through her continual intercessions, Mary was seen as the dispensatrix (Lat.) who distributed and applied the graces of Christ. Finally, Mary's ontological mediation was perceived to be rooted in her divine motherhood and the fullness of grace she possessed from the moment of her conception.

The Second Vatican Council (1962–65) noted, however, that Mary's role in humanity's salvation is entirely subordinate to that of Christ, who is "the one Mediator" for all (Dogmatic Constitution on the Church, n. 62). *See also* Mary, Blessed Virgin.

medical ethics, the recognition, classification, justification, and assimilation of the value dimensions in the practice of medicine. These dimensions include the virtues of the medical professional, as well as the rights and wrongs of acts and practices.

Only in the twentieth century did truly systematic Catholic treatises on medical ethics appear. Included in this group would be Charles McFadden's *Medical Ethics,* Gerald Kelly's *Medico-Moral Problems,* Thomas O'Donnell's *Morals in Medicine,* and Edwin Healy's *Medical Ethics.* The approach of these authors built heavily on the moral theology textbooks used at the time. Most of the subjects covered related to either the Decalogue (Ten Commandments) or the sacraments.

In 1969 Daniel Callahan and psychiatrist Willard Gaylin founded the Institute of Society, Ethics, and the Life Sciences, now known as The Hastings Center, in New York State. In 1971 André Hellegers founded the Joseph and Rose Kennedy Institute for the Study of Human Reproduction and Bioethics,

now known as The Kennedy Institute of Ethics, in Washington, D.C. These sister institutes brought together theologians, philosophers, physicians, lawyers, and nurses for the sustained and systematic study of medical ethics. They were the precursors of other such centers around the world and have given shape and impetus to research and reflection in the Catholic community. *See also* bioethics.

Medical Mission Sisters (M.M.S.), a congregation of female medical personnel founded in 1925 in Washington, D.C., initially to care for Muslim women in India. Anna Dengel, an Austrian woman who studied medicine, was frustrated when sisters were prohibited by canon law from helping her in surgery and obstetrics. With the encouragement of missionary bishops, she founded the congregation and was instrumental in obtaining a change in canon law so that her sisters could practice medicine in its full scope. In 1993 there were about seven hundred sisters, two hundred and eighty from India, working in India, the United States, Africa, Asia, and Latin America, engaged in healing ministries that include agricultural and community development, the empowerment of women, and the support of Islamic peoples, as well as medical ministries. The generalate is in London.

Medical Missionaries of Mary (M.M.M.), a congregation founded in Ireland in 1937 by an Irish woman, Mary Martin, to provide medical care, particularly for women and children. Fortunately, Vatican restrictions on medical training for sisters had just been lifted. Clinics, general and maternity hospitals, and leprosaria were established. The emphasis today is on primary health care, nurses' training, and the care of AIDS patients. In 1993 this international community of more than four hundred members from thirteen countries works in Nigeria, Liberia, Kenya, Tanzania, Uganda, Malawi, Angola, Ethiopia, Sudan, Brazil, and the United States. About one-sixth of the members are African. The motherhouse is in Drogheda, Ireland.

Medina, Bartolomeo (meh-deen'uh, bahr-toh-loh-may'oh), 1527–80, Spanish Dominican theologian. In a commentary on Thomas Aquinas in 1577, he was the first to propose probabilism by holding that, when two opinions concerning the moral licitness of an action are both probable, the one less probable may be followed if it is held by wise theologians and supported by good arguments. *See also* probabilism.

meditation, mental prayer of surrendered silence and listening. Discursive meditation, thinking about religious material, Scripture, or devotional reading, is a beginner's technique. *Lectio divina* (Lat., "divine reading") may be practiced discursively. Pure meditation involves abandoning discursive thought for simple awareness. It has two major characteristics: sustained attention to its object and bright, clear awareness. Meditation has two basic forms: concentration and awareness.

Concentration practice, an imaging technique, holds attention on a single chosen object. One gently returns to the object whenever the mind wanders. The object can be mental, visual, or auditory, such as a sacred word, an icon, or a chant. Concentration practice produces great serenity and gradually transforms the mind into its object. It is used in centering prayer techniques. One must avoid falling into a comfortably foggy state that is relaxing but abandons clarity.

In awareness practice, a nonimaging technique, one tries to maintain continuous, alert attentiveness to all one's experiences. One must not "tune out" repetitious experiences or lose clear focus, and one must neither reject nor encourage any particular experience. This practice may bring unfinished psychological business into awareness; suitable techniques safely manage this eruption. Awareness practice purifies the mind of contents incompatible with experiencing God. This form is found in Christian *vipassana* (Pali, "insight") practice.

At heart, meditation is a spiritual practice to bring one to union with God. However, it may also produce medical and psychological benefits, such as reduced heart rate and blood pressure, more restful sleep, less emotional turmoil, greater ability to concentrate, and improved self-control. *See also* prayer.   MARY J. MEADOW

Medjugorje (med-joo-gaw'ree), a village in the Catholic Croatian region of what was formerly Yugoslavia. On June 24, 1981, six Croatian youths reported a vision of the Blessed Virgin Mary. Since then the apparitions have allegedly continued both at the original site and at the village church of St. James. The visionaries claim to have seen, heard, and touched Mary and to have been given ten secret messages related to world events. Mary has called for greater faith, prayer, penance, fasting, and personal conversion.

Although no official judgment has been made regarding the authenticity of the apparitions, some bishops have spoken favorably about the new devotion, and in 1986 John Paul II approved travel to Medjugorje for prayer, fasting, and conversion. By contrast, the local bishop, Pavao Zanic, dismissed the apparitions as a case of "collective hallucination" and accused the Franciscans of exploiting the situation for self-interest. By the early 1990s, however, pilgrimages to Medjugorje began to compete in popularity with those to Lourdes and Fátima, even though a violent civil war in the area disrupted the flow of visitors. *See also* apparitions of the Blessed Virgin Mary.

Meinrad, St., d. 861, a Benedictine priest, renowned for his holiness, who taught near Zurich and later assumed the life of a hermit. An abbey in Einsiedeln, Switzerland, stands on the site of his last hermitage. Feast day: January 21.

Mekhitarists, or Mechitarists, the name for Armenian Catholic monks in two congregations, of Venice and Vienna, following a rule modeled on that of St. Benedict. The order was founded at Constantinople in 1701 by the monk Mekhitar (1676–1749) (Arm., *Mxit'ar*, "Consoler," "Paraclete"), an Armenian Orthodox vadarpet (priest-monk with the honorary title "doctor"). In 1702 he transferred the congregation to Morea in the Peloponnesus, then under Venetian rule, and in 1717 to the Island of San Lazzaro in Venice. A promoter of church unity, it seems that Mekhitar considered himself in communion with both the Armenian Orthodox and Catholic churches, and apparently he and his monks became exclusively Catholic only after moving to the Catholic Venetian dominions. In 1772 dissensions caused a split, with some monks breaking off to found a separate congregation, centered in Vienna since 1809. The scholarship and publications of the Mekhitarists have rendered an enormous service to the cultural renaissance of the Armenian nation. *See also* monasticism.

Mel, St., d. ca. 488, first abbot-bishop of Ardagh, in Ireland. He is reputedly one of the four missionary-nephews of St. Patrick. Feast day: February 6.

Melanchthon, Philipp (meh-lank'tuhn), 1497–1560, Lutheran theologian and Reformer. Called to teach Greek at Wittenberg in 1518, he became Luther's follower and by 1521 had produced the first comprehensive statement of Reformation theology, the *Loci Communes Rerum Theologicarum* (which he reedited in 1535, 1544, and 1559). He also composed the Augsburg Confession (1530) and its Apology (1531) against the Catholic *Confutation* (1530), which remain to this day the central Lutheran confessions. Melanchthon's irenic personality and clarity of thought and expression suited him well for this work—he attended or submitted opinions for every major colloquy attended by the Lutherans—but made him less able to handle situations of leadership and conflict. Although others suspected his resolve, he never lost the trust and deep affection of Luther. When Luther died in 1546, Melanchthon naturally emerged as the leader of the Lutheran Reformation, but he quickly undermined his influence by his response to the Augsburg Interim (1548) after the defeat of the Protestants in the Schmalkaldic War (1545–46), allowing for the reimposition of Catholic ceremonies by the emperor as matters of indifference (Gk., *adiaphora*). Other controversies erupted concerning the Lord's Supper, justification, good works, election, and free will, bringing pain and sadness to his later years from "the rage of theologians." *See also* Lutheranism; Protestantism; Reformation, the.

Melania, "the Elder," St., ca. 342–ca. 410, and Melania, "the Younger," St., ca. 383–ca. 439, ascetics; among the wealthy Roman matrons who shared the fourth century's explosion of interest in ascetic life and the sites of the Bible and so, with prominent churchmen as advisers and friends, left the structures of aristocratic family life to travel among holy figures and settle in the Holy Land. "The Elder," widowed young, visited Egyptian saints before founding a double monastery with Rufinus on the Mount of Olives. Her granddaughter, "the Younger," entered ascetic life with her husband; together, they distributed their own wealth as they founded monasteries at Augustine's home at Tagaste in North Africa and then entered monastic communities in Bethlehem with Jerome. When widowed, Melania "the Younger" established another monastery in Jerusalem. Feast days: Melania, "the Elder," June 8; Melania, "the Younger," December 31.

Melchizedek (mel-ki'zed-ek), a Canaanite priest-king, whose name means "My king is Zedek" (a Canaanite deity). According to Gen 14:18–20, Melchizedek, the king of Salem and priest of God Most High (El Elyon), blessed Abram after his victory over a coalition of four kings. Ps 110:4 cites Melchizedek as the model for the Davidic king. In the NT, the Letter to the Hebrews (7:1–28) interprets both OT texts and finds in Melchizedek a model of Christ, the High Priest of the new covenant. Later exegetical traditions found in Melchizedek's offer of bread and wine to Abram a foreshadowing of the Eucharist. In fact, he is mentioned explicitly in Eucharistic Prayer I (the old Roman Canon of the Mass).

Melitian Schisms. *See* Melitius of Antioch, St.; Melitius of Lycopolis.

Melitius of Antioch, St., d. 381, originally bishop of Sebaste, then, from 360 to 381, of Antioch. His orthodoxy, the cause of his being thrice exiled from Antioch, was suspect to another group of orthodox, old partisans of Eustathius, bishop of Antioch deposed by the Arians ca. 327. Lucifer of Cagliari (d. ca. 370) ordained one Paulinus for them, thus initiating the schism, sometimes called Melitian, at Antioch. Melitius presided over the Council of Constantinople until his death. Supported unwaveringly by Basil, but not by Athanasius or the West, Melitius was vindicated when the Eustathian party recognized his successor. Feast day: February 12. *See also* Arianism; Nicaea, First Council of.

Melitius of Lycopolis, d. early fourth century, schismatic bishop of Lycopolis in Egypt. He opposed the leniency of Peter of Alexandria (bishop 300–11) toward Christians lapsed under persecution. He began to ordain bishops schismatically, was deposed by an Egyptian council (ca. 306), but continued in schism even after the martyrdom of Peter. The Council of Nicaea (325) attempted reconciliation, but this failed when, with Arian encouragement, the Melitians opposed Athanasius's election (328) and the renewed schism persisted for several centuries. This "Melitian Schism" is to be distinguished from that associated with Melitius of Antioch. *See also* lapsi; Nicaea, First Council of.

Melito of Sardis, St., d. ca. 190, bishop of Sardis and prolific writer. He traveled in Palestine and was a Quartodeciman, i.e., he celebrated Easter on the fourteenth of Nisan, date of the Jewish Passover. His writings, which include "On the Pasch," may have influenced Irenaeus, Tertullian, Clement of Alexandria, and Origen. Feast day: April 1. *See also* Quarto-decimans.

Melkite Catholic Church, the Byzantine Catholic counterpart to the Orthodox patriarchate of Antioch, concentrated in Lebanon and Syria. Other Byzantine Catholic communities within the boundaries of the Orthodox patriarchates of Jerusalem and Alexandria are also included in this church.

Origin and Early History: The word "Melkite" comes from the Syriac and Arabic words for king and was used to refer to those in the Middle East who shared the Christological faith professed by the Byzantine emperor in accord with the Council of Chalcedon (451), as opposed to those who did not accept the Chalcedonian definition.

While there was little opposition to Chalcedon in the Jerusalem patriarchate, only a minority accepted it in Alexandria (those opposed gave rise to the Coptic Orthodox Church) and about half accepted it in Antioch (those contrary evolved into the "Jacobite" or Syrian Orthodox Church). The Chalcedonian Orthodox patriarchates of Antioch, Jerusalem, and Alexandria gradually adopted the Byzantine liturgical tradition of Constantinople.

Jesuits, Capuchins, and Carmelites had been engaged in missionary activity among the faithful of the Orthodox patriarchate of Antioch since the mid-seventeenth century. Although a number of these (including some bishops) formally become Catholic, by and large they remained mixed with Orthodox communities. Strictly speaking, the Melkite Catholic Church originated in a schism that took place within the patriarchate of Antioch in the early eighteenth century. This division was exacerbated by a rivalry between the cities of Aleppo and Damascus.

Patriarch Athanasios III Debbas, who died on August 5, 1724, had designated as his successor a Cypriot monk named Sylvester. His candidacy was supported by the Aleppo party and the Constantinople patriarchate. But on September 20, 1724, the Damascene party elected as patriarch a strongly pro-Catholic man who took the name Cyril VI. A week later, the patriarch of Constantinople ordained Sylvester as patriarch of Antioch. The Ottoman government recognized Sylvester, while Cyril was deposed and excommunicated by Constantinople and compelled to seek refuge in Lebanon.

In 1729 Cyril's election as patriarch of Antioch was recognized as valid by Pope Benedict XIII. But it was only in 1744 that Cyril was given the pallium, a woolen vestment worn around the neck, as a sign of full communion with Rome.

In the beginning this new Catholic community was limited to what is now Syria and Lebanon. But later Melkite Catholics began to immigrate to Palestine and especially to Egypt after that country rebelled against Turkish control. For this reason the Melkite Catholic patriarch was given the additional personal titles of patriarch of Jerusalem and Alexandria in 1838.

At first the Ottoman government had been very hostile to this new church and took strong measures against it. But conditions improved with the passage of time. In 1848 the government formally recognized the Melkite Catholic Church, and the patriarchate itself was moved to Damascus from Holy Savior Monastery near Sidon, Lebanon, where it had been established by Cyril VI after he fled there. This was followed by a period of growth, enhanced by the popular perception that the Melkite Church was becoming a focus of Arab resistance against the Turks. The Orthodox patriarchate of Antioch, on the other hand, was viewed by many as dependent upon Constantinople and therefore upon the Ottoman government.

In the nineteenth century the Melkite Church experienced tensions in its relationship with Rome because many Melkites felt that their Byzantine identity was being threatened by those who favored greater integration into the Roman Catholic Church. This uneasiness was symbolized at Vatican I (1869–70) when Melkite patriarch Gregory II Youssef voted against the constitution *Pastor Aeternus,* which defined papal infallibility and universal jurisdiction.

Vatican II to Today: At the Second Vatican Council (1962–65), Melkite patriarch Maximus IV Sayegh spoke forcefully against the latinization of the Eastern Catholic churches and urged a greater receptivity to the oriental Christian traditions, especially in the area of ecclesiology. Some Melkite bishops, including Patriarch Maximus IV, have supported the idea that, in the event of a reconciliation between the Catholic and Orthodox churches, their church should be reintegrated into the Orthodox patriarchate of Antioch.

Today there are five Melkite Catholic male religious orders, all of them with headquarters in Lebanon. Three of them are of monastic origin but later became involved in active ministry: the Basilian Order of the Most Holy Saviour (Salvatorians) was founded in 1683, the Basilian Order of Saint John the Baptist (Saorites) was founded at the beginning of the eighteenth century, and the Basilian Aleppine Order was separated from the Salvatorians in 1829. The Melkite Paulist Fathers were founded in 1903 as a missionary community modeled on the White Fathers. More recently, the Monastery of the Resurrection has been established in Lebanon for the purpose of living out the Eastern monastic ideal.

Three Melkite women's communities correspond directly to the men's orders: the Salvatorian Sisters of the Annunciation, the Basilian Saorite Sisters, and the Basilian Aleppine Sisters. Of more recent foundation are the Missionaries of Our Lady of Perpetual Help and the Sisters of Our Lady of Good Service.

Melkite religious orders are involved in many pastoral efforts in the parishes, schools, and centers for social assistance. A number of them have followed the faithful into the emigration.

St. Anne's Seminary in Jerusalem, under the direction of the White Fathers, was the main seminary for the Melkite Church until it had to be closed in 1967 because of the political situation. Candidates for the priesthood now study at the patriarchal seminary of Raboué, Lebanon. Moreover, the Melkite Paulist Fathers direct an important theological institute at Harissa, and run a well-known publishing house.

Today the Melkite Catholic Church is one of the largest and most prosperous Catholic communities in the Middle East. It is the largest Catholic Church in Syria and second only to the Maronites in Lebanon. Smaller communities are found throughout the region.

Significant emigration from the Middle East in recent years has created flourishing Melkite communities in the West. Dioceses have been established in Brazil, the United States, Canada, Mexico, Australia, and Venezuela. Altogether in 1994 the Melkite Catholic Church had just over a million members. *See also* Antioch; Byzantine rite; Eastern churches; Eastern rites.

Bibliography

Descy, Serge. *The Melkite Church: An Historical and Ecclesiological Approach.* Newton, MA: Sophia Press, 1993. RONALD G. ROBERSON

Memorare (mem-ohr-ahr'ay; Lat., "remember"), an intercessory prayer to Mary by an unknown author. Appearing in texts from the fifteenth century, it begins, "Remember, most gracious Virgin Mary." It was made popular by Claude Bernard (1588–1641)

and its use was promoted by Pope Pius IX, who attached indulgences to it in 1846.

MEMORARE

Remember, most gracious Virgin Mary, that never was it known that anyone who fled to your protection, implored your help, or sought your intercession was left unaided. Inspired by this confidence, I fly to you, O Virgin of virgins, my mother. To you I come; before you I stand, sinful and sorrowful. O Mother of the Word Incarnate, despise not my petitions, but in your mercy, hear and answer me. Amen.

memorial, a liturgical day commemorating a saint or blessed (one not yet canonized but already beatified). Memorials are designated "optional" or "obligatory" depending upon the saint's significance for the Church. Memorials are lower in rank than feasts or solemnities. They are never observed during Holy Week, Easter Week, or the week before Christmas. *See also* feasts, liturgical; solemnity.

memorial acclamation, the acclamation sung by the assembly during the Eucharistic Prayer immediately following the Institution Narrative, the passage from the NT that describes Christ's institution of the Eucharist at the Last Supper. The most common acclamation—"Christ has died. Christ is risen. Christ will come again."—indicates the vivid and active recollection ("memorial") of the saving events of Christ's life and ministry made by the Church at Mass.

Menaion (men-ay'awn; Gk., "lunar," i.e., "monthly"), Byzantine-rite liturgical book containing the liturgical propers for the major hours (on ordinary days, Matins and Vespers) of the fixed cycle, i.e., those days that fall on a fixed date in the calendar. Arranged in twelve volumes, one for each month, the cycle begins with the Byzantine New Year on September 1.

mendicant orders, also known as friars, religious with the privilege of begging (Lat., *mendicare*) in the dioceses where they are established since they were vowed to corporate poverty as well as to the personal poverty of monks. The Benedictine domination of monasticism in the West gave way in the twelfth century to new varieties of monasticism.

These new forms of religious life and the urbanization of Europe paved the way for the introduction of the mendicant orders at the beginning of the thirteenth century under the inspiration of Francis of Assisi (d. 1226) and Dominic de Guzman (d. 1221), founders of the Franciscans and the Dominicans. The friars (from the Lat., *fratres*, "brothers") became evangelists carrying out the pastoral mission outlined by the Fourth Lateran Council (1215). The friars were the preachers, confessors, and theologians needed by this mission. The friars were also mobile, as distinguished from other monks who remained in monasteries. They were also centralized and international. Moreover, they modified monastic observances to facilitate study and ministry.

The success of the friars raised opposition among bishops and clergy. The two ablest friars of the thirteenth century, Thomas Aquinas (d. 1274) and Bonaventure (d. 1274), spearheaded the defense of the friars. At the Second Council of Lyons (1274) the Dominicans and the Franciscans received full approval. The Carmelites and the Augustinian Hermits, who became friars in 1247 and 1256, respectively, were to continue till final provisions could be made; they received full approval in 1298. After Lyons II other mendicants had to cease accepting candidates until they died out. The bull *Supra Cathedram* in 1300 set a pattern for mendicant and episcopal relations by requiring friars to seek licenses from bishops to preach and hear confessions in their dioceses. The Servites also became mendicants, and in 1578 Pope Gregory XIII accepted others as mendicants, e.g., the Minims and Mercedarians. *See also* Augustinian Hermits; Dominican order; Franciscan order; Mercedarians; Minims; Servites.

KEITH J. EGAN

Menno Simons, 1496–1561, leader of the Mennonites. Troubled by infant baptism and the Catholic Eucharist, Menno, a priest, was rebaptized in 1537 and became the leader of a group of Anabaptists who would later be known as the Mennonites. *See also* Anabaptism; Mennonites.

Mennonites, a pacifistic branch of sixteenth-century Anabaptism. Taking their name from Menno Simons, one of the early leaders, the Mennonites practiced believers' (adult) baptism. Because they held to a complete separation of Church and state, they refused to serve the state in any way. To maintain the purity of the community they used the ban. Seeing the "world" as corrupt, they withdrew from it. Since the Mennonites suffered merciless persecution in western Europe, they emigrated to Russia, South America, and North America. *See also* Anabaptism; Menno Simons; sectarianism.

mental prayer. *See* meditation.

mental reservation, the addition of a modifying phrase in the mind of a speaker that restricts the meaning of spoken words. The dilemma between the absolute prohibition of lying and the duty to keep a secret gave rise eventually to the doctrine of mental reservation. Some taught the permissibility of strict mental reservation, in which one mentally added a qualification to which the audience had no access. This teaching was condemned by Pope Innocent XI in 1679. However, broad mental reservation, involving the use of equivocal language that was intended to deceive, yet that had a secondary meaning available to the audience, was permitted by virtually all Catholic writers. This teaching has all but disappeared from contemporary moral theology because the conflict between the duty to speak the truth and to preserve secrets is approached differently. *See also* lying; truthfulness.

Mercedarians, a religious order founded in Spain ca. 1220 by Peter Nolasco dedicated to Our Lady of Mercy (Merced). Originally a Crusader military order whose members vowed to accept captivity in exchange for Christian prisoners, it later became a clerical order with apostolates to the sick and imprisoned. *See also* Crusades; Nolasco, St. Peter.

Mercier, Désiré Joseph (mair'see-ay), 1851–1926, cardinal-archbishop of Malines (Belgium). Following Pope Leo XIII's encyclical *Aeterni Patris* (1879), he sought to harmonize Aquinas's philosophy with contemporary thought. He argued for the independence of philosophy from apologetic concerns and founded the Institut Supérieur de Philosophie, Louvain, as a center of neo-Thomism. As archbishop, he presided over the Malines Conversations (1921–25), which explored the conditions for union between Catholics and Anglicans. *See also* philosophy and theology; Thomism.

mercy, active compassion toward another in unfortunate circumstances; an essential form of Christian charity. Mercy requires not only a feeling of sympathy but also an intention to ease the other's misfortune if possible. Mercy is based on a recognition of the shared human condition before God and a willingness to do one's duty to alleviate the suffering of others. Acts that express mercy are categorized as spiritual and corporal works of mercy. The corporal works of mercy require the Christian to feed the hungry, give drink to the thirsty, clothe the naked, shelter the homeless, visit the sick and the imprisoned, and bury the dead (Matt 25:34–40). The spiritual works of mercy are concerned with preserving the faithful in their faith and maintaining harmony in personal relationships; they enjoin Christians to counsel the doubtful, instruct the ignorant, admonish the sinner, comfort the sorrowful, forgive injuries, bear wrongs patiently, and pray for the living and the dead. *See also* charity; justice; mercy, corporal works of; mercy, spiritual works of.

mercy, corporal works of, actions directed toward fulfilling the physical and related needs of a neighbor. The emphasis is not on specific actions but on an overall attitude toward people in a disempowered condition. Matt 25:34–40 and Isa 58:6–10 are the scriptural sources for the teaching on the corporal works. A relationship with God is judged in terms of behavior toward the lowly. There is a close relationship between social justice and the works of mercy. Justice serves the rights of individuals and the demands of the common good. Mercy is loving gratuity.

The corporal works of mercy are as follows: (1) To feed the hungry: The hungry are those starved for food, but besides giving food to the poor, Christians are called to improve the economic and social structures so as to eliminate poverty and bestow a sense of dignity on the marginalized. Fasting as a means of fostering empathy with the poor and sharing a meal with the poor create attitudes that diminish the sense of social alienation suffered by the poor. (2) To give drink to the thirsty: Alleviating thirst includes providing unpolluted water for poverty-stricken areas and restoring ecological balance. This work of mercy also serves those seeking righteousness, which seeks to accomplish the will of God by going beyond a mere fulfillment of law. (3) To clothe the naked: The naked are those stripped of human dignity and power, as well as those in need of sufficient clothing, bedding, and necessary tools for labor or work. Undertaking any measures that meet the immediate needs of the poor and instituting changes that address this state of physical and psychological impoverishment are central to this particular work. Treating all people with dignity

and sensitivity on a daily basis is an important application of this act of mercy. (4) To visit the imprisoned: Captivity takes a variety of forms. Imprisonment for political, criminal, and religious reasons are overt forms. Victims of domestic violence, sexism, racism, and class distinction also experience oppression and captivity. Measures to release political and religious prisoners and intervene in cases of domestic violence constitute this work of mercy. Opportunities for education, counseling, job training, and religious services in prisons provide hope and a constructive outreach for the incarcerated. (5) To shelter the homeless: Street people, migrants, refugees, orphans, and foster children are counted among the homeless. Alienated, marginalized, abused, and misunderstood people suffer a state of emotional dispossession, and those totally lacking belief in God suffer a sense of exile. For all these forms of homelessness, providing shelter entails fostering a sense of belonging to others. (6) To visit the sick: Supplying companionship and housekeeping for the sick, elderly, and homebound, and accommodating the needs of the physically and mentally disabled are principal avenues of serving the sick. Meeting the needs of the emotionally troubled or sharing kind words with a stranger or friend in need comes under this work of mercy. (7) To bury the dead: Providing companionship, pastoral counseling, and professional advice to the dying and the family of the dying are considered part of burying the dead. Spiritual direction and religious ritual also play a key role at the time of death. Helping survivors forgive themselves and others for unfinished business in major relationships is of particular importance. *See also* mercy; mercy, spiritual works of.

PATRICIA M. VINJE

mercy, spiritual works of, acts of charity and compassion rooted in Scripture and the constant practice of the Church on behalf of those with special emotional and spiritual needs. As manifestations of mercy, they are done freely, without the obligatory demands of justice. Like all acts of mercy, they are acts of love, but they may initiate discomfort as well as comfort. These seven expressions parallel the corporal works of mercy. (1) To admonish the sinner (Matt 18:15–20; Col 3:5–17; 1 Thess 5:12; 2 Thess 3:15): Believing that sin can lead a person away from God and neighbor, the first act of mercy risks telling a person what he or she may not wish to hear. Admonishment may take the form of good example or of disciplinary action. (2) To instruct the ignorant (Rom 11:25; 1 Cor 10:1; 1 Tim 4:6–16; 2 Tim 4:1–5; 1 Thess 4:13): The goal of instruction is to inform and to correct misunderstandings and prejudices based on ignorance and fear. Instruction helps people to see things from a different point of view and invites them to conversion and transformation. (3) To counsel the doubtful (Luke 24:36–53; John 20:26–29): Doubt assumes various forms: doubt about one's faith, about oneself, and about one's relationships with others. Counsel may also take various forms: direct spiritual advice, good example, patient presence to the other. (4) To comfort the sorrowful (John 11:19; 1 Thess 4:13–18): It requires an empathetic presence and attentiveness to meet the emotional needs of another. The energy and time that one shares with the bereaved, the lonely, or the alienated focus on those actions and attitudes that strengthen and empower them to grow through their struggles. (5) To bear wrongs patiently (Matt 16:24; Jas 5:7–11): It requires fortitude to endure strain, stress, and evil without causing more suffering and evil. Humility and a sense of reality help a person keep the underlying needs of others in mind when their needs are inadequately or inappropriately expressed and when there are no immediate or easy solutions. (6) To forgive all injuries (Matt 6:15; 18:21–35; Col 3:13): Injuries are harmful acts received from another that often generate bitterness, resentment, and a spirit of vindictiveness. Love and forgiveness can transform an injurious event by restoring health and integrity to a relationship or at least by mitigating the injurious effects. (7) To pray for the living and the dead (Jas 5:16; Col 1:3,9; 2 Macc 12:45): The act of intercession for the living and the dead unites the prayers of the Church on earth with the ongoing intercession of Jesus and the saints in heaven and is expressive of the permanent bond that unites all Christians in the communion of saints. *See also* mercy, corporal works of.   PATRICIA M. VINJE

Mère Angélique. *See* Arnauld, Jacqueline Marie Angélique.

Merici, St. Angela. *See* Angela Merici, St.

merit, a term denoting just reward from God; used in Catholic theology since Tertullian (d. ca. 225) to indicate the human contribution to salvation. Discussed extensively in the Middle Ages, the Catholic affirmation of merit was bitterly contested during the Reformation, revealing differing conceptions of justification and grace. Reaffirmed at Trent (1545–63) and championed throughout the Catholic Reformation as implied by biblical discussions of "reward," merit has been criticized by more recent Catholic theologians as predicated on an overly legalistic view of God-human relations.

Theological Development: The principal reward of merit is eternal life, life with God in heaven. Catholic theologians of various stripes agree that good acts performed in this life can be meritorious of heaven, provided these acts are done in grace. The schools disagree, however, why precisely morally good acts done in grace are meritorious of eternal life. In Aquinas (d. 1274) and his followers, the emphasis is on grace as the transformative power of the Holy Spirit, who moves people to morally correct action. As the Spirit's, grace is of great intrinsic value, elevating the human act, which it makes possible, to equal value to the reward rendered by God; here, theologians speak of "condign" merit. While they, too, speak of condign merit, Duns Scotus (d. 1308), William of Ockham (d. 1347), and their followers prefer to describe grace as something created, as a created habit. Nothing created can be equal of itself in value to God, nor can it necessitate anything from God, including God's reward. That good acts done in grace are condignly meritorious is due, rather, to a further decision by God to accept these graced good works as if they were condignly meritorious of eternal life.

Catholic theologians have speculated about other possible rewards of human merits. A guiding metaphor is life as a "journey," which begins with the individual in the state of sin, then moving into the state of grace, performing good actions that keep one in grace and moving closer to life with God, and finally reaching the culmination of the journey in the next life, in heaven. Many theologians insist that the first step on the journey, the movement into the state of grace, can itself be meritorious. From the twelfth century on and repeated by Scotus, Ockham, and the young Thomas Aquinas, this affirmation was closely connected to the axiom *facientibus quod in se est* (Lat., "to those who do their best, God does not deny grace"), that is, God grants first grace to those who make the effort to reform their lives. Here, theologians speak of a "congruent" merit. Because the actions of one who lacks grace must by necessity fall short in value of any reward given by God, there is no condign merit at this stage of the journey. Rather, grace is granted as a reward only by the mercy of God: it befits God, it is congruent with the mercy of God, to recognize any effort at reformation in this way. The Aquinas of the *Summa Theologiae* abandoned this position; in the light of his reading of certain treatises of Augustine against the Massilians (later known as "semi-Pelagians"), who had themselves advanced an early version of the *facientibus,* Thomas came to describe the first step to God as itself due to the wholly unmerited grace of God that achieves the conversion of the sinner. He restricts talk of a "congruent" merit to the state of grace. One and the same moral act can be viewed from two angles: as due to God's grace, it is condignly meritorious; as the result of the correct use of human freedom, it is meritorious congruently.

Theologians gave much less attention to the role of merit in keeping a person in the state of grace; distinctive positions on perseverance in grace are thus revealing. Scotists, Ockhamists, and Thomists agree that good actions done in grace have a secondary reward: in addition to eternal life, they also merit the increase of habitual grace. For Scotus and Ockham, the increase of habitual grace is simply equivalent to persevering on the right path to God. The Aquinas of the *Summa Theologiae* adds, however, that a second grace, distinct from habitual grace, is needed to keep one in the state of grace and on the road to God; this grace is wholly unmerited, granted solely in accordance with God's saving will for the individual. This grace of perseverance, which permits the individual to overcome the temptations that arise from the remnants of past acts and stands at the head of every good act, is again probably championed by Thomas in the light of his reading of Augustine's later writings. *See also* condign merit; grace; justification; salvation; sanctification.

JOSEPH WAWRYKOW

Merry del Val, Rafael, 1865–1930, cardinal and diplomat. Son of a Spanish marquis and diplomat and an English mother, he studied in England, Belgium, and Rome, where he was ordained. In the papal diplomatic corps, he served in London, Berlin, Vienna, and Canada. In 1903 Pope Pius X named him cardinal and papal secretary of state, in which office he served until 1914. Noted for his personal integrity, he was politically unpopular in France. Though he was reputed an extremist in the struggle against Modernism, some think he may actually have moderated Pius X's policies. *See also* Modernism; Pius X, St.

Mersch, Émile (ay-meel' mairsh), 1890–1940,

Jesuit philosopher and theologian. He contributed significantly to the early-twentieth-century renewal in ecclesiology occasioned by a return to biblical and patristic images of the Church. Mersch produced a massive two-volume study of the historical development of the doctrine of the Mystical Body and a draft of another two-volume dogmatic synthesis of the same subject, published posthumously. Mersch was killed in an air attack during the early years of the Second World War.

Merton, Thomas, 1915–68, Trappist monk, author, peace activist, and ecumenist. A precocious and undisciplined youth with no religious education, he proclaimed himself an atheist and pursued a hedonistic life-style. After an academically and morally disastrous year at Cambridge University, Merton attended Columbia University in New York. He toyed with communism but became progressively attracted to Catholicism through reading and discussion. Baptized a Catholic in 1938, he astonished his friends by entering the Cistercian (Trappist) Abbey of Gethsemani in Kentucky three years later. As a young monk he wrote a dramatic autobiography, *The Seven Storey Mountain,* which became a bestseller and a classic. It made Merton a religious figure of international prominence and established him as a Catholic writer. During the next twenty years he wrote prolifically on a vast range of topics

Thomas Merton, Trappist monk and peace activist, whose writings have exercised a wide and profound influence on Catholic and secular thought in the second half of the twentieth century.

His earlier books dealt exclusively with religious matters such as prayer, asceticism, and interior growth. Later writings ventured into controversial issues connected with social problems and Christian responsibility: race relations, violence, war, economic injustice. Merton's ecumenical concerns predated and intensified ideas of Vatican II on interreligious understanding. He interpreted the great religions of the East to Catholics. Thomas Merton's accidental death occurred while he was attending a conference in Bangkok on December 10, 1968. He is regarded as a spiritual master, a brilliant religious writer, and a man who embodied the quest for God and human solidarity in the modern world.

messiah (Gk. transliteration *messias* of Heb. *mashiakh;* Gk., *christos,* "anointed one"), title used for the Israelite king (2 Sam 1:14) and for the high priest (Lev 4:3; cf. Zech 4:14). Kings and high priests were appointed at God's command by having their heads anointed with oil (1 Sam 9:15–10:1; 16:1–13; 2 Kings 9:3; Lev 8:12). Other figures appointed by God were occasionally spoken of as anointed by God, such as Cyrus (Isa 45:1) and prophets (1 Kings 19:16; Isa 61:1). Psalms speak often of a favored, anointed (Davidic) king (Pss 2, 45, 89, 132). The prophets seldom speak of an anointed one but they often look forward to an ideal ruler (Isa 7, 9, 11; Jer 23:5–6; Mic 5:2–4). The book of Daniel alludes to two anointed ones (probably the high priests Joshua and Onias III) as rulers (9:25–26).

In the Greco-Roman period, the rise of Jewish apocalyptic eschatology brought with it the expectation of a variety of "messianic" or angelic figures sent by God to intervene decisively in history and bring about the end of evil. A distinction should be made between figures explicitly called "anointed one" (messiahs in a strict sense) and similar figures called "Son of Man," "Chosen One," "Righteous One," "Branch of David," "Prince," etc. (messianic figures in a loose sense). Scenarios concerning God's intervention in the world varied greatly and did not always include a messianic figure. Such figures were understood as an ideal Davidic king or Levitical high priest or as heavenly intermediaries. For example, Daniel 7 speaks of a heavenly figure "like a son of man." *Jubilees* 31 and the *Testaments of the Twelve Patriarchs* hope for descendants of Judah and Levi. Various Dead Sea Scrolls speak of two anointed ones of Israel and Aaron, as well as of a Prophet like Moses, a Branch of David, Prince of the Congregation, and Melchizedek. *Psalms of Solomon* 17 looks forward to an anointed one, as do the late first century A.D. apocalypses *4 Ezra* and *2 Baruch.* The *Similitudes of Enoch* (*Enoch* 37–71) speaks of a son of man, chosen one, and righteous one. Later rabbinic Judaism settled on a Davidic Messiah, who would appear at the end of the world. During the first centuries B.C. and A.D. a number of popular leaders claimed to be prophets or messiahs sent by God to lead Israel to freedom.

The centrality of Jesus in the NT caused eschatological thought to focus on the Messiah and other royal and eschatological figures. Jesus was identified early as Messiah (Christ), son of David, prophet, Son of Man, and Son of God (a royal title). Paul's Letters in the 50s already use "Christ" as a name (Rom 1:1, 7–8; 5:8 and often) rather than as a title (Rom 9:5). The Gospels understand Jesus as the Christ (Mark 1:1; 8:29) and contain reflections on Jesus as son of David (Mark 12:35–37; Matt 1–2; Luke 1–2), King of the Jews (Mark 15:32; Matt 2:2), and Savior (Luke 2:11). Because Jesus was executed by the Romans, early Christians used Isa 53 and other passages to develop the figure of a suffering Messiah (Mark 8:31; Luke 24:26; Acts 3:18; 26:23) who subsequently rose from the dead. The expectation that Jesus the Messiah will return at the end of the world permeates the NT, though the returning Messiah is sometimes called by other titles (Mark 13:26; 1 Thess 4:16; 1 Cor 15:23; Rev 20:4). *See also* Christ; Jesus Christ; titles of Christ. ANTHONY SALDARINI

metania (me-tah'nee-ah; Gk., *metanoia,* "change of mind," "penance"), penance. Metania, or metany, also refers to the reverential bow or prostration used in the Byzantine rite upon entering the church, or in reverence to an icon or relic. It is called "metania" because it is often performed repeatedly as a penance, especially by monks. *See also* penance.

metanoia (me-tah-noy'ah; Gk., "change of heart"), a conversion from sin to God. In Catholic theology, *metanoia* includes sorrow for sin, amendment of sinful ways, and satisfaction or payment of the penalty for sin when possible. *See also* conversion.

metaphysics (Gk. "beyond the physical"), philosophical science of being or the study of first principles governing existence. According to Parmenides and Plato, physical realities persist in being what they are because of unchangeable, immaterial being. For Aristotle, metaphysics, as first philosophy, seeks to understand being as that which makes any

seeks to understand being as that which makes any being real. In medieval Christianity, both Aquinas and Duns Scotus related metaphysics to certain doctrines of Christian faith, explaining how all of creation depends on the existence of God. Today, Catholic theologians hold that the being of God is the object of human desire and first principle of existence. *See also* philosophy and theology.

metempsychosis, otherwise known as the transmigration of souls or reincarnation, name given to the doctrines of various religions and philosophies that posit both the preexistence of the human soul before union with the body and the soul's subsequent return to life on earth in human, animal, or inanimate form. *See also* reincarnation; soul.

Methodism, an evangelistic renewal movement composed of various churches numbering about 55 million members in over 100 countries, as of 1994. In general, the principle prevails that the best governed churches are autocephalous churches in individual nations, and churches in mission territories tend to become independent in time. Most are represented in the World Methodist Council.

The origins of Methodism are in the life and work of John Wesley (1703–91), a priest of the Church of England. Beginning with the Holy Club in Oxford, Methodism represented a disciplined or methodical approach to the Christian life in a time of great laxity in English Christianity. After a fruitless missionary experience in Georgia, Wesley returned to England. In 1738, after a particularly intense religious experience, he began preaching to the coal miners and other workers in the fields and wherever he could gain a hearing. His gifts as a preacher were equaled by those as an organizer. Where converts were made, he immediately developed a system of pastoral supervision, usually administered by laypeople.

Throughout his long life, Wesley remained a priest of the Church of England and never desired separation from it. His vision of the people called Methodists was basically that of a third order within the state church and for this he prescribed "Rules." Wesley's evangelistical zeal was matched by a strong emphasis on sacramental life. In the time of the Enlightenment, he represented a countercultural movement, insisting on "constant," i.e., frequent, Communion and faithful attendance to the other means of grace: Scripture, prayer, the Lord's Supper, fasting, and Christian conference (spiritual direction). In many ways, it was a Catholic reaction within the Church of England, coupled with evangelical zeal.

Basically a pragmatic traditionalist, Wesley often turned to his background as a patristics scholar to find solutions for contemporary problems. In worship, this meant a revival of the *agape* as a love feast, the vigil as watch night, and a great devotion to hymn singing. He published the first Anglican hymnal in 1737 and his brother Charles Wesley (1707–88) produced a prodigious amount of hymnody. Much of it was theological treatises set to music, such as the 1745 *Hymns on the Lord's Supper.*

John Wesley agreed with medieval theologian Peter Lombard (d. 1160) that bishops and presbyters were not different orders. He argued that only ordained presbyters could celebrate the Eucharist and so, when English bishops were unwilling to ordain men for North America, he took this step himself in 1784. He also provided an ordinal with rites for deacons, elders, and "superintendants." Three years later, American Methodists changed this last term to bishops. Most of American Methodism has been episcopal, with a strong connectional emphasis in contrast to the prevailing American congregationalism. Methodist bishops have the power of appointing elders to parishes.

Various black Methodist churches split from the American Methodist Church in the nineteenth century, and the Methodist Episcopal Church divided in 1844 over slavery. Many of these divisions have been healed as issues shift. English Methodism has never had bishops, but European Methodism and most mission territories reached by North Americans have. Methodists in many parts of the world, beginning in Canada in 1925, have joined in mergers with other churches. A distinctive feature has been the strong social conscience of American and English Methodism, generally expressed through a liberal agenda. In the United States in 1994, 126 colleges and universities reflect Methodist origins. Methodist theology has been deeply involved in the ecumenical movement. *See also* Protestantism; Reformation, the.　　　　　　　　　　*JAMES F. WHITE*

Methodist-Catholic dialogue, theological conversations between delegates appointed by the World Methodist Council and the Vatican Secretariat for Promoting Christian Unity (now the Pontifical Council for Promoting Christian Unity) since 1967. Each partner in these discussions is represented by bishops, presbyters, and laypeople from various continents.

To date, a series of reports at five-year intervals have been submitted to the respective churches. Topics such as the mission of the Church, evangelism, social problems, morality, ecclesiastical discipline, and spirituality have been the subjects of these reports. More extensive work began on the Eucharist and ministry. Both sides have agreed that bread and wine in the Eucharist become "efficacious signs of the body and blood of Christ," yet transubstantiation remains a stumbling block to further accord. Both sides affirm an apostolic ministry within the wider ministry of the whole Church, but disagree on how historical the current concepts of apostolic succession are and how essential they must remain for the life of the Church.

More recent discussions have been concerned with the Holy Spirit and ecclesiology, resulting in "Towards an Agreed Statement on the Holy Spirit" in 1981 and "Towards a Statement on the Church" five years later. In the early 1990s discussion revolves around the topic "The Apostolic Tradition," particularly with aspects of the apostolic faith and ministry and ministries.

Other regional discussions between Methodists and Catholics have occurred at regular intervals in the United States, the United Kingdom, and New Zealand. Both partners are deeply involved in World Council of Churches projects such as *Baptism, Eucharist and Ministry* (1982) and the resulting discussions. *See also* Methodism.   JAMES F. WHITE

Methodius of Olympus, St., d. 311, theologian, probably bishop of Olympus in Lycia. He practiced allegorical exegesis after the method of Origen but attacked some of Origen's teachings (e.g., on the resurrection body). His *Symposium* survives in the entire original Greek and other works survive in translation, but his scriptural commentaries, a major rebuttal of Porphyry (an anti-Christian philosopher), and many other works are lost. Feast day: September 18 (West); June 20 (East). *See also* Origen; Porphyry.

metropolitan, adjective referring to the chief local church of a region or to its bishop. Most often a metropolitan see is based in a city important because of its size, history, or political status. This see is headed by an archbishop who has certain responsibilities for governance in the dioceses attached to the archdiocese. Although in the West these responsibilities are very limited, in the Eastern churches they are greater. The metropolitan archbishop is given the pallium, the same stolelike vestment worn by the pope, as a sign of union with the Roman church and, through that church, with the universal Church. *See also* archbishop; pallium.

Metz, Johannes, b. 1928, German Catholic theologian. Ordained a priest for the diocese of Munich-Freising, he served as a professor of theology at the University of Münster from 1963 until his retirement in 1993. Author of numerous writings on theology and politics, he is credited with coining the term "political theology" to emphasize the close connection between faith and the temporal order.

Mexico, Catholicism in. The Christian faith was brought to the Aztecs and the many other tribes of the region now known as Mexico (formerly, "New Spain") from Spain in the 1500s by Augustinian, Dominican, Franciscan, and Jesuit missionaries. The peoples residing in the central plateau accepted the Church's teachings, and in 1530 Mexico City became a diocese. On December 9, 1531, the evangelization of New Spain received a lasting impetus when Juan Diego is reported to have received a vision of the Virgin Mary at Tepeyac, a hill northwest of Mexico City. By her words and countenance, Our Lady of Guadalupe conveyed that the indigenous peoples of Latin America could embrace Christian belief as fully as the peoples of Europe. Early evangelization was also aided by the exemplary lives and visionary leadership of Fray Juan de Zumárraga (1468–1548), the bishop of Mexico, and Don Vasco de Quiroga (ca. 1470–1565), the bishop of Michoacán. The Tribunal of the Inquisition, established in Mexico City in 1571, worked (for the next three hundred years) to keep the faith from incorporating pagan beliefs and practices and also to prevent the spread of Protestantism.

The faithful gathered for the celebration of the Eucharist, as the procession of clergy and other altar ministers enters the Basilica of Our Lady of Guadalupe, Mexico City.

Eighteenth and Nineteenth Centuries: As Spain declined as a world power in the eighteenth century, so, too, did its support for the Catholic Church in Mexico. As a result, evangelization waned and ecclesiastical discipline became lax. The misconduct of ecclesiastical officials eroded the Church's credibility among the people. Acting on controversies within Europe, the Spanish government expelled the Jesuits from Mexico in 1767, thereby weakening or eliminating their educational institutions and other apostolates. Nevertheless, the University of Mexico, established by the Jesuits in 1553, continued to develop. The country was also served well by the newspaper *Gaceta de México* (Sp., "Mexican Gazette"), founded in 1720 by Juan Ignacio de Castorena y Ursúa (1668–1733), who eventually became the bishop of Yucatán.

During Mexico's wars of independence (1810–21), the Church's hierarchy wanted to maintain Mexico as the Viceroyalty of Spain. However, some priests like Miguel Hidalgo y Costilla (1753–1811) and José María Morelos y Pávon (1765–1821) assumed leadership among the revolutionaries. After independence from Spain on September 28, 1821, the Mexican empire headed by Augustín de Iturbide

regarded the Catholic faith as one of the pillars of the society and the state. Soon after the Mexican republic was established (1823), the government negotiated a concordat with the Holy See concerning Church-state relations, thereby ending the practice of *patronato real* (Sp., "royal patronage"). Yet conflicts persisted regarding the actual working relationship between the Church and the state. After the revolution that started in 1854, a new federal republic was founded on a liberal constitutional charter (1857) that ended special privileges and secularized Church property. The liberal government of Benito Juárez, which came to power after the War of Reform (1858–61), severed official ties with the Vatican. While the subsequent relations between the government and the Catholic Church were in general hostile, tensions lessened during Porfirio Díaz's dictatorship (1876–1910).

Twentieth Century: After the revolution that began in 1910, President Venustiano Carranza sponsored the constitution of 1917 that called for the separation of Church and state. The Catholic Church was virtually suppressed under the political leadership of Plutarco Elías Calles, who controlled the Mexican government from 1924 until 1934. As Mexico's president (1924–28, 1931), Calles's policy against the Church was so severe from 1926 through

1929 that in response the clergy went on strike. However, Calles kept the churches open without priests, who either went into hiding or were persecuted. Mexican Catholics in some regions revolted against the government by joining the militant organization *Cristeros,* named because of its motto, *Vivo Cristo Rey!* (Sp., "Long live Christ the King"). One martyr of the government's repression was the Jesuit priest Miguel Pro (b. 1891) who was executed by a firing squad on November 23, 1927. (He was beatified by Pope John Paul II on September 25, 1988, at St. Peter's in Rome.) In 1929 Calles organized the *Partido Revolucionario Institucional* (Institutional Revolutionary Party) that since then has been Mexico's dominant political party. The government of Lázaro Cárdenas (1934–40) ended the persecution of the Church and instituted a more lenient policy toward the Church. Nevertheless, according to law the Church was forbidden to own property and establish schools, priests were disfranchised and forbidden to wear clerical attire in public, and religious processions were prohibited.

In the early 1970s, President Luis Echevarría Álvarez sought to revive the spirit of the revolution of 1910 by opening the government to wider popular representation, and in this endeavor he received public support from liberal Catholic bishops, priests, and lay leaders. As a result, relations between the government and the Church were improved, even though some conservative Catholics resisted reform efforts. A new phase in the cooperation between the Catholic Church and the Mexican

A young Mexican girl portrays the Blessed Virgin Mary on her way to Bethlehem to give birth to the Savior, in Las Posadas, Jocotopec, Mexico.

government commenced on February 17, 1990, when the government and the Vatican agreed to exchange permanent personal representatives. In September 1992, after a lapse of 131 years, full diplomatic relations between the Holy See and Mexico were resumed. The Mexican government now sends an ambassador to the Vatican and receives an apostolic nuncio, an official diplomatic representative of the Holy See. Legal restrictions against the Church were also lifted.

In 1993, 90 percent of Mexico's approximately 90 million people are nominally Catholic. There are fourteen archdioceses and fifty-seven dioceses. While Catholicism remains strong among the Mexican people, some Mexicans have responded positively in recent years to the evangelization and recruitment of Protestant churches, especially the fundamentalists, as well as the Mormon church. *See also* Guadalupe, Our Lady of; Latin America, Catholicism in.

Bibliography

Callcott, W. H. *Church and State in Mexico, 1822–1857.* Durham, NC: Duke University Press, 1926.

Braden, C. S. *Religious Aspects of the Conquest of Mexico.* Durham, NC: Duke University Press, 1930.   ROBERT A. KRIEG

Meyer, Albert Gregory, 1903–65, cardinal-archbishop of Chicago (1958–65). A native of Milwaukee, he was appointed bishop of Superior, Wisconsin, in 1937, archbishop of Milwaukee in 1953, and archbishop of Chicago in 1958, becoming a cardinal the following year. Meyer was a reserved and dutiful bishop, ponderous in speech and cautious in action. His prominence as a figure in the U.S. hierarchy came during his years in Chicago when he attacked the evils of racism in the Church and gave support to priests involved in civil rights and ecumenical activities. A biblical scholar, he was also an important American figure at Vatican II, aligning himself with the progressive wing at the council.

Michael the Archangel, St., the leader of the ranks of angels and the guardian and protector of the people of Israel (see Dan 10; 12). Michael is also depicted in Jude 9 as having conducted warfare with the devil over the body of Moses. According to early Christian custom and cult, Michael defeated Satan and his followers and banished them from heaven. The feast of archangels Michael, Gabriel, and Raphael is celebrated on September 29, also known as Michaelmas Day. *See also* angel.

Michael the Archangel, traditionally regarded as the guardian of Christian armies against the enemies of the Church (thus the sword in hand) and as the protector of individual Christians against the power of Satan, especially at the moment of death; fifteenth-century Florentine sculpture by Andrea della Robbia, Metropolitan Museum of Art, New York.

Michel, Virgil, 1888–1938, a Benedictine monk of St. John's Abbey, Collegeville, Minnesota, and an American liturgical pioneer. After initial contacts with the liturgical movement in Europe, he founded the influential liturgical periodical *Orate Fratres* (now, *Worship*), as well as The Liturgical Press. Michel's editorials constantly linked the liturgy, social justice, and other areas of contemporary living and critiqued excessive American individualism. He promoted the liturgical movement in the United States by lecturing widely and by writing a textbook series (*Christ-Life Series*) that attempted to integrate liturgy and life. *See also* liturgical movement.

Michelangelo [Michelangelo Buonarroti], 1475–1564, Italian High Renaissance sculptor, painter, architect, and poet. He was recognized as a genius by his contemporaries, who called him the *divino* (It., "divine one"). Michelangelo's work reflects Renaissance humanism, particularly the Neoplatonic philosophy encountered among the intellectuals at the Medici court, and the Catholic Reform movement, beginning with the preaching of the Florentine Dominican Savonarola and culminating in the profound personal faith of Michelangelo's later years. The heroic *David* (1505), the *Moses* (1513–15, part of the tomb for Pope Julius II), and the sculptures for the Medici tombs in San Lorenzo in Florence (1524–34) embody the tension between action and repose, the dualism of body and spirit that preoccupied the artist. The recently cleaned paintings of the Sistine Chapel ceiling (1508–12), together with the *Last Judgment* on the end wall (1536–41), brilliantly depict the creation of the world, the fall of humanity, and the ultimate reconciliation of all creation to God. Architectural commissions include the Capitol of Rome (1537–39) and the new design for St. Peter's Basilica (1546–64).

Michelangelo, the most famous and most accomplished Catholic artist in history. He produced the *Pietà*, the sculptures of David and Moses, the frescoes on the ceiling of the Sistine Chapel, and the designs for St. Peter's Basilica.

His self-portrait in the flayed skin of St. Bartholomew in the *Last Judgment* and Michelangelo's face as that of Joseph of Arimathea in an unfinished *Pietà* for the artist's own tomb (ca. 1555) intimately show the aged Michelangelo dependent on God's mercy, yearning for union with God. *See also* Catholicism and architecture; Catholicism and the visual arts; Saint Peter's Basilica.

Middle Ages, the historical period that spans the milennium between the collapse of the Roman Empire in 476 and the birth of the modern world at the end of the fifteenth century (others date it to the beginning of the twelfth century). As a historical concept, it is the invention of fifteenth-century humanists who regarded the time between the glories of Rome and their own rebirth of classical culture as a long middle age of darkness and superstition. The pejorative lables of "medieval" and "Gothic" are as inaccurate as was the excessively romantic view of the Middle Ages popular in the nineteenth and early twentieth centuries. In its broadest terms medieval Europe emerged as the combined result of Rome's classical legacy, barbarian settlements within the boundaries of the old empire, and the Christian religion. Christian and political expansion were often coterminous and fostered the broad unity of Christendom stretching from Britain to Byzantium until

Constantinople's fall in 1453 and the subsequent division of Christendom during the Reformation. Its limits were also fixed by the rise of non-Christian religions such as Islam and the internal tensions between the spiritual and temporal destinies of Christian nations. The Middle Ages witnessed the birth of Europe, the rise of most modern European states, and the development of many European cultural, political, and social institutions. These include Romance languages and vernacular literature, bicameral forms of political government, much of canon and civil law and their judicial structures, the Christian intellectual life, the university, religious life, and ecclesiastical institutions including the papacy. The Gothic cathedral is the artistic triumph of medieval engineering and design. *See also* canon law; Holy Roman Empire; papacy, the; Rome; Scholasticism.

WILLIAM J. DOHAR

midrash (Heb., "inquiry, interpretation"), most properly rabbinic biblical interpretation, used more loosely for the process and results of all inner biblical, Jewish, and Christian interpretation. The word is used three times in the Bible with uncertain meaning (2 Chr 13:22; 24:27; Sir 51:23). The Dead Sea Scrolls use "midrash" to mean instruction, judicial inquiry, study of the law, and biblical interpretation. Rabbinic *midrashim* (pl.) are collections of interpretations arranged either verse by verse or thematically in sermonic compositions. Midrashic interpretations of biblical passages are scattered throughout other works. Many writings are called midrashic in the wider sense, including biblical books and passages that interpret earlier ones, Greek and Aramaic translations of the Bible (Septuagint and Targums), Qumran pesharim, *Jubilees*, the *Genesis Apocryphon,* and many passages of the NT.

Migne, Jacques-Paul (meen'), 1800–75, publisher. Ordained in Orléans in 1824, he moved to Paris and in 1836, fearing censorship, set up his own publishing house, Ateliers Catholiques, to produce an affordable, complete, 2,000-volume library for priests and educated laity. Though an 1868 fire prevented the completion of this project, he helped renew patristics with a 221-volume Latin patrology extending from Tertullian (d. ca. 225) to Innocent III (d. 1216) and a 161-volume Greek patrology extending from Pseudo-Barnabas (first century) to the Council of Florence (1438–45). He copied the best editions or had new ones made; many have yet to be superseded.

Milan, Edict of. *See* Constantine, Edict of.

military ordinariate, Church structure established to bring pastoral care to members of the military and their dependents. In brief, the military ordinariate functions like a diocese whose membership is determined not on the basis of residence within certain geographic boundaries, but on the basis of membership in the military service. Headed by a bishop who is assisted by a staff comparable to that of a diocesan bishop, the ordinariate oversees the religious care of military personal and their dependents worldwide. The priests who serve are drawn from a number of dioceses and religious communities; their ecclesiastical superiors have released them for such service. In the military of the United States these chaplains hold rank as officers. Before the creation of the military ordinariate, the archbishop of New York was the head of the military vicariate, whose offices were connected with the archdiocesan offices. Now bishop and offices are separate and independent from the archdiocese.

millenarianism, within Christian eschatology, the belief in the future establishment of a thousand-year period (the "millennium") either in preparation for, or subsequent to, the Second Coming of Christ. During this time, it is held, the martyrs and all the saints will be raised to life and share in Christ's messianic reign. Based largely on interpretations of Rev 20:1–15, the history of the teaching has been long and controversial. Recurrent literal readings of the text, especially in the second century and in the later Middle Ages, have never found favor within Catholic theology (cf. Thomas Aquinas, *Summa Theologiae* 3.77.1–4), which has tended instead to stress the allegorical meaning of the passages, the millennium symbolizing the temporal duration of the Church, from Christ's Resurrection to the final judgment (cf. Augustine *City of God* 20.7–9). *See also* eschatology, individual; eschatology, universal.

Mill Hill Missionaries (M.H.M.), known officially as St. Joseph's Society for Foreign Missions, religious order founded in 1866 in England by Cardinal Herbert Vaughan. The society came to the United States in 1951. Its main purpose is to train and provide priests for ministry in foreign missions. It currently operates in twenty-one mission territories in Africa, Asia, and South America. Headquarters is located in London and the

American headquarters is in St. Louis. *See also* Vaughan, Herbert.

Mill Hill Sisters, officially known as the Franciscan Missionaries of St. Joseph (F.M.S.J.), a congregation founded in 1883 by Alice Ingham in England originally to work in parish and charity ministries. These sisters received their popular name from the location of a seminary in London, where they collaborated with the Mill Hill priests. When the Mill Hill priests invited these sisters to join them in Malaysia in 1894, they became missionaries. An important work has been the nurturing of indigenous communities of sisters in Malaysia, Ecuador, Kenya, and the Philippines, but only in recent years have indigenous women joined the Mill Hill Sisters' congregation. In the 1990s about two hundred and fifty sisters minister in England, Scotland, Ireland, the United States, Kenya, and Ecuador. The generalate is in Manchester, England. *See also* Mill Hill Missionaries.

Milosz, Czeslaw (ches'law mee'wawsh), b. 1911, Lithuanian-born Polish poet and man of letters. After an early diplomatic career and exile in France, he came to the United States in 1960. He is emeritus professor of Slavic languages at the University of California (Berkeley). Author of the antitotalitarian work *The Captive Mind* (1950), he is the premier poet in the Polish language. His work gained him the Nobel Prize for literature in 1980.

mind/body, the philosophical problem of whether or not a valid substantial distinction can be drawn between the human mind and the human body. The question is a practical one because it bears on our survival as human persons after death. Is there a soul, or mind, that continues to exist after the body no longer exists? Although there are important historical and philosophical differences between the framing of this question in terms of "mind" or "soul," the pivotal divide is basically between some form of naturalism and some form of dualism. Naturalism construes human beings as complex physical systems that are continuous with the rest of the natural order, whereas dualism locates the distinctively human in a spiritual principle (a mind or a special kind of soul) that is discontinuous with the natural order and, therefore, capable of survival after separation from the body.

Most traditional accounts of distinctiveness and survival are grounded in dualistic accounts of mind or soul. On the other hand, many in the Christian tradition today construe distinctiveness and survival in terms of salvation history and the resurrection of the body without invoking the core metaphysical distinction of mind and body. Belief in eternal life is not based finally on philosophy but on the gospel of Jesus Christ. *See also* eternal life; immortality; resurrection of the body; soul.

Mindszenty, József (joh'zef mind-zen'tee), 1892–1975, Hungarian cardinal and active anti-Communist. Arrested by the Hungarian government in 1948, he pleaded guilty to the charge of treason after being drugged by his captors. Sentenced to life in prison, he received asylum in the United States embassy during the failed Hungarian uprising of 1956. As relations between Hungary and the West, including the Vatican, began to improve, his presence in Hungary became something of an embarrassment. In 1971 the Vatican arranged for his departure from Hungary to Rome, and in 1974 he relinquished his title as primate of Hungary. He became a symbol of anti-Communist sentiment in the United States and a heroic figure for conservative Catholics. *See also* Hungary, Catholicism in.

Minims (O.M.), a religious order of men founded by Francis of Paola in 1435 with an accent on humility and a Franciscan orientation. Minims in Latin means "the least." A second order of nuns and a third order of lay members were founded later. The order's headquarters is in Rome. *See also* Francis of Paola, St.

minister, extraordinary. *See* extraordinary minister of the Eucharist.

minister, ordinary. *See* ordinary minister.

ministry (Lat., *ministerium,* "service"), the public service rendered by members of the Church. Ministry is the work of those gifted with charisms and appointed by the Church to act in the name of Christ and of the Church with a view to continue the mission of Christ in the Church and in the world. In a more general sense, the term also designates works of service in the Church or in the world done in the name of Christ by any of the baptized. Throughout the Church's history, and especially since Vatican II (1962–65), ministry has undergone profound changes in response to new needs and new situations.

The Beginnings of Ministry: It is the belief of the Church that ecclesial ministry has its beginnings in the ministry of Jesus, who proclaimed the saving presence of the kingdom of God and called others to be associated with him in his God-given mission. Gospel accounts of post-Resurrection appearances make it clear that experience of the Risen Jesus involved a call to mission in his name.

The earliest documents of the NT, the Letters of Paul, show both that all the baptized are called to continue the mission of Christ and that certain persons have, by the gift (charism) of the Holy Spirit, a recognized ministry (Gk., *diakonia*) within the community to assist it in its life and mission. Names and roles of ministries vary greatly, though they are all seen as gifts of the Spirit and meant to build up the community of the faithful (1 Cor 12:4–11; 28–30; Rom 12:4–8). There are ministries of the word, of healing and of leadership; there are missionary leaders and local leaders. There is ample evidence for the role of women in ministry: in the founding of churches, in leadership roles, in teaching roles and as prophets, and in public worship.

Other NT documents give further evidence of the widespread presence of various specific ministries in the Church. In the pastoral Letters there are indications of efforts to describe the qualities needed for ministers and to order them for the good of the community.

Ministry in the Tradition of the Church: A wide variety of ministries continued to exist in the Church in its early centuries. In addition to bishops, presbyters, and deacons, there were, among others, teachers, prophets, widows, women deacons, confessors, doorkeepers, lectors, acolytes, and gravediggers. The type and exercise of ministry differed from place to place according to local need. Two dynamics of ecclesial ministry that continued to recent times began in the patristic period: the tendency of clerical roles to absorb ministry and the continuing birth of new expressions of ministry to respond to new needs.

With the rise of monasticism, many church ministries were taken over by monastic communities both of men and of women. Further changes came in response to the needs of developing feudal cul-

ture and again with the rise of urban society in the eleventh and twelfth centuries. Guilds organized for works of mercy and the care of the urban poor. When existing church structures were unable to respond to the needs of the masses, mendicant orders of laity, women and men, and clergy emerged and adapted new ministries of evangelization and care of the poor. Because many mendicants operated under the aegis of papal directives, tensions rose sometimes between ministries related to local episcopal structures and those of religious orders, especially as regards preaching responsibilities. It was tension, in part, between evangelical ministry and clerically dominated liturgical ministry that influenced debates between Reformers and the Catholic hierarchy in the sixteenth century.

In response to Reform focus on the ministry of the word and opposition to separation of clergy and laity, the Council of Trent (1545–63) defended the clerical ministries of minor orders, subdiaconate, diaconate, and priesthood. Sacramental ministry was based on the power of orders and preaching, teaching, and governing ministries on the power of jurisdiction. All were restricted to clerics. Yet post-Tridentine Catholicism also was marked by a multiplicity of religious orders of women and men and lay organizations that undertook ministry in many forms: education on all levels; health care; care for the poor; spiritual direction and counseling; missionary efforts; and care for the social, economic, and religious needs of immigrants. Even with the increasing clerical centralization in the late nineteenth and early twentieth centuries, new forms of lay ministry continued to develop among various groups: youth, families, workers, students, and those in the communications media.

Vatican II: The watershed of contemporary Catholic understanding of ministry came in Vatican Council II (1962–65). Developments, in both practice and theory, that had emerged in the decades before the council received official recognition. Basic to its understanding of ministry in the Church is the council's recognition that all the faithful, by Baptism and Confirmation, are called to take an active responsibility for the community and mission of the Church. All the baptized participate in the mission of Christ, who was himself the minister of God's presence and purpose in the world. Several Vatican II documents—the Pastoral Constitution on the Church in the Modern World, the Dogmatic Constitution on the Church, and the Decree on the

Apostolate of the Laity—speak of the Church's call, especially to the laity, to serve in the name of Christ the many needs of humankind in the world.

Other conciliar positions also contribute to current Catholic understanding of ministry, in both its specific and general sense. In several instances the council recognized that the Holy Spirit guides and directs the Church in communion and in ministry by both hierarchic and charismatic gifts. The council restored the permanent diaconate, in part, to grant the grace of office to those who were in fact doing diaconal ministry. Recalling ancient traditions of the Church, the council promoted the role of lay ministries in the liturgy of the Church, thus reversing the medieval and post-Tridentine restriction of liturgical ministries to clerics and those preparing to be clerics. It also recognized, most especially in the Decree on the Church's Missionary Activity, the contribution made by lay ministers of various types who contribute to the growth of the Church and the fulfillment of its mission. The call for a revised catechumenate involved a further recognition of the role of nonordained ministries in the Church.

Most of the council's explicit teaching on ministry focused on the ordained ministries of episcopacy, priesthood, and diaconate. In this teaching the council made significant shifts from previous Catholic understanding. The council's express teaching on lay ministries is ambivalent. At times it sees lay ministries in terms of Church functions to which laity are appointed by the hierarchy or which laypeople exercise only because there are too few or no clerics. In other instances, the council recognizes ministries that have their basis in a divine call and make a necessary contribution to the growth of the community.

Post–Vatican II: The tentative directions of the council have been pursued in subsequent papal documents, the revised code of canon law in 1983, and in the statements of various episcopal conferences. Pope Paul VI abrogated minor orders and the subdiaconate in 1972 and assigned the liturgical functions of the subdeacon to the lay ministries of lector and acolyte, restricting these ministries to men. The pope also invited the establishment of other ministries according to need. In his 1975 statement on evangelization, Pope Paul VI clearly recognized the place of nonordained ministries in the Church and suggested that norms for them be guided by the origins of the Church, its present needs and those of humankind. Pope John Paul II addressed the issue of ministries in the Church in his 1989 document on the laity, *Christifideles Laici.*

Developments in the actual function of church ministries have outpaced their official recognition in the Church. Lay ministries function in many areas of the life of the Church: religious education; pastoral work; liturgy and music; the catechumenate; care for the youth, the elderly, the sick; social ministry; spirituality; evangelization; and parish administration. While a rite of ordination is presently restricted to deacons, priests, and bishops and the formal rite of installation is reserved to those entering the canonical ministries of lector and acolyte, various types of rituals have been adopted to recognize the women and men who engage in lay ministries. The increasing presence of women in ministry has major implications not only as regards numbers but also in the understanding and practice of ministry.

In the face of rapid developments in ecclesial ministry, conclusions are premature. Certain directions do emerge, however. All the baptized share in the responsibility to build up the community and carry on the mission of the Church in the world. In this broad sense, all the baptized share in the ministry of the Church. Within this wider meaning is the more specific meaning of public ministry in the name of the Church. The Catholic Church recognizes, in the specific sense of public ministry, the presence of both ordained and lay ministry in the Church. The development of the latter is one of the more significant features of twentieth-century Catholic church life. *See also* Church; laity; priesthood.

Bibliography

Cooke, Bernard. *Ministry to Word and Sacraments: History and Theology.* Philadelphia, PA: Fortress Press, 1976.

Lawler, Michael G. *A Theology of Ministry.* Kansas City, MO: Sheed & Ward, 1990.

O'Meara, Thomas Franklin. *Theology of Ministry.* New York: Paulist Press, 1983.

Osborne, Kenan B. *Ministry: Lay Ministry in the Roman Catholic Church.* New York: Paulist Press, 1993.

Power, David N. *Gifts That Differ: Lay Ministries Established and Unestablished.* New York: Pueblo Publishing, 1980.

Schillebeeckx, Edward. *The Church with a Human Face: A New and Expanded Theology of Ministry.* New York: Crossroad, 1985.

FREDERICK J. CWIEKOWSKI

minor basilica. *See* basilica, minor.

minor orders, the orders of porter, lector, exorcist, and acolyte. For many centuries minor orders functioned as transitional ministries for those preparing for diaconate and priesthood. These orders have their origins in the ministries that, responding to diverse local pastoral needs, developed without set pattern in the third and fourth centuries. Porters had maintenance and security responsibilities; lectors read during worship; exorcists assisted at rites of initiation and repentance; subdeacons assisted the deacons; acolytes, initially, served as secretaries and messengers for the bishop. There were also other ministries, varying in different places, such as psalmists, teachers to instruct catechumens, orders of widows and virgins, and those who buried the dead. In time, these ministries became increasingly regulated, reduced in number, and eventually reserved to candidates for priesthood. By the time of the Council of Trent (1545–63), the minor orders were four: porter, lector, exorcist, and acolyte. The order of subdeacon, with its obligations of the Liturgy of the Hours (breviary) and celibacy, came to be regarded in the West as a major order.

The Second Vatican Council called for a revision of the ceremonies of the rites of these orders in the Latin Church. In 1972 Paul VI abrogated the four minor orders and replaced the subdiaconate with the lay ministries of lector and acolyte, though reserving their reception to men. The revised Code of Canon Law of 1983 authorizes men and women, even if they are not lectors or acolytes, to fulfill certain of their functions when designated ministers are lacking and the needs of the Church call for them. *See also* Holy Orders; major orders; subdeacon.

FREDERICK J. CWIEKOWSKI

Minucius Felix, third-century Latin Christian Apologist. A Roman advocate, possibly of African origin, Minucius wrote the *Octavian,* a sophisticated defense of Christianity modeled on Cicero's *On the Nature of the Gods.* This stylized debate between the young pagan Caecilius and the Christian Octavius on the providence of God and the end of the world was much admired by Jerome, the influential biblical scholar.

miracles [in the Bible], divine actions performed directly by God or through human beings that provoke wonder and amazement. The biblical vocabulary is much more diverse than the English "miracle." Key Hebrew terms in the OT include *'ôt,* "sign," which emphasizes the function of the action or specified object; *môpēt,* "wonder, portent, miracle," most frequently associated with God's wonders in Egypt; and *nîpĕlā'ôt,* "great deeds," which stresses

the extraordinary character of the deed. The psalmists regularly praise God for divine *nîpĕlā'ôt.* The actions or objects to which these terms refer are often but not always "miraculous," e.g., both the plagues in Egypt as well as Isaiah and his children are called "signs and wonders/portents" (*'ōtôt* and *môpĕtîm* [Deut 4:34; Isa 8:18]). NT texts employ a variety of Greek terms: *sēmeion,* "sign," points to the significance of the event and is the word for miracle in John; *teras,* "wonder," is associated with *sēmeion* in the NT and draws attention to the extraordinary character and even terror of the deed; *dynamis,* "deeds of power," accents the divine source; *ergon,* "work," has a specialized meaning, primarily in Johannine texts, indicating the miraculous activity of God and Jesus. The NT uses the verb *thaumazō,* "to be amazed," to express the reaction of bystanders. As in the OT, the NT terms sometimes refer to nonmiraculous events or objects. The biblical text, therefore, presents miracles within a broad frame of reference.

Three Clusters of Miracles: There are three major clusters of miracles in the Bible. The most important in the OT is the series of acts by which Yahweh delivered Israel from Egypt and led the people to Canaan. These demonstrate Yahweh's sovereignty over the gods of Egypt and care for Israel through the control of the forces of nature. A second collection appears in the Elijah-Elisha stories, which present the confrontation between Yahwism and Baalism. The last major set consists of the miracles of Jesus and the early Church, which are linked with the inbreaking of the eschatological kingdom.

Since many of these stories were told orally before they became part of texts, scholars have used form criticism to analyze them. Most miracles in the OT are sagas or legends celebrating Israel's origin and heroes. NT scholars group miracles into the large category of "miracle story" and then subdivide it into exorcisms, healings, epiphanies (i.e., the manifestations of divinity), rescue miracles (stories of deliverance from danger), gift miracles (extraordinary provisions), and rule miracles (reinforcement of religious rules). The basic pattern of a miracle story is threefold: a description of the problem, the miracle, and confirmation.

NT authors use miracle stories to make specific theological points. Mark's Gospel counterbalances miracle stories in the first half with the Cross in the second half. The message is that Jesus' true identity as the Son of God is recognized at the Cross. Matthew's fondness for systematic collections is evident in the ten miracles of chapters 8–9, which show that Jesus the Messiah is not only a teacher (the Sermon on the Mount) but a miracle worker. Luke-Acts connects miracles with the Spirit in the unfolding of salvation history. The seven "signs" in the first half of John are set beside related discourses as events that reveal Jesus' true identity.

The historicity of biblical miracles has been disputed, especially since the Enlightenment. The Catholic Church upholds the general reality of Jesus' miracles as signs of the kingdom, while permitting historical investigation to make independent judgments about specific miracle stories. *See also* miracles [theology of]. GREGORY E. STERLING

miracles [theology of], unusual and unexpected manifestations of the presence and power of God in human history. The First Vatican Council (1869–70), in its Dogmatic Constitution on the Catholic Faith (*Dei Filius,* ch. 3), affirms that, along with the internal help of the Holy Spirit, God wanted to join external demonstrations to divine revelation. These divine deeds, miracles, and prophecies are certain signs of that revelation made understandable to all. The council listed Moses and the prophets Christ the Lord, and the apostles as primary examples of miracle workers. With the development of modern science and the Enlightenment insistence on the autonomy of reason, miracles, along with the revelation they are intended to demonstrate, have been strongly questioned as nothing more than mythic stories from a primitive past. While not adhering to an earlier apologetic notion that miracles "prove" anything (such as Jesus' divinity) in a strict empirical sense, contemporary biblical criticism does recognize that miracles are integral to God's self-communication (or revelation) as recorded in the Judeo-Christian biblical witness. In other words, miracles belong to the substance of the proclamation about God's saving action in Christ. There are three foundational miracles, on the basis of which all other claims to the miraculous must be tested. They are Creation, Exodus, and Resurrection.

Creation—The Wonder of Human Existence: The philosophical question as to why things exist receives its biblical answer in the personal self-involvement of God in the shaping of human history from its very beginning. The Scriptures do not include the modern concept of "nature" with its Newtonian ideas of constancy and fixity that do not allow interventions or contraventions of nature's "laws." Such a view is questioned today even by science. In the Bible, the world and all that is in it belongs to God. There is no hard and fast distinction between nature and history. The world is the arena of God's surprising and unexpected actions. The sin of Adam and Eve has consequences for the relationship between humans and the rest of creation (Gen 3:15). God is everywhere interacting with the created world. A miracle (for which there is no word in Hebrew) is a "sign" (Heb., *'ôt*), a "wonder or portent" (*môpēt*), an "unusual or unexpected event" (*pālā'*) that manifests the presence and power of God.

Exodus—The Power and Will of YHWH to Save: The biblical notion of miracles cannot be understood apart from the centrality of faith. While the miracle stories exhibit the characteristics of popular tradition, as would be expected, their purpose is not to dwell on the phenomenal character of the miraculous as such but to call the community to faith in YHWH, who is Lord of all that exists. The "miracle" of the Exodus is the covenant, God's personal relationship to the people and the consequences that it bears for their relationships to one another. "Signs" like the burning bush, "wonders and portents" like the plagues in Egypt, "unusual and unexpected events" like crossing the Red Sea, while containing a historical core or factual base, are primarily intended to manifest and communicate this new and wonderful relationship of YHWH with the beloved community of Israel.

Resurrection—The Final Transformation of Creation: For the Christian, all of God's promises are fulfilled in the death and Resurrection of Jesus. This is the final and definitive action of God for the sake of the whole of reality. It is a divine embrace that reaches back to the very origins of the universe, affirms the history of Israel culminating in the history of Jesus, and reaches forward to the final transformation of all things in Christ. For the believer, the miracle lies in God's all-inclusive and transforming love. It is within this embrace that one must locate the miracles of Moses and the prophets, of Jesus in his historical ministry, and of the apostles in the continuing life of the Church.

The Christian Scriptures, like the Hebrew Bible, have no word for miracle. They speak of a "sign" (Gk., *sēmeion;* Heb., *'ôt*), a "wonder or portent" (*teras; môpēt*), a "work of power" (Gk., *dynamis*), and frequently in John a "work" (*ergon*). However, the notion of "signs" as things that legitimate Jesus' ministry or prove his divinity is rejected (Mark

8:11–12) unless it is understood as a God-given sign pointing beyond itself to the central miracle of Jesus' death and Resurrection (Matt 16:1–4; Mark 8:11–13; Luke 11:16, 29–32; 12:38–42, 54–56; John 2:18–22; 6:25–34). This is the interpretation of the Evangelists. For Jesus, in his historical ministry, there can be no question that he was perceived to be a healer of infirmities and an exorcist who had the power to drive out demons. These miracles are not unique, as can be seen from parallel stories in rabbinic and Hellenistic literature and from Jesus' response to the charge (Mark 3:22–30) that he casts out demons by the prince of demons: "... by whom do your own exorcists cast them out?" (Matt 12:27b; Luke 11:19b). What is important is Jesus' understanding of his miracles as signifying the arrival of the kingdom of God and so the triumph of the Spirit of God over Satan: "But if it is by the Spirit of God that I cast out demons, then the kingdom of God has come to you" (Matt 12:28; Luke 11:20). The miracles are authentic signs of the kingdom when faith is integral to the experiences either of those healed or their intercessors (see, e.g., Matt 8:5–13; 15:21–28; Mark 5:21–43; 9:14–29; 10:46–52; Luke 7:36–50; 17:11–19). This idea is developed, particularly in John, so that explicit faith in Jesus Christ is required for the signs or works to be adequately seen or understood. The important thing, then, is not just the phenomenon but the personal relationship with Jesus that it points toward (John 20:29, 31).

There are many today who can accept the fact that Jesus was a healer and exorcist, but who cannot accept the so-called nature miracles because they appear to contravene the "laws" of nature. Certainly, stories of miraculous feedings, walking on water, and raising the dead appear more mythic than factual to the contemporary mind. There can be a certain freedom of belief with regard to their factual character, but they, too, must remain integral to the Church's proclamation of the Risen Lord, who has power over all our fears and uncertainties and finally over death itself (1 Cor 15:24–27). Have miracles continued since the time of Jesus? Paul claims as a firsthand witness that he and others, too, worked miracles (Rom 15:18–19; 1 Cor 12:9–10; 2 Cor 12:12; Gal 3:5). There is no reason to think that miracles have not occurred even to the present day. But their authenticity depends on whether, with Paul, they serve to proclaim "the good news of Christ" (Rom 15:19). *See also* apologetics; faith; miracles [in the Bible].

Bibliography

Fuller, R. H. *Interpreting the Miracles.* London: SCM Press, 1963.

Kee, H. C. *Medicine, Miracle, and Magic in New Testament Times.* New York: Cambridge University Press, 1986.

Lewis, C. S. *Miracles.* New York: Macmillan, 1947.

Monden, Louis. *Signs and Wonders: A Study of the Miraculous Element in Religion.* New York: Desclee, 1966.

Moule, C. F. D., ed. *Miracles: Cambridge Studies in Their Philosophy and History.* London: A. R. Mowbray, 1965.

MICHAEL L. COOK

Miraculous Medal, religious sacramental. Inspired by the visions of Catherine Labouré in 1830, a medal in honor of the Immaculate Conception was struck in 1832. One side depicted the Blessed Virgin Mary standing on a globe crushing a serpent's head; on the other side was the letter M, under which were the twin hearts of Jesus (circled by thorns) and Mary (pierced by a sword), circled by twelve stars. The figure of Mary had the invocation, "O Mary, conceived without sin, pray for us who have recourse to thee." Many miracles were attributed to the devotion, which accounts for its name.

The medals were extraordinarily popular before the Second Vatican Council (1962–65), and their use was encouraged by the Church. The popularization of the devotional use of the medal was a particular

The Miraculous Medal, struck in 1832 in honor of the Immaculate Conception, a dogma defined by the Church in 1854, is called miraculous because of the miracles that were said to have been performed for the benefit of those who wore it.

apostolate of the Vincentian Fathers. *See also* Labouré, St. Catherine.

Mirari Vos (mee-rah'ree vohs; Lat., "You wonder"), encyclical letter of Pope Gregory XVI, August 15, 1832, condemning (without mentioning by name) the social and political principles espoused in *L'Avenir*, the Catholic newspaper edited by F. de Lamennais, C. Montalembert, and J. Lacordaire, e.g., social liberty, separation of Church and state, and freedom of religion and of the press.

Mishnah (Heb., "repetition, study"), the authoritative, early-third-century collection of rabbinic legal teachings assembled by Rabbi Judah the Prince and his colleagues. Laws and disputes concerning tithes, festivals, marriage, civil law, sacrifices, and ritual purity are collected, expanded, and systematized so that the details of the law form a coherent whole that reflects the rabbinic view of an orderly and sanctified world.

Missal, General Instruction of the Roman. *See* General Instruction of the Roman Missal.

Missal, Roman. *See* Roman Missal.

missalette (mi-sah-let'), a small missal or booklet to assist the assembly in following the words and actions of the Mass. Because monthly or seasonal missalettes with musical selections are often printed on recycled paper and may break down quickly with frequent use, these pamphlets may stand in marked contrast to the presider's grand liturgical books. Successful attempts to restore integrity to the assembly's liturgical books have been made with the publication of dignified music books, which at the same time supply scriptural readings and pastoral aids for catechesis and evangelization. *See also* Roman Missal.

Missa pro populo. *See* Mass for the People.

missiology, a specialization within theology that focuses on the missionary activity of the Church toward non-Christians. Drawing upon anthropological and cultural data, missiology studies the pertinent teachings and norms of the Church as well as the history, present condition, and methods of missionary activity (Decree on the Church's Missionary Activity, n. 26). *See also* missions.

mission, the purpose for which the Church has been "sent." Mandated by Christ to preach the gospel to every nation, the Church sees itself as sent, like Jesus, to bring the good news of God's love to people throughout the world. This task implies and requires that the Church give witness to this love by works of charity, teach the implications of this love by proclaiming respect for each human person and an ethic based on God's love, and celebrate this love in public and private worship. The organization of the Church exists to support the Church's mission. Areas of the world that have received the gospel relatively recently are at times called "mission" lands. *See also* Church; missions.

mission, parish. *See* parish mission.

Missionary Sisters of Our Lady of Africa (M.S.O.L.A.), sometimes called "The White Sisters" because of their white habits, a congregation founded in Algiers, North Africa, by Archbishop (later Cardinal) Charles Lavigerie in 1869 to care for orphans and provide medical care, combatting in particular eye diseases. Twenty-two indigenous sisterhoods have been founded by these sisters. As of 1993 they worked in seventeen countries in Africa, empowering women, training leaders, and doing pastoral work. There are about fourteen hundred members, from twenty-four different countries. Half of those in formation are Africans. The generalate is in Frascati, Italy.

Mission Helpers of the Sacred Heart (M.H.S.H.), a congregation founded in Baltimore, Maryland, in 1890 by Mary Frances Cunningham and Anna Hartwell to teach religion to African-American children who were not allowed to attend classes with white children. Evangelization and catechetics have always been the focus of the group. In the early years of the twentieth century they began work in catechizing the deaf. By 1993, about 120 members worked in pastoral ministry, catechetics, telecommunications, parish visiting, and hospital ministry, among both minority and majority populations. They minister in several dioceses in the United States, in Puerto Rico, and in Venezuela. The motherhouse is still in Baltimore.

MISSIONS

issions, or simply mission, is what the Church does for the sake of furthering God's reign in the world; more specifically, the announcing the gospel to those who have not heard it, either in one's own country (home missions) or abroad (foreign missions). Missions also sometimes refers to parish renewal programs. The term is now used most frequently in the singular form "mission." "Evangelization" and "evangelize" are roughly equivalent terms for "mission" and "missionary activity."

Missionary activity goes back to Jesus himself, who sent out disciples two by two to proclaim his message (Matt 10:1–15; Mark 5:7–13) to Israel and commissioned the Eleven to carry his gospel to all nations (Matt 28:19–20). The Acts of the Apostles can be read as a highly idealized account of the earliest missionary movement in Christianity. Paul is presented as the greatest of the early missionaries.

The Old Mission in Santa Barbara, California, a monument to the missionary efforts of Spanish clergy to bring the gospel to the New World. In 1994 the largest number of U.S. Catholics was in the state of California—over 7.5 million.

MISSION HISTORY

The Church has carried out its mission in a variety of ways and with differing levels of intensity throughout history. In the earliest period, monks and occasionally bishops were the missionaries. Some of these are commemorated as "apostles" to their specific regions: St. Augustine, to England; St. Patrick, to Ireland; St. Boniface, to Germany; and Sts. Cyril and Methodius, to the Slavic peoples. An alternative method in this period, used especially by the Merovingian kings (sixth–ninth centuries), was forced mass conversions as a policy for the pacification of northern European tribes.

In the medieval period, argument and moral persuasion were used to convert Jews and Muslims by figures such as Raymond of Peñafort (d. 1275) and Ramón Lull (d. ca. 1315). Forced conversions of Jews were common, however, in the same period. The thirteenth century saw the first European missionary forays into China, especially by the Franciscans. Nestorian missionaries had reached there earlier, however.

The so-called voyages of discovery, beginning in the 1490s ushered in a new missionary era, associating mission with imperial conquest. In 1493 Pope Alexander VI divided the new territories discovered by Christopher Columbus between Portugal and Spain, with the mandate to convert the peoples in the New World (the Caribbean islands, Central and South America) to Christianity. Christianity spread to Latin America and parts of Asia and Africa, with the missionaries, drawn mainly from the mendicant religious orders (Franciscans, Dominicans, Augustinians), serving as agents of the crown. Some missionaries, however, such as Bartolomé de las Casas (d. 1566), criticized imperial policy.

The newly founded Jesuits contributed important figures to mission;

principal among them was Francis Xavier (d. 1552), considered the patron saint of Catholic missions along with Thérèse of Lisieux (d. 1897). The Jesuit Matteo Ricci (d. 1610) and companions used European technology and the adoption of Chinese ways and thought patterns to launch a successful mission in China. This mission came to an end in the Chinese rites controversy, i.e., whether Chinese rites of ancestor veneration could be incorporated into Christianity. Pope Clement XI decided against the rites in 1704 and 1715, but these decisions were overturned by Pope Pius XII in 1939.

In 1622, Pope Gregory XV founded the Vatican office called the Sacred Congregation for the Propagation of the Faith (*De Propaganda Fide*; commonly known as the Propaganda; renamed Congregation for the Evangelization of Peoples in 1969) to centralize missionary activity and to provide for those new churches where the hierarchy had not yet been established. Missionary activity went into decline immediately before the French Revolution, especially with the suppression of the Jesuits (1773).

The modern missionary period begins with Europe's expansion into Africa and Asia at the beginning of the nineteenth century. A host of religious orders were founded to carry out missionary work (e.g., the Marists for the South Pacific, the White Fathers for Africa). National missionary societies were also founded (e.g., the Columbans in Ireland, Maryknoll in the United States).

The United States was itself considered a mission territory by the Propaganda until 1908, although American religious men and women had already been sent out to missions abroad. U.S. missionary efforts grew between the two world wars as the Propaganda entrusted more than thirty mission territories to American missionaries. But the largest U.S. missionary wave came after World War II, when Pope Pius XII appealed for U.S. missionaries to go to Latin America to help save that continent from Communism. This wave peaked in 1968 with more than 9,600 U.S. missionaries abroad. By 1992, there were fewer than 6,000 U.S. foreign missionaries.

Up to World War II, most U.S. missionaries were men and women religious, with the Jesuits and Maryknoll providing the largest numbers. Beginning in the late 1950s, a significant number of diocesan priests began to serve as foreign missionaries. Since the 1960s many laymen and laywomen have become missionaries, either in association with religious orders or in independent lay mission organizations.

MODES OF MISSIONARY ACTIVITY

Missionary activity in the modern period is carried out in a number of ways. First among these is a direct proclamation of the message of Jesus Christ. Throughout the nineteenth and twentieth centuries education, medicine, and social development have also been modes for carrying out mission. While this has brought Christianity and improved the lot of many people, it has often led to confusing Christianization with Westernization, both in the minds of missionaries and those they reached.

A priest gives absolution to a penitent in Joballar, Dominican Republic, where evangelization began almost immediately after the arrival of Christopher Columbus in 1492 and where there are now over 6.5 million Catholics, or more than 91 percent of the population.

These methods continue to be used, but with more caution. Since the 1960s other methods have been emphasized. Among these are dialogue with non-Christian religions, the witness of Christian life (especially in areas where other forms of missionary work are not permitted), and solidarity in the liberation of the poor from oppression. In all instances, there is a greater emphasis on allowing the message of the gospel to be expressed in forms known to, and appropriate in, the culture where it is being proclaimed. This is known as the process of "inculturation." Missionaries now recognize that conversion is a much slower and more complex process than was once imagined.

MISSIONARY ORGANIZATION

Through long periods of the Church's history there was no systematic organization of missionary activity. Papal patronage was often sought for undertaking missionary work, but this was not necessary. Secular rulers often provided both protection and material support.

The medieval religious orders used their own internal structure of provinces and houses to provide organization. From 1622, the Propaganda assigned geographical regions to different orders, a practice that continued into the 1960s. The Propaganda continues to collect and distribute funds through the Pontifical Aid Societies (Society for the Propagation of the Faith, the Holy Childhood Association, Society of St. Peter the Apostle) to aid newer and poorer churches. These societies each have a national and a diocesan organization and also carry out mission education as well as collect funds.

The religious orders worked largely independently of one another in their missions. In 1950 the Propaganda authorized setting up national mission secretariats for coordinating services, training, and publication.

Such a secretariat was established in the United States and continued until 1969. It was replaced in 1970 by the U.S. Catholic Mission Council, which jointly represented the U.S. bishops and men and women religious. This continued until 1976, when the bishops withdrew their support and consolidated their efforts within the Missions Committee of the National Conference of Catholic Bishops. In 1982, the U.S. Catholic Mission Association was established as a means of communication among religious orders, lay mission associations, and interested individuals.

CATHOLIC MISSION TEACHING

Although missionaries had developed manuals for mission activity at various points in history, comprehensive thinking and teaching about mission began with Pope Leo XIII (d. 1903), who wrote six encyclicals relating to mission, most of them on specific issues. On the academic side, the discipline of missiology began among Protestants in the latter half of the nineteenth century, with the first Catholic professorship of missiology established at Münster, Germany, in 1911. Faculties of missiology were established subsequently at the Gregorian and Urban universities in Rome and in other European universities.

Contemporary mission teaching dates from Pope Benedict XV's encyclical *Maximum Illud* (1919). It reminded Catholics that the purpose of missionary activity was to bring about the conversion of souls and to provide the Church in other lands with its own native leadership as quickly as possible. These themes of conversion and establishing the Church were elaborated upon in missiology down to the time of Vatican II (1962–65). Pope Pius XI (d. 1939) carried Benedict XV's policies forward with his encyclical *Rerum Ecclesiae* (1926) and by ordaining Chinese, Indian, and Japanese bishops. Pius XII (d. 1958) continued in the same vein with two encyclicals, *Evangelii Praecones* (1951) and *Fidei Donum* (1957). There was in these works a growing emphasis on what would later be called inculturation.

The watershed in mission teaching came with the Second Vatican Council. Three important developments took place. First, a more dynamic understanding of the Church in itself and in relation to the world was presented in the Dogmatic Constitution on the Church (*Lumen Gentium,* 1964) and the Pastoral Constitution on the Church in the Modern World (*Gaudium et Spes,* 1965). The Church no longer saw itself as separated from the world, but as deeply engaged in it. A theological balance was likewise restored by making proper distinctions between the Church and the reign of God (the two are not identical) and between Christ's Church and the Catholic Church (the former "subsisting" in the latter).

The second development was the relation of the Church to mission. The Decree on the Church's Missionary Activity (*Ad Gentes Divinitus,* 1965) roots the basis for mission not so much in the Church or even in the Great Commission (Matt 28:19–20), but in the dynamic activity of the Trinity itself in the world, through the sending of the Second Person in the Incarnation, and in the sending of the Holy Spirit following the Resurrection. The Church participates in this sending inasmuch as it is sacrament of God in the world. The Church is thus by its very nature missionary; or put another way, the Church does not have missions, it is mission. Missionary activity is therefore not the work of a designated few but is incumbent upon all the baptized.

The third development affecting mission was a new attitude toward other great religious traditions, expressed in *Lumen Gentium* and *Ad Gentes Divinitus,* but especially in *Nostra Aetate* (The Declaration on the Relationship of the Church to Non-Christian Religions, 1965). The good things found in other religions are affirmed, and it is now taught that those who follow those traditions and through no fault of their own do not know Christian faith, achieve some measure of salvation. What exactly the council fathers meant by this remains controverted and has opened a debate about the relation of Christianity to other religions. Its effect has been to support dialogue with other religions, but it has also called into question for some people whether Christianity should attempt to convert members of other religions at all.

The most influential postconciliar document for mission has been Pope Paul VI's apostolic exhortation on evangelization in the modern world, *Evangelii Nuntiandi,* published in 1975. It provides an extensive reflection on what evangelization is and how it takes place. It emphasizes not only the evangelization of individuals, but also of cultures. It also gives cautious support to liberation theologies and small ecclesial communities if properly understood. For many, *Evangelii Nuntiandi* remains the handbook for modern missionary activity.

"Inculturation" grew as a concept in the 1970s and was first used in a papal document in Pope John Paul II's *Catechesi Tradendae* in 1979. John Paul II also issued an encyclical on mission in 1991, *Redemptoris Missio.* It reiterates conciliar and postconciliar teaching, with a special emphasis on proclamation as the central mode of evangelization. He has also urged a "New Evangelization" in Christian countries that have lost the fervor of earlier commitment, especially in western Europe and Latin America.

Contemporary mission thought rests on the triad of evangelization, inculturation, and liberation. Evangelization is about the bringing of the gospel into a culture. But the process is not complete without inculturation, the gospel's taking root and assuming the form of the culture. And that cannot happen until there is a genuine "renewal of humanity" (Paul VI) that is brought about by the liberation of the poor from their oppression.

See also Church; evangelization; inculturation; liberation theology.

Bibliography

Jenkinson, William, and Helene O'Sullivan, eds. *Trends in Mission: Toward the 3rd Millenium.* Maryknoll, NY: Orbis Books, 1991.
Motte, Mary, and Joseph R. Lang, eds. *Mission in Dialogue.* Maryknoll, NY: Orbis Books, 1982.
Scherer, James A., and Stephen B. Bevans, eds. *New Directions in Mission and Evangelization.* Maryknoll, NY: Orbis Books, 1992.

ROBERT SCHREITER

Mit brennender Sorge (miht bren'nen-dehr zawr'gay; Ger., "With searing anxiety"), papal encyclical attacking Nazism. This scathing denunciation by Pope Pius XI of racism and other unchristian tenets of Nazism was smuggled into Germany and read from all pulpits in March 1937. The encyclical infuriated Nazi leaders, who were caught wholly offguard and afterward stepped up their already intense pressure against the Church and its priests. *See also* Nazism.

mitre (mi̱'tuhr; Gk.; Lat., *mitra*, "headband"), the headcovering that bishops and some abbots wear during liturgical rites. Two triangular pieces of stiffened material are sewn together on the sides with an opening for the head at the base. Two strips of fringed material, known as fanons or lappets, hang from the back base of the mitre. Three forms may be worn: a high mitre with jewels, a shorter less ornate mitre made of gold cloth, or a simple mitre covered with white silk or linen. The mitre is removed whenever its wearer leads the assembly in a spoken or sung prayer.

mixed chalice, the chalice or cup of wine prepared for Eucharist by mixing a small amount of water with the wine. Early liturgical texts refer to it in rubrics or directions before the mixing or in the prayers that accompany it. The ritual action spawned allegorical interpretations: the water is the baptized people whose sins are absorbed into the saving blood of Christ; both water and blood flowed from the side of the crucified Christ; water and wine represented the human and divine natures in Christ. Some Reformed churches reject this practice, while the Roman Catholic Church retains it. *See also* unmixed chalice.

mixed marriage, a marriage between a Catholic and a person of another faith. Church law shows a reluctance to allow a Catholic to marry a non-Catholic because of fear concerning the difficulty of such a marriage. A distinction is made between a mixed marriage in which the non-Catholic partner is baptized and a marriage in which that spouse is not. In both cases, however, the bishop's approval is required after the Catholic partner has promised to remain faithful to Catholicism and to raise the children Catholics. The non-Catholic need not make such a promise but must be told of the other's promise. Permission may be given for the ceremony to take place with non-Catholic rites. *See also* marriage law.

mixed religion, impediment of, a marriage impediment found in the 1917 Code Canon of Law that forbade marriage between a Catholic and a baptized non-Catholic. That impediment did not invalidate the marriage, but simply forbade it. The present code of canon law (1983) still requires a Catholic to obtain permission to marry a non-Catholic, although the condition is no longer considered an impediment. It is common to give such permission as long as the Catholic promises to remain faithful to the Church and to do all within his or her power to raise the children as Catholics. *See also* marriage law.

Modalism, an extreme form of Monarchianism, called Sabellianism in the East and Patripassianism in the West, and condemned by Dionysius of Alexandria (d. ca. 264) because of its exaggerated emphasis on the unity of the divine Being. According to Modalists, God is triune only in that creation, redemption, and sanctification represent three manifestations of God in history. Modalists deny any real distinction of the divine Persons, holding that Father, Son, and Holy Spirit are merely modes, aspects or energies of the one divine Person, who exercises three distinct functions on behalf of humanity. As a reaction to subordinationist beliefs of the second century, many early Modalists emphasized the uni-

Mitre

mitre

lappets

ty of God so as to oppose any view that the Son is God only in a secondary or subordinate way. The resulting view, however, affirmed that the distinctions among Father, Son, and Spirit belong entirely to the economy of salvation, not to the eternal essence of God. Early opponents of Modalism, notably Tertullian in the third century and Augustine in the fifth century, attempted to correlate the events of salvation history with the divine Being through the development of a doctrine of appropriations and a theology of divine relations emphasizing the eternal, ontological relations of Father, Son, and Spirit. Today, locating the unity of God either within only one of the divine Persons or within a substance shared by them remains highly problematic. The perennial struggle between orthodox trinitarian theology and Modalism seems to revolve around the difficulty of speaking about the oneness of God while maintaining three real relations in God. *See also* Monarchianism; Trinity, doctrine of the.   JANICE POORMAN

moderator of the curia, priest or bishop appointed by the diocesan bishop where expedient to assist him as coordinator of diocesan administration and as curial supervisor. This optional office may be particularly suitable for larger dioceses with complex administrative tasks, but in the case of larger dioceses, it is recommended that the vicar general hold the office. *See also* diocesan curia.

Modernism, the name given to the doctrinal and disciplinary crisis in the Catholic Church in the early years of the twentieth century, a crisis that was created by the efforts of Catholic intellectuals to reconcile Catholic faith with modern rationality and that eventually, in 1907, provoked Pope Pius X to condemn these efforts as heretical.

Modern rationality mediated by industrialization (science, technology) and democracy (emancipatory reason) challenges the world religions, including Christianity, by threatening to secularize their sacred Scriptures, invalidate their metaphysical concepts, and undermine their traditional hold on society. The first temptation of these religions is to resist modern rationality. The Catholic Church did so in the course of the nineteenth century (see Pius IX's "Syllabus of Errors" of 1864). When intellectuals among believers try to reconcile their faith with modern culture, they often embrace modern rationality uncritically and then are unable to de-

fend the foundation of their faith. At the turn of the century, Catholic intellectuals challenged traditional Catholicism with their scientific approach to the biblical books, their repudiation of classical metaphysics, and their call to the laity to become politically active independently of the hierarchy.

Pope Pius X believed that these challenges represented a dangerous movement guided by a heretical theology that he called Modernism. In the decree *Lamentabili* (1907) he condemned a long list of Modernist opinions, and in his encyclical *Pascendi Dominici Gregis* (1907) he presented a striking theological synthesis drawn from the ideas of various Modernist authors that defined the essential nature of the modern heresy. Modernism, according to *Pascendi,* was derived from two false principles. The first was the rejection of metaphysical reason, which led to skepticism regarding the rational proofs for God's existence. The second, the rejection of "the supernatural" (God's gratuitous self-communication in divine revelation), led to the idea that Christian doctrine was derived from religious experiences responding to people's deep psychological needs. Since the synthesis created by the encyclical did not as such exist in the minds of any of the Modernist authors, they thought they had been gravely misunderstood.

Biblical Modernism: Rome defended the historical veracity of the biblical books against the biblical scholars who relied more on symbolic or allegorical interpretations. In 1907, a new guideline strengthened the authority of the Pontifical Biblical Commission. The most famous biblical scholar condemned as a Modernist was Alfred Loisy (d. 1940). In response to Adolf von Harnack's liberal Protestant proposal that reduced Christianity to a simple, original message and rejected later Christian beliefs as extraneous additions, Loisy defended the Catholic tradition by showing that the Christian message was a living force that unfolded its meaning in the early Church and summoned forth new responses in subsequent history. Rome put Loisy's work on the Index of Forbidden Books as an example of vitalism and immanent evolutionism that ignored the conceptual truth contained in divine revelation. After his excommunication Loisy left the Catholic faith to embrace a more general belief in the universal divine presence. To this day historians disagree whether Loisy still held to the Catholic faith when he was condemned by Rome, or whether he was already skeptical of biblical revelation.

Theological Modernism: The best-known speculative authors condemned as Modernists were the French philosopher Lucien Laberthonnière (d. 1932) and the English theologian George Tyrrell (d. 1909). Following the modern (Kantian) rejection of metaphysics, Laberthonnière turned to Maurice Blondel's philosophy of action, which held that truth was implicit in human willing and choosing. Yet while Blondel (d. 1949) protected the gratuity of divine revelation, Laberthonnière seemed to assign human religious creativity to the vital forces immanent in humanity. A similar turn to immanent vitality was taken by Tyrrell, who sought to make the Church and its message more credible in modern culture. For him Christian truth was founded on religious experience and was articulated in symbols and rituals. The Church moving through the ages was an evolving historical community sustained by the religious experiences of its members. In the age of democracy, Tyrrell argued, the Church should be guided by the free discussion among its members rather than by an ecclesiastical magisterium. After dismissal from his religious order and excommunication, Tyrrell became increasingly hostile to what he called "Romanism" or "the Roman heresy." Two well-known Modernists in England, Tyrrell's friends Baron Friedrich von Hügel (d. 1925) and Maude Petre, both laypeople, escaped condemnation and remained believing Catholics.

Social Modernism: In his own review and later through a political organization, the Italian priest Romolo Murri promoted the concept of Christian democracy, in which Catholic laypeople, freed from intellectual and disciplinary control of the hierarchy, would assume Christian responsibility for their society. Rome condemned these liberal ideas as Modernist. Murri was suspended from his priestly function in 1907 and excommunicated in 1909. In France, similar democratic ideas were promoted by Marc Sangnier's Sillon movement, dissolved by Pius X in 1910.

Rather than a system, Modernism was an intellectual orientation of Catholics who wrestled with the questions posed by modernity. This orientation was successfully crushed by the ecclesiastical condemnations, the anti-Modernist oath demanded of every priest prior to ordination (a rule no longer in force), and the notorious spying organization *Sodalium Pianum,* directed by Monsignor Benigni, which was later suppressed by Pope Benedict XV. Since then theological progress has been made, especially during and after Vatican Council II (1962–65), but the religious questions raised by modernity have not yet received their definitive answers. *See also* Benedict XV; Pius X, St.

Bibliography
Loome, T. M. *Liberal Catholicism, Reform Catholicism, Modernism.* Mainz: Matthias Grunewald, 1979.
Ranchetti, M. *The Catholic Modernists.* London: Oxford University Press, 1969.
Reardon, B. M. *Roman Catholic Modernism.* Stanford, CA: Stanford University Press, 1970.
Vidler, A. R. *A Variety of Catholic Modernists.* London: Cambridge University Press, 1970.   GREGORY BAUM

Modernism, oath against. *See* oath against Modernism.

modes, Gregorian, arrangement of the notes of the musical scale of chant according to certain set patterns. *See also* chant, Gregorian.

Möhler, Johann Adam (mer'luhr), 1796–1838, major German theologian and doctrinal historian. He taught Church history at the University of Tübingen and is considered the central figure of the important Catholic Tübingen School. In his early but widely read *Die Einheit in der Kirche* ("The Unity of the Church," 1825), Möhler drew on themes from romantic idealism to treat the Church as a living tradition and an organic unity. In addition to his many writings in patristics and Church history, his *Symbolik* (1832) provided a comparative analysis and assessment of the beliefs of, and basic differences between, Protestants and Catholics. Appointed professor in Munich in 1835, he lectured for only three years before his death. Möhler's ecclesiology and understanding of tradition had considerable influence at Vatican II, through the work of twentieth-century Tübingen theologians and the French Dominican Yves Congar. *See also* Congar, Yves; Tübingen.

Mohrmann, Christine, 1903–88, Dutch historian of primitive Christianity and specialist in early Christian Latin. Her *Atlas of the Early Christian World* (co-authored with F. van der Meer; Eng. ed., 1958) is still a standard reference work. In 1947 she launched *Vigiliae Christianae,* a scholarly, ecumenical journal of Christian life and language.

Molina, Luis de, 1535–1600, Spanish Jesuit theologian. He entered the Jesuits in 1553 and later taught philosophy and theology. Preeminent among Catholic moral theologians of his day, Molina is best known for his *Concordia,* or *Harmony of Free Will with the Gifts of Grace* (1588), in which he reconciled divine grace with human free will through a process of *scientia media* (Lat., "middle knowledge"), according to which God foreknows specific human acts in different hypothetical situations and then confers grace according to foreseen merits. He was opposed by the Dominican theologian Domingo Báñez. The ensuing controversy between the Jesuits and the Dominicans about grace and human abilities (known as *De Auxiliis*) led to papal silencing of all involved parties. *See also* Báñez, Domingo; *De Auxiliis;* Molinism.

Molinism, the theory of Luis de Molina, a seventeenth-century Spanish Jesuit theologian, concerning the relationship of divine grace to free will. This theology emerged during a time that saw a greater emphasis upon the human being, humanist education, and new theories of meditation and religious life. Molina's theology, appearing in *Concordia,* or *Harmony of Free Will with the Gifts of Grace* (1588), highlighted human freedom, deemphasized divine grace prior to freedom, and fashioned a novel theory of God's knowledge of future events. Particularly novel was his theology of a "middle knowledge": in the vast realm of free human decisions God sees every decision in all its conditions and ramifications and so grasps all possible arrangements, but God leaves the individual choice of direction to human freedom. Dominicans beginning with Domingo Báñez argued that this did not represent the real teaching of Thomas Aquinas (d. 1274), who viewed grace as a prior, efficaciously divine force, albeit in a real human freedom. This Spanish debate began the wider controversy *De Auxiliis* (lit., "concerning the helps" [toward salvation]), which ended in Rome in 1607. Issues were left undecided and Molinism was allowed to be taught alongside various Thomisms and other Catholic systems. The Society of Jesus espoused Molinism until Jesuit theologians in the twentieth century (Henri de Lubac, Karl Rahner) recovered and newly emphasized patristic and modern theologies. *See also De Auxiliis;* grace. *THOMAS F. O'MEARA*

Molinos, Miguel de, 1640–97, Spanish spiritual director and writer. He was called a Quietist because he advanced a spirituality of self-abandonment before God that required complete annihilation of one's will. Because of the disruptive effects of this teaching in convents, he was condemned and, even

after he repudiated his ideas, imprisoned for life. *See also* Quietism.

Monarchianism, designation for certain second- and third-century teachings emphasizing God's oneness in divine rule (Gk., *monarchia*) at the expense of God's trinitarian character. Following the German theologian Adolf von Harnack (d. 1930), scholars distinguish "Modalist Monarchianism" from "Dynamic Monarchianism." Tertullian (the first to use the designation "Monarchians") and Hippolytus attacked the former, first taught by Noetus of Smyrna (ca. 200), then at Rome by his pupil Epigonus, by Praxeas (ca. 200), and by Sabellius (ca. 220), whose name became especially associated with this heresy ("Sabellianism"). For the Modalists, "Father," "Son," and "Holy Spirit" were merely names for modes or manifestations of one and the same God. Their critics allege they maintained that in Jesus the Father was incarnate, suffered, and died, "Son" being merely the name of the one God when incarnate. They were thus mocked as "Patripassianists," i.e., for teaching that the Father suffered.

The Dynamic Monarchians (also called Adoptionists) preserved God's monarchy by denying that "Son" was the name of anything divine—it was merely the designation of a man, Jesus, after his receipt of divine power (Gk., *dynamis*) at his baptism. Ancient critics accused such teachers, including Theodotus the Leather Merchant (ca. 190), Theodotus the Banker, Artemon (ca. 230–50; all of whom taught at Rome), and Paul of Samosata, of "psilanthropism," i.e., of teaching that Jesus was "merely a human being," adopted into his stature as God's son. *See also* Adoptionism; God; Modalism; Patripassianism; Sabellianism; Trinity, doctrine of the.

 JOHN C. CAVADINI

monastery (Gk., *monos,* "alone"; "hermit's cell" or "group of protected cells"), currently designated in the 1983 Code of Canon Law as the dwelling place of monks (can. 613), clerics living a communal life (can. 613), or nuns (cans. 609, 614). In the West, the term is generally reserved for Benedictine houses or houses derived from the Rule of St. Benedict. Defining characteristics of a monastery are separation from the world; the monk's permanent attachment to the place of profession; virtual autonomy of government of the individual house (cans. 586, 591–96); and commitment of members to a classical monastic rule. Monasteries are commonly designated

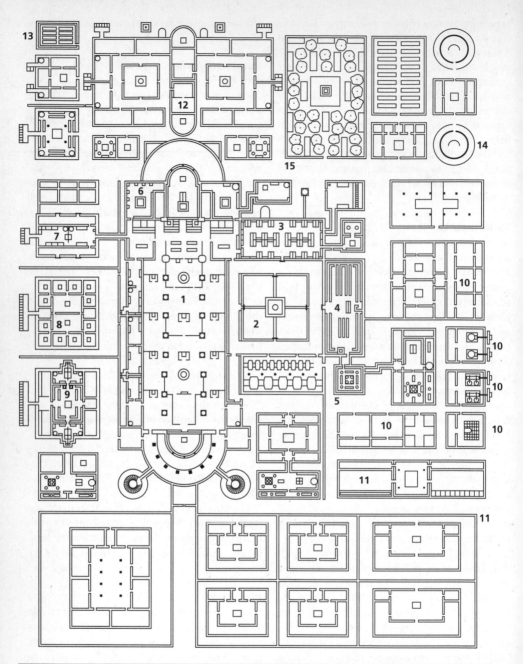

1 church	**6** scriptorium	**11** barns and stables	
2 cloister	**7** abbot's house	**12** infirmary-novitiate	
3 dormitory	**8** school	**13** gardens	
4 refectory	**9** guest house	**14** poultry houses	
5 kitchen	**10** workshop	**15** cemetery-orchard	

The plan for an ideal monastery, developed ca. 820 at the Benedictine abbey of St. Gall in modern-day Switzerland, reconstructed by Walter Horn and Ernest Born from the manuscript in the library of St. Gall. The monastery site was to have been 480 feet by 640 feet, housing 120 monks and 170 serfs. This plan, although never realized in stone, exercised a major influence on monastic construction in subsequent centuries.

St. Scholastica Monastery in Subiaco, Latium, Italy. Scholastica (d. ca. 543) was the sister of Benedict of Nursia, one of the founders of Western monasticism. She established this monastery only a few miles from Benedict's Monte Cassino.

by the superior's rank (abbey, priory) or the work undertaken therein (mission, house of studies). While all monasteries are named in honor of a sacred mystery or a patron saint, they are more often known by the name of the local town. *See also* monasticism.

monastic spirituality, the whole complex of attitudes and practices that characterize the life of men and women living according to a monastic rule. Although St. Anthony of Egypt (d. 356) is often called "the father of monks," monastic spirituality cannot properly be understood without reference to its roots in the NT and in the history of the Church prior to Anthony. Many early Christians who desired to follow the gospel in a particularly intense way embraced celibacy "for the sake of the kingdom" (cf. Matt 19:12). This later came to be regarded as an essential component of monastic spirituality, so

much so that many scholars believe that the original Greek word for "monk," *monachos* (Lat., "one living alone"), referred not to a hermit but to someone living without a spouse.

Another essential component from the beginning was a significant degree of retirement from the world. Anthony's early biographer, Athanasius (d. 373), notes that already before Anthony there were many ascetics living near the outskirts of villages in Middle Egypt; what differentiated Anthony from the others was that he set out for "the faraway desert" and lived in almost complete solitude for some years before emerging to give instruction to those who wanted to embrace this way of life. Critics of the monastic movement have often judged such retirement harshly as being fueled by an unchristian, Platonic disdain for the temporal order, but in its original intent it served as a way of simplifying one's life, thereby enabling the monk or nun to focus more sharply on the clear challenge of the gospel, putting on the mind of Christ. This is why references to the great commandments of love of God and neighbor recur so frequently in early monastic literature, as in the *Ascetikon* of Basil the Great (d. 379).

Other integral aspects of monastic spirituality are the meditative pondering of the Scriptures (Lat., *lectio divina*), the ideal of constant mindfulness of God (*memoria Dei*), poverty (at least in the sense of the communal ownership of goods), obedience to a spiritual guide (who came to be known as abbot or abbess in monastic communities), and, for those living in community (as distinct from hermits), regular periods of common prayer (called the *opus Dei* in the Rule of St. Benedict).

Benedict (d. ca. 550) assumed in his rule that the life of prayer and work would be practiced within the enclosure of the monastic precincts, but already in the early Middle Ages the pressing needs of society often called monastics out of their cloisters to serve as missionaries, preachers, and Church reformers, with the result that long ago there arose great diversity in the kinds of work undertaken by monastic men and women. The call of Vatican II (1962–65) for members of all religious orders to return to the spirit of their founders has led to vigorous discussion among monastics as regards what kinds of work and life-styles are genuinely compatible with monastic life. *See also* Benedict, Rule of St.; monasticism; spirituality, Christian.   JAMES WISEMAN

Monenergism, a seventh-century Christological heresy that posited only one divine energy, or action, in Christ. It was developed by Sergius (d. 638), patriarch of Constantinople, in an attempt at theological reconciliation with the Monophysites, who persisted in their belief that in Christ there is only one divine nature, a position condemned by the Council of Chalcedon (451). Monenergism was the companion heresy to Monothelitism, which held that there is only one divine will in Christ. Monenergism and Monothelitism were condemned by the Third Council of Constantinople in 681. *See also* Constantinople, councils of; Monophysitism; Monothelitism.

Monica, St., ca. 331–87, mother of Augustine of Hippo. She lived in North Africa near Carthage, where she generously served the poor while raising her own family. She became concerned about young Augustine's dissolute life-style and prayed constantly for his conversion. She followed him to Rome in 383 and later to Milan, where she came under the influence of Ambrose, its bishop, and eventually witnessed her son's conversion. She died at Ostia, in Italy, while traveling back to Africa with her son.

Her feast day is August 27. *See also* Augustine of Hippo, St.

monitum, an official "warning" (Lat.). The term may be used when an official warning is given regarding a particular teaching or when an author is suspected of error on matters of doctrine. The same term is also used to indicate one of the warnings that must clearly be given a person in the process used before a penalty or sanction is imposed.

monk, a word commonly used to refer to any vowed member of a religious community of men adhering to the monastic rule of life. Derived from the Latin word *monachus,* a transliteration of the Greek for "one who lives alone," the term has been applied broadly and imprecisely throughout history to hermits and members of religious communities alike. Early medieval monastic reforms designated it as appropriate to Benedictines, Cistercians, and Carthusians, but not to less strictly contemplative groups. Such precision of usage was never the norm, however, and after the Reformation precise application became even more elusive. In modern practice, "monk" is also used to designate male members of non-Christian religious bodies, e.g., Buddhist monks. *See also* monasticism.

Monks of St. Hormisdas, the Antonine Order of St. Hormisdas of the Chaldeans, a Chaldean Catholic monastic congregation, founded in 1880 by Gabriel Dembo beside the ruins of the ancient East-Syrian monastery of Rabban Hormuzd near Alqosh in northern Iraq. The order follows a rule and organization borrowed from the Maronite Antonine monks. *See also* monk.

monogenism, the theory of human origin from one individual. The Bible seems to suppose monogenism (Gen 1–3; Rom 5), but, scientifically, polygenism seems more probable. The inspired biblical texts seem to say only that humankind is one in nature, sin, and grace. Although Pope Pius XII's encyclical *Humani Generis* (1950) supported monogenism, Catholics are not required to hold such a position today. *See also* creation; evolution; original sin.

monophony (Gk., "one voice"), music that consists of one melodic line as opposed to polyphony, which has several melodic lines. *See also* liturgical music.

MONASTICISM

Monasticism (Gk., *monos*, "one, alone") is an institutionalized form of ascetic religious life in which individuals take vows of poverty, chastity, obedience, and (as in the Benedictines) stability, separating themselves from society either singly (eremitic form) or in community (cenobitic form). The goal of monasticism is to pursue, under the guidance of a formal rule, a life of prayer and work for the glory of God, for personal sanctification, and for the good of the Church and the world.

BACKGROUND

Although Anthony of Egypt (d. ca. 356) is generally regarded as the founder of monasticism, having given away all of his possessions and devoted himself to a life of asceticism in the desert, monasticism has its roots in the earliest Christian tradition. The care of widows mentioned, e.g., in 1 Tim 5:3–16 seems to have been institutionalized by the second century as a kind of "order" in which women lived on the alms of the community and were responsible for intercessory prayer and service (see Polycarp *Philippians* c. 4). By the end of the third century, "Sons and Daughters of the Covenant," celibates who practiced austerities in their own homes and offered spiritual leadership in the churches, populated Syria. The Greek word *monachos*, "monk," which begins to appear in papyri in the fourth century, may derive from the designation used of these Syriac-speaking ascetics, the "single ones" (Gk., *monos*, "one"). The origins of monasticism may have been influenced by the Essenes or the Therepeutae, both Jewish groups, as suggested as early as the fourth century by Eusebius of Caesarea. Others postulate Manichaean influence, observing the ascetic character of the Manichaean elect, who scorned the things of the world and pursued a life of severe austerity.

Sometimes the influence of Buddhist monasticism is even suggested. Palladius, the fourth-century monastic historian, wrote a treatise on the Indian brahmin ascetics, *De Gentibus Indiae et Bragmanibus* (On the People of India and the Brahmins). Surely traditions of non-Christian asceticism, especially the Neoplatonic, were also influential as the monastic movement gained ground.

THE DESERT TRADITION

Monasticism is in its origins Egyptian, lay, Coptic-speaking, and of peasant roots. In ca. 285 Anthony of Egypt retired to the desert to encounter the demons who were said to inhabit those waterless places. He soon attracted disciples. He came out of the desert ca. 305 to organize these disciples under a rule according to regular patterns of life, although

Anthony's contemporary Pachomius (d. 347) is generally credited with giving the movement its communal character. Anthony returned to the desert five years later, and for the next forty years his influence as a spiritual leader grew. He was a strong supporter of the teaching of the Council of Nicaea (325) that Jesus Christ was of the same substance (Gk., *homoousios*) as God the Father, and not simply the greatest of creatures, as Arius had held. He also became thereby a close associate of Athanasius, one of the staunchest defenders of the Nicene dogma. Indeed, the most important text for understanding Anthony and the beginnings of monasticism is the *Life of Anthony*, written by Athanasius just after Anthony's death.

Anthony, however, was only the leading figure in the first wave of those withdrawing from society. The life of an anchorite (Gk., *anachoresis*, "withdrawal") was largely a reaction against the gradual establishment of Christianity following the triumph of the emperor Constantine (d. 337) over his rival Maxentius in 312. Ironically, many Christians protested against the newly privileged status of the Church conferred immediately thereafter by Constantine. They warned that Christians would become too comfortable in their new situation and would no longer proclaim and live by the high moral demands of the gospel. In its origins, therefore, monasticism had a prophetic edge to it. It also had an almost immediate impact on the Church. Bishops began to be recruited from among those with some monastic training. Athanasius (d. 373), a disciple of Anthony, was an outstanding example.

Sayings and anecdotes of the various desert Christians were collected in the fifth century and circulated, in various forms, under the title *Sayings of the Fathers*. The desert tradition spread outside the Nile valley to other locations, especially into Palestine, which produced a rich literature and deeply rooted monastic tradition of its own. Pachomius was the first to organize monks into a communal (cenobitic) life; by the mid-fourth century there were eleven Pachomian monasteries in Egypt, including two for women, all emphasizing obedience to a superior and a highly regimented community life of prayer and work.

Basil the Great (d. 379) reinterpreted monasticism to make it more pastoral, that is, concerned especially with care for the poor, and to place it in the milieu of urban life. With Gregory of Nazianzus (d. 390), he took up the "philosophic" life of retirement and prayer in 358, spending time at various Eastern monasteries. A theorist of cenobitic monasticism, Basil produced rules and commentaries promoting a vision of a community of shared goods inspired by Acts 4:32–35 that have been one of the principal sources of monastic discipline to this day.

THE RISE OF WESTERN MONASTICISM

Eastern monasticism was transferred to the West when Martin of Tours (d. 397) established a monastery near Poitiers in 362. The promotion of monasticism was spread through Martin's biography, written by Sulpicius Severus about the time of Martin's death. But several other factors were influential in its taking root in the West. Ambrose (d. 397), in Milan, and Jerome (d. 420), first in Rome and later in Palestine, promoted monasticism along with a number of ascetic women. Ambrose's knowledge of Greek put him in touch with the theology of the East and he himself wrote on ascetical subjects and encouraged the development of monasteries in northern Italy. Jerome had taken up the life of a hermit for four or five years in Syria before being ordained a priest in ca. 380. After the death in 384 of Pope Damasus, whom he had served as secretary, Jerome returned to the East, settling in Bethlehem where he ruled a newly founded monastery.

Eusebius (d. 371), bishop of Vercelli, had also lived in the East for a time in exile. When he returned he preached ascetic ideals for his clergy and lived with them under a common rule. The work of John Cassian (d. 435) was another important factor in the acceptance of monasticism in the West. Trained in the East, he mediated its spirituality to the West after he settled and established a monastic foundation at Marseilles. His *Conferences* and *Institutes* had a particularly strong impact on the later Benedictine tradition. Augustine of Hippo (d. 430) applied ideas about the ascetic life he had learned in Milan (see his *Confessions* 8 for references to *The Life of Anthony* and other sources he had encountered there). He also had a firsthand acquaintance with Roman monasteries. In North Africa he encouraged the life of those styled *servi Dei* (Lat., "servants of God," celibate laymen who practiced the sharing of goods), supported the communal life of women ascetics, and also promoted the *vita apostolica*, or the communal life of the bishop with his cathedral clergy.

Western monasticism, however, was given its distinctive shape by Benedict of Nursia (d. ca. 550). After a period as a hermit, he established a community at Monte Cassino in ca. 529 under a rule of poverty, chastity, obedience, and stability. In the final chapter of his Rule he acknowledged the influence of John Cassian's *Conferences* and *Institutes* as well as the various *vitae* (Lat., "lives," biographies) of the early monks and the Rule of St. Basil, which he probably knew in a Latin translation by Rufinus. The Rule of St. Benedict especially commends the reading of Scripture and itself quotes Scripture profusely. It depends heavily on an early anonymous work, three times as long, known as the *Regula Magistri* (Lat., "The Rule of the Master"). According to Benedict, the purpose of the monastery is to honor God by worship and to benefit the community by prayer. But since the monastery had to be self-sustaining, the monks were also required to work in the fields and to do other manual labor. Thus, the essence of the Rule of St. Benedict was *ora et labora* (Lat., "pray and work").

In his *Dialogues* (ca. 594), Pope Gregory the Great (d. 604) praised Benedict's rule for its discernment and clarity of language, but it remained only one of many rules in the West until the early medieval period, when Charlemagne (d. 814) imported it into the land of the Franks in order to establish a degree of uniformity among the monastic establishments in his kingdoms. The systematization of the Rule of St. Benedict in the West is due mainly to a monk entrusted by Charlemagne with his projects of monastic reform, Benedict of Aniane (d. 821), whose monastery in the Languedoc became a center for reform. His *Capitulare Monasticum* was approved at the Synod of Aachen in 817; he also compiled a catalogue of all monastic rules then known to him, the *Codex Regularum Monasticorum et Canonicarum*. Largely through his foundational efforts, by the tenth century the Rule of St. Benedict was normative in the West, except in Ireland.

THE CELTIC TRADITION

Monasticism was at the heart of early Irish Christianity, introduced by Patrick (d. ca. 461). It had a strongly ascetic character, emphasizing fasting, penance, and the ascetic discipline of *peregrinatio* (Lat., "wandering," "exile"), which explains why Irish monasticism had outposts in Scotland, England, and on the continent as far south as Italy (e.g., Bobbio). The Irish monks had a keen interest in evangelization, and in Ireland the faith was spread not from cities, since Ireland was not urbanized at all, but from monastic centers, from which preaching radiated out to surrounding populations. The bishops themselves were associated with monasteries. The Rule of St. Benedict, however, never gained a foothold in Ireland.

LATER WESTERN DEVELOPMENTS

The role of the monastery as the center of scholarship developed only gradually. Benedict was concerned that his monks should be sufficiently literate to read the Bible and the Fathers of the Church. Later, with the Carolingian renaissance, many of the monks were relieved of manual labor and were encouraged to devote themselves to scholarly pursuits. One of the most practical was the copying of the texts of the classics of Western civilization.

Medieval monasticism may be viewed, in shorthand, by the four "Cs": Cluny, Camaldolese, Carthusians, and Cistercians. Cluny, founded in 910, is a Burgundian monastery that in the eleventh and twelfth centuries was a center of monastic and of Church reform. From Cluny many dependent monasteries were founded and many older monasteries (even Monte Cassino) were reformed. The repression of simony and the enforcement of celibacy, mandated by Pope Gregory VII (d. 1085), were ideals inspired by this monastic reform movement. The Cluniacs were known as the "Black Monks" from the color of their cowls. As they became more successful and more powerful, they in turn became the object of criticism from the "White Monks" of the Cistercian reform.

The Camaldolese were a monastic movement that combined the communal life of the Benedictine rule with the eremetical life of the solitary living singly in a cell. Inspired by Romuald (d. 1027) and Peter Damian (d. 1072), both from Ravenna, the movement emphasized what almost seems an oxymoron: missionary, cenobitic, and eremetical existence. The Camaldolese had a long history of monastic exchange with the larger culture, and among their number were Gratian (codifier of canon law), Lorenzo Monaco (Renaissance painter), and Ambrogio Traversari (fifteenth-century humanist and theologian).

The Carthusians were founded by Bruno (1032–1101), whose vision of reform for monasticism emphasized withdrawal from the world, solitary living combined with some elements of the cenobitic life inspired by the Rule of St. Benedict, contemplative prayer, and silence. It has always been a small order, but its monks have contributed much to spiritual literature, often anonymously. They pride themselves on having never needed a reform of their life—*numquam reformata quia numquam deformata* (Lat. "never reformed because never deformed").

Finally, the Cistercians were founded as a reform of the Benedictines at Citeaux ("Cistercium") in Burgundy ca. 1098. By the thirteenth century it numbered 750 houses in Europe. Among its early founders was Bernard of Clairvaux (d. 1153), who is often called the "last of the [Church] Fathers," as well as the admonisher of popes for their use of temporal power. The Cistercians put a high premium on the cenobitic life, agricultural labor, uni-

Trappist monks at St. Bernard's monastery, Snowmass, Colorado, bow during the singing of the Divine Office; Trappists are in the Cistercian tradition of monasticism, dating back to the late eleventh century.

formity of discipline for all houses, and a high degree of monastic culture. Beside Bernard, they produced a number of important spiritual writers whose influence would be felt for centuries after. In the seventeenth century, Cistercian life was reformed under Armand de Rancé at the monastery of La Trappe, thus giving the name "Trappist" to the strict branch of the current Cistercian family.

Western monasticism suffered major losses during the Reformation, although the decrees of the Council of Trent (1563) requiring all monasteries to be affiliated with congregations fostered a renewal that gave rise to the traditions of learned monasticism associated with the Maurists (the French Benedictine congregation of St. Maur) and of missionary work associated with other congregations. But the French Revolution (1789) suppressed all monastic life in France, and similar restrictions elsewhere, up to and including those imposed by Communism, have made the history of modern monasticism a story of repression and reconstruction.

A revival, however, did take place in the mid-nineteenth century in almost all of the countries of western and central Europe, and monastic life was carried to North America and elsewhere, continuing to spread throughout the twentieth century.

LATER EASTERN DEVELOPMENTS

Unlike the West, monasticism in the East had never divided into different orders. There remained two main forms of one tradition: those in community (Lat., *coenobium*), within a common enclosure, and a small group of individuals (Lat., *lavra,* "street," "alley") living both a community and an individual life.

Monasticism had spread with Christianity itself to the Slavic countries: in Kiev, where Prince Vladimir (d. 1015) became an ardent promoter and builder of monasteries, and then in Radonezh, near Moscow, where Sergius, Russia's most revered saint, and his brother Stephen founded in 1354 the famous monastery of the Holy Trinity and reestablished the monastic life in Russia that had been lost in the Mongol invasions. Altogether Sergius founded forty monasteries before his death in 1392. A secularization of the monasteries took place in 1764 when the wealth of the large monasteries caught the attention of Peter the Great. But, as in the West, a strong revival of monasticism took place in the nineteenth century, continuing until the virtual elimination of monasticism in Russia with the Communist Revolution of 1917. But with the collapse of Communism after 1990, yet another revival was underway.

See also Anthony of Egypt, St.; Augustine, Rule of St.; Basil, Rule of St.; Benedict, Rule of St.; Benedictine order; Camaldolese; Carthusian order; Cistercian order; Cluny; double monasteries; monastery; monastic spirituality; religious orders and congregations; Russia, Catholicism in; Trappists.

Bibliography

Burton-Christie, D. *The Word in the Desert: Scripture and the Quest for Holiness in Early Christian Monasticism.* New York: Oxford University Press, 1993.

Chitty, D. *The Desert a City.* Oxford: Blackwell, 1966.

Knowles, David. *Christian Monasticism.* New York: McGraw-Hill, 1961.

Lawless, G. *Augustine of Hippo and His Monastic Rule.* Oxford: Clarendon Press, 1987.

LeClerq, Jean. *The Love of Learning and the Desire for God: A Study of Monastic Culture.* New York: Fordham University Press, 1982.

Pennington, M. Basil. *Monastic Life: A Short History of Monasticism and Its Spirit.* Petersham, MA: St. Bede's Publications, 1989.

Voobus, A. *History of Asceticism in the Syrian Orient.* 2 vols. Louvain: Secretariat du Corpus Scriptorum Christianorum Orientalium, 1958, 1960.
                                                            JOHN C. CAVADINI

Monophysitism (Gk., *mono* "one"; *physis*, "nature"), the view held by those who claim that, after the Incarnation, Christ had only one (divine) nature. The earliest forms of Monophysitism were not condemned as heretical but rather were espoused by Alexandrians following the lead of Cyril. After condemning Nestorius for promoting a view that, according to Cyril, would lead to the error of implying two persons in Christ, Cyril adopted the formula, "the one nature of the Incarnate Word." Cyril attributed this phrase, which is actually Apollinarist in origin, to his predecessor, Athanasius of Alexandria. Cyril's use of an ambiguous Greek word for "nature," however, led to further confusion that was eventually clarified at the Council of Chalcedon (451). To avoid the danger of any implication of two distinct persons in Jesus Christ, Chalcedon justified Cyril's usage but adopted earlier trinitarian terminology refering to "two natures" in the one person of Jesus Christ without mixture or confusion. After the Council of Chalcedon, some Monophysites, like the archimandrite Eutyches, continued to hold the position that Christ's humanity is subsumed by his divinity in such a way that only one nature exists. However, for many of those initially involved in the so-called Monophysite revolt or schism, rejection of the Chalcedonian formulation was hardly revolutionary or schismatic. Followers of Severus of Antioch, for example, clearly maintained the integrity of the two natures in Christ after the Incarnation, but sought to clarify further the Christological language used by Chalcedon. Monophysitism hardened into a schismatic movement when its proponents refused obedience to the proscriptions of the Second Council of Constantinople (553), which called for unconditional acceptance of Chalcedon's formula. *See also* Chalcedon, Council of; Christology; hypostatic union; Incarnation, the; Jesus Christ; Nestorianism.

JANICE POORMAN

monotheism, belief in one, personal, transcendent deity as opposed to belief in and worship of many deities (polytheism), or worship of one deity without denying the existence of others (henotheism), or belief that the deity is indistinguishable from the world (pantheism). In the religion of Israel the beliefs of those (priests, prophets, sages) who gave us the OT were different from what people were actually thinking and doing in the religious sphere of their lives. At the level of popular religion, both biblical texts and archaeological data attest to the belief that, while Yahweh was the principal deity for Israel, the existence and efficacy of other deites (El, Baal, Asherah) were also acknowledged; hence the frequent denunciations of such beliefs and practices in the prophetic literature (esp. Hosea, Jeremiah, Ezekiel) and in the historical record (e.g., 1 Kgs 18; 2 Kgs 1:1–4; 17:7–20; 23:4–14). There is also evidence for the assimilation of characteristics and attributes of Yahweh to those of other deities (syncretism) and for belief in the territorial restriction of the jurisdiction of deities in general, including Yahweh (e.g., 1 Sam 26:19; 2 Kgs 5:15–19; Ps 137:4). The link between deity and territory was broken in principle during the Babylonian exile in the sixth century B.C., with the development of belief in Yahweh as creator and sustainer of the world. This belief comes to expression most clearly in the exilic Isaiah (e.g., Isa 40:12–26; 42:5; 44:24) and in the Priestly source (the narrative and legal portions of the Pentateuch composed by priests), especially the creation narrative in Gen 1:1–2:3. *See also* God.

JOSEPH BLENKINSOPP

Monothelitism (Gk., *monos*, "one"; *theleis*, "will"), a seventh-century heresy that held that Jesus Christ possessed only a divine will. In an effort to reconcile the Monophysites with the Church, Pope Honorius I (625–38) followed the advice of Sergius, the patriarch of Constantinople (610–38), and spoke of Christ as possessing "one will." This expression was adopted in the *Ecthesis* (Gk., "exposition of faith"), a Monothelite document probably drafted by Sergius and then promulgated by Emperor Heraclius in 638. It was opposed by Sophronius of Jerusalem. Though synods in Constantinople (638 and 639) confirmed the teaching of only one will in Christ, the Lateran Synod of 649 condemned it. This decision was confirmed by the Third Council of Constantinople (680–81), which declared that Christ possesses two wills, one divine and one human, as well as two natures. The council also posthumously excommunicated Pope Honorius. *See also* Constantinople, councils of; Honorius I; Monophysitism.

monsignor (Fr., "my lord"), an honorary ecclesiastical title ordinarily bestowed by the pope on diocesan clerics in recognition of service rendered to the Church. Monsignors are designated as members of one of three ranks: Apostolic Prothonotaries, Honorary Prelates of His Holiness the Pope, or Chaplains of His Holiness the Pope. The honorary title is sometimes given in the United States to the vicar general of a diocese, but many dioceses have abandoned the practice of conferring honorary titles on priests, regarding it as an inappropriate relic of the past. In some European nations, the title "monsignor" is commonly used in reference to bishops. *See also* prelates of honor.

monstrance (mon'struhnts), a vessel used to expose to view the eucharistic bread. The monstrance is usually made of a precious metal. It has a broad base, a stem with a node, and a round opening usually surrounded by some design. A round flat window—known as a lunula, luna, or lunette—encases the consecrated Host. The monstrance is placed on the altar or in some place of reverence for adoration during the rite of exposition and benediction of the Blessed Sacrament and is sometimes carried in processions. The use of this vessel originated in fourteenth-century France and Germany, where eucharistic devotion outside of Mass flourished. The term "monstrance" and its synonym, "ostensorium," derive from the Latin verbs *monstrare* and *ostendere,* which mean "to show" or "to display." Reminiscent of the earlier ostensorium or reliquary, which was a glass cylinder for the viewing of the whole or part of a martyr's body, the monstrance houses the Real Presence of the body of Christ, the premier martyr, and provides a secure and reverent place for

Monstrance

a prolonged exposition of the host. *See also* Benediction; Blessed Sacrament; eucharistic adoration; Real Presence.

Montalembert, Charles René, 1810–70, French historian, developer of Catholic social doctrine. A devout Catholic influenced by contacts with English liberalism and associated with Félicité de Lamennais and Henri Lacordaire, Montalembert worked vigorously to reconcile Catholicism with democratic liberalism.

Montanism, a mid- to late-second-century apocalyptic and charismatic movement within Christianity that threatened to undermine traditional authorities such as Holy Scripture and the office of bishop. Montanus emerged in Phrygia ca. 155–60 claiming to be directly inspired by the Holy Spirit. As the Holy Spirit incarnate he recruited numerous followers including two prophetesses, Maximilla and Priscilla, whose prophecy was regarded as the first fruits of the eschatological outpouring of the Spirit (Joel 2:28–32). They prophesied a speedy end of the world and preached the need to restore rigorous ascetic practices to Christianity. Most of their writings have been destroyed, but the accusations recorded by Eusebius and Epiphanius indicate the Montanist doctrines were not readily susceptible to attack on matters of dogma. Therefore, the Church stressed traditional sources of authority and raised character issues in order to combat the Montanists. However, their extreme asceticism continued to have strong appeal and attracted their most famous convert, Tertullian, ca. 207. *See also* apocalypticism; charism; Tertullian.

Monte Cassino, the chief monastery of the Benedictine order, situated on a prominent mountain midway between Rome and Naples. It was here that Benedict of Nursia (d. ca. 550) wrote his monastic rule ca. 540. The buildings were destroyed several times in the course of the centuries, most recently during World War II, but they have been restored. *See also* Benedict of Nursia, St.

Montfort, St. Louis Grignion de, 1673–1716, French priest and mission preacher. Ordained in 1700, he first became a hospital chaplain but a few years later abandoned that ministry and began preaching missions. Not long before his death, he founded the Missionaries of the Company of Mary, known today as the Montfort Fathers. His manuscript, discovered in 1842 and entitled "True Devotion to Mary," gained great popularity. His feast day, April 28, is no longer observed universally. *See also* Montfort Fathers.

Montfort Fathers, Missionaries of the Company of Mary, also known as the Society of Mary of Montfort (S.M.M.), a group founded in France in the early eighteenth century by Louis Grignion de Montfort. Although founded as a preaching and missionary society, the Montfort Fathers established seminaries in the mid and late nineteenth century—a ministry they have continued to the present. Throughout its history, the community has fostered a special devotion to the Blessed Virgin Mary. In 1903 the Montfort Fathers established their first house in the United States and later began publishing the *Queen of All Hearts* magazine. *See also* Montfort, St. Louis Grignion de.

Month's Mind Mass, a memorial Mass one month after the date of death or burial of a person with the explicit intention of keeping the deceased in mind. The practice is reminiscent of early observances of anniversaries of the deceased, marked with Masses celebrated at regular intervals beyond the date of death. Mass was ordinarily said at the graveside, followed by a meal in the cemetery. When such an observance became impossible due to frequency and cultural shifts restricting its occurrence, the custom of donating a stipend or a fixed amount of money to the clergy for the celebration of the Month's Mind Mass became an acceptable substitute. *See also* prayers for the dead.

Montserrat, mountain near Barcelona that is the site of a Benedictine monastery founded at the beginning of the eleventh century. Ignatius of Loyola went to Montserrat in 1522 after his recovery from the wound that led to his conversion. The monks there are celebrated for their scholarship and especially for their interest in sacred music. *See also* Ignatius of Loyola, St.

Mont-Saint-Michel, a Benedictine monastery originating in the late tenth century on an island off the coast of Normandy. Its abbey, an exquisite example of Medieval French architecture, became a prison during the French Revolution and later a museum. A religious community was recently restored to the abbey.

moral certitude. *See* certitude, moral.

morality, magisterium and. *See* magisterium and morality.

morality plays, medieval dramas with a heavily didactic character. These plays, the most famous being *Everyman,* typically contrast virtues and vices in a heavily allegorical manner.

moral law and civil law. *See* civil law and morality.

moral matter, that aspect of a human act that makes the act what it is, e.g., a theft rather than a murder.

moral person. *See* juridical person.

moral theology, the theological discipline that studies the moral life and action of Christians. Catholic insistence that the human person is an image of God with intellect, free will, and the power of self-determination, the importance of works as well as faith, and the practice of the sacrament of Reconciliation have given great importance to morality. Catholic insistence on reason and theology in general contributed to the development of a reflexive, thematic, and critical study of moral life called moral theology. All Catholics are called to discern and make responsible human judgments, but moral theology as a discipline seeks a systematic, coherent, and adequate understanding of all aspects of the moral life and actions of the Christian.

Content and Method: Moral theology discusses not only the morality of particular actions but also the basic orientation, motivation, and imagination of the person; the virtues, attitudes, and dispositions that should mark the Christian person (e.g., hopeful, just, compassionate); the values that should be present in society (e.g., justice, concern for the poor); the principles that direct our lives (the preferential option for the poor, the Golden Rule); and the concrete norms that give greater specificity to decision making (the obligation to tell the truth), conscience formation, and discernment. Casuistry, which determines the morality of a particular action or case in relationship to general principles and to other cases, has been developed at great length in the Catholic tradition, but moral theology includes more than just casuistry. Moral theology has typically been divided into general moral theology, which deals with those principles and aspects common to all moral life and issues, and special moral theology, which deals with the particular areas of concern such as personal, sexual, medical, and social ethics.

The method of Catholic moral theology finds moral wisdom in Scripture, tradition, hierarchical Church teaching, human reason, and experience, with official Church teaching and human reason (natural law) constituting distinctive Catholic emphases. This discipline is related to three publics—the Church, the academy, and society or the world in general. The discipline of moral theology traditionally found its home in the seminary and was aimed at training priests for their ministry. In more recent years, especially in the United States, moral theology has been taught as an academic discipline in Catholic colleges and universities and as ministerial preparation for service in the Church. Whereas ministerial preparation sees the discipline primarily from a more pastoral perspective, colleges and universities view moral theology in a more academic light. Until the mid-1960s the teachers of moral theology were priests who taught especially in the seminary or theologate. Today religious women and lay women and men are professors of moral theology, often in colleges and universities but also in some seminaries.

Historical Development: Moral theology as a separate discipline distinct from all other theology came into existence at the end of the sixteenth and the beginning of the seventeenth centuries. The first six hundred years of Christian existence are referred to as the patristic age since the Fathers of the Church, most of whom were pastors, were the major authors. In their writings they often discussed particular moral issues (lying, participation in the military, sexuality), but primarily from a pastoral perspective and did not elaborate a systematic discipline of moral theology. The *Libri Poenitentiales* (Lat., "Penitential Books") came into existence in the sixth century and flourished until the eleventh century. They were attempts to guide priests in giving a precise penance for each particular sin confessed in the rite of private penance that came into existence at this time. Systematic theology as a discipline began to develop in the twelfth century and Thomas Aquinas (d. 1274) stands as the most significant Catholic theologian to propose an integrated discipline of theology; the consideration of morality is found in the second part of his *Summa Theologiae.* Subsequent theologians wrote commentaries on the work of Aquinas. At the same time a new genre of practical handbooks geared to the

sacrament of Penance arose and flourished, the *Summae Confessorum;* these often dealt with subjects according to an alphabetical arrangement with no attempt at systematic presentations.

After the Council of Trent (1545–63), with its call for all Catholics to celebrate the sacrament of Penance once a year and its establishment of seminaries to prepare priests, the *Institutiones Theologiae Moralis* came into existence, originally within the Society of Jesus, to help prepare confessors to serve as judges in the sacrament of Penance. These books, which became the standard textbooks of moral theology until the Second Vatican Council (1962–65), provided a brief discussion of the principles of fundamental moral theology and of particular aspects of the moral life, arranged according to the Ten Commandments and the seven sacraments. In the seventeenth and eighteenth centuries a serious controversy arose between laxists and rigorists, which was settled by the moderate approach of Alphonsus Liguori (d. 1787), who was later named a saint, a Doctor of the Church, and the patron saint of moral theologians.

These textbooks of moral theology, with their heavy emphasis on casuistry, constituted a marvelous pastoral adaptation to the needs of a particular time, but they did not constitute an adequate and comprehensive approach to moral theology. The renewal of moral theology before, during, and after the Second Vatican Council called for a number of different emphases in an attempt to develop a more adequate moral theology—a life-centered, rather than an exclusively act-centered approach; a strong dependence on Scripture and on all theology; an emphasis on the total Christian life and not just its minimum requirements; an ecumenical dialogue with other Christians and all religions; a critical openness to dialogue with contemporary philosophical ethics; a more positive appreciation of the human and empirical sciences; and a strong emphasis on the social mission of the Church. *See also* magisterium and morality; theology.

Bibliography

Curran, Charles E. *Toward an American Catholic Moral Theology.* Notre Dame, IN: University of Notre Dame Press, 1987.

Grisez, Germain. *The Way of the Lord Jesus. Vol. 1: Christian Moral Principles.* Chicago: Franciscan Herald Press, 1983.

Gula, Richard M. *Reason Informed by Faith: Foundations of Catholic Morality.* New York: Paulist Press, 1989.

Mahoney, John. *The Making of Moral Theology: A Study of the Roman Catholic Tradition.* Oxford: Clarendon Press, 1987.

CHARLES E. CURRAN

moral virtues. See cardinal virtues.

Thomas More, who suffered martyrdom rather than deny the pope in favor of King Henry VIII, wearing the symbol of his office as Lord Chancellor, a post he resigned after opposing the king in the matter of his divorce from Catherine of Aragon.

More, St. Thomas, 1478–1535, Lord Chancellor of England, executed for refusing to accept King Henry VIII's supremacy over the Church in England. More studied law at Oxford and was a close friend of Erasmus. He refused to sign an oath that declared Henry's marriage to Catherine of Aragon invalid and that repudiated the pope. He resigned as chancellor in 1532 and was imprisoned in 1534. Though he remained silent regarding the Act of Supremacy, he was convicted on perjured evidence and beheaded on July 6, 1535. More was a humanist who argued for moral and social reform through education and sacred literature. His most famous works include *Utopia,* a social satire written in 1516, and his letters from the Tower of London, which reveal a deep devotion to the suffering Christ. More maintained an affection for Henry VIII to the end and hoped that his death would somehow serve the king. Feast day: June 22. *See also* England, Catholicism in.

Mormons, the Church of Jesus Christ of Latter-day Saints, founded by Joseph Smith, Jr., (1805–44) at Manchester, New York. In 1827 Smith announced that in a divine revelation he had received a sacred text, the *Book of Mormon.* Over the next few years, Smith, with the help of Sidney Rigdon, organized

churches in Ohio, Missouri, and Nauvoo, Illinois, where Smith was killed in 1844. In 1846–47 Brigham Young (1801–77) led the Mormons to Salt Lake City, Utah, which became the church's permanent headquarters. Polygyny was instituted in 1852 but was officially ended in 1890.

Mormonism is polytheistic, claiming that human beings can develop into gods. It acknowledges the divinity of Jesus Christ but insists that every person is responsible for his or her salvation, which is attained by undergoing Mormon baptism and living according to the laws of the church. In this view, traditional Christians lack the true faith, for they have not been touched by the authentic Spirit. Mormonism permits baptism by proxy, thereby assuring the possibility of the salvation of people who died without the Mormon baptism. In areas where Mormons are numerous, Catholics have found it very difficult to enter into ecumenical relationships with them.

Morning Offering, prayer of devotion. It is the practice of beginning the day with a prayer by means of which one offers the day to God and accepts, as from the hands of God, all that comes in the course of the day.

Inspired by Christ's requests to Margaret Mary Alacoque, the devotion was begun by a Jesuit, Father Gaurelet, in 1844 and has been popularized since 1860 by the Apostleship of Prayer (League of the Sacred Heart). *See also* Apostleship of Prayer; Sacred Heart, devotion to the.

MORNING OFFERING PRAYER

"O Jesus, through the immaculate Heart of Mary, I offer You all my prayers, works, joys and sufferings of this day, for all the intentions of Your Sacred Heart, in union with the Holy Sacrifice of the Mass throughout the world, in reparation for my sins, for the intentions of all our associates, and for the general intention recommended this month."

Morning Prayer, part of the Liturgy of the Hours. Formerly called Lauds (Lat., *laus,* "praise"), it is prayed in the early morning hours to praise God for the beginning of another day. One of the two hinges on which the day's prayer pivots, along with Evening Prayer or Vespers, Morning Prayer begins with an invitation to prayer. A hymn of praise is sung followed by a morning psalm, an OT canticle, and another psalm of praise, each with an antiphon. A passage from Scripture is read and a homily may be given, followed by silence, a responsory, and the Canticle of Zechariah or the Benedictus (Luke 1:68–79). Prayers of intercession consecrate the day and its work to God. The Lord's Prayer follows immediately. A concluding prayer, blessing, and dismissal close the rite. *See also* Liturgy of the Hours.

Morse, St. Henry, 1595–1645, English Jesuit martyr. Ordained in Rome, he was arrested after returning to England. Released from prison and banished in 1630, he returned again to England, where he worked for fifteen years, only to be arrested and executed for high treason in 1645. Feast day: December 1.

Mortalium Animos (mohr-tahl'ee-oom ahn'ee-mohs; Lat., "souls of mortals"), encyclical of Pope Pius XI, issued January 6, 1928, that negatively assessed the nascent ecumenical movement and insisted that Catholicism could not be considered on a par with other religions.

mortal sin (Lat., *mors,* "death"), a violation of God's will (the moral order) that is considered so serious that it brings death to the soul, the rupture of the relation of the individual to God. For the commission of such a sin traditional theology has required three conditions: grave matter (Lat., *gravitas materiae*), sufficiently full knowledge, and full consent or freedom. Any significant diminution in one of these conditions would usually render the sin less than mortal. For truly mortal sins, the Church's law demands (outside of emergency situations) specific confession for forgiveness. There are references in Scripture (Matt 12:31; Mark 3:29; Luke 12:10) to a sin "against the Spirit" or an "eternal sin" that is not forgiven, but these remain the object of continuing theological debate.

Since the mid-1960s theologians have been somewhat uncomfortable with the sharp and neat categorization of sins as either mortal or venial. Some have suggested that a more realistic division would be mortal, serious, or venial (slight). In this division serious sins would indeed be more than slight (everyday failures) but not such as to rupture the relationship with God; this would be similar to situations in which families suffer rather severe tests but still survive intact. Other theologians have insisted that any serious moral act, whether virtuous or sinful, derives its seriousness from the de-

gree of liberty in the act. Only an act that also involves, beyond explicit freedom of choice, self-disposing fundamental freedom is a serious moral act in the sense of a mortal sin or a conversion from it. It is often difficult to know whether such freedom was involved or not. This constitutes another reason why individuals are in no position to judge others before God. *See also* fundamental option; *gravitas materiae;* sin; venial sin.   RICHARD A. McCORMICK

mortification (Lat., *mors,* "death"; *facere,* "to make"), the process of "killing" sinful desires and practices in order to draw closer to God. While mortification suggests a denial of illicit and even licit pleasures that might distract one from the demands of the gospel, it is also a discipline that is self-imposed and joyfully embraced. Jesus invited Christians to this sort of self-discipline when he told the disciples that following him meant denying one's very self and taking up the Cross (Matt 16:24). Paul echoed Christ's teaching in Romans (8:13). As the practice is commonly understood, the object of mortification is the senses. If, for example, one is easily tempted to the sin of theft, mortification might involve denying oneself the otherwise legitimate pleasure of browsing in a store. To take the act of mortification a step further, this person might choose to donate a prized possession, legally purchased, to the poor. The goal of mortification is to create a sense of detachment from inclinations that habitually lead to sin. The practice requires patience and prayer and is best undertaken with the help of a spiritual director. In every case, excess should be avoided. *See also* penance.

mosaics, art form consisting of colored pieces of glass (called *tesserae,* Lat.) pressed into soft plaster to form pictures. Such art was widely used in church decoration, especially in the Byzantine Church and in Italy during the so-called Italo-Byzantine period. *See also* Catholicism and the visual arts.

Moschus, John, ca. 550–619, a monk who traveled to monasteries in Palestine, Egypt, Cyprus, and Rome. His *Spiritual Meadow,* with its monastic lore, became immensely popular as a devotional manual and was expanded and revised by others after his death.

Moses, the leader of the Exodus and lawgiver of the OT. He was born in Egypt, perhaps ca. 1300 B.C., and was rescued from the death sentence on Israelite

Sixth-century Byzantine mosaic of the head of John the Apostle and Evangelist; in the Church of St. Apollinaris, Ravenna, Italy.

Michelangelo's *Moses*, on the tomb of Pope Julius II (d. 1513), in the Church of St. Peter in Chains, Rome.

male babies by being placed in a basket on the Nile. There the pharaoh's daughter found him and raised him in the palace. After he killed a man, he fled Egypt and hid in Midian, where he married Jethro's daughter Zipporah and served him as shepherd. At the burning bush the Lord commissioned Moses to return to Egypt and lead the people into the wilderness. He did so, and after the ten plagues he led them across the Reed (Red) Sea and to Mount Sinai (the site of the burning bush), where the covenant was made with the Lord. Despite frequent complaints from the people, he led the nation through the wilderness for forty years, but was not permitted to enter Canaan because of his disobedience (Num 20). He died at age 120, after addressing the people and viewing Canaan from Mount Nebo. Because Moses is the major character in Exodus, Leviticus, Numbers, and Deuteronomy, and because he is pictured as writing (e.g., Exod, 24:4), he came to be considered the author of these books already in OT times and eventually of Genesis as well. He acted as prophetic spokesman for the Lord and served as a model for a succession of prophets (Deut 18:15–22). In Matthew and John, Jesus is pictured as a new Moses, and Peter, James, and John see Moses during the Transfiguration. Moses represents the old covenant in these works, in Paul's Letters, and in Hebrews.

motet. 1 A thirteenth-century composition in which words were added to fragments of Gregorian melodies. 2 In the sixteenth century, a four- or five-voiced sacred musical composition using a Latin text and usually sung without accompaniment. *See also* Catholicism and music.

Mother Angelica. *See* Angelica, Mother.

Mother of God (Gk., *Theotokos*), a title applied to Mary at the Council of Ephesus in 431. Nestorius had claimed that Jesus was two persons, one divine and the other human, and as such Mary was not properly to be called *Theotokos*, "Mother of God," but *Christotokos*, "Mother of Christ." Under the leadership of Cyril of Alexandria, the fathers of Ephesus rejected Nestorius's position, claiming that Jesus, although fully human in nature, was a divine person. Consequently, Mary was truly the Mother of God. The title was upheld by the Council of Chalcedon in 451. *See also* Ephesus, Council of; Mary, Blessed Virgin.

mother of Jesus, the primary role of Mary in the history of salvation. References to Jesus' mother in the NT are shaped primarily by theological concerns about the mission and identity of her son. Paul mentions her to emphasize the saving entry of God's Son into human existence: "God sent his Son, born of a woman, born under the law, in order to redeem those who were under the law, so that we might receive adoption as children" (Gal 4:4–5; similar bipolar formulations in Phil 2; 2 Cor 5:21; 8:9; Rom 1:3–4). Mark locates the meaning of being Jesus' "mother" or "brother" in relation to following Jesus (Mark 3:31–34; cf. Matt 12:46–50; Luke 8:19–21, 11:27–28) and emphasizes that mere knowledge of Jesus' family relations can be an obstacle to faith (Mark 6:3; cf. Matt 13:55; John 6:42). For Matthew, Jesus' birth from a virgin fulfills the promise of "God with us" (Matt 1:18–25; Isa 7:14). For Luke, it constitutes the high point of divine interventions in history, following the pattern of Samuel's birth from the barren Hannah (Luke 1:47–55; 1 Sam 2:1–10). The criterion that to be Jesus' "mother" one must "hear the word of God and do it" (Luke 8:28) is fulfilled by Mary in becoming Jesus' mother (Luke 1:38; 2:19, 51; cf. 10:39). John never names her "Mary" (though the name "Mary" appears to have symbolic resonances in 11:1–53, 19:25 and 20:11.16) but, as in other cases, such as "the Beloved Disciple," uses a standard phrase that expresses her role: "the mother of Jesus" or, more poignantly, "the mother" (19:26). He gives her a prominent place at the beginning (2:1–12) and at the end (19:25–26) of Jesus' public ministry as "the woman," the nucleus of the new community that flows from Jesus. The sign of the woman in Rev 12:1–6 refers to this community (see 12:17), though a reference to the individual mother of the Messiah may also be included. *See also* Mary, Blessed Virgin.   MICHAEL WALDSTEIN

Mother of the Church, a title conferred on the Blessed Virgin Mary by Paul VI on November 21, 1964, in response to a number of bishops who felt that the significance of Mary had not been sufficiently stressed by the Second Vatican Council (1962–65). The title accents Mary's role as mother of all Christians through her role as mother of the Savior. *See also* Mary, Blessed Virgin.

Mother Teresa. *See* Teresa of Calcutta, Mother.

motu proprio (moh'*too* proh'pree-oh; Lat., "on his own initiative"), papal document originating from the pope's own office. Such a document might be used to address several different kinds of matters. Many of the changes brought about by Vatican II (1962–65) were given practical application by this type of document.

Mount Carmel. *See* Carmel, Mount.

Mount Carmel, Our Lady of. *See* Our Lady of Mount Carmel.

movable feasts, solemnities and feasts whose annual dates vary, depending on the date of Easter. Twelve such dates shift each year: Epiphany (in countries where it is not observed as a holy day of obligation, e.g., the United States), Baptism of the Lord, Ash Wednesday, Easter Sunday, Ascension Thursday, Pentecost Sunday, Trinity Sunday, Solemnity of the Body and Blood of Christ (Corpus Christi), Solemnity of the Sacred Heart of Jesus, Solemnity of Christ the King, First Sunday of Advent, and Feast of the Holy Family.

Mozarabic chant. *See* chant, Mozarabic.

Mozarabic rite (mohts'ah-rah-bik), the liturgical order of the churches of the Iberian peninsula. The term "mozarabic" refers to Christians living in Muslim lands, though the formation of the Mozarabic liturgies predates the Islamic conquest. Isidore of Seville (d. 636) is the earliest witness to the practices of the Hispanic churches. The Roman rite generally followed the Christian reconquest of the peninsula, entering Catalonia during the eighth century; Avalon, Castile, and León, late in the eleventh. The Mozarabic rite was suppressed in 1085, when Toledo, the primatial see of Spain, was recaptured and the Roman rite was imposed on Spain by the newly appointed French archbishop. Because of the restoration efforts of Cardinal Jiménez de Cisneros in the fifteenth century and Cardinal Lorenzana in the late eighteenth, a form of the Mozarabic rite was restored to a chapel of the Cathedral of Toledo, Spain, where it is observed in the 1990s. *See also* rite.

Mozarabs, Christians living in Spain under Muslim rule from the invasion in 711 until 1492. *See also* Mozarabic rite.

Mozart, Wolfgang Amadeus, 1756–91, Austrian composer. Mozart's early experiences of performed music and his first position as composer came from the court of the prince-archbishop of Salzburg. His church music includes over twenty Masses or parts of Masses (including the unfinished *Requiem*), several settings of litanies and parts of the Divine Office (now called the Liturgy of the Hours), eighteen organ sonatas for use during the Mass, and many individual pieces like the well-known *Ave Verum* and *Exsultate, Jubilate*. Although sympathetic to the Enlightenment's critique of Church power, his religious music displays not only a delicate maturity but a joy and exuberance born of, and suited to, late Baroque Catholicism.

Mundelein, George W., 1872–1939, cardinal-archbishop of Chicago (1915–39). A vigorous centralizer, Mundelein astutely drew power into his hands and imposed a strict uniformity in archdiocesan discipline, especially with priests. This was aided by the development of an effective minor and major seminary program. He also improved the financial condition of the Chicago see, expanded its programs of elementary and higher education, and attempted to curtail some of the independence of ethnic groups. He deliberately used the trappings of power and ecclesiastical pomp to accentuate the status of Catholics in Chicago and was known as a supporter of President Franklin Delano Roosevelt.

Munificentissimus Deus (moon-i-fi-chen-tees' i-moos day'oos; Lat., "The Most Munificent God"), the apostolic constitution issued by Pope Pius XII on November 1, 1950, defining the dogma of the bodily Assumption of the Blessed Virgin Mary into heaven. *See also* Assumption of the Blessed Virgin Mary.

Münster, Sebastian, 1488–1552, Hebraist and geographer. A Franciscan who converted to Lutheranism around 1524, as professor of Hebrew at Basel he published works on geography and cosmography. His *Biblia Hebraica* (1534–35) provided the Hebrew text of the OT and a Latin translation that was widely influential.

Müntzer, Thomas, also Münzer, 1488/9–1525, radical reformer and revolutionary. A Catholic priest, then Lutheran minister at Zwickau (1520) and Allstedt (1523), Müntzer relied on direct divine revelation and sought an apocalyptic purge of Church and state. Caught up in the Peasants' War (1524–25) he was captured, tortured, and executed.

Muratorian fragment, a list of scriptural books from the early Church. The fragment, discovered in 1740, survives in a corrupt Latin translation from a Greek work composed between the second and fourth century A.D. The list, the beginning of which is lost, includes Luke, John, Acts, twelve Pauline Letters, Revelation, Jude, and 1 and 2 John. It acknowledges the Wisdom of Solomon and the *Apocalypse of Peter,* although noting that some exclude the latter from public reading. It allows the *Shepherd of Hermas* to be read, but not in public, and it rejects a pseudo-Pauline *Letter to the Laodiceans* and the works of heretics. *See also* canon of the Scriptures.

Murphy, Roland E., b. 1917, leading OT scholar and pioneer in biblical renewal. Ordained a Carmelite priest (1942) he received the S.T.D. (1948) and M.A. degree in Semitics (1949) at The Catholic University of America, and the S.S.L. from the Pontifical Biblical Institute (1958). He taught Semitic languages (1949–55) and Old Testament (1956–70) at Catholic University, and is presently George Washington Ivey Emeritus Professor of Biblical Studies at Duke University, where he taught from 1971 to 1987. He is former president of the Society of Biblical Literature and Catholic Biblical Association. The author of major studies of OT wisdom literature, he is editor, with R. E. Brown and J. A. Fitzmyer, of *The Jerome Biblical Commentary* (1968) and *The New Jerome Biblical Commentary* (1990).

Murphy-O'Connor, Jerome, b. 1935, Dominican biblical scholar. Born in Ireland and ordained a Dominican in 1960, he received his Th.D. at the University of Fribourg, Switzerland (1962), and his S.S.L. from the Pontifical Biblical Commission, Rome (1965). Beginning as a lecturer in 1967, he has been professor of New Testament at the École Biblique et Archéologique Française, Jerusalem, since 1972. He is author of many books, including *The Theology of 2 Corinthians* (1991), *The Holy Land: An Archaelogical Guide* (1992), and *Paul: A Critical Life* (1995). *See also* École Biblique.

Murray, John Courtney, 1904–67, American Jesuit theologian, the most important contributor to Catholic reflection on Church and state and the question of religious liberty in the twentieth century. His early work, written in the early to mid-1940s, focused on ecumenical and interfaith cooperation and argued that persons of different faiths could

John Courtney Murray, Jesuit priest, one of the leading twentieth-century Catholic theologians in the United States and the principal architect of the Second Vatican Council's Declaration on Religious Freedom.

collaborate in the post-World War II reconstruction of the social order. In the late 1940s he turned his attention to the question of Church and state, and began to make the case that constitutionally protected religious freedom was consistent with Catholic teaching. Conflict on this point with Cardinal Alfredo Ottaviani, head of the Holy Office, led, in 1954, to the request by Murray's superiors that he refrain indefinitely from writing on Church-state relations. He turned his attention to a range of social issues and brought together the writings in *We Hold These Truths* (1960).

His work on Church and state received new life when, at the intervention of Cardinal Francis Spellman of New York, he was invited to be an expert (Lat., *peritus*) at the Second Vatican Council (1962–65). Here, he was instrumental in the drafting of the Declaration on Religious Freedom (1965), which affirmed religious freedom as a human right for all and the freedom of the Church as the fundamental principle governing relations between the Church and governments. Murray's later writing, cut short by his death, began to apply the concept of religious freedom internally to the Church. *See also* Church and state; Declaration on Religious Freedom; religious liberty.
TODD D. WHITMORE

music. *See* Catholicism and music; liturgical music.

Muslims. *See* Islam.

mustum (Lat., "new [unfermented] wine"), the unfermented juice of ripe grapes. It may validly be substituted for altar wine, but its use is illicit without permission from the Apostolic See. Priests who are recovering from alcoholism and who cannot take even a small amount of wine, as by intinction (dipping the consecrated host into the wine), may seek permission through their ordinary (diocesan bishop) to use *mustum* instead of wine. *See also* wine, eucharistic.

mutual aid society, a benevolent organization founded to provide aid to needy parishioners or to raise funds for the establishment of new parishes.

mystagogy (Gk., *muein,* "to teach a doctrine, to instruct into the mysteries"), the period of special instruction on the sacramental life immediately following catechumenal formation and initiation into the Christian community. The period of instruction is also known by its Greek form, *mystagogia.* The catechumenal process that began to evolve in the second century in the Eastern and Western churches instructed candidates on the Christian moral life and God, Christ, and the Spirit. The Scriptures were explained and the catechumens were taught how to pray. During this period, which could last three years or longer in some communities, the catechumens were probably not permitted to take part in worship, except the Liturgy of the Word, the first part of the Eucharist. Some scholars have suggested that secrecy was maintained by the baptized on the inner life of worship in the community. Thus, the Holy Saturday vigil celebrations, during which these candidates were initiated through Baptism, anointing, and the Eucharist into full participation in the life of the Christian community, had not been previously explained. The mystagogia were instructions or homilies on these sacraments, usually given by the bishop in the early Church to the neophytes in the week following their initiation. Among the mystagogical homilies still extant are those of Cyril of Jerusalem, Theodore of Mopsuestia, Ambrose, John Chrysostom, and Augustine.

In today's practice, the period of mystagogia explains how the new Christian is to live the new life into which he or she has been initiated. According to the Rite of Christian Initiation of Adults, the period should begin at Easter and should continue for "a suitable period." *See also* Rite of Christian Initiation of Adults.

Mysteries of the Rosary, fifteen incidents from the life of Jesus or Mary that are divided into three groups and meditated upon while reciting the Rosary. When prayed publicly, a mystery is usually announced before reciting each decade of the rosary. The three groups of mysteries are (1) the joyful mysteries: the Annunciation, the Visitation (Mary's visit to Elizabeth), the birth of Our Lord, the Presentation of Jesus in the Temple, and the finding of Jesus in the Temple; (2) the sorrowful mysteries: the agony of Jesus in the garden, the scourging of Jesus at the pillar, the crowning of Jesus with thorns, the carrying of the cross, and the Crucifixion and death of Jesus; and (3) the glorious mysteries: the Resurrection of Jesus, Jesus' ascension into heaven, the descent of the Holy Spirit at Pentecost, the Assumption of Mary into heaven, and the coronation of Mary as Queen of Heaven.

Three-Stage Development: The development of the mysteries took place in three stages, which roughly correspond to the development of the Rosary itself.

The first stage occurred in the twelfth century when it became customary to cite a phrase referring to an important incident in the life of Jesus or Mary before the recitation of a psalm. Although originally intended to supplement the praying of the psalms, the psalms were eventually discontinued, and the phrases that once introduced the psalms developed into brief reflections on the Annunciation, Jesus' life, death, Resurrection, and the glorification of Jesus and Mary in heaven. Retaining the original structure given by the psalms, the reflections were organized in groups of 50 and usually consisted of 150 meditations.

The second stage occurred in the thirteenth and fourteenth centuries. While initially limited to the joy of the Annunciation, it soon became customary to focus on other Marian joys. Often, the recitation of each joy was accompanied by a "Hail Mary." For example, one would recite 50 joyful meditations accompanied by 50 "Hail Marys." During the fourteenth century, parallel developments took place concerning Mary's sorrows and her heavenly joys.

Once again, the number of sorrows and heavenly joys multiplied, and were accompanied with "Hail Marys." Eventually, it became common to recite 50 earthly joys, 50 earthly sorrows, and 50 heavenly joys in conjunction with 150 "Hail Marys."

The final stage occurred during the fifteenth century. As long as the meditations were sets of 50, those who used them had to be literate and possess a text, since it was impossible to recall 150 separate meditations. In order to make the meditations universally accessible, their number was reduced to 15; 5 for each set, combined with 150 "Hail Marys." Now the meditations functioned as focal points for the recitation of the "Hail Marys," which had now evolved into the Rosary by being combined with the "Our Father" and the "Glory be to the Father, the Son, and the Holy Spirit...."

This structure, first recorded in *Our Dear Lady's Psalter* (1483), is used today. It is now customary to focus on particular mysteries during certain days of the week: the joyful mysteries on Mondays and Thursdays, the sorrowful mysteries on Tuesdays and Fridays, and the glorious mysteries on Wednesdays, Saturdays, and Sundays. *See also* Rosary.

MICHAEL O'KEEFFE

Mysterium Ecclesiae (mis-stehr'ee-oom ek-klayz'ee-ay; Lat., "Mystery of the Church"), "Declaration in Defense of the Catholic Doctrine on the Church Against Certain Errors of the Present Day," declaration issued by the Sacred Congregation for the Doctrine of the Faith on June 24, 1973, in response to Hans Küng's *Infallible? An Inquiry* (1970). The declaration is remarkable for its recognition that even dogmatic pronouncements are historically conditioned and must be interpreted in light of the language, concepts, and circumstances of the time in which they were formulated. On the other hand, it rejects a "dogmatic relativism" that holds that such pronouncements "cannot signify truth in a determinate way, but can only offer changeable approximations...."

Mysterium Fidei (mis-tehr'ee-um fi'day-ee; Lat., "Mystery of Faith"), encyclical on the Eucharist by Pope Paul VI in 1965 to counter erroneous opinions and practices that had arisen. The encyclical noted that there are many ways in which Christ is present in the Church and that this presence is in every case real. But the encyclical maintained that Christ's presence in the Eucharist is real *par excellence* because it is substantial, the Eucharist being the presence of the whole Christ, divine and human. The encyclical also reaffirmed the doctrine of transubstantiation. *See also* Real Presence; transubstantiation.

mystery, a term that refers to the infinite incomprehensibility of God. God is not provisionally mystery, God is essentially mystery; not just unknown, but unknowable, literally incomprehensible. While "mystery" is also used in Catholic theology to refer to those things that merely confound the finite intellect, mystery in its most fundamental sense refers to the permanent character of God's incomprehensibility. Even in the Beatific Vision, God will remain mystery.

In the NT, mystery (Gk., *mustērion*; Lat., *mysterium*) is used in reference to God's saving plan for human history (Col 1:1–2:6; Eph 1–3). Similarly, in the early Church, the rites of the Easter Vigil are called mysteries, as rites that incorporate the believing community into salvation history. In this use, mystery is linked with a providential plan that gradually is being revealed.

The theologian Karl Rahner (d. 1984) orders the second of these two related understandings of mystery to the first. Rahner insists that there is only one fundamental mystery with two aspects: the mystery that is the being of God and the mystery that is the saving presence of the incomprehensible God in human history. All positive knowledge exists only in reference to this unfathomable mystery of God's life with us, a mystery that is expressed by three mutually implicated doctrines of the faith: the Trinity, the Incarnation, and the doctrine of grace. These three doctrines are formally declared by the Church to be mysteries in the strict sense (Lat., *mysteria stricte dicta*), terminology that refers to Vatican I's assertion (1869–70) that some doctrines of the faith are products of divine revelation, not deducible from human reason alone; *See also* faith and reason; God; sacrament. NANCY DALLAVALLE

mystery plays, a form of medieval European religious drama that evolved out of liturgical services after the tenth century. Mystery plays were performed during festal seasons; in them biblical subjects were acted out in cycles before outdoor audiences. Dramas with an ethical theme were called morality plays.

mystic, a person whose experience of the presence of God is intense, direct, and transforming, but not necessarily accompanied by extraordinary phenomena. Mystics experience a deep communion of love and of knowledge with God and, in God, with other people and all reality. Today, the mystical potential of all Christians is increasingly emphasized. *See also* mysticism.

mystical marriage. *See* marriage, spiritual.

mystical theology, a systematic reflection on the deepest levels of human experience of God. In the early Church, and consistently in Eastern Christianity, all theology was regarded as "mystical," as no sharp division was made between religious experience and doctrine. In the West, during the later Middle Ages, a growing separation arose between experience and intellectual knowledge. By the nineteenth century, "mystical theology" became a discipline concerned with the higher reaches of contemplation. Mystical theology was distinguished from "ascetical theology," which was concerned with "ordinary" Christian life. Contemporary theologians reject such distinctions and favor a reintegration of spirituality with doctrinal and moral theology. *See also* mysticism; theology.

mystical vision, a dimension of mystical experience. In the narrow sense, it refers to ecstatic phenomena, for example, apparitions of Jesus Christ, angels or saints, experienced by some, but by no means all, mystics. More broadly, it refers to the general transformation of consciousness and deepened awareness associated with mysticism. *See also* mysticism.

Mystici Corporis (mis'ti-chee kohr'pohr-is; Lat., "Of the Mystical [Body] of Christ"), encyclical of Pope Pius XII, issued on June 29, 1943. Although the encyclical described the relationship of head and members in hierarchical and juridical terms, it also emphasized the interior reality of grace and the role of the Holy Spirit as the soul of the Mystical Body of Christ. Thus, it is composed of both hierarchical and charismatic elements, which "complement and perfect one another." "Real" membership in the Church, however, belongs only to those who have been baptized, profess the true faith, and are in union with the pope. Therefore, the Mystical Body of Christ is identical with the Catholic Church. This teaching was modified by the Second Vatican Council (Dogmatic Constitution on the Church, n. 8). *See also* Body of Christ; Church.

mysticism, in Christian terms, an element of religion involving the explicit experience of the immediate presence of God. Despite the large body of modern literature on mysticism, the term is notoriously difficult to define.

The Problem of Definition: Definition involves three related factors. First, mysticism exists in all world religions. Therefore, a major question is whether there is something, "mysticism as such," that transcends the boundaries of particular religions and is open to generic definition. However, attempts at inclusive definitions are often criticized as inadequate in relation to specific traditions.

Second, the implication that there is a common "mystical core" in all religions raises serious questions about the possibility of distinguishing experiences from interpretation. In fact, they are interdependent because one can only experience within a framework of meaning. Thus, Christian mysticism is the way it is because mystics experience what they do within, rather than despite, a framework of Christian belief. Christian mystics may be said to be those who believe in and practice their faith with particular intensity. One attitude to this inclusiveness also determines whether to limit the term "mystic" to persons who speak of firsthand experiences, for example, Julian of Norwich (d. ca. 1420), or to include writers whose style is more theoretical, for example, Bernard of Clairvaux (d. 1153).

Third, if mysticism is defined as an explicit experience of God, is it limited to *particular kinds* of experience that are valid in every context? In fact, while mystical experience has a quality of immediacy, it is in some sense a mediated experience because it is always particular and contextual. It is not only within a faith tradition but also within the framework of the mystic's individual consciousness, temperament, life-style, and ideas about God, the world, and the self.

Context also implies historical factors. Mystics live at particular times and in particular places. The history of Christian mysticism includes a variety of different emphases because of specific social, historical, and religious conditions. For example, the emergence of a more Christ-centered mysticism during the twelfth and thirteenth centuries can only be properly understood in relationship to general shifts in religious and cultural sensibilities and contemporary reform movements in the Church.

The Basis of Christian Mysticism: Christian mysticism is rooted in the baptismal call of all Christians to enter into the divine mystery through exposure and response to the Scriptures, liturgy, and sacraments. This, rather than an interest in subjective experiences, was the understanding of "mysticism" in the early Church. The anonymous fifth- or sixth-century writer, known as Denys the Areopagite, whose works had such an influence on medieval Western mystical theology, sums up this early tradition. This approach underlines that mysticism, in its most general sense, is potentially a dimension of every Christian life. It also emphasizes that mysticism is a baptismal gift rather than something achieved through individual effort.

Yet, some people have intense experiences that are more usually described as "mystical" and have reached a deep level of communion with God. The latter is more important because not all mystics experience ecstacy, visions, or other altered states. On their own, these are not reliable indicators of mysticism. Equally, mysticism, even in the narrow sense, is essentially a process or way of life rather than isolated experiences. It is the Christian life lived with a particular commitment and intensity.

The word most frequently used by mystics and commentators to describe the heart of Christian mysticism is "union." However, union with God is, in some degree, the precondition of all spiritual development, rather than simply its deepest level. In addition, mystical union has often been understood in terms of human passivity and absorption. Apart from the difficulty of relating this factor, without qualification, to Christian understandings of the relationship of God to the human person, it does not correspond to the lives of the great mystics. Rather, the deep union of, say, Bernard of Clairvaux, Francis of Assisi (d. 1226), or Catherine of Siena (d. 1380) led them into greater activity and service of others. It may also be the case that the narrower understanding of union reflects the religious culture of male celibates who generated most of the language of mystical theology. Either a much broader understanding of "union" with God is needed or one must seek other, less exclusive, phrases such as "an immediacy of divine presence."

Types of Mysticism: In all Christian mysticism there is a movement toward greater simplicity and stillness and a growing realization of the inadequacy of human images for God. However, because mysticism is always particular and contextual, it is possible to speak of various types of Christian mysticism in which the emphases differ. No typology of Christian mysticism will be totally adequate but the most common types usually involve some variation on a simple, twofold distinction between the way of imagelessness, stillness, and wordlessness (apophatic) or the way of imaging God by the use of imagination or words (kataphatic). This distinction derives ultimately from Denys the Areopagite. Thus, Meister Eckhart (d. 1327) or the author of *The Cloud of Unknowing* would be in the first category and Julian of Norwich or Francis of Assisi would be in the second. In fact, there is no basis in Denys for such an absolute distinction because, for him, God is revealed in and through images and yet is always beyond them.

There is a balance between images and imagelessness in all Christian mysticism. The mysticism of "unknowing" or imagelessness cannot bypass the role of Christ, "the image of the unseen God," in the Christian life. Equally, Christ-centered mysticism employs imagination and imagery merely as doorways into divine presence where one is, ultimately, simply to be. Finally, while someone like Ignatius of Loyola (d. 1556), the sixteenth-century founder of the Jesuits, may be seen as espousing a "mysticism of service" in a special way, no Christian mystic would suggest that one can leave behind the demands of charity and service of others in pursuit of purely introspective and isolated contemplation. *See also* contemplation; English Mystics; mystical theology.

Bibliography

Dupré, Louis *The Deeper Self: An Introduction to Christian Mysticism.* New York: Crossroad, 1981.

Egan, Harvey. *What Are They Saying About Mysticism?* New York: Paulist Press, 1982.

Katz, Stephen, ed. *Mysticism and Religious Traditions.* New York: Oxford University Press, 1983.

McGinn, Bernard. *The Foundations of Mysticism: Origins to the Fifth Century.* New York: Crossroad, 1991.

Woods, Richard, ed. *Understanding Mysticism.* New York: Doubleday, 1980.   PHILIP SHELDRAKE

myth (Gk., *mythos,* "word," "speech," "story," "fiction"), a traditional story that deals with a character or characters from remote antiquity who are more than merely human. For Aristotle, myths encapsulate the truth "that the divine holds nature as a whole in its embrace." Fictional elements were added "with a view to the persuasion of the many and to the use [of myths] in laws and in what is advantageous [for the city]" (*Metaphysics* 12.8). Augustine (d. 430), like other Christian apologists, criticizes Roman civic-mythical religion on the grounds that peace or happiness is the goal of a community. If such a goal is not to be imaginary, the first demand to be made of a religion is that it be true (*City of God* 4.27; 6.1–8).

Some modern theologians continue to assess myth negatively. For Rudolf Bultmann (d. 1976), all forms of speech that objectify the nonobjective God, including stories or dogmas, are mythical. By contrast, God is the nonobjective challenge heard in the moment of decision. Demythologizing reverses objectivation: it allows the word of God to be heard. Others assess myth more positively. Karl Rahner (d. 1984) sees the tension between myth and concept as arising from the very nature of human knowledge: no transcendental knowledge is possible without "phantasms," images created by the mind but rooted in sense experience. On similar premises Hans Urs von Balthasar (d. 1988) sees myth as story, realized in worship and ritual, arising from both human longing and divine self-communication, irreducible to concepts. Carl Jung (d. 1961) maintains the permanent validity of myths as expressions of the collective unconscious.

Some contemporary biblical critics adopt a literary-sociological paradigm. Émile Durkheim's (d. 1917) pioneering sociological work has shown that in all societies religion and myth are central regulative institutions. As an agnostic, Durkheim understood religions as mythical (fictional) symbol-systems regulating the moral progress of society. Only society itself was real. On the more radical premise that all "reality" is socially constructed, some literary-sociological approaches to the Bible see the Christian myth in its various forms as one such construction, beyond the distinction between fact and fiction. These samples of reflection on myth point to issues that have been central in recent debates.

Historical-critical studies have shown the Bible to be deeply rooted in mythical traditions. In appropriating these studies, Catholic theologians have tended to resist attempts to reduce faith to metaphysical truth or existential decision. They have also resisted attempts to reduce faith to a symbol system expressing and furthering social values: the distinction between truth and fiction is relevant for a communal faith that acknowledges the gift of peace and happiness in the person of Jesus Christ. *See also* Bultmann, Rudolf; Scripture, interpretation of.

MICHAEL WALDSTEIN

name of Jesus. *See* Jesus [name].

Name of Jesus, feast of the, a day no longer commemorated as a separate feast in the Roman liturgical calendar of Vatican II. January 1, the Solemnity of Mary, Mother of God, recalls the conferral of the name of Jesus. The feast of the Name of Jesus originated in 1721 and was suppressed in 1969 as part of a general effort to eliminate duplication of feasts and to highlight the feasts that celebrate the central mystery of redemption.

Nantes, Edict of, grant of toleration to French Protestants (1598). Issued by Henry IV, the edict allowed Huguenots to worship in certain areas, granted civil liberties, and provided fortified cities of refuge. In the seventeenth century these concessions were eroded until Louis XIV revoked the edict (1685). *See also* Huguenots.

narthex. *See* vestibule.

National Assembly of Religious Women (NARW), successor in 1978 to the National Assembly of Women Religious, founded eight years earlier by Sister Ethne Kennedy. The assembly is a visible and vocal network of feminist women and men of Catholic and other traditions who share a vision of a world of peace with justice. NARW's agenda addresses a broad range of justice issues affecting women and children. Participation of people in decisions that affect their lives is emphasized. Social analysis is adopted as a tool for social change. NARW encourages collaboration with other women's groups to build coalitions for action on local, national, and international levels. Organized into local groups, members gather to discuss issues and use their collective power to effect justice in Church and society. The national office provides current resources and program materials; publishes annual reports and the bimonthly newsletter *Probe,* and sponsors workshops and annual national conferences.

National Black Catholic Congress, an organization founded in 1986 to encourage participation of black, or African-American, Catholics in the Church. The NBLC drafted the National Black Catholic Pastoral Plan in 1987. The central office is in Baltimore, Maryland.

National Black Sisters' Conference (NBSC), an organization of African-American nuns. It was founded in August 1968 by an international gathering of 155 black Roman Catholic sisters from 79 different religious congregations. By 1993, the NBSC provided a forum through which some 500 black sisters cooperate across congregational lines to confront individual and institutional racism in the Church, religious congregations of women, and society.

National Catechetical Directory, also known as Sharing the Light of Faith (1977), guidelines adapted from the General Catechetical Directory (1971) to the pastoral experience and needs of the U.S. Catholic Church; approved by the National Conference of Catholic Bishops after extensive consultation and review. It presents catechesis as a lifelong process, the stages of which are tailored to the experiential level of catechumens. *See also* catechesis; catechetics.

national Catholic churches, various church groups, distinguished by nationalities, that separated from the Roman Catholic Church. In the eighteenth century some Dutch Catholics in Utrecht separated from Rome because of their pro-Jansenist leanings. The nineteenth century saw certain national churches arise in Germany, Switzerland, and Austria because of a resistance to the doctrine of papal infallibility proclaimed at the First Vatican Council (1870). In the United States, some churches separated from Rome mainly because of ethnic discontent. The most important of these was the Polish National Church (1897) and a smaller group of Croats in 1924.

European churches of this type are also called Old Catholic churches. They accept the authority of the first eight ecumenical councils, have a vernacular liturgy, and a married clergy and episcopate. They entered into full communion with the Church of England (Anglican) in 1932. In the 1990s formal dialogue was started between the Polish National Church and the Roman Catholic Church. *See also* Old Catholics; Polish National Church.

National Catholic Coalition for Responsible Investment (NCCRI), a joint project of concerned Catholic organizations founded in 1973. Its purpose is to educate Catholic institutions about corporate social responsibility in their investments.

National Catholic Conference for Interracial Justice (NCCIJ), a federation of Catholic Interracial Councils (CIC) established in the United States in 1960 to bring Catholic teachings to bear on racial and ethnic issues. John LaFarge (d. 1963), a Jesuit, founded the first of these councils in 1934.

National Catholic Educational Association (NCEA), voluntary organization of more than fourteen thousand Catholic educational institutions and educators. Founded in 1904 as the Catholic Educational Association, it changed its name in 1927. The main purpose of the NCEA is to improve Catholic education at all levels. The association holds an annual convention and publishes a quarterly journal.

National Catholic Register, a weekly newspaper published by Twin Circle Publishing Company of Denver and Los Angeles. First published in 1955, its positions reflect a conservative point of view on theological, pastoral, and social issues.

National Catholic Reporter, a weekly newspaper published by NCR Publishing Company of Kansas City, Missouri. Founded in 1964 by Michael Greene, it provides analysis and commentary on secular and church news. The weekly is owned and edited by laypeople. Its positions on current pastoral, theological, social, and political issues are progressive in orientation.

National Catholic Welfare Conference (NCWC), the precursor of the National Conference of Catholic Bishops (NCCB). Founded in 1919, it was designed to draw all the bishops of the United States into voluntary consultation on matters of common interest and to provide an organizational framework for the participation of the laity in the national public life of the Church. The bishops of the midwestern sees of Cincinnati, Cleveland, Chicago, and Detroit chaired the conference through most of its history. The conduct of its daily business was left to the discretion of the general secretary and his staff in Washington, D.C. The plan for drawing the laity into national federations of men and women had uneven results. Catholic men's organizations resisted pressure to affiliate with the NCWC. Catholic women responded with some enthusiasm, and their volunteer efforts were among the more notable achievements of the organization. With the establishment of the NCCB in 1966, the NCWC passed out of existence.

National Conference of Catholic Bishops (NCCB), the organization of the U.S. hierarchy mandated by Vatican II. It is empowered as a canonical body to make policy, subject to Vatican review, for the Church in the United States. Since its organization in 1966, the conference has made major decisions regarding the English liturgy, sacramental practices, religious education, and church discipline. The body of U.S. bishops also exercises public influence on a national and international level through its civil incorporation as the United States Catholic Conference (USCC). The USCC has been the source of policy statements and practices pertaining to a range of public issues, including nuclear war, the economy, and abortion. Participation in the assembly of the NCCB is limited to bishops. Until the debate over the proposed pastoral letter on women (1992), there had been a noteworthy degree of consensus among the bishops on most major issues. This consensus has been created through discussion and negotiation rather than being imposed from the top down. The NCCB/USCC has its national headquarters in Washington, D.C. Its activities are administered by a general secretary and staffed by professionals who may be nuns, priests, or laypersons. It has maintained continuity with its predecessor, the National Catholic Welfare Conference, by making the welfare of the family a consistent foundation for its public policy considerations. It has carried forward the ambitions of those Catholic leaders of an earlier period, who saw the importance of creating a central forum for coordinating the activities of the Church in the United States. *See also* episcopal conference.   ELIZABETH MCKEOWN

National Council of Catholic Men (NCCM), a federation of all lay male societies in the United States. It was conceived by the organizers of the National Catholic Welfare Council in 1920. The chief national success of the NCCM lay in its sponsorship of the radio program "The Catholic Hour." After Vatican II and a short-lived merger with the National Council of Catholic Women, the NCCM concentrated its efforts largely on assisting its affiliates to develop and carry out religious and social programs on the local level.

National Council of Catholic Women (NCCW), a federation of existing women's societies organized in 1920 under the National Catholic Welfare Council. The NCCW has come to define its mission as the support, education, and empowerment of all Catholic women. Currently, the council is engaged in a variety of issues, including housing, racism, the environment, and international peace.

National Federation of Priests' Councils (NFPC), an association of more than 110 priests' councils, religious congregations, and other priests' associations, founded in Chicago in 1968. Stated purposes of the federation include the promotion of collaborative efforts to advance the Church's social teachings, the development of national and universal perspectives in Church and ministry, and a commitment to the renewal of priestly life. National headquarters are in Chicago, Illinois.

National Office of Black Catholics, an organization founded in 1970 to make the Church's presence more effective in the black, or African-American, community and to foster participation of black Catholics in the Church. The central office is in Washington, D.C.

national parish, a parish whose membership is based not on geographical boundaries, but on belonging to a given ethnic group. National parishes have been common in the United States during those periods of immigration when, for a significant number of Catholics, English was a second language. Among the more common national parishes in the United States, for example, are those for Italian-, Polish-, German-, Spanish-, and French-speaking Catholics.

nativism, a form of xenophobia directed especially at Catholic immigrants to the United States in the nineteenth century. Nativists prompted the burning of the Charlestown (Massachusetts) Convent (1834), the Philadelphia riots (1844), and the formation of the Know-Nothing movement (1850s). The Civil War eased nativist tendencies, but massive immigration in the late nineteenth century rekindled the movement. Nativists spurred the formation of the American Protective Association (1887), the resurgence of the Ku Klux Klan, and immigration restrictions in the 1920s. *See also* anti-Catholicism.

Nativity, feast of. *See* Christmas.

natural family planning, any of several nonartificial methods that make use of a woman's physical symptoms to determine her fertile period each month, used in spacing the births of children. As a method of birth control natural family planning is accepted by the Catholic Church because it does not involve disruption either of the act of sexual intercourse or of the natural process of conception. One form of natural family planning was the so-called rhythm method of past decades, which relied upon a calendar calculation of fertility based upon menstrual cycles and was sometimes inaccurate as a result. In its most complete modern form, also called the symptothermal method, natural family planning involves daily charting of a woman's basal body temperature (taken immediately upon awakening), the shape and position of her cervix, and the quantity and consistency of vaginal mucus, in addition to menstrual cycle and sexual activity data. This method is said to have enjoyed great success among married couples whether they are attempting to achieve or avoid pregnancy.

Natural family planning is of particular interest to Catholics as a nonartificial method of spacing births. Official Catholic moral teaching unequivocally condemns abortion and still regards artificial means of birth control as unacceptable for a variety of reasons, although this latter teaching, reaffirmed in *Humanae Vitae* (1968), remains controversial. Traditionally, children have been regarded as gifts from God to the married couple and to human society in general, and their conception was not to be inhibited by methods that disrupt the normal biological processes of the female, e.g., by the use of the contraceptive pill. Methods such as the so-called morning-after pill and the intrauterine device are regarded as abortifacients, which act by preventing the fertilized egg from being implanted in the uterus. Because human life is held by Catholic teaching to be sacred from the time of conception, these methods constitute the direct and unjustified termination of human life. Use of condoms is disallowed, according to this teaching, because such use prevents the sexual act from being completed in the manner ordained by God. For the same reason, premature withdrawal by the male (Lat., *coitus interruptus*) is not permitted. Natural family planning, by contrast, makes use of naturally occurring periods of infertility when practiced as a method of spacing children. Proponents of the method argue that the beneficial nature of the method is not limited to its acceptability as a means of birth control, but involves as well the good effects brought about by shared responsibility for decision making about the appropriateness of sexual intercourse on a particular occasion. The periodic abstinence necessitated by natural family planning is also considered to be beneficial by its practitioners, because abstinence during the woman's fertile period allows spouses to find other ways to express their love and reminds them of the importance of nonsexual reaffirmations of their commitment to each other. *See also* birth control.   ALISON LIDSTAD

natural law, the sum of those universally binding moral principles that can be discerned by human reason, understood as analogous to a legal code. The natural law has been understood in a variety of different ways by its proponents and opponents alike.

History of the Natural Law: the Classical Period. The natural law tradition originated in the late Roman Republic, through the reflections of political thinkers like Cicero (d. 43 B.C.), as well as many of the early Church Fathers. Following Aristotle (d. 322 B.C.), these thinkers attempted to evaluate the institutions of society according to what is natural to the human person, in contrast to the conventions of particular societies. What distinguished the natural law tradition from Aristotelianism, however, was its different account of what is natural to the human person. Whereas Aristotle had argued that barbarians, slaves, and women are naturally incapable of independent moral judgment, and therefore are justly subject to the authority of male citizens, the natural lawyers insisted that all mature, normal human beings are equal in their fundamental capacities for moral virtue, and that the institutions of domination structuring society are therefore unnatural. In this light, slavery, property, the state itself, and even marriage in its actual form were all seen as problematic.

Nonetheless, it was held that these institutions enjoy limited moral legitimacy, on the grounds that they represent necessary compromises with the natural ideals of equality and noncoercion. For example, the state, which maintains public order, was legitimated on the grounds that only through its exercise of force can the state protect the weaker members of society from the oppression of the strong; thus, through its violations of the ideals of noncoercion and equality, the state was paradoxically justified because it secured the nearest approximations to these ideals possible in an imperfect world.

The main lines of the account of the natural law sketched above would have been generally accepted by Christian as well as non-Christian political theorists in this period. It was given its most influential Christian expression, at least in the West, by Augustine (d. 430), who appropriated it to lay the foundations for what would later develop into the theory of the just war.

Medieval Period: Throughout the Middle Ages, the tradition of the natural law continued to function primarily as a means by which to evaluate the central institutions of society against the criteria of equality and noncoercion, ideals that could never be realized fully in this world, but could nonetheless be approximated. The natural law tradition could and did function either as a force for conservatism or as an impetus for reform. For some thinkers, it served to justify structures of dominion, on the grounds that one could now do no better, but for others, it provided a set of criteria by which to challenge at least some aspects of these same institutions, on the grounds that even in this postlapsarian world, one could approximate natural equality more nearly than one actually does. At the same time, medieval thinkers also appealed to the natural law in ways that are familiar to Catholics today, as a source for evaluating the morality of sexual and medical actions against the criterion of what is proper to human biological nature. But these sorts of arguments did not have the centrality that they later came to have.

Medieval natural law theory is associated above all with the figure of Thomas Aquinas (d. 1274), who provided one of the most complete influential accounts of this tradition in the medieval period. However, the association of medieval natural law with Aquinas can be misleading, since he attempted to synthesize this tradition with the recently rediscovered moral and political theory of Aristotle. As a result, the Catholic theory of natural law after Aquinas was perhaps less inclined to see the central institutions of society as being problematic and needing paradoxical justification than was the Augustinian natural law tradition of the Middle Ages itself.

Modern Period: After the Reformation and the Enlightenment, the natural law tradition divided into two strands. Under the influence of philosophers such as Thomas Hobbes (d. 1679) and John Locke (d. 1704), it was incorporated into the political thought of the Enlightenment as the basis for the emergent doctrine of universal human rights.

Within the Catholic community, under the influence of the reforms in moral theology and penitential practice mandated by the Council of Trent

(1545–63), the natural law was increasingly applied to questions of personal morality, and as a result, its distinctively political character was increasingly obscured. It was during this period that Catholic natural law reasoning took on the characteristics that are most commonly associated with the natural law today. During this period the natural was increasingly contrasted with the unnatural, which was straightforwardly prohibited, rather than with the conventional, which could be ambiguously tolerated. Correlatively, the natural was increasingly equated with the given biological structures of the human species, particularly the structures of the human person, which were then seen as unconditionally normative.

The Natural Law Today: Official magisterial statements still incorporate the understanding of the natural law that emerged within the Catholic community after the Counter-Reformation. However, very few moral theologians today would accept the conception of the natural law just described. It is widely seen as both philosophically untenable, in its assumption that there is an essential human nature that is normative for all times and places, and theologically suspect, in that it seems to leave little room for Scripture and Church tradition in Christian moral reflection.

Nonetheless, almost every Catholic moral theologian would agree that the natural law tradition is essentially valid and important for contemporary moral reflection. This tradition would be understood today as including at least the claim that there is a core of universally binding moral precepts that can be discerned, at least in principle, through human reason unaided by special revelation. The foundations of this invariant core, its content, and its extent are widely debated. *See also* faith and reason; moral theology.

Bibliography

Carlyle, Sir Robert Warrand, and Alexander James Carlyle. *A History of Mediaeval Political Theory in the West.* 3d ed. Edinburgh: William Blackwood and Sons, 1923.

d'Entreves, Alessandro P. *Natural Law: An Introduction to Legal Philosophy.* London: Hutchinson and Company, 1970.

Troeltsch, Ernst. *The Social Teachings of the Christian Churches.* Trans. Olive Wyon. Chicago: University of Chicago Press, 1931; reprinted by Westminster/John Knox Press, 1981.   JEAN PORTER

natural rights, those fundamental rights grounded in the dignity of the human person and pertaining therefore to all persons. Human dignity is based on the *imago Dei* doctrine that the human person is created in the image of God.

Natural rights cannot be revoked legitimately by any governmental or other social power. However, this does not mean that these rights are without limit. For instance, while the right to private property is a natural right, it is limited by concern for the common good.

In addition to the right to private property, the Catholic tradition lists as natural rights the right to life and bodily integrity; the right to work, a just wage, and adequate working conditions; and the right to religious belief, among others. The recognition of both those rights considered to be "civil rights" (for instance, the right to associate) and those considered "economic rights" (for instance, the right to food) means that the Catholic understanding of natural rights encompasses both liberal democratic and socialist understandings. The document that spells out these rights most clearly is Pope John XXIII's encyclical, *Pacem in Terris* (1963). *See also* Catholic social teachings; human rights; *imago Dei;* right to die; right to life.

natural theology, the study of God solely through the use of human reason. Typically, theology relies upon God's revelation for knowledge about God, as in the doctrines of the Trinity and the Incarnation. Natural theology, however, works independently from the content of revelation. Processes observable by any human person, along with human reason, provide the sources for the knowledge of God gained by natural theology.

One of the traditional concerns of natural theology has been to show that human reason unaided by revelation can arrive at the conviction that God exists. Natural theology has offered several proofs for the existence of God. Anselm's (d. 1109) ontological proof, the five ways of Thomas Aquinas (d. 1274), and Cardinal Newman's (d. 1890) moral argument are some of the most famous proofs for God's existence.

Religious and philosophical objections have been raised concerning the possibility of practicing natural theology. The religious objection states that the act of faith is its own justification and that rational demonstration has no place in justifying faith. This position is known as fideism. The philosophical objection, of which Immanuel Kant (d. 1804) is the most prominent representative, argues that human reason is limited to that knowledge which comes from sense experience. This limitation to human knowledge makes any proof that God exists impossible. In opposition to these objections, the First Vatican Council affirmed in 1870 that human reason can know of God's existence with certainty (*Dei Filius*). *See also* faith and reason; philosophy and theology; Vatican Council I.

nature (Lat., *natura;* Gk., *physis*), that which is basic and unifying in anything existing independently of human action or chance, contrasted to what in it is superficial or transient; also, the total visible creation. Greek philosophers sought to discover the dynamic essential structure of things as the principle of their stability and activities, classifying them into species of elements, compounds, and vegetable and animal organisms, with special interest in the question, "What is the human person?" These became the fundamental questions of science. Theology extends this questioning to ask, "What is the nature of God?"

Because scientific and theological answers to such questions, even when true, are partial and inadequate, some philosophers claim we can never know the natures or essences of things, but only their behaviors, measurements, or appearances. Others denounce "essentialism," i.e., the denial of the reality of activity, change, and process. In fact, activity, change, and process presuppose the relative stability of acting, changing units such as atoms, molecules, and other organisms independent of human thought and manipulation.

When theology speaks of "one divine nature in Three Persons," "Christ's human and divine natures," or "the natural law," these concepts are derived by analogy from our knowledge of material objects, but must not be understood univocally and reductively. God's "nature" is not an "object" but the pure act of absolute personal life, wisdom, and love. Similarly the "nature" of human persons differs from that of nonpersonal objects in its subjectivity (self-consciousness), freedom, and historicity. *See also* nature and grace.   BENEDICT M. ASHLEY

nature and grace, a traditional Catholic distinction. It is intended to emphasize that grace (the relationship of friendship with God and the radical transformation of the person that results from that divine love) is totally gratuitous; it is neither owed to human beings, nor is it something we could obtain through our own capacity. In the Scriptures, the basic distinction drawn is not between nature and grace, but rather between persons as graced and persons in sin. Augustine of Hippo (d. 430) uses the terminology of nature and grace in some of his writings, but more frequently he contrasts grace and sin.

Historical Development: The systematic development of the distinction occurred during the Scholastic period when Thomas Aquinas (d. 1274) drew on Aristotle's notion of nature to speak of the divinizing power of grace (recipients of grace "become participants of the divine nature"; 2 Pet 1:4). Aristotle explained reality in terms of a system of natures with inbuilt capacities that empower operations to achieve the final end (Gk., *telos*) of the nature. Because the final end of human nature is union with God, Aquinas concluded that a "renovation" of human nature was necessary in order for human beings to reach their goal. Habitual or sanctifying grace is precisely this new life-principle. It enables human persons to operate at the level of knowing and loving that is beyond their own power through the virtues of faith, hope, and love. By the central Thomistic expression that "grace builds on nature," Aquinas meant that grace transforms human nature so that human persons can participate in the divine nature, yet human nature retains its powers and individuality.

Unfortunately, in later centuries the Thomistic distinction became a clear separation of two orders. To preserve the gratuity of grace, Thomas Cajetan (d. 1534) spoke of "pure nature" with its own finality. In response to the Baianist and Jansenist positions that grace was a necessary completion of humanity, the theological hypothesis of "pure nature" took hold. Grace, while necessary to heal and elevate human nature, was considered totally extrinsic to human nature or experience.

Modern Period: The twentieth-century renewal of biblical and patristic studies enabled theologians to restore the focus of the theology of grace to God's self-communication—the offer of a share in the trinitarian life of love extended to humankind. Henri de Lubac (d. 1991), Karl Rahner (d. 1984), and other Catholic theologians proposed alternative ways of preserving both the inner desire for grace and the sheer gratuity of God's offer. De Lubac stressed that relationships between persons are never "deserved" or "owed," even among human beings. Rahner used the term "supernatural existential" to explain that the offer of grace, located in the depths of every human heart, remains sheer gift. In Rahner's view, "pure nature" remains an important hypothetical concept to remind us that human beings could have been created differently and to protect the gratuity of grace, but it is not, and has never been, the state of any historical human being. Pope Pius XII's encyclical *Humani Generis* (1950) reaffirmed Catholic teaching on the gratuity of grace.

The return to biblical, relational, historical, and personalist categories of language for grace has offered various new perspectives incorporating distinction and interplay, but the key point remains: relationship with God is sheer gift, not something "owed" to human beings. *See also* grace; supernatural.   MARY C. HILKERT

nave (Lat., *navis*, "ship"), ecclesiastical architectural term referring to the space between the church entrance and the sanctuary; this space includes the main aisle and the space for congregants to sit or stand. Typically, the supporting pillars distinguish the nave from the side aisles.

Nazarene, a designation for Jesus. The NT uses two related Greek forms, *Nazarenos* (Mark, Luke) and *Nazoraios* (Matthew, Luke, John, Acts). Both probably identify Jesus as a resident of Nazareth, although the latter may relate Jesus to a Jewish sect. The term came to be used of early Christians as well (Acts 24:5).

Nazareth, a village in Galilee. Nazareth was a small village to the north of the Jezreel Valley (the Plain of Esdraelon) near Sepphoris, an important provincial center. The NT records that it was Jesus' home as a youth (Matt 2:23; 4:13; Mark 1:9; Luke 4:16).

Nazism, German fascism under Adolf Hitler, from 1933 until 1945. A combination of differing ideologies, Nazism was held together by its core of anti-Semitic racism and by the adulation of Hitler, who took over the National Socialist party after World War I, but experienced little or no political success until the worldwide depression of the 1930s. Named chancellor in January of 1933, Hitler was able to achieve dictatorial powers partly because of the Catholic Center party, which supported the Enabling Act of April 1933, giving Hitler emergency powers. The Catholic Center party thought its support would have a moderating influence on his future actions. On July 8, three days after the dissolution of the Catholic Center party, a Concordat was signed between Germany and the Vatican that was to have protected the Church's rights under Fascism but failed to do so. Almost four years later Pope Pius XI issued an encyclical letter *Mit brennender Sorge*

in which he scathingly denounced Nazism as racist, neo-pagan, and anti-Christian. *See also* Fascism; Germany, Catholicism in.

negative way, an approach to theology that emphasizes that all language about God is radically inadequate. Because God is revealed in creation and in human experience, it is possible to speak of God using human categories such as "goodness." However, God transcends all such concepts. Therefore, the path to a deeper knowledge of God is one of "negation," whereby one denies that any name, affirmation, or image is God. Historically, this approach originates in elements of Neoplatonist philosophy adopted by the sixth-century theologian known as Denys the Areopagite, who had considerable influence on both Eastern and Western Christianity. *See also* Denys the Areopagite; language, religious; mysticism; Neoplatonism.

neophyte (Gk., *neophutos*, "new growth, new convert"), the newly baptized. As a baptismal term, it dates back to third- and fourth-century Greek Christian usage (the Latin churches spoke of *infantes;* see 1 Pet 2:2). It has recently been recovered by the Rite of Christian Initiation of Adults (1972). *See also* Rite of Christian Initiation of Adults.

Neoplatonism, a philosophical school beginning with Plotinus (205–70) that was the dominant philosophical trend in late antiquity, shaping the thought of Christian and pagan alike. Plotinus regarded himself as an interpreter and systematizer of Plato, drawing out what was implied or "veiled" in Plato's thought and reconciling contradictions. To this end Plotinus drew heavily upon his wide reading in the philosophical tradition, freely using Aristotelian, middle-Platonic, and Stoic thinkers, many of whom had themselves commented on Plato. In addition, he incorporated traditional religious elements, so that his "Platonism" was highly syncretistic, in some ways a summation of classical ideals, and thus of widespread appeal.

Plotinus's *Enneads* describes a system focused on three hypostases (substances): the One, fount of all being but itself beyond being and predication; Mind, emanating eternally from the One as its image, containing the eternal ideas on which the sensible universe is modeled; and World-Soul, which penetrates and enlivens the sensible world on the basis of the rational principles it receives in its generation from Mind. Against the Gnostics, Plotinus taught that the sensible universe is not evil. Evil is equivalent to nonbeing, but even matter, in itself a kind of nonbeing and therefore evil, participates in the form, beauty, and intelligibility of the whole universe. Thus consideration of even the sensible world can direct the soul to the contemplation of Mind and, ultimately, beyond speech and thought, of the One.

Plotinus's successors Porphyry (ca. 232–ca. 305, biographer of Plotinus), Iamblichus (ca. 250–330, who strongly influenced the emperor Julian), and Proclus (410–85, most famous for his *Platonic Theology*) extended and even further enlarged the syncretism of Plotinus, especially in a religious direction. The thought of Church Fathers from the Cappadocians and Pseudo-Dionysius in the East to Augustine and Boethius in the West turned Neoplatonic themes to Christian use and served to transmit a Christian/Neoplatonic synthesis to the Middle Ages. *See also* Plato; Plotinus.   JOHN C. CAVADINI

neo-Scholasticism, a term used for the revival, from 1860 to 1960, of the philosophical tradition of the medieval and baroque universities. After the rise of the Enlightenment, Catholic theology found difficulty in using the empiricist and idealist philosophies to express orthodox theological concepts. By 1850 some were suggesting that a return to the "Scholastic" tradition of the older Catholic universities might be the best solution. This received papal approbation in Leo XIII's encyclical *Aeterni Patris* (1879), which held up the "Christian philosophy" of Thomas Aquinas (d. 1274) as the best model of a *philosophia perennis* (Lat., "perennial philosophy") for all Catholic education but urged that it be freed of obsolescent elements and that it assimilate the best of modern thought.

Catholic schools were quick to accept forms of neo-Scholasticism, but two difficulties remained: (1) the need for historical research and analysis to understand the authentic thought of Aquinas and the other great Scholastics; and (2) the discovery of the proper way to assimilate modern thought without distortion of the old. The period from 1870 to Vatican II (1962–65) made progress in these two areas, but resulted in a wide spectrum of interpretation of what an authentic and creative Thomism might be, ranging from the "existential Thomism" of Jacques Maritain (d. 1973) and the "historical Thomism" of Etienne Gilson (d. 1978) to the "traditional Thomism" of Reginald Garrigou-Lagrange (d. 1964) and the "transcendental Thomism" of Joseph Marechal (d. 1944) and Bernard Lonergan

(d. 1984). These differences centered on how or whether the "turn to the subject" that underlies modern philosophy since Descartes (d. 1650) can be reconciled with the Aristotelian epistemology of Aquinas. Differing explanations of the relation of the modern empirical sciences to metaphysics contributed to this spectrum of interpretations.

The enforced teaching of what were often eclectic or grossly oversimplified versions of Thomism led to a reaction favoring a "return to patristic thought" or adaptations to contemporary pragmatism, existentialism, phenomenology, process philosophy, Marxism, or hermeneutic and analytic philosophy. Vatican II opened the door to better solutions.

By the time of the council the weaknesses of neo-Scholasticism were generally recognized by Catholic theologians: its lack of historical perspective and the eclectic confusion of Thomism with the alien doctrines of Francisco de Suarez (d. 1617), Duns Scotus (d. 1308), René Descartes (d. 1650), G. W. Leibniz (d. 1716), Immanuel Kant (d. 1804), and idealism; its failure to deal adequately with the findings of modern science and to recognize human historicity and subjectivity; and its teaching methods that tended to conceptualism, while neglecting to ground principles and definitions in experience.

On the other hand, neo-Scholasticism did provide Catholic theology with a common philosophical language that facilitated teaching and dialogue; it offered clarity in definition and argumentation; and it provided some metaphysical grounding for those natural truths that prepare for Christian faith, namely, the existence of God, the spirituality of the human soul, and the natural moral law.

In the end, however, the documents of Vatican II largely avoided dependence on technical neo-Scholastic terminology and argumentation, even though the Decree on Priestly Formation (1965) continues to recommend the *philosophia perennis* (n. 15) and the guidance of Aquinas in systematic theology (n. 16). *See also* philosophy and theology; Scholasticism; theology; Thomism. BENEDICT M. ASHLEY

neo-Thomism, the various interpretations of the thought of Thomas Aquinas (d. 1274) intended to enable it to assimilate the best of modern thought. Neo-Thomism developed after 1860, and especially after Pope Leo XIII's 1879 encyclical *Aeterni Patris*. The movement was particularly strong in France during the first half of the twentieth century. *See also* Thomism.

Nepomucen, St. John. *See* John Nepomucen, St.

Nereus, St. (nay'ray-uhs), Roman martyr of unknown date whose commemoration is linked with St. Achilleus. Feast day: May 12.

Neri, St. Philip. *See* Philip Neri, St.

Nestorianism, the heretical belief that there were two separate persons in Christ, one divine and the other human, in contrast to the orthodox teaching that in Christ there is only one divine Person.

Nestorius (d. ca. 451) was bishop of Constantinople from 428 to 431. His pastoral zeal for orthodoxy led him to reject both Arianism and Apollinarianism, according to which the one Person (Christ) had only one nature (the divine). In contrast, Nestorius insisted that Christ had two natures (human and divine) that were always distinct but conjoined in a metaphysically unique manner. His affirmation agreed with the eventual orthodox position that the two natures of Christ were not synthesized or (con)fused in his one Person, but disagreed with it in that it denied the hypostatic union of the two natures in the one divine Person.

Three implications of Nestorius's Christology led to its denunciation prior to, and at, the Council of Ephesus (431). The first had to do with salvation: If the human nature of Christ is metaphysically unique, then it is not the same as humanity, and hence has no capacity to save humanity. The second implication had to do with the Eucharist: If Christ is not consubstantially divine and human, then there is no way in which the physical elements in Holy Communion can impart spiritual life to humans. Finally, the third implication had to do with Mary: If Christ's two natures were conjoined in a metaphysically unique manner, then Mary could not have been *Theotokos* (Gk., "God-bearer") since by definition the "borne" cannot be metaphysically different from the "bearer." This third consequence precipitated the charges against Nestorius that led to his removal from the see of Constantinople. *See also* Apollinarianism; Arianism; Chalcedon, Council of; Christology; Ephesus, Council of; hypostatic union; *Theotokos*.   KERN R. TREMBATH

Nestorius, d. ca. 451, heretical bishop of Constantinople (428–31). He was an Antiochene monk who possibly had studied under Theodore of Mopsuestia. Theodosius II, prompted by his reputation as a preacher, appointed him to the see of Constantino-

ple in 428. Declaring himself a defender of orthodoxy, he opposed the use of *Theotokos* (Gk.), "Godbearer," for Mary, which sparked a violent controversy not only because of the Christological implications, but also because of the growing devotion to the Virgin. Cyril of Alexandria and the Egyptian monks sided against Nestorius. His teaching was condemned in 430 by a Roman synod and in 431 by the Council of Ephesus. He was deposed and sent back to the monastery at Antioch from which he was later exiled. In 435 his writings were condemned, so few fragments of his letters and sermons survive. However, one of his writings, the *Bazaar of Heracleides,* discovered in 1895, has prompted some reevaluation of Nestorius's claim to orthodoxy. *See also* Antioch; Christology; Cyril of Alexandria, St.; Ephesus, Council of; Nestorianism; *Theotokos*.

Ne Temere (nay tem-air'ay; Lat., "Do not fear"), papal decree issued in 1908 by Pope Pius X requiring all Roman Catholics to marry before a properly authorized priest and two witnesses.

Netherlands, Catholicism in the. Christian presence in what is now the Netherlands dates to Roman times (ca. sixth century), when the Rhine was the northern boundary of the empire. Irish monks (Willibrord, d. 739, and Boniface, d. 754) evangelized the north. Willibrord became bishop of Utrecht in 695, and it was the only bishopric until modern times. In the ninth century Normans sacked cities and ejected the clergy. During the Middle Ages monastic life flourished, preserving Christian culture.

The Reformation had a profound effect on Holland. William of Orange's overthrow of Spanish rule brought the rejection of Catholicism in the north and gradual acceptance of Calvin's doctrine. Catholic churches became Dutch Reformed; statues were destroyed and frescoes painted over. Catholics practiced their faith in hiding. The southern provinces remained overwhelmingly Catholic, but the Netherlands was considered a Protestant country, both by its own government and by Rome. It lost its hierarchy in 1580 and was administered by the Vatican office of the Propagation of the Faith until 1853. From 1583 until 1795 the Catholic Church was subjected to severe penal restrictions. In 1702 a minority of Catholics associated with Jansenism, a French movement that stressed human sinfulness and imposed a rigorous moral code, were censored by

Rome and later formed the Church of Utrecht (also known as Old Catholics) in 1724. By 1853 the self-emancipation of Dutch Catholics had begun in earnest, by means of a Catholic press, schools, and political life.

Before World War II nearly 40 percent of the Dutch population was Catholic. With Vatican II a period of renewal began, especially in catechetics, ecumenism, and pastoral methodology. The National Pastoral Council's proposal of a married priesthood was unacceptable to Rome. Appointments of very conservative bishops since the 1970s, intended to overcome divisions, served instead to exacerbate the situation. A synod of the Dutch bishops, held in the Vatican in 1980, was unsuccessful in resolving the problem of polarization. A once flourishing Catholic Church declined under the weight of pastoral demoralization and frustration.

In 1993 there are over 5.5 million Catholics in the Netherlands, or under 37 percent of the total population. There are six dioceses and one archdiocese. *See also* Alfrink, Bernard Jan; Old Catholics.

JACINTA VAN WINKEL

Network, national Catholic lobby to promote social justice legislation in the United States. Founded in 1971 by forty-seven women religious, it is a nonprofit membership organization of women and men that seeks just access to economic resources, fairness in national funding for the poor and others in need, and justice in global relationships. Beyond lobbying, it provides print and electronic resources and organizes educational programs and internships.

Neumann, St. John Nepomucene, 1811–60, U.S. bishop. Born in Bohemia and educated at Prague's Charles-Ferdinand University, he was ordained a priest for the diocese of New York in 1836. After ministering in western New York, he joined the Congregation of the Most Holy Redeemer (Redemptorists) in 1842 and served in his order's churches in Baltimore and Pittsburgh. Appointed bishop of Philadelphia in 1852, he presided over the diocese's rapid development. He had gained admiration for his humility and saintliness by the time of his death. He was beatified in 1963 and canonized in 1977. Feast day: January 5.

New American Bible. *See* Bible, English translations of the.

New Jerusalem Bible. *See* Bible, English translations of the.

Newman, John Henry, 1801–90, English cardinal, Catholic and Anglican apologist, and man of letters. Born in London and raised with Bible religion, Newman experienced conversion at age fifteen: luminous awareness of himself and God, impressions of creed and dogma, and a calling to single life. He studied classics and mathematics at Trinity College, Oxford, there developing his evangelical beliefs along Calvinist lines. Ordained an Anglican priest, he became vicar of the university church, St. Mary the Virgin. Fellow and tutor of Oriel College, Oxford, he was influenced by rationalist scholars whose methods included logic and evidences to prove religious matters. Patristic studies, Joseph Butler's *Analogy of Religion,* friendships, illness, and his sister's death gradually separated him from the liberal leanings of Oriel, centering him in high church or Anglo-Catholic tradition. In 1832 he published *The Arians of the Fourth Century* and, on a Mediterranean voyage, wrote many religious poems (*Lyra Apostolica*). Recovering from a grave illness in Sicily, he returned to England to become leader of the Oxford movement.

Religious Odyssey: From 1833 to 1841, Newman defended the Via Media of the Anglican

Cardinal John Henry Newman, one of the great Catholic thinkers of the nineteenth century; he was largely responsible for the renewal of interest in the writings of the Fathers of the Church and for a deeper appreciation of the role of the laity in the development of doctrine.

Communion. The far-reaching "Tracts for the Times against Popery and Dissent" were complemented by his *Parochial and Plain Sermons* delivered at St. Mary's. He published *Lectures on the Prophetical Office viewed relatively to Romanism and Popular Protestantism,* and became editor of the movement's journal, *The British Critic.* His and the movement's last tract, the ninetieth, proposing a Catholic reading of the "Thirty-nine Articles," was denounced by church and university. This blow, other disappointments and doubts, and further study of the early Church resulted in Newman's resignation from his position and clerical status. After years of intellectual and spiritual struggle, Newman became a Catholic in 1845 while completing *An Essay on the Development of Christian Doctrine,* which showed continuity from the Church of antiquity to the Catholic Church of the nineteenth century.

Newman went to Rome to study theology for Catholic priesthood, entered and brought to England the Oratory of St. Philip Neri, published two novels of conversion, *Loss and Gain* (1848) and *Callista* (1855), and two volumes on ecumenical relations in England, *Lectures on Certain Difficulties felt by Anglicans in submitting to the Catholic Church* (1850) and *Lectures on the Present Position of Catholics in England* (1851).

From 1851 to 1858, Newman founded and presided over the Catholic University of Ireland, justifying Catholic liberal education in *The Idea of a University.* In 1859 he founded the Birmingham Oratory School for boys, became editor of *The Rambler,* and published "On Consulting the Faithful in Matters of Doctrine" (1859). He was reported to Rome for it and asked to resign the editorship.

Newman's Reemergence: After four years of relative silence, Newman was aroused by Charles Kingsley's published accusation that Newman and the Roman Catholic clergy were indifferent to truth and cultivated deception. Newman responded with the *Apologia pro Vita Sua* (1864), disclosing the history of his religious opinions from childhood and magnificently defending both reason and authority. Enthusiastic response from Anglicans and Catholics reinstated Newman in the public mind. In 1865 he published "The Dream of Gerontius," a long poem about immediate life after death, and "Letter to Pusey" on Marian devotion. His most philosophical work, *An Essay in Aid of a Grammar of Assent* (1870), aimed at justifying religious faith by describing how ordinary minds reach certitude.

Newman declined the invitation by bishops and pope to serve as theological consultant for the First Vatican Council. As a Catholic, he believed in papal infallibility but opposed its conciliar definition, saying the Church was not yet ready and episcopal intrigue for the doctrine was too dominant. His "Letter to the Duke of Norfolk" (1875) defended both the doctrine of infallibility and the freedom of the Catholic conscience. His last major contribution to ecclesiology was the 1877 preface to *The Prophetical Office,* now retitled *The Via Media,* in which he detailed the Church's three offices and their interrelations: the prophetic, exercised by theologians; the priestly, by laity; the governing, by pope and bishops.

In 1878 Newman became first honorary fellow of Trinity College, Oxford. In 1879 Pope Leo XIII made him cardinal and, in accepting, Newman singled out as his lifelong work the battle against the usurpations of reason in matters of religion. After physical decline, Newman died in 1890. Newman's *Letters and Diaries* (posthumously published from 1961 to 1984), when complete, will comprise thirty-one of his nearly eighty published volumes.

Thought and Spirituality: A thinker of great assimilative power, originality, and genius, Newman is one of the foremost stylists of the English language. His writings are rich in psychological subtlety, illustration, and satire. He was interested in the personal character of all mental acts; the influence of mind upon mind; the sacred duty of developing one's gifts; and liberal education as the cultivation of the healthy mind.

Newman's spirituality emphasized conscience as the connecting principle between self and God, the Holy Spirit's indwelling in individuals and Church, the gospel "Image of Christ," God's particular providence, devotion to Mary and the saints, and patience. He celebrated the reality of the invisible world, the sacramentality of the visible world, the holiness of everyday life in consistent fulfillment of one's duties, through friendship and personal influence, not so much by words as by actions.

Newman's thought had significant influence on the Second Vatican Council, particularly his ecclesiology, ecumenism, theory of doctrinal development, defense of conscience, and theology of the laity. Pope John Paul II declared him "venerable" in 1991. *See also* Anglicanism; Anglo-Catholicism; doctrine, development of; Oxford movement; *sensus fidelium.*

Bibliography
    Bouyer, Louis. *Newman: His Life and Spirituality.* London: Burns & Oats, 1958.

Lash, Nicholas. *Newman on Development: The Search for an Explanation in History.* Shepherdstown, WV: Patmos Press, 1975.

Newman, John Henry. *Newman the Theologian: A Reader.* Notre Dame, IN: University of Notre Dame Press, 1990.

MARY KATHERINE TILLMAN

Newman movement, the network of organizations for Catholic students on secular college and university campuses. Committed to providing pastoral care and religious education for Catholic students, the Newman movement also represents Catholicism to the wider university community. The first Newman club, named in honor of John Henry Newman (d. 1890), was formed at the University of Pennsylvania in 1893, with similar organizations soon developing at other schools. Chaplains were appointed by and responsible to local bishops and received minimal national coordination. Many bishops feared that too much Catholic religious activity at non-Catholic schools would encourage Catholics to attend them, to the disadvantage of Catholic colleges. This attitude changed gradually, and in 1962 Newman clubs were recognized as part of the Church's national educational effort. A federation of Newman clubs was formed in 1915, and today it is part of the United States Catholic Conference.

New Testament. *See* Bible.

New Testament theology, a branch of biblical theology that attempts to describe historically and to synthesize what the NT says about God and God's relation to humanity. An important contribution of New Testament theology has been the production of numerous biblical dictionaries that describe the literary heritage, historical background, and contextual meaning of fundamental NT concepts, e.g., justification, redemption, grace. In the 1950s German Protestant scholars, especially Joachim Jeremias and W. G. Kümmel, proposed synthetic NT theologies, organized around the teaching of Jesus or the religious perspective of particular authors (especially Paul and John). Rudolf Bultmann (d. 1976) produced the most influential work, *Theology of the New Testament.* Bultmann first described the evolving faith and practice of the early Church and then argued that this faith came to its most authentic expression in the Pauline teaching on the justification of the sinner through grace by faith. He then interpreted this in terms of existentialist philosophy as the move from unauthentic to authentic existence. Despite justifiable criticisms, Bultmann's work remains a model for the proper method of NT theology: solid exegesis of the text, awareness of the historical setting and development of NT traditions, a conscious and philosophically grounded theory of interpretation, and sensitivity to the religious questions of a given age. Within the last two decades NT theology has turned away from synthesis and concentrated on individual NT traditions (e.g., the theology of Q) and on particular Bible books, especially those previously considered to be the least theological, e.g., the synoptic Gospels. *See also* biblical theology.

JOHN R. DONAHUE

New Theology. *See* Nouvelle Théologie.

New Zealand, Catholicism in. Catholics have composed about 15 percent of the total population of New Zealand throughout most of its *pakeha* (Maori, "white") history. Early missionaries were French, usually Marist Fathers, yet the Church quickly took on an Irish tone. The first bishop, Jean Baptiste Pompallier, arrived in 1838. The dioceses of Auckland and Wellington were formally established in 1860, followed by Dunedin in 1869 and by Christchurch in 1887. Missions to indigenous Maoris, first in rural areas and later in cities, were given high priority. Marist and Mill Hill priests specialized in this apostolate. From the last quarter of the nineteenth century, the principal pastoral strategy was to build the parish school. Each parish supported its own school, which aimed to find a place in the classroom for every Catholic child. Schools were staffed by religious, principally women, so that women religious made up some three-quarters of total church professionals. Lay teachers now staff the schools, which are integrated into the national system. There is also a strong tradition of Catholic hospitals and social services. Most Catholics were working class and supported the Labour party. The first Labour government (1935) was headed by a Catholic, Michael Savage. In recent years, this traditional political alignment has diminished as Catholics entered the middle class. A Jocist (Young Christian Workers) movement, founded in Belgium in 1925 and begun in New Zealand in the 1940s, provided lay leadership to the post–Vatican II Church, as the sense of the Church as a clerically led parallel society faded. The best-known New Zealand Catholic of modern times is James K. Baxter, poet and civil dissident. In the 1990s Catholics constitute 15 percent of the total population of more than 3.5 million.

EDMUND CAMPION

Nicaea, First Council of, the first ecumenical or universal council of the Church. It met from late May until late August, A.D. 325, in the city of Nicaea, located in modern-day Turkey, and defined orthodox trinitarian belief.

The council was convened by the emperor, Constantine, to resolve several controversies, the chief of which was the controversy created by the presbyter (priest) Arius. Arius taught that the Son is not God in the same way as the Father is God. To be divine means above all to be unoriginated, or to have no origin. The Son and the Father could not both be unoriginated, since there is only one God. Thus, only the Father is unoriginated and truly God; the Son originates from the Father. Although the Son exceeds all other creatures in perfection, nevertheless, the Son has the status of a creature in relation to the Father.

Excommunicated in 320 from his home diocese of Alexandria by a synod of Egyptian and Libyan bishops, Arius traveled to Syria and Palestine and found support from Eusebius of Caesarea and Eusebius of Nicomedia, who helped promote Arius's teaching.

Estimates of the number of bishops who attended the council range from 228 to 318. The number 318, mentioned by Ambrose and Hilary of Poitiers, is thought to symbolize the 318 servants of Abraham mentioned in Gen 14:14 and not to represent the actual number of participants. Among those in attendance was the deacon Athanasius, the future bishop of Alexandria and a leading anti-Arian spokesperson. No official minutes of the council were kept. Knowledge of the proceedings comes from later writings of three conciliar participants, Eustathius of Antioch, Athanasius, and Eusebius of Caesarea.

To make its opposition to Arianism explicit, the council formulated a creed containing expressly anti-Arian elements, followed by a series of Arian beliefs to which those who subscribed were declared anathema. Specifically, the council in the creed declared the Son "from the substance of the Father," and "begotten not made," "of one substance with the Father" (Gk., *homoousios*). With these phrases, and especially with the term *homoousios,* the council stipulated the proper interpretation of the Son's divinity. The Son is truly God, just as the Father is truly God.

In addition to the Arian controversy, the council decided against the practice of celebrating Easter on the date of the Jewish Passover, as was the custom of certain Eastern churches. Twenty canons (rules) resolving questions of specific Church practices were also passed. Several canons concerned the status within the Church of Christians who had lapsed during persecutions. Others provided regulations related to clerical life and practice. Three canons outlined the selection procedures for future bishops, as a response to the practices of the schismatic bishop, Melitius, who had ordained bishops without consulting his fellow bishops.

At the council's conclusion, two bishops, Secundus of Ptolemais and Theonas of Marmarica, refused to sign the council's creed and, along with Arius, were banished to Illyricum. Controversy over the use of *homoousios* in the creed continued until the Council of Constantinople (381).

The creed of Nicaea was expanded into the Nicene-Constantinopolitan Creed that is today recited by the congregation at Mass. *See also* Arianism; *homoousios;* Jesus Christ; Nicene Creed.

ANTHONY W. KEATY

Nicaea, Second Council of, seventh ecumenical council of the Church. Convened in 787, it restored the practice of icon veneration and affirmed belief in the value of intercession by saints. The Byzantine empress, Irene, in the name of her young son, Constantine VI, convened the council with the support of Pope Hadrian I. Political disturbance forced a change of location from Constantinople to Nicaea where three hundred bishops deliberated for three weeks (eight sessions), from September to October 787. Although opposed by the Frankish king, Charlemagne, the Western Church recognized the acts of the Second Council of Nicaea on January 26, 880. This was the last ecumenical council to be recognized by the Eastern Church. *See also* ecumenical council; iconoclasm.

Nicene-Constantinopolitan Creed. *See* Nicene Creed.

Nicene Creed, also known as the Nicene-Constantinopolitan Creed, a statement of Christian belief, originally formulated by the Council of Nicaea in 325 and later affirmed, with modifications, by the Council of Constantinople in 381. The Council of Nicaea was called, in part, to end the controversy created by Arianism. The gathered bishops produced the Nicene Creed to insure unity in fundamental beliefs. The creed consists of three sections—one section for each Person of the Trinity—

and concludes with four statements contradicting the central tenets of Arianism. The council based the creed upon an already existing baptismal formula. Traditionally ascribed to Eusebius's church at Caesarea, scholars are unsure as to the precise origins of the baptismal formula.

In composing the Nicene Creed, the bishops made two significant insertions into the text of the baptismal formula, namely: "that is, from the substance of the Father" and "true God from true God, begotten not made, of one substance with the Father." These two insertions make clear that the Son is equal in status with the Father, since the Son is of the same substance as the Father. Not intended to replace local baptismal formulas, the creed was a test of orthodoxy for bishops.

This creed issued at the Council of Nicaea is not the creed that is popularly known as the Nicene Creed. What is commonly called the Nicene Creed is the creed affirmed by the Council of Constantinople in 381 and called the Nicene-Constantinopolitan Creed. Traditionally thought to have been based upon the creed issued at Nicaea, the creed affirmed at Constantinople is now thought to have been derived from a baptismal formula used by the church in Antioch or Jerusalem. Longer than the creed issued at Nicaea, the creed of Constantinople includes a fuller treatment of the Holy Spirit by affirming the divine status of the Holy Spirit, which certain Christian groups called Pneumatomachoi denied. The identification of the creed of Constantinople with that of Nicaea occurred at the Council of Chalcedon (451), where the bishops understood the Council of Constantinople as essentially affirming the faith of Nicaea with an expanded teaching on the Holy Spirit.

The creed of Constantinople was incorporated into baptismal and eucharistic liturgies. By the sixth century, the creed affirmed at Constantinople had become the baptismal creed used in the Eastern churches. In the sixth century, Rome began using the Constantinople version for its baptismal creed, with other Western churches soon adopting this practice. During the Middle Ages, the creed from Constantinople was eventually displaced as a baptismal creed by the Apostle's Creed. The Constantinople version was incorporated into the eucharistic liturgies in the East soon after the Council of Chalcedon and was made official by an ordinance of the emperor Justin II in 568. In the West, the third council of Toledo (589) in Spain introduced the practice of reciting the Constantinople creed at the Eucha-

rist. Rome eventually adopted the practice in the eleventh century. The Latin text of the creed used in the West added the phrase, "and the Son" (Lat., *Filioque*), so that the creed read that the Holy Spirit "proceeds from the Father and the Son." The Eastern churches maintained the more primitive practice, refusing to add "and the Son." This difference in creeds became a major source of tension between the Eastern and Western churches. *See also* Arianism; Constantinople, councils of; creeds; *Filioque;* Jesus Christ; Nicaea, First Council of.   ANTHONY W. KEATY

NICENE CREED

We believe in one God,
the Father, the Almighty,
maker of heaven and earth,
of all that is seen and unseen.
We believe in one Lord, Jesus Christ,
the only Son of God,
eternally begotten of the Father,
God from God, Light from Light,
true God from true God,
begotten, not made, one in Being with the Father.
Through him all things were made.
For us men and for our salvation
he came down from heaven:
by the power of the Holy Spirit
he was born of the Virgin Mary, and became man.
For our sake he was crucified under Pontius Pilate;
he suffered, died, and was buried.
On the third day he rose again
in fulfillment of the Scriptures;
he ascended into heaven
and is seated at the right hand of the Father.
He will come again in glory to judge the living and the dead,
and his kingdom will have no end.
We believe in the Holy Spirit, the Lord, the giver of life,
who proceeds from the Father and the Son.
With the Father and the Son he is worshiped and glorified.
He has spoken through the prophets.
We believe in one holy catholic and apostolic Church.
We acknowledge one baptism for the forgiveness of sins.
We look for the resurrection of the dead,
and the life of the world to come. Amen.

Nicholas I, St., d. 867, pope from 858 to 867. Nicholas was elected pope the same year that the legitimate patriarch of Constantinople, Ignatius, was deposed in favor of Photius. The resulting controversy was one of several that preoccupied Nicholas. In a noted pastoral letter to the Bulgar khan, he tried to bring the newly Christianized Bulgars into allegiance to Rome. Feast day: November 13. *See also* Photius.

Nicholas of Cusa, 1401–64, German theologian, mathematician, and reformer. Following a successful ecclesiastical and academic career, he was made a cardinal in 1448. Best known for his negative approach to God as expounded in *On Learned Ignorance*, Nicholas made substantial contributions to mathematics, science, philosophy, and Church reform.

Nicholas of Lyra, ca. 1270–1349, Franciscan master of theology at Paris and influential biblical commentator. Renowned for his knowledge of Hebrew, Lyra drew extensively from rabbinic exegetes, especially Rashi. He glossed the entire Scriptures according to the literal sense in his *Postilla Litteralis*, insisting with earlier Scholastics that in argument only the literal sense can be used. He also wrote a much shorter spiritualizing gloss, *Postilla Moralis*, for devotional and pastoral use, which similarly proved popular in the later Middle Ages. *See also* Scripture, senses of.

Nicholas of Myra, St., d. ca. 350, patron saint of sailors and children, as well as of Greece, Sicily, and Russia, and bishop from whom the Santa Claus tradition developed. Born somewhere in Asia Minor, he became bishop of Myra, where he was famous for his holiness and pastoral zeal. He was imprisoned during the persecution of the emperor Diocletian and was alleged to have been present at the Council of Nicaea (325), but his name appears on none of the lists. Legends developed around him after his death, and his popularity in the West increased greatly when his relics were brought to Italy in 1087 and his shrine at Bari became one of the great pilgrimage centers of all Europe. Stories of his miracles led to the practice of gift giving in his name at Christmas and to the change of his name, St. Nicholas, into Sint Klaes by the Dutch and then to Santa Claus. Feast day: December 6. *See also* Christmas; Santa Claus.

Nicholas of Tolentino, St., 1245–1305, Augustinian friar and patron saint of mariners. Born in Italy, he was an exceedingly popular preacher and confessor and was especially devoted to the sick and the poor. He is depicted in paintings by Raphael and others, often with a basket of bread, called St. Nicholas's Bread, that was distributed to the sick or to women in labor. Feast day: September 10.

Nicodemus (nik-oh-dee'muhs), a Pharisaic leader sympathetic to Jesus. In the Fourth Gospel, Nicodemus is instructed about entry into the kingdom (John 3), protests that one accused must have an opportunity to respond (John 7:50–51), and participates in Jesus' burial (John 19:39). The fourth-century *Gospel of Nicodemus* recounts Jesus' harrowing of hell.

Nietzsche, Friedrich (nee'chee), 1844–1900, German philosopher. The son of a Lutheran pastor, Nietzsche was appointed to the chair of classical philosophy at the University of Basel when only twenty-four. He became an intimate associate of Richard Wagner, with whom he later broke violently, and through him was introduced to the pessimistic philosophy of Arthur Schopenhauer. After teaching at Basel for ten years (1869–79), he resigned because of increasingly ill health. For the next ten years he traveled in Germany, Italy, and Switzerland, always alone and incessantly writing. In 1889 he collapsed into madness from which he never recovered.

Nietzsche is both one of the most insightful critics of modernity and one of the most influential opponents of religious belief. An acute analyst of psychological motivation, he attempted to trace "the genealogy of morals," demonstrating that morality is an attempt by the powerless to control the creative energies of the powerful. He attacked bourgeois European and especially German society of his time as controlled by a "slave morality" based in the "resentment" of the weak for the strong. His proclamation that "God is dead" was intended to force his contemporaries to realize that disbelief in Christian doctrine inevitably undermines the Christian ethic. Most humans, he argued, find it impossible to live with the impersonality and indifference of a Godless world; thus, one must become "superhuman." His principal works are *The Gay Science* (1882), *Thus Spake Zarathustra* (1883–85), *Beyond Good and Evil* (1886), *The Genealogy of Morals* (1887), and *The Anti-Christ* (1888). *See also* faith and reason; Modernism; philosophy and theology.   MICHAEL J. HIMES

Night Prayer. *See* Compline.

nihilism (ni'uhl-iz-uhm; Lat., *nihil,* "nothing"), a philosophical position that denies the meaningfulness of morality and human existence. Nihilists maintain that moral decisions cannot be justified by rational argument but result from emotion or social pressure. Existentially, nihilists despair over life's emptiness. *See also* despair; hope.

nihil obstat (nee'hil ahb'staht; Lat., "Nothing stands in the way"), term indicating approval for given process to proceed. It is often used for the approval given to a book by a censor prior to a bishop's granting of an imprimatur (Lat., "It may be printed"). *See also* imprimatur; imprimi potest.

nimbus. *See* halo.

Noah, a figure of primordial history. According to Gen 5:28–9:29, God preserved the righteous Noah, son of Lamech, from the Flood. The NT recalls that event (Matt 24:37–38; Luke 17:27–28) and remembers Noah as righteous and faithful (2 Pet 2:5; Heb 11:7). His preservation foreshadowed baptism (1 Pet 3:20).

Nobili, Robert de. *See* de Nobili, Robert.

Noble Guards, aristocratic bodyguards of the pope, founded in 1801. They were distinguished by their plumed helmets and military dress. Made up of seventy-seven men of the Roman nobility, the corps was dissolved by Pope Paul VI in 1970. They are not to be confused with the Swiss Guards, founded in 1505, who still serve the pope. *See also* Swiss Guard.

Nocturn (nok'tuhrn; Lat., *nocturnus,* "by night"), the first service in the Liturgy of the Hours, formerly called Matins. Nocturn is prayed in monasteries at the beginning of the new day between midnight and daybreak, at times divided into first and second Nocturns at two intervals through the night. The term may also be used, although precariously, in reference to one or the other of two readings in the Office of Readings, the first from Scripture, the second from the Fathers of the Church, ecclesiastical writers, or lives of the saints. *See also* Liturgy of the Hours.

Noetus, a native of Smyrna condemned ca. 200 by a local synod of presbyters. He taught the earliest form of the antitrinitarian Monarchianism, i.e., that there is only "one ruler" in God. *See also* Monarchianism.

Nolasco, St. Peter, ca. 1189–1258, French-born founder in 1218 of the Mercedarians (Order of Our Lady of Mercy) in Spain, an order dedicated originally to offering its own members in exchange for slaves, and later, to helping the sick and the imprisoned. Feast day: January 31. *See also* Mercedarians.

nominalism, a philosophical theory developed in the fourteenth century that denies the existence of universal concepts and principles apart from the human mind. For example, resemblance among human beings does not mean they share a common human nature. Nominalists hold that only individual things, like particular human beings, actually exist.

Nominalism had its most profound effect on moral theology. If there are no universal moral principles rooted in human nature, all that remains are individual laws and rules created by the absolutely free (and perhaps arbitrary) will of God. Morality, therefore, is simply conformity to the will of God as expressed in commands.

The most famous nominalist was the Franciscan friar William of Ockham (ca. 1285–1349), whose nominalist school opposed traditional Thomism. *See also* legalism; moral theology.

nonconformism. *See* Free churches.

nonconsummation of marriage. *See* consummated marriage.

None (nohn; Lat., *nona hora,* "ninth hour"), the last of the three daytime hours of prayer, or minor hours, in the Liturgy of the Hours. It is now called Midafternoon Prayer. None marks the ninth hour from dawn, or 3 P.M., when 6 A.M. is considered the first hour. None is preceded by Terce, the third (Lat., *tertia*) hour, at approximately 9 A.M., now known as Midmorning Prayer, which is followed by Sext, the sixth (*sexta*) hour, around noon. Sext is known now as Midday Prayer. *See also* Liturgy of the Hours.

Norbert, St., ca. 1080–1134, founder of the Premonstratensians (Norbertines) and archbishop of Magdeburg from 1126. Ordained a priest in 1115, Norbert was famed for his preaching, and in 1121 he and his followers founded the Canons Regular of Prémontré. Feast day: June 6. *See also* Norbertines.

Norbertines, known also as the Order of the Canons Regular of Prémontré (O. Praem.), Premonstratensians, and as White Canons (from the color of their habit), an order founded by St. Norbert in 1120 at Prémontré near Loan, France. It adopted the Rule of St. Augustine with variations. Norbert was a friend of Bernard of Clairvaux, which resulted in Cistercian influence on the Norbertine way of life. Canonesses have constituted a Second Order of nuns from the time of St. Norbert and eventually Third Order members were associated with the Norbertines. In the United States a Norbertine abbey at De Pere, Wisconsin, sponsors St. Norbert's College. *See also* canons regular; Norbert, St.

North American College, a residence in Rome, Italy, for American Catholic priests and seminarians studying at various Roman theological universities. Founded in 1859 by Pope Pius IX, it was located in a seventeenth-century monastery on Via dell'Umiltà. A new spacious facility was dedicated in 1953 on the Janiculum Hill overlooking St. Peter's Basilica and the Vatican City palaces. It has a very active and loyal alumni and these include over 150 bishops and more than a dozen cardinals. The rector of the college has often served as a liaison between American bishops and the Vatican. The college has served as a host to countless numbers of American Catholics who have visited Rome as tourists and pilgrims. It has also hosted many notable Americans, including seven U.S. presidents. The building on Via dell'Umiltà is now used exclusively by American priests doing graduate work in Rome and by bishops and priests in continuing education.

North American Martyrs, six French Jesuit priests and two laymen *donnés* (assistants) who were killed by the Iroquois between 1642 and 1649 and who were canonized in 1930. They were, at Ossernenon (Auriesville, N.Y.), Sts. René Goupil, *donné* and surgeon (d. 1642); Isaac Jogues, priest (d. 1646); John de la Lande, *donné* (d. 1646); and, in Canada, the priests Anthony Daniel (d. 1648); John de Brébeuf (d. 1649); Gabriel Lalemant (d. 1649); Charles Garnier (d. 1649); and Noël Chabanel (d. 1649). They were caught in the middle of a fierce Iroquois-Huron rivalry, in which the French and English took sides. There are shrines to the martyrs at Midland, Ontario, and Auriesville, New York.

Jean de Brébeuf and Gabriel Lalement, two of the eight French Jesuits who are collectively called the North American Martyrs, being tortured at the stake by Iroquois Indians near Georgian Bay, Canada, in 1649.

Feast day: October 19. *See also* Brébeuf, St. Jean de; Jogues, St. Isaac; Lalement, St. Gabriel.

Nostra Aetate (nohs'trah ay-tah'tay). *See* Declaration on the Relationship of the Church to Non-Christian Religions.

notes, theological, qualifying phrases employed in pre–Vatican II manuals of theology to indicate the positive degree of authority one might attach to a theological proposition or thesis. The negative counterparts are called theological censures. The fundamental purpose of the notes was to safeguard the faith and prevent confusion between binding doctrines and theological opinions. Understood in the broadest sense, theological notes can be traced back to the very origins of Christianity in which it became necessary to distinguish between the authentic apostolic message and that which was opposed to it. Designations regarding divine truth and heresy were used quite broadly well into the Middle Ages and did not receive their more specialized meanings until after the Council of Trent (1546–63).

The Counter-Reformation saw the first systematized gradations of theological notes and censures in the works of theologians like Melchior Cano (1509–1560) and Francisco Suarez (1548–1617). Here we find the practice of identifying the varying degrees to which a proposition may be said to agree or conflict with divine revelation. A teaching was taught as *de fide* (Lat.), "of the faith," if it was believed to be found explicitly in divine revelation. A doctrinal proposition was considered *de fide definita*, "of defined faith," if it was solemnly defined by the pope or an ecumenical council. The rejection of a *de fide definita* teaching was denoted as *heretica*, a "heretical" proposition. One may find notes identifying teachings that "border on the faith" (*proxima fidei*) or that are "theologically certain" (*theologice certa*), and censures regarding teachings involving "proximate error." The lowest level of authority was that of a probable opinion. The flourishing of neo-Scholasticism in the nineteenth and early twentieth centuries brought with it an expansion of this system, identifying subtle distinctions by the employment of lesser notes that specified the safety or danger of a theological position. *See also* theology.

RICHARD R. GAILLARDETZ

The University of Notre Dame's Main Building with its famous Golden Dome, and Sacred Heart Basilica to its left, as seen from the Hesburgh Library.

notes of the Church. *See* marks of the Church.

Notre Dame, University of, the most famous Catholic university in the world. Located just outside South Bend, Indiana, it was founded in 1842 and 150 years later had just over ten thousand undergraduate, graduate, and professional students and a full-time faculty of about nine hundred.

In reaching its sesquicentennial in 1992, Notre Dame passed through several stages. Like other American Catholic colleges, it was modeled on European secondary schools, such as the French *lycée,* and throughout the nineteenth century it remained a combination secondary and collegiate institution. But Edward F. Sorin, the French missionary priest who founded Notre Dame and shaped its development for half a century, greatly admired American ways and was quick to adopt them. When Sorin died in 1893, collegiate programs in the humanities, natural sciences, engineering, law, and commercial subjects were well established, and Notre Dame already enjoyed a national reputation among American Catholics.

Key leadership in the next era came from John A. Zahm and James A. Burns, both priests of the Congregation of Holy Cross, the religious community that established and operated Notre Dame. As U.S. superior of the community (1898–1906), Zahm sent his younger confrères to graduate school, thus laying the groundwork for true university development in the future. His protégé, Burns, built on that foundation when he became president of Notre Dame in 1919. He eliminated the preparatory academy, attracted foundation support, conducted the first great fund drive, and built up the lay faculty. The impetus his reforms lent the university was redoubled by the success of Knute Rockne's football teams, which gave Notre Dame national visibility and made it a familiar symbol of American Catholicism.

Academic growth, though slowed by the Great Depression, picked up in the late 1930s with the arrival of several prominent refugee scholars from Europe. Graduate work, begun in 1918 in the summer school and carried on mainly at the master's level, was reorganized in 1944 and grew consistently thereafter; by 1992, twenty-three departments offered doctoral programs. By the same date, externally funded research, which began with defense-related work during World War II, amounted to about $25 million annually. World War II training programs for Navy personnel also marked the beginning of Notre Dame's involvement in ROTC programs, under which some six hundred undergraduates now receive scholarship assistance.

Three Holy Cross priests have guided Notre Dame's development since World War II. Systematic fund-raising and the building program began in the presidency of John J. Cavanaugh (1946–52), but during Theodore M. Hesburgh's unprecedented thirty-five-year term (1952–87) Notre Dame was transformed in physical facilities, financial resources, faculty size and quality, and academic prestige. In 1967, juridical control of the university was transferred from the Congregation of Holy Cross to an autonomous, lay-dominated board of trustees, but the president of the university must be a Holy Cross priest. In 1972 women were admitted to the formerly all-male undergraduate body. Edward A. Malloy succeeded Father Hesburgh as president in 1987. *See also* Hesburgh, Theodore Martin.

PHILIP GLEASON

Notre Dame Cathedral, located in Paris, one of the most famous churches of Catholic Christianity. It is built on the site of a Gallo-Roman temple, which was replaced by a Frankish cathedral in 528. The present structure, a monument of the early Gothic style, was begun by Bishop Maurice de Sully in 1163; although basically completed by 1250, construction continued for another eighty years. Much of the original artwork fell victim to eighteenth-century alterations and severe vandalization during the French Revolution of 1789; in 1845 a neo-Gothic "restoration" was begun. The church has witnessed many events of French history, including the coronation of Napoleon in 1804. *See also* France, Catholicism in; Paris.

Notre Dame Sisters, international congregation of apostolic women religious dedicated to education and other ministries according to local need. Founded in 1833 in Bavaria by Mary Theresa Gerhardinger, the congregation drew inspiration from the Rule of St. Augustine and devoted its initial energies to educating poor girls. The School Sisters came to the United States in 1847 and taught children of German immigrants principally in the upper Midwest. In 1993 there are over eight thousand members in thirty-two countries, with the most recent expansion in Kenya and Guatemala. The members continue to educate, that is, to help people develop their gifts for a better world. When accepting new apostolic fields, they prefer to work among the poor, especially women and youth. *See also* School Sisters of Notre Dame; Sisters of Notre Dame de Namur.

Nouvelle Théologie (Fr., "New Theology"), a French Catholic theological movement of the 1940s that sought to overcome the limitations of neo-Scholastic theology through a return to biblical, patristic, and medieval theological sources. It reintegrated pastoral experience with theology, challenged the dominant rationalistic exegesis of Scripture, and investigated the development of dogma. Pope Pius XII's encyclical *Humani Generis* (1950) was aimed at ending this movement, but the *Nouvelle Théologie* proved to be an essential preparation for Vatican II (1962–65), where its methods were vindicated and its theological approaches adopted.

Novatianism, rigorist movement that arose at Rome in response to the restoration of Christians who had apostatized during the Decian persecution (249–51). Led by Novatian, a presbyter (priest) who in 251 became a rival bishop (antipope) to Cornelius in Rome, they refused to readmit into communion the lapsed, i.e., those who had compromised with paganism under persecution. Although theologically Orthodox, the Novatianists were excommunicated because of their schismatic origin and their refusal to grant pardon or penance for any serious sin. The Council of Nicaea (325) gave the terms under which they could be readmitted into Catholic communion. Scattered Novatian communities survived into the seventh century. *See also* Nicaea, First Council of.

novena (noh-vee'nah; Lat., *novem,* "nine"), a public or private devotion repeated nine successive times. The succession may consist of continuous days (nine days prior to a special feast), specific weekdays (nine Mondays), or specific days of the month (nine First Fridays). Public novenas consist of specified prayers recited in common, often followed by Benediction; they may precede or follow Mass. Novenas may be made for special intentions and may be repeated without limit. Devotional novenas arose in France and Spain in the early Middle Ages as a preparation for Christmas, though novenas of mourning were known much earlier. *See also* devotions.

novice, individual in a probationary period preparing for first vows in a religious institute. Both the general law of the Church and the particular law of a religious community regulate the qualities needed before a person can be admitted as a novice. *See also* novitiate; religious institute.

novitiate, probationary period preparatory to initial incorporation of persons (novices) into a religious institute. The period must last at least one year, be supervised by a formation staff, and take place in a religious house approved by the highest authority of the institute for this purpose. The major moderator may approve another house of the community to be used for part of the year. The program is to instruct the novices in the meaning of the vows that they are about to take, the spiritual life, and the history and particular charism of the given institute. *See also* religious institute; vows.

nullity, legal nonexistence. Canon law presumes that acts have been validly accomplished. It is possible, however, to prove that acts have not been done in such a way that the law should acknowledge them. Marriage, Holy Orders, and a given ecclesiastical procedure are examples of such acts whose nullity might be proven. *See also* validity [canon law].

number of the beast (666). *See* beast of the Apocalypse.

nun, in the strict sense, women in religious orders who take solemn vows of poverty, chastity, and obedience. Nuns observe the papal cloister and live a life of silence, contemplation, and prayer. Choir nuns chant the Divine Office daily. Vatican II (1962–65) called for modifying the cloister, eliminating outmoded customs, and modifying the habit.

The word "nun" is also popularly used for women in religious congregations who take simple vows and who do not observe the cloister. It is also used as a synonym for "sister." *See also* religious life; sisters, congregations of.

Nunc Dimittis (nuhnk dee-mit'tis; Lat., "now you are dismissing [your servant]"), title of the Canticle of Simeon (Luke 2:29–32). The hymn is sung at Vespers in the East and at Compline in the West. *See also* Simeon.

nunciature (nuhn'see-ah-choor; Lat., *nuntius,* "messenger"), the diplomatic headquarters of a papal nuncio or pronuncio, that is, of a legate who represents the pope to a civil government and who enjoys ambassadorial status in the nation to which he is sent. *See also* nuncio; papal legate.

nuncio (Lat., *nuntius,* "messenger"), a specific type of papal legate (Code of Canon Law, cans. 363–67) who represents the Apostolic See to a state or civil government and also represents the pope to particular churches in that state or nation, in contrast to papal legates (called apostolic delegates) who relate only to particular churches. A papal legate promotes relations with a state or civil government and holds the title of nuncio if he has the rank of ambassador and also acts as dean of the diplomatic corps. If he has the rank of ambassador but is not dean of the diplomatic corps, his title is pronuncio. If he lacks ambassadorial rank, the legate's title is internuncio. As the representative to the particular churches, a nuncio is not subject to the jurisdiction of any bishop but acts in a spirit of cooperation with each bishop as well as the episcopal conference. He is also instrumental in the selection of new bishops. *See also* papal legate.

nuptial blessing, the blessing given by the priest on behalf of the Catholic Church to the spouses at a wedding. "Nuptial" is derived from the Latin *nubere,* which literally means "to marry [a man]." The blessing applies, therefore, directly only to the bride. When the nuptial blessing first appeared in the Roman liturgy of Marriage, it was exclusively a bridal blessing and, though the Second Vatican Council (1962–65) prescribed that it be amended to reflect the equal obligation of both spouses to remain faithful, the blessing in the revised Catholic rite retains traces of bridal focus. Immediately after the Lord's Prayer at Mass, or after the Prayer of the Faithful outside of Mass, the priest extends his hands over the couple and prays that they may grow in love of and fidelity to one another and to Christ, of whom they are to be living examples. *See also* Marriage.

nuptial Mass, the Mass within which the wedding of Catholics traditionally takes place. It has marriage-related readings from the OT and NT along with prayers for the spouses and their future children. It also includes, after the Lord's Prayer, the special nuptial blessing from which it takes its name. *See also* Marriage; Marriage, liturgy of.

O Antiphons, a series of seven antiphons, each beginning with the invocative "O," appointed for the Magnificat at Vespers celebrated between December 17 and 23. The texts are a mosaic of biblical verses from prophetic and wisdom books. Already known to Amalar of Metz (d. ca. 850), both texts and music probably date from the eighth or even the seventh centuries.

The O Antiphons are *O Sapientia* (Wisdom), *O Adonai* (Lord), *O Radix Jesse* (Root of Jesse), *O Clavis David* (Key of David), *O Oriens* (Radiant Dawn), *O Rex Gentium* (King of All Nations), and *O Emmanuel* (literally, God-with-us). *See also* Advent.

oath, an invocation of God's name in witness to the truth of a statement. An oath may be either assertory, referring to the validity of a past or present fact, or promissory, referring to the reliability of a future commitment. The taking of oaths, especially ecclesiastical oaths of office, is often surrounded with solemnity and ritual. Oaths are not to be taken or imposed lightly. The swearing of an oath imposes the weight of a new and different religious obligation with more substantial ramifications than those implied by either a profession of faith or a simple promise to fulfill an accepted responsibility. *See also* promise.

oath against Modernism, an oath once required of clerics prior to the reception of the subdiaconate, as well as by all those appointed confessors, preachers, pastors, canons, seminary professors, religious superiors, and officials in Roman congregations and diocesan curias. Incorporated into the pontifical letter of Pius X titled *Sacrorum Antistitum* (September 1, 1910), the oath was conceived as a method to unmask any clerics who might attempt to evade the proscriptions of views the same pope had previously condemned as "Modernism, the synthesis of all heresies." The first part of the oath required agreement to five distinct affirmations taught explicitly or implicitly by the First Vatican Council (1869–70): (1) that God can be known and proved to exist by arguments of natural reason; (2) that external signs of divine revelation, specifically miracles and prophecies, bring with them certainty, and are adapted to all persons and all times, including the present; (3) that the Church as an institution was founded by Christ; (4) that there exists a constant deposit of faith, so that the avowal that dogmas change from one generation to the next and with a meaning different from that taught by the Church is heretical; and (5) that faith involves a real assent of the intellect to truth revealed from an external source, rather than a blind and inherent sense brought to the surface of human consciousness by a morally ordered will. By swearing the second part of the oath a cleric promised submission to the teachings of the decree of the Holy Office, *Lamentabili* (July 3, 1907), which condemned sixty-five Modernist propositions on the nature of the Church, on revelation, on the person of Christ, and on the sacraments, and of the papal encyclical *Pascendi Dominici Gregis* (September 8, 1907), which elaborated on these themes. The imposition of the oath was considered juridically a personal ratification by Pius X of his earlier authoritative decisions. It was imposed throughout the Catholic world, and only about forty of those asked to swear it refused to do so. The only notable exception occurred in Germany, where professors in the state faculties of Catholic theology, not engaged in the pastoral ministry, were, at the behest of the German bishops, dispensed. The oath against Modernism was rescinded by a decree of the Congregation for the Doctrine of the Faith (the former Holy Office) in July 1967. The official text of *Sacrorum Antistitum* is printed in *Acta Apostolicae Sedis* (1910), 2:655–80 (the oath itself, 669–72). An English translation can be found in *American Catholic Quarterly Review* 35 (1910): 712–31. *See also* Modernism; Pius X, St.   MARVIN R. O'CONNELL

oath of fidelity, an official promise to preserve communion with the Church, carry out the duties of office, preserve the deposit of faith, foster the Church's common discipline, and obey and collaborate with bishops. The Congregation for the Doctrine of the Faith issued the oath of fidelity, which took effect March 1, 1989. Most provisions of this new oath repeat canons in the 1983 Code of Canon Law. The oath also draws on a longer version that new bishops must take, which emphasizes fidelity to the pope.

This oath is to be taken when assuming certain church offices. Vicars general, episcopal, and judicial are bound to take the oath; other diocesan officials are not. Pastors, rectors of seminaries, and seminary theology and philosophy teachers must take the oath of fidelity, but not other parochial leaders or seminary teachers and administrators. Candidates for the diaconate must take it, but not candidates for presbyteral ordination. Rectors of ecclesiastical universities (which grant Vatican-sanctioned degrees) and of Catholic universities properly so-called, are bound to take it; other university administrators are not. Teachers of disciplines that deal with faith and morals are bound to take the oath if they teach in seminaries, ecclesiastical universities, and other universities under direct church control; teachers in other universities do not seem to be so bound. Superiors in clerical religious institutes and clerical societies of apostolic life are to take a slightly modified version; other superiors are not bound to take it. *See also* profession of faith.

JAMES H. PROVOST

obedience, the submission of one's will and conduct to an authority. This submission is unconditional to God, but conditional to humans. In the OT morality centers on obedience to the will of God (Deut 1–4; Eccl 12:13). Persons are charged with observing the commandments of the Lord (Gen 17:9; Exod 19:5). The very heart of sin is disobedience (Gen 3:1–7). A similar emphasis is present in the NT, as is clear in the submission by Jesus of his life to God. This is especially clear in John where Jesus did not come to do his own will but the will of him who sent him (John 4:34; 6:38; 10:18; 12:49; 15:10). In Paul, Christ's obedience is the source of our salvation, just as disobedience was the source of sin.

All obedience is founded on authority that is understood to be derived from God and ordered to the good (John 19:11). Therefore, obedience to God includes obedience to duly established human authorities. Since human authorities share God's authority in different ways, obedience to such authorities takes on different forms (e.g., child to parents, pupil to teacher, citizen to the state, believer to Church authority) and is subject to differing requirements, conditions, and limits.

In the Church religious men and women vow obedience in imitation of Christ crucified. Diocesan priests promise obedience to their bishop. At times in the Church's history these bonds have been distorted by overstatement, much as in modern times obedience can be minimized by an imbalanced exaltation of autonomy. *See also* authority.

ALISON LIDSTAD

Oberammergau (oh-bair-ahm'air-gow), a village in Bavaria where, since 1634, the villagers have performed a passion play every ten years in the summer to express their gratitude for the ending of a plague in 1633. In 1680 the play was switched to decimal years. For the 350th anniversary the play was also held in 1985, at which time some lines were reworded in order to eliminate anti-Semitic implications.

oblates (Lat., *oblatus*, "offered"), persons associated with religious communities. In the early Middle Ages, the term was applied to children "offered" to a monastery by their parents and raised there, often with the understanding that they would remain bound to the monastic way of life as adults. Later, the term was applied as well to adults who did not take vows, but who chose to live in close connection to a monastery, integrating the spirit of the monastic rule into their daily lives. Groups of such "secular oblates" persist today in various forms. In modern usage, members of several religious congregations founded since the Council of Trent (1545–63) are also referred to as oblates, e.g., the Oblates of Mary Immaculate and the Oblates of St. Francis de Sales. *See also* religious life; religious orders and congregations.

Oblates of Mary Immaculate (O.M.I.), a congregation of men founded in 1816 by Charles Joseph de Mazenod in Aix-en-Provence, France. The Oblates received episcopal approbation in 1818, but conflicts with local bishops concerning the validity of their vows moved them to seek and receive papal approbation in 1826. They were first known as Missionaries of Provence, then as Oblates of St. Charles. The name change to O.M.I. occurred when papal approbation was secured.

Strong opponents of Jansenism and supporters of papal infallibility, the Oblates take the three vows of poverty, chastity, and obedience and add a fourth, a vow of perseverance until death, even if circumstances force the congregation to disperse. Originally founded for parochial and mission work, the Oblates also established seminaries for the improvement of clergy education. The first such seminary was founded in Marseilles in 1826. Others were established in Asia, Africa, Europe, and North America. Missions were founded in Canada in 1841 and in the United States the next year. Oblates in the United States formed a separate province in 1883.

Today the Oblates conduct missions, retreat houses, and parishes and emphasize ministry to the poor and most abandoned. They care for Marian shrines, including the Shrine of Our Lady of the Cape, Quebec, Canada. They assist the diocesan clergy in the care of the National Shrine of the

Immaculate Conception in Washington, D.C. The generalate is in Rome.

Oblates of St. Francis de Sales (O.S.F.S.), a religious community of priests and brothers founded in 1871 in Troyes, France, by Father Louis Brisson. The community's rule is according to the spirit of St. Francis de Sales who, 160 years earlier, had been asked to found a group of men in the spirit of the women's Order of Visitation. The oblates' main works are education, foreign missions, and pastoral ministry. The motherhouse is in Rome. There are seven provinces: French, Austrian, American, German, Dutch, Swiss, and Italian. *See also* Francis de Sales, St.

oblations (Lat., *oblatio,* "offering"), the gifts that the participants in the Eucharist present for use in the liturgy (bread and wine) or—in accord with ancient practice—for distribution to the poor and sick. Offerings are also made for the Church and clergy. *See also* offertory.

obligation, holy days of. *See* holy days of obligation.

obligation, moral, the state of being bound or required as a moral agent to perform an action. Obligation binds someone to restrict and direct personal freedom by making a choice. Obligation arises from the human person's status as a free creature: because God is Creator, existence has the character of a debt to God; and because persons can control their actions, they are accountable for how they direct themselves. Moral obligation imposes itself from within, i.e., from human nature directed by reason and will to participation in God.

O'Brien, John Anthony, 1893–1980, priest, convert maker, author. A priest of the diocese of Peoria, he gained prominence early in his ministry by creating an extensive center for Catholic students at the University of Illinois. After 1940, he lived as author-in-residence at the University of Notre Dame. His writings—forty-five books and hundreds of pamphlets—were apologetical and pastoral in orientation. *The Faith of Millions* (1938) was his most popular work; many others dealt with timely topics such as evolution and the need for Catholic scholarship. He was also active in convert work, i.e., in encouraging non-Catholics to join the Catholic Church. He did so not only through his writings but also through street preaching, especially throughout the American South.

occasion of sin, a place, thing, or relationship likely to lead a person into sin. In Catholic moral theology discussion of responsibilities concerning occasions of sin usually focuses upon occasions of serious (mortal) sin. The principle involved is that since Christians have an obligation to avoid serious sin, they are obliged by reason of prudence to avoid whatever will lure them into sin or is likely to provide an easy opportunity for sin. Thus, someone might know by experience that association with a certain group will probably involve using drugs or engaging in sexual misconduct. Moralists argue that voluntarily choosing to associate with such persons would be wrong. The assumption is that the likelihood of sin would be removed, or greatly reduced, were the individual not exposed to this particular occasion of sin.

Catholic moralists distinguish between proximate and remote occasions of sin based on whether the probability of doing evil is great (proximate) or slight (remote). Occasions of sin are also distinguished as necessary or voluntary occasions of sin. To voluntarily place oneself in the proximate occasion of serious sin is considered morally wrong. A necessary occasion of sin is one that cannot be avoided because of other obligations. To enter into a necessary occasion of sin as part of one's job, for example, would not ordinarily be considered immoral. But, as always, it depends upon the circumstances.

Variations in judgment about what constitutes an occasion of sin indicate that occasions of sin are relative to particular persons, communities, and cultures. *See also* sin. *DANIEL KROGER*

occult compensation, the act by which a person secretly takes what belongs to her or him from the goods of one in debt to her or him. While not against strict justice, it was and is viewed as ordinarily illicit for several reasons. First, one takes the law into one's own hands. Public order demands that such claims generally be settled openly. Second, if the sum is great, the solvency of the debtor may be unjustifiably jeopardized. Third, one may imprudently risk prosecution, with damage to one's own reputation and that of others (family, profession, business firm).

Occult compensation was and is regarded as licit:

(1) if that which is owed is owed in strict justice (not only out of gratitude, for example); (2) if the debt is morally certain; and (3) if there is no other way of recovering the debt.

Ockham, William of. *See* William of Ockham.

O'Connell, Denis Joseph, 1849–1927, American bishop and key figure in the Americanist controversy. Born in Ireland, but raised in South and North Carolina, he was ordained in Rome for the diocese of Richmond, Virginia, in 1872. He was rector of the American College in Rome (1885–95) and was influential in establishing the apostolic delegation (1893). His partisan support of Cardinal James Gibbons and Archbishop John Ireland led Pope Leo XIII to demand his resignation as rector. He played a key role in the controversy over Americanism. In 1903, he began an undistinguished rectorship at The Catholic University of America. Named auxiliary bishop of San Francisco in 1909, he became bishop of Richmond in 1912. In 1926, he resigned and was named titular archbishop of Mariamne, a defunct see in Syria. *See also* Americanism; Gibbons, James; Ireland, John.

O'Connell, William Henry, 1859–1944, archbishop of Boston, 1907–44; cardinal, 1911. O'Connell's career represented a major step in the "romanization" of the American hierarchy in the twentieth century. He was influential in local politics and society, but lost his influence within the Church over a 1920 financial scandal involving archdiocesan personnel, particularly his priest-nephew, who was also discovered to have been secretly married.

O'Connor, Flannery, 1925–64, American Catholic writer. Born and raised in the South, she created brilliant fictional characters of fundamentalist convictions and habits. These characters formed the stories (what she called "the very large letters") with which she challenged the self-assurance of her Catholic and secular readers ("the near-blind"). Her stories expressed her sense of sacrament and of the possibility of redemption in the midst of the strangeness of ordinary life. She published two novels, *Wise Blood* and *The Violent Bear It Away,* and two collections of short stories before her death at age thirty-nine of lupus.

O'Connor, John J., b. 1920, cardinal-archbishop of New York since 1984 and the most influential

Flannery O'Connor, twentieth-century novelist from the American South whose literary work reflects the Catholic principle of sacramentality, that is, of seeing the presence and activity of the divine in the human and of penetrating through the material world to its spiritual ground and source.

member of the American Church hierarchy. Ordained a priest in 1945, consecrated a bishop in 1979, and created a cardinal in 1985, he served as chief of chaplains for the U.S. Navy, attaining the rank of rear admiral. He holds a Ph.D. in political science from Georgetown University (1970) and served on the U.S. bishops' committee that produced the 1983 pastoral letter "The Challenge of Peace."

octave (ok'tiv; Lat., *octavus,* "eighth"), a period of eight consecutive days that extends the celebration of a solemnity. The Christian year has two solemnities with octaves: Easter and Christmas. Easter's octave derives its tone from the celebration of Christ's life, death, and Resurrection, as well as from the attention given to the neophytes, those newly baptized at the Easter Vigil. The eighth Sunday of Easter, or Pentecost Sunday, concludes what has been called the great octave of eight Easter weeks. The Christmas octave concludes with the Solemnity of Mary, Mother of God, on January 1.

October Devotions, devotions to the Blessed

Virgin Mary during the month of October, regarded as the month of Our Lady because the Feast of Our Lady of the Rosary was celebrated on October 7. The devotions can take various forms, but almost always include the public recitation of the Rosary and Benediction and various Marian hymns.

Octogesima Adveniens (ahk-toh-jay'zi-mah ahd-vayn'ee-enz; Lat., "the eightieth anniversary"), "A Call to Action," apostolic letter of Pope Paul VI, written to Cardinal Maurice Roy, president of the Council of the Laity and of the Pontifical Commission for Justice and Peace. The letter was issued on May 14, 1971, eighty years after the publication of Leo XIII's *Rerum Novarum*. Although the letter covers many topics, its distinctive contribution may have been its recognition that the social teachings of the Church have a political as well as an economic dimension (nn. 46–47).

odes, a ninefold series of poetic refrains of the Byzantine-rite liturgy, modeled on the themes of nine biblical canticles. These odes, called the "canon," now a characteristic element of Byzantine *orthros* (Gr., "dawn") or Matins, replaced in the Divine Office the original biblical canticles on which they are based. The second ode of the canon is always omitted outside of Lent. Furthermore, Lenten ferial (weekday) canons have fewer odes, often three, which is why the book of Lenten propers is called the Triodion or "[book] of three odes." *See also* canticle.

Odes of Solomon, a collection, perhaps from the second century, of forty-two Christian hymns preserved in Syriac, perhaps originally written in Greek. The *Odes* were once characterized as Gnostic, but the absence of cosmic dualism and the reverence for the OT and for God as Creator rule out such an interpretation. Rich in baptismal imagery, the *Odes* probably had a liturgical use.

Odilia, St., d. ca. 720, abbess. Other than her founding and presiding over a nunnery (later a pilgrimage site) at what is now Odilienberg in the Vosges Mountains, little is known about her. Her role as patroness of the blind derives from a legend that she was born sightless. Feast day: December 13.

Odilo of Cluny, St. (oh'duh-loh), 962–1049, fifth abbot of Cluny. During Odilo's abbacy, Cluniac usages spread throughout France, Italy, and Spain. He was noted for his charity, selling his monastery's treasures to feed the poor in famine. He also established the Feast of All Souls. Feast day: April 29 (for Benedictines). *See also* Cluny.

odious law, in canon law a law falling into the category of those that are to be considered "hateful" and consequently to be interpreted as narrowly as possible. Laws establishing penalties, providing exceptions to the law, or limiting rights are so considered.

odium theologicum (oh'dee-oom tay-oh-loh'jee-koom; Lat., "theological hatred"), a term used to describe the bitterness with which theological disputes are sometimes argued.

Odo of Cluny, St., 879–942, second abbot of Cluny. Under his able leadership Cluny grew in size and prosperity. He wrote hymns, moral treatises, and a life of St. Gerald. Feast day: November 18 (April 29 for Benedictines). *See also* Cluny.

Oesterreicher, John Maria, 1904–93, founder and director of the Institute of Judeo-Christian Studies at Seton Hall University, South Orange, New Jersey (1953–93). Born a Jew, he converted to Catholicism under the influence of the writings of Cardinal John Henry Newman (d. 1890). Ordained in Vienna in 1927, he opposed Adolf Hitler and the Nazi movement and was forced to leave his native Austria in 1938, moving to the United States two years later. He served as a consultor of the Vatican Secretariat for the Promotion of Christian Unity (1961–68) and contributed to the Second Vatican Council's Declaration on the Relationship of the Church to Non-Christian Religions (*Nostra Aetate*).

offertory (awf'uhr-tohr-ee), a transitional rite in the Mass in which the gifts of bread and wine are presented with the collection of money or other goods. The rite bridges the Liturgy of the Word with the Liturgy of the Eucharist. Since the reform of Vatican II, the preferred term for this rite is the Preparation of the Altar and the Gifts. The term "offertory" is no longer used as a noun, only as an adjective. The actual offering of the bread and wine takes place within the Eucharistic Prayer or Canon of the Mass. The purpose of the presentation rite is simply to prepare the altar, the gifts, and the community for the offering that is to come during the Eucharistic Prayer. *See also* Eucharist.

office, a stable ministerial position within the Church. Some ministerial positions are always necessary for the Church and are considered to have been established by divine law; others, while useful and even necessary for the Church at a given time and place, have been established by human law. The former includes such positions as bishop, pope, and priest (presbyter); the latter includes those such as finance officer or music minister. In the 1917 Code of Canon Law, officeholders were limited to the clergy alone, because "office" was strictly defined; it included the exercise of jurisdiction, the governing power within the Church. Because clerics alone could possess jurisdiction, positions requiring it were limited to them alone. In the current code (1983) the term "office" is understood in a broader sense; any permanent ministry for the good of souls is considered to be an office. Broadening the definition of office not only allows members of the laity the opportunity to hold office, but also places additional positions under many of the same norms as clerical offices, thus protecting the rights of lay ministers. *See also* ministry.

Office, Divine. *See* breviary; Liturgy of the Hours.

Office, Holy. *See* Holy Office.

offices of Christ (Lat., *officium,* "dutiful action"), Christ's saving roles as prophet, priest, and king. As prophet, Jesus Christ reveals the Father's will (John 17:3; Matt 11:27). As priest, he mediates between God and humankind (Heb 4:14–7:28). As king, he is the bearer of God's kingdom, possessing a sovereignty above all earthly rulers (John 18:37; Rev 5:13). Reference to Christ's offices developed in the late Middle Ages and was elaborated especially by the Reformer John Calvin (1509–64). *See also* Jesus Christ.

officialis (oh-fee-chee-ahl'lis). *See* judicial vicar.

O'Hara, Edwin Vincent, 1881–1956, bishop, educator, and sociologist. Ordained for the diocese of Oregon City (now Portland), he promoted Catholic education and labor reform in Oregon and served as the first chairman of the National Catholic Rural Life Bureau. As bishop of Great Falls, Montana (1930–39) and of Kansas City, Missouri (1939–56), he was active in revising the *Baltimore Catechism* and a new English translation of the Bible. *See also* *Baltimore Catechism.*

oil, substance extracted from olives after the harvesting in late summer and one of the principal agricultural products of Palestine during the biblical period and after. In addition to secular uses in food preparation and as an unguent, it was used in the anointing of kings (1 Sam 10:1; 2 Kgs 9:3) and priests (Lev 8:30) and was an important ingredient in certain sacrifices (Lev 2:4).

oil of catechumens, oils used to anoint catechumens during the Christian initiation process. This anointing takes place either at the Easter Vigil or on Holy Saturday. Children are anointed during the rite of infant Baptism. The purpose of the oil, made from the olive or other plant, is to "give wisdom and strength to all who are anointed with it" (Prayer for Anointing of the Catechumen). *See also* chrism; holy oils.

oil of the sick, oil used for the Anointing of the Sick. It is generally consecrated by a bishop on Holy Thursday but may be blessed by a priest in an emergency. Its purpose is stated in the prayer from the Rite of Anointing of the Sick: "Make this oil a remedy for all who are anointed with it; heal them in body, in soul, and in spirit, and deliver them from every affliction." *See also* chrism; holy oils.

oil stocks, a storage container for holy oils. The case has three compartments, each marked with an initial indicating the chrism, oil of the catechumens, and oil of the sick. Many churches display the holy oils in an ambry, a boxlike structure placed in a prominent position in the church near the baptismal font. *See also* chrism; oil of catechumens; oil of the sick.

Oktoechos (awk-toy'ee-kaws; Gk., "eight-toned"), Byzantine-rite liturgical book containing the liturgical propers (prayers assigned to particular Sundays and feasts) of the mobile cycle (i.e., those whose date depends each year on the date of Easter) throughout the liturgical year except for the cycles of Lent, Easter, and Pentecost, which are found in separate books, the Triodion and Pentekostarion. In the Oktoechos the proper texts for each day of the week, Sunday through Saturday, are arranged according to eight musical tones. Since not only the music but also the texts for each tone differ, the Oktoechos contains fifty-six complete daily propers. The Oktoechos cycle takes eight weeks to complete, one week per tone, and is repeated throughout the year from All Saints' Day on the first Sunday after Pentecost, until fully replaced in Lent by the propers in the Triodion. The Oktoechos also overlaps with the monthly Menaion propers for the Divine Office. The Byzantine liturgical *ordo* or Typikon contains the rules regulating the precedence of these competing propers. In present Greek usage, this complete cycle of the "Great" or "New Oktoechos" is often called the *Paraklitike,* the name "Oktoechos" reserved to the Sunday propers only. The West Syrian rite also has an Oktoechos. *See also* proper, liturgical; Proper of the Mass.

Olaf, St., 995–1030, patron saint of Norway. He became king in 1016 and attempted to Christianize the land. The zealous harshness of his methods alienated many, however, and a revolt deposed him from the throne in 1029. Although unpopular in his lifetime, Olaf was later venerated as a champion of Norwegian unity, independence, and Christianization. *See also* Scandinavia, Catholicism in.

Old Catholics, schismatic Catholic churches, also known as "National Catholics." There are three such groups of Catholics in the West who have separated themselves from papal authority: Dutch Old Catholics, centered in Utrecht; small groups of German, Dutch, and Austrian Catholics who went into schism in the nineteenth century over the issue of papal infallibility; Polish Catholics who separated from Rome because of ethnic tensions in the United States.

Old Catholics keep formal relationships with the Church of England. Recent ecumenical efforts, especially between Rome and the Polish National Church, have sought to heal the schism. *See also* National Catholic churches.

Old Church Slavonic, or Old Bulgarian, earliest literary language of the Slavs. It originated as a southeastern dialect of Late Common Slavic but continues to undergo modernization and russification. Like Latin in the West, it long functioned as a supranational language in the Slavic world, and was the official liturgical language of all Slavic Byzantine-rite churches until the second half of the twentieth century, when some of them began to introduce the vernacular. *See also* liturgical language.

Old Roman Creed, a short, trinitarian confession that originated in the church of Rome in approximately A.D. 150 and eventually developed into the Apostles' Creed. Its content was similar to Hippolytus's interrogatory baptismal creed. *See also* Apostles' Creed; creeds.

OLD ROMAN CREED

Do you believe in God, the Father almighty?

Do you believe in Jesus Christ, the Son of God, who was born of the Virgin Mary by the Holy Spirit, has been crucified under Pontius Pilate, died [and was buried], who on the third day rose again, alive, from the dead, ascended into heaven and took his seat at the right hand of the Father, and shall come to judge the living and the dead?

Do you believe in the Holy Church and the resurrection of the body in the Holy Spirit?

[The text is from The Apostolic Tradition of Hippolytus, ca. 215, which is based on the Old Roman Creed. The format is still used today in the sacrament of Baptism and is recited by the entire congregation at the Easter Vigil and on Easter Sunday. Other early creeds, e.g., the Creed of Marcellus (340), also considered to be based on the Old Roman Creed, add the words "the forgiveness of sins" and "life everlasting" in the third paragraph. The Creed of Rufinus (ca. 404) adds only "the forgiveness of sins."]

Old Testament. *See* Bible.

Olga, St., d. 969, widow of the Grand Duke of Kiev, honored as one of the earliest of Russia's Christian people. Prior to her conversion, Olga was known as a barbarous woman. A missionary journey to Kiev, made at her request around 959, failed. Her grandson, Vladimir, was more successful at promoting the new faith in Russia. Feast day: July 11. *See also* Russia, Catholicism in.

Olier, Jean-Jacques, 1608–57, French priest and founder of the Society of St. Sulpice (Sulpicians). He is best known for his establishment of the seminary at Saint-Sulpice parish in Paris and other seminaries founded by members of his society. His spiritual teaching is in the tradition of St. Vincent de Paul and St. John Eudes. Sulpicians today are still engaged in seminary education. *See also* Sulpicians.

Olives, Mount of, a hill overlooking Jerusalem on the east. Jesus approached Jerusalem for the last time over the mount (Matt 21:1; Mark 11:1) and wept upon seeing the city (Luke 19:41). He foretold Jerusalem's destruction on the mount (Matt 24:3; Mark 13:3–4) and from it ascended to heaven (Luke 24:50; Acts 1:12).

Olivi, Petrus Joannis, ca. 1248–98, Spiritual Franciscan and writer of exegetical and doctrinal treatises. Born in Languedoc, Olivi entered the Franciscan order at the age of twelve, later attending the University of Paris. Consulted by the pope in 1279 on the controversial matter of Christ's poverty, Olivi's conclusions drew opposition from the moderate members of his own order, and the General Chapter of 1282 condemned his writings. Reinstated five years later, he had already become the intellectual champion of the Spiritual Franciscans. In later years, as the controversy raged, his writings were suspect once again. *See also* Franciscan order; Spiritual Franciscans.

ombrellino (ohm-brel-lee'noh; It., "little umbrella"), a canopy, usually made of white silk with gold fringe, carried over the Eucharist in procession.

omnipotence of God, the attribute of God that God is all-powerful. This divine attribute means, strictly speaking, that there can be no limits on what God can do. However, this strict meaning is rarely invoked in theology. As soon as one asks whether God can do anything, for example, commit a sin, one realizes that there must be some boundaries on the assertion that God is all-powerful. The most common way of formulating those boundaries has been a logical one: it would make no sense to say that God could do things that were self-contradictory or incompatible with the nature of divinity, such as sin. By invoking logic in this way, one does not limit God's power by another force, but by the bounds of sense or meaning. Thus, God cannot be said to be able to do anything at all, but only what is consonant with being God. *See also* God.

omniscience of God, the attribute of God that God is all-knowing. God knows all things past, present, and future, but God knows everything from the standpoint of eternity. The idea that there could be something hidden from God offends theological sensibilities.

The greatest difficulties in understanding God's knowledge have to do with how God knows the future. The normal way of formulating this question leads quickly to a picture of predestination in which God "already knows" what will take place. But a future known to God and therefore predetermined by God is antithetical to human freedom, which to some extent must leave the future open-ended. Theologians have sought different ways to correct this picture without compromising God's omniscience, notably by reminding us that God's knowledge is eternal while events take place in time. We can never expect to know how it is that God knows all there is to know. *See also* God.

omophorion (oh-moh-faw'ree-ahn; Gk., "borne on the shoulder"), Byzantine-rite pallium, the symbol of episcopal office worn around the neck. Though similar in form and worn in the same way, it is much wider and longer than the Western pallium. Once reserved to patriarchs and metropolitans, it is now worn by all bishops. There is also a less ancient "small *omophorion*," a broad, short stole that the bishop wears over his black monastic mantle (*mandyas*) at lesser services, when not fully vested, or, when celebrating the Eucharist, from the Gospel until Communion. *See also* pallium.

Onesimus, St. (oh-nee'si-muhs; Gk., "beneficial"), a slave. Paul wrote to Philemon on behalf of Onesimus. He may have been bishop of Ephesus in the early second century. Feast day: February 16.

ontological argument, a proof for the existence of God arguing from the nature of being. The term comes from Immanuel Kant (1724–1804), who used it to distinguish this form of argument from arguments for God's existence that begin with the world, so-called cosmological arguments. The most famous example of an ontological argument comes from the eleventh century in Anselm's *Proslogion*. In this work, Anselm sought a "single formula" whose own logical structure would contain a proof for God's very existence. The formula was to name God as "that than which nothing greater can be thought." Anselm proceeded to show how anyone using that expression would have to be speaking of a perfect being whose very perfection would entail that it exist not only in the human mind (as an idea of God) but also exist "in reality." *See also* five ways of St. Thomas Aquinas; God.

ontologism, the idea that the human intellect has a direct, intuitive perception of Being and that this Being is God. Ontologism was condemned by the Holy Office in 1861 because it confuses natural and supernatural knowledge. Ontologism is associated with N. Malebranche (d. 1715), V. Gioberti (d. 1852), and A. Rosmini-Serbati (d. 1855).

ontology (Gk., *on-logos,* "study of that which is"), a branch of metaphysics that deals with being in general. Other philosophical disciplines investigate the identifying characteristics of a limited set of beings while ontology considers the underlying principles present in all existing things simply because they exist.

Ontological thinking was more characteristic of pre–Vatican II neo-Scholastic theology and philosophy than it is of present-day theology and philosophy. *See also* metaphysics; philosophy and theology.

Opening Prayer. *See* Collect.

Optatum Totius (ahp-tah'tahm toh-tsee'uhs). *See* Decree on Priestly Formation.

Optatus of Milevis, St., d. ca. 370, bishop of Milevis in Numidia, Roman Africa. Around 366 Optatus authored a Catholic defense, in six books, against the treatise on Baptism by Parmenian, the Donatist bishop of Carthage. With a seventh book added in 385, Optatus argues for the validity of Catholic Baptism and the unity and universality of the Church. Much admired by Augustine of Hippo, Optatus's work is enhanced by a collection of church documents appended to his book. Feast day: June 4. *See also* Africa, the Church in Roman; Donatism.

optimism, in Catholic theology the confidence that, despite the corrosive and debilitating effects of sin and evil, human beings and the world are essentially good. Optimism ultimately is grounded in faith and hope in the one supremely good God, through whose salvific grace all things are created. *See also* hope.

Opus Dei (Lat., "work of God"). **1** phrase used to indicate the liturgical prayer of the Hours in monastic communities. **2** Religious movement founded by Monsignor Josemaría Escrivá de Balaguer (1902–75) in Spain. Begun as a pious association of laypeople (and clergy) dedicated to their sanctification

and that of society, the movement went through various phases. Declared a Pious Union in 1941, it became a secular institute in 1947 (with final approbation in 1950). Pope John Paul II established it as a personal prelature in 1982. It has both priestly and lay members.

The current structure of the organization has various levels of commitment: (1) Numeraries, who are celibate, live in the organization's centers and work full-time at the apostolate. (Female numeraries do administrative/domestic chores for the houses.) (2) Oblates embrace a celibate life but live outside the centers. (3) Supernumeraries, who are married members, live independently, and have professional careers. (4) Cooperators support the work of the organization but do not have formal ties to it.

The spirituality of Opus Dei is shaped by Escrivá's work *The Way* (1935; enhanced edition 1939), which is a series of 999 spiritual maxims. Often criticized for their alleged secrecy, their theological conservatism, and their rigorous spirituality, Opus Dei members have sometimes been controversial in the Church. They sponsor university faculties in Spain, Rome, and Latin America and student residences in widespread areas of the world. Their founder was beatified by Pope John Paul II in 1992. *See also* prelature, personal; Spain, Catholicism in.

opus operantis (oh'puhs oh-pur-ahn'tis). *See ex opere operantis.*

opus operatum (oh'puhs oh-pur-ah'toom). *See ex opere operato.*

oracle, a generic term corresponding to several Hebrew expressions for a prophetic utterance of well-being, judgment, or information about the future. The frequent introductory formula, "Thus says Yahweh," indicates that the oracle communicates a divine message verbatim by means of a specially designated intermediary. *See also* prophet.

Orange, Council of, council convened in 529 by Caesarius of Arles, to resolve a century of Gallic debates concerning divine grace. Orange (Arausio) is in southern France. This "council" was actually a small gathering of bishops who met for the consecration of a basilica. Caesarius, supported by a letter of Pope Felix III, presented to the assembly a list of twenty-five *capitula* (Lat., "chapters"), which generally upheld Augustine's teachings on original sin, the need for grace, and predestination. The approval of these propositions represented the final rapprochement between Augustine's doctrine of grace and the Gallic church. Many of fifth-century Gaul's leading theologians (John Cassian, Vincent of Lérins, Faustus of Riez) had refused to endorse fully Augustine's predestinarianism, thereby incurring the suspicion of having harbored Pelagian sentiments. The bishops of Orange accepted Augustine's teaching of the absolute priority of grace to any human striving, but rejected the harshest implications of Augustine's teaching on predestination, explicitly rejecting, as Augustine had, predestination to evil. *See also* grace; predestination; semi-Pelagianism.

orans (Lat., "one praying"), the symbol of a human figure with outstretched arms representing a praying or interceding person. In the Roman catacombs, the figure is found on Christian tombs, sometimes combined with that of the Good Shepherd or with biblical scenes, signifying prayer as a means to salvation. *See also* catacombs.

orarion (aw-rah'ree-ahn), Byzantine-rite deacon's stole, a long narrow band of vestment cloth worn over the left shoulder, and (except among the Russians) wrapped around the body under the right arm, with the two ends of the stole extending to the floor in back and front. The origin of the name is obscure. *See also* stole.

Oratorians (C.O.), the Oratory of St. Philip Neri and the French Oratory, groups of priests organized in the spirit of the Council of Trent (1545–63) to improve the quality of clerical leadership. The Oratory of St. Philip Neri, established in Rome in 1564, was named after its founder and inspiration. Philip Neri (1515–95) was respected as a holy priest and popular spiritual director. Called Oratorians because they gathered in the oratory of the Church of St. Girolamo, the Italian Oratorians emphasized holiness of life, sound preaching, and well-prepared worship services. The French Oratorians, founded in 1611 by Pierre de Bérulle (1575–1629), were modeled after their Italian counterpart. Their chief ministry became the education of seminarians and, though they shared many of the purposes of the Italian group, they were independent. The Oratorians represent a constructive response to the need for genuine reform of priestly life in the sixteenth century. *See also* Philip Neri, St.

oratorio, an extended musical composition on a

The interior of Brompton Oratory, a major Catholic center in London, founded in 1849 through the efforts of Frederick William Faber and John Henry (later Cardinal) Newman and moved to Brompton Road in 1854; nineteenth-century painting by Herbert A. Gribble. The Oratory of St. Philip Neri, from which the name is derived, is a congregation of priests living in community without vows.

sacred subject for solo singers, chorus, and orchestra. The first oratorios were composed in the late sixteenth century and were a staple of the later Baroque musical repertory. *See also* Catholicism and music.

oratory, a place (other than a church) designated for divine worship. Each religious house is to have a chapel (public oratory) where the Blessed Sacrament is reserved. Each bishop is allowed to have a private oratory. *See also* chapel.

Oratory of Divine Love, Catholic reform movement of the sixteenth century founded under the inspiration of Catherine of Genoa (d. 1510) to serve charitable purposes. The Roman branch was the nursery of Church reformers: Gian Matteo Giberti, St. Cajetan, Gian Pietro Caraffa (Paul IV), Jacopo Sadoleto, and Gasparo Contarini. Cajetan and Caraffa (then bishop of Chieti, or "Theate") later founded the Clerks Regular of the Divine Providence, also known as the Theatines, in 1524. *See also* Catherine of Genoa, St.; Theatines.

Order of Preachers. *See* Dominican order.

Order of St. Basil the Great, Byzantine-rite monastic order. Metropolitan Joseph Rutskyj (appointed in 1617) centralized the men's monasteries in the Ruthenian (Ukrainian and Belorussian) Catholic Church and promoted theological studies. The order influenced all church life, guiding people spiritually and providing all bishops until the nineteenth century. In the 1830s the order was suppressed in territories under the Russian empire, surviving only in western Ukraine. Another reform begun in 1882 led to a notable expansion in Ukraine and among Ukrainian immigrants. A Romanian branch was aggregated in the 1920s. The nuns were organized into an order in 1951. *See also* Basil, Rule of St.; Basilians.

orders. *See* Holy Orders.

ordinariate, military. *See* military ordinariate.

ordinary, title for an individual who holds one of a certain class of offices within the Church. Although in common parlance the term often refers to the bishop of the diocese, canon law includes a greater number of officeholders under this title. Canon 134 gives a taxative list. The term includes the pope, diocesan bishops, vicars general and episcopal vicars of a diocese, those in charge of groups legally equivalent to a diocese (e.g., a vicariate apostolic), and major superiors in pontifical clerical institutes. All but those in the last category are also called "local ordinaries."

The law frequently uses the term "ordinary" and reserves certain powers to those who hold an office so designated. All of these officeholders have executive power of governance. Superiors in institutes that are classified as lay are not considered "ordinaries" because such superiors might be themselves laypersons, and canonical tradition excludes laypersons from the power of governance in the strict meaning of that term. *See also* diocesan bishop; local ordinary.

ordinary, liturgical, the part of the Mass, the Liturgy of the Hours, and other sacramental rites that does not vary. Musical compositions of the Mass, both classical and contemporary, render these parts chorally: the Kyrie or "Lord, Have Mercy," the Gloria or "Glory to God," the Credo or creed or profession of faith, the Sanctus or "Holy, Holy, Holy" and the Agnus Dei or "Lamb of God." Ordinaries supply a consistent structure that is filled out by the liturgical proper, or parts that vary. *See also* proper, liturgical.

ordinary/extraordinary means, terms used to describe operations, treatments, and medicines as obligatory or nonobligatory for physical health and survival.

Catholics view the meaning of both life and death within the context of the Paschal Mystery (the life, death, and Resurrection of Christ). This has a relativizing effect on both life and death. Thus, while life is a basic good as the condition of all other experiences, it is not an absolute one. It may be sacrificed for other, more urgent or higher goods. For this reason Catholic tradition has put a limit on the means that must be used to preserve life. As Pope Pius XII noted in 1957 in an allocation to an international congress of anesthesiologists: "But normally one is held to use only ordinary means—according to circumstances of persons, places, times and culture—that is to say, means that do not involve any grave burden for oneself or another. A more strict obligation would be too burdensome for most and would render the attainment of the higher, more important good too difficult."

Recent Catholic tradition has therefore distinguished between ordinary means (obligatory) and extraordinary means (generally nonobligatory) to preserve life. Ordinary means are understood to include all means (medicines, surgery, etc.) that offer a reasonable hope of benefit and can be had and used without grave inconvenience. Extraordinary means are understood as those that offer no reasonable hope of benefit or, even if they do, involve an excessively grave burden. Examples of grave burden given in the textbook tradition were pain (in preanesthetic days), expense, disfigurement, risk, recuperative travel to a distant land, and climate.

The terms "ordinary" and "extraordinary" have been widely used even outside Catholic circles, but they have been so badly misunderstood and misused that many authors in bioethics prefer different language. For instance, in its Declaration on Euthanasia (1980) the Congregation for the Doctrine of the Faith noted this fact and cited the possibility of using "proportionate" and "disproportionate" to avoid the misunderstandings associated with "ordinary" and "extraordinary." Whatever the language employed, the key judgment anchors in a weighing of burdens and benefits for the particular patient. *See also* bioethics; medical ethics; quality of life.

RICHARD A. MCCORMICK

ordinary jurisdiction, the power of governance attached by canon law to a particular office. Certain positions within the Church include certain governance powers. The office of diocesan bishop, for example, carries with it all of the powers necessary to perform the tasks required by the ministry of bishop. *See also* jurisdiction.

ordinary magisterium. *See* magisterium.

ordinary minister, the minister prescribed by canon law as the one authorized to celebrate a particular sacrament without special permission. For example, the ordinary ministers of the sacrament of Anointing are priests and bishops. Bishops alone are the ordinary ministers of the sacrament of Holy Orders. *See also* extraordinary minister of Eucharist; sacrament.

Ordinary of the Mass, the term used, prior to Vatican Council II, to describe the invariable parts of the Mass, as distinguished from those parts that varied with the ecclesiastical calendar (called the Proper of the Mass). The Ordinary comprised the priest's preparatory prayers ("prayers at the foot of the altar"); the Kyrie; the Gloria and Creed (on most Sundays and feasts); the Canon (Eucharistic Prayer from the "Sanctus" onward); the Lord's Prayer; the Agnus Dei; the priest's prayers before Communion; and the last Gospel. Musical settings of the Ordinary (whether plainchant or polyphonic) commonly included five parts: Kyrie, Gloria, Credo, Sanctus, and Agnus Dei. *See also* Proper of the Mass.

Ordinary Time, the days of the Church year that are not Advent, Christmas, Lent, or Easter. The longest period of the year, Ordinary Time is so called not because it is set apart from the "extraordinary" times, but because it is time ordered for, or ordained to, the everyday living of a Christian life. This is clearer in the Latin title, *tempus ordinarium,* "measured time." There are two discrete periods of Ordinary Time. The first is the five to eight weeks between Epiphany and the beginning of Lent (Ash Wednesday). The second is the twenty-three to twenty-seven weeks following the feast of Pentecost and concluding with the Solemnity of Christ the King, the final Sunday of the liturgical year. The liturgical color for days in Ordinary Time is green. *See also* liturgical calendar.

ordination, the sacramental rite of the Church in which the Spirit of God is invoked on candidates for the office of bishop, priest, and deacon as they are initiated into ministry in the Church. Ordination points to two fundamental beliefs in the Church's understanding of itself and of its ministry: that the ministry of the Church in any age is always linked with the ministry of Jesus and of the apostles; and that the Church and its ministry must always draw on the power of the Holy Spirit if it is to be true to itself.

The form of ordination has a long and varied history. Its origins are found in NT references to the designation of ministers for service in the Church, sometimes accompanied by references to prayer and the imposition of hands. A pattern of imposition of hands and prayer over the candidate appears in the earliest extant ordination rites, found in the *Apostolic Tradition* (ca. 215) of the Roman writer Hippolytus.

Ordination rituals of the late patristic period add elaborate allusions to high priests, priests, and Levites of the OT. Roman prayers of the same period introduce a preoccupation with gradations of honor and dignity in the ranks of the ordained. Medieval Gallican and Germanic influences contributed a ceremony of anointing, a ritual of vesting, and the presentation of symbols of office. The liturgical books of William Durandus the elder, thirteenth-century bishop of Mende, France, give a highly ornate ordination ritual for bishop, priest, and deacon. This ritual inspired the Roman pontifical books, which became the norm for the post-Tridentine Church.

Catholic ordination rituals were revised after the Second Vatican Council (1962–65), with efforts made to reflect the council's teaching on the offices of the ordained. Emphasis is placed on the imposition of hands and the prayer over the candidate to be ordained. The meaning of the office is incorporated in the suggested text for the address to the congregation and the ordinand and in the prayer following the imposition of hands. Although rites of vesting, anointing, and presentation of symbols remain, they are ancillary to the imposition of hands and the prayer that follows.

While the revised rite of ordination of a bishop draws upon the ancient prayer of Hippolytus, the ordination prayer of a presbyter retains much from the liturgical books of the post-Tridentine Church. That prayer's emphasis on the honor and dignity of the presbyter contrasts with the stress on service of Vatican II. The rite does recognize, symbolically, the responsibility of the entire congregation to approve the choice of the ordinand. Ordination rites teach that ordained ministry exists to assist and enable all the baptized to carry on the serving mission of Christ.

Catholic teaching holds that in addition to the grace of office, the ordained receives a sacramental "character." While the understanding of character varies in the tradition, the notion of character implies that ordination confers a sacramental union with Christ and the ecclesial community such that ordination cannot be repeated. *See also* Holy Orders; sacramental character.   FREDERICK J. CWIEKOWSKI

ordination of women, a proposition that has met with controversy about the possibility of ordaining women to the priesthood or presbyterate. Current practice in the Catholic Church prohibits the ordination of women. Little is known of any organized movement to change that practice until the twentieth century. In the 1930s, however, a British organization called Saint Joan's Alliance submitted a petition to the Vatican stating that, "should the Church in her wisdom and in her good time decide to extend to women the dignity of the priesthood, women would be willing and eager to respond." The alliance has continued to submit petitions in this vein yearly since. In the United States, the movement is usually traced to Mary Lynch, who began in the mid-1960s to append to her Christmas cards messages about the timeliness of the ordination of women. In 1974 the Women's Ordination Conference (WOC) came into being at a meeting in Detroit. Organizers were anticipating about 600 women and 1,200 actually arrived. The founding of WOC led to a series of dialogues between a committee of the National Conference of Catholic Bishops (NCCB) and leaders of the Women's Ordination Conference on topics related to the possibility of a change in the practice. These talks eventually broke down in the wake of the 1976 Vatican declaration *Inter Insignores,* which defended the Church's position, and the subsequent pressure on bishops to uphold what the document declared to be an "unbroken tradition."

Irregular ordinations of Episcopal women as priests in 1974, followed by the 1976 decision of the Episcopal Church in the United States to approve women as priests, made for increasing models of an ordained ministry of women in a tradition close to Catholicism. A scientific survey of U.S. Catholics in 1974 reported that 29 percent of those polled were in favor of ordaining women; by 1992 that percentage had risen to 67 percent. In the interim, the National Conference of Catholic Bishops committed itself to writing a pastoral letter on the concerns of women, one of which was their exclusion from ordained priesthood. Over the course of nine years and four drafts, the pastoral letter shifted from discussing the possibility of ordaining women to the diaconate to reiterating the official arguments against admitting women to any of the sacramental orders. In the fall of 1992, the fourth draft of the proposed pastoral letter failed to attain a majority when put to a vote of the bishops, and the project was abandoned, though not before some U.S. bishops had publicly expressed their support for the ordination of women.

As the numbers of ordained men decline, however, more parishes are being administered by women. Women are also acting as pastoral associates, chaplains, and spiritual directors, as well as carrying out many of the liturgical functions previously reserved to men. The decision of the Church of England in 1992 to ordain women increases the ecumenical strain over the issue and leaves the Catholic and Orthodox Churches the remaining opponents to a change in official policy. *See also* Holy Orders; ordination; priesthood; women in the Church.
MARY AQUIN O'NEILL

ordinations, liturgy of, the rituals by which the Church calls out and consecrates one or more of its members for specific service of the Christian community. The earliest such ritual still extant is that of the *Apostolic Tradition* of Hippolytus (ca. 215), which provides instructions and prayers for the ordination of bishops, presbyters, and deacons. From the fourth century there is a succession of such rituals in the Eastern and Western churches well into the early Middle Ages. Two assumptions are attached to these rituals in the first centuries: that the celebration takes place on a Sunday or major feast day when the whole community is gathered and that a person is always ordained for a specific community (consultation with and approbation by the community is the norm).

Other general elements of these rituals are: some

form of proclamation of what is about to happen and an invitation to pray for the candidates; the prayer of the people; the imposition of hands on the candidates by the ordaining bishop, followed by a prayer of ordination; some concluding rituals (the kiss of peace, the handing over of the symbols of office). The ordinations of bishop, priest, and deacon also have special rituals to point up the specific role of each of these offices. In the case of the bishop, other bishops in addition to the ordaining bishop participate in the laying on of hands silently, and the Gospel book, containing the portions of the four Gospels read at Mass, is placed on the head of the candidates. The ordination prayer is distinct for bishop, priest, and deacon. The ordination rituals were revised in 1968 and reflect the theology of Vatican II (1962–65). *See also* Holy Orders; ordination.

REGIS DUFFY

ordo (Lat., *ordo* [pl., *ordines*], "order," "plan," "arrangement"), a liturgical handbook or calendar that describes and/or regulates the celebration of Mass, the sacraments, the church year, or the Canonical Hours. An *ordo* presents the outline or blueprint of a liturgical action and the sequence of its component parts. The *ordo*'s description of ritual acts complements the sacramentary's prayer texts. The most influential examples are the *Ordines Romani,* ancient collections of ceremonial directions for the papal liturgy that began circulating in the late eighth century and that helped spread the Roman rite throughout Europe.

O'Reilly, John Boyle, 1844–90, author, promoter of Irish freedom from British rule. Born in Ireland, O'Reilly was court-martialed by the British Army for his association with the Fenian Brotherhood, a secret revolutionary society in Ireland and the United States organized to achieve Irish independence from England by force. He was exiled to Australia, but in 1869 he escaped to America, where he found work with the *Pilot* newspaper in Boston. He eventually owned and edited the paper, acquiring a wide reputation as a poet, essayist, and orator. He is best known for a volume of poems, *In Bohemia,* and for *The Ethics of Boxing and Manly Sport* (both 1888). O'Reilly was a leader in the movement that sought to achieve respectability for Irish immigrants.

organ, a winded-pipe instrument with keyboard(s) used in liturgical worship since at least the twelfth century. The most common use of the organ in church has been for the accompaniment and elaboration of liturgical song. In recent decades electronic instruments designed to simulate the tone of pipes have been purchased by churches, primarily for economic reasons.

organ transplantation, the removal of a bodily organ from a living person, from a cadaver, or (rarely) from an animal and its transfer to a living person. Catholic teaching on this issue has undergone significant change since transplantation became common in the 1940s. At first moral theologians tended to oppose all living donor transplants, arguing that they were forbidden by the principle of totality, which allowed a mutilation of a living body only for the total good of that same body. But gradually this opinion shifted, largely due to American Catholic medical ethicists, who began to support those procedures that brought great benefit to recipients with little or no harm to donors. Some defended the practice on the basis of an extended principle of totality that would include the human race and not just the donor's body; others argued on the basis of Christian charity. Today Catholic moral teaching generally supports organ transplantation.

However, certain cautions are required. Living donor transplants require the free and informed consent of the donor and recipient, a proportionality of harms and benefits, and the use of alternative therapies when available and equally beneficial. All transplants must be judged in the context of scarce medical resources; these expensive procedures ought not unjustly limit access to basic care. Catholic moral theology need not oppose interspecies transplants (from animal to human), provided the usual requirements are met. Transplants from fetal cadavers should be subject to the same criteria, but are often rejected because of a claimed connection to immoral abortion. *See also* bioethics; medical ethics.

DAVID KELLY

Oriental Institute. *See* Pontifical Oriental Institute.

Orientalium Ecclesiarum (oh-ree-en-tahl'ee-oom ek-klay-zee-ah'room). *See* Decree on Eastern Catholic Churches.

Origen, ca. 185–ca. 254, theologian and biblical commentator. Born in Alexandria, where he lived until 231, Origen spent the last twenty years of his life in Caesarea in Palestine with travels taking him across the empire from Roman Arabia and Asia Minor to Rome. The greatest teacher of Christian doctrine of his time, he has exercised an enduring influence as an interpreter of the Bible for Christianity in East and West. The son of well-to-do and devout Christian parents, Origen was deeply affected by the martyrdom of his father, Leonides, during the persecution of Severus in 201. He completed his education in the circle of a rich Alexandrian woman, where he had direct encounters with Valentinian Gnostics. A few years later he came under the influence of Alexandrian Platonists, like Ammonius Saccas, and read extensively the works of Philo the Jew, who was a contemporary of Jesus and who had written philosophical and deeply religious commentaries on the Torah.

Teaching Career: While still in his late teens, Origen was appointed catechetist by Demetrius, bishop of Alexandria. The young man's fiery mysticism, combined with a rigorous intellectualism, led him to divide his mixed audience of Christian catechumens and pagan sympathizers into two groups, one for beginners whom he entrusted to Heracles, his assistant, and a second level of students whom he led through a program of Christian instruction reflecting the advanced studies of the Alexandrian academia of his time. It was Origen's conviction, two centuries before Augustine conceived his own program of Christian instruction, that a proper interpretation of Scripture required a grounding in many secular studies such as arithmetic, music, geometry, astronomy, grammar, and rhetoric. He introduced his students to the major philosophical currents, teaching them to apply Christian discernment in retaining the truth compatible with the Bible. Master and pupils shared a semimonastic life-style with the possibility of martyrdom ever in mind. Origen's fame as a learned layman spread far beyond the local community. Invited to give homilies in Palestine and ordained to the priesthood ca. 230 by Theoctistus of Caesarea and Alexander of Jerusalem, Origen incurred the wrath of Bishop Demetrius and was banished from the Alexandrian church. In Caesarea he started a new teaching career, in addition to intensive preaching in the local churches. He was invited as theological advisor to a synod in Arabia (Jordan) and traveled to Cappadocia and to Athens before suffering imprisonment in the persecution of the Roman emperor Decius (250–51). Broken in health, Origen died some time after his release.

Literary Legacy: Origen did not begin the authorship of his vast works until he was in his early forties. Dictating to secretaries provided by his patron, Ambrose, Origen became the most prolific commentator on Holy Scripture in the ancient Church. With many of Origen's writings lost even in the first century after his death, Jerome, in the fourth century, could still enumerate hundreds of titles. The majority of the works surviving today are known only through Latin translations by Jerome, Rufinus, and other Western commentators. In order to secure a critical text for his exegetical works, Origen carefully compared the Greek translations of the Bible circulating among the Christian and Jewish communities with the Hebrew Scripture available to him. His intention was to verify and correct the Septuagint version, which was standard in the Alexandrian tradition. He juxtaposed "six columns" of text (Gk., *Hexapla*) in an immense papyrus volume, of which only one copy survived by the fourth century. The biblical verses were transcribed word by word, first in the original Hebrew, then in Greek transliteration of the Hebrew, then in the remaining columns, the Greek versions of Aquila, Symmachus, the Septuagint, and Theodotion. In the fifth column, the Septuagint, critical signs helped to secure a corrected text, in showing what had been added to or subtracted from the Septuagint text by different generations of copyists. This enormous enterprise continued over a period of at least twenty years. While there can be no certainty that the whole Bible came under the scrutiny of Origen and his assistants, there can be no doubt that through all these labors Origen acquired an uncommon familiarity with Scripture. Origen's earliest commentaries were on the Psalms and the Gospel of John. Other extended commentaries, preserved in Latin, were those on Matthew, the Letter to the Romans, and the Canticle of Canticles, all of which were to have an enduring impact on later generations. A greater number of Origen's exegetical works (twenty-eight in Greek, but the majority in Latin translation) were in the form of homilies, such as those on Genesis, Exodus, Leviticus, Numbers, Joshua, Judges, 1 Samuel, Isaiah, Jeremiah, Ezekiel, and the Gospel of Luke. A distinctive mark of Origen's genius is to have inaugurated his literary production by dictating the treatise *On First Principles* (*Peri Archon*), by which he meant a theological articulation of the most basic Christian beliefs. The notion of divine Trinity serves as a central focus for the doctrinal analyses of creation and salvation, as well as the final recapitulation at the end of book four. A synthesis of Christian Platonism and biblical thought, the work immediately attracted controversy. It is very possible that it contributed to his banishment from Alexandria in 231. Although it continued to be used against him long after his death, its seminal influence can be traced through the centuries, as is evidenced in the work of Erasmus of Rotterdam in the sixteenth century. Origen wrote an *Exhortation to Martyrdom* for his friend and patron, Ambrose, an essay *On Prayer,* and another essay *On Easter,* as well as an extensive apologetic work, *Against Celsus,* a refutation of a pagan philosopher of the second century. Some letters and many fragments of his works have also survived the attacks on his literary legacy at the end of the fourth century, as well as the proscription of his works by the emperor Justinian in the sixth century.

Origenian Doctrine: Origen taught that God, almighty, provident, and saving, is known only through Jesus Christ, as announced in Jewish Scripture and witnessed in the NT. Jesus Christ, preexistent as the Eternal Word of God (Gk., *Logos*), originated the universal creation in producing a purely spiritual world. Celestial powers and human souls experienced a precosmic fall in that spiritual world. Fallen angels, according to Scripture, became evil powers. Fallen souls needed to undergo the hardship of existing in a material world, which was created for their spiritual reeducation and ultimate reintegration into the divine unity of all things. Thus salvation is a divine pedagogy by which Jesus, the perfect model and accomplished teacher of virtues, illuminates and transforms the souls of believers. Many would make only limited progress, receiving the Scriptures in a simplistically literalistic manner. But the more gifted would climb to the highest contemplation and enjoy an ever-deepening knowledge of the divine mysteries. While later tradition rejected Origen's mythic notion of preexistent human souls and his speculation about the final consummation of the universe, as well as the elitism of his spirituality, the riches of Origen's exegesis and theological accomplishment have contributed to all major schools of thought of the ancient Church in both East and West. *See also* Logos; Origenism; Scripture, interpretation of; Septuagint; soul.

Bibliography

Balthasar, Hans Urs von. *Origen: Spirit and Fire. A Thematic Anthology of His Writings.* Washington, DC: Catholic University of America Press, 1984.

Crouzel, Henri. *Origen.* Trans. A. S. Worrall. San Francisco: HarperCollins, 1989.

Kannengiesser, Charles, and W. L. Petersen, eds. *Origen of Alexandria: His World and His Legacy.* Notre Dame, IN: Notre Dame University Press, 1988.

Origen. *On First Principles.* Trans. G. W. Butterfield. London: SPCK, 1936.

Trigg, J. W. *Origen: The Bible and Philosophy in the Third Century Church.* Louisville, KY: John Knox Press, 1983.   PAMELA BRIGHT

Origenism, a pejorative designation for Origen's teaching or teachings derived from it. Origen's influence was massive and fundamental for fourth-century Orthodox theology, all of which with some justice could be called "Origenism." But the term as usually used refers to certain heterodox themes allegedly taught by Origen, themes later exaggerated and incorporated into rigid spiritual systems based on his thought. These include the doctrines of the preexistence of souls, the transmigration of souls (metempsychosis or reincarnation), the "apocatastasis" or restoration of all souls including that of the devil, and the teaching that the final, resurrected state will be bodiless. Origen himself is also accused of teaching that the Son was subordinate to the Father, that creation was eternal, and that Christ's sacrifice was not unique but will be repeated in future worlds.

Origen's Teaching: Of these doctrines, Origen did teach the preexistence of all rational beings and that their "cooling off" from contemplation of God resulted in their fall and differentiation into human beings, angels, devils, etc. But in his own day such speculation was not heretical and was advanced as a theodicy to counter Marcionite charges against the Creator God based on the inequality of humans at birth. For Origen this inequality was a result of a prenatal free choice to fall away from God, the degree of fallenness determining what sort of body one fell into. Further, against Marcionite and Gnostic denigration of matter, the material bodies into which souls "fell" are good, created by God as an accommodation to the fall and as a means for return. The "spiritual" resurrection body, following Paul (1 Cor 15:35–50), will be continuous with these bodies but not identical, as a plant is continuous but not identical with a seed. And, if God has created from eternity, it is clear that creation is dependent upon God, is not divine, and at any rate is eternal only as its idea or plan exists in the eternally generated Logos. Origen denies metempsychosis and explicitly affirms the uniqueness of Christ's sacrifice, and, although the salvation of the devil must be left open as a logical possibility in a system emphasizing the divine pedagogy and human freedom of will to the degree that Origen's does, there are passages in which he rules it out. Finally, Origen's subordinationism is in part an illusion created by interpreting his vocabulary through later, fourth-century specialization of terminology and, for the rest, is orthodox for a time and place when the distinctions of Nicaea (325) were still seventy-five years in the future.

Controversies: Controversies over "Origenism" began quite early. Methodius of Olympus (d. 311), Peter of Alexandria (d. ca. 311), and Eustathius of Antioch (bishop, ca. 324–27) objected to what they believed to be Origen's teaching on the resurrection body, on the preexistence of souls, and on the eternity of creation. But the most significant and most bitter controversy began in the late fourth century, when the monk Evagrius of Pontus (345–99) incorporated his own scholastic systematization of Origen's teaching into a spiritual system adopted by many monks both in Palestine and Egypt. Controversy between Origenist monks and non-Origenist monks in Egypt led to a condemnation of Origen by a synod convened at Alexandria (400) by Theophilus, the bishop, and ca. 402 Theophilus excommunicated the four "Tall Brothers," leaders of the Origenist monks. Meanwhile, Epiphanius, bishop of Salamis, had included a one-sided version of Origen's teachings in his collection of heresies, the *Panarion*. By 395 he had persuaded Jerome (in his monastery in Bethlehem) to agree and to press for the condemnation of John, bishop of Jerusalem and sympathetic to Origen. Rufinus of Aquileia, who also admired Origen, supported John from his monastery in Jerusalem, thus alienating himself from Jerome. His translation of Origen's *On First Principles*, published in 398 after his return to Rome, infuriated Jerome because it pointed out that Jerome had also initially been an enthusiastic supporter of Origen. Jerome's countertranslation (399) and bitter accusations ensured that the controversy, and Theophilus's condemnation, would travel to the West, where Pope Anastasius I condemned Origen's teaching in three letters.

Another major controversy developed in the sixth century, again stemming partly from a controversy among monks, initiated in this case by the anti-Origenist monks in Palestine against their "Origenist"—actually radical Evagrian—counterparts. The anti-Origenists were able to secure from the emperor Justinian the *Letter to Menas* (Menas was patriarch of Constantinople) condemning Origen; it was approved, together with extracts from the *On First Principles* and anathemata, by a synod

convened at Constantinople in 543 and subscribed by Pope Vigilius and the other patriarchs. Following this condemnation, a division arose among the Origenist monks. The most radical, the "Isochrists," were virtual pantheists who believed that all souls will be equal to the soul of Christ in the apocatastasis; they were opposed by the "Protoctists," who believed in the permanent superiority of Christ's mind. These latter eventually gave up belief in the preexistence of souls and joined orthodox opposition to the Isochrists. The controversy was ended by the Second Council of Constantinople (553), which included Origen in a list of heretics condemned, almost as an afterthought, in the anathemata associated with a different dispute (the Three Chapters). The precise value of this condemnation is uncertain: it seems clear that it is actually the Isochrist doctrine that is condemned under Origen's name, and that the council fathers may even have believed that Origen, who actually confessed his faith under the persecuting emperor Decius despite torture, was an apostate. *See also* apocatastasis; Gnosticism; Jerome, St.; Marcion; Origen; subordinationism.   JOHN C. CAVADINI

original justice, or original righteousness, the theological term describing the perfect, prefallen human condition. Prior to the first instance of sin—in the Genesis narrative, Adam's rebellion—humankind theoretically existed in a state of complete happiness, free from sin and its consequences. The concept of an original justice thus provides a theological counterpoint to the present sinful condition of the human race, indicating the authentic, divinely intended mode of human existence. Neither Scripture nor theology shows an interest in humanity's prefallen state in itself; rather, original justice suggests that the justification brought about in Christ is essentially a restoration of humanity. *See also* original sin.

original sin, the state into which, owing to the first sin of Adam and Eve, all human beings are born. The term original sin is actually used in two senses: in reference to the initial, "originating" Adamic sin (Lat., *peccatum originale originans*) and, in its more generally understood sense, to describe the subsequent "originated" universality of human sin (Lat., *peccatum originale originatum*).

History: A doctrine of universal human sin might be implied by certain scriptural texts, especially some Pauline writings (Rom 5:12–19; Eph

2:3), but developed notions of original sin took shape only after some centuries, and were by no means uniform in their portrayal of how the human race participates in the first sin. Original sin does not figure prominently in the earliest Christian writings outside the NT. References to Christ's redemptive work in writers like Clement of Rome (d. ca. 101) and Ignatius of Antioch (d. ca. 107) feature only sparse allusions to the source of the evil from which we are redeemed.

From the second century onward, one can speak broadly of a distinction between Greek and Latin Christian writers concerning the consequences of Adamic sin. Early Greek writers from Justin Martyr (second century) to John Chrysostom (fourth–fifth centuries) denied that human beings bear the guilt for Adam's transgression. Rather, they believed that humans are culpable only insofar as they willingly imitate the first parents by sinning; Adam's sin is a model or prototype. By contrast, early Latin writers beginning with Tertullian (d. ca. 225) tend to portray a much more direct and deleterious connection between Adam's sin and the subsequent human condition. Tertullian speaks of a propensity to sin sown in each soul through the parent (*On the Soul* 16.39–41). Cyprian of Carthage (d. ca. 250) was the first to argue that infants are baptized because of a "contagion of death" inherited from Adam (*Letters* 64.5).

This rather severe view was continued in the West by Ambrose (d. 397) and Ambrosiaster (late fourth century), but the Western view received its fullest and most enduring development in the writings of Augustine of Hippo (354–430), who coined the term *peccatum originale*. The Pelagian controversy, which occupied the later years of Augustine's life, supplied the context for his seminal writings on original sin. Pelagius denied that infant baptism imparted forgiveness of sin, since infants could not be guilty for sins they did not commit. Augustine responded by asserting that the guilt of Adam's sin is passed on to his posterity through the *libido* (Lat., "lust") involved in procreation. The human liability to death is the most evident penalty for the first sin. Augustine identifies original sin with concupiscence, the yearning for self-gratification in humans that turns them away from God, such that the human will invariably fails to choose the good. Because all human beings both inherit the guilt and penalty for Adamic sin and experience its presence as concupiscence, the human race as a whole stands condemned, a *massa damnata* (Lat., "condemned mass" [of human beings]). God might with complete justice have left humanity to its collective condemnation, but through Christ some receive, *gratis* (Lat., "freely"), the transformation needed to reorient them toward the good. Augustine's anti-Pelagian views on original sin were endorsed in the canons of the Sixteenth Council of Carthage (418), which were in turn approved by Pope Zosimus (d. 418).

Through the Middle Ages discussion about original sin in the West preserved many Augustinian themes, but also departed from Augustine's profound analysis in important ways. From Anselm (d. 1109) onward discussion of original sin focuses not on concupiscence but on the lack of that sanctifying grace (or original justice) forfeited by Adam in the first sin. Thomas Aquinas (d. 1274) speaks of original sin as a weakened, disordered condition but does not fully follow Augustine's pessimism about original sin's effects on human nature. Original sin is taken away in Baptism, while concupiscence and death remain. The Council of Trent (1545–63) argued precisely this point against the Protestant Reformers, who tended to follow Augustine's identification of original sin with concupiscence (sixth session, 1547). One sees little development in subsequent centuries, though post-Tridentine Catholic theologians (including John de Lugo, d. 1660, and Louis Billot, d. 1931) elaborated theories as to how Adam's sin could be imputed to humanity.

Theology: Catholic theologians today, in a world inclined to see both concupiscence and death as simply constitutive elements of human existence, go beyond the difficulties of theories regarding original sin as either the sin of the first humans or as an inherited collective guilt. In an age that has witnessed unspeakable human evil on a massive scale, theologians have attempted to revivify a doctrine that for many has become abstract and peripheral to Christian thought. The most influential modern Catholic theologian on this question, Karl Rahner (d. 1984), echoes the Scholastic and Tridentine equation of original sin with the lack of sanctifying grace, but frames his treatment in existential terms. The lack of sanctifying grace, i.e., the absence of the indwelling of the Holy Spirit, is, contrary to God's will, the universal interior condition of humanity. The offer of grace reveals to us the negativity of our situation. We are born fallen or wanting, into a world in which the presence of evil circumscribes our freedom. The purely Augustinian view fails, for it never established carefully the difference between original sin and the voluntary, personal sin for which one can be accountable. Original sin is merely analogous to personal sin, and therefore its designation as "sin" can be somewhat misleading. Recent formulations underscore the tendency to view original sin in terms of the concrete situation of human life and society rather than as a taint transmitted biologically through human history. The doctrine of original sin is thus expressed in contemporary Catholic thought less as a "catechism truth" valorizing infant baptism and more as a useful category for the analysis of the tragic human condition. *See also* Adam and Eve; concupiscence; grace; redemption; sin.   THOMAS A. SMITH

Origins, a weekly journal published by the National Catholic News Service of Washington, D.C. First published in 1971, it reprints papal and episcopal addresses and exhortations, statements from Catholic and ecumenical groups, speeches of prominent individuals, and reports on current events. Articles are published with prefaces, marginal notations, and summaries.

Orthodox Christianity, the original Apostolic churches, and the later churches they founded, in the Eastern half of the Roman Empire and in other Eastern territories beyond the imperial frontiers: Armenia, Ethiopia, Persian Mesopotamia, Georgia. Originally the epithet "orthodox" applied only to those who accepted the Council of Chalcedon (451). In the East this included the churches of the Orthodox patriarchates of Constantinople, Alexandria, Antioch, Jerusalem, and the Byzantine Orthodox churches derived from them. Today the pre-Chalcedonian Eastern churches also call themselves "Orthodox," and in contemporary ecumenical discourse it is customary to distinguish between the

A Russian Orthodox worship service in the seventeenth-century Church of the Holy Spirit, Moscow.

The celebration of Orthodox Christmas, January 7, 1992, in Red Square, Moscow. The Russian Orthodox follow the Julian rather than the Gregorian calendar.

orthodoxy (Gk., *orthos doxa*, "right praise," "right belief"), a pattern of belief and worship that is consistent with the fundamental teachings of the Church. Orthodoxy is the opposite of heresy. The term is also used of Eastern churches (Greek Orthodox, Russian Orthodox) that acknowledge the honorary primacy of Constantinople, but are not in union with Rome.

Although the word "orthodoxy" does not appear in the NT, concern for sound doctrine and right belief was evident already therein (Rom 16:17; 1 Cor 11:2, 28; 15:1–3; 1 Tim 1:10; 6:3–4; 2 Tim 4:3; Titus 1:9; 2:1). In the early centuries orthodox faith was expressed in creeds, especially the Apostles' Creed, the Nicene Creed, and the so-called Athanasian Creed. Other criteria of orthodoxy include an appeal to the consensus of the Fathers of the Church and to the universally held beliefs of the Church down through the centuries as embodied in the formula attributed to Vincent of Lérins: "that which has been believed everywhere, always, and by everyone." Solemn conciliar and papal teachings are yet another source of orthodox belief. The main practical criterion of orthodoxy, however, is the liturgy: *lex orandi, lex credendi* (Lat., "the rule of prayer is the rule of belief"). Indeed, the Greek word for orthodoxy itself can mean either "right praise" or "right belief."

The word is often used today as a polemical term by ultraconservative Catholics to describe the body of teachings they recall from their own pre–Vatican II catechetical formation. By contrast, the council used the word only once (Dogmatic Constitution on the Church, n. 66).

Eastern (i.e., Byzantine) Orthodox and the Oriental (i.e., pre-Chalcedonian) Orthodox churches. The latter include the Armenian, Coptic, Syrian, and Ethiopian churches. Eastern or Oriental Orthodox churches comprise the majority of the Christians in what was the Eastern and later the Byzantine Empire (present-day Albania, Armenia, Belarus, Bulgaria, Cyprus, Georgia, Greece, Macedonia, Romania, Russia, Serbia, Syria, Turkey, Ukraine), and in most of the Middle East except Lebanon and Iraq. There is also a strong representation outside of the home countries, i.e., in the diaspora, including the United States. Statistics are inaccurate and reliable data are impossible to obtain. There were certainly over 200 million Eastern Orthodox in 1993, and this figure will probably be revised upward as people return to the churches as a result of the newfound freedom in the former Communist bloc. In addition, there are about 4.5 million adherents of "noncanonical" Eastern Orthodox churches not recognized by the others. Estimates of Oriental Orthodox adherents also vary widely (e.g., the Copts claim over 12 million, others estimate their entire membership at less than a third as many), but they probably number at least 30 million. *See also* Eastern churches; Eastern rites; uniatism.   *ROBERT F. TAFT*

orthopraxy (Gk., *orthos praxis*, "right practice"), a pattern of Christian behavior that is consistent with the practice of Jesus and the spirit of the gospel. The term grew out of liberation theology in Latin America and political theology in Europe during the 1960s and 1970s. It complements orthodoxy as practice complements belief and as doing complements knowing.

orthros (awr'thraws; Gk., "dawn," "daybreak"), Byzantine-rite Matins, including both nocturns and Lauds. It is characterized especially by the long liturgical poetry of its nine-ode canon. *See also* Matins; odes.

Ortynskyj, Soter (soh'tair ohr-tin'skee), 1866–1916, first Ukrainian Catholic bishop in the United

States. Born in Ukraine, he became a Basilian monk and was ordained priest in 1891. In 1905 he was named ritual bishop for immigrants in the United States, but without the power of governance, which greatly hampered him in organizing parishes.

O Salutaris Hostia (oh sahl-*oo*-tahr'is hoh'stee-ah; Lat., "O Saving Victim"), the words that begin the last two stanzas of the hymn "*Verbum Supernum Prodiens*," written by Thomas Aquinas (d. 1274) for the Feast of Corpus Christi. These stanzas are also sung at Benediction of the Blessed Sacrament. *See also* Benediction; Corpus Christi, Feast of.

O SALUTARIS HOSTIA

LATIN TEXT

O Salutaris hostia,
Quae caeli pandis ostium,
Bella praemunt hostilia:
Da robur, fer auxilium.
Uni trinoque Domino,
Sit sempiterna gloria,
Qui vitam sine termini
Nobis donet in patria.

ENGLISH TEXT

O Saving Victim, opening wide
The gate of heav'n to all below!
Our foes press on from ev'ry side:
Thine aid supply, Thy strength bestow.
To thy great name be endless praise,
Immortal Godhead, One in Three;
O, grant us endless length of days
When our true native land we see.

Osservatore Romano (aw-sair-vah-tohr'ay roh-mahn'oh), Italian-language newspaper of the Holy See. Founded in 1861, it appears each day (except Sunday) and serves as the authoritative voice of the Vatican. It publishes news of the Vatican, official statements of the pope and Curia, as well as news from the Catholic world, book reviews, etc. In recent decades various foreign language editions have also been made available on a subscription basis. A weekly English-language edition began in 1968. The contents of the paper run from the informational (e.g., the papal schedule for a given day) to editorial comments reflecting papal policy.

ostensorium (ah-sten-saw'ree-uhm). *See* monstrance.

Ottaviani, Alfredo (al-fray'doh ah-tah-vee-ahn'ee), 1890–1979, cardinal, canonist, and head of the former Holy Office. A native Roman, he spent his entire life in the service of the Church in Rome. After a distinguished career in Church law, he became prefect of the Holy Office (now the Congregation for the Doctrine of the Faith). Named a cardinal in 1953, Ottaviani was a central figure at the Second Vatican Council (1962–65) as one of the most articulate and intransigent conservatives, especially on issues concerning religious liberty and papal authority. Despite his reactionary attitudes, he was also known in Rome as a zealous priest whose spare time was spent in the care and education of orphans at the Oasis of St. Rita (near Frascati), which he founded and supported.

Otto, St., ca. 1062–1139, bishop of Bamburg. He was deeply involved with missionary activity in Pomerania. Feast day: July 2.

Otto of Freising, ca. 1114–58, Cistercian historian and bishop of Freising. His historical writing modifies the Augustinian notion of the two cities (the City of God and the earthly city) by unifying them in the Catholic Church as the continuation of the Roman Empire. *See also City of God*; Roman Empire.

Our Father. *See* Lord's Prayer.

Our Lady, common title given to the Blessed Virgin Mary, usually followed by some special designation associated with a place, a devotion, or some service rendered by her, e.g., Our Lady of Hungary, Our Lady of Grace, Our Lady Help of Christians.

Our Lady, Mother of the Church, a title personally given to the Blessed Virgin Mary by Pope Paul VI during his speech at the end of the third session of the Second Vatican Council (1964). This was a gesture of healing on his part toward the council's minority that had wanted a separate document on Mary and then, failing that, wanted the chapter on Mary in the Dogmatic Constitution on the Church (*Lumen Gentium*) to be entitled, "Mary, Mother of the Church," a title with medieval roots. This proposal also failed. Because the Church itself is the Mother of all, most felt it better to speak of Mary as the preeminent member of the Church, a disciple *par excellence*, and as a type, or exemplar, of the Church.

Our Lady of Czestochowa. *See* Czestochowa, Our Lady of.

Our Lady of Guadalupe. *See* Guadalupe, Our Lady of.

Our Lady of La Salette. *See* La Salette, Our Lady of.

Our Lady of Lourdes. *See* Lourdes.

Our Lady of Mount Carmel, a Marian title derived from a community of twelfth-century hermits who lived on Mount Carmel in the Holy Land and expressed their special devotion to Mary by wearing brown scapulars. *See also* Mary, Blessed Virgin.

Our Lady of Sorrows, a Marian title pertaining to the spiritual martyrdom of Mary, particularly in the Passion and death of her son. By the fourteenth century her sorrows (Lat., *dolores*) were fixed at seven: the circumcision of Jesus in the Temple, the flight into Egypt, Jesus being lost in Jerusalem, the encounter with Jesus on the way to Calvary, the crucifixion, the taking of the body down from the cross, and Jesus' burial. *See also* Mary, Blessed Virgin.

Our Lady of the Rosary. *See* Rosary.

Our Lady of the Snows, a Catholic liturgical feast, also known as the Dedication of the Basilica of St. Mary Major, celebrated on August 5. The feast originated in a tenth-century legend claiming that, during the pontificate of Liberius (352–66), a Roman couple who had vowed their wealth to the Blessed Virgin Mary had their vows confirmed when Mary appeared to them in a dream, instructed them to build the Basilica of St. Mary Major, and caused a miraculous midsummer snowfall. *See also* Mary, Blessed Virgin.

Our Sunday Visitor, a weekly newspaper published by OSV, Inc., of Huntington, Indiana. Founded in 1912 by Father (later Archbishop) John F. Noll to refute anti-Catholic bigotry and provide adult Catholics with ongoing catechesis and news

analysis, its positions on pastoral, theological, and social issues reflect a generally conservative point of view.

Oxford movement, religious reformation begun at Oxford University in 1833, also known as the Tractarian movement and Puseyism. It aimed at and effected spiritual, doctrinal, and liturgical renewal in the Anglican Communion by returning to the Church Fathers and seventeenth-century Anglican theologians. In pamphlets and treatises, such as the ninety popular and controversial "Tracts for the Times," and in sermons, poetry, lectures, and articles the movement relentlessly attacked the secularism (religious indifference), liberalism (the view that reason alone can cure all evil) and Erastianism (the idea that final authority in religious matters belongs to the state) of university, church, and country. Affirming doctrine and devotion, the movement promoted the Holy Catholic Church as a supernatural, divinely authorized institution, a visible unity on earth possessing sacraments and unbroken apostolic succession of bishops.

The movement's leaders were noted for their intellectual, moral, and spiritual stature and for their personal attraction and influence: John Keble, poet of Anglican devotion; Richard Hurrell Froude, zealous apologist for Catholic truths; Edward Bouverie Pusey, devout, erudite aristocrat; John Henry Newman, acknowledged leader and genius of the movement, who developed its foundational position, the Via Media. Reaching its zenith in 1838, the movement, though antipapal, was increasingly attacked by church and university for its Romanism. Nonetheless, it survived Newman's conversion to Rome (1845) and spread fragmentedly to urban centers, there emphasizing social, pastoral, and liturgical matters over doctrinal ones. Besides bringing many converts to Catholicism, the Oxford movement was a renaissance of catholicity in the universal Church. *See also* Anglicanism; Anglo-Catholicism; Newman, John Henry.   *MARY KATHERINE TILLMAN*

Ozanam, Antoine Frédéric, 1813–53, French intellectual and founder of the Society of St. Vincent de Paul. He distinguished himself as a literary scholar, a professor of rhetoric, and a defender of doctrine against its opponents. A political liberal, he founded the Society of St. Vincent de Paul in 1833 as a religious association of laymen for the service of the poor. *See also* Society of St. Vincent de Paul.

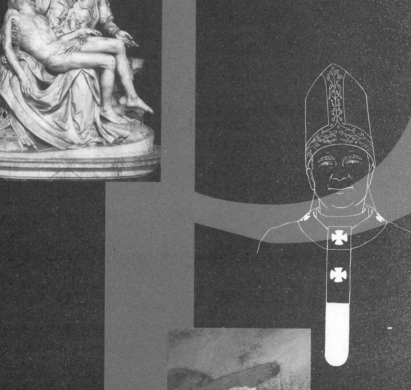

Pacem in Terris (pah'chem in ter'ees; Lat., "Peace on Earth"), encyclical on peace issued by Pope John XXIII in 1963. It provides the most systematic presentation of rights and duties of all the documents in Catholic social teaching. These rights and duties are grounded in the claim that there is an "astonishing order" in the universe created by God. This order is reflected in human persons and is the basis of their inviolable dignity. This dignity is the basis for a wide array of rights, for instance, the right to life, to a just wage, to worship, and to form associations. These rights have corresponding duties, particularly the obligation to "contribute to the establishment of a civic order in which rights and duties are more sincerely and effectively acknowledged and fulfilled" (n. 31).

Because the recognition of these rights and duties requires protection and promotion, there stands a need for public authority. Therefore, John addressed the basis for legitimate authority. All rightly ruling authority serves the common good, which is the sum total of the conditions that allow persons to seek their perfection "more fully and more easily." Such conditions are specified in the rights and duties.

Pope John XXIII extended the range of modern Catholic social teaching in two additional ways. First, he applied his social theory to the relations between states. Previous documents focused primarily on the relations within states. Second, this emphasis on international relations led him to address more fully the problem of war and the conditions of peace. Previous social teaching accented the economic sphere. *See also* Catholic social teachings; encyclicals, social; peace.   TODD D. WHITMORE

Pachomius, ca. 290–ca. 347, founder of the first organized monasteries in Upper Egypt at Tabennisi ca. 320. His emphasis on disciplined obedience contrasted with greater individualism among the solitaries. Soon he had a following of about nine thousand monks and nuns in several monasteries. The texts of his rules are probably mainly written by successors.

pacifism, the belief that human beings ought always to seek peaceful, nonviolent ways of living together and resolving conflicts and ought never to kill other human beings.

In Christian teaching, pacifism is the starting point even for positions that allow for justifiable exceptions. Jesus taught, "Do not resist an evildoer," but rather "Love your enemies and pray for those who persecute you"; turn the other cheek if struck (Matt 5:39–43). Among Protestants, Mennonites and Quakers have been especially committed to nonresistance; among Catholics, monastic orders, such as the Franciscans, have been particularly engaged with it.

Christian pacifists note that Jesus did resist evil, though without lethal violence. They practice a more activist form of pacifism, or active nonviolence. Its most important exemplar, however, was a Hindu admirer of Christ, Mahatma Gandhi. In leading India to independence from British rule, he developed strategies of nonviolent coercion, protest, and social mobilization. Martin Luther King, Jr., later appropriated these in the U.S. civil rights movement of the 1950s and 1960s. Dorothy Day, her Catholic Worker movement, Thomas Merton, and peace activists such as Daniel and Philip Berrigan also modeled such a pacifism.

Some representatives of the Catholic Church's just-war tradition have concluded that warfare in the nuclear age has become so destructive that no modern war can meet the criteria for a just war. They speak of their position as nuclear pacifism. *See also* just-war doctrine; peace; peace movement, Catholic.

PADRES (Span., "fathers"), the organization of Catholic Hispanic clergy in the United States.

Palamas, St. Gregory, ca. 1296–1359, monk and mystical theologian in the Orthodox Church. Gregory convinced his sisters, brothers, and widowed mother to enter religious life. On Mount Athos he encountered firsthand the Hesychast tradition of which he became a prime defender and exponent, especially against Barlaam of Calabria and Western theology. Gregory systematized the thought of Simeon the New Theologian; both he and Simeon found the liturgy a normative resource for theology. Gregory emphasized the need for theology to be apophatic, i.e., restrained in its speech about God, because of the transcendence of God, but with a firm affirmation of the reality of divine revelation. He put special emphasis on the Transfiguration and on the light seen there by the disciples, a light that was a divine reality. For Gregory God's grace brought to the faithful the gift of deification. Gregory Palamas became archbishop of Thessalonica in 1347 and was canonized in the Orthodox Church soon after his death in 1368. Feast day: November 14, also the second Sunday of Lent (East). *See also* mystical theology.

Pall

Paleo-Christian art, Christian artifacts made before Constantine's Edict of Toleration in the early fourth century. These consist mainly of such artifacts as carved gems, catacomb frescos, tomb decoration, some pieces of sculpture, and architectural remains that predate the period when Christians were not subject to persecution. *See also* Catholicism and the visual arts.

Palestrina, Giovanni, ca. 1525–94, foremost liturgical composer of the sixteenth century. Brought to Rome in 1551 by Pope Julius III, Palestrina created rich and complex polyphonic settings of the Mass (e.g., *Missa di Papa Marcello*) that were important artistic expressions of the Counter-Reformation. *See also* Catholicism and music.

pall (pawl; Lat., *pallium,* "cloak"), 1 a sacred cloth, usually a square piece of cardboard covered with linen, placed over the chalice at Mass. It derives from a larger altar cloth, capable of being folded over the chalice. 2 The term also designates the cloth covering for the coffin at funeral Masses.

Palladius, ca. 365–425, historian famous for his *Lausiac History* (419–20), one of the most important sources for the history of ancient monasticism. He was accused, perhaps unjustly, of Origenism and exiled (406–12) for his support of John Chrysostom. His *Dialogue* on the life of Chrysostom is both a defense and biography of his friend. *See also* Chrysostom, St. John; monasticism; Origenism.

pallium, a narrow circular band of white wool, marked with six dark purple crosses, with two hanging strips front and back. It is worn around the neck and shoulders of the pope, signifying the plenitude of the pontifical office. The pope may grant its

use to archbishops (and occasionally bishops). *See also* archbishop.

Pallotti, St. Vincent, 1795–1850, founder of the Society of the Catholic Apostolate (Pallottine Fathers) in Rome in 1835. He later founded the Sisters of the Catholic Apostolate. Pallotti supported artisan guilds and schools for young workers. He has been called the second Philip Neri because of his ministries during a cholera plague. Feast day: January 22. *See also* Pallottine Fathers.

Pallottine Fathers, popular name for the Society of the Catholic Apostolate (S.A.C.), founded in Rome in 1835 by Vincent Pallotti. Members strive to be a bridge between diocesan and religious priests. They are an exempt (i.e., from the control of the local bishop) society of clerics and lay brothers who live a common life and make promises, not vows, of poverty, chastity, obedience, and perseverance. In 1854 their name was changed to the Pious Society of the Missions because it was asserted that the "apostolate" belonged to the hierarchy alone. The name was restored in 1947. Works include education, parish ministry, missions, and publication. The generalate is in Rome and there are five provinces in the United States. *See also* Pallotti, St. Vincent.

Palm Sunday, the first day of Holy Week, the

Pallium

pallium

Sunday before Easter. This day's distinctive ceremonies—especially the procession commemorating Christ's triumphal entry into Jerusalem shortly before his death—are already attested in the fourth-century *Peregrinatio Egeriae*, the travel diary of a woman who saw this ritual performed in Jerusalem. Such rites were adopted slowly in the West, where they are first met in an eighth-century Gallican sacramentary known as the Bobbio Missal. Originally separate from Mass, the Palm Sunday procession was eventually attached to the beginning of the eucharistic celebration. Since Vatican Council II (1962–65), this day also has been called Passion Sunday. *See also* Holy Week.

Palmieri, Domenico (doh-men'i-koh pahl-myair'ee), 1829–1909, Jesuit philosopher and theologian. He taught at the Gregorian University in Rome before falling out of favor with neo-Thomists because of his rejection of hylomorphism, the belief that every being is constituted of form and matter.

Panagia (pah-nah-gee'ah; Gk., "all-holy [one]"), Byzantine title for the Mother of God and, by extension, for the loaf of bread blessed at table in Greek monasteries and elevated in her honor. It is also the Russian term for the Byzantine episcopal "pectoral" (Gk., *enkolpion*), an oval-shaped medallion worn by Byzantine-rite bishops and more recently adopted by bishops of other Eastern churches. It usually bears a small icon of the *Panagia* holding the Christ child. *See also* Mother of God; *Theotokos*.

Pancras, St., d. ca. 304, martyr. His cult was established in Rome and spread to England after Augustine of Canterbury (d. ca. 605) built a church there in his honor. Nothing reliable is known of him. Feast day (with Sts. Nereus and Achilleus): May 12.

Panentheism (Gk., *pan,* "everything," *en,* "in," *theos,* "God"), the belief that the being of God is "in" the whole universe, but that God's Being is more than the universe (unlike the view of Pantheism that God and the universe are one). Traceable to Plato in his discussion of the problem of the one and the many, various forms of Panentheism have stressed that contained in the Absolute God are both infinity and limitation, abstract possibility and concrete realization, the unchanging and the essential, as well as the dynamic and the accidental. Twentieth-century theorists such as Alfred North Whitehead, Charles Hartshorne, and the Jesuit Pierre Teilhard de

Chardin have given formal expression to Panentheism in views espousing belief in a dipolar or evolving God, at once eternal and temporal, encompassing and transcending the world. *See also* Pantheism.

Pange Lingua (pahn'jay ling'wah; Lat., "Sing, my tongue"), a hymn composed by Venantius Fortunantus (d. 610). Another version of it, composed by Thomas Aquinas (d. 1274), is sung on Holy Thursday and Corpus Christi, and its last two verses, *Tantum Ergo,* are sung at Benediction of the Blessed Sacrament. For the full English text, see *The Raccolta* (1957) or P. Klein, ed., *Catholic Source Book* (Dubuque, Iowa: Brown-ROA, 1990). *See also* Benediction; Corpus Christi, Feast of; Holy Thursday; *Tantum Ergo.*

panniculus (pan-ik'yuh-luhs; Lat., *panis,* "bread"), a small morsel of bread, like a Host. Alternatively, in ancient sources, a small rag, an altar linen, or gremial (a bishop's ceremonial lap cloth).

Pantaleon, St. (pan-tay'lee-ahn), also known as Panteleimon, d. ca. 305, martyr and patron saint of physicians. A physician whose patients included the emperor Galerius, he was beheaded during the Diocletian persecutions. He is venerated widely in the East as a great martyr and wonder-worker; in the West he is considered one of the Fourteen Holy Helpers, and his blood at Ravello, Italy, is believed to liquefy on his feast day like that of St. Januarius. Feast day: July 27. *See also* Fourteen Holy Helpers.

Pantheism (Gk., *pan,* "all"; *theos,* "God"), belief or theory that identifies God with the world and the world with God. In the Hindu literature of ancient India, the absolute deity is immanent in all reality and animates humanity. Buddhism, Jainism, and Taoism likewise reflect varying degrees of identification of God with the world. For Christianity, the relationship between God and the world, between Creator and creature, is characterized as both unity and difference, maintained in tension so as to affirm God's transcendence while stressing the participation of creatures in the infinite being of God. Although Catholic doctrine clearly upholds the unity of Creator and creature "in the Holy Spirit," teachings about the reality of grace never negate or suppress belief in the finitude of the human soul or the otherness of God. Such a tension is virtually eliminated in religions with strong pantheistic tendencies. *See also* Panentheism.

THE PAPACY

The papacy is the office and jurisdiction of the Bishop of Rome (the pope). In the history of Christianity, the papacy has always been considered one of the most important and con-troversial issues. Because of the tradition that Peter and Paul (the two main leaders of the apostolic Church) were martyred in the imperial city of Rome, the bishop of the local church of Rome has been considered the possessor of a specific authority associated with the mission and well-being of the whole Church. This mission implies a specific power of jurisdiction for the oversight of all the other bishops and the churches these bishops serve as vicars of Christ (cf. Dogmatic Constitution on the Church, n. 27). But even as early as the time of Cyprian (d. 258), the relations between the bishop of the principal episcopal see and the other bishops were never exempt from tensions and even conflicts. It has been said that, because a relationship between power and freedom is always involved, the papacy is a gift of God difficult to manage evangelically. On many occasions it has been at the root of Christian division and remains an important stumbling block on the way to full visible unity of all the disciples of Christ. Nevertheless, it belongs to the structure of the Church.

The Roman papacy changed considerably between its quite rudimentary beginnings in the first centuries and the form it assumed following the Middle Ages. But it is important to understand that any such changes have always been linked to the evolution of the whole Church and its relation to the whole of human history. Sometimes many tasks assumed by the Bishop of Rome were the consequence of political and social conditions, as, for instance, the government of the so-called Papal States. Quite often external pressures obscured the authentic nature of the papacy. One of the main challenges of the papacy is to judge all tasks in the light of the gospel in order to avoid transforming ecclesiastical jurisdiction into political power. It is clear that during the nineteenth and twentieth centuries the papacy has been led, because of political circumstances as well as some evangelical streams of renewal, to give up most of its worldly power. The papacy is now universally perceived as a spiritual reality and not as a political one, even if it intervenes more often than in the past for the promotion of social justice, peace, human rights, and political freedom. Since the pontificate of Leo XIII (1878–1903), the papacy has been considered a very strong voice in concert with the voices of all those who work for the defense of the poor and of workers. The influence of Paul VI (1963–78) and John Paul II (elected 1978) on the political scene has been acknowledged by political experts. The papacy is seen as a spiritual power, grounded in a long history of service to humanity, counterbalancing the political games of the worldly powers.

For many centuries, the papacy has been considered by non–Roman

Catholics as a source of intractable problems. These have been central to the separation between Rome and Constantinople and between Rome and the so-called Reformed and Protestant churches. Nevertheless, thanks especially to the entry of Roman Catholicism into many bilateral ecumenical dialogues and the World Council of Churches' Commission on Faith and Order, significant steps forward have been accomplished. The papacy is no longer seen as an incarnation of the antichrist and on many occasions the leaders of other Christian bodies address the Bishop of Rome as one of their brothers. During the Seventh Assembly of the World Council of Churches at Canberra, Australia (1991), it was said (not only by Orthodox delegates but also by representatives of Protestant churches) that now it is no longer the presence of the papacy but its absence from the World Council of Churches (except for the Commission on Faith and Order) that is the main problem of the ecumenical movement.

During the first centuries, when the Eastern churches and the Western churches were in communion, papal power was exercised mainly by giving authoritative answers to controversial questions (like the date of Easter), by protecting the rights of the other bishops, by arbitrating conflicts, and sometimes by excommunicating those refusing to accept the decisions of the Roman see (as Victor I did in 198 and Stephen I in 257). But slowly the Roman see came to take initiative in leading other churches toward what it understood to be the will of Christ for the Church. Pope Leo I (d. 461)—following the policy of Siricius (d. 399), Innocent (d. 417), and Zosimus (d. 418)—gave the papacy the high profile it kept for the next centuries. It was Gelasius I (d. 496) who opened the way to the theology of "the two powers," according to which political and temporal power was subordinated to spiritual power. It is this theory that was expressed very harshly by Boniface VIII in the bull *Unam Sanctam* (1302), a source of many problems for Western Christianity. Before the separation between East and West, the existence of the patriarchates and their officially recognized authority within their own juridical structure were powerful moderators of the papacy's growing desire to control and direct the whole life of the churches, an enterprise that the see of Rome had felt, in many circumstances, was in harmony with its mission. After the split in 1054, the shape of the papacy changed considerably. Only one patriarchate remained in the West. Thus, because its patriarch was the same person as the primate of the universal Church, the patriarchal leadership came to be entirely absorbed by the power of the papacy. Western Christianity became what some Orthodox describe as a papal church, that is, a church that relates so predominantly to the see of Rome that the relationship to the local bishop is somehow swallowed up. The traditional vision of the Church of God as a "communion of local churches" was in danger of being entirely absorbed into the vision of a "universal Church under a universal primate."

Against this background, Vatican I's (1869–70) constitution *Pastor Aeternus* and the original draft of it sound very moderate. Because of the strong theological positions of the so-called minority, the council tried to propose a vision of the papacy that did not restrict the authority of the other bishops over their own local churches. It stressed the fact that the Bishop of Rome is not the bishop of any other local church. Moreover, during the discussions it became clear that supreme papal authority cannot be exercised in a purely worldly manner; it is the authority of the *servus servorum Dei* (Lat., "servant of the servants of God"). The correspondence between Pius IX and the German bishops, provoked by the intervention of German chancellor Bismarck (1875), shows very clearly that, according to Vatican I, the authority of the local bishops is essential to the life of the Church and cannot be considered a pure concession. The papacy is not a religious form of monarchy, in which the bishops are the vassals of the Roman Pontiff.

At Vatican II (1962–65) *Pastor Aeternus* was reread by placing it within the main insights of the ecclesiology of communion. It became very clear that the Church is neither a monarchy in which the supreme head delegates authority to the vassals, nor a confederation of local churches whose bishops give to a president a certain amount of authority in view of their "being together." It is a communion of local churches to which Christ himself gives, in the person of the bishop of the see of Peter and Paul, a ministry of unity in order to keep the churches in authentic unity of faith, charity, mission, ministry, and sacraments. Since Vatican II the Catholic Church has been experiencing a new stage in the history of the papacy. On one side, through his apostolic trips all over the world, the Bishop of Rome has made his personal presence more and more important; on the other, since Paul VI, the World Synod of Bishops has been periodically convoked in order to work with the Bishop of Rome in an advisory capacity and, if necessary, to exercise deliberative power.

See also collegiality; communion, Church as; infallibility; Papal States; Petrine ministry; Petrine succession; primacy, papal; Vatican Council I; vicar of Christ; Vicar of Peter.

Bibliography

Bertrams, Wilhelm. *The Papacy, the Episcopacy and Collegiality.* Westminster, MD: Newman Press, 1958.
Brezzi, Paolo. *The Papacy: Its Origins and Historical Evolution.* Westminster, MD: Newman Press, 1958.
Caragounis, Chrys C. *Peter and the Rock.* New York: W. de Gruyter, 1990.
Dionne, J. Robert. *The Papacy and the Church.* New York: Philosophical Library, 1987.
Granfield, Patrick. *The Limits of the Papacy: Authority and Autonomy in the Church.* New York: Crossroad, 1987.
Miller, J. Michael. *What Are They Saying About Papal Primacy?* New York: Paulist Press, 1983.
Tillard, Jean-Marie Roger. *The Bishop of Rome.* Wilmington, DE: Michal Glazier, 1983.

JEAN-M. R. TILLARD

papal audience. *See* audience, papal.

papal blessing, 1 a benediction or blessing bestowed by the pope. Cardinals and bishops may be delegated to bestow the papal, or apostolic, blessing on solemn occasions. It may also be given by abbots, retreat masters, and priests at the hour of death. It carries with it a plenary indulgence, i.e., the remission of all temporal punishment due to sins that have already been forgiven. 2 The term also applies to the parchment certificate bearing the words of the blessing for particular persons on special occasions, such as a wedding anniversary.

papal chamberlain, commonly known as a monsignor, formerly one of several ranks, some merely honorary, conferred on ecclesiastics attached to the papal household. In 1968, Pope Paul VI eliminated or altered many such categories, with papal chamberlains renamed as "Chaplains of His Holiness." *See also* Honorary Prelate of His Holiness; monsignor.

papal election, the election of a pope by the College of Cardinals in conclave, a closed meeting. The conclave must begin between fifteen and twenty days after the death of the previous pope. In 1970 Pope Paul VI restricted participation to those cardinals who are less than eighty years old, and in 1973 he limited the number of cardinals who could participate in a conclave to 120. The dean of the College of Cardinals convokes the conclave, and prior to it, a committee of the cardinal chamberlain (Camerlengo) of the Apostolic *Camera* (Lat., "chamber"; office that administers the Holy See during the vacancy in the papal office) and three cardinals (a cardinal-bishop, cardinal-priest, and cardinal-deacon, each chosen by lot from the 120 cardinal-electors) determines dates for mandatory daily general sessions preparatory to the conclave. The dean presides over the preliminary sessions, which decide necessary details, review pertinent legislation, and administer required oaths of secrecy. After entrance to, and sealing of, the conclave, election takes place in the Sistine Chapel with only cardinal-electors present. Election is permitted by acclamation (spontaneous, unanimous, vocal proclamation) or by compromise (entrusting the choice to a group of nine to fifteen cardinals), but the usual manner is by scrutiny (secret ballot). Actual voting is governed by detailed norms for the size, shape, and appearance of ballots as well as how they are cast, counted, and

destroyed. Two scrutinies are held per day, and a vote of two-thirds plus one is required for election. Ballots from inconclusive scrutinies are burned with straw and chemicals, producing dark smoke. Ballots from a conclusive scrutiny are burned without straw, producing the white smoke that signifies election of a pope to those outside the conclave. *See also* Cardinals, College of; conclave.   *ELIZABETH MCDONOUGH*

papal enclosure. *See* enclosure.

papal flag, the national standard of Vatican City State, consisting of two equal-sized vertical stripes of yellow and white, with the insignia of the papacy on the white stripe (a triple crown, or tiara, over two crossed keys, one gold and one silver, tied with a red cord and two tassels). *See also* Vatican City State.

papal legate, a representative of the pope to a particular church or civil government or to an international council or conference (Code of Canon Law, can. 363). Legates to civil governments are emissaries of the Holy See recognized as an international entity having a worldwide spiritual mission. *See also* Holy See; nuncio.

papal nuncio. *See* nuncio.

papal primacy. *See* primacy, papal.

papal resignation. *See* resignation.

Papal States, parts of central Italy and the territory of Avignon and Venaissin in France that once acknowledged the temporal sovereignty of the pope. Although popes claimed temporal sovereignty over

PAPAL STATES

Rome

PAPAL STATES (CA. 1100)

certain areas in Italy beginning in the fourth century, it was not until the eighth century that the papacy assumed juridical and administrative control. The center of its territories was the former Byzantine Duchy of Rome. In 1791 the papal territories situated in France were absorbed by the Republic. In 1861 the remaining lands under papal control, except for Rome itself, became part of the Kingdom of Italy, and in 1870, after the withdrawal of French protection, Rome itself became part of the Kingdom of Italy.

After 1870 the "Roman Question" became a major problem in Italian politics. Pius IX (d. 1878) rejected the concessions offered by the Italian state, which granted the pope a pension and control over the basilicas and palaces of the Lateran and the Vatican. Final resolution was not reached until 1929 when Vatican City was recognized as a separate state. *See also* Lateran Treaty; Vatican; Vatican City State.

Papias, early-second-century bishop of Hierapolis. Irenaeus calls him "a man of old," who knew "John" and was a friend of Polycarp. His five books of *Expositions of the Lord's Sayings* are lost apart from fragments, the most famous of which concern the origin of the Gospels of Mark and Matthew. *See also* synoptic Gospels, problem of.

parable (Gk., *parabolē*, "a casting alongside of," hence, "comparison"), a story, metaphor, or simile drawn from ordinary life or nature and often used by Jesus to make a religious point. The NT "parable" translates the Hebrew *mashal,* which is used in the OT for a wide variety of literary forms such as proverbs (1 Sam 10:12; Prov 1:1, 6; 10:1; 26:7–9), riddles (Judg 14:10–18), taunt songs (Mic 2:4; Hab 2:6), and allegories (Ezek 17:3–24) and in the intertestamental literature for long revelatory discourses such as the similitudes of Enoch (*1 Enoch* 39–71). The NT exhibits similar variety; "parable" describes proverbs (Luke 4:23), wisdom sayings (Luke 5:36–39), allegories (Mark 12:1–11; Matt 22:1–14), and the more familiar narrative parables (Luke 18:9–14). Passages not explicitly called parables can be considered as such when they contain introductory formulas such as "it is like" (Matt 11:16), "the kingdom of heaven is like" (Matt 13:31, 33), or "to what shall I compare" (Luke 7:31; cf. Mark 4:30) or because of their context (Luke 15:11–32; see 15:1–3). Teaching in parables was characteristic of the historical Jesus, especially in his proclamation of the kingdom of God (see Mark 4:26–32; Matt 13:24–30, 33, 44–46;

18:23–35; 20:1–16). *See also* allegory; kingdom of God [in the Bible].

paraclete (par'uh-kleet; Gk., "one called to the side"), a counselor or an advocate. The Fourth Gospel uses the term for the Spirit that Jesus promises to send to instruct his disciples (John 14:16, 26; 15:26; 16:7). 1 John 2:1 uses the term "paraclete" of Jesus himself ("advocate" in NRSV). *See also* Holy Spirit.

Paraclete, the, monastery of nuns in Troyes, France, founded by Peter Abelard, confirmed by Pope Innocent II in 1131, with Héloïse as its first prioress and abbess. Abelard accommodated the Benedictine rule to the needs of women, provided directives for *lectio divina* (Lat., "spiritual reading") and for studies, composed a treatise on the origin of nuns as well as hymns, sermons, prayers, and a breviary. After Abelard's death in 1142, Héloïse founded several daughter houses. In 1147 the Paraclete received canonical status as a religious order and survived until the French Revolution. *See also* Abelard, Peter; Héloïse.

paradise, in the NT (Luke 23:43; 2 Cor 12:3; Rev 2:7) and in common Christian usage, the realm of God into which the righteous enter after death. It also refers to the garden of Eden as symbolic of that realm (Rev 2:7). The Hebrew word (*pardēs*) is a loanword from Old Persian, meaning a private park or enclosure. *See also* heaven.

paraliturgy, a service of public prayer modeled on the liturgy but not found in the official books. Paraliturgies originated in post–World War II France as biblically and liturgically inspired prayer services that were created locally, in the vernacular, and authorized by the local bishop. The liturgical reforms of Vatican II made them largely redundant. *See also* extraliturgical service.

parents, duties of, the general and particular obligations that the Church specifies to be those that mothers and fathers have toward their children. Canon law states that "Parents have the most serious duty and the primary right to do all in their power to see to the physical, social, cultural, moral, and religious upbringing of their children" (can. 1136). The documents of Vatican II speak of the family as the domestic church (Dogmatic Constitution on the Church, n. 11), where parents are the first to communicate the faith to their children (Decree on the

Apostolate of the Laity, n. 11). Parents must set an example by their own faith, as well as by their conjugal love and fidelity. Parents also have the task of educating their children to recognize God's love for everyone and to show concern for the material and spiritual needs of their neighbor. In this sense, family life is an apprenticeship for the Church's mission (n. 30). It is also the duty of parents to help their children in vocational choices generally and to promote religious vocations when these are discerned (n. 12). Parents are obligated to send their children to Catholic schools whenever possible (Declaration on Christian Education, n. 8) and to safeguard their children against those elements in society that threaten their faith or morals (Decree on the Instruments of Social Communication, n. 10). *See also* family.

Paris, a Christian center beginning in the third century. According to Gregory of Tours (d. 594), historian of the Franks, St. Denis, the first bishop of Paris, was one of seven bishops sent to evangelize Gaul in the mid-third century (by the end of the second century there was already a Christian community at Lyons, in east-central France). Several key institutions that flourished during the Middle Ages made Paris an important Christian center: the Benedictine abbey of Saint-Germain-des-Prés, founded in the sixth century; Notre Dame Cathedral, begun and consecrated in the eleventh century; and the abbey of St. Victor and the University of Paris, both founded in the twelfth century. In the thirteenth century Paris was the chief center of Scholasticism, including among its outstanding theologians members of the new mendicant orders (the Dominicans Albertus Magnus and Thomas Aquinas and the Franciscans Alexander of Hales, Bonaventure, and John Duns Scotus) and diocesan priests (William of Auxerre and Henry of Ghent).

By the end of the fourteenth century, however, Paris began to recede as a theological center with the decline of Scholasticism, the Great Schism (1378–1417), and the war with England, during which the city was occupied by English forces (1420–36). In the seventeenth century Paris was the center of a religious renewal under the leadership of Francis de Sales, Vincent de Paul, Pierre de Bérulle, and Jean-Jacques Olier, in reaction against Gallicanism and Jansenism. In the eighteenth century, however, Paris became a center of rationalism and the Enlightenment. With the French Revolution of 1789 and subsequent revolutions of 1830 and 1848, Catholicism in Paris went largely into eclipse. The theology faculty of the University of Paris, abolished since the revolution of 1789, has been represented since 1875 by the Institut Catholique. *See also* France, Catholicism in; Institut Catholique; Notre Dame Cathedral; Saint-Germain-des-Prés; Scholasticism; Victorines.

RICHARD P. MCBRIEN

parish, a defined, stable community of Christian faithful usually established locally within a geographical section of a diocese and entrusted by the diocesan bishop to the pastoral care of a priest called a pastor. If circumstances should warrant, diocesan bishops may organize parishes nonterritorially, in accordance with special religious or sociocultural needs, like rite, nationality, or language. Canon law safeguards the stability of parishes, endowing them with the status of a juridical person, requiring bishops to consult the presbyteral council of the diocese when opening, closing, or changing them, and instituting special procedures for removing and transferring pastors. *See also* pastor.

parish council, a body of representatives chosen or appointed for the purpose of sharing administrative and ministerial responsibilities with the pastor. Parish councils had their origin in Vatican II's Decree on the Apostolate of the Laity (1965), which called for lay involvement in diocesan councils and encouraged a parallel development on the parish level (n. 26). The Directory on the Pastoral Ministry of Bishops (1973) further specified the responsibilities of these councils: they were to assume temporal administrative tasks (n. 135) and works proper to their apostolate (n. 179), and their formation was intended to foster a sense of community and to promote zeal for the apostolate among the laity (n. 147). Parish councils can be required by a diocese, but they are not mandated by canon law (can. 536). Canon law further stipulates that parish councils are to be governed by norms determined by the bishop, while their immediate president is the pastor. Their authority and vote are to be consultative.

In the first decade after Vatican II (1962–65), more than ten thousand councils were founded. By the late 1980s approximately 75 percent of U.S. parishes had a council in place. Councils are often organized into committees responsible for the various administrative and pastoral ministries of the parish: administration, finance, liturgy, education, social justice, spiritual development, ecumenism, and parish activities. They function variously as advisory or decision-making bodies. Tensions over the relative authority of council and pastor and the assignation of tasks proper to each have emerged in the years following the council and continue to inform the ongoing definition of ministry and of lay vocation in the Church.

Among the issues that such councils face as they enter their second generation are the continuing need for committed volunteers and adequate training, the challenge to realize collaborative models of interaction, and the mandate to articulate and enable leadership at the parish level. *See also* laity; parish.   CATHERINE MURPHY

parish mission, a technique of evangelization that originated in the Catholic Reform era of the sixteenth century. Promoted by religious orders, especially the Jesuits, it sought to strengthen the religious faith and devotion of the people. Itinerant missionaries would arrive in a parish and remain there for a week, two weeks, or even longer; they would follow a regular schedule of sermons, always seeking to convert their listeners to a life of holiness. It was very similar to revivals taking place in Protestant churches at this time. The preaching was emotional and the message of sin and salvation inspired every sermon. After flourishing in the sixteenth and seventeenth centuries, the parish mission went into decline in the eighteenth century. It was revived in the nineteenth century and was brought to the United States by immigrant clergy. The parish mission was a key element in the renewal of Catholicism in the nineteenth century. *See also* revivalism, Catholic.

parish team, a group of people working in partnership to exercise the ministry of leadership on behalf of a parish community. Typically, a parish team consists of both lay and ordained ministers whose collaborative efforts are aimed at facilitating the teaching, preaching, sacramental celebration, and action on behalf of justice and peace, which together create an authentic, local actualization of the Church of Christ. *See also* parish.

parochial school, general term for a Catholic elementary school, but specifically a Catholic school attached to a particular parish. The first Catholic schools in the United States were operated by congregations of women religious who used the proceeds from their academies to fund free schools. St. Mary's School in Philadelphia, founded in 1782, is generally considered the first parochial school in the United States. Intensive development of parochial schools began in the 1840s, as Catholics battled Protestants unsuccessfully for a share of state educational funds. Catholics objected to the distinctly Protestant bias of the public or common school, and so established a separate school system to protect the Catholic faith of their children. Essential to the development of parochial schools was the hard work and devotion of countless groups of teaching sisters, who provided the inner strength of the Catholic educational system. In 1852 the First Plenary Council of Baltimore encouraged each parish to establish a school, and in 1884 the Third Plenary Council of Baltimore mandated that each parish open a school within two years, and set the ideal as "every Catholic child in a Catholic school." Though the ideal was never realized, a massive Catholic school system did develop throughout the country. Catholic schools reached their peak in the post–World War II era. The 1960s brought a severe questioning of Catholic schools, highlighted by Mary Perkins Ryan's challenge, *Are Parochial Schools the Answer?* (1964). The biggest challenge facing the post–Vatican II parochial school was financial. With the reduction in the number of teaching sisters, more lay teachers had to be hired, entailing a dramatic increase in school budgets. The increased costs, plus the flight of older Catholic groups from the inner cities, led to the closing of many urban Catholic schools in the 1980s. *See also* Catholicism and education.   JEFFREY M. BURNS

parochial vicar, associate parish priest assigned by the diocesan bishop to collaborate with the pastor in parish ministry. Diocesan law and policy may define the assignment process and the specific rights and duties of parochial vicars. The diocesan bishop may remove and transfer them for just cause. The parochial vicar was formerly known as a curate. *See also* parish team; pastor.

Parousia (pahr-*oo*-see'uh; Gk., "presence," "arrival"), the coming of Christ in glory. In the Hellenistic period the term was used for the visit of an official to a city or territory. Paul thus speaks of his own parousia to his congregations (Phil 1:26). From that use derives the application to the Second Coming of Christ, described in detail in 1 Thess 4:15–18 or Matt 24:3–41. Parousia then becomes the standard designation for the event in Paul (1 Cor 15:23; 1 Thess 2:19; 3:13; 5:23; 2 Thess 2:1, 8) and other early Christian writers (Jas 5:7–8; 2 Pet 1:16; 3:4, 12; 1 John 2:28). *See also* Second Coming.

Parsch, Pius, 1884–1954, Austrian canon of St. Augustine, promoter of pastoral liturgy, and author of the influential *The Church's Year of Grace*. Realizing how removed the liturgy of his day was from the life of the average Catholic, Parsch began a publishing house that generated popular biblical and liturgical materials. *See also* liturgical movement.

Parsons, Robert, also Persons, 1546–1610, Jesuit missionary. A fellow at Oxford, Parsons left England and converted to Catholicism at Louvain, becoming a Jesuit in 1575. Along with Edmund Campion, he led the first Jesuit mission to England in 1580, but left for the Continent after Campion's arrest. He continued his diplomatic activity in Rouen on behalf of the English Catholics, promoting for twenty years the Spanish invasion of England and formulating ideas about a Catholic successor to Elizabeth I. His most influential writing was an exhortation to the way of salvation by faith and good works, *The Christian Directory* (1582). From 1597 until his death, he was rector of the English College in Rome. *See also* England, Catholicism in.

partes inhonestae (pahr'tays in-oh-nest'ay; Lat., "dishonorable parts"), euphemism for the genitals. Based on 1 Cor 12:23–24, this phrase was used in the Vulgate to translate Greek equivalents. Augustine, who regarded the genital organs as instruments for the transmission of original sin, and other Latin writers handed down the term to the Scholastics. From there it was incorporated into the Latin manuals of moral theology in use up to the Second Vatican Council (1962–65).

particular church, canonical term for local church. The code of canon law identifies particular churches "first of all" as dioceses. Others include territorial prelatures, territorial abbacies, apostolic vicariates, apostolic prefectures, and apostolic administrations "which have been erected on a stable basis" (cans. 368–74). Groupings of particular churches include ecclesiastical provinces and regions (cans. 431–34). *See also* diocese; parish; prelature, territorial.

particular judgment. *See* judgment, particular.

particular law, canon law norms legislated for a specified group of the faithful. Contrasted to universal law, which is laid down for the entire Church, particular law might exist for a given group such as a diocese, a country, or a religious institute.

parvitas materiae (pahr'vi-tahs mah-tair'ee-ay; Lat., "smallness of matter"), a technical term in Scholastic moral theology referring to the "smallness" or "slightness" of the moral content of an act. Following Scripture (1 John 5:16–17), Catholic moral theology maintains that most sins are not mortal. One reason a sin could be venial is that the moral "matter" involved is slight. For example, the theft of two dollars is of "slight" moral seriousness in comparison with a murder.

Pascal, Blaise, 1623–62, French mathematician, scientist, and religious thinker. Born in Clermond-Ferrand and educated at home by his father, Etienne, Pascal was brought into contact with leading scientists when the family moved to Paris in 1631 and his father joined the Society of Scientists. Pascal published his first mathematical treatise at age seventeen, and soon thereafter invented a calculating machine. His analysis of the mathematics of chance resulted in probability theory, and in physics Pascal's law has become the basis of modern hydraulic operations.

Pascal exerted a singular influence on the Christian spiritual tradition after he encountered Jansenism at Port-Royal. An initial "conversion" in 1646 was followed some years later by a second conversion during the night of November 23, 1654, when an intense religious experience profoundly altered his life. Pascal became more involved with the teachers of Port-Royal (Arnauld, Nicole, Le Maitre de Saci), supporting Arnauld during his controversy with the Jesuits and the papacy. Pascal's defense, published pseudonymously in a series of eighteen articles (*Provincial Letters,* 1656–57), quickly became a classic and was placed on the Index of Forbidden Books.

Pascal's most enduring legacy, however, is another classic: the *Pensées,* a collection of notes intended as an *apology* in defense of Christianity for unbelievers. Pascal drew from the experience of paradox that lies at the heart of the human condition and that he expressed as tension between human power and frailty. When faced with ultimate questions, reason and science are powerless. God is finally known (i.e., experienced) not by human striving but by God's gracious self-disclosure, not through reason but in the heart. Pascal's views mediated against the optimism of the Enlightenment and were opposed by Diderot, Voltaire, and others. *See also* apologetics; faith and reason; Jansenism.

EILEEN KEARNEY

Pascendi Dominici Gregis (pah-shen'dee doh-mee'nee-chee gray-jis; Lat., "Feeding the Lord's Flock"), an encyclical of Pius X condemning Modernism, published on September 8, 1907. The various points of the Vatican's understanding of what it called "Modernism" were presented sharply and synthetically. It defended the transcendence of God and the reality of the Incarnation and revelation; it examined the philosophical, moral, and practical aspects of agnosticism and immanentism; and it commended the teaching and study of Scholasticism as well as the censorship of writings. Alfred Loisy (d. 1940), a French biblical scholar, was an implied target of the document. German scholars insisted that the papal charges did not correspond to German thought. *See also* Modernism; Pius X, St.

Paschal I, St., d. 824, pope from 817 to 824. In 817 Emperor Louis the Pious confirmed for Paschal the privileges accorded the papacy by Charlemagne, and the emperor also promised not to interfere in the papal domains or in papal elections. Paschal actively promoted the evangelization of the Danes and crowned Louis's son Lothair I as coemperor in 823. Although he made many efforts to renew the city of Rome and its monuments, Paschal's manner of governing was harsh, and he made many enemies. After his death, his body could not be buried in St. Peter's Basilica because of the disfavor he had incurred among the Roman people. His feast day, May 14, was dropped from the liturgical calendar in 1963.

Paschal II, d. 1118, pope from 1099 to 1118. More flexible than some of his predecessors, he was able to develop compromises that ended the investiture controversy in England and France; his attempts to come to an agreement with the German emperor, however, failed. *See also* investiture controversy.

Paschal Baylon, St., 1540–92, lay Franciscan brother and Spanish ascetic. He lived a life of self-denial and deep devotion to the Blessed Sacrament. He was known for his staunch defense of the doctrine of Christ's real eucharistic presence against the Protestants. Feast day: May 17.

paschal candle, Easter candle, marked and lit at the opening of the Easter Vigil. It was in widespread use as early as the late fourth century. Its symbolism is best understood from the *Exultet* (Lat., "exult") sung in its honor, usually by the deacon. It is the Easter proclamation of Christ's resurrection from the dead for our salvation. Though the paschal candle used to be extinguished after the Gospel reading on Ascension Day, it now remains near the ambo until Pentecost and is kept near the font through the year. It is used for its resurrection symbolism at baptisms and funerals.

paschal lamb (Aram., "passover"), the lamb sacrificed and eaten by Jews on the Feast of Passover to commemorate the liberating event in which God "passed over" the homes of the Hebrew people (who had sprinkled their doorposts with lamb's blood) and then brought them, led by Moses, out of Egypt and into Canaan (Exod 12:3–11). Christians have applied this name to Jesus Christ (1 Cor 5:7; John 1:29). *See also* Passover.

Paschal Mystery (Gk., *pascha,* Hebrew *pesah,* "passover"; Gk., *musterion,* "secret reality" or "rite"), the unified total event of Christ's Passion, death, Resurrection, Ascension, and sending of the Holy Spirit, insofar as it reveals and accomplishes God's previously hidden plan of salvation. The term reflects the Hebrew Passover, God's act of delivering Israel from Egypt, anticipating God's redemptive action in the Christ event. In the Paschal Mystery, Christ "passed over" to the Father, drawing all humankind and history with him. Christians remember, celebrate, and share in this Paschal Mystery in the liturgies of Holy Week/Easter Season and in each sacrament. *See also* Holy Week; Jesus Christ; salvation.

Paschal season, or Easter season, a fifty-day period beginning with Easter Sunday and concluding on the fiftieth day, called, since the fourth century, Pentecost Sunday. This liturgical period celebrates the Easter mystery of new life in Christ inaugurated by the Lord's Passion, death, and Resurrection, and bestowed by the Spirit. The Paschal season, a week of weeks, is a time of festival and, for the newly baptized, is the period of mystagogy, a fuller understanding and living of the Easter sacraments. *See also* Easter; Easter duty; mystagogy.

Paschasius Radbertus, St. (pash-kay'zhee-uhs rad-bair'toos), ca. 785–ca. 860, abbot and theologian. Abbot of the Benedictine monastery of Corbie from 843 to 849, he wrote the first treatise devoted exclusively to the Eucharist (831, revised in 844). He took an extreme realist view of eucharistic presence (identifying it with the human flesh of Jesus) and was excessively credulous regarding eucharistic miracles. His position was criticized by Ratramnus and Rabanus Maurus but remained influential throughout the medieval period. Feast day: April 26. *See also* Real Presence.

Passaglia, Carlo (kahr'loh pas-sahl'yah), 1812–87, influential theologian at the Roman College from 1844 to 1858. He left the Jesuits in 1859 and was suspended from the priesthood by Rome in 1862 because of his advocacy on behalf of priests sympathetic to Italian nationalism.

Passion, the (Lat., *passio*, "suffering"), the suffering and death of Jesus; a shorthand reference to the Passion narratives (Matt 26–27; Mark 14–15; Luke 22–23; John 18–19). Prior to these narratives, the suffering and death of Jesus were the subject of early Christian preaching and confession (Acts 2:23, 36; 4:10; 5:30; 10:39; Rom 8:32; 1 Cor 1:23; 15:3) and were liturgically celebrated (Phil 2:6–11; Rom 6:3–5; 1 Cor 11:23–26). Other more concrete terms are used for the Passion of Jesus: (1) the Cross (1 Cor 1:18; Gal 6:12, 14; Phil 3:18; Col 1:20); (2) the [saving] death (1 Cor 15:3; Rom 6:3); (3) blood and the shedding of blood (Rom 3:25; 5:9; 2 Cor 10:16; 11:27; Eph 1:7; 2:13; Heb 9:14; 10:19; 1 John 1:7; 1 Pet 1:2); (4) the "handing over" of Jesus (Rom 4:25; 1 Cor 11:23; Mark 9:31; 10:33); and (5) the "lifting up" of Jesus (John 3:14; 12:32) with the double meaning of lifting up on the cross and exaltation or return to the Father (John 14:28; 16:16; see Luke 9:51, Acts 2:33).

The Jewish Scriptures provided the major influence on the language of the Passion. Faced with "the offense of the cross" (Gal 5:11; Deut 21:23) and the absence of any OT expectation of a suffering messiah, early Christians mined the OT to argue that the Passion was "according to the Scriptures" (1 Cor 15:3; see Mark 14:21). Some of the major motifs are (1) Jesus' death as the Passover sacrifice (1 Cor 5:7) and Jesus himself as the Passover Lamb (John 19:36; see 1:29, 36; Rev 5:6, 12; 7:14; 12:11), or as a propitiation (Rom 3:25) taken from the liturgy of the Day of Atonement; (2) Jesus as the "righteous just one" who, like other figures from Jewish history, is unjustly persecuted but vindicated by God (Gen 37:39–41; Dan 3, 6; 2 Macc 7; Wis 2, 4–5; see also Psalm 22), and as the "suffering servant" of Isaiah (esp. 52:13–53:12); (3) Jesus as the high priest according to the likeness of Melchizedek who, by his death, offers the definitive sacrifice for sin (Heb 5:1–10; 7:1–27; 9:1–28; 13:11–12, 20).

Though the Passion narratives are the principal historical source for the final days of Jesus, they are written from the perspective of post-Easter faith. Mark stresses the paradox of faith: the Cross is the revelation of Jesus' true status (15:39); Jesus the true Messiah (royal figure) is mocked as a king (15:16–20); the lowly one is the risen one (16:6). Matthew portrays a Jesus who goes to death as lordly master of his own fate (26:53–55), and his removal by death is the way to an enduring presence with the community (28:16–20). In Luke, Jesus is a model martyr who is judged innocent by Pilate (23:22), forgives his persecutors (23:34), and dies with a prayer of confidence (23:46). John mitigates the harsher aspects of the Passion (19:2–3), which is less a story of degradation than the triumphal return of the Word to the Father and Jesus' hour of glorification (17:1). *See also* crucifixion.   JOHN R. DONAHUE

Passionists, popular name for the Congregation of the Passion (C.P.), founded in Rome in 1720 by St. Paul of the Cross, who wrote the rule and constitution when he was twenty-six years old and still a layman. The purpose of the congregation is twofold: the sanctification of the self and the sanctification of others. The first foundation was established in 1737; papal approval was granted in 1741.

In the same year, Pope Clement XIV entrusted to them the care of the Basilica of Sts. John and Paul on the Coelian Hill in Rome. Their motherhouse is located on the grounds. When religious institutes in Italy were suppressed by Napoleon, the Passionists were totally destroyed since all of their houses were in that country. After being restored in 1814, the congregation flourished.

Passionists are an exempt (i.e., from the control of the local bishop) clerical order who take simple perpetual vows of poverty, celibacy, and obedience. They vow obedience first to the pope and then to the superior. Brothers and priests share the same status in their common life. They chant the Divine Office daily. The coarse black wool habit, with a leather belt, bears a heart-shaped insignia with the words *Jesu, XPI Passio* ("The Passion of Jesus Christ"). Passionists are committed to preach and to center their ministries and spiritual lives on the suffering and death of Jesus Christ. The spirit of the congregation is prayer, penance, and solitude. Their primary work is preaching missions and retreats; catechetical instruction is secondary. The Passionists in the United States conduct television programs and published the *Sign* magazine until 1982. *See also* Paul of the Cross, St.   REGINA COLL

passions, faculties and acts of the sense appetites, e.g., love, hatred, hope, fear, desire, aversion, joy, and sadness. In Scholastic psychology, the passions are understood to be tendencies of the human person, grounded in the physiological responses of the organism toward its environment as those are experienced affectively, toward what is perceived to be beneficial or pleasurable, and away from what is perceived to be hurtful or unpleasant. Human passions cannot function unless they have first been informed by cognitive judgments that certain things are desirable, and others are undesirable or hurtful. Nonetheless, they can be misdirected toward what is not good overall. In contemporary moral theology, the language of the passions has largely been superseded by discussions of the emotions, understood developmentally. *See also* concupiscence; emotions, moral aspects of; appetites, concupiscible and irascible.

Passion Sunday, the Sunday opening Holy Week, popularly termed "Palm Sunday" because palms are blessed and distributed in commemoration of the Lord's entry into Jerusalem. This commemoration, derived from fourth-century Jerusalem, is the first part of the liturgy and may include a procession. Of Roman origin, the second part focuses on the Cross and Passion of Christ. One of the synoptic Passion accounts is proclaimed as the Gospel. The 1969 calendar revision suppressed "passiontide," renaming Palm Sunday (then the second Sunday of passiontide) Passion Sunday. *See also* Holy Week.

Passover, a major Jewish feast celebrated on the evening of 14 Nisan (i.e., March–April, the first month of the Jewish calendar during the spring equinox) commemorating the deliverance from Egyptian bondage (the Exodus). The English term derives from the Hebrew *pesah*, Exod 12:13, "I will *pass over* you . . . when I strike the land of Egypt," while the Greek loanword *pascha* is the basis for the English "Pasch" and "paschal." Exod 12:1–13:16 offers evidence that the feast developed from the joining of the Passover sacrifice (Exod 12:2–13) with a seven-day spring Festival of Unleavened Bread (Heb., *maṣṣot*, Exod 12:14, 18–20; see also Lev 23:4–9; Num 9:1–14; Deut 16:1–8; Ezra 6:19–22). Passover became a pilgrimage feast celebrated in Jerusalem as a ritual meal with the extended family. According to the synoptic Gospels (Matt 22:17–29; Mark 14:12–25; Luke 22:7–38) Jesus celebrated Passover with his followers before his death and is subsequently identified with the Passover lamb (1 Cor 5:7; John 1:29–30; Rev 5:12).

pastor, priest responsible for the pastoral care of a parish community entrusted to him by appointment of the diocesan bishop, under whom he exercises his duties by collaborating with his parishioners and his ministers. Besides fulfilling their sacramental and catechetical ministries, pastors are responsible for finances, building maintenance, parish programs, and coordinating the entire parish mission, fostering lay ministries in particular. While pastors serve under the authority of the bishop, appointments, transfers, and removals are procedurally safeguarded by a consultative process. *See also* parish.

Pastor Aeternus (pahs'tohr ay-tair'nuhs; Lat., "Eternal Pastor"), "First Dogmatic Constitution on the Church of Christ," constitution issued by the First Vatican Council on July 18, 1870, defining the primacy and infallibility of the pope. *See also* infallibility; primacy, papal.

pastoral associate, collaborator with the pastor or pastoral coordinator in parish ministry. The pastoral associate may be a nonclerical ministerial assistant to a coordinator of sacramental, administrative, educational, or social activity in a parish. The proper term for a priest assigned to assist the pastor is "parochial vicar," although "associate pastor" is common. *See also* parish; parish team; pastor.

Pastoral Constitution on the Church in the Modern World (Lat., *Gaudium et Spes,* "joy and hope"), one of the sixteen documents of Vatican II. Approved on December 7, 1965, it was the last and the longest document of the Second Vatican Council. It was a truly conciliar text not only in its formal character, but also because the idea for such a document was a product of conciliar reflection and debate. As the bishops reflected on the nature and mission of the Church, the need for an explicitly theological address to the world became imperative.

Gaudium et Spes, along with the Declaration on Religious Liberty (*Dignitatis Humanae*), fulfilled this need. The theology of the pastoral constitution is rooted in two sources: the papal social teaching of the twentieth century and the theology developed in Western Europe from the 1930s through the 1950s.

The social encyclicals from the pontificate of Leo XIII (d. 1903) through that of John XXIII (d. 1963) had elaborated a social philosophy and a moral assessment of the socioeconomic order. They did not provide, however, a theological or ecclesiological foundation for the social teaching. This more explicitly theological writing was produced after World War II in Europe particularly in the work of Yves Congar, Henri de Lubac (d. 1991), and Gustave Thils. When the decision was made at Vatican II to develop a document on the Church in the world, much of the basic theological work had been done. The conciliar text, nonetheless, was an advance beyond the previous theological work.

The nature, methodology, and tone of *Gaudium et Spes* all contributed to its distinctive character. First, the idea of a "pastoral constitution" meant that it was rooted in doctrinal principles but extended its analysis to contingent issues in the sociopolitical order. Second, the methodology of *Gaudium et Spes* required that the first step of theological reflection be an assessment of the empirical situation the Church sought to address. Then the assessment of this data "in the light of the gospel" followed. This approach influenced much theological reflection in the post-conciliar period, including the theology of liberation and the pastoral letters of the U.S. bishops in 1983 and 1986.

Gaudium et Spes has two parts. The enduring theological contribution is contained in Part One, where the conciliar text synthetically presents a Christian anthropology, a theology of human work, and a reflection on the Church's role in the world. Part Two is essentially a development of the themes found in the social encyclicals.

The chapters on marriage and the family and on the international community have had a major impact on the life of the Church since Vatican II. The chapter "Fostering the Nobility of Marriage and the Family" established the framework of the postconciliar debate on contraception by recasting the relationship of the unitive and procreative dimensions of sexuality.

The chapter "The Fostering of Peace and the Promotion of a Community of Nations" gave Catholic theology on war and peace a major impetus. By reaffirming traditional restraints on war in the face of the technology of the nuclear age and by legitimizing a nonviolent position for Catholics, *Gaudium et Spes* provided the foundation for Catholic theology of war and peace in the 1970s and 1980s.

The influence of *Gaudium et Spes* extended beyond any single issue. It is impossible to understand the highly active and effective social engagement of the Catholic Church in the postconciliar era apart from this document. *See also* Catholic social teachings; Vatican Council II.

Bibliography
Group 2000, ed. *The Church Today: Commentaries on the Pastoral Constitution on the Church in the Modern World.* Westminster, MD: Newman Press, 1967.
Murray, J. C. "The Issue of Church and State at Vatican II." *Theological Studies* 27 (1966): 580–606.
Vorgrimler, H. *Commentary on the Documents of Vatican II.* Vol. 5. Freiburg: Herder, 1968.   *J. BRYAN HEHIR*

pastoral council, representative diocesan or parish consultative body. Strongly recommended by canon law (cans. 511 and 536), a pastoral council collaborates with the bishop and the pastor, and all those ministerially associated with them in fulfilling the total mission and ministry of the diocese and the parish.

Members of such councils are either elected or appointed. Some members may be elected and others appointed. The function of the councils is advisory only. *See also* diocesan pastoral council; parish council.

pastoral counseling. *See* counseling, pastoral.

pastoral letter, a document, sometimes of considerable length, issued by a bishop to address matters of pastoral concern in a diocese. The term also refers to similar documents issued by a conference of bishops (Code of Canon Law, can. 447) that deal with pastoral matters in the territory of a particular episcopal conference. Examples of pastoral letters issued by the U.S. Catholic bishops include "The Challenge of Peace" (1983) and "Economic Justice for All: Catholic Social Teaching and the U.S. Economy" (1986).

pastoral Letters, a term referring to three NT Letters: 1–2 Timothy and Titus. They are called "pastoral" because they are addressed to "pastors" and because they are concerned with the pastoral life and welfare of churches. These three Letters purport to be by the apostle Paul to two co-workers. All three, however, probably come from the late first century A.D. They are likely the product of a Christian group that saw itself carrying on the traditions of Paul (a "Pauline school"), located, perhaps, in Ephesus. They also reflect a sense of a developing Christian tradition. *See also* catholic Letters.

pastoral ministry, commonly described as the

self-realizing activity of the Church whereby the saving and shepherding care of God for all peoples is made present in the world. In its commitment to gospel proclamation, liturgy, administration of the local church, and acts of service, pastoral ministry is concerned not merely with the communication of theological principles but also with how those principles can be applied to concrete and changing circumstances. It aims to aid human persons and communities to recognize in all circumstances a depth dimension indicative of the salvific presence of God. *See also* ministry.

Pastoral Provision, also known as the Anglican Use, a canonical arrangement, approved by the Vatican's Sacred Congregation for the Doctrine of the Faith in June 1980, whereby married Episcopal (Anglican) priests who enter into full communion with the Catholic Church and who are eligible for ordination as Catholic priests may be dispensed from the discipline of clerical celibacy and whereby Episcopal (Anglican) parishes that enter into full communion with the Catholic Church may maintain a "common identity reflecting certain elements of their own heritage" through the use of Vatican-approved liturgical rites for the sacraments, the Liturgy of the Hours, and other forms of worship contained in the *Book of Divine Worship.* Each such parish, however, remains subject to the pastoral jurisdiction of the diocesan bishop. *See also* Anglicanism; Anglican ordination; Episcopal Church.

Pastor Bonus (Lat., "good pastor"), the apostolic constitution by Pope John Paul II ordering changes in the Roman Curia. Published on June 28, 1988, and made effective on March 1, 1989, the constitution was based on the broad outline of Pope Paul VI's (d. 1978) four-year reorganization study of the Roman Curia, beginning in 1963 and ending with the publication of *Regimini Ecclesiae Universae* (Lat., "On the governance of the universal Church") in 1967. The reorganized Curia consists of the Secretariat of State, nine congregations, three tribunals, twelve councils, and three offices, as well as many other departments and agencies attached to the Holy See. *See also* Roman Curia.

Patarag (pah-tah-rahg'; Arm., "offering," "sacrifice," "gift"), one of the common names for the Armenian eucharistic liturgy.

Patarenes, radical Church reform movement orig-

inating in Milan in the 1050s seeking to end clerical marriage and simony (buying and selling of Church offices and spiritual goods) and hostile to lay involvement in the Church. Though supportive of papal reforms, they were criticized by Pope Alexander II for their violence and extremism. "Patarene" eventually became a general label for heretics.

paten (Lat., *patena,* Gk., *patane,* "dish," "plate"), a small, circular, flat dish that holds the presider's host at Mass. Originally made of glass, it is presently made of gold-plated metal. Before the ninth century, the paten was large enough to hold sufficient bread (unleavened) for Communion of the faithful.

Pater Noster (pah'tair nah'stair). *See* Lord's Prayer.

patience (Lat., *patientia,* "endurance"), the virtue that enables one to bear suffering over a long period of time, courageously and without rancor. It is part of the cardinal virtue of fortitude and is to be distinguished from indifference, or insensitivity to misfortune.

patriarch [biblical], in a strict sense, any of the male ancestors of Israel mentioned in Genesis, both before and after the Flood. More commonly, however, the term is restricted to the descendants of Abraham, principally Isaac, Jacob, and Joseph. As heirs of Israel and its traditions, early Christians saw themselves as "children of Abraham." *See also* Abraham; Isaac; Jacob.

patriarch [ecclesiastical], title for the highest-ranking bishop of an autonomous church or federation of local eparchies (dioceses), with effective jurisdiction over all its bishops. The title "patriarch" (Heb., *nasi*) originally referred to the spiritual head of the Jewish Diaspora in the Roman Empire, and was also employed by the heretical Montanists. After 429, when Emperor Theosodius II suppressed the Jewish patriarchate, the title was applied to the principal bishops of a region. In 451 the Byzantine emperor Justinian I determined the five chief patriarchal sees as Rome, Constantinople, Alexandria, Antioch, and Jerusalem, and in the East the title became restricted to those sees. In the six Eastern Catholic churches with a patriarchal structure (Armenian, Chaldean, Coptic, Maronite, Melkite, West Syrian) the patriarch is subordinate to the pope. The Ukrainian Catholic Church also claims a patriarchal structure, but this has not yet been recognized by Rome. *See also* patriarchate; pentarchy.

patriarchal basilica. *See* basilica, patriarchal.

patriarchate, an autonomous, self-governing federation of dioceses under the jurisdiction of a chief bishop, called "patriarch," and his synod. The five most ancient patriarchates of Rome, Constantinople, Alexandria, Antioch, and Jerusalem were considered to form a ruling "pentarchy." Later developments, like the schisms following the councils of Ephesus (431) and Chalcedon (451), and the creation of national churches consequent upon the rise of new political entities from the sixteenth century on, led to the creation of numerous other Eastern and Oriental Orthodox patriarchates. Though the Catholic Church established nominal Latin patriarchates in the Middle Ages, the patriarchal system is basically an Eastern phenomenon. *See also* Latin patriarchates.

Patrick, St., ca. 390–ca. 461, bishop and apostle to Ireland. Born the son of a deacon and the grandson of a priest in Britain, he spent some years in slavery in Ireland after having been captured by border raiders. Returning to Britain (perhaps after spending

Patrick, known as the Apostle of the Irish, a fifth-century British missionary bishop who endured great hardships to plant the Catholic faith in Ireland and who remains the country's most popular saint and patron; sculptured stone, St. Patrick's Cathedral, New York.

time in Gaul), he was ordained to the priesthood and returned to Ireland to evangelize the country from his see in the north (Armagh), where he seems to have had a residence and a school. While not a monk himself, he strongly supported monasticism. We possess two authentic texts, both obscure and in bad Latin, from his own hand: a *Confessio*, an autobiographical apology, and the *Letter to Coroticus*, which protests British slave trading. The famous *Lorica* (Lat., "breastplate"), a work praising Christ attributed to Patrick, is probably his.

The traditional folk tales about Patrick (e.g., his using the shamrock to illustrate the concept of the Trinity, driving snakes from the island) are all pious elaborations of a later time. Feast day: March 17. *See also* Ireland, Catholicism in.

Patrick's Cathedral, St. *See* Saint Patrick's Cathedral.

Patrimony of St. Peter, lands in Italy under direct papal rule until 1870, also known as the Papal States. In 754 Pepin the Short gave the land between Rome and Ravenna taken from the defeated Lombards to the papacy instead of returning it to its former rulers, the Byzantine emperors. Papal control over these lands was sporadic until Pope Julius II (1503–13) established Rome's authority in a series of military campaigns. Many of the states joined the new Italian kingdom in 1860, and the remainder were seized by Italy in 1870. *See also* Papal States.

Patripassianism (Lat., "the suffering of the Father"), the belief that, in Christ's suffering and death, God suffered and died. It derived from Monarchianism, which emphasized unity in the Godhead. Patripassianism regarded the Son as merely a different mode of God and not a Person distinct from the Father. Thus, the Son's death meant God's death. This view was espoused by Praxaes (d. ca. 200), a theologian who was denounced by Tertullian. The trinitarian doctrine of the Second Council of Nicaea (787) excludes Patripassianism from Christian faith. *See also* Monarchianism.

patristics, a designation dating from the seventeenth century for the branch of theology dealing with the thought and culture of the Fathers (Lat., *patres*) of the Church, generally in the West up to Gregory I (d. 604) and in the East up to John of Damascus (d. 749). *See also* Fathers of the Church.

1. OCCUPATIONS AND GROUPS

accountants	Matthew
actors	Genesius
advertisers	Bernardino of Siena
altar boys	John Berchmans
anesthetists	René Goupil
architects	Thomas the Apostle
artists	Luke
	Catherine of Bologna
	Bl. Angelico
astronomers	Dominic
athletes	Sebastian
authors	Francis de Sales
aviators	Our Lady of Loreto
	Thérèse of Lisieux
	Joseph of Cupertino
bakers	Elizabeth of Hungary
	Nicholas
bankers	Matthew
barbers	Cosmas and Damian
	Louis
blacksmiths	Dunstan
bookbinders	Celestine V
bookkeepers	Matthew
booksellers	John of God
Boy Scouts	George
brewers	Augustine of Hippo
	Luke
	Nicholas of Myra
bricklayers	Stephen
brides	Nicholas of Myra
builders	Vincent Ferrer
butchers	Anthony of Egypt
	Luke
cabdrivers	Fiacre
cabinetmakers	Anne
canonists	Raymond of Peñafort
carpenters	Joseph
catechists	Viator
	Charles Borromeo
	Robert Bellarmine
children	Nicholas of Myra
clerics	Gabriel of the Sorrowful Mother
communications personnel	Bernardino of Siena
confessors	Alphonsus Liguori
	John Nepomucen
cooks	Lawrence
	Martha
coppersmiths	Maurus
dairy workers	Brigid of Ireland
dentists	Apollonia
dietitians, hospital	Martha
ecologists	Francis of Assisi
editors	John Bosco
engineers	Ferdinand III
farmers	George
	Isidore
firefighters	Florian
First Communicants	Tarcisius
fishermen	Andrew
florists	Thérèse of Lisieux
funeral directors	Joseph of Arimathea
	Dismas
gardeners	Adalhard
	Trypho
	Fiacre
	Phocas of Sinope
glassworkers	Luke
goldsmiths	Dunstan
	Anastasius
gravediggers	Anthony of Egypt
grocers	Michael
hairdressers	Martin de Porres
homemakers	Anne
hospital administrators	Basil the Great
	Frances Xavier Cabrini
hunters	Hubert
	Eustachius
immigrants	Frances Xavier Cabrini
innkeepers	Amand
	Martha
jewelers	Eligius
	Dunstan
journalists	Francis de Sales
jurists	John Capistrano
laborers	Isidore
	James
	John Bosco

967

lawyers	Ivo	preachers	John Chrysostom
	Genesius	priests	Jean-Baptiste Vianney (Curé
	Thomas More		d'Ars)
librarians	Jerome	printers	John of God
locksmiths	Dunstan		Augustine of Hippo
maids	Zita		Genesius
marbleworkers	Clement I	prisoners	Dismas
mariners	Michael		Joseph Cafasso
	Nicholas of Tolentino	public relations	Bernardino of Siena
medical technicians	Albertus Magnus	radiologists	Michael
messengers	Gabriel	radio workers	Gabriel
metalworkers	Eligius	sailors	Cuthbert
military chaplains	John Capistrano		Brendan
mothers	Monica		Eulalia
	Gerard Majella		Christopher
motorcyclists	Our Lady of Grace		Peter Gonzales
motorists	Christopher		Erasmus
	Frances of Rome		Nicholas
mountaineers	Bernard of Montjoux		Elmo
musicians	Gregory the Great	scholars	Brigid of Ireland
	Cecilia		Bede
	Dunstan		Jerome
notaries	Luke	scientists	Albertus Magnus
	Mark	sculptors	Four Crowned Martyrs
nurses	Camillus of Lellis	secretaries	Genesius
	John of God	seminarians	Charles Borromeo
	Agatha	servants	Martha
	Raphael		Zita
nursing and	Elizabeth of Hungary	shoemakers	Crispin and Crispinian
nursing services	Catherine of Siena	silversmiths	Andronicus
orators	John Chrysostom	singers	Gregory I "the Great"
painters	Luke		Cecilia
paratroopers	Michael	skaters	Lydwina
pawnbrokers	Nicholas	skiers	Bernard of Montjoux
pharmacists	Cosmas and Damian	social workers	Louise de Marillac
	James the Greater	soldiers	George
philosophers	Justin		Ignatius of Loyola
physicians	Pantaleon		Sebastian
	Cosmas and Damian		Martin of Tours
	Luke		Joan of Arc
	Raphael	speleologists	Benedict
pilgrims	James the Greater	stenographers	Genesius
plasterers	Bartholomew		Cassian
poets	David	stonecutters	Clement I
	Cecilia	stonemasons	Stephen
police officers	Michael	students	Thomas Aquinas
porters	Christopher	surgeons	Cosmas and Damian
postal employees	Gabriel		Luke
		tailors	Homobonus
		tax collectors	Matthew

teachers	Gregory the Great	watchmen	Peter of Alcantara
	Jean-Baptiste de La Salle	widows	Paula
telecommunications workers	Gabriel	wine merchants	Amand
		workers	Joseph
television workers	Gabriel	writers	Francis de Sales
		yachtsmen	Adjutor
theologians	Augustine	young boys	Dominic Savio
	Alphonsus Liguori	young girls	Agnes
travelers	Anthony of Padua	youth	Aloysius Gonzaga
	Nicholas of Myra		John Berchmans
	Christopher		Gabriel of the Sorrowful Mother
	Raphael		

2. SPECIAL CATEGORIES

animals	Francis of Assisi	hospitals	Camillus of Lellis
art	Catherine of Bologna		John of God
charitable societies	Vincent de Paul		Jude
Church	Joseph	missions, foreign	Francis Xavier
crops, protector of	Ansovinus		Thérèse of Lisieux
Eucharistic congresses and societies	Paschal Baylon	missions, parish	Leonard Casanova
		retreats	Ignatius of Loyola
expectant mothers	Raymond Nonnatus	schools, Catholic	Thomas Aquinas
	Gerard Majella		Joseph Calasanz
greetings	Valentine	television	Clare of Assisi
		universities	Bl. Contardo Ferrini
		vocations	Alphonsus Liguori

3. SPECIAL NEEDS

barren women	Anthony of Padua	heart patients	John of God
	Felicity	invalids	Roch
beggars	Martin of Tours	learning	Ambrose
blind	Odilia	mentally ill	Dymphna
	Raphael	orphans	Jerome Emiliani
blood banks	Januarius	poor	Lawrence
bodily ills	Our Lady of Lourdes		Anthony of Padua
cancer patients	Peregrine of Auxerre		Giles
		possessed	Bruno
convulsive children	Scholastica		Denis
deaf	Francis de Sales	rheumatism	James the Greater
desperate situations	Jude	searchers of lost articles	Anthony of Padua
	Rita of Cascia	sick	Michael
dog bites	Vitus		John of God
epilepsy	Vitus		Camillus of Lellis
	Willibrord	snake bites	Vitus
eye diseases	Lucy	throat ailments	Blaise
falsely accused	Raymond Nonnatus	women in labor	Anne
headache sufferers	Teresa of Ávila		

4. COUNTRIES AND REGIONS

Americas	Our Lady of Guadalupe
	Rose of Lima
Angola	Immaculate Heart of Mary
Argentina	Our Lady of Lujan
Armenia	Gregory the Illuminator
Australia	Our Lady Help of Christians
Belgium	Joseph
Bolivia	Our Lady of Copacabana ("Virgen de la Candelaria")
Brazil	Nossa Senhora de Aparecida
	Immaculate Conception
	Peter of Alcantara
Canada	Joseph
	Anne
Chile	James the Greater
	Our Lady of Mount Carmel
China	Joseph
Colombia	Peter Claver
	Louis Bertrand
Cuba	Our Lady of Charity
Cyprus	Barnabas
Czech Republic	Wenceslas
	John Nepomucen
	Procopius
Denmark	Ansgar
	Canute
Dominican Republic	Our Lady of High Grace
	Dominic
East Indies	Thomas the Apostle
Ecuador	Sacred Heart
El Salvador	Our Lady of Peace
England	George
Ethiopia	Frumentius
Europe	Benedict
	Cyril and Methodius (co-patrons)
Finland	Henry
France	Our Lady of the Assumption
	Joan of Arc
	Thérèse of Lisieux
Germany	Boniface
	Michael
Greece	Nicholas
	Andrew

Hungary	Blessed Virgin ("Great Lady of Hungary")
	Stephen of Hungary
Iceland	Thorlac
India	Our Lady of the Assumption
Ireland	Patrick
	Brigid and Columba
Italy	Francis of Assisi
	Catherine of Siena
Japan	Peter Baptist
Korea	Joseph and Mary
	Mother of the Church
Lithuania	Casimir
	Cunegund
	John Cantius
Luxembourg	Willibrord
Malta	Paul
	Our Lady of the Assumption
Mexico	Our Lady of Guadalupe
Monaco	Devota
Netherlands	Willibrord
New Zealand	Our Lady Help of Christians
Norway	Olaf
Papua New Guinea	Michael the Archangel
Paraguay	Our Lady of the Assumption
Peru	Joseph
Philippines	Sacred Heart of Mary
Poland	Casimir
	Cunegund
	Stanislaus Kostka
	Stanislaus of Cracow
	Our Lady of Czestochowa
	Florian
Portugal	Immaculate Conception
	Francis Borgia
	Anthony of Padua
	Vincent of Saragossa
	George
Russia	Andrew
	Nicholas of Myra
	Thérèse of Lisieux
Scandinavia	Ansgar
Scotland	Andrew
	Columba

Slovakia	Our Lady of Sorrows	Uruguay	Blessed Virgin Mary ("La Virgen de los Treinte y Tres")
South America	Rose of Lima		
Solomon Islands	Most Holy Name of Mary	Venezuela	Our Lady of Coromoto
Spain	James the Greater	Wales	David
	Teresa of Ávila	West Indies	Gertrude
Sri Lanka	Lawrence		
Sweden	Bridget		
	Eric		
Switzerland	Gall		
Tanzania	Immaculate Conception		
United States	Immaculate Conception		

patron saint, a saint venerated as a special protector or intercessor. Individual persons, occupations, churches, dioceses, countries, or particular problems may be under the protection of patron saints. A person's patron saint is the saint whose name is received at Baptism. The patron saint of the United States, for example, is Mary, under the title Immaculate Conception.

Saints usually become patrons of countries, professions, and special needs through popular devotion and custom rather than by any official designation. They may be closely associated with the history of a country, or have been engaged in some form of work associated with a particular profession, or have performed certain ministries or healings related to special needs. Sometimes, however, the connection is difficult, if not impossible, to ascertain. *See also* saints.

Paul I, St., d. 767, pope from 757 to 767, brother to Stephen II (III; d. 757), who received the Papal States from the Frankish king Pepin. Paul's diplomacy ensured their preservation. He assailed the iconoclasm of Emperor Constantine V, restored Roman churches, and translated many relics of saints from the catacombs to churches. Feast day: June 28. *See also* Papal States.

Paul III [Alessandro Farnese], 1468–1549, Counter-Reformation pope from 1534 to 1549. He was educated in Florence and was a friend of Medici pope Leo X. Alexander VI named him a cardinal (1493), but Farnese postponed ordination until 1519. He indulged in Renaissance Rome's lax morality and nepotism, but upon becoming pope, he also embarked decisively upon Church reform, calling unsuccessfully for a general council (1535, 1538). Paul finally convened the Council of Trent in 1545, suspending it in 1549 after noteworthy but incomplete reforms. He also endorsed reforming religious orders, notably the Jesuits (1540), and commissioned Michelangelo to paint the *Last Judgment* and to supervise the work on the new St. Peter's Basilica. In 1538 he excommunicated Henry VIII and placed England under interdict. *See also* Trent, Council of.

Paul IV [Gian Pietro Carafa], 1476–1559, Counter-Reformation pope from 1555 to 1559. He came to the Roman Curia from the Neapolitan nobility through his uncle Oliviero's influence. He participated in the Oratory of Divine Love (1520–27), was a model bishop of Chiete (where he founded the Theatines), and reorganized the Roman Inquisition against Italian Protestants (1542). As pope, he refused to reconvene the suspended Council of Trent, believing that he could carry on the necessary reforms on his own initiative more effectively and more quickly. Although he enforced some needed reforms, such as insisting that bishops live in their dioceses and monks in their monasteries, his approach was often harsh and severe. In 1559 he intensified censorship and his own unpopularity through the Roman *Index Librorum Prohibitorum* (Lat., "Index of Forbidden Books"). He also allowed the Inquisition to harm many innocent people, such as Cardinal Giovanni Morone (d. 1580), who was wrongly imprisoned for heresy. And it was also Paul IV who confined Roman Jews to a ghetto on the suspicion that they were somehow aiding Protestants. *See also* Index of Forbidden Books; Inquisition; Theatines.

ST. PAUL

S t. Paul was the prominent early Christian missionary and "apostle to the Gentiles." Paul, whose Jewish name was Saul, was born in Tarsus in Asia Minor of a Hellenistic-Jewish family probably between A.D. 1 and 5. He received both Greek and Jewish education and probably possessed Roman citizenship. Paul described himself as a Pharisee (Phil 3:5) and received some of his Jewish education in Jerusalem beginning around A.D. 30. Shortly afterward he "persecuted" the early believers in Jesus because of his zealousness as a Pharisee (Gal 1:13–14; 1 Cor 15:9). Contrary to Acts 9:1–2, this probably involved only subjecting them to the normal punishments of the synagogue, including flogging and exclusion from the Jewish community, rather than either imprisonment or capital punishment. About A.D. 35, on the way to Damascus, Paul experienced what he described as a revelation by God of the risen Jesus (Gal 1:15–16). Paul interpreted this experience as a call to preach the risen Jesus to the Gentiles. After spending three years in the area around Damascus (A.D. 35–38), Paul spent the next ten years (A.D. 38–48, his first missionary journey) preaching in Syria and Asia Minor. In 48 he was part of a delegation sent from Antioch to Jerusalem to discuss with the leaders of the Jerusalem community the status of gentile believers (Gal 2:1–10; Acts 15:1–35). The two groups finally agreed that gentile Christians did not have to be circumcised or observe Mosaic law but that Jewish Christians would continue to do both. Paul spent the next eight years establishing Christian communities around the eastern Mediterranean. The center of operations for his second missionary journey (A.D. 49–52) was Corinth in Greece; the center for the third missionary journey (53–57) was Ephesus in Asia Minor. While Jewish members were prominent in these Christian communities, the majority were of gentile origin. During these journeys (especially the third), he wrote the letters that form part of the NT. In A.D. 57 he returned to Jerusalem, where he was arrested and imprisoned for two years. In 59, exercising his prerogative as a Roman citizen to appeal his case to Caesar, he was sent by the procurator, Porcius Festus, to Rome (59–60) and was held there under house arrest for approximately two years. Between A.D. 62 and 67 he was executed in Rome by the Roman authorities.

St. Paul, the greatest missionary in the history of the Church; painting by Masaccio, Civic Museum, Pisa, Italy.

WRITINGS

Paul made extensive use of letters to maintain contact with and direct the communities he had established. Of the thirteen Letters attributed to Paul in the NT, seven are generally agreed on as written by Paul: 1 Thessalonians, Galatians, 1–2 Corinthians, Philippians, Philemon, and Romans. The Letters were written between A.D. 51 and 57. 1 Thessalonians was written in 51 from Corinth on Paul's second missionary journey; its purpose was to assure the Thessalonian Christians that those of their number who had already died would not be at a disadvantage at Jesus' coming in power. The other Letters were written during Paul's third

Paul, newly converted to Christ after he himself had persecuted Christians, disputes with the Jews of Damascus about the Christian claim that Jesus is the Messiah (Acts 9:19–22); when the Jews plot to kill him, his disciples take him by night and "let him down through an opening in the wall, lowering him in a basket" (9:25); mosaic in the Palatine Chapel, Palermo, Italy.

missionary journey. Galatians (A.D. 53–54) was written from Ephesus to oppose the preaching of Jewish-Christian missionaries who claimed that Christians were obliged not only to believe in Jesus but also to be circumcised and observe at least part of Mosaic law. 1–2 Corinthians (A.D. 54–56), written partly from Ephesus and partly from Macedonia, reflect the complex and rocky relationship between Paul and the Corinthian Christians over a number of issues, including the Corinthians' interpretation of their Christian beliefs on the analogy of Greek mystery cults (1 Corinthians) and their fascination with mystically oriented Hellenistic-Jewish interpretations of the Scriptures (2 Corinthians, which combines

Twelfth-century mosaic depicting four scenes from the life of Paul: his baptism, his preaching, his escape from the city of Damascus by being dropped over the wall in a basket (Acts 9:25), and his handing over of his letters to Timothy and another disciple.

several letters). Philippians (A.D. 55–56), also a composite, again deals with the problem of Christians and the observance of Mosaic law. Philemon, written during the same period, deals with the problem of the runaway slave Onesimus. Paul's last extant Letter is to the Romans, written from Corinth in 57. In it Paul assures the Roman Christian community that his controversial views about the observance of Mosaic law were ultimately in accord with the Jewish Scriptures and tradition.

THEOLOGY

Although Paul was controversial both during his lifetime and subsequently, many of his basic convictions were traditional, rooted in Judaism and early Christianity. Two of his basic convictions were belief in Jewish monotheism and belief in the revelation of God in the Jewish Scriptures. Hence Paul always thought of himself as a Jew, both ethnically and religiously. From Christian tradition and his own experience on the road to Damascus came his conviction about the centrality of Christ, especially of his death and Resurrection. Also characteristic of Paul is his conviction, rooted in his experience of the risen Jesus, about the relationship between Jews and Gentiles and the status of Mosaic law. For Paul there was "in Christ" no longer any distinction between Jews and Gentiles (Gal 3:28; Rom 3:22); all are saved through faith in Christ rather than through the observance of Mosaic law (Rom 3:21–30). Through faith in Christ there is no longer any need for either Jewish or gentile Christians to observe Mosaic law as such. Although there is some dispute, Paul seems to have included in this both the ritual and the ethical sections of the law. Christian conduct was now to be guided by the presence of the Spirit, by faith working through love, and by Christians becoming servants of one another (Gal 5–6). Paul also had a belief, based on but expanded from early Christian eschatology, that in the consummation of the world all things would be subjected to Christ and to God. For Paul this included the Jewish people (Rom 9–11). Although the precise manner of this inclusion remains uncertain, it is clear that Paul could not imagine a consummation of the world in which the Jewish people were not included. Paul's reputation in the second and third centuries remained controversial, especially for Jewish Christians. Interpretations of Paul's Letters were central to the thought of Augustine, Aquinas, Luther, and Calvin. Feast days: January 29 (Conversion) and June 29 (Peter and Paul).

Bibliography

Bultmann, Rudolf. *The Theology of the New Testament.* 2 vols. New York: Scribner, 1952–55. 1.185–352.

Fitzmyer, Joseph A. *Paul and His Theology: A Brief Sketch.* 2d ed. Englewood Cliffs, NJ: Prentice Hall, 1989.

Meeks, Wayne. *The First Urban Christians: The Social World of the Apostle Paul.* New Haven, CT: Yale University Press, 1983.

Sanders, E. P. *Paul and Palestinian Judaism.* Philadelphia: Fortress, 1977.

Segal, Alan E. *Paul the Convert: The Apostolate and Apostasy of Saul the Pharisee.* New Haven, CT: Yale University Press, 1990.

THOMAS H. TOBIN

Paul V [Camillo Borghese], 1552–1621, Counter-Reformation pope, from 1605 to 1621. Important for completing work on St. Peter's Basilica, for rebuilding the aqueduct of Trajan in Rome, and for enforcing the reforms of the Council of Trent, he placed Venice under interdict for rejecting papal claims to temporal power and for trying clerics in secular courts (1606–7). Although he published a revised *Roman Ritual*, tightened discipline in religious orders, and approved the use of the vernacular in the Chinese liturgy, he was also infamous for having censured Galileo (1616) and placing Copernicus's treatise on the movement of the earth around the sun on the Index of Forbidden Books. *See also* Galileo.

Paul VI [Giovanni Battista Montini], 1897–1978, pope from 1963 to 1978, who guided the Church during its difficult post–Vatican II transition. He was prepared for the papal office by working intimately with popes Pius XI (d. 1939) and Pius XII (d. 1958). He assisted then-Cardinal Pacelli (later

Pope Paul VI, whose task it was to carry forward the work of the Second Vatican Council following Pope John XXIII's death and then to guide the implementation of its reforms in the face of misunderstanding and opposition from conservatives and progressives alike.

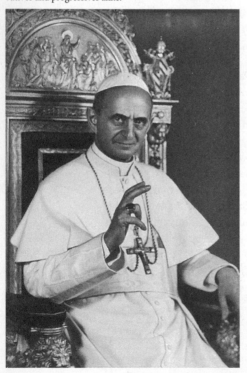

Pius XII) in the Secretariat of State, became pro-secretary in 1952, and archbishop of Milan in 1954. A liberal in liturgy, ecumenism, and social questions, he had long advocated the "internationalization" of the Curia. But he had not expected the council called by his friend Pope John XXIII and thought at first that it would stir up "a hornet's nest of problems." His spiritual adviser told him to relax in the Holy Spirit.

So Paul VI—his name was chosen to express the adventurous, outgoing spirit of Paul the missionary to the Gentiles—had to conclude a council that he would not himself have called. He had already helped rescue the first session from chaos by providing it with an architecture that he realized in his pontificate. He had to be won over to collegiality, reassured that it did not undermine the primacy. But once convinced, he loyally accepted the council's authority.

His hesitations on documents concerning religious liberty, ecumenism, and the Jews were all motivated by his desire to ensure that the defeated minority was not simply crushed. He wanted them to be *convaincus, pas vaincus* (Fr., "convinced, not vanquished"). Sometimes he made too many concessions to achieve this end, notably with the *nota praevia* (Lat., "prefatory note," which really served as an appendix) on collegiality, which tried to dilute the Dogmatic Constitution on the Church's emphasis on episcopal authority at the alleged expense of the pope's.

Papal Journeys: Paul influenced the council by his journeys, infrequent and well thought out. He went first to the Holy Land, from which St. Peter came, and there embraced the ecumenical patriarch of Constantinople, Athenagoras (d. 1972). This "return to the sources" had great ecumenical potential. With the assistance of Father Theodore M. Hesburgh, president of the University of Notre Dame, Paul established Tantur in Israel, an ecumenical project to reflect on salvation history in an atmosphere of study and prayer. His second visit was to India, a land of ancient religious traditions that welcomed him as a holy man. Then he went to the United Nations in New York on the feast of St. Francis, 1965, met the whole world in miniature and proclaimed, "Never again war!" In 1966 he longed to go to Poland for the millennium celebrations, but the Polish government denied his request.

Apart from their intrinsic significance, these journeys spoke of the Church's relations with non-

Christian religions and with nonbelievers—the outer circles he had spoken of in his first programmatic encyclical, *Ecclesiam Suam* (1964). Paul set up secretariats to deal with both of these matters. They joined the Secretariat for Christian Unity and the Justice and Peace Commission to form the "new Curia," which was contrasted with the old in its readiness to listen and the fact that it had corresponding local bodies. It proved more difficult to renew the habits of the old Curia, but by shrewd appointments Paul tried to make it more responsive. He was greatly aided from 1969 by Cardinal Giovanni Benelli, the human dynamo who was *sostituto* (Ital., "substitute" [secretary of state]). Benelli's power grew when Paul appointed that same year a French secretary of state, Cardinal Jean Villot.

Paul's most important innovation was to found the Synod of Bishops as an instrument of collegial consultation. Elected representatives of the episcopal conferences were to offer "advice and information" to the pope. In 1971 the synod dealt with justice in the world (and produced a fine text) and the ministerial priesthood (at which a proposal for the ordination of married men was narrowly defeated). Though the 1974 synod on evangelization ended in confusion, it provided Paul with the raw material for his finest apostolic exhortation, *Evangelii Nuntiandi* (1975). The 1977 synod on catechesis came too late for him to do more than accept it.

The Pope and Controversy: Little collegial consultation, however, took place before his famous encyclical on birth control, *Humanae Vitae* (1968). The withdrawal of contraception from the competence of the council had been justified on the grounds that a pontifical commission existed to deal with it. However, the advice of the commission was then set aside, so that *Humanae Vitae* looked like a solo exercise of the primacy. The Extraordinary Synod of 1969 dealt with the aftermath of reconciling primacy and collegiality. *Humanae Vitae* was never presented as irreversible, still less infallible, and Paul resisted attempts to make it the be-all and end-all of his pontificate. Insofar as it posits a permanent element in human sexuality and insists on the equal importance of the unitive and procreative aspect of human sexuality, it contained a valuable insight.

Clerical celibacy was the other topic withdrawn from the council's competence. This was harder to justify. Paul's encyclical *Sacerdotalis Caelibatus* (1967) showed the fittingness of celibacy, but could do no more, given the existence of married priests in the Eastern Catholic churches. Besides, by restoring the permanent diaconate, Paul ensured that there would be married clerics in the Church. In his apostolic letter *Ministeria Quaedam* (1972) we hear for the first time of "lay ministries," and episcopal conferences were invited to be "creative." Though the Congregation for the Doctrine of the Faith's *Inter Insignores* (1976) said no to women's ordination, it was not presented as a definitive statement for all time.

In the Third World Paul's most important encyclical was *Populorum Progressio* (1967), which spoke of "development as the new name for peace." It also cautiously stated the conditions under which there might be a "just revolution." Right-wing papers dismissed it as "souped-up Marxism." Even more acceptable to the liberation theologians of Latin America was *Octogesima Adveniens* (1971), which finessed on "socialisms" and admitted that such was the complexity of the modern world that no universal teaching could be provided. The task of "discerning the signs of the times" fell to the local churches.

Paul believed that relations with the Orthodox were crucial, for this was the original schism. His relations with the ecumenical patriarch were good. The excommunication of 1054 was lifted. Koinonia (Gk., "communion") was made the basis for theological unity. The brother patriarchs exchanged the kiss of peace in Rome and Constantinople, thus indicating that they belonged to "sister churches." The same language was used of the Anglican communion. Paul received two archbishops of Canterbury, Dr. Michael Ramsey (1966) and Dr. Donald Coggan (1977), by which time the Anglican/Roman Catholic International Commission (ARCIC) had revealed "convergences that were as happy as they were unexpected," as the common statement read.

Paul died on the feast of the Transfiguration, August 6, 1978. Though much criticized, even ridiculed, in his lifetime, nostalgia for his pontificate has increased notably in the years since his death. *See also* Ecclesiam Suam; Evangelii Nuntiandi; Humanae Vitae; Octogesima Adveniens; Populorum Progressio; Vatican Council II.

Bibliography

Hebblethwaite, Peter. *Paul VI: The First Modern Pope.* New York: Paulist Press, 1993.   *PETER HEBBLETHWAITE*

Paula, St., 347–404, ascetic. A married Roman noblewoman under Jerome's guidance, she devoted herself to a life of charity and penance and founded a convent and monastery in Bethlehem. She is the patron saint of widows. Feast day: January 26.

Paul and Thecla, Acts of, second-century apocryphal work describing, in the style of Hellenistic romance, the miraculous missionary adventures of Paul, not always appearing to advantage, and Thecla of Iconium, a convert and companion of Paul whom Paul commissioned to teach and to baptize. According to tradition she established a ministry in Seleucia of Isauria, where she taught, cared for the poor, and healed the sick. While Tertullian (d. ca. 225) denied that her example provided warrant for baptisms by women, fourth-century evidence shows her faith and ascetic virtue commended by both women and men, and her name was often taken by vowed virgins including Macrina (d. 379), older sister of Basil the Great and Gregory of Nyssa. Thecla's feast day was celebrated in the East on September 24 and in the West on September 23, but her name was dropped from the calendar of saints at the time of Vatican Council II (1962–65).

Paul Chong Hasang, St. (pawl chong hahsahng'), d. 1846, Korean seminarian and martyr. The Korean martyrs were collectively canonized in 1984 by Pope Paul II. Feast day: September 20.

Pauline privilege. *See* Privilege of the Faith.

Paulinus of Nola, St., ca. 355–431, bishop of Nola (409–31). From a family of noblest rank, Paulinus was baptized (389), withdrew from public office, and with his wife, Teresia, gave away an immense fortune, retiring to the shrine of St. Felix at Nola where they founded an ascetic community. Many of Paulinus's poems and letters survive. Feast day: June 22.

Paulists, formally known as the Missionary Society of St. Paul the Apostle (C.S.P.), an order founded by Isaac Thomas Hecker (d. 1888) dedicated to serving English-speaking Catholics and winning American converts to the Catholic Church. Hecker, an American convert, evangelist, and Redemptorist priest, visited Rome to seek permission to expand the work of parish missions among English-speaking Catholics in the United States. The Redemptorists were strongly identified with work among German-Americans. Dismissed from the Redemptorists for coming to Rome without permis-

sion, Hecker appealed to the pope and, together with four Redemptorist associates, won permission to establish a new religious order. The original Paulist band included Augustine F. Hewit, Francis Baker, and George Deshon. They made solemn promises rather than vows and emphasized individual initiative and flexibility in the apostolate. Their rule was given final approval by the Holy See in 1940.

Under Hecker's leadership, they established St. Paul the Apostle Parish in New York City, offered missions in English-speaking parishes, and initiated efforts to attract non-Catholics by means of lectures, a magazine (*The Catholic World*), and a publishing house, later known as the Paulist Press. Always a small community, the Paulists continued this combination of internal and external evangelization, the former through their own parishes, parish missions, and ministry on non-Catholic university campuses in the United States and Canada. They achieved recognition for innovative missionary work among non-Catholics through publications, urban information centers, home missions, and use of the mass media. *See also* Hecker, Isaac Thomas.

DAVID O'BRIEN

Paulists, Melkite, a men's missionary society of the Melkite Catholic Church founded in Lebanon in 1903 by Bishop Germanos Mouaccad to preach retreats and missions, work for the "return" of the Orthodox to Rome, staff schools, and maintain a Catholic publishing house. Since Vatican II (1962–65) the society has worked to strengthen both the Orthodox and Melkite Catholic churches. *See also* Melkite Catholic Church.

Paul Miki, St., d. 1597, Jesuit brother and martyr. One of twenty-six martyrs for the faith who were crucified in Nagasaki and canonized in 1862. Feast day: February 5.

Paul of Samosata, third century, bishop of Antioch from ca. 260 to 268, when he was deposed. Paul taught an Adoptionist Monarchianism, advocating a consubstantiality between Father and Logos (perhaps even using the Gk. *homoousios*) that conceded no independence whatsoever to the Logos, which he conceived as God's governing power. Because it indwelt Jesus, he became God's "Son." There is no preexistent "Son." Jesus differs from the prophets and saints only in the degree of indwelling. *See also* Monarchianism.

Paul of Thebes, St., also known as Paul the Hermit, d. ca. 340, an early Christian hermit. Jerome provides all that is known about Paul, namely, that he lived a hermit's life until he was 113 and that Anthony of Egypt buried him in a cloak owned by Athanasius. Feast day: January 15.

Paul of the Cross, St., 1694–1775, founder of the Passionists. Born in Italy as Paul Francis Danei, he is said to have had a vision of Our Lady in a black habit with the name Jesus and a cross in white on the chest. She told him to found a religious order devoted to the preaching of the Passion of Christ. Paul himself became one of the most celebrated preachers of his time. He also founded an institute of Passionist nuns. Feast day: October 19. *See also* Passionists.

Paul the Deacon, ca. 720–ca. 799, Carolingian monk and scholar. A Lombard nobleman educated at Pavia, Paul entered the monastery of Monte Cassino when Charlemagne conquered Lombardy (774), later (ca. 782–84) visiting Charlemagne's court. Among other works, he wrote a *History of the Lombards* and compiled a *Homiliary* based upon patristic sources. *See also* Charlemagne; Monte Cassino.

Pax Christi USA, an affiliate of the Catholic European peace organization, Pax Christi International. In 1972 Pax Christi USA grew out of the American Pax Association. Pax Christi USA's primary orientation is gospel-inspired nonviolence; the organization is committed to making the Church an instrument of peacemaking. Two bishops, Carroll T. Dozier (d. 1985) of Memphis and Thomas J. Gumbleton of Detroit, agreed to act as its first episcopal moderators.

The organization publishes a quarterly magazine, organizes an annual national assembly, publishes and disseminates informational literature, and encourages local and regional development with peace groups and parishes. In 1992 the organization had over eleven thousand members, ninety-two of whom were bishops. *See also* pacifism.

Payne, St. John, d. 1582, one of the Forty Martyrs of England and Wales canonized in 1970. Ordained at Douai in 1576 and sent to Essex, he was arrested in 1581 and executed in 1582. Feast day: April 20. *See also* Forty Martyrs of England and Wales.

Pazzi, St. Mary Magdalen Dei, 1566–1607, virgin and nun. Spurning an arranged marriage, she entered a Carmelite convent against her parents' wishes. She fasted on bread and water except on Sundays and holy days and cured many sick people. Her body lies in the church attached to the Carmelite convent in Florence. She was canonized in 1669. Feast day: May 25.

peace, a state of ordered tranquility. In the Catholic tradition, peace is not merely the absence of overt conflict, but the result of right relationships with God and neighbor. This is evident in three key sources for reflection on peace: Scripture, the writings of Thomas Aquinas (d. 1274), and Catholic social teaching.

In the OT the term for peace is *shalom* (Heb.), which is best understood as the spiritual and material well-being of both persons individually and the community as a whole that results from fidelity to the covenant with God. The covenant, and thus peace itself, is initially a gift from God. The close link between peace and the covenantal relationship with God is evident in Isa 54:10: "My covenant of peace shall not be removed." The gift of the covenant is to the community as a whole, and includes, therefore, right relationship with the neighbor. In the NT, Jesus Christ becomes the means of this peace. He offers peace (John 14:27) and, ultimately, is this peace (Eph 2:14).

In the work of Thomas Aquinas, peace is tranquility both within and between persons. Within the individual, it is the harmony of the desires when the soul is directed by charity to its true good, that is, God. Full peace is not attainable in this lifetime, but a partial peace is possible when the will and the intellect control and guide the desires. Charity prompts peace to extend beyond the person when it directs her to love her neighbor as herself. This leads the person to desire to fulfill the neighbor's will as if it were her own. Justice, motivated by charity, regulates the external relations between persons and thus describes the order of peace.

Catholic social teaching since Pope Leo XIII (d. 1903) continues to understand peace as the fruit of a right relationship grounded in justice and directed by charity. Because justice concerns the external ordering of charity, the social teaching often makes an explicit link between justice and peace. Pope Pius XII's (d. 1958) motto was *Opus iustitiae pax* (Lat., "Peace is the work of justice"). Pope John XXIII (d. 1963) picks up this concern for the relationship between peace and justice, particularly in *Pacem in Terris* (1963), where a social order based on truth, justice, charity, and freedom is the source of peace. Pope Paul VI (d. 1978) argues in *Populorum Progressio* (1967) that economic inequality leads to violence and that a just economic development of poorer peoples is "the new name for peace." Pope John Paul II sums up the idea of right relationship with neighbor under the term "solidarity" and writes, *"Opus solidaritatis pax"* ("Peace is the work of solidarity").

In the event of an outbreak of war, Catholic teaching recognizes two legitimate responses. The first is that of the just-war tradition, which holds that for the sake of justice it is sometimes legitimate to use carefully circumscribed lethal armed force. The second is pacifism, which holds that it is never legitimate to take human life. Both pacifist and just-war traditions seek peace, but they diverge on the question of the appropriate means. *See also* Catholic social teachings; *Pacem in Terris;* pacifism; peace movement, Catholic. TODD D. WHITMORE

peace movement, Catholic, organizations and initiatives devoted to peace and nonviolence. In 1927 John A. Ryan founded the first Catholic peace organization in American history and called it the Catholic Association for International Peace (CAIP). Prior to World War II it had grown in size to five hundred members. When the United States entered World War II, the organization sanctioned the actions of the government and declared that the nation was engaged in a just war. After the war, the CAIP declined in significance.

The first Catholic group in the United States to identify with the American peace movement and to challenge the just-war doctrine was the Catholic Worker, when its cofounder, Dorothy Day (d. 1980), first proclaimed Catholic pacifism during the Spanish Civil War and maintained this position through all subsequent wars. Dorothy Day and the Catholic Worker supported the 223 Catholic conscientious objectors during World War II.

After World War II, the Catholic Worker added nonviolence to its Catholic pacifist position and in the 1960s fostered the growth of Catholic peace groups. In 1962 the American Pax Association (PAX) was founded. Its aim was to have the Catholic Church in the United States recognize conscientious objection. In 1964 the Catholic Peace Fellowship (CPF), an affiliate of the interfaith Fellowship of Reconciliation, was formed to provide draft counseling and oppose the war in Vietnam. When Daniel and Phillip Berrigan, priests and brothers, left CPF to perform the draft board action at Catonsville, Maryland, Catholics emerged at the forefront of the American peace movement.

In November 1968, the U.S. Catholic hierarchy in the pastoral letter "Human Life in Our Day" declared that Catholic teaching supported conscientious objectors and selective conscientious objectors. By 1969, 2,494 Catholics had received conscientious objector status, representing the single largest percentage of all American religious bodies. Finally, in November 1971 the bishops condemned the war in Vietnam as unjust. It was the first time in history that a Catholic hierarchy had condemned its own nation's war effort.

The organization of Pax Christi USA in 1972 was one of the most important developments in the post-Vietnam phase of the Catholic peace movement. Its aim was to make the Catholic Church an instrument of peacemaking. In their 1983 pastoral letter "The Challenge of Peace: God's Promise and Our Response," the U.S. bishops for the first time condemned nuclear warfare and indicated that pacifism and nonviolence are as valid a position to hold in response to war as the just-war doctrine, specifically, that pacifism and the just-war doctrine "support and complement one another, each preserving the other from distortion" (n. 121). *See also* Catholic Worker movement; Day, Dorothy M.; just-war doctrine; pacifism; Pax Christi USA. PATRICIA MCNEAL

Peace of Westphalia, treaty ending the Thirty Years' War (1618–48). Westphalia reconfirmed the religious articles of the Peace of Augsburg (1555), including the *cuius regio, eius religio* principle (Lat., "whose region, his religion"), but extended legal recognition to the Calvinists and gave individuals greater freedom of worship and belief. The papacy condemned the treaty, but it remained in effect until 1806. *See also Cuius regio, eius religio.*

Peasants' Revolt, or Peasants' War (1524–25), a rebellion in Germany against the Catholic Church and feudal lords. Appealing to the message of Martin Luther, German peasants attacked monasteries and castles seeking redress of traditional economic and political grievances. Rejected by Luther, the revolt was put down with ferocity by the armies of the Protestant princes. *See also* Luther, Martin.

Peckham, John, ca. 1225–92, master in theology at Oxford and Paris, Franciscan, and archbishop of

Canterbury (from 1279). He was much concerned with pastoral care and clerical reform, although his Augustinianism led him to reject (1286) some teachings of Thomas Aquinas as heretical. *See also* Canterbury.

pectoral cross, a cross of precious metal worn by bishops and abbots on the chest and suspended from a chain around the neck. In some Eastern churches, it is worn also by priests.

Péguy, Charles (pay-gee'), 1873–1914, French poet, dramatist, essayist. Born in Orléans, Péguy was educated at the École Normale Supérieur, where he embraced socialism. Péguy soon abandoned Catholicism, opened a socialist center in Orléans, became a disciple of Henri Bergson, and actively crusaded against the injustices of the Dreyfus affair. Péguy founded the *Cahiers de la Quinzaine* (1900–1914), a journal for uncensored political and philosophical discussion. In 1908 Péguy reclaimed his Catholic heritage and, until his death at the Battle of the Marne, worked to bring about an alliance between Catholicism and socialism. His poetry and poetic drama were designed to express the mysteries of faith, e.g., *Le Mystère de la Charité de Jeanne d'Arc.*

Pelagianism, the body of teaching about divine grace connected with Pelagius (ca. 350–ca. 425), an ascetic teacher in Rome. Pelagius, probably a British Celt by birth, emphasized in his reformist teaching the freedom of the human will and the necessity of good works for the Christian. His teaching asserts human freedom against Manichaean fatalism, emphasizing the human capacity or ability to do good. The freedom to choose rather than to act by natural necessity separates humans from all other creatures. This ability, given by God, is grace according to Pelagius; the desire for, and the realization of, the good lies within human nature. Because all people are fundamentally free to choose good or evil, one could theoretically live without sin, though such a case would be exceedingly rare. Humans are born without an inherent proclivity to sin, though the force of habit gives sin a particular power over us. No special, supernatural grace is needed for one to choose the good. For Pelagius, the grace needed to live a holy life consists in: the primal gift of free will; the law of Moses; Christ's redemptive death; and the teaching and example of Christ.

Around 409 Pelagius left Rome, and passed through Carthage on the way to Palestine. His disciple Celestius was condemned at Carthage in 412 for asserting the sinlessness of infants prior to baptism, and Pelagius's own teaching was first attacked directly by Jerome in 413. Pelagius's treatise *On Nature,* written ca. 414, drew a reply in Augustine's *On Nature and Grace* (415), the first of his many explicitly anti-Pelagian tracts. Successive synods in 415, first in Jerusalem, then in Diospolis, failed to find anything objectionable, at least to Eastern opinion, in Pelagius's teaching. The North African bishops condemned Pelagius and Celestius in synods at Carthage and Milevis (416) and requested a judgment from Innocent, bishop of Rome. Innocent excommunicated Pelagius and Celestius in three letters of January 417, saying that *On Nature* blasphemously denied the need of divine grace. In 418, in the wake of the Sixteenth Council of Carthage and an imperial banishment of Pelagius and Celestius, Pope Zosimus issued his *Epistola tractoria* renewing their excommunication. Eighteen Italian bishops led by Julian of Eclanum refused to subscribe to Zosimus's letter, and until Augustine's death in 430 Julian was the main spokesman for the Pelagian viewpoint. Monastic writers like John Cassian (d. 435) and Faustus of Riez in Gaul (d. ca. 490), while not endorsing Pelagius's doctrine, continued to express reservations through much of the fifth century about the more extreme elements of Augustine's anti-Pelagian works. *See also* grace; nature and grace; semi-Pelagianism; sin.   THOMAS SMITH

pelican, ancient symbol for Christ. Attested as early as the sixth century, the symbolism derives from the folk belief that pelicans pierced their breasts with their beaks to nourish their young with their own blood.

Pelletier, St. Mary Euphrasia, 1796–1868, French founder of the Sisters of Our Lady of Charity of the Good Shepherd to care for girls and women who were considered "wayward." In 1835 she received papal approval to centralize the government of a group of independent convents involved in this work. She was canonized in 1940. Feast day: April 24.

penal law, norms that regulate penalties for the violation of Church laws. Although the Church is a society based on forgiveness, it is argued that some form of penal law is necessary to facilitate the conversion of the wrongdoer and to maintain public order. The first of these ends is met by what are called censures or medicinal penalties; the second, by what are called expiatory penalties. In addition, there are lesser penalties called penances that are also regulated by penal law.

Penal law is considered "odious" in the canonical tradition, and so is to be interpreted strictly. It is to be understood in as narrow a manner as possible so that there are as few ecclesiastical crimes as possible and consequently as few ecclesiastical penalties as possible. Penal law considers certain causes to diminish, at least partially, the culpability of a given individual. When the moral culpability is diminished, there is a consequent diminishment of the gravity of a crime. Such diminishment can result in the total abolition or diminution of a penalty.

The censures levied in Church law are three: excommunication, suspension, and interdict. Suspension is a penalty that limits the ability of a cleric to perform his ministry. Both excommunication and interdict in varying degrees distance a person from the life of the Christian community and the celebration of the sacraments. Although in the former law (1917) interdict could be levied against a whole group of the faithful, current law (1983) understands it as a penalty appropriate for use only against an individual.

The commission of some crimes automatically incurs a given penalty. These are *latae sententiae* (Lat., "concealed [automatic] sentences") penalties. In the 1983 revision of the code of canon law their number has been considerably lessened; Pope Paul VI ordered that they be fewer in number and used only for more serious offenses.

At times a penalty is inflicted as the result of a trial or an administrative procedure; such a penalty is called a *ferendae sententiae* ("imposed sentences") penalty. In such a trial or procedure there are provisions in canon law to guard the rights of the accused. Failing to follow procedure might result in the invalidity of the sentence rendered.

Penalties are ordinarily pardoned by the local bishop or someone to whom the bishop has entrusted such remission. Some penalties for the most serious matters can be lifted only by the Holy See. Examples of the latter include desecration of the Eucharist, violation of the seal of confession, and laying violent hands upon the pope. Permission to lift penalties for crimes confessed in secret is to be obtained in a fashion that does not violate the confidentiality of the confessional. *See also* censure.

JOHN F. LAHEY

penalties. *See* penal law.

penance, 1 the sacrament of Penance, or of Reconciliation; **2** the prayers or works one performs at the direction of one's confessor after receiving the sacrament; **3** a prayer or work one does, independently of the sacraments, to express sorrow for sin. In almost all religious movements, the realization of sin, i.e., a transgression against God, has stirred followers to lead lives in which they realign themselves with a religiously correct set of moral standards. In the Christian framework, there are clearly defined elements: (1) a transcendent personal God has created the world and established a normative structure; (2) through the gift of free will and the presence of original sin human beings deliberately transgress this normative structure; and (3) Jesus Christ alone has provided redress (redemption) for human sinfulness. Christian life, therefore, is basically penitential: Christians freely acknowledge their sinfulness and their dependence on Jesus. Following Jesus often requires moral behavior that is at odds with the prevailing culture and that demands sacrifice, suffering, and even death, patterned after Jesus' own Passion and crucifixion. It also involves an attempt to minimize both sin and the temptation to sin. In medieval Catholic life, Penance became a common name for the sacrament of Reconciliation. In the renewed rite of this sacrament, after Vatican II (1962–65), each form of the ritual is called a "rite of Reconciliation," and the entire ritual an "order of Penance." *See also* Reconciliation.

penance service, communal, the sacrament of Reconciliation observed within a liturgical assembly of more than two members. The Book of Rites allows for two forms of communal penance. Form two is celebrated whenever there are several penitents. A Liturgy of the Word is held in common followed by the private confession by each penitent and individual absolution bestowed by a single confessor. Form three is celebrated in emergencies or whenever the number of penitents disproportionately exceeds the number of available confessors. Following the Liturgy of the Word, form three concludes with a communal confession of sins and general absolution pronounced over the entire assembly. Form one is the rite for the reconciliation of individual penitents. *See also* Reconciliation.

penitential books, catalogues compiled for confessors specifying the appropriate penance for various sins. Appearing first in Welsh and Irish monasteries in the sixth century, they exerted influence through the eleventh. Penitentials by Vinnian (ca. 549), Columbanus (ca. 590), Cummean (ca. 650), and Theodore (ca. 700) prescribed fasting, psalm recitation, and often permitted monetary commutations to substitute for rigorous physical satisfactions.

In the eighth century, following Irish and Anglo-Saxon missions, penitential books became influential throughout Latin European Christianity, bringing confusion as disparate compilations judged sins and penances in widely different fashion, some overemphasizing the possibility of monetary commutation. Carolingian reformers sought to base practice on ancient church canons, but penitential books continued to be widely used until they were superseded by the appearance of more sophisticated general guides for confessors such as that by Alan of Lille (d. 1203). *See also* confession, auricular; Irish tariff penance; moral theology.

Penitential Rite, part of the opening rite in the celebration of the Eucharist. After the entrance hymn and the greeting by the presider there are three possible forms that this prayer may take. The Confiteor ("I confess to Almighty God") may be recited by all, a short call and response to awareness of our sinfulness may be prayed, or a threefold invocation echoed by "Lord, have mercy . . . Christ, have mercy . . . Lord, have mercy" may be used. At other times an alternative form of prayer is in order: at a Eucharist in which a baptism, marriage, or funeral is celebrated, the Penitential Rite gives way to appropriate prayers for these celebrations, and in the Easter period, the sprinkling of blessed water with its recollection of one's baptism is used. *See also* Eucharist.

Penitentiary, Apostolic, that tribunal of the Apostolic See with responsibility for all matters of the internal forum, both sacramental and nonsacramental, including absolutions, dispensations, commutations, sanctions, condonations, and other favors, as well as over granting and usage of indulgences (*Pastor Bonus*, 1988, nn. 117–20). *See also* internal forum; Reconciliation.

penitentiary, canon. *See* canon penitentiary.

penitents, those who acknowledge their sinfulness. In the early Church, penitents formed a special order, like catechumens. When private confession prevailed, the order disappeared. In current Catholic theology, every Christian is a penitent, i.e., in continual need of God's forgiving grace. Liturgically, penitents today are those participating in the rite of Reconciliation. *See also* penance; Reconciliation.

pentarchy (Gk., *pentarchia*, "rule of five"), a theory of church governance, gradually developed in the fourth- and fifth-century Byzantine East, according to which the five patriarchs of Rome, Constantinople, Alexandria, Antioch, and Jerusalem are invested with supreme authority in the universal Church. In 451 the theory received ecclesial sanction in canon 28 of the Council of Chalcedon (a canon never accepted by Rome) and civil confirmation in Novella 109 of Emperor Justinian I. Some Byzantine theologians considered a council to be "ecumenical" only if all five patriarchates were represented. This raises questions in the 1990s about the possibility of an Orthodox ecumenical council without Rome. In the Orthodox pentarchial system the Bishop of Rome is "first among equals," neither superior to nor in command of the others. Some Catholic theorists advocate distinguishing more clearly the distinct levels of the pope's jurisdiction as Bishop of Rome, Primate of Italy, Patriarch of the West, and Pope of the universal Church. But in Catholic ecclesiology such distinctions are largely nominal, and can be considered an Eastern system that has never been an effectively operative part of Western ecclesial consciousness, much like Western views of centralized papal authority are in the East. Though these two views of church governance coexisted peacefully in the undivided Church during the first thousand years of its existence, their implicit tensions, never adequately resolved, formed the basis of later conflicts. *See also* patriarchate.

Pentateuch (pen'tuh-took), the first five books of the Bible. They are unified by a story line that begins with creation and ends with Moses' death. The books combine narrative (Genesis; Exod 1–19; parts of Numbers) and law (Exod 19–40; Leviticus; Num 1:1–10:10; other parts of Numbers; Deut 12–26). Some of both types of material are contained in Deut 1–11; 27–34. The narratives relate how the people were chosen and promised a land; the laws define how life in the land was to be lived.

Though the belief that Moses had written these five books arose in OT times and is echoed in the NT, modern scholars divide them into four sources or documents, all of which were written after Moses' time. In the classical form of the Documentary Hypothesis, the sources are identified and dated as follows: (1) J (the Yahwist source), the work of a ninth-century B.C. author who wrote a narrative from creation (beginning in Gen 2:4) to Moses' time and always referred to the deity as Yahweh ("Lord"); (2) E (the Elohist source), an eighth-century B.C. narrative in which the deity is called God (Heb., 'elohim) until the burning bush scene; (3) D (Deuteronomy), a seventh-century B.C. collection of speeches and laws; and (4) P (the Priestly source), a combination of laws and editorial notes, with a few stories (such as Gen 1). The J, E, and P sources were combined to produce Genesis, Exodus, Leviticus, and Numbers; to these Deuteronomy was added.

Pentecost (Gk., "the fiftieth day"), the descent of the Holy Spirit upon the apostles (Acts 2:1–41) fifty days after Easter and the liturgical feast that celebrates the event. It is popularly regarded as the birthday of the Church because from that point on the apostles carried the message of Christ to the whole world. The feast of Pentecost is also known as Whitsunday. The Greek name was originally given to the Feast of Weeks (Tob 2:1), which fell on the fiftieth day after Passover. So important is the feast of Pentecost that, until 1969, the Sundays between Pentecost and Advent were identified as Sundays after Pentecost. Since 1969 they are called Sundays in Ordinary Time. *See also* Holy Spirit; liturgical calendar.

Pentecostal churches, Christian charismatic churches founded on the conviction that believers should have a religious experience similar to that of Pentecost (Acts 1:12–2:13). The primary manifestation of this experience is glossolalia, speaking in tongues, similar to that of the first Christians (Mark 16:17; Acts 2:4–11; 10:46; 19:6; 1 Cor 14). These loosely affiliated Protestant churches came into existence primarily in the United States beginning in the late nineteenth century. Instrumental at the outset of this movement were Bethel Bible College (Topeka, Kansas) and the Apostolic Faith Gospel Mission (Los Angeles, California), where the Azusa Street Revival occurred in 1906. Today, many of these charismatic churches are connected with the Pentecostal World Conference in Wales. *See also* Charismatic Renewal movement; evangelicalism; fundamentalism, biblical; Protestantism.

Pentekostarion (pen-tuh-kaws-tah'ree-ahn; Gk., "Pentecost [book]"), Byzantine-rite liturgical book of hymnody containing the prayers assigned to Sundays and feast days (propers) for the second half of the Paschal-Pentecostal cycle, from Easter Matins to All Saints' Day on the Sunday after Pentecost inclusive. Formerly included in the Triodion, this hymnody first appears in a separate Pentekostarion anthology in the fourteenth century. *See also* Pentecost.

People of God, biblical image of the Church; by extension, the whole human race. In the OT there are some three hundred uses of the Hebrew word for people ('am). The classic text is Ezek 37:26–27: "I will make a covenant of peace with them; it shall be an everlasting covenant with them; and I will bless them and multiply them, and will set my sanctuary among them forevermore. My dwelling place shall be with them; and I will be their God, and they shall be my people."

The NT identifies the People of God with the Church in Rom 9:25–26; 2 Cor 6:14–16; Titus 2:14; and Heb 8:10. The notion of the Church as the new eschatological People of God is the guiding theme of the Letter to the Hebrews. However, the classic text is 1 Pet 2:9–10: "But you are a chosen race, a royal priesthood, a holy nation, God's own people, in order that you may proclaim the mighty acts of him who called you out of darkness into his marvelous light. Once you were not a people, but now you are God's people; once you had not received mercy, but now you have received mercy."

Nowhere is the Church spoken of explicitly as the "new" People of God, but there is explicit mention of the "new" Covenant (Luke 22:20; 1 Cor 11:25; 2 Cor 3:6; Heb 8:13; 9:15; 12:24), and that covenant is connected, at least implicitly, to a new community (Heb 8:8–12 cites Jer 31:31–34, where such a link is made).

A tension remains, however, between the old and the new People of God, and it is most strongly portrayed in Paul's Letters, especially in Rom 9–11. Unbelieving Israel is "Israel according to the flesh" (1 Cor 10:18), but believing Israel is "the Israel of God" (Gal 6:16). God calls us, Jew and Gentile alike (Gal 3:28–29). But even in the NT the new People of God are not identical with the community of the elect. In other words, membership in the Church is no guarantee of participation in the final kingdom of God. False prophets will be rejected by the Lord at the end (Matt 7:22–23) when all evildoers will be cast out (13:41–43). On the other side, many who did not belong to the new People of God will be acknowledged by the Son of Man as his brothers and sisters (Matt 25:31–46; Mark 13:27).

The Second Vatican Council (1962–65) made the People-of-God image its dominant image of the Church, more prominent even than Body of Christ, meriting an entire chapter in the Dogmatic Constitution on the Church. The placement of this chapter generated one of the most dramatic conflicts at the council. It was finally decided that it should be placed before, rather than after, the chapter on the hierarchy to emphasize that the Church is a community with a hierarchical structure rather than a hierarchical body with spiritual subjects.

The People-of-God image reminds us that we are saved not merely as individuals but as a community (n. 9) and that everyone in the community—laity, religious, and clergy alike—participates in the threefold mission of Christ as prophet, priest, and king (nn. 11–12; Decree on the Apostolate of the Laity, n. 2). The image, therefore, introduces a principle of coresponsibility that some Catholics, contrary to the council itself, find threatening to the Church's traditional structure of governance. *See also* Body of Christ. *RICHARD P. MCBRIEN*

Pepin III, "the Short," 714–68, king of the Franks. Succeeding his father, Charles Martel, as Frankish Mayor of the Palace (741), he later persuaded Pope Zacharias and the Frankish nobles that he should take the place of the nominal king, Childeric III. Pepin was succeeded by his son Charlemagne. *See also* Charlemagne; Franks.

Percy, Walker, 1916–90, American novelist and man of letters. Born to a prominent Southern family, he trained as a physician and took up fiction relatively late in life. His *The Moviegoer* (1961) won the National Book Award the following year. His corpus of fiction reflected his keen interest in philosophy and his deep Catholic faith, to which he converted in 1947. His close study of semiotics, psychiatry, and existentialism is reflected in such nonfiction collections as *Lost in the Cosmos* (1983).

Peregrine of Auxerre, St. (pair'uh-green uhv oh-sair'), d. ca. 261, bishop, martyr, and patron saint of cancer patients. Regarded as the first bishop of Auxerre, he was martyred for opposing the dedication of a local temple to Jupiter. Feast day: May 16.

Perfectae Caritatis (pair-fek'tay cah-ree-tah'tis). *See* Decree on the Appropriate Renewal of the Religious Life.

perfect contrition, a form of contrition in which love for God moves a sinner to repent of sin, ask for forgiveness, and promise not to sin again. Perfect contrition became a technical theological term in medieval Scholasticism. Peter Abelard (1079–1142) noted that whenever a sinner makes an act of perfect contrition, sin is forgiven. This position seemed to minimize the need for sacramental confession. Subsequent medieval theologians tried to relate the two. Theologically, the term "perfect" is added to "contrition" to indicate that contrition is made perfect by grace (D 1676, 1677). The Council of Trent (1545–63, D 1704) considered contrition, along with confession and satisfaction, as part of the matter of the sacrament. (The form is the absolution by the priest.) In contemporary post–Vatican II theology, there has been no major discussion of perfect contrition; nonetheless, some studies have been made on the issue of conversion, which involves the basic elements of perfect contrition. *See also* attrition; confession, auricular; contrition; imperfect contrition; Reconciliation.

perfection, a spiritual quality, proper to God alone, of being without any moral defect of any kind or to any degree whatever. Christians, however, are called by Jesus to strive for perfection: "Be perfect, therefore, as your heavenly Father is perfect" (Matt 5:48). This saying is a fusion of Deut 18:13, "You must remain completely loyal to the Lord your God," and Lev 19:2, "You shall be holy, for I the Lord your God am holy." Luke 6:36 reads, "Be merciful, just as your Father is merciful." Thus, the biblical notion of perfection is an ideal of imitating God's goodness, holiness, and mercy. Jesus expressed this ideal in his challenge to love God fully and to love one's neighbor as oneself (see Mark 12:28–34).

In the Christian tradition, the goal of Christian life is union with God in love, and it recognizes love, expressed as virtuous life, as the means to this goal. Thomas Aquinas (d. 1274) taught that the perfection of the Christian life consists of acts of charity inspired, first, by a love of God and, second, by a love of neighbor.

Because the human person, even with the help of grace, has a capacity for love of God and neighbor that has been weakened by original sin, persons can achieve only certain degrees of perfection on earth. If the obstacles to perfection are selfishness and sin, the aids to perfection are self-knowledge, prayer, and the sacraments. A misinterpretation of spiritual and moral perfection as a life without any flaw or failure whatever has discouraged some from pursuing the ideal of perfection given by Jesus in the Gospels.

This perfection in love differs from what was once called a state of perfection, which pertained to members of religious orders and congregations who took vows of poverty, chastity, and obedience. Given the Second Vatican Council's teaching that the call to holiness is for everyone, not just for clergy and religious and those who take vows, the term "state of perfection" is no longer used (see Dogmatic Constitution on the Church, n. 40). *See also* discipleship; love; perfection, state of.   PATRICIA M. VINJE

perfection, state of, a pre–Vatican II term describing the canonical status of members of religious orders and congregations who had taken the vows of poverty, chastity, and obedience in pursuit of the perfection to which Jesus had called his disciples (Matt 5:48). However, the Second Vatican Council (1962–65) taught that the call to holiness is universal, namely, "that all the faithful of Christ of whatever rank or status are called to the fullness of the Christian life and to the perfection of charity" (Dogmatic Constitution on the Church, n. 40). Consequently, the term "state of perfection" fell into disuse because of its spiritually elitist overtones. *See also* perfection; religious life.

perichoresis (per-ee-kor-ay'sis). *See* circumincession.

pericope (pair-ih'koh-pee; Gk., "cut around"), any self-contained unit of Scripture, e.g., the pericope on the calling of the disciples (Mark 1:16–20).

peritus (Lat., "expert"), a consultant with special knowledge or skill. In some cases canon law requires that experts in behavioral science be called to assist a judge by their testimony. At Vatican II (1962–65) many bishops had *periti* in theology, Scripture, or canon law to assist them in theological understanding and decision making.

permanent diaconate. *See* deacon, permanent.

Perpetua, St., d. 203, North African martyr. The *Passion of Perpetua and Felicitas* provides not only an exemplary account of suffering and triumphant death under the emperor Diocletian but also, in its concentration on the plight of two young mothers separated from their nursing infants because of their faithfulness to Christ, one of the earliest records of the experience of Christian women. Perpetua was a visionary in whom the continuing and authoritative presence of the Holy Spirit was manifest. Feast day: March 7. *See also* Felicity, St.

perpetual vows, final vows in a religious institute by which people make their lifelong consecration to God and become definitively incorporated into a religious community. The candidate for final vows must be at least twenty-one years of age and have spent a probationary period of at least three years in temporary vows. As with any religious profession, to be considered valid it must be free from coercion, fraud, or grave fear and must involve the free approval of the appropriate authorities. The pronouncing of perpetual vows is considered a very significant life passage and the ceremony is often performed with great solemnity. *See also* religious institute; vows.

Perrone, Giovanni (joh-vahn'ee pair-roh'nay), 1794–1876, Jesuit theologian. He exerted a profound influence on Pope Pius IX (d. 1878) and other curial officials as dogmatic theologian and rector of the Roman College. A Scholastic theologian only in the broadest sense of the term, Perrone was well versed in patristic studies. He wrote an influential multivolume dogmatic manual and prepared for the definition of the Immaculate Conception in 1854.

persecutions, acts of harassment and violence directed against Christians. The sectarian, apocalyptic Judaism that was the background of Christianity often predicted persecution. The righteous would suffer, perhaps in a final confrontation with the forces of darkness, variously identified with the Jewish or Roman establishment. The suffering of the righteous could serve as atonement for the sins of the people, righteous and unrighteous alike (Isa 53; 2 Macc 7:32–38), and Jesus himself died the death of a martyr/prophet, speaking of his own death accordingly (Mark 14:24; Matt 26:28; 23:37–39). The Gospels warn would-be disciples that they, too, could expect persecution (Mark 10:39; Matt 10:16–25).

Christians and Rome: The Romans did not distinguish earliest Christianity from Judaism, a *religio licita* (Lat., "a religion authorized by the empire"), but Christians were cast out of synagogues and persecuted by the Jewish establishment. Stephen was martyred ca. 35 (Acts 7:60); ca. 44 Herod Agrippa I, Rome's client, executed James the brother of John and detained Peter (Acts 12); Paul himself confesses he had persecuted the Church (Gal 1:13); in turn he was opposed and harassed both in the Diaspora and at Jerusalem (e.g., Acts 17:10–13; Acts 21; Acts 24). James, "brother" of the Lord, was executed ca. 62 by the high priest Ananias.

As Christianity gained more gentile converts, the Romans learned to distinguish it as a separate, unauthorized religion. The emperor Nero initiated a gruesome persecution ca. 64, perhaps scapegoating the Christians for the great fire at Rome, blamed by some on himself. Hostility between Jews and Christians may have played a role here. The Jews, in popular imagination misanthropes and incendiarists who insulted the Roman gods, would have been natural scapegoats; they may have in turn suspected and accused the renegade hostile sect from whom they wished to dissociate themselves. Whatever the cause, Christians were now placed in a legally precarious position, henceforth vulnerable to popular prejudice, which regarded them, like the Jews, as antisocial. They were also charged with secret incest, cannibalism, and atheism (refusal to worship the gods of Rome). All of these, especially the last, only amplify the original charge; in failing to worship the gods of Rome, the Christians seemed to be assaulting the very character and aspirations of Roman society.

The emperor Domitian, according to the historian Eusebius, banished certain Christians from Rome (95). But the emperor Trajan's correspondence with Pliny, his governor in Bithynia, provides the first clear statement of official policy toward Christians (112). Christianity in itself is a capital offense; recantation earned one's release; but Christians should not be sought out or anonymous denunciations accepted, a provision strengthened under Trajan's successor Hadrian (ca. 125). Later, Marcus Aurelius's reign (161–80) marked the rise of mob violence against Christians, with particularly vicious outbreaks at Vienne and Lyons (177), preceded by executions in Asia Minor (including that of Polycarp, bishop of Smyrna), Athens, and Rome (e.g., Justin Martyr, ca. 165). Under Septimus Severus (193–211) persecution seemed directed particularly at converts (Perpetua and Felicitas, ca. 203, catechumens at Carthage; at Alexandria six students of Origen, ca. 206, besides Origen's father Leonides, ca. 204). Under Alexander Severus (222–35), however, persecution subsided and the Church even began to own property, although Maximinus Thrax (235–38) exiled Pope Pontian (230–35) and Hippolytus from Rome and violence broke out in Cappadocia and Pontus and in Caesarea.

The Final Phase: Decius (249–51) was the first emperor to institute an officially sponsored empire-wide persecution against the "atheism" responsible for the declining fortunes of the empire under his predecessors. Early in 250 he required all to obtain a certificate (Lat., *libellus*) proving sacrifice to the gods. In Caesarea Origen was tortured; the bishops of Jerusalem (Alexander) and Antioch (Babylas) were martyred. The most savage phase of this persecution, and perhaps of all early persecutions, began in 257 under Valerian (253–60). Imprisonment, torture, loss of property, exile, reduction to forced labor in chains, and death were the fates of many, including Cyprian, bishop of Carthage, Pope Sixtus II, and several prominent women of Rome. Fructuosus, bishop of Tarragona, and two deacons, Augurius and Eulogius, were burned alive at the stake (259). The accession of Gallienus (260), however, began some forty years of relative peace for the Church. These came to an abrupt end with the final "Great Persecution" begun by the emperor Diocletian (303). As part of his general reform platform reinstating fundamental Roman values, Diocletian aimed to eliminate Christianity. At his abdication (305) the persecution virtually ceased in the West except in Africa. In the East persecution continued brutally, especially in Egypt, ending only with the Edict of Constantine (313). *See also lapsi;* martyr; martyrdom.

JOHN C. CAVADINI

perseverance, final, the divine gift of continuance in the grace of justification until and at the time of death. Catholic theologians traditionally have distinguished final perseverance from the virtue or habit of perseverance by describing the latter as a potential power and the former as the act brought to completion at the end of life. The doctrine expresses the necessity of special divine help and, second, cooperation with God in attaining salvation. This position stands in opposition to the semi-Pelagian estimate of the complete sufficiency of the natural power of free will for perseverance and in opposition to the general disregard of the

Reformers for the role of the human will in salvation. Hence, the teaching must be seen as chiefly the product of theological reflection on the efficacy of grace and divine predestination, though it has been ascribed various scriptural roots (e.g., Phil 1:3–6; Matt 10:22). The Council of Trent (1545–63) followed Augustine (d. 430) in calling it a "great gift" that fixes the free will in choosing the good and followed Thomas Aquinas (d. 1274) in teaching that it is beyond merit and, therefore, beyond the certainty of our knowledge; nevertheless, the just may be confident of obtaining it through prayer. *See also* grace; salvation.

personal law, in canon law norms whose force applies to a given individual rather than a particular geographical territory. These laws are said to "cling to the bones" of a person. Their force follows an individual regardless of where he or she might be.

personalism, Christian, a philosophical orientation that emphasizes the value and dignity of each individual human person, the importance of dialogue (the I-thou relationship), and the notion of human solidarity. Rooted in the teachings of Jesus, the approach is particularly strong in the writings of the French Catholic philosopher Gabriel Marcel (d. 1973). It is also central for the Lublin School of philosophy, with which Pope John Paul II was once associated and whose philosophical orientation continues to influence his thinking and writing, especially his 1981 encyclical *Laborem Exercens* (On Human Work).

person of Christ, the divine Logos (Word) made flesh. According to the Christian tradition, the Logos is the person in whom the divine nature and human nature are united. The person, or *hypostasis* (Gk.) of the Second Person of the triune God, is the unifying subject in Jesus Christ, who is truly God and truly a human being. Christ's human nature did/does not exist on its own but "subsists" by virtue of participating in the existence of the Word, the Son of God.

This understanding raises such questions as: Was Jesus conscious of himself as the Son of God during his earthly life? Could he have sinned? Did he enjoy the Beatific Vision throughout his life? In Catholic theology of the mid-twentieth century the issue of the self-consciousness of Jesus Christ was considered by theologians like J. Galot, E. Gutwenger, B. Lonergan, and K. Rahner. It was ad-

dressed, too, by Pius XII in his encyclical *Sempiternus Rex Christus* (1951), which, though setting some limits, left the way open for critical inquiry. Such inquiries require that one clarify such notions as person, experience, and consciousness, distinguishing between their psychological meaning and their ontological/metaphysical meaning. *See also* Christology; hypostasis; hypostatic union; Jesus Christ; subsistence theory.

Persons, divine, the Father, Son, and Holy Spirit as named in the NT. Although "person" is often thought of as an individual center of consciousness, applied to the Trinity this would be tantamount to tritheism. In contemporary theology, philosophy, and psychology the relational characteristics of personhood are emphasized. Thus, a person, whether divine or human, is one who comes to self through another, who is free, who loves and is loved, and who knows and is known. All persons, whether divine or human, are ineffable, unique, and unrepeatable. By definition, a person is "ecstatic," oriented toward others. Finally, all persons are made for communion with other persons. Thus, what is "unnatural" for persons is to be self-focused or self-absorbed. Indeed, contemporary philosophers and theologians view the self-reflective self as a false self.

In the history of trinitarian theology, "person" was a fluid term, defined differently at various stages of doctrinal history and in contrast to nature or essence. Boethius's (d. 524) definition is classic: a person is an individual substance of a rational nature. Thomas Aquinas (d. 1274) used Boethius's definition and thus it had perduring influence in Latin theology. According to Scholastic theology, the one divine nature is differentiated by three divine Persons who subsist in perfect equality, alike in Godhead.

In Eastern Christianity, personhood is predicated as the rudimentary ontological category. Person logically precedes nature, because the originating principle of all reality is a personal (not a substantial) God. The primary truth about God is that God is not a substance that can be metaphysically determined, rather, God is "someone" who meets us in a redemptive history.

In sum, "person" is a central category in trinitarian theology. The claim that God is "personal" is, of course, an analogy. The point is that God is capable of relationship with a people throughout salvation history. *See also* God; Trinity, doctrine of the.

CATHERINE MOWRY LACUGNA

pertinacity, persistent and tenacious obstinacy. It traditionally characterizes the denial or doubt of heretics concerning articles of faith.

Perugino (pair-*oo*-jee'noh) [Pietro Vannucci], 1448–1523, Italian artist. An Umbrian painter, he did important frescos in the Vatican (most lost) and in Perugia. He taught Raphael for one year.

pessimism, the philosophical doctrine that this is the worst possible universe or, less extremely, that in this universe evil outweighs good. It runs counter to the Catholic affirmation that the universe, taken in its entirety, is intelligible and good because it has been created by an infinitely wise and loving God. *See also* despair; hope.

Petavius, Dionysius (di-uh-nee'shuhs peh-tay' vee-uhs), 1583–1652, also known as Denis Pétau, Jesuit theologian and patristics scholar. He taught theology at the Collège de Clermont in Paris for much of his career. An accomplished student of the early Church writers, Petavius edited numerous collections of ancient theological texts and, in his multivolume work of dogmatic theology, sought to demonstrate the biblical and patristic origins and development of Church doctrines.

Peter Baptist, St., 1545–97, Franciscan missionary and martyr and patron saint of Japan. Spanish-born, he worked as a missionary in Mexico, the Philippines, and Japan, where he was crucified with twenty-five other Christians, all of whom were canonized in 1862 as the Martyrs of Japan. Feast day: February 6. *See also* Japan, Catholicism in.

Peter Canisius, St. *See* Canisius, St. Peter.

Peter Chanel, St. *See* Chanel, St. Peter.

Peter Chrysologus, St. *See* Chrysologus, St. Peter.

Peter Claver, St., 1581–1654, Spanish Jesuit missionary known as "the Saint of the Slaves." He entered the Society of Jesus in 1602 and was inspired by Alphonsus Rodriguez to become a missionary in South America. In 1610 he went to the seaport of Cartagena, Colombia, to begin his practice of meeting ships arriving from West Africa and going into

Peter Claver, seventeenth-century Spanish Jesuit, devoted minister to African slaves brought forcibly to the New World (modern-day Colombia in South America), and minister to the native peoples as well.

their holds in order to care for the physical and spiritual well-being of the slaves. He is said to have instructed and baptized over 300,000 slaves. In 1616 he was ordained a priest in Bogotá. During his last years, he suffered a paralysis and mistreatment by his servant. In 1888 he was canonized by Pope Leo XIII. Feast day: September 9.

ST. PETER

S t. Peter was Jesus' leading disciple, traditionally regarded as the first pope. The synoptic Gospels indicate that Simon was the first disciple chosen by Jesus, on which occasion Jesus either gave him a new symbolic name (Cephas, or Peter, "rock"; Matt 16:18) or designated him as "fisher of men" (Mark 1:17; see Luke 5:10). Respect and authority reside for the ancients in the first of a line, firstborn or first chosen. Peter was a fisherman from the village of

Peter, with John the Evangelist (right), is instructed by Jesus, "Go to the sea and cast a hook; take the first fish that comes up; and when you open its mouth, you will find a coin; take that and give it to them for you and me" (Matt 17:27). When he first called Peter to be his disciple, Jesus said to him, "Follow me, and I will make you fish for people" (Matt 4:19); fifteenth-century painting by Masaccio, in the Brancacci Chapel, Santa Maria del Carmine, Florence, Italy.

Capernaum, son of Jonah (Matt 16:17) and brother of Andrew. He worked his father's trade, possibly in a consortium with Zebedee and sons. He was married (Mark 1:30) and apparently traveled with his wife (1 Cor 9:5). Acts 4:13 records a public verdict that he was an "uneducated common man."

Peter receiving the keys of the kingdom of heaven from Jesus in Caesarea Philippi (Matt 16:19), a scene traditionally regarded as the basis of Peter's and his successors' pastoral authority over the Church; medieval English enamel plaque (ca. 1185).

STATUS AND ROLE

In Matthew's Gospel Peter enjoys a special status and role. The traditional elements of his call by Jesus are supplemented with charismatic phenomena such as walking on water (14:28–29), special revelations (16:17), and miraculous events (17:27). Peter asks key questions and so becomes the unique conduit of information from Jesus about an important range of topics (15:15; 17:25–26). Thus his status is a blend of traditional commissioning stories and unusual charismatic demonstrations. Only in Matthew is Peter formally designated "rock" of the new church, given keys of authority to admit or exclude, and promised that his role in the group would survive death (16:18–19).

All the Gospels record many unflattering remembrances about Peter. He is the disciple who rebuked Jesus when he first began to speak of his impending death in Jerusalem; Jesus called him a "Satan" (Mark 8:33). Peter's faith failed after he began to walk on the water (Matt 14:30–31). Finally, Peter is famous for his boasts of loyalty to Jesus (Mark 14:29, 31; John 13:37) and his subsequent shameful denial of the Lord (Mark 14:66–72). One Gospel identifies him as the disciple who drew his sword in the garden to defend Jesus (John 18:10). That his insight is inferior to that of the Beloved Disciple is noted twice (John 20:6–9; 21:7). Yet for all that, Jesus prayed for him that his faith be strengthened (Luke 22:31–32). Like Paul, who is remembered as the one who "persecuted the church," Peter is remembered as the disciple who denied the Lord.

Many NT documents testify to the importance of Peter, which confirms our appreciation of his unique position among the earliest churches. Among the Twelve there seems to have been an elite inner circle consisting of Peter, James, and John. They accompanied Jesus to the raising of Jairus's daughter (Mark 5:37), to the Transfiguration (Mark 9:2), to the Mount of Olives for a special farewell discourse (Mark 13:3), and to close association with Jesus in the garden (Mark 14:33). Yet Peter is more typically presented as the spokesman for the disciples, asking about the interpretation of parables (Luke 12:41) or offering the correct confession about Jesus (Mark 8:29).

Paul, either willingly or reluctantly, admits Peter's special position; he mentions that Jesus appeared first to him (1 Cor 15:5) and that he functioned not only as a "pillar" of the Jerusalem church, but as the leader of the mission to the circumcised (Gal 2:7). Luke describes Jesus at the Last Supper commissioning Peter as leader of his disciples (22:32) and notes that the risen Jesus appeared first to him (24:34). John's Gospel is more complicated, as it indicates a rivalry for leadership between Peter and the Beloved Disciple. But even here, Jesus formally commissions Peter as "the noble shepherd" (21:15–19), namely, his successor and leader of the group.

It cannot be underestimated how important is the pervasive witness to the tradition that Jesus appeared to Peter after the Resurrection. Luke indicates that Jesus appeared first to Peter (24:34), a primacy supported by Paul's list of witnesses (1 Cor 15:5). And the angel at the tomb instructs the women to tell their message to "the disciples and Peter" (Mark 16:7), mentioning him by name. Finally, Matthew (28:16–20), Luke (24:36–49), and John (20:19–23; 21:15–19) all record a formal commissioning of Peter, either in the group or individually, as witness. If such Resurrection appearances function as commissioning stories, Peter is the most commissioned of the Twelve.

PETER AND THE EARLY CHURCH

Peter's role in the early Church is described in Acts. To outsiders, he functioned as chief witness about Jesus, either heralding the good news to the crowds (2:14–36) or defending the gospel before legal courts (4:7–12). To insiders, he enjoyed the role of judge (5:1–10), missionary (9:32–42), and arbiter of conflict (15:7–11). He articulates the need to replace Judas with a new, qualified apostle (1:15–22). Acts records him receiving an important vision of foods descending from heaven, with the accompanying explanation that Jewish rules for kosher food no longer apply to Jesus' disciples (10:13–15). On the same occasion, Peter was designated by God to begin the mission to the Gentiles by approving the admission of Cornelius and his spirit-filled household into the Church (10:44–48). Acts mentions his imprisonment and apparent flight from Jerusalem (12:17). The mention of a "Cephas party" at Corinth might indicate his migration there (1 Cor 1:12), but this seems doubtful.

He is credited with writing two Letters, 1 and 2 Peter. While a case can be made for Petrine authorship of 1 Peter, it seems unlikely that he is the author of the second Letter. Nevertheless, the author of 2 Peter is privy to a host of stories about Peter that indicate a common and widespread appreciation of his stature in the early Church. 2 Peter knows that Jesus revealed his death to him (1:12–15; see John 21:18–19); Peter's witness of the Transfiguration is noted (1:16–18; see Matt 17:1–7); like the Peter of the Gospels, he is credited with inspiration (1:20–21; see Matt 16:17). He receives revelations about future false prophets (2:1–3; see Matt 24:11, 24), the unknowability of the time of the Parousia (3:8; see Matt 24:8, 36), special traditions about the Parousia (3:10–13; see Matt 24:29–31), the thief in the night (3:10; see Matt 24:43), and the regeneration of the world (3:11–12; see Matt 19:28). This document, then, is a compendium of traditions about Peter and a witness to his importance.

The NT records that Peter did not stay in Jerusalem, as seems to be the case with the other apostles. He traveled to Lydda, Joppa, and Caesarea (Acts 9–10). Peter and Paul eat together with the church at Antioch (Gal 2:11). He probably visited Corinth (1 Cor 9:5); and there is solid support for his eventual travel to Rome and martyrdom there; the Roman leader Clement describes Peter's trials in Rome (1 *Clem.* 5:4), and Eusebius reports an ancient story about Peter's crucifixion in Rome (*Ecclesiastical History* 2.25.5, 8).

There is even less evidence of how Peter functioned while in Rome. It would be wrong, however, to read back into first-century Rome the existence of the papacy as we know it today. Ignatius of Antioch (d. ca. 107) did assume that Peter and Paul exercised special authority over the church in Rome, and Irenaeus (d. ca. 200) claimed that they jointly founded the church there and inaugurated its succession of bishops. Historical evidence suggests that not until the mid-second century did the monarchical episcopate (a single bishop presiding over a diocese) finally replace the Roman system whereby a body of presbyter-bishops functioned in the presidential role. By the late second or early third century, however, the tradition identified Peter as the first Bishop of Rome, and the tradition continues to this day. Feast day (with St. Paul): June 29.

See also papacy, the; Petrine ministry; Petrine succession; pope; primacy, papal.

Bibliography

Brown, Raymond, Karl Donfried, and John Reumann, eds. *Peter in the New Testament.* New York: Paulist Press, 1973.

Brown, Raymond, and John Meier. *Antioch and Rome: New Testament Cradles of Catholic Christianity.* New York: Paulist Press, 1983.

Brown, Raymond. *The Churches the Apostles Left Behind.* New York: Paulist Press, 1984.

JEROME NEYREY

Peter Comestor, d. 1179, exegete. Born in Troyes, where he became dean of the cathedral, he then studied and taught in Paris. His major work is *Historia Scholastica (Scholastic History)*, a continuous history from creation to the end of Acts utilizing Scripture and the Church Fathers to weave a consecutive narrative.

Peter Damian, St., 1007–72, Doctor of the Church, reformer, and theologian. Born in Ravenna, after studying and teaching the liberal arts he converted to the monastic life, joining a group of hermits at Fonte Avellana in the Apennines. Called to Rome in 1057 and made cardinal-bishop of Ostia, he was sent on several missions on behalf of the reform papacy. His writings urged clerical reform. He was an early proponent of apostolic poverty for the clergy and wrote in favor of clerical celibacy. He was a moderate on the question of simony, the buying and selling of spiritual goods, including Church offices. While insisting that it is a sin and that simoniacal priests should be punished, he concluded that their sacraments were valid. Feast day: February 21.

Peter Gonzales, Bl., 1190–1246, Benedictine preacher and patron saint of sailors. Spanish-born, he served as King Ferdinand III's chaplain, preached a crusade against the Moors, then counseled mercy. He was particularly concerned with the welfare of sailors. Feast day: April 14.

Peter Lombard. *See* Lombard, Peter.

Peter Martyr, St., ca. 1200–1252, Dominican preacher and martyr. Born of Cathar parents, Peter was admitted to the Dominicans in 1221 by Dominic de Guzman himself and spent the rest of his life trying to convert heretics. Appointed inquisitor for northern Italy in 1251, he suffered martyrdom the next year and was canonized the year after that. Feast day: April 29. *See also* Cathari; Inquisition.

Peter of Alcántara, St., 1499–1562, founder of the Spanish Discalced Franciscans. Peter studied at the University of Salamanca and lived a life of solitude and austerity. His followers were known as Alcantarines. A trusted adviser to Teresa of Ávila, Peter was canonized in 1669. Feast day: October 19.

Peter of Alexandria, St., d. ca. 311, bishop of Alexandria (ca. 300–311). Imprisoned under Diocletian and freed ca. 306, he fled renewed persecution and returned in 311, but was beheaded shortly thereafter under Maximinus Daia. His leniency toward the *lapsi* (Lat., "those who denied the faith under persecution") prompted Melitius of Lycopolis to try to take over in Peter's absence, ultimately provoking the Melitian schism. Peter's works are lost. Fragments show he disputed Origen's teachings on the soul and resurrection body. Feast day: November 24 (East); November 25 (Ethiopia); November 26 (West). *See also lapsi.*

Peter's Pence, an amount of money contributed annually by Catholics worldwide for the support of the Holy See, revived by Pope Pius IX in 1860 after the fall of the Papal States. Its origin can be traced to England in 787 as a tax of one penny that was levied on all but the poorest families and given to the pope. The practice spread to other nations and should not be confused with the feudal tribute, or *census* (Lat., "assessment"), paid for papal protection at a time when the Holy See was a temporal power. The *census* was abolished in England by Henry VIII in 1534 and did not survive in any nation after the Reformation. *See also* Holy See.

Peter the Chanter, ca. 1130–97, exegete and theologian. He was canon and master of theology in Paris at the cathedral school, where he also became the cantor. Principally concerned with moral, pastoral, and sacramental theology, he also wrote commentaries on biblical books.

Peter the Venerable, ca. 1092–1156, ninth abbot of Cluny and leader of twelfth-century revival of monastic life. His writings include treatises against Christian heretics, Muslims, and Jews. He had the Qur'an translated into Latin. Though honored as a saint, he was never canonized. He is listed in some books of saints with a feast day of December 29. *See also* Cluny.

petitioner, party initiating action in canon law. The petitioner must have some direct involvement in the case. Hence only a spouse (or the promoter of justice, the diocesan prosecutor) can introduce a marriage case. The petitioner need not be Catholic. Minors and certain mentally incompetent persons, however, can only stand trial through parents or guardians since procedural capacity is required.

Petrine ministry, the ministry that the Bishop of Rome (the pope) exercises in his capacity as Vicar of Peter. The Spirit of God gives the bishop of the see where, according to tradition, Peter and Paul were martyred a specific mission and some important prerogatives. Their purpose is the serving of the communion formed by all the local churches (presided over by the local bishops) and indeed by all the disciples of Christ. This ministry is the ministry of the one among the bishops called by Christ to fulfill the declaration that Luke inserts into his account of the Last Supper: "I have prayed for you that your own faith may not fail; and you, when once you have turned back, strengthen your brothers" (Luke 22:32). The ministry of Peter as leader of the apostolic community in the first part of the book of Acts is the model and the norm of this ministry, precisely because it is Peter himself who continues to preside and serve through his vicar, the pope. Like Peter, the Bishop of Rome has to witness to the faith that Peter (and Paul) confessed, to watch over the way the local churches keep and transmit this faith with integrity, to help his fellow bishops defend the content of this faith when its authentic meaning is at stake, to promote and coordinate the activities of the churches in their missionary task, to speak in the name of all the bishops and all their local churches when (guided by the Holy Spirit) he knows it is necessary, and to declare officially and solemnly the meaning of a revealed truth in the name of the whole Church with the guarantee of the charism of infallibility and under precise and very strict conditions. Because the whole Church is the communion of all the local churches and each local church is under the oversight of one bishop, the ministry of the Bishop of Rome is necessarily connected with the authority each bishop possesses in his own diocese. In order to safeguard the communion of all the local churches in faith, charity, and mission, the Bishop of Rome has the duty to watch over the inner unity and cohesion of the whole episcopal college, to help his brothers in their tasks, to make known their needs, and sometimes to speak for them when they are unjustly accused or prosecuted. His ministry is the ministry of the *servus servorum Dei* (Lat., "servant of the servants of God"), an old episcopal title that describes at one and the same time the pope's relation to his fellow bishops and to the whole People of God. *See also* collegiality; communion, Church as; papacy, the; Peter, St.; Petrine succession; pope; primacy, papal; vicar of Christ; Vicar of Peter.   JEAN-M. R. TILLARD

Petrine privilege. *See* Privilege of the Faith.

Petrine succession, an expression pertaining to the complex process by which the bishops of Rome (popes) follow in the line of St. Peter as his vicars and as earthly heads of the universal Church. The process is complex because it is clear that in his function as founder, with Paul, of the apostolic see of Rome, Peter cannot have a successor. It is also clear that as one of the Twelve he cannot have any successor in the basic apostolic function of bearing witness to the fact that the Risen Lord is really the Jesus in whose company they spent some years of their life. Moreover, no one may succeed Peter and the other apostles in the eschatological privilege of surrounding the Christ at the time of the judgment (cf. Luke 22:30) and of being the foundations of the eschatological Jerusalem (Rev 21:14). It is indeed possible for him to have inheritors in the responsibility of evangelizing the whole world and of keeping in communion all the baptized people. But these inheritors will be continuators, not replacements, and his death will not prevent him from presiding over the destinies of the Church founded on the rock of his faith. These inheritors will fully succeed each other, but their link with Peter will only be a succession in an analogical way. Because in Rome they are continuing the mission once for all given to Peter, their relation to the other bishops will be the same as the relation of Peter to the other apostles; their authority over the whole college of bishops will be the same as the authority exercised by Peter in the midst of the apostolic group; their responsibility for the leadership of the Church will be the same as the responsibility of Peter over the apostolic community. But it is the once-for-all nature of the office of Peter that remains present through all those who successively occupy the apostolic see of Rome.

It is important to remember that for Cyprian (d. 258) every bishop in his own episcopal see is in some sense Peter's successor: the other apostles were what Peter was (i.e., signs of unity and bearers of the tradition); Peter was in every apostle. Hilary of Poitiers (d. 367) calls all the local bishops "successors of Peter and Paul" (Migne *Patrologia Latina* 10.645). Augustine (d. 430) says that in Peter the whole Church, not only Peter, was receiving the keys of the Kingdom (*Tract on John* 27.9; *tract.* 118.4; *tract.* 124.5). Theologians of the Orthodox churches maintain that Rome is not the only see in which Peter exercised his apostolic primacy and in which an episcopal succession may be found. They affirm that according to the Scriptures the apostolic see of Antioch is one of the Petrine churches enjoying a Petrine succession. *See also* apostolic succession; papacy, the; Peter, St.; Petrine ministry; pope; vicar of Christ; Vicar of Peter. JEAN-M. R. TILLARD

pew, wooden church benches. Pews, arranged in rows, are used by the congregation or individuals for worship and private prayer.

pew rent, a contribution for the use of a particular pew in a church. Sometimes the term has been used for a contribution solicited from worshipers as they enter the door of a church. Both practices are no longer extant in the United States. The 1917 Code of Canon Law mandated free entry to divine worship.

Peyton, Patrick J., 1909–92, Irish-born Holy Cross priest who promoted the Rosary on radio and television and also through diocesan "crusades." His motto was "The family that prays together stays together."

Pharisees (fair'uh-seez; Heb., "separated ones"), a Jewish sect during the time of Jesus. The group was active from the late second century B.C. through the destruction of Jerusalem in A.D. 70. They are mentioned in the NT, the works of the Jewish historian Josephus (*Jewish War* 2.162–66, *Antiquities* 18.12–15), and the literature of rabbinic Judaism.

At the core of the Pharisaic program is God's injunction to Israel to be holy (Lev 19:2). Through a tradition of interpretation (the oral Torah) of the Pentateuch, the Pharisees extended law (Heb., *halakah*) applicable to the priests and the Temple to all of Israel. Such traditions were eventually codified in the Mishnah.

The NT portrays the Pharisees as models of conventional piety (Luke 18:10) but criticizes them for concern with superficial matters (Matt 23:13–29; Luke 11:38–52). Matthew records Jesus' admonition to abide by Pharisaic teaching but to avoid their example (Matt 23:2–3). The Pharisees often appear as hostile questioners of Jesus (e.g., Matt 9:11; 16:1; 22:15; Mark 9:11; 10:2; Luke 6:2; 11:53; 17:2). John suggests that their hostility led some to conspire with the high priests against Jesus (John 7:32; 11:47, 57). Yet some Pharisees apparently were well disposed toward Jesus (Luke 13:31; John 3:1; 7:45–52). Acts 5:33–40 records that a distinguished teacher, Gamaliel, advised tolerance for the new community.

Before his experience with the risen Christ, the Apostle Paul was a Pharisee (Phil 3:5). On trial in Jerusalem he used the Pharisaic belief in resurrection to his advantage (Acts 23:6–11).

HAROLD W. ATTRIDGE

phelonion (fay-loh'nee-ahn), also *phenolion,* Byzantine-rite liturgical chasuble, principal outer vestment worn by priests. Like the Western chasuble, it evolved from the Roman *paenula,* from which its name derives. *See also* chasuble.

phenomenology (Gk., *phainomenon,* "what appears"; *logos,* "study of"). 1 A general type of inquiry that objectively describes the subject matter and the experiences associated with it, without attempting to explain the cause(s) of these experiences. 2 A philosophical method, developed principally in Germany in the first half of the twentieth century. The primary representative of this philosophical school was Edmund Husserl (1859–1938). The phenomenological approach, emphasizing the material world as the bearer of the sacred, has been especially prominent in sacramental theology, particularly in the writings of Edward Schillebeeckx, the author of *Christ the Sacrament of the Encounter with God* (1963). *See also* philosophy and theology; sacrament.

Philemon (fi-lee'muhn), an early Christian convert of Paul (Phlm 19) and recipient of a letter from him. Philemon was a wealthy resident of Colossae, at whose house an early Christian community met (Phlm 2). He also owned the slave Onesimus, who had run away to Ephesus and had been of great service to Paul during Paul's imprisonment (Phlm 13). Paul then sent Onesimus back to Philemon. In his letter Paul urged Philemon to receive Onesimus back no longer as a slave but as a beloved brother (Phlm 16). It is unclear whether Paul was asking for Onesimus's emancipation or simply for Philemon to treat him kindly.

Philip, St., one of the twelve apostles. Philip is listed with the Twelve in the synoptic Gospels (Matt 10:3; Mark 3:18; Luke 6:14; Acts 1:13). He plays a significant role only in the Fourth Gospel, where, along with Peter and Andrew and like them an inhabitant of Bethsaida, he is among the first disciples called by Jesus (John 1:43–44). At the feeding of the five thousand he comments that two hundred denarii worth of bread would not suffice to feed the crowd (John 6:5–7). Because he has a Greek name, it is appropriate that "the Greeks" come to him looking for Jesus (John 12:21–22). At the Last Supper, he asks Jesus to show the Father to the Twelve, eliciting the response that the one who has seen Jesus has seen the Father (John 14:8–9).

Philip the Apostle is often confused in tradition (e.g., Eusebius *Ecclesiastical History* 3.31.2) with Philip the deacon (Acts 6:5), who evangelized Samaria (Acts 8:5–13) and converted the Ethiopian eunuch (Acts 8:26–40). Acts 21:8 gives this Philip the epithet the Evangelist and places his home in Caesarea Maritima.

At least two apocryphal works attributed to Philip circulated in the early Church. Epiphanius (*Panarion* 26.13.2–3) cites a *Gospel of Philip* used by fourth-century Egyptian Gnostics. A Coptic *Gospel of Philip* was discovered in the Nag Hammadi collection, without the material cited by Epiphanius. The latter text contains disparate materials, many of which share an interest in sacramental symbolism.

Philip is the patron saint of Uruguay. Feast day: May 3. *See also* apostle; Twelve, the.

HAROLD W. ATTRIDGE

Philip II, 1527–98, king of Spain from 1556 to 1598. Champion of Catholicism against the Reformation and of Catholic reform, he suppressed religious dissent throughout Spanish territories, provoking Dutch revolt. His effort to restore English Catholicism ended with the defeat in 1588 of the Spanish Armada.

Philip Neri, St., 1515–95, Italian priest, founder, and confessor. Known as a man of prayer and generosity, he was regarded as a living saint by contemporaries. It was reported that he experienced spiritual ecstasy. His most notable accomplishments include the cofounding of the Confraternity of the Most Holy Trinity, dedicated to assisting pilgrims and the sick, and his inspiration for the Congregation of the Oratory, an association of priests whose aim it was to promote holiness of priestly life and to foster good preaching. Feast day: May 26. *See also* Oratorians.

Philip the Chancellor, d. ca. 1236, theologian, chancellor of the University of Paris by 1218, and author of *Summa de Bono* (*Concerning the Good*), a comprehensive statement of Christian theology widely read by thirteenth-century Scholastic theologians.

Philippines, Catholicism in the. Catholicism was introduced to the Philippines in 1521, when Spain claimed the islands as a colonial outpost. For over 350 years, the Philippines were under Spanish rule. A variety of religious orders including Augustinians, Franciscans, Jesuits, Dominicans, and Augustinian Recollects evangelized the islands. The archdiocese of Manila was established in 1578, and was made a Metropolitan See in 1595. The first bishop was Domingo de Salazar, appointed in 1579. In order to provide better instruction of the native Filipinos, the widely scattered *barangays* (Sp., "clans") were encouraged to resettle in larger villages. Despite evangelical efforts, popular non-Christian religious practices, particularly ancestral worship, continued to flourish. As a result, Filipino spirituality has always been attracted to sacramentals—relics, holy water, medals, and devotions to saints.

While the institutional Church grew, it failed to develop a native clergy; native Filipinos were not allowed to become priests until the late seventeenth century. As the number of native clergy increased, tensions grew between Filipino diocesan priests (directly subject to the local bishop) and Spanish religious order priests. In 1872, several nationalistic Filipino priests were accused by Spain of rebellion and were executed; a repression of the native clergy ensued. The Revolution of 1896 against Spain

PHILIPPINES

contained significant anticlerical feeling, though anticlericalism was directed primarily at the Spanish clergy. In 1898, as a result of the Spanish-American War, the Philippines and the Philippine church came under American control. At the same time, a strong push was made for the appointment of Filipino bishops; with no appointments forthcoming, a movement led by a guerilla hero, Father Gregorio Aglipay, split from the Catholic Church to form the Independent Filipino Catholic Church in 1902. The schism claimed close to one-fourth of the islands' Catholics, though by the 1930s and 1940s the numbers had declined precipitously. In 1906, a Filipino bishop, Father Jorge Barlin, was appointed, and more Filipino bishops were subsequently named. The Filipino church also confronted increasing Protestant proselytization as a result of American occupation, but few inroads were made.

Over the course of the twentieth century the Church in the Philippines has grown in size and strength, and so has popular religiosity in the form of fiestas, processions, and devotions to saints, such as the Santo Nino. In 1994, it was estimated that over fifty million Catholics live and worship in the Philippines, 83 percent of the total population.

JEFFREY M. BURNS

Philocalia (fi-loh-kay'lee-uh; Gk., "love of things beautiful"). **1** An anthology of Origen's writings collected by Gregory of Nazianzus and Basil of Caesarea ca. 359, preserving the original Greek of many passages otherwise extant only in translation. **2** A 1782 collection of spiritual writings from the fourth to the fifteenth centuries focused on hesychastic themes, especially the Prayer of the Heart (the Jesus Prayer). *See also* Jesus Prayer; Origen.

Philomena, St., revered in the past as virgin and martyr. Because virtually nothing is known about her, the Church suppressed her feast (August 11) in 1960. Philomena's veneration flourished in the nineteenth century and Jean-Baptiste Vianney, in particular, was devoted to her.

Philo of Alexandria, ca. 20 B.C.–ca. 50 A.D., leading figure of the Jewish community in Alexandria and major source for understanding diaspora Judaism. Although Philo wrote more than seventy tractates, only fifty survive: thirty-eight in Greek and twelve in Armenian. His commentaries on the Pentateuch are divided into "Questions and Answers," the "Allegorical Commentary," and the "Exposition

of the Law"; the other works are apologetic and philosophical treatises. His insistence on both literal and allegorical meanings of the Bible allowed him to create a synthesis of Jewish faith and Middle Platonism. Central to his thought is the divine Logos, an intermediary between God and humanity. Both his method of exegesis and his thought significantly influenced the development of Christian theology, especially through Clement of Alexandria, Origen, Eusebius, Gregory of Nyssa, Gregory of Nazianzus, and Ambrose. *See also* Logos.

philosophy and theology. Since the time of the Greeks, philosophy and theology have sometimes been seen as complementary to each other and at other times in opposition. In Greek "philosophy" literally means "love of wisdom," while "theology" means "knowledge of God," so it would be natural for believers in God to consider them to complement each other, while unbelievers would try to find wisdom apart from belief in God. Any attempt to relate the two raises questions about the relation of reason to faith. For the Greeks, theology was equivalent to a study of the most fundamental causes of the universe and so represented the culmination of a philosophical inquiry. For Jews and Christians, on the other hand, theology had as its subject the God who was self-revealed to human beings—at Sinai or in Jesus—and so required a prior assent of faith.

It was inevitable that Jews or Christians in the Hellenic world should find themselves at odds intellectually. These differences account for the various senses given to the two expressions as time went on: unconverted Greeks complained that their philosophy comprised all there was to know about the universe and about God, and converted Greeks insisted that their theology was the only true philosophy. Finding the proper way to distinguish between philosophy and theology, so that they could also be related, was the work of signal Christian thinkers, notably Augustine of Hippo in the fourth century and Thomas Aquinas in the thirteenth. Augustine used the current philosophy of Plato to show how one might understand the God of Abraham, Isaac, Jacob, and Jesus not as something outside the universe but as the source of its very life and goal-directedness. Aquinas employed Aristotle to show how Christians' faith, in a universe that is freely created by God, permeates the world we observe and seek to understand. In other words, the philosophy of the Greeks can be incorporated into Christian inquiry as the "handmaid of theology." In both cases, however, relating philosophy to theology in this fashion required these authors to restrain the pretensions of philosophy to offer a total explanation of the universe. That claim also contains the seeds of their opposition.

Later thinkers found themselves less able to conceive of these modes of inquiry as complementary. The period of European thought associated with Immanuel Kant (d. 1804) and called the Enlightenment revived the totalizing pretension of philosophy just at the time in which the Reformation introduced distrust of the claims of human reason. So a new form of opposition between philosophical and theological inquiry was generated. Christian thinkers have insisted, however, that one never begins any inquiry without presupposing something. Therefore, a hybrid discipline of "Christian philosophy" may well be legitimated, even in the academy. Herein, the creative tension continues in a new form. *See also* theology.   DAVID B. BURRELL

philosophy of religion, the study of religion from a philosophical perspective. The philosophy of religion is a relatively recent phenomenon. Its predecessor, philosophical (or natural) theology, sought to probe the most philosophically vexing issues of theology, while the new discipline limited itself to those points where religious questions link up with other human concerns: the meaning of language about God, the problem of evil, and similar questions. *See also* philosophy and theology; theology.

Phocas of Sinope, St., possibly fourth century, martyr and patron saint of gardeners. His name is surrounded by legend, and he is sometimes made into three different saints (Phocas of Antioch, Phocas of Sinope, and Phocas the gardener). Because of the confusion, it is impossible to cite one single feast day; it is most commonly given as September 22 or July 14.

Phos hilaron (faws hee-lah-rahn'; Gk., "O joyous light"), opening words of the "hymn of light" sung at Byzantine-rite Vespers in honor of Christ, the Light of the World. Called the "thanksgiving for the light," it was already considered ancient in the fourth century. *See also* Vespers.

Photius, ca. 810–ca. 893, courtier, scholar, and patriarch of Constantinople. When the patriarch Ignatius of Constantinople opposed Bardas, uncle and chief minister of the young emperor Michael III, he

was soon exiled. The brilliant aristocratic civil servant Photius, a layman, was quickly tonsured, ordained, and installed on the patriarchal throne (Christmas, 858). Ignatius, however, claimed that he had been deprived of his see without sanction of a Church council; Pope Nicholas I consequently refused to recognize Photius. So began the Photian Schism between East and West. The basic problem was aggravated by attempts of the Bulgar khan to play Rome and Constantinople off against each other, by political rivalries between the Frankish emperor and the Byzantine, and by long-standing disagreements about papal authority over the patriarch. In the end, however, palace politics were decisive. In 867, Michael's favorite (and coemperor), Basil, murdered both Bardas and Michael and, as sole ruler, exiled Photius and recalled the elderly Ignatius. In 874, Photius was recalled and given a post in the palace; when Ignatius died in 875, Photius succeeded unchallenged to the patriarchate. In 887, Basil's son, Leo VI, accused Photius of conspiracy; exiled a second time, he died in retirement. Feast day: February 6 (East). *See also* Constantinople.

physical person [canon law], an individual who is the subject of rights and duties in Church law. The 1983 Code of Canon Law addresses itself to members of the Catholic Church and those seeking membership in the Catholic Church. Non-Catholics are affected at those points where they interact with Catholics, e.g., marriage situations.

physico-theologies, seventeenth- and eighteenth-century tracts for God's existence based on the new mechanical science. Each tract, e.g., Robert Boyle's *A Disquisition About the Final Causes of Natural Things* (1688), attributed to divine intervention phenomena believed to be inexplicable by the new mechanics. Advances in mechanics, and especially widespread acceptance of Darwin's evolutionary theory, undermined this movement in natural theology.

Pico della Mirandola, Giovanni, 1463–94, Italian humanist and mystical writer. An accomplished linguist, he was the first scholar to seek in the Jewish Cabbala a way of access to the meaning of the Christian mysteries. In part to reconcile humanism with Scholasticism, he developed a set of some nine hundred theses on a great variety of religious topics, but when Pope Innocent VIII found many of them to be heretical, Pico abandoned the project. He died soon after being received into the Dominican order by Girolamo Savonarola (d. 1598), a Dominican preacher and reformer who would later be tortured and hanged as a heretic.

Pierozzi, St. Antony. *See* Antoninus of Florence, St.

Pierre d'Ailly. *See* d'Ailly, Pierre.

pietà (pee-ay-tah'; It., "pity"), artistic depiction of the Virgin Mary holding the dead Christ after his body is taken down from the cross. The most famous is Michelangelo's marble sculpture in St. Peter's Basilica in the Vatican. *See also* Michelangelo.

Pietism, reform movement in Protestantism that focused on personal devotion and experience, ethical conversion, literal interpretation of the Bible, and the imitation of models from primitive Christianity (e.g., small groups, especially in the beginning, met in homes). Characteristics like these often led to opposition by Church authority; separatism was a constant temptation.

Pietism has been linked with the publication in 1675 of the *Pia Desideria* by the Lutheran Philip Spener (1635–1705). The beginnings and expression of Pietism, however, were more diverse and

La Pietà (the Blessed Virgin Mary cradling the crucified body of her Son), Michelangelo's masterpiece in St. Peter's Basilica, Rome.

more widespread than Spener's Lutheran version. The original impulses of Pietism were effective through the late seventeenth century and the first half of the eighteenth century. Associated with early Pietism were August Francke (1663–1727), Friedrich Lampe (1683–1705), and Count Nikolas von Zinzendorf (1700–1760). The last named influenced the formation of the Moravian Brethren at Herrnhut.

Pietism has had a lasting impact on Protestantism to this day. Modern interest in Pietism has brought considerable refinement of its varieties, affinities, and exponents. Pietism opposed and was influenced by the Enlightenment. Moravian Pietism had an effect on John and Charles Wesley and subsequent Methodism. Pietism was a major force in the formation of American Protestantism, and the Pietist tradition shaped the thought of the influential theologian Friedrich Schleiermacher (1768–1834). *See also* Enlightenment, the; Methodism; Protestantism; Schleiermacher, Friedrich Daniel Ernst.

piety (Lat., *pietas,* "dutifulness"), a virtue that calls for faithfulness in relationships to others, e.g., to family and kin (familial piety) and to country (patriotism). Piety is also one of the gifts of the Holy Spirit. This gift moves a person to venerate God with generosity and affection and to be responsible in one's relationships with others. Sometimes the words "piety" and "pious" describe devotional practices. "Piety" and "pious" have also been used pejoratively as indications of insincerity, hypocrisy, or religiosity, but these are caricatures of authentic piety, which is expressed with gladness. *See also* gifts of the Holy Spirit.

Pighi, Albert, ca. 1490–1542, Dutch theologian and humanist. An opponent of Luther and champion of papal infallibility, he participated in the effort at reunion with the Protestants at Ratisbon (1541).

Pignatelli, St. Joseph, 1737–1811, Spanish Jesuit who lived for forty years in exile in Italy after the Jesuits' expulsion from Spain. Following the suppression of the Society of Jesus in 1773, Pignatelli worked tirelessly for its restoration. He was made provincial of Italy in 1803; he died three years before the order was fully restored. Feast day: November 28.

pilgrimage, a religiously motivated journey to a

specific location to visit a holy person or to commemorate a special event that occurred there. The journey to and from this special place, along with the stay, comprise the pilgrimage.

Three requisites constitute an authentic pilgrimage: (1) the belief that God responds to prayer, (2) the conviction that God is present at holy sites, and (3) the desire to make a sacred journey to a holy site. People undertake pilgrimages to seek guidance for direction in life, to thank God for favors received, to petition God for spiritual and physical favors, or to atone for sin.

The practice of pilgrimage has often been regarded with skepticism in the Christian tradition. Early Christianity considered it a form of pagan worship. However, with the legalization of Christianity in the fourth century, resulting in an upsurge of public devotions, pilgrimage became popular. Once pilgrimages became fashionable they played a considerable role in influencing liturgical practices. For example, the procession of palms and veneration of the cross were brought to the West by pilgrims to Jerusalem, where these practices had originated. Devotion to Mary, Mother of God, developed when pilgrimages to the sites of Jesus' life were undertaken. In the Middle Ages, Christian crusaders were sent by popes and Catholic temporal rulers to the Holy Land to win back the holy places from the Muslims so that pilgrims could visit them safely once again.

The Church promoted pilgrimages to Jerusalem, Rome, and Santiago de Compostela as a form of penance. The spirit of exile imposed by the journey was meant to be a deterrent against future sins that might place one in a permanent state of exile from heaven. From ascetical-spiritual perspectives, extended pilgrimages were more a form of flight from the world. Like the hermits of the desert, the pilgrim left home and possessions and all superficial concerns.

Contemporary spirituality fosters the notion of an inner journey, but this is not a new concept. Philosophers and spiritual writers such as Boethius, Bonaventure, Teresa of Ávila, and John of the Cross advocated interior ascents or descents within the inner self to find God. The symbolic interpretation of life on earth as a pilgrimage enables the Church to see itself on a journey to the heavenly Jerusalem. *See also* Egeria, Pilgrimage of; People of God; pilgrim Church.   PATRICIA M. VINJE

pilgrim Church, an expression emphasizing the transitory, changeable, and imperfect phase of the Church's life on earth as it moves through history on its way toward the final kingdom of God.

pious association. *See* associations of the Christian faithful.

pious foundation, endowment established for works of religion or charity. Such a foundation is governed by a number of norms in canon law. These norms reflect concern that the foundation be under proper Church supervision in order that the donor's wishes be respected. *See also* foundations.

pious union. *See* associations of the Christian faithful.

pious will. *See* wills [canon law].

Pisa, Council of, 1409–10, first of three reform councils (the others are Constance and Basel) dealing with the crisis of papal authority provoked by the Great Schism (1378–1417). Cardinals from the Roman (Gregory XII) and Avignon (Benedict XIII) obediences convened the council (1409) without papal approval. Approximately 200 prelates, 287 abbots, and 700 theologians supported the council, which declared Gregory and Benedict deposed (June 5) and elected Peter of Candia as Pope Alexander V (June 26). Supporters of the other claimants refused to recognize the validity of Alexander's election. Pisa had failed to end the Great Schism and had indeed complicated matters further, because now there were three rival popes rather than two. The crisis was resolved at the Council of Constance (1414–18), which deposed Alexander's successor, John XXIII, brought about the resignation of Gregory, and elected Martin V. The third claimant, Benedict, fled. *See also* Great Schism.

Pius I, St., d. ca. 155, pope from ca. 142 to ca. 155. He was perhaps native to Aquileia, perhaps a brother of Hermas, author of the *Shepherd*. Evidence for Pius's martyrdom, like all else about him, is uncertain. Feast day: July 11. *See also* Hermas, Shepherd of.

Pius II [Aeneas Sylvius Piccolomini], 1405–64, Renaissance pope from 1458 to 1464. Born in Pienza (near Siena), Italy, he was a conciliarist and renowned humanist. He served antipope Felix V at the Council of Basel and then the emperor Frederick III in Germany (1442), where he defended Roman superiority in letters and civilization against German humanists. As pope, Pius II abandoned his earlier conciliarism and decisively strengthened papal power in the bull *Execrabilis* (1460), which prohibited any appeal of papal decisions to a future council. He encouraged the patronage of arts and letters and the lavish pageantry popularly associated with the Renaissance papacy.

Pius IV [Gian Angelo Medici], 1499–1565, pope from 1559 to 1565. His most important achievement was in reconvening the Council of Trent (1562), suspended since 1552, and bringing it to a successful conclusion (1563). He published a new edition of the Index of Forbidden Books, approved Communion under both kinds (consecrated bread and wine) for the laity of Germany, Austria, Hungary, and other regions where Protestantism was strong, and initiated work on the *Roman Catechism* to be based on the "Profession of the Tridentine Faith." *See also* Trent, Council of.

Pius V, St. [Antonio Ghislieri], 1504–72, Dominican Counter-Reformation pope from 1566 to 1572. He served the Inquisition in Milan and Bergamo. Elected pope with the support of Charles Borromeo, Pius made monastic austerity a model for Counter-Reformation Rome. He strengthened the Index of Forbidden Books, the Roman Inquisition, and carried through the reforms of the Council of Trent. He also published the *Roman Catechism* (1566), the *Roman Breviary* (1568), the *Roman Missal* (1570), and a new edition of Thomas Aquinas's works (1570). Pius excommunicated Queen Elizabeth I of England and promoted the military alliance with Spain and Venice that defeated Turkish naval power at Lepanto (1571). He was canonized in 1712 by Pope Clement XI. Feast day: April 30. *See also* Counter-Reformation/Catholic Reformation.

Pius VI [Giovanni Braschi], 1717–99, pope from 1775 to 1799. His was one of the longest pontificates in history, but at its end many thought the papacy had reached its nadir. He died in exile, having been removed from Rome by French Napoleonic forces. Throughout his pontificate, Pius had difficulties with various temporal powers as secularism, atheism, and nationalism grew: the kingdom of Naples, the Austrian emperor Joseph II, and especially France following the Revolution of 1789. In 1786, when he tried to establish a nunciature at Munich, even the German bishops defied him on the

grounds that they did not want any intervention from Rome. After the invasion of the Papal States by Napoleon in 1796, the pope was forced to hand over valuable manuscripts, artworks, and a substantial portion of his territories, and then formally to recognize the new French Republic. *See also* Febronianism; Gallicanism; Josephinism.

Pius VII [Luigi Barnaba Chiaramonti], 1742–1823, pope from 1800 to 1823. He was one of the first popes to oppose modernity. Forced to give concessions to Napoleon in areas of French church life, he nonetheless furthered the period of the Romanticist restoration of Catholicism by encouraging tolerance of some modern approaches and ideas, by expanding Asian missions, and by encouraging priestly education and pastoral life in the aftermath of the secularizing Enlightenment. He worked to make Rome a center of culture through restored and new museums and schools. *See also* Romanticism.

Pius IX [Giovanni Mastai-Ferretti], 1792–1878, longest-reigning pope in history, from 1846 to 1878. His pontificate was characterized by civil and religious controversy. By nature a warm and open person, Pius began his pontificate with a positive attitude toward the political and economic changes that swept over Europe during the first half of the

Pope Pius IX, the longest-reigning pope in history (1846–78), who promulgated the dogmas of the Immaculate Conception of the Blessed Virgin Mary (1854) and of papal infallibility (1870).

nineteenth century. But the revolution in Italy and in Rome itself, along with the nationalistic confrontation between Italians and Austrians, compromised Pius's position. Unable to take sides in a nationalistic dispute, Pius saw his popularity with the Italian people vanish almost overnight. Forced to leave Rome late in 1848, Pius was able to return only after the Austrian army overthrew revolutionary governments in the provinces and when French expeditionary forces defeated the new Roman Republic in the city of Rome itself in 1850. In the opinions of Italians the papacy had stood in the way of national unification. The Papal States straddled the country from west to east, making a union between northern and southern Italy impossible. In the years that followed his restoration, however, Pius saw his worldly sovereignty over the entire "Patrimony of St. Peter" (Papal States) evaporate as one church province after another chose to become part of the new Italian nation. In 1859 Rome itself was left unprotected by the French, at which time it, too, joined Italy. The future of the pope's earthly sovereignty over the Papal States—the so-called "Roman Question"—remained unresolved for the rest of Pius's pontificate and for the rest of the nineteenth century. Pius refused to recognize the new Italy and forbade the Italian faithful to participate in it.

Corresponding to his turn to political conservatism, Pius's church leadership tended toward the reactionary. In contrast to the nineteenth century's trend toward shared political power, Pius centralized the Church and asserted his own authority over that of other bishops. This culminated in the calling of the First Vatican Council (1869–70) and in its declaration of the dogma of papal infallibility. Reaction to the dogma was immediate and massive. Austria disclaimed its Concordat with the Vatican. Religious confrontations broke out in Switzerland. A minority of the faithful broke off from Rome, formed their own church, and became known as the "Old Catholics." The pronouncement on infallibility helped kindle the *Kulturkampf* (church-state political struggle) in Germany. Already incensed over Pius's earlier document, "The Syllabus of Errors" (1864), which condemned many tenets of nineteenth-century Liberalism, such as freedom of speech and of religion, German liberals joined forces with the conservative, Protestant chancellor Otto von Bismarck in an all-out attack upon the Church. The controversy was centered in Prussia, the largest German state, whose population counted the second highest number of Catholics, but spread as well to

other central European states. Only the death of Pius allowed the *Kulturkampf* to subside.

A second Church dogma, the Immaculate Conception of Mary (1854), also emerged from Pius's pontificate. This teaching gave encouragement to the strong Marian movement in France and beyond. The Confraternity of the Immaculate Conception spread with alacrity throughout the Western hemisphere. Thus, Pius laid the foundation for the broad development of Marian devotion in the twentieth century.

In other Church teachings Pius was equally conservative. Shunning modernity and the new scientific and religious ideas that developed during the nineteenth century, Pius also laid the foundation for the neo-Scholastic emphasis in Church teaching that dominated much of the twentieth century.

Although unpopular with the educated, Pius IX enjoyed support among the masses, who recognized his sincerity and his pastoral and spiritual concern, even in the midst of great temporal upheavals. Pius died amid the controversy that his leadership had brought to the Church in Italy and on the Continent. *See also* Immaculate Conception; infallibility; *Kulturkampf*; Syllabus of Errors; Vatican Council I.

MICHAEL PHAYER

Pius X, St. [Giuseppe Sarto], 1835–1914, anti-Modernist pope from 1903 to 1914. A parish priest, seminary spiritual director, bishop of Mantua (1884–93), and patriarch of Venice (1893–1903), he inclined more toward the inner life than toward Church leadership. Concentrating on problems within the Church, he showed little interest in pursuing or expanding the contacts with society established by his predecessor, Leo XIII. Unsympathetic toward the Orthodox churches, rigidly opposed to cultural adaptation in the missions, and tireless in securing political rights for the Church, he developed the public image of a man of prejudice and negation. Hostile to democracy in Italy and the United States, he argued for support of the poor while at the same time weakening the labor movement. He saw the ensemble of philosophical and biblical trends the Vatican came to call "Modernism" as dangerous to Christian revelation and the Church and was convinced that modern forms of culture were generally irreconcilable with Catholicism. This attitude produced a flood of measures: condemnations of individuals (Herman Schell) and of movements (Le Sillon in France). At the same time he tolerated the right-wing, monarchist movement Action Française.

Pope Pius X, early-twentieth-century pope well known for his personal sanctity and his encouragement of frequent reception of Holy Communion. He was also responsible for the harsh repression of Catholic scholarship that set the Church's intellectual life back nearly fifty years, until the pontificate of John XXIII (1958–63) and the Second Vatican Council (1962–65).

The decree *Lamentabili* and the encyclical *Pascendi Dominici Gregis* (1907) became the central documents of several anti-Modernist campaigns and remained influential until Vatican II (1962–65). These documents opposed the reduction of revelation to logic or human consciousness, the absorption of the event of Christ in the flow and laws of history, and the replacement of Church authority by democracy. To enforce these views he established a secret network of informers whose reports on theologians, historians, and biblical scholars led in many cases to dismissal from their teaching positions.

Other Vatican measures were similarly ill informed, such as the conscious ignoring of the pastoral leader of the Church in the United States, John Ireland, or the inflammatory encyclical on Charles Borromeo, which, because of its vulgar polemics against German Protestantism, was quickly withdrawn. On the positive side the pope established realistic relationships with Italy, proposed Christian measures for the improvement of society, insisted upon a deeper spiritual formation for priests, and worked for improved preaching, more suitable liturgical books, and a restoration of Church music (Gregorian chant in particular). He reformed aspects of

the central administration of the Church and initiated the process for the codification of canon law in 1917. He became popular as the "pope of frequent Communion" and is remembered for having lowered the age for First Communion to the "age of discretion" (approximately seven). He was canonized in 1954. Feast day: August 21. *See also* Modernism.

THOMAS F. O'MEARA

Pius XI [Ambrogio Achille Ratti], 1857–1939, pope from 1922 to 1939. A seminary professor, librarian, and diplomat, he was cardinal-archbishop of Milan when elected to the papacy. Strongly opposed to modern liberalism, communism, and secularism, Pius XI turned to fascism in the hope of increasing the influence of the Church on modern-day life and out of fear of communism. He signed agreements or concordats with both of the most successful and notorious twentieth-century fascist leaders, Adolf Hitler and Benito Mussolini.

The Concordat with Italy allowed Pius to reach a favorable solution to the "Roman Question," the name given to the conflict between Church and state in Italy since 1870, when Italian forces occupied Rome and incorporated the city into the new Italian state. The 1929 Lateran Accords gave the pope sovereignty over Vatican City, a small enclave within the city of Rome itself. Furthermore, many anticlerical laws were repealed and religious instruction in

Pope Pius XI, who signed the Lateran Treaty with Mussolini in 1929, walking in the Vatican Garden to the rear of St. Peter's Basilica.

secondary schools became obligatory. In return, the Church recognized Italy as a kingdom with Rome as its capital and did not object to Mussolini's invasion of Ethiopia or to Italy's antidemocratic intervention in the Spanish Civil War.

During the 1930s Pius became critical of anti-Christian aspects of fascism and, specifically, of its racism. Pius is celebrated for his denunciation of Nazi excesses in the encyclical *Mit brennender Sorge* (1937). Written largely by the cardinal-archbishop of Munich, Michael Faulhaber, the letter soured the already difficult relationship between Hitler and the Church in Germany when it was publicly read in churches throughout the country in March 1937.

Pius took at least four important steps to increase Christian influence over modern life: (1) He invited greater lay initiative and participation in the life of the Church through the Catholic Action movement. (2) He emphasized Christian social teachings in his encyclical *Quadragesimo Anno,* published in 1931, in the midst of the worldwide economic depression. (3) He doubled the number of missionaries by requiring every religious order to engage in missionary work, and founded a faculty of missiology at the Gregorian University in Rome. (4) He promoted science and scholarship, founding the Pontifical Institute of Christian Archaeology in 1925 and the Pontifical Academy of Sciences in 1936. He also installed a radio station in the Vatican in 1931 and was the first pope to use radio for pastoral purposes. *See also* Fascism; Lateran Treaty; Nazism.

MICHAEL PHAYER

Pope Pius XII, although somewhat aloof, one of the most prominent of the twentieth-century popes, having governed the Church during the Second World War and prepared the way for the reforms of the Second Vatican Council through his encyclicals on the renewal of biblical studies, the liturgy, and the Church.

Pius XII [Eugenio Pacelli], 1876–1958, pope from 1939 to 1958. Ordained in 1899, he entered the papal service two years later, working on the codification of canon law while teaching international law at the school for papal diplomats in Rome. In the midst of the First World War, he became nuncio to Bavaria in 1917 and to the new German Republic in 1920, subsequently forging concordats with Bavaria and Prussia. As papal secretary of state (1930–39), he also fashioned concordats with Austria and National Socialist Germany (the latter was repeatedly violated by Adolf Hitler, and relations with the Church deteriorated). With the world on the verge of another war, he was elected pope on the third ballot in a one-day conclave, the first secretary of state chosen as pope since 1667. Dedicating his pontificate to the cause of peace, two months after his election he called for an international conference to settle differences. His pontificate faced the problem of dealing directly with many authoritarian regimes: the Italian state, Nazism and various other fascisms, as well as Communism.

The Pope and the Germans: While living in Germany during the 1920s as nuncio, Pacelli came to admire German culture and German Catholicism. A known Germanophile, he would later as pope choose Germans as his close advisers and confidants. The future pope was less familiar with the U.S. Catholic Church, although he traveled through the United States in 1936. The trip also provided the opportunity for Pacelli to make the acquaintance of President Franklin D. Roosevelt.

His respect for things German kept him from recognizing the dangerous rise and then ruthless oppression of Hitler; his generous financial support of refugees and Jews was counterbalanced by a reluctance to denounce the Axis enslavement as forcefully as demanded. Uppermost in the mind of Pius XII (as with Pius XI) was the need to preserve the benefits that previous concordats with Germany had won, but the signing of a new concordat at the beginning of Hitler's chancellorship lent the German leader international prestige.

The question regarding the attitude of Pius XII toward the Nazi persecution of the Jews did not arise until after his death. His supporters pointed to his efforts to rescue Italian Jews through financial assistance and by dispensing with Church regulations so that Jews could be hidden in ecclesiastical institutions, including monasteries. On the other hand, he did not speak out plainly regarding atrocities but only in general terms (the style, for example, of his otherwise strong Christmas address of 1942). Even before the end of the war the pope challenged the notion of the collective guilt of the German people, and the appearance of the Cold War soon after 1945 seemed to confirm Pius's view of Germany as a bulwark against Communism.

The Pope and Church Renewal: Pius adopted a moderate attitude toward modernity's relationship to the Church; he approved a limited use of the historical-critical method for biblical studies (*Divino Afflante Spiritu,* 1943), a modest beginning for the liturgical movement (*Mediator Dei,* 1947), and a theology of the Church that promoted positive relationships with nonbelievers (*Mystici Corporis,* 1943). At the same time, he held himself aloof from ecumenism and from any theology in dialogue with modern philosophy. He did not appreciate the intellectual need within Catholic life to pass beyond the simple categories of neo-Scholasticism and the false dichotomies between grace and world (the "new theology" in France, censored in the encyclical *Humani Generis,* 1950). He did not grasp the dramatic effects of secularization in Europe in the twentieth century (e.g., the further loss of working classes), and he was unsympathetic toward new pastoral theologies ranging from religious education to the use of abstract art. He used personal appearances, radio, and newsreels to contact millions of people; his addresses, invested with varying levels of papal formality and authority, brought Catholic ideas to bear on a large number of topics ranging from architecture to sports. He worked tirelessly for the expansion of institutions conducted by members of religious orders, particularly schools. His efforts to hold back Communism in Eastern Europe were unrelenting, but he distinguished between the subjected peoples in their culture and religion and the atheist ideology forced upon them. His many writings and addresses on Mary found their climax in the infallible proclamation in 1950 of her Assumption into heaven.

Having presided over an extraordinary growth of the Church throughout the world, Pius XII must be seen as one of the most powerful popes in modern history. Despite the tightly centralized mode of Church authority, his authoritarian personality did not reject the emergence of democracies and secular institutions, and he gained considerable credibility and influence for the papacy and the Church among non-Catholic powers throughout the world. This was strengthened and advanced by three facets of an immature theology: the presentation of his own person as an aloof "Holy Father"; the theology of his office as the basic and immediate pastor for every Catholic; and the implication that the charism of infallibility was easily accessible to all of his major decisions.

At the same time he prepared for the theological event of Vatican II (1962–65) by furthering Catholic intellectual life, by multiplying dioceses (the number rose from 1,696 to 2,048), by appointing numerous native bishops in Asia and Africa, and by internationalizing the College of Cardinals. *See also* Jews, Catholicism and.

THOMAS F. O'MEARA

Placet (plah'chet; Lat., "it is pleasing"), affirmative response or vote given to a particular proposal, nomination, or proposition. In some circumstances the word refers to a vote cast in a collegial body such as an ecumenical council; in other circumstances it refers to an approval given by proper authority.

Placet iuxta modum (plah'chet yooks'tah moh' doom; Lat., "it is pleasing to a certain extent"), conditional affirmation given to a particular proposal, nomination, or proposition.

plate. *See* paten.

Plato, d. ca. 347 B.C., familiar name of Aristocles, ancient Greek philosopher. Plato wrote thirteen letters and twenty-seven dialogues, of which *Apology, Phaedo, Republic,* and *Timaeus* are the most popular. The dialogue style enabled him to present the different views held by philosophers of his time and to draw readers into thinking through their own philosophical positions. A fictionalized Socrates is his spokesman and model philosopher. A sequential arrangement of his dialogues shows the beginning, development, and critique of a philosophical system. There is a hint of a secret and unwritten philosophy.

The main features of Plato's philosophy can be summarized thus: Truth emerges in ongoing dialogue; knowledge is contrasted with unreflective opinion, and is arrived at by questioning (the Socratic method); the sensible world of experience is a limited imitation of, and participation in, a higher world of eternal ideas or forms. Plato used myth to suggest that the human soul possessed these ideas in a previous existence but forgot them when it descended into a human body. Learning is the gradual recovery, usually through questioning, of these innate ideas (theory of reminiscence). Education prepares the soul to free itself from the tyranny of the senses and rise to philosophical insight (dialectic). These ideas laid the foundation for liberal education in the West.

Ethics is the major concern in the early dialogues, including the *Socratic Dialogues, Protagoras,* and *Republic.* Plato argued that virtue is knowledge; growth in virtue is growth in the understanding of ethical ideas (values); on the other hand, moral failure is not a matter of will but of ignorance. The good state models the good man; justice is the proper functioning of various social classes and groups: workers, warriors, philosophers. The proper virtues of the philosophers are temperance, fortitude, and wisdom (cardinal virtues). Therefore, the king should be a philosopher who has knowledge of ideas, especially the idea of the good, the highest in the hierarchy of ideas and cause of all being and all knowledge. The ascent to the good begins in the love (eros) of beauty. Though a mythmaker himself, Plato criticizes the works of imagination (poetry, art) because they stand between the soul and the ideas (mathematics, values, being, the real world).

The human soul is eternal, and though it does not remember its previous existence, it desires to be free of the body and return to its origins and the world of ideas. The soul alone, using the body and its organs as an instrument, like a boatman using a boat or a rider using a horse, forms the essence of the human being. Aristotle (d. 322 B.C.), a pupil of Plato, reacted against the philosophy of ideas and developed a philosophy that relied more fundamentally on sensible experience. Religious thought in the West, particularly Christian thought, has swung back and forth between Plato and Aristotle even to modern times. Later Platonists, preeminently Plotinus (ca. A.D. 200), developed a synthesis of Plato, Aristotle, and the Stoics called Neoplatonism, which heavily influenced the philosophy of early Christianity, the Middle Ages, and much of modern philosophy. Christian leaders in the development of Neoplatonism were Augustine (d. 430), Pseudo-Dionysius the Areopagite (d. ca. 500), and Bonaven-

ture (d. 1274). Thomas Aquinas (d. 1274) gave a strong Aristotelian twist to this development, which formed much of Renaissance Scholasticism in the sixteenth century and neo-Scholastic philosophy between 1879 and Vatican Council II (1962–65). *See also* Neoplatonism.   ROBERT F. HARVANEK

pleasure, any form of joy, satisfaction, or gratification at the anticipation or attainment of something good. In this sense, pleasure can be not only morally neutral but morally good, e.g., if it accompanies virtuous activity. In a more restricted sense, pleasure is understood as the sensual gratification of one of our basic appetites, e.g., for food or sexual intercourse. Even in this sense, pleasure in itself has been viewed as morally neutral, but some theologians have viewed it with suspicion as an inducement to sin. Others have viewed even physical pleasure as morally desirable when it accompanies morally praiseworthy actions. *See also* concupiscence; passions.

plenary council, an ecclesiastical assembly, convoked by the conference of bishops, with authority to enact particular law for the dioceses of a nation. Only bishops have a deliberative vote in the council, although others participate. Three plenary councils were held in Baltimore, Maryland, in the latter half of the nineteenth century. *See also* council; ecumenical council.

plenary indulgence, forgiveness of all temporal punishment due to sin, often conferred at the moment of death, and related to the sinner's prior prayers and good works. The idea of a plenary indulgence derives from the time of Urban II, who granted plenary indulgences (1095) to those who took part in the Crusades. Alexander II may have also granted plenary indulgences (ca. 1063) to those Christians fighting the Saracens. Boniface VIII in 1300 extended plenary indulgences to those Christians who took part in the first "holy year" by making a pilgrimage to the Roman basilicas. At the time of Vatican II (1962–65), Paul VI restricted plenary indulgences to those Christians who rejected all sin, including venial sin. *See also* indulgences.

plenitude of power (Lat., *plenitudo potestatis*), fullness of power exercised by the pope in religious matters, compared to the partial power of other bishops. First used by Pope Leo I (440–61), the term refers, according to Vatican I (1869–70), to the pope's legal authority over other bishops. *See also* papacy, the.

pleroma (Gk., "fullness" or "totality"), a theological term used by early Christian and Gnostic writers. In Paul, *pleroma* describes the fullness of divinity in Jesus (Col 2:9). Later Christian writers, notably Origen and Tertullian, applied it to the fullness of divine revelation experienced by Christian faith.

Plessington, St. John, d. 1679, one of the Forty Martyrs of England and Wales canonized in 1970. Ordained in Spain in 1662 and sent to England the next year, he was hanged at Chester in 1679 as a member of the popish "plot" against the king. Feast day: July 19. *See also* Forty Martyrs of England and Wales.

Plotinus, ca. 205–70, first of the Neoplatonist philosophers. A Greek who studied under Ammonius Saccas, Plotinus developed from the Platonic system his own metaphysics that was the basis of his mysticism. For him the human ascent or return to the source of all being culminates in the presence of the One. Contemplation or ecstasy is for Plotinus the highest of human activities, not totally a work of grace as Augustine would teach. His pupil Porphyry posthumously edited the six *Enneads* of Plotinus. Christian thinkers like Augustine of Hippo and Denys the Areopagite found the mysticism of Plotinus congenial, adapting it to fit their own articulation of Christian mysticism. *See also* Neoplatonism.

Plunket, St. Oliver, 1629–81, Irish bishop and martyr. After studies at the Irish College in Rome and ordination (1649), he taught at the Propaganda Fide College in Rome until he left for Ireland as archbishop of Armagh in 1669. An indefatigable pastor, he was arrested as a conspirator against the crown after the Titus Oates plot and was imprisoned in Newgate jail (London) for three years. Falsely accused, he was executed for high treason in 1681. He was canonized in 1976. Feast day: July 1. *See also* Ireland, Catholicism in.

pluralism, in moral theology, the existence of disagreement concerning the method and/or content of moral reflection. Ethical pluralism is largely a product of cultural or social pluralism. New moral problems may also generate ethical pluralism while the Church investigates their implications and at-

tempts to develop new moral norms to address them. Pluralism itself has become a matter of disagreement in recent times; some theologians and other Church members believe ethical pluralism to be disruptive of the unity that ought to characterize the Catholic community, while others consider tolerance of disagreement to be compatible with unity at a deeper level. Similarly, some Church members are concerned that the faithful will be confused by the multiplicity of opinions on moral matters; others view ethical pluralism as a necessary stage in the process of growth in understanding. Moral theologians who consider ethical pluralism healthy often attribute suspicion of pluralism to a confusion of levels of moral discourse. These theologians argue that legitimate disagreement on the applicability of general moral norms to specific cases need not imply disagreement on the norms themselves. Disagreement about the validity of ethical pluralism is thus often a disagreement about the level of moral discourse at which Christian unity ought to be located. *See also* moral theology.

pneumatology (Gk., "study of the Spirit"), the branch of systematic theology that deals with the Person and work of the Holy Spirit. While biblical references to the Holy Spirit are important sources for pneumatology, the discipline itself cannot be said to have developed prior to the fourth century, when a controversy arose over the divinity of the Holy Spirit. *See also* Holy Spirit.

Pneumatomachians (noo-mah-toh-mahk'ee-uhns; Gk., "fighters of the Spirit"), a term used to designate Christians, otherwise orthodox, who in the second half of the fourth century denied the divinity of the Holy Spirit. They are also called Macedonians, after Macedonius (bishop of Constantinople ca. 342–60), perhaps the first to explicitly defend this position. *See also* Holy Spirit.

Poland, Catholicism in. Beginning with the introduction of Christianity in the territories of the western Slavs in the tenth century by missionaries aligned with Rome, the fortunes of the Catholic Church have closely mirrored those of Poland itself. Championed initially by the nobility, the Catholic religion in time completely displaced the native paganism, and for most of the past thousand years Catholics have formed the overwhelming majority of the population. While Poland, and its church, has

POLAND

(Map labels: Warsaw, Czestochowa, Auschwitz (Oświęcim), Cracow)

enjoyed periods of great prosperity—especially under the leadership of strong kings in the later Middle Ages, when Polish intellectuals and churchmen played prominent roles in the broader cultural and religious life of Western Christendom—the country has suffered greatly throughout much of its history, with severe repercussions for the Catholic Church.

Poland's great misfortune has been its close proximity to powerful nations with expansionist tendencies. The late eighteenth and nineteenth centuries brought the partition of Poland at the hands of Prussia, Russia, and Austria, and it was only at the end of World War I (1918) that Poland regained its independence, only to lose it again with the German invasion that initiated World War II. The years under foreign rule imposed severe hardships on the Polish people and the Catholic Church. While the Austrian conquerors tended to leave their coreligionists in peace, the religious commitments of Poles under the rule of Protestant Prussians and the Orthodox Russians were repeatedly put to the test. Nevertheless, foreign oppression did not defeat the Polish people, and, aided immeasurably by the spiritual and intellectual resources of the Church, a distinctive Polish identity has emerged unscathed. A more serious challenge than foreign occupation to the continued fidelity of the people to the Church came from within during the Reformation, when factions among the nobility adopted different sides in the great religious conflict of the age as part of the struggle for power in Poland. The attraction of the Protestant cause, strong in some quarters for much of the sixteenth century, in the end proved fleeting and Poland has been steadfastly Catholic ever since.

Piety: A special mark of Polish Catholic piety has been the vibrant devotion to the Blessed Virgin Mary, who is seen as the protectress of Poland. Most prominent of the many Marian shrines that dot the countryside is that of the "Black Mother of God" at Czestochowa, the icon credited with saving its monastery from foreign attack in 1655. Thousands travel yearly to this and to other shrines to express their gratitude and to seek Mary's favor. Providing structure to such religious expressions is the Polish ecclesiastical hierarchy, which has demonstrated a remarkable resiliency, going underground during the worst oppression, but quickly reemerging and expanding when conditions became more favorable. Even under Communist rule after World War II, the Polish hierarchy was well articulated and widespread: over seventy bishops distributed over a number of ecclesiastical provinces, and thousands of priests and nuns, now serve the pastoral needs of the people.

Modern Period: The history of Poland from the onset of World War II (1939) to the present encapsulates the suffering and the glory of the country, underscoring as well the centrality of the Catholic Church in the maintenance of Polish identity. World War II brought unprecedented brutality. Millions of Poles died during the war, including most of the sizable pre-war Jewish population in the Nazi death camps. Recovery after the war was slow and the establishment of a Communist government in Poland, closely tied to the Soviet Union, created new challenges for both the people and the Church. The early years of Communist rule were marked by persecution of Catholics and their leaders. Eventually, however, the Church was able to work out a more tolerable mode of coexistence with the state. More recent events have disclosed the irrepressible vitality of Catholicism in Poland. The election in 1978 of the first Slav pope, Cardinal-Archbishop Karol Wojtyla of Cracow as John Paul II, was a matter of enormous national pride and itself provided a stimulus to the growing political and social reform movement in Poland. The success of the reformers in overthrowing Communist rule and establishing democratic institutions was in no small measure due to the alliance between the reformers, especially those in the Solidarity labor movement, and the leaders in the Church. The coming years promise new challenges, as the Polish people attempt to develop a society that avoids the pitfalls of both their former Communism and the excesses of capitalism of the West. On the basis of its history it seems clear that the Catholic Church will continue to play a leading role in the life of Poland.

In 1994 there were almost 37 million Catholics in Poland, comprising more than 96 percent of the total population. There are fourteen archdioceses and twenty-six dioceses. *See also* Czestochowa, Our Lady of.   JOSEPH WAWRYKOW

Pole, Reginald, 1500–58, archbishop of Canterbury and humanist. Opposed to the divorce of Henry VIII and shocked by the executions of Thomas More and John Fisher, Pole wrote a treatise censuring the king, which led to the imprisonment of his family and the execution of his mother. Made cardinal in 1536, Pole sought unsuccessfully to mediate between Protestant and Catholic views of justification, both as councilor of Contarini at Ratisbon (1541) and as legate to the Council of Trent (1545). Sent by Pope Julius III as legate to England in 1553, Pole absolved Parliament of schism in 1554 and was made archbishop of Canterbury in 1556. He died in 1558, caught between the policies of the pope and Mary Tudor. *See also* England, Catholicism in; Mary Tudor.

Polish National Church, late-nineteenth-century schismatic group. Struggles between Polish ethnic parishes and their non-Polish hierarchy led, in 1897, to a breakaway Polish parish in Scranton, Pennsylvania. The divisive issues were not doctrinal but questions of jurisdiction and ethnic pride. Other parishes joined the dissidents, with the pastor eventually receiving episcopal ordination from an Old Catholic prelate. In this century there eventually grew a national church movement with approximately a quarter of a million members and an outreach into Poland itself. After World War II the church made ecumenical links with both the National Council of Churches and the World Council of Churches. In the late 1980s ecumenical conversations began with Catholic authorities.

politics. *See* Church and state.

Polycarp of Smyrna, St., ca. 69–ca. 155/6, bishop of Smyrna. A disciple of John, according to Irenaeus, he bridged the apostolic age and the second century. His *Letter to the Philippians* gives early witness to certain NT writings. The *Martyrdom of Polycarp* records his execution at Smyrna. Feast day: February 23. *See also* apostolic age; Apostolic Fathers.

polyglot Bibles, printed Bibles in which the Hebrew and Greek biblical text is accompanied by translations in several languages. The first was the Complutensian Polyglot (1521–22); others were published in Antwerp (1569–72), Paris (1629–45), and London (1654–57).

polyphony (Gk., *polyphonia,* "many tones"), musical term denoting the simultaneous interweaving of many melodic lines into a single whole in a musical composition. Its opposite form is monophony, which uses only one melodic line. Polyphonic church music reached its apex in the Renaissance and Baroque periods, although its roots go back to the late Middle Ages. *See also* Catholicism and music; liturgical music.

Pomponazzi, Pietro, 1464–1525, influential Italian Renaissance philosopher. Distrustful of the Scholastic appropriation of Aristotle, he insisted on the limitations of reason in teaching Christian doctrine and on the need for the Church to rely on supernatural revelation to guarantee the truths inaccessible to unaided reason.

Pontian, St., d. 235, pope (230–35) and martyr. After five years as pope, he was banished by the new anti-Christian emperor Maximinus Thrax to Sardinia where he died of harsh treatment. Before dying, however, he abdicated his office to make possible the election of a successor. He was the first pope to abdicate. Feast day (with St. Hippolytus): August 13.

Pontifex Maximus (pon'tee-fex max'ee-muhs; Lat., "Supreme Pontiff," "bridge-builder"), a title of honor accorded the Bishop of Rome, the pope, since the late fourth century, stressing his ministry of bridging the gap between heaven and earth, the divine and the human. It was originally a pagan title given the emperor as head of the college of priests in Rome. *See also* papacy, the; pope.

Pontifical Biblical Commission, commission established in 1902 by Pope Leo XIII to encourage biblical studies in the Church. The commission soon became a vigilance committee, seeking to safeguard the Bible's authority against Modernist criticism. It consisted of five cardinals and thirty-nine consultors. From 1903 to 1933 the commission published thirteen *responsa* (misentitled "decrees"), replies to intricate questions on biblical topics (e.g., Mosaic authorship of the Pentateuch, historicity of Gen 1–3, authorship of Hebrews). These replies cast a cloud of conservatism over Catholic biblical scholarship. After Pius XII issued *Divino Afflante Spiritu* (on promoting biblical studies, 1943), the commission changed its activity and image. Its secretaries issued in 1955 a quasiofficial explanation, making it clear that the *responsa* touching on literary questions (e.g., authorship, date, integrity) were time-conditioned and that Catholic interpreters could pursue research in such matters "with full freedom" (*Catholic Biblical Quarterly* 18 [1956]: 23–29). In 1964 the commission published an instruction titled "On the Historical Truth of the Gospels," obliging Catholic interpreters to expound the Gospels according to the sound principles of form criticism and the three stages of Gospel tradition. This Gospel interpretation was adopted by Vatican II (Dogmatic Constitution on Divine Revelation, 1965, n. 19). In 1971 Paul VI restructured the commission, appointing twenty biblical scholars instead of cardinals as members. The commission is no longer a vigilance committee and acts as an advisory board to the pope and the Congregation for the Doctrine of the Faith. *See also* Bible, Church teachings on the.

JOSEPH A. FITZMYER

Pontifical Biblical Institute, a graduate-level institution of teaching, research, and publication founded in Rome by Pope Pius X in 1909. The pope intended the institute to be a positive response to Modernism, a center under papal supervision for studying and teaching biblical exegesis based on firsthand control of the sources. The institute was entrusted to the Society of Jesus. A Jerusalem branch was opened in 1926, and a faculty for ancient Near Eastern studies was established in 1932. Degrees given are the licentiate (S.S.L., equivalent to a rigorous M.A.) and the S.S.D. (doctorate in Sacred Scripture). An average of sixty-five licentiate degrees and six doctorates are granted every year.

Pontifical Commission for Latin America, a department of the Roman Curia related specifically to the Congregation for Bishops, whose prefect is its president, and that has responsibility for advising, assisting, and studying questions of interest to the dioceses in Latin America (*Pastor Bonus* [1988], nn. 83–84). *See also* Latin America, Catholicism in; Roman Curia.

Pontifical Council for Promoting Christian Unity, the office of the Roman Curia responsible for contacts and dialogues with other churches and ec-

clesial communities and for fostering ecumenical activity within the Catholic Church.

On May 30, 1960, Pope John XXIII announced the establishment of a secretariat that was to host non-Catholic observers at Vatican II. But in the end the new office was also given responsibility for drafting important conciliar documents. In 1966 Pope Paul VI confirmed the Secretariat for Promoting Christian Unity as a permanent office of the Holy See. In 1974 a special Commission for Religious Relations with the Jews was set up in association with the secretariat.

The presidents of the secretariat have been Augustine Cardinal Bea (1960–68), Cardinal Johannes Willebrands (1968–89), and Edward Cardinal Cassidy (since 1989). In 1989 the name of the office was changed to Pontifical Council for Promoting Christian Unity.

Currently the council sponsors theological dialogues with ten different communions and cooperates with the World Council of Churches through the Joint Working Group. It also provides and updates ecumenical guidelines for Catholics in an ecumenical directory (1967, 1969). *See also* ecumenism.

Pontifical Council for the Family, a department of the Roman Curia that promotes pastoral care of families, fosters studies on marriage and family spirituality, strives for acknowledgment and defense of family rights, including protection of the unborn, and encourages associations that serve families (*Pastor Bonus,* 1988, nn. 139–41). *See also* family; Roman Curia.

Pontifical Council for the Interpretation of Legislative Texts, department of the Roman Curia authorized to issue authentic (i.e., authoritative) interpretations of Church laws. It reviews the documents of curial departments, synods, and episcopal conferences regarding their juridic form and content and assesses conformity of other legislation with universal law (*Pastor Bonus,* 1988, nn. 154–58). *See also* canon law; Roman Curia.

Pontifical Council for the Laity, a department of the Roman Curia responsible for promoting lay participation in the mission of the Church. It coordinates the lay apostolate, fosters cooperation in catechetics, liturgy, the sacraments, and charitable works, and regulates international associations of the faithful (*Pastor Bonus,* 1988, nn. 131–34). *See also* laity; Roman Curia.

Pontifical Gregorian University. *See* Gregorian University.

Pontifical Marian Academy, international institute for the promotion of multidisciplinary Marian studies and devotion to Mary. Founded in 1946 by Carlo Balic, this Rome-based academy holds congresses and publishes the acts of its meetings and other Mariological literature. In 1959 Pope John XXIII bestowed upon the academy the title "Pontifical," commissioning it to coordinate Marian studies by worldwide Mariological societies. *See also* Mariology.

Pontifical Oriental Institute, a graduate school for Eastern Christian studies founded in Rome by Pope Benedict XV in 1917 and given over to the direction of the Jesuits in 1922. In addition to its degree programs, it is noted for the high level of its scholarly publications and for its renowned library, considered by many the best in the world on Eastern Christianity. The "Orientale," as it is called, forms part of the consortium of Jesuit Roman institutions, along with the Pontifical Gregorian University and Pontifical Biblical Institute. The post–Vatican II (1962–65) era of East-West ecumenism and, more recently, the demise of Communism in the East have greatly increased its student body and given a new impetus to its work.

pontifical right, status of a religious institute or society of apostolic life that has a decree of approval from the Holy See. Such approval allows more autonomy to an institute because its internal affairs are then mostly free from the supervision of the diocesan bishop. *See also* religious institute; society of apostolic life.

pontifical universities, schools that have particular approval by the Holy See. In some cases schools that have one or more approved departments or faculties in particular academic disciplines are also called "pontifical," even though the approval has been given only to those departments. These schools can grant "pontifical degrees," i.e., degrees approved by the Holy See, and are governed by particular norms approved by Rome.

Poor Clares, religious order of women. Originally called the Poor Ladies, the Poor Clares were founded at Assisi, Italy, in 1212 by Clare of Assisi. In the beginning, they adopted the ideal of poverty espoused by Francis of Assisi, having the custom that neither individual religious nor the given community might hold property of any sort. In time, this interpretation of poverty was modified. The Poor Clares were established as a canonical religious community in 1215 under Pope Innocent III. Brought to the United States from Italy by Mother Maria Maddalena Bentivoglio and Mother Maria Costanza Bentivoglio, the order established its first American monastery in Cleveland, Ohio, in 1875. The members of the community take the three vows of religious life—poverty, chastity, and obedience—as well as a vow of enclosure. As a contemplative community, the sisters engage in the recitation of the Divine Office, contemplative prayer, and mental and manual labor. Worldwide in 1994, the order of Poor Clares numbers more than 17,000 sisters in a thousand autonomous monasteries. Contemporary followers of St. Clare are known as Poor Clares (P.C.), the Order of St. Clare (O.S.C.) and Poor Clares of St. Colette (P.C.C.). *See also* Clare of Assisi, St.; Franciscan spirituality.

pope (Lat., *papa,* "father"), the Bishop of Rome and the earthly head of the Catholic Church. In earlier centuries the term was used of any bishop in the West, while in the East it seems to have been used of priests as well, and was a special title of the patriarch of Alexandria. In 1073 Pope Gregory VII formally prohibited its use for all except the Bishop of Rome. *See also* papacy, the; pope, titles of the.

pope, titles of the, Bishop of Rome, Vicar of Peter, Vicar of Jesus Christ, Successor of the Chief of the Apostles, Supreme Pontiff of the Universal Church, Patriarch of the West, Primate of Italy, Archbishop and Metropolitan of the Roman Province, Sovereign of Vatican City State, and Servant of the Servants of God. *See also* papacy, the.

Pope Joan. *See* Joan, "Pope."

popular religion, term denoting a wide range of practices (e.g., pilgrimages, novenas; devotion to the Virgin Mary, the saints, shrines) not directly tied to the official liturgy of the Church. These practices tend to differ according to locale and are not infrequently connected to customs and practices that may predate Christianity or were absorbed from the surrounding non-Christian culture. Official statements of the Church tend to support such practices since they reflect the experience of the poor and the marginalized. *See also* devotions.

The following list of popes—262 in all—is based on the annual Vatican directory, known as the *Annuario Pontificio*, and on J. N. D. Kelly's *The Oxford Dictionary of Popes* (New York: Oxford University Press, 1986). When there is a minor discrepancy between the dates given by the two sources for the beginning and end of individual pontificates, especially in the case of the earliest popes, Kelly is generally preferred.

Alternate names are given in brackets; nationalities other than Italian are given in parentheses. The dates in the second column refer to the beginning and end of individual pontificates. The second date almost always coincides with the pope's death. The dagger symbol (†) following the dates indicates that there is a separate entry on that particular pope elsewhere in the encyclopedia.

1. Peter, Apostle, St. (Galilean)†	d. ca. 64	Although the terms "first pope" and "first Bishop of Rome" are traditionally associated with Peter, the monoepiscopal, or single-bishop, system of governance in the church of Rome only gradually emerged and did not become clearly identifiable until the pontificate of Pius I (ca. 142–ca. 155).
2. Linus, St.†	ca. 66–ca. 78	Although he and several other early popes are regarded as martyrs, the historical evidence is, in most cases, lacking.
3. Anacletus, St. [Cletus]	ca. 79–ca. 91	Very little is known about him, but he is mentioned in the ancient Canon of the Mass.
4. Clement I, St.†	ca. 91–ca. 101	Author of the most important first-century document outside the NT, *1 Clement*, sent to Corinth to resolve a dispute about authority.
5. Evaristus, St. (Greek)	ca. 100–ca. 109	There is little reliable historical information about him.
6. Alexander I, St.	ca. 109–ca. 116	Little is known about him except that he played a leading role in the church of Rome.
7. Sixtus I, St.	ca. 116–ca. 125	Little is known about him.
8. Telesphoros, St. (Greek)	ca. 125–ca. 136	The only second-century pope whose martyrdom is historically verifiable.
9. Hyginus, St. (Greek)	ca. 138–ca. 142	A philosopher who, like his contemporary Justin Martyr, came to Rome from the East.
10. Pius I, St.†	ca. 142–ca. 155	With his pontificate the monarchical episcopate becomes a settled reality in Rome.
11. Anicetus, St. (Syrian)†	ca. 155–ca. 166	He erected a popular memorial shrine for St. Peter on Vatican Hill.
12. Soter, St.	ca. 166–ca. 174	During his pontificate Easter became an annual feast in Rome.
13. Eleutherius, St. [Eleutherus] (Greek)	ca. 174–ca. 189	Although his reign was peaceful, he seems to have ignored Irenaeus's warnings about the growth of Montanism, a movement that stressed the imminent end of the world.
14. Victor I, St. (African)†	189–198	He enforced the Roman date for the celebration of Easter and was the first pope to have dealings with the imperial household.
15. Zephrynus, St.†	198/9–217	During his pontificate, Rome was torn by debates about the divinity of Christ.
16. Callistus I, St. [Calixtus]†	217–222	His pontificate was marked by conflicts over doctrine and discipline with the Church's first antipope, Hippolytus, who thought Callistus too lax in both areas.
17. Urban I, St.	222–230	Although the antipope Hippolytus was still alive during much of Urban's reign, his pontificate was relatively peaceful because there were no persecutions under the emperor Severus.

18. Pontian, St.†	July 21, 230–Sept. 28, 235	The first pope to abdicate, after being arrested and deported in 235 by the new emperor Maximinus Thrax.
19. Anterus, St. (Greek)	Nov. 21, 235–Jan. 3, 236	The first pope to be buried in the new papal crypt in the cemetery of Callistus.
20. Fabian, St.†	Jan. 10, 236–Jan. 20, 250	One of the great popes of the early Church—an outstanding administrator and reformer.
21. Cornelius, St.†	Mar. 251–June 253	He was bitterly opposed by the antipope Novatian, a disappointed candidate for the papacy, who thought the pope too lax in his attitude toward those who had weakened under persecution and were seeking readmission to the Church. Cornelius excommunicated Novatian.
22. Lucius I, St.	June 25, 253–Mar. 5, 254	Banished from Rome by the emperor Gallus almost immediately after his election as pope, he returned under the emperor Valerian. Little is known about him thereafter.
23. Stephen I, St.†	May 12, 254–Aug. 2, 257	He was best known for his clashes with Cyprian, bishop of Carthage, especially over the question of the rebaptism of those baptized by heretics. Stephen vigorously opposed rebaptism.
24. Sixtus II, St. (Greek)†	Aug. 30, 257–Aug. 6, 258	He took a more conciliatory stand on the issue of rebaptism, apparently allowing both practices to coexist. Beheaded while presiding at liturgy, he became one of the most revered martyrs of the early Church.
25. Dionysius, St.	July 22, 260–Dec. 26, 268	One of the most important popes of the third century, he was not elected until two years after the death of Sixtus II because of the continued persecutions. He held a synod in Rome to clarify the relationship between the Father and the Son and proved to be a vigorous administrator and reformer.
26. Felix I, St.	Jan. 3, 269–Dec. 30, 274	Very little is known of him or of his pontificate.
27. Eutychian, St.	Jan. 4, 275–Dec. 7, 283	The last pope to be buried in the papal crypt in the cemetery of Callistus.
28. Caius, St. [Gaius]	Dec. 17, 283–Apr. 22, 296	Little is known of him except that his pontificate was peaceful.
29. Marcellinus, St.†	June 30, 296–Oct. 25, 304	During the Diocletian persecutions, he complied with imperial orders to hand over copies of Sacred Scripture and to offer incense to the gods. Some scholars think he was deposed before his death. His name was omitted for a time from the official list of popes.
30. Marcellus I, St.†	Nov./Dec., 306–Jan. 16, 308	He was so much of a rigorist in his attitude toward those who compromised their faith under persecution that the emperor banished him from Rome as a disturber of the peace.
31. Eusebius, St. (Greek)	Apr. 18–Oct. 21, 310	He adopted a more compassionate policy toward apostates, but the split in the community over the issue deepened and the emperor Maxentius deported him.
32. Melchiades, St. [Miltiades] (African?)	July 2, 311–Jan. 10, 314	During his pontificate, all confiscated Church properties were returned. The emperor Constantine presented him with the empress Fausta's palace (the Lateran) as a papal residence.
33. Sylvester I, St. [Silvester]†	Jan. 31, 314–Dec. 31, 335	Pope during the reign of Constantine the Great, when Rome acquired the trappings of a Christian city, but he does not seem to have exercised great influence, particularly on the Council of Nicaea (325).
34. Mark, St.	Jan. 18–Oct. 7, 336	He had a short, uneventful pontificate.
35. Julius I, St.†	Feb. 6, 337–Apr. 12, 352	A vigorous supporter of the teaching of the Council of Nicaea and of Athanasius.
36. Liberius†	May 17, 352–Sept. 24, 366	A weak pope, he at first opposed the excommunication of Athanasius by the Arian party with the support of the emperor Constantius, but later relented under pressure. He returned to orthodoxy after the emperor's death. He was the first pope not to be listed among the saints.

37. Damasus I, St.†	Oct. 1, 366–Dec. 11, 384	Active in the fight against heresies and in promoting the primacy of Rome, he restored the catacombs and authorized Jerome to do a new translation of the Gospels based on the Greek.
38. Siricius, St.†	Dec. 384–Nov. 26, 399	The first pope to issue decretals in the style of imperial edicts, he ruled that no bishop should be consecrated without the knowledge of the Apostolic See.
39. Anastasius I, St.†	Nov. 27, 399–Dec. 19, 401	Although he did not understand Origen's writings, he acquiesced in their condemnation.
40. Innocent I, St.†	Dec. 21, 401–Mar. 12, 417	No previous pope had made the claim so strongly that the Apostolic See possesses supreme teaching authority.
41. Zosimus, St. (Greek)†	Mar. 18, 417–Dec. 26, 418	Temperamentally impulsive and politically inept, he generated bitter conflicts and upon his death left Rome torn by factions.
42. Boniface I, St.	Dec. 28, 418–Sept. 4, 422	A dedicated opponent of Pelagianism and a vigorous advocate of the authority of the papacy. "It has never been lawful for what has once been decided by the apostolic see to be reconsidered" (*Roma locuta est; causa finita est;* Lat., "Rome has spoken; the cause is finished").
43. Celestine I, St.	Sept. 10, 422–July 27, 432	He took a firm stand against Nestorius, who posited two persons in Christ, but played little part in the Council of Ephesus (431), which condemned Nestorianism. As the successor of Peter, he claimed oversight over the whole Church, East and West alike.
44. Sixtus III, St. [Xystus]	July 31, 432–Aug. 19, 440	He acted as a peacemaker in the aftermath of the Council of Ephesus (431) and directed a major rebuilding program in Rome in the aftermath of the invasion by the Visigoths in 410.
45. Leo I, "the Great," St.†	Aug./Sept. 440–Nov. 10, 461	One of only two popes called "the Great" (the other being Gregory I), he was especially strong in claiming supreme and universal authority for the papacy and was a firm supporter of the teachings of the Council of Chalcedon (451). He personally persuaded Attila the Hun to withdraw from his advance toward Rome.
46. Hilarus, St. [Hilary]	Nov. 19, 461–Feb. 29, 468	A supporter of Christological orthodoxy, he frequently intervened in Church matters in Gaul (France) and Spain.
47. Simplicius, St.	Mar. 3, 468–Mar. 10, 483	He interacted primarily with the East in trying to maintain Christological orthodoxy and the prerogatives of Rome.
48. Felix III (II), St.†	Mar. 13, 483–Mar. 1, 492	A vigorous opponent of Monophysitism (the denial of a human nature in Christ), his authoritarian personality kept alive the first schism between East and West. He excommunicated the patriarch of Constantinople, Acacius. (St. Felix II had served as antipope 355–65.)
49. Gelasius I, St. (African)†	Mar. 1, 492–Nov. 21, 496	The first pope to be called "Vicar of Christ," he was, after Leo the Great, the outstanding pope of the fifth century.
50. Anastasius II	Nov. 24, 496–Nov. 19, 498	Unlike his two predecessors, he took a conciliatory attitude toward the Acacian Schism, but this provoked dissension among the clergy and then schism in Rome itself.
51. Symmachus, St.†	Nov. 22, 498–July 19, 514	The first pope to bestow the pallium (a symbol of episcopal authority worn around the neck) on a bishop outside of Italy.
52. Hormisdas, St.†	July 20, 514–Aug. 6, 523	He ended the Acacian Schism between Rome and the East. His son Silverius later became pope.
53. John I, St.†	Aug. 13, 523–May 18, 526	The first pope to leave Italy for the East (Constantinople), he also ratified the Alexandrian computation of the date of Easter, which came to be accepted throughout the West.
54. Felix IV (III), St.	July 12, 526–Sept. 22, 530	A strong opponent of semi-Pelagianism, which held that the beginning of faith is the result of human effort, not grace.

55. Boniface II	Sept. 22, 530–Oct. 17, 532	Though born in Rome, he was the first pope of Germanic stock. His record as pope was mixed: at times he was vindictive, at other times conciliatory. He confirmed the teaching of the Second Council of Orange (529), which ended the controversy on grace.
56. John II	Jan. 2, 533–May 8, 535	Because his name from birth was that of a pagan god (Mercury), he was the first pope to take a different name upon election to the papacy. He was also famous for contradicting, under pressure from the Eastern emperor, the teaching of a previous pope (Hormisdas) on a matter of doctrine: he accepted the Theopaschite formula, "One of the Trinity suffered in the flesh."
57. Agapitus I, St.†	May 13, 535–Apr. 22, 536	He had to pawn sacred vessels to finance a peacekeeping mission to Constantinople, where he died.
58. Silverius, St.	June 8, 536–Nov. 11, 537	Because he and the senate had surrendered Rome peacefully to the Gothic army, he was charged by the Monophysite empress Theodora (wife of Justinian) with being pro-Goth and was stripped of his pallium, degraded to the rank of a monk, deposed, and deported. Justinian relented and let him return, but his enemies (including his successor) kidnapped him to an island in the Gulf of Gaeta, where he was forced finally to abdicate on November 11, 537. He died Dec. 2.
59. Vigilius†	Mar. 29, 537–June 7, 555	A devious and weak person in league with the Monophysite empress Theodora, he was elected under the most dubious of circumstances in which he compelled his predecessor's abdication. His vacillation on the teaching of the Council of Chalcedon caused great consternation in the West, leading even to his excommunication by a synod of African bishops.
60. Pelagius I	Apr. 16, 556–Mar. 3, 561	Although he was a gifted administrator, dedicated reformer, and generous pastor, his pontificate was marked by great frustration because of his association with the emperor Justinian (who seems to have named him without an election) and rumors about his role in the death of Vigilius, his predecessor.
61. John III	July 17, 561–July 13, 574	As the invading Lombards marched on Rome, the pope fled to Naples to beg Narses, the emperor's viceroy in Italy, to take charge of the resistance. This created such a negative reaction in the city that the pope had to take up residence outside of Rome.
62. Benedict I	June 2, 575–July 30, 579	Little is known of his pontificate, except that he died while the city was under siege by the Lombards.
63. Pelagius II	Nov. 26, 579–Feb. 7, 590	His pontificate, too, was marked by the crisis of the Lombard invasion. At the same time, the Visigoths in Spain were converted and a controversy erupted with the East over the bishop of Constantinople's use of the title "ecumenical patriarch," to which the pope objected as an encroachment upon papal supremacy.
64. Gregory I, "the Great," St.†	Sept. 3, 590–Mar. 12, 604	The first pope to have been a monk. With the breakdown of temporal authority in Italy, he became its virtual civil ruler. An ardent reformer and gifted administrator, he dispatched the first missionary band to England under Augustine of Canterbury. He was a prodigious writer; his most enduring work, *Pastoral Care*, became a textbook for medieval bishops.
65. Sabinian	Sept. 13, 604–Feb. 22, 606	Unlike Gregory, he promoted diocesan (secular) clergy rather than monks. Also unlike Gregory, he sold grain to the hungry rather than give it away. He was so unpopular at the time of his death, his funeral procession had to be diverted outside the city walls to reach St. Peter's.

66. Boniface III	Feb. 19–Nov. 12, 607	He received from the new emperor, Phocas, a formal declaration that Rome, as the see of Peter, was head of all the churches. He also held a synod to regulate papal elections. The penalty of excommunication would be imposed on anyone discussing a successor to a pope or bishop during the pope's or bishop's lifetime and until three days after his death.
67. Boniface IV, St.	Sept. 15, 608–May 8, 615	A disciple of Gregory the Great, he turned his house into a monastery. His reign, too, was marked by famine, plague, and natural disasters. He also displayed a special interest in the English church.
68. Deusdedit, St. [Adeodatus I]	Oct. 19, 615–Nov. 8, 618	The first priest to be made pope since John II (533–35). Unlike Gregory the Great and his predecessor, Boniface IV, he was partial to diocesan clergy rather than to monks and religious.
69. Boniface V	Dec. 23, 619–Oct. 25, 625	A compassionate and kindly pastor, he continued the pro-clergy policies of his predecessor as well as the special interest of Boniface IV in the English church.
70. Honorius I†	Oct. 27, 625–Oct. 12, 638	An admirer of Gregory the Great, he, too, turned his house into a monastery and employed monks rather than diocesan clergy on his staff. He became an unwitting adherent of Monothelitism, which held that there is only one (divine) will in Jesus Christ. After his death he was formally condemned by the Third Council of Constantinople (680).
71. Severinus	May 28–Aug. 2, 640	An elderly man, he resisted the emperor Heraclius's pressure to endorse Monothelitism, but paid a high price in the form of an imperial siege of the Lateran Palace and a plundering of the papal treasury. He died two months after consecration.
72. John IV (Dalmatian)	Dec. 24, 640–Oct. 12, 642	He held a synod in 641 that condemned Monothelitism.
73. Theodore I (Greek)	Nov. 24, 642–May 14, 649	An uncompromising opponent of Monothelitism, which continued to find favor in the East.
74. Martin I, St.†	July 5, 649–June 17, 653	Another determined opponent of Monothelitism, he paid a high price in the form of capture, deposition, deportation, humiliation, ill-treatment, flogging, imprisonment, and death (Sept. 16, 655) at the hands of the emperor. The church of Rome, which had abandoned him during his ordeal, later revered him as a martyr, the last pope to be so honored.
75. Eugenius I, St. [Eugene]	Aug. 10, 654–June 2, 657	Even though condemned by the Third Council of Constantinople (680), Monothelitism continued to divide Rome and Constantinople. The pope tried to reconcile the two sides by prematurely accepting a compromise that seemed to posit three wills in Christ. The clergy and people of Rome rejected it and demanded that the pope reject it as well. He died before the emperor Constans II could do to him what he had done to his predecessor.
76. Vitalian, St.	July 30, 657–Jan. 27, 672	He restored good relations with the emperor, but not without serious compromises. After the emperor's murder, the pope supported the claims of his son, Constantine IV, for which the new emperor was grateful. The pope was able to profess orthodox doctrine more freely against Monothelitism.
77. Adeodatus II	Apr. 11, 672–June 17, 676	An elderly man upon election, he did little more than reaffirm orthodox doctrine on the question of the two wills in Christ, but he had a good reputation as a kind and generous pastor.
78. Donus	Nov. 2, 676–Apr. 11, 678	Even less is known about his pontificate than about that of his predecessor's. He died before efforts to restore harmony between Constantinople and Rome could bear fruit.
79. Agatho, St.†	June 27, 678–Jan. 10, 681	His pontificate was marked by the definitive end of imperial support for Monothelitism in the East and the restoration of good relations between Rome and Constantinople.

80. Leo II, St.†	Aug. 17, 682–July 3, 683	An accomplished singer and patron of church music, he ratified the Third Council of Constantinople's condemnation of Monothelitism and anathematized (censured) its adherents, including Pope Honorius I.
81. Benedict II, St.†	June 26, 684–May 8, 685	A man devoted to the poor, he secured agreement from the emperor to allow the imperial exarch (viceroy) in Ravenna, Italy, to ratify papal elections instead of having to wait for approval from Constantinople.
82. John V (Syrian)	July 23, 685–Aug. 2, 686	He was so ill during his brief pontificate that he established little or no significant record.
83. Conon	Oct. 21, 686–Sept. 21, 687	An elderly compromise candidate, he was weak and ill during his year-long pontificate.
84. Sergius I, St. (Syrian)†	Dec. 15, 687–Sept. 8, 701	He successfully resisted pressures from the emperor Justinian II, who was eventually overthrown and exiled. He restored churches in Rome, including St. Peter's and St. Paul's, and introduced the singing of the *Agnus Dei* (Lat., "Lamb of God") at Mass.
85. John VI (Greek)	Oct. 30, 701–Jan. 11, 705	He had to spend great sums of money ransoming prisoners and bribing invaders so they would not enter Rome.
86. John VII (Greek)	Mar. 1, 705–Oct. 18, 707	The first pope to be the son of a Byzantine official. He was known for his building projects and for being a patron of the arts.
87. Sisinnius (Syrian)	Jan. 15–Feb. 4, 708	Already old and crippled upon election, he established no record of accomplishment.
88. Constantine (Syrian)	Mar. 25, 708–Apr. 9, 715	Summoned by the emperor, he made a year-long journey to Constantinople to normalize relations between the two sides. The meeting was a success. Justinian II was later murdered and replaced by a fanatical Monothelite, but he was himself overthrown and replaced by an orthodox emperor.
89. Gregory II, St.†	May 19, 715–Feb. 11, 731	The first Roman to be elected pope after five popes of Greek or Syrian background, and the most accomplished pope of the eighth century. He opposed iconoclasm (antipathy to icons and other sacred images), promoted monasticism, and was a liturgical innovator.
90. Gregory III, St. (Syrian)	Mar. 18, 731–Nov. 28, 741	The last pope to seek approval for his consecration from the Byzantine exarch (viceroy) in Italy. He made a pact with the Franks to protect Rome against the Lombards, supported Boniface's mission to Germany, promoted monasticism, and beautified Rome.
91. Zacharias, St. [Zachary] (Greek)†	Dec. 3, 741–Mar. 15, 752	The last of the Greek popes. He, too, supported Boniface's mission to Germany and solidified the alliance with the Franks, agreeing to the transference of the crown from the Merovingian to the Carolingian line.
92. Stephen II (III)†	Mar. 26, 752–Apr. 26, 757	He established the independence of the papacy from the Byzantine empire and placed it under the protection of the Frankish kingdom. He also formed the Papal States. (An elderly Roman priest who would have been Stephen II had been elected pope on Mar. 22 or 23, 752, but died before being consecrated. In those years consecration rather than valid election was the essential requirement.)
93. Paul I, St.†	May 29, 757–June 28, 767	He defended the young Papal States and strengthened the papacy's ties with the Franks.
94. Stephen III (IV)†	Aug. 7, 768–Jan. 24, 772	He directly replaced not Paul I, but the antipope Constantine, a layman who illegitimately reigned from July 5, 767, to August 6, 768. A subsequent synod at the Lateran formally invalidated that election. Stephen's reign was marked by political vacillation.

95. Hadrian I [Adrian]†	Feb. 1, 772–Dec. 25, 795	He supported Charlemagne, even when he interfered in the Papal States and elsewhere in Italy, and he approved the Second Council of Nicaea (787), which condemned iconoclasm.
96. Leo III, St.†	Dec. 26, 795–June 12, 816	He crowned Charlemagne as emperor on Christmas day, 800, and was the first and only pope to offer obeisance to a Western emperor. Nevertheless, he resisted Charlemagne's efforts to add the *Filioque* (Lat., "and the Son") to the creed.
97. Stephen IV (V)	June 22, 816–Jan. 24, 817	The first pope to anoint an emperor (Louis the Pious), suggesting thereby that papal approval was necessary for the exercise of full imperial authority.
98. Paschal I, St.†	Jan. 24, 817–Feb. 11, 824	The practice of crowning the emperor in Rome took hold during his reign. He was so detested by the people that his body could not be buried in St. Peter's. His feast day, May 14, was dropped from the liturgical calendar in 1963.
99. Eugenius II [Eugene]	June 824–Aug. 827	Upon election he acknowledged the emperor's authority over the Papal States and swore an oath of allegiance to him, but he maintained his independence on matters of Church doctrine and discipline.
100. Valentine	Aug.–Sept. 827	He was elected with the participation of the laity, as mandated by the imperial constitution of 824, ratified by Eugene II.
101. Gregory IV	late 827–Jan. 25, 844	He was elected with the support of the lay Roman nobility; his pontificate was undistinguished.
102. Sergius II	Jan. 844–Jan. 27, 847	Elderly and gout-ridden when elected by his fellow Roman aristocrats, he engaged in simony and other dubious practices to raise funds for his ambitious building program. Muslim pirates plundered St. Peter's and St. Paul's during his reign— acts many saw as divine retribution for papal corruption.
103. Leo IV, St.†	Apr. 10, 847–July 17, 855	He restored papal prestige through successful military expeditions against the Saracens who were threatening Rome.
104. Benedict III	Sept. 29, 855–Apr. 17, 858	Little is known of his brief reign, but he reasserted Rome's primatial authority over Constantinople.
105. Nicholas I, St.†	Apr. 24, 858–Nov. 13, 867	He viewed himself as God's representative on earth with authority over the whole Church, including all bishops (regardless of rank) and the East generally. He and Photius, the patriarch of Constantinople, excommunicated each other, thereby contributing to the final separation of East and West.
106. Hadrian II [Adrian]	Dec. 14, 867–Nov./Dec. 872	When the Fourth Council of Constantinople (869–70) placed Constantinople second in rank behind Rome, relations between East and West temporarily improved. He consecrated Methodius as archbishop of Sirmium and legate to the Slavs.
107. John VIII	Dec. 14, 872–Dec. 16, 882	Although elderly, he personally led military expeditions against the Saracens. To win support from the East, he accepted the decisions of a council in Constantinople presided over by Photius in 879, including the lifting of the anathematization of Photius. He was the first pope to be assassinated.
108. Marinus I	Dec. 16, 882–May 15, 884	He was the first bishop of another diocese to be elected bishop of Rome, in violation of canon 15 of the First Council of Nicaea (325).
109. Hadrian III, St. [Adrian]	May 17, 884–Sept. 885	He maintained friendly relations with the East but died under dubious circumstances that suggested assassination.
110. Stephen V (VI)	Sept. 885–Sept. 14, 891	Mainly involved in political activities and in military defense against Saracen raids, he unwittingly pushed the Slavs away from Rome and into the arms of Orthodoxy when after the death of Methodius, he forbade the Slavonic liturgy.

111. Formosus	Oct. 6, 891–Apr. 4, 896	He was most famous for what happened to him after death. His body was exhumed, propped up on a throne in full pontifical vestments, and subjected to a mock trial (the so-called Cadaver Synod) in which he was found guilty of perjury, coveting the papacy, and having violated the canons forbidding translation from one diocese to another. His acts and ordinations were declared null and void, and three fingers of his right hand (by which he swore oaths and gave blessings) were cut off. He was reburied in a common grave and then exhumed and thrown in the Tiber. A hermit retrieved the body and gave it a third burial. Pope Theodore II exhumed the body and gave it a fourth, and final, burial with honors.
112. Boniface VI	Apr. 896	Although defrocked twice from the priesthood, he was elected under pressure of riots. He died after only fifteen days. A Roman synod two years later prohibited such uncanonical elections.
113. Stephen VI (VII)	May 896–Aug. 897	He was most famous for his role in the mock posthumous trial of Pope Formosus. He himself was deposed, stripped of his papal insignia, imprisoned, and strangled to death.
114. Romanus	Aug.–Nov. 897	Little or nothing is known of his reign. Some say that he was deposed by a faction partial to Formosus who wanted a stronger pope in order to rehabilitate their hero.
115. Theodore II	Nov. 897	Although he reigned only twenty days, he held a synod invalidating the so-called Cadaver Synod, which degraded the dead Formosus. He also rehabilitated and reburied Formosus (the fourth and final burial) with honors.
116. John IX	Jan. 898–Jan. 900	He, too, convened a synod in Rome annulling the Cadaver Synod and burning its acts, pardoning some participants and deposing others. It also prohibited trials of dead persons and decreed that, while the pope should be elected by bishops and clergy at the request of the senate and people of Rome, his consecration should take place in the presence of imperial representatives.
117. Benedict IV	May/June 900–Aug. 903	Very little is known of his reign other than that Rome continued to be torn by partisan conflict.
118. Leo V	Aug.–Sept. 903	After only thirty days in office he was overthrown by an antipope, Christopher, imprisoned, and murdered.
119. Sergius III	Jan. 29, 904–Apr. 14, 911	He was elected pope after leading an armed force against Rome and imprisoning the antipope Christopher. He had both Leo V and Christopher strangled to death. He held a synod that reaffirmed the Cadaver Synod, including its declaration that all the episcopal ordinations of Formosus were invalid. This threw the Church into a state of confusion and turmoil. He was the pawn of Roman noble families, especially the Theophylact.
120. Anastasius III	ca. June 911–ca. Aug. 913	The domination of the papacy by the Theophylact family continued during his brief reign.
121. Lando [Landus]	ca. Aug. 913–ca. Mar. 914	Also a product of the Theophylact family's influence, his brief reign was undistinguished.
122. John X	Mar./Apr. 914–May 928	With his election, also supported by the Theophylact family, the resistance to translating bishops from one diocese to another subsided because of the growing recognition of the unique significance of the see of Rome. He took an active role in the defeat of the Saracens, who had been plaguing Italy for sixty years. Because he tried to distance himself from the noble families, he was deposed, imprisoned, and suffocated to death (929).
123. Leo VI	May–Dec. 928	An elderly man who was elected to keep the papal throne warm for a son of the Theophylact family; nothing of any consequence is known of his short reign except that he himself died before his deposed predecessor was murdered.

124. Stephen VII (VIII)	Dec. 928–Feb. 931	His election and reign were marked by the same forces that controlled his predecessor's brief pontificate.
125. John XI	Feb./Mar. 931–Dec. 935 or Jan. 936	He is generally regarded as the illegitimate son of Pope Sergius III and Marozia, head of the house of Theophylact. He officiated at an unpopular marriage of his widowed mother, for which he and his mother were imprisoned. He was later released but kept under house arrest as a virtual slave of his half brother Alberic II, the self-declared prince of Rome.
126. Leo VII	Jan. 3, 936–July 13, 939	A creature of Alberic II, he, too, was limited to ecclesiastical functions. He supported major monasteries like Cluny and Subiaco and promoted reform of the clergy.
127. Stephen VIII (IX)	July 14, 939–Oct. 942	Supported also by Alberic II, he was confined to ecclesiastical duties. He seems at the end to have incurred the wrath of Alberic. He was imprisoned and mutilated and died soon thereafter.
128. Marinus II	Oct. 30, 942–May 946	Also controlled by Alberic II, he did little during his reign.
129. Agapitus II	May 10, 946–Dec. 955	Elected with the support of Alberic II, he promoted, like his immediate predecessors, Alberic's interest in monastic reform. On his deathbed, Alberic made the pope and others swear, in violation of the decree of Pope Symmachus in 499, that the next pope would be Alberic's son Octavian.
130. John XII†	Dec. 16, 955–May 14, 964	Elected at age eighteen, he was the second pope in history to change his name (from Octavian). He restored the Holy Roman Empire, crowning the German king Otto I in 962, and allowed the emperor to reassert his influence over papal elections. His private life was marked by gross immorality. He was deposed by a Roman synod Dec. 4, 963, at the urging of Otto, but resumed the papacy in Feb. 964 after deposing Leo VIII, Otto's candidate. He died in May 964.
131. Leo VIII	Dec. 4, 963–Mar. 1, 965	The legitimacy of his election is a matter of canonical debate because of the deposition of John XII and later reinstatement. After John XII's death, the Romans elected Benedict V. But Otto deported Benedict and reinstated Leo in June 964.
132. Benedict V	May 22–June 23, 964	A reformer rather than a libertine, his pontificate was marked by strife and confusion because of the political power plays involving John XII, Leo VIII, and the emperor Otto I. He was deposed and exiled to Germany, where he enjoyed a reputation for personal holiness. He died July 4, 966.
133. John XIII	Oct. 1, 965–Sept. 6, 972	He was elected and reigned with the full support of the emperor Otto I, whose political and ecclesiastical bidding he did.
134. Benedict VI	Jan. 19, 973–July 974	When his protector, the emperor Otto I, died, he was seized, imprisoned, and strangled to death by order of the antipope Boniface, a tool of the powerful Crescentii family in Rome.
135. Benedict VII	Oct. 974–July 10, 983	Favored by both the emperor Otto II and the Crescentii family, he promoted monastic reform as well as the emperor's political and ecclesiastical programs. The latter included the prohibition of simony, i.e., the buying and selling of spiritual goods. The practice of *ad limina* (Lat., "to the thresholds" of the tombs of Peter and Paul) visits to Rome by bishops from around the world became more common during his pontificate.
136. John XIV	Dec. 983–Aug. 20, 984	He was appointed by the emperor Otto II, whose former archchancellor he had been, without consultation with the clergy and people of Rome. Because his baptismal name was Peter, he changed it to John to avoid using the name of the first pope. When Otto died, John was left at the mercy of his enemies. He was seized, beaten, and imprisoned and died either of starvation or of poisoning.

137. John XV   Aug. 985–Mar. 996

Elected with the support of the powerful Crescentii family, he was the first pope formally to canonize a saint: Ulric of Augsburg in 993. He was hated by the clergy for his greed and nepotism.

138. Gregory V (Saxon)   May 3, 996–Feb. 18, 999

The twenty-four-year-old relative of Otto III, he was the first German pope. He took the name Gregory because of his admiration for Gregory the Great. He crowned Otto emperor and named him protector of the Church. Gregory died of malaria before he reached the age of thirty.

139. Sylvester II [Silvester] (French)†   Apr. 2, 999–May 12, 1003

The first Frenchman to become pope, taking the name Sylvester, a fourth-century pope who had forged a close working relationship with the emperor. Opposed to simony, nepotism, and clerical marriage, he was a man of keen intellect and great cultural breadth.

140. John XVII   May 16–Nov. 6, 1003

A relative and agent of the Crescentii family, he left little or no trace of a record of his pontificate. (In between John XV and John XVII there was an antipope who took the name John XVI.)

141. John XVIII   Dec. 25, 1003–June/July 1009

Another creature of the Crescentii family; his pontificate has left few historical traces and the manner of his leaving office remains shrouded in obscurity.

142. Sergius IV   July 31, 1009–May 12, 1012

Another product of the Crescentii family's influence, he, too, changed his name from Peter out of deference to the first pope. The fact that he died within a week of his patron Crescentius and the fact that his successor came from the rival Tuscalan family (in the line of the Theophylact family) have led historians to speculate that both the pope and Crescentius were murdered.

143. Benedict VIII   May 17, 1012–Apr. 9, 1024

Elected while still a layman with the support of the Tuscalan family, he changed his name from Theophylact to Benedict. He restored relations with the German royal house and crowned the king, Henry II, emperor in 1014. He spent much of his time in military expeditions but, at the instigation of the emperor, also initiated ecclesiastical reforms. He is said to have wielded more power than any of his predecessors.

144. John XIX   Apr. 19, 1024–Oct. 20, 1032

The younger brother of Benedict VIII, he, too, was a layman upon election. He was accused of gaining the papacy through bribery.

145. Benedict IX   Oct. 21, 1032–Sept. 1044; Mar. 10–May 1, 1045; Nov. 8, 1047–July 16, 1048

Another layman and another member of the ruling Tuscalan family who gained the papacy through bribery, he had an ignoble personal reputation. He was the only pope to have held office for three different periods.

146. Sylvester III [Silvester]   Jan. 20–Mar. 10, 1045

After Benedict IX was expelled from Rome, Silvester was elected. Benedict, however, returned and expelled Silvester, who returned to his diocese of Sabina as bishop. He died in 1063. The legitimacy of Sylvester's election is open to question.

147. Gregory VI   May 5, 1045–Dec. 20, 1046

Given the circumstances of his election, upon abdication of Benedict IX, he was accused of simony by the emperor and synod and deposed. The emperor took him back to Germany where he died in 1047.

148. Clement II (Saxon)   Dec. 24, 1046–Oct. 9, 1047

He was the first of four German popes imposed upon the Church by King Henry III of Germany in order to rescue the papacy from the power of the feuding Roman families. Clement crowned Henry and his wife as emperor and empress on the same day he was consecrated as pope. Significantly, he remained bishop of Bamberg during his pontificate. Upon his death Benedict was restored to the papacy for a third time, until forcibly ejected upon orders of King Henry III. He died 1055/6.

149. Damasus II (Bavarian) — July 17–Aug. 9, 1048

The second of the German popes imposed by King Henry III; his reign was brief and uneventful. He continued as bishop of Brixen after his election.

150. Leo IX, St. (Alsatian)† — Feb. 12, 1049–Apr. 9, 1054

The third and best of the German popes imposed by King Henry III, he retained the see of Toul until 1051. He arrived in Rome dressed as a pilgrim, to the delight of the Romans. He deliberately selected the name Leo to recall the ancient and still pure Church. He proved to be a great reformer pope, although his last years were marked by failure.

151. Victor II (Swabian) — Apr. 13, 1055–July 28, 1057

The last of the German popes nominated by Henry III, he remained bishop of Eichstätt during his pontificate. Like his predecessor he was a reformer, combatting simony, the alienation of Church property, and abuses of clerical celibacy.

152. Stephen IX (X) (French) — Aug. 2, 1057–Mar. 29, 1058

He was the abbot of Monte Cassino when elected and remained so during his brief pontificate. He committed himself to Church reform and surrounded himself with leading reformers.

153. Nicholas II (French) — Dec. 6, 1058–mid-July 1061

A leading reformer, he remained bishop of Florence during his pontificate. At a Lateran synod in 1059, simony was prohibited in papal elections but, more significantly, the election of a pope was restricted to cardinal bishops, with the clergy and people giving their subsequent assent. The synod also legislated against clerical concubinage and produced the first prohibition against lay investiture (the conferral of ecclesiastical offices by laypersons).

154. Alexander II† — Sept. 30, 1061–Apr. 21, 1073

A reformer pope, he also supported the liberation of Christian lands from the Muslims, as well as Duke William of Normandy against Harold of England in the battle of Hastings in 1066.

155. Gregory VII, St.† — Apr. 22, 1073–May 25, 1085

One of the greatest popes in history; his pontificate marks the real turning point between the first Christian millennium and the second. In an effort to free the papacy and the Church generally from temporal control, he claimed temporal as well as spiritual power over the whole Christian world. He opposed simony, clerical marriage, and lay investiture and insisted that metropolitan archbishops come to Rome to receive the pallium.

156. Victor III, Bl.† — May 24, 1086–Sept. 16, 1087

The abbot of Monte Cassino when elected (and until three days before his death), he took the name Victor as a gesture of reconciliation with the emperor Henry IV, whose father Henry III had supported a candidate by that name. Partisan conflicts (including the presence of an antipope) made his pontificate very difficult.

157. Urban II, Bl. (French)† — Mar. 12, 1088–July 29, 1099

To win support from the antireformers, he moderated Gregory VII's methods. He issued a summons to the First Crusade (1095–99) to liberate Jerusalem from the Muslims. He also established the Roman Curia.

158. Paschal II† — Aug. 13, 1099–Jan. 21, 1118

Under pressure from the emperor Henry V, he reversed many of the reforms initiated by Gregory VII, and the papacy itself suffered a decline in prestige.

159. Gelasius II — Jan. 24, 1118–Jan. 29, 1119

An elderly man, he was attacked and imprisoned immediately after election by the head of a patrician family that detested his predecessor. When the emperor left Rome, Gelasius returned but found it controlled by hostile forces, including an antipope. He fled to France and died at the monastery in Cluny.

160. Callistus II [Calixtus] (French) — Feb. 2, 1119–Dec. 14, 1124

He agreed to the Concordat of Worms in 1122, which settled the investiture controversy. The Church retained all spiritual rights in the appointment of bishops and abbots while the emperor's role was largely limited to Germany. The concordat was ratified by the First Lateran Council in 1123.

161. Honorius II	Dec. 21, 1124–Feb. 13, 1130	Like his predecessor, he was a member of the younger generation of Church reformers, more open to compromise than were the so-called Gregorians. (Although usually classified as the antipope Celestine II, a cardinal priest by the name of Teobaldo was canonically elected to succeed Callistus. Troops broke into the conclave and forced Teobaldo to resign in favor of Honorius II.)
162. Innocent II	Feb. 14, 1130–Sept. 24, 1143	One of two cardinals elected to succeed Honorius II; Innocent represented the new reformers; the antipope Anacletus represented the old Gregorians. An eight-year schism followed, ending only upon the death of Anacletus. Innocent II called the Second Lateran Council in 1139, which annulled all of Anacletus's acts and reaffirmed the reform legislation of the past.
163. Celestine II	Sept. 26, 1143–Mar. 8, 1144	An elderly scholar, he supported the internal reform of the Church.
164. Lucius II	Mar. 12, 1144–Feb. 15, 1145	He faced serious political problems in Rome where a senate, independent of the papacy and critical of the clergy, was established under the leadership of the brother of the late antipope Anacletus.
165. Eugenius III, Bl. [Eugene]†	Feb. 15, 1145–July 8, 1153	A Cistercian who retained the habit and life-style of a monk while pope. He was committed to monastic and clerical reform and also proclaimed the Second Crusade in 1145.
166. Anastasius IV	July 8, 1153–Dec. 3, 1154	A very old man upon election, he had good relations with the popular commune in Rome and with the civil authorities generally.
167. Hadrian IV [Adrian] (English)	Dec. 4, 1154–Sept. 1, 1159	The first and only English pope; his reign was marked by conflict with the German king Frederick I Barbarossa.
168. Alexander III†	Sept. 7, 1159–Aug. 30, 1181	The first pope who was a lawyer. His election provoked an eighteen-year schism between those loyal to him and those loyal to the antipope Victor IV, including the Holy Roman emperor, Frederick I Barbarossa. Only after the emperor's defeat by the Lombard League and the subsequent peace treaty of 1177 did he acknowledge Alexander as pope. Alexander called the Third Lateran Council in 1179, which decreed that a two-thirds majority of cardinals is necessary for papal election.
169. Lucius III	Sept. 1, 1181–Nov. 25, 1185	Because of the hostility of the Roman citizenry, he spent most of his papacy residing outside the city. In concert with the emperor, he established a charter of the Inquisition to repress and punish heretics.
170. Urban III	Nov. 25, 1185–Oct. 20, 1187	An avowed opponent of the emperor, he retained his archbishopric of Milan while pope so that the revenues of the archdiocese would not pass into the imperial treasury, as was customary during a vacancy. His confrontational policy, however, was largely a failure.
171. Gregory VIII	Oct. 21–Dec. 17, 1187	Elected because of his better relations with the emperor, he devoted himself in his short reign to reform of the clergy and Curia, and especially to the preparation of the Third Crusade to liberate the holy places in Jerusalem.
172. Clement III	Dec. 19, 1187–Mar. 1191	Weakened by poor health, he nevertheless brought the papacy back to Rome after a six-year exile, establishing a relatively cooperative relationship with the popular commune and the emperor, but at a high price in financial and other concessions. He was preoccupied with mounting the Third Crusade (1189–91).
173. Celestine III	Mar./Apr. 1191–Jan. 8, 1198	Elected at age eighty-five, he had a surprisingly long reign marked by delicate relations with the new young king, Henry VI. The emperor challenged the pope's authority, even in Church matters, but the pope responded by supporting the emperor's opponents in Germany and elsewhere.

174. Innocent III†	Jan. 8, 1198–July 16, 1216	One of the most powerful popes in history, claiming authority not only over the whole Church (as Gregory VII had done) but over the whole world as well. His principal concerns were with two crusades, reform of the clergy and Curia, and the combatting of heresy, especially Albigensianism in France. He also called the Fourth Lateran Council in 1215, which decreed, among other things, that Catholics should make an annual confession and that Jews and Muslims should wear distinctive dress.
175. Honorius III†	July 18, 1216–Mar. 18, 1227	Although he was old and in poor health, his reign lasted almost eleven years. He was preoccupied with the Fifth Crusade (1217–21), but he also launched a crusade against the Moors in Spain, continued the battle against Albigensianism in France, promoted the Inquisition, and approved the establishment of the Dominican order.
176. Gregory IX†	Mar. 19, 1227–Aug. 22, 1241	A friend of Dominic and Francis of Assisi and a protector of the Franciscan order. The beginning and end of his reign were marked by conflict with the emperor Frederick II. He established the papal Inquisition under the direction of the Dominicans.
177. Celestine IV	Oct. 25–Nov. 10, 1241	An aged and sick man, he was elected as a compromise candidate by eight other cardinals who were forcibly confined for sixty days. He died about two weeks later.
178. Innocent IV†	June 25, 1243–Dec. 7, 1254	A distinguished jurist, in 1245 he called the First Council of Lyons (to which he had secretly escaped from his enemies), which was concerned with the liberation of the holy places and other matters. The papacy suffered during his pontificate because of nepotism, bribery, and other financial misdeeds.
179. Alexander IV	Dec. 12, 1254–May 25, 1261	He supported the new mendicant orders, especially the Franciscans, and founded the Augustinian Hermits.
180. Urban IV [French]	Aug. 29, 1261–Oct. 2, 1264	When elected, there were only eight cardinals left. He himself was an outsider, the patriarch of Jerusalem, who happened to be in Italy on business related to the Holy Land. He appointed fourteen new cardinals, six of them French. Because of civil strife, he never resided in Rome as pope.
181. Clement IV (French)	Feb. 5, 1265–Nov. 29, 1268	Another Frenchman, he, too, resided outside Rome (in Perugia and Viterbo) during his pontificate because of civil unrest. He centralized the authority of the papacy by decreeing that appointments to all benefices in the West were papal appointments.
182. Gregory X, Bl.†	Sept. 1, 1271–Jan. 10, 1276	He was elected at the famous conclave in Viterbo, where the civil authorities locked the cardinals in the papal palace, then removed its roof and threatened them with starvation. He was in the Holy Land at the time on a crusade (hence he was not consecrated until March 27, 1272, in Rome), and he made the liberation of the holy places the central concern of his pontificate. He also called the Second Council of Lyons in 1274, affirming a short-lived union with the Greek church. He also decreed that papal elections be held within ten days after the death of the pope, in the city where he died, and with the cardinal-electors having no contact with the outside world.
183. Innocent V, Bl. (French)†	Jan. 21–June 22, 1276	A Dominican scholar and collaborator of Albertus Magnus and Thomas Aquinas, he was the first Dominican pope. He was also a friend of the Franciscan Bonaventure and preached at his funeral. The papal custom of wearing a white cassock began with this pontificate, since the Dominican habit is white.
184. Hadrian V [Adrian]	July 11–Aug. 18, 1276	A nephew of Innocent IV, he suspended Gregory X's rules for a papal conclave but died before he himself was ordained a priest and consecrated. In *The Divine Comedy*, Dante placed him in purgatory for the sin of avarice.

185. John XXI (Portuguese)	Sept. 8, 1276–May 20, 1277	A Portuguese-born scholar with a medical background, he left the administration of his papacy to Cardinal Orsini (later Pope Nicholas III). It was as the result of his papal bull, however, that the bishop of Paris condemned nineteen propositions of Thomas Aquinas. He died when the ceiling of his newly built study collapsed on him. Dante placed him in paradise in *The Divine Comedy*. (No pope took the name John XX.)
186. Nicholas III	Nov. 25, 1277–Aug. 22, 1280	To preserve the independence of the papacy in Rome, he decreed that no outside prince could be a senator without papal approval and he had himself elected to the senate for life. He was the first pope to make the Vatican palace his residence. Dante placed him in hell in *The Divine Comedy* for nepotism and avarice.
187. Martin IV (French)†	Feb. 22, 1281–Mar. 28, 1285	Because the Romans refused him entry into the city, he was consecrated in Orvieto and for most of his pontificate resided there. He excommunicated the emperor Michael VIII Paleologus in 1281 and thereby voided the union with the Greek church forged at the Second Council of Lyons in 1274. He was unabashedly pro-French in his policies and appointments. (He was actually the second Martin, not the fourth. Popes Marinus I and II were incorrectly given as Martin III and IV in the official lists of the thirteenth century.)
188. Honorius IV	Apr. 2, 1285–Apr. 3, 1287	The grandnephew of Pope Honorius III; his election was greeted positively in Rome. He was crowned there and maintained his residence in the city. He was a strong supporter of religious orders, especially the Dominicans and Franciscans.
189. Nicholas IV	Feb. 22, 1288–Apr. 4, 1292	The first Franciscan pope. To solidify his standing in Rome, he forged close and compromising ties with the Colonna family. During his pontificate, the Catholic Church was established for the first time in China.
190. Celestine V, St.†	July 5–Dec. 13, 1294	A hermit who was elected at age eighty, he proved to be an ineffective, easily manipulated pope. He resigned voluntarily but was prevented by his successor from returning to his retreat. He died under virtual house arrest on May 9, 1296.
191. Boniface VIII†	Dec. 24, 1294–Oct. 11, 1303	Few popes made greater claims for the authority of the office. He engaged in constant battles with the temporal powers, especially Philip the Fair of France. In 1302 he issued *Unam Sanctam* (Lat., "One Holy"), asserting papal supremacy over the temporal as well as spiritual orders and declaring that every creature is subject to the pope. He also proclaimed the first holy year in 1300. (Boniface VII was antipope June–July 974 and Aug. 984–July 985.)
192. Benedict XI, Bl.	Oct. 22, 1303–July 7, 1304	A Dominican, he took the name Benedict after his predecessor's baptismal name, Benedetto, but he weakly acceded to most of Philip the Fair's demands, in spite of the latter's enmity toward Boniface. He created three cardinals—all Dominicans. (Benedict X was antipope April 1058–Jan. 1059.)
193. Clement V (French)†	June 5, 1305–Apr. 20, 1314	Elected by the pro-French cardinals, the first nine of ten cardinals he created were French, including four of his nephews. The French king insisted he reside in France, and thus began the seventy-year "Babylonian captivity" of the papacy in Avignon.
194. John XXII (French)†	Aug. 7, 1316–Dec. 4, 1334	He expanded papal power in the appointment of bishops and the imposition of papal taxes. He was severe in his condemnation and punishment of the Spiritual Franciscans (who held to a strict form of poverty), but he himself was accused of heresy for his stated belief that the saints do not see God until after the final judgment.

195. Benedict XII (French)† Dec. 20, 1334–Apr. 25, 1342

A monk by vocation, he was a careful and competent administrator. He insisted that clergy live in clerical residences and monks in monasteries, improved their training, reorganized the Curia, and prohibited the flow of income from benefices during vacancies. His bull *Benedictus Deus* (Lat., "Blessed God") decreed in 1336 that the saints see God face to face (the Beatific Vision).

196. Clement VI (French) May 7, 1342–Dec. 6, 1352

His bull *Unigenitus* (Lat., "Unbegotten") defined the treasury of merits won by Christ and the saints that could be drawn upon by the faithful. This laid the groundwork for the doctrine of indulgences. He proved to be the most French of the Avignon popes, naming mostly Frenchmen to the College of Cardinals and enlarging the papal palace, where he lived the life of a secular prince.

197. Innocent VI (French) Dec. 18, 1352–Sept. 12, 1362

He promoted the reform of the clergy and of monasteries, but was particularly severe toward the Spiritual Franciscans, because of which Bridget of Sweden withdrew her support of him and denounced him as a persecutor of Christ's flock. He had hoped to return the papacy to Rome but died before he could do so.

198. Urban V, Bl. (French)† Sept. 28, 1362–Dec. 19, 1370

He retained his Benedictine habit and life-style while pope and continued his predecessor's reforms. He founded universities in Cracow and Vienna and was a generous patron of the arts. In 1367 he left Avignon and returned the papacy to Rome, which he found in miserable condition. He devoted himself to rebuilding and renovation, including St. John Lateran Church, which had burned down in 1360. He returned to Avignon just before his death.

199. Gregory XI (French)† Dec. 30, 1370–Mar. 27, 1378

The last of the Avignon popes. Upon appeal from Catherine of Siena, he returned the papacy to Rome in 1377. He devoted himself to the reform of religious orders and employed the Inquisition to stamp out heresy. Because of political factors, he had to leave Rome for Anagni under pressure from a hostile citizenry.

200. Urban VI† Apr. 8, 1378–Oct. 15, 1389

Historians believe him to have been mentally unstable, volatile, and abusive. So intransigent and unreasonable was he that the French cardinals elected an antipope, Clement VII, thereby inaugurating the Great Western Schism of 1378–1417. Urban solidified his place in Rome through force, but he eventually alienated the people and it is said that he died of poisoning.

201. Boniface IX Nov. 2, 1389–Oct. 1, 1404

Though he ruled like a benevolent despot, he was popular in Rome because his personality was so different from his predecessor's. He took no steps, however, to resolve the schism, even rejecting the conciliatory gestures of the antipope Benedict XIII. His reputation was marred by charges of nepotism and the selling of ecclesiastical offices and indulgences.

202. Innocent VII Oct. 17, 1404–Nov. 6, 1406

Although he had promised to work toward the resolution of the schism, he rebuffed the efforts of the antipope Benedict XIII to reach some settlement.

203. Gregory XII Nov. 30, 1406–July 4, 1415

In his eighties when elected, he at first attempted to heal the schism, but it became clear that neither claimant to the papal throne was ready to abdicate. He broke a preelection pledge and named new cardinals, including two nephews. This enraged some of his cardinal-supporters who then held a council at Pisa in 1409 where a third claimant was elected, Alexander V, who was succeeded the following year by John XXIII. Eventually Gregory resigned as part of a plan to end the schism and died on Oct. 18, 1417, three weeks before Martin V was elected.

204. Martin V† Nov. 11, 1417–Feb. 20, 1431

His election at the Council of Constance ended the Great Western Schism. He entered a devastated Rome three years later and set about the task of rebuilding churches and public buildings and of restoring order to the Papal States.

205. Eugenius IV [Eugene]†   Mar. 3, 1431–Feb. 23, 1447

He tried to dissolve the Council of Basel in 1431, but it refused to disperse and instead appealed to the Council of Constance (1414–18) in declaring a general council superior to a pope. The pope had to withdraw his decree of dissolution and accept the council's validity. A revolt in Rome forced him to Florence where he remained for nine years. The Council of Florence in 1439 ratified a short-lived union with the Greek church.

206. Nicholas V   Mar. 6, 1447–Mar. 24, 1455

A conciliatory and politically astute man, he brought peace to Rome and the Papal States. The first of the Renaissance popes, he was a patron of literature, the arts, and architecture. When Constantinople was sacked by the Turks in 1453, Europeans were terrified. The pope tried unsuccessfully to mount a crusade of liberation.

207. Callistus III [Calixtus] (Spanish)   Apr. 8, 1455–Aug. 6, 1458

His pontificate focused on the recapture of Constantinople, but the costs were regarded as too high by others and the campaign never received the necessary military and political support in the West. His nepotism was especially resented. One of two nephews he made cardinals was the future infamous Alexander VI.

208. Pius II†   Aug. 19, 1458–Aug. 15, 1464

He, too, was preoccupied with the effort to combat the Turkish advance into Europe, but like his predecessor he could not muster the necessary forces or resources. He died while waiting to set sail for battle.

209. Paul II   Aug. 30, 1464–July 26, 1471

A very unpopular pope, he refused to implement the program of reform expected of him by the cardinal-electors. He loved luxury, sport, and entertainment. Many humanists detested him for his treatment of scholars and the suppression of the Roman academy. He installed the first printing press in Rome. Like his immediate predecessors, he failed to marshal support for a crusade against the Turks.

210. Sixtus IV†   Aug. 9, 1471–Aug. 12, 1484

A Franciscan, he supported the mendicant orders and canonized Bonaventure. He focused too much, however, on temporal power over the Papal States and on the interests of his own family, making six nephews cardinals. His profligate ways left his successor with a huge deficit, but he transformed Rome from a medieval to a Renaissance city. He also built the Sistine Chapel and established the Vatican archives.

211. Innocent VIII   Aug. 29, 1484–July 25, 1492

The papacy sunk to the depths of worldliness in this pontificate; Innocent left Rome insolvent and the Papal States in anarchy.

212. Alexander VI (Spanish)†   Aug. 11, 1492–Aug. 18, 1503

The nephew of Callistus III, he lived a dissolute life before and after election and fathered several children. At first he restored order in Rome and made promises to address other problems such as the Turkish threat, but it soon became clear that the interests of his own family had the highest priority. Nepotism and unbridled sensuality were the hallmarks of his pontificate. He was pope when Christopher Columbus landed on American soil in 1492. (Alexander V was antipope 1409–10.)

213. Pius III   Sept. 22–Oct. 18, 1503

A compromise, or stopgap, candidate in poor health, he died ten days after his coronation.

214. Julius II†   Nov. 1, 1503–Feb. 21, 1513

His election ensured by exaggerated promises and bribes, he strengthened the Papal States and secured the independence of the Church from foreign powers. He was a patron of artists such as Michelangelo and Raphael, and he commissioned plans for the new St. Peter's Basilica, to be funded by the "sale" of indulgences.

215. Leo X†   Mar. 11, 1513–Dec. 1, 1521

His personal extravagance, military campaigns, and engagement in the construction of St. Peter's led the Church into deep debt that he tried to reduce through the selling of offices and indulgences. The Dominican John Tetzel and the Augustinian monk Martin Luther reacted, and the Protestant Reformation soon followed. Leo excommunicated Luther in 1521.

216. Hadrian VI [Adrian] (Dutch)†	Jan. 9, 1522–Sept. 14, 1523	The only Dutchman elected to the papacy and the last non-Italian until John Paul II in 1978. His nationality was resented by the Romans and his efforts to bring reforms and financial belt-tightening to the Curia were resisted by the cardinals. He also failed in efforts to deal with the Turkish threat or to deal effectively with Luther's challenge to Rome.
217. Clement VII†	Nov. 19, 1523–Sept. 25, 1534	During his pontificate Rome was invaded and sacked by the imperial forces and he had to live away from the city for nearly a year. He did not recognize the gathering clouds of the Reformation and refused the emperor's request to call a council in order to deal with the crisis. England and northern Europe drifted away from the Catholic Church during his reign.
218. Paul III†	Oct. 13, 1534–Nov. 10, 1549	A Renaissance pope in the best and worst senses of the word: a patron of the arts and a nepotist. He recognized the crisis of the Reformation and began laying out a program for renewal, including the reform of religious orders and the development of new congregations such as the Jesuits. But he also established the Congregation of the Roman Inquisition (Holy Office). He called the Council of Trent in 1545, but suspended it in 1548.
219. Julius III	Feb. 8, 1550–Mar. 23, 1555	Like his predecessor, a quintessential Renaissance pope. The Council of Trent reconvened in 1551, but had to be suspended a second time in 1552 because of political and military problems. He encouraged the Jesuits and welcomed the temporary return of England to Catholicism under Queen Mary. He appointed Michelangelo chief architect of St. Peter's.
220. Marcellus II	Apr. 9–May 1, 1555	One of the few popes in modern times to retain his baptismal name (Hadrian VI, the Dutchman, had also done so). His pontificate began on a note of promise with a modest coronation rite, a reduction of the size of his Curia, and the discouragement of nepotism (he ordered his relatives to stay away from Rome). As he prepared to publish a comprehensive reform program, he died of a stroke after only twenty-two days in office.
221. Paul IV†	May 23, 1555–Aug. 18, 1559	At first reformers were delighted with his election at age seventy-nine, but they soon found him to be a pope in the triumphalistic, medieval mold. He was vehemently opposed to Protestants and Jews (confining them to a special quarter in Rome and requiring them to wear distinctive headgear), and he lent his strong personal support to the Inquisition. He created the Index of Forbidden Books in 1557. Upon his death crowds stormed the Inquisition and toppled his statue.
222. Pius IV	Dec. 25, 1559–Dec. 9, 1565	In personality and policies his pontificate was in striking contrast to Paul IV's. He reconvened the Council of Trent in 1562 (it had been suspended for ten years). He worked thereafter to have the council's decrees and teachings accepted throughout the Catholic world. In one of the few successful instances of nepotism in the papacy, he chose his nephew Charles Borromeo to be cardinal and archbishop of Milan.
223. Pius V, St.†	Jan. 7, 1566–May 1, 1572	A Dominican, he enforced the decrees of the Council of Trent, published the *Roman Catechism*, reformed the breviary (Divine Office) and the Roman Missal, and declared Thomas Aquinas a Doctor of the Church. His excommunication of Queen Elizabeth in 1570 had a very negative impact on Catholics in England, but the victory over the Turks at Lepanto in 1571 also occurred during his reign.
224. Gregory XIII†	May 14, 1572–Apr. 10, 1585	A firm promoter of the decrees of the Council of Trent and of Catholic reform generally. A strong supporter of the Jesuits, he reconstructed and endowed the Roman College, later called the Gregorian University in his honor. His name is more notably associated with the reform of the Julian calendar, completed in 1582, involving the dropping of ten days and the introduction of a leap year. It is still in use and is known as the Gregorian calendar.

225. Sixtus V†	Apr. 24, 1585–Aug. 27, 1590	A Franciscan, like Sixtus IV, he restored order to the Papal States by harsh and repressive means. He set the maximum number of cardinals at seventy, a total that was not exceeded until the pontificate of John XXIII (1958–63). He also reorganized the Roman Curia, which remained basically unchanged until Vatican II (1962–65). Through his building projects, including the completion of St. Peter's dome, he transformed Rome into a great Baroque city.
226. Urban VII	Sept. 15–27, 1590	He contracted malaria the night after his election and died before his coronation.
227. Gregory XIV	Dec. 5, 1590–Oct. 16, 1591	He made his incompetent nephew a cardinal and then secretary of state, which created resentment and opposition among the other cardinals. While he was pope, Rome suffered from plague, food shortages, and lawlessness.
228. Innocent IX	Oct. 29–Dec. 30, 1591	An elderly man when elected as a stopgap candidate, he had a short and undistinguished pontificate.
229. Clement VIII	Jan. 30, 1592–Mar. 5, 1605	Despite his faults, which included nepotism and a love of display, he restored prestige to the papacy. He reduced the influence of Spain in Church affairs, issued a corrected edition of the Vulgate, and reformed various liturgical books. But he also expanded the Index of Forbidden Books and intensified the severity of the Inquisition. The holy year of 1600 brought millions of pilgrims to Rome.
230. Leo XI	Apr. 1–27, 1605	A nephew of Leo X, he was elected with French support and in the face of Spanish opposition. However, he was already old and in poor health and died before the month was over.
231. Paul V†	May 16, 1605–Jan. 28, 1621	The pope who censured Galileo for teaching that the earth revolves around the sun. On the other hand, he promoted Church reform and encouraged missions, approving the use of the vernacular in the liturgy for China.
232. Gregory XV	Feb. 9, 1621–July 8, 1623	He decreed that papal elections should be conducted by secret ballot (a practice that remains in force today) and founded the Sacred Congregation for the Propagation of the Faith. He canonized Teresa of Ávila, Ignatius of Loyola, Philip Neri, and Francis Xavier.
233. Urban VIII†	Aug. 6, 1623–July 29, 1644	Historians refer to him as a "reckless nepotist" who created a brother and two nephews cardinals, advanced other family members, and enriched his relatives generally. He consecrated the new St. Peter's in 1626 and selected Castel Gandolfo for summer retreats—a place still used by popes to escape the summer heat of Rome.
234. Innocent X†	Sept. 15, 1644–Jan. 1, 1655	He was an elderly man when elected; his pontificate was dominated by his ambitious sister-in-law. He opposed the use of Chinese ritual in the liturgy in that country and condemned Jansenism.
235. Alexander VII	Apr. 7, 1655–May 22, 1667	Although he showered his family with Church offices and properties, he did permit the Jesuits in China to use Chinese rites and dispensed Chinese priests from praying the Divine Office in Latin. He confirmed the condemnation of Jansenism. He also commissioned Bernini to enclose St. Peter's piazza with two semicircular colonnades.
236. Clement IX	June 20, 1667–Dec. 9, 1669	He spent much of his short pontificate trying to resolve existing tensions and disputes involving Spain and France, and in assisting Venice (unsuccessfully) to recover Crete from the Turks.
237. Clement X	Apr. 29, 1670–July 22, 1676	He was elected at age seventy-nine, and his pontificate was marred by the nepotistic and avaricious behavior of his cardinal-assistant, related to him through a niece's marriage. Clement canonized an unusually large number of saints, including Rose of Lima, South America's first saint.

238. Innocent XI, Bl.†	Sept. 21, 1676–Aug. 12, 1689	Although a morally upright, antinepotist pope, he manifested Jansenist leanings, an impression accentuated by an apparently anti-Jesuit bias. He was in constant conflict with Louis XIV of France and the French church generally. He is regarded as the outstanding pope of the seventeenth century.
239. Alexander VIII	Oct. 6, 1689–Feb. 1, 1691	Elected at age seventy-nine, he was welcomed by the Romans as a pleasant contrast with Innocent XI. The Romans delighted in his worldly ways and blatant nepotism. He also lowered their taxes and food prices.
240. Innocent XII	July 12, 1691–Sept. 27, 1700	A reformer pope in the style of his hero Innocent XI, particularly in his campaign against nepotism. He reached a compromise with Louis XIV, ending a fifty-year political and religious impasse between France and the papacy.
241. Clement XI	Nov. 23, 1700–Mar. 19, 1721	His long and relatively ineffective pontificate was preoccupied with political troubles in Spain and continued debates about Jansenism in France. It was he who finally settled the argument between the Jesuits and Dominicans by siding with the latter in forbidding the use of Chinese rites (1704; reiterated in 1715). Persecution of Chinese Christians and the closing of missions followed. The prohibition was not lifted until 1939 by Pius XII.
242. Innocent XIII	May 8, 1721–Mar. 7, 1724	He disliked the Jesuits and even thought of suppressing the order when he learned that they were still using Chinese rites. His short pontificate, however, was marked by constant illness.
243. Benedict XIII	May 29, 1724–Feb. 21, 1730	A Dominican who retained his monastic life-style after election, he remained archbishop of Benevento but also took a direct pastoral interest in the diocese of Rome. Unfortunately, former associates from Benevento formed a corrupt inner circle around him, much to the detriment of his pontificate and popularity among the Roman citizenry.
244. Clement XII	July 12, 1730–Feb. 6, 1740	Elected at age seventy-nine and blind from the second year of his pontificate, he relied on poor advisers, especially his cardinal-nephew, and the international standing of the papacy continued to decline. He erected the famous Trevi Fountain in Rome.
245. Benedict XIV†	Aug. 17, 1740–May 3, 1758	He was elected after the longest conclave in modern times: six months. He cultivated good relations with many foreign countries and improved the financial condition of the Papal States. He also won the respect of non-Catholics for his generally tolerant and cultured ways.
246. Clement XIII	July 6, 1758–Feb. 2, 1769	His pontificate was dominated by the Jesuit issue. He was under heavy pressure from Portugal, and then France, Spain, Naples, and Sicily, to dissolve the order. He summoned a special consistory to discuss the matter but died the day before it met.
247. Clement XIV	May 19, 1769–Sept. 22, 1774	A Franciscan who had been friendly with the Jesuits before election, he saw his task as one of satisfying the Catholic powers' insistence that the Jesuit order be suppressed. After delaying his decision for four years, he finally acceded to their demands in 1773.
248. Pius VI†	Feb. 15, 1775–Aug. 29, 1799	He was pope during the French Revolution and denounced the Civil Constitution and the Declaration of the Rights of Man. Thereupon Napoleon Bonaparte invaded the Papal States and imposed arduous terms of peace. Pius was deposed as head of state and withdrew to Florence. He was later taken across the Alps and died as a prisoner.
249. Pius VII†	Mar. 14, 1800–July 20, 1823	A Benedictine, he entered into concordats with the Italian Republic and with France, but when he later excommunicated all "robbers of Peter's patrimony," he was arrested by Napoleon's forces, imprisoned near Genoa, and then taken to Fontainebleau. His captivity was severe, but his manner of bearing it enhanced his personal prestige. He restored the Jesuit order in 1814.

250. Leo XII	Sept. 28, 1823–Feb. 10, 1829	Elected with the support of conservative cardinals, he replaced Pius VII's liberal secretary of state and condemned indifferentism, religious toleration, and Freemasonry. He reinforced the Index of Forbidden Books and the Holy Office, reestablished the feudal aristocracy in the Papal States, and confined Jews once again to ghettos. He died an unpopular figure.
251. Pius VIII	Mar. 31, 1829–Nov. 30, 1830	He returned to the spirit and policies of Pius VII, generally opposing liberal movements in Ireland and Poland, but supporting the July (1830) revolution in Paris against King Charles X. He approved the decrees of the First Council of Baltimore in the United States in 1830.
252. Gregory XVI†	Feb. 2, 1831–June 1, 1846	A Camaldolese monk elected with the support of the conservatives, he banned railways in his territories, opposed Italian nationalism, and crushed an uprising in the Papal States with the help of Austria. Although he condemned freedom of conscience, freedom of the press, and the separation of Church and state, he also denounced slavery and the slave trade and encouraged a native clergy and hierarchy in mission lands.
253. Pius IX†	June 16, 1846–Feb. 7, 1878	He was elected as a moderate liberal, but his reputation soon changed when he refused to support the expulsion of Austrian forces from Italy. The Papal States were annexed to the new kingdom of Italy, and he refused thereafter to set foot outside the Vatican. He defined the Immaculate Conception (Mary was born without original sin) and called the First Vatican Council (1869–70), which defined papal primacy and papal infallibility. His was the longest pontificate in history.
254. Leo XIII†	Feb. 20, 1878–July 20, 1903	The first pope to attempt to bring the Church into the modern world. He called for a renewal of the thought of Thomas Aquinas and opened the Vatican archives to scholars. He supported biblical research and gave tentative support for democracy. His most famous encyclical, *Rerum Novarum* (Lat., "Of New Things"), promoted social justice and the rights of workers. During his pontificate, there was a vast missionary expansion of the Church.
255. Pius X, St.†	Aug. 4, 1903–Aug. 20, 1914	Taking an entirely different approach from Leo's, he emphasized the rights of the Church against temporal authorities and the purity of Catholic doctrine. He enforced the latter with an oath against Modernism and a vigorous prosecution of those suspected of heresy. He also reorganized the Curia, prepared a new code of canon law, encouraged early and frequent Communion, and reformed the liturgy.
256. Benedict XV†	Sept. 3, 1914–Jan. 22, 1922	His pontificate was overshadowed by the First World War, in which he maintained neutrality and was reduced to an observer. He called a halt to the internecine warfare between traditionalists and progressives in the Church, promoted reunion with the separated churches of the East, and promoted the missions.
257. Pius XI†	Feb. 6, 1922–Feb. 10, 1939	He encouraged lay participation in the mission of the Church, condemned contraception, and concluded a Lateran Treaty with Mussolini establishing the Vatican City State as a separate political entity. He opposed both Communism and Nazism and supported Franco in Spain. The number of missionaries doubled during his pontificate. He was the first pope to use the radio for communication.
258. Pius XII†	Mar. 2, 1939–Oct. 9, 1958	Pope during the Second World War, he was a firm opponent of Communism in the postwar years. He promoted biblical studies, liturgical renewal, and Marian devotion, defining the Assumption (Mary was taken bodily into heaven) and declaring a Marian Year. He was the first pope to be heard widely on radio and seen on television.

259. John XXIII†	Oct. 28, 1958–June 3, 1963	He called the Second Vatican Council (1962–65) to update the Church and brought a whole new pastoral and personal style to the papacy. Although elected at age seventy-seven and in office less than five years, he was one of the most beloved popes in history, by Catholics and non-Catholics alike. He was a strong proponent of ecumenism, peace, and social justice.
260. Paul VI†	June 21, 1963–Aug. 6, 1978	He continued the Second Vatican Council begun by his predecessor and assumed responsibility for implementing its decrees. He was the first pope to travel by airplane and to visit countries thousands of miles away from Rome. Although progressive in theology and social thought, his pontificate was forever marked by his divisive encyclical condemning contraception.
261. John Paul I†	Aug. 26–Sept. 28, 1978	Although he died after only thirty-three days in office, this humble man left his mark on history by being the first pope in centuries to refuse to be crowned. He was invested instead with the simple pallium of an archbishop.
262. John Paul II (Polish)†	Oct. 16, 1978–	The first Slavic pope and the first non-Italian since Hadrian VI (1522–23), he is also the most traveled pope in history. Although committed to the Second Vatican Council, much of his pontificate thus far has been dedicated to the containment of progressive ideas and practices following from that council. For that reason, it has been called a restorationist papacy. Others see him as the first postmodern pope, a strong and deeply spiritual leader guiding the Church toward a new century and a new millennium.

RICHARD P. MCBRIEN

Populorum Progressio (pah-poo-lohr'uhm prohgres'ee-oh; Lat., "Progress of Peoples"), social encyclical issued in 1967 by Pope Paul VI. It expands Catholic teaching's concern about the gap between rich and poor to the differences and tensions between wealthy and impoverished countries. Therefore, the encyclical focuses on the problem of international development. Pope Paul is forceful in his insistence that development is spiritual and cultural, as well as economic. He urges a "complete humanism" that accentuates "the fully rounded development of the whole man and of all men" (n. 42).

Backing the call to development is the theological claim that God intends the earth and its goods for use by everyone. A growing gap between rich and poor nations inhibits God's intention from being realized. Therefore, *Populorum Progressio* emphasizes the necessity of aid to poor nations and that trade between nations be regulated by the principle of social justice.

Pope Paul also picks up and carries forward Pope John XXIII's insistence in *Pacem in Terris* (1963) that peace is intimately bound up with economic justice. Peace is not the mere absence of war, but a quality of relationship between persons and nations. For this reason, Pope Paul argues that "the new name for peace is development" (nn. 76–87). *See also* Catholic social teachings; encyclicals, social.

Porphyry, ca. 232–ca. 303, Neoplatonic philosopher who was biographer and popularizing successor of Plotinus; author of commentaries on classical philosophy influential for the Middle Ages. His direct importance for Christian literature is twofold: a consistent opponent of religious credulity, he wrote a now-lost, sophisticated and fierce attack on Christian beliefs, including biblical interpretation, which elicited elaborate apologetic refutations, notably from Eusebius of Caesarea. While Augustine joined the criticisms in his mature work, Porphyry's writings were likely among the "Platonist books" to which his religious development was indebted. *See also* Neoplatonism.

Porras y Allon, St. Rafaela Maria (paw-rahs' ee i-ohn'), 1850–1925, Spanish-born founder of the Handmaids of the Sacred Heart, devoted to teaching children and to retreat work. Feast day: January 6.

Porres, St. Martin de. *See* Martin de Porres, St.

portal (Lat., "gate"), the main door of a church or cathedral.

porter, the first and lowest of the old minor orders. Originally the porter's duties included guarding the doors of the church from entry by unauthorized people, calling the community to worship by the ringing of the bells, and assisting the preacher. The office was abolished by Pope Paul VI in 1972. Laypersons now perform its functions. *See also* minor orders.

Portiuncula, chapel near Assisi, Italy, also known as St. Mary of the Angels, the main church of St. Francis.

Port-Royal, Cistercian convent and Jansenist center near Versailles, founded in 1204. The convent in 1602 came under the direction of a ten-year-old abbess, Jacqueline Marie Angélique Arnauld (1591–1661). Through her spiritual director, the Abbé de Saint-Cyran (1581–1643), Port-Royal attracted devout laypersons who took no vows (known as "Solitaires"), including Antoine Arnauld (1612–94), and became a center of Jansenism, a morally rigorist movement. In 1661 the nuns refused to acknowledge the papal condemnation of five Jansenist propositions contained in Cornelius Jansen's *Augustinus,* which led to their persecution. Some nuns were transferred (1664), others forbidden the sacraments. In 1679 the archbishop of Paris prohibited new novices to Port-Royal, and in 1709, when the nuns again refused to condemn Jansenism unconditionally, the convent was closed. *See also* Arnauld, Jacqueline Marie Angélique; Jansen, Cornelius; Jansenism.

Portugal, Catholicism in. It is traditionally believed that Catholicism was brought to Lusitania, the Portuguese area of the Iberian Peninsula, through the missionary work of St. James during the apostolic age. By the beginning of the fifth century the majority of the population in the peninsula was Christian. In A.D. 409 the Swabians and later the Visigoths settled in Portugal. The Lusitanians suffered a religious crisis until the Swabians were converted by Martin of Braga in the 550s.

Muslims invaded the Iberian Peninsula in 711 and ruled for over five hundred years. Christian Crusaders drove them out beginning in 1212. The reconquest of Portugal by the Christians under Alfonso III (d. 1279) was concluded in 1249 with the victorious battle for Algarve. To this day the liturgical feast of the *Vitória dos Cristãos* (Port., "Christian's Victory") is celebrated in Portugal in commemoration of the expulsion of the Moors.

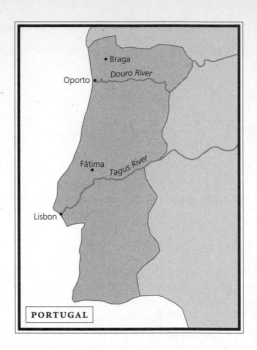

PORTUGAL

In the fifteenth and sixteenth centuries, while the unity of the Church was being challenged throughout Europe, Portugal and Spain remained loyal to the Church. In the age of exploration, Portugal established colonies in Indonesia, India, Malaysia, China, Japan, Africa, and Brazil, opening the way for evangelization therein. However, these missionary efforts were sometimes corrupted by an unholy alliance between the Church and business and political interests.

The Church suffered a major anticlerical attack from 1750 to 1777 under the Marquis of Pombal. Pombal expelled the Jesuits in 1759 and restricted the activity of the clergy. Pombal's sanctions were temporarily lifted during the reign of Maria I. Anticlericalism continued through the nineteenth century, but Catholicism prevailed in the Concordat of 1886. With the emergence of the Portuguese Republic in 1910, the Law of Separation of Church and State was passed to eliminate Catholicism from the country. The Church was disestablished the following year. However, the people from the north continued to support the Church, and the reported apparition of the Blessed Mother at Fátima in 1917 strengthened the Catholic faith of the Portuguese people.

Relations with the Vatican were resumed in 1918. The political separation of Church and state was finalized by Antonio Salazar (d. 1968) with the Concordat with the Vatican in 1940. The Catholic Church was once again allowed to maintain private schools, and most of its property was restored.

Among the most prominent Portuguese saints are Anthony de Padua, John of God, John de Britto, Eulália of Mérida, Rudesind, and Theotonius. Elizabeth of Portugal was originally from Saragossa, Spain. Our Lady of the Immaculate Conception was proclaimed the patron saint of Portugal in 1645 by King John IV.

In 1994 Catholics constituted about 93 percent of the total population of over 10.5 million. There are one patriarchate, two archdioceses, and seventeen dioceses.   *MARIA L. CARRANO*

positive theology, theological inquiry based on historical facts and concrete data (e.g., liturgical practice, religious customs). It is characterized by an inductive approach in contrast to the more deductive methods of natural theology, philosophical theology, and systematic theology. One form of positive theology is historical theology. *See also* theology.

positive way. *See* ways of the spiritual life.

positivism, a type of philosophy according to which the human intellect can know only that which can be apprehended by the human senses and tested empirically. As a result, it denies the possibility of metaphysics and theology. It is exhibited in the positive philosophy of Auguste Comte (1798–1857) and the "logical positivism" of Alfred Jules Ayer (1910–89). *See also* philosophy and theology.

Possevino, Antonio, 1534–1611, Italian Jesuit missionary and diplomat. One of the most versatile and gifted Jesuits of his age, he worked to obtain the conversion of Protestant Sweden through King John III, and obtained papal absolution for Henry of Navarre. He was one of the first Westerners to visit Muscovy in 1581 as a papal emissary, where he unsuccessfully discussed church union with the staunchly Orthodox Czar Ivan IV, "the Terrible."

Postel, St. Mary Magdalene, 1756–1846, French-born founder of the Sisters of Christian Schools of Mercy. She worked in the field of religious education. Feast day: July 16.

postulancy, program to prepare a candidate for the novitiate in a religious community. Many religious communities attempt to assist the emotional, intellectual, and spiritual development of their candidates even before the novitiate. Such programs vary considerably from one religious community to another, and often the term itself might not be used for such a program. *See also* novitiate; religious institute.

postulant, a candidate for the novitiate in a religious institute who is participating in a formal program called a postulancy. *See also* novitiate; postulancy; religious institute.

poverty, a state of material deprivation and dependence. Poverty is usually considered a lack of physical necessities, such as food, clothing, and shelter. The greatest poverty is loss of life.

Early in OT history, the Israelites considered poverty a sign of divine chastisement; however, their experience of exile gradually transformed that understanding to one in which the poor became the faithful who humbly relied on God for all needs. Christ manifested the religious character of poverty. The giving of his own life for the sake of others revealed the redemptive value of sacrifice.

Involuntary poverty embodies the real, though often unacknowledged, human condition of reliance on God. Voluntary poverty freely embraces this state of dependence for the purpose of providing more generous service of others, in imitation of Jesus. Spiritual poverty is a form of voluntary physical poverty in which one acknowledges dependence on God for material and spiritual needs. Sensitivity to the spiritual and material needs of others is a fruit of spiritual poverty.

The evangelical counsels of poverty, chastity, and obedience, and the religious vow of poverty underscore human dependence on God and the interdependence of all creatures. Francis of Assisi (d. 1226) gave a special meaning to institutional poverty through the Franciscan order, which he founded. Franciscans commit themselves to a life of poverty and simplicity, and to the service of the poor. *See also* counsels, evangelical; Franciscan order; Franciscan spirituality; Spiritual Franciscans.

power, the capacity to effect action. The OT contains no speculation on the nature, origin, or exercise of power. Israel was, of course, familiar with the reality of political power, as a result of subjection by the superpowers of the day, successively Egypt, Assyria, Babylonia, Persia, Macedonia, and Rome. The political power of its own rulers was also a present and sometimes oppressive reality. A steady refusal to grant such power ultimate validity is evident, especially in the prophetic writings. Psalms in particular often express a sense of powerlessness in the face of not only political realities but also cosmic forces threatening the return of chaos, variously symbolized as Leviathan, Rahab, Tannin, Behemoth (Pss 74:13–14; 89:10; Job 3:8; 9:13). Ultimate power rests with God, a conviction generally expressed in terms of the political realities of kingship and imperium (e.g., Isa 6:1–5). The idea of divine power focuses on creation, to which appeal is made in speaking of divine control of nature (e.g., Amos 4:13; 5:8–9; 9:5–6; Job 38–39), the powerlessness of other gods, and the folly of those who worship them (e.g., Isa 44:9–20; 45:9–13).

The NT adds nothing new to this belief in divine power but affirms that God has made his power available for salvation in Jesus (Matt 28:18–20). Early Christians were aware of contemporary belief in autonomous cosmic forces ("rulers and authorities in the heavenly places"; Eph 3:10) but denied either their autonomy or their reality. The endowment of Jesus with power is revealed in miracle (for which the Greek word *dynamis,* "power," is often used; e.g., Matt 7:22) and exorcism, the casting out of Satan and voiding of his power. At the same time, the Gospels relay the message that the exercise of power and authority is to be eschewed in favor of service (Luke 22:25–26; John 13:14–15). Indeed, Jesus charged his disciples not to be engaged in any struggle for power among themselves (Matt 20:20–28; Mark 10:35–45). *JOSEPH BLENKINSOPP*

power of the keys. *See* keys, power of the.

Praemunire (pray-moo-neer'ay; Lat., "to fortify in front"), English statute (1353) forbidding appeals to courts outside of England in cases where royal courts could exercise jurisdiction. Originally aimed at appeals to the papal Curia in cases involving English benefices, the statute was infrequently invoked until Henry VIII (d. 1547), who used it for political ends. It was finally repealed in 1967. *See also* benefice; England, Catholicism in.

Praepositinus of Cremona (pray-pahz-i-teen' uhs), ca. 1140–1210, theologian and liturgist at the University of Paris, whose writing on the symbolism of the Offices exerted considerable influence.

Pragmatic Sanction of Bourges (1438), a decree governing the relations of the Church and state in France. Negotiated with the Council of Basel by King Charles VIII, the sanction curtailed papal rights to award French benefices, interfere in French canon law cases, and levy taxes in France. Gallicanism, the movement in support of independence of the French church from Roman interference, appealed to the Pragmatic Sanction. *See also* Gallicanism.

pragmatism, a school or perspective in philosophy that holds as its central claim the notion that ideas are authentic or true only insofar as they have practical consequences that verify the ideas. Widely considered to be an American branch of philosophy, pragmatism was nurtured by utilitarian thought, and is represented by William James (1842–1910) and John Dewey (1859–1952). Pragmatism may have influenced the Catholic Modernists, since they judged that the Church needed to restate its teachings to make their meaning more relevant to the concerns of twentieth-century Christians.

Prague, Infant of, statue of the child Jesus in kingly crown and robes. Smaller reproductions were popular objects of devotion before Vatican II (1962–65). The original eighteen-inch-high statue was donated by Princess Polixena to Our Lady of Victory Church, Prague, in 1628.

Prat, Ferdinand (prah), 1857–1938, French scripture scholar. After ordination as a Jesuit in 1885, and studies in oriental languages and exegesis in Beirut, Paris, and Rome, he taught in France, Belgium, and Lebanon. He was one of the first consultors to the Pontifical Biblical Commission (1902–7), and is author of the influential *The Theology of St. Paul* (Eng. trans. 1926) and *The Life and Teaching of Jesus* (Eng. trans. 1950).

praxis (Gk., "doing," "performing"), the aspect of Christian discipleship expressed through actions and choices. Liberation theologies and religious education theorists (e.g., Thomas Groome) in particular have emphasized the importance of reflective activity, maintaining that the content of faith must be formed not only by acts of worship and intellectual assent to a body of truth-claims but also by participation in efforts aimed at transforming human persons and communities. A commitment to praxis does not depreciate worship or theological reflection but challenges them to become ever more consistent parts of an inseparable whole, leading to, issuing from, and enriching one another. *See also* liberation theology; religious education.

PRAYER

rayer is the act by which one enters into conscious, loving communion with God. Prayer acknowledges the existence of a relationship between God and humanity and, more specifically, that God relates to each human being with ongoing solicitude and benevolence. All prayer is based on the underlying reality of personhood and the ability of persons to be present to one another. A divine Person interacts with human persons who reach out to the One who sustains all creatures. When prayer is directed to the mother of Christ or a saintly intercessor, the one prayed to is viewed as connected with God.

The basic sense of the word "prayer" as entreaty, supplication, and petition is the introductory phase of approaching the One who is infinite power and limitless goodness. In addition to petition, prayer is also intercession, thanksgiving, repentance, adoration, and praise. Scriptural phrases to describe the way in which people pray include "call upon," "intercede with," "meditate on," "consult," "cry out to," "draw near to," "rejoice in," and "seek the face of."

Definitions of prayer from the great teachers of the Christian tradition include raising the mind to God (John Damascene), conversation and discussion with God (Gregory of Nyssa), affectionate directing of the mind to God (Augustine), intimate sharing between friends (Teresa of Ávila), and loving attentiveness to God (John of the Cross).

All Christian explanations of prayer agree that the initiative comes from God, who moves people to the act of praying. Grace disposes the mind and heart and energizes the praying throughout. The human spirit is raised to enlightenment and love through the guidance of the Holy Spirit. The objects of prayer can be temporal or spiritual goods for oneself or for others. A person cannot request something evil, since that would deny the intrinsic nature of an all-good God and be a perversion of prayer.

In praying, people acknowledge divine truth, mercy, and power. Christian pray-ers celebrate the Good News of Jesus Christ, revealing God as Father, Son, and Holy Spirit. Their pleas for God's help or praise of the divine goodness are rooted by faith in Christ. This faith moves toward hope and reaches out to embrace God in love. They believe in the divine willingness to come to their aid, they trust in the salvation made available to them, and they are moved to love the One who pours out infinite love on them.

The power of prayer is affirmed throughout Scripture. It does not reverse the divine will, but in the eternal designs prayer is causally connected to the outcome desired. Prayer, then, is part of the decrees whereby providence works unto good. Strength, comfort, and resignation are given to the pray-er even if what is asked does not come to pass exactly as requested.

By praying, individuals are changed, raised to a new level of spiritual being that affects understanding and behavior. Increase in virtue should be the fruit of praying. Interaction with other people should be marked by greater charity, compassion, and willingness to be of service. A new freedom from deep-rooted, self-centered attachments begins to emerge. Selfishness gives way to an awareness of others that is based on deeper awareness of God. Perceptions are cleansed and capacities for joy increased. Suffering and pain are linked to the central mysteries of redemption. Earthly passage is directed toward its goal in eternity. Prayer, then, is meant to influence the way people live by turning their attention to the divine dimension of earthly existence.

VOCAL PRAYER

Vocal prayer uses words that are recited, spoken, or sung. It may draw on already composed material with a long history in a particular culture or community. It may also be spontaneous. The Lord's Prayer, the Hail Mary, liturgical texts, psalms, litanies, and ejaculations are examples of centuries-old vocal prayers. In public worship, words combine with gestures to make up the ritual of the Church's official ceremonies.

Vocal prayer is particularly expressive in devotions, with their more individualistic, expansive character. Less strictly regulated than liturgical worship, public devotional practices lack the power and austerity of liturgy. But they have a warm emotional immediacy. Private devotions, the choice of the suppliant, are able to focus on what evokes the strongest personal response. However, devotional prayer alone can keep one at a less profound and even superstitious level of religious awareness.

Liturgical celebration rises out of the local Christian community but unites it to all believers on earth and to the Church Suffering in purgatory and the Church Triumphant in heaven. It represents the praying congregation at its highest level of worship. Sacramental reality joins heaven and earth in a union that empowers physical being with the transcendent dynamism of Christ's living mysteries. Ritual observances, especially when linked to the Eucharist, educate the pray-er through symbol and bodily action. Without a connection to the Church, prayer can become idiosyncratic.

MENTAL PRAYER

Mental prayer refers to a reflective process that involves mind, imagination, and will. Beginning as meditation on divine realities, it pulls in the wandering mind in order to focus it. For authentic prayer to take place, eventually the heart must be moved. Meditation methods like the Ignatian and Sulpician are made up of considerations, affections, petitions, and resolutions. Methods with such carefully laid out schemas did not appear until the fifteenth century. Contemporary practices like journaling, imaging, and narrative techniques have a strong psychological component that aims at self-understanding in order to facilitate spiritual development and its expression in praying.

Monastic approaches to mental prayer still draw on ancient customs, echoed in the twelfth century, that speak of *lectio* (Lat.), reading, as seeking the sweetness of the blessed life, meditation as finding it, prayer as asking for it, and contemplation as tasting it.

Meditation practices should gradually move into a more affective mode. Thinking decreases and the heart is easily aroused to fervor. Charismatic renewal is an example of the power of affective prayer on the group level. Eventually affective prayer simplifies even more and is increasingly drawn to interior stillness. The multiplicity of acts by mind or heart are silenced into one single act of longing that is more like a state of being. This stage is aptly called the prayer of simplicity. Other names given to it are the prayer of faith, of repose, of simple regard, or of the simple presence of God. It has also been designated as active contemplation, a phrase used less frequently today.

Contemporary prayer methods focus increasingly on this stage of simplification. The Jesus Prayer, or Prayer of the Heart, which comes from the Christian Eastern monastic tradition, and the various forms of centering prayer deal with praying in the simplified mode. Non-Christian spiritual techniques from Asia, with their emphasis on mindfulness and interior emptying, have influenced some Christian simplification practices. A mantra's power to focus interior attention is analogous to the teaching of the fourteenth-century *Cloud of Unknowing*. However, a Christian word or phrase repeated in order to hold the mind's attention always bears some theological content. Active recollection, described by Teresa of Ávila, while appropriate to all stages, is especially helpful when interior calming occurs. In Teresa's practice, the Christian mysteries always play a dominant role.

PASSIVE PRAYER

Simplified prayer reaches out to contemplation. In some spiritual literature, the term "contemplation" can mean an inward summarizing glance of love that is still in the active mode of praying. But monastic teachers and especially the Carmelite school always use contemplation to describe infused passive prayer. Pure gift of God and wholly beyond the power of human effort to generate, it initiates the mystical encounter with the divine Beloved.

Contemplation in its earliest form is passive recollection, sometimes considered the prayer of simplicity with an infused element. The pray-er at this stage needs at times to reach out actively to make contact with God. Therefore, it is a transitional phase in which the infused gift, still weak, does not occupy the inner attention entirely. The prayer of quiet is a deeper form of passive recollection. The heart is held, but mind and imagination are often free to wander.

Simplified prayer before the onset of infused contemplation and even in the first passive stages often bears with it the suffering of aridity and distractions. The radical decrease of material that the mind finds nourishing leaves the understanding open to the onslaught of useless imaginings. Prayer, as it simplifies, cleanses excessive attachments to what is less than God and increasingly demands greater purity of conscience. Temptations can seem stronger than before because the cleansing effect of more advanced prayer uncovers the psychic compromises people make with their imperfections. To someone used to the sweetness of the earlier stages, especially in affective prayer with its high emotional content, the bleak desert of contemplative purgation can seem like moving backward.

Longing for God continues and deepens in the desert. A simple gaze of love unifies one's being, overflowing into one's life. One looks at ordinary existence with new eyes, seeing the mark of God on everyone and everything. Prayer, no longer a set time on the clock, permeates all activity and all rest. Awareness of the Divine Presence transforms perceptions.

In the prayer of full union, the inflowing of contemplation controls the interior faculties of mind, imagination, and will so powerfully that a person is wholly caught up in God. In the next stage of ecstatic union, absorption or rapture seizes the pray-er so that the senses can no longer communicate with the outside world. Spiritual betrothal and spiritual marriage are the last phases of mystical prayer. Here transformation in God reaches its completion, but the pray-er still retains his or her distinct being.

Intoxicating fulfillments in passive prayer are granted at the cost of intense suffering. A person advances in holiness and virtue through the strengthening discernment of contemplation. But the path can be enveloped in deep, crucifying darkness. John of the Cross describes this passage as the "night of the senses" and the later, much more terrible "night of the spirit." Spiritual purification is exquisitely fitted to each person's particular temperament and personal history. Just as the final transformation in God realizes a unique, unrepeatable beauty in each human being, so the preparatory cleansing is apportioned in degree and kind by a God who knows how to apply the process of purification with infinitely loving precision.

Extraordinary phenomena like private revelations, visions, locutions, unexplained fragrances, levitation, and the stigmata are peripheral to holiness. If communicated by God, they instruct and encourage but are not of the essence of mystical contemplation, which always proceeds in faith. They can be a hindrance when valued possessively.

Contemplative experience, even at its lowest levels of passive recollection and quiet, exhibits characteristics that are manifested later in greater fullness. Mystics describe these qualities in experiential phrases: the perception of God's living presence; felt inward quiet; the taste of everlasting life; love burning but not consuming; the wine of inebriating joy; blessedness irradiating every passing moment with eternity.

Mystics testify to the apostolic power of prayer, which serves the Church and the world by drawing down divine blessings. Even when prayer is not in the distinctly intercessory form, the saints attest to its efficacy for achieving good and conquering evil.

Prayer stages are not distinct divisions. A person does not pass beyond an early stage, never to return there. Earlier characteristics can appear in more advanced prayer. One must pray as one can since God has infinite adaptability. The great teachers of spirituality urge never giving up a practice that is the source of so much goodness.

Prayer at every stage is the conversation of heaven already begun on earth. It realizes human potential through a deepening perceptual process. This takes individuals to the dimension of earthly existence where the divine exemplar is already imprinted on their creaturehood. In prayer, the indwelling Trinity calls to persons, conforming them more and more to the image of the Incarnate Word.

See also spirituality, Christian.

Bibliography

Balthasar, Hans Urs von. *Prayer.* San Francisco: Ignatius Press, 1986.
The Classics of Western Spirituality. Mahwah, NJ: Paulist Press, 1978.
Cunningham, Lawrence. *Catholic Prayer.* New York: Crossroad, 1989.
Foster, Richard J. *Prayer: Finding the Heart's True Home.* San Francisco: HarperCollins, 1992.
Wright, John H. *A Theology of Christian Prayer.* 2d ed. New York: Pueblo Publishing Co., 1988.

MARGARET DORGAN

Prayer, Apostleship of. *See* Apostleship of Prayer.

Prayer After Communion, a prayer concluding the Communion rite; formerly termed the "post-communion." After the Communion of the people, a period of silence may follow. The prayer after Communion, usually beginning with a reference to the assembly's Communion and then moving to the effects of this union in Christ, concludes the rite.

Prayer of the Faithful, the litany of general intercessions at Mass or during the Liturgy of the Hours. Appropriate subjects for the Prayer of the Faithful include the Church and its ministers, civil authorities, the world and its peoples, the health and physical well-being of the ill or physically challenged, those who are dying, the faithful deceased, those who mourn, those who are receiving special rites such as Baptism or Matrimony, and those observing anniversaries or birthdays. On Good Friday, the Prayer of the Faithful assumes an especially solemn character as each intercession is followed by silent prayer and what was formerly (before 1965) called a Collect, or prayer recited by the priest in which the intentions of the congregation are "collected" together and presented to God.

Prayer over the Gifts, formerly termed the "Secret," a silent oration, prayed after the bread and wine are placed on the altar, that concludes the rite of Preparation of the Altar and the Gifts. The prayer generally mentions presenting gifts to God with a petition for their transformation.

Prayer over the People, an extended form of blessing used on certain occasions (e.g., the Sundays of Advent). Part of the dismissal rite, this prayer in the form of a Collect, in which the priest "collects" the prayers of the congregation and presents them to God, precedes the simple blessing formulary. Its content relates to the season or mystery celebrated. *See also* blessing.

prayers for the dead, the custom of praying that God will admit into heaven the souls of the departed still in purgatory. According to Catholic doctrine, people who die in the state of sanctifying grace may have committed unabsolved venial sins or still owe temporal punishment for other sins already forgiven in the past. In these cases, atonement must be made before the soul can enjoy the Beatific Vision in heaven. By praying for the "poor souls" in purgatory, the Church Militant (living members of Christ's Body on earth) intercedes for the Church Suffering (deceased members of the Church as yet unperfected). In this way, the living help to hasten the admission of the dead into the company of the saints. The liturgical celebration of All Souls' Day on November 2 each year is an example of this ancient practice. So are Masses of Christian Burial and anniversary Masses for departed relatives and friends. Prayers for the dead, however, need not be restricted to liturgical celebrations. One may offer a prayer such as: "Lord, have mercy on her soul," or "May his soul and all the souls of the faithful departed, through the mercy of God, rest in peace." In defending this custom, Catholics refer to 2 Macc 12:42; 45–46 where the text seems to encourage such prayers. Christians have prayed for their dead from the time of the Roman persecutions. *See also* purgatory.

Preachers, Order of. *See* Dominican order.

preaching, canon law concerning, norms regulating preaching, which is the proclamation of the word of God by one authorized to do so, usually a bishop, priest, or deacon (cans. 762–72). Canon law is concerned with the regulation of preaching in order to ensure that the word of God is properly proclaimed; it is considered one of the chief duties of ordained ministers. Bishops may preach anywhere in the world, and universal canon law allows priests and deacons to do the same unless the local bishop explicitly forbids them to do so.

In Church law two kinds of preaching are considered: the homily, a sermon based on the scriptural readings of the day's Mass, which is part of the liturgy itself, and other preaching, such as at a prayer service, a parish mission, a retreat, or a day of recollection. The first kind of preaching is reserved to an ordained minister. People other than clerics, however, may speak at Masses, for example, where many children are present if they may be better understood by the children. The second kind of preaching is to be regulated by norms established by the bishops' conference in each country; this kind of preaching is open to qualified laypersons as well as clerics. Preaching is not only for instruction, but also to bring people to faith. *See also* homily.

preambles of faith, introductory premises or conditions of the act of faith. This phrase, not common in present-day Catholic theology, had its home in apologetic theology prior to Vatican II (1962–65).

It was part of an analytical account of the conditions and logic of the act of faith. The preambles of faith are those things that can be known historically and through reason; together they generate the reasonableness or credibility of the object of faith. Since faith is a free act and its object transcends all this-worldly knowledge, the preambles of faith do not establish faith but only lead one to its threshold.

A good example of the preambles of faith is the use of Jesus' miracles in neo-Thomistic fundamental theology. The Gospel miracles were taken at face value to be overt manifestations of the divine in history that established the divinity of Jesus, his authority, and the authority of the Church he founded. The content of Jesus' revelation remained the transcendent object of a free act of faith. But as a preamble to that faith Jesus' miracles established reasonably and with a degree of certainty that Jesus' teachings were expressions of divine revelation. *See also* apologetics; faith and reason.

precedence, ranking given a member of the hierarchy, clergy, or a religious community in accord with law or custom. Such a ranking might determine the place of an individual in ceremonies or in voting groups. It might even determine the outcome of a tied election. The ranking is determined according to universal or particular norms.

precept, a canonical decree given to an individual by a legitimate authority (e.g., a bishop or religious superior). The decree obliges a person to act or enjoins a person from acting. A precept often urges the observance of an existing law.

Precepts of the Church. *See* Commandments of the Church.

preces (pray'chez; Lat., "prayers"), brief prayers of intercession. Preces may be said responsively, with an opening phrase delivered by a minister and a concluding phrase by an assembly. A common example is the prayer (versicle) "Rest eternal grant unto them, O God"; (response) "And may light perpetual shine upon them." Another (versicle) "Pray for us, O Blessed Virgin Mary"; (response) "That we may be made worthy of the promises of Christ."

Precious Blood, devotion to the, veneration of the blood of Jesus Christ as a symbol of his self-giving life (e.g., 1 Pet 1:18–19; Matt 26:28; John 19:34). The veneration of relics of Christ's blood began at Mantua in 553, Weingarten in 1090, and

Bruges in 1158. Special devotions to the Precious Blood developed in the early 1800s, and in 1849 Pope Pius IX dedicated the first Sunday in July for the celebration of the feast of the Precious Blood. In 1960 Pope John XXIII approved the Litany of the Precious Blood. The Second Vatican Council (1962–65) encouraged Christians to venerate the whole person of Jesus Christ and, as a result, the feast has been dropped from the liturgical calendar. For the full text of the litany, see *The Raccolta* (1957) or P. Klein, ed., *Catholic Source Book* (Dubuque, Iowa: Brown-ROA, 1990). *See also* blood of Christ.

Precious Blood Fathers (C.Pp.S.), religious community founded in Italy in 1815. The society's founder, Gaspare del Bufalo, envisioned a community of priests and brothers dedicated to the task of giving missions and fostering devotion to the Precious Blood, i.e., the blood shed by Christ on the cross for the redemption of the human race. The bond among the members was not a vow, but a charity. Their only distinguishing feature was a large crucifix on a gold chain, worn over a cassock and cincture. Although severely criticized by some as too novel, Gaspare's rule was approved by Pope Gregory XVI in 1841. The first American foundations began in Ohio in the 1840s. Eventually, the society spread to several states, and missions were also founded in South America.

predella (pray-dehl'ah; It., "footstool"), the platform at the top of several steps upon which an altar may be installed. *See also* altar.

predestination, the eternal, gracious, and infallible decree of God conferring human salvation. Using the language of such texts as Rom 8:29–30 and Eph 1:5, 11, this doctrine refers to the Church's faith that the salvation of the saints is the result of the knowledge (foreknowledge) and the unmerited, gratuitous, and sovereign act of God (election) and, therefore, is part of God's eternal will (decree). At the same time, because human beings are endowed by God with free will, salvation is consequent not only upon the free self-offer of God in love, but upon its free acceptance by the individual. The basic underlying issue is how to conceive the relationship between divine grace and human freedom.

Classic Formulations: The classic formulation of this problem arose in Augustine's (d. 430) disputes with Pelagius (d. ca. 425), who contended that the grace necessary for salvation is already given to all men and women in the free will with which they are endowed by God. Augustine countered that human nature had become so radically disordered by sin that only God's gratuitous decision to save could provide the unique grace necessary to liberate, empower, and guarantee true freedom (*On Nature and Grace* 53.62). But his theology so emphasized the power of grace and the utter dependence of human freedom upon it, that it became difficult to see how human self-determination was preserved. This emphasis led Augustine to speak at times of a double predestination, that of the saints to salvation and that of sinners to damnation (*City of God* 15.1). The Second Council of Orange (529), however, taught that no one is predestined by God to sin.

Thomas Aquinas (d. 1274) emphasized that God desires all to be saved (1 Tim 2:4) and is ready to give grace to all. While affirming that God's will in predestination is infallibly effective, Aquinas insisted that God is able to move the human heart to the love of God in a manner that in no way diminishes human freedom (*Summa Theologiae* 1–2.113.3). God rejects only those who refuse grace (*Summa Contra Gentiles* 3.159.2). But at times, Aquinas can be read as leaning to a more Augustianian position. Appealing to texts such as Mal 1:2–3, Aquinas spoke of those whom God predestined to receive grace (thus revealing divine mercy) and those whom God reprobated in permitting them to remain in their sins (thereby revealing divine justice). Simply put, God frees some sinners from their sins and leaves others in them, according to the prerogative of God's sovereign freedom. In Aquinas's view, God is not unfair, for in bestowing a favor on some, God does not deprive others of what they are due. (*Summa Contra Gentiles* 3.161, *Summa Theologiae* 1.23.3, 5).

From the Reformation to the Twentieth Century: The doctrine of double predestination became central among several Reformers, notably John Calvin, who believed that God predestines not only to salvation but also to damnation. This doctrine represents a major break with the single predestination doctrine, found in the works of Aquinas and Augustine, and was condemned by the Council of Trent (1545–63). Its Decree on Justification (1547) is the most important formulation of official Church teaching on the necessity and gratuity of grace and the freedom of the individual under grace. Debate continued as evidenced in the extreme Augustinian writings of Michael Baius (condemned in 1567), in the "*De Auxiliis*" controversy about how grace aids human freedom to do good that developed in the

late sixteenth century between the Dominicans (following Domingo Bañez) and the Jesuits (following Luis de Molina), and in the struggles with the Jansenists, who denied that Christ died for all human beings (condemned in 1653).

In the twentieth century, Karl Rahner (d. 1984) posed the question in somewhat different terms, insisting that God's eternal plan is the salvation of the whole world, not the salvation of some and the damnation of others. In Pauline terms, one should speak of predestination for salvation alone (Rom 8:29–30; cf. 1 Cor 15:22). God wills and effectively offers salvation to all (1 Tim 2:4, 4:10; Tit 2:11). Christ is the revelation that God has created human freedom in such a way that it is oriented toward divine life as its final goal. The term predestination, then, is simply a way of expressing God's universal saving will and eternal purpose as accepted by human freedom. History and free human decisions are not superfluous, because God cannot predetermine how individual free creatures will respond to the grace of Christ.

There has never been an undisputed consensus among theologians on the subject of predestination. Two things must be borne in mind concerning the relationship between divine grace and human freedom. First, as the tradition has stressed since Augustine, human freedom must be and is liberated by God's grace from the power of sin in order that it may become truly free and therefore able to respond to grace. Second, the necessity of a human response in freedom is in no way diminished by the action of God's grace in liberating human freedom. The Church has permitted a considerable range of opinion on the question, while always requiring that in some way both the necessity of the divine initiative and the reality of human self-determination and responsibility be maintained. *See also De Auxiliis;* election, divine; nature and grace; providence; salvation.

Bibliography

Jüngel, Eberhard. *God as the Mystery of the World.* Grand Rapids, MI: Eerdmans, 1983.

Kasper, Walter. *The God of Jesus Christ.* New York: Crossroad, 1984.   JOHN R. SACHS

preevangelization, those pastoral activities that prepare the way for the direct preaching of the gospel to those who are not yet ready or able to hear it. These may include works of charity, justice, and education designed to remove existing obstacles to evangelization, e.g., chronic illness, poverty, ignorance, and oppression. Some of these activities are now seen as "a constitutive dimension of the preaching of the gospel" (1971 World Synod of Bishops, "Justice in the World," par. 6). *See also* evangelization.

preexistence of Christ, the existence of the person of Christ prior to the Incarnation. Belief in Christ's preexistence developed within the early Church. Christians perceived Jesus Christ to be the Son of God who existed from all eternity (1 Cor 8:6; 2 Cor 8:9; Phil 2:5–11; John 1:14; Col 1:15–17; Heb 1:2–3). This biblical witness was affirmed in a condensed form in the creed of the Council of Nicaea (325), that from eternity the Son of God "was begotten" from the Father, "came down," "was made man," and "ascended." *See also* Jesus Christ.

Preface (pre'fis), the varying prayer of the Mass that immediately follows the Prayer over the Gifts and initiates the Eucharistic Prayer or Canon of the Mass and is an integral part of it. A dialogue precedes it and an acclamation ("Holy, Holy, Holy") follows. More than ninety prefaces are available for various feasts and seasons. An extended poem of praise and thanksgiving, each preface elaborates on God's work in creation and redemption while focusing on a particular aspect of God's saving work in Christ. *See also* Eucharistic prayer.

prefect apostolic, a priest in charge of a geographical area in which the local church has not grown sufficiently to be a diocese. The prefect apostolic has many of the same responsibilities as a diocesan bishop.

preferential option for the poor, an expression used in liberation theology, in the documents of the Latin American Bishops' Conference (CELAM), and in the social encyclicals of the pope to underscore the Church's primary commitment to the service of the poor, motivated by both charity and justice. "The Church's love for the poor," Pope John Paul II writes in his 1991 encyclical *Centesimus Annus,* "which is essential for [the Church] and a part of its constant tradition, impels it to give attention to a world in which poverty is threatening to assume massive proportions in spite of technological and economic progress. . . . [L]ove for the poor . . . is made concrete in the promotion of justice" (nn. 57, 58). *See also* Catholic social teachings.

prelate, a priest who has the power of governance in the external (public) forum. Such a classification includes all those considered ordinaries and certain officials of the Roman Curia. There are also honorary prelates, e.g., priests called by the title "monsignor" in the United States. *See also* external forum; Honorary Prelate of His Holiness; ordinary; prelates of honor.

prelate nullius, literally, the prelate without a diocese. He is the head of a territory independent from and equivalent to a diocese. The prelate nullius governs with powers similar to those of a diocesan bishop. The current term for a prelacy nullius is territorial prelacy.

It has also served as an honorary title, carrying no jurisdiction but entitling the bearer to the wearing of a special ecclesiastical costume and to a place of distinction in ceremonies. *See also* prelate.

prelates of honor, one class of priests commonly called "monsignors" in the United States. The title is purely honorary and is usually given by the Holy See at the request of a diocesan bishop. The bearer has the right to wear ecclesiastical garb similar to a bishop's. *See also* monsignor.

prelature, personal, a society of secular clergy (priests and deacons) established by the Apostolic See for the purpose of providing an equitable distribution of clergy or to perform particular apostolic works. It is governed by its own statutes and presided over by a prelate as its proper Ordinary, a bishop or priest who has authority over the society. The prelature's relations to the local Ordinary (the diocesan bishop) are defined in the statutes. The prelate has the right to establish seminaries, incardinate (formally enroll) the students, and promote them to Holy Orders. Laypeople can be affiliated with a personal prelature and share in its apostolic works and spiritual activities, as in Opus Dei, an organization of laity and clergy to bring the faith into ordinary life and especially the professions. *See also* Opus Dei; prelature, territorial.

prelature, territorial, and also territorial abbacy, "a certain portion of the people of God which is established within certain territorial boundaries and whose care, due to special circumstances, is entrusted to some prelate or abbot who governs it as its proper pastor, like a diocesan bishop" (can. 370). *See also* abbot nullius; pastor; prelate; prelature, personal.

Premonstratentian Canons. *See* Norbertines.

premoral evil, the undesirable dimension or disvalue of a human action that is relevant to, but not always determinative of, the act's morality, e.g., the loss of fertility in a necessary surgical procedure.

Premoral evil becomes morally evil when it is caused or permitted without a sufficient reason. *See also* evil, moral; proportionalism.

Preparation of the Gifts. *See* offertory.

Presanctified Liturgy, a Communion service in which the reserved eucharistic gifts, previously consecrated at a eucharistic liturgy (hence the name "presanctified"), are consumed. A Presanctified Liturgy is found in the Roman, Byzantine, and Maronite rites, and was once used in the Armenian, West Syrian, and East Syrian rites as well. In the Roman rite it is restricted to Good Friday, and is preceded by a Liturgy of the Word. In the Byzantine rite it is celebrated with Vespers. Intended for use on "aliturgical days" when the Eucharist was not celebrated, the Presanctified Liturgy results from the fourth-century practice of prohibiting the Eucharist, deemed festive, on Lenten ferias (weekdays without a special feast) and other days of fast and penance. In the East, Presanctified was an afternoon service, often celebrated with Vespers, because only one meal, taken in the evening, was allowed to those fasting; even Holy Communion was considered to break the fast. In Latin and Eastern monasteries, which usually had no daily Eucharist (and often no priest), it was customary for the religious to have Communion made available to them daily at a short monastic Presanctified service. The apocryphal attribution of the Byzantine Presanctified to Pope Gregory I does not antedate the twelfth century. *See also* Good Friday.

presbyter (prez'beht-uhr; Gk., *presbyteros*, "elder"), a term used for Church officials in the NT and early Church and currently, on occasion, as an alternative term for priest. Christian use of this term quite probably derives from postexilic Judaism, where councils of elders, lay leaders distinct from Jewish priestly families, functioned as synagogue leaders. When the term was applied to Christian community leaders, it sometimes was used interchangeably with the term *episkopos* (Gk., "overseer"), from which comes the English term bishop. Only at the end of the first century did the presbyter's role become distinct from that of the "overseer."

The presbyter of the second and third centuries functioned as a member of a council of advisors to the bishop and does not seem to have had a regular liturgical function. With the expansion of Christianity into rural areas, the presbyter came to have a distinctive role as community leader and presider at Eucharist. In the process, his role as advisor to the bishop was diminished. Gradually the presbyter came to be identified as a priest. It is likely that the English word "priest" comes from the Latin form *presbyter* and its contracted form, *prester.*

The term "presbyter" was used by Vatican II when it spoke of priests: the council desired to reflect NT usage; it wished to distinguish the priest from the bishop, in whom, the council teaches, the fullness of priesthood resides; and it sought to promote a notion of priestly ministry more extensive than one focused predominantly on worship. *See also* priest; priesthood.

presbyteral council, mandatory representative body, or senate, of priests serving as chief advisers to their diocesan bishop. For some matters the bishop must consult with the council to act validly, e.g., the erection, suppression, division, or merger of parishes, and in the determination of remuneration for the diocesan clergy. Following ancient tradition, however, the diocesan bishop should regularly consult the presbyteral council in all important matters of governance.

Statutes approved by the bishop according to the norms of the episcopal conference determine membership, about half to be elected by the priests. Most members will be diocesan priests. Some should serve *ex officio;* others may be appointed by the bishop. The bishop convokes and presides over the council and proposes its agenda. Items for discussion and consideration may, however, be received from any of its members.

presbyterate (prez-bit'uh-ruht), union, based upon ordination, of all the priests (presbyters), including religious priests, with the diocesan bishop. Antecedents of this understanding are found in second-century councils of presbyters united with the local bishop. After centuries of neglect, the Second Vatican Council (1962–65) revived an appreciation of the sacramental bond between priests and bishop. *See also* priesthood.

Presbyterianism, a movement among Christian churches whose form of polity depends upon councils composed of presbyters (Gk., "elders"). This form of governance is less hierarchical than the Church of England and the Catholic Church, but it is more structured than Congregationalism. The Protestant Reformers of the sixteenth century sought to recover the communal decision making of the early Church (e.g., the council of Jerusalem, Acts 15). According to John Calvin (d. 1564), the risen Christ calls a local church to be a community that ministers in his name, and, therefore, the congregation itself must select its specific ministers by means of a governing council (presbytery) composed of elected elders. Guided by this understanding, churches overseen by boards of pastors and presbyters were established beginning in the middle 1500s in Switzerland, the Netherlands, England, and Scotland. Under the leadership of John Knox (1513–72), Presbyterianism flourished in Scotland, and in 1557 the Presbyterian Church was recognized as the Church of Scotland.

Presbyterianism came to North America with the colonists. In 1706 the first church with a presbytery was established in Philadelphia by the Irish missionary Francis Makemie, and in 1716 a Presbyterian synod was constituted. In 1746 Presbyterians founded the College of New Jersey, now Princeton University. At the time of the Civil War, the Presbyterian churches in the United States affiliated with either the United Presbyterian Church in the U.S.A. (with offices in New York City) or the Presbyterian Church in the United States (with offices in Atlanta, Georgia). In 1983 these two bodies merged into a single organization, the Presbyterian Church of the U.S.A. The Presbyterian Church of Canada was formed in 1875. Worldwide membership in the Presbyterian churches as of 1994 has been estimated at fifty million. *See also* Calvinism; Protestantism; Reformation, the. ROBERT A. KRIEG

presbyterium (Lat., "body of presbyters"), the area of the church building reserved to the seating of clergy. In Roman basilicas, this was the apse; in later churches, it became synonymous with the choir. "Presbyterium" may also refer to the priest's senate (more commonly, the presbyteral council) or diocesan chapter, an advisory body to the bishop. It is also synonymous with "rectory," the house for one or more members of the clergy, although that is more commonly called the "presbytery." *See also* presbyter; presbyterate; sanctuary.

Presbyterorum Ordinis (pres-bee-tair-aw-*room* awr'dee-nees). *See* Decree on the Ministry and Life of Priests.

Presence, Real. *See* Real Presence.

presence of God, an affirmation in the Christian tradition of divine involvement in the universe and human affairs, called immanence as opposed to transcendence. A current task of theology is the exploration of the connectedness of immanence and transcendence. Even with Israel's emphasis on transcendence, belief was in a God who is near (Ps 119:51). Jesus is the presence of God in the world through the Incarnation and as the Body of Christ (Church and Eucharist). Jesus promised: "I am with you always" (Matt 28:20). It has been suggested that the presence of God is the most appropriate model for mystical experience. *See also* mysticism; transcendence.

Presentation, the ceremony in which the infant Jesus was brought to the Temple and Mary was purified after childbirth. According to Luke 2:22–40 Mary came to fulfill the requirements of the Torah (Exod 13:2, 12; Lev 12:6–8). Simeon greeted them and pronounced the prayer that came to be known as the Nunc Dimittis ("Now you are dismissing [your servant]"), and the prophetess Anna spoke of Jerusalem's redemption. The feast of the Presentation of the Lord is celebrated on February 2.

Presentation, Sisters of the. *See* Sisters of Mary of the Presentation.

presidential chair, the seat from which the presider leads the assembly in prayer. The chair's significance in each parish church is derived from the *cathedra* (Lat., "chair") in the cathedral from which the bishop of the diocese presides. Only the bishop uses the *cathedra,* which may be imposing in the cathedral though it should never resemble a throne. The presidential chair in the parish church should be placed prominently in a presiding position without suggesting domination or remoteness. The chair is to stand alone, not crowded by chairs of other liturgical ministers.

presidential prayers, prayers or orations that the presider voices in the name of the entire assembly. The premier presidential prayer in the Mass is the Eucharistic Prayer or Canon of the Mass, which is sung or spoken by the presiding priest. Other presidential prayers at Mass are the Opening Prayer, the c se of the General Intercessions or Prayer of the Faithful, the Prayer over the Gifts and the Prayer After Communion. Rites of other sacraments, the Liturgy of the Hours, and other liturgical celebrations include presidential prayers spoken by the one who leads the praying assembly.

presider (pree-zi' duhr), the one who oversees any act of public worship. The presider's responsibility is to animate the ritual texts and inspire the assembly to active participation. The presiding priest at Mass has often been called the principal celebrant or PC, which sometimes has caused the people to forget their role as celebrants along with the priest. The illusion was created that the priest was the sole celebrant, while the assembly watched him celebrate. The use of the term "presider" offers a corrective, in an attempt to alert the people to their active role in worship. But the term could prove unsatisfactory if it were to diminish the role at Mass of the priest, who alone acts in the person of Christ. *See also* Eucharist.

Presov. *See* Pseudo-Synod of Presov.

Prester John, fabled medieval Christian king of the East who, according to differing legends, lived in the Far East, India, or Ethiopia. He was thought to have defeated the Muslims in the Holy Land.

Preston, Thomas Scott, 1824–91, priest and administrator. Born in Hartford, Connecticut, and ordained an Episcopal priest, he converted to the Catholic Church in 1849. A prolific preacher and polemicist (author of fifteen volumes and numerous articles), the rigidly orthodox Preston was successively secretary, chancellor, and vicar-general to three New York prelates (Hughes, McCloskey, and Corrigan) until his death. With Mother Mary Veronica Starr, he cofounded in 1886 the Sisters of the Divine Compassion (R.D.C.), who work in education, retreats, social services, and related ministries. In the 1990s there are over one hundred members serving in the Archdiocese of New York.

presumption, in Catholic moral theology, the distortion or vice directly opposed to the theological virtue of hope. Where the vice of despair is the lack or absence of hope, presumption, at the opposite extreme, constitutes an unwarranted and exaggerated hope. In general, the vice of presumption rests on a misinterpretation of the relation between divine

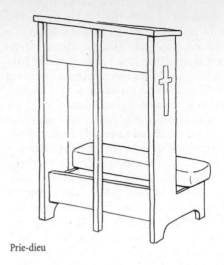

Prie-dieu

mercy and human freedom, and is classically described as either the habitual expectation that eternal life will be gained without God's assistance, or that salvation will be granted regardless of one's personal responses to God's gifts of grace. Both expectations are traditionally held to be gravely sinful. *See also* hope.

pride, the disordered love of self or one's own success to the exclusion of others or God. Pride is a capital sin because it is often the source of other sins. Pride may be the cause of the allied sins of presumptuousness, undue ambition, and vainglory, which is the exaggerated striving to demonstrate one's real or imagined excellence to others. Because of the malice involved, pride that seeks directly to disregard God and rightful authority is more serious than pride that only occasionally disregards God or the worth of others by making too much of one's own worth. *See also* capital sins.

prie-dieu (pree'dyuh; Fr., "pray-God"), a kneeling bench. The prie-dieu remains a common liturgical furnishing for weddings and the Mass. A standalone bench with a padded cushion for kneeling and a small bookrest, prie-dieus are often placed in the sanctuary area in front of and around the altar, where there are typically no pews.

Prierias, Sylvester (pree-air'ee-ahs), 1456–1523, Italian Dominican theologian. He was an early opponent of Luther and author of the compendium of moral theology *Summa Summarum Quae Silvestrine Dicitur.* As Pope Leo X's adviser (1515), he formulated the first theological attack on Luther's Ninety-five Theses and supported papal authority.

priest, one who performs the basic ordained ministry in the Catholic Church. The English word "priest" is used to translate both the Latin word *sacerdos* and the Greek word *hiereus,* both of which suggest ritual responsibilities pertaining to worship, an emphasis that served to express medieval and post-Tridentine Catholic associations between priesthood and Eucharist. "Priest" also translates, and in fact derives from, the Greek *presbyteros* ("elder"), a term suggesting a broader range of pastoral responsibilities, both in the NT and in the documents of Vatican II. The term also designates Christ (Letter to the Hebrews) and, collectively, all the baptized (1 Pet 2:5 and 9). *See also* presbyter; priesthood.

priesthood, the identity and role of Jesus and of the entire community of the baptized; also, the identity and role of the most common of the ordained ministries within the Church. While the latter usage is most common, Catholicism since Vatican II (1962–65) has tried to give due recognition to all of these meanings of the term.

Biblical Background: Certain details of Jewish priesthood figure in the historical development and understanding of Christian priesthood. Three items are of particular importance. The first is the priestly tribe of Levi, regarded as one of the twelve tribes of Jacob. In ancient times, the Levitical priesthood had responsibility in three areas: proclamation of the divine will, instruction and interpretation of the Law, and responsibilities associated with worship and ritual sacrifice (Deut 33:8–10). In the time of the monarchy, prophets assumed the first responsibility. In the exile, scribes became Israel's teachers. In postexilic Judaism, the priests' basic function centered around sacrifice and offering. In this narrower meaning, the term influenced Christian usage.

A second item is the figure of the high priest, associated with Aaron and his sons in the book of Exodus and with Zadok, appointed high priest by King David. The principal religious function of the high priest occurred on the annual solemn feast of the Atonement when the high priest entered the innermost sanctuary of the Temple to offer sacrifice for the sins of the people.

Thirdly, along with the priestly tribe of Levi and the high priesthood, the entire nation, because of God's covenant, was seen as a priestly people (Exod 19:5–6): the people as a whole were to live so that by their lives, regarded as sacrificial offerings to God, all nations would come to know the goodness of the God of Israel.

Two of these Jewish notions are background for two understandings of priesthood in the NT, that of the risen Christ and that of the entire body of the faithful. In the Letter to the Hebrews, and only there, Jesus is called priest. It is the risen Christ, interceding for us at the right hand of God, who is said to fulfill the functions of the Aaronite priesthood: he is the mediator between God and humankind; he is compassionate; and he is appointed by God to this office. By a line of reasoning using the figure of Melchizedek, the author of Hebrews argues that Jesus surpasses the high priesthood of the Aaronite line. While Jesus' sacrifice of himself as a holy and unblemished victim on the cross achieved definitive atonement for all and renders obsolete the annual sacrifices offered by the high priest in the Temple, it is in his present intercession for us that Christ is priest.

A second understanding of priesthood, as it applies to the entire Christian community, appears in 1 Pet 2:4–12. The author, using the imagery of Exod 19:5–6, identifies the community of those baptized in Christ as a "body of priests" and calls the people to offer their lives as spiritual sacrifices acceptable to God. By seeing the example of such lives, the nations of the earth will come to glorify God.

NT writings, while recognizing divinely authorized leadership roles within the Christian communities, do not designate as priest any who hold such roles. It was only at the end of the first century when Christians came to see themselves as a religious body distinct from Judaism and the Eucharist as an unbloody sacrifice replacing Temple sacrifices that they began to apply the notion of priesthood to Christian leaders.

Priesthood in the Tradition of the Church: In the early centuries of the Church, the leadership of the community and its worship centered on the bishop. In the conviction that Jewish priesthood and worship were types of Christian realities, the bishop came to be called high priest and priest of the Christian Church. With the growth of the Christian population, especially in rural areas, presbyters increasingly came to function as community leaders and presiders at Eucharist and so they, too, were called priests.

As Christianity became a legal religion of the Roman Empire and then its official religion, Christian priests were also seen as replacing the priesthood of the Roman cults. With this development came an increasing emphasis on the ordering of different groups within the Church, analogous to the diverse orders of groups distinguished from the general populace in the empire. Heightened stress on priesthood lessened appreciation of the role and responsibility of the laity. Application of monastic ideals to priesthood also contributed to the separation of clergy from laity.

The patristic idea of priesthood was further influenced by the anti-Arian reaction in which the Eucharist was experienced less as a sacrifice of the Church than as a holy theophany. The liturgy became the preserve of the priest, whose role as ritual minister increasingly was emphasized.

Early medieval emphasis on the Eucharist further promoted an understanding of priesthood in terms of liturgical power to change bread and wine into the body and blood of the Lord and diminished the notion of priesthood understood in relationship to the community. Bishops, in turn, were seen as priests who had additional power of jurisdiction by which they could ordain and exercise ecclesial authority. The writing of Pseudo-Dionysius, with its great emphasis on spiritual and ecclesiastical hierarchy, influenced the medieval emphasis on the divinely ordered hierarchy of bishop and priest in the community and further separated the priesthood from the laity.

It was in reaction to these developments that the Reformers insisted on ministry as basically a power to preach, on a lack of distinction between clergy and laity in the priesthood of all believers, and on what they believed to be a lack of biblical warrant for a divinely ordered hierarchy within the ministry of the Church. In response, the Council of Trent (1545–63) reaffirmed the distinction between clergy and laity, the presence of a divinely constituted sacramental priesthood with power to offer sacrifice and to forgive sins, and a hierarchical ordering of ministers in the Church. Although Trent's teaching on priesthood dealt only with the most pressing questions of the day, the emphases of that teaching dominated Catholic thought and practice until the mid-twentieth century.

Priesthood in the Teaching of Vatican II: The Second Vatican Council (1962–65) sought to present Catholic teaching on the priesthood in relation to the biblical, liturgical, and historical traditions of the Church. In so doing, the council presented an understanding of the priesthood and priestly ministry that differs significantly from the emphases of post-Tridentine Catholicism.

Two teachings of Vatican II are basic to its teaching about ordained priesthood: its reaffirmation of the priority of the priesthood of Christ and its teaching that the entire community of the baptized is a priestly people sharing, by the power of the Holy Spirit, in the threefold mission of Christ as prophet, priest, and servant of the kingdom of God. Only within the context of these truths does one properly appreciate the role of ordained priesthood in the Church.

The council's principal teachings on ordained priesthood included the idea that the fullness of the priesthood resides in the episcopate. Through sacramental ordination, bishops receive the office of sanctifying, teaching, and governing in the Church. The order of priests shares with the bishops in the one and same priesthood and ministry of Christ, though it does so in its distinctive way. In ordination, priests receive the power of the Spirit to act sacramentally in the person (role) of Christ, the head and shepherd of the Church.

The council deliberately broadened the notion of priestly ministry: rather than defining the priest in terms of his relationship to the Eucharist and his power to forgive sins, priesthood is seen in terms of a threefold ministry, that of the word, of the sacraments, and of community leadership. The priest exercises these functions in union with the bishop and the college of priests of which the bishop is the head. Priests are cooperators of the episcopal order, necessary helpers and advisers in the ministry and office of the bishops.

The ordained priesthood and the laity share, through Baptism, a common dignity, a common grace, and a common vocation to perfection. Within that framework, the council teaches that ordained priesthood differs essentially from the priesthood of the faithful, though the two are ordered one to the other and each in its own way shares in the one priesthood of Christ. Basic to the function of ordained priesthood is the charge to so minister in the name of Christ to the entire body of the faithful that the entire Church sees itself and acts as a prophetic people, a priestly people, servants of the kingdom of God.

The understanding and practice of priesthood within the history of Catholicism show both continuity and development. Past history suggests that both characteristics will continue to be present in the future. *See also* Holy Orders; ministry; ordination.

Bibliography

Cooke, Bernard. *Ministry to Word and Sacraments: History and Theology.* Philadelphia: Fortress Press, 1976.

Donovan, Daniel. *What are They Saying About the Ministerial Priesthood?* New York: Paulist Press, 1992.

Galot, Jean. *Theology of the Priesthood.* San Francisco: Ignatius Press, 1984.

Osborne, Kenan B. *Priesthood: A History of the Ordained Ministry in the Roman Catholic Church.* New York: Paulist Press, 1989.

FREDERICK J. CWIEKOWSKI

priesthood of all believers, the belief that the corporate body of the baptized are, in Christ, a priestly people, sharing in the one priesthood of Christ. The term has its biblical foundations in Exod 19:6, where Israel is called a priestly people by virtue of the covenant, and in 1 Pet 2:5 and 9, where the Exodus imagery is applied to believers in Christ. After a long period of neglect, largely because of negative Catholic reaction to teaching of the Reformers, the notion was revived at Vatican II (1962–65). "For their part, the faithful join in the offering of the Eucharist by virtue of their royal priesthood. They likewise exercise that priesthood by receiving the sacraments, by prayer and thanksgiving, by the witness of a holy life, and by self-denial and active charity" (Dogmatic Constitution on the Church, n. 10). *See also* Baptism; laity; priesthood.

priests' senate. *See* presbyteral council.

primacy, papal, the honorary and jurisdictional authority possessed by the Bishop of Rome (the pope) and exercised over the universal Church. The Roman Catholic doctrine on papal primacy has been at the heart of the last two ecumenical councils of the Church: Vatican I (1869–70) and Vatican II (1962–65). Its authentic meaning has to be discovered not only in the affirmations of Vatican I but also in the very important clarifications of Vatican II. The ecclesiological language of Vatican I was strongly juridical. This council was the culmination of a long process of development in Western theology that had, since 1054, been isolated from any vital dialogue with the Eastern churches. By contrast, Vatican II was deeply influenced by the old ecclesiology of communion where, without being denied, the primacy of the Bishop of Rome is related to the collegiality of all the bishops, and this collegiality of the bishops is related, in turn, to the synodality of their local churches. Nevertheless, the strongest affirmations concerning the primacy of the Bishop of Rome are in the so-called *Nota Explicativa Praevia* (Lat., "Prefatory Note of Explanation") of the Dogmatic Constitution on the Church (*Lumen Gentium*), where it is asserted that collegiality does not contradict papal primacy.

See of Rome: The constitution *Pastor Aeternus* of Vatican I states, in one of its principal paragraphs, that the primacy of the Bishop of Rome cannot be separated from the primacy of the local church of Rome: "We teach and declare that in the disposition of God the Roman Church holds the pre-eminence of ordinary power over all the other Churches and that this power of jurisdiction of the Roman Pontiff which is truly episcopal is immediate" (DS 3060). This link between the see of Rome and the bishop who occupies this see of "the Church of Peter" (and Paul) is reaffirmed when the constitution deals with infallibility, which the Bishop of Rome possesses when he speaks *ex cathedra* (Lat.), "from his see (or his chair)" (DS 3074). The constitution quotes the Second Council of Lyons (1274), which affirms: "The holy Roman Church possesses the supreme and full primacy and authority over the universal Catholic Church which it recognizes in truth and humility to have received with fullness of power from the Lord himself in the person of Blessed Peter, Prince or head of the Apostles of whom the Roman Pontiff is the successor. And as it is bound above all to defend the truth of faith, so, too, if any questions should arise regarding the faith, they must be decided by its judgment" (DS 3067; it is important to remember that this council was convoked to bring about the restoration of communion with the Eastern churches). Moreover, Vatican I affirms that the charism of truth and never-failing faith was conferred on those presiding "in this Chair" (or see) of Rome (DS 3071). Even if the same Vatican I document includes statements that stress the reverse relationship (the importance of the see of Rome depending on the primacy of its bishop), it is ecumenically crucial to point out that *Pastor Aeternus* does not forget the most traditional way of understanding the Roman primacy. The primacy of the church of Rome and the primacy of the Bishop of Rome cannot be dissociated; they are mutually dependent.

During the first centuries and until the Second Council of Nicaea (787), in spite of many doctrinal and political tensions, it is evident that the church of Rome is concretely considered the first among the local churches dispersed throughout the *oikumené* (Gk., "the whole wide world"). It is from the see of Rome and its bishop that other churches ask for help, for solution of conflicts, for guidance. While, according to Pope Zosimus (d. 418), no other church can judge the church of Rome, this Roman church is convinced that it is called by God to a *sollicitudo omnium Ecclesiarum* (Lat., "pastoral care of all the churches"). This unique position among the other churches (and not over them) comes from what Irenaeus (d. ca. 200) calls "its more powerful principality," having its source in the martyrdoms of Peter and Paul. Peter showed the link with the people of the OT; Paul showed the link with the evangelization of all the nations (*Against Heresies* 3.3, 2), and both were explicitly called by Christ for a specific mission. Clement of Rome (d. ca.101), Ignatius of Antioch (d. ca.107), Dionysius of Corinth (d. ca. 170), Tertullian (d. ca. 225), and many other Christian writers of the first centuries associate Peter and Paul, inseparable from each other, with the destiny and the prerogatives of the church of Rome. Rome, indeed, is not the only church grounded in the faith of the two apostles. Moreover, Peter and Paul were not the first disciples of Christ to come to Rome. Nevertheless, since both shed their blood in this city because of their confession of Christ, the church of Rome carries more weight than other apostolic churches. The charism of Peter and Paul together with the blood of their "confession" are forever part of the identity of the local church of Rome. It belongs to this see.

Role of the Bishop of Rome: It is because of this charism and these prerogatives of his local church that the bishop of the see of Rome has a specific role concerning the communion of all the local churches in the apostolic faith and everything attached to this faith (charity, mission, sacramental life, eschatological hope). He is the first among the bishops because he is the minister and the representative of the local church that, among all the local churches, has been called to be the guardian of the supreme confession of the apostolic faith. To be in communion with him means for another bishop (and for the local church that this bishop serves and represents) to be in communion with all the bishops and all the churches who confess, have confessed, and will confess this faith. Vatican I's *Pastor Aeternus* affirms that his mission is communion in faith "in order that the episcopate itself might be one and undivided, and that the whole community of believers might be preserved in unity of faith and communion by

means of a closely united priesthood" (DS 3051). But other bishops are not the vicars of the Bishop of Rome, and no detriment may be done to the ordinary and immediate jurisdiction of the bishops in their own local churches (DS 3061). Vatican II adds that in his local church each bishop is "vicar of Christ" (Dogmatic Constitution on the Church, n. 27) and that the power of jurisdiction he possesses in this local church is given through his sacramental ordination and not through the Bishop of Rome.

College of Bishops: The primacy of the Bishop of Rome is a primacy of jurisdiction, but Vatican II states that the college of bishops, together with the Bishop of Rome who is its head, also has a full and supreme power over the whole Church. The college of bishops does not possess this jurisdiction because it has been conceded to it by the Bishop of Rome, but because of Christ himself.

When a local bishop exercises his own jurisdiction in his local church or in a collegial action (as in a general council), he is necessarily acting in communion with the Bishop of Rome and consequently with all those in communion with the see of Rome. But the Bishop of Rome himself, even when he speaks alone without consulting the college, is never out of essential communion with his brothers. He cannot act as if he were not the head of the college. What he has to say or to declare is either the faith confessed by all his fellow bishops (as the faith of Peter was the faith of all the apostles) or the answer to a need he has seen in the life of the communities assigned to the bishops. Even when he performs actions "which in no wise belong to the bishops, for example, convoking and directing the college, approving the norms of action" (*Nota praevia* 3), or acts on his own initiative without any explicit cooperation of other bishops, he is acting as head of the episcopal college and not as a private leader. Nevertheless, although the consent of the Bishop of Rome is required for every decision of the college as such, the consent of the college is not required for every decision of the Bishop of Rome (DS 3074). Even if the Bishop of Rome is morally bound to consult with the college before making an important decision, he is not canonically obliged to do so. Vatican II stressed the unity that exists between the head of the college and the college as such, but did not deal with concrete situations.

As primate, the Bishop of Rome has a jurisdiction that is not delegated (it is ordinary) and can be exercised directly for the whole Church without having to go through an intermediate body (it is immediate). This power is episcopal, given in the sacramental grace of episcopacy. *See also* collegiality; communion, Church as; infallibility; papacy, the; Peter, St.; Petrine ministry; Petrine succession; pope; vicar of Christ; Vicar of Peter.

Bibliography

De Satge, John. *Peter and the Single Church.* London: SPCK, 1981.
Dionne, J. Robert. *The Papacy and the Church.* New York: Philosophical Library, 1987.
Granfield, Patrick. *The Limits of the Papacy: Authority and Autonomy in the Church.* New York: Crossroad, 1987.
Tillard, Jean-Marie Roger. *The Bishop of Rome.* Wilmington, DE: Michael Glazier, 1983.
———. *Church of Churches: The Ecclesiology of Communion.* Collegeville, MN: Liturgical Press, 1992. Pp. 256–318.

JEAN- M. R. TILLARD

primate, an honorary title reserved usually for the archbishop or bishop of the oldest diocese in a country or region. In most instances, the title is purely honorary, although historically it often carried with it certain jurisdictional responsibilities. For example, the archbishop of Armagh is primate of all Ireland. But in the United States, although Baltimore is regarded as the country's primatial see, the archbishop of Baltimore is not considered a primate, even for honorary purposes.

Prime (Lat., *prima,* "first"), the first hour (*hora prima*) of the monastic office, celebrated at 6 A.M. In the Rule of St. Benedict (ch. 17), it was to consist of a hymn, three psalms, a brief Scripture reading, versicles and responses, and concluding prayer. Later, longer *preces* (litanic prayers) and the reading of the Martyrology were added. Prime was abolished by Vatican II (Constitution on the Sacred Liturgy, 1963, n. 89, d). *See also* Liturgy of the Hours.

Primitive Rule, the foundational rule of the Carmelite order, laid down in 1209 by Albert of Vercelli, the Latin patriarch of Jerusalem. The rule was one of rigorous asceticism. It prescribed absolute poverty, total abstinence from flesh meat, and solitude. After the order was reorganized in the mid-thirteenth century along the lines of the mendicant friars (Franciscans and Dominicans), the rule became less stringent. In the sixteenth century the Primitive Rule was restored in many houses under the leadership of Teresa of Ávila (d. 1582) and John of the Cross (d. 1591). Those living under the Primitive Rule were called Discalced ("without shoes") Carmelites in contrast with the Calced, who continued to follow the less stringent rule. *See also* Carmelite order.

prior, title for a religious superior in certain religious orders of monks, mendicants, and canons regular. For example, the Servites, Augustinians, and Carmelites call the superior of the house the "prior"; the major superior of a province, the "prior provincial"; and the supreme moderator of the order, the "prior general." *See also* religious orders and congregations.

prior bond, impediment of, invalidating obstacle to a marriage because of a previous marriage while the previous spouse is still living. The impediment stems from the nature of marriage as a monogamous and indissoluble union. From the twelfth century on, this prohibition has been known as the impediment of ligamen. *See also* ligamen, impediment of; marriage law.

prioress, title for a superior in certain communities of women religious, roughly corresponding to the position of prior in men's communities. Originating in the Middle Ages, the title is still used today by various religious institutes of women, most of them cloistered orders of nuns. *See also* religious orders and congregations.

priory (Lat., "the first"), a type of residence for a community of vowed religious. The community is under the leadership of a prior, i.e., the "first" (of the community). In some religious orders a priory is a house that is not yet firmly established; when further growth occurs, the status of the house is upgraded, e.g., to that of an abbey under the direction of an abbot. Other religious orders call their fully established houses priories.

Prisca, St. *See* Priscilla, St.

Priscilla, St., also known as Prisca, a first-century Christian who, along with her husband Aquila, was praised by Paul (Rom 16:3–5) in A.D. 58 for hosting the Christian assembly in her home. She is mentioned five more times in the NT (Acts 18:2, 18, 26; 1 Cor 16:19; 2 Tim 4:19). Feast day: July 8.

In Roman tradition, two other women have this same name. One is St. Prisca, a martyr whose relics are enshrined in the fourth-century church bearing her name on Rome's Aventine Hill. Feast day: January 16. The other person is Priscilla, a noblewoman, who in the first century established a catacomb for Christians on Rome's Via Salaria.

Priscillianism, a heresy of the fourth to sixth

centuries. It takes its name from Priscillian, a rigorous ascetic who taught in Spain beginning ca. 375 a dualistic doctrine reminiscent of Gnosticism and Manichaeism. Although such teachings were denounced at the Council of Saragossa in 380, Priscillian was elected bishop of Ávila shortly thereafter. In 386 he was brought to trial, convicted of sorcery, condemned by the emperor, and executed. Thus, much to the dismay of some Church officials, including Martin of Tours and Ambrose of Milan, Priscillian became the first heretic to suffer capital punishment. The movement he inspired, however, persisted until its condemnation at the Council of Braga in 563. Its adherents taught that while human souls came from God, because of their sins they were united to bodies, which were the creation of the devil. It followed that Christ could not have had a real human body (Docetism). Their doctrine of the Trinity was Modalist, i.e., the belief that there are not three distinct Persons in God but only three modes of divine existence and activity. *See also* dualism.

private vows. *See* vows, private.

privilege, a special favor granted by Church authority. The favor given is not required by law. It can be given to a person or to a group of persons. Unless otherwise specified, a privilege continues until it is revoked by the one granting it, by that person's successor, or by higher authority.

Privilege of the Faith, the dissolution of a non-sacramental marriage for the sake of the living out of the faith. The privilege encompasses two models. The first of these is called the "Pauline Privilege" and is based on 1 Cor 7. The initial marriage is between two nonbaptized parties, one of whom converts to Christianity. Under specified conditions the convert may enter into another marriage, which dissolves the first marriage.

The second model, sometimes called the "Petrine Privilege," involves a marriage between a baptized party and a nonbaptized party. Under given circumstances the pope may dispense from the first union so that a second marriage can take place. *See also* indissolubility of marriage.

Pro, Bl. Miguel, 1891–1927, Mexican Jesuit. He exercised his priestly ministry even though it was illegal at the time for priests to do so. He was accused of an assassination plot against the Mexican presi-

dent and was arrested and executed. Feast day: November 23 (United States).

probabiliorism, a moral system for resolving doubts about the moral character of actions by following the "more probable" opinion. Probabiliorism became a favored response of Jansenists and Dominicans in the seventeenth century against what they regarded as the abusive laxness of probabilism. Probabilism held that one may follow a moral opinion if supported by a sound argument, even if this were not the more probable argument. Probabiliorism maintained that one must follow the more probable opinion or argument amid diverse positions. Effectively, however, probabiliorism demanded that one always follow the present law rather than any more benign opinion. *See also* equiprobabilism; probabilism; tutiorism.

probabilism, a system for forming a certain conscience in cases of doubt about the lawfulness of an action by following any probable opinion. Probabilism asserts that the opinion favoring freedom from obligation, if it is solidly probable, may be followed with moral integrity even if the opinion favoring obligation or the law is more probable. The need for some moral system is rooted in the universally held conviction that it is wrong to act when one is in doubt about the rectitude of one's act. A person who acts with uncertainty is said to act with an uncertain conscience. Some reflex or indirect way must be found to bring certainty to the agent's conscience. Probabilism fills this role by maintaining that a doubtful obligation is certainly no obligation.

Any number of arguments have been used to establish this certainty. The following is fairly standard: "No one is bound by any precept except through the knowledge [Lat., *scientia*] of the precept" (Thomas Aquinas *On Truth* 17.3). But there is no true knowledge of a precept when the opinion supporting it is only probable.

Central to the understanding of probabilism is the meaning of probability. Probability can be either intrinsic or extrinsic. It is intrinsic when the reasons for the opinion are cogent but not conclusive. It is said to be extrinsic when its probability is grounded in the authority, learning, and prudence of the authors who hold it. A rule of thumb often cited is that if five or six truly reputable authors hold an opinion, that is a sign of its intrinsic probability.

Probabilism was first systematically presented by the Dominican Bartholomeo Medina in 1577. It became a matter of bitter dispute in the Church and the system was accused of being laxist. The great moral theologian Alphonsus Liguori (d. 1787) favored equiprobabilism in his later years, but frequently proposed the basic tenets of probabilism (a doubtful law does not bind, an uncertain law cannot induce a certain obligation). For the last three centuries, the Church has imposed no particular system on theological schools and indeed has tolerated the presentation of probabilism throughout the world.

While probabilism, like any other system, can be, and has been, abused, it is still of great theological and pastoral significance in the Church. No purification or renewal of Christian morals can do away with the fact and urgency of concrete decisions. As long as these decisions are to be made and as long as uncertainty adheres to some of them, some reflex principle like probabilism is essential for the achievement of certainty of conscience. In broader perspective, probabilism remains a tribute to the claims of human freedom against all systems or ideologies that would attempt unduly to restrict this freedom. Furthermore, it has indirectly benefitted moral theology by preventing premature closure of difficult moral questions.

The use of probabilism is not without risk. It is often difficult to determine what is a genuinely probable opinion, who is a reputable theological authority, and what weight is to be given to past and present magisterial pronouncements. *See also* certitude, moral; equiprobabilism; probabiliorism.

RICHARD A. MCCORMICK

pro-cathedral, church used by a bishop (e.g., in a newly erected diocese) as his cathedral until a suitable cathedral is built or designated. *See also* cathedral.

process theology, a term applied to any theological system that emphasizes becoming over being as a metaphysical ultimate, but particularly those systems that are heir to Alfred North Whitehead's "philosophy of organism" (*Process and Reality: An Essay in Cosmology,* 1929). Originally a mathematician, Whitehead was influenced by the observations of Albert Einstein; his thought is both a highly speculative philosophical cosmology and an empirical reflection on human nature. Process theologians tend either to emphasize Whitehead's metaphysical system, first rigorously clarified by Charles Hartshorne, or to read Whitehead in the company of William

James and Charles Sanders Pierce, sometimes under the heading American empirical theology.

For Catholic theology, the distinguishing feature of process thought is its rejection of the Aristotelian basis of Scholastic metaphysics of being in favor of a metaphysics of becoming, in which the ultimate units of reality are events and relationality is prized over philosophical simplicity. Key to this is Whitehead's reversal of the usual pattern of causality. Rather than seeing causes as the producers of effects, effects generate themselves by their selection of causes. Each entity, including God, is *causa sui* (Lat., "a cause of itself"); God is, therefore, the supreme exemplar of a relational cosmos, not the supreme exception. God's vision or will is but one of the causes that may or may not be appropriated by a moment of becoming. Thus God's power to effect change in the world is persuasive and not coercive, making process thought fertile ground for theological issues such as evil, divine omnipotence, and the relationship between God and creation. *See also* philosophy and theology.   NANCY DALLAVALLE

procession, divine (Gk., *ekporeusis;* Lat., *processio,* "to emanate from another," "to have one's origin from another"), term used in trinitarian theology to signify the origin of one divine Person from another. According to Latin theology there are two processions, the Son from the Father, and the Spirit from the Father and the Son (Lat., *Filioque*). In Greek theology the Son proceeds from the Father, but the Holy Spirit proceeds from the Father through the Son. Latin and Greek theologies agree that God the Father does not proceed since the Father is unbegotten and unoriginated, coming from no one.

Processions are distinguished from missions. Though the two processions of begetting and spirating are said to take place immanently ("within" God), the two missions of Incarnation and the sending of the Holy Spirit take place within the economy of salvation. At the same time, because of the identity of economic and immanent Trinity, the divine missions presuppose the intradivine processions. *See also* Filioque; Trinity, doctrine of the.

procession, liturgical, the ordered movement of a liturgical assembly or its ministers from one location to another. Often accompanied by religious song, processions occur regularly during liturgical worship. The most frequent are the Entrance, Gospel, Offertory, and Communion processions, which are made, even in abbreviated form, during almost every Mass. Solemn processions are performed on Presentation of the Lord (February 2), Palm Sunday, the Feast of Corpus Christi, at the Stations of the Cross, or during the Rite of Christian Burial. The religious procession provides a vivid image of the Church: a body of pilgrims moving through time following the lead of its Lord in concerted action toward and on behalf of the world.

Proclus, St., d. 446, patriarch of Constantinople (434–46). The Council of Ephesus (431) included in its acts a homily he preached (428) in Nestorius's presence defending the *Theotokos* (title for Mary as "Mother of God"). His "Tome" (435) to the Armenian bishops attacks the teaching of Theodore of Mopsuestia (without his name) using the formula "God the Word, one of the Trinity, became incarnate," but the controversial sixth-century ("Theopaschite") formula, "one of the Trinity was crucified in the flesh," is not his. Feast day: October 24 (West); November 20 (East). *See also* Ephesus, Council of; *Theotokos.*

Procopius, St., d. 303, martyr and patron saint of the Czech Republic. Born in Jerusalem, he was beheaded in the Diocletian persecutions and was later revered as a great martyr by the historian Eusebius of Caesarea. Feast day: July 8.

profession, religious. *See* religious profession.

profession of faith, the public recitation of the creed, usually during the liturgy. A creed is a concise statement of the central beliefs of the Church. It is both a doxology that proclaims the glory of God and a hymn of thanksgiving for all God has done in and through Jesus Christ. The creed is used liturgically at the eucharistic celebration and during the rite of Baptism. Its public recitation on these occasions narrates the saving events that form the basis of Christian faith, identifies the assembly as a Christian community, and expresses the willingness of the members of the community to live as followers of Christ. The profession of faith is thus the assembly's verbal response to the salvation proclaimed in the Scriptures and memorialized in the Eucharist. A profession of faith is also recited by bishops and pastors before taking office. *See also* creeds.

pro-life movement, in the United States, a popular organized opposition to abortion. It receives substantial support from the National Conference of Catholic Bishops (NCCB) and from other religious bodies. Since the 1973 U.S. Supreme Court decision affirming a woman's right to abortion (*Roe v. Wade*), pro-life activists have sought to defeat pro-abortion legislation and overturn public policies and judicial decisions. Cardinal Joseph Bernardin of Chicago and the U.S. bishops generally have exhorted Catholics to broaden their pro-life position to include other issues affecting human dignity and human rights. This is the so-called "consistent ethic of life" position, also known as the "seamless garment" approach. Many in the pro-life movement reject it, or are highly critical of it, because they feel it diminishes, or even undermines, their fight against abortion. *See also* abortion; civil law and morality; consistent ethic of life; right to life.

promise, a commitment made to another that one will do or refrain from doing something, to the benefit of the other. In moral theology, the obligation to keep promises is usually discussed in the context of unilateral and gratuitous commitments rather than mutually binding contracts. A promise is morally binding in justice if both parties understood it in that way. More usually, promises are binding in fidelity. Promises binding in fidelity ought still to be kept because truthfulness requires conformity of actions to words.

promoter of justice, mandatory diocesan prosecutor for all penal and contentious cases involving the public welfare as determined by the bishop, canon law, or circumstances. The bishop must appoint a priest or layperson of sound temperament and reputation with at least a canonical licentiate. Some cases are considered as invalidly tried unless the promoter of justice is involved, e.g., a case involving the imposition of penalties on a cleric, such as a suspension imposed in a judicial proceeding.

Promoter of the Faith, once popularly known as the "devil's advocate," an office within the Sacred Congregation for the Causes of Saints whose purpose is to investigate thoroughly any objections raised against a cause for beatification and canonization and to safeguard the integrity of the procedure. *See also* beatification; canonization.

pro-nuncio, the papal ambassador in countries where the representative of the Holy See is not head of the diplomatic corps. The pro-nuncio not only represents the Holy See to the government of the country, but also has certain responsibilities toward the Catholic Church in that country and toward its hierarchy. *See also* papal legate.

proofs of God's existence. *See* five ways of St. Thomas Aquinas; God.

Propaganda Fide (prah-pah-gahn'-dah fee'day). *See* Congregation for the Evangelization of Peoples.

proper, liturgical, the part of any liturgical rite that varies from day to day or from season to season. Solemnities, feasts, memorials, and the seasonal cycles of Lent/Easter and Advent/Christmas often have their own proper parts, i.e., presidential prayers or orations, readings, prefaces, antiphons, psalmody, responsories, and intercessions, which do not belong to the liturgical ordinary. *See also* ordinary, liturgical.

Proper of the Mass, the variable parts of the Mass. The proper parts of the Mass are taken either from the Proper of the Season (Sundays and other feast days without fixed dates) or from the Proper of the Saints (feast days of fixed dates). The parts of the Mass included in the Proper are the entrance antiphon, the Opening Prayer, the chant after the first reading, the preface, the Prayer over the Gifts, the Communion antiphon, and the Prayer After Communion. *See also* Ordinary of the Mass.

property, an object of ownership. Ownership, seen in Catholic thought as fundamental for the autonomy and development of the human person, is the right to dispose freely of something as one's own, unless otherwise prohibited. Catholic social teaching on property distinguishes between the right and the use of the right. Thus, "unless otherwise prohibited" means that the use of the right is limited by the duty to observe the other virtues, legitimate laws, and contracts. These limitations are centuries old in Catholicism (see *Summa Theologiae* 2–2.66) and are presented repeatedly in papal encyclicals (*Mater et Magistra* [1961], 43; *Populorum Progressio* [1967], 23–24; *Centesimus Annus* [1991], 30.2). Such limitations are rooted in the universal or common destination of human goods. John Paul II, after asserting the right to private property as "valid and necessary," added: "Private property, in fact, is under a 'social mortgage,' which means that it has an intrinsically social function based upon and justified precisely by the principle of the universal destination of goods" (*Sollicitudo Rei Socialis* [1987], 42.6). *See also* Catholic social teachings.

property law, norms concerning Church property and Church-related property. The Church's reasons for its possession of material goods are that they are for: (1) divine worship, (2) works of religion and charity, and (3) the just remuneration of its ministers. Canon law understands Church property to be any property belonging to a public juridical person (similar to a corporation). So, for example, each diocese, parish, or religious institute holds property under the supervision of Church leaders but not at their free disposal. Indeed, Church property is not to be administered solely by one person but with the advice and sometimes the required consent of councils and financial experts. These must respect the purpose for which property has been given the Church.

prophecy, divine communication through a human agent, variously defined depending on whether the emphasis is placed on prediction, emotional preaching, social protest, religious enlightenment, or charismatic endowment. Among evangelicals and, to some extent, sociologists, the emphasis tends to be placed on millenarian and apocalyptic sects and their beliefs. The predictive understanding of prophecy, with reference to the new reality of Christ and the Church, has prevailed throughout most of Christian history, while in Judaism the predictive function has been subordinated to a close connection between prophecy and the law. The modern critical study of prophecy concentrated on identifying the message of the prophets, a message focused on the present rather than the future and proclaiming a religion at once individualistic and ethical in contrast to contemporary popular religion centered on sacrificial rituals. This typical nineteenth-century view has since given way to a more objective and nuanced understanding of prophecy in relation to the institutional life of Israel, especially Temple ritual and worship, and one that could assume different forms in different historical circumstances.

Both early Christianity and the Qumran community read the prophetic books and other biblical compositions, especially Psalms, as predictive of their own identity and as corroborating their own self-understanding. Several early Christian churches prized the charismatic gift of prophecy, meaning insight into the Christian reality communicated effectively to the community (1 Cor 12:28–29; 14). The names of several early Christian prophets have been preserved (Acts 11:27; 15:32; 21:9–10); some served in leadership roles in churches (e.g., Acts 13:1), while others were itinerant (e.g., *Did.* 11–13). The consolidation of Church structures and hierarchy, together with the threat posed by prophetic-millenarian movements (e.g., Montanism in the second century), led to the gradual disappearance of prophecy as a distinct social phenomenon.

JOSEPH BLENKINSOPP

prophet (Heb., *nābî*; Gk., *prophētēs*), one of a class of intermediaries who transmit communications from God to particular individuals or to the people as a whole. While the designation is commonly taken to refer primarily to the putative authors of the twelve books of Latter Prophets, in the course of time its scope was enlarged to refer to any important figure from the past, e.g., Abraham (Gen 20:7) and Moses (Deut 18:15–18; 34:10). It is therefore not surprising that John the Baptist (Mark 11:32) and Jesus (Mark 6:4; Luke 24:19) were thought of as prophets. The gift of prophecy was highly prized in many early Christian churches (e.g., 1 Cor 12:10) and prophets both male and female are often referred to in the NT (e.g., Acts 11:27; 13:1; 15:32; 21:9) and other writings down into the second century (e.g., *Did.* 11–13). *See also* prophecy.

propitiation, the act of appeasing another human being or the deity. In the latter sense, it was an important function of sacrificial ritual in antiquity, though the primary function of sacrifice in Israel was the removal of sin. The Greek term *hilasterion* used by Paul in Rom 3:25 should be translated "expiation" rather than "propitiation" to avoid the idea that the sacrifice of Jesus was needed to assuage the anger of God. *See also* atonement, biblical view of; atonement, doctrine of.

proportionalism, a type of analysis for determining the objective moral rightness and wrongness of actions in conflict situations and a procedure for establishing exceptions to behavioral norms. It began in the mid-1960s as a revision of both the principle of double effect and the doctrine on intrinsic moral evil. "Proportionate reason" is the moral principle used to determine concretely and objectively the rightness or wrongness of acts and the various exceptions to behavioral norms. Proportionalists argue that no judgment of moral rightness or wrongness of acts can be made without considering all the circumstances of the action. Because the human act is a structural unity, no aspect of the act can be morally appraised apart from all the other components. Consideration of the agent's intention, all foreseeable consequences, institutional obligations, and a proportion between the premoral values and disvalues are necessary before making a moral judgment.

The proponents make a distinction between moral and premoral values/disvalues. Moral values and disvalues describe qualities of persons as they confront situations, e.g., just or unjust. Premoral evils or disvalues refer to the harms, lacks, deprivations, etc., that occur in, or as a result of, human agency, e.g., death. Premoral values refer to those conditioned goods that we pursue for human and nonhuman well-being, e.g., life, health, etc. This distinction is used by proportionalists in their application of the principle of proportionate reason. The principle contains two elements. First, the word "reason" means a premoral, i.e., a conditioned, and thus not an absolute, value that the agent seeks to promote in the total act. Second, the term "proportionate" refers to a proper relation that must exist between the premoral disvalue(s) contained in, or caused by, the means and the end or a proper relation between the end and the premoral disvalue(s) in the consequences of the act.

In making exceptions to negative behavioral norms, e.g., no killing, proportionate reason is used to discern if the premoral disvalue contained in, or caused by, the means (killing) stands in due proportion to the premoral value in the act (self-defense). If a proportionate reason is present, the norm as stated does not apply to this act under its terms of reference. Exceptions to behavioral norms that prohibit premoral evil, then, are made on the basis of the presence of a proportionate reason.

Proportionalists claim that the distinction between direct and indirect in the principle of double effect is not always morally decisive. The distinction can be merely descriptive in that it only indicates what agents are doing, what they are aiming at, and with what means. *See also* double effect, principle of; evil, intrinsic; premoral evil; values, moral.

JAMES J. WALTER

proselyte (prah'sel-it; Gk., "one who has newly arrived or come near"), in the religious sense, a "convert." In the NT it refers primarily to full converts to Judaism (Matt 23:15; Acts 2:10, 6:5, 13:43), distinguished from "a worshiper of God" (Acts 16:14, 18:7) who did not obey the whole law. Though proselytism ("convert-making") has a negative connotation today, the original term is neutral. *See also* conversion; convert; evangelization.

prosopon (proh'soh-pahn; Gk., "face," "mask"), a term used by ancient theologians to distinguish the members of the Trinity by describing each member as a distinct *prosopon,* or person. Originally, the term referred to the mask worn by a Greek actor. Its lack of philosophical precision forced theologians to use the more precise term, *hypostasis* (Gk., "substance," "person").

Prosper of Aquitaine, St., ca. 390–after 455, lay theologian who defended Augustine's teachings on grace against John Cassian and the other semi-Pelagians. His defense was somewhat moderated after Augustine's death (430), following the lead of Pope Celestine I, whom Prosper had consulted in 431. His *Call of All Nations* defends God's universal salvific will. His *Book of Sentences,* perhaps the earliest florilegium of extracts from Augustine, was influential at the Council of Orange (529). Feast day: July 7. *See also* Augustine of Hippo, St.; grace; Orange, Council of; semi-Pelagianism.

prosphora (praws-faw-rah'; Gk., "offering," "gift"), a loaf of leavened, Byzantine-rite eucharistic bread. The form of a cross-in-square with the seal ICXCNI-KA ("J[esus] Ch[rist] conquers") is stamped on top of the prosphora. A cube-shaped section of the loaf bearing the stamp, called the "lamb," is cut out by the priest during the Prothesis, or rite of Preparation of the Gifts, and is used for the eucharistic consecration. *See also* bread, eucharistic.

Protestantism, a sixteenth-century religious movement that originated in western Europe over against the prevailing Roman Catholicism; it has spread over most of the world during the last four and a half centuries. Conceived originally by its leaders in northern Europe and the British Isles as a reform of Catholicism, it soon broke with the Catholic Church, which had dominated Europe for the eleven centuries after its establishment as the religion of the Roman Empire. Some of the reform leaders quickly removed themselves from obedience to Rome. Others worked harder to remain within the Catholic orbit but undertook actions that forced

their early excommunication. By the 1550s Protestantism had taken shape.

Protestantism derives its name from a document at the Diet of Speyer in Germany in 1529. The name, however, suggests a unity the protest causes never had. Even those who signed that document spoke for only a couple of parties, which did not represent many others. Protestantism in the British Isles, whether in the form of what became Anglicanism after the break with Rome under King Henry VIII (d. 1547) or in what became Presbyterianism under John Knox (d. 1572) in Scotland, developed quite independently from the way continental Lutheran, Reformed, or Anabaptist movements took shape.

Indeed, from the viewpoint of Catholics in 1529 or even at the end of the twentieth century, Protestantism has had only two distinguishing marks: it is divided, fragmented, and ever capable of generating more offshoots and divisions, and it has no positive set of common doctrines or practices that characterize its life. Only one aspect is universally present: the rejection of obedience to the hierarchical system that finds its pinnacle in papal authority, personified by the Bishop of Rome, the pope.

The Divisions of Protestantism: According to reference books such as the *World Christian Encyclopedia* (1982), near the end of the twentieth century there are almost twenty-five thousand separate Christian church bodies or what in North America would be called denominations. That number grows by about five per week, thanks to the vitality of independent and often prophetic or Pentecostal movements in sub-Saharan Africa, Latin America, parts of Asia, and the Pacific Island world. All of these groups are considered Protestant groups because of the nature of Protestantism itself: there is no central jurisdiction such as the papacy to determine the legitimacy of one group or another.

In Protestant theory, while all Christians are members of the single and undivided Body of Christ or one, holy, catholic, and apostolic church, in the world of appearances this church inevitably takes on many forms and embodiments. In the twentieth century an ecumenical or church-unity movement, largely of Protestant orientation, has worked to bring the separate churches into communication and communion with one another, usually through the forming of councils and federations. Ecumenism, however, has not inhibited the tendency of Protestant bodies to be independent of one another.

The *World Christian Encyclopedia* projects that by the beginning of the twenty-first century, there will be 1.144 billion Catholics and 386 million Eastern Orthodox; there will be 61 million Anglicans, 24 million "marginal Protestants," 204 million "nonwhite indigenous Christians," and 386 million just plain "Protestants" of the sort most European and North American Catholics know: Presbyterians, Lutherans, Methodists, Baptists, and the like.

The four-way clustering does not begin to suggest the varieties of Protestantism. For example, not all Anglicans (Christians who are connected to the see of Canterbury in England, whose bishop presides as "first among equals" of the Anglican or Episcopal bishops), consider themselves Protestants. They are "Anglo-Catholics" or simply "Catholics" of Anglo background, wherever they reside. They seek friendly relations with Rome but will not yield obedience to the pope. "Marginal Protestants" are offshoot movements such as the Mormons, Jehovah's Witnesses, and Christian Scientists, who are completely separated from ecumenical Protestantism and are considered heterodox across the spectrum.

"Nonwhite indigenous Christians" are offspring of missionary endeavors, for example, in Africa; they are thus derivative of western European impulses. But in postcolonial nations, as the missionaries left the scene voluntarily or were made to feel unwelcome on the soil they had prepared, indigenous and independent movements took shape. They are the most rapidly growing sector of Protestantism. Meanwhile, the just plain "Protestants" also flourish everywhere, though their heartland remains western Europe, the British Isles, and North America.

No one can prevent a prophet in Mozambique or Chile or a splinter group in Tennessee or Texas from forming as an independent Protestant denomination. That independence looks chaotic and anarchic to Roman Catholics but is a feature of church life with which Protestants have lived from the beginning, from times when Martin Luther (d. 1546) and Reformed leaders like John Calvin (d. 1564) and Ulrich Zwingli (d. 1531) agreed to disagree—or even disagreed on the terms of disagreement. If they and the Anglicans constituted a kind of Protestant "mainstream," often remaining established by law even after the break with Rome, they were nagged from the beginning by more radical and anti-establishment groups, some of which they exiled or persecuted. Most of these were Anabaptist, which means they rejected infant baptism and then rebaptized Christians. They represented what we might see as a protest against the protest.

Despite the apparent chaos of division, from some distance one can see coherences in the form of Protestant families in approximately this order of size: Lutheran, Reformed (including Presbyterian), Baptist (which is currently the most rapidly growing group worldwide), Methodist, mainstream Pentecostal, United Church of Christ, and Disciples of Christ. Then follow various Holiness, Adventist, Mennonite, Moravian, Friends, and other groups, such as Unitarians and Universalists. Few of them follow the Anglicans in having an authoritative council or episcopal leadership, though many have formed international federations.

Antipapacy and Protestant Doctrine: While early Protestantism found its identity in rejection of the papacy, there were varying degrees of distancing. Thus in the middle of the sixteenth century, many Lutheran leaders were still willing to picture a reunion with Catholicism in which the Bishop of Rome would be first among equals. But they would not submit to papal authority on terms that would have satisfied Rome. For Luther and many other Protestant leaders the pope was the fulfillment of the prophetic biblical pictures of the antichrist. They saw him usurping roles that only God in Christ through the Holy Spirit rightfully could claim.

Centuries later, especially since the appearance of modern popes after the model of John XXIII (d. 1963)—bishops of Rome who were more friendly to conciliar and synodical governance and who in their attitudes were concerned to show regard for the Christian expression of Protestants—there has been a great diminishing of opposition to the papacy. Antagonism has often been replaced by genuine signs of positive concern and affection. Still, whoever canvasses the whole range of Protestant teaching will find that the only common bond across the entire range has been an unwillingness to surrender to papal authority.

Lacking such authority, most Protestants from the beginning have insisted that the only source and norm of their doctrine has been the Bible, made up of the Hebrew Scriptures, called the OT, and the NT. They respect the Apocrypha, but regard these noncanonical writings as inferior and not "inspired" by the Holy Spirit the way the sixty-six canonical books are. Of course, interpretations of the Bible vary widely. Therefore, when the majority of Protestants cry the Reformation motto *sola Scriptura* (Lat.), "Scripture alone," they solve very little in the eyes of other Protestants, to say nothing of Catholics.

Battles over how to interpret the Bible have

marked the life of Protestantism. While the seeds of "private interpretation" were present in the sixteenth century, especially among the more radical groups, most leaders and movements were "churchly," which meant they regarded the communal character of interpretation to be vital. However, in the eighteenth century, when a philosophical movement called the Enlightenment took shape and as political freedoms grew, the freedom to interpret the Bible apart from community came to characterize much of Protestantism. In Catholic eyes, Protestants are people who are quite free to go their own way undisturbed with the interpretations of the Bible they favor.

If the eighteenth century saw an increase in freedom, independence, and autonomy, the late nineteenth and early twentieth centuries saw develop a new polarity that cut through or divided denominations. On the left have been modernist or liberal movements that granted more to the Enlightenment and private judgment. Thinkers and actors in the leadership encouraged adapting of the faith to modernity, being up to date, and embracing reason and science and progress. Over against them are the currently burgeoning movements on the right, from the extremes of fundamentalism to the more moderate forms of evangelicalism and Pentecostalism. Most of them insist that the Bible is inerrant in all details and that they alone interpret it correctly.

Protestant doctrine is not only about the Bible, however. Most Protestants retain the Lord's Supper, attaching a wide range of meanings to it. All but the Quakers, who also do not regularly celebrate Holy Communion and may utterly reject such ordinances, also keep Baptism as a sacrament. Most Protestants continue to baptize infants and some, like the Lutherans, see in the act the imparting of grace. But Baptists and many others insist on "believers' baptism" and consider the act a sign of commitment, covenant, or obedience to a command.

Protestants in the main will say that alongside the devotion to the Bible they are constituted by an equal devotion to its main theme: that God is gracious and that through faith believers are grasped by divine grace and, as a corollary, made members of the Church. Over against what they saw and still often, though with diminishing warrant or passion, regard as Catholic dependence or partial dependence on the good works and merits of humans who would be right with God, the Protestants were "evangelical," or gospel-centered. As they saw it, this meant they would stress the entirely unmerited grace of God as the initiative and fulfillment of the divine transaction with humans. Works of love were to follow the response in faith, but they did not "save" the sinner.

Most Protestants, at least until the Enlightenment and outside the modern liberal movements, have held to views of human nature in which the human is "fallen," inescapably given over to sin apart from the works of God in Christ. Most Protestants have continued to teach and believe in the atoning work of Jesus Christ on the cross and the reality of his Resurrection as the grounding of reasons for faith. While not all of them share the majority preference for retaining the Apostles' and Nicene creeds (Baptists, for example), most would, in the words of the end of a creed, share faith in "the life of the world to come."

Protestant Practices: If the practices of faith differ widely from place to place even within such an ordered and regulated body as Catholicism, it is easy to see that practices will vary drastically from place to place and from communion to communion across Protestantism. Yet there are at least some means of grasping the varieties. For instance, just as most Protestants administer and receive two sacraments, so they also expect the living of a godly life, however described; that is, believing has consequences. Protestants stressed this so much that some Catholics, looking at them from the viewpoint of a sacramentally graced faith, have equated Protestantism with grim moralism, a series of many "don'ts" alongside numbers of "do's." Some of these moralist Protestant movements such as Puritanism serve as stereotypes by which Catholics often miss the vision of exuberance and the presence of joy in much Protestant worship.

Protestants, given their devotion to the Bible, have been promoters of translation of the Scriptures (into many hundreds of languages) and of literacy directed to biblical and other texts. This has meant that they stress education of the young and have often been originators of colleges and universities in newly missionized territories. Like Catholics, they have been devoted to healing, often establishing the first clinics or hospitals in an area.

Attitudes toward the arts vary. In general, Protestantism has been suspicious of Orthodox icons and Catholic statuary, visual representations that evangelicals feel can often attract devotion bordering on idolatry. Yet names like Johann Sebastian Bach, Rembrandt van Rijn, and John Milton signal Protestant devotion to the sundry arts. Protestantism has made a particular contribution to church music. Protestants like to build and use churches, "houses of God," and have developed many indigenous styles of architecture to match their concepts of worship.

Some leaders have defined Protestantism, given its origins in protest and its often unestablished or outsider status, as an extension of biblical prophetic movements. While many if not most Protestants, like their Catholic and Orthodox counterparts, become defenders of the status quo, they also frequently respond to calls for justice. They have developed movements called the social gospel, Christian socialism, social Christianity, or various conservative evangelical but socially radical programs. The liberals did so to "bring in the kingdom of God" and the more conservative types did so because they believe that Protestant Christians are to be responsible citizens and supporters of earthly government.

Such conservatism and support have not meant mere acquiescence to the powers that be. For example, in Britain and the United States, Protestant impulses developed into movements for the abolition of slavery over against other support for slavery, often by Protestants. Movements to extend suffrage, to work for equity in the economic realm, to extend health care to the poor, and to work for world peace have issued from Protestant groups. Often relatively small groups like Quakers, Mennonites, and the Church of the Brethren, historically "peace churches," have led the way, to be joined by their larger and more adapted Protestant counterparts.

The Future and Fulfillment: Mainstream Protestantism in Europe and North America is generally not an expanding group, but given the fire of Pentecostal and prophetic movements, it grows almost wildly in Africa and Latin America. So dramatic has been the spread in many Latin American nations that the Protestants have unsettled Catholic communities and created antagonisms that could mean that the twenty-first century may see, in some places, renewed hostility between Protestants and Catholics—hostility compensated for by continuing growth in the ecumenical spirit in most places.

While original Protestantism saw itself as a reform within Catholicism and while the language of sixteenth-century evangelical movements often spoke of reunion with Rome, the terms for such reunion have been such that neither side expects it to occur. The vast majority of Protestants have settled for ever-changing patterns of church life in which "return to Rome" or reunion with Rome has not been a practical or vivid expectation. While they

seek ever better relations except where there is open competition for souls, as in Latin America, they try to find ecumenical expression in forms that will not find them yielding what they see to be a spirit of freedom and independence and a rejection of the human authority they find in the papacy.

Protestants tend to be eschatologically minded; that is, they have their mind and eye on "the last things." Literalists expect a literal second coming of Christ, and often talk in millennial terms, expecting a thousand-year reign of Christ. The nonliteralists have no such vivid pictures of visible returns, comings, or endings in mind. Yet they also believe that history is worked out under God through the lordship of Christ. Such history has beginnings, central points—the Crucifixion and Resurrection of Christ and the coming of the Holy Spirit—and the expectation of a fulfillment or a consummation when the fullness of God's love and care for all believers will be made evident. They expect that such a consummation will involve all sorts of Protestant believers with the Catholics and Orthodox from whom they may remain divided for many ages to come. *See also* Catholic Church; Catholicism; Reformation, the.

Bibliography

Barrett, David B., ed. *World Christian Encyclopedia.* Oxford: Oxford University Press, 1982.

Bouyer, Louis. *The Spirit and Forms of Protestantism.* London: Harvill Press, 1956.

Brown, Robert McAfee. *The Spirit of Protestantism.* Oxford: Oxford University Press, 1961.

Forell, George. *The Protestant Faith.* Englewood Cliffs, NJ: Prentice-Hall, 1960.

Marty, Martin E. *Protestantism.* New York: Holt, Rinehart, and Winston, 1972.   MARTIN E. MARTY

Prothesis (proh'thes-ihs; Gk., "offertory"), Byzantine-rite offertory or rite of preparation of the bread and wine, a separate *akolouthia* (Gk.) or office performed by the priest and deacon before the public beginning of the Eucharist. The rite is also called *Proskomidia* (Slav.) or *Proskomide* (Gk., "offering," "anaphora"), though that is more properly the name of the prayer preceding the anaphora, or eucharistic prayer, in the Byzantine rite. *See also* offertory.

protodeacon, "first deacon," an honorary title conferred on a nonmonastic Byzantine-rite deacon. The term also refers to the first deacon of a cathedral church of the same rite. *See also* deacon; hierodeacon.

Protonotary Apostolic, an official of the Roman Curia who notarizes certain documents. The title is also given other priests as an honorary title. Until 1968 protonotaries could on occasion wear bishops' vestments when presiding at Mass, but this privilege is no longer given.

protopresbyter (Lat., "first presbyter"), a Byzantine-rite archpriest, an honorary title similar to monsignor. Among Russians it is the highest title conferred on a nonmonastic priest, and is granted to very few. *See also* monsignor; presbyter.

prototype (Gk., *proto*, "first"; *typon*, "of a kind"), a soteriological term designating Jesus Christ as the savior of all people because he is the archetypal human being in relation to whom all other human beings can be formed or renewed by the Holy Spirit. Paul speaks of Jesus Christ as the new Adam (1 Cor 15:20–21), and Colossians describes Christ as the "firstborn" of the new creation (Col 1:15–20). In his theory of recapitulation Irenaeus (d. ca. 200) presents Christ as the "new head" of the human family. *See also* Jesus Christ.

providence, the divine plan by which God brings creation to its goal. Derived from Latin, it means literally "foresight." Providence was a technical term of Stoic philosophy to express divine rule over all events. Although providence is not a biblical term (but see Wis 14:3; 17:2), the idea of a loving, wise, and powerful God at work in the world is everywhere present. In contrast to Stoicism, however, the emphasis is on loving care rather than on power. Early Christian writers used "providence" to express the biblical idea. But gradually it came to have Stoic connotations, emphasizing power. This was especially true in Augustine of Hippo (d. 430).

The Stoic view encountered two main problems: human freedom and evil. Augustine confronted the first when opposing the Pelagian error that free will without any further grace enables human beings to achieve salvation. He taught that God's grace decides who is saved and who is lost. He recognized that this imposes necessity on human activity, but he did not wish to deny human freedom (*City of God* 5.9).

Augustine dealt with evil by making all suffering punishment for sin. The sin of Adam and Eve made the whole human race a "lump of clay damned in its root." From this lump God mercifully chooses to make some vessels destined for eternal life, the rest God justly lets go to eternal damnation (*Admonition*

and Grace 7, 16). However, God is so powerful that God would never let any evil enter creation if God could not draw good from it (*Enchiridion of Faith, Hope and Love* 11).

John of Damascus (d. ca. 749) suggested another view. He distinguished between the antecedent and the consequent will of God (*The Orthodox Faith* 2, 29). The first makes salvation possible for everyone; the second condemns only unrepentant sinners. This view regards providence as "contingency planning": God does not predetermine events or choices, but directs whatever occurs to the infallible realization of God's gracious purpose.

Thomas Aquinas (d. 1274) described providence as the order of creation to its end as this order preexists in the mind of God (*Summa Theologiae* 1.22.1). He, too, presupposed "contingency planning" in explaining how God's will is always fulfilled (*Summa Theologiae* 1.19.6).

Aquinas maintained that infallible divine knowledge does not necessitate human choice because God does not foresee events as future, but eternally sees all things as present. Knowledge of what is present can be infallible without imposing necessity on what it knows (1.14.13).

Aquinas basically accepted Augustine's solution to the problem of evil (*Summa Theologiae* 1.48.5). However, recent thought does not see all human suffering as a consequence of sin. Rather, some things happen that God does not directly intend (though God intends their possibility in willing to make a universe where there is emergent freedom), whether these be sins and their effects or natural contingent events, and God is present to draw good from them. *See also* creation; evil; God; providence [in the Bible]; salvation history. JOHN H. WRIGHT

providence [in the Bible], God's care for all creatures and the chosen people in particular. The classical examples of the latter occur in the Exodus from Egypt and the forty-year sojourn in the wilderness during which time the Israelites were provided with food (Exod 16:1–36; Num 11:4–35) and drink (Exod 17:1–7; Num 20:2–13) and guided to their destination by means of an angel, or the divine presence (face) itself, or the fire and cloud that descended on the ark and the tent. This theme is repeated often in the homiletic material in Deuteronomy (e.g., 6:31; 8:16). Numerous other instances occur illustrating God's solicitous care for creatures: God clothes the man and the woman before their expulsion from Eden (Gen 3:21), provides Cain with a protective mark (4:15), takes care of Jacob during his twenty-year exile in Mesopotamia (28:15), and provides for the future of the midwives who put themselves at risk by protecting the Hebrew male infants in Egypt (Exod 1:20). The story of Jonah illustrates how God's care even extends to the animal world (Jonah 4:11). God's providence is especially in evidence in narratives about holy men and women; Elijah is fed miraculously by ravens (1 Kgs 17:6), as Anthony of Egypt, in the biography by Athanasius, is fed by angels.

God's action in leading events toward a predestined end, often in defiance of the will of human agents, also comes to expression in some of the most accomplished literary compositions in the OT. In the so-called Succession History (2 Sam 11–1 Kgs 2), for example, Solomon ends up on the throne in spite of his low ranking and the morally tainted circumstances leading to his conception and birth. In the Joseph story (Gen 37–50), the protagonist attains the highest distinction in Egypt and succeeds in saving his family in spite of the hostility of his brothers. In this case the point is made explicitly: "Even though you intended to do harm to me, God intended it for good, in order to preserve a numerous people, as he is doing today" (Gen 50:20). This deep sense of a divine purpose at work does not, however, entail a doctrine of fate, an idea that comes to expression only in the philosophical reflections of Qoheleth (Eccl 2:14; 3:19; 9:2).

Explicit allusion to divine providence (Gk., *pronoia*) occurs for the first time in Jewish authors writing in Greek in the postbiblical period, especially in the Wisdom of Solomon (14:3; 17:2). By this time influences from Greek philosophy, especially the Stoics, may be detected, though in the latter providence tends to be of a more impersonal and cosmic nature. In the Gospel tradition Jesus recommends laying aside anxiety in dependence on divine providence and even appeals to God's care for the birds of the air and the lilies of the field (Matt 6:25–33). Providence is related to other NT passages that speak of God's plan (Acts 4:28) or predetermined purpose (Rom 8:29–30; Eph 1:5, 11). *See also* providence.   JOSEPH BLENKINSOPP

Providence, Sisters of. *See* Sisters of Providence.

Providentissimus Deus (prah-vi-den-tis'i-muhs day'uhs; Lat., "The Most Provident God"), encyclical of Leo XIII on the study of Sacred Scripture, promulgated on November 18, 1893, in response to emerging higher biblical criticism and new archaeological discoveries. Though it inaugurated a new era in Catholic biblical studies by urging the study of biblical languages and methods of exegesis, it remained cautious by affirming that Scripture was written "at the dictation" of the Holy Spirit, by stating that all exegesis must proceed on the basis of the analogy of faith, and by stressing the normative role of Church doctrine in interpreting Scripture. After Leo XIII's death and in the wake of the anti-Modernist reaction, it was interpreted in an increasingly conservative sense. *See also* Bible, Church teachings on the.

province, a grouping of a number of dioceses under the supervision of a metropolitan archbishop. The term is also used for a major division, usually geographical, of some institutes of consecrated life under the governance of a provincial superior.

provincial council, gathering of bishops of an ecclesiastical province for the purpose of deciding matters concerning the Church in that province. The term is also used to designate the group of advisers to the provincial superior of a religious institute required by canon law.

provincial superior, official with authority over, and responsibility for, a province, i.e., a significant portion of an institute of consecrated life or society of apostolic life. Assisted by a council, which gives advice and consent on given issues, the provincial superior has personal authority over the individual communities within the province (known as houses) and each of the members of the province. Not all communities use the terms "provincial" or "province" to designate their major divisions. *See also* religious institute; society of apostolic life.

Provisors, Statute of, English law (1351) forbidding papal appointments to English ecclesiastical offices, a practice known as "papal provision." The statute stated that only local electors and patrons had the right to fill positions in the English church. *See also* England, Catholicism in.

prudence, one of the four cardinal virtues, also known as the "rudder" virtue because it "steers" all other virtues. Prudence, together with temperance, fortitude, and justice, has traditionally been viewed as one of the four qualities of character necessary to live a humanly good life, as well as a fully Christian life. The centrality of prudence for the Catholic moral tradition is difficult to understand today, since many people tend to equate prudence with a morally dubious tendency toward caution and shrewdness.

However, for Thomas Aquinas (d. 1274) and for the moral tradition that follows him, prudence is understood in a more comprehensive way. Aquinas, following Aristotle (d. 322 B.C.), holds that in order to live morally, it is necessary both to know what is a humanly good life, and to have the intelligent discernment necessary to translate this general knowledge of the good into concrete actions. This capacity of discernment, by which the individual translates the general demands of morality into concrete actions, is prudence. Prudence is, strictly speaking, an intellectual virtue, but it is counted among the moral virtues because without it, full moral virtue is impossible. Prudence can only be acquired through experience and reflection. At the same time, Aquinas claims that God bestows prudence directly on those who receive grace, together with the other infused cardinal virtues, even though some of those who are graced would not have the intellectual capacities to acquire prudence on their own. *See also* cardinal virtues; discernment of spirits; fortitude; justice; temperance.

Prudentius, Aurelius Clemens, ca. 348–ca. 410, Christian Latin poet. Born in Spain, a lawyer and civil administrator, he devoted his retirement to poetry. His collection (404/5), with an autobiographical preface, includes "Hymns for Every Day," the *Peristephanon* ("Martyrs' Crowns," the passions of fourteen martyrs, most Spanish or Italian), the *Psychomachia* ("Spiritual Combat," an allegory with personified virtues and vices), and other works of theological interest. He is the only lay Latin Father of the Church. *See also* Fathers of the Church.

psalmody, the musical style for the liturgical singing of psalms at Mass or, more typically, at the Divine Office. Psalmody is responsorial (as at Mass) when a leader sings the verse and the congregation sings a refrain or response. It is antiphonal (as in the Divine Office) when the congregation is divided into two groups that alternately sing the verses. Psalmody is direct when all sing the verses together. *See also* liturgical music.

Psalms, the (Gk., *Psalmoi,* "songs sung to a stringed instrument"; *Psalterion,* "stringed instrument"), or Psalter, a compilation of 150 Israelite religious lyrics, poems, and prayers by many authors. The Psalter consists of five books (Pss 1–41, 42–72, 73–89, 90–106, 107–50) compiled from earlier collections and individual compositions. The numeration of the psalms in English versions derived from the Hebrew Bible (RSV, JB, NAB) differs from those dependent upon the Septuagint and Vulgate (earlier Catholic Bibles, including Douay, Knox, and Confraternity). The compositions are of several types, such as wisdom psalms (Ps 1), royal psalms (Ps 2), and laments (Ps 22).

Several Psalms scrolls from Qumran differ from the traditional Hebrew Psalter in content, arrangement, or both. These manuscripts indicate that the Psalter was gradually assembled from psalms written earlier. Pss 1–89 were mostly in their present order by the first century B.C., and the whole collection (Pss 1–150) was finalized in the second half of the first century A.D. The psalms have continued to play an important role in Jewish tradition, prayer, and communal worship.

Psalms are frequently quoted and messianically interpreted in the NT, especially Ps 22 in relation to the Crucifixion (Mark 15:34), and were the model for several NT hymns or prayers. For the early Church, the psalms were both prayerbook and hymnbook and are featured in the writings of many patristic authors. The Psalter is prominent in Catholic and most Protestant liturgies. For the Liturgy of the Hours, the complete Psalter is recited during the course of a one- or four-week cycle; the psalms also play an important role in the celebration of the sacraments. *See also* Psalter. PETER W. FLINT

Psalter, a liturgical book containing the psalms and biblical canticles used in divine services.

pseudepigrapha (sood-e-pig'rah-fah), books whose authors assume the names of famous ancient characters. Pseudepigraphy was widely practiced in antiquity and is attested in Judaism and Christianity. Examples are the books of *Enoch,* which were composed from the third century B.C. on, and the book of *Jubilees* (ca. 150 B.C.), which claims Moses as its author. Some biblical works are pseudepigrapha, e.g., Wisdom of Solomon (first century B.C. or A.D.) in the OT and perhaps 1–2 Timothy and Titus in the NT. The motivation for the practice varied but it need not have been unethical. It may have been a way of acknowledging the tradition in which one's ideas belonged.

Pseudo-Dionysius. *See* Denys the Areopagite.

Pseudo-Synod of Lvov (Lviv), a Communist-orchestrated pseudo-synod held on March 8–10, 1946, in Lviv, capital of Galicia in western Ukraine, at which the Ukrainian Greek Catholic Church was forcibly integrated into the Russian Orthodox Church.

Western Ukraine was incorporated into the USSR (Union of Soviet Socialist Republics) at the end of World War II. Lviv was the metropolitan see of the Ukrainian Catholic Church, to which most of the population of western Ukraine belonged (the Polish Orthodox parish in Lviv was the only Orthodox church in the entire region). In the winter of 1944–45 the Soviet regime prohibited all contact of the hierarchy with its clergy and faithful, and initiated a campaign of forced meetings and propaganda in favor of union with the Russian Orthodox Church. Opponents were arrested and tortured. In April 1945 the entire hierarchy was imprisoned, and the regime recognized an "Initiative Group" of three Catholic priests, formed to carry out the government plan, as the sole authority over the Church. The government instructed them to make lists of all clergy who refused to recognize their authority.

Under police protection this group carried out a campaign of propaganda and threats. The NKVD (Soviet secret police) pressured the unwilling Greek Catholic clergy to sign the petition for union with Orthodoxy. Those who refused were arrested. At the end of February, thirteen Catholic priests were received into Orthodoxy secretly in Kiev, and the two celibate members of the "Initiative Group" were consecrated as Orthodox bishops. Their leader, Havriyjil Kostel'nyk, a married priest, was made a mitred archpriest, the highest dignity open to the married clergy (he was assassinated September 20, 1948). On March 8–10 a "synod" of 216 terrorized priests (many were married men who, like Kostel'nyk, had received threats against their families) and nineteen laypersons, orchestrated in Lviv under the leadership of this group, abolished the Union of Brest (1596), by which millions of Eastern Christians entered into communion with Rome. This purported to be a synod of the Ukrainian Greek Catholic Church, but its entire hierarchy was in prison, and the thirteen-priest presidium of the synod had in fact already become Orthodox in Kiev on February 22–23, 1946, though this was kept secret until the action was completed. Some claim that Patriarch Alexis I of Moscow never recognized the legitimacy of this action (the congratulatory telegram sent in his name has been said to be a forgery). The "reunion" was followed by massive arrests, interrogations, abuse, trials, banishment, and deportations, causing incalculable suffering and death. Of over three thousand Ukrainian Catholic priests, Orthodox sources claim that 986 submitted to Orthodoxy. Some three hundred fled west; the others were arrested or went underground.

The acts of the synod were published in Ukrainian in Lviv in 1946, and in 1982, for the forty-fifth anniversary of the synod, the Moscow patriarchate, which by then had become embarrassed by the realities, issued bowdlerized versions in Ukrainian, Russian, and English, much to the derision of the scholarly world. The publication of the acts of the synod also provoked a large body of scholarly studies in the West and, from the Russian Orthodox side, a relentless campaign of propaganda until the late 1980s, when the public admission of the truth, even by Soviet government officials and police agents who had participated in the "synod," revealed the synodal proceedings as shameful. It had been neither free nor representative of the Ukrainian Greek Catholic Church.

On May 16, 1992, the synod of the Ukrainian Catholic Church in Lviv unanimously declared the pseudo-synod of 1946 canonically invalid. But despite repeated Catholic appeals since 1980, Russian Orthodox authorities have defended the action as a legitimate abolition of the "forced" Union of Brest, and have refused to disclaim or condemn it, saying that they may not annul a "Catholic Synod," though it is common knowledge that its presidium and the two bishops present at it were already Russian Orthodox.

Since the granting of religious freedom in Ukraine, the return to the Greek Catholic Church of an estimated five million faithful and at least four hundred Orthodox priests would seem to disprove Orthodox claims that the union with Rome was artificial and forced, without popular or religious roots, and that it dissolved itself in 1946 as soon as its external political props were removed. *See also* Russia, Catholicism in; Ukrainian Catholic Church.

ROBERT F. TAFT

Pseudo-Synod of Presov, a Communist-orchestrated assembly on April 28, 1950, in the city of Presov in Slovakia, which incorporated the 305,000-member Greek Catholic Church into the Orthodox church. Until 1950, the minority Orthodox Church in Slovakia had only 20 churches to the Greek Catholics' 434 churches and 72 chapels. Relations between the two churches were good, and there was freedom of religion. Orthodox proselytism among Greek Catholics was intense, and any Greek Catholic who wished to join the Orthodox was free to do so.

At the end of World War II the 35,000-member Orthodox Church of Czechoslovakia came under the jurisdiction of Moscow, and a Russian was named Orthodox bishop of Presov. After a government-coordinated propaganda campaign that won over only nine Greek Catholic priests, a "Greek Catholic Conference" (Slovak, *sjazd*) was convoked. Though later called "The Historical Synod of Greek Catholic Priests and Laity," the 820 delegates who gathered, including 100 priests, had not been informed about the purpose of the meeting. After speeches praising the USSR (Union of Soviet Socialist Republics) and the Russian Orthodox Church and attacking the Catholic Church and the Vatican, resolutions liquidating the union with Rome were accepted "by acclamation." The Greek Catholic cathedral in Presov was seized by force, and an Orthodox service of thanksgiving was celebrated. A government decree of May 27 confirmed these actions, handed all Greek Catholic property over to the Orthodox Church, and declared that "From now on, therefore, in all matters concerning the former Greek Catholic priests, whether there is question of their person, their salary, or their residence, all civic and state agencies shall have recourse to the bishops of the Orthodox Church."

By this fiat all Greek Catholic priests, most of them married men with families, were placed under Orthodox authority for their homes and livelihood. Those who accepted this transfer to the Orthodox Church were allowed to remain in their parishes; the rest were evicted, confined for about a year, then banished. A hundred diocesan priests, one-third of the total, eventually converted to Orthodoxy. The two bishops were imprisoned. In 1950 it was estimated that 50 percent of the people had remained loyal to the Catholic Church, including 230 priests; all were forced to reside in exile in the Czech regions outside their native Slovakia. Over four hundred thousand recusants who opposed the suppression were deported west to the Sudetenland, from which three million ethnic Germans had been expelled in 1945–46.

During the "Prague Spring," a brief period of political freedom under Alexander Dubček, later suppressed by the Soviet military, the Greek Catholic

Church was legalized by government decree of June 13, 1968. Plebiscites were held in the parishes, and the people returned to the Greek Catholic Church en masse. There were sporadic incidents of intolerance and violence by both sides when the Orthodox, having lost the vote, refused to deliver the church. The discredited and collaborationist Orthodox Church was reduced to a critical position. Hopes that the Soviet invasion of 1968 would crush the Catholic resurgence were not fulfilled, but the government halted the plebiscites in the summer of 1969, after the Orthodox had won in only 5 out of 210 parishes. An imposed settlement prohibited further voting. The 205 parishes that had declared themselves Catholic were assigned to the Greek Catholics; another 87 remained Orthodox, only 5 by a free vote. Seventy-eight Orthodox priests became Catholic, joining the 166 surviving priests who had remained Catholic at the suppression. The Greek Catholic Church is estimated to have recovered 90 percent of its faithful, with about ten to fifteen thousand choosing to remain Orthodox. The Czecho-Slovak census of 1991 listed 188,397 Greek Catholics and 53,613 Orthodox in the country. *See also* Greek Catholic Church.   ROBERT F. TAFT

Pseudo-Union of Alba Iulia, the forced reintegration of the Romanian Greek Catholic Church into the Romanian Orthodox Church by the Communist regime at Alba Iulia in 1948.

In 1947 the Romanian government reorganized the Orthodox hierarchy. The metropolitan of Moldavia was replaced by Justinian Marina (1901–77), who was then elected patriarch on May 24, 1948. On August 4, the new law on cults (outlawed religious groups) forbade relations with any foreign religious body, severing Catholics from the Vatican, and provided for the withdrawal of legal recognition from a religious body for a good reason. All property of the outlawed cult would pass to the state.

The government orchestrated an intense campaign and the patriarch made threatening appeals to the Greek Catholics to return to Orthodoxy for reasons of national unity. Greek Catholic priests were harassed, arrested, and tortured. During September 1948, about 430 priests were coerced into signing a declaration empowering delegates to engineer the return to Orthodoxy. On October 1, 1948, thirty-eight priests were brought to Cluj for a "congress" under police surveillance. Thirty-six priests (two had escaped) "unanimously" signed a government-prepared "decision" to join the Orthodox

Church. This was "accepted" by the patriarch and synod and then confirmed in Alba Iulia on October 21 before a large rigged assembly, after which Marina celebrated a thanksgiving service in the "former" Greek Catholic cathedral there. Later a plaque was affixed to the cathedral to commemorate this sham. The statistics and the dates expose this action as a contrived response to the act of union with Rome signed by thirty-eight Orthodox clergy in Alba Iulia 250 years earlier on the same date.

All who opposed went into hiding or were arrested, including all the Greek Catholic bishops. On December 1, the thirtieth anniversary of the Union of All Romanians in 1918, the government decreed that the 1,562,980-member Greek Catholic Church, with five dioceses and 1,834 priests, had ceased to exist. The government confiscated its property except for the parishes, which were handed over to the Orthodox. "Certificates of Orthodoxy" were required of Greek Catholic priests even for civil purposes. Since most of them were married men, they were forced to acquiesce in order to support their families. It is estimated that some three hundred of them, mostly in the countryside, adjusted to the situation and were left in their parishes. Many of them are known to have remained Catholics in conscience, and witnesses hold that only a few Catholic priests accepted Orthodoxy willingly.

The "reintegration" was accomplished with extraordinary brutality. Some six hundred priests were arrested. Estimates claim that two hundred were imprisoned and four hundred executed. All the bishops died in confinement. But the Greek Catholic Church continued a precarious underground existence. The faithful resisted the takeover of churches: on October 31, 1948, the Orthodox metropolitan of Sibiu needed the help of the Communist police to enter the Catholic cathedral in Blaj. Continuing resistance and greater audacity as the illegal church increased its underground activities led to new clergy show trials in 1957, with sentences of up to twenty-five years.

The Romanian Orthodox Church was largely a passive spectator in the forcible reunion. Seventy-eight Orthodox priests went to prison rather than take over Catholic churches assigned them, and Romanians in exile publicly condemned the suppression. But Patriarch Marina had campaigned openly for the "reintegration," a few of the higher clergy openly supported it, not one of them spoke out against it, and for over forty years Orthodox exponents have systematically lied about its true nature.

Marina's statements to the press during a 1972 visit to Belgium provoked widespread scandal and indignation in the free world. In 1973, Orthodox bishops demanded that the government be more severe with the uniates. But times had changed, and by then the government wished to integrate the recusants into the Latin rite.

Upon the overthrow of the Ceausescu regime in Romania in 1989, the instantaneous resurgence of this church, despite Orthodox protests and slander, disproved Orthodox claims that the "reintegration" of 1948 was free. *See also* Romanian Catholic Church.

ROBERT F. TAFT

Pseudo-Union of Uzhorod, the Soviet-orchestrated forcible incorporation into the Russian Orthodox Church of the Greek Catholic Church in Subcarpathia in 1949. In June 1945, the Subcarpathian region of Czechoslovakia was incorporated into the Ukrainian Soviet Republic, a Russian Orthodox bishop was named to the region, all churches were declared state property, and Greek Catholic churches began to be seized and delivered to the Orthodox. On November 1, 1947, the Byzantine Catholic bishop Theodore G. Romzha of Mukachevo was assassinated by the Soviets. In June 1948, Russian Orthodox archbishop Makarij Oksiiouk of Lviv, the Soviet government's agent in the 1946 Lviv "reunion," was sent to the largely Catholic region. In February 1949, the regime relinquished to him the Catholic cathedral in Uzhorod, and the following August he declared the Union of Uzhorod at an end without holding a pseudo-synod like the one he had helped orchestrate in Lviv in 1946, a service that had earned him his promotion to archbishop. The outcome was the same as in Galicia (western Ukraine): arrests, persecution, deportations, with the Church driven underground to reemerge and reclaim its faithful when granted freedom in 1990. *See also* Uzhorod, Union of.

psychiatry. *See* Catholicism and psychology/psychiatry.

psychology. *See* Catholicism and psychology/psychiatry.

psychology and spirituality, two disciplines, as well as processes, that intersect most pointedly in questions of human interiority and the nature of the self. Psychology studies mental and emotional states and their interplay in the emergence of the self. Spirituality is concerned with the total lived response of a person to the presence of God in life.

Psychology studies and facilitates a process of self-appropriation. Spirituality supports a process of self-transcendence. It identifies a dynamism within the human personality to go beyond itself to know and love the other. A Christian perspective understands this self-transcending dynamism to be the result of Christ's Spirit enabling the human spirit to grow into consciousness, responsible living, and a loving union with God, others, and creation.

Two extremes are possible in the relationship between psychology and spirituality. One extreme reduces spirituality to psychology and locks the person in the psychological self with no other resource. Spirituality, however, addresses realities for which psychological categories become inadequate. Nor can psychology responsibly escape these deeper questions of the human spirit.

The other extreme denies any relationship between psychology and spirituality and thereby is unable to find in psychological processes an indication of God's grace, or identify any psychological determinants that impinge on a person's response to God, such as early childhood factors, unconscious motivations, or psychic factors in shaping images of God.

Psychological wholeness and spiritual holiness are not linked inseparably, nor are they totally unrelated. Psychological readiness for a full and faithful response to God is always a relative matter. Individuals who are psychologically impaired may evidence heroic faith in God. Such individuals remind us that all psyches are limited and that a life of faith is a gift unmerited by anyone. On the other hand, Christian mystics testify that their experience of God transformed and healed their psychic structures. Desires warring within them were reoriented and put at the service of God's will in their lives.

Psychology attempts to name specific issues that arise in the unfolding of personality. Christian spirituality addresses the origins of this life, the power that sustains and impels it, and the goal of its growth. The Christian spiritual tradition has generally affirmed that knowledge of self is required for knowledge of God. However, the tradition also holds that one's true self is only revealed in relationship with God.

Developmental psychologists chart human development through crises, passages, and seasons as the personality undergoes transformation. Spirituality understands freedom and authentic personhood to be the result of a process of conversion underlying these personality changes. From a Christian perspective, developmental theories explore not simply personality transformation, but manifestations of what is, at root, a graced invitation to surrender a life in trust to God's empowering love and mercy. Psychological constructs may be understood as a tracing of the Paschal Mystery, the dying and rising of Christ, inbuilt in human development.

The Christian mystics, paradigms of humanity, teach that authentic human development is ultimately a process of divinization, a participation in the knowing and loving of God. The mystics report a graciousness at the core of life, a transcendent source of identity and empowerment within the psyche, which nurtured and guaranteed their personhood. *See also* Catholicism and psychology/psychiatry; spirituality, Christian.   JOHN F. WELCH

psychology of religion, the rational or scientific study of the psychological and philosophical aspects of beliefs and practices of religion. Two early pioneers were William James (1842–1910) and Pierre Janet (1859–1947), although best known are the theories of Sigmund Freud (1856–1939) and Carl Jung (1875–1961).

Included in the study of the psychology of religion are the role of the emotions in the origins of belief, the psychological dynamics of religious conversion, comparative phenomena in Eastern and Western religions, and the relationship of religious belief and practice to psychopathology. Psychology of religion has enjoyed a surge of interest in Christian churches since the 1960s, especially in the training of pastoral counselors. *See also* Catholicism and psychology/psychiatry.

public vows. *See* vows, public.

publican (Lat., *publicanus,* translated, somewhat inaccurately, from *telones,* "tax or toll collector"), a generally wealthy individual who purchased the right to collect taxes, often in a brutal and exploitative manner. The Gospel "tax collectors," befriended by Jesus (e.g., Mark 2:15–16), were petty bureaucrats, often scorned as agents of an occupying power.

Puebla, the city in Mexico where the Third General Conference of Latin American Bishops (CELAM, the acronym for *Conferencia Episcopal*

Latinoamericana) was held in January 1979 and attended by Pope John Paul II. Building on CELAM II (in Medellín, Colombia, in 1968), CELAM III endorsed the notion of "integral liberation," approved of the formation of "base communities," and committed the Church to a "preferential option for the poor." The documents are available in J. Eagleson and P. Scharper, eds., *Puebla and Beyond* (Maryknoll, NY: Orbis Books, 1979). *See also* base communities; Latin America, Catholicism in; liberation theology; preferential option for the poor.

Pulcheria, St. (pul-kair'ee-uh), 399–453, empress and consecrated virgin, elder sister of Emperor Theodosius II (408–50). She succeeded him at his death, taking the elderly Marcian as consort. An able and pious stateswoman, she had the bones of John Chrysostom returned to Constantinople (438) and took an active part in theological controversies, arranging and organizing the Council of Chalcedon (451). She bequeathed her wealth to the poor. Feast day: September 10. *See also* Chalcedon, Council of.

pulpit, an elevated wooden or stone stand for the preacher or reader. In early Christian times the bishop preached from the cathedra, or episcopal chair. Later the ambo, an elevated platform structure, was used. Pulpits, often ornately decorated, became popular in medieval times. Currently, the lectern has replaced the pulpit, for the most part. *See also* ambo; homily; lectern.

Purcell, John Baptist, 1800–1883, U.S. archbishop. Born in Ireland, he served as instructor and then president of Mount St. Mary's Seminary in Emmitsburg, Maryland. He was appointed bishop of Cincinnati (1833) and later promoted to archbishop (1850). He was an ardent supporter of Catholic schools.

purgative way. *See* ways of the spiritual life.

purgatory, an intermediate state of purification between death and heaven that provides for the removal of remaining personal obstacles to the full enjoyment of eternal union with God. According to Catholic doctrine, such purification continues and completes the process of sanctification (or divinization) that makes intimate union with the triune God possible for persons justified and reconciled in Christ. The obstacles in view here are both venial

sins, unrepented at the time of death, and any enduring dispositional consequences of the repented and forgiven serious sins committed during one's earthly life. There is no question of a reversal of the direction that one has taken in the course of earthly life. Purgatory is not an opportunity for conversion where none has transpired in earthly life. The eternal destiny of the "holy souls" is not in question. Given that individual judgment follows immediately upon death, purgatory affords an interval of final purification for erasing conditions that would prevent justified persons from enjoying full fellowship with God in the communion of saints.

The doctrine of purgatory, as it came to be formulated by Church councils, articulates the basic assumptions of an unbroken liturgical tradition in the Christian community of intercessory prayer offered on behalf of "those who have gone before us." This is evident in conciliar affirmations of the doctrine, notably at the councils of Florence (1439), Trent (1563), and Vatican II (1965; Dogmatic Constitution on the Church, nn. 49–50). Through prayer, the pilgrim Church on earth affirms its solidarity with the Church on the threshold of glory.

Christian art, preaching, and exhortatory literature have pictured purgatory as a place of fire and torment to be endured for a definite duration. But these imagistic conceptions, though significant for understanding the cultural setting of the doctrine, are by no means central to its affirmation. At its core, the doctrine affirms simply a transitional spiritual state (possibly instantaneous and coincident with death) of transformation in view of the assured prospect of the Beatific Vision. *See also* Beatific Vision; eternal life; heaven; last things.   JOSEPH A. DINOIA

purification, a cleansing that restores a person to life in the community, or to communion with God. Primitive belief held that people could be contaminated by contact with certain profane or sacred objects. In the OT, purification rites cleansed people who had contracted a legal uncleanness through an impurity such as a skin disease, or through contact with the divine, as in childbirth. Jesus Christ emphasized the importance of faith and loving service of brothers and sisters rather than ritual purifications.

Traditionally, spiritual writers have spoken about a purification needed to overcome resistance to God's love. John of the Cross (d. 1591), for example, pointed to God's love at work freeing the soul through the purification of the dark night. More generally, one can speak of the purification that comes through the faithful living of one's commitments. *See also* absolution; Presentation; sanctification.

purificator (Lat., *purificare,* "to purify"), a small cloth used for wiping the paten and drying the chalice (after rinsing the latter with water) at Mass. It is made of white absorbent linen, 16 inches by 8 inches, the width being folded in thirds. A small red cross decorates it at one end.

Puritanism, a term covering a number of groups from the time of Elizabeth I (1558–1603) to that of Charles II (1660–85) seeking to purify the Church of England of all vestiges of Catholicism. The first Puritans rejected the Lutheran/Anglican claim that ceremonies are indifferent matters (Gk., *adiaphora*), insisting on the removal from worship of all that obscures the once-for-all sacrifice of Christ, such as vestments, altars, and prayers for the dead. The next generation sought to restore the worship and polity of the early Church, rejecting episcopacy for a presbyterian polity and making discipline a third mark of the Church. The movement further diversified with the creation of the Congregationalists or Independents under Robert Browne (1582) and the Baptist movement under John Smythe and Thomas Helwys (1612). Suppressed by the Act Against Puritans (1593) under Elizabeth I, the Puritans set their hopes on James I, to whom they presented their Millenary Petition on his way to London. The king frustrated their hopes at the Hampton Court Conference of 1604, but he did agree to a new Bible translation, the Authorized Version of 1611 (the King James Version). Charles I and archbishop of Canterbury William Laud pursued an expressly anti-Puritan policy, mandating the "Roman" ceremonies Puritans found offensive. The execution of Laud and Charles I by the Long Parliament and the Solemn League and Covenant with Scotland (1643) led to the creation of the Westminster Confession of 1649, a synopsis of seventeenth-century Puritan theology. The Civil War under Oliver Cromwell gave ascendancy first to the Presbyterians, then to the Independents. With the Restoration of 1660, the Puritans were excluded from the Church of England, although they were protected under the Toleration Act of 1689 and had established communities in Holland and New England. *See also* Protestantism; Reformation, the.

RANDALL C. ZACHMAN

purity, living as a sexual person in accord with God's will. The Church has vigorously taught the moral obligations related to human sexuality. At times, however, these obligations have been associated with an un-Christian understanding of sexuality. This dualistic perspective regarded even appropriate sexual expression as tainted or somewhat "dirty." This was because bodily activity of its nature was not so good or so pure as spiritual activity. In the 1990s, Pope John Paul II and others have tried to present a more holistic understanding of purity. *See also* chastity; sexual morality.

purity of heart, a spiritual state that is gained, according to the Desert Fathers, by ascetic practices and attainment of tranquility. Those who enjoy purity of heart are free from self-serving desires of the spirit, mind, and flesh. Their will is transformed by the will of God alone so that all expressions of egoism cease. *See also* asceticism.

putative marriage, in canon law an invalid marriage that is presumed valid if celebrated in good faith by at least one party. Historically, this concept was instituted to avoid the adverse consequences of illegitimacy and invalidity on innocent parties. *See also* marriage law.

pyx (piks; Gk., *puxis,* "wood container"), small metallic receptacle used by a priest or other eucharistic minister to carry Holy Communion to those who, by reason of sickness, are unable to attend Mass. The term is less frequently used to designate the container of the Host used for public veneration of the Eucharist; that is more properly known as a lunette. *See also* Communion, Holy.

Q, the designation, mostly likely derived from the abbreviation of the German *Quelle* ("source"), given to roughly 235 verses that the Gospels of Matthew and Luke share in common, but that are not found in Mark. Advocates of the Two-Source Hypothesis argue that Matthew and Luke composed their Gospels by combining Mark and Q, along with special material from their own traditions, designated as M and L. Following the Lucan order, a widely accepted list of Q passages would be the following verses (with slight variations in the Matthean parallels): Luke 3:7–9, 13–17; 4:1–13; 6:20–23 (the Beatitudes and woes) 27–49 (the Sermon on the Plain, cf. Matt 5–7); 7:1–10, 18–35; 9:57–62; 10:2–16; 21–24; 11:2–4, 9–20, 23–26; 29–35, 39–52; 12:2–12, 22–31, 33–34, 39–46, 51–53, 57–59; 13:18–21, 23–30, 34–35; 14:16–24, 26–27, 34–35; 15:4–7; 16:13, 16–18; 17:3–4, 6, 23–24, 26–30, 33–37; 18:14; 19:12–27; 22:28–30. Q contains mainly sayings of Jesus, has only one miracle (the healing of the centurion's servant in Luke 7:1–10), and has no Passion or Resurrection narrative. Many contemporary scholars argue that Q itself underwent different editions, with the earliest version consisting of wisdom sayings of Jesus (e.g., Luke 6:43–49; 11:34–36) and the later portions having a high proportion of eschatological sayings (e.g., sections from Luke 12), reflecting the delay of the Parousia (the expected return of Jesus). Jesus, the prophetic wisdom teacher, is awaited as the coming Son of Man and judge. The collection and preservations of Q may be the work of a community that followed the itinerant life-style of Jesus (Luke 10:1–16) and lived in expectation of the imminent return of Jesus.   *JOHN R. DONAHUE*

Quadragesimo Anno (kwah-drah-jay'zee-moh ah'noh; Lat., "After Forty Years"), social encyclical written in 1931 by Pope Pius XI. It sought to develop Pope Leo XIII's social teaching as articulated in *Rerum Novarum* (1891), the encyclical credited with inaugurating modern Catholic social teaching.

Quadragesimo Anno first assesses the impact of *Rerum Novarum* on both Church and society. The Church turned more to the plight of the worker. Civil authority responded by following Pope Leo's positive understanding of the role of the state, leading to policies to protect and aid the worker. Pope Leo's emphasis on the right of workers to associate facilitated the formation of unions.

Pope Pius XI then applied *Rerum Novarum* to the circumstances of the era. Issued in the midst of the Depression and the rise of Communist totalitarianism, *Quadragesimo Anno* critiques both capitalism and socialism. The former can lead to an excessive individualism that leaves the worker unprotected, while the latter can oppress human freedoms through a damaging collectivism. An understanding of private property as a qualified right allows Pope Pius XI to avoid both errors. While an individual has a right to private property, the use of that property is limited by its social character. God created the goods of the world for the well-being of everyone within it.

Pius XI offers a concrete alternative to both capitalism and socialism, a society based on vocational—that is not to say class—groupings. Relationships between these groups are regulated by the principle of subsidiarity: do not do through large-scale institutions what can be performed by smaller, more intimate ones. *See also* Catholic social teachings; encyclicals, social; subsidiarity, principle of.

TODD D. WHITMORE

Quakers, also known as Friends or the Religious Society of Friends, a religious community devoted to listening to and obeying Christ speaking within. They emerged under the leadership of George Fox (1624–91) during a time of great religious ferment in Commonwealth England under Oliver Cromwell. By 1647, Fox began to travel throughout northern England, declaring to Christian assemblies in "steeplehouses" that Christ had come to teach his people himself, so that they might know Christ and God by the Spirit in themselves and speak the word of God to others in a fellowship of love by the same Spirit that had spoken through the prophets and apostles in Scripture. The followers of Fox, called "Friends" by him but "Quakers" by others because "we bid them tremble at the word of God," were mainly dissatisfied Independents and Baptists. They would gather for worship in silent meetings, listening for Christ speaking within and often speaking to others on his behalf. The movement gained momentum in 1652 and rapidly spread to Ireland, Scotland, North America, and the Continent. Its most famous representatives are William Penn, who founded Pennsylvania in 1682, and Robert Barclay, who wrote its greatest defense in his *Apology for the True Christian Religion* (1676; Eng. trans., 1678). Quaker opposition to tithes, oaths, military service, and hierarchical social conventions brought persecution and often execution. Quakers have been dominant in the antislavery movements, law and prison reform, as well as opposition to war and religious persecution. *See also* pacifism.

quality of life, judgments about the kind of life a patient experiences before or after the application of medical technology. The term originated in the 1950s with the advancements of medical science and technology. There are disagreements about the meaning of the term, but quality-of-life judgments should not be understood as evaluations of the individual's ability to contribute to society. Life itself is valuable because it is created by God. However, physical life is not an absolute value, but it is only the condition for the pursuit of other values. It provides us with the possibility or opportunity to pursue material, moral, and spiritual values. Quality-of-life judgments, then, are assessments about the patient's current or future medical condition in relation to his or her abilities to pursue these other important values that transcend physical life. Any decision to use medical technology must consider whether the application of this technology will enhance or worsen the patient's ability to pursue life's values beyond merely physical existence. *See also* bioethics; medical ethics.

Quam Singulari (kwahm· sin-goo-lah'ree; Lat., "That with a particular [love]"), decree issued by the Sacred Congregation of the Sacraments, August 8, 1910, requiring that children who have reached the "age of discretion" (understood to be approximately seven) be permitted to receive Holy Communion.

Quanta Cura (kwahn'tah koo'rah; Lat., "How much concern"), encyclical of Pope Pius IX, December 8, 1864, accompanying the "Syllabus of Errors." It condemned liberalism, socialism, communism, secularism, and what Pius IX viewed as other contemporary social evils. *See also* Syllabus of Errors.

Quartodecimans (kwohr-toh-dech'i-muhnz; Lat., "fourteenth"), the designation used by Hippolytus and later heresiologists for Christians who celebrated Easter on the date of Passover, the fourteenth day of the Jewish month Nisan, instead of the following Sunday. This practice, followed especially by the churches in Asia Minor, was essentially the celebration of a Christian Passover. Prominent Quartodeci-

mans include Polycarp of Smyrna, Melito of Sardis, Apollinaris of Hierapolis, and Polycrates of Ephesus, whom Pope Victor I (d. 198) threatened to excommunicate, although he was rebuked for this by Irenaeus (d. ca. 200). The Council of Nicaea (325) settled on the Sunday celebration of Easter, but Quartodeciman practice continued until at least the fifth century. *See also* Asia Minor; Easter; Passover.

quasi-domicile, temporary residency within a given diocese or parish. Canon law is concerned that each person be attached to a Christian community in a diocese and/or parish, even on a temporary basis, in order that the person may receive the pastoral ministrations of the Church. One must have the intention to stay within a given territory for at least three months or actually stay there for at least three months in order to acquire a quasi-domicile. *See also* domicile.

Queen of Heaven, a Marian title pertaining to the belief that, after her Assumption, Mary was crowned Queen of Heaven. The feast of Mary the Queen, celebrated on May 31, was instituted by Pius XII in 1954. The queenship of Mary is now observed as a memorial in the liturgical calendar on August 22, the octave of the Solemnity of the Assumption (August 15). *See also* Assumption of the Blessed Virgin Mary; *Regina Coeli.*

Quiercy, synods of, a series of important Church councils (754, 838, 849, 853, 857, 858). In 754 Pope Stephen II concluded an alliance with King Pepin III that resulted in the foundation of the Papal States. Quiercy also saw condemnations of the German monk Gottschalk (849, 853) for denying the universal salvific will of God, and an attack on Amalarius of Metz (838) for his fanciful and artificial explanations of ritual. *See also* Amalarius of Metz; Papal States.

Quietism, heretical spiritual movement of the sixteenth and seventeenth centuries. The Quietists insisted on the annihilation of all human desires in the spiritual life so that a disinterested love of God could flourish. This view fostered the teaching that even the desire for salvation must be abandoned. Further, their passive spirituality led some Quietists to reject as unimportant active works of charity. Quietist ideas were expressed most fully by Miguel de Molinos, who was imprisoned in 1685. Charges of Quietism surfaced in France with the works of Jeanne Marie Guyon and François Fénelon. Guyon's writings were condemned in 1695, and Fénelon's *Maxims of the Saints* was condemned in 1699.

Quinquagesima Sunday (kwin-kwah-jehz'ee-mah; Lat., *quinquagesimus,* "fiftieth"), formerly the Sunday before Ash Wednesday. Quinquagesima refers to both a day (the fiftieth before Easter) and a season (the penitential period marked, in ancient times, by abstinence from meat). Following Vatican II, Quinquagesima was eliminated from the Roman Catholic calendar.

quinquennial report, mandatory diocesan status report to the pope filed by the diocesan bishop every five years in a manner and time determined by Holy See. Most bishops submit their report on the form provided by the Sacred Congregation for Bishops detailing diocesan administrative, financial, educational, and personnel organization, pastoral and ecumenical activities, and pertinent statistics.

Qumran (koom-rahn'), the name of a dry riverbed (wadi Qumran) and site of the ruins (khirbet Qumran) of a community compound built next to the wadi, near the northwest shore of the Dead Sea, about 8 miles south of Jericho and about 13 miles east southeast of Jerusalem. The Dead Sea Scrolls were discovered in eleven caves immediately west and north. A predominantly male cemetery lies east of the buildings. Pottery and coins found there suggest that the site was occupied ca. 150 B.C. to A.D. 68. Qumran is the only archaeological site north of Engedi on the west side of the Dead Sea that can correspond to Pliny's description of the Essenes' settlement. *See also* Dead Sea Scrolls

quodlibet (kwahd'li-bet; Lat., "anything [whatsoever]"), an academic exercise held at regular intervals at a medieval university at which masters were expected to respond to topics raised at random by students and other masters. It required considerable mental agility, and some written versions are extant, revealing much about contemporary concerns in theology. *See also* Scholasticism.

Quo vadis? (kwoh vah'dis; Lat., "Where are you going?"), according to legend, words addressed to Christ on the Appian Way by Peter, who was fleeing Rome during Nero's persecution (A.D. 64). Christ re-

plied that he was heading to Rome. Peter returned to Rome and was martyred. *See also* Peter, St.

Qurbana (kuhr-bah'nah; Syr., "sacrifice," "oblation"), East (*Qurbana*) and West (*Qurobo*) Syrian variants of a common Syriac name for the eucharistic service.

Rabanus Maurus, also known as Hrabanus Maurus or Raban Maur, 780–856, abbot and archbishop. Born at Mainz, educated at Fulda and Tours (where he studied under Alcuin), Rabanus served Fulda as master of the school and as abbot (822–42), becoming archbishop of Mainz in 847. His commentaries, homilies, and other writings are based on careful selections from patristic sources. *See also* Fulda.

rabat (rab'bee), the cloth or silk material that is attached to a clerical Roman collar and is worn under a suit or cassock. The rabat of a bishop or monsignor is purple, a cardinal's is red, the pope's is white. For all other clerics and seminarians, it is black.

Rabbi (Heb., "my great one"), title of respect in ancient Judaism, particularly for a teacher. The title, or its equivalent Rabbouni, is applied occasionally to Jesus (Matt 16:49; Mark 9:5; 11:21; 14:45; John 1:38; 6:25; 11:8; 20:16). Jesus, however, prohibited his disciples from accepting such a title (Matt 23:8).

Raccolta (It., "collection"), anthology of prayers. Common title for the book of prayers to which indulgences have been attached. The first such collection was published in the early nineteenth century, but such publications are now obsolete. They have been supplanted by the much briefer *Enchiridion Indulgentiarum* of 1968. *See also* indulgences.

racism, discrimination against persons on the basis of their racial or ethnic origin. The first Vatican document to deal solely with racism is the Pontifical Justice and Peace Commission's 1988 statement, "The Church and Racism: Toward a More Fraternal Society." It understands racism as "contempt for a race characterized by its ethnic origin, color, or language." The first section traces the history of racism. Although racism is rooted in the reality of human sin, its rise is due primarily to colonialism from the sixteenth century forward. It was not until the eighteenth century that a clear ideological basis for racism developed. While the Catholic Church often made statements condemning racial prejudice, at times missionaries "even gave it encouragement on the basis of false interpretations of the Bible."

"The Church and Racism" cites several forms of contemporary racism. Institutional racism encodes the practice in a country's constitution, excluding persons from participation in the political order. In other instances, there may be participation on a limited basis. Elsewhere, customary practices, not encoded in law, exclude persons of minority races. Finally, "spontaneous racism" often erupts, particularly in places where there is a high rate of immigration.

Church teaching counters racism with its emphasis on the dignity of the human person and the unity of the human family. The *imago Dei* (Lat., "image of God") doctrine backs both of these emphases. Because persons are created in the image of God, they have an inalienable dignity. Since all persons are so created, there is a unity to the human family. Such dignity and unity forbid discrimination on the basis of race. According to the Catholic Church's moral teaching, racism is a sin. *See also* imago Dei. *TODD D. WHITMORE*

radical sanation. *See* sanation.

Rahner, Hugo, 1900–68, German Jesuit historian, theologian, and elder brother of the theologian Karl Rahner. At the University of Innsbruck (Austria), Rahner taught primarily in the field of patristics. He was best known for his early theological study of preaching, his book presenting Mary as the symbol of the Church (at the time of Vatican II), and his studies on Ignatius of Loyola.

Rahner, Karl, 1904–84, probably the most prominent and influential Catholic theologian of the twentieth century. A German Jesuit ordained in 1932, his education in neo-Scholasticism was complemented by philosophical studies with Joseph Maréchal (who was among the first to develop a connection between the thought of Kant and Aquinas) and Martin Heidegger (who fashioned an existential metaphysics from neo-Kantian and Husserlian origins). This educational background offered Rahner the opportunity to fashion a new style of theology out of the approaches of Thomist, transcendental, and existentialist philosophies.

Theological Career: As Rahner began his teaching at Innsbruck in 1936, the Nazis closed Catholic schools. During the war he worked in the religious education of clergy and laity in Vienna. Returning to Innsbruck in 1948, he wrote creative essays that liberated Catholic theology from an increasingly rigid neo-Scholasticism. These collected essays began to appear in 1954 in *Schriften zur Theologie* (Eng. trans., *Theological Investigations*), a series that would continue for two decades through more than twenty volumes. Their method and content were an example for many theologians of how Catholic theology need not flee originality and development in order to remain true to Church tradition. In the 1950s some of Rahner's ideas incurred Vatican censorship, but in 1962 he was named a theological adviser (Lat., *peritus*) to Vatican II. Two years later he became the successor of Romano Guardini at the University of Munich. During the conciliar years (1962–65) he worked on commentaries on the conciliar documents, a new edition of the encyclopedia *Lexikon für Theologie und Kirche (Lexicon for Theology and Church),* theological dictionaries, and multivolume handbooks of pastoral and systematic theology. He presented his own system, later published as *Foundations of Christian Faith,* first at Munich in 1964, and then at the University of Münster, where he taught from 1967 until retirement in 1971.

The Elements of His Theology: Rahner drew upon Aquinas's thought even as he related

Karl Rahner, German Jesuit priest generally regarded as the greatest Catholic theologian of the twentieth century, who, like Thomas Aquinas in the thirteenth century, attempted to reconcile Christian faith and contemporary thought.

Catholicism successfully to idealism, phenomenology, and existentialism, but without falling into modern tendencies to derive grace and revelation solely from human consciousness. Rahner's theology found expression in several genres: there are the essays on theological topics considered historically and pastorally; the *Foundations* is a presentation of what is most basic in Christianity for an educated but nonspecialist audience; and there are also books of sermons, meditations on the mysteries of Christ, and reflections on faith in daily life.

One can see in Rahnerian thought three areas of focus: the analysis of the human person; the self-communication of God as the ground of revelation and grace; and the history of self and of culture. The human person becomes the place where revelation occurs. Human structures of knowing and of ordinary life make possible the reception of divine revelation and grace. Divine self-communication comes first in a universal and unthematic way to all; later, human beings and society make it concrete in life and religion. What is called "salvation" is a primal presence of God, including what emerges as "grace" and "revelation." Different cultural and theological epochs emerged in history because an incarnational revelation disclosed itself in the forms of a particular age.

Rahner developed his theology to meet basic contemporary challenges: the development of a Catholic theology that took seriously modern thought; a description of how God's presence touched nonbelievers in secular northern Europe; the existence of grace in the world religions; perdurance and change within the historical forms of Catholicism occurring after Vatican II; and, finally, the monumental shift in the Catholic Church from European Christendom to a world Church.

Rahner insisted that he wrote not for scholars but for ordinary Christians, for all religious people. He wanted to explain what was most basic in the gospel, the reality of the mystery of a special presence of God in each individual life and in the history of humanity. The transcendental and existential side of Rahner's theology was modified after Vatican II by his attention to history and to praxis. Despite his use of terminologies from modern philosophy and a vivid, if dense, German style, his works have been translated into many languages and have attracted a wide following around the world. In this century he pioneered the project of rethinking Catholic dogmatic theology in modern philosophical categories,

and he became after Vatican II the Catholic Church's most important theologian.

Bibliography

Rahner, Karl. *Theological Investigations.* Baltimore and New York: Helicon, 1961–69; Seabury/Crossroad, 1977–.

———. *Foundations of Christian Faith: An Introduction to the Idea of Christianity.* New York: Seabury Press, 1978.

Vorgrimler, Herbert. *Understanding Karl Rahner.* New York: Crossroad, 1986.

Weger, Karl H. *Karl Rahner: An Introduction to His Thought.* New York: Seabury Press, 1980.   THOMAS F. O'MEARA

Ramsa (Syr., "evening"), East (*Ramsa*) and West (*Ramso*) Syrian variants of the term for Vespers. *See also* Vespers.

Ranke, Ludwig von, 1795–1886, Protestant German historian. A professor of history at the University of Berlin at only thirty years of age, he gained fame through his balanced and detached history of the modern papacy from the sixteenth century to the First Vatican Council (1869–70).

rape, impediment of. *See* abduction, impediment of.

Raphael [Raffaello Sanzio], 1483–1520, Italian Renaissance artist. Noted for his classical idealism, harmonious forms, and profound spirituality, Raphael was painter at the papal courts of Julius II and Leo X, and architect of St. Peter's Basilica for Leo X. Significant works include the *Sistine Madonna* and paintings and tapestries for the Vatican apartments. *See also* Catholicism and architecture; Catholicism and the visual arts.

Raphael, St. (Heb., "God heals"), archangel. In the story of Tobit, Raphael heals Tobit's blindness and provides Sarah with a husband (Tob 3:16–17). Raphael is God's messenger, who hears people's prayers and brings these before God (Tob 12:12, 15). Feast day (with Michael and Gabriel, archangels): September 29, also known as Michaelmas Day. *See also* angel; archangel.

rapture. *See* ecstasy.

rash judgment, the attribution of moral inadequacy or fault to another without sufficient evidence. Rash judgment is imprudent because it decides without sufficient reflection; it is judgment rather than suspicion or doubt because of the certainty with which the view is held. Because rash judgment results in a lowering of the esteem in which another person is held, without a sufficient basis in fact, an injury is done to the person judged. As such it is a violation of justice and charity. *See also* calumny; detraction; justice; slander.

ratified marriage. *See* marriage law.

rationalism, any worldview that either explicitly or implicitly requires that all claims to truth either be based on clearly and scientifically demonstrable premises or be unambiguously derived from what can be so demonstrated. Because the processes of the mind determine the criteria for demonstrability, nothing can claim the status of truth that is not already given in the content or structure of the mind or positivistically through the five senses. Consequently, rationalism stands in opposition to any religious tradition oriented toward mystery and claiming access to revealed truth. Rationalism and its opposite, fideism, were condemned by the First Vatican Council (1869–70). *See also* faith and reason; fideism.

Ratisbon, Conference of, or Conference of Regensburg (1541), the last attempt to reconcile Protestants and Catholics during the Reformation. Participants on the Catholic side included John Eck and Gasparo Contarini; on the Protestant side, Martin Butzer and Philipp Melanchthon. Compromise articles on the condition of humans before the Fall, free will, the cause of sin, and original sin were rejected by both Luther and the papacy. *See also* Reformation, the.

Ratramnus (ruh-tram'nuhs), d. ca. 868, theologian and Benedictine monk of the monastery of Corbie who criticized the extreme realist eucharistic theology of Paschasius Radbertus and advanced a symbolic understanding of eucharistic presence. His teaching, wrongly attributed then to John Scotus Eriugena, was condemned by a synod at Vercelli in 1050. The treatise was placed on the Index of Forbidden Books in 1559, after some Protestants appealed to it in support of their own doctrines, but it was removed again in 1900. He also wrote on predestination. *See also* Real Presence.

Ratzinger, Joseph, b. 1927, German Catholic

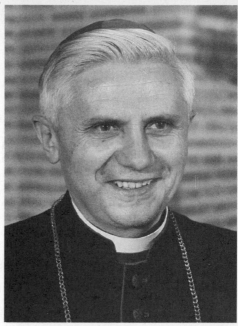

Cardinal Joseph Ratzinger, Prefect of the Sacred Congregation for the Doctrine of the Faith, who has served as Pope John Paul II's principal defender and enforcer of orthodoxy and as the principal architect of the *Catechism of the Catholic Church* (1992).

theologian and cardinal. Ordained a priest for the diocese of Regensburg (1951), he was awarded his doctorate in theology from the University of Munich (1953) and served as professor of theology at the universities of Bonn (1959–63), Münster (1963–66), Tübingen (1966–69), and Regensburg (1969–77). During Vatican II, as a theological adviser to Cardinal Joseph Frings of Cologne, he was known for his progressive views. In March 1977, he was chosen by Paul VI to succeed Cardinal Julius Döpfner as the archbishop of Munich, and in June 1977 he was named a cardinal. In November 1981, he was appointed prefect of the Congregation for the Doctrine of the Faith by John Paul II, where he has led an effort to maintain doctrinal orthodoxy and clerical discipline in the post–Vatican II Church. *See also* Congregation for the Doctrine of the Faith.

Raymond Nonnatus, St., ca. 1204–40, Cistercian abbot and patron saint of expectant mothers and those falsely accused. Spanish-born, he led military expeditions against the Moors, forming the military order of the Knights of Calatrava. Feast day: February 6.

Raymond of Peñafort, St. (payn'yuh-fohr), 1180–1275, Dominican canon lawyer. Commissioned by Pope Gregory IX to prepare an official codification of canon law, Raymond finished the *Quinque Libri Decretalium* (Lat., "Five Books of Decretals") in 1234, which remained in effect until 1917. Feast day: January 7. *See also* canon law.

raza (rah'zah; Syr., "mystery"), ecclesiastical term for sacrament. In the Syro-Malabar tradition, *raza* is the proper name for the most solemn form of the *Qurbana* or eucharistic liturgy. The plural *raze,* "mysteries," is the common term for eucharistic services, including the Presanctified Liturgy. *See also* sacrament.

RCIA. *See* Rite of Christian Initiation of Adults.

reader. *See* lector.

reading, spiritual. *See* spiritual reading.

Real Presence, the teaching of the Catholic Church that Jesus Christ is present at and in the Eucharist in his body and blood, humanity and divinity, under the form of bread and wine.

The NT attests to the faith of Catholics and other Christians that Christ is present in and to his Church in a variety of ways. As the Risen Lord, he is no longer bound by the constraints of a particular time and place and thus can be present when his disciples gather to pray, invoke his name for healing, proclaim his gospel, forgive sins, suffer for his sake, and assemble to remember his Last Supper with his disciples. Fundamental to the recognition of this presence was the Church's experience of the power of the Spirit of the Lord transforming it into the community of his body and empowering it to continue his mission.

The accounts of the Last Supper in the three synoptic Gospels (Matt 26:26–30; Mark 14:22–26; Luke 22:14–20), as well as in Paul's First Letter to the Corinthians (11:23–25) and the Bread of Life discourse in the Gospel of John (ch. 6), attest to the celebration of the Lord's Supper in the NT Church. Paul and John also speak of the bread and wine in terms strong enough to evidence the belief of the first-century Church in the presence of the body and blood of Christ: Paul speaks of sharing in the body and blood of Christ (cf. 1 Cor 10:16–17; 11:27) and John speaks of eating the flesh of Christ and drinking his blood (6:52–56).

Throughout the first millennium, the faith of the Church in the presence of the body and blood of Christ went relatively undisturbed. Diverse terminology was used to describe the change of the bread and wine into the body and blood of Christ, and theologians sought to relate this presence of the body and blood of the Lord to his historical and risen body as well as to his ecclesial body. But some controversy erupted in the ninth century and developed further in the eleventh century between extreme positions that saw the bread and wine either as mere signs or as totally changed even in their physical elements. Out of these controversies came the Church's teaching on transubstantiation, which held that the substances of the bread and wine are changed into the body and blood of Christ. This was taught by Lateran IV (1215) and Trent (1551). In the latter case, the council reiterated the doctrine in response to perceived distortions of the tradition by the Reformers.

Contemporary Church teaching and theology has placed the doctrine of the Real Presence within the context of the many ways in which Christ is present in the Church. In his 1965 encyclical *Mysterium Fidei* Pope Paul VI identifies these as prayer, works of mercy, preaching, governance, the sacraments, and finally the Eucharist, "a way that surpasses all others" (n. 38), because this presence "is substantial and through it Christ becomes present whole and entire, God and man" (n. 39). Vatican II's Constitution on the Sacred Liturgy (1963) spoke of Christ's presence not only in the consecrated bread and wine but also in the proclaimed word, the person of the minister, and the worshiping assembly itself (n. 7).

The Real Presence of Christ in the Eucharist flows from his total self-gift on the cross and his will to make that gift effective for all people throughout history. Thus the purpose of his presence is communion with his Church through his body and blood. *See also* Eucharist.   JOHN J. STRYNKOWSKI

reason and faith. *See* faith and reason.

recapitulation (Lat., "summing up" or "summary"), used in Eph 1:10, where God is said to "sum up" all things in Christ. Irenaeus (d. ca. 200) proposed a theory of recapitulation in which God restored fallen humanity to full communion with God through the full obedience of Christ, who in turn "summed up" all divine revelations prior to the Incarnation. *See also* Jesus Christ.

Reception into Full Communion,

liturgical rite used to receive baptized Christians into full communion with the Catholic Church by a simple profession of faith. Equating a candidate with a catechumen, an unbaptized person undergoing catechesis for entrance into the Church, should be avoided. Full reception should occur within a liturgical context clarifying the connection between the reception and eucharistic communion (Rite of Christian Initiation of Adults, n. 476). Preparation for this profession of faith should include spiritual formation.

Although it is the office of the bishop to receive baptized Christians into full communion, he may entrust this celebration to a priest who thereby has the faculty to confirm the candidate within the rite of reception, unless the person had already been validly confirmed (Rite of Christian Initiation of Adults, n. 481). *See also* convert; profession of faith; Rite of Christian Initiation of Adults.

reception of doctrine

(Lat., *recipere*, "to take up," "accept," "adopt"), a process whereby the faithful accept a teaching or decision of the Church; an ecclesial community or institution accepts a dogmatic tradition or decision that did not originate within itself and makes this tradition or decision its own. Examples of items received are the decisions of a council, doctrines concerning matters of faith and morals, disciplinary ordinances, liturgical decrees, even the transfer of persons from one ecclesiastical office to another. The recipients can be local churches, conferences, councils, the pope, or the entire Church. Reception can also occur between separated churches.

In the NT, reception is a basic act of faith and is characterized by *lambanein* (Gk., "to take in") and *dechestai* (Gk., "to receive graciously"). It concerns the acceptance of the word of God (Mark 4:20), the message of Jesus (Rev 2: 41), and the gospel (1 Cor 15:1). It also concerns the acceptance of Jesus and God by accepting those whom Jesus has sent (Matt 10:40; John 13:20) and whom he himself has first of all accepted (Rom 15:7). This acceptance is a life process effected by the Spirit (1 Cor 2:10–16).

In the ancient Church confessions of faith, liturgies, and the decrees of councils attained general recognition and authority by means of reception. The formation of the biblical canon also took place in this way. The general reception of a writing or doctrine by local churches was understood as a demonstration that it agreed with apostolic tradition. Recognition by reception is a form of consensus formation in a Church that understands itself as a community of local churches.

In the Catholic Church, as the particular role of the local churches diminished and the role of a centralized "lawgiver" became more prominent, reception was reduced to obedience. Since the Second Vatican Council (1962–65) the Church is being rediscovered as community and the role of reception is regaining respect.

Reception does not legitimate or validate the decision of the ecclesial teaching office. It is the confirming witness of the sense of the faith by the People of God regarding a decision's truth and serviceableness. When nonreception occurs, those responsible for the decision need to examine the reasons for the lack of acceptance. A responsibly acting pastoral and teaching office will review the preparation of its decision in relation to the belief of the People of God and the legitimate requirements of decision making in order to avoid nonreception. Regarding the infallible decisions of the teaching office, the Second Vatican Council says: "The assent of the Church can never be lacking to such definitions on account of the same Holy Spirit's influence, through which Christ's whole flock is maintained in the unity of the faith and makes progress in it" (Dogmatic Constitution on the Church, n. 25).

An example of reception in the recent history of the Church is the acceptance of the aims of the biblical, liturgical, and ecumenical movements by Vatican II. In the realization of the vision of the Second Vatican Council, reception is currently being experienced as a longer, more difficult, and more creative process than anticipated. An example of nonreception or partial reception is the anti-birth control encyclical *Humanae Vitae* (1968) by Paul VI. The great majority of married Catholics do not accept the teaching that the use of artificial means to prevent conception is always morally wrong. In the ecumenical movement the processes of reception are acquiring ever more significance. Convergence and consensus of opinion are first worked by commissions into documents, which then must be accepted by the participating churches. With the acknowledgment of the historical character of the Christian faith and the Church, all churches maintain that formulations of the faith that were received earlier by the Church are always to be appropriated again and communicated anew (rereception). *See also* doctrine; reception of law; *sensus fidelium.*   HERMAN J. POTTMEYER

reception of law, the process by which the laws of the Church are appropriated by the community and become a vital force in shaping its life.

Every human law has its own life cycle, which divides into two principal stages. In the first one, the actor is the legislator, conceiving the law by identifying a specific value that is either necessary or beneficial for the community, and ascertaining that the community has the capacity to reach out for it. The legislator then formulates the law; that is, a proposition is construed in an imperative mood (ordinance) directing the subjects to act accordingly. Finally, the legislator promulgates the law; that is, it is brought to the notice of those for whom it is intended. The end result of this stage is an abstract, general, and impersonal command that carries a binding force but does not as yet shape the life of the community.

In the second stage, the actors are the subjects. From the words of the law they must understand the meaning of the law, that is, the action or order the legislator wishes to impose. Then, as they encounter concrete, particular, and personal situations, they must come to a conscious decision to implement the law. In this act of implementation, the original norm of action meets the demands of real life and, as in a crucible, it reveals its suitability or its shortcomings. Finally, the subjects must form a critical judgment about the law, either by affirming it through steady observance, or by bringing to the legislator's notice the difficulties the law may generate; all this must be done in the living spirit of *communio* (Lat., "communion").

When this process is completed and the law is observed throughout the community, its reception is achieved: it has become a vital force that shapes the life of the Church.

For the perfection of this process, the legislator must be disposed to explain the values that it intends to uphold and promote, so that the subjects have all the information that is necessary to grasp the full meaning of the law and become able to appreciate it rationally and implement it responsibly.

Further, the subjects must be aware that the ultimate criterion for an act of obedience to any law is in the judgment of a well-informed practical con-

science. To surrender with dignity to its dictate it is necessary to know, or to sense, the value behind the positive rule. By embracing freely that value, the members of the community ready themselves to accept also the hardships that the observance of the law may entail. Through such attitudes and acts the law is intelligently and freely received.

The reception of the law, as described, should never be confused with its juridical ratification by the subjects. A correct act of promulgation can impose a legally binding norm; yet, its effective reception alone can make it into a vital force, leading to a pleasing sacrifice to God. *See also* canon law; reception of doctrine.   LADISLAS M. ORSY

recidivism (Lat., "a falling back"), in moral theology, the pattern of behavior established by one who repeatedly commits the same kind of sin without attempting to avoid doing so; the moral disposition resulting in this pattern. Behavior resembling recidivism may result from extreme immaturity or repeated and severe temptation, but the true recidivist is characterized by a lack of intention to amend the sinful behavior. *See also* habit [moral].

recollection, an inward focus of attention on the presence of God. It involves maintaining a clear alertness regarding the object of recollection throughout the day. Recollection also includes an awareness of how thoughts, speech, and actions affect spiritual life. To remain centered interiorly may require withdrawing attention from exterior objects that arouse sensory or other desires.

Recollection conserves energy for spiritual practice and keeps attention and desires from being dispersed. Some people use short prayers, particular actions, scheduled breaks in activity or other aids to recollection. Silence, solitude, and recollection support each other. *See also* meditation; prayer.

Recollects, a designation of two religious orders. One was a reformed branch of the Franciscan Observants begun in France during the late sixteenth century. In 1897 Pope Leo XIII incorporated them and other Franciscan groups into the Franciscan order (O.F.M.). The other Recollect order was a reform branch of the Augustinian Friars begun during the sixteenth century in Spain. They became a congregation in 1621 and an independent order in 1912. They are known as the Order of Recollect Hermits of St. Augustine (O.A.R.). The prior general resides in Rome. *See also* Augustinian Hermits; Franciscan order.

RECONCILIATION

T he sacrament of Reconciliation is the ritual of the Christian community, under the leadership of the bishop or priest, in which sinners are reconciled both to God and to the Church. Reconciliation is found on almost every page of the NT; it is an essential part of the gospel message. Jesus preached a message of reconciliation both in his parables and in his healings. His life, death, and Resurrection were all part of revelation: the good news of God's gift of reconciliation. The entire life of a disciple of Jesus is essentially a life of reconciliation. Nonetheless, in the course of history, the Church developed a ritual of reconciliation, which came to be called a sacrament. In the NT three specific passages have often been used to substantiate the sacramental ritual: Matt 16:16; 18:18; and John 20:23. Major biblical scholars today, however, do not find either in the text or in the context of these passages an account of an institution of a reconciliation ritual. Rather, there is in these passages a power, present in the Church at large, to isolate and negate sin. Sin is removed by every prayer, by fasting, by charity to one's neighbor, by all good works, and by every sacramental act, especially the Eucharist.

RECONCILIATION IN THE PATRISTIC CHURCH

In early Church history one does not find any record of a reconciliation ritual until ca. 150. This first written record of a ritual stems from Hermas, a layperson, whose mystical writings include mention of a rite of reconciliation as a sort of sabbatical. Hermas, however, indicates that a sinful Christian could receive this ritualized forgiveness only once in a lifetime and the rite was a public one. Hermas does not indicate which sins required this ritual, nor does he describe the rite. However, in the churches, both East and West, this form of reconciliation very quickly became the official form: the ritual was public in nature, i.e., a communal ritual, and a sinner could receive reconciliation only once during a lifetime. If a Christian fell into a publicly known serious sin a second time, the Christian community prayed for this sinner on his or her deathbed, but the sinner did not receive the sacraments of Reconciliation, of Anointing, or of the Eucharist. Records indicate that major, publicly known sins such as apostasy, murder, and adultery were the more common sins that required this form of reconciliation. Other publicly known sins were at times also included, but these varied from region to region. Moreover, this ritual was a process that often lasted three years. For some sins, such as murder, however, fifteen years were prescribed in some local churches. The process itself was not uniform throughout the Christian world; various local churches developed their own forms of the ritual. Generally, however, the final act of this ritual included the silent laying on of hands by the bishop or priest. The penitent could then join the Eucharist with the community. In the West, more than in the East, an additional penance was added to this ritual: namely, those who received this form of Reconciliation had to remain celibate for the remainder of their lives. This caused the breakup of marriages, and the rule of celibacy was resisted by many Christian communities. The length of time, the severity of the penances, and the inclusion of celibacy made this form of Reconciliation so odious to the majority of Christian laity, that from about the year 700 onward Reconciliation was deliberately postponed, and it became more often than not the sacrament of the dying. Bishops continued to urge the reception of this public form of Reconciliation, but the laity did not respond.

THE CELTIC FORM OF RECONCILIATION

In England and Ireland, this public ritual of Reconciliation was never used, according to historical records. There is no indication in the early documents of any alternate form of Reconciliation. Among the Celtic monks, however, a form of spiritual direction began to take place, in which monks and nuns privately and frequently discussed both their sinfulness and their need of reform with the abbot or abbess. Precisely when and how this form of spiritual direction regarding sin, conversion, and amendment became the actual form for the sacrament of Reconciliation remains shrouded in undisclosed history. When the Celtic monks came as missionaries to continental Europe in the latter part of the sixth century, this form of private and frequent confession became popular and gradually was considered the normal sacramental rite of Penance. Early records do not describe any precise ritual, but they do indicate the listing of sins.

The Celtic form of Penance, which was private and frequent, clashed with the Roman form of Penance, which was public and available only once in a lifetime. Slowly, however, the unofficial Celtic form became so widespread that the public form almost disappeared from the local churches. In 1215 at the Fourth Lateran Council, church leadership officially adopted the Celtic form of Reconciliation. This was done in an indirect manner, through the decree *Omnis Utriusque*, in which each baptized Christian was required to confess his or her sins and receive the Eucharist once each year. Only in the Eastern churches have public forms of Penance continued down to the present time. In the twelfth and thirteenth centuries Scholastic theologians provided a theological base for this private form of confession, utilizing the process, developed by Peter of Poitiers (a.k.a. Peter the Chanter, d. 1197) and popularized by Alexander of Hales (ca. 1186–1245), namely contrition, confession, absolution, and satisfaction. Among the major theologians were Alexander of Hales, Albertus Magnus (ca. 1200–1280), Thomas Aquinas (ca. 1225–74), Bonaventure (ca. 1217–74), and John Duns Scotus (ca. 1265–1308). Each of these formulated the theology of Penance in different ways, and the Franciscans and Dominicans, in particular, shaped their theologies of

Reconciliation in quite opposite directions. Nonetheless, they all followed the fourfold process—contrition, confession, absolution, and satisfaction—a theological mode that eventually became standard within Catholic thought down to the renewal of the sacrament in the post–Vatican II period.

THE REFORMATION AND THE COUNCIL OF TRENT

The Reformation leaders Martin Luther and John Calvin accused the Roman Catholic Church of extolling good works over God's grace. In a special way they found this accusation realized in the way the sacrament of Penance was presented by the Catholic Church, both in its official documents and in the Roman form of theology. In particular, the Reformers focused their accusation on the detailed confession of sin, the need to make an act of perfect contrition, and above all the *ex opere operato* (Lat., "from the work worked") words of absolution by the priest, as well as the "penances" imposed on confessing sinners. All of these seemed in their eyes to be good works, which denied the absolute gratuity of grace. The Reformers also accused past Church leadership of "inventing" this sacrament and imposing it on the Church community, because unlike Baptism and Eucharist, the institution of this ritual did not appear to have scriptural basis. The bishops at Trent reacted against the Reformers' denial that bishops had any authority to determine the form of sacramental rituals that were binding on the baptized. They also insisted that the sacrament of Penance was indeed scriptural, although they realized that this ritual was not as clearly indicated in Scripture as were Baptism and Eucharist. The bishops also struggled to present the sacrament of Penance in conformity with the teaching on the absolute gratuity of grace. However, the two issues, grace and Penance, were discussed separately: the decree on justification appeared in 1547; the decree on the sacrament of Penance in 1551. No effort was made by the bishops to unite these two decrees in a unified way. Nonetheless, the bishops at Trent officially taught that God's grace is absolutely gratuitous and that we do nothing to gain it. The bishops indicated that good works, including the act of contrition, the confession of sins, priestly absolution, and the penance or satisfaction after confession, must and can be explained within the framework of the decree on justification. After Trent, the Scholastic, rather than the patristic, understanding of this sacrament became common, and frequent confession of sin was encouraged. Jansenism, a movement that emphasized the need for severe forms of penance, abetted the frequent confession of sin.

TWENTIETH-CENTURY RESEARCH ON PENANCE

In the twentieth century, the history of this sacrament began to be studied in depth, particularly the rich understanding of reconciliation in the patristic period, and with this research came a call for pastoral renewal of the sacrament. In several areas of Europe, just prior to Vatican II, new forms of the Penance ritual were introduced and some of them included general absolution. There occurred at the same time a rethinking of sacramental theology, recognizing Jesus, in his humanity, as the primordial sacrament and the Church as a basic sacrament. The bishops at Vatican II mandated a renewed ritual, and in 1973 the new ritual was finally promulgated. This new ritual was based on criteria taken from Vatican II's Constitution on the Sacred Liturgy (*Sacrosanctum Concilium*): (1) the rite should clearly express both the nature and effect of the sacrament; (2) the role of the church community must be emphasized; (3) the reading of the word of God should be central; (4) because liturgical services are not private functions but celebrations of the Church, a public form of worship should predominate over a private form; and (5) the rite should be short and clear, free from useless repetitions, and formulated within the ordinary person's power of comprehension, i.e., not requiring extensive explanation.

The revised ritual includes four distinct forms: the first is an individual ritual; the second is a communal ritual with individual confession and absolution; the third is a communal ritual with general absolution; the fourth is an abbreviated, emergency ritual to be used at the time of immanent death. The theology behind all of these new forms is twofold: sin is basically an offense both against God and against one's community; and reconciliation, therefore, is reconciliation with God and with the community. In this approach the social nature of sin and the social nature of the ritual of Reconciliation are officially stressed. With the exception of the emergency form for time of death, the other three forms are presented in the ritual in a way that does not make any one normative over the other. In accord with the Vatican II Constitution on the Sacred Liturgy, the preferred or normative form would always be communal, since liturgical rites are never private rituals. Even more profound, however, is the emphasis on prayer throughout the renewed rite. There is a prayer of welcome, a prayerful reading of the Scriptures, a prayerful reflection on the word of God, a prayerful examination of one's conscience, and a prayer of absolution followed by a prayer of praise, a prayer of blessing, and dismissal. Whenever the ritual of Reconciliation becomes a time of communal prayer, the sacrament of Reconciliation is indeed renewed.

In the *Praenotanda* (introduction) of the new ritual, one finds an important overview of the theology undergirding the new ritual. These *Praenotanda* begin with Jesus himself as reconciliation, both in his message and in his life, death, and Resurrection. In this way, it is indicated that Jesus himself is the primordial sacrament of Reconciliation. Second, the text moves to the Church as a basic sacrament of Reconciliation, indicating that in every ecclesial activity reconciliation is present. Only then does the document focus on the sacramental ritual of Reconciliation. This indicates that the new ritual must be understood within the framework of Jesus as fundamental sacrament of Reconciliation and the ecclesial community itself as basic sacrament.

ISSUES OF CONTINUING PASTORAL CONCERN

There remain today, however, several issues in need of further discussion: namely, the frequency of confession; the age of First Confession; the use of general absolution; and the need to confess privately to a priest. The new ritual, if celebrated properly, does take more time, and this tends to run at odds with an emphasis on frequent confession. A stress on frequent confession will have the effect of curtailing key prayer elements in the ritual, thereby thwarting the intended renewal. Second, the regulation from Lateran IV on the necessity for confession, i.e., once a year if one has committed a mortal sin, remains the basic law of the Church binding a Christian of any age to receive the sacrament of Penance, if morally and physically able. A blanket requirement of First Confession prior to First Communion on the part of baptized children runs counter to the regulation of Lateran IV. Third, bishops of various conferences are not in agreement with regards to the occasions when general absolution is licit within their jurisdictional area. This lack of uniformity arises from the theological uncertainty behind such key words as "case of necessity" (Lat., *casus necessitatis*), "for a long time" (*diu*), and "integral confession" (*confessio integra*). Moreover, some Church leaders, counter to the ritual, wish to make the first form, the individual form, "normative." Until these issues are clarified, the role of a Reconciliation ritual that includes general absolution in the daily life of the Christian will remain ambiguous. Finally, in the case of general absolution, the ritual requires that those conscious of mortal sin confess such sins when they next make their confession privately to a priest (the first and second forms). Since such mortal sins are already forgiven and the person in question can receive not only the Eucharist but all pertinent sacraments licitly and validly, the reason behind the regulation of "confessing such sins privately to a priest" remains unclear. Moral theologians are also discussing in a deeper way the nature of sin, particularly the social nature of all sin, because such an emphasis seems to indicate that the more socially destructive a sin is, the more evil it is in comparison with other sinful situations.

See also absolution; Celtic spirituality; confession, auricular; contrition; general confession; Jansenism; penance; penance service, communal; Reconciliation, liturgy of; sacrament; satisfaction; sin.

Bibliography

Dallen, J. *The Reconciling Community: The Rite of Penance.* New York: Pueblo, 1986.
Gula, R. *To Walk Together Again: The Sacrament of Reconciliation.* New York, Paulist Press, 1984.
Kennedy, R. J., ed. *Reconciliation: The Continuing Agenda.* Collegeville, MN: Liturgical Press, 1987.
Orsy, L. *The Evolving Church and the Sacrament of Penance.* Danville, NJ: Dimension Books, 1978.
Osborne, K. *Reconciliation and Justification.* New York: Paulist Press, 1990.   KENAN OSBORNE

Reconciliation, liturgy of, ordinarily refers to the rite of Penance promulgated in 1973. The rite has three distinct ritual forms. The first is the reconciliation of individual penitents; the second, the reconciliation of several penitents with individual confession and absolution; and the third, the reconciliation of several penitents with general confession and absolution. Although early witnesses testify to the Eucharist as the premier liturgy of Reconciliation, current popular Catholic parlance would more often refer to the liturgy of Reconciliation as the rite of Penance in one of its threefold sacramental expressions. Less often would it refer to nonsacramental prayer services with a penitential theme but without sacramental confession and absolution, which were included in an appendix in the 1973 reformed rite of Penance.

The four parts of penance (contrition, confession, act of penance or satisfaction, and absolution) are operative within each of the three official forms of the liturgy of Reconciliation. Contrition is the heartfelt desire in the life of conversion to turn from the darkness of sin to the light of Christ. Confession refers to that part of the rite when the penitent, moved by the inner attitude of contrition, expresses in honest and coherent language the ways in which he or she has participated in the darkness of sin since the last celebration of the sacrament. The priest proposes the act of penance or satisfaction; the penitent accepts the penance as an exercise to amend conduct, repair injury, or restore order. Absolution, the tangible expression of God's forgiveness, includes two simultaneous parts: the imposition of the priest's hands on the penitent's head (or at least the extending of the priest's right hand over the penitent's head) and the priest's praying of the prescribed absolution formulary that affirms God as the agent of forgiveness, Christ as its means, and the Church's minister as its mediation.

The Rite for Individuals: The rite for individual penitents is made up of six moments: (1) the reception of the penitent by way of the priest's greeting, a sign of the cross, and an invitation to contrition and trust in God; (2) a reading of the word of God that the confessor or the penitent chooses; although this reading is optional, it is encouraged, if only a sentence from Scripture read from the text or recalled from memory; (3) the penitent's confession of sins and acceptance of an act of penance or satisfaction that the priest assigns or both determine in light of the penitent's need or circumstance; (4) the prayer of the penitent expressing sorrow for sin in a fixed form (act of contrition) or spontaneous words of the penitent's own choosing; (5) the priest's praying of the formula of absolution with imposition of hands; and (6) a proclamation of praise of God and a farewell or dismissal.

While face-to-face exchange between the penitent and priest in a reconciliation room is encouraged, the revised rite retains the option for a private confession in a confessional box or behind a confessional screen to secure anonymity. This option continues to serve as a necessary form in response to pastoral need. However, several empirical studies have noted a marked decline in its use well before the revised rite's promulgation. Critics of the rite claim it reinforces the larger culture's tendency to individualism and privatization, securing a sense of personal sin as one's own private affair and thus limiting the penitent's awareness of participation in sinful social structures and the sinful condition of the world.

The Rites for Groups: More frequently used is the rite for several penitents with individual confession and absolution. Custom has situated its celebration during Advent and Lent, although it is not restricted to those seasons. The second rite is similar to the first with some variance due to its public nature: (1) introductory rites (song, greeting, opening prayer); (2) the celebration of the word of God (first reading, responsorial psalm, second reading, gospel acclamation, Gospel, homily, examination of conscience); (3) the rite of Reconciliation itself (call to penance, prayer of contrition or confiteor, litany of forgiveness, the Lord's Prayer, closing prayer); (4) individual confession and absolution; (5) the proclamation of praise for God's mercy; (6) a concluding prayer of thanksgiving; (7) the concluding rite (blessing and dismissal). This rite is favored because of the communal experience and expression of solidarity in sin and grace. Reservations about the rite concern the often limited time for individual confession, which minimizes opportunity for ample exchange between the priest and penitent.

Least frequently used is the rite for several penitents with general confession and absolution. The rite is permitted in two cases: in danger of death when there is no time for the priest(s) to hear confessions of individual penitents (soldiers going off to battle, for example) and in circumstances of serious necessity (too many penitents and too few priests to hear confessions within a reasonable span of time, thus depriving people of sacramental grace or the Eucharist for an extended period of time). Ecclesiastical restrictions discourage the celebration of this rite. Its shape is almost the same as the second, with the omission of individual confession and absolution and the inclusion of a communal act of penance, an act of contrition, the Lord's Prayer, and the extended absolution formulary provided for this occasion. In addition to the three rites, a short rite is provided in dire situations of emergency or accident in which the short form of the absolution is sufficient.

No other sacrament historically witnesses to the intensity of development in liturgical forms and expression as do the liturgies of Reconciliation that make up the rite of Penance. The Church faces another critical historical juncture. Negotiating this transition successfully will demand adaptation of current rites in response to the continuing pastoral need in people's lives to express Christ's forgiveness and reconciliation in sacrament. *See also* Reconciliation.

Bibliography

Dallen, James. *The Reconciling Community: The Rite of Penance.* New York: Pueblo Publishing, 1986.

Gula, Richard. *To Walk Together Again: The Sacrament of Reconciliation.* New York: Paulist Press, 1984.   DANIEL P. GRIGASSY

reconciliation room, or chapel, a space in the main body of a church where the rite of Penance in its first form (Individual Confession of One Penitent) is celebrated. Located near the baptismal area, the room is designed to safeguard the penitent's anonymity or to allow the option of an informal face-to-face exchange between the penitent and the priest. It is furnished with two chairs, a fixed grill or screen and a kneeler, and a table with a simple cross and a Bible. The two options for reconciliation should be immediately recognizable to the penitent entering the room. Never a multipurpose room, but a space solely for the prayerful celebration of the sacrament, it is more appropriately called the reconciliation chapel. *See also* confession, auricular; confessional.

rector, title for the supervising office of a religious institution. The title of rector is used with reference to a church, chapel, cathedral, school, or religious house. In the United States, a rector commonly refers to a priest who has the pastoral responsibility for the cathedral parish. It is often used in Europe for the head of a school.

recusancy (Lat., *recusare,* "to refuse"), adherence to the Roman Catholic Church in Anglican England.

In 1559, the Uniformity Act, issued by Queen Elizabeth I, made attendance at services of the Established Church mandatory for all subjects of the English monarch. Those who refused to attend such services, recusants, were subject to large fines. Later versions of the law added further penalities, such as confiscation of land and denial of burial in consecrated ground. The crime of recusancy for not attending the services of the Church of England was abolished by the Catholic Relief Act of 1791. *See also* England, Catholicism in.

redeemer (Lat., *redimere,* "buy back"), literally one who buys back property that has been sold or a relative who has been enslaved (Lev 25:23–26; 48–49). Metaphorically, when used of God (Job 19:25; Pss 19:14; 78:35; Isa 41:14; 49:26), it takes on the nuance of one who rescues a person from oppression or some other grave danger (Exod 6:6; 15:13; Pss 25:22; 26:11; 119:34–35; Jer 15:21; Mic 4:10). In the NT Jesus is never called "redeemer," but his saving work is described as "redemption" (Luke 2:38; 21:28; Rom 3:24; 8:23; 1 Cor 1:30, Eph 1:7, 14; 4:30; Heb 9:12). It is also related to the notion of "ransom" or the price paid to free a slave (Exod 21:8; Mark 10:45; 1 Tim 2:6). Irenaeus (ca. 130–ca. 200) and Origen (ca. 185–ca. 254) developed the theory that the human race was enslaved by Satan and that the death of Jesus was the "price" of release. This theory remained popular until it was replaced by the satisfaction theory of Anselm (ca. 1033–1109). Today "redeemer" and "redemption" have lost their technical sense and are used for the saving action of God conceived often as rescue from human alienation or from evil social structures. *See also* redemption.

redemption (Lat., *redemptio,* "buying back"), God's saving activity through Christ in delivering humankind from sin and evil. Unlike the doctrine of the one person of the Son of God in two natures (divine and human), the redemption Christ effected for all did not provoke theological debate and teachings from general councils during the first centuries of the Church's existence. From NT times on, it was taken for granted that it was only through Christ that human beings could be saved (Acts 4:12), and that the purpose of everything from his Incarnation to his Second Coming was, as the creeds stated, "for us and for our salvation." The Fathers of the Church, in particular the Greek Fathers, often used the belief that human beings had been healed and divinized through the Incarnation (and Cross) of the Son of God as a premise from which to argue that he must therefore have become fully human by assuming a complete human nature (and not just a body). Since he was fully human and fully divine, Christ could act as mediator between God and the human race in effecting redemption.

Creation and Redemption: The NT associated God's redemptive work with creation by acknowledging Christ to be not only the redeemer but also the agent through whom all things were originally made (John 1:3, 10; 1 Cor 8:6; Col 1:16; Heb 1:2). Redemption entails "a new creation" (2 Cor 5:17; see Rev 21:1–5). The biblical vision of Irenaeus (d. ca. 200) held together the orders of creation and redemption as two distinguishable but inseparable moments in God's one saving plan for all humanity. John Duns Scotus (d. 1308), Pierre Teilhard de Chardin (d. 1955), and others maintained the unity in God's creative and redemptive work—a unity challenged by the view encouraged by Athanasius of Alexandria (d. 373), Thomas Aquinas (d. 1274), and others that if human beings had not sinned, the Second Person of the Trinity would not have come among humanity. Vatican II's Pastoral Constitution on the Church in the Modern World (*Gaudium et Spes, 1965*) linked creation and redemption by describing redemption as God's renewing of creation (n. 9), and presenting Christ as being actively present in the whole, universal work of salvation from creation to the end (n. 45). Paul VI's apostolic exhortation *Evangelii Nuntiandi* (On Evangelization in the Modern World) of 1975 expounded the divine redemptive work as beginning during the life of Christ, being definitively accomplished by his death and Resurrection, and realized fully at his final coming (n. 9). But in his first encyclical, *Redemptor Hominis* ("Redeemer of Humankind," 1979), John Paul II returned to the vision of *Gaudium et Spes* by explaining redemption as the renewal of creation (n. 9).

The Nature of Redemption: Through the centuries official Church teaching has rarely addressed directly the issue of redemption. Even Vatican II's summary of Christ's redemptive work (Pastoral Constitution on the Church in the Modern World, n. 22) occurs "indirectly"—reaffirming teachings on the dignity of the human person. Faith in Christ as redeemer of the human race has usually been accepted by all Christians. Such issues as original sin (see, e.g., the Pelagian controversy in the fifth century), the ecclesial nature of grace and the axiom

"outside the Church no salvation," the issue of predestination of the elect, and the Council of Trent's teachings on justification and on the Mass as a sacrifice that "re-presents" the bloody, once-and-for-all sacrifice of Calvary inevitably introduced teaching on redemption—at least under the aspect of its subjective appropriation.

The objective dimension of redemption has been expressed by the Church's Scriptures, liturgy (see, e.g., the *Exultet,* or Easter Proclamation) and theology in three characteristic ways: (1) as Christ the second Adam conquering the power of sin, death, and all evil, and so through a new exodus liberating fallen human beings for new and eternal life (1 Cor 15: 25, 54–57, Col 2:15: 1 John 3:8); (2) as Christ the great high priest expiating sin and cleansing human defilement through his sacrificial death and Resurrection (Rom 3:24–25; Heb 2:17–18); and (3) as Christ the universal mediator whose act of reconciliation has brought humanity a new covenant of love with God and one another (Rom 5:6–8, 10; 2 Cor 5:18–20; Heb 9:15). In these terms Christian visual art, hymns, and poetry have persistently interpreted Jesus' Cross as the flag or standard of victory, the means of atonement, and the great sign of divine love toward humankind.

The NT recognizes that redemption through Christ embraces not only the human race but also the cosmos. Christ has reconciled all things to God—a reconciliation to be consummated at the end of history (Col 1:20; Rom 8:18–23). Such recent Church teaching as John Paul II's *Redemptor Hominis* recalls that the whole world shares the human need for final recreation (n. 8).

Along with the Bible, the official texts from the Church's public worship, together with popular devotions, offer the fullest range of concepts, symbols, images, and narratives in response to those who ask: What is redemption? When and where did and does it occur? Who brought and brings it? The liturgy bears witness, above all, to the utter centrality of Christ (and his Holy Spirit) in the work of humanity's redemption, which has brought to humankind justification, adoption as God's sons and daughters, incorporation into the Body of Christ, the gift of the Holy Spirit, and a divinized existence that lets human beings share in the life of the tripersonal God. *See also* atonement, doctrine of; Christology; crucifixion; expiation; Resurrection of Christ; sacrifice; salvation.

Bibliography

O'Collins, Gerald. *Interpreting Jesus.* New York: Paulist Press, 1983.

Schillebeeckx, Edward. *Christ: The Experience of Jesus as Lord.* Trans. John Bowden. New York: Seabury Press, 1980.

GERALD O'COLLINS

Redemptor Hominis (ray-demp'tohr hom'ee-nees; Lat., "Redeemer of Humankind"), first encyclical letter of Pope John Paul II, issued on March 4, 1979. The letter emphasizes the gospel's affirmation of the "worth and dignity" of the human person, rooted in the redemption (n. 10). At the same time, it acknowledges the threat posed by the abuse of technology and modern means of production, which so often involve the "exploitation of the earth" and the destruction of the environment (n. 15). The document is especially strong in its condemnation of consumerism, that is, the accumulation and misuse of goods by privileged social classes and rich countries "to an excessive degree" (n. 16). It also condemns the arms race, which diverts essential resources from the poor, as well as the widespread violation of human rights around the world (n. 17).

Redemptoris Mater (ray-dem-tohr'is mah'tair; Lat., "Mother of the Redeemer"), sixth encyclical letter of Pope John Paul II, issued on March 25, 1987, in preparation for the Marian year (June 7, 1987–August 15, 1988).

Redemptorists, Congregation of the Most Holy Redeemer (C.SS.R.), an order founded in Naples, Italy, by Alphonsus Liguori in 1732 and approved by Pope Benedict XIV in 1749. A community of Redemptorist nuns was similarly approved in 1750. Members take the three traditional vows of poverty, chastity, and obedience and add a fourth of perseverance.

The congregation was originally founded to work with poor and abandoned Catholics in remote districts of the Italy. Their main work is retreats, parish missions, and foreign missions. Following the example of their founder, they have made significant contributions in the area of moral theology, reflected in the work of Bernard Häring. Asceticism, prayer, a commitment to community living and apostolic works are the hallmarks of the Redemptorists. The generalate is located in Rome. There are three American provinces (Baltimore, Maryland; St. Louis, Missouri; and Oakland, California) and two vice-provinces (New Orleans, Louisiana; and Richmond, Virginia). *See also* Alphonsus Liguori, St.; Häring, Bernard.

red hat, the wide-brimmed red hat with tassels that was conferred upon a newly appointed cardinal at a public consistory. It was not used again during his lifetime. At his death, the hat was hung from the ceiling of the cathedral church. The practice of conferring the red hat was discontinued in 1967. *See also* cardinal.

Red Mass, a votive Mass of the Holy Spirit offered to invoke wisdom and guidance during the coming term of a school, legislative, or judicial year. The custom originated in thirteenth-century Europe with members of the legal profession, receiving its name from the red vestments worn by presiding clergy and the scarlet robes donned by judges and academicians in attendance.

reduction of wills. *See* wills [canon law].

Reformation, the, political and religious event in the sixteenth century that divided the Western Christian Church into Catholic and Protestant.

The fourteenth and fifteenth centuries were among the darkest in the history of the Church in the West. The papal monarchy that had developed in the twelfth and thirteenth centuries had become a bloated bureaucracy with an insatiable appetite for money and power. The disaster of the Avignon papacy (1305–78) and the Great Schism (1378–1417) brought the papacy into such disrepute that the councils of Constance (1414–18) and Basel (1431–39) sought to replace it as head of the Church. During these years the clergy became increasingly corrupt. Church offices (benefices) were for sale. Careerists accumulated numbers of benefices (pluralism) that made it impossible to serve them all personally (absenteeism). Ill-paid substitutes who were often uneducated and negligent provided for the needs of the people. Clerical immorality, greed, and arrogance were blamed for what was perceived as a religious decline. The need for reform was universally acknowledged but was thwarted by the self-interest of the hierarchy and of secular rulers who profited by the abuses. As a result, popular dissatisfaction and anticlericalism assumed threatening proportions, creating a powder keg awaiting the spark of Martin Luther.

Central and Northern Europe: In 1517 Luther posted his Ninety-five Theses against indulgences. Though the theses themselves were rather conservative, in the months and years that followed Luther developed a theological critique of the Catholic Church that denied any human contribution to

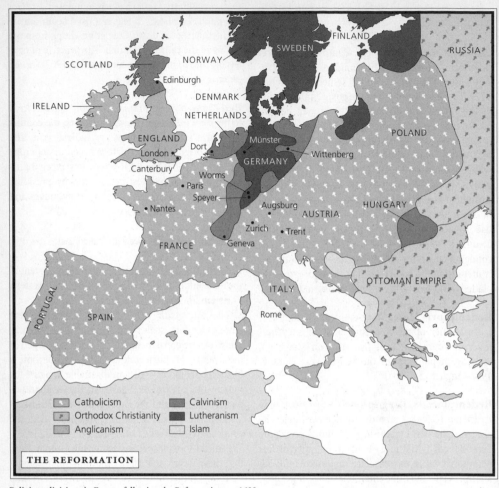

THE REFORMATION

Religious divisions in Europe following the Reformation, ca. 1600.

salvation, the Catholic teaching on the sacraments, papal authority, the Catholic priesthood, monasticism, the cult of the saints, and the right of the hierarchy to interpret Scripture. Unlike earlier reformers Luther saw the problems of the Church as primarily theological, not moral. By arguing that the corrupt state of the Church was simply the product of false doctrine, Luther provided an ideological weapon that undermined the Catholic Church's authority, opening the door for wide-reaching theological, institutional, and spiritual change. In Germany Luther's message fell on fertile soil. He was viewed as a liberator from foreign papal domination and exploitation. A popular movement spread rapidly through Germany in the 1520s. Churches and Church property were seized. Monks, nuns, and

priests who did not join the reform were expelled. The Catholic liturgy was revised and the sacraments reduced to only two: the Lord's Supper and Baptism. Fearful of the social unrest (especially after the Peasants' War in 1524–25 and the Anabaptist Kingdom of Münster in the mid-1530s) local princes and city councils coopted the movement and proceeded to construct territorial or city-state churches. In Sweden, Olaus Petri, a married priest who had studied at Wittenberg, began preaching Lutheranism in 1519. The new king Gustavus Vasa adopted the new movement with the support of most of the bishops. In 1527 the Swedish church broke with Rome, and in 1544 the kingdom became officially Lutheran, though the episcopal form of church government under the king's rule was retained. Denmark followed in 1536. When Denmark conquered Norway the same settlement was imposed, as it was in Iceland.

Alongside the Lutheran movement in northern Europe and northern and central Germany, there arose a competing Protestant movement in the cities of southern Germany and Switzerland. Beginning with Ulrich Zwingli in Zurich and achieving its classic form under John Calvin in Geneva, this Reformed Protestantism agreed with Lutheranism on most points, e.g., justification by faith alone and the role of Scripture. But the Reformed were more radical in their demands, rejecting all of Catholic worship as idolatry, emphasizing predestination, and instituting a rigorous system of religious and moral discipline. In 1525 the Reformed and the Lutherans divided over the interpretation of the Eucharist. Calvinism spread down the Rhine to the Netherlands where it became wedded to a movement for national independence from the Spanish crown. Charles V and his successor, Philip II, had been particularly uncompromising in the suppression of heresy, particularly during the regency of the Duke of Alva (1567–73). The northern provinces (Holland) achieved their independence in 1584 after Calvinism had been accepted at a synod at Dort (1574). Despite its Calvinism, Holland became one of the few places in Europe to allow religious diversity.

A third stream of Protestantism is usually referred to as the Radical Reformation. The largest segment, the Anabaptists (the ancestors of modern Baptists and Mennonites) rejected infant Baptism, insisting that only those who had faith be baptized. Anabaptists were condemned as heretics by Protestants and Catholics alike. More than fifty thousand were executed in the sixteenth century.

The existence of Protestantism created a political problem. The Edict of Worms in 1521 had made Protestantism illegal. Nonetheless, many princes and city-states became Protestant in the 1520s, making enforcement of the ban impossible. Fearing war, the Imperial Diet of Speyer in 1526 issued a new edict that left enforcement of the Edict of Worms to individual princes and cities, in effect granting toleration to the Protestants. In 1529, again at Speyer, that toleration was rescinded, a move that provoked a "Protestation" from which "Protestantism" gets its name. After Charles V invited and then rejected Protestant confessions of faith at Augsburg in the following year, the Protestants formed the military and political Schmalkaldic League. Frus-

trated in his attempts to reach a compromise and momentarily freed from outside distractions, Charles V finally launched the Schmalkaldic War (1545–46). The Protestants were defeated and forced to accept a compromise religious settlement, the Augsburg Interim. Popular resistance rendered the Interim ineffective, however. In the Princes' War (1552–53) the Protestants struck back. The Peace of Augsburg (1555) divided the empire into Protestant and Catholic territories and brought peace until the Thirty Years' War (1618–48).

England: The course of the Reformation in England was idiosyncratic. Though there were disciples of Luther at the universities and coastal cities already in the 1520s, it was the desire of King Henry VIII to divorce Catherine of Aragon that gave the early impetus. Henry broke with Rome and had himself declared the head of the Church in England (1534). This was followed by the dissolution of the monasteries (1535–40). Though Henry and many of his bishops and courtiers remained Catholic in doctrine and practice, Protestantism spread, fostered by the prime minister Thomas Cromwell. Nonetheless, Henry executed Protestants as heretics at the same time as he executed Catholics (e.g., Thomas More, John Fisher) as traitors. Under Henry's son Edward VI (1547–53) Protestantism became the official religion with both English (Thomas Cranmer, Nicholas Ridley, Hugh Latimer) and foreign (Martin Butzer, Peter Martyr Vermigli) leaders. A new liturgy—*The Book of Common Prayer* (1549, 1552)—and Forty-Two Articles of faith (1553) were promulgated. The Catholic "Bloody Mary" (1553–58) reinstated the Catholic hierarchy and the Mass. Protestantism was outlawed and she executed 273 men and women, among whom were 5 bishops (including Cranmer, Ridley, and Latimer). Many others fled abroad. Protestant Elizabeth I (1558–1603) and parliament issued the Acts of Supremacy and Uniformity (1559), which maintained the episcopal organization of the church but placed it under the headship of the throne. Both the reissued *Book of Common Prayer* and the revised Thirty-Nine Articles were a compromise between conservative Anglicans and radical Protestants (Puritans), many of whom had returned from exile in Reformed Protestant centers. The tensions between these two branches of the national church would lead to civil war in the seventeenth century. In Scotland John Knox introduced a Calvinist church order (1560–61) and a simple Reformed liturgy (1564).

France: Protestantism made little headway in the 1520s and 1530s in France, but under the guidance of John Calvin and Theodore Beza, the Huguenots grew rapidly in the early 1550s. The first Reformed congregation in Paris appeared in 1555 and by 1559 the city saw France's first Calvinist National Synod. The Catholic forces were powerful, however, and France was torn asunder by the Wars of Religion (1562–94). Henry IV, a Protestant who had returned to Catholicism in order to hold his throne, issued the Edict of Nantes (1598) granting Protestants toleration. Never more than a strong minority, their numbers slowly dwindled until Louis XIV revoked the edict in 1685, when most fled or went underground.

Eastern Europe: Bohemia (the former Czechoslovakia) proved fertile ground for Protestantism, given its Hussite heritage, and it spread widely among the nobles and city dwellers. The defeat of White Mountain (1620) at the hands of the Habsburgs resulted in the crushing of the movement, though some remnants remained to rise again in the eighteenth and nineteenth centuries. Hungary was influenced first by students of Luther and Melanchthon (Synod of Erdöd, 1545) and then by Calvinism, the Calvinists and Lutherans winning religious toleration by force of arms in 1606. Poland was introduced to Lutheranism already in 1518. After 1540 Calvinism also spread. King Sigismund Augustus (1548–72) favored Protestantism. It achieved its high-water mark at the Synod of Sendomir (1570). Divisions among the Protestants, however, and the pressure of the Catholic Counter-Reformation thoroughly undermined the movement by the seventeenth century. *See also* Counter-Reformation/Catholic Reformation; Protestantism.

Bibliography

Dickens, A. G. *The English Reformation.* University Park, PA: Pennsylvania State University Press, 1991.

Kingdon, Robert M. *Geneva and the Coming of the Wars of Religion 1555–1563.* Geneva: Librairie E. Droz, 1956.

Ozment, Steven. *The Age of Reform, 1250–1550.* New Haven, CT: Yale University Press, 1980.   R. EMMET MCLAUGHLIN

Reformed churches, in general, all Christian churches whose beliefs have been shaped by the Reformation, but specifically those Protestant churches that have adhered in some manner to John Calvin's teachings, especially regarding the Lord's Supper. These churches, frequently also called "Presbyterian," stand separate from the Lutheran churches. In this specific sense, there are numerous associations of Reformed churches throughout the world, including the Church of Scotland, Germany's Reformed Alliance, which formed the Confessing Church during the Third Reich, the Hungarian Reformed Church, the Netherlands Reformed Church, the Presbyterian Church of Ireland, the Reformed Church of France (also known as the French Calvinists or Huguenots), the Swiss Reformed Church, and in the United States and Canada the Reformed and Presbyterian churches. Reformed and Presbyterian churches also exist throughout Africa and Asia. *See also* Calvinism; Protestantism; Reformation, the.

Reformed Church of America, Protestant denomination also known as the Dutch Reformed Church. It was originally brought to what is now the state of New York by colonial settlers from Holland, where it began in 1571 in conformity with the teachings of John Calvin (d. 1564). Formally established in the colonies by Jonas Michaelius in 1628, it became independent from the church governing body (classis) in the Netherlands in 1754. It founded Queens College, now Rutgers University, in 1792. In 1867 it officially changed its name from "Reformed Protestant Dutch Church" to "Reformed Church of America." In the second half of the nineteenth century, the new Dutch immigrants to the midwestern United States established congregations of the Reformed Church that tended to be more doctrinally conservative than the congregations on the East Coast that dated from the colonial period. Today, the Reformed Church sponsors Hope College (Holland, Michigan) and Central College (Pella, Iowa). *See also* Calvinism; Protestantism; Reformation, the.

Regensburg. *See* Ratisbon, Conference of.

Regimini Ecclesiae Universae (rej-i'meen-ee ek-klayz'ee-ay *oo*n-ee-vair'say; Lat., "On the governing of the universal Church"), apostolic constitution, promulgated by Pope Paul VI on August 15, 1967, reforming and modernizing the Roman Curia. It decreed some changes of names, e.g., Propaganda Fide became the Congregation for the Evangelization of Peoples; new curial appointments were limited to a five-year term; all prelates, including cardinals, were to resign at age seventy-five; all offices were to lapse upon the death of a pope; the main modern languages were to be used in official documents; and all curial departments were declared juridically equal (n. 1, sec. 2), although the Secretariat of State was assigned the task of overall coordination (n. 19, sec. 1). *See also* Roman Curia.

Regina, St., second-century virgin and martyr. Regina was imprisoned, tortured, and beheaded when she refused to marry a pagan, sacrifice to idols, and deny her faith. Feast day: September 7.

Regina Coeli (reh-jee'nah chay'lee; Lat., "Queen of Heaven"), an ancient title that honors Mary as Queen of Heaven and emphasizes her role as queenly intercessor. Because she is Mother of God, Mary is queen of the kingdom of God. The feast of the queenship of Mary is celebrated on May 31. *Regina Coeli* is also the title of an anthem to the Blessed Virgin recited during the Easter season in place of the Angelus. It probably dates from the twelfth century; its author is unknown. *See also* Queen of Heaven.

Reginald of Piperno, ca. 1230–90, Dominican, companion and secretary of Thomas Aquinas, responsible for compiling, from Thomas's earlier writings, the "Supplement" to the unfinished *Summa Theologiae. See also Summa Theologiae.*

regulae iuris (reg'oo-lay yoor'ees; Lat., "rules of law"), rules developed to aid the interpretation and application of canon law.

Regula Magistri (reg'oo-lah maj-is'-tree; Lat., "Rule of the Master"), a monastic rule written in the vicinity of Rome in the first quarter of the sixth century. Benedict of Nursia (d. ca. 550) incorporated considerable portions of it into his own monastic rule but avoided the anonymous "Master's" wordiness and his extreme suspicion of human nature. *See also* Benedict, Rule of St.

reign of God. *See* kingdom of God.

reincarnation, a doctrine held by various religions and philosophies that generally includes belief in the preexistence of the soul prior to its union with the body and the soul's return to life after death in some other human or nonhuman form, perhaps depending on the deeds of the prior life. Reincarnation differs considerably from Christian doctrine, which teaches the eschatological resurrection of the body, in which ultimate personal destiny is inseparable from one's original integrity of body and spirit. Reincarnation may presume a different conception of the soul, i.e., as a life force or energy rather than as the center of individual identity. Reincarnation is particularly incompatible with Aquinas's doctrine of hylomorphism, which asserts that the soul is the form of the body. Reincarnation often accompanies cyclical models of history rather than the Christian eschatological understanding of history, which envisions history moving toward a final consummation. The latter coincides with Christian doctrines of individual and general judgment, which attribute eternal significance to human decision in one's life. In spite of these difficulties, assertions of total incompatibility should be moderated by awareness that both the doctrine of purgatory and the concept of reincarnation attempt to allow for a process of purification after death. *See also* hylomorphism; immortality; soul.

relativism, the view that morality varies according to differences in cultural or individual attitudes. There are two broad types of relativism. Cultural relativism points out the differences in moral norms from one culture to another and draws the conclusion that no moral norm is objectively correct for all cultures. Individual relativism, sometimes called "subjectivism," avers that the moral rightness of an action depends on conformity with one's motives at a particular time and place. On this view, an action that is wrong for someone in one situation can be right in another situation, even when the morally relevant circumstances are the same. *See also* situation ethics.

relativity, Albert Einstein's (1879–1955) theory revolutionizing previously held concepts of space and time. The strongly confirmed special theory (1905) weds space to time in a four-dimensional space-time continuum such that measurements of distance and duration vary according to the observer's motion: there is no absolute length or time scale. The general theory (1916), still undergoing crucial testing, constitutes a revision of Isaac Newton's (1642–1727) theory of gravitation and implies this space-time continuum is curved. *See also* eternity; space; time.

relics (Lat., *reliquiae*, "remains"), in the strict sense, material remains of the bodies of canonized and beatified saints; in a wider sense, those things used by canonized or beatified persons during their lifetime or objects that have touched their material remains (cans. 1186–90). The old Code of Canon Law (1917) further distinguished major relics (whole body, head, arm, hand, heart, tongue, or part of the body that suffered martyrdom) from minor relics (can. 1281.2).

In the early Church, relics emerged alongside the development of the cult of saints/martyrs. On saints' feast days, Eucharists were celebrated at their graves. In the sixth century, martyrs' bones became required elements in church altars (see can. 1237.2). This mandate led to the transfer and division of remains.

Medieval theologians drew careful distinctions between the worship (Gk., *latria*) appropriate to God and the veneration (*dulia*) appropriate to saints. They further distinguished the *cultus absolutus* (reverence paid to God and to God through saints) from the *cultus relativus* (honor paid to things related to the holy person). These distinctions were often inoperative in the Church at large, however, where relics were thought to possess an inherent power parallel to Christ's redemptive act.

Sixteenth-century Reformers opposed the veneration of relics, seeing them as images prohibited in the OT. The Council of Trent (1545–63) reaffirmed Catholic practice but encouraged bishops to avoid past extremes. Vatican II's Constitution on the Sacred Liturgy (1963) articulated the place of relics, relative to the mysteries of salvation (n. 111). *See also* reliquary; saints.   CATHERINE MURPHY

religious, a member of a religious institute, i.e., a group of individuals who live life together as brothers or sisters and publicly profess religious vows. Religious vows are the evangelical counsels of poverty, chastity, and obedience.

There is considerable variation in the manner of living the vows and of sharing the common life depending not only on the particular purpose of a religious community but also upon its historical development. Although a religious may be either a layperson or an ordained minister within the Church, canon law applies many of the rules of clerical conduct to religious. The reason for this is that a religious, by public profession of vows, is seen to represent the Church in a way not unlike that of a public minister of the Church.

Together with the obligations they have assumed, religious have certain rights, especially within their communities. Chief among these is the right to the common life, i.e., the life of sharing as sisters or brothers, considered one of the essential elements of religious life. Once finally professed, a religious cannot be dismissed from the community or denied community rights without cause and proper process. *See also* counsels, evangelical; religious life; vows.

religious education. There is little consensus about the precise meaning of the widely used term "religious education." Specifically, it designates an academic and school-based study of religious tradition(s). Its pedagogy is more intellectual inquiry than religious socialization; its intent is more sympathetic understanding than confessional commitment. In this sense, religious education is clearly distinct from "catechesis" or "Christian education," the favored Catholic and Protestant terms for forming people in Christian identity.

This distinct meaning suggests a convenient division of labor between parish and school and would seem to encourage rigorous and critical study without confessional interest or restraint. It is clearly helpful in a social context like Britain where "religious education" is a required discipline in the curriculum of government-supported schools but where the law (1944) mandates an academic study of various religions and forbids any attempt to influence people's religious identity.

However, this specifically academic meaning also reflects the myth of objective and disinterested knowledge and presumes a dichotomy between "knowing" and "being," as if religious study is not to impinge on people's lives. Furthermore, posing catechesis as nonscholarly and nonreflective tends to forget the Catholic wisdom that faith is deepened by understanding and that revelation is enhanced by reason.

The more generic meaning of "religious education" refers to the whole educational enterprise of enabling people to learn about, to learn from, and to learn to be religious persons by studying religious tradition(s). When religious education is sponsored by a particular tradition or denomination, as is typical in the United States, it can be further designated as, e.g., "Christian," or "Jewish," or "Muslim" religious education. However, all particular expressions reflect the common intent to inform and form people in faith by studying the traditional ways of being religious.

As a generic term, "religious education" signals that the general enterprise and specific instances should be good "education" that draw from educational research and literature to inform practice (a value not carried by the term "catechesis"); that there should be an ecumenical bond and partnership between all efforts to educate people religiously; and that it should avoid the pretext of value-free study and recognize that all religious education should inform and form people's religious identity.

All religious traditions do "religious education" in one way or another; from the beginning, Christianity believed it had the mandate of the Risen Christ to "go therefore . . . and teach. . ." (Matt 28:19–20). As a field of study and research, however, religious education is relatively new and its formal beginnings are typically linked with the founding of the Religious Education Association in 1904. Under the initiative of William Rainey Harper, and with many of the academic leaders of the era as founding members, the REA stated its purpose as: "to inspire the religious forces of our country with the educational ideal; to inspire the educational forces of our country with the religious ideal." This still-urgent purpose continues to be carried on by the Religious Education Association today. *See also* catechesis.

THOMAS GROOME

Religious Formation Conference, formerly the Sister Formation Conference, founded in 1953, a national organization providing initial and ongoing intellectual and spiritual formation for men and women religious through an annual national congress and newsletter, *In-Formation*.

religious house. *See* religious life.

religious institute, a group approved by competent Church authority who live in community and profess the public vows of poverty, chastity, and obedience. A religious institute may be of diocesan right (mainly under the authority of the local bishop) or pontifical right (for the most part under the direct authority of Rome). It may be clerical (founded to be engaged in the work of ordained ministry) or lay (founded for a number of works, but excluding that of ordained ministry). It may be contemplative (devoted mainly to the pursuit of prayer) or active (given to the works of the apostolate).

Canon law has a considerable number of regulations concerning the foundation, supervision, and administration of religious institutes. In addition, each institute has its own norms approved by Church authority. One of the major goals continued from the post–Vatican II reforms into the current canon law is to allow each institute the freedom needed to live out its own particular identity. *See also* counsels, evangelical; religious orders and congregations; secular institute; society of apostolic life.

religious law. *See* religious life.

religious liberty, the freedom to exercise one's religious beliefs, even in the public forum, according to one's conscience. Catholic understanding of the problem of religious freedom has developed through three stages. In the first stage, extending up until Pope Pius IX's "Syllabus of Errors" in 1864, Catholic teaching held that the establishment of Catholicism as the official state religion was the only acceptable arrangement between Church and state. Pius IX listed as error no. 77 this statement: "It is no longer expedient that the Catholic religion should be treated as the only religion of the state, all other forms of worship whatever being excluded."

This statement, suggesting that Catholicism be the only official religion in every state, struck many commentators as excessive. This inaugurated the second stage of Catholic thought on religious liberty. The French bishop, Félix Dupanloup, qualified Pope Pius's statement in a commentary that developed a "thesis-hypothesis" distinction in the relations between Church and state. The Catholic state is to remain the ideal, or "thesis." Still, historical circumstances might require an altered relationship, or "hypothesis," at least until the situation changes so that a Catholic state is once again a viable option. This allowed for the toleration of the arrangements in the United States, Latin America, and Belgium.

The American Jesuit John Courtney Murray (d. 1967) is the person most responsible for the shift from the second to the third stages of Catholic teaching on religious liberty. His argument was that a variety of Church-state arrangements, with no one arrangement being preferable, best protects the freedom of the Church. Which arrangement is best in a particular instance depends upon the concrete historical circumstances. In a pluralistic society like that in the United States, the best arrangement is one of constitutionally protected religious liberty. Any attempt to bring about a Catholic state would provoke a backlash that would limit the freedom of the Church.

Thus religious freedom, for Murray, is a protection against interference by the state and other associations in the practice of religious communities. It is, in Murray's words, "simply a negative, namely, immunity from coercion in religious matters." Religious freedom "contains no positive evaluation of the religious phenomenon in any of its manifestations. It simply defines the immunity of these manifestations from interference."

In making his case for religious liberty, Murray is careful not to condemn earlier teaching. His approach is to place such teaching in its historical context. Earlier cases for a Catholic state were legitimate because the populace was not ready to be self-directing, and thus needed a paternal government. However, persons are now more literate and capable, and therefore more aware of their human dignity. This required a development in Church teaching. The development occurred in Vatican II's Declaration on Religious Freedom (1965), for which Murray himself was largely responsible. *See also* Church and state; Declaration on Religious Freedom; Murray, John Courtney. TODD D. WHITMORE

religious life, a way of living the Christian life that includes communal living and the profession of the public vows of poverty, chastity, and obedience in a community approved by competent Church authority. Religious life has a rich history of development that produced various models, many of which continue today. The forms include (1) the monastic life, in which the community lives together and is bound by the celebration of the Liturgical Hours; (2) the mendicant life, which was established to give members more mobility to preach the gospel where needed; and (3) the Counter-Reformation and later apostolic communities, which maintain a major focus on apostolic works. Religious life embraces communities given to the works of the apostolate (preaching, teaching, nursing, publishing, foreign missions, social work, etc.) as well as communities devoted solely to contemplation. Every religious institute has its distinctive mixture of the above elements, and Vatican II (1962–65) called each community to renew itself by rediscovering that founding charism (inspiration) that is its specific distinctive mixture of a particular spirituality, way of life, and work. That special charism is seen as a gift to the Church, not only because of the apostolic work an institute accomplishes, but mainly because of the particular manner in which the way of life itself witnesses to the gospel. This renewal was accompanied by considerable change and tension in many religious communities. At present, however, not only do the older forms of religious life continue, but new forms continue to develop as well.

Religious life is governed by general Church law that applies in principle to each individual religious and to each religious community. It is also governed by particular law, approved by Church authority, which applies to a given religious community and to its members. The laws have as their purpose the protection of the rights of the members, the safeguarding of the ideals of the given community, and the harmony between religious communities and the Church.

The way of life in any religious institute entails prayer in common and private prayer, accountability for the use of material resources (which are all to come from the common fund), participation in social interaction with others in community, doing one's part in work, sharing in the decision-making processes of the group, obedience to the authority of the institute, and observance of the vows. In communities devoted to the apostolate, it also means having involvement in a ministry commissioned by the community.

Some communities are approved by Rome and have a degree of exemption from the authority of the local bishop (of pontifical right), while others have been established by a local bishop who retains a greater role in their governance (of diocesan right). The institutes approved by Rome have a certain degree of autonomy from the local bishop, especially in regard to their internal affairs, while those of diocesan right look to the bishop as a superior even in matters internal to the living of the religious life. Some institutes whose way of life involves the exercise of the ordained ministry are called clerical institutes; others are called lay institutes. *See also* counsels, evangelical; religious institute; religious orders and congregations. JOHN F. LAHEY

religious profession, the pronouncement of vows in a religious institute approved by the Church. These vows consecrate persons to God and make them members of religious community. The person professing vows must be of sufficient age and have had the requisite period of formation in order for the vows to be recognized as valid by the Church. The candidate must be admitted to profession by competent authority and must make the profession freely and without grave fear or fraud. The vows must be received by an authority competent to receive them. Initial religious profession is made for a temporary period of time; final profession for the whole of life. *See also* religious institute; vows.

RELIGIOUS ORDERS AND CONGREGATIONS

Religious orders and congregations are groups living under a religious rule and publicly professing the vows of poverty, chastity, and obedience or their equivalents. Technically, the terms refer to groups who are recognized by Church authorities, are subject to canon law, and have central authority structures. However, there are "noncanonical" groups that are considered under this heading. Equally, the terms are understood to include associations of autonomous monasteries (e.g., the Benedictines) following a common rule. The outdated distinction between "orders" and "congregations" was based on technical differences concerning the status of their vows.

At their most fully developed, religious orders are a Roman Catholic phenomenon. In the Eastern Orthodox churches, a variety of patterns exist within a single monastic tradition. Anglican religious life and the small number of communities within some Reformed churches have not generally developed the centralized features of Roman Catholic orders.

ORIGINS OF RELIGIOUS COMMUNITIES

A visibly distinctive, consecrated life within the Christian community existed from earliest times. Precisely how to define "religious life" is a matter of dispute. Some authorities suggest that celibate community is the common core. However, Celtic monasticism was not exclusively celibate and community life means different things to an enclosed nun and a missionary priest.

Traditionally, religious life is dated to the end of the third century when groups of women and men ascetics retired to the Egyptian desert in search of a purified gospel life-style. They did not see themselves as other than ordinary Christians, living out the full implications of Baptism. Early monasticism was a lay movement. However, there was an earlier tradition of ascetics in the Palestinian and Syrian wilderness. There were also autonomous virgins or widows alongside deaconesses within local Christian congregations at a very early stage. By the fourth century, virgins lived increasingly in communities. Community life under a rule originated in Egypt primarily with Pachomius (ca. 290–ca. 347). The monastic ideal traveled to the West through such Easterners as John Cassian (ca. 365–ca. 435), whose writings, based on the Egyptian tradition, influenced the Rule of St. Benedict.

A SINGLE LINE OF DEVELOPMENT?

It was once thought that religious orders developed in a single line from primitive monasticism to modern international missionary congregations. In that sense, all religious life was a kind of monastic derivative. This view was oversimple.

First, while the Benedictine model (strong abbot, stable residence, centrality of the Liturgy of the Hours) eventually prevailed, early Western monasticism was pluriform. Monastic founders such as Martin of Tours (d. 397) were not in the Benedictine tradition. Celtic monasticism, such as that of Columba (d. 597) on Iona, Cuthbert (d. 687) on Lindisfarne, Hilda (d. 680) at Whitby, and Columbanus (d. 615) in Gaul and Italy, had different values and structures from the well-ordered world of a Benedictine abbey.

Second, there is another ancient stream of religious life in the West, the so-called canonical life. Its nature has often been misunderstood and treated as a subspecies of monasticism. By tradition, Augustine (d. 430) founded the first monastic community at Hippo in North Africa at the end of the fourth century. The rule named after him had considerable influence during the Middle Ages, particularly from the eleventh century. Its spirit contrasted in significant ways with that of the Rule of St. Benedict and was adopted by more active communities such as canons and canonesses, friars and nursing sisters.

Third, an understanding of religious life depends on whether one includes the solitary life. After the early solitaries and single virgins, the solitary life continued in the Western Church although it was not always formally recognized by Church law. The recent revision of canon law (1983) once more gives it a formal status and there has been a striking revival of the solitary life in recent years.

During the Middle Ages, "hermits" or "solitaries" were not necessarily enclosed recluses. The majority had fairly close contact with the local community and some served it as guides to travelers, hostel-keepers, and guardians of bridges or coastal beacons. Others made pilgrimages to the great shrines of Christendom. In contrast, "anchorites" had a more secluded, contemplative vocation. Among these may be counted the fourteenth-century English mystic Julian of Norwich (d. ca. 1420).

After the thirteenth-century foundation of the mendicant orders, groups of associated tertiaries (Third Orders) were established for those unable to take on the full life of the parent religious order. Some gathered in communities, but others lived autonomously at home. The same mixture may be found among the women's movement, the Beguines of Flanders, northern Germany, and northern France, from the end of the twelfth century. These developments offered an alternative to the traditional structures of religious life.

IMPORTANT DEVELOPMENTS AND REFORMS

There have been three particularly important periods of development associated with social and cultural change and movements of Church reform. The first, from the eleventh to thirteenth centuries, was a period of greater centralization and increased freedom of the Church from political control. At the same time there were major cultural developments such as the "twelfth-century Renaissance" as well as social changes involving the gradual development of towns and a new mercantile class. Alongside all this grew a complex movement of spirituality with particular emphasis on gospel simplicity and radical poverty.

During the eleventh and twelfth centuries, the reforms were largely within the traditional structures of religious life. Thus many groups joined the canonical life under the Rule of St. Augustine and there were various attempts by men and women to return to the original spirit of the Rule of St. Benedict. This produced reformed monasteries and new orders such as the austere and physically isolated Cistercians and Camaldolese. The latter, and the better-known Carthusians, balanced solitude with community.

During the early part of the thirteenth century an entirely new form of religious life emerged, the mendicant orders with their emphasis on preaching and poverty. The Dominicans, Franciscans, Augustinians, Carmelites, and Servites had varied origins. The common style that emerged can broadly be described as urban, conventual but not enclosed, with a strong emphasis on university teaching and popular preaching.

Women participated in most of these movements but were increasingly subject to restrictive legislation. For many centuries attempts had been made to impose strict enclosure on women with varying degrees of success. The participation of women in groups of wandering preachers during the twelfth and thirteenth centuries provoked strong reactions from Church authorities that went hand in hand with the restriction of all ministerial roles to a celibate priesthood with enhanced status. Mendicant women, in the end, were unable to share exactly in life-style of their male counterparts.

The second period of significant development came in the sixteenth century. In response to social and religious upheaval, there arose a new form of religious life freed from enclosure and lengthy public liturgies, mobile and espousing a spirituality strongly oriented toward service. New clerical communities under a rule became known as clerks regular. Perhaps the best known example is the Society of Jesus, or Jesuits. From these roots stemmed what became known, somewhat unfortunately, as "apostolic religious life," embracing all orders and congregations whose primary focus was active ministry. Women, however, were once again limited in their roles. For example, the initiatives of Angela Merici's Ursulines in the sixteenth century and Mary Ward's Institute of the Blessed Virgin Mary in the early seventeenth century in creating mobile groups of women were severely hampered until modern times by an imposed degree of enclosure.

Although new, mostly active religious congregations of women and men continued to be founded throughout the seventeenth and eighteenth centuries, the third great period of expansion in religious life was during the nineteenth century. This development is closely associated with the growing distance between the Church and large sections of new industrial city populations and the acute social and educational needs produced by industrialization. There was an extraordinary proliferation of women's communities involved in catechesis, education, and various forms of social and medical work. Finally, European colonial expansion in Africa and Asia saw the development of many specialized missionary congregations.

THE CONTEMPORARY SITUATION

The Roman Catholic Church has inherited four broad categories of orders and congregations: monastic, canonical, mendicant, and fully active (or "apostolic"). Some of the striking, if superficial, differences between orders have blurred in recent years with the move toward less institutional life-styles and the breakdown of rigid distinctions between contemplation and action. Since the Second Vatican Council (1962–65), the recovery of a theology of one, common baptismal vocation and the rejection of a spirituality of separation from the world as the precondition of holiness have also blurred the distinction between religious life and the laity and clergy. New religious movements and groups are increasingly open to single and married people alike. In this context, the precise future of the traditional structures of religious orders has become more uncertain.

See also Augustine, Rule of St.; Augustinians; Benedict, Rule of St.; Benedictine order; Carmelite order; Cistercian order; Dominican order; Franciscan order; Jesuits; mendicant orders; monasticism; religious life; vows.

Bibliography

Brown, Peter. *The Body and Society: Men, Women and Sexual Renunciation in Early Christianity.* New York: Columbia University Press, 1988.
Hostie, Raymond. *The Life and Death of Religious Orders: A Psycho-sociological Approach.* Washington, DC: CARA, 1983.
Schneiders, Sandra. *New Wineskins: Reimagining Religious Life Today.* New York: Paulist Press, 1986.
Sheldrake, Philip. *Spirituality and History.* New York: Crossroad, 1992.

PHILIP F. SHELDRAKE

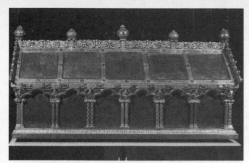

Ornate twelfth-century medieval reliquary containing the bones of Archbishop Anno of Cologne (d. 1075); made of oak, gilded copper, bronze, precious stones, and rock crystal; in the Abbey of St. Michael, Siegburg, Germany.

reliquary, a vessel used to contain and expose relics, frequently made of precious metal and decorated with gems. Forms include caskets, capsules, crosses, and monstrances. Whole bodies are often enclosed in gabled shrines. The shape of the reliquary may correspond to the shape of the relic (arm, leg, head, bust). *See also* relics.

Rembert, St., d. 888, archbishop of Hamburg and Bremen beginning in 865 who also evangelized the northern Slavs in Sweden and Denmark. He worked to free Christians enslaved by the northern Slavs and Norsemen and inaugurated the conversion of the former to Christianity. Feast day: February 4.

remedial penalty, a penalty in canon law whose purpose is to seek some kind of repair for the damage done to the common good. It is contrasted with a "medicinal penalty," whose purpose is to seek the correction of the wrongdoer.

Remigius, St., or Remi, ca. 438–533, bishop and evangelist of the Franks. A Gaulish nobleman appointed bishop of Reims at twenty-two, sometime around 496 he baptized Clovis I, king of the Franks, and many followers. Feast of the translation of his relics: October 1 (no longer universally observed). *See also* Franks.

Renaissance (Fr., "rebirth"), ca. 1300–1550, a renewal movement in arts and letters associated primarily with Italy. Scholars, however, now discount views that the Italian Renaissance broke decisively with medieval culture. Historians point to other "renaissances" in European history, notably the eighth-century "Carolingian Renaissance" led by Al-cuin of York (d. 804) and the "Renaissance of the Twelfth Century" leading to the rise of European universities. Common to all was a rediscovery of classical Roman and Greek texts.

The Italian Renaissance is conventionally dated from the time of the Italian poet and humanist Petrarch (d. 1374), also known as Francesco Petrarca, who championed the study of ancient classics, particularly Cicero, and the liberal arts of poetry and rhetoric. This intellectual emphasis distinguished humanists from the Scholastics, who stressed dialectics. Later humanists included Giovanni Boccaccio (d. 1375), Lorenzo Valla (d. 1457), Pico della Mirandola (d. 1494), and Niccolò Machiavelli (d. 1527). They valued the active over the contemplative life and rejected what they called Christian escape from the world. Renaissance artistic styles favored realism, perspective, and secular themes. Although the personal corruption of individual popes and their involvement in artistic patronage had led some to view the Renaissance as anti-Christian and pagan, the age was strongly, even conventionally, pious. In northern Europe, Christian humanists such as Desiderius Erasmus (d. 1536) and Thomas More (d. 1535) employed humanist techniques to advance piety and biblical studies. *See also* humanism, Catholic; humanism, secular.   DAVID MYERS

Renan, Joseph Ernest, 1823–92, French orientalist and philosopher. He became estranged from the Church, becoming a skeptic in matters of faith, and denying the divinity of Christ and the existence of a transcendent God. His chief work is a seven-volume history of the origins of Christianity. The first volume, *The Life of Jesus,* for which Renan is most famous, denies the divinity of Jesus and presents him merely as a great moral teacher. Renan made more significant contributions to Semitic philology than to theology. *See also* Modernism.

renewal of marriage vows. *See* convalidation; sanation.

reparation, penitential and devotional acts that allow an individual or community to participate in Christ's redemptive work of restoring all things to God. In the sacrament of Reconciliation, acts of reparation for personal sin are made by the penitent after receiving absolution from the presiding priest in order to mend the damage created by personal sin. These acts of reparation, usually in the form of prayers suggested by the priest, are intended to honor God whom sin has offended, to remind the penitent that sin is a grave matter deserving punishment, and to guard against future sin. Acts of reparation form an important part of the devotion to the Sacred Heart inspired by the visions of Margaret Mary Alacoque (d. 1690). The Morning Offering prayer and the holy hour meditation seek to unite one's daily actions and one's affections to the sufferings of Christ in order to share in Christ's work of making satisfaction for sin. *See also* Morning Offering; penance.

repentance, a response to the experience of the gracious love and forgiveness of God. The term originates from the Old French *repentir,* "be sorry for" (Lat., *paenitere*), and translates principally the Hebrew *šub,* "turn back to the right path," and the Greek *metanoia,* "a change of heart" or "disposition," or *epistrephein,* "turn around or toward." It is central to prophetic preaching (Amos 4:16–13, Hos 5:15–6:5; Jer 3:12–24), and to the preaching of John the Baptist (Mark 1:4; Matt 3:2; Luke 3:3) and Jesus (Mark 1:14–15; Matt 4:17; Luke 13:3, 5). The early Church proclaims repentance and forgiveness of sin in the name of Jesus (Mark 6:12, Acts 2:39; 3:19; 26:18, 20; 2 Pet 3:9). *See also* contrition; conversion.

repose, altar of (Lat., *repositorium,* "storehouse"), a side altar where hosts, consecrated at the Holy Thursday Mass of the Lord's Supper, are reserved for Communion on Good Friday. Believers are encouraged to pray there until midnight, contemplating Christ's Passion, death, and Resurrection. The space should be suitably decorated. *See also* altar.

reprobation, in Catholic theology, the divine decree whereby sinners are excluded from grace in this life and from the final vision of God in the next. Reprobation refers both to God's foreknowledge of spiritual failure and the divine intention to abandon unrepentant sinners to damnation. Reprobation can be understood as the negative side of predestination but, according to Catholic theology, only insofar as it is taken as a function of God's foreknowledge. God wills the damnation of those who are foreseen as freely and definitively rejecting the divine offer of grace. This reprobation is said to be positive and consequent, that is, it entails God's positive intention to punish as a response to human sin. There has been considerable debate within Catholic circles

concerning negative reprobation (the denial of divine election as an undue gift, apart from considerations of punishment). The debate, which centers on the question of in what sense God could will that human beings die in the state of mortal sin, has been polarized in the teachings of two sixteenth-century Spanish theologians: the Jesuit Luis de Molina and the Dominican Domingo Báñez. Strict Molinists take the less rigorous position, refusing to admit antecedent reprobation of any sort. Nevertheless, Catholic theologians are unanimous in rejecting any understanding of reprobation that posits God's condemnation antecedent to human guilt. This includes a rejection of the Jansenist position, which states that foreknowledge of original sin alone is sufficient to justify God's positive reprobation prior to individual sin. *See also* damnation; *De Auxiliis;* predestination.   GERARD JACOBITZ

reproductive technologies, medical procedures used to overcome infertility in the male or female. In its broadest sense the term includes artificial insemination by husband (AIH), artificial insemination by donor (AID), *in vitro* (Lat., "in glass") fertilization with embryo transfer (IVF-ET), gamete intrafallopian transfer (GIFT), surrogate mothers and carriers, and all the ancillary techniques that are part of or supportive of such procedures, for example, cryopreservation (freezing) of sperm and preembryos, various micro techniques to improve efficacy, for example, zona drilling (the making of a hole in the outer layer of the ovum to facilitate access by the sperm).

The medical indications for such procedures are related to the cause of infertility. For example, *in vitro* fertilization can be used where the woman's fallopian tubes are blocked or when she suffers from pelvic endometriosis. Donor insemination is often suggested when the husband is genetically at risk as a carrier, or when he is oligospermic (produces too few sperm) or azoospermic (produces immobile or dead sperm). Donor preembryos might be used when both husband and wife are incapable of fertilization.

World attention focused on *in vitro* fertilization on July 25, 1978, when Louise Brown was born in Oldham, England. She was the first so-called test-tube baby, the culmination of the work of the late Patrick Steptoe, a physician, and Robert Edwards, a research scientist. Since that time, thousands of babies have been born around the world as a result of

IVF. It is no longer regarded as an experimental procedure; several states in the United States have legislated its inclusion in insurance coverage. Rates of success (defined as carry-home babies) differ according to the technology and the experience of the team involved. Quality control has been a problem. Some practitioners, for example, offer IVF-ET, yet have never achieved a success in this procedure.

Over the years any number of commissions have addressed the ethical aspects of the reproductive technologies. Some of the more important are the Ethics Advisory Board of the former U.S. Department of Health, Education, and Welfare (1979); Waller Report from Australia (1983–84); Warnock Report from England (1984); Ontario Law Reform Commission (1985); Benda Report of the Federal Republic of Germany (1985); American Fertility Society (1986 and repeatedly updated).

The Church and Reproductive Technologies: The official Catholic response to the new reproductive technologies appeared in March 1987. The document is entitled "Instruction on Respect for Human Life in its Origin and on the Dignity of Procreation" (*Donum Vitae*), and was drawn up by the Congregation for the Doctrine of the Faith.

The Congregation first proposes a criterion for judging these technologies: the dignity and integral good of the human person. Reproductive technologies, therefore, cannot be assessed and rejected merely in terms of their artificiality.

The ethical assessment of these technologies is complex and can involve any number of considerations. Three, however, stand out: the moral status of the preembryo, the use of third parties in these technologies, the simple procedure of IVF-ET ("simple" meaning that the semen of the husband and ovum of the wife are used).

(1) The status of the preembryo is a key moral issue because of preembryo discarding, freezing, and experimentation. Such procedures are not inseparable from IVF-ET, but often accompany it. Many of the commissions listed earlier concluded that the preembryo deserves profound respect, but not necessarily that due to persons.

Donum Vitae refers to "unconditional respect." The preembryo must be "treated as a person from the moment of conception," for "how could a human individual not be a human person?" It views destruction of preembryos as abortion, and nontherapeutic experimentation on them as a "crime against their dignity as human beings."

Some contemporary Catholic theologians have raised doubts about this doctrine. Pointing to certain phenomena of the preimplantation period (twinning, recombination of fertilized ova, totipotentiality [capacity to become an integral individual] of the preembryo, spontaneous loss), these theologians believe that while genetic individuality is present from fertilization, developmental individuality is not.

(2) Third-party participation is a broad category that includes sperm donation, egg donation, embryo donation, and uterus donation (surrogacy). While these procedures differ markedly, present official Catholic teaching would reject them all as violations of the unity of marriage. *Donum Vitae* states: "Human procreation has specific characteristics by virtue of the personal dignity of the parents and of the children: the procreation of a new person, whereby the man and the woman collaborate with the power of the Creator, must be the fruit and the sign of the mutual self-giving of the spouses, of their love and of their fidelity. The fidelity of the spouses in the unity of marriage involves reciprocal respect of their right to become a father and a mother only through each other."

While this statement appears in the section on heterologous artificial insemination (AID), it touches in principle all third-party donations in reproductive technology.

(3) The simple procedure. *Donum Vitae* begins its consideration as follows: "The Church's teaching on marriage and human procreation affirms the 'inseparable connection, willed by God and unable to be broken by man on his own initiative, between the two meanings of the conjugal act: the unitive meaning and the procreative meaning.'"

The citation within the above quote is drawn from Pope Paul VI's encyclical letter on birth regulation, *Humanae Vitae* (1988). The Congregation for the Doctrine of the Faith refers to this "inseparable connection" as a "principle based on the nature of marriage and the intimate connection of the goods of marriage." It goes on to note that just as contraception separates the unitive and procreative dimensions, so does IVF-ET in an analogous way. Because this is the case, procreation by IVF-ET is "deprived of its proper perfection" and is not "in conformity with the dignity of the person" because it fails to respect the body-soul unity of the human person.

Thus official Catholic teaching rejects any reproductive technology (e.g., AIH) that replaces sexual intercourse. This is the most controversial aspect of this teaching and has been challenged by many Catholic theologians who agree that not everything that is "deprived of its proper perfection" is necessarily morally wrong. Thus, while many accept the inseparability of the unitive and procreative, they apply this to the marriage relationship, not to individual acts. *See also* bioethics; *in vitro* fertilization; Marriage; medical ethics.

Bibliography

Kelly, Kevin T. *Life and Love.* San Francisco: HarperCollins, 1987.

Shannon, Thomas A., and Lisa Sowle Cahill. *Religion and Artificial Reproduction.* New York: Crossroad, 1988.

RICHARD A. MCCORMICK

reputation, moral right to, the moral claim of an individual to the esteem of others. In traditional Catholic moral theology this right was treated in relation to its most prominent violations, detraction and calumny. Detraction is the unjust violation of another's reputation by revealing to others some true but hidden fault of the person. Calumny is the imputation to another of a fault that is false in fact and known to be false. It adds to the injustice the sin of lying.

Detraction is serious if the defamation has been serious (a cause of great harm) and unjust. It has always been admitted in Catholic tradition that the revelation of another's fault is not unjust where it is in the circumstances necessary or very useful. Thus, it is usually not unjust to reveal a child's faults to its parents or those of a religious to the superior. Nor is it considered detraction to reveal a fault that is already juridically notorious. Detraction and calumny give rise to the duty of restitution. *See also* calumny; detraction.

Requiem (Lat., "rest"), the funeral Mass. The first word ("Requiem") of the Introit of the older funeral Mass became a shorthand description of the Mass itself. The Requiem Mass is now called the Mass of Christian Burial, or simply the Mass for the Dead, when celebrated apart from the funeral rites. In the larger sense the term now means any valedictory on the occasion of a death. *See also* burial, Christian; funeral Mass.

reredos (Old Fr., *arrière, dos,* "behind the back"), the decoration of the space behind (and above) the altar, e.g., in the form of hangings or wooden panels or painted scenes. The reredos presupposes an altar

at which the priest stands with his back to the people. *See also* altar.

Rerum Novarum (ray'ruhm noh-vahr'uhm; Lat., "Of new things"), "On the Condition of the Working Person," encyclical of Pope Leo XIII, issued on May 15, 1891. The first of the major social encyclicals, it sought to apply traditional Catholic teaching to the new conditions created by the Industrial Revolution. The pope's deep concern over the growing alienation of workers from the Church and the widening and increasingly bitter division between the classes added urgency to his message.

The encyclical defended the right to private property and condemned socialism, but it also supported the right of workers to form labor unions for collective bargaining, insisting on the worker's right to a just wage and to decent working conditions. The pope made it clear that the Church has the right and the duty not only to teach the principles of justice, but also to apply its teachings to the temporal order, that is, "to point out the remedy" (n. 26). Indeed, the Church is not "so preoccupied with the spiritual concerns of her children as to neglect their temporal and earthly interests" (n. 28).

The Church's intervention, however, was not to be limited to the activities of the hierarchy and clergy. There was an important and indispensable place for the laity as well (nn. 54–55). At the same time, the state has its own proper role to play, but bound always by the Church's teachings on justice and human rights (nn. 32–49).

The encyclical inspired a century of papal, conciliar, and episcopal pronouncements, for example, Pius XI's *Quadragesimo Anno* ("Forty Years After"), Paul VI's *Octogesima Adveniens* ("The Eightieth Anniversary"), and John Paul II's *Centesimus Annus* ("The Hundredth Year"). *See also* Catholic social teachings.

RICHARD P. MCBRIEN

rescript, a response to a question or request by proper ecclesiastical authority. The term is most often used to refer to a response given by the Holy See. The response might clarify a point of law or grant a dispensation or a privilege to one requesting it.

reservation, mental. *See* mental reservation.

reservation of the Eucharist, the practice of retaining the remainders of the consecrated bread and wine beyond the time of the Mass itself. According to the 1967 document, *Eucharisticum Mysterium* (Lat., "Eucharistic Mystery"), "the primary and original purpose of the reserving of the sacred species in church outside Mass is the administration of Viaticum." Viaticum is Communion for the dying. Other purposes for the reservation of the eucharistic foods include the distribution of Communion outside of Mass, as during the Liturgy of the Presanctified in Eastern rites and on Good Friday in the West. The eucharistic foods are reserved for the purposes of worshiping and adoring Christ, who remains present and available to communicants in his body and blood, even after the Mass itself has ceased. Normally, the eucharistic bread alone is reserved. Most Catholic churches reserve a modest supply of consecrated breads in a solid and secured tabernacle attached to an altar in a side chapel. Occasionally, consecrated wine may be reserved for specific purposes, e.g., the Communion of one unable to consume solid foods, but ordinarily its reservation is forbidden. The Catholic and Orthodox practice of eucharistic reservation stands in contrast to the practices and pieties of Protestant denominations. Ecumenical dialogues have suggested that Protestant Christians will, in charity, move toward greater reverence in the disposal of the eucharistic foods. Catholics and Orthodox have been asked to minimize devotional exaggerations, and to emphasize the primary purposes for eucharistic reservation. *See also* Blessed Sacrament; eucharistic devotions; Holy Communion; Viaticum. JEFFREY T. VANDERWILT

reserved censures. *See* penal law.

reserved sins, those sins for which forgiveness of is reserved to a bishop or to one designated by the bishop, or even to the pope alone. The reservation of sins is basically a canonical rather than a theological issue. The first recorded appearance of a reserved sin occurred in England in the eleventh century. As canon law developed following the original codification by Gratian (d. ca. 1159), the regulations for the reservation of sins also became more specific. Reservation of certain sins depended on their gravity, and Germanic law influenced the way in which canon law defined such gravity. The revised code of canon law discusses the reservation of canonical penalties (cans. 1354–63) but abrogated former laws on the reservation of sins. Church law, not divine law, determines both reservation of sins and of penalties; consequently, such laws can vary from one period of time to another, and from one place to another. *See also* confession, auricular; Reconciliation; sin.

res et sacramentum (rez et sah-krah-men'toom; (Lat., "the reality and the sacrament"), in classical sacramental theology, a shorthand way of referring to the inner reality of a sacrament, as distinguished from its outward rite (*sacramentum*) and its ultimate purpose (*res sacramenti*). The *res et sacramentum* of the Eucharist, for instance, is the Real Presence of the body and blood of Christ. *See also* sacrament; *sacramentum tantum; res tantum.*

resignation, the loss of an ecclesiastical office by one's own initiative. Canon law (can. 187) recognizes resignation from office "for a just cause" as a right, to be exercised even by the pope. Although a papal resignation is not accepted by anyone, it must be manifested to those who are responsible for filling the vacancy of office (can. 332.1), namely, the College of Cardinals. A papal resignation takes effect immediately, but a pope who resigns could be eligible for reelection (can. 189.4). The older term for resignation is abdication. The first pope to abdicate was Pontian (235), and the last pope to resign was Celestine V (1294). *See also* abdication.

respondent, the nonpetitioning party summoned to a nonpenal ecclesiastical trial. Sometimes called the defendant, though more appropriately so in penal trials, the respondent must answer a legimately executed summons. Canonical procedures protect the rights of respondents to be heard and be informed throughout the trial.

Responsorial Psalm, the portion of a psalm sung in a responsorial manner between the first and the second readings from Scripture at Mass. To sing responsorially is to alternate between a response (or antiphon) sung by the entire assembly and a verse sung by cantor(s) or choir. Responses are either sentences from the designated psalm or some other biblical phrase appropriate to the day or occasion. *See also* psalmody; Psalms.

responsory, a liturgical chant that follows the reading from Scripture during the Liturgy of the

Hours. Responsories follow this structure: A two-part sentence forms the response, followed by a scriptural verse and the "Glory be to the Father." An abbreviated response, i.e., only the second half of the response, concludes the chant.

res tantum (rez tahn'toom; Lat., ("the reality itself"), technical expression in classical sacramental theology that refers to the grace conferred by the sacrament and hence to its ultimate goal or purpose. In the case of the Eucharist, the *res tantum* is the unity of the Church and the indwelling of Christ in the soul of the communicant. *See also* sacrament; *sacramentum tantum; res et sacramentum.*

restitution, an act of commutative (or strict) justice by which the injury of another's right is repaired. The proper or formal source of the obligation to restore or to do something to repair harm that has been done is not the wrong of injustice as such, but rather the undue inequality that has been created by the injury. It can happen, for instance, that an inequality exists without there being any wrongful act of injustice on anyone's part—for example, a person in total good faith has what actually belongs to another.

Catholic tradition has recognized two proximate sources of restitution: the wrongful possession of another's goods and harm unjustly done to another.

Over the centuries a virtual encyclopedia of casuistry developed around the duty to restore. Undoubtedly this can be traced to the very complex situations in which people found themselves. For instance, for an obligation of restitution to exist as a result of unjust damage, three conditions were stipulated: (1) the action had to violate strict justice; (2) the action had to have been the efficacious cause of the injury; and (3) the action had to be theologically culpable.

By and large it can be said that the detailed treatises on restitution were composed for the direction of confessors who had to make sure that in forgiving a penitent they were not further harming the victim. Some of the solutions arrived at might strike modern readers as the kind of dogged and logical pursuit of judicial rules that occasionally compromised fairness. *See also* casuistry; justice.

restorationism, a pejorative term used to describe the effort of some church officials to restore Catholicism as fully as possible to its pre–Vatican II condition (before 1962). The restorationist agenda includes a powerful and unchallenged papacy, weak national episcopates, strong individual bishops uncritically loyal to the Holy See, traditional gender roles in ecclesiastical life and ministry, and a spirituality that separates the life of faith from the struggle for justice.

restrictive interpretation of law. *See* canon law, interpretation of.

Resurrection of Christ, Jesus' return to divine life with God on Easter (e.g., Rom 1:4). The Resurrection of Jesus is the basis for the Catholic belief that all faithful Christians will share a glorious, heavenly life with God (e.g., Phil 3:20–21; Rev 21:1–22:5).

Resurrection in the Time of Jesus: Most of the OT speaks only of this life. God rewards, punishes, protects, and rescues people from death while they are alive (e.g., Ps 23). By the time of Jesus, centuries of suffering, exile, and persecution had led some Jews, notably the Pharisees (e.g., Acts 23:6–8), to believe that God would raise up and reward good people who had suffered in this life. Dan 12:1–3 speaks of persons who had taught others holiness

The Risen Christ; panel from the sixteenth-century *Isenheim Altarpiece* by Matthias Grünewald, Unterlinden Museum, Colmar, France.

and were transformed like angels or stars. Stories of Jews who had suffered martyrdom for God promised that the martyr's tortured body would be given a new life with God (e.g., 2 Macc 7).

Other Jewish teachers insisted that it was impossible to believe in resurrection because it was not part of the ancient tradition. Mark 12:18–27 describes Jesus arguing against such teachers, saying that it would be absurd to imagine that people in heaven had exactly the same physical bodies they have on earth. Jesus uses the imagery of Daniel to make the point that resurrection life is like that of angels, not of earthly humans. He suggests that when God spoke to Moses, God referred to Abraham, Isaac, and Jacob as living. Therefore, even the law teaches that God raises the dead.

Some passages in the OT speak as though God takes people into new life as soon as they die (e.g., Wis 3:1–9). Others look foward to a future judgment when God will punish the wicked and reward the righteous. Resurrection to new life with God is part of the future reward (e.g., Dan 12:1–3; 2 Macc 12:43–46). At that time, death will be abolished (e.g., Isa 25:6–9).

The Resurrection of Jesus: Since belief in resurrection was usually linked to the end of the world, Jesus' disciples did not expect to encounter the Risen Lord on Easter (e.g., Luke 24:13–35). Even in ancient times, skeptics accused the disciples of inventing the story of Jesus' Resurrection (e.g., Matt 27:62–66; 28:11–15). Christians have always insisted that the Resurrection of Jesus was unexpected, a new experience of God's saving power.

When Jesus was raised from the dead, he did not return to the human life he had lived with his disciples. Jesus returned to a divine life. Christians worship the Risen Jesus as Lord (Phil 2:6–11). They turn to Jesus in prayer (Heb 4:14–5:10; 1 John 2:1–2). The Holy Spirit, which inspires and shapes Christian life, is the spirit of the Risen Jesus (Rom 8:9–17; John 14:15–26). Throughout the NT, the Christian experience of living a new life in Christ depends upon the belief that Jesus was raised from the dead. Christians are baptized into Christ. Baptism is an experience of dying and rising with Christ (e.g., Rom 6:3–11; Eph 2:4–7). The Risen Christ is present at the Eucharist (Luke 24:30–32).

How did the disciples come to believe that Jesus rose from the dead on Easter? No one actually witnessed the corpse of Jesus returning to life or being taken out of the tomb. The proof came as a revelation from God. Some women, who had gone to mourn Jesus at the tomb, were told by an angel (e.g., Mark 16:7; Luke 24:5–7). Other disciples had visions of the Risen Lord (e.g., 1 Cor 15:3–8). When Paul saw the Risen Lord, he was firmly convinced that Christians were corrupting the Jewish tradition. He was persecuting the Church (e.g., Gal 1:13–16). One of Jesus' relatives, James, who did not believe during Jesus' lifetime, was apparently converted by a vision of the Lord (e.g., 1 Cor 15:7). The cases of Paul and James indicate that visions of the Risen Lord were not merely subjective wish fulfillment. All of the earliest witnesses are convinced that the one who appeared in this vision was Jesus of Nazareth, the human being who had died on the cross.

The earliest evidence for early Christian belief comes from the Letters of Paul. He refers to those who had seen the Lord, Jesus' heavenly exaltation, and the activity of the Spirit in the community. Paul does not use details of his own experience to prove the truth of Christian belief. The proof that God raised Jesus is found in the transformation of Paul's life from persecutor to apostle (Gal 1:13–17; 1 Cor 15:8–10). Several decades later the Gospel writers provided narrative accounts of appearances of the Lord.

Such stories are secondary to the belief that Jesus has been raised and is exalted as Lord. The differences in details, timing, place, and persons present show that these accounts are not dependent upon a single source. Some refer to Jesus appearing to disciples in Galilee (Mark 14:28; 16:7; Matt 28:16–20; John 21:1–14); others to appearances in Jerusalem (Matt 28:9–10; John 20:1–29; Luke 24:13–49). Each Evangelist has shaped the stories to suit the narrative emphases of the particular Gospel account. Though they do not provide eyewitness evidence for the Resurrection of Jesus, the Gospel narratives show what early Christians believed about Jesus' Resurrection.

Just as Paul claims that God called him to be an apostle through the vision of Jesus, so the Risen Jesus commissions the other disciples to preach the gospel (e.g., Matt 28:19–20; Luke 24:47–49). Other sayings refer to the foundations of the early community (e.g., John 20:21–23; 21:15–17). The stories in John and Luke also suggest a need to affirm the reality of the Risen Lord. John 20:24–29 contains an episode said to occur a week later. Thomas demands and receives tangible evidence that the Risen Lord is identical with the crucified Jesus. In Luke 24:36–43, physical evidence reassures the disciples, who initially think that they are seeing a ghost. By the second century some Christians held the false belief that Jesus was a divine being who had only used a body to appear in our world. His divine, spiritual self returned to God prior to the Crucifixion. The appearance narratives provided evidence for the Catholic arguments against this attempt to deny the humanity of the Savior.

Another story that only appears in the Gospel narratives concerns the tomb of Jesus. A visit by female disciples finds the tomb empty (Mark 16:1–8; Matt 28:1–8; Luke 24:1–10; John 20:1–2). Those Gospels in which Jesus' male disciples are still in Jerusalem report that Peter confirmed the women's account (Luke 24:12, 24; John 20:3–10). All the stories emphasize the perplexity caused by this discovery. Matt 28:13 alleges that enemies of Christianity spread rumors that the disciples had stolen the body. In John 20:2, 13, Mary Magdalene voices the suspicion that someone else has removed the body. An empty tomb of itself would not lead anyone to believe that Jesus was alive. However, the earliest traditions show that Christians believed that the Risen Jesus was the crucified person, not merely the inner spirit of the Lord. Therefore, early Christians certainly believed that the tomb of Jesus was empty. The glorious body of the Risen Lord (Phil 3:21; 1 Cor 15:22–23, 47–49) could not coexist with the corpse buried in the tomb.

Resurrection of the Believer: The earliest traditions about Jesus' Resurrection spoke of resurrection as glorification. Jesus assumes the divine name "Lord." Christians whose lives were shaped by the Risen Lord clearly expected to share the same heavenly life. However, 1 Cor 15 and 1 Thess 4:13–18 show that some early Christians were confused about whether and how resurrection applied to them. Christ's return as judge signals the resurrection of the dead and the transformation of the living from material to spiritual existence.

At the time of Jesus, resurrection was primarily considered a reward for those who had remained faithful to God. Occasionally, the wicked were said to be resurrected for judgment (e.g., John 5:28–29). Their fate is generally understood to be eternal death because they are separated from God's presence (e.g., Wis 5; Rev 20:4–15). 1 Thess 4 and 1 Cor 15 describe the gathering of the faithful at the end time. Their resurrected existence reflects the divine life of Jesus. Catholics do not believe that 1 Thess 4:13–18 refers to a gathering up of the righteous before the end of the world and the judgment, a phenomenon that many evangelical and fundamentalist Christians refer to as "the rapture."

Greek philosophers believed that human beings are composed of a mortal, material, and emotional bodily reality and an immortal soul, and have a rational element that is capable of learning truth and of acquiring moral discipline. Immortality of the soul is a consequence of its nature. Christians believe that the human person, body and soul, was created by God. Resurrection is not a natural consequence of perfecting human nature. It is a gift of God that represents the goal of the transforming work of God's Spirit (e.g., 1 Cor 15:42–55). Natural phenomena such as near-death experiences do not prove or disprove Catholic belief in the resurrection. Since Catholics believe that the whole person, including those elements of the person dependent upon our bodily and emotional individuality, is transformed in Christ, resurrection excludes the possibility of reincarnation. God perfects what remains imperfect and incomplete at the end of this life for those in who are "in Christ" (e.g., Rom 8:12–39; Phil 3:12–21). *See also* Easter; Jesus Christ; redemption; resurrection of the body.

Bibliography

Brown, Raymond E. *The Virginal Conception and Bodily Resurrection of Jesus.* New York: Paulist Press, 1974.

O'Collins, Gerald. *What Are They Saying About the Resurrection?* New York: Paulist Press, 1978.

Perkins, Pheme. *Resurrection: New Testament Witness and Contemporary Reflection.* Garden City: Doubleday, 1984.

Williams, Rowan. *Resurrection.* London: Darton, Longman & Todd, 1982.   PHEME PERKINS

resurrection of the body (see Apostles' Creed) or of the dead (see Nicene Creed), the everlasting life of the whole human person. OT hope in resurrection (Wis 3; Job 19:25–27; Dan 12:2; 2 Mac 7:9, 14) was disputed among Jews in NT times (Mark 12:18–27; Acts 23:6–10). For Christians, this belief is grounded in the Resurrection of Jesus and is central to the faith, as evidenced in the appearance stories of the Gospels, the early kerygmatic formulas found in Acts, and the ancient creeds of the Church. In the Bible, the most extensive treatment of its nature and significance is in 1 Cor 15. Paul understands the raising of Jesus as the inauguration of the end time that brings God's judgment and promised salvation. In Christ, all shall be made alive. He is the first fruits; then at his coming, all believers (v. 23). Paul opposes those who deny the resurrection, but he does not advocate the idea of the immortality simply of the soul, a concept familiar in Greek philosophy of the time but very different from biblical thought, which views the human person as an integral whole. Here Paul is not interested in contrasting soul with body, but human life in its entirety as it is threatened by sin and death (flesh) with the new life of the Spirit.

It would be wrong simply to read the Pauline distinction flesh/spirit as body/soul. Our hope for eternal life is not based on an inherent immortality of the human soul, but on the life-giving Spirit of God, who alone is immortal and raises the dead. Human persons, not simply "souls," are saved by God and raised to new life. This will not be a resuscitation and prolongation of life as we know it. Even from a scientific point of view, what we call the body is an ever-changing constellation of atoms, none of which persist throughout a mortal life. Resurrection of the body does not mean the survival of a matrix of particular atoms, but identity and continuity of persons and lives in a process of final transformation.

The Resurrection Stories: The resurrection stories, which stress the bodiliness of the Risen Lord, are just as insistent that his body has been radically transformed. Paul concludes that God, who provides us with the kind of body appropriate to this life, will also transform it in a way appropriate to the new life of the kingdom of God (15:42–50). How this happens remains a mystery.

Christians of Paul's generation believed that the Lord's coming, and with it the resurrection of the dead, was imminent. As this expectation faded, the question about the fate of the faithful departed, still in their graves, became acute. Later NT writings offer assurance that they are with God, and gradually a Christian teaching, heavily dependent upon Greek philosophy, arose about the soul as the human self that survives after death, deprived, until the time of the final judgment and resurrection, from the complement of its body (councils of Toledo, 675; Lateran IV, 1215; Lyons II, 1274; Vienna, 1312; Florence, 1439; Congregation for the Doctrine of the Faith, 1979). Although any dualistic reading of a body/soul opposition, found in Western philosophy since Plato, is problematic, especially given the Church's own insistence upon the integrity and unity of the human person (Vatican II, *Gaudium et Spes*, n. 14), many Christians today speak of "saving one's soul," which, unlike the body, can "go to heaven." This view can lead to a depreciation of the body, individualism, and a flight from our responsibilities

in this world. The biblical doctrine of the resurrection of the body can remind the Church that God does not wish to save our souls from this world, but to save our souls and our world from sin and death. The body symbolizes the connection that human beings have with each other and with the earth. Thus, the life of the resurrection must be seen in its communal and cosmic dimensions. There can be no salvation apart from the body, the community, and the world. The time of the resurrection is a subject of continuing theological dispute involving various understandings of history and eschatology. Some, like Karl Rahner (d. 1984), hold for resurrection at the time of individual death. Others, like Cardinal Joseph Ratzinger, maintain a more traditional position, i.e., that it happens universally at the end of history. *See also* eternal life; Resurrection of Christ; salvation.   JOHN R. SACHS

resurrection of the dead. *See* resurrection of the body.

retreat, a personal or group withdrawal for prayer, meditation, or study. A retreat is both a place and a spiritual experience.

Almost a million people each year come to the six hundred retreat centers in the United States and Canada in search of religious experience. The phenomenon is repeated in many other countries as well. Often in solitude, sometimes in dialogue, retreatants are guided through reflections on life's mystery and meaning.

About 80 percent of these centers are run by religious orders of men and women. Each religious order has imprinted its unique spirituality on the programs at its retreat center. Programs range in length from a three-day weekend to a week or a month. The retreat movement was lay initiated and was begun in the late nineteenth century responding to a widespread need for formation in spirituality. The purpose of a retreat is religious awakening and the deepening of spiritual living. It is an invitation to prayerful listening and responding to the spirit of God in the contemporary world.

Reuchlin, Johannes (roykh'leen), 1455–1522, German humanist. Reuchlin championed the study of cabala and Jewish mystical literature, opposing the destruction of Hebrew books proposed by the Jewish convert Johannes Pfefferkorn and other

Cologne Dominicans. Reuchlin's work stimulated the study of the OT in the original language. He was tried for heresy, and his satirical pamphlet *Augenspiegel* (Ger., "ophthalmoscope") was condemned by Pope Leo X in 1520. Though many Reformers took his side in the controversy, Reuchlin remained a loyal Catholic and tried to dissuade his grandnephew Philipp Melanchthon from drawing close to Martin Luther.

revelation (Lat., *revelare*, "to take away the veil"), the disclosure of persons, events, and things previously hidden or only partly known; ultimately, the self-disclosure of God. Against Gnostic claims that they enjoyed special revelations that added to the truth already manifested through Christ and his apostles, orthodox writers in the early Church insisted on the complete and once-and-for-all nature of NT revelation. But revelation (its existence, nature, and mediation) did not become a theological issue for many centuries. Not even the Council of Trent (1545–63) was as much concerned with revelation itself, which can be identified with "the gospel" that the council announced to be "the source of all saving truth and rule of conduct," as with its transmission through the inspired Scriptures and the various traditions going back to the apostolic age.

The debate about revelation really began with the emergence of deism at the end of the seventeenth century. Can or do we know everything that there is to be known about God, as well as about the nature and destiny of human beings, simply by using our natural, created powers of reason? Or did the coming of Christ reveal something substantially new?

In one of its two major documents, the First Vatican Council (1869–70) addressed the theme of faith, the human response to God's revelation. It taught that, by the light of human reason, both the existence of God and basic divine attributes can be certainly known (the "natural" way). But it insisted on the "supernatural" way by which God has revealed to humans the divine "mysteries" (plural) of which humans were ignorant. Through revelation humanity has been given a certain knowledge of other truths which humans alone would only imperfectly grasp. Vatican I, although it spoke of divine self-revelation, highlighted God's communication of truths previously unknown or at best only inadequately known. In this version of faith, human beings, with the help of the Holy Spirit and acknowledging God's supreme authority, give an intellectual assent to the divinely revealed truths.

Vatican II: Developments in biblical, liturgical, patristic, ecumenical, and philosophical studies, along with wider theological, cultural, and historical shifts, made it possible for Vatican II to produce richer teaching in its Dogmatic Constitution on Divine Revelation (*Dei Verbum*) of November 1965. At least eight points merit attention.

(1) Revelation is essentially God's self-communication, a loving and utterly gratuitous invitation to enter a dialogue of friendship (nn. 2–4, 14, 17). That self-revelation also has a content; it manifests truths about God and human beings that can be summarized as "the treasure of revelation" (n. 26) or "the deposit of faith" (n. 10).

(2) Human beings are called to respond in faith totally and not merely intellectually to the divine self-disclosure (n. 5). This dialogue of faith expresses itself in biblically based prayer (n. 25).

(3) The divine self-revelation is understood to be utterly centered on Christ, who is the Revealer and the Revelation (nn. 2, 4, 17). Although the Dogmatic Constitution on Divine Revelation refers twenty-three times to the Holy Spirit (e.g., nn. 4, 5), many Eastern Christians think its emphatic Christocentrism led it to neglect somewhat the role of the Spirit in revelation.

(4) From the outset the document considers revelation and salvation as practically synonymous: the "economy" of revelation coincides with the history of salvation and vice versa (nn. 3, 4, 6, 7, 14, 15, 17, 21). God's self-manifestation and gift of grace are two sides of the same coin, which can be expressed together as the divine self-communication (n. 6). The essentially salvific impact of revelation relates to its sacramental nature. Like the sacraments themselves, God's saving self-disclosure takes place through words, deeds, and events associated with the person of Christ (nn. 2, 4, 14, 17).

(5) The Dogmatic Constitution on Divine Revelation makes use of Pauline language to speak of the divine "mystery" (singular) disclosed in Christ—i.e., God's final plan of salvation for all human beings (n. 2). This unifying sense of the one, historic revelation contrasts with Vatican I's revealed "mysteries" (plural). This language shift has been maintained in the encyclicals and other major documents of Pope John Paul II. He consistently speaks of the one mystery of redemption or revelation in Christ.

(6) For the Dogmatic Constitution on Divine Revelation, as well as for the Church's liturgy and the earliest Christian proclamation, revelation and salvation reached their full, definitive climax with the dying and rising of Christ, along with the coming of the Holy Spirit. It is neither with the Incarnation nor with the ministry of Jesus but with the Paschal Mystery that God "completed and perfected" revelation (n. 4).

While recognizing the fullness of foundational revelation "back there and then" with Christ and the apostolic Church, the Dogmatic Constitution on Divine Revelation does not relegate revelation simply to the past. Revelation remains a reality, which involves more than just a growing understanding of the full, divine self-disclosure in Christ (n. 8). The living voice of God continues to speak (nn. 8, 25). As a call to faith, the event of divine revelation is repeated every time God invites a human being into an interpersonal dialogue of friendship. This endlessly repeated event of divine self-disclosure remains dependent on the revelation completed through Christ (and his apostles) and adds nothing essential to its content.

(7) Much of the Dogmatic Constitution on Divine Revelation (five out of six chapters) discusses the transmission of revelation (in its primary and secondary senses—as event and content, respectively) through the inspired Scriptures and tradition, understood to be strictly united in this process. The experience of spiritual realities enjoyed by the faithful (n. 8) appears as one factor in the growth of the Church's living tradition. But, in general, the document pays little attention to human and Christian experience, nor does it address the relationship between the transmission of revelation and the wider events of human history and world religions. Likewise it has little to say about the consummation of revelation at Christ's final coming (nn. 4, 7).

(8) The document does not develop the roles of the magisterium (the bishops) and theologians in transmitting, interpreting, and helping to actualize revelation. Yet it includes items of great importance: the magisterium "is not above the word of God but serves it" (n. 10); theologians should find the soul of their discipline in the study of the Scriptures (n. 24), the inspired record and interpretation of foundational revelation.

The Integral Doctrine: The Dogmatic Constitution Divine Revelation drew together most significant issues of Catholic doctrine and theology on divine self-manifestation. Respect for Vatican II's integral doctrine of revelation requires, however, that we incorporate the teaching on revelation found in other conciliar documents. At least three complex themes should be mentioned.

(1) Vatican II texts such as the Dogmatic Constitution on the Church (*Lumen Gentium,* 1964), the Decree on the Church's Missionary Activity (*Ad Gentes Divinitus,* 1965) and the Declaration on the Relationship of the Church to Non-Christian Religions (*Nostra Aetate,* 1965) reflect on the knowledge of God found through other religions. These documents provide commentary on major world religions and the implications of Christ being "the true light" who "enlightens everyone" (John 1:9).

(2) Concern for the post–NT experience of revelation and salvation leads the Pastoral Constitution on the Church in the Modern World (*Gaudium et Spes,* 1965) to examine various themes: the deeper questions and desires of the human condition itself (which open human beings to God's redeeming manifestation in Christ); the dynamics of history and world cultures; the present signs of the times through which, if they are interpreted in the light of the original gospel, humans can hear God speaking now; the mission of the Church in mediating to all people the saving revelation of God; and the way all things converge toward the final manifestation of Christ (nn. 39, 45).

(3) Along with the bishops, theologians have a special responsibility to discern the voices of our times (Pastoral Constitution on the Church in the Modern World, n. 44). They should also constantly be concerned to use common language so as to communicate more adequately the essential truths of revelation (n. 62).

Post–Vatican II: Since Vatican II, official documents and dialogues of the Catholic Church have developed further teaching and reflection on at least two major themes concerned with revelation. The first is the way in which such primordial and universal experiences as that of suffering correlate with and can become privileged places where God speaks to and saves humanity; see, for instance, John Paul II's *Dives in Misericordia* (1980) and *Salvifici Doloris* (1984). Second, the role of non-Christian religions as imperfect and provisional ways of revelation and salvation has been addressed not only by such papal texts as Paul VI's *Evangelii Nuntiandi* (1975) and John Paul II's *Redemptor Hominis* (1979) and *Dominum et Vivificantem* (1986), but also in interfaith dialogues and much theological writing. Usually issues have been articulated in terms of salvation and grace. But any position taken on the means of redemption necessarily carries implications for a theology of revelation.

Finally, Avery Dulles, Aylward Shorter, and others have developed a theme that has preconciliar roots in the theology of Karl Rahner (d. 1984): revelation as God's symbolic self-communication. The Dogmatic Constitution on Divine Revelation used the language of divine self-communication (n. 6); further, its sacramental version of revelation approached the language of symbolism. Contemporary theology of revelation speaks to an age that seems to be regaining a richer sense of the power and reality of symbols. The flourishing science of social communications can enrich the approaches to the divine self-communication found in Rahner's theology of grace and John Paul II's encyclical on the Holy Spirit (*Dominum et Vivificantem*). *See also* faith; revelation, biblical.

Bibliography

Dulles, Avery. *Models of Revelation.* Garden City, NY: Doubleday, 1983.

O'Collins, Gerald. *Fundamental Theology.* Mahwah, NJ: Paulist Press, 1981.

Shorter, Aylward. *Revelation and Its Interpretation.* London: Geoffrey Chapman, 1983.   GERALD O'COLLINS

revelation, biblical (Lat., *revelare*, "to unveil"), the disclosure of what is hidden or obscure; theologically, the self-manifestation of God to humans. Divine revelation in word and deed is central to the OT. God's word is revealed through the Torah (Deut 6:20; 29:29), through self-manifestation to figures of destiny (Gen 12:1–3; 17:1–22; Exod 3:1–4:31), by prophetic calls (Isa 6:6–13; Jer 1:6–9; Ezek 3:1–11) with accompanying divine communications (Isa 1:10–31; Jer 2:1–4:4), and through the gift of divine wisdom to humans (Prov 2:6–15; Wis 7:7–8). Early creedal statements (Deut 6:20–25; 26:5–10; Josh 24:2–13), hymns (Exod 15:1–18), Psalms (Pss 78, 105, 106) and narrative accounts (Joshua-Kings) affirm God's self-disclosure in history. God is also revealed in the glory of nature (Pss 8, 104) and in religious experience, especially in a cultic setting (Pss 18:6; 48:9). In the postexilic period (after 539 B.C.) a distinct genre of literature developed, which contemporary scholars call apocalyptic (Gk., *apokalypsis*, "uncovering"). Arising among a persecuted and often marginalized people, apocalyptic literature is characterized by an emphasis on the hidden plan of God that explains the historical suffering of a peo-

ple. This plan is revealed to a specific prophet or seer (e.g., Dan 7:15–16; *1 Enoch* 1:1–2; 37:1–5), with assurance that God favors those persecuted (Dan 7:23–27) and with hope for future vindication through a final cataclysmic judgment (Dan 8:18–27; 12:1–13). Revelation in the NT builds on the OT. God is revealed in word (John 3:34; 6:63, 68), in history (Acts 7:2–53), and in religious experience (2 Cor 12:1–9), but all these assume a marked Christological focus (1 John 1:1–2). Jesus' life and teaching reveal God's nature and purpose (Acts 2:22–36) and Jesus becomes the preeminent "word" (John 1:1–18). Apocalyptic motifs are also very strong especially in Mark 13 (and parallel texts), in parts of Paul (1 Thess 4:13–5:11; 1 Cor 15:35–58) and in the book of Revelation (the Apocalypse). Essential to all expressions of revelation is the freely given self-communication of the hidden God which transcends human capacity, along with an invitation to enter more deeply into the divine presence and mystery. *See also* revelation.   JOHN R. DONAHUE

Reverend (Lat., *reverendus*, "worthy of respect"), a title used for the clergy since the fifteenth century. Bishops are addressed as "Most Reverend" and monsignors as "Reverend Monsignor." Older titles for monsignors were "Right Reverend" (for a domestic prelate) and "Very Reverend" (for a papal chamberlain). Abbesses, prioresses, and superiors of religious communities of women are often addressed as "Reverend Mother." The word is an adjective, not a noun. Therefore, the definite article "the" precedes it in formal correspondence.

revivalism, Catholic, a style of religion that stressed personal conversion, promoted by Catholic preachers, most often members of religious orders. This development was first noticeable in the Catholic Reform era that took place after the Protestant Reformation of the sixteenth century. Religious order preachers traveled across Europe conducting revivals, also known as parish missions. These missions or revivals stressed the need for personal conversion that would be ratified through reception of the sacraments of Penance and Eucharist. Like their Protestant counterparts, these revivals nurtured an evangelical piety that was rooted in the religious experience of conversion, but their emphasis on the sacraments of Penance and Eucharist gave this evangelical piety a decidedly Catholic quality.

Such revivals flourished in the sixteenth and seventeenth centuries; after a period of decline in the eighteenth century they experienced a renewal in the nineteenth century throughout the Catholic world. They declined once again in the mid twentieth century. *See also* parish mission.

reviviscence (ree-viv'uh-sens), a later, delayed reception of the grace of a sacrament once the obstacle to that grace—often seen as ignorance or a culpable resistance to the grace of the sacrament—has been removed. This teaching is especially applied to those sacraments that cannot be repeated because they impart a particular character: Baptism, Confirmation, and Holy Orders. For example, after being baptized as an infant but never raised in the faith, individuals who undergo a conversion to Christ and the Church later in life cannot be rebaptized, but because of their conversion, the grace that had been "blocked" becomes operative in their lives. *See also* grace, sacramental; sacrament.

Revue Biblique, the oldest Catholic quarterly of biblical studies, edited at the École Biblique in Jerusalem and published in Paris. It covers archaeological, epigraphic, and patristic studies as well as exegesis. Founded in 1892, it continues to be a major scholarly journal. Articles are published in the major European languages. It maintains a regular archaeological chronicle that enables the researcher to follow the progress of excavations throughout a region on an annual basis.

Reynolds, St. Richard, ca. 1492–1535, Brigittine monk; canonized as one of the Forty Martyrs of England and Wales. Learned friend of leading Catholic humanists, his refusal to take the oath of supremacy recognizing Henry VIII as supreme head of the Church in England led to his execution by hanging. Feast day: October 25. *See also* Forty Martyrs of England and Wales.

rhipidion (rih-pih'dee-ahn; Gk., "fan"), a Byzantine-rite flabellum or liturgical fan of wood or metal, also called *hexapterygon* (Gk., "six-winged") because it symbolizes and often bears the image of the six-winged Seraphim worshiping before the throne of God (Isa 6:2–3). The use of such fans in the liturgy dates from the fourth century. They are carried in processions and the deacons agitate them

over the eucharistic gifts during the anaphora, or eucharistic prayer.

rhythm method. *See* natural family planning.

Ricci, Matteo, 1552–1610, scientist and Jesuit missionary to China. Born in the Papal States, Ricci joined the Jesuits (1571). In 1582 he studied Chinese language and culture, which he mastered to an extent unheard of by a foreigner. He entered China (1583) along with Michele Ruggier (1543–1607). Ricci attracted converts using Western science. Arriving at the imperial court (1601), Ricci became a favorite of the emperor and an important scientific and literary figure. He published in Chinese a catechism (1595), "On Friendship" (1595), "Twenty-Five Sayings" (1604), a work on ethics (1604), along with polemics against the Buddhists and translations of Euclid. In order to missionize, Ricci adopted the controversial method of adapting to Chinese culture, e.g., referring to God as the "Lord of Heaven," promoting the use of Chinese rites, and assuming the status and style of a mandarin. An acrimonious controversy between Jesuits and Dominicans about his methods followed his death, and his approach was definitively forbidden by Pope Benedict XIV in 1742. In 1939, however, Pope Pius XII reopened the case and declared the practices "licit and commendable." *See also* China, Catholicism in; Chinese rites controversy; inculturation.

Richard, Gabriel, 1767–1832, missionary. A Sulpician priest, he fled revolutionary France and came to the Old Northwest Territory as a missionary (1792). He labored throughout the Michigan Territory; he ministered to Native Americans, established schools, hospitals and churches, introduced the first printing press to Detroit, and published the first Catholic newspaper in the United States, *The Michigan Essay* (1809). One of the founders of the University of Michigan (1821), he served the institution as vice president, professor, and trustee. As Michigan's territorial delegate, he was the first Catholic priest to serve in the U.S. Congress. While caring for cholera victims, Richard died from the disease.

Richard of Chichester, St., ca. 1197–1253, bishop of Chichester. Having studied at Oxford, Paris, and Bologna, Richard served as chancellor of

Oxford and later of Canterbury. He was noted for his generosity to the poor and his zeal in promoting clerical discipline. Feast day: April 3.

Richard of St. Victor, d. 1173, exegete, theologian, and disciple of Hugh at the abbey of St. Victor in Paris. His treatise *De Trinitate (On the Trinity)* stresses the empirical basis for the proof of God's existence and indicates that it is possible to arrive at the doctrine of the Trinity through speculative reasoning. Richard wrote treatises on Scripture such as *Benjamin Maior,* which emphasizes the biblical narrative as the basis for the ascent of the soul in contemplation. In *De Quattuor Gradibus Violentae Caritatis* Richard stresses love as the basis of all contemplation. *See also* contemplation; Trinity, doctrine of the; Victorines.

Richelieu, Armand Jean du Plessis, 1585–1642, French cardinal, minister of Louis XIII from 1624 to 1642. A defender of Catholicism and opponent of the Huguenots and Jansenists, Richelieu was interested mainly in strengthening French independence from Rome. He therefore sided with German and Swiss Protestant princes against the Catholic Habsburgs during the Thirty Years' War (1618–48), precluding Catholic restoration in Germany. *See also* Gallicanism.

Rienzo, Cola di, ca. 1313–54, Italian humanist who sought to restore ancient Roman glory during the Avignon papacy. Rienzo appointed himself tribune in 1347, but his dictatorial behavior and imperial pretensions led to his expulsion by the Roman nobility. Returning to Rome as senator in 1353, he again offended the people, who revolted and killed him in 1354.

Rievaulx (ree-voh'), Cistercian abbey in Yorkshire, England, founded 1131 by Walter Espec and monks sent from Clairvaux by Bernard. Rievaulx's third abbot, Aelred, presided over considerable growth and the building of a new church. The last abbot, Edward Kirkby, was removed by Henry VIII's Royal Commissioners, and the house was dissolved in 1538.

Rigby, St. John, d. 1600, one of the Forty Martyrs of England and Wales canonized in 1970. A Catholic layman born in Lancashire, he was executed for refusing to attend Protestant services. Feast day: June 21. *See also* Forty Martyrs of England and Wales.

righteousness, a quality predicated in Scripture of both God and human beings. God is declared righteous (Exod 9:27; Jer 12:1; Ps 116:5) and is said to judge with righteousness (Isa 3:13; Ps 9:9; 98:9). This divine judicial quality becomes in postexilic writings that whereby God manifests divine salvific bounty in a sentence of acquittal (Isa 46:13, where "my righteousness" is parallel to "my salvation"). The Pauline understanding of God's righteousness echoes this postexilic understanding (Rom 1:17; 3:21–26; 10:3). The Hebrew equivalent of Paul's phrase is not found in the OT, but is known from Qumran texts (1QM 4:6; 1QS 11:12). Paul, however, uses the same phrase to describe the status of justified Christians, "that in him we might become the righteousness of God" (2 Cor 5:21; cf. Phil 3:9). It thus denotes the gift of righteousness coming from God to human beings, an alien righteousness given to Christians by God as an effect of what Christ has done for humanity in his life, Passion, death, and Resurrection. Among NT writers Paul also speaks of human beings as righteous (Rom 5:19; Gal 3:11), by which he means the status of acquittal that sinners have acquired before God's tribunal through faith in the gracious merits of Christ Jesus. Matthew, too, speaks of the Christians' righteousness, denoting their moral conduct in keeping with God's will (Matt 3:5; 5:20; 6:1; 10:41; 21:32).

rights and obligations in canon law, those goods and benefits to which members of the Church are entitled together with the duties by which they are bound. Many of these rights and obligations are listed in the Western and Eastern codes of canon law. The primary listing for the rights and obligations of all the Christian faithful is found in canons 208–23 in the Western code and canons 7–26 in the Eastern code; these apply to all the baptized in full communion with the Catholic Church. In addition, because of their proper roles in the Church, there are listings of rights and obligations for laypeople alone, for clerics, and for religious. It is only after the post–Vatican II reform of canon law that we see such listings. The original contemporary enumeration was found in a document called the *Lex Ecclesiae Fundamentalis* ("Fundamental Law of the

Church"), which was an attempt to write a legal constitution for the Church. Although the attempt was not successful, the list of rights and obligations from this proposal was used in both codes. These rights and obligations are virtually the same as those articulated in the documents of Vatican II, and much of the language the codes use is taken directly from those documents. Although articulated by the council, the bases for these rights and obligations are, for the most part, to be found either in the natural law (and thus they are common to all human persons) or in the dignity of Christians, which derives from their Baptism and from the nature of the Church (thus they are common to all those baptized in full communion with the universal Church). These rights and obligations are, therefore, neither granted as a concession nor imposed as a burden by ecclesiastical authority; they would exist whether or not they were specified in the code of canon law.

The rights and obligations include: the fundamental equality of all believers, the obligation to seek the truth, the right to freedom of inquiry, the obligation to remain in communion with the Church, the right to express pastoral needs and opinions to the pastors of the Church, the obligation to support the Church with material assistance, the right and duty to participate in the Church's missionary endeavors, the right to the Church's spiritual ministrations, the right to a Christian education, the duty to pursue holiness, the right to a good reputation, and the right to vindicate one's rights within the Church.

Given that clergy and laity, although sharing a fundamental equality, are seen as having different roles within the Church and within secular society, some of their rights and obligations differ. After a general list of rights and obligations applying to all the faithful, there are separate listings for the laity and the clergy found in both codes (see cans. 224–31, 273–89 in the Western code and cans. 399–409, 367–93 in the Eastern code). Some, though not all, of the rights and obligations in those lists are considered matters of Church discipline and tradition that are subject to change. As such, they are less fundamental than the rights and obligations mentioned above.

All rights and obligations form part of the context for the interpretation of other laws, and it would be a violation of canonical equity to disregard them in understanding canon law. It is important to note, however, that they are not always to be taken absolutely and in a manner indifferent to other rights, duties, and concerns for the individual and common good. One of the rights a member of the Church has is to vindicate rights. In the judicial area this right is well provided for in those places where the ecclesiastical tribunal system is functioning. In places where that system is not established, as well as in other areas of Church administration, the ability to vindicate rights has been, at times, more difficult because of the drawbacks of distance or confusion concerning the procedure to be followed, or outright resistance to it in principle. There was a proposal that the 1983 code establish administrative tribunals in order to ameliorate this situation. Although it was turned down, there is evidence of ongoing concern for the vindication of rights at the highest levels of Church administration. *See also* canon law, interpretation of; due process. JOHN F. LAHEY

right to die, the claim that persons have a legal or moral right to die if and when they so choose. The phrase "right to die" is ambiguous. It may refer only to the choice to reject treatment or it may include the claim that (active) euthanasia is morally right and ought to be legally right as well.

The Catholic position is based on two essential moral distinctions. First, persons have an obligation to use "ordinary" means of preserving their lives, but are not required to use "extraordinary" means. The difference is based on the burdens and benefits of the treatment and of its results. This right of a dying person to be free of useless or overly burdensome treatment is sometimes called the right to die, and in this sense it is supported by Catholic moral theology.

Second, though persons may sometimes reject treatment, they may not directly kill themselves or be killed by others. The withholding and the withdrawing of extraordinary means of preserving life is not (active) euthanasia, nor is the sedation of a dying patient from pain, even if the medication indirectly hastens the moment of death. But persons may not intend to kill innocent persons or actually kill them. Some theologians suggest that euthanasia may in some cases be licit, but even most of these oppose its legalization because of the social harm it would cause. The Church has consistently opposed the movement to legalize euthanasia. If "the right to die" includes the option for (active) euthanasia, the claim is denied by Catholic moral teaching. *See also* euthanasia.

right to life, a term in general use to characterize the position of opponents of abortion. It also refers to a political advocacy group, the National Right to Life Committee (NRLC), formed in the late 1960s to combat abortion. The NRLC, formed and organized with substantial support and direction from the leadership of the U.S. Catholic Church, was and remains the largest antiabortion organization in the United States. The NRLC severed its formal connection with the Catholic Church in 1973 but continues to draw support from it. Right-to-life activists express their opposition to abortion by means of local protests and national political initiatives. *See also* abortion; civil law and morality; consistent ethic of life; pro-life movement.

rigorism, an attitude in moral theology whereby the law is always applied severely. Rigorism, strong among the Jansenists of the seventeenth century, offered an image of God as harsh and intimidating. For the rigorist, the only way to overcome human depravity was through "rigorous" obedience to the will of God as expressed in God's laws. *See also* Jansenism; laxism; tutiorism.

Rimini, Council of (359), council called, together with an Eastern council at Seleucia, by the Arianizing emperor Constantius to solve the Arian controversy. The majority of the four hundred bishops present approved the *homoousios* (Gk., "of one substance") for the Son, but subsequently, pressured by Constantius and the Arian delegation, the council reversed itself, accepting a vague formula (also approved at Seleucia) describing the Son as "like the Father according to the Scriptures." Use of *ousia* and cognates was banned. Jerome commented that "the whole world groaned, amazed to find itself Arian." *See also* Arianism; *homoousios*.

rings, metal (usually precious) bands worn on the finger(s) of the hand. Such insignia mark fully professed religious sisters, some members of male religious orders, and prelates such as bishops and abbots. The pope wears a special ring known as the "Fisherman's Ring." Traditionally such jewelry signified a symbolic marriage to the Church or to Christ. Couples exchange rings at marriage as a sign of mutual fidelity.

Rita of Cascia, St., 1381–1457 Italian widow and nun. She lived with a brutal husband until he was murdered. Then she became an Augustinian nun. She is the patron saint of desperate situations. Feast day: May 22.

rite, any repetitive ceremonial activity with fixed rules; also, a particular ritual ceremony ("the rite of Baptism"). The term "rite" is also used for a distinct liturgical family, comprising all the liturgical rites and usages of a particular tradition or historic liturgical family (e.g., Roman rite, Byzantine rite). This broad meaning of rite is to be understood not only in the external, ritual sense, but also as the particular ethos that sustains the rite, and which the rite expresses. Without this spirit that animates it and that alone justifies its celebration, the liturgy of a rite is little more than superficial ritualism. In pre–Vatican II Catholic usage, "rite" in this latter sense was also used to designate the particular Catholic tradition to which one belonged. Since Vatican II (1962–65), Catholic documents refer instead to the particular church.

In addition to the Roman (Latin) rite, there are seven Eastern Catholic rites (statistical estimates of their adherents in 1993 in parentheses): Armenian (142,853); Byzantine (8,840,000); Coptic (152,584); Ethiopian (118,550); Maronite (2,176,152); East-Syrian, including Chaldean (469,764) and Syro-Malabar (2,887,050); West Syrian, including Syro-Antiochene (100,245) and Syro-Malankara (281,868). *See also* Eastern rites; Latin rite; Roman rite.

rite, change of, an expression often used to mean transferring from one Catholic church to another of a different rite. Such transfers are governed by canon law and generally require the consent of the Apostolic See of Rome. In marriages where the spouses belong to different churches, the wife is free to transfer to the church of her husband.

There are at present twenty-one Eastern Catholic churches in full communion with the Apostolic See of Rome (e.g., the Chaldean, Maronite, Melkite, Ruthenian, Syro-Malabar, Ukrainian). Each of these churches possesses its own rite, which is described in the Code of Canons of the Eastern Churches as the liturgical, theological, spiritual, and disciplinary patrimony peculiar to each church because of culture and historical circumstances. *See also* Eastern rites; rite.

RITE OF CHRISTIAN
INITIATION OF ADULTS

T he Rite of Christian Initiation of Adults (RCIA) is the liturgical and formational process of Christian initiation. The Rite of
Christian Initiation was revised and restored in 1972 in accordance with the mandate of the Second Vatican Council (Constitution on the Sacred Liturgy, n. 64) and by decree of Pope Paul VI.
National statutes for the catechumenate were approved in the United
States by the National Conference of Catholic Bishops in 1986. And,
finally, the Rite of Christian Initiation of Adults was mandated for use in
the United States beginning on September 1, 1988.

THE ORIGINS OF THE RCIA

During the first and second centuries there was no formal process of initiation into the Church. Faith in Jesus Christ and in God as Father of
Jesus Christ, conversion of life-style, and signs of concern for the needy
were the only requirements for Baptism. In time some elementary theology and moral instruction were imposed. The *Didache* (Gk., "The Teaching," an early document on Church practice from ca. 100) presents two
ways: the way of life and the way of death. By the third century the
process of initiation was formalized. In the *Apostolic Tradition* (ca. 215)
Hippolytus defines two stages of preparation:
those being introduced to God's word for the first
time, called *catecumeni* (Lat., "catechumens") or
audientes ("hearers"), and those who have been
chosen for initiation. The latter had been observed
by the community and deemed worthy of the
sacrament.

A candidate for initi-
ation into the
Church, also known
as a catechumen,
stands with her
sponsor (left) during
the Rite of Election
on the First Sunday
of Lent, at which
time she is deemed
worthy of admission
to the sacraments of
initiation (Baptism,
Confirmation, and
Eucharist), to be
administered at the
Easter Vigil.

Although the rites were always developing and
fluctuating depending on the local church, a
highly structured and unified rite of initiation
evolved. A signing with the cross, claiming the
inquirers for Christ, and welcoming them into the
catechumenate constituted the first step in the
process. Catechumens could have spent as many as three years in a
period of catechetical, liturgical, and spiritual formation. The roles of
catechists and sponsors were clearly defined: catechists were to explain
the history of salvation from the beginning of time to the present, and
sponsors were to walk the way of conversion with the catechumen and
then testify to the catechumen's sincerity of intention and readiness to
continue the process of initiation.

Thereafter, catechumens were urged to enter a more intense period of preparation, usually coinciding with the season of Lent. Once chosen, they were presented to the bishop and given a new name. Lent took the form for the whole community of a lengthy annual retreat before Baptism. The period was one of intense prayer, fasting, and continued study. The Apostles' Creed and the Lord's Prayer were handed over to the chosen. The Gospel stories of the Samaritan woman (John 4:16–42), the man born blind (John 9:1–41), and the resurrection of Lazarus (John 11:1–45) formed the basis of the scrutinies, the purpose of which is the strengthening of the catechumens' ability to overcome temptation as well as the purifying of their intentions.

An Easter Vigil baptism at Holy Cross Church, Onamia, Minnesota. Baptism is a climactic moment in the process of Christian initiation, the liturgical culmination of which is the Eucharist.

Tertullian (d. 225) and Hippolytus both identified the great vigil of Easter as the most appropriate time for Baptism. There was much diversity in how the churches celebrated Baptism, but among the consistent elements were the renunciation of Satan, the proclamation of the Apostles' Creed, prebaptismal anointings, the bath of new birth with a trinitarian profession of faith, bestowal of white garments, and anointing and imposition of hands. Following these initiatory rites the newly baptized were welcomed at the eucharistic table.

From the beginning there was a strong linkage between liturgy and catechesis. Catechetical readiness determined the time of the liturgical rite. The rites expressed what the catechumens were experiencing in their faith development. Certain core elements of the faith were not shared until the converts had been initiated. Catechesis on the Eucharist was only possible after full initiation. A period of *mystagogia* (Gk., "deepening of faith") provided the community with time to continue the formation of the newly baptized.

THE DECLINE OF INITIATION RITES

The fourth and fifth centuries saw an increase in the number of converts after Christianity became the official religion of the empire. This resulted in a shortened initiation process, relaxed requirements, and unverified conversions.

With the universal acceptance of infant Baptism during the fifth century and indiscriminate baptisms of conquered "barbarians," the adult catechumenate became nearly defunct. Despite efforts to renew the process, the catechumenate was relegated to one season of Lent, seven weeks at first, later only four. Only missionary territories retained some semblance of a process of initiation within a community context.

RITE OF CHRISTIAN INITIATION OF ADULTS

PERIOD OF EVANGELIZATION AND PRECATECHUMENATE
A time, of no fixed duration or structure, for inquiry and introduction to gospel values, an opportunity for the beginnings of faith.

FIRST STEP:
ACCEPTANCE INTO THE ORDER OF CATECHUMENS
The liturgical rite, usually celebrated on some annual date or dates, marking the beginning of the catechumenate proper, as candidates express and the Church accepts their intention to respond to God's call to follow the way of Christ.

PERIOD OF THE CATECHUMENATE
A time, in duration corresponding to the progress of the individual, for the nurturing and growth of the catechumen's faith and conversion to God; celebrations of the word and prayers of exorcism and blessing are meant to assist the process.

SECOND STEP:
ELECTION OR ENROLLMENT OF NAMES
The liturgical rite, usually celebrated on the First Sunday of Lent, by which the Church formally ratifies the catechumen's readiness for the sacraments of initiation and the catechumens, now the elect, express the will to receive the sacraments.

PERIOD OF PURIFICATION AND ENLIGHTENMENT
The time immediately preceding the elect's initiation, usually the Lenten season preceding the celebration of this initiation at the Easter Vigil; it is a time of reflection intensely centered on conversion, marked by celebration of the scrutinies and presentations, and of the preparation rites on Holy Saturday.

THIRD STEP:
CELEBRATION OF THE SACRAMENTS OF INITIATION
The liturgical rite, usually integrated into the Easter Vigil, by which the elect are initiated through Baptism, Confirmation, and the Eucharist.

PERIOD OF POSTBAPTISMAL CATECHESIS, OR MYSTAGOGY
The time, usually the Easter season, following the celebration of initiation during which the newly initiated experience being fully a part of the Christian community by means of pertinent catechesis and particularly by participation with all the faithful in the Sunday eucharistic celebration.

SOURCE: *Rite of Christian Initiation of Adults: Study Edition*, Liturgy Training Publications, 1988.

From the sixth through the ninth centuries parents of infants to be baptized were invited into a catechumenal process. In the sixteenth century there were attempts by Dominicans and Augustinians to restore an adult catechumenal process, if only for seven to forty days. In 1552 Ignatius of Loyola established catechumenate houses where converts gathered for three months.

Modern missionary efforts to renew the catechumenate were heroic, but all failed by the beginning of the twentieth century. The only place that kept a catechumenal model alive was North Africa, where the White Fathers recognized the need to build the Church from the grass roots. North Africa's experience drew the attention of the European churches, especially of France, with its large number of nonpracticing Catholics. The revival of the catechumenate in Africa and Europe was the principal basis for the Vatican's reinstatement of the Rite of Christian Initiation of Adults.

THE REFORM OF VATICAN II

The Second Vatican Council (1962–65) mandated the restoration of an adult catechumenate, and in 1974 a provisional text was published for use in the United States. The reinstatement of the Rite of Christian Initiation of Adults restored a vision of Christian community embraced by the early Church, the vision of a people with conversion as its primary focus, the faith community as its context, and discipleship as its goal. The Church recognized once again that conversion cannot be artificially induced, that motives for initiation must be questioned and evaluated, and that the whole community needs to be renewed. "The initiation of catechumens is a gradual process that takes place within the community of the faithful. By joining the catechumens in reflecting on the value of the Paschal Mystery and by renewing their own conversion, the faithful provide an example that will help the catechumens to obey the Holy Spirit more generously" (RCIA, n.4).

There was a major shift also in the understanding of who is responsible for initiation: "the people of God, as represented by the local Church, should understand and show by their concern that the initiation of adults is the responsibility of all the baptized" (RCIA, n.9). The rite reclaims the roles of catechists, sponsors, godparents, the pastor, and the whole faith community. While each individual's ministry is unique, it is part of a fuller, more comprehensive process of initiation.

PASTORAL REFLECTIONS

The RCIA was designed specifically for the initiation of unbaptized persons. These, and only these, are called catechumens upon entrance to the catechumenate. The rite also supports preparation of baptized uncatechized Catholic adults for Confirmation and the Eucharist, and for other baptized Christians seeking full communion with the Catholic Church. However, all these people are called candidates, and the document clearly states that the dignity of their Baptism is to be respected.

A priest lays his hands on the head of a catechumen during a Lenten ceremony known as the scrutinies, intended to purify the cate-chumen's mind and heart, to strengthen her against temptation, to purify her intentions, and to solidify her decision to enter the Church.

The 1988 mandate decreed that whenever an adult or anyone of cate-chetical age is prepared for Baptism, the RCIA is to be used. The RCIA, therefore, has become the norm of formation. Consequently, it has had impact on the process of preparation for all the other sacraments by emphasizing the need for evangelization, by introducing liturgical and lectionary catechesis, and by contributing to a catechumenal model of the Church, which includes also a call to conversion, personal and com-munal prayer, and participation in apostolic activities.

See also Baptism; catechumenate; conversion; Easter Vigil; Holy Week; Lent.

Bibliography

Duffy, Regis. *On Becoming Catholic: The Challenge of Christian Initiation.* San Francisco: Harper & Row, 1984.

Duggan, Robert, ed. *Conversion and the Catechumenate.* New York: Paulist Press, 1984.

Ivory, Thomas P. *Conversion and Community: A Catechumenal Model of Total Parish Formation.* New York: Paulist Press, 1988.

Morris, Thomas H. *The RCIA: Transforming the Church: A Resource for Pastoral Implementation.* New York: Paulist Press, 1989.

Yarnold, Edward. *The Awe-Inspiring Rites of Initiation: Baptismal Homilies of the Fourth Century.* Slough, England: St. Paul Publications, 1972.

Rite of Christian Initiation of Adults: Study Edition. Chicago: Liturgy Training Publications, 1988.

BEVERLY M. BRAZAUSKAS

Ritual, Roman, a liturgical book containing those special rites and blessings, other than the Mass, that are commonly performed by priests. One of the last books to be revised since Vatican II (1962–65), the Roman Ritual is now called the Book of Blessings. The rites and blessings have been newly revised for use in Christian assemblies, large or small, actively participating, with simple and clear vernacular prayers and gestures. The revised rites are marked by a more prolific use of Scripture. *See also* blessing; liturgical books.

Robert Bellarmine, St. *See* Bellarmine, St. Robert.

Robert of Melun, d. 1167, English logician, theologian, and bishop of Hereford from 1163 to 1167. A student of both Peter Abelard and Hugh of St. Victor, Robert founded his own school at Melun in France in 1142 and taught theology there until recalled to England by Henry II in 1160. Robert promoted the development of theology as a science, especially through his teaching and writing, e.g., his *Sentences* (1152–60).

Robert of Molesmes, St. (moh-lem'), ca. 1027–1111, abbot of Molesmes and cofounder of Cîteaux. He left the monastery of Molesmes, which he had founded, when its life-style became lax to found Cîteaux, later the motherhouse of the Cistercian order. He eventually returned to Molesmes. Under Robert's leadership, Molesmes became a famous Benedictine center. *See also* Cîteaux.

Roberts, St. John, ca. 1577–1610, one of the Forty Martyrs of England and Wales canonized in 1970. Raised a Protestant in Wales, he joined the Benedictines and was ordained in 1602. Especially known for his services during the London plague of 1603, he was arrested and expelled from England a number of times before he was executed in 1610. Feast day: December 9. *See also* Forty Martyrs of England and Wales.

Roch, St. (rahk), 1350–80, French layman, devoted to the care of plague victims. He is invoked against epidemics. Feast day: August 16.

Rogation Days, days of special public intercession in the Roman liturgy, marked by litanies and processions. The Great Litany, held on April 25, originated in Rome in the fourth century; the Lesser Litanies originated in Gaul in the fifth century and were held on the three days before Ascension Thursday. In the Roman Calendar of 1969, the Great Litany was abolished. The Rogation Days were retained, though the time and manner of their celebration was left to episcopal conferences. *See also* Litany of the Saints.

Rolle, Richard, ca. 1300–49, English hermit and author of biblical commentaries and didactic treatises on prayer, asceticism, and mystical experience. His works include his letters to those under his spiritual direction and his Latin treatise *Incendium Amoris* ("Fire of Love"). Rolle was an enormously popular English mystical writer in the late Middle Ages. *See also* English Mystics.

Roman Catholic, an alternate post-Reformation designation for a member of the Catholic Church. Before the sixteenth century the Church universal was simply the Catholic Church. The adjective had its origin in Ignatius of Antioch (early second century) and was found also in the writings of the early Fathers of the Church and in the creeds. When the authority of the Bishop of Rome became a source of contention between West and East in the eleventh century, and between Catholics and Protestants in the sixteenth, the adjective "Roman" served to distinguish those Christians who remained in union with Rome from those who did not.

However, the adjective "Roman" tends to confuse rather than define the reality of Catholicism. The history of the Church begins with Jesus' gathering of his disciples and with the eventual post-Resurrection commissioning of Peter to be the chief shepherd and foundation of the Church—in Jerusalem and in Caesarea Philippi, not in Rome. Therefore, it is not the Roman primacy that gives Catholicism its distinctive identity within the family of Christian churches, but the Petrine primacy.

The adjective "Roman" applies more properly to the diocese of Rome than to the worldwide Church that is in union with the Bishop of Rome. Indeed, it strikes some as contradictory to call the Church Catholic and Roman at one and the same time.

Eastern-rite Catholics who are in union with Rome (sometimes pejoratively called "Uniates") also find the adjective "Roman" objectionable. They prefer to speak of their churches as Catholic and then to distinguish particular ecclesial traditions (e.g., Roman, Byzantine, Maronite) within the Catholic communion. In addition to the Latin, or Roman, tradition, there are seven other non-Latin, non-Roman ecclesial traditions: Armenian, Byzantine, Coptic, Ethiopian, East Syrian (Chaldean), West Syrian, and Maronite. *See also* Catholic Church; Catholicism; Eastern Catholics and Rome; Eastern churches; Eastern rites. *RICHARD P. MCBRIEN*

Roman Catholic Church. *See* Catholic Church.

Roman Catholicism. *See* Catholicism.

Roman congregations, major departments or offices through which much of the executive business of the Holy See is conducted. The congregations are an important part of the Roman Curia, which assists the pope in his responsibilities governing the universal Church. Each is presided over by a cardinal-prefect assisted by an archbishop-secretary who is second in command. These, in turn, are assisted by a number of functionaries who handle the day-to-day business. The actual members of the congregations are cardinals and bishops drawn both from those resident in Rome and those living elsewhere. The cardinals are also chosen in such a way that an individual cardinal might be a member of a number of congregations whose concerns overlap. A full meeting of a congregation is called a *plenarium* and discusses more important matters.

The Congregation for the Doctrine of the Faith (formerly the Holy Office) is concerned with matters touching upon doctrine. The Congregation for Bishops deals with bishops and their ministry. The Congregation for the Evangelization of Peoples (also called Propaganda, from *Propaganda Fide,* Lat., "Propagation of the Faith") handles the Church's missionary activity. The Congregation for Institutes of Consecrated Life and for Societies of Apostolic Life covers religious communities and other similar groups publicly recognized by the Church. The Congregation for the Oriental Churches relates to those Eastern churches in communion with Rome. The Congregation for the Clergy deals with the life and ministry of clerics and with catechetical matters. The Congregation for Catholic Education (also called "for Seminaries and Universities") handles the Church's schools. The Congregation for the Causes of Saints oversees the processes of beatifica-

tion and canonization. The Congregation for Divine Worship and the Discipline of the Sacraments oversees public worship and dispensations from clerical obligations. *See also* Roman Curia. *JOHN F. LAHEY*

Roman Curia, bureaucracy that assists the pope in his responsibilities of governing the universal Church. Although early in the history of the Church bishops of Rome had assistants to help them in the exercise of their ministry, it was not until 1588 that formal organization of the Roman Curia was accomplished by Pope Sixtus V. The most recent reorganization of the Curia was completed in 1988 by Pope John Paul II in the apostolic constitution *Pastor Bonus.*

The Curia is organized into offices of various ranks and importance. Chief among them is the Secretariat of State, which not only deals with diplomatic relations with various states, but also is in charge of the overall supervision of the other departments (discateries) of the Curia. These include various councils, tribunals, and prefectures that handle matters ranging from the economic patrimony of the Holy See to the liturgical celebrations of the pope. The higher officials of the Curia are cardinals or archbishops.

In relatively recent times, beginning especially under Pope Paul VI (d. 1978), the Curia has become more internationalized as the number of officials, even higher officials, from countries other than Italy grows. Some concern that more women be included among curial officials has been addressed, though the tradition that higher officials be archbishops or cardinals has meant that the few women in positions of leadership currently cannot aspire to higher positions. With a growing emphasis on the role of the local (diocesan) church, concern has also been expressed over the centralizing tendency of a large curial operation.

The offices and officials of the Roman Curia are listed in the official publication *Annuario Pontificio. See also Pastor Bonus;* Vatican. *JOHN F. LAHEY*

I. THE SECRETARIAT OF STATE TO HIS HOLINESS:

Assists the pope in the care of the universal Church and in his dealings with the Roman Curia.

First Section: For General Affairs:

Assists the pope in matters not within the competence of other dicasteries, or departments, within the Roman Curia and coordinates the activities of, and fosters relations with, these other departments and also with the bishops and with the diplomatic missions of the Holy See.

Second Section: For Relations with States:

Formerly the Council for Public Affairs of the Church. Assists the pope in all matters relating to civil governments, diplomatic relations of the Holy See with other governments, and diplomatic missions of the Holy See.

II. THE CONGREGATIONS

Congregation for the Doctrine of the Faith:

Responsible for the safeguarding of Catholic faith and morals, for all matters pertaining to the Petrine Privilege, or "privilege of the faith" (dissolution of a valid and consummated marriage between a baptized and an unbaptized person), and for safeguarding the dignity of the sacrament of Reconciliation, or Penance. Attached to this Congregation are the Pontifical Biblical Commission and the International Theological Commission.

Congregation for the Causes of Saints:

Responsible for all matters pertaining to the beatification and canonization of saints and the preservation of relics.

Congregation for the Oriental Churches:

Responsible for all matters pertaining to persons, discipline, or rites of the Oriental churches (Eastern-rite Catholic churches in communion with Rome), with authority over territories in which the majority of Catholics belong to Eastern rites (e.g., Egypt, Greece, Iraq, Lebanon, Syria) and over minority communities of Oriental Catholics, no matter where they live.

Congregation for Bishops:

Responsible for all matters having to do with the naming of bishops and the establishment of dioceses and provinces, except what is subject to the authority of the Congregation for the Oriental Churches and the Congregation for the Evangelization of Peoples.

Congregation for Divine Worship and the Discipline of the Sacraments:

Responsible for all matters pertaining to the seven sacraments, except what is specifically reserved to the authority of other offices of the Holy See, particularly the Congregation for the Doctrine of the Faith. It deals with the causes for nullifying ordinations and for granting dispensations from the obligations of ordination to deacons and priests.

Congregation for the Evangelization of Peoples or for the Propagation of the Faith:

Responsible for the direction and coordination of missionary work throughout the world, including the proposing of candidates for bishop, the establishment of episcopal conferences, and the mobilizing of financial support for missionary activity.

Congregation for Institutes of Consecrated Life and for Societies of Apostolic Life:
Responsible for institutes of religious, societies of the apostolic life, Third Orders, and secular institutes. It is divided into two sections; the second is responsible for societies of the apostolic life; the first is responsible for the rest.

Congregation for the Clergy:
Responsible for everything pertaining to clergy and the clerical life. It is divided into three sections; the first is concerned with diocesan priests; the second, with preaching, catechesis, and religious education; the third, with the temporal goods of the Church, except where other Congregations have authority over them.

Congregation for Catholic Education:
Responsible for all that pertains to the formation of the clergy and the Catholic education of both clergy and laity. It is divided into three sections; the first is concerned with seminaries and whatever concerns the education of diocesan clergy, and with the formation of religious and secular institutes; the second, with Catholic universities and institutes of higher learning; the third, with parochial and diocesan schools and other educational institutes below the level of a university.

I. TRIBUNALS

Apostolic Penitentiary:
Has authority over anything pertaining to the internal forum (i.e., matters of conscience) and to the granting and use of indulgences.

Supreme Tribunal of the Apostolic Signatura:
The supreme court of the Church and of Vatican City State. It is divided into two sections; the first is concerned with the proper administration of justice and other matters assigned to it by the code of canon law; the second, with matters referred to it, including the resolution of conflicts of authority among various departments of the Holy See.

Sacred Roman Rota:
Hears appeals from decisions of lower tribunals, primarily on matters pertaining to the nullification of marriages.

. PONTIFICAL COUNCILS

Pontifical Council for the Laity:
Responsible for the apostolate of the laity and their participation in the life and mission of the Church.

Pontifical Council for Promoting Christian Unity:
Responsible for relations with non-Catholic Christian communities and with Judaism (via the Commission for Religious Relations with Jews) and promotes ecumenical dialogue and other activities.

Pontifical Council for the Family:
Responsible for the promotion of family life.

Pontifical Council for Justice and Peace:
Responsible for the promotion of justice and peace, especially through the social teachings of the Church.

Pontifical Council "Cor Unum":
Provides information and coordinating services for Catholic aid and human development organizations and projects throughout the world.

Pontifical Council for the Pastoral Care of Migrants and Itinerants:
Concerned with pastoral assistance to migrants, nomads, tourists, and sea and air travelers.

Pontifical Council for the Pastoral Care of the Health Care Apostolate:
Fosters the work of formation, study, and action by international Catholic health-care organizations.

Pontifical Council for the Interpretation of Legislative Texts:
Provides official interpretation of the universal laws of the Church.

Pontifical Council for Interreligious Dialogue:
Responsible for relations with non-Christian religions and for promoting study of, and dialogue with, them. The Commission for Religious Relations with Muslims is attached to the Council.

Pontifical Council for Dialogue with Nonbelievers:
Studies atheism and promotes dialogue with nonbelievers.

Pontifical Council for Culture:
Responsible for promoting dialogue between the Church and the many cultures of the world.

Pontifical Council for Social Communications:
Responsible for matters pertaining to the communications media.

V.   OFFICES

Apostolic Camera:
Cares for and administers the temporal goods and rights of the Holy See during a vacancy in the papal office.

Prefecture of the Pontifical Household:
Responsible for the Apostolic Palace, including the papal chapel, for papal audiences, papal trips outside the Vatican, and nonliturgical papal ceremonies.

Administration of the Patrimony of the Holy See:
Responsible for the estate of the Holy See under direction of papal delegates. It is divided into two sections; the Ordinary Section performs regular administrative tasks assigned to it; the Extraordinary Section fulfills duties assigned to it by the pope.

Central Office of Statistics:
Gathers and organizes statistics relevant to the condition and mission of the Church.

Prefecture for the Economic Affairs of the Holy See:
Coordinates and supervises the administration of the possessions of the Holy See.

Office of Pontifical Ceremonies:
Responsible for everything pertaining to liturgical and other sacred ceremonies done by the pope or in his name.

Archives of the Second Vatican Council:
Maintains records and documentation pertaining to the Second Vatican Council (1962–65).

VI. COMMISSIONS AND COMMITTEES

Commission "Ecclesia Dei":
Responsible for facilitating the return of full communion with the Catholic Church those priests, seminarians, and religious who went into schism with the late Archbishop Marcel Lefebvre (d. 1991).

Commission of the Roman Curia:
Responsible for matters of discipline.

Council of Cardinals for the Study of Organizational and Economic Problems of the Holy See:
Responsible for monitoring the financial problems of the Holy See.

International Theological Commission:
Advises the Congregation for the Doctrine of the Faith on matters pertaining to Catholic theology and doctrine.

Commission of Cardinals for the Pontifical Shrines of Pompeii, Loreto, and Bari:
Responsible for the care of these three shrines.

Pontifical Biblical Commission:
Advises the Congregation for the Doctrine of the Faith on matters pertaining to the study and interpretation of the Bible.

Pontifical Committee for the International Eucharistic Congresses:
Responsible for international eucharistic congresses.

Pontifical Commission for the Revision and Emendation of the Vulgate:
Responsible for matters pertaining to the Latin Vulgate Bible.

Pontifical Commission for Vatican City State:
Responsible for the care of Vatican City State.

Pontifical Commission for Sacred Archaeology:
Responsible for matters pertaining to archaeological exploration of Christian antiquity.

Pontifical Committee for Historical Sciences:
Responsible for matters pertaining to the history of the Church.

VII. INSTITUTIONS CONNECTED WITH THE HOLY SEE

Vatican Secret Archives:
Responsible for the care of Vatican documents not open to public review, but since 1881 open to scholars.

Vatican Apostolic Library:
Responsible for the care of the Vatican libraries.

Pontifical Academy of Sciences:
Honors pure science and its practitioners, promotes freedom of pure science, and fosters research.

Vatican Radio:
Responsible for the operation of Vatican Radio.

Vatican Television Center:
Responsible for the operation of Vatican Television.

Fabric of St. Peter's:
Responsible for the administration, care, and preservation of St. Peter's Basilica.

Office of Papal Charities:
Distributes alms and aid in the name of the pope.

Vatican Polyglot Press:
Responsible for all printing done by the Vatican.

Vatican Publishing House:
Responsible for the preparation of books and other documents for publication.

Institute for the Works of Religion:
Responsible for the banking and administration of funds for the work of religion.

L'Osservatore Romano:
The daily newspaper of the Holy See.

Press Office:
Handles day-to-day relations with the world's communications media.

Commission on Latin America:
Concerned with matters pertaining to the Church in Latin America. Attached to the Congregation for Bishops.

Commission for the Preservation of the Artistic and Historic Patrimony of the Church:
Responsible for the care and preservation of the artistic and other historic possessions of the Holy See.

Commission on Russia:
Responsible for all ecclesiastical matters pertaining to Russia. Attached to the Secretariat of State.

Commission on Religious Relations with Jews:
Responsible for dialogue and the fostering of ecumenical contacts with Jews. Attached to the Council for Promoting Christian Unity.

Commission on Religious Relations with Muslims:
Promotes, regulates, and interprets relations with Muslims. Attached to the Council for Interreligious Dialogue.

Commission for the Protection of the Historical and Artistic Monuments of the Holy See:
Responsible for the protection of the artistic and other historic possessions of the Holy See.

Commission for the Preservation of Faith, Erection of New Churches in Rome:
Responsible for matters pertaining to the faith of Catholics in Rome and for the building of new churches in the city.

Labor Office of the Apostolic See:
Responsible for those who are employed by the Holy See and for settling labor disputes with them.

Catechism Commission:
Responsible for the drafting and translations of the *Catechism of the Catholic Church* (published in 1992; English translation, 1994).

Roman Empire, the territory around the Mediterranean and in Europe that was ruled by Rome from the first century B.C. to the fourth century A.D. Ancient Christian historians often pointed out the coincidence of Christ's birth with the reign of Augustus (27 B.C.–A.D. 14), the first emperor, but Christian attitudes regarding the empire varied. The book of Revelation pictures Rome as "Babylon the great . . . drunk with the blood of the saints . . ." (17:5–6). Hippolytus (d. ca. 236), among others, agreed, and Revelation continued to inspire apocalyptic protest in groups as diverse as the Montanists and Donatists, but more often Christians protested imperial policy toward Christians along with various aspects of imperial culture without actually impugning the empire itself as evil. This is the attitude of the Apologists, and even Tertullian (d. ca. 225) insists that Christians pray for the good of the empire (although his fellow African Minucius Felix denounced it altogether). Origen (d. ca. 254), while exhorting his students and congregation to martyrdom and himself dying as a result of torture, nevertheless felt that the empire had a providential character, intended by God to make it easier to "Go and teach all nations," as Jesus had commanded. Eusebius of Caesarea (d. ca. 340) agreed, extending this logic in the wake of Constantine's accession and portraying the Constantinian empire as the fulfillment of God's intentions from the time of Augustus and Christ. In the West, Ambrose (d. 397) and Prudentius (d. ca. 410) represent this view (somewhat modified), but Augustine (d. 430) came to be much less sanguine, regarding the empire, Christian or not, as at best a neutral reality where the destinies of the City of God and the city of this earth were ambiguously intertwined.

At any rate, despite the antipagan legislation of Theodosius I, Christians at the end of the fourth century had no reason to believe any given emperor would be Christian. The fourth century had seen a succession of Arian emperors, and the memory of Julian's pagan revival loomed large. It is not until the time of the Council of Ephesus (431) that one can begin to think of a "Christian" empire. In the East the "Byzantine" empire survived until the fall of Constantinople in 1453; in the West it soon gave way to the new Germanic kingdoms, but the imprint of the empire persisted even there, in the organization and polity of the Western Church. The diocese as an ecclesiastical territorial unit had its precedent in Roman civil territorial divisions; the insignia of Roman officials passed into use among the various

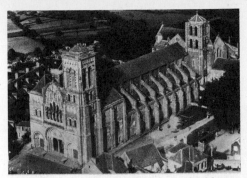

The Romanesque basilica of Vézelay, France, with its characteristically thick walls, barrel vaults, and relatively simple ornamentation.

ranks of clergy; and regulations for transfer and promotion of clergy were patterned after those for Roman civil servants. The legacy of Roman law was especially enduring in the area of appeals procedures, procedures for councils, marriage regulations, and the structure of papal legislative authority. *See also* Constantine, the Great; persecutions; Rome.

JOHN C. CAVADINI

Romanesque style, an architectural term designating the church architecture that emerged in the West ca. A.D. 1000. Characterized by massive, thick walls and piers, relatively small windows, and heavy barrel vaults and arches, Romanesque architecture derives from a style that looked similar to Roman architecture. *See also* Catholicism and architecture.

Romanian Catholic Church, the Byzantine Catholic community centered in Transylvania, one of the three major regions of modern Romania. It is the counterpart of the Romanian Orthodox Church.

Early History: Transylvania became part of Hungary in the early eleventh century. Although the principality was home to large numbers of Hungarians and Germans who were mostly Latin Catholics, Orthodox Romanians made up the majority of the population. Soon after the province was taken by the Turks in the sixteenth century, Calvinism gained ground among the Hungarians and Lutheranism among the Germans.

In 1687, the Habsburg emperor Leopold I drove the Turks from Transylvania and annexed it to his empire. It was his policy to encourage the Orthodox faithful within his realm to become Byzantine Catholics. For this purpose the Jesuits began to work as missionaries among the Transylvanian Romanians in 1693. Their efforts, combined with the denial of full civil rights to the Orthodox, and the spread of Protestantism in the area, which caused growing concern among the Orthodox clergy, all contributed to the acceptance of a union with Rome by Orthodox metropolitan Atanasie of Transylvania in 1698. He later convoked a synod that formally concluded the agreement on September 4, 1700.

At first this union included most of the Romanian Orthodox in the province. But in 1744, the Orthodox monk Visarion led a popular uprising that sparked a widespread movement back toward Orthodoxy. In spite of government efforts to enforce the union with Rome—even by military means—resistance was such that Empress Maria Theresa reluctantly allowed the appointment of a bishop for the Romanian Orthodox in Transylvania in 1759. In the end, about half of the Transylvanian Romanians returned to Orthodoxy.

It proved difficult for the new Byzantine Catholic community, known popularly as the "Greek Catholic Church," to obtain in practice the religious and civil rights that had been guaranteed it when the union was consummated. Bishop Ion Inochentie Micu-Klein, head of the Greek Catholic Church from 1729 to 1751, struggled with great vigor for the rights of his church and of all Romanians within the empire.

The Romanian Greek Catholic dioceses had originally been subordinate to the Latin Hungarian primate at Esztergom. But in 1853 Pope Pius IX established a separate metropolitan province for the Greek Catholics in Transylvania. The diocese of Fagaras-Alba Iulia was made the metropolitan see, with three suffragan dioceses at Gherla (Cluj), Lugoj, and Oradea. Since 1737 the bishops of Fagaras had resided at Blaj, which had become the church's administrative and cultural center. Romanian Greek Catholic synods were held at Blaj in 1872, 1882, and 1900, which drafted legislation governing the life of the church.

At the end of World War I, Transylvania was united to Romania, and for the first time Greek Catholics found themselves in a predominantly Orthodox state. By 1940 there were five dioceses (a fifth diocese had been erected at Maramures in 1930), over 1,500 priests (90 percent of whom were married), and about 1,500,000 faithful. Major seminaries were functioning at Blaj, Oradea, and Gherla. The Pontifical Romanian College in Rome received its first students 1936.

From World War II to the Present: But the establishment of a Communist government in Romania after World War II proved disastrous for the Romanian Greek Catholic Church. On October 1, 1948, thirty-six Greek Catholic priests met under government pressure at Cluj-Napoca. They voted to ask for reunion with the Romanian Orthodox Church and to terminate the union with Rome. On October 21, it was formally abolished at a ceremony at Alba Iulia. On December 1, 1948, the government issued a decree that dissolved the Greek Catholic Church and gave over most of its property to the Romanian Orthodox Church. The six Greek Catholic bishops were arrested on the night of December 29. Five of the six later died in prison. In 1964 the bishop of Cluj-Gherla, Iuliu Hossu, was released but placed under house arrest in an Orthodox monastery, where he died in 1970. Pope Paul VI revealed in 1973 that he had made Hossu a cardinal *in pectore* (Lat., "in the breast," or secretly) in 1969.

After forty-one years underground, the fortunes of the Greek Catholic Church in Romania changed dramatically after the Ceausescu regime was overthrown in December 1989. On January 2, 1990, the 1948 decree that dissolved the church was abrogated. Greek Catholics began to worship openly again, and three secretly ordained bishops emerged from hiding. In March 1990, Pope John Paul II reestablished the hierarchy of this church by appointing bishops for all five dioceses.

Unfortunately the reemergence of the Greek Catholic Church has been accompanied by a confrontation with the Romanian Orthodox Church over the restitution of church buildings. The Catholics insisted that all property be returned as a matter of justice, while the Orthodox held that any transfer of property must take into account the present pastoral needs of both communities.

As of mid-1992 the impasse continued with only about fifteen churches, including the Blaj cathedral, having been returned. However, even though they had very limited resources and elderly professors, seminaries had begun functioning in Blaj, Cluj, and Baia Mare.

The new head of the Romanian Greek Catholic Church, Metropolitan Alexandru Todea, was created a cardinal by Pope John Paul II in June 1991. Todea had spent eighteen years in prison under the Communist regime.

Before the suppression there were two orders of sisters unique to the Romanian Catholic Church. The Contemplative Nuns of Moreni were founded in 1938 and numbered twenty-eight sisters when the monastery was closed. Some Sisters of the Holy Mother of God of Obreja, involved in education and works of charity, survived and the community is now receiving new vocations.

The size of the Romanian Catholic Church as of 1992 is disputed. The Greek Catholics themselves have claimed that they now number almost 3 million. But according to a government census carried out in January 1992, those declaring themselves Greek Catholics were only 1 percent of the population, or less than 250,000. In Romania the church calls itself "The Romanian Church United with Rome."

An apostolic exarchate for Romanian Greek Catholics in the United States was created in 1982. In 1987 it was elevated to the rank of eparchy (diocese). *See also* Byzantine rite; Eastern Catholics and ecumenism; Eastern Catholics and Rome; Eastern churches; Eastern liturgies; Eastern rites.

Bibliography

Georgescu, Vlad. *The Romanians: A History.* Columbus, OH: Ohio State University Press, 1991.   RONALD G. ROBERSON

Roman Martyrology, the official listing of martyrs (and other saints) and their feast days, issued by Gregory XIII in 1584 and subject to several subsequent revisions. It is currently being revised once again in conjunction with the post–Vatican II renewal of the Roman liturgy. *See also* martyr; martyrdom; martyrology.

Roman Missal, the book containing the introductory documents and prayer texts for the celebration of Mass according to the Roman rite; also known as the sacramentary. Prior to Vatican II (1962–65), the Missal of Pope Paul V (1605–21), also called the Tridentine Missal, contained all the elements of Mass, both the "proper" elements, i.e., the Introit, Collect, Epistle, Gradual, Alleluia, Gospel, Offertory, Secret, Communion and Post-communion, and the "ordinary," i.e., the Order of Mass. Since 1970, when the Roman Missal containing the liturgy that was revised following Vatican II was promulgated by Pope Paul VI, the missal has consisted of two books. The Roman Missal proper contains the three presidential prayers (Opening Prayer, Prayer over the Gifts, Prayer After Communion), the entrance and Communion antiphons, and the Order of Mass. A second book, the Lectionary for Mass, contains the Scripture readings. The lectionary follows a three-year cycle of OT readings, NT readings, chants, and Gospels for Sundays, and a two-year cycle of first readings and Gospels for weekdays. Readings for feasts

and votive masses are also included. *See also* Mass; sacramentary.

Romanos Melodos, St., d. ca. 560, acclaimed hymn writer, master of the "kontakion," a metrical sermon form he invested with a depth of feeling and drama that remains unsurpassed. Feast day: October 1. *See also* kontakion.

Roman Pontifical, the liturgical book containing the prayers and ceremonies for Latin rites presided over by a bishop, e.g., Confirmation, ordinations, the dedication of churches. The first printed edition was published in Rome in 1485 and an authoritative edition was issued in 1596 by Pope Clement VII. A partial revision was undertaken during the pontificate of Pius XII (d. 1958), and the remainder was revised after, and at the direction of, the Second Vatican Council (1962–65). *See also* bishop; sacramentary; worship.

Roman Question. *See* Lateran Treaty.

Roman rite, sometimes inaccurately called the Latin rite, principal ancient liturgical tradition of the Western Church and of the entire Catholic Communion, and the most widely used rite in Christendom.

Origins and Formative Period: Originally, the Roman rite prevailed only in the area around Rome and in "Suburbican Italy," i.e., southern Italy and the islands of Sicily, Sardinia, and Corsica. Roman liturgical usages gradually came to predominate throughout Europe in the eighth and ninth centuries, under the Carolingian and Ottonian emperors. In the seventh century, Roman missionaries under Augustine of Canterbury had established it in the British Isles. In the following century, Rome-oriented missionaries from Britain returned to the Continent to reform the Gallican church and evangelize the Germans. They brought with them a Roman-type liturgy and found that Roman liturgical books and customs had already penetrated north of the Alps. These "Gelasian" and "Gregorian" Roman usages amalgamated with local Gallican and Visigothic customs to form a Franco-Germanic-Roman synthesis.

It is this hybrid rite, reintroduced to Rome in the late tenth century during the Germanic hegemony of the Ottonians, that is the immediate ancestor of what is called the "Roman rite" today. The original Roman rite was one of great sobriety; what is considered most "Italianate" in Roman Catholic liturgy is actually the product of this Nordic transfusion.

The Gregorian Reform: From Gregory VII (d. 1085) to the Council of Trent (1545–63), a reformed papacy, invigorated by the investiture victory that prevented lay princes from installing bishops, Cluniac monastic renewal in Rome, which included the repression of simony and enforcement of clerical celibacy, and the Gregorian reform (1073–85) that encompassed all of these measures, regained liturgical leadership in the West. Although under Gregory, the Roman rite was imposed in Spain, it spread more by the power of example: itinerant Franciscan friars and the peregrinations of the papal court carried it across Europe.

The Period of Tridentine Catholicism to Vatican II: A period of consolidation followed the Council of Trent, which reformed and codified the Roman liturgical books and imposed them throughout the West. Exceptions were allowed where an ancient tradition still prevailed, and some dioceses of France and northwestern Germany did not accept the Tridentine books until the nineteenth century.

In modern times, beginning with the nineteenth-century romantic revival, the liturgical movement and the twentieth-century liturgical reforms of several popes culminate in those of the Second Vatican Council (1962–65) and beyond. *See also* Latin rite; Roman Catholic.

Bibliography

Bishop, Edmund. "The Genius of the Roman Rite." *Liturgica Historica*. Oxford: Clarendon Press, 1918, 1–19.

Klauser, T. *A Short History of the Western Liturgy*. London, New York, Toronto: Oxford University Press, 1969.

van Dijk, S. J. P., and Joan Hazelden Walker. *The Origins of the Modern Liturgy*. Westminster, MD: Newman Press, 1960.

ROBERT F. TAFT

Romanticism, a movement in literature and art beginning in the late eighteenth century and continuing in different forms through the nineteenth century. Going beyond the Enlightenment's emphasis on reason and classicism, it emphasized intuition and emotion, individualism and history. By 1790 in Germany there was a new appreciation of human history (Johann Gottfried von Herder), emotional individualism in literature, enthusiasm for Plato and Shakespeare (August and Friedrich von Schlegel), and for Eastern cultures and folktales (Jacob and William Grimm). Friedrich von Schelling developed a philosophy that appealed to people such as Johann von Goethe and the Schlegels: the

absolute realizes itself through central ideas in intuitive consciousness, bringing about a unity of science, art, and the history of religion.

This romantic idealism influenced not only Protestants such as Schleiermacher, but also Catholic thinkers, from theologians to politicians, in southern Germany. Although Catholicism had found the rationalism and secularity of the Enlightenment alien to its tradition, it was more sympathetic to the characteristics of Romanticism, such as organic diversity and unity, intuition and mysticism, universality-within-diversity, incarnation and sacramentality. This influence could be detected in the work of Joseph von Görres in Munich and of Johann Adam Möhler in Tübingen.

Just as after 1860 one sees a "late Romanticism" (less historical and optimistic, but psychological and darkly morbid) in the operas of Richard Wagner or the theories of Sigmund Freud, so one finds in the Catholic devotions and spiritualities of the nineteenth century a particular kind of Romanticism, less substantive, theologically shallow, and more focused upon visions, death, suffering, penance, and similar themes. *THOMAS F. O'MEARA*

Rome, the capital of the Roman Empire, traditionally founded 753 B.C. by the twins Romulus and Remus.

First and Second Centuries: Christianity was well established before the arrivals of Peter and Paul; Paul's Letter to the Roman church (A.D. 57–58) includes a list of twenty-four individuals prominent enough to be known by name (Rom 16), some wealthy enough to provide their houses as meeting places. The tension between these Judeo-Christians and the Roman synagogues is probably to be credited for the disturbance, "instigated by a certain Chrestus," which Suetonius mentions (*Life of Claudius* 25.4) as responsible for Claudius's expulsion of the Jews from Rome ca. 49 (cf. Acts 18:2). Paul was martyred under Nero, probably in the persecution associated with the great fire at Rome in 64 (Tacitus *Annals* 15.44). Tradition uniformly reports that the apostle Peter also arrived in Rome and was martyred there, although the dates are unknown. Another glimpse of the early Roman church at the end of the first century is afforded in the letter Clement, its bishop, sent to the Corinthian church on matters of church discipline (*1 Clement*).

There is much better information about the second century. The bishop Telesphorus (ca. 125–ca. 136) was probably a martyr. Rome was a missionary center for the evangelization of Italy, and probably for Gaul and North Africa as well. Until Victor I (ca. 189–98) all the bishops spoke Greek, and thus links with the Eastern churches were retained and extended. Anicetus (ca. 155–66) received Polycarp of Smyrna, with whom he discussed the contentious matter of the date of Easter. Dionysius of Corinth wrote to Soter (ca. 166–74) to defend himself against accusations that had caused Soter to censure him; Victor attempted to regulate the date of Easter for the whole Church, although Irenaeus, who himself may have lived at Rome for a time before becoming bishop of Lyons (ca. 178), reproved him when he excommunicated Asian churches for their Quartodeciman practice. The second century also saw the confluence of Christians of all stripes at Rome, from Justin Martyr (d. ca. 165), his pupil Tatian, and Hegesippus (ca. 110–80), to Marcion (excommunicated ca. 144 by Pius [ca. 142–ca. 155], brother to Hermas who wrote the *Shepherd*), and Valentinus (in Rome ca. 140–ca. 160). In 177 Montanists were excommunicated by Eleutherius (174–89), although Irenaeus, still a presbyter, came to Rome with a request for toleration of them on behalf of the church at Lyons. Later, Theodotus the Leather Merchant, an Adoptionist Monarchian from Byzantium teaching in Rome, was condemned by Victor, followed by his disciple Theodotus the Banker, also from Byzantium, condemned by Zephyrinus (198/9–217).

Third Century: In the third century, Hippolytus (d. ca. 235), in his recently recovered *Apostolic Tradition,* provides valuable information regarding Baptism, the catechumenate, the Eucharist, and forms of assistance including the agape and a collection taken up to provide for burials. Under Zephyrinus, the deacon Callistus, as one of seven deacons set in charge of charitable works in each of the city's seven districts, maintained for the Church the catacomb on the Appian Way. Eusebius attests to a numerous clergy and a relief system serving fifteen hundred needy, although there is no evidence for any churches apart from private homes.

A dispute, and perhaps a schism, resulted when Callistus (217–22), who succeeded Zephyrinus, seemed to Hippolytus to be dealing too leniently with penitents and to have incorrectly approved marriages of Christians of unequal rank. Hippolytus was reconciled with Callistus's successor Pontian (230–35, after Urban, 222–30) only after they were exiled together and about to be martyred. Later, a more serious schism arose after the Decian

persecution, when in 251, the presbyter Novatian led a community in opposition to the bishop Cornelius (successor, after a thirteen-month vacancy, to the martyred Fabian [236–50]), whom Novatian felt had dealt too leniently with the *lapsi* (Lat., those who had lapsed under persecution). Cornelius was able to assemble a synod of some sixty bishops against him. A related issue divided Stephen I (254–57) and the more rigorist Cyprian of Carthage, who objected to Stephen's reinstatement of two Spanish bishops accused of yielding under persecution and who insisted on rebaptizing persons baptized by heretics or schismatics (e.g., Novatianists). In the persecution of Valerian, Sixtus II (257–58) and his deacon Lawrence were martyred (258). Dionysius (ca. 260–ca. 268), who succeeded Sixtus, criticized the trinitarian theology of Dionysius of Alexandria, although he ultimately accepted the Alexandrian bishop's defense.

Fourth Century and Later: Little is known of the Roman church during the persecution of Diocletian, but after the victory of Constantine (312), there is a blossoming of church construction: the basilica, later St. John Lateran, founded by Constantine to serve as the episcopal church and papal residence; St. Paul's Outside the Walls, erected by Constantine and rebuilt as a basilica by the emperor Honorius (395); St. Peter's, erected by Constantine; St. Mary Major, founded by Liberius (352–66) and rebuilt by Sixtus III (432–40); and Santa Croce in Gerusalemme, founded by St. Helena.

The great popes of the fourth century—e.g., Julius I (337–52), who sheltered Athanasius in 339 and called the Council of Sardica (342–43) which pronounced Athanasius the rightful holder of his see; Damasus (366–84), who adorned the tombs of the martyrs with poetic inscriptions, commissioned Jerome's revision of the Latin Bible, and condemned the Pneumatomachians at a Roman council in 377; and Siricius (384–99)—advanced the Nicene cause and enhanced papal prestige. In the fifth century this tradition was continued especially by bishops such as Innocent (401–17), who condemned Pelagius at the request of the African bishops; Boniface (418–22), who secured the claim of Rome to immediate jurisdiction over Illyricum; Celestine (422–32), who intervened on behalf of Cyril of Alexandria in his dispute with Nestorius; and finally Leo the Great (440–61), whose *Tome* was canonized by the Council of Chalcedon (451), and who, with Damasus and Gelasius (492–96), was one of the foremost theorists of the papacy.

By the sixth century the empire in the West had fallen (the last Roman emperor was deposed in 476), and Rome, sacked for three days in 410 by Alaric and for seventeen days in 455 by the Vandals, was almost completely abandoned during the Gothic War (537–53) between the Goths and the Byzantines. As Byzantine power waned and the Lombards invaded Italy (from 568), the population relied on the popes to negotiate treaties, prisoners, etc. Pelagius II (579–90) and Gregory the Great (590–604) were crucial in the survival of Rome through this, its lowest period. Rome remained within the dominion of the Lombards until Pepin III defeated them in 754 and again in 756 and donated the duchy of Rome, the exarchate of Ravenna, and other territories to the Holy See, thus formally creating the Papal States. *See also* Byzantine Italy; Constantinople; Latin rite; papacy, the; Papal States; Paul, St.; persecutions; Peter, St.; Roman Catholic; Roman Empire; Roman rite; Rome, churches of.

Bibliography

Alfoldy, Geza. *The Social History of Rome.* Baltimore, MD: Johns Hopkins University Press, 1985.

Claster, Jill. *The Medieval Experience: 300–1400.* New York: New York University Press, 1982.

Garnsey, P., and R. Saller. *The Roman Empire: Economy, Society and Culture.* Berkeley, CA: University of California Press, 1987.

Meeks, Wayne. *The First Urban Christians.* New Haven, CN: Yale University Press, 1983.

Salmon, E. T. *The Making of Roman Italy.* Ithaca, NY: Cornell University Press, 1982.   JOHN C. CAVADINI

Rome, churches of, places of Catholic worship located in the city of Rome. Excluding nonpublic chapels or oratories, there are well over one hundred Catholic churches within the city of Rome. The buildings themselves reflect the long history of Christianity's presence in the city.

Rome's cathedral is St. John Lateran, which sits on a site given to the Church by the emperor Constantine in the fourth century. St. John Lateran is also a major basilica; the other three in the city are St. Peter's in the Vatican, St. Mary Major, and St. Paul's Outside the Walls. Those churches, along with the basilicas of St. Lawrence Outside the Walls, Holy Cross in Jerusalem, and St. Sebastian, constitute the seven pilgrimage churches that were the obligatory parts of the pilgrimage visit to the city in ancient times.

The oldest of the Roman churches were called *tituli* (Lat., *titulus,* "name" or "title"). These were places of worship known by the name of their location or of the person who donated the land and monies for the place. After the fourth century these churches assumed the names of saints. Venerable churches like Santa Sabina, Santa Cecilia, and Sts. John and Paul have the remains of earlier *tituli* under their present foundations. Of similar antiquity are those churches, like that of St. Agnes, that were built over the tombs of early Roman martyrs.

Some Roman churches commemorate historical events: the seventeenth-century Baroque church of Santa Maria della Vittoria was built in honor of the end of the Thirty Years' War (1620). Other churches, like the Jesuit Sant' Ignazio and the church of the Gesú, were inspired by religious orders. Small churches and oratories dot the city because they were annexed to either palaces (San Lorenzo in Damaso) or monasteries. Craft guilds had their own places of worship, like the tailor guild's St. Omobono. A pious confraternity, like that dedicated to the care of condemned prisoners, had a church dedicated appropriately to the beheaded St. John the Baptist (San Giovanni Decollato).

Many historic churches in Rome, which once served particular purposes, now serve as "home" churches for various nationalities: e.g., Santa Susanna (United States), San Luigi dei Francesi (France), San Silvestro in Capite (England), and Santa Maria in Campo Santo (Germany). Other churches serve various rites of the Church, like the small Abyssinian (Coptic) church on the grounds of the Vatican.

Most of the ancient churches of Rome reveal layers of rebuilding. St. Peter's in the Vatican, for instance, was designed by Michelangelo in the sixteenth century (with additions in the seventeenth) but was built over the site of an ancient church begun in the period of Constantine (fourth century), which rested, in turn, over a burial chapel for the tomb of St. Peter. The oldest church dedicated to the Blessed Virgin, Santa Maria in Trastevere, started as a third-century oratory, with elaborations done in the twelfth century, followed by restorations and additions in the fifteenth, sixteenth, and seventeenth centuries. The present portico (porch) was added in the nineteenth century during the pontificate of Pius IX.

The plethora of churches in the city is a challenge in terms of maintenance and restoration. It is also a pastoral problem. The diocese of Rome needs churches for the burgeoning population in the suburbs, where both clergy and buildings are scarce, while the historic center of the city has too many churches. *See also* basilica; Lateran Basilica; Rome; Saint Mary Major; Saint Paul's Outside the Walls; Saint Peter's Basilica.   LAWRENCE CUNNINGHAM

Romero, Oscar Arnulfo, 1917–1980, martyred archbishop of San Salvador. Born in Ciudad Barrios, El Salvador, Romero entered the minor seminary in 1930, studied theology at Rome's Gregorian University beginning in 1937, and was ordained in Rome in 1942. Returning to El Salvador in 1943, he became the bishop's secretary for the diocese of San Miguel. Serving in this capacity for twenty-three years, he was appointed the editor of the diocesan newspaper, the pastor of the cathedral parish, and the rector of the minor seminary. In 1967 he was elected secretary of the national bishops' conference for El Salvador, and in 1968 he was chosen to be the executive secretary of the Central American Bishops' Secretariat. He became the auxiliary bishop of San Salvador in 1970, and was named the bishop of the diocese of Santiago de Maria in 1974. He was installed as the archbishop of San Salvador in 1977. Though known to be politically cautious, he took seriously the documents of Vatican II (1962–65), and of the Latin American Bishops Conferences (CELAM) at Medellín, Colombia (1968), and Puebla, Mexico (1979), as well as Pope Paul VI's *Evangelii Nuntiandi* (On Evangelization in the Modern World, 1975). As a result, he increasingly spoke

Archbishop Oscar Arnulfo Romero of San Salvador, one of the unofficial martyrs of the twentieth century, who was gunned down in 1980 while celebrating the Eucharist because of his vigorous defense of the poor and the powerless against the military and the wealthy classes.

in behalf of the human rights of the poor and the powerless. As the violence increased in El Salvador amid efforts for land reform, Romero read aloud each week at Mass a roll call of the week's dead. He also publicly condemned abuses of human rights and pleaded that foreign military aid cease, writing a letter in this regard to President Jimmy Carter. He was assassinated on March 24, 1980, while celebrating Mass in the chapel of San Salvador's Hospital of Divine Providence. His tomb, erected in the cathedral of San Salvador, has become a popular site for prayer and pilgrimage.   *ROBERT A. KRIEG*

Romuald, St., ca. 952–1027, hermit and founder of the Camaldolese order. Of noble birth, Romuald became a monk to do penance for his father's slaying of a kinsman in a duel. Seeking a rigid life-style, he constantly moved about, founding hermitages and monasteries, including Camaldoli. Feast day: June 19. *See also* Camaldolese.

rood screen (Old Eng., *rood,* "cross"), an architectural term denoting the wall-like structure that divides the choir from the sanctuary area (or the choir and sanctuary from the nave) of, mainly, English cathedrals. It is so called because a cross *(rood)* figured prominently in the decoration of such screens.

Rosary, the most common of Catholic devotional prayers. The term derives from the Latin *rosarium* ("rose garden"), which by the fourteenth century had come to mean a collection of devotional texts. Today it generally refers to the so-called Dominican Rosary, which consists in the recitation of fifteen decades of Hail Marys, each introduced by the Lord's Prayer and concluded with the Doxology. Each decade is accompanied by a meditation on some aspect of the life of Christ or the Virgin Mary, called a mystery. These are divided into three groups of five, known as the Joyful, Sorrowful, and Glorious Mysteries, focusing on the Incarnation, Passion, and glorification of Christ respectively; the whole is a virtual epitome of the liturgical year. Ordinarily only one of these sets, or five decades, is recited at a time; to assist the memory, the prayers are commonly counted on a string of beads.

A legend dating from the late fifteenth century attributed the Rosary to St. Dominic. This opinion can no longer be historically sustained; in fact the Rosary as we know it received its present form only in the sixteenth century. On the other hand, its roots extend into the distant past. The use of beads or

Rosary beads

Both the contemporary liturgical movement and a renewed emphasis on the reading of Scripture have reduced the dominance of the Rosary in Catholic devotional life, but because of its practical simplicity and warmth it remains widely popular. *See also* devotions; Marian devotion. DOMINIC MONTI

Rose, Golden. *See* Golden Rose.

Rose of Lima, St., 1586–1617, first canonized saint of the Americas and patron saint of South America and the Philippines. Reputed to have extraordinary mystical gifts, Rose modeled her life after St. Catherine of Siena, living the life of a recluse and adopting extreme practices of mortification and penance. She joined the Third Order of St. Dominic at the age of 20. Feast day: August 23.

Rose of Lima (lower right), Peruvian mystic and patron saint of South America, has a vision of the Blessed Virgin Mary and two other Dominican saints: Catherine of Siena (holding the cross) and Agnes of Montepulciano (holding the child Jesus); eighteenth-century fresco by Tiepolo, in the Church of St. Mary of the Rosary, Venice.

knotted strings as a device for keeping count of prayers is found in many religious traditions, and from patristic antiquity Christians also utilized such means to assist in the continuous repetition of biblical passages or other texts. By the eleventh century, the custom of saying 150 Our Fathers as a substitute for the psalms was widespread among devout laity. This "poor person's breviary" was often divided, as was the Psalter, into three sets of fifty; the strings of beads used to count them were called "paternosters."

In the twelfth century, as Marian piety increased, the Angelic Salutation from Luke's Gospel was added to these, and soon the words of Elizabeth at Mary's Visitation as well. Gradually, popular piety created "psalters" dedicated to Jesus or Mary, concentrating the devotee's attention on biblical scenes. Much of this development, especially a "rosary" consisting primarily of Hail Marys, originally took place in Carthusian circles. However, the term "Dominican Rosary" is very accurate, as the friars of that order did the most to make it a general, popular prayer by propagating it through their preaching and the foundation of rosary confraternities, as well as by introducing a number of simplifications that standardized the prayer in its present form. The Dominican pope Pius V did much to foster the devotion and in 1572 instituted an annual celebration to give thanks to the Blessed Virgin for having delivered Christendom from the Turks by the decisive sea battle of Lepanto the preceding year. This feast, titled Our Lady of the Rosary since 1573, was eventually fixed on October 7.

Rose Philippine Duchesne, St. *See* Duchesne, St. Rose Philippine.

Rosmini-Serbati, Antonio (ahn-tohn'ee-oh raws-meen'ee-sair-bah'tee), 1797–1855, Italian philosopher. Ordained in 1821, Rosmini founded the Institute of Charity (Rosminians) and an academy dedicated to the study of Thomas Aquinas. His metaphysics and epistemology were grounded in the immediate intuition of ideal being as the basis for every act of knowledge. It was this line of thought that led to the periodic accusations of ontologism leveled against him. But he was best known for his writings on behalf of Church reform. His *Five Wounds of the Church* was condemned by the Congregation of the Index [of Forbidden Books] in 1849. His influence was strong in Italy, but only negligible elsewhere.

Rossello, St. Josepha, 1811–80, founder of the Daughters of Our Lady of Mercy [Pity] in Italy in 1837 to care for abandoned girls. She was canonized in 1949. Feast day: December 7.

Rota (Lat., "wheel"), the second-highest (and most active) court of the Holy See. Different theories as to the derivation of the name are: the auditors (judges) hear the cases in turn, the documents are wheeled from judge to judge, or there was a wheel design on the floor of its courtroom. This is the court of third instance for most marriage cases and has been the source of important developments in matrimonial jurisprudence.

Rousselot, Pierre (roos'suh-loh), 1878–1915, French Jesuit philosopher and theologian. Despite his untimely death in the First World War, his two doctoral theses were significant contributions to the twentieth-century revival of Thomism. The first thesis asserted the primacy of the intuitive intellect over discursive reason. The second examined the relationship between love of self and love of God, reconciling the two. *See also* philosophy and theology; Thomism.

rubrics (Lat., "red text"), directives for liturgical actions or gestures. Rubrics are printed in red so as to distinguish directions for action from spoken texts, which are printed in black. Rubricism, the scrupulous regard for correct performance of rubrical minutiae, derives its name from this term.

Rudd, Daniel, 1854–1933, the leading African-American Catholic spokesman of the late nineteenth century. In 1886, he began publishing the *American Catholic Tribune.* He also initiated the black Catholic lay congress movement, which brought black Catholics together in national conventions five times between 1889 and 1894. *See also* black Catholics.

Rudesind, St., also known as Rosendo, 907–77, Portuguese saint who founded the monastery of Celanova. Feast day: March 1.

Ruether, Rosemary Radford, b. 1936, Georgia Harkness Professor of Applied Theology at Garrett-Evangelical Theological Seminary in Evanston, Illinois, and theologian known for her work in feminist theology (*Sexism and God-Talk: Toward a Feminist Theology,* 1983). Ruether's academic specialty is historical theology; her doctoral dissertation at Claremont was on Gregory of Nazianzus.

Rufinus of Aquileia, ca. 345–410, translator. Educated at Rome, where he became friends with Jerome, Rufinus later lived in Egypt (373–80), subsequently founding a double monastery on the Mount of Olives (381) with Melania the Elder. Jerome, in Bethlehem by 386, sided against him in the controversy over Origenism, precipitating a bitter enmity that persisted until Rufinus's death. In 387 Rufinus moved back to Rome. He undertook a series of extraordinary translations, including works of Origen that would otherwise have been completely lost: *On First Principles* and homilies on Genesis, Exodus, Leviticus, Numbers, Canticle of Canticles, and Romans. Rufinus also translated (and supplemented) Eusebius's *Ecclesiastical History;* homilies of Basil and Gregory of Nazianzus and the Pseudo-Clementine *Recognitions. See also* Jerome, St., Origen; Origenism.

Rule of St. Augustine. *See* Augustine, Rule of St.

Rule of St. Basil. *See* Basil, Rule of St.

Rule of St. Benedict. *See* Benedict, Rule of St.

Rule of the Master. *See Regula Magistri.*

Rupert, St., d. 717, Benedictine abbot-archbishop. He spread Christianity in southern Germany, rebuilding an old town, Juvanum, and renaming it

Salzburg. He founded an abbey and a school there. He is venerated as an apostle of Bavaria and Austria. Feast day: March 27.

Rupert of Deutz, ca. 1075–1129, Benedictine theologian, biblical commentator, and abbot of Deutz, near Cologne. Experiencing as a young man a divine call to interpret God's word, he produced works filling four volumes of J.-P. Migne's *Patrologia Latina*. His exegetical writings are characterized by original allegorical interpretations and emphasis upon the history of salvation. Rupert opposed the encroachment of dialectic in theology and entered into disputes over the Eucharist and predestination with leading masters at Paris, Laon, and Liège. *See also* allegory.

Rusin, Rusyn, an ethnic name designating the East Slavic inhabitants of Austria-Hungary and their descendants in the United States. Today it applies more specifically to the Eastern Slavs living in the Transcarpathian district of the Western Ukraine. *See also* Ruthenian Catholic Church.

Russia, Catholicism in. Christian missionaries from Europe first evangelized Russia in the ninth and tenth centuries. Prince Vladimir of Kiev (d. 1015) embraced the Christian faith in 988 and subsequently established Christianity as the official religion within the territories under his control, including Kiev, Polotsk, and large areas of White Russia (Belorussia). He built many churches and placed great pressure on his people to accept baptism. Because of his desire to forge closer relationships with Europe, he brought in priests from the Byzantine Empire, centered in Constantinople, and established a Greek hierarchy under a metropolitan. From the outset, however, the Slavic tongue was used in worship and a Russian clergy gradually replaced the Greeks.

Monasticism, perhaps Russia's most spiritually powerful religious institution, began with the monk Antony, who had come from Mount Athos in Greece in the middle of the eleventh century, establishing himself in a grotto near Kiev from which the great monastery of Kievo-Petcherskaja would develop. By the next century there were seventeen monasteries in Kiev alone. Sergius of Radonezh (d. 1392), a monastic reformer and one of the most revered of Russian saints, gave added impetus to the monastic movement all over the country. It was the monaster-

ies that supplied the bishops, while the married diocesan clergy tended to be uneducated.

It was during the early years of the fourteenth century that the metropolitan see, originally established by Vladimir in Kiev, was moved to Moscow. In 1461 the Church in Russia was divided between two metropolitans, one in Moscow and one in Kiev. Moscow was entirely Russian and firmly Orthodox. Kiev was more exposed to Western influences. When the Council of Florence (1442) forged what proved to be a temporary agreement (the Decree of Union) between Rome and Constantinople on such issues as the double-procession of the Holy Spirit from the Father and the Son (the *Filioque* controversy), the Eucharist, papal primacy, and purgatory, the Russian church, under Basil II of Moscow, rejected it. In 1448 a council of Russian bishops elected a metropolitan of Moscow without any reference to Greek ecclesiastical authorities, thereby laying the foundation for an autocephalous (Gk., "oneself the head"), or independent, Russian church.

Those Christians who remained faithful to Rome were severely repressed in Orthodox Moscow after the Council of Florence, while Russians in the metropolis of Kiev (which came within the territory of Poland and Lithuania) found themselves under pressure from their Roman Catholic rulers. Although a large part of the Russian church in this region acknowledged the authority of the papacy at the Synod of Brest-Litovsk in 1596, the Orthodox metropolis of Kiev continued in existence, in spite of persecution, and was in constant conflict with those loyal to Rome.

Growing Estrangement and Reduced Presence: Early conflicts between the Prince of Novgorod, Alexander Nevsky, and the Germanic Knights, together with Catholic Sweden, hardened Russian feeling toward the West. As a member of the Hanseatic League (a late-fourteenth-century mercantile alliance based in northern Germany), Nevsky's own Republic of Novgorod remained a focal point of Western culture during the Russian Middle Ages. Here an edition of the Bible was prepared using the Latin Vulgate.

Estrangement from Western culture in Muscovy resulted from the Tartar yoke, as well as growing hostility between Orthodox Muscovy and Catholicism's Eastern bulwark, the Polish-Lithuanian Commonwealth. Ill feeling culminated during the occupation of Moscow by the Poles at the end of the sixteenth century, during the "Time of Troubles." Popular Russian Orthodoxy identified the Catholic

Church with Poland—a tendency already present during the Kievan period of the eleventh and twelfth centuries when there was a state centered in Kiev.

In 1473, Zoe Sophia Paleologa, the Greek bride of Ivan III, arrived at the Kremlin with her suite, including several Italians. Scion of the Imperial House of Byzantium and ward of the Greek cardinal Bessarion, Sophia was at least a nominal Catholic. Soon after her wedding by proxy with the Muscovite sovereign, arranged by Pope Sixtus IV (d. 1484) and held in Rome at St. Peter's, she exchanged Catholicism for Orthodoxy in Russia. In 1583 Czar Ivan IV received the Italian Jesuit Antonio Possevino in Moscow. Possevino successfully concluded the Treaty of Yam-Zapolsky but was unsuccessful in fermenting papal plans for church unity or in organizing a common crusade of Orthodox and Catholics against the Turks.

Under Austrian protection, the Jesuits were able to establish a foothold in Russia, first under the reign of Czar Alexis (1629–76) and later during that of his son Peter the Great (1672–1725). Jesuit influence in Russia reached its apogee under Catherine II (1729–96) and her son Paul (1754–1801). Banned in Europe, the order survived in Russia thanks to Catherine's admiration of the Jesuit system of education, their quick acceptance of Russian rule after the Polish partitions, and their dislike of revolution or abrupt social change. The Jesuits were permitted to administer colleges in the Belorussian lands and a school for the nobility—both Orthodox and Catholic—at St. Petersburg. They were finally expelled in 1820 by Alexander I.

Despite limited patronage of the Jesuits and some interest in Catholic ritual, Czar Peter turned Russia toward Protestantism and the secularized West rather than to the papacy. Peter's grandfather, Patriarch Philaret, a Polish captive during the Time of Troubles, ordered the rebaptism of Roman Catholic and "Uniate" converts to Orthodoxy, but the anti-Nikonian Council of 1666–67 declared this to be unnecessary.

Catholics as Subjects of the Czars: While Catholics in Russia until the time of Catherine II (d. 1796) were generally foreigners who dwelt and worshiped in segregated areas of the larger towns, the first partition of Poland in 1772 incorporated 100,000 Latin Catholics and 800,000 "Uniates" with their ancestral lands into the Russian Empire. Always hostile to those who accepted the Union of Brest, Catherine II and her successors eventually

succeeded in destroying the latter's link with Rome and incorporating them into Russian Orthodoxy.

Russia's Latin Catholics, on the other hand, were organized into the monolithic diocese of Mogilev, an unimportant town in Belorussia, which served as the center of the largest ecclesiastical province in the world. Despite the adverse influence of the sycophantic metropolitan of Mogilev, Stanislaus Siestrzencewicz-Bohusz, under whose jurisdiction all Latin Catholics of the empire fell, an apostolic nunciature was established at St. Petersburg in 1798. Three successive nuncios, Andrea Archetti, Lorenzo Litta, and Tommaso Arezzo, were able to visit or reside in Russia.

Catherine's son, the eccentric Paul I, sponsored the Jesuits and Knights of Malta and declared himself in favor of union with Rome, but these plans came to naught.

A few conversions to Catholicism among the Westernized nobility occurred under Czar Alexander I (reigned 1801–25), but penal legislation against abandoning Orthodoxy for Catholicism hardened under Nicholas I (reigned 1825–55) and his successors in conjunction with the Polish rebellions. Despite Nicholas I's general dislike of the Catholic Church, which he equated with revolutionary Poland, he enjoyed a papal audience in 1845. This visit laid the basis for a concordat between Russia and the Vatican that was signed two years later.

Catholics in nineteenth-century Russia were almost exclusively of foreign origin. At St. Petersburg they were divided into four nations: Germans, French, Italians, and Poles. By the time of the revolution of 1917 there were about a million and a half Catholics in Russia, organized into 680 parishes, including about twenty-six in the areas of the empire with a mainly Russian population and thirteen in Russian Asia.

Nicholas II was forced to concede the Edict of Toleration in 1905, which allowed Orthodox to change their religion and resulted in the mass conversion of a quarter of a million Polonized Belorussian peasants to Catholicism.

Russian Catholics, the Revolution, Today's Situation: The end of the nineteenth century saw the beginnings of the Russian Catholic movement, which attempted to reconcile Catholic dogma with Russian ritual and ecclesiastical tradition in accordance with the teachings of Vladimir Solov'ev. Always small in number, these Byzantine-rite Russian Catholics included several intellectuals, including the Dominican nun Catherine Abrikosov, the laywoman Julia Danzas, and their pastorally gifted exarch Leonid Feodorov. While relations were difficult with the almost exclusively Polish Latin Catholic hierarchy in Russia, Russian Catholics enjoyed the support of Andryj Sheptyckyj, metropolitan of the Greek Catholics in Galicia. The Russian Catholic movement did not survive the revolution and forthcoming Stalinization but continued to exist among emigrants. Traces of their teachings survived in the Soviet Union.

The Latin hierarchy was likewise decimated through persecution following the Revolution of 1917. An attempt to restore it by the French Jesuit Michel d'Herbigny during the 1920s ended in disaster. By 1934 only three Catholic churches remained open in the Soviet Union.

The situation changed after the Second World War, when significant numbers of Catholics in formerly Polish Belorussia and the Baltics and Greek Catholics of the Western Ukraine were incorporated into Soviet territory. These groups became subject to many restrictions.

With the fall of Communism after 1990, the Catholic Church in the former Soviet Union attempted to regroup its losses. Rome appointed an apostolic administrator for European Russia, a bishop for Siberia and Central Asia, and other nominations in Ukraine and Belarus, despite the protests of Russian Orthodox hierarchs who feared Catholic proselytism.

Catholics are still a somewhat foreign element in Russian society, despite a tendency toward increased assimilation and growing acceptance on the part of some Russian intellectuals. There are fewer than 400,000 Catholics in a total population of some 150 million. *See also* Communism; Byzantine rite; Russian Catholics in the Diaspora.

Bibliography

Just, Sister Mary. *Rome and Russia*. Westminster, MD: Newman Press, 1954.

Mailleux, Paul. *Exarch Leonid Feodorov*. New York: P. J. Kennedy and Sons, 1964.

Stehle, Hansjakob. *Eastern Politics of the Vatican; 1917–1979*. Athens, OH: Ohio University Press, 1981.

Zatko, James. *Descent into Darkness*. Notre Dame, IN: University of Notre Dame Press, 1965.   CONSTANTINE SIMON

Russian Catholics in the diaspora, those Russian Catholics living outside of Russia. They are estimated as of 1993 at about 3,500 and have an apostolic visitor, a papal representative, based in Paris, whose responsibility is to visit Russian Catholics living outside of Russia and to determine their pastoral needs. He can exercise no canonical or pastoral authority over these Catholics, however. They remain subject always to the authority of their local Roman Catholic bishop. In pre-revolutionary Russia they numbered only about 400 in three communities. Immediately after the revolution, Russian Catholic parishes were established in the principal centers of Russian emigration in France, Berlin, New York, and in Manchuria. They were placed under a Russian Catholic bishop of Lithuanian origin, Peter Bucys. In 1923, French Dominicans opened a seminary in Lille for training Russian Catholic clergy. The Russicum, or Russian College, was opened in Rome for this purpose in 1929. In 1921, the French Jesuit Louis Baille opened a school for Russian boys at Istanbul, an early center of Russian emigration. Later transferred to Namur in Belgium and then to Meudon, a suburb of Paris, the school continued to exist until 1969. Both Jesuits and Marian Fathers worked among the Catholic Russians in Manchuria. The English Jesuit Frederick Wilcock organized the evacuation of the Russian community at Shanghai in 1949 in the wake of the Chinese Communists. In 1950 he helped found the Russian Center at Fordham University in New York. A parish was later founded for Catholic Russians at El Segundo near Los Angeles and a smaller center in San Francisco. Other parishes were organized for them in Australia and in South America at São Paolo, Buenos Aires, and Santiago. Distinguished Russian Catholic laypeople include the poet Vyacheslav Ivanov, the historian Helen Iswolsky, the opera singer Nicola Rossi-Lemeni, the religious activist Catherine de Hueck Doherty, and Irina Posnov, a publisher of Russian religious literature. *See also* Russia, Catholicism in.   CONSTANTINE SIMON

Russicum, the Pontifical Russian College in Rome, founded by Pope Pius XI in 1929 and entrusted to the Jesuits. Its original purpose was to train Catholic clergy of the Byzantine-Slavonic rite for missionary activity within the confines of the Soviet Union, where all Christians were suffering persecution. Although courses in Russian and liturgics were offered to its students, the Russicum served mainly as living quarters for seminarians who attended theology lectures at pontifical universities. From the beginning, Russians comprised only a small part of the student body. After Vatican II, the Russicum enjoyed many fruitful contacts with the Russian Orthodox Church in the Soviet Union. The original aim of the Russicum has been reexamined in the light of ecumenical dialogue and the new religious freedoms offered to the faithful, both Orthodox and Catholic, within Russia. *See also* Russia, Catholicism in.

Ruthenian Catholic Church, a Byzantine Catholic community centered in the extreme western part of the Ukraine, an area known variously in the past as Carpatho-Ukraine, Carpatho-Ruthenia, Carpatho-Russia, and Subcarpathia, and presently Transcarpathia. Although the ecclesiastical term "Ruthenian" was formerly used more broadly to include Ukrainians, Belarusians, and Slovaks, it is now used by Church authorities in a narrower sense to denote this specific Byzantine Catholic Church. In terms of ethnicity, Ruthenian Catholics prefer to be called Rusyns. They are closely related to the Ukrainians and speak a dialect of the same language. The traditional Rusyn homeland extends beyond Transcarpathia into northeast Slovakia and the "Lemko" region of extreme southeast Poland.

Early History: In the late ninth century, most of this area came under the control of Catholic Hungary, which later began to promote Catholic missionary work among its Orthodox population, including the Rusyns. This activity culminated in the reception of sixty-three of their priests into the Catholic Church on April 24, 1646, at the town of Uzhorod. The Union of Uzhorod affected the Orthodox population of an area that roughly corresponds to present-day eastern Slovakia. In 1664 a union took place at Mukachevo that involved the Orthodox in today's Transcarpathia and the Hungarian diocese of Hajdúdorog. A third union, which included the Orthodox in the county of Maramaros to the east of Mukachevo, took place in about 1713. Thus within a hundred years after the 1664 Union of Uzhorod, the Orthodox Church virtually ceased to exist in the region.

Early on there were jurisdictional conflicts over who would control this new Byzantine Catholic Church. In spite of the desire of the Ruthenians to have their own ecclesiastical organization, for more than a century the Ruthenian bishop in Mukachevo was only the ritual vicar of the local Latin bishop, and Ruthenian priests served as assistants in Latin parishes. The dispute was resolved in 1771 by Pope Clement XIV who, at the request of Empress Maria Theresa, erected the Ruthenian eparchy of Mukachevo and made it suffragan of the primate of Hungary. A seminary for Ruthenian Catholics was set up at Uzhorod in 1778.

After World War I, Transcarpathia became part of the new republic of Czechoslovakia. By this time there were two Ruthenian Catholic dioceses at Mukachevo and Presov. Although in the 1920s a group of these Ruthenian Catholics returned to the Orthodox Church, Rusyn ethnic identity remained closely tied to the Ruthenian Catholic Church.

World War II to the Present: At the end of World War II, Transcarpathia, including Uzhorod and Mukachevo, was annexed to the Soviet Union as part of the Ukrainian Soviet Socialist Republic. Presov, however, remained in Czechoslovakia. The Soviet authorities soon initiated a vicious persecution of the Ruthenian Church in the newly acquired region. In 1946 the Uzhorod seminary was closed. In 1949 the newly named Orthodox bishop of Mukachevo declared the union with Rome dissolved and the integration of his diocese into the Moscow patriarchate. Rusyns on the other side of the Czechoslovakian border were also forced to become Orthodox, while those in the Polish Lemko region were deported en masse in 1947 either to the Soviet Union or other areas of Poland. In all three countries, an attempt was made to wipe out any residual Rusyn national identity by declaring them all to be Orthodox and Ukrainian.

The collapse of Communism throughout the region had a dramatic effect on Ruthenian Catholics. The first changes took place in Poland in the mid 1980s, where Lemko organizations began to surface and press for recognition of their rights and distinct status. In Czechoslovakia, the much-diminished Ruthenian Catholic minority began in November 1989 to campaign for recognition within the predominantly Slovak Greek Catholic diocese of Presov. And finally, in the Transcarpathian heartland, the Ruthenian Catholic eparchy of Mukachevo was reestablished when the Holy See appointed a bishop and two auxiliaries in January 1991. In late 1990 it was estimated that there were about a half million Ruthenian Catholics in Transcarpathia with 100 priests and 120 registered communities with 60 churches. After an unpleasant confrontation with the Orthodox, the old Greek Catholic cathedral in Uzhorod was returned to its pre-1949 owners in early 1992. At that time a new seminary was being built in Uzhorod.

A continuing issue for Ruthenian Catholics will be their relationship with the much larger Ukrainian Catholic Church. With the restoration of religious freedom in the Soviet Union and now in newly independent Ukraine, the Mukachevo diocese for the first time is functioning openly within the same country as the Ukrainian Catholic Church. Although the Mukachevo diocese is not a part of the Ukrainian Catholic metropolitanate, Ruthenian Catholic bishops have attended recent Ukrainian Catholic synods. The bishop of Mukachevo has made it clear, however, that he opposes integration into the Ukrainian Catholic Church and favors the promotion of the distinct national and religious identity of his Rusyn people. It remains to be seen what type of relationship will develop between Ukrainian and Ruthenian Catholics. Much will depend on the uncertain future political status of Transcarpathia itself.

Many Ruthenian Catholics had immigrated to North America in the late nineteenth and early twentieth centuries. Because of strained relationships with the local Latin hierarchy who would not recognize such legitimate Ruthenian Catholic traditions as a married clergy, large numbers of these Catholics returned to the Orthodox Church. In 1982 it was estimated that out of 690,000 people of Rusyn descent in the United States, 225,000 were still Ruthenian Catholics, 95,000 were in the Carpatho-Russian Orthodox diocese, 250,000 were in the Orthodox Church in America, 20,000 were in Orthodox parishes directly under the Moscow patriarchate, and 100,000 belonged to various other Orthodox, Ukrainian Catholic, Roman Catholic, and Protestant denominations.

In many areas of the world, including Australia, Great Britain, and Canada, Ruthenian Catholics are not distinguished from Ukrainian Catholics. In the United States, however, the Ruthenians had in 1994 four dioceses and about 200,000 members. This church, generally known simply as "Byzantine Catholic," emphasizes its American character and celebrates the liturgy in English in most parishes. *See also* Byzantine rite; Ukrainian Catholic Church.

Bibliography

Warzeski, Walter C. *Byzantine-Rite Rusins in Carpatho-Ruthenia and America.* Pittsburgh, PA: Byzantine Seminary Press, 1971.

RONALD G. ROBERSON

Ruysbroeck, Bl. Jan van (roiz'brook), 1293–1381, Flemish mystical writer. Ordained a priest in Brussels in 1317, he remained there another twenty-six years before retiring to a more secluded location at Groenendaal. Many of his eleven treatises were motivated by a desire to combat the Quietist (spiritually passive) tendencies of his day, but their tone is generally not polemical. Rather, Ruysbroeck enunciates a positive understanding of the entire

Monsignor John A. Ryan, known during the Franklin D. Roosevelt administration (1932-45) as "Monsignor New Dealer," gave the benediction at Roosevelt's second and fourth inaugurations.

course of the spiritual life, from its humblest beginnings to the deepest mystical union with God. *See also* mysticism; Quietism.

Ryan, John Augustine, 1869–1945, American moral theologian and economist. Inspired by Pope Leo XIII's encyclical *Rerum Novarum* (1891), Monsignor Ryan's life's work focused on the relationship of Christian ethical principles to the nation's socioeconomic conditions. Ordained in 1898, he studied at The Catholic University of America (1989–1902), received his S.T.D. (1906), and served as a member of Catholic University's faculty (1915–39). Prior to that appointment, he taught moral theology at St. Paul Seminary in Minnesota, lectured on labor issues, and worked for minimum wage laws for women in Wisconsin and Minnesota. His book *The Living Wage* (1906) was the first of many publications that addressed the plight of the wage earner. In 1919, Ryan wrote the policy statement of the National Catholic Welfare Conference, known as the "Bishops' Program of Social Reconstruction." It contained eleven proposals that anticipated New Deal legislation. Ryan was so zealous a supporter of Franklin D. Roosevelt's New Deal that he was sometimes referred to as "Monsignor New Dealer." *See also* Catholic social teachings.

S

Sabas, St., also known as Sava, 439–532. **1** A monk born in Cappadocia, the founder of the large lavra (colony of monks) known as Mar Saba, located between Jerusalem and the Dead Sea. The monastery, with few monks, still functions. Its best known resident was John of Damascus (d. ca. 749). Sabas opposed Origenism and Monophysitism. He is buried at Mar Saba. Feast day: December 5. **2** Patron saint of Serbia, d. 1235. Feast day: January 14 (Serbian Orthodox Church).

Sabbath (Heb., *shabbat,* "to stop, rest"), the seventh day of the Jewish week. On the Sabbath no work is to be done, according to early biblical laws (Exod 23:12; 34:21; Lev 23:2–3) and both versions of the Ten Commandments (Exod 20:8–11; Deut 5:12–15). The prophets and later books praise observance and condemn violations of the Sabbath rest (Isa 56:1–6; Neh 13:19–21). Concern for keeping the Sabbath and the development of more detailed rules are evident in Second Temple literature (1 Macc 2:32–38), the NT (Mark 2:23–3:6), and rabbinic literature. Sabbath observance was a well-known Jewish practice during the Greco-Roman period.

Sabbath was a festival marked by a holy convocation and special sacrifices (Lev 23:2–3; Num 28:9–10) and symbolically associated with creation (Gen 2:2–3; Exod 20:11), the covenant (Exod 31:16), and holiness. The origins of Sabbath observance are unclear: the term may be connected with a Mesopotamian word for the day of the full moon or derived from the root *sbt* ("completion, cessation"). Or the practice may reflect a cultural preference for periods of seven days. Followers of Jesus continued the observance of every seventh day as holy but soon transferred the day to Sunday, the day of Jesus' Resurrection (Acts 20:7 and often in early Christian literature). From the fourth century on, councils and Christian legislation frequently mandated cessation from work and attendance at worship on Sunday. *See also* Sunday.

Sabbatine Privilege, a promise of Mary's to bring to heaven, on the Saturday after their death, the wearers of the Carmelite brown scapular, a tradition based on a papal bull now considered spurious. *See also* scapular.

Sabellianism, third-century trinitarian belief denying any real distinction of the divine Persons. It has been variously defined as Modalism or as a form of Monarchianism and was condemned by Dionysius of Alexandria (d.ca. 264) because of its exaggerated emphasis on the unity of the divine Being. The chief spokesperson for this doctrine, a Roman cleric named Sabellius, developed a theme from the writings of Noëtus of Smyrna, whose work was largely a reaction to subordinationism. Like other Monarchianists, Sabellius held that Father, Son, and Holy Spirit are merely modes, aspects, or energies of one divine Person, who exercises three distinct functions or activities on behalf of humanity. *See also* Modalism; Monarchianism; Trinity, doctrine of the.

sacrament (Lat., *sacramentum,* "oath," "pledge"), one of the seven principal liturgical rites of the Church through which participants experience the love and power of God (grace) that flows from Christ's Passion, death, and Resurrection. Prior to the determination of the present list of seven sacraments in the twelfth century, the term "sacrament" had a much broader meaning. Used originally to name any manifestation of God's power and love in space and time, sacrament (Gk., *mysterion,* "mystery") also conveyed a sense of hiddenness. This usage stems from the use of the word *mysterion* in the Greek version of the Scriptures to indicate the hidden plan of God manifested in human history and made accessible to those who have faith (see, e.g., Wis 6:22; Matt 13:11; Rom 16:25–26; Eph 1:9–10). The life of Jesus Christ, culminating in his suffering, death, and Resurrection (the "Paschal Mystery") is the realization of God's loving intention to save humanity and the basis not only for the Church's sacramental worship, but also for its existence.

Tertullian (d. ca. 220), a lawyer from North Africa, was the first to translate *mysterion* into Latin as *sacramentum.* In secular usage, a *sacramentum* was the pledge or oath a soldier made upon entering military service. Sometimes this oath was accompanied by branding the new soldier on the arm with a sign of the general he was to serve. Tertullian spoke of Baptism using this image of *sacramentum* as a permanent consecration to God's service through word (oath) and visible sign (brand) made possible through sharing in the Paschal Mystery of Christ. Augustine (d. 430) further developed a notion of *mysterion/sacramentum* that would prove very influential in the writings of later theologians. He described a sacrament as a sacred sign or "visible word" composed of word and material element. This distinction would help later theologians develop the distinction between matter (the material substance) and form (the verbal formula).

During the Scholastic period (eleventh–thirteenth centuries) a more systematic approach to the sacraments was introduced, influenced by the newly recovered philosophy of Aristotle. There was a concern to distinguish the principal ways in which God builds up the Church and brings its members to salvation. The seven sacraments were thus distinguished from sacramentals in that the sacraments are "instrumental causes" of grace, the means by which God chooses to sanctify humanity and unify the Church. God unfailingly acts in these signs because they were instituted by Christ himself. The Church's present list of seven sacraments dates from this period, as does the familiar definition of a sacrament as "an outward sign, instituted by Christ, to give grace." The seven sacraments are: Baptism, Confirmation, Eucharist, Reconciliation (or Penance), Anointing of the Sick, Marriage (or Matrimony), and Holy Orders.

In recent years, modern sacramental theology, while not disagreeing with the Scholastic definition, has emphasized that the Incarnation of Jesus Christ is the "first" sacrament. It is from the Word taking flesh in the person of Christ—in his living, suffering, dying, and rising again—that all sacraments ultimately derive their power. The Church is also a sacrament insofar as it is a continuation of Christ's presence on earth until the end of time, for it is the Church, existing in time and space—the Body of Christ in this world—that proclaims God's powerful love for humanity in and through the Paschal Mystery of the Risen Lord. *See also* Anointing of the Sick; Baptism; Confirmation; Eucharist; Holy Orders; Marriage; Reconciliation; sacramental character; sacramentals.

MARK R. FRANCIS

sacrament, form of a, the verbal formula determined by the Church that so "shapes" the material element and ritual action prescribed by the rite that the sacrament is truly celebrated. Thus, for example, the form in the Roman rite for the sacrament of Baptism is the declarative sentence, "I baptize you in the name of the Father, Son, and Holy Spirit" while the minister immerses the person being baptized in water or pours water over the candidate's head. The words defined by the Church as the form of the sacrament are the absolute minimum necessary for those present to be sure that the sacrament was indeed celebrated. *See also* sacrament; sacrament, matter of a.

sacrament, matter of a, the material element and/or gesture used in the celebration of the sacrament. For example, the matter of the Eucharist is the bread and wine; of Baptism, the threefold immersion or pouring of water; of Holy Orders, the imposition of hands on the head of the ordinand. The sacrament of Reconciliation is the only sacrament to which this definition does not strictly apply. In Reconciliation the matter is not a gesture or material element, but the penitent's contrition, confession, and satisfaction. Matter is often discussed with its correlative term, "form": the words used to announce God's saving action in the sacrament. *See also* sacrament; sacrament, form of a.

sacramental character (Gk., *karakter,* "distinctive mark"), the traditional teaching, affirmed by the Council of Trent (1545), that in the sacraments of Baptism, Confirmation, and Holy Orders "a character is imprinted on the soul, a certain spiritual and indelible mark, and for this reason these sacraments cannot be repeated" (D 1609).

A scriptural basis for this affirmation was found in the interpretation given to certain biblical texts by Greek patristic writers who interpreted the Greek word "seal" (*sphragis*) as a description of how Christians are marked by Baptism. Rev 7:2–8; 2 Cor 1:22; and Eph 1:13, 4:13 are all cited as supporting the notion that the Holy Spirit permanently seals or marks as God's servants those who are baptized.

The teaching regarding the nonrepeatability of certain sacraments is found as early as Augustine (d. 430), who sought to explain the common practice of not rebaptizing persons who had received the sacraments of initiation at the hands of heretics. He maintained that in the conferral of the sacraments of initiation as well as in Holy Orders it is really Christ who acts. Therefore, the fact that the minister is in error or sin does not affect the permanent, public, and lasting value of Baptism (including Confirmation) and Holy Orders.

It was not until the thirteenth century that theologians began to discuss the nature of the sacramental character itself. Pope Innocent III (d. 1216) distinguished between the sacramental character and the grace bestowed by these sacraments. Alexander of Hales (d. 1245) and Bonaventure (d. 1274) taught that sacramental character was a *habitus* (Lat., "condition") that marks the soul and disposes it to the grace of the sacrament. Thomas Aquinas (d. 1274), on the other hand, described character more in functional terms, emphasizing that it is a *potentia*

(Lat., "power") or spiritual power that conforms an individual more to Christ, forever changing one's relationship to God and the Church, giving one a share in Christ's priesthood, and deputing the Christian to engage in acts of worship.

The Council of Florence in 1439 affirmed the existence of a character imparted by the sacraments of Baptism, Confirmation, and Holy Orders, speaking of character as an "impress" on the soul (D 1313). It was this definition that was essentially repeated by the Council of Trent to answer Luther's denial of the existence of the sacramental character.

Contemporary theological treatment of the sacramental character has tended to move away from discussing character as a "thing" conferred at Baptism, Confirmation, and Holy Orders, and has emphasized that the reception of these sacraments publicly and irrevocably changes one's relationship to Christ and the Church. Vatican II's Dogmatic Constitution on the Church (1964, n. 11), for example, speaks in dynamic terms of the character conferred by Baptism as that which appoints all Christians to religious worship and witness to the faith.

The teaching on sacramental character underscores the Church's deeply held conviction that, despite any possible infidelity on our part, God is always true to the divine promises incarnated in Christ and celebrated in the sacraments of Baptism, Confirmation, and Holy Orders. *See also* Baptism; Confirmation; Holy Orders.   MARK R. FRANCIS

sacramental grace. *See* grace, sacramental.

sacramentality, principle of, the notion that all reality, both animate and inanimate, is potentially or in fact the bearer of God's presence and the instrument of God's saving activity on humanity's behalf. This principle is rooted in the nature of a sacrament as such, i.e., a visible sign of the invisible presence and activity of God. Together with the principles of mediation (God works through secondary agents to achieve divine ends) and communion (the end of all of God's activity is the union of humanity), the principle of sacramentality constitutesoneofthecentraltheologicalcharacteristics of Catholicism. *See also* Catholicism; sacrament.

sacramentals, sacred signs instituted by the Church, similar to the seven major sacraments in that they "signify effects, particularly of a spiritual kind, that are obtained through the Church's intercession. They dispose people to receive the chief effect of the sacraments and they make holy various occasions in human life." This definition of sacramentals, taken from the Constitution on the Sacred Liturgy (1963, n. 60), points to a renewed understanding of the way in which sacramentals help sanctify human life and how they are intrinsically related to the sacraments themselves.

Unlike older definitions of sacramentals, such as the one found in the previous code of canon law that referred to sacramentals as objects and actions usually "done by" the clergy, this new definition identifies sacramentals as dynamic signs used in celebration. They are first and foremost liturgical actions in which the faithful are invited to participate (Constitution on the Sacred Liturgy, n. 79). Thus, holy water, ashes, palms, candles, and the like serve legitimate liturgical purposes and are not simply static objects but elements that enhance individual and communal prayer. It is true that some sacramentals, such as rosaries and medals, are not used in a specifically liturgical context, but they too remind individuals of God's presence in their lives and call them to prayer.

Among those signs named as sacramentals by the Constitution on the Sacred Liturgy are liturgical prayers and rites used in administering the sacraments, funerals, exorcisms, blessings of persons, and consecrations and blessings of objects. All sacramentals are intercessory prayers of the Church. They ask for God's grace and blessing on persons— for example, on a religious woman or man consecrating themselves to Christ in the context of a religious community—or on objects such as ashes, holy water, rosaries, sacred images (and on those who are to use these objects). Blessings of secular objects or places used daily by the faithful, such as homes, cars, and places of business, also fall under the category of sacramentals.

Sacramentals are distinguished from sacraments in that they have been instituted by the Church and do not find their origin in Christ. While sacraments produce their effect *ex opere operato* (Lat., "from the work done") because it is Christ himself who celebrates them, sacramentals confer grace because of the Church's power of intercession (*ex opere operantis ecclesiae,* Lat., "by the work of the working Church"). They exist in order to make holy almost every event in the lives of believers and, like the sacraments, draw their power from the Paschal Mystery of Christ's Passion, death, and Resurrection, the only source of the Church's power. Sacramentals, like the sacraments, also underscore the Church's deeply held conviction that all of creation is a potential medium for the revelation of God's presence and blessing. In speaking about sacramentals, the Constitution on the Sacred Liturgy (n. 61) affirms the goodness of the material world and plainly states that "there is hardly any proper use of material things that cannot be directed toward human sanctification and the praise of God."

Although the Apostolic See reserves to itself the regulation of all sacramentals (can. 1167), the 1983 Code of Canon Law recognizes the age-old practice of the Christian people in administering some sacramentals. Many of the practices of popular religion, of exchanging blessings and the like, are now legally allowed by the 1983 code (can. 1168); laypersons can be legitimate ministers of some sacramentals in accord with the provisions in the liturgical books, e.g., parents blessing their children, laypersons distributing ashes on Ash Wednesday. Non-Catholics can also now be the recipients of some sacramentals.

Along with the sacraments themselves that hallow the key moments in human life—the Liturgy of the Hours (Divine Office) that sanctifies the Christian day and the liturgical year that relates the annual cycle of seasons to God's grace—sacramentals address the myriad of occasions in the lives of individuals, families, and communities where there is need for the Church's prayer and the blessing of God. *See also* sacrament.   MARK R. FRANCIS

sacramentary, the liturgical book containing all the prayers needed by the presider (priest or bishop) for Mass, for the celebration of sacraments (e.g., Baptism), for the Liturgy of the Hours, and for occasional services (e.g., funerals). As the presider's book, the sacramentary does not include material needed by other ministers in the liturgy (e.g., it contains neither Bible readings nor music, because these are assigned to readers, deacons, or cantors). Nor does the sacramentary provide "rubrics" (detailed directions about how the service is to be conducted), since these are contained in books known as *ordines* (Lat., singular, *ordo*). The sacramentary did not appear all at once in developed form; its historical evolution is complex. It was preceded by small booklets or leaflets (Lat., *libelli missarum*), which contained formulas for one or more Masses (e.g., the texts for Christmas day). Eventually these booklets were collected into larger groups. An early example is the sixth-century collection called the Leonine or Verona Sacramentary. Although the Ve-

rona Sacramentary followed the civil calendar, later sacramentaries, such as the Old Gelasian (manuscript, ca. 750) and the Gregorian (manuscript, late eighth century), usually followed the church calendar. As early as the tenth century, the sacramentaries began to be replaced by books called "missals" or "pontificals," which contained all parts of the service (including readings and music) in a single portable volume. By the thirteenth century the sacramentary had all but disappeared. It was restored as a functional liturgical book following Vatican Council II (1962–65). *See also* Roman Missal; sacrament.
                                    NATHAN MITCHELL

sacrament house, a late Gothic tower-shaped receptacle for reservation of consecrated hosts (Blessed Sacrament). It was freestanding or attached to the sanctuary wall. Used universally in German-speaking countries until the seventeenth century (Cologne until the nineteenth), it was prohibited by Church law in 1917 in favor of the tabernacle. *See also* tabernacle.

Sacrament of the Sick. *See* Anointing of the Sick.

sacramentum tantum (sah-krah-men'toom tahn' toom; Lat., "the sacrament itself"), in classical sacramental theology, the external rite and symbol perceptible to the senses. For example, in the Eucharist, the *sacramentum tantum* is the consecrated bread and wine; in Baptism, the pouring of water and the invocation of the Trinity. *See also* res et sacramentum; *res tantum;* sacrament.

sacrarium (Lat., "sacristy"), a basin or sink located in the sacristy that drains directly into the soil. The sacristy is a preparation and vesting room usually located near the sanctuary or wherever the liturgical rite is to be celebrated. The sacrarium is used for the cleaning of Mass linens, purificators, and eucharistic vessels. It is also used for the disposal of blessed ashes, oils, or holy water. Consecrated wine, however, is never to be poured down the sacrarium.

Sacred College. *See* Cardinals, College of.

Sacred Heart of Jesus, Congregation of the (S.C.J.), a nonexempt (i.e., subject to the local bishop) clerical religious institute with pontifical status whose members take the traditional vows of poverty, chastity, and obedience. Founded in 1877 by Father Leon Dehon, their constitution received approbation from Rome in 1923. Its priests and brothers are committed to devotion and reparation to the Sacred Heart of Jesus, and their works include education of young boys, seminaries, retreats, parishes, and missions. In the United States they minister especially among African Americans, Hispanics, and Native Americans. The Sacred Heart Fathers also conduct missions in South Africa. *See also* Sacred Heart, devotion to the.

Sacred Heart, devotion to the, a form of devotion to Jesus Christ as the Word of God Incarnate, consisting of veneration of his physical heart, united to his divinity, as the symbol of his redemptive love. Anchored in Jesus' assertion that living water would flow from his heart (John 7:37–39) and the patristic tradition that the Holy Spirit flowed out upon the Church from Jesus' pierced side (John 19:33–37), this devotion draws upon the popular sense of the heart as the seat of a person's inner life, both natural and supernatural. Christ's threefold love—human, infused, and divine—is epitomized by the pierced heart of Jesus hanging on the cross. The Middle Ages saw a transition from the wound in Jesus' side as a source of grace to the Heart of Jesus as the express object of a particular, more personal devotion. Coupled with a subjective piety that emphasized

A type of depiction of the Sacred Heart of Jesus that was common in pre–Vatican II Catholicism. It is one of many mass-produced devotional items in an art style in which Jesus is portrayed as effeminate, if not sexless.

Christ's Passion, the devotion was taken up by the Devotio Moderna and was bequeathed to the Society of Jesus and the Sisters of the Visitation by their founders, Ignatius of Loyola (1491–1556) and Francis de Sales (1567–1622). John Eudes (1601–80) composed a Mass and Office of the Sacred Heart, and the private revelations of Margaret Mary Alacoque (1647–90) at Paray-le-Monial, France (1673–75), promoted the devotion and shaped its practice, especially acts of reparation and consecration. In 1765, the bishops of Poland were allowed to celebrate a feast of the Sacred Heart, which was extended to the universal Church in 1856. It is celebrated on the Friday after Corpus Christi. The practice of enthroning an image of the Sacred Heart in homes began at Paray-le-Monial in 1907. Pope Pius XII described the theological foundation of the devotion in the encyclical *Haurietis Aquas* (1956).

JAMES T. CONNELLY

sacred minister, technical term used in canon law for an ordained minister. Ordained ministry is considered sacred not only because of the responsibilities of the minister, but also because it is conferred through a sacred sacrament. *See also* ministry.

sacrifice, anything offered to God. The positive function of sacrifice was to appease the deity by offering a gift, while the negative function was to remove sin. Priestly theory (as expressed in the narrative and legal portion of the Pentateuch composed by priests) distinguished between inadvertent and deliberate sin ("acting high-handedly," Num 15:27–31), and it remains unclear to what extent sacrifice could expiate the latter (see Heb 9:22). The biblical narrative records sacrifices made from the earliest times, e.g., by Cain and Abel (Gen 4:3–5) and Noah (Gen 8:20–22), but according to the Priestly view sacrificial ritual was instituted at Sinai. Lev 1–7 is a manual of instruction for the performance of sacrificial ritual, with the respective roles of priesthood and laity clearly specified. The principal types of sacrifice were the burnt, cereal, and peace offerings, which were unscheduled and ad hoc, and the mandatory sin (purgation) and guilt (reparation) sacrifices, which were essential for the removal of sin. Sacrifice also accompanied the making of covenants (Gen 31:54; Exod 24:3–8) and the Passover is explicitly designated as a sacrifice (Exod 12:27). The near-sacrifice of Isaac by Abraham (Gen 22) may have had the purpose of discouraging the practice of human sacrifice, which, however, was not unknown in Israel (Judg 11:30–40; 2 Sam 21:1–14; 1 Kgs 16:34; 2 Kgs 16:3; 21:6). Infant sacrifice associated with Molech, common in Phoenicia and its colonies, was practiced in Judah and proscribed during the reign of Josiah (2 Kgs 23:10).

The sacrificial cult came to an end with the destruction of the Temple in A.D. 70. In the NT, sacrificial language serves to bring out the meaning of the self-offering of Jesus by his death (1 Cor 5:7, Heb 9–10). *See also* Eucharist; priesthood.   JOSEPH BLENKINSOPP

sacrifice of the Mass, the doctrine of the Church that Christ's sacrifice on the cross is made present in the celebration of the Eucharist. Late Judaism had already developed the principle that the sacrifice most pleasing to God was the obedience of a person to the divine law and will and that fidelity to God, even to the point of martyrdom, could be a source of salvation for others. Jesus would have been aware of this tradition. His words regarding the cup of his blood being poured out for the many have definite sacrificial overtones (cf. Mark 14:24). The setting of the Last Supper within the context of the Passover celebration—with the sacrificed lamb as the center of the meal—would have heightened awareness of Jesus' sacrificial intentions.

Certainly the first-century Christians did not hesitate to understand Jesus' death as a sacrifice (cf. 1 Cor 5:7). Paul's contrast of the Eucharist with pagan sacrifices (1 Cor 10:14–22) hints at the fuller identification of Eucharist as sacrifice in the future. So, too, does the Bread of Life discourse in the Gospel of John (cf. especially 6:51).

In the second century there was increasing application of sacrificial terminology to the Eucharist, culminating in the identification of the Eucharist as a sacrificial action in the beginning of the third century. Patristic thought saw this action as the Church's, which could make this offering only in the power of Christ's own sacrifice made present through the Church's remembrance of the Paschal Mystery. The Church's engagement of itself in remembrance of the death and Resurrection of the Lord is made possible by that very mystery, which makes itself present through the Church's action and assumes that action unto itself so that the Church's offering is ultimately Christ's offering of himself through and with the self-offering of the members of his ecclesial body.

The Reformers of the sixteenth century, reacting against abuses and exaggerations in the role of the priest and the multiplication of Masses, denied that the Eucharist is a sacrifice because such a teaching took away from the unique and infinitely abundant sacrifice of Christ on the cross. The Council of Trent responded in 1562 by declaring that "in the Mass, the same Christ who offered himself once in a bloody manner on the cross is contained and is offered in an unbloody manner." Christ's offering is one and unrepeatable, but it is made present in every Eucharist.

It has been in the twentieth century that scholars have recovered the rich notions of memorial in the Scriptures and the patristic era. The remembrance of divine action opens space and time to the presence of that divine action, fulfilled once historically but in the eternity of God always available to subsequent generations. Thus Christ continues to make his sacrifice on the cross present and effective for the Church, which through his Spirit gathers to remember and give thanks for his death and Resurrection.

The recovery of the ancient notion of memorial has led to increasing ecumenical agreement on the presence of Christ's sacrifice in the Eucharist. *See also* crucifixion; Eucharist; priesthood.

JOHN J. STRYNKOWSKI

sacrilege, the violation or profanation of any sacred person, place, or thing. There are three categories of sacrilege: personal, local, and real.

A personal sacrilege is the violation of persons who have dedicated themselves to God by Holy Orders or religious vows. Canon law establishes penalties for the use of physical force against clerics and religious. The penalty for assault against the Holy Father is automatic excommunication reserved to the Apostolic See; against a bishop, the penalty is automatic interdict, an ecclesiastical censure imposed without a hearing or other process. Physical force against a cleric or religious out of contempt for the faith, the Church, ecclesiastical power, or ministry is punishable by a just penalty. Also considered sacrilegious are wrongfully imprisoning or suing clergy and religious, or engaging in sexual conduct with them.

A local sacrilege is the violation of a sacred place—a dedicated or blessed church, oratory, private chapel, altar, or cemetery. The violation occurs by the commission of certain crimes in them, such as murder or theft of precious or sacred objects, or by engaging in sexual acts in them. Sacrilege also occurs by illicitly using the sacred place for a profane purpose.

A real sacrilege is the violation of a sacred thing that has been dedicated to God or reserved for divine worship. A standard example is simony, i.e., the selling of spiritual goods. Another is sacrilegious Communion—the reception of Holy Communion when one is conscious of serious sin and has not made an act of perfect contrition with the intention of confessing the sin. Such examples of sacrilege are considered mortally sinful.   JOHN HUELS

sacristan, person charged with the care and maintenance of sacred vessels, vestments, altar linens, candles, oils, holy water, and other liturgical items. The sacristan may be lay, religiously professed, or ordained. In larger churches and shrines, the sacristan may be a full-time ministry, though in most parishes the duties of sacristan are shared among volunteers.

sacristy, a preparation and vesting room, often located to one side of the sanctuary. Vestments, altar linens, eucharistic vessels, and other liturgical wares are stored in the sacristy. It is the place where the presider and other liturgical ministers proximately prepare for liturgical ceremonies by vesting and by sharing last-minute instructions and a brief prayer.

Sacrosanctum Concilium   (sah-kroh-sahnk' toom kahn-chee'lee-oom). *See* Constitution on the Sacred Liturgy.

Sadducees (sad'joo-seez), a Jewish religiopolitical party in the last two centuries B.C. and the first A.D. No Sadducean writings have survived, but the Sadducees' views were described by the first-century historian Josephus and by NT writers. Their name, which apparently derives from Zadok, the leading priest in the time of David and Solomon, suggests a priestly orientation. In legal matters, they considered only the written law of Moses to be authoritative, not the oral tradition of commentary accepted by their opponents, the Pharisees. They denied the existence of fate and believed that individuals are responsible for their own actions. They are mentioned several times in the NT in connection with other denials. In Matt 22:23–33 Jesus refuted their thesis that there would be no resurrection of the dead. The same issue figured in a dispute between Paul and Sadducean members of the council reported in Acts 23:1–10. When Paul mentioned the resurrection of the dead (which the Pharisees accepted),

there was a violent disagreement between Pharisees and the Sadducees who "say there is no resurrection, or angel, or spirit; but the Pharisees acknowledge all three" (23:8). The Sadducees, according to Josephus, thought the soul died with the body and that there was no afterlife. Josephus also reports that the Sadducees were men of high standing in society and the group attracted only the wealthy. Some high priests are known to have been Sadducees, and they exercised strong influence on the state at different times, though the Pharisees were usually more popular. *See also* Pharisees; scribes.

Sadoleto, Jacopo (jah-koh'poh sah-doh-lay' toh), 1477–1547, Italian cardinal, classical scholar, reformer. An influential adviser to Pope Paul III, in 1537 Sadoleto became a member of a special commission on Church reform and for the preparation of a general council (to be held eventually at Trent). He tried to reconvert Protestants, notably Philipp Melanchthon (1537) and the city of Geneva (1539), without force but also without dogmatic compromise. Extremist Catholics suspected his orthodoxy, charging that his theology of grace and original sin reflected a semi-Pelagianist bias, ascribing too much to human effort and too little to grace in the attainment of salvation.

Sailer, Johann Michael (zi'luhr), 1751–1832, German pastoral theologian. Ordained in 1775, he served as professor of theology at Ingolstadt, Dillingen, and Landshut. In 1829 he became bishop of Regensburg. He is considered one of the founders of the science of pastoral theology, which seeks to understand and develop the implications of faith for the actual situation of the Church, specifically for preaching, counseling, and various other ministries.

Saint-Cyran, Abbé de, 1581–1643, a founder of Jansenism. Born Jean Duvergier de Hauranne, he was Cornelius Jansen's friend and an important supporter of Jansenism as the spiritual counselor to the convent of Port-Royal and Antoine Arnauld, brother of Mère Angélique, the abbess of the convent. He was incarcerated from 1638 to 1643 for his Jansenism and for opposing Cardinal Richelieu, the chief minister of France. His influence continued through his spiritual direction and his *Lettres chrétiennes et spirituelles* (1645), which contained the basic teachings of the Jansenist movement, namely, an emphasis on the irresistible power of grace, the

Sainte-Chapelle, thirteenth-century chapel and masterpiece of Gothic architecture and medieval glass, was built in Paris for King Louis IX to house various relics of the Passion of Christ, including allegedly the Crown of Thorns.

An abbey church founded in Paris in the sixth century, Saint-Germain-des-Prés became a center of historical scholarship in the seventeenth century, but most of the abbey, like other Catholic properties, was destroyed in the French Revolution of 1789.

difficulty of attaining salvation, and the need for a life of moral severity and rigorism. *See also* Jansenism; Port-Royal.

Saint-Denis, abbey in Paris founded ca. 625 on the reputed site of the martyrdom of the patron saint of France who during the Middle Ages was assimilated to the Dionysius reported in Acts (17:34) to have been converted by Paul. Known as the first Gothic church from the twelfth-century renovations under Abbot Suger, Saint-Denis served as the burial site for the kings of France. *See also* Denis, St.

Sainte-Chapelle (sant shah-pel'), chapel built in Paris ca. 1245 for King Louis IX of France to house relics of the Passion, including the Crown of Thorns. Desecrated in 1791, it still retains much of its original character despite heavy remodeling in the nineteenth century.

Saint-Germain-des-Prés (san jher-manh' deh preh'), Benedictine abbey founded in the middle of the sixth century. Located in Paris, the abbey is named after its benefactor, Germain (d. 576),

bishop of Paris. The abbey became a great center of learning during the seventeenth century.

Saint Joan's Alliance, originally called the Catholic Women's Suffrage Society, an international organization founded in London in 1911 to secure legal and true equality of women in the Church and in society. Since 1915, they focus especially on the Church. The Alliance holds consultative status at the United Nations.

Saint John Lateran. *See* Lateran Basilica.

Saint Mary Major, also known as Santa Maria Maggiore, one of Rome's four major basilicas. Founded in the fourth century by Pope Liberius on the Esquiline Hill, the present church was built by Pope Sixtus III in the fifth century. Relics of Christ's manger are reputed to be held in the basilica. The feast commemorating its founding is August 5, which was formerly called Our Lady of the Snows because, according to legend, the pope built on a site where snow fell in August. *See also* basilica.

The interior of the basilica of Saint Mary Major in Rome. According to a medieval legend, the Blessed Virgin Mary left her footprints on the site during a miraculous snowfall one August evening; thus the feast of Our Lady of the Snows.

Saint Patrick's Cathedral, New York City landmark and the cathedral church of the archdiocese of New York. The present structure superseded the Old Cathedral and was the personal dream of Archbishop John Hughes, who was determined to erect a cathedral "worthy of the increasing numbers, intelligence, and wealth" of the Catholic community.

Architect James Fenwick was commissioned to build the Gothic Revival church. In preparation for the groundbreaking in 1858, Hughes circulated a letter to raise the funds "for the glory of God . . . Holy Mother Church . . . the honor of the Catholic name in this country." It was left to his successor, Cardinal John McCloskey, to complete the task; the formal dedication was held on May 25, 1879. The orator Bishop Patrick John Ryan delivered the sermon to a crowd of seven thousand, commending both the rich and the "children of toil" who gave generously to build the "greatest church edifice of the New World," a testimony to the great spirit of the "faith of the ages."

Expansion of the scope and structure of the cathedral continued over the years with the construction of the famous spires in 1885 and the lady chapel in 1906. The mortgage finally cleared, St. Patrick's was solemnly consecrated to the service of God by Cardinal John Farley in 1910.

Saint Patrick's Purgatory, a pilgrimage center on an island in Lough (Lake) Derg, County Donegal, Ireland. Nothing can be said of a connection with St. Patrick since pilgrimages probably began in the twelfth century. To this day it is a popular center of pilgrimage and penance during the summer months. *See also* Ireland, Catholicism in; Patrick, St.

Saint Paul's Outside the Walls, one of the four major basilicas in Rome. Its full name derives from

The imposing facade and spires of St. Patrick's Cathedral, New York City, one of American Catholicism's most recognizable symbols and one of the city's most popular tourist attractions. It is the largest Catholic cathedral in the United States.

The interior of the basilica of St. Paul's Outside the Walls in Rome, one of the city's four major basilicas and the place where, on January 25, 1959, Pope John XXIII first announced his intention to call the Second Vatican Council.

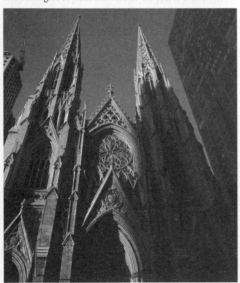

its location on the Via Ostia outside the walls of the city. First built over the relics of St. Paul by Constantine in the fourth century and later enlarged, the basilica burned to the ground in 1823. It was rededicated (after a complete rebuilding) in 1854. Only the mosaics in the present church survived the fire. The church has been maintained over the centuries by Benedictine monks who live in an adjacent monastery. *See also* basilica; basilica, major.

Saint Peter's Basilica, Catholicism's principal church. Built over the site on Vatican Hill in Vatican City State where St. Peter was said to have been buried, the original building was constructed during the reign of the emperor Constantine (d. 337). The original church was built in the basilica style with a large courtyard (atrium) at its entrance. The present church was begun in 1506 under the direction of a succession of architects (Bramante, Raphael, Peruzzi, and Sangallo). The final shape of the church derives from Michelangelo (d. 1564), who did not live to see the erection of the great dome. (The dome stands 404 feet from the pavement and has an interior diameter of 137 feet.) The long nave and facade, designed by Carlo Maderno, was added in the seventeenth century; it was not planned by Michelangelo, who had envisioned the church as having the shape of a Greek cross. Over the main entrance, Maderno also installed a loggia for public blessings. Now 619 feet in length, the church was dedicated by

St. Peter's Basilica, Vatican City, Catholicism's mother church; Bernini's famous columns embrace St. Peter's Square, with the obelisk at its center; the papal residence is behind the columns to the right and the Vatican Gardens are to the rear of the basilica. Various administrative offices are to the left, including the papal audience hall.

Pope Urban VIII (d. 1644) in 1626. Gianlorenzo Bernini (d. 1680) further decorated its interior with the famous baldachino over the main altar, and the baroque "altar of the chair" was added. He also designed the piazza in front of the basilica. Set off by a semicircle of four rows of columns, the piazza is centered by an Egyptian obelisk excavated from the nearby Gardens of Nero. The obelisk, in turn, is flanked by two fountains.

Excavations begun in this century have shown that the church is built over a large Roman necropolis. Archaeologists think they have discovered the ancient marker (Lat., *tropheum*) that was placed over the grave of Peter before the building of the Constantinian basilica in those excavations. The "confessio" (Peter's grave) is under the main papal altar. The crypts and altars of the basilica contain the burial places of over a hundred and thirty popes. *See also* basilica; Michelangelo; Vatican City State.

LAWRENCE CUNNINGHAM

saints, in a strict sense, those officially recognized (canonized) by the Church as persons who have lived a holy life, who now share in the Beatific Vision (i.e., face-to-face experience of the presence of God), and who may be publicly venerated by the faithful. To be sure, there are countless more saints than those who have been formally offered for public veneration. Anyone who may reasonably be believed to have lived a good life and who, therefore, may be presumed to be enjoying eternal life with God can be considered a saint. Devotion to the saints is an expression of the doctrine of the communion of saints, a belief that even death does not break the bonds that tie Christians together. Holiness of life and heroic virtue mark a saint; miracles and wonders worked are not necessarily signs of saintliness.

Saints do not witness to one model of sanctity. The list of canonized saints provides a wide variety of models of holiness. Saints come from all walks of life and provide creative instances of living a Christian life in different times and in response to different challenges. The faithful are encouraged to follow the example of the virtuous lives of the saints according to the lights of their own day.

History: Paul used the word "saint" to refer to all the Christian faithful (2 Cor 13:12; Eph 1:1). Neither the OT nor the NT speak explicitly about invocation of the saints. In the early Church, however, veneration of the original disciples of Jesus and of martyrs became widespread. Soon, persons who suffered for the faith (confessors) but who were not martyred were also venerated. After the era of persecution subsided, virgins, hermits, and monks were honored as saints. In time, holy persons who led exemplary Christian lives, especially those who practiced great austerity and penance in the spirit of the martyrs, were added to the list.

Over the course of centuries, the number of persons proclaimed as saints by the faithful grew to enormous proportions. Each locality had its own list of saints and devotions to them. Abuses arose and the Church established a process whereby a bishop made the final decision after studying a biography and an account of miracles presented to him. If the bishop approved, the person was declared a saint and a feast day assigned in that diocese or province, usually the anniversary of their death.

The custom grew of asking the pope to formally approve the canonization, since papal approval had greater prestige than that of bishops. In 993, Ulric of Augsburg (d. 973), a bishop, was declared a saint in the first papal canonization (by Pope John XV). Gregory IX formalized the process and in 1234 papal canonization became the only legitimate form of canonization. Veneration of the saints was one of the controversial practices rejected by the Protestant Reformers because it seemed to detract from devotion to Christ. The Council of Trent (1545–63) reaffirmed the Catholic doctrine.

Veneration of Saints. The juridical process whereby a person, already declared blessed, is proclaimed a saint involves beatification (when public veneration is permitted) and canonization (the definitive declaration that the individual is in heaven). If, after a person has been beatified, additional miracles are alleged, a further process of investigation and verification is undertaken. Upon a positive completion of this process, the pope issues a bull of canonization declaring the blessed to be a saint and extending veneration of the saint to the whole Church. An elaborate and solemn ceremony celebrates the canonization.

Once a person has been declared a saint, a feast day is assigned, and churches and shrines may be dedicated to the saint. The person may be declared patron saint of a country, a diocese, or other religious institution. Statues and images may be struck, prayers said publicly in his or her honor, and relics venerated. A Mass is composed in the saint's honor.

Catholics pray only to God; they ask the saints to intercede for them with God. They do not believe that healing, forgiveness, or other blessings come through the power of the saint, but from God through the saint's intercession. Veneration afforded saints is considered praise and glory of God since holiness is impossible without the gift of God's grace. The veneration given to saints (Gk., *dulia,* "service or veneration") and to Mary (Gk., *hyperdulia,* "more than veneration") is distinguished from the adoration and worship due to God alone (Gk., *latria,* "worship"). Honor given to the saints is honor given to God. The Second Vatican Council (1962–65) teaches that while it is fitting to love the saints who are our brothers and sisters in Christ, devotion to the saints is ultimately directed toward God. "For by its very nature every genuine testimony of love which we show to those in heaven tends toward and terminates in Christ, who is the 'crown of all saints'. Through Him it tends toward and terminates in God who is wonderful in His saints and is magnified in them." (Dogmatic Constitution on the Church, 1964, n. 50). *See also* beatification; canonization; *dulia; hyperdulia;* patron saint; saints, devotion to.

Bibliography
Delaney, John J. *Dictionary of Saints.* New York: Doubleday, 1980.
Farmer, David Hugh. *The Oxford Dictionary of Saints.* 3rd edition. New York: Oxford University Press, 1992.
Woodward, Kenneth. *Making Saints: How the Catholic Church Determines Who Becomes a Saint, Who Doesn't, and Why.* New York: Simon and Schuster, 1990.   REGINA COLL

saints, canonization of. *See* canonization.

saints, devotion to, private and public practices that honor or venerate holy men and women. These holy people are ordinarily, though not necessarily, properly canonized, i.e., their names placed on the official list (canon) of saints. Never to be confused with adoration (Gk., *latria,* "worship"), which is due God alone, devotion to a saint acknowledges his or her life of virtue as a model of holiness that provides a path to God through the one doorway, Jesus Christ. The saint was a holy person insofar as his or her life conformed to Christ's, manifested the inherent values of the gospel tradition and provided a paradigm for the Christian life. At certain junctures in the Church's history, confusion about the relationship between the saints and Christ caused the misconception that Catholics actually worship the saints. Church teaching retains the important distinction: God is worshiped; Mary and the saints are venerated and appropriately honored in private and public devotions.

In the earliest days of the Church's persecution,

special homage was paid to the memory of martyrs who suffered to the point of death. The cult of martyrs united people in a common memory and cultivated devotional practices that invoked the martyrs' intercession. When the age of persecution ended with the Peace of Constantine (ca. 313), the cult of martyrs extended beyond "red martyrdom" to "white martyrdom." The latter included those who did not die but suffered imprisonment and torture because of their faith or those who purposely severed themselves from the mainstream of life in the world and took up the discipline of ascetics as monks in the desert or some other place of solitude. The cult of Mary as Mother of God and Mother of Christ also grew in the early centuries.

Both the "red" and "white" martyr came to be honored annually on the anniversary of his or her death, the day of birth to a new life in heaven. Churches were named in honor of saints and placed under their patronage. Special prayers to saints were added to the Mass and readings about them were inserted into the Liturgy of the Hours. Eastern churches venerated their images, while Western churches revered their relics. Hagiographical literature, or lives of the saints, came to be more familiar than Sacred Scripture and thus formed the Catholic imagination of the Middle Ages, when popular devotions to the saints flourished with pilgrimages to places where relics reposed. Saints' names were assigned to people and places as patrons, and feast days were often regarded as civic festivals.

Changes in Devotional Practices: There were excesses, and exaggerated stories and practices brought protests from within the Church itself (Lateran IV, 1215). In 1530, Martin Luther contested the intercessory role of saints as detrimental to Christ's role as the unique mediator between God and humankind. The Council of Trent (1545–63) countered Luther's stance by encouraging Catholics to invoke the saints as sources of grace from God through Christ, who alone is redeemer. The following centuries witnessed a steady increase in the canonization of saints and devotions to them, especially in Italy, Spain, and France.

Vatican II (1962–65) warned against abuses that detract from the praise of God in Christ. At the same time, the council encouraged devotion to the saints as a way to enrich the worship of God through Christ in the Holy Spirit. Postconciliar reforms addressed both public and private devotion to the saints by way of the church's official liturgical life and its public popular devotions, as well as the individual's private devotion. The liturgical life of the Church manifested the renewal in its liturgical calendar and books. The Sanctoral Cycle or Proper of Saints ensures the annual liturgical remembering of past figures who loom large in the corporate consciousness of Catholics. Obscure saints have been eliminated from the calendar, which was restructured on principles of universal and local devotion and need. The Lectionary (1969) and Sacramentary (1970) offer a common (a proper of the Mass that can be used by saints without a special Mass) of the Blessed Virgin Mary, of martyrs, pastors, Doctors of the Church, virgins, and holy men and women, as well as votive Masses for particular saints and one for all saints. The Office of Readings includes the writings of saints and hagiographical texts about them. Private devotions are encouraged by way of image and prayer, ultimately directed through the saint to Christ as the source of all holiness. Always a hallmark of the Catholic tradition, devotion to the saints is cutting across ecumenical lines in an increased awareness of the communion of saints among all Christian peoples. *See also* canonization; communion of saints; saints. *DANIEL P. GRIGASSY*

Saint-Sulpice, Society of. *See* Sulpicians.

sakkos (sah'kaws), Byzantine-rite episcopal dalmatic. Originally an imperial garment, its use as a liturgical vestment was extended to patriarchs and, progressively, to all ranks of bishops. *See also* dalmatic.

Salamanca. *See* Salmanticenses.

Salesians, the Society of St. Francis de Sales (S.D.B.), a community of priests founded in Turin, Italy, by John Bosco in 1859 dedicated to the education of boys and young men. John Bosco had a lifelong interest in helping poor youth with their material needs and in seeing to their religious education. At first, he gathered boys for evening classes where they could learn trades in a religious atmosphere. Later, with the help of other interested priests, he established a "pious society" named after St. Francis de Sales (1567–1622) to develop this ministry to youth throughout Italy. It was Bosco's hope that some of the youngsters trained by the Salesians would eventually enter religious life. In 1772, he established the Daughters of Our Lady Help of Christians to work with girls in the same capacity. Today, both congregations have members all over the world. *See also* Bosco, St. John.

Salmanticenses (sahl-mahn-tee-chen'sez; Lat., "those of Salamanca"), collective name for the Spanish Discalced Carmelite authors of the commentary *Cursus Theologicus Summam d. Thomae Complectens* (1631–1701). This theological textbook, a huge running commentary on the *Summa Theologiae* of Thomas Aquinas (d. 1274), helped Salamancan Thomism attain influence throughout Europe. Its authors, professors at the University of Salamanca in Spain, were Antonio de la Madre de Dios (d. ca. 1640), Domíngo de Santa Teresa (d. 1654), Juan de la Anunciación (d. 1701), and three others. *See also Summa Theologiae.*

salt, symbol used in religious rituals from early times because of its seasoning and preservative qualities. The Rite of Blessing and Sprinkling of Holy Water in the Sacramentary contains the blessing for salt added to holy water. A blessing is also found in the Book of Blessings. *See also* blessing.

salvation, the condition of the ultimate restoration and fulfillment of humanity and all creation effected by God's action in Jesus Christ through the Holy Spirit; also, the process by which this condition is brought about.

The Theology of Salvation: As the condition of humanity and the cosmos at the end of history, salvation is the final triumph over sin and death and, therefore, the ultimate accomplishment of God's purpose for creation. Sin is the rejection of God's will. It is made actual in the evil free decisions of individuals and embodied in unjust social arrangements. Sin results in disorder experienced variously as pride, alienation, enmity, oppression, and violence, as well as destruction of the environment. History, Christian tradition, and personal experience agree that human capability alone cannot bring about the needed reconciliation and restoration.

But in Jesus Christ through the Holy Spirit, God is restoring and reconciling the world. God's work will be brought to completion at the end of history. This end will not be arbitrary; rather, it will be the consummation of history when all creation enters into the destiny intended for it by its Creator. Then all that is good, true, and beautiful in human nature and achievement will not be obliterated, but will be purified and transfigured.

Salvation as experience means perfect fulfillment and happiness. As such, God is its content as well as its cause. But complete and eternal union with God can never be adequately understood and expressed, because God's reality transcends human comprehension. While the Bible apparently depicts the experience of salvation quite explicitly (e.g., Matt 25, Rev 21), the pictorial details in passages like these cannot be taken as a descriptive report. "Heaven" and "Hell" are not places but rather the joy of union with God or the anguish of separation from God. The images are not meant to satisfy curiosity about the final state but to foster participation in it. Taken seriously but not literally, they are reminders of the ultimacy involved in one's everyday decisions.

Popular devotions, saints' testimonies, and theological reflections have also depicted the ultimate salvation in various ways. Official Church teachings, however, say essentially no more and no less than what the Bible affirms. They have been developed when needed to protect the mystery of salvation from being reduced to spatiotemporal categories and particular culture-bound models.

As a process, salvation is God's work of reconciliation and restoration in Jesus Christ in the Holy Spirit. As God Incarnate, Jesus is God's total self-gift to humanity. As human, Jesus makes humanity's complete and irrevocable acceptance of God's gift. This acceptance became definitive in his self-surrendering death on the cross and was vindicated in his Resurrection. The Church as the Body of Christ continues Jesus' saving work in the world. It expresses and brings about people's reconciliation with one another and with God.

Meaning of Salvation Today: Membership in the Catholic Church is, however, neither a requirement nor a guarantee of salvation. After the Protestant Reformation (sixteenth century) and prior to Vatican II (1962–65), many Catholics held Church membership to be necessary for salvation: "Outside the Church, no salvation." But the Church never definitively taught that Church membership was necessary for salvation and condemned the view that it was. Vatican II recovered a fundamental affirmation of the Catholic tradition in teaching that those who strive to do God's will as it is made known to them in conscience can be saved (e.g., Dogmatic Constitution on the Church, n. 14).

Despite the Nicene Creed's confession of faith in the "resurrection of the body," Catholic theology before Vatican II tended to exalt grace over nature and spirit over matter. Salvation was taken as the healing and final condition of the soul, which survived death. The destiny of the body, along with the rest of material creation, was depreciated. So Christianity was attacked by some as a narcotic. By preaching a blissful hereafter, it seemed to render Christians uncaring and blind to the dehumanizing injustices of this world.

Vatican II recovered the more traditional and comprehensive meaning of salvation as transformation and restoration of the entire universe (Pastoral Constitution on the Church in the Modern World, n. 39). Latin American liberation theology, European political theology, and feminist theologies have led the Church to insist that the process of salvation necessarily includes (but is not limited to) transformation of unjust and oppressive social conditions. Wherever people's God-given dignity and rights are denied, God's salvation is needed and awaited.

The mystery of salvation lies not in the impenetrable darkness of the future but in the omnipotent love of the God who is beyond human comprehension. To experience that love is to experience the essence of salvation's meaning and mystery. *See also* salvation outside the Church; universal salvific will of God.   JON NILSON

Salvation Army, Protestant denomination and social service agency. Founded by William and Catherine Booth in 1865 to spread evangelicalism in the London slums, the Salvation Army emphasizes individual conversion, holy living, and social welfare activity among the poor. By the early 1990s the Salvation Army was functioning in over one hundred countries, and in the United States had over four hundred thousand members and over four thousand facilities serving more than five million people.

salvation history (Ger., *Heilsgeschichte,* "sacred history"), the pattern of events in human history that realize God's salvific activity. The notion of salvation history as a theological category was originally formulated in the nineteenth century to express the biblical teaching that God acted in the history of the divinely covenated community to bring salvation to the entire world. The key events recounted in the OT include God's promise to Abraham, the liberation of the Israelites from slavery, the Sinai covenant, the conquest of Canaan, and the establishment of the Davidic kingdom. The NT sees this history as culminating in the person of Jesus Christ, whose life, death, and Resurrection constitute God's definitive act of redemption. In much of Scripture, the believing community expresses the content of its faith precisely by reciting the story of these mighty deeds of God (e.g., Deut 26:5–9; Ps 105; Acts 10: 36–43).

In this understanding of salvation history in its special sense, contemporary Catholic theology contends that all history is the arena of God's salvific action, even if unrecognized. Further, Catholic theology affirms that salvation is a matter not just of an individual's inner religious experience, but also of a communal response to the concrete historical process wherein faith discerns the saving activity of God. The Church's ministry participates in that process: through word and sacrament and through the sacrifical love that meets evil with good. The Church serves as a divine instrument in liberating the human race from the effects of sin and ushering it into communion with the triune God. *See also* history, theology of; salvation.

salvation outside the Church, a topic of debate throughout the Church's history—whether people can be saved if they are not members of the Catholic Church. This question and possible answers to it must be understood in terms of the traditional axiom, "no salvation outside the Church" (Lat., *extra Ecclesia, nulla salus*). Taught by such early Church Fathers as Irenaeus (d. ca. 200) and Origen (d. ca. 254), this axiom reached its classic expression in Cyprian (d. 258) and Fulgentius of Ruspe (d. 527). Affirmed by Church councils (e.g., Lateran IV, 1215; Florence, 1442), and by papal documents through the centuries (e.g., *Unam Sanctam,* 1302; *Quanto Conficiamur Moerore,* 1863), this axiom states that salvation is granted only within the community of believers and highlights the biblical and Catholic view that salvation is a communal and not merely private event. Negatively, the most severe interpretation of this doctrine stated that salvation was possible only for visibly incorporated members of the Catholic Church, excluding from salvation Jews, Muslims, pagans, apostates, and members of Christian churches not in union with Rome. This interpretation was repeatedly rejected by Pius IX as invalid for those "invincibly ignorant of the true religion" (1854, 1863), and condemned by the Holy Office in *Suprema Haec Sacra* (1949). Pius XII in *Mystici Corporis* (1943) taught that non-Catholics can be saved by being "ordained to the mystical body of the Redeemer by some kind of unconscious desire or longing." Vatican II distinguished various ways in which diverse religious cultures are related to the Church and taught that all those "who seek

God with a sincere heart, and, moved by grace, try in their actions to do his will as they know it through the dictates of their conscience may achieve eternal salvation" (Dogmatic Constitution on the Church, n. 16). Awareness of divine mercy and the desire to extend the possibility of salvation have prompted theologians to devise ways to account for salvation outside of visible membership in the Church, e.g., a baptism of desire available for those who have not been baptized; implicit faith for those to whom the gospel has not been effectively presented; or a special moment of final choice at the time of death. After Vatican II, new developments in ecclesiology and soteriology, along with an increasingly acute awareness of the growing, not decreasing, number of non-Christians around the globe, led many theologians to assert more boldly that salvation is available outside the visible Church. To support this view some simply postulated that each religion is the place of salvation for its members. Others distinguished between the Church and the kingdom, between Christ and the Church, or between Christ (who saves Christians) and God (whose salvific will extends to all) and used these distinctions to explain how salvation is available to all. Karl Rahner (d. 1984) maintained that those who do not know Christ explicitly can nevertheless encounter him anonymously and live mysteriously in his grace and thus be in communion with the Church. By the end of the twentieth century, the terms of the debate were once again changing, as increasing familiarity with the world religions created a new context in which the issues related to "salvation outside the Church" were being rethought with respect to specific religions, their distinctive characteristics, and their own theologies of salvation. *See also* Church; salvation; universal salvific will of God.

FRANCIS X. CLOONEY

Salvatorians, the Society of the Divine Savior (S.D.S.), a society founded in Rome in 1881 by Father Franziskus Maria Jordan. They are priests and brothers who take vows of poverty, chastity, and obedience, as well a fourth vow promising fidelity to the apostolate. The society's purpose is the spread of the faith through education, retreats, and missionary activity. The Salvatorians, who have missions in several foreign countries, arrived in the United States in 1896; their principal work has been the education of young people in seminaries and high schools. They also staff parishes, give retreats, and run programs for adult vocations. Father Jordan,

with Baroness Theresia von Wüllenweber, also founded the Sisters of the Divine Savior in 1888.

Salve, Regina (Lat., "Hail, Holy Queen"), opening Latin words of an antiphon in honor of the Virgin Mary. The text was probably composed by Herman of Richenau (d. 1054). It was sung or recited after various hours in the Divine Office. During the Middle Ages laity joined with monks and friars in singing the *Salve, Regina* at the end of the day. From the fourteenth century it was usually sung after Compline in the Roman rite. Pius V directed that it also follow other hours of the Office. Leo XIII assigned it as a prayer to follow low Masses, a practice discontinued in 1964.

SALVE, REGINA

English text:

"Hail, Holy Queen, Mother of mercy! Hail, our life, our sweetness, and our hope! To you do we cry, poor banished children of Eve. To you do we send up our sighs, mourning and weeping in this valley of tears. Turn then, most gracious advocate, your eyes of mercy toward us; and after this, our exile, show unto us the blessed fruit of your womb, Jesus. O clement, O loving, O sweet Virgin Mary! Amen."

Salvian of Marseilles, ca. 390–ca. 480, theologian, best known for his *Governance of God,* a defense of providence (God's guiding care for the world) in the face of barbarian invasions and an important historical source. *See also* providence.

Samaria, a city and district in north-central Palestine. The city was the capital of the Northern Kingdom, Israel, until its fall in 721 B.C. and was later a provincial center. Jesus passed through the territory (John 4:4); Philip the deacon evangelized the city (Acts 8:5). It is the traditional site of John the Baptist's burial.

sanatio in radice (sah-nah'tsee-oh in rah-dee' chay; Lat., "healing in the root"). *See* sanation.

sanation, the validating or, literally, healing of a marriage previously considered invalid in Church law. The marriage might be considered invalid because a Catholic married outside a Catholic ceremony without the Church's permission or because the marriage labored under an undispensed impediment. Validation usually takes the form of the couple's exchanging consent before a properly authorized deacon or priest and two witnesses. This is commonly called the "blessing of marriage." A marriage may also be validated by a legal decree of the diocesan bishop as long as matrimonial consent is still mutually present on the part of each spouse. In these cases there is no obligation for the couple to formally exchange the consent before a Church officiant and two witnesses. This manner of validating a marriage can be used when one of the spouses is reluctant to exchange consent publicly.

Sanchez, Thomas, 1550–1610, Spanish Jesuit moral theologian. His major work, *Disputations on the Sacrament of Holy Matrimony,* enjoyed great authority during the seventeenth century. One volume of the Venetian edition was listed on the Index of Forbidden Books until the nineteenth century because it omitted a passage defending the pope's right to legitimize illegitimate children without interference from the civil authorities. The Venetian Republic objected to the passage. In his *Opus Morale in Praecepta Decalogui* (Lat., "Moral Opus on the Precepts of the Decalogue"), published after his death, Sanchez developed a moral system based on the Ten Commandments, but he did not go much beyond the Second.

sanctification (Lat., "making holy"), the transforming effect of divine love and presence in an individual's religious and moral life. Jesus' teaching about the "reign of God" and his metaphors about water and life, banquet and family, as well as Paul's theology of the presence of the Spirit in the Christian life are developed in theologies of human sanctity. Holiness follows upon God's gift of forgiving grace, i.e. justification, which not only overcomes sin in its source, if not in all its effects, but also interiorly transforms the individual. Catholic theology after the Middle Ages, however, has distinguished between a transient grace, which inspires a prophet or a leader, and an ordinary grace, i.e., sanctifying grace, which brings to an individual faith and love.

Sanctification is the perduring, personal effect of grace: it brings about an interior transformation and renders God silently but constantly present; it also overflows into distinct facets of grace called virtues and gifts of the Holy Spirit. Sanctity, therefore, is not a collection of miraculous phenomena in an odd or unhappy life, but the lived, individualized Christian life enabled by grace and modeled after the teaching and practice of Jesus. The active holiness of God created in humans is only driven out by serious, lasting activity that is directly counter to God's presence.

Some important differences between Protestants and Catholics have focused upon sanctification, and its links to human freedom and an ethical life (good works). Catholicism has always stood between a sole emphasis upon justification (as in Lutheranism) and a fascination with supernatural charisms (charismatic and fundamentalist churches). Ecumenical discussion and recent pastoral movements since Vatican II (1962–65) have brought to Catholicism a richer theology that grounds sanctification in the sovereign initiative of God in Christ in light of the Reformers' theology; assimilates the theologies of grace in Eastern Christian theologians; reflects on grace in the human personality in terms of modern psychologies; takes seriously the charismatic manifestations of grace; and insists that grace is the source of all offices in the Church and leads normally to service.

Only God can be the proper cause of sanctification. Any created means of holiness like the sacraments, devotions, or self-discipline are either instrumental, directive causes of God's grace or simply conditions, themselves inspired by grace, which enable personally deeper responses to the present invitation of God. *See also* grace; justification.   THOMAS F. O'MEARA

sanctifying grace. *See* grace, sanctifying.

sanctity. *See* holiness.

Sanctorale, the Proper of Saints, governing both Mass and Divine Office, running through the whole year alongside the Temporale. The earliest example is the Philocalian Calendar (ca. 354), listing the dates of death and burial places of the bishops and martyrs of the city of Rome. Continuing additions to the Sanctorale have tended to overshadow the Temporal Cycle and led to significant pruning from time to time, most recently in the 1970 Roman Calendar. *See also* liturgical year; Temporale.

sanctuary (Lat., "building for religious worship"), that space in a church immediately around the altar. Until the Second Vatican Council (1962–65), it was separated from the remainder of the church by the altar rail; the sanctuary may also be called the "chancel," or "choir." The common-law notion of "sanctuary" is related to that separation; the sacred precincts of the altar are not to be desecrated by violence or the spilling of blood. *See also* sanctuary, right of.

sanctuary, right of, the privilege of refuge from persecution or law enforcement offered in a consecrated place, such as a church, and guaranteed by law or custom. Catholic churches have historically provided places of sanctuary for those fleeing persecution; in the late twentieth century the concept of sanctuary enjoyed a resurgence in the United States because of its use in offering shelter to refugees from violence in Central America. These refugees have been considered illegal aliens and have on occasion been pursued by agents of the U.S. government.

The right of sanctuary is rooted in the reverence for places of worship and an abhorrence of any violation of sacred space.

Although an explicit right of sanctuary was not included in the 1983 revision of the Code of Canon Law, the long tradition of the Church in providing sanctuary has encouraged some Catholic communities to continue to provide haven for refugees, whether in the church building itself or in the homes of parishioners.

Sanctus (sahnk'tuhs; Lat., "Holy"), title for the acclamation sung following the preface of the Eucharistic Prayer at Mass. The text is based upon Isa 6:3, Ps 118:26, and Matt 21:9: "Holy, Holy, Holy Lord, God of power and might, heaven and earth are full of your glory. Hosanna in the highest. Blessed is he who comes in the name of the Lord. Hosanna in the highest."

San Lazzaro, a small island in Venice, home monastery of the Venetian Congregation of Armenian Catholic Mekhitarist monks, who moved there in 1715 when their refuge in the Venetian colony in the Peloponnesus was occupied by the Turks. *See also* Mekhitarists.

Santa Claus, name derived from St. Nicholas (mid-fourth century), bishop of Myra in Lycia (Turkey), patron saint of Russia, sailors, and children. The North American custom of giving gifts to children at Christmas was introduced in the 1600s by Dutch Protestants in New York, where the Dutch "Sint Klaes" was changed to the English "Santa

Claus." Feast day of St. Nicholas: December 6. *See also* Christmas; Nicholas of Myra, St.

Santa Maria Maggiore. *See* Saint Mary Major.

Santeria (sahn-tair-ee'ah; Sp., "pertaining to the saints"), a syncretic religion developed in Cuba, combining elements of African religion (primarily Yoruba) and popular Catholicism. It developed as an adaptation of the ancestral religion of the slave population to their new circumstances in the Ibero-American world. This was done primarily by identifying the divinities of the Yoruba pantheon (Yoruba, *orishas,* "gods") with saints whose attributes matched those of the gods or goddesses, so that the thunder god Shango, for example, is identified with St. Barbara, who was invoked as a protectress during thunderstorms. Contact between the believer and the supernatural world is thought to be achieved by means of rituals that culminate in the devotee's possession by the divinity. Devotees of Santeria in the United States have encountered difficulties with the civil law because of their ritual sacrifice of animals.

Santiago de Compostela (sahn-tyah'goh day kohm-pohs-tay'lah), pilgrimage shrine and metropolitan see in Galicia, Spain. Location of the relics of St. James the Great, who was said to have evangelized Spain, it served as a major pilgrimage site in the Middle Ages as well as a symbol of the resistance of Spanish Christianity against Muslim rule. *See also* James the Great, St.

Sapra (Syr., "dawn," "morning"), East (*Sapra*) and West (*Safro*) Syrian variants of the term for Matins. *See also* Matins.

sarcophagus (Gk., *sarx phagein,* "to eat flesh"), stone coffin, usually made of limestone, used for above-ground burial in the ancient world. Highly decorated ones are important sources for an understanding of early Christian art, especially in the fourth century and later. *See also* burial, Christian.

Sardica, Council of (343), a council summoned to deal mainly with the orthodoxy of Athanasius. It was intended by emperors Constans I and Constantius II to be an ecumenical council, but the Easterners withdrew when the West insisted on seating Athanasius and others deposed in the East. The

The sarcophagus of a Roman prefect, Junius Bassus; an example of fourth-century Christian art, in the Vatican.

Western bishops reaffirmed their reinstatement (341, Council of Rome) of Athanasius and Marcellus of Ancyra, forbidding, like the Creed of Nicaea (325), a distinction of *hypostases* (substances), language favored by the East. The council also made provisions allowing bishops condemned by provincial synods to appeal to Rome. *See also* Arianism; Athanasius; St.; hypostasis.

Sarpi, Paolo, 1552–1623, Venetian scholar, Servite theologian. He was an opponent of papal power and the author of the *Istoria del concilio Tridentino* ("History of the Council of Trent"). As official theologian of the Republic of Venice (1606–22), Sarpi brilliantly and successfully opposed Pope Paul V's interdict of Venice for attacking ecclesiastical liberties, for which he was excommunicated in 1607.

Satan (Heb., "accuser," "adversary"), head of the demons and evil spirits. Satan only appears in the postexilic books of the OT, Job 1–2 and Zech 3:1–2, and in a more general sense, in 1 Chr 21:1. Satan is a member of the court of God and his role is to act as accuser of humankind. It is he who initiated all the sufferings of Job. In the intertestamental literature and the NT there was a clear development of the concept of Satan. This arose particularly because of the belief in dualism, the polarity of good and evil. Satan was known variously as Satan, Belial, Beliar, Mastema, Sammael, Asmodeus, Apollyon, and Beelzebul, the devil, ruler of this world (John 12:31); later he was identified with the serpent in the garden of Eden. Subsequent mythology tells of his expulsion from heaven because he would not acknowledge the superiority of humankind (see Rev

Satan, the fallen angel who refused to serve God, smitten by Michael the archangel; engraving illustrating John Milton's *Paradise Lost*, Book VI, vv. 320–24.

12:7–12). His female counterpart is Lilith, queen of demons. Satan and his angels are opponents of God and his angelic host (see esp. the Qumran *War Scroll*). In the NT he tempts Jesus in the desert (Matt 4:1–11; Mark 1:12–13; Luke 1:1–13; see Matt 16:23) and enters into the heart of Judas Iscariot (Luke 22:3; John 13:27). He is associated with physical and mental diseases. Revelation predicts that God will conquer him in the last days and throw him into the lake of fire (Rev 20:2, 7, 10). Throughout the centuries the Christian churches possessed a strong belief in Satan, influenced not so much by the Bible as by literature such as John Milton's *Paradise Lost* (1667). Many modern theologians consider Satan a symbol of evil forces and inclinations rather than a personal spiritual figure. *See also* devil.   J. MASSYNGBAERDE FORD

Satis Cognitum (sa'tis cog'nee-toom; Lat., "Known Enough"), encyclical of Pope Leo XIII, issued on June 29, 1896, on religious unity. Reflecting the spirit of Counter-Reformation theology, it insisted on the acceptance of papal primacy as a necessary condition of Christian reunion.

satisfaction (Lat., *satis,* "enough"; *factio,* "a doing"; hence, "making amends"). **1** In moral theology, the third moment in the process by which sins are forgiven. Following contrition and confession, a penitent must make reparation for sin by engaging in some form of satisfaction (e.g., prayer, almsgiving, fasting, restitution, or good works). **2** In soteriology, Christ's act of reparation for sin. Anselm (1033–1109), using the feudal motif of vassal and master metaphorically, reasoned that the "offense" done to God's "honor" by Adam's sin could only be remedied by someone who was both God's equal and also a human being, though without sin. In his Incarnation and life of obedience to God, Jesus Christ has vicariously made amends to God for the dishonor and the disruption done by Adam. As a result of the saving activity of Jesus Christ, harmony has been objectively restored to the relationship between God and creation. Anselm did not intend this "satisfaction theory" to present God as legalistic and punitive. Rather, by the use of the feudal language of honor, he sought to highlight God's love and mercy, for God has done what a master did not need to do, namely, God took the initiative to remedy the alienation. Also, Anselm intended to affirm God's respect for the rational, natural order, wherein offenses cannot merely be forgotten but must be forgiven. This soteriological view is limited by its neglect of the Resurrection (Rom 4:25), and also by the fact that it can easily be misunderstood when used by those unfamiliar with the thought patterns of the medieval world. *See also* Anselm of Canterbury, St.; atonement, doctrine of; Jesus Christ; redemption.

ROBERT KRIEG

Satolli, Francesco, 1839–1910, first apostolic delegate to the U.S. hierarchy. A leading Thomist in Perugia and later Rome, he was named archbishop in 1888. In January 1893, he became the first apostolic delegate to the U.S. hierarchy. In 1895, he became a cardinal and prefect of the Congregation of Seminaries and Universities in Rome, where he opposed Americanism. *See also* Americanism; apostolic delegate.

Saulchoir, Le (luhr sohl-shwahr'), named for the nearby willows (Fr., *saules*), a *studium generale* ("study center") of the Dominicans of the province of France, established in Belgium in 1903 when religious orders were expelled from France. In the years 1937–39 it was transferred to Étiolles, near Paris, then in 1971 to Paris. Its important library was moved to Paris in 1972, but in 1974 its teaching functions ceased. Its innovative historical method for studying theology was described in 1937 by M.-D. Chenu in a prophetic book that aroused Vatican censure in 1942. In addition to training many

Dominic Savio, a young Italian peasant who was a disciple and collaborator of John Bosco in his ministry to boys in need; he was canonized by Pope Pius XII in 1954.

students, its remarkable staff produced the *Bulletin thomiste* ("Thomist bulletin"), the *Revue des sciences philosophiques et théologiques* ("Review of the philosophical and theological sciences"), and many other important studies.

saving history. *See* salvation history.

Savio, St. Dominic, 1842–57, confessor of the Church and patron saint of young boys, especially juvenile delinquents. Born in Italy, he was trained under the wise and temperate influence of John Bosco, who was deeply impressed with Dominic's piety and goodness. In 1954 Dominic became the youngest nonmartyr to receive official canonization. Feast day: March 9.

Savonarola, Girolamo, 1452–98, Florentine Dominican priest and religious reformer. He employed apocalypticism and prophecy to preach against the ruling Medici family and papal corruption. After Savonarola correctly prophesied the French invasion of Italy in 1494, Florence exiled the Medici and reestablished the Florentine republic under Savanarola's stringent moral guidance. He convinced Florentines to destroy art, jewelry, and literature. In 1497, his attacks on papal immorality brought his excommunication by Pope Alexander VI. When his attempt to demonstrate miraculous powers in public failed, his popularity declined, and his political protection vanished. On May 23, 1498, the Florentine government hanged and then burned him in the Florentine piazza.

Scalabrini Fathers, Congregation of the Missionaries of St. Charles Borromeo (C.S.), a congregation founded in Italy in 1887 by John Baptist Scalabrini. As bishop of Piacenza, Scalabrini recognized the expediency of providing for the spiritual and temporal needs of Italian emigrants to America when he encountered large numbers of them in the railroad station in Milan. To this end, the congregation provided priests, established churches and schools, and set up committees of assistance in Italian settlements in North and South America.

Scala Sancta (Lat., "holy stairs"), stairs near the Lateran Basilica in Rome, traditionally thought of as having been ascended and/or descended by Christ when he went before Pilate. Allegedly brought to Rome from Jerusalem by Helena, mother of Constantine, in the early fourth century, they are a popular place of pilgrimage, many pilgrims making the ascent on their knees.

scandal (Gk., *skandalon,* "stumbling block"), conduct that gives moral offense to others, incites others to do evil, or provides others with an occasion for morally wrongful conduct. How we act or do not act may encourage or discourage the virtuous conduct of those who belong to the same families, institutions, and communities. Giving scandal amounts to doing wrong against our neighbors, because love for our neighbor dictates that we encourage one another to virtuous conduct.

A common problem is that some people appear to see scandal in anything, maliciously construing innocent actions as perverse. Jesus was a source of scandal for the Pharisees because he ate with the prostitutes, tax collectors, and sinners, thus, the term "pharisaical scandal." Nevertheless, Jesus continued his mission, challenging those who were scandalized to realize that he came to call sinners, not the righteous. Thus, for sufficient reason a Christian might rightly take some action though some members of the Church or community will be scandalized by it. Sensitivity to local customs and culture is required for responsible decisions about actions that may cause others to perceive scandal.

An external action or omission that gives scandal may or may not be sinful in itself. For example, Paul urged those Corinthians eating meat offered in pagan temples to refrain from doing so. Paul told them that loving concern for their neighbors prohibited them from allowing their liberty be a stumbling block, a scandal, for those of weak conscience (1 Cor 8:9). Thus, charity might oblige a person to refrain from conduct foreseen to lead others to evil, though the conduct in question may not be wrong in itself. *DANIEL KROGER*

Scandinavia, Catholicism in. Christianity took hold slowly in the Scandinavian lands, introduced first in Denmark and then Norway, later spreading to Sweden and Finland. Although a Danish chief had been converted while visiting Louis the Pious in the ninth century, only in the first quarter of the eleventh century was the Christianization of Denmark complete. Olaf Haraldssön, king of Norway from 1016 to 1030 (he was subsequently canonized), sponsored the evangelization of that country. Beginning in the eleventh century, English missionaries were especially prominent in Sweden; missionaries from Sweden, as well as from England and Russia, converted Finland over the course of the twelfth century. The experience of medieval Scandinavian Catholicism mirrored that in the rest of Europe. Along with its saints, such as Bridget of Sweden (d.1373), conflicts between secular and ecclesiastical officials were common, and there was often a perceived gap between apostolic ideal and clerical performance.

The Reformation virtually destroyed the Scandinavian Catholic Church. Scandinavian kings and their subjects converted to Lutheranism by the end of the sixteenth century, although small communities of Catholics survived. Catholics were granted religious toleration by 1849, but few Scandinavians converted to Catholicism; in the 1990s, 95 percent of Scandinavians are Lutherans. *See also* Reformation, the.

Scanlan, Patrick F., 1894–1983, journalist. As editor of the Brooklyn *Tablet* (1917–68), he was a highly influential ultraconservative voice in the American Catholic press before Vatican II (1962–65). He was a fierce anti-Communist and polemicist.

scapular (Lat., *scapulae,* "shoulders"), a narrow

Carmelite monk in a brown scapular, the model for the personal scapular, which is only slightly bigger than a large postage stamp; it is held by strings and worn around the neck by pious Catholics, but was more common in the pre–Vatican II era than today.

cloak with an opening for the head that hangs down the front and back of a body. Such a garment was standard apparel for a monk in the Benedictine tradition and was later adopted by a number of other orders like the Dominicans and Carmelites. Lay affiliates of these orders often wear a stylized scapular (two small decorated patches of cloth connected by two strips of ribbon) under their ordinary clothes as a devotional practice. The use of the brown scapular of the Carmelites was especially popular as a devotion before the Second Vatican Council (1962–65). *See also* devotions.

Scheeben, Matthias Joseph (shay'buhn), 1835–88, German theologian. He drew not only on Scholasticism but on the early Greek Fathers, along with contemporary developments in German theology inspired by Romantic idealism. In the area of ecclesiology, he offered a positive appraisal of the role of the laity; his understanding of the Church included the animating presence of the Holy Spirit. At the same time he was a vigorous defender of the papacy and of papal infallibility. In his consideration of the relationship between nature and grace, his commitments to the gratuitous self-offering of the divine life led him to appear to posit nature and grace as two distinct realms. His major work in English was *The Mysteries of Christianity*, originally published in German in 1865.

Schelling, Friedrich Wilhelm Joseph von, 1775–1854, German philosopher who merged the transcendental philosophy of Immanuel Kant and Johann Fichte into Romanticism and idealism. In 1800 he developed an initial systematic presentation of a philosophy of the self, of the absolute, of nature manifest in chemistry and electromagnetism, and of art. After 1810 this system influenced Johann Sebastian Drey of the Catholic Tübingen school of theology and, through Johann Adam Möhler, Vatican II (1962–65). After 1827 a final system unfolded a trinitarian dynamic in religion and Christianity. He distinguished three elements in God: (1) necessary being; (2) unconscious and natural will, and the unity of the two; and (3) the three Persons who evolve from (1) and (2). Schelling's Protestant origins are shown in a God of will and struggle, and in a Christology of the Cross; after 1960 he became prominent again among Catholics because of his understanding of presences of the ideal in the real. He distinguished three periods in the history of the Church: Petrine (Western Catholic), Pauline (Protestant), and Johannine (charismatic or Orthodox).

schema (Gk., "dress," "habit"), Byzantine-rite monastic habit of monks and nuns. The "small schema" is the mandyas or monastic mantle (cappa in the Western Church). The "great schema" is the monastic cowl (Gk., *koukoulion*) and scapular adorned with embroidered symbols. In Orthodox usage very few attain to the "great habit," usually only in old age. *See also* cowl; mandyas; scapular.

Schervier, Bl. Mary Frances, 1819–76, German founder of the Sisters of the Poor of St. Francis. She showed concern for the poor and the sick from childhood. In 1844 she joined the Third Order Franciscans and organized soup kitchens, the beginning of her institute. Her sisters came to the United States in 1858. She was beatified in 1974.

Schillebeeckx, Edward (skil'eh-bayks), b. 1914, world-renowned Dominican theologian and a major theological influence on the renewal of Catholic life and thought during and since the Second Vati-

Edward Schillebeeckx, Belgian Dominican noted for his writings on Christ, the Church, faith, revelation, and ministry, who ranks with Jesuit Karl Rahner and fellow Dominican Yves Congar among the leading Catholic theologians of the twentieth century.

can Council (1962 65). Born in Antwerp, Belgium, he entered the Dominican order in 1934 and was ordained a priest in 1941. At Le Saulchoir, the Dominican faculty in Paris where he pursued doctoral studies under the direction of M.-D. Chenu (d. 1990), Schillebeeckx learned the importance of interpreting theological positions in their historical context and of the theologian's active engagement with political and social movements of the day.

He taught dogmatic theology at the University of Louvain from 1947 to 1958, and occupied the chair of Dogmatics and History of Theology at the Catholic University of Nijmegen in the Netherlands from 1958 to 1983. While not an official *peritus* (Lat., "expert") at the Second Vatican Council, he exercised a significant influence on the council through his well-attended theological lectures in Rome.

His commitment to relate the Christian tradition to human experience is reflected throughout his writings on sacramental theology, the Church/world relationship, revelation and the mystery of God, eschatology, ethics, spirituality, hermeneutics, Christology, and ministry. While the radical secularization of Western culture has remained a constant concern in his work, Schillebeeckx's later writings

focus more critically on Christian claims that Jesus is the universal Savior in the face of radical suffering in the world; crises of ministry, ecclesiology, and authority within the Catholic Church; and the liberating power of Christian faith.

He founded the Dutch-language theological journal *Tijdschrift voor Theologie* and was a founding editor of the international theological journal *Concilium*. In 1982 the Dutch government awarded him the Erasmus Prize for contributions to the development of European culture.

His major writings include *Christ: The Sacrament of Encounter with God* (Eng. trans., 1963), *Jesus: An Experiment in Christology* (Eng. trans., 1979), *Christ: The Experience of Jesus as Lord* (Eng. trans., 1980), and *Church: The Human Story of God* (Eng. trans., 1990).   MARY C. HILKERT

schism (Gk., *schisma*, "tear"), a formal breach in Church unity brought about when a particular group willfully separates itself from the larger faith community. As distinguished from heresy, schism is not directed against orthodoxy but communion. Thus, Augustine (d. 430) accused the Donatists of the sin of schism because they abandoned the one Body of Christ by establishing a rival altar and a competitive Eucharist.

The East-West Schism is traditionally dated from 1054, when mutual hostilities were exchanged between Michael Cerularius, patriarch of Constantinople, and Pope Leo IX. However, it was the sacking of Constantinople by the Crusaders in 1203 that sealed the divisions between the two churches.

The Great Western Schism occurred in 1378 when the election of Urban VI was declared null and void by the College of Cardinals. When Urban refused to abdicate in favor of the newly elected Clement VII, two rival claimants to the papal office emerged, establishing rival sees at Avignon and in Rome. The schism did not end until the Council of Constance deposed two claimants, witnessed the abdication of a third, and then elected Martin V as pope in 1417.

In traditional Catholic theology, all those who are not in communion with the Holy See were regarded to be in material schism and thus guilty of sin. This included the Orthodox and all Protestant communities. This theology was changed by the Second Vatican Council (1962–65), particularly in its Decree on Ecumenism (1964), which acknowledged that there are degrees of unity among Christian churches and called for the restoration of Christian unity rather than the return of non-Catholics to the Catholic Church. *See also* Eastern Schism; Great Schism.

MICHAEL O'KEEFFE

Schism, Eastern. *See* Eastern Schism.

Schism, Great. *See* Great Schism.

Schlegel, Friedrich (shlay'guhl), 1772–1829, German philosopher and literary historian. His religious convictions were prominent in his later writing. His *Philosophie des Lebens* ("Philosophy of Life," 1827) contrasted the vacuity of materialism with a biblical spirituality. In *Philosophie der Geschichte* ("Philosophy of History," 1828), he configured the epochs of world history around biblical revelation.

Schleiermacher, Friedrich Daniel Ernst (shli'uhr-mah-kuhr), 1768–1834, German Protestant theologian and philosopher. He was appointed head of the theological faculty at the newly established University of Berlin in 1810, where he remained until 1834. In numerous writings, he developed a philosophy of human knowing, an ethics, and a theory of hermeneutics, all of which contrasted with the influential philosophies of Kant, Fichte, and Schelling. He is remembered above all as "the father of modern theology" because of his apologetic defense of religion and Christianity in *Religion: Speeches to Its Cultured Despisers* (1799; Eng. trans., 1893), his articulation of the nature of theology in the modern university in *Kurze Darstellung des theologisches Studiens* ("A Concise Presentation of Theological Studies," 1811, 1830), and his dogmatics, *The Christian Faith* (1821–22, 1830; Eng. trans., 1928).

Schleiermacher's theology received only minimal attention from his Catholic contemporaries; exceptions include J. S. Drey, J. A. Möhler, and F. A. Staudenmaier. Catholic theologians have criticized Schleiermacher's doctrine of revelation, Christology, and ecclesiology. But his apologetic defense of the religious nature of the human person and of the nature of Christianity against deists and rationalists and his organic understanding of doctrinal development and the Church are points of common interest. The growing influence of the Hegelian and Ritschilian paradigms among Protestants and the rise of neo-Scholasticism among Catholics caused interest in Schleiermacher to wane in the second half of the nineteenth century. Because of the Second Vatican Council (1962–65), the decline of neo-Scholastic theology, and the work of Karl Rahner (d. 1984), numerous Catholic theologians have taken a renewed interest in Schleiermacher's thought. *See also* theology.

BRADFORD E. HINZE

Schmalkaldic Articles, theological statement by Luther that is foundational for the Lutheran church. Prepared in response to a proposed Catholic Church council to meet at Mantua in 1537, the articles stated clearly the key Lutheran doctrines and disagreements with the Catholics. They were included in the *Book of Concord* (1580). *See also* Concord, Book/ Formula of; Lutheranism.

schola cantorum (skoh'lah cahn-taw'room; Lat., "school of singers"), a school for the training of singers of liturgical chant. *Schola cantorum* is now synonymous with "choir," a small group of singers appointed to support the singing of the liturgical assembly and to perform more difficult chants and pieces in their stead. In the Middle Ages the *schola* represented the earliest model for the liberal education of boys. *See also* choir.

Scholastica, St., ca. 480–543, virgin, sister of Benedict of Nursia, and patron saint of Benedictine nunneries. The *Dialogues* of Pope Gregory the Great are the source of our scanty information on the saint. At the time of her death, she was living near Benedict's abbey, Monte Cassino; brother and sister

Scholastica, sister of Benedict of Nursia, with her brother, other members of the Benedictine community, and some of the sisters from the convent she founded nearby. She and Benedict met annually to discuss spiritual matters at Monte Cassino; medieval manuscript illustration, Condé Museum, Chantilly, France.

were eventually interred in one grave. Feast day: February 10. *See also* Benedict of Nursia, St.

Scholasticism, a method of intellectual inquiry that was prominent until the sixteenth century in Western medieval thought, especially in universities, in contrast with the *lectio divina* (Lat., "divine reading," i.e., meditative reflection on the Bible and other classical sources) and more rhetorical type of thought usually found in monastic schools. Scholasticism is described by M.-D. Chenu as "a rational form of thinking, consciously and voluntarily working from texts it held to be authoritative" (*Toward Understanding St. Thomas*, p. 63).

Methods: In the eleventh-century, dialectics (posing one text off against another) was increasingly applied in philosophy and theology by teachers such as Berengar of Tours and Lanfranc of Bec, the teacher of Anselm. Anselm's program of "faith seeking understanding" could be understood in two ways, either as a search for devout contemplative understanding of the divine mysteries or as an understanding the intellect sought within faith by using all the resources of human reason. Abelard, a textual critic of the Bible, furthered the use of dialectics, drawing upon himself the wrath of Bernard of Clairvaux and William of St. Thierry, who disagreed not only with his teachings but also with what they viewed as his rejection of the pious use of reason they espoused. Nevertheless, dialectics and Scholastic methods came to be used universally in cathedral schools and universities.

In the universities, a Scholastic master would apply himself to *lectio* (Lat., "reading"), reading a text and commenting on it in a logical, somewhat artificial manner, often reducing examples and metaphors to abstract concepts. Or he would undertake systematic inquiry into every conceivable problem, usually by *quaestiones* (Lat., "questions"). These brought out different aspects of a question through arguments on both sides of the issue, which were followed by the master's solution or "determination" of the question. His replies used the method of distinctions, which allowed the master to accept some part of the arguments while rejecting the rest. The appeal to distinctions, useful for such clarification, became in later Scholasticism an excessively subtle display that ended in sterility and provoked derision from sixteenth-century humanists. Even when masters wrote systematic *summae* (Lat., "syntheses"), they usually used the question format as the building blocks of the whole work.

Authorities: When commenting or questioning, Scholastic authors showed deference to authorities—texts of Scripture, the Church Fathers, ancient secular authors, or revered masters who had such great prestige in some fields that their writings would regularly be quoted in arguments pro or con. If the texts seemed to be opposed to a master's views or in conflict with other authorities, they could not simply be dismissed; they were brought into harmony with the master's position or were shown to agree with other authorities—in either case by explanations that could be legitimate or creative (the latter were called "benign" or "reverential interpretations"). Gratian's work in canon law, the *Concordia Discordantium Canonum* ("Harmonization of Discordant Canons"), was a model for this aspect of Scholasticism, as was Peter Lombard's *Sententiae* ("Sentences"), although Lombard sometimes simply gathered texts and left their concordance to others. Abelard's *Sic et Non* ("Yes and No") called attention to many apparently discordant patristic texts; he did not resolve the discordances but prefaced these texts with an important introduction on textual interpretation meant to guide those wishing to resolve such differences.

Scholastic inquiry involved impersonal, formal reasoning, breaking texts into small logical components, using repetitious formulas, divisions, and distinctions. Language, especially "speculative grammar," which saw grammar as a faithful mirror of underlying metaphysical or theological truths, was a major tool of Scholasticism in different periods. The fairly common use of similar methods masks the rich variety and originality of persons and positions that flourished in the Middle Ages. If the method lacked elegance, imagination, or rhetorical flourish, when used moderately it provided a scientific basis for free investigation of every sort of question. It served to clarify issues, to make language precise, and to foster critical inquiry, logical exactness, and objectivity. *See also* neo-Scholasticism; Thomism.   *WALTER PRINCIPE*

schools, Catholic. *See* Catholic colleges and universities—statistics; parochial school.

School Sisters of Notre Dame (S.S.N.D.), an international congregation founded in Bavaria in 1833 by Mother Theresa Gerhardinger and Bishop George Wittmann for the ministry of education. In response to a call to preserve the faith among German immigrants, the School Sisters came to the

United States in 1847 and established themselves in Milwaukee, Wisconsin, where, under the leadership of Mother Caroline Friess, the community learned to adjust to national cultures. This enabled the congregation to spread rapidly to other countries. In 1993 there were more than six thousand sisters in Europe, Asia, Africa, Latin America, and North America engaged in educational work at all levels. The motherhouse was in Munich from 1843 until 1957, when it was transferred to Rome. *See also* Notre Dame Sisters.

Schoonenberg, Piet, b. 1911, Dutch Jesuit theologian. Noted for his work on the *Dutch Catechism* and writings in Spirit Christology, Schoonenberg was trained at Maastricht and has taught at the universities of Louvain, Nijmegen, Fordham, and the Jesuit School of Theology at Berkeley, California.

Schrader, Klemens (shray'duhr), 1820–75, German Jesuit theologian. Professor at the Roman College, he provided a more historical orientation to contemporary Scholastic theology, drawing upon the work of the Tübingen theologians. His increasingly papal-centered views influenced his authorship of the theocratic first draft of Vatican I's Dogmatic Constitution on the Church.

science. *See* Big Bang; Catholicism and the social sciences; creation; creationism; Darwinism; evolution; faith and reason; Galileo; materialism, scientific; nature; nature and grace; scientism.

scientia media (shee-en'see-ah may'dee-ah), Lat., "middle knowledge"), a theory within sixteenth-century Molinist thought explaining the knowledge by which God infallibly knows what a free creature would do in any circumstance before any action of God and without presupposing that action. This theory attempts to reconcile human freedom with the themes of God's foreknowledge, providence, predestination, and efficacious grace. *See also De Auxiliis;* Molinism.

scientism, the belief that empirical science provides sole access to truth. In opposing scientism, the Church teaches that although empirical science legitimately studies connections of cause and effect in the natural world, there are truths to which empirical science has no direct access, including, especially, moral and religious truths. *See also* faith and reason.

Scotland, Catholicism in. Christianity reached Scotland by the fifth century through the efforts of British and Irish monks, notably Columba (d. 563). Brought into conformity with the Roman hierarchy and calendar in the seventh century, the Church of Scotland withdrew its allegiance from the Holy See in 1560, adopting Calvinist theology and Presbyterian government and outlawing the Catholic Church. A large body of Catholic loyalists remained in the Gaelic-speaking highlands and in the nineteenth century many Irish Catholic immigrants settled in the industrial cities. The hierarchy was restored in 1878, with archbishops at Edinburgh and Glasgow. In the 1990s, Catholics make up only about 15 percent of the population of over 5 million.

Scotus, Eriugena. *See* Eriugena, John Scotus.

Scotus, John Duns, ca. 1266–1308, Franciscan philosopher and theologian, known as the "Subtle Doctor." Of Scottish birth, he studied theology at Oxford and Paris; after holding the Franciscan chair in theology at the University of Paris (1305–07), he moved to Cologne, where he died. In addition to his writings on the *Sentences* of Peter Lombard, Scotus's literary production includes quodlibetal (freely

John Duns Scotus, medieval philosopher of the thirteenth and early fourteenth centuries, who combined Aristotelianism with Augustinianism, thereby emphasizing love and the will more than knowledge and reason, as in Thomas Aquinas's system.

posed) and disputed questions, as well as commentaries on some of Aristotle's books.

Scotus's deeply metaphysical thought has been immensely influential down to the present. Such characteristic teachings as the univocity (single meaning) of being, the primacy of the will and of love over reason and knowledge have contributed to the development of distinctive doctrines of God and the human person. Not all, however, have found him so appealing. His dogged attempts to work out every implication of his main insights can be wearing and seen, ultimately, as irrelevant. The word "dunce" is a later play on his name.

Perhaps his most lasting contribution is his championing of the Immaculate Conception. Earlier theologians had argued against this notion, stating that Mary had been conceived in the normal way and thus had been stained by original sin; to say that she had always been free of sin would have been to imply that she did not need redemption. Scotus's advance was to ascribe the Immaculate Conception to the grace of Christ, styling the total preservation from sin as a first and distinctive application of Christ's redemptive work. *See also* Immaculate Conception; philosophy and theology; Scholasticism.

screens, partitions made of various materials (stone, wood, metal) that divide a church into two or more sections, e.g., a screen dividing the choir of a church from its nave. Screens were elaborate or simple, high or low. A screen mounted with a cross is called a rood screen. *See also* choir; nave.

scribes, governmental officials and, later, scholars in the law of Moses. In the OT some scribes were officials employed by the royal government (e.g., 2 Kgs 18:18; 22:3; Isa 22:15). Baruch, however, who wrote down Jeremiah's prophecies, is also called a scribe (Jer 36:26, 32); and Ezra, who was "a scribe skilled in the law of Moses" (Ezra 7:6), enforced provisions of that law in Judea. Sirach, who may also have been one, praises the scribe in glowing detail (Sir 38:24–39:11): he has the leisure to devote "himself to the study of the law of the Most High" (38:34); he ponders prophecies, wise sayings, and parables; he advises rulers, travels, and acts piously. In the NT, scribes, who are legal experts, figure often as opponents of Jesus and his followers. They are closely associated with the Pharisees and are even called "scribes of the Pharisees" (e.g., Mark 2:16). With the Pharisees they are the objects of Jesus' woe sayings in Matt 23; here their legal views are strongly op-

posed. Jesus recognized their authority as experts in the law of Moses; however, he taught that they should be obeyed but not imitated. Some scribes with the chief priests and elders participated in Jesus' hearings or trials and were present at the Crucifixion (Mark 14:43, 53; 15:1, 31). These and other passages indicate that some scribes were members of the council, also known as the Sanhedrin, composed of chief priests and leaders in Jerusalem (see also Acts 23:9). *See also* Pharisees; Sadducees.

scriptorium, the workroom, generally in monasteries, where manuscripts were written; by extension, a center of literary and artistic production with its own proper calligraphic style. Often located near the library, the scriptorium, sometimes divided into carrels for individual scribes, was oriented so as to admit the maximum of light. General management of the scriptorium and scribes was entrusted to the *armarius* (Lat.) or librarian. *See also* monastery.

scripture, literally, that which is written. As used in theological and ecclesiastical circles, the term connotes either a small part of the biblical text, for example, a single verse (scripture), or the entire Bible (Scripture). When the term appears in the NT, it designates what would later be called the OT or the Jewish Scriptures. In its specifically theological usage, the term serves to identify the written and authoritative word of God (see Dogmatic Constitution on the Church, n. 9) rather than any specific textual content. It is insofar as they are Scripture that biblical texts are read during the celebration of the Church's liturgy. *See also* Bible

Scripture, accommodation of, the use of a biblical text for a purpose other than that for which it was originally intended and other than that for which the biblical text was incorporated into the canon. As such, the accommodated sense of Scripture is a result of *eisegesis* (Lat., "reading into" a text), rather than a result of exegesis ("reading out" of a text). Exploiting a more than literal sense of the text, it has appeared in a variety of fashions throughout the ages.

Origen (d. 254) had recourse to an accommodated use of Scripture when he found in the three decks of Noah's ark (Gen 6:15) a warrant for his doctrine of the three senses of Scripture: corporeal, psychic, and spiritual. Gregory the Great (d. 604) used the Scripture in accommodated fashion when he used the five talents of the Matthean parable (Matt

25:14–30) in reference to the five senses. Throughout the patristic era the Scriptures were often used in an accommodated fashion since they served as the principal catechetical text for the instruction of the faithful.

The liturgy frequently uses the texts of Scripture in an accommodated fashion, especially on feasts and memorials, for example, in applying the lover's canticle (Cant 3:1–4) to Mary Magdalene or a reading about God's choice of David (1 Sam 16:6–13) to saintly pastors. Homilists often use the Scriptures in an accommodated manner. Caution should be exercised when doing so, lest the faithful confuse the product of the homilist's imagination with the true meaning of the text. According to Pius XII's 1943 encyclical *Divino Afflante Spiritu,* a homilist's use of an accommodated sense of the sacred text may be useful but it is "extrinsic and adventitious to Holy Scripture." *See also* Scripture, interpretation of.

RAYMOND COLLINS

Scripture, authority of. Vatican II (1962–65) recognized that the role of the Scriptures in the life of the Catholic Church is somewhat different from what it is in the churches that are not united with Rome: "When Christians separated from us affirm the divine authority of the sacred books, they think differently from us—different ones in different ways—about the relationship between the Scriptures and the Church. In the Church, according to Catholic belief, an authentic teaching office plays a special role in the explanation and proclamation of the written word of God" (Decree on Ecumenism, n. 21).

The authority of the Scriptures derives from the fact that the Scriptures have been inspired by the Holy Spirit and are revered as the word of God. Thus, the authority of the Scriptures is an expression of the authority of God. The Scriptures bear witness to the word of God and have influenced the lives and actions of believers throughout the centuries.

In Protestantism: The authority of the Scriptures is a focal point in the teaching of the various Protestant churches. At the time of the Reformation the doctrine of the authority of the Scriptures was initially promoted in an argumentative fashion, taking issue with the authority of the Church in matters of faith and morals.

The polemical thrust of the doctrine has disappeared from most contemporary Protestant writings, but the authority of the Scriptures continues to be a central focus in Protestant teaching. For Protestants, the Bible is the source of Christian faith; the teachings of the Scriptures are considered to be authoritative for faith and morals.

Since the development of the historical-critical method of biblical interpretation during the eighteenth-century Enlightenment, much discussion has taken place within the different Protestant churches as to the nature of biblical authority. Some churches and various writers see the historical-critical interpretation as an attack upon the authority of the Bible. Among many, a biblical fundamentalism is seen as a way to safeguard the authority of the Scriptures. Other churches and other writers, especially those representing mainline Protestant denominations, view the historical-critical approach as a contemporary form of fidelity to the Scriptures, in keeping with the spirit of early Reformers such as Luther and Calvin. The precise nature of scriptural authority continues to be a point of discussion among contemporary Protestants.

In Catholicism: Generally Catholics do not reflect on the "the authority of the Scriptures" as Protestants do. The expression occurs in Vatican II's Decree on Ecumenism, but it is not otherwise used in conciliar texts; nor is it employed in the *Catechism of the Catholic Church* (1992). It is almost as if Protestantism has preempted the use of the expression "authority of Scripture." Nonetheless, the realities to which the expression points are central to the teaching of the Catholic Church on the Scriptures.

The inspiration and the inerrancy of the Scriptures are an important element of Catholic doctrine. That *Dei Verbum* (Lat., "the Word of God"), Vatican II's document on divine revelation, has the status of a dogmatic constitution (Dogmatic Constitution on Divine Revelation) is a forceful expression of the authority the Church attributes to the Scriptures, as the word of the living God.

This constitution teaches that the Church venerates the Sacred Scriptures just as it venerates the body of Christ, particularly within the context of the eucharistic liturgy (n. 21). By describing the Scriptures as the soul of theology (n. 24; Decree on Priestly Formation, n. 16) and as the supreme norm of faith (Dogmatic Constitution on Divine Revelation, n. 21), the Church expresses its teaching that the Scriptures are authoritative in matters of faith and morals.

What distinguishes a Catholic view of the authority of the Scriptures from a Protestant view is the relationship between the Scriptures and the Church. Catholic doctrine links tradition, the Scriptures, and the teaching authority of the Church together so that one cannot stand without the others (n. 10).

It teaches that the Scriptures must be read within the living tradition of the Church and that they be interpreted within the context of "the analogy of faith." From the perspective of divine revelation all of the truths of faith cohere with one another. According to Catholic doctrine, responsibility for authentically interpreting the word of God has been entrusted to the teaching authority of the Church, the magisterium, which is called to serve and to faithfully explain the word of God. *See also* Bible and doctrine; inspiration of Scripture; magisterium; Scripture and tradition.   *RAYMOND COLLINS*

Scripture, canon of the. *See* canon of the Scriptures.

Scripture, inerrancy of. *See* inerrancy of Scripture.

Scripture, inspiration of. *See* inspiration of Scripture.

Scripture, interpretation of. Concern for the proper interpretation of the Scriptures has always been part of the life of the Church. The canonical Gospels themselves portray Jesus as being in conflict with the Pharisees over the proper interpretation of the Scriptures (Matt 15:1–9; Mark 7:1–13). 2 Peter warns its readers about those who twist the meaning of Paul's letters and the other Scriptures (2 Pet 3:15–16). On the other hand, the Gospels repeatedly make reference to the Scriptures being fulfilled in Jesus (e.g., Matt 1:22–23; Luke 4:21) while the Letters interpret various scriptural passages in the light of the Christian experience (Gal 4:21–31; Hebrews).

Patristic Interpretation: Interpreting Scripture in light of the gospel continued in the patristic period. The *Letter of Barnabas* tries to show that the OT scriptures point to Christ, as does Justin Martyr (d. ca. 165) in his *Dialogue with Trypho the Jew*. On the other hand, Marcion, a second-century Roman heretic, read the OT in a very literal way and rejected both it and its God in the name of a Christianity he had misconstrued on the basis of Paul's writings. In opposition to Marcion, Irenaeus (d. ca. 200) highlighted the OT's use of anthropomorphic language and had a vision of the Scriptures that accorded a pride of place to the four Gospels. In the Scriptures he found a "norm of truth."

From the end of the second century until the fifth century, there were two main schools of interpretation in the Eastern church. The school of Alexandria stressed the harmony between the OT and NT but often allegorized the biblical text in order to do so. Clement of Alexandria (d. ca. 215), for example, interpreted the biblical division between clean and unclean animals as a reference to the separation between the Church and Jews and/or heretics. Origen (d. ca. 254) developed a theory of scriptural interpretation in which he distinguished the corporeal, psychic, and spiritual senses. Origen's approach was inspired by a Platonic anthropology that distinguished body, soul, and spirit, but he found a biblical warrant for it in the three decks of Noah's ark (Gen 6:15) and the three loaves of bread offered to a friend (Luke 11:5).

The school of Antioch was more literalist and historicist in its approach to the Scriptures. Theophilus of Antioch, for example, developed a chronological table of the biblical events beginning with creation and ending in his own day. In the West, Jerome (d. 420), the renowned biblical scholar, was strongly influenced by the Alexandrians, especially by Didymus the Blind. Augustine (d. 430), Jerome's contemporary, worked out a system of biblical interpretation in *On Christian Doctrine,* one of his major works. He claimed that the goal of the entire process was knowledge of the love of Christ and warned against interpreting literal expressions figuratively and figurative expressions literally, but he was prone to allegorize many biblical texts.

Medieval Interpretation: The goal of the allegorical method, used in the interpretation of Canticle of Canticles and many other biblical texts, was to extract a spiritual meaning from the text. Due attention was to be paid to the literal or historical meaning of the text (Lat., *litera*). In the case of narrative material, this was not "history" in the modern sense of the term, but the story line of the text. In the twelfth century, the school of St. Victor especially emphasized the importance of the literal meaning of the text.

Generally, however, medieval authors believed that a spiritual sense flowed from the literal meaning of the words. In this regard they were dependent upon the great patristic writers. They distinguished an allegorical, a tropological, and an anagogical sense of the text. These senses more or less correspond to a Christological, ethical, and mystical reading of the text.

The medieval dependence upon patristic exegesis

was, in this regard, fostered by the way in which biblical texts were copied. Typically there appeared along with the transcription of the text itself interlinear or marginal comments (Lat., *glossae*) or fairly large blocks of interspersed commentary (*postilla*). To a large extent the comments were comprised of citations of patristic authors. Notwithstanding this tendency, some medieval theologians, for example, Abelard (d. 1142) and Thomas Aquinas (d. 1274), made use of philosophy in the interpretation of various biblical texts.

Historical-Critical Interpretation: The doctrinal interpretation, with a relatively heavy emphasis on points of ecclesiology and sacramentology, led the Reformers to seek out the "plain sense" of the Scriptures. The way for this approach had been prepared by Jacques Lefèvre d'Étaples ("Stapulensis," ca. 1461–1536), whose commentary on the Psalms (1524) had distinguished between the literal historical sense and the literal prophetic sense of those scriptures. It was abetted by the Renaissance, whose fascination with classical learning led to a desire to have available the texts of the Scriptures in their original languages. The French Oratorian Richard Simon (1638–1712) and the Dutch humanist Erasmus (1469–1536) were pioneers in this movement.

Erasmus's edition of the NT, appropriated by the Reformers, ultimately served as the basis for the translations of the NT found in the popular King James Version and Luther's German Bible. In reaction to the new movement, the Council of Trent, on April 8, 1546, reaffirmed the Catholic Church's acceptance of the Latin Vulgate as the authentic text of the Scriptures and the authority of the Church to judge the "true sense and interpretation of the Holy Scriptures."

With the eighteenth-century Enlightenment came the development of a critical sense of history. From that time on a variety of questions have been raised regarding the historicity of the traditions narrated in the Scriptures. These questions dealt with the development of the biblical tradition even more than they dealt with the brute facticity of the scriptural data. These questions gave rise to the historical-critical method of scriptural interpretation. The new method was principally developed and refined in the schools of theology of continental European, and especially German, universities. Gradually it made its impact on the interpretation of the Scriptures in theological seminaries and came to be used by Catholic interpreters as well as by those of the various Reform movements.

The historical-critical method of interpretation, in fact, comprises various methodologies. A first endeavor focuses on the establishment of a critical edition of the scriptural texts. This is the task of text criticism, once known as "lower criticism" to distinguish it from "higher criticism," which was concerned with the historical meaning of the text. Higher criticism (exegesis) seeks to establish the meaning of the biblical text within its proper historical context. It is concerned with what the text meant at the time it was written, as distinct from what the same text might mean for people of faith at the present time.

Source criticism was an important component of the new approach. Questions as to whether or not a biblical author made use of written sources help to identify the potentially oldest witnesses to the events and to clarify how biblical texts came into existence in their present form. Along with these kind of questions were those that critically examined traditions attributing, for example, the entire Torah (Genesis through Deuteronomy) to Moses and the Letter to the Hebrews to the Apostle Paul. Before the end of the eighteenth century it had been suggested that the book of Isaiah was a two-part composition, with the second part (chs. 40–55) coming from the sixth century B.C. By the end of the nineteenth century scholars were writing about the documents on which the Pentateuch was based and proposing various theories as to which of the three synoptic gospels (Matthew, Mark, Luke) served as the principal source for the other two.

The historical-critical interpretation of the Bible was refined during the twentieth century with the development of a form-critical and a redaction-critical approach. The former concentrates on individual units of material (genealogies, miracle stories, legal collections, etc.) and seeks to relate them to their presumed social settings. Redaction criticism focuses on the way in which the biblical authors worked creatively with the documentary material at hand as well as with the oral traditions known to them in order to weave these materials into the literary compositions we now have as books of the Bible.

Catholic scholars were at first reluctant to espouse the historical-critical method of biblical interpretation, but the principle of form criticism was endorsed by Pius XII's encyclical *Divino Afflante Spiritu* (1943), and that of redaction criticism was supported by the Pontifical Biblical Commission's instruction "Holy Mother the Church" (*Sancta*

Mater Ecclesia, 1964) and Vatican II's Dogmatic Constitution on Divine Revelation (*Dei Verbum,* 1965).

Other Approaches: The historical-critical method of biblical interpretation does not answer all the questions raised by those who seek to understand the Bible fully. Consequently some interpreters elucidate the text by paying attention to the communication techniques taught in the rhetorical schools of old as well as to the impact of an author's words upon the presumed readership (rhetorical criticism). Others focus on the way in which the biblical stories are narrated, with attention drawn to what they say and how they say it (narrative criticism). Other scholars focus their attention on particular points of view, asking about the social structures to which the biblical texts refer and the social circumstances in which they were written (sociological reading). Feminist hermeneutics studies critically the role, or lack thereof, of women in the Bible.

This wide variety of approaches to biblical interpretation is partially due to the size of the Bible, with seventy-two different books, whose component parts were written over the greater part of a full millennium. It is partially due to the fact that those who read the Bible have many different kinds of questions and all of these questions must be answered as completely as possible if the Bible itself is to be more fully understood. *See also* Alexandria, school of; allegory; Antioch, school of; Bible; biblical criticism; hermeneutics; Scripture, senses of; Scripture and tradition.

Bibliography

Collins, Raymond F. *Introduction to the New Testament.* Garden City, NY: Doubleday, 1983. Ch. 2, "Historical Critical Methodology." Pp. 41–74.

Morgan, Robert, with John Barton. *Biblical Interpretation.* The Oxford Bible Series. New York: Oxford University Press, 1989.

Neill, Stephen, and Tom Wright. *The Interpretation of the New Testament 1861–1986.* 2d ed. New York: Oxford University Press, 1989.

Schneiders, Sandra M. *The Revelatory Text: Interpreting the New Testament as Sacred Scripture.* San Francisco: HarperCollins, 1991.

RAYMOND COLLINS

Scripture, private interpretation of, the practice associated with Martin Luther and other Reformers, whose numbers later included John Wesley and some Puritan leaders, who claimed that the meaning of the Bible is plain enough for ordinary Christians to understand. These Christians were therefore encouraged to read the Bible on their own. In response, the Council of Trent (1546) affirmed that it is the responsibility of the Church to interpret the Scriptures. The Scriptures are to be interpreted within the context of the community of faith that is the Church. The Catholic tradition maintains that the understanding of Scripture involves more than personal insight; it includes the role of the community exercised through the teaching office of the bishops and the insights of scholars and pastoral ministers. *See also* Scripture, interpretation of.

Scripture, senses of, the multiple meanings of a biblical text. The early Christian attribution of more than one meaning to a biblical text arose from two convictions: all Scripture preaches Christ and, therefore, OT texts have a hidden Christological meaning; all biblical texts are revelatory and, therefore, those whose apparent meaning is banal or even irreligious have another deeper meaning. This led to the development of the theory of two, three, or four senses in every text. In modern times, especially during the Modernist crisis in the Catholic Church in the early twentieth century, biblical scholars were pressed to find current Church teaching and/or contemporary relevance in texts that did not, literally, support such readings. This led to the revitalization of theories of typological sense and *sensus plenior* (Lat.), or the "fuller sense" of Scripture. Contemporary literary and hermeneutical theories provide more solid grounds for multiple interpretations of texts.

History: Origen (d. ca. 254), the Church's first great biblical scholar, distinguished between the "body" of the text (the literal/historical meaning); its "soul" (moral meaning); and its "spirit" (spiritual/allegorical meaning). In practice, he usually distinguished literal from allegorical, or letter from spirit. Sometimes Origen used "literal" to refer to the historical meaning that he always considered important as a vehicle of deeper meaning. But often "literal" meant the most naïvely materialistic (mis)reading, which he showed to be absurd, God's way of hiding the meaning so that the believer might search more deeply by means of allegorical interpretation. For Origen "allegory" included symbolism, metaphor, and allusion, which today would be considered part of the literal or literary meaning. His allegorical interpretation, although sometimes fanciful, was a scholarly attempt to attain the sense of the text intended by God through the human author, i.e., its spiritual sense. Origen's influence dominated biblical scholarship until modern times.

From Augustine (d. 430) and John Cassian (d. 435) through the Middle Ages, most interpreters held to a fourfold sense of Scripture: the literal, i.e., historical sense; the allegorical, i.e., the doctrinal/

spiritual sense; the moral, i.e., behavior-guiding sense; and the anagogical, i.e., eschatological sense. Although some scholars (e.g., Aquinas) defended the priority of the literal sense, most interpreters regarded the four senses as equal.

Until quite recently, modern critical scholars distinguished between the literal sense, i.e., the meaning intended by the biblical writer as that is ascertained by historical critical research, and more-than-literal senses, which included dogmatic, pastoral, and other senses, namely, any meanings not actually intended by the human author. Catholic scholars favored the theories of the typological sense and the fuller sense. A "type" is an OT reality (e.g., Isaac carrying the wood on which he would be sacrificed up Mount Moriah) whose full (i.e., Christological) meanings could only be grasped in light of its NT "antitype" or fulfillment (e.g., Jesus carrying his cross up Mount Calvary). The fuller sense of a text is a meaning that the human author could not or did not intend but whose God-intended meaning could only be recognized in light of subsequent developments in salvation history, e.g., that Isa 7:14 was a reference to the virgin birth of Jesus.

Increasingly, contemporary scholars recognize that all texts, including biblical ones, carry multiple meanings because meaning is an event of interaction between text and reader, not a fixed "content" established by the author. They also recognize that a variety of interpretive methods, eliciting diverse meanings, can legitimately be applied to a text. This is a post-critical reappropriation of the ancient insight that the biblical text is a many-layered mine of meaning. *See also* Scripture, interpretation of.

SANDRA M. SCHNEIDERS

Scripture, versions of, translations of Scripture from the original languages (e.g., the King James Version, the Douay-Rheims Version). While any translation can be called a version, the most important are the ancient Aramaic and Greek versions of the OT. These versions provide information on the history and establishment of the biblical text and evidence of the Hebrew text accessible to and used by the ancient translators, a text older than any extant Hebrew manuscripts, sometimes including departures or deviations from the standard Masoretic Text of the Hebrew Bible. Translations of the biblical books from their original languages (Hebrew, Aramaic, Greek) are termed primary versions. Early translations of the primary versions are called secondary versions. The other principal versions are in Syriac, Latin, Coptic, Ethiopic, and Armenian. While the Septuagint and the Jewish Aramaic Targums represent only the OT, the other versions contain complete Bibles. By the second century A.D., the consonantal Hebrew text had been fixed in the form still used today.

Aramaic Versions: Beginning in the postexilic era (after 539 B.C.), Aramaic gradually replaced Hebrew as the language of Jews in Palestine and Mesopotamia. It was for these Jews that translations of the Hebrew Bible into the Aramaic vernacular were produced. Probably originating as oral translations and paraphrases of the Scriptures when Jews gathered for prayer, these translations were ultimately committed to writing in what are called Targums, the Aramaic word for "translation." The Targums contain not simply translations of the Hebrew text but exegetical and homiletic expansions of the text as well.

The *Targum Onqelos,* an Aramaic translation of the Pentateuch, is the most literal and authoritative of the Targums. Originally produced in Palestine in the first or early second century A.D., it was taken to Babylonia where, after extensive revision in the second and third centuries, it became the official Babylonian Targum. The authoritative Targum of the Former and Latter Prophets is *Targum Jonathan.* Like *Onqelos,* it had its origin in Palestine and was revised in Babylonia in the fourth and fifth centuries A.D. More paraphrastic than *Onqelos, Jonathan* contains expansions of the text chiefly in the poetic sections.

Greek Versions: The oldest Greek version is the Septuagint (LXX), so-called from the legendary account of its origins in the *Letter of Aristeas,* which speaks of seventy-two Jewish translators producing a Greek version of the Pentateuch in Alexandria in the third century B.C. The translation of the rest of the books of the Hebrew canon (Former and Latter Prophets; Writings) followed, from the second century B.C. to the first century A.D. The Septuagint also includes books not part of the Hebrew canon (Wisdom of Solomon, Sirach, Baruch, Tobit, Judith, 1–2 Maccabees) as well as additions in Greek to the translations of Daniel and Esther.

The use and veneration of the Septuagint by the early Christian Church and its deviations from the current Hebrew text occasioned several other Greek translations of the Hebrew Bible in the second century A.D. for Jews, which survive only fragmentarily.

Syriac Versions: The Syro-Palestinian Bible is a Western Aramaic (not Syriac) version that survives primarily as a Melkite Christian lectionary text. Extensively adapted to the septuagintal tradition, the surviving parts of the Syro-Palestinian OT are rooted in older Syriac and (possibly) Jewish Aramaic texts. While extant Syro-Palestinian Gospel lectionaries date from A.D. 1029 and later, there is some evidence that the Syro-Palestinian version arose in the sixth century.

Several different, usually interdependent, Syriac translations of the OT and NT are known. One of these, the mid-second-century *Diatessaron* (Gk., "[One] through four"), was probably composed in Greek by Tatian, a Syrian disciple of Justin Martyr, and soon thereafter translated into Syriac. It is a continuous harmony of the four Gospels and some apocryphal material that circulated widely, apparently as the official Syrian Gospel text (rather than the four Gospels). It was eventually replaced by the four Gospels in Syriac.

Harmonies similar to the *Diatessaron* (or translations of it) have come down in various other languages. The Armenian and Georgian Gospels were influenced by it and traces may be found in patristic citations.

The Old Syriac OT is known only from incidental citations and some early traces that survive in the Peshitta. The Old Syriac Gospels are known from two fifth-century manuscripts with variant forms of a Syriac text that is later in origin than the *Diatessaron*. Citations from Acts and the Pauline corpus in early writers suggest a similar Old Syriac version for them too, but no continuous Old Syriac texts survive.

In both OT and NT, the Peshitta is a compilation and careful reworking of earlier materials. Firmly established by the early fifth century, it remained the Bible of all Syriac-language Christians. The Peshitta OT, mainly a series of somewhat uneven translations from the Hebrew, was also influenced by the Septuagint. The NT books of Revelation, 2 Peter, 2–3 John, and Jude were not transmitted in Peshitta manuscripts; their Syriac versions in modern editions are of later origin.

The Syro-hexaplar OT is a partially surviving early-seventh-century translation of the Septuagint text in column five of Origen's six-column Greek *Hexapla* with an apparatus of variant readings from other columns, all transposed from Greek into an awkward Syriac that reflects the source as closely as possible.

Contemporary with the Syro-hexaplar OT is a similarly stiff and mechanical rendering of the NT edited by Thomas of Harkel, bishop of Hierapolis in Syria. This Harclean NT, based on a revision of the Peshitta done a century earlier, was reworked for use in later West Syrian lectionaries.

Latin Versions: Except for Jerome's OT from the Hebrew, all early Latin renderings of the OT and NT were made from the Greek. The place of origin for the Latin Gospels and, indeed, for much of the Old Latin Bible can no longer be established with certainty; alongside North Africa, both Rome and Gaul have been suggested as early European centers for the Old Latin Scriptures.

No complete Latin OT version based on the Greek survives from the early period. The five OT books known best in the Old Latin form (1–2 Maccabees, Wisdom, Sirach, and Baruch) are those that Jerome judged uncanonical and refused to revise or retranslate. Preserved in the Vulgate anyway, each exists in a full text that is the work of a single translator. In general, surviving Old Latin versions were reworked in the centuries after Jerome's time and reflect mutual contamination of the Vulgate and the Old Latin.

Around the end of the fourth century, Jerome broke with the Septuagint–Old Latin tradition to produce the Vulgate rendering based directly on the Hebrew OT text preserved among the Jews. The parts of Esther and Daniel not included in the Jewish canon he supplied from the Greek; for Daniel, he drew on the book's "Theodotionic" form, which also influenced his rendering of the Aramaic sections. Tobit and Judith were translated on the basis of Aramaic recensions rather far removed from the lost Aramaic and Hebrew originals, respectively.

The Vulgate recension of the Gospels, a correction and adaptation of the existing Old Latin text in the light of good Greek manuscripts, was prepared in Rome by Jerome; the extent of his influence on the remaining NT in the Vulgate is unclear. The thirteen Pauline Letters (exclusive of Hebrews) go back to a single, early translator. The varying forms of Acts seem to derive from one early North African version. Two renderings are known for Hebrews, and possibly three for Revelation.

Other Versions: The complete OT does not survive in any one Coptic dialect. Like the Aramaic Targums, the Coptic OT versions were sometimes paraphrased or simplified to clarify the Hebrew OT. In contrast, the Coptic NT translations are fairly literal and often reflect the Alexandrian Greek text. The earliest versions reflect Greek manuscripts older than most of those used to establish the critical text of the Greek NT.

The Ethiopic OT, based on the Greek and sometimes a good witness to the unrevised Alexandrian Septuagint, is the only complete source for apocryphal *Jubilees* and *1 Enoch*. The Ethiopic NT (translated partly from Greek, partly from Syriac) has fifth-century origins, but few manuscripts antedate the fourteenth century. While the Ethiopic Gospels were reworked under Egyptian Arabic influence in the thirteenth century, two manuscripts of the unrevised fifth-century Gospel survive.

The early fifth-century Armenian translation, based on pre-Peshitta Syriac forms, was subsequently revised to match the Greek. The fifth-century Georgian version, based on Armenian texts with Syriac origins, was similarly revised by the seventh century. The Arabic versions are late and represent Greek, Hebrew, Syriac, Coptic, and even Latin prototypes.

Modern and contemporary vernacular translations of the Bible also reflect choices about meaning and interpretation, but they are not versions in the strict sense, since they do not provide independent evidence for the earliest biblical text. Such translations may shed new light on the meaning or implications of biblical passages, however, and each can be consulted with profit. No version, ancient or modern, can be absolutized or regarded as the exclusive bearer of the biblical message. It is advisable to consult a variety of translations about any biblical passage in order to reach a deeper and more nuanced insight into its meaning. *See also* Bible.

Bibliography

Ackroyd, P. R., and C. F. Evans, eds. *The Cambridge History of the Bible.* 3 vols. Cambridge: Cambridge University Press, 1963–70.

Bruce, F. F. *The Books and the Parchments: How We Got Our English Bible.* Rev. ed. Old Tappan, NJ: Revell, 1984.

Jellicoe, Sidney. *The Septuagint and Modern Study.* Oxford: Clarendon Press, 1968.

Metzger, Bruce. *The Early Versions of the New Testament: Their Origin, Transmission and Limitations.* Oxford: Clarendon Press, 1977.

JOHN KSELMAN AND KEVIN G. O'CONNELL

Scripture and tradition, the relationship between the Bible and the process of handing on the faith within the Church. In the life of the Church Scripture and tradition are not two realities radically distinct from one another; together they form a single copenetrating reality. Because some proponents of the Protestant Reformation denied the value of tradition and extolled Scripture as the only authoritative expression of the word of God (Lat., *sola Scriptura,* "Scripture alone"), the Council of Trent strongly emphasized the importance of tradition (1546). As a result, some Catholic theologians spoke of Scripture and tradition almost as if they constituted two distinct sources of revelation.

Vatican II (1962–65), however, explained that, "there exist a close connection and communication between sacred tradition and sacred Scripture. For both of them, flowing from the same divine wellspring, in a certain way merge into a unity and tend toward the same end" (Dogmatic Constitution on Divine Revelation, n. 9). Again, "sacred tradition and sacred Scripture form one sacred deposit of the word of God, which is committed to the Church" (n. 10).

The conciliar texts, as do many Catholic theologians, reflect on the relationship between the NT and tradition more clearly and systematically than they do on the relationship between the OT and tradition. To some extent this concentration is based upon the faith conviction that the Christ event constitutes the fullness of revelation. Given the unity of the two Testaments, however, what can be said about the NT can be analogously applied to the OT.

Through his teaching, activity, and very being Jesus Christ revealed God and the kingdom to the disciples. Called to be apostles, the disciples witnessed to what they had seen and heard. Their oral preaching transmitted to others what they themselves had received from Christ and learned through the prompting of the Holy Spirit. In turn, this tradition was passed along to others. The living tradition develops within the Church with the help of the Holy Spirit who enables the Church to have an ever fuller understanding of the tradition that has been passed down. In this fashion the living tradition of the Church witnesses to divine revelation.

Under the inspiration of this same Holy Spirit, the apostolic message was committed to writing. These writings came to be known as the scriptures of the NT. The living tradition of the Church has shaped the tradition written in these Scriptures. In the life of the Church the writing of the Scriptures is a privileged moment in the handing on of tradition. They are a product of and a witness to the tradition in its earliest stages.

The tradition to which the Scriptures bear witness is the apostolic tradition, which is constitutive of and normative for the life of the Church. Those entrusted with the teaching office in the Church, the magisterium, have a particular responsibility and the grace of office in the handing down of this divine revelation. Normative apostolic tradition is to be distinguished from the various traditions, dogmatic, liturgical, pastoral, and devotional, that have developed in various places at different moments in the Church's history. *See also* Bible, Church teachings on the; Bible and doctrine; Scripture, authority of; tradition. RAYMOND COLLINS

scrupulosity, the condition of a person who sees and fears sin where there is none. It is not simply a fear of sin, or even a great fear of sin, which is characteristic of the delicate conscience. Scrupulosity is morbid, i.e., fear of sin for unreasonable motives. Thus the person is unable to formulate a practical judgment concerning the morality of action.

Scruples can settle in any area of the moral life, or in many areas together, or in the whole moral attitude. The most common types of scrupulents are those who are apprehensive that they are about to sin or that they are always sinning. *See also* sin.

scrutinies, the catechumenal rituals that mark the final preparation of candidates to receive the sacraments of initiation (Baptism, Confirmation, Eucharist). These rituals are normally celebrated during the Eucharist on the third, fourth, and fifth Sundays of Lent. The Gospel readings for these Sundays are from John 4, 9, and 11. The ritual takes place after the readings and homily. The candidates (now called the "elect," or the chosen) come before the presider and kneel to pray silently. Then everyone stands for the prayers of intercession for the elect, to which they respond "Lord, hear our prayer." A prayer of exorcism then follows, in which God is asked to free them from the power and wounds of sin in their lives, and then the presider lays his hands on the head of each candidate. The readings from the Gospel of John, which deal with the Samaritan woman (Third Sunday), the young man born blind (Fourth Sunday), and the raising of Lazarus (Fifth Sunday), reflect the meaning of these rituals, a profound conversion to Christ's offer of healing and salvation, themes that resonate in the prayers of exorcism. *See also* Baptism; Rite of Christian Initiation of Adults.

seal of confession, the injunction placed on a priest to maintain absolute silence about matters discussed within the sacrament of Reconciliation. The issue arose when private confession to a priest became acceptable. In the first nine hundred years

of the Church, the official form of Reconciliation was public, and it affected only those whose sins were publicly known. A seal of sacramental secrecy, therefore, had no meaning. From the end of the sixth century onward, a private form of confession began, unofficially at first, to develop. The privacy of the confession ritual and the requirement that private sins be confessed eventually raised the issue of sacramental secrecy. Only in the ninth century is there evidence of a church law requiring secrecy, i.e., the seal of confession. Eventually, the law of the sacramental seal became standard in late medieval canon law. The law of the seal affected only the priest, not the penitent. The revised code of canon law calls this seal "inviolable" (can. 983). A priest who directly discloses confessional matter is automatically excommunicated, and the removal of the excommunication is reserved to the pope (can. 1388). Indirect disclosure of confessional matter is also punishable in accordance with the seriousness of the situation. Those who act as interpreters for a penitent or who have knowledge of confessional matter from another source are also held to secrecy. If such people reveal confessional matter, they may be punished by church law (cans. 983, n. 2; 1388, n. 2). *See also* confession, auricular; Reconciliation.

KENAN B. OSBORNE

seamless garment. *See* consistent ethic of life.

Sebastian, St., d. ca. 288, a widely venerated Roman martyr and saint; in his honor a basilica was erected on the Appian Way. Later legend has him dying of arrow wounds. Feast day: January 20.

Second Coming (Gk., *parousia,* "arrival," "coming"), the expectation among Christians of a return of the exalted Jesus. In the earliest extant Christian writing, 1 Thessalonians, Paul uses apocalyptic imagery to indicate that Christians who have died will rise to greet the Lord at his coming (1 Thess 4:13–18). At the Parousia, Jesus will be manifest in his glory (e.g., Mark 13:26). That day will see Christ revealed as judge; the wicked will be destroyed (2 Thess 1:7–10) and the righteous vindicated (Rev 20:4–6). That an imminent return of the exalted Jesus was eagerly awaited by the early Christians is evident in the expectant prayer *Maran atha,* "Come, Lord" (1 Cor 16:22; see also Rev 22:20) and in Paul's instructions to remain in one's present state since the "time has grown short" (1 Cor 7:25–31).

The belief in a proximate Parousia and the hope

that God would triumph over civil powers gave rise to the notion of an earthly millennial reign of Jesus, based on Rev 20:4–6. Such millenarian beliefs continued with varying intensity through the early centuries of Christianity but were rejected by some, including the allegorists of Alexandria and Eusebius of Caesarea. With the ascendancy of Constantine in the fourth century, an emperor sympathetic to Christianity, greater emphasis is placed on the historic successes of the Church. Such concerns, together with the increasingly evident delay in Jesus' return, effectively quashed active hope in an imminent Parousia, although anticipation of Jesus returning as heavenly judge continued and is enshrined in early creedal statements. Chiliastic expectations have, indeed, recurred at significant junctures in the history of Christianity. *See also* apocalypticism; Parousia.   SUSAN MYERS

Second Vatican Council. *See* Vatican Council II.

Secret. *See* Prayer over the Gifts.

Secretariat of State, the office in the Roman Curia that provides special assistance to the pope in the care of the universal Church and in his dealings with the Roman Curia (see *Pastor Bonus* 39). Divided into two sections, it has responsibilities dealing with a wide range of issues including diplomacy. It is considered one of the most important offices of the Holy See. *See also* Roman Curia.

secretarium (seh-creh-teh'ree-uhm; Lat., "secret place"), the room near the entrance of a cathedral, distinct from the sacristy, for the vesting of the bishop and other ministers prior to the opening procession of the Mass or other liturgies. From historical studies of Christian architecture, it can be determined that the development of the secretarium was prior to that of the sacristy. *See also* sacristy.

sect (Lat., *secta,* "faction"), a religious body that has separated itself from a larger religious body, or denomination. The term is usually associated with moral rigor and exclusivity, enforced through a variety of social or religious means. Sects often appeal to some specific religious experience as a basis for membership and separation. *See also* sectarianism.

sectarianism, a type of religious adherence and practice associated with the spirit or attitude of sects. The term is often used in reference to certain elements or factions within mainline Christian churches that embody the negative characteristics of a sect, namely, the desire to be separated from the larger Christian community by appealing to individualistic aspects of Christianity, stressing the importance of moral purity, and defining true Christianity as incompatible with membership in established Christian churches or with engagement with modern culture. Sectarians tend to reject the value of diversity and define themselves in opposition to others. They are not instinctively drawn to ecumenism and dialogue.

Sectarianism pertains particularly to the relationship between the Church and the wider society. A sectarian group is one that is detached from the world and resistant to any involvement in the sociopolitical problems that exist outside the Church. Indeed, the sectarian defines the Church as the exclusive locus of God's activity, and the mission of the Church as limited to a countercultural, otherworldly salvation. Although sectarianism is diametrically opposed to Catholicism, a certain sectarian orientation has emerged in recent years in portions of the Catholic peace movement and in some younger Catholic moral theologians influenced by Protestant sectarian ethicists. *See also* catholicity.

secular institute, group of persons who live a consecrated life in the world. Its members work for their growth in Christian charity and for the sanctification of the world. They often do not live a common life similar to that of a religious community, but such a life is not precluded by the general law of the Church. Both laypersons and priests, depending on a given secular institute's rules, may be members of a secular institute. A number of the general laws of the Church concerning secular institutes are similar to those of religious communities. *See also* religious institute.

secularism, the general attitude, form of life, or philosophical system that excludes or denies the existence and relevance of any values beyond those of the natural order. Secularism focuses exclusively on this finite world. As a philosophical system, secularism typically asserts the possibility of human perfection within the context of a self-sufficient, though evolving, natural order, and often holds the natural sciences to be the highest forms of human knowing. Though it is not always explicitly hostile to the Church, secularism's consistent denial of the supernatural directly contradicts traditional Christian faith in God and divine providence.

sede impedita (sed'ay im-ped-ee'tah; Lat., "when the see is impeded"), a situation that occurs when the bishop of a diocese is prevented from exercising his ministry. Such a situation might arise in times of war or persecution. Canon law provides regulations for the governance of a diocese when its bishop is prevented from governing.

sede vacante (sed'ay vah-kahn'tay; Lat., "when the see is vacant"), a situation when there is no bishop in a diocese. It can arise through the death of the bishop, through his resignation and acceptance of the resignation by the pope, or through the removal of the bishop from office. Canon law has certain regulations concerning the interim governance of the see; chief among them is that the interim pastoral leader is only a caretaker and that nothing new is to be undertaken (Lat., *nihil innovetur,* can. 428.1).

sedia gestatoria (sed'ee-ah jes-tah-tohr'ee-uh; Lat., "portable chair"), the chair on which the pope can be carried through a crowd in such a way that he can easily be seen by the people. It was last used by Pope John Paul I (d. 1978), who originally discarded it but resumed its use when told it would allow more people to see him.

sedilia (seh-dee'lee-uh; Lat., "seat" or "chair"), the chair for the presider of the Eucharist. The sedilia was constructed either as a single seat to hold three ministers or as a combination of three seats. When combined, the presider occupied the center chair, and his assisting deacon and subdeacon sat on either side. Most American churches use a single presider's chair. Assisting ministers sit elsewhere in the sanctuary, the space surrounding the altar.

Sedulius Scotus, Irish scholar active in the middle of the ninth century on the Continent. He was a poet and a grammarian. His writings include a *Collectaneum,* from works of classical and Christian authors; a treatise, *On Christian Rulers;* and commentaries on Matthew and the Pauline Letters.

see (Lat., *sedes,* "seat"), a local church. The Latin word from which the term is derived refers to the chair of the bishop. This chair is symbolic of the apostolic office of presiding over, and teaching, the Christian community. At times the first occupant of the see gives the name to the see, e.g., Rome as the See of Peter. *See also* diocese.

self-defense, protecting oneself from unjust physical attack through the use of force. Basing its argument on natural law, Catholic moral theology has generally maintained that individuals and societies may rightly defend themselves against such attack. However, the instinct of self-preservation should not be allowed to develop into hatred or excessive violence. Love of neighbor must constrain any necessary use of force, keeping it proportionate to the attack. The example and teaching of Jesus leads some Catholics to adopt a peaceable life-style that rejects violence and employs nonviolent means of self-defense. *See also* just-war doctrine; pacifism.

self-denial, the disciplinary practice of foregoing legitimate bodily pleasures for the purpose of gaining spiritual strength to combat temptation and overcome the power of sin. Fasting for brief periods and abstaining from certain kinds of food are examples of self-denial that are familiar to many Catholics, especially during the season of lent. *See also* mortification.

semi-Arianism, a fourth-century theological movement positioned between Arianism and Catholic orthodoxy. Identified with Basil of Ancyra, the movement rejected extreme Arian views that stripped Christ of any claim to a unique relationship with God. The semi-Arians spoke of Christ as having a substance "like" the Father's (Gk., *homoioúsious* rather than *homōoúsious,* "of the same substance"), and their whole tendency was toward orthodoxy. Their writings had a positive influence on the Cappadocian Fathers and the subsequent defeat of Arianism at the Council of Constantinople in 381. *See also* Ancyra; Arianism; *homoousios.*

seminary (Lat., *seminarium,* "seedbed"), the program of training candidates for the priesthood; also the building(s) in which the program in conducted. The seminary originated in the Council of Trent's decree *Cum Adolescentium Aetas* (1563) that enjoins each bishop to sponsor a college at his cathedral to train poor youth for the priesthood. The decree prescribes a general education and instruction in the tasks of ministry for seminarians. The bishop was free to determine the length and content of studies according to diocesan resources and needs. The decree does not address the training of religious-order priests. Subsequent developments influenced the operation of the diocesan seminary. The seventeenth-century French school of spirituality provided a method of spiritual formation stressing mental prayer and the candidate's identity with Christ. In the nineteenth-century United States, the diocesan seminary developed in several formats: within bishops' households, combined with lay colleges, sponsored by religious orders, and in institutions devoted solely to priestly formation. At the Third Plenary Council of Baltimore (1884), the bishops outlined six-year programs of studies for minor and major diocesan seminaries. Roman centralization is reflected in the seminary canons of the 1917 Code of Canon Law that outlined the seminary's operation, named its officials, listed courses, determined the years for study, and made seminary studies a prerequisite for ordination. Thereafter, the Sacred Congregation of Seminaries and Universities issued additional regulations based on these canons. Vatican Council II in 1965 issued the Decree on Priestly Formation directing each national hierarchy to devise its own national program of priestly formation. *See also* Baltimore, councils of; seminary, major; seminary, minor; Trent, Council of.   JOSEPH M. WHITE

seminary, major, an institution, with a six-year program of studies in philosophy (two years) and theology and related sciences and disciplines (four years), established for the educational, pastoral, and spiritual formation of candidates for the ordained priesthood. Some, but not most, seminarians will have attended a minor seminary before entering the major seminary. The students are in residence at the major seminary where they receive their spiritual and pastoral formation, but may take some of their academic courses of study elsewhere. The final, or deacon, year is usually taken in a pastoral assignment away from the seminary campus. *See also* seminary; seminary, minor.

seminary, minor, an institution, with a four- or six-year program of studies in the humanities and the sciences, established for the education and spiritual formation of candidates for the ordained priesthood. During the four years of high school, the students may be in residence at the seminary or live at home with their own families. During the first two years of college, however, they usually reside in community and attend classes on or off the seminary campus. Following completion of their studies at the minor seminary, the candidates for the priesthood enter a major seminary for the remainder of their education and spiritual formation. *See also* seminary; seminary, major.

semi-Pelagianism, modern name for the teaching of certain fifth-century monastic theologians in southern Gaul who reacted against what they considered the extremes of Augustine's teaching on grace. It originated from two monasteries, at Lérins and Marseilles, founded by Honoratus and John Cassian, respectively, both of whom had Eastern ascetic formation. The principal documents of semi-Pelagianism are Cassian's *Conference* 13, Vincent of Lérins' (probably) *Ojectiones Vincentianae*, the *Capitula Gallorum* (these last two being responses to the Augustinian Prosper of Aquitaine), and *On Grace* of Faustus of Riez (ca. 400–ca. 490, sometime monk of Lérins). The so-called semi-Pelagians held that the first step toward salvation was independent of grace, which, however, was operative thereafter. The Council of Orange (529) decided against semi-Pelagianism, in favor of a somewhat modified Augustinian view of grace and predestination. *See also* Augustine of Hippo, St.; Cassian, St. John; grace; Orange, Council of; Pelagianism.

Sempiternus Rex Christus (sem-pi-tair'noos reks krees'toos; Lat., "Christ, the Eternal King"), an encyclical of Pius XII, commemorating the fifteenth centenary of the Council of Chalcedon, October 8, 1951. *See also* Chalcedon, Council of.

senses of Scripture. *See* Scripture, senses of.

sensus fidelium (sen'soos fid-ay'lee-oom; Lat.), "the sense of the faithful." Other phrases for the same idea are *consensus fidelium,* "the consent of the faithful," and *sensus fidei,* "the sense of faith." The last phrase, the sense of faith, points to an aspect of the knowability of faith; faith possesses what is called a "connatural," or instinctive, spontaneous, and intuitive knowledge of its object (God). This is called a supernatural sense because it comes from the inner presence and working of God as Spirit in the person of faith. This makes the community of faith a pneumatological community, anointed and animated by God as Spirit (1 John 2:27). The sense of the faithful is thus the intuitive grasp on the truth of God that is possessed by the Church as a whole, as a consensus. It is both an adherence to the public teachings of the Church and an active charism of discernment, a power of practical and possessive knowledge belonging to the body of the faithful by virtue of their concrete living of the faith in response to God as Spirit.

This concept is found implicitly in the Fathers of the Church when they insist that Church teaching can never contradict the universal and corporate faith of the Church. John Henry Newman drew this teaching out in his essay of 1859, *On Consulting the Faithful in Matters of Doctrine.* Yves Congar developed it further in his influential *Lay People in the Church* prior to Vatican II (1962–65).

Vatican II teaches that this sense of the faithful is infallible: "The body of the faithful as a whole, anointed as they are by the Holy One, cannot err in matters of belief" (Dogmatic Constitution on the Church, n. 12). This unerring quality is manifested when the whole Church, sustained by the Spirit of truth, "shows universal agreement in matters of faith and morals" (n. 12). This does not mean that in every matter of detail a majority or even a consensus of opinion in the Church at any given time is theologically sound. But it does mean that the experience of the faithful is a source for theology and that, in the terms of Newman, the faithful should be consulted in the teaching of the Church.

This concept of the sense of the faithful is fruitful because of its bearing on many other areas of Catholic theology. It enriches the notion of tradition as something mediated by the corporate living of applied faith by the whole Church. Thus, tradition as the historical process of the *sensus fidelium* provides a basis for understanding the dynamics of the development or reinterpretation of doctrine. The *sensus fidelium* forms part of a theology of the laity which must be an integral part of ecclesiology. The reality of the *sensus fidelium* also recommends a theology of reception to complement the teaching authority of the Church. *See also* reception of doctrine; tradition.

ROGER HAIGHT

sensus plenior (sen'soos playn'ee-ohr; Lat., "fuller sense"), the deeper meaning of the words of Scripture that is intended by God but is not fully understood by its human authors. The term was in vogue among Catholic exegetes from ca. 1925 to ca. 1970. The idea of a *sensus plenior* is dependent upon an instrumental theory of inspiration, according to which human authors serve as God's instruments in the composition of biblical texts. *See also* Scripture, senses of.

Sentences, collections of scriptural sayings and the opinions of the early Church Fathers ordered topically, a favorite genre of twelfth-century theologians. The most successful collection was that compiled by Peter Lombard (d. 1160) in the 1150s. Drawing on mostly Western materials, most notably the writings of Augustine (d. 430), Lombard's *Sentences* fall into four books: on God, on human beings under sin and grace, on Christ and the virtues, on sacraments and the last things. Originally divided only into chapters, the division of the four books into distinctions was the work of Alexander of Hales (d. 1245), who did much to popularize the genre. A handy compendium of theological opinions, by the end of the first third of the thirteenth century and for centuries thereafter, Lombard's *Sentences* had been incorporated into the theological curriculum: commenting on the *Sentences* marked the final stage in the formal training of the Scholastic theologian, required before becoming a regent master. Numerous commentaries, including those of Aquinas, Bonaventure, and Duns Scotus, are extant. *See also* Lombard, Peter; Scholasticism.

Septuagesima Sunday (sep'too-ah-jeh'sih-mah), "the seventieth" day before Easter, the tenth Sunday before Easter, and third Sunday before Lent. Septuagesima once marked the beginning of the pre-Easter penitential season. The pre-Lenten season, once begun on Septuagesima, has been suppressed following the revision of the Roman Calendar in 1969.

Septuagint (sep'too-ah-jint), the original Greek translation of the Hebrew Bible, often designated as LXX. The name derives from the tradition, begun in the legendary *Letter of Aristeas,* that seventy-two or seventy (Gk., *septuaginta,* "seventy") Jewish elders translated the Pentateuch into Greek. Quotations by early writers and manuscript evidence suggest that the Torah was translated as early as ca. 250 B.C., the Prophets by ca. 200 B.C., and several of the Writings by ca. 150 B.C. The Septuagint was the first translation of the Hebrew Bible into another language, and it is the best single witness, after the Masoretic Text, to the ancient Hebrew text. The Septuagint includes all the books in the rabbinic Bible, as well as the apocryphal or deuterocanonical books. In contrast to the threefold division found in the Masoretic Text (Law, Prophets, Writings), the earliest Septuagint codices display a messianic four-part arrangement (Pentateuch, Historical, Poetic, and Prophetic books), though early lists differ in contents and order. While some of these books are similar to their counterparts in the Masoretic Text (Isaiah), others are substantially shorter (Jeremiah) or longer (Daniel), thus attesting to different editions or editorial stages in the development of the books. Several revisions of the Septuagint were made up to the mid-third century, both Jewish (Aquila) and Christian (Origen). Until it was eclipsed by the Latin Vulgate, the Septuagint was the first testament in the Bible of the Christian Church, and it remains such for the Greek Orthodox Church. *See also Hexapla.*   EUGENE ULRICH

Sepulchre, Holy. *See* Holy Sepulchre, Church of the.

sequence, a hymn sung after the second reading and before the gospel acclamation at Mass. Only four are presently appointed for liturgical use: *Victimae Paschali Laudes* (Lat., "Praises to the Paschal Victim") on Easter Sunday, *Veni, Sancte Spiritus* ("Come, Holy Spirit") on Pentecost, *Lauda Sion* ("Praise Sion") on Corpus Christi, and *Stabat Mater* ("The Mother Stood") on the feast of Our Lady of Sorrows. Perhaps the most famous sequence is the *Dies Irae* ("Day of Wrath"), though it is no longer sung at funerals.

seraphim, celestial beings around the throne of God who take part, with the cherubim, in the heavenly liturgy. Isa 6:1–7 describes them as having three pairs of wings and intoning the praises of the holy God. Etymologically, the word might mean "burning ones" and may go back to the representation of a winged serpent common in ancient Near Eastern iconography. *See also* angel.

Serapion of Thmuis, St. (suh-rap'ee-awn; thum-wees') fourth-century Egyptian bishop (d. after 360). An important collection of early liturgical texts—called the *Euchologion of Serapion*—is attributed to him.

Sergius I, St., d. 701, pope from 687 to 701. Elected by clergy and people over two rivals, he resisted attempts by the emperor Justinian II to coerce him into signing canons (Trullan Council, Constantinople, 692) that would have given the see of Constantinople the same authority as Rome. Feast day: September 8. *See also* Constantinople.

Sergius of Radonezh, St. (rah-doh'nesh), 1314–92, the most popular Russian saint and first Russian mystic, venerated by Orthodox and Catholics alike. Considered the patron saint of Russia, Sergius is often called "the Russian Orthodox Francis of Assisi." Born of noble parents, after their death in 1334

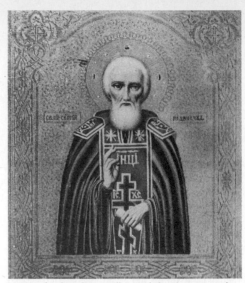

Sergius of Radonezh, generally regarded as the greatest of Russian saints, founder of some forty monasteries, and mediator and peacemaker in political disputes; depicted here as an abbot.

Sergius withdrew to the forests of Radonezh just north of Moscow to live a life of monastic solitude. In 1336, he built a chapel in honor of the Trinity, and soon attracted disciples who lived a "lavriot," or semieremitical, monastic life. In 1354, Sergius and his disciples adopted a cenobitic (community) rule, and the great monastery that developed, now known as the Trinity-St. Sergius Lavra, became a center of pilgrimage, the principal center of Russian spirituality, and the spiritual heart of Russian Orthodoxy. Sergius refused election to the patriarchate of Moscow in 1378, and became a national hero when he gave his blessing to Prince Dimitri to repel the Mongols at the famous Battle of Kulikovo in 1380 during the Tatar domination of Rus' (early name for Russia) and Muscovy. Because he lived before the Orthodox rejection of the Union of Florence (1439), the feast of St. Sergius on September 25 is also found in the Eastern Catholic sanctoral. *See also* Russia, Catholicism in.

Seripando, Girolamo, 1492–1563, Italian theologian, archbishop of Salerno, and influential Catholic reformer. A member and later vicar-general (1538) of the Augustinian order, he strongly opposed Lutheranism but nevertheless espoused a biblical and Augustinian view of justification and Scripture. At the Council of Trent (1545–63), Seripando failed in his effort to elevate Scripture above tradition as a source of Catholic truth; however, he was influential in formulating final decrees on justification and original sin. As archbishop (1554–63), Seripando fulfilled the Tridentine ideals of episcopal residence (living in his diocese), visitation, and preaching.

sermon. *See* homily.

Sermon on the Mount, sayings of Jesus in Matt 5–7 (111 verses), with parallels in Luke 6:20–49 (the Sermon on the Plain). The sermon begins with Beatitudes that praise those virtues and dispositions that characterize the new eschatological community (Matt 5:3–12). After statements on the abiding validity of the law (5:17–20), there follow six antitheses (5:21–43) contrasting the old law with the teaching of Jesus (e.g., "You have heard that it was said ... but I say to you"). Since these do not describe accurately the OT (e.g., nowhere does the OT say "hate your enemy," as Matt 5:43 suggests), emphasis should be put on the positive exhortation. After instructions on the practice of Christian discipleship, including the Golden Rule (Matt 7:12), the sermon concludes with exhortations to both hear and do Jesus' words (7:24–27). Though often called "utopian," in Matthew the sermon describes those attitudes and actions which constitute discipleship in response to the love of God manifest in Jesus (see Matt 4:23–25).

Serra, Bl. Junipero (hoo-ne'pair-oh sayr'ah), 1713–84, Spanish Franciscan priest, founder of the California missions. He established the first mission in present-day California at San Diego in 1769, and went on to establish eight more missions, serving as president of the missions until his death. He was beatified in 1987, but his cause for canonization became the source of controversy between the Catholic Church and Native American activists, who objected to the missionaries' treatment of those whom they sought to convert.

Sertillanges, Antonin-Gilbert, 1863–1948, French Dominican theologian. A thinker characterized by breadth and openness of thought, Sertillanges wrote on Thomistic philosophy, moral theology, ecclesiology, and exegesis; he taught Scripture at the École Biblique (Jerusalem) and theology at Le Saulchoir in France. For his time, he was unusually irenic and well-informed as he sought to explain faith and Church to modern philosophy,

literature, and science. He is perhaps best known to many Catholics for his book *The Intellectual Life* (1946).

servant of the Lord, "servant" referred to in certain passages in the later, exilic part of the book of Isaiah (42:1–4; 49:1–6; 50:4–11; 52:13–53:12). The passages speak of a chosen instrument of God with a mission to Israel and the nations, in which the servant perseveres in spite of opposition, and in pursuit of which he suffers ignominy and, possibly, death. The standard Jewish interpretation connects these passages to Israel's mission to the world, but there are indications that at least one of them must allude to an individual or collectivity within Israel, thought by some to be the exiled ruler and by others a prophet or prophetic group. The last of the passages, which speaks of the suffering and (probable) death of the servant, has left a deep imprint on the NT representation of the mission and death of Jesus (Matt 12:15–21; Mark 10:45; 1 Pet 2:22–24).

server, altar, an assistant to the presider at Mass. The principal functions of the altar server are to hold the sacramentary for the bishop or priest as he prays with extended arms at Mass, to bring the sacred vessels to the altar at the presentation of the gifts, and to minister the wine and water for the presider. Altar servers originated in the ninth century, as young boys assumed the role of ordained acolytes. They carried the Mass Book (missal), placed it on the altar, responded to the priest's prayers, and ministered the wine and water to the presider. The revised Code of Canon Law (1983) allowed in principle for women and girls to fulfill this function, but not until 1994 was a definitive interpretation rendered by the Vatican, with the approval of Pope John Paul II, authorizing national conferences of bishops to permit women and girls to serve at the altar. *See also* acolyte.

Servetus, Michael, ca. 1511–53, Spanish physician and antitrinitarian. The author of *De Trinitatis Erroribus* (*On the Errors of the Trinity;* 1531), *Dialogorum de Trinitate Libri Duo* (*Two Books of Dialogues on the Trinity;* 1532), and *Christianismi Restitutio* (*The Renewal of Christianity;* 1553), in the latter revealing the pulmonary circulation of the blood, Servetus was executed for heresy at Geneva at Calvin's instigation. *See also* Trinity, doctrine of the.

servile work, physical labor forbidden on Sundays

and holy days, contrasted with mental work, like reading or music, which was allowed. The distinction, however, scarcely suits modern life. In the encyclical *Laborem Exercens* (1981) Pope John Paul II identifies labor in all its forms as a defining characteristic of what it is to be human. Accordingly, the 1983 Code of Canon Law, unlike the 1917 code, focuses on the purpose and spirit of the Sunday rest, directing that Catholics, except in cases of necessity, refrain from any work or business concerns that hinder their worship of God and the celebration of the day (can. 1247). *See also* Sunday.

Servites, the Order of Friar Servants of Mary (O.S.M.), a religious community including priests and brothers, contemplative nuns and tertiaries. Servites lead a monastic life in the tradition of the mendicant orders and undertake various apostolic works. The order was founded in Cafaggio, Italy, in 1233 by cloth merchants from Florence. Now known as the Seven Founders, their original intent was to live in the spirit of the early Church, according to the Rule of St. Augustine. The order was given papal approval in 1256. There have been American foundations of Servites since 1870. *See also* Seven Holy Founders of the Servants of Mary.

Servus Servorum Dei (sair'voos sair-vohr'oom day'ee; Lat. "Servant of the Servants of God"), papal title. First used by Pope Gregory the Great (590–604), it has been in general use since the pontificate of Gregory VII (1073–85).

Seton, St. Elizabeth Ann Bayley, 1774–1821, the first American-born saint. Born in New York City of a wealthy and devout Episcopalian family, the daughter of a professor of anatomy at King's College (now Columbia University) in New York and the stepsister of Archbishop James Roosevelt Bayley of Baltimore, in 1794 she married William Magee Seton, a wealthy merchant, with whom she had five children. She became involved in social work and established the Society for the Relief of Poor Widows with Children in 1797. Six years later, during a trip to Italy with the entire family, her husband died. Inspired by the kindness of an Italian family, she converted to Catholicism in 1805, upon her return to the United States. The rector of St. Mary's Seminary in Baltimore invited her to open a school for girls, and in 1809 with four companions she founded a re-

Elizabeth Ann Bayley Seton, the first person born in America to be canonized (Frances Xavier Cabrini was the first American citizen to be so honored) and founder of the Sisters of Charity, a religious community devoted to the poor and the sick.

ligious community, the Sisters of St. Joseph, and also a school for poor children near Emmitsburg, Maryland.

Her community's rule, based on the rule of Vincent de Paul, was approved by the archbishop of Baltimore in 1812. She was elected superior and, with eighteen other sisters, took vows the following year. Thus began the first American religious society, the Sisters of Charity of St. Joseph, devoted primarily to the education of the poor and to teaching in parish, or parochial, schools. That is why historians often credit her with laying the foundation for the Catholic parochial school system in the United States. The new order spread throughout the United States, the rest of North America, South America, and Italy. By the time of her death at Emmitsburg, there were already some twenty communities in existence. With extraordinary support from the Catholic communities in and around Philadelphia and Baltimore, she was beatified by Pope John XXIII and later canonized in 1975 by Pope Paul VI—the first American-born saint. In his canonization talk, Pope Paul VI praised her for her contributions as a wife, mother, widow, and consecrated religious, and her witness to an authentic spirituality in a land where "temporal prosperity seemed to obscure and almost make

[it] impossible." Feast day: January 4. *See also* Bayley, James Roosevelt; Sisters of Charity.   RICHARD P. MCBRIEN

seven capital sins. *See* capital sins.

Seven Holy Founders of the Servants of Mary, thirteenth-century Florentine youths who founded the Servites. Their names were Buonfiglio Monaldo, Alexis Falconieri, Benedict dell'Antello, Bartholomew Amidei, Ricovero Uguccione, Gerardino Sostegni, and John Buonagiunta Monetti. Feast day: February 17. *See also* Servites.

Seven Sorrows of the Blessed Virgin Mary. *See* Our Lady of Sorrows.

Seventh-Day Adventists, members of the largest Protestant denomination to emerge out of the Millerite movement in the United States. Organized in 1863 by James and Ellen G. White, Seventh-Day Adventists believe in reading the Bible literally, Saturday as the Sabbath, the imminent return of Christ, and the prophetic nature of Mrs. White's writings. They emphasize health, abstaining from alcohol, tobacco, and often meat. Like other evangelicals, Seventh-Day Adventists promote individual conversion, and often have coupled their evangelistic efforts with the founding of health-care institutions. In the 1990s, there were 783,000 Seventh-Day Adventists in North America and 7.3 million worldwide.

Severinus Boethius, St. *See* Boethius, St. Severinus.

Severus of Antioch, ca. 465–538, bishop of Antioch (512–18), whose moderated Monophysite teaching approached, in effect if not in language, the teaching of the Council of Chalcedon (451). *See also* Chalcedon, Council of; Monophysitism.

Sexagesima Sunday (seks'uh-jeh'sih-mah), "the sixtieth" day before Easter, it is actually the sixty-third. Sexagesima is the second Sunday before Lent and the ninth before Easter. As with Septuagesima, the preceding Sunday, and Quinquagesima, the following Sunday, its observance has been suppressed under the reformed Roman Calendar (1969).

sexism, patterns of discriminatory attitudes and practices based on gender. The habits of consider-

ing one sex inferior to the other and of evaluating a person's worth on the basis of sex have come to be known as sexism. Though the term could theoretically apply to either sex, in practice it usually conveys the meaning of discriminatory attitudes toward women. Often compared to racism, it is considered by many theologians to be a form of social sin. *See also* feminism; inclusive language.

Sext (Lat., "sixth"), second of the three daytime hours of liturgical prayer. Sext is prayed at the "sixth" hour, roughly 12:00 noon. Like its companion offices, Terce and None, it is brief, and its texts and songs vary far less frequently than those of the major hours: Matins, Lauds, and Vespers. *See also* Liturgy of the Hours.

sexton (seks'tun), the person charged with the day-to-day care and maintenance of the physical structure and environment of a church building and its properties; the janitor. Because sextons cared for church-owned cemeteries and belltowers, they once had to possess ancillary skills in undertaking and bell ringing.

sexual morality, an understanding of the moral obligations associated with human sexuality. Unlike some other ethical traditions, Catholicism holds that there is an objective moral order that is greater than the sum of individual moral choices. In the very act of creation God gave to all aspects of creation a purpose or a finality. Often spoken of as the "natural law," this purpose gives meaning to human activity and also establishes moral obligations for human living.

The purpose of human sexual activity is to express love and create new life in the context of marriage. Any sexual activity or expression that is not consistent with, or violates, this purpose is considered to be morally wrong because it opposes the divine plan. This is why artificial means of birth control, masturbation, fornication, and premarital intercourse have been viewed in the Catholic tradition as always immoral actions. The reason these actions are always immoral, it has been argued, is that the nature of these activities is such that neither human intention nor circumstances can change or mitigate their violating the purpose of human sexual activity. For that reason these actions are said to be intrinsically evil.

Many theologians disagree with some aspects of

this traditional teaching. While affirming the purpose or finality of human sexual activity, they say that there are circumstances in which, for example, artificial birth control would be morally correct. The Church's hierarchical magisterium has rejected this position. At the same time Paul VI and John Paul II have taught the positive value of human sexuality. This teaching is grounded in a deep appreciation of humanity having been created in the image and likeness of God, a God who is love. Consequently, human sexuality is good and is most authentic when it is an expression of committed love in marriage. *See also* chastity; fornication; homosexuality; masturbation; purity.   MICHAEL D. PLACE

Shakers, members of a millennialist offshoot of the Quakers. They derived their name from the shaking which possessed them through spiritual exaltation. Ann Lee, revered for her prophetic visions, led a small group of Shakers from England to America in 1774. Early Shakers emphasized celibacy, communal living, and ecstatic, yet simple, worship. They were innovative farmers and superb artisans. Around 1850 nineteen communities housed perhaps 3,600 members. In the early 1990s there were only a handful remaining in New Hampshire.

shalom (Heb., "peace," "well-being"), a common greeting. It achieves a special resonance in the context of epistolary greetings in early Christianity (e.g., Rom 1:7).

Shea, John Gilmary, 1824–92, Church historian, considered by some to be the "father of American Catholic history." His four-volume *History of the Catholic Church in the United States* covers the period from the earliest settlements to 1852 and in certain respects has never been superseded. After a vocation with the Jesuits, Shea remained a layman. He never held a teaching position and was bitterly disappointed when he was not named to the Church History chair at The Catholic University of America when it opened in 1889. He wrote popular history and journalism to support his family, but also published a history of Georgetown University and many works on Indian missions.

Sheed, Francis Joseph, 1897–1981, writer, lecturer, publisher, and lay theologian. Born in Australia and educated there and in England, he was a street preacher before he and his wife, Maisie Ward, founded the Catholic publishing house of Sheed and Ward in London in 1929. His public speaking led to his writing; he is the author of more than ten books, including *Theology for Beginners* (1957).

Sheen, Fulton J., 1895–1979, archbishop, preacher, author, and radio and television personality. Ordained for the diocese of Peoria in 1919, he continued his education at The Catholic University of America, and received a Ph.D. from the University of Louvain in 1923.

Appointed to the faculty at Catholic University in 1926, he taught philosophy and theology until 1950. Sheen attracted widespread attention as a dynamic preacher, anti-Communist, and intellectual popu-

Archbishop Fulton J. Sheen, before the Second Vatican Council the most popular Catholic radio and television speaker in America, having reached millions of listeners and viewers via his "Catholic Hour" and "Life Is Worth Living" broadcasts from the 1930s through the 1950s.

larizer. A pioneer of the electronic church, he was the featured speaker on "The Catholic Hour" radio broadcasts (1930–52), with an estimated four million listeners. He was also celebrated for his "Life Is Worth Living" television show (1951–57), which reached an audience of some thirty million viewers.

In 1950, he became national director of the Society for the Propagation of the Faith, raising millions of dollars for the missions. He was the author of more than sixty books, and was instrumental in receiving prominent people, such as Congresswoman Clare Booth Luce and former Communist Louis Budenz, into the Catholic Church.

Named bishop of Rochester, New York, in 1966, Sheen focused his attention on ecumenism and urban poverty. After a short and stormy tenure, marked by controversy over his style of leadership, he resigned in 1969. He became increasingly critical of certain post–Vatican II developments in the Church and gradually receded from the public scene.

Sheerin, John B., 1906–92, Paulist priest, editor, and ecumenist. Ordained in 1937, he was editor of *The Catholic World* (1948–72), a syndicated columnist in the Catholic press (1956–82), an official Vatican observer to the World Council of Churches (1957–63), a *peritus* (Lat., "expert") at the fourth session of the Second Vatican Council (1965), and the author of several books, including *Christian Reunion: The Ecumenical Movement and American Catholics* (1966).

Shenoute (sheh-noo'tay), also known as Shenudi, ca. 350–ca. 450, abbot of the White Monastery in Upper Egypt and one of the greatest Coptic writers of homilies, letters, and treatises. His severe adaptations of Pachomius's rules prescribed floggings and required a written profession of obedience. He collaborated with patriarchs of Alexandria from Athanasius to Dioscorus, even accompanying Cyril to Ephesus (431). Feast day: July 1 (Coptic). *See also* Copt, Coptic.

Sheol (shay-ohl'), ancient poetic Hebrew term for the underworld, translated "grave," "pit," or "hell" (cf. Job 17:13–16; Vulgate, *infernus*). It originally designated a place of confinement, but not punishment, for all the deceased. During the Hellenistic era, it became associated with Greek *Hades* and the notion of judgment developed. It is to be distinguished from the NT *Gehenna* (e.g., Matt 5:22).

Shepherd of Hermas. *See Hermas, Shepherd of.*

Sheptyckyj, Andryj (ahn-dree' shep-titz'kee), 1865–1944, Ukrainian Catholic metropolitan of Halych and archbishop of Lviv. Of noble origin, he entered the Order of St. Basil in 1888, was ordained a priest in 1892; he became bishop of Stanyslaviv in 1898 and metropolitan in 1900. As head of the Ukrainian Catholic Church, he combined deep spiritual life with tireless pastoral activity, and an ecumenial spirit far in advance of his times.

shrine (Lat., *scrinium*, "coffer"). **1** A container for relics exhibited in a church or chapel. **2** A church location holding a sacred statue or painting that people visit for devotional purposes. **3** A separate complex near a church that houses, typically, a statue or other object of devotion. **4** A pilgrimage destination (e.g., Guadalupe or Lourdes) that may encompass a complex of buildings but whose main focus is a cult site or cult figure, like a statue or an altar with relics. *See also* relics; reliquary.

shrines, Marian, holy places devoted to Mary that are the destinations of pilgrimages. Although many places in medieval Europe and elsewhere had shrine destinations connected with devotion to Mary (e.g., the cathedral of Chartres, which held the relic of the tunic of Mary, or the Shrine of Our Lady of Walsingham in pre-Reformation England), there have been any number of shrines connected to the cult of Mary that have continued to draw large numbers of pilgrims. These shrines are also the loci of purported Marian apparitions. They include the Mexican shrine of Our Lady of Guadalupe (famous since the late-sixteenth century), or more modern Marian apparition shrines like Lourdes (France), Knock (Ireland), Fátima (Portugal), and La Salette (France). Recent alleged Marian apparitions (e.g., those in Medjugorje in Croatia) have developed into objects of pious pilgrimage. Some Marian shrines are more important for their miraculous images than as the sites of apparitions: e.g., Our Lady of Montserrat (Spain) or the Black Madonna shrine on Jasna Gorna (Pol., "Shining Mountain") in Poland. *See also* apparitions of the Blessed Virgin Mary; Marian devotion.

Shroud, Holy. *See* Holy Shroud.

Shrove Tuesday, Tuesday before Ash Wednesday. Also known as Mardi Gras (Fr., "fat Tuesday"), the

The Marian shrine of Our Lady of Montserrat in Spain.

day in question was named "Shrove" from the Old English word *scrifan,* meaning to hear or make confession. It is a day for confessing and feasting. *See also* Holy Week.

Shuster, George Nauman, 1894–1977, educator, publicist, and government official. A graduate of Notre Dame and Columbia University, Shuster served on the staff of *Commonweal* magazine (1924–37), was president of Hunter College in New York (1940–60), and was assistant to the president at Notre Dame (1961–77). A prolific author, he published important works on German history and culture and on American Catholicism. *See also Commonweal;* Notre Dame, University of.

Sic et Non (sik et nohn; Lat., "Yes and No"), a medieval text, first drafted by Peter Abelard in 1121, that provided students and teachers of theology with a resource for resolving apparently contradictory teachings. The brief prologue, a collection of patristic and classical rules for interpreting problematic texts, is followed by 158 questions, each of which presented patristic, conciliar, and scriptural sayings on a controversial theological issue.

While Abelard's debt to others in this work is well-known, *Sic et Non* is a distinctive work. It is a significant early championing of a place for dialectic in theological inquiry, thus furthering the development of theology as a "science." *See also* Abelard, Peter; Scholasticism.

Siger of Brabant (see'zhay), ca. 1240–ca. 1284, Belgian philosopher. Active as a teacher and writer at the University of Paris in the 1260s and 1270s, he is considered the founder of Latin Averroism. After 1270, he progressively modified his views in the direction of orthodoxy; nevertheless, he was a prime target of the Parisian condemnation of 1277. Bishop Stephen Tempier listed a number of Averroist errors, particularly the idea that, when in conflict, truths of philosophy are superior to truths of the Catholic faith. *See also* Averroism.

Sigismund, St., d. ca. 523, king of Burgundy from 516 to 523, son of the Arian king Gundebald.

Sigismund converted to Catholicism ca. 499. Feast day: May 1.

Signatura, Apostolic, the highest tribunal in the Church judicial system. The court's responsibilities include the adjudication of procedural issues raised in other tribunals and administrative procedures, as well as the supervision of all other tribunals in the Catholic Church. Some think that the court's name derives from the fact that its early meeting room was the place where documents were signed. *See also* Roman Curia.

sign of peace, the phrase used since Vatican Council II (1962–65) to describe the liturgical greeting exchanged among Christians as a sign of neighborly love and unity. At Mass, it follows the Lord's Prayer and precedes Communion. The sign of peace may also be exchanged at other services: e.g., the Liturgy of the Hours, ordinations, baptisms, and during the liturgy of Reconciliation (Penance). Because cultures differ in their manner of expressing unity and peace, this liturgical sign may take many forms: a kiss, an embrace, bowing, touching one another, a handshake. The handclasp is common in many parishes in the United States.

sign of the cross, the private or public act of tracing an image of the cross on persons or things. Tertullian (d. ca. 225) already attests to the use of this gesture as a way for Christians to sanctify daily life or signal mutual recognition during periods of persecution. Soon the personal gesture was extended to Baptism and Eucharist, and then to other liturgical blessings of persons and objects. In early times the cross was drawn on the forehead with the right thumb. Later, in the Roman rite, it was made by drawing the right hand from forehead to breast, then from left shoulder to right shoulder. *See also* cross.

signs of the times, a phrase referring to the activity of God in the world and in the changing events of human history. It is taken from the Bible (Matt 16:3) and is found also in Pope John XXIII's 1963 encyclical *Pacem in Terris* (nn. 126–29) and in the Second Vatican Council's *Gaudium et Spes* (Pastoral Constitution on the Church in the Modern World, n. 4). To carry out its role as a servant, the council declared, "the Church has always had the duty of scrutinizing the signs of the times and of interpreting them in the light of the gospel."

Silas, short form of the name Silvanus, a companion of Paul. He is mentioned in Acts 15:22–18:5, under the name of Silas, as a fellow evangelist of Paul and Timothy. He is called Silvanus in 1 Cor 1:19. He is the coauthor of 1 and 2 Thessalonians, and is the scribe of 1 Peter (1 Pet 5:12).

silence, the quieting of one's being. The first requirement is not speaking. True exterior silence also includes refraining from eye contact, gesturing, reading, writing, touching, and other forms of communication. Deep interior silence requires recollection, stilling thought, calming emotion, and acceptance of experiences without judgment.

Silence centers one in the ability to listen without reaction or distraction. It is important in contemplative living and required in some monastic codes. It is essential for concentration, awareness, self-understanding, and prayer life. Deep silence aids recollection and makes possible the primarily receptive prayer that ripens spiritual life. Ultimately, silence is being still in order to know God. *See also* prayer.

Sillon, Le (luh see-yohn'; Fr., "the furrow"), French lay movement founded by Marc Sangnier (1873–1950) to reconcile Catholicism with the French Republic. It was condemned by Pope Pius X in 1910 because of its desire to be free of hierarchical control, its acceptance of theories about the revolution, and its alleged Modernist tendencies. *See also* Modernism.

Silvester [name of popes]. *See* Sylvester.

simandron (Gk., *simantron,* "bell"), a wooden beam (or metal bar) used in Byzantine monasteries in place of a bell. It is struck with a bar or baton to signal the beginning of the chanting of the Divine Office and other liturgical services.

Simeon, a character in Luke's Gospel. Simeon was a pious old man who recognized the significance of Jesus at his Presentation in the Temple (Luke 2:25–35). Upon seeing Jesus he pronounced the prayer that came to be known as the Nunc Dimittis. Another Simon, "The Black," was a leading figure in the Christian community at Antioch (Acts 13:1). *See also* Nunc Dimittis.

Simeon Stylites, St. (sti-lee'teez), also known as Simeon "the Elder," ca. 390–459, first "stylite" or pillar saint, from northern Syria. After living in a monastery and then as a hermit, Simeon from ca. 423 lived on top of a succession of pillars, the last one about fifty-five feet high. His holiness was admired worldwide, and he exerted significant influence on contemporary events. His disciple Daniel (d. ca. 493) and his namesake Simeon ("the Younger," d. ca. 596) were also both famous stylites. Feast day: January 5 (West); September 1 (East). *See also* stylite.

Simon, Richard, 1638–1712, the founder of modern biblical criticism and the greatest biblical scholar of his day. He was ordained an Oratorian priest (1670), and, partly to answer Protestant claims about the sole authority of Scripture, published *Histoire critique du Vieux Testament* (1678), which denied the Mosaic authorship of the Pentateuch. He was opposed by Jacques Bénigne Bousset and was later expelled from the Oratorians because of his controversial views.

Simon, St., one of the twelve apostles. His nickname, "the Cananaean" (Matt 10:4; Mark 3:18), Aramaic for "Zealot," is used in Luke 6:15 and Acts 1:13. Simon may have been zealous for Israel's independence or for the law. Tradition relates his missions to Egypt and Persia followed by his martyrdom. Feast day: October 28. *See also* apostle; Twelve, the.

Simon Bar Jonah. *See* Peter, St.

Simon of Cyrene, the bearer of Jesus' cross. From the capital of Cyrenaica in North Africa, Simon was probably in Jerusalem for Passover when impressed into service (Matt 27:32; Mark 15:21; Luke 23:26). Mark also notes his sons Alexander and Rufus. Paul may have greeted the latter in Rome (Rom 16:13).

Simon Stock, St., ca. 1165–1265, prior general of the Carmelite order about whose life very little is known. Late medieval traditions attributed the granting of the brown scapular to Simon by the Blessed Virgin. Relics are venerated at Bordeaux and Aylesford, England. Feast day: May 16 (Carmelite order). *See also* scapular.

simony, the buying or selling of Church offices, named after Simon Magus, who tried to buy the power of laying on hands from Peter (Acts 8:9–24). Simony has been a recurrent problem in the history of the Church, and a significant portion of canon

law is given over to measures to eradicate it. The eleventh-century Gregorian reformers made simony one of their main targets, and the investiture controversy had its roots in disputes about the simoniacal character of lay investiture. Many of the conditions that made simony prevalent no longer exist, and the abuse is rare today. *See also* Gregorian reform; investiture controversy.

Simplicianus, St., d. 400, bishop of Milan who succeeded Ambrose, his pupil, in 397. He played a crucial role in the conversions of both Marius Victorinus and Augustine. Feast day: August 16. *See also* Augustine of Hippo, St.

sin, a general term that covers several different realities: actual sin (a violation of the moral order); habitual sin (the sinful state that results from actual sin); and original sin (the sin of the first humans, resulting in the fallen condition into which all are born),

Scriptural Basis: In the OT (Gen 3) sin appears as a deliberate act against the divinely established order, but even more as internal pride and rebellion against God whose supremacy the human person refuses to acknowledge. In the Synoptics sins are acts that contravene the moral order in different ways, but beyond this it is the heart from which they proceed that is sinful. Therefore, conversion of heart is required. John speaks not only of sins, but of sin (Gk., *anomia*), which refers to hostility to God, the internal state of the sinner. In Paul's Letters there is the distinction between sin transgressions (in the plural, generally referred to as *paraptomata*) and sin (in the singular, generally referred to as *hamartia*) which is a kind of power in the sinful person. Sin transgressions are manifestations of the sinful condition of the person and from this condition redemption is had only through the death and Resurrection of Christ.

Mortal and Venial Sins: Sin properly so called refers to actual sin. In Catholic tradition actual sin was categorized as mortal (death-dealing) or venial (slight) sin. There is a fundamental difference between the two because what is said of mortal sin (that it involves a radical rupture in the person's union with God) cannot be said of venial sin.

Some contemporary theologians have suggested that there should be a threefold division of sin: mortal, serious, and venial. They base this suggestion largely on the unfortunate popular tendency to interpret venial sin as "only" venial sin in a way that makes light of it. Not only is this theologically and spiritually regrettable in itself, but it obscures the fact that some venial sins, like offenses in a family, can be very serious without rupturing the relationship with God.

The characteristics of sin are most perfectly realized in mortal sin. Traditionally the requisites for the commission of mortal sin were said to be serious (grave) matter, sufficiently full knowledge, and full consent of the will. For many centuries the difference between mortal and venial sin was traced to the matter; that is, if the matter was slight (e.g., a small theft, a relatively harmless white lie), the sin was all but automatically judged venial. With the recovery of the notion of fundamental freedom, there has been an adjustment in this analysis, although not all theologians accept it. The matter of the violation is now related to fundamental freedom. Only serious matter is likely to provoke an individual to the profound self-disposition known as a fundamental option. Therefore, many modern theologians see a sin as mortal if the opposition to God proper to every sinful act is penetrated from the central depths of the person by self-disposing freedom. Therefore, it is not unthinkable, even if unlikely, that such a self-disposition could occur where only slight matter is involved. Venial sin, committed at a less central depth of personal freedom, remains compatible with the love of God alive in the depths of the soul.

There are important practical implications to the contemporary view of the distinction between mortal and venial sin as based on the intensity of the personal disposition involved. First, in contrast to the view of the moral life as above all a series of discrete actions or omissions, this view lays greater stress on subjectivity and views the moral life as above all a growth process, the deepening of the biblical "adhering to God," and of the love of Christ poured into our hearts. This avoids an excessive objectivism.

Second, this approach avoids a kind of "security-ism," the view that avoidance of materially grave violations is equivalent to justification before God. Actually our internal disposition before God, rooted as it is in our fundamental freedom, is not available to our awareness with absolute security. However, we do have a certain conjectural certainty about our true internal disposition, a certainty necessary for a basic optimism and joy in the spiritual life. For instance, Christian tradition believes that the experi-

ence of peace and consolation testifies to the efficacious presence of the Spirit of Christ.

Finally, since external acts are not sure signs of internal dispositions, there is every reason for a nonjudgmental attitude toward the neighbor. *See also* fundamental option; mortal sin; venial sin.

RICHARD A. MCCORMICK

sin against the Holy Spirit, the final repudiation of God's grace. The synoptic Gospels (Matt 12:31–32; Mark 3:28–30; Luke 12:10) report Jesus' saying that all sins against people can be forgiven, but that blasphemy against the Holy Spirit cannot. Apostasy is viewed similarly in Heb 6:4–6. 1 John 5:16 mentions a "mortal sin" that may be related.

The precise meaning of the "sin against the Spirit" has been much debated. Patristic authors favored the notion of apostasy or the rejection of the Gospel. Moderns tend to emphasize the final and obdurate rejection of God's forgiveness itself.

Sinai (si'nī), the sacred place where the covenant between God and the Israelites was inaugurated. Sinai is the name of the triangular peninsula between Africa and Asia. It designates the wilderness in which Mount Sinai is located (Exod 16:1; 19:1). On the mountain itself God delivered the law to Moses (Exod 19–34). *See also* Commandments, the Ten; covenant.

sinlessness of Christ, the belief that Jesus Christ, being free from sin, remained in perfect communion with God the Father throughout his earthly life. Rooted in the NT (Heb 4:15), this belief has been continually affirmed by the Church, beginning with the Council of Chalcedon in 451.

Because Jesus Christ was without sin (Lat., *impeccantia*), he was able to embody in himself the perfect union between God and humanity. On the one hand, he perfectly discloses the divine for humankind. Being without sin, he is the perfect image of the invisible God (Col 1:15). On the other hand, Jesus Christ is the fulfillment of the human movement toward God. Through him, humans have access to God, and in Jesus' life, death, and Resurrection is a paradigm of how humans are to be in relation to God and to one another.

Neo-Scholasticism claimed that because Jesus Christ was a divine person, he was not capable of sinning (Lat., *impeccabilitas*). Today, theologians claim that because Jesus Christ is fully human, he had the capacity to sin. He remained sinless because he chose not to sin; he refused to alienate himself from the Father by an act of his will. *See also* Jesus Christ.

Siricius, St., d. 399, pope from 384 to 399. His letter to Himerius of Tarragona (385), first letter in the papal decretals, promotes the authority of Rome, insists on celibacy for deacons and priests, and recommends clemency toward public penitents. Another letter regarding matters of church order was sent to the African churches (386). He condemned Jovinian (392). Feast day: November 26. *See also* celibacy, clerical.

sister. *See* nun.

Sister Formation Conference. *See* Religious Formation Conference.

sisters, congregations of, institutes of women who profess the simple vows of poverty, chastity, and obedience, live a common life, and are engaged in ministering to the needs of society. The strict rule of enclosure does not hold for sisters as it does for nuns.

Common life involves sharing material things and traditionally has meant living together in a monastery or convent and sharing an horarium (daily schedule). Recent developments in the definition of community focus more on unity of spirit and of values rather than sharing daily life. As a result, some sisters live in small self-chosen communities, and some live alone. Communities also may include members of other congregations and persons who do not belong to any congregation. These auxiliary members are often called associates; they accept the vision of the congregation and share in the ministry.

Authority: Congregations of sisters may be pontifical, under the authority of the pope, or diocesan, under the authority of the local bishop. The constitutions of the congregations are approved by the appropriate authority.

Congregations are usually governed by a president or superior, assisted by a council. Some congregations have adopted a conciliar model of governance without one person acting as president or superior. The leaders of congregations are ordinarily elected by a general chapter. The chapter is the highest governing body while it is in session.

History: While cloistered orders of women have existed since the fifth century, in the sixteenth century women united to form a new kind of religious commitment. They strove to unite the practice of prayer, meditation, spiritual reading, and silence common in cloistered congregations with ministerial activity in response to the needs and sufferings of the day.

Early efforts by women like Angela Merici, founder of the Ursulines (1535), and Jane Frances de Chantal, founder with Francis de Sales of the Visitation Sisters (1610), were halted as the cloister was imposed by Church authorities. Vincent de Paul insisted that the Daughters of Charity, which he founded, would have no convent but the hospital, no chapel but the parish church, and no cloister but the streets.

It was not until 1900 that the Church, in Pope Leo XIII's *Conditae a Christo,* recognized congregations committed to the active apostolate as true religious.

Recent History: In 1950, Pope Pius XII convoked a meeting of the superiors of religious congregations under the title of the First General Congress of the States of Perfection. Two years later, he called the First World Congress of Mothers General and suggested updating certain aspects of the sisters' lives so they would be able to respond to the needs of the times. The pope issued two documents on women in religious congregations: *Sponsa Christi* (1950) and *Sacra Virginitatis* (1954). Among the issues considered were the modification of the habit, the abolition of class distinctions that existed among some sisters, and the use of the vernacular in praying the Divine Office.

Pope Pius XII also encouraged the creation of national congresses of heads of religious congregations. In the United States, the Conference of Major Superiors of Women (today, the Leadership Conference of Women Religious, LCWR) was established.

Vatican II: In 1965 the Second Vatican Council issued the Decree on the Appropriate Renewal of the Religious Life (*Perfectae Caritatis*) calling for "two simultaneous processes: a continuous return to the sources of all Christian life and to the original inspiration behind a given community and an adjustment of the community to the changed conditions of the times" (n. 2). The document also provided five principles for this renewal: (1) the fundamental norm of religious life is the gospel; (2) each order's uniqueness is best served by a return to the spirit of the founder; (3) each community should participate in the enterprises and objectives of the Church; (4) members should develop an appropriate awareness of the contemporary human condition as well as the needs of the Church; and (5) interior renewal must inform exterior changes.

The Council of Trent (1545–63) spoke of religious life as superior to marriage. The documents of Vatican II avoid all such language and insist on the universal call to holiness.

After Vatican II: Congregations were founded to answer a particular need in society, but over the years some of those needs have changed as society has changed. In response to the challenges of Vatican II, sisters respond to new needs according to the spirit of the founder rather than simply maintaining the particular works envisioned by the founder. Thus, congregations dedicated to teaching may educate outside the formal school system; hospital sisters have begun to minister in clinics and other noninstitutional ways. Some work in business or government. Many sisters minister on parish and diocesan staffs. Sisters have become involved in justice ministries.

In the years immediately after Vatican II, changes in the habit and life-style, changes in the understanding of community, and the appropriation of new ministries have contributed to a new definition of sisters as well as diminishment in the number of sisters. As numbers decrease and the median age rises, some congregations are uniting with others of similar background and vision.

Taking seriously the model of the Church as the People of God and the challenge of the 1971 Synod of Bishops for "action on behalf of justice and participation in the transformation of the world" as constitutive of the mission of the Church, sisters are more involved in ministries aimed at changing oppressive structures in society. Direct service to the poor and needy is supported by efforts toward the transformation of society. At the same time, congregations of sisters are continuing many of the institutional ministries sponsored by the Church (schools, orphanages, and hospitals). *See also* Decree on the Appropriate Renewal of the Religious Life; religious orders and congregations.

Bibliography

Foley, Nadine, ed. *Claiming Our Truth: Reflections on Identity.* Washington, DC: Leadership Conference of Women Religious, 1988.

Neal, Marie Augusta. *From Nuns to Sisters: An Expanding Vocation.* Mystic, CT: Twenty-third Publications, 1990.   REGINA COLL

Sisters for Christian Community   (S.F.C.C.), founded in 1970 by Lillanna Kopp, one of the largest noncanonical communities of women. As such, the community is not constituted as a juridical person under canon law. It is not subject to any control by the Vatican or the local bishop. The degree of commitment is decided by each individual member within the framework of a profile that presents the scriptural, theological, and historical focus of the community. Their purpose is to provide an experience of communal life, marked by prayer, mutual support, and service to those in need. Each member is self-supporting and responsible for her own living arrangements. There is no presiding officer, motherhouse, rule, or constitution. Most members were once in canonical institutes. There are sisters in the United States, Canada, Australia, Europe, and Central and South America.

Sisters of Charity, a generic term used especially in the United States and England to denote any Catholic sister engaged in works of charity. There are many congregations of Catholic sisters around the world who are called Sisters of Charity. Many originally used some form of the rule of St. Vincent de Paul's Daughters of Charity, which allowed them to go out of their convents to work among the poor and avoid the cloistral prescriptions of traditional religious life for women. Thus there are German congregations of Sisters of Charity of St. Vincent de Paul in Freiburg, Fulda, and Heppenheim, and one in Zams, Austria. Irish and Australian Sisters of Charity stem from a group founded by Mary Aikenhead in Dublin in 1815. There are Belgian groups of Sisters of Charity at Kortemark, Roeselare, Ghent, Namur, and Kortrijd, and a Canadian group in Quebec. Many groups add additional titles after "Sisters of Charity" such as: "and Christian Instruction" (Nevers, France); "of Lovere" (Italy); "of St. Joan Antida" (Rome); "of Ivrea" (Italy); "of St. Augustine" (United States); "of the Blessed Virgin Mary" (United States); "of the Cross" (Canada); "of the Incarnate Word" (United States).

United States: In the United States several groups of Sisters of Charity trace their origin to the first active sisterhood founded in the United States by a U.S. citizen. Elizabeth Bayley Seton (d. 1821), a prominent New York widow and convert, founded these Sisters of Charity in Emmitsburg, Maryland, in 1809. Her community wore the simple black widow's garb and bonnet that Seton wore. She and her mentor, Bishop John Carroll, rejected the constitutions of the French Daughters of Charity of St. Vincent de Paul because they were not suited to the American situation. A modified version of this rule was adopted. The sisters operated schools, orphanages, and hospitals, and nursed in epidemics and wars.

In 1850 the Emmitsburg motherhouse affiliated with the French Daughters of Charity of St. Vincent de Paul. They doffed the simple bonnet to don the elaborate cornette of this community. Their new rules dictated, among other things, that they could not care for male orphans over age five. Many sisters objected to the adoption of French ways, and bishops who needed the sisters to staff orphanages for boys were furious. At this point independent branches of Mother Seton's original Sisters of Charity were established in New York City under Mother Elizabeth Boyle and in Cincinnati, Ohio, under the leadership of Mother Margaret George. This latter group sent missionaries to China in 1928. In 1855 the Sisters of Charity of Halifax, Nova Scotia, Canada, became independent of the New York group. The Sisters of Charity of St. Elizabeth (Convent Station, New Jersey) became independent of the New York group, with help from Cincinnati in 1859 under Mother Mary Xavier Mehegan. The Greensburg, Pennsylvania, Sisters of Charity of Seton Hill became independent of Cincinnati in 1870, lead by Mother Aloysia Lowe. The Sisters of Charity of Nazareth, Kentucky, were founded in 1812 by Father John David, to provide education and works of charity for the people of the area. Mother Catherine Spalding was the first superior general. These sisters have conducted schools, hospitals, orphanages, and other works of charity, including nursing in epidemics and wars. In 1947 they began notable missionary work in India, where there is now a separate Indian province. The Sisters of Charity of Leavenworth, Kansas, branched off from this community and established themselves in Kansas in 1858, under the leadership of Mother Xavier Ross. *See also* Daughters of Charity of St. Vincent de Paul; Seton, St. Elizabeth Ann Bayley; Vincent de Paul, St.   MARY EWENS

Sisters of Holy Cross (C.S.C.), a congregation founded by Father Basil Moreau in Le Mans, France, in 1841, providing graduate education in theology for women when it was not available elsewhere. In 1843 four members came to Indiana, where they established a motherhouse at Notre Dame, Indiana. In 1869 they became independent of the French motherhouse, with Mother Angela Gillespie as the first American superior general. Health care is also an important ministry of the congregation. They nursed in both the American Civil and Spanish-American wars and claim the distinction of being the first U.S. Navy nurses. Mission work was begun in India in 1889. These sisters have also done mission work in Bangladesh, Brazil, Uganda, Ghana, Mexico, and Peru.

Sisters of Loretto at the Foot of the Cross (S.L.), a congregation founded in 1812 by pioneer women of Kentucky—Mary Rhodes, Christina Stuart, and Nancy Havern—with help from Father Charles Nerinckx, a Belgian emigré. He gave the community extremely penitential rules that were later mitigated to suit American conditions. The sisters were notable for opening schools in sparsely settled territories, particularly in the American Southwest. They also provided education and access to Catholic religious life for young African Americans. In 1923 Loretto Sisters became missionaries to China.

Under Sister Mary Luke Tobin, they were leaders among American sisters in the renewal of religious communities and the Church during and after the Second Vatican Council and supporters of the civil rights and peace movements beginning in the 1960s.

Sisters of Mary of the Presentation (S.M.P.), a congregation founded in Broons, France, in 1828 by Mother St. Louis Le Marchand and Father Joachim Fleury to educate people in the faith following the suppressions of the French Revolution and to care for the poor, the sick, and the needy. Mother St. Andre Petitbon, who became superior general in 1838, guided the development of the congregation for forty-eight years. At various times in its history this congregation suffered from the effects of anticlericalism. Sisters were expelled from their schools in the early years of the twentieth century, which caused some to emigrate to Canada and the United States. In 1914, by a decree of dissolution, the sisters were expelled from their motherhouse, and it was turned into a military hospital—at which some of the sisters later nursed. When the decree was revoked in 1923, the sisters returned from their exile on the Isle of Guernsey in the English Channel. In 1956 a mission was begun in Cameroon, Africa. There are about four hundred sisters in the congregation in the 1990s, with provinces in France, Belgium, Canada, and the United States. Health care and education continue to be its chief areas of ministry.

Sisters of Mercy, religious community of women.

Founded in 1831 in Dublin, Ireland, by Catherine McAuley, the Sisters of Mercy are dedicated to the service of the "poor, sick and ignorant," as the original wording of their fourth vow of service indicates. Popularly known as the "walking sisters," the women who gathered around Catherine McAuley nursed the sick poor in their homes, gave shelter to young women harassed by their employers, and engaged in other corporal and spiritual works of mercy as the need arose. Though Catherine herself never intended to establish a religious order, the expectations of the Catholic Church of the day, as well as her desire to give lasting form to the work her associates were doing, led her to do so. Foundation Day, December 12, 1831, marks the day the first Sisters of Mercy took vows of poverty, chastity, and obedience. Mother Catherine McAuley identified as characteristic of the institute "a most serious application to the instruction of poor girls, visitation of the sick, and protection of distressed women of good character."

History: Between 1831 and 1841, the year of her death, Catherine McAuley personally opened twelve of the fourteen original Convents of Mercy. In time, the Sisters of Mercy became the largest group of women religious established in the English-speaking world. Mercy congregations are now found in Ireland, Australia, Great Britain, New Zealand, Newfoundland, South Africa, Philippines, and the Americas.

The Sisters of Mercy came to the United States in 1843. The first American congregation was founded when Sister Frances Warde, with seven companions, traveled to Pittsburgh, Pennsylvania. By 1854, Sisters of Mercy from Ireland had settled in New York, Pittsburgh, and San Francisco and from these cities moved throughout the country. By the end of the Civil War, in which Sisters of Mercy served as nurses for wounded soldiers on both sides of the conflict, the community could be found throughout the Northeast, down the Atlantic seaboard, in the South, the Midwest and along the West Coast. So numerous were the foundations by 1929 that Sister Carmelita Hartman suggested an amalgamation to gather the autonomous houses into a single canonical structure. The move was only partially successful; approximately one half of the Sisters of Mercy in the United States joined the new Sisters of Mercy of the Union, and the others remained independent. Later in the century, however, the desire to be in close communication led to the establishment of a Federation of Sisters of Mercy. That experience made possible a new move toward unity in the 1980s. After a series of community chapters considered a new structure that would unite the Sisters of Mercy in the United States and in the Latin American/Caribbean region, the Sisters of Mercy of the Americas came into existence on July 20, 1991.

In the new institute, there are 25 regional communities with approximately 7,400 sisters in 1994. Through the regional communities, the institute has international partnerships with congregations in Argentina, Belize, Chile, Guam, Guyana, Honduras, Jamaica, Panama, Peru, and the Philippines. Education, health care, social work, and parish service constitute the major forms of serving the "poor, sick and uneducated," as the modern terminology phrases it. The Sisters of Mercy serve in parish schools and eighteen colleges in the United States and Guam. They sponsor more than a hundred health care facilities in more than a hundred cities, as well as operating emergency shelters, food banks, and soup kitchens for the poor. Providing financial support, technical assistance and management expertise is a new form of the original concern for sheltering the homeless. Ministries with battered women and children, pregnant teenagers, persons with AIDS, the chemically dependent, and those in prison continue the work of the "walking sisters." They are joined by more than 1,300 Mercy associates who make annual formal commitments to share in the work of the order while maintaining their lives as clergy, married, or single persons. Others have joined in the works of the Sisters of Mercy through Mercy Corps, a full-time volunteer program. The central office for the Sisters of Mercy of the Americas is located in Silver Spring, Maryland. *See also* McAuley, Catherine; Warde, Frances.

MARY AQUIN O'NEILL

Sisters of Notre Dame de Namur (S.N.D.), a congregation founded in 1803 by Julie Billiart for the education of the poor in Amiens, France. Because innovations in the rule were not acceptable in France, the motherhouse was moved to Namur, Belgium. The congregation spread to the United States in 1840 and to England in 1845. Education at all levels has been the special work of this congregation. Sisters became missionaries to the Congo in 1894, to Rhodesia (now Zimbabwe) in 1899, to Japan in 1924, to China in 1929, and to Italy in 1931. By 1993 these sisters could also be found in Zaire, Brazil, Kenya, Nicaragua, Nigeria, Peru, and Sudan. The generalate is now in Rome.

Sisters of Providence (S.P.), several congregations with this name, including those in France at Alençon, Annonay, Arras, Chartres, Corenc, Douai, Evreux, Langres, Laon, Pommeraye, Lisieux, La Jumelliere, and Gap; at Gosselies in Belgium; and in Amsterdam. One group was founded in Montreal, Canada, in 1843 by Mother Emilie Gamelin. An offshoot in Kingston (Canada) established another group in Holyoke, Massachusetts, that became independent in 1894. In 1856 Mother Joseph Pariseau and four other sisters established an American province in Washington Territory (now Seattle) dedicated to education and health care. Mother Joseph was an intrepid designer and builder of schools, hospitals, and orphanages; her statue stands in the rotunda in the Capitol in Washington, D.C. The congregation began work in Argentina and Chile in 1852, and in Haiti, Cameroon, Egypt, and Nigeria in 1960. The American congregation of Sisters of Providence of St. Mary of the Woods, Indiana, was founded from that of Ruille-sur-Loire in France in 1840, with Mother Theodore Guerin at its head. Education is their chief work.

Sisters of St. Dominic (O.P.), officially the Order of Preachers, apostolic religious communities of women affiliated with the Dominican family founded by Dominic de Guzman (1170–1221) in Prouille, France, in 1206. The Dominican family, with its international headquarters in Rome, is comprised of priests, contemplative nuns, brothers, sisters, and lay members not living in community. Dominic revolutionized religious life by taking it out of secluded monasteries into the newly developed towns and among the people, where he preached the gospel to combat the Albigensian heresy.

"To contemplate and give to others the fruits of one's contemplation" is the goal of these sisters, and "Truth" their motto. Study and contemplation inform and inspire their ministries in schools at all levels, in health care, pastoral, missionary, and social service work. Since Vatican II (1962–65) they have expanded their roles as members of the Order of Preachers to include direct preaching of the gospel. Democracy and the principle of dispensation from rules for the sake of ministry characterize Dominicans. The leader is called "prioress," "first among equals."

Apostolic congregations of Dominican Sisters blossomed in the nineteenth and twentieth centuries, when contemplative groups established new foundations in North America, Australia, South America, and Africa, where conditions forced them to develop into active communities. Thus, for example, Holy Cross Convent in Regensburg, Bavaria, with fewer than fifty members itself, sent groups to the United States, which eventually developed twelve different congregations with thousands of members. Congregations such as these struggled to find a balance between practices of the contemplative life, such as rising at midnight to recite the Divine Office, and the demands of teaching and nursing. The number of congregations changes as groups merge or separate, but in 1991, a total of 148 women's congregations were affiliated with the Dominican family in Europe, Asia, Africa, North and South America, Australia, and New Zealand. At that time, there were thirty-six congregations in the United States, with 10,205 members. *See also* Dominican order.

MARY EWENS

Sisters of St. Joseph (S.S.J.), congregations of women religious within the Catholic Church who trace their origin to LePuy, France, where they were founded originally as a single community in the mid-seventeenth century. There, several women, inspired by Father Jean Pierre Médaille's preaching, assembled to live in community and to profess simple vows. On March 10, 1661, Bishop Henri de Maupas du Tour granted official approbation to the Sisters of St. Joseph, then composed of Francoise Eyraud and five companions. Father Médaille prepared *Constitutions, Reglements and Maxims of Perfection* for their guidance. Dedicated to the Holy Trinity, the sisters were encouraged to acquire personal perfection and to assist their neighbors by all the works of mercy of which women are capable. Membership was open to all classes of women. Living in small communities, the sisters ministered in hospitals and reformatories, conducted schools, and taught catechism and a trade to young women. Each autonomous motherhouse maintained a novitiate for the formation of new members. Bishops and pastors in south central France sought the presence and service of the sisters and thus contributed to the spread of the congregation.

The French Revolution of 1789 disrupted religious life by anticlerical decrees. Forced to leave their convents in 1792, the sisters returned to their families. Some were imprisoned and five Sisters of St. Joseph were martyred in 1794. After Napoleon's Concordat of 1801 women's congregations were gradually restored. In 1807 Cardinal Joseph Fesch, archbishop of Lyons, summoned Mother St. John

Fontbonne, a Sister of St. Joseph, to direct some women desirous of becoming religious. Having entered the community in LePuy in 1778, she had become superior at Monistrol from 1785 to 1792. After that she had lived with her family except during her imprisonment in 1794. The women whom she trained in the spirit of the Sisters of St. Joseph received the habit on July 14, 1808. This date marks the restoration of the congregation at Lyons. Here and at other centers, including LePuy, sisters worked to meet the pressing religious, educational, and social needs of the people. The congregation spread within France and beyond. By 1900 the Sisters of St. Joseph had missions in the United States, Canada, India, Italy, Denmark, Norway, Sweden, Russia, Iceland, Armenia, Algeria, Argentina, and Brazil.

United States: In the United States the apostolic needs of the growing Catholic population caused bishops to seek financial support and religious personnel from agencies and congregations in Europe. Bishop Joseph Rosati of St. Louis, Missouri, appealed to the Society of the Propagation of the Faith at Lyons and to Mother St. John Fontbonne. She appointed six sisters, including her nieces, Sister Delphine Fontbonne and Sister Febronie Fontbonne, to go to America. Bishop Rosati welcomed these pioneer sisters on March 25, 1836. With few exceptions, the present twenty-nine congregations in North America have originated, either directly or indirectly, from this initial establishment at St. Louis. For instance, sisters sent to Philadelphia in 1847 later made foundations at Toronto in 1851 and at Brooklyn in 1856. These motherhouses, in turn, responded to requests for sisters. Brooklyn sent sisters to Baden, Pennsylvania, in 1869, to Rutland, Vermont, and Boston, Massachusetts, in 1873, and to Springfield, Massachusetts, in 1883. Education on all levels, instruction of the deaf, and health care became the characteristic ministries of the Sisters of St. Joseph. Their increase in membership, geographic expansion, and mission activities reflected developments in Church and society. Empowered by their educational attainments, influenced by the Sister Formation Movement of the 1950s, and called to renewal of religious life by the Second Vatican Council (1962–65), the Sisters of St. Joseph in the United States and throughout the world examined the spiritual, communal, and ministerial aspects of their lives. Research into their history and the founder's original inspiration was facilitated by federations established in Canada and the United

States in 1966 and in collaboration with the French Federation, an organization of individual congregations. Translations of Father Médaille's documents and renewed awareness of their charism assisted renewal among the sisters. Through general chapters and revised constitutions, the Sisters of St. Joseph have reaffirmed their vocation "to serve God and their neighbors without distinction" and to become "the congregation of the great love of God and neighbor." While many sisters continue in educational and health-related service, others engage in religious and adult education, pastoral ministry, social service, and advocacy for women and children. The sisters serve in Japan, Australia, Papua New Guinea, Hawaii, Kenya, Puerto Rico, Nassau, Guatemala, and Peru. *See also* Joseph, St.; religious orders and congregations.

MARGARET QUINN

Sisters of the Holy Names of Jesus and Mary (S.N.J.M.), an order of nuns canonically established in 1843 in Quebec, Canada, for the education of children and young women. Eulalie Durocher, later known as Mother Marie-Rose, adapted the Marseilles S.N.J.M. rule to the situation in Canada to better respond to unmet needs in the Church and society. She became the order's first superior. Sisters came to the United States in 1859. They conduct elementary schools, high schools, and colleges emphasizing education in the faith, spiritual growth, and Catholic social justice principles. In South Africa, they conduct schools and dispensaries. *See also* Durocher, St. Marie-Rose.

Sisters, Servants of the Immaculate Heart of Mary (I.H.M.), an order of nuns founded in 1845 in Monroe, Michigan, by Louis Florent Gillet, C.SS.R., and Mother Teresa Maxis Duchemin in the spirit of Alphonsus Liguori (d. 1787), Italian founder of the Redemptorists. Originally founded for education and health ministry, today they are also engaged in pastoral ministries, campus ministry, and social service. In 1978, they initiated a program for associate members. The sisters serve in about fifty dioceses in the United States and in Central and South America, the West Indies, and Africa. The motherhouse is in Monroe, Michigan. *See also* Alphonsus Liguori, St.

Sistine Chapel, named for Pope Sixtus IV (d. 1484), the principal chapel of the Vatican palace in Rome. Famous for its frescoed walls by various

The Sistine Chapel in Vatican City, known for its frescoes by Michelangelo, especially his *Last Judgment*, which covers the wall behind the altar; the chapel is used by cardinals for the election of a new pope.

artists (including Botticelli), the Sistine Chapel is best known for the ceiling and altar wall painted by Michelangelo, the ceiling showing scenes from the book of Genesis (including the famous *Birth of Adam*) and the altar wall depicting the Last Judgment. Many papal ceremonies are conducted in the chapel, but the most famous is the gathering of cardinals in consistory when they meet to elect a new pope.

Recently cleaned and restored, Michelangelo's frescos are considered to be the epitome of High Renaissance art of the sixteenth century. The chapel is accessible through the Vatican museum and attracts thousands of visitors each year. *See also* Michelangelo; Sixtus IV; Vatican.

situation ethics, a system of ethics in which acts are judged according to their contexts rather than by a set of absolute principles. Sometimes called "contextual ethics" or "the new morality," situation ethics refers more to certain general philosophical tendencies than to a coherent moral theory. In a broad sense, all ethics can be called situational because circumstances do make a moral difference. Aristotle and Aquinas claimed as much. Although situation ethics takes many forms, three tenets distinguish it from other approaches: (1) the loving intention has priority over law; (2) a preexisting objective moral order that yields concrete absolute norms rendering some actions intrinsically wrong in every situation is questionable; and (3) moral principles find significance only in the situation and not in an abstract, fixed human nature.

The philosophical roots of situation ethics lie in nominalism and existentialism. Historically, situation ethics grew out of the collapse of the post–World War II social world in Germany and France where people were becoming aware of historical change and were left free and fully responsible for their decisions. In that context, it endorsed the actualizing of human freedom and the interpreting of laws in relation to human needs rather than to abstract human nature.

Pope Pius XII in 1952 and again in 1956 condemned any version of situation ethics that rejected an objective moral order, and that claimed that moral decisions have their ultimate foundation in an individualistic and subjective appeal to immediate intuitive judgments based on the situation but not on any universal, objective moral law, either natural law or God's revealed law.

Situation ethics became popular in the United States with Joseph Fletcher's *Situation Ethics* (1966). His method falls between antinomianism and legalism. It has three characteristics: (1) love is the only universally binding principle and is served by the principle of utility, that is, the greatest good for the greatest number; (2) other moral principles illumine moral obligation but do not prescribe an absolute and universal obligation; and (3) the absolute moral obligation (God's will, or what love demands) arises from within the situation and is not subject to abstract law. Thus, Fletcher's method demands that each person discover the most loving deed by calculating its consequences in the situation. The moral quality of the deed derives from maximizing love.

Situation ethics has been criticized for setting love in opposition to rules, and for being naive about human ability to control consequences. It does not adequately appreciate the role of principles and is vulnerable to the dangers of self-deception. Actions and situations are sufficiently similar and continuous to warrant a prescriptive use of principles.

Yet the discussion of situation ethics has directed attention to neglected aspects of decision making. It has forced a clearer refinement of the relationships of love, law, and freedom and the relationship of context to principles. It has taught that decision making is more than the reasoned application of objective norms, but that is also includes some form of intuitive judgment or moral instinct. It has also shown that objectivity in morality means that moral standards must be based on the way things are, and not on the way we would like things to be. It has led Catholic morality to rethink basic concepts of natural law and to include the discernment of spirits in the process of making decisions. It has also given rise to further considerations regarding the binding force of magisterial teaching on moral matters, on the debates between deontological versus teleological methods, and between holding firm to exceptionless concrete moral absolutes versus proportional moral judgments. *See also* magisterium and morality; moral theology; natural law.

RICHARD M. GULA

Sixto-Clementine Vulgate. *See* Scripture, versions of.

Sixtus II, St., d. 258, pope from 257 to 258. He restored relations with Cyprian, broken by his predecessor, Stephen I, yet continued the Roman practice of not rebaptizing those baptized by heretics. Given Sixtus's less confrontational style, he apparently accepted the coexistence of both practices. Martyred under Valerian, he was highly venerated. His name is in the Canon of the Roman Mass. Feast day: August 6. *See also* lapsi.

Sixtus IV [Francesco della Rovere], 1414–84, Franciscan pope from 1471 to 1484. He transformed Rome from a medieval to a Renaissance city through a number of physical improvements. He built the Sistine Chapel, founded the Sistine choir, established the Vatican archives, and enriched the Vatican library. His priorities as pope, however, seemed to be focused on the Papal States and the advancement of his own family. His brother Girolamo drew the pope into the Pazzi conspiracy of 1478 in which two members of the Medici family, Lorenzo and Giuliano, were attacked (Lorenzo was wounded, Giuliano was killed), apparently with the pope's knowledge. This drew the pope, in turn, into a politically and financially debilitating war with Florence (1478–80), the power base of the Medici family. *See also* Sistine Chapel.

Sixtus V [Felice Peretti], 1520–90, Counter-

Reformation Franciscan pope, from 1585 to 1590. As pope, Sixtus strictly enforced the disciplinary demands of the Council of Trent, especially against simony, strengthened and expanded both the Inquisition and censorship, and supported overseas missions. He fixed the maximum number of cardinals at seventy (not exceeded until Pope John XXIII, 1958–63), reorganized the Roman Curia (not changed until Vatican Council II, 1962–65), and required all bishops to visit the Holy See at least every five years and to submit reports on the state of their dioceses (the *ad limina* visit). Through ambitious building projects, he transformed Rome into a magnificent Baroque city. He rebuilt the Lateran palace and completed the dome of St. Peter's. He also established the Vatican press.

skete (skeet; Gk., "small monastery"), a small monastery, generally the dependency of a lavra or large independent house.

slander, the violation of another's reputation by false accusation. Slander differs from detraction, which harms the good esteem of another by revealing true but hidden faults. Slander is also distinct from libel in that it is defamation in spoken words rather than in writing. It is practically indistinguishable from calumny.

Slander adds the sin of lying to that of injustice. Its seriousness is measured by the harm done, and this harm is determined by the character and position of the slanderer and the slandered. Slander generates the duty of restitution. *See also* calumny; detraction.

slavery, the possession of persons as property for the purpose of unrecompensed use of their labor. Because slavery was an integral part of the social system at the time when Christ lived, the practice was largely unchallenged by the early Christians. The NT treats slavery primarily from a religious rather than a social perspective, preaching the elimination of distinctions before God between master and slave (Gal 3:28; 1 Cor 12:13; Philemon).

For many centuries Catholic theologians did not question the morality of slavery. Some, like Leonhard Lessius (d. 1623) and John de Lugo (d. 1660), justified slavery if it arose out of birth or a contract, or in punishment for a crime or as the result of a just war. However, their fellow Jesuits were among the strongest opponents of slavery in the mission territories of South America. In Paraguay they established a model colony without slaves before being expelled in 1768. Pope Gregory XVI's widely cited condemnation of the slave trade (1839) was interpreted by bishops in the southern United States as referring to the transatlantic slave trade. If it can be said that Catholicism was slow and relatively late in its rejection of slavery, it is clear today that Catholic teaching condemns slavery as a direct violation of both the gospel and the natural law.

Slipyj, Josyf (joh'sif slip'ee), 1892–1984, metropolitan of Halych and archbishop of Lviv. He was ordained a priest in 1917, was rector of Theological Academy, was ordained bishop-coadjutor to Andrew Sheptyckyj in 1939, under Soviet rule, and became Sheptyckyj's successor in 1944. In 1945 he was arrested; freed in 1963, he had to leave the Soviet Union. He was named cardinal in 1965.

sloth. *See* capital sins.

Slovak Byzantine Catholic Church, a Byzantine Catholic community located in present-day Slovakia arising from the Union of Uzhorod (1646). It has had a separate identity since 1818, when the diocese of Presov was created for the area, then a part of Hungary.

Slovakia became part of the republic of Czechoslovakia after World War I. (In 1992 the republic split into the Czech Republic and Slovakia.) In April 1950, under pressure from the new Communist government, the church was dissolved and incorporated into the Orthodox Church. But most of the former Byzantine Catholic parishes opted to become Catholic again when conditions permitted during the 1968 "Prague Spring."

The Presov diocese in 1993 had about 363,000 faithful. The Canadian diocese of Sts. Cyril and Methodius, with 30,000 members, is the only jurisdiction of the church outside of Slovakia. *See also* Byzantine rite; Eastern churches; Eastern rites; Ruthenian Catholic Church.

Smith, Alfred E., 1873–1944, first Catholic candidate for president of the United States. Born and raised in New York City, he became a major figure in New York State politics. He served as governor of New York for four terms in the 1920s and in 1928 became the first Catholic to be nominated by a major party for the presidency of the United States. His candidacy as the Democratic party nominee inspired a national debate on the compatibility of Ca-

tholicism and American democracy. The Republican party nominee, Herbert Hoover, easily defeated Smith after a campaign marked by considerable anti-Catholic bigotry. *See also* anti-Catholicism.

Snows, Our Lady of the. *See* Our Lady of the Snows.

sobornost (soh-bohr'nawst; Russ., *sobornaja,* "catholic"), Russian theological neologism that defines an ideal of ecclesiology that is conciliar and collegial (Russ., *sobirat',* "to gather, congregate" from which is derived Russ., *sobor,* "cathedral," or Gk., *katholikon*) based on an interior spiritual communion of freedom and love. Apparently coined by the Russian Orthodox Slavophile and lay theologian Alexis S. Khomyakov (1806–60), the term is untranslatable, which is why it has entered other languages. *Sobornost* is claimed to be characteristic of Orthodox ecclesiology, and to provide a *via media* (Lat., "middle way") between the two Western extremes of excessive individualism (Protestantism) and the legalism of an ecclesial communion based on external authority (Catholicism). This claim is only partly true. In the Orthodox communion of national churches, often in disarray and conflict with one another, *sobornost* exists more in theory than in practice. *See also* communion, Church as.

Sobrino, Jon, b. 1938, Jesuit theologian of El Salvador. Born in Barcelona, Spain, and ordained a Jesuit priest, he was awarded a doctorate in theology at the Hochschule Sankt Georgen in Frankfurt am Main, Germany (1975). He is professor of theology at the Universidad José Siméon Cañas of Central America in San Salvador and a leading figure in Latin American liberation theology. *See also* liberation theology.

social action movement, a general term describing the coordinated effort of Catholics, especially laity, to effect a greater measure of justice in society. Leo XIII (d. 1903) and the twentieth-century popes have taught that social reconstruction requires not only the reform of morals but also the reform of social institutions. They have urged Catholics to organize in social action groups to achieve institutional change, especially regarding the distribution of wealth, the rights of labor, human rights, and world peace. *See also* Catholic social teachings.

social encyclicals. *See* encyclicals, social.

social gospel, a movement among American Protestants in the late nineteenth and early twentieth centuries that interpreted salvation as a process of social and economic transformation. In response to the social problems of modern industrial life and *laissez-faire* capitalism, advocates stressed the Bible's prophetic call for justice and the teachings of Jesus Christ. They believed Christ had proclaimed the kingdom of God on earth in order to create a society of love, justice, and cooperation. They often joined forces with labor and other social movements. The social gospel movement as such had little direct impact on Catholicism, but Catholics have responded in analogous ways to modern social problems.

socialism, a politicoeconomic system based on common ownership (or centralized regulation) of productive economic resources. Adam Smith (d. 1790) thought that if the regulation of the national economy were left to the free market (Fr., *laissez-faire*), reasonable demands would be met at the lowest possible prices.

Although industrial free market capitalism proved immensely productive, it was also subject to cycles of inflation and unemployment, widening the gap between rich and poor. Hence, before 1848 many "utopian socialist" schemes were proposed by reformers, to be instituted simply through education and the example of successful models. Socialism took a political, revolutionary turn with Marx and Engels' *Communist Manifesto* (1848). This "scientific socialism" claimed to prove that the demise of capitalism through class struggle was inevitable.

In the 1990s, Socialist or Social Democratic parties still advocate centralized economic control and state ownership of large industries, to be achieved through nonviolent political action. Yet, against the resistance of free market ideologists, many socialist reforms have already been incorporated into modern capitalism.

Catholic social doctrine, as expressed, for example, in Pope John Paul II's 1991 encyclical *Centesimus Annus,* defends private property, but also demands that the state regulate the economy to achieve social justice. Sometimes this is called "Christian socialism." *See also* Catholic social teachings.

social justice, virtue pertaining to the structural requirements for a just society focused on the human rights and needs of each person. The paradox of the concept of social justice is the major role it has in the Church's life and ministry contrasted with its recent appearance in Catholic teaching. The paradox is resolved when its is understood that the idea of social justice has an ancient lineage in the Catholic tradition, but its precise designation is found in Pius XI's encyclical *Quadragesimo Anno* (1931).

Catholic Teaching Before 1931: Catholic teaching on justice prior to *Quadragesimo Anno* was shaped by two major influences. On the one hand, biblical conceptions of justice, especially as they are found in the teaching of the prophets, served as a point of reference for Church teaching on justice. The biblical influence, however, was not a dominant theme of social teaching. It held a secondary role to the natural law ethic through which the Church expressed its teaching on the political, economic, and international orders. This second source of moral wisdom, the natural law ethic, found its classical exposition in Thomas Aquinas (d. 1274). Aquinas developed his theory of justice by drawing directly from Aristotle (d. 322 B.C.), as well as the insights of the Stoics and the Scriptures.

The clear link between Aristotle and Aquinas is the basic understanding of justice as *suum cuique* (Lat.), giving each his due, and the elaboration of this highly formal notion through the three types of justice: commutative, distributive, and legal justice. In the development of a theory of justice, Catholic teaching identified it as the proximate norm to govern all social relationships. The three types of justice are distinguished by the relationships they govern in society.

Types of Justice: Commutative justice sets standards for social and economic relationships between individuals. Often the model implied in commutative justice is that of a contractual relationship involving a private transaction. The standards of commutative justice are rooted in Catholic thought in the principle that every human person shares equal dignity and is invested with equal rights. The relations between such persons are conceived in terms of strict equality, a standard Aristotle described as arithmetical proportion. The moral conviction supporting commutative justice is that duties can be precisely defined and that failure to fulfill one's precise obligation requires restitution to the party who has been harmed.

Distributive justice governs public relationships in society; more precisely, it is the standard that measures the fair allocation of benefits and burdens to individuals and groups in society. The relationship envisioned by distributive justice is too complex to admit of arithmetical precision. Distributive justice envisions individuals as citizens and seeks to determine what access to public goods each citizen needs and deserves to protect his personal dignity. The state's role in guaranteeing a fair distribution of benefits and burdens, e.g., through taxation and social programs, is a major aspect of distributive justice, but it does not exhaust the category.

For Aquinas, legal justice, sometimes called "general justice", is the broader objective norm within which the demands of "particular justice," i.e., commutative and distributive justice, are determined. Legal or general justice, in the Thomistic scheme, directed the action of citizens toward the common good. It also served to relate the virtue of justice to other virtues exercised in society. These other virtues are directed to the common good by legal justice. The notion of legal or "general justice" thus fulfilled a broad regulative function in society; its content was never as precisely defined as the two forms of "particular justice."

Catholic Teaching After 1931: The decisive contribution of Pope Pius XI to Catholic teaching on justice was the way in which he replaced the idea of legal justice with that of social justice. The development occurs in *Quadragesimo Anno* and it is a good illustration of the way in which social science influenced Catholic moral teaching in the twentieth century. Pius XI's encyclical demonstrated a much clearer grasp of the structured, institutional character of modern society than earlier Catholic teaching had shown. Building upon this understanding, Pius XI took over the notion of legal justice, i.e., its focus on the common good, and then focused social justice on the assessment of the structural organization of society. The fruit of these two notions is that social justice is designed to evaluate and redirect those public institutions of society that hinder the achievement of the common good. Just as commutative justice is focused on the contractual relationship between individuals, so social justice is focused on the functioning of major public institutions of the social, legal, economic, or political orders.

The function of social justice is to evaluate the essential institutions of society in terms of their ability to satisfy the minimum needs and basic rights of the citizenry. Because social justice is directed to the achievement of the common good, the obligation to

pursue it falls, in different ways, upon all in society: the state, voluntary associations, business and professional groups, religious and cultural organizations, and citizens themselves. It is usually expected that social justice will be accomplished through organized activity rather than individual actions.

From the publication of *Quadragesimo Anno,* the term "social justice" has assumed a central role in the development of Catholic social teaching. While retaining the specific demands of commutative and distributive justice, the emphasis in papal teaching is directed by the concept of social justice. The character of the teaching stresses the need to shape the institutional patterns of social life in accord with the demands of justice so that commutative and distributive justice may be more easily fulfilled. Pius XI had focused his teaching on economic justice within a nation; his successors placed growing emphasis on the structure of international society, e.g., in *Pacem in Terris* (1963), *Populorum Progressio* (1967), and *Centesimus Annus* (1991). The Third International Synod of Bishops (1971) referred to the concept of "international social justice." Pope John Paul II in his encyclicals *Redemptor Hominis* (1979), *Sollicitudo Rei Socialis* (1987), and *Centesimus Annus* has criticized the trading and financial institutions of the international economy as failing to provide an adequate distribution of goods and services for developing countries.

The demand of social justice in contemporary Catholic social teaching is to reform those institutions at the national level that do not meet the needs of the national common good and to create new institutions at the international level that will be directed toward the emerging needs of the international common good.

The scope of social justice is determined today by both the increasing complexity of domestic societies and the increasing demands of the international common good. The other major influence on the Church's teaching since Vatican II has been the systematic use of biblical perspectives to shape the understanding of social justice. The biblical categories are less precise and less analytical than the teaching of Aquinas and the earlier encyclicals, but they add a power and passion the philosophical categories do not possess.

The influence of the teaching on social justice may best be assessed in light of the fact that the entire social ministry of the Church is today often described simply as the work of social justice. *See also* Catholic social teachings; justice.

Bibliography

Calvez, J. Y., and J. Perrin. *The Church and Social Justice: The Social Teaching of the Popes from Leo XIII to Pius XII (1878–1958)*. Chicago: Henry Regnery, 1961.

Hollenbach, D. *Claims in Conflict: Retrieving and Renewing the Catholic Human Rights Tradition*. New York: Paulist Press, 1979.

J. BRYAN HEHIR

social ministry, also called justice ministry, service that aims to alleviate human suffering by working to transform those structures that cause or promote oppression, poverty, war, racism, or sexism. *See also* ministry.

social sciences. *See* Catholicism and the social sciences.

social teachings. *See* Catholic social teachings.

society of apostolic life, a group whose members live together in common to pursue some apostolic end, but who do not take religious vows. A society of apostolic life may be very similar to a religious community and may be subject to many of the same norms as religious communities.

Society of Jesus. *See* Jesuits.

Society of Missionaries of Africa. *See* White Fathers.

Society of St. Peter. *See* Fraternity of St. Peter, Priestly.

Society of St. Vincent de Paul, religious congregation founded in Paris by Frederic Ozanam in 1833. Ozanam, a layman, was deeply moved by the poverty and disorder that gripped Paris in the early stages of industrialization. With a desire to blunt the efforts of the Saint-Simonians (followers of the French socialist Claude Saint-Simon, 1760–1825), he and his companions formed a Catholic organization of laypersons devoted to individual holiness, personal contact with the poor, and the distribution of alms. The new group took Vincent de Paul as its patron saint and was organized into conferences on local levels. Eventually diocesan, national, and international councils formed the framework for broader cooperative endeavors. As urban poverty and social dislocation spread throughout Western society, the need for the work of the Society grew. It expanded rapidly in France and in 1845 made its first appearance in the United States in St. Louis. It eventually spread to 112 countries.

Vincentians, as the members are called, devote themselves not only to personal contact with the poor, but to the creation of institutions to care for the needy, such as orphanages and hospitals. More commonly, the Vincentians' used-clothing and furniture stores are found in many American cities. *See also* Vincent de Paul, St.; Vincentians.

Society of the Divine Word (S.V.D.), a clerically exempt society, independent of the local bishop, whose members take the evangelical vows of poverty, chastity, and obedience, founded in 1875 by Arnold Janssen in Holland and approved by the Vatican in 1905. Members include both priests and brothers.

The main work of the society is evangelizing in non-Christian areas. To this end, they are involved in education on all levels and the publication of magazines and pamphlets. Emphasis is placed on the education of native clergy. In the United States, their ministry includes work among African-Americans.

The generalate is located in Rome and the American headquarters is in Techny, Illinois.

Society of the Sacred Heart (R.S.C.J.), formerly known as the Madams of the Sacred Heart, a community of sisters devoted to religious and academic education. Founded in France by Madeleine Sophie Barat (d. 1865) in 1800 for the education of girls, the community established itself in the United States in 1818 devoting itself for many decades to educating the daughters of the wealthy. It is engaged today in religious and academic education in parishes and schools, and is also involved in social and health care ministries. In 1994 there were about six hundred sisters in the United States. *See also* Barat, St. Madeleine Sophie.

sociobiology, the scientific study of the biological basis of social behavior. Sociobiology studies the evolutionary basis of prosocial behavior, e.g., cooperation, reciprocity, and altruism, as well as antisocial behavior, e.g., aggression and bias against groups other than one's own. Sociobiology (also called "neo-Darwinism") focuses attention on ways in which specific traits (e.g., incest avoidance) bestow adaptive advantages on their organisms, whose reproductive success in turn promotes the continuation of the species. Human sociobiology tends to depreciate the spiritual dimension of human beings as well as human freedom.

Sociobiological accounts of the place of human beings in nature raise questions for Catholic theology in several areas, including the doctrines of providence, creation, and the *imago Dei* (the human person as the image of God). Theories of "kin altruism" (doing good for one's own relatives) and "reciprocal altruism" (doing good for those who have done good to oneself) pertain to the natural bases of neighbor love and justice. The adaptive significance of morality, territoriality, loyalty to one's own group, homosexuality, and sexual promiscuity provide interesting, if not determinative, evidence relevant to moral norms.

Socrates "Scholasticus," ca. 380–450, ecclesiastical historian. Socrates intended his *Historia Ecclesiastica* (Lat., "Ecclesiastical History") to continue the work of Eusebius, chronicling events from 306 to 439. Both the Arian controversy and the Novatianist sect are addressed in some detail. The writings of church leaders in the East, official ecclesiastical and imperial documents, and oral testimony served as his sources. *See also* Arianism; Novatianism.

sodality, an association of Catholics to promote the spiritual life of its members, apostolic works of evangelization, and aid to those in need (see can. 298). Jesuit John Leunis organized the first sodality in Rome (1563). Sodalities, under the patronage of the Blessed Mother, offered Catholic men a well-defined program for spiritual formation, prayer, and Christian service. During the nineteenth century, sodalities in the United States served as a basic parish organization for both women and men. The sodality's monthly meeting emphasized Marian devotions, frequent Communion, and social action. In the twentieth century, Jesuit Daniel S. Lord, editor of the *Queen's Work,* the movement's publication, promoted the development of sodalities throughout the nation. In 1931, Lord instituted the Summer Schools of Catholic Action. These sessions, attended by Catholic youth, consisted of intensive prayer, lectures, and social activities. In 1956, the U.S. bishops approved the formation of the U.S. National Federation of Sodalities. Pope Paul VI promulgated revised norms for these sodalities in 1971, and their name was changed from Sodalities of Our Lady to Christian Life Communities. Although the *Spiritual Exercises* of Ignatius of Loyola remains the specific source of the movement's spiritual life, the emphasis in the post–Vatican II years (after 1965) has been on Scripture, liturgy, and ecumenism rather than on personal piety, as in the preconciliar period.

Soisson, councils of, several Church councils or synods held at Soisson, France, during the late eleventh and early twelfth centuries. Only two of these councils are considered significant; both concern trinitarian doctrine. In 1092 the nominalist Roscelin of Compiègne was condemned for tritheism. In 1121 Peter Abelard, Roscelin's pupil and opponent of nominalism, was condemned for Sabellianism and forced to burn his book *On the Divine Unity and Trinity. See also* Trinity, doctrine of the.

sola fide (soh'lah fee'day; Lat., "by faith alone"), a Reformation principle that justification by God in Christ comes from "faith alone" and cannot be earned, or "merited," by good works. Catholic doctrine insists that, while faith is indeed the beginning of salvation, faith must issue in good works and those good works are meritorious of salvation to the extent that they are expressions of faith. *See also* faith.

sola gratia (soh'lah grah'ztee-ah; Lat., "grace alone"), the Reformation principle that we are saved by "grace alone," that is, by God's action and not at all by our own. Catholic doctrine insists that God requires our free cooperation, although it is God alone who makes that cooperation possible. *See also* grace.

sola Scriptura (soh'lah skrip-toor'ah; Lat., "Scripture alone"), a foundational principle of Protestantism that Scripture as God's word mediates faith and is the final arbiter of theology. Other correlative authorities such as tradition, reason, and experience are not independent sources of revelation but assist in the interpretation of Scripture. Catholic doctrine insists that the Bible is itself the Church's book and that all official teachings are subject to its authority. However, the task of "authentically interpreting the word of God . . . has been entrusted exclusively to the living teaching office of the Church" (Dogmatic Constitution on Divine Revelation, n. 10). *See also* Scripture, authority of.

solea (soh-lay'ah; Gk.), that part of the raised sanctuary platform in front of the iconostasis (sanctuary screen covered with icons) in Byzantine-rite churches. The term originally referred to the enclosed processional pathway that led from the sanctuary chancel to the ambo (pulpit) in early Constantinopolitan churches in the fourth through sixth centuries.

Solemn Blessing, part of the concluding rite at Mass, the Liturgy of the Hours, the Liturgy of the Word, and other sacramental rites that may expand the presider's simple blessing over the assembly. The Roman Missal offers twenty solemn blessings, with additional texts for specific solemnities, feasts, and seasons. The deacon (or in his absence, the priest) invites the people to bow their heads and pray for God's blessing. With hands extended, the presider prays a threefold invocation, to which the assembly responds "Amen." The usual blessing in the name of the Trinity follows. *See also* blessing.

Solemn High Mass (Lat., *Missa Solemnis*), the third and most solemn form of the Tridentine Mass (excepting the Pontifical High Mass, which is a Solemn High Mass celebrated in the presence of a bishop). The Tridentine Mass was the Latin-rite Mass in general use by the Roman Catholic Church from the Council of Trent (1545–63) until the Second Vatican Council (1962–65). The Solemn High Mass, like the High Mass, was chanted from beginning to end. It was marked by a proliferation of ministers and assistants, notably by the mandatory deacon and subdeacon, who were often priests vested in dalmatic (the outer vestment of the deacon) or tunic (the outer vestment of the subdeacon). During the Solemn High Mass, incense was used and special ceremonies were added, such as the Asperges (the sprinkling of the people with holy water) and the Gospel procession. With the revision of the Mass in 1969, the tripartite ranking of ceremonial elaboration has been abandoned to the more flexible principle of "progressive solemnization," the idea that the Mass might be progressively solemnized according to the relative importance of its various portions. *See also* High Mass; Low Mass; Mass.

solemnity (soh-lem'ni-tee), a principal day with the highest rank in the liturgical calendar. A solemnity eclipses all other feasts or memorials. Its observance begins with Evening Prayer I, or First Vespers, on the evening of the preceding day. Some solemnities have their own vigil Mass. All Sundays throughout the year are solemnities. Easter and Christmas are the two greatest solemnities, with Easter being the Sunday of Sundays. Principal days of local significance may be raised from a memorial or feast to a solemnity in regions, dioceses, or religious institutes. *See also* feasts, liturgical; memorial.

Solemnity of Mary, the most important liturgical celebration honoring the Blessed Virgin Mary in the Catholic Church: the Immaculate Conception (December 8); Mary, Mother of God (January 1); the Annunciation of the Lord (March 25); and the Assumption of Mary (August 15). In addition to the solemnities, the liturgical calendar dedicates three feasts, five memorials, and four optional memorials to Mary. *See also* liturgical calendar.

Solesmes (soh-lem'), Benedictine abbey of Solesmes, France. Founded as a priory in 1010, it remained so until 1791. Dom Prosper Guéranger (d. 1875) refounded the monastery in 1833. Because of Guéranger's efforts at liturgical renewal, Solesmes became foremost among centers for the research and revival of Gregorian chant. Its roster of chant scholars boasts a continuing legacy: Canon Augustin Gontier (d. 1881), Dom Paul Jausions (d. 1870), Dom Joseph Pothier (d. 1923), Dom André Mocquereau (d. 1930), Dom Joseph Gajard (d. 1972), Dom Jean Claire (choirmaster since 1971). More than simply its chant scholars, Solesmes produced the first and many subsequent typical editions of the Kyriale (containing the chants for the ordinary

Solesmes, famous eleventh-century French Benedictine monastery that contributed significantly to liturgical renewal in the twentieth century, especially the renewal of liturgical music.

prayers of the Mass), Graduale (containing the Gradual prayers), Antiphonal (containing the chants for the antiphons), and the Graduale Triplex. Gregorian scholarship continues at Solesmes with inquiries into Gregorian semiology, rhythm, and the origins of the Western modal system. *See also* chant, Gregorian; Guéranger, Prosper.

solitude. *See* desert.

Sollicitudo Rei Socialis (soh-lis-ee-too′doh ray′ee soh-shee-al′uhs), "On the Social Concern [of the Church]," social encyclical issued in 1988 by Pope John Paul II. The document celebrates the twentieth anniversary of Pope Paul VI's encyclical, *Populorum Progressio.* John Paul assesses the originality of Paul VI's encyclical, which includes the latter's recognition of the spiritual and cultural dimensions of international development and its linkage of peace with economic justice. Then, *Sollicitudo* analyzes the present conditions of the international economy. Pope Paul's hope for development remains unfulfilled. The gap between rich and poor is widening, and this is due in large part to the East-West superpower rivalry that diverts human energy and resources from meeting basic human needs. The institutions that structure the rivalry are "structures of sin" driven by the desire for profit and the thirst for power. John Paul II also extends Paul's concern for the environment. *Populorum Progressio* is the first encyclical to accent the limits of the earth's natural resources. *Sollicitudo* picks up this point and makes it a key theme.

To respond to these problems, John Paul II sets out guidelines for ecclesial and social action, though he is careful to point out that he is not advocating a third ideology alongside capitalism and socialism. Rather, the guidelines reflect theologically-based criteria for reflection. The main guideline is the "option for the poor." This option arises out of the fact that the goods of the world are intended for all persons. Righting the present imbalance regarding access to the goods of the world requires giving the poor priority in policy and action. *See also* Catholic social teachings; encyclicals, social.   TODD D. WHITMORE

Solomon, David's son and successor (ca. 961–922 B.C.). He was one of David's younger sons yet he became a candidate for the throne and, through his mother's intrigues, obtained it. The Lord granted him wisdom, riches, and other gifts when he asked for understanding (1 Kgs 3). He built and dedicated

Solomon renders his most famous judgment in the dispute between two women who claim to be the mother of the same child (shown lying on the ground). When he orders that the baby be cut in half to be shared equally, only the real mother begs him not to do it, and Solomon in his wisdom grants her the child (1 Kgs 3:16–28); fifteenth-century painting by Giorgione da Castelfranco, Uffizi Gallery, Florence, Italy.

the Temple and wrote proverbs, songs, and scientific lists. After his many foreign wives led him into idolatry, he was punished with revolts, and his son lost most of the kingdom. He is credited with parts of the book of Proverbs and with the Canticle of Canticles, also known as the Song of Solomon, while Ecclesiastes and the Wisdom of Solomon imply that he wrote them.

Solomon, Odes of. *See Odes of Solomon.*

Solov'ev, Vladimir Sergeevich (vlah-dee′meer sair-gay′vitch soh-law-yawf′), 1853–1900, Russian religious philosopher, poet, and mystic. Although a brilliant student, his teaching career was ruined after he pleaded for clemency for the assassins of Czar Alexander II. He was influenced early by the German Romantics and Spinoza, as well as by the Gnostics and early Christian mystics. Later he evolved into a forerunner of the ecumenical movement, urging the reunion of the Orthodox Church with Rome. This earned him the ire of the Slavophiles, who preferred Slavic culture to Western culture, and the Holy Synod. Whether or not he died a Catholic is a moot point. His thought enjoyed an even greater resonance after his death, especially throughout the recent religious renaissance in the former Soviet Union, when it particularly influenced intellectuals who admired the West. *See also* Russia, Catholicism in.

Somaschi (soh-mahs'kee), order of clerks regular founded in 1534 at Somasca, Italy, by Jerome Emiliani. Their continuing apostolate is directed to the care of orphans and the teaching of the poor. They are known today as the Somascan Fathers (C.R.S.), with headquarters in Rome. *See also* Jerome Emiliani, St.

Song of Songs, also known as the Song of Solomon, a book of the OT. Divided into eight chapters, this collection of love songs, so filled with erotic symbolism, has rarely been interpreted literally. The most consistent tradition has been allegorical, spiritual, or mystical, beginning with Origen (d. ca. 254). In the Middle Ages, Bernard of Clairvaux (d. 1153) composed eighty-six influential sermons on these songs. In the sixteenth century John of the Cross's "Spiritual Canticle" was a mystical rewriting of the Song of Songs. Modern scholars, however, call for a reading of these songs that keeps the literal and spiritual traditions of interpretation in creative tension.

Son of David, a designation for Jesus. The claim of Davidic lineage indicates that Jesus fulfilled Nathan's oracle (2 Sam 7:14) that a Son of David would forever sit on David's throne. The Annunciation (Luke 1:32) and the speeches of Peter and Paul (Acts 2:29–30; 13:22–23) recall that oracle.

Jesus' Davidic lineage is frequently emphasized in the genealogies (Matt 1:2–17; Luke 3:23–38), the requests for healing (Matt 9:27; 15:22; 20:30; Mark 10:47; Luke 18:38), and the symbolism of Revelation (Rev 5:5; 22:16).

Some texts question the title. Jesus is portrayed as suggesting that the Messiah is more than David's son (Matt 22:41–45; Mark 12:35–37; Luke 20:41–44). Paul notes that Jesus was of the Seed of David according to flesh, but Son of God by the Resurrection (Rom 1:3). John, perhaps ironically, minimizes the connection of Jesus to David and Bethlehem (John 7:42). Heb 7:14 contrasts Jesus' Davidic lineage with his heavenly high priesthood. *See also* David.

son of God, in biblical literature an individual in a special relation to God. In the OT "sons of God," as in Canaanite myth, were heavenly beings (Gen 6:2, 4;

Job 1:6; 2:1; 38:7). The image is also used of Israel (Exod 4:22–23; Deut 1:31; 8:5; Hos 11:1; Mal 1:6) and the king (2 Sam 7:14; Ps 2:7; 89:26–27). Eventually the title applied to righteous individuals (Wis 2:18). The Davidic title was extended to expected messiahs (4QFlor 10–14; *1 Enoch* 105:2; 4 Ezra 7:28–29).

The confession of Jesus as Son of God is partly based on his own intimate address to God as Father (Matt 11:25–27; 26:39; Mark 14:36; Luke 10:21; 22:42). Experience of the Resurrection also grounded early Christian belief (Acts 9:20; Rom 1:4; 2 Cor 1:19; Gal 1:16; 4:4; 1 Thess 1:10; Heb 1:5; 4:14).

The synoptic Gospels situate the confession of Jesus' divine sonship within narratives of his baptism (Matt 3:17; Mark 1:11; Luke 3:22), temptation (Matt 4:3; Luke 4:3), Transfiguration (Matt 17:5; Mark 9:2; Luke 9:35), and encounters with demons (Matt 8:29; Mark 5:7; Luke 8:28). Several texts, particularly in Matthew, report Jesus' own language claiming to be God's Son (Matt 7:21; 10:33; 12:50; 16:16–17; 18:19, 35).

The Fourth Gospel shifts from a functional toward a metaphysical notion of Jesus' sonship. Jesus is not simply a messiah (John 1:34, 49), but the Son who was in the Father's bosom (John 1:18), who descended from heaven (John 3:13) and yet remains one with the Father (John 10:30, 36–38).

Creedal affirmations of the early Church tended to rely heavily on the Christological perspective of the Fourth Gospel. *See also* Christology; Jesus Christ; Son of Man; titles of Christ.   *HAROLD W. ATTRIDGE*

Son of Man, a designation for Jesus. In Hebrew and Aramaic, the phrase "son of man" is an idiom for "man" or "someone." In the book of Ezekiel, the prophet is regularly addressed as "son of man." In this context, the point is that he is a mortal creature in contrast to the immortal God. In the vision of Dan 7, four beasts symbolize four kingdoms, and the ancient of days represents God. The significance of the figure described as "one like a son of man" who receives kingship is disputed. In this context, "one like a son of man" means a figure with a human appearance. Angels are regularly described as "men" in Daniel. The figure would thus seem to be an angel, the agent of God and patron of the people of Israel, probably Michael. Other theories propose that he is a collective symbol for Israel or the idealized Messiah. In the Similitudes of Enoch (*1 Enoch* 37–71), a Jewish apocalypse written in the first century A.D., "that son of man" in Dan 7 is interpreted as the heavenly Messiah. Another Jewish apoca-lypse composed around A.D. 100 also alludes to the figure in Dan 7 and interprets him as the Messiah (4 Ezra 13).

The book of Revelation preserves the sense of the Semitic idiom and implies that the Risen Christ is the one "like a son of man" in Dan 7:13 (Rev 1:13; see 14:14). Elsewhere in the NT (Mark, Matthew, Luke, John, Acts), the phrase has become definite rather than indefinite and a title or fixed nickname, rather than a descriptive phrase intelligible only as an allusion to Dan 7. *See also* Christology; Jesus Christ.   ADELA Y. COLLINS

sophia. *See* wisdom.

Sorbonne (sohr-buhn'), originally a college for secular theologians at the University of Paris founded by Robert de Sorbon in 1257 and mirroring the provisions for members of the mendicant orders studying at Paris. By the mid-sixteenth century, the term came to refer to the entire theological faculty at the university and more recently to the University of Paris itself.

Sorrowful Mysteries of the Rosary. *See* Mysteries of the Rosary.

Sorrows, Our Lady of. *See* Our Lady of Sorrows.

soteriology (Gk., *soter,* "salvation"; *logos,* "word about"), critical reflection upon the salvific activity of Jesus Christ. This branch of Christology asks: What does it mean to say that Jesus Christ "saved" us? From what and/or whom has Jesus Christ "saved" humankind and creation? Why did/do we need to be "saved"? In answering these questions, soteriology gives serious consideration to the testimony of the OT (e.g., Gen 3:1–4:16) and the NT (e.g., Mark 14:24; John 11:49–52; Rom 4:25; 5:6–11; 1 Cor 15:3; 1 Pet 1:3).

The Church Fathers tended to see Jesus as the *Christus Victor* (Lat., "Christ the Victor"), who freed creation from Satan's power. In the Middle Ages, Anselm proposed his satisfaction theory, and Abelard offered his view of exemplarism. During the Reformation, Martin Luther, John Calvin, and Philipp Melanchthon accentuated Jesus Christ's saving work for humankind and proposed theories of imputation and substitution. Today, some theologians (e.g., Karl Rahner), retrieving Abelard's view,

have presented a sacramental understanding in which the entire life, death, and Resurrection of Jesus Christ disclose God's love for humankind and Christ's complete surrender to God, even in the face of absurdity. In recent years, some theologians have proposed that, when used in light of the Gospels, "liberation" is another word for "salvation." *See also* atonement, doctrine of; Christology; exemplarism; imputation; Jesus Christ; redemption; satisfaction; substitution of Christ.

Soto, Dominic de, 1494–1560, Spanish Dominican theologian. Professor at the University of Salamanca in Spain (1532–45), he became Charles V's imperial theologian at the Council of Trent (1545–63) and later his confessor (1547–50). He subsequently returned to his native Salamanca and was elected to the University's principal chair of theology, whose previous occupant was Melchior Cano (d. 1560).

Soubirous, Marie Bernarde. *See* Bernadette of Lourdes, St.

soul, the principle of life in a human being. Christian reflection on the nature of the human soul attained clarity only gradually. Thus early theologians adopted positions that from a later standpoint must be judged erroneous: Tertullian (d. ca. 225), for example, took the human soul to be in some sense corporeal, and Origen (d. ca. 254) held that it preexists the creation of the body.

The notion of soul that has predominated in Catholic theology since the late thirteenth century is that of Thomas Aquinas (d. 1274). Following Aristotle, he conceived of soul in general as the pattern of interrelatedness ("substantial form") that integrates the many parts and processes of an organism into a functioning whole. In human beings, this integrating or formal element manifests itself not only in the activities that Thomas referred to as "vegetative" (e.g., nutrition, growth) or "sensitive" (e.g., seeing, hearing), but also in the higher-order activities he designated as "intellectual" or "rational" (e.g., questioning, understanding, deciding, loving). On this view, the human soul is naturally and intrinsically related to the body; it is not a spiritual captive in a material prison.

The Catholic Church affirms that each human being has only one soul; that the human soul is spiritual, for, as Aquinas explained, its higher-order activities are neither material nor intrinsically dependent upon matter; that it is created directly by

God and simultaneously with the body; and that it is immortal, although whether this attribute is natural or a gift of grace has never been defined. *See also* eternal life; holy souls; immortality; mind/body.

MICHAEL STEBBINS

Southwell, St. Robert, 1561–95, one of the Forty Martyrs of England and Wales canonized in 1970. A native of Norfolk, ordained a Jesuit in 1584, he had a successful mission in London from 1586 until his arrest in 1592 and his execution in 1595. He was widely known for his poetry. Feast day: February 21. *See also* Forty Martyrs of England and Wales.

Southworth, St. John, 1592–1654, one of the Forty Martyrs of England and Wales canonized in 1970. Ordained at Douai in 1618, he was especially known for his ministry during the London plague of 1636. He was executed in 1654; his relics were hidden and then rediscovered in 1927. Feast day: June 28. *See also* Forty Martyrs of England and Wales.

Sozomen, early fifth-century ecclesiastical historian. Sozomen's *Historia Ecclesiastica* (Lat., "Ecclesiastical History") covers the period A.D. 324–421, roughly the same span chronicled by Socrates "Scholasticus," his main source. However, Sozomen includes material from other sources, e.g., concerning the Church in the West and biographies of monks, etc. He depicts the emperors as defenders of orthodoxy and stresses the role of divine providence in history.

space, according to common sense, the three-dimensional expanse in which material objects exist and move. The major philosophical and scientific controversy concerns whether space is "absolute," like a container, or "relative," merely a set of relations between objects. The theory of relativity denies that space by itself is absolute but has not resolved the controversy with respect to space-time. Regardless, theology traditionally holds that, as Creator, God is present to all points of space (space-time), not subject to its constraints. *See also* relativity; time.

Spain, Catholicism in. Catholicism has been a key element in shaping Spain's national identity. Christianity arrived in Spain in the late Roman period. By the fourth century Spain had produced major Christian figures such as Bishop Hosius and Pope Damasus I (366–84). In 587 the Arian Visigoths who had invaded Spain converted to Catholicism. A symbiosis between the state and the Church destined to last into modern times soon developed. The Church exerted considerable influence on law and customs while the state controlled the appointment of bishops.

After Spain had fallen to Muslim invaders in 711, the remnants of the Visigoths in northern Spain initiated a protracted War of Reconquest, seeking to restore the land to the monarchy and Christianity. This enterprise was seen as a crusade, especially after the discovery in Compostela of the supposed tomb of St. James. He was named patron saint of the country, and his tomb became a major center of European pilgrimage. As the beneficiary of substantial land grants, the Church had the resources to build numerous churches, cathedrals, and monasteries in the Romanesque and Gothic styles, a reflection of heavy influence from the French Cluniacs and Cistercians.

Missionary Expansion: This militant character did not abate with the completion of the Reconquest in 1492. The Catholic rulers Ferdinand and Isabella enhanced the role of Christianity by making it the essential factor in unifying under one crown a politically and culturally diverse country. Jews were forced to convert or leave the country, and the recently created Inquisition, an ecclesiastical tribunal controlled by the state, watched for heresy and false conversions. In the sixteenth century Spanish Catholicism reached its apex. Under the effective leadership of Cardinal Ximénez de Cisneros, a general reform of both religious and diocesan clergy raised their standards of education. In the newly created universities, Catholic thought flourished in a general climate of openness strongly influenced by Erasmus (d. 1536), the outstanding Christian humanist of his time. The Church also played a prominent

A Palm Sunday procession in the small Spanish town of Mohernado, Guadalinara; one of the world's oldest Catholic countries, Spain was first evangelized around the year 200 and by 1994 had more than 39 million Catholics, or almost 95 percent of the total population.

role in Spain's imperial expansion into the New World, where the religious orders (mostly the Franciscans, Dominicans, Augustinians, and later the Jesuits) achieved the most important missionary enterprise since early Christianity. They converted and educated a large number of the native population and frequently protected them from common abuses by civilians.

Tensions Between Church and State: In the seventeenth century Spanish Catholicism declined in intellectual and moral vigor, although popular and artistic religiosity continued to thrive. The number of clergy reached an all-time high—close to 3 percent of the population—and religious orders dominated secondary schools. The first tensions between the state and the Church developed in the eighteenth century. The Bourbon monarchs sought to increase their control of the Church by confiscating its vast landholdings, a process that was not completed until the 1860s. The Jesuits, feared because of the power they exercised through their vast network of secondary schools, were expelled from Spain and Spanish America in 1767. A more profound split developed between the enlightened lay class, which favored a moral and educational renewal of the Church, and the church hierarchy, which tended to cling to the traditional ideology. The split intensified in the nineteenth century, as the liberal ideology grew in strength and some of its followers became radically anticlerical. The Concordat, signed in 1851, reflected a compromise between the moderate liberals and the church hierarchy, for the state still acknowledged Catholicism as the national religion, although its control of the Church increased by appointing and paying the diocesan clergy directly. A Catholic renewal at the end of the century failed to stop the increasing alienation of intellectuals, urban workers, and landless southern peasants, who increasingly viewed the Church as a natural ally of reactionary forces. With the powerful emergence of leftist revolutionary movements in the twentieth century, opposition to Catholicism took a new and violent form, crystalizing in the revolutionary violence of the Civil War (1936–39), during which thousands of clergy were killed and many religious buildings were destroyed.

Post–World War II Spain: The Church overwhelmingly supported Generalissimo Franco's victorious side by terming the war a modern crusade and then helping the authoritarian regime attempt to build a reactionary form of the traditional national Catholicism. This effort ultimately failed in the 1960s, when a significant part of all levels of the clergy and many Catholic lay organizations clamored for reform and supported a wide variety of political options, including the radical Left. After Franco's death in 1975, the Church by and large supported the peaceful transition to democracy, which ultimately brought about the first complete separation of Church and state in the history of Spanish Catholicism.

Although Spain remains largely a Catholic country, increasing desacralization of the country has considerably undermined the traditional influence of the Church. Church attendance has decreased substantially, the number of vocations has reached a critically low level, and strong opposition to divorce and abortion legislation by the hierarchy failed to bring results. Nevertheless, customs, rituals, and celebrations of a religious character remain as popular as ever.

As of 1994 Catholics constituted nearly 95 percent of the total Spanish population of thirty-nine million. *See also* Latin America, Catholicism in.

Bibliography

Glick, Thomas F. *Islamic and Christian Spain in the Early Middle Ages.* Princeton, NJ: Princeton University Press, 1979.

Payne, Stanley G. *Spanish Catholicism. An Historical Overview.* Madison, WI: University of Wisconsin Press, 1984.

ANGEL DELGADO-GOMEZ

Spalding, John Lancaster, 1840–1916, bishop, writer, educator, and poet. Born in Kentucky and educated at Louvain and Rome, he was ordained for the diocese of Louisville and worked there and in New York before being named the first bishop of Peoria, Illinois (1877–1908). As bishop he was an ardent promoter of parochial schools and of the Irish Catholic Colonization Association, which sought to settle Irish immigrants in rural areas in America. A proponent of a Catholic institution of higher learning for the United States, he chaired the bishops' committee to found, in Washington, D.C., The Catholic University of America in 1888, refusing appointment as the first rector. He also supported the establishment, in Washington, D.C., of Trinity College for women (1900) and Sisters' College at Catholic University (1911).

Spalding, Martin John, 1810–72, archbishop of Baltimore and author. Born in rural Kentucky, alumnus of the Urban College of the Propaganda, he was ordained in Rome in 1834. In 1848 he was named coadjutor to Bishop Benedict Flaget of Louisville, Kentucky, whom he succeeded in 1850. He authored historical and apologetical books and a host of articles. In 1864 he became archbishop of Baltimore, where he provided the Church in the United States with a comprehensive legislative code at the Second Plenary Council. At Vatican Council I (1869–70) he proposed a compromise definition of papal infallibility. He was the most productive and perhaps the most influential U.S. Catholic bishop at mid-century. *See also* Baltimore, councils of; United States of America, Catholicism in the.

speaking in tongues. *See* glossolalia.

Spellman, Francis Joseph, 1889–1967, cardinal-archbishop of New York. Born in Whitman, Massachusetts, he graduated from Fordham College and studied at the Urban College in Rome, where he was ordained on May 14, 1916. Relegated to minor positions by Cardinal William O'Connell of Boston, he was appointed to the Vatican Secretariat of State in 1925. Through his friendship with Eugenio Pacelli, later Pius XII, he became auxiliary bishop to

Cardinal Francis J. Spellman, one of the best known, and, because of his personal friendship with Pope Pius XII, one of the most influential American bishops in the twentieth century.

O'Connell in 1932. In 1939, he was named archbishop of New York by Pius XII.

Spellman was also military ordinary, a position that gave him influence with President Franklin D. Roosevelt and other world leaders. Though he failed to obtain formal U.S.-Vatican diplomatic relations, he was instrumental in having Roosevelt appoint a personal representative to the pope in 1940. Named a cardinal in 1946, he frequently provoked controversy in his public attempts to defend Catholic interests. Yet, he also had John Courtney Murray (d. 1967) invited to Vatican II to help draft the council's Declaration on Religious Freedom. *See also* military ordinariate; Pius XII.

Spiritans. *See* Holy Ghost Fathers.

spiritual bouquet, an enumerated collection of prayers, devotional exercises, and acts of self-denial offered to an individual for spiritual benefit. This pious custom, in vogue before the Second Vatican Council (1962–65), was especially popular with parochial school children. The listing, or bouquet, of pledged spiritual activities was presented usually in some artistic form, to the local pastor, a nun, or member of one's family on some special occasion, such as an anniversary of ordination, religious profession, or marriage. The custom passed out of favor after the council because it tended to view spiritual realities, including Mass, as quantifiable entities whose spiritual benefits are readily transferable to others.

spiritual combat, theme in the NT using language of war and athletics, e.g., "Take up the whole armor of God" (Eph 6:13), to describe the individual Christian's inner struggle between the flesh and the spirit. An element in desert spirituality, it gave a name, *Spiritual Combat,* to a book by Lorenzo Scupoli.

Spiritual Communion, the desire to receive the Eucharist as a substitute for the actual, physical reception of Communion. Known in the fourth century, it developed in the Middle Ages together with looking at, and adoring, Christ in the Blessed Sacrament. Overemphasis on Christ's divinity and an exaggerated sense of personal unworthiness fostered this practice. *See also* Communion, Holy.

spiritual direction, a guided process of understanding one's relationship with God. A common form of spiritual direction occurs when a spiritual director listens to the prayer experiences and life experiences of one under his or her direction and asks significant questions, encouraging growth and honesty in facing personal strengths and weaknesses. Communal liturgy, friendships with members of the Christian community, and spiritual reading (*lectio divina*) also serve as major sources of spiritual direction because they deepen one's relationship with God and raise significant questions about one's spiritual journey. *See also* discernment of spirits.

Spiritual Exercises, a pattern of contemplations, meditations, examination of conscience, and other forms of prayer, considerations, and instructions framed by Ignatius of Loyola (1491–1556) as indicated by the experience of the working of God in his own life. The Exercises, normatively made in solitude over thirty days under the guidance of a spiritual director, dwell initially upon God's gracious forgiveness of sin and then upon the life, Passion, and Resurrection of Christ. Their purpose is "to prepare and dispose the soul to remove from itself all disordered affectivity in order to seek and find the divine will in the disposition of one's life." The Exercises place great emphasis upon the discernment of the various religious movements and influences ("spirits") within one's life and, above all, upon allowing God to work immediately with the "exercitant." The Exercises have historically been adapted according to need. The book, *The Spiritual Exercises,* was written from 1521 to 1548. *See also* Ignatius of Loyola, St.; Jesuit spirituality.

Spiritual Franciscans, those who sought to separate from the ruling body of Franciscans, the Conventuals, in the late thirteenth and early fourteenth century, believing that the order had deviated from the strict poverty of the rule and testament of St. Francis. This rebellious minority, originally called Zealots (Zelanti), adhered to the prophecies of Joachim of Fiore (d. 1202) and viewed themselves as ushering in the age of the Holy Spirit. The Spirituals faced alternately persecution and toleration until their movement was formally condemned by Pope John XXII in 1317, 1318, and 1323. *See also* Franciscan order; Fraticelli.

spiritual healing, the forgiveness of sin and the resolution of spiritual and emotional difficulties.

There are four kinds of sickness that require healing: physical illness, emotional distress, sin, and demonic affliction. The sacrament of Penance, and in some cases the sacrament of the Anointing of the Sick, along with counseling, are avenues of spiritual healing. *See also* Anointing of the Sick; forgiveness; Reconciliation.

spiritual life. *See* ways of the spiritual life.

spiritualism, a practice, rejected by the Church, which involves contacting the dead through a living person (a medium) and sometimes using this contact to learn about the future (necromancy). Popular in ancient China, spiritualism (also known as spiritism) is noted with disapproval in 1 Sam 28:8 and condemned in Deut 18:11. Spiritualists believe that mediums possess powers and efficacious techniques, like turning tables and involuntary writing that provide access to the spirit world. No evidence exists to support such claims.

Spirituality, American Catholic, the network of human experiences that form a lived faith commitment within the U.S. context. Pluralism emerges as significant in forming this spirituality. Catholics encounter pluralism in U.S. society and in their own ethnically diverse communities. Despite a constitutional guarantee of religious liberty, the nineteenth- and early-twentieth-century immigrants experienced the constraints of U.S. culture's anti-Catholicism. The challenge for nineteenth-century Catholics was to retain their ethnically mediated religious identities while shedding foreign traits that thwarted political and economic aspirations. Parishes often bridged the gap between the ethnically familiar and culturally new. Parish associations adapted the essentially Protestant notion of voluntarism to meet adult immigrants' diverse religious needs. Parish schools diminished children's ethnicity by creating American patriots and Catholics faithful to uniform sacramental practices. Individual piety retained unequivocally Catholic forms, with abundant choices among popular devotions featuring a saint, Mary, or the Eucharist. Socially engaged spirituality emerged in the twentieth century, including Benedictine Father Virgil Michel's justice-oriented liturgical reform, the Catholic Worker movement, and Thomas Merton's socially conscious contemplative writings. The post–Vatican II emphasis on Scripture radically affected American Catholic spirituality, minimizing private piety and declericalizing communal piety, as in the charismatic renewal and the development of small Christian communities. Still, the parish-celebrated Eucharist remains the primary lay religious experience in American Catholicism. Adapting worship to the spirituality of Hispanics and African-Americans reflects an effort toward integration of diversity. Liberation theologians, feminists, and others continue to call the Church to greater inclusiveness in determining whose experiences will define future American Catholic spirituality. *See also* spirituality, Christian. *SANDRA Y. MIZE*

spirituality, Celtic. *See* Celtic spirituality.

spirituality, Dominican. *See* Dominican spirituality.

spirituality, Franciscan. *See* Franciscan spirituality.

spirituality, Jesuit. *See* Jesuit spirituality.

spirituality, lay. *See* lay spirituality.

spirituality, liberation. *See* liberation spirituality.

spirituality, monastic. *See* monastic spirituality.

spiritual reading, a traditional Christian practice that involves setting aside some time each day to explore the spiritual life by reading works of respected authors in the field. The point of spiritual reading is to benefit from the insights and experiences of others and to deepen one's own sense of the sacred.

spiritual sense. *See* Scripture, senses of.

spiritual theology. *See* ascetical theology.

spiritual works of mercy. *See* mercy, spiritual works of.

Spiritus Paraclitus (spir'i-tuhs pahr-ah'klit-uhs; Lat., "the Holy Spirit, the Comforter"), encyclical on biblical studies by Pope Benedict XV, issued on the fifteenth centenary of St. Jerome's death (September 15, 1920). While encouraging biblical studies, it is more cautious than Leo XIII's *Providentissimus Deus* (1893). *See also* Bible, Church teaching on the.

CHRISTIAN SPIRITUALITY

Christian spirituality is the daily, communal, lived expression of one's ultimate beliefs characterized by openness to the self-transcending love of God, self, neighbor, and world through Jesus Christ and in the power of the Spirit. "Spirituality" is a term that describes realities related to the Spirit of God. The OT speaks of the "breath" of God and in the NT, especially in Paul's Letters, "spirit" often refers to the Spirit of the Risen Christ in the community. Throughout the tradition, the term "spiritual" has had intellectual, juridical, and philosophical connotations, but it has referred consistently to that aspect of human life characterized by grace, that is, by the presence and activity of the Holy Spirit.

During and after the Middle Ages, many spiritual writers emphasized the interior, affective aspects of the spiritual life and advocated spiritual practices intended to nurture a life of perfection and heroic virtue that exceeded the demands of the ordinary Christian life. This view has changed dramatically and the journey toward holiness is now seen as an integral outcome of the baptismal commitment of every Christian.

Since Vatican II (1962–65), the Catholic Church has experienced a renewed interest in spirituality that encompasses a wide range of elements: the primacy of religious experience; biblical spirituality; renewed liturgy; recovery of the tradition's spiritual classics; interest in Eastern forms of the spiritual life; the relationship between spirituality and psychology; liberation and feminist spiritualities; and mysticism. Other signs of this renewal include the retreat movement, charismatic renewal, prayer, and Bible study groups; spiritual direction; the study of spirituality; and intensified social justice activity. In addition to a number of single volumes on spirituality, several publishing houses have inaugurated multivolume series on Christian and world spiritualities, making this material readily available to a wide audience. Such renewal is visible among many groups of Protestants as well. This abundance of material suggests the rich and varied ways in which one can experience and understand spirituality. On the negative side, it can lead to confusion, lack of coherence, and uncertainty about how to discern the wheat from the chaff.

In the past, treatises on the spiritual life were, in the main, written by and for members of clerical and monastic communities. This understanding of the spiritual life did spill over and affect the laity, but too often lay spirituality was seen as peripheral and inferior to the primary spiritual business of the Church. At Vatican II, the Church emphasized the primacy of Baptism for all Catholic Christians and issued a clarion call to universal holiness (Pastoral Constitution on the Church in the Modern World, nn. 40–41). The shift has significantly altered the discussion about the contours of the spiritual life and has broadened the audience to whom spiritual counsel is addressed. Every baptized Catholic is now encouraged to become conscious of, and to develop, her or his own spiritual life.

A satisfactory, comprehensive definition of spirituality is elusive. A marked pluralism leads one to speak of spiritualities rather than a single Christian spirituality. Definitions reflect various starting points, emphases, and perspectives, revealing the broad horizon in which the spiritual life is situated. All aspects of existence, even sin, have the potential to be part of one's search for spiritual meaning. For some, spirituality deals primarily with prayer and explicit religious experience, but for others it encompasses one's entire life in all its diversity—relationships, work, love, suffering, creativity, and so on.

But one can identify spirituality on at least three levels. The first is the originating experience—an individual or group of individuals have an encounter with God that develops into a sustained relationship. Second, although this primordial experience of God is ineffable and beyond human grasp, it may find outward expression in a way of life, a text, a set of images, or even music. This expression varies depending on its context, e.g., historical period, geographic location, age, sex, background, and experience. Third, students of the spiritual life analyze, categorize, and communicate in an organized fashion elements of this outward expression. In turn, persons are led anew to their own personal encounter with God, continuing the cycle of originating experiences.

TYPES OF SPIRITUALITY

Scholars reflecting on religious experience have categorized what appear to be different types or approaches to the spiritual life. One of the most common distinctions uses terms derived from the Greek, "kataphatic" and "apophatic." "Kataphatic" denotes a positive spirituality that finds God primarily in created things and uses analogy to speak of God, e.g., God is like the dawn or God is a friend. The term "apophatic" describes a negative spirituality that speaks of God in ways that call attention to the transcendent otherness of God, e.g., God is *not* like the dawn or God is *not* a friend as we experience these realities in human life.

In the past, God's transcendence was often emphasized more than God's immanence, and many thought that God could be spoken of more adequately through the negative way. Today, there are two changes in this way of thinking. First, these two ways to God are no longer seen in a hierarchical way, placing one above the other. It would seem, in fact, that the positive way is the way that most persons experience God. Many surveys on religious experience in the United States, for example, show that the majority of persons find God enmeshed in the very fiber of their daily life, with its personal relationships, struggles, and joys. Second, these two ways to God are seen not in opposition to each other but as different facets of the same religious experience. Most persons will experience both the positive and the negative approaches to God. Indeed, it could be said that one can only fully appreciate one way when it is seen in light of the other. They go hand in hand, reflecting the fullness of the human experience of God.

The terms "action" and "contemplation" are used to denote a second major distinction in the way one speaks about the spiritual life. Leah and Rachel in the OT and Martha and Mary in the NT have been seen as "types" of these two modes of the spiritual life. Here, too, one often encounters a misunderstanding. Because the Christian spiritual life has been so rooted in monasticism, it was sometimes thought that action was a necessary, but inferior, form of spirituality. This hierarchical understanding led the Christian community to see those members who dedicated themselves to formal contemplation as superior and more holy than those members whose lives were filled with activity.

As with the positive and negative ways, there has been a reevaluation of the dichotomy between action and contemplation. Movement and rest are two different, but crucial, rhythms in human life and both are required for survival. Most Christians spend most of their lives in some kind of activity. Occasionally it is important to step back and reflect on the meaning and intention of life and to engage full attention on God. But for the most part, one experiences God within the very matrix of existence. Jesus is a model. Occasionally he withdrew to pray and to discern God's will, but for the most part he was engaged in an active and demanding ministry.

Active and contemplative modes are being drawn closer and closer to each other. For Christians, active involvement in the world need not be seen as a distraction from, but rather as the very core of, the spiritual journey. Work, family, education, disappointment, illness, leisure, friendship, celebration—all are at the heart of the journey of holiness. Beholding the world at any given moment with an attentive, loving gaze is also at the heart of a contemplative existence. On the other hand, contemplation can be experienced as profoundly cosmic, relational, engaged, and committed to the world.

SPIRITUAL DEVELOPMENT

During the course of the twentieth century, the study of psychology made enormous strides in its understanding of how the human psyche functions. Much of this information proved relevant and helpful to an understanding of spirituality. Rather than seeing self and world as divided into separate compartments and eliminating certain elements from the spiritual life, such as bodiliness and sexuality, there is a more holistic view. The world and the human person are seen and valued in their totality. Nature and grace are not at war with each other but build on each other in a mutual and reciprocal way.

Foremost among these discoveries is the idea of human psychic growth and development. While the stages of growth should not be regarded in confining or rigid ways, they can be helpful in explaining the periods and kinds of growth and/or decline one is likely to experience in the spiritual life.

Growth in the spiritual life will not be divorced from the stages of life, even though each person experiences these stages in a unique way. The experiences of birth, childhood, adolescence, adulthood, old age, and dying are the moments of spiritual development. Spirituality can never be inimical to the depths of genuine human existence. The classic spiritual writers often recorded their own experience of God in order to provide guidance for others in their spiritual quest. These texts can be of assistance, provided the necessary adjustments are made to accommodate them to the present.

For hundreds of years, Catholic spiritual theology has delineated three major stages in the spiritual life: purgation, illumination, and perfection. In the first stage, the person strives to root out sin and to nurture a life of virtue. In the second stage, one reaches enlightenment; a life in conformity with God makes it possible for God to be known. In stage three, one experiences union with God, characterized by a knowledge of God that is tender and loving. These stages are not intended to be followed in an exact temporal sequence; rather, they describe aspects of the spiritual life that are present in different ways as one progresses toward final union with God.

Today, many spiritual writers caution against taking sin (purgation) as the starting point and focus of the spiritual life. A renewed theology centered on creation and incarnation has led to an emphasis on the goodness and value of the created, finite, material order. Catholics are invited to see themselves and all of creation as expressions of God's image and therefore as sacred. This is what is meant by a sacramental view of reality. From this renewed starting point, one is moved, second, to recognize sinful behavior and to experience genuine sorrow and the need for forgiveness from a generous and loving God. Third, spirituality views the person as graced by God, invited to participate in and extend God's creative activity in the world. Through this process, one's human existence is transformed and holiness is understood in terms of one's full, authentic humanity.

FUTURE TRENDS

The understanding of spirituality will continue to develop in a global context. National and political units are breaking down at an accelerated pace, demanding a reorientation of thought about and action toward people of all beliefs. Almost overwhelming are all the new voices that are part of the base of experience from which the spiritual life must be understood. Not only are there black, Hispanic, Asian, and female Christian voices, there are also the voices of Hindus, Buddhists, Jews, Native Americans, Confucians, and New Agers. As the awareness, knowledge, and practice of one's own tradition deepens, the dialogue with other voices in a spirit of inquiry and openness continues.

Second, many authors emphasize the connections between the practice of the Christian life and efforts to preserve the ecosystem. As the nuclear threat wanes, problem areas such as global warming, acid rain, the destruction of rain forests, and the pollution of air and water systems demand attention. Spiritual practices can never be at odds with the genuine welfare of the planet and of each person who inhabits it.

Third, spirituality takes seriously the mandate to identify with the poor, working in solidarity with them and for them. Action for justice, as the fruit of an authentically lived Christian spirituality, takes many forms—from the immediate alleviation of food and housing needs, to care of AIDS patients, to lobbying for just legislation, to paying a just wage, to improving education, and so on. In his Letter to the Ephesians (4:25–5:20), Paul captures the true spirit of the Christian life, the test of authentic spirituality.

Fourth, it remains to be seen how the inclusion of women's experience will eventually affect an understanding of the spiritual life. In general, women's spirituality emphasizes personal relationships, focuses on process and inclusive categories, moves toward synthesis, is oriented toward nature, takes seriously the body and sexuality, is concerned with the concrete as well as the abstract, and includes the affective as well as the intellectual. In the past these elements were often marginalized. Now they stand nearer to the center, thanks to feminist theology and feminist spirituality.

Finally, a renewed theology of the Holy Spirit has opened doors to new and broader ways of imaging God and to a fresh, more inclusive understanding of the person of Jesus. As awareness of the power and dynamism of the Holy Spirit at work in each member of the Church increases, words and images for the Third Person of the Trinity will need to be attended to anew.

See also Asia, spirituality of; Benedictine order; body and spirituality; Carmelite order; Carthusian order; Celtic spirituality; Dominican spirituality; feminism; Franciscan spirituality; Holy Spirit; Jesuit spirituality; lay spirituality; liberation spirituality; monastic spirituality; mysticism; spirituality, American Catholic; ways of the spiritual life; women in the Church.

Bibliography

Classics of Western Spirituality. New York: Paulist Press, 1978–.

Conn, Joann Wolski. *Women's Spirituality.* New York: Paulist Press, 1986.

Fox, Matthew. *Original Blessing.* Santa Fe, NM: Bear, 1983.

Woods, Richard. *Christian Spirituality.* Chicago: Thomas More, 1989.

World Spirituality: An Encyclopedic History of the Religious Quest. Vols. 16, 17, 18. New York: Crossroad, 1985, 1988, 1989.

ELIZABETH DREYER

sponsor, the person who, during the process of Christian initiation, stands as witness to the candidate's moral character, faith, and intention. Sponsors are significant ministers for both catechumens, unbaptized persons undergoing catechesis for entrance into the Church, and young people preparing for Confirmation.

The Rite of Christian Initiation of Adults distinguishes sponsors from godparents. The sponsor must give witness before admission to the catechumenate. Meeting the necessary qualifications, this same person may also serve as the godparent (nn. 10–11). Furthermore, the Code of Canon Law recommends that the one who undertook the role of sponsor at Baptism be the sponsor for Confirmation (can. 893.2). *See also* Baptism; godparent; Rite of Christian Initiation of Adults.

Spy Wednesday, Wednesday in Holy Week. The term is believed to have originated in Ireland. Given the reference in the Scripture reading for the day to Judas Iscariot as a traitor, the day is so called to commemorate the betrayal of Jesus by Judas. *See also* Holy Week.

S.S.D., *Sacrae Scripturae Doctor* (Lat.), doctorate in Sacred Scripture, granted only by an official ecclesiastical faculty, such as the Pontifical Biblical Institute in Rome, or by the Pontifical Biblical Commission (can. 817). It usually requires advanced studies in theology and in Sacred Scripture as well as some teaching experience.

S.S.L., *Sacrae Scripturae Licentiatus* (Lat.), licentiate in Sacred Scripture, granted only by an official ecclesiastical faculty, such as the Pontifical Biblical Institute in Rome, or by the Pontifical Biblical Commission (can. 817). It usually requires two years of course work after a licentiate in Sacred Theology (S.T.L.). A licentiate is a graduate-level degree, comparable to a master's degree, granted by faculties authorized to do so by the Holy See.

Stabat Mater Dolorosa, (stah'baht mah'tair dohloh-roh'sah; Lat., "the sorrowful Mother stood"), a thirteenth-century poem describing Mary, the Blessed Mother, that begins, "At the cross her station keeping, stood the mournful Mother weeping." The author of the poem is unknown. In the 1990s, the poem is used for the feast of the Seven Sorrows (September 15) and for the Stations of the Cross.

For the English text, see *Catholic Source Book,* P. Klein, ed. *See also* Stations of the Cross

stability, the practice of perseverance as prescribed by the Rule of St. Benedict and other early monastic rules. It implies not merely remaining in the community of one's profession throughout life (sometimes called "stability of place") but observing all the sound monastic practices followed in that community ("stability of heart"). *See also* Benedict, Rule of St.

stalls, the rows of seats, often ornately carved, situated in the choir of churches. Accompanied by a prie-dieu (kneeling bench with book rack), they are outfitted with a seat that may be folded up and with armrests in two positions.

Stanislaus Kostka, St. *See* Kostka, St. Stanislaus.

Stanislaus of Cracow, St., 1010–79, bishop, martyr, and patron saint of Poland and the city of Cracow. He was slain by King Boleslaus's own hand after Stanislaus, as bishop of Cracow, reproved and excommunicated him. Pope Gregory VII placed Poland under interdict and the king eventually fell from power. Feast day: April 11. *See also* Poland, Catholicism in.

Stapleton, Thomas, 1535–98, Counter-Reformation Catholic theologian. As canon of Chichester, after studies at Oxford and travels to Paris and Rome, he refused to take the oath of supremacy and left England in 1563 to teach at Douai and Louvain. Influenced by Augustine (d. 430) and Melchior Cano (d. 1560), his writings defended the teaching authority of Rome and the importance of tradition.

Starr, Eliza Gates, 1859–1940, American Catholic social worker. After visiting the world's first settlement house, Toynbee Hall (London), Starr and Jane Addams established Chicago's Hull House in 1889. Starr was active in the union movement and Chicago politics. Inspired by her aunt, Eliza Allen Starr, a noted Catholic educator, she converted to Catholicism in 1920.

state of perfection. *See* perfection, state of.

stational liturgy, a type of urban processional liturgy, first seen in fourth-century Jerusalem, in which the worshiping community, headed by its bishop and clergy, went in procession to one or more sanctuaries or sacred sites, making a stop (Lat., *statio*) at each for a liturgical service adapted to the shrine or feast. During the procession it was customary to chant antiphons. Such outdoor, mobile liturgical services involving stational processions and rogational (prayers for the harvest) services, especially with litanies, were characteristic of the liturgy in Jerusalem, Rome, Constantinople, and other major urban centers from the fourth century through the Middle Ages.

Stations of the Cross, one of the more familiar Catholic devotional exercises in which participants focus their prayer on representations of fourteen scenes of Christ's Passion. Its origins are ultimately traceable to pilgrims' visiting the various sites in Jerusalem associated with Christ's suffering and death, a practice that began in patristic antiquity and continued throughout the Middle Ages. Not all could make such a journey: by the twelfth century the fervor of the Crusades and a heightened devotion to the Passion created a heavy demand in Europe for pictorial representations of the last events in Jesus' life. When the Franciscans took over the custody of the shrines in the Holy Land in 1342, they saw it as part of their mission to propagate devotion to these places; soon in western Europe a series of shrines erected to commemorate Christ's Passion became commonplace. There was for many years a considerable variety in both the number and the title of these "stations"; the current number of fourteen first appeared in the Low Countries in the sixteenth century, becoming standard in the eighteenth century with a series of papal pronouncements. The chief promoter of this devotion was the Franciscan Leonard of Port Maurice (d. 1751), who set up more than five hundred sets of stations, the best known being the one in the Colosseum of Rome. Modern liturgists have emphasized that devotion to the Passion is incomplete without reference to the Resurrection and to this end have fostered the addition of a "fifteenth station." *See also* devotions.

statue, a three-dimensional image of Christ, an angel, Mary, or other saint. Statues may be regarded as merely decorative, didactic, or, more significantly, as devotional objects. Fashioned as expressions of faith, they are honored by the faithful because they represent persons who share God's holiness. Against misunderstandings and abuses, the

Statue of the Blessed Virgin Mary and the child Jesus; fourteenth-century French sculpture in limestone, Metropolitan Museum of Art, New York.

Church has supported the use of statues, maintaining that veneration of statues (and other sacred images) is directed not to the material itself, but to the person represented; and that veneration of statues and the persons mirrored by them is appropriate, being distinct from the adoration due to God alone.

Staudenmaier, Franz Anton (stow'den-mi-yuhr), 1800–56, German theologian. Ordained in 1827, he became professor of dogmatics in Giessen in 1830 and in Freiburg in 1837. His theology reflects the influence of the Tübingen theologians J. A. Drey, J. A. Möhler, and J. B. Hirscher as it treats the religious nature of the human person in relation to the historical character of revelation.

Stauffenberg, Claus Schenk Graf von (shtohf'en-berg), 1907–44, leader in the German resistance against Hitler. From old Catholic Swabian nobility, his enthusiasm for social reform had turned to anti-Hitler resolve by 1942. He prepared three assassination attempts on Hitler's life, the last ending in a bomb explosion in the headquarters of the eastern front from which, nevertheless, Hitler escaped. Von Stauffenberg was later executed.

S.T.D., *Sacrae Theologiae Doctor* (Lat.), doctorate in Sacred Theology. This is the highest degree conferred after the licentiate in Sacred Theology and requires advanced study at a pontifical university, one under the authority of the pope. The licentiate is a graduate-level degree, comparable to a master's degree, granted by faculties authorized to do so by the Holy See.

Stein, Bl. Edith, 1891–1942, philosopher, feminist, and convert. Stein, assistant to the philosopher Edmund Husserl, gave up her Jewish faith and became a Catholic in 1922. She was a teacher and lectured widely on pedagogical and women's issues. She entered the Carmelite order in 1923 at Cologne where she was known as Sister Teresa Benedicta of the Cross. She published philosophical and religious writings such as her book on John of the Cross, *The Science of the Cross,* and an autobiography, *Life in a Jewish Family.* Nazi persecution sent her to the Netherlands. Arrested there and executed at Auschwitz, Stein was beatified in 1987. Feast day: August 9.

Stephen, St., d. ca. 35, the first Christian martyr and one of the seven chosen by the twelve apostles to serve tables (Acts 6–7). A Greek-speaking Jew living in Jerusalem, he was converted to Christ and became a leader of the Hellenist Christians. This group argued that the new faith could not develop except by separating itself from Judaism, and in particular by putting distance between itself and the Temple and the Mosaic law. The Hellenists also urged a more expansive approach to the mission of the Church so that the gospel would be preached to the Gentiles as well. Feast day: December 26. *See also* Hellenism; martyr.

Stephen I, St., d. 257, pope from 254 to 257. He incurred the ire of Cyprian of Carthage for his leniency in reinstating two Spanish bishops who had lapsed under persecution and, later, for insisting that those baptized by heretics did not need to be rebaptized to be admitted to full communion. In 256, Stephen refused to receive legates from Cyprian. He was formerly believed to be a martyr. Feast day (until 1969): August 2. *See also* Cyprian of Carthage, St.; *lapsi.*

Stephen II (III), d. 757, pope from 752 to 757. Confronted by the Lombards, who were expanding into central Italy and threatening Rome, Stephen appealed to Byzantium for aid, but the emperor was unable to help. The pope next turned to the Frankish king Pepin, who defeated the Lombards in the campaigns of 754 and 756, thus transferring the papacy from the Byzantine sphere of influence and to that of western Europe. *See also* Pepin III.

Stephen III (IV), d. 772, pope from 768 to 772. Restoring order in the Roman church after the brief reign of the antipope Constantine through a synod in 769, Stephen soon became involved in Lombard politics. His mishandling of affairs left Rome open to Lombard attack and the city was saved only by the pro-Frankish policy of his successor, Hadrian I. *See also* Hadrian I.

Stephen Harding, St., d. 1134, abbot of Cîteaux and cofounder of the Cistercian order. Of English origin, Stephen left the austere community of Molesmes to found another at Cîteaux. His writings formed the core of the *Carta Caritatis,* the constitution of the order. Feast day: July 16. *See also* Cistercian order; Cîteaux.

Stephen of Hungary, St., ca. 975–1038, national saint. After ascending to the throne in 997, he undertook the task of uniting and Christianizing the Magyar people, aided by the German emperor and Pope Sylvester II. Feast day: August 16. *See also* Hungary, Catholicism in; Sylvester II.

sterility, the incapacity to have offspring. It differs from impotence, which is the incapacity to have sexual intercourse. Sterility does not establish an impediment to marriage in canon law; impotence, however, does. *See also* impotence, impediment of.

sterilization, a medical or surgical intervention that renders procreation impossible or very unlikely. Sterilization may be of the male (e.g., double vasectomy) or the female (e.g., tubal ligation). It can be either permanent or temporary (e.g., by pill). Traditional Catholic theology has distinguished between direct, or contraceptive, sterilization (where the contraceptive effect is desired and intended as a means or end) and indirect sterilization (where the contraceptive effect is not intended but occurs as the result of a necessary or highly desirable therapeutic procedure, e.g., the removal of cancerous ovaries or uterus).

Early Christian tradition was unfamiliar with the forms of sterilization now practiced. However, as early as Augustine (354–430) the "poisons of sterility" were rejected. Medieval theologians continued this usage, though it is not always clear what means they intended to include under "poisons of sterility."

While Pope Pius XI's *Casti Connubii* (1930) condemned contraception, it remains very doubtful whether sterilization can be included in this solemn condemnation. During the 1920s the key issue involving sterilization was compulsory eugenic sterilization. Twenty-three states had laws permitting sterilization of persons classified as feeble-minded or insane. The U.S. Supreme Court in 1927 upheld the constitutionality of such laws. *Casti Connubii* was explicitly concerned to reject such practices when it asserted that the individual's right over his or her sexual faculties was superior to the welfare of the community.

Pius XII was very explicit in his condemnation of direct sterilization. "Direct sterilization—that is, sterilization which aims, either as a means or as an end at rendering procreation impossible—is a grave violation of the moral law and therefore illicit" (Address to the Midwives, 1951). Paul VI's *Humanae Vitae* repeated this condemnation in 1968.

Since many theologians dissented from the central assertion of *Humanae Vitae,* it was to be expected that many would also hold that direct sterilization could also be justified, at least as a last resort. Many did. Aware of this, the Congregation for the Doctrine of the Faith repeated the absolute condemnation of direct sterilization on March 13, 1975, in its document on sterilization in Catholic hospitals. It acknowledged the existence of widespread dissent, but denied "that this fact as such has any doctrinal significance, as though it were a theological source which the faithful might invoke, forsaking the authentic magisterium for the private opinion of theologians who dissent from it." Many theologians continue to believe that the overall good of the person can justify sterilization.

This division of opinion continues to create problems for Catholic hospitals. Tubal ligation remains a hospital procedure but is prohibited by official teaching. Sisters of Mercy of the Union, sponsors of the largest group of nonprofit hospitals in the country, finished a painstaking study in 1980 with the conclusion that tubal ligations could be allowed when they are determined by patient and physician to be essential to the overall good of the patient. The General Administrative Team came under intense pressure from the Holy See to reverse this conclusion, and eventually did so rather than forfeit other valuable aspects of their ministry. The practice of Catholic hospitals remains uneven with regard to tubal ligation. Some permit it for grave reasons; others tolerate it as a form of material cooperation; others forbid it. *See also* bioethics; medical ethics.

RICHARD A. MCCORMICK

sticharion (stih-kah'ree-ahn), Byzantine-rite liturgical vestment. The term is used for the alb or undertunic worn by priests and bishops, as well as for the deacon's outer garment or dalmatic. *See also* alb; dalmatic.

stigmata (stig-mah'tuh; Lat., "marks"), bodily signs borne in commemoration of Christ's Passion. The word is used by Paul in Gal 6:17, "I carry the marks of Jesus branded on my body," but in the Middle Ages referred to actual wounds corresponding to those of Christ. Although not the first to carry such marks, the most famous stigmatic was Francis of Assisi, who received wounds on his hands, feet, and side during an ecstatic experience in 1224, two years before his death. Since then, hundreds of cases of stigmata have been claimed, usually

Francis of Assisi receiving the stigmata; illustration in a fifteenth-century French manuscript, Metropolitan Museum of Art, New York.

accompanied by an ecstatic experience of the Passion of Christ.

Stigmata can take many forms; they may be visible, as in the case of Francis, or invisible as in the case of Catherine of Siena (d. 1380). They may appear in different shapes and in different places on the body; they may appear only at certain times and represent all or only some of the wounds of Christ.

On very rare occasions, the Catholic Church has accepted an occurrence of stigmata as authentic, but has never defined their origin or nature, thus allowing for physical, psychological, and preternatural explanations for these phenomena.

Stigmatines, Congregation of the Sacred Stigmata (C.S.S.), a congregation of priests and brothers founded in Italy in 1816 by Gaspare Bertoni, a priest in the Verona diocese. The early rule was based on that of the Jesuits; the rule and constitutions were approved by Pope Benedict XV in 1916. They arrived in the United States in 1905, eventually settling in New York and Massachusetts. The major work of the Stigmatines is education, but they also carry on missionary work, direct summer camps, and do preaching and retreat work.

Stimmen der Zeit (shti'men dehr tzit; Ger., "Voices of the Time"), a German Jesuit journal of religion and culture. Begun in 1871 as *Stimmen aus Maria-Laach,* it became *Stimmen der Zeit* with the return of Jesuit institutions to Germany in 1914; contributors such as Erich Przywara and Karl Rahner indicate its depth and contemporaneity in addressing Catholic encounters with society and Church.

stipend, an offering (the preferred term today) given on the occasion of requesting a special remembrance in the Eucharist. It is to be distinguished from a stole fee, which is a voluntary offering on the occasion of the administration of sacraments and sacramentals other than the Eucharist. The custom originated in the offerings of bread and wine by the people at the Eucharist (mentioned already by Justin Martyr in the second century). An offering of money eventually replaced such offerings. It came to be a supplemental means for the financial support of the clergy. Canon 848 insists, however, that the poor and the needy are never to be denied access to the sacraments because of their lack of material resources. *See also* Mass stipend.

stipend, Mass. *See* Mass stipend.

S.T.L., *Sacrae Theologiae Licentiatus (sive) Lector* (Lat.), licentiate or instructor in Sacred Theology. This is an intermediate graduate degree conferred after the baccalaureate (S.T.B.) by a pontifical university, one under the authority of the pope.

stock, holy oil, a small vessel in use since the Middle Ages to store the three sacramental oils: oil of catechumens for prebaptismal rites, oil for Anointing of the Sick, and chrism for Baptism, Confirmation, and ordination rites. *See also* holy oils.

stole, a long narrow strip of fabric worn over one or both shoulders by bishops, priests, and deacons, normally under an outer garment. Its remote origins are obscure; it may be related to a kerchief or, alternatively, to a festal ceremonial garland. Its Christian use derives from rank-signifying scarves worn by Roman officials. *See also* vestments.

stole fee, offerings given upon the celebration of certain liturgical functions other than Mass. The term is not currently used because it gives the impression that a fee must be given for these ministrations. Canon law requires pastors to provide these services to all regardless of the ability to pay.

Stone, St. John, d. 1539, an Augustinian friar of Canterbury canonized in 1970 as one of the Forty Martyrs of England and Wales. Arrested in 1538 during the visitation of the monasteries under Henry VIII, he was executed sometime in 1539. Feast day: December 27. *See also* Forty Martyrs of England and Wales.

stoup, a vessel for holding holy water. Fonts were located at the entrances to ancient churches and monasteries so that individuals could wash their hands prior to entering the church. Possibly due to medieval developments surrounding the *Asperges* rite (sprinkling with holy water during the opening rites of the Mass), the act of washing evolved into blessing oneself with holy water. *See also* asperges; holy water.

straw, liturgical, a tube that may be used in Communion to ingest the eucharistic wine. The communicant purifies the tube by sipping some water, then places the tube on the paten. The General Instruction on the Roman Missal permits drinking from the chalice directly, using a tube or spoon, or intinction (n. 200). The 1970 Instruction prefers drinking from the chalice directly (n. 6). *See also* Communion, Holy.

Stritch, Samuel A., 1887–1958, cardinal-archbishop of Chicago (1940–58). After service in Memphis and his native Nashville, he was made bishop to Toledo in 1921. In 1930 he became archbishop of Milwaukee, where his term of office coincided with the Great Depression. In 1940 he was appointed archbishop of Chicago and was created a cardinal in 1946. A bookish man, Stritch was a conservative and genial prelate, known as the "bishop of charity" and the "bishop who never said no." Under his tolerant policies, priests were often given ample leeway to pursue innovative approaches to racial justice, urban affairs, Christian education, and family life. He died in Rome on May 26, 1958, soon after assuming the Vatican post of Pro-Prefect of the Sacred Congregation for the Propagation of the Faith.

Studites, a federation of Byzantine Orthodox monasteries founded in Constantinople under the leadership of Theodore of Studios (759–826) that flourished and dominated Orthodox monasticism from the ninth to the thirteenth centuries. The liturgical synthesis of Palestinian and Constantinopolitan monastic usages the Studite monks created was an important phase in the formation of the Byzantine rite. The name "Studite" is also used by a congregation of Ukrainian Catholic monks formed by a group of peasants in 1900 and developed under the direction of Andryj Sheptytskyj, metropolitan of Lviv, who remained their archimandrite or general superior, though he confided them to the care of his brother, the Studite hegumen (abbot) Klimentij, in 1915. They numbered 225 when dispersed after World War II, and have emerged again since 1990 in the new religious freedom in Ukraine.

Stuhlmueller, Carroll, 1923–94, biblical scholar. A member of the Congregation of the Passion since 1943, he was professor of Old Testament studies at Catholic Theological Union in Chicago and the only male member of the steering committee of the Women's Ordination Conference. A past president of the Catholic Biblical Association, he served as general editor of *The Bible Today,* as editor of *Old Testament Message,* a twenty-three-volume international commentary series, and on the editorial boards of the *Journal of Biblical Literature* and the *Catholic Biblical Quarterly.* He was the author of twenty-three books and many scholarly and popular articles on the Bible.

stylite (Gk., "pillar"), a solitary monk who lived on a platform on top of a pillar. The pillars were of varying heights, and sometimes the platforms were covered to form a small hut. Disciples would bring the stylite food. Stylites were especially common in Syria and Egypt between the fifth and tenth centuries. Simeon Stylites (d. 459) is regarded as the founder of the practice. *See also* Simeon Stylites, St.

Suárez, Francisco de, 1548–1617, Spanish Jesuit philosopher and theologian. Suárez was the foremost representative of the Jesuit tradition in philosophy and theology as it took shape in the golden age of Spain and Portugal. His philosophical doctrine, broadly Aristotelian-Thomist, yet incorporating many Scotist and nominalist elements, has had a major influence on modern metaphysical thought. His *Disputationes Metaphysicae* (1597) was the first modern systematic treatise in metaphysics. In theology, Suárez was a major systematizer of the Jesuit position, first developed by Luis de Molina, in the *De Auxiliis* controversy about free will and grace. An original political and legal theorist, Suárez explored the nature of civil society and the relationship between civil authority and the Church in his *Defensio Fidei Catholicae* and *De Legibus,* rejecting divine right theories of kingship. With his ideas of the natural community of nations and the law of peoples, Suárez was one of the founders of international law. *See also De Auxiliis;* Molinism.

subdeacon, until recent times in the Western Church, the first of the major orders. With the reception of this order, one was entrusted with certain functions in the solemn liturgy and undertook the obligations of praying the Liturgy of the Hours (Divine Office, breviary) and of observing clerical celibacy. The earliest evidence for the subdeacon, as liturgical assistant to the deacon, comes from the third century. In the thirteenth century the subdiaconate came to be regarded as the first of the major orders, though held only in transition to diaconate and priesthood and not regarded as part of Holy Orders. In 1972 Pope Paul VI abrogated the order of subdeacon in the Roman Catholic Church. The liturgical functions of the subdeacon were transferred to the lay ministries, reserved to men, of reader and acolyte. The function of subdeacon continues to exist in Eastern-rite Catholic churches. *See also* deacon; major orders.

submersion, an ancient method of baptism whereby the whole body is plunged under water three times. With time, the more common form of baptism became the pouring of water over the head. The Rite of Christian Initiation of Adults (RCIA) has revived an appreciation of submersion. Churches are encouraged to consider the construction of baptismal fonts suitable for this practice. *See also* Baptism.

subordinationism, an understanding of God in which the Son is made inferior in status to the Father and in which the Holy Spirit is made inferior in status to both the Father and the Son. This understanding of God sought to ensure a monotheistic expression of Christian belief by limiting divinity to the Father alone. The writings of such esteemed authors of the first three centuries as Hermas, Justin Martyr, Irenaeus, Tertullian, Clement of Alexandria, and Origen contained elements of subordinationism. The councils of Nicaea (325) and of Constantinople (381) condemned the subordinationist teachings associated with the Alexandrian priest Arius. *See also* God; Trinity, doctrine of the.

subsidiarity, principle of, a modern Catholic social teaching, first articulated by Pope Pius XI in *Quadragesimo Anno* (1931), that the best institutions for responding to a particular social task are those that are most proximate to it. Properly understood, subsidiarity cuts in two directions. First of all, it carries a presumption against direct involvement by large-scale institutions. The role of large-scale institutions is to support, not replace, the smaller ones. The root meaning of the Latin word *subsidium* is "support." Larger institutions have difficulty discerning and responding to the unique textures of human life. If they usurp the prerogative of the smaller, more intimate institutions, the result can be the opposite of what was intended. Second, subsidiarity affirms that the role of larger institutions in the form of support is positive and necessary.

The words of *Quadragesimo Anno* are direct: "It is an injustice and at the same time a grave evil and a disturbance of right order to transfer to the larger and higher collectivity functions which can be performed and provided for by lesser and subordinate bodies. Inasmuch as every social activity should, by its very nature, prove a help to its members of the body social, it should never destroy or absorb them" (n. 79).

The two dimensions of subsidiarity are evident in the treatment of private property. While one has the right to private property, if it is not used for the common good, then the state can intervene and even expropriate the property. *See also* Catholic social teachings; common good. TODD D. WHITMORE

subsistence theory, an explanation of the hypostatic union that holds that the human nature of Jesus Christ, substantially complete in itself, did not exist on its own but existed ("subsisted") out of its union with the divine Logos. This theory is meant to safeguard the total unity of the humanity and the divinity of Jesus Christ. *See also* hypostatic union; Jesus Christ.

subsistent relations, the idea that divine Persons (constituted by their relations) are identical to the divine substance. According to the trinitarian doctrine of Thomas Aquinas (d. 1274), everything in God is identical with the divine essence or nature. God's wisdom, for example, is not predicated of any of the divine Persons in particular, but of the divine essence. At the same time, each of the divine Persons possesses this wisdom because of the inseparability of person and nature.

Relation is the fundamental category of trinitarian doctrine. Relations are said to be either logical or real; a logical relation is one that does not constitute the reality of something (for example, one's relation to one's desk), whereas a real relation is constitutive of the essence of something (for example, creation would not exist at all or be what it is except for God's agency to create). In God there are no accidents, thus there are no logical, only real, relations. Further, in God, real relations result from an activity immanent in God.

There are four real relations in God: Begetter to Begotten (Father to Son), Begotten to Begetter (Son to Father), Spirator to Spirated (Father and Son to Spirit), Spirated to Spirator (Spirit to Father and Son). Only three of these relations are person-constituting: Begetting, Being Begotten, and Being Spirated. The three divine Persons "subsist," that is, they exist as what they are, because of their relations to another. In a sense there are no discrete "persons" who have relationships to other persons, rather, to be a divine Person is to *be* a relation. Relations in God, paternity, filiation, and spiration, are thus not accidental but are as real as the divine nature itself and, while distinct, are inseparable from the divine nature. *See also* Persons, divine; Trinity, doctrine of the.   CATHERINE MOWRY LACUGNA

substance, a philosophical concept derived from Aristotle (d. 322 B.C.) that describes pure existence independently of the changeable "accidents" inhering to it. The categories of substance and accidents are traditionally used to describe the transformation of the bread and wine into the body and blood of Christ. This is the doctrine of transubstantiation, which speaks of the Real Presence in such a way as to explain why we do not taste flesh or blood when we consume the Eucharist. The whole substance of the bread and wine is replaced with the substance of the body and blood of Christ; the accidents (the outward appearance of the bread and wine perceptible to our senses) remain unchanged. *See also* accident; transubstantiation.

substitution of Christ, a theory of atonement derived from the ancient Israelite practice on the Day of Atonement of burdening a goat with the sins of the people and then releasing it into the desert (Lev 16:20–22), where it would perish. In this view, Jesus Christ assumed responsibility for the sin and guilt of all human beings and endured God's punishment in our place, thereby reconciling humankind with God. This theory relies on disputed interpretations of Luke 22:27b and Mark 10:45. *See also* atonement, biblical view of; imputation; Jesus Christ; redemption.

Suenens, Leo Josef (*soo'*nenz), b. 1904, former cardinal-archbishop of Malines-Brussels and one of the leading figures at the Second Vatican Council. Ordained a priest in 1927, he was made bishop in 1945, archbishop and primate of Belgium in 1961–1979, and cardinal in 1962. He served as a moderator of the Second Vatican Council (1962–65) and received the Templeton Foundation Prize in 1976. Former vice-rector of the University of Louvain 1940–45, he is the author of many books, including *Coresponsibility in the Church* (1968). He became active in the Catholic charismatic movement after the council and wrote frequently on it, including *A New Pentecost?* (1974).

suffering, a painful and often mysterious aspect of human life, embraced by Jesus Christ. Before his own Passion, Jesus closely associated himself with

Cardinal Leo Josef Suenens, Belgian cardinal-archbishop who was one of the leading figures at the Second Vatican Council (1962–65); he placed particular emphasis on the active role of the Church in the modern world.

those who suffer by befriending, defending, and healing them. Jesus also said, in reference to the hungry, thirsty, sick, and imprisoned, that whatever one did for these, one did for him (Matt 25:31–46).

The types and causes of suffering are manifold. Suffering can be emotional, physical, spiritual, or mental. Some suffering is freely chosen as a form of self-discipline or as a necessary component of serving others. Other suffering is caused by human errors and sins. On occasion, however, people endure tragedies that have no apparent cause or purpose. Only by faith can such people believe that "all things work together for good for those who love God" and nothing "will be able to separate us from the love of God" (Rom 8:28, 39).

Catholic social teaching emphasizes the need to serve the suffering as Christ served them, and to serve them with the same devotion one would serve Christ. In the Catholic spiritual tradition, those who suffer can draw consolation by uniting themselves with Christ, uniting their current suffering with Christ's redemptive suffering. *See also* redemption.

sufficient grace. *See* grace.

suffragan, a diocesan bishop considered in relationship to the archbishop of his ecclesiastical province. The term is not widely used; the Western Church does not put a great deal of emphasis on the role of the bishops in the province vis-à-vis the metropolitan archbishop.

Suger, Abbot (soo'zhay), ca. 1080–1151, abbot of the monastery of St.-Denis, near Paris, and an important adviser of King Louis VII. The new church he built for St.-Denis was the first great example of Gothic architecture. *See also* Gothic style.

Sulpicians, a community of diocesan priests on leave from their dioceses to teach in seminaries. The Society of St. Sulpice, one of the Church's smallest communities of priests, originated in 1641 when Jean Jacques Olier assembled a small group of clergymen dedicated to the religious formation of aspirants to the priesthood. Within a short time the community of priests who were attached to the church of St. Sulpice in Paris and to its nascent seminary were known as Sulpicians. They became identified with the revival of parish life, reform of seminary education, and the revitalization of spirituality of the priests. The Sulpician system entailed a rigid schedule of prayer, spiritual conferences, and study. Each Sulpician was an educator as well as a spiritual director.

Olier sent Sulpicians to the Canadian settlements of New France in 1657, but it was not until 1790, during the period of the French Revolution, that fear for their survival led them to enter negotiations with Bishop John Carroll to establish a seminary in the United States. Arriving in Baltimore in the summer of 1791, four Sulpicians and five seminarians founded the first American seminary, just two years after establishment of the first diocese in the new republic.

In addition to St. Mary's Seminary, the Sulpicians founded St. Mary's College for lay students, assumed ownership of Mount St. Mary Seminary and College until 1826, and became missionaries in the West and South.

From the origins in 1791 to the closing of St. Mary's College in 1852, when they opened St. Charles minor seminary, thirty-five Sulpicians served the Church in the United States, ten of whom became bishops and archbishops. They opened seminaries in Boston (1884), New York (1896), and San Francisco (1898). Seminaries were also opened in Seattle, Hawaii, Detroit, and Louisville, but in recent years a decrease in vocations led to the closing

of many Sulpician seminaries; St. Mary's in Baltimore and St. Patrick's in San Francisco (Menlo Park) are the two remaining Sulpician seminaries. The Sulpician Seminary in Washington, D.C., is now Theological College, a residence for seminaries under the spiritual direction of the Sulpicians. A few Sulpicians serve in seminaries in Zambia.

In 1992 there were ninety-two Sulpicians in the American province. Though always a small community, the Sulpicians have had a significant influence in the U.S. Catholic Church. *See also* Olier, Jean-Jacques.   CHRISTOPHER J. KAUFFMAN

Sulpicius Severus, ca. 360–ca. 420, historian and ascetic known chiefly for his biography of Martin of Tours (d. 397), which exerted wide influence in the burgeoning Western monastic movement. His *Chronicle*, or history from creation to 400, offers important evidence regarding Gallic Arianism and the condemnation of Priscillian, a Spanish layman who was associated with ideas at odds with the official teachings of the Church. *See also* Martin of Tours, St., Priscillianism.

Summa Contra Gentiles (Lat., "Summa [Synthesis] Against the Pagans"; the more correct title is *The Truth of the Catholic Faith Against the Errors of Unbelievers*), a selective synthesis of Catholic theology written by Thomas Aquinas between 1259 and 1264, possibly for Dominican missionaries to Muslims but more likely for Christians to help present their faith to infidels or to argue against "paganizing" philosophers. A work of theology, not apologetics, its first three books examine God, creation, and the human return to God, employing reason without recourse to Scripture or the Fathers; these, however, are used abundantly in the fourth book where Aquinas explores the Trinity, the Incarnation, sacraments, and eschatology—mysteries of faith inaccessible to unaided human reason. *See also* Aquinas, St. Thomas; *Summa Theologiae*.

Summa Theologiae (Lat., "Summa [Synthesis] of Theology"), Thomas Aquinas's most important systematic work in theology, written at Rome and Paris for "beginners," that is, for Dominican students trained in philosophy and studying Scripture concurrently with systematic theology. The *Summa Theologiae* therefore presupposes a reader's competence in biblical theology and Scholastic philosophy. Having begun in 1266 to revise his *Scriptum Super Sententiis,* Aquinas decided that the "order of doctrine" or "order of teaching" for students required a different plan and method from those of a commentary on Lombard's textbook, the *Sententiae* ("Sentences"). He also wanted a more solid doctrinal base for the predominantly moral-pastoral training being given to Dominican students. It is uncertain whether he actually taught the sections of the *Summa* that he wrote in Rome; it is known that he never taught the other parts.

The work has three parts. The first part, written in Italy (1266–68), examines God, the procession of creatures from God, and some aspects of the creature's return to God; the second part deals with the return to God of human beings insofar as they are images of God; it itself is divided into two parts (the first, Paris, 1268–70; the second, Paris, 1270–71); the third part (1271/72–73) presents Christ and his sacraments as the Way of creaturely return to God (we come from God in birth and return after death): incomplete, it breaks off within the study of the sacrament of Penance.

The *supplementum*—texts from his earlier *Scriptum* arranged by Thomas's disciples after the pattern of the *Summa* so as to complete the work—is not authentic and should not be attributed to Aquinas, especially since he later changed some positions he had held in the *Scriptum*.

The *Summa Theologiae* is not, as are later theologies, a series of treatises, tracts, or theses to be proved, but rather it is an organic whole in which the different questions or parts must be read with reference to the whole. It is a grave error in reading this or any medieval *summa* to presume one has the whole doctrine by isolating a few articles or questions while disregarding the relationship and complementarity of many other questions or parts. This is particularly true of the *Summa Theologiae* concerning Christ: all that is said in the first and second parts must be seen in relation to Christ, who in our history provides the only access to God and to the Trinity's personal saving work through justification, missions, indwelling, and gracious guidance to beatitude. *See also* Aquinas, St. Thomas.   WALTER PRINCIPE

Summi Pontificatus (*soo' mee pahn-ti-fi-kah' toos*; Lat., "great pontificate"), the first encyclical of Pius XII, issued October 20, 1939, on the threshold of the Second World War. It presents a Christian vision of a harmonious human society.

Sunday, the first day of the week. Originally named to honor the Sun (or solar deity), Sunday was cho-

sen later by Christians as the day for weekly worship in honor of Christ's Resurrection. In the Jewish system, days were simply numbered ("first day," "second day," etc.); only the final day of the week was honored with a specific title ("Sabbath") and preceded by a "preparation day" (Friday). As a day of rest and (eventually) liturgical assembly, the Sabbath established the precedent and pattern for a weekly day of worship. The earliest Christians (at least those of Jewish origin) probably continued to observe the Sabbath as their day of rest and worship.

At a very early period, however, Christians began emphasizing the connection between Sunday, the "first day of the week," and Jesus' Resurrection (see Mark 16:2). So prominent did the Resurrection motif become that by the end of the first century, Sunday was known simply as "the Lord's day" (Rev 1:10). There is evidence that in some first-century Christian communities Sunday (evening) was already being singled out as a particularly appropriate time for communal worship and "the breaking of bread" (see Acts 20:7, possibly 1 Cor 16:2). Still, the NT offers no conclusive proof that Christians considered Sunday a day of rest, or that they chose it as an exclusive day for worship (a replacement for the Jewish Sabbath), or that they held eucharistic meals on Sunday only. The earliest Christians may simply have viewed Sunday as *primus inter pares* (Lat., "first among equals") because it memorialized the Lord's Resurrection.

By the mid-second century, however, Sunday had clearly become the preferred day for weekly Christian assembly and Eucharist. Describing practices in Rome (ca. 150), Justin Martyr noted that every Sunday a common assembly was held, the "apostles or prophets were read," the presider offered instruction, prayers were said, and bread and wine were blessed with thanksgiving, then distributed to the faithful (*First Apology* 67). The pattern for Sunday as a day of Eucharist was thus set.

Meanwhile, the connection between Sunday and Christ's Resurrection was ever more strongly stressed. Christian teachers like Clement of Alexandria (ca. 150–215) spoke of Sunday as the "eighth day," that is, the eschatological fulfillment of that "first day" who is really Christ, the Dawn of a new creation and the Light of the world. Increasingly, the resurrectional character of Sunday was seen as incompatible with labor, penitential fasting or kneeling. In 321, Constantine decreed abstention from work and legal matters on Sunday. Similarly, the first ecumenical council of Nicaea (325) forbade kneeling on Sunday and during the fifty days of Eastertide.

From the sixth century onward, the obligation to attend Mass on Sunday became the object of increasingly strict ecclesiastical legislation. Catholics are still bound to it according to the 1983 Code of Canon Law (can. 1246), which notes that the Lord's day, on which the Paschal Mystery is celebrated, is to be observed everywhere as the primary holy day of obligation. *See also* Easter.   NATHAN D. MITCHELL

Sunday observance, practices used to mark the Lord's day among Christians. Early Christian practice observed Sunday to mark the day of the Lord's Resurrection. Today Church law requires that Catholics participate in the celebration of the Eucharist on Sunday or on Saturday evening. Although the liturgical observance of Sundays and greater feasts had for centuries started with the celebration of First Vespers the evening before, it was only with the 1983 code of canon law that the fulfilling of the Sunday obligation on Saturday evening was universally permitted. The custom of starting the Sabbath on the evening prior is of course reminiscent of the Jewish practice of starting the Sabbath on Friday evening. In addition, Catholics are to refrain from unnecessary work on Sunday. *See also* Sunday.

supererogation, works of, actions which exceed the demands of morality. Catholic moral theology, like other theories of morality that give a central place to a conception of a moral law, recognizes a category of praiseworthy actions that exceed the minimal demands of morality. These sorts of actions are described as supererogatory. Within the Catholic context, discussion of acts of supererogation tends to focus on the so-called evangelical counsels, but not all supererogatory actions are of this sort; for example, the heroic action of a woman who saves a child by throwing it out of the path of a truck, knowingly sacrificing herself in the process, would also be a work of supererogation. *See also* counsels, evangelical.

superior, official with authority and responsibility. The term is used for an official at the parish, diocesan, or universal level. Within a religious institute or society of apostolic life a superior may have authority on the local, provincial (regional), or general level. A superior has personal authority, but at times must obtain the advice or consent of a council.

superior general, the highest official in an institute of consecrated life or society of apostolic life. The superior general, assisted by a council that gives advice and consent on given matters, has authority over all the provinces, houses, and individuals in the institute. Particular law determines the term of office, manner of selection, and particular areas of authority. The title is not used by every religious community or society of apostolic life.

supernatural, that which pertains to whatever absolutely exceeds the power and capacity of human nature and any created natural reality, apart from the grace of God. In Christian theology the supernatural is the divine plan for the human race beyond its biological and psychological resources. What Jesus called "the reign of God" and what the Pauline author of the Letter to the Ephesians described as God's mysterious "plan," theologians express as a level of being or a horizon of consciousness that is above the natures, powers, and claims of creation. With roots in the NT and the writings of theologians of the fourth and fifth centuries, the dialectic between the natural and the supernatural in the human person reaches in the writings of Thomas Aquinas (d. 1274) a theology that emphasizes both distinction and harmony in the interplay of nature and grace. The Enlightenment, idealism, science, and some Protestant theologies have sought to reduce the supernatural to the natural or to meld the two into one reality, thereby denying the supernatural (against which the papal anti-Modernist documents protested). Some authors drew all powers and energies, human and divine, into one system, realizing in human history God's unfolding life (Schelling); others asserted that the scientifically formed individual would no longer believe in any supernatural intervention of God but would find in Christianity an existential psychology drawn from religious narratives, or myths (Bultmann). Catholic theologians such as Henri de Lubac (d. 1991) and Karl Rahner (d. 1984) criticized the widespread mentality in Catholicism in the nineteenth and early twentieth centuries that conceived of "two layers" in reality: the natural and the supernatural. Drawing on medieval and patristic sources, theologians at Vatican II (1962–65) emphasized the variety of God's (supernatural) presence in the world, the notion of revelation in history and not only in religious texts, and a divine grace which intimately touched individual lives and social movements. *See also* grace; nature; nature and grace.   THOMAS F. O'MEARA

surplice

Surplice

superstition, a morbid or submissive attitude toward objects or processes of nature, an exaggerated belief in luck, or any irrational attitude toward nature or the mysterious, which is subversive of true religion. Superstition may involve worship of an object other than God, which is a form of idolatry. More common among religious persons is a disordered attachment to particular rituals or persons in the context of worship of God. Such attachments usually do not involve any irreverence to God, but reveal the frailty of the human spirit.

supreme moderator. *See* superior general.

surplice, originally a wide-sleeved white linen alb-like vestment adopted in northern countries for wear over fur-lined cassocks in the twelfth century. It became the lower clergy's distinctive dress outside of Mass. Later it became a waist-length, lace-decorated vestment worn over the cassock. Today the alb is considered the appropriate vesture for liturgical ministers. *See also* vestments.

Susanna, St., reputedly a virgin martyred in

Rome during the third century. Her existence is based on the primitive Hieronymian Martyrology, which contained the notice: "In Rome, at 'Two Houses' beside the baths of Diocletian, the birthday of St. Susanna." The ambiguity of the notice has given rise to many legends. Feast day: August 11.

Suso, Bl. Henry, *See* Henry Suso, Bl.

suspension, penalty imposed on clerics that restricts the exercise of ministry. The penalty might totally restrict a cleric's ministry or might prohibit a cleric from a specific act or acts of ministry. In some cases, canon law automatically suspends a cleric for the commission of an ecclesiastical crime. A suspension can be imposed by a competent Church authority with a published declaration that a certain act has been committed and that this act carries with it a certain penalty. In other cases, a suspension is imposed through the sentencing of a Church court. In these cases, the commission of an unlawful act must be proven and the punishment decided by the court. In still other cases, suspension can be a punishment for violation of a penal precept, a decree given by a legitimate authority to which a penalty is attached for noncompliance. In such a case the competent superior gives a command under the pain of suspension. If the command has been violated, the punishment of suspension may then be inflicted.

As with all ecclesiastical penalties, laws are to be interpreted strictly. In addition, many factors can diminish an individual's imputability for personal actions and thus lead to a decision that a person has not been guilty of violating the law and is not subject to the penalty of suspension. *See also* penal law.

Swiss Guard, soldiers in the employ of the Vatican as a small security force for the papal palace and the person of the pope. Originally recruited from Switzerland as mercenaries in the service of the papacy in the early sixteenth century, these soldiers are still recruited from Switzerland today. Their colorful uniform of red, yellow, and dark blue, originally designed by Michelangelo (d. 1564), is one of the best-known features of Vatican life today. New recruits to the corps must be Swiss, Catholic, unmarried, and under twenty-five years of age. *See also* Michelangelo; Noble Guards.

Swithbert, St., 647–ca. 713, Anglo-Saxon bishop,

The Swiss Guard, composed of about one hundred Swiss men serving as military guards of the pope and the papal palace; the uniforms were designed by Michelangelo.

scholar, and missionary in the Netherlands. Feast day: March 1.

Switzerland, Catholicism in. The Christian faith came to the area now known as Switzerland in the fourth century. By the late fifth century, bishops were seated in Geneva and Chur, and the monasteries of Romainmotier and Saint-Maurice were established. The pagan Alamanni repressed Christianity in central Switzerland from the sixth through the ninth centuries. Throughout the Middle Ages, religious foundations were begun by the Cistercians, Franciscans, and Dominicans. Beginning with the Reformation, Catholics lived in tension with the followers of Ulrich Zwingli (d.1531) and John Calvin (d. 1564) until the twentieth century. There are six Swiss dioceses that, lacking a metropolitan see, are directly responsible to the Holy See. In April 1991, Pope John Paul II met with the Swiss bishops to discuss pastoral issues, including Rome's controversial appointment of the bishop of Chur. In 1994 Catholics made up nearly half of the nation's approximately seven million people. *See also* Reformation, the.

Syllabus of Errors, document containing eighty previously condemned theses, attached to Pope Pius IX's encyclical *Quanta Cura,* of December 8, 1864. The Syllabus itself was never signed by the pope. The origin of the document can be traced to 1849 when the Provincial Council of Spoleto requested that the pope draw up a list of new errors threatening the Church. The final form of the Syllabus contained eighty condemned theses and was modeled on a similar list of eighty-five errors found in an 1860 pastoral instruction of Bishop Gerbet of Perpignan. The condemned propositions coalesced around three themes. A number of the propositions were concerned with Pantheism and naturalism, either the attempt to identify God with the world or to exclude God from it. A second theme concerned the interplay between faith and reason and condemned were the various forms of rationalism that tended to identify the act of faith with the processes of human reason. A third theme directly addressed the fruits of political liberalism as they affected the civic prerogatives of the Church. In an age when the Church's possession of the Papal States and its temporal authority in general were being threatened, the Syllabus sought to preserve the legitimate autonomy of the papacy and of the Church itself with respect to its right to property, to elect bishops, to regulate the life of the faithful, and to communicate Church teaching. While the listing of many of the condemned propositions was aimed at correcting specific abuses associated with modern liberalism, the wording of these propositions was often vague and led to misunderstandings and abuse. The document must be read now in light of its original political context and of twentieth-century developments in the Catholic Church's teaching on religious freedom and Church/state relations as articulated at the Second Vatican Council (1962–65). *See also* Pius IX.

RICHARD R. GAILLARDETZ

Sylvester I, St., pope from 314 to 335. An important figure in the period after the Peace of Constantine, he had representatives at the First Ecumenical Council, Nicaea, in 325 and oversaw the building of St. Peter's Basilica as well as of St. John Lateran. The claim that he received lands from Constantine (the "Donation") in thanksgiving for a miracle has no factual basis. Feast day: December 31.

Sylvester II [Gerbert of Aurillac], 940–1003, scholar and pope from 999 to 1003. After being a student and master at Reims (and, briefly, abbot of Bobbio), Gerbert became archbishop of Reims in 991 in a disputed election. Under imperial patronage, he was elected archbishop of Ravenna in 998 and pope in 999. Several of his letters and mathematical and logical treatises survive.

symbol, something through which something other than itself is incarnated and encountered. A symbol runs deeper than a mere sign, which arbitrarily points to some other thing extrinsic to itself. A symbol in various ways embodies and mediates the other, as does a dream the subconscious or an artifact a vision of life. Such symbols are of different kinds: they may be concrete things, linguistic concepts, or ritual actions. Symbols are multivalent; they open up different meanings that cannot finally be circumscribed. Symbols are also realistic; they bear the reality poured into them; they often communicate what can be reached in no other way. Religious symbols embody transcendent reality.

Because of these various qualities, the category of symbol is particularly relevant to theology and commonly used in its subdisciplines. Some theologians understand revelation as having a symbolic structure: God is always encountered as mediated through things of this world. Faith as a human response expresses itself in objective beliefs such as the creeds, traditionally referred to as symbols of faith. Jesus is the Christ because he mediates God. Sacrament is a subspecies of symbol. The Church, as the sacrament of Christ, mediates God through Christ symbolically. The concept of symbol is as important in Catholic theology today as the idea of analogy was in the Middle Ages. *See also* analogy; mystery; sacrament.

Symmachus, St. (sim'uh-kuhs), d. 514, pope from 498 to 514. His first years were troubled by schism when the pro-Byzantine party of his predecessor, Anastasius II, elected a rival, Lawrence. With this behind him after ca. 504, Symmachus rejected Zeno's *Henoticon,* expelled the Manichees from Rome, protected African Catholics persecuted by Arian rulers, confirmed the primacy of Arles over Spain and Gaul, and introduced the singing of the Gloria on Sundays. Feast day: July 19. *See also* Henoticon; Manichaeism.

synagogue (Gk., "assembly"), a Jewish gathering place for prayer and religious instruction or the congregation assembled in it. Although their origins are unclear, synagogues certainly existed by the first century A.D., when they are attested in the NT and in Jewish sources (Philo, Josephus, inscriptions). Synagogues are found both in the land of Israel and in the Greek Diaspora.

Jesus is portrayed as teaching in synagogues (Matt 4:23; 9:35; 13:54; Mark 1:21; 3:1; Luke 4:15–16; 6:6; John 6:59). Paul, too, is said to have preached in Jewish synagogues in his missionary activity (Acts 13:5, 14; 14:1; 17:1, 17; 18:4). *See also* Church.

synaxis (sin-ak'sis; Gk., "assembly" or "congregation"), the gathering of the Christian community for public prayer or liturgical celebration. In the early Western Church, it referred to noneucharistic services, while in the Eastern Church it was used for the eucharistic assembly. Since Vatican II (1962–65) official documents have adopted the latter usage.

syncretism, the mixing of elements from different religious traditions. Gnosticism combined Jewish, Christian, Zoroastrian, and Platonic elements without achieving any stable synthesis. Catholicism has been accused by Protestants of syncretistic distortions of the pure gospel in its efforts to inculturate the gospel, e.g., different liturgical rites or the veneration of Mary.

synderesis, habitual knowledge of the first principle of practical reasoning. (The word is a corruption of the Greek word for "conscience".) According to Thomas Aquinas (d. 1274), rational reflection, whether speculative or practical, proceeds from first principles that are naturally known, specifically, the principle of noncontradiction in speculative matters, and the principle that good is to be done and evil is to be avoided in practical matters; knowledge of the latter is called synderesis. As such, it is the foundation of all moral reflection, even though the first principle of practical reason should not be understood as applying to moral good and evil alone, but to any sort of goodness or noxiousness. *See also* conscience.

Synod of Bishops, World, a consultative assembly drawn from the whole Catholic episcopate to discuss matters of concern to the Church universal and to provide opportunities of collaboration between the bishops of the world and the Bishop of Rome. Chartered by Pope Paul VI on September 15, 1965, in the document *Apostolica Sollicitudo* (Lat., "Apostolic Solicitude"), the synod was originally mandated by the Second Vatican Council's Decree on the Bishops' Pastoral Office in the Church (n. 5). The pope serves as its president, determines its agenda, and can grant it deliberative power, if he so chooses. Although the synod only meets every few years at the call of the pope, it is a permanent body, with a permanent general secretariat presided over by a general secretary appointed by the pope, and with the assistance of a council of bishops. The Code of Canon Law treats of the synod's structure, responsibilities, and powers in canons 342–48.

The synods, in ordinary and extraordinary sessions alike, have addressed a variety of topics, including the unfinished business of the council (1967), collegiality and the relationship of episcopal conferences to the Holy See (1969), priesthood and justice (1971), evangelization (1974), catechesis (1977), the Christian family (1980), Penance and Reconciliation (1983), the Second Vatican Council (1985), the laity (1987), priestly formation (1990), and religious life (1994). *See also* synods.

synods, gatherings of Church leaders to decide or advise on matters touching the life of the Church. A synod can also be a gathering of bishops of a country, a region, or a church organized on the basis of rite, e.g., Byzantine or Maronite. After Vatican II (1962–65) Pope Paul VI established the Synod of Bishops. Drawn from the worldwide episcopate, a group of bishops, some elected by fellow members of their conference, some appointed by Rome, gather to advise the pope on matters of current importance to the Church. Before such a synod, *lineamenta*, or discussion topics, are mooted; the preparation for the synod, therefore, can involve the wider Church. Topics covered by synods have included: the family, ordained ministry, the effects of Vatican II, the laity, and the religious life.

Yet another type of synod is found on the level of the local church. Diocesan synods are to involve certain leaders within each diocese, clerical, religious, and lay. They are to offer the bishop advice. The current code of canon law does not require the celebration of the diocesan synod but allows it. Some dioceses have used it in such a way as to involve a wide number of Christians in the process of renewal in the local church. *See also* collegiality; council.

synoptic Gospels, problem of, the issue of accounting for the similarities and differences among the Gospels of Matthew, Mark, and Luke. The first three Gospels share much of the same traditional material about Jesus and recount the events of his life in much the same general sequence. Important differences are also apparent. Matthew and Luke, for example, contain more of Jesus' teaching than

does Mark. The content of that teaching is the same in many details, but the order of its presentation varies. Matthew and Luke also have accounts of the birth of Jesus, but these are quite different.

Numerous theories have attempted to account for these similarities and differences. Some scholars have argued that the Gospels rely on different forms of oral tradition. Most assume that there is a literary relationship between the Gospels and that one or more used the others as sources. Some theories also incorporate data external to the Gospels, particularly the testimony of Papias (in Eusebius *Ecclesiastical History* 3.39.16) that Matthew composed a collection of sayings of Jesus in Aramaic that others translated. Augustine (d. 430) held that the canonical order was the order of composition: Matthew was indeed first; the account was abbreviated by Mark, then expanded by Luke. In the eighteenth century J. J. Griesbach (1745–1812) proposed a theory that has recently been revived, that Matthew wrote first, that Luke used and expanded his work, and that Mark wrote an epitome or conflation of the other two. This theory is known as the Griesbach or Two-Gospel Hypothesis.

The most widely held contemporary theory is based upon arguments developed in the nineteenth century that Mark was the first Gospel to have been written. Matthew and Luke independently used Mark for their narrative framework. Into that framework they inserted teachings of Jesus derived from a collection of sayings that scholars have labelled Q, from the German word for "source" (*Quelle*). Luke is thought to have preserved more faithfully the original order of Q, while Matthew often better preserves the original wording. Both also had access to special traditions. These are often designated M for the Matthean special material and L for the Lucan. There is considerable debate about whether such sources were oral or written. This general theory is known as the Two-Source Hypothesis or the theory of Marcan Priority. Numerous other more complicated theories have also been developed.

The synoptic problem played a role in the Catholic controversies about biblical scholarship that took place in the early part of the twentieth century. At one time (1911–12) the Pontifical Biblical Commission decreed that Catholic scholars should defend the priority of Matthew. That restriction has long since been lifted and Catholic scholars now may be found defending all the major alternative theories.

See also apocryphal Gospels; gospel; infancy Gospels; Luke, St.; Mark, St.; Matthew, St.   HAROLD W. ATTRIDGE

Syriac, a northwest Semitic language evolved from the Aramaic dialect of Edessa and Osrhoene, the traditional ancient liturgical language of the Chaldean, West Syrian, and Maronite rites, and, until after Vatican II (1962–65), of the Syro-Malabar and Syro-Malankara rites as well. Beginning in the second and third centuries it became the medium of a brilliant and flourishing Christian literature. With the breakup of Syriac Christianity into the Nestorian (East Syrian) and Jacobite (West Syrian) churches, Syriac evolved two variants, Eastern and Western, differing chiefly in alphabet and pronunciation. Modern dialects of Syriac are still spoken among the Syriac Christians of Iraq, Iran, Turkey, the Caucasus, and in the United States, including large communities in Detroit, Chicago, Los Angeles, and San Francisco.

Syrian Catholic Church, the ecclesiastical community of Syro-Antiochene, or West Syrian–rite, Catholics who are in communion with Rome and who are principally located in Syria, Iraq, and Lebanon. It is the Catholic counterpart of the Syrian Orthodox ("Jacobite") Church which, not having accepted the teaching of the Council of Chalcedon (451) that in Christ there are two natures, one human and one divine, has not been in full communion with the Catholic Church since that time.

During the Crusades there were many examples of warm relationships between Catholic and Syrian Orthodox bishops. Some Syrian bishops seemed favorable to union with Rome, but no lasting results were achieved. Similarly, a Decree of Union between Syrian Orthodox and Rome at the Council of Florence (1439) did not endure.

Jesuit and Capuchin missionaries began to work among the Syrian Orthodox faithful at Aleppo in 1626. So many Syrians became Catholic that in 1662, when the patriarchate had fallen vacant, the Catholic party was able to elect one of its own, Andrew Akhidjan, as patriarch. This provoked a split in the community, and after Akhidjan's death in 1677 two opposed patriarchs were elected, an uncle and nephew, representing the two parties. But when the Catholic patriarch died in 1702, this brief line of Syrian Catholic patriarchs died out with him.

The Ottoman government supported the Eastern Orthodox against the Catholics, and throughout the eighteenth century the Catholic Syrians underwent much suffering and persecution. There were long periods when no Syrian Catholic bishops were functioning, and the community was forced underground.

In 1782 the Syrian Orthodox Holy Synod elected Metropolitan Michael Jarweh of Aleppo as patriarch. But shortly after he was enthroned, he declared himself Catholic, took refuge in Lebanon, and built the still-extant monastery of Our Lady at Sharfeh. After Jarweh there has been an unbroken succession of Syrian Catholic patriarchs.

In 1829 the Turkish government granted legal recognition to the Syrian Catholic Church, and the patriarchal residence was established at Aleppo in 1831. Catholic missionary activity resumed. Because the Christian community at Aleppo had been severely persecuted, the patriarchate was moved to Mardin (now in southern Turkey) in 1850.

Steady Syrian Catholic expansion at the expense of the Syrian Orthodox was ended by the persecutions and massacres that took place during World War I. In the early 1920s the patriarchal residence was moved to Beirut, to which many Syrian Catholics had fled.

The patriarch always takes the name Ignatius in addition to another name of his choosing. Although Syrian Catholic priests were bound to celibacy at the Synod of Sharfeh in 1888, there are now a number of married priests.

A patriarchal seminary and printing house are located at Sharfeh monastery in Lebanon. Efforts have been made to revive the "Ephremite" tradition of male religious life (after Ephraem the Syrian), and the Ephremite Sisters of Mercy were founded in 1958.

The largest concentrations of Syrian Catholics, who in total number just over 100,000, are found in Syria, Lebanon, and Iraq. Their common language is Arabic, but Syriac is still spoken in some villages in eastern Syria and northern Iraq. There are no Syrian Catholic bishops outside the Middle East. See also Antiochene rite; Chalcedon, Council of; Eastern Catholics and ecumenism; Eastern Catholics and Rome; Eastern churches; Eastern liturgies; Eastern rites; West Syrian rite.   RONALD G. ROBERSON

Syrian spirituality, a spiritual tradition linked with Syria and Syriac-speaking Christians, evolving from the second to the thirteenth century. Up to the fourth century it had an emphasis on the imitation of Jesus, a commitment to virginity, and its own style of small-group monasticism. From this era the best known author was Ephraem of Syria (d. 373), biblical commentator and composer of hymns, who wrote only in Syriac. *See also* Ephraem the Syrian, St.

Syro-Antiochene rite, also called the West Syrian rite, the liturgical tradition of the Syrian Orthodox in the patriarchate of Antioch and in India, as well as of the West Syrian and Syro-Malankara Catholics. Though called "Antiochene," the rite is actually a synthesis of native Syriac compositions with Greek elements from the Antiochene and Jerusalem liturgies. *See also* Syro-Malankara Catholic Church; West Syrian rite.

Syro-Malabar Catholic Church, a Syro-Malabar-rite church deriving from the Christian community tracing its roots back to the Apostle Thomas (Thomas Christians) that the Portuguese encountered in 1498 while exploring the Malabar coast of India (now the state of Kerala). Although the Thomas Christians were then in full communion with the (Nestorian) Assyrian Church of the East, they greeted the Portuguese as fellow Christians and as representatives of the Church of Rome, whose special status they recognized despite centuries of isolation.

But the Portuguese, with the assistance of Catholic missionaries (especially Jesuits), began to impose Latin customs and rituals on the Thomas Christians. At a synod held at Diamper in 1599 under the presidency of the Portuguese archbishop of Goa, a number of such latinizations were adopted, including the appointment of Portuguese bishops, changes in the eucharistic liturgy, the use of Roman vestments, the requirement of clerical celibacy, and the setting up of the Inquisition. This provoked widespread discontent in the community and finally culminated in a decision by most of them in 1653 to break with Rome. In response, Pope Alexander VII sent Carmelite friars to Malabar to deal with the situation. By 1662 the majority of the dissidents had returned to communion with the Catholic Church.

European Carmelites served as bishops in the Syro-Malabar Church until 1896, when the Holy See established three vicariates apostolic for the Thomas Christians (Trichur, Ernakulam, and Changanacherry) under the guidance of indigenous Syro-Malabar bishops. A fourth vicariate apostolic (Kottayam) was established in 1911. In 1923 Pope Pius XI set up a full-fledged Syro-Malabar Catholic hierarchy.

This new autonomy initiated a strong revival of the church. While in 1876 there were only about 200,000 Syro-Malabar Catholics, this number had more than doubled by 1931. By 1960 there were nearly 1.5 million faithful, and by 1992 they numbered just under 3 million. Presently there are 2 metropolitan sees with equal rank at Ernakulam and Changanacherry, and nineteen other dioceses in India. Vocations to the priesthood have been very strong, and the church has over 20,000 religious women belonging to sixteen different Syro-Malabar congregations, five of pontifical right. There are major seminaries at Alwaye (interritual), Kottayam, Satna, Bangalore, and Ujjain.

In 1934 Pope Pius XI initiated a process of liturgical reform in view of a restoration of the oriental nature of the heavily latinized Syro-Malabar rite. A restored eucharistic liturgy, drawing on the original East Syrian sources, was approved by Pius XII in 1957 and introduced in 1962. Despite a reaffirmation of the main lines of the 1962 rite by the Congregation for the Oriental Churches in 1985, however, there has been strong resistance to this reform. The majority of Syro-Malabar dioceses still use a rite that in externals is hardly distinguishable from the Latin Mass.

Relations between the Syro-Malabar and Latin churches in India have often been marked by tension, particularly regarding the question of the establishment of Syro-Malabar jurisdictions in other parts of India to care for the many who have emigrated there. In 1987 the Holy See began to establish Syro-Malabar dioceses throughout India, even where Latin dioceses already exist. *See also* Eastern Catholics and Rome; Eastern churches; Eastern liturgies; Eastern rites; India, Catholicism in; latinization; Syro-Malabar rite; Thomas Christians.   RONALD G. ROBERSON

Syro-Malabar rite, the liturgical usages of the Catholic "Thomas Christians" of Kerala in southwest India, who trace their origins to the Apostle Thomas. These Christians came under East Syrian ecclesiastical influence in the fourth century, receiving bishops from the Mesopotamian "Church of the East" and adopting their Chaldean (or Assyro-Chaldean) rite with local variants. They celebrated it in Syriac, which only the clergy understood. This apostolic church underwent Latin influence in the era of Portuguese colonization beginning in 1498, especially under Jesuit influence at the Synod of Diamper in 1599. Since the time of Pope Pius XII (1939–58), efforts, hitherto only partly successful, have been made to restore, modernize, and inculturate the Syro-Malabar liturgical traditions. Since Vatican II (1962–65), Syriac in the liturgy has been abandoned in favor of the local vernacular, Malayalam. *See also* Syro-Malabar Catholic Church; Thomas Christians.

Syro-Malankara Catholic Church, a Syro-Malankara-rite church that originated in the Malankara Orthodox Syrian Church in India, established in the seventeenth century by Thomas Christians, evangelized by the Apostle Thomas, who rejected the latinizations imposed by Portuguese colonialists. They had subsequently established full communion with the Syrian Orthodox (Jacobite) patriarchate of Antioch.

In 1926, five Malankara Orthodox Syrian bishops opposed to the jurisdiction of the Syrian patriarch commissioned one of their own number, Mar Ivanios, to open negotiations with Rome with a view to reconciliation on the condition that their liturgy be preserved and that the bishops be allowed to retain their dioceses. Rome proposed that the bishops make a profession of faith and that their baptisms and ordinations be proven valid in each case.

In the event, only two of the five bishops accepted the new arrangement with Rome, including Mar Ivanios, who had founded the first monastic communities for men and women in the Malankara Orthodox Syrian Church. These two bishops, a priest, a deacon, and a layman were received into the Catholic Church together on September 20, 1930. Later in the 1930s two more Malankara Orthodox bishops were received into communion with Rome.

This triggered a significant movement of faithful into this new Syro-Malankara Catholic Church. By 1950 there were some 65,588 faithful, in 1960 112,478, and by 1970 the community had grown to 183,490. By 1992 there were three dioceses (Trivandrum, Battery, and Tiruvalla) for nearly 300,000 faithful, all in Kerala State, India.

An interesting development in this church was the foundation of the Kurisumala Ashram in 1958. This is a monastic community based on a strict Cistercian interpretation of the Benedictine monastic rule, the observance of the Syrian liturgical tradition, and forms of asceticism in use among Hindu ascetics. It has become a spiritual center for Christians and Hindus alike. *See also* Eastern Catholics and Rome; Eastern churches; Eastern liturgies; Eastern rites; India, Catholicism in; latinization; Syro-Malankara rite; Thomas Christians.   RONALD G. ROBERSON

Syro-Malankara rite, the West Syrian rite practiced with some local variants by the Syro-Malankara churches, Orthodox and Catholic, centered in Kerala in southwest India. This rite was introduced into India after a group of Syro-Malabar Catholics abandoned Catholic unity in 1653 to escape the Jesuit domination of their Church. They eventually received bishops from the Syrian Jacobite church and adopted their rite. A group of these Christians reunited with Rome in 1930. Since Vatican II (1962–65), they have abandoned Syriac in the liturgy in favor of the local vernacular, Malayalam. *See also* Syro-Malankara Catholic Church.

systematic theology, an area of Christian theology that addresses and develops the interconnectedness of mysteries and doctrines. Since Origen in the third century some theologians have sought to arrange, usually by drawing on a particular philosophy, the totality of Christian teaching in a framework that focuses upon certain organizing points and has a certain order. Although Christianity is based upon the unsystematic elements of God's plan and upon the history of Jesus of Nazareth in particular, an arrangement of teachings can and has been made on the basis of their relationship to one another and to the core of the gospel and the history of salvation. Contemporary examples are found in the Protestant theologies of Paul Tillich, Karl Barth, and Wolfhart Pannenberg and in that of the Jesuit theologian Karl Rahner (d. 1984). The term "systematic theology" can also apply to the part of theology that treats the central doctrinal and dogmatic areas of Christianity other than moral theology; indeed, prior to the 1960s Catholics called it simply "dogmatic theology." *See also* theology.

systems, moral. *See* moral theology.

tabernacle (ta'buhr-nak-uhl; Lat., *tabernaculum*, "tent"), a container or cupboard in the church in which the eucharistic bread is reserved. The box is secured and stationary; its door is locked with a key. The tabernacle holds bread primarily for the purpose of Viaticum (Holy Communion) for the dying and secondarily for Communion outside Mass and for adoration and devotion.

From the early days of the Church, the sacrament has been reserved for the sick and dying in a variety of ways and locations. A pyx suspended over the altar, a sacristy cupboard, or a sacrament house provided reverent repose for the eucharistic bread. The sixteenth century showed a preference for reservation on the altar, but the practice was never legislated. By the nineteenth century, the custom of building the tabernacle into the high altar was legislated and all other forms were forbidden.

Reforms following Vatican II (after 1965) changed pastoral practice. Each church is to have one tabernacle, preferably located in a chapel separate and distinct from the body of the church. If a separate chapel is not possible, the tabernacle is placed in a significant location, conspicuous and conducive to prayer. Its form and design are consistent with local usage and artistic creativity. Placed on a pedestal, pillar or column, or in a recessed wall niche, the form of the tabernacle should be solid and unbreakable, dignified and appropriately ornamented, always mindful of the function of eucharistic reservation. *See also* Communion, Holy; Real Presence; reservation of the Eucharist.

Tabernacle

Tablet, the (London), English Catholic periodical under lay editorship. Founded in England by Frederick Lucas in 1840, it is the oldest Catholic weekly journal of opinion in the English-speaking world.

Taizé (ti-zay'), a religious community in France, founded by Roger Schutz (b. 1915) in 1940 to revive the tradition of monasticism in Protestantism. Now an ecumenical order whose members live under a rule dating from 1952, the community takes its name from its location, the town of Taizé in southeastern France. One of the principal works of Taizé is the fostering of unity among all Christian denominations. The celebration of the Liturgy of the Hours three times each day exemplifies both the community's grounding in monasticism and its effort to root ecumenism in a life of common prayer. The church at Taizé is called Church of the Reconciliation.

Talbot, Matt, 1856–1925, Irish layman, model for recovering alcoholics. At age twenty-eight, he underwent a conversion, took "the pledge" against further drinking, and embarked upon a life of penance and devotion, in accordance with Louis Grignion de Montfort's "True Devotion." *See also* alcoholism; Montfort, St. Louis Grignion de.

Tall Brothers, four Egyptian Origenist monks. John Chrysostom's reception of them after their condemnation by Theophilus of Alexandria helped bring about John's deposition in 403. *See also* Origenism.

Talmud (Heb., "teaching, study, learning"), a collection of Hebrew and Aramaic interpretations of the Mishnah, exposition of Scripture, rabbinic traditions, and stories. There are two Talmuds, the Palestinian and Babylonian, of which the Babylonian is more lengthy and thoroughly edited. The Babylonian Talmud is the basis for numerous commentaries and law codes and is normative for most of Judaism.

Tametsi (tahm-et'see; Lat., "nevertheless"), first word of the decree of the Council of Trent that established (in 1563) the canonical form of marriage for Catholics. Before this decree there were no canonical requirements for entering into marriage in the Roman Catholic Church, other than consent. *See also* marriage, form of.

Tanakh, traditional Jewish designation for the Hebrew Bible. The word is derived from the names of the three major divisions of the OT, the *Torah,* or Pentateuch; the *Nebi'im,* or Prophets, which includes both the historical books and the prophets proper; and the *Kethubim,* or the Writings. *See also* Bible.

Tanquerey, Adolf Alfred, 1854–1932, theologian and priest of the Society of St. Sulpice. He was born in France, where he taught theology and performed various priestly ministries. He also taught dogmatic and moral theology as well as canon law at St. Mary's Seminary, Baltimore, Maryland (1887–1902). Tanquerey composed manuals of dogmatic, moral, and spiritual theology that were widely used in the seminaries of France, the United States, and elsewhere. His *The Spiritual Life: A Treatise on Ascetical and Mystical Theology* (English trans., 1930) served seminaries and novitiates until Vatican II (1962–65) as a standard manual for spiritual theology. *See also* ascetical theology.

Tantum Ergo (tahn'toom air'goh; Lat., "come adore"), the opening words, and title, of a eucharistic hymn. The text is sung in Latin or English form to various melodies at Benediction of the Blessed Sacrament. The text is usually attributed to Thomas Aquinas (ca. 1263), who was invited by Pope Urban IV to compose the hymn for the Solemnity of the Body of Christ (Corpus Christi). The two verses cited below are actually the last verses of a longer eucharistic hymn known as the *"Pange lingua [gloriosi Corporis mysterium]"* ("Praise [my] tongue the mystery of [his] glorious Body"). The longer hymn is sung during eucharistic processions, especially on Corpus Christi and at the close of the Mass of the Lord's Supper on Holy Thursday, when the eucharistic bread is reposed overnight for Communion at the celebration of the Passion of the Lord on Good Friday. The text rehearses the entire history of redemption in Christ and should not be confused with the *"Pange lingua [gloriosi lauream certaminis],"* ("Praise [my] tongue his victory in the glorious contest"), an earlier hymn (ca. 569) composed by Venantius Fortunatus to honor a relic of the True Cross. *See also* Benediction.

Taparelli d'Azeglio, Luigi. *See* d'Azeglio, Luigi Taparelli.

Tantum ergo Sacramentum
Veneremur cernui:
Et antiquum documentum
Novo cedat ritui:
Praestet fides supplementum
Sensuum defectui.

Genitori, Genitoque
Laus et jubilatio,
Salus, honor, virtus quoque
Sit et benedictio:
Procedenti ab utroque
Compar sit laudatio.

Come adore this wondrous presence,
Bow to Christ the source of grace.
Here is kept the ancient promise
Of God's earthly dwelling place.
Sight is blind before God's glory,
Faith alone may see his face.

Glory be to God the Father,
Praise to his coequal Son,
Adoration to the Spirit,
Bond of love, in Godhead one.
Blest be God by all creation
Joyously while ages run.

Taparelli d'Azeglio, Massimo. *See* d'Azeglio, Massimo Taparelli.

Targum (Heb., *trgm,* "translate," "explain"), the Aramaic translation of the Hebrew Bible. Targums were produced for most books of the Hebrew Bible, especially the Pentateuch (Targums *Onqelos, Pseudo-Jonathan, Neofiti*). Some Targums are literal translations, others paraphrastic and interpretive; as such they differ in form from midrash, which presents scriptural verses followed by commentary. Originating in the late–Second Temple period for synagogue use, the Targums underwent heavy revision as late as the fifth century A.D. Targums of Leviticus and Job were found among the Dead Sea Scrolls.

Tarsicius, St., third or fourth century, martyr and patron saint of altar boys and First Communicants. He was stoned to death while transporting the

Blessed Sacrament to Christians in prison. Feast day: August 15.

Tatian (tay'shen), second-century Apologist and native of East Syria famous for his *Diatessaron,* a harmony of the Gospels that became the standard Gospel text of the Syriac churches until the fifth century. Visiting Rome, Tatian became a disciple and perhaps convert of Justin Martyr. Later he founded a school in Mesopotamia, increasingly adopting a strict, Encratite asceticism opposed to marriage and perhaps veering toward a Gnostic distinction between the true God and the Creator. The *Oration to the Greeks,* a critique of Greek civilization, is his only extant work. *See also* Apologists; *Diatessaron.*

Tauler, John, ca. 1300–61, German Dominican mystic and spiritual writer. A disciple of Meister Eckhart, Tauler belonged to a "Friends of God" circle. His *Conferences* interpret in an orthodox sense Eckhart's negative theology, which the Church had censored. These German sermons had a wide influence and were admired by Martin Luther.

tax collector. *See* publican.

teaching authority. *See* magisterium.

tears, gift of, spontaneous sign of repentance. With precedents in the OT and with the example of Jesus who wept over Jerusalem and for Lazarus, early Christianity considered tears a normal expression of sorrow for sins or for the suffering of Christ. Authenticity, however, depends on tears as an expression of inner sorrow. *See also* repentance.

Te Deum (tay day'oom; Lat., "You [are] God"), title of the hymn of praise: "You are God, we praise you." Once attributed to Ambrose of Milan and Augustine of Hippo, it is now considered to be the composition of Nicetas, fourth-century bishop of Remesiana. Once part of Sunday Lauds, the canticle now concludes the Office Readings on Sundays and solemnities.

TE DEUM

You are God: we praise you;
You are the Lord: we acclaim you;
You are the eternal Father;
All creation worships you.

To you all angels, all the powers of heaven,
Cherubim and Seraphim, sing in endless praise:
Holy, holy, holy, Lord, God of power and might,
heaven and earth are full of your glory.

The glorious company of apostles praise you.
The noble fellowship of prophets praise you.
The white-robed army of martyrs praise you.

Throughout the world the holy Church acclaims you:
Father, of majesty unbounded,
your true and only Son, worthy of all worship,
and the Holy Spirit, advocate and guide.

You, Christ, are the king of glory,
the eternal Son of the Father.

When you became man to set us free
you did not spurn the Virgin's womb.

You overcame the sting of death,
and opened the kingdom of heaven to all believers.

You are seated at God's right hand in glory.
We believe that you will come, and be our judge.

Come then, Lord, and help your people,
bought with the price of your own blood,
and bring us with your saints to glory everlasting.
Save your people, Lord, and bless your inheritance.
Govern and uphold them now and always.
Day by day we bless you.
We praise your name forever.
Keep us today, Lord, from all sin.
Have mercy on us, Lord, have mercy.
Lord, show us your love and mercy;
for we put our trust in you.
In you, Lord, is our hope;
and we shall never hope in vain.

Teilhard de Chardin, Pierre, 1881–1955, French Jesuit paleontologist and theologian. Ordained a priest in 1911 and appointed professor of geology at the Institut Catholique in Paris, he went on paleontological expeditions in Africa and China from 1923 to 1946. There he evaluated the sites where important human fossil remains had just been found and trained the first Chinese paleontologists. In the midst of scientific fieldwork and writing, he began in the 1920s outlines of a theology whose directions and parameters were drawn from a scientific milieu. He viewed Christianity from an evolutionary

Pierre Teilhard de Chardin, pioneering French Jesuit priest and scientist whose theological and spiritual writings, although controversial during his lifetime, have grown in influence since his death in 1955.

cal institutions, were published to worldwide acclaim. This unusually imaginative thinker in theology, paleontology, and the cultural implications of science offered in a vivid and elegant style a worldview linking human evolution in the widest sense to themes from the Gospel of John, Paul's Letters to the Colossians and Ephesians, and the Greek theologians of the first Christian centuries. His optimistic thought helped to set aside conflicts between religion and science, inspired the spiritual journeys of many men and women in diverse areas of life, and stimulated countless studies of the Christocentric sacramentality of the universe. *See also* evolution; process theology.

Bibliography

Lukas, Mary Ellen. *Teilhard: A Biography.* New York: Doubleday, 1977.

Teilhard de Chardin, Pierre. *The Phenomenon of Man.* Trans. by Bernard Wall. New York: Harper & Row, 1965.

————. *The Divine Milieu.* Trans. by Bernard Wall. New York: Harper & Row, 1960.

THOMAS F. O'MEARA AND JOHN H. WRIGHT

Tekakwitha, Bl. Kateri, 1656–80, Native American holy person, also known as "Lily of the Mohawks." Born in Ossernenon (Auriesville, New

perspective, in which the movement is always toward greater complexity and higher levels of consciousness. He identified the Risen Christ as the future center of a higher level of human society propelled by the invisible force of charity. After 1951 he worked at the Wenner-Gren Foundation in New York City, where he died on Easter Sunday, 1955.

Some questioned the orthodoxy of his thought, and his speculative writings were published only after his death. They said he regarded the spiritual soul as resulting from materialistic evolution; but, though the human soul as a center within does result from the complexification of matter, this is due to the causal influence of God. Also, God as Omega seems to result from the convergence of the universe upon its goal; but "Omega" has two meanings. God as Omega, while intimately present to the universe, is distinct from it. The final state of the universe may also be called Omega, but this must not be confused with God. Some said he did not take evil seriously enough; but his concern was to see it in evolutionary perspective, not to deny it.

Nevertheless, throughout his life he was forbidden by the Vatican to publish works outside of science, but immediately after his death his theological writings, entrusted to friends outside of ecclesiasti-

Kateri Tekakwitha, Native American holy person, known as the "Lily of the Mohawks."

York), she was the daughter of a Christian Algonquin mother and a Mohawk warrior. She survived a smallpox epidemic that claimed the lives of her parents but suffered from facial disfigurement and poor health. Jacques de Lamberville, a Jesuit missionary, instructed Tekakwitha in the Catholic faith and on Easter Sunday, 1676, she was baptized and received the name Kateri (Catherine). Because her Christian commitment and refusal to marry angered her kin, Kateri fled the village and found refuge at the Mission of St. Francis Xavier near Montreal. There she taught children, cared for the sick and aged, and lived a life of penance and prayer. Kateri, known for her great holiness, died at the age of twenty-four (1680). The bishops of the Baltimore Council (1884) petitioned to begin Kateri's beatification process; she was beatified in 1980. Feast day (in the United States): July 14.

teleology (tee-lee-ah'luh-jee; Gk., *telos,* "end"), a way of thinking about right or wrong according to the end to which an action leads. Various forms of teleology are present in ethics. Thomas Aquinas (d. 1274) is teleological in holding that whatever leads to the person's ultimate end, union with God, is morally right. The traditional Catholic understanding of the natural law is teleological in holding that conduct must correspond to the ends of human nature. Situation ethics is teleological in its utilitarian quest for the greatest good for the greatest number. Proportionalism is a moderate form of teleology with its concern for the relation of means to ends and in its assessment of the totality of an act in light of its effect on total human wellbeing.

The strength of this approach is that it challenges us to hold in view the big picture. It takes seriously the future implications of an action as part of the action's moral meaning. Its weakness is apparent when it ignores other aspects of the act that may be involved in creating the future. Also, there is no unanimity on the way to order goods or to choose among competing goods. Since no one is an expert on the future, this method is limited by human ability to predict what will happen. Teleology needs to be complemented by considerations of deontology and an ethics of virtue. *See also* deontology; virtue.

temperance, the proper control of one's desires, one of the four cardinal virtues. The word "temperance" is today often associated with abstinence from alcohol. Originally, however, it directly translated the Latin *temperantia,* for which "self-restraint" or "self-control" is a more accurate meaning. According to Thomas Aquinas (d. 1274), a moral virtue is a habit directed toward a good work well done. In the case of temperance, the habit is attained by educating one's passions—as in the desire for food, drink or, in part, sexual pleasure—to the point that one more or less spontaneously and easily chooses the right action, not allowing temptations to deflect the choice. A person assaulted by strong emotions or desires may exercise self-control in the situation, but this is not yet the complete virtue or habit of temperance. Temperance is a quality of character that is dependable because one's desires have been disciplined to respond to the truly good. Furthermore, unless one acts for a truly good end, temperate behavior is imperfect because the full act cannot be considered good. Thus, fasting, which is the temperate control of one's desire for food, is not fully virtuous if the person knows that sickness will result. To the objection that emotions are fundamentally spontaneous, one must answer that human beings can both choose good aims or goals and learn to guide their desires according to these good ends. Thus, the cardinal virtues of prudence, justice, temperance, and fortitude, as consciously chosen, require implementation through careful training. *See also* cardinal virtues.   MARK MILLER

Templars. *See* Knights Templar.

Temple, the sacred complex in Jerusalem. Solomon (ca. 961–922 B.C.) constucted the first Temple in Jerusalem ca. 950 B.C. (1 Kgs 5–7). It functioned until the Babylonians destroyed it in 587/86 (2 Kgs 25:9). When exiles returned to Jerusalem in 538, they built a new Temple on the same site (Ezra 1–6). It stood from 516 B.C. until A.D. 70 when the Romans burned it down. King Herod had begun remodeling the Temple in about 20 B.C., and the process continued for many years (John 2:13–22). The Temple consisted of three rooms (Holy of Holies, holy place, nave) in the building proper, with surrounding courtyards and structures.

Temporale, the Temporal Cycle of the Church's calendar, which divides the year into three seasons celebrating the mystery of redemption: the Christmas Cycle (Advent and Christmastide), the Paschal Cycle (Lent, the Triduum, and Eastertide), and Ordinary Time, with its Sundays and moveable feasts

(Trinity, Corpus Christi, Sacred Heart, and Christ the King). *See also* liturgical year; Sanctorale.

temptation, an inducement to sin. In its most general sense, temptation is any sort of inducement that could lead an individual to act sinfully, or in nontheological terms, to act in a way that is contrary to the demands of morality. The specific conceptions of temptations found within the Catholic tradition have varied with changing conceptions of grace, sin, and the nature of the moral life. For those theologians who have emphasized the dangers of sensuality, and of sexual sins in particular, physical pleasure, pleasant or stimulating circumstances, or even the presence of other human beings have been stigmatized as occasions of sin. Others, following Thomas Aquinas (d. 1274), have tended to emphasize the intellectual dimension of the moral life, and have identified inducements to sin as those forms of persuasion that appeal to the intellect and to the wider emotional life, presenting a way of life that is superficially attractive but ultimately destructive.

Earlier moral theologies tended to put a great deal of weight on the importance of recognizing and avoiding temptations. More recently, however, moral theologians have deemphasized temptations, preferring instead to consider difficult situations as opportunities for moral growth. There is a greater awareness of the possibility that the culture as a whole can present temptations, by what it obscures from our consciousness and by the inducements that it offers us. *See also* sin.

temptations of Christ, specifically, the narrative of Jesus' temptations or testings in Mark 1:12–13 and in the sayings Gospel Q incorporated in Matt 4:1–11; Luke 4:1–13; generally, Jesus' testings throughout his ministry (Luke 22:28), especially in his suffering (Heb 2:18; 4:15). The origin of the narrative is disputed. The symmetry of the temptations and the unrealistic details rule out a literal understanding. Some think the account goes back to Jesus, who told parabolic stories to illustrate his victory over the lure of political messiahship or related inner experiences in figurative language. Others believe the early community created the story to correct false messianic expectations or to hold Jesus out as a model for Christian behavior. The narrative probably arose in response to the demand for signs (Luke 11:16). Either way, the story has religious value. The Marcan version is a brief narrative introducing Jesus' conflict with Satan and demonic forces. The Q account is a dialogue between Jesus and the Devil, which draws on Deut 6–8 to contrast Israel's failure in the wilderness with Jesus' success. Matthew inserted Q into the Marcan frame, while Luke placed a genealogy between the baptism and temptation and reversed the last two temptations to emphasize Jerusalem's importance. By juxtaposing the baptism and the Q form of the temptation, Matthew and Luke accentuate Jesus' filial obedience to God's will. *See also* Jesus Christ.

Ten Commandments. *See* Commandments, the Ten.

Tenebrae (Lat., "darkness"), the popular term for Matins and Lauds of the last three days of Holy Week. These morning offices were anticipated, i.e., celebrated, on the evening before. The term came into use because candles were gradually extinguished during the service and all departed in darkness (*tenebrae*) and silence. *See also* Holy Week; Liturgy of the Hours.

Terce (Lat, *tertia,* "third"), the monastic office celebrated at the third hour (*hora tertia*), or 9 A.M. Probably originating in the early Christian practice of commemorating different moments in Christ's Passion at the third, sixth, and ninth hours of the day, Terce was traditionally associated with the Crucifixion (Mark 15:25). *See also* Liturgy of the Hours.

Teresa of Ávila, St. , 1515–82, mystic, founder of the Discalced Carmelites, and first woman Doctor of the Church (1970). Born Teresa de Cepeda y Ahumada near Ávila, Spain, Teresa came from a large family with Jewish ancestry. In 1535 she entered the Carmelite monastery of the Incarnation at Ávila. During the next two decades Teresa led a prayerful life, but she felt that she had not surrendered fully to God and later commented that she had not felt fully alive. In 1554, while she prayed before a statue of the wounded Christ, she underwent a profound conversion.

Inspired by the memory of thirteenth-century Carmelites, Teresa founded her first reform convent of Carmelite nuns in 1562 at Ávila. In the same year Teresa composed the first draft of her *Life,* which included a nearly independent treatise on the growth of mystical prayer using the imagery of water (chs. 11–22). In 1566 she wrote the first, and probably the second, edition of *The Way of Perfection* as well as her *Meditations on the Song of Songs.*

In 1567 she met for the first time the newly ordained John of St. Matthias (later known as John of the Cross), whom Teresa convinced to remain a Carmelite and to collaborate in her reform of the order. Teresa admired John's holiness and wisdom. Although she and John act in the tradition as complements and interpreters of one another, Jerome Gracian was her closest friend among the friars. In 1568 Teresa saw to the inauguration of the first of the reform houses of the friars at Duruelo, and in 1577 she began the composition of her masterpiece, *The Interior Castle,* a disguised autobiography in the third person written while her *Life* was in the hands of the Inquisition. This book describes the mystical life through the symbolism of seven mansions, with the first three mansions as the premystical journey to God and the next four mansions as growth in the mystical life. With the imagery of the Song of Songs in the background, Teresa saw spiritual betrothal occurring in the sixth mansion and spiritual marriage in the seventh mansion.

For Teresa the test of growth in the mystical life is love of neighbor. Teresa stressed the importance of rooting prayer in Christ, and she emphasized the wholly gifted nature of the mystical life. Although Teresa was profoundly contemplative with regular manifestations of mystical phenomena, she was very active as the leader of the Discalced reform, making numerous foundations of nuns and friars. She was adviser, spiritual and otherwise, to countless people, as her warm and informative letters show; in fact, these letters reveal the lively and down-to-earth personality of Teresa. This Spanish mystic had a strong ecclesial sense. She died saying: "Finally, Lord, I am a daughter of the Church." Modern writers find Teresa's spirituality a complement to that of Ignatius of Loyola (d. 1556). She was beatified in 1614 and canonized in 1622. She is a patron saint of Spain. Feast day: October 15. *See also* Carmelite order; John of the Cross, St; mysticism.

KEITH J. EGAN

Teresa of Calcutta, Mother, b. 1910, founder of the Missionaries of Charity (M.C.). Born Agnes Gonxha Bojaxhiu at Skopje in the former Yugoslavia, she joined the Sisters of Loretto in Ireland at the age of seventeen, and within a year she was sent to teach in Calcutta, India. There she became acquainted with the poor who lived and died in the streets. In

Mother Teresa, one of twentieth-century Catholicism's most inspiring examples of Christian ministry to the poor, the sick, and the dying.

1948 she left the Sisters of Loretto to serve the sick and the dying in the city's slums. She became known as Mother Teresa. In 1949 she founded the Missionaries of Charity, a community of sisters, priests, and brothers who serve the poor by providing food, clothing, shelter, and medical care. Within thirty years there were eighty foundations of this community in thirty-two countries. She was the recipient of the 1979 Nobel Peace Prize, the Nehru Award, and the 1981 Père Marquette Discovery Award.

Térèsa of Lisieux, St. *See* Thérèse of Lisieux, St.

terna, list of three candidates proposed to fill a vacated office. Many offices, including that of bishop, require a terna from which electors or the responsible authority can choose. The list is usually presented by those authorized to do so (e.g., the bishops of a province) and is given in order of preference. In some cases the electors or authorities are bound to choose from the list; in other cases they may choose a person not on the list. *See also* bishops, appointment of.

territorial law, in canon law a law whose authority is limited to a geographical territory. Such law can be said to "cling to the stones" of the territory. Territorial law is designed to meet the needs of a given region. It has no force outside of a given diocese, province, or country.

tertianship, the third and last stage of probation in the Society of Jesus (Jesuits). It is a year of spiritual training and study required of members after ordination to the priesthood and some years of experience in ministry. This year of renewal includes a thirty-day retreat. *See also* Jesuits.

tertiary, popular term for membership in the only secular associations (third orders) of the faithful still explicitly mentioned by the Code of Canon Law (can. 303). Traditionally, members of secular third orders associate themselves with either first order or second order communities of women or men to live under their guidance and according to their spirit, but without the bonds of public vows or common life. Although twelfth-century records refer to groups of devout persons receiving spiritual guidance from Benedictines and Premonstratensions, such tertiaries were initially formalized by Francis of Assisi (d. 1226). Currently, several tertiary orders observe papally approved rules of life affiliated with the Augustinian, Benedictine, Carmelite, Dominican, "Norbertine," Servite, and Trinitarian traditions. *See also* third orders.

Tertullian, ca. 160–ca. 225, Latin Christian writer and Apologist from Roman Africa. While a large body of Tertullian's writings have come down to us, few details of his life are known with any certainty. He was born in Carthage and, like many of his countrymen, probably practiced law in Rome for some years. He converted to Christianity in his maturity and, according to Jerome, was ordained presbyter. In later life Tertullian was attracted by the uncompromising rigor of the apocalypticists who proclaimed that the heavenly Jerusalem would soon descend upon the earth and became Montanist. (A century later, Augustine reconciled to the Catholic Church a group of Christians called Tertullianists.) By 197, Tertullian had placed at the service of Christianity his skills in rhetorical composition, his bilingual ability in Latin and Greek, his ironic wit, his incisive mind, and his abundant energy. For more than twenty years he defended Christianity against paganism (the *Apology* and *To the Nations*), exhorted his fellow Christians to ever more rigorous standards of moral life (*On Penitence, On Modesty, On Fasting Against the Psychicos* [*the Catholics*]), attacked heresy and defended the Scriptures (*Against Marcion* in five books, *Against Hermogenem, On the Prescription Against Heretics*, among numerous other titles). Tertullian wrote profoundly on doctrinal issues, including seminal works on Trinity (*Against Praxeus*) and Christology (*On the Flesh of Christ*) that were to be points of reference for fourth-century pro-Nicene theologians like Hilary of Poitiers. Tertullian's writings illuminate many aspects of church life in the second and third centuries, its spirituality (*On Prayer, On Patience*), its sacramental life (*On Baptism, On the Crown*), its inner tensions (*On Flight during Persecution*), and its suffering (*To the Martyrs*). While Augustine (d. 430) places him with Cyprian (d. 258) among the admired Christian writers, Tertullian stands beside Augustine himself in infusing Christianity with a distinctive Latin genius. *See also* Africa, the Church in Roman; Montanism.   *PAMELA BRIGHT*

Testem Benevolentiae (test'em ben-eh-voh-len'see-ay), apostolic letter of January 22, 1899, condemning Americanism. While praising American patriotism, Leo XIII warned against religious indifference, watering down doctrine, denigration of religious vows, and the rejection of external authority in the Church—positions attributed in Europe to Isaac Hecker (d. 1888, founder of the Paulists). *See also* Americanism; Leo XIII; United States of America, Catholicism in the.

tetragrammaton (tet'ruh-gram'uh-tahn; Gk., "[the word with] four letters"), the four Hebrew consonants Y(J)HWH for the name of God (Exod 3:14), generally in English translations written as LORD. Because the divine name was not pronounced, 'adonai (Heb., my Lord) was substituted. "Jehovah" is a sixteenth-century combination of the consonants of YHWH and the vowels from 'adonai.

Tetzel, John, ca. 1465–1519, German Dominican preacher. In 1516 he was commissioned by Pope Leo X to preach in Magdeburg and Halberstadt (in modern-day Germany) to secure financial donations for the rebuilding of St. Peter's in Rome, in return for which donors would receive spiritual benefits known as indulgences. His approach outraged

Martin Luther because of its assumption, widely believed at the time, that the payment of money could secure the release of souls from purgatory. In response, Luther issued his Ninety-five Theses on October 31, 1517, the day commonly regarded as the beginning of the Protestant Reformation. *See also* indulgences; Luther, Martin; purgatory; Reformation, the.

Thaddeus, St. *See* Jude, St.

Theatines (Lat., *Theate*, "[from the town of] Chieti"), Italian religious order founded in 1524 by Cajetan, an Italian priest, and Gian Pietro Carafa, bishop of Chieti and later Pope Paul IV. Both were members of the Oratory of Divine Love, a group committed to the spreading Catholic reform throughout Europe. The ascetic Theatines observed the practice of absolute poverty, but were not allowed to beg. They dedicated themselves to evangelization, helping the poor, and parish work. They are known today as the Congregation of Clerks Regular (C.R.), with headquarters in Rome. *See also* Cajetan, St.; Oratory of Divine Love.

Thecla. *See* Paul and Thecla, Acts of.

theism, the belief that the universe originates from a unitary source and cannot be presented as its own explanation. Theism is contrasted with monism, according to which the universe contains its own principles within itself. Theism relies on a "distinction" of God from the world, while monism finds God immanent within the universe. Theism is also distinguished from deism, which considers the divine origin as initial and remote and thus practically severs the universe, once originated, from its divine source. The term theism broadly characterizes a family of religious faiths that includes Judaism, Christianity, and Islam, even though each of these holds quite distinctive teachings regarding God's free origination of the universe. But since theism would be compatible with the idea of a God who necessarily brought forth the world, the philosophical system of Plotinus (third century), presented as an alternative to Christianity, could count as a form of theism. While it is tempting to think of theism as a generic term that comprehends all those religions that avow creation, the term is far too inclusive to countenance such use. Most accurately, it intends a position opposite to atheism or to monism, yet in itself it is too vague to indicate which God (or gods) are intended. *See also* God.

theocracy (Gk., "rule by God"), a term coined by the first-century historian Josephus to describe Mosaic law. As is the case in some contemporary Islamic states, ancient Israel was ruled directly by religious leaders. Another form of theocracy was the submission of temporal rulers to the papacy in the Christian Middle Ages (see *Unam Sanctum*, Boniface VIII, 1302).

theodicy (Gk., *theos*, "God"; *dikē*, "justice"), the attempt to justify belief in the goodness of God in the face of the evil and suffering in the world. The existence of evil requires that one modify either the belief that God can do all things or the belief that God wills only good. Faced with the question of theodicy, theologians tend to stress human free will and responsibility for evil, the limits of human ability to discern the full meaning of an event, the ineffability of God, and the fact that the world is still on the way to perfection. *See also* God; natural theology; theology.

Theodore of Mopsuestia, ca. 350–428, bishop of Mopsuestia from 392 to 428, pupil of Diodore of Tarsus, and staunch defender of the trinitarian theology of the Council of Constantinople (381). Against both Arians and Apollinarians, his Christology developed Diodore's doctrine of two natures and (in effect) two subjects in Christ, the "man assumed" and the divine Word who assumed and indwelt him by grace. They were united in one *prosopon* (Gk., figure, presentation, "person"), a description of unity that seemed weak to Cyril of Alexandria, who viewed it as an early form of Nestorianism. Theodore was condemned at Constantinople II (553), a victim of Justinian's efforts to placate the Monophysites.

Theodore's brilliant but strongly antiallegorical exegesis, typically Antiochene, severely restricted not only allegory but even typology in the OT, regarding only four Psalms (2; 8; 45; 110) as Christological, excluding prophecy of Christ from all of the prophets except Malachi, and finding in Zerubbabel and the Maccabees the fulfillment of most of the messianic prophecies. *See also* Antioch, school of; Christology; Constantinople, councils of; Monophysitism; Nestorianism.

Theodore of Studios, St., 759–826, Byzantine monastic reformer and opponent of iconoclasm. In 799, he and his monks took over and revived the dying Studios monastery in Constantinople. His tightly organized monastic confederation of Studite monasteries under the leadership of the abbot of Studios was much like a Western monastic congregation. Its Typikon, or rule, and the spread of Studite liturgical usages from the tenth through the thirteenth centuries were crucial influences in the formation of the Byzantine rite. *See also* Studites.

Theodore of Tarsus, St., ca. 602–90, archbishop of Canterbury from 668. Theodore reformed and unified the government of the English church, establishing the metropolitan authority of Canterbury, and presiding over important synods in 673 (Hertford) and 680 (Hatfield). Feast day: September 19.

Theodoret of Cyrrhus, ca. 393–ca. 466, bishop of Cyrrhus from 423. He supported Nestorius and two-nature Christology against Cyril of Alexandria, even after Nestorius was condemned. Responding to accusations of dividing the Son, he composed a confession supporting the use of *Theotokos* (Gk.), "God-bearer," for Mary. Nevertheless, he was condemned by Dioscorus, Cyril's successor, and was deposed in 449. At the Council of Chalcedon (451), he reluctantly anathematized Nestorius and regained his see. He wrote apologetic works, biblical commentaries in the Antiochene tradition, and historical works, including a *History of the Monks of Syria* and a *Church History* (covering the period 323–428). His writings against Cyril (one of the "Three Chapters") were condemned by the Council of Constantinople in 553. *See also* Christology; Cyril of Alexandria, St.; Nestorianism; *Theotokos.*

Theodosius I, "the Great," 346/7–95, Roman emperor from 379 to 395 and architect of the Catholic empire, enacted through a series of decrees outlawing Arianism and other heresies and progressively restricting pagan sacrifice. As part of his anti-Arian agenda, he called the Council of Constantinople (381). In 390 he was obliged by Ambrose to do public penance for a punitive massacre at Thessalonica. *See also* Arianism; Constantinople, councils of.

Theodulf of Orléans, ca. 750–821, abbot and bishop. Probably born in Visigothic Spain, Theodulf served as abbot of Fleury, Micy, and St. Aignan as well as bishop of Orléans (from 781). Active at Charlemagne's court, especially after Alcuin's retirement, he was accused of conspiracy by Louis the Pious (817) and died in exile. He is the probable author of *Libri Carolini,* books attributed erroneously to Charlemagne containing teachings critical of the iconophile Second Council of Nicaea (787). *See also* Libri Carolini.

theologian, professional practitioner of theology, which is the scientific study of God and of God's relationship to the world. A person of faith, the theologian needs scientific training, so to approach theology both positively (through knowledge of data from the Bible and religious traditions) and speculatively (through a developed capacity for evaluation and reflection). Eastern Christians call attention to the indispensable role of prayer for the theological enterprise. They give the name of "the Theologian" to John the Evangelist, traditionally identified by them as the Beloved Disciple who appears in prayerful intimacy at Jesus' side in John 13–21. The methods and standards of theologians are inevitably affected by the setting of their work, whether university, seminary, or monastery, their audiences, whether the general public, students of theology, or the Church at large, and their philosophical systems, whether Platonism, Aristotelianism, or some form of existentialism or other system.

Whatever the setting, Catholic theologians need to cultivate a sense of their ecclesial role, showing genuine responsibility towards the members of the hierarchical magisterium and the wider faith community. As was indicated in the 1990 "Instruction on the Ecclesial Vocation of the Theologian," published by the Congregation for the Doctrine of the Faith, the prophetic function of theologians in the service of the Church will involve some fruitful tensions with the magisterium. *See also* magisterium; theology.

theological notes. *See* notes, theological.

Theological Studies, a scholarly journal published quarterly by Theological Studies, Inc., under the sponsorship of the U.S. Jesuit Conference. Established in 1940, it publishes articles and book reviews representing a broad range of theological reflection: systematic theology, moral theology and ethics, biblical studies, historical theology, and spirituality. Its two most prominent editors have been John Courtney Murray (d. 1967) and Walter Burghardt.

theological virtues, faith, hope, and love, grouped together by Paul in 1 Cor 13:13. Their proper and immediate object is God. Unlike other virtues, they are not acquired by personal effort but are received as gifts. Like other virtues, they require exercise to be perfected and can be squandered by neglect. Though each has a distinct activity, they cannot be fully isolated from one another. Different historical periods have emphasized different virtues. Augustine (d. 430) saw love as the ordering virtue. Martin Luther (d. 1546) placed faith at the center of Christian life. Recent theology has seen an increased emphasis on the virtue of hope. *See also* charity; faith; hope.

theologoumenon (theh-aw-law-goo'men-ahn; Gk., "that which is said about God"), a nondoctrinal theological interpretation that cannot be verified or refuted on the basis of historical evidence, but that can be affirmed because of its close connection with some defined doctrine about God. Belief in the virginal conception of Jesus or in the procession of the Holy Spirit from the Father and the Son *(Filioque)* are two examples of theologoumena (pl.).

theology (Gk., "the science of God"), any scientific, or methodical, attempt to understand and interpret divine revelation mediated through the data of Scripture and tradition. Classically described as "faith seeking understanding," theology begins with faith and uses the resources of reason, drawing in particular upon the disciplines of history and philosophy. In the face of the divine mystery, theology is always seeking, and never reaches final answers and definitive insights. Theology may be practiced within an academic setting. Yet unlike the philosophy of religion or religious studies, it should be done in and for (not outside or merely alongside) the believing community.

Systematic theology, often coinciding in practice with dogmatic theology, attempts to expound in a coherent and scholarly fashion the main Christian doctrines. Its branches include: Christology, which interprets the nature and significance of Jesus Christ; the doctrine of God, with special focus on the Trinity; Christian anthropology, which examines the creation, fall into sin, redemption through grace, and final destiny of human beings and their world; ecclesiology, which systematically reflects on the origin, nature, distinguishing characteristics, and mission of the Church; and sacramental theology, which interprets the seven visible signs instituted by Christ that reveal and communicate grace.

Fundamental theology studies foundational issues, in particular, God's definitive revelation in the history of Israel and Jesus Christ; the conditions that make human beings accessible to this divine self-communication; the signs that make faith in and through Christ a reasonable and responsible option; the transmission, through inspired Scripture and Church tradition, of the experience and content of God's self-manifestation.

Moral theology methodically examines the nature and norms of responsible human and Christian conduct. Pastoral or practical theology reflects on the Church's religious mission to the world in preaching, catechetics, and liturgical and sacramental celebration, involvement in struggles for justice and peace, and care of people facing special problems in different life situations.

Interests and Approaches: Particular interests or methodologies have always shaped theology. In addition, new movements have arisen, such as the theology of hope, the theology of the Cross, and narrative theology (in which biblical and Christian history and stories play a leading role). New realizations shape theologies such as black theology, which opposes racism and promotes full civil and ecclesial rights; feminist theology, which opposes masculine bias in theology and biblical interpretation and promotes full equality of women and men in civil and ecclesial life; and liberation theology, which opposes institutionalized injustice and the impoverishment of masses of people and promotes the integral liberation of human beings through structural change.

Approaches to theology frequently (but not always) have varied according to their geography. European and North American academic theologians typically raise questions about meaning, look for truth in dialogue with professional colleagues, place great importance on written texts, and often use criteria elaborated by speculative reason. Many recent Latin American theologians represent another theological method, which seeks justice, works in a very public context, privileges the voices of the poor and suffering, and respects the criterion of praxis, reflection that is linked with actual practical experience. North American feminist theological method recovers the contributions of women in the history of Christianity, privileges women's experience, and uses the criterion that whatever promotes the full humanity of women and men is redemptive. A liturgical and monastic approach to theology contemplates divine beauty and glory, finds its home in the setting of prayer, and takes its texts and criteria from the Church's worship. Ideally, Catholic and indeed all Christian theology can only be enriched by a proper pluralism in which the academic, practical, and liturgical styles work to complement each other, and are pursued in an ecumenically sensitive way. Like all human beings, theologians should be open to the true, the good, and the beautiful.

"Religion," John Henry Newman (d. 1890) stated in the nineteenth century, "cannot do without theology." He saw theology as "the fundamental and regulating principle of the whole Church system." Newman appreciated the essential service that theology, practiced with deep faith and impeccable intelligence, should render within the Church and for the Church and the world. *See also* faith; feminism; liberation theology; magisterium; philosophy and theology; praxis; revelation.

Bibliography

Congar, Yves. *A History of Theology.* Garden City, NY: Doubleday, 1968.

Dulles, Avery. *The Craft of Theology: From Symbol to System.* New York: Crossroad, 1992.

Lonergan, Bernard. *Method in Theology.* New York: Crossroad, 1972.

Newman, John Henry. *Idea of a University.* Oxford: Oxford University Press, 1976.   GERALD O'COLLINS

theopaschite clause, a fifth-century Monophysite text, "who was crucified for us," added to the Trisagion hymn, "Holy God holy mighty holy immortal," by patriarch of Antioch Peter Fuller ca. 468–70. The addition is found in all Eastern Christian liturgies except the Byzantine and East Syrian. Much disputed during the sixth century, the addition was condemned at the Council of Trullo in 692. It is now agreed that the clause can have an orthodox meaning provided the hymn is being addressed to Christ. *See also* Monophysitism; Trisagion.

Theophany (Gk., "divine manifestation"), common early Eastern Christian name for the January 6 feast; in the West called the Epiphany (Gk., "manifestation"). In the East this was the original Incarnation feast, celebrating both the Nativity of Jesus and his manifestation as Son of God at his baptism in the Jordan. In the West, the Nativity is December 25, and Epiphany celebrates the manifestation of Jesus to the Gentiles represented by the Magi. When the East adopted the Western Nativity feast of December 25 at the end of the fourth century, the two scenarios, Bethlehem (including the visit of the Magi) and the Jordan River, were split, the former assigned to December 25, the latter to January 6. But the mystery celebrated in both is the same: the manifestation of God's salvation in Jesus Christ. The Armenian Orthodox Church did not accept the December 25 feast; it maintains the ancient Jerusalem tradition of Christmas on January 6. *See also* Christmas; Epiphany.

Theophilus of Alexandria, d. 412, patriarch of Alexandria (385–412). He campaigned against paganism and destroyed its shrines, most notably the Sarapeum. At the urging of Egyptian monks, he opposed Origenism. His latter years were marked by bitter confrontation with John Chrysostom, bishop of Constantinople. Feast day: October 15 (Coptic); October 17 (Syrian). *See also* Chrysostom, St. John; Origenism.

Theophilus of Antioch, St., late second century, bishop of Antioch and Christian Apologist. His apologetics develops the doctrine of the Logos by distinguishing between the *logos endiathetos* (Gk.), God's Word prior to creation, and the *logos prophorikos,* God's Word spoken to form creation. He is the first known theologian to apply the word "triad" (hence, "triune") to God. *See also* apologetics; Apologists; Logos.

Theotokos (thay-oh-taw'kaws; Gk., "God-bearer"), the title given to the Blessed Virgin Mary at the Council of Ephesus (431). The council taught that because Jesus is one divine person, not two as the Nestorians had argued, Mary is truly the Mother of God and not only the mother of the human Jesus. *See also* Ephesus, Council of; Mother of God.

Theotonius, St., 1086–1166, Spanish-born Portuguese saint. Honored by the people as a very holy man, he persuaded King Alphonsus of Portugal to release the Mozarabic captives, Spanish Christians who practiced their faith under Muslim rule. Feast day: February 18.

Thérèse of Lisieux, St. (tuh-rayz' uhv leez-yoo'), 1873–97, saint popularly known as the Little Flower. She was born Thérèse Martin in Alençon, France, the youngest of five sisters who became nuns. She entered the Carmelite monastery of Lisieux at age fifteen and subsequently became Thérèse of the Child Jesus and the Holy Face. Told to write the story of her life, she composed an autobiography she said reflected not on what had occurred but on grace at work in the events. She declared she had suffered much, but even in the excruciating darkness of

Thérèse of Lisieux, better known as the Little Flower, a highly influential spiritual force for Catholics in the first half of the twentieth century because of the simplicity and practicality of her approach to sanctity.

mystic purification she continued to rejoice in the outpouring of divine love for her. Thérèse makes her story a canticle of gratitude to Jesus Christ, whom she sees present with her in every experience.

Her teaching shows how the most ordinary human existence contains material for extraordinary holiness. Thérèse invites others to follow her "little way" of spiritual childhood, which she describes as an attitude of unlimited hope in God's merciful love.

Her spiritual nourishment came especially from Scripture and the works of John of the Cross (d. 1591). She emphasized the apostolic power of prayer, hidden but far-reaching in serving the Church and the world.

All major languages have translations of the writings of this most beloved of modern saints. Thérèse's profound and joyous simplicity conveys original insights into the theology of grace.

She died of tuberculosis at age twenty-four.

Countless miracles attributed to her intercession fulfill her promise to spend her heaven doing good upon earth. Feast day: October 1. MARGARET DORGAN

thesis-hypothesis. *See* Church and state.

Thierry of Chartres (teer'ee uhv shahrtr), d. 1151/6, Scholastic philosopher and theologian. A teacher at the school of Chartres, and in 1141 its archdeacon and chancellor, Thierry sought to reconcile Platonic philosophy with Christian revelation, as in his work on the creation. He also wrote important commentaries on Cicero and Boethius.

Thils, Gustave, b. 1909, theologian. Ordained a priest for the archdiocese of Malines, Belgium, in 1931, he obtained his doctorate and *Magister theologiae* (Lat., "Master of theology"), a degree beyond the doctorate, at the University of Louvain (1935, 1937) and taught theology (1939–47) in the major seminary of Mechelen (Malines) and at the University of Louvain (1947–77). Author of more than twenty books and many scholarly and popular articles on the Church, ecumenism, spirituality, and related topics, he was an expert (*periti*) at the Second Vatican Council and a major contributor to the Decree on Ecumenism (*Unitatis Redintegratio*) and the Pastoral Constitution on the Church in the Modern World (*Gaudium et Spes*).

Third Order Regular of St. Francis, religious congregations tracing their origins to the third order secular established by Francis of Assisi in 1221. Though Franciscan tertiaries did not initially take public vows of poverty, chastity, and obedience, and did not live together in community, many fourteenth- and fifteenth-century Franciscan tertiaries of Italy began to do so. They were accorded official approbation as third order regulars by Pope Nicholas V in 1447. Congregations of third order Franciscans, both male and female, having arisen throughout Europe and the United States, now take public vows and live under a common rule of life in the spirit of St. Francis, as do the other principal orders of Franciscans: the Friars Minor, Conventuals, and Capuchin[esse]s. *See also* Franciscan order; tertiary; third orders.

third orders, associations of laity (third orders secular) or of religious women and men (third orders regular). The latter are religious institutes whose members take public vows and follow the spirit and rule of an order, e.g., the Third Order Regular of St. Francis. Traditionally men belonged to a first order and women to a second order, e.g., Second Order Dominicans. Third order has been a category for laity who seek to attain holiness by following a way of life in the world but under the inspiration and spiritual guidance of a papally approved religious institute. Diocesan priests can also belong to third orders. Most third-order members, sometimes called tertiaries, make promises but some members take vows. Promises and vows in third orders, as among first and second orders, are a renewal of baptismal promises. The religious practices of third orders are meant to suit life in secular society, but third orders challenge members to take seriously the gospel of Jesus in the context of the traditions of the order to which they are affiliated.

The third-order movement attained formal structure with Francis of Assisi, and the Franciscans spread the movement throughout Europe. However, during the Middle Ages there was great variety in the kinds of affiliation that the laity had with the first and second orders. Secular third orders, since Vatican II (1962–65), often go by other names, e.g., Lay Carmelites. Canon law accords official recognition to third orders as corporate juridical persons. *See also* tertiary; Third Order Regular of St. Francis.

Thirty-nine Articles, the doctrinal summary of the Church of England. Passed by Convocation in 1563, the Thirty-nine Articles represent the teaching of the reformed Church of England, based on a revision of Cranmer's Forty-two Articles of 1553, combining Lutheran and Reformed themes in a way characteristic of the Elizabethan settlement. Founded on the material norm of Christ's once-for-all sacrifice for sin (Articles 1–4) and the formal norm of Scripture alone (6–8), the articles present a Lutheran understanding of justification (9–16) and a Reformed understanding of election (17) and the sacraments (25–31), along with the Erastian (state over church) ecclesiology of Elizabeth I (19–21, 34–39), who personally deleted the article on sacramental eating (29, restored in 1571) and wrote a preface to Article 20 on rites and ceremonies in order not to offend Catholic piety. *See also* Anglicanism.

Thirty Years' War (1618–48), last European religious war and first "world war." Beginning with the Defenestration of Prague and ending with the Peace of Westphalia, the Thirty Years' War destroyed central Europe, undermined the Holy Roman Empire, and ushered in the modern era of secularized international relations. *See also* Holy Roman Empire.

Thomas, St. (Aram., "twin"), one of the twelve apostles. Thomas is mentioned in all the lists of the apostles (Matt 10:3; Mark 3:18; Luke 6:15; Acts 1:13), and he plays a prominent role in the Fourth Gospel. There he is designated not only by the name Thomas, but also by its Greek translation, Didymus (John 11:16; 20:24; 21:2). Thomas first appears as one who is ready to die with Jesus (John 11:16). At the Last Supper he admits that he does not know where Jesus is going (John 14:5). After the Resurrection he plays his most famous role as the doubting Thomas (John 20:24–29).

The tradition of the early Church connects Thomas with Parthia and India. In particular, the *Acts of Thomas* tells of his legendary missionary activity in the East. The *Acts of Thomas* portrays Thomas as an extreme ascetic who preached total sexual renunciation. Thomas is supposed to have been martyred in India and his bones transferred to the Syrian city of Edessa. There the fourth-century pilgrim Egeria visited his memorial. Thomas's mission to India is venerated by the Thomas Christians of the Malabar Coast and relics are preserved in the Cathedral of St. Thomas at Mylapore.

The *Gospel of Thomas* is a collection of sayings of Jesus that Thomas supposedly transcribed. Like the *Acts of Thomas,* it has Syrian connections and ascetical leanings. The distinct *Infancy Gospel of Thomas* says nothing about the apostle.

The Syrian traditions represented by the *Gospel of Thomas* and the *Acts of Thomas* understood Thomas's name to indicate that he was the "twin" of Jesus. Feast day: July 3. *See also* apocryphal Gospels; apostle; Thomas Christians; Twelve, the.

Thomas à Kempis, ca. 1380–1471, author of the *Imitation of Christ,* a book that expresses the spirituality of the Modern Devotion (Devotio Moderna). This renewal movement was begun in the latter half of the fourteenth century by Geert de Groote (d. 1384) and spread through the Netherlands and Germany. Thomas was born in Kempen in the Rhineland and schooled by de Groote's Brothers of the Common Life at Deventer. In 1399 he joined the Canons Regular of St. Augustine at Mount St. Agnes. He was elected subprior in 1425 and was responsible for training novices. First published anonymously, *Imitation* is commonly attributed to Thomas. He wrote other devotional works, sermons, and biographies of the founders of the Modern Devotion. *See also* Devotio Moderna.

Thomas Aquinas, St. *See* Aquinas, St. Thomas.

Thomas Becket, St. *See* Becket, St. Thomas.

Thomas Christians, common epithet for the Malabar Christians of India, mostly concentrated in the state of Kerala on the southwest coast, who trace their origins to the evangelization of India by the Apostle Thomas. Today these Christians belong to the Syro-Malabar and Syro-Malankara Catholic churches and to their Orthodox counterparts, or to various offshoots from these historic churches. *See also* Syro-Malabar Catholic Church; Syro-Malankara Catholic Church.

Thomas More, St. *See* More, St. Thomas.

Thomas of Villanova, St. *See* Villanova, St. Thomas of.

Thomism, the thought of Thomas Aquinas (d. 1274) and of the succession of individuals and schools that interpreted and applied his ideas. Expositions of Aquinas are found in universities (Louvain, The Catholic University of America), religious orders (Dominicans, Jesuits), periods (the Baroque, the early twentieth century), and in orientations (political, historical, philosophical, transcendental). Thomism has four periods: the age of defenses (thirteenth–fifteenth centuries); the age of commentaries (1450–1630); the age of disputations, encyclopedias, and systems (1500–1720); the Thomist revival (1860–1960). The last three, particularly the most recent, are "neo-Thomisms." Neo-Thomism in turn is a development within neo-Scholasticism, the revival of Scholastic, that is, medieval theology. Modern neo-Thomism (rarely discussed outside of Catholicism and mandated by papal documents like Pope Leo XIII's encyclical *Aeterni Patris* of 1879) sought to transcend the Enlightenment and Reformation by proposing that the thought-world of medieval Scholasticism, and particularly that of Thomas Aquinas, could hold solutions to contemporary problems.

Important moments in the history of Thomist interpretations occurred, for instance, in the sixteenth century with the Salamancan Dominicans defending human rights, the controversy between Jesuits and Dominicans over grace and free will, and the interpretation of grace and personality employed by the Carmelite mystics. Less positive were the unimaginative Church responses, mired in a dated Scholasticism, to both the Renaissance and the Reformation, and the widespread but superficial and often oppressive study of Thomist textbooks prior to Vatican II (1962–65). The "fourth Thomism" (1860–1960) was excessively philosophical, a sign of which is the attempt through "Twenty-four Theses" to establish one set of philosophical principles that would encapsulate all of Aquinas. At the turn of the century various scholars (Martin Grabmann, Étienne Gilson, and Marie-Dominique Chenu) initiated the study of the Middle Ages, locating Aquinas's theology in its cultural context; others (Pierre Rousselot, Joseph Maréchal) brought the thought of Aquinas into dialogue with modern philosophies. Along with the reemphasis in Catholicism on the Bible and the Fathers, these scholarly initiatives led to a greater appreciation of Aquinas as a theologian.

Basic Elements: Throughout its many metamorphoses Thomism remains a philosophical theology where human life remains in active touch with the worlds of nature and of grace. Fundamental to this school of thought are the following: each nature reveals its being through activity, and it acts for a goal; God bestows upon creatures the reality and dignity of true causes; human knowing grasps and forms the external world; human beings are created images of God's intelligence and goodness; the life of the Trinity is shared with women and men through grace; this graced life, theologically explored from Aristotle's psychology, is an invitation for all to virtue and meditation; in this life Jesus is both casual influence and model and his power continues in sacraments of grace. One can find these characteristics at work in modern theologians such as Edward Schillebeeckx and Karl Rahner (d. 1984), painters such as Fra Angelico (d. 1455) and Raphael (d. 1520), novelists such as Graham Greene (d. 1991) and Flannery O'Connor (d. 1964), or in papal encyclicals on social justice.

The most recent Thomism, with its own pluralism (Jesuits and Dominicans, Reginald Garrigou-Lagrange and Antonin-Gilbert Sertillanges), succeeded by 1935 in making known the texts and philosophy of Aquinas and in extending the influence of his thought. But many sought through Vatican power a monopolistic and dictatorial control over Catholic thinking, and, in the name of Thomism, warred against modern philosophy, science, and politics as well as ecumenism, vernacular liturgy, and modern art. But the mind of Aquinas was, in fact, remarkably open to diverse movements and sources. This monopoly of thought ended when Vatican II (1962–65) affirmed modern biblical, patristic, systematic, and pastoral theologies, many of which were rooted in Aquinas's historical openness and positive depiction of God and humans. *See also* Aquinas, St. Thomas; neo-Scholasticism; Scholasticism; transcendental Thomism.   THOMAS F. O'MEARA

Thompson, Francis, 1859–1907, English poet and critic. The son of converts to Catholicism, his early life was a series of failures: he dropped out of seminary, ended medical studies at Manchester University, quit as a salesman, and was not accepted by the army. When his mother died in 1880, he became an opium addict and a derelict. In 1889 the monks at Storrington took him in, and his masterpiece, "The Hound of Heaven," was written the following year. His last ten years were quite productive: he wrote over five hundred reviews. His poetry is metaphysical in its interests, mystical, and somewhat florid.

Thorlac Thorhallsson, St., 1133–93, patron saint of Iceland. He founded a monastery at Thykkviboer and became its abbot. Later he was named bishop of Skalholt, one of two dioceses in Iceland. Feast day: December 23.

Three Chapters (ca. 544), strictly speaking, an edict of the emperor Justinian, but the name is usually transferred to the three subjects it anathematizes. Justinian attempted to appease the Monophysites by condemning the person and works of Theodore of Mopsuestia, the writings of Theodoret of Cyrrhus against Cyril of Alexandria, and Ibas of Edessa's letter to Maris—all representatives of the Antiochene theology inherited and developed by Nestorius. Pope Vigilius protested but, summoned to Constantinople, reversed himself (548). The Western churches objected vehemently, and Vigilius withdrew his support, but Constantinople II (553) condemned the Three Chapters and excommunicated Vigilius. When Vigilius, condemned to prison or exile, confirmed the council's decision (December 553), the Western bishops again protested, the patriarchate of Aquileia even withdrawing from communion. The schism persisted until ca. 689. *See*

also Antioch, school of; Constantinople, councils of; Justinian I; Monophysitism; Vigilius.

throats, blessing of, the practice of placing two crossed candles, accompanied by the recitation of a prayer, on the throats of the faithful. This practice arose as part of the cult of St. Blaise, a fourth-century bishop of Sebaste (modern Armenia). When Diocletian ordered the persecution of Christians, Blaise hid in a forest. Legend describes wild animals gathering in his cave where, unharmed, he fed them all. When hunters came upon his hiding place and saw him surrounded by lions and bears, they decided he was a magician and took him captive. While in prison, he saved the life of a boy who was choking on a fishbone. The boy's mother rewarded Blaise with food and candles. Blaise was later beheaded. After his martyrdom he was invoked, as one of the Fourteen Holy Helpers, on behalf of people suffering from throat infections. The blessing of throats with candles on his feast day began in the sixteenth century when his cult was at its peak. Feast day: February 3. *See also* Blaise, St.

throne, bishop's. *See cathedra.*

thurible (thur'ih-bul; Lat., "censer" or "incense"), the vessel containing hot coals in which incense is

Thurible

thurible

Papal tiara

burned. It may also be called a censer. Thuribles are made of metal, suspended upon a short chain, and swung gently to create the most smoke. Some vessels for burning incense are stationary, but these are more properly called braziers. *See also* incense; thurifer.

thurifer (thur'ih-fur; Lat., "thurible carrier"), the minister or acolyte charged with holding the thurible and incense boat during liturgical ceremonies. The thurifer maintains the lighted charcoals within the thurible. The thurifer is always the first member of any procession, proceeding either the cross or the Gospel book. *See also* incense; thurible.

tiara, papal, extraliturgical papal headdress that evolved from a kind of cap in the early Middle Ages. It assumed a coronet and then, in time, two and finally three coronets with two cloth strips (lappets) hanging behind. The final, beehive shape took its form in the fifteenth century. The symbolism of the tiara was closely associated with both sacred and secular papal power. With the Second Vatican Council (1962–65), however, that symbolism, plus its increasingly ornate and costly character, came to be regarded as inappropriate. The use of the tiara (and any "crowning" with it for new popes) was ended by Pope Paul VI after the council, and no pope has used it or been crowned with it ever since. *See also* coronation, papal.

Tillich, Paul, 1886–1965, German Protestant theologian who influenced both Protestant and Catholic thinkers, especially in the United States.

Tillich's experiences in World War I modified his education in liberal Protestantism, while his life in Berlin expanded his cultural horizons. He was a pioneering advocate within Protestantism for a more positive attitude toward modern art and psychotherapy. After influencing generations of students at Union Theological Seminary in New York, his university-wide lectures at Harvard University and the University of Chicago were exceedingly popular, and during this time he composed his three-volume *Systematic Theology* (1951–63). With Catholic theologians in the United States, he initiated a dialogue that spread to Germany, France, and Italy, and then to Africa and Asia. Catholics were particularly attracted by Tillich's appreciation of philosophy and mysticism, his knowledge of the history of Christianity outside of Protestantism, and his theology's openness to the divine in the finite (the principle of sacramentality).

time, duration wherein events are ordered as earlier than, simultaneous with, or later than one another. Philosophers and scientists debate, for example, time's relationship to change, how time as subjectively experienced relates to time as an objective measure, and whether, in view of its relativistic connection to space, time "flows." Augustine (d. 430) and Thomas Aquinas (d. 1274) formulated the traditional position that, as its eternal Creator, God exists "outside" time, whatever its ultimate nature. Divine "timelessness" is, however, much debated by contemporary theologians. *See also* eternity; relativity; space.

time [canon law], computation of time according to legal rules. Some canonical rules seem quite obvious, such as "A day is composed of twenty-four hours." Others are more complicated and legislate the amount of time within which certain procedures must or may take place. Still others lay down the manner in which time should be calculated for certain actions.

There are two kinds of time in canon law (cans. 200–203): continuous time (the usual way of calculating the lapse of time) and available time (sometimes called useful time). Terms of office are calculated continuously, as is the six-month interval between ordination to the diaconate and ordination to the priesthood. On the other hand, if a person is elected to an office, the law provides eight days of available time from the receipt of notification to the time when the person informs the authority whether he or she accepts the office. However, if the person is unaware of this legal provision or is unable to respond within its limits, the time within which the response is to be made does not run. Available time also applies to appeals against judicial sentences and for recourse against administrative decrees.

Timothy, St., early Christian missionary and co-worker of the Apostle Paul. Timothy came from Lystra in Asia Minor, the son of a Jewish-Christian mother and a Greek father (Acts 16:1). Paul first met him during Paul's second missionary journey. Timothy accompanied him during parts of his second and third missionary journeys. During the second missionary journey, Timothy was sent by Paul to strengthen the Thessalonian Christians (1 Thess 1:1; 3:2, 6). During the third he was sent by Paul from Ephesus to Corinth (1 Cor 4:17; 16:10) and to Philippi (Phil 2:19) as an emissary to deal with the problems of these two communities. Paul joined Timothy again in Macedonia (Acts 19:22; 2 Cor 1:19), and he accompanied Paul to Corinth (Rom 16:10) and at least as far as Troas on Paul's return to Jerusalem (Acts 20:4). Timothy's prominence is indicated not only by the delicate tasks that Paul gave him but also by his being listed by Paul in the openings of 1 Thessalonians, Philippians, and 2 Corinthians. Timothy was also the supposed recipient of two letters from Paul (1–2 Timothy), both of which probably came from a "Pauline school" toward the end of the first century A.D. In later Christian tradition Timothy was considered the first bishop of Ephesus (probably based on 1 Tim 1:3). Feast day: January 26.

Tisserant, Eugene Gabriel, 1884–1972, French orientalist, Oriental Scriptor, and later Prefect (head librarian) of the Vatican Library. Created a cardinal and bishop in 1937, Tisserant is esteemed for his years (1936–59) as Prefect of the Vatican Congregation for the Oriental Churches, where he manifested his knowledge, love, and support for Eastern Catholics. He was dean of the College of Cardinals when John XXIII was elected (1958).

tithing, the setting aside of a tenth of one's income for sacred purposes. A common practice in the ancient Near East, it appears in several OT law codes. Some texts suggest it was associated with shrines (Gen 28:22; Amos 4:4) or served as a royal tax (1 Sam 8:15, 17). The Deuteronomistic code modified regulations in an effort to create a central sanc-tuary (Deut 14:22–29). The priestly code and post-exilic texts stressed clerical support (Lev 27:30–33; Num 18:21–32; Neh 10:32–39). Later attempts to harmonize variations in these codes resulted in multiple tithes (Tob 1:6–8). NT writers mention tithing only in passing (Matt 23:23; Luke 11:42; Heb 7:1–10). Paul's instructions on the Jerusalem collection urge voluntary giving (1 Cor 16:1–4; 2 Cor 8–9), which became the practice of Christians until religious and civil authorities (sixth and eighth centuries) initiated legislation mandating tithing. Although the Council of Trent (1545–63) upheld the practice, civil authorities have abolished it since and ecclesiastical practice has moved back toward voluntary contributions.

title, a classical inscription (*titulus*, Lat.) denoting a claim to a particular building or territory. Thus, the term applies to a church or deaconry assigned to a cardinal. Because the College of Cardinals has its origin in the clergy of Rome, each cardinal is assigned to a church or deaconry (section of that city) in remembrance of this fact. The term was also used in the past to indicate the source of support for a cleric receiving Holy Orders, e.g., the title to remunerated service of the diocese, or to daily meals at the common table. *See also* titular church.

titles of Christ, biblical references to Jesus Christ. The name "Christ" is the English translation of the Latin *Christus* or the Greek *Christos,* both of which are references to "the anointed one," or the Hebrew word for "messiah." Shortly after Jesus' death, the disciples called him "the Christ" to express their belief in him as the unique Messiah, but this title became shortened to "Christ." The NT uses "Jesus Christ" and "Christ Jesus" interchangeably. Additionally, the Christian tradition includes the following biblical references as titles of Christ:

son of Joseph (Mark 6:3)
son of Mary (Luke 3:23)
the Son of Man (Matt 8:20)
the Bread of Life (John 6:35)
the Master (Luke 8:24)
the High Priest (Heb 5:10)
prophet (Matt 21:46)
bridegroom (Mark 2:19)
the Alpha and the Omega (Rev 22:13)
Logos (John 1:1)
the Just One (Acts 3:14)
Lamb of God (John 1:29)
the Way, the Truth, and the Life (John 14:6)

the Good Shepherd (John 10:11)
the Lord (Rom 10:9)
the Head of the Body (Col 1:18)
the Vine (John 15:1)
the Savior (Titus 3:7)
Redeemer (Luke 24:21)
Servant (Luke 22:26)
the Light of the World (John 8:12)
the Resurrection (John 21:23)
the firstborn (Col 1:15)
He-Who-Comes (Luke 13:35)
the Son of God (Matt 14:33)
See also Jesus Christ.

titular bishop, bishop given an honorary diocese. Auxiliary bishops, together with those in diplomatic or administrative posts and who are not heads of dioceses, are given the title of an extinct see (e.g., Hippo, St. Augustine's diocese in North Africa) as a reminder that the office of bishop has its primary purpose in caring for the people of a Christian community. Most of these extinct sees are in areas of the world in which there are no longer large numbers of Christians. See also auxiliary bishop; titular see.

titular church, Roman church assigned to a cardinal for honorary purposes. Because the College of Cardinals has its origin in the clergy of Rome, each cardinal is given an honorary position among the Roman clergy. Titular churches usually display the coats of arms and portraits or photographs of the cardinal to whom they have been assigned. Many cardinals take an interest in their Roman churches and offer them financial assistance. Cardinal deacons' churches are known as diaconal rather than titular churches. See also title.

titular see, extinct diocese given to a bishop who is not the head of an extant see. The bishop might be an auxiliary or have another administrative or diplomatic position. Titular sees (e.g., Hippo in North Africa) are in a part of the world (e.g., Turkey, Syria, North Africa) where there is no longer a Christian community (at least not one large enough to be recognized as a diocese). See also titular bishop.

Titus, St. (tī'tuhs), early Christian missionary and co-worker of the Apostle Paul. Titus was of Greek origin and perhaps a native of Antioch on the Orontes. In A.D. 48 he accompanied Paul and Barnabas from Antioch to Jerusalem to meet with the leaders of the Jerusalem church about whether gentile Christians

had to be circumcised and observe Mosaic law. As an indication of his success, Paul claimed that Titus, although a Greek, was not compelled to be circumcised (Gal 2:3). Titus was Paul's co-worker at least during Paul's stay at Ephesus on his third missionary journey. In Paul's sometimes bitter dispute with the Corinthian Christians, Titus was sent to Corinth to serve as intermediary. He was successful in mediating the dispute for, when Paul rejoined Titus in Macedonia, he was comforted by the news that Titus brought from Corinth (2 Cor 2:13; 7:6, 13–14). Titus was also the supposed recipient of a Letter from Paul (Titus), which probably came from a "Pauline school" toward the end of the first century A.D. Titus also appears in several of the apocryphal Acts of the apostles and, based on Titus 1:5, was later thought to be the first bishop of Crete. Feast day: January 26.

Toledo, councils of, apart from the relatively insignificant first and second councils (ca. 397 and 527), a series of sixteen Visigothic councils meeting at Toledo from 589 to 702. They embody a uniquely Visigothic symbiosis between Church and state. Convened by the king, but under the presidency of a bishop, they issued professions of faith and canons pertaining to church discipline, but could also promulgate law codes and other legislation pertaining to national affairs. See also Spain, Catholicism in.

tolerance, religious, respect for the consciences of others in matters of religious faith and practice and acknowledgment of their legal right to express and practice their faith. Catholic teaching on religious tolerance developed significantly at Vatican II in the Declaration on Religious Freedom (1965). Before the council, the Church called upon states to protect the religious freedom of the Church when Catholics were a minority, but did not call for tolerance toward other faiths when Catholics were a majority. At the council the Church went far beyond merely advocating tolerance and held that religious freedom is a natural right. The foundation of this right is twofold: the dignity of free and rational human persons, which requires that individuals assume personal responsibility for their actions and omissions (n. 2); and the freedom of the act of faith (nn. 9–10). The full exercise of human responsibility requires freedom from both coercion and restraint in all matters of religion. Since human responsibility is inalienable, this right may not be removed or impeded, except to protect the public order (n. 4). The council further held that this natural right to religious freedom should be given constitutional protection and hence become a civil right (nn. 2, 6).

The Church's prior official teaching was rooted in the proposition that error and evil have no rights and in the fear that an endorsement of toleration would support religious indifferentism or relativism. The council avoided this problem by seeing religious freedom as a negative right, a freedom from coercion, not a freedom to believe what is false and do what is evil. *See also* Declaration on Religious Freedom; religious liberty.   *THOMAS POUNDSTONE*

toleration of evil, the allowance or noneradication of wrongful practices or institutions. The context for discussing toleration of evil is that of the use of authority, and most especially (though not exclusively) civil authority. Civil authorities are charged with protecting the rights of individuals and promoting those conditions favorable to their flourishing. In brief, they are charged with promoting the common good. This means that they will work to stamp out evil and its causes wherever feasible.

However, the eradication of evil is not always practically feasible. At times the attempt to do so will induce even greater evils or sacrifice indispensable goods. Catholic tradition has, therefore, accepted the general notion that the toleration of evil by civil authorities is sometimes morally permissible.

The classic statement on the matter is that of Thomas Aquinas (d. 1274) in the *Summa Theologiae*: "Human governance is derived from divine governance, and it ought to imitate this divine governance. Although God is omnipotent and good in the highest degree, nevertheless he permits certain evil things to develop in the universe, which he would be able to prevent except that, if these things were taken away, greater goods would be eliminated or even greater evils would follow as a consequence. So also in human governance, those who govern rightly tolerate certain evils lest certain goods be impeded or also lest some greater evil obtain, as Augustine said in the second book of his *De Ordine*" (2–2, 10.11).

Theologians have accepted this general principle but they have disagreed vigorously at times about its application to this or that evil, e.g., prostitution and abortion. *See also* civil law and morality; evil.

RICHARD A. MCCORMICK

Tolton, Augustus, 1854–97, the first African-American priest to identify with, and to be ac-

Augustus Tolton, a priest whose courageous example in the face of racial prejudice has inspired African-American Catholics in the United States ever since.

claimed by, black Catholics. Born a slave, Tolton was ordained in Rome in 1886. Denis J. O'Connell, rector of the North American College in Rome, said that Tolton's ordination "opens the door wider here for colored candidates." After an initial period of acceptance, however, his trials as a pastor in Quincy, Illinois, and in Chicago, where he endured severe racial prejudice, portended the fate of many black priests. Bishop James Ryan of Alton, Illinois, explained to Rome that Tolton's trouble in Quincy resulted because "he wants to establish a kind of society here that is not possible (integration)." Even the great archbishop John Ireland of St. Paul, Minnesota, once said of a prospective young black seminarian, "I want no Toltons." Tolton's ministry, however, inspired increased black Catholic activism in the Church and in society and his name is still held in high esteem among African-American Catholics today. *See also* black Catholics.

Tome of Leo, the letter sent in June 449 by Pope Leo the Great to Flavian, patriarch of Constantinople, condemning Eutyches's Christology; it is the classical articulation of the Western Christology of two natures, one person. The *Tome* was canonized by the Council of Chalcedon (451), and many of its phrases were adopted into the council's formula. It teaches that the one subject in Jesus is the person of the Word of God, in whom two natures are permanently but unconfusedly united. Each nature retains its characteristic properties (e.g., it is the humanity, properly speaking, that suffers), but because of the unity of person, it is also appropriate and indeed necessary to say, e.g., that God's eternal Son was crucified. *See also* Chalcedon, Council of; Christology; Leo I, "the Great," St.

tongues, gift of. *See* glossolalia.

tonsure, a now-abandoned rite of initiation to the clerical state. The rite involved the ceremonial cutting of a portion of the candidate's hair on the crown of the head. Originally a monastic practice, tonsure later emerged as a distinct rite of admission to the clerical state in the sixth and seventh centuries. Paul

Traditional full tonsure of a monk; other forms were much smaller in size or, in the case of candidates for the diocesan priesthood, involved only a symbolic clipping of a few hairs from the crown of the head.

VI eliminated tonsure and all minor orders in 1972. Admission to the clerical state now occurs at ordination to the diaconate. *See also* clergy; deacon.

Torah (tohr'ah; Heb., "instruction"), the traditional Jewish designation for the Pentateuch. Torah can be used generically to refer to commands and rulings (Gen 26:5; Exod 18:16) or to instruction, particularly for priests (Deut 17:10–11; 33:10). The term epitomized the instruction that God gave through Moses (Josh 1:7; 1 Kgs 2:3). It came to be applied to the collection of such instruction found in the book of Deuteronomy (Deut 1:5; 4:8; 28:58, 61; 31:26), a version of which was found in the Temple under Josiah (2 Kgs 22:8; 23:25). From that application arose the more comprehensive reference to the whole of the Pentateuch. *See also* Pentateuch.

Torquemada, Juan de, also known as Juan de Turrecremata, 1388–1468, Spanish Dominican bishop, cardinal, and theologian. He attended the councils of Constance (1414–18) and Basel-Ferrara-Florence (1431–43), defending the rights of the papacy, opposing conciliarism, and presenting the first systematic exposition of the pope's universal pastoral jurisdiction. He also played an important role at the Council of Florence in the negotiations for reunion with the Greek Church. His magisterial work, *Summa on the Church* (1489), was a major step in the development of ecclesiology. Although it defended papal infallibility and the fullness of the pope's spiritual power, it took a moderate position on temporal papal power. He supported the Thomist tradition in opposing the doctrine of the Immaculate Conception.

Torquemada, Tomas de, also known as Tomas de Turrecremata, 1420–98, Spanish Grand Inquisitor and Dominican confessor of Isabella I and Ferdinand. Though himself of Jewish descent, he encouraged the expulsion of the Jews from Spain. In spite of papal attempts to restrain him, he pursued people accused of heresy with unprecedented rigor. *See also* Inquisition.

totality, principle of, the principle that justifies the sacrifice of an organ or its function for the overall good of the whole person (thus, "totality").

Pope Pius XII discusses this principle in many places in his essays on medical ethics. He rejects its application to the individual's relation to the community, as if the person could be subordinated to the good of the community. While the name "principle of totality" is relatively new, the concept is not. Thomas Aquinas (d. 1274) wrote: "Since any member is a part of the whole human body, it exists for the sake of the whole as the imperfect for the sake of the perfect. Hence a member of the human body is to be disposed of according as it may profit the whole. *Per se*, the member of the human body is useful for the welfare of the whole body; *per accidens,* however it can happen that it is harmful, for example, when a diseased member is injurious to the whole body. If, therefore, a member is healthy and continuing in its natural state, it cannot be cut off to the detriment of the whole" (*Summa Theologiae* 2–2, 65.1c).

Clearly, contemporary theologians, with greater medical knowledge, realize that even healthy organs and functions can be a "detriment to the whole." *See also* bioethics; medical ethics.

Toth, Alexis (tawth), 1845–1909, first Ruthenian Catholic priest in America to convert to Russian Orthodoxy. This conversion happened after an interview with Archbishop Ireland of St. Paul, during which he requested and was refused permission to function as a priest. In all, about 300,000 Catholic Ruthenians became Orthodox as a result of the movement that the Hungarian-born Toth started. Posthumously, he was hailed by the Russian Orthodox as the "Father of American Orthodoxy." *See also* Ireland, John.

tract, a psalm chanted after the first reading in the Tridentine Mass by a soloist on certain more solemn penitential days in which the Alleluia is not sung. *See also* Tridentine Mass.

Tracy, David W., b. 1939, a leading American theologian and professor at the University of Chicago. Ordained in 1963, he received an S.T.D. from Gregorian University, Rome, in 1965. He has taught at The Divinity School, University of Chicago, since 1969 and has, since 1987, occupied the Greeley Distinguished Service Professorship of Catholic Studies. He is the author of major works in foundational theology, including *Blessed Rage for Order* (1975) and *The Analogical Imagination* (1981).

tradition, the process and content of the transmission of beliefs, doctrines, rituals, Scriptures, and life of the Church. As process, tradition constitutes the teaching, life, and worship of the Church through which the truth and reality communicated by Christ and the Spirit to the apostles is passed on to succeeding generations. As content, tradition comprises the whole life of the Church, everything that contributes to holiness of life, all that the Church is and believes (Vatican II, Dogmatic Constitution on Divine Revelation, n. 8). This content is more than a message; it is the whole life and activity of the Church, the totality of Christian revelation.

General usage distinguishes between Tradition (capital "T") as the process of transmission, tradition (small "t," singular) as the content of what is transmitted, and traditions (small "t," plural) as the particular customs of separate churches or movements.

Council of Trent: The relationship between Scripture and tradition has been a critical point of discussion in the history of the Church. When Martin Luther insisted that the word of God in Scripture was the only source of Christian truth, the Church was faced with the task of articulating the relationship between Scripture and tradition. After rejecting a preliminary draft that stated that revelation is contained "partly in written books, partly in unwritten traditions," the Council of Trent (1543–65) taught that the gospel, the source of saving truth and rule of conduct, is "contained in the written books and unwritten traditions" that have come down to us. (D 1501)

Sometimes Trent is interpreted as teaching that revelation is contained in two separate, parallel sources, Scripture and tradition, and this was, in fact, the general interpretation of the Counter-Reformation, which interpreted revelation as a series of propositions contained either in Scripture or handed down by oral tradition, so as to imply two different sources of Tradition. This was the position of Melchior Cano, Peter Canisius, Robert Bellarmine, and H. Lennerz. J. R. Geiselmann, on the other hand, held that divine revelation is contained entirely in tradition and entirely in the Scriptures. J. Beumer developed an intermediate theory according to which tradition encompasses all that Scripture contains and interprets it.

Today it is generally agreed that Scripture itself is a product of tradition (upper and lower cases alike). In the early Church an oral tradition preceded the written tradition collected in the Scriptures. In this sense tradition logically and chronologically precedes Scripture.

Trent does not explicitly consider tradition in the

modern sense of the whole life of the Church. Nor does it refer to traditions as a collection of traditions, that is, ecclesiastical customs. Rather, "traditions" refer to apostolic traditions, what is essential to faith. Examples of traditions in the Tridentine sense would include the sacraments, particularly the Eucharist.

Second Vatican Council: The Second Vatican Council (1962–65) clarifies this relationship in the Dogmatic Constitution on Divine Revelation when it teaches that sacred Tradition and Sacred Scripture form one sacred deposit of the word of God, which is entrusted to the teaching authority of the Church for authentic interpretation (n. 10). Vatican Council II refused to adopt the expression "two sources of revelation." It spoke of a single deposit of the word of God expressed in written form or in the form of Tradition (n. 10). Significantly, the document does not oppose oral traditions to written traditions. Vatican II no longer identified revelation with propositions, but with the word of God in its entirety. Further, Tradition is seen as encompassing the whole life, witness, and worship of the Church.

Scripture and tradition are intimately interrelated; both of them, "flowing out from the same divine well-spring, come together in some fashion to form one thing, and move towards the same goal" (Dogmatic Constitution on Divine Revelation, n. 9). The correlative relationship between Scripture and tradition is evident in the fact that Scripture is the critical norm to which tradition is subject, while Scripture itself is one form of apostolic tradition because it represents the Christian community's experience of the life and teaching of Jesus.

As the relationship between Scripture and tradition has been a focal question in the Church, so, too, is the relationship between tradition and change. Tradition demands continuity with the past, yet because it is living, it also develops. Vatican II teaches that Tradition continues through the apostolic succession and develops with the help of the Holy Spirit with the result that revelation is received with greater understanding. Growth in insight into what is being passed on occurs through the contemplation and study of believers, their intimate sense of spiritual realities, and preaching (n. 8).

"The authentic interpretation of the Word of God, whether in its written form or in the form of Tradition, has been entrusted to the living teaching office of the Church alone" (n. 10). It is the responsibility of the teaching office to ensure that any growth in the tradition is continuous with the Tradition and with original revelation. This teaching office is limited by what has been handed on to it. *See also* revelation; Scripture and tradition; traditionalism, Catholic.

Bibliography

Congar, Yves. *Tradition and Traditions*. London: Burns and Oates, 1966.

Mackey, John P. *Tradition and Change in the Church*. Dayton, OH: Pflaum Press, 1968.

Moran, Gabriel. *Scripture and Tradition: A Survey of the Controversy*. New York: Herder and Herder, 1963.

Tavard, George H. *Holy Writ or Holy Church*. New York: Harper, 1959.

SUSAN K. WOOD

traditionalism, Catholic, a teaching of certain Catholic philosophers and theologians in the eighteenth and nineteenth centuries that human reason can attain to knowledge of God and of moral and religious truth only by God's revelation. Revelation is passed down within a tradition that provides instruction through the written and spoken word. There were two main schools of traditionalist thought. The rigid school was represented by L. de Bonald (d. 1840), who taught that the Creator had to provide the human mind with both ideas and language and had done so by speaking to a particular man who then instructed others. Similar teachings were put forth by F. de Lamennais (d. 1854) and by J. de Maistre (d. 1821). A moderate traditionalism was closely associated with the University of Louvain. Moderate traditionalists considered instruction a necessary condition for human reason to come to understanding of divine truth, though the capacity for such knowledge resided in reason itself.

Traditionalist doctrine was formulated against the extremes of Enlightenment rationalism, which denied any value to Christian tradition and fostered the idea that reasoning alone would lead to an understanding of all truth, even divine truth. Traditionalism itself, however, tends to the error of promoting blind faith, suggesting that faith is irrational and disregarding the value of human rationality.

Numerous provincial councils and several papal encyclicals during the first half of the nineteenth century condemned traditionalist writings. Nonetheless, the doctrine continued to attract adherents. Against extreme traditionalism, the First Vatican Council (1870) officially declared that without external revelation, human reason is capable of reaching the conclusion that God exists. The conciliar document, however, retains the values found in traditionalist emphasis on the importance of faith. It asserts that revelation, tradition, and instruction are important aids to full and correct understanding of God. Today Catholic traditionalism applies to those opposed to the central reforms of Vatican II (1962–65). *See also* tradition; Ultramontanism; Vatican Council I. *CORINNE WINTER*

tradition of the instruments. *See* instruments, tradition of the.

traditors (Lat., *traditor,* "one who handed over"), persons who surrendered the Scriptures when possession of them was outlawed in Africa during the Diocletian persecution (303–311). When peace was restored to the churches, controversies began concerning the validity of sacraments celebrated by traditors. *See also* persecutions.

traducianism (Lat., *tradux,* "vine branch"), the doctrine that human souls are derived from their parents' souls, either by direct generation (Tertullian) or by God's individual shaping of spiritual substance derived from the parents' souls (admitted by Augustine as a possibility). *See also* soul.

transcendence (Lat., *transcendere,* "to climb over," "to surpass"), the divine, or supernatural, order. God is described as transcendent because God's existence surpasses creaturely existence. Transcendence is often contrasted with immanence. The latter emphasizes the presence of God within human existence rather than above and beyond it. *See also* supernatural.

transcendental Thomism, an approach in philosophy and theology that combines modern philosophy with the thought of Thomas Aquinas (d. 1274). Transcendental philosophy, which has origins in the works of Immanuel Kant but includes the range of modern philosophy from Friedrich Schelling to Henri Bergson and Martin Heidegger, focuses on the conditions of knowledge and on the nature of the human subject. Despite a century of hostility from Church authorities, after 1900 a few Catholic thinkers began to point out the similarities between this modern philosophy of the free human subject and that of Aristotle (d. 322 B.C.) and Aquinas. The latter two had addressed the dynamics of human knowledge. In the modern Francophone world the same issues were addressed by Pierre Rousselot, Joseph Maréchal, and Maurice Blondel; after World War I, in Germany other Catholic scholars continued the same approach: Gustav Siewerth, Johann Baptist Lotz, Max Müller, Bernhard Welte, and Karl

Rahner. In Rome, the Canadian Bernard Lonergan examined philosophy, theological method, and ways of knowing. The more conservative orientation of Hans Urs von Balthasar also had some sources in transcendental thought. Karl Rahner's theology in particular has shown how to consider the most basic truths of Christianity from the point of view of the human subject without sacrificing the divine initiative and the reality of revelation and grace. The Church is at times viewed by Vatican II (1962–65) as a collective self (People of God) or as a symbolic sacrament for history and the world. When an area of Christianity is explored through an analysis of the human subject, whether in psychology or existential philosophy, and when the historical and cultural context of knowledge and life is taken seriously, such a theology is really building upon the work of the transcendental Thomists. *See also* Thomism.

THOMAS F. O'MEARA

Transfiguration, the appearance of Jesus to his disciples in glorified form. The synoptic Gospels all record the episode (Matt 17:1–9; Mark 9:2–10; Luke 9:28–36). Jesus took Peter, James, and John with

Jesus is transfigured with Moses and Elijah, while Peter, James, and John cover their faces; sixteenth-century painting by Raphael, Villa Albani, Rome.

him onto a mountain. There he appeared before them in a luminous form with Moses and Elijah at his side. Peter reacted by proposing to build three tabernacles. A heavenly voice then declared Jesus to be the "beloved son" and enjoined the disciples to heed him. Jesus then appeared in his usual form and commanded his disciples to keep silence.

Numerous interpretations of the episode have been proposed. Some view it as a misplaced account of a resurrection appearance; others as a report of a mystical experience that Jesus' disciples had in his presence; others as a symbolic account devised by the first Evangelist or the tradition on which he relied. Whatever its origin, the episode serves as a literary device to place Jesus on the same level as the Law and the Prophets. He is the authentic source of divine truth for those who would listen to him. The feast of the Transfiguration is celebrated on August 6. *See also* Jesus Christ.

transfinalization, philosophical theory developed in the latter part of the twentieth century maintaining that the substance of a thing is its finality, or ultimate purpose; sacramental theory that in the Eucharist the finality of bread and wine as food to be eaten is changed into a new finality of nourishing Christians with the body and blood of Christ. In *Mysterium Fidei* (1965) Pope Paul VI insisted that the new finality is grounded in a new ontological reality, i.e., there is not only a change in ultimate purpose of the consecrated bread and wine but also in their very being. *See also* Real Presence; transubstantiation.

transignification, philosophical theory developed in the latter part of the twentieth century maintaining that the substance of a thing is its meaning; sacramental theory that in the Eucharist the meaning of bread and wine as the ordinary nourishment for human beings is changed into a new meaning of communion with the body and blood of the Lord. In *Mysterium Fidei* (1965) Pope Paul VI insisted that the new meaning is grounded in a new ontological reality, i.e., there is not only a change in the meaning of the consecrated bread and wine but also in their very being. *See also* Real Presence; transubstantiation.

transitional diaconate. *See* deacon, transitional.

transmutation, word used in the patristic era to describe the change that takes place in the bread

and wine at the Eucharist; also used by Guitmond of Aversa (late eleventh century), who described the change of the bread and wine as a transmutation of their substance into that of Christ's body and blood. *See also* Real Presence; transubstantiation.

transubstantiation, teaching of the Church that the substance of the bread and wine offered at the Eucharist is changed into the substance of the body and blood of Jesus Christ. The term emerged out of medieval attempts to resolve the conflict between seeing bread and wine as mere signs or asserting their change into the body and blood of Christ even in their physical components. In the late eleventh century theologians described the change that takes place at the Eucharist in terms of a change in the substance of bread and wine, which undergoes transformation into the substance of the Lord's body and blood. The term "transubstantiation" itself is found only in the twelfth century and was subsequently used at Lateran IV (1215).

Under the influence of Aristotelian thought, theologians gradually came to distinguish between the substance of the Eucharist (the body and blood of the Lord) and the accidents of bread and wine (their weight, texture, color, etc.). These remain, even as the substance of bread and wine changes into the substance of Christ's body and blood.

In response to opposition to transubstantiation from the Reformers of the sixteenth century, the Council of Trent in 1551 affirmed that the substance of bread and wine is changed into that of Christ's body and blood, adding that "this change the holy Catholic Church has fittingly and properly named transubstantiation."

Trent's use of the word was intended not to explain how the change takes place but to provide a term that describes what takes place. Theological attempts in the latter part of the twentieth century to define the substance (transignification and transfinalization) led Pope Paul VI to insist in *Mysterium Fidei* (1965) that the new meaning and finality of the consecrated bread and wine are grounded in the new ontological reality of the presence of the body and blood of the Lord. *See also* Real Presence.

JOHN J. STRYNKOWSKI

Trappistine Sisters, officially known as Cistercian Nuns of the Strict Observance (O.C.S.O.), an order of Cistercian women who trace their origins to the founding of a cloister for women at Tart, near the Cistercian monastery at Cîteaux, France, in the early

Trappist monk, also known as a Cistercian of the Strict Observance, fulfilling a normal daily task of service to his community and the Church with the use of modern technology.

twelfth century. The Trappistines represent a reform movement instituted by Dom Augustin with the 1796 founding of the convent La Sainte Volonté de Dieu in Switzerland. Today the Trappistines have convents throughout Europe and Africa, as well as two houses in the United States: in Wrentham, Massachusetts, and in Dubuque, Iowa. They are cloistered nuns, living a contemplative life of prayer, spiritual reading, and manual work. *See also* Cistercian order.

Trappists, the popular name for the main branch of the Cistercians, the Order of Cistercians of the Strict Observance (O.C.S.O.). It was formed in 1892 by the consolidation of three congregations of Cistercian monks and nuns who had resisted mitigation of monastic customs. The Strict Observance developed against the backdrop of seventeenth-century Gallicanism and Jansenism. Gallicanism claimed for the Catholic Church of France almost total autonomy from Rome. The crown made all ecclesiastical appointments and adjudicated disputes. A morally rigorous Jansenism opposed both papal centralism and state control of the Church, as well as aristocratic extravagance and Jesuit theology. In this environment, young reform-minded Cistercians declared their determination to observe the Rule of St. Benedict to the letter. The symbolic dividing line of reform—the refusal to eat meat—led to the nickname "abstinents," as against the "ancients," or followers of a long-standing relaxation of this rule.

Historical Development: Under Cardinal Richelieu, chief minister of France and commendary abbot general of the Cistercian order, and his successor, Cardinal Mazarin, the Strict Observance became increasingly influential, despite opposition from other Cistercian congregations and from Rome. When Richelieu died in 1642, the Ancients became defenders of the papacy against secular involvement in religious affairs and the Abstinents enjoyed the protection of the French queen, Anne of Austria (d. 1666), who traded papal acquiescence for royal opposition to Jansenism. The apostolic constitution *In Suprema* (1666) recognized the Strict Observance as a legal entity within the Sacred Order of Cistercians and fruitlessly imposed perpetual silence over the dispute.

The best known of the Strict Observance abbots was Armand-Jean Bouthillier de Rancé (d. 1700). A nobleman with connections to the royal court, Rancé had become commendatory abbot of five monasteries at age twelve, one of them the delapidated La Trappe. Having decided to introduce strict reform to La Trappe, he entered the Cistercians and in 1664 became the regular abbot of a community of nine. Modeled on early Cistercian ideals but strongly imbued with desert spirituality, the penitential life of La Trappe elicited awe and admiration in an age of indulgence.

The French Revolution (1789) abolished monastic orders as relics of medieval superstition and appropriated their properties. Disdaining both proffered pension and the requisite oath to the revolutionary government, the last novice-master of La Trappe, Augustin de Lestrange (1754–1827), fled with twenty-one monks to La Valsainte, Switzerland. Austerities were intensified, diet and rest restricted, and manual labor increased. Among the several small foundations Lestrange sent out, two groups bound for Canada were diverted by war to Westmalle, Belgium, and to Lulworth, England.

Breaking with Cistercian custom, Lestrange opened a school for boys and formed the teachers, children, and refugee nuns of various orders into a Third Order of Cistercians. At the French invasion of Switzerland, Lestrange set off with his monks, nuns, and schoolchildren—some 542 strong—on a two-year odyssey through eastern Europe to White Russia, back to Germany, on to America and finally, with the fall of Napoleon, back to France and La Trappe.

Some newly refounded Strict Observance houses abandoned the stringent "new reform" of Lestrange for the "old reform" of La Trappe. In a new war of observances, Cistercians divided between Ancient and Strict Observance, and among new reform, old reform, and new reform without Lestrange's oversight. By 1892 Pope Leo XIII insisted on the consoli-

dation of the Strict Observance, and the Order of Reformed Cistercians of the Strict Observance, popularly called "Trappists," came into being.

Postconciliar Changes: Until the Second Vatican Council (1962–65), Trappist monks and lay brothers as well as nuns were strictly enclosed and supported themselves chiefly by agricultural work and cottage industries. Since the council, Trappist have emphasized the founding ideals of the Cistercian order more than the seventeenth-century austerities that gave rise to their distinctive observance. Work is still done within the enclosure, although monks and nuns now go out for medical, business, and educational reasons. Private "cells" have replaced common dormitories at most monasteries. The distinction between choir monks/nuns and lay brothers/sisters has been discontinued, and strict silence and sign language have given way to necessary speaking.

The order maintains close bonds through triennial general chapters and regional meetings. New constitutions have recognized the cultural diversity of members in Europe, Asia, the Americas, and Africa by authorizing a "more authentic monastic life through legitimate diversity." Separate general chapters of monks and nuns have been supplemented since 1990 by a triennial meeting of abbots and abbesses with equal voice and vote. *See also* Cistercian order.

Bibliography

Krailsheimer, A. J. *Rancé and the Trappist Legacy.* Kalamazoo, MI: Cistercian Publishcations, 1985.

Lekai, Louis J. *The Rise of the Cistercian Strict Observance in Seventeenth-Century France.* Washington, DC: The Catholic University of America Press, 1968.

Shank, Lillian Thomas, and John A. Nichols, eds. *Hidden Springs: Medieval Religious Woman.* Vol. 3. Kalamazoo, MI: Cistercian Publications, 1993.   E. ROZANNE ELDER

traveler [canon law], a person who is outside his or her place of residency. Canon law places certain obligations upon travelers, namely, to obey the universal laws of the Church, and releases travelers from other obligations, namely, particular laws that apply to their home diocese or to the diocese in which they happen to be, so long as no harm to the public order of the Church occurs (can. 13). Thus, a Catholic traveler from Ireland, while visiting the United States in March, would be bound by the Sunday obligation to attend Mass each week but would not be bound to attend Mass on St. Patrick's Day, even though it is a holy day of obligation in Ireland.

Travelers are distinguished from wanderers (Lat.,

vagi) in that the former have a domicile, or residence, whereas the latter have no fixed residence anywhere. *See also* domicile; quasi-domicile; wanderer.

Trent, Council of, ecumenical council held from 1545 to 1563 in response to the Protestant Reformation.

The papal and imperial condemnations of Martin Luther (1521) were followed by the demand by the Diet of Nuremberg (1523) for an immediate "free Christian Council on German soil." The popes, however, were leery of Church councils because of their experiences with the councils of Constance (1414–17) and Basel (1431–49). They feared that the council would contend for control of the Church and introduce reforms to curtail papal power and diminish papal revenues. Under pressure from Charles V, Pope Paul III finally convened a council in the northern Italian city of Trent. It met in three convocations (1545–48, 1551–52, 1562–63) comprising twenty-five sessions. By its conclusion the council had defined Catholic doctrine in a way that made the split with the Protestants irrevocable.

From the beginning, the council was badly divided. The papacy and the Italian bishops dependent upon it wanted the council to limit itself to issues of doctrine to meet the Protestant challenge and to leave the reform of corruption and abuses within the Church hierarchy to the pope. The "ultramontane" churches (Germany, France, and Spain) wanted to begin with reform since they laid the blame for most of the abuses at the feet of the papacy itself. They decided to deal with doctrine and reform simultaneously.

Doctrine: The council (session 4) declared, in contrast to the Protestant reliance on Scripture alone, that Scripture and tradition were to be received with "equal reverence." The Latin Vulgate text of Scripture was declared the authentic version upon which Church teaching was to be based. These decrees rendered impossible any dialogue with the Protestants.

Session 5 further hardened the lines separating the two confessions. The council rejected Luther's teaching that Baptism did not eliminate original sin in its entirety. For Luther the concupiscence that remained was itself sin. For the council it was only a "scar," but not actually a sin. After months of heated discussion the council (session 6) rejected justification by faith alone. While asserting the necessity for grace at all stages of salvation, free will and human dispositions to receive grace were also affirmed.

Faith is the fundament, but good works are required and increase grace. The Protestants had distinguished sanctification from justification and had seen in the latter solely the remission of sins. By contrast, the council defined justification as including the "sanctification and renovation of the inner man."

Session 7 saw the reaffirmation of the Church's teaching on the sacraments as efficacious signs that confer grace through their proper execution (Lat., *ex opere operato*) independently of the faith of the recipient. The council maintained the traditional seven sacraments, rejecting the Protestant claim that only Baptism and the Eucharist had scriptural warrant.

Session 13 affirmed the Real Presence of Christ in the consecrated bread and wine of the Eucharist, thus rejecting the purely symbolic sacrament of Zwingli and Calvin. The council also defined that presence in terms of transubstantiation, implicitly rejecting Luther's consubstantiation.

Session 14 defined the sacrament of Penance and upheld the juridical nature of sacerdotal absolution. It also maintained Extreme Unction as a sacrament. Session 21 affirmed that in the Eucharist Christ was wholly present in each of the two elements. In Session 22 the pope was authorized to handle the practical question of whether the laity should receive only the Host or both Host and Precious Blood. Papal permission for the laity to receive both was eventually given for a time to several areas in Germany. Also in Session 22 the council reaffirmed that the Mass was a propitiatory sacrifice that may be offered to venerate the saints and to help the living and the dead. Session 23 defined the sacrament of Holy Orders as a divine ordinance conferring an indelible character. Session 24 reaffirmed the sacramentality of Matrimony and for the first time required that it be solemnized before a priest.

The council failed to issue a decree on the Church or to define the nature of the Roman primacy. The council was badly divided on the status of the bishops within the hierarchy. While extreme papalists, reflecting the growth of papal monarchy in the later Middle Ages, tended to view the bishops as deriving their power from the pope, the Ultramontane bishops retained the older tradition of the bishops as deriving their authority directly from God. For the Ultramontanes the pope was merely the first among equals. These two contrasting outlooks clashed over the issue of the residency of bishops in their dioceses. One of the gravest abuses of the late medieval

Church was the practice of bishops failing to reside in their dioceses, usually preferring to dwell at royal courts or urban centers. They normally received papal dispensations to do so. The reformers at Trent believed that declaring residency a divinely established responsibility would prevent papal liberality in this regard. The papal party opposed it for that reason and because it implied that bishops derived their being directly from God. A compromise was formulated in Session 23 that failed to resolve the matter.

Reform: The council also issued reform measures. For the first time Session 5 obligated bishops and pastors to preach on Sundays and holy days. Session 7 saw a number of measures designated to reestablish episcopal authority in the dioceses. Session 23 ordered the establishment of episcopal seminaries to train priests. Previously priests had received no formal training. Candidates simply presented themselves after a period of private study or apprenticeship. No spiritual preparation was provided. It was only in the seventeenth century that seminaries were established in great numbers, but they proved to be the most successful of the council's reforms. The council also commissioned the pope to carry out certain tasks after its closing: the Index of Forbidden Books (1564), the Tridentine Catechism (1566), a new Roman Breviary (1568), a reformed Roman Missal (1570), and a revised edition of the Vulgate (1597). The decrees of Trent were confirmed by Pius IV in 1564 and became the law of the Church despite the resistance to certain of its reform decrees in France and Germany. The dogmatic decrees clearly delineated the Church's theological position over against Protestantism. The result was the form of Roman Catholicism that endured into the second half of the twentieth century, yielding finally to the modern reforms of the Second Vatican Council (1962–65). *See also* Counter-Reformation/ Catholic Reformation; justification; Protestantism; sacrament; Scripture and tradition; seminary.

Bibliography

Jedin, Hubert. *A History of the Council of Trent.* New York: Herder, 1957–61.   *R. EMMET MCLAUGHLIN*

trial of Jesus, the process in which Jesus was condemned to death. The Gospels report that after his arrest Jesus was brought before the Sanhedrin or supreme council of Jerusalem for what apparently was a hearing (Matt 26:57–68; Mark 14:53–65; Luke 22:54–71; John 18:13–24), the precise purpose of which remains obscure. Thereafter Jesus was

brought to the Roman prefect, Pontius Pilate, who questioned him about the politically dangerous claim that Jesus was king of the Jews (Matt 27:11–14; Mark 15:2–5; Luke 23:2–5; John 18:29–38). Luke 23:6–12 adds that Pilate sent Jesus for a hearing to Herod Antipas, tetrarch of Galilee, who returned Jesus to Pilate, who found him innocent of any wrongdoing (Luke 23:13–16). The prefect, after proposing to release the insurrectionist Barabbas (Matt 27:15–23; Mark 15:6–14; Luke 23:17–23; John 18:39–40) delivered Jesus to be crucified (Matt 27:24–26; Mark 15:15; Luke 23:24–25; John 19:16).

The Gospel accounts preserve important historical data, although they recount that data with obvious biases. It is clear that Jesus was executed as a perceived threat to the Roman imperial order, as a Jewish royal pretender. Nonetheless, the role of Pilate and the political character of the charges against Jesus are minimized. The role of the Jewish leadership is highlighted and their religious opposition to Jesus stressed, whereas they probably shared Pilate's concern in maintaining public order. *See also* Jesus Christ; Passion, the.

tribunal, an ecclesiastical court. The term applies to courts on all levels of the Church's judicial system. There is to be a tribunal in every diocese. In addition, there are appeal courts for diocesan courts, and courts of the Holy See. None of these courts set precedents but decide matters of Church law for individual cases. Although a number of issues are brought before tribunals, the majority of cases deal with the validity of marriage. Personnel who staff the courts must have degrees in canon law (judges are required to have at least the J.C.L.) or have acquired needed expertise in canon law.

Tridentine (Lat., *tridentinus,* "of Trent"), adjective describing the liturgical, disciplinary, theological, and cultural contours of the Catholic Church resulting from the reforms and spirit of the sixteenth-century council held in the northern Italian city of Trent. Those characteristics include a baroque religious mind-set and a preference for firm discipline centralized in Rome. As used today, the term has a pejorative meaning, denoting an old-fashioned or reactionary attitude. *See also* Trent, Council of.

Tridentine Mass, the name given to the Latin Mass celebrated according to the ritual prescribed by the Missal of Pope Pius V (1570) following the

The trial of Jesus before Pilate, who washes his hands of the matter, saying to the crowd, "I am innocent of this man's blood; see to it yourselves" (Matt 27:24); fourteenth-century painting by Duccio, Cathedral Museum, Siena Italy.

Council of Trent (1545–63). The Tridentine Mass remained in force (with minor changes and variations) until the reforms of Vatican Council II (1962–65) were codified in the Missal of Pope Paul VI (1970). In 1984, Pope John Paul II permitted celebration of the Tridentine Mass under certain strictly controlled circumstances. In the opinion of some, this permission constitutes a concession to ultraconservative Catholics who question (or even repudiate) the liturgical reforms of Vatican Council II.

triduum (tri'doo-oom; Lat., *triduum*, "a space of three days"), a span of three consecutive days reminiscent of biblical periods of gestation and rebirth. The term is used most often when referring to the Easter Triduum, which includes the three days prior to Easter Sunday: Holy Thursday, Good Friday, and Holy Saturday. Some usage embraces the entire sa-cred three days of the crucified, buried, and Risen Lord, from Holy Thursday evening to Easter Sunday inclusive. The Easter Triduum begins with the evening Mass of the Lord's Supper on Holy Thursday, reaches its high point at the Easter Vigil and closes with Evening Prayer on Easter Sunday. Since the core and center of the Paschal Mystery (the life, death, and rising of Jesus Christ) is celebrated in these sacred three days, the Easter Triduum is considered the culmination of the entire liturgical year. The term is less often used in a general sense for any three-day period of special observance to prepare for the celebration of a feast by prayer and fasting, to give thanks for special blessings, or to acknowledge and honor extraordinary occasions or events. *See also* Holy Week.

trikirion (tri-keer'ee-ahn). *See* dikirion, trikirion.

trination, the practice of a priest's presiding at the Eucharist three times in one day. For pastoral need a diocesan bishop may allow trination on Sundays and holy days of obligation. *See also* bination.

Trinitarians, popular name for the Order of the Most Holy Trinity for the Redemption of Captives (O.SS.T.) founded by John of Matha and Felix of Valois and approved by Innocent III in 1198. The original purpose of the order was the redemption of Christians captured by the Muslims. There is no accurate record of the number of captives ransomed, but the estimates go as high as 140,000. When that need was over, Trinitarians ministered in schools, hospitals, missions, and prisons. The Trinitarians are an exempt mendicant order (i.e., not under the authority of the local bishop) whose rule is modeled after that of the Monastery of Saint Victor in Paris; they are committed to combining the contemplative life and the active life. In addition to the three vows of poverty, chastity, and obedience, they add a fourth: not to aspire after ecclesiastical honors. They recite the Divine Office, or Liturgy of the Hours, daily. The habit is a white tunic with a white scapular and hood. There are provinces in Canada, Italy, Spain, and the United States; the motherhouse is in Rome. *See also* John of Matha, St.

Trinity, doctrine of the, the specifically Christian way of speaking of God. The doctrine of the Trinity, which stands at the center of Christian faith, summarizes the basic truth of Christianity: that people are saved by God through Jesus Christ by the power of the Holy Spirit. The triune mystery of God is the central mystery of Christian faith and life; thus the doctrinal formulation about the nature of this God is the source of all other mysteries of the faith.

Scriptural Basis: The doctrine of the Trinity as such is not revealed in either the OT or the NT; however, the essential elements of what eventually became the doctrine are contained in Scripture. For example, the OT depicts God as Father of Israel and personifies God through the concepts of Word (*dabar*), Spirit (*ruah*), Wisdom (*hokmah*), and Presence (*shekinah*). In the NT God is called the Father of Jesus Christ 170 times: 4 times in Mark, 15 in Luke, 42 in Matthew, and 109 in John. The word "Abba" (Aram., "Father") is used only 3 times in the Scriptures: once in Mark's Gospel (14:36) and twice in Paul's Letters (Rom 8:15; Gal 4:6).

In addition to the *pater* (Lat., "father") texts, the opening greetings in the Pauline and Deutero-Pauline (those attributed to Paul, but not written by him) Letters direct that praise be offered to God through Jesus Christ. The most explicit triadic texts include the baptismal formula in Matt 28:19, the

The three Persons of the Trinity; fifteenth-century icon by Andrei Rublev, Tretyakov Gallery, Moscow. Inspired by the account in Gen 18 where Abraham is visited by three men, taken to be three divine beings who become one (vv. 10, 13), the icon situates the Father on the left, the Son at the center, and the Holy Spirit on the right.

benediction in 2 Cor 13:14, the account of Jesus' baptism in Matt 3:16–17, the fragments of prayer in Gal 4:6 and Rom 8:15, and the description of the whole economy of salvation in Eph 1:3–14. The purpose of searching the Scriptures for testimony to God's triune mystery is not to find passages that contain "three" names, but to discover those that testify to the saving works of God who redeems through Christ by the power of the Spirit.

Liturgical Origins: Alongside the biblical roots of trinitarian doctrine, its liturgical origins are also important. Christian prayer was normally mediatory and directed to God through Christ (cf. Rom 1:8; 1:8; 16:27, 7:25; 1 Cor 15:57; 2 Cor 1:20; Eph 5:20; Col 3:17; 16:27; 7:25; Heb 13:15; 1 Pet 4:11). The same mediatory pattern was found in common eucharistic prayers. Eventually this mediatory pattern was eliminated because it was open to heretical misinterpretation about the status of Christ. In many prayers the Holy Spirit was not mentioned but was assumed to be the power by whom the prayer was offered.

The baptismal formula in Matthew is important from both scriptural and liturgical points of view, but later doctrinal developments should not be read into it, as if Matthew is affirming a metaphysical unity of Father, Son, and Spirit. Still, Matthew's injunction to baptize "in the name of the Father, the Son, and the Holy Spirit" quickly became normative for baptismal practice.

Development of Doctrine: Trinitarian doctrine as such emerged in the fourth century, due largely to the efforts of Athanasius and the Cappadocians (Basil, Gregory of Nazianzus, Gregory of Nyssa), who responded to the doctrinal challenges of Arius and Eunomius about the status of Jesus Christ. In the West, these Christological and trinitarian questions were taken up by Augustine.

Arius and his successors claimed that Jesus Christ was less than God—higher than other creatures, but still less than God. To Athanasius and the Cappadocians this threatened human salvation, since Jesus Christ was believed to be essential to accomplishing salvation. These theologians took technical concepts such as person (Gk., *hypostasis*) and substance (*ousia*) and refined them to accommodate theological concerns in order to affirm that the nature of the one God is unthinkable apart from God's concrete existence in the economy of redemption in the Persons of the Father, Son, and Holy Spirit. The doctrine of the Trinity formulated in the late fourth century thus affirms that the one God exists as three Persons. The purpose of this formulation was to profess that God, Christ, and the Spirit are equally responsible for our salvation, thus each must be "divine."

This formulation does not contradict the fundamental religious assertion that God is one. Indeed, trinitarian doctrine is a guard against tritheism as well as Modalism. The Fourth Lateran Council (1215) notes that each divine Person *is* the divine nature. Further, the Council of Florence (1442) formulated the principle that "everything in God is one except where there is opposition of relationship." Thus, the doctrine of the Trinity simultaneously affirms both "unity of substance" and "diversity of persons." The divine Persons are said to be really distinct and utterly unique in their personal identity. The Father is Unbegotten, the Son is Begotten, and the Holy Spirit Proceeds from the Father and, or through, the Son. At the same time, the divine Persons are who they are by virtue of relationship to each other. "The Father is wholly in the Son and wholly in the Holy Spirit; the Son is wholly in the Father and wholly in the Holy Spirit; the Holy Spirit is wholly in the Father and wholly in the Son" (Council of Florence).

The trinitarian synthesis worked out by the Cappadocians in the East and Augustine in the West was refined by medieval theologians such as Gregory Palamas in the East and Anselm and Thomas Aquinas in the West. Once the main tenets of trinitarian doctrine had been formalized in the medieval synthesis, it underwent very little change and attracted very little notice, until recently, when there has been a resurgence of interest in the doctrine of the Trinity and an effort to reconnect it with the themes of salvation and the daily demands of Christian life. *See also* Arianism; *Filioque*; God; Modalism; Persons, divine; subsistent relations; tritheism.

CATHERINE MOWRY LACUGNA

Trinity Sunday, an annual solemnity celebrated on the first Sunday after Pentecost Sunday. Trinity Sunday explicitly acknowledges the threefold revelation of God as Father, Son, and Holy Spirit. Special emphasis on the Trinity in preaching and devotion emerged as a result of the Christological and trinitarian controversies of the fourth and fifth centuries. This emphasis escalated in the seventh and eighth centuries, formulating a proper preface and votive Mass by the ninth century. Testimony before the year 1000 suggests a solemnity of the Trinity with its own proper and office observed in some monasteries on the Sunday after Pentecost. Although the Trinity is celebrated every Sunday, and in fact every day, the solemnity of the Trinity was extended to the universal Church in 1334. This "idea feast" commemorates an aspect of doctrine, rather than an event in salvation history. The readings and presidential prayers focus on the mystery of redemption by God through Christ in the power of the Holy Spirit. *See also* Trinity, doctrine of the.

Triodion (tree-oh'dee-ahn; Gk., "[book] of three ōdes"), Byzantine-rite liturgical book containing the seasonal propers, prayers assigned to Sundays and feasts, of the Lenten cycle from the tenth Sunday before Easter until the Holy Saturday midnight-office inclusive. Its name comes from the fact that the poetic canon of Matins during this period often has only three odes instead of the usual nine. Early Triodia also included the propers of the Pentecost cycle, now found in the Pentekostarion.

Trisagion (tri-sah'gee-ahn; Gk., "thrice-holy"), a fifth-century liturgical refrain, "Holy God holy mighty holy immortal (who was crucified for us), have mercy on us!" The section in parentheses is the famous "theopaschite clause," a much-disputed fifth-century Monophysite addition accepted by all rites but the Byzantine and Chaldean. Though the origins of the Trisagion are disputed, it is traditionally held to be a synthesis of the biblical Sanctus ("Holy, holy, holy"; Isa 6:3) with elements of Ps 41:3. *See also* Sanctus.

tritheism (Lat., "three gods"), the doctrine that there are three gods who share one divine essence. No theologians have deliberately taught tritheism, but a number have been properly accused of it because of their inadequate attempts to explain the relationship of divine Persons and divine nature. Christian apologists of the second and third centuries often had to defend Christianity against false accusations of tritheism because the Christian practice of using the names Father, Son, and Holy Spirit in worship seemed to some outside observers to oppose the strict monotheism of the OT. *See also* God; Trinity, doctrine of the.

triumphalism, the tendency to exaggerate the achievements and good points of the Church and to minimize or deny its mistakes and weaknesses. The term was popularized by Bishop Emile de Smedt of Bruges, Belgium, in a highly publicized speech, critical also of the clericalism and legalism of the preconciliar Church, given during the first session of the Second Vatican Council (1962).

True Devotion. *See* Montfort, St. Louis Grignion de.

trusteeism, lay, a development in the republican period of U.S. history (1780–1830) that sought to adapt European Catholicism to American republican values. Trusteeism emphasized the participation of laymen in the government of the local church. Called "trustees" and elected annually by members of the congregation, these men were responsible for the temporal affairs of the parish, such as salaries of clergy and church personnel and the maintenance of the church and its properties. The most widespread implementation of this system of church government was in the diocese of Charleston, South Carolina, where the bishop, John England, was an ardent supporter of lay involvement in church government. The emphasis on republican values, such as election of trustees and lay involvement in church government, came into conflict with the tradition of clerical control of church affairs. Nu-

merous trustee controversies occurred in the republican period and eventually the hierarchy, with the support of the papacy, was able to suppress this republican lay initiative. But the suppression was never complete because each new immigrant group that came to the U.S. sought to implement this style of local church government. This desire for democracy in the Church never failed to create tension and conflict in the immigrant communities. Each new controversy only served to intensify the demand by the hierarchy for strong centralized episcopal control of church affairs. *See also* laity; United States of America, Catholicism in the. *JAY P. DOLAN*

truthfulness, veracity, the virtue of making oneself and one's thoughts known both accurately and in a manner appropriate to the circumstances. Truthfulness primarily concerns the presentation of who one takes oneself to be. Hence, for example, the president of a country ought to act and speak as a president in order to be truthful. To pretend or claim either to be more than one is (boastfulness) or to be less (false modesty) is a failure in truthfulness, though understatement is not inimical to the virtue as is boasting.

Veracity includes a disposition against lying, but its demands extend much farther than a rule against false speech. For instance, it requires both the habit of judging things according to their real worth as well as a due regard for the nature of the audience and the particular circumstances. *See also* lying.

Trypho, St., also known as Tryphon, third-century, martyr and patron saint of gardeners. He is said to have been martyred at Nicaea under the emperor Decius, but much of his life is legendary. Feast day: November 10.

Tübingen, a city in southwest Germany whose prestigious university, founded in 1477, included among its students the astronomer Johannes Kepler (later a professor there), the philosophers Georg Hegel and Friedrich Schelling, and the poet Friedrich Hölderlin. Led by Ferdinand Christian Baur (1792–1860), the university's "Tübingen school" in Protestant theology applied Hegel's philosophy to the study of early Christian history. The university's "Catholic Tübingen school," established by Johann Sebastian von Drey (1777–1853) in 1817, is committed to fashioning a theological synthesis of Scripture and tradition, historical inquiry, and contemporary thought. Its best-known Catholic professor is Hans Küng. *See also* Küng, Hans.

Tunstall, Cuthbert, 1474–1559, bishop of London and Durham. Loyal to the crown, Tunstall accepted Henry VIII's break with Rome, but remained an unrelenting opponent of Protestantism. Under Edward VI he was imprisoned (1551) and deposed (1552). Restored by Mary, he was deposed by Elizabeth and died in prison.

Turibius of Mogrovejo, St. (toor-eeb'ee-oos uhv moh-groh-vay'yoh), 1538–1606, Spanish-born archbishop of Lima (Peru) known for his pastoral zeal. He is one of the first saints of the New World. Feast day: March 23.

tutiorism (Lat., *tutior,* "safer"), a mode of moral decision making, similar to rigorism, whereby one chooses to follow the "safer" way, that of the law. One may doubt a moral law either because its wording is unclear or its application to a particular situation is uncertain. Tutiorism proposes that obedience to the law is always the safer and required choice. As a strict form of probabiliorism in the sixteenth and seventeenth centuries, it tended to make certainty more important than the search for truth, relying upon a notion of morality as obedience to the will of another, particularly God, as expressed in laws. Tutiorism was condemned by Pope Alexander VIII in 1690. *See also* probabiliorism; rigorism.

Twelve, the, a designation of Jesus' intimate disciples. Although Jesus sent many disciples on mission (Luke 10:1), he chose twelve apostles, who have come to be called the Twelve. This number imitates the sacred twelves in Israel's history: twelve sons of Jacob, twelve tribes of Israel, twelve guardians of the shrines corresponding to the twelve months of the year (Rev 21:12–14). Although no mention of the Twelve is found in the Q source, a very early tradition, the four Gospels indicate that Jesus chose twelve men (Mark 3:16–19), gave them special instructions (Mark 4:10), sent them on preaching tours of Galilee (Mark 3:14), and designated them judges (Matt 19:28). Mark 3:16–19 lists their names, a tradition repeated in Matt 10:2–4, except for the different placement of several names on the list. The Gospels signal the Twelve's importance, not simply by recording their choice by the earthly

Jesus, but by their formal commission by the Risen Christ (Luke 24:46–48; John 20:21; 1 Cor 15:5). Their role in the early Church is mentioned sparingly. Acts 6:2 describes them functioning like elders of the group. Paul visits Jerusalem and sees only Peter, James, and John (Gal 2:9), "pillars" of the Church. This correlates with the Gospel description of an inner circle among the Twelve, Peter, James, and John, to whom Jesus gave special revelation, took on special occasions, and with whom he prayed before his death. The NT records that only Peter left Jerusalem, traveled to Antioch (Gal 2:11), possibly to Corinth (1 Cor 9:5), presumably to Rome. Legends abound concerning the travels and missions of the rest of them. *See also* apostle; disciple. *JEROME NEYREY*

Twelve Great Feasts, the most important liturgical feasts of the Byzantine rite. The list, variable in earlier sources, eventually comprised the following twelve, given here in Byzantine calendar order: Nativity of Mary (September 8), Exaltation of the Cross (September 14), Entrance of Mary into the Temple (November 21), Nativity of Jesus (December 25), Theophany (January 6), Hypapante (February 2), Annunciation (March 25), Entrance into Jerusalem (Palm Sunday), Ascension, Pentecost, Transfiguration (August 6), Dormition (August 15). The principal feasts as depicted in a series of festive icons will also include Resurrection (Easter), which is the feast beyond all lists, and Crucifixion (Good Friday), though the latter is never listed liturgically among the Great Feasts. *See also* feasts, liturgical.

Two-Source Hypothesis, an explanation of the relationships between and among the three synoptic Gospels, Matthew, Mark, and Luke. According to this theory Mark was the first Gospel to have been written. Matthew and Luke each independently drew upon Mark for the framework of their accounts of Jesus' ministry. Each also combined with Mark a collection of sayings of Jesus, usually designated "Q," from the German word for "source," *Quelle.* Hence, the two sources of the synoptic Gospels are, according to this theory, Mark and Q.

The Two-Source Hypothesis accounts for most of the similarities and differences among the synoptic Gospels. Originally elaborated by German Protestant scholars in the mid-nineteenth century, it is widely accepted today among Catholic as well as Protestant scholars, although some specialists defend other solutions to the "synoptic problem." *See also* synoptic Gospels, problem of.

two-swords theory, the medieval belief that the pope has power not only in the spiritual realm but also in the temporal. It found its highest expression in Boniface VIII's papal bull *Unam Sanctam* (1302), which held that "there are two swords, the spiritual and the temporal, in the control of the Church. . . . One is used by the hand of the priest, the other by the hand of the kings and knights at the command and with the permission of the priest." Therefore, "for every human creature to be submissive to the Roman pontiff is absolutely necessary for salvation." *See also* Church and state.

Tyconius, d. ca. 400, lay theologian of the Donatist church of Roman Africa. Tyconius authored at least four books, the most influential being a biblical commentary challenging the literal interpretation of the book of Revelation, and another, the *Book of Rules,* in which obscure prophecies regarding the Church were explained in terms of seven mystical rules. Censured by Parmenian, Donatist bishop of Carthage, Tyconius influenced the development of Augustine's ecclesiology and interpretation of Scripture. *See also* Africa, the Church in Roman; Donatism.

Typikon (ti-pee-kahn'; Gk., "model," "rule"), a Byzantine-rite monastic and/or liturgical rule or custom-book. Byzantine monastic rules, like the Rule of St. Benedict, also contained prescriptions regulating fasting and liturgy, especially the Divine Office and its psalmody. In addition, early Byzantine liturgical calendars included norms for the readings, commemorations, and particular services of each day. From these rudimentary liturgical prescriptions the present Byzantine-rite liturgical Typikon evolved. It is essentially a liturgical calendar to which have been added instructions for each day's liturgy, especially when there are special services not found on ordinary days. Adherents of the Byzantine rite use the term "Typikon" for the Byzantine rite, much as Western monks will use "the Rule" as shorthand for the monastic way of life. *See also* Byzantine rite.

typology, a way of interpreting the Scriptures whereby older realities (types) are seen as having foreshadowed, according to God's plan of salvation, future realities (antitypes). One clear example of typology is in Rom 5:14, where Paul identifies Adam as "a type [Gk., *typos*] of the one who was to come," that is, Christ. In similar fashion Paul portrays the Israelites' passage through the Red Sea as foreshadowing Baptism (1 Cor 10:2). The author of Hebrews sees Melchizedek as a type of Christ (Heb 6:20–7:28; cf. Gen 14:18–20). The author of 1 Peter presents the salvation of Noah and his family as foreshadowing Baptism (an *antitypos;* 1 Pet 3:21).

The Fathers of the Church such as the author of the *Letter of Barnabas,* Justin, Melito of Sardis, and Irenaeus used typology to argue in favor of the unity of the two Testaments. Their interests were largely polemical, but later Fathers of the Church used the approach to provide for a Christian understanding of the OT. Typology is closely related to the allegorical reading of the OT promoted by the Fathers of the Church and various medieval authors. In the mid-twentieth century attention to the patristic exegesis of biblical texts led to a new interest in typology among some prominent Catholic scholars such as Jean Daniélou (d. 1974) and Henri de Lubac (d. 1991). *See also* Scripture, interpretation of.

Tyrrell, George, 1861–1909, English theologian associated with the Modernists. Raised Anglican, he was received into the Catholic Church in 1879, entered the Jesuits in 1880, and was ordained in 1891. An outspoken critic of neo-Scholasticism, he wrote on the development of doctrine, the nature of the Church, and the importance of religious experience. Because of his controversial writings he was expelled from the Jesuits and suspended from the priesthood in 1906. After publicly criticizing the encyclical *Pascendi Dominici Gregis* in 1907, he was excommunicated. He received the Last Rites of the Church before his death, but was denied Catholic burial. *See also* Modernism; neo-Scholasticism.

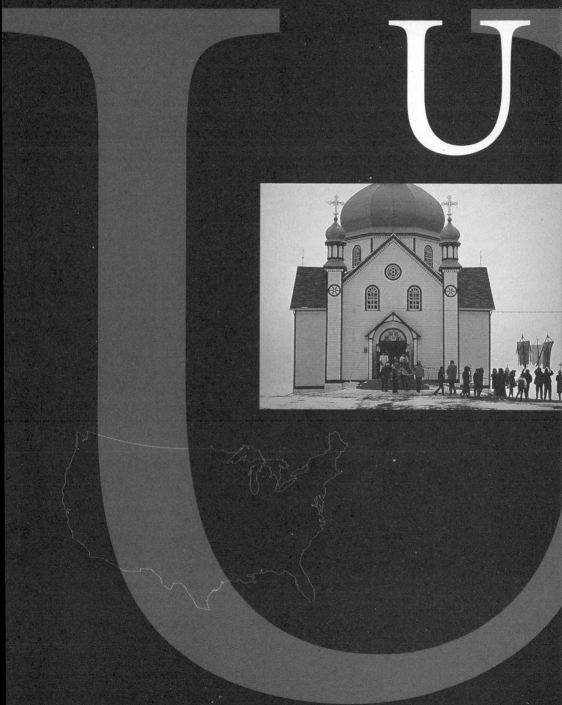

Ubertino of Casale, 1259–1330, Franciscan preacher. Entering the Franciscans in 1273, he studied at Paris and served in Italy as preacher and lector. An ardent and uncompromising Spiritual Franciscan, Pope John XXII transferred Ubertino to a Benedictine house for refusing to be reconciled with his own order. *See also* Spiritual Franciscans.

Ukrainian Catholic Church, a Byzantine Catholic Church centered in Galicia in western Ukraine, a former republic of the Soviet Union.

Early History: The Ukrainians received the Christian faith in its Byzantine form, and their church was originally linked to the patriarchate of Constantinople. But by the fourteenth century most Ukrainians were under the political control of Catholic Lithuania. Metropolitan Isidore of Kiev attended the Council of Florence and agreed to the 1439 Decree of Union between Catholics and Orthodox. Although many Ukrainians within Lithuania initially accepted this union, within a few decades they had rejected it.

In 1569, Lithuania and Poland united to form a single commonwealth, and most of Ukraine passed to Poland. By this time Protestantism was expanding rapidly in the Ukrainian lands, and the Jesuits had begun to work for a local union between Catholics and Orthodox as a way of reducing Protestant influence. Soon many Orthodox also began to view such a union favorably as a way of improving the situation of the Ukrainian clergy and of preserving their Byzantine traditions against the expansion of Latin Polish Catholicism.

These developments culminated in a synod of Orthodox bishops at Brest in 1595–96 that proclaimed a union between Rome and the metropolitan province of Kiev. This event sparked a violent conflict between those who accepted the union and those who opposed it. The dioceses of the far western province of Galicia, which lie at the heart of what is now the Ukrainian Catholic Church, adhered to the union much later (Przemysl in 1692 and Lvov [Lviv] in 1700). By the eighteenth century, two-thirds of the Christians in western Ukraine had become Byzantine Catholic.

As Orthodox Russia expanded its control into Ukraine, however, the union was gradually suppressed. In 1839, Czar Nicholas I abolished it in all areas under Russian rule with the exception of the eparchy of Kholm, which was itself disbanded in 1875. Thus by the end of the nineteenth century Byzantine Catholicism had virtually disappeared from the empire.

Easter procession at the Ukrainian Catholic Church of the Blessed Virgin Mary, in Saskatchewan, Canada, where there are large concentrations of Ukrainian Catholics; in 1993 there were almost 150,000 Ukrainian Catholics in the United States.

But the Ukrainian Catholic Church survived in Galicia, which had come under Austrian rule in 1772 and passed to Poland at the end of World War I. The church flourished for a time under the energetic leadership of Metropolitan Andrew Sheptyckyj (1900–1944). The situation changed dramatically at the beginning of World War II, however, when most of Galicia was annexed by the Soviet Union.

Post–World War II: The Soviet government acted decisively to liquidate the Ukrainian Catholic Church. In April 1945 all its bishops were arrested, and the following year they were sentenced to long terms of forced labor. In March 1946 a "synod" was held at Lvov (Lviv) that officially dissolved the union and integrated the Ukrainian Catholic Church into the Russian Orthodox Church. Those who resisted were arrested, including over 1,400 priests and 800 nuns. Metropolitan Joseph Slipyj, the church's head, was sent to prison in Siberia. In 1963 he was released and exiled to Rome. In the same year he was given the unique title "Major Archbishop" of Lviv of the Ukrainians. He was made a cardinal in 1965 and died in 1984.

Although the exact role played by the Moscow patriarchate in the suppression has not been clearly established, the events of 1946 would poison the atmosphere between Ukrainian Catholics and Orthodox for decades to come. All this came to the surface in the late 1980s when new religious freedoms inaugurated by Mikhail Gorbachev enabled the Ukrainian Catholic Church to emerge from hiding.

On December 1, 1989, Ukrainian Catholic communities were given the right to register with the government. With the support of the local authorities, Ukrainian Catholics gradually began to take possession of their former churches. All this led to a strong Ukrainian Catholic resurgence in the region. In March 1991, Cardinal Myroslav Lubachivsky, the head of the Ukrainian Catholic Church, was able to take up residence at his see in Lviv. In December 1991 he reported that his church had 11 bishops, 1,100 priests, 300 religious, 700 nuns, and 5 million faithful with 2,176 churches in the newly independent Ukraine. Seminaries set up in Lviv and Ivano-Frankivsk and monasteries were receiving many vocations.

As the Ukrainian Catholic Church was reestablishing itself, the Moscow patriarchate protested that violence had been used in repossessing some churches (which the Catholics denied) and that Ukrainian Catholics were attempting to expand at the expense of the Orthodox. A series of high-level contacts between the Vatican and the Moscow patriarchate began in 1990, but the talks have not yet been able to resolve the dispute satisfactorily.

Also affected was the fate of Ukrainian Catholics in Poland. When the Soviet Union annexed most of Galicia during World War II, about 1,300,000 Ukrainians remained in Poland. In 1946 the new Polish Communist authorities deported most of these Ukrainians to the Soviet Union and suppressed the Ukrainian Catholic Church. Approximately 145,000 Ukrainian Catholics dispersed around the country were able to worship openly only in the Latin rite. Only in 1957 were pastoral centers opened to serve the Ukrainian Catholics. In 1989 Pope John Paul II appointed a Ukrainian bishop auxiliary to the Polish primate. He was named bishop of Przemysl of the Ukrainians in January 1991, thus providing Ukrainian Catholics in Poland with their first diocesan bishop since the war.

Two men's religious orders are unique to the Ukrainian Catholic Church: the Studite Monks and the Basilian Order of St. Josaphat. The Redemptorists also have a Ukrainian province. Women's communities include the Basilian Sisters, the Studite Nuns, the Sister Servants of Mary Immaculate, the Holy Family Sisters, the Sisters of St. Joseph, the Sisters of Charity of St. Vincent de Paul, the Sisters of Mercy, the Sisters of St. Josaphat, and the Catechists of St. Anne. The Catechists of the Sacred Heart exist only in the diaspora (those Ukrainian Catholics living outside the country).

There are major seminaries for Ukrainians in the diaspora in Washington, D.C., Ottawa, Canada, and in Curitiba, Brazil. A Ukrainian College has existed in Rome since 1897.

The Ukrainian Catholic diaspora, 700,000 strong, played a significant role in preserving Ukrainian traditions during the suppression. There are four dioceses in the United States, five in Canada, one each in Australia, Brazil, and Argentina, and apostolic exarchates in Great Britain, Germany, and France. *See also* Brest, Union of; Byzantine rite; Poland, Catholicism in; Russia, Catholicism in.

Bibliography

Dyrud, Keith P. *The Quest for the Rusyn Soul: The Politics of Religion and Culture in Eastern Europe and in America, 1890–World War I.* Philadelphia: Balch Institute Press, 1992.

Himka, John-Paul. *The Greek Catholic Church and Ukrainian Society in Austrian Galicia.* Cambridge, MA: Ukrainian Studies Fund, Harvard University, 1986.   RONALD G. ROBERSON

Ulfilas (uhl'fuh-luhs), ca. 311–83, evangelizer of the Goths. Consecrated bishop in 341 by the Arian

Eusebius of Nicomedia, Ulfilas worked among the Goths both north of the Danube and within the empire, and thus the Christianity transmitted to the Goths and the other peoples who later settled in the Western empire was Arian. Using an alphabet he invented, Ulfilas translated the Bible into Gothic. *See also* Arianism.

Ullathorne, William Bernard, 1806–89, Benedictine monk and bishop. He worked as a missionary in Australia from 1832 to 1840, especially among convicts, and was vicar apostolic for western, later central, England from 1846 to 1850 and bishop of Birmingham from 1850 to 1888. In 1888 he resigned his see and became titular archbishop. He was a friend of John Henry Newman; his correspondence during the First Vatican Council (1869–70) has been an important source for that council's history. *See also* Newman, John Henry; Vatican Council I.

Ulric of Augsburg, St., 890–973, the first saint to be formally canonized. He succeeded his uncle as bishop of Augsburg in 923. When he named his own nephew to succeed himself, he was accused of nepotism. Nevertheless, he was canonized by Pope John XV in 993. Feast day: July 4. *See also* canonization.

Ulric of Cluny, St., ca. 1018–93, Cluniac monk and prior at a number of monasteries. Godson of Emperor Henry III, Ulric joined the monks at Cluny after a pilgrimage to the Holy Land and wrote a three-volume work on the customs of Cluny. Feast day: July 14. *See also* Cluny.

Ultramontanism (Lat., "beyond the mountains"), a nineteenth-century intellectual and political movement in European countries beyond the Alps (France, Germany, Spain, England) that exalted the papacy as the bulwark against political liberalism and modern philosophical and scientific trends. Until their destruction during the French Revolution and the Napoleonic wars, European ecclesiastical structures, especially in Germany and France, were rooted in feudalism and contained limits that held in check centralizing forces in the Church. After the revolution, governments sought to subsume the now weakened Church under claims of national sovereignty. By means of concordats the popes succeeded in arranging ecclesiastical structures in new ways and securing a degree of civil freedom for Catholics. Because of this success and

in reaction to the spiritual and intellectual insecurity within the Christian faith, many Catholics looked to the papacy for reassurance. Since many Catholics saw the pope as the guardian of the Church's political independence and the source of its internal security, they wanted papal authority strengthened, even at the expense of the local churches. Initially, even many liberal Catholics were strongly Ultramontane. They did not, however, support the program of political restoration and intellectual defensiveness pursued by Gregory XVI (1831–46) and Pius IX (1846–78). This restorationist and anti-modern Ultramontanism sought to oppose the Enlightenment and liberalism through the strengthening of papal authority. The movement found its programmatic voice in several influential journals, e.g., *Civiltà Cattolica*, and *L'Univers*. The Ultramontane movement provided strong support and incentive for the doctrines of papal primacy and infallibility at Vatican Council I (1869–70). *See also* Pius IX; Vatican Council I.   HERMANN J. POTTMEYER

Unam Sanctam (*oon'*ahm sahnk'tahm; Lat., "One Holy"), bull of Pope Boniface VIII, promulgated in 1302, that insists on the absolute primacy of the pope. Written during the conflict with King Philip IV of France, it concludes with the declaration that submission to the pope is necessary for salvation. *See also* Boniface VIII; papacy, the.

uncreated grace. *See* grace.

unction. *See* anointing.

Underhill, Evelyn, 1875–1941, English mystic. Her many writings, especially *Mysticism* (1911), demonstrate the complementarity between theology and mysticism. She functioned as a spiritual director and was popular as a director of retreats. In addition to her books, she also translated and edited *The Cloud of Unknowing,* Walter Hilton's *Scale of Perfection,* and other works. In her later years she was active in the pacifist movement against World War II. *See also* English Mystics.

uniate churches. *See* Eastern churches; uniatism.

uniatism, a pejorative term for a method of union between Eastern Christians and Rome, considered by its critics as politically rather than religiously motivated and contrary to the communion ecclesiology of the undivided Church. In "uniatism" one church is seen as the aggressor against a "sister church" with which it is at the moment in schism, deceptively absorbing groups of the "sister's" faithful by allowing them to retain their own rite and a certain autonomy. Some historical instances of uniatism are seen as the result of political pressure reinforced by violence, which created not unity but new divisions in an already fragmented Christendom.

Origins and Nature of Uniatism: Though uniatism is considered to have begun with the Union of Brest in 1596, its application to all cases of reunions of Eastern Christians with Rome is without justification either historically or ecclesiologically. The Maronites and Syro-Malabarians, for instance, resumed union with Rome without having formally broken it and without having entered into any formal reunion. The Italo-Albanians, too, are not "uniates," the result of a union. They are the ancient Byzantine church of southern Italy, within the territory of the Roman patriarchate. Their continued ecclesial communion with that patriarchate is in full accord with all the norms of the traditional ecclesiology of the undivided Church of the first millennium.

Uniatism is considered in the 1990s to be a questionable phenomenon both historically and ecclesiologically, apart from the exaggerations, anachronistic reductionism, and falsehoods with which the topic is often treated. To understand this negative judgment one must understand the nature of the reunions of the sixteenth and later centuries, and of the uniate churches that resulted. Regardless of the intentions behind them, these reunions were not, except in the most formal theological sense, a restoration of the communion that had existed before the schism between East and West. They represented something new in the history of the Church, a departure from the past.

Had the Union of Florence in 1439 been successful, the phenomenon of uniatism would never have emerged. For at Florence the Latin West and the Byzantine East tried to deal with each other directly. But the later Orthodox repudiation of the Union of Florence (a repudiation definitively sealed by the fall of Constantinople to the Turks in 1453) resulted in a clear, though perhaps unconscious, shift in tactics by the Latin church. Disillusioned by the failure to achieve a general union, the Roman Catholic Church began to sign separate union agreements with individual groups of Orthodox, thus nibbling away at the fringes of Orthodoxy in areas under the political control of Catholic powers. For the Orthodox, this was perfidious. Rome could respond that they were simply entering into union with a local church, which indeed they had every right to do. But phenomenologically, the churches had evolved beyond the pre-Nicene system in which one could legitimately view the universal Church as a federation of local churches with no intervening higher structures. The Orthodox groups that entered into union with Rome were not simply restoring the former, broken unity between a local church and the Church of Rome, even if this was their intent. Rather, they were separating themselves from one entity, their Byzantine Orthodox Mother Church, and being absorbed into another, the Latin Catholic Church of the West. In short, they were leaving the Eastern Church and being assimilated into the Western Church. Instead of restoring the broken communion between the two, this led to new divisions.

The "uniates" not only separated themselves from the living roots of the Oriental tradition, they united to a Latin majority quite different from themselves in religious culture and outlook, and not at all accustomed to more than one way of doing things. Inevitably, a process of latinization set in, and the Eastern tradition began to erode as the "uniates" gradually began to lose the spirit of their heritage.

Uniatism as an Ecumenical Problem: This highly emotional issue is the major stumbling block in relations between the Catholic and Orthodox churches. It is much discussed today, often with distortions and oversimplifications of history, rarely with fairness and objectivity. The Orthodox accuse Catholics of practicing uniatism, but the Orthodox, too, have practiced it in both the past and present, in the forced unions of Armenians with the Byzantine church, for example, in 590 under Emperor Maurice; the "Western-rite" Orthodox jurisdiction in France; and the receiving of some disaffected Latin Catholic parishes in northern Italy into the Russian Orthodox Church in the 1970s.

The problem of uniatism has become especially acute since the late 1980s and the restoration of religious freedom in the former Soviet bloc. The emergence from the underground of the persecuted Eastern Catholic churches has led to conflicts and a resurgence of traditional Orthodox anti-Roman sentiment.

In Search of a Solution: Catholics have begun to

struggle with the issue through a painful examination of conscience. Discussions of the topic with the Orthodox have begun, with tangible results, as the public forum serves to instill some fairness, objectivity, and courtesy in those with otherwise intemperate views. Pope John Paul II has already enunciated the three inalienable and inseparable principles with which this issue and every community and person involved in it must be treated: truth, justice, and charity. Those of good will on both sides of the debate are in agreement on two fundamental principles: (1) uniatism is to be rejected as a no longer valid method for the future; and (2) the religious liberty of both individuals and communities is an absolute right that excludes all violence or coercion, physical or moral. Four other necessary principles have not yet been sufficiently recognized by some: (1) judging past events in the light of newly acquired principles is considered by some an anachronism devoid of ethical or historical validity; (2) the dignity, rights, and very existence of an ecclesial community *today* cannot be impugned on the basis of problems and injustices at its historical origins; (3) one cannot challenge a church's right to continued existence because it ill accords with another's ecclesiology, or with new advances in theological and ecumenical consciousness; and (4) ecumenism is a dialogue in which each side must judge itself by the same criteria and standards of behavior with which it judges the other.

Only the reestablishment of communion between the Catholic and Orthodox churches will solve these problems satisfactorily. But if, in the meantime, solutions remain provisional, interim answers to the pastoral and ecumenical problems posed by the existence of Eastern Catholic churches must be sought with charity, objectivity, and realism, without the bigotry and reductionist simplifications of history to which these communities are too often subjected. *See also* Church; Eastern churches; Eastern Schism; Florence, Council of; latinization; Orthodox Christianity; unity of the Church.

Bibliography

Suttner, Ernst C. *Church Unity: Union or Uniatism? Catholic-Orthodox Ecumenical Perspectives.* Rome: Centre for Indian and Interreligious Studies/Bangalore: Dharmaram Publications, 1991.

ROBERT F. TAFT

Unigenitus (oon-ee-jay'nee-toos; Lat., "Only Begotten," a reference to the Son of God). 1 Papal bull of Clement VI in 1343 granting remission of sins to all who visited Rome during the Jubilee year of 1350. The bull formally set out the doctrine of the "treasury of merit," which stated that Christ and the martyrs had built up by their acts a vast reserve of merit that the papacy could dole out to lesser mortals to offset the burden of sin. 2 Papal document issued in 1713 as the constitution of Clement XI condemning 101 propositions drawn from the contemporary Jansenist writings of Pasquier Quesnel (d. 1719). *See also* Jansenism; Jubilee, Year of; merit.

Union of Brest. *See* Brest, Union of.

Unitarianism, a religious movement teaching the one good God and the goodness of humanity against Augustinian pessimism and against Trinitarianism. It developed out of three distinct yet loosely related movements. The first was sixteenth-century opposition to the Trinity, initially expressed by Martin Cellarius, Michael Servetus, and Bernardino Ochino and culminating in the anti-Trinitarian movements in Hungary and Poland. The second began in England with the anti-Trinitarian tracts and conventicles of John Biddle (1615–62), often called the father of Unitarianism, and emerged as a denomination in 1774. The third movement began in America when Jonathan Mayhew challenged the doctrine of the Trinity in 1755. The formation of the American Unitarian Association (1825) under the leadership of William Ellery Channing gave greater momentum to the movement, as did the writings of Ralph Waldo Emerson and James Martineau. In 1961, the American Unitarian Association merged with the Universalist Church of America to form the Unitarian Universalist Association. *See also* Trinity, doctrine of the.

Unitatis Redintegratio (oo-nee-tah'tis ray-din-tay-grah'tsee-oh). *See* Decree on Ecumenism.

United Church of Christ, an American Protestant denomination that was formed at a synod in 1957 through the union of the General Council of Congregational Christian Churches (Congregationalism) and the Evangelical and Reformed Church (Presbyterianism). It recognizes the autonomy of the local assembly and simultaneously organizes these churches into regional associations and state conferences, which elect representatives to the General Synod (convened biennially). The Statement of Faith, adopted in 1959, is regarded as a nonbinding witness to the faith of the affiliated churches. It affirms two sacraments, Baptism and the Lord's Supper, and it recognizes ordination through the imposition of hands. At the same time, it acknowledges the autonomy of each local congregation regarding worship, doctrine, and government. *See also* Protestantism; Reformation, the.

United Methodist Church. *See* Methodism.

United States Catholic Conference (USCC), the civilly incorporated (1967) operational secretariat and service agency of the National Conference of Catholic Bishops (NCCB). The USCC replaced the National Catholic Welfare Conference (1919), itself the successor to the National Catholic War Council (1917), and provides the organizational structure, in the words of its certificate of incorporation, "to unify, coordinate, encourage, promote, and carry on all Catholic activities in the United States; to organize and conduct religious, charitable and social welfare work at home and abroad; to aid in education; to care for immigrants and generally to enter into and promote, by education, public action and direction, the objects of its being." Day-to-day management is the work of a general secretary, who is also general secretary of the NCCB. Principal officers of the USCC are the same bishops who fill the positions for the NCCB. An administrative board of bishops is identical with the administrative committee of the NCCB. There is an executive committee and a national advisory board composed of bishops, priests, religious, and laypeople. Three major departments, on communications, education, and social development and world peace, are chaired by bishops and operated by secretariats under supervision of a committee having equal numbers of episcopal and nonepiscopal members. Many Catholic organizations are affiliated with the USCC. The USCC, its administrative board, executive committee, and several departments periodically issue statements on social and political matters.

unitive way. *See* ways of the spiritual life.

Unity Brothers (Lat., *Fratres Unitores*), a medieval Catholic Armenian religious congregation originally associated with the Dominicans, whose rule and habit they borrowed and whose missal and breviary they used in Armenian. Founded around 1331 by an Armenian monk and a Dominican, they eventually became autonomous with their own superior, then were absorbed into the Dominican order in 1583.

unity of humankind, the concept that despite national, cultural, ethnic, and sexual differences the human race is essentially one. The idea is foundational in Catholic theological anthropology and constitutes a basic presupposition of the Church's social teaching. At its heart is the doctrine that every human being is created equally in the image of God, is redeemed by the death and Resurrection of Jesus Christ, and is destined for eternal life in the heavenly kingdom of God.

unity of the Church, the oneness of the Church, both in the sense that there can be only one Church of Christ and in the sense of its communion in faith, worship, and charity, brought about by the Holy Spirit. From the fact that the Church is the Body and Bride of Christ, it follows that there can be only one Church of Christ. The communion that is the work of the Holy Spirit is described by Vatican II in the following terms: "It is the Holy Spirit, dwelling in those who believe, pervading and ruling over the entire Church, who brings about that marvelous communion of the faithful and joins them together so intimately in Christ that He is the principle of the church's unity" (Decree on Ecumenism, 1964, n. 2).

The same council further declares that the unity that Christ wishes his Church to have requires visible communion in the confession of the one faith, in the common celebration of the sacraments, and in the fraternal harmony of the family of God. It is through the preaching of the gospel by the successors of the apostles, through their administration of the sacraments, and through their exercise of authority that Christ perfects his people's fellowship in unity under the influence of the Holy Spirit (see Decree on Ecumenism, n. 2).

While Vatican II insisted that the visible unity that Christ bestowed on his Church subsists in the Catholic Church as a gift that it cannot lose (cf. Decree on Ecumenism, n. 4), it also recognized that a real, though imperfect, communion binds together all the Christian churches and ecclesial communities, which in various ways participate in the reality of the one Church of Christ. *See also* Church; ecumenical movement; ecumenism; marks of the Church.

FRANCIS A. SULLIVAN

Universal Catechism. *See* Catechism of the Catholic Church.

CATHOLICISM IN
THE UNITED STATES
OF AMERICA

R oman Catholics in 1994 numbered 59,858,042, or 23 percent of the U.S. population of 259,353,627. Most American Catholics are of European descent, but 350,000 Native Americans and 2.5 million African Americans also belong to the Catholic Church. Of an estimated 22.4 million Hispanic Americans, 80 percent are baptized Catholics. Recent immigration has added Filipino, Haitian, and Southeast Asian Catholics. The Church in the fifty states and the District of Columbia is divided into thirty-three metropolitan archdioceses, the archdiocese for the military services, and 150 dioceses. Thirteen Eastern-rite dioceses have 500,000 communicants. Catholics in the United States are 80 percent urban or suburban and primarily in the middle to upper income range. Over 70 percent have a secondary school education, and about 20 percent are college graduates.

A small U.S. country church, Old St. Hilary's in Tiburon, California (now a Historic Site); in 1994 there were almost 60 million Roman Catholics in the United States, over 7.8 million of whom were in California.

COLONIAL PERIOD TO THE PRESENT

Catholics came to the present United States as Spanish and French explorers in the late sixteenth and seventeenth centuries. Spanish settlements stretched in a long arc from Florida to California. The legacy of Spain is evident in placenames, in "mission-style" architecture, and in Native American and Hispanic Catholics who trace their ancestry to colonial days. Spain's arc was intersected by a French one, anchored at Quebec and New Orleans. Spaniards planted missions and presidios, but settlements were few on the French arc. Except in Arizona, a Jesuit mission until 1767, Franciscans founded the Spanish missions. Jesuits and Franciscans, together with Carmelites and Quebec seminary priests, evangelized along the Great Lakes and the central river system.

The first permanent Catholic presence was established in 1565 by diocesan priests at St. Augustine, Florida. Franciscans were more successful with Florida tribes than the Jesuits who preceded them, but in 1763 the missions ended when Florida became British. Catholics in Florida were few after the 1821 U.S. occupation. The twentieth century has seen Catholic growth in Florida with retirees from the north and refugees from Cuba, Haiti, and elsewhere.

The original colonists in the southeast were Low Church Anglicans, followed by Scotch-Irish Presbyterians, Baptists, and Methodists. African-American slaves were generally evangelical Protestants. The twentieth-century movement of industry to the Sun Belt has modified the picture as Catholics follow jobs south, but Catholics remain few

except in Louisiana, where Creole and Cajun descendants of the French live, as does the country's largest concentration of African-American Catholics. Catholics in Texas are growing, fed by immigration from Mexico and migration from the north.

New Mexico and Arizona have retained a strong Spanish-Mexican patina. Many southwestern Catholics are of mixed Mexican and Native American heritage. Though after 1848 missionaries from France and elsewhere organized the Church on a European model, the twentieth century has seen a reassertion of Latino style, together with an influx of sun-seeking Catholics from elsewhere in the United States.

What is now the state of California was neglected by the Spanish until Russian moves southward from Alaska in 1768 prompted attention.

Members of a congregation exchange handshakes at Mass, following the Lord's Prayer and the presider's invitation, "Let us offer each other the sign of peace." The handshake replaces the kiss of peace (a ceremonial embrace) exchanged only by priests in the pre–Vatican II solemn High Mass.

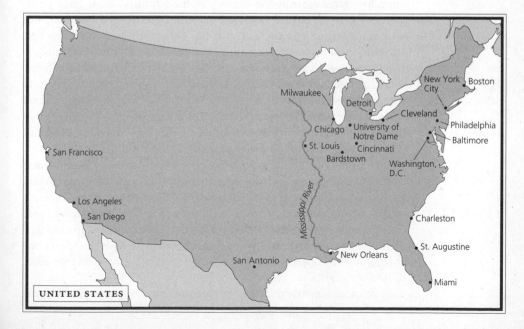

UNITED STATES

Junipero Serra (d. 1784) was the planner of the Franciscan chain of twenty-one missions in which more than one hundred thousand natives were baptized between 1769 and 1834. California became a U.S. territory in 1847, in time for the gold rush, which brought adventurers from around the world. The dominant religious culture was Protestant, although a wide cross section of Catholics were among the settlers. The lingering Spanish-Mexican tradition was reinforced with the beginning in the 1890s of massive Mexican immigration.

France's colonial empire left little trace, save for placenames and a late-nineteenth-century immigration from Canada, chiefly into New England. In the Midwest, Catholicism came with pioneer settlers and later

immigrants. Cities such as Cincinnati, St. Louis, Milwaukee, and Chicago became Catholic urban centers, while farmers from Maryland settled in rural Kentucky after 1785. Cities along the industrial Great Lakes drew increasing numbers of Italian and Slavic Catholics as the nineteenth century progressed.

A lay minister of the Eucharist offers the chalice to the communicant. The distribution of Holy Communion under the species of both consecrated bread and consecrated wine and the reception of Communion while standing rather than kneeling are the results of the liturgical reforms of the Second Vatican Council (1962–65).

ORGANIZATION OF THE CHURCH AND RELIGIOUS TOLERATION

Church organization in the United States stemmed from Lord Baltimore's Maryland colony (1634). Catholics were never a majority, not even aboard the ships the *Ark* and the *Dove,* which brought the first colonists, but for twenty years they held social and political control, and during those years a policy of complete religious toleration was in force. Religious freedom finally ended in 1692 when the Church of England became the established church in Maryland. Legislation was then passed that penalized the Catholic minority. Similar toleration existed from 1683 to 1689 in New York under Catholic governor Thomas Dongan, but Catholics were then proscribed until after the Revolution.

Most of the thirteen seaboard colonies were hostile to Catholics, and they were found only in Maryland, in Pennsylvania (thanks to Quaker tolerance), and scattered in New York, New Jersey, and Virginia. The only priests, apart from some Franciscans during one fifty-year period, were Jesuits who supported themselves on slave-operated farms and exercised an itinerant ministry. Most were English, twenty-one were American-born, and a half dozen Germans ministered to Catholics among Pennsylvania Dutch farmers.

In colonial New England, Congregationalist, Unitarian, and Baptist descendants of the original Puritan settlers predominated. Until the Revolution, there were few Catholics, except for the Abenaki in Maine, converted by French Jesuits. Nineteenth-century immigration from Ireland, Quebec, Italy, and Portugal changed the religious face of the region. In its southern tier of states Catholics developed their strongest regional concentration in the United States, especially in Connecticut, Massachusetts, and Rhode Island.

REVOLUTION AND THE FEDERAL PERIOD

In 1776 Catholics numbered 25,000, or 1 percent of the population. There were twenty-three priests, all ex-Jesuits. Their religious order had been suppressed in 1773 by Pope Clement XIV; they were subject to a bishop in London, but in practice governed by their last Jesuit superior until in 1784 Rome named ex-Jesuit John Carroll superior of the mission. In 1789 the priests elected him as the first bishop of Baltimore, and in 1808 he became archbishop. Carroll had a strong sense of the newness of America and the challenge it offered. A partisan of the Revolution, he advocated universal religious toleration and separation of Church and state. His efforts to introduce republican styles in church government were less successful. He retreated from support of vernacular liturgy and failed to involve the laity in choosing of pastors. While he argued that "an ordinary national church" had the right to choose its own bishops, he failed to organize a system to do that and acquiesced in a "mission" status that left matters in Rome's hands and set a model later imposed on the whole Church.

Refugees from the French Revolution included Sulpician priests who founded the nation's first seminary, St. Mary's in Baltimore (1791). Elizabeth Ann Bayley Seton (d. 1821), American founder of the Sisters of Charity, symbolized the Church's commitment to education and health-care institutions. Disputes with lay trustees, often triggered by less-than-exemplary clergy, plagued port cities, but the church of Boston prospered under Bishop Jean Cheverus, as did the frontier diocese of Bardstown (later Louisville) under Benedict Flaget.

CATHOLIC POPULATIONS OVER 500,000 IN U.S. ARCHDIOCESES (*) AND DIOCESES

*Los Angeles	3,559,816	Cleveland	815,608	Brownsville,	
*Chicago	2,322,000	*Hartford	802,688	Tex.	652,214
*New York	2,286,187	Pittsburgh	792,178	San Diego	647,094
*Boston	1,993,126	Buffalo	758,313	Providence	645,653
Brooklyn	1,630,013	Galveston-		*San Antonio	628,776
*Detroit	1,480,116	Houston	748,781	*Milwaukee	616,276
*Philadelphia	1,428,395	Trenton	701,987	Orange, Calif.	598,663
Rockville Centre,		*Miami	694,558	San Bernardino	570,040
N.Y.	1,340,279	*St. Paul–		*St. Louis	558,775
*Newark	1,301,838	Minneapolis	691,180	*Cincinnati	544,100

SOURCE: *1995 Catholic Almanac* (Huntington, IN: Our Sunday Visitor Publishing Division, 1994).

EXPANSION AND THE IMMIGRANT PERIOD

The 1803 Louisiana Purchase doubled the land area of the United States. Texas was annexed in 1845; Idaho, Washington, and Oregon came by agreement with Great Britain in 1846; and the Mexican cession in 1848 added another half million square miles. By the mid-nineteenth century immigrants were transforming the Catholic body. Ten million Catholics arrived from Europe between 1820 and 1920. They settled in coastal and midwestern cities; some few became farmers. Archbishop John Hughes of New York (d. 1864) was an aggressive Irish immigrant leader; Bishop John Nepomucene Neumann of Philadelphia (d. 1860) was an example of earlier German-speaking immigrants. By 1850 the Roman Catholic Church was the largest single denomination in the country, but the national culture remained resolutely Protestant. Converts, like the philosopher Orestes Brownson (d. 1876) and the founder of the Paulists, Isaac Hecker (d. 1888), explored the compatibility of Catholicism and Americanism, but the pre–Civil War years were marked by antiforeign and anti-Catholic nativism, which abated only with the war, in which Catholics fought and Catholic sisters nursed on both sides.

A soup kitchen at Blessed Sacrament Church in Seattle, Washington, highlights the traditional commitment of U.S. Catholics to the service of those in need as well as the increased involvement of lay Catholics in the mission and ministries of the Church.

American bishops attended Vatican I (1869–70), where most opposed a definition of papal infallibility. They had a strong collegial tradition, developed in the seven provincial (1829–49) and three plenary (1852, 1866, 1884) councils of Baltimore, that ran counter to contemporary Roman ideas, but they failed to put into place permanent supporting structures like those envisioned by Bishop John England (d. 1842) of Charleston, who wrote a constitution for the diocese and held regular conventions of clergy and laity.

Post–Civil War reconstruction began with the Second Plenary Council's failure to take initiatives on behalf of the freed slaves. Work among Native Americans was hindered by the government's "Peace Policy," which turned many Catholic tribes over to the ministry of Protestants. Urbanization and industrialization brought prosperity to many Irish and Germans. Archbishop John McCloskey (d. 1885) of New York became the first American cardinal in 1875, but the reigning churchman for a half-century was Cardinal James Gibbons (d. 1921), archbishop of Baltimore from 1877 until his death.

STATE CATHOLIC POPULATIONS OVER 1 MILLION

California	7,827,156	Florida	1,821,941
New York	7,331,820	Wisconsin	1,548,632
Texas	3,974,688	Connecticut	1,368,962
Pennsylvania	3,617,998	Louisiana	1,311,458
Illinois	3,561,715	Minnesota	1,165,523
New Jersey	3,250,180		
Massachusetts	2,978,321		
Michigan	2,267,063		
Ohio	2,223,714		

SOURCE: *1995 Catholic Almanac* (Huntington, IN: Our Sunday Visitor Publishing Division, 1994).

Catholic numbers grew with the influx of immigrants from Italy and eastern Europe. They formed ethnic neighborhoods served by national parishes and schools. There was conflict with established Catholics, and small groups of Lithuanians and Poles separated from the Roman Catholic Church, as did an estimated quarter-million Eastern-rite Ukrainians. Italian adaptation was helped by the arrival of priests and sisters from Italy, including Frances Xavier Cabrini (d. 1917).

The Catholic Church in the United States has been characterized by development of educational and social-welfare institutions paralleling those of the state. The Third Plenary Council (1884) declared that "no parish is complete until it has schools adequate to the needs of its children." Secondary schools, colleges, and universities followed. The Catholic University of America in Washington, D.C., opened in 1889. Other institutions included vocational and industrial schools, orphanages, protectories, and hospitals, chiefly staffed by religious sisters, who became the backbone around which the Church grew.

Catholics at the turn of the century were torn by conflict over the pace and extent of Americanization. In the Midwest, an activist, optimistic religious approach flourished. The "Americanists" endorsed Church-state separation, championed organized labor, and were less enthusiastic about parochial schools. Opposition to them centered in the church of

A young member of a Christian service group at Resurrection Church in Tempe, Arizona, assists in the construction of houses for poor families near Tijuana, Mexico.

New York and among the midwestern Germans, who resisted assimilationist tendencies. Two papal encyclicals by Leo XIII cooled the Americanists' ardor: *Longinqua Oceani* (1895), which mingled caution with praise for American accomplishments, and *Testem Benevolentiae* (1899), which criticized an excessively activist religious approach. Pope Pius X's crusade against Modernism (1907) had lasting effects in discouraging intellectual advances in the U.S. Church.

A CHURCH CONSOLIDATED

Post–World War I restrictions on immigration slowed Catholic growth from that source and allowed stabilization. Major building projects were undertaken: seminaries, churches, and cathedrals were built. The 1920s were marred by an outbreak of anti-Catholicism, largely spurred by the Ku Klux Klan. Broader Protestant fears contributed to the 1928 defeat of the first-ever Catholic major-party presidential candidate, Alfred E. Smith. Catholics suffered with everyone else in the 1930s depression, but became influential in the labor movement and had better political

A sister and lay teacher interact with young students in a Catholic school; in 1994 there were over 600,000 students enrolled in Catholic high schools and almost 2 million in Catholic elementary schools.

connections than ever before with Franklin Roosevelt's New Deal. Groups like the personalist, communitarian Catholic Workers, led by Dorothy Day, took root. A growing liturgical movement was understood as an expression of social Catholicism. Interracial committees and organizations in support of marriage and family multiplied. The Legion of Decency, publishing moral evaluations of moving pictures, had a substantial impact on the film industry. The 1930s were also notable for the popularity among many Catholics of the right-wing populist radio priest Charles E. Coughlin.

Wholehearted Catholic participation in World War II was followed by a decade of religious revival. The Catholic population increased between 1940 and 1960 from 21 to 42 million. An estimated 70 percent regularly attended Sunday Mass, and seminaries and convents were filled. Bishop Fulton J. Sheen (d. 1979) popularized religious philosophy as a national television personality. Lay Catholics were socially and economically upwardly mobile, a process aided by the GI Bill (1944) and the economic successes of the labor unions.

American Catholicism's contemporary era was introduced by the pontificate of John XXIII (1958–63), the Second Vatican Council (1962–65), and the election (1960) of the first Catholic American president, John F. Kennedy (d. 1963). Idealism among Catholic youth found new outlets in the Peace Corps and similar agencies. All this was prelude to American involvement in the worldwide societal convulsion of the 1960s, which found expression in growing agitation for civil rights and disillusionment with the war in Southeast Asia. Catholics were among the most radical antiwar activists.

With the exodus of Americans from cities to suburbs, the role of the parish as social center diminished. Parish schools declined as costs rose and Catholics moved away from close-knit neighborhoods. The downward trend in religious vocations and the broader range of ministries open to sisters and laypeople have been major factors in altering the institutional face of the Church. The feminist movement affected church life, and women took on administrative and pastoral responsibilities, but without ordination. In half the country's 19,000 parishes, 20,000 laypeople (85 percent women) and sisters function as ministers in several pastoral roles.

American Catholics run the ideological spectrum. There are small groups who reject liturgical reform and in general "Vatican II Catholicism." Most are religiously centrist. There is greater liberalism in ethics, in judging what is and is not sinful. Both social-activist liberals and right-wing intellectuals are active. The hierarchy speaks out more frequently, usually through the National Conference of Catholic Bishops and its operational secretariat, the United States Catholic Conference, both organized in 1967. While a national "Call to Action" Conference (Detroit, 1976) was less influential than anticipated, the appointment of pastorally oriented younger bishops during the tenure as apostolic delegate (1973–80) of Archbishop Jean Jadot, combined with a perceived liberal bent in the bishops' Washington staff, resulted in publication of pastoral letters on topics like the United States economy, war and peace, and the Hispanic presence in American Catholicism. Heightened consciousness on the part of bishops of their collegial teaching responsibility provoked some tensions with Rome in the restorationist pontificate of John Paul II. A "third age" of American Catholicism, following the colonial and immigrant phases, has begun. It finds American Catholics better integrated into the national life and less defensive about their religion than ever before. But structures and style appropriate to the "third age" are still very much in process.

See also Americanism; Baltimore, councils of; Brownson, Orestes Augustus; Cabrini, St. Frances Xavier; Calvert, Cecil; Calvert, Charles; Calvert, George; Calvert, Leonard; Carroll, John; Coughlin, Charles Edward; Day, Dorothy M.; Flaget, Benedict Joseph; Gibbons, James; Hecker, Isaac Thomas; Hughes, John Joseph; Kennedy, John Fitzgerald; McCloskey, John; Neumann, St. John Nepomucene; Serra, Bl. Junipero; Seton, St. Elizabeth Ann Bayley; Sheen, Fulton J.; Smith, Alfred E.

Bibliography

Dolan, Jay P. *The American Catholic Experience: A History from Colonial Times to the Present.* Garden City, NY: Doubleday, 1985.

Ellis, John Tracy. *American Catholicism.* Chicago: University of Chicago Press, 1969.

Hennesey, James. *American Catholics: A History of the Roman Catholic Community in the United States.* New York: Oxford University Press, 1981.

JAMES HENNESEY

universal salvific will of God, God's intention to save human beings. The classic text indicating the scope of God's salvific will is 1 Tim 2:3–4: "God our Savior, who desires everyone to be saved and to come to the knowledge of the truth." The universal scope of God's saving mercy is shown in many other texts as well, e.g., Rom 11:32, John 3:16, 1 Cor 15:21–22, 2 Cor 5:14–15.

But what does it mean for God to will the salvation of everyone if conceivably not everyone is saved? Augustine (d. 430), from the time of the Pelagian controversy, emphasized the infallible efficaciousness of God's will. Augustine took it for granted that many were lost. Hence, he gave these universal texts a restricted scope. He said they meant that God wills the salvation of all who are saved, or the salvation of people of all kinds and classes. But God does not actually will everyone to be saved; for if God did, no one would be lost.

A more satisfactory explanation was given by John of Damascus (d. ca. 749), who said that God antecedently wills the salvation of all, i.e., prior to a consideration of sinners who die unrepentant, but that God consequently wills the salvation only of those who freely accept and persevere in divine grace. Salvation is a divine gift that only God can confer; but God wills to give it to everyone who does not refuse it. This is the common opinion of Catholic theologians today. *See also* predestination; salvation; salvation outside the Church; will of God.

universities, Catholic. *See* Catholic colleges and universities—statistics.

universities, pontifical. *See* pontifical universities.

unmixed chalice, the ancient Armenian custom of consecrating at the Eucharist pure wine unmixed with water. Given a later Monophysite interpretation as signifying that Jesus had only one nature, it was a source of frequent controversy and condemned more than once, notably at the Council in Trullo in 692. Recent restoration of the Armenian Catholic Eucharist has reinstated the original Armenian custom. *See also* mixed chalice.

Urban II, Bl. [Odo], ca. 1042–99, pope from 1088 to 1099. After serving as canon and archdeacon of Reims, France, and prior of Cluny ca. 1070, he was made cardinal-bishop of Ostia and served as papal legate to France and Germany. As pope, Urban II was occupied with reform of the Church and con-

flicts with the emperor, Henry IV. He presided over the Council of Clermont (1095), where he inaugurated the First Crusade, and the Council of Bari (1098), where he attempted an unsuccessful reconciliation of the Greek and Latin churches. *See also* Clermont, Council of; Crusades.

Urban V, Bl. [Guillaume de Grimoard], 1310–70, pope from 1362 to 1370. A French Benedictine and professor of law, he attempted as pope to reform the Avignon curia and, unsuccessfully, to move the papacy back to Rome. He was beatified in 1870. Feast day: December 19. *See also* Avignon.

Urban VI [Bartolomeo Prignano], ca. 1318–89, pope from 1378 to 1389. Urban succeeded Gregory XI, who had returned the papacy from Avignon to Rome. Taking advantage of his violent demeanor, which led some to think him deranged, the French cardinals elected a second pope, Clement VII, claiming Urban's election had been invalid because the Romans had coerced them into electing an Italian. Clement immediately returned to Avignon, beginning the Great Western Schism (1378–1417). Urban's reign was marked by disorder and war. He executed five cardinals who plotted against him, and he himself may have died by poisoning. *See also* Avignon; Great Schism.

Urban VIII [Maffeo Barberini], 1568–1644, pope from 1623 to 1644. As pope he revised the Roman Breviary (1632), enforced the Council of Trent's decrees on the residence of bishops in their sees, and built extensively in Rome. He was also a nepotist, issued the second condemnation of Galileo, and condemned Jansen's *Augustinus* (1642).

Urbi et Orbi (oor'bee et ohr'bee; Lat., "to the city and to the world"), the blessing given by the pope, ordinarily in public (e.g., from the balcony of St. Peter's Basilica in Rome) and on a major feast day, such as Christmas or Easter, intended for both the people of Rome and for all of the faithful of the world.

Ursula, St., ca. fourth-century virgin and martyr. In legend, she was a British princess who fled to Cologne to preserve her virginity and was martyred there along with an unknown number of companions. Her cult grew with the discovery of her bones in 1155. She is a popular figure in religious art and iconography. Feast day: formerly October 21 (no longer observed).

Ursulines (O.S.U.), a general title for various institutes of religious women that are the monastic heirs to the Company of St. Ursula, founded by the Italian Angela Merici in 1535.

The original Company of St. Ursula had the goal of educating girls. Under the Primitive Rule set forth by Angela Merici, the members continued to live with their families, until a 1585 revision appropriated the Brescian rule's vision for community life. A 1612 bull of Paul V made the community into a formal religious order of cloistered nuns taking solemn vows.

In the seventeenth century the major Ursuline monasteries were in France, at Paris and Bordeaux. These monasteries were the sources for foundations in Quebec (1639) and New Orleans (1727). Ursuline communities in Tildonk, Belgium, and Mt. Calvary, Ahrweiler, Germany, also have foundations in the United States. At the initiative of Pope Leo XIII, many Ursuline convents banded together into the Roman Union of the Order of St. Ursula in 1900, under a single prioress general, Mother St. Julian. Other Ursuline communities are under pontifical jurisdiction as independent monasteries or under diocesan jurisdiction as convents.

While embracing many apostolates, the education of women has continued to be a distinctive hallmark of the Ursuline order in the United States. In 1848 the Cleveland community added a fourth vow, that of instruction, to their profession. The Ursulines of Cleveland run Ursuline College, which has undertaken to revamp its curriculum to reflect the particular ways in which women learn. *See also* Angela Merici, St.

usher. *See* hospitality, minister of.

usury, the charging of an excessive payment (interest) for the use of money. Many Fathers of the Church condemned interest on loans absolutely because, according to their interpretation of Mosaic law, the practice originates in lenders' greed and leads to exploitation of the poor. Some early councils forbade only clerics from charging interest, but others made the prohibition absolute. There is no analysis in these texts of the meaning of interest, nor is there consideration of the question of moderate rates of interest.

Early Scholastic philosophy based its analysis on the notion that the value of money consisted in its being a commodity directed to immediate consumption, like food or drink. Early Scholastics, therefore, classified monetary loans as gratuitous by nature. Moreover, following Aristotle (d. 322 B.C.), they thought of money as essentially sterile, so that charging interest was a violation of commutative justice. However, they did acknowledge that there could be extrinsic reasons for charging interest, such as compensation for loss due to late payment.

In the sixteenth century, a large number of Catholic authors distinguished loans for consumption from loans for production. By rejecting the Aristotelian notion of money, they could affirm that the same amount of money could have a different value at different times and, consequently, that there could be intrinsic reasons for charging interest.

Although Benedict XIV made the Scholastic teaching part of Church doctrine by his encyclical *Vix Pervenit* of 1745, the rationale behind the distinction between intrinsic and extrinsic justifications of interest has become obsolete. The Scholastics themselves recognized that the value of different currencies depended on the agreement of traders in the market, and thus that market forces could determine a just price for loans. ROBERT P. KENNEDY

utilitarianism, any of several moral systems that maintain that the moral rectitude of an action is determined by its overall utility or usefulness, measured on a previously determined scale of value. In its classic form, as developed primarily by Jeremy Bentham (d. 1832), utilitarianism held that utility refers to an action's contribution to the general welfare; classical utilitarianism identified human pleasure as the only absolute good and pain the only evil. Subsequent modifications of utilitarianism advocate some system of maximization of human welfare. Utilitarianism has been criticized by Catholic moral theologians because of the inadequacy of its value structure and its incomplete understanding of human action. *See also* moral theology.

utraquism, the teaching of John Hus and his disciples in the fifteenth century that Christians must receive the Eucharist under the forms of both bread and wine, since Christ's words in reference to the bread speak only of his body and in reference to the wine only of his blood. This teaching was rejected by the councils of Constance (1415), Basel (1432), and Trent (1551). *See also* Communion under both kinds.

Uzhorod, Union of (1646), the first of three unions between the Catholic Church and Orthodox faithful, who had long coexisted within the Catholic kingdom of Hungary.

Because no act of union was formally documented, the precise date and other details of this event are obscure. The majority opinion is that on April 24, 1646, a group of sixty-three Ruthenian priests made a profession of Catholic faith at the castle of Uzhorod. This was done without the knowledge of the Holy See or any higher Catholic ecclesiastical authority, but was simply accepted by the Latin bishop of Eger. According to a letter written by six Ruthenian archdeacons to Pope Innocent X in 1652, the group acknowledged the primacy of the pope and added three conditions: that they retain the Byzantine rite, elect their own bishop who would then be confirmed by the Holy See, and have the free enjoyment of ecclesiastical immunities.

The evidence indicates that these Orthodox asked for full communion with the Catholic Church because they felt that union would offer a defense against the advance of Protestantism, improve the level of clerical culture, and liberate the Ruthenians from social and economic servitude.

The seed sown at Uzhorod in 1646 took root and spread. In 1664 and 1713 other unions took place that resulted in the virtual disappearance of Orthodoxy within the Hungarian kingdom.

These unions gave rise to the Byzantine Catholic churches that are now located in Slovakia, Transcarpathia (Ukraine), and Hungary, as well as in the Maramures area in Romania. *See also* Hungary, Catholicism in; Pseudo-Union of Uzhorod; Ruthenian Catholic Church; Slovak Byzantine Catholic Church.

RONALD G. ROBERSON

vagus (vah'guhs). *See* wanderer.

Vaison, councils of, two interprovincial synods of the church in Gaul important for the history of the liturgy. The first (442) specified regulations for penitents. The second (529), under the presidency of Caesarius of Arles, gave to rural priests the right of preaching and ordered the singing of the threefold Sanctus at Mass.

Valdés, Juan de, ca. 1500–1541, Spanish humanist and writer. His Erasmian piety, emphasizing inner religious feelings over hierarchical authority, inspired prominent laypeople and clerics in Italy, where he had moved in 1531. Although devoutly Catholic, his spiritual writings were posthumously condemned by Counter-Reformation Church leaders. Some of his followers became Protestants, notably Bernardino of Ochino and Peter Martyr.

Valentine, St., the name of two saints about whom very little is known. One was reportedly a priest from Rome, beheaded in 269 by the Emperor Claudius II (d. 270) for refusing to worship Roman gods. The other, martyred several years earlier, was bishop of Terni, renowned for his gift of healing. Feast day: February 14.

Valentine's Day, St., a popular feast celebrated on February 14 by the exchange of signs of love. Its origins are found in the Roman martyrology, the earliest listing of martyrs, where two Valentines were commemorated on February 14, both beheaded on the Flaminian Way. One was a Roman priest, the other, a bishop of Terni. Whether there were one or two Valentines remains an open question. Neither has a clear connection with courting couples or those in love. The custom of sending love notes and gifts probably originated in the Middle Ages from the belief that February 14 marked the mating season of birds. This day is no longer acknowledged or celebrated as a memorial or feast in the liturgical calendar. *See also* Valentine, St.

Valentinus, ca. 100–ca. 175, founder of a Gnostic Christian school of thought that included Heracleon, Ptolemy, Florinus, Theodotus, and Marcus among its followers. He came to Rome from Alexandria, ca. 136–40, where he earned great respect for his learning. His failure to be elected the Bishop of Rome may have prompted the founding of his school. Only fragments remain of Valentinus's own writings, but the *Gospel of Truth, Tripartite Tractate, Gospel of Philip,* and *Epistle to Rheginum* reflect the thought of the Valentinian school. *See also* Gnosticism.

validation, in canon law the rectification of an act previously not recognized as legal. Validation may take place by repeating the act in the proper manner or, under certain conditions, by decree of an authority competent to rectify the act.

validity [canon law], the quality of an act that determines whether it is recognized as legal. At times canon law requires that an act be performed in a certain manner in order to be valid; in such cases the law states this explicitly. The presumption of canon law is that all acts are valid until proven otherwise.

validity of sacraments, juridical concept, used along with liceity in speaking about sacraments. Validity refers to the minimal requirements necessary for the Church to recognize that an action or celebration has resulted in a true sacrament. For example, in Baptism the minimum requirements for validity are the pronouncement of the prescribed form (the trinitarian formula) and the use of the correct matter (water). If either of these minimum requirements is not met—for example, the form only invokes one person of the Trinity or water is not used—the sacrament is not celebrated and is considered invalid.

Other conditions also affect validity. The administration of any sacrament other than Baptism on someone not baptized is considered invalid. The reconferral of those sacraments that leave a character and hence can only be celebrated once—Baptism, Confirmation, and Holy Orders—is impossible and therefore also invalidates the sacrament.

Finally, the intention of both the minister and recipient of certain sacraments may also play a role in their validity. Minimally, the minister must intend to do what the Church intends in celebrating a sacrament. In Marriage, for example, since the spouses minister the sacrament to each other, their intention to celebrate the sacrament is a *sine qua non* (Lat., "absolutely necessary condition") for validity. *See also* liceity [canon law]; sacrament.

Valla, Lorenzo, ca. 1406–57, priest, Italian humanist scholar, and opponent of Scholastics. A champion of Renaissance classicism, Valla pioneered textual criticism, seeking by philological methods to expose medieval "corruptions" of important texts such as the Bible and the Donation of Constantine, which Valla claimed was a complete forgery.

Vallumbrosan order, contemplative order of monks, nuns, and lay brothers known for its ascetic life-style, founded ca. 1035 by St. John Gualbert near Vallumbrosa, twenty miles east of Florence. A few houses remain active. *See also* John Gualbert, St.

values, moral, those worthy (Old Fr., *valoir*) things that are essential to proper human living, e.g., the capacity for love. Moral values include such virtues as honesty, justice, chastity, fortitude, and temperance.

The broadest and most essential difference in understandings of value is that between the subjective and the objective. For subjectivists, the value of something depends on how people esteem it. For objectivists, things have intrinsic worth, so that evaluations must respect the relative worth of their objects and can thus be correct or incorrect. In Catholic ethics, value translates the Latin *bonum,* "good," and therefore has objective reality.

Values are either properly moral, related directly to the morality of the person (e.g., justice, chastity), or, more commonly, morally relevant effects of human action. Properly moral values are absolute and inviolable because to act against them involves violation of one's own or another's conscience. In the second sense, values are identical with premoral goods, e.g., knowledge, health, friendship, beauty.

Judgments about intrinsic value find expression in moral norms or rules. If the value is moral in the strict sense, it yields a formal, inviolable norm, such as the injunction to be just or truthful. Formal norms do not, however, specify what particular actions accord with them. If the value is premoral, then the norm is specific and may admit of exceptions; whether specific norms, such as the rule forbidding contraception, are in principle open to exception is a matter of contention.   ROBERT P. KENNEDY

Vandals, Germanic people who in 429 invaded North Africa and by 439 had captured Carthage. Arian Christians, they persecuted the orthodox Catholic population, confiscating property, exiling people, and raiding ships and ports throughout the Mediterranean. They seized and "vandalized" Rome in 455. Their kingdom in Africa fell in 534–35. *See also* Arianism.

Vatican, an independent state in Italy where the Bishop of Rome (the pope) resides. The term is often used as a shorthand expression for the central authority of the Catholic Church: the pope, the Roman Curia, and the Vatican City State together. It takes its name from the Vatican hill, which in classical Rome was located outside the city walls and was the site of Nero's circus and a cemetery. Tradition holds that the Apostle Peter was martyred in Nero's circus and buried in the nearby cemetery. A shrine over the tomb of the apostle was reported in the second century, and the fourth-century emperor Constantine leveled the previously hilly site of the cemetery and built a basilica in honor of the apostle. This church was replaced in the Renaissance by the present St. Peter's Basilica (dedicated, 1626).

Because of the deterioration of the palace at the Lateran, the papal residence at the Vatican became the principal residence of the bishops of Rome after the Avignon papacy in France (1309–77), though the popes also used other residences, including the Quirinal Palace until the unification of Italy and the fall of the Papal States in 1870. At that time the pope became a "prisoner of the Vatican" until the solution of the "Roman Question" in 1929. The Lateran Treaty with the Italian government recognized the independent sovereignty of the Vatican City State, compensated the papacy for the loss of the Papal States, and granted official recognition and privileges to the Catholic Church in Italy. The treaty was renegotiated in 1985, with the Catholic Church relinquishing most of the privileges granted in 1929, including compulsory religious instruction in government schools and the payment of clergy salaries by the Italian government. *See also* Saint Peter's Basilica; Vatican City State.   *JOHN F. LAHEY*

Vatican City State, the political entity that governs the territory where the Holy See is located. The smallest sovereign state in the world (108.7 acres in all), it is completely surrounded by the city of Rome. It contains St. Peter's Basilica, the Vatican Palace (the residence of the pope), the Vatican Museum, the Vatican Library (containing 70,000 manuscripts and almost 800,000 books), Vatican Radio, Vatican Television Center, the Vatican Observatory, Vatican Polyglot Press, the Vatican Gardens, art galleries, archives, a post office, a bank, a newspaper, a railroad

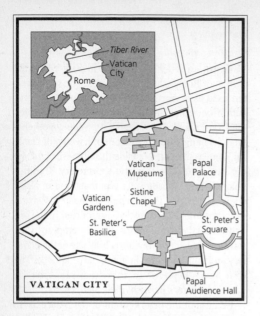

Map labels:
Tiber River
Vatican City
Rome
Vatican Museums
Papal Palace
Sistine Chapel
Vatican Gardens
St. Peter's Basilica
St. Peter's Square
VATICAN CITY
Papal Audience Hall

temporal authority that could allow him to fulfill his ministry to the universal Church, free from coercion. As part of the settlement the Vatican City State was created as an independent political entity. This Lateran Treaty was signed on February 11, 1929, and ratified on June 7 of the same year, by the Italian government and Vatican City. The agreement recognized Catholicism as the religion of Italy and provided financial compensation for the loss of the Papal States. A new concordat was ratified on June 3, 1985, ending the official status of Catholicism in Italy, the mandating of Catholic instruction in government schools, and the payment of clergy salaries by the Italian government.

Vatican City State and the Holy See are not synonymous. The Holy See is the sovereign spiritual and diplomatic authority exercised by the pope. Vatican City State is the political entity and territory in which the Holy See is located and that guarantees the Holy See's independence. Over one hundred nations have formal diplomatic relations with the Holy See, not with Vatican City State. *See also* audience, papal; basilica, major; Holy See; Lateran Treaty; papacy, the; papal flag; Roman Curia; Saint Peter's Basilica; Vatican Library; Vatican Radio. JOHN F. LAHEY

station, and various offices, apartments, and service facilities. Its extraterritorial rights also extend to various other buildings in Rome, including the major basilicas of the St. John Lateran, St. Mary Major, and St. Paul's Outside the Walls; office buildings for various Congregations of the Roman Curia; and the papal villa at Castel Gandolfo, fifteen miles southeast of the city. The pope is the head of the government, with full executive, legislative, and judicial power. The administration of its daily affairs, however, is in the hands of the Pontifical Commission for the State of Vatican City. The territory's normal population is about one thousand, but it employs about four thousand in all. One could walk across the territory in thirty minutes or less.

Located outside the walls of classical Rome, the Vatican hill is revered as the site of the Apostle Peter's martyrdom and his burial place. Although the term "Vatican" has come to refer to the pope as well as to those offices of the Roman Curia that assist the pope in his teaching and pastoral ministry, the Vatican City State was established only in 1929 as part of the Lateran accords that regularized the relationship of the Holy See with the government of Italy. The pope had been a temporal sovereign until the fall of the Papal States in 1870. The "Roman Question" then became a vexing concern especially between the new state of Italy and the Holy See. The question involved a number of issues, including a concern to grant the pope an independence from

Vatican Council I, the twentieth (according to customary enumeration) general, or ecumenical, council of the Church, which met from December 1869 to October 1870 at Rome in St. Peter's Basilica. It approved two dogmatic constitutions: *Dei Filius*, on the relationship of reason and faith, and *Pastor Aeternus*, on the papacy's juridical primacy and on the infallibility of the papacy's teaching office.

Historical Background and the Preparation for the Council: Pope Pius IX and his advisers intended the council as a bulwark against the modern spirit and the principles of the Enlightenment and the French Revolution of 1789. They wanted to combat rationalism, materialism, and atheism, since these ideologies undermine religion; liberalism as a worldview and as a political movement, since it calls into question the authority of the Christian faith and the Church and, together with nationalism, threatens the unity and independence of the Church and its existence as an institution; and theology insofar as it had become open to modern ideas. The plan for a council stood in close relation to the encyclical *Quanta Cura* and its well-known "Syllabus," the list of "modern errors." Two days before the encyclical's publication, on December 6, 1864, in the presence of some cardinals, Pius IX declared for the first time his intention to convene a council. The preparatory commissions began their work in 1865. It became increasingly clear that the pope intended the council to solemnly confirm the condemnation of the errors listed in the "Syllabus."

The commissions that prepared the council were composed predominantly of supporters of Ultramontanism, a movement that opposed the Enlightenment and liberalism through the strengthening of papal authority. Their goal was the declaration of the dogma of papal infallibility and the papacy's juridical primacy. Nevertheless, there was at the outset no agenda for the preparatory work. Since 1867, Bishop Senestrey of Regensburg and Archbishop Manning of Westminster, along with Rome's Jesuit journal *Civiltà Cattolica,* had promoted the definition of papal infallibility. From the point of view of the Ultramontanists and their supporters, opposition groups appeared to be forming, headed by J. J. I. von Döllinger in Germany, Acton and Newman in England, Gratry and C. de Montalembert in France. Many of these opponents regarded the definition as impossible for historical reasons, others as inopportune in the current situation. To the latter group belonged Archbishop Spalding of Baltimore and fourteen German bishops, who informed Rome in late summer 1869 of their lack of support for a decree on papal infallibility. Since the beginning of 1867 the preparatory commission for the dogma was preoccupied with this opposition.

The Course of the Council: In June 1867 it was officially announced that Pius IX planned to convoke the council the following year. The invitation to the Orthodox bishops and Anglicans and Protestants was *pro forma* (Lat., "according to form"), i.e., perfunctory, and not acted upon by the pope. The solemn opening occurred on December 8, 1869. Of the approximately 1,050 possible participants, 774 were present, of which two-thirds were Europeans and one-third Italians. Most of the missionary bishops also were Europeans. The United States was represented by forty-eight bishops and one abbot. The five presidents of the council were named by the pope.

Of the fifty-one schemas, or proposed decrees, prepared by the commissions, only six were discussed and only two—in part—acted upon. The council treated the schema on the erroneous teachings of rationalism, traditionalism, and semirationalism, the last of which represented by the theologians Georg Hermes from Bonn and Anton Günther from Vienna. The schema was severely criticized, reworked, and finally unanimously approved on April 24, 1870, as the Dogmatic Constitution on the Catholic Faith (*Dei Filius*).

The council fathers, differing on the definition of papal infallibility, can be divided into three groups. The small group of active infallibilists under the leadership of Manning and Senestrey represented an extreme view, upholding the infallibility of all papal teachings, especially of the Syllabus, and also advocating papal infallibility as the source of the Church's infallibility. The majority of the council was not primarily interested in declaring a formal definition of papal infallibility, but these bishops wanted to strengthen the principle of papal authority and were, therefore, receptive to the propaganda of the infallibilists. The third group, the minority in opposition to the definition of papal infallibility, comprised a fifth of the council fathers and was composed primarily of bishops from Germany, France, and Austria-Hungary. Archbishop Kenrick of St. Louis and Archbishop Connelly of Halifax also belonged to this group. Their opposition was based partially on ecclesial-political and ecumenical reasons and partially on principle. Many rejected the Ultramontane-centralist model of the Church because it conflicts with the ecclesial structure of the ancient Church.

The infallibilists succeeded in filling the important delegations on the dogmatic statement with their members and presenting to the pope a list of four hundred supporters of a definition of papal infallibility. In light of this support, the pope decided that the schema on the Church would be expanded with a chapter on papal infallibility. When public discussion grew sharper, the majority of the council pressed for a quick decision. At the request of approximately a hundred council fathers, the pope chose to separate from the schema on the Church the chapter on papal primacy and papal infallibility and to allow this chapter to be acted on separately as the Dogmatic Constitution on the Church of Christ.

In conciliar debate, the minority hardened in its resistance to the proposed constitution. Minimally, these bishops wanted it stressed that the pope could only be infallible if he was supported by the infallible tradition of the faith of the whole Church. This was the understanding of the majority, but in light of earlier conciliar and Gallican tendencies, they did not want to introduce procedural conditions for the validity of a papal decision (e.g., that the pope must poll the episcopacy prior to declaring a pronouncement infallible). Neither the extreme infallibilists nor the minority could win in the final version of the text. Out of protest sixty-one members of the minority left Rome before the final vote. On June 18, 1870, the Dogmatic Constitution on the Church of Christ (*Pastor Aeternus*) was passed, with only two negative votes.

The minority of bishops, who had not voted for the decree, gradually accepted the decision on condition of its reception by the Church as a whole and in the sense of its interpretation that was indirectly clarified by the pope. In German-speaking lands protest within the Church led to the formation of the Old Catholic community.

Because of the outbreak of the Franco-Prussian war, Pius IX adjourned the council on October 20, 1870, for an indefinite time. It was never reconvened.

The Results of the Council: Because of its premature ending the council remained incomplete. Fortunately, it did not accomplish the intended goal of making the Syllabus into a dogma. Although conditioned by the concerns of its time, the constitution *Dei Filius* can be regarded as effective. In opposition to rationalism, which makes the value of revelation dependent upon the judgment of human reason, it teaches the proper truth of revelation. In opposition to fideist traditionalism, which denies to human reason any capacity for religious and ethical knowledge, it defends reason and the rational credibility of Christian faith.

The one-sided emphasis of the constitution *Pastor Aeternus* is regrettable. As the minority anticipated, this document has proved harmful to the Church. It was also unnecessary, because the supreme pastoral and teaching authority of the papacy was not contested at the time. Nevertheless, the minority did prevent the acceptance of the extreme definition of papal infallibility, and eventually the views of the minority were confirmed by Vatican II (1962–65). *See also* faith and reason; infallibility; Manning, Henry Edward; Newman, John Henry; Old Catholics; Pius IX; primacy, papal; Syllabus of Errors; Ultramontanism.

Bibliography

Butler, Cuthbert. *The Vatican Council, 1869–1870.* Westminster, MD: Newman Press, 1962.

Ellis, John Tracy. "The Church Faces the Modern World: The First Vatican Council." *The General Council: Special Studies in Doctrinal and Historical Background,* edited by William J. McDonald. Washington, DC: Catholic University of America Press, 1962.

Hennesey, James J. *The First Council of the Vatican: The American Experience.* New York: Herder and Herder, 1963.

HERMAN J. POTTMEYER

Vatican Library, founded by Pope Nicholas V (d. 1455), a collection of some 70,000 manuscripts, almost 800,000 printed books, and 7,500 *incunabula* (Lat., "cradle [books]") housed in Vatican City State. (The *incunabula* are products of the so-called cradle days of printing, i.e., the fifteenth century.) The oldest public library in Europe, it also contains the Vatican archives, which were opened to scholars by Pope Leo XIII in 1881. *See also* Vatican City State.

Vatican Radio, the electronic voice of the Vatican, inaugurated in 1931 by Pope Pius XI. Designed by Guglielmo Marconi, the inventor of radio, and supervised by him until his death in 1937, the station broadcasts in thirty-four languages to every part of the world. It has a staff of over four hundred broadcasters and technicians, including thirty-five Jesuits. The Vatican Television Center was founded by Pope John Paul II in 1983. *See also* Vatican City State.

Vaughan, Henry, 1622–95, English spiritual poet. He had a conversion experience early in life, which diverted his attention from the practice of medicine to the writing of spiritual poetry. His best-known work is the *Silex Scintillans,* published in two parts in 1650 and 1655.

Vaughan, Herbert, 1832–1903, English cardinal, founder of the Mill Hill Missionaries. Appointed archbishop of Westminster in 1892, he obtained permission from Rome for English Catholics to attend Oxford and Cambridge universities and built Westminster Cathedral, begun in 1895. *See also* Mill Hill Missionaries; Mill Hill Sisters.

Vawter, Bruce, 1921–86, biblical scholar, leader in the Catholic biblical renewal. He entered the Congregation of Mission (Vincentians) in 1942; was ordained in 1947; received S.S.L. (1952) and S.S.D. (1957) degrees from the Pontifical Biblical Institute, in Rome; and taught principally at Kenrick Seminary in St. Louis, St. Thomas in Denver, and De Paul University in Chicago (1968–86). He was president of the Catholic Biblical Association (1961–62). His influential books *A Path Through Genesis* (1956) and *The Conscience of Israel* (1961) were models for the presentation of solid scholarship to a wider audience.

VATICAN COUNCIL II

Vatican Council II was the twenty-first general, or ecumenical, council of the Church (October 11, 1962–December 8, 1965). The council is regarded by many as the most significant religious event since the sixteenth-century Reformation and certainly as the most important of the twentieth century.

Gathering of all the Catholic bishops of the world in the nave of St. Peter's Basilica, Vatican City, for the ceremony opening the Second Vatican Council, October 11, 1962; Pope John XXIII enters the basilica in procession down the middle aisle.

St. Peter's Basilica during the Second Vatican Council, with a view of the altar, Bernini's classic baldachino overhead, the sanctuary, the enthroned Bible in the center aisle, and many of the bishops and official observers.

GENERAL FACTS ABOUT THE COUNCIL

Pope John XXIII first announced his intention to call a council on July 25, 1959, and convoked the council on December 25, 1961, in an apostolic constitution, *Humanae Salutis* ("Of Human Salvation"). There were four separate sessions, all held in St. Peter's Basilica: October–December 1962, September–December 1963, September–November 1964, and September–December 1965. Each day began with Mass celebrated in as many different rites as were represented at the council—twenty-six by one estimate—and by the enthronement of the Sacred Scriptures.

The total number of delegates (or "fathers") at this council greatly exceeded the number attending any of the preceding twenty. The largest previous ecumenical council had been Vatican Council I (1869–70), with 737 in attendance. Vatican II had more than 2,600 bishops from all over the world (2,908 would have been eligible to attend the first session). The total number of participants exceeded 3,000, counting theologians and other experts. These experts, *periti* in Latin (as distinct from the bishops' private advisers), numbered about 200 in the first session and 480 by the end of the council.

The council was not only the largest in terms of numbers but also the most ecumenical (meaning, lit., "the whole wide world") in terms of nations and cultures. Vatican I, for example, was dominated by Europeans, including European bishops in mission territories. Because of the Church's success in building native clergies between Vatican I and the mid-twentieth century, most of the bishops from mission countries attending Vatican II were themselves natives of those lands and products of those cultures. Among eligible bishops, 1,089 were from Europe, 489 from South America, 404 from North America, 374 from Asia, 296 from Africa, 84 from Central America, and 75 from Oceania. All speeches and discussions were conducted in Latin, however. Cardinal Richard J. Cushing of Boston offered to pay for a system of simultaneous translation, similar to the one used at the United Nations, but the Vatican declined.

The council was also more ecumenical than previous councils in terms of non-Catholic and lay observers. Some forty non-Catholic observers were present from the start, although none from the Eastern Orthodox churches. By the beginning of the second session in 1963, there were sixty-three observers from almost every major Christian denomination, including three newly arrived representatives of the Russian Orthodox Church. By the end of the council, there were eighty in all. These observers had some of the best seats at the council, in the tribune of St. Longinus, close to the moderators' table. Once a week they met with one of the *periti* to discuss matters under consideration, but their influence was indirect rather than direct, as they had no right to speak or to vote at the council. Eleven laymen were invited to attend the second session, but by the beginning of the fourth and final session in 1965 there were fifty-two lay auditors, twenty-nine of whom were men and twenty-three women, including ten nuns.

This was also the first ecumenical council in history to have available to it electric lights, telephones, typewriters, and other modern means of communication and transportation (although it did not yet have access to computers and satellite technology). It was also the first council to be covered by newspapers, magazines, radio, and television from all over the world, although the media were not allowed in St. Peter's during the sessions. They relied on press handouts that usually reflected the views of the conservatives and on the reports of friendly bishops and *periti.*

The council was unique in its stated purpose as well. Unlike so many previous councils, Vatican II had not been called to combat heresy or to deal with some serious threat to the unity of the Church. On the contrary, Pope John XXIII, in his opening address of October 11, 1962, said that the council's goal was to eradicate the seeds of discord and to promote peace and the unity of all humankind, not to repeat traditional doctrinal formulations or to condemn errors.

The preparation for this council was the most extensive in the history of the Church. Ideas for the conciliar agenda were solicited from every bishop, from the heads of clerical religious orders (but not orders of religious women), from Catholic universities and theological faculties, as well as from members of the Roman Curia. Over 9,300 proposals were submitted. The material was indexed and distributed to eleven preparatory commissions appointed by Pope John XXIII in June 1960 to prepare draft documents for discussion. These commissions met between November 1960 and June 1962 and produced over seventy documents, or schemata. These documents, in turn, were reduced to twenty separate texts, each of which was reviewed and revised by the Central Preparatory Commission before being submitted to the pope for approval. In July 1962 seven of these documents were circulated among the bishops of the world in preparation for the opening of the council in October. The documents were concerned with the sources of revelation, the moral order, the deposit of faith, the family and chastity, liturgy, media, and unity. By contrast with the final documents approved by the council itself, these schemata were very conservative in orientation. Fearful of the impact of the council on its traditional ways of conducting the business of the Church, the Curia had seen to it that only the safest, mostly Rome-based theologians were appointed to serve on the preparatory commissions.

THE FIRST SESSION (1962)

The most dramatic and most important of the four sessions was the first. There were at least five significant moments in this session: Pope John XXIII's opening address, the refusal of the bishops to accept the Curia's organization of the conciliar commissions, the initial debate over the document on the liturgy, the debate over the document on revelation, and the rejection of the Curia's draft document on the Church. Together these developments signaled a new mood and direction for the Catholic Church.

In his opening speech on October 11, 1962, Pope John XXIII underscored the positive purposes and opportunities of the council; namely, to work toward the unity of humankind so that "the earthly city may be brought to the resemblance of that heavenly city where truth reigns [and] charity is the law." Indeed, he explicitly rejected the advice of those close to him who "can see nothing but prevarication and ruin," who regard the modern era as worse than others and getting worse all the time, and who are "always forecasting disaster." He called them "prophets of gloom." He also rejected their view that the council should simply reaffirm traditional doctrines of the Church, while condemning errors that undermine those teachings. "For this a council was not necessary," he said. Instead these doctrinal formulations should be presented in new forms that reflect modern thought. And the most effective way to combat error is through "the medicine of mercy rather than that of severity." The Church must show herself always as "the loving mother of all, benign, patient, full of mercy and goodness toward the brethren who are separated from her."

The second key moment in this first session came two days later, on October 13, when Cardinals Liénart of Lille and Frings of Cologne successfully urged the council to reject the Roman Curia's plan for election of members to the ten conciliar commissions. Instead of voting immediately, they suggested that regional groups of bishops should meet to choose the best qualified candidates. The loud applause indicated that the council would not be under the Curia's control.

The third key moment occurred on October 22 when the document on the liturgy was brought up for discussion. There was an obvious and immediate division of the council between traditionalists and progressives, the former rejecting any change, especially in the language of the liturgy, and the latter upset by the obvious tampering with the document between the time it was approved by the Central Preparatory Committee and the time it reached the council itself. A few days later Cardinal Ottaviani, prefect of the Holy Office, complained about revolutionary tendencies in the council and charged that these would cause scandal among the faithful. When he went over his time, he refused to stop. When his microphone was turned off, the assembly applauded, another indication of a major change in the balance of power.

Pope John XXIII, who called the council, addresses the opening session of the Second Vatican Council on October 11, 1962, in a speech in which he criticized conservative "prophets of gloom" in the hierarchy and the Roman Curia; Cardinal Francis Spellman of New York is at the pope's right.

A fourth development concerned the document on revelation. At the opening of debate on November 14, Cardinal Liénart attacked the schema on the grounds that there is only one source of revelation (the word of God), not two (Scripture and tradition). The following day Cardinal Döpfner of Munich complained that the schema was too one-sided and should be rejected. On November 20 a vote to reject the schema had the support of 60 percent of the Fathers, but not enough under the rules of the council to scuttle the document. The following day the pope ordered its withdrawal and directed that it be considered by a new commission jointly chaired by Cardinals Ottaviani and Bea, the latter of the Secretariat for Promoting Christian Unity.

Finally, on December 4, three days after Cardinal Ottaviani presented the schema on the Church, Cardinal Suenens of Belgium called for a complete redrafting of the document. His speech was greeted by prolonged applause. The council was on a different course from the one marked out by the Curia.

THE SECOND, THIRD, AND FOURTH SESSIONS (1963–65)

Pope John XXIII died the following June and was succeeded by Cardinal Montini of Milan, one of the council's leading progressives, who took the name Paul VI. One of his first acts was to determine September 29, 1963, as the opening day of the council's second session. In his opening address he listed four aims of the council: the development of a clearer idea of the Church, its renewal, the unity of all Christians, and dialogue between the Church and the world. The most contentious issue in this session had to do with the doctrine of collegiality, but the most dramatic moment came on November 8 when Cardinal Frings of Cologne openly criticized the Holy Office for its dealings with theologians and called for reform of the Curia. Cardinal Ottaviani took the floor to denounce Cardinal Frings's attack as an attack on the pope himself, but that afternoon Pope Paul VI telephoned Cardinal Frings to express his approval of what he had said. At the end of the session, on December 4, the first two council documents were formally approved: the Constitution on the Sacred Liturgy and the Decree on the Instruments of Social Communication.

The pace quickened in the third session, leaving many with the suspicion that the conservative minority was trying to rush matters in order to leave some business unfinished. There were discussions on a wide variety of complex topics: religious liberty, the Jews, the laity, the Church in the modern world, marriage, culture, the missions, and the formation of priests. After an "Explanatory Note" (Lat., *Nota praevia*) reaffirming the authority of the pope was added to the Dogmatic Constitution on the Church, conservative opposition to the document disappeared and the constitution was approved on November 19 with only ten negative votes. Other late developments in the session added to the pessimism of the progressive majority: the sidetracking of the document on religious liberty, last-minute changes ordered by the pope in the Decree on Ecumenism to satisfy the conservative minority, and the postponing of a vote on the document on non-Christian religions. The mood was somber at the closing of the third session on November 21. When a grim-faced Pope Paul VI was carried into St. Peter's, there was no applause.

The fourth and final session began on September 14, 1965, with an announcement by Pope Paul VI that he would establish the long-awaited Synod of Bishops. He did so the next day, which also marked the beginning of debate on religious liberty—a document drafted in large part by the American Jesuit John Courtney Murray and rescued from curial burial through the efforts of Cardinal Spellman of New York and others. Discussion resumed also of documents on the missions, religious life, priestly formation, priestly life and ministry, and non-Christian religions. The bulk of this session was devoted, however, to a section-by-section discussion of the document on the Church in the modern world. On

December 6 the document was approved by an overwhelming vote, and a major reform of the Roman Curia was announced. The final public session was held on December 7, at which the pope removed the excommunication of 1054 against the patriarch of Constantinople. The next day there was a closing ceremony in St. Peter's Square.

DOCUMENTS OF VATICAN II

There are sixteen documents in all: the Dogmatic Constitution on the Church (*Lumen Gentium*), the Dogmatic Constitution on Divine Revelation (*Dei Verbum*), the Constitution on the Sacred Liturgy (*Sacrosanctum Concilium*), the Pastoral Constitution on the Church in the Modern World (*Gaudium et Spes*), the Decree on the Instruments of Social Communication (*Inter Mirifica*), the Decree on Ecumenism (*Unitatis Redintegratio*), the Decree on Eastern Catholic Churches (*Orientalium Ecclesiarum*), the Decree on the Bishops' Pastoral Office in the Church (*Christus Dominus*), the Decree on Priestly Formation (*Optatam Totius*), the Decree on the Appropriate Renewal of the Religious Life (*Perfectae Caritatis*), the Decree on the Apostolate of the Laity (*Apostolicam Actuositatem*), the Decree on the Ministry and Life of Priests (*Presbyterorum Ordinis*), the Decree on the Church's Missionary Activity (*Ad Gentes Divinitus*), the Declaration on Christian Education (*Gravissimum*

Another view of the Second Vatican Council meeting in St. Peter's Basilica in the presence of Pope Paul VI; the non-Catholic observers are seated on the right, in the Tribune of Longinus, diagonally opposite the altar.

Educationis), the Declaration on the Relationship of the Church to Non-Christian Religions (*Nostra Aetate*), and the Declaration on Religious Freedom (*Dignitatis Humanae*).

Constitutions touch substantively upon doctrinal and universal pastoral matters that pertain to the very essence, or "constitution," of the Church. Decrees and declarations are directed at practical questions or specific pastoral concerns. As such, these latter presuppose the doctrine, theology, and pastoral directives of the constitutions.

Among the distinctive teachings of Vatican II, by contrast with some common beliefs of the pre–Vatican II era, are the following:

1. The Church is, first and foremost, a mystery, or sacrament, and not primarily an organization or institution.
2. The Church is the whole People of God, not just the hierarchy, clergy, and religious.
3. The Church's mission includes action on behalf of justice and peace and is not limited to the preaching of the word and the celebration of the sacraments.
4. The Church includes all Christians and is not limited exclusively to the Catholic Church.
5. The Church is a communion, or college, of local churches, which are not simply administrative subdivisions of the Church universal.
6. The Church is an eschatological community; it is not yet the kingdom of God.
7. The lay apostolate is a direct participation in the mission of the Church and not simply a sharing in the mission of the hierarchy.
8. There is a hierarchy of truths; not all official teachings of the Church are equally binding or essential to the integrity of Catholic faith.
9. God uses other Christian churches and non-Christian religions in offering salvation to all humankind; the Catholic Church is not the only means of salvation.
10. The dignity of the human person and the freedom of the act of faith are the foundation of religious liberty for all, over against the view that "error has no rights."

See also separate entries on each of the council documents and Bea, Augustine; constitution, conciliar; declaration, conciliar; decree, conciliar; ecumenical council; John XXIII [Angelo Roncalli]; Murray, John Courtney; Ottaviani, Alfredo; Paul VI; Spellman, Francis Joseph; Suenens, Leo Josef.

Bibliography

Hastings, Adrian, ed. *Modern Catholicism: Vatican II and After.* New York: Oxford University Press; London: SPCK, 1991.
Miller, John H., ed. *Vatican II: An Interfaith Appraisal.* Notre Dame, IN: University of Notre Dame Press, 1966.
Vorgrimler, Herbert, ed. *Commentary on the Documents of Vatican II.* 5 vols. New York: Herder and Herder, 1967–69.

RICHARD P. MCBRIEN

Vázquez, Gabriel, 1549–1604, Spanish Jesuit moral theologian. He was critical of fellow Jesuit Francisco de Suarez's congruism, which held that God gives grace in accordance with circumstances that God foresees as most favorable, or congruent, to its use. Vázquez instead defended a strict Molinism, holding that the efficacy of grace is rooted not in the divine gift itself, but in human free will which God foresees will be present when the grace is given. *See also* Molinism; Suarez, Francisco de.

veil, a head-covering worn by some religious congregations of women to symbolize their separation from the world. Traditionally, novices wear white veils and professed sisters, black.

Venantius Fortunatus, St., ca. 530–609, bishop of Poitiers and poet. Fortunatus composed *Vexilla Regis Prodeunt* ("The Royal Banners Forward Go") and *Pange Lingua Gloriosi* ("Sing, My Tongue, the Glorious Battle") to mark receipt, by a convent in Poitiers, of a fragment of the True Cross. He was elected bishop ca. 599. Feast day: December 14 (local observance). *See also Pange Lingua.*

Venerable, a traditional title given to a deceased person whose holiness is under investigation with a view toward beatification and eventual canonization. The title is conferred on those who have been judged to have lived a virtuous life to a heroic degree. The most famous historical figure bearing that title was the Venerable Bede (ca. 673–735), biblical scholar and "Father of English History." *See also* beatification; canonization.

veneration of the cross, devotional practice. Known principally as part of the Good Friday service, the veneration of the cross entails the unveiling of the cross to the congregation with the invitation to come forward to show some sign of respect for it. Participants often bow and/or kiss the cross at this time. *See also* cross; Good Friday.

venial sin, a moral transgression not considered serious enough to rupture a person's relationship with God; thus, one where pardon (Lat., *venia*) is relatively easy. The distinction between mortal and venial sin, while not formally present in the biblical sources, is foreshadowed there in the gnat and the camel (Matt 23:24), a speck and a log (Matt 7:3), sins of daily occurrence (Matt 12:36), and those that exclude from the kingdom (1 Cor 6:9–10). The mag-

isterium asserted against the fifth-century Pelagians and later against the sixteenth-century Reformers that not all sins strip one of the spiritual effects of justification, i.e., of being made righteous in the sight of God. Catholic tradition has struggled to explain the possibility of venial sin in an analytically satisfactory way. Some (e.g., Baius and the Nominalists) appealed to a decree of God. Others traced the mortal-venial distinction to the matter of the action. But neither of these analyses explains why any sin, as a negative response to God, is not a total perversion of the relation of Creator and creature. Many contemporary theologians find the difference in the type of freedom (basic, peripheral) present in the act. *See also* imperfections; mortal sin; sin.

Veni Creator (veh'nee cray-ah'tohr; Lat., "Come, Creator"), Pentecost hymn. The text is attributed to Rabanus Maurus (d. 856). Its seven verses are sung for Evening Prayer on Pentecost Sunday, at the dedication of a church, for Confirmation, and at ordination. English translations may be found in most Catholic and many Protestant hymnals.

Veni Sancte Spiritus (veh'nee sahnk'tay spee' ree-toos; Lat., "Come, Holy Spirit"), Pentecost sequence hymn. Informally called "The Golden Sequence," the hymn was written by the archbishop of Canterbury, Stephen Langton (d. 1228). It is sung at Mass on Pentecost Sunday between the second reading and the Gospel acclamation. *See also* Pentecost.

vernacular (Lat., "native"), the native language of a particular country, region, or culture. The term refers particularly to the use of a community's native language in the liturgy. This is by way of contrast with the use of a so-called dead language (such as Latin) in worship.

Veronica, St., legendary figure. Preserved in Catholic imagination and memory by the sixth Station of the Cross, Veronica is the woman who is thought to have wiped Jesus' face with her veil as he carried his cross through the streets. She subsequently discovered on her veil an impression of the face of Jesus. Feast day: July 9. *See also* Stations of the Cross.

Verot, Jean-Pierre Augustin Marcellin (vairoh'), 1805–76, bishop of Savannah, Georgia, and first bishop of St. Augustine, Florida. Born in France, he entered the Sulpician community and

Veronica, a woman of Jerusalem who, legend tells us, wiped the face of Jesus on his way to Calvary on Good Friday; fourteenth- or fifteenth-century painting, National Gallery, London.

was ordained in 1828. Two years later he came to the United States and taught at St. Mary's College and the Sulpician Seminary in Baltimore. In 1858 he was consecrated a bishop and appointed vicar apostolic of Florida. In 1861, he was given the additional post of bishop of Savannah while retaining the Florida jurisdiction. He was caught up in the politics leading to the Civil War and was an unabashed Southern nationalist, winning the sobriquet "the Rebel Bishop." He also endorsed the property rights of slaveowners in an 1861 sermon entitled: "A Tract for the Times: Slavery and Abolitionism." In the Reconstruction era, he undertook an ambitious missionary program among the freedmen and at the Second Plenary Council of Baltimore in 1866 called for a major Catholic effort among the newly freed slaves. At Vatican I (1870) he opposed the definition of papal infallibility and absented himself from the final vote. *See also* Baltimore, councils of; infallibility; Sulpicians.

versicle, in the Mass, a sentence from Scripture that is divided into two phrases. The first phrase is sung by the presider or cantor, the second, in the manner of a response, by the choir or assembly. One of the most common versicles is used in the funeral liturgy and other rites for the dead: "Eternal rest grant unto him/her, O Lord"; the response to which is "And let perpetual light shine upon him/her."

versions of Scripture. *See* Scripture, versions of.

Vespers (Lat., "evening star"), or Evening Prayer, the liturgy of the Church celebrated in the early evening as daylight ends. One of the two principal Hours of prayer, Vespers includes a hymn, two psalms and an NT canticle, a reading from Scripture (usually the Pauline Letters), a proper responsory, the Magnificat with its antiphon, a litany of intercessory prayer, the Lord's Prayer, a concluding blessing, and dismissal. *See also* Liturgy of the Hours.

vestibule (Lat., *vestibulum,* "entrance-court" or "courtyard"), the entrance hall between the front doors of a church and its main interior.

vestments, the special garments worn by liturgical ministers indicating the proper function of the wearer. In the first centuries of the Church, there was no special clothing for liturgical ministers. Gradually a fairly complex set of vestments became mandated, especially for bishop, priest, and deacon. The alb, a white tunic reaching to the ankle, is common to all liturgical ministers. The stole, a long scarf placed over the alb, is worn over the left shoulder by the deacon and over both shoulders by a priest or bishop. The chasuble, a long, sleeveless outer garment, is worn over the alb by a priest or bishop. *See also* alb; chasuble; stole.

Vetus Latina (Lat., "Old Latin"), the Latin translation of the Bible prior to Jerome's Vulgate. It was probably made in the Roman province of Africa. The earliest evidence of the Vetus Latina is from such North African Christian writers as Tertullian (d. 225) and especially Cyprian of Carthage (d. 258), who quotes it more than fifteen hundred times. No codex of the entire Bible exists, but there is a large number of manuscripts of the Gospels and Acts. *See also* Scripture, versions of.

Veuillot, Louis François (*loo'*ee frahn-swah' vuh-yoh'), 1813–83, journalist and editor of *L'Univers* from 1843 to 1883, a strongly Ultramontane French newspaper that gradually became a semiofficial Vatican medium. He enjoyed the confidence of Pope Pius IX, passionately argued for defining papal infallibility, and strongly defended papal temporal authority even when it conflicted with French foreign policy. For the latter he was arrested in 1844 and had to suspend publication of his paper from 1860 to 1867. *See also* infallibility; Ultramontanism.

Via Antiqua, Via Moderna, rival late medieval realist and nominalist schools. The Via Antiqua (Lat., "Old Way") can be identified with the moderate realist tradition, whether Thomist, Scotist, or Augustinian, which views linguistic structures as mirroring reality and argues that universal terms represent real things. The Via Moderna ("New Way") followed the nominalism of Ockham, holding that only individuals exist in reality, universals being merely names (*nomina*). In theology, the Old Way continued the tradition of natural arguments for God's existence and attributes. The New Way stressed God's absolute freedom to the point where nature, which could be utterly different, provided no base for reasoning to God. In the fifteenth century, the New Way came to dominate in the schools. It has been suggested that by its separation of physics from metaphysics and by its belief that reality encompasses only individual things, the Via Moderna fostered the rise of empirical science.

Via Dolorosa (vee'ah doh-loh-roh'sah; Lat., "sorrowful way"), the original stations of the cross in Jerusalem, which trace the path of Jesus on the way to Calvary. Metaphorically, the term refers to the way Christians must walk to follow Christ. *See also* Stations of the Cross.

Via Media, theory developed by John Henry Newman (d. 1890) during the Oxford movement concerning a distinctive Anglican identity. It proposed that the Church of England was a middle way (Lat., *via media*) between the accretions and centralized authority of Catholicism and the subtractions and privatized pluralism of Protestantism. Later rejected by Newman as "paper religion," the theory was based on the principles of dogma, sacrament, and anti-Romanism. *See also* Newman, John Henry; Oxford movement.

Via Moderna. *See* Via Antiqua, Via Moderna.

Vianney, St. Jean-Baptiste. *See* Curé d'Ars.

Viaticum (vi̱-a'ti-kum; Lat, "food for the journey"), the reception of Communion by a dying person, specifically as provision for the passage through death to eternal life. This is properly the last sacrament of Christian life. It may be celebrated within or outside Mass. In the latter case the minister may be a deacon or an unordained minister entrusted with the care of the sick. In addition to the reception of Communion by the dying, the rite includes a Liturgy of the Word, renewal of the baptismal profession of faith, and the exchange of the sign of peace by the dying person with the minister and others who are present. *See also* Anointing of the Sick; Communion, Holy.

Viator, St., fourth-century deacon, patron saint of catechists. Little is known about him except that he went to Alexandria in 381 in the company of Justus of Lyons (d. ca. 390) and joined a monastery in Egypt.

Viatorian Fathers, Clerics of St. Viator (C.S.V.), an order founded in 1835 by Louis Joseph Querbes of Lyons to enhance the religious literacy of post-Revolutionary France. After the suppression of religious schools in France (1903), most Viatorians emigrated to Belgium or Canada, where they continue to administer and teach in several schools for the hearing impaired. After a short-lived first mission in the United States, at Carondelet, Missouri (1842–57), they opened schools for boys in Illinois and established in 1868 St. Viator College at Bourbonnais. Though the college closed in 1938, Viatorians continue to administer and teach throughout Illinois and have also been assigned by U.S. bishops to missions in Japan, Taiwan, and several South American countries. *See also* Viator, St.

vicar, one who has, by office, the authority to act in place of another. The authority to act comes from the nature of the office that a person holds and thus is not given by way of delegation to the vicar. A vicar may have the authority to act in all matters pertaining to an office or may have authority limited to a certain class of persons or to given subject matter. Vicars are found in dioceses and in religious institutes. A vicar must not act contrary to the will of the one for whom she or he is a vicar. The pope and bishops have been called vicars of Christ, although the more traditional title for the pope is Vicar of Peter.

vicar, episcopal. *See* episcopal vicar.

vicar, judicial. *See* judicial vicar.

vicar, parochial. *See* parochial vicar.

vicar apostolic, prelate who governs, in the name of the pope, a territory equivalent to a diocese. The territory has not yet become a diocese because of particular circumstances, e.g., insufficient ministerial and material resources.

vicar capitular, under the 1917 code of canon law, the priest who was elected to govern a diocese when a see became vacant. He was called "capitular" because he was elected by the cathedral chapter in those countries that had chapters. Currently the interim administrator is elected by the college of consultors and is called diocesan administrator. *See also* cathedral chapter; consultors, college of.

vicar forane, the priest who functions as the head of a deanery. Appointed by the bishop, this priest has very limited responsibility for a vicariate forane or deanery, i.e., a particular geographical territory of the diocese. The more common term for this person is dean. *See also* deanery.

vicar general, the priest who functions as the bishop's deputy. He has wide-ranging responsibility for the executive functioning of the diocese. In some circumstances there can be more than one vicar general in a diocese, but usually there is only one.

vicar of Christ, a traditional title for a bishop, although recently applied only to the Bishop of Rome (the pope). The title has a very long and complicated history. This history shows that it is a mistake to understand it only as a specific or characteristic title of the Bishop of Rome in his capacity of Universal Primate of the Church. When Vatican II declares that "bishops govern the particular churches entrusted to them as the vicars of Christ and his ambassadors" (Dogmatic Constitution on the Church, n. 27), it is not innovating; this has been part of the Western tradition since Cyprian (d. 258). During the Middle Ages the title was usually employed to characterize the specific mission of all the bishops. Only during the pontificate of Eugenius III (1145–53) did the title begin to be officially seen as a specific designation for the function of the Bishop of Rome. In the past, the use of this title as a papal title

was connected with the strong conviction that the most characteristic title of the Bishop of Rome was "Vicar of Peter." Innocent III (d. 1216) found in the title "Vicar of Christ" the root of his universal power, even over temporal authorities. "Although successor to the Prince of the Apostles, we are not his vicar nor that of any man or apostle but we are the vicar of Jesus Christ himself." Great defenders of the authority of the pope like Robert Bellarmine (d. 1621) propagated the theory that Vicar of Peter is an incorrect title and, therefore, that the Bishop of Rome has to be called Vicar of Christ. This title implies that the pope is acting in the place of Christ (Lat., *Christi vices*), with the power corresponding to this function. In light of recent historical studies, however, Vicar of Christ must be understood as an implication of the traditional title Vicar of Peter. It expresses the episcopal relation to Christ of the one who, as bishop of the local church of Rome, is charged by the Lord to watch over, in faith and love, the communion of all the local churches of the world. It is a consequence of the episcopal grace of one among all other vicars of Christ. But this bishop is the head of the local church of Rome, which enjoys an unparalleled claim to apostolicity because of the martyrdom of Peter and Paul there. The pope is Vicar of Christ, however, insofar as he is a bishop, not insofar as he is a pope. *See also* papacy, the; Vicar of Peter.

JEAN-M. R. TILLARD

Vicar of Peter, the most traditional title designating the function of the Bishop of Rome (the pope) and theologically the most adequate. The title was commonly accepted by popes themselves from the end of the fourth century. The title is important for two reasons. First, it shows that in the apostolic witness there was an untransmittable element that is precisely the most important component of the rock on which the Church is built, namely, the eyewitness experience of the Risen Christ (Acts 1:21–22). Through the oversight of the Bishop of Rome and the other bishops in communion with him, it is this faith in the Risen Christ that is kept alive in the proclamation and pastoral ministry of the Church. The Bishop of Rome and his brother bishops do not take the place of Peter and the other apostles. The Bishop of Rome and the other bishops are not apostles. They are not eyewitnesses of the Resurrection. They can only be the vicars of Peter and the other apostles by keeping alive what they have transmitted. But, second, even concerning what was transmittable in the apostolic mandate, i.e., the proclamation of faith in the Risen Christ, the pastoral care of the community, and especially maintaining it in authentic communion, the mandate and power of the Bishop of Rome and his fellow bishops are the same as those given to Peter and his fellow apostles, always judged and measured by reference to them. The Bishop of Rome perpetuates within the communion of bishops and for the whole Church the "once for all" of Peter's apostolate. *See also* papacy, the; Peter, St.; Petrine ministry; Petrine succession; vicar of Christ. *JEAN-M. R. TILLARD*

vice, a habitual disposition to act evilly; the opposite of virtue. Vice results from repeated actions at either extreme from the moderate course represented by the virtues. The traditional list of capital sins represents instances of character-shaping patterns of sinful behavior, or vice. Vice is thus typified in patterns of pride, sloth, lust, envy, anger, gluttony, and covetousness. The number of vices is greater than that of virtues because in each case both extremes of disordered behavior constitute vice. One lacking in prudence and temperance may demonstrate a lack of courage, e.g., by a disposition either to rash action or to cowardice. *See also* capital sins; virtue.

vice-chancellor, the assistant to the diocesan chancellor. In the United States, the office of chancellor, which is primarily responsible for record keeping in a diocese, has traditionally been more significant than in other countries. *See also* chancellor, diocesan.

Victor I, St., d. 198, pope from ca. 189 to 198. Victor's attempt to regularize the date of Easter throughout the universal Church was a milestone in the development of papal prerogative. His efforts met with general agreement except among the Quartodecimans (those who celebrated Easter on the day of Passover) of Asia Minor, whom he threatened to excommunicate. He also excommunicated the Adoptionist Monarchian Theodotus. Feast day: July 28. *See also* Quartodecimans.

Victor III, Bl. [Desiderius of Monte Cassino], ca. 1027–87, pope from May 24, 1086, to September 16, 1087. He was the most powerful abbot of his day and was elected pope against his wishes several months before his death. As abbot of Monte Cassino, Desiderius served as the chief negotiator be-

tween the Holy See and the Norman forces in Italy. Feast day: September 16. *See also* Monte Cassino.

Victorines, canons regular (semi-monastic clergy) of the abbey of St. Victor in Paris. A group of clergy originally following the leadership of the Parisian scholar William of Champeux organized the Augustinian abbey of St. Victor in 1113. Although the abbey remained active until 1790, it is best known for the brilliant school of theology centered there in the twelfth century. The most outstanding and influential of the Victorine scholars was Hugh of St. Victor (d. 1142), whose students included the biblical scholar Andrew of St. Victor (d. 1175), the mystical theologian Richard of St. Victor (d. 1173), and the liturgical poet Adam of St. Victor (d. ca. 1180). *See also* Adam of St. Victor; Andrew of St. Victor; Hugh of St. Victor; Richard of St. Victor.

Victorinus Afer. *See* Marius Victorinus.

Vienne, Council of (1311–12), ecumenical council. Convened by Clement V in the French city of Vienne, the council refused to condemn the Order of the Knights Templar despite the French king Philip IV's insistence; Clement unilaterally disbanded the order by a special decree. Both the council and the pope, however, rejected the king's demand that they condemn Pope Boniface VIII (d. 1303). The council did condemn the radical Spiritual Franciscans, as well as the Beguines and the Beghards. It limited the pastoral activities of the mendicant orders, placed restrictions on the Inquisition, and legislated against usury and attacks on the clergy. *See also* Beghards/Beguines; Boniface VIII; Inquisition; Knights Templar; mendicant orders; Spiritual Franciscans.

vigil (Lat., *vigilia*, "watch"), a prayerful watch on the eve of a solemnity. The term has many and varied meanings. Its most important usage refers to the Easter Vigil, the mother of all vigils, which begins after nightfall on Easter Saturday and ends before the dawn of Easter Sunday. Each Sunday of the year is reminiscent of Easter Sunday. In several dioceses, a vigil Mass is held on Saturday at 4:00 P.M. or later, using the same liturgical proper as the Sunday Mass. Other solemnities that do not fall on Sunday may also have a vigil Mass with liturgical propers differing from those of the solemnity itself. The Order of Christian Funerals (1989) prefers a Vigil for the Deceased to a wake service because the vigil anticipates the approaching funeral Mass. The term "vigil" is also used in monastic communities to refer to the night office, Matins or the Office of Readings, which is prayed communally in the first hours of the day. *See also* Easter Vigil.

Vigil for the Deceased. *See* wake service.

Vigilius, d. 555, pope from 537 to 555. He is remembered principally for his role in the Three Chapters controversy. *See also* Three Chapters.

Vigilius of Thapsus, late-fifth-century bishop of Thapsus, anti-Arian polemicist, and defender of the Council of Chalcedon (451). His surviving works include the *Against Eutyches* and the *Dialogue Against Arians, Sabellians, and Photinians*. *See also* Chalcedon, Council of.

vigil light, a burning wax candle, usually contained in glass, or an oil lamp kept near a tabernacle in which the Eucharist (Blessed Sacrament) is reserved. The light indicates the eucharistic presence of Christ, reserved for Communion of the sick, and reminds Christians of the reverence due the Sacrament. *See also* candle; votive candle.

Villanova, St. Thomas of, 1486–1555, archbishop of Valencia and outstanding figure of Catholic reform in Spain. Thomas became an Augustinian in 1516 and was ordained the following year. As provincial, he sent Augustinian missionaries to the New World. He was known as a powerful preacher and devoted himself to the care of the poor and sick. He founded colleges for young students in need and was canonized in 1658. Feast day: September 22. *See also* Augustinians.

vimpa, a veil worn over the shoulders and hands by an attendant who holds the crosier at episcopal functions. *See also* crosier.

Vincent de Paul, St., 1580–1660, French priest and founder of the Congregation of the Missions (Vincentians). After escaping enslavement by pirates in 1607, he began a life of charitable works that led to his founding of the Sisters of Charity. In 1625 he established the Congregation of the Mission, a religious order of men known as the Lazarists, now more commonly called Vincentians. The Lazarists worked as mission preachers and seminary educators. Before he died, Vincent distinguished himself

as a preacher against Jansenism. Feast day: September 27. *See also* Jansenism; Sisters of Charity; Vincentians.

Vincent de Paul Society, St. *See* Society of St. Vincent de Paul.

Vincent Ferrer, St. (fair'uhr), ca. 1350–1419, a Spanish Dominican priest, he is best known for his preaching missions in Europe and for his labors in bringing unity to the Church during the Great Schism. Feast day: April 5.

Vincentians, the Congregation of the Mission (C.M.), founded in France by Vincent de Paul in 1625 to do missionary work among peasants. The aims of the congregation include preaching to the poor, administering parishes, training seminarians, and promoting Catholic education. The beginnings of the congregation lay in Vincent's awareness of the need for religious instruction among the peasants on the estates of the nobles in the area around Paris. Because its early headquarters was the former priory of St. Lazare in that city, the Vincentians are known in France as Lazarists. Vincentians are secular (diocesan) priests who take simple vows and live in community. After the Louisiana Purchase in 1803, the Vincentians came to America, eventually establishing parishes, schools, and seminaries across the country, including St. John's University on Long Island, Niagara University in upstate New York, and DePaul University in Chicago. In their parish work, Vincentians follow their founder, Vincent, who gave new meaning to the Catholic parish as a center of the spiritual life and also of the charitable and communal activities of its members. In this holistic approach to parish life, Vincent anticipated by three hundred years the parish revitalization envisioned by Vatican II (1962–65). From their earliest days, Vincentians have been deeply involved with the training of priests and have staffed various diocesan seminaries in addition to their own institutions.

Vincent of Beauvais, ca. 1190–1264, Dominican author of the encyclopedia *Speculum Maius* (Lat., "Greater Mirror") and of *On the Education of the Sons of Nobles*, a pedagogical treatise.

Vincent of Lérins, St., d. before 450, a monk and priest on the island of Lérins involved in the debate over semi-Pelagianism. His *Objections* against Augustinianism, now lost, were the subject of Prosper of Aquitaine's rebuttal, *Responsiones.* Vincent's *Excerpts* is one of the earliest florilegia of Augustine, a short collection of passages compiled against Nestorius. But Vincent's best-known work, the *Commonitorium,* is the most influential early statement of the character and authority of tradition and its relation to Scripture and of the possibility of the development of doctrine. Tradition is *quod ubique, quod semper, quod ab omnibus* (Lat., "what [has been believed] everywhere, always, and by all"), but Vincent carefully points out that this is subject to growth in understanding and explication. Feast day: May 24. *See also* doctrine, development of; Lérins.

Vincent of Saragossa, St., d. 304, deacon, martyr, and patron saint of Portugal. Spanish-born, he is known almost exclusively through his martyrdom by the Romans. His memory was revered by Christians throughout the Roman Empire, relics were venerated, and several churches were dedicated to him. In art he is depicted as a deacon holding a palm or suffering the torture of a gridiron. Feast day: January 22.

vincible ignorance, a type of ignorance that should be removed by the exercise of ordinary care. Ignorance of this kind implies some degree of subjective fault for performing a wrong act. The agent is morally responsible for not exercising diligence in discerning a moral obligation that applies in the situation or for not knowing the circumstances of the action. Because the agent is culpably negligent, the act is considered voluntary and imputable. The handbooks on moral theology generally divide vincible ignorance into simple, crass, and affected. If the agent makes some minimal but insufficient effort to overcome the ignorance, it is simple vincible ignorance. The ignorance is crass or supine when virtually no effort is made to dispel the ignorance. Affected or studied vincible ignorance is the most serious; it is directly voluntary, and there is the desire to remain in ignorance so that the person may remain free from any moral obligation. *See also* ignorance; invincible ignorance.

vipassana (vi-pahs'suh-nuh; Pali, "insight"), insight meditation, a practice of Theravadan (early) Buddhism. It involves sharp, clear awareness of the changing contents of one's mind and purification of the mind of negative contents. It has been adapted

for Christian use as a method for pursuing the teachings of Carmelite mystic St. John of the Cross (d. 1591).

virginal conception of Jesus, the belief and teaching of the Church that Jesus Christ was conceived by the Blessed Virgin Mary through the power of the Holy Spirit without a human father. It is commonly equated with the virgin birth. *See also* infancy Gospels; Jesus Christ; virgin birth of Christ; virginity of Mary.

virgin birth of Christ, the belief that Jesus became a human being without the participation of a human father. Since its beginnings, the Church has attested in its Scripture and tradition to the virginal conception and birth of Jesus Christ.

The Biblical Witness: Biblical evidence for the virginal conception can be found in the infancy narratives in chapters 1 and 2 of both Matthew and Luke. It is widely believed that these narratives are the latest part of the Gospel tradition, because interest in the human origin of Jesus arose later in the Church. Most scholars hold that the Gospel formation began with the death and Resurrection of Jesus and grew backward to include his public life and ministry. Mark's Gospel (ca. A.D. 70), which opens with Jesus' baptism by John the Baptist, is the example of this stage. Around A.D. 80, when the Gospels of Matthew and Luke were written, the belief that Jesus was Messiah and Son of God from his conception onward was firmly established. Few historical facts were available, as is evident in these two Gospels. The points of agreement between their infancy narratives are the names of Mary and Joseph, the fact that they were engaged (though not yet living together), the name of Jesus, his conception from the Holy Spirit, angels as messengers (in Luke to Mary, in Matthew to Joseph), the birth in Bethlehem, and the return to Nazareth. The differences are much more numerous, though noticed less because of the harmonization in the telling of the Christmas story. The agreement of Matthew and Luke on the matter of Jesus' conception from the Holy Spirit without the participation of a human father is, therefore, especially important.

Matthew opens his Gospel with "the genealogy of Jesus the Messiah, the son of David, the son of Abraham" (1:1), thereby rooting Jesus in the Davidic Messiah tradition. His ancestry is traced through the male line until the final verse where a significant change occurs: "Joseph the husband of Mary, of whom Jesus was born, who is called the Messiah" (1:16). Matthew then begins his narrative: "Now the birth of Jesus the Messiah took place in this way. When his mother Mary had been engaged to Joseph, but before they lived together, she was found to be with child from the Holy Spirit" (1:18), an expression that Matthew repeats in the message of the angel in Joseph's dream (1:20). Matthew summarizes the events in the fulfillment formula, "All this took place to fulfill what had been spoken by the Lord through the prophet [i.e., Isaiah]: 'Look, the virgin [Gk., parthenos, in the Septuagint] shall conceive and bear a son, and they shall name him Emmanuel,' which means, 'God is with us'" (1:23). Joseph then "took her as his wife, but had no marital relations with her until she had borne a son; and he named him Jesus" (1:24–25). The use of "until" neither disproves nor proves Mary's virginity post partum (Lat., "after giving birth").

In the Gospel of Luke the account of the conception and birth of Jesus parallels and surpasses that of John the Baptist in many details. John's miraculous birth from a barren mother and aging father is transcended by Jesus' conception from a virgin. Most significant in Luke is the conversation between Mary and the angel Gabriel (Luke 1:26–38). Mary is told not to be afraid, because she has found favor with God. The angel's announcement does not explicitly say that the child will not have a human father, but Mary's request for an explanation, "How will this be since I am a virgin?" receives this assurance from the angel: "The Holy Spirit will come upon you, and the power of the Most High will overshadow you; therefore the child to be born will be holy; he will be called Son of God" (1:35). This statement reiterates what is explicitly said in Matthew: Jesus was conceived in the Virgin Mary by the Holy Spirit without the participation of a human father.

The names and titles given to the child (in Matthew: Jesus [God saves], Messiah, Savior, Emmanuel, God with us; and in Luke: Jesus, Son of the Most High, descendant of David, holy, Son of God) make clear that the Gospel accounts of the virginal conception have primarily a Christological significance. They have become, in the tradition of the Church, affirmations of the holiness, obedience, and commitment of the Virgin Mary as well.

The Teaching of Tradition: Church tradition has persistently recognized Mary's singular role within God's salvific activity and, specifically, the virgin birth as a particularly clear manifestation of the mystery of the Incarnation. During its first centuries the Church refined its reflections on the birth of Jesus Christ, especially through the writings of Ambrose (d. 397) and Augustine (d. 430). Since the end of the fifth century the virgin birth has usually been considered according to three aspects: (1) the virginal conception of Jesus Christ in the womb of the Blessed Virgin Mary through the power of the Holy Spirit without the participation of a human father (also referred to as ante partum, Lat., "before giving birth"); (2) the virginal parturition of Jesus Christ in which Mary gave birth to her son without the loss of her virginity (also referred to as in or durante partu, Lat., "during the giving of birth"); and (3) the perpetual virginity of Mary, that is, that she remained a virgin throughout her entire life, with the result that Jesus had no siblings (also referred to as post partum).

This threefold understanding is manifest in the Second Vatican Council's primary statement on the Blessed Virgin Mary. Placing its reflections on Mary within the Dogmatic Constitution on the Church (Lumen Gentium, 1964), the council (1962–65) presented the Church's view (initially promoted by Ambrose) that Mary is the paradigm or model of the Church, for her purity of heart and faith exemplify the perfect human response to God's love. Within this perspective the council affirms, with differing degrees of emphasis, the three traditional aspects of the virgin birth. (1) It attests to the virginal conception of Jesus: "This union of the mother with the son in the work of salvation was manifested from the time of Christ's virginal conception up to his death" (n. 57). (2) The council witnesses to Jesus' virginal parturition: "This association [of the mother with her son] was shown also at the birth of our Lord, who did not diminish His mother's virginal integrity but sanctified it" (n. 57). (3) It refers to Mary's perpetual virginity when it appeals to the "Easterners, who with ardent emotion and devout mind concur in reverencing the Mother of God, ever Virgin" (n. 68).

Over the centuries, the Church's witness to the virgin birth has been prompted not by a curiosity about the biology of Jesus' conception and birth but by a concern to express key theological convictions: the gracious and free act of the Father in sending the Son into the world, the uniqueness of Jesus Christ, the inability of the human family to provide its own savior, and the Church's vocation to become like Mary, who "stands out in eminent and singular fashion as exemplar of both virginity and motherhood" (n. 63). In support of this theological focus, the Congregation for the Doctrine of the Faith (formerly the Holy Office) issued an instruction on July 27, 1960, in which it warns against inappropriate considerations of the biological dimensions of the virginity of Mary and urges that the Church's reflections on this mystery remain theological.

The early Church's first formal testimonies to the virgin birth are located within its Christological confessions. The Roman Symbol, for example, as found in the Interrogatory Creed of Hippolytus (215), asks, "Do you believe in Christ Jesus, the Son of God, Who was begotten by the Holy Spirit from the Virgin Mary, Who was crucified. . . ." While the phrase "begotten by the Holy Spirit" denies Adoptionism, the phrase "from the Virgin Mary" opposes Docetism. The same twofold Christological emphasis also occurs in the full Apostles' Creed (ca. 700): "And in Jesus Christ, His only Son, our Lord, Who was conceived by the Holy Spirit, born of the Virgin Mary, suffered under Pontius Pilate . . ." Mary is not included in the Nicene Creed (325), but she is mentioned in the Nicene-Constantinopolitan Creed (381): the Son of God "was incarnate by the Holy Spirit and the Virgin Mary and became man." With the inclusion of this Christological tenet, the creed specifically refutes Apollinarianism, the belief that Christ had no rational soul. The Council of Chalcedon (451) also views Mary within a Christological perspective: "As to his deity, he was born from the Father before the ages, but as to his humanity, the very same one was born in the last days from the Virgin Mary, the Mother of God, for our sake and for our salvation . . ." By using the title "Mother of God," the doctrine specifically opposes Nestorianism, the belief that in Christ there were two persons, one human and one divine.

Although the Catholic Church has never offered a dogmatic formulation on the virgin birth, it does consider this belief among its dogmas. It does so because it recognizes that this belief has its origins in Scripture and the early Church and has persisted in Christian faith over the centuries. At the same time, the Church allows a limited spectrum of theological opinions concerning both the place of this belief within the Church's "hierarchy of truths" and also the exact content of this belief. In the twentieth century support for belief in the virgin birth and theological refinements of this belief have been offered by such highly respected theologians as the Protestant Karl Barth (d. 1968) and the Catholic Karl Rah-

ner (d. 1984). *See also* Chalcedon, Council of; Docetism; Ephesus, Council of; infancy Gospels; Jesus Christ; Mary, Blessed Virgin; virginity of Mary.

Bibliography

Brown, Raymond E. *The Birth of the Messiah.* Garden City, NY: Doubleday, 1977. Rev. ed., 1993.

Brown, Raymond E. *The Virginal Conception and Bodily Resurrection of Jesus.* New York: Paulist Press, 1973.

Fitzmyer, Joseph A. *The Gospel According to Luke I–IX, The Anchor Bible.* Vol. 28. New York: Doubleday, 1981.

Graef, Hilda. *Mary: A History of Doctrine and Devotion.* 2 vols. New York: Sheed and Ward, 1965.

Jelly, Frederick. *Madonna: Mary in the Catholic Tradition.* Huntington, IN: Our Sunday Visitor, 1986.

ROBERT A. KRIEG
JACINTA VAN WINKEL

virginity, the condition of never having had sexual relations. In the patriarchal society of early Israel, female virginity was prized, as legal traditions attest. It was expected that a bride would be a virgin. If her husband found her to be otherwise, she could be stoned to death; if he complained falsely, he would merely be whipped (Deut 22:13–21). Rape of a betrothed virgin was punishable by death; violation of one not betrothed simply required payment of a bride price and marriage (Deut 22:23–29; Exod 22:16–17). Priests could only marry virgins (Lev 21:13–15; Ezek 44:22).

Virginity, symbolizing the status of Yahweh's daughter or bride, was used metaphorically of Jerusalem or Israel (Amos 5:2; Isa 37:22; 62:5; Jer 14:17; 18:13; 31:4).

The NT values virginity as suitable for service of the kingdom of God. Paul praises, but does not require, maintenance of virginity in view of the "impending distress" (1 Cor 7:7, 25–38). He also portrays the Church, like Israel, as a pure, i.e., virginal, bride (2 Cor 11:2; Eph 5:27). The martyrs in Revelation are virgins (Rev 14:4). Some of these attitudes may reflect Jesus' own preference for celibacy. His comment that some make themselves eunuchs for the kingdom (Matt 19:12) may be ironic, given the low status of eunuchs. Yet the saying apparently supports sexual renunciation.

The traditions about Jesus' birth (Matt 1:23; Luke 1:34–35) affirm the virginity of Mary when she conceived her son. These passages form the basis for later beliefs in the perpetual virginity of Mary. Such doctrines in turn reinforced the preference for celibacy that has characterized Christian asceticism. *See also* brothers of Jesus; celibacy, clerical; chastity; virgin birth of Christ; virginity of Mary; widow.

HAROLD W. ATTRIDGE

virginity of Mary, the doctrine that Mary was bodily a virgin before, during, and forever after the birth of Jesus Christ.

Before (Lat., *ante partum,* the virginal conception): NT infancy narratives testify that Mary conceived Jesus by the power or overshadowing of the Holy Spirit without male intervention (Matt 1:18–25 and Luke 1:26–38). The focus of these narratives is Christological. They attest that Jesus' origin is in God, that what is special about him cannot be explained by human parentage alone but is due to God's creative initiative.

During (*in partu,* the virgin birth): post-biblical apocryphal literature such as the *Protevangelium of James* extends Mary's virginity to include her giving birth painlessly without biological rupture.

After (*post partum,* perpetual virginity): developed in tandem with the patristic Church's prizing of lifelong, consecrated celibacy, perpetual virginity refers to Mary's having no sexual relations after Jesus' birth. Jesus' brothers and sisters (Mark 6:3) are then interpreted as step-siblings or cousins.

The subject of some patristic argument, this belief in its tripartite form was officially taught by a Lateran council in 649. In devotion it interweaves with belief in Mary's sinlessness and Christ's divinity. Critical NT study today questions whether the infancy narratives reflect history or legend; available evidence makes a definitive answer unlikely. While presuming Mary's virginity to be historical, Vatican II also interprets it symbolically as wholehearted fidelity to Christ that the Church, by the power of the same Holy Spirit, is called upon to emulate: "the Church herself is a virgin" (Dogmatic Constitution on the Church, 1964, n. 64). *See also* brothers of Jesus; Mary, Blessed Virgin; virgin birth of Christ; virginity. *ELIZABETH JOHNSON*

Virgin Mary, Blessed. *See* Mary, Blessed Virgin.

virtue, an enduring quality of character or intellect, through which an individual is enabled to act in praiseworthy ways or to live a morally good life. This general definition is compatible with many different theories of virtue. Within the Catholic tradition, the most influential theory of virtue is that of Thomas Aquinas (d. 1274), which is in turn deeply indebted both to Augustine (d. 430) and to Aristotle (d. 322 B.C.).

For Aquinas, a virtue is a *habitus* (Lat., "habit"), a stable quality of the intellect, will, or passions through which an individual can do what morality demands in a particular instance, and do it in the right way, i.e., with the appropriate motivation. The usual translation of *habitus* as "habit" is misleading in this context, however, since it suggests that virtue could be acquired and maintained through unreflective good actions that become customary over time. While some theorists have indeed understood virtue in this way, Aquinas, following Aristotle, insists that the virtues must be grounded in a rational apprehension of what it means to live a morally good life. At the same time, a general knowledge of the good alone is not enough to produce fully virtuous behavior. The virtuous individual must also be able to apply one's knowledge of the good to concrete circumstances through the virtue of prudence. Since fully virtuous behavior involves responding in accordance with the true human good, as well as acting in accordance with it, the passions of the virtuous individual must be formed in such a way that one responds appropriately, that is, in a way that is congruent with one's overall understanding of the good; the relevant virtues here are temperance, which regulates sensual desires, and fortitude, which regulates fear, aversion, and aggressiveness. Finally, one must maintain appropriate relationships with those around oneself, with one's community as a whole, and with God, through the virtue of justice. Thus the four cardinal virtues, prudence, justice, fortitude, and temperance, are jointly necessary if one is to lead a humanly good life.

While the cardinal virtues are sufficient to direct their subject to a humanly good way of life, they are not sufficient to bring one to union with God in the Beatific Vision. This requires the theological virtues of faith, hope, and charity, which have direct union with God as their object. Through faith, the individual comes to believe in God, to accept God's revelation in Christ, and to begin to understand that one's ultimate good consists of union with this God. (Today, however, a majority of theologians argue that faith consists of an implicit belief in, or orientation toward, God that is not explicitly recognized as such.) Hope is the orientation of the will toward the attainment of this union with God, and finally, charity is the love of God for God's own sake, and of oneself and others for the sake of God.

Because of the growth of legalism in the fourteenth century, reaching its high point during the first half of the twentieth century, the virtues were reduced to tendencies to obey the laws of morality. The importance of the emotions to the moral life, and the significance of the quality of one's life, apart from one's particular actions, were obscured in moral theology. This trend was reversed by the Second Vatican Council (1962–65) and the biblically based moral theology it promoted. Consequently, a number of scholars have turned away from an exclusively rule-and-act-oriented account of moral life and are attempting to recover some sense of the importance of the virtues for Christian morality. *See also* cardinal virtues; moral theology; theological virtues.   *JEAN PORTER*

virtue, infused, a virtue given directly by God rather than acquired by natural means. While some moral virtues direct us toward a purely natural form of happiness, and may be acquired by natural means, others direct us toward personal union with God, and exceed the natural capacities of any creature, whether human being or angel. These latter virtues include both the theological virtues of faith, hope, and charity, and the cardinal virtues of prudence, fortitude, justice, and temperance as they exist and function in an individual who possesses the theological virtues. Both the theological and the cardinal virtues were traditionally said to be infused directly by God, and were therefore referred to as infused virtues. *See also* virtue.

Visigoths, Germanic people settled by the Romans in Gaul as a federated people in 418. Expanding into Spain after King Euric declared himself independent of Rome in 475, they were restricted to the Iberian peninsula when Clovis defeated them in 507. The Arian Visigoths ruled the Hispanic Roman population, who were Catholic, with tolerance, maintaining a degree of cultural continuity almost unparalleled at a time when learning was dying out in many other regions of the West. The conversion of King Reccared to Catholicism in 589 and the unique succession of councils of Toledo established the Visigothic kingdom of Hispania as one of the foremost centers of Catholic civilization until its fall to the Muslims in 711. *See also* Spain, Catholicism in.

vision of God, usually a clear, although not comprehensive, intuitive knowledge of the divine essence. In the OT, Jacob, Moses, and Isaiah "saw" God in theophanies that were understood as an experience of God present yet essentially hidden. In the NT, Jesus Christ is the full disclosure, the icon, of God. He revealed that God is in a loving relationship with this world. Therefore, God is truly known in Jesus Christ, in the brother and sister participating in God's life through the divinizing work of the Spirit, and in God's creation. We know God's essence, indirectly, in this mediated fashion. Because God's self-communication can never be received fully by us, God remains ineffable. Church teaching affirms that God is seen face to face in the Beatific Vision only after death and by the light of God's glory. *See also* Beatific Vision; contemplation; mysticism.

visions, extraordinary phenomena including images, ideas, and words, which may accompany and express the activity of God. God's self-communication at the core of a person's life may result in physical, psychological, or intellectual manifestations. Therefore, visions may be physical apparitions, or occurrences in the imagination, or deeply experienced intuitive understandings.

Visions seen with the eyes and heard with the ears occur rarely in the tradition. Events such as the Marian apparitions at Lourdes and Fàtima have been approved by the Church as credible but not as objects of Catholic doctrine. Catholic mystics generally mistrusted visions apprehended by bodily senses.

Visions that occur solely in the imagination are most probably conditioned by factors such as a person's religious education, age, and psychic structure. Intellectual visions represent an intuitive knowledge beyond form and image. These deeply interior expressions of God are less open to distortion and are therefore more trustworthy, according to the mystics.

Visions are not of the essence of the spiritual life, but they may be integral to a particular individual's journey. They are generally absent in the later stages of union with God. Visions that contain a message do not add to revealed doctrine but may specify God's will in particular situations. A healthy skepticism regarding the authenticity of visions may be more prudent than a naive credulity. However, an openness to the possibility of visions is in accord with the nature of Christianity, which is, after all, based on historical revelation. *See also* contemplation; mysticism.   *JOHN F. WELCH*

visitation, canonical, an official inquiry into a Church organization such as a diocese or religious institute. The inquiry could be one regularly established by law or one instigated because of special circumstances. Depending upon the law or the particular mandate, the visitor might have a wide range of powers touching upon investigation, recommendation, and decision making.

The Blessed Virgin Mary visits her cousin Elizabeth, who greets her with the words "Blessed are you among women, and blessed is the fruit of your womb." Mary replies, "My soul magnifies the Lord, and my spirit rejoices in God my Savior ..." (Luke 1:42,46–47); fifteenth-century painting by Fra Angelico, Prado, Madrid.

Visitation, the encounter of Mary and Elizabeth in the Gospel of Luke. According to Luke 1:39–56, Mary, having learned that both she and her aged cousin had conceived, visited Elizabeth and remained with her for three months. Upon arrival Mary uttered the song of praise known as the Magnificat. The event is commemorated as one of the joyful mysteries of the Rosary. The feast of the Visitation is celebrated on May 31. *See also* Magnificat.

Visitation order (V.H.M.), congregation of contemplative women founded in France in 1610 by Francis de Sales and Jane Frances de Chantal. They were established at Georgetown, Washington, D.C., in 1799 by Father Leonard Neale, later bishop of Baltimore. In 1815 Pope Pius VII granted the Georgetown foundation the rights and privileges of the Visitation Nuns. Humility before God and meekness toward one's neighbor constitute their spirit. The strictest form of separation from the world, known as papal enclosure, is observed. Autonomous monasteries in the United States are grouped into two federations, loosely knit organizations of independent monasteries, based on nonteaching or teaching activities. *See also* Chantal, St. Jane Frances de; Francis de Sales, St.

vitandus (vi-tahn'doos; Lat., "one to be avoided"), according to the 1917 Code of Canon Law, an excommunicated person under the most severe censure. The punishment restricted the interaction that could be had with members of the Church. The punishment is no longer in force under the current law (1983). *See also* excommunication.

Vitoria, Francisco de, 1486–1546, Spanish Dominican theologian. He held the first chair of theology at the University of Salamanca from 1526, and was the forerunner of the Salmanticenses. Among his treatises was the famous *De Indis* (1532, "Concerning the Indians"), which defended human rights for all peoples and is considered the origin of international law. He criticized papal plans for distribution of the newly discovered lands in America and Spanish methods of colonization, holding that indigenous people were not necessarily damned by their social structures, religion, or lack of Christian faith. He laid down the conditions of a just war, basing his views on Augustine (d. 430) and Aquinas (d. 1274), but going beyond them. He held that no war would be just if it endangered the world or Christendom. *See also* just-war doctrine; Salmanticenses.

Vitus, St., d. ca. 303, martyr and patron saint against epilepsy and a nervous disorder known as St. Vitus's Dance. Also patron saint of dancers and patron saint against dog and snake bites. Feast day: June 15.

Vladimir, St., 956–1015, ruler and baptizer of Kievan Rus', the land and people from which present-day East Slavic peoples (e.g., Ukrainians, Russians, Belorussians) derive. After fratricidal fighting, Vladimir became ruler of Kiev in 980. At first a fervent pagan, in 987, with the opportunity of marrying the sister of the Byzantine emperor, he became a Christian, accepting baptism from Byzantium. For the rest of his reign he promoted the evangelization of Rus' and the organization of the Church in his realm. He was canonized in the thirteenth century. *See also* Russia, Catholicism in.

vocation (Lat., *vocare*, "to call"), the inclination toward a particular state of life that the Christian accepts as a call from God. Vocation has a general and a particular meaning in Catholic parlance. In general, the term refers to the call of Christ, offered to all the baptized, to follow him and to become signs and witnesses of the reign of God. In this sense, all Christians share a common vocation. The word, however, also has a particular meaning. It refers to a specific state of life to which believers understand that God is calling them. Some people are inclined, by God's grace, to follow Christ as husbands and wives. Others feel called to the single state without seeking Holy Orders or taking vows as religious women or men. Still others hear God inviting them to become sisters, brothers, priests, or deacons. No one vocation is superior to another. Each leads to a manner of life and specific tasks that are essential for building up the Body of Christ and the reign of God.

voluntary, term for that characteristic of an act whereby it proceeds from the will. Voluntary demands two features: an act must proceed from the will as an act of the will or as an act of another faculty led by the will, and it must involve intellectual knowledge of the means as means or the end as end, the type of knowledge thought to be exclusive to creatures endowed with intellect. An act can be involuntary in two different ways: first, it can be nonvoluntary, e.g., one accidentally discovers a lost friend; second, it can be positively involuntary, e.g., when one accidentally kills a friend, an act to which one would be positively opposed.

Many other distinctions about voluntary (necessary vs. free, perfect vs. imperfect, in itself vs. in its cause, etc.) are of concern mostly to specialists. *See also* free will.

von Balthasar, Hans Urs. *See* Balthasar, Hans Urs von.

von Hügel, Friedrich. *See* Hügel, Friedrich von.

voodoo (Fr., *vaudoux;* Dahomey, *vodu,* "sorcery"), a syncretic religion developed in Haiti, combining elements of African (primarily Dahomean) religion and Catholic popular religiosity. The popular association of malignant magic and witchcraft with voodoo has a certain amount of truth to it, but is often exaggerated and sensationalized; like any other religion, voodoo is primarily a vehicle for its adherents to access the transcendent.

votive candle, a burning candle, usually set in a glass container, which, by pious custom, is placed before some representation of Christ, Mary, or the saints as a way of prolonging a prayer.

votive Mass, a Mass in which the proper parts (readings and presidential prayers) are directed not to a particular solemnity, feast, or season but to a particular devotion (Lat., *votum*). The liturgical books of Vatican II (1962–65) offer sixteen votive Masses: Holy Trinity, Holy Cross, Holy Eucharist, Jesus Christ the High Priest, Holy Name of Jesus, Precious Blood, Sacred Heart of Jesus, Holy Spirit, Blessed Virgin Mary, Angels, Joseph, Apostles, Peter, Paul, One Apostle, All Saints. Other Masses for various needs and occasions and Masses for the dead are also included, which are often referred to as votive Masses. A votive Mass may be celebrated on weekdays in Ordinary Time when there is no particular memorial or in place of an optional memorial. Pastoral need may also displace obligatory memorials of saints, weekdays of Advent, Christmas season, and Easter season in favor of a votive Mass. Serious need or pastoral advantage may also suggest the use of a votive Mass on any day of the year with the permission of the local bishop, except on Sundays of Advent, Lent and the Easter season, on Ash Wednesday, and during Holy Week. *See also* Eucharist; Mass.

votum (voh'toom; Lat., "a wish, a vow"), an opinion, usually of the bishop or superior, sought before action is taken in a given case. The case might be, e.g., a request for a dispensation or the filling of an office. The term can also refer to a vow. *See also* vows.

vows, promises made to God. The term most often refers to the vows of religion, i.e., those made in religious institutes. These are vows recognized as public in Church law and are regulated not only by the law of a given religious order, but also by the general law of the Church. Certain requirements as to the age, condition, and preparation of the one making the vows, as to the content of the vows, and as to the authority of those who allow the vows to be taken and who receive them in the name of the religious community and of the Church are laid down in Church law.

The vows themselves most often include those of consecrated chastity, poverty, and obedience. Some religious orders also have particular vows, for example, to serve in mission lands, to be at the special disposal of the pope, to live out one's life in the same monastery. The meaning of any of these vows is spelled out not only in Church law, but also in the legislative documents of a given religious community. Under Church law vows are first taken for a temporary probative period before final or perpetual vows are pronounced.

The term can also refer to private vows and is used commonly, though inaccurately, to refer to the promises made by diocesan priests, specifically to the requirement of celibacy, which binds diocesan priests. *See also* counsels, evangelical; religious institute; religious life; vows, private; vows, public.

vows, private, vows that do not have the public juridical effects of public vows. The term includes both those promises made to God singly and privately by individuals and promises made within the context of a community. The latter are not considered public because they are not recognized as such in canon law. *See also* vows.

vows, public, promises made to God that are recognized as public by the Church and that fall under the supervision of the Church. The Church supervises these vows, first of all, by regulating the conditions under which they may be made and by determining who is competent to receive them and to make them. Second, the Church supervises the conditions under which the vows are lived and the ongoing observance of the vows. *See also* vows.

Vulgate, the Latin Bible containing the translation of Jerome (347–420). Jerome's earliest biblical work was a revision of the Old Latin Gospels (382–85, in Rome), which he corrected on the basis of the Greek manuscripts available to him. Moving to Bethlehem after 387, Jerome undertook a Latin translation of the Greek OT, using the Septuagint from Origen's *Hexapla,* available to him at the library established at Caesarea by Origen and Eusebius. Jerome began

this undertaking with a translation of the Psalms; this translation, known as the Gallican Psalter (because of its liturgical use in Gaul), was to become the Psalter of the Vulgate. Job, 1–2 Chronicles, the Canticle of Canticles, and parts of Proverbs were the next fruits of this project.

Jerome abandoned his translation of the Septuagint ca. 390, in favor of a translation of the Hebrew OT. This decision was reached on the basis of his principle of *Hebraica veritas* (Lat., "Hebrew truth," i.e., the superiority of the Hebrew OT to its Greek translation, as containing the truth of the word of God). For Jerome, this principle determined not only his decision to translate the Hebrew text rather than the Greek; it also determined for him what was canonical and therefore authoritative. Excluded from canonical status were the books found only in the larger Greek OT (1–2 Maccabees, Wisdom of Solomon, Sirach, Baruch, Tobit, and Judith).

Jerome translated the following books from the Hebrew OT ca. 390–405: 1–2 Samuel; 1–2 Kings; the Psalms, the so-called *juxta Hebraeos* ("according to the Hebrews"), a version that never achieved the popularity and use of his earlier Gallican Psalter; the Prophets (including Daniel) and Job by 392–93; 1–2 Esdras (Ezra-Nehemiah) by 394; 1–2 Chronicles by 396; the "Books of Solomon" (Proverbs, Ecclesiastes, the Canticle of Canticles) by 398; and the Pentateuch, Joshua, Judges, Ruth, and Esther (with its Greek additions) by 405. Tobit and Judith he translated from the Greek OT, with the help of the Old Latin.

Apart from his revision of the Old Latin Gospels, Jerome did not translate the rest of the NT (Pauline Letters, Catholic Letters, Acts, Revelation). The Latin version of these books in the Vulgate is probably the work of Jerome's disciple, Rufinus (400–405).

The authority of the Vulgate as authentic (i.e., canonical and authoritative) was affirmed by the Council of Trent in its fourth session (1546). The council also mandated a new edition of the Vulgate. This edition, published by Pope Sixtus V (1590) and improved by Pope Clement VIII (1592), came to be known as the Sixto-Clementine Vulgate. It was this version, and its translation into other languages, that remained authoritative for Roman Catholics until Pope Pius XII's encyclical *Divino Afflante Spiritu* (1943), which allowed and encouraged modern translations of the Bible from the original languages. *See also* Scripture, versions of.   JOHN S. KSELMAN

WX
YZ

wake service, the principal rite following death and preceding the funeral liturgy, or if there is no funeral liturgy, preceding the rite of committal. The preferred term is the Vigil for the Deceased. The vigil may take place in the home of the deceased, in the funeral home, in the chapel of rest, or in some other suitable place. It may also be celebrated in the church in due time before the funeral liturgy. The Order of Christian Funerals (1989) offers the vigil in the form of a Liturgy of the Word consisting of introductory rites (greeting, opening song, invitation to prayer, pause for silent prayer, opening prayer), the Liturgy of the Word (first reading, responsorial psalm, Gospel reading, homily), the prayer of intercession (litany, Lord's Prayer, concluding prayer, eulogy), and a concluding rite (blessing, hymn, silent prayer). The rite may be adapted to incorporate other devotions, depending on popular custom and pastoral need. *See also* prayers for the dead.

Walafrid Strabo, ca. 808–49, abbot of Reichenau and poet. Student and editor of Rabanus Maurus, Walafrid wrote *Visio Wettini* ("The Vision of Wettin"), on visions of heaven and hell. The *Glossa Ordinaria* was for a long time erroneously ascribed to him. *See also* Rabanus Maurus.

Waldensians, Christian sect that traces its origin to a lay preacher of the late twelfth century, Valdes of Lyons (Peter Waldo). After his conversion in 1173 to the apostolic life, Valdes gave away the wealth he had acquired as a merchant and took up the life of a beggar and preacher. When he and his followers sought recognition from Pope Alexander III in 1179, the pope urged these Poor Men of Lyons to be obedient to their local bishop and priests and would not grant them permission to preach in public. The Waldensians nevertheless continued to preach and gain followers. Persecuted as heretics from 1184, the Waldensians eventually became strident in their criticism of the Roman Catholic Church, accusing it of apostasy and refusing to swear oaths or bear arms. Waldensian communities still exist.

Wallburga, St., ca. 710–79, abbess and sister of St. Willibald and St. Winnebald. English-born, she was asked to help Boniface in his missionary work in Germany. She became abbess of the double monastery at Heidenheim upon the death of her brothers, who had founded it. Feast day: February 25. *See also* double monasteries.

Walpole, St. Henry, 1558–95, one of the Forty Martyrs of England and Wales canonized in 1970. A native of Norfolk, ordained at Paris in 1588, he returned to England after working in Europe, but he was arrested the day after he arrived in England in 1593 and executed in 1595. Feast day: April 7. *See also* Forty Martyrs of England and Wales.

Walsh, James Anthony, 1867–1936, cofounder of Maryknoll. Ordained a priest for the archdiocese of Boston in 1892, he served as archdiocesan director of the Society for the Propagation of the Faith from 1907 until 1911, when he and Father Thomas Price organized the Catholic Foreign Mission Society of America, also known as Maryknoll. He was its superior general from then until his death in 1936. He was named a titular bishop in 1933. *See also* Maryknoll.

Walter of St. Victor, d. after 1180, theologian. A member of the famous Parisian abbey of St. Victor, he wrote (after 1179) *Contra Quattuor Labyrinthos Franciae (Against the Four Labyrinths of France)* attacking Peter Abelard, Peter Lombard, Peter of Poitiers, and Gilbert de la Porrée for their use of dialectical method in theology. *See also* Victorines.

wanderer (Lat., *vagus*), a person without a fixed residence. Church law makes certain provisions for the pastoral care of wanderers (e.g., can. 383). *See also* domicile; quasi-domicile; traveler [canon law].

Wanderer, The, conservative U.S. Catholic lay-owned weekly newspaper, based in St. Paul, Minnesota. Originally printed in German, it was one of many German Catholic newspapers founded in the nineteenth century to preserve German Catholic allegiance to the faith. Its adversarial tone was sharpened when it took a firm stand against the Americanizers in the U.S. hierarchy, including the ordinary of its own city, Archbishop John Ireland (d. 1918). Despite its highly touted rejection of Hitler, the fortunes of the paper sank dismally in the 1930s and during World War II. By 1945 its total subscriptions sank to 1,800. The onset of the cold war revived its fortunes when its strong anticommunism seemed to harmonize with the new mood of the country. It was one of the few Catholic publications that did not support John F. Kennedy in 1960. The paper's national reputation and circulation soared when it served as one of the main organs of criticism of the reforms of Vatican II. In the 1990s it reaches about 40,000 subscribers.

war, holy, warfare as a ritual activity in which the gods of the respective combatants are involved. Campaigns of this kind are often rounded off with the ban, i.e., the dedication by destruction of the persons and property of the conquered to the deity (e.g., Num 21:1–3). The idea of holy warfare is not confined to Israel. In certain parts of the Muslim world today, it is referred to as *jihad.*

war, morality of. *See* just-war doctrine.

Ward, Barbara, also known as Lady Jackson, 1914–81, economist. Trained at Oxford, her international influence came from her many books and articles on the political and economic challenges facing poor and developing nations, and from her role as foreign editor of *The Economist* (from 1946). Her influence in the Church before and after the Second Vatican Council (1962–65) was rooted in her application of Christian values and teachings to modern economic and political problems. Her many writings include monographs on the social thought of Pope Pius XII and on the 1967 encyclical *Populorum Progressio* of Pope Paul VI, and such books as *Faith and Freedom* (1954), *My Brother's Keeper* (1959), and *The Rich Nations and the Poor Nations* (1962).

Ward, St. Margaret, d. 1588, one of the Forty Martyrs of England and Wales canonized in 1970. She was executed for helping a priest escape from Bridewell Prison and for refusing to divulge his hiding place. Feast day: August 30. *See also* Forty Martyrs of England and Wales.

Ward, Wilfrid, 1856–1916, writer and journalist. Son of William George Ward, he was editor of *The Dublin Review* from 1906 until his death. After the condemnation of Modernism, he tried to exercise a restraining influence on intemperate anti-Modernism and opposed its anti-intellectual excesses. He wrote biographies of his father and of Cardinals Wiseman and Newman.

Ward, William George, 1812–82, apologist and writer. Ordained an Anglican priest in 1840, he was a disciple of John Henry Newman (d. 1890) and a zealous member of the Oxford movement. He became a Roman Catholic in 1845. He edited *The Dublin Review* from 1863 to 1878 and made it the leading English-language Ultramontane journal. A supporter of an extreme interpretation of papal infallibility, he became alienated from Newman, whom he regarded as insufficiently loyal to Rome. *See also* infallibility; Newman, John Henry; Oxford movement; Ultramontanism.

Warde, Frances, 1810–84, American founder of the Sisters of Mercy. Born in Ireland, she worked in Dublin with Catherine McAuley at her Baggott Street center for needy children and women. When McAuley founded the Sisters of Mercy in 1831, Frances Warde was one of her first postulants; her chosen name in religious life was Mary Frances Xavier. She came to the United States in 1843 with six other Sisters of Mercy and in Pittsburgh, Pennsylvania, she established parish schools, academies, and a House of Mercy for young women, along with an orphanage and a hospital. She led the Sisters of Mercy in the United States through a period of rapid growth and was responsible for establishing thirty-nine convents in thirty-seven years throughout the United States. *See also* McAuley, Catherine; Sisters of Mercy.

washing of feet. *See* Mandatum.

water, an ancient symbol for life and sometimes for chaos. Jesus speaks of water he will give the believing person as "a spring of water gushing up to eternal life" (John 4:14). *See also* Baptism; holy water.

Waugh, Evelyn, 1903–66, English novelist and man of letters. Known for his well-crafted satirical novels, he was a convert, in 1930, to the Catholic faith. An inveterate traveler (and travel writer), he never lost his insular British sensibility. His Catholicism is most clearly reflected in his finest novel, *Brideshead Revisited* (1945). His biography of his friend Ronald Knox (1959) reflects his conservative and very English conception of Catholicism. He never reconciled himself to the changes of the Second Vatican Council (1962–65); indeed, his natural pessimism led him to lament loudly the changes both in the liturgy and the social program of the renewed Church. A prodigious letter writer, diarist, and writer of fiction, he is considered one of the finest British prose writers of the twentieth century.

ways of the spiritual life, the three stages of the spiritual journey as understood by many Christian writers from Origen in the third century onward.

The theoretical and practical interpretation of the threefold way was developed further by later mystical theologians such as John of the Cross (d. 1591). Traditionally, the three stages were described as purgative (for beginners), illuminative (for the experienced or proficient), and unitive (for the perfect). The initial purgative stage involved conversion from sin and detachment from the senses or material reality. The second, the illuminative stage, was one of deepening knowledge and love of God within a contemplative experience. According to some writers, movement to the third, unitive, stage was marked by a further experience of purgation ("dark night"). In the unitive way, desire is dominated by love of God and all things in God. The typical prayer is characterized as "loving attentiveness," in which an intense union with God is experienced without complete loss of personal identity.

Some mystics adopt other titles for the three ways. For example, Jan van Ruysbroeck (d. 1381), in *The Spiritual Espousals,* did not focus on union with God exclusively in the final stage. He wrote, rather, of three kinds of union. The "active life" was for beginners and involved "union with God by intermediary." The "interior life" was more inward and union with God was "without intermediary." The "contemplative life" was the highest point and union was "without distinction."

In general, the threefold way has been criticized in recent times both from a theological and a psychological standpoint. Most modern spiritual writers regard any notion of absolutely distinct, successive stages, with universal application, as far too rigid. It conflicts with the uniqueness of each person and the uniqueness of grace. The understanding of union with God as a final stage has also been criticized. As Ruysbroeck argues, union with God in some sense must be present from the very beginning as the precondition of all spiritual growth. Union, too, is a gift that is not achieved by human effort. An Anglican expert on mysticism, Evelyn Underhill (d. 1941), has also pointed out that, in the greatest Christian mystics, union becomes not an end in itself but leads quite naturally to selfless service of others.

Theologians such as Karl Rahner (d. 1984) have suggested that the traditional scheme of distinct stages depends too much on a Neoplatonist understanding of the human person. According to this understanding, derived from Origen, growth involves detachment from all human passions and ascent away from the material world. However, in-terpreted flexibly and particularly not as a set of completely distinct and unrepeatable stages, the threefold way remains a useful guide to the spiritual journey. People are at different stages in their relationships with God and in prayer and it is important to identify distinctive needs. Equally, the characteristics that identify the traditional ways—conversion, enlargement of vision, growth in selfless love—are recognized as the major challenges present in different proportions at all points in the spiritual journey. *See also* mysticism; spirituality, Christian.   *PHILIP SHELDRAKE*

Wearmouth and Jarrow, twin monasteries in Anglo-Saxon Northumbria (modern Yorkshire, England). Founded (673) and enriched by Benedict Biscop, the community of Wearmouth-Jarrow had many ties to Rome: Codex Amiatinus of the Bible, written here ca. 715, was meant as a gift for the pope. Bede was a monk of Jarrow. *See also* Bede, St.

Weigel, Gustave, 1906–64, Jesuit priest and ecumenical theologian. He taught theology in Santiago, Chile (1937–49) and at Woodstock College, Maryland (1949–64). His openness, warmth, and tolerance of differences won acceptance among Protestants despite his conservative theology. He was named consultant to the Vatican Secretariat for Promoting Christian Unity in 1960 and served as interpreter for Protestant observers at Vatican II (1962–65).

Weil, Simone, 1909–43, French essayist and mystic. Born in Paris of a distinguished Jewish family, Weil was educated in classics and philosophy at the École Normale Supérieur, where she embraced Marxism. Her commitment to social causes led to personal involvement, e.g., she joined the March of Miners (1933), served with the International Brigade against Franco during the Spanish Civil War, and worked as a laborer on farms and in factories.

Weil's writings, now in collections such as *The Need for Roots, Gravity and Grace,* and *Waiting for God,* reflect her experience of God's absence in the midst of suffering and the need to wait for God's return. While she was visiting Assisi (Italy) and Solesmes (France) in 1937, Weil had several mystical experiences. Although never baptized, she espoused Christianity, believing that Christ's Passion continued in the suffering of each person.

Wells, St. Swithun, 1536–91, one of the Forty

Martyrs of England and Wales canonized in 1970. He was a married schoolmaster who aided the underground Catholic Church in England. Feast day: October 25. *See also* Forty Martyrs of England and Wales.

Wenceslas, St., ca. 907–29, king, martyr, and patron saint of Bohemia. A Christian who sought to extend the Church's influence in his realm with the support of Emperor Henry I, he issued policies that met with strong opposition from the nobles, many of whom were pagan. Killed by a band of conspirators that may have included his brother, he is venerated as a martyr. He was memorialized much later in the famed Christmas carol. Feast day: September 28.

Wesley, Charles, 1707–88, preacher and writer of hymns and brother of John Wesley. Ordained a priest in the Church of England (1735), he underwent a conversion on Pentecost in 1738 that shaped his ministry as an itinerant preacher. He eventually became attached to the City Road Chapel, London. He wrote over five thousand hymns, including "Love Divine, All Loves Excelling," "Hark, the Herald Angels Sing," and "Christ the Lord Is Risen Today." *See also* Methodism.

Wesley, John, 1703–91, founder of the Methodist movement (originally within the Church of England) and brother of Charles Wesley. Ordained a priest for the Church of England (1728), he underwent a conversion in 1738, after which he undertook an itinerant ministry to the poor and uneducated throughout the British Isles. Wesley's reliance on lay preachers and his ordination of priests and bishops created tensions between his ecclesiastical organization and the Church of England. After his death, the Methodist church was founded. *See also* Methodism.

Wessel [Gansfort], ca. 1419–89, Dutch theologian. Though often viewed as proto-Protestant because he criticized papal infallibility, indulgences, and purgatory, Wessel was a pious Catholic.

Western Schism, Great. *See* Great Schism.

Westminster Abbey, the London church that has, since William the Conqueror in 1066, been the site of English royal coronations. Already a Benedictine monastery by the end of the eighth century, it was refounded by Edward the Confessor (1003–66); the monastery was dissolved under Henry VIII in 1540, reestablished by Mary I in 1556, and again dissolved by Elizabeth I in 1559.

Westminster Confession, the confession of faith of the Westminster Assembly. It was drafted by an assembly meeting in Westminster Abbey and was approved as the confession of faith by the English Parliament in 1647 and the Scots Parliament in 1649. It remained the central confession of English-speaking Presbyterians. Based on the witness of the Holy Spirit in Scripture (Article 1), the confession follows the temporal enactment of God's predestinating will (Art. 3) in the election of some of fallen humanity to salvation by Christ (Art. 4–9) through their calling, justification, adoption, sanctification, and perseverance (Art. 10–17). The confession is noteworthy for subsuming the work of Christ under limited election (Art. 8), for distinguishing between the covenants of works and grace (Art. 7), for making the practical syllogism foundational for assurance (Art. 18), and for equating the Sabbath observance with Sunday (Art. 21). *See also* Presbyterianism.

Westminster version. *See* Scripture, versions of.

Westphalia, Peace of. *See* Peace of Westphalia.

West Syrian rite, also called Syro-Antiochene rite, the liturgical tradition of the Syrian Orthodox in the patriarchate of Antioch and in India, as well as of the West Syrian and Syro-Malankara Catholics. Antioch and Jerusalem were the principal liturgical centers at the origins of the West Syrian rite. It is a synthesis of native Syriac elements, especially hymns and other choral pieces, with material translated from the Greek liturgical texts of the early Jerusalem and Antiochene traditions. This synthesis was the work of the Syriac, non-Chalcedonian, monastic communities in the Syriac-speaking hinterlands of Syria, Palestine, and parts of Mesopotamia, beyond the Greek-speaking cities of the Mediterranean littoral (coast). These Syriac Christians were organized into an independent church under Jacob Baradai (d. 578), after whom they are sometimes called "Jacobites." The Divine Office of this rite is closely related to that of the Maronite rite, and all three Syrian rites—the latter two plus the Chaldean—have basically the same liturgical year. Its eucharistic liturgy, however, is based on the

Jerusalem Liturgy of St. James. *See also* Syro-Malankara Catholic Church.

Whitby, Synod of [Streanaeshalch], Anglo-Saxon church council (664). Mid-seventh-century Northumbria had two provinces, two kings, and two churches—Roman and Celtic—separated by differences over the date of Easter and other observances. King Oswy and his son King Alchfrid summoned Roman and Celtic spokesmen to St. Hilda's Abbey at Whitby; after hearing them debate, Oswy opted for Rome, lest the gatekeeper of heaven deny him entrance. The chief Roman spokesman was Wilfrid of Ripon. *See also* Wilfrid, St.

White, Andrew, 1579–1656, Jesuit priest and missionary. Ordained a secular priest at Douai, France, in 1605, he served as a missionary in England, was expelled after the Gunpowder Plot (1605), entered the Jesuits (1607), taught philosophy, and then returned to missionary work in England. He founded the Maryland mission (1634), was deported to England in chains (1644), and was then exiled. He returned to England and died. His works include *A Narrative of the Trip to Maryland* and pamphlets encouraging colonization.

White Fathers, Missionaries of Africa (M. Afr.), a society founded in Algiers in 1868 by Cardinal Charles M. Lavigerie, archbishop of Algiers. The name White Fathers (dropped in 1984) was derived from the white habit they traditionally wore. The first aim of the society was care of orphans following the typhoid epidemic of 1867. Missions were soon established in other parts of the area around the northern fringes of the Sahara, although two attempts to cross the Sahara and establish missions in the interior of Africa failed, ending with the massacre of six White Fathers by their Touareg guides. In 1878, in response to his plan for the evangelization of Central Africa, Lavigerie was appointed apostolic delegate to Equatorial Africa. That same year, the first of what were to become annual caravans of missionaries left Tanganyika and headed toward the interior. The society faced great hardships, including persecution by tribal chiefs and slave traders. Many priests, brothers, and lay associates gave their lives for the work of the missions; twenty-two Christians martyred in Uganda were canonized in 1964. Slowly, however, Lavigerie's visions became reality. The goal of building up an indigenous clergy bore its first fruit with the ordination of two priests in Uganda in 1913. Dedicated to their apostolic work in Africa, the White Fathers may not accept any other apostolic work outside of that continent, unless requested to do so by the Holy See. An American province of the White Fathers was established in Washington, D.C., in 1948. *See also* Africa, Catholicism in.

White Sisters. *See* Missionary Sisters of Our Lady of Africa.

widow, a married or (in Jewish tradition) betrothed woman whose husband has died. The care of widows and orphans in the ancient world was an important duty of the community because the widow rarely possessed means of support. Hence there are constant exhortations in the Scriptures pleading for care and justice for widows, e.g., Exod 22:22. A childless widow in the Jewish tradition was expected to marry her husband's nearest male relative. The practice was known as levirate marriage. In the primitive Church widows played an important role. Indeed, there may have been an order of widows that later merged with that of deaconesses. The older widows were formerly registered as ministers of charity within the community (1 Tim 5:3–18). The widow enjoyed greater independence than other women. Exonerated from the patriarchal system, childbearing, and household responsibility, she was free to use her own wealth, to travel, and to play a vital and often influential part within the community. This is seen especially in the corpus of apocryphal acts of the Apostles (e.g., the *Acts of Paul,* the *Acts of Thomas*). The status of consecrated widow was of greater prestige than the consecrated virgin in the first three centuries of the Church. Gradually, however, virginity became the preferred status. *See also* virginity.

Wilfrid, St., 634–709, bishop of York from 664 to 709. He advocated the Roman position on the date of Easter at the Synod of Whitby (664), promoting closer ties with Rome generally, both with regard to liturgical practice and to papal authority. Feast day: October 12. *See also* Whitby, Synod of.

will of God, a notion about God's infinite capacity to desire the good. Scripture teaches that the creation of the universe and the Incarnation of Jesus were the results of God's will, and that God "desires everyone to be saved" (1 Tim 2:4). The Christian tradition has repeatedly directed Christians to discover and to follow God's benevolent will for them. Thomas Aquinas (d. 1274) argued that where there is an intellect there is a will, that the one who knows has the capacity to choose the good known. As one who has all perfections, a knowing God is also a God who wills.

Considering the will of God raises numerous questions. The will of God, like God's very self, is a mystery. Thus, those who want to conform their lives to God's will must seek ways to discover what God's will is for them. The Scriptures and the Catholic tradition contain much discussion about this process of discovery. The existence of evil, natural and moral, also raises questions that theologians have tried to answer for centuries. If God wills only good and knows the good perfectly, how can the existence of evil be explained? Some theologians have argued that in some cases God wills only indirectly. Thus, God's will for justice indirectly wills the punishment attendant to the implementation of justice. God does not will moral evil, but God permits its existence as a result of human free will. Indeed, Christian faith consistently affirms the existence of God's loving will despite the presence of physical and moral evil in the world. Since the time of Jesus, Christians have prayed daily that the will of God be accomplished: "Your will be done on earth as it is in heaven" (Matt 6:10). *See also* nature and grace; providence; salvation; universal salvific will of God.

PATRICIA M. VINJE

William of Auvergne, ca. 1180–1249, theologian, bishop of Paris from 1228, and prolific author. His efforts to reconcile the newly recovered Aristotle (d. 322 B.C.) with the Platonism of earlier theology anticipated the more successful work of later theologians at Paris. *See also* Aristotle; Plato.

William of Auxerre, d. 1231, theologian at the University of Paris and author of the *Summa Aurea* (Lat., "Golden Synthesis"), a comprehensive statement of Christian theology employing Aristotle (d. 322 B.C.) in the service of Christian truth that was influential throughout the thirteenth century. *See also* Aristotle.

William of Champeaux, ca. 1068–1122, French logician and bishop of Châlons-sur-Marne from 1113 to 1122. Renowned as the finest teacher of dialectic in Paris at the turn of the twelfth century, William, a logical realist, became embroiled in debate

on the problem of universals with his former student, Peter Abelard. Although William retired from teaching in 1108, he soon resumed the task, and, with other Augustinian Canons, founded the School of St. Victor. *See also* Scholasticism; Victorines.

William of Moerbeke, ca. 1215–ca. 1286, Flemish Dominican, archbishop of Corinth (1278–86), and translator from Greek into Latin. Besides classics of mathematics, physics, optics, and medicine, he translated previously unavailable works of Aristotle (d. 322 B.C.) and many commentaries thereon. His literal translations directly from Greek often replaced versions made from Arabic and Syriac intermediaries; this made possible a more accurate reading of Aristotle, the fruits of which appear in Thomas Aquinas's (d. 1274) theology. His translations of Proclus shaped German Dominican mysticism. *See also* Aquinas, St. Thomas; Aristotle; mysticism.

William of Ockham, ca. 1285–1347, Franciscan philosopher and theologian; known as the "Venerable Inceptor" because, although academically qualified, he never secured a position as regent master of theology at a university. After entering the Franciscan order at an early age, the English-born William studied theology at Oxford, lecturing on the *Sentences* of Peter Lombard from 1317 to 1319. Next serving as a lecturer in a Franciscan house (probably in London), his literary energies were focused on logic and natural philosophy, as well as on more overtly theological issues. In 1324 he was summoned to Avignon to respond to charges that some of his theological positions, including those on the Eucharist, were heretical; there he met Michael of Cesena, the minister general of the order, who had come to the papal court to champion a stricter Franciscan line on spiritual poverty. As he studied papal pronouncements on poverty at Michael's urging, William concluded that Pope John XXII had himself lapsed into heresy. Fleeing the papal court in 1328, he was received by the rival of the pope, Emperor Louis of Bavaria, and lived out his life in Munich. His later works, including the "Work of Ninety Days," were more political in tone and highly critical of papal pretensions. He was never, however, formally condemned as a heretic.

Ockham's philosophical and theological teachings exerted tremendous influence in the later Middle Ages. Although not the originator of the concept, he made great use of the distinction between the absolute power of God, which refers to the vast range of possibilities open to the omnipotent God, and God's ordained power, which designates the course of action on which God has, in fact, settled. By virtue of the distinction, which was widely employed in subsequent theology, Ockham was able to insist on both divine transcendence and the radical contingency of the creation: the world need not be the way it is, for God could, in absolute power, have decided to establish things differently; that the world takes its present form is due to God's ordained will.

Ockham, however, is now probably best known for his "razor," which advocates economy in argument. "Ockham's razor" is a rule in science and philosophy stating that, because entities should not be multiplied needlessly, the simplest of two or more competing theories is preferable. *See also* nominalism; philosophy and theology; Scholasticism.

JOSEPH WAWRYKOW

William of Saint-Thierry, ca. 1085–1148, theologian, mystic, and abbot of the Benedictine monastery, Saint-Thierry, in Champagne, France, from 1119 to 1135. While abbot he argued for a strict observance of the Rule of St. Benedict. In 1135 he was released from his duties, at his request, to retire to the stricter Cistercian monastery of Signy. *See also* Benedict, Rule of St.

William of Tyre, ca. 1130–86, chancellor of the Latin Kingdom of Jerusalem, archbishop of Tyre, and historian. Commissioned by King Amaury to write a history of the kingdom, he also led the delegation of Jerusalem to the Third Lateran Council (1179).

Willibald, St., 700–786, bishop of Eichstätt (742–86) and associate of St. Boniface, who consecrated him bishop. Feast day: July 7. *See also* Boniface, St.

Willibrord, St., 658–739, missionary to the Frisians (in western Germany). An oblate under Wilfrid at Ripon, England, and later ordained a priest in Ireland, he left in 690 for West Frisia with eleven companions. Visiting Rome in 692, he received the support of Pope Sergius I, who in 695 consecrated Willibrord as archbishop of the Frisians. He established his cathedral outside Utrecht on land granted by Pepin II, and in 698 established a Benedictine monastery at Echternach, which became a base for further missionary activity extending as far as Denmark. Feast day: November 7. *See also* Germany, Catholicism in.

wills [canon law], gifts to the Church and to Church-related institutions. Church law is concerned not only with gifts given by way of last will and testament, but also with gifts given while the donor is still alive. A major concern of the law is to follow the intention of the donor. The bishop, or in some cases the competent religious superior, has the duty of ensuring this, and consequently the responsibility of oversight; of interpreting the meaning of the donor's intent when it is not expressed clearly; and, under certain conditions, of making changes in the intent when it is impossible to fulfill.

Windesheim Congregation, association of Augustinian Canons Regular committed to the Devotio Moderna movement inspired by Geert de Groote (d. 1384). Eventually spreading from Windesheim through the Low Countries and Germany, the congregation had about one hundred monasteries before its suppression by the Protestants. *See also* Augustinian Canons; Devotio Moderna.

wine, eucharistic, the wine consecrated during the Eucharistic Prayer and distributed during the Communion rite at Mass. The sacrifice of Christ is recalled by the words "the blood of Christ," which are spoken both during the Eucharistic Prayer and as the consecrated wine is distributed to the faithful during the Communion rite. *See also* mixed chalice; unmixed chalice.

wisdom (Old Eng., *witan*, "to know"; Lat., *videre*, "to see"), a gift of the Holy Spirit that, according to Catholic theology, is a special grace of the Spirit to help one practice virtue more perfectly. Wisdom is a kind of knowledge in the sense that it allows one to understand God's purposes and the divine will. In the Hebrew Scriptures, wisdom (a feminine noun) is God's first creation (Sir 1:4) and is frequently associated with "fear of the Lord" (Ps 111:10; Prov 1:7; Sir 1:12–14)—an expression that means reverence for the Lord. In the NT, Paul identified Christ with God's wisdom (1 Cor 1:24) when he attempted to express Christian reliance on Christ crucified and to distinguish Christian faith from the empty wisdom of Greek learning. Relating wisdom to God's incarnate Word, as Paul does, and to divinity itself, as Sirach suggests, indicates that wisdom is not a human virtue or a skill that can be acquired through self-effort. As the author of Proverbs put it, God gives birth to wisdom (8:22). While creatures can discover and understand valuable knowledge, wisdom always originates with the creator God. *See also* gifts of the Holy Spirit.

witchcraft, the use of supernatural powers with the aid of evil spirits. Condemned in both the OT (Exod 22:18; Deut 18:9–14) and NT (Gal 5:20) as opposed to the worship of God, the early Church considered witchcraft to be superstition. By the thirteenth century, witchcraft was condemned as heresy and subject to the Inquisition and prosecution by secular justice. Persecution of witches grew in the following centuries and continued in both Protestant and Catholic countries into the eighteenth century.

Wittenberg, a university town in Germany. With both Martin Luther and Philipp Melanchthon as professors, the University of Wittenberg (established 1502) became the center of the new Protestant movement in the sixteenth century. Luther nailed his *Ninety-five Theses* on Wittenberg's Castle Church, in which both he and Melanchthon are buried. *See also* Luther, Martin; Melanchthon, Philipp.

Wolff, Madeleva, 1887–1964, a Sister of the Holy Cross and third president of St. Mary's College, Notre Dame, Indiana, from 1934 to 1961. Distinguished educator and poet, she was the author of *My First Seventy Years* (1959).

Wolfgang, St., ca. 924–94, bishop of Regensburg, monk, missionary, and educator. He was noted for his zeal in church reform and pastoral care. Feast day: October 31.

Wolsey, Thomas, ca. 1474–1530, cardinal from 1515, who as privy councilor to Henry VIII attained great power, being named bishop of Lincoln and then archbishop of York (1514), lord chancellor (1515), and papal legate. His failure to procure a papal dispensation for the divorce of Henry VIII from Catherine of Aragon in 1529 led to his arrest in 1530 for high treason, but he died before his trial.

woman deacon. *See* deacon, woman.

Women for Faith and Family, an organization founded in 1984, with headquarters in St. Louis, Missouri, to provide Catholic women with the means to express support for the hierarchy and the teaching of the Church.

Women's Ordination Conference (WOC), an international grass-roots movement of women and men committed to the ordination of Roman Catholic women to a renewed priestly ministry. Officially established in 1976, WOC had its beginnings in Chicago, where two years earlier Mary Lynch had gathered a small group of women to discuss raising the question of the ordination of women during the International Year of Women.

The general office is in Fairfax, Virginia, and local WOC chapters exist in many major cities. WOC is a clearinghouse of research and information. It sponsors workshops and conferences, conducts surveys, and provides speakers to local groups. The official bimonthly publication is *New Women, New Church. See also* ordination of women.

word of God, a verbal expression of God's power, will, and purpose; a frequent Christian description of the Bible. In the ancient Near East, "word" carries the nuance of "expression of power," and in Hebrew *dabar* means both "word" and "event." The Bible opens with the creative word of God: "Then God said, 'Let there be light': and there was light" (Gen 1:3; see Pss 33:6, 9; 147:4, 15–18; Isa 40:26). The OT uses the expression "word of the Lord" over two hundred times, most often for the powerful advent of God that transforms human history, especially in the calling and activity of the prophets (1 Kgs 17:1–5; Isa 6:6–13; Jer 1:6–9; Ezek 3:1–11; Amos 3:1; 4:1). The decalogue is literally the "ten words" of God (Deut 4:13; Exod 20:2–17; Deut 5:6–21), and in Deuteronomy the word of God is virtually identical with the "decrees and the statutes and the ordinances that the Lord our God has commanded you" (Deut 6:20). The Gospels refer to the OT as the word of God infrequently (Matt 15:6; Luke 1:38, 45; 3:2), but the phrase appears in Acts and the Pauline writings as a virtual synonym for the early Christian proclamation (Acts 4:31; 6:2, 4, 7; 8:14, 25; 11:1; 1 Thess 2:13; 1 Cor 14:36; 2 Cor 2:17; Col 1:25). The OT legacy of the powerful word is captured by Heb 4:12, the word of God as "living and active, sharper than any two-edged sword." As revealer and expression of God's presence Jesus is "the word" (John 1:14–18; Heb 1:2).

The biblical background is a caution against calling Scripture the literal word of God. The Bible is God's word as the written witness to the powerful presence of God manifest in the history of Israel and in the Christ event (i.e., the life, teaching, death, Resurrection, and abiding presence of Christ). *See also* Bible; inspiration of Scripture; Scripture, authority of. JOHN R. DONAHUE

WOMEN IN THE CHURCH

From the beginning of Christianity, women have played a significant role in the Church, some according to the customs and mores of the times and others in sharp contrast to the conventions of their day. In the twentieth century, the women's movement and the Church's sensitivity to issues of human dignity and justice raised expectations among women and encouraged them to assume greater responsibility for the Church's mission.

WOMEN IN THE NEW TESTAMENT

Recent research by Scripture scholars has unearthed new insights concerning women and their involvement in the life of Jesus and the early Church. Jesus welcomed women among his disciples and treated them in a manner that differed from the accepted norms of his religious and social milieu. Women followed him from town to town and some provided for him out of their own means (Luke 8:3). There is no indication that he ever dealt with women as inferiors or tried to control or manipulate them. Women remained at the cross and the Risen Christ appeared to them and sent them as apostles to announce the Resurrection to the other disciples (Mark 15:40–41; 16:7). Women were present at Pentecost and received the Holy Spirit (Acts 1:14).

Paul refers to women as fellow workers in the service of Christ and as fellow prisoners for Christ. He commends Phoebe as sister, patron, and deacon (Gk., *diakonos*) of the church of Cenchreae (Rom 16:1–2). She is the only person in the NT who is called deacon of a particular church, yet she has remained relatively unknown. Significantly, when the Church uses Romans 16 in the liturgy, the Roman lectionary omits the two verses about her and begins the reading with v. 3. Paul mentions many other women by name who served as "fellow workers" (Rom 16; 1 Cor 16:19; Phil 4:2–3).

The baptismal formula cited in Galatians 3:28 expresses the understanding of Pauline communities that there is no distinction of race, status, or sex among the baptized. "There is no longer Jew or Greek, there is no longer slave or free, there is no longer male and female; for all of you are one in Christ Jesus."

The Fourth Gospel presents a story of women's leadership role in the community. Martha assumed leadership in the community in the story of the raising of Lazarus from the dead, sending for Jesus and professing faith in him, and in the resurrection of the dead (John 11). In this Gospel it is Martha who professes faith in Jesus, as Peter does in the synoptic Gospels. Luke presents Martha and her sister Mary as symbolizing the ministries of the table and of the word (Luke 10:38–40).

While Scripture may provide positive models, it also includes negative insights concerning the role of women. The household codes, prescriptions for behavior, present another picture of the role of women in the early Church. They are instructed to keep silence in the churches (Cor 14:34), to be submissive (Titus 2:5) even as children (1 Tim 3:4) and slaves are (Titus 2:8), to listen in silence and not act as teachers (1 Tim 2:11–12), and to find salvation through childbearing (1 Tim 2:15). Arguments for women's silence and submission are given in 1 Timothy: Adam was created first, then Eve, and it was she who was led astray (2:14). These arguments have been repeated over the centuries in efforts to silence women.

The contributions of women to the Church have frequently been overlooked because of emphasis on their roles as mother, wife, or harlot. For instance, Mary is honored as the virgin mother; little is said about her role as disciple. The Samaritan woman is remembered more for her five husbands than for the fact that many in her town believed in Jesus on the strength of her word (John 4:39). Magdalene, faithful to the end (Luke 24:10), is known as a repentant sinner, even though Scripture does not describe her thus (Luke 8:2).

Christ in the home of Mary and Martha, two types of personalities, the one (Mary) contemplative and the other (Martha) active; "Mary has chosen the better part," Jesus said to Martha (Luke 10:42); seventeenth-century Dutch painting by Jan Vermeer, National Gallery of Scotland, Edinburgh.

WOMEN IN THE EARLY CHURCH

Women in the early Church assumed leadership roles for groups of Christians in the cities of the Mediterranean world by opening their homes to members of the Church and serving those in need. During the persecutions, women courageously professed the faith and died as martyrs along with their brother Christians. Later, holy women and men looked to desert mothers as well as desert fathers for guidance in their lives of prayer, penance, and study.

The *Apostolic Constitutions,* a fourth-century document, describes a ceremony for ordaining deaconesses. When the bishop laid hands on a woman, he was to pray, "Do Thou look down on this Thy servant, who is to be ordained to the office of woman deacon and grant her Thy Holy Spirit." Later councils forbade the practice of ordaining women as deacons. Numerous reasons were given, the final one being "because of the weakness of their sex." The discipleship of equals established by Jesus was overcome by societal and cultural forces of patriarchy.

THROUGH THE AGES

Abbesses in medieval times exercised jurisdiction over double monasteries of both women and men. They shared in the responsibilities and symbols of episcopal office. Abbesses were ordinarily women from royal or powerful families and often wielded a kind of power that was usual in their day but that has been criticized as inappropriate as a model for today's women.

Mystics of the Middle Ages such as Julian of Norwich (d. ca. 1413), Mechtild of Magdeburg (d. ca. 1280), and Hildegard of Bingen (d. 1179) exerted great influence over their contemporaries. The many revisions and recent publications of their works testify to the esteem in which they are still held. Catherine of Siena (d. 1380) and Teresa of Ávila (d. 1582) have been declared Doctors of the Church.

Before the seventeenth century all convents were strictly cloistered, but the founding of active communities of women dedicated to the works of mercy radically changed the nature of religious life. These communities of religious sisters assumed responsibility for education, health care, and social outreach while maintaining many of the practices of the cloistered communities. Sisters assumed positions of authority in schools, hospitals, orphanages, and social agencies, often in conflict with both social customs and the hierarchy.

WOMEN IN TODAY'S CHURCH

Education, especially higher education, has prepared women to assume more public roles and responsibilities in society and the Church. Madeleva Wolff, president of St. Mary's College, Notre Dame, Indiana, established the first doctoral program in theology for women in the United States in 1943. Nine years later, Pope Pius XII founded Regina Mundi, a pontifical institute in Rome to prepare women to teach theology in women's colleges. Since that time, women have earned graduate degrees and teach in universities and seminaries throughout the world. Women are earning Master of Divinity (M.Div.) degrees preparing them for pastoral ministry. The number of women in professional theological and biblical societies has increased dramatically in recent decades. Women theologians are making significant contributions not only in the field of feminist theology but in all areas of theology and biblical studies.

The challenge of Vatican II (1962–65), coupled with the shortage of priests, has increased women's involvement in the life of the Church. The Notre Dame Study of Catholic Parish Life (1986) indicated that women are engaged in ministry in greater numbers than men. Women comprise over 80 percent of those who minister as teachers and sponsors of the catechumenate and who serve

A laywoman distributes Holy Communion at Mass in St. Stephen's Church, Anoka, Minnesota. Before the Second Vatican Council, the distribution of Communion was a function restricted to priests and deacons.

the poor, visit the sick, and comfort the grieving. Half of parish council members, lectors, and eucharistic ministers are women. In practice, however, men are called on more often to serve in these capacities.

The documents of the Second Vatican Council (1962–65) locate the call to ministry in Baptism and charge all Christians to minister. The theology that has developed since that time has provided the foundation for women and laymen to assume more public roles as ministers in the Church. Involvement of laypeople is not just to make up for the shortage of priests. Ministry is recognized as the right and responsibility of all Christians.

Some women minister in a general way. In families as well as in parishes, the majority of teachers and catechists are women. Women volunteers keep many parish projects afloat. Mothers, wives, and single women comprise the largest group of women whose faith, love, and generous service nourish and build up the Church. While sisters make a great contribution, they are fewer in number.

More women are currently involved as paid professionals in the Church than in the past and are assuming responsibilities once closed to them. Parish administrators and pastoral associates are but two of the more recent ministries that women provide. Women serve as hospital chaplains, campus ministers, religious educators, liturgical coordinators, and vicars in dioceses as full-time professional ministers.

In priestless parishes (now more than 10 percent of all parishes in the

United States) women carry out the ministries of a pastor with two exceptions: they do not celebrate the Eucharist or hear confessions. They are the liturgical and prayer leaders of the community as well as spiritual directors. They counsel parishioners, conduct Scripture studies, visit the sick, and care for the suffering. In some remote areas, women have been commissioned by the local bishop to preside at weddings and funerals.

Women teach and serve as administrators in seminaries and in pro-

A Native American nun speaks with Native American Catholics.

grams preparing men for the diaconate. Wives of candidates for the diaconate are encouraged to accompany their husbands in the training process. Some dioceses admit women to the training program but do not promise that they will be ordained permanent deacons.

WOMEN IN RELIGIOUS CONGREGATIONS

Pope Pius XII issued *Sponsa Christi* in 1950, in which he discussed the need for professional and religious formation of sisters. He also noted that modern life demanded that sisters be able to support themselves and not depend on gifts. Under the impetus of the Sister Formation Movement (1951), the process of transformation was begun. When Vatican II's Decree on the Appropriate Renewal of the Religious Life mandated a return to the intention of the founders, revision of constitutions, and examination of life-styles, sisters were already prepared for the challenge.

In 1966, two-thirds of all sisters were teaching in elementary schools, high schools, and academies. Others were serving in hospitals, orphanages, and homes for the elderly and persons with physical and mental disabilities. Since that time, large numbers of sisters have left their orders. Those who remain are involved in less institutional ministries and many have responded to the call for a "preferential option for the poor."

OFFICIAL STATEMENTS REGARDING WOMEN

The Church gets mixed reviews for its treatment of women over the centuries. In some times and places it has protected them by curbing the power and authority of patriarchal rulers, totalitarian governments, and of abusive husbands and fathers who would deny them full human dignity. In other situations, it has contributed to abuse and exploitation by perpetuating degrading stereotypes and condoning abusive situations with appeals to biblical passages on suffering, submission, and patience. Recent documents indicate a growing awareness by the hierarchy of women's changing role in society and the Church. The ideals these documents contain have, for the most part, not yet been accomplished.

Pope John XXIII, in *Pacem in Terris* (1963), cited women's participation in public life as one of the three most significant signs of the times to which the Church should attend. The Second Vatican Council's Pastoral Constitution on the Church in the Modern World also noted the changing role of women in society (nn. 9, 52, 60). The Decree on the Apostolate of the Laity states: "Since in our times women have an ever more active share in the whole life of society, it is very important that they participate more widely also in the various fields of the Church's apostolate" (n. 9). In 1971, the Third World Synod of Bishops called for women to participate in, and share responsibility for, the life of society and of the Church ("Justice in the World").

The ministries of acolyte and lector were restored to the laity in 1972 when the apostolic letter *Ministeria Quaedam* was published. While women were given permission to serve in both capacities, formal commissioning to those offices was reserved to men. Many dioceses have discontinued the practice of commissioning because of this discrimination.

In 1976, the Pontifical Biblical Commission reported that Scripture alone did not support the exclusion of women from ordination. In the same year and in spite of that report, the Congregation for the Doctrine of the Faith issued the "Declaration on the Question of the Ordination of Women," presenting arguments against the ordination of women to the priesthood. The main arguments were that the Church is following the mind of Jesus who chose only men as apostles; that it has been the constant tradition of the Church; and that the "natural resemblance" between Christ and the celebrant of the Eucharist would be difficult to see if the role were not taken by a man.

In 1983, the National Conference of Catholic Bishops agreed to write a pastoral letter in response to the concerns of women. Over the next nine years, four drafts of the document were submitted to the NCCB. The fourth draft was voted down in November 1992. One of the main points over which the bishops disagreed was the question of the ordination of women. The bishops referred the concerns addressed in the drafts to various committees in the NCCB, which were to issue statements on particular issues rather than attempt to write a more encompassing pastoral.

On August 15, 1988, Pope John Paul II issued *Mulieris Dignitatem* ("On the Dignity and Vocation of Women"). This encyclical was released shortly after the first draft of the NCCB document. The foundational anthropology was complementarity, suggesting that there are unique roles, abilities, and characteristics for women that are different from those of men. The theory of complementarity holds that it is God who determines woman's unique nature to complement man. The subsequent drafts of the U.S. bishops' document drew on that anthropology rather than that of partnership, as in the first draft.

The U.S. Bishops' Committee on Marriage and Family Life and the Committee on Women in Society and the Church issued "A Pastoral Response to Domestic Violence Against Women" in November 1992. In doing so they followed the example of bishops in Canada and New Zealand. The document identifies violence against women as sinful, decries the use of Scripture to support abusive behavior, and encourages pastors and other ministers to provide support for abused women. In November 1994 the U.S. bishops approved a pastoral reflection on women in the Church and in society, "Strengthening the Bonds of Peace," which rejects sexism in Church teaching and practice and commits the bishops to enhance the participation of women "in every possible aspect of church life."

WOMEN'S ORGANIZATIONS

Organizations of Catholic women span the spectrum from liberal to conservative. Some of the more active organizations are St. Joan's Alliance (1911); the National Council of Catholic Women (1920); the Grail (1921); the Leadership Conference of Women Religious, formerly the Conference of Major Superiors of Women (1956); the National Assembly of Religious Women, formerly the National Assembly of Women Religious (1968); National Coalition of American Nuns (1969); the Women's Ordination Conference (1974); the women-church movement (1977); the Women's Alliance for Theology, Ethics, and Ritual (1982); and Women United for Faith and Family (1984).

See also deacon, woman; feminism; ordination of women.

Bibliography

Carmody, Denise Lardner. *Responses to 101 Questions About Feminism.* New York: Paulist Press, 1993.
Carr, Anne E. *Transforming Grace: Christian Tradition and Women's Experience.* San Francisco: Harper & Row, 1988.
Coll, Regina. *Christianity and Feminism in Conversation.* Mystic, CT: Twenty-Third Publications, 1994.
LaCugna, Catherine Mowry, ed. *Freeing Theology: The Essentials of Theology in Feminist Perspective.* San Francisco: HarperCollins, 1993.

REGINA A. COLL

work, theology of, an understanding of human labor most thoroughly developed in Pope John Paul II's 1981 encyclical, *Laborem Exercens* ("On Human Work"). The primary text for grounding John Paul II's theology of work is the book of Genesis. He draws from this text two fundamental doctrines. The first is the *imago Dei* doctrine, which affirms that all persons are created in the image of God. Because God is our Creator, and persons are created in the image of God, persons are to live out that image by working with creation. "The word of God's revelation is profoundly marked by the fundamental truth that [the human person], created in the image of God, shares by his [or her] work in the activity of the creator, and that, within the limits of his [or her] own human capabilities, [the human person] in a sense continues to develop that activity and perfects it as he [or she] advances further and further in the discovery of the resources and values contained in the whole of creation" (n. 25). Work is participation in the activity of God.

The call to work with God in creation leads to the second doctrine underpinning the theology of work: God's charge to humanity to "subdue the earth." Because God is active in creation, humanity, created in the image of God, should be so as well. Moreover, it is precisely through the activity of subduing the earth that humanity realizes and fulfills its true nature as being in the image of God. In Pope John Paul's words, "[The human person] is the image of God partly through the mandate received from the creator to subdue, to dominate, the earth. In carrying out this mandate, [the human person], every human being, reflects the very action of the creator of the universe" (n. 4).

Centrality of the Human Person: The force of these two doctrines in interpreting the nature of work is to place the human person at the center. This theologically grounded understanding of the nature of work has two corollaries, one philosophical, the other social. The philosophical corollary is the priority of the subject over the object in the understanding of work. While work may have indispensable external, objective purposes—particularly the production of material goods to meet human needs—the primary purpose is to serve as a means for humanity to realize its true nature. John Paul II makes the link between the theological doctrines and the philosophical corollary clear: "In order to continue our analysis of work, analysis linked with the word of the Bible telling [us] that [we are] to subdue the earth, we must concentrate our attention on work in the subjective sense, much more than we did on the objective significance. . . . [The human person] is to subdue the earth and dominate it, because as the 'image of God' he [or she] is a person, that is to say, a subjective being capable of acting in a planned and rational way, capable of deciding about himself [or herself] and with a tendency to self-realization. As a person, [the human being] is therefore the subject of work. As a person he [or she] works, he [or she] performs various actions belonging to the work process; independently of their objective content, these actions must all serve to realize his [or her] humanity, to fulfill the calling to be a person that is his [or hers] by reason of his [or her] very humanity" (n. 6).

Priority of Labor: The social corollary of the theological doctrines and the centrality of the subject of work is the priority of labor over capital. In highlighting this priority, John Paul II is not criticizing market economies per se, but rather the tendency in some market economies for capital—the external means of objective production—to take precedence over the human work that makes production, and even the accumulation of capital, possible. According to John Paul II, human labor created the means of production in the first place. This makes human labor the "primary efficient cause" of production, while capital "remains a mere instrument or instrumental cause." Therefore, human labor should have priority in Catholic reflection on the nature of work. Capital is only "a collection of things" that results from human labor.

The theological understanding of work and its philosophical and social corollaries have concrete implications for the economic sphere of life. The first is a view of the relationship between the owners of capital and labor that does not place them in opposition. If capital is dependent on prior labor and continues to be so dependent, then the relationship between the two is more interdependent than either traditional capitalism or socialism allow. The second implication is that recognition of this interdependence leads to specific proposals for embodying it in the workplace. John Paul II recommends joint labor-management ownership of the means of production, worker-management sharing in the profits of business, and shareholding by labor. Behind these recommendations is an understanding of the nature of private property that rejects both socialist and capitalist extremes. Unlike socialism, persons have a right to private property. In contrast to capitalism, the right to private property is not absolute.

It is subordinate to the right of all persons to the use of the things of creation. If private ownership is not meeting this more comprehensive criterion, then state involvement and even ownership is allowable in certain cases. State-directed compensation for unemployment is an example of such redirection of private property for the common good. The preference, however, is for meeting problems of distribution through coordination of intermediate, nongovernmental institutions if possible.

Ultimately, the person, created in the image of God, participates not only in God's creative activity, but also in God's salvific activity through work. This becomes most evident when one takes into account the fact of human toil, which "marks the way of human life on earth and constitutes an announcement of death." At this point, John Paul II places the theological significance of work in the context of the Paschal Mystery. Through toil, persons participate in the redemptive activity of the Cross. "The Christian finds in human work a small part of the cross of Christ and accepts it in the same spirit of redemption in which Christ accepted his cross for us" (n. 27). *See also* Catholic social teachings; creation; *imago Dei; Laborem Exercens;* property.

Bibliography

Baum, Gregory. *The Priority of Labor: A Commentary on "Laborem exercens," Encyclical Letter of Pope John Paul II.* New York: Paulist Press, 1982.

Baum, Gregory, ed. *Work and Religion.* New York: Seabury Press, 1980.

Chenu, Marie-Dominique. *The Theology of Work: An Exploration.* Chicago: Henry Regnery, 1966.

Kaiser, Edwin. *Theology of Work.* Westminster, MD: Newman Press, 1966. TODD D. WHITMORE

Worker Priests, French and Belgian priests who joined the workforce to evangelize alienated Catholic workers. The idea seems to have originated with priests who had done forced labor in Germany during the Second World War. Between 1944 and 1954 well over one hundred priests involved themselves in this ministry, supported and encouraged by prominent members of the French hierarchy and the intellectual elite. Rome began to suppress the experiment in 1954 and so restricted it by 1959 (because of what was seen as a compromise of the priestly life) that its original intent was compromised. Little was left of the movement when the Second Vatican Council opened (1962), but a guarded tribute to its work did appear in the Decree on the Ministry and Life of Priests (n. 8). The 1971 World Synod of Bishops in Rome left the possibility of secular employment for priests to the discretion of the local ordinary. The Code of Canon Law (can. 285) only forbids "unbecoming" employment for clerics.

world, end of the material, a theological metaphor pointing to the "new creation" or the fullness of God's salvific activity. Salvation brings the material order not to destruction, as though it were an evil to be overcome, but to completion. The material order is truly caught up in the mystery of redemption initiated in creation through the Word and united eternally with the divine in the Word-made-flesh, Jesus Christ.

From the perspective of cosmology, the metaphor "the end of the material world" must be interpreted within an understanding of the innate goodness of creation and of the full flowering of that goodness through the divine will to save.

From the perspective of anthropology, the metaphor is linked with the redemption of the human race and finds its primary paradigm in Christ's death and Resurrection, "the first fruits of those who have died" (1 Cor 15:20). It underscores the openness of the material world to the activity of God's life-giving Spirit.

The fullness of life, flowing from Jesus' relation to the Father, is only available to us in history through our embodied openness to human interaction and relationship, self-giving, and mutual love. Our hope in the transformation of the whole of creation, with its manifold cultural, social, and political structures, in accordance with God's revealed desire for this world can lead the reflective Christian to see what is lacking or distorted in human relationships and the created order and to participate in the process of this transformation. *See also* eschatology, individual; eschatology, universal; eternal life; salvation history.

world, responsibility for the, commitment to, and moral accountability for, the welfare of the planet. Arising with the exponential expansion of technological and scientific power in the modern period, the phrase reflects both an increased sense of the vulnerability of nature to human actions as well as a deepening awareness of human dependence on the natural world.

"Responsibility for the world" refers primarily to moral accountability on the part of both individual persons and collectivities (e.g., corporations) for the negative impact of human actions (e.g., industrialization and consumption patterns) on the natural world. This responsibility is not total, but rather proportioned to the degree of control and power that human agents can exert.

The proper ordering of competing claims posed by various objects of responsibility (e.g., the needs of the poor vs. the needs of a local biosphere) constitutes the major problem in moral deliberation over responsibility for the world, as in the ongoing debate over sustainable development. The Church's prohibition of artificial birth control has been criticized for contributing to environmental destruction by undermining efforts to control population expansion.

The Bible's characteristic "desacralization" of nature, in which nature is separated from God, contributed to the flourishing of technology and the subjugation of nature in the West. Following the works of Francis Bacon (d. 1626) and René Descartes (d. 1650), the dominion over creation granted to humanity in Genesis was used to justify the tyrannical domination of nature. Acknowledging a degree of complicity in the legacy of Western ecological exploitation, the Church today strives to retrieve a sense of stewardship and interdependence with nature and advances a moral vision of the universal common good that encompasses nature as well as human societies ("planetary common good"), a theology of cocreation and cooperation with nature, and a sacramental understanding of nature. *See also* creation; history, theology of.

STEPHEN J. POPE

World Council of Churches (WCC), the most visible international expression of the ecumenical movement in the twentieth century. It was constituted at its first general assembly in Amsterdam in 1948, when 147 national churches became members; there were 317 members at the seventh assembly in 1991 (Canberra, Australia).

A precondition for membership is a church's acceptance of the WCC basis: "a fellowship of churches which confess the Lord Jesus Christ as God and Savior according to the Scriptures, and therefore seek to fulfill together their common calling to the glory of the one God, Father, Son and Holy Spirit." With no intention to be an incipient "world superchurch" or to legislate for the churches, the WCC since 1948 has notably advanced in its self-understanding, structures, and programs. The 1975 assembly (Nairobi) agreed that the "common calling" of the churches is "to advance towards visible unity in one faith and in one eucharistic fellowship, expressed in worship and in common life in Christ."

The WCC organizes its studies and activities around four focal points: (1) Unity and Renewal: ecclesial unity, inclusive community, theological education, worship, and spirituality; (2) Mission, Education, and Witness: evangelism, health and healing, gospel and culture, theological significance of religions, and dialogue with peoples of other world faiths; (3) Justice, Peace, and Creation: ethics and creation, racism, churches in solidarity with women and with youth, international affairs, development and socioeconomic justice, peace, and human rights; and (4) Sharing and Service: relief in emergencies and work with refugees, advocacy and action with the poor, sharing ecumenical resources, linking churches in service.

In these tasks the WCC works together with national and regional councils of churches, world confessional bodies such as the Lutheran World Federation, and other ecumenical groups.

Geneva is the headquarters of the WCC general secretariat and staff of about 270 persons. A 150-member central committee exercises governance between the general assemblies (every seven years) of delegates from each of the member churches (at Canberra in 1991, there were 842 delegates).

Prior to Vatican Council II (1962–65), the Catholic Church had kept deliberate distance from the WCC. Pope Pius XII (1939–58) forbade Catholics to attend its program meetings and assemblies. After Pope John XXIII founded the Secretariat for Promoting Christian Unity in 1960, he delegated official observers to the 1961 third general assembly (New Delhi). Paul VI in 1965 approved the Joint Working Group, an official consultative forum of the World Council of Churches and the Roman Catholic Church that initiates, evaluates, and sustains collaboration between its respective organizations and programs. Although not a member church, the Catholic Church participates in various ways in almost all WCC programs. For example, twelve Catholic theologians are full members of the Faith and Order commission.

The Catholic self-understanding as "a universal fellowship with a universal mission and structure," which differs from that of the mainly national churches in the WCC, was offered as the main (but not the only) reason why the Roman Catholic Church in 1972 declined to request WCC membership "in the immediate future." But Catholic membership might also have a destabilizing effect on the organization. Given its status as the world's largest church and the requirement of proportional representation, it would inevitably dominate all of the WCC's governing bodies.

The success of the WCC in carrying out its various purposes over four decades in ever-changing regional and world arenas has uncovered both the strengths and the weaknesses of ecumenism in the member and nonmember churches, as well as in the WCC. Called "a privileged instrument of the one ecumenical movement," the WCC in fact remains the focal point for positive evaluations and negative criticisms of the ecumenical movement itself: its vision and motivations, its intermediate goals, its activities, and its institutional forms. *See also* Church; ecumenical movement; ecumenism; unity of the Church.

THOMAS F. STRANSKY

worlds, possible, complete cosmic histories that might have taken place. The philosopher Leibniz (1646–1716) speculated that, apart from God's actual decision to create, God must know all such "possible worlds" and how much value would be realized in each. In virtue of that knowledge and of God's goodness, the actual world must then be the best of all possible worlds, containing the maximum achievable good despite the concomitant evil. This view has affinities with the theory of God's "middle knowledge" (Lat., *scientia media*), devised by the sixteenth-century Jesuit theologian Luis de Molina to reconcile the infallibility of divine providence with human freedom. Not all Catholic thinkers admit the feasibility of the concept of possible worlds or that of "middle knowledge," but many contemporary philosophers employ the former as a convenient way of discussing possibility and necessity as modes of being. *See also* creation; Molinism.

Worms, Diet of (1521), German Parliament that condemned Martin Luther. Summoned to the Diet after his condemnation by the papacy, Luther refused to retract any of his theology unless proven wrong by Scripture. On May 25 he was proclaimed an outlaw and went into ten-months' hiding at the Wartburg, a twelfth-century German castle. *See also* Luther, Martin.

worship (Old Eng., worth-ship, "honor"), the praise, thanksgiving, and acknowledgment given to God by believing individuals and communities through actions and words.

The Scriptural Notion of Worship: The Gospels describe Jesus as a devout Jew who participated in the worship of the synagogue and in the Temple

feasts at Jerusalem. Recent scholarship has emphasized the importance of Jewish worship for understanding Jesus' unique prayer and some of the origins of early Christian worship. In Jesus' time, the sacrifice of animals was only performed at the Temple in Jerusalem. Sacrifice, whether of animals or food, was a major form of worship whose importance increased after the Babylonian exile (sixth century B.C.). Except for the high holy days, most Jews worshiped in their local synagogues where a prayer service was conducted in the morning, afternoon, and evening. The core of these services was short citations from Scripture and a series of blessings that originally may have been improvised. The daily Temple worship included the sacrifice of two male lambs as well as meal and drink offerings, the sacrifice of incense, and the burning of lamps. God's Commandments were recited as well as the scriptural citations and blessings used in the synagogue services. The most sacred part of the Temple, the Holy of Holies, with its ark of the covenant was the symbol of God's presence to and covenant with Israel. In brief, Israel's worship in Christ's time was expressed in a number of ways but was always addressed to the God of the covenant made with the Jewish people.

The uniqueness of Christian worship is expressed by comparison with Temple worship. The Letter to the Hebrews argues that since Christ's death was a perfect sacrifice, no further sacrifice is needed (Heb 9:11–12, 24–28). With his death, Christ became the unique High Priest who entered the Holy of Holies once for all to offer the perfect sacrifice. In place of the physical structure of the Temple, Christians had become the temple of God and a royal priesthood in which the Holy Spirit dwelt. Christ had established a new covenant (Heb 9:15). The people of this new covenant are continually to offer "a sacrifice of praise to God, that is, the fruit of lips that confess his name" (Heb 13:15).

The earliest Christians at Jerusalem continued the familiar Temple and synagogue worship while retaining their own communal forms of instruction and worship (Acts 2:42–47). The baptism of John had been transformed into a baptism into the death and Resurrection of Christ, and his last meal with his disciples before his death continued to be celebrated as a principal form of worship. In 1 Corinthians a new stage of development is described, occasioned by Paul's formation of Christian communities with both Jewish and gentile converts. Unlike their Jewish or pagan contemporaries,

Christians had no sacred space such as a temple, not only because of practical reasons, but because the community itself was the Body of Christ. Worship was celebrated in "house churches," that is, usually the commodious homes of more affluent converts. The Greek term "to come together" assumes a special Christian meaning of a gathering to pray, sing, hear the Word of God, and celebrate the Lord's Supper. Scholars have pointed to examples of hymns probably used in early worship in the NT (Col 1:15–20; Eph 1:3–14; 1 Tim 3:16).

Paul's practical rule for solving problems of order in worship (e.g., the potential disruptive conduct of charismatic Christians) is simple: whatever is for the "upbuilding" of the community is permissible (1 Cor 14:26). In other words, Paul connects the worship of the community with its God-given tasks to announce the gospel and its message of reconciliation. In giving praise and thanks to God, the Christian community is enabled to live out the gospel message and give a credible witness to the world. These practical corollaries of worship are tested in the situations Paul faces in the Corinthian community. The Eucharist was normally preceded by a meal shared by rich and poor Christians. Inequalities in food and drink had caused divisions among these Christians (1 Cor 11:17–22). Paul draws the obvious conclusion: the Corinthians had missed the point of their worship. For Paul, all worship of God has been transformed by the death and Resurrection of Christ. With this event the new covenant marked by a redeeming oneness has been established: "Because there is one bread, we who are many are one body, for we all partake of the one bread" (1 Cor 10:17). Authentic worship brings about a unity of life and purpose that effectively announces the reign of God.

The Historical Development of Christian Worship: Aside from general references to worship and the celebration of Baptism and Eucharist, the NT does not offer great detail about the ways in which worship was carried out. In part this is due to the different cultural backgrounds of Christian communities spread throughout the Roman world and also to the improvised character of much Christian prayer. Even the *Apostolic Tradition* of Hippolytus (third century) in giving the text of a eucharistic prayer reminds its readers that it is only an example of how the prayer might be improvised. In the fourth century, with the end of the persecutions and official recognition by the state, the Christian communities were free to develop their own traditions of worship and sacrament in their communities. The result was families of liturgical traditions in the East and West that incorporated the cultural traditions and the theological emphases of their communities.

Two trends mark the historical development of worship from the early Middle Ages to Vatican II (1962–65). First, the liturgical participation of the laity was gradually reduced to a passive role with ritual language and actions becoming the exclusive domain of clerics. Second, in addition to the sacraments of initiation, Baptism, Confirmation, and Eucharist, there was a gradual development of other sacramental expressions that were not definitively clarified as among seven sacraments until the Middle Ages. With the final demise of the catechumenate by the early Middle Ages, the preparation for worship and sacraments was no longer formed by catechumenal and symbolic training, and popular devotions began to replace communal worship as the mainstay of peoples' religious life.

Vatican II's Renewal of Worship: With the promulgation of the Constitution on the Sacred Liturgy in 1963, the council in its first document placed liturgical reform at the head of its pastoral agenda. It situated the dying and rising of Christ at the center of all worship and the presence of Christ in the Eucharist and the other sacraments, in the word of God, and in the assembly gathered for prayer. It called for a full, conscious, and active participation of all the faithful in liturgy and a reform of worship so that it would be more accessible to peoples of every culture. This liturgical reform has served as a model for other Christian churches as well. *See also* Constitution on the Sacred Liturgy; liturgical movement; liturgy; liturgy, theology of.

Bibliography

Duffy, Regis A. *Real Presence, Worship, Sacrament, and Commitment.* San Francisco: Harper & Row, 1982.

Kavanagh, Aidan. *On Liturgical Theology.* New York: Pueblo, 1984.

Power, David. *Worship: Culture and Theology.* Washington, DC: Pastoral Press, 1990.

Vorgrimler, Herbert. *Sacramental Theology.* Collegeville, MN: Liturgical Press, 1992.

REGIS A. DUFFY

worship [in the Bible], actions in veneration or service of a deity. Throughout most of the history of Israel worship was carried out at sanctuaries scattered around the land. The biblical texts, archaeological data, and place names attest that, in addition to Yahweh, other deities were the object of veneration, especially those indigenous to Canaan (El, Asherah, Baal). Worship is essentially a public and social phenomenon, and we are not well informed about personal piety at any time during the biblical period. The principal form taken by worship was sacrifice, accompanied by prayer, which came to assume greater importance from the time of the Babylonian exile in the sixth century B.C. Psalms constitutes our principal source of information on prayer and, indirectly, the ritual acts of which it formed a part. The Deuteronomic program (Deut 12) restricted sacrifice to the Jerusalem Temple and its priesthood, though local cults continued in operation into the postexilic period. The details of worship were organized and codified by the Jerusalem priesthood (see esp. Leviticus and Numbers), creating a system that continued until the destruction of the Temple in A.D. 70. Early Christian worship preserved many of the forms and formulas of Jewish worship, which, however, were transformed by the new reality of Christ expressed in the ministries of word and sacrament. *See also* Bible and liturgy; sacrifice; worship.

Wounds, the Five Sacred, the wounds incurred by Jesus during his Passion and Crucifixion, namely the four nailmarks in his feet and hands and the lance wound in his side from the soldier's spear (John 19:34). Devotion to the Five Wounds has included special graphic emphasis on Christ's endurance of the pain of the cross and symbolic allusions to blood and water flowing from his side. *See also* crucifixion.

wrath of God, the metaphor of anger employed by the ancient Israelites to describe God's attitude toward sin. This anthropomorphism occurs in the OT when God is described as punishing sinners (Exod 15:7; Pss 2:12; 29:6) and also as inflicting trials upon the innocent (Job 14:13). The prophets, too, speak of God's anger toward Israel and Judah (Jer 25:7–38). This anthropomorphism is implied in the NT when Jesus says "Woe to you" (Matt 3:7). Paul speaks about the day of judgment as the "day of wrath" (Rom 2:5). The book of Revelation refers to "the wrath of the Lamb" and "the wrath of the Almighty God" (Rev 6:16; 19:15). *See also* judgment, general; judgment, particular.

Wright, John Joseph, 1909–79, American prelate. Bishop of Worcester, Massachusetts, 1950–59; bishop of Pittsburgh, 1959–69; cardinal, 1969; prefect, Sacred Congregation for the Clergy, 1969–79, Wright was the most prominent American ecclesiastic in Rome in the years following the Second Vat-

ican Council (1962–65). He was a doctrinal conservative but a liberal on social issues.

Wycliffe, John, ca. 1329–84, Oxford theologian and critic of the temporal authority of the Church and much of Catholic theology. He insisted that the right to rule, in both state and Church, came from personal piety and not from the office, and on biblical grounds he rejected transubstantiation, purgatory, and indulgences. Twenty-four propositions from his writings were condemned by the Blackfriars Council called by the archbishop of Canterbury, William Courtenay, at London in 1382, yet he was never excommunicated and died of natural causes at Lutterworth. Because of his continuing influence among the Hussites and Lollards, his works were formally condemned by the Council of Constance (1414–17), and his remains were ordered by the council exhumed from consecrated ground and burned. *See also* indulgences; Lollards; Protestantism; purgatory; Reformation, the; transubstantiation.

Xavier, St. Francis. *See* Francis Xavier, St.

Xaverian Brothers, Brothers of St. Francis Xavier (C.F.X.), a community of laymen who take vows of poverty, chastity, and obedience and who participate in the Church's mission of evangelization. Theodore James Ryken, a Dutch layman, established the first community in Bruges, Belgium, in 1839 to serve the needs of the Church, especially in missionary countries. Over the last one hundred fifty years the Xaverian apostolates have included teaching on all levels; the running of homes for needy youth; college and university work in Belgium, England, and the United States and in mission areas of Zaire, Bolivia, Kenya; and home missionary work among Native Americans in South Dakota and African Americans in South Carolina. The brothers' ministries include religious and adult education, campus ministry, and prison ministry. Administrative centers are located in Milton, Massachusetts, and Ellicott City, Maryland. *See also* brothers, religious.

Ximénes de Cisneros, Francisco (zi-may'nez), 1436–1517, Spanish scholar and reformer. Confessor to Queen Isabella (1492), he became archbishop of Toledo (1495) and cardinal (1507). Pious and ascetic, he spiritually renewed the Spanish church by vigorously reforming monastic and mendicant orders. Cisneros advanced the goal of Spanish religious purity by expelling nonconverting Moors in

Francisco Ximénes de Cisneros on horseback and in cardinal's attire leading a Spanish force into Oran, Morocco (1509); sixteenth-century Juan de Borgoña mural in the Mozarabic Chapel, Cathedral of Toledo, Spain.

1502 and supporting the Inquisition. He became grand inquisitor of Castile in 1507. As a scholar, Cisneros produced a landmark in biblical studies: the Complutensian Polyglot Bible, which consisted of Latin, Greek, and Hebrew versions of the Bible arranged side by side; it was the first Christian edition of the Hebrew Scriptures. *See also* Complutensian Polyglot Bible.

Yahweh, a name used for God in the OT. It was revealed to Moses, to whom God is identified as "I am who I am" (Exod 3:14)—a wordplay on Yahweh. It is an archaic form of the Hebrew verb "to be" and may mean "he causes to be." Many OT names are compounded with abbreviated forms of Yahweh such as -*iah* (e.g., Hezekiah) or *Jeho-* (e.g., Jehoshaphat). Later the name was considered too sacred to pronounce and other words, especially the word *adonai* ("my Lord"), were substituted for it. It was then translated into Greek as *kyrios* ("Lord") and subsequently into English as Lord.

year, liturgical. *See* liturgical year.

YMCA (Young Men's Christian Association), community-service agency sponsoring educational and recreational activities. Founded by George Williams in 1844 as a nondenominational organization to spread Protestant evangelicalism among young men in London, the YMCA no longer has an explicitly religious mission. For that reason Catholics are no longer discouraged from membership as they once were. Today it serves 30 million people in 110 nations. In the United States it has over two thousand local organizations.

yoga (Sanskrit, "union"), Eastern methods (with origins in Hinduism) for union with God. They include selfless action, physical postures, controlling vital energies, and meditation. Yogic techniques, originating in India and first codified by Patanjali in about the second century B.C., characterize much Asian spirituality. Various yogic disciplines have been adapted to Christian spiritual practice.

Yom Kippur (Heb.), the Day of Atonement. Special sin offerings marked this holiest day of the Jewish year (Lev 16). According to Heb 9, it prefigured Jesus' sacrificial death. The day is still celebrated as the holiest Jewish holiday of the year on the tenth day of Tishri (September–October).

Yorke, Peter C., 1864–1925, Irish-born priest, educator, and labor leader. Ordained in Baltimore for the diocese of San Francisco in 1887, he gained legendary status by vanquishing the anti-Catholic American Protective Association, acting as union spokesman during the successful teamster strike of 1901, founding and editing the Irish newspaper *The Leader,* publishing a series of textbooks on religion, and supporting the fight for a free Irish state.

Young Men's Christian Association. *See* YMCA.

Young Women's Christian Association. *See* YWCA.

Yugoslavian Byzantine Catholic Church. *See* Byzantine Catholic Church of the Diocese of Krizhevci.

YWCA (Young Women's Christian Association), community service agency sponsoring educational and recreational activities for girls and women. Founded in London in 1877 to assist young women without family support, the YWCA originally promoted the values of Protestant evangelicalism. Today the organization serves people regardless of religious faith in eighty nations; there are four hundred affiliates in the United States.

Zabarella, Francesco, 1360–1417, Italian canonist. He wrote standard commentaries on the twelfth-century Decretals of Gratian. He supported antipope John XXIII (1410–15), who created him a cardinal, and held conciliarist views. His collection of proposals for ending the Great Schism, *De schismate* (Lat., "On schism"), was placed on the Index of Forbidden Books because the work placed the power of a general council over that of a pope. *See also* conciliarism; Great Schism.

Zacharias, St., d. 752, pope from 741 to 752. A supporter of St. Boniface, Zacharias defended images against the iconoclast emperor Constantine Copronymus and translated Gregory the Great's *Dialogues* into Greek. Feast day: March 15 (West, formerly); September 5 (East). *See also* iconoclasm.

Zachary [name of pope]. *See* Zacharias, St.

Zahm, John Augustine, 1851–1921, Holy Cross priest and professor at the University of Notre Dame. He was the author of *Evolution and Dogma* (1896), which argued that evolution was compatible with Catholic teaching. It was condemned by Rome, largely because Zahm had identified himself too closely with the liberal faction in the controversies then raging over "Americanism," the loosely structured movement that sought to accommodate Catholic faith and practice to American culture. *See also* Americanism.

Zealots, a Jewish group or party that played a prominent part in the revolt against Rome (A.D. 66–70). They may have begun in A.D. 6 under Judas the Galilean. They appear to have agreed with the Pharisees in many respects but differed from them in their violent refusal to serve anyone as lord or king except God. Their opposition to Roman rule, which may have continued sporadically after A.D. 6, exploded just before and at the beginning of the revolt when Zealots took Jerusalem and Masada. Luke 6:15 names a disciple of Jesus "Simon, who was called the Zealot."

Zechariah, father of John the Baptist. According to Luke 1:5–25, 57–80, Zechariah, while performing priestly duties in the Temple, learned of John's forthcoming birth from the angel Gabriel. Temporary dumbness answered his doubting request for a sign. Upon his son's birth and naming, Zechariah recovered his speech and pronounced the prophetic oracle now known as the Benedictus. *See also* John the Baptist, St.

Zen Buddhism, a blend of early Buddhism with Taoism. This mainly Japanese form of Mahayana Buddhism has two major schools. Soto Zen teaches meditating with simple awareness of all one's experiences. Rinzai Zen uses "koans," mental puzzles defying rational solution, to bring experience of the mind's limitations.

Zen's goal is enlightenment, direct experience of reality simply as it is. This nonconceptual state is beyond dualism. It destroys ego-centeredness and flows naturally into compassion. It is sometimes called *sunyata* (emptiness) or *tathata* (thusness), and is seen by some Christian practitioners as analogous to the unmanifest Godhead. Some Jesuit priests are Zen masters.

Zeno of Verona, St., d. 375, bishop of Verona in northern Italy from 362 to 375. A collection of ninety homilies, divided into two unequal books and primarily liturgical and exhortatory in nature, is attributed to him. Feast day: April 12.

zeon (zay'ahn; Gk., "hot"), the custom, peculiar to the Byzantine rite, of adding hot water to the consecrated chalice just before Communion. The origins of the custom are obscure, but it was usual for the ancients to drink wine cut with hot water. Later liturgical symbolism interprets the *zeon* to mean that in Communion one receives the warm blood of the living, Risen Christ. *See also* Communion, Holy.

Zephyrinus, St., d. 217, pope from 198/9 to 217. Information about him comes mostly from the hostile testimony of Hippolytus, bitter enemy of Callistus, Zephyrinus's close associate and successor. Hippolytus alleges that Zephyrinus was uneducated and a virtual Modalist, even though he excommunicated two Monarchians (both named Theodotus) for heresy. Origen visited Rome during Zephyrinus's pontificate. Feast day: August 26.

Zion, a hill symbolizing Jerusalem and its Temple. Zion designated the Jebusite city captured by David (2 Sam 5:6–10), then the Temple Mount immediately to the north (Pss 2:6; 46:4; 78:68–69). In the Byzantine era the name came to designate a ridge southwest of the current walled city, traditional site of David's tomb and the Last Supper. *See also* Jerusalem; Temple.

Zita, St., 1218–78, Italian-born patron saint of

domestic servants. She herself was in domestic service for forty-eight years. Feast day: April 27.

zone (zoh'nay; Gk., "cincture"), a belt of vestment cloth used as the liturgical cincture in the Byzantine and Armenian rites. *See also* cincture.

Zoroastrianism, religion of ancient Persia founded by Zoroaster (Zarathustra, sixth century B.C.), who reformed an older warrior-based cult related to the Vedic religion of India. Zoroaster's religion was, within the confines of an ultimate monotheism, dualistic and antisacrificial. After a period when the old cult was reintroduced, it was reformed and systematized under the Sassanids (from the third century A.D.). Small groups of believers still survive in India, Iran, and the United States.

Zosimus, St., d. 418, pope from 417 to 418. Revoking Innocent I's condemnation, Zosimus readmitted Pelagius and Celestius to communion (417), but under pressure from the African bishops he reversed himself, provoking Julian of Eclanum's schism. Feast day: December 26.

zucchetto, a skullcap worn since the thirteenth century by bishops, cardinals, and the pope. The color indicates the rank of the wearer: purple (bishop), scarlet (cardinal), white (the pope), and black (others, such as abbots).

Zwingli, Ulrich, 1484–1531, Reformer of Zurich. Educated in Basel, Bern, and Vienna and ordained in 1506, he served as priest in Glarus and then at Einsiedeln. In Einsiedeln he came under the influence of Erasmus. Zwingli's reputation as a powerful humanist preacher grew and he was called to be People's Preacher at the Great Minster in Zurich (1519). By 1522, Zwingli emerged as an evangelical Reformer, preaching Christ crucified as the sole source of grace and the gospel in Scripture as the sole norm of truth, against what he perceived to be the abuses of the Catholic Church. Stirred by his preaching, the people of Zurich called for reform, which was taken up by the city council of Zurich in two debates (January and October 1523), both of which upheld the reform agenda of Zwingli while claiming sole authority for its implementation. By 1525, canon law was annulled, images and organs were removed from churches, monasteries were dissolved, and the Latin Mass was replaced by a Lord's Supper in German. From 1525 to his death in the

Second Battle of Kappel in 1531, Zwingli was involved in constant controversy. Against the Catholic and Lutheran theologians, Zwingli argued that the sacraments do not confer grace. Nor is the body of Christ present in the Lord's Supper, given Jesus' statement that "the flesh is useless" (John 6:63) and the article of faith that he has ascended to the right hand of the Father. Philip of Hesse tried and failed to attain unity on this issue between Luther and Zwingli at the Marburg Colloquy of 1529, leaving Zwingli isolated at the Diet of Augsburg (1530), where he was forced to submit his own account of faith for Zurich. *See also* Protestantism; Real Presence; Reformation, the.

Alinari/Art Resource, NY: 53, 90, 117, 134, 140, 144, 191, 235 (left), 260 (upper left), 305, 507 (upper), 539, 551 (upper), 596, 608 (detail), 610, 649 (middle right, detail), 669 (detail), 685 (lower left), 716 (detail), 743 (upper), 752, 764, 773, 776, 830, 895 (right), 949 (upper), 972, 973 (detail), 974, 1000, 1166 (detail), 1263, 1269, 1293 (lower), 1318; Kirk Amyx: 869; courtesy Archives Canada: 903 (lower, detail), 920; T. Arruza/Image Works: 873; Art Resource, NY: 1005; Alan Becker/Image Bank: 1282; Bettmann Archive: 35, 158 (left), 213, 231, 707, 925 (middle), 929, 1163 (right), 1170; Boltin Picture Library, Georges Rouault: 695; Bord Fáilte: 381; Bridgeman Art Library, London: 388, 599 (middle, detail), 631 (detail), 632 (detail), 649 (lower left), 653, 949 (lower, detail), 990, 1013 (detail); Bridgeman Art Library/Art Resource, NY: 1331, Dan Budnik/Woodfin Camp: 1145 (middle left), 1155; Bulloz: 507 (middle), 531, 591; Karen Callaway/Catholic News Service: 1119; Cap-Viollet: 1131; Luis Castañeda/Image Bank: 1212, 1145 (middle right); Catholic News Service: 153, 208, 234, 351, 386, 387, 389, 395, 437 (upper), 475, 483, 486, 627, 708, 740, 744, 828, 856, 898, 976, 1144, 1164, 1188, 1213, 1239 (bottom), 1239 (middle right), 1243 (right), 1259, 1299, 1300, 1303, 1305; Kay Chernush/Image Bank: 556; Collection Viollet: 903 (upper), 913, 1004 (right), 1207; Crosiers/Catholic News Service: 487, 1123, 1283, 1284, 1333; Michael Dyer/Stock Boston: 1288; John Eastcott/Yva Momatiok/Image Works: 1275, 1276; Victor Englebert: 756, 825; Fabian/Sygma: 713 (left); Fathers of London Oratory/ Bridgeman Art Library/Art Resource, NY: 925 (upper), 935; Les Fetchko/Catholic News Service: 1286; Chuck Fishman/Leo de Wys, NY: 36; Mimi Forsyth/Catholic News Service: 59; Foto Marburg/Art Resource, NY: 278, 551 (lower), 589, 731 (upper), 733, 743 (middle), 774, 798, 803 (middle), 806, 817, 843; Stuart Franklin/Magnum Photos: 306, 428; Fratelli Bonella: 599 (lower), 618 (upper left, upper right); Robert Frerck/Woodfin Camp: 595; Frick Collection, NY: Giovanni Bellini, *Saint Francis in the Desert*: 542; Hans Holbein: 893; Robert Fried/Stock Boston: 137; Gene Plaisted/Crosiers/Catholic News Service: 61, 348, 437 (middle), 446, 840, 1120; Alexis Georgeon/Gamma Liaison: 375, 1265; Gerhard Gscheidle/Image Bank: 860; Giordani/Catholic News Service: 1002; Giraudon/Art Resource, NY: 325 (right), 383 (lower right), 391 (upper, detail), 413 (detail), 430, 576, 698, 1145 (upper), 1153 (left), 1168, 1208, 1260; Ulysse Gosset/Sygma: 685 (middle), 688; Spenser Grant/Photo Researchers: 823; Jeff Greenberg/Photo Researchers: 945; Harlingue-Viollet: 1243 (left); Michael Hoyt/Catholic News Service: 600, 731 (lower), 738; Hulton Deutsch Collection Limited: 151, 652, 678, 862 (right), 1184; courtesy International Melkite Catholic Union: 844; J. B. Co.: 618 (lower); Bob Kalman/Image Works: 182; Shinichi Kanno/FPG International: 1154 (lower left); Lisa Kessler/Catholic News Service: 665; KNA-Bild-Rollik/Catholic News Service: 796, KNA-Bild/Catholic News Service: 742, 1073 (lower), 1077, 1079, 1137, 1176; Lauros-Giraudon/Art Resource, NY (detail): 125 (middle), 170; Erich Lessing/Art Resource, NY: 15, 31, 56, 64, 74, 132, 158 (right), 235 (right), 260 (lower right), 325 (left), 360, 380 (lower right), 601, 629, 650, 651, 690, 697, 751, 799 (detail), 803 (lower), 805, 832, 834, 838, 895 (left), 991, 1073 (middle), 1103, 1108, 1138 (right), 1154 (upper left), 1163 (left), 1293 (upper), 1308; Mary Ellen Mark: 1239 (middle